WEST AFRICA

THE ROUGH GUIDE

ROUGH GUIDE CREDITS

Series Editor	Mark Ellingham
Editorial	Jonathan Buckley, Martin Dunford, John Fisher, Jack Holland, Richard Trillo, Greg Ward
Production	Susanne Hillen, Kate Berens, Andy Hilliard
Layout and Design	Greg Ward, Gail Jammy and Richard Trillo

A large number of people have been involved in making this book.
We want to thank Susanne Hillen and Kate Berens for tireless toil, Gail Jammy for massive quantities of creative and efficient typesetting, Greg Ward again for first-class typesetting, but also for sound advice always on tap, Catherine Mulvenna for fast and superlative proof-reading, Jules Brown for rapid keying of proof corrections (and not a few editorial oddities zapped), Andy Hilliard for swift paste-up and scanning and Henry Iles for inspired artwork. We also owe a huge debt to the combined editorial talents of Jonathan Buckley, John Fisher, Jack Holland, Greg Ward and Mark Ellingham who knocked extra sense into it all. Special thanks to Mark for agreeing it was a good idea in the first place and being unflaggingly enthusiastic and supportive throughout.

Richard: Many thanks to Cathy Driver and Khalil Ibrahimi for coming to the rescue so often, to Andy Fisher for coming to the rescue in The Gambia, and to Dick Porter.
To Teresa and Alex, for endurance, all my love and gratitude.

Jim: All my thanks to Irma Hudgens, for her support and encouragement, and to Arba and Sallee.

Illustrations for "Basics", "Contexts" and the country title pages are by **Henry Iles**; the small illustrations in "Basics" and "Contexts"are by **Edward Briant**.

First published by Harrap Columbus Ltd, 1990.
This reprint published 1992 by Rough Guides Ltd, 149 Kennington Lane, London SE11 4EZ.
Distributed by Penguin Books, 27 Wrights Lane, London W8 5TZ.

Typeset in Linotron Univers and Century Old Style to an original design by Andrew Oliver.
Printed by Cox & Wyman Ltd, Reading.

1232p, includes index

British Library Cataloguing in Publication Data
A catalogue recored for this book is available from the British Library.

ISBN 1-85828-014-1 (previously published by Harrap Columbus Ltd under ISBN 0-7471-0087-X).

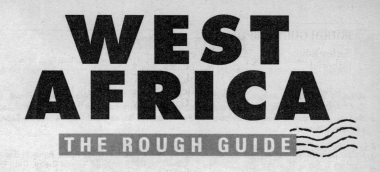

WEST AFRICA

THE ROUGH GUIDE

WRITTEN AND RESEARCHED
by
JIM HUDGENS and RICHARD TRILLO

Additional research and accounts by
Daniel Jacobs, Jane Bryce and Dave Muddyman
with
**Chris Scott, Bill Jackson, Teresa Driver,
Phillip Martin and Jim Taylor**

Edited by
Richard Trillo

THE ROUGH GUIDES

THANKS FOR HELP

Many people have been involved in creating this book, either with practical help, or by keeping our information up-to-date to the last minute. To everyone we extend our warmest thanks.

Jointly we thank

Adenike Adedoyin, James K. Anaman, Tricia Barnett, Bolgatanga Tourist Office, Grant Carstairs, Luc Denesle, Kate Dawson, Colette Gallie, Henry Iles, Bill Jackson, Daniel Jacobs, Kudum, Fran Loots, Musée Provincial de Poni (Gaoua), Helen Scadding, Fatimatou Tchabana and David Warne

Jim thanks

Didier Agbedivlo, P. U. Agunenye, Eric K. Anim, Edward Apanah, Duke Apou, Agbessi Boniface, Reuben T. Azzu, Muntaka Bello, Seidou Coulibaly, Julia Bromhead, Ismail Dicko, Gata Djima, Assoumane and Adamou Garkai, Xolani Mafeje, Dogbe K. Mensah, Kouadio Kouame Olivier, Hamidou Soumah , Omar Touré and Gotzon Zaritiega

Richard thanks

Sigrid Allen, Joanna Bell, Richard Bursby, Jane Bryce, Kate Calvert, Kabba Camara, Simon Clarke, Helene Cloutias, David Constable, Bud Crandall, Clementine Deliss, Anne Dordal, Andrew Dordal, Charles Easmon, Marc Etienne, Paul Everett, Hank Evers, Andrew Frankel, Samba M. Fye, Tricia Gilchrist, Anne Hammick, Tim Harrison, Carole Hartley, Paul Hayward, Wendy Hillary, Rowena Hopkins, Abdul Iscandri, Demba Keita, Boubacar Kouyateh, Mssrs C. Latridge and C. Perrrot, Kelly Lesperance, Brian Luckett, Monica Mackaness, Kevin Malone and Rory, Phillip Martin, Patrick Matturi, Alistair McKinroy, Dave Muddyman, Viban Ngo, Robert Norman, Terry O'Leary, Dayo Okunlola, Helen Pickering, Moukarim Ossam, Manfred Prinz, Alison Robbs, Chris Scott, George Senger, Chris Seward, Caroline Shaw, Patrick Sothern, Abdou Sourang, Paul Spring, Phil Stanton, Pat Sutton, Rachel Swann, Jim Taylor, Daphne Topouzis, Simon Underwood, Jacques Verrier, Marc Vicens, Steve Wallis, Jaime Ward, Elaine Wattam, Karen Wenzel, Paul Williams, Nicky Young, Nancy Zlotsky and Anthony Zurbrugg.

HELP US UPDATE

We've done our best to make sure that this first edition of **West Africa: the Rough Guide** is as useful, accurate and up-to-the-minute as possible, credit for which is due in large part to the contributors among the names above. But events move fast in West Africa and we can only keep it all current in future editions by hearing from readers. We are conscious of the fact that, while we have had some African contributors, the book has been largely put together on the basis of the research and opinions of white travellers, and we are therefore particularly keen to have the input of feedback from black readers.

If we've got it wrong, or you feel there are places we've overrated or under-praised, or find we've missed something good or covered something which has gone, then **please write and tell us**. Letters about obscure routes off the beaten track are as welcome as details of your favourite club or hotel, and we are always trying to improve our maps.

Because of the work involved in future editions (and our intention to cover certain countries in individual books) we are keen to establish permanent, or semi-permanent, correspondents in as many countries as possible. We would welcome hearing from anyone interested in this – either nationals or expatriates.

We will acknowledge all information used in the next edition and will send a free copy of this or any other Rough Guide for the best (and most legible!) letters.

**Richard Trillo, Africa Editor, Rough Guides,
149 Kennington Lane, London SE11 4EZ, UK**

NOTE THAT EACH OF THE COUNTRY PARTS (2–19) BEGINS WITH A PRACTICAL INFORMATION SECTION SPECIFIC TO THAT COUNTRY, AND ALSO HAS ITS OWN DETAILED INDEX.

CONTENTS

WEST AFRICA: MAIN ROADS

To

Dakhla

To Morocco

WESTERN
SAHARA

Nouadhibou

Atar

MAURITANIA

MALI

NOUAKCHOTT

Néma

Timbuktu

River Niger

St-Louis

River Senegal

DAKAR

SENEGAL

Kayes

Mopti

THE
GAMBIA

BANJUL

Tambacounda

BURKINA
FASO

Ziguinchor

BAMAKO

OUAGADOUGOU

GUINEA
BISSAU

BISSAU

Labé

Bobo-
Dioulasso

GUINEA

Kankan

CONAKRY

Tamale

SIERRA
LEONE

COTE
D'IVOIRE

GHANA

FREETOWN

Bo

Nzérékoré

Man

Yamoussoukro

Kumasi

MONRIVIA

LIBERIA

ABIDJAN

Sassandra

0   500 km

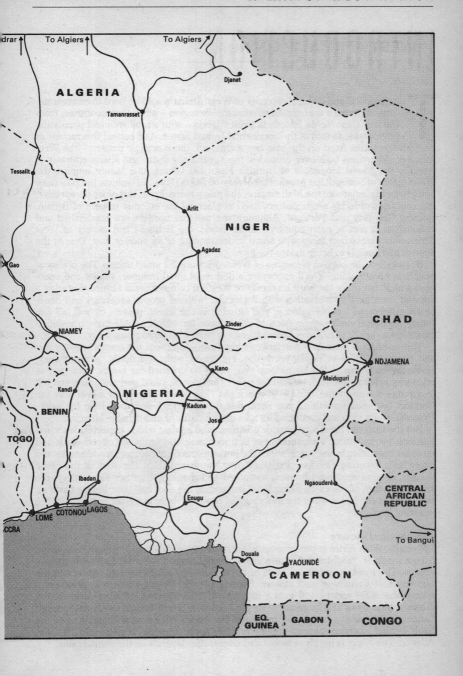

INTRODUCTION

The physical and cultural diversity of **West Africa** would be hard to exaggerate. This is perhaps the world's most complex region – seventeen countries, from the tiny Cape Verde Islands to giant Nigeria – with a total area and population comparable to that of the continental United States. And behind this mosaic of modern territories fixed on the map lies a different, more organic pattern – the West Africa of old nations built over centuries: the Yoruba city states and Hausa emirates of Nigeria; the Mossi kingdoms of Burkina Faso and Ghana; the Asante empire; the Wolof states of Senegal; the Muslim theocracy of Fouta Djalon in Guinea; the Bamiléké chiefdoms of Cameroon; the Mali empire; and many more. From this older perspective, the countries of today are imposters fixed in place by the colonial powers of Britain, France, Germany and Portugal. Although the national borders are established and nationalism a part of each country's social fabric, the richness and variety of West Africa only comes into focus with some understanding of its ancient past. One of the aims of this book is to bring that to the fore.

But some of the biggest pleasures of West Africa are the small things. The civility of people is breathtaking. You'll encounter a degree of good humour, vitality and openness which can make the hard insularity of Western cultures seem absurd. Entering a shop or starting a conversation with a stranger without proper greetings and hand-shaking becomes inconceivable. If you stumble in the street, passers-by will tell you "sorry" or some similar expression of condolence for which no adequate translation exists in English. You're never ignored; you say hello a hundred times a day.

This intimacy – a sense of barriers coming down – sharpens the events of every day and eases the more mundane hardships. For travel, without a doubt, is rarely easy. Going by bus, shared taxi or pick-up van, you'll be crushed for hours, subjected to mysterious delays and endless halts at police roadblocks, jolted over potholes, and left in strange towns in the middle of the night. The sheer physicality never lets up. Comfort becomes something you seek, find, leave behind, and then long for again. Cold water, dry skin and clean clothes take on the status of unattainable luxuries.

But the material hardships provide a background against which **experiences** stand out with clarity. Africa's sensuousness is undeniable: the brilliance of red earth and emerald vegetation in the forest areas; the intricate smells of cooking, wood smoke and damp soil; towering cloud-scaped skies over the savannah at the start of the rains; villages of sun-baked mud houses, smoothed and moulded together like pottery; the singing rhythm of voices speaking tonal languages; the cool half-hour before dawn on the banks of the Niger when the soft clunk of cowbells rises on a haze of dust from the watering herds...

The physical picture

Physically, West Africa is predominantly flat or gently undulating. Although most countries have their **"highlands"**, these are generally rugged hills rather than mountain ranges. The most mountainous parts of the region are Guinea's Fouta Djalon and the highlands of Cameroon and eastern Nigeria (where Mount Cameroon peaks at a respectable 4000 metres and gets a little frost). The big river of West Africa is the **Niger**, which flows in a huge arc from the border of Sierra Leone, northeast through Guinea, into Mali and to the very fringes of the Sahara (where sand dunes rise on the bank behind snorting hippos) before turning south through Nigeria and into the Atlantic. The Niger is highly seasonal and river traffic depends on the annual rains.

As for the scenic environment, expectations of tropical forest are usually disappointed, at least to begin with. While the natural **vegetation** across the whole southern coastal belt is rainforest – with a gap in the Ghana-Togo area where grasslands come nearly to the coast – by far the commonest scene in the densely populated parts is of a desolate, bush-stripped landscape where dust and bare earth figure heavily. True rainforest, however, is still present in parts of Guinea and Ghana, in southeast Nigeria and especially in Cameroon. Guinea also features beautiful **savannah** lands, as does Burkina Faso. Along the **coast**, creeks and mangroves make many parts inaccessible. The best beaches are in Sierra Leone and Côte d'Ivoire, with Ghana, Senegal, The Gambia and Cameroon creditable runners-up. The currents tend to be strong, though, making many shorelines unsuitable for swimming – take care.

Where to go

If you have the time, by far the most satisfying way of visiting West Africa is **overland**, traversing the yawning expanse of the **Algerian Sahara**, arriving in the dry northern reaches of the Sahel in Mali or Niger to the ravishing shock of an alien culture, and then acclimatising to a new landscape, a new climate and new ways of behaving.

Choosing **where to go** is no easy task: the region offers so much and Africa repeatedly confounds all expectations and assumptions. In the main section of the guide, the individual country introductions give an idea of what to look forward to. However, at the risk of reinforcing stereotypes, it's possible to make a few generalisations about the feel of the countries.

Of the eleven francophone, **ex-French colonies**, the three nations most dominated by French culture and language are Senegal, Côte d'Ivoire and Cameroon; these are also expensive countries, and their relatively westernised cities are inclined to be hustly. In many ways, though, **Senegal** is an obvious choice to launch your travels, especially for English-speaking visitors flying into The Gambia: facilities for travellers are relatively good and the verdant **Basse Casamance** region has a remarkable network of village-based accommodation. **Côte d'Ivoire** provides an at times bizarre melange of the traditional and modern, African and French. **Cameroon** – which has an English-speaking region – blends magnificent scenery, and wildlife parks similar to those of East Africa, with an extraordinary richness of culture, running the whole African gamut from "Pygmy" hunting camps to Arabic-speaking trading towns and taking in the colourful kingdoms of the western highlands.

If you're crossing the desert, resist the temptation to rush through **Algeria** and the republic of **Niger**, both of which offer considerably more than desert track, with their isolated mountain ranges and startling evidence of prehistoric inhabitants. Vast and land-locked **Mali** is blessed with the great inland delta of the Niger river and, again, striking cultural contrasts – the old **Islamic cities** of Gao, Timbuktu and Djenné (on, or near the river), and the traditionally non-Muslim **Dogon country** along the rocky cliff of the Bandiagara escarpment. Other francophone countries include the narrow strips of **Togo** and **Benin**, both easy-going and fairly undeveloped as far as tourism is concerned; the marvellously laid-back, revolutionary republic of **Burkina Faso**; and the remote and dramatic expanse of **Mauritania**. Perhaps the most impressive of the *pays francophones*, however, is the republic of **Guinea** – one country in the region which demands the adjective "authentic".

Four West African countries are anglophone – **former British colonies**, divided from each other by the speed of the French invasion in the nineteenth century. **The Gambia** is an easy place to set out from, a winter holiday destination that's small and personable enough to feel accessible for the least adventurous visitor. **Sierra Leone** is a more demanding destination and, unless you fly in, somewhat hard to reach too, but it has some of the best beaches in the world – only minutes away from the raffish tumble of Freetown. The distinctive personality of **Ghana** provides flamboyant cultural experiences and a splendid, palm-lined coast, dotted with old European forts. The big travel incentives of **Nigeria**, by contrast, lie inland – in the fine uplands of the plateau and the old cities of the north. It's a hard country to come to terms with but, once away from the slightly psychotic manifestation of Lagos, there's no denying the ease and peace which accompany travels even here. Tragically, the same can no longer be said for **Liberia** – a former vassal state of the USA, nominally independent since 1847 – whose ugly civil war has all but destroyed a country that was already on its knees. We have retained Part Thirteen almost exactly as it was written, but it's all sad history for now.

The **former Portuguese colonies** are West Africa's least-known destinations. The **Cape Verde Islands** are immediately beguiling: volcanic outcrops and desert islands in the mid-Atlantic, with a scenery and lifestyle that make them hard to leave. **Guinea-Bissau** has its own island highlights – the Bijagos – luxuriant green forests in the warm, inshore sea, as different from the Cape Verdes as it's possible to imagine.

The first recommendation in all this, is to give yourself **time**. It's tempting to try to cover as much of this fascinating region as possible. But the rewards become thinner the faster you go and, beyond a certain pace, the point of being there is lost in the pursuit of the next goal. While it may be hard to stop completely, or just to limit yourself to a small corner, that is precisely the way to get the most out of your trip – and, incidentally, also how to put the most in. In such a poor region, the idea of some kind of reciprocity is one worth keeping. At the risk of sounding mysterious, everything comes back to you in the end. Patience and generosity always pay off: haste and intolerance tend to lead to disaster.

If you're travelling alone – and it's really the best way if you want to get to know West Africa rather than your travelling companion/s – it may be useful to know about the main **travellers' crossroads** in the region, where you might team up for a while or swap experiences: Agadez and Gao at the edge of the desert, Mopti in Mali, Lomé in Togo, and Busua in Ghana on the south-facing coast.

When to travel

Individual **climate** details are given for each country. The big consideration is not the **heat** – temperatures, in fact, only occasionally climb very much higher than you might experience in Europe – but the **humidity** and particularly the timing of the **rainy seasons**. Broadly the rains come in the "summer" months, some time between April and October. Although travel is rarely out of the question during the rains, it's obviously not an ideal time. You can be pretty sure of dry weather everywhere from mid-November to the end of January. Where the rainy seasons are very marked, the very end of the dry season is best avoided as it can be stiflingly humid. The best time to leave on an overland trip planned to last several months is September.

THE LAYOUT OF THE BOOK

This book is designed to be as much use if you're visiting a single country, as for travelling widely in several. Part One, *Basics*, covers many of the **practical details and much of the background information** useful to know before arrival in Africa. If you can't find the information you're looking for anywhere else in the book, it should be in *Basics*.

Parts Two to Nineteen cover **the countries**, starting from the north with the Algerian Sahara, followed by Niger, Mali and Burkina Faso, and the fifteen **coastal states** from Mauritania to Cameroon. Each part begins with specific, **practical information** on that country and a short **history**. Following this is the **guide** proper, starting with the capital or largest city. Again, if something seems to require explanation, you should find it covered in "Practical Information". Each country has its own **index**.

The book's concluding section – *Contexts* – has an article on **music**; an annotated **reading list**, both for the whole region, and country by country; an introduction to West African **cinema**; an indexed **chronology**; and a brief survival guide for speaking **French**.

PART ONE

THE
BASICS

GETTING THERE

The most straightforward – and usually the cheapest – way to get to West Africa is by air. If you have the time, though, making your way overland, either with your own vehicle or using public transport, gives rewards of its own – and an unbeatable introduction to the region.

You can travel in similar style, with most of your needs looked after, by going on an organised overland tour. These, however – like inclusive package holidays to West Africa – are fairly limited in choice.

FLIGHTS FROM BRITAIN

In London, and increasingly in other cities, travel agents offer tickets for scheduled flights at substantially **discounted rates** – well below the official fares agreed by *IATA*, the association to which most airlines belong. Airlines prepared to sell off their tickets through these agents have in the past been generally the less reputable ones left with the most unsold seats. But more and more major carriers are cashing in, some albeit as part of a "restricted eligibility" arrangement where the passenger has to be a student, for example, or under a certain age.

BOOKING AND BUYING

The so-called **"bucket shops"** are, almost without exception, respectable travel agents, even if first impressions sometimes indicate otherwise. If you phone around, you quickly get an idea of the set-up by throwing a few destinations at them.

When booking, note whether the agent reserves seats directly with the airline by telephone or on a computer system, or has to go through another agent. Fraud isn't a problem but confusion and delays are common enough. Don't expect to see your ticket until you've paid in full. While many agents have ticketing agreements with certain airlines and can write tickets on the premises, they may have to order some tickets from the nominated "consolidator" of the airline concerned – usually another agent.

Always ask what **refund** you'll get if anything goes wrong and find out how easy it will be to **change your reservation dates** once you've got your ticket. You can sometimes leave a round-trip ticket "open-dated" on its return portion, but in that case you'll have to make a seat reservation yourself with the airline. It's just as easy, and safer, to have a confirmed seat and change the date if necessary (and if seats are available). Note that if you book through a discount agency, you cannot deal direct with the airline on your booking until you have your ticket, though you can always quote them the details and ask them to check the reservation is held under your name. If it's not, don't panic. It will probably be held under the agent's block seat allocation.

Airline "seasons" for West Africa vary considerably but many discounted fares are non-seasonal. They don't vary. Most student and youth fares do have a seasonal structure to tie in with summer and Christmas holiday periods. **Book as far in advance as you can.** Some routes are full to capacity at peak periods, especially Christmas, and disounted seat availability is often snapped up quickly.

FARES

Return fares are generally of three types – short excursions (usually one month), three month excursions and one year (never more). A **one-way** fare (valid a year) is normally half the "yearly" fare. You may be able to fly out to one destination and back from another (an "open jaw"), depending on the airline and the agent's contract. In rare cases, you may also be able to purchase a ticket *back* from West Africa, before you leave – useful if you're travelling out overland. *Balkan Bulgarian Airlines* and *Egyptair* tickets can be bought like this, though in the case of *Egyptair*, the ticket is collected from their office in the city in question. Such arrangements are often surprisingly reliable.

As regards **prices** to West African destinations, you can pay anything from under £400 return to nearly £700. Most discounted return fares fall between £400 and £500. One-ways are rarely less than £200. The cheapest fare to many destinations is often on the Soviet Airline, *Aeroflot*, via Moscow. Many *Aeroflot* schedules, however, only operate once or twice a month and most require a stopover in Moscow (basic hotel at their expense).

For an idea of the saving over the airlines' own fares, make a few calls to their fares departments (see box). Current IATA one month excursion fares in the region go from £744 (Bissau) to £936 (Douala). If you want to try some detective work, ask the airline to give you their consolidators' details. Some are only too happy, others refuse (see box, "The Airlines").

CHARTERS AND NON-SCHEDULED FLIGHTS

From London, the only regular **charter flights** to West Africa are to **The Gambia**, between October and April. The Gambian government isn't disposed to the idea of "flight-only" tourists, so details about taking a holiday in The Gambia that doesn't include pre-paid accommodation don't figure very highly in the **package holiday** brochures. Nevertheless, when flights threaten to take off unfilled, the charter operators (see box, "Packages from the UK", p.8) are keen to sell off the unsold seats. Prices over the last few seasons, for stays of from one to four weeks, have ranged from a last-minute £59 snip to around £300. Whether you fly back or not this isn't bad value. But you'll have to keep checking the situation with the operators – it changes from year to year and even through the season. Promotions are often introduced to clear seats, and these can be really excellent value, even with a hotel included.

From France, alternatives to the scheduled airlines are more promising. Until its demise in 1987, the non-profit-making charity airline **Le Point** offered a wonderfully cheap and laudable service to Ouagadougou, Lomé and Cotonou (plus Bangui in the Central African Republic). Profits were ploughed back into development projects in the countries concerned. Sadly, it perished under the onslaught of the outpriced commercial airlines *UTA* and *Air Afrique*.

Le Point's legacy is three national operations, *Nord-Sud Burkina*, *Nord-Sud Benin* and *Nord-Sud Togo*. Under the wing of adventure travel giant *Uniclam*, these offer four or five flights a month from around £150 one-way and from £250 to £400 return depending on the date and the flight (Ouagadougou is cheapest). Unfortunately, precise details aren't available in advance (these flights operate on a "day of departure" basis) so you need to be based in Paris for a few days at least. Write or phone (**Nord-Sud Découverte/ Espace Afrique** – see p.9) for as much advance information as they can offer.

UK DISCOUNT AGENTS

STA Travel, 74 Old Brompton Rd, London SW7 (☎071 937 9962, autoqueue). Huge range of cities and airlines for West Africa, from 20 UK offices and 120 worldwide. Special fares for students and young people and a specialist Africa Desk at 117 Euston Rd (☎071 465 0486, Telex 25951).

Africa Travel Centre, 4 Medway Court, Leigh St, London WC1H 9QX (☎071 837 3154, Telex 266686, Fax 071 387 1211). Helpful and resourceful.

African Travel System, 6 North End Parade, North End Rd, London W14 (☎071 602 5091). Specialists with particularly good deals on direct flights to Accra and Lagos.

Redcoat Express, Unit 12, Gatwick Metro Centre, Balcombe Rd, Horley, Surrey RH6 9GA (☎0293 774141). Specialists in direct flights to Banjul and Freetown.

Trailfinders, 42–48 Earl's Court Rd, London W8 6EJ (☎071 938 3366). Respected discount flights agency with a convenient range of other services. Some reasonable fares, but not especially geared up for West Africa.

Soliman Travel, 233 Earl's Court Rd, London SW5 (☎071 370 6446). Particularly good on flights via Cairo.

Sam Travel, 14 Broadwick St, London W1V 1FH (☎071 434 9561) and 805–7 Romford Rd London E12 5AN (☎081 478 8911). Specialists in flights via Moscow.

Wexas, 45 Brompton Rd, London SW3 1DE (☎071 589 3315). If you're unable to visit others, this membership-only organisation handles everything competently by post. Detailed brochures and fare and airline information.

PLANNING AHEAD

If you're planning travels in West Africa and are uncertain where to fly in, this rundown of the airports might help to narrow down your choice.

● Some **airports are simply best avoided**. **Lagos** (Nigeria), **Douala** (Cameroon) and **Monrovia** (Liberia) will not make for promising first impressions. All are likely to be swelteringly hot and they are notoriously corrupt. Lagos, after dark, is downright unsafe and the journey to the city by taxi can be unnerving, while Monrovia's airport at Robertsfield is 60km from the city.

● Smaller capitals, naturally enough, have the most agreeable airports. Good candidates include **Banjul** (The Gambia), **Bissau** (Guinea Bissau), **Sal** (Cape Verde), **Bamako** (Mali), **Ouagadougou** (Burkina Faso) and **Niamey** (Niger).

● Among medium-sized capitals, **Abidjan** (Côte d'Ivoire) is well-organised and convenient and **Accra** (Ghana), **Dakar** (Senegal) and **Conakry** (Guinea) aren't bad. **Freetown** airport tends to be fairly shambolic and it's very incoveniently located.

● **Lomé** (Togo) is probably the best all round choice. The airport is modern enough but small and well-run, pretty much unaffected by hassles and chaos and very close to the city. Moreover, **Togo** is a good country to start your travels, whichever direction you're headed. Many nationalities don't need visas here either – another factor to consider before you buy an air ticket (see "Red Tape", p.14).

OVERNIGHT FLIGHTS

An additional factor is the time you will arrive. It's obviously preferable to **arrive by day**, especially in a large city – but, unfortunately, overnight flights to West Africa are in the minority. Most flights arrive in the evening, or at best the late afternoon.

These airlines operate at least **some flights by night**, to arrive in West Africa the next morning:

Abidjan
British Airways, TAP, UTA and *Air Afrique*

Accra
British Airways, Ghana Airways and *Balkan*

Bamako
Air Afrique

Banjul
British Airways

Bissau
Aeroflot

Conakry
Sabena

Cotonou
Aeroflot, UTA and *Air Afrique;*

Dakar
Sabena, Aeroflot, and *Air Afrique;*

Douala
Aeroflot and *UTA;*

Freetown
British Airways, Aeroflot;

Lagos
Sabena, Iberia, UTA, Balkan and *Nigeria Airways;*

Monrovia
British Airways;

Niamey
UTA, Air Afrique;

Nouadhibou
Aeroflot

RESERVATIONS-SPEAK

Apex Advance purchase excursion fare – usually the cheapest return deal an airline will offer to you direct

Charter A flight chartered from an airline by a tour operator to ferry tourists.

Confirmed What your reservation has to be to get a seat (written as "OK" on the ticket), a guarantee in Europe, not always in Africa.

Flight number Every scheduled flight has one, made up of the two-letter airline code and three digits. It's unique to that airline on that route but not specific to the date.

MCO Miscellaneous Charges Order. A refundable receipt for funds held in your name by an airline, no longer of any use in immigration situations where you need an onward ticket.

PTA Passenger Ticket Advice. Pre-payment for a ticket back home to be collected in the city of departure.

Reconfirm What some airlines insist you do direct with them within 48 hours of departure. It's vital to do this in Africa or you'll find your seat bumped. Note that your ticket nearly always remains a valid travel voucher even if you miss your confirmed reservation or lose your seat.

Requested (RQ) A booking which has this status isn't even on the waiting list.

Scheduled A flight operated by the airline to a regular timetable regardless of demand. In Africa sometimes cancelled, diverted or simply unknown.

Stop-over A voluntary stay in a city/country en route to your destination where you would otherwise make a simple connection.

Waitlisted (WL) On a waiting list for cancellations in a particular class, or empty seats from other agents' expired allocations.

Yclass The usual designation for economy class – the cheapest seats.

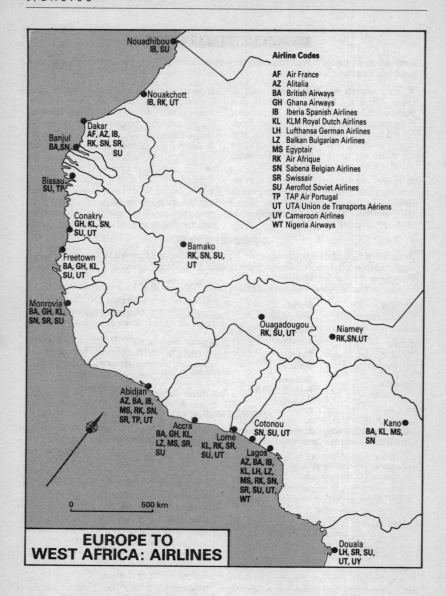

Nouadhibou
IB, SU

Nouakchott
IB, RK, UT

Dakar
AF, AZ, IB,
RK, SN, SR,
SU

Banjul
BA, SN

Bissau
SU, TP

Conakry
GH, KL, SN,
SU, UT

Freetown
BA, GH, KL,
SU, UT

Monrovia
BA, GH, KL,
SN, SR, SU

Bamako
RK, SN, SU,
UT

Ouagadougou
RK, SU, UT

Niamey
RK, SN, UT

Abidjan
AZ, BA, IB,
MS, RK, SN,
SR, TP, UT

Accra
BA, GH, KL,
LZ, MS, SR,
SU

Lomé
KL, RK, SR,
SU, UT

Cotonou
SN, SU, UT

Kano
BA, KL, MS,
SN

Lagos
AZ, BA, IB,
KL, LH, LZ,
MS, RK, SN,
SR, SU, UT,
WT

Douala
LH, SR, SU,
UT, UY

0   500 km

Airline Codes

AF Air France
AZ Alitalia
BA British Airways
GH Ghana Airways
IB Iberia Spanish Airlines
KL KLM Royal Dutch Airlines
LH Lufthansa German Airlines
LZ Balkan Bulgarian Airlines
MS Egyptair
RK Air Afrique
SN Sabena Belgian Airlines
SR Swissair
SU Aeroflot Soviet Airlines
TP TAP Air Portugal
UT UTA Union de Transports Aériens
UY Cameroon Airlines
WT Nigeria Airways

EUROPE TO
WEST AFRICA: AIRLINES

THE AIRLINES

Check with the airlines for schedules and full fares. Because they persist in discounting while publicly agreeing not to, airlines don't like to be publicly associated with particular agents. So they don't as a rule quote discounted fares but may refer you to their "consolidator" agent. Such tie-ups are not specified here but addresses for these agents are given in the "Agents" box. Phone around and you'll quickly learn what's what.

Aeroflot (SU), 70 Piccadilly, London W1 (☎071 355 2233). Heavily discounted one year fares available on most of their routes through many bucket shops.

Air Afrique (RK), c/o *UTA*, 177 Piccadilly London W1V 9DE (☎071 629 6114). The multinational francophone African airline, run by an Abidjan-based consortium. Flights originate in Paris. No discounts available ex-London.

Air Algérioe (AH) 10 Baker St, London W1M 1DA (☎071 487 5709).

Air France (AF), 158 New Bond St, London, W1 (☎071 499 9511). Flights to Dakar only, via Paris. Discounted seats available.

Alitalia (AZ), 205 Holland Park Ave, London W11 (☎071 602 7111). Via Rome. Rarely discounted.

Balkan Bulgarian Airlines (LZ), 322 Regent St, London W1 (☎071 637 7637). Overnight flights to Accra and Lagos via Sofia. Not a pleasant journey but reliable enough and among the cheapest fares. Student fares too.

British Airways (BA), shop at 156 Regent St, London W1 (central res. ☎081 897 4000). Includes the network of the now-defunct *British Caledonian*. Good student fares available through selected agents. Specially discounted (and unrestricted) fares have also recently been on offer.

Cameroon Airlines (UY), 44 Conduit St, London W1R 9FB (☎071 734 7676). Discounted fares to Douala available through agents.

Egyptair (MS), 31 Piccadilly, London W1 (☎071 734 2395/437 6426). Flights to Abidjan, Accra, Lagos and Kano via Cairo (with an overnight at the airline's expense). Extended stop-overs in Cairo are possible, which makes this an interesting alternative. Discounted fares are widely available.

Ghana Airways (GH), 12 Old Bond St, London W1 (☎071 499 0201). Twice-weeekly flights to Accra (good fares from the airline), plus an unusual weekly run between Las Palmas and Accra, via Monrovia, Freetown and Conakry (no discounts on that from the UK, but possibly in the Canaries). Increasingly reliable.

Iberia (IB), 29 Glasshouse St, London W1 (☎071 437 5622). Flights via Madrid to Abidjan, Dakar and Lagos (the latter continuing to Malabo, Equatorial Guinea), but only Lagos offered through the discount agencies. Also flies from the Canary Islands to Nouadhibou and Nouakchott.

KLM Royal Dutch Airlines (KL), Time Life Building, New Bond St, London W1 (☎081 568 9144). Daytime flights only, via Amsterdam, out of Belfast, Birmingham and Manchester as well as London. One of the best airlines. Many agents offer discounted excursion fares. One or two have longer validities, and "open jaws", available at very competitive prices.

Lufthansa German Airlines (LH), 28 Piccadilly, London W1 (☎071 488 0322). Flights to Lagos and Douala via Frankfurt. Rarely discounted.

Nigeria Airways (WT), 12 Conduit St, London W1 (☎071 629 3717). Overnight flights direct to Lagos, but phenomenally unreliable and unaccountable. Occasionally good discounted fares.

Sabena Belgian Airlines (SN), 36 Piccadilly, London W1 (☎071 437 6950). Flights via Brussels include some less common destinations (Bamako and Niamey, for example). Generally full fare only, but some discounted yearly fares.

Swissair (SR), Swiss Centre, 10 Wardour St, London W1 (☎071 439 4144). Daytime flights only, via Zurich and Geneva. Slightly discounted one month excursion fares available.

TAP Air Portugal (TP), 38-44 Gillingham St, London SW1 (☎071 828 0262). Via Lisbon to Bissau, Sal and Abidjan. Their "discounted" excursion fares are remarkably expensive.

UTA Union de Transports Aériens (UT), 177 Piccadilly, London W1V 9DE (☎071 493 4881). A French carrier, all flights originate in Paris. *UTA* has the best West African coverage and a new charter service to Agadez, Niger. They offer "Challenge" fares which have slightly restricted eligibility. Ask agents for details.

PACKAGES FROM THE UK

The Gambia is the best-known (almost the only) West African destination from Britain. Most high street travel agents will have a fair choice of brochures to leaf through and if it's a shortish winter holiday you're looking for (7, 14, 21 or 28 days only), with guaranteed sun and heat, and a low-key African atmosphere that's by no means over-exploited, The Gambia can be thoroughly enjoyable. Don't go too early in the season (good chance of rain), nor too late (chokingly dry and dusty). Take a meals-included option (you'll spend a lot more otherwise, even if you save on the odd night out) and read the brochures carefully. The final cost of packages can vary remarkably. There's almost always a spate of good, last-minute offers available around Easter if you, or the travel agent, call to check. And note, there's a real distinction between the handful of hotels near Banjul at the mouth of the Gambia river, and the better feel and facilities on the west-facing Atlantic coast. Full details in the Gambia chapter.

● Currently, the only UK package alternatives are to **Senegal's Cap Skiring** coast (with flights into Banjul) or to **Sierra Leone**. The latter is a particularly appealing proposition – or would be if the facilities on the wonderful Freetown peninsula were more reliable. Sierra Leone was offered a few years ago *Kuoni* and then dropped. Hopefully the new operators will have more luck.

●The best "package" news, though not really a package, is the highly recommended **Ghana homestay** programme operated by *Insight Travel*, 6 Horton Rd, Garstang, Preston, Lancs, PR3 1JY (09952 6095).

THE GAMBIA

Serenity, 17 Bell St, Romsey, Hampshire, SO51 8GY (☎0794 514646). Gambia specialists with some offbeat hotels and off-season offers. Excellent flight only and "basic accommodation" deals. Long-stay offers too.

Vacations for Wildlife Ltd, 2 Elizabeth Cottage, Mead Lane, Bognor Regis, Sussex, BO22 8AB. A new set-up specialising in no frills, local stay, bird-watching holidays in The Gambia. Flexible and good value.

Kuoni, Kuoni House, Dorking, Surrey, FH5 4AZ (☎0306 885 717/0306 740 500) is up at the top end of the market with one week Gambia packages from around £450. They also do a more unusual "Bird Watcher's Safari" up-river by yacht (about £650).

Select Holidays, Centurion House, Hertford, SG14 1BH (☎0992 554144). Summer and winter holidays. Some good value summer offers.

Thomson, Greater London House, Hampstead Road, London NW1 7SD (☎071 387 8484). Less beating about the bush, one week Gambia holidays from around £350. Flight-only deals up to 28 days.

Horizon, Broadway, Edgbaston Five Ways, Birmingham B15 1BB (☎081 200 8733 or 021 632 6282). Much the same as *Thomson*, and owned by them, but a shade cheaper. For flight only (max. 14 days) check their *Airsavers* brochure.

Intasun, Intasun House, Cromwell Ave, Bromley, Kent BR2 9AQ (☎081 290 1900). Good prices to The Gambia, on a B&B basis, and competitive four-week deals.

Hayes and Jarvis, 200 Sloane St, London SW1X 9QV (☎071 245 1051). An upmarket image, over-priced for The Gambia. Features some off-season deals.

THE GAMBIA AND SENEGAL

Enterprise, Groundstar House, London Road, Crawley, West Sussex RH10 2TB (☎0293 517866, Telex 87891, Fax 0293 25225) A good choice of Gambian hotels at competetive prices. Senegal packages are good value. There's also a 2-week Gambia and Casamance "River Trip" – under £700.

Sunmed, Groundstar House, London Road, Crawley, West Sussex RH10 2TB (☎0293 561444, Telex and Fax as *Enterprise*). Much the same as *Enterprise* – both are owned by *Redwing Holidays* – but slightly pricier.

SIERRA LEONE

Tana Travel, 2 Ely St, Stratford-upon-Avon, Warwickshire, CV37 6LW (☎0789 414400, Telex 31430). Established operator in a new country. Prices from £470 for a week's B&B at the *Cape Sierra Hotel* up to £900 for 10 nights HB at the *Africana Tokey Village*.

Tradewinds Faraway, 81–83 Fulham High St, London SW6 3JP (☎071 731 8000, Telex 21264, Fax 071 736 9371). In West Africa offers a limited choice of hotels in Sierra Leone, at substantially higher rates than *Tana Travel*.

FRENCH TOUR OPERATORS AND TICKET AGENTS

If you're happy making travel arrangements in the francophone environment, then you may find it's worth a trip to Paris. The variety of outlets and options far exceeds anywhere else in Europe.

Airtour Afrique, 29 rue du Colisée, 75008, Paris (☎42 25 71 69). The holiday wing of *Air Afrique* with packages to francophone West Africa from around FF5000 for a week.

Club 7L Afrique, 3 rue Mandar, 75002, Paris (☎42 21 15 30). Bucket shop with some good prices on scheduled airlines (e.g. Dakar via Madrid from just over FF3000).

Club Méditerranée, 106–8 Brompton Rd, London SW3 1LJ (☎071 581 1161, Telex 299221, Fax 071 581 4769). West African holiday camps in Senegal (Cap Vert, Cap Skiring) and Côte d'Ivoire (Assinie). Only hedonists need apply.

Déserts, 6–8 rue Quincampoix, 75004, Paris (☎48 04 88 40, Telex 212 395). "You don't "do" the desert, it does you . . ." they say. Specialists offering Algeria, Niger and Mali (for example 28 days by camel from Tamanrasset to Illizi doing you at just under FF1000 per day . . .). Lesser journeys somewhat cheaper; some have specialist themes – astronomy, prehistory, natural history.

Explorator, 16 place de la Madeleine, 75008, Paris (☎42 66 66 24). Expensive and exotic overland adventures in Algeria, Niger, Mali and Mauritania. Competently organised.

Moto-contact Evasion, 26 route de Grasse, 06800 Cagnes-sur-mer, France (☎93 22 50 31). Escorted motorbiking across the Sahara and in the hinterland of San Pedro, Côte d'Ivoire.

Nord-Sud Découverte/ Espace Afrique, at a branch of *Uniclam*, 54 rue des Ecoles, 75005, Paris (☎46 34 21 17, Telex 204 488, Fax 46 33 55 96). *Le*

Point lives on. Scheduled and non-scheduled return flights;to Dakar from FF2000, to Ouagadougou from around FF2500, and to Abidjan, Bamako or Cotonou from about FF3000. Cheapest one-way (very limited availability) is to Dakar from FF1000.

Nouvelles Frontières, 87 blvd de Grenelle, 75738, Paris (☎47 73 05 68); also UK office, 1–2 Hanover St, London W1 (☎071 629 7772). The biggest independent travel organisation in France with jolly impressive catalogues. In West Africa they specialise in 1–4 week excursions on scheduled airlines (most from FF3000–4000) plus Dakar charters from FF2000. Hotel nights, car hire and tours available off the peg.

Terres d'Aventure, 16 rue St Victor, 75005, Paris (☎43 29 94 50, Telex 201 545, Fax 43 29 96 31). Walking trips in Algeria, Niger, Mali and Mauritania. Wide variety of good value treks in southern Algeria (from around FF8000 for 10 days, including a week's walking, or FF12,000 for twice as long).

Uniclam, 63 rue Monsieur-le-Prince, 75006, Paris (☎43 29 12 36). Innovative operator/agents offering flights and packages in Senegal and The Gambia, Sierra Leone, Cameroon, Benin, Togo and Guinea-Bissau. Mountain-biking in Senegal's Basse Casamance (from FF6000 all in), sailing through the Bijagos islands. Charter operators to Banjul. Cheap flights to Guinea-Bissau and Cape Verde. Agents for *Nord-Sud Burkina*. Half-price seats on *Air Burkina* flights ex-Ouagadougou. Moped hire in Ouagadougou (FF300 per week).

FLIGHTS FROM AUSTRALIA AND NEW ZEALAND

You'll have the most options if you **fly first to Europe**, and then connect with a flight to West Africa, though you could fly to **Cairo** and then on to Kano, Lagos, Accra or Abidjan on *Egyptair*.

The only possible **"direct" flight from Australia** or New Zealand to Africa incorporates the Monday and Thursday flights on *Qantas/Air Zimbabwe* from Sydney and Perth to **Harare**, Zimbabwe. There you can connect (after a suitable rest) with one of the two flights from Zimbabwe to West Africa – *Balkan Air's* Sunday night departure for **Lagos**, en route to Sofia and London, or *Ghana Airways'* Monday night flight (it doesn't connect wth the incoming flight from

Australia) to Lagos and Accra. If you'd prefer to tie in your destinations with travels in East Africa, read on.

FLIGHTS FROM NORTH, EAST AND SOUTHERN AFRICA

From **East Africa**, **Nairobi** is the natural hub for flights, though even here, where discount ticket agents thrive, special fares to West Africa, apart from the odd Apex, are unknown. There are direct flights on *Ethiopian Airlines* to Abidjan (shared with *Air Afrique*), Accra, Douala, Lagos and Monrovia, and also – with a change of planes in Addis Ababa – to Bamako, Dakar and Ouagadougou. *Cameroon Airlines* runs flights twice a week between Douala and Nairobi.

From **central southern Africa**, flights from Harare to Lagos and Accra, and Lusaka to Monrovia (see "Flights from Australia" above) are the only direct connections. There are flights from Harare to Nairobi four times a week on *Air Zimbabwe* and *Kenya Airways* – fare about £160.

If you're in **North Africa**, it seems a shame not to traverse the Sahara and experience the gradual shift into West Africa. But if you're pressed for time, there are direct flights **from Casablanca** to Abidjan, Bamako, Conakry, Dakar, Lomé, Nouakchott and – once a month – Bissau; **from Algiers** to Bamako, Dakar, Nouakchott and Ouagadougou; and **from Tunis** to Dakar. Prices, even one-way, seem high, from around £200 to £350 on these routes, and you'd be lucky to find anything discounted.

VIA THE CANARIES

One off-beat route to West Africa is **via the Canary Islands** (which are part of Spain and the European Community). You can pick up exceptionally cheap last-minute **package holidays to Gran Canaria**, then cancel, or possibly sell off, your seat back to Britain. Going on from Las Palmas on Gran Canaria, the shortest (and cheapest) flight to West Africa is to **Nouadhibou** in Mauritania (twice weekly on *Iberia/Air Mauritanie*, around £160 one way). *Ghana Airways* flies Las Palmas–Conakry–Freetown–Monrovia–Accra every Thursday (stop-overs not possible) and *Air Afrique* and *Iberia* fly three times a week to Dakar (some £280).

If you're bent on trying the **coastal trans-Sahara route** though Moroccan-held Western Sahara (which some Moroccan tourist offices seem to think is open through to Mauritania) then the Canary Islands also provide an escape route to continue your journey without having to go back over 1000km to Casablanca if the *piste* turns out to be mined or otherwise impassable. *Royal Air Maroc* flies from Layoune to Las Palmas, every Wednesday, Friday and Sunday, for about £60

(though added to the Las Palmas–Nouadhibou fare this is more expensive than a flight straight from Casablanca to Nouakchott at around £200).

WEST AFRICA BY FREIGHTER

Taking **a berth on a cargo ship** to "the Coast" is not quite history. *Polish Ocean Lines/Gdynia American Shipping Lines* (238 City Road, London EC1V 2QL, ☎071 259 3389) run from Hamburg to Antwerp, Rotterdam, Dunkirk, Rouen, Las Palmas, Dakar, Banjul, Freetown, Monrovia, Abidjan, Tema, Lagos, Apapa, Douala and Pointe Noire and back again every ten days or so (total voyage around 80 days). One-way fares start from £420 single/£764 twin. *The Grimaldi Line* (Eagle House, 109/110 Jermyn St, London SW1Y 6ES, ☎071 930 5683) operates brand new Italian container ships (much bigger and specifically designed with passengers in mind, even with swimming pools!) from Tilbury to Hamburg, Rotterdam, Dakar (12 days), Conakry, Monrovia, Tema, Lomé, Lagos, Douala (20 days), Rio de Janeiro, Santos, Paranagua and back across the Atlantic to Tilbury. One-way fares, Europe to West Africa start at £370 sharing a four-berth inside cabin (£490 sharing twin). Car tarifs are £300 or £390 and motorbikes £120. Departures are every 3–4 weeks. Brochures and bookings through *Weider Travel*, Charing Cross Shopping Concourse, The Strand, London WC2N 4HZ (☎071 836 6363).

OVERLAND

Travelling overland to West Africa is the best way to get there if you want to become fully immersed in the identities and landscapes of the region. There's a resounding satisfaction in **crossing the Sahara** which flying to a West African airport can't provide. As you finally arrive on the far side of the sea of sand and rock, the first sensations of another world are ones that endure.

TRANS-SAHARA ROUTES

The two main routes across the Sahara are covered in detail in Chapter One. The **western route** (Adrar–Gao) connects Algeria with Mali; the **eastern route** (Tamanrasset–Agadez) links Algeria with Niger. Two routes much **further to the west**, one from Algeria through Tindouf to Mauritania, and the coastal one from Morocco, through Western Sahara to Mauritania, both remain of highly doubtful status until the plight of the Saharawi refugees and the war between Polisario and Morocco is settled. For adventurous and persistent drivers the *possibility* of using these routes still exists. If you're setting off without your own wheels however you may as well forget them. There's more information in Chapter five: Mauritania. Keep your ear to the ground.

WEST AFRICA AND EUROPE

If you're setting off on extensive travels, the **best time to leave** is at the end of the European summer. Especially if you plan to hitch and use public transport, you should aim to be in North Africa in September and across the Sahara in October. Throughout most of the region, this gives you at least six months before you can realistically expect to be rained upon.

The practical information at the beginning of each country section has details on overland **arrival** *from that country's neighbours, including transport availability, road conditions and the kind of treatment you might expect from border officials. As a general rule, borders close at dusk and often on public holidays. Very few are open 24 hours.*

DRIVING YOURSELF

Crossing the Sahara isn't a difficult feat in itself. Many people set off with more or less unmodified road vehicles. Even a *Citröen 2CV* can make it if you're prepared to go slowly, take care as you drive and let it cool – and its physical lightness can be a positive advantage. But all motorised travellers (whether on two, four or six wheels) agree that the comfort and independence of their **own vehicle** is a mixed blessing. It insulates you from the life of Africa, it's a permanent security headache, especially in towns, and it says one thing – money – to everyone you meet along the way, whether in uniform or not. You can feel like a travelling circus after a few weeks of this. Taking account of fuel, maintenance and insurance, it is a fairly expensive business, too. And unless you have someone aboard who knows the vehicle inside out (and even then) any serious breakdown can be immensely tedious and costly.

The outstanding **advantages** of taking your own vehicle are that you can get off the beaten track (assuming the vehicle is sturdy enough) and visit areas that see a local vehicle only once in a toddler's lifetime. To a great extent, you can avoid towns and cities, or at least avoid staying overnight in them, by driving out into the wilderness and camping. And you can thus avoid the expense of hotels and restaurants if you really want to.

If you decide to drive, one consideration can't be stressed enough – give yourself **time**. Rushing around in Africa is a bad enough idea using local transport. But to try to drive yourself with a fixed number of days and weeks is to court disaster. Allow a month, at the very least, to get from the Mediterranean to the Atlantic. It's simply not worth the work, in any case, to rush through at a breakneck pace.

If you intend to **sell your vehicle** in West Africa, your best investment would be a three-year old *Peugeot 504 familliale* station wagon – semi-automatic, petrol engine and of course left hand drive. Most end up in service as *taxis brousse*. The weekly bring-and-buy car sale in Utrecht, Netherlands, is a good place to find one. The best West African countries in which to sell vary depending on current import laws and economic conditions. Togo has been a straightforward market for many years.

Further **details and checklists for drivers** are given on p.79.

HITCHING AND USING LOCAL TRANSPORT

If you're going to travel **under your own steam**, it's worth considering a cheap, one-way flight to Morocco or Tunisia (under £100) to get started. Bearing in mind the possible cost of even a few days travel through Europe (plus ferry fares across the channel and Mediterranean) this can be a positive saving. Unfortunately there are no cheap flights direct to Algeria (£200 one way economy class).

Of course, you can do it the hard way. Not a few Timbuktu-bound travellers have begun the trip **hitching** to a channel port for the crossing to France and the unpredictable haul through Italy or Spain to North Africa. Of the **Mediterranean ferries**, **Algeciras** is the cheapest and easiest embarkation point for **Morocco** with several ferries a day to Tangier, around £15, and to the Spanish enclave of Ceuta on the Moroccan coast. Ferries from **Sicily to Tunisia** cost around £30.

If you camp, and have the stamina to keep hitching, there's no reason you shouldn't get to the Algerian side of the Sahara at remarkably little cost. The ease of hitching in North Africa compensates for the common misery of the roadside in southern Europe. Morocco is very cheap, Algeria expensive and Tunisia moderate. Alternatively, take the ferry from Sète or Marseille in France. Note there are *Rough Guides* to France, Spain, Italy, Sicily, Tunisia and Morocco – invaluable travelling companions and marketable commodities as you move on!

The empty section of the **Sahara** will usually cost you to cross. Though motorised travellers sometimes have room for hitchers, vehicles are generally packed to the gills. The usual transport is in the back of an Algerian or West African lorry for two or three days, maybe sharing with camels and petrol drums. More details in Part Two.

UK-BASED OVERLAND TOUR OPERATORS

The "overland tour" catch-all covers most of the organised holidays that don't feel like packages. Not all of them are *overland* the entire way. The fly out, tour around by truck, fly back option is an increasingly popular one. Note that operators sometimes run trips "in association" with each other. The number of trips offered each year is actually quite small.

If you're interested in one of the more inexpensive (sometimes regrettably one-off) expedition companies that advertise in the classified columns, it's worth paying them a visit. It seems unfair to throw blanket disapproval over them, but even more unfair on you if things go disastrously wrong. They're often just a private trip hoping to minimise costs by taking others. Scrutinising their blurb gives a good indication of their probable preparedness and real know-how. And if the blurb looks cheap or hasty, forget it.

Africa Travel Centre, 4 Medway Court, Leigh St, London WC1H 9QX (☎071 387 1211, Telex 266686, Fax 071 837 3154). Offers an unusual 3 week trip through Ghana, Togo and Benin.

Dragoman, 10 Riverside, Framlingham, Suffolk (☎0728 724124). Personal and creative operators with notably good trucks and competitive prices. Regular trans-African departures include passage through Mali, Côte d'Ivoire, Ghana and Togo.

Encounter Overland, 267 Old Brompton Rd, London W5 (☎071 370 6951). Specialists in long trips; several pass through Algeria and Niger.

Exodus Expeditions, 100 Wandsworth High St, London SW18 (☎081 870 0151). Runs several trips a year between Nairobi and London via eastern parts of West Africa.

Explore Worldwide, 7 High St, Aldershot, Hampshire, GU11 1BH (☎0252 319448, Telex 858954, Fax 0252 343170). Highly respected small groups operator; offers southern Algeria expeditions.

Guerba Expeditions, 101 Eden Vale Rd, Westbury, Wiltshire BA13 3QX (☎0373 826611, Telex 449831). The acknowledged African experts, running a four-week trans-Sahara trip (Tunis-Lomé), several trips in West Africa and London to Nairobi journeys via more of the West African region than most.

Tracks Africa, 12 Abingdon Rd, London W8 6AF (☎071 937 3028-30). Offers a London to Nairobi (or vice versa) trip via West Africa.

Truck Africa, Field House, Hockering Rd, Woking, Surrey GU22 7HJ (☎04862 61357). Small operator offering trans-Africa trips via a large part of West Africa.

African Trails, Glendower, Furzefield Chase, Dormans Park, West Sussex RH19 2LY (☎034287 541). Another small outfit, specialising in running London–Zimbabwe trips via Burkina Faso and Nigeria.

CYCLING IN WEST AFRICA

The invention of the **mountainbike** opened a new chapter in African travel. On condition that you have enough **time** (the most precious commodity), it's quite feasible to consider cycling through Europe in the summer, down through North Africa in the autumn, loading your machine aboard a lorry for the hardest part of the Sahara crossing and then cycling where your fancy takes you through the dry season. It's not necessary to be super-fit or to have done anything more than cycle to the shops before.

It is of course possible to take a sturdy touring bike, or even use a locally bought roadster. A tourer is much faster on the main roads and a fit cyclist could expect to cover 120km a day or more. But you're likely to suffer more from broken spokes and punctures at unexpected potholes

and you're much less free to leave the highways. Some routes and regions for which a mountainbike is ideal are beyond the scope of other bikes.

More cycling practicalities are detailed in "Getting Around" on p.40. If you still need convincing, write to *Bicycle Africa*, 4247, 135th Place Southeast, Bellevue, Washington 98006 USA (☎(206) 746 1028) for details of their escorted cycle tours.

BIKES BY AIR

If your time is limited, you can **fly your bike** to West Africa. If you plan to do this without paying excess baggage charges, you should do everything to facilitate your transit from check-in desk to plane: write in advance to the ground operations manager of the airline, pack as many heavy items into your hand luggage as possible and arrive several hours before the flight to get to know the check-in staff. It's rare that you'll be obliged to pay.

It's much harder, as a rule, to avoid excess fees on charter flights. Let them know in advance and plead your case. The 20kg weight allowance, which your bike and luggage is likely to exceed, is a notional figure with no bearing on air safety, used to extract more profit from the passengers.

Few airlines will insist your bike be boxed or bagged. But it's best to turn the handlebars into the frame and tie them down, invert the pedals and deflate the tyres. Probably the most helpful airline for bikes (so long as you don't take them for granted) is *KLM*. But which airport to choose for a flight home, bike and all, is a difficult matter. Lomé in Togo seems the safest bet.

RED TAPE AND VISAS

It may be obvious, but it's still worth stating: check that your passport is current. It must be a full ten-year passport, and it should remain valid for at least six months beyond the end of your travels. Some West African countries will not allow you in with less. Allow at least one blank page per country to be visited.

Stamps indicating visits to Israel or South Africa are reason to get a new passport, though some countries (most likely the coastal states between The Gambia and Benin) will overlook Israeli stamps. Evidence of any sort that might be used to deduce that you've been in South Africa can lead to problems. If your passport gives an occupation, student, teacher or business person is best. Avoid journalist, photographer and anything similar that might be misconstrued.

GETTING VISAS BEFORE YOU LEAVE

If you're flying out to a limited number of countries on a short trip, you're best advised to get **visas** in advance. Few visas remain valid beyond three months, however, and if you'll be away for longer you'll have to procure them at the respective embassies in West Africa.

Visa regulations in West Africa are notoriously fickle and hard to pin down. While there are few rules that can't be broken in an emergency, cases do occur – too often – of people sent back hundreds of kilometres for want of a stamp. It pays to plan ahead if you're travelling extensively.

It's always important to bear in mind also that a visa only constitutes "permission to apply to enter". This isn't mere pedantry. You can be turned away despite having a visa (for arriving on a one-way ticket, for example, in the case of Cameroon) and the length of **validity** of a visa may have no connection with how long you're allowed to **stay** in the country when you arrive. It's almost always possible to **extend** a first stay, but in several countries it can be a serious issue if you overstay without extending.

There seems to be little sense to the who-does and who-doesn't of **visa requirements** (see table). The French get off lightly, with visa-less entry to most of the thirteen francophone ex-colonies. Italians and West Germans have an even easier time. Britain's relations with the five anglophone ex-colonies are less easy-going and, of these, British passport holders are visa-exempt only for The Gambia. Six countries – **Cape Verde, Guinea-Bissau, Guinea, Sierra Leone, Liberia** and **Nigeria** – require all non-West Africans to have visas.

VISA CHECKLIST

The table shows which nationalities from the main countries of Western Europe, North America, Australasia and Japan require visas (✔) and which don't (blank). Further details are given under the "Red Tape" sections in each country's chapter.

	Britain	Eire	France	West Germany	Bene-lux	Scandi-navia	Italy	Spain	Switz-erland	Japan	Canada	USA	Australia–NZ
Morocco					✔								
Algeria	✔	✔	✔	✔	✔					✔	✔	✔	✔
Tunisia					✔								✔
Niger		✔						✔	✔	✔	✔	✔	✔
Mali	✔	✔		✔	✔	✔	✔	✔	✔	✔	✔	✔	✔
Burkina Faso	✔	✔	✔			✔		✔	✔	✔	✔	✔	✔
Mauritania	✔	✔		✔	✔	✔		✔	✔	✔	✔	✔	✔
Senegal					✔	1		✔	✔	✔	✔	✔	✔
The Gambia			✔							✔		✔	
Cape Verde	✔	✔	✔	✔	✔	✔	✔	✔	✔	✔	✔	✔	✔
Guinea-Bissau	✔	✔	✔	✔	✔	✔	✔	✔	✔	✔	✔	✔	✔
Guinea	✔	✔	✔	✔	✔	✔	✔	✔	✔	✔	✔	✔	✔
Sierra Leone	✔	✔	✔	✔	✔	✔	✔	✔	✔	✔	✔	✔	✔
Liberia	✔	✔	✔	✔	✔	✔	✔	✔	✔	✔	✔	✔	✔
Côte d'Ivoire					✔			✔	✔	✔	✔	✔	✔
Ghana	✔	✔	✔	✔				✔	✔	✔	✔	✔	✔
Togo						2		✔	✔	✔	✔	✔	✔
Benin	✔	✔			✔	3		✔	✔	✔	✔	✔	✔
Nigeria	✔	✔	✔	✔	✔	✔	✔	✔	✔	✔	✔	✔	✔
Cameroon	✔	✔		✔	✔	✔		✔	✔	✔	✔	✔	✔

(1) Denmark: visa not required (2) visas not required except Finland (3) Denmark and Sweden: visa not required

To get a visa in your home country you'll fairly often be asked to provide evidence of a return air ticket and occasionally show an invitation or a covering letter stating the purpose of your trip. Tourist visas and business visas are always distinct. The latter usually require a letter from your company and often a letter from an African contact. It's always worth asking for a **multiple entry visa** (which often costs more). Should you need to go back from a neighbouring country it saves a lot of hassle.

Overlanders who need visas for **Algeria** should get it from the embassy of their home country if one exists. Algerian embassies in Africa often refuse visas to non-residents.

VISA SERVICES

If you're in a hurry, need a visa for a country which doesn't have a representative in your home country, or anticipate a hassle getting it, it may be worth using a commercial **visa service**. These have application forms and set fees. You sign the forms and post them your passport and they do the legwork. If you're flying straight into a country you may have little choice, since personal applications abroad by post can take several months to process.

Visaservice, 2 Northdown St, King's Cross, London N1 9BG (☎071 833 2709, Fax 071 833 1857). One of the largest visa agents. They charge £10 for the first and £7 for each subsequent visa, plus visa fees. If your passport has to be sent abroad you also pay courier fees (£50) — or registered post (£3) for a less speedy delivery.

Thames Consular Services, 363 Chiswick High Rd, London W4 4HS (☎081 995 2492). Offers a slightly more expensive, but more personal service.

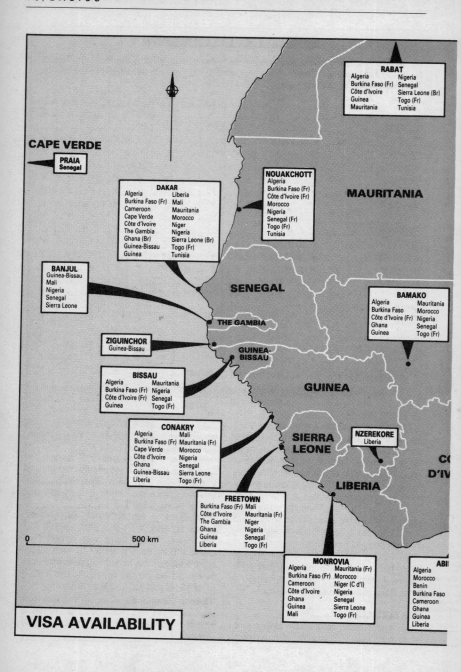

RABAT

Algeria	Nigeria
Burkina Faso (Fr)	Senegal
Côte d'Ivoire	Sierra Leone (Br)
Guinea	Togo (Fr)
Mauritania	Tunisia

CAPE VERDE

PRAIA
Senegal

MAURITANIA

NOUAKCHOTT
Algeria
Burkina Faso (Fr)
Côte d'Ivoire (Fr)
Morocco
Nigeria
Senegal (Fr)
Togo (Fr)
Tunisia

DAKAR

Algeria	Liberia
Burkina Faso (Fr)	Mali
Cameroon	Mauritania
Cape Verde	Morocco
Côte d'Ivoire	Niger
The Gambia	Nigeria
Ghana (Br)	Sierra Leone (Br)
Guinea-Bissau	Togo (Fr)
Guinea	Tunisia

BANJUL
Guinea-Bissau
Mali
Nigeria
Senegal
Sierra Leone

SENEGAL

BAMAKO

Algeria	Mauritania
Burkina Faso	Morocco
Côte d'Ivoire (Fr)	Nigeria
Ghana	Senegal
Guinea	Togo (Fr)

THE GAMBIA

ZIGUINCHOR
Guinea-Bissau

GUINEA-BISSAU

BISSAU

Algeria	Mauritania
Burkina Faso (Fr)	Nigeria
Côte d'Ivoire (Fr)	Senegal
Guinea	Togo (Fr)

GUINEA

CONAKRY

Algeria	Mali
Burkina Faso (Fr)	Mauritania (Fr)
Cape Verde	Morocco
Côte d'Ivoire	Nigeria
Ghana	Senegal
Guinea-Bissau	Sierra Leone
Liberia	Togo (Fr)

SIERRA LEONE

NZEREKORE
Liberia

CÔTE D'IV

LIBERIA

0   500 km

FREETOWN

Burkina Faso (Fr)	Mali
Côte d'Ivoire	Mauritania (Fr)
The Gambia	Niger
Ghana	Nigeria
Guinea	Senegal
Liberia	Togo (Fr)

MONROVIA

Algeria	Mauritania (Fr)
Burkina Faso (Fr)	Morocco
Cameroon	Niger (C d'I)
Côte d'Ivoire	Nigeria
Ghana	Senegal
Guinea	Sierra Leone
Mali	Togo (Fr)

ABI
Algeria
Morocco
Benin
Burkina Faso
Cameroon
Ghana
Guinea
Liberia

VISA AVAILABILITY

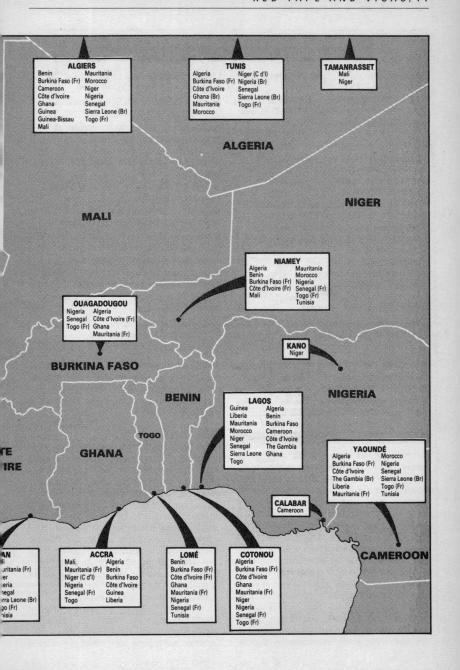

ALGIERS

Benin	Mauritania
Burkina Faso (Fr)	Morocco
Cameroon	Niger
Côte d'Ivoire	Nigeria
Ghana	Senegal
Guinea	Sierra Leone (Br)
Guinea-Bissau	Togo (Fr)
Mali	

TUNIS

Algeria	Niger (C d'I)
Burkina Faso (Fr)	Nigeria (Br)
Côte d'Ivoire	Senegal
Ghana (Br)	Sierra Leone (Br)
Mauritania	Togo (Fr)
Morocco	

TAMANRASSET

Mali
Niger

ALGERIA

NIGER

MALI

NIAMEY

Algeria	Mauritania
Benin	Morocco
Burkina Faso (Fr)	Nigeria
Côte d'Ivoire (Fr)	Senegal (Fr)
Mali	Togo (Fr)
	Tunisia

OUAGADOUGOU

Nigeria	Algeria
Senegal	Côte d'Ivoire (Fr)
Togo (Fr)	Ghana
	Mauritania (Fr)

KANO
Niger

BURKINA FASO

BENIN

NIGERIA

LAGOS

Guinea	Algeria
Liberia	Benin
Mauritania	Burkina Faso
Morocco	Cameroon
Niger	Côte d'Ivoire
Senegal	The Gambia
Sierra Leone	Ghana
Togo	

YAOUNDÉ

Algeria	Morocco
Burkina Faso (Fr)	Nigeria
Côte d'Ivoire	Senegal
The Gambia (Br)	Sierra Leone (Br)
Liberia	Togo (Fr)
Mauritania (Fr)	Tunisia

TOGO

GHANA

CALABAR
Cameroon

CAMEROON

ACCRA

Mali	Algeria
Mauritania (Fr)	Benin
Niger (C d'I)	Burkina Faso
Nigeria	Côte d'Ivoire
Senegal (Fr)	Guinea
Togo	Liberia

LOMÉ

Benin
Burkina Faso (Fr)
Côte d'Ivoire (Fr)
Ghana
Mauritania (Fr)
Nigeria
Senegal (Fr)
Tunisia

COTONOU

Algeria
Burkina Faso (Fr)
Côte d'Ivoire
Ghana
Mauritania (Fr)
Niger
Nigeria
Senegal (Fr)
Togo (Fr)

EMBASSIES, HIGH COMMISSIONS AND CONSULATES IN THE UK AND EIRE

Algeria 54 Holland Park, London W11 (☎071 221 7800), 9.30am–12.30.

Benin 125–129 High St, Edgware, Middlesex HA8 7HS (☎081 951 1234, telex 24620), 10–12.30, 2–5.

Burkina Faso 150 Buckingham Palace Rd, London SW1W 9TR (☎071 730 8141, telex 296420), 9am–1pm, 2–5pm. Multiple entry visa, immediate issue.

Cameroon 84 Holland Park, London W11 3SB (☎071 727 0771-4, Telex 25167), 09.30–12.30 for visa application, noon–4pm for visa collection. Return ticket required.

Côte d'Ivoire 2 Upper Belgrave St, London SW1X 8BJ (☎071 235 6991, telex 23906), 9–12, 1–4.

The Gambia 57 Kensington Court, London W8 5DG (☎071 937 9618, telex 23229), 9.30am–5pm (closes 1pm Fri).

Guinea-Bissau 8 Palace Gate, London SW8 4RP (☎071 589 5253). 3 months visas in 24 hrs.

Ghana 13 Belgrave Square, London SW1X 8PR, (☎071 235 4142, telex 28827), 9.30am–1pm. Return ticket routinely demanded.

Liberia 2 Pembridge Place, London W2 4XB (☎071 221 1036, telex 915463), 10am–2.30pm.

Morocco 49 Queen's Gate Gardens, London SW7 5NE (☎071 581 5001-3), 9.30am–1pm.

Nigeria Nigeria House, 9 Northumberland Ave, London W2 (☎071 839 1244, telex 8814318), 9.30am–2pm; 3–11 North St Andrew's St, Edinburgh 2 (☎031 557 0275, Telex 727524), 9am–1pm, 2–5pm; 56 Leeson Park, Dublin 6 (☎01 604 366, Telex 93235). Return ticket or covering documentation required.

Senegal 11 Phillimore Gardens, London W8 7QG (☎071 937 0925/6, telex 917119), 9.30–3pm.

Sierra Leone 33 Portland Place, London W1N 3AG (☎071 636 6483-5, telex 27640), 9.30–1pm for visa application, 2.30–3.30pm for visa collection.

Togo 30 Sloane St, London SW1 (☎071 235 0147, telex 8952650), 9am–1pm, 1.30–4.30pm.

Tunisia 29 Prince's Gate, London SW7 1QG (☎071 584 8117), 9.30am–1pm.

Mauritanian visas can be issued by the French embassy in London but for Cape Verde, Guinea, Mali and Niger contact the appropriate embassies in Europe (see box on p.20).

Visa Shop Ltd, 1 Charing Cross Undergorund Concourse, London WC2 (☎071 379 0419, Fax 071 497 2590). The biggest by far, with a walk-in shop and agent in Brussels for the tricky visas. £12 plus visa fee, or £50 all-in if it's done in Brussels.

GETTING VISAS ALONG THE WAY

On an **overland trip**, it would seem to be simplest to pick up the visas you need along the way – were it not for the fact that some West African embassies in the region may on occasion refuse to issue visas to passport holders who could have obtained them in their own country. A further obstacle – though one that's steadily diminishing – is the lack of representation for a number of countries which have very few embassies. Plan ahead to see where you should be getting your next visa. The **visa map of West Africa** on the previous page indicates in which cities you should be able to obtain which visas. Certain nationalities will have hassles getting some of these (Germans with Algeria, Britons with Nigeria, most nationalities with Guinea) so it's worth trying at the first opportunity. Even an

expired visa can be a help in getting another for the same country, though reckless applications can be an expensive hobby. Take plenty of passport photos – allow three or four for each visa you expect to need.

VISA ADVICE

Once you've located the embassy in question (addresses are given in as much detail as possible in the directory section of each capital. Where you've any choice it's the *consulate* you want), **obtaining visas** is fairly straightforward in most cases. It's often a good deal easier than doing so at home. Be prepared for an average 2–3 days wait from application to delivery though, and have a handy hotel address to use as your intended address in the country (nothing too slummy).

A **letter of introduction** from your own embassy is sometimes required (this can usually be provided on the spot, for a fee). Ask about this in advance if you're unsure – you may not be told it's necessary. Countries for which a letter of introduction is either helpful or mandatory include Algeria, Cape Verde, Guinea, Mauritania, Cameroon and Nigeria, but it's hard to generalise as rules and norms vary enormously from embassy to embassy. It's always a help to already have a visa for the country you intend to go to *after* the one for which you're applying.

The person whose signature is required is invariably the **consul**. If you sense you're going to be delayed or messed around, ask to see him or her in person. Never give up. If you get stone-walled, or you're in a hurry and told to come back next week, try putting in an hour or two in the waiting room. This often has miraculous effects, especially combined with persistent whining.

Visa fees can be high (up to £20 equivalent or more) and sometimes vary mysteriously from one applicant to the next, not always depending on different passports. Visas are often issued with *fiscal stamps* stuck in your passport, or a hand-written sum of money. The value should be what you paid. If it differs, it's worth complaining and asking for a receipt. There may have been an accidental overpayment . . .

In cities where they have no direct representation, visas for Mauritania, Senegal, Burkina Faso, Côte d'Ivoire and Togo are often available from the **French Embassy** (Fr). There's one in every country except The Gambia. Where Niger has no embassy, Côte d'Ivoire embassies (C d'I) process Niger visas. **British Embassies** (Br) in Rabat, Algiers, Tunis, Dakar, Abidjan and Yaoundé provide a similar service, in principle, to unrepresented Commonwealth countries (The Gambia, Sierra Leone, Ghana and Nigeria). British High Commissions (the mutual embassies of Commonwealth countries) cannot do this.

Lastly, a few West African countries issue (or have an official policy to issue, which is slightly different) **visas on arrival** at the airport. There are details in relevant country sections. Don't risk it unless you have to – it always delays the arrival formalities.

Further kinds of red tape which may entangle you on your travels include "currency declaration forms", "tourist cards", "photography permits" and international vaccination certificates. Currency rules, health formalities and photography are dealt with in detail further on. Other pieces of paper are mentioned in the practicalities sections of relevant country chapters.

BRITISH DIPLOMATIC REPRESENTATIVES IN NORTH AND WEST AFRICA

For general enquiries, the Consular Department at the Foreign and Commonwealth Office, Clive House, Petty France, London SW1H 9HD (☎071 270 4129) can be helpful. Other countries' embassy and consulate addresses are given in the listings section for each capital city.

Algeria British Embassy, BP 43 Alger Gare, Algiers, (Résidence Cassiopée, Batiment "B", Chemin de Glycines ☎2605601).

Burkina Faso British Honorary Consulate, BP 1918, Ouagadougou (☎33 63 63).

Cameroon, British Embassy, BP 547, Yaoundé (ave Winston Churchill, ☎22 05 45, Telex 8200).

Côte d'Ivoire British Embassy, 01 BP 2581, Abidjan 01 (Immeuble "Les Harmonies", angle blvd Carde/ave Dr Jamot, Plateau, ☎22 68 50/52, Telex 23706).

The Gambia British High Commission, PO Box 507,Banjul (48 Atlantic Rd, Fajara, ☎95133, Telex 2211).

Ghana British High Commission, PO Box 296, Accra (Osu Link, off Gamel Abdul Nasser Ave, ☎221665, Telex 2323).

Guinea British Honorary Consulate, BP 834, Conakry.

Guinea-Bissau British Honorary Consulate, CP 100, Bissau (c/o *Mavegro*, ☎21 15 29, Telex 259).

Liberia British Embassy (mini-mission), PO Box 120, Monrovia (Mamba Point, ☎221491, Telex 44287).

Morocco British Embassy, BP 45, Rabat (17 Blvd de la Tour Hassan, ☎20905-6).

Niger British Honorary Vice Consulate, BP 942, Niamey (☎72 20 32).

Nigeria British High Commission, PMB 12136, Lagos (Chellarams Building, 54 Marina, ☎667061, 666413, Fax 666909), responsible for **Benin**.

Senegal British Embassy, BP 6025 Dakar (20 rue du Docteur Guillet, ☎239971), responsible for **Mali, Mauritania, Cape Verde**.

Sierra Leone British High Commission, Freetown (☎23961, Telex 3235).

Togo British Honorary Consulate, BP 60958 BE, Lomé (*Agence Maritime Atlantique du Togo SARL*, 1 rue l'Hotel Miramar, Ablogamé 2, ☎214082).

Tunisia British Embassy, 5 Place de la Victoire, Tunis (☎245 100). Visa Section, 141–3 ave de la Liberté, Tunis (☎287 293).

NORTH AND WEST AFRICAN EMBASSIES AND CONSULATES

FRANCE

Algeria Consulate, 11 rue d'Argentine, 75016 Paris (☎45 00 99 50).

Benin Consulate, 89 rue de Cherche-Midi, 75006 Paris (☎42 22 31 91).

Burkina Faso Embassy, 159 blvd Haussmann, 75008 Paris (☎43 59 21 85) 09–13.00, 15–18.00.

Cameroon Embassy, 73 rue d'Auteuil, 75016 Paris (☎46 51 89 00).

Cape Verde Consulate, 92 blvd Malesherbes, 75017 Paris (☎42 25 63 31, Telex 26696).

Côte d'Ivoire Consulate, 8 rue Dumont-d'Urville, 75016 Paris (☎47 20 35 09).

The Gambia Consulate, 57 rue de Villiers, 92200 Neuilly-sur-Seine (☎47 57 31 60), 10–12.00, 14.30–16.00.

Ghana Embassy, 8 Villa Said, 75116 Paris (☎45 00 09 50).

Guinea Embassy, 24 rue Emile Meunier, 75016 Paris (☎45 53 72 25) 09–16.00.

Guinea-Bissau Consulate, 91 ave de la République, 75011 Paris (☎48 06 69 66).

Liberia 12 pl. Gén. Catroux, Paris 75017 (☎47 63 58 55).

Mali Embassy, 89 rue Cherche-Midi (next to Benin), 75006 Paris (☎45 48 58 43) 09–13.00, 14–16.30.

Mauritania Consulate, 89 rue Cherche-Midi (next to Mali), 75006 Paris (☎45 48 23 88) 09–13.00.

Morocco 5 rue Le Tasse, Paris 75016 (☎45 20 69 35).

Niger Embassy, 154 rue de Longchamp, 75016 Paris (☎45 04 80 60) 09.30–12.30.

Nigeria Embassy, 173 ave Victor Hugo, 75016 Paris (☎47 27 31 89).

Senegal Consulate, 22 rue Hamelin, 75016 Paris (☎45 53 75 86) 09–13.00, 14–18.00.

Sierra Leone Embassy, 16 ave Hoche, 75008 Paris (☎42 56 14 73).

Togo Embassy, 8 rue Alfred-Roll, 75017 Paris (☎43 80 12 13) 09–13.00, 15–18.00.

Tunisia Consulate, 19 rue de Lubeck, 7016 Paris (☎45 53 50 94).

GERMANY

Algeria 2 Reinallee 32, 5300 Bonn, (☎228 87 07-0).

Benin 2 Rudiger 10, 5300 Bonn (☎228 34 40 31).

Burkina Faso 2 Wendelstrasse 18, 5300 Bonn (☎228 33 20 63).

Cameroon 2 Rheinallee 76, 5320 Bonn (☎228 36 19 22).

Cape Verde 1 Meckenheimerallee 113, 5300 Bonn (☎228 65 16 04).

Côte d'Ivoire 1 Konigstrasse 93, 5300 Bonn (☎228 22 90 31).

The Gambia Kurfürstendamm 102, 1000 Berlin (☎030 88 60 51).

Ghana 2 Rheinallee 58, 5300 Bonn 2 (☎228 35 20 11).

Guinea 3 Reifenberg 21, 5300 Bonn (☎228 23 10 98).

Liberia 2 Hohenzollern 73, 5300 Bonn (☎228 35 23 94).

Mali 2 Bastei 86, 5300 Bonn (☎228 35 70 48).

Mauritania 2 Bonner 48, 5300 Bonn (☎228 36 40 25).

Morocco 2 Goten 7, 5300 Bonn (☎228 35 50 44).

Niger 2 Durenstrasse 9, 5300 Bonn (☎228 35 60 57).

Nigeria 2 Goldbergweg 13, 5300 Bonn 2 (☎228 32 20 71).

Senegal Munchernerstrasse 7, 6000 Frankfurt 1 (☎69 23 26 91/2).

Sierra Leone 2 Rheinallee 20, 5300 Bonn (☎228 35 20 01).

Togo Beethovenallee 13, 5300 Bonn 2 (☎228 35 50 91).

Tunisia 2 Godesbergerallee 103, 5300 Bonn (☎228 37 69 83).

ITALY

Algeria 26 v. B Oriani 00197 (no. 3 Linee Urbane), Rome (☎6 80 41 41, Telex 680846).

Burkina Faso 26 v. Alessandria, Rome (☎6 86 31 94).

Cameroon 82 av. Pietra, Rome (☎6 678 35 46, Telex 611558).

Côte d'Ivoire 4/6 v. Spallanzani, 00161 Rome (☎6 884 05 65, Telex 610396).

Ghana 4/6/8 v. Ostriana, Rome (☎6 83 46 87, Telex 610270).

Guinea 9/15 v. Ristori, Rome (☎6 37 89 89), 66 v. Iannialli, Rome (☎6 376 69 21, Telex 611487).

Liberia 64 v. Buozzi, Rome (☎6 80 58 10/12, Telex 612569).

Morocco 8/10 v. Spallanzani, Rome (☎6 884 86 53, Telex 620854).

Nigeria 14/16/18 v. Orazio (no. 4 Linee Urbane), Rome (☎6 653 10 48, Telex 610666).

Senegal 12 v. Bastolomé Eustachio, Rome (☎6 844 55 04, Telex 612522).

Togo 18 Corso Vitorio Emmanuele, Turin (☎11 87 17 19).

Tunisia 7 v. Asmara (no. 3 Linee Urbane), Rome (☎6 839 0748).

THE BENELUX COUNTRIES

BRUSSELS

Algeria av Molière 207, B6 (☎2 344 99 19).
Benin av Observatoire 5, B8 (☎2 374 91 92/375 03 17).
Burkina Faso pl G. d'Arezzo 16, B6 (☎2 345 06 12).
Cameroon av Brugmann 131, B6 (☎2 345 18 70).
Côte d'Ivoire av Franklin Roosevelt 234, B5 (☎2 672 23 57).
The Gambia av Franklin Roosevelt 126, B5 (☎2 640 10 49).
Ghana rue Gachard 44, B5 (☎2 649 01 63).
Guinea ave R Vanderdriessche 75, B15 (☎2 771 01 26).
Guinea-Bissau av Franklin Roosevelt 70, B5 (☎2 647 08 90).
Liberia av Franklin Roosevelt 55, B5 (☎2 648 13 49).
Mali av Molière 487, B6 (☎2 345 75 89).
Mauritania rue P. Lauters 1, B5 (☎2 640 76 75).
Morocco bd St Michel 29, B4 (☎2 736 11 00).
Niger av Franklin Roosevelt 78, B5 (☎2 648 61 40).
Nigeria av Tervueren 288, B15 (☎2 762 52 00).
São Tome av Brugmann 42, B6 (☎2 347 53 75).

Senegal av Franklin Roosevelt 196, B5 (☎2 673 43 97).
Sierra Leone av Tervueren 410, B15 (☎2 771 00 53).
Togo av Tervueren 264, B15 (☎2 770 17 91).
Tunisia av Tervueren 278, B15 (☎2 771 73 95).

THE HAGUE

Algeria V. Stolkin 1/3 (☎703 52 29 54).
Cameroon Amaliastr. 14 (☎703 46 97 15).
Cape Verde Koninginnegr. 44 (☎703 46 96 23).
Morocco Oranjestr. 9 (☎703 46 96 17).
Nigeria Wagenaarwg. 5 (☎703 50 17 03).
Tunisia Gentsestr. 98 (☎703 51 22 51).

ROTTERDAM

Cape Verde Consulate Mathenesserin 326 (☎10 77 89 77).

LUXEMBOURG HONORARY CONSULATES

Niger 29 bd Roosevelt, L-2450 (☎2 19 75).
Senegal 11 bd Royal, L-2449 (☎2 82 84).
Togo rue de la Forêt, L-8065 (☎45 04 72).

SCANDINAVIA

COPENHAGEN

Burkina Faso Svanemøllevej 20, DK2100 (☎01 18 40 22).
Côte d'Ivoire Gersonssvej 8, Hellerup, DK2900 (☎01 62 88 22).
Ghana Egebjerg Allé 13, 2900 Hellerup (☎01 62 82 22, Telex 19471).
Guinea Hølmemarksvej 6, Tastrup, DK2630 (☎02 99 32 42).
Liberia Storekongensgade 114, DK1264 (☎01 13 98 00).
Mali Skodsborgvej 188, Naerum, DK2850 (☎02 80 53 33).
Morocco Øregårds Allé 19, 2900 Hellerup (☎01 62 45 11, Telex 22913).
Senegal Valkendorfsgade 22, DK1151 (☎01 13 61 88).

Tunisia Strandboulevarden 130, DK2100 (☎01 62 50 10).

STOCKHOLM

Algeria Danderydsgt. 3–5 POB 26067, 10041 (☎(8)21 1070, Telex 14734).
Guinea-Bissau Sturegt. 8, POB 10141, 100 55 (☎(8) 10 93 05, Telex 12290.
Morocco Kungsholmstorg 16, 11221 (☎(8) 54 43 83).
Nigeria Tyrgt. 8, POB 628, 10128 (☎(8) 24 63 90, Telex 17649).
Senegal Skeppsbron 8, POB 2036, 10311 (☎(8) 14 32 35, Telex 12833).
Tunisia POB 3219, 10364 (☎(8) 23 64 70, Telex 19193).

SPAIN AND PORTUGAL

MADRID

Algeria General Oraa 12, 28006 (☎411 6065).
Cameroon Roasrio Pino 3, 28020 (☎571 1160, Telex 27772).
Côte d'Ivoire Palace Hotel, Plaza Cortés 7, Madrid, CP 50-221 (☎261 1607).
Equatorial Guinea Claudio Coello 91 (☎ 276 1249, Telex 46800).
Mauritania Velazquez 90, 28006 (☎575 7007).
Morocco Serrano 179, 28002 (☎458 0950, Telex 27799).
Nigeria Segre 23, Aptdo 14287, 28002 (☎458 0650, Telex 44395).
Tunisia Pl Alfonso Martinez 3 (☎447 3516).

LAS PALMAS, CANARY ISLES

Mauritania Rafael Davila 10 (☎28 23 4500).
Senegal Explanada tomas Quevado s/n (☎28 26 5069).

Morocco Juan Manuel Duran Gonzalez 41 (☎28 22 5494).
Sierra Leone E. Benot 1 (☎28 26 5162).

LISBON

Algeria Ave do Restelo 31, 1400 (☎88 79 66, Telex 15490).
Cape Verde 33 Av Restelo, Lisbon 13 (☎1 61 34 00/24/54, Telex 13765).
Guinea-Bissau Rua de Alconene 17, Lisbon 14 (☎61 53 71, Telex 14326).
Morocco Rua Borges Carneiro 32, Lisbon 12 (☎67 91 93, Telex 16770).
Nigeria 50-A Fernão M. Pinto, Lisbon 14 (☎ 61 61 91/89, Telex 18418).
São Tome 2 Rua da Junqeira, Lisbon 13 (☎63 82 42/63 86 58, Telex 13796).

SWITZERLAND

Algeria Willandingweg 74, 3006 Berne (☎031 44 69 61, Telex 912623)

Cameroon Brunnadernrain 29, 3006 Berne (☎031 44 47 37):

Côte d'Ivoire Thormannstrasse 51, 3005 Berne (☎031 43 10 51, Telex 912 718), 33 Chemin de Lavanchet, Cointrin, Geneva (☎022 98 46 44).

Ghana Belpstrasse 11, Post Lach, 3007 Berne (☎031 257 852, Telex 912 993).

Mauritania 4 rue Petitot, 1204 Geneva (☎022 21 72 90).

Morocco Helvetiastr. 42, 3005 Berne (☎031 44 82 26, Telex 912620).

Nigeria Zieglerstrasse 45, 3007 Berne (☎031 26 07 26, Telex 912995).

Senegal 10 Monbijoustrasse, 3011 Berne (☎031 26 12 02/3), 22 rue François Lehmann, 1218 Geneva (☎022 98 21 77).

Togo 6 rue Bellot, Geneva.

MOROCCO

Algeria 46 blvd Tariq Ibn Ziad, Rabat (☎65092).

Côte d'Ivoire BP 192, 21 Zankat Tiddas, Rabat (☎63151, Telex 31070).

France 3 rue Sahnoun, Rabat (☎77822, Telex 31013) issue various West African visas.

Guinea 2 Zankat Mokla, Orangers, Rabat (☎32705, Telex 31796).

Mauritania 6 rue Thami Lamdouar, Souissi, Rabat (☎56817).

Nigeria BP 347, 70 ave Omar ibn al-Khattab, Agdal, Rabat (☎71856, Telex 31976).

Senegal 17 rue Cadi ben Hamadi Senhaji, Souissi, Rabat (☎54148, Telex 31048).

Tunisia 6 ave de Fass (☎25644).

United Kingdom BP 45, 17 blvd Tour Hassan, Rabat (☎20905) issue Sierra Leone visas.

TUNISIA

Algeria 18 rue de Niger, Tunis (☎238 166, Telex 13081).

Côte d'Ivoire 84 Ave Hé di Chaker, Tunis (☎238 878).

France place de l'Indé pendance, Tunis (☎245 700, Telex 12553) issue various West African visas.

Mauritania BP 62, 17 rue Fatma Ennechi, al-Menzah, Tunis (☎234 935, Telex 12234).

Morocco 39 ave du 1er Juin, Tunis (☎782 775, Telex 14460).

Senegal 122 ave de la Liberté, Tunis (☎282 544, Telex 12477).

United Kingdom Visa Section, 141–3 ave de la Liberté, Tunis (☎287 293) issue visas for Ghana, Nigeria and Sierra Leone.

JAPAN

Algeria 10-67 Mita 2-chome, Meguro-ku, Tokyo 153 (☎03 (711) 2661).

Cameroon 9-12 Nanpedai-cho, Shibuya-ku, Tokyo 107 (☎03 (408) 2101).

Côte d'Ivoire Aoyama Tower 19-68, 2 Chome Uehara Plaza, appt 2C, Tokyo (☎03 402 8371).

The Gambia Hon. Cons., Hayama Building A-1, 3-14, Hiroo 1-chome, Shibuya-ku, Tokyo 150 (☎03 (444) 7806).

Ghana 11th Fl, Dai 28 Morai Building, 16-13 Nishiazabu 4-chome, Minato-ku, Tokyo 106, Tokyo (☎03 (400) 1830).

Guinea 12-6 Minamiazabu 1-chome, Minato-ku, Tokyo 106 (☎03 (769) 0451).

Liberia 6th Fl, Odakyu Fudosan, Minamiaoyama Building, 8-1, Minami Aoyama 7-chome, Minato-ku, Tokyo 107 (☎03 (499) 2451).

Mauritania 17-5 Kitashinagawa 5-chome, Shinagawa-ku, Tokyo 104 (☎03 (449) 3810).

Mali Hon. Cons. c/o Kanematsu Corp, Tokyo head office, 14-1 Kyobashi 2-chome, Chuo-ku, Tokyo 104 (☎03 (562) 8256).

Morocco 5 & 6th Fl, Silver Kingdom Mansion, 16-3 Sendagaya 3-chome, Shibuya-ku, Tokyo 151 (☎03 (478) 3271).

Niger Hon. Cons. c/o Overseas Uranium Resources Devt. Co., Landic Akasaka Building, 3-4 Akasaba 2-chome, Minato-ku, Tokyo 107 (☎03 (505) 6371).

Nigeria 19-7 Uehara 2-chome, Shibuya-ku, Tokyo 151 (☎03 (468) 5531).

Senegal 3-4 Aobadai 1-chome, Meguro-ku, Tokyo (☎03 464 8451).

Sierra Leone Hon. Cons. same address as Mali but (☎03 (567) 7111).

Tunisia 18-8 Wakaba 1-chome, Shinjuku-ku, Tokyo 160 (☎03 (353) 4111).

AUSTRALIA

Ghana PO Box 338, Manuka, Canberra (☎62 95 1122).

Nigeria 7 Terrigal Crescent, O'Malley, Canberra (☎62 86 1322).

MONEY AND COSTS ·

Travel in West Africa can become dominated by economic considerations, especially if you arrive unprepared. Eleven different currencies are used by the countries covered and it pays to know what the score is wherever you are. Even where sophisticated banking systems operate you may not be able to change certain foreign currencies. And in some countries a parallel "black market" in hard currencies still thrives.

CURRENCIES

The currency of all the **francophone countries** in West Africa, with the exceptions of Mauritania and Guinea, is the **CFA franc**. CFA stands for *Communauté Financière Africaine*. Cameroon's currency is also CFA, but of a different regional grouping – the *Coopération Financière en Afrique Centrale* – which includes Chad, Central African Republic, Gabon, Equatorial Guinea and Congo. CFA francs are guaranteed by the French treasury and have a fixed value of 50:1 against the French franc (FF).

The two types of CFA can't be spent outside their own region but are easily exchanged in a bank. In Europe, major banks will normally exchange CFA francs at their French franc equivalent. Because of the French backing, the CFA (commonly pronounced "Sefa") is a hard currency in the region – Africa's strongest – and currency laws in the countries which use it are generally relaxed. In theory there are limits to the value of CFA you can export, even from one CFA state to

another, but in practice these limits are very rarely enforced. CFA comes in 1, 5, 10, 25, 50 and 100 coins and notes of 500, 1000, 5000 and 10,000, making it easily the most convenient African currency.

The countries outside the franc zone have their own, usually weaker ("soft") currencies. Algeria uses the Algerian **Dinar**, Mauritania, the **Ouguiya**; Cape Verde Islands, the Cape Verdean **Escudo**; The Gambia, the **Dalasi**; Guinea-Bissau, the **Peso**; Guinea, the **Guinean franc**; Sierra Leone, the **Leone**; Liberia, the **Liberian Dollar**; Ghana, the **Cedi**; and Nigeria, the **Naira**. Guinea could both become part of the CFA zone in the next few years.

MONEY

If you're travelling widely in West Africa, you're probably best off carrying a large part of your funds in **French franc travellers cheques**. Apart from any commission on exchanging them for cash, if you're using them in CFA countries, you've already effectively made the exchange when you bought the travellers cheques. In the CFA zone you'll always know how much you've got in local currency and your funds won't vary in value as you travel.

You generally end up better off if you have French francs to convert to CFA, rather that going straight from, say, **sterling** to CFA, because the national banks of the CFA zone normally set their own rates for exchanges with non-franc currencies. In some towns in the CFA zone, banks will not deal in non-franc currencies – frustrating in a business-minded place like Côte d'Ivoire. Hotels and some shops and traders will take French franc travellers cheques but it's essential to have some **French francs in cash** as a standby.

In the neighbouring, *non*-CFA countries, your surplus CFA cash can generally be changed with ease as it's commonly used by people crossing the borders to buy goods (though note the details below on declaring your currency). But if you're heading directly for one of the **soft currency countries**, or intending to spend most of your time there, then either **dollars** (US$) or **pounds sterling** (£) is probably the best currency to carry. Again, carry at least some in cash – you'll often need it at borders and airports for your first food or transport.

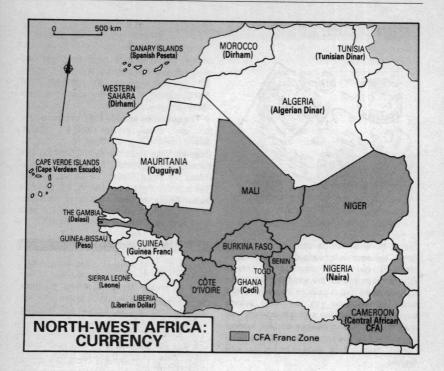

NORTH-WEST AFRICA: CURRENCY

☐ CFA Franc Zone

0 — 500 km

CANARY ISLANDS
(Spanish Peseta)

MOROCCO
(Dirham)

TUNISIA
(Tunisian Dinar)

WESTERN
SAHARA
(Dirham)

ALGERIA
(Algerian Dinar)

CAPE VERDE ISLANDS
(Cape Verdean Escudo)

MAURITANIA
(Ouguiya)

MALI

NIGER

THE GAMBIA
(Dalasi)

GUINEA-BISSAU
(Peso)

GUINEA
(Guinea Franc)

BURKINA FASO

BENIN

NIGERIA
(Naira)

SIERRA LEONE
(Leone)

LIBERIA
(Liberian Dollar)

CÔTE
D'IVOIRE

TOGO

GHANA
(Cedi)

CAMEROON
(Central African
CFA)

Denominations of travellers cheques and cash should be as small as you can manage, bearing in mind the bulk that a large sum of exchange will amount to. If you take mostly US$50 or FF500 denominations for convenience, make sure you have plenty of US$10 and 20 or FF100 and 200 as well. A small stash of really low value hard currency notes (US$1 and 2) is always very useful too.

Travelling through the CFA zone, the issuing authority of your travellers cheques isn't of much consequence, so long as they're in French francs. Outside the CFA countries, however, *American Express* is by far the most widely recognised brand and, should the need arise, also the fastest to supply replacements for lost cheques.

CARRYING AND KEEPING FUNDS

How you physically carry your funds around is something to which you should give serious consideration, especially if you're travelling for a long duration. In certain cities, travellers are vulnerable and it only takes one piece of bad luck (or simple carelessness) to terminate your trip prematurely.

It's wise to carry valuable hard currency cash (as opposed to local soft currency) in a very safe place, ideally in a soft **leather pouch** under your waistband, hanging from a loop around your belt. This is comfortable and virtually impregnable to ordinary theft – even in the unlikely event it's noticed. It's probably worth wearing shorts, skirts or jeans with strong waistbands and a belt just for this purpose. Larger, strong, leather belt-pouches worn on the outside are good for passport, local money, travellers cheques and anything replaceable. They can be hard to find in useful shapes and at reasonable cost. A home-made version (old shoe leather, suede offcuts) may be the answer. While belt pouches are hard to mislay, **wallets** are a disaster because they're not attached to anything. Hanging **neck**

pouches worn beneath a shirt are vulnerable, but fairly safe if the loop is strong. Nylon **money belts** are painfully hot and bulky.

Bank notes and travellers cheques (and airline tickets) need **protection from sweat** with small plastic bags. Defaced, they can all become worthless.

DECLARATIONS

On arrival in many soft currency countries you'll have to make a **declaration** of the money you're carrying in cash and travellers cheques. This may be accompanied by a search, varying from the cursory to the intimate. Mostly, you simply say what you've got and then show some of it.

You may also be issued with a **currency declaration** or **exchange control form**, which you retain until departure. This shows the money you imported and is supposed to be stamped and amended every time you change money at an authorised bank, hotel or *bureau de change*. In theory, when you leave the country, your currency declaration form is checked against the money you have on you and any discrepancy (which must have been exchanged unofficially, or lost, or given away . . .) has to be accounted for. In practice, CD forms are taken much more seriously on arrival than on departure. It's wise to assume, however, that your experience will turn out to be the exception.

None of this applies if you're travelling to, or within, **CFA zone countries only**. Here the fiscal arrangements commonly leave you feeling you're merely in an overseas French *department* and there's rarely any interest in the money you have on you (apart from a purely private interest), nor any currency declaration forms or concern about where you change your money.

BANKS

Banking systems are generally slow and limited. The capital city is often by far the best place, if not the only one, to change money. Always try to arrive early in the day and remember your passport. Never start the transaction without checking the rate of exchange, the commission and any other charges. It's best to establish how much you'll receive in advance, before the paperwork starts. In the CFA zone there can be marked differences in the rates offfered by different banks and their scales of commission, and rates are often well behind the latest American and European swings.

WIRING

Try to avoid **sending home for money**. It's expensive and even telexed draft orders can take weeks to reach you at the counter – even though the normal delay should be four or five working days. You probably won't be able to receive hard currency except in the CFA zone, and not necessarily then. It's far better to have all you'll need, and more, in travellers cheques.

CREDIT CARDS

VISA, *American Express*, *Access-Mastercard* and *Diners' Club* are of some use in cities and large towns for tourist services such as upmarket hotels and restaurants, flights, tours and car hire. *American Express* has offices or agents in Morocco, Tunisia, Senegal, Sierra Leone, Liberia, Côte d'Ivoire, Ghana, Togo, Nigeria and Cameroon.

Don't count on **cash advances** against credit cards outside the CFA zone, and even in francophone capitals you'll have to find the right local bank.

BLACK MARKETS

An unofficial, **parallel exchange rate** (the "black market") exists wherever there's a local demand for hard, foreign currency that can't be met through official channels. Except in the CFA zone, you can't usually walk into a bank and buy dollars, sterling, or other hard currency over the counter. Hard currency is kept in state control and sold to private citizens only reluctantly and with all sorts of conditions. Local currencies are worthless beyond these countries' borders and local people have enormous difficulty in obtaining hard currency to travel abroad, conduct business or support relatives.

In most of the non-CFA countries, you can, threrefore, exchange your hard currency for local money at higher-than-bank rates. **Black market rates** vary from a few percentage points better to several *hundred* per cent better than the bank rate. At the time of writing the only countries in West (and North) Africa with major black markets are Nigeria, Guinea-Bissau, Liberia, Sierra Leone and Algeria.

It may seem unfair on strangled economies to squeeze even harder for the sake of cheap local currency by depriving the banks of foreign exchange. But on the other hand it's naïve to hold exaggerated views of the importance of your hard currency to the national development of the coun-

EXCHANGE RATES

As we go to press the following official exchange rates (£1) apply:

ALGERIA *Dinar* 14.23	GUINEA-BISSAU *Guinea-Bissauan Peso* 3500
BENIN *CFA Franc* 488	LIBERIA *Liberian Dollar* (no value)
BURKINA FASO *CFA Franc* 488	MALI *CFA Franc* 488
CAMEROON *Central African CFA Franc* 488	MAURITANIA *Ouguiya* 140
CAPE VERDE *Escudo* 122	NIGER *CFA Franc* 488
CÔTE D'IVOIRE *CFA Franc* 488	NIGERIA *Naira* 14
THE GAMBIA *Dalasi* 13.5	SENEGAL *CFA Franc* 488
GHANA *Cedi* 650	SIERRA LEONE *Leone* 280
GUINEA *Guinean Franc* 1200 (GF700 : US$1)	TOGO *CFA Franc* 488

(CFA rates vary from bank to bank and should be measured against the equivalent in French francs)

try you're in, or of the net benefit to local people of putting your money into a bank rather than private hands. Sometimes the official exchange rate is simply set at an unrealistically high level that makes the place swingeingly expensive. It's worth noting that most prices tend to adjust to black market levels and that some services (especially hotels) may, in any case, be payable only in hard currency at the official rate of exchange. Questions of altruism and morality apart, it needs to be said, whatever else you do on your travels, *never change money on the street*. You run a high risk of being skilfully ripped off in public, even if the police informer scenario rarely comes to pass. If you must change money illegally, you'll obviously need to hide cash for the purpose when you enter the country. Shops and businesses are the usual places to change. If you ask around you'll soon pick up on the whos and wheres. Always be accompanied, always count every note yourself before handing over anything (there are some brilliant conjurers, though usually they're street sharks, not in legitimate business), and for obvious reasons, don't change travellers cheques. Indications are that the remaining black market dominated economies in West Africa will be progressively "legitimised" over the next few years as treasuries come to accept the need to devalue their overrated currencies.

COSTS AND BARGAINING

It's perhaps surprising to find that, in general, West Africa is an expensive part of the world. The point to hang onto is that mere **survival** can be dirt cheap, but anything like a Euro-American lifestyle costs as much, if not more, than in

Europe or America. In between these extremes you can mix the cheapest transport, market food and cheap restaurant meals with nights either camping in the bush, staying with people or in budget hotels. Travelling like this it's possible to get by on **£300 a month** (though £600 split between two is a good deal easier). It's clearly much harder to keep costs down in cities such as Dakar and Abidjan, where a panoply of tempting comforts and consumables is available in every direction and where it's hard to avoid staying in **hotels** – likely to be your biggest single expense.

The best way to keep costs *really* low is to **cycle**, which not only gives you free transport but also enables you to seek out cheap or free accommodation or tent space. A cycle tour of West Africa need not cost more than £5 a day. If you were hardy and avoided cities altogether you could do it for even less.

As a very general guideline to budget planning, a double room in a **cheap hotel** can usually be had for under £15, often under £10 but rarely under £5. Long-distance **road transport** works out, on average, at about 100km for £2–3 though it varies with the quality and speed of the vehicle. Rail tends to be cheaper, river more expensive. As for **food**, you can always fill yourself with calories for under £1 if you eat street food or sit at a market or lorry park chop house.

Travelling on a different budget, **car hire** rates are some of the highest in the world (in a number of countries it's not difficult to work up bills of £100 a day or more *without* taking the air-conditioned *Range Rover*). **International standard hotels**, too, are very expensive in most cities.

BARGAINING

You'll need to get into **bargaining** quickly. It's expected and is the normal way of conducting business. Moreover every time you pay an unreasonable price for goods or services you contribute to local inflation. **In markets** there's generally a "fixed price" which the seller has in mind. You can assume the one you're quoted is more but a few good natured offers will establish the fact. Try offering a bulk price for several items at once, or add some "presents" to the thing you're negotiating over. Loads of good humour counts for much.

General stores, groceries and supermarkets invariably have **fixed prices**, though there's never any harm in trying to pay less. Transport costs are usually subject to state control and almost always fixed – at least your travelling companions will be paying the same as you – but baggage can be haggled over. Pretty well every other service (including cheap hotel rooms in some countries) can and should be bargained for. This is often just a case of showing reluctance to pay what you're told is the going rate and getting some sort of **"discount"**.

It's in **buying major items** – particularly **craftworks** – that you'll have the most fun bargaining. There's enormous flexibility around a few immutable rules. The most important is never to engage in bargaining if you've no intention of buying the item at any price. To offer what you thought was a silly price and then refuse to pay it can cause grave offence. Nor should you embark on negotiations when you're in a hurry to go somewhere else, or if you have period pains or malaria or are otherwise feeling less than one hundred per cent – it's an exhausting business.

When negotiating, don't automatically assume you're in the clutches of a rip-off artist. Concepts of **honour** are very important, and stalls are often minded by friends and relatives with whom, if you're quick and convincing, you can sometimes strike *real* bargains. Don't forget, from the trader's point of view, you're selling *money*.

Most importantly, men should make **physical contact** – hand-clasping is usually enough to emphasise a point. Be as jocular as possible and don't be shy of making a big scene – the bluffing and mock outrage on both sides is part of the fun. Women can't pursue these negotiating tactics in quite the same way, except when buying from women – which is invariably much tougher anyway).

Getting down to figures, try to **delay the moment when you have to name your price**. When you hear "One hundred how much you pay?", you say nothing. It's amazing how often the seller's price drops way below your expectation before you've made any offer, so forget those "offer-a-third-come-up-to-a-half" formulae. If you do arrive at an unbridgeable gap you can always drop the matter and come by later. With stalemates, a **disinterested companion** tugging your sleeve is always a help.

If you're conducting all this in a language you don't speak, then a **calculator** is helpful for both parties to communicate prices.

HEALTH AND INSURANCE

Those who perspire readily, feel fittest in the tropics ... If the right food is bought, prepared and served thoroughly clean and fresh, water boiled and filtered, insects kept out of homes, the usual prophylactics and daily exercise taken, sensible light clothes worn and strong alcohol avoided or drunk in moderation, then anyone with normal blood pressure should keep very fit.

R.J Harrison Church, *West Africa* (1957)

It's not easy, of course, to maintain such zealous standards when you're on the move, though this old handbook advice holds good in principle. There's no reason to expect to get ill in West Africa, but plenty of opportunities to do so if you're unlucky or careless. The most likely hazards are stomach problems and malaria. Health details given in the practicalities sections for each country, include a brief run-down on local problems and issues. The only required inoculations for travel throughout the region are yellow fever and cholera, for which you should have *International Vaccination Certificates.*

VACCINATIONS

Plan ahead and start organising your shots at least **six weeks** before departure. A first-time cholera inoculation needs at least two weeks between the two injections of the course. A yellow fever certificate is only valid ten days after you've had the shot.

The validity of a cholera inoculation is a nominal six months, and it doesn't provide a great deal of protection against the disease, but the risks of contracting cholera are negligible unless you're based in the middle of an epidemic. If you're *not* travelling widely, it's worth knowing that the only country for which a **cholera inoculation** is currently an *entry requirement* is Niger. **Yellow fever** jabs are good for ten years and confer high immunity. Countries for which **yellow fever vaccination** is *always* a requirement are Benin, Burkina Faso, Cameroon, Côte d'Ivoire, Ghana, Niger, Senegal and Togo. Several others require to see the yellow fever certificate if you're staying over two weeks. **All West African countries** require the certificate if you've arrived by way of an infected area – i.e. any other sub-Saharan country. If you lose a vaccination certificate, you can buy blank ones in many stationery stores. Explain your situation at a hospital or clinic and have it stamped and signed by someone (there'll probably be a small charge).

Doctors recommend you have both the cholera and yellow fever shot in any case as a protection. Similarly, you shouldn't consider major travels without a **typhoid vaccination** (which lasts three years) or **polio** and **tetanus** boosters.

Nor is there any reason not to have a more expensive pain in the backside – a shot of **gamma globulin** which protects you from three to six months against the common form of **hepatitis** ("A") spread by contaminated food and water. It's a lot nicer having the jab than catching the disease, which seriously damages your liver and can leave it permanently scarred. Hepatitis "B" isn't a worry for most people. Like HIV, it's caught through the transfer of blood products, usually from dirty needles.

Whether you have the hepatitis "A" shot or not, be extra careful about cleanliness and in particular about contamination of water – a serious problem where, for example, a single water tank or barrel holds the whole water supply in a cockroach infested toilet-cum-bathroom.

MALARIA

Protection against **malaria** (*le paludisme* or *"palu"* in French) is absolutely essential. The disease, caused by a parasite carried in the saliva of *Anopheles* mosquitos, is endemic in tropical Africa – many Africans have it in their bloodstream and get occasional bouts of fever. It has a variable **incubation period** of a few days to several weeks so you can become ill long after being bitten. If you go down with malaria, you'll probably know. The fever, shivering and headaches are something like severe flu and come in waves, usually beginning in the early evening. Malaria is not infectious but it can be dangerous and sometimes even fatal if not treated quickly.

IF YOU GO DOWN WITH MALARIA

You'll need to take a cure. Don't compare yourself with local people who may have considerable immunity. The priority, if you think you might be getting a fever, is **treatment**. Delay is potentially risky.

First, confirm your diagnosis by getting to a doctor and having a blood test to identify the strain. If this isn't possible take two **quinine** tablets (600mg) twice daily for five days and then 3 *Fansidar* tablets. This should clear up any strain. If you don't have quinine tablets (you'd probably need to have obtained them abroad) then take ordinary **chloroquine** tablets at the rate of 10mg per kilo body weight up to a maximum of 600mg (usually 4 tablets) immediately, then half as much (usually 2 tablets) eight hours later.

Assuming you feel an improvement, take this second dose again on the second and third days. If you notice no improvement after the *initial* dose, try again to see a doctor or take 3 *Fansidar* tablets if you have them – *your malaria is chloroquine resistant*. The *Fansidar* should clear it up within a few hours.

TABLETS

It's vital to take **preventative tablets** and important to keep a routine and cover the period before and after your trip with doses (doctors can advise on which kind – it's generally the latest anti-resistant creation, but you can buy most of them without a prescription at a pharmacy). Once in West Africa, the chloroquine-based tablets (e.g. *Nivaquin*, *Aralen* and *Resochin*) and proguanil-based *Paludrin* and pyrimethamine-based *Daraprim* can be bought in small shops and from street drug stalls all over, but *Maloprim*, *Fansidar*, and some of the newer drugs to which **falciparum** malaria – the common African strain – is less often resistant, are only available in big towns. Chloroquine-resistant malaria has now been reported all over West Africa, so complacency isn't in order.

Common preventative combinations are a small daily dose of proguanil and a weekly dose of chloroquine, or chloroquine alone with a supply of *Fansidar* to be used immediately if chloroquine-resistant malaria is suspected and you can't get to a doctor.

Chloroquine is safe **during pregnancy** but *Maloprim* and *Fansidar* sometimes have side effects and the latter isn't recommended (whether you're pregnant or not) as a prophylaxis. *Mefloquine*, a safer variation on *Fansidar*, which is only taken once a week, is worth asking your doctor about, but it's not recommended for stays of over three weeks. It's worth knowing that there are sometimes side effects with anti-malarial drugs – itching and rashes are the most common – but they're always preferable to malaria.

NETS AND MOSQUITOS

Sleep under a **mosquito net** when possible – they're not expensive to buy locally – and burn **mosquito coils** (which you can buy everywhere) for a peaceful night. Don't use *Cock Brand* or *Lion Brand* which are said to contain DDT and are banned in many countries. Whenever the mosquitos are particularly bad (and that's not often) cover your exposed parts with something strong. So-called *"Neat Deet"* (the insecticide diethyltoluamide) works well and you can mix it 1:9 with water to soak clothes and make them repellant. **Best repellant** of all, remarkably enough, is *Avon* Bath oil. . . Electric **mosquito destroyers**, which you fit with a pad every night, are less pungent than mosquito coils but more expensive

in use – and you need electricity. Mosquito **"buzzers"** turned out to be useless.

Female *Anopheles* mosquitos – the agressors – prefer to bite in the evening. They can be distinguished by their rather eager head-down position. In various parts of West Africa, the local or seasonal malaria risk is low but you shouldn't break your course of pills as it's vital to keep your parasite-fighting level as high as possible.

OTHER DISEASES

BILHARZIA

Bilharzia is a potentially nasty disease. The usual recommendation is never to swim in, wash with, drink or even touch lake or river water that's not been vouched for. On a long trip, out in the bush, this isn't always possible, particularly if you're drinking with local people. Snail-free water that's stood for two days, or has been boiled or chlorinated, is safe, as is salt or brackish water.

Bilharzia – also known as **schistosomiasis** – comes from tiny flukes which live in freshwater snails and which, as part of their life cycle, leave their hosts and burrow into animal (or human) skin to multiply in the bloodstream. The snails themselves favour only stagnant water (though the flukes can be swept downstream) and the chances of picking up bilharzia are fairly small unless you repeatedly come into contact with infected water. It is possible, though, to pick it up from one brief contact. If infected, you'll get a slightly itchy rash an hour or two later where the flukes have entered the skin.

Bilharzia is most prevalent in the **savannah regions** and particularly in **artificial lakes and dams**. If you have severe abdominal pains and pass blood – the first symptoms after 4–6 weeks – see a doctor: it's easily curable.

SLEEPING SICKNESS

Sleeping sickness – trypanosomiasis – is mainly a disease of wild animals, but it also affects cattle and horses and to a much lesser extent people. It's carried by tse-tse ("setsy") flies which crowd streams and riverbanks in deep bush areas. They're determined, brutish flies with a painful bite, attracted to large moving objects like elephants or land-rovers. They tend to fly in the windows of vehicles driving through game parks.

Infection is extremely uncommon among travellers – fortunately, because the drugs used to treat it aren't very sophisticated. But a boil which suddenly appears, several *days* after a tse-tse fly bite *might* indicate an infection you should get examined. Untreated, sleeping sickness results in infections of the central nervous system and drowsiness. Not amusing.

RIVER BLINDNESS

River blindness – onchocerciasis – is common along several river systems. It's spread by tiny **blackflies**, which have a vicious bite and pass on minute worms. These move to the eyes and can eventually cause blindness. Travellers virtually never pick this disease up. Impaired vision, however, can be caused by long-term use of chloroquine against malaria – nothing to do with onchocerciasis.

SEXUALLY TRANSMITTED DISEASES AND AIDS

The only other real likelihood of your encountering a serious disease is if it's **sexually transmitted**. Assorted venereal diseases are widespread, particularly in the larger towns, and the HIV virus which causes **Aids** is alarmingly prevalent and spreading all the time. It's very easily passed between people suffering relatively minor, but ulcerous, sexually transmitted dieseases, and the very high prevalence of these is thought to account for the high incidence of heterosexually transmitted HIV. So there you have it: not exactly an encitement to throw caution to the winds.

On the associated topic of receiving **blood transfusions** or injections in an emergency, although you might want to carry a sterile emergency kit to be used by a doctor if you get into trouble, there's no point in carrying a pint of your own blood with you as some travellers have – it's not enough to be much help in a serious emergency.

WATER AND BUGS

In many places, the **water** you drink will have come from a tap and is likely to be clean. Since bad water is the most likely cause of **diarrhoea**, you should be fairly cautious of drinking rain or well water if you can't get clean tap water.

In truth, **stomach upsets** don't plague many travellers badly. If you're visiting West Africa for a short time only, it makes sense to be scrupu-

---

MEDICINE BAG

There's no need to take a mass of drugs and remedies you'll probably never use – and best not to plan a pharmaceutical relief number and give away a lot of miscellaneous pills. Various items, however, are immensely useful, especially on a long trip, and well worth buying in advance.

On a local level, if you're interested in herbal and other natural remedies, you'll find a wealth of examples in markets. Intuition, common sense and persistent enquiries are all you need to judge whether they're worth trying.

Paracetomol Safer than aspirin for pain and fever relief.

Water purifying (chlorine) tablets Taste horrid but do the trick. Shop around – they vary greatly in price.

Anti-malaria tablets Enough for prophylactic use plus several courses of *Fansidar* and/or quinine tablets in case of attack.

Codeine phosphate This is the preferable emergency anti-diarrhoeal pill but is on prescription only. Some GPs may oblige. *Lomotil* is second best.

Antibiotics *Flagyl* is good in a lower bowel crisis. *Amoxil* is a broad spectrum antibacterial drug useful against many infections. Neither should be used unless you cannot see a doctor.

Zinc oxide powder Useful anti-fungal powder for sweaty crevices.

Antiseptic cream *Cicatrin* is good but creams invaribly squeeze out sooner or later so avoid metal tubes. Bright red or purple *mercurochrome* liquid dries wounds.

Alcohol swabs *Medi-swabs* are invaluable for cleaning wounds, insect bites and infections.

Sticking plaster, steri-strip wound closures, sterile gauze dressing, micropore tape You don't need much of this stuff. If you use it, supplies can be replenished in most capital cities.

Lipsalve/chapstick Invaluable for dry lips.

Thermometer Very useful. Ideally you'll be 37.5°C. A *Feverscan* forehead thermometer is unbreakable and gives a ready reckoning (from chemists).

Lens solution If you wear contact lenses you'll need a good supply of solution.

DISABLED TRAVELLERS

Only the most intrepid would consider West Africa, but it's not an impossible notion. The Gambia and Togo are two countries sufficiently low-key, accessible and accustomed to visitors to make extra difficulties surmountable. Actual facilities are non-existent, even wheelchairs pretty well unknown. But most hotels are single storey or have ground-floor rooms and you'll at least have no problems recruiting local help. You can expect overwhelming consideration.

Campbell Irvine Ltd (48 Earl's Court Rd, London W8 6EJ, ☎071 937 6981-3) is one company that offers insurance for disabled travellers.

lous – purifying tablets and/or boiling kill most things. For longer stays, and especially if you're travelling widely, think of re-educating your stomach rather than fortifying it. It's virtually impossible to travel around the region without exposing yourself to strange bugs from time to time. Take it easy at first, don't overdo the fruit (and wash it in clean water before peeling), don't keep food too long and be very wary of salads. If you travel across the desert, particularly if you do so by hitching/public transport, gradually acclimatising, you'll most likely find you can survive without ill effect most of the bugs you must be consuming. Ironically, perhaps, if you're travelling on a shoestring budget and rarely eat restaurant meals,

your chances of picking up stomach bugs are considerably reduced.

If you do have **a serious attack**, 24 hours of plain tea and nothing else may rinse it out. The important thing is to replace your lost fluids. Most upsets resolve themselves. If you feel in need you can make up a **rehydration mix** with four heaped teaspoons of sugar or honey and half a teaspoon of salt in a litre of water. If the diarrhoea seems to be getting worse – or, horrifically, you have to travel a long distance – any pharmacy should have name brand anti-diarrhoea remedies. These (*Lomotil*, codeine phosphate etc) shouldn't be over-used. A day's worth of doses is about the most you should take.

GENERAL HEALTH TIPS

Some people **sweat** heavily and lose a lot of salt. Salt tablets are a complete waste of money. Sprinkle extra salt on your food. Even if you're not a great perspirer it's important to keep a healthy salt balance. The body can't function without it and it's not uncommon to experience sudden exhaustion and collapse a few days after arrival. The contrast between a European winter and the dry season in West Africa is a big shock to the system

About **pawpaws** (papaya): these, if you like them, can be eaten as a kind of tonic. They contain excellent supplies of invigorating minerals and vitamins and are reckoned to help the healing process and to aid digestion. Pawpaw pips – which taste like watercress – are good for you too. The smaller and more fragrant mountain varieties are delicious but in many parts of West Africa, pawpaws aren't even sold. They grow as giant weeds, left for the children, and not relished as proper fruit at all. If you don't see them for sale, approach the people of a house where they're growing in the compound.

MEDICAL TREATMENT

If you need **medical treatment** in West Africa, you'll discover a frightening lack of well-equipped **hospitals**. In each country, we've tried to indicate which are the best and to give general practitioners and dentists in city listings. For serious treatment you're almost certain to want to come home. Blood and urine tests can be performed locally but needles and other instruments may not be fresh from a sealed package. Insist on paying for new ones.

Moderate injuries can be treated locally. In remote areas, missions are usually the first recourse. If you require treatment, it's normally proficient and the charges low, though comforts fairly rudimentary.

CONTRACEPTIVES

Condoms are available from most pharmacies, or alternatively from some clinics and dispensaries. But they tend to be expensive or Korean. Take some with you. If you use oral contraceptives, get your doctor to prescribe a supply. And don't forget an alternative method to fall back on if you have a stomach upset or take a course of antibiotics, as either can leave you unprotected for the rest of the month.

In Britain your first source of advice and probable supplier of jabs and prescriptions is your general practitioner. Family doctors are often well-informed and some won't charge you for routine injections. For yellow fever and other exotic shots you'll normally have to visit a specialist clinic, often in a county town health authority headquarters.

In London, advice and low-cost **inoculations** are available from the **Hospital for Tropical Diseases**, 4 St Pancras Way, London NW1 0PE (☎071 388 8989). They produce a series of useful fact sheets and you can get most jabs without prior appointment any weekday morning. With a referral from your GP, the Hospital for Tropical Diseases will also give you a complete **check-up** on your return if you think it may be worth it.

Also in London, the *British Airways Travel Clinic*, 75 Regent St, London W1 (☎071 439 9584/5) is open Monday to Friday 09–19.00. They can provide a wide variety of unusual shots like plague, anthrax and rabies as well as the usual ones, anti-malarial tablets and various hardware.

If you can't make it to London, you may want to check out the services of **MASTA** *(Medical Advisory Services for Travellers Abroad,* Bureau of Hygiene and Tropical Diseases, Keppel St, London WC1E 7HT) who provide very detailed, personalised "Health Briefs" for whichever country or countries you're visiting. They advise on which inoculations you need and when you should get them, give rundowns on all the diseases you're (not) likely to fall victim to and include up-to-date health news from the countries concerned. The "Concise Brief" seems pretty complete but the "Comprehensive" one is amazingly so and a delight for hypochondriacs (students half-price). *MASTA* also sell Neat Deet insect repellant (brilliant stuff), various mosquito nets and *Sterile Emergency Kits* – basically sterile needles and drip.

Other major tropical disease centres in the UK are:

Liverpool School of Tropical Medicine, Pembroke Place, Liverpool L3 5QA (☎051 708 9393);	**Communicable Diseases Unit**, Ruchill Hospital, Glasgow G20 9NB (☎041 946 7120).	**Department of Communicable and Tropical Diseases**, East Birmingham Hospital, Bordesley Green Rd, Birmingham B9 5ST (☎021 772 4311);

Avoid jumping for **antibiotics** at the first sign of trouble. They annihilate what's nicely known as your *gut flora* (most of which you want to keep) and will not work on viruses such as those which cause amoebic dysentery. By the time you're considering their use, you should really seek a doctor. If you've definitely got blood in your diarrhoea and *it's impossible to see a doctor*, then this is the time to take a course of metronidazole (*Flagyl*). You'd have to arrange this on prescription with your GP before your trip. Antibiotics and anti-diarrhoeal drugs shouldn't be used as preventatives – this is potentially very dangerous. Women using **contraceptive pills** have another reason to fear diarrhoea – it reduces hormone absorption and can leave you unprotected.

Lastly, two common gynaecological problems. **Cystitis** can be relieved, if not eradicated, with acidy fruit juice. Oranges and pineapples are available in abundance over much of the region. Don't fail to get medical treatment as soon as possible however, as cystitis can be very dangerous in a hot climate. **Thrush** responds well to a good dose of yoghurt (both eaten and applied).

Take more care than usual over minor **cuts and scrapes** – the most trivial scratch can become a throbbing infection if you ignore it. Take a small tube of antiseptic cream with you – *Cicatrin* is recommended. Otherwise, there are all sorts of potential **bites**, **stings** and **rashes** which rarely, if ever materialise.

Many people get a bout of **prickly heat** rash at first, before they're acclimatised. It's an infection of the sweat ducts caused by excessive perspiration which doesn't dry off. A cool shower, **zinc oxide powder** and cotton clothes should help. On the subject of heat, it's important not to overdose on **sunshine** – at least in the first week or two. The powerful heat and bright light can mess up your system. A **hat** is strongly recommended and sunglasses are almost required.

As for animal attacks, **dogs** are usually sad and skulking and pose little threat, though like captive **monkeys** they may carry rabies. **Scorpions** and **spiders** abound but are hardly ever seen unless you go turning over rocks or logs.

Scorpion stings are painful but almost never fatal – and scorpions usually need considerable goading before they'll bring their tail into service. Spiders are mostly quite harmless. The large, terrifyingly fast and active **solifugids** (also known as camel spiders or wind scorpions) do sometimes have a painful bite, but you're not likely to sit around and find out. **Snakes** are common but, again, the vast majority are harmless and to see one at all you'll need to search stealthily – walk heavily and they obligingly disappear. For reassurance about larger beasts, see "Wildlife and National Parks" on p.62.

TEETH

Get a thorough **dental check-up** before leaving and take extra care of your teeth while in West Africa. Stringy meat, acid fruit and too many soft drinks are some of the hazards. The answer is to take dental floss and brush at least once in the middle of the day. You could get into the habit of using a fresh "toothbrush stick" cut from a branch, as many locals do. Some varieties (for sale at markets) contain a plaque-destroying enzyme and they're not a bad oral substitute for a cigarette.

If you lose a filling and aren't inclined to see a dentist locally, try and get hold of some *gutta percha* – a natural, rubbery substance – which is available from some pharmacies. You heat it and then pack it in the hole as a temporary filling. Your dentist could get you some to take with you. **Emergency dental packs** are available from some vaccination centres (see box). Using chewing gum for the same job is a bad idea.

INSURANCE

Insurance, in the light of all this, is too important to ignore. Though it's unlikely you'll need to call on it for medical reasons, *ISIS* travel insurance – available to everyone up to the age of 65 through branches of *STA Travel* or *Endsleigh* (☎071 589 6783) – is one of the cheapest available in Britain. An outlay of £15–20 per month will cover you against all sorts of calamities as well as lost baggage, flight cancellations and hospital charges.

Whatever insurance you go for, make sure you're not paying a high premium for cover you don't need – too much baggage cover, or a huge sum for personal liability – and make sure you *are* covered for what you intend to do. Some activities (climbing for example) are usually specifically excluded but can often be included as a supplement.

If you need to claim, you *must* have a police report in the case of theft or loss, and supporting evidence in the case of hospital and medication bills. Keep photocopies of everything before you send it to the insurer and don't allow months to elapse before informing them. Write immediately and tell them what's happened. You can usually claim later.

> For a book on your health in tropical countries you couldn't do better than Richard Dawood's *Travellers' Health*, (OUP, £5.95); exceptionally sane, detailed and well-written, it covers just about every imaginable symptom.

MAPS, INFORMATION AND SOURCES

Although you will find maps of individual countries, and even certain cities, when you get to West Africa, they're almost always expensive and hard to obtain. Buy what you need in advance. As for tourist offices, there are few around and those that exist – usually attached to embassies or airlines – rarely offer more than a few vague leaflets. For addresses see the "Information and Maps" details at the front of each country section. Specialist bookshops and libraries are the best sources of pre-departure information. For general pre-departure reading have a look at the "Books" section on p000.

MAPS

The single most useful item to take is the **Michelin** map **#953** *Africa North and West*. It covers all of northwest Africa with the exception of southern Cameroon (on the #955 *Africa Central and South*). A fairly recent edition of the #953 takes account of most roads built in the 1980s, showing water and fuel sources, roads liable to flood, ferry crossings and a mass of other details at a scale of 40km to 1cm (63 miles to the inch). It's indispensable for crossing the Sahara. The only serious competition is *Kummerly & Frey's* "Africa North & West" map – on the same scale but less detailed and altogether less user-friendly.

For individual countries, the French **Institut Géographique National** (IGN – 107 rue de la Boétie, 75008, Paris) has maps currently in print for a number of Francophone countries (plus Guinea-Bissau) but several of them are out of date. There are good *Michelin* maps of Algeria-Tunisia (north) and Côte d'Ivoire, a number of road maps of Nigeria, and a good new one of Cameroon by *Macmillan*. Other maps, where they exist, are hard to obtain abroad. Again, details for each country are given under "Information and Maps".

Lastly, get hold of a copy of the international *Thomas Cook Overseas Timetable* (£5.95, bi-monthly from branches of *Thomas Cook*). The West African coverage is sparse and rarely updated, but it does mention pretty well every country and provides the closest impression you'll ever see of railway timetables, with incomplete bus details thrown in for reasonable measure.

MAP AND BOOK SUPPLIERS

Stanford's, 12–14 Long Acre, Covent Garden, London WC2E 9LP (☎071 836 1321). Centrally located and one of the world's best map and guide book suppliers.

Robertson McCarta, 122 King's Cross Rd, London WC1X 9DS (☎071 278 8276). IGN agents.

Africa Bookcentre, 38 King St, London WC2E 8JT (☎071 240 6649). Located in the Africa Centre, Mon–Sat 11am–5.30pm. A very wide selection of books from and about the continent, with an emphasis on African writers and academic works.

The Travellers Bookshop, 25 Cecil Court, London WC2N 4EZ (☎071 836 9132). New shop, with enthusiastic, well-travelled staff and "buyback" offer on used books.

Daunt Books for Travellers, 83 Marylebone High St, W1M 4AL (☎071 224 2295). A huge selection of guides and maps, plus history, novels and more.

If you're in **Paris**, *Ulysse* at 35 rue St Louis en Ile, 75004 Paris (Metro, Pont Marie) is crammed full of guides, old books and maps.

LIBRARIES AND RESOURCE CENTRES

Africa Centre, 38 King Street, London WC2E 8JT (☎071 836 1973). Office and reading room open Mon–Fri 9.30am–6pm. Britain's best independent charity institute for African affairs, open to allcomers – reading room with magazines and newspapers, exhibitions, music, theatre, cinema, language teaching. Bar and restaurant open seven days. A good place to meet people.

School of Oriental and African Studies Library, Thornhaugh St, Russel Square, London WC1H 0XG (☎071 637 2388). A vast collection of books, journals and maps in a modern building. Day visits are allowed but membership to borrow costs £10 with a £50 deposit and a reference.

Commonwealth Institute, Kensington High Street, London W8 6NQ (☎071 603 4535) Large centre offering library and resource services, shop, exhibitions, workshops. Performance venue

Royal Geographical Society, 1 Kensington Gore, London SW7 2AR (☎071 581 2057). Helpful Expedition Advisory Service provides a wealth of information, including maps and technical guides.

WARRI, WOLÉ, OURIL – THE GAME OF HOLES AND SEEDS

There's an ancient game for two people played all over Africa with two opposing rows of holes and a handful each of seeds, cowries or pebbles. It goes under dozens of different names and the rules vary locally. But the principle is always the same. Seeds are deposited in each hole and then the players take turns to pick up a pile from one of their holes and "sow" them, usually one by one, around the board. Depending on the rules, the hole the last seed is sown into determines the continuation of play, and, if it makes up a certain number of seeds in that hole, then they're captured. The player with the most seeds at the end, wins. It's a game that's devastatingly simple and, at the same time, mathematically highly complex in its endless chain of cause and effect – financial analysts love it.

GETTING AROUND IN WEST AFRICA

Details of local route and transport conditions in each country are given under "Arrivals" and "Getting Around" at the beginning of each country part. Specific transport practicalities are also covered in the *Arrivals* sections for each capital city and in "Moving On" details throughout. What follows here is a general user's guide to West African transport practicalities, highlighting various options and pitfalls.

BUSH TAXIS

The classic form of West African public transport is the **bush taxi** (*taxi brousse* in French, plus numerous local terms). This can vary from a reasonably comfortable ***Peugeot* station wagon** seating five or six plus driver, to the same thing seating nine or ten in discomfort, to a converted **Japanese pick-up** with slat-wood benches and a canvas awning jammed with fifteen people or more. A basket of chickens stuffed under the bench, and maybe a goat or two tied to the roof are regular fare-paying additions. Larger French **box vans**, increasingly replaced by Japanese and Korean **minibuses**,

are no less zoo-like, though padded benches or seats help, as does the extra ventilation. Most vehicles have roof-rack luggage carriers. Most also have a more expensive seat or two at the front with the driver.

If you spend any time in West Africa travelling by public transport, bush taxis are vehicles you'll have to get used to. The **chaos** which seems to accompany their journeys is an illusion. They are nearly all licenced passenger vehicles, serving approved routes at fixed rates. Many even have notional schedules, though these are never published and rarely adhered to.

Peugeot taxis generally sell their places and drive straight from A to B, if possible without stopping. They often do the trip in half the time it takes a more beat-up bush taxi, which may drop people off and take fares en route. But the converted pick-ups (*bâchés* in French, after their tarpaulins) are often the only way to get to more obscure destinations, or to travel on the roughest roads. Not suprisingly they're cheaper.

Beware of inadvertently *chartering* a bush taxi for private hire (a *déplacement* in French). Once you've done it, there's no way of avoiding paying for *all the seats*.

TAXI PARK TACTICS

Most towns have a **transport park** ("station" "stand", *gare routière*, *autogare*) where vehicles assemble to fill with passengers. Larger towns usually have several, each serving different routes and usually located on the relevant road out, at the edge of town.

Practice varies slightly from country to country, but usually on arrival you'll find you're quickly surrounded by **taxi scouts** trying to get you into their vehicle. This can be trying and sometimes unnerving – when there's lots of competition and you're physically mobbed. It pays to behave robustly and to know exactly where you're going,

---

BUSH TAXI SURVIVAL

They're probably the most dangerous vehicles on the roads so don't be afraid to make a very big fuss if the driver appears to have lost all sense. Ask and then shout at him to **"Slow down!"** ("Ralentir!" in French) and try to enlist the support of fellow travellers – which is rarely forthcoming. In *Peugeots* it's nice to have a couple of **cassettes** for the stereo. In any vehicle, and in most parts of West Africa, sharing some **kola nuts** goes down well (see p.55). Lastly, if you're in a van with an engine mounted behind the front cab, be sure not to sit near it – you'll melt.

and the names of any towns en route or beyond. It's often the case that your destination is not where all the vehicles are headed. You may have to change, or get out earlier. The best time to travel is early in the morning. By an hour after sunrise the best vehicles have gone. In many parts there won't be another until the next day.

Before long on your travels, you'll run into a situation where you seem to be **the only passenger** in a vehicle you were assured was about to leave. Beware of this. It's true your presence will encourage others to take a seat in the vehicle — which is why they wanted you there in the first place. But sometimes it's better to forget over-ambitious travel plans (especially any time after noon) or to take a shorter journey with a vehicle that's nearly ready to go. Taxi parks are full of interest for up to an hour or so. But a half day spent as passenger bait in one is a waste of time.

From passenger confidence to **fares**: in order to guarantee you'll stay and attract others, drivers, owners and scouts will often try to get you to pay up front. Again, practice varies from country to country. Your luggage tied on the roof generally ought to be sufficient sign of good faith and, unless you see others paying, it's always best to delay. Make sure you pay the right person when you do.

Over-charging is almost unheard of. It's your **luggage** that will cost you if you don't fight. You'll often have to argue fiercely about how small, light and streamlined it is. Fellow passengers are just as likely to suffer but aren't in such a good position to create a scene. Shout, compare and contrast, tell the crowd how he's trying to kill you with his grasping ways. Make them laugh, make him happy to give you a good price. If you get nowhere, go to one side with him and be conspiratorial — this sometimes works because people like to show off business acumen and it draws attention again. If you pay more than **one third** of the head price (the fare) for a back pack or large bag of any size, you've been

taken. It's normally much less. Remember, you can argue forever about what you're *going* to pay, but once you've paid it, the argument is over.

During **long waits** it's a good idea to keep an eye on your luggage. Anything tied on the roof is safe, but taxi parks are notoriously thievey and bags sometimes get grabbed through open windows. Keep valuable items round your neck. Don't worry unduly, however, if the vehicle, while waiting to fill, and with booked passengers scattered around, suddenly takes off with all your gear on top. While it's obviously good practice to make a discreet mental note of the vehicle registration, you should avoid offence by appearing suspicious. Make friends with other passengers and relax. Maybe nobody knows where they've gone (probably to buy petrol), but they'll be back.

BUSES

Bus travel, when you've the option, is usually more comfortable, though certain manifestations are little better than gigantic bush taxis and not always much faster. Algeria, Niger, Burkina Faso, Cape Verde, Mali, The Gambia, Sierra Leone, Côte d'Ivoire, Ghana and Nigeria have more or less well-developed bus services. Ghana's state-run service is particularly good, and not expensive. Côte d'Ivoire even has video coaches.

The big advantage of most buses is having your own seat (even *Peugeot* bush taxis usually sell more places than there are seats) and being able to buy tickets in advance for a departure at a set time. There's still some room for discussion over luggage, but it's rarely a big issue.

Whether travelling by bus or bush taxi, it's worth considering your general direction through the trip and **which side to sit on for the shadiest ride**. This is especially important on dirt roads when the combination of slow, bumpy ride, dust and fierce sun can be horrible. If you're travelling on a *busy* dirt road with lots of other traffic, you don't want to be seated on the left of the vehicle in any case.

POLICE AND ARMY CHECKPOINTS

It's worth paying some attention to the condition of driver and vehicle before deciding to give him your custom. It's rare to undertake any journey over 20km in West Africa without encountering a posse of uniforms at the side of the road. A neatly turned-out *Peugeot* with a well-tied load and quite possibly some persons of influence inside is likely to pause for a greeting and move on. Conversely, a bruised and shaken *camion bâché* with 19 passengers, no lights and the contents of someone's house on the roof may be detained for some hours. During which time you'll have to extract what interest you can from the situation. See "Trouble – getting in and out".

TRUCKS

On all main routes – and in the remotest regions too – you'll be able to travel by **lorry**. Pick up a lift in small villages or along the road. You'll rarely find a truck ride in a large town as it's usually against the law. Once aboard, you can expect the lorry to stop at every checkpoint – slow progress.

There's sometimes a spare seat or two in the cab, but more often space in the back. **Travelling in the back** of panelled vehicles is pretty miserable, but many older trucks are open at the back with wood frame sides. When loaded with suitable cargo, these can be a delight to travel in. You get great views and even, on occasions, a comfortable ride in a recumbent position. Do bear in mind your safety however (look out for low branches) and avoid getting the driver in police trouble by being conspicuous or foolhardy.

Travelling in an empty goods lorry on bad roads can be close to intolerable. They go much faster unladen and you're typically forced to stand and clasp the sides as the vehicle smashes through the pot holes, causing severe discomfort to loose parts of the anatomy. For truck travel, you need to know your fares and distances or you'll find yourself paying over the odds. Occasionally you might rib or plead with a driver into giving you a free lift. Lorries often drive late into the night too. If you're carried outside, be sure to have **something warm to wear** for later.

HITCHING

This is how the majority of rural people get around – by **waving down a vehicle** – but they invariably pay, whether it's public transport, a truck or a private car with a spare place. Private vehicles are still comparatively rare and usually full. Travelling for nothing is often considered to be rather improper and most people will assume your car's broken down or something. There's some sense, however, in hitching in and out of large cities, especially if you're stuck for money or can't find a bus or taxi. The kinds of drivers who respond positively are usually foreign-educated business types or expatriates.

Hitching **techniques** need to be exuberant. A modest thumb is more likely to be interpreted as a friendly, or rude, gesture than a request. Beckon the driver to stop with your palm. You'll feel like a policeman but that doesn't matter. Always explain first if you can't – or won't – pay. You will sometimes be left at the side of the road.

Best chances for conventional hitch-hiking are in Senegal, Côte d'Ivoire, Ghana, Nigeria and Cameroon. Algeria is a slightly special case – marvellously easy and rewarding hitching in the north, but much harder in the desert proper. Your only chance of a free lift north or south across the Sahara is with generous or lonesome tourists.

Hitching with overland tourists can be a good change of pace, and – more calculatingly – if you're in the right vicinity can throw you in with people visiting game parks, which tend otherwise to be inaccessible to the wheel-less.

TRAINS

For many (colonial) years there was a French plan to push a **railway** across the Sahara. Had it succeeded, it might have have altered today's network, in which only two of the nine West African railway systems cross borders. And of those nine rail systems most are single lines running from the coast to the interior.

In practice only three lines are much used by travellers: in Cameroon between **Douala and Ngaoundéré**; the *Niger-Océan* line between **Bamako and Dakar**; and the line between **Abidjan and Ouagadougou**. Timed right, you could do a trip of as short as a couple of weeks, substantially by rail, through Senegal, Mali, Burkina Faso and Côte d'Ivoire.

Details are given on all these railways through the book. The *Thomas Cook* Overseas Timetable (monthly, from travel agents) also covers them, but is often out of date. It's worth knowing that travelling by rail in West Africa is usually slower than road and that while you can always get **street food** through the windows at stations, you should have **drinking water** for the duration. It's also worth remarking that **toilets** on the trains are rarely usable by the time you've left the city – maybe you should prepare in advance for that too.

Although **other railway lines** exist, not all of them are running and some are freight only. The ones marked on our map operate passenger services. Some offer student discounts, though these are usually intended for nationals.

FERRIES

There are still hundreds of small, hand-hauled or spluttering diesel ferries pulling people and vehicles across the rivers of West Africa. But river transport upstream or down is very limited. The most attractive **ferry services** run on the Niger

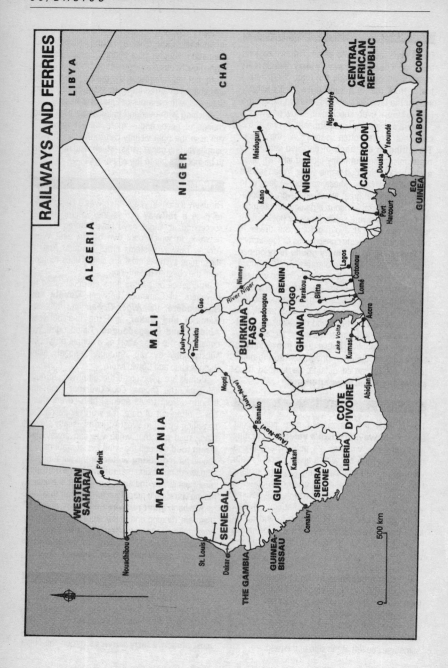

RAILWAYS AND FERRIES

river in Mali, from the height of the rainy season to a couple of months after it finishes. Apart from the Ghanaian services on Lake Volta, there are few other significant car ferries operating in the region. The Gambia river no longer has a ferry service. Nor does the Senegal.

On the Niger, more or less anywhere between Kankan in Guinea and Niamey in the republic of Niger, you can usually negotiate a passage in a **pirogue** (a dug-out/plank canoe) or a **pinasse** (a larger freight carrying vessel) at any time of year, but in parts of Mali this has now become an expensive, tourism-stained affair.

There's virtually no scheduled inter-state **sea transport**. Ferries connect the Cape Verde islands with each other and Dakar and there's minor shipping on the coasts of Sierra Leone, Guinea-Bissau, and Nigeria.

PLANES

If you're in a hurry, **flying** is usually the only way to go. But West African inter-state flights are expensive, and travel by air not automatically the quickest option. On several coast connections the combination of flying time, formalities and transfers to and from the airports are enough to counteract any advantage over fast road transport. Freetown–Monrovia and Abidjan–Accra can be done in a day and Dakar–Banjul, and hops between Accra–Cotonou–Lagos, in a few hours.

Aviation in West Africa is in financial trouble and changes happen often. Currently the big West African inter-state **airlines** are *Air Afrique*, owned by a consortium of francophone governments, and *Ghana Airways*. Together they more or less cover the region. Other up-and-running state airlines (the larger of which operate inter-state services) include *Nigeria Airways*, *Cameroon Airlines*, *Air Ivoire*, *Air Sénégal*, *Air Mauritanie* and *TACV* of Cape Verde. Airlines in less certain state of repair include *TAGB* of Guinea-Bissau, *Air Guinée*, *Air Mali*, *Air Niger*, *Air Benin*, *Sierra Leone Airlines* and *Air Liberia*. Several of them are virtually defunct.

A number of other airlines (mostly private) operate domestic services. Most flights on the private airlines are operated on a charter basis, though sometimes with regularity, so you can buy a seat, in effect, from the charterer.

You can expect domestic flights to cost in the order of twice the surface transport rate. Also, beware of lower-than-expected baggage allowances on some internal flights.

AIR TICKET TACTICS

The air ticket set-up in West Africa is quite different from Europe's. There's little unofficial discounting of **fares**. Most tickets get sold at the approved rate, though some airlines operate anomalously, in which case you'll find it hard to discover what those fares are. If you possess an *ISIC* **student card** it's always worth requesting a student reduction. Several airlines offer them.

You can expect some problems in **getting a reservation**, further problems at the airport getting a boarding pass and (occasionally) problems yet again in exchanging the boarding pass for a seat. Many domestic and regional flights in West Africa are heavily and permanently blockbooked by government and not-so-government departments. Only when the actual number of required seats is notified to the airline can they open normal reservations to the public. In many cases notification comes on the day of departure, in the airport.

There's little you can do to un-burden yourself of this state of affairs. Obviously, book as soon as you can and re-book if plans change, rather than wait until you're certain. This anyway gives you leverage in terms of personal recognition at the airline office, and airline bookings don't require a deposit as a rule. Be utterly sceptical of a "confirmed seat" until you're sitting in it. Arrive at the airport long before the flight if you've any doubt about your status, and use every angle and pull every string you can to improve your chances. Clearly this is a worst-case scenario, but even when there appears to be no problem and no question of not getting on, always **re-confirm your seat** in person two days before the flight.

CAR HIRE

Car hire is available in nearly every capital city, at most of the larger airports and in one or two provincial towns in a number of countries. *Hertz*, *Avis* and *Europcar* have a fair network, enabling you to pre-book. *Hertz*, for example, offers Benin, Cameroon, Côte d'Ivoire, Nigeria, Niger, Senegal and Togo (with Guinea and Mauritania possibly still available too). Outlets are local licensed firms and, apart from being more expensive, not necessarily much different from others which don't have the international trademark. Where possible we've given details in city listings to enable advance booking of those too.

There are several general **points to bear in mind**. Firstly, hired cars cannot as a rule, be driven into **neighbouring countries**. In a number of countries, private self-drive car hire is a novelty and authorities feel uneasy about it beyond the city limits. You may be obliged to take a **driver** with the car and this inevitably puts the price up, though it isn't always a bad arrangement in itself – and can work out brilliantly. Some firms insist on four-wheel drive (4WD) if you'll be departing from surfaced highways. The **costs** can be astronomical and you may spend in a day what would pay for a week's self-drive in Europe.

An alternative is to consider simply hiring a **taxi** on a daily basis. Buy the fuel separately or you'll never get anywhere and settle every other question in advance – bed, board, cigarettes too. And however good the price, don't take on a vehicle that's unsafe or a driver you don't like and can't communicate with.

Whether you're driving or being driven, you should have your **national driving licence** with you and an **international licence** too. At delicate moments, British driving licences count for little as they lack the important identity photo. Minimum age for hiring varies from 21 to 25 (18 for Nigeria) with one or two year's experience.

DRIVING

Don't automatically assume the vehicle is roadworthy. **Before setting off**, have a look at the engine and tyres and don't leave without checking water, battery and spare tyre (preferably two) and making sure you've a few tools. Except on certain main highways, it's important to keep jerricans of water and petrol on board. As for breakdowns, local mechanics are usually excellent and can apply creative ingenuity to the most disastrous situations. But spare parts, tools and proper equipment are rare away from the *Michelin* map's red highways – and not really common along them.

When **driving**, beware of unexpected rocks and ditches – not to mention animals and people – on the road. It's accepted practice to honk your horn stridently to warn pedestrians, though be cautious of doing so in built-up areas which may have local laws you'd quickly fall foul of.

All of West Africa **drives on the right**, though in reality vehicles keep to the best part of the road until they have to pass each other (ill-positioned potholes account for many head-on collisions). Right- and left-hand **signals** are conventionally used to say "Please overtake" or "Don't overtake!", but you shouldn't assume the driver in front can see. In fact, never assume anything about the behaviour of other drivers. Driving licences are obtained by various methods in West Africa, not all of them after a dozen lessons with a School of Motoring. Road death statistics are horrifying – Nigeria, famously, takes the lead in this respect.

You're unlikely to be kept for long by **police** or other security forces at the roadside, but you should *never* pass a check-point or barrier without stopping and waiting to be waved on. Nor should you ever drive anywhere without all your documents.

CYCLING

In many ways **cycling** is the ideal form of transport in West Africa. It gives you total independence, with no loss of contact. You can camp out all the time if you prefer, or take your bike into hotel rooms with you. When you're cycling in rural areas you can often leave your bike unattended for a short while if you're eating in a chop house or visiting a market – a crowd of onlookers will make sure no one touches it. If you get tired of pedalling you've the simple option of transporting your bike on top of a bush taxi or bus (reckon on paying about half-fare) or even "cycle-hitching".

And a bike gives you great scope for exploring off the beaten track and getting round cities. Routes that can't be used by motor vehicles – even motorbikes – because they're too rough, or involve crossing rivers by small craft, are open to you. With a tough bike, you can explore off the roads altogether, using bush paths – though remember to give ample verbal warning to people walking in your direction ahead of you, who may otherwise be seriously frightened by your appearance.

A rear-view **mirror** is close to essential on busy roads.

PRACTICALITIES

You won't get any **spares for mountainbikes** in West Africa. But take only what you're sure to need – spare tubes, spare spokes and a good tool kit. If you need to do anything major, you can always borrow large spanners and other heavy equipment. Don't bother with spare tyres if you're going for under six months. On a long trip, it's worth depositing some money with a reputable dealer before you leave so that, in an emergency, you could telex from a public telex office and have a part sent out by a courier service like *DHL*.

You can hire bicycles and mopeds in a number of places, including The Gambia, Basse Casamance (Senegal) and Ouagadougou (Burkina Faso). But they're not usually well-adapted for touring, as they lack the necessary carriers. Anywhere you fancy cycling, however, you can often make informal arrangements to lease a bike for a few days.

You can forego these hassles by buying one of the heavyweight **roadsters on sale locally**. There are bike shops and market areas devoted to cycling in most large towns. Ouagadougou in Burkina Faso has long been one of the cheapest places to buy, with a vast area devoted to bikes and good second-hand possibilities from about £60. You should be able to get a new bike for under £100. Bikes with three-speed hub gears (usually *Raleighs*) come somewhat more expensive. If you go for the gearless mount, console yourself with the fact that hub gears are fiddly to adjust and almost impossible to mend if anything packs up inside.

If you're taking a bike with you, then you'll probably want to **carry your gear** in panniers. These are fiendishly inconvenient when not attached to the bike, however, and you might consider sacrificing ideal load-bearing and streamlining technology for a backpack you can lash down on the rear carrier. An arrangement like this is probably what you'll have to do if you buy a bike in West Africa. Locally, with the kind of cane that is used for cane furniture plus lashings of inner tube rubber strips, you can create your own highly un-aerodynamic **carrier**, with room for a box of food and a gallon of water underneath.

With a bike from home, do take a battery **lighting system** (dynamo lighting is a pain) – it's surprising how often you'll need it. The front light doubles as a torch and getting batteries is no problem.

Take a **U-bolt cycle lock**. In situations where you have to lock the bike, you'll always find something to lock it to. Out in the bush it's less important. Local bikes can be locked with a padlock and chain in a hose which you can buy and fix up in any market.

Finding and carrying **water** is a daily chore on a long cycle trip. You'll need at least one five-litre container per person (more if you're camping out and want to wash) but you shouldn't often need to carry it full. Empty plastic oil jars and jerricans, available all over North and West Africa, are convenient.

Lastly, **distances**: depending on your fitness and enthusiasm, expect to cycle around 1000km a month, including at least two days off for every three on the road. During periods when you're basically cycling from A to B (often on a paved road, which is somewhat slow on a mountain-bike), you'll find 40–50km in the early morning and 20–30km more in the afternoon is plenty.

OTHER FORMS OF LOCOMOTION

Clearly, if you're hardy and not tied to any schedule, you can simply **walk**. All over the region, you'll come across local people walking vast distances because they have no money at all to pay for transport. If you're hiking for a few days you can fall in with them (if you can keep up), but they'll rarely speak any French or English.

From a more recreational angle, we've covered a number of **hiking possibilities** throughout West Africa. These are mostly in upland and mountainous regions. You need good footwear – heat, sweat and water take a heavy toll.

It's an attractive idea also to use a **beast of burden** for your travels. Unfortunately, **horses** succumb quickly in the more southern tse-tse fly regions and a horse in good shape is expensive. If you know what to look for and how to a look after a horse, the most promising districts are sub-Sahelian – most of southern Mali, Burkina, southern Niger, northern Nigeria and further south into highland Cameroon. If you ride south towards the coast, however, and sell your animal, it's likely to end up in a pot.

Donkeys are a lot tougher, cheaper and will happily go further south in the dry season. They're used to long treks. You'd need three donkeys between two with luggage, however. Then there are **camels** (dromedaries: *méharis* in French). It's not impossible to join a caravan in the desert or northern Sahel, though fewer and fewer such journeys are made these days. But buying, equipping and travelling with your own animals is not to be undertaken lightly even by the most qualified romantics. For salutary advice read Michael Asher's *Impossible Journey* (Viking, 1988).

SLEEPING

There's not a huge diversity of accommodation options in West Africa. A good range of hotels is found only in the cities, and in several countries hotels themselves are rather uncommon outside the capital. Hostels of various kinds are usually an urban phenomenon, often permanently full and so not to be relied upon and there are no IYHA youth hostels. In some countries you'll find government rest houses and in remote parts where tourists are rare you may be able to stay in volunteer rest houses and missions.

Campsites are very rare. *Campements*, in several of the French-speaking countries, are more West African. The options of staying with local people or camping in the bush are usually there depending on how you travel.

HOTELS

In large towns, and specifically capitals, you'll want and probably have to stay in **hotels**. There tends to be a gap between the expensive places and the dives and you sometimes need to look hard to find something good at a reasonable price. If you're splurging there's usually a clutch of **international establishments** bookable from abroad. There are local star ratings but they're not much used and about as useless an indication of value for money as anywhere. Hotel listings throughout this book are simply categorised by price.

There's not much local market for western-style hotels (with reception, bars, restaurant) except in countries with a mobile, salaried middle class. **Mid-range hotels** are usually well-run and nice enough places to stay. But **small town hotels** – and of course the cheapest joints in the cities – are usually equated with drinking and sex. Rooms are often taken for a few hours only. These places sometimes have a vaguely brothel-ish feel about them, with a gang of women and toddlers permanently in residence. Don't be put off unduly. They can be terrific fun to stay at – and by no means all are intimidating places for female travellers – though you may have to pick a room carefully (not easy) for anything like a quiet night.

It's hard to generalise about **prices** across the region. Hotels are generally expensive throughout the CFA zone, with Togo and Burkina Faso more reasonable. Prices in soft currency countries may depend on where you change your money. Broadly, for a decent, simple twin room with clean sheets, air-conditioning and bathroom, expect to pay upwards of £20. You can often get a fairly mediocre place, usually without air-conditioning and certainly without hot water, for about £10. But the $5 hotel room (even a single of the most basic kind with showers down the corridor) is nearly history. To put some kind of perspective on all this, hotels in Morocco are perhaps a third or a quarter of the cost of any in West Africa.

HOSTELS

Although there are no internationally affiliated youth hostels in West Africa, you'll find **YMCA** and **YWCA** hostels in several anglophone cities (notably Freetown, Monrovia, Accra, Lagos) where they're usually permanently full with students and single professionals. If you can get in they're great places to meet people and, though they're generally run by slightly pious types there are few limiting restrictions on what you do and when.

CAMPEMENTS AND REST HOUSES

For non-camping travellers, alternative types of "hotel" accommodation are popular options in the rural areas. *Campements*, in French-

CHEAP HOTEL PRACTICALITIES

● Always ask to **see the room** first and don't be surprised if it looks like a tornado's passed through, especially in the morning before it's been cleaned.

● Unless there's a proper tariff sheet, it's always worth haggling over the **price** of a room. If there's air conditioning or a fan but no electricity, ask for a discount. Check there'll be no **tax** on top.

● In highland regions or during the *harmattan* it's normally expected you'll ask for a bucket of **hot water** to supplement the cold tap – but it may not be offered.

● You usually **pay** on taking the room and may have to leave your **passport** with the person in charge if there's no registration card to fill out.

● Always ask for clean sheets and towel if you're not happy with them.

● Use discretion about leaving your **keys** with the management and, if your door locks by padlock, use your own instead and check the fixture.

● If you suspect **bedbugs** may lurk behind the plaster, pull the beds away from the wall. Keeping the light on deters them.

ACCOMMODATION ABBREVIATIONS

AC Air-conditioning, air-conditioned

S/C Self-contained, with private shower and toilet

B&B Bed and breakfast

HB Half board, meaning dinner, bed and breakfast

FB Full board, meaning all meals included

CFA3000/5000 for example, means CFA3000 for a single, CFA5000 for two people sharing, usually a twin room. Double beds are unusual.

---

speaking countries, have a fairly loose definition. They're certainly not camping sites, though you can sometimes camp at them, but they represent more the modern equivalent of a colonial caravanserai or "encampment" in the bush, often associated with game parks and areas of natural beauty. They tend to consist of huts or small room blocks made of local materials (often mud bricks and thatch) with shared washing and toilet facilities. At the top end they're effectively hotels. But at their most innovative, in Senegal, they're *campements rurals integrés* ("rurally integrated"), built with government loans by the people of a village in order to host independent travellers.

In the English-speaking countries a network of **government rest houses**, for the use of officials on tour, is theoretically at the disposal of travellers when rooms aren't occupied. There's a similar *réseau* of government *villas* in Guinea. In fact, these places are very often unused for long periods and need a good airing. Water and electricity are often turned off or disconnected. First, in any case, you have to find the caretaker.

And lastly there are the **aid and development organisation rest houses** and **rest houses of voluntary organisations** like the United States Peace Corps (some 1400 of whose graduate volunteers are on placements in thirteen West African countries at any one time) and, somewhat thinly these days, **missions**. If you're travelling extensively, you may find some of these alternatives helpful and generous in certain countries. In some cases – a few of the Peace Corps rest houses for example – there's a special tarif for "outsiders". But in general you'll be staying explicitly as a guest, using facilities intended for others. Where such arrangements are based on informal invitations and strictly word-of-mouth, we've usually kept them that way. It would be unfair to suggest that such accommodation is universally open to all, and it's sometimes abused.

CAMPING

The few **campsites** that exist are covered in the main body of the guide. There's a number at the end of the trans-Saharan arteries in Mali and Niger, several on the coast in Togo and virtually no others.

Bring the lightest **tent** you can afford or consider making your own. A few weekends messing about with a sewing machine, rip-stop nylon and some netting should see the job done if you've a little dexterity. Nylon netting with a sewn-on groundsheet is the basic tent. The flysheet is a separate roof. Make a scale model in paper first and be sure your fly-sheet doesn't stretch too much when wet (camping in the rain doesn't make much sense, but you may have no choice). The main purpose of a tent is to keep the insects out and give you some privacy. Outside poles back and front can be used for guys and tension but you'll probably resort to trees wherever they're convenient...

If you'd rather **buy a tent**, here's the best. It's called the *Skeeter*, made by *The North Face (Scotland) Ltd*, PO Box 16, Industrial Estate, Port Glasgow, PA14 5XL, (**☎0475 41344**), sold through branches of *Alpine Sports* in the UK and costs most of £300. But it uses "no-see-um" mosquito netting in a geodesic design to give you ample room for two, total insect protection and all round visibility when the flysheet is off, and it only weighs 3kg.

Camping rough depends much on your style of travel. Clearly, **if you're driving** your own vehicle it's only necessary to find a good spot for the night. Note that some countries – Benin is quite explicit – do not permit wild camping. Don't assume you can always do this anonymously. A vehicle in the deep bush is unusual and noisy and people will often come to watch your activities.

If you're cycling or walking, bush-camping is a lot less obtrusive in this respect. For safety's sake, always get right away from the main road to avoid being accidentally run over or exciting the interest of motorised pirates (every country has a few, West Africa fewer than most). You may still be visited by delegations of machete-wielding villagers, especially if you light a fire, but satisfaction that you're harmless is usually their first concern. Some cigarettes or a cup of tea breaks any ice.

If you're travelling by public transport, it's a lot harder to camp effectively night after night. Vehicles go from town to town and it's rare you can get dropped off at just the right spot in between, all ready and supplied for a night under the stars. **Walking out of town** in search of a place to camp is an exercise which soon palls, and it can be miles. If you really want to camp out – and it's one of the best West African experiences – you have to get independent transport or be fit enough to walk those centimetres across the *Michelin* map.

STAYING WITH PEOPLE

In this context there's not much to be said. Experiences vary enormously and depend as much on the guest as the host. But all over the region you'll run into **people who want to put you up for the night**. A warm, but more especially a *dutiful* hospitality characterises most of these contacts. Most open to them are single travellers who get into conversation on public transport. Your hosts are typically a low-income family with ambitions whose son has been away and has brought you home. You'll be expected to correspond later and send photographs.

It's sometimes difficult to know how to **repay such hospitality**, particularly since it often seems so disruptive of family life, with you set up in the master bedroom and kids sent running for special things for the guest. While it's impossible to generalise, for female guests a trip to the market with the woman/women of the household is an opportunity to pay for everything. Men can't do this, but buying a sack of rice or a big bundle of yams (get it delivered by barrow or porter) would be a generous gift.

In Benin and Mali it's illegal for foreigners to stay with *indigenes* (as the authorities call local people) and there's strong official disapproval in Niger also.

CAMPING MATTERS

In more heavily populated or farmed districts it's usually best to ask someone before pitching a tent. Out in the wilds, hard or thorny ground is likely to be the only obstacle. Fill your water bottles from a village before looking for a site. During the dry seasons, you'll rarely have trouble finding wood for a small fire so a stove isn't absolutely necessary. But it's very useful for wet or barren conditions. You can find *camping gaz* butane cartridges in most capital cities. Petrol stoves are more convenient once you've shelled out for them. If you're cycle-camping, a small kerosene lamp is perfectly feasible. Be sure to buy kerosene however, and not petrol . . . Another safety consideration, wild animals, isn't likely to worry you much when you're there (see "Wildlife and National Parks" further on). Night-time noises, especially in forest regions – some spectularly eerie and sinister shrieks and calls – merely add to the atmosphere.

EATING AND DRINKING

While West Africa has little in the way of well-defined cuisines this is in large part because supplies are erratic, recipes aren't written down, and no two meals ever taste quite the same. Nevertheless, there's a considerable variety of culinary pleasures and a probably infinite range of intoxicating drinks. Describing it all is complicated by the variety of terms used for common ingredients. Indigenous food and drink was one area in which colonial interests were limited. As far as possible, "Food and Drink" sections in the "Practicalities" for each country give an indication of what you can expect and any local specialities.

FOOD

The great thing about West African food is its massive calorific value. Hearty appetites are rarely disappointed. Although less bulky alternatives are usually available, most meals consist of a pile of the staple diet plus a sauce or stew often called "soup".

The **staple** varies geographically. **Rice** predominates everywhere from Mauritania to Liberia and across the Sahel and is expanding as a commercial staple. **Root crops** (varieties of yam and cassava) and **plantains** figure heavily along the coast from Côte d'Ivoire through Nigeria to Cameroon. In the Sahara, **couscous***, tiny grains of durum wheat flour, is common.

Sauces can be based on **palm oil** (thick and copper-coloured, all along the south coast from Sierra Leone eastwards), on **groundnut paste** (which is peanut butter, found mostly in Sahelian regions), **okra** ("gumbo" or "ladies' fingers" – five-sided, green pods with a high slime content which is much appreciated), various **beans** and the **leaves** of sweet potatoes and cassava among others. All of them are usually heavily spiced, often with chillis – "hot pepper" – though the emphasis on this ingredient tends to be exaggerated. It's rarely too much and only southern Nigeria is really dangerous territory for tender mouths. Whatever else they consist of, sauces are made with *bouillon* cubes – invariably *Maggi* cubes. *Maggi* sauce, too, is a ubiquitous presence in every cheap restaurant.

The more expensive, or festive, "sauces" have an emphasis on their **animal protein** content. **Fish** and **mutton** are probably the most common. **Eggs** are rarely very popular (they're sometimes attributed with contraceptive powers) but they're always available. **Beef** tends to be reserved for special occasions. **Chicken** is pricey, but a favourite meat for guests. **Pork** is very localised and hogs foraging at the roadside are a sure sign you're in a non-Islamic district. Various kinds of **"bush meat"** are widely eaten except in the most devoutly Muslim regions, and often bought and sold. Large, herbivorous rodents ("bush rat", "cutting grass", "agouti") are the commonest and usually delicious, but antelopes, monkeys, even cats, dogs and giant snails are eaten in various parts of West Africa.

---

* *Couscous* (*kus-kus*, *coos-coos* etc) is a confusing term and refers to the preparation of the flour as much as anything else. It can be made from other flours, not just wheat, but the principle of making tiny grains of flour, and then steaming them, is the same.

WHERE TO EAT

If you're lucky enough to be staying **with a family**, you're likely to experience consistently well-prepared and tasty food – though according to their means this may depend on how much you contribute. In homes, or when travelling on long-distance trucks, or by trading canoe, eating around a **communal dish** (in strictly Islamic regions always males at one, females at another)

COMMON WEST AFRICAN FOOD PLANTS

There's a multitude of names in different languages for the same few foodplants. Some of the names appear in the "Food and Drink" sections at the beginning of each country part. This section is an attempt to clarify things a little (botanical and French names in brackets).

Cassava (*Manihot*; *Manioc* in French). This is the spindly 2-metre shrub from South America, with hand-like leaves, seen growing all over. The tubers, which tend to have a bitter taste, are large and coarse and have to be boiled and then usually pounded in a mortar to reduce them to an edible glob of nearly pure starch (*fufu/foufou/eba*). Cassava leaves taste much nicer and are full of vitamins. They're finely shredded and used like spinach. *Gari* is cassava flour (from which tapioca is made), but the word gets used quite broadly.

Yam (*Dioscorea*; *ignames* in French). Yams are massive tubers which grow singly beneath a climbing, vine-like plant with spade-shaped leaves, commonly grown in southern parts of the region, especially in Nigeria. They come in white (the preferred) and yellow varieties and are used like cassava to make pounded yam *fufu*, but they have a better flavour.

Cocoyam (*Colocasia*). Tastier than yams or cassava, but easily confused. Grown mostly in wet, forest regions, the plants have unmistakably huge, heart-shaped, edible leaves. Tubers are rounded with a fleshy stalk and commonly known as "koko", "mankani", "taro", "eddo" or "dasheen". Similar names are often given to the introduced **Tannia** (*Xanthosoma*). This "new cocoyam" has giant arrow-shaped leaves and tasty, smaller, dark, hairy tubers.

Potatoes (*Ipomoea*; *Patate* in French). Unless specified as *Irish*, these are always the *sweet* variety with pink skins, known in America, confusingly, as "yams". They're grown in mounds and ridges and have a mass of creeping vines. They tend to be something of a luxury, used to add flavour to stews and sauces. The leaves are good and widely used. **Irish potatoes** (*Solanum*) only grow in West Africa above an altitude of about 1200 metres.

Millet (*Pennisetum*). Looks like bulrushes, with a maize-like stalk, grown mostly in the Sahel. *Gero* in Hausa. Used for porridge and gruel but, again, especially for making beer.

Sorghum (*Sorghum*; *Sorgho* in French). Tall plants (2 to 4 metres) similar to maize but with feathery, white or red grained flower heads. Also known as "guinea corn" and "giant millet", sorghum is grown mainly in the savannah zone, and is made into porridge or pap and, outstandingly, "millet beer".

Cowpeas (*Vigna*). The commonest type of bean ("black-eye beans"), cowpeas come in many varieties and are grown throughout the region. They're usually dried and stored for use, or made into flour, but you often see them freshly harvested in their long, pale pods. Mashed cowpeas are used for *akara* – "deep-fried balls" sold nearly everywhere. Common names include *wake* and *niebe*.

Maize (*Zea*; *Maïs* in French). Grown a lot in forest region clearings, this is exactly the same as "corn" and "sweetcorn" and used widely on the cob as a stop-gap and a roasted or boiled snack. Maize flour is used quite extenisvely in some parts as a staple – in Ghana for fermented corn dough (*kenkey*) for example.

Groundnut (*Arachis*; *Arachide* or *cacahouètes* in French). Groundnuts (peanuts, monkey nuts) are grown widely to be used as the basis of sauces, and you'll see little dollops of peanut butter on leaves, for sale in markets everywhere.

Melon seeds (*Cucumeropsis*). Certain types of melon are good only for their large, oily seeds, commonly known by the Yoruba name, *egusi*, and widely used in soups.

Plantain (*Musa*). These mega-bananas are found all over the rainier southern part of West Africa. They're not eaten raw, but cooked (fried when ripe, boiled and sometimes pounded to a tasty *fufu* when hard).

Aubergine (*Solanum*). These are grown on garden plots all over and come in many shapes and colours (round, white, yellow, red) but rarely in the familiar large, purple variety. Known variously as egg-plants, garden eggs or bitter balls, they can be identified as aubergines by the star-shaped, leathery, leafy bits at the stalk end.

Other common food plants include **onions** and **tomatoes** (available everywhere, even in the driest districts, but often tiny and sold in piles of four), **lettuces** (wash very carefully), short but tasty **cucumbers**, **avocados** (wonderful, huge specimens in Cameroon), **tiger nuts** (*chufa* – tiny coconut-flavoured tubers like shrivelled beans), **pigeon peas** (small, round brown and white beans), **white haricot**, **lima** and **butter beans**, and various kinds of **gourd**, **pumpkin** and **squash**.

is the typical way meals are consumed. You commonly finish in order of age, the eldest first. It's not normal to eat from separate dishes, and so restaurants, where someone goes and buys a meal for themselves, are not the institution they've become in the Euro-centric world.

But it's wrong to assume you can't eat well at the cheapest **street food stalls** and roadside or **market restaurants**. The secret is to eat early — this means late morning (11am–noon) and early evening (5–6pm), when most people eat and food is freshly prepared. Street food (most often offered by women) isn't usually a take-away — there's commonly a table and benches, plastic bowls, spoons and cold water. Anything extra you want — soft drinks, instant coffee — can be got for you from nearby.

If you want to eat in more privacy, most towns, even the smallest, have at least one or two **basic restaurants** (these are more commonly run by men). Much of the menu or blackboard is likely to be unavailable, however, and there's probably more cause for hesitation over what you eat in small restaurants where you can't be certain of the freshness or provenance of your food, than there is from street stalls where it all has to be cooked, or has just been cooked, before your eyes.

Large towns, and the capital cities of course, have a wide variety of restaurants and, in general, less street food options. Eating chop house cooking at inflated prices in a silver service restaurant seems odd at first, but it's sometimes a real treat and not necessarily to be sneered at. The eating out alternative to African food, in cities, is usually **French** or vaguely continental,

international **Chinese**, or **Middle Eastern**. **Lebanese food**, in the shape of snacks and sandwiches, is found all over at street level too, where it fills the niche that would otherwise be occupied by the menace of franchised burger joints (still thankfully little known).

STREET EATS

Street food varies widely from country to country and regionally too, and is covered in more detail for each country. One snack that's pretty well universal is the **brochette** — a tiny stick of kebabed meat. This is often eaten as a sandwich in a piece of French **bread**.

Bread is found everywhere and tends to conform to the colonial recipe. In the francophone countries it's a *baguette* a French stick, though rarely as long or as crunchy as the real thing. In the anglophone countries you have to search hard to find good bread. Mostly it's spongey white stuff, far worse than anything pumped out of British supermarket bakeries in the 1970s, sometimes very sweet, often dyed a horrid yellow, or even pink. Bread isn't a staple food in West Africa, it's almost a luxury, often something to eat on long journeys.

In the French-speaking countries you're likely to adopt the habit of eating **breakfast in the street**. Practice and adroitness vary, but in several countries you'll get excellent hot, whipped *Nescafé* with *pain beurre* (and real butter) for a set price (about 40–50p). But be ready with appropriate French if you want your coffee black or — big shock — without sugar. As it's made with sweetened condensed milk, white-no-sugar is a problem.

VEGETARIAN WEST AFRICA

It's perhaps a little unfair to devote a special section to the needs of vegetarians, because the region makes no concessions to them. Eating ready-prepared food, whether on the street, or in any category of restaurant, is unrewarding: animal protein is the focus of most dishes, and even where it's apparently absent there's likely to be some stock somewhere (rice is often cooked in it, or fat is added to the vegetables). This means, if you're strictly vegetarian, you're mostly going to have to stick to market fruit and veg and any food you cook for yourself. Peanuts and locally ground **peanut butter** are a good source of vegetable protein. Groundnuts (peanuts) can be found boiled as well as roasted.

If you consume them, **milk** in various forms (and milk powder) and **hard-boiled eggs** are usually obtainable. Cheese is largely unheard of, except in its processed and E-supplemented, foil-packaged variety. **Bread** and canned **margarine**, are available everywhere.

Vegetarians who are the guests of African families have a hard time — with such status attached to meat, vegetarianism for health's or animals' sake is regarded as an untenable philosophy. Avoiding meat is particularly trying if you consent to have eggs with every meal instead, as you can find yourself presented with six or more, specially prepared for you, every day.

COMMON WEST AFRICAN FRUITS AND NUTS

The most satisfying eating in West Africa is **fruit**. There's a magnificent variety in the markets south of the Sahel, though even in the drier regions you'll find citrus most of the year, mangoes in season and the odd pawpaw.

The main ones to watch out for are:

Oranges and tangerines. These – often bright green – are the main juicy fruits of West Africa. If you travel widely you'll rarely find them unavailable for long, though they do go out of season in the rains. Oranges are always available for immediate consumption for a few pence from girls and women with trays and sharp knives. The outer skin is shaved off, leaving the orange in its pith, then the top is lopped off and you squeeze the juice into your mouth and discard the emptied orange. You can easily go through a dozen or twenty in a day like this – diabolical on the front teeth.

Grapefruit. Not to be ignored even if you'd commonly reject a grapefruit as it is. African varieties are often exceptionally sweet and really big. Skin them, pith them, separate the segments and leave them to dry for a while. You can then peel off the inner skins to reveal hundreds of little packets of grapefruit juice. A fine pleasure.

Mango. A royal fruit this, and available and rightly esteemed everywhere, it comes in hundreds of varieties. The thick green foliage of the trees gives glorious shade. The mango season coincides with the end of the dry season and the first rains (roughly March–June depending on where you are). They're expensive at first and rapidly drop in price until they're two a penny (sometimes literally). Whole villages devote themselves to eating and selling the fruit. The very best are long and narrow with bright green skins and very firm, orange, stringless flesh (we found them near Yaoundé in Cameroon).

Pineapple. Quite a local fruit, pineapples grow on the ground, with a spikey fringe of long sisal-like leaves around them. Commonest in coastal districts of Côte d'Ivoire and eastwards to Cameroon. Available throughout the dry season.

Pawpaw. Not much eaten but widely obtainable. Very good (and good for you) with lime juice. Non-seasonal. See "Health".

Banana. If you spend long in West Africa, you may find you never eat a banana again. But local varieties are often wonderfully flavoured compared to the imported, white-fleshed supermarket type. Look out for very thin-skinned dwarf bananas in huge bunches, and for very fat, squat varieties with pale orange flesh and sometimes red skins.

Guava. Don't buy unripe ones. They should have a very strongly perfumed scent. The best ones have pink flesh.

Cashew. Not just a nut, the cashew also has a fruit attached. The arrangement of the nut at the apex of the cashew "apple" is hard to believe when you first see it. You can't eat the apple because the fibrous flesh is bitter, but curiously you can *chew* it to extract the delicious, light juice. In some parts this stuff is made into a potent hooch. Beware of feasting off cashew trees. They only have a small number of valuable nuts each and owners get very upset.

Coconut. Another surprise, the familiar brown "nuts" ofcoconut shies are contained within a thick husk and the whole thing is green and about the size of a football. Coconuts are very hard to open without a machete, but all along the coast (they're not happy above 500 metres) you'll have the opportunity to try them in several, satisfying conditions as the flesh changes from a thin jelly to a thick layer of coconut. They're not seasonal.

Sugar cane. Sometimes sold in markets, you simply strip off the shiny outside and chomp on the pith, which oozes sucrose. Another dental nightmare.

You'll also come across **starfruit** (attractively shaped but tasteless), **custard apples** or **soursops** (lovely pear-drop flavour in the roughly heart shaped, green fruit) and **mangosteens** (amazing taste inside the small, round, brownish fruit with very thick skin). Towards the Sahara **dates** in all their different grades and lastly, at certain times and places, quite a variety of **wild-collected fruit**, some of which (like the *ditak* in Senegal) is good, and not merely edible.

DRINKING

Probably the most widely consumed beverage in the region – after water – is **green tea** (in reality yellow). In the Sahel, from Senegal to northern Cameroon, it's an essential part of every day and no long journey is completed without it. It's common further south, too, in all regions where Islam predominates. Rock sugar in huge lumps, China tea leaves and water are brought to the boil in a little kettle on a handful of coals, then poured out repeatedly to infuse and froth the brew. It's traditional to drink three glasses – strong and bitter, sweet and full-bodied, and sweet and mild – and considered rude to refuse a glass. But like everything in real life, form isn't always followed. The tea has to be *Green Gunpowder*, however, a tin of which makes a very good little gift.

Coffee is much less popular, and *real* coffee uncommon except in the big hotels. *Nescafe* is pretty ubiquitous, though as mentioned earlier ("Street Eats") most widely in French-speaking countries. Various **infusions** are locally common. One which has wide popularity in the western part of West Africa (as a base for mixing in a lot of *lait concentré sucré*) is *Kenkeliba* (also spelled "Quinceliba" and various other ways). It's OK on its own straight from the hot bucket or kettle, but don't mistake it for water and have *nescafé* added. That's disgusting.

When you can't get cold water, **soft drinks** – especially fizzy orange and lemonade and *coke* – are permanent standbys and in remote areas any establishment with electricity is almost bound to have a fridge of battered bottles. In deference to your teeth, it's always worth asking for **soda water** (*eau gazeuse* in French), but you won't often be lucky. In the francophone countries, supermarkets and some general stores carry large bottles of French-style **mineral water** but, like soda water, you'll rarely find this in roadside fridges. On the street, however, you'll often see **locally made fruit juices**, cold water and ices, in plastic bags, sold from buckets of ice by children. Ginger is refreshing, as too is the white sherbert made from baobab fruits. Don't assume the soft drinks bottling plant necessarily applies any more hygienic methods of manufacture than local outlets. The water they use is almost certainly the same as what comes out of the village pump.

BEER AND SPIRITS

The most *obvious* drink in the region is **beer**. Almost every country has a brewery. Nigeria has many, and a whole host of competing brands. Only the Islamic Republic of Mauritania is dry. Beer, usually in half litre bottles, is mostly strong, lager-ish, sometimes quite bitter in flavour and, most of the time, cold, including *Guinness*, brewed under licence.

You can sample **home-made beer** under many different names. It's as varied in taste and colour as its ingredients – basically a fermented mash of sugar and cereal, usually sorghum or millet, sometimes with herbs and roots for flavouring. It's always made by women. The results are frothy and deceptively strong, and can easily cause you to alter your travel plans for the rest of the day. Home-made beer is usually drunk in the round, each person taking their turn with the dipper, from a central calabash.

In coastal parts, **palm wine** is produced from oil palms, tapped for their sap, which ferments in a day or two from a very pleasant, mildly intoxicating juice to a ripe and pungent brew with seriously destabilising qualities. The flavour is aromatic and slightly acidic. There are usually laws controlling tapping because it hinders the production of the palm nuts used in vital palm oil manufacture, but it's available wherever you see the stumpy, dark green palms. Taller *borassus* and coconut palms can also be tapped, but in West Africa rarely are.

Spirits distilled from beer, palm wine or sugar cane are locally much in evidence (in Ghana, Sierra Leone, Burkina and Cape Verde for example) and normally only alcoholically dangerous, rather than actually denatured with unknown toxic additives, as in parts of North Africa. But beware.

If you're moved to drink **imported spirits**, you'll find them excessively expensive. **Imported beer**, too, is rarely worth the extra. Cheap French **wine**, on the other hand, is fairly affordable in Senegal and Côte d'Ivoire (unless you're French when it'll seem extortionate) where you can often buy it from ordinary general stores.

MEDIA

Local press and broadcasting isn't likely to give you much of an idea of what's going on in the world – though we've tried to uncover the best and most intrepid of the output in the "Communications and Media" details at the beginning of each country section. And the availability of imported English language newspapers and magazines is very limited throughout West Africa, even in the most cosmopolitan capitals. If you're travelling for any length of time, it's definitely worth investing in a short-wave radio in order to listen to the BBC World Service – quite an institution in West Africa.

MAGAZINES AND PERIODICALS

Worthwhile Africa-centred magazines, worth checking through for news before you go, and sporadically available in major cities once you're there, include:

West Africa (43–45 Coldharbour Lane, London SE5 9NR, ☎071 737 2946). Independent weekly magazine available in some newsagents or by subscription. The best – the only – English language specialist news magazine, relied upon throughout the region. Particularly strong on Nigeria and Ghana.

Africa (Kirkman House, 54a Tottenham Court Rd, London W1P 0BT, ☎071 637 9341). Mainstream news and business magazine.

Africa Confidential (Miramoor Publications, 33 Rutland Gate, London SW7 1PD, ☎071 584 9141). Fortnightly 8-page newsletter with solid inside info. Subscription only (£100, £35 students).

Africa Events Comment and analysis with a Muslim flavour

African Business (IC Publications, PO Box 261, Carlton House, 69 Great Queen St., London WC2B 5BN, ☎071 404 4333). Good general coverage.

BBC WEST AFRICAN FREQUENCIES AND WAVELENGTHS

All times are GMT. At any time between 5am and 11pm you can find a signal at two or more different wavelengths, depending on local conditions. Early and late, the best signals are received at lower frequencies/higher wavelengths, and during the middle of the day at higher frequencies/lower wavelengths. Kilohertz (kHz) is the same figure as Megahertz (MHZ) only 1000 times bigger (e.g. 25750 kHz).

	MHz	metres		MHz	metres
11am–4.15pm	25.750	11.65	8–9.15am and	15.070	19.91
9am–5.45pm	21.710	13.82	4–8.30pm		
6.30–7pm	17.880	16.78	7.30–9.15am	11.860	25.30
7–11.30am and	15.400	19.48	5.45–8.15am	9.600	31.25
3–11pm			5–7.30am and	9.410	31.88
7.30–8am and	15.105	19.86	6–11pm		
1–1.45pm			5–5.45am	6.005	49.96

VOA WEST AFRICAN FREQUENCIES AND WAVELENGTHS

Voice of America broadcasts from 3–7am and from 4–10pm.

3–4.30am and 5.30–10pm	621 kHz, 484 metres (medium wave)	5–7am	9.540 MHz
3–4.30am and 6–7pm	3.990 MHz	6–7am	6.080, 6.125, 9.530, 9.550, 11.915 MHz
3–7am	6.035, 7.280 MHz	4–6.30pm	15.600 MHz
3–5am	9.525 MHz	4–7pm	11.920 MHz
3–6am and 4–7pm	9.575 MHz	4–10pm	7.195, 15.410, 15.445, 15.550, 17.785, 17.800, 17.870 MHz
3–4.30am	11.835 MHz	6–10pm	21.485 MHz
		7–10pm	6.045, 9.620 MHz

Jeune Afrique (51 ave des Ternes, 75017 Paris, ☎47 66 52 42). Influential weekly in the *Newsweek* mould with African and international news.

Jeune Afrique Magazine. From the same publishers – a glossier, colour supplement-style monthly famed for its photography.

Africa Report (833 UN Plaza, New York, NY 10017, ☎212 949 5666). Bi-monthly American heavyweight newsmag, published by the African-American Institute with good analyses and in-depth reporting.

Apart from general BBC World Service coverage (which ranges from Andy Kershaw to The Archers) there are several excellent Africa Service programmes to listen out for, including the morning magazine **Network Africa** at 6.35am and 7.35am, the vital **Focus on Africa** repeated four times every afternoon Monday to Friday, the Saturday morning news review **Saturdays Only** and the weekend arts and literature forum, **Arts and Africa**.

You can also listen to the BBC in French, Hausa and Portuguese. Write to BBC African Service, PO Box 76, Bush House, London WC2B 4PH and they'll send you the details.

VA has a less interesting output and not such good reception. **Daybreak Africa** is the morning show at 6.10am. and there are several Africa angle programmes on Sunday evening.

POST AND TELEPHONE

Post and telecommunications have improved enormously over the last ten years. Ordinary letters posted at main post offices rarely go astray if they're carefully addressed. Recieving mail is a little more variable. As for phoning, all the West African countries are now theoretically on International Direct Dialling. Specifics for each country are covered in each case under "Practicalities". A few general points are worth making however.

POST

In French-speaking countries the post office is the **PTT** (*Postes, Télécommunications et Télédiffusion*), in English-speaking ones, the **GPO**. Post offices in francophone countries usually have **separate counters** (*guichets*) for different services, so make sure you're in the right queue.

SENDING MAIL

It's easiest and most secure to use **aerograms** for writing home. Although these are often in high demand and always running out, they're usually postage pre-paid, so you don't have to worry about weighing and handing over letters.

If you have **urgent mail** to send, the best place is usually not the main post office, but the airport, whence mail is often sent on the next flight to Europe. There may not be much of a post office, just a post box. For similar reasons, if you're sending slightly heavy, or valuable items, it's worth doing so with a friend or contact who's flying. A lot of ordinary mail is sent this way too and posted in Europe. It's always quicker. Leave it unsealed for customs.

If you've the option, it's worth looking ahead to the next country before. sending your mail. **Postal rates** vary widely, especially in comparison between CFA and non-CFA countries.

POSTE RESTANTE

It's not wise to have mail sent anywhere except the **capital city**, not just to maximise your chances of getting it, but to speed up the delivery. (Kano, Nigeria is an exception). Note, too, that some post offices only hold mail for a few weeks before returning it to sender. From Europe, allow two weeks for mail to be received and one week or at most ten days to post out. For the rest of the world allow three days longer.

Post Office staff are often remarkably uncivil, even rude, so if you find yourself returning repeatedly, go prepared to smile and plead. To collect mail, write your name on a piece of paper as you'd expect it to appear on the letter, and go armed with your passport, without which you'll rarely be allowed to receive mail.

For clarity's sake, ask people to write your address in this form:

DRIVER, Teresa
Poste Restante
PTT
Ouagadougou
BURKINA FASO

and to put their own address on the back.

Alternatives to public *Poste Restante* are your embassy or high commission (some of which will hold mail for up to three months) or ***American Express*** offices, all of which will hold mail for customers, even if you only have their travellers' cheques. Local addresses are given in the guide.

TELEPHONES

Despite IDD, most international phone calls from the region take a while to fix up. There always seems to be someone "occupying" the line, or an operator in the ether somewhere. If you have to go through an operator, always insist on "station to station" (number to number) rather than a personal call. The latter costs more and will only connect you if the person you name is available.

Reverse charge ("collect", *PCV* in French) calls are possible – but not easy to make – in most countries of the region. In principle, there should be no problem, but you may have some pleading to do. It's often easier, if you want to have a phone conversation, but aren't up to the very high likely cost, to arrange in advance to *receive* a call at a certain time and number.

To **call the UK** from West Africa, dial the international access code, followed by 44, then the UK area code (without the initial "0") and then the number.

WEST AFRICAN IDD COUNTRY CODES

Benin 229 plus six digit number

Burkina Faso 226 plus six digit number

Cameroon 237 plus six digit number

Cape Verde 238 plus six digit number

Côte d'Ivoire 225 plus six digit number

The Gambia 220 plus five digit number

Ghana 233 plus area code plus number

Guinea 224 plus six digit number

Guinea-Bissau 245 plus six digit number

Liberia 231 plus six digit number

Mali 223 plus area code and number totalling six digits

Mauritania 222 plus six digit number

Niger 227 plus six digit number

Nigeria 234 plus area code plus number

Senegal 221 plus six digit number

Sierra Leone 232 plus area code plus number plus luck

Togo 228 plus six digit number

TELEX AND FAX

It's very useful to have access to a **telex** number at home through which urgent messages can be relayed to friends or family. Telex is often quicker and more flexible than telephone – and usually works out cheaper so long as you avoid a live "conversation". Contact a local telex bureau (yellow pages) before you leave. Every capital in West Africa has a public telex office at which you can send and receive messages via an operator (the cost of receiving a telex is nominal). Most large hotels have telex services, too, at slightly more expensive rates.

Fax is still relatively unknown in the region.

HOLIDAYS, FESTIVALS AND TIME

In addition to the main Christian and Islamic religious festivals, each country has its own national holidays, listed at the start of each country section. These are rarely as established as you would find, for example, in Europe. Some, commemorating no longer respected events, are quietly ignored. In one or two countries, the practice of mounting national celebrations for the president's birthday and similar annivesaries adds a bizarre and unfamiliar quality. Traditional, community festivals, connected either to annual agricultural cycles or to life cycle events, are more attractive but less accessible. Details are given wherever possible.

ISLAMIC HOLY DAYS

Every West African country, with the exception of Cape Verde, has a significant Muslim population. Islam is the dominant religion in most, but Mauritania is the only nation to dub itself an Islamic Republic. In other countries, the Muslim holy days are variably observed – devoutly in strictly Muslim districts, perhaps only vaguely in the capital city.

The **principle events** of which to be aware are the ten days of the Muslim New Year which starts with the month of Moharem (**Ashoura** on the 10th of Moharem celebrates, among other events, Adam and Eve's first meeting after leaving paradise), **Muhammad's birthday** (known as Mouloud, or Maulidi), the month-long fast of **Ramadan** and the feast of relief which follows immediately after (known as Id al-Fitr or Id al-Sighir), and the **Feast of the Sacrifice** or *Tabaski*, which coincides with the annual *Hajj* pilgrimmage to Mecca, and when every Muslim family with the means available slaughters a sheep.

The last of these festivals, (known as the *fête des moutons* in French) can be a lot of fun to participate in. **Ramadan** isn't an entirely miserable time either. Fasting applies throughout the daylight hours, and covers every pleasure (food, drink, tobacco and sex). While non-Muslims are not expected to observe the fast, it's highly affronting in strict Muslim areas to contravene publicly. Instead, switch to the night shift, as everyone else does, with special soup to break the fast at dusk, and applied eating and entertainment through the night.

The **Islamic calendar** is lunar, divided into twelve months of 29 or 30 days (totalling 354 days). The twelfth month has 29 days and a thirtieth day eleven times every thirty years. The calendar dates from 622AD, the "Year of the *Hijra*" (AH), when the prophet fled from Mecca to Medina. The Islamic year 1411AH began on July 20 1990.

ISLAMIC FESTIVALS – APPROXIMATE DATES			
	1991	1992	1993
Beginning of Ramadan (1st Ramadan)	Mar 18	Mar 7	Feb 24
Id al-Fitr/Id al-Saghir (1st Shawwal)	Apr 17	Apr 6	Mar 26
Tabaski/Id al-Kabir (10th Dhu'l Hijja)	Jun 26	Jun 15	Jun 4
New Year's Day (1st Moharem)	Jul 9	Jun 29	Jun 18
Ashoura (10th Moharem)	Jul 19	Jul 8	Jun 28
Mouloud/Maulidi (12th Rabial)	Oct 3	Sep 23	Sep 12
Islamic dates in brackets			

CHRISTIAN HOLIDAYS

Christmas and to a much lesser extent Easter are observed as religious ceremonies in Christian areas and, on a more or less secular, national basis, in every country. But if you can't find a bank or post office open, you'll have no trouble finding street food and limited transport.

Christmas and New Year are the occasion of street parades and carnival festivities in a number of cities. On the downside, Christmas is a time to avoid contact, as far as possible, with people in uniform. This most applies to the police in the English-speaking countries, where a misappropriated tradition of "Christmas Boxes" survives and is relentlessly cultivated from mid-December to the middle of January.

Lastly, both Guinea-Bissau and Cape Verde have inherited and elaborated upon the Portuguese-Brazilian institution of *Carnaval* and there are float parades and street festivals in February or March.

THE PARIS–DAKAR RALLY

Apart from the religious festivals, the biggest trans-national annual event is the **Paris–Dakar rally**, which takes place along an annually fixed route in the first two weeks of January.

Such is the level of prestige and expectation attached to this twelve-year-old race that teams and drivers have seemed prepared to risk almost anything, including their lives and the lives of uninterested villagers along the route.

Nearly every race sees a clutch of fatal accidents and embittered bystanders. Every year sees renewed pressure for the show to be cancelled. Principle objector is the campaigning organisation Pa'Dak ("Paris–Dakar pas d'accord"). But with a record of empathy with West Africa like France's and considering the kudos and financial stakes at play, an early demise seems unlikely. How long before an African driver participates?

TIME

Most of West Africa is conveniently on **Greenwich Mean Time** (GMT). Cape Verde is two hours earlier (10.00 when it's 12.00 GMT), Guinea-Bissau is one hour earlier (11.00), Benin, Niger, Nigeria and Cameroon are all one hour later (13.00). The **24-hour clock** is widely used in the French and Portuguese-speaking countries, and always used by airlines. The 12-hour system is usual in the English-speaking countries.

Although all of West Africa lies north of the equator, the coastal region from Monrovia to Douala, just a few degrees north, has roughly the equatorial twelve hours of **daylight** – a little more in summer, a little less in winter. Sunrise comes earlier in the west (about 05.00 GMT) and later in the east (about 07.00 GMT). Latitudes further north experience greater seasonal variation, with slightly longer summer days, though it's almost always going to be light by the time you wake, and dusk still comes before 20.00GMT.

The notion that the **tropical dusk** is extraordinarily brief is true. With the sun tracing a nearly perfect arc through ninety degrees most of the year, it plunges vertically below the horizon and is lost in minutes. In more extreme latitudes it slides obliquely into night leaving a long period of twilight.

TIME-KEEPING

People and things are usually late. That said, if you try to anticipate **delays** you'll be caught out. Scheduled transport can and does leave on time – at least some of the time. More importantly, transport may leave early if it's full. Even planes have been known to take off before schedule.

Although a surprising number of people now wear digital watches – which have flooded the region in the last decade – they're essentially jewellery. Notions of time and duration are pretty hazy. Outside the cities, dusk and dawn are the significant markers. You'll soon find you, too, are

NATIONAL INDEPENDENCE DAYS		
Algeria Jul 3 1962	**Ghana** Mar 20 1956	**Niger** Aug 3 1960
Benin Aug 1 1960	**Guinea** Mar 6 1957	**Nigeria** Oct 1 1960
Burkina Faso Aug 5 1960	**Guinea-Bissau** Sep 10 1974	**Senegal** Jun 20 1960
Cameroon Jan 1 1960	**Liberia** Jul 26 1847	**Sierra Leone** Apr 27 1961
Cape Verde Jul 5 1975	**Mali** Jun 20 1960	**Togo** Apr 27 1960
Côte d'Ivoire Aug 7 1960	**Mauritania** Nov 28 1960	**Tunisia** Mar 20 1956
The Gambia Feb 18 1965	**Morocco** Mar 2 1956	

judging time by the sun, and reckoning how long before dark.

Note that in remote areas, if a driver tells you he's going somewhere "today", it doesn't neces-sarily mean he expects to *reach* the place today. Always allow extra time. There's no better way of ruining West African travel than to attempt to rush it.

GREETINGS, BODY LANGUAGE AND SOCIAL NORMS

You can't hope to avoid social gaffes on a West African stay, but humour and toler-ance aren't lacking, so you won't be left to stew in embarrassment. Getting it right really takes an upbringing, but people are delighted when you make the effort.

GREETINGS

Greetings are fundamental. No conversation starts without one. This means a handshake followed by polite enquiries, even as you enter a shop. Traditionally, such exchanges can last a minute or two, and you'll often hear them, performed in a formal, incantatory manner between two men. Long greetings help subse-quent negotiations. In French or English you can swop something like "How are you? Fine, How's the day? Fine, How's business? Fine, How's the family?, Fine, Thank God". It's usually considered polite, while someone is speaking to you at length, to grunt in the affirmative, or say thank you at short intervals. Breaks in conversation are filled with more greetings.

Shaking hands is normal between all men present, on arrival and departure and it's easily adopted. Women shake hands with each other, but with men only in more sophisticated millieux. Soul brother handshakes and variations on the terminal finger snap are popular among young people. Less natural for Westerners (certainly for men) is an unconscious ease in physical contact. Men need to get used to holding hands with strangers as they're shown around the house, or guided down the street, and, on public transport, to hands and limbs draped naturally wherever's most comfortable in a fashion that ensures you'll never see tube travel in the same way again.

SOCIAL NORMS

Be aware of the **left hand rule**. Traditionally the left hand is reserved for unhygienic acts and the right for eating and touching, or passing things to others. Like many "rules" it's very often broken. Don't think about it then.

Don't **point** with your finger. Such actions are equivalent to obscene gestures. For similar reasons, beckoning is done with the palm down, not up.

Don't be put off by apparent shiftiness in **eye contact**, epsecially if you're talking to someone much younger than you. It's fairly normal for those deferring to others to avoid direct looks.

Hissing ("Tsss!"), is an ordinary way to attract a stranger's attention. You'll get a fair bit of it, and it's quite in order to hiss at the waiter in a restaurant.

Answering anything in the negative is often considered impolite. If you're asking questions, don't ask yes-no ones. And don't phrase things in the negative (Isn't the lorry leaving?) because the answer will often be yes (It isn't leaving).

There's a host of **unexpected turns of phrase** which pop up into English. "I am coming", is often said by someone just as they leave your company – which means they're going, but coming back.

KOLA NUTS

Kola nuts are the chestnut-sized fruit from the pods of an indigenous tree, cultivated widely all over the forest belt and traded on a grand scale throughout West Africa. Before tobacco, cannabis, tea and coffee arrived, kola was the main non-alcoholic drug of the region, an appetite depressant and a mild stimulant. It comes in dark red, pink and white varieties, of which the latter are the best and more expensive. Kola should be fresh and hard, not old and rubbery, and you chew it – you don't swallow – for the bitter juice. Buy a handful for long journeys, as much to share among fellow passengers as to stay awake. Giving and receiving kola is a traditional exchange of friendship.

TROUBLE – GETTING IN AND OUT

It's easy to exaggerate the potential hassles and disasters of travel in West Africa. Keep in mind while reading this section that bad experiences are unusual. True, there is a scattering of urban locations, easily enough pinpointed, where snatch robberies and muggings are common. But most of the region carries minimal risk to personal safety compared with Europe and North America. The main problems are sneak thieving and corrupt people in uniforms. The first can be avoided. And dealing with the second can become a game once you know the rules.

AVOIDING TROUBLE

If you flaunt the trappings of wealth where there's **urban poverty**, somebody will want to remove them. There's always less risk in leaving your valuables in a securely locked hotel room or, judiciously, with the management, than in taking them with you. If you clearly have nothing on you (this means not wearing jewellery or a wrist watch), you're unlikely to feel, or be, threatened.

Public transport rarely produces scare stories. Apart from the standard of driving, which is another matter, you haven't much to worry about on the roads – except in Lagos, which is acquiring notoriety for hold-ups (exaggerated, even so). Trains provide thieves with more opportunities. People fall asleep and robbers have been known to climb aboard and steam through the carriages. Establish a rapport with your fellow passengers as soon as possible.

If you're flying into West Africa, or arriving overland in your **first big city**, it's obviously wise to be very cautious to begin with. If you're looking after yourself, 24 hours is usually enough to get the feel of a place. There's always a lot going on and it's important to distinguish harmlessly robust, up-front interaction (commonly part of the public transport scene) from more dangerous preludes. At the risk of sensationalism, the box below outlines some good strategies for big city survival in Dakar, Abidjan, Lagos or Douala – the most difficult to deal with. Praia, Bissau, Nouakchott, Banjul, Bamako, Niamey, Lomé and Freetown are mostly very relaxed.

Don't feel unnecessarily victimised, but be rationally suspicious of everyone until you've caught your breath. It doesn't take long. Every rural immigrant coming to the city for the first time goes through exactly the same process, and many are considerably less streetwise than you, easier pickings for never having been in a big town before.

Lastly, don't forget that impoverished fellow travellers are as likely – or as unlikely – to rip you off as anyone else. None of this is meant to induce paranoia. But a controlled rise in your adrenalin level is a good thing. New York, London, Paris, Rome – if you can cope with any of them, you can handle a West African city.

BIG CITY SURVIVAL

Mere **pick-pocketing** can happen anywhere, and it's usually the work of pocket-high thieves, hanging around in markets or other places where people's attention is focused. If your valuables are secure it can't be done.

Heavier attacks usually take place in specific areas of the city – downtown shopping streets, docks and waterfront, city centre parks and central markets. Less threatening districts include transport parks (full of tough young men with jobs) and, surprisingly perhaps, the lower income suburbs and slums away from the city centre.

When walking – assuming you have money or valuables on you – have a destination in mind and stay alert. Be aware of what's going on around you. Scan ahead. Don't dawdle or dream. Keep your hands to yourself; loose hands are likely to be caught. In heavy places, a handshake from a stranger in the street, or a knicknack pressed into your hand or some murmured offer or suggestion can foreshadow a more aggressive act. If you want to give off strong defensive vibes, hands in pockets or round the straps of a backpack are effective.

Steer clear of creepy-looking street sharks in jeans and running shoes (every robbery ends in a sprint). And don't be steered down an alley or between parked cars.

DRUGS

Grass (marijuana, cannabis) is the biggest illegal drug in the region, much cultivated (clandestinely) and as much object of confused opprobrium and fascination as anywhere else in the world. Many social problems are routinely attributed to smoking the "grass that kills" and it's widely believed to cause insanity. In practice, if you indulge discreetly, it's not likely to get you into trouble. The usual result of a fortuitous bust is on-the-spot fines all round.

An altogether different state of affairs exists with heroin and cocaine, which are smuggled though West African airports en route to Europe (often inside hapless female "swallowers"). Some of the consignments are now getting on to the streets of capitals like Accra and Lagos, together with the associated tensions and paranoia you'd expect. It's sufficient to know it's happening. Stay clear. Very long prison sentences and the death penalty are not unknown for those involved.

THIEF GRIEF

Hotel room **burglaries** and car break-ins do occur. If you get **mugged**, it will be over in an instant and you're not likely to be hurt. But the hassles, and worse, that gather as soon as you try to do something about it, make it doubly imperative not to let it happen in the first place. Robbers and pick-pockets caught red-handed are usually dealt with summarily by the crowd – often killed – so when you shout "Thief!" (or "Voleur!" in French), be swift to intercede once you've retrieved your belongings

Usually you'll have no chance, or desire, to catch your assailant(s), and the first reaction is to go to the **police**. Unless, however, you've lost a lot of money (and cash is virtually irretrievable) or irreplaceable property, think twice about doing this. They rarely do something for nothing – even stamping an insurance form may cost you – and you should consider the ramifications if you and they set off to try to catch the culprits. If you're not certain of their identities, pointing the finger of suspicion at people is the worst possible thing to do. If they're arrested, as they probably will be, a night in the cells usually means a beating and confiscation of possessions.

In smaller towns, or where you have some contacts, a workable alternative to police involvement is to enlist **traditional help** in searching for your stolen belongings. Various diviners and traditional doctors operate nearly everywhere. If the culprits get to hear of what you're doing you're likely to get some of your stuff back. Or you could offer a reward. Local people will often go out of their way to help.

DEALING WITH THE POLICE

Police in West Africa are probably no worse than most. But, badly paid, and often poorly educated as they are, it's wise to stay clear as far as possible. You will inevitably come into a fair amount of **contact** even in those countries where you're no longer obliged to check in at the local police station in every town (now the vast majority), the notion of "control" still remains highly developed. Checks on the movement of people (police and security services) and goods (customs, *douanes*) take place at junctions and along highways in most countries. Many capital cities have major checkpoints on the access roads.

Police forces vary considerably from one country to the next. In Côte d'Ivoire they're not excessively corrupt but can be unnervingly conscientious and pedantic. In Guinea they're outrageously on the make and seemingly unfazed by the question of upholding laws. It's worth knowing that most police forces constitute a separate entity from the rest of the people: they have their own compounds and staff villages and receive – or procure – subsidised rations and services.

If you have **official business** with the police, smiles and handshakes always help, as do terms of address like "Sir", "Officer" or (in a French-speaking country), "Mon Commandant". If you're expected to give a bribe – as you often are – wait for it to be hinted at and haggle over it as you would any payment. A pound or two is often enough to oil small wheels. Infringements of currency laws or drug possession will land you a large fine, possibly deportation. Don't expect to buy yourself easily out of this kind of trouble. If you're driving, you'll rarely be forced to pay sweeteners, except sometimes on entry to and exit from the country. If you're travelling by lorry or bush taxi, it's the driver who pays. If you're singled out, *remind them* it's the driver who pays. Avoid any show of temper. Aggressive travellers always have the worst police stories.

BRIBERY AND CORRUPTION

It is indeed a way of life. But probably not yours. If you find yourself confronting an implacable uniform, you don't have to give in to tacit demands for gifts or money. The golden rule is to **keep talking**. Most laws, including imaginary ones about the importation of backpacks, the possession of two cameras or the writing of diaries, are there to be discussed rather than enforced. If you haven't got all day, a *dash* or **"small present"** – couched in exactly those terms – is all it usually takes. If you can't, or won't give gifts to officials, give words. On extensive West African travels, you have literally hundreds of police, army, customs, immigration and security checkpoints to cross and you'll sail through ninety per cent of them. With patience and good humour, the other ten per cent can be negotiated relatively painlessly too. When you know they know your "infraction" is bogus, keep joking, keep pleading and hang on. If you think you may be in breach of a law (or someone's interpretation of it) you might suggest paying the "fine" (*amende*) immediately, or "coming to an agreement" (*faire arrangement* or *s'arranger* in French).

In **unofficial dealings**, the police, especially in remote outposts, can go out of their way to help you with food, transportation and accommodation. Try to reciprocate. Police salaries are always low and often months overdue and they rely on unofficial income to get by. Only brand new police forces and realistic salaries could alter the entrenched situation which now exists in most countries.

BEHAVIOUR

- Never go out without identification. You don't have to carry a passport at all times, but a photocopy of the first few pages in a plastic wallet is very useful. Not carrying an ID (*carte d'identité*, *papiers* or *pièces* in French) is usually against the law, as it is in a number of European countries.

- If you're heading for remote regions, to hike for example, it's worth leaving some details behind with your embassy or the honorary consul.

- Be warned that failure to observe the following points of **public etiquette** can get you arrested or force you to pay a bribe:

  Stand still on any occasion a national anthem is played or a flag raised or lowered. If you see others suddenly cease all activity do the same.

  Pull off the road completely if motorcycle outriders and limos appear, or stand still.

  Never destroy banknotes, no matter how worthless they may be.

  And don't urinate in public.

WOMEN'S WEST AFRICA

Machismo, in its fully-fledged Latin varieties, is rare in West Africa. Male egos are softened by reserves of humour and women do travel widely on their own or with each other, without suffering the major problems sometimes experienced in parts of Asia and Latin America. Women's groups flourish in some countries, occasionally under the aegis of a government ministry – though in several they've hardly taken off. Where they exist, they're concerned more with improvement of incomes, education, health and nutrition than with social or political emancipation.

TRAVELLING ALONE

Travelling on your own or with a woman companion is by turns frustrating and rewarding. You'll usually be welcomed with generous hospitality, though occasionally you'll seem to get a run of harassment and hassles because of your gender. It's well to know, if you're overlanding from Europe, that the biggest difficulties will occur in North Africa – especially Morocco – and that Muslim regions south of the Sahara are altogether different.

On **public transport** a single woman traveller causes quite a stir and fellow passengers don't want to see you badly treated. They'll speak up on your behalf and get you a good seat or argue with the driver over your baggage payments. In the francophone countries, if your French isn't good, people will wait patiently for you to explain. You can speak your mind, be open and direct and nobody takes offence. Fellow male passengers always assume protective roles. This can be helpful but is sometimes annoyingly restictive and occasionally leads to misunderstandings (see "Sexual Atitudes" below).

Women get offers of **accommodation** in people's homes more often than male travellers (and most of them without strings attached). And, if you're staying in less reputable hotels, there'll often be female company – employees, family, residents – to look after you. And of course, the opportunity to team up with other travellers arises from time to time.

The **clothes** you wear and the way you look and behave get noticed by everyone and they're more important if you don't appear to have a male escort. Your **head** and everything from **waist to ankles** are the sensitive zones, particularly in Islamic regions. Long, loose hair is extraordinarily provocative, and doubly so if blonde. Pay attention to these areas by keeping your hair fairly short or tied up (or by wearing a scarf) and wearing long skirts or, at a pinch, very baggy pants.

In the heat it can be hard to be that disciplined, however, so if you have to wear **shorts** try to make them long ones. If you find it's too hot to wear a **bra**, it's not going to interest anybody. Breasts aren't an important issue and topless bathing is rarely offensive. If you'll be travelling much on rough roads, however, you'll need a bra for support. Seriously.

Teresa Driver writes:

I relished the opportunity to be with women but they continually made me feel dowdy. While gara (indigo tie-dyed damask) is becoming more fashionable, traditional West African dresses are made from brilliantly colourful printed cloth, used in vast quantities.

Senegalese women have to be the best dressers in the world. Their clothes are amazing, off-the-shoulder creations tailored to accentuate slim waists and sexy bottoms, and to show off long necks and broad backs (working backs). With towering headdresses the whole ensemble has an impressive, swaying grace. Or else they wear flowing, embroidered boubous. At parties and on festive occasions the women look stunning – decked in jewellery and flower-scented gowns and often wearing high heels that just add to the total effect. Even in the villages, women change into their best clothes to go market-shopping. The importance of your "look" can't be over-emphasised. If you make the effort to dress up it won't go unappreciated.

I took earrings and necklaces as small presents to give away (every woman has pierced ears). Blue eyeliner is becoming popular too. Body Shop cosmetics in small containers make excellent gifts.

MEETING OTHER WOMEN

It's often very difficult **getting to know women** in West Africa. Most contact is mediated, at least initially, through their male relatives, with whom you'll take on the role of honorary man, at least in the way you're treated socially. In the small towns and villages women are usually less educated than men and rarely speak English or French. They don't hang out in bars and restaurants either and are much more often to be found in their compounds working hard. Their fortitude as **housewives** is something to behold – always in total control of the family's food and comfort, from chopping wood to selling home-made produce in order to make ends meet. Even school-educated professional women dominate their household affairs and make sure everything runs smoothly. The extended family and the use of the younger girls as helpers is a major contribution. Men are away a great deal of the time.

For their part, West African women will try to picture themselves in your position, traipsing around *your* homeland – a scenario that most find hard to imagine. Family obligations are everything. Conveying the fact that you, too, have a family and a home is a good way of reducing the barriers of incomprehension but, assuming you're over fifteen, explaining the absence of **husband and children** is normally impossible. You can either invent some or expect sympathy instead – and perhaps the offer of fertility medicine.

BROADER ISSUES

Despite widespread paper commitments to **women's rights**, West Africa remains a powerfully male-dominated part of the world and the region's first woman president seems many years away. Women do the large proportion of productive labour and most subsistence agriculture is in their hands, though this varies among different ethnic groups. Women have the explicit support of government ministries (for what it's worth) only in Cameroon, Côte d'Ivoire, Mauritania, Niger and Togo. In other countries there's usually a non-governmental women's organisation working to improve the lot of women as mothers, agricultural labourers and crafts workers. Professional market women usually run their own informal unions in the cities.

Matrilineal cultures, which once held sway over large parts of the region, are on the decline, under joint assault by paternalistic Islam and Christianity. Matrilineal inheritance doesn't, in any case, necessarily imply *matriarchal* social structures but simply inheritance by a man from his mother's brother rather than his father.

Current major **women's issues** in West Africa are primarily concerned with rights over women's bodies – contraception, abortion and the practices of genital mutilation, known, in a classic bit of male "anthopologese" as "female circumcision".

Tragically few West African countries have successful **family planning** programmes, though there may be substantial improvements in the near future. Men are unwilling to co-operate by using condoms and women are pushed out-of-date pills at market stalls (sold singly if they prefer . . .).

Abortion is virtually a taboo subject in some parts, though abortions by traditional methods (and less traditional backstreet operations) are believed to be widely performed. Few governments permit abortion on demand. Both contraception and abortion (especially as encouraged by Rich World development agencies) are topics which can incense women as well as men, so be wary of crashing into conversation.

Genital mutilation is widespread and occurs to some degree in every mainland West African country. It's traditionally carried out by female practitioners on the occasion of a girl's initiation into womanhood. Today, although on the decline, it's also performed under aneasthetic in hospital and often at an early age. It varies from clitoridectomy, to excision of the inner labia, to excision of most of the outer labia as well (a major operation known as infibulation nearly confined, in West Africa, to Mali). The sexual and psychological issues for women and men are complex. Women campaigning to eradicate the practises have met resistance from traditionalist women. And mutilations can't be analysed just in terms of male sexual demands (a tighter vagina, loss of sexual response and consequent presumed fidelity). Unfortunately, it's an issue that many governments would prefer not to address.

WOMAN TO WOMAN

● Carry pictures of your family.

● Beware of big men in small towns. Don't accept an invitation to the disco from the local commandant unless you're on very firm ground.

● Clothing – it's legs and bottoms that are the big deal. If you want to wear shorts, keep them loose and knee-length and have a wrap handy to cover yourself when necessary.

● Keep your hair short.

● Always lock your door at night.

● Take a supply of condoms. Don't tell yourself it will never happen. Be prepared, because he will never have any.

● Never meet someone as arranged if you're uncomfortable about it.

● And three useful French phrases for pesistent clingers: *J'en ai marre de toi* (I've just about had enough of you), *Laisse-moi tranquille!* (Leave me alone!), or, in a crisis, *Va te faire foutre!* (Go and fuck yourself!).

SEXUAL ATTITUDES

Don't make any assumptions about puritanism on the basis of Islamic society in West Africa. It's the church which has successfully repressed sexuality. Otherwise, sexual attitudes are liberal (though you'll rarely see open displays of affection between men and women) and sex is openly discussed except in the presence of children. It's rarely the subject of personal hang-ups either, though sexual violence is surely as prevalent in the family as it is anywhere. You'll be treated as a sexual person wherever you go. If you travel with a companion of the opposite sex, you'll find the relationship tends to insulate you – but not completely.

WOMEN TRAVELLERS

Flirting is universal in West Africa and in order to avoid it you'd have to be perspicacious about where you go in towns. The fantasy inventory of black-white sexual relations tends to get played out whenever you find yourself in a bar, or on a dance floor. And whether you're inclined to put the mythology to the test or not, there are plenty of men who are forthrightly curious about the equally myth-bound allure of white women. If a man asks you to "come and see where I live", he means you should come and see where he and you are going to sleep together. "Tell your husband you have to go outside for some air". You'll have no shortage of offers. They're usually easy to turn down if you refuse as frankly as you're asked. Unwanted physical advances are rare. But it always helps to avoid offence and preserve a friendship if you make your intentions (or lack of them) clear from the outset. If you're not with a man, a fictitious husband in the background, much as you might prefer to avoid the ploy, is always useful.

If you're in a certain mood, all this can be fun. There's no reason you can't spend an evening dancing and talking and still go back to your bed alone and unharassed.

MALE TRAVELLERS

Much of what applies to women travellers applies equally to men, though of course questions of personal safety and intimidation don't arise in the same way. It's common enough for women, and especially unmarried girls, to flirt with strangers. And many town bars and hotels are patronised by women who more or less make a living from **prostitution**.

This is not the secretive and brutally exploitative transaction of the West and pimps are unknown. Unfortunately, **sexually transmitted diseases**, and the Aids virus, are rife.

Attitudes in West Africa are waking up to this new reality, but you should be aware of the very real risks – and prepared for the occasion – if you accept one of the many propositions which, travelling alone, or with a male friend, you're likely to receive.

GAY LIFE

Beyond the big cities, **homosexuality** is more or less invisible. People from a more traditional African background almost always deny it exists, find the notion laughable or childish, or describe it as a phase or a harmless peculiarity. As for the legality of gay sex, it's not *illegal* in Burkina Faso. Most countries, however, including all the anglophone ex-colonies, inherited the laws of 1950s Europe and have hardly changed – though in practice prosecutions are almost unheard of.

For gay male visitors, the only parts of the region you'll find like-minded company are the big capital cities and the resort areas. Contacts, however, tend to be exploitative on both sides. Gay women can't hope to find any hint of a lesbian community anywhere.

It's worth knowing that the ex-patriate community has a statistically high gay constituency. The Lebanese community, too, has a fairly visible proportion of gay men.

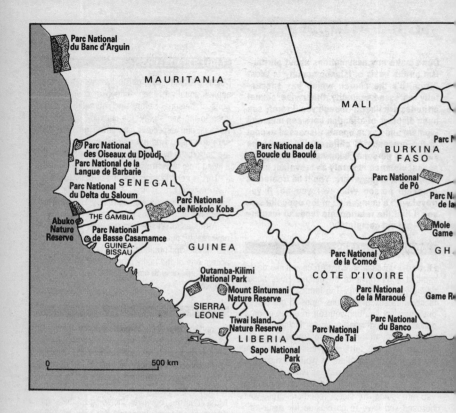

MAURITANIA

MALI

Parc National
du Banc d'Arguin

Parc National de la
Boucle du Baoulé

BURKINA
FASO

Parc N

Parc National
de Pô

Parc National
des Oiseaux du Djoudj

Parc National de la
Langue de Barbarie

Parc National
du Delta du Saloum

S E N E G A L

Parc N
de la

Parc National
de Niokolo Koba

Mole
Game

Abuko
Nature
Reserve

THE GAMBIA

Parc National
de Basse Casamamce

GUINEA-
BISSAU

G U I N E A

Parc National
de la Comoé

G H.

CÔTE D'IVOIRE

Outamba-Kilimi
National Park

Mount Bintumani
Nature Reserve

SIERRA
LEONE

Tiwai Island
Nature Reserve

Parc National
de la Maraoué

Game R

Parc National
du Banco

L I B E R I A

Parc National
de Tai

Sapo National
Park

0   500 km

WILDLIFE AND NATIONAL PARKS

West Africa doesn't have the game reserves and wildlife concentrations of East or Southern Africa. But it offers a number of major national parks that are worth taking in if you're an enthusiastic naturalist. Outside them, too, it's possible to see a good variety of Africa's birds and mammals in habitats ranging from desert to swamp and floodland, savannah, dry woodland and dense, moist forest – both lowland and mountain. Travelling by public transport, it always pays to spend a little more on a seat in the front. That way you can reckon on seeing a lot more animals, mostly crossing the road – or squashed upon it.

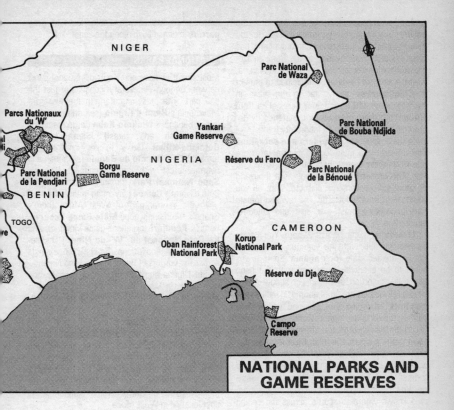

NATIONAL PARKS AND GAME RESERVES

Map labels: NIGER, Parc National de Waza, Parcs Nationaux du 'W', Yankari Game Reserve, Parc National de Bouba Ndjida, NIGERIA, Réserve du Faro, Borgu Game Reserve, Parc National de la Bénoué, Parc National de la Pendjari, BENIN, TOGO, CAMEROON, Korup National Park, Oban Rainforest National Park, Réserve du Dja, Campo Reserve

The large animals you'll see most often out on the road, or in the bush, are **monkeys** and **baboons**. **Gazelles** and other small antelope are also quite common, especially in the Sahel. Larger grazing animals are localised and unusual sights. Along the Niger north of Niamey there are **giraffes**, and **buffalo** inhabit pockets of forest and bush thicket in various parts.

Elephants hang on in dwindling numbers in Cameroon, Ghana, Côte d'Ivoire and Burkina Faso. Most other countries have populations amounting to no more than a few hundred while in Mauritania and Guinea-Bissau they may well be extinct. The **black rhino** hasn't inhabited more than the far east of the region in historical times. You can still see them in Cameroonian parks.

None of these animals, even outside the confines of the parks, poses any threat to you as a traveller, even if you choose to camp out and hike or cycle. More threatening wildlife – the big cats, crocodiles, hippos – are very localised. You're extremely unlikely to see any large predators outside the parks. And even in a national park, seeing a **lion**, **cheetah** or **leopard** is cause for some celebration. **Crocodiles** are hard to spot and are mercilessly hunted where they live because they do occasionally grab people at the water's edge. Be somewhat cautious by rivers and lakes. **Hippos**, too, have a justified dangerous reputation, especially when accidentally trapped on dry land or panicked in the water while dozing. You're most likely to see them from a boat on the Niger in Mali, along the upper Gambia, along the Comoé in Côte d'Ivoire, or in Cameroon.

Another supposedly dangerous animal – the **gorilla** – is really very timid. It lives in the remote, southern forests of Cameroon and has recently been re-discovered, to the frank amazement of zoologists, across the border in Nigeria, where a new park is being established to protect it. **Chimpanzees** survive far to the west, in patches of remote forest from Senegal to Côte d'Ivoire, but their existence is threatened by deforestation and the pet and laboratory trade.

In the smaller range, **spiders and scorpions** and various other multi-legged invertebrates are less often encountered than you might expect, or fear. The **butterflies** – as many as a thousand different species in some districts – are all you could wish for in a butterfly. The lowland forests harbour Africa's most extensive and colourful lepidoptera.

Lizards are common everywhere. You'll soon become familiar with the vigorous push-ups of the red-headed male **rock agama**. Some towns seem to be positively swarming with them, no doubt in proportion to the insect supply. Large lizards (all species are quite harmless) include the **monitors**, of which the grey and yellow Nile monitor grows to an impressive two metres. They live in the vicinity of water, but you can often see them dashing across the road. **Chameleons** too, are often seen making painfully slow progress across the road, or wafer-thin, squashed on the tarmac. In some areas, at night, little **house geckos** come out like translucent aliens from who knows where to scuttle across the ceiling and walls in pursuit of moths and mosquitos.

West Africa's **birdlife** is astonishingly diverse – nearly eleven hundred species ranging from the diminutive pygmy woodpecker to the ostrich. Characteristc sights are the urbanite **pied crows** of the Sahel and savannah, electric blue **Abyssinian rollers**, perched on telephone wires in the grasslands, the marvellous, lurching flight of **hornbills** swooping across the road in forest areas, and quite unmistakeable flocks of **grey parrots** in dense bush along the coast.

NATIONAL PARKS

Most countries have some sort of national parks network, though in several it consists of just the one park. The most important in the west are Mauritania's **Banc d'Arguin** (sea and migratory birds), Senegal's **Niokolo-Koba** (large mammals of savannah and forest), Sierra Leone's **Outamba-Kilimi** (bush thicket and swamp forest), Mali's **Boucle de Baoulé** (savannah and riverine forest with large mammals), Liberia's **Sapo National Park** (primary rain forest) and Côte d'Ivoire's **Comoé** (savannah mammals).

In the central part of West Africa there's Ghana's surprisingly good **Mole Game Reserve**, Benin's **Pendjari** (excellent game-viewing), and the **Parc National du "W" du Niger** ("Double-U" of the Niger National Park) which extends across the borders of Benin, Burkina and Niger.

But Nigeria and Cameroon have probably the best parks in West Africa. Nigeria's **Borgu** is bush thicket while the smaller **Yankari** has well-organised game-viewing and quantities of animals. The new **Oban** is a remote rain forest gorilla refuge bordering **Korup National Park** in Cameroon. Cameroon's other parks include some fine, highland savannah reserves in the north – **Faro**, **Bénoué** and **Bouba Ndjida** – and **Waza** in the floodlands near Lake Chad, which for faunal diversity and large herds of elephant is the best location in West Africa.

Parks vary quite widely in **entrance fees**, **seasonality** (many are closed during the rains) and **facilities**. Of those included above, only Mole and Yankari are really accessible on a budget. Some of the smaller parks and reserves, however – in The Gambia, southern Senegal and Sierra Leone for example – are low-key enough to permit entrance on foot. Vital, if you're visiting parks, is a pair of good, light binoculars.

PHOTOGRAPHY

West Africa is immensely photogenic but to get good pictures takes skill and confidence. While parts of the region have huge landscape potential at the right time of year, and there's obviously a wealth of opportuni- ties for wildlife enthusiasts, you'll probably find people, villages and towns are your most compelling subjects – as well as being the trickiest. Except for wildlife photography, for which a telephoto is essential, you

don't really need cumbersome equipment. It's often easier and less intrusive to take a small compact and keep your money for extra film.

Whatever you decide, if you take a camera, **insure it** and make sure you've a dust-proof bag to keep it in – film in the camera gets scratched otherwise. Take spare batteries, too – miniatures are hard to obtain.

Film tends to be very pricey so bring all you'll need. Try to keep it cool by stuffing it inside a sleeping bag. If you'll be away for some time, posting it home, or preferably sending it with someone flying back, is a good idea. Local black and white or colour print processing tends to be hit and miss. The opportunity to process slides is rare.

TECHNICAL BUSINESS

Getting (slightly) **technical**, use skylight or UV filters to block haze and protect your lens. Take several speeds of film – don't let anyone tell you it's unnecessary to have fast film – in rolls of twenty so you don't get stuck at the wrong speed too long. Unless you intend to do some bird or game park photography (and you have to be quite determined about this, tracking and patiently setting up your prey) it's probably not worth taking a telephoto or zoom lens. Long lenses are very difficult to use in public places. But if you feel it's worth taking a camera bag of lenses for your SLR, then it really makes no sense not to take two camera bodies as well – less lens changing and two film speeds available. Alternatively, take two compact cameras.

Early morning and late afternoon are the **best times for photography**. At midday, with the sun almost directly overhead, the light is flat and everything is lost in a formless glare. In the morning and evening the contrast between light and shade can be huge, so be careful to expose for the subject and not the general scene. A flash is very useful to fill in shade, even in bright sun. Remember too, as you negotiate for your next master portrait, that black skin usually needs a little more exposure. Think of people as always back-lit – a half stop is normally enough.

The **rainy seasons** are rewarding, especially when the first rains break. Months of dust are settled, greenery sprouts in a few hours, the countryside has a lush, bold sheen and the sky is magnificent.

CAMERAS, PEOPLE AND THE STATE

At the risk of generalising, West Africa is hostile to the camera's probing eye. There's considerable **mistrust of your motives** from three main sectors. Firstly, there are the people in markets, along the road and in the villages, who may resent you photographing them uninvited – with some justification. Secondly, there are others, often teachers or civil servants, who may take it upon themselves to protect the state from your unwelcome inspection and ask you to stop taking pictures, or report you to the police. And third are the security forces themselves, who will often hassle you about photography if they see you doing it – usually on the pretext that you were taking pictures of them.

None of this is intended to cause alarm. During the months of research for this guide, never was a film confiscated or a camera opened. But disturbing encounters are not infrequent.

TAKING PHOTOS OF PEOPLE

There are two options if you want to get **photos of people**. Firstly, you can adopt a gleefully robust (or blithely arrogant) approach, take pictures before anyone knows it's happened and deal with the problems after the event. But this is the kind of crassly journalistic manner which will almost inevitably get you into trouble and spread bad feeling in your wake. Some travellers – few – seem to get away with it. Go to a busy market place at home and try the same thing. It's difficult.

Far better is a more interactive approach. **Ask people first.** Summoning the confidence and humour to ask to take peoples' portraits, and accept refusal with equanimity, is at least half the affair. If they insist on posing, so be it. If purist irritations detract, try to come to terms with the reality of your position. To get anywhere close to a fly on the wall, you'd have to be able to take photos in your sleep. Shooting with a telephoto in crowded streets or a market, or using a sneaky right-angle fitting is almost always a failure.

Be prepared to pay something or to send a print if your subjects have addresses. If you're motivated to take a lot of pictures of people, you should seriously consider lugging along a **Polaroid** camera and as much film as you can muster, in order to offer a portrait immediately. Very few people have a photo of themselves. Or you could have a lot of photos of you and your family printed up with your address on the back, which should raise a few laughs at least when you try the exchange. The exchange is what counts. A family you've stayed with is unlikely to refuse a photo session and they may even ask for it. The same people might be furious if you jump off the bus and immediately start taking photos. Or worse, if you stay on the bus and do it through the window. Photos from Africa are full of examples of people who didn't want to be photographed. That you might have taken some of their soul is not an explanation, but it's a good metaphor.

SECURITY

A "risk to state security" is the explanation for why you shouldn't take photos of anything that could be construed as strategic or military — including any kind of army or police building, police or military vehicles and uniforms, prisons, airports, harbours, ferries, bridges, broadcasting installations, national flags and, of course, presidents. For subtler reasons, some countries are specifically ill-disposed to tourists taking photographs of scenes reflecting poverty — and with this kind of discretionary caveat, you can more or less rule out photography in the towns. It all depends on who sees you of course. Protesting your innocence won't appease small-minded officials. The Gambia, Senegal and Cape Verde are less uptight about these subjects. Cameroon and Nigeria are notoriously touchy.

One or two countries still have "photography permits" — Niger and Guinea for example. Details are given under " Practicalities" for each country.

VIDEO CAMERAS

Everything that applies to still photography applies ten-fold to videos. The sight of people wandering around with them is very new indeed, everywhere except the Gambian beaches. So new, in fact, that it would be well worth asking permission in advance through the nearest embassy and trying hard to get something in writing from the country's Ministry of Information. Most of the laws allowing amateur filming apply to non-broadcast quality 8mm filming and haven't yet caught up with videos.

PEOPLE AND LANGUAGE

Whether called peoples, ethnic groups, nations or tribes, West Africans have a multiplicity of racial and cultural origins. Distinctions would be simple if similarities in physical appearance were shared by those who speak the same language and share a common culture. The term "tribe" tends to imply this kind of banal stereotype.

But "tribes" have never been closed units and appearance, speech and culture have always overlapped. Even in the past, families often contained members of different ethnic groups. Over the last fifty years or so, "tribal" identities have broken down still further in many parts, as broader class, political and national ones are beginning to emerge.

The most enduring and meaningful ethnic distinction is **language**. A person's "mother tongue" is still important as an index of social identity. A *tribe*, if the word means anything, is best defined as a group of people sharing a common first language. But in the towns and among affluent families, even language is increasingly unimportant. Many people speak two or three languages (their own, French or English and sometimes a third or even fourth lingua franca like Hausa, Bambara or Krio). And for a few, the old metropolitan languages — French, English or Portuguese — have become a first language.

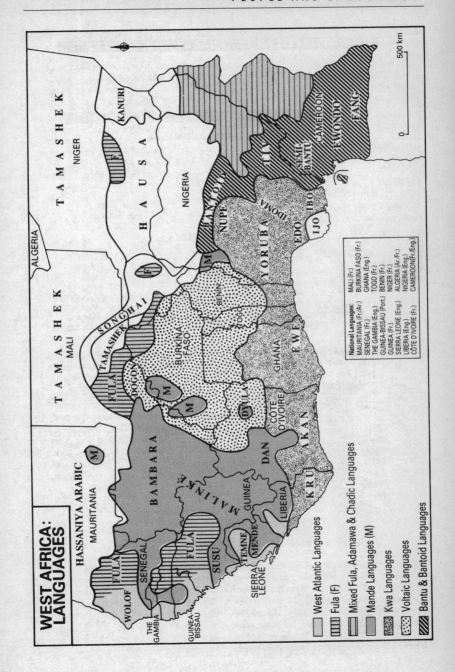

WEST AFRICA: LANGUAGES

500 km

National Languages:
MAURITANIA (Fr./Ar.)
SENEGAL (Fr.)
THE GAMBIA (Eng.)
GUINEA-BISSAU (Port.)
GUINEA (Fr.)
SIERRA LEONE (Eng.)
LIBERIA (Eng.)
CÔTE D'IVOIRE (Fr.)

MALI (Fr.)
BURKINA FASO (Fr.)
GHANA (Eng.)
TOGO (Fr.)
BENIN (Fr.)
NIGER (Fr.)
ALGERIA (Ar./Fr.)
NIGERIA (Eng.)
CAMEROON (Fr./Eng.)

West Atlantic Languages
Fula (F)
Mixed Fula, Adamawa & Chadic Languages
Mande Languages (M)
Kwa Languages
Voltaic Languages
Bantu & Bantoid Languages

HASSANIYA ARABIC
MAURITANIA
WOLOF
THE GAMBIA
GUINEA-BISSAU
SENEGAL
FULA
SUSU
TEMNE
MENDE
SIERRA LEONE
LIBERIA
GUINEA
DAN
KRU
AKAN
MALINKE
BAMBARA
DOGON
FULA
TAMASHEK
SONGHAI
MALI
TAMASHEK
ALGERIA
TAMASHEK
NIGER
KANURI
HAUSA
HAUSA
NIGERIA
BURKINA FASO
BENIN
TOGO
GHANA
EWE
CÔTE D'IVOIRE
YORUBA
EDO
IJO
IBO
NUPE
IDOMA
BANTOID
TIV
SEMI-BANTU
CAMEROON
EWONDO
FANG
CÔTE D'IVOIRE

WEST AFRICAN LANGUAGES AND PEOPLES

The following loose classification is a broad and selective breakdown of West Africa's larger people and language groups into separate ethno-linguistic identities. Although listed together by languages, not all the names here are distinct languages. These lists are intended only to provide anchorages for the different names you'll encounter. Additional names are closely related dialects. Names in brackets are alternatives.

Southern Area of Wider Affinity – "Niger–Congo" Languages

● WEST-ATLANTIC LANGUAGES ●

Fula (Fulani, Peul, Fulbe), Tukulor, Bororo
Wolof
Temne
Serer
Sherbro, Bulom
Kissi
Limba

Jola (Diola), Fogny, Banjal
Balante
Pepel, Manjak
Gola
Baga
Tenda, Basari
Bijago (Bidyago)

● VOLTAIC LANGUAGES ●

MORE/MOLE
Mossi
Dagomba
Mamprusi
Wala

SENUFO
Senoufo, Djimini, Karaboro
Minianka

GURMA
Gourmantché
Bassari, Tchamba
Moba

GRUSI
Gourounsi, Kassena, Sissala
Dagara (Dagarti)
Lilse, Fulse (Kurumba)
Frafra
Builsa
Wagala

TEM
Kabré (Kabyé) Logba, Tamberma, Lamba
Tem (Kotokoli, Cotocoli)

LOBI
Loron
Nabe
Gan
Koulango

HABE
Bobo, Bwaba, Kos, Siby
Dogon

BARGU
Somba (Betammaribe)
Bargu (Bariba)
Yowa

● KWA LANGUAGES ●

KRU
Bete
Dida
Grebo
Krahn
Bakwe
Bassa

EDO
Edo
Bini
Isoko, Urhobo (Sobo)
Kukuruku

NUPE
Nupe
Igbira
Gwari, Koro

YORUBA
Yoruba, Oyo
Egba
Ijebu
Ekiti
Ife
Bunu
Itsekiri
Ana

IDOMA
Idoma
Igala
Egede
Iyala

IGBO
Igbo (Ibo), Onitsha

TWI LANGUAGES

AKAN
Twi (Asante)
Baulé
Fante
Agni
Abron
Akwapim
Guang

EWE
Fon, Adja, Xwala, Xuéda, Maxi
Ewe, Ang-lo
Ga-Adangme
Mina, Popo
Gun, Tofinu

CENTRAL TOGO
Akposso

LAGOON
Abé
Ajukru
Abidji
Alladian
Assini, Nzima
Ebrie

● EASTERN NIGRITIC LANGUAGES ●

ADAMAWA

Fali	Mbum	Namshi	Longuda	Vere
Massa	Mundang	Chamba	Mumuye	Yungur

● IJO LANGUAGES ●

Ijo (Ijaw)	Brass	Kalabari

● BANTOID LANGUAGES ●

Ibibio, Efik, Anang	Birom	Jerawa
Mada	Ekoi, Oban	Anyang
Katab	Orri, Ukelle	Basa-Kaduna
Boki	Korup	Yergum
Kamberi	Dukakari	Jukun

MACRO-BANTU

Tiv	Jarawa	Mambila

NORTH-WESTERN BANTU		CAMEROON HIGHLANDS BANTU ("SEMI-BANTU")'	
Ewondo (Yaoundé)	Duala (Douala)	Ba-Miléké, -Djou, -Fang, -Foussam, -Mendjou, -Ngangté	
Bulu, Fang, Eton	Bassa, Bakoko	Ba-	Ba-Fut
Gbaya	Batanga	Moun (Bamoum, Bamum)	Tikar
Sango-Ngbandi	Bakweri, Bimbia	Fia (Bafia)	Widekum
Bakundu		Nso (Bansaw)	Fungom
		Li (Bali)	Ndop

Northern Area of Wider Affinity – "Afro–Asiatic" Languages

● ARABIC ●
HASSANIYA

● CHADIC LANGUAGES ●

HASSANIYA	Hausa, Adrawa, Tazarawa	Wakura
Berabish	Angas	Toupouri (Tuburi)
Imragen	Bura	Wajawa
Kunta (Kounta)	Kotoko (Longone)	Gude
Regeibat, Rehian	Tangale	Gerawa
Tajakant, Arosien	Mandara (Wandala)	Guizica, Mofou
Trarza	Kapsiki (Margi)	Podoko
Zenaga, Chorfa, Tichit	Matakam (Mafa)	Bata
Choa (Shoa)	Mauri	Mousgoum (Musgu)

● BERBER LANGUAGES ●
Tamashek (Tuareg, Touareg)

● SAHARAN LANGUAGES ●
Kanouri (Kanuri, Beriberi)

Songhaic Languages

Songhai (Sonray)	Dendi	Djerma (Zerma)

Mande Languages

NUCLEAR MANDE		*PERIPHERAL MANDE*	
Malinké (Mandinka,	Kuranko	Mende	Bussa (Busa)
Mandingo)	Diallonke (Yalunka)	Kpelle (Gerse)	Ngere (Guerze)
Bambara	Kasonke	Vai (Gallinas)	Kono
Soninke (Sarakolé)	Konyanke	Dan, Gio, Mano, Guro	Sia
Susu (Sousou)	Bozo	Loma (Toma), Buzi	Loko
Dyula	Kagoro	Samo	Gbande

NAMES AND GROUPS

West Africa is the most linguistically complex region in the world. There are dozens of **major languages** and literally hundreds of less important languages and distinct dialects. Some 400 of these are spoken in Nigeria alone. Most of West Africa's languages are viable and thriving and very few are in any danger of extinction.

For an outsider, the confusion is exacerbated by the fact that, until Europeans and the Bible colonised the region, almost none of these languages was written. Today, many are written, in the Roman alphabet, sometimes with additional phonetic symbols. But in the early days, even the language and ethnic **names** first recorded varied according to the nationality and ear of the researchers and the identity of the person asked (a similar, but simpler situation exists in Europe with, for example, the words for *German: deutsh, allemand, allemão,* etc). Often enough in West Africa the name of the language and of the people who speak it are genuinely distinct.

We have tried to be as consistent and simple as possible in this book, without sweeping distinctions away. Generally, we've used the **names** used locally (for example Mandingo in Liberia, Malinké in Guinea, Mandinka in The Gambia). On the other hand, varieties of names for the people and language often called *Fulani* are so diverse that we've gone for simple *Fula* throughout except in Nigeria, where "Fulani" is in common usage.

Some understanding of differences and relatedness is worth achieving in order, at the very least, to come to grips with what can otherwise seem an incomprehensible and unfathomable cultural region. Most West Africans speak languages of one of **three great groups** – "Niger-Congo" (recently re-named the Southern area of wider affinity – Sawa), "Afro-Asiatic" (the Northern area of wider affinity – Nawa) and Mande. African language classification (the attempt to assess the way the languages are presumed to have evolved from common ancestral languages) is immensely complicated and linguists have recently tried to get away from the notion of "families" of languages, in case it turns out they have things in common through long association rather than common ancestry.

In trying to work out where everyone fits in, it helps, especially when reading different sources, to keep a flexible attitude to **spellings** (try pronouncing the word in as many ways as possible). Two sets of much interchanged sounds are p, b, v, f, w and d, gh, r, l. And of course anything spelled "qu" might just as well be spelt "kw" or, for that matter, "cou" or "kou". Likewise, "j" is commonly spelt "dy" or "di" in French transcription. The French are keen on apostrophes everywhere, too. they don't usually mean anymore than that someone found the word hard to pronounce. Finally, look out for prefixes or suffixes that may mean "people" ("Ba-" in the Bantu languages for example, or "-nke" in the Mande languages).

THE "SOUTHERN AREA OF WIDER AFFINITY"
The **Sawa group** includes the 400 **Bantu** languages that are spoken all over central and southern Africa. In West Africa, Bantu languages are only spoken in parts of southern Cameroon. Further west, the picture is much more complicated. The so-called **"West Atlantic"** languages, which include Wolof, Temne and Fula, are part of this grouping, though fairly distantly related to Bantu. Also part of the Sawa group is the **Kwa sub-family** of language clusters, which include the **Akan languages** (of which the Asante are the most famous speakers), the **Ewe languages** of Ghana and Togo and the **Yoruba** and **Ibo** language groups of Benin and Nigeria. To the north, the **Voltaic sub-family** of language clusters includes the **Senoufo**, **More** and **Lobi** groups of Côte d'Ivoire, Ghana and Burkina.

Many of the languages in the Sawa group have **class systems** (something like genders in French in that everything must agree) with up to 20 or more classes – Bantu languages are the classic examples. Many Sawa languages, too, are **tonal** – in which the pitch of a spoken word determines its meaning – and extra notations are often necessary when writing them.

THE "NORTHERN AREA OF WIDER AFFINITY"
The **Nawa group** includes most of the languages of North Africa, and the Middle East, including Hebrew, Arabic, Berber and Tamashek (the language of the Tuaregs). The most important languages in the area as far as West Africa is concerned are known as "Chadic", the biggest of which is **Hausa**, spoken by some twenty million people as a first language. Nawa languages are mostly non-tonal and classless, though many have masculine and feminine genders.

UNRELATED LANGUAGE GROUPS

The **Mande cluster of languages** doesn't belong to either area of wider affinity and, linguistically, it's on a classification level with both of them. The languages in this group are closely related and very old. Geographically, they're quite compact and appear to be centred in the Mali-Guinea border region – which, historically, was the heartland of the old Mande/Manding/Mali empire. From the linguistic point of view, the "nuclear Mande" family includes **Bambara**, **Mandinka** and **Dyula**. This group is also known as "Mande-Tan" (after their word for "ten") The languages of "Peripheral Mande" (or "Mande-Fu"), which deviate much more from the heartland languages, and from each other, include **Susu**, **Mende**, **Dan-Gio** and **Vai**. Tones are important in this southern section, less so in the more mainstream languages.

The **Songhai** of the middle Niger River are another old imperial people, with a language quite distinct from any other in Africa.

DIRECTORY

ADDRESSES The postman never comes in West Africa. Mail is sorted into PO Boxes (*BP* in French, *CP* in Portuguese) or sometimes into *Private Mail Bags* (*PMB*). The lower the number, usually, the older the address – sometimes a useful indication of credentials when making bookings or enquiries. *Your* address is likely to be much in demand – a stack of small address labels is very useful.

BEGGARS Beggars are part of town life, though not as much as you might realistically expect. Most are visibly destitute and many are blind, or victims of polio or accidents, or lepers or homeless mothers and children. Some have established pitches, others keep on the move. They are harassed by the police and often rounded up. Many people give to the same beggar on a regular basis and, of course, alms-giving is a requirement of Islam supposed to benefit the donor. Keep small change handy all the time – it will hardly dent your expenses.

There's no question of confusing real beggars with the incessant demands – in the more touristy parts of several of the francophone countries – for "cadeaux", usually from children. These you simply have to devise a strategy to deal with. Like heat and mosquitos, they seem to trouble new arrivals most.

CLOTHES Cotton is obviously the main criterion. Dirty colours are best and clothes should be tough enough to stand repeated hand washing. Mostly you'll want to wear the minimum, but pack at least one warm jacket or sweater. Though you can buy clothes as you go, they'll rarely be cheaper than at home. Even "junk clothes" – "deadmen's clothes" shipped in bulk from Europe and the USA – which you'll find in every town, may be cheaper bought nearer to source. If you fancy kitting yourself up in local style, expect to pay. Cloth is expensive but tailoring cheap.

People are generally very clothes-conscious. Ragged clothes and long hair on men don't go down well. Avoid absolutely any military-style, or army surplus, gear. Camouflage prints are out. And, however you dress, pack a set of "smart" clothes for difficult embassies and other important occasions.

Take the lightest, toughest, airiest footwear you can afford. Forget about waterproofs. You won't go out in the rain, and if you do, you'll get wet anyway. All that plastic and nylon is too hot.

ELECTRICITY When there is some, it is usually 220V AC 50Hz. Niger has 220V/380V AC 50Hz and Liberia 110V AC 60Hz. Only top hotels have shaver points or outlets in the rooms.

GIFTS It's very useful to have some tokens to give to people. Postcards from home are appreciated by people who have little or no chance of possessing colour pictures. Pictures of you and your family are of tremendous value. Think about getting a pile of prints done before you go. Ball point pens are also nice to give away, to kids at school mostly.

IVORY The elephants of West Africa are in such a dire predicament that little international effort is being made to save those isolated pockets of a once large population still hanging on in remote bush against the poachers. Park boundaries aren't always much safeguard. Ivory is for sale in many West African cities, much of it carved in Hong Kong. And bracelets and bangles are widely touted. Tragically, it seems it's still a viable way to earn a living and will likely remain so as long as ivory itself remains unstigmatised.

The following are West Africa's latest elephant population estimates: Mauritania – 30, Guinea – 50, Senegal – 54, Sierra Leone – 100, Liberia – 100, Mali – 400, Niger – 400, Benin – 500, Ghana – 600, Nigeria – 1500, Burkina Faso – 1500, Côte d'Ivoire – 1600, Cameroon 17,000.

LAUNDRY Washing is always done by hand, in a stream with flat rocks by preference. You won't find laundrettes, but there are plenty of people willing to do the job. Even the smallest hotel can arrange it. If you have any choice, dry your clothes indoors. Avoid spreading them on the ground if you can – they may be infested by the Tumbu fly which lays its eggs on wet clothes. Ironing kills the eggs.

STUDENT CARDS If you're 32 or under, do what you can to obtain an International Student Identity Card (ISIC) before you go. Student unions and a number of student-minded travel agents sell them. They're valid from the start of the autumn term until December 31 the following year. They're no guarantee of cheap deals, but are worth waving for many official payments (airlines, railways, museum entrance) you may make. If you are a student it's useful also to have a rubber-stamped letter substantiating the fact.

TOILET PAPER This is usually provided by the user of the facilities rather than the owner. Never run out – alternative methods take more time to get used to than most people have.

WORK Exceptions are noted in one or two places in the book, but in general there's no way you can work your way through West Africa. Bed and board in return for your help is sometimes available on development projects, in schools or through voluntary agencies, but such arrangements are entirely informal and word-of-mouth. Teachers and engineers have the best chances. Direct, personal approach to the appropriate ministry might open some doors. But under-employment is a serious problem and work permit regulations everywhere make your getting a wage nearly impossible without pulling strings. You usually sign a declaration that you won't seek work when you obtain the visa or fill in the arrival card.

A FEW FINAL SUGGESTIONS

● A **pocket French dictionary** is extremely useful.

● **Binoculars** (the small, fold-up ones) are invaluable for game- and bird-watching.

● **Sunglasses** are a health precaution worth bringing even if you're not used to them, and they're expensive to buy locally.

● Multi-purpose **penknife**. Avoid blades longer than a palm-width. They're sometimes confiscated.

● A **torch.**

● A small **alarm clock** – handy for pre-dawn starts.

● A **padlock** – vital in cheap hotels where doors don't lock properly.

● **Plastic bags** are invaluable – bin liners to keep dust off clothes, small sealable ones to protect cameras and film.

● If driving or hiking in remote areas, a **compass** is immensely useful.

● **Camping gas stoves** are light and useful even if you're not camping. The cylinders are fairly expensive (about £2) but you'll find them somewhere in every capital city.

● You might want to take your own pair of **flip flops** for hotel bathrooms and generally padding about, but these can be bought cheaply locally.

● A **sheet sleeping bag** (sew up a sheet) is essential for low budget travel.

● A **sleeping bag** isn't of much use if you'll be staying in hotels. If you plan on other sleeping arrangements, or anticipate some long journeys, then get the best one you can afford – light and compressible – since you'll sleep on top of it nine times out of ten anyway.

● If you shave, bring disposable **razors** (available only at import supermarkets) or preferably an old fashioned razor blade holder.

● **Tampons** are expensive and only available in big cities. Bring as many as you can bear to.

ALGERIAN SAHARA

THE ALGERIAN SAHARA

The **Sahara** is the largest desert in the world: a territory whose scale is difficult to comprehend. Saying that it spreads over ten million square kilometres – an area which is larger than the USA – hardly conjures an image you can get a grip on. But driving for day after day across the desert, you do begin to feel its immensity.

Travelling the **Hoggar route**, for example, the main Saharan artery, you are – by the time you reach the outpost of Tamanrasset – about halfway across the desert, but further from Algiers than that city is from London. On the wilder **Tanezrouft route**, to the west, you cover desolate expanses of flatness where the only detectable feature is a feeling of the earth curving away on the distant horizon. Stop for a break and, unless it's windy, the only sound is your own breathing, or your oddly loud voice. But if images like these of the void are the Sahara's most memorable aspects, it's mistaken to equate the desert solely with nothingness. Within the relatively small Algerian sector described here, there are **mountains** rising to nearly 3000m, **cave paintings** dating to 6000 BC, remote **oases** and almost-forgotten **cities**.

Algeria as a whole has been shaped inevitably by its colonial past, its close ties with France; its long and bitter war for independence, attained only in 1962; and subsequent rule by the socialist FLN, the old Liberation Front. Algerians consequently have a high level of political consciousness and a broad commitment to traditional Muslim values – characteristics which make the country seem at once more progressive and more conservative than either Morocco or Tunisia.

Widespread anti-imperialist sentiments don't, however, translate into hostility to individuals from the capitalist world; in fact the notable absence of tourism, compared with neighbouring countries, makes this a place where contact is sincere and the people open and quite extraordinarily generous. But the veil is still commonly worn by Algerian women, who have little public presence in society outside the northern cities – particularly with fundamentalism on the increase. A very strong strand of male arrogance runs through every level of Algerian society and you may be amazed at the way women are treated in a state that claims to follow socialist principles. As a result, it's a country that male and female travellers tend to experience in quite different ways, women travelling alone quite often having a tough time.

The people

The **Arabs**, who stormed North Africa soon after the death of Muhammad in the seventh century, today comprise the majority of the Algerian population. However, over the centuries, many have intermarried with the earlier Berber inhabitants and with the Europeans – mainly French and Spanish – who settled in the last century.

The **Berbers**, who were the original inhabitants of Africa's northern fringe, today make up about 25 percent of the country's population. Their customs and languages vary greatly across the regions and groups. The **Kabylie** live in the mountainous region of the same name, centred around Tizi Ouzou, some 100km east of Algiers. Further south, the **Mozabites** are ardent defenders of a rebel Muslim sect and ambitious business people. The **Tuareg**, also of Berber origin, are traditionally nomadic, traversing the desert with their camels through Algeria, Mali, Niger and beyond.

Lastly, significant numbers of **West Africans** have settled in Algeria over the last twenty years, escaping from drought and poverty to the comparative affluence of the oil-rich, socialist economy. Their presence is tolerated but they're generally the poorest people of the desert and always in danger of being expelled.

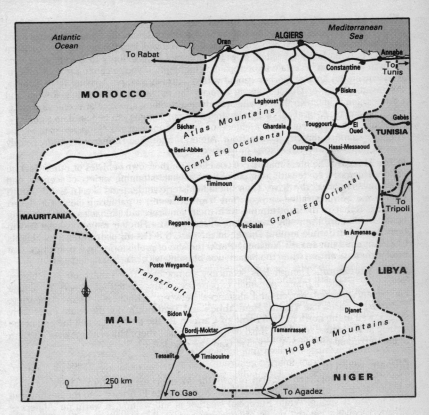

DESERT SOCIETY

There are two main **Tuareg groups** living in the Algerian Sahara: the **Kel Ahaggar**, who occupy the Hoggar near Tamanrasset, and the **Kel Ajjer**, who live in the Tassili near Djanet. Further afield, other groups are scattered throughout the desert. Among them are the Kel Aïr and Kel Gress in Niger, and the Kel Tademaket in the Timbuktu region of Mali.

The Tuareg speak **Tamahaq** (or *Tamashek*, or numerous other spellings), a Berber dialect that's one of the few African languages with its own script. Traditionally, they controlled trans-Saharan trade, offering protection to caravans or raiding those that refused their services. Their society was highly stratified, with classes ranging from nobles to slaves, and the **Harratin**, blacks who formerly worked as indentured servants, still live in virtual chatteldom in many of the desert oases. The Tuareg have become increasingly sedentary, due in part to a government plan to settle them, and in part to the crippling effects of the drought of the mid-1980s.

Another group of nomads – the **Chaamba** – live in the northern desert between the towns of Ouargla and El Goléa. Traditional enemies of the Tuareg, they allied themselves with the French in their attempts to pacify the Sahara at the beginning of the century. Their armies were instrumental in winning the Battle of Tit, which dealt a decisive blow to the Tuareg's anti-colonial resistance.

Where to go: the trans-Saharan routes

Once you've crossed the Mediterranean to Algiers or Oran, the Sahara is just a day's drive to the south – and a couple of days will see you well into the heart of it. **Northern Algeria** is remarkably unvisited; however, despite its proximity to Europe, and time spent in the region is certain to be repaid. A highlight, if you're coming from Morocco, is Tlemcen, an ancient Berber capital with a Turkish history. Arriving from Tunisia, the beautiful city of Constantine is a focus for exploring the region's Roman and Carthaginian ruins, with the Kabylie mountains providing spectacular scenic and cultural complement. A brief survival guide to the city of **Algiers** can be found on p.80.

Setting out south, you have a choice of just two main **trans-Saharan routes**: the **Hoggar** (almost directly south from Algiers) and the **Tanezrouft** (more easily approached from western Algeria or Morocco).

● **The Hoggar.** The great majority of travellers (in their own vehicles or otherwise) go via the Hoggar, a route with long portions of asphalt, stunning variety of scenery, and more towns to break the drive. These include historic settlements like **In Salah** and **El Goléa** and administrative outposts like **Tamanrasset**, a gathering point for desert nomads. But it is the **mountains**, with their sun-scorched pinnacles and balancing boulders, that are the really compelling attraction. The Hoggar range peaks at 2908m near **Assekrem**, while around Djanet, in the east, the **Tassili** plateau reaches heights of 2154m amid the **Tassili National Park**, the site of prehistoric **cave paintings** that bear witness to an age when the Sahara was bursting with plant and animal life.

● **The Tanezrouft.** Though less scenically compelling, the Tanezrouft is a bigger adventure – and a more personal experience. This stretch of desert is almost completely flat and barren and distances between settlements seem staggering. Picturesque oases like **Taghit, Beni-Abbès** and **Timimoun** dot the route in its early stages, well to the north of the **Tropic of Cancer**. By the time you reach the end of the tarmac at **Reggane**, roughly a third of the way across, there still remains over 1300km of uninterrupted *piste* before arrival at **Gao**, the next town.

Climate: when to go

The climate in **northern Algeria** follows the Mediterranean pattern. There's a good amount of rain – especially abundant from November to February – so the best overall time to visit is spring. While European weather is still waiting to warm up, Algiers is already receiving healthy doses of sunshine and the surrounding countryside looks amazingly green: be forewarned, however, that showers continue through to May, and in March and April it can bucket down. But the summer months, from June to September, are uncomfortably hot, especially in the big cities where the air seems more stagnant. Temperatures in Algiers often rise above 30°C in July and August.

Weather **in the Sahara** is somewhat more predictable. Some regions receive no rain for decades, and those that do are hit by torrential storms that turn dry *oueds* (wadis) into rushing river beds. All year round, the daytime is hot and dry, though in the summer months, temperatures can be staggering as they push towards 45°C in the

ALGERIAN STATISTICS

Algeria is huge, extending over **2.3 million square kilometres**, making it Africa's largest country after Sudan. **The Sahara** – Algeria's most resoundingly dramatic region – spreads over most of it, though containing less than a million of the thirty million **population**– the vast majority of whom live in the Mediterranean hinterland. Since independence in 1962, **government** has been by a single party, the *Front de Libération Nationale*, engineers of the nationalist victory over the French. The current president, **Chadli Bendjedid**, was elected to his third consecutive term in 1989.

shade. Inside a vehicle, it gets a lot hotter. **Nights** can, however, be cool. In the winter, temperatures commonly drop to 10°C – often lower in mountainous regions like the Hoggar or the Tassili – while mornings can be crisp and cool; but, as the day warms up, temperatures usually rise to 25–30°C. Take note that, although the northern reaches of the desert do get cold at night between October and February, the much-repeated folk-knowledge about the temperature dropping below freezing at night is something of an exaggeration. The lowest temperature ever recorded in In Salah was minus 3°C. The overriding impression is a hot one.

If you're **driving**, the heat will obviously affect your car's performance. Vehicles tend to overheat anyhow when travelling through sand, which acts like a continuous brake to forward momentum. In the summer months, your driving time may be limited to a couple of hours in the early morning and late afternoon. Progress will be slow.

AVERAGE TEMPERATURES AND RAINFALL

ALGIERS

	Jan	Feb	Mar	Apr	May	June	July	Aug	Sept	Oct	Nov	Dec
Temperatures °C												
Min (night)	9	10	11	13	15	18	21	22	20	17	13	10
Max (day)	15	16	18	20	23	26	29	29	27	23	19	16
Rainfall mm	112	84	74	41	46	15	0	5	41	79	130	137
Days with rainfall	11	9	9	5	5	2	0	0	4	7	11	12

IN SALAH

	Jan	Feb	Mar	Apr	May	June	July	Aug	Sept	Oct	Nov	Dec
Temperatures °C												
Min (night)	6	8	12	17	21	27	28	28	25	19	12	7
Max (day)	21	24	28	33	37	43	45	44	41	34	27	22
Rainfall mm	3	3	0	0	0	0	0	3	0	0	5	3
Days with rainfall	0	0	0	0	1	0	0	0	1	1	1	1

TAMANRASSET

	Jan	Feb	Mar	Apr	May	June	July	Aug	Sept	Oct	Nov	Dec
Temperatures °C												
Min (night)	4	5	9	13	17	21	21	21	19	15	10	6
Max (day)	19	22	26	30	33	35	35	34	33	30	25	21

Arrivals

Unless you're flying to Algiers, it makes sense to consider the Mediterranean ferries as a means of access to Algeria. Travelling through Europe and Morocco or Tunisia won't save time and can easily end up costing more.

■ Flights to/from West African cities

Despite the importance of Algiers airport, it is linked direct with only a handful of countries in West Africa. All the useful West African services are on **Air Algérie**, which flies regularly between Algiers and Bamako (weekly), Dakar (twice weekly), Niamey (twice weekly) and Ouagadougou (weekly).

■ Ferries from France and Spain

The *Compagnie Nationale Algérienne de Navigation* (*CNAN*) runs **ferries from Marseille** to Algiers, Annaba, Bejaïa and Oran. Seasonal ferries also run from **Sète** (France) and **Alicante** (Spain) to Oran. The voyage from Marseille to Algiers takes about twenty hours, so, in timing your arrival, a morning departure is best. The *CNAN* works in conjunction with the French *Société Nationale Corse-Mediterranée* (*SNCM*) which represents them in Europe.

Though **France–Algeria** is an expensive trans-Mediterranean option, ferry prices and schedules change with the season; summer fares are up to twenty percent higher than winter. If you do travel in the **summer months** (not a great time for the Sahara!), beware that ferries are heavily booked and it's essential to reserve well in advance.

Arriving in Marseille with no booking and a car you may find yourself, due to lack of space, travelling on a passenger ferry and your **car on a separate cargo vessel**, scheduled to arrive a day or two later in Algiers. Items from vehicles sent this way are frequently found to be missing when the cars are retrieved from customs. If you're loaded down with gear, it's therefore advisable to wait a couple of days for a ferry on which you and your car can travel together. Even so, **once docked in Algeria**, cars have to be left on board, unlocked, keys in ignition, to be disembarked by dockworkers. Don't leave valuables inside.

One-way **passenger fares to Algiers** start from around £70 economy class, or £110 in a cabin with meals included. **Cars** up to 3.8m cost from £172 one-way, rising to £208 for vehicles up to 4.92m. **Motorbikes** are £55 one-way. Return fares are slightly less than twice the one-way price. There are a few **special deals** which some agents can offer; for example a small car and up to five passengers for £244 return, low season.

For additional information, **SNCM** has the following offices in Europe:

BRITAIN: *Continental Shipping & Travel*, 179 Piccadilly, London W1V 9DB (☎071-491 3502, telex 297248, Fax 071-491 3502)

FRANCE: *SNCM*, 12, rue Godot-de-Mauroy, 75009 Paris (☎42.66.67.98)

SNCM, 62, Boulevard des Dames, Marseille 13222 (☎91.56.32.00)

BELGIUM: *Centre International Rogier*, Bureau 314, 1000 Brussels (☎219.47.88)

■ Overland via Morocco or Tunisia

Many overland travellers route through Spain, then take a shorter ferry crossing to **Morocco**, crossing into Algeria from the west. This saves money if you're hitching, but little if you're driving, given the extra time and expense of the detour (three days driving – 2000–2500km depending on ferry). Still, it's a great journey if you've time to take it slowly, as, too, is the slightly shorter route down through Italy, across to **Tunisia** on the ferry from Palermo and into Algeria from the east.

From Morocco

There is a choice of four main **ferry crossings from Spain to Morocco**: Algeciras–Ceuta, Algeciras–Tangier, Málaga–Mellilla and Almería–Melilla. If you are driving, and your main concern is getting into Algeria fast, then the Melilla crossings are by far the most convenient, leaving just a 166-km haul to the border at Oujda. Travelling by local transport, Tangier is probably the best starting point, with good rail links to the medieval city of Fes and thence to Oujda.

In past years, the **Oujda** border was confined to car drivers, with everyone else being directed 380km south to the desert crossing at **Figuig**. Since the improvement of Moroccan–Algerian relations in 1989, however, the Oujda border seems firmly open to all. If you want to travel on the Tanezrouft route through the Sahara (and you already have a Malian visa), you might actually prefer to enter at Figuig, which offers a fairly straight run to Béchar on the main highway.

DRIVING ACROSS THE SAHARA

Saharan travellers have strong views on suitability of vehicles for the crossing – and it's easy to become motor-obsessive at the planning stage. Some people would never consider crossing the desert in anything other than a brand new 4-wheel drive (4WD) vehicle with enough new equipment on board to start a spare parts store. Others bring tired VW minibuses or trusty and marketable Peugeot 504s and odd scrap parts from a worn-out engine.

There's really no right way to cross the Sahara and your choice of vehicle has as much to do with mentality as with monetary limitations. Still, you can't afford to be too casual. The enterprise is dangerous – people get lost and die every year – and there are major financial risks attached, too, if things go wrong. That said, with reasonable care, even light cars such as Citroen 2CVs can and do make it across the routes described in this chapter, usually with no great difficulty. Precautions should include having the time to drive slowly, stopping every hour or two to allow the engine to cool and travelling with someone capable of making ordinary car repairs and of improvising when replacement parts are unavailable.

DESERT DRIVING: SOME SERIOUS HAZARDS

Wherever there's *erg* or **sand dunes** (not often on the Hoggar route) sand may blow across the road. It is cleared regularly, and likely danger spots are indicated by the incongruous warning triangle with exclamation mark and the legend *SABLE* (sand). If you hit soft sand at speed you'll lose control of the steering, possibly break a suspension member or even roll over.

If you're driving after fairly **recent rains** (say in the previous week), beware sections of road completely washed away, without warning.

Camels tend to stand in the middle of the road and just stare at you. Where this is a recognised danger there are dromedary warning signs, but absence of signs doesn't mean no camels.

FUEL

Petrol (*essence ordinaire*) is around DA3 (about 25p) a litre in Algeria, the cheapest on the continent. *Super* (when you can get it) is a little pricier. **Diesel** is amazingly cheap (less than DA1/litre).

Oil, exploited and refined in Algeria and sold under the name *Naftilia*, is good quality and costs about DA10 (80p) a litre. All fuel supplies become extremely irregular in the far south.

PARTS AND EQUIPMENT

The following list is by no means exhaustive.

Spare battery

Bulbs for headlights, brakes and indicators.

Cables for accelerator, clutch and speedo.

Carburettor

Condensor

Distributor cap with a set of points and rotor.

Fan belt

Fuel pump

Clutch and brake cylinder repair kits

Hoses for radiator and heater; supply of clips.

Jerry cans Always overestimate the quantitiy of petrol required, remembering that consumption is dramatically increased when driving on sand. On the Tanezrouft, you should ideally have enough petrol to get you the 1500km from Adrar to Gao.

Oil Algeria is a good place to stock up on spare cans

Plastic water containers As a general rule, reckon on 10 litres of water per passenger per day. It seems like a lot, but leaves extra in case of radiator problems – and for *some* washing.

Footpump

Water pump and gasket

Nylon rope

Sand ladders or PSP (perforated steel plating). Essential for getting out of the sand, the *protection civile* in Adrar requires you to have this equipment if you're going down the Tanezrouft.

Shock absorbers

Spark plugs

Tyres At least two spares are mandatory, before gaining permission to cross at the Sahara at the *protection civile* in Adrar. More are desirable – those you don't need can easily be sold once you reach tarmac again. Also include extra **tubes**, **spare valves** and, of course, a **puncture repair kit** with plenty of patches.

Clothing It's well worth kitting yourself out with a **headscarf** of lightest muslin – a *shesh* or *cheche* – which are worn by locals and available throughout Algeria.

ALGIERS: A ROUGH GUIDE

Algiers (El-Djazir in Arabic; Alger in French) is a stately bowl of a city, swooping from suburban and residential heights, through steep, upmarket hillsides down to the old Turkish quarter known as the Kasbah and to the western-style city centre and port.

Though founded around 600 BC, the city no longer feels like an ancient metropolis, with pollution and congestion taking their toll. But the shabby old French centre, cut through by wide boulevards and dotted with *boulangeries* and cafés, has its attractions, and there are some excellent museums to while away the hours between waiting for visas.

ARRIVAL AND ORIENTATION

Algiers seems huge at first, and the replacement of French road names with Arabic ones is frustrating. The city's topography, however, is a major aid to orientation, with the huge Mémorial du Martyr a useful landmark on the south side of the centre.

● Arriving by air you'll find yourself at **Houari Boumedienne Airport**, 20km southeast of the city centre at El Harrach. Taxis from the airport should cost no more than DA200; airport buses run from dawn to midnight for DA10, taking you right to the centre by the *Hôtel Es-Safir*.

● Arriving by **ferry**, the *Nouvelle Gare Maritime* is below and just to the south of the Kasbah and,

again, right by the *Es-Safir* – along with most of the airlines and shipping agents on split-level **Bd Zirout Youcef**. The **railway station** is here too.

You're likely to spend a good deal of your time around this lower **Eastern Quarter** of the city – the pedestrian shopping area around Place Port Said, with shops and cinemas and, at its centre, bd Khemisti and the *Grande Poste*. The **Kasbah** area has preserved much of its architectural heritage. Its oldest buildings date from the sixteenth century. The majority of embassies are up the hill out of the centre in **Hydra** and **Bouzaréah**.

CITY TRANSPORT

● **Taxis**. Relatively easy to find, but settle the fare first: it should be a flat DA5 by day, DA7.5 by night, then under DA2 per km.

● Buses are efficient and cheap, and operate from dawn until about 8.30pm. Useful routes include:
#45/59 *Grande Poste* to Bouzaréah

#15 *Grande Poste* to Marché 1er Mai
#27 Marché 1er Mai to Palais de la Culture
#88 Marché 1er Mai to Hydra Central
#32 Place Audin to Mémorial du Martyr
#31 Place Audin to Hydra Central
#44 Hydra Central/Ben Aknoun to Cité des PTT/ Cité des DNC.

ACCOMMODATION

You can run into difficulties with accommodation in Algiers. Many of the hotels seem to be permanently *complet* and those that admit to having rooms are generally expensive. For cheapish lodgings, look in the vicinity of Place Port Saïd. Two reliable standbys are:

Hôtel El-Badr, 31 rue Amar el Kamar, off Sq. Port Saïd (☎62.08.12). A real gem, with double rooms from under DA60.
Hôtel Es-Safir (☎63.50.40, telex 52142). Best of the expensive addresses, and at DA300–400 for a double, reasonable enough value. High standards – and views out to sea or onto the Kasbah.

FOOD

Algiers restaurants can be excellent, though keep in mind that many are closed on Saturdays.

A dozen or more of the city's famous fish restaurants are to be found down on the **Rampe de la Pécherie**, off the Place des Martyres. For a splurge *Le Sindbad* (☎62.10.65) is hard to beat: fish cooked any way you like and bottles of underrated Algerian plonk for around DA180 a head.

For **cheaper meals**, head for the alleys between Place Emir Abdelkader and Place Port Saïd, where you can eat ordinary fare for under DA20. And if you want to investigate where the moneyed youth of Algiers hang out (there are some), go down to the **Victory Park** (Riad el Fet'h) for burgers, ice cream and the rest.

AROUND THE CITY

Algiers' **Kasbah** may not be the exotic warren of shops and alleys of myth, but it's a pleasantly unintimidating place to wander for an hour or two. You may possibly find yourself adopted by a "guide", though in a much more low-key way than in Morocco; if you hit it off, you'll probably appreciate the extra knowledge on the quarter.

Of the various museums, the **Bardo** (rue F. Roosevelt; 9am–noon & 2–5pm; closed Fri & Sat) is the city's finest, with huge ethnographic and archaeological collections and lots to look at if you're planning some diversions in the desert.

Other city highlights include the rambling **Jardin d'Essai** botanical gardens, conveniently en route to the collossal and brutish **Mémorial du Martyr** (the *Makam ech Chahid*), which, with the **Victory Park** at its foot, sounds a slightly premature congratulatory note in reinforced concrete over the bay.

Other **museums** include:
Museum of Popular Arts and Traditions, 9 rue Malek Mouhand Akli (10am–noon & 2.30–5pm; closed Sat).

National Museum of Islamic and Classical Antiquities, Parc de la Liberté, 124 rue Didouche Mourad (10am–noon & 2–5pm; closed Fri am, Sat); Roman mosaics, Islamic art.

Museum of Fine Arts, Place de Dar es Salam (summer 9.30–11.30am & 2.30–6pm; winter 9.30–11.30am & 2–5pm; closed Fri am, Sat, Sun am).

Djihad Museum, Riadh El Fet'h, by the Mémorial du Martyr (Mon–Wed 9am–6pm, Thurs, Fri 9am–7pm; closed Sat & Sun). Exhibits relating to the independence struggle.

DIRECTORY

Airlines main offices include:
Aeroflot, 7 rue Malki Nassiba (☎60.56.61)
Air Algérie, 1 Place Audin (☎63.12.82)
Air France, Immeuble Mauritanie, bd Colonel Amirouche (☎649.0 2.10)
British Airways, 40 Didouche Mourad (☎64.12.20)
Egyptair, 4 rue Didouche Mourad (☎63.05.05)
Lufthansa, 10 rue Didouche Mourad (☎64.27.36)
Sabena 61, rue Larbin Ben M'Hidi (☎63.20.12)
Swissair, 19 rue Didouche Mourad (☎63.33.67)
Tunis Air, 6 rue Emir El-Khettabi (☎63.25.73)

Cinemas The city has about 40 cinemas, mostly showing European films, for about DA15 entrance. The *Cinématique* on Rue Ben Mehidi shows films from the Maghreb and francophone Africa.

Discos Try *El Aurassi*, bd Frantz Fanon/La Sqifa, *El Djazair*, 24 ave Souidani, Boudjemâa, or the very upmarket *Le Triangle* at the Riadh el Fet'h.

Embassies Most embassies and consulates are closed Thursday and Friday. See "Red Tape" on p.83 for addresses in Algiers of African embassies and visa details. *Embassies include:*
Australia: 12 ave Emile Marquis, Djenane el-Malik, Hydra (☎60.28.46, telex 66105)
Canada 27 bis rue Ali Massoudi, BP225, Hydra (☎60.66.11, telex 66043)
Denmark 29 bd Zirout Youcef, BP 500, DZ-16000 Alger-Gare (☎63.88.71, telex 67328)
France 6 av Larbi Alik, Hydra, Algiers (☎60.44.88, telex 52644)
German Fed. Rep. 165 chemin Sfindja. BP 664. Algiers (☎63.48.45, telex 67343)
Italy 18 rue Muhammad Ouidir Amellal, el-Biar (☎78.33.99, telex 61357)

Netherlands 23 chemin Cheikh Bachir Ibrahimi, BP 72, el-Biar (☎78.28.29, telex 61364)
Spain 10 rue Azil Ali (telex 67330)
Sweden BP23 Place Allendé Bir-Mourad Rais B (☎59.42.90, telex 66069)
Switzerland 27 blvd Zirout Youcef (☎63.39.02, telex 67342)
United Kingdom 7 chemin Capitan Slimane Hocine (ex-des Glycines), El-Mouradia BP43 (☎60.56.01, telex 6615, fax 60 44 10)
USA 4 chemin Cheikh Bachir Ibrahimi (☎60.11.86, telex 66047)

Ferries to Marseille Bookings at *CNAN*, 6, bd Mohammed Khemisti (☎63.26.98/☎64.04.20, Telex 52241) and 7 bd Colonel Amirouche (☎57.93.12). *SNCM* at 28 bd Zirout Youcef (☎63.03.33, Telex 67067)

Maps of Algiers are available in newsagents. More serious maps, including satellite sheets, are available from the *Institut géographique* in rue Abane Ramdane, parallel to boulevard Zirout Youcef above the main railway station. As a precaution against your using the maps for espionage purposes you have to write your name and address (any expensive hotel will do) in their book.

Post office (PTT) Reliable *poste restante*, open 8am–7pm (closed Fri all day & Sat from 1pm).

Telephone office Open 24hr a day near the *Grande Poste*.

Tourist office The head office of ONAT is located at 25–27 rue Khelifa Boukhalfa.

Visa extensions (Algeria) *Bureau des Étrangers*, 19 bd Zirout Youcef.

From Tunisia

Border post openings between Algeria and Tunisia change as erratically as relations between the two countries. Currently, however, you can cross at Babouch, Ghardimao, Hazoua-El Oued, Sakiet Sidi Youssef and Bou Chebka.

The .quickest way to **Ghardaïa** and the Sahara routes is via Hazoua-El Oued, across the oil-producing region centred around Ouargla. If you're heading to **Algiers**, take the route through the northern cities which leads through some spectacular mountain scenery and close by **Timgad**, one of the best preserved and most extraordinary Roman towns anywhere.

You can also enter Algeria by **train**, on the **Trans-Maghreb Express**, but it can be quite a squeeze to get a place.

Red Tape

With the exception of citizens of Denmark, Finland, Norway, Sweden, Switzerland, Italy and Spain, everyone must have a visa to enter Algeria. Exemptions for the British were removed in April 1990.

■ Visas

Visas must be obtained **in advance**, as they aren't issued at any of the border points or at the airport. Some nationals are required to obtain the visa in their country of residence. Thus, an American travelling to Europe before heading to Africa may be denied a visa at the embassy in Paris, for example. But it's not a hard and fast rule, and embassies in **Madrid**, **Rabat** and **Tunis** (see p.21) usually issue a visa whether or not you're a resident of those countries.

If you have a stamp from **South Africa** or **Israel** in your passport, you stand virtually no chance of getting a visa or entering the country.

Visa extensions

Most tourist visas are valid for one month. If you want to stay longer, you can extend them once in the country. Generally, this is done in Algiers at the *Département des Etrangers*. But in the capital of each *wilaya* (administrative regions corresponding to a *préfecture* in France) you can prolong your visa at the *Daira*. *Wilaya* capitals include Béchar, Tamanrasset, Adrar and Ghardaïa.

To qualify for a visa extension, you have to prove you've changed the necessary DA1000 (see

"Money"), provide two passport photos and pay DA60 in fiscal stamps (available at post offices).

■ Vehicle Documents

Travelling by private vehicle drastically increases the red tape you'll have to deal with. First and foremost, you must be able to produce the vehicle's **log book**, stating ownership, country of registration and the registration, chassis and engine numbers. All these details are checked thoroughly at customs. If you're not the owner of the car you're driving, you'll need a notified document (known in Algeria as an *attestation du propriétaire*) stating permission to use the car.

Your national **driver's licence** is acceptable in Algeria, but many people get an **international driving licence**, not a bad idea, especially considering how easy to obtain and cheap they are (the AA and other motoring organisations sell them over the counter). Their size and the official-looking stamps seem to confer extra legitimacy to border officials, and as they're translated into French and Arabic they're instantly recognisable.

A *carnet* is also taken by many motorists. These documents (again issued by associations like the AA) allow you to take your car into a country without paying import duties or a deposit. They're expensive, however, since the motoring clubs require a bank guarantee (that may be substantially more than the value of your car) before handing them out. The *carnet* is not required for Algeria, nor for Morocco or Tunisia, and is specifically not valid in Nigeria. You will find you need one, however, or an alternative *laissez-passer*, in many countries.

Insurance

Algerian **motor insurance** is obligatory. The cost for a car or "Tourist Vehicle" is DA145 (£12) for 10 days, and DA155 (£13) for 20 days. Since extending insurance involves a visit to the *Daira* as well as the local *Sociéte Algérienne d'Assurance* office, and an expired insurance certificate can get your vehicle impounded, it makes sense to insure for the longer period. Motorbike insurance is approximately half the cost of cars, and commercial vehicles (including minibuses with eight seats plus driver) twice as much.

This insurance is valid only in Algeria. As soon as you cross one of the southern borders, you need to buy a new policy that will cover you for all *ECOWAS* (*Economic Community of West African States*) countries.

VISAS FOR ONWARD TRAVEL

Most West African countries have embassies in Algiers and the British and French embassies cover for those which don't. It's also useful to know that you can now get **visas for Mali and Niger in Tamanrasset**, which means you no longer have to make a special trip to the capital for the sake of this formality.

Before you try to obtain a visa, it's not a bad idea to call at your own embassy and check: a) if you need a letter of introduction (which costs DA225 from the British Embassy), and b) if the embassy is still at the address given here (they change often).

Most are closed Thursday and Friday.

AFRICAN EMBASSIES IN ALGIERS

Benin 16 Lot du Stade, Birkhaden (☎56.62.71)

Burkina Faso 12 rue Mouloud Belhouchat (☎6.38. 97)

Burundi 116 bis bd des Martyrs. Algiers (telex 53501)

Cameroon 35 rue J. Apremont, Bouzaréah (☎78.81.95) 9am-4pm, Sun-Thurs; visas for 20-day stays, valid 3 months.

Chad 18 chemin Ahmed Kara, Hydra/Cité des DNC (☎60.66.37) 9am-4pm, Sun-Thurs; letter required, visa issued 24 hrs, 1-month stay, valid 3 months

Congo 107 Lot Cadat, Djenane Ben Omar, Kouba (☎58.38.88)

Côte d'Ivoire Immeuble "Le Bosquet", Le Paradou, Hydra (☎60.23.78, telex 52881)

Gabon 30 rue Ali , El-Hamadya, Bouzaréah BP85 (☎78.02.64, telex 52242)

Ghana 62 rue des Frères Benali Abdellah, Hydra (☎ 60.64.44, Telex 62234)

Guinea: 43 bd Said Hamdine, Hydra (☎60.00.59, telex 53451)

Guinea-Bissau 17 rue Ahmad Kara, Hydra/Cité DNC (☎60.01.56)

Libya 15 chemin Cheikh Bachir Ibrahimi (telex 52700)

Madagascar 22 rue Abd al Kader (☎ 62.31.96, telex 61156)

Mali 15, chemin Ahmed Kara, Hydra (☎60.61.18, telex 52631)

Mauritania 107, Lot Baranès, El-Hamadya, Bouzaréah (☎79.20.44, telex 53437)

Morocco 8 rue des Cèdres (☎60.74.08)

Niger 54 rue du Vercors, Rostomya, Bouzaréah (☎78.89.21, telex 52625) 9am-2pm, Sat-Wed

Nigeria 77 Cité des PTT, Hydra BP629 (☎ 59.32.98, telex 52523) 9am-4pm Sun-Thurs; generally require introductory letter from a Nigerian citizen

Senegal 1 rue Mahieddine Bacha, El-Mouradia (☎ 66.13.48, telex 52133)

Somalia 11 impasse Tarting; bd des Martvrs (telex 52140)

Tunisia 11 rue du Bois de Boulogne, Hydra (☎60.15.67, telex 52968)

Zaire 104 Lot Cadat, Djenane Ben Omar, Kouba (☎58.06.79)

Zimbabwe 24 rue Arab Si Ahmad, Birkhadem

Maps and information

There's an increasing supply of information about travel in Algeria. You can get a free foretaste and some ideas on the options for travel and exploration by writing to some of the desert specialist tour operators mentioned in *Basics*.

■ Maps

The ***Michelin*** West Africa Map (#953) offers the best overall coverge of the entire Sahara region. Because of its small scale coverage of the region, though, it isn't exceptionally detailed and, certainly in the desert, you don't have enough information to travel safely off the main routes. *Michelin's* Tunisia and Algeria (#172) is no better, as it doesn't cover the desert.

In Algiers, you can get **topographical maps of the desert regions** at the *Institut National de Cartographie*. These are made from aerial photographs and are at scales of 1:500,000 (1cm: 5km) and 1:200,000 (1cm: 2km).

■ Information

The few Algerian national **tourist offices** abroad are not stuffed with useful information. But this situation may change in the near future as the government has recently hit on the idea of promoting the country overseas.

Main addresses include:

UNITED KINGDOM: *Algerian National Tourist Office*, Time-Life Building, New Bond St, London W1 (☎071/493 7494).

FRANCE: *ONAT*, 28 av de l'Opéra, Paris 75002 (☎42.96.12.09).

GERMANY: *Algerisches Verkehrsburo*, Taunusstrasse 20, Frankfurt-6 (☎230.76.41).

Advice and reports

You can pick up useful advice and reports from recently returned desert travellers through the **153 Club** (Cruck Cottage, Long Wittenham, Abingdon, Oxon, OX14 4QP, England). They publish a quarterly newsletter.

The **Royal Geographical Society**, 1 Kensington Gore, London SW7 2AR (☎071/581 2057) offers a helpful *Expedition Advisory Service* with maps and technical guides on desert travel.

Money and Costs

The Algerian dinar (DA) is a weak, non-exportable currency. It's divided into 100 *centimes*, just like the French franc. The current exchange rate is £1 = DA14.24.

■ Currency, cheques and plastic

French francs were the currency in Algeria until the early 1960s, and older people still think in tems of **francs**, a term used interchangeably with dinars. You will often hear people talking in terms of *ancien francs*, too, multiplying everything by 100. By this reckoning, FF10 = 1000 anciens francs (which would be "mille") = DA10.

French francs in cash are recognised everywhere, though **travellers' cheques** are safer and can be changed in banks throughout the country. Sterling, dollars and other major currencies are fine too. You can't bring dinars into the country, in any case, even if you were able to buy them abroad.

Credit cards are accepted in some hotels in Algiers, but even then you're more or less limited to *American Express*. Elsewhere, plastic is all but useless.

■ Money regulations

Upon entering the country, you'll be required to declare all your money – noting travellers' cheques and cash on a **currency declaration form**. Every time you change money at a bank, this will be registered on the form, which you present to customs on departure.

The money you have left and the money you've changed should add up, and it's important to keep all **bank receipts** during your travels. Although they may seem like useless scraps of paper, they're often demanded at customs when you leave. Again, if you want to extend your visa, you may be required to show receipts. If you plan on using the **black market**, whose exchange rate is three to four times the official bank rate, you shouldn't declare – or be discovered with – all your foreign cash.

All travellers must **change currency to the value of DA1000** during an Algerian visit. Formerly, exceptions were made for students, but this hasn't applied for several years now. You may be required to change the entire sum immediately when you enter, but often customs allows you to change it in small amounts over the period of your stay. In any case, it must be done before you exit – especially critical if you're leaving at one of the Sahara border posts where the nearest bank is hundreds of miles away.

■ Costs

Costs vary greatly depending on how you change your money, though the DA1000 obligatory exchange starts everyone off on an equal footing – with rather a small number of dinars.

The DA1000 gets used up quickly if you're driving, travelling on buses or sleeping in hotels, even cheap ones. **Government-controlled prices** are graded by "priority" – milk and bread are priority 1 (and cheap), meat and fridges fall into priority 2 (less so), while beer and perfume are expensive priority 3 numbers. After Morocco, Algeria seems very expensive, as even local produce – oranges for example, earmarked for export – can be pricey.

Public transport over the long distances can be a major expense, too, and even hitching may cost you as soon as you get down near the desert. **Accommodation** is also fairly pricey at the official rate – a single in a cheap hotel runs at about DA60–80 and most of those in the Sahara from about DA120 a room.

Johnny Walker and Levi Strauss

In addition to the parallel market for currency, there's also a thriving **black market for goods**.

Whisky is in high demand and worth bringing in to resell: though you're only allowed to import one litre, that'll buy you enough dinars for several nights' accommodation. **Western clothes** are readily bought too; original Levis or brand-name running shoes are worth a small fortune. Even hand-me-downs fetch rather more than you'd expect, especially considering they're usually resold at a profit in local markets.

If you've come with a car, virtually unobtainable **spare parts** are widely sought after – though you'd be unwise as well as mercenary to sell anything on your outward journey. Also, parts like these usually have to be declared on your currency declaration form and, unless you can bluff your way though, you'll have serious problems when you try to leave the country. Remember too, that all these items make excellent **gifts** – a much appreciated thank you, say, if someone's invited you to stay in their home.

Getting around

Travel within Algeria is mostly by road or air. In the north, a good system of trunk roads extends from the coast to the Atlas mountains, making for fast and easy driving. Improvements are constantly being made on the routes across the Sahara, but it will still be a while before you can cross the desert entirely on tarmac – thankfully, perhaps. Detailed descriptions of routes and possible hazards are given throughout the guide.

■ Public transport

Public transport is good and not too expensive, making a trans-Saharan route quite feasible if you're prepared to **hitch rides** with either overland tourists or truckers once you reach Tamanrasset or Adrar.

Buses

Buses, much like express coaches in Europe, run to all towns of any size. The national company, called either the *Société National de Transport de Voyageurs* (**SNTV**) or the *Entreprise Publique de Transport de Voyageurs* (**EPTV**) – is divided into regional enterprises, each again with its own acronym. Branch offices are found in virtually every town covered in the guide; for the sake of convenience, they're referred to as *SNTV* offices, though they may have other names.

Buses run directly from Algiers to the capital of each *wilaya*, except Tamanrasset for which you change in Ghardaïa. Regular coaches go **as far south** as Adrar in the Tanezrouft, and Tamanrasset in the Hoggar. The *SNTV* also operates large **Mercedes trucks** to assure transport right to the borders at In Guezzam and Bordj Moktar.

Trains

The 4000km **railway** network is confined mainly to the north – the only "Saharan" branch is the stretch linking Oran with Béchar.

Flights

Because of the size of the country, planes are an option worth considering. Flights are often not much more expensive than the bus fare.

The national airline, *Air Algérie*, has at least a small booking office in nearly every town, and operates even to remote locations in the Sahara. You are, however, required to pay for tickets in

---

■ ALGERIAN VEHICLE REGISTRATION PLATES

As it's possible to hitch widely in Algeria, it's worth noting vehicle number plates. The "domicile" is coded in the last two digits. White or yellow plates are private vehicles, red ones are company or *société* and green are *corps diplomatiques*.

01 Adrar, **02** Chlef, **03** Laghouat, **04** Oum Bouaghi, **05** Batna, **06** Bedja, **07** Beskra, **08** Béchar, **09** Blida, **10** Bouira, **11** Tamanrasset, **12** Tebessa, **13** Tlemcen, **14** Tiaret, **15** Tizi Ouzou, **16** Algiers, **17** Djelfa, **18** Djidjil, **19** Sétif, **20** Saida, **21** Skikda, **22** Sidi Bel Abbès, **23** Annaba, **24** Guelna, **25** Constantine, **26** Medea, **27** Mostaganem, **28** Msila, **29** Mascara, **30** Ouargla, **31** Oran, **32** Baid, **33** Illizi, **34** Bordj Boureredj, **35** Bounerdess, **36** Taref, **37** Tindouf, **38** Tissinsilt, **39** El Oued Souf, **40** Kenchla, **41** Souk Ahras, **42** Tipaza, **43** Mila, **44** Ain Defla, **45** Naana, **46** Ain Temouchent, **47** Ghardaïa, **48** Relizane.

foreign currency at the official rate of exchange. Most travel agencies demand a special bank receipt called an *attestation de cession de devises* before issuing a ticket, but some may settle for your currency declaration form showing you have changed DA1000. Though flying will obviously save you travelling time, it's not a spontaneous option, since you normally have to **book well in advance**.

Most flights originate **from Algiers**, which is linked to the following cities in the guide: Adrar and Béchar along the Tanezrouft route; and Djanet, El Goléa, Ghardaïa, In Guezzam, In Salah and Tamanrasset on the Hoggar route. It is possible, though, to fly **between many of these towns** without passing through Algiers.

Accommodation

The Algerian government classifies hotels from luxurious five-star palaces (mainly in Algiers) to hole-in-the-wall one stars. Most have pretty high standards. Prices are government-controlled, too, and range from around DA60 to DA400 for a single, DA80 to DA600 for a twin or double room.

■ Camping, hostels and *hammams*

Travelling overland lends itself to **camping** – especially in the desert where distances between towns are great. No-one would prevent you pitching a tent in the Sahara or at a reasonable distance from a desert town. Remember to sleep well away from the road, however, and to mark your site clearly so that night truckers avoid running over you in the darkness.

Most towns along the desert routes have **campsites** (*campings*) as well – places to shower and get some washing done. They usually charge around DA20 per person and DA10 per vehicle. Some towns – notably Algiers and Ghardaïa – also have **youth hostels**.

For men on a low budget there's the additional option of staying in *hammams* (bath houses: see entry in "Directory", p.88). They're cheap, simple and safe and you get on the road extremely early, because they kick you out. They usually provide just bedrolls and blankets on the floor.

■ Staying with people

It's very common to end up staying with local people in Algeria, which is, simply, one of the world's most hospitable countries. If they offer hospitality, your hosts won't expect payment, but may be interested in engaging in a little black market activity. It would be prejudicial to assume this, but gifts will be welcome in any case.

Food and Drink

Though the French left a restaurant legacy in the north, eating out has never been a serious event in the Sahara. Eating places in the desert, commonly called *gargottes*, tend to be basic, serving fare that is virtually indistinguishable from one place to the next – simple chicken, meat, fish and vegetable dishes kept warm through the day.

■ Food dishes

Main courses typically consist of a starchy staple dish – like *couscous*, pasta or beans – with a little meat and a hot peppery sauce. More expensive are plates of meat (or chicken) served with fried potatoes. Bread (*khoubs*) always accompanies, along with a plate of hot red sauce (*loobia*). If there's a **starter**, it will probably be *chorba* – an oily soup.

There's rarely much to follow the main course, and you'll also find that servings tend to be on the mean side. By way of compensation you're almost bound to have at least one enormous **couscous with an Algerian family**, in the course of which you forget what it ever felt like to be hungry.

Local **Tuareg diet** in the desert is based mainly on milk (from goats and camels), cereals, dates and occasionally meat. Wheat and millet are essential ingredients for making bread or, when steamed, *couscous*. *Tagella* is a type of unleavened bread commonly eaten by the nomads on caravan. Made from water and a mixture of flours, it is cooked in a hole in the sand – coals are placed on the bottom, the dough added and the whole thing covered over and left to bake. Once dug up and brushed or washed off, it tastes as good as if it had just come from a bakery.

■ Drinks

In the desert, you won't find **alcohol** outside of western style-hotels in large towns like Ghardaïa, Tamanrasset or Adrar. And across the country many of the new FIS local councils have banned booze from non-tourist hotels. In the local cafés,

FOOD AND DRINK

DISHES

Salade mechouia	Mixed roasted vegetables	**Ojja**	The same, with more egg – like a messy omelette.
Brik à l'oeuf	Deep-fried pastry containing egg and sometimes vegetables and tuna	**Couscous**	Steamed cracked wheat or semolina base, served with meat or fish and vegetables
Chorba	Soup: various flavours often hidden by pepper	**Tadjine**	Soup, stew, or just "dish" in general
Chakshuka	Onions, peppers, tomatoes, egg, fried and sometimes chopped		

MEAT

Mechoui	Roast meat	**Poulet roti**	Roast chicken
Merguez	Spicy sausage	**Poulet haricot**	Chicken with beans
Mermez	Stewed mutton		
Kefteii	Meat balls		
Tajine haricot	Stew		

SWEETS

Baklava	Pastry with honey	**Pasteque**	Watermelon (with nuts)
Loukoum	Turkish delight	**Makrouf**	Traditional wheat biscuit
Youyou	Ring doughnut	**Figues**	Pomegranate
Halva	Sweet sesame seed cake	**Grenade**	Figs
Mesfuf	Sweet couscous	**Dattes**	Dates
Mille feuille	French cream pastry	**Raisins**	Grapes

or *gargottes*, choice of drinks is limited to mineral water or fizzy drinks (known as *gazouz* from French *gaseuse*). *Sirops*, distilled from fruit (pomegranate, orange, lemon, mint), are sickly and garish but they make excellent mixers.

The big culinary event of the desert is **tea**. Most travellers soon acquire a taste for the golden thimble-fulls with their bitter-sweet sustaining qualities. And there are few better ways to pass an hour summoning the energy to dig a vehicle out of the sand.

Communications: post and phones

Mail is reliable in Algeria and all towns of even moderate size have an office of the PTT. Letters get home quickest from Algiers where you can usually count on delivery within two weeks; delivery in London two days after posting isn't unknown. Add an extra week when posting from the south.

■ Poste restante

The **poste restante** in Algier's *Grande Poste* is dependable and they hold letters for up to a month. Other large PTTs around the country also have *poste restante* services.

■ Phones

Telephoning abroad is straightforward, by IDD, but costs around DA20 per minute to Europe. In the past, reverse charge calls were possible to the UK, but recent enquiries suggest this is no longer the case. **Service numbers** include Regional ☎15, International ☎16, Enquiries ☎12.

حذر انتباه
للجمال

PRUDENCE

ATTENTION aux CHAMEAUX

■ Media

Freedom of the press is burgeoning, by all accounts, in Algeria's newly "democratising" political climate. The main French-language **newspapers** are *Horizon* and *El Moudjahad* and weekly newsmags *Libre Algérie* and *Algérie Actualité*. The **monthly magazines** *Jeune Afrique* and *Nouvel Observateur* are also available in larger towns.

Entertainment and Sport

Algeria has two massively popular entertainments: Rai music and football. If you appreciate either, you'll enjoy the country, and if you can communicate your appreciation in French you'll be very well received — to be able to do so in Arabic, even haltingly, would be spectacular.

■ Music: Rai, Chaabi and Kabylie

Rai was originally the music of working-class Oran, derived out of traditional shepherds' songs. Its modern form grew out of 1950s and 1960s street life, wedding songs and dance dens. The word *Rai* means "opinion", but that's not as important (unless you speak Arabic) as the incessant beat and soaring singing. In many ways the punk music of the Maghreb, it's danceable and swiftly infectious, even to ears that have never heard it before. Among the star **singers** to see if given half a chance are: Cheb Khaled, Cheb Mani, Cheb Zahouani, Cheb Mohammed Sghir, Cheb Tahar and Cheb Nourdine (men), and Cheba Fadila, Cheba Zehouania, Cheba Zohra Relizania and Cheba Ouardia (women).

More mainstream Arabic ***Chaabi*** music stars include El Hachni Geurouabi, El Hadj El Aunka, Kanel Bourdib, Abdelkader Adjadj and El Koubi.

On your way south to the desert, listen out for **Kabylie Berber** music and in particular for the following exponents: Takfariness, Att Menguellet, Fahin, Matoub, Karina and Idir.

■ Le Futbol

Algerian football needs no introduction if you're a serious fan of the sport. The Algerians regularly field world-class teams in international events and always provide one of the top African sides. The country hosted, and to their consummate delight, won, the 1990 Africa Cup — the continent's top competition. Shining players include Madjer, El-Ouazani and Menad.

Directory

AIRPORT TAX None

EMERGENCIES Police ☎17

ETIQUETTE Among the less obvious pitfalls, the wearing of shorts by men is considered particularly odd and objectionable. You'd be wise not to when dealing with police, immigration or customs officials in the south; "Stopping to put long trousers on" becomes established routine.

FEMINISM Algerian feminists have struggled hard against the betrayal of promises made to them at independence. Today, however, there's a widening gulf between the "progressive" women old enough to have participated in the independence war and young, working class fundamentalists who wear robes and the *hijab* veil with pride. The *Union Nationale des Femmes Algériennes*, 22 avenue Franklin Roosevelt, Algiers, produces a journal *El Djazairia*.

HAMMAMS The civilised institution of the public bath is one of Algeria's finest features. You'll find one in virtually every town, though it may not be marked, or perhaps only in Arabic. Men and women have separate hours or days of admission, though times for women are limited. Once inside, you strip down to pants or swimming trunks (not, usually, completely), then collect towel and soap and enter the steam room, where you sluice down with cold water, and can get an innocent rub-down or back scrub.

OPENING DAYS AND HOURS The Algerian week runs from Sunday to Thursday. Friday is a bank and office holiday, though shops and markets are open; on Saturday almost everything is closed. Shops and offices are usually open from 8am to 7.30pm (shops) or 4.30pm (offices), with a long lunch break.

PHOTOGRAPHY Taking photos, you'll often encounter animosity in remote or untouristy parts if people are included in your frame. It's also easy to snap the wrong building by accident, and, if seen, police will simply confiscate your film. There is no official photography permit.

PUBLIC HOLIDAYS Apart from the moveable Islamic feasts, all doors are closed and most services shut-down or minimal on: **Jan 1** New

Year's Day; **May 1** Fête du Travail; **June 19** Anniversary of overthrow of Ben Bella in 1965; **July 5** Independence Day; **Nov 1** Anniversary of the Revolution.

SHOPS Government-controlled supermarkets, called *galeries nationales*, are found all over, selling an increasing range of goods at set prices.

TROUBLE The threat of violence or robbery is minimal in Algeria, and if you get into trouble with the police it will generally be of your own causing. It will also, more than likely, be a fairly serious matter; corruption is less widespread than people imagine and if you've committed an offence you can expect to be brought to trial. Drugs offences are viewed harshly and seaches are common on arrival from Morocco.

ARABIC GLOSSARY

Ain/in spring, water source

Bab door or gate

Berrani foreigner

Bir well

Bordj fort

Chott flat, dry area, salt lake

Dar house, palace

Djebel/jebel mountain

Djemm/djemaa Great Mosque, or Friday Mosque, the central place of worship in any town

Erg sand dunes

Feche-feche deep sand, disguised by a firm crust

FIS *Front Islamique de Salvation*, a fundamentalist party, the main opposition

FLN *Front de Libération National*, the ruling party

Fondouk inn and storehouse, known as a caravanserai in the eastern part of the Arab world

Hadj pilgrimage to Mecca

Hammam Turkish-style steambath

Imam Prayer leader and elder of mosque

Kasbah palace-centre or fortress of an Arab town

Ksar, Ksour (pl.) village or tribal stronghold

Maghreb "West" in Arabic – used of Algeria and the other Northwest African countries

Masjid small, local mosque

Mechouar assembly place, court of judgement

Medressa student residence and teaching annexe for the old mosque-universities

Minaret tower attached to mosque

Mouloud festival of the birth of the Prophet

Moussem pilgrimage-festival

Muezzin, Mueddin singer who gives call to prayer

PAGS The Algerian communist party

Oued, Wadi river or river course

Ramadan month of fasting

Ras source: **Ras El Ma**, water source

RCD *Rallye pour Culture et Démocratie*, a secular Berber opposition movement

Reg flat, gravel and stone plain

Ribat monastic fortress

Sebkha salt flat

Shia heretical Islamic sect, whose split from the Sunni majority in the seventh century is still the biggest sectarian division in Islam

Souk market, or market quarter

Sufi unorthodox sects in Islam, often with mystical associations

Sunni Islamic orthodoxy, divided into a number of different schools

Tanout well

Tizi mountain pass

Zaouia "monastic" centre of a Sufi brotherhood

Zeriba grass and wood hut in the desert

A Brief History of Algeria

Algeria never controlled the great empires of the Maghreb, and through medieval times large parts of the country were ruled by the Moroccan Almohad and Almoravid dynasties. In the early sixteenth century the territory became part of the Turkish Ottoman empire and remained so for 300 years, until a French diplomatic dispute with the *dey* of Algiers in 1827. In that year, France blockaded the port of Algiers and, within a short time, the Turks capitulated. French colonial rule was to last for the next 135 years.

■ Abd El-Kader

The French, it seemed, were at first uncertain what to do with their victory, and clear ideas of conquest hadn't fully materialised. As they hesitated, a **nationalist movement** was brewing in the west under the leadership of **Abd El-Kader**, who, at the age of 24, had already been elected sultan of the Arabs and carved out a foothold in the Mascara region. His authority soon stretched from Oran to the Kabylie Beber country and from Biskra to the Moroccan border.

The French had acquiesced to Abd El-Kader's armies on several occasions in the past and in 1835, after failing to take **Constantine**, where the Turks had retreated, they signed the **Treaty of Talna** which recognised Abd El-Kader's authority over two-thirds of Algeria.

The size and importance of Abd El-Kader's movement, however, and the threat of a united and organised **Arab state**, soon caused French alarm. For the first time, they defined a clear political strategy to dominate the region and in 1837 set about retaking Constantine. This time successful, they allied themselves with local feudal leaders and committed over half the French army to the decade-long campaign against Abd El-Kader. In 1847, Abd El-Kader was seized and exiled to a French prison, and opposition from the Arabs was temporarily crushed.

■ French colonialism

Resistance continued meanwhile among the **Berbers** and it took a further decade to "pacify" the mountainous Kabylie region. In the isolated reaches of the Sahara, too, the Tuareg held out against French rule until 1902, when they were defeated in the **Battle of Tit**. By then, the French had succeeded in occupying the entire country.

From the outset, France viewed its new **Algerian colony** as an extension of the metropole. Land was appropriated to European settlers, who by 1871 were 272,000 strong –

roughly ten percent of the total population. In 1881, Algeria was divided into *départements d'outre-mer* ruled directly from Paris without any participation of the Muslim population. The **Arabo-Berbers** were treated as outsiders in their homeland, grew quickly hostile to the foreign occupants and found room for reconciliation among themselves. Yet even the Europeans frequently felt ignored. Though the majority were French, many of these residents – *colons* as they were known – were naturalised citizens from Spain, Italy and Malta. Their allegiance to Paris was always fickle and they tended to view themselves as Algerian when there were problems with France and as French when conflict arose with the Muslims.

■ Nationalist stirrings

Despite the tensions, the colonial apparatus continued to be constructed through the early part of this century, and more and more peasants were displaced from the countryside, moving into the cities and sometimes to Europe. Through this process, people gradually gained something of a proletarian understanding of their own postion and impoverished condition and of the hypocrisy of western democracy. In 1926, North African workers in France formed the *Etoile Nord-Africaine* – a communist-inspired party that stood for socialism and Maghreb unity.

The Arab population underwent a simultaneous reawakening as the Islamic **Association of Algerian Ulema** sought to bolster the sagging pride in traditional values. The group was founded with the motto: "Islam is my religion, Arabic my language, Algeria my homeland". The Ulema avoided politics, but they were avowedly anti-French and they succeeded in stirring patriotic ideals. As the movement intensified, the *Parti Populaire Algérien* was founded in 1927, and began calling for independence and the nationalisation of industry.

Changes, however, were slow to materialise. Although the French government granted a few reforms after World War I (in which tens of thousands of Muslim Algerians had fought and died for France: thousands are buried in unnamed graves at Verdun), it was not ready to consider the right of independence, or even citizenship.

■ World War II: the turning point

After **Hitler's invasion of France**, Algeria was brought under the nominal rule of the Vichy government. But in 1942, French troops loyal to Petain surrendered to an American-British offensive and the Algerian colony was returned to the Free French. In the light of events, however, their claims to legitimate rule in Algeria were harder than ever to justify. France was no longer in a moral or physical position to act as a colonial power and, in 1942, nationalists drew up the **Manifesto of the Algerian People**, which called for an autonomous state.

It was clear that **concessions** had to be made to stave off a rebellion. In 1944, de Gaulle offered an olive branch of sorts by finally granting citizenship to certain elite groups of Algerians. But it was too little and too late. Algerians had stopped thinking in terms of increased rights within the colonial system. The nationalist spirit had taken over; integration was impossible.

In 1945, during celebrations marking the end of the war, **riots** broke out around **Constantine**. Members of the PPA and Reformist Ulema came to demonstrate and clashes broke out with the police. The protesters then went on the rampage, murdering European settlers and pillaging property; over a hundred Europeans were killed.

Not surprisingly, the police and army wreaked a brutal revenge. But the scale of the onslaught was unprecedented in colonial history. For several days, Constantine was besieged as wave after wave of air and naval attacks shattered the city. The toll of death has never been conclusively established, but at least 6000, and perhaps as many as 80,000, Algerians were killed. Disillusionment with the colonial government turned to scathing indignation and hatred.

The attack on Constantine was the point of no return, but the government in Paris made last ditch efforts to salvage the situation. In 1947 it ratified the **Statute d'Algérie**, granting French citizenship to all Algerians and establishing an Algerian parliament. But this was controlled closely by the *colons*, who had become increasingly racist and reactionary. Muslims, despite the reforms, had gained little political ground.

■ Revolution

Given the hard line the *colons* had adopted, and the failure of successive French governments to override their unenlightened politics, insurrection was inevitable. In 1948 the *Organisation Spéciale* – an underground military organisation – was formed, only to be dismantled in 1950, following their armed attack on the Oran post office and the arrest of one of the leaders, Ben Bella.

Ben Bella later escaped and fled to Cairo while OS members stayed in contact with each other. In October 1954, they met on the outskirts of Algiers. With their formation of the **Front de Libération Nationale** they launched the armed struggle, plotting attacks on French installations and police stations across the country.

The **uprising**, on November 1, 1954, went as planned, and, though little damage was done, the FLN caught the French sharply by surprise. Their attacks brought sensational coverage to the unknown group that demanded "the restoration of the Algerian State, sovereign, democratic and social in the framework of Islamic principles". Within a short space of time all but one of the major Muslim political parties had rallied behind them and by 1956 it was estimated that half the Muslim population were FLN supporters.

The French government responded with more repression. As the **revolution** grew, they looked increasingly for military responses – including torture, terrorism and resettlement. By 1956, there were 400,000 French troops in Algeria. Militarily, they were effective in ferreting out pockets of resistance, but on a diplomatic front their presence resulted in repeated setbacks.

France's unflinching, and well-publicised, brutality helped to bolster international support for the **Gouvernement Provisoire de la République Algérienne** which had been established in Cairo. In 1958, the United Nations' Political Commission recognised Algeria's right to independence. Even the normally conservative United States seemed to show sympathy for the rebel cause when Senator John Kennedy gave a speech strongly attacking French repression and advocating negotiation. (For an understanding of the events, Italian director Pontecorvo's resoundingly good film, *Battle of Algiers* – made in 1965 – focuses on the years 1954–57.)

■ De Gaulle and the OAS

While the war was still being fought in Algeria, its conclusion was being orchestrated in Paris. In 1958 the hardline right wingers among the *colons* and in the army staged a putsch and threatened to declare war on France. The Fourth Republic fell and **General de Gaulle** was voted into the presidency with greatly increased powers.

The *colons*, with their slogan *Algérie Française*, supported de Gaulle massively at first. But despite his rhetoric, it seems clear the general had already given up the idea that France could hold on to Algeria, or even that it would be desirable. He moved increasingly towards coming to terms with the FLN and in 1959 gave the colony three options: integration; independence in co-operation with France; or complete independence. De Gaulle openly favoured the second.

The European settlers were outraged. Anti-Gaullist demonstrations broke out in Algiers, and in 1961 the **Organisation de l'Armée Secrète** was formed. This paramilitary organisation was formed of a desperate combination of *colons* and embittered army officers determined to hang on to French Algeria at any price. Acting independently of the national army, they carried out gruesome massacres and even plotted to assassinate de Gaulle. In April 1961 intransigent officers in Algiers staged an insurrection that brought France near to civil war. But the OAS really only succeeded in dividing and deepening the crisis among the *colons*, and further isolating them from a shocked international community.

De Gaulle weathered all attempts to overthrow him and in 1962 was able to negotiate a settlement at the **Evian Peace Talks**. As a result, France agreed to recognise Algerian sovereignty following a referendum. The Algerians voted overwhelmingly for complete independence. Guarantees were given to the Europeans for their protection after independence, but the overwhelming majority left Algeria for France.

■ Independence

The first years of independence were difficult ones for the new Algeria. One million Algerians had died during the conflict; three million *colons* (representing most of the skilled labour) had fled; and two million people from the rural areas had been forcibly resettled by the French military.

The economic, social and human problems ensuing from these statistics were compounded by a **political malaise**: for the first time since fighting had begun eight years earlier, rivalries were developing within the FLN. **Ben Bella** ultimately took over the reins of government, but not without isolating himself from most of the *historiques*– the leaders who had initiated the revolution.

Ben Bella pushed through a new constitution and helped lay the framework of Algerian socialism, but opposition mounted to his style of leadership – opposition which he in turn didn't hesitate to suppress. Critics accused him of creating an authoritarian state; of eliminating leaders and thereby depriving the nation of its best minds; and of moulding the FLN in his own image. In 1965, he was overthrown in a quiet **coup** by his Minister of Defence, **Colonel Houari Boumedienne**.

Boumedienne came to power with the wider support of the party leadership. He suspended the constitution and dissolved the National Assembly, replacing it with a **Revolutionary Council** to assist him in governing. In 1967 he began building communal and provincial assemblies. But his most important objective was to rebuild the economy in an effort to create real independence. He was aided by revenue generated by national reserves of **oil and gas**, which enabled the creation of an industrial base. In the 1970s, the president tried to bolster the lagging agricultural sector by increasing productivity and raising the standard of living in the rural areas – though today the country still imports up to sixty percent of its food requirements.

The Spanish Sahara – and Morocco

Since independence, Algeria has supported liberation struggles and revolutionary movements throughout the world, offering moral or material support over the years to groups as varied as the American Black Panthers and freedom fighters in the former Portuguese colonies. In 1976 Algeria nearly went to war with Morocco over the future of the newly decolonised **Spanish Sahara**. Boumedienne naturally sided with the region's **Polisario** guerrillas who waged war on Morocco when it occupied the former Spanish territory.

Today, **relations with Morocco** remain volatile, though fighting in the region has decreased and the two Maghreb neighbours reached a kind of accord in a reconciliation conference in 1989.

But the question of another, quite unrelated and long-standing dispute between the two countries over the unclear **colonial frontier** in the south-west is one which is bound to surface again.

■ The 1980s

Boumedienne died in 1978. The following year, a special FLN congress named **Colonel Chadli Bendjedid** as the sole presidential candidate — confirmed by a national election in February 1979.

In the 1980s Chadli steered the country along much the same course as his predecessors. But the drop in world oil prices has put the economy in a rather more precarious position. Though still dedicated to socialism, the president also started a cautious process of liberalisation. In 1986, a new **National Accord** moved the country away from rigid centralised planning, while legislation removed many public companies from government control and relaxed the banking system.

On an international level, the president emphasised **Maghreb Unity**, seeking to smooth over relations with Libya and Morocco. In 1983, the country signed treaties with both Tunisia and Niger, fixing borders long disputed. The same year, Chadli sought to improve **relations with the west**, and became the first Algerian president to visit France. Two years later, he was the first Algerian head of state to visit Washington — for a summit meeting with Ronald Reagan.

■ Entering the 1990s

Though Algeria has achieved rapid growth since independence, it has paid a price. Social welfare and democracy have typically taken a back seat to longer-term economic goals. As the government sought to develop industry, it shielded itself from foreign imports, leading to shortages of manufactured goods. From time to time, this has triggered unrest, even outbreaks of violence. Even under Boumedienne's rule, the wave of popular criticism led him to draw up a **National Charter**, which, as early as 1976, resolved to give higher priority to improving the living conditions of all citizens.

But the situation hasn't much altered, and Chadli's term has been punctuated by occasional **protests against austerity measures** which his government has continued to impose, albeit unenthusiastically, under IMF conditions. When oil prices dropped dramatically in 1986, the president withdrew a number of hefty food subsidies, a move which prompted **rioting**, primarily among

university students and young unemployed. The outburst was quickly contained, but when subsidies were removed again in 1988, the action triggered a wave of unrest the like of which hadn't been seen since colonial days. Thousands of people rallied in Algiers to protest against the hardship and the army was called in to restore order. In these nationwide demonstrations, official figures claimed 179 people were killed in clashes between demonstrators and the military, and the figure may have been as high as 500. Perhaps 3000 more were detained.

Subsidies were quickly reinstated but the government had to shuffle to change an image which has suffered much in recent years. In 1989, a **new liberal constitution** was proposed and approved. It provided for **multiple political parties** — of which there are presently more than twenty — and human rights guarantees.

These recent gains had a dramatic result in the municipal elections of Spring 1990, which brought a landslide victory for the biggest opposition grouping, the **Islamic Salvation Front** (FIS). Ruling FLN party deputies (who are currently the only representatives in parliament), have claimed the surprise local election results represented only a protest vote against sliding living standards. And, while fundamentalist activists in the FIS are likely to do everything possible to hold onto the iniatives seized so far, further economic reforms by the government may result in a quite different poll at the **general elections** promised for 1992. Chadli, who was re-elected to his third five-year term in 1989, now faces both pressure to bring the elections forward and the temptation to delay in order to trumpet intended reforms.

An additional factor in the political future is posed by the increasingly confident political voice of the ten-million-strong **Berber community**, who largely oppose the strengthening of Islam's role in the state. Their main political party, the social-democratic **Assembly for Culture and Democracy**, is calling for greater local autonomy, secularism and cultural freedom and the deletion of constitutional references to Algeria as an Arab state. The Berber constituency has financial support from Algerians working in France, eighty percent of whom are Berber.

Lastly all is not well, either, within the ruling camp of the **FLN**. Having sacked the prime minister who pushed through the new constitution, Chadli is engaged in a fierce struggle over the way the country should proceed. One wing of the FLN wants party government in a liberal constitution, while Chadli himself seems to envisage an executive presidency above all the parties. Resolving not just this contradiction but also coming to terms with fundamentalism, ethnic cleavages and the changes in eastern Europe and the Soviet Union (traditional supporters of Algeria), are likely to bring Algeria increasingly into the headlines in the Maghreb region.

THE HOGGAR ROUTE

The **Hoggar route** is preferred by most trans-Saharan travellers on account of its scenery – which ranges from the sun-scorched pinnacles of the namesake **Hoggar Mountains** to the shifting sands of region's great *ergs* – and for the presence of a scattering of towns breaking up the 1950-kilometre haul from **Ghardaïa**, 630km south of Algiers, to **Arlit** in northern Niger. If you're driving, it's also the route where your car will likely suffer the least wear and tear.

Nonetheless, it's not always easy going. Though the road is paved well past **Tamanrasset**, the heat has eaten up large chunks of tarmac, forcing you to travel through narrow *oueds* with high crumbling banks or rugged foothills lined with loose volcanic rock. A major resurfacing project in 1989–90 has improved much of this route, but wear and tear is constant and rapid and the road condition unpredictable for more than about six months.

As soon as you climb beyond the coastal ranges, 50km or so south of the Mediterranean, you're effectively in the **desert**, which in its initial stages is a high, windy plateau of unremitting landscapes and bleak towns. The beauty of the **Sahara proper** begins as you drop down again south of the Atlas mountains.

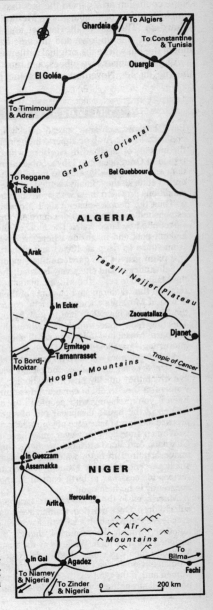

Ghardaïa

GHARDAÏA – the so-called "Gateway to the Sahara" – does have a feeling of being on the edge of something ominous, but as the **M'zab** *oued* (river) carves its way through the rocky hills of this barren region it breathes life into a vast and beautiful **oasis**.

This is the traditional domain of the **Mozabites**, a Berber people known for their religious fervour (see box overpage), commercial drive and architectural genius. Over the past thousand years they have built up one of the most visually striking towns in the Sahara – a place well worth taking a few days to explore.

Orientation and practicalities

Some confusion arises from the fact that what is commonly called Ghardaïa is really a conglomeration of five towns – **Melika, Beni Isguen, Bou-Noura, El Atteuf** and **Ghardaïa**. The last is the largest and the one where you'll spend most time. It's divided into the old town and the *ville basse*, a modern district that spreads out at the foot of the hill where the original settlement was founded.

All the administrative offices, and most hotels and services are in the *ville basse*.. On the rue du 1er Novembre, one of the principal streets, you'll find the **post office**

THE MOZABITE BERBERS OF GHARDAÏA

Early **Islamic schisms** spread quickly in North Africa, where Berbers were often in conflict with the Arab occupiers. In the ninth century, the **Kharedjite** sect spread under the impetus of the **Ibadite Berbers**, who created an empire that spread from the coastal region of Oran deep into Libya. Subsequent Shi'ite invasions, however, toppled the kingdom and forced the Ibadites to move further south towards the desert. In the early eleventh century, they finally settled in the **M'zab** region, where the hills and harsh conditions provided them with protection from persecution.

Thus the people – later called **Mozabites**, a name derived from the M'zab *oued* – established the five towns of Ghardaïa. Originally, these were individual fortified cities, surrounded by large walls. The mosque that crowned each of the five hills doubled as a lookout post and magazine where arms were stored in case of attack. Wells were dug (sometimes as deep as 100m) and elaborate irrigation systems devised to support the vast **palm groves** and **gardens** that supported the population.

Self-sufficient and effectively isolated, the Mozabites became one of the few peoples of the Maghreb to resist the Muslim mainstream, and for nearly a thousand years they have retained the traditions and customs of their rebel sect. **Religion** is taken very seriously here and Mozabite society is strictly controlled by it. Though well protected, however, the Mozabites have long had to look beyond their oasis for wealth to support the town. This they have done, traditionally, through trade – and for most of this century as **shopkeepers**. Mozabites today run small shops throughout Algeria and France: a monopoly interestingly paralleled by the Djerbans of Tunisia and Soussi of Morocco.

Male foreigners will have no contact at all with **Mozabite women**. Those you pass on the streets cover themselves completely with their white cotton *hawli*, exposing only one eye which they quickly turn away should you have the temerity to stare. (Photographing women on the streets is considered extemely rude and will provoke hostile reactions.) Even if you're staying with people in town, your arrival will be announced so that the women of the house disappear out of sight before you walk inside. Though they may prepare meals and take care of your needs, you'll never see them or speak to them.

Women travellers, however, may have access to the world of their counterparts in Ghardaïa. And since Mozabite women's contact with the outside is almost exclusively an image acquired through watching television, they are generally very eager to talk; a small percentage speak French. Women travellers report discussing everything from recipes for *couscous* to birth control methods – the pill is impossible to find here and apparently in high demand.

Marriages in the M'zab are pre-arranged, with the couple-to-be often matched while still children. Once married, women live most of their lives behind closed doors – very few ever leave the M'zab. It's said that women are the glue that has held Mozabite society together through the centuries, though this laudable role would seem to have been assigned them by men. While away for business (and they may be gone years at a time), Mozabite men can easily shed social restrictions they would always abide by at home. Woman obviously don't share the same freedom. Yet men are not allowed to marry foreign women and, if they did so, the wife would never be accepted in the M'zab. Small consolation, but it strengthens women's role as guardians of tradition – the pillars men return to.

(winter 8am–noon & 2–6pm; summer 7am–noon & 4–6pm), which has an unreliable *poste restante* service (it's a much better idea to pick up your mail in Algiers or otherwise wait until Agadez or Niamey); if **telephoning**, you can call long-distance to Europe, though expect long delays. Near the post office, the *BNA* **bank** will change travellers' cheques.

For information on travel in the region, contact the *ONAT* **tourist office** (☎89.17.51), located on the rue Emir Abdel Kader.

Accommodation

The range of **accommodation** takes all tastes into account.

If you're on a very tight budget, one of the cheapest places is the *Auberge de Jeunesse*, located right in the centre of the *ville basse*, within easy walking distance of the market. They've dormitories full of sagging spring beds, but the prices are reasonable. Despite the good location, the hostel closes at around 9pm, which means you may be out of luck if you arrive in town late. Another inexpensive possibility (especially practical if you've come by car) is to stay at one of the town's two **campsites**. The first, the *Oued M'zab* , is on the road from Algiers; the second, the *Oasis* (☎89.48.93), on the road to Beni Isguen. Both have showers and clothes-washing facilities, plus rudimentary shelters if you've no tent.

Inexpensive **hotels** are clustered around the Place des Andalous, near the *SNTV* bus office. One of the least expensive is the *Hôtel de la Paix* where a non-S/C double costs DA60. In an attractive if dilapidated old building next door, the *Hôtel Essada* (☎89.16.59) has doubles from DA70. The *Hôtel Napht* is another well-known place in the area and has spacious rooms for up to three people from about DA80. Slightly more upmarket, the *Hôtel les Rochers*, off the main road to Algiers, has furnished non-S/C rooms from DA110 for two and a decent restaurant – one of the few places in town where you'll be served beer, though it costs about DA15 for a small can.

The **expensive** league is dominated by the *Hôtel les Rostémides*, located on a hilltop with striking views of the old towns. It's built in a modern variant of traditional style with heavy stucco arches. The cheapest doubles cost DA180. The hotel has a swimming pool and terrace bar which makes for an excellent place to come for a drink at dusk when the sun throws a superb burnt orange light on Melika town.

The oasis towns

With a history spanning a thousand years, Ghardaïa is a fascinating place to wander. The pastel-coloured old towns have changed little over the centuries, their crooked houses crowding the twisted streets that lead up to the mosques. Simone de Beauvoir compared them to Cubist pictures and the architect Le Corbusier called them perfect *machines à habiter* – "machines for living".

Ghardaïa Town

The most accessible of these original settlements is that of **Ghardaïa Town** itself. As you stroll through, be sure to stop at the **market**, on a large square near the *ville basse*. In addition to the fruits and vegetables (beautiful dates) brought in daily you'll find a wide selection of **artisan goods**, ranging from heavy wooden *couscous* bowls to the intricately woven rugs for which the town has a reputation.

Down in the *ville basse*, Ghardaïa's small **museum** is to be found near the *Auberge de Jeunesse*, on the road leading up to the *Rostémides* hotel. It's built in the traditional style of a Mozabite house and contains furnishings and utensils used in the home, as well as a display of rugs, basketwork and pottery. Opening hours appear to be rather arbitrary, though the caretaker is rarely far away; if you let it be known you're interested in visiting, he'll come and open up for you.

Beni Isguen

Beni Isguen, 3km from the centre, is considered a *ville sainte* – the holiest of the old towns. For that reason, it can't be visited freely: you will only be allowed to enter with a guide; it's off limits after sunset and during prayers; and photography is not allowed.

You can arrange a visit at the *ONAT* office in Ghardaïa, or simply show up at the town entrance and pick up a guide at the gate. They'll tell you some of the history, explain how the houses are made and show the original wells dug by hand over a period of generations. The tour ends with a climb up to the mosque and the adjoining *bordj*. You can climb to the top of this fortification for a view of the palm grove.

Melika

Melika is sited near Ghardaïa's *ville basse* and therefore easy to visit; it has neither the crowds of Ghardaïa nor the visitor restrictions of Beni Isguen.

Inside the **cemetery**, near the town gate, you'll find the fabulous tomb where Cheik Sidi Aïssa is buried. The miniature towers crowning his resting place are painted an intense white that seems to shine under the hot desert sun. There's usually an old man guarding the tomb and you're expected to give him a small donation. In exchange, he'll tell you a bit about the cemetery, Sidi Aïssa and the way Mozabites bury their people.

Bou-Noura and El Atteuf

Further afield are **Bou-Noura** and **El Atteuf**. Founded in 1014, El Atteuf was the first of the Mozabite towns; the smooth lines of its Sidi Brahim mosque inspired Le Corbusier's Ronchamp chapel in France.

The palm groves

While in Ghardaïa, be sure to take in one of the **palm groves**, or *palmeraies*, that border each of the old towns. The largest are at Ghardaïa and Beni Isguen.

Full of flowers and fruit trees – oranges, pomegranates, figs, dates – they are cool even when the temperature in town is scorching. Note the dams and aqueducts that feed a complicated irrigation system designed to assure an equitable distribution of water. The M'zab *oued* builds into a rushing river for only a few days out of the year and then dries up completely; its waters are harnessed and their distribution strictly controlled by the mosque.

MOVING ON FROM GHARDAÏA

Ghardaïa is the last big town before the desert and a good place to arrange transport south. The road is paved all the way to EL GOLÉA, and the only potential problem is sand dunes blowing onto the tarmac, sometimes unforeseeable after a bend.

Around 6km south of El Goléa, a branch road heads west to TIMIMOUN – an oasis town with hotels and campgrounds (see p.116). This paved road is extremely narrow and full of potholes, but traffic moves fairly well and it is the easiest way from Ghardaïa if you want to cut over to the Tanezrouft route.

Buses

Coaches are probably the most convenient and comfortable way to travel unless you've got a car. They can get you to all major towns in the north, or to **El Goléa** (three daily departures) and **Tamanrasset** if you're crossing the desert. From Tamanrasset, your chances are especially good of finding continuing transport with tourists or truckers heading down to Niger. You can also get coaches to **Timimoun** and **Adrar** (daily departures) if you're planning on crossing the desert on the Tanezrouft into Mali.

For complete information on schedules and prices, call in at the *SNTV* office on the Bd Ahmed Talbi (☎89.47.50).

Hitching
If you're planning to hitch across the Hoggar, check around the campsites and hotels for cars heading to Tamanrasset, or wander out to the lorry park on the Algiers road and ask the drivers if they can take a passenger. Alternatively, take a taxi out to the **roundabout** south of the town centre, where the road to Bou-Noura and El Atteuf branches off from that heading to El Goléa and Ouargla; all truckers pass by here and may be more willing to pick you up than they would be in town. Whichever, you'll have to come to an agreement on price; truckers won't take you for nothing.

By Plane
There are daily flights from Ghardaïa airport (18km out of town) to Algiers, plus one or more a week to Tamanrasset (DA370), Oran, Adrar, Timimoun, El Goléa and Djanet, and other destinations; no flights go directly south across the desert beyond Tamanrasset.

Air Algérie has an office in the *ville basse* on the av du 1er Novembre. For full schedules and price information, stop by or call them (☎89.40.62).

El Goléa (El Meniaa)

With about a quarter of a million date trees, **EL GOLÉA** (or EL MENIAA, as it has been officially renamed) is the largest **oasis** in the Sahara. The town is completely surrounded by palmeries, and every householder has a palm or two in his garden, as well as apricots and other fruit trees, vegetables, and often formally laid out flower beds. The huge **palm groves** and gardens to the east of town are beautiful to wander through, and the area is also one of the best places in the Sahara to find the remarkable pink sugar crystals known as **sand roses**.

Orientation and accommodation

El Goléa's **ville nouvelle** has a **bank**, **post office** and *ONAT* **tourist office**, all grouped around the central Square du Port Saïd. The town **market** is well-stocked with food, though it closes during the heat of the day from noon to 4pm.

The best **accommodation** in town is at the *Hôtel el Boustan*, an elegant place built in an attractive neo-Sudanic style. Rooms here are comfortable and, at DA140 for an AC double, *petit déjeuner* included, not at all bad value. There's a **swimming pool** open even if you're not a guest for a charge of DA25. On the road to In Salah, the *Hotel Vieux Ksar* (☎73.63.19) is cheap and friendly, clean enough and with air conditioning in the bar. On the same road are a couple of small cheap hotels and, a couple of kilometres from the centre, a **campsite** – the cheaper (and more run-down) of the town's two *campings*. The other, bordering the palm grove on the road to Ghardaïa, offers hot water and well-tended grounds. If you want to camp out in the desert, and have an hour or two left in the day, follow the route into the dunes detailed below.

There are numerous **restaurants** in the general area of the Square du Port Saïd, all modestly priced. Directly on the square, the *Port Saïd* offers basic dishes like *poulet frites* or *couscous*. Just north of the square, the *Restaurant des Amis* is a frequent stop-off for overlanders who fill up for around DA25. Ice creams and milk shakes are readily available around the square, too – your last chance before Tamanrasset. In the extreme northern quarter of the new town, the *Café du Peuple* has a shady terrace that makes an excellent afternoon base to drink and sit out the heat.

The Ksar and other sights

El Goléa means "The Citadel" – a reference to its remarkable ninth-century **Ksar**, which dominates the region from a hilltop on the eastern outskirts. The fortress commands a view of the entire oasis, a green blanket of vegetation, pierced by dozens

of white marabout domes. It was built by Zenete Berbers, soon conquered by belliger-
ent Chaamba nomads, and saw its last battle in 1960 when Algerian freedom fighters
held the Foreign Legion at bay for several weeks.

You can visit the citadel without a guide, though kids from town will offer to lead
you. To get there, take the southeastern road heading out from the *Hôtel Boustan* and
follow it for 1km; you'll then have to climb the stark cliff on foot. Inside the fort, notice
the well – incredibly deep if dropping pebbles are anything to go on – near the tower.

Just outside of town are a couple of odd, minor sights. Two kilometres north, in a
little-used churchyard, is the tomb of the French missionary-explorer **Charles de
Foucauld**. Two kilometres south is the **El Mellah Lake**, home to several species of
large water birds. Neither site is easy to find without a guide.

An excursion to the Erg

Surprising though it may seem, El Goléa – at the edge of the **Grand Erg Occidental** –
is the only point on the easterly trans-Saharan route where you will be close to an
appreciable area of *erg* – **sand dunes**. If you're heading west for Timimoun and Beni
Abbès you'll see much more spectacular dunes there, but if you are travelling south (or
north) and want to spend just one night in real *erg*, this is the place to do it.

It's extremely easy to get lost in *erg*, even without a sandstorm to obliterate your
tracks. The one route into the dunes from El Goléa runs to **Hassi Nebka** – a 60km
drive. Take the turning to the west just south of the petrol station on the In Salah road,
and ask for directions through the maze of back-streets; you'll eventually pass through
a small *palmerie* and onto the unmarked but well-established *piste*; follow it until you
feel far enough away from civilisation, turn off at a likely looking dune, and camp down.
If you really want to be in the middle of nowhere, you could drive *through* the dunes,
but this will require deflation of your tyres and skilful driving if you're not to get stuck.

TRANSPORT SOUTH FROM EL GOLÉA

Buses passing through from Ghardaïa stop in El Goléa as they head south to In Salah
and Tamanrasset, though you may have to fight your way on for a seat. The same applies
for buses over to Timimoun and Adrar. The *SNTV* office is on rue de la Liberté.

Prospects for **hitching** aren't too bright, although you could try your luck at the campsites and hotels. Most overlanders are still loaded down with food, water and other
supplies at this point; your chances of a lift south increase once down at Tam.

Moving on by **plane**, *Air Algérie* (rue de la Liberté; ☎73.61.00) have flights from El
Goléa to Algiers and Tamanrasset on Tuesdays and Sundays.

Ghardaïa to In Salah: the Tademait Plateau

The paved road south from El Goléa starts off well, the only hazard being sand that
occasionally piles up on the surface as you pass between the Grand Erg Occidental and
Grand Erg Oriental. At 63km from town you arrive at the junction (with a small café) of
the road to **Timimoun** and **Adrar** – the quickest way over to the Tanezrouft route.

Tademait Plateau and Aïn el Hadjadj

Even before you reach the junction, the road begins climbing up the **Tademait
Plateau**, a featureless plain, stretching most of the way to In Salah, that's the least
interesting section of the Hoggar route. From the start of the climb onwards, the road
has recently been replaced and runs parallel to the dreadful old strip. Only a section of
about 50km, beginning about 150km before In Salah, was still bad at the last check,
and this has probably been repaired or replaced by now.

A café standing in the middle of nowhere near the **Aïn el Hadjadj** pass offers some relief from the plateau. Truckers and tourists stop here for lemon drinks, cooled in a generator-powered fridge, and excellent meat, fish and vegetable stews. If you got a late start, the *patron* will likely let you spend the night on the café floor. Beyond, some 90km from In Salah, the road begins winding its way back down off the plateau and then across a pan-flat plain for the approach to In Salah.

In Salah

IN SALAH feels on the knife-edge of survival. Its position in the centre of the Sahara, which makes it oppressively hot, also ensures it's a mandatory stopping point for the collection of water in one of the world's most arid areas. The water source, allegedly conjured up by the magic flute of one Salah Ben Azzi, enabled it to grow rich as a slave market, and now supports vast **date groves**, alongside some light industry, on the town's western periphery. The palms can survive on the water, which is said to contain bilharzia. It is certainly unpleasantly salty and comes through the tap – rationed to two half-hours a day at around 8am and 8pm – heavily chlorinated.

The palmeries must also struggle against the encroaching dunes, and in the centre of town the streets are piled high with sand. The large **Sudanic gates** surrounding the mud-brick houses are typically veiled in a dense desert haze as sandstorms kick up from the surrounding wilderness. Few locals walk the streets, preferring the protection and relative coolness of their thick-walled houses. Daytime and night-time both, In Salah feels like a ghost town.

The Town

The *wilaya* authorities have made brave attempts to restore In Salah's natural role as a stopping point for travellers, installing a tourist office and an office of *Air Algérie* (flights to Algiers three times a week), both just off the main boulevard near the Daira. There's a new hotel for better-off travellers, and free official camping for everyone else. Most incongruously, the approach road and the pedestrianised main boulevard have been painted in pastel colours and adorned with civic statues, brick paving, flower beds, and globe lampposts; post-Modernists would be proud. Underneath the lime and jonquil paint, the walls are ochreous mud.

The **old town** quarters built by Arab and Tuareg traders have been somewhat transformed by cables for lighting and TV antennas. But you can still see the red walls of the Sudanic-style buildings, 1–2m thick at the base, curving elegantly to narrow and simply decorated parapets at the roof. The old-established **market** still occupies the town centre. At the centre of the boulevard is a small market entrance where slaves have been supplanted by vegetables (plump and juicy, but very expensive), as well as meat, and the occasional sand rose or carpet. The market is open from dawn to near dusk, although stallholders bed down near their goods or in a café during the hottest hours.

Hassi Terraga
From In Salah it's possible to visit the **petrified forest** at HASSI TERRAGA, a drive of about four hours along *piste*.

Practicalities

Shops and services are gathered around the market, on one or other of the two main streets running parallel to its eastern and western sides. A *BNA* **bank** for exchange, a **post office** and the *ONAT* **tourist office** are to be found in this area.

If you're driving, it's well to know there are several **mechanics** in town, and bulk oil is available from a store opposite *Le Carrefour* restaurant, open from 8am to noon and from 3pm to dusk; you need to supply your own containers. This is sometimes the last oil for sale before Niger.

Accommodation

Until recently the *Hôtel Badjouda* was the town's only one, which may explain its relatively high price (rooms start at DA80) and unreliable toilet facilities. It has a crusty charm, though, runs a good restaurant and is in a lively location on the boulevard opposite the market. The Badjouda's newer rival, the *Hôtel Tidi Kelt* (☎73 03 93), on the El Goléa road, is part of the *EGT* luxury chain, but doesn't live up to the splendour of the flagship *Hôtel Tahat-Tam* in Tamanrasset. Rooms start at DA200 for a S/C twin, with working AC but no private water supply – remember to take a shower at the appointed times. There's a swimming pool too, but it's most unlikely to have water.

The **campsite**, *Camping Tidikelt*, is on the main street to the south of the town centre. Facilities are rudimentary, but it's only DA15 a night.

Food

In Salah's several **restaurants** are generally mediocre, if cheap, offering considerably less choice than their menus suggest. The *Restaurant du Carrefour* on the main street near the market is the traditional eating place for overlanders, much appreciated for its food and the friendliness and helpfulness of its eccentric proprietor. If you're hitching, stop in and he'll likely be able to make suggestions about lifts, but, alas, latest reports are universal in describing the food itself as stodgy and gristly and the restaurant dirty.

L'an 2000, on the boulevard, is probably a better bet – clean and with outside tables, which could be pleasant after sundown. Their menu offers a wide choice of European as well as Arabic food.

Alternatively, make your way to the *Hôtel Tidi Kelt*, which serves pricey beers, cheap and excellent tea, and a good French meal in the restaurant or on the "pool" terrace (around DA60–100).

TRAVELLING SOUTH FROM IN SALAH

Coaches connect In Salah with Ghardaïa, Adrar and Tamanrasset, the last served three times weekly by a large Mercedes bus, for which you should book a day in advance at the *SNTV* office. It's about a twenty-hour trip to Tamanrasset, so stock up on food and water before leaving; there are stops along the way (notably at Arak), but provisions are hard to come by.

In Salah is a notoriously bad place to **hitch** from, but virtually every long-distance driver has to stop at the petrol station on the main road. Alternatively, try your luck at the hotel and campsite, or ask at the *Restaurant du Carrefour*. If nothing works out, consider taking the bus to Tamanrasset, where chances of getting a lift increase.

Road conditions

The road was paved all the way to Tamanrasset some years ago, but only recently has it once again become fair to call it a tarred highway. For years, from only some 80km south of In Salah, **potholes** were a vicious menace and progress slow as drivers tried to avoid the jagged tarmac to save precious shock absorbers. By early 1990, the Algerian army units who have done so much to improve the Hoggar route had resurfaced, or relaid, almost the whole stretch from In Salah to Tamanrasset.

The worst parts of the road are the section from 50 to 100km **south of In Salah**; parts of the **Arak Gorge** (often washed away by flash floods); and the initial 50km stretch south from the tomb of the **Marabout Moulay Hassan to In Ecker**.

In Salah to Tamanrasset: the Arak Gorge

Travelling south from In Salah, the mountains gradually close in and the scenery changes from long stretches of sand to rugged rocky terrain. After recent surfacing, drivers may make good time, but the 650-odd kilometres is still best tackled over two days.

Arak Gorge

After driving about 270km, you enter the **Arak Gorge**, a beautiful mountain pass with stark cliffs rising up on either side of the road. The new road passes right through the gorge, bypassing a café made out of bits of old cars. A couple of kilometres further, the road turns south between spectacular cliffs, past an army base and a little further, on the right, a **filling station** (quite reliable). Behind, the settlement of ARAK comprises a **café** (with cold drinks) and a **campsite**, sometimes flanked by a Tuareg encampment. Some 4km east from here – an easy walk – there's a small, clean **lake**, perfect for an unexpected swim. Further south along the gorge there are good **places to camp** and plenty of firewood.

Marabout Moulay Hassan

South of Arak, the tarmac used to be really bad and this is still the stretch where the road is most likely to deteriorate into a jumble of smashed tarmac. Unless it's regularly repaired (after every flash flood), you could well be driving most of this stretch on *pistes* running parallel to the main road.

About 110km from Arak, tracks lead west of the main road to the tomb of **Marabout Moulay Hassan**. It's customary for desert crossers to pay respect to the marabout by driving around his mausoleum three times. It's said that bad luck – even tragedy – awaits those who don't honour the tradition. There's an ancient painting of an elephant on the nearby rocks. Even if you don't find it, the diversion is worth the effort for the surrounding rock formations, which look like something conceived by Salvador Dali.

Since the new road was built in 1989, the three-kilometre detour to the tomb is no longer marked by the "Tam 268k" signpost – as indicated in most older guides – and the burnt-out VW combi landmark has disappeared from sight, too. However, a new piste is being created by pilgrims, and there is a café by the tomb.

In Ecker Fort

The next landmark, 95km on from the marabout turn-off, is the old Foreign Legion post of **IN ECKER FORT**, later used by the French in the early 1960s when they carried out underground nuclear tests in the region. The fort is well preserved and still in use and there's a **café** and **petrol station** (supplies almost always available) nearby. Forty kilometres further, the deserted IN AMGUEL FORT is marked by a cluster of mud brick houses and another café. A *piste* to DJANET branches eastward, 7km down the road from here. It's a reasonable track, at least in its early stages, and gives access to the rock paintings at MERTOUTEK (see p.107).

A remote sidetrack to Mali

Forty-two kilometres before Tamanrasset (which by now, like all overland travellers, you'll be referring to as Tam) another set of tracks leads west to ABALESSA: a route which continues all the way to BORDJ MOKTAR on the **Malian border**. Beyond SILET (86km along it) this *piste* is no longer *interdite* as indicated on the *Michelin* map, and is now marked clearly with red and white oil drums every kilometre. It was along this stretch that a certain Mark Thatcher lost his bearings during the 1982 Paris–Dakar rally.

Tamanrasset

Amid the barren moonscapes of the Hoggar, **TAMANRASSET** appears with an almost hallucinatory character: a large town with avenues of trees and a constant flow of cars, camels and people. The settlement was originally founded by the **Kel Ahaggar Tuareg**, nomads who now share the space with an army of civil servants from the north and caravans of European, Australian, American and Japanese overlanders.

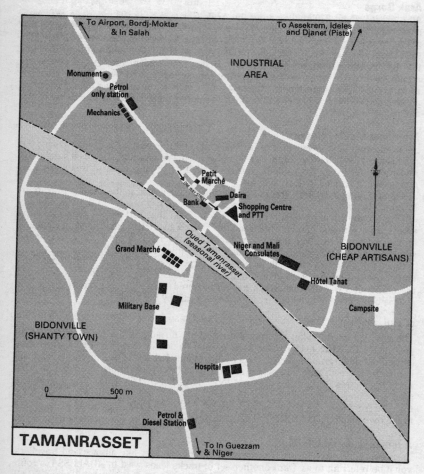

The Town

With all its outdoor cafés and boutiques for the overland trade, Tam is no longer the isolated desert outpost people spoke of even ten years ago; to those arriving by land and having other oases with which to compare, it seems almost like a Saharan theme park. If you happen to have flown in from Europe, though, and you've come at the right season, it can nevertheless all feel rather wonderful: a town of legendary name, which has served for centuries as the junction of Arab and Black Africa. Proud Kel Ahaggar Tuareg still stroll the streets with their camels, albeit dressed in their finest clothes mainly to stop and offer their best profile if you produce a camera.

As part of the government drive to reclaim the south, Tam has grown dramatically over the last few years, and the population now stands at over 30,000. Small industries have been launched and street lights illuminate the night. The wealth brought in by the adventure tourists has been used to build luxury apartments and shopping centres in red, mud-covered breeze blocks which, with a little weathering, blend reasonably well with the old buildings. They've built on the sites of the fast-disappearing shanty towns, inevitable accompaniment of the too rapid expansion since 1978, when the asphalt from the north was first completed.

The centre nonetheless has its charms and in certain respects has benefited from the upswing. The **market** is well stocked and the stores – including a supermarket – full of provisions from throughout the country. There's a new **post office** and a *BNA* **bank** just off the market on the Place de la Poste. Along the centre's main street, the rue Emir Abdel Kader, there's *Air Algérie* and the *Altour* **tourist information office** and all around numerous **crafts boutiques** full of Tuareg handicrafts.

Further down the main street you'll find the Daira and the old **Bordj**, or fort. This structure, a well-known landmark, is now used by the military and you could be arrested (people *are* arrested) for trying to take pictures of it.

Accommodation and practicalities

Though there are a couple of good hotels in town, most overlanders head directly to the **campsite** – *Les Zéribas* – about 2km east of the centre on the road to Adriane. The grounds here are well-kept, the showers and toilets very clean. They charge DA25 per person to camp (plus DA20 per car); cold drinks and some food are served.

A few hundred metres from the *camping*, back towards town, the *Tahat-Tam* (☎09/75.44.74, telex 63072) is the town's nicest **hotel** – in fact one of the Sahara's finest, with fountains, marble floors, spacious lounge bar, attentive staff, and everything working. Despite the elegance, they don't look askance at travellers arriving dirty and tired, nor at overlanders repairing their cars in the car park round the back, and you're welcome to fill up with as much water as you can carry. Rates are from DA200 for a S/C twin room with running water and working AC; in the high season (Oct–Feb) you should book some time in advance, as rooms are usually block-booked by *ONAT* and tour agencies. The *Tahat* is authorised to change money, and is open for this service until 8pm.

In the centre, the more modest *Hôtel Tinhinane* has rooms at about DA60/120. This place, also block-booked when the *Tahat* is full, dates from colonial times, and has an air of faded gentility. The restaurant does decent Algerian and European-style meals, and there's a popular bar. The manager runs the *auberge* at Assekrem (see below), and you may get a free beer if you offer to take some supplies out there on your way. Another small hotel, the *Ilamane* (☎73.48.66) is located near the Place Abdel Kader, across from the fort. They have singles for DA50 and doubles for DA100.

Food and drink

Evenings are pleasant in Tam as everyone heads outdoors. **Restaurants**, of which the town has many, are busy, though some of the smaller ones close at dusk, and excellent *chorba* and *couscous* can be had for DA5–6. In the square around the police station (at the northern end of the main street) there are perhaps a dozen cafés and restaurants. *Le Palmier* here is popular with locals and tourists alike – as well as *couscous* they sell chicken and chips, for about DA10.

Much **café** business is done from lunch until mid-afternoon, when men rest out of the heat, drinking tea, and listening to loud music. One of the most popular locales for travellers is the *Café de la Paix* next to the *ONAT* office with *couscous* and other meals from DA25. Nearby are a couple of other places with similar fare – the *Restau Assekem* and the *Café-Restaurant Tassili*. Back by the Place de la Poste, the *Ali-Baba* is an expensive Italian-run restaurant and *salon de thé* with pizzas and spaghetti bolognaise on tables under the pavement arches. Behind the same square near the *gendarmerie*, *Chez Amar – Restaurant de l'Est* serves copious meals and fresh salads on a patio shaded by canopies and exotic plants.

For a more special event, the restaurant near the *oued* on the northern side of the Ain Guezzam road serves good local and European food (and alcohol) till late, either inside or on the pavement underneath the colonnade. Alternatively, the *Hôtel Tahat* serves good, somewhat pricey meals for non-residents, and there's an expensive Italian-run restaurant in the shopping centre opposite the *bordj*.

Formalities

If you haven't changed the equivalent of DA1000 by now, Tam is the last place to do so – there are no **banks** further south. The *Banque Nationale* is in the new shopping centre, as is the **PTT**.

Before leaving town, you no longer have to have your **passport and visa** checked, or currency declaration form stamped, as older guidebooks suggest. You can also now get **visas** for both **Mali** and **Niger** in Tamanrasset. The consulates are near the TV station (easily located by the large satellite dish). Visas for both countries cost DA65; you must provide three passport photos and show your vaccination card and currency declaration form. The consulate will not issue visas unless you have the equivalent of US$500 in travellers' cheques or cash. Driving north, **motor insurance** has to be bought in Tamanrasset by those entering from Niger. The *Société Algérienne d'Assurances* is newly located at the rear of the new triangle opposite the *bordj*, on the northeast side.

Petrol isn't a problem in Tam, with several filling stations reliably stocked. **Water**, however, can be more problematic. Most hotels won't let you fill your jerry cans unless you're a guest, and even then, they may let you take no more than a token five litres. You may be obliged to head out of town to one of the water sources in the surrounding area. Ask around at the filling stations or hotels.

Into the Hoggar: excursions from Tam

For trips into the **Hoggar Mountains**, you may want to engage the services of one of the town's travel agencies: the sites are not feasible without your own transport, and tourists are reluctant to take along hitchers as roads are difficult. **Organised tours** are expensive but usually rewarding, covering itineraries you choose at a pace you set. Common targets are **Assekrem** and treks through the haunting, spiked mountains, some of whose peaks rise to over 2900m. Further afield, **Djanet** and the nearby **Tassili National Park** (see further on) are compelling attractions.

Closer to Tam, if you're staying at the campsite, it's a simple matter to take a morning hike up **Mount Hadriane**, self-evident to the southeast and only a thirty-minute walk.

Assekrem

If you have the means for a visit, **ASSEKREM** is a must – a dramatic mountain-top site that's likely to be a highlight of a desert crossing. It's perhaps best explored by organised tour (through the *Hôtel Tahat* and the *Altour* office, or informally with local 4WD owners; about DA200 if you get a group together). Going it alone with your own vehicle, be aware that this is one of the most punishing roads in the Sahara. It starts with

ONAT, Bd Abdel Kader (☎73.41.17). The government-run agency offers a variety of *raids* through the Hoggar region. Well-organised but expensive.
Agence Akar Akar, BP164 (☎73.43.40). Run by the manager of the *Zériba* campsite. Programmed tours and individualised excursions.
Mero Nman, rue de la Poste (☎73.40.32). Knowledgeable and friendly guides for personalised tours of the region.

soft sand, and progresses through gravel and *ornières* to a boulder-strewn road, which, for the last kilometre, is at an incline to test the mettle of any 4WD aficionado.

The Algerian tourist authorities are begining to realise Assekrem's potential and the road is being levelled, and will perhaps be asphalted before long. Out of season, you might just be the only visitor, but from October to February, expect to share the experience with up to three hundred others. The drive takes about three hours, but you need to allow time for a puncture or three. As one of the main points of a visit is to watch the sun set and rise, it's advisable to leave Tam with perhaps five hours in hand – another half-hour is required for the final ascent by foot to the mountain top.

Once at the summit, you'll come upon the laid-back **auberge**, run by staff from the *Hôtel Tin Hinane*, which charges DA10 to sleep in the car park and use the hole-in-the-ground toilet, or DA100 for a rough stone hut with half a dozen dirty foam mattresses. They do however cook an excellent soup and stew or *couscous* meal for about DA15 a head; you supply your own water.

Nearby is **L'Hermitage**, the hermitage church of Charles de Foucauld. A simple and austere building, it is looked after by three *Petits Frères de Jésus*, who spend five years here in between acting as worker-priests in the poorest parts of Europe and South America. Every morning at sunrise they celebrate mass, to which entry is now by invitation only, although anyone is welcome inside the tiny chapel after the service is over. Should you request and be given an invitation to the mass, the priest may take you back for breakfast at his house, a bare stone building cut into the mountainside. A gift of bottled water is appreciated, as he has to walk the donkeys some considerable distance to collect brackish water from *gueltas*.

It's possible to **return to Tamanrasset by a different route**, completing a circular tour, but this road is difficult and sometimes doesn't get another vehicle for many days. If the main road worries you, don't attempt the alternative route.

Mertoutek: rock paintings

About 5km **east of Assekrem**, the main road forks to the pretty villages of HIRHAFOK and MERTOUTEK (signposted in Arabic only). Mertoutek is the only site of **rock paintings** (*gravures rupestres*) close to the Hoggar route. You should be able to hire a guide there to show you the site.

Alternatively, you can head out of Tam, north along the Hoggar route for 130km, turning right along a good *piste* to Hirhafok, and then (15km beyond it), north along a lonely track to Mertoutek.

South from Tamanrasset to Niger

Tamanrasset is the last Algerian town before the **border with Niger**, 400km to the south at **Assamakka** – a route which may well work out longer if you have to deviate from the tracks. Obviously, it's important for drivers to take on adequate supplies of fuel and water. See overpage for transport details.

TRANSPORT SOUTH FROM TAM

Buses

Buses from Tam are mainly northbound. There's a regular service to **Ghardaïa** with stops at In Salah and El Goléa. To the south, a weekly bus runs as far as **In Guezzam**, though it's usually better to try and arrange a ride further south – Tam is a much more enjoyable place to wait for a lift than the dismal border post. The new *SNTV* **bus station** is at the entrance to Tamanrasset, near the monument that marks the so-called geographical centre of the Sahara.

Hitching

In season (Oct–Feb), you stand a good chance of getting a ride south from Tam with motorised **overlanders**. If you're staying at the *camping*, ask everyone who comes in if they have room for an extra passenger (if you're travelling in a pair, you'll have a much more difficult time). You may wait between a couple of days to a couple of weeks, but you will eventually find a ride.

If you're in a hurry, it may be better to ride with a **lorry**. You can usually find them near the filling station on the In Guezzam road (100m from the police station), though on Thursdays and Fridays traffic dwindles to nothingness. Cost of a place in a lorry to Assamakka should be around DA400; most truckers are also happy to take French francs (about FF100) or dollars (about $30).

Flights

Air Algérie (rue Abdel Kader; ☎73.44.63) have **flights** to Algiers, Ghardaïa, El Goléa, In Salah and In Guezzam, or to Adrar and Bordj Moktar if you want to cross over to the Tanezrouft route. There's also a weekly flight (Thursdays) to Djanet for around DA150. Whatever your destination, book well in advance.

Tam to In Guezzam

South of Tam the paved road has been extended for a stretch of some 50km – and is at present in very good condition. After that, it deteriorates and there's little sign of the work needed to carry it – as planned – to the Niger border. In the meantime, you have to drive alongside the tarmac, following markers of piled stones. Gradually the mountains cede to flatter sandscapes (roughly 90km from Tam). The crust is generally pretty hard, but there are stretches of soft patches you can't see. Keep your speed up.

Dunes de Laouni

It should be fairly smooth sailing until the dreaded **Dunes de Laouni** – some 280km from Tamanrasset. A signboard marks their spot and, as you reach them, you'll see a graveyard of burnt-out cars, half buried in soft sand. If you try driving through the dunes, you'll almost certainly get bogged down and spend most of the day digging your way back out – usually advancing no further than the length of your sand ladders. The trick is to wait for a truck to pass: these regular drivers generally know the easiest way around the dunes, which varies from year to year. Watch to see how they go and, if they get by without problem, follow their lead.

Gara Eckar Mountains

After this obstacle, the worst is over, though you'll still encounter lengths of painful washboard. At around 360km from Tam, the **Gara Eckar Mountains** rise up from the flat desert floor. Chiselled by the wind and smoothed by the blowing sand, they are easily recognised and have become a popular place for overlanders to camp before continuing to IN GUEZZAM, which lies only fifty-odd kilometres further on. You may want to deflate your tyres to negotiate the 20km of soft sand before In Guezzam. There'll usually be a truck driver or two at the border from whom you can borrow a compressor to reinflate them with.

A major diversion: Djanet and the Tassili

Though justly famed for its beautiful location in the Tassili Mountains, **Djanet** suffers from too much tourism, and a positive deluge of bureaucracy. On arrival you have to check in at the *Daira*, whence you're directed to stay at the expensive *Hôtel Zeribas*, because camping in the palm grove isn't allowed. To visit the Tassili plateau itself, you have to take a guided tour, as individual excursions are forbidden. Finally to further encourage you, you may even be refused permission to photograph in the region without special authorisation, obtainable only in Algiers.

Proof of the Tassili's exceptional pull is the fact that none of this puts anyone off visiting – and even less so in retrospect. The exuberant scenery – like sketches for an experimental planet – is merely the backdrop to a string of striking prehistoric sites containing some of the world's most extensive, varied and expressive displays of ancient rock paintings.

The route from Tamanrasset

The route from **Tam to Djanet** covers some difficult stretches, but it's feasible even in an ordinary car like a *Peugeot 504* in two to three days. It's a particularly scenic *piste*, with astounding variation in landscapes and colours.

Tam to Hirhafok

From Tamanrasset, one of the easier approaches is to head out on the northern road towards In Salah. About 7km before Ain Amguel, turn off on the eastbound *piste* leading in 93km to **HIRHAFOK**, a Tuareg town on the road to Djanet.

An alternative, beautiful, but very much more difficult route to Hirhafok branches from the main road 8km north of Tam and passes through **ASSEKREM**, where the **Père du Foucauld** (see Beni-Abbès) built his religious hermitage in the mountains. Although he was there to convert the Tuaregs, the Father was a valuable informant to the French army. He was murdered in the fortified retreat in 1916 by rebel nomads determined to force the French out of the region. The tortuous *piste* winds its way straight through the Hoggar Range, amid loose rock and across narrow sandfilled *oueds*, but it's the most beautiful route from Tam.

Idèles and Serouenout

Thirty-five kilometres east from Hirhafok, the oasis of **IDELÈS** appears – a large settlement with irrigated palm groves, and a filling station but no hotel. Try to avoid the place as the police there tend to be sticklers.

Beyond, the tracks continue another 195km to **SEROUENOUT**, where there's an abandoned fort. It's generally good going on a hard corrugated surface along this stretch, though the soft sand increases over the last 30km, and rises at times to low-lying dunes. At 48km east of Serouenout, a marker indicates the turn-off to AMGUID to the north: take instead the eastern tracks for Djanet.

The final stretch: Zaouatanlaz

From the turning, the *piste* leads across a *oued* with deep sand. Keep up your speed and stay out of other tracks. It's a 93-kilometre-haul to **ZAOUATANLAZ**, where the old outpost of **Fort Gardel** is located. The village has occasional fuel and a *zériba* hotel with expensive food, but you have to stomach the disgusting local water. It's worth stopping, however, to enquire about the possibility of excursions to rock paintings in the region. They're organised privately in town and are much cheaper and more relaxed than the those of the bigger tour outfits in Djanet.

It's 164km further to Djanet – a glorious stretch – with the Tassili mountains to the north and the rolling dunes of the **Admer Erg** to the south. The road is mostly hard washboard.

Djanet

DJANET is Algeria's most remote and expensive town – a strange combination. For all its commercialisation, the people are warm and contacts are easy to make, especially outside the Christmas-peaking tourist season. As for sights and facilities, there's a small **museum** near the *Daira*; an **artisanal centre** near the **post office** (calls to Europe no problem); numerous overpriced restaurants; and a cinema for evening entertainment if the night sky isn't diverting enough for you. There is, however, *no bank*, so you need to plan ahead. A possible fallback, if you haven't, is the customs office, which is authorised to change travellers' cheques, providing they have cash.

The compulsory **accommodation** at the *Hôtel Zéribas* (sadly, no longer in grass hut *zéribas*) costs around DA200 per person per day, with unexceptional meals included, though you can sometimes pay in FF which helps a little. If you're travelling in a vehicle adapted for sleeping, you may be allowed to "camp" in the hotel gardens.

THE TASSILI: DJANET TOUR OPERATORS

Excursions into the **Tassili National Park** must be arranged through a **tour operator**. All offer tours by Land Rover, with camels and donkeys or on foot; most run throughout the year, except in the sandstorm season between mid-April and mid-July. All-in prices are from around DA2500 per person (minimum group of six) for a six-day tour, starting and finishing at Djanet airport. If you elect to go *sans prise en charge* (which means that food, camping gear, etc are your responsibility) you'll get around 40 percent reduction.

Recommended operators include:

Voyages Tim Buer, BP27 Djanet (Djanet office telex 42024, Algiers office ☎56.12.22, telex 62313). This is probably the most professional outfit, but also the most expensive.

Agence Sefar, BP4 Djanet (☎73.54.13 telex 42021).

Agence Admer, BP19 Djanet (☎73.52.78).

Altour located near the market and *Hotel Zéribas.*, can do one-day camel treks for around DA200.

If you can't afford the price of a tour, you can still see some **engravings** at the much-visited **Oued Indebirene**, just a few kilometres south of Djanet en route to the airport.

The Tassili National Park

Entrance DA100, only with official guide (Warden and information, BP 11, Djanet)

The engravings and paintings in the **Tassili Mountains** were identified and brought to the notice of Europeans in the 1930s but it was only in 1956 that one Henri Lhote realised their significance, identifying at least thirty distinct styles painted over several clear eras. Tens of thousands of paintings have been uncovered in the area and presumably thousands more await discovery: the Tassili is by far the richest source of prehistoric art in the world.

Sadly, the paintings are fading fast and the caves they were made in are eroding. Efforts are being made to protect them, but it seems clear they won't last forever. Within the next couple of centuries, almost all of these ancient relics may be lost. Though painfully heavy-handed, some of the tourist restrictions in the Tassili are justifiable. People used to bounce around in Land Rovers as they visited the region's **prehistoric rock paintings**, already suffering natural destruction from the pernicious natural elements. Worse still, they used to throw water on the engravings to make them temporarily brighter.

Some history

The earliest **rock paintings** in the Tassili date from between 6000 and 4000 BC – a period known as the **"hunting"** or **"round-headed men"** era. They were painted by black Africans who lived here at a time when the mountains flowed with rivers, and game animals – hippos, rhinos, elephants, giraffe, antelopes – teemed in the forests and on the plains. A second, pastoral period, of the **"cattle herders"** lasted from around 4000 to 1500 BC. The people who drew them were also black, but apparently with different origins from the artists who preceded them. They may have been the ancestors of the **Fula**, a diverse people (though predominantly nomadic) who live across the Sahel region from Senegal to Sudan, maintaining a clear identity through their very old language.

The following period, designated **"chariots and horses"**, spanned the millennium 1500 to 500 BC and marked, for the first time, the suggestion of contact with the Mediterranean world, with the depiction of Caucasian figures. One theory has it that these may have been Greeks who, failing to conquer Egypt, turned their sights on the Sahara. It seems possible that a chariot route ran from Tripoli all the way down to Gao on the Niger.

Over time, the Tassili region dried up and the rocks eroded into sand. Vegetation in the Sahara could no longer support horses, and so began the last period, known as **"Cameline"**, which started around 500 BC. Some of these late drawings are accompanied by writing in the *Tifinar* script, related to that used by present-day Tuaregs.

The paintings: highlights

Most of the paintings are small, but a few, exceptionally, are nearly life-size. Among them is the famous cyclops-like **"Great Martian God"** which helped inspire Erik Von Daniken's excited popular theses. One of the most beautiful is **"The White Lady"** or **"Horned Goddess"** at Aouanrhet, a sublimely graceful form dancing through a flock of tiny figures.

If you have to choose – and your time is almost bound to be limited – some of the best sites are only 20km east of Djanet. Aim to go first to the **Wadi Jerat** and **Sefar**, where some 4000 paintings are located in a zone of a few square kilometres. In the deep rock shelters to the south of Sefar, at **Jebbaren**, there are 5000 more. **Aouanrhet**, a rewarding site for more than just the Horned Goddess, is across the wadi from Jebbaren.

The Niger border: In Guezzam

IN GUEZZAM is a military outpost in the middle of nowhere – a way station for unlucky service personnel and government officials who'd rather be stationed almost anywhere else. It gets so hot here, they say, that the rare birds flying overhead sometimes get heatstroke in mid-air and fall dead to the ground, a story all too believable out in the afternoon sun.

The settlement consists of a scattering of mud-brick houses, a café or two, and a filling station (which sometimes runs out of petrol, but at least has no shortage of water to fill jerry cans). There's little to do, other than work your way through the border formalities. For waiting about, the most pleasant café is second left, driving south down the main street from the fuel station; they do excellent coffee, tea, cold drinks and home-made cakes, as well as meals.

Border formalities: Algeria

The Algerian police and customs are located just south of the town. They open at 8.30am but break for lunch and a siesta from noon to 2pm. Best to arrive early in the hopes of finishing the formalities before the break. If you're driving, unless your vehicle happens to be Algerian-registered, hand in (or collect, if you're heading north) your pink *Temporary Importation* document. Don't show a *Carnet de Douane*, or it may be stamped, causing you problems on your return home. Then head to the police for a stamp in your passport and verification of your **currency declaration form**. Agents may demand to see bank receipts for every currency exchange listed on the form and can really hassle you if one is missing; and if you've not changed DA1000 in Algeria by now, you'll be sent back to Tam.

After the police, you head to customs, who invariably ask vehicles to unload *everything* on board. Remember that most of the *agents* are not happy to be stranded in this wasteland and may take pleasure in making life difficult for you. It sometimes helps to have a few beers or a bottle of whisky openly visible and to casually mention that you don't think you can travel any further with it and ask if they'd mind terribly if you left it behind; they won't and the process goes much quicker. During the month of Ramadan, however, you might try thinking of an alternative gift.

Generally speaking, formalities proceed in a protracted and orderly fashion and, if you're heading north, you generally won't be hassled unduly. Depending on how many other cars and trucks are waiting, you might get through in about an hour. If they decide to hassle you, over what may seem a technicality, it could take all day or possibly overnight; the worst thing you can do is get angry or aggressive.

Across the border: Assamakka

From the Algerian border, it's only 25km to **Assamakka**, the border post for Niger. If you're unlucky, though, it could take the better part of an afternoon to get there. The desert here is completely flat, the type of landscape where you can see the curve of the globe. Drivers need to keep up speed and avoid other tracks, as the sand can be soft.

Soon after leaving In Guezzam, you'll see on the horizon a small wart on the world. Head straight for it – that's the hill Assamakka is built on. The Niger border post here is surrounded by deep soft sand and many people get really bogged down on the way in. Maintain speed, but do not, as the travellers' grapevine sometimes advises, take a run-up at the hill to ensure getting to the fort and flagpost on top – you'll drive into a ditch and annoy the soldiers.

Assamakka

Godforsaken **ASSAMAKKA** is a small mound in the middle of the desert. Its foul-tasting, sulphurous bore water supports a few stunted trees, providing no shelter from the wind for the few miserable huts belonging to the population of army and police, on two-year postings. Among the few buildings on the sandy hillock is a **restaurant-bar** with warm *Flags* for CFA600. And that's the big event – your first taste of West African beer. Of course there's no bank, so you must either have CFA or French francs.

The **customs and police posts** are housed in the inconspicuous huts at the bottom of the mound, on the east side. They're notorious here (and they know it) and you'll hear horror stories of people getting turned back to Tam or waiting days or weeks to be cleared – most, for some reason, involving Swiss travellers. Material inducements to the authorities can be effective, but the stakes tend to be high. Much obviously depends on the mood of the official you're assigned to and on how you behave. If you click, you could be through in a couple of hours. If not, there's always the bar with the warm *Flags*.

Border formalities: Niger
The police and customs offices at Assamakka are open from 8am to noon and from 4 to 6pm. Head first to the **police** to show your passport, vaccination certificate and proof that you are travelling with at least the equivalent of US$500. Under no circumstances should you attempt to enter Niger without a **vaccination certificate** that's been duly stamped for cholera and yellow fever. Authorities are unbending about this regulation and will send you back north if you're without it. Bribes don't seem to help.

Customs are next and can be agonising. Expect to unload everything from your vehicle and open every bag. If you have camera equipment, especially expensive-looking stuff, you may be asked to show a **photography permit** which you must have if you intend to take pictures in the country. It's pretty hard to see how you could have obtained a permit between In Guezzam and here (though you can get them at Nigérien embassies) but more realistically you might try explaining that you won't be taking pictures until you arrive in Agadez where you will definitely buy the permit. It helps to show that your camera is empty, so use up the film before arriving in Assamakka.

Formerly it wasn't necessary to buy **car insurance** until Agadez, but now there's an insurance office in Assamakka and you won't be allowed to proceed until you get some. You can pay in most major currencies but rates of exchange are somewhat arbitrary.

On to Arlit

The drive on to **Arlit** takes about six hours. You shouldn't attempt to set off after around midday: if you lost your way in the dark, you could drive for 2500km in a straight line before seeing tarmac – and probably never would. Best, then, to reckon on staying overnight at Assamakka. There's a **car park** for tourists as well as an ordinary **lorry park**. The latter offers better shelter although the police flash torches around at night and may ask you to move to the tourist park if you're the wrong category of person.

West and North African lorry drivers stay at Assamakka for days, as it's a goods *entrepôt* and a meeting place for West Africans hitching north to Algeria or France. If you're heading north, you may be asked for a lift by someone with a visa but no money. If you were to lend him CFA50,000 to be returned after he cleared immigration in In Guezzam, you'd have that much currency for the Algerian black market and he'd have the coveted stamp to enable him to melt into Algeria. Nigérien authorities have no interest in this kind of transaction – but it's not easy to be sure he doesn't also melt off with your money.

The road to Arlit and piste to Agadez
The 200-kilometre stretch of tracks leading from **Assamakka to Arlit** should cause few problems. It's mainly washboard, with the odd sandy patch – easily crossed if you keep up a decent, but not reckless, speed. There are markers (*balises*) every kilometre.

If you're into more *piste*, there's a longer route that leads **direct to Agadez** (375km), passing through the village of TEGGUIDDA-N-TESSOUM, known for its salt evaporation ponds. Camel caravans still stop here to take the salt south to the Hausa country, but this route is not open during the rains and is difficult at other times of the year. There are markers every 5km – further route details on p.154.

THE TANEZROUFT ROUTE

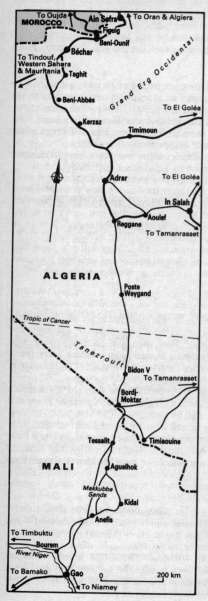

Tanezrouft means "the great thirst" – a fitting name for this vast, achingly flat expanse. With its sporadic wells, the route inspires humility even in the Iforhas Tuaregs who make marathon treks across the region to sell their flocks. And the first traverse by a European occurred only in 1913, when the French Capitaine Cortier led an expedition from Aoullen to the Niger with three men and eight camels.

Today, despite the featureless landscapes, the Tanezrouft has its devotees. It is far less touristed than the Hoggar, and the enormous 1300-kilometre length of unpaved desert tracks between **Reggane** in Algeria and **Gao** in Mali do provide a greater challenge, for some almost spiritual. The crossing is like an ocean voyage. There's nowhere else on earth that feels as remote, as pure, as silent and as utterly peaceful. The absence of towns and villages adds to the sense of individual adventure, and when you make it to the banks of the Niger after several days of travel, you really know you've crossed the Sahara.

The flatness of the Tanezrouft generally makes for a reasonably smooth drive, and you can often make better time than across the Hoggar – despite the greater distance of unpaved surface. If you're coming from Morocco, it's also more accessible. On the *piste*, solar-powered beacons every 10km have upstaged the oil drums that were formerly the only route markers.

Béchar

A modern town with a large industrial zone and suburbs of box-like apartment blocks, **BÉCHAR** conspicuously lacks appeal. But it's the administrative capital of the Saoura region and has numerous services – **banks**, a **PTT**, a **supermarket** and a few **filling stations**. In addition, its position on the main road from Oran – and on a major travel route from Morocco – makes it a convenient stopping point when heading down to the desert, even if other oases further south offer finer scenery.

Béchar accommodation

The best **accommodation** in Béchar is at the three-star *Hôtel Antar* (☎23.71.61) where comfortable, furnished singles go for DA120. It's on the south side of town, off the road to Beni-Abbès. The *Hôtel Transat*, on the avenue du Sahara, is in the same price range and has a swimming pool.

In the centre, near the Place de la République, clean, less expensive lodgings (DA60 for a single) can be found at the *Hôtel de la Saoura* (rue Kada Belahrech ☎23.80.07).

Taghit

If the prospect of a night at Béchar doesn't thrill you – and you have transport – it is worth heading out to **TAGHIT**, 93km south on a small road that loops back onto the Tanezrouft highway near Beni-Abbès. The route out from Béchar involves some rather rough patches of road – normally passable but often washed out after heavy rains.

Taghit itself is a beautiful oasis, built on the edge of the mountainous dunes of the Grand Erg Occidental. It has a vast date grove and first-rate, if moderately expensive, **accommodation** at the *Taghit Hôtel*. Just 17km from the town (ask any kid to direct you), there are ancient **rock paintings** of lions, cattle and other animals.

MOVING ON FROM BÉCHAR: TRANSPORT OPTIONS

Buses and trains
Béchar's bus station is by the town market. **Coaches** head north to Oran and south to Taghit, Timimoun, Beni-Abbès and Adrar if you're continuing across the desert. Béchar is also the terminus of the **train** from Oran, which calls en route at the dull towns of Saïda and Aïn Sefra. The railway station is on the northeast side of town, near the military base.

Driving and hitching
Heading to **Beni-Abbès**, first main town on the Tanezrouft route, you can either take the fast **southern highway** through ABADLA (where a highwa – closed to casual visitors – heads off for 700km to the Saharawi refugee camps around TINDOUF) or detour through **Taghit** (see above).

If you've been **hitching** up to now, there's no need to stop, though it is something of a haul to get yourself out of Béchar on the road south: you need to get to the junction of the by-pass and the road out of town, where you'll catch every vehicle.

Flights
Air Algérie has an office on the Place de la République (☎23.52.52). There are daily flights to Algiers and one or more a week to Adrar, Ghardaïa, Oran and Tindouf.

Beni-Abbès

After the stodgy modernity of Béchar, it's worth making a detour from the main road (after 253km) and taking the turning to the wonderful oasis of **BENI-ABBÈS**. Founded in the eleventh century, the town rambles along the Oued Saoura, wedged between a plateau and the magnificent dunes of the Grand Erg Occidental. Desert-style mud-brick houses and the groves of some ten thousand palms and fruit trees give the place a brooding, Mesopotamian feel, especially at sunset when the *oued* is in flood and a lattice of reflections shaft through the palms. Along the riverbanks, the old **Ksars** – one of which is in ruins – emphasise the ancient tranquility.

The spell may be cracked somewhat by the sight of dozens of local kids tobogganing on the amazingly steep slope of the nearest dune – something between 50 and 100m high. No doubt you could borrow a car bonnet or a sheet of plastic and follow suit. Beni-Abbès might even become a sand-skiing resort.

The museum and zoo

The town also has an interesting **museum**, sited near the *palmeraie*. Run by the *Centre National de Recherche sur les Zones Arides*, this contains exhibits on the prehistory of the region and desert geology. There are also a few displays of regional handicrafts like weaving and basket-making. Adjacent is a small **zoo**.

The Foucauld Hermitage

In 1901, **Père du Foucauld** built a religious *hermitage* in Beni-Abbès, the first of three he established in the Sahara. A figure of fascinating contradictions, he led a colourful and apparently carefree life as a viscount in France before being ordained into the priesthood. He spent the rest of his life in Algeria, seeking ever greater degrees of discomfort and solitude, trying to absolve himself from earlier sins. He was a champion of desert peoples, notably tne Tuareg, but also of French imperialism, delighting in colonial military victories (such as the one in Tit in 1902, a decisive battle for control of the Hoggar). Ultimately, and ironically, his death was at the hands of Tuareg bandits who killed him in his isolated retreat in the mountains at Assekrem, near Tamanrasset.

The **chapel** at Beni-Abbès, beautiful in its simplicity, is still run by the *Petites souers de Jésus*, the order founded by du Foucauld.

Practicalities and accommodation

The showiest **accommodation** is offered by the *Hôtel Rym* (☎23.32.03), on the north side of town, overlooking (or, more accurately, looking onto) the gigantic dunes. They have AC rooms (DA180 a double), a **swimming pool** and tennis courts. Operated by *Altour*, the hotel also organises excursions in the region – **trips on camel** through the *erg* for example. The more modest *Hôtel du Grand Erg* (☎23.34.39) is down near the palm groves and *ksars*. Rooms are simple – showers but no toilets. A night costs DA120 for a double, which is steep, but they do allow camping in the courtyard for DA20.

With a little discretion, not to menntion some caution if you're here in the rains, you can also **camp out** among the palms near the *oued*.

As to other practicalities, there is a *BNA* **bank** on the east side of town near the cinema. The **post office** is in the centre next to a quite well-stocked supermarket. Petrol and water are both freely available.

MOVING ON: THE BENI-ABBÈS TO ADRAR ROAD

The **road to Adrar** passes through a number of picturesque oases – **Guerzim, Kerzaz, Foum-el-Kheneg**. Though the road is good, you may encounter stretches where sand from the *erg* has completely covered the tarmac, especially between Guerzim and Kerzaz. 244km from Béchar, you arrive at the junction of the N51 which heads off east towards Timimoun and El Goléa. This is your chance to cut over if you're intending to cross the desert via the Hoggar route into Niger.

Travelling **by coach**, the SNTV station is near the market. Main destinations are Taghit (daily), Béchar (twice daily), Adrar (daily) and Timimoun (daily).

Timimoun

With its Sudanic-style gateway and numerous red earth buildings, **TIMIMOUN** oasis has architecture reminiscent of African towns much further south, along the banks of the Niger. It is a quite remarkable site, too, overlooking a vast *sebkha*, or dried salt lake, and nestled against an extensive palm grove that reaches out to meet the flowing dunes of the Grand Erg Occidental. In the west of town near the *palmeraie*, you can still see the old **ksar**.

Timimoun is the main town of the Gourara region, relatively prosperous from its agriculture. It's populated mainly by ex-slaves to the Tuareg – the Harratine – and by Chaamba peoples.

Accommodation

The *Hôtel Rouge de l'Oasis* – a landmark palace in the centre of town – suffered severe structural damage in the early 1980s and was closed down. Hopefully it has by now re-opened, since it's an architectural treat, built in Sudanic style, with Berber patterning in the hall, and a lot of fun to stay at – even if the rooms seem a little run-down compared to the luxury they provided in the 1920s when they housed such European guests as the Grand Duchess of Luxembourg.

If it remains closed, the best place in town is the *Hôtel Gourara*. A modern hotel with AC rooms, it commands a beautiful view of the *sebkha* and palm groves and is worth visiting just for a drink on the patio near the swimming pool. If you're not operating on a big budget, head to the **campsite**, *La Palmeraie*. Facilities here include showers and washbasins; the grounds are well kept and the staff exceptionally friendly.

Practicalities

You'll find most of the shops and offices in town grouped near the Place de la République, where the *Hôtel Rouge de l'Oasis* is located. Across from the hotel is a *BNA* bank. Many restaurants are also in the vicinity. Up the main street past the mosque, you'll find the **market**, which has a good selection of produce.

There's also a **Syndicat d'Initiative** (tourist office) near the Place de la République and an adjoining **crafts boutique**. You can get tourist information here and organise excursions through the *sebkha* – a 50km circuit that takes in many of the oases in the Gourara region – or arrange to see the nearby **petrified forests** and sites where the pink, crystalised rocks known as *roses de sable* abound.

Moving on, the **SNTV office** is on the main street, near the Place de la République. **Coaches** are regularly scheduled for Adrar and Ghardaïa. *Air Algérie*, also on the *place* (☎23.45.55), has weekly flights to Ghardaïa, Adrar and Oran, and may even have started flights to Bordj Moktar.

Adrar

Like Timimoun, **ADRAR** is built along Sudanic lines, with impressive entrance gates, a vast *place*, and red earth walls and buildings. But this administrative town has grown rapidly in recent years and lacks the rural charm of its more northerly sister. It is, however, the last big market town on the Tanezrouft route and so the place to pick up **supplies**, food, water and petrol.

Though some supplies are available further south in Reggane and even at Bordj Moktar, you can't guarantee availability of anything. Most people prefer to play it safe, making sure they have enough of everything (especially petrol and water) to make it all the way to Gao – a distance of over 1500km and a journey time that can vary from three days to a week or more. The last **bank** along the way is also in Adrar, off the main town square; make sure by now you've changed the equivalent of DA1000. Beyond Adrar, there's little to spend it on, so try to estimate closely.

Accommodation

On the Place des Martyrs – Adrar's main public square – the *Hôtel Touat* (☎25.99.33) is the best in town. It's a new hotel with AC rooms and bar; comfortable but expensive at around DA200 a double. A cheaper option (DA100) is the *Hôtel Timmi*, a block south of the *place* near the arches.

SOUTH FROM ADRAR: TRANSPORT PRACTICALITIES

The **road south from Adrar** is paved and fast as far as Reggane. Known as the *route des palmeraies*, it runs through the **Tohat region**, dotted with small oases – Tamentit, El Mannsour, El Ahmar – irrigated by a vast network of *foggaras*; it's one of the best parts of Algeria to see the underground water storage system used extensively in the country.

Departure formalities
Before heading off south, it's wise to call in at the **police and customs** to see if they're interested in controlling your passport and currency declaration forms. Formerly this was mandatory here, but now it seems these formalities may only be necessary in Reggane and Bordj. Best to check anyhow to avoid any misunderstandings and the nightmare of being told to *faire demi-tour* – turn back – later.

If you're **driving**, stop by at the *protection civil* to register your intent to cross the desert. Officials will verify that your **car is in proper condition** (in fact they examine it to make sure it's functioning properly in every particular) and that you have two spare tyres and sand ladders. They also insist you drive in a convoy of at least two vehicles, advice that must be followed. If you set off alone, you will be stopped at Reggane.

Buses and trains
The *SNTV* office is on the main square in town. Buses run to Béchar, Timimoun, In Salah and Reggane and *SNTV* even operates irregular trucks to Bordj Moktar.

Hitching
If you hitched into Adrar, it's about as far as you'll normally get standing at the roadside, but ask around town and you may be able to fix up a ride to **Gao** – your best bet is simply to approach every party of overlanders you see. Alternatively, most trucks (Algerian, Malian and occasionally European) pay an initial visit on arrival at one of the service/petrol stations on the north side of town; if you chat up the staff they may keep you in mind when vehicles come in.

There are vehicles departing pretty well daily, except, generally, between May and July – when high winds and severe sandstorms may force the closure of the route by the police. When you do manage to fix up a lift, consider the **life-support arrangements** quite carefully. It's a good idea to be as self-sufficient as possible in water and (especially) food. Relations with strangers can quickly sour over such issues. **Dates**, though surprisingly expensive here, are good for the trip, as is simple **bread** (though it's often in short supply in Adrar), halved and tied in plastic bags. Buy enough cans of food to have some left over, and don't bother with fruit. Buy extra water containers if necessary.

Flights
Air Algérie has an office on the *grand place*: flights to Bordj Moktar via In Salah (Tues and Sat mornings) are around DA250 (about the same as the route transport fare). Flights to Algiers go non-stop, Tuesday and Thursday morning and Saturday evening.

Reggane

Though it's still more than 640km from the Malian border, **REGGANE** feels a lot like a frontier town – an effect emphasised by having to go through a perfunctory police and customs check, formalities which are repeated once you arrive at the true border at Bordj. The town maintains a sizeable military camp and has a notorious history: it was from this base that the French carried out nuclear tests in the Sahara in the early 1960s.

Arriving, drive into town slowly and avoid shooting past **customs**, which are located on the main road, near the spot where the pavement ends. Staying overnight, you can get a room at the *Hôtel du Tanezrouft*, but it's expensive and most overlanders simply head to the *palmeraie* to the south of town and camp.

Onwards from Reggane

If you change your mind about the Tanezrouft, or want to join the Hoggar route, you can do so from Reggane quite easily today on a tarred road to AOULEF and a resonable *piste* thereafter that takes you to IN SALAH via the petrified forest 60km west of that town.

The Tanezrouft piste: Reggane to Bordj

The fifty-kilometre stretch immediately south of Reggane promotes a swift involvement in the pleasures of desert travel. A treacherous **soft sandpit**, this bogs down many drivers almost immediately, who then have to spend the day getting acquainted with their sand ladders practically within sight of the customs post. If you're aware of the situation, you can get through with little difficulty, but you must keep up speed and stay out of the wheel ruts of other vehicles – especially trucks. If people in your convoy get stuck, keep going until you arrive on a hard patch before walking back to help.

As you move on, you gradually learn to read the colour and texture of the sand, and will instinctively recognise bits to avoid. You should in fact encounter no major problems after this, as the featureless floor of the Tanezrouft has few obstacles and rolls relatively well. But occasional soft stretches do pop up from time to time and it pays to be constantly vigilant.

Most of the landmarks along the route are artificial. One of the first you come to is **Poste Weygand**, 272km from Reggane. There's nothing left of this outpost but some old corrugated metal structures. A sign marks the distance to Gao – 1112km. The **Tropic of Cancer** is the next progress marker, but beware that the churning around of other vehicles looking for the big notice board has added to the unstable nature of the surface around here and it's easy to get stuck in the vicinity.

A stretch of soft sand also ushers in the next landmark, **Bidon V**, 515km from Reggane. The site gets its name from the first vehicle crossing of the desert by one Georges Estienne. Having gone down to the Niger, he returned north and marked his route, placing a large drum every 50km from Tessalit. The fifth drum was at this site (*bidon cinq* means "drum no. 5"). In its heyday in the 1940s and 1950s it was used as a reserve for water and petrol and a landing strip was even added along with a light tower to guide aircraft. Since the late 1970s it has consisted merely of sun-scorched ruins, but it's lately been opened again as a rough and ready overlanders' service station.

It's 120km from here to Bordj Moktar. Shortly after Bidon V, the **Oued Tamanrasset** traverses the *piste*. There are stretches of soft sand and you may also notice the odd sprout of vegetation – desperate thorn bushes or tufts of optimistic-looking grass – depending when water last coursed down the wadi. After days without flies, without birds, without a sign of life anywhere, the knowledge that this vegetation is part of tropical Africa can be an exciting thought.

Bordj Moktar

Once no more than a collection of army barracks – a little island of the state in a sea of sand and gravel – **BORDJ MOKTAR** now has a sizeable community. Most of them, though, are unhappy civil servants from the north and the town still has the feeling of an overgrown military outpost. Currency forms and formal exit from Algeria are dealt with here, and, as it's all a military zone, they like to move travellers on south (or north) as soon as the formalities are concluded. There is nowhere to stay.

The settlement, though, is functional enough for travel requirements. The **filling station** is usually kept well supplied (if you're unlucky to find it dry you will have to wait a day or two for the refuelling) and there's no limit on the amount you can fill up with – a good way of dispensing with those last dinars. Water is also available so you can top up your jerry cans. The town even has a *galeries* **supermarket** where you can spend surplus dinars on whatever might be in stock.

Across the border into Mali

Once you leave Algeria, the *piste* is no longer clearly marked and the initial road through Mali has many stretches of soft sand. The flatness of the Tanezrouft soon ends and you'll find yourself travelling at reduced speeds as new obstacles arise. Small **mountains** appear on the horizon before Tessalit, and crossing them is a bit of an adventure. The winding tracks are covered with bone-shaking washboard and littered with jagged rocks that can tear apart the belly off a low-clearance vehicle. Flat tyres (and far worse) are common along this stretch. Go easy.

Tessalit

One hundred and twenty kilometres from the border (and over 150km from Bordj Moktar), **TESSALIT** is the first checkpoint in Mali. The post is situated in an attractive *palmeraie*, but the village is more or less off-limits to travellers. That's not an official rule – it just seems to be more the will of the townspeople, devoutly religious and reserved. Around the customs and police posts, however, you'll find a restaurant and a rudimentary *campement*. There's no petrol officially available nor any bank.

Formalities and practicalities

Customs and police procedures are relaxed at Tessalit, especially when compared to the trials of Assamakka – the Niger border post on the Hoggar route. If you need a **visa** for Mali, though, you should officially have one before entering the country. Immigration officials have been known to permit entry to those without, sending them on to Gao, but don't count on their benevolence.

On arrival, go first to the **police** in the fort on the hill. They'll check your passport and visa. You'll also have to present your **international vaccination certificate**, stamped for yellow fever. Cholera vaccinations may be required if there's an epidemic (not so uncommon along the Niger River). If you're driving a vehicle, you also need to buy a **laissez-passer** (CFA2200 for eight days), and **insurance** (up to CFA10,000 or more, also for eight days).

Next, head down the hill for **customs**. The *agents* will make you take everything from your car, eyeing up your possessions while inspecting and making clear the things they'd like. Car parts and tyres are popular and you may be coerced into selling some for prices that seem somewhat low. Of course you're under no obligation to do so, but they're not obliged to make the process a quick one either.

If you are forced or have chosen to **stay the night**, a crop of new *campings* and restaurant-bars has mushroomed in the last few years. South of the town, *Etoile Bleu* charges around CFA500 to sleep in a hut, CFA200 to park a vehicle, CFA100 for a meal. They even have a pool (CFA400).

While there's no licensed **petrol** supply in Tessalit, privately you can get dirty fuel – with a lot of messing about – for around CFA250–300 a litre, not too much over the odds. And lastly, from here to Gao it's just about essential to have either **French francs** or **CFA** in cash to finance your trip. Try to change money in the town, or with travellers, if you haven't obtained either currency in advance.

Moving on to Gao

The stretch of *piste* from **Tessalit to Gao** is particularly bad. Not only are there long patches of deep soft sand accompanied by loose rock, but acacia trees now figure in the landscape, and they have treacherous thorns that easily work their way into hot, soft tyres. Punctures occur frequently, sometimes several times a day.

Tilemsi Valley route

An alternative to the main piste, and often proposed by "guides" in Tessalit, is the **Tilemsi Valley route**. It's marked clearly enough on the *Michelin* map and provides a smoother surface and lots of wildlife-viewing opportunities – mainly gazelles. But beware two possibilities: one, that it's recently rained and the Tilemsi is muddy; and two, that your guide is so interested in a paid ride to Gao that he's unconcerned at never having been down the Tilemsi route before. Such things happen.

The main piste

If you opt for the main *piste* south, the first settlement you come to is the Tuareg town of **AGUELHOK**, 100km from Tessalit. Here you present your travel documents to the police. There's a small restaurant nearby.

A very difficult stretch known as the **Makubba** begins around 100km south of Aguelhok. It consists of about ten kilometres of soft sand, often scattered with clumps of grass which are too solid to drive over in a car. Consequently a fair amount of "weaving" is necessary to avoid them, which makes you liable to bog down. If you get stuck in the Makubba, you'll spend the rest of the day trying to get out. To avoid such a scenario, keep away from the tracks of other vehicles and maintain your speed, and, ideally, get off the main *piste* altogether and make a sweeping detour to the west. It's best, too, to cross this stretch in the early morning when there's still a hard crust of sand. Once through, you have another 75km to the village of **ANEFIS**, where, once again, you have to have your papers "controlled" by the police.

There's still another police check at the town of **TABANKORT**, 40km beyond. From here, **two southern pistes run to Gao**. The most direct is open only in the dry season; 195km long, it rolls well, though the last fifty-odd kilometres before Gao are bedevilled with more stretches of soft sand. During the rains, you'll be obliged to go via **BOUREM**, a small town with a terrific market on the banks of the **Niger River**. Check in at the police there (it soon becomes a habit) before continuing the remaining 95km to **GAO**. Route details continue on p.237–238.

index

NIGER

NIGER

Smothered by the advancing Sahara and mostly very poor, **Niger** creates a strong initial impression of inertia, especially if you enter the country from the north, where the wide-open spaces of the desert and slow pace of life are particularly characteristic. **Agadez** is the main town of the region, an ancient desert metropolis, seat of a powerful sultanate, and one of the most obvious targets in the southern Sahara. It's also the base for determined, and usually costly, visits to more isolated oases in the **Erg du Ténéré** and the **Grand Erg du Bilma**, where camel caravans still cross the shifting dunes to the salt mines of Bilma. Other villages with historic names – Timia, Iferouâne, Assodé – lie hidden in the harsh volcanic mountains of the **Aïr region**, and can only be reached with special preparation from Agadez.

In contrast with the north, an image of relative prosperity begins to take shape only when you reach the agricultural regions and commercial centres of the south. The **River Niger**, flowing over 500km through the southwest, is one of the few bodies of water in the country – which in itself makes it an attraction. Cosmopolitan **Niamey**, straddling the banks of "La Fleuve", draws a mix of local traders, international business people, and overlanders pausing to shake the dust out of their boots. Air-conditioned hotels and restaurants provide welcome relief, while the modern high-rises coexist nicely – at least at the aesthetic level – with the city's sprawling markets and low-rise neighbourhoods of mud-brick homes. From the capital, you can travel by road (or in stages by river) along the Niger to the Malian border, passing Songhai villages and the commercial centres of **Tillabéri** – where some of the last giraffes in West Africa still wander through the surrounding bush – and **Ayorou**, which has a spectacular market that unites all the regional peoples. South of Niamey, the Niger is navigable only in short sections as it closes in on the **"W" National Park**.

A third main pole of travel lies along the southern border with Nigeria and the **Hausa** towns of **Birni Nkonni**, **Maradi** and **Zinder**. These historic centres lie in the country's relatively green belt and have been bolstered by agriculture – a regional mainstay. The road from Zinder is paved all the way to **Nguigmi**, a Kanouri settlement on the banks of **Lake Chad**.

FACTS AND FIGURES

The **République du Niger** has a confusing name for English-speakers. Pronouncing it like an unfinished "Nigeria" means nothing to *Nigériens* – the people of the country – who pronounce it "Nee-zhé". It is a vast country on the map, spreading over 1,270,000 square kilometres – twice the size of Texas and five times as big at the UK. In reality, however, the Sahara covers most of the northern region, making a vast extent of it uninhabitable. A population of some seven million people is concentrated in a fairly high density, mainly along the borders with Nigeria, Mali and Benin. About 600,000 people are reckoned to live in the capital, Niamey. The government is led by a military council headed by Colonel Ali Saïbou, who replaced the long-standing head of state Seyni Kountché after his death in 1986. Though France has cancelled its debts, Niger has a **foreign debt** in the order of £700M – about the same as British Steel's pre-tax profits for 1990. Yet, despite the disastrous recent droughts and a drop in the world price of its unhealthy principal resource – **uranium** – the country remains politically fairly stable.

People

Nearly half the population of Niger are **Hausa**-speaking. Engaged principally in agriculture and commerce, the Hausa are mostly based in the south, where they long ago established large urban centres such as Maradi and Zinder. The overwhelming majority of Hausa are Muslim, but small splinter groups have retained traditional religious beliefs, notably in the Birni Nkonni district. If you don't have a chance to get further south to the original Hausa city states in Nigeria, you can still see the brilliant **durbar festivals** – cavalry charges, clashing costumes and all – in Zinder, which retains its sultanate and beautiful quarters of traditional architecture.

The **Djerma** and **Songhai** speak the same language and probably have common origins. Numbering about one and a half million, they're the second largest group in Niger and have tended to be politically dominant. Descendants of those who fled the collapse of Gao's great Songhai empire, today's Songhai live mostly along the banks of the Niger as far downstream as Tillabéri, and retain the basic class structure – nobles, commoners, slaves, and crafts people – of the old empire. The Djerma live further south in the regions of Niamey and Dosso.

Another large group, the **Fula** (Peul or Peulh in French), make up some ten percent of the population. Spreading east from the west-facing Atlantic coast, they founded large kingdoms in Senegal and Guinea, with splinter groups heading east towards Macina around the eleventh century. By the end of the nineteeth century, a group of town Fula (as opposed to nomads), led by Uthman Dan Fodio, had established a huge Islamic theocracy centred on Sokoto in Nigeria. In Niger today, the Fula are still divided into townspeople (Fulani) and nomadic herders, commonly called Bororo or Wodaabe. The urbanites are Muslim while the pastoralists tend to follow traditional beliefs.

The **Tuareg** represent less than a tenth of Niger's population. They're of Berber origin, and migrated to the desert regions of the Aïr some time around the seventh century, when they came to control large portions of the Saharan routes, either pillaging passing caravans, or offering protection to them, or both. Some Tuareg still take camel caravans to the salt mines of **Bilma**, but an increasing number have been forced to seek jobs in the towns by the droughts of recent years. The Tuareg have a rather exaggerated reputation as sharp operators: they often work as guides and also produce some of Niger's finest crafts – especially leather and silver work.

In the region of Lake Chad, the **Kanouri** are one of Niger's smaller groups. These people are part of the legacy of the great neighbouring empires of **Kanem** and **Bornu** which reached a peak in the sixteenth century. With the advent of colonialism, their territory was divided into parts of Chad, Nigeria, Niger and Cameroon. Today, they're principally farmers and fishers, and in towns like Zinder they have mixed substantially with the Hausa. Descendants of the two groups are known as **Beriberi** – a term applied equally to Hausa-speaking Kanouri.

Climate

With the Sahara creeping up on all sides and covering about half of the country, Niger is hot most of the year. If weather is a concern when deciding **when to visit**, the best you can do is to aim for the period when the heat is least oppressive, usually from about October or November through to March. If you're travelling overland from Gao to Niamey, it's also worth trying to avoid the **rainy season**, which in the Sahel falls roughly between July and September. Note also that when the *harmattan* winds blow down from the north in November, they kick up blinding clouds of dust and sometimes cause morning temperatures to tumble near to freezing point, especially in the north near Agadez and Bilma.

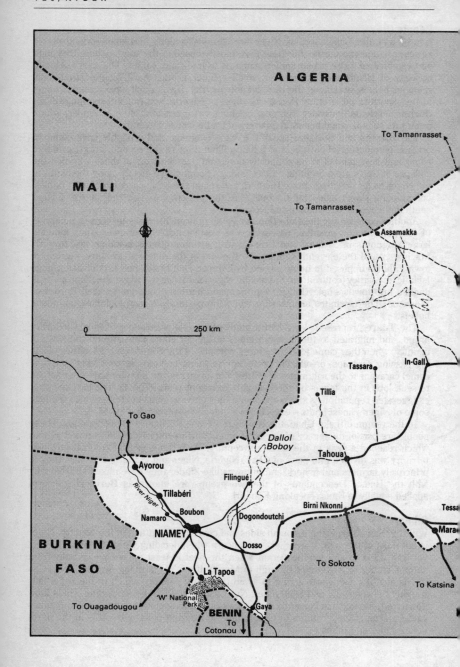

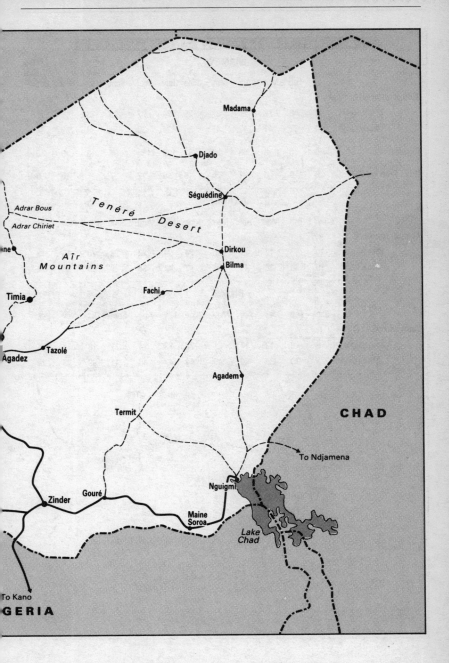

Madama

Djado

Séguédine

Ténéré Desert

Adrar Bous

Adrar Chiriet

Aïr Mountains

Dirkou

Bilma

Fachi

Timia

Tazolé

Agadez

Agadem

CHAD

Termit

To Ndjamena

Zinder   Gouré

Nguigmi

Maine Soroa

Lake Chad

To Kano

GERIA

AVERAGE TEMPERATURES AND RAINFALL

NIAMEY

	Jan	Feb	Mar	Apr	May	June	July	Aug	Sept	Oct	Nov	Dec
Temperatures °C												
Min (night)	14	18	22	26	27	25	24	22	23	23	19	15
Max (day)	34	37	41	42	41	38	34	32	34	38	38	34
Rainfall mm	0	0	5	8	33	81	132	188	94	13	0	0
Days with rainfall	0	0	0	1	4	6	9	12	7	1	0	0

AGADEZ

	Jan	Feb	Mar	Apr	May	June	July	Aug	Sept	Oct	Nov	Dec
Temperatures °C												
Min (night)	10	13	17	21	25	24	24	23	23	20	15	12
Max (day)	29	33	38	41	44	43	41	38	40	39	35	32

BILMA

	Jan	Feb	Mar	Apr	May	June	July	Aug	Sept	Oct	Nov	Dec
Temperatures °C												
Min (night)	6	8	13	17	21	22	23	24	21	16	11	8
Max (day)	26	29	35	40	43	44	42	40	41	39	33	28

Arrivals

Located astride the easiest route across the desert, Niger is the commonest overland entry point to sub-Saharan Africa. If you're not driving or hitching across the Sahara, there are sometimes cheap flights from Algiers or occasionally direct ones from Europe.

■ African Flights

From **North Africa** *Air Algérie* often has very good deals on its twice weekly flights to Niamey, especially if you qualify for the youth fares. Within **West Africa**, there are direct flights from **Abidjan** (twice weekly with *Air Afrique* and weekly with *UTA*), **Bamako** (*Ethiopian Airlines*), **Cotonou** (weekly with *Air Afrique* and *UTA*), **Dakar** (*Air Afrique*), **Lomé** (*Air Afrique*), **Nouakchott** (weekly with *Air Afrique*), and **Ouagadougou** (*Air Burkina* and *Air Afrique*). Flights from **Accra** or **Bangui** go via Abidjan.

Air Afrique also has a weekly flight from **Ndjamena** in Chad, and *Ethiopian Airlines* provides a link from East Africa with flights from **Addis Ababa** and **Nairobi**.

■ Overland

Complete trans-Saharan information is given in the Algerian Sahara section (Part Two). Additionally, however, it's worth knowing that the only approved route into Niger from the north is through the frontier at **Assamakka**. *Touristes* who try obscure routes from Tamanrasset or Djanet (or even, as they have, from Libya) risk a lot of trouble, and are invariably turned back.

From Mali, the main overland traffic follows the Niger River between Gao and Niamey. It's a difficult stretch for drivers, awash with deep soft sand and dreaded thorn trees (endless punctures), but motoring frustrations are more than compensated by Sahelian scenery at its best – dust-shrouded sunsets over the broad river and numerous fishing villages along the banks. Customs formalities have never been a terrific problem at **Labbezanga**, though agents on the Niger side can be fussy about health certificates.

The road linking Ouagadougou with Niamey has recently been paved, hugely simplifying travel **from Burkina Faso**. But you need an early start from Ouaga as the borders close at 6pm. Formalities are pretty routine.

The road **from Benin** is also paved, at least the stretch from Parakou. Until resurfacing on the section linking Dassa-Zoumé to Parakou is completed, travel from Cotonou may be easier by making a loop to Lomé and Kara – a rather wide detour, but at least it saves a deal of wear and tear if you're driving your own vehicle. The offices on both sides of the border at Malanville (bridge over the Niger) also close at 6pm.

Numerous paved roads feed into Niger **from Nigeria**, assuring a Hausa-land commercial unity despite the frontier dividing it. Main lines of entry are Sokoto to Birni Nkonni, Katsina to Maradi and Kano to Zinder. A major effort has recently been undertaken to upgrade the desert routes linking Algeria with Nigeria across Nigérien territory. And arriving from Nigeria, it's now just as easy to get all the way north to Arlit via good paved roads as it is to cut over far to the west via Niamey.

Red Tape

Niger cultivates one of the most irksome bureaucracies in the world. Customs officials have a reputation for being painfully no-nonsense: it's the only country in West Africa where you're likely to be thoroughly searched as a matter of course. You can find yourself emptying everything – while they quiz you on every medicine bottle or bit of unrecognised technology (telephoto lenses in particular don't go down well) – only to repeat the entire process for the police. Don't expect jocular exchanges or upbeat conversation. The situation is especially bad at the Assamakka border post, where travellers have been known to wait a couple of days before obtaining permission to carry on.

Once in the country, the best advice is always to assume you need to make one more official visit before proceeding. Remind yourself you're never "free" to travel anywhere here.

■ Visas

Visas for Niger are not required by Ecowas members and citizens of the UK, France, West Germany, Belgium, Netherlands, Luxembourg, the Scandinavian countries or Italy. Niger has no representation in Britain; the closest **embassies** are in Brussels or Paris.

For passport-holders who need them, visas are most easily obtained in neighbouring West African countries – Algeria (Algiers and Tamanrasset); Benin; Côte d'Ivoire; Nigeria (Lagos and Kano); and Senegal. Note that French embassies don't handle visas for Niger but some Ivoirian embassies do; and that Niger has no representation in Bamako. If you're arriving from Mali and need a visa, plan ahead. In general, Niger officials are literate and well-versed in the rules and regulations. Bluffing in any situation is rarely effective.

If you apply for a visa outside Africa, Nigérien embassies ask for strict **guarantees** in case of an accident – either proof of a costly insurance package promising emergency repatriation, or a letter from your bank confirming funds frozen in your account (usually around US$500). In addition, you have to show a return air ticket or, at the very least, the registration details of the vehicle you'll be travelling with. To avoid these headaches, you're better off getting the visa in Africa where embassies routinely ask only to see $500 in cash or travellers' cheques.

To enter Niger you need a **yellow health card** with yellow fever (except infants under 12 months) and cholera certificates. All visitors must pay the *Taxe Touristique* of CFA500 at a police station (tourist cards are no longer required), for which you'll be given a yellow, general purpose receipt. This has to be shown when you leave Niger, and there are stories about tourists being sent back to the nearest town to get one. (If you're exiting at Assamakka, that's 200km back.)

Visas for onward travel

You can get visas with little problem to all neighbouring countries in Niamey. Burkina Faso, Togo and Chad have no representation, but the French consulate handles their visas. If you're travelling overland **to Algeria**, it's useful to know that, in addition to the embassy in Niamey, there's a consulate in Agadez that can deliver visas.

■ Photography permits

Before **taking pictures**, you should know that a **photography permit** is required and taken very seriously by officials. Even civilians may stop you and demand to see a permit if they see you taking pictures. Religious or cultural objections aside, most people in towns are uneasy about being photographed unless they know you have

government authorisation. Permits can be obtained in most **Nigérien embassies**, or at the *Offices du Tourisme* in Niamey or Agadez. If you're travelling overland, especially across the desert, try to get a permit before entering the country or be extremely discreet. It's a wise precaution to finish and remove films before crossing Nigérien borders.

■ Vehicle papers

If you're driving, a **carnet** is required and expected by police. If for some reason you don't have one, they'll issue you with a Temporary Importation document. You'll also be issued with a *laissez-passer*, a form filled in with the same details as your Vehicle Registration Document (V5) or *Carte Grise* (French and West African equivalent), to be surrendered on exit. There's no charge.

Third party **insurance** is compulsory, and the police like to check it. It's not available at frontier posts, but the police allow travel without it to the nearest town. Entering from Kano and Magaria, buy insurance in Zinder; from Assamakka, in Arlit. The large and efficient *Société Nigérienne d'Assurances et de Réassurances*, Avenue de la Mairie, Niamey BP426 (☎73 55 26) has branches throughout the country. Insurance costs about CFA1000 a day for a car or Land Rover staying for a short period, and is valid in all the **Conseil de l'Entente** countries (Niger, Burkina Faso, Benin, Togo and Côte d'Ivoire).

It's relatively easy to **sell vehicles** in Niger. Report to a police station for official stamping of your documents – purchase receipt (*Autorisation d'achat en course de validité*), registration document (*Carte Grise*), insurance certificate (*Attestation d'assurance*) and tax disc (*Vignette de l'année en cours de validité*).

■ Other headaches

Tedious bureaucracy doesn't stop once you've crossed the border. Officially, you're required to **report to the police station in every town** you visit. This usually takes twenty minutes or thereabouts, and you shouldn't miss having your passport stamped in major towns (Arlit, Agadez, Maradi, Niamey, Tahoua and Zinder), though there are rarely any ill effects from missing one or two small ones. In some places, they like to keep your passport until your specified day of departure.

Money and Costs

Niger is in the CFA Franc zone (CFA50 always equals 1 French Franc; CFA450–500=£1). It's essential, arriving either by air, across the Sahara, or from Nigeria, to have some French Francs in cash to tide you over until you reach a bank where you can change travellers' cheques. If you're coming overland by car you'll need money for fuel and other necessities, so plan ahead.

The two main **banks** in Niger are the *BIAO* and the *BDRN*. Outside Niamey, one or the other has branches in Zinder, Tahoua, Birni Nkonni, Maradi, Agadez and Arlit. Changing money at the bank costs four percent commission.

Credit cards are pretty much limited to use in Niamey, and even then only for major expenses such as car hire, luxury hotels and a handful of upmarket restaurants. Major ones that are accepted are *American Express* and *Diner's Club*.

■ Costs

Everything in Niger has a **price**, generally an expensive one. Passing through, a few days in the towns can eat deeply into your pocket. Spending any length of time in Niger, and visiting places off the beaten track, can cost a small fortune.

Information and Maps

Tourist information on Niger is virtually non-existent outside the country; there are no tourist offices abroad. The office in Niamey has a good plan of the capital, with many of the city's restaurants and hotels indicated.

Other information they supply isn't especially useful except as an appetite-whetter for organised excursions – say to the Aïr. The entire Saharan region is, in fact, off-limits to fully independent travel. A second tourist office in Agadez also has information on routes and can fix you up with the obligatory guide.

The *IGN* publishes road maps in scales of 1:2,500,000, 1:1,000,000, 1:500,000 and 1:200,000. You're not supposed to use the latter two without authorisation, which you can apply for at any Niger embassy. In Niamey, maps are available at the *Direction de la Topographie*.

Health

In Niamey and other large towns, tap water is usually suitable for drinking. Cholera epidemics, however, occur frequently along the Niger and you should use purifying tablets, or boil it. In case of an epidemic, even town water is suspect. Driving on the Gao to Niamey road, the river or wells may be your only source of water, and you should always treat it before drinking.

Health care facilities are generally bleak. For minor ailments you can be treated at Niamey's **hospital**, but you may never figure out what you were suffering from, since the Chinese doctors don't speak much French or English and write prescriptions in Chinese.

If you have a medical problem, embassies will always recommend a **private clinic**. For anything serious – surgery for example – they're sure to suggest repatriation.

Getting Around

Niger has some good roads and there's a decent public bus system if you're not driving, plus perfectly feasible hitching prospects at checkpoints. In addition, you have the less convenient options of flying and, in the southwest of the country, using the Niger River.

■ Roads and driving

Surfaced roads link the main cities of Niamey, Tahoua, Zinder and Agadez. The *Route de l'Uranium* – from Niamey to Agadez and Arlit – and the *Route de l'Unité* – connecting Maradi, Zinder and Lake Chad in the southeast – were resurfaced in the years following the 1980s' droughts, and in 1990 were in superb condition, straight, level and unpotholed. The only section in this triangle still unfinished at the end of 1989 was some 200km midway between Agadez and Zinder, easily negotiated by two-wheel-drive vehicles.

On tarmac, experienced local drivers tank along at 150kph. If you're driving yourself you can keep up a good speed too; visibility is excellent and all bends and hazards are marked well in advance. **Night driving** is now legal. Driving **off the paved roads** is still subject to police jurisdiction, though in practice they're rarely fussed about it in the south.

The entire **northeast**, however, is a domain of tough desert *pistes* traversing the Ténéré desert. The *Office du Tourisme* in Agadez hires out Land Rovers and guides for **excursions** through the colossal desert dunes to such isolated places as Bilma. Even if you're fully equipped in your own 4WD vehicle, you're required to submit an itinerary with the Agadez tourist office, and obtain an authorisation from the *préfecture* and *gendarmerie* before heading off through the Ténéré or the Aïr. Invariably they'll insist you take an official guide (not cheap). Failure to comply with every condition will lead to serious problems with the police in desert settlements and oases.

Once you've dealt with town paperwork, there are few **roadblocks** in Niger, and they're generally clearly marked at the edge of town – not too much of a problem.

Petrol and diesel are generally plentiful, but are so far apart on the roads to the Sahara that you need to be sure of your supplies. Fuel can be bought from either a filling station – dependent on electricity – or from an entrepreneur with half a dozen fifty-gallon drums at the roadside. Maps aren't generally a good guide to fuel supplies; fuel station attendants, police and lorry drivers know where the next supply is and how likely it is to have fuel. Check regularly.

North of Zinder, **lubrication oils and transmission fluids** can be hard to come by.

■ Buses and taxis

The state-run *Société Nationale des Transports Nigériens* operates a good system of **buses** between major towns. Inexpensive and relatively comfortable, they run on fixed schedules. Because of their popularity with local and foreign travellers, it's imperative to **reserve in advance** at the local *SNTN* office. *Taxis de brousse* soak up the excess passengers; they're slightly more expensive and always overcrowded. **Trucks** also run between certain centres and often take travellers for a fee – an especially useful option for the stretch between Agadez and Zinder, where bush taxis and buses are scarce, and from Arlit north across the Sahara.

■ Hitching

Roadblocks and police checks at the entrance to every large town help to make **hitching** a viable alternative. Cars are obliged to stop at these controls and while the *gendarmes* are checking the papers you can ask drivers if they're headed your way. Often the police will help. Foreign aid workers usually take hitchers for free; Nigérien drivers will routinely expect you to subsidise the trip.

Many foreign **women**, accompanied by men, hitch through Niger without any major problems. However, lorry drivers have been known to pressurise female travellers for sex, even when they're accompanied by a man. This isn't likely to happen if you say you're married to your male companion.

Hitching is fast. On the three main axes you can expect a vehicle going to one of the big towns or a neighbouring country at least once an hour, and most vehicles will stop. But lorry drivers sometimes turn off at a junction which only they recognise as such, so check the final destination and any detours to be made.

A hitch on a lorry usually means standing in the back for several hours under the blazing sun; hats and/or *cheches* are essential plus **at least two litres of water**. A lift in the cab is noisy and muggily hot, and gets exhausting if you're also trying to make conversation in unfamiliar French or Arabic.

■ Air and river

Internal **flights** tend to be expensive and infrequent. *Air Niger* operates Boeing 737 and Fokker 27 planes between Niamey and Tahoua, Maradi, Zinder, Agadez and Arlit (several flights a week to most destinations). For complete information on schedules and prices, contact the airport in Niamey (☎73 23 84). In addition to scheduled flights, it's possible to hire small planes from the *Transniger* company (☎73 20 55) in Niamey.

Large steamers don't ply the Niger below Gao, but motorised *pirogues* do venture along the river between Ayorou (near Mali) and Gaya (near Benin). They operate only during the rainy season when the water level is high enough. Deals have to be struck on your own in the river towns. Between March and September, it may also be possible to canoe-hop downstream from Gaya to Port Harcourt in southern Nigeria; rapids and artificial barriers block the way at numerous points and prevent a continuous journey in the same vessel.

Sleeping

Hotels tend to be expensive in Niger, but at least you'll find comfortable places with toilets and air conditioning in all the major towns – Niamey, Arlit, Agadez, Zinder, Maradi. Budget accommodation seems especially bad value: you'll usually have to pay upwards of CFA4000, even for a non-self-contained room, with a fan at best. You can do slightly better in *chambres de passage*, but here you pay in terms of peace and privacy.

Camping sites are an idea that's caught on in Niger and you'll find them scattered lightly throughout the country. They usually cost around CFA1000 per person plus extra for each vehicle – which means, if you're travelling in a large group, that it's about as cheap to sleep in a moderate hotel. Crossing the desert, of course, you can sleep under the stars so long as you stay at least 20km outside the limits of the northern towns.

Officially, **staying with people** is not allowed, but authorities don't seem as strict in enforcing this law as in neighbouring Benin or Mali. An exception to this rule is Tahoua, where people probably won't invite you anyhow. In Niamey or other large towns, no one seems to notice if you stay with Nigériens for short periods, though you obviously need to use discretion.

Nigérien Food and Drink

Though Niger has concentrated heavily on improving its agriculture, food shortages occur in years of bad harvest or drought. Staples tend to be less varied than in countries to the south, meals being usually based around millet, rice or *niébé* – a type of bean that has become an important crop. Along the river, these are usually eaten with sauces and fresh or smoked fish.

The Songhai often make a cornmeal stodge (or *pâté*) eaten with a baobab leaf sauce perked up with fish or meat. Beef and mutton is more common in the Hausa country and the nomadic regions of the north. In both areas, *brochettes* are sold everywhere on the streets. Stuffed into a *demi-baguette* and doused with a bit of *Maggi* sauce, they make a quick and satisfying meal.

A more traditional speciality, *foura*, is one of the most common dishes, and eaten throughout the country. It consists of small balls of ground and slightly fermented millet, crushed in a calabas with milk, sugar and *piments* added.

Niamey has a surprisingly good selection of **foreign restaurants**, ranging from European to Asian. Outside the capital, eating places tend to be much more modest, the selection of dishes usually something like grilled chicken or *steack frites*. **Street food** is still common (more so than in Niamey, where it's recently been subject of official disapprobation) with vendors selling omelettes, salads, *riz gras* and a variety of other cheap meals.

As for **drinks**, Niger's great beverage – in common with other Sahel countries – is **tea**, drunk on most occasions, especially on the road whenever a little time is available to fix up a fire. You'll also find *Flag* **beers** in most towns, though they're rather expensive.

Communications, Media and Language

Niamey's new PTT is quite modern and efficient. The *poste restante* is reliable, although mail sometimes winds up in the old *Grande Poste* – so if your letters don't arrive, check both post offices.

Phoning abroad should now be possible with IDD, though operator-assisted calls were until recently still the rule. Usually they can put you through quite quickly. It's expensive, but the connections are good. You may be told that reverse-charge calls (*PCV*) are possible only to France; in that case, ringing ☎16 from a payphone puts you through to the foreign operator, who will connect a reverse-charge call to the UK. Persistence may be needed.

■ Press and broadcasting

There's nothing much in the way of **newspapers** in Niger: *Le Sahel* (circulation 5000) is published daily in Niamey and a new independent monthly news magazine, *La Marché*, was launched in 1989. You can find French papers and news mags in some of the bigger Niamey hotels, but nothing in English.

Nigérien radio, *La Voix du Sahel*, broadcasts in French, Hausa, Songhai-Djerma, Kanouri, Fulfuldé (Fula), Tamashek, Toubou, Gourmantché and Arabic. The TV service, *Télé-Sahel*, aims to come on air four evenings a week.

BASIC HAUSA

Surpassing even French and English, **Hausa** is the most international language in West Africa, and is spoken by anything from 25 million to 100 million people. The language developed into a regional *lingua franca* in the fifteenth century, when Hausa traders led caravans to North Africa. Through their widespread commercial liaisons, Hausa became a trade language throughout northwest Africa and, in terms of the area over which it's spoken, Hausa is today second only to Swahili in sub-Saharan Africa. Though there are many dialects, the two most important are **Kano** and **Sokoto**. Differences are primarily phonetic and discrepancies don't prevent speakers of different dialects from understanding each other. The following words and phrases are based on the Kano dialect, which is generally considered to be standard Hausa.

NUMBERS

1	*daya*	8	*takwas*	30	*talatin*	90	*casa'in* (or *tamanin da goma*)
2	*biyu*	9	*tara*	40	*arba'in*		
3	*uku*	10	*goma*	50	*hamsin*	100	*dari*
4	*hudu*	11	*goma sha daya*	60	*sittin*	200	*dari biyu*
5	*biyar*	12	*goma sha biyu*	70	*saba'in*	250	*dari biyu da hamsin*
6	*shida*	20	*ashirin*	75	*saba'in da biyar*	1000	*dubu*
7	*bakwai*	25	*ashirin da biyar*	80	*tamanin*		

In Niger, money is commonly counted in multiples of CFA5 (*dela*) – which can be difficult to calculate even if you're thinking in English. For example:

CFA100	*dela ashirin*	CFA200	*dela arba'in*	CFA500	*dela dar*
CFA150	*dela talatin*	CFA450	*dela tamanin da goma*	CFA1000	*jikai*

GREETINGS

If the following list seems long and trivial, it barely gives a taste of the extended formal exchange that's so important in Hausa, as in most African languages. Just learning the three words *sanu*, *lafiya* and *yauwa*, will permit you to carry on a surprisingly lengthy conversation.

All purpose greeting (men)	*Salamu alaikum*	Are you tired? (how's the tiredness)	*Ina gajiya?*
(Response)	*Alaika salamu*		
Greetings	*Sanu*	No, I'm not tired	*Ba gajiya*
(Response)	*Yauwa, sanu kadai*	What's the news?	*Ina labari?*
Are you in good health?	*Kazo lafiya?*	Everything's fine	*Labari sai alheri*
(Response)	*Lafiya lau*	Good afternoon	*Barka da yamma*
How's the household/your family?	*Ina gida?*	(Response)	*Barka kadai*
		See you tomorrow	*Sai gobe*
Good morning (how was the night)?	*Ina kwana?*	Okay, see you tomorrow	*To, sai gobe*
		See you later	*Sai an juma*
How are your children?	*Yaya yara?*	Okay, see you later	*To, sai an juma*
Fine (general response)	*Lafiya lau*		

SHOPPING

How much?	*Nawa nawa ne?*	I'll give you CFA100	*Zan biya ka dela ashirin*
Do you have oranges?	*Akwai lemo?*		
Yes I do/no I don't have them	*I, akwai/ah ah babu*	No deal (seller refusing)	*Albarka*
How much are your oranges?	*Lemo, nawa nawa ne?*	Give the money (offer accepted)	*Kawo kudi*
They're expensive!	*Kai, suna da tsada*		

A SHORT NIGÉRIEN GLOSSARY

Azalai Camel caravans.

Baba Old man, a term of respect.

Birni Hausa word meaning a formerly fortified town.

Boro Bi Black person or people.

Canaris Large clay pots for storing water.

Djoliba Malinké name for the Niger. Literally "River of Blood" since the body of water was as vital to life as blood flowing in the veins.

Erg Shifting sand dunes common in the Ténéré.

Fech-fech Soft sand hidden beneath a hard crust.

Gravures Rupestres Rock paintings (Fr), common in the Aïr and Djado regions.

Kaya-kaya Wandering salesmen.

Kori Seasonal river course or wadi (Hausa).

Razzia Slave raid.

Reg Stony wastes.

Wonki-wonki Launderers, common along the banks of the Niger in Niamey.

Zongo Section of a town or village where newly arrived strangers live.

Sports, Arts and Entertainment

Wrestling and one-armed boxing (fist wrapped in cloth) attract big crowds, but there's not a great deal going on in terms of national "culture" in Niger – no theatre except the odd event in Niamey, and little happening musically. The film tradition, brief as it is, shows more promise.

Cinema in Niger has been dominated by three film makers, none of whose work you're very likely to come across abroad. **Oumarou Ganda** began his career as an actor in a Jean Rouch film, *Moi, un Noir*, and went on to become a cinéaste in his own right and one of the great cultural archivists of African cinema. You're more likely to see his (largely autobiographical) works abroad or at Niamey's Franco-Nigérien Cultural Centre than in any ordinary Nigérien cinema.

Rouch also inspired another relatively well-known director, **Moustapha Alassane** whose most famous feature film is *Femme, Villa, Voiture, Argent* (1972), a popular comedy dealing with the issue of cultural identity.

Another film maker to gain international acclaim is **Djingary Maïga**, producer of *l'Etoile Noire*, in which he also starred, which deals with the clash between western and traditional values.

■ Music

In the realm of **music**, Niger remains rooted in tradition and the country has produced no international stars. In Niamey, look out for performances of the national music and dance troupe, **Karaka**. You might also catch a less worthy, mimed, Top of the Pops thing that goes out on *Télé-Sahel* TV. For a taste of Nigérien music, the *Agence de Cooperation Culturelle et Technique* has put out two volumes of a record entitled *Festival de la Jeunesse Nigérienn*. Further nuggets are given in the "Music" section in *Contexts*.

LE BOXEUR
VENTE AU NIGER

Directory

CONTRACEPTION Birth control was only legalised in Niger in 1988. There's an active *planification familiale* programme now, but contraception still isn't widely available.

CRAFTS AND MARKETS Niger has a wealth of mostly inexpensive and portable crafts. Agadez is well known for its **silversmiths** who turn out some fine jewellery; popular items are the pendants known as desert crosses, particularly the *Croix d'Agadez*. The Hausa towns, and notably Zinder, specialise in **leather goods** – sandals, bags and boxes. Fula weavers (*tisserands*) are noted for their geometrically patterned **blankets**. And there's a lot more. To get a better overview, the National Museum in Niamey shows a wide range of the country's artisanal output. Best buys are in local markets, though for guaranteed quality and variety you should also check out the official *Centres Artisinales* in Niamey, Agadez and Zinder (see appropriate pages in the guide).

HOLIDAYS Muslim holidays are of key importance, with Niger's Islamic population at upwards of 85 percent of the total. For festivities, the best place to be for one of these celebrations is in the Sultanate of Zinder. Other national holidays are: **January 1**, **April 15** (Anniversary of the 1974 coup), **August 3** (Independence Day) and **December 18** (Proclamation of the Republic). Christmas and Easter are also office holidays.

OPENING HOURS Due to the heat, business starts early in the morning and generally closes down for at least three hours in the sweltering afternoon. Banking hours vary from one institution to the next but roughly they're Mon–Fri 7.30–11.30am & 3.30–5.30pm. Government offices are open Mon–Fri 7.30am–12.30pm & 3.30–6.30pm. Most businesses are open Mon–Fri 8am–12.30pm & 3–6.30pm, plus Sat mornings.

PETROL Expensive generally in Niger, except along the southern border between Birnin Konni and Zinder, where there's a thriving black market in Nigerian petrol. Virtually no one buys from the stations here.

WILDLIFE Niger's harsh climate and terrain has preserved some rare species from the vicissitudes of habitat spoilation and hunting (which was outlawed in 1964). Even in the south, hippos can nearly always be seen in the Niger river and there are giraffes in the vicinity of Tillabéri. The *parc du "W"* has a good cross-section of savannah fauna, including possibly 200–300 elephants. One beast of special note is the beautiful Addax antelope: completely at home in almost waterless conditions, the Addax is being reintroduced into the Aïr region, where it was formerly common. Recent reports of officials turning a blind eye to hunting parties from Saudi Arabia aren't encouraging, however.

WOMEN TRAVELLERS Though Niger is a Muslim country, women don't wear the veil and their public presence is strongly felt – something you notice immediately if you arrive from southern Algeria. Women travellers generally have few problems and western volunteers, for example, feel comfortable making trips across the country unaccompanied. Advances are frequent but harmless and easily turned away – though hitching alone can be uncomfortable (see above).

A Brief History of Niger

After the demise of the Songhai empire, whose territory spread into western Niger, two spheres of influence predominated in the region. In the twelfth century, the Tuareg settled in the north around Agadez, and soon controlled regional trade. The Hausa spread from the original seven city-states founded in Nigeria in the tenth century to settle southern towns like Zinder and Maradi. Unlike the western Sudan, where trans-Saharan trade focused mainly on gold, slavery was the mainstay of the eastern routes and the basis of local economies.

■ European Explorers

For centuries, news of cities like Timbuktu, Gao and Djenné had circulated in Europe, but although the Portuguese had been along the West African coast since the fifteenth century, no western power had penetrated the interior. It wasn't until the eighteenth century that expeditions were launched into a region notorious for its hostility to Christians. In 1796 Mungo Park reached the Niger near Ségou and described its eastern course. Until that time, Europeans believed the mysterious river flowed west – as incorrectly documented by Leo Africanus in the sixteenth century – or that the Niger was a branch of the Nile.

It was another thirty years before the Europeans saw Timbuktu. In 1826, **Gordon Laing** became the first white man to return from the legendary city alive. In 1850, **Heinrich Barth** led a new expedition into the interior, his eastern route from Tripoli taking him through Agadez, Zinder and the Hausa country south to Kano. He thus became the first European to explore the region of present-day Niger.

■ Colonialism

The information gleaned by these explorers opened the doors to colonial conquests. France, anxious to link colonial settlements in west and central Africa, was the most ambitious usurper of Sahelian territories. In 1854, General Louis Faidherbe became governor of Senegal and plotted the eastward expansion of France's West African empire. He sent troops up the Senegal River and east to the Niger. Following its course, they broke the resistance of such formidable adversaries as **Samory Touré** and **El Hadj Omar**, who had founded the Tukulor empire of Ségou.

By the end of the nineteenth century, the French had established a military presence at **Niamey**, which they quickly turned into the most important army post east of Bamako.

In 1898, spheres of influence were established between France and Great Britain, the principal powers vying for control of the Niger. The following year, the French sent an expedition to Lake Chad to demarcate borders between Niger and Nigeria. Led by two generals, **Voulet and Chanoine**, it was to be one of the bloodiest of the colonial missions. As the two soldiers pushed east with troops of Senegalese infantry, they embarked on a series of massacres, torching villages in their path and slaughtering the people. Birni Nkonni was virtually razed. Reports of the brutality reached France and the government sent an expedition led by Colonel Klobb to investigate. Infuriated that their tactics should be questioned, the generals went over the edge, murdered Klobb, broke with France and apparently set about conquering the territories for themselves. Their madness was only stopped when they were killed by their own infantrymen. Replacements were sent out and Lake Chad was finally reached in 1900.

■ French Rule

With the territory's southern borders established, Niger became part of French West Africa in the following year. But the nature of this territory differed from that of other West African neighbours: officially, it was an **autonomous military territory**, and its importance was strategic, rather than commercial. Outside the army, the French presence was minimal: there was no French settlement and development was barely considered.

"Pacification" was a difficult process in Niger, as resistance sprouted in pockets across the country. One of the most serious **uprisings** was that of the **Kel Gress Tuareg**, who occupied Agadez from 1916 to 1917 and controlled most of the Aïr highlands. Then, in 1919, a rebellion broke out in the region of Tahoua, which was only quelled in 1921, the same year that Niger was finally upgraded to the status of a colony.

World War II was a turning point in West African politics, and following the Brazzaville Conference of 1944, reforms were enacted which provided African representation in the national assembly, the senate and the assembly of the French Union. In 1956, the famous *Loi Cadre* was passed, establishing local government for the French colonies.

In the wake of these reforms, two political movements developed in Niger. The most radical was embodied in the the *Union Nigérienne Democratic* – also known as **Sawaba** – which dominated political life in the 1950s. Led by **Djibo Bakary**, the party fought vigorously against close ties with France and de Gaulle's proposed constitution, the main provision of which was for a Franco-African Community with limited autonomy for individual colonies, but continued economic dependence on Paris. For a while, it seemed probable that Niger would join Guinea in saying "No" to de Gaulle's proposal and in opting for immediate independence "with all its consequences".

In the event, the new constitution was approved in the landmark **1958 referendum** – a victory for the *Parti Progressiste Nigérien* of **Hamani Diori**, who had advocated the alternative of close links with France. It's generally believed the election results were falsified. According to the official count, 370,000 people voted for the union compared to 100,000 who voted against; that left 750,000 people who ostensibly didn't exercise their voting rights.

Despite its wide support, the Sawaba party was banned in 1959, and Bakary forced into exile. With the implicit backing of the French, the PPN was thus poised to dominate post-independence politics and Diori was assured the presidency of the new nation, formed in 1960.

■ Independence

Conservative politics prevailed in the days after independence, as Diori aligned his country with France and developed close ties with moderate neighbours, notably Côte d'Ivoire. Diori ruled with a small Council of Ministers, carefully selected to maintain the status quo. Sawaba tried to operate from abroad (its foreign backers included Algeria, Ghana and China), but opposition to government policies was rigorously suppressed. Various plots to overthrow Diori's regime in the early 1960s led to mass arrests and

violence. When Sawaba was accused of leading a series of guerrilla attacks near the Nigerian border in 1964, seven of the presumed assailants were publicly executed in Niamey.

By the late 1960s, the PPN – by then the only political party – was in a state of disarray and subject to a wave of mounting criticism. Diori made an effort to reorganise it, but was careful to stack the party leadership with faithful pre-independence politicians – and ensured that it remained ineffective as a forum for the discussion of opposing views. Despite his tight control over the political reigns, however, he began to loose his grip on power as the economic situation deteriorated drastically in the late 1960s.

Diori was given a political reprieve when the mining of **uranium**, discovered in 1968, gave new financial hope to a nation that had previously gained seventy percent of its export earnings from groundnuts. Eager to take advantage of the new source of revenue, Diori accepted a minimal seventeen percent share for the national mining company, *Société des mines de l'Aïr* (SOMAÏR), which was controlled by the French Atomic Energy Commission. However, 1968 also saw the start of the first great **Sahel drought**. Lasting until 1974, the natural catastrophe brought Niger to its knees.

By the early 1970s, over a million head of livestock (nearly two-thirds of the national herd) had died, and the pasturelands of the northern nomads had disappeared. International organisations helped establish emergency refugee camps and sent food supplies, but rumours began circulating that government officials were hoarding food and selling it off at hefty profits, rather than distributing it to those facing starvation. These were quickly confirmed by the discovery of emergency food aid, stockpiled in the homes of several of Diori's ministers.

■ Kountché's Coup

Disillusion with the government turned to anger. When Lieutenant-Colonel **Seyni Kountché** overthrew Diori in April 1974, there was widespread satisfaction, and even the French conceded they could do business with the new order. Kountché established a *Conseil Militaire Suprême* which made a priority of dealing with corruption and reinvesting the government with credibility. In a conciliatory move, hundreds of political prisoners were released and Djibo Bakary, Sawaba's leader, returned home from exile. In 1975, Kountché pulled off an economic coup, when he managed to renegotiate the terms under which uranium was mined, raising SOMAÏR's share to 33 percent and making the national company the biggest single partner.

Fuelled by uranium revenues (prices for which soared following the oil crisis of the 1970s) and aided by the end of the drought, the economy began to pick up. Government workers received wage increases, roads were improved and prestigious building projects undertaken in Niamey. Even the agricultural sector improved dramatically. Niger, one of the countries hardest hit by the drought, was also one of the quickest to recover, and by the end of the decade, it could boast self-sufficiency in food production – no mean feat.

Niger had become something of an economic oasis in the middle of a poverty-stricken region, and that alone was enough to lend stability to Kountché's military regime. But policy and personality conflicts within the CMS threatened his authority, and he repeatedly reshuffled the ruling council and expelled critics. Following a new outbreak of political activity, Bakary was rearrested in 1975. A coup attempt the following year led to the execution of its alleged protagonists. Even as he tightened the screws, however, Kountché made a number of good-will gestures. In 1980, Diori and Bakary were granted a degree of freedom, along with many of their supporters. And by 1982, the president appeared to be making plans for a return to a constitutional government.

■ The 1980s

A *Conseil National de Développement* was established in 1983 as a means of granting greater participation on a local level. But the CND had barely started functioning when another coup attempt, this time led by some of Kountché's closest aides, nearly toppled the government while he was abroad.

Reforms thereafter proceeded at a slower pace, though the president eventually announced that a **National Charter**, or draft constitution, would be drawn up and submitted to a referendum. Approved by the government in 1986, the charter was submitted to voters in May 1987 – the first time elections had been held in the country since independence – and received overwhelming approval.

But even as Kountché was setting about reorganising the government, the **economy** took an unexpected dive. Already in 1980, a combination of the world recession and cuts in nuclear power programmes had led to a drop in the price of uranium. Production in Niger has since continued to fall off and plans to mine some of the country's unexploited reserves have been scrapped. Hopes that Niger would become one of the world's leading uranium producers faded rapidly. And as revenues dwindled and the national debt grew, another drought struck the country in the early 1980s. By 1984, the number of livestock had dropped by a half and, as cereal shortages climbed to nearly 500,000 tons, the country again found itself importing vast quantities of food, depending much on the USA. At about the same time, Nigeria closed its land borders and cut off some of Niger's important markets.

The downswing was accompanied by tensions with Niger's northern neighbour, **Libya**, which claims some 300 square kilometres of territory in northern Niger, an area with certified uranium deposits. After the Libyan army occupied northern Chad in 1980, Kountché's government had become wary of possible destabilisation – with some justification after Gaddafi told reporters "We consider Niger second in line". Gaddafi accused the Niger government of persecuting its **Tuareg** population – an issue about which Niamey is acutely sensitive – and may have encouraged dissent among the nomads, who have generally been sold short since independence. Many observers suspected Gaddafi of behind-the-scenes support for the 1983 coup attempt and although relations have subsequently improved between the two countries, they remain strained. Relations with other Maghreb countries – Morocco, Algeria and Tunisia – were strengthened over this period, however, and Niger has developed close ties with Saudi Arabia, Kuwait and other Arab states in the Gulf, Muslim confrères who have proved reliable sources of aid.

■ Recent events: into the 1990s

In 1986, Kountché travelled abroad to countries that had been traditional sources of political and financial support. He made his first official trip to France, during which he suffered a brain haemorrhage and subsequently died, after an operation in Paris, in November 1987.

Kountché's chosen successor as head of state – **Colonel Ali Saïbou**, the military Chief of Staff and a long-time supporter – has followed the same orientation as his predecessor. In mid-1988 Saïbou announced the creation of a one-party state (the PPN and all the other parties were disbanded when Kountché came to power), a move which he said would "normalise" political expression and which was generally perceived as a step to further reforms started in the early 1980s. In 1989, the first congress was held of the military council's **National Movement for a Society of Development** (*MNSD*), a supra-political organisation which promised great things, but within a party-state order that threatened to be elitist and almost exclusively urban-based. The government's fear of ethnic divisions in the country is so great that even acknowledging the plurality is viewed as a danger.

The IMF-ordered economy has forced in austerity measures which have hit poor urban dwellers very hard. Students, too, have felt the full impact of rising prices and reductions in already strapped services. There were student protests in 1988, and in February 1990 the university in Niamey was the scene of large-scale **student demonstrations** that ended in a violent clash with security forces and the deaths of three students and many serious injuries. A week later there was a mass protest rally through the streets of the capital. In further response, the Lagos-based opposition, the Niger Movement of Revolutionary Committees (*MOUNCORE*), issued statements demanding a popular uprising in Niger and the overthrow of the Saïbou clique.

Niger was thrown under the spotlight in June 1990, after *Le Monde* reported a **massacre** of about 200 Tuareg civilians in reprisal for a Tuareg raid on Tchin-Tabaradene near Tahoua. Amnesty International has evidence of other outrages near Tchin-Tabaradene and at In-Gal, in which dozens of people were summarily executed.

Niger has been a classic case of a country over-dependent on a **single resource** and held hostage to the fickleness of world market prices. The importance of improving agriculture is critical as only three percent of the land is arable. In addition to the vast **irrigation projects** that have been undertaken in regions around Tillabéri, Birni Nkonni and Dosso, there's been a positive trend towards smaller-scale projects involving co-operatives for individual farmers. With its huge public debt and limited possibilities for further credit, the military council will have to look increasingly to Niger's untapped resources to underwrite both future development and better prospects for stability and the **democratisation** still barely hinted at.

NIAMEY

As uranium money showered on Niger in the 1970s, **NIAMEY** changed almost overnight. Many of its dusty roads were paved, and a Voie Triomphale was traced through town, its bright streetlights blotting the Sahelian nights from memory. Avant-garde buildings like the Palais des Congrès and, fittingly, the Office National de Recherches Minières appeared, to be joined by futuristic hotels, banks and offices. The renaissance didn't go as far as in Abidjan or Lagos, and the conflict between modernity and tradition – and between city and country – is therefore less unsettling. In fact, the juxtaposition works remarkably well here. The sight of camel caravans crossing the Niger River on the Kennedy Bridge hardly seems incongruous, and neither does the spectacle of Fula, Hausa, Tuareg and Djerma traders gathering at the Petit Marché under the shadow of western-style high-rises.

Some history

Before the colonial era, Niamey was no more than a small village whose origins probably didn't predate the eighteenth century. When French troops swarmed into the desert in the 1890s, they recognised the strategic importance of this spot on the river and dug in their heels. By 1902, the unlikely village had grown into one of the most important military and administrative posts east of Bamako. When Niger officially became a colony, the larger urban centre at Zinder was chosen as the new capital, but the French administrators preferred Niamey's climate, and in 1926 they transferred the capital back again.

Throughout the colonial era, Niamey never developed much beyond the **European quarter** built in the plateau district. The population in the 1930s was under 2000, though by independence it had increased to around 30,000. Still, real growth only occurred in the 1970s, with the population surging to over a quarter of a million by the end of the decade.

A great deal of the influx was caused by the **drought** of the mid-1970s, which sparked a rural exodus of Biblical proportions. Niamey, fattened on uranium income, flourished as immigrants from the devastated provinces poured into the city where they could hope to find food, housing and work. A second drought in the mid-1980s produced a new wave of immigration, forcing population figures sky-high. Today, it's estimated over 600,000 people live in Niamey, and virtually every ethnic group is represented here. This rapid growth, combined with the recent fall in the world price of uranium, has put huge strains on the city. Though Niamey provides a comfortable escape for travellers and expatriates with cash in their pockets, the benefits of modernisation are now tempered by the spectre of shantytowns, mass unemployment and other urban blights.

Arriving

Coming in by *taxi brousse* you're most likely to be let off at the *gare routière* in the **Wadata district**, a good 5km from the centre. It's not difficult or expensive to get a taxi into town: **collective taxis** cost an average of CFA150 each, though at night drivers often ask twice that. If you hire a cab it will cost at least CFA500 per short trip. Taxis are now licensed to operate until midnight. City buses run during daylight hours and work out a little cheaper than taxi shares.

Niamey's **airport** is 12km from town on the Dosso road. Unfortunately, buses don't shuttle into the centre, so you'll have to take a cab. Expect to pay about CFA1500.

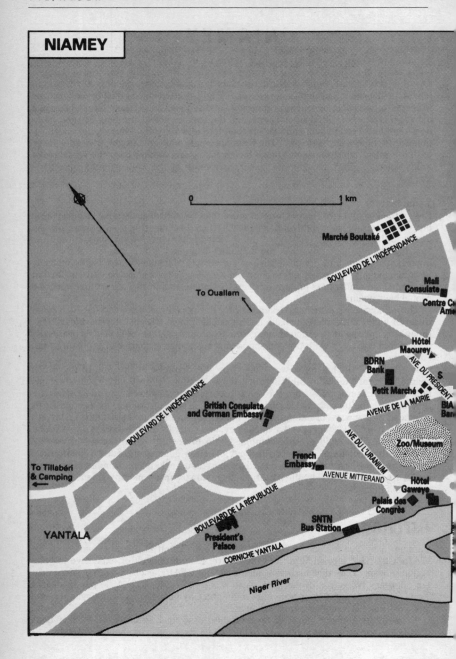

NIAMEY

0 _____ 1 km

Marché Boukaké

BOULEVARD DE L'INDÉPENDANCE

Mali
Consulate

Centre Cu
Amé

To Ouallam

Hôtel
Maourey

BDRN
Bank

AVE. DU PRESIDENT

Petit Marché

BIA
Ban

AVENUE DE LA MAIRIE

BOULEVARD DE L'INDÉPENDANCE

British Consulate
and German Embassy

Zoo/Museum

AVE DU L'URANIUM

To Tillabéri
& Camping

French
Embassy

AVENUE MITTERAND

Hôtel
Gaweye

YANTALA

BOULEVARD DE LA RÉPUBLIQUE

Palais des
Congrès

SNTN
Bus Station

President's
Palace

CORNICHE YANTALA

Niger River

To Filingué

Mosque

Gare routière

WADATA

Hôtel Moustache

NIAMEY HAUT

Hôtel Sabka Lahiya

...emique

BOULEVARD DE L'INDÉPENDANCE

Grand Marché

AVENUE DE L'AMITIÉ

To Airport, Dosso

BOULEVARD DE LA LIBERTÉ

Hôtel Le Dé

Hôtel Ténéré

Stadium

AVENUE DE L'AMITIÉ

Sûreté Nationale

Hôtel des Postes

Hôtel Rivoli

LUEBKE

Le Vietnam

GAMKALÉ

Tourist Office

AVENUE DE L'AFRIQUE/ROUTE DE GAMKALÉ

Le Tapoa

Feu du Bois

Hôtel Terminus

RUE DU SAHEL

Grand Hôtel

NIAMEY BAS

Hôtel Sahel

CORNICHE GAMKALÉ

To Kollo

Le Bateau

Niger River

To Say, Tapoa

Passport formalities

As soon as possible after arriving, you must check in with the authorities and get your **passport stamped** at the *Sûreté Nationale*, in the Place de la République, near the new *Hôtel des Postes* (Mon–Fri 7.30am–12.30pm & 3.30–6.30pm). It's another bureaucratic headache, but one you can't really circumvent. Sooner or later you'll have problems if you don't take care of this formality – without a stamp you most likely wouldn't get further than the roadblocks at the town exits. In addition to the paperwork, you must provide **passport photos**, which normally take a minimum of 24 hours to get developed in Niamey if you don't already have some.

Orientation

Niamey spreads along seven kilometres of the Niger's left (north) bank, and has now expanded to the other side of the river. The size of the town makes it difficult to get an immediate grip on its layout – a problem compounded by the French-style planning, with numerous roundabouts and streets that rarely run parallel.

You'll spend virtually your whole time on the left bank. To define a centre, use the **Kennedy Bridge** as a landmark. To the north of the bridge, rue de Gaweye leads straight up to the **Grand Marché**, bordered by the boulevard de la Liberté. The entire **commercial centre** lies between this new market and the river, and this is where you'll come to shop, eat, change money, and visit sights such as the **National Museum**.

To the **west of the Kennedy Bridge**, avenue François Mitterrand runs past the impressive *Hôtel Gaweye* and Palais des Congrès as it heads towards the tree-lined avenues of the **Plateau district**. This colonial-looking neighbourhood is where most government ministries are located, along with the Palais du Président and many of the embassies. Continuing west, you come to the underdeveloped **Yantala district**, which you'll become familiar with if you stay at the *camping* near the entrance to town on the Tillabéri Road.

East of the bridge, the rue du Sahel leads to the residential neighbourhoods known collectively as the **Niamey Bas** district. Streets are comfortably shady in this area, where you'll find a good number of hotels and restaurants. Further east, Niamey Bas gives onto the **Gamkalé district** and then to the capital's **industrial zone**.

Accommodation

Though you'll find many good places in the moderate and expensive levels, budget travellers are left in the lurch in Niamey. Some relief is provided by the *camping* and there are one or two shabby places in the centre that can put you up at relatively reasonable rates.

Camping and other cheap places

Camping Touristique, on the road to Tillabéri in the Yantala district. A well-run site with decent showers and toilets. It's ideal if you have a car, but a little distant from the centre for those without, though taxis are frequent enough in the daytime. What you do with tent and other gear while you're in town is another problem. They charge CFA1000 per person plus CFA750 per vehicle, so it's no special bargain either. If you're travelling alone, you will save money here, but couples could do just as well by heading to one of the rare budget hotels.

Le Dé, on a small sidestreet near the intersection of bd de la Liberté and rue du Maroc, has rooms starting as low as CFA2200. It's admittedly grotty and the downstairs bar may be the source of more raucous activity than you'll want, but this is one of the town's cheapest, and within walking distance of the centre.

Le **Moustache**, rue du Cameroon, north of bd de la Liberté (☎73.42.82). Another cheap alternative, a bit further from downtown. The comfort of their rooms also leaves a bit to be desired, but they charge only CFA3225 for one or two people. Some AC rooms are available.

Moderate

Le **Rivoli**, av du Président Luebke (☎73.38.49). A popular place among overlanders, often seen drumming up business with local hustlers – notably car dealers – in the bar. With rooms starting at CFA6500 a single, it's almost as pricey as some of its more upmarket competitors. Perhaps they feel the central location is worth it; you may not.

Le **Maourey**, Rond Point Maourey (☎73.35.75). Also in a good location about halfway between the Nouveau Marché and the Petit Marché, the *Maourey* has eleven S/C rooms with AC. Not nearly up to the standards of hotels like the *Terminus*, its prices nonetheless start at CFA9500.

Slightly upmarket

Le **Terminus**, rue du Sahel, near rue du Terminus (BP 882; ☎73.26.92, telex 5425). Though hardly more expensive than hotels in the preceding category, *Le Terminus* is much nicer, with 38 AC bungalows around a well-kept garden, swimming pool, bar and restaurant. Rooms start at CFA9200.

Le **Sahel**, rue du Sahel, near the Olympic pool (BP 627; ☎73.24.31, telex 5330). Recently renovated and comfortable, with 35 AC rooms (from CFA10,000), restaurant, disco and crafts boutiques.

Sabka Lahya, off bd Tanimoune in the Poudrière district (BP 1030; ☎74.09.33, telex 5427). Far from the centre, but a likeable place with its own pool, restaurant and outdoor bar. Fifty S/C rooms with AC from CFA10,000.

Les **Roniers**, Tondibia road, about 7km from the centre (BP 795; ☎72.31.38, telex 5428). The furthest of the lot from the centre, which is perhaps why it's not bad value. Bungalows here are grouped around a park near the river and cost from CFA9000; has its own pool.

Expensive

Le **Gaweye Sofitel**, place Kennedy (BP 11008; ☎72.34.00, telex 5367). The most distinguished and luxurious of Niamey's hotels, this giant rises near the river and the *Palais des Congrès*. It boasts 248 rooms – some overlooking the river – and has a pool, tennis courts, restaurants, bars and nightclubs. It costs upwards of CFA25,000 to stay here – you can settle with your *Amex* or *Diner's Club* card.

Le **Ténéré**, bd de la Liberté (☎73.39.20, telex 5330). Part of the *PLM* chain, the *Ténéré* has 55 AC rooms of international standing, a pool, conference rooms and the usual abundance of restaurants and bars. Prices upwards of CFA15,000.

Le **Grand Hôtel**, place de la Fraternité (BP 471; ☎73.26.41, telex 52.39). This colonial-style hotel is holding its own against larger, more modern competitors, partly because of its striking location overlooking the river. It has 36 comfortable rooms and 35 bungalows plus pool and restaurant (from CFA12,000). Best value in this category.

The Town

Niamey isn't brimming with pleasures and pastimes, but it's not difficult to find ways of passing the day. The obvious place to start is the *Musée National* complex, which apart from exhibits on national peoples and culture incorporates extensive gardens, a zoo and shopping boutiques. Niamey also boasts a couple of innovative cultural centres that regularly feature exhibitions, films and performances of theatre and dance. The markets, too, each with its own character, provide active diversions – if you're headed south, the Grand Marché is bigger than anything you'll find in northern Nigeria.

The Musée National

Inaugurated in 1959, the **Musée National** (☎73.43.21; Nov–March daily 9am–noon & 3.30–6pm; April–Oct 9am–noon & 4–6.30pm) was a radical breakthrough at the time and is still out on its own. Remarkably for a museum, you really feel this place is alive – at weekends especially, the grounds and exhibition areas are thronged with an eclectic mixture of young and old, foreign and local, scholarly and illiterate.

The main museum entrance leads into the park from a sidestreet off the avenue de la Mairie. Before heading into one of the stylised Hausa pavilions where the exhibition spaces and boutiques are located, take a stroll around the zoo – especially popular with the young kids from town. A big draw are the hippos in a man-made pond, but cages scattered around the grounds display the other fauna of Niger – lions, hyenas, various monkeys, crocodiles and tortoises, all in a reasonable state of health. Aviaries contain vultures and a variety of more colourful birds. In a far corner of the park there's a set of examples of some of Niger's traditional housing types – a good chance to compare the difference between Fula, Hausa, Djerma and other styles.

Each of the buildings that comprise the museum is dedicated to a theme – costumes and jewellery, weapons, handicrafts and musical instruments. One of the pavilions contains palaeontological and botanical displays, including **dinosaur skeletons** from **Gadoufaoua**, in the Agadez region. Discovered accidentally by geologists prospecting for uranium, these skeletons are around 100 million years old, making this remote zone one of the most exciting sites outside the western USA. Also here is the amazing **Arbre du Ténéré**, a tree that once stood solitarily in the Ténéré desert and became a famous overlanders' landmark – until it was knocked over by a lorry driver. Formerly the only living thing for hundreds of miles around, the tree was transported to the museum and a sturdy steel replacement erected in the desert.

While at the museum, be sure to check out the **crafts centre**. Goods sold here are usually more expensive than on the streets (in certain cases substantially so), but profits help keep the museum going. Quality is controlled, so your silver jewellery won't turn green hours after you buy it or the camel-hide bag smell suspiciously of goat when it gets wet.

The markets

Niamey's **Grand Marché** (open until sunset daily) – also called the Nouveau Marché – reopened in 1986 after being completely reconstructed after a fire. It's decidedly modern, with monumental entrance gates and a fountain or two for show, yet the smooth lines and earth tones still respect the more traditional Sahelian styles. Within the market, paved alleyways lead through a maze of merchant stalls grouped into sections according to wares – clothing and fabrics; soaps, cosmetics and pharmaceuticals; hardware; ironmongery and utensils, and so forth. Along with the new market in Ouagadougou, this is one of West Africa's finest.

Further south in the **Zongo district**, where rue du Président Luebke and avenue de la Mairie intersect, the **Petit Marché** has a more casual flavour. Merchants who didn't get a space in one of the market stalls simply clear room on the ground and set up shop. It's primarily a **food** market, and you'll find a good selection of fruits and vegetables, meat, fish and grains. People from all over the country converge here to buy and sell – a wide mixture of Fula, Djerma, Tuareg and Hausa. Nearby streets give way to **crafts** stands, an excellent place to pick up jewellery, leather goods or blankets. Dealers tend to be aggressive and bargaining can turn into a battle; to take off some of the pressure, try saying you left your money at the hotel and are just interested in getting an idea of prices. There's another small market, devoted entirely to **pottery**, across from the tall *BDRN* bank down avenue de la Mairie – look for the beautiful hand-painted water pots produced in the village of Tondibia, just outside Niamey.

Several communities have their own **neighbourhood markets**, usually specialising in everyday domestic goods. At the Marché Boukoki, north of boulevard de l'Indépendance near the *Lycée*, vendors sell firewood, calabashes, mats, scrap metal and small animals such as chickens and goats. In other districts, you'll find the **Marché Yantala** (along bd de la République) and the **Marché Gamkalé** (on the Kollo road).

Cultural centres and sports events

Across from the museum, the **Centre Culturel Franco-Nigérien** (Tues–Sat 9am–12.30pm & 4.30–7.30pm) has an active schedule that includes exhibits of local artists and craftsmen, performances of dance and theatre and regular film screenings. You can stop by and pick up their events programme, or check the pages of *Le Sahel*.

Also check the paper for the schedule of the **Centre Culturel Oumarou-Ganda**, named after the late, great film maker and native son. Located on boulevard Mali Bero near the Grande Mosquée, the centre has an open-air amphitheatre where concerts of traditional music, ballet and theatre are often staged. The **Centre Culturel Americain**, on rue de Kalley near the Grand Marché, also sponsors a variety of events.

Just down from the Centre Culturel Oumarou-Ganda, on boulevard Mali Bero, the **Arène des Jeux Traditionels** is a good place to check out West African **wrestling** (*la lutte traditionelle*), at which Niger excels. Again, scan the paper for announcements.

Restaurants and Nightlife

Niamey has a remarkable selection of eating places, including classy restaurants specialising in exotic cuisines such as Russian or Vietnamese. If you've just blown in from the desert, you won't have seen such variety in a long time. Street food is increasingly rare, but many local eateries and snack bars will set you up with square meals that aren't too expensive.

Inexpensive

You can still find the occasional morning *caféman* and evening stalls for *fufu*, rice, macaroni or *to* (cornmeal dough), but **street vendors** are becoming scarcer, and are apparently subject to official harassment. After sunset, you'll still find a good amount of street food – notably beef *brochettes* or fried omelettes with onions, tomatoes and *Maggi* sauce – around rue de Kabekoira, especially in the general area of the *Vox* cinema. Daytimes, of course, you can get really cheap eats at the Petit Marché, the Nouveau Marché or the motor park.

Bottom bracket restaurants

La Croisette, av du Président Luebke, across from the *Rivoli*. Africanised French place (or is it the other way round?). Good steak and outdoor eating for around CFA1500, or you can come just for a beer.

Marhaba, off rue de Kalley, near the American Cultural Centre. "Discovered" by Peace Corps workers and other ex-pats, this one's become popular with overlanders. Chop-house meals at around CFA1500 seem pricey, but it's a good place to meet people.

An Na Chouwa, close by the Petit Marché. More of a beer hall than an eating place, but you can get snacks such as *brochettes*. Good music to go with an upbeat ambience.

L'Islam, av de l'Arewa, near av Soni Ali Ber. No alcohol, but copious servings of a daily African *plat du jour*. Good value for money.

Bar-restaurant Damo, av Soni Ali Ber, near the rue du Cameroon. Another inexpensive eatery convenient for those staying at the *Moustache*.

Tabacady, near the Palais de Justice (☎73.58.18). Moderately priced African meals.

Le Refuge, rue du Maroc, near *Hôtel Le Dé*. Courtyard African place, where the *plat du jour* will set you back CFA700.

Le Mbacke, off rue du Sahel, behind the *Hôtel Terminus*. Specialities from Senegal with large servings and reasonable prices.

Tapoa, rue du Terminus. Outdoor joint with North and West African food.

Damsi, Sonara I Building, near the Kennedy Bridge. Snack bar with *bistro* type French food. A good view of the river from the terrace.

Moderate to expensive

AFRICAN

Au Feu du Bois, rue du Sahel (☎73.28.18). Nicely served meals from throughout the region for around CFA3000.

Diamangoup, Corniche Gamkalé (☎73.51.43). French and African specialities served on a boat docked in the Niger – one of the town's more interesting venues.

L'Oasis, ground floor of the El Nasr building (☎73.30.30). African dishes like *poulet aux arachides* (groundnut chicken) or *bouef aux gombos* (glutinous beef okra) in the evening. Sandwiches and ice cream during the day.

EUROPEAN AND MIDDLE EASTERN

L'Oriental, near the Rond Point Kennedy, towards the rue du Président Luebke (☎72.20.15). Lebanese.

La Cascade, in the Zongo district near the *Vox* cinema (☎73.28.32). Best French dining in town, specialising in fish with a variety of interesting sauces; meals from a very reasonable CFA4000. Good wine list.

La Flotille, Corniche Yantala (☎72.32.54). Unusual to find Russian food in this part of the world, but here you have it, and cooked by a native. French specialities are also on the menu of this very good – and accordingly expensive – restaurant.

ORIENTAL

Le Vietnam, rue du Terminus (☎73.26.46) The best oriental food in town though it gets stiff competition from another Vietnamese restaurant, *Lotus Bleu*, located nearby on av de l'Afrique (☎73.21.05). Both restaurants cost around CFA3000 for a full meal.

Dragon d'Or, rue du Grand Hôtel (☎73.41.23). Wide variety of Chinese food including soups, spring rolls, sweet and sour pork and the like.

Nightlife

Eating is the principal after-dark pleasure, as **Niamey nights** are very low-key. The bigger hotels have **discos** – the *Kakaki* at the *Gaweye* and the *Fofo* at the *Sahel* – with high covers and expensive drinks; the latter is the looser of the two, and on weekends can be quite fun. The *Takoubakoyé*, near the *Rivoli*, usually draws a more enthusiastic crowd and is one of the most popular of the **downtown clubs**; others include the *Hi Fi* and *Le Satellite* (in the El Nasr Building). Up near *Hôtel Le Dé*, the *Akalan* is another well-known venue where you'll find a young crowd of *ambianceurs*.

Directory

Airlines Most of the following are in the area of the Petit Marché, near the *Rivoli*.
   Air Afrique, Immeuble Air Afrique, av Président Luebke (BP 11090; ☎73.30.11).
   Air Algérie, Immeuble Rivoli (BP10818; ☎73.38.98).
   Air Mali (BP8; ☎73.31.89).

Air Niger (BP 865; ☎73.38.40).
Ethiopian Airlines, Immeuble Sonara (BP 11051; ☎73.50.52/53).
Nigeria Airways, Immueble El Nasr (BP 714; ☎73.32.58).
Sabena, Immeuble El Nasr (BP 11656; ☎73.23.20/21).
UTA, Immeuble Sonara (BP10935; ☎73.31.61).

Banks Banks are on or near av de la Mairie. The two most convenient are the *BIAO* and the *BDRN*. *Citybank* has a branch in Niamey (☎73.36.20).

Bus information Try calling the *SNTN* (☎72.30.23).

Car Hire *Hertz* is represented at the *Hôtel Gaweye* and has an office at the airport. For additional information, contact *Niger-Car* in the El Nasr Building (☎72.23.31) or *Sonauto* at the *Hôtel Terminus*.

Cinema The *Studio* (☎73.37.69) – an air-conditioned place with perhaps the town's newest films – and the *Vox* (☎73.32.19) – an outdoor theatre where old Charles Bronson's often play – are downtown near the Petit Marché. In other districts, you'll find the *Cinema Soni Ali Ber* (Haut Niamey), the *Cinema Zarbakan* off the av de l'Entente (Poudrière), and the *Cinema HD* (Yantala).

Embassies and consulates include:
  Algeria, av du Président Luebke (BP 142; ☎72.31.65, telex 5262);
  Belgium, Immeuble Sonara, 4th floor (BP 10192; ☎73.34.47, telex 5329);
  Benin, Plateau district (BP 11544; ☎72.39.19);
  Canada, Immeuble Sonara, 2nd floor (☎73.36.86);
  Egypt, Nouveau Plateau (☎73.33.55, telex 5245);
  France, Tillabéri road, Yantala district (BP 10660; ☎72.24.31); the French consulate is by the hospital roundabout (BP 607; ☎72.27.22/33) and handles visas for Côte d'Ivoire, Togo, Burkina Faso and Chad;
  Germany, av du Général de Gaulle, (BP 629; ☎72.25.34, telex 5223);
  Italy, consulate (☎72.32.91);
  Mali, representation and visas on the bd de la Liberté next to the Grand Marché (☎72.28.83);
  Mauritania, Yantala district (BP12519; ☎72.38.93);
  Morocco, av du Président Luebke (BP 12403; ☎73.40.84, telex 5205);
  Nigeria, av du Président Luebke (BP 11130; ☎73.24.10, telex 5259);
  Netherlands, consulate (☎72.29.29);
  Tunisia, av du Général de Gaulle (BP 742; ☎72.26.03, telex 5379);
  United Kingdom, honorary vice consulate (BP 942; ☎72.20.32);
  USA, Yantala district (BP 11201; ☎72.26.21, telex 5444);
  USSR (BP10153; ☎73.27.40, telex 5539).

Newspapers and Magazines A sprinkling of international papers (mostly French) and news magazines such as *Time* and *Newsweek* are sold in the *Hôtel Gaweye* bookshop. Check also the *tabac* in the Rivoli Arcade and the *Camico Papeterie* near the *Score* supermarket. For browsing, there's also the library of the American Cultural Centre.

Post Office The new PTT is on rue de Kabekoira, down from the *Sûreté National*. Efficient *poste restante* (CFA100 per letter) and phone services. Formerly, the main post office was at the intersection of av de l'Uranium and av des Ministères – this is now a branch office for the Plateau district.

Swimming Pools Non-guests may pay to use the pools of the three major hotels – the *Ténéré*, the *Grand* and the *Gaweye*. The last is the nicest, most central and most expensive at CFA1000. Cheaper than any of the above is the **public pool** on rue du Sahel, near the *Hôtel Sahel*.

Supermarkets The best of the European-style supermarkets is *Score* on av de la Mairie. It's completely air-conditioned and a carbon copy of a Parisian *supermarché* – from the shopping trolleys down to the boxed Camembert. Vegetables and fruit are flown in directly from France – for which you'll pay prices two to three times higher than at source.

Tourist Office The *Office National du Tourisme* on av du Président Luebke (BP612; ☎73.24.47) is especially useful for organising excursions to places like the Ténéré desert or the "W" game park. Their prices for these trips compare favourably with travel agents'. But as for helping you figure out Niamey, they aren't much good. A city map costs CFA1000, with a sketchy *Guide des Hôtels* thrown in free.

Travel Agents *Transcap Voyages* (☎73.36.36) and *Temet Voyages* (☎72.34.00) specialise in trips to the Aïr Mountains and Ténéré desert.

MOVING ON FROM NIAMEY

From the *gare routière* you'll find **taxis** or privately run **buses** to all major destinations in Niger and beyond – to Ouagadougou, Kano and Lomé, for example.

The depot for the more comfortable and expensive *SNTN* **coaches** is on the Corniche Yantala (☎72.30.20), west of the *Hôtel Gaweye*. Domestic destinations include Gaya near the Benin border, Zinder and Maradi in the Hausa country, and Agadez and Arlit in the north. There are also three buses a week to Gao and to Ouagadougou.

Niamey's **airport** (☎73.23.81), 12km southwest of the city centre on the bd de l'Amitié/bd du 15 Avril, is small but modern and functional. You can often get good deals on flights to Europe from here, notably with *Air Algérie*. For the most current information, contact the airlines given in the "Directory". *Air Niger* handles flights to Arlit, Agadez, Tahoua, Maradi and Zinder.

ALONG THE NIGER

The route from Gao to Niamey is a logical continuation of the trans-Saharan journey across the Tanezrouft, and one frequently taken by overlanders heading to the coast via Benin, Togo or Nigeria. Within Niger, it's a scenic road that hugs the river all the way from **Ayorou** to the capital. From **Tillabéri** onwards, a good paved road leads through Niamey and down to the Niger-Nigeria-Benin border at **Gaya**. Alternatively, a *piste* traces the river's west bank to Niger's only game reserve, the **Parc National du "W"**.

Ayorou

After crossing the border from Mali, if you're driving, you initially have to contend with a difficult road that involves stretches of soft sand and tiring tracks. The first town of any size is **AYOROU**, a quiet Songhai fishing village on weekdays. But on Sundays the population is swelled by a diversity of Sahelian peoples who, having crossed the river by *pirogue* or the savannah by mule, camel or on foot, converge for the weekly **market**. Famous throughout West Africa, it's an event well worth catching.

An important element is the **animal market**, the main draw for nomads – Fula cattle herders, Tuareg with their camels, and Bello with mules. Songhai, Djerma and Sorko people bring fruits and vegetables, various grains, fish, goats and chickens, while Moorish (Mauritanian) merchants, in distinctive light blue robes and white headscarves, run their typical general stores. Traders also sell traditional medicine and a variety of **regional crafts**, especially jewellery and leather work.

Though most of Ayorou crouches along the eastern bank of the river, the oldest part of town, with traditional *banco* houses, spreads over the island of **Ayorou Goungou**. You can rent a *pirogue* to visit it, or one of the surrounding islands, at the mooring point near the market square. Your chances of seeing **hippopotamus** along this stretch of the river are good, and exotic **birds** are common, especially near the island of **Firgoun**, 12km north of town. During the rainy season, you may even be able to hire a *pirogue* to take you as far as Niamey.

Accommodation

Ayorou's sole hotel is the *Hôtel Amenokal* (reservations through the *Hôtel Ténéré* in Niamey; ☎73.39.20). Part of the French *PLM* chain, it's only open from November to April, but offers more than you'd expect in such a small town. Though expensive – expect to pay upwards of CFA12,000 for an AC room – it's got charm too, with a good location on the river bank, plus its own swimming pool, bar and restaurant.

Tillabéri

If you've come across the desert via Gao, you'll appreciate **TILLABÉRI** for one important reason – **asphalt**. Running into the paved road after hundreds of miles of thundering desert *piste* is some cause for celebration; fingers crossed, it's smooth sailing from here all the way to the coast. This Djerma town is an important agricultural centre surrounded by fields of rice and millet, but there's not much to do besides taking in the **market** – notably on the big trading days, Sunday and Wednesday (though on a Sunday you'd more likely want to be in Ayorou).

Tillabéri's main claim to fame is its **giraffe herds**. The wooded savannahs stretching north of the town harbour some of West Africa's last free-roaming troops of these marvellous, graceful animals. Sometimes kids from town will agree to take you to areas where they've recently been spotted; it's possible to get quite close before they sail off with their extraordinary, slow-motion canter.

Practicalities

Tillabéri has a number of small **restaurants** and **bars**, some with fridges, making it a good place for a roadside stop. There are modest and affordable rooms at the *Relais Touristique*.

Farié, Namaro and Boubon

Midway between Tillabéri and Niamey, the town of **FARIÉ** used to be an important crossroads, as the only point between Gao and Gaya where cars could cross the river. A **ferry** still links the Niger's banks, and at the end of the dry season there's usually a passable ford, but the Kennedy Bridge in Niamey has removed the crossing's main significance. Still, you could cross here and continue to the Niger border at TERÁ and then on to DORI in northeast Burkina Faso. Transport is going to be fairly slow along these routes, but northeast Burkina has some pleasant compensations and, as the pied crow flies, it's about half the distance to Ouagadougou compared with going via Niamey.

Continuing downstream, a *campement* perches on a hilltop above the village of **NAMARO** on the west bank. Comprising bungalows, a pool and restaurant, it's reached by taking a *piste* off the main road and then crossing by *pirogue*. Namaro's market is held on Saturday – a colourful event with many traders arriving by boat. Reservations can be made at the *Office National du Tourisme* in Niamey.

A small village on the banks of the Niger, **BOUBON** has become a popular weekend rural getaway for Niamey's expatriates. The town is some 25km north of the capital, approached by a small *piste* leading west from the main paved road; **taxis from Niamey** leave for Boubon from in front of the Petit Marché. The village is especially known for its handmade pottery, sold in vast quantities in Niamey's market, and is also good for bird-watching. **Accommodation** is located on **Boubon Island**, reached by *pirogue* from the mainland. Here you'll find a government-run *campement* with nicely set-up huts, a swimming pool, bar and restaurant. Note that the camp is effectively open only at weekends; again, reservations can be made in Niamey.

South of Niamey: Dosso to Gaya

South of Niamey, the main road and river drift apart, joining up again only at the Benin border. Along the way, the road passes through the important trading town of **DOSSO**, which occupies a crossroads position between Niamey, Benin, Maradi and Zinder. The motor park is frenetic and there's a large market. Dosso still has its traditional Djerma chief who lives in the *Djermakoye* – a compound built in the Sudanic style. With authorisation you should be able to visit it. **Accommodation** is pretty much limited to the *Hôtel Djerma* (☎65.02.06), a rotten place with rooms from around CFA5000 (some AC). Slightly cheaper, and even more rudimentary, is the *Auberge du Carrefour*.

GAYA is the last town in Niger before crossing the river into Benin. The border post closes at 6.30pm here, so if you're rolling in after dark, you'll have to spend the night. There are rooms without electricity or water at the town hotel, but you may notice people in your taxi heading to a house near the motor park, where they get mats to sleep on the earth floor inside. People pay about CFA100 for this and there's no reason not to join them, though you'll elicit some embarrassed laughter.

The "W" National Park

Part of the vast reserve that spreads across into Burkina Faso and Benin, the **PARC NATIONAL DU "W"** (named after the bends of the Niger river) covers 2200 square kilometres in Niger alone. It's one of West Africa's better game parks and relatively good for animal watching, with herds of **elephant** concentrated in the Tapoa valley and **buffalo** on the wooded savannahs. Reports still come in of **lions** and **leopards** roaming the park, but they stay very well hidden. Easier to spot are antelope – **cobs** and **duiker** especially – and large troops of **baboons** scampering through the bush, often near the camp (see below). **Warthogs** and **hippos** are also quite common. The park counts some 300 species of **birds**, with good showings of storks, herons and ibises. During the June to September rainy season the park closes down, and doesn't usually reopen until early December, after the 400-odd kilometres of *piste* have been groomed.

The main **park accommodation** is the comfortable but expensive *Hôtel de la Tapoa*, at the village of **LA TAPOA**, on the edge of the reserve. (You can make reservations at the *Office National du Tourisme* in Niamey, or at the *Hôtel Gaweye*.) At the entrance you pay for a visitor's permit valid for the duration of your stay. You can also pick up a road map that is quite detailed and useful for orientation, though an accompanying guide is obligatory.

THE NIGÉRIEN SAHARA

To travel through the north of Niger takes some determination. It's a region with a stifling climate, great expanses of emptiness between the towns and very little water. From the boomtown of **Arlit** – the northermost major settlement – a paved road now leads directly to Niamey, passing through the historic Tuareg stronghold of **Agadez** and the commercial centre of **Tahoua**. Other interesting sites are extremely hard to reach, but the effort is rewarded by beautiful **desert oases** which eke out a living from the **salt trade**, and the continued spectacle of **camel caravans**. Trips through the volcanic moonscapes of the **Aïr region**, or through the awesome dunes of the **Ténéré desert** also provide opportunities to visit a wealth of **prehistoric sites** – including the rock paintings near **Iferouâne** – and a number of **springs and waterfalls**.

Arlit

Approaching from the Hoggar, **ARLIT** appears from nowhere, like a vast aberration on the fringes of the Sahara. As little as twenty years ago there was virtually nothing here, but after the discovery of uranium in the mid-1960s a town burgeoned beside the vast complex built for the *SOMAÏR* company. Despite its recent origins, Arlit's prosperity has drawn a wide mix of people, making it an attractive stopping point.

Arlit is really **two towns**. The first, built entirely for the mining company and its employees, is well planned and exclusive, with villas for engineers and executives, supermarkets stocked directly from France, a well-equipped hospital, and the town's best restaurants. The obvious divisions between the African and European workers – unequal housing, salaries and living standards – make this a disturbing spectacle, and you won't really have access to the facilities unless you know or befriend someone working here. The nearest you'll get to the high life is an overpriced, past-sell-by-date tub of caviar in a local shop.

A more **traditional town** has grown in a chaotic fashion alongside the mining complex. For many travellers, this offers a first taste of life in sub-Saharan Africa. The large **market** – a maze of tiny stalls covered by mats and corrugated iron – contains items you'll be seeing a lot of from here on south: vegetables such as *gombo* (okra or ladies' fingers), dried tomatoes and *piments* (hot peppers); fresh meat cut before your eyes in the open-air abbatoir; household items like decorated calabashes, pottery and basketware. And coming from Algeria, it's at first a surprise to see unveiled women drumming up their own business in the market place, walking openly in the streets and engaging in spirited conversation with men.

Practicalities

For most practical purposes, you'll be confined to the African town, where, in addition to accommodation and restaurants (see below), you'll find most necessities. Two **banks** – the *BDRN* and the *BIAO* – provide the country's first money exchanges. If you need to do emergency work on your vehicle after the desert crossing, several **mechanics** operate from makeshift garages and may be able to dig up some usually expensive and dubious spare parts. (For major work, try to get in to see the mechanics at the *SOMAÏR*.) The town has its own post office and **airport**, with flights to Agadez and Niamey.

On arrival, you should head straight to the **police** and **get your passport stamped** – the station is at the north end of the main street on the east side. The officers here aren't pleasant about the formality and generally keep your passport until the day you leave – and when you are ready to leave, you'll normally be given thirty minutes to clear the city boundary after bidding fond farewell to the police. If you need identification to change money, go to the bank before the police. **Driving** south from Arlit you're likely to be asked for insurance documents, so buy insurance here if you've not already done so: cost is about CFA1000 a day for short-stay saloons and Land Rovers.

You're also expected to **report to customs** after arriving – in a compound at the south end of the main street past the petrol station – although they're not always interested. Petrol and diesel are usually available here, and the filling station has good water on tap (it's worth noting that Arlit's water is pure). There are several small supermarkets and market stalls where, if you're northward-bound, you ought to dispose of your CFA small change.

A couple more warnings: driving around town after dusk is forbidden and cameras are disliked – keep it at the bottom of your bag here, even if you have a photography permit. There are no suitable subjects in Arlit.

Accommodation and eating

Arlit has a pleasant **hotel**, the *Tamesna*, on the main street near the market. The bar is a major meeting place for townspeople hiding from the heat (cold beer and soda with ice cubes), and the tables spill over into the shaded interior courtyard. The rooms are nothing to write home about, especially given the elevated prices, but some of them do have AC. Vendors continuously pass through, selling local crafts and jewellery.

Alternatively, two **campsites** are especially convenient if you've come by car. The first is about 3km out of town, along the signposted road to Agadez; facilities don't go much beyond the showers, but the place only charges about CFA1000 plus CFA1000 per vehicle. The second *camping*, some 3km to the north of town, has a similar set-up and prices. If you're alone and without a car, you'll have to rely on other people in the campsites to give you lifts back and forth.

The **restaurant** at the *Tamesna* does European-style meals (chicken, chips, canned peas) that aren't bad. Down the street, the popular *Sahel i*s good for inexpensive meals – *steack frites*, rice and sauce – and has a lively bar at night. Also on the main drag, the *Restaurant N'Wana* prepares good couscous and salads that go down well on the patio with a cold beer. Lastly, you could ask around town to discover if anything's on at the *Cheval Blanc*, an outdoor bar-disco that often has **live music**.

THE ROAD NORTH FROM ARLIT TO ASSAMAKKA

The 200-kilometre drive to Assamakka will take three to six hours, depending on your vehicle and desert driving experience. It's forbidden to enter Assamakka after dusk, and anyway the customs post closes at 6pm, so you should leave Arlit as early as possible. If this is your first time driving in the desert, the *piste* will cruelly expose any inadequacies in the securing of jerry cans, luggage, the battery fixings, and anything else that might come loose. It takes a little time to get used to the desert heat, and to driving techniques imposed by a mixture of bed-rock, *fech-fech* and *reg*.The main *piste* runs at some distance from the *balises*, which have often been replaced with piles of tyres or rocks, but you can nearly always see the next marker even though they may be 2–3km to either side. If it appears you won't make Assamakka by dusk, it's as well to camp off the *piste* – choose a spot on a mound or in a gully where you won't be squashed by a night-driving smuggler's lorry.

Agadez

Unlike Arlit, **AGADEZ** has been a major stopping point on the trans-Saharan routes for hundreds of years. You can read its history through buildings like the **Grande Mosquée** – a monument known throughout West Africa – or the more prosaic **camel market**, which has been drawing Sahelian peoples here for generations. While the salt caravans still come from Bilma, they do so very rarely, and many of the visitors are now serious tourists, cross-Sahara travellers, and even film crews. The discovery of uranium to the north, and the roads linking Agadez to Niamey and (almost) Zinder have brought hopes of additional prosperity. Yet the town has retained a dusty old charm, characterised by narrow streets of *banco* houses displaying Sudanic and Hausa influences.

Some history

In the fourteenth century, Agadez was a small but expanding town, a **centre of commerce** where Arabs from Tripoli traded with the Hausa from Nigeria and the Songhai from Gao. By the fifteenth century it was on its way to becoming the **capital** of the Tuareg – as far as such a thing existed for the nomads – and in 1449, a **sulta-nate** was established under the leadership of **Ilissaouane**. Fifty years later, the town came to be controlled by the Songhai and throughout the sixteenth century, Agadez marked the northernmost point of their great empire, with a relatively massive population of perhaps 30,000.

After the Songhai were defeated by the Moroccans, the Tuareg regained the town, but like other trading posts in the region it was already entering a period of long decline. Agadez fared better than most, however, thanks in large measure to its location near the salt mines of Bilma; trade continued, especially with Hausa-land to the south. Nonetheless, by the time the German explorer **Heinrich Barth** arrived in 1850, the population had dwindled to about 7000 and many of the old buildings were in ruins.

With the coming of the twentieth century, Agadez was incorporated into the French Territory, but not without resistance. One of the most serious threats to colonial rule was led by the Targui reformer **Kaocen Ag Mohammed**, who swooped down from Djanet to take Agadez in 1917, aiming to reunite all Muslims of the region and to terminate foreign domination. Supported in his efforts by the Germans and the Turks, Kaocen held the town for three months before being ousted by the French, who sent up emergency reinforcements from Zinder. The rebellion quelled, the colonials killed over 300 suspected conspirators and guillotined many of the town's marabouts.

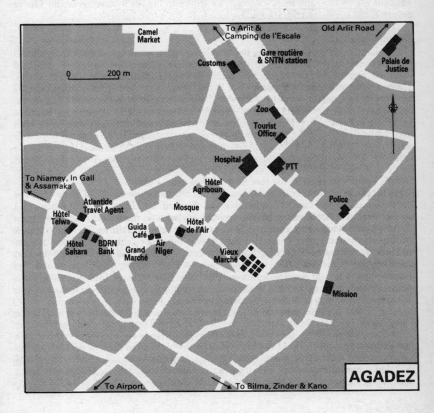

Since independence, the population of Agadez has zoomed up for two important reasons. The first was the discovery of uranium in Arlit, which provided an economic boost to the entire north. The second was the drought of the 1970s, when tens of thousands of nomads converged on Niger's cities. Agadez swelled with so many dispossessed Tuareg and Bororo herders that the population of the town and surrounding shanty city hovered at around 100,000. Though many returned to the plains when the rains started again, a similar rural exodus occurred again after the drought of the mid-1980s.

Practicalities

In Agadez, as in other towns, you need to **check in with the police** and have your passport stamped. You'll find the *commissariat* near the main post office – go there as soon as possible to fill out the necessary forms; they may keep your passport overnight.

As the main administrative town in the north, Agadez has a number of government buildings plus a **bank**, **PTT**, **service stations**, **hospital** and a small **air field**. It also has a decent range of hotels and restaurants, making it the most convenient place to spend time in the region. The tourist office can be quite helpful with information and advice if you've time and money enough for trips into the Aïr mountains or the Ténéré desert.

Accommodation

Situated at the foot of the mosque, the most interesting **accommodation** in Agadez is the *Hotel de l'Aïr*(☎44.01.47), formerly the **sultan's palace** and still quiet, cool and dignified. Except the bar, that is, which has a wide selection of booze and customers. There may be drivers practising for the Paris–Dakar rally, or ex-pats up from Niamey for a break, or even the seriously rich who these days fly in from Paris for a long weekend. Such wealth attracts its acolytes – young men and women working their way to a better life in France drop in to sell drugs or sex, while traditionalist Tuareg hawk what they say are family heirlooms. Outside there's a permanent crowd of small boys who speak fluent English, American and German and will conduct you round the town for a small fee. Despite the architectural grandeur and the clientele, the *Aïr* 's rooms aren't really that fancy, with cheaper singles starting from around CFA6000 (some rooms with AC). You can sleep on the roof for a third of that, or less.

As for the other **hotels**, *Hôtel Telwa* (☎41.01.64) lacks the nostalgia of the *Aïr*, but the accommodation is more comfortable and the tariff no higher. *Hôtel Agriboun* is a recommended cheaper place, where unsophisticated S/C rooms with fans start from CFA4000, and bargaining usually gets good results, especially if you're in a group. If you've come by car, they'll let you park inside the fenced courtyard. *Hôtel Sahara* (☎44.01.97) is the traditional haunt of overlanders, but overrated. Conveniently located opposite the Grand Marché, its rooms are looking shabby these days, and the management has a frustrating *laisser-aller* attitude. They charge from CFA4000 for a single, though you may be able to sleep on the rooftop for CFA1500 – in that case, you pay extra for showers or to have your washing done.

Agadez also has two **campsites**. The closest, and the one overlanders prefer, is the *Camping de l'Escale*, about 4km out, on the Arlit road. Despite its shady setting, the older *Camping de l'Oasis* has seen its popularity decrease in recent years – perhaps it's the distance from town, 7km from the centre on the old road to Arlit, or perhaps it's the less attentive staff. Both places have similar facilities – showers and restaurants included – and charge about CFA1000 per person and per vehicle. The *Oasis* has a pool, though it never seems to have water in it these days.

FESTIVALS IN THE AGADEZ REGION

Agadez itself celebrates the Muslim holidays in style, especially the end of **Ramadan**, the **Tabaski** and the **prophet's birthday**. Festivities marking these events begin with a morning prayer led by the *imam*, who then kills a lamb according to tradition. Families return to their homes for a feast, after which the entire town reassembles along the streets between the mosque and the sultan's palace, as drummers announce the recommencent of festivities. Already men on horseback are beginning to gather, among them the sultan's guards with their bright red turbans. The event everyone's come out to see is the **cavalcades**, the highlight of celebrations that last until sundown and then pick up again the next day. When the signal is given, the riders race their horses at a frenzied pace, kicking up clouds of dust in their wake. Men, women and children all strain for a better look, pressing dangerously close to the horsemen, who end their charge in front of the palace, where the sultan and dignitaries are gathered. The elaborate costumes, the music and the excitement of the races leave an indelible impression – you won't regret making an effort to be in town for the festivities.

THE CURE SALÉE

Along with the Muslim festivals, one of the more interesting celebrations of the nomadic Fula and Tuareg is the **Cure Salée**, a traditional homecoming that takes place sometime after the rains, between July and September. Herders who have migrated to the far south in the dry season then return to the region around **In-Gall**, west of Agadez, whose large salt flats fill with water at this time. It's a period for fattening the animals and giving them the "salt cure", punctuated by various festivities including music, dancing and, frequently, camel races.

During the month of September, the **Bororo** – a nomadic Fula people – stage a remarkable ceremony called the *Gerewol*. Often likened to a beauty pageant, this is a party for unmarried men, who spend hours adorning themselves with jewellery and putting on make-up – red ochre on the face, white outlines for features like the nose and mouth, black on the lips and round the eyes. Elaborate hairpieces are also concocted with scarves, beads, braids and feathers. Having prepared themselves to emphasise Bororo ideals of male beauty – long slender bodies, bright white teeth and eyes, straight hair – the bachelors line up in the festival arena to dance, roll their white eyes, flash their broad smiles and chant a droning melody. The young women, who also spend a considerable amount of time beautifying themselves, look on, and one by one come forward and take their choice of the most handsome man. According to custom, if a girl doesn't like the husband proposed to her by her parents, she can marry the man she desires, chosen at the *Gerewol*. Men who aren't happy with their partner have some difficulty getting out of the social obligation to spend a night with her, but numerous weddings do take place over the course of the *Cure Salée*.

Another *Cure Salée* event is the virility test known as the **Soro**. Here men stand in front of their girlfriends and allow other men to strike them several times across the chest. To show their courage to their loved one, they're expected to smile as they're beaten. These elaborate demonstrations of manliness are part of an extensive and complex **codified social life**, which characterises many pastoral peoples – it's similar in many respects, for example, to that of the Maasai, Samburu and Dinka in East Africa – and which finds expression in a mesh of taboos and ritual behaviour maintaining extraordinary social cohesion and group identity.

Although the events at the Bororo *Cure Salée* have been filmed and photographed often enough to make them relatively familiar images, the occasion is not a tourist spectacle and it's difficult to get to witness it. Increasingly, government bureaucrats are setting the agenda, however, so you might find that you can visit on an official tour. If you have time enough to be persistent, the best would be to make friends first in Agadez or In-Gall.

Eating

Apart from the hotel restaurants, there are several small places to get inexpensive meals. Near the mosque, the *Tafadak* serves copious helpings of couscous and other regional specialities in a pleasant interior courtyard. The nearby *Restaurant Chez Nous* is also recommended – *riz sauce* for CFA400, full Niger eats for CFA2000 and cheap, help-yourself coffee. Behind the market near the bank, the *Restaurant Islamique* is well known among travellers for friendly service, good salads and inexpensive main courses. Similar in style is the town centre *Restaurant Senegalais*. For sandwich-type snacks and *gelati* there's an Italian ice cream place – *Vittorio's /Guida* – next to the *Air Niger* office.

The Town

Agadez is sprawling town, so if you are not here long enough to orientate yourself, one of the young guides may be invaluable. You might find yourself invited into houses (men should avoid looking at the women within the courtyard), and you'll see all the sights you ask about.

Spiring through the one-storey skyline to a height of 27 metres, the tower of the **Grande Mosquée** is a landmark whose fame has spread even beyond West Africa. Built in 1515, the mosque is a classic example of medieval Sudanic, with wooden beams protruding from the minaret like quills from a porcupine. Over the years the structure has been much renovated and was completely rebuilt in 1844, following the original style. In former days, the tower doubled as a sentry post, and it's worth climbing today for views of the town and surrounding coutryside. Though the mosque is normally off limits to non-believers, there's a guardian who, in exchange for a *cadeau*, will lead you to the top, providing you don't arrive at prayer time. He's recently become accustomed to *cadeaux* from wealthy tourists in the order of CFA10,000, and you may not be let in for much less.

The nearby *Hôtel de l'Air* served as the **Kaocen Palace** early this century. It's a beautiful building, and even if you don't stay here you should stop by for a look. The large dining hall is where the sultan formerly received his audiences and, it's said, where subversives were hanged after the 1917 Targui uprising. You can go upstairs to the rooftop terrace for an interesting perspective on the mosque and town.

Also in the centre, the massive *banco* structure of the **Sultan's Palace** is the current residence of the traditional city ruler. The Nigérien government has left the basic structure of the sultanate intact, but although he's often called upon to mediate in local disputes, the sultan has at best blunted powers at the state level. Agadez's main festivals always culminate at the informal public square in front of the palace.

The markets

Not far from the mosque, the **Grand Marché**, often called the Marché Moderne, is the town's main commercial venue. Tumbledown corrugated iron sheds sell a variety of goods, loosely divided into **food** sections (expensive, as most fruit and vegetables have to be trucked in), **tools**, **fabric** and so on. Many traders sell **crafts** aimed at the tourist trade, and this is one of the cheapest places to get Tuareg and Fula **jewellery** – quality is often wanting, however, since the shiny trinkets are often made from melted-down Algerian dinars or other alloys that quickly acquire a dull green patina. Leather goods – sandals, pouches and bags – also abound.

On the eastern side of the main north–south road that splits the town in two, the **Vieux Marché** is much less hectic, but worth visiting, since it lies in one of the town's oldest quarters. The dusty streets surrounding the market are tightly hemmed in by *banco* houses bearing the stamp of Sudanic and Hausa influence, with their smooth lines and decorated facades.

The town's most interesting trade takes place at the **camel market**, on the town's northwestern outskirts. In the mornings, camels, donkeys, sheep and goats are bought and sold in an open field bordered by stalls specialising in nomadic goods – mostly salt pillars, rope, water containers and mats. If you've never sat on a camel, you can do so here by approaching one of the Tuareg traders. In exchange for a small handout, he'll likely help you into the saddle and let you circle the area – not exactly an adventure, but it gives you a taste.

Silversmiths and saddlemakers

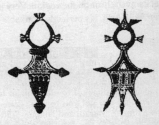

The refined craftsmanship of the Agadez **silversmiths** has become something of a byword in West Africa and even in some European circles. Though these artists make a variety of innovative jewellery and other objects from precious metals, they're best known for the **desert cross** pendants, especially the renowned *Croix d'Agadez*. (Other towns with their own unique crosses include Bilma, In-Gall, Iferouâne, Tahoua and Zinder.)

The smiths still work out of small *ateliers*, which you won't have to seek out, as young boys make it a point to propose a **tour of the workshops** to every tourist passing through. They say there's no obligation to buy, but once you're in the shops, the pressure to do so is pretty intense. If you're fairly certain you're not interested in making a purchase, perhaps you should decline the whole show. This said, watching the *forgerons* producing jewellery by the time-honoured **lost wax process** is genuinely interesting. A wax form of the intended object is used to make a clay mould, which is then baked in a charcoal fire until all the wax has trickled out of the holes made for that purpose; liquid silver is poured into the mould, which after cooling is broken to free the the hardened metal. Detailed carving and polishing can then take place.

The craftsmen are known not only for the quality of their work, but also for the honesty of their materials. Unlike the market vendors, they have a reputation for straight dealing – when they say something is pure silver, it usually is. Many of them still have silver coins from such unlikely origins as the Austro-Hungarian empire, which they'll show you, and – if you pay the price – transform into pieces of jewellery.

Other artisans specialise in the **leather work** for which Agadez is also famous. The workshops still produce *rahlas* (camel saddles), covering the wooden frames with treated hides that are then decorated. They also make colourful sandals, with red and green leather in the design, and Tuareg "wallets" – stylised pouches worn round the neck with compartments for money, tobacco and other necessities.

Directory

Air Niger The Agadez office of *Air Niger* is across from the *Hôtel de l'Air*. There are roughly two flights a week to Niamey.

Banks The only bank in town is the *BDRN*, located across from the Grand Marché, near the *Hôtel Sahara*.

Cinemas Check out the open-air *Cinéma du Sahel*, near the *aerodrome*: films are generally bad but the crowd reaction adds a little excitement to quiet Sahel nights.

Consulates There are **Libyan** and **Algerian consulates** in the town centre. You're not likely to be making last-minute arrangements to visit the former, but the Algerian consulate should be able to provide visas to those who need them.

Post Office Across from the tourist office on the main road (Mon–Fri 8am–noon & 3–5pm); *poste restante* service.

Supermarket You can find European canned and dry goods plus a selection of wine at *Ruetsch*, across the main road from the *Hôtel Agriboun*.

Tourist information The government-run *Office National du Tourisme* can set you up with tours of the town and surrounding region. Trips to the Ténéré or Aïr range from four to fourteen days (special arrangements can be made for longer excursions); a guide costs CFA12,000 per day.

Travel Agents One of the most efficient agencies is *Temet Voyages* (☎44.00.51), which hires out vehicles and guides for trips to the Ténéré and Aïr. They can even organise travel by camel caravan through the region. Very professional and expensive.

Water As in Arlit, it's perfectly drinkable straight from the tap.

MOVING ON FROM AGADEZ

The **gare routière** is on the asphalt road to Arlit, across from customs. Most of the *taxis brousse* from here seem to be heading to Niamey via Tahoua, though with patience you can also find transport to other major towns. *SNTN* **coaches** leave from next to the *gare routière* and can get you to Arlit (three times a week), Zinder (once or twice), Tahoua (three times), Maradi and Niamey (ditto). From the adjoining **lorry park** you can sometimes arrange to pay for a lift north to Tamanrasset and occasionally eastwards all the way to Bilma. If you have no luck here, you could try asking the truckers when they go through customs.

Driving south, Agadez to Zinder can be accomplished pretty comfortably in a day. The road is paved as far as the **Falaise de Tiguidit**, an escarpment with a wonderful view back across the plain. At the little village of ADERBISSINAT, halfway along the laterite stretch that follows, there's sometimes a cursory police check, and foreigners stopping here are regarded with interest and curiosity by traders in the market (leather goods, sweets and basic food). There's usually a fuel dump with diesel and petrol on the left of the road, before you enter the village. The small town of TANOUT (back on tarmac again – the whole section should soon be finished) is 140km north of Zinder and makes a suitable last stopping point for a cold drink at the one bar, and fuel if there is any. There's okay water at several wells – out with that forty-metre rope.

It's worth taking your time on this stretch, as it's a relatively narrow band of the Sahel, with sights you won't get elsewhere. The **Kel Gress Tuareg** live here in their mat huts. There are tall **Sodom apple trees** as well as many smaller, sometimes colourful, plants, and you might see an **ostrich** or two. Be careful walking in what appears to be tufts of grass – the seeds are contained in a small casing like a very spiky horse chestnut. These spikes draw blood, and if your shoelaces get tangled up with them it takes hours to get your shoes off.

The Aïr Mountains and east of Agadez

Two classic journeys from Agadez lead through the volcanic **Aïr Mountains** and the rolling dunes of the **Ténéré Desert**. *Pistes* wend through both areas, but in general they're extremely demanding. Roads get washed away during the rainy season or obliterated from sight when unheralded winds kick up a desert sandstorm. Partly because of the danger and partly because the scenic areas are potential sources of foreign exchange, the government requires all travellers to set off with an official guide, assigned to you at the tourist office. You'll also have to submit an itinerary of the places you plan to visit and specify the time you expect to take. Such formalities may cramp your adventurous spirit, but you can't forego them without running into serious problems (possibly arrest) later in your travels. And, of course, there are good reasons – dehydration and death in the desert – for following them meticulously.

The Route de l'Aïr

The **Route de l'Aïr**, accessible from the old Arlit road northeast from Agadez, is relatively good *piste* apart from the jostling washboard surface and one or two other unexpected hazards. The road forks at TELOUA (take a left), and about 15km later there's the possibility of a diversion left to TAFADEK, a wonderful deep spring that's great for swimming and diving, and reckoned to possess curative properties. Back on the main *piste*, 77km out of Agadez you branch off to the right from the Arlit road, and follow the sign to ELMÉKI, 125km from Agadez. This small town lies in a district whose tin deposits support the local population, and is also on the In Sarek *oued*, the water supply for the town gardens.

Just outside Elméki, you'll notice a number of tracks leading off the main route – they head to the mines and nowhere else. Follow instead the large *piste* to the village of KREB KREB, 72km from Elméki. (About 15km before Kreb Kreb, an alternative route leads directly north to ASSODÉ, a short cut that bypasses Timia.) Just after Kreb Kreb, the tracks lead through the beautiful **Agalak Range** – difficult driving, as the route crosses dry river beds (*kori*) and hidden stretches of sand.

Timia to Iferouâne

Roughly 220km from Arlit and a little more from Agadez, **TIMIA** is a large Tuareg-controlled village nestled between the Agalak mountains and a wide desert *kori*. On the outskirts of town the **Cascade de Timia** is a trickling waterfall for most of the year, but during the rains it develops into something quite spectacular. The town itself is one of the most beautiful oases in the Aïr, with extensive gardens and palms. Away from the box-like *banco* houses that spread over the valley, **Fort Timia**, built by the French colonials in the 1950s, commands a striking view of the *oued* and mountains.

North of Timia, the road continues some 30km to the **ruins** of ASSODÉ. Founded as long as 1000 years ago, it preceded Agadez as **capital of the Tuareg** and was once the most important town in the Aïr mountains. As trans-Saharan trade declined, so did the fortunes of Assodé. Kaocen dealt the final blow to the struggling community when he sacked it in 1917. The townspeople never returned, and today the site is a ghost town – its ruins lie east of the *piste* and you'll need sharp eyes to spot them. Many of the larger buildings – including the **grande mosquée** – are remarkably well preserved; a maze of empty streets winds through abandoned houses and squares.

Beyond Assodé, the tracks are progressively easier. After 90km, they lead to Niger's northernmost settlement of any size, **IFEROUÂNE**, a marvellous oasis on the fringes of the striking **Tamgak Mountains**. The *kori* running through town breathes life into some of the most beautiful **gardens** in the Aïr. Iferouâne has a small *campement*, the only bona fide accommodation on this route. And the town's craftsmen, especially the Tuareg **silversmiths**, have a reputation for excellence. It's a good stop-over for a day.

Iferouâne is also the starting point for visiting the Aïr region's wealth of **prehistoric sites**. Just north of the town along the Zeline *kori*, neolithic rock paintings of giraffes, cattle and antelopes can be seen on a distinctive boulder outcrop. More such paintings are found in the valley of the Aouderer *kori* near TEZIREK, 90km from Iferouâne.

The Ténéré

The route to Bilma takes you through what's often described as the most beautiful desert in the Sahara – the **Ténéré**. This is an arduous, 620-kilometre journey, with a great deal of very soft sand and hardly any supplies or water along the way – so it's strictly for the well-equipped. The brooding graves of victims of the crossing are among the markers along the route. You must have a guide, and usually be in convoy, before the police will let you go.

Leaving Agadez, take the Zinder road and, after roughly 2km, follow the eastern branch towards Bilma. The first 200-odd kilometres run through the Aïr, with alternating stretches of sand and rock-strewn *piste*. After 270km, you arrive at the site of the **Arbre du Ténéré**, formerly the only tree growing in a region the size of France. For over a hundred years it served as a landmark for desert crossers, until it was knocked over by a truck driver in 1973. A scrap-metal sculpture now marks the spot.

After 500km, you arrive at FACHI, a small Toubou and Kanouri village with a few hundred inhabitants and cool groves of date palms. In the centre, the fortified palace (*ksar*) is built of salt blocks – you can visit the **salt mines** on the eastern outskirts of town. The road covering the remaining 110km to Bilma is the same as that used by the *Azalai*, or camel caravans, that still ply the region. It's full of long stretches of soft sand, making the going tough at times.

Bilma and the pillars of salt

With around 1000 Kanouri, Tuareg and Toubou inhabitants, the small fortified town of **BILMA** is nearly a miracle out here in the middle of nowhere. Set against the backdrop of the **Kaouar Cliffs** – and as picturesque and hospitable as you could wish – Bilma owes its existence to natural water sources, which support a sizeable *palmeraie* and gardens. People in Bilma often refer to themselves, distinctively, as **Beriberi** (or Blibli), a term which has various interpretations but usually implies Hausa-Kanouri. Many Beriberi families are Hausa in all but name and some speak Hausa most of the time.

Bilma is best known for its **salt manufacture**, which just about maintains the viability of one of the desert's last camel caravan routes. Perhaps twenty to forty caravans a year make the trek from Agadez, with altogether up to a thousand camels in train – though in living memory the figure was sometimes 50,000 or more. Drought has now wiped out much of the livestock and changing priorities are attracting nomads to a settled lifestyle. And even on some of the hardest caravan trails, motor vehicles seem to make more sense. To make matters worse, the demand for Bilma's commodity has slackened in the traditional Hausa markets of southen Niger and Nigeria, where so much livestock has been lost in recent years. Bilma, meanwhile, is filled with unsold sixty-centimetre pillars of dirty brown, rock-hard animal salt. They continue to make them in moulds of saline mud, piling up vast reserves for a fatter future.

Tahoua

Niger's fourth largest town, **TAHOUA** is a major stopping point on the main road between Agadez and Niamey. Despite a large population of over 40,000 and a wide mix of peoples, the town hasn't really warmed up to travellers – indeed it was expressly closed to them until the mid-1980s, and could well be again (see "Recent Events" p.140). Your first clue of this is a signboard at the entrance to town with a list of everything that's forbidden, including taking pictures and sleeping with inhabitants. Such restrictions would be frustrating if there were any good reason to contravene them, but there's little to detain you here except the authorities. The rosy dunes that have settled permanently on the edge of town are pretty examples of their kind, but not worth a special detour.

Primarily a commercial centre, Tahoua does, however, boast a singularly animated **market**. It's one of those places where everyone in Niger – Djerma, Hausa, Bororo Fula, Tuareg, the odd tourist – comes together. The nomads bring salt pillars, dates, livestock and leather, which they sell to regional farmers who provide grain, cotton, spices, peanuts, tobacco and locally made indigo fabrics. Look out for the intermediaries called *dillali*, who bring together traders, help them strike a deal and even serve as translators. The market building is itself an attractive example of Sahel-inspired archi-tecture. Sunday is the main trading day.

Though Tahoua strikes you neither as modern nor traditional on first appearance, it does have some interesting older quarters, notably around the market place, where the house facades sport bas relief designs in the characteristic Hausa fashion.

Practicalities

Even if you don't stay in Tahoua, you're expected to stop at the **gendarmerie** for some paperwork. **Accommodation** is limited. On a budget, head to the *campement* and do your best to ignore the lack of hygiene and comfort – conditions especially hard to endure when you're paying CFA1500 to sleep on the ground and substantially more for a dingy room. The alternative is *Les Bungalows de la Mairie*, across from the town hall and surrounded by pleasant gardens. The set-up here is very good, with furnished, AC bungalows, but not so cheap at CFA8000. There's a good restaurant with European food.

SOUTHERN NIGER

As one of the country's rare green regions, **southern Niger** is the nation's richest agri-cultural belt. It also has the highest population density and is home to the biggest ethnic group, the **Hausa**. Renowned traders, with a long history of regional statehood, they are energetically commercial, the vigour of their towns being enhanced today by the region's proximity to Nigeria.

Dogondoutchi

Two hundred and thirty kilometres from Niamey, DOGONDOUTCHI (commonly shortened to "Doutchi") is a small town surrounded by sculpted red cliffs reminiscent of a western movie backdrop. It's inhabited by the **Maouri**, a people of Hausa origin who consistently refused to adopt Islam, even in the nineteenth century when the Sokoto *jihad* led to the conversion of the entire region. Islam has made some inroads in recent years, but this is still a stronghold of traditional beliefs, and local fetishers – notably the old chief of the nearby village of BAOURA BAWA – are said to have control even over the elements. Their powers are respected and feared.

The small *campement* on the edge of town – Doutchi's only place to stay – recently underwent renovations and should now be open. Lodgings are simple and cheap, with an adjoining restaurant and courtyard bar.

Birni Nkonni

Much of **BIRNI NKONNI**'s Hausa prosperity is owed to its position on the border. Some neighbourhoods actually spill into Nigeria, and a paved road pushes through the town to Sokoto, only 93km away. There's a lot of **trafficking** going on in these parts – most notably of petrol, which you can buy on the streets for a fraction of the price you'd pay at the pumps. Birni Nkonni also lies in one of the country's most fertile regions – the main streets are shaded by towering trees which were planted during the colonial period, and the **market** has a range of goods and produce that are expensive and scarce further north (Wednesday is the main day). It's an attractrive and soulful town, with traditional *banco* houses and characteristic dome-shaped granaries in the older neighbourhoods around the market.

Accommodation

Having a couple of comfortable and affordable places to stay, Birni Nkonni makes a suitable stopping point. The *Relais Touristique* is popular with overlanders – moderate rooms plus camping facilities at CFA1000 per person and CFA500 per vehicle. Their bar and restaurant are pretty good and they sometimes pull the TV onto the terrace in the evenings – a chance to see Niger's tiny TV station (*Télé-Sahel*) at work.The more upmarket *Kado Hôtel* has S/C rooms from CFA5000. Finally, there's a simple *campement* on the fringes of town as you head out on the Niamey road.

Maradi

With a population approaching 50,000, **MARADI** ranks as Niger's third largest town. Sometimes dubbed Niger's "groundnut capital", as over half the country's crop is grown in the surrounding region, it lies in an area of nascent industrialisation, and has already surpassed Zinder in economic importance. Formerly it was a province of Katsina – one of the original seven Hausa city-states – which lies over the Nigerian border, just 90km to the south. After the nineteenth-century Sokoto *jihad*, Hausa refugees fled to Maradi and eventually overthrew the Fula here. Sokoto and Maradi remained at odds for years afterwards. Despite these historical links, Maradi has lost much of its traditional flavour. After World War II, the streets were retraced on an anonymous-looking grid layout, since the older neighbourhoods had been subject to flooding after the rains.

This isn't to say that Maradi is devoid of interest. Foremost among the "sights" is the **Dan Kasswa Square**, bordered by the **Grande Mosquée** and the **Chief's Palace** – a colourful and typically Hausa confection. The **marketplace** is also impressive, spreading over a couple of blocks along the main Katsina road. You'll find a vast array of produce grown in the region or imported from Nigeria, at prices much lower than in Niamey (Monday and Friday are the main days). Over by the Hôtel de Ville there's a shady public garden, with gazebo-like bar in the middle and a church nearby.

Practicalities

Maradi has a number of useful facilities. There are two **banks** – the *BIAO* across from the *Sûreté*, and the *BDRN*, on the Katsina road across from the market. The **post office** is also on the Katsina road near the Palais de Justice. One street north of the *Sûreté*, you can get **car parts** at the *SONIDA* store, or try *Auto Service* near the *BDRN*. For medical needs, head to the *Pharmacie Populaire*, on the same square as the Grande Mosquée, or to the **hospital**, in the south of town.

There's a good selection of **hotels** in Maradi, foremost of which is the *Jan Gorzo* out near the airport (☎41.01.40). The government gives this one a four-star rating, though the standards have dropped rather dramatically since the days when it opened. But with a nightclub, one of the town's better restaurants and a **swimming pool** (open to non-guests for a fee, assuming it has water), it's still the best. In the town centre, the *Hôtel Niger* (☎42.02.12) is a much more modest affair, but not bad value with rooms starting around CFA4000. Cheaper still is the African-style *Hôtel Liberté* near the Petit

---

MOVING ON FROM MARADI

The main *gare routière* is right next to the market on the Katsina road. Vehicles head off from here to all points, but if you're heading for Kano or Katsina, note that you won't get into Nigeria without a visa and there are no issuing facilities at any of the border posts. Maradi's **airport** is east of the town, past the *Jan Gorzo* hotel. *Air Niger* has an office in the centre near the market and can give you prices and information on flights to Niamey.

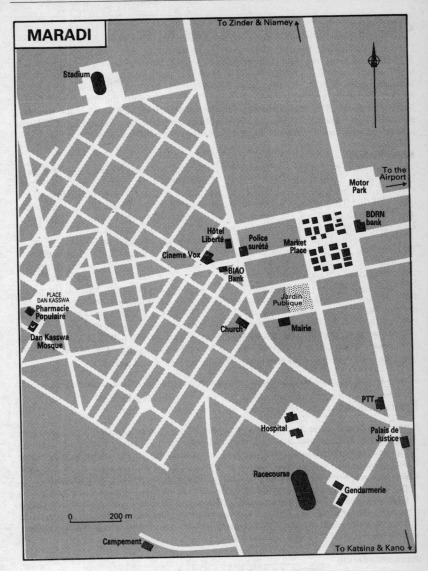

MARADI

Stadium

To Zinder & Niamey

To the Airport

Motor Park

BDRN bank

Hôtel Liberté

Police sûreté

Market Place

Cinema Vox

BIAO Bank

PLACE DAN KASSWA

Pharmacie Populaire

Jardin Publique

Church

Mairie

Dan Kasswa Mosque

PTT

Hospital

Palais de Justice

0   200 m

Racecourse

Gendarmerie

Campement

To Katsina & Kano

Marché: single rooms cost CFA2500 with shower and fan. On the south side of town, you'll also find the *Campement Administrative* – decent and fairly priced rooms.

The best place **to eat**, beyond the hotels' confines, is the well-known Afro-Lebanese *Chez Naoum*, for good and generous steaks, chicken and fish. There are loads of cheaper Nigérien eating houses in and around the market. *Le Yorumba*, just north of the motor park, is recommended.

Zinder

Formerly the largest town in Niger and briefly capital of the French colony, sleepy **ZINDER** has more recently seen its influence slide. It's still Niger's second city, but much of the commerce with Nigeria – long the main source of its wealth – now bypasses it via Maradi, on the faster Kano–Niamey highway. But even in decline, Zinder remains a centre of trade, as a quick stroll through the impressive Grand Marché confirms. Nor has it lost all its former glories: it retains some of the best and most satisfying **traditional Hausa architecture** anywhere, and the old town of **Birni** is even better preserved than its Nigerian counterparts in Kano, Zaria or Katsina.

Some history

The **Sultanate** of Zinder was founded by the Kanouri, descendants of the Kanem Bornu empire of the Lake Chad region. They settled here after being chased from northern territories by Tuareg invaders, and mixed with the Hausa population which itself had fled the region of Sokoto under pressure from the Fulani. In the eighteenth and nineteenth centuries, the Kanouri and Hausa joined forces to found the powerful **Damagaram state**, of which Zinder was capital. The sultan is still Kanouri.

Zinder reached its apogee in the mid-nineteenth century under the reign of **Tamimoum**, who greatly enlarged the boundaries of Damagaram, introduced new crops and developed trade. Under his rule, a vast wall or *birni* was erected around the town. Originally ten metres high and fourteen deep, this wall has long since crumbled, but ruins of it can still be seen around the old town. According to legend, the structure's invincibility was ensured by incorporating into the walls a number of Korans and several virgin girls. Under subsequent rulers, however, Zinder's fortunes were tied more to those of the slave trade than to the success of magic. By the end of the century one of the Sahel region's biggest **slave markets** was regularly held here. To support his empire, the sultan led frequent raids on vassal villages; captives were sold in town, taken to Kano and then force-marched down to the coast.

The **French** captured Zinder in 1899. With a population well in excess of 20,000, it was by far the region's biggest metropolis and remained the effective capital until 1927.

Practicalities

Zinder comprises three separate districts, so distinct they're almost individual towns. To the north, **Zengou** was the original Hausa settlement, formerly a stopping point for camel caravans. **Birni** – the old fortified town and site of the sultan's palace and Grande Mosquée – lies about a kilometre to the southeast. Between the two is the **new town**, with administrative buildings laid out in characteristic French colonial style.

Services are entirely concentrated in the new town. They include the hotels and better restaurants, three **banks** (*BIAO*, *BDRN* and *BCEAO*), the **post office** and a couple of **supermarkets**. There's also an outdoor cinema, *L'Etoile*. At some point during your stay (and the sooner the better), you're expected to check in at the **police**, whose office is on the avenue des Banques .

Accommodation

For such a large town, Zinder doesn't have an overabundance of **hotels**. The two main ones are both located off the central Place de la Poste. The *Hôtel Central* (☎51.20.13) is the cheaper alternative, a colonial-style pile with average comfort – single room with shower and fan from CFA3000. The outdoor bar-restaurant is a popular place in the evening; people often hook up here before going to the cinema or out on the town. Up the street, the *Hôtel Damagaram* (☎51.06.19) is bigger, nicer and correspondingly

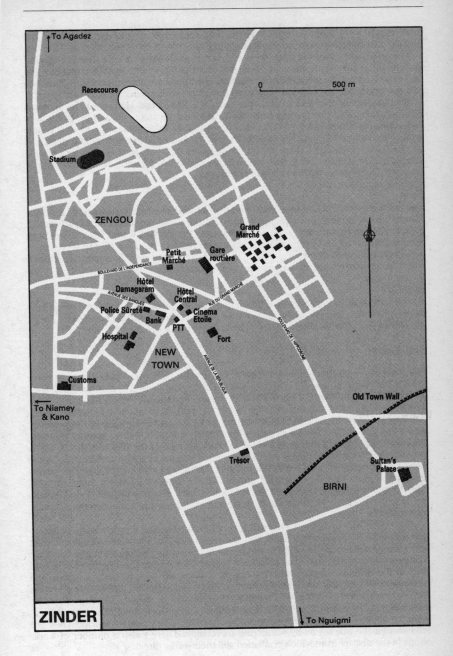

To Agadez

Racecourse

0   500 m

Stadium

ZENGOU

Grand
Marché

Petit   Gare
Marché   routière

BOULEVARD DE L'INDÉPENDANCE

Hôtel
Damagaram   Hôtel
Central
AVENUE DES BANQUES

RUE DU GRAND MARCHE

Police Sûreté   Cinema
Étoile

Bank
PTT
Fort

Hospital

NEW
TOWN

BOULEVARD DE L'INDÉPENDANCE

AVENUE DE LA RÉPUBLIQUE

Customs

To Niamey
& Kano   Old Town Wall

Trésor   Sultan's
Palace

BIRNI

ZINDER

To Nguigmi

more expensive – singles from CFA7000. Its furnished AC rooms are considered the best in town and the restaurant is excellent too.

The **cheapest places** in town are a number of small hotel-bar-restaurants clustered in Zengou, about twenty minutes' walk past the *Central* in the Agadez direction. The two rooms at the *Restaurant Dar-es-Salaam* are highly recommended (the food too) and the kindly *patron* is a good source of knowledge (in English) about Zinder.

Heading out of the centre the other way, the Kano road leads past the customs house (where, if you're driving, you may or may not be stopped), and on to the new *Hôtel Amadou Kourandaga* (☎51.07.42). Nice features are spacious Hausa-style rooms around a courtyard (from CFA7500/9000), and its own reliable water supply (the hotel was built over a spring) – there's even hot water on tap. This is where Zinder's middle classes go for a quiet drink; you might meet the chief of police or the mayor. The restaurant does good meals at a slight premium.

Food

Street food is easy to find in town, especially in the Place de la Poste, across from the *Hôtel Central*. Among the fare you'll find cheap salads, omelettes and *brochettes*. A popular African **restaurant** is the *Scotch Bar* near the market, where you can get large servings of rice or *pâté* with various sauces. Also reliable, the *Dan Kasina* serves inexpensive chicken and *steack frites*. Watch the hygiene everywhere, however, as **Zinder's water** is considered suspect and usually needs purifying.

Nightlife

For night-time drinking and sometimes a dance, the *Damagaram* and the *Central* both have night clubs. Popular spots you could check out in town include the *Moulin Rouge*, the *Oiseau Bleu* and the *Tropicana* – let us know what they're like.

The Town

The most obvious attraction in town is the old quarter of **Birni**, reached from the new town by following avenue de la République south beyond the old French fort (still used by the Nigérien military). This will take you past the **Grande Mosquée**, the front of which gives onto a large public square facing the **Sultan's Palace**, a two-storey *banco* building set apart by its size. There are tombs of the former sultans in the grounds, which you should be able to visit with authorisation from the Mairie. Another noteworthy residence is that of the Fulani chief, located just east of the mosque; the facade is decorated with colourful raised motifs, a common feature of Hausa architecture. All of Birni's buildings have been left in the traditional style, and walking through the narrow streets you get a real sense of what life was like in Zinder's heyday a hundred years ago. An unobtrusive house behind the mosque is marked with a bronze plaque indicating that the explorer Heinrich Barth stayed there during his mid-nineteenth-century visit to Zinder.

Also interesting is Zinder's **Grand Marché**, in the **Zengou** district. Long an important way-station between the Sahel and the regions to the south, the Zengou market still unites a wide range of peoples and is one of the country's biggest centres of trade (Thursday is the main day). Salt pillars are brought down from the Ténéré and are sold next to the **animal market**, with its Tuareg, Fulani and Bousou traders. Hausa and other peoples from the south sell a variety of local and imported goods in and around the arcaded market building, which dates from the colonial period. This is perhaps the best place in the country to get quality **leather** – for which the Hausa have a long-standing reputation – at inexpensive prices; sandals, bags, pouffes and pouches are sold around the market or by wandering merchants. There's also a number of workshops in the district from which craftsmen sell their wares direct.

Zengou has seen the introduction of modern cement buildings and corrugated iron roofs – elements that are completely absent in Birni – yet the **traditional flavour** is still strongly felt here. The oldest house in Zinder is in this quarter, and some of the town's showiest examples of Hausa architecture have been built here by the wealthier merchants. The pride in this style of decoration is by no means dead, and new – even quite innovative – examples are commissioned all the time.

Lastly, seek out the Zinder **regional museum**. It specialises in colonial history and has recently been granted £40,000 by Germany for the construction of a new wing – in homage, naturally, to Heinrich Barth.

On to Nigeria and Lake Chad

There's a good road the whole way from Zinder **to Kano**, but by public transport it's cheaper to break the journey at the border rather than do the whole trip in one vehicle.

In the **Chad** direction, road improvements have been undertaken as far as Nguigmi. The infrequently travelled route heads through a region that was part of the Kanem Bornu empire up to the nineteenth century, and today is peopled mainly by Hausa, Kanouri, Dangara and Manga. Just 22km from Zinder you arrive at the first **oasis** in these arid parts – MIRIA. The gardens here harbour date palms and groves of mango and guava. Sunday is the main **market day**; look out for local pottery.

A further 144km brings you to the small *sous-préfecture* of **GOURÉ**, where the rudimentary *campement* provides one of the few caravanserais along this route. It's another 330km to MAINE-SOROA, the next place of any size, where they make a living drawing salt from the saline earth. The desert is felt strongly east of this town, and you can see large dunes from the roadside. DIFFA, an administrative town on the banks of the **Komadougou River** – which sometimes flows into Lake Chad – is 75km further.

Finally you arrive at **NGUIGMI**, a full 1500km from Niamey and nearly 600km from Zinder. An important town during the days of the Kanem Bornu empire, when it was home to the semi-nomadic Kanouri princes, Nguigmi became wealthy from its position on the trade routes to the **Kaourar oases** (whence salt was brought by caravans) and, of course, from its site on the shores of **Lake Chad**. Today access to the lakeshore is difficult: it has shrunk much farther south and virtually disappears in periods of drought. Nguigmi is devoid of basic facilities (including petrol stations), so stock up in Diffa. A very arduous *piste* leads north of here to Bilma. If you're heading **into Chad**, Nguigmi is where you take your official leave of Niger and drive or find a ride east, then south, around the lake zone to Ndjamena.

MALI

MALI

Historically, geographically and from a travel perspective, **Mali** is West Africa's centrepiece. Long a bridge between the north and the south, the area outlined by the butterfly shape of the present country formed the meat of three great **empires**, the oldest of which was **Ancient Ghana** which flourished as early as the third century. The region's location on the main **caravan routes** and the banks of the **River Niger** later fuelled the rise of the powerful **Mali** and **Songhai** states, which lasted until the sixteenth century and the Moroccan invasion. The political stability and unity of previous centuries was never recovered thereafter.

Reminders of the country's great past are remarkably intact. Camel caravans still make their way from salt mines in the Sahara to **Timbuktu**, where you can visit a fourteenth-century mosque built when the town was one of the world's most prestigious centres of learning and culture. Wooden *pinasses* continue to carry their cargo along the river from here to **Djenné** – a great commercial town that spawned numerous technical innovations including the Sudanic style of architecture now common throughout the region. Boats also ply the river to the Sahelian town of **Gao** – formerly the capital of the Songhai Empire and final resting place of the **Askia kings**.

Tempering the romance of the country's opulent past is the more immediate spectre of **poverty**, evident even in the capital **Bamako**, a city virtually devoid of modern symbols of prosperity. Mali lacks substantial mineral resources and is almost wholly dependent on its agricultural and animal production, but recent droughts have devastated the country. Between 1983 and 1985 harvests failed almost entirely, and as much as three-quarters of the livestock was lost. People swarmed from the countryside to already crowded towns and, having lost everything, nomads were forced into a sedentary lifestyle and a cruelly inadequate wage economy. Faced with a growing crisis, the government took pragmatic steps to increase production and denationalise state enterprises – only one of which was profitable in the early 1980s. The long-maintained socialist veneer was rubbed off, in 1985 rain returned to the country and, by 1987, Mali was achieving a small grain surplus.

Despite these encouraging signs, the effects of drought are still visible today and the country's position remains extremely precarious. Mali is faced with a staggering and seemingly irreducible debt and, every year, the Sahara creeps south, converting arable land, only twenty percent of which is cultivable even now, to dust.

Travel in Mali

In the absence of other resources, the government took notice of Mali's abundance of tourist sites. The sinister sounding *SMERT* tourist bureau has had a heavy-handed control of the industry, forcing visitors to pay for organised excursions and sleep in expensive state-run hotels. They hold an almost complete monopoly in popular regions where it's very difficult for travellers to move about freely or escape the mandatory guided visit.

Recent signs, however, indicate a more relaxed and confident attitude to tourism. You no longer need to obtain the once obligatory tourist card, for example, and the photo permit has been abolished. Fewer towns require that you register with the police during your stay, though too many still insist that you do. This fraying bureaucracy means that travelling independently through Mali requires more imagination and persistence and, above all, more good humour on your part than usual.

In the end, however, it is indubitably worth the effort, because Mali breathes the very essence of West Africa and condenses more good reasons to visit than any other coun-

FACTS AND FIGURES

The **Rzfepublic of Mali** was known as **Soudan Français** – the French Sudan – during the colonial period. The name Mali was chosen for its historical resonance and significance for the Mande- (or Malinké-) speaking people of the region. Spreading across nearly 1,240,000 square kilometres, an **area** five times the size of the UK and three times as big as California, much of Mali lies in the Sahara or Sahel regions and the **population** barely tips eight million. The military government is controlled by a single party, the *Union Démocratique du Peuple Malien*, with **General Moussa Traoré** acting as head of state since his coup d'état of 1968. Mali's **foreign debt** stands in excess of £1 billion, equivalent to about one sixth of the estimated cost of building the European channel tunnel.

try in the region. The **River Niger** is magnificent (unforgettably so at dawn) and offers the chance to make the last great **river journeys** in West Africa. Several of the **old cities** carry their ragged history with immense grace – though Timbuktu itself can strike a depressing note. But remarkable **visual and cultural contrasts** in close proximity are Mali's hallmark. Hiking through the fractured **Dogon country** – where traditional culture has survived to a remarkable degree – is a goal of most travellers. If you approach it carefully it's possible to get right inside this fascinating district and to some extent into one of the region's most interesting non-Islamic cultures. Mali's **musical output** – currently stoking the pistons of the international record industry with the likes of Salif Keita, Ali Farka Touré and Tata Bambo Kouyaté – is another major attraction, enough on its own to draw music lovers. Finally, Mali is the country best placed for **onward travel** to virtually anywhere in the region – by rail to Dakar, by trans-Saharan *piste* to the Mediterranean, or by road to the south-facing coastal states.

The country

The outstanding geographical feature of Mali is the **River Niger**. Known to the Greeks and Romans (who called it *Nigris*, whence Niger – a word which incidentally doesn't mean black, but rather comes from a Berber expression, *gher nigheren*, meaning "river of rivers"), the Niger long fascinated Europeans. But it took them nearly 2000 years – until the nineteenth-century exploits of Mungo Park, Gordan Laing, René Caillié and Heinrich Barth – to figure out its source and the place where the river emptied into the ocean. Today, 1300km of the river, from Koulikoro near Bamako to Gao, is navigable, and most of the population is concentrated on or near the Niger's banks. Without any exaggeration, the river is the nation's lifeline.

The headwaters of the **Senegal River** also flow through the western tip of the country, but despite these great waterways much of Mali lies in the **Sahara**. The extreme north is uninhabited desert, empty except for a few stranded oases and Tuareg camps. Between the desert and the river stretches the **Sahel zone**, mostly flat plains with scruffy bush and thin trees that are especially resistant to the arid climate.

Only a few ripples interrupt the overall impression of flatness you get as you travel across the country. West of Bamako, the **Manding Highlands** provide a rare hilly spectacle as they rise to heights of 500 to 1000m, and the **Bandiagara escarpment**, which winds across the landscape for some 200km east of Mopti, is striking for the sheer cliffs that drop some 500–600m to the plain. Other dramatic formations are found in the solid stone **Hombori Hills** a little further east, towering sheer to heights of nearly 1200m.

The people

Numbering roughly a million, the Mande-speaking **Bambara** are the largest linguistic community in Mali. Though concentrated in the region surrounding Bamako and Ségou, their influence spreads much further, due in large part to their language, which is one of the most widely spoken in West Africa. To the west, the **Malinké** are closely

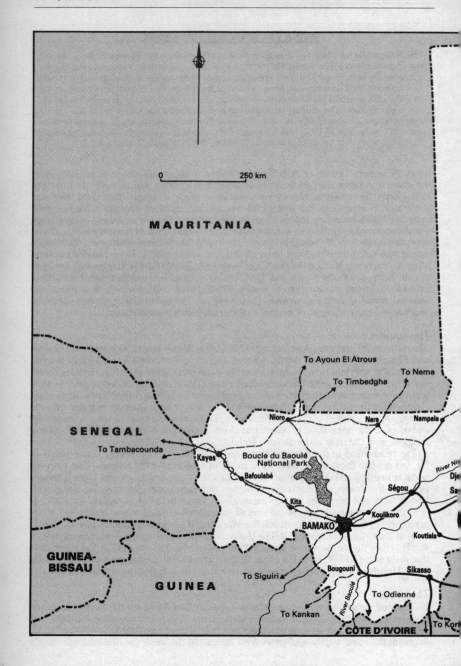

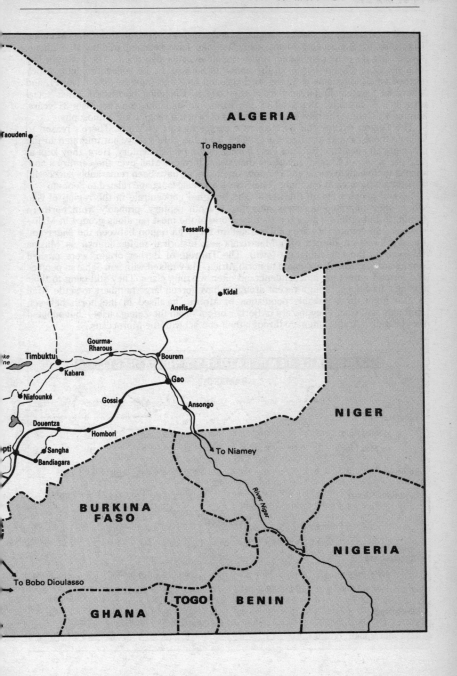

related and share a similar language and customs. Spread from the Manding Highlands to the Senegal River, many Malinké have retained traditional religions, despite Islam's early penetration in the region and repeated *jihads*. The **Senoufo** live near the Côte d'Ivoire border in the region of Sikasso. In the sixteenth century, they formed small kingdoms at Kong, Korhogo and Odienné (now in Côte d'Ivoire), and when the Songhai Empire collapsed they began expanding northward. Their social structure is strongly influenced by the *poro* – an initiation rite that lasts 21 years, during which time the men learn the secrets of Senoufo religion and philosophy.

The **Dogon** occupy the Bandiagara escarpment east of Mopti. There's reason to believe these people may have originated from the Nile Valley, but migrated to the isolated cliffs near the Burkina Faso border in the twelfth century. Here, they kept at bay the waves of Muslim invasions that swept through Mali over the centuries and, thanks to their tight social and religious organisation, have been remarkably successful at maintaining ancient traditions. They speak a Voltaic language related to Senoufo.

Several peoples live in the north. The **Songhai** concentrate in the region of Gao where they migrated in waves after the seventh century, probably from northern Benin. **Fula** herders – after the Bambara, one of the most populous groups in Mali – traverse the country but are concentrated in the delta region between the Niger and the northwestern border with Mauritania – a historical region known as Masina (Massina is the contemporary town). The **Tuareg**, of Berber origin, were pushed southward after the Arabs came to north Africa. They mixed with sub-Saharan peoples and formed numerous independent, and often warring, clans. They still cling to their nomadic traditions, though recent droughts have forced large numbers to settle. Mali is also home to a sizeable population of **Moors**, localised in the north between Timbuktu and Gao. They too are of Berber origin (from the Zenaga tribe), but adopted the Hassaniya Arabic language through their contact with the Moroccans.

AVERAGE TEMPERATURES AND RAINFALL

BAMAKO

	Jan	Feb	Mar	Apr	May	June	July	Aug	Sept	Oct	Nov	Dec
Temperatures °C												
Min (night)	16	19	22	24	24	23	22	22	22	22	18	17
Max (day)	33	36	39	39	39	34	31	30	32	34	34	33
Rainfall mm	0	0	3	15	74	137	279	348	206	43	15	0
Days with rainfall	0	0	1	2	5	10	16	17	12	6	1	0

TIMBUKTU

	Jan	Feb	Mar	Apr	May	June	July	Aug	Sept	Oct	Nov	Dec
Temperatures °C												
Min (night)	13	14	19	22	26	27	25	24	24	23	18	13
Max (day)	31	34	38	42	43	43	39	36	39	40	37	32
Rainfall mm	0	0	3	0	5	23	79	81	38	3	0	0
Days with rainfall	0	0	1	0	2	5	9	9	5	2	0	0

Climate

Without taking into account seasonal variations, it's tempting to sum up Mali's climate in two words – gaspingly hot. Rains generally last from June to September. The dry season takes over the rest of the year. Between October and February the **Harmattan** has a drastic influence on the weather, causing temperatures to drop quite low in the evenings (sweaters in the Sahara). Climate-wise, this is probably the best time to plan a trip, and it's also the period when the Niger is most easily navigable.

Arrivals

Despite being at the very heart of the region, Mali's transport links with other parts of West Africa aren't brilliant: from the north, desert tracks; from Senegal, a twice-weekly rail link but no real road; from Burkina and Niger, rough *pistes*; and only from Côte d'Ivoire a good highway.

■ Flights from Africa

Air Afrique handles most of the traffic from other capitals in **West Africa**. They offer regular direct flights from Abidjan, Cotonou, Dakar, Douala, Lomé, Niamey and Ouagadougou. In addition, *Aeroflot* has about two flights a month passing through from Monrovia, *Air Mauritanie* a weekly flight from Nouakchott and *Sabena* a weekly link from Banjul.

From **North Africa**, *Air Algérie* has a weekly flight from Algiers. They also complement *Air Afrique*'s flights from Niamey.

A link from **Central Africa** is assured by *Air Afrique* with a weekly flight from Brazzaville. *Ethiopian Airlines* can get you from Ndjamena, which they pass through en route from **East Africa** with flights from Addis Ababa (direct) and Nairobi (via Abidjan or Addis).

■ Overland

Coming from the north, one of the main **trans-Saharan routes** passes through southern Algeria and eastern Mali to Gao, from which point a new paved road leads all the way to Bamako. For the complete run-down, see Part Two "The Algerian Sahara", p.73–122. Other routes connect southern and western Mali with its neighbours.

From Niger

Despite the long border running between Mali and **Niger**, only one main road cuts through this difficult sandy region of the Sahel. From Niamey it passes through Tillabéri (where the tarmac ends) and up to Gao. It's a beautiful stretch that follows the **Niger River** and passes through numerous villages along the banks, but the tracks are bad and there are frequent patches of deep soft sand. Niger's state-run *SNTN* as well as private buses regularly ply between the two towns. From Gao, a good paved road leads all the way to Bamako. The alternative is to travel through Burkina, via Fada Ngourma, Ouagadougou and Bobo-Dioulasso.

From Burkina Faso

The quickest **routes linking Burkina and Mali** originate in **Bobo-Dioulasso**. From here, you can travel either to **Sikasso** (tracks are extremely shoddy on the Burkina side, especially during the rains) or to **Ségou** on a paved road. You can also get direct transport **from Bobo to Mopti via San**. Formalities present no special problem, but the *agents* seem particularly gung-ho to check your Health Card, so make sure you're up to date on cholera and yellow fever. Burkina border posts close at 6pm.

In the dry season it's possible to go directly into the **Dogon country** – setting out from **Ouahigouya** and passing through Tiou and then Koro. Vehicles rarely pass along this stretch, so if you're without your own car you'll face long waits for the occasional goods truck or tourist. As a compensation, this is one of the most rewarding ways of entering the Dogon country through one of the few corners not to be overrun with tourists.

From Côte d'Ivoire

The main point of entry from **Côte d'Ivoire** is along the road from Korhogo and Ferkessédougou to Sikasso, regularly linked by bus. Traffic along the stretch between Odienné and Bougouni (from where there's a good paved road to Bamako) is much less frequent.

From Guinea

After the Niger has swelled with seasonal rains (roughly August to December) it's possible to travel down the Milo tributary from **Kankan to Bamako by barge**. The 385-kilometre trip takes you past Niandakoro, where the Milo joins the Niger, and Siguiri, before terminating some five days later at Bamako. As adventure this is rewarding travel, but it's no pleasure cruise: you sleep on mats and share mediocre toilets; food is provided. The boats leave every two weeks or so (when water levels permit) and reservations can be made through the *CMN* in Bamako.

In the dry season, the main alternatives are by **bush taxi** from Kankan or Kouroussa (the latter an especially pretty route).

From Senegal and The Gambia

From Dakar, you can travel by road as far as **Tambacounda**, after which the best means of transport is the **train** to Bamako. Coming from **The Gambia** or **Basse Casamance**, you can also pick up the train in Tambacounda but it's routinely stuffed to overflowing. Full details in Part Seven "Senegal" p.351.

From Mauritania

The main overland route from Mauritania to Bamako starts at **Néma** (sealed road all the way from **Nouakchott**) and passes through **Nara** and **Kolokani**. Nara is busy and has pretty well everything but a bank. Water is usually paid for, fuel expensive, travellers very few and local people and officials friendly enough. The tracks between Néma and Nara may be impassable during the rainy season. It's best to get up-to-date information from other travellers before heading out.

From **Ayoun el Atrous**, you may also be able to get transport to **Nioro** (*campement*), from which point you can continue to Bamako, or to **Kayes** along a bad, beautiful track. Again, rains can make this route impassable and even in other seasons the frequency of vehicles may not add up to much. More on the Mauritanian parts of these routes on p.304 and p.332.

Red Tape

Basically, everyone needs a visa for Mali except the French. There's no embassy in London, the closest ones being Paris or Brussels (see *Basics* for addresses).

Coming overland, travellers without visas are often let into the country anyhow and allowed to obtain them upon arrival in the nearest *préfecture* (this most likely means Gao, Kayes or Bamako). It's a risk (you never know when you'll happen on an unbending immigration officer), and one that hardly seems worth taking, especially if coming over the Sahara (can you imagine going back to Algiers for a formality?). Unless you're flying into Bamako, it's advisable to pick up your visa en route in one of the neighbouring West African countries (offices in Dakar, Banjul, Conakry, Freetown, Monrovia, Abidjan, Accra, Niamey, Algiers or Tamanrasset) as they're usually issued with less fuss and cost a lot less.

■ Visas for onward travel

You can get visas in Bamako for Algeria, Burkina, Ghana, Guinea, Mauritania, Morocco, Nigeria and Senegal: Côte d'Ivoire and Togo entry permits are available at the French embassy. **Niger** is a problem since there's no representa-

tion, and the ease (or rather difficulty) with which visas for **Guinea** are obtained seems to be arbitrary and variable. Currently, however, the embassy in Bamako is one of the least troublesome places to get a visa – usually valid for a single entry of fifteen days, though you may persuade them to give you a month.

■ Other official hassles

The only **vaccination** normally required for Mali is yellow fever, although outbreaks of **cholera** occur from time to time, in which case this shot is necessary too. Best to take care of it before leaving.

Mali has in the past been notorious for its red tape, and it's still not the easiest place to travel, but some of the hassles are being abolished. **Photography permits**, for example, have been eliminated, as has the once obligatory **tourist card**. And although formerly you had to **report to the police** and get your passport stamped and signed in every town and village you stayed in, using up pages of passport in the process, this is no longer the case, with certain exceptions – notably everywhere east of Mopti.

SMERT

The national tourist organisation, **SMERT**, is obnoxiously overactive in the places travellers head to most – namely Djenné and the Dogon country. Here their employees try to impose guided tours, entry fees and limitations on your freedom of movement and generally act like unsuccessful pirates. SMERT's agents are in many other towns – Bamako, Mopti, Timbuktu, Gao – but fortunately keep a lower profile. While there are some exceptional staff and occasionally inspired guides, it seems likely much of their zeal in harassing tourists will increasingly be seen by the government as counterproductive.

Money and Costs

In 1984, Mali abandoned it's *Franc malien* in favour of the CFA franc (CFA50 always equals 1 French franc; CFA450–CFA500 = £1). Prices remain high, and you'll find the cost of transport and accommodation a definite drain on your resources. Given the long distances between towns (nearly 1000km separates Gao and Bamako) taxis will represent a big chunk of your budget.

Banks are rare throughout the country so you have to plan ahead. The *Banque de Développement du Mali* (BDM) has the most branches – in Bamako, Kayes, Sikasso, Ségou, Nioro, Mopti and Gao – but commission outside Bamako can be as high as 20 percent. Outside these towns, you can't expect to change money. This means that if you're coming across the desert make sure you've brought some CFA or at least French Francs (most places take them or you can always find someone to change) to tide you over until Gao.

Health

Outbreaks of cholera occur almost annually along the Niger so inoculation against it, along with the mandatory yellow fever, is well worthwhile: if there's an outbreak just before or during your visit you'll probably be required to have one anyway.

Bilharzia is another disease that remains all too common, especially in rural areas with slow streams and brackish water. Don't swim in such areas – especially if they're bordered by grass – if you want to avoid the disease. Even stretches of the Niger can be dubious, notably in the dry season when the low waters stagnate in many places. Along the entire course of the river, you'll see people bathing, doing their wash and bringing their animals to drink. Swimming in the river is, in fact, usually safe, and you'll probably find yourself doing it at some point. But keep in mind that while the river is a source of life, it can also carry disease; if you come to a place where no one from the area goes into the water, stop and ask yourself why.

Tap **water** is drinkable in Bamako and other big towns. In distant villages, wells and river water are commonly used for drinking and the purity may be suspect. Bottled water is available in the large towns. In places like the Dogon country, which receive a lot of foreign visitors, you can also find it, though the price of a 1.5 litre bottle may be as much as CFA2000. Purifying tablets or filters are a cheaper alternative.

Hospitals aren't promising as they tend to be under-equipped and overcrowded. For a serious problem, your best bet is either the *Hôpital du Point G* or the *Hôpital Gabriel Touré*, both in Bamako. Anything requiring surgery or setting may prompt ideas of repatriation. Consult your embassy (or the American embassy) for advice.

Maps and Information

There's little information about Mali available abroad and no real tourist offices. Maps are few. The *Société Malienne d'Exploitation des Réssources Touristiques* (*SMERT*) is the government-run tourist office, with branches throughout the country.

In places like Bandiagara or Djenné, your main preoccupation will probably be avoiding their "services", but consider taking advantage of their other offices, especially the one in Bamako. Here the staff are low-key and will give you information on car hire, route conditions or visa formalities. They also arrange excursions. Sometimes they have Bamako **city maps** kicking around the office and they'll give them to you free of charge along with a brochure, entitled *Le Mali Touristique*, that seems to date from the 1970s.

Michelin coverage of Mali on the #953 map is always fairly up to date. But the *IGN* also does a more detailed **national map** at 1:2,500,000, best picked up before leaving Europe as you may not be able to get your hands on one in Mali.

Getting Around

The longest navigable stretch of the Niger flows through Mali, and you can travel by boat virtually from one end of the country to the other, stopping along the way at historic towns like Ségou, Mopti, Timbuktu and Gao. It's an exciting – if at times tiring and uncomfortable – way to see the country, and the regular steamer service is almost unique in West Africa. To take advantage of the boats, however, it's crucial to time your trip with the rains (see below). If you can't schedule it, Mali does have alternatives to get you around the country, including a regular train service from Bamako to Dakar, flights linking the main towns and, of course, bush taxis.

■ Bush Taxis and Buses

Most Malians rely on *taxis de brousse* to get around the country and if you're without your own transport you will too, especially in the dry season when boats don't operate. Most of the vehicles seem particularly old and overcrowded relative to neighbouring countries. Prices are relatively high too – CFA20 or more per kilometre. In addition, drivers tend to charge quite steeply for baggage and you'll have to bargain hard.

The *Compagnie Malienne de Transports Routiers* (*CMTR*, ☎22.33.64) covers a limited number of routes by **coach** – notably Bamako to Ségou and Mopti. Although slightly cheaper than taxis, their buses tend to be old clunkers that go slowly and take forever to fill at the motor parks. You often see them broken down on the road. *SOMATRA* buses are faster and better.

■ Trains

The *Régie des Chemins de Fer du Mali* (☎22.59.67) provides the **rail link from Bamako to Dakar**. Trains cover the stretch between the two capitals twice weekly, leaving Bamako on Wednesday and Saturday mornings at 8am. First-class sleeper tickets cost nearly CFA30,000 for the thirty-hour trip (though you can pay for a berth once on board if you choose); second class CFA12,000. You can also put your vehicle on the train – an option that's not unreasonable at least to **Tambacounda** where you reach a paved road to Dakar. Even if you don't have transport, you might consider getting off at Tambacounda and continuing by bush taxi, to reduce both the cost of the trip and the boredom of the long stretches.

There are also trains from Bamako to **Kayes** (daily at 9am except Wed & Sat; 9hr) and to **Koulikoro**, the upper terminus of the Niger River steamers (daily at 5pm, arriving 7pm).

There are **student reductions** on the train fares at the start and end of term.

■ River travel

It's possible to travel over 1300km **along the River Niger**, between Koulikoro (60km from Bamako) and Gao. Such a trip can only be made, however, in the period during and just after the rains – roughly from July/August to the end of November between Gao and Koulikoro or from July to January/February downstream between Mopti and Gao – when waters are high enough for the steamers. The exact dates vary each year with the timing and volume of the rains. Aim for months in the middle if you want to be sure of travelling by boat.

Three **boats** now ply the waters: the *General A Soumare*, operating since 1965 and now refurbished; the *Tombouctou*, which has been going since 1979; and the *Kankou Moussa*, operative since 1982. The latter, being the newest, has by far the best accommodation. Reservations for the trip can be made through the *Compagnie Malienne de Navigation* (CMN) in each of the port towns.

According to the schedule, one boat leaves weekly in each direction, from Koulikoro on Friday evening and from Gao Thursday evening. In practice this only happens if at least two out of the three vessels are operable, which is not often. The only fairly predictable elements of the service are the **approximate journey times** between ports if there are no delays. The entire stretch takes five days from Koulikoro to Gao (downstream) and six days back again. Mopti–Kabara services should depart Sunday evening and arrive Tuesday morning. In the other direction, boats should leave Kabara Saturday evening and reach Mopti Monday morning; but these are indications only, not to be planned around.

There's a choice between **five classes** of accommodation: *first class A*, a double cabin with beds and wash basin; *first class B*, same as A, but with bunks; *second class*, four people to a cabin with two bunks; *third class*, rather cramped cabins with eight to twelve people but permission to sleep on the cooler upper deck; *fourth class*, floor space (if you're lucky) on the lower deck with the cargo. The last option is hot and dirty and a completely miserable way to travel.

Food is included in the price of first, second and third class accommodation. If you take fourth class, you fend for yourself, buying whatever's available (and it's often not much) in the ports of call. There's a **bar** serving cold drinks, but in theory fourth class passengers don't have the right to use it.

Smaller vessels

Anywhere along the Niger, and virtually year-round, you can find local **pirogues** to get you from A to B. These are rowed – or poled much of the time – and sometimes venture quite long distances with large consignments of rock salt or other goods. Details are given through the guide, but you can expect to pay from CFA1000 per person per day (50–100km) with food shared with the crew included. They provide the best, and perhaps the hardest means of seeing the Niger – from 10cm above its surface.

It's also possible to get **pinasses** along certain stretches of the river. These are large handmade boats covered with a type of matted overhang and run by motors. They operate mostly in the area around **Mopti** and you can get them from here to **Djenné** and sometimes as far as **Gao**.

Although comfort is rudimentary, there's a nostalgic sort of attraction to this type of transport which has been operating for centuries along the Niger. Some people even arrange to travel along the river in **barges** used to carry goods (especially grain) and even pile their vehicle on board. This last option is spur of the moment, however, and can't be counted on.

■ Planes

For domestic travel, *Air Mali* operates flights between Bamako, Goundam, Timbuktu, Gao, Kayes, Kenieba and Nioro. Due to severe financial difficulties and limited equipment, their schedules are frequently interrupted by delayed or cancelled flights. You won't normally find them included in the ABC world timetable. Frequencies of planes to the destinations listed above vary according to the size of the town, but there are normally at least a couple a week. You need to make Herculean efforts to get seats.

Sleeping – where to stay

Although Mali doesn't have much of what you could describe as luxury lodgings, the price of accommodation seems inordinately high for what you get. Much of the time, your choice is limited pretty much to the government-operated *campements* which jealously guard their monopoly.

In Timbuktu, for example, rooms in the shabby *campement* start at CFA7000, and the only alternative is the international class *Sofitel*. Private *pensions* do exist in some of the small towns, but it's rare to find anything for much under CFA3–4000.

The government has made **staying with Malians** illegal in towns where accommodation exists. They're quite serious about this and even if you don't particularly mind a brush with the *gendarmes*, note that your hosts will likely pay a higher price for this "offence" than you. In much-visited places – Mopti, Djenné, Timbuktu – a black market for rooms has arisen and people will offer to lodge you in their houses for a fee that you agree on beforehand. It works out cheaper, but leads to a ridiculous situation where you find yourself sneaking around corners and looking over your shoulder on your way home.

Coming across the desert, **camping** is allowed as long as you stay well away from urban centres (Gao and Timbuktu). Some towns also have *campings* (different from *campements*) where you can sleep quite cheaply on mats in the courtyard or in simple rooms.

Food and Drink

Mali's main staple, rice, is the favoured dish virtually throughout the country. It's often eaten with a thin beef broth mixed with tomatoes which you get in restaurants by ordering *riz gras*.

Obviously, there are numerous regional variations on this common standby. In the Dogon country, **millet**, or *petit mil*, provides the basis of nearly every meal and is prepared in hundreds of ways. Most commonly, it's served in a boiled mush called **tô**, and eaten with sauce. The Senoufo tend more towards tubers (**yams** and **cassava**), supplementing the rice and millet dishes which they eat less frequently than other peoples.

Food in Djenné has retained a strong Moroccan flavour. A type of **couscous** is eaten here, as is a noodle-like dish, known as **kata**, which is accompanied by meat. **Nempti** is a type of *beignet* (fritter) mixed with hot peppers, while **fitati** is a kind of thin pancake. During special celebrations the people make a pastry called **tsnein-achra** from rice flour and honey. The Tuareg, too, make a variant of couscous from a wild grain known as *fonio* or "hungry rice".

All along the river, of course, the people eat **fish**. One of the most common varieties is *capitaine* (Nile perch) – a boney little creature that's quite good when deep fried in oil or grilled over coals. In the northern regions of the Fula herders, beef, mutton and goat outsell fish, although for many people red **meat** is still a luxury.

The main **Malian beer** is *Flag*, expensive (and too rarely cold) relative to other countries. Beer and soft drinks – called *sucreries* – are worth a small fortune north of Gao. **Home-brewed beer**, made from corn or millet, is common to many different peoples – especially non-Muslims like many Dogon and Senoufo – and is known variously as *konjo*, *dolo* or *chakalo*. Lastly, sweet, yellow China **tea** is drunk all over the country, but with particular devotion in the north, and above all by the Tuareg.

Communications

Contact with Europe can be slow even out of Bamako. Though letters are inexpensive to send, they usually take their time arriving; estimate two weeks from the capital, as much as a month from the provinces. The PTT in Bamako has a *poste restante* service which seems to work relatively well.

Although Mali is connected to the IDD system, only in Bamako can you guarantee international direct dialling. From the rest of the country you can only make operator-assisted calls to Europe and **phones** are rare. It takes a while to get through, and it's often easier to call from the big hotels rather than small post offices, where queues tend to be long and obstructions many.

■ Languages

French is the official language and the one you'll have to deal with for all administrative preoccupations. A very small percentage of the population speaks it fluently, but it will always see you through.

The most widely spoken national language is **Bambara** (not very dissimilar from Malinké), used throughout the country, but especially in the

region around Bamako. Other languages include Pulaar (Fula), Senoufo, Songhai and Dogon.

■ The Media

The **press** offers nothing very promising. In French there's a news monthly called *l'Essor – la Voix du Peuple*, a weekly culture and sports journal called *Podium*, and a trimestral cultural magazine, *Jamana*.

Government-controlled **radio** goes out in nine languages but **TV** is broadcast – now to several solar-powered public viewing centres – only two hours a week.

BASIC BAMBARA

Compare these with the "Minimal Mandinka" words and phrases in Part Eight "The Gambia".

GREETINGS

Hello	*Aye ni ké*	How's the family?	*Den Baya ka kendé?*
Good morning	*Aye ni sogoma*	How's it going?	*Hera bé?*
Good afternoon	*Aye ni télé*	See you later	*An bé sogoma*

NUMBERS

1	*kélén*	6	*woro*	20	*mugan*	100	*kémé*
2	*fila*	7	*woronfila*	25	*mugan ni lolu*	120	*kémé ni mugan*
3	*saaba*	8	*seguin*	30	*bi sabi*	150	*kémé ni bi lolu*
4	*nani*	9	*konondo*	40	*bi nani*	200	*kémé fila*
5	*lolu*	10	*tan*	50	*bi lolu*	five franc piece	*dorem*

USEFUL EXPRESSIONS

How much?	*Jeli/joli?*	Where are you going?	*I bi taa min?*
I'll take it (give it to me)	*A di yan*	I don't know	*N'ta lou*
It's too expensive	*A songo ka gbélé*	I don't understand	*N'ma fahamuya*
Do you know of a cheap restaurant?	*I bi resitoran da duman don wa?*	Excuse me	*Ya fan ma*
Where's the bank?	*Bank bé min fan?*	What did you say? (please repeat)	*Aw kodi*
Show me the way	*Sila jira kan na*	Thank you	*I ni se*

MALIAN TERMS – A GLOSSARY

Azalai Desert caravans that formerly dominated Saharan trade. They continue today in small numbers, notably between the salt mines of Taoudenni and Timbuktu.

Cadeauter Transformation of the French word *cadeau* meaning gift, into a verb. Sometimes used by children in the expression: *il faut me cadeauter*, meaning "give me something".

Dourou-dourouni *Camion bâché*, pick-up or bush taxi.

Ghana In the historical context, usually refers to Ancient Ghana, the earliest Mande-speaking kingdom (precursor of Mali), the ruined capital of which, Koumbi Saleh, is located in southeast Mauritania. The name "Ghana" was the title used by its Soninke rulers.

Hogon Dogon priests who live in isolation. These elderly men represent the highest spiritual authority in the Dogon Country.

Mali An old empire (based southwest of Bamako) as well as the modern state, "Mali" is synonymous with "Manding" just as the language Malinké is the same one as Mandinka. Mali in Malinké means "hippo".

Oued Pronounced "wed"; French version of Arabic word designating a rocky river bed, dry except in the rainy season. The English equivalent is "wadi".

Pinasse Large wooden boat originally invented in Djenné to carry cargo. Though the basic covered design hasn't changed over the centuries, motors are often added today.

Pirogue Smaller boat that looks somewhat like a canoe. Used the length of the river for fishing and transport.

SMERT *Societé Malienne d'Exploitation des Ressources Touristiques*: the state tourist board.

Sudan/Soudan Former colonial name for the territory encompassing Senegal, Mali and Burkina Faso. Sometimes used today to refer to the same basic area. Thus Sudanic architecture refers to the style that originated in Djenné and has nothing to do with the modern state of Sudan.

UDPM The *Union Démocratique du Peuple Malien* – the single national party created in 1979 by Moussa Traoré.

Arts and Entertainment

Mali is world-famous for its music and a major part of the *Contexts* section on music is devoted to it. But Malian cinema is also thriving and, like music, making an impact across the world.

◼ Cinema

The government of Mali, like that of Burkina Faso, has an enlightened attitude to film. It has tried to encourage film makers by nationalising cinemas (it manages 25 out of Mali's 28) and controlling distribution.

The most famous name in Malian cinema is **Souleymane Cissé**. After studying film in the Soviet Union, he returned to Mali and launched his career with *Cinq Jours d'Une Vie* (1971), a film short that met with some acclaim. It was followed in 1978 by *Baara*, a full-length look at the relationship between workers and *patron* in a textile factory – a symbol of the injustices arising in a changing Africa. Cissé's second feature, *Finye* ("The Wind", 1982) was filmed entirely in

the Bambara language, yet became an international success. In it, the wind symbolises a new generation of post-independence youth, struggling against the repression of the military government. It was presented at Cannes, Carthage and Ouagadougou, where it won first prize. Cissé followed *Finye* with *Yeleen* ("Brightness", 1986) which was an international hit and at last saw his recognition as a major film maker. Through the main character, Nianankoro – an initiate possessed of magical powers – the film looks at the conflict of generations in Africa and gives non-African movie-goers an insight (at times spine-tingling) into traditional values.

Like Cissé, two other early Malian film makers also received their training in the USSR – **Djibral Kouyaté** and **Kalifa Dienta**. Kouyaté was the first Malian to make a fiction film, *Le Retour de Tiéman* (1970) – the story of a young agriculturalist who runs into the resistance of traditionalists when he tries to implement modern methods in his village. Dienta is best known for his feature *A Banna*, in which the main character, Yadji, takes his new bride from Bamako to meet his family in the village. The clash between urban and rural values comes into focus as Yadji's wife has to contend with everything from the authority of the griot to old-fashioned divisions between men and women.

Alkaly Kaba was another pioneer, best known for films portraying the conflict between western and African worlds. Early films (1970s) in this vein include *Wallanda* and *Wamba* .

Sega Coulibaly comes from a new generation of film makers whose experiences are rooted in post-independence society. Born in 1950, he briefly studied film in Paris before returning to Mali where he helped Kaba shoot *Wamba*. Coulibaly's first feature, *Mogho Dakan* (1976) follows a city teacher stationed in a village. His success with women (because of his status), backfires when one of them gets pregnant. Coulibaly's second feature, *Kasso Den*, is all-action, a prisoner wrongly jailed seeking vengence on the men who framed him.

Another new name, **Issa Falaba Traoré**, gained recognition for *An Be Nodo* (1980), the story of a promising student. Too poor to continue her studies, she brings shame on her family when she drops out of school and becomes pregnant.

Directory

AIRPORT TAX CFA2500.

BARGAINING The first price on tourist items in Mali is invariably huge. If you make a dismissive offer expecting it to be turned down, you an be caught out. Beware. It's easy to cause offence if, in the end, you refuse to buy the item.

HOLIDAYS Muslim holidays are celebrated with fervour in Mali, and during the month of **Ramadan** virtually everything closes down during the daytime – though night-time feasts make up. **Christian celebrations** – Christmas Day and Easter – are also public holidays as is New Year's Day and Labour Day (May 1). **National holidays** include January 20, the *Fête de l'Armée*; Africa Day on May 25; Independence Day on September 22; and the anniversary of Traoré's coup on November 19.

NAMES The same ones crop up all the time and it doesn't mean everyone is related; these are great, clan branches incorporating many strands and complex class and caste hierarchies. Classic Manding names are **Diabaté/Jobarteh** and **Traoré** (which are historically related), **Keita** (with its royal associations), **Kanté/Konté/Kondé** and **Kouyaté**. Fula names include **Bari/Barry**, **Diallo/Jalo** and **Cissé**. Many people have at least one Arabic name – Fatima, Moussa, Ali, etc.

OPENING HOURS Businesses tend to open weekdays from 8am to noon and from 3 to 6 or 7pm. Many are closed on Friday afternoons, most on Saturday afternoons. Government offices open weekdays from 7am–2pm and Saturdays from 7am–noon.

PHOTOGRAPHY Permits are no longer required, but as elsewhere discretion and good sense should be used before snapping away. In certain areas, such as the Dogon Country, there are still many taboos associated with taking pictures. Taking shots of people bathing in the river is a good way to get your camera confiscated: such voyeurism is not appreciated.

WOMEN'S ISSUES Women travellers don't find Mali a special hassle (beyond the interminable nuisance, for men and women, of bureaucracy and "cadeaux"). In the West African context, there's a good deal of proud, feminine freedom in the country, coupled paradoxically with the highest incidence of initiatory **genital mutilation**, including the horrific practice of infibulation. Look out for *Mali Muso* ("Women of Mali") published quarterly by the *Union des Femmes du Mali*.

A Short History of Modern Mali

The outstanding features of Mali's history are the old empires. Much of the modern country was part of the ancient Mali (or Manding) empire during its maximum extent in the thirteenth and fourteenth centuries. When the Moroccans crushed the Askia dynasty of the Songhai empire in 1591, they left Mali with a political vacuum, partially filled from time to time by the rapid rise and fall of mini-empires. The first was the kingdom of Ségou (Segu in many history books), founded in the early eighteenth century and almost immediately eclipsed by the Fula jihad that spread from Masina (Macina). This kingdom was founded in 1818 by Cheikou Ahmadou Hammadi Lobbo – a religious zealot inspired by Dan Fodio's religious war that had spread from Sokoto in present-day Nigeria. And from Senegal, the Tukulor marabout Al Hadj Omar Tall launched his own holy war, setting out in 1852 to conquer animist Mandinka districts to the east.

■ Arrival of the French

The Tukulor cavalry spread across the Niger belt with lightning speed, carving out an empire headquartered at **Ségou** that extended from Masina to Bandiagara. Increasingly, it came to be seen as a threatening obstacle to the designs of French colonials in St-Louis, Senegal, bent on commercial and military penetration into the Soudanese interior.

The governor of Senegal, **General Louis Faidherbe**, opted in the first instance for a diplomatic repsonse to Tukulor expansion and sent an expeditionary mission to Ségou. Arriving in 1868, the French signed a treaty with the new ruler **Ahmadou**, son of Omar who had been killed in battle in 1864. By 1880, the French were back to renew the treaty, but, although Ahmadou was increasingly suspicious of their motives and this time had the emissary locked up, it was too little too late. **French forces** had now advanced as far east as Kita and brought with them the parts of an armed gunboat which they assembled and launched at Koulikoro. They thus managed to control the river as far down as Mopti. But the Tukulor Empire based at Ségou refused to cede. Finally, the capital fell in 1890 and the other towns in the interior toppled like dominos in their turn – Djenné and Bandiagara in 1893 and, after fierce Tuareg resistance, Timbuktu in 1894.

Tieba and Samory

Meanwhile, resistance was already being fomented in the Senoufo country around Sikasso. The Malinké chief **Samory Touré** had been carving out his own small empire since 1861 and had taken the Senoufo strongholds of Kong, Korhogo and Ferkessédougou. He ran into conflict with

Tieba, king of Sikasso. Samory attacked Sikasso in 1887 and beseiged it for fifteen months, but the town resisted. The French, watching the rivalry with close attention, eventually allied themselves with Tieba, helping him reinforce his regional power. Tieba died in battle in 1893 and was replaced by his brother **Ba Bemba**. The new king, however, mistrusted the French and refused to follow through on the kingdom's commitment to help the colonials destroy Samory's influence. In May 1898 the French attacked and took Sikasso, and in September they captured Samory as he dashed southwest towards Liberia, hoping to get more weapons from the British; the same year, El Hadj Omar's son Ahmadou died in exile in Sokoto. France was now the sole power in the region.

■ The French Soudan

Confident of eventual victory, the French had already declared the **Soudan** an autonomous colony in 1890. Later it was incorporated into the colony of **Haut Sénégal-Niger**, of which **Bamako** was made the capital in 1908. The railway had been extended from Dakar to Koulikoro in 1904 and, with the creation of the *Office du Niger* – a national agricultural agency based in Ségou – the French hoped to turn Mali into the breadbasket of West Africa and even make the colony turn a profit through the production of cash crops like groundnuts and cotton. *Pistes* were traced through the interior to facilitate the transportation of crops and, in 1932, a dam was built near Ségou in the hope of turning hundreds of thousands of square kilometres into irrigable land.

From the beginning, however, the ambitious designs were frustrated. In the first place, the colonial authorities soon ran into a shortage of labour which they solved by forcibly recruiting volunteers from neighbouring countries, notably the region of the Upper Volta (Burkina Faso). In addition, much of the soil in the Sudan turned out to be too poor to support cotton production and rice was substituted. Finally, the *Office du Niger* had restrictive financial limitations. As a result, only a small fraction of the territory destined to become an agricultural miracle was ever exploited. Not that it made much difference to Malians at the time, since the production was almost exclusively destined for export to France.

World Wars I and II – African Participation

Of all the colonies in the AOF (*Afrique Occidentale Française*), Mali paid the highest price with the outbreak of World War I. The Bambara, especially, were recruited in large numbers to fill the ranks of the famous *Tirailleurs Sénégalais* – the **Senegalese Infantry**. These troops had already experienced European war as early as 1908 when they had been used by France to "pacify" Morocco. After 1914, tens of thousands of Africans were sent to Verdun where one in three died in the muddy war of attrition. Back in the Soudan, uprisings that sprouted to protest the draft of native soliders for a foreign war were brutally suppressed by the French authorities.

As if the price wasn't high enough, when the war was over, the new colonial governor, Just Van Vollenhoven, began mobilising civilians in the Soudan to develop agricultural production and the regional infrastructure. It was a move he deemed necessary to make the colony profitable after the stagnant period during the war.

Parallel to this, the French made minimal concessions to give Africans an extended role in the **politics** of their countries. By 1925, Africans could be elected to sit on the governor's advisory councils, although this of course gave them no direct political power. From the 1930s, laws were made to facilitate access to **French nationality** – a status considered by the government to be a great honour despite the sacrifices Africans had made during the war. But by 1937 only some 70,000 people in the entire AOF had been granted French citizenship and the vast majority of these were Senegalese. World War II had the effect of nipping political and social development in the bud.

Postwar Political Developments

The Second World War acted as a catalyst that gave rise to a new political consciousness in Africa and a determination to achieve political rights. Independence was still only envisaged by a very few, and de Gaulle himself ruled out this possibility at the 1944 **Brazzaville conference**, although he did say France was willing to make concessions, including greater African involvement in the respective governments.

In the aftermath of Brazzaville, three **political parties** were formed in Mali: the *Parti Soudanais du Progres* (PSP) headed by **Fily Dabo Cissoko**; a Soudanese afiliate of the *Section Française de l'Internationale Ouvrière* (SFIO) with **Mamadou Konaté** at the helm; and the *Parti Démocratique du Soudan* (PDS) founded by French Communists living in Mali. Though Cissoko came out ahead in elections to a constituent assembly in 1945, the first year of government was characterised by infighting among the parties – notably the PSP and the SFIO.

In 1946, Bamako hosted the ***Rassemblement Démocratique Africain*** – a vast political convention that brought together over 800 delegates from Senegal, Côte d'Ivoire, Guinea, Benin, Togo, Cameroon, Chad and Mali. The main theme was **union**: so that West Africa could speak with one voice, it was imperative the Soudan have a single voice within the RDA. Rather to the surprise of everyone, the three parties agreed to form a single *Union Soudanaise* within the RDA (USRDA). But within a couple of days, Cissoko announced that a bloc with what he called "unrepentant communists" was impossible and he reformed the PSP.

The Soudan swings Left

The next decade saw an intense **rivalry** between the PSP and the USRDA but, by 1957, the latter had clearly won the upper hand. This was in large part because the USRDA had more effectively distanced itself from Paris and had better grassroots organisation in Mali. After the elections of 1959, in which the PSP had fared so badly, they were constrained to join forces with the USRDA. On the eve of independence, there was no effective opposition to this party.

Changes had occurred within the USRDA when Konaté died in 1956. A moderate voice on the left, Konaté had advocated union of all the peoples of Mali. The void he left in the party ranks was quickly filled by more radical elements headed by **Modibo Keita**.

In the same year, the *Loi Cadre* drafted in Paris had opened the door to semi-autonomous governments in each of the territories of AOF. This led to divisions in the formerly united RDA as a cleavage arose between leaders like Sekou Touré and Leopold Senghor – who advocated the maintenance of a federal government in Dakar – and those such as Houphouët-Boigny, who advocated the maximum autonomy for each of the territories.

Federalists and Federation

Modibo Keita stood firmly in the camp of the Federalists, mainly because, as a poor country, the Soudan had a lot to gain from uniting itself with other territories (many of the country's colonial projects had been financed by AOF funds that originated outside Mali). Senghor's motives were more ideological and he pleaded for a politically united West Africa that would maintain good relations with France. It became more pressing to decide on the pros and cons of a federation after the **1958 referendum** where AOF nations voted to continue self-government within the French Union.

Sekou Touré was the only African leader who, for better or worse, had the courage to storm out of the French Union. Guinea was therefore excluded from any West African federation as well. Côte d'Ivoire was also out since Houphouët-Boigny had already stated loud and clear that he wouldn't have his country become "the milk cow" to feed the mouths of hungry neighbours.

In January, 1959, the four remaining members of the former AOF – Soudan, Senegal, Upper Volta and Dahomey – met in Dakar and drew up the constitution for a **federation** of their territories. Under pressure from Côte d'Ivoire, Upper Volta eventually backed out of its commitment and Dahomey followed suit. Hopes for a broad-based political union in the region had been pared down to two nations, but it was still an important step for pan-African ideals. The **Mali Federation** of Mali and Senegal was born.

Unhappy Union with Senegal

From the beginning, the alliance was uneasy. Keita was eager that Mali be granted independence. Senghor was more methodical, less hurried. De Gaulle himself helped sort out this problem by recognising in 1959 that it was possible for the federation to be granted **independence** while staying in the French Community. The Mali Federation did, in fact, become independent – on April 4 1960 – but the honeymoon between Senghor and Keita lasted barely two months.

Although numerous social and economic inequalities existed between the two former territories (which without doubt had an adverse effect on the union), the most glaring divergences were political and symbolised by the **clash of personalities** of the two leaders. Keita championed a Marxist approach to "African socialism". He was a man of (often admirable) principles who liked decisive action and who was unused to compromise. Senghor's approach was more measured and tended to favour dialogue and diplomatic action. He was especially cautious and pragmatic in his attitude to France which he hoped to keep as a friend and ally.

The stand-off between the two men – and as a consequence the territories they presided over – came to a head during the 1960 elections for President of the Federation, a powerful office that the Soudanese were wary of Senghor occupying. Senegal ruled out any alternative nominee and the brief federal arrangement collapsed.

■ Birth of the Mali Republic – a difficult labour

After the failure of the Federation, Keita set about creating the basis of the independent Malian state – a task of Promethean proportions at such short notice. He was helped, however, by the wave of **nationalist pride** and unity that swept the country, now destined to stand alone. Even Keita's former opponent, Cissoko, threw his support behind the USRDA in the name of the national cause. In September 1960, a special congress of the USRDA announced the implementation of a **planned socialist economy**. Shortly afterwards, Keita closed French military bases in Mali. He then set up state enterprises, starting with SOMIEX. This company had a monopoly on all imports and exports of primary products – an advantage French companies operating in the country hardly appreciated. In 1962, Keita pushed his country further into **isolation** by taking it out of the franc zone and creating a national currency, the Franc Malien. In the same year, a **Tuareg revolt** in the Adrar des Iforhas mountains northeast of Gao was savagely repressed by the army.

It was a difficult start, made even worse by the fact that Senegal stopped trains to Bamako for three years after the rupture and closed its borders with Mali. As Keita continued down his radical path (and he was sincere in his belief that Mali could be the spearhead of a new brand of "African socialism", though his conception of what this meant differed from that of other regional leaders) he distanced himself from other African nations. And the West, too, turned an icy shoulder as, in the middle of the Cold War he chose to ally his country with the Soviet Union. Opposition mounted grimly at home as the business community saw their economic privileges being eroded into state assets.

By the mid-**1960s**, Keita had created a heavy state machinery that dragged mercilessly on the nation's already fragile economy. The situation was characterised by numerous national enterprises (almost all of them running a deficit), a plethora of civil servants clogging the administrative machinery, a soaring balance of trade deficit and foreign debt, and a rapid weakening of the currency. Inflation soared and wages were frozen – a combination that wasn't calculated to enthuse Malians. By 1967, taking his queue from Peking, Keita was engaged in a **"cultural revolution"** to purge the nation of enemies within. He was supported in this by radical students, some of the unions, and by some lower grades in the civil service who resented the corruption of senior officials and business profiteers. But in the same year, Keita was obliged to devalue the Malian franc by fifty percent. The public outcry was immediate; the government's entire direction came under attack from all sides.

The coup

Keita seemed not to notice that opposition was sprouting up all around him. Believing the monumental role he'd played in his country's development absolved him from criticism by a populace faced with a deepening economic crisis, he was apparently surprised and aggrieved when a group of young military officers staged a **bloodless coup** in 1968.

The **Comité Militaire de Libération Nationale** (CMLN) was quickly formed, headed by a 32 year-old lieutenant, **Moussa Traoré**. Keita and senior members of his government were arrested and the former president died in prison ten years later.

Initially the military didn't challenge the nation's socialist orientation. The officers did, however, recognise the need to correct certain errors committed by the previous regime, to bring new order to the management of the economy and to boost production. To this end, Traoré continued to rely on Soviet and Chinese technical aid.

■ The Traoré Years

The first years of military rule brought little relief to the country. Overnight revival of the economy was impracticable, and the **drought** that ravaged the nation in 1973 and '74 had a disastrous effect on agriculture. Industrial development didn't fare much better and the **border war** with Burkina Faso, in 1974, put an extra drain on human and financial resources. Despite discouraging signs in the political and economic spheres, the military drew up a new constitution in 1974 that was approved in a plebiscite by what the government claimed was 99.7 percent of the population.

The new constitution, however, didn't go into effect until 1979 when a single party, the **Union Démocratique du Peuple Malien** (UDPM) was charged with running the country. Traoré remained at the head of government.

This symbolic transformation to civilian rule (cosmetic as it may be) was accompanied by a softening of the rigid socialist philosophy. This trend has been accelerated since a second drought devastated the country from 1983–85. In an effort to assure continued foreign aid, Traoré has worked hard to improve relations with the West, notably with France. Most of the state organisations and companies that were a tremendous financial burden have been privatised in an effort to dynamise the economy. Additionally, Traoré brought Mali into the CFA fold in 1985 which has encouraged investment.

Into the 1990s: hopes and fears

All these steps are signs that Traoré is seeking to bring his country out of the quarter century of political and economic isolation into which it retreated after the so-called Balkanisation of French West Africa on the eve of independence, and especially after the final rupture with Senegal. There have been i**mprovements in the agricultural sector**, and in 1987 Mali began to produce a small surplus. The industrial sector is still embryonic and the country hardly has money to exploit the few resources it possesses (small deposits of phosphates, uranium, gold and bauxite).

So Mali remains in a precarious situation. Traoré has never reconciled the supporters of Keita's socialist programmes to the need for pragmatic readjustments and he faced serious **student protests** from 1977 to 1981 which have continued, sporadically, ever since. How the military regime will react to the **pressure for democratic reforms** across the region, and from France, is uncertain. An unwelcome blip for the government has been the formation of a **Front for the Liberation of the Azwod Region**, a secessionist Arab-Tuareg group based in the north Malian Sahara, which has lately attacked a number of government targets.

But after more than two decades in power, Traoré faces few other political obstacles and has easily put down the coup attempts that have surfaced over the last twenty years. The relative upswing in the economy seems to have legitimised recent reforms and if the trend continues, Traoré is likely to be around for some time.

STOP PRESS: THE TUAREG

As this book goes to the printers, reports are coming from Gao of serious conflict between the Tuareg population of northeast Mali and government forces. Amnesty International has claimed there have been several extra-judicial executions. Gao has been under curfew and its phone lines restricted. These developments may have significant repercussions for the freedom to travel in the area.

BAMAKO

Although **BAMAKO** has grown quickly since independence, evidence of modernisation has hardly penetrated the dusty townscape, with its constant crowds of mopeds and people. Apart from a single highrise building, the *Hôtel de l'Amitié*, and a few other oddities like the *Banque Nationale* and the new Korean-built *Palais de la Culture* near the bridge, the most impressive structures in town date from the colonial era. Monuments to French administration – like the beautiful Ministry of Geology, the Ministry of Public Works and the *Grande Poste* – stand out among the single-storeyed trading houses and compounds (many of which are still made of *banco*) that line the broad avenues.

SOME HISTORY

As rock paintings (notably at the **Point G caves**) attest, Bamako is the site of ancient settlements, peopled as early as the African Paleolithic and Neolithic ages. Oral history traces the roots of the present town back to **Seribadian Niaré**, who sought refuge in the Bambara empire after being chased from the region of Nioro du Sahel in the seventeenth century. Upon arrival in the capital town of **Ségou**, Niaré married the sister of the king, **Soumba Coulibaly**. The couple had a son, **Diamoussadian Niaré**, and moved to the region around the present capital of Mali. A hunter of heroic dimensions, the son eventually killed a giant crocodile that had long terrorised the people of the area, thus fulfilling a prophecy and laying the basis for the establishment of a dynasty (also prophesied) that would grow up on the site. The Niarés thereby became rulers of the chiefdom at Bamako (crocodile-river).

An alternative version traces the beginnings to a hunter from Kong (Côte d'Ivoire), **Bamba Sanogo**. After killing an elephant at the spot, he received permission from the Bambara prince who had authority over the region to found a town which he named Bamba-Kong, after himself and his city of origin. After Bamba's death, with no offspring to inherit his position, Diamoussadian Niaré became chief.

The town grew to be a prosperous trading centre. By the time European explorers **Mungo Park** and **René Caillié** arrived in the early eighteenth century the population had grown to about 6000. By 1883 the French had built a fort here and soon afterwards colonised the region. In 1904 the railway line was pushed through from Kayes and in 1908 the town was made capital of the colony of **Haut Sénégal-Niger**. When independence was returned to the country in 1960, Bamako became the Malian capital. At the time, the town's population was some 160,000, but in the following years of rapid growth that figure has probably quadrupled.

Arrival

If you arrive by **bush taxi** (and note that if you're coming up-river from Mopti or beyond you'll get only as far as Koulikoro, 60km east of Bamako, which has a rail link to the capital), chances are you'll be let off at the **gare routière de Sogoniko**, about 8km from the centre on the wrong side of the Niger River. You can either hire a taxi from here to town (you'll get many offers from drivers who reckon you can't have had time to find out the going rate – under CFA2000 for a *déplacement*) or jump on a *Peugeot bâché* that takes passengers along a fixed route into town, over the magnificent bridge spanning the Niger. Once in the centre, either walk to a hotel or hire another taxi if you want to lodge in the outskirts. **Arriving by train**, the station is walking distance from most of the cheap places.

Bamako's **airport** is 15km south of town at Senou. After going through formalities, you'll have to hire a taxi to town: check the tariff with someone who looks knowledgeable – it shouldn't exceed CFA3000, except after midnight when it's CFA5000.

Around town: orientation and daily needs

Bamako is an easy town to walk around, and its centre conveniently compact. To get your bearings, the **Niger Bridge** serves as a useful reference point: the main road from here leads to the **Square Patrice Lumumba**, with the large French embassy and airline offices (*UTA, Air Afrique*). The avenue du Fleuve leads northward from this square changing names after a couple of hundred metres to become the **avenue Modibo Keita** – one of the town's main streets along which you'll find many banks, restaurants and stores. If you follow this street all the way to the end, you'll run into the **rue Baba Diarra** running parallel to the railway tracks. This passes by the **train station** and American embassy before arriving at a junction with the **boulevard du Peuple**. If you turn right, you can follow this street all the way back down to the Square Lumumba. These three streets form a triangle within which you'll find all the main elements of Bamako's commercial centre, including the large **Grand Marché** (central market) with its seductive Sudanese lines.

Hotels

Accommodation in Bamako is generally low quality and prices disproportionately high. Fortunately for budget travellers, a couple of hostels exist to help take the sting out of what would otherwise be a big drain on finances.

Budget class

La Maison des Jeunes, at the foot of the bridge spanning the Niger, provides a cheap overnight in a complex surrounded by a vast park. They offer bouncy spring beds in large unfurnished rooms with fans from CFA1000 per person. Collective showers and toilets are bearable. If you have a vehicle, you can **camp** in the park for CFA500 plus an extra CFA1000 per car. Different African educational groups often stay here and it could be a place to meet students.

Le Centre d'Accueil des Religieuses (*Centre d'Acceuil Catholique des Soeurs Blanches*), a salmon-coloured building towards the centre of town on rue El Hadj Ousmane Bagayoko (behind the Vox Cinema), also takes in travellers, though not enthusiastically. Their dorm rooms are clean and they provide mosquito nets, but doors are open only 8am–noon and 4–10pm, meaning you'll have to turn in early.

Inexpensive (for Bamako)

Pension Djoliba rue Testard (☎22.63.77). Just down from the American Embassy in a quiet neighbourhood near the railway station, this is the best of the "inexpensive" places and often full. Spacious ventilated rooms from CFA5000 or bedspace on the terrace for under CFA2000. Recommended.

Hôtel Majestic av du Fleuve (BP 321; ☎22.52.60). This boasts the best location of any in its class, but the dingy rooms seem overpriced, starting at CFA4500 for a single with fan. Some rooms have AC.

Bar Mali av Mamadou Konaté (BP 104; ☎22.27.81). A brothel with over-priced and dirty rooms (from CFA5500 with fan), the only advantage is its central location. A look in the dank downstairs bar gives enough idea of what the place is all about.

Buffet Hôtel de la Gare (BP 466). At the railway station, this is *the* place to stay for committed Rail Band and Ambassadeurs addicts.

Moderate

Les Hirondelles route de Koulikoro, 4km from downtown (BP 1026; ☎22.44.35). Like most of the hotels in the moderate range, this one's distance from the centre makes it practical only if you have a vehicle. Colonial-style S/C lodgings with swimming pool, restaurant and disco.

Le Lido av Kassé Keita, 5km from centre (BP 133; ☎22.21.88). An extremely popular hotel and, due to its small size, often full. S/C rooms with AC (from CFA12,000) plus a restaurant, bar and pool in a cool green setting.

Le Motel av Follereau (BP 911; ☎22.56.22). Another hotel with a large garden and setting near the river, though about 4km from the centre. The distance aside, the S/C rooms from CFA7000 aren't bad value.

Les Jardins de Niarela Niarela district (BP 2031; ☎22.36.67). Formerly known as the *Dakan Hôtel*, this place has pleasant bungalows grouped around gardens, from around CFA10,000.

Top notch

L'Amitié (BP 1720; ☎22.43.21/52, telex 433). Bamako's only skyscraper (construction started in 1963 by the Soviets), the *Amitié* is at an awkward age, too old to be modern and too new to be quaint. Still, as part of the Sofitel chain, it's the most comfortable hotel in town and boasts many functioning amenities: pool, cinema, tennis, mini golf and shopping gallery. Rooms from CFA25,000.

Grand Hôtel av Van Vollenhoven near the railway station (BP 104; ☎22.24.81, telex 578). Recently renovated, this colonial style hotel is smaller than the *Amitié* and has a charm the larger chain lacks. Swimming pool, tennis courts, restaurant, bar and disco; rooms from CFA20,000.

Food

Street food is getting increasingly rare in Bamako, but you can still find the occasional *caféman* in the mornings and roadside stalls in the daytime and evenings. A heavy concentration of such places can be found in front of the *Vox cinema*. Also try the motor park on the boulevard du 22 Octobre, opposite the *Comanav* office by the river.

Inexpensive food

Restaurant Central rue Loveran. One of the town's popular terrace restaurants with a daily *plat du jour* for about CFA1000. Open late in the evening for meals or drinks.

Le Berry Bar, across from the cathedral. Very near the *Central* and similar to it, although a little more expensive. Popular with ex-pats.

Patisserie Phoenicia av Mohammed V. With fresh croissants and other pastries, this is a good breakfast address. At lunchtime they serve sandwiches and *chawarmas*; in the evening ice cream, pastries and drinks.

Sabbaque corner of bd du Peuple/rue Gouraud. Another bar-patisserie with sandwiches and light meals at affordable prices. And another popular ex-pat hangout.

Dining

Most of the town's better **French restaurants** are in the hotels (the *Grand* has a good reputation for eating, as does *l'Amitié* with its three restaurants). Other restaurants of note are:

Les Trois Caïmans bd du 22 Octobre next to *Maison des Jeunes* (☎22.23.80 but only open Oct–June). Outdoor eating (bring a mosquito coil and put it under your table, the beasts are fierce) with specialities like braised *capitaine*.

Le Vietnam Near the *Caïmans* on the bd du 22 Octobre. A small restaurant near the river featuring very affordable oriental cuisine.

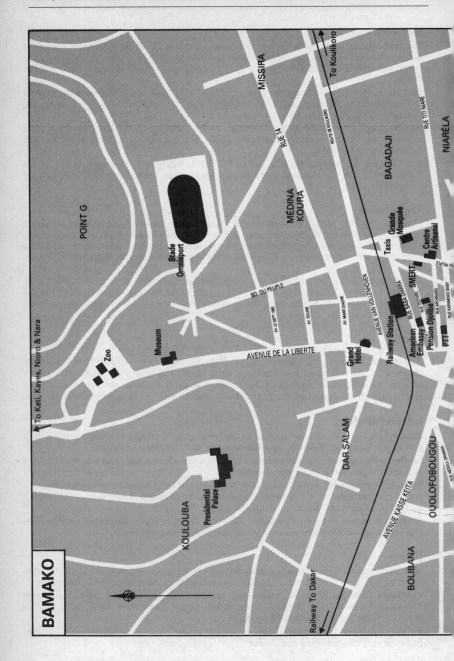

BAMAKO

POINT G

To Kati, Kayes, Nioro & Nara

Zoo

Museum

Stade
Omnisport

RUE 14

MISSIRA

To Koulikoro

ROUTE DE KOULIKORO

BAGADAJI

RUE TITI NIARÉ

NIARÉLA

MÉDINA
KOURA

Grande
Mosquée

Taxis

Centre
Artisanal

RUE LE PEUPLE

BD. DU PEUPLE

AVENUE VAN VOLLENHOVEN

AV 22 SEPT 1960

AV ROUME

RUE BABA DIARRA

SMERT

RUE TESTARD

RUE ARCHINARD

AV MARR DIAGNE

Railway Station

American
Embassy

Pension Djoliba

RUE KARAMOKO DIABY

PTT

AVENUE DE LA LIBERTE

Grand
Hotel

DAR SALAM

KOULOUBA

Presidential
Palace

AVENUE KASSE KEITA

OUOLOFOBOUGOU

RUE ABDOUL DRAMAN

BOLIBANA

Railway To Dakar

To Dakar

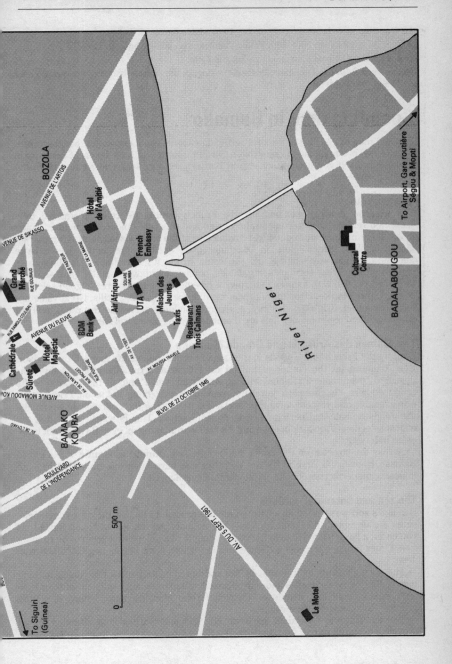

To Siguiri
(Guinea)

0   500 m

BOULEVARD
DE L'INDEPENDANCE

AV. DE L'OVAO

BAMAKO
KOURA

AVENUE MOMADOU KO

AV. DE LA NATION

Sureté

Cathédrale

Hôtel
Majestic

RUE FONGASE

AVENUE DU FLEUVE

RUE DE TAMOLO COULIBALY

RUE GOURAUD

Grand
Marché

VENUE DE SIKASSO

RUE PASTEUR

AV. DE LA MARNE

BDM
Bank

AV. DE L'IGER

AV. MOUSSA TRAVELE

BLVD. DE 22 OCTOBRE 1946

AV DU 5 SEPT. 1961

Le Motel

BOZOLA

AVENUE DE L'ARTOIS

Hôtel
de l'Amitié

French
Embassy

Air Afrique

SQUARE
LUMUMBA

UTA

Maison des
Jeunes

Taxis

Restaurant
Trois Caïmans

River Niger

Cultural
Centre

BADALABOUGOU

To Airport, Gare routière
Ségou & Mopti

La Gondole av de la Nation (☎22.52.23). Dependable European dishes.

L'Ecuelle av de l'Yser. Nice, with Franco-Antillean specialities, but not cheap.

Bol du Jade. The best Vietnamese cooking in town.

Restaurant Asia rue Titi Niare. Oriental cooking, in the capable hands of the owner of the *Nuits de Chine* in Mopti.

Spending time in Bamako

Bamako may not be one of the most gripping capitals you'll encounter, but the centre of the town is compact and enjoyable to stroll through – at least before it heats up in the afternoon. If you do nothing else in Bamako, be sure to spend some time in the excellent museum.

The markets

The **marché central** was built by the French during the colonial era, but they respected regional architecture in the design and this rose-coloured structure, which looks like a mosque from outside, remains one of the most visually satisfying market places in West Africa. Built in triangular plan, each of the angles has a large Sudanic-style gateway leading into the souk. Inside it's a veritable Aladdin's cave, divided into different sections – vegetables, poultry, basketwork, pottery and so on. A large part is filled with a range of hardware type goods. There's a really good selection of **rugs and blankets**, too, though you need fierce bargaining skills. Great value are local **cassettes** (CFA600). Nearby, a separate building serves as the **meat market** where neither customers nor flies are dissuaded by the blood and stench.

The Maison des Artisans and Grande Mosquée

Built by the French in the 1930s in the same Sudanic style as the market, the **Maison des Artisans** (at the corner of the bd du Peuple and rue Karamoko Diaby) was designed to promote traditional Malian art. Today you'll find all the various **crafts** produced here – leatherwork, jewellery, weaving, woodcarving and so on. Prices aren't unreasonable and you can have the satisfaction of meeting the craftspeople who make the goods on sale and perhaps seeing them in action. This is where you'll find the widest selection of artwork in town and it's well worth taking in, even if you're not interested in buying.

Across the street from the crafts market, the new **grande mosquée** was a gift to Bamako from Saudi Arabia. It's not one they can have been too enthralled by – an imposing modern concrete pile, of little architectural merit.

The zoo and botanical gardens

Bamako's **zoo** was a good idea whose time has passed. In theory, the cages and enclosures are designed to resemble closely the animals' natural habitats, and indeed, as you enter, a large fenced-in field harbours a couple of antelope that seem to be running free. Other inmates are less fortunate and the whole place seems neglected and run-down.

The scraggly **lions** look terminally hot and bored as they mark time doing nothing between feeds, while **gorilla** and **chimpanzee** will momentarily snap out of their lethargy in exchange for peanuts or (heaven forbid) chewing gum, before retreating grumpily to a corner of their cages.

The surrounding **botanical gardens** are vast and, with a little attention, could provide a beautiful retreat from the city. But these too are suffering from neglect.

The Museum

Banish the tawdry zoo from your mind, for Bamako's brand new **museum** is extraordinary. Housed in a low-rise building with smooth lines inspired by the architecture of Djenné, it contains remarkable masterpieces of African art. Inside, objects are beautifully displayed, with photographs discreetly lining the walls around the exhibits to put them in a broader context. Lighting is subtle and the museum comfortably air-conditioned – in short, it's more than you could hope for.

Something of a pioneering institution, the museum is engaged in efforts to repatriate some of the vast treasure-store of artefacts taken abroad in colonial times. They conduct research here and perodically round up materials from different parts of the country. The textiles collection – some of the cloth was restored in the museum workshop – is particularly strong. The collections are relatively small, however, and you can easily visit them in half a day. Part of the museum concentrates on objects from daily activities – **domestic utensils** as well as **forging** and **weaving** – and a large section is dedicated to the techniques involved in making some of the many types of **cloth** for which the region has a wide reputation; spinning, weaving, tie-dyeing and preparation of dyes. A separate section displays religious objects from Mali's various ethnic groups. Highlights include the stylised antelope **tyiwara** (chiwara) masks of the Bambara; various **Senoufo statuary**; and, of course, the world-renowned antique **Dogon sculptures**.

Point G

From the museum and zoo, you can walk up to the **north of the city** and to the hill known as **Point G**, the location of the main hospital. There are wonderful views from here, though they're possibly better still from Kolouba (which is mostly Presidential palace nowadays). Point G has abandoned cliff dwellings with old **rock paintings**.

A day at the races

Out at the dusty *course hippique* (racetrack) in Missira, off the route de Koulikoro 3km from the town centre, you can watch horse-racing most Sunday afternoons. It's a popular pastime with Bamako's more influential citizens. Between gallops, there's usually a bout or two of *lutte* – traditional wrestling.

Nightlife

Despite its slow pace during the day, Bamako has a satisfying nightlife, and one where the action only really gets going late. The most noteworthy venue, the **Buffet Hôtel de la Gare** – at the railway station – was an early showcase for the **Rail Band**, a government-sponsored group that went on to massive stardom and launched Mali's first international superstar, **Salif Keita**. Though Keita left the Rail Band to form the **Ambassadeurs** in the early 1970s, the *Buffet Hôtel de la Gare* remains a classic and popular spot and a good place to catch up on what's currently taking shape in Malian music. The Rail Band only plays now on Saturdays.

In the same area, near the American embassy, the **Cotton Club** is a newer place that has caught on in recent years. Open daily, it has a sizeable ex-pat clientele out to enjoy the latest in African music. In the centre near the cathedral, the **Black and White** is a long-standing haunt that is still packed to overflowing almost every night. **Antipodes** is part of the French cultural centre complex, with a bar and occasional music to add to its mainly theatrical reputation.

Canoë Club, near the bridge, and **Blue Notes**, on the route du Sotuba/rue Titi Niare, are favoured hang-outs of young Bamakois and French volunteers.

Among the **hotel discos**, *Le Village* at the *Grand Hôtel* draws the largest crowds and features a good mix of music. Western disco figures more prominently at *Le*

Dogon, the slick and expensive nightclub at the *Hôtel de l'Amitié*. Outside the centre, *l'Africana* at the *Hôtel les Hirondelles* is one of the town's cheaper venues and, for that reason, usually lively even on slow weekdays.

Directory

Airline offices
Aeroflot rue Loveran (BP 93; ☎22.56.93).
Air Mali Immeuble Hachkar, av de la Nation (BP 27; ☎22.33.36/22.57.41, telex 2568).
Air Afrique Square Lumumba (☎22.49.39).
Sabena 6 av Kassé Keita (BP 2056; ☎22.63.61/22.37.92).
UTA Square Lumumba (☎22.22.12).

Banks Hours are short – weekdays from 8am to noon. The best bank for changing money or travellers' cheques is the *BIAO* on av Mohammed V; quick service and no problem, especially for FF. The other three banks – the *BDM* and the *Banque du Mali* (opposite one another on av du Fleuve), and the *BMCD* (av Modibo Keita) are likely to look confused when you say you want to change money and will probably send you to the *BIAO*.

Car Hire In addition and in preference to *SMERT*, car hire is available from: *Gamby-Auto*, av de la Nation (☎22.24.46); *Europcar, Grand Hotel* (☎22.24.81); *Falaye Keita, Hôtel de l'Amitié* (☎22.43.25).

Cinemas The nicest cinemas are at the *Hôtel de l'Amitié* and the newer cultural centre on the other side of the Niger from downtown. Besides being more comfortable, they also show the most recent films. Dated action movies are more common in the smaller theatres of which the *Vox*, near the market, is the most central.

Cultural Centres The *Centre Culturel Français*, off the bd de l'Indépendance, has a good library including French newspapers and magazines. They also organise sporadic exhibitions, shows and movies. Similar activities are arranged at the *USIS* – the cultural branch of the American embassy – located near the train station.

Embassies and Consulates include:
Algeria Badalabougou district, behind the river.
Belgium place du Souvenir (BP 187; ☎22.51.44).
Burkina Faso Consulate (BP 9022). Visas CFA7500, available next day.
Canada route de Koulikoro (BP198; ☎22.22.36, telex 2530).
Egypt Badalabougou (BP 44; ☎22.35.03, telex 2407).
France Square Lumumba (BP17; ☎22.28.36).
German Fed. Republic av de Farako, Badalabougou (BP100; ☎22.32.99, telex 22529).
Ghana 125 av de la Nation (☎22.31.55).
Great Britain Honorary Consul Mr Harvey Smith (BP 2069; ☎22.20.64).
Guinea (BP 118; ☎22.29.75, telex 2576).
Italy (☎22.35.40).
Mauritania rue Titi Niare, Bagadadji (BP135; ☎22.48.15, telex 2415).
Morocco (BP 2013; ☎22.21.23, telex 22430).
Netherlands Bureau de Coopération Néérlandais (BP 2220; ☎22.43.27, fax 22.36.17).
Nigeria Badalabougou (BP57; ☎22.57.71).
Senegal av Kassé Keita. Visas CFA2500, available next day.
USA av Mohammed V (BP34; ☎22.58.34, telex 2948).

Football Sundays at the *Stade Omnisport*.

Post and Telephones The *poste centrale* is on rue Karamoko Diaby, not far from the market. There's a reliable **poste restante** service here.

Supermarkets *Malimag* and *Somiex*, the two main supermarkets, are both located near the *Hôtel Majestic*. They have canned goods and toiletries, but the relatively paltry selection reflects import difficulties in Mali.

Swimming pools *L'Amitié* has the nicest pool in the centre of town, but it costs CFA1200. The one at the *Grand* is small, but okay for cooling off and only CFA700.

Tourist information *SMERT* has its main office in the bd du Peuple, opposite the grande mosquée (BP 222; ☎22.59.42, telex 2433) as well as a branch in *l'Amitié*. The office in Bamako is a bit more relaxed than those in Mopti or Djenné and the staff are happy just to give you information rather than force excursions or guided tours at you. *SMERT* handles everything from car hire to hotel or airline bookings, and can help with papers (including visa extensions). Of course they also offer a wide range of excursions if that interests you.

Travel Agencies Common destinations for organised tours include the game parks, Dogon country, Timbuktu and Djenné. In addition to *SMERT*, other agencies (which often have cheaper excursions) include *Manding Voyages* (BP 2224; ☎22.47.36) and *Dogon Voyages*, near the cathedral (BP 2442).

Visa Extensions These are available at the *Sûreté Nationale* on the av de la Nation (Mon–Thurs 8am–2pm, Fri–Sat 7.30am–12.30pm). They may require a couple of days to deliver – you can get the necessary forms at *SMERT*.

MOVING ON

Bamako has four main **motor parks**. The most central, and the smallest, is located near the bridge on the boulevard du 22 Octobre 1946, near *les Trois Caïmans* restaurant. Vehicles leave from here for **Kayes and Guinea**, and it's also the *SOMATRA* bus station for **Ségou**, **Mopti** and **Gao**. Vehicles for most other destinations – and all bush taxis – go from the larger *gare routière*, 8km from the city centre at **Sogoniko**. To get there, pick up a shared *bâché* or charter your own taxi *déplacement*. There are also two smaller *autogares* in Bamako; one, which serves **Nara**, behind the grande mosquée, and another at the Nouveau Marché by the Stade Omnisport for **Nioro**. For **bus** schedules, call the *Compagnie Malienne de Transports Routiers* (BP 208; ☎22.33.64, telex 2539).

By Train

The **train to Dakar** leaves Bamako on Wednesday and Saturday mornings. Saturdays are preferable, since this is when the newer, more comfortable Senegalese train runs. The thirty-hour trip costs around CFA30,000 in first class and CFA12,000 in second. Sleeping berths are available (though barely worth it due to disturbances at the border through the night) and it's also possible to put cars on the train to avoid wear and tear on the miserable roads that link Mali and Senegal.

Daily trains also leave for **Kayes** in the west, and **Koulikoro** to the east of Bamako – the main embarkation point for the Niger River ferries. There are further details in Part Seven "Senegal" on p.351. For the latest information on schedules and prices, stop by the train station, or call the *Régie du Chemin de Fer de Mali* (*RCFM*), rue Kassé Keïta (BP 260; ☎22.29.67, telex 2586).

By Boat

Ferries to Gao depart from Koulikoro, 60km from Bamako. Rapids between the two towns make it impossible to travel directly by water from the capital and you must take the train or a taxi to get around them. Boats from Koulikoro operate roughly from late July or early August until November, when the rains swell the river to a suitable level. Boats from Koulikoro leave on Tuesdays and Fridays. For reservations (get them early, especially for second and third class) and up-to-date information on departures, contact the office of the *Compagnie Malienne de Navigation* (Mon–Thurs 7.30am–2.30pm, Sat 7.30am–12.30pm) on the boulevard du 22 Octobre 1946, on the river bank across from the motor park. You could also try calling the head office in Koulikoro on ☎26.20.34 (BP 10 Koulikoro).

CMN can also give you information on **barges to Guinea**, which leave Bamako about once every two weeks between August and December (or when the water level permits). The 385 kilometre-trip to Kankan lasts about five days – a period entirely devoid of creature comforts since the boats were designed to transport cargo, not people. If you can put yourself in the right frame of mind, however, it's a cheap and exciting way to travel. For more information on boats operating in Mali, refer to the "Basics" section.

Flying out of Bamako
Flights within Mali are frequently delayed or cancelled, and *Air Mali* schedules for flights to Goundam, Timbuktu, Gao, Kayes, Kenieba and Nioro should be taken with a pinch of salt. Each of these towns is serviced by at least one departure a week from the airport, 15km southeast of central Bamako in the suburb of Senou. Shuttles are meant to run there from in front of the *UTA* office on the Square Lumumba, but you'll need to confirm that information as well as schedules and prices at the *Air Mali* office on av de la Nation.

KAYES AND THE WEST

Often ignored by travellers, **western Mali** contains some of the country's most beautiful scenery. It's a region of woodlands and rivers where the Baoulé, Bakoye and Bafing rivers rush from the **Manding Mountains** through the hilly landscapes of the **Malinké country** before joining forces to form the **Senegal** river. This was the heartland of the thirteenth-century Mali kingdom under Sundiata Keita, before it expanded into an empire to include Djenné, Timbuktu and Gao.

The Senegal flows through the realm of the Fula-speaking **Tukulor** people, which extends west from Kayes – the regional capital and an important commercial town of 50,000 people. In the northwest, **Nioro du Sahel**, sweltering in pre-desert heat, attracts a wide mixture of **nomads** – Tuareg, Fula, Moors – who converge for the large market. The route from these northern parts back to Bamako leads through **Bambara country** and numerous farming villages. Along the way, the road skirts the **Boucle du Baoulé** national park – a huge reserve with the nation's best game viewing.

Unfortunately – and this is the reason that so few people head out this way – **"roads"** through the region are among Mali's worst, and many of them aren't even open after the start of the rains. In this case, the only reliable means of transport is train, and the railway won't get you off the beaten track.

Kayes

The last major town before Senegal, **KAYES** (pronounced "Ky-eh") is an important administrative centre. It served as capital of the Haut Sénégal-Niger colony, until the seat was transferred to Bamako when the rail tracks pushed through from Dakar in the early part of the century. With the arrival of the **railway line**, river traffic along the Senegal dwindled dramatically and so did Kayes' importance as the last major port in the interior. Even so, it's still a large town and a big trading centre. Its market attracts a wide range of regional peoples – Tuareg, Fula, Sarakole and Moors, who mix freely with the Malinké population – and the place has a nice feel. The actual climate, though, is less inviting – Kayes has the dubious honour of being Mali's, and Africa's, hottest town, with afternoon shade **temperatures** between March and May crackling into the high 40°s centigrade (say, 120°F). Indeed, Kayes adds a whole new dimension to the notion of staying inside because of the weather.

Accommodation and practicalities

Due to its size, Kayes is graced with a bank, airport, pharmacy and a couple of reliable if unfancy hotels. Before checking into one, you should stop by at the **police** and have your passport stamped. The best **accommodation** in town is the Moorish-style *Hôtel du Rail* (☎22.55.86) located across from the station. Spacious S/C rooms are reason-

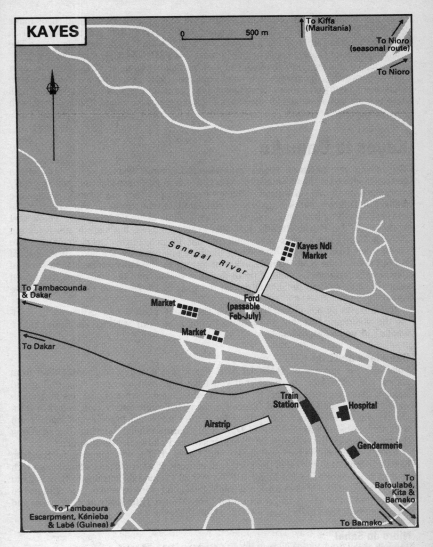

able, with cheaper ones starting at CFA5000. Near the market is a local hotel, the *Amical*, fairly standard for its type – a double bed with fan in a stark room here costs from CFA2500.

Moving on

The obvious form of transport out of Kayes is the **train**, which will get you to Bamako or Dakar in any season. When heading **towards Senegal**, you may consider taking the train only as far as **Tambacounda** (285km from Kayes) from where good roads make travel to the coast by bush taxi quicker and cheaper than continuing by rail. Disembarking in Tamba is also a good way to avoid Dakar if you're heading for the The Gambia or Basse Casamance. The border post is at **KIDIRA**, 105km from Kayes.

During or shortly after the rains, you may be able to negotiate a trip down the River Senegal, travelling **by pirogue**. Conceivably, you could get as far as **Bakel** or even **Matam** by this means. From these towns, you can continue to St-Louis by road. You'll have to work out all details for the trip, including price, accommodation and food, with your prospective *piroguier*.

Kayes to Bamako

The railway line **between Kayes and Bamako** passes through scenic hills with a denser bush cover than you might expect. If you're entering Mali by train the early morning scene makes a welcome change from the previous day's bleak, Senegalese plains.The **Bakoye** and **Senegal rivers** run parallel to the tracks for a good part of the journey, thrashing into rough rapids at several points along their courses. The lowest of these are the **Felou Rapids**, just 10km east of Kayes, but slightly disappointing since a hydroelectric dam was built by the French further up-river. The more spectacular **Gouina Falls** are 65km further up, towards Bamako. Just east of **Bafoulabé** are the **Kale Rapids** followed in turn by the **Billy Falls**, 270km short of Bamako. Unfortunately, none of these rapids is visible from the train, and you'd need your own transport to be able to get off the road that follows the railway line to see them.

If you travel by bus or taxi from Kayes, the "main" **road** heads further north, skirting the Mauritanian border, and passing through the town of **Nioro du Sahel** before winding its way south to Bamako.

Bafoulabé and Kita

Following the rail tracks, **BAFOULABÉ** lies in a scenic region about 130km from Kayes, rife with places to discover if you have your own transport. The Bafing and Bakoye rivers converge at this town to form the Senegal, which continues northwestwards to Kayes and the ocean. There's a cheap but rudimentary *campement* in town should you decide to use it as a base for further travels. A branch road leads south from Bafoulabé towards the **Fouta Djalon highlands** in neighbouring Guinea. Along the way, it passes the striking cliff formations of the **Falaise de Tambaoura**.

Roughly midway between Bamako and Kayes, **KITA** was founded as Sundiata Keita's second Mali capital in the thirteenth century. It's a small agricultural town with its own *campement*, *Le Chat Rouge* (BP 43; ☎57.30.45), and daily trains to Bamako and Kayes. If you're into Malian **music**, it might be a good place to stop over a night or two – many traditional griots hail from round here. **Mount Kita Kourou**, with caves and rock paintings, rises quite impressively behind the town.

Nioro du Sahel

Though the *piste* leading to Bamako via **NIORO DU SAHEL** is more travelled and normally in better condition than the one that passes through Bafoulabé and Kita, both roads are frequently washed out in the rainy season. In that case, you may be restricted to train travel.

Some 250km from Kayes, Nioro is a seventeenth-century town built on a plateau. It is famed for its **mosque**, one of the most important in the country after Djenné. The heat here can be oppressive, and shade from the few trees provides little respite.

Despite its relative isolation, Nioro has a police and customs post, petrol stations, a hospital and an airport. **Accommodation**, though, is limited to a modest *campement*.

Nioro is a common departure point for **Mauritania**, but traffic along the 212-kilometre *piste* that leads to the desert town of AYOUN EL ATROUS (see p.332) is thin at the best of times and can dwindle to nothing between July and October – the rainy season. Check for trucks around the market place.

If you're driving, you can short cut the route to Bamako, saving nearly 100km and bypassing Nioro, by forking east at SANDARÉ for DIÉMA.

Nioro to Bamako

From Nioro there are still 430 or so kilometres to go before you reach the capital. Just after DIÉMA the road passes through the **Vallée du Serpent**. This valley gets its name from the tortuous route followed by the **Baoulé River** as it snakes down from the Manding Mountains near Bamako to join the **Bakoye River**.

About 125km before Bamako, the Nioro road passes through the small administrative village of KOLOKANI. There's a *campement* here where you can spend the night before heading out to visit (providing, again, that you've got your own transport) **Ouenga** and **Kolani** lakes. These twin bodies of water are located 15km southwest of the TIORIBOUGOU, a Bambara village on the Bamako road, 24km south of Kolokani. During the rains, the lakes swell to a length of 5km and are the site of traditional fishing activities.

The Parc National de la Boucle du Baoulé

The **BOUCLE DU BAOULÉ NATIONAL PARK** covers 3300 square kilometres, but it's actually part of a larger conglomeration that includes three game reserves – **Fina**, **Badinko** and **Kongassambougou**. In total this ensemble covers more than 7700 square kilometres of wooded savannah that lie only 100km from Bamako as the pied crow flies.

The park is open during the dry season, from November to May. The most common entrance from Bamako is via Kati and Negala – a small village on the Kayes road, from where a *piste* branches northward to Faladyé. Before arriving at this latter village, another *piste* leads westward to the *campement* at the entrance to the park on the Baoulé River. On entering the park, the tracks lead to another *campement* at the village of MADINA. From here, *pistes* head out in all directions for game viewing. Another *campement* – less frequently visited than the former two – is located in the northeast of the park at the village of MISSIRA.

The Boucle du Baoulé derives its name from a huge bend, or "buckle", in the **Baoulé River** as it heads north from the Manding Mountains towards Diéma before making a sharp hairpin turn and heading back south to join the Bakoye. The course of the river forms the northern borders of the park and contains a forested area harbouring numerous Bambara villages and a significant animal population.

Common among the wildlife are a variety of **antelope** species, **buffalo** and **warthogs**. With more luck, you might hope to spot **giraffe** and possibly **lions** as well, though these latter beasts have been victims of widespread poaching, even since the park was founded in 1954. Boucle de Baoulé is also the home of most of Mali's estimated 400 surviving **elephants**.

All three *campements* in the park are tiny, and you should therefore book accommodation in Bamako – it's possible to do so through *SMERT* (see Bamako "Directory"). If you don't have your own transport, it may be worth checking with them anyway as they operate excursions to the park.

SÉGOU AND AROUND

Between Bamako and the Delta Region lies a broad expanse of territory where numerous kingdoms rose to power after the demise of the Songhai Empire. The most important were the **Bambara Empire** of Ségou and the **Kénédougou Empire** in the **Senoufo country**, with **Sikasso** its capital. Although they were fated to be eclipsed almost as quickly as they sprang up, these towns, together with **San**, have remained commercially important thanks to their positions on well-travelled routes, and the surrounding districts count among the nation's most agriculturally productive. Mali's best **road** runs east from Bamako through Ségou to San and Mopti, with connections south to Sikasso.

Ségou

Arguably the second largest town in Mali, **SÉGOU**, 240km northeast of Bamako, was capital of a vast empire in the eighteenth century, and in more recent history became an important French outpost and headquarters of the *Office du Niger* – an irrigation scheme originally planned for the exploitation of cotton. Reminders of the colonial period still stand out in graceful administrative buildings in the neo-Sudanic style at which the French excelled. Traditional Bambara architecture has also held its own against more modern and easily maintained cement buildings, and today whole districts of this quiet tree-lined town are filled with rust-coloured *banco* houses. Away from the busy **market** (the main day is Monday), much of the modern activity focuses on the banks of the **Niger**, with its *pirogues* and crowds. It's a very pleasant stopover.

The history

The **kingdom of Ségou** had its roots in the seventeenth century when a Bambara chief, Kaldian Coulibaly, brought his people to settle in the area. In 1620 his son established the village of Ségou-Koro (old Ségou), about 10km from the present town. In 1712 the able and despotic **Biton Coulibaly**, widely considered the true founder of the kingdom, became *fama*, king. The army he formed carved out a huge kingdom stretching from Timbuktu to the banks of the Senegal River, and the enemy soldiers captured during the conquests were marched to ports in Senegal and Ghana where they were traded with slavers for firearms. Along with the Songhai to the north, the Ségou Empire was one of the earliest in the Sahara to obtain guns, which were used effectively to subdue rival powers. The kingdom thus continued to grow under the reign of **Ngolo Diarra** (1766–1787) and his son **Monzon Diarra** (1792–1808).

The Ségou rulers developed a **nationalist policy** where all rights were accorded to loyal Bambara subjects but the conquered peoples were excluded from the system altogether. It was a tenuous situation based purely on force of arms, and when the Fula empire of Masina arose in the northeast, disgruntled elements in the Bambara country rallied to it, assuring the demise of Ségou. In 1861, El Hadj Omar conquered Ségou and forced the inhabitants – who had remained one of the few **non-Muslim** groups in the Sahel – to convert to **Islam**. The French took the city in 1892.

Sleeping, eating and other practicalities

The traditional place for **inexpensive** accommodation has been the *Office du Niger's Campement* (☎32.00.78), at the entrance to town near the Mairie (follow the signs to the *Centre d'Acceuil*). A small colonial building with tidy rooms with fans (from CFA3000), and a good restaurant and bar, this place is often full. If you don't mind searching a little, ask for the *Maison des Jeunes*, north of town, where you can get

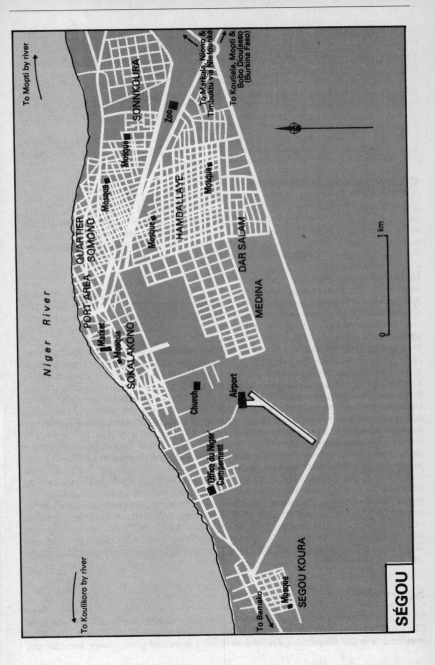

SÉGOU

simple lodgings from CFA1000 a night. There's also a new privately run hotel in town, the *Bakaridjan*, which is more central (between the *BDM* and the river) and slightly less expensive (rooms from CFA2500–8000). The management is very friendly and they have a good restaurant and nightclub set in the courtyard.

Of the moderate places, *L'Auberge* (☎32.01.45) is a popular choice, due to its location near the river: clean S/C rooms (some with AC) from CFA7000. The restaurant and bar here are popular with ex-pats. Slightly upmarket, the *GTM* (*Grand Toit de Medine*, BP 107; ☎32.02.79) has AC rooms from CFA5500 plus a popular **disco** with occasional live music and a restaurant recommended for fish.

Besides the hotel restaurants, try *Tantie J'ai Faim*, near the centre, for well-prepared local specialities or the popular *Snack Golf* (CFA750/dish). Other places for inexpensive **Malian food** near the motor park are *La Gargotte* and *Au Bon Coin*.

Moving on and travel information

Frequent **bush taxis** along Mali's main highway link Ségou with Bamako in the west, and San and Mopti in the east. Taxis also head to Sikasso in the Senoufo country, further south, from where you can continue to **Burkina Faso**, although you'll make better time if you head to Bobo Dioulassa via San. In the rainy season, you can of course travel **by boat to Koulikoro** (port of call for Bamako) or all the way up to Gao. For more information on the river boats, see "Getting Around" p.181.

To Timbuktu by road

During the dry season, it's possible to zig-zag all the way across the delta by road. Although this alternative involves tackling long stretches of tortuous *piste*, it allows you to take in fascinating scenery along a little-travelled route. From Ségou, take the northern road to MARKALA, and then follow the road to MASSINA, 105km further. This route passes through the old city of SANSANDING, "the great marketplace of the Western Sudan" by the nineteenth century, according to Heinrich Barth. From Massina, you can make an interesting side trip (44km) to DIAFARABÉ – a small village located on one of the narrowest points of the Niger. In December, **Fula herders** descend on this village en masse as they lead their cattle from the Sahel grazing grounds to the southern banks of the Niger to await the return of the rains. The spectacle of hundreds of head of **cattle** crashing simultaneously into the water and swimming to the other side as herders prod them along is not quickly forgotten. Music and festivities accompany the event, but there's no set date. Check it out in Ségou.

From Massina, tracks lead north towards NAMPALA. After 154km, however, rather than turning west towards this latter town, follow the eastern road to LERE – a small village with a Friday **livestock market** that unites Moorish, Tuareg, Bella and Fula herders from the region. Lere is 136km from NIAFOUNKÉ, a village surrounded by dunes on the banks of the Niger, whose most famous sometime resident is guitarist Ali Farka Touré, currently building a big family house here. Accommodation is available at the town's small *campement*. A ferry crosses the river at Niafounké, making it possible to connect with the road leading to KORIENTZE and on to MOPTI. Alternatively, you can continue 90km northeast to the Songhai town of GOUNDAM (see "Around Timbuktu", p.222). A sandy track (four-wheel-drive vehicles only) leads over the remaining 100km **to Timbuktu**.

San

SAN is an important commercial town on the main road to Burkina Faso and Côte d'Ivoire and on the banks of the **Bani River** (a major branch of the Niger). The town **market** (main day Monday) is the largest in the region and people come from far and wide to trade everything from livestock to agricultural produce and imported goods. The beautiful **grande mosquée** already evokes the renowned Sahelian style more common to the Delta region further northeast.

Accommodation and transport practicalities

San doesn't have much in the way of places to bed down, although you can always count on the modest rooms at the *campement* from CFA3500. In addition, there are a couple of small hotels – the *Banzani* and the *Hôtel Concorde* near the *autogare*.

San is the main departure point for **Burkina Faso** and **Côte d'Ivoire**. Taxis head regularly to Bobo Dioulasso and Ferkessédougou from the large *autogare* in town. They also link San to towns on the main road – Ségou and Bamako to the west and Mopti to the northeast. A small road branches from the main route to Mopti, 110km from San, and continues 23km over a raised earth dike to Djenné.

Sikasso

A large town in one of the country's most fertile regions, **SIKASSO** was the last capital of the **Kénédougou Empire**, a kingdom founded by Dyula (Dioula) traders in the seventeenth century. There aren't many reminders left, even of the period after 1870 when Sikasso was capital, but you can still see remnants of the fortifications – known as *tata* – that, despite their impressive dimensions, couldn't hold out against the onslaught of French forces at the end of the last century.

The largely **Senoufo** town grew to become a colonial outpost, as many administrative buildings from the period attest. Today, its proximity to Burkina Faso and the Côte d'Ivoire assure a good deal of international activity, centred around the market, held each Sunday. In general, however, life seems slow on the shady streets where *banco* huts crowd alongside colonial buildings and *Peugeot 504*s nudge donkey carts for road space.

History

Sikasso was founded in the nineteenth century by members of the Traoré family who came from the region of Kong (now in the Côte d'Ivoire). Towards the end of the century, a warrior named **Tieba** began to impose his authority over the region, thanks to decisive military victories. In 1876, he was proclaimed *fama* by the Traoré, and thus became head of the **Kénédougou empire**.

Tieba turned Sikasso, his mother's birthplace, into his capital and transformed the tiny agricultural village into a fortified town. He expanded his empire through military conquest, and developed trade and agriculture in his territory. During the same period, **Samory Touré** was expanding his own influence in the region and thus came into conflict with the Senoufo. Relations remained tense between the forces of Touré and those of Tieba, especially after the former destroyed the historical town of Kong, and Senoufo strongholds in Korhogo and Ferkessédougou. After escaping **French troops** (a new force to be reckoned with by the end of the nineteenth century) led by Gallieni, Samory attacked Sikasso in 1887. After a siege that lasted fifteen months, the Kénédougou capital – thanks to its fortifications and a highly skilled army – still had not yielded, and Samory decided to call off his attack.

In his retreat, Samory ran into the forces of French lieutenant **Binger** who was leading a mission in the area. Samory hoped to ally himself with the French army against his rival, but the French threw their support behind Tieba, helping him to become the most important regional power. On January 23, 1893, Tieba died in an attack on the Bobo village of Bama. The *fama* was replaced by his son **Ba Bemba**. Relations with the French – who in the eyes of the new king were not keeping their engagements to check the power of Samory (now marching towards Bobo) – deteriorated. Despite improved fortifications that Ba Bemba had erected at Sikasso, the capital fell to French forces on May 1, 1898 and the king committed suicide. He thus escaped the fate of Samory who was captured in September of the same year and sent to exile in Gabon, where he died.

Accommodation and practicalities

For cheap accommodation, there are *chambres de passages* right in the *autogare*: CFA500 for a bed in a room without electricity or water, but they're often full. For washing, there's also a cement structure in the motor park with toilets and stalls for showers (you pay for a bucket of water). Unless you really need to save money, you'll be more comfortable in one of the town's **small hotels** such as the *Hôtel Loto* on the Bamako road. Rooms, from CFA2000, are still pretty rudimentary here. The *Hôtel Solo Kahn* next to the motor park is another inexpensive place, and convenient if you arrive late by taxi. The more upmarket *Mamelon* has S/C rooms (some with AC) from around CFA6000.

Onwards from Sikasso

Sikasso's *autogare* is located a good kilometre from town on the Ferkessédougou road, and you can reach it by walking or taking a collective taxi. **Bush taxis** leave regularly for **Ferkessédougou** (Côte d'Ivoire), **Bobo Dioulasso** (Burkina), **Bamako** and **Ségou**. If you're heading to Burkina, note that the *piste* is extremely difficult and it's often worthwhile making a detour to Koutiala (sleep in this large town on the main paved road at the *Motel Huicoma*). If you do go direct from Sikasso, border posts close at 6pm, so get an early start. This same recommendation holds for Côte d'Ivoire.

MOPTI AND THE DELTA REGION

The Niger's extraordinary **inland delta** is one of the most compelling places in West Africa, and bound to leave a lasting impression. As the Niger forges its way through these arid parts, it passes near medieval towns like **Djenné** and **Timbuktu** – once renowned as centres of commercial prosperity and Islamic piety. Today their economic importance has been overshadowed by Mopti, with its bustling port at the confluence of the Bani and Niger Rivers.

STEAMER TRAVEL ON THE NIGER

By far the most fascinating way to travel through the region is **by steamer**, an option that requires a bit of planning. Ferries operate only after the rains – roughly from July to January or February between Mopti and Gao. From Mopti to Koulikoro, near Bamako, they stop as early as November, when the Niger is already too low to be navigable. Details are given in "Getting Around", on p.181.

Along the river, the *gares routières* are replaced as the centres of trade by **steamer ports**, and wherever you arrive it will be amid a rush of activity as merchants from throughout the country scramble to buy whatever goods are available before the boat pulls out and continues its slow journey.

Small towns and villages dot the river bank, their ground-hugging mud buildings cowering before the inevitable Sudanic style mosque. Occasionally, fields of rice and other cereals can be seen from the decks of the boat – evidence of government attempts to irrigate large portions of the delta before they are irretrievably claimed by the advancing Sahara. Although Fula and Tuareg nomads still lead their flocks through the region, vegetation is remarkably sparse and the landscapes often flat and barren.

Mopti

MOPTI isn't immediately gripping. Its **Old Town** lacks aesthetic harmony, and the **New Town** is neither modern nor impressive. It doesn't take long, however, before the **port** and **canals** – busy with the traffic of the handmade wooden *pinasses* and smaller canoe-like *pirogues* – begin to work their magic. The more time you spend wandering through Mopti, built on three islands (now connected by dykes) where the **Bani** and **Niger** rivers join, the more it grows on you. As a consequence of its setting on the water, Mopti has become the coutnry's major route intersection, where the commerce pulls together all the peoples of Mali – Bambara, Songhai, Fula, Tuareg, Moor, Bozo and Dogon.

The mix of cultures and the town's buoyant pace add to the charm, making this one of the most fascinating stopovers anywhere in Mali. It seems to be the centre of everything and it's a major travellers' focus. If you can, aim to come on a market day – Thursday.

Some background

Originally Mopti was a cluster of islands inhabited by **Bozo fishing people**. It became an important site in the region early in the nineteenth century when, with the jihad proclaimed by the Fula scholar and ascetic **Cheikou Ahmadou Lobbo**, it gained strategic significance as an outpost of his Masina Empire, centred on Djenné and the Fula pasturelands around. Mopti was later captured by the Tukulor warmonger **El Hadj Omar** who turned the settlement into his principal military base, from where he launched attacks against his Fula rivals. A small town grew up around the site, but Mopti remained largely overshadowed by Djenné.

It wasn't until the beginning of this century that Mopti found commercial importance – at first in the export of white egret feathers to the *belle époque* couturiers of Paris, which must have baffled the feather collectors. Economic development was largely due to the French, who exploited Mopti's position at the confluence of the **Bani** and **Niger** rivers and its accessibility from the main overland routes. When the railway line connecting Bamako to Dakar was built, Mopti became the largest river port in the **French Sudan**. Its population has grown steadily since and today, with around 50,000 people, it rivals Ségou as Mali's second town.

Police formalities and other headaches

Assuming you plan to spend the night in Mopti, one of the first orders of business is to stop by the **police headquarters** near the *campement* to get your passport stamped. You'll need two passport photos and will be charged a very unofficial tax that ranges from CFA500–1000, though if you say you work for an international aid agency and need a receipt, the tax is waived. Some people skip this formality with no apparent consequence, but if you stay long in town, the police will catch up with you sooner or later and will drag you to the headquarters. After serious grilling, you'll be required to fill out endless forms and will likely be stung with a heavy fine. Even if you don't get caught in town, over-zealous police and customs agents later in your travels may demand to know why you don't have a Mopti stamp in your passport, and in some cases have sent people back to get it.

Mopti's heavy tourist influx has also resulted in another headache – that of pestering kids who try to earn a living guiding people through town. Mopti is straightforward enough not to need that kind of assistance, but the children persist. They're harmless, even funny companions if you're in the mood, but otherwise, if you're not firm from the outset you'll have shadows following you for the rest of your stay.

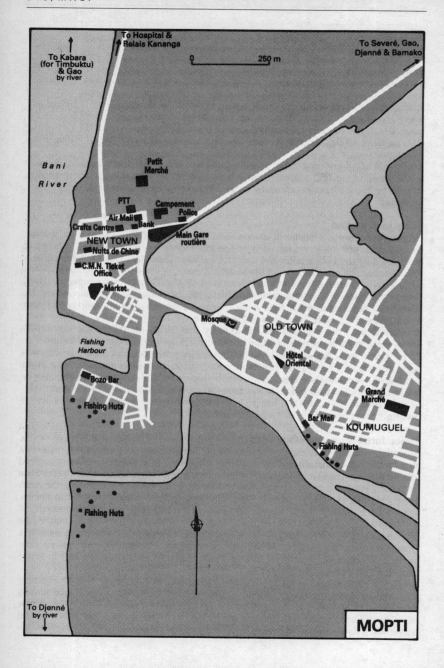

To Hospital &
Relais Kananga

To Kabara
(for Timbuktu)
& Gao
by river

To Sevaré, Gao,
Djenné & Bamako

0   250 m

Bani

River

Petit
Marché

PTT

Campement

Air Mali   Police

Crafts Centre   Bank

NEW TOWN   Main Gare
routière

Nuits de Chine

C.M.N. Ticket
Office

Market

Mosque   OLD TOWN

Hôtel
Oriental

Fishing
Harbour

Grand
Marché

Bozo Bar

Bar Mali   KOUMUGUEL

Fishing Huts

Fishing Huts

Fishing Huts

To Djenné
by river

MOPTI

Accommodation and other practicalities

Although the new town has conveniences like a **bank** that changes money, a couple of **travel agencies** for **car hire** or excursions (see "Moving on" below) and an *Air Mali* office, Mopti offers surprisingly little choice when it comes to **accommodation**. Since the popular *Oriental* closed – along with the abandoned river boat that formerly took in lodgers – the *Bar Mali* is the last of the inexpensive places and, in the absence of serious competition, its prices have risen: rooms are at least CFA2500 (plus CFA500 hotel tax). For a supplement, you can have one with ceiling fan, but since the electricity is normally cut at 11pm, this convenience hardly makes a difference. The place is a bit grotty, but not shockingly so; at night the atmosphere heats up in the popular bar with its plethora of unambiguous *femmes libres*. Food in the **restaurant** is notoriously bad, but inexpensive.

The more expensive alternative is the *campement* near the *autogare*. It offers attractive if simple colonial-style accommodation, but nothing to justify the elevated price of rooms, from about CFA8000. The restaurant, on the other hand, serves good European food. If you have transport, you can **camp** on the grounds, but again, the price per person and per vehicle is inexplicably high.

Upmarket accommodation is also available in the *Relais Kananga* (reservations in Bamako, BP 2473; ☎22.33.18), located near the waterfront in the New Town. Part of the *Sofitel* chain, this place has very comfortable AC rooms with showers from CFA20,000.

If none of these officially sanctioned hotels suits you, there's also the possibility of **staying with people**, usually sleeping on a mat on a rooftop terrace. Kids will make such offers, and the prices (negotiable) are usually very reasonable. There was even an unofficial **camping site** – a large privately owned courtyard in the Old Town where travellers with cars could park and sleep for a small fee. All these possibilities are of course illegal, but if you need to save money, they're there. The longer you stay in town, however, the more likely are the police to find out and set you up for a fine.

If Mopti's atmosphere seems a litle intimidating, there's less hassle involved in spending the night at the *Motel* (BP 911; ☎22.50.22) in Sevaré, Mopti's base on the "mainland" and site of the airport. It's a little expensive, but quite a few people do this, as it's an easy base from which to visit the river town on brief excursions.

Eating

Street food is plentiful in Mopti, especially near the harbour and the motor park. **Tea stalls** are open mornings and evenings for omelettes and bread with *Nescafé* or tea. One of the most popular **restaurants** is the *Nuits de Chine* near the *BP* filling station at the harbour. Although the decor is oriental, food now is of the *steak frites* or braised chicken variety – well prepared and not overpriced. Another favourite haunt is the *Bozo Bar*, an outdoor terrace restaurant nicely located on the harbour overlooking the activity of the riverside. There's nothing particularly fancy about the rice and fish dishes, but it's good value. If you don't want to eat, you can come just for a beer and watch the *pirogues* slopping between the port and surrounding islands. Much less classy is the nearby *Restaurant N'Benida*. They have rice and chicken or *capitaine* (fish) – a whole meal for about CFA500. Lastly, check out *Chez Maman* for fresh dairy produce.

Around town

Given its size, Mopti has an energy and variety of things to do that make it easy to pass a couple of days in town. Most of the sights centre around the **harbour**, from where you can hire *pirogues* to take you to various Bozo or Tuareg camps. **Markets** in Mopti are colourful and famous for a wide range of crafts, including hand-woven Sahelian blankets.

The harbour

Mopti's *raison d'être*, the **harbour**, built by the French in the early part of the century, is always the centre of life in town. Large wooden *pinasses* with their canvas covers and colourful flags waving in the breeze tie up regularly to unload cargo and passengers. Smaller *pirogues* taxi back and forth transporting people from different points in the islands that make up the town.

A **fish market** occupies the southern edge of the port near the *Bozo Bar*. Behind it is a large open-air **"factory"** where craftsmen build the traditional *pinasses* from large planks imported from the south. On the northern edge of the harbour (the opposite side from the *Bozo Bar*), Moorish traders mill around stacks of marble-like **salt slabs**, brought by camel caravan from the desert to Timbuktu and then transported by boat to Mopti. Formerly one of the desert's great riches, salt is still a precious commodity for herders who need it for their livestock.

The harbour is the place to get boats to take you along the river to see the **Bozo and Tuareg "camps"**. Kids will find you and propose the trip (just hang around the *Bozo Bar*); their brothers or uncles are inevitably **boatmen** who will give you a "special rate" – the going price seems to be CFA1000–1500.

The **Bozo** are a fishing people who build circular thatched huts, clustered in small *campements*, around Mopti during the rainy season when the catch is most prolific. If you take a *pirogue* to one of these communities, you'll see them repairing their boats and nets and engaged in other piscatorial activities. Although interesting, you ultimately end up feeling a bit like a voyeur.

The **Tuareg camp** is nothing more than a few huts where women sell **crafts** –bracelets, necklaces and leather goods – at elevated prices. Buying brings twinges of conscience as you deliberate whether you're being stupid to pay so much or stingy for trying to beat down the price – especially considering the economic and social upheaval the Tuareg have undergone since the recent Sahelian droughts. Paying more than the market norm, however, only encourages people to give up productive occupations and try to survive on the tourist industry instead.

Even if the visit to these camps adds up to a rather artificial experience (it is, after all, a touristy thing to do), the boat ride is enjoyable and gives an interesting perspective of the town.

The old town and markets

From the harbour, the **grande mosquée** is easily visible to the east. As you cross over the dyke leading to it, you enter into the **Old Town** with its narrow pedestrian streets and grey *banco* houses. The mosque itself is a relatively recent construction, but faithful to the regional style that originated in nearby Djenné. Unfortunately, it's off limits to non-Muslims.

The **grand marché** is also in the Old Town, to the southeast of the mosque in the Komuguel district. It's the main place for **foodstuffs** including grain, fruits and vegetables. There's also a large covered **fish market**. More intimate is the **petit marché** in the New Town near the bank. You'll find more food here, plus various household items like **pottery** or **calabash** utensils. The main market day is Thursday, when commerce is especially brisk.

The best place for **crafts** is the *Hall des Artisans* near the *petit marché*. Blankets are a regional specialty and Mopti has a wide selection at relatively low prices – costs vary according to the quality of the wool or cotton threads. At the crafts centre, you'll find weaves of local peoples including the Dogons, the Fula and the Songhai. Each of these peoples also has characteristic **jewellery** – earrings, bracelets and necklaces – handcrafted in gold, silver, copper and bronze.

MOVING ON: MOPTI TRAVEL DETAILS

From Mopti there's onward transport in all directions. Besides being the major port of call on the **Niger River route** (tickets and schedules from the *Compagnie de Navigation Malienne*, near the port), it's also a quick twelve-kilometre drive along the dyke to SEVARÉ – a more modern town on the newly surfaced **Bamako–Gao road** – making it quite easy to get to all the big towns in Mali. In addition, it's the most convenient springboard for trips to **Djenné** (via river or road) and the **Dogon Country**. If you're heading for the latter, *Bar Mali* provides a reasonably safe lock-up **luggage store**, CFA200 per night for a large bag, payable on safe return.

By Boat

Downstream, from July or August to January (depending on the rains), you can travel by steamer to **Gao**. During this period, boats also provide the quickest link to **Kabara**, the port of call for **Timbuktu**. Upstream, to **Koulikoro** (port of call for **Bamako**), they usually stop running sometime in November due to the low waters. You may also be able to get a *pinasse* to Kabara. When enquiring at the port, specify that you want a place on a goods boat, otherwise they'll think you want to hire the whole *pinasse* to yourself, a rather pricey alternative (say CFA250,000 to Timbuktu). Non-motorised *pinasses* or *pirogues* to Timbuktu should charge around CFA5000 for the four-day voyage, but even these don't operate much after February. The journey varies from spell-binding (when you push off at dawn) to alarmingly uncomfortable (early afternoon out on the river), and it's fair to say the romance can wear thin given the restricted space and unpredictable nature of the whole trip. This, in retrospect at least, is why it's such a wonderful adventure: birdlife is prolific and hippos easily seen.

It's also possible to travel **up the Bani to Djenné**. *Pinasses* leave from the harbour Friday mornings and take a full day to get there (local price, around CFA2500). Hiring a motor *pinasse,* count on about CFA100,000 for two days. Non-motorised charters can be arranged for as little as CFA20,000 for the same period. You can usually arrange to have your food prepared for you on these wooden boats – otherwise bring your own provisions. Beware, they can take three days to pole and paddle to Djenné. Lastly, motor *pinasses* also operate up the Niger **to Ségou** – a three-day journey.

By Road

As an alternative to the boats, you can take a **bush taxi to Djenné**. Vehicles leave from the station across from the *campement* and take about two-and-a-half hours for the 130-kilometre trip. Your best chance of finding taxis is on Sunday and early Monday morning – Djenné's market day. Other times there may be nothing, and during the rains the overland route may be out altogether.

The main **motor park** for other destinations is opposite the *Bozo Bar* near the harbour. Here you'll find regular vehicles for Gao, San, Ségou and Bamako. In addition, a mail **bus**, the *courier postal*, leaves Saturday mornings for Gao and is slightly cheaper than the taxis. Enquire at the post office.

Mopti is the main departure point for the **Dogon Country** (see p.223). You can get bush taxis to Bandiagara or Bankas from where you can proceed by foot, donkey cart, bicycle or mobylette. See overleaf for *SMERT* tours and less organised trips.

By Air

From the **airport** in Sevaré, *Air Mali* operates regular flights (once or twice a week) to Bamako, Gao, Goundam and Timbuktu. If you're in town during the dry season, this may be your only hope of getting to Timbuktu. Note, however, that flights out of Timbuktu are rare and you could find yourself stranded for several days in this isolated outpost. Get full details of schedules – including those out of Timbuktu – from the *Air Mali* office, next to *SMERT* in Mopti.

Tours out of Mopti with Smert – and unofficial entry into the *Pays Dogon*

SMERT organises **tours to the Dogon country** – Bandiagara, Songo and Sanga – and to **Djenné**. The trip includes Land Rover, chauffeur and accommodation, but costs at least CFA50,000 for a two-day excursion. Mopti's other travel agency, *Manding Voyages*, does a similar tour at prices that work out almost exactly the same. Both of these agencies have offices in the New Town.

Young kids in Mopti also take guided tours through the Dogon Country, all claiming to be from there. If you select a guide, you normally pay his transport to and from Mopti and a negotiable daily fee. Although there are **no guarantees** (when you get there, you may discover your guide knows surprisingly little about the area, or that he can't arrange to get you to places he promised) it will cost you a fraction of the official excursions.

Most of the youngsters turn out to be quite informative and work hard, leading you on foot through the villages and down the escarpment, to give you your money's worth. But people do wind up with undesirable brats more interested in pocketing the pay than showing you anything interesting. Read the section on the Dogon Country that follows, figure out what you want to see, and question your potential guide to see if he seems to know the area and if he can get you through it for a reasonable price. It's often wise to pay for your trip in one fully-inclusive lump sum (that you agree upon *before* setting out) to include transport, accommodation, food and your guide's fee. Pay part before leaving and the rest when you come back. If you don't do it this way, in addition to the daily rate you pay your guide, you'll have to haggle over everything once you arrive in the Dogon Country – the price of sleeping, eating, even the baggage charge for the taxi you take there. This obviously becomes tedious, and your trip will be much more pleasant if you leave these details to your guide.

You can also simply go on your own to Bandiagara or Bankass. At these two towns, you'll surely find boys to guide you; in fact, you'll be assaulted by them upon arriving. Full coverage of the Dogon region begins on p.223.

Djenné

DJENNÉ is unquestionably the most beautiful town in the Sahel and a superbly satisfying place to visit. On an island for most of the year, the buildings are shaped in the smooth lines of the Sahelian style, moulded from the grey clay of the surrounding flood plains. In the main square, the famous **grande mosquée** dominates the townscape. People from throughout the region gather in town for the festive market day on Monday – the best time to plan a trip. Despite unnecessary meddling on the part of the police and *SMERT*, this is one of the most rewarding towns in the country, and one where you can easily imagine what life in the Sahel must have been like a century or more ago.

Originally a **Bozo settlement**, Djenné was founded around 800 AD, according to the *Tarikh es-Soudain* – one of the earliest written records of the Sahel. The original site was at a place called Djoboro, but it may have moved to the present location as early as 1043 (other sources put the date two centuries later). In the reign of the Soninke king **Koï Kounboro**, Djenné converted to Islam: the king himself dutifully rased his palace to make place for the town's first mosque in the thirteenth century. The town became a way-station for gold, ivory, lead, wool, kola nuts and other precious items from the south. Merchants had their depots in Djenné, and sold from outlets they operated throughout the region, notably in Timbuktu. They developed a large flotilla of boats – some up to twenty metres long – capable of transporting tens of tons of these goods to Timbuktu from where they made their way to the north.

In 1325, Djenné was incorporated into the **Mali Empire** under which it enjoyed a period of stability and continued prosperity. In 1473 – after a seige that purportedly lasted seven years, seven months and seven days – it was conquered by the **Songhai Empire**. The intellectual and commercial exchanges with Timbuktu were reinforced during this period until, in 1591, Djenné fell to the Moroccans, under whose domination it remained until the nineteenth century. The town went into a slow decline that successive invasions were powerless to stop. **Cheikou Ahmadou** – a religious zealot from Masina – ousted the Moroccans in 1810, and destroyed Djenné's famous mosque. The **Tukulor Empire** briefly swallowed up the town in 1862, but held it only until 1893 when **French troops** arrived and took control.

Practicalities and problems: the Police and SMERT

You're supposed to register with the police on arrival. Officially you must then take a tour of town with a guide from *SMERT* (CFA2000) who have an office next to the *gendarmerie*. Some people get away without guides but *SMERT* agents are likely to

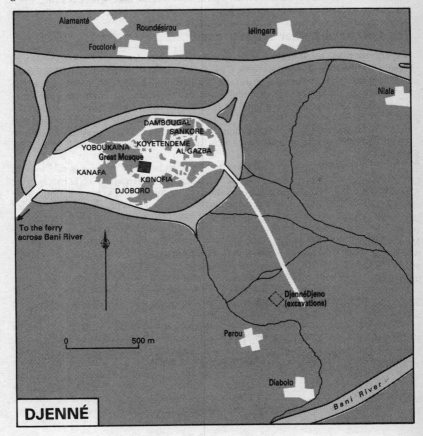

DJENNÉ

smell you out in town and demand to see your receipt. It's the same frustrating scenario encountered in just about every other place of interest in Mali where the authorities try to control your every movement, including where you sleep and what you see. On the brighter side, they do point out the highlights in town, and after you've paid the money, which seems to be all anyone's really interested in, you can take your leave of the guide. (The very latest report is that *SMERT* in Djenné may have closed.)

Accommodation and food

Accommodation is limited to *Le Campement*, well sited near the grande mosquée. Rooms are nothing fancy, but clean and well maintained. Unfortunately it tends to be stuffed with tourists on Mondays. Prices, at least, aren't excessive, and you can even sleep on the rooftop terrace or **camp** for CFA1500 (including the CFA500 hotel tax). Order in advance for meals from the **restaurant**. It's not the best food you'll eat in West Africa, but you don't have many alternatives in town. Kids may also offer to put you up on the terrace of their homes. Some try to charge as much, or more than the *campement*, so check the price. *SMERT* spies, however, are everywhere in town, and if you stay more than a night or two, are bound to catch up with you.

The mosque and other things to see

Arriving by road, you'll see Djenné's **grande mosquée** from some distance as you travel over the dyke leading to town. This architectural masterpiece only dates from 1905, but was built in the style of the original mosque constructed in the reign of the Soninke king Kounboro. The rounded lines of the facade are dominated by three towers, each eleven metres high and topped with an ostrich egg. The beams protruding from the edifice serve more than an aesthetic function; like scaffolding they are essential for the upkeep of the building. Each year rains wash away the building's smooth *banco* outer layer and the people from town work to restore it in the dry season.

Inside is a forest of pillars connected by sturdy arches. The mosque is said to hold up to 5000 worshippers – not bad considering Djenné's entire population is barely twice that number. For a fee, the guardian will take you up to the rooftop terrace from where you get a beautiful view of the town and surrounding flood plains. For a much smaller fee, you can get on the rooftop opposite and have much the same view – enter the "daily" market, turn left after the gate, and climb the ladder in the corner.

The weekly **market** is the other main sight, and it's worth making every effort to time your trip for a Monday when traders from throughout the region make a commercial pilgrimage to town. They spread their wares on the main square in front of the mosque in much the same way that French explorer **René Caillié** described in the nineteenth century in his *Travels through Central Africa to Timbuktu*. There are few if any markets as animated, as colourful and as *rich* – those colossal swaying earrings are solid gold – as Djenné on a Monday morning.

If you take *SMERT's* guided tour, they'll also lead you through the maze of streets in town, pointing out the most interesting of the two and three storey **banco houses** with wooden Moroccan-style shutters and doors. Still a pious community, the largest homes belong to the *marabouts* – the most important of whom is said to live in the town's oldest house. *SMERT* also run you around the workshops and boutiques of local **artisans** – no surprise there. And, finally they point out the spot where a young Bozo virgin was sacrificed to ensure the town's prosperity. After you've finished the tour, it's much more satisfying to wander through the dusty streets on your own, admiring the exquisite architecture and soaking up the way of life.

Sites surrounding Djenné

A number of **villages** surround Djenné, built on small elevations in the flood plains. One of the most interesting is SENNISSA – peopled mainly by Fula and just 4km from Djenné as the crow flies (ask a kid to take you there). The village boasts two beautiful **mosques** and an abundance of artisans working along the small streets lined with single storey *banco* homes. You're likely to see women here wearing the huge gold heirloom earrings that were once common in the region. Bigger ones may be the size of a rugby ball and hang down to the woman's breasts; some are so heavy they have to be strung from a cord that passes over the woman's head.

In the late 1970s, a team of American archaeologists discovered an ancient village 2km from town at a spot now called **Djenné-Djeno** (old Djenné). The foundations of buildings they uncovered here, along with terracotta statues, utensils and jewellery, date back as far as the third century BC and prick holes in a blanket of ignorance about archaic Africa – a highly developed, commercial society (the town counted over 10,000 inhabitants) that existed long before the arrival of Islam. For reasons still unclear, the town went into decline in the early Middle Ages and was abandoned by the fourteenth century. You need permission from the police to visit the site, although kids will sometimes agree to take you there.

MOVING ON FROM DJENNÉ

Taxis run to Mopti on Monday afternoons when the market closes down. Alternatively, you can take a motor *pinasse*. They leave early Tuesday morning and arrive in Mopti in the evening, transporting goods in time for Mopti's market day on Thursdays. Any kid in town can take you to the water's edge from where the boat departs. The *piroguier* will sell you a ticket (even a couple of days in advance if you like) that includes the price of transport plus food if you specify. The lowlying boats hug the water's edge, passing numerous villages on the river. The landscape, however, is remarkably flat and unvaried. Outside these two possibilities, there's no guaranteed transport out of Djenné. And it's a full, long day's hike along the dyke to the main road.

Timbuktu (Tombouctou)

> *If I told you why it is mysterious then it would not be mysterious*
> Minister of Sports, Art and Culture

> *Is that it?*
> Bob Geldof, after looking around

Long associated with mysterious beauty, learning and above all wealth, **TIMBUKTU**, "the forbidden city", has always fascinated outsiders. From the time of the crusades, it was one of the main entrepôts through which came the West African **gold** on which European finance relied. From the fourteenth century, when Mansa Musa, Emperor of Mali, passed through Cairo on his way to Mecca, (stunning the city with his fabulous entourage and selling so much gold that its price slumped for decades), to the sixteenth, when Leo Africanus from Granada in Spain visited and described Timbuktu's opulent royal court, to as late as the eighteenth century when a lemming-like "explorers' rush" broke out to settle the enigma of the city roofed with gold, Timbuktu has achieved a near-legendary reputation. "Going to Timbuctoo" is still synonymous with going to the ends of the earth – or to hell – and only in the last few years has a more prosaic recognition forced itself into popular awareness.

Of course the town couldn't live up to the myths which disguised it so long and any illusions of grandeur you harbour are bound to be frustrated. As long ago as 1828, René Caillié wrote:

I found it neither as big nor as populated as I had expected. Commerce was much less active than it was famed to be. . . Everything was enveloped in a great sadness. I was amazed by the lack of energy, by the inertia that hung over the town. . . a jumble of badly built houses. . . ruled over by a heavy silence.

This frank assessment rings true today and, walking through the streets of deep sand, lined with pale grey stucco-covered mud-brick houses, you're more likely to be struck by the poverty and sense of despair that seem endemic in the district, than by the historical monuments evoking a prouder past.

A long and turbulent history

Towards the end of the eleventh century, a group of **Tuareg** who came to the Niger to graze their herds discovered a small oasis on the north bank where they set up a permanent camp. When they went off to pasture their animals, they left the settlement in the care of an old woman named Tomboutou – which means "the woman with the large belly button". Other versions have it that the woman's name was Buktu (or alternatively *bouctou* may derive from the Arabic for "dune") while *tim* in Berber signifies "place of".

The camp quickly developed into an important commercial centre where merchants from Djenné set up shops and acted as middlemen between the salt caravans coming down from the north (and general dealers from across the Sahara) and the river traffic bringing goods downriver from the south. Although the Tuareg herders didn't live permanently in the town, they continued to control it, levying heavy and arbitrary taxes from the increasingly wealthy traders. Eventually, in response, the inhabitants invited the great Mali ruler **Mansa Musa** to liberate the town from Tuareg domination and he annexed it in 1330. To commemorate the occasion, the king visited Timbuktu and built a palace and the **Djinguereber mosque**.

Under the hegemony of the **Mali Empire**, Timbuktu enjoyed a period of stability and prosperity, but as the kingdom declined in the fifteenth century, the town again slipped into Tuareg control.

Extortions began again, and by the sixteenth century the merchants turned to the Songhai ruler **Sonni Ali** who chased the Tuaregs west to the desert post of Oualata. Ali laid the foundations of the **Songhai Empire** which grew under the impetus of **Askia Mohammed**. Timbuktu reached its zenith at this point and became one of the Sahel's principal centres of commerce and learning. Reports of unimaginable wealth trickled back to Europe. The **Moroccan invasion** of 1591, however, when firearms were used in the Sahel for the first time, was a catastrophe for Timbuktu. The expedition's Andalusian leader, Djouder Pasha, had a number of senior scholars executed, exiled most of the others to Fez, and caravanned out the bulk of the city's wealth. Under the descendants of marriages between the invaders (some of whom were conscripted Scots, Irish and Spanish soldiers) and Songhai women – a group who came to be known as the Arma, after their guns – Timbuktu went into a steady decline that lasted throughout the seventeenth and eighteenth centuries. At different times it was attacked by the Mossi, the Fula, the Tukulor and the Tuareg. Subjected to pillage and oppression, the townspeople retreated behind the heavy, metal-studded wooden doors characteristic of Timbuktu houses. These were one of the few symbols of the city's former wealth that endured until the final arrival of the Europeans in the nineteenth century.

The European explorers

On the strength of a few translated books and a skein of rumours, Europeans set about uncovering Timbuktu's fabled riches. Between the late sixteenth century (by which time the city was, unknown to them, already nearly destitute) and 1853, at least forty-three travellers attempted to reach it, of whom just four succeeded.

The race really began in 1824, when the Geographical Society of Paris offered a prize of 10,000 francs for the first explorer to return with a verifiable account of the city.

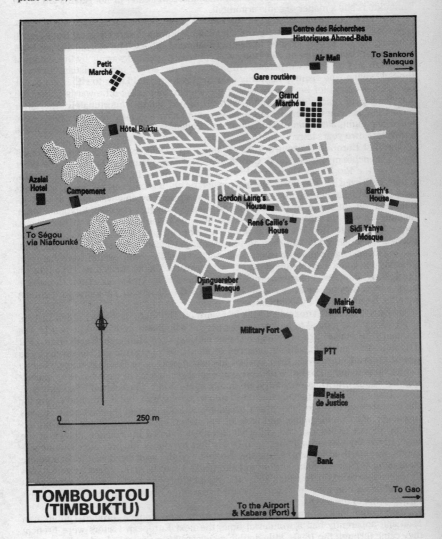

TOMBOUCTOU
(TIMBUKTU)

The earliest first-hand account by a non-Muslim, however, had already been given, not by an explorer, but by an illiterate American sailor, **Robert Adams**, who had been sold into slavery after his ship was wrecked off Mauritania, and who almost certainly spent several months in Timbuktu in 1811. But the story he related to the British Consul in Morocco in 1813, wasn't given much credibility as Adams wasn't aware of the mystique surrounding the city and his dreary description was too flat to be believed – except by Moroccan Muslims who themselves had been there. Whether or not Adams did get to Timbuktu is still a matter of some argument.

The first explorer to succeed conclusively – a prudish Scot named **Gordon Laing** – reached Timbuktu on August 13, 1826, after a hazardous desert crossing from Tripoli in which he was almost slashed to death by Tuareg robbers. The squalid slaving town was a bitter disappointment. But Laing was apparently greeted warmly by the sheikh of Timbuktu and by the townspeople. On hearing of the arrival of a Christian, however, the Fula sultan who claimed authority over the town ordered Laing to either get out or be killed. Worried for his guest's safety, the sheikh sent Laing off towards Ségou (he was hoping to reach Sierra Leone) with an armed guide. Unfortunately, the latter turned out to be in the service of the sultan, and Laing and most of his servants were killed one night, 50km out of Timbuktu. One trailed back to Tripoli with Laing's notes and letters, two years later.

The first European to return from Timbuktu to write about the adventure himself was a Frenchman named **René Caillié** whose fantastic journey started on the West Coast on the Rio Nunez (now in northwest Guinea). Prior to taking off for Timbuktu, Caillié had lived in a Moorish village further north, learning Arabic and immersing himself in Muslim culture. Amazingly, he was sponsored by no government or association, and set off alone to the unexplored interior, disguised as an Egyptian. After making his way through the Fouta Djalon hills, he reached the Niger at Kouroussa, then continued to Tiémé (Côte d'Ivoire), where he fell gravely ill. After recovering, he pushed on to Tangrela and then to the devoutly Muslim town of Djenné where he made a deep and favourable impression on the sheikh – who would have had him instantly executed had his disguise been discovered. Caillié arrived in Timbuktu on April 20, 1828 and was received by Sidi Abdallahi Chebir. Two weeks later, the adventurer joined a camel caravan and headed across the Sahara to Tangiers. In eighteen months, he had crossed 4500km alone.

Caillié's book wasn't considered the last word on Timbuktu, however, and in Britain, especially, it was judged to be bogus. The person who finally convinced the world was the fourth to make it, the German polyglot and explorer **Heinrich Barth**. Barth left Tripoli in 1850 on an expedition financed by the British government. He survived the desert crossing to Agadez, then worked his way down to the Hausa country, his two companions dying en route. With delays and long residences in various towns, including diversions into Dogon country, he finally made it into Timbuktu on September 7, 1853. Like Caillié, he originally disguised himself as an Arab, but it didn't take long for the townspeople to discover he was Christian, and from then on the explorer's life was in danger. Barth, phlegmatic and undeterred, stayed eight months under the protection of Sheikh El Backay and collected the most detailed information known at the time. El Backay was virtually beseiged by his Fula overlords and only after long negotiations, was Barth at last able to escape. He followed the river back east to Gao before continuing to Sokoto, Kano and on to Lake Chad. From here, he again set out across the Sahara, arriving in Tripoli in 1855. His explorations had lasted five-and-a-half years and had taken him over 16,000km. And the five-volume book he published at last overturned some of the myths.

Apart from a lucky young German, **Oskar Lenz**, who skipped through Timbuktu in 1880 and apparently had a wonderful time, the next European visitors were French: they came through the 1890s, little doubting success, to conquer and colonise.

Timbuktu's mosques and other sights

The oldest and most famous mosque in Timbuktu is the Friday **Djinguereber mosque.** It was first built in 1327 by El Saheli – an Andalusian architect whom Mansa Musa met in Cairo during his pilgrimage to Mecca – who is credited with the invention of mud bricks. Before bricks, all building was done using mud and straw, slapped on a wooden framework. Appropriately covered up and respectful, you may be able to climb the minaret here – but permission isn't always granted. The **Sankore** mosque dates from the fifteenth century. During Timbuktu's golden era, this mosque doubled as a **university**, renowned throughout the Moslem world, that specialised in law and theology. Up to 25,000 students were studying here in the sixteenth century. The **Sidi Yahya** mosque was first constructed in 1400 by a marabout named El-Moktar Hamalla. It was intended to serve a saint whose imminent arrival had been prophesied. Four decades later, Sherif Sidi Yahya crossed the desert and asked for the keys to the mosque. He was declared *imam*, and is today one of the most revered of the town's **333 saints**.

Though the mosques are today the main sights, it's really more rewarding to spend some time walking through the confuison of narrow streets to take in the unique **architecture**. The finest homes – usually owned by Moorish merchants – are made of carved limestone brought from a desert quarry. Again, the basic design of these homes may date to El Saheli; the columns of square pilasters that decorate the facades are reminiscent of those in Egyptian temples, an element he may have picked up in Cairo. The small shuttered windows and heavy wooden doors with geometric ironwork designs also bear an Arabic stamp, though they seem to hark back to the Moroccan invasion of the late sixteenth century. Plaques still mark the homes where **Laing**, **Caillié** and **Barth** stayed during their exploits in Timbuktu. The first two were on the same street in the **Sankore district**; and any kid can point them out to you. Heavy rains reduced Caillié's house to rubble recently, but there's every reason to believe it will be repaired again for the sake of Timbuktu's precarious tourist industry – building in mud guarantees an authentic, weathered, historical look.

More modest houses are made of *banco* in a style that originated in Djenné. Along the streets you'll also notice dome-shaped **clay ovens** where women bake round loaves of bread – a speciality of the town, traditionally made from wheat grown near Lake Faguibine. The outskirts of Timbuktu are bordered by circular straw huts – the domain of Tuareg, Bella and Fula nomads. Walk out past the *Hôtel Azalai* in the west to see them, or climb one of the **dunes** at dawn to watch the sun rising above the town: the city looks best in silhouette.

Also near the *Hôtel Azalai* on the west side of town, **terraced gardens** challenge the intense heat. Looking something like Greek amphitheatres, they're built around large craters dug deep into the earth, at the bottom of which stands a pond of brackish water.

To the north of the centre is the **Abaradio district** where the *azalai* or camel caravans formerly arrived in great numbers (even when the first European explorers arrived, as many as 60,000 camels a year unloaded their goods here). Apart from goods from North Africa and the Mediterranean, the Sahara's biggest prize was salt from the oasis of **Taoudenni**. This ultra-remote desert post, 700km due north of Timbuktu, is famous for its salt mines – a Malian Siberia where the former president Modibo Keita was detained until his death and political undesirables were, until recently, banished. The occasional caravan of salt slabs still makes its way down to Timbuktu, but in 1989 Taoudenni ceased to be a prison camp.

The *CEDRAB* and the crafts centre

While in town, try to stop by at the **Centre des Recherches Historique Ahmed Baba**. One of the greatest remaining legacies of Timbuktu's former glory is the wealth of **Islamic literature** that was produced here. Traditionally, families wrote their histories in chronicles known as *tarikh* – one of the most important of which was the *Tarikh es-Soudain*, written by El Sadi in the seventeenth century. These and other related writings have provided invaluable information about the scientific, legal and social practices of the seventeenth, eighteenth and nineteenth centuries throughout the region, and indeed the entire Muslim world. In addition, they've helped trace Mali's history back to the empire of Ancient Ghana.

Countless volumes still remain in private family collections and, exposed to dust, damp and insects, the works (some of which may be 400 years old or more) could soon be lost forever. The centre is trying to persuade reluctant families to part with these priceless documents – at least long enough to let them be restored and copied on microfilm. To date, it has collected over 2500 volumes (they estimate that Timbuktu alone harbours easily 5000 unseen works) and have made copies of 600 others. About eighty percent of these are written in Arabic, the rest in Songhai. Enquire at the *direction* and they'll show you some of the older handwritten documents, the most beautiful of which contain ornate geometric artwork and gold lettering.

Next to the *Centre Ahmed Baba*, the town has recently opened a brand new **crafts centre**, housed in a traditional building with imposing wooden doors.

Practicalities

Timbuktu is a first-rate rip-off as far as the police are concerned. It's pretty hard to avoid their tax and *réglementation des pieces* (and they know everyone wants a nice "TOMBOUCTOU" in their passport), but it does grate that you're then directed to approved lodgings.

Budget **accommodation** has become a real problem in Timbuktu, since the government-run *campement* (BP 49) has squeezed out most competition. They now charge an outrageous CFA7000 for a room in this dilapidated colonial hotel located on the edge of the desert. If there are any available, you can get rooms at the *Hôtel Buktu*, in the northwest part of town, from about CFA5000. Otherwise, if you get stuck with no transport out of town for a couple of days, Timbuktu the mysterious can be a severe financial drain. As a possible alternative, the owner of *Le Senegalais* restaurant – Abdoulah Arafa – has in the past lodged travellers in his home for a reasonable CFA2000 or so. He seems to have an arrangement with the police, and you can try tracking him down at his restaurant, across the street from SONATAM (the national tobacco company) in the main market building. If you pay a little more, Abdoulah will provide your day's meals. Otherwise, **staying with people** is risky indeed. Most people are reluctant, since there are now too many kids in cahoots with the *campement* manager. They'll alert him if they see you staying elsewhere, and he'll alert the police.

If you have money to spend, Timbuktu has been a great deal more comfortable since the opening of the *Relais Azalaï* (reservations in Bamako, BP 2473; ☎22.33.18, telex 994), part of the French *Sofitel* chain. They offer comfortable AC rooms (kept going by their own generator) from CFA17,000 and have a restaurant with reputable French food for CFA5000.

There's surprisingly little in the way of other **eating-houses** or bars. The market doesn't offer a great deal either, but as you'll either be staying in one of the hotels, or unofficially with a family who will provide meals in any case, it's not a big problem.

Around Timbuktu

Lake Faguibine is a beautiful stretch of water surrounded by soft sand dunes, 100km west of Timbuktu. Though its size varies greatly with the seasons, the lake can swell to 120km long by 25km wide, making it one of the largest natural lakes in West Africa. In 1984, however, it dried up completely.

The approach to the lake is via **GOUNDAM** – an important agricultural town in the middle of a region considered to be the breadbasket of Mali. Rice, millet, corn and, remarkably, even **wheat**, are all grown in the area. Situated on the much smaller **Lake Télé**, Goundam has a *campement* and is linked to the river by a 34-kilometre road from DIRE, a sizeable port on the Niger, 100km upstream from Timbuktu. From Goundam, continue to Lake Faguibine via the *piste* that passes through the village of BINTAGOUNGOU.

If you don't have **transport**, *SMERT* organises excursions out of Timbuktu to these parts, but prices are steep. You'd need luck on your side to make much headway on local transport.

MOVING ON AND TRAVEL INFORMATION

If you weren't impressed by Timbuktu's isolation during your stay, you will be when you try to leave. Unless you're travelling with your own vehicle, the options for **onward travel** are pretty much limited to river craft or the plane. The **river journey** from Timbuktu (Kabara port) to Gao is beautiful – the Niger snakes between high yellow dunes – and hippos are often seen along the way. The last known **flight schedule** consisted of a single weekly plane (on Sunday) to Bamako. For up-to-date information, check at *Air Mali* (☎92.11.09) near the *grand marché*.

To Gao by Road

A picturesque route that follows the Niger, the road to Gao is nonetheless very demanding. It would be folly to attempt it with anything less than a 4WD vehicle, as serveral parts are blocked by soft sand dunes that extend right to the water's edge. During the rains, the road is impassable. It's 195km to **BAMBA** – a difficult stretch with deep soft sand, especially just before Bamba. One of the first major villages along the route, Bamba is an **oasis** sandwiched between the road and the river, said to have been founded by the Moroccan invaders of the 1590s. Another 135km brings you to **BOUREM**, a Songhai village with characteristic *banco* homes and a large market – and also the southern terminus of the trans-Saharan Tanezrouft route between May and September. From here, the road continues along the river to Gao, 95km away. If you're without transport, it's sometimes possible to pay for a place on a lorry. Traffic, however, is very irregular and you definitely can't count on this alternative.

It's worth noting, however, that a feasible route exists from GOURMA-RHAROUS, (about 100km east of Timbuktu on the south bank), to the new, paved, Gao-Bamako road. There's a basic car ferry across the river at Gourma-Rharous, though unless you're driving you won't need to worry much about the crossing as *pirogues* cross on demand.

THE DOGON COUNTRY

Until the end of the colonial era, the **Dogon** were one of the African peoples who had most successfully retained their culture and traditional way of life. This was in large part due to the isolation of their territory in the remarkable and picturesque **cliffside villages** they built along the **Bandiagara escarpment** – the *falaise* – south of Mopti.

They're still dogged defenders of their customs, religion and art, but in more recent years they have become the object of an intense **touristic exploitation**. Even today, much of the **Dogon country** can only be visited on foot or at best with a donkey cart, and the area you can cover with a 4WD vehicle is limited. Yet despite the difficulty of getting through the region, the place is swarming with travellers. The official government tourist agency, *SMERT*, has actively encouraged the boom. They control the most popular sites, and you won't be able to discover them without linking up with an official guided tour. Off the main circuit you can often hire kids to take you around, but since the area is now big business in Malian terms, you'll have to fork out a lot of cash even for this alternative. With patience and a lot of time, you can still manage to get completely **off the beaten track**, but only the most intrepid and persistent travellers can today hope to avoid the bad-tasting obduracies of a money-talks trip and discover the real beauty of the Dogon people's outstanding civilisation.

Some background

Recent **archaeological research** has uncovered caves dug into the cliffs around the Dogon town of SANGA that date to around the third century BC. The Dutch scientists who discovered these caves called the people who made them the **Toloy**, but there seems to be a rather large gap between this culture and the next known inhabitants of the escarpment, the **Tellem**, who arrived in the eleventh century. The Tellem were a people of small stature, often said to have been "pygmies", although they probably weren't related to the contemporary Central African people of small stature. They're generally thought to have shared the escarpment for a couple of centuries with the **Dogon**, who arrived in the fifteenth century. Some time around the seventeenth century, the Tellem were pushed out of the Dogon country and migrated to Burkina Faso.

SEX, SPEECH AND WEAVING: DOGON COSMOLOGY

The Dogon believe in a single God, **Amma**, who created the sun, moon and stars. Afterwards, he created the earth by throwing a ball of clay into space. The ball spread to the four points of the horizon and took on the shape of a woman with an anthole for her vagina and a termite mound for her clitoris. Alone in the universe, Amma attempted to make love to the earth, but the termite mound blocked his path and he tore it out. Because of this violence, the earth could not bear the twins that would have resulted from a happy union and instead gave birth to a jackal.

Amma again had intercourse with the earth, and a pair of twins resulted, known as **nommo**. They were born of divine semen, the precious water found in everything in the universe. Green in colour, their upper bodies were human and their lower bodies like snakes. The *nommo* are present in all water. Living in the heavens with their father, the *nommo* looked down on their mother and, seeing her naked, made a **skirt** into which they wove the **first language**. Thus the earth was the first to possess speech.

Meanwhile, the jackal was running loose. His mother was the only woman, and he raped her. The earth bled and became impure in the sight of Amma. It's for this reason that today, menstruating women are considered impure in Dogon society – as they are in nearly all African cultures. When he forced himself upon the earth, the jackal also touched her skirt and thus stole language.

Having turned from his wife, Amma decided to create a human couple from clay. The couple had elements of both sexes – the foreskin being the feminine part of the man, and the clitoris the masculine part of the woman. Foreseeing that problems would arise from this ambiguity, the *nommo* circumcised the male and later an invisible hand removed the clitoris from the woman (circumcision of men and clitoridectomy of women is still an important step into adulthood for the Dogon). The couple was thus free to procreate and produced eight children, the original **Dogon ancestors**. After creating **eight descendants** of their own, the ancestors were purified and transformed into *nommo*, then went to join Amma in the sky. But before his ascension, the seventh ancestor was charged with giving the **second language** to humans. Using his mouth as a loom, he spat out a cotton strip from which the new speech was transmitted to humanity.

The eight ancestors didn't get along with Amma and the *nommo* and they were eventually sent back to earth. On the way, the eighth ancestor came down before the seventh,

The Dogon may originally have come from the region of the Nile, but before moving to the Bandiagara escarpment they lived in the Mande country to the west. Determined to preserve their traditional religion in the face of Muslim expansionism and religious jihads, they migrated to the safety of the *falaise* in the fifteenth century. Even with this natural shelter as a homeland, they had to fight off numerous agressors over the centuries. In the 1470s the country was invaded by the **Songhai**, and in the early eighteenth century it was attacked by the **Ségou kingdom**. Much later, in 1830, the Fula from **Masina** marched on the region and, in 1860, the Tukulor ruler **El Hadj Omar** brought his holy war to the escarpment, making Bandiagara his capital: he died in Deguembere near Bandiagara. The **French** occupied the region of Sanga in 1893, but it wasn't until the battle of Tabi in 1920 that the colonial army finally "pacified" the Dogon people.

In the 1930s Reverend Francis McKinney, an American, established the first **Christian mission** in Sanga. Several years later Marcel Griaule, a French anthropologist, came to the same town to study traditional Dogon religion and customs. He spent a quarter of a century living in Dogon country and helped them to set up dams for irrigation and introduced the onion crop that's now one of the only exports of the region to the rest of Mali and Burkina. Respected by the Dogon, he also helped open the eyes of the rest of the world to the complexity and integrity of a civilisation that had long been regarded by Muslim and Christian invaders as merely primitive.

---

who was angry as a result. He turned himself into a snake and set about disturbing the work of the other ancestors. They told the people to kill the snake – which they did. But this seventh ancestor – whose name was Lebe – held the **third language**, needed for mankind, since the second wasn't adequate. The oldest of the eight original descendants thus had to be sacrificed and was buried with the head of Lebe the snake. Humans then received the third language in the form of a drum and found it to be complete and perfectly adapted to the new times.

Traditional religion has a profound effect on Dogon art and **symbolism** to this day, and is incorporated into the smallest item. Villages are laid out in human shape. They're frequently divided into twin parts – as in Sanga which incorporates Ogol-du-haut and Ogol-du-bas and Sanga-du-haut and Sanga-du-bas – that signify the original twin ancestors. Facades of the characteristic **Dogon houses** contain niches as reminders of primitive ancestors and **granaries** are divided into a complex series of inner compartments that represent the cosmos.

The villages are filled with "**temples**" – maybe a simple rock or a clay pilaster, covered with sacrifices of chicken blood or millet paste. Carvings (such as on Dogon doors or locks), clothes and skin markings are all charged with meaning. It was formerly common to file the teeth in the shape of a weaver's comb, since speech is an action that weaves the world and should thus pass through a worthy loom. Even the baskets used by the Dogon are symbolic, the square bases representing the four cardinal points and the round top the celestial dome of the sky.

Symbolism from the story of creation also carries over into **Dogon dances. Masks** are an important element of the dances and the Dogon use over eighty different varieties according to the celebration. The biggest ceremony is the **Sigui**, celebrated every sixty years to commemorate the passing of a generation. The frequency of *Sigui* is calculated by the periodicity of an invisible satellite of the "dog star", Sirius. Sirius itself appears brightly between mountain peaks exactly when expected, suggesting a level of astonomical knowledge which has long baffled outsiders. The event serves to venerate the Big Mask, made in the shape of a serpent in reference to **Lebe**, who is credited with leading the Dogon to the Bandiagara escarpment as well as bringing them speech and, simultaneously, death. The last Sigui festival was held in the 1960s; the next – without undue optimism – should be in the 2020s.

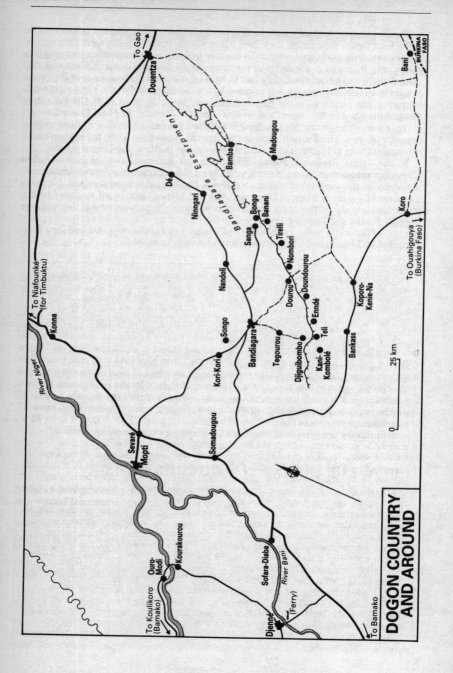

DOGON COUNTRY AND AROUND

Into the *pays Dogon*: what it takes – and what to take

A trip to the Dogon country involves hours of trekking in the sweltering sun, and is likely to entail climbing up and down the 300-metre escarpment and walking over rocky terrain. You'll want to go as light as possible therefore and you're recommended to leave all but the essentials in Mopti. You can **consign your bags** to the sweet care of the *Bar Mali* in Mopti who, for a small daily fee, will guard them while you're gone. Other hotels will do the same.

Bring a water bottle or canteen for the long hot stretches between villages. Dogon villages have no running water, and you'll be drinking from local wells. It's a good idea in principle to try to boil or purify it: when stocks are low in the dry season, water can take on a murky colour that's more than enough persuasion. Guinea worm is a severe problem, though crude filtering (through a tee-shirt for example) removes the parasites.

Although the terrain is rough, you won't need any special **walking shoes**. Tennis shoes or even sandals should be fine. Due to the scorching sun, you may want to think about taking a hat. You can take some fruit or light snacks from Mopti, but most of your **food** will be bought in Dogon villages.

If you have your own **vehicle**, you're better off leaving it in Mopti, unless it's four-wheel-drive. At some point in the Dogon country, you're likely to have to abandon it in order to visit villages hanging on the cliffs of the escarpment and it's best to leave it where you know it'll be safe.

Guides are essential. Without one, you'll have real problems just communicating with the people, since few of them speak French. Additionally, you'll have trouble locating villages and the quickest footpaths between them, or those that lead up and down the escarpment. Guides will also help when it comes to figuring out village market days, and they can make arrangements for sleeping and eating in isolated places where, unaided, you might not make your intentions clear. Except in the most remote communities you will in any case be expected to have a local escort: it says something for Dogon cohesion that such an understanding, with its long-term benefits for all concerned, has been achieved. Or at any rate it says something for the vigor of local entrepeneurs faced with official tourism policy. If you have a Dogon friend, he'd be the ideal person to show you around. If not, you'll have to pay a young Dogon or, much worse, take an official *SMERT* guide. As a rough indication, you should expect private guides (who know all too well that their services are indispensible) to want at least CFA3–4000 per day. Alone, you've most bargaining power, though it's usually cheaper per person in a group.

Sanga and the *SMERT* circuits

Much has been written about **SANGA** and it is indeed a striking example of a classic Dogon village, sited on the plateau above the escarpment, with traditional homes and granaries. This is the town where Reverend McKinney set up the first mission in the Dogon country in the 1930s and where, soon after, Marcel Griaule lived and studied this civilisation. The work of these two men went a long way towards focusing interest on the Dogon. Overflowing down the cliffs of the Bandiagara escarpment, the town was too picturesque to go unnoticed and has become the main *SMERT* domain in the district. Some of the best and most popular **walking tours** through Dogon country start at Sanga, but it's virtually impossible to do them without a *SMERT* guide.

Arrival and other practicalities

If you don't sign up for a full-fledged *SMERT* excursion in Mopti, you can get to Sanga by taking a bush taxi to BANDIAGARA. From here, it's possible to get transport to Sanga, notably on the town's market day. Markets in the Dogon Country are held

A FEW WORDS OF DOGON							

Most Dogon, especially younger people, speak some French. A few words in the Dogon language, however, are bound to help comunication.

Hello	*Po*	1	*Ti*	5	*Noonay*	9	*Tuwa*
Boy	*Ah*	2	*Loy*	6	*Kuray*	10	*Peo*
Girl	*Ñe*	3	*Tahnu*	7	*So*	And, of course	
God	*Amma*	4	*Nay*	8	*Sira*	millet beer	*Konjo*

(Not that you'll be able to say "Hello, boy, girl, God" and count to ten after a couple of bowls of *Konjo*.)

every five days so try and find out when Sanga's will be before leaving Mopti. Sanga is actually a conglomeration of villages and your introduction will be at one called **OGOL-DU-HAUT**. This is where you'll find the *SMERT* office, the Gendarmerie and the government-run *campement* (**accommodation** from CFA4500). At the *campement*, you can hook up with a guide for a walking tour. You can also stay at the *Bar de la Dogonne* near the Protestant church. Besides more comfortable lodgings than the *campement*, they also have a good **restaurant** and cold beer.

Around Sanga

SMERT arranges three different day trips. The first, called the *petit tour,* includes a visit of Sanga and a seven-kilometre roundtrip trek to GOGOLI. The ten-kilometre *moyen tour* continues from these villages to BANANI, located partly on the *falaise* and partly on the plain below. The descent to this village from the plateau takes you through a strange tunnel carved into the cliff near the village of BONGO. All along the escarpment, you see caves – originally used by the Tellem as granaries or for defence in case of attack – cut into the rocky face. The fifteen-kilometre *grand tour* extends the loop to include TIRELLI, another village located both on the cliff and the plain. These treks last roughly between three and ten hours. Along the way, guides point out important aspects of Dogon village structure: the *toguna* open air "huts" covered with millet stalks where elders meet to chat and confer; the round huts where women stay during their periods; and the *gina,* a type of sanctuary reserved to honour the ancestors. At some point, you're bound to stop for a calabash full of *konjo* – bittersweet millet beer. It's also possible to arrange longer walking trips that could last up to a week.

Bandiagara and non-*SMERT* circuits

Although *SMERT*'s tours are convenient if you want a perfunctory overview of Dogon territory, you may prefer less organisation and the flexibility of following your own plans and pace. In that case it's usually better to head directly to **BANDIAGARA**, a seventy-kilometre taxi ride from Mopti over decent tracks. A sizeable **administrative town**, Bandiagara is nothing like more traditional villages in the region (as the large mosque testifies) although the population is sixty percent Dogon. There's a good deal of commerce by Dogon standards, plus a hospital, mission and police headquarters. It's a convenient point of entry, where you can arrange to visit villages on the plateau, the escarpment face and on the plain below. Although *SMERT* has a firm presence in town, you don't necessarily have to arrange your trip with them as is the case in Sanga. That doesn't mean you've worked your way off the tourist route, as you'll discover immediately upon entering, or that you can forego a guide. Even the young kids who hire themselves out are starting to ask for a lot of money, but they're still cheaper than official guides and, with them, you'll have more say about how you go and what you see.

Accommodation and practicalities

At some point during your stay in Bandiagara, if not immediately on arrival, you'll be expected to **register with the police** at their post just outside town on the Sanga Road. As for **somewhere to stay**, the government-run *campement* here costs from CFA4000 for ordinary, none-too-clean rooms. Some *auberges* and bars in town also offer cheap accommodation. The most popular is the *Hôtel Kansaye* at the town exit, just before the bridge. Rooms are well maintained and, at CFA1500, much cheaper than the *campement*. Kansaye, the owner, can fix you up with a guide and will let you leave baggage while you're hiking.

Bandiagara is a pleasant enough town, but brace yourself for a blunt introduction to Dogon tourism. Besides the no-lodging-with-locals law and the mandatory police check-in, kids swarm around you from the minute you arrive, offering their services as guides. Be careful when choosing one, making sure he knows the terrain and will take you around for a reasonable price. As you go through the villages oultined here, you'll encounter numerous **expenses** in addition to what you pay your guide. Many Dogon villages now charge a flat **entry fee** for visitors, usually around CFA500. And staying in people's homes will cost you extra, as will food.

From Bandiagara to Djiguibombo

Twenty-five kilometres of walkable tracks separate Bandiagara from Djiguibombo at the edge of the *falaise*. This relatively flat road over the plateau passes through sparse vegetation of bush savannah with the occasional baobab rising up to dominate the rocky landscape: *SMERT* and their works are rapidly left behind. After about 12km you pass the town of TEGOUROU. Nearby is a dammed stream and the terraced fields of the Dogon's famous onions. Before continuing the trip down the escarpment most guides will stop at **DJIGUIBOMBO**, the last town on the plateau. The town stands in an extremely rocky area near the cliff: a stone wall surrounds it and many of the houses use stone in their construction as well.

Along the plain from Kani-Kombolé to Teli

A couple of kilometres south of Djiguibombo, you finally arrive at the cliff: from the edge of the plateau, there's a sweeping vista onto the plains below. Although the cliff drops suddenly, there are walkable paths down it that your guide will lead you along, and the 300m descent poses no special problem. Once on the plain, KANI-KOMBOLE – with a reasonable little *bar-resto* and somewhere to stay if you need it – isn't too far off.

Following the *falaise* eastwards, you come next to **TELI**, a four-kilometre walk over a flat, sandy stretch bordered by millet fields. If you didn't manage to get to Sanga (or decided to avoid it), Teli is a satisfying substitute that is still a lot less visited, with some of the most spectacular **cliffside houses** along this part of the escarpment. If you take this route, it's worth coming at least this far. Some guides are better than others at getting you permission to climb up to the cliff-dwellings, but the people living on them don't seem too enthralled at having visitors. Go in your lowest key and look out for the old lady up on the rock face, with her macabre "souvenir" skulls in the wall.

Enndé to Bandiagara via Douru

Having reached Teli, you can consider you've had a pretty good overview of the Dogon country and will have seen villages on the plateau, in the cliffs and on the plains. At this point, you could either return to Bandiagara retracing the route described above, or continue east to **ENNDÉ**. Here, you can spend the night on the roof of the house of the village chief's son, who's quite accustomed to putting up travellers. You can also pay to have meals of chicken and rice prepared and wash it down with home-brewed millet beer.

YAMBO OUOLOGUEM – A POEM

Yambo Ouologuem, who is Dogon, is Mali's best known writer (see "Books" in
Contexts).

WHEN NEGRO TEETH SPEAK

People think I'm a cannibal
But you know what people say

People see I've got red gums but who has
White ones
Up the tomatoes

People say there are not nearly so many tourists
Now
But you know
This isn't America and nobody
Has the money

People think it's my fault and
*   are scared*
But look
My teeth are white not red
I've not eaten anybody
People are rotten they say I scoff
Baked tourists
Or maybe grilled
Baked or grilled I asked
They didn't say anything just kept
*   looking uneasily at my gums*
Up the tomatoes

Everyone knows in an agricultural country there's agriculture
Up the vegetables

Everyone knows that vegetables
Well you can't live on the vegetables
*   you grow*
And that I'm quite well developed
*   for someone underdeveloped*
Miserable scum living off the tourists
Down with my teeth

People suddenly surrounded me
Tied me up
Threw me down
At the feet of justice

Cannibal or not cannibal
Answer

Ah you think you're so clever
So proud of yourself

Well, we'll see I'm going to settle
your account
Have you anything to say
Before you are sentenced to death

I shouted Up the tomatoes

People are rotten and women curious
you know
There was one of these in the
curious circle
In her rasping voice sort of bubbling like
a saucepan
With a hole in it
Shrieked
Slit open his belly
I'm sure father is still inside

There weren't any knives
Naturally enough among the vegetarians
Of the western world
So they got a Gillette blade
And carefully
Slit
Slat
Plop
Slit open my belly

Inside flourishing rows of tomatoes
Watered by streams of palm wine
Up the tomatoes

Translated from the French by Clive Wake and John Reed in *A New Book of African Verse* (Heinemann 1988) and reproduced with permission of the translators.

After Enndé, the road continues through a number of villages on the plain. One of the more picturesque is DOUNDOURU, known for the spectacular homes carved in the cliff. Still following the escarpment to the east, you next come to KONSAGOU, and finally GIMINI. After this village, you can climb back up the *falaise* and walk along the edge of the plateau to **DOUROU**.

Dourou has one of the most important **markets** so near the escarpment, and a **motorable** road from Bandiagara. Every five days, vehicles arrive here from Bandiagara and Mopti bringing traders and goods to the heart of Dogon country. In addition to ubiquitous Dogon onions, grown nearby and sold in large quantities, you'll find cereals, Fula milk and rough cotton weaves of indigo-dyed material, a common element in Dogon dress. If you time your visit to coincide with **market day**, you can hope to get a ride back to Bandiagara, 25km to the north.

Approaches from the south: Bankass

An alternative route into Dogon country from Mopti and Sevaré bypasses Bandiagara altogether, entering the Dogon region via **BANKASS**, reached from the road that passes through Somadougou. This way you start the trek from down on the plains, and approach the escarpment from below. Bankass is a large market village with a mixed population, less centrally placed than Bandiagara for visits to the traditional villages. Hiking access to the *falaise* is more difficult from here, but in the dry season it's just about possible to go by car (or hire a donkey cart or moped) to Kani-Kombolé, Enndé and Teli. Although this is easier, the visit from Bandiagara is really more interesting and, approaching the scarp edge from above, certainly more impressive.

Accommodation and transport

Accommodation in Bankass is pretty much limited to *Ben's Bar* which is cheap and basic but increasingly complacent. Toilets are a hole in the ground, and showers are taken outdoors with buckets. Prices vary depending whether you sleep without frills on the roof (as little as CFA250) or take a room (CFA1000). You can leave baggage here while hiking. Ben can fix you up with guides, will prepare meals for you and get kids to do your wash if need be. If you're without transport, ask him about the possibility of hiring a moped to Kani-Kombolé, at the base of the *falaise*. Once you reach this village, you can visit others along the escarpment by following the routes described above.

Koro

Coming **from Burkina Faso**, you can also enter the Dogon country by taking the road from Ouahigouya to the border post at TIOU. From here a very bad *piste* (often impassable during the rains) leads some 55km to **KORO** where you go through Malian police and **customs formalities**. Although Koro has a large **market** and beautiful **mosque**, it's far from the heart of the Dogon country and sees few tourists. It's one place where you certainly won't encounter the tender mercies of *SMERT* or have kids swarming around you like flies. The town could reasonably be used as a springboard for a trip through some of the less-visited Dogon villages, but you'll have to allow yourself extra time to work out transport and other details.

Accommodation and travel ideas

Across from the market, the *Tolo Bar* puts up travellers cheaply. There should, by now, be rooms around the courtyard (outdoor shower and toilet) or you may still be able to sleep on the terrace. They'll fix you up with meals and cold drinks and, while facilities are rudimentary, the reception is very warm. If you're heading out of the Dogon country towards Burkina, it can come as a welcome relief. Near the Gendarmerie the newly renovated *campement* rooms from CFA2000 are more comfortable than Tolo's, and if you catch the owner on a good day he can be very helpful. You can also find a bed at the *Le Point* bar or the *Bar de la Jeunesse* near the mosque.

To visit the *falaise* from Koro, you could head up to Bankass and follow the routes outlined above. Alternatively, you could make for DOUENTZA in the northeast (see p.239). This last route is virtually untravelled by foreigners and passes through the Dogon villages of MADOUGOU and BAMBA and a wild, duney area. EVERI, a seven-kilometre hike from Douentza, is built on a high mesa at the end of the escarpment. Rare vehicles link these villages on market days. Talk to people at the *Tolo Bar* for ideas of other places to visit along this road: they may be able to get you through the entire Dogon country without ever running into *SMERT* or the police.

If you're heading to Gao with your own vehicle, the Douentza *piste* provides a kind of "rear view" of the Dogon country. The tracks, however, are very difficult (with taxing stretches of soft sand and boulders) and it's hard to follow their endless branches. *Peugeot 404* taxis do ply between Douentza and Madougou for the market, so you should be able to go by normal car, although a 4WD vehicle is obviously preferable. It would probably prove just as quick to follow the longer but more obvious route via Somadougou and the main Bamako–Gao highway.

MOVING ON

Transport out of Koro is somewhat problematic. Taxis head fairly frequently to Bankass (at least every couple of days), but are extremely rare to Tiou and Burkina Faso. Even in the dry season you may be stranded several days in Koro waiting for the occasional goods truck or tourist heading south. During the rains, the road may be unpassable for weeks on end.

GAO AND THE NORTHEAST

Arid and inhospitable, northeastern Mali is only habitable at all thanks to the River Niger, along which life in the area concentrates. Coming south out of the desert, you reach the river – and a parting of the ways – at **Gao**, formerly the capital of a great kingdom and now the administrative and commercial centre for the region. From here you can follow the river south **to Niamey** (in Niger) along a difficult but scenic *piste* leading through small fishing villages; head upstream, along even more difficult tracks, **to Timbuktu** in the west; or go west the easy way, on a recently paved road **to Mopti and Bamako**. Alternatively **the river** itself can serve as your highway, certainly a more memorable way to travel – providing you time your travels to coincide with the rains.

Gao – the town

Arriving from the void of the desert, **GAO** seems like a small miracle of civilisation emerging from the wasteland. After the last stretch of soft sand thrown up by the Sahara around the town, entering the dusty tree-lined avenues, fringed by busy shops and thronging with crowds, stirs certain exhilaration. The physical sensations of admission into a new world are strong and enchanting – though not unsullied by bureaucracy. Desert-crossers usually celebrate their arrival in West Africa by heading straight to the *Hôtel Atlantide* – a grand, tatty colonial pile that might as well be the Ritz out here – and downing a few cold beers. The first few hours are intoxicating.

Behind the hotel is the source of all this vigor, the **River Niger**, normally encountered here for the first time by travellers arriving from the north. If you've come up from the south you get a rather different view of the place: the river, which from this direction is neither new nor unusual, is unlikely to stir much excitement, while the town itself resembles any other Sahelian town, bigger than most but neither especially beautiful nor unusually dynamic. All is relative.

Formalities and time-fillers

You must **register with the police** on arrival. Their office is next to the market and central mosque. You'll be given forms on which you must state date of arrival and departure and your address in Gao, and your passport is then stamped. This is generally a frustrating and time-consuming process. If you managed to get admitted through the border post at Tessalit without a visa, you can get it here – tourist cards and photo permits are no longer required.

There's hours more fun to be had in the **bank** if you need to change money. The system here hasn't changed for years and involves repeated visits to various *guichets* for different signatures. The place is always stacked full of money and full of back-country people trying to perform once-yearly transactions before it closes at noon.

And lastly, there's more time-wasting if you had the presence of mind to suggest people write to you at **Poste Restante**, Gao. Delays generally run to three weeks from posting and there's no accounting for the bitterly abject misery of the *fonctionnaires* in the office. You need exceptional powers of diplomacy if you plan on going in there every morning to repeat your request.

Some history

The original founders of Gao, known in its early days as Kawkaw, were **Sorko fishermen** who migrated in waves from Benin between the sixth and eleventh centuries. They mingled with the rural Gabili peoples living along the banks of the Niger, and eventually this mixture evolved into a people known as the Songhai. The first **Songhai** monarch at Gao was Kanda, who founded the **Za (or Dia) dynasty** in the seventh century. He quickly opened the town to trans-Saharan trade and to Berbers who wanted to settle there for commercial reasons.

The fifteenth king of Songhai, Za Kossoi, converted to **Islam** in 1009. The town prospered to the point where it rivalled all the great regional trading centres in power and wealth, even surpassing the capitals of Ancient Ghana and later Mali. Rulers of the Mali Empire coveted Gao's success and potential and annexed the town in 1325, although the Songhai princes managed to flee from their clutches. One of them, **Ali Golon**, went on to found the **Sonni dynasty** still based at Gao. The greatest of the Sonni rulers was the despotic Sonni Ali Ber, or **Ali the Great.** It was he who, towards the end of the fifteenth century, expanded the kingdom at Gao to the dimensions of an empire (see below). The capital continued to flourish under the reign of the **Askias**, founders of a new dynasty that lasted throughout the sixteenth century. At the time, Gao had 70,000 inhabitants and in the busy harbour were crowded over 1000 war boats from the Askia's flotilla, 400 barges and thousands of *pirogues*.

With the **Moroccan invasion** of Songhai in 1591, the empire collapsed and Gao was virtually rased. The town never recovered and when the German explorer **Heinrich Barth** arrived in 1854, he described the once ostentatious city as "a desolate abode with a small and miserable population". Much of the town's present look dates to the beginning of this century. The **French** built up the port, traced new streets (which explains the rather uniform grid layout) and established an administrative district with characteristic colonial buildings still used by the present government. With a population of some 20,000, Gao still hasn't returned to its former grandeur, but as a commercial town at the crossroads, it's holding its own.

Getting by in Gao: places to stay

It's worth knowing that **camping sauvage** (what you've been doing across the desert) is prohibited within a 12km radius of Gao. The last opportunity to do something similar is provided by *Camping Bangu* (ex-*Askia*, ex-*Dominque*), on the way into town on the left of the Tessalit route (not the Bourem one).

Gao's finest **hotel** is the *Atlantide*. But once you've got over the initial post-desert impression of grandeur, the comforts turn out to be something of an illusion: some of

THE SONGHAI EMPIRE

Towards the end of the fourteenth century, Mali's influence and power had diminished greatly and the stage was set for **Sonni Ali Ber** – nineteenth ruler in the Sonni dynasty and the effective founder of Songhai as an empire – to embark on his great conquests. A shrewd administrator, Ali was also a brilliant and ruthless strategist and it is said he never lost a battle. A half-hearted Muslim, Ali quickly set about terrorising the Fula and Tuareg nomads – his bitter enemies in the region. His expansionist designs were greatly facilitated in 1468 when he was invited by the governor of **Timbuktu** to liberate that town from Tuareg domination.

Historians of the period reported that Ali's conquest of Timbuktu was brutal, and many of the townspeople who had longed for the Songhai "liberation" fled north to Oualata for fear of persecution. After an initial period of purging religious leaders who stood in his path, however, Ali brought stability to the town which once again prospered under his rule. At the same time, he managed to neutralise the **religious influence** of Timbuktu's powerful marabouts who exercised considerable political power over the entire region.

Ali next turned his sights on **Djenné**, but it proved a harder target. The Sonnis besieged the town for seven years, seven months and seven days before it finally fell in 1423. Rather than taking vengence on the ruling class as he had in Timbuktu, Ali married his fortunes with those of Djenné by taking the queen mother to be his wife. **Masina** was his next objective, and he conquered this Fula stronghold shortly afterwards.

All the chief strategic points of the Niger and the Delta region were now in Songhai control. The nation's military strength was founded in its **navy** and Ali depended so heavily on his flotilla that, at one point, he envisaged digging a canal from the port town of Ras al-Ma to the desert oasis of Oualata in order to attack the Tuareg there. Although work started, the plan was eventually abandoned as Ali extended his control southwards to the villages of Bandiagara, Bariba and Gourma.

After he died, Sonni Ali was succeeded by his son Bakari, but the new king followed his father's example of keeping a distance from the faith and thus incited religious disapproval. He was overthrown by Mohammed Torodo, the governor of Hombori, who formed a new dynasty known as the **Askia** or usurper.

Though he had no hereditary claim to the throne, Askia Mohammed legitimised his rule through religious channels, soliciting the backing of powerful **marabouts**. He received the ultimate benediction to his rule after making the pilgrimage to Mecca with 500 horsemen and 1000 footsoldiers. There he requested and was granted the title of Khalif for the entire Sudan.

Returning to Mali, he set about expanding his empire into Mossi country, then pushed eastward to Hausaland and into the Aïr as far as Agadez.

While away on a campaign, Mohammed was forced out of power in 1528. Internal intrigue followed and a number of Askias succeeded one another until the reign of **Ishak I** who ruled from 1539–49 – a decade which marked the Songhai Empire's apogee. The country now extended from Senegal to the Aïr mountains and from the Taghaza salt mines in the desert to the Hausaland in what is now Nigeria.

Meanwhile **Morocco** far to the north was in a period of crisis. Ejected from Andalusia and hemmed in to the east by the Turks, the Moroccan sultan turned his sights towards the south, where he sought to gain control of the salt and gold trade. In 1591 he sent an army to wrest the Sudan from Songhai control. Thanks to a combination of Moroccan firearms and the disarray of the Askia rulers, the Sultan's army won a decisive battle at **Tondibi**, 60km north of Gao: Gao, Djenné and Timbuktu all fell soon afterwards.

Es Sadi, writing in the *Tarikh es-Soudin*, described the invasion in these terms: "Everything changed after the Moroccan conquest. It signaled the beginning of anarchy, theft, pillage and general disorganisation". And indeed the entire Sahelian region suffered a blow from which it never recovered.

the rooms have AC, but in general they're uninviting. Prices range from under CFA5000 to over CFA11,000. There's no other permanent, cheap place to stay in the town centre, though one or other of the restaurants periodically risks letting out rooms – until police demands become excessive.

For **budget travellers**, the best value is at *Tizi Mizi Camping*, though this is quite a distance from the centre, about 4km down the Niamey road. Rooms are comfortable and impeccably clean; or you can pitch a tent next to your car or sleep on the rooftop terrace for less than CFA1000. They have a pleasant outdoor bar and restaurant as well as a disco. The long-established *Camping Yarga* is also about 4km from the centre, off the paved road leading to the Mopti road ferry. Buildings are of traditional mud bricks or *banco* – dried mud on a wooden frame. Prices are slightly below those at *Tizi Mizi*, but the rooms are less comfortable. You can have meals prepared. *Yarga's* is close to good swimming beaches along the Niger – the river is considered schisto-free in these parts.

Eating and drinking

Gao doesn't boast very classy **restaurants** except, with a stretch of imagination, the *Atlantide's* where you can sit down to French-style *steak frites* or *poulet* and vegetables – unexciting and rather pricey. A cheaper alternative, the *Restaurant Senegalais*, near the place de l'Indépendance, is a more popular overlanders' joint: they serve copious plates of jollof rice on their patio. Cheaper still is a string of chop houses on the road running parallel to the principal boulevard des Askias – two blocks east as you walk away from the river. The *Blackpool* is a well-known and recommended place for local fare such as Nile perch and *riz sauce*. Just across the street is the *Restaurant Dikou* which has an almost identical menu and pricelist. Down the street towards the place de l'Indépendance, the *Oasis* is another popular place. And be sure to sample Gao's delicious, long spicy sausages – always a reliable evening street food fallback.

Due to the Muslim influence, **nightlife** is concentrated in out of the way, but well-known clubs with bars and coolish beer. During the month of Ramadan, even some of these close down, and finding a cold beer outside the *Atlantide* could be a problem. *L'Escale* near the place de l'Indépendance, counts as one of the better places for dancing. Another popular night spot is *Le Twist Bar* near the police. And if you're staying at the *Tizi Mizi*, their full-scale disco isn't likely to escape your notice.

Around town: museum, markets and minor monuments

Considering the centuries of history through which Gao has played a leading role, the **Musée du Sahel** is disappointingly small. In any case, rather than concentrating on the Songhai Empire, the museum is dedicated to the different **peoples of the Sahel**, with displays of their art and domestic implements. You'll see farming and fishing tools (some rather impressive harpoons), musical instruments, and household items used by the **Tuareg**, **Fula**, **Chamba** and **Arma** (descendants of Moroccan-Songhai marriages). There are different prices for guided or unguided tours: the guides are extremely enthusiastic and their personal comments are probably worth a couple of extra coins, but if you want to go it alone you'll find that most of the exhibits are explained relatively well.

In the town centre, Gao boasts two outstanding **markets**. The *grand marché*, just opposite the *Atlantide*, has an entire section devoted to **crafts**, for which the region is well known. The most common items are Tuareg **leather boxes**, knives and swords; on sale too are numerous examples of **Sahelian sandals** – flat and wide to facilitate walking on the sands. Some pairs incorporate intricate weaving and green or red dyed leather in the design. Fula and Tuareg **jewellery** can also be a good buy here, but vendors generally set astronomically high starting prices: bargaining tends to be more of a headache than the good-humoured exchange you're hopefully used to.

Behind the crafts section, women bunch around desert wares – anonymous spices, dollops of peanut butter, sour milk, fish and meat, pyramids of miniature tomatoes, onions, peppers, lettuces carefully washed (in the river) and, in season if you're lucky, the full range of tropical fruits and vegetables. After the Saharan dearth, the exotic variety is impressive. The *petit marché*, next to the police, specialises in cloth. Dozens of tailors – all men of course – treadle ancient *Singers* and will take orders if you want to have loose-fitting Sahelian clothes made to measure.

In physical terms, Gao has few reminders of its glorious past. The **mosque** in the centre of town near the police was initially built by Kankan Moussa after he annexed the town in the fourteenth century but, its origins apart, it's unimpressive compared even to those in Timbuktu and certainly to the mosque in Djenné.

Following the boulevard des Askias to the northeast brings you to the **Askia tomb** – a fifteen-minute walk from the centre. Now used as a mosque, you can visit this strange fifteenth-century mud structure and climb to the top of the odd-shaped pyramid with wild wooden crossbeams sticking out porcupine style from the facade: from the top, you get a good view of town and of the river. You're expected to tip the guardian something for the visit.

MOVING ON

Now that the road has been paved **from Gao to Bamako**, getting out of town is a great deal easier. During and after the rains, you can also take advantage of the **steamers** that pass along one of the most interesting stretches of the **Niger** between here (their terminus) and Mopti. Conditions are much tougher for travel **to Niamey** or of course **to Algeria** via Tessalit. Expect long waits for vehicles heading in these directions.

By River
Apart from the main August–November steamer services (see p.181), it's possible to use smaller river craft for transport most of the year round. Upstream, poled *pirogues* set off for **Bourem** (all day and half the next), **Bamba** (3–4 days), **Gourma-Rharous** (4–5 days) and Timbuktu (one week). Downstream, *pirogues* rarely go much beyond **Gargouna** (one day away, Tuesday market) or **Ansongo**, two days away (splendid Thursday market). This latter trip, below Gao, is especially rewarding from a natural history viewpoint, as the boats crush through marvellous deep reedbeds harbouring a wealth of **birdlife**, and then break onto open water where they regularly pass several herds of snorting **hippos**. *Pirogue* fares have increased enormously in recent years, but a place on an ordinary transport vessel shouldn't cost you more than CFA1500 per day, including communal rice and fish.

By Air
Air Mali operates **flights** from Gao airfield (7km from the centre) to Timbuktu, Mopti, Goundam and Bamako. There are one or two flights a week to each of these destinations. For more details, check out the *Air Mali* office which is in the centre of town next to the *Atlantide*.

By Road to Mopti and Bamako
You can frequently arrange to travel out with tourists heading by car to Mopti or Bamako by asking around at the *Atlantide* or one of the *campings*. There's also a **mail bus** that leaves for Mopti once a week from in front of the PTT. Check at the post office for schedules and information.

By Road from Gao to Niamey
The best way to get to Niamey if you don't have your own transport is with the *SNTN* **bus** that leaves every Monday, Wednesday and Friday morning. It's wise to book the day before as it's often full. The bus leaves Gao around 11am and gets into Niamey the following afternoon. As an alternative, check with overlanders staying at the *Atlantide* or at the campsites. They, however, will still be loaded down with Algerian fuel to get at least as far as Tillabéri, and are often reluctant to add to their weight. Try to look light, offer to share costs (*partager le frais*) and be ready to help dig the car out of the soft sand in which it may become repeatedly bogged.

Trans-Sahara and Timbuktu
Overlanders driving north **across the Sahara** are rare, so your best bet for transport is with truckers. The owner of the *Tizi Mizi* often seems to know what's going north, or you can enquire at the *Atlantide*. Kids can also be a help finding out about transport through the desert if you give them a small *cadeau* (after you've scored a ride, of course). You can expect to pay in the order of CFA20,000 for the crossing to Adrar, meals included (take this option; it's a poor idea to be excluded at meal times). If you want to save money, you should head out with the first vehicle you find, even if the driver quotes you an unusually high price. In certain seasons, you can wait a long time to find transport and if you're paying out for a hotel and food, it adds up quickly. The route between the border and Gao is covered in detail in Part Two, "The Algerian Sahara" p.120–121.

The strategy of checking at the hotels and with children also applies for tracking down rare vehicles heading **to Timbuktu**. This destination involves the longest wait from Gao and at times there's nothing at all heading in that direction. If you get fed up, take a vehicle to BOUREM and try waiting there. Some traffic crosses the desert and turns right there to Timbuktu.

Along the Mopti Road

Heading out of Gao, the only way to reach the new paved road to Bamako is by taking the **ferry** across the Niger; a regular service with fixed prices. The departure point is 7km south of town, but boats stop running at nightfall, around 6pm. This is usually more of a problem if you're coming in the other direction, from Mopti to Gao. Plan on arriving in time or you'll be forced to sleep on the wrong side of the river.

The early stages of the Mopti road are pretty dull, with long stretches of monotonous Sahel landscape. After 90km you arrive at DORO, a small town in a region where lions are said to exist. If these reports are true, you'd have to follow tracks a good 40km south of town to have any hope of seeing them. Ask in Doro if any have been spotted recently and, if so, enquire about the possibility of taking someone along as a guide.

GOSSI is the next large Songhai village along the road, 160km from Gao. It's on the shore of a muddy lake and is the site of a sizeable reafforestation and agricultural project headed by a Norwegian church fund. Many **Tuareg** are making the uneasy transition to a sedentary lifestyle in this area. Gossi has no accommodation but makes for a pleasant place to stop off for a lukewarm drink and bite to eat. Grilled meat is sold in large quantities at the marketplace and quite cheap.

After Gossi, the scenery shifts from neutral into top gear, with large and spectacular **stone outcroppings** in the vicinity of **HOMBORI**, 250km from Gao. A strikingly beautiful village, Hombori itself is built partially on the rocky slopes of **Hombori Tondo** – a flat-topped mountain that rises to 1150m. Many of the homes here are built of stone, a rarity in West Africa, and there are a number of small **restaurants** and bars scattered along the section of highway that passes through town. Then, 11km out of Hombori, the road slides past the dramatic rock formation known as **La Main de Fatima**, since it resembles the symbolic hand – with outstretched thumb and finger – of the prophet's daughter.

Just under 400km from Gao, **DOUENTZA** is a town with an important market and an impressive **mosque**, poised at the northeastern periphery of the **Bandiagara escarpment** which stretches some 200km south through the Dogon country. Just before arriving at Douentza, a signboard marks the turning for KORO. If you have transport, this *piste* provides an excellent means of getting to the Dogon villages of Bamba, Madougou and Koro (p.232). From here you can head back up to Bandiagara, and will have visited a good chunk of the Dogon country without ever running into police or government tourist agents. Few overlanders take this route, however, and with good reason. The tracks are extremely difficult, combining long stretches of soft sand with hard stone – a nightmare for your car's belly, though understandably battered *Peugeot 404* bush taxis do make the trip out from Douentza.

Back on the main paved road to Mopti, BORÉ (458km from Gao) boasts an unusually large and beautiful **mosque** for such a small place. A further 56km and you arrive at KONA, a market town on the junction of the road to Niafounké and Timbuktu. From here, it's a quick jog to Sevaré – the highway junction for Mopti.

The road to Niamey

The road to Niamey hugs the banks of the **Niger** through some exceptionally beautiful scenery. It's a well-travelled route, but full of sandy pitfalls and thorn trees whose wicked spines pass readily through hot, soft rubber. Although only 443km separate Gao and Niamey, the trip involves a good two days' drive – longer in the rains, or if you take a leisurely pace and stop off at the numerous fishing villages.

The initial 95km presents few problems until you arrive at ANSONGO – a picturesque village with an important **market** on Thursdays. The town is essentially Songhai, but you'll also see numerous Tuareg who make their way through the entire region. After Ansongo, the road becomes progressively worse, with stretches of treacherous sand that may become impassable during the rains. Despite the difficulties, it's a beautiful stretch that the government has officially classified as a protected natural area. Your chances are good of seeing **hippos** at some point along the river: in many instances they come quite close to the villages and the areas where people swim. **Giraffes** and numerous varieties of **gazelle** also roam through the region, though you're unlikely to spot them from the road.

FAFA is the next village, 140km from Gao. There's a pleasant *campement – Chez Fafa* – with a restaurant and rooms from around CFA4000, though it's closed from the end of July to the end of August. You can arrange here to take a river ride on a *pirogue* to see nearby hippos.

The road continues tortuously until you arrive at LABBEZANGA, 191km from Gao, the Mali-Niger **border post** where you'll be subjected to marvellously protracted formalities. There's a bar and **restaurant** near the customs post. It's another 44km to AYOROU, a large market town where you pass through Niger customs, and 132km to Tillabéri where a surfaced road picks up – in blissful comfort by comparison – the rest of the way to Niamey. For more detail on this route, see "Niger" p.150.

index

BURKINA FASO

"Burkinabe stand up! We are going to work to make our country better!"

BURKINA FASO
LA DIMENSION
HUMAINE
DU TOURISME

BURKINA FASO

There are few such unlucky countries as **Burkina Faso**. But for a twist of administrative fate in colonial times, it would never have existed. It is desperately, and famously, poor, with an almost total lack of raw materials or natural resources. Although it shares its land-locked predicament with Niger and Mali, unlike them it does not have direct access to the important trans-Saharan routes. And its experiments with radical forms of government, under young and ideological leadership, have unfortunately cost it dear in terms of foreign relations and investment.

Added to these national difficulties are several superficial disadvantages from the traveller's point of view: the country is boringly flat, and offers little of the natural spectacle and traditional cultural colour of its neighbours; it has a bare minimum of places to stay and roads to travel on, and it suffers from an image problem in the foreign press which acts as an unreasonable deterrent.

Despite what sounds an uninviting prospect, however, most visitors really enjoy Burkina. Although there are endless military checkpoints throughout the country, soldiers and customs agents treat you with respect, and even familiarity, as they venture a *Bonne arrivée, ça va?* while verifying your passport.

For all the slogging poverty, there's a climate of almost youthful **optimism**, and you'll encounter a refreshing lack of complexes and considerable vitality in popular culture. You can travel by bush taxi to small towns in the back country, and not have people stare at you the whole time. Getting business done is perhaps no easier than anywhere else, but as a place to travel, or simply hang out, Burkina leaves an exceptionally good taste.

These impressions are given certain official sanction by a committedly interventionist tourist policy, which emphasises Burkina's "Human Dimension of Tourism". The efforts of the French charity airline, *Le Point*, in the early 1980s, to offer the cheapest flights to West Africa and plough the profits back into the region, soon placed Burkina in the centre of many overland travel plans. Before its demise, the company developed a philosophy, loosely defined as "a different kind of tourism", that placed contact between peoples above jet-setting between five-star hotels, and the government has taken up the call.

Specific targets for travel include **Bobo-Dioulasso**, unquestionably one of the most pleasant towns in West Africa, the hilly and prettily wooded **Banfora region** in the southwest, and the remote and fascinating **Lobi country** in the south with its mysterious stone ruins. The appeal of **Ouagadougou**, the capital, isn't especially strong, but it improves with some background knowledge of the venerable **Mossi kingdoms**, of which Ouagadougou was formerly one of several in the central region. Solid insights are scattered through this chapter.

The land

Burkina is nearly all flat and most of the country is swathed in semi-arid **grasslands**. The further north you go, the drier things become until you arrive at the denuded **Sahelian landscapes** of the extreme north. Only in the southern regions of Banfora and the Lobi country will you find much greenery. Around Banfora, the forests are run through by streams that fall in striking waterfalls from the cliffs.

BASIC FACTS ABOUT BURKINA FASO

The country's official name, **Burkina Faso** is a hybrid of a More word meaning dignity-nobility-integrity and a Dioula word meaning homeland. The name, changed in 1984 from Haute Volta (Upper Volta), thus means, roughly, "Land of the Honourable". The **population** of Burkina (the *Burkinabe*) numbers perhaps nine milllion people, around 400,000 of whom live in the capital, Ouagadougou. With an **area** of 275,000 square kilometres, the country is slightly larger than Great Britain. Since August 4 1983, it has been ruled by a military regime overseen by the *Conseil National de la Révolution*. Blaise Compaoré has been head of state since 1987 when he succeeded Thomas Sankara in a coup in which Sankara was killed. On the economic front, even with the cancellation of its French debt, Burkina's **foreign debts** total above £500 million – but that's still a piffling amount in international terms, about the cost of a very modest aircraft carrier for example.

Although the Red, White and Black Volta Rivers all rise in Burkina, only the *Volta Noire* flows in the dry season. The three meet up much further south in Ghana where they form a navigable river the Portuguese called *Rio da Volta*, or "River of Return".

The people

With some sixty different language groups living within its borders, Burkina has the usual ethno-linguistic mosaic. But most of them speak languages of the big *Voltaic* group, and it's unusual in having an overwhelming majority of a single people. The More-speaking **Mossi**, who live in the central plains around Ouagadougou, make up over half the population. They are related to the **Gourmantché**, who live in the east around Fada Ngourma, and less closely to the Grusi or Gourounsi from around Pô and Léo.

Main peoples of the north include the **Fula**, the **Hausa** and the **Bella**. Near the northwestern border with Mali, live small enclaves of **Dogon**, **Samos** and **Pana**. In the south, different **Bobo** peoples – Bwaba, Kos and Siby – populate the area around Bobo-Dioulasso. The **Senoufo** occupy the southwestern tip near Côte d'Ivoire and Mali, while the **Lobi**, towards the border with Ghana, remain one of the most isolated peoples in the country today.

Burkina's population has suffered mightily over the last two or three generations. It was from the region of the Upper Volta that the French recruited much of the **labour** to work plantations in their Ivory Coast colony, and the Burkinabe continue to look south for work in relatively prosperous Côte d'Ivoire as the land at home becomes impoverished. Burkina has been one of the countries most blighted by the recurrent Sahel droughts and it remains a main focus of many aid and development agencies.

Climate

Burkina's climate is characterised by two main seasons. The rains last from June to October, with violent storms gathering quickly, inundating everything and blowing away to leave clear blue skies behind. It's a period of hard work on the farms and, for travellers, one when many of the country's *pistes* are impassable. Except on the main routes, you can have trouble getting around the country by car or *taxi brousse* during this period.

The dry season lasts from November to May. This is when the **Harmattan** blows across the country, whipping up dust and smothering everything in a dreary ochre haze. At night it can get quite chilly, especially in the north. The **best period to travel** is from December to February – after the rains have finished, but before the ground gets hot and temperatures reach oppressive levels.

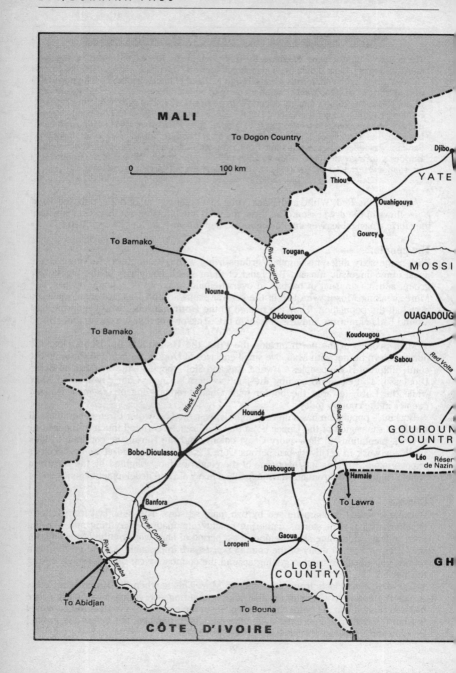

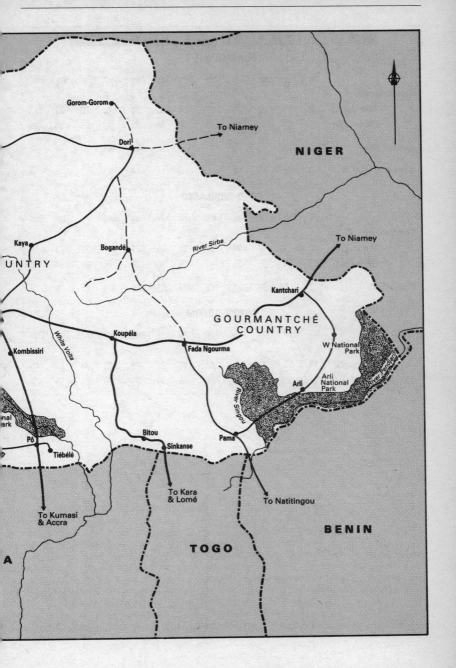

AVERAGE TEMPERATURES AND RAINFALL

OUAGADOUGOU

	Jan	Feb	Mar	Apr	May	June	July	Aug	Sept	Oct	Nov	Dec
Temperatures °C												
Min (night)	16	20	23	26	26	24	23	22	23	23	22	17
Max (day)	33	37	40	39	38	36	33	31	32	35	36	35
Rainfall mm	0	3	13	15	84	122	203	277	145	33	0	0
Days with rainfall	0	1	1	2	6	9	12	14	11	3	0	0

BOBO-DIOULASSO

	Jan	Feb	Mar	Apr	May	June	July	Aug	Sept	Oct	Nov	Dec
Temperatures °C												
Min (night)	18	21	23	24	24	22	21	21	21	21	20	18
Max (day)	33	34	35	35	34	31	30	29	31	32	34	32
Rainfall mm	3	5	28	54	119	124	253	310	219	65	18	0

GOROM-GOROM

	Jan	Feb	Mar	Apr	May	June	July	Aug	Sept	Oct	Nov	Dec
Temperatures °C												
Min (night)	12	17	22	26	28	26	25	23	25	25	18	15
Max (day)	32	35	38	42	41	38	36	33	38	38	35	32

Arrivals

There are no direct flights from London to Ouagadougou. *UTA* and *Air Afrique* share a monopoly on regular flights from Western Europe (Paris) and it often works out cheaper to go via Moscow with *Aeroflot* although this route, with stops in Libya and Mali, can add up to a long trip. An even cheaper alternative is *Burkina Nord-Sud's* charters from France (once or twice weekly). Details in the "Getting There" section of *Basics*.

■ Flights from Africa

There are **flights** pretty well daily from **Abidjan**, but other West African capitals have airlinks only two or three times a week at most. *Air Burkina* flies in from Niamey, Abidjan, Bamako, Lomé and Cotonou. These same routes are covered by *Air Afrique* which also flies twice weekly from Dakar and once a week from Lagos. *UTA* flies once a week (Tuesday) from Conakry. *Air Ivoire* flies from Bouaké and Abidjan to Bobo and Ouaga. *Air Algérie* handles flights from Algiers and Niamey. There are no direct flights from Accra or Freetown.

For connections from east and southern Africa, there's a weekly (Saturday) flight on *Ethiopian Airlines* from Addis Ababa to Ouagadougou.

■ Overland from Niger

A 520-kilometre surfaced road now links Ouaga with **Niamey**, passing via Fada Ngourma. *Taxis brousse* and buses regularly make the trip in about twelve hours, or twice as long if you have to sleep at the border. It costs CFA6500–8500 depending on whether the vehicle is a bus, truck or car.

■ Overland from Mali

The usual route **from Mali** is from Bamako to Bobo via Sikasso, although you can also enter from Mopti to Bobo. Taxis link these destinations regularly and take about twelve hours. It's also possible to come down through the Dogon Country via Koro. This route is often unpassable during the rains and, even at other times, there's no regular taxi service. If you don't have your own car, you'll be dependent on passing tourists or goods trucks. Approaching from this direction gives an interesting first perspective on Burkina through Ouahigouya and the historical Yatenga region, but you can't expect to rush it.

■ Overland from Côte d'Ivoire

The *Régie Abidjan-Niger*, or *RAN*, assures daily **train** connections between Abidjan and Ouaga. There are usually two a day in both directions. The *Gazelle* and *Antelope* are the *rapide* trains while the *Autorail* and *Express* take much longer. Even in the best of cases the trip takes over 22 hours, but it's a better option than **bus** or **bush taxi**, though these also run from Abidjan and are competive pricewise. Couchettes are available on the night trains.

■ Overland from Ghana

The *Ghana State Transport Corporation* has buses to Ouagadougou from **Accra**, **Kumasi** and **Tamale**. Taxis also cover this stretch, passing via **Bolgatanga**, **Navrongo and Pô**. The 1000-kilometre paved road between Accra and Ouaga is good on the (short) Burkina stretch and has been undergoing repairs on the Ghana side.

■ Overland from Togo

Regular taxis ply between Lomé and Ouaga. They take about twenty hours to cover the 1000km and cost around CFA12,000. The surfaced road is in general very good, except for periodic patches on the Togo side that are undergoing repairs.

■ Overland from Benin

The usual route from Cotonou is via Lomé. If you're coming from northern Benin, vehicles link Natitingou with Fada Ngourma from where you can change to Ouaga.

Red Tape

Unless you're from West Germany, Belgium, the Netherlands, Italy or Luxembourg you'll need a visa before entering Burkina. Burkinabe embassies are few and far between, but in many countries where Burkina lacks representation, the French embassy can process the visa.

■ Visas for Onward Travel

Although there are relatively few diplomatic missions in Ouagadougou, the **French embassy** handles visas for several West and Central African countries (see Ouagadougou "Directory"). Note that they don't take care of visas for Mali, Benin, Niger, Cameroon or Guinea, none of which have representation in Ouaga. And there's no

British representation above the level of Honorary Consul, so no visas are issued for The Gambia or Sierra Leone. Ghana visas can be a hassle for UK nationals. If you are travelling through Burkina to any of these countries, be sure to plan ahead.

■ Photography Permits

In theory, before taking any pictures in Burkina you need to obtain a photo permit at the *Direction du Tourisme et de l'Hotellerie* in Ouaga on the rue Augustino Neto (near the *Hôtel Indépendance*) – a process which may use up a full working day.

Money and Costs

Burkina Faso is part of the CFA zone (CFA50 always equals 1 French franc; CFA450– CFA500 = £1). In Ouaga and Bobo, you'll have little trouble changing travellers' cheques or cash (FF are best) although banks can be fussy in other towns, refusing to change travellers' cheques without the original receipt, for example.

Banks in small towns in the extreme north of the country may refuse to change even cash, including FF, although if you're in a jam, you can usually pay for transport and commodities with French currency in any case. Banks in towns throughout the country are the *Banque Internationale pour le Commerce, l'Industrie et l'Agriculture* (BICIA), the *Banque Internationale du Burkina* (BIB) and the *Banque Nationale de Développement* (BND).

Prices in Burkina are reasonable and even Ouagadougou is inexpensive for a West African capital. Cheap hotels around the country will cost you from CFA2000–4000. Eating street food, you can fill up on *riz sauce* or *tô* for as little as CFA200. **Transport costs**, which are relatively high, range from CFA15–25 per kilometre, depending on whether the road is paved or *piste* and the type of vehicle.

Health

You'll need a yellow fever vaccination certificate in Burkina as elsewhere in West Africa. During outbreaks of cholera, you may (unpredictably) need that vaccination too. Malaria prophylaxis is esential.

Tap water is treated in Bobo and Ouagadougou. It smells of chlorine, but otherwise is drinkable. In the bush, progress has been made in water purity, but some supplies are still dubious. If you have any doubts, use purifying tablets. The only other real worry is **bilharzia**. Except around Bobo, where a number of water bodies are clean, you should be careful of swimming, especially where the water is stagnant or grassy.

Note too that Burkina has one of the world's highest incidences of *onchocerciasis* and whole villages have been evacuated where this **river blindness** has run its course (notably near streams where the simulium blackflies breed). A giant WHO project has been launched to wipe out the disease and allow the resettlement of these areas. Oncho rarely affects short-stay visitors.

Information and Maps

In the last couple of years, the government has begun promoting Burkina Faso in quite a big way at tourism fairs and similar events, and you may be able to find a few moderately useful leaflets and booklets. There are no overseas tourist offices as such. The best map of the country is the *Institut de Géographie Burkinabé*'s map, styled after the French IGN maps. It's available anywhere that stocks IGN.

In Burkina, the *Institut de Géographie Bukinabé* on Ouagadougou's Ave de l'Indépendance also has good city maps of Ouaga and Bobo. For tourist information, the tourist office in Ouaga is near the *Indépendance Hôtel* (☎33.67.64). In Bobo, there's a provincial office (☎98.26.09). *Burkina Nord-Sud* (back in the days when it was *Le Point*) published a **guide booklet on Ouaga and environs** in French. It dates from 1985, but has some good information and is available at their office on the Ave Bassawarga.

Getting Around

With the exception of the Lobi Country near the Ghanaian border, a decent road system connects Ouaga with most places in the south of the country. The north is still a problem area, however, and many towns are virtually impossible to get to during the rainy season.

■ Bush Taxis, Trucks and Buses

Bush taxis are usually 504 *breaks* (estate cars) or 404 *bâchés* with boarded up back ends. The latter are cheaper and, given the level of comfort, rightly so. You won't see much of the countryside in them unless you arrange to have a seat in the cabin – a possiblity that a small supplement usually fixes.

The *Régie X9* operates **buses** to most towns in Burkina. It's a far more comfortable option than the taxis and highway checkpoints are much less of a hassle. Prices are competitive. X9 is planning to expand its service to include Dori, Gorom-Gorom, Niamey, Bamako, Cotonou and Lomé.

Faso Tours runs regularly scheduled buses to Ouahigouya, Bobo-Dioulasso and Fada Ngourma plus excursions to the Arli National Park. *FT* also acts as the agents for Niger's *SNTN* buses to Niamey.

Routes, frequencies and sample fares

There's a good amount of traffic to all neighbouring capitals. It's only really to northern towns – and other isolated areas such as the Lobi Country – that you'll experience long waits (several days in some cases) for vehicles.
Ouagadougou–Lomé 970-km surfaced road, CFA12,500 (20hr).
Ouaga–Niamey 500-km surfaced road, CFA8100.
Ouaga–Bolgatanga 200-km surface road, CFA4000 (4hr).
Ouaga–Bobo 360km by good paved road, CFA27500–3500 (5hr).
Ouaga–Gorom-Gorom 300-km tracks, CFA6000.

■ Trains

Before arriving in Côte d'Ivoire, the **train** passes through Ouagadougou, Koudougou, Siby, Bobo, Banfora and Niangoloko – the Burkinabe border post. Check prices and schedules by calling the RAN (in Ouagadougou ☎33.37.51). A new line is projected from Ouaga to the manganese mines in the northern town of Tambao. Eventually, it will pass through Kaya and Dori. However, barely 30km of this line has been completed, and without foreign financing, it's doubtful the project will advance quickly over the next few years.

■ Domestic Flights

Air Burkina (☎30.61.44 in Ouaga; ☎98.18.87 in Bobo) flies from Ouaga to: **Bobo** (CFA15,000);

Djibo (CFA6000); **Sebba** (CFA10,000); **Gorom-Gorom** (CFA12,000); **Gaoua** (CFA8500); and **Dori** (CFA11,000). These last available prices indicate one-way fares. Frequencies vary according to the destination.

■ Other forms of Transport

Car hire works out as an expensive means of getting around the country. You'll find agencies in Ouaga and Bobo (see the directories for those towns).

Another option that is more economical, and potentially much more satisfying, is to rent a **bicycle**, **moped** or **motorbike**. It's an excellent way to see the sights around Ouaga, Bobo and Banfora, all of which towns have people around their market places who hire out machines.

Sleeping – where to stay

In Ouaga and Bobo there are international class hotels, but anywhere beyond Koudougou, the country's third largest town, accommodation is much more basic. In smaller towns, expecially in the extreme north, electricity and running water are luxuries indeed. Prices for accommodation are reasonable – CFA2000–4000 for simple rooms, usually with fans.

A network of *Auberges populaires* is being worked out by the newly empowered Ministry of Environment and Tourism, which is supposed to put at least a basic hotel in each of Burkina's thirty main towns.

Off the few beaten tracks, **staying with people** is a viable, permissible and recommended option. In the bush, so too is **camping**: most of the country is ideal.

Food and Drink

The staples in Burkina are rice and millet. After grinding, these are boiled in water and mixed into a mealy-meal mush known here as *tô*. One of the most common sauces to accompany *tô* is made from manioc leaves with palm oil, fresh fish and seasonings. Gumbo (okra) is also common.

Despite its drought-land reputation, most towns in Burkina have an array of **street food** and throughout the country, you'll find women selling bean or banana fritters, yam chips, fried fish and *brochettes*.

Nationally brewed **beers** include *Sobra*, *Brakina* and *Flag*. When serving you, the waitress may place the bottle on the bar and wait. You're supposed to be feeling to see if it's cold enough. Different homemade drinks are enjoyed in the various regions. Around Banfora, you'll find a lot of palm wine, *banji*, which you can order by the (beer) bottle in most small bars (*cabarets*). Sweet and frothy, it goes down easily and has the added advantage of being cheap. Also cheap is the deadly African gin known here as *patasi or "qui me pousse"*. Further north, these drinks give way to *chapalo*, locally made millet beer.

The usual foreign soft drinks compete against hideously coloured *Spark* (in lemon, orange and banana). *Savanna* is a non-gassy bottled fruit drink in exotic flavours like mango – but far too sugary. Throughout the country (especially in motor parks), you'll run into *Lemburgui*, thirst-quenching homemade ginger beer frozen in small plastic bags.

Communications: PTT, media and language

You can make international phone calls from Ouagadougou. Go to the building three doors down from the main post office on the Ave Mandela (open 7am–8pm). You can dial directly to the UK, North America and most of Europe.

Ouaga's ***poste restante*** works well, although you should be careful to have your letters addressed with the exact name that appears in your passport.

■ Languages

French is the official language of Burkina, although it's estimated that only fifteen percent of the population speak it with any degree of fluency. That percentage is noticeably higher in the large towns, where you'll have no problem fumbling through in French. The most widely spoken African language is **More**, mother tongue

---

A LITTLE MORE

GREETINGS

Good morning (early)	*Neyibeogo*	Response	*Yung soab*
Reponse	*Yibeoog soab yeaala*	How are you?	*Yibeoog yaa laafi?, laafi beeme?, lafi bala?*
Further response (men)	*Naaba*		
Further response (women)	*Eyn*		
		Goodbye	*Wend na tasse*
Good day	*Neywindaga*	See you later	*Wend na kodnindaare*
Response	*Windg soab yeaala*	See you tomorrow	*Wend na kodbeogo*
Good evening	*Neywungo*	Response: the same, or	*Ammi*

LIMITED CONVERSATION

Excuse me	*Ysugri*	Yes	*Nye*	How much?	*Wanwana?*
Sorry	*Ykabre*	No	*Ayo*	Water	*Koom*
Thank you	*Barka*				

DAYS

Today	*Dunna*	Monday	*Fene*	Friday	*Arzuma*
Tomorrow	*Beoogo*	Tuesday	*Falato*	Saturday	*Sibri*
Yesterday	*Zaame*	Wednesday	*Arba*	Sunday	*Hado*
This evening	*Zaabre*	Thursday	*Lamusa*		

NUMBERS

1	*Aye*	4	*Anaase*	7	*Yopoe*	10	*Piiga*
2	*Ayiibu*	5	*Anu*	8	*Anii*	100	*Koabga*
3	*Ataabo*	6	*Ayoobe*	9	*Awe*	1000	*Tusri*

BURKINABE GLOSSARY

Américain General term for a missionary regardless of nationality or religious affiliation. Early missionaries in the region were anglophone Protestants.

Brousse Common term for bush or countryside, but to the Mossi in particular, it means anywhere outside the Mossi country, especially outside the purlieu of Ouagadougou. Thus someone who has gone to study in Côte d'Ivoire or France is said to be *en brousse*.

Burkinabe (or Burkinabé). Man or woman from Burkina Faso; there is no masculine or feminine form.

Cabaret A rural bar (especially in Lobi country).

CDR *Comités pour la défense de la Révolution* – first established by Sankara to implement government policy and organise local affairs on a regional level.

FESPACO Pan African Film Festival held every odd-numbered year in Ouagadougou.

Ghanéenne A popular term for a prostitute, equally insulting to Ghanaian women and barmaids.

Koure Mossi funeral ceremony.

Kwara Gourounsi chief's sacred insignia, equivalent of a staff of office.

Mogho Naba Also spelled *Moro Naba*; traditional leader of the Mossi people who resides in Ouagadougou. *Mogho* signifies the traditional cultural realm of Ouagadougou.

Naba King of a Mossi state, and also village chief.

Nassara Common appelation for white people and other foreigners.

Marabout Muslim holy man who may use his spiritual powers for devination.

Ouédraogo The most common surname in Burkina, it's derived from the More *ouefo* (horse) and *raogo* male. It is the Mogho Naba's name and that of other important political and cultural leaders. The Burkina phone book contains pages of Ouédraogos.

Zaka Round house in the countryside with banco walls and thatched conical roof. The plural is *zaksé*.

---

of the Mossi and spoken by over half the population. Other widely spoken languages are **Pulaar**, spoken by the Fula herders of the north, and **Dioula** (Dyula), which has become the major commercial lingua franca spanning most of the borders in this part of West Africa.

■ The Media

The national press consists principally of a government daily, the French language **Sidwaya** ("Truth") – not exactly a paragon of free speech. *Dunia*, *Lolowulein* ("Red Star") and *Notre Combat* are others you might come across.

The weekly magazine **Carrefour Africain** is another mouthpiece of the information ministry but the weekly **L'Intrus** attempts a satirical treatment of current events and is worth getting hold of a copy.

Listening to **RTB** government radio (in sixteen Burkinabe languages) or watching TV (very limited transmission and audience) aren't likely to be major leisure activities. **REP** and **Horizon FM** in Ouaga and **Radio Bobo-Dioulasso** are commercial radio stations that sound more promising.

The Arts and Entertainment

In the arts, Burkina has carved itself an international image with its African film festival and there's a thriving, though severely underfunded, popular cultural life.

The biennial **Festival Panafricain du Cinéma** is held in Ouaga every odd-numbered year at the end of February (Feb 23–Mar 2 1991). FESPACO was founded in 1969 and is dedicated to promoting African film makers throughout the world. If you happen to be here during the festival, it's hard to find a hotel room as the city fills with an international crowd of film makers and movie-hacks flocking to the ten-day event. Names of Burkinabe producers whose careers have been germinated by the festival include **Gaston Kaboré** who won a French César award in 1985 for *Wend Kuuni*, and **Idrissa Ouédreago** whose film *Yaaba* won three awards at the 1989 festival and was presented the same year at Cannes.

Drama has received a boost in recent years and major towns (Ouaga, Bobo, Koudougou) all have well-equipped theatres. The country has over a dozen drama troupes that give regular performances. Check out what's going on by calling in at the French cultural centres in Ouaga or Bobo.

■ Music

Despite the country's cultural richness and the ease with which you can hear local **music** in Burkina Faso, very few artists have reached a wide African or international audience. A couple of good albums of traditional music are available, including *Haute Volta* – a compilation of Mossi, Peul (Fula), Bambara, Lobi and Gan music – put out by the *Agence de Coopération Culturelle et Technique* (ACCP).

In a more popular vein, **Hamidou Ouédraogo** – the self-proclaimed *Vedette Voltaïque* – is one of the nation's better known stars. A Fula-speaker from the region of Dori, he moved to Ouagadougou in the 1970s and formed the group **l'Orchestre Super Volta**. Popular albums from the period include *Le Vedette Voltaïque* and *Le Chanteur Voltaïque* both on Sonodisc.

The best known artists outside the country are the brilliantly watchable (if occasionally musically monotonous) percussion group **Farafina**, and the very exciting **Coulibaly Twins**. All are based, when at home, in Bobo-Dioulasso, the town to head for if you want to get to grips with Burkinabe music. There's a big **percussion festival in Bobo** early each year in February or March, which is attracting increasing interest from drummers around West Africa.

Directory

AIRPORT TAX CFA3000.

CRAFTS Crafts are an important industry in Burkina, ranging from those intended for everyday use (pottery, basketwork, wooden utensils) to those used in ceremonies (masks, statues) or as tourist fodder/decoration. **Bronze statues**, cast using the lost wax method, were traditionally made for the royal court, but are now widely available in Ouaga. **Pottery** is the most widespread craft in Burkina and is used everywhere. **Leatherwork** is also widespread, an offshoot of the country's large livestock industry. Traditional sandals, bags and pouches are sold in village markets, and in Ouaga, you can see new uses for old materials – things like leather covered chessboards – at the *Société Burkinabé de Manufacture de Cuir*.

EDUCATION Burkina was for a long time one of the most poorly educated countries in the world. Though primary education was in theory compulsory for all children aged seven to thirteen, until the 1980s less than ten percent of kids ever made it through primary school. That number has today risen to nearly thirty percent and should increase after a recent restructuring of the school system. Secondary schools (*lycées*) have a good reputation and, in fact, attract a number of foreign students, notably from Côte d'Ivoire where the cost of education is much higher. The country has one university, in Ouagadougou.

HOLIDAYS Office holidays include all the usual Muslim and Christian celebrations and New Year's day is also a national holiday.

Additional Christian holidays include **Ascension** Thursday, **Pentecost** and **Assumption**. **New Year's Day** is also a bank holiday.

Principal **national holidays** are January 3 (1966 Revolution), May 1 (Labour Day), August 4 (Revolution Day), August 5 (Independence Day) and December 11 (Proclamation of the Republic).

OPENING HOURS Businesses open from 8am–12.30pm and 3–6pm on weekdays. Many are open Saturday mornings too. Government offices operate from 7am–12.30pm and 3–5.30pm weekdays only.

WILDLIFE AND NATIONAL PARKS Burkina's flat, over-grazed, relatively over-populated lands offer poor refuge for the country's natural savannah fauna. A conscientious conservation programme does exist (with controlled tourist hunting part of its policy), though its best chances of success lie with the Burkinabe ethic stressing community before individual. Hippo and crocodile "pools" are recognised tourist assets. Encouraging reports indicate a relatively large elephant population in the Burkina sector of the Parc National du W, in the Parc National d'Arli (both in the remote southeast) and in the little visited Pô and Nazinga reserves south of Ouagadougou.

Recent History of Burkina

The Mossi empires dominated the Volta region's politics until the French usurped the independence of their states in the 1890s. For two decades the colonials simply merged their new territory with the *Colonie du Haut-Sénégal Niger*, and it wasn't until 1919 that they divided this huge mass into two separate colonies – *Soudan Français* and *Haute Volta* – the latter corresponding to present-day Burkina Faso. In 1932, commercial considerations (primarily a need for manual labour in neighbouring colonies) led the French to divide Upper Volta again, annexing half the colony to Côte d'Ivoire and dividing the rest between the French Sudan and Niger. It wasn't until September 4 ,1947 that Upper Volta re-emerged as an entity.

■ Independence

Maurice Yaméogo, the prominent figure in pre-independence politics, founded the *Union Démocratique Voltaïque* – **a local section of Félix Houphouët-Boigny's *Rassemblement Démocratique Africain*** – shortly after World War II. By 1958, Upper Volta had become an autonomous territory with Yaméogo the prime minister. When full independence was granted on August 5, 1960, he was elected the country's first president.

During the years when the French governed Upper Volta, little was done to upgrade the country or give it an infrastructure capable of spurring economic development. Admittedly, Yaméogo had inherited a desperate situation, but he did little to reverse the trend and outside of Ouagadougou, the country had few roads or communications systems. As the economic situation deteriorated, Yaméogo introduced austerity measures unpopular with increasingly disgruntled workers and civil servants. In the face of rising opposition, he banned political parties outside UDV and adopted an autocratic style. He was ousted, on January 3, 1966, in a coup led by the army chief of staff, **Sangoulé Lamizana**.

■ A Decade of Coups

The army, with Lamizana at its head, ruled the country during a four-year period in which the nation was ostensibly being prepared for a **return to civilian rule**. Parties were formed and a new constitution was drafted. In 1970, a semi-civilian government was elected with the UDV winning a majority of the seats in parliament.

But the UDV's leadership was split, with a rivalry developing between **Joseph Ouédraogo** and **Gérard Ouédraogo** – both of Mossi origin though unrelated. After a period of political infighting, it was agreed that Gérard would serve as prime minister and Joseph as president of the assembly. Lamizana remained in office as head of state and the army retained real power.

By the early 1970s, drought had struck the country and the economic outlook was bleaker than ever. As parts of the north were struck with the prospect of starvation, a scandal erupted with the discovery of **food aid embezzlement** by members of the government distribution committee. The event seemed to confirm rumours that administrative corruption was widespread. The government suffered a further crisis in 1973, when conflict developed between civilian leaders and the militant teacher's union and a **general strike** swept through the public sector. As the situation deteriorated, the national assembly refused to pass further legislation until the prime minister stepped down. Gérard Ouédraogo refused to do so and the army decided to take control of the country once again, on February 8, 1974. They dissolved the parliament and suspended the 1970 constitution.

A new crisis hit Haute Volta in 1975, when **war** broke out with Mali over the **Agacher Strip**. Their rival claims to this 150km-wide border strip in the desolate northern regions of the Sahel – believed to be rich in mineral deposits – were based on legal documents dating back to the days when Upper Volta had been divided and redivided between Côte d'Ivoire, the French Sudan (Mali) and Niger. Before the dispute was settled with OAU mediation, a new generation of popular military heroes had arisen, including a young officer, **Thomas Sankara**.

■ New Stab at Democracy

Under pressure from the labour unions, **elections** were once again held in 1978, and on May 28 of that year, the Third Republic was proclaimed. Lamizana was elected president, but his UDV party didn't have an overall majority in the parliament and his tenure was habitually challenged by the trade unions (at the time, an unusually powerful force since half of all wage earners belonged to one of the four national unions and their opposition could bring down governments) and students. He was overthrown in a quiet palace coup on November 25, 1980, by **Colonel Saye Zerbo** who became head of the new "Military Committee for Recovery and National Progress" (CMRPN).

The coup was initially supported by the unions, but they quickly became disgruntled after the CMRPN's **banning of political activity**, and relations deteriorated utterly when the Military Committee withdrew the right to strike in 1981. Serious cleavages began to become apparent within the party, and in 1982 Sankara – whose popular appeal was growing – was removed from the influential position he had been given in the Ministry of Information.

Unrest quickened, and the coups d'état struck one after another. On November 7, 1982, a group of military officers forced out Zerbo and set up the "Provisional People's Salvation Council" (CSP) with an army doctor named **Jean-Baptiste Ouédraogo** at its head. The new regime let fire a volley of denunciation at Zerbo's corrupt and repressive government and took a radical pro-union position, championing the right to strike. In January 1983, Sankara was named prime minister.

By early 1983, it was clear that the new government was divided between **traditionalists** – led by the army chief of staff, Colonel Gabriel Somé – and **radicals**, headed by Sankara. The two factions came into open conflict when

Sankara invited Colonel Gaddafi to Upper Volta in May 1983. The day after the Libyan leader's departure, Ouédraogo ordered Sankara's arrest on the grounds that he had dangerously threatened national unity.

The arrest of the prime minister triggered a rebellion in Sankara's commando unit at Pô, a small town near the Ghanaian border. The commandos, led by **Captain Blaise Compaoré** believed the move to have been instigated by Somé and encouraged by France. They took control of Pô and refused orders from the capital until Sankara was unconditionally released. But Ouédraogo refused to dismiss Somé and gradually the rebellion spread to other commando units in the country. On the eve of the 23rd anniversary of independence – August 4, 1983 – Sankara seized power. Ouédraogo had lasted less than a year as head of state.

■ Changes: Burkina Faso

Sankara settled in as president of the new governing body, the "Counseil National de la Revolution", and as head of state. Compaoré was nominated minister of state to the president. The country was renamed Burkina Faso. With the logistic help of the previously underground **Patriotic Development League** (LIPAD), the CNR quickly set about reorganising the administrative regions of the country and ousting **traditional rulers** from their positions of power and influence. Revolutionary **"people's courts"** were established to try former public officials charged with political crimes and corruption. One of the first to be tried was Lamizana, who was acquitted. But several former ministers were convicted and sentenced to prison, as were ex-president Zerbo (who was also ordered to repay $200,000 in public funds) and Gérard Ouédraogo, former UDV leader.

The style of Thomas Sankara

Only 34 years old when he came to power, **Sankara** symbolised a new generation of leaders with innovative ideas, but his popularity went beyond his ability to compose revolutionary music on his guitar or eloquent denunciations of capitalism and imperialism. Sankara may have had a penchant for facile rhetoric, but he could also transform words into **action**. He waged war on desertification, women's inequality and children's diseases (creating a "vaccination-commando'").

When foreign investors refused to finance a railway line to magnesium deposits in the north of the country, he launched the *bataille du rail* – encouraging peasants to build the tracks themselves. (Although critics said his recruitment methods were hauntingly reminiscent of French *travaux forcé*, Sankara was too young to remember that.) But perhaps his greatest achievement was the virtual elimination of **corruption** and government waste, proving his commitment to the cause by having himself chauffered around in the back of a Renault 4, rather than the customary black Mercedes.

In another popular move, Sankara early in his term announced free housing for all Burkinabe and called a moratorium on rents (an incautious decision from which he later had to retreat). But even though the young president seemed to prove himself as a capable, if unpredictable leader, he was gaining a long list of enemies.

Detractors – at home and abroad

By early 1984, there was growing **opposition** to Sankara's radical style, and in May of that year a plot to overthrow the government was uncovered. The leaders were hastily arrested and tried. Unlike the people's courts, these proceedings took place in secrecy and the penalties were severe. Seven of the alleged plotters were executed and five others sentenced to hard labour.

In light of these events, **relations with France** soured, and Sankara accused the French government of supporting exiled political rivals. Other western nations also viewed the new regime with scepticism, though the fact that Sankara made efforts to distance his government from Libya and the Soviet Union was interpreted as an encouraging sign. Gradually, the "revolution" came to be identified less with Marxist ideology, and was seen more as a means of unifying a wide cross section of society. The success of the CNR and the genuine popularity of the movement hinged primarily on the dynamic personality of its founder.

War with Mali flared up again in late 1985. Over fifty people were killed and better-armed Mali did major damage in Burkina. In December 1986, the International Court of Justice in The Hague divided the disputed Agacher Strip between the two countries and peace was regained.

But relations were also deteriorating with other West African neighbours – especially **Côte d'Ivoire** and **Togo**. Close ties between Sankara and Jerry Rawlings of Ghana were regarded suspiciously by these conservative nations – especially after 1986 when the two socialist neighbours decided to work towards political integration by the late 1990s (see p.825). Relations with Togo were nearly broken off after an attempted coup in Lomé shook President Eyadema's regime in September 1986. Both Ghana and Burkina were accused of involvement and of harbouring Togolese dissidents. And despite a 1987 visit to Ouagadougou by François Mitterrand, **France** (still the country's most important potential ally) continued to treat Burkina with reserve – a wait and see attitude generally shared by Western powers.

At home, Sankara was frequently criticised by intellectuals, labour unions and business leaders, though he had a charismatic knack for diffusing enmity from all these groups. In January 1985, opposition to the austerity measures Sankara introduced led unions to wage a "leaflet war", but the tumult quickly died down and no major dissent ensued. Even salary cuts for civil servants and the military were accepted on the grounds that they were necessary to raise the level of social services among the poor. In the absence of serious opposition from **traditional political forces,** it was a growing lack of consensus within the governing CDR and resulting rifts that ultimately proved Sankara's downfall.

■ The New Regime

Thomas Sankara was killed in a botched and bloody coup on October 15, 1987. It was precipitated by a group of soldiers loyal to **Blaise Compaoré** (Sankara's companion in arms and partner in the government), who opened fire on Sankara after arresting him. The precise nature of the overthrow is still shrouded in mystery. It did not, at any rate, take a planned course and it doesn't seem likely that Compaoré intended to come out of it looking like a murderer. He has since said "Thomas confiscated the revolution and brought untold suffering to the people", and it's clear at least that Sankara had allowed himself to become fatally isolated. But Compaoré's image as a West African leader with the blood of a brother on his hands won't easily be erased.

Sankara's death sent shock waves through the region and chilled progressive movements round the world. For even if his methods were often open to question (something he never denied), he had demonstrated sincerity and righteousness in his aims and proved himself a credible friend of the people. Most importantly he had managed to instil **national pride** and create a realistic **sense of hope** in one of West Africa's most brutalised countries. Most West African, and not a few Western governments seemed relieved with the change, but the people's response varied from mournful to muted – not a good sign for the new president.

The basis of the revolutionary system Sankara set in place remains intact, although the new head of state quickly announced that "rectifica-

tions" would be made, signalling a willingness to deal pragmatically with the inevitablities of World Bank and IMF loan negotiations.

However, there has been an almost continuous rumble of **rumour and incident** within the *Front Populaire* (high level disagreements, coup attempts and a number of subsequent executions). Everything suggests considerable latent support for Sankara and serious threats to the survival of the current leadership, which can hardly have been forgiven. Compaoré is now attempting to bring disenfranchised political groupings into the fold. He wants to achieve peace with the powerful unions and plans a new constitution for the end of 1990. But he will have a difficult time obtaining the respect accorded to his former friend.

CENTRAL AND NORTHEAST BURKINA

Lying in the centre of Burkina, **Ouagadougou** is an inevitable stopping point and a pleasant place to rest up for a few days before heading off to some of the country's more isolated outposts. Ouaga is relatively small for a capital city, though it generates a satisfying amount of commercial and cultural activity.

This is Burkina's undisputed hub, from which main roads head to all major national and international destinations. The eastern route to Niamey passes through the **Gourmantché country** and the important market town of **Fada Ngourma**. Another busy junction along this route is **Koupéla**, where the highway to **Dapango** in neighbouring Togo starts its southern course. West of Ouaga, the route to **Bobo-Dioulasso** is lined with small Mossi towns and villages such as **Sabou**, famed for its sacred crocodile pond, while a branch road leads off to **Koudougou** – the nation's third-largest town and a centre of Burkina's textile industry.

Ouagadougou

On the surface, **OUAGADOUGOU** has little to offer. Capital of one of the world's poorest countries, it seems more like a shambling provincial town. The heat is oppressive; the flat, dirt streets are filled with choking red dust in the dry season and muddy morasses during the rains, while overhead vultures wheel on the lookout for scraps and bats flutter from roosting sites.

But despite its unpromising appearance Ouaga turns out to be exceptionally animated – and more attests to this than simply the clouds of exhaust that sputter from the thousands of mopeds crushing into traffic jams at rush hour. Over the last ten years, drastic measures have been taken to try to improve the city's image. New roads have been paved in the centre, more efficient sewerage systems are being laid and the government has encouraged people to clear the streets of garbage and goats, both of which had come to be recognised as permanent fixtures by Ouagalais and visitors. As the town modernises, building projects have included the striking *nouveau marché* – an attractive and spacious brick complex in the city centre. Thankfully, there's a noticeable absence of the kind of strutting skyscraper architecture so popular in other West African capitals but, for better or worse, Ouagadougou's act is coming together.

Ouaga is the traditional capital of the **Mossi empire**, but all the country's major ethnic groups, religions and languages coexist here with remarkable harmony. A good number of international organisations, and the nation's only university, are also based in Ouaga. Life moves at a brisk pace, but as a visitor, you'll find that **contact** with the people is much more immediate than in other West African cities.

The rise of Ouagadougou – and some name derivations

Mossi oral literature traces the beginning of the **Mogho** or **Moro** (the Mossi empire: *Mogho* literally means "the world") to the thirteenth century and a chief named Gbewa or Nédéga who ruled over Pusiga in present-day Ghana (see p.871). In the course of a battle, Gbewa's daughter, a horsewoman named **Yennenga**, was separated from the clan when her horse took fright and fled into the Bitou woods. She chanced upon the forest's one inhabitant, an elephant hunter named **Rialé** (a corruption of the More words *ri*: "to eat", and *yaré*: "anything", since bush-dwellers ate anything they found). The couple eventually returned to Gambaga and had a baby, which they named **Ouédraogo**, after Yennenga's steed – from *ouefo*: "horse", and *raogo*: "male".

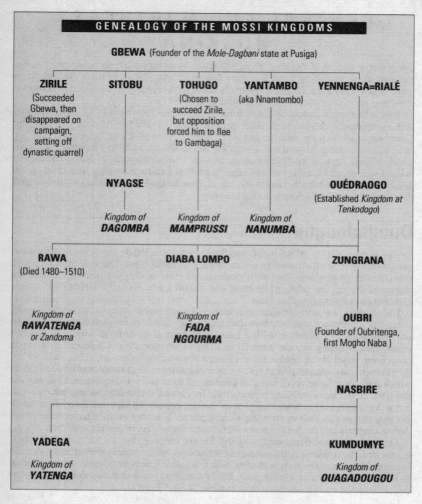

GENEALOGY OF THE MOSSI KINGDOMS

GBEWA (Founder of the *Mole-Dagbani* state at Pusiga)

ZIRILE
(Succeeded Gbewa, then disappeared on campaign, setting off dynastic quarrel)

SITOBU

TOHUGO
(Chosen to succeed Zirile, but opposition forced him to flee to Gambaga)

YANTAMBO
(aka Nnamtombo)

YENNENGA=RIALÉ

NYAGSE

OUÉDRAOGO
(Established *Kingdom* at Tenkodogo)

Kingdom of
DAGOMBA

Kingdom of
MAMPRUSSI

Kingdom of
NANUMBA

RAWA
(Died 1480–1510)

DIABA LOMPO

ZUNGRANA

Kingdom of
RAWATENGA
or Zandoma

Kingdom of
FADA NGOURMA

OUBRI
(Founder of Oubritenga, first Mogho Naba)

NASBIRE

YADEGA

Kingdom of
YATENGA

KUMDUMYE

Kingdom of
OUAGADOUGOU

But the territory of Pusiga became overpopulated and Ouédraogo set off with a company of his father's cavalry to conquer the northern territories. He established a kingdom at **Na Ten Kudugo** (Tenkodogo). Much later, Ouédraogo's grandson **Oubri** set off in conquest of new territories and founded the statelet of **Oubritenga**, later known as Wogodogo or Ouagadougou. A grandson of Oubri broke off to form another small state, **Yatenga**, with Ouahigouya as its capital.

The autonomous Mossi states or kingdoms (see box for genealogy) remained remarkably stable for over four centuries, but by the end of the nineteenth century, the French, Germans and British were pressing in on the region. In 1898, the French occupied Ouagadougou, and within a short time subjugated the surrounding empires which they integrated into their colony of *Haut-Sénégal Niger*.

THE *NABAYIUS GOU* – OR FALSE START CEREMONY

Ouagadougou's answer to the changing of the guard, the **Nabayius Gou** is a re-enactment, every Friday at 7am by the western side of the Mogho Naba's palace, of events that took place in the early eighteenth century, in the reign of Ouarga, the twentieth Mogho Naba, when the kingdom's frontiers were under threat by raids from Yako.

The Mogho Naba's favourite wife had obtained his permission to visit her family, but hadn't returned on the agreed date. Heartbroken, he prepared to set out and find her, but his courtiers, fearing war, begged him to stay. With a heavy heart, the king concurred that his duty to his subjects came before personal concerns and, dismounting from his horse, he returned to his palace. The ceremony reaffirms this commitment to his people.

The present-day Mogho Naba comes out of his palace dressed in red for war, but then returns inside to re-emerge in white and mount his horse. His courtiers surround him, begging him to stay, and eventually he heeds their pleas and returns to the palace.

This isn't a spectacle put on for tourists and it's rather a solemn affair, which needs to be witnessed with some respect. Nonetheless it's a fascinating ceremony, well worth getting up early for. Photographs aren't usually allowed, but you may be able to get special permission by applying (in advance, with a normal photo permit) to the Naba's secretariat.

Arrival

Ouagadougou spreads across a considerable area, though the centre is fairly compact. It's officially divided into thirty, flat, dusty *sectors* (like Paris' *arrondissements*), of which you're likely to spend time only in the few at the centre.

Even the **international airport** is well within the city limits. **Flying in**, you're gently introduced to Burkina's revolutionary spirit even before you descend from the aircraft. Bright red slogans on the airport walls spell out *Honte à l'imperialisme* ("Shame on Imperialism") and a banner was recently added warning, *Protegez-vous et protegez les autres: préservatifs* ("Protect yourself and others: condoms") – a bold call in a region where few countries recognise the problem of Aids.

Collecting your baggage and going through **customs and immigration** is normally an untraumatic experience, but you'll be asked your place of residence; (just say the *RAN Hôtel* or any other that comes to mind). There's no bank. **Getting into town** is easy. Taxi prices are marked up outside the airport (check, and tell the driver before setting off what you're prepared to pay). A quick zip up the avnue Yennenga gets you to the centre in a matter of minutes. Alternatively you can take a route #6 bus and get dropped at Place des Nations Unies.

Arriving **by train** is even more straightforward as the **RAN station** lets you off a stone's throw from Avenue Nelson Mandela and the *zone commerciale* in the heart of the city. You could reasonably walk to a hotel from here, but if you've got a lot of luggage bear in mind that the taxis are cheap.

Arriving **by taxi brousse** or **bus**, the main *gare routière*, commonly known as *Ouaga Inter*, is some 8km south of the city on the Route de Pô. If you get into town after dark, you'll have to rely on urban taxis. In the daytime, you can get buses to the centre: they stop on the Route de Pô across from the *gare routière*.

SECURITY

Ouagadougou is generally very safe, but incidents, especially bags snatched by moped pasengers, do happen to inattentive amblers. If you need to have all your valuables in one bag, make sure you've a good grip on it and walk on the left side of the road against the traffic. If you pay modest attention, it's very unlikely that anything will befall you.

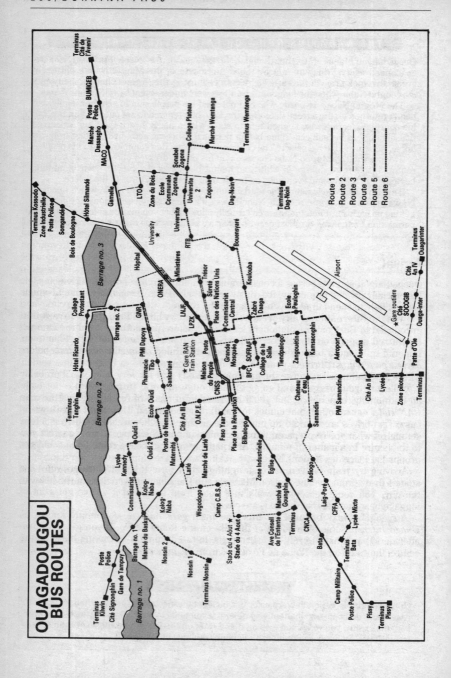

OUAGADOUGOU
BUS ROUTES

Route 1
Route 2
Route 3
Route 4
Route 5
Route 6

Transport around town

Although you can walk around much of the town centre, you may want to take **buses** to some of the further extremities (the *gare routière*, the museum, the *Hôtel Silmandé*'s pool). Since 1984, Ouagadougou has had a reasonably good system that will get you almost anywhere for CFA100 – see route map. Ouagalais know where the buses are going out of habit. In the centre, most depart from the Place des Nations Unies, or from in front of the nearby PTT.

The alternative is to share a **taxi** – in Ouaga, that's likely to mean a battered Renault 4L. Flag it down on the road and shout your destination. If the other passengers on board are headed the same way, the driver will pick you up. Prices are fixed within the centre, so find out beforehand what they are. To certain destinations (the airport, train station, luxury hotels and outer suburbs) a higher tariff is normal. And at night, the price doubles.

Orientation

The precise centre of Ouaga's fairly uncomplicated geography could be considered the **Place des Nations Unies**, with its incomprehensible lightning-bolt sculpture. All the major roads seem to start from this square. To the east, Boulevard de la Révolution (formerly known as the Champs Elysées) leads through the **administrative quarter** down to the *style coloniale* **Palais Présidentiel**. The Avenue d'Oubritenga leads off to the northeast, past the **hospital** and **museum**, and on to the **Zone du Bois** (ex-"de Boulogne"). This road then joins the main route to Niamey. West of the United Nations roundabout, Avenue Nelson Mandela passes through the **zone commerciale** and continues to the semi-modern **Maison du Peuple** and the **Place de la Révolution** where speeches and political gatherings take place. To the south, av Kwame Nkrumah runs parallel to av Yennenga. This latter is one of the most animated streets in town, running past the **Grande Mosquée** in a neighbourhood of small *commerçants* before ending near the **airport.**

These are the main arteries, and even if you don't stay for very long, you'll probably get to know them well.

But the town also has distinctive *quartiers* each with its own flavour. Behind the train station, **Moemmin** is the traditional Muslim neighbourhood. Home of Ouaga's grand Imam, it was also the site of the town's first mosque. Further north, **Niogsin** is a residential area known for its metal workers, many of whom still work here in small *ateliers*. Nearby **Paspanga** has a reputation for harbouring the best *dolotières* – women who make millet beer (*dolo*). Bars and small *cabarets* are common here. In the centre, the av Yennenga passes through **Tiendpalogo** ("the newly arrived"), **Zangouetin**, and **Peuologhin**. The latter two are respectively the Hausa and Fula neighbourhoods with Muslim-style homes and Koranic schools.

Accommodation

Accommodation is unlikely to be a problem. From camping sites to four-star hotels, Ouaga has a wide range of places to stay and budget travellers are as well served here as businesspeople.

Camping

Ouaga Camping on the route de Pô, 500m from the *Gare Internationale* (signs mark the way from the *gare routière*). Quiet setting with inexpensive bungalows and plenty of space to pitch your tent. They also have a good restaurant and bar plus a small swimming pool. CFA2000/bungalow, or CFA1000 per person to camp.

Cheap sleeps

YENNENGA

Avenue Yennenga is one of the liveliest streets in town and, conveniently, has a good number of cheap places to stay. Heading towards the centre, these include:

Oubri rue de la Mosquée near place Yennenga and the airport (☎33.29.36). Clean AC rooms (from CFA5000) and a bar loaded with ambience – maybe more than you'd want. There's a nice airy *terrasse*.

Hôtel de la Paix (☎33.30.23) Formerly known as *de l'Amitié*, this hotel was recently renovated and now boasts some of the cleanest and comfiest S/C budget rooms – with AC or fans from CFA5000.

Pension Guigsème. Nothing fancy – non S/C rooms grouped around a pleasant courtyard – but the CFA3500 starting price is about the centre's most reasonable. Clean and good value.

Idéal, (☎33.57.65) an older hotel with AC rooms (from CFA6000) that would be quite comfortable if better maintained.

Relais Near the *Idéal* but on the other side of the street, an unmarked hole-in-the-wall recognised only by the morning and evening *caféman* outiside. Ask him if he's got a *chambre*. The building behind his table gives onto a courtyard with several simple rooms. For CFA2000 you get a bed and fan. Friendly service, but filthy collective showers and toilet.

Hôtel Yennenga Similar price and standards to the *Idéal*. The courtyard restaurant and bar is a sometime favourite among Ouaga and Bobo intellectuals who come to converse and unwind – though latest reports suggest that watching *Dallas* on TV is a more common pursuit.

FURTHER AFIELD

Hostellerie des Soeurs Blanches White sisters' Catholic mission down a passage to the left of the cathedral, separate men's and women's dorm beds. Good value if you're broke.

Hôtel Delwende Rue Brunnel near the Grand Marché (☎33.63.14). Excellent location is the main draw. Not outstanding S/C, AC rooms from CFA5000. The ones on the street have balconies from where you can take in the busy life around the market.

Le Pavillon Vert av de la Liberté, Moemmin (☎33.44.16) A popular, but less central place with a nice courtyard and rooms from CFA6000.

Hotel Wend Kouni Off the av Bassawarga in the Kamsaoghin district near the Mogho Naba's palace (BP 2134; ☎30.80.79). CFA4000 for clean rooms with fan.

Moderate

Hotel de France av de la Liberté (☎33.45.96) Some way from the centre in the animated Paspanga district, the *France* has comfortable AC rooms from CFA7000.

Ricardo North of *barrage* no. 1 (☎33.30.42) It's a shame this hotel is so far from the centre, because the comfort and friendly reception are worth the effort. Near a fishing reservoir to the north of town. Good disco and restaurant. AC rooms CFA10,000 and up.

Tropicale av Frobenus in the Tiendpalogo district (BP 1758, ☎33.21.29) Clean and comfortable, this place is in a busy neighbourhood near the centre. Brace yourself for 5am prayer calls from the nearby mosque. Doubles from around CFA9000.

Central Place du Marché (☎33.34.17) A colonial-style hotel, the *Central* could hardly be better located. Prices seem slightly high (CFA9000) given the deteriorating standards, but it's always got plenty of clients and action.

Chic and/or expensive

Hôtel Silmandé (BP 4733; ☎33.36.35, telex 5345). One of the few high-rises in town, the *Silmandé* is Ouaga's luxury base with total comfort and facilities to unwind – tennis courts, pool, disco, and the rest – at prices far in excess of anywhere else (from CFA22,000). It's a good 3km from the centre, near the reservoir and the *Bois de Boulogne*, and not a place you'll feel Ouaga around you.

RAN Hôtel av Mandela (BP 62; ☎33.42.55, telex 5273). The colonial era's best, the *RAN* has aged with a certain grace. No longer the poshest, it still offers good service and facilities (rooms and comfortable bungalows from CFA10,000), with a pool, French restaurant and bars.

Hôtel Indépendance av Coulibaly (BP 127; ☎33.41.86, telex 5201, fax 30.67.67) Top hotel in the centre, the *Indépendance* recently underwent a very necessary renovation, making its rooms and bungalows quite good value (upwards of CFA12,000) and the poolside bar a popular hangout. Groups of four or five can take a junior suite with extra mattresses for around CFA25,000 – a budget way to Ouaga's luxury levels.

OK Inn Route de Pô near the international *gare routière* (BP 5397; ☎33.67.66, telex 5418). Attractive rooms and bungalows around a garden and pool, but quite a distance from the centre. Starting at CFA11,000, their rooms are good value nonetheless.

Nazemse Off the av Boumedienne in the centre (☎33.53.28). Privately run hotel with AC, S/C rooms from CFA10,500. Modern and quite comfortable.

Eating

Good, and reasonably priced, **eating** is no problem in Ouaga. The town is full of small **café terrasses** separated from the dusty streets by brightly painted fences. There's a host of such places along av Yennenga and they all serve similar fare – spaghetti, rice and meat sauce, couscous, potato stew. Most of them also do large bowls of homemade **yoghurt** – delicious, especially at breakfast time when it's freshly made. More upmarket restaurants are rarely overpriced and Ouaga has some very good ones.

But the city excels at **street food**. In the evenings, the streets fill with **brochette vendors** gathered around the glow of their charcoal fires. You can get beef and lamb, beautifully cooked, but if you want to savour the smokey flavour, be sure to ask for *sans piment*. Kerosene lamps light the tables of *les cafémans* who also emerge in the morning to whip up omelettes and sticky Nescafé concoctions.

Inexpensive restaurants

Chez Bawa av Loudun, 150m from airport. Popular with overlanders for moderately priced burgers, pizzas, salads, shakes and fresh fruit juices in a casual, thatched *paillotte* with taped jazz and reggae accompaniment. A trained musician, Bawa makes large drums (*djembé*) and balafons by hand, and for sale, and gives percussion lessons (CFA1000/hr). If you want a rural experience, he also puts people up in his *maison de brousse* (40km from Ouaga); lodgings are free and you pay CFA750/day for meals.

Le Soir Au Village On the corner of the av Yennenga and the av Boumedienne, this small restaurant has a long and varied menu, mostly of French food. Meals for about CFA1000 and the best murals in town.

Café de la Paix av Loudun near Ciné Burkina. Mostly African food; baked chicken a specialty (CFA500 and up).

Le Terminus av Loudun, Sector 4. Well known volunteer-patronised eating house, with excellent *brochettes* and grilled chicken.

Restaurant Photolux av Loudun near the Oubri Cinema. African and some European dishes served in a small interior courtyard; CFA500–1000.

More expensive restaurants

AFRICAN

L'Harmattan The disco doubles as a popular restaurant with specialties from throughout West Africa. Pleasant courtyard and friendly service included in the price (from CFA1500).

Le Marquis 8 av Coulibaly, 300m from the airport. Specialties from Côte d'Ivoire and other West African countries served under outdoor *paillotes*; CFA1000 and up.

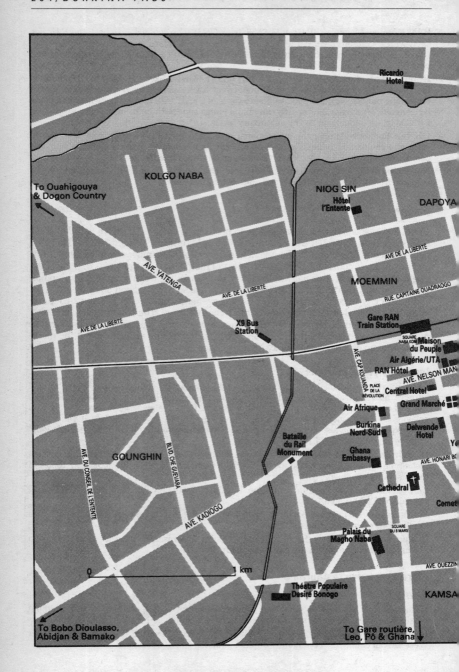

To Ouahigouya
& Dogon Country

KOLGO NABA

NIOG SIN

Hôtel
l'Entente

DAPOYA

Ricardo
Hotel

AVE. YATENGA

AVE. DE LA LIBERTÉ

AVE. DE LA LIBERTÉ

MOEMMIN

RUE. CAPITAINE OUADRAOGO

AVE. DE LA LIBERTÉ

XS Bus
Station

Gare RAN
Train Station

SQUARE
NABA KOM
Maison
du Peupie

Air Algérie/UTA

RAN Hôtel

AVE. NELSON MAN

AVE. CAP KOUANDA

PLACE
DE LA
RÉVOLUTION

Central Hotel

Grand Marché

Air Afrique

Burkina
Nord-Sud

Delwende
Hotel

Yé

GOUNGHIN

BLVD. CHE GUEVARA

AVE. DU CONSEIL DE L'ENTENTE

Bataille
du Rail
Monument

Ghana
Embassy

AVE. HONARI BO

Cathédral

Cemet

AVE. KADIOGO

0   1 km

SQUARE
DU 8 MARS

Palais du
Magho Naba

AVE. OUEZZIN

To Bobo Dioulasso,
Abidjan & Bamako

Théâtre Populaire
Desiré Bonogo

KAMSA

To Gare routière,
Leo, Pô & Ghana

To Kaya

Silmande

To Fada Ngourma,
Niamey & Lomé

Hôtel
de France

RUE MON GREMASSOM

Museum

PASPANGA

AVE. DIM DOLOROM

Nigerian
Embassy

Stadium

AVENUE D'OUBRITENGA

BLVD. DU FASO

Centre
des Arts

ost and
lephone

PLACE DES
NATIONS UNIES

BLVD. DE LA RÉVOLUTION DU 4 AOUT

French
Embassy

Hôtel de
l'Indépendance

Grande
Mosquée

AVE. RAOUL FOLLEREAU

German
Embassy

American
Embassy

KOULOUBA

el
nga

ENNE

Hôtel Idéal

Hôtel
de la Paix

AVE. RESISTANCE DU 17 MAI

ZANGOUETIN

AVE. LEO PROBENUS

AVE. NKRUMAH

AVE. LOUDUN

AVE. YENNENGA

Hôtel
Tropicale

PEULOGHIN

Airport

BALY

Hôtel
Aéroport

HIN

Oubri
Hôtel

OUAGADOUGOU

FRENCH:

La Chaumière av Mandela across from the *Ran Hôtel*. Trying-to-be-Norman restaurant as reflected by the bare beams and whitewashed walls. Fish and meat dishes from CFA2500. Attentive and friendly service. Closed Monday.

Le Belvédère Across from the International School and near the American Embassy. Continental food from CFA3000.

Le Vert Galant Next to Photolux, this restaurant features fish and meat dishes accompanied by salads and soups, crêpes and sorbets and a small wine list. Around CFA2500.

L'Eau Vive Place du Marché (☎33.35.12), closed Sunday. Most famous if not the best restaurant in Ouaga, this is an appealing place where the sister-waitresses pause mid-service to belt out the *Ave Maria*. More international than French, the daily rotating menu shifts between African, European and American specialties (from CFA2500).

ITALIAN

Le Vesuvio av Boumedienne. Pizza, lasagne, spaghetti and other *cucina Italiana* served in an attractive setting. Meals from about CFA3000.

ORIENTAL

Le Mandarin av Boumedienne in the Koulouba district. Vietnamese specialties with a *menu* for CFA4000.

Le Printemps en Chine A Chinese restaurant with real Chinese chef (from Beijing). Specialties like prawns *à la pekinoise*; CFA1000–3000 *à la carte*.

PÂTISSERIES

Le Bonbonnière av Mandela near the PTT. The best pastry shop in Ouaga and a great breakfast address. Fresh and flakey *croissants* to go with juices and yoghurt. Magazines on the tables for browsing while you eat.

Gourmandise, southeast corner of the market. Good pastries and hot drinks.

Boulangerie/pâtisserie de Koulouba av du 17 Mai (☎33.54.52). Great pastries plus ice cream and non-alcoholic drinks.

Around town – the nouveau marché and crafts markets

After Sankara rased the old market in 1985, Ouagadougou had a gaping hole in its heart for three years. Then the **Nouveau Grand Marché** opened, and Ouaga now boasts the most modern (and perhaps the most attractive) marketplace in West Africa. The variety of stock ranges from Chinese bicycles to American beauty products and local *gris gris*. This is by far the best place to shop for fresh **fruit and vegetables**, meat and poultry (live), and cereals. Basketry (of which Burkina produces some of the region's best), like the round multi-coloured **baskets** with leather-wrapped handles, are sold beside Asian-made enamel bowls, commonly used for eating throughout Africa. Much of the market is reserved for **fabric sellers**, who sit by stacks of much-prized Holland wax prints – very often made in England. They also sell quite decent, and substantially cheaper, prints made down the road in Koudougou and Côte d'Ivoire plus a good selection of Indigo tie-dyed cloth from Guinea and Mali. Tailors work inside the market to the hum of lovingly-tended, foot-operated Singers, and will make clothes to order. They're adept at European styles (shirts, trousers, dresses) if you don't think you'll get much wear out of more African designs. But the best way to get what you want, as always, is to take along a garment to be copied.

A good place to start shopping for **crafts** is at the state-operated **Centre Artisanal** (3 av Dimdolobsom, near the PTT, weekdays 8am–noon and 3–6pm). The quality of the bronze castings, carvings and weavings is quite good, and prices are fixed, while

Burkinabe artists have mastered the exotic **batik** form better than any others in the region, mixing beautiful colours with striking village scenes. Come to get an idea of how much items should be before heading off to bargain in the **nouveau marché** or at the **antiquaires de l'Hôtel RAN**. These latter operators sell from tables set up along the av Nelson Mandela in front of the hotel. Despite their name, they don't deal in antiques, but do offer one of the widest selection of **bronzes** in town. **Masks**, imported from the Côte d'Ivoire and Mali, may be treated in workshops in Laglin or Dapoya to give them an ancient look, which is often aesthetically effective if nothing else. Other wooden objects include **Senoufo chairs** and **Dogon carvings**. You'll also find jewellery – desert crosses and terracotta beads from Niger for example, and the ubiquitous old glass trade beads. Vendors can also be found in front of the *Casino* supermarket, where there tends to be more of an emphasis on **Tuareg leather boxes**.

Try too, the **Centre de formation féminine et artisinale** at the exit of town on the Bobo road (Gounghin district). This is a religious-sponsored organisation, where the women make a variety of crafts like Tuareg-inspired **woollen rugs**, and less compelling tablecloths and napkins embroidered with African motifs. Finally, for **leather goods**, you should try the **Centre du Tannage** on the Fada road opposite the prison.

The museum

Tues–Sat 9am–12.30pm and 3.30–5.30pm

The **musée national** is located in the *Lycée Bogodogo* on the av d'Oubritenga. Primarily an **ethnographic collection**, it contains household utensils, tools and weapons used by various peoples in Burkina. Numerous **clay pots** are on display, including ones made specifically to store clothing, jewellery or grain. Among the most interesting are the magic pots used for keeping medicines. Their potency was protected with sacrifices. **Basketmaking** and **weaving exhibits** from around Burkina are complemented by **regional costumes**, including a Mossi chief's regalia – compare it with what the Mogho Naba wears on a Friday morning at the *Nabayius Gou* ceremony. A good part of the display is dedicated to sculptures in wood, including **ancestral statues** of the Bobo, Mossi, Lobi and Gourounsi. These are accompanied by carved stools and sceptres (*kwara*) symbolising the authority of chiefs, and a fantastic collection of **masks** showing the different regional styles: abstract and geometric in the north; exaggerated animal shapes in the Senoufo country; cylindrical helmets used by the Mossi; and horizontally shaped *masques papillon* ("butterfly masks") common among the Bobo-Bwa.

Nightlife

Ouagadougou lives for the night. Energy suppressed by the day's heavy heat is ecstatically released when the sun sets. The streets fill with thousands of Ouagalais walking to the cinema, checking out the clubs or just looking for conversation and a breath of night air (staying inside, of course, is mostly too hot). One of the few Sahelian towns that's predominantly non-Muslim, Ouaga's bars and discos don't suffer any taboo. They pack out nightly and often feature live music and dancing. As an extra bonus, they're cheap (cover charges and drink prices are fixed by law). It all adds up to a good time – and some credit to the revolution. Some of the better addresses include:

L'Escale av Yennenga near the Idéal. More of a bar (overstuffed armchairs and low tables inside) than a disco, but it often relaxes into dancing. Ghanaian waitresses so you can speak English; they shake your hand before taking your order. The DJ, Boots, keeps it happening.

Palladium av Yennenga near the *grande mosquée*. Popular outdoor *dancing* with live music and inexpensive drinks. Latest salsa and African tunes; small cover charge.

Maxim's av Loudun. Another open-air disco popular for its central location and low prices.

Bar de l'an II Far from the centre on the route de Pô this is a well-landscaped (exotic plants) outdoor disco with two dance floors and tables for drinking under thatched *paillotes*.

Lux Bar In the northern district of Kolgo Naaba this one requires a taxi if you're staying in the centre. Live bands most nights and a hot environment.

L'Harmattan Off the av Yennenga near the Palais de Justice. An indoor disco aiming for chic, with blinking lights and dark corners. Heavier emphasis on American pop (driving beat essential), but African and Antillean hits are also popular. Cover charge.

L'Unesco Bar Another outdoor *dancing* in the Dapoya district. Live bands and small cover.

Silmandé In the hotel past the *Zone de Bois* this is a stuffier disco where you're supposed to look like you have huge sums of money. The CFA3000 cover charge includes a cold buffet and a similar ambience.

Directory

Airlines The main ones are:
Aeroflot rue Josef Badoua (☎33.36.93/33.36.88).
Air Afrique 3 av G. A. Nasser (☎33.45.01).
Air Algérie av Nelson Mandela.
Air Burkina av Yennenga (☎33.61.55).
Air Ivoire rue Maurice Bishop (☎33.36.60).
Ethiopian Airlines (☎31.00.82).
Burkina Nord-Sud (formerly *Le Point*) 17 av Bassawarga (☎33.41.51).
UTA 12 av Mandela (☎33.30.86).

American cultural centre av Kennedy near av Boumedienne (Mon–Fri 7.30am–12.30pm and 2.30–5.30pm). They have an exhibition space here and show videos of last week's ABC news, but the library has moved to the university, off the av de Gaulle.

Banks Banks are open Mon–Fri 7am–noon and 3–6pm. Note that there's no bank in the airport. In town, major branches are *BICIA* av Nkrumah (BP 8; ☎33.69.50) and at *l'Hôtel Indépendance*; *BIB*, rue Patrice Lumumba; *BND* Place de la Révolution (☎33.29.96).

Bicycle and moped rental A possibility (and a good one given the flat landscapes) for loco-motion throughout Burkina – and further afield if you like it. In Ouaga, try at SOBA (☎33.34.36) near the *Grand Marché*. A bike should cost around CFA1500 per day and a moped CFA2500. Also ask any of the bicycle vendors around the *Grand Marché*. You can pick up hardly used second-hand bicycles for under CFA30,000.

Books and magazines English press is hard to find, but try the bookstore of the *Hôtel Indépendance*. In town, the *Librarie Attié* on the av Yennenga has French papers and books, plus some other foreign press. Also try the *Librarie Générale* near the *Nouveau Marché* next to *Mini-Prix*. Along the streets (notably av Yennenga) vendors sell second-hand books from *pousse-pousse*. You'll find the occasional outdated English novel which you can buy or exchange for your unwanted books.

Cinema Even in the capital of African cinema, you're not likely to see a film by an African film maker (unless you come for the FESPACO film festival), but Ouaga is full of cinephiles. The best cinema with A/C and the newest films is the *Ciné Burkina* near the *grande mosquée*. Cheaper places include *Ciné Oubri* on the rue Maurice Bishop; *Riale* on the rue Patrice Lumumba; and the *Ciné Gounghin* in the *quartier* of the same name.

Car hire In Ouaga, count on at least CFA10,000/day to rent a car plus CFA100/km and taxes, although prices vary depending on the agency. It all adds up to at least CFA25,000 a day for say 100km, and you may be strongly persuaded to take a driver. In descending price order, outlets include:
Rentacar rue de la Chance, (☎33.32.29), branches at the *Hôtel Silmandé* and the airport;
Burkina Auto Location, *Hotel Indépendance*, (☎33.55.52);
Express Auto Location, *RAN Hôtel* , (☎33.42.55).

Embassies and consulates include:

Algeria Place des Nations Unies (BP3893; ☎30.64.01, Telex 5359).

Austria (BP 620; ☎33.33.66).

Belgium 231 rue Patrice Lumumba (BP118; ☎33.59.63).

Canada (BP 548; ☎30.00.30).

Egypt (BP 7042; ☎30.66.67).

France av de l'Indépendance (BP 504; ☎30.67.74/33.22.70, telex 5211). Visas issued for **Côte d'Ivoire, Togo** and **Mauritania** plus **Gabon, Chad, CAR** and **Djibouti**. Two photos required, prices vary.

Germany FR av Raoul Follereau (BP 600; ☎30.67.31/2, telex 5217).

Ghana av Bassawarga (BP 212; ☎30.67.75). On the subject of visas for British passport holders, see p.810, "Overland from Burkina Faso".

Nigeria av d'Oubritenga (BP 132; ☎30.67.71, telex 5326).

Netherlands (BP 1302; ☎30.61.34, Telex 5303).

Senegal , west of av Yennenga, just south of *Hôtel Aéroport* (BP 91; ☎33.37.14).

Spain (BP 23; ☎33.23.72).

Sweden (BP 362; ☎33.33.75).

Switzerland (BP 578; ☎30.67.29).

United Kingdom Honorary Consulate (BP 1918; ☎33.63.63).

USA av Raoul Follereau (BP 35; ☎30.67.24).

Film and developing: You can buy film or have it developed (B&W only) at *Photolux* which you'll find across from the *Ciné Oubri*. They also do **passport photos**. For colour development you could try *Fuji Film* on av Boumedienne not far from the market (CFA9000 for 36 exposures).

French cultural centre With a vast library, exhibition space and theatre, this is an excellent place for cultural information.

Hospital The only hospital is the *Hôpital Yalgado Ouédraogo*, av Oubritenga(☎30.66.43, 33.46.41).

Maps The *Institut de géographie* on the av de l'Indépendance has decent city maps of Ouaga and Bobo, plus a good national map with routes.

Pharmacies Two central pharmacies are *Pharmacie du Sud* on av Yennenga (☎30.65.37, 33.36.31) and *Pharmacie Keneya* across from the market.

Supermarkets Main supermarkets in town are: *Casino* on av Mandela; *Socibe*, *Mini-Prix* and *Self Service* – all near the *nouveau marché*. The best shopping is at Mini-Prix. Also try *FASO Yaar*, the government-run store on the route de Ouahigouya; although not as well stocked, you find some occasional bargains (for example, sugar).

Swimming pools The cheapest pool in the middle of town is at the *RAN Hôtel*. More expensive, but generally with cleaner water, are the *Hôtel Indépendance* and the *Hôtel Silmandé*. On the outskirts, the *OK Inn's* is another good, and often empty, pool.

Theatre It's worth checking out what's on at the National Theatre in the southwest part of Ouagadougou.

Tourist information The *Ministère de l'Environnement et du Tourisme*, (BP 624; ☎33.43.15) situated next to the *Hotel Indépendance*, is friendly, but doesn't have that much in the way of brochures and information to offer. They do, however, organise excursions to the game reserves at Pô and Arli, plus a number of other trips.

Travel agents *Burkina Nord-Sud*, 17 av Bassawarga (☎33.41.51), organises interesting tours to the Dogon country and Timbuktu in Mali, to Togo, Côte d'Ivoire and Ghana's Asante country. Also try *Faso Tours* , 3 rue Amiron Thombiano, Cité III (BP 1318; ☎30.66.71, telex 5377), who operate a number of trips round the country.

MOVING ON FROM OUAGA

By Road

Leaving Ouaga **by taxi**, the station for international traffic, *Ouaga-Inter*, is on the Route de Pô, 8km from the centre. Paved roads link Ouaga with Abidjan (1300km), Accra (1000km), Lomé (1000km), Cotonou (1150km via Lomé) and Niamey (550km). When heading to Lomé, remember that the border closes at 6pm, so leave early. Travelling by *taxi brousse* you can knock about a third off your costs by changing taxis at Dapango, but that often involves an overnight wait there.

Heading by taxi **to Kaya and northern Burkina**, vehicles often leave from the city centre, near the filling station by the *Centre Artisanale*. Check there before trekking out to the *Ouaga-Inter* station. There's also another *autogare* at Tampouy, near the X9 station on av Yatenga – vehicles to Ouahigouya, Yako and Djibo, even to Bobo and Dori.

Buses also run to many destinations. The **Régie X9** (BP 2991; ☎30.42.96) runs services to **Bobo-Dioulasso** (7am and 2pm daily), **Ouahigouya** (8am daily except Sun), **Pô** (8am daily) **Nouna**, for San, Mali (8am Mon, Wed & Sat), **Léo** (8am Tues, Thurs & Sat), and **Sinkanse**, for Togo (2pm, Wed & Sat).

In addition the **SBTR** (*Société Burkinabe des Transports* ☎33.54.12) has a regular service between Bobo and Niamey (via Ouaga and Fada Ngourma). They leave from near the train station. *Faso Tours* also has buses to Bobo (with a stop to clock the crocs at Sabou), Niamey and other destinations.Their office in Cité III quarter, northwest of the railway station, is at 3 rue Amiron Thombiano (BP 1318; ☎30.66.71).

Internationally, if you're **Ghana-bound**, Ghana's state transport corporation office in Ouaga is at the junction of av Nkrumah and av Boumedienne. They run six bus services a month to Accra, from the Ouaga-Inter station (every Mon and every second and fourth Fri in the month). Headed for **Abidjan**, the new luxury coaches are really much better than the train, but more expensive too.

Getting out by Train

The *Régie Abidjan-Niger*, or RAN, has trains to Koudougou, Bobo, Banfora and through to Côte d'Ivoire.Trains are relatively comfortable but slow and often late. Since schedules change often, you should check them at the station (or try to call ☎33.37.51). Note that at certain times of the year (notably when schools start up), you can get a fifty percent student discount on second class by showing an *ISIC* card.

And Plane

Air Burkina (☎33.61.55) has the cheapest **domestic flights**. Daily flights connect Ouaga to Bobo, but they are far less frequent to other destinations. For full details on prices and times, contact the airline.

For **flights to Europe**, basically France, *Naganagani* (*Burkina Nord-Sud*; see address on p.268) still offers the cheapest flights on a weekly basis. The other airlines with regular service to Europe are *Aeroflot*, *UTA* and *Air Afrique*.

Around Ouaga – the route to Koudougou

West of Ouaga, the **road to Koudougou** passes through a number of villages where you could reasonably stop if you've got your own transport and aren't pressed for time. Barely out of the city, you arrive in the small town of **TANGUIN-DASSOURI** which has a lively market on a three-day cycle. A *piste* leads 6km north of this town to a village renowned for its sacred crocodiles – **BESOULE**. When you arrive here, pay respects (and CFA500) to the chief and he'll have you shown to the lake where the *caimans* live. After sacrificing a chicken, you can touch and photograph the reptiles (should you be wondering, the oldest male is the most docile). If you're using public transport, you're likely to have to walk the 6km from Tanguin-Dassouri, but by way of compensation you'll find the people here very friendly. The place is much less visited than the lake at **SABOU** – about 90km down the main road to Bobo, a staple destination for the tour operators. Sabou has become a ghastly trap, although at least it's in a pleasant setting and there's accommodation in a modest *campement*.

Koudougou

Before reaching Sabou, the main road to Bobo branches in the direction of **KOUDOUGOU**, Burkina Faso's third-largest town. It's a quiet place with wide tree-lined avenues, but a certain level of activity is assured by the country's largest textile factory, **Faso Fani**, and no less than three secondary schools (*collèges*). Koudougou is also the hometown of the first president of Upper Volta, Maurice Yaméogo.

Sleeping and eating

There's a choice of several hotels in Koudougou – nothing very luxurious, but there are several comfortable places with AC and a number of more inexpensive lodgings:

Hôtel l'Oasis Ideally situated next to the market. Simple rooms grouped around a mango-shaded courtyard. From CFA3000–3500 according to amenities.

Hôtel Yaleba On the same street as the old mosque. Friendly management and rooms from CFA3000–5500, the latter with AC. Very good courtyard restaurant with a wide range of inexpensive dishes.

Relais de la Gare 100m from the train station. Rooms with fan or AC go from CFA3500–5500. There's a spacious bar/restaurant and a *dancing*.

Hôtel Photo-Luxe Perhaps the nicest hotel in town, though a bit far from the centre on the junction of the old and new roads to Ouaga. Many rooms are S/C AC and start at CFA5000. Clean and friendly, the hotel has an excellent bar and small **pool** (CFA500 for non-guests).

Hotel Toulourou In the centre near the motor park (☎44.01.70), convenient and comfortable with S/C rooms, some AC (CFA5000–7000). European-style restaurant with meals from around CFA1500.

For **meals**, try *Au Coin du Plaisir* just across from the *gare*. This bar has a shady courtyard with *paillotes* and cheap eats on sale in front. Another such place is the *Gazelle Bar* next to the *Oasis*. Apart from the hotel restaurants, plenty of cheap **street food** is sold near the market or at the railway station. A Koudougou speciality is *pintade* (guinea fowl) which you see being grilled on roadside braziers in the evening.

Things to do around town

During the day, wander around the **market** which is well supplied with fruit – mangos, pineapples, avocados, bananas – vegetables and cereal. There's a reasonable selection of **handicrafts** too; woven goods (hats and baskets), leather (handbags, wallets and shoes) and pottery (jugs and bowls of all sizes). You'll also find ready-to-wear outfits made from locally handwoven and embroidered cloth.

Evening diversions include a couple of **cinemas** – the *Nelson Mandela* on the main road to Ouaga, and a second one north of the market near the mosque. The town also boasts an impressive new **théâtre populaire** in the west beyond the *palais de justice*. Koudougou has its own troupe that puts on periodic performances (mostly in More); worth seeing if you're in town at the right moment. On other nights, the theatre doubles as an open-air cinema. Good **discos** in town include the *Okinawa* on the Old Ouaga Road near the Photo-Luxe; and *Au Joie du Peuple* in the north of town.

Practicalities and moving on

Change money in Bobo or Ouaga, not Koudougou. The *BICIA* changes cash (FF) only and the *BIB* wants to see receipts (!) before changing even major travellers' cheques.

There are two **trains** a day out of Koudougou in each direction: Ouaga, second class, CFA800; Bobo, second class, CFA2400. The **autogare** for Bobo and Côte d'Ivoire is next to the train station. Vehicles leave for Ouaga and the north from near the market.

East of Ouaga – the route to Fada

The route to Niamey runs from Ouagadougou through the **Gourmantché country**. The first town of any size on this road is **KOUPÉLA**, which, on the main road to Togo, seems like one large and very busy intersection.

Koupéla

The flow of traffic through Koupéla makes for a lively scene. If you want or need to pass a night here you have several options. Behind the post office, the *Bon Séjour* has dirty non-S/C *chambres* for CFA2000. For preference, try the *Calypso Hôtel* on the main Ouaga road. It's a clean and pleasant abode with a bar, *dancing* and fan-ventilated rooms from under CFA2000. You can also eat in their patio restaurant and watch vultures land on neighbouring tables to snaffle leftovers. **Food** is no problem in town as countless vendors line the streets waiting for taxis and buses to roll in. Buy a grilled *pintade*, take it to the *Amicale Bar* on the eastern edge of the market, and wash it down with a cold *Brakina*.

Other practicalities

Koupéla has a large daily **market** renowned for its pottery, most of which is displayed at the southern end. There's also a small *centre artisanale* on the junction of the Ouaga and Togo roads. It's got a very limited selection of leather and weaving by disabled artisans. Across from the centre is a BICIA **bank**, though there's no guarantee you can change travellers' cheques here. If you spend the night and want to take in a movie, the *Buuru Cinema* is right next to the *Calypso* on the main road: no recent releases.

Fada Ngourma and beyond

Midway between Niamey and Ouagadougou, **FADA NGOURMA** is another of Burkina's junction towns, the eighth largest in the country in fact. It was founded by Diaba Lompo, who is variously claimed to be the son, maternal uncle or cousin of Ouédraogo (see the Mossi genealogy). The town was originally called Bingo, meaning a slave settlement, but Fada Ngourma is a Hausa appelation, mysteriously meaning "The place where you don't pay tax". It happens to be twinned with Epernay, the champagne capital of France, where the prosperous burghers certainly do pay tax. A more unlikely match is hard to imagine.

Fada is a pleasant, tranquil focus, but does host a colourful **market** with a wealth of goods from across the Sahel region. The beautifully woven **blankets** and **rugs** on sale are invariably better buys here than in Ouagadougou.

Sleeping, eating and other important matters

The *Auberge* at the eastern end of the market is the only **accommodation** in town and seems rather pricey with plain rooms (with fan) from CFA3000 (CFA4500 with AC). They do have a good restaurant however, with grilled chicken and chips and similar fare going for around CFA1500. Next door, the *Restaurant de la Paix*, has a peaceful courtyard for eating. North of the market, the *Restaurant du Gourma* is the other mealtime venue. They formerly had rooms to rent and may have started up again. North of the *Auberge* there's a small **cinema** which sometimes gets a movie in.

The *BIB* **bank** in town won't change your travellers' cheques unless you can show receipts from where you bought them: they will take cash. You'll find the *autogare* on the main road near the modern **cathedral** (an edifice that's particularly strange looking). For Ouagadougou (CFA2500) and Niamey (CFA4500) there are direct, frequent departures.

Out of Fada Ngourma to Benin and Arli National Park

Besides the main, paved Ouaga–Niger highway, however, an important *piste* to NATITINGOU and northern Benin leads out from Fada and goes past the **Arli National Park** (open dry season only, stay at the village of PAMA at the western end, where there's a cheap *campement*).There are fairly infrequent taxis down here. If you're driving – and without plenty of luck, there's really no other way of looking around the park itself independently – you might do better to continue to KANTCHARI and then skirt south through DIAPAGA (there's a *campement de chasse* there) to ARLI village and the district's moderately expensive (CFA16,000/20,000), pretty lodge, the *Safari Hôtel*, which is the base for game-viewing trips around the park.

Northeast to Gorom-Gorom

Gorom-Gorom is actually closer to Ouaga than Bobo, yet the 300km of dirt roads and tracks separating this town in the **Sahel** from the capital can take considerable time to cover, even in the dry season. You might break the trip with stopovers in **Kaya** and **Dori** – the two major towns en route. Along the way you'll notice a change in the peoples as Mossi-speakers give way to northerners – principally Fula, Tuareg and Bella – and the Muslim influence becomes more predominant. The vast majority of the people of the north are farmers and herders. Their livelihoods are especially sensitive to the drought conditions that recently plagued the country and continue to threaten them.

From Ouagadougou to Kaya

Before reaching **KAYA**, the route to Gorom passes a couple of villages with important roles in Mossi tradition. To the first, the Muslim fief of **LOUMBILA**, a **blacksmith** is sent on the death of the Mogho Naba, in order to cast a bronze effigy of the deceased ruler. Since the death of Ouédraogo, 36 sets of five statues (each representing the Mogho Naba, one of his wives, a servant and two musicians) have been cast in this town where the assigned blacksmith is confined for three years. Today these statues are carefully guarded in the chief's compound. The other village, nearby **GUILONGOU**, marks the spot where, according to Mossi legend, pottery was first invented. It's still an important industry here.

Kaya practicalities

Only 98km from Ouaga, **KAYA** is the last major Mossi town on this route. With a population of some 17,000 it has a certain infrastructure – including some banks – and hotels, the best of which is the *Hôtel de l'Oasis* with large S/C rooms. If you feel like making the effort, try also the *Mission Catholique* on the Kongoussi road, where the rooms are a sight cleaner and cheaper than the *Oasis'*. There's nowhere special to eat in town, but the market has no shortage of cheap eats.

Kaya's flourishing **market** sells many of the **crafts** for which the region is widely reputed; there are weavers, tanners and leather workers in town and more pour in from neighbouring villages to sell their wares.

From Kaya to Dori

Sixty-eight kilometres beyond Kaya, TOUGOURI marks the northern limits of the Mossi country. A short distance further, **YALOGO** is a Fula village with a large Tuesday market. And another 60km brings you to the Islamic stronghold of **BANI** with its solid large banco *mosquée* and an important regional market held every Wednesday. Only 35km remain to Dori.

Dori details

Despite its small size, **DORI** is an important administrative centre in the north. There's a **bank** (though as usual no promise they'll change travellers' cheques) and numerous bars, but not much in the way of **rooms**. In the absence of anything better, you'll have to fall back on one of the *chambres de passage* adjoining the bars. The owners of *Chez Jean* next to the market are used to putting up overlanders. They'll give you a bed and a bucket for showers. Dori's **market day** is Sunday and, according to the German explorer, Heinrich Barth, who passed through in July 1853, it's supposed to be really good for blankets. If you're there on a Sunday, perhaps you could write to verify that.

From Dori, there's a rough, but pretty route through hilly bush to Djibo, and OUAHIGOUYA. **DJIBO** was founded in the sixteenth century. It became capital of the Peul (Fula) kingdom of Djilgodji and, in the nineteenth century, came under the control of the Muslim state of Masina, in present-day Mali. Little evidence of that remains outside the handed-down memories of a few old men and women. Djibo today is a livestock market, at the mercy of the encroaching desert.

Gorom-Gorom

Less than thirty kilometres separate Dori from **GOROM-GOROM**, a large Sahelian village with a **market** – one of the biggest in the north – that draws a vast array of northern peoples. Tuareg, Fula and Bella nomads trek into the mostly Songhai-run market on Wednesday, the main trading day. In addition to the foodstuffs, you'll find a variety of leather goods, jewellery and textiles, all produced locally. A short distance away is the **animal market** where camel, goat, sheep and donkeys are bought and sold. The town itself is a picturesque blend of banco houses and narrow dusty streets with numerous mosques.

Accommodation and practicalities

The *Campement Hotelier* was built by *Le Point* (since taken over by *Naganagani/ Burkina Nord-Sud*) and reflected the airline's philosophy that tourism should ideally work to benefit both the inhabitant and the visitor. *Le Point* envisaged the place as "the cornerstone of 'a different kind of tourism' based on dialogue and exchange." Not only did construction of the site provide villagers with months of work, but the people of Gorom-Gorom help run the *campement* and will eventually take it over as the sole operators. Contacts here are direct and motivated by the people's genuine desire to open their town to you. The complex is modelled after a Sahelian village, with houses and thatched lean-tos surrounded by a large mud wall. House interiors match the local style. There's a bar on the premises and a restaurant, though, admittedly, meals are slightly more expensive than you would normally expect to pay in these parts.

Air Burkina has two **flights** a week to Gorom-Gorom and the *campement* runs a weekly **shuttle** (4WD vehicle) from Ouaga. The centre closes, however, in July and August. The *campement* also organises **excursions** throughout the area if you want to get out to explore the region and its people. Ask about the possibility of visiting on camel.

Among the offerings are trips to nearby Songhai villages (Korya, Zena, Tin Akof) or to cave paintings near ARBINDA. Emphasis is placed on getting to know regional life-styles and the relationship between the people and the Sahel's fragile ecosystem. With the continuous threat of desertification, the **agro-ecological centre** opened in conjunction with the *campement* is designed to provide local farmers with information and technical advice with the aim of self-sufficiency in food production. For complete information on prices and and organised trips, contact the *Burkina Nord-Sud* office in the capital (see Ouagadougou "Directory").

Ouahigouya and the Yatenga state

Sparse and mostly bone dry, but historically important, **Ouahigouya** is the capital of northern Burkina. It was founded in the eighteenth century as capital of **Yatenga**, the northernmost Mossi kingdom, which had broken away from Ouagadougou some three hundred years before. It's a relaxed and pleasant place to mooch around, perhaps dallying in its large market, or taking in some of the 37 picturesque mosques. Most of Yatenga's sights, however, lie outside it in the villages of the region: its original capitals at **La** and **Gourcy** in the south; the burial sites of many of its *nabas* at **Somniaga**; and the region's most impressive mosques at **Ramatoulaye** to the west, and **Yako** to the south. All these places are worth a look, but you'll be back in Ouahigouya by sunset if you value cold beer and music.

The Yatenga region is an arid, undulating **plateau**, not quite a plain but too flat to rate hilly. Barren for most of the year, the rains in May lay a green carpet on the earth that lasts until October, during which time the region's main crops, particularly millet and sorghum, but also maize, cotton, groundnuts and indigo, are sown and harvested. Outside this season, Yatenga reverts to a scrubby savannah of tree–dotted thornbush – shea-nut, *neré* (carob) and false mahogany trees – with tamarind and types of plum (*nobega*) and fig (*kankanga*) among the wild fruits.

The animal life is unimpressive (there was still the odd lion in the region fifty years ago, but you'd be lucky to see as much as a gazelle today) but **birds** are much in evidence – especially vultures, which seem even more overbearing here than in the rest of Burkina. A good deal more agreeable are the electric blue **Abyssinian roller birds**, perched on telegraph wires in the barren landscape. They're like the traveller's herald in West Africa, as unmissable as magpies over a motorway.

Ethnography

The main ethnic group is the Mossi, who were living around here by the end of the 1330s, when they sacked Timbuktu. They took political power probably in the second half of the fifteenth century (some claim several centuries earlier). The Dogon, then living in the north of the region, fled up to the Bandiagara escarpment in Mali, while the Samos, based in the east, stayed on and have now more or less assimilated with the Mossi.

The principal state was run by the **Kurumba** or Fulse. They claim to have come from the region of Say and Niamey some two hundred years before the Mossi, to set up the Kingdom of Lurum, with its last capital at Mengao, now in Djibo district. Just as the Dogon hadn't resisted the Kurumba invasion, so the Kurumba hardly opposed the Mossi, and the two communities have merged into the dual socio-political system largely still existent today, in which the **Mossi** hold political power (as "masters of the sky") while the Kurumba have authority over agriculture and the land (the "masters of the earth"). Each village has a Kurumba "earth chief", whose functions complement those of the Mossi *naba*. There's a third element in this system, the **blacksmiths** (*saaba*), who never marry out, usually live in their own wards (*zaka*) inside Mossi villages (though they have one or two villages of their own, like Séguénéga) and have special ceremonial duties such as performing circumcisions. Only the men are smiths; women are generally potters.

Within this same system are the captives (*Yemse*). Descendants of prisoners of war, and loyal to the Yatenga Naba, they live in their own section of town called the *bingo*. Ouahigouya's *bingo* consists of half the city and captives form more than half its population. Village chiefs and court dignitaries are often captives by descent.

HISTORY OF YATENGA

The first great Mossi conqueror, **Naba Rawa**, eldest son of Ouédraogo, founded the kingdom of **Zandoma** or Rawatenga, maybe around 1470. His great nephew Ouemtanango, son of Oubri, perhaps jealous of Rawa's success, expanded his father's Oubritenga kingdom (later Ouagadougou) to the north, moving its capital from Tenkodogo to La.

The kingdom of Yatenga was probably founded around 1540 on the death of the fourth Mogho Naba, **Nasbire**. It happened thus. Nasbire's son and heir, **Yadega**, who was away, heard about his father's death and rode straight to La to claim the kingdom. He arrived, however, to find that his brother Kumdumye had taken power, kept the news from reaching him and moved south to Ouagadougou. Yadega followed but found Kumdumye's authority already well established. He returned angrily to La, where he was soon followed by his sister Pabre, who'd managed to seize the **royal amulets** embodying the Mogho Naba's power. With these, Yadega declared a new kingdom and had himself enthroned at La. His new state was known after him as **Yatenga** (from *Yadega tenga*: Yadega's land). A legacy of the dispute is the continued mutual avoidance of the holders of the offices of Mogho Naba and Yatenga Naba who to this day refuse to set eyes on each other.

Oral history is a bit confused on some of these points. Ouagadougou tradition inserts a fifth Mogho Naba between Nasbire and Kumdumye, making the latter the sixth Naba, and also claims that the royal amulets were recovered from Pabre – though Yatenga tradition says they got nothing more than her horse's droppings. It's possible that Nasbire had named Kumdumye his heir in any case. But why Yadega was away from La, and where he was, are also disputed, as is his relationship to Kumdumye, who may have been his cousin. The date of Yatenga's foundation could have been as much as four hundred years earlier.

THE RISE OF YATENGA

At first the Yatenga statelet was the runt of the Mossi litter. Consisting of the towns of La, its first capital and **Gourcy**, its second, plus a few surrounding villages, it lay sandwiched between Zandoma to the north and Oubritenga to the south. When Yadega's brother Kouda jumped on the bandwagon and set up his own kingdom of Risiam, to the southeast (independent until the nineteenth century), it was bigger than Yatenga. What changed this balance was a tradition of conqest and expansion that commenced with the activities of the ninth Yatenga Naba, **Vanteberegum**. He moved the Yatenga capital to **Somniaga**, extending the kingdom to do so, and his son set out on a campaign of aggrandisment that gobbled up most of Zandoma and established Yatenga as the second most powerful Mossi kingdom. However, it was the twenty-fifth *naba*, **Naba Kango**, famous for his cruelty as much as his conquests, who really fixed Yatenga in the oral histories.

Deposed almost as soon as he took power in 1754, Naba Kango returned after three years, aided by the formidable advantage of **firearms**, to retake power with an army of mercenaries. He then built a new capital at **Ouahigouya**, with an enormous **palace**, and summoned all Yatenga's chiefs (including the *naba* of Zandoma) to pay homage to him there. Those who failed to do so received a visit from his troops, who then went on to invade neighbouring territories, leading to a vast expansion of Kango's kingdom. Within it, he maintained an impressive unity, largely by burning down any villages that defied

The **Peulh** (Fula) are the region's other main group. Although based in Djibo and outside the Mossi-Kurumba system, they've played an often major role in Yatenga's history. The **Silmi-Mossi**, descendants of a union, considered somewhat disreputable, of Fula and Mossi, live in their own villages, mainly isolated in the south and southeast of the region. Lastly, members of three Islamic trading nations, the **Songhai**, **Bambara** and Mande-speaking **Yarse**, also live in Yatenga. The Mossi themselves, despite having resisted the advances of Islam for so long, are nowadays mostly Muslim here too.

his authority. He had criminals publicly burnt to death and even massacred his own Bambara troops when they misbehaved. He was succeeded in 1787 by his nephew, **Naba Sagha**, but the large kingdom was growing unwieldy and and, within forty years, Yatenga had plunged into the series of civil wars that were to destroy it.

CIVIL WAR AND DISSOLUTION

The wars concerned the succession of Sagha's 133 sons, the first of whom, **Tougouri**, managed to succeed him in 1806. Following his death in 1825, war broke out between those of Sagha's sons who were next in line. Only after 1834 was there a lull in the strife. On the death of Naba Yende, in 1877, however, the dynastic conflicts flared up once more.

This time the dispute was between Sagha's grandsons. The sons of his first-born and successor, Tougouri, claimed that they alone were entitled to rule. The sons of Tougouri's brothers and successors disagreed, pointing out that the intended *naba*'s mother had been a concubine, and that in any case, each branch of Sagha's family should take a turn. The two groups formed opposing parties called **Sons of Tougouri** and **Sons of Sagha**.

When two Sons of Sagha were successively enthroned as *nabas*, the Sons of Tougouri went to war against them. Baogo, the incumbent *naba*, turned to the **French** – who, although new on the scene, had just taken Bandiagara, and were hovering on Yatenga's borders. **Desteneves**, the leader of the French expeditionary force, offered only to mediate. Undeterred, Baogo went into battle against the Sons of Tougouri in 1894 and was killed.

All other eligible branches of Sagha's family having had their turn, the kingdom now returned to Tougouri's family. His senior son, Naba Boulli, took the throne but predictably the Sons of Sagha refused to accept him and set up a rival *naba* in **Sissamba**. Boulli turned to the French, who this time seized the opportunity and, on 18 May, 1895, declared Yatenga a protectorate, thus usurping its independence.

The French sacked Sissamba, but the Sons of Sagha successfully recaptured Ouahigouya as soon as they had left. The French bailed out Boulli and put him back on the throne twice more, by which time half Ouahigouya was in ruins. The rebellion of the Sons of Sagha wasn't put down until 1902, and violent incidents in connection with it continued as late as 1911.

MODERN YATENGA

French military occupation ended in 1909 when Yatenga passed to civilian colonial rule, and the region was generally quiet during the 1916 anti-conscription rebellion. With the 1932 division of Upper Volta, Yatenga became part of the French Sudan until the recreation of Upper Volta in 1947. The 1930s and 40s saw the rise of **Hammalism**, a reformist Muslim cult which the French considered anti-colonial (it was). The movement was largely responsible for the spread of Islam in Yatenga (hitherto strongly resisted because of its association with hostile empires, especially Songhai to the north). This in turn became the base for opposition to the traditionalist, chief-led *Union Voltaïque* in the region. A *UV* breakaway, the *MDV* (*Mouvement Démocratique Voltaïque*) carried Yatenga in the 1957 election with a base of Muslim support.

Since independence, Yatenga has been a *département* of Burkina, divided into four *cercles*: Ouahigouya, Gourcy, Séguénéga and Titao. Yako lies outside it in the département of Koudougou.

Ouahigouya

OUAHIGOUYA's wide streets and low buildings give a lazy feeling of space, especially after the dust and shimmering heat of day. The market sprawls, the *autogare* sprawls, the main square sprawls: you can't rush about here.

The town's lack of specific "sights" belies its significant **history.** Most important buildings were destroyed in the nineteenth-century **Yatenga civil wars.** Ouahigouya was founded in 1757 – the last of Yatenga's capitals – and marked the northern limit of the state's expansion. King Kango's summons to the chiefs of Yatenga to pay him homage gives the town its name (from *Waka yuguya!* – "Come and greet"). Unfortunately, the great palace where this took place was destroyed in 1825 during one of the struggles for the throne, in which the city was rased to the ground.

Kango may originally have built Ouahigouya as a salt depot; he certainly had his eye on trans-Saharan commodities (gold and kola for example) and hoped to make money by channelling more of their trade through Yatenga. Another motive in building the town could have been to escape from the power of the Mossi aristocracy which had always resented his rule and may well have been repsonsible for usurping him in the first place. At any rate, Kango populated the new city with captives and ethnic minorities, from whose number he chose many of his officials.

As well as the dynastic struggles of the 1820s and 30s, Ouahigouya suffered serious damage in the later wars between Sons of Sagha and Sons of Tougouri (see box on previous page). By the time the French managed to secure their stooge Boulli on the throne at the end of 1896, it was half in ruins again, but they needed a base for eastward conquest and "pacification" of Yatenga, and so constructed a fort and rebuilt the town as the regional capital.

Ouahigouya practicalities

Ouahigouya's **hotels** range form cheap and seedy to French-style deluxe. Arriving at the *autogare*, the lower end of the scale is first on offer. The *Hôtel du Nord*, opposite the gare's northern corner has the very cheapest lodgings in town, but it's very basic and not clean. Its bar is a meeting place for prostitutes and their clients but the management is friendly and they don't run out of cold beer (or music) till midnight. A little further along the main drag, towards the *quartier administratif*, the *Auberge Populaire* is much the same (midnight closing), but a touch less sleazy. The rooms with fans, showers and nets are looked after and it's cheaper than the *Nord*. More upmarket, the *Hôtel de l'Amitié*, half a kilometre down the Mopti road, has a more polished, less friendly, and much less Burkinabe atmosphere. They have various rooms at different prices depending on quality, the cheapest singles at the same rate as the *Populaire*, but some S/C, AC ones too. Meals are available, as too is a late-running disco that does draw a crowd. If you don't like the look of the *Amitié* and have seen the others, you'll want the Lebanese-run *Hôtel Dunia* which offers AC luxury and even a pool. The *Hôtel Receuil* (BP 131; ☎55.00.09) is exceptionally cheap (less than CFA2000 for a double with fan, less still without) and an ideal backpacker's retreat – though 2km out of town.

You can have satisfying **meals** at either the *Dunia* or the *Amitié*. The *Dunia's* excellent French-Middle Eastern food make it the first choice of local ex-pats. Smaller places, where you pay for the food and not the service, include the *Ciné Restaurant*, the *Restaurant du Centre* and the *Faso Benie* – rice, yam, pasta, soup, chicken, liver, beans and salad. First thing in the morning, try the *Alpha Café and tape shop*, behind the autogare, and breakfast on omelettes, sandwiches and strong black coffee to the sounds of the Congo, the Mersey and the Hudson. If you'd rather hear some strictly local **music**, call at the shack just round the corner from *Alpha*, where you can get cassettes of traditional Yatenga bands such as **Troupe Ouamagilosa**.

To Koumbri, Bani & Douentza (Mali)

To Djibo, Dori & Gorom-Gorom

Hospital

Yatenga Naba's Compound

Tomb of Naba Kango

To Séguénéga & Kaya

Mairie

Market

PTT

'X9' Bus Stop

Caiman Bar

Boulangerie

Restaurant Faso Benie

Police Station

Hôtel de l'Amitié

Hôtel du Nord

Auberge Populaire

To Dogon Country & Mopti (Mali)

BICI Bank

Cinema

BND Bank

Ciné Restaurant and Restaurant du Centre

Autogare

Restaurant Famille

Sports Ground

Alpha Café

Gendarmerie

0   200 m

OUAHIGOUYA

To Tougan & Bobo Dioulasso

To Yako & Ouagadougou

By day, Ouahigouya lends itself to gentle meanderings. A community as laden with history as this bursts with presence. But the only sight as such is **Naba Kango's tomb**, an imposing white edifice situated between the Mairie and the present Naba's compound. According to popular legend, anyone who walks all the way round it will die (by Burkinabe standards, not very unlikely).

Moving on, you come to the **Yatenga Naba's compound** on the old site of Kango's palace. With luck, you may even get to meet the Naba, who's said to be an expert on Yatenga history – as well he would need to be to justify his position. On the way back, you could check out the market, always worth a wander. Ouahigouya also boasts no less than 37 **mosques**, built in a pretty and distinctive style.

In the evenings, **cold beer and hot music** at the *Nord* and the *Populaire* take you through to midnight – and later if you move on to the *Amitié*'s disco. The *Amitié* is where it all happens in Ouahigouya and it can be a bit of a thrash. So for a quieter drink, the *Bar Caiman*, next door keeps a well-stocked bar and does brochettes.

Around the Yatenga district

Most of Yatenga's **sites of interest** are spread around the villages. Its first capital, and the Mossi capital before Yatenga's secession, was La, now called **LA-TODIN**, beyond the borders of modern Yatenga, 22km west of Yako.

The fourth Yatenga Naba, Guéda, moved his capital north to **GOURCY**, where you can see the **sacred hill** on which his successors are still enthroned. Here, too, are the royal amulets stolen by Pabre on behalf of her brother Yadega. In the civil wars of the

1890s, the Sons of Sagha kidnapped the amulets to prevent the French from crowning Naba Boulli until they were returned at the end of 1897. Gourcy is on the main Ouagadougou–Ouahigouya road, 42km south of Ouahigouya.

The kingdom's third and penultimate capital, **SOMNIAGA**, was seized from the kingdom of Zandoma by Naba Vanteberegum as part of his campaign to enlarge Yatenga. Seven kilometres south of Ouahigouya on the Ouaga road, it makes an easy walk first thing in the morning, or can even be hitched , but don't forget to carry a few litres of water. Most of Yatenga's *nabas* are buried here in the **royal cemetery** (*nayaado*) and looked after by the Yaogo Naba, the man to find if you want to see it. One quaint little Yatenga burial custom was the internment of the *naba's* court jesters with their dead king – alive.

Of the capitals of neighbouring traditional states, **YAKO** is the easiest to visit. Some 70km south of Ouahigouya, it marks the end of the tarmac on the road from Ouagadougou. The most striking first impression is of its **mosque**, but its main claim to local fame goes further. Capital of a kingdom founded by Naba Yelkone – son of the same Kumdumye who split with Yadega over the question of the Mossi throne – it was a perpetual object of Yatenga-Ouagadougou rivalry, generally a fief of the latter. Naba Kango managed to force its submission and the flight of its *naba*, who was only allowed to stay on condition that he planted a sacred grove of thorn bushes (*kango* in More) outside the town. The French also found Yako a tough nut to crack. More recently, **Thomas Sankara** was born here; with some discretion, you may be able to get someone to show you exactly where.

ZANDOMA, the region's very first Mossi capital, is now a tiny village some 40km southwest of Ouahigouya, northwest of Gourcy. The chief still claims descent from **Naba Rawa**, whose tomb can be seen close to his compound.

Other places of interest in and around Yatenga include: **Ramatoulaye**, 25km east of Ouahigouya on the road to Rollo, with another impressive **mosque**, a major centre of Hammalism in colonial days; **Lago**, some 30km south of Ouahigouya (but 41km by road from Zogoré), **burial site** of the first Yatenga *nabas*; **Sissamba**, 11km southwest of Ouahigouya and en route to Lago, where the Sons of Sagha installed their pretender to the throne on Naba Boulli's accession in 1894 and which the French sacked the following year; and **Mengao**, 82km northeast of Ouahigouya on the road to Djibo (27km further), which was the last capital of the kingdom of Lurum and is still the home of the **Kurumba paramount "earth chief"**, the counterpart of the Yatenga Naba – the Mossi paramount sky chief.

If you're **heading for Ouaga**, you have plenty of choice of vehicles, including a *Faso Tours* bus most days and *Régie X9* bus (they have their own stop by the market and leave at 3pm Mon–Fri, 8am Sun, not on Sat). The road is a corrugated *piste* most of the way to Yako and paved from there onwards; allow four or five hours for the trip. You should also be able to find the odd *occasion* to **Djibo**, something to **Bobo-Dioulasso** most days (weather permitting), and even the odd **Abidjan**-bound truck. **Into Mali**, however, transport is scarcer and there's no through service to Mopti, just a vehicle every couple of days or so to KORO, where you'll have to change.

THE GOUROUNSI COUNTRY

The area **around Pô** on the Ghanaian border **south of Ouagadougou** is dominated by the Grusi or **Gourounsi**, a name which usually includes the **Kassena**, the **Nouna** and the **Sissala** from around **Léo**. Their distinctive **architecture** provides the region's main attraction. The Gourounsi country also boasts a couple of **national parks** – though access to them is difficult if you don't have your own transport – and there are some interesting archaeological remains near Léo.

THE GOUROUNSI

How long the people known as **Gourounsi** (originally a Mossi term of denigration) have lived in this region isn't clear, but Mossi tradition claims they were pushed back across the Red Volta River by the thirteenth Mogho Naba, Nakiem, at the end of the seventeenth century. Never united, the various strands of Gourounsi-speakers have long existed in a state of near-permanent village war. More seriously, their lack of central government has always made them vulnerable to attack from more organised groups, especially the Mossi who often made kidnapping raids for slaves. Many Mossi dissidents set themselves up as chiefs in Gourounsi-land, and their families continue to live here. Gourounsi chiefs possess sacred objects called *kwara* – insignia of office – which are handed down from generation to generation.

At the end of the nineteenth century, the Gourounsi were the targets of Djerma Muslim zealots from the Niamey region, who stormed down on horseback and engaged in heavy slave-raiding under a *jihad* banner. They converted the son of the chief of Sati and set up shop there, almost decimating the lands of the Sissala, Nouna and Kassena, before being defeated by a Gourounsi-French alliance in 1895.

The Gourounsi build their **houses** from mud in smooth, sand-castle shapes, often painted with striking diamond patterns. Larger compounds may consist of whole labyrinths of submerged rooms and doorways through which people weave and duck. Buildings are not expected to last more than a few seasons and new houses are built around the foundations of older dwellings, resulting in a characteristic organic appearance. Another typical feature is the presence of forked and notched logs, leant against the walls as ladders to the **flat roofs** where grain is commonly dried, out of goat-reach. Women gather up here to chat and smoke during the day, the whole family often sleep here, and all sorts of occasional items are stored. Village chiefs usually have the largest and most impressive compounds – though not necessarily the prettiest. You can often tell the status of a family from the height of its walls.

The Gourounsi traditional **capital**, TIÉBÉLÉ, has the finest architecture, but it characterises all the villages along the roads parallel with the frontier on both sides. You won't see it, however, in the more modern centre of PÔ, the main town of the region.

On the way to Pô from Ouagadougou, you pass through KOMBISSIRI, 40km south of the capital. This town became a Muslim centre following the settlement here of a community of **Yarse** (Mande-speaking traders) in the eighteenth century. Its religious status was developed by the pro-Muslim 25th Mogho Naba, Sawadogho, who ruled from 1825–42 and had the mosque built. It's 4km east of the town: follow the *piste* from the police checkpoint at the northern end of Kombissiri.

The **Pô national park** lies across the road to Pô and, south of NOBÉRÉ, you may see representatives of the district's elephant herd – one of the few places in West Africa where *elephants on road* is a delightful possibility.

THE GOUROUNSI LANGUAGE

If you learn no other Gourounsi, at least learn to say *Din le*, the all-purpose greeting, which means "Thank you". The following sampler comes from "Kassem", the main dialect of Gourounsi, spoken by the *Kassena*.

Good	*Tim paga*	1	*Kalo*	6	*Trodo*	20	*Finle*	
morning		2	*Inle*	7	*Tirpai*	50	*Finnu*	
Good	*Tim dadan*	3	*Nto*	8	*Nana*	100	*Bi*	
evening		4	*Nna*	9	*Nogo*	500	*Bi yennu*	
		5	*Unu*	10	*Fuga*	1000	*Moro*	

Pô

What **PÔ** lacks in traditional architecture it tries to make up for with a selection of **fountains** with revolutionary names – "Nelson Mandela", "Enver Hoxha", "Les Trois Luttes". If this is your last town in francophone Africa, make the most of plentiful cold beer and relative lack of petty corruption. Coming the other way, it's a gentle introduction to some of French Africa's more tiresome aspects – high prices and an obsession with *papiers*. The Pô **police** are fond of asking for these and you can expect a fair number of spot checks, but like most of the townspeople they're friendly enough and there's no big hassle. Pô is also a garrison town with a chequered recent history. But the soldiers don't obtrude. The vibe is happy and Pô bursts into life in the **evenings**, despite the fact that electricity's mainly confined to the north end of town. Note there's no bank: people in the market or around the *autogare* will change Ghana cedis for CFA (at the standard border rate of around one for one) as well as FF and dollars, but not sterling.

Sleeping, eating and hanging out

Don't expect much comfort in Pô – all the **accommodation** is pretty basic. Arriving from northern Ghana, you'll find it pricey too, but, as a frontier town, there is at least some choice. Up from Ghana, your first option is the *Bar la Montagne* opposite the customs about a kilometre south of the town. There's a variety of rooms and prices, from cheap and grotty to half decent, with a bucket shower and murals by a passing Ghanaian artist – but no *courant*, water off from dusk to dawn, warm beer and limited food. Press on to the *Kora Bar Restaurant*, a bar/hotel half way to the town centre. And if this doesn't appeal either then make for the *Restaurant Bar Koubassary*, behind the market, which seems to be top of the league. Despite rather poky rooms, there are compensations in an electricity supply, a good restaurant, a friendly *patron* and a pet gazelle. You might also try the *Jaochan Bar*, behind the *BP* station

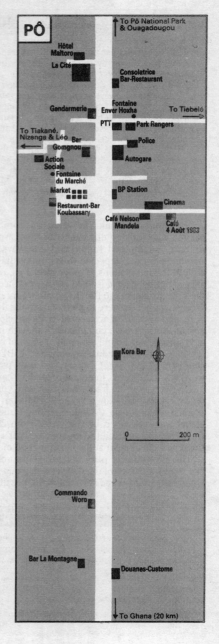

PÔ

To Pô National Park & Ouagadougou

Hôtel Maltoro
La Cité
Consolatrice Bar-Restaurant
Gendarmerie
Fontaine Enver Hoxha
To Tiebelé
PTT
Park Rangers
To Tiakané, Nizenga & Léo
Bar Gomgnou
Police
Action Sociale
Autogare
Fontaine du Marché
Market
BP Station
Restaurant-Bar Koubassary
Cinema
Café Nelson Mandela
Café 4 Août 1983

0   200 m

Kora Bar

Commando Woro

Bar La Montagne

Douanes-Customs

To Ghana (20 km)

A SHOT OF PÔ HISTORY

According to legend, Pô was founded around 1500, by a Mossi man, **Nablogo**, son of Mogho Naba Oubri. He started cultivating a field (*pô*) but got into a land rights dispute with Kassena neighbours. About this time, a certain **Gonkwora** from Kasana near Léo turned up in Pô, having left his village after being disinherited of his rightful chiefship. He brought three magic bracelets with him (still looked after by his descendants in Pô) and fell in with Nablogo, who helped him, and in whose dispute with the Kassena he interceded. Gonkwora's brother then arrived from their home village with the village *kwara*, and became the ancestor of the present chief. Gonkwora meanwhile married Nablogo's daughter and they all lived happily ever after. Gonkwora's tomb is supposed to be under a sacred baobab in the Kasno quarter of town.

More recent and less halcyon history has also been made in Pô. In 1976, **Thomas Sankara** set up the *Centre Nationale d'Entrainement* here, taken over by Blaise Compaoré in 1982. The following year the Ouédraogo regime arrested Sankara and fellow officers. Pô became a radical focus for students, young workers and academics, who came to join the commandos. In August 1983, the coup that toppled Ouédraogo, fired the revolution and put Sankara in power, was launched here. And it was from Pô that Compaoré planned a second takeover in 1987, that led to Sankara's untimely death and put Compaoré in power.

in the town centre which has rooms among the music, beer and loose women. Lastly, if you're arriving from Ouaga, or have reasons to want special luxuries, you could check out the *Hôtel Maltoro*, behind the *cité* north of the town, whose 24 aid workers' houses (built by Sankara) are looked after by an elusive caretaker.

Street **food** is your most likely calorie source. Try near the market and especially around the cinema. Every evening, there's good fried fish from the Black Volta, brochettes, guinea fowl, roast mutton and plenty of other choice morsels. Sit-down eateries include: the *Koubassary* for couscous, sandwiches, omelettes, rice, spaghetti, *tô* and brochettes; the *Commando Woro* down near the customs post (look for the "Honte a l'Imperialisme" sign) whose military atmosphere (it's an army club) is worth braving for the ice cold beer, music till midnight and edible food; the *Bar Gomgnou*, across from the *autogare* which definitely gets only a low score (flying insects, sheep's head soup and warm beer don't add up to an enviable evening); and the *Consolatrice Bar Restaurant*, opposite the *cité* which plays music till 11.30pm and although not incredibly inspiring, does have some food (brochettes maybe) and an awful lot of *consolatrices*. When you want to pull yourself together again, visit the blue shack opposite the *BP* station for real filter **coffee** (amazing!) or check out the *Nelson Mandela* café opposite the cinema.

MOVING ON FROM PÔ

There are frequent *taxis brousse* to **Ouagadougou** (2–3hr) from the *autogare* in front of the police station. *Régie X9* goes every afternoon at 2pm. South **into Ghana**, there are taxis to PAGA and even as far as BOLGATANGA, especially on Friday (market day in Bolga). Alternatively you could reasonably expect to hitch from the customs post just south of town. The Ouagadougou–Accra bus also halts in Pô.

Vehicles to TIÉBÉLÉ only operate on market days there (Tues, Wed, Thurs) and to LÉO likewise (Sun). On other days, and to other destinations such as the reserves (see overleaf), you'll have to make private arrangements with taxi drivers or car or moped owners, though taxis are expensive if you want to do a *déplacement*. To hire, ask around the *autogare* or market, or see if your hotel proprietor knows anyone. Women might try the *Action Sociale* women's movement, 100m up the Léo road (an active organisation running an advice centre and working in the areas of family planning, domestic economy and child care).

Out of town: Pô National Park and Nazinga reserve

The two **reserves** near Pô are a problem to get into unless you have your own transport. Otherwise, you'll have to make private arrangements. Cycling down from Ouagadougou isn't a bad idea (see the Ouaga "Directory").

PÔ NATIONAL PARK (main gate 31km north of Pô, 5km south of the bridge over the Volta Rouge) is open from November to May only. To visit, you first need a permit from the rangers' office by the PTT, behind the police station. The park *pistes* aren't currently in good shape and rangers have been advising moped riders against using them. The sector **east of the main road** does have a feasible circuit of about 35km however, which you could ride around, preferably in the early morning from the un-staffed south gate – some 9km north of Pô – to the north gate. Baboons and antelope are the most obvious inhabitants but the elephants are there if you keep looking and there are buffalo and warthog too. Tracks are mostly rather sandy, the vegetation tall rank grasses, thick bush, stands of dense forest near the water courses and occasional clearings of more open country savaged by fire. Going round the park alone is an exciting business, but if you try it by bicycle, be sure to take at least ten litres of water per person and leave word of your intentions in Pô. And don't go alone.

The **NAZINGA RESERVE** south of the Léo road (its north boundary runs along the road from about 15km to about 40km west of Pô) is an easier target, and you may have better game-spotting luck there. Set up by the Canadians to study wildlife resource management, the place is (comparatively) bursting at the seams with **elephants**, and also harbours several species of monkeys, baboons, antelopes, gazelles and warthogs and also, rather surprisingly, **lions**. You'll have to get a ranger to accompany you from the office but he'll know where you're likely to find animals. It's even possible to do a tour on foot, though entirely at your own risk. Accommodation is available but it's rudimentary and you'll need a mosquito net and mattress or sleeping bag.

Tiébélé

TIÉBÉLÉ, the traditional Gourounsi capital, 31km east of Pô, is something of a tourist attraction, but worth the visit. The chief here is the most important *chef de canton* in Gourounsi country and you should go and see him on first arriving: his compound is, in any case, the town's main attraction.

Coming into town from Pô, you'll find yourself travelling down an avenue of large trees which unexpectedly cleaves off from the road, leaving you on an obviously much more recent avenue. To find the chief, however, you want to leave the road and follow the original avenue of trees which will take you to his compound. You have to sign the visitor's book and pay for a guide and authorisation to take photos (a steep CFA2000). This naturally doesn't stop women and kids pestering you for more money when you do start wielding your *appareil*, but they probably recieve little if any of the visitors' fees. Tiébélé's houses are better built and decorated than others in Kassena country and the Tiébélé chief's is a magnificent maze of mud-pie huts. For a good view of the whole compound, scale the refuse heap behind it.

Tiakané

TIAKANÉ, 7km west of PÔ, is more laid-back. Its houses aren't as striking as those in Tiébélé but you'll feel more like a visitor and less like a punter. The *Cage de Binger* in the chief's compound is a mini underground labyrinth where the villagers hid the nine-teenth-century French explorer from a party of Mossi who were out to kill him. Binger went on to become governor of Cote d'Ivoire. His family have evidently not forgotten Tiakané: recently they sent funds from France to build a village school. The chief provides a guide to show you round Binger's hide-out and both will expect a reasonable tip. Tiakané makes a nice early morning walk from Pô, especially after it's rained.

Léo and the Djerma-Gourounsi ruins

If you can find transport from Pô (tricky except on Sunday, market day), a trip to LÉO might be worthwhile. A small border town with a couple of hotels, Léo's main attraction is the nearby **ruins** in the villages of **Satí and Yoro**. They date from the period of the **Djerma invasions** at the end of the nineteenth century, when the Djerma made alliances with Gourounsi Muslim chiefs. Satí became the capital of a Djerma mini-state and Yoro was fortified as a warehouse for slaves and booty acquired in raids on the local "infidel" Gourounsi. Later, the Gourounsi Muslim leaders had a change of mind about their Djerma business partners and revolted against them – a resistance which eventually involved collusion with a Djerma renegade called Hamaria who successfully enlisted French support to defeat the Djerma. French involvement led, as everywhere, to a colonial sell-out and the formal "protection" of the Gourounsi.

Satí, 22km northwest of Léo, should still have the remains of fortifications and battlements, especially on the eastern side, while a kilometre to the south, the chief's personal mosque and compound may still be visible. Back, 7km down the road to Léo, are the ruins of more fortifications – including triangular loopholes and a well, used by the Djerma while besieging Satí. Yoro, 32km west of Léo on the way to DIÉBOUGOU, still preserves a long stretch of wall, part of the Djerma treasure house.

None of this is very impressive archaeology, but the search for the ruins makes a good hook from which to hang idle wanderings. And if you have your own transport (public means aren't very promising), Léo is a reasonable night stop en route from Gourounsi to **Lobi country** (see p.292).

BOBO, BANFORA AND THE SOUTHWEST

Fed by the **Comoé** and other lesser rivers, the southwest is the most densely forested, and hilliest, region in Burkina and a pleasant change from the relentless grasslands covering most of the rest of the country. A rich vegetation camouflages a wealth of natural sites, ranging from **waterfalls** and lakes to striking cliff formations. But the southwest also contains important urban centres – **Bobo-Dioulasso** and **Banfora** – that grew up on the Abidjan railway line in a productive agricultural region.

Bobo-Dioulasso and around

Burkina's second city, with over 300,000 inhabitants **BOBO-DIOULASSO** ("Home of the Bobo and the Dioula") was long the country's economic capital, a position which has only in recent years been convincingly usurped by Ouagadougou. Yet life moves at a slow pace here, and Bobo has *style* and real ambiance. Sweeping avenues roofed by the foliage of cool mango trees, colonial buildings in the *style-soudanais* and a rich mixture of peoples give it a unique character that makes it one of the most inviting places to unwind anywhere in West Africa. It's also a traditional music centre with balafon orchestras and electric bands adding night-time action to the town's many bars.

Brief background

Bobo was founded in the fifteenth century, when it was known as **Sya**, meaning "island". According to oral history, a man named Molo Oumarou came here and, after founding villages in Timina and Sakabi, built a house in a clearing of the woods by a stream called the Houet. A village of Bobo-Fing and Bobo-Dioula people grew up around this original home. The French arrived in the late nineteenth century, and set up their first administrative headquarters here in 1897. In 1928, Pépin Malherbe broadened the town limits as Bobo awaited the arrival of the **railway line** from Abidjan. The RAN pushed through in 1934, two decades before the line was extended to Ouaga, and a large colonial town grew up around the station, a short distance from the original settlement (the graceful Sudanic-inspired architecture of the *gare*, market and *palais de justice* dates from this period). Thus Bobo gained a large economic jump on the present capital, a fact which today helps to explain its commericial importance. On the main routes to Mali and the Côte d'Ivoire, too, the town has acquired an international flavour with numerous foreign workers and students.

Places to stay

Lodgings in Bobo range from dormitory beds to AC hotels with pools. In between there's a good number of inexpensive *auberges*, lacking in luxury but usually well maintained.

Low cost lodgings

Foyer des Scouts About 1.5km from the town centre on the av Philippe Zinda (sector 4). Dorm beds for CFA900 or CFA500 to sleep outside (beware of thieves and rain). Used by students at exam time, so you may have to sleep on floor in the hall. Friendly caretaker who loves practising his English.

Hôtel Hamdalaye, behind the *gare routière*, has a nice management and very clean, S/C, AC rooms in terraces from under CFA5000/double. Only possible disadvantage is the very loud disco right next door (featuring bad music), from which you should distance your chosen room. Otherwise, top-of-the-line Bobo budget boarding. Bicycle hire too.

Hotel Okinawa, near the train station in the Accart Ville district (sector 9). Simple but clean and friendly. Rooms without fan start at CFA2000. Nice courtyard with nightly disco (no cover) and restaurant with meals from CFA1000.

Hotel Liberté Same owner as the *Okinawa* and very similar in terms of price and standards. Also near the train station.

L'Amitié In the south of town at the end of the bd de la Révolution. Some way from the centre, but quiet and inexpensive with rooms from CFA2500.

L'Unité On the rue de l'Unité (☎98.08.42). A popular place with overlanders, this hotel offers good value, clean, friendly accommodation – from CFA2500, fan included.

Bar-Restau-Club Nouvelle Renaissance av de la République. This popular restaurant and *dancing*, brilliantly located in the very heart of town, has clean, adjoining rooms, grouped around an attractive courtyard, from CFA5000.

Hôtel de la Paix Neither the cleanest nor most comfortable accommodation in town (and that's a generous assessment), this place is right next to the *gare routière* and dead handy if you arrive by taxi at night. With rooms from CFA3000, it's cheap at least.

Hôtel du Commerce Near the market on the av Roumé. Comfortable and calm with an ideal location. Single rooms start at CFA4000 or CFA5000 for a double.

On the expensive side

Hôtel Watinoma rue Pépin Malherbe, near the police *Commissariat Central* (☎98.21.62). Clean AC rooms start at CFA6500. They also have an excellent restaurant with European food for around CFA2500.

Auberge Restaurant (☎99.01.84) Centrally located near the market, this restaurant (French cooking from CFA1500) also has nice, S/C, AC rooms (singles start at CFA7000), a clean pool in the shaded courtyard (CFA1400 for non-guests) and billiards in the bar. But it's utterly European and more or less remote from the life of Bobo.

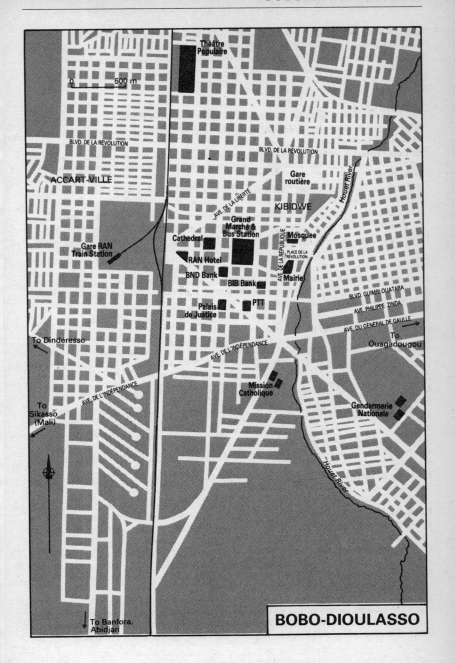

0   500 m

BLVD. DE LA RÉVOLUTION

ACCART-VILLE

BLVD. DE LA RÉVOLUTION

Théâtre
Populaire

Gare
routière

KIBIDWE

AVE. DE LA LIBERTÉ

Grand
Marché &
Bus Station

Mosquée

Gare RAN
Train Station

Cathedral

PLACE DE LA
RÉVOLUTION

AVE. DE LA RÉPUBLIQUE

RAN Hotel

BND Bank

BIB Bank

Mairie

PTT

BLVD. GUIMBI OUATABA

Palais
de Justice

AVE. PHILIPPE ZINDA

AVE. DU GÉNÉRAL DE GAULLE

To Dinderesso

To
Ouagadougou

AVE. DE L'INDÉPENDANCE

AVE. DE L'INDÉPENDANCE

To
Sikasso
(Mali)

Mission
Catholique

Gendarmerie
Nationale

Houet River

Houet River

To Banfora,
Abidjan

BOBO-DIOULASSO

Relax Hôtel (☎98.02.93) Swimming pool and S/C rooms with AC from CFA7000.

Soba Hôtel Near the post office (BP 185; ☎99.10.48) Colonial style with single rooms, some with AC, from around CFA6000. Free use of the *Auberge*'s pool (same management).

RAN Hôtel (☎98.18.45) Near the train station, this three-star place is supposed to be the best in town. S/C , AC rooms start at CFA11,000. Pool.

Restaurants

Bobo has good eating, with especially wonderful beef. Besides the hotel restaurants, some of the better places include:

Le Loup Blanc A bit far from the centre in the *zone des écoles*, but convenient if you're staying at the *Foyer des Scouts*. African food and good salads, sometimes to the accompaniment of live music.

L'Eau Vive Sister restaurant (literally) to the *Eau Vive* in Ouaga with similar international specialties and waitressing nuns. Across from the *Relax Hôtel*.

Yan Kady av de l'Unité. A good address for inexpensive and well-prepared African food.

Le Transfo Popular restaurant-cum-disco with European food (moderately expensive).

Café des Amis, between the Grand Marché and the av de la République, has fresh yoghurt daily and is a really nice place to sit and eat.

Café Central Excellent.

Avocado sandwich ladies Well, it's not a restaurant, but *ça ne fait rien* in Bobo. Huge and delicious avocado salad submarines for about next to nothing, from a group of ladies opposite the cinema south of the market.

Sights around town

In the heart of Bobo, the **grand marché** was built in 1951 in a pleasing neo-Sudanic style. It's still today the very centre of activity in town and among the fruit, vegetables and manufactured goods, you'll find a wide selection of **crafts**, including many woven blankets and cloth from the region. Follow the road leading out of the market's eastern end two hundred metres to the **old town** in the **Kibidwé** district. As you arrive, you'll notice the porcupine silhouette of the **grande mosquée** – a banco construction originally built in 1880. Except during prayers, it's possible to visit; ask the guardian and leave him a small dash after the tour, but beware of photography. Apparently the city council had planned to tear down the mosque and build a new one in its place, but the thick banco walls stood firm against the bulldozer – proof that Allah is more powerful than Caterpillar.

From here, kids will doubtless pick you up and want to show you around the historic core of town.

First on their list of worthy sites is the "Konsa", the **oldest house** in town, said to date from the fifteenth century. As you follow them through the narrow streets of the ancient neighbourhoods, they'll point out **traditional artisans** – mostly blacksmiths and weavers – and finish the tour with a stop at the **sacred fish pond** – the murky backwaters of the Houet stream where oversized mudfish peer up for food. No telling what makes them sacred: fishy totems are a Bobo speciality.

Bobo by night

Like the Ouagalais, the people of Bobo are great night-timers. The percussionists **The Coulibaly Twins** and **Mahama Konate**, founder of Farafina, are from Bobo and regularly play the town clubs when home from Paris. Some venues worth a visit are mentioned above under restaurants and hotels – including *Nouvelle Renaissance* and *Okinawa*. Other places of note include:

Makhno (is it really named after the anarchist revolutionary whose army held the Ukraine until 1921?). Opposite the post office and a little touristy, but has good live traditional music Thurs–Sat until midnight. Smallish cover but pricey beers. The restaurant serves African and European specialties on a lively *terrasse* to a well-heeled French clientele .

Memphis av de la République across from the Mairie. Bar-restaurant-disco with good food and frequent live music.

Le Golfe Dancing On the other side of av de la République, a little north of the *Memphis*, near the *Commissariat*. Pleasant garden and dance floor under *paillotes*.

Others you might investigate are *Le Black and White*, near the market and *Le 421*, on bd de la Nation.

Outside Bobo

Some rewarding **side-trips** are within easy distance of Bobo, convenient if you have a car. If not, perhaps the best way to see them is by renting a bicycle or moped from the place next to the *Total* station on the west side of the market towards the railway station (prices for mopeds around CFA2–3000/day depending on duration).

Top on the list of Bobo excursions is a swimming hole called **La Guinguette**, 18km west of town in the **Kou Forest**. You can splash around in bilharzia-free waters, though it's sometimes crowded, especially at weekends.

Some 15km on the Sikasso (Mali) road takes you to the village of **Koumi**, with characteristic, pseudo-fortified, Bobo architecture. Now frequently visited, your presence will surprise no one; check with the chief if you want to take pictures (whether you've a permit or not).

If you've had your fill of sacred crocodiles, **Dafra**, 8km southeast of Bobo, boasts a **pool of sacred fish**, in beautiful surroundings, much more important than the underwhelming mud hole in Bobo itself. The enormous catfish, some even wearing earrings (a miracle), to which sacrifices of chickens are made, are the symbol of Bobo and reproduced on the Mairie wall in town. Either take a taxi most of the way, or walk, taking a **path** from the junction of the Ouaga road and av du Gouverneur Général Eboué, right on the edge of town. It's a tricky route to follow and you'll probably need a guide (kids en route would no doubt oblige for the customary *cadeau*) but it's worth it for the scenery. If you do this, set off early and take water. Remember, too, to **wear nothing red** – it's prohibited. Unfortunately, there have been some recent muggings: *attention*!

Another popular attraction, the **hippo lake** (*mare aux hippopotames*), is located some 60km from Bobo on the Dédougou/Ouahigouya road – though it's a little far for a moped and the difficult tracks (even in the dry season) just about rule it out. To get there, take a Dédougou-bound taxi from the main *gare routière*, or head to the *gare de Satiri* on the intersection of the bd de la Paix and the av Général Merlin (taxis here from the main *autogare* for CFA100). The Satiri taxi stops in small villages along the way and takes up to three hours (as opposed to less than two for the Dédougou-bound taxi) to cover the scenic route. Picturesque **Sahelian-style mosques** crown villages like Kouentou and Satiri. Then you still have to get to the lake from Satiri. At weekends, you could hope to hitch with passing tourists or, if you're alone, you could probably find someone to take you on the back of his bike (fix an arranged price for the return trip). Fishermen at the lakeside will take you out by *pirogues* for as close an inspection of the hippos as you're likely to want. Again, fix the fee in advance – they appreciate aspirins and cigarettes as a tip. If you're extremely lucky, they say, you may spot elephants; we didn't.

Bobo-Dioulasso Directory

Airlines *Air Afrique* (☎98.19.23); *Air Burkina* (☎98.18.87).
Airport Information Bobo airport (☎98.03.68).
Banks *BIB*, *BICIA* and *BNB* all have branches near the central market (sector 1). Changing travellers' cheques is usually no problem.
Car hire *Auto-Location* has an office on the bd de la Nation.
Cinemas There are three in Bobo: *Ciné Guimba*, *Ciné Sya* and *Ciné Houet*.
Emergencies and Hospital ☎98.00.79/82.
Tourist information *Houet Direction Provincial de l'Environnement et de laTourisme* (BP 18; ☎98.25.12).
Trains Schedule information from the station (☎98.29.22/98.23.91).
Travel agents *Faso Tours* (BP 18) has an office next to the Mairie. Their buses depart from nearby.

ONWARDS FROM BOBO

Bobo is a springboard for Ouagadougou, Mali (Mopti, Bamako) and Côte d'Ivoire. Different possibilities for reaching these destinations include: **by train**, two daily for **Ouaga**. Check at the station or call the RAN (☎98.29.50) for schedules. There are also two daily trains to **Abidjan**, via Ferkessédougou for northern Côte d'Ivoire, also a convenient means of reaching **Banfora**.

Travelling **by bush taxi**, the main *gare routière* has just moved to the edge of town. This is the quickest means to points in Mali (punishing *piste* as far as Sikasso if you go that way, reasonable tarmac to Ségou if you go that) and Côte d'Ivoire (good sealed road) as well as to Ouagadougou and Dédougou, Banfora and Boromo. Bobo is also a possible departure point for the **Lobi Country** via a difficult *piste* to Diébougou.

The *Régie X9* in Bobo (☎99.07.86) has **buses to Ouaga** from next to the Mairie (daily at 7am and 2pm) to **Gaoua** (8am Mon, Thur & Sat), to **Ouessa** and **Hamale** for Ghana (8am Mon, Wed & Sat) to **Dédougou** (8am Mon and Thur) and to Banfora and Niangoloko, for Côte d'Ivoire (8am daily except Fri). Nearby, *Faso Tours* ' buses leave for Ouagadougou from the bottom of the av Concorde.

By air, there are direct flights three times weekly to Abidjan on *Air Ivoire* or *Air Burkina*, every Wednesday to Bamako and four flights a week to Ouagadougou.

Banfora and around

With a population of some 17,000, **BANFORA** is Burkina's fifth-largest town. Its development during colonial times was due to its position on the railway line, but today, the economic importance of the region springs from the vast **sugar cane** projects that have made Burkina a net exporter of manufactured sugar. Although the town itself lacks the spark of Ouaga and Bobo, it lies in a beautiful region of cliffs and forests. Even coming from Bobo by train or taxi, you see streams and **waterfalls** from the roadside and notice the vegetation getting denser. Banfora's **market day** is Sunday.

Sleeping, eating and other practicalities

The only paved road in Banfora is the main street – centre of the limited commerce in town. For accommodation, the best address is the *Comoé Hôtel* (☎88.01.51) in the southern part of town about 1km from the *gare routière*. Rooms are grouped around a shady courtyard that serves as restaurant, bar and nightclub. The cheapest ones go from CFA2500. The *Hôtel Fara* – near the train station – is slightly more expensive (☎88.01.17). Banfora's top hotel is the two-star *Canne à Sucre*. Clean and comfortable AC rooms here start at CFA6500. Since Banfora has become a major attraction in

Burkinabe terms, enterprising young people have started renting rooms in their homes (you may be asked at the motor park upon arrival). A bed and bucket shower will probably cost about CFA1000, which means if you're alone, about half the price of a hotel room. A companion to take you to the various sights in the surrounding countryside is usually part of the deal – but work out how much you want to pay for each individual trip, and, when bargaining, don't feel bound by bonds of new-found friendship; this is business.

There are few distractions in Banfora itself. In the evening, you could take in a film – or more likely *the* film – at the *Paysan Noir* cinema (near the stadium), or go to one of the many open-air nightclubs. One to recommend is the *Banji Bar* with garden seating and a large dance floor. They specialise in palm wine (*banji*) but also have the full range of drinks from softs to spirits. Note that while there is a **bank** in town, they have **no exchange** service for travellers' cheques or anything else. Plan ahead if you're coming in from Côte d'Ivoire. The nearest bank with change is in Bobo-Dioulasso.

Around Banfora

To see the region around Banfora, it's best to **rent a moped** or motorcycle at the market. It should cost around CFA2000–3000 for the day; you pay for fuel. The **lake and waterfall** are surprisingly difficult to find (numerous tracks lead through a tall growth of sugar cane most of the year), so you might consider taking someone from town along with you.

Tengréla Lake

Take the road leading west out of Banfora towards the village of Tengréla (signs in town mark the way, but are often confusing and don't stay the distance). The lake is some 10km from Banfora. On arrival, you'll see fishermen along the shore who'll take you around the lake in their *pirogues*. Settle on a price before heading out. It's sometimes possible to spot **hippos** that live in the waters. At the edge of the lake, an abandoned cement house provides an ideal place for **camping** if you've the equipment.

Karfiguéla Falls

These waterfalls, located in a beautiful, verdant setting, are only about 3km from the lake, though again, the way is difficult to find (ask the fishermen or people in the vicinity to point you to the *cascades*). Note that the river has been dammed as a source of irrigation for the cane plantations and be warned, too, that in the dry season, the falls are a disappointing trickle. During the rains, they swell to thunder impressively over the solid rock formations. From the main track, you approach the falls by means of a narrow path bordered with huge mango trees. Apparently bilharzia is a risk if you want to swim, but it's difficult to resist the temptation.

Further afield – to Sindou and the Lobi country

Fifty kilometres from Banfora towards the Malian border, **SINDOU** is accessible only by tortuous tracks. A moped won't manage them so you'll have to rent something with greater horsepower if you don't have your own transport. The scenery is spectacular along the way, the cliffs around Sindou turning into giant rock formations, sculpted by the wind and rains. There's another large cascade 10km from Sindou. It's a difficult excursion, but a great escape.

Onwards from Banfora

Vehicles out of Banfora to LOROPENI in the Lobi country go on Loropeni's market day (which happens on a five-day cycle, useless for planning to outsiders). There are daily afternoon departures for Bobo (except Friday) on *Régie X9*.

THE LOBI COUNTRY

A green and pleasant corner of Burkina, nestling between the Ghanaian and Ivoirian frontiers, the **Lobi country** is a favourite travellers' destination and an interesting diversion en route from Bobo and the southwest into Ghana. It's all hilly, tree-scattered savannah, and rich enough in wildlife for the elephant stories to be just about credible.

Although the strange ruins of **Loropeni** are the region's only real tourist sight, the Lobi themselves, with their traditions and their *cabaret* drinking bars, not to mention their friendliness, make their corner of the country one of the best to visit, in spite of the fact that transport in the region is often difficult.

The Lobi believe in maintaining their **traditions**. Lobi men for example still hunt with bow and arrows for hares, guinea fowl and gazelles, and it's common to see men carrying bows and arrows – traditionally poison-tipped – with them along the road. Another notable aspect of Lobi culture is the cutlery embedded in gravestones: the Lobi are buried with their fork, spoon, plate and saucepan. Every seven years, too, the new generation of young people still take part in the **djoro** initiation ceremony. Some customs, however, are disappearing. Few Lobi women nowadays wear the disc plugs through their lips which used to be so admired. And the old-fashioned, all-in-one method of house building is giving way to easier mud brick construction.

The traditions the Lobi maintain best are the ones with widest appeal – booze, music and markets. No Lobi town or village would be complete without its **cabarets** – not nightclubs but places where *chapalo* and *qui-me-pousse* or *patasi* (home-brewed firewater) are consumed in serious quantities and **traditional music** is often played. Many *cabarets* brew their own *chapalo*, a process that thankfully only takes three days. And it's so much cheaper than bottled beer that you could afford to shout the whole place a drink for the same price as a bottle of *Brakina* in a bar. Many *cabarets* keep a drum and a balafon handy in case anyone feels like playing, which they often do. Even in the unlikely event you don't acquire a taste for *chapalo* and Lobi music, *cabarets* are the best places to go and be sociable with the locals – there's never any shortage of welcome. The **markets** are traditionally held on a five-day cycle, though now increasingly on the same day every week. In more remote ones, you can still use cowries if you have any (you could buy some).

Food in the Lobi country is generally of the rice and sauce variety though there are other staples, such as fish and guinea fowl, if you look for them. More typically Lobi is millet *tô* with a sauce of baobab leaves, shea nuts or *néré* fruit.

The region's main town is **Gaoua** – whose chief attraction is its enormous number of *cabarets* – and it's here that you'll probably want to base yourself, though the principal reasons for coming are the **ruins** and bustling five-daily **market** at Loropeni. Outside Lobi country proper, and not especially interesting in itself, **Diébougou** is a pleasant enough stopover on the way to Ouaga or Bobo, or into Ghana via **Hamale**.

Gaoua

GAOUA, whose colourful market takes place on Sunday, is the main town of the Lobi country and absolutely shaking with *cabarets*. It's almost certainly the best place to get thoroughly acquainted both with *chapalo* and traditional roots music, though obviously the sounds in Bobo-Dioulasso are more refined.

As for **staying**, there are basically two **hotels** in town – the *Pony Bar*, in the centre by the market, for budget beds, reasonably comfortable either with or without fans but with no choice about the reggae and soukous sounds till midnight; and the *Hala Hôtel* (1km out on the Diébougou road) for a little high living where CFA8000 gets you an ultra-clean, super comfortable, air-conditioned sit-down loo room with even a laundry

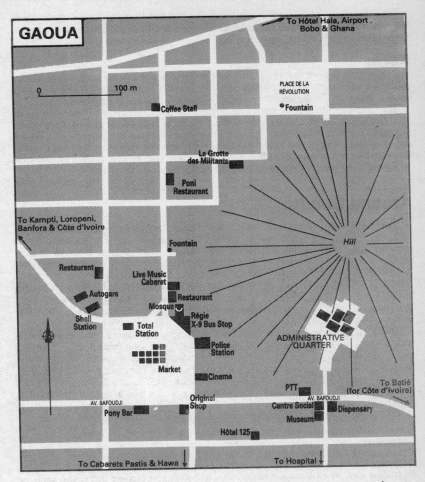

GAOUA

0   100 m

To Hôtel Hala, Airport,
Bobo & Ghana

PLACE DE LA
RÉVOLUTION

●Fountain

■Coffee Stall

La Grotte
des Militants

■Poni
Restaurant

To Kampti, Loropeni,
Banfora & Côte d'Ivoire

Fountain

Hill

Restaurant■

Live Music
Cabaret

■Autogare

■Restaurant

Mosque■

Shell
Station

■Régie
X-9 Bus Stop

Total
Station

ADMINISTRATIVE
QUARTER

Police
Station

Market

To Batié
(for Côte d'Ivoire)

Cinema

PTT

AV. BAFOUDJI

Original
Shop

Centre Social

Museum

■Dispensary

Pony Bar

Hôtel 125■

To Cabarets Pastis & Hawa

To Hospital

service (extra) if you want to make a fresh start. A third hotel, the *125*, may have re-opened.

   Food-wise you'll find plenty of stalls doing roast meat and fried fish and there are two restaurants on the road to Diébougou. The first of these, a shack selling rice and rather salty sauce, is on the right just as you leave the market square. And two blocks further, also on the right, is the *Poni Restaurant* (not to be confused with the *Pony Bar*, but both named after Gaoua's small river, tributary of the Volta Noire). Full of anti-malaria and anti-apartheid posters this offers an inexpensive menu of rice, beef, omelette, not very good yoghurt and the ubiquitous national slogan "La patrie ou mort, nous vaincrons!" If that's too brisk for **breakfast** (or closed), there's a little bar two blocks further on the left that does tea, real coffee, nescafé, omelettes and *pain beurre*. And for a splurge you won't need reminding about the extravagant selection of Lebanese, African and French cuisine on offer at the *Hala Hôtel*.

Drinking is mainly a *cabaret* sport with the *Cabaret Pastis* and the *Cabaret Hawa* both open until late, or until the *chapalo* runs out, and both with sporadic live music. There are dozens of others, located by ear.

In Gaoua

The main draw in town though, apart from the drinking dens, is the magnificent Sunday **market**, a maelstrom of colour and activity, if less rustic than Loropeni's. There are, too, some **ruins** near Gaoua, but not much left, even if you manage to find them.

The *Centre Sociale* is set to open a **museum** in an old, colonial-style house with exhibits of traditional art, Lobi lifestyles, and homes typical of local ethnic groups. They're also hoping to open an *Action sociale* welfare centre, and to run a library and crafts centre, and they aim to offer trips to the Loropeni ruins and the statues of the Gan kings of Obiré, to Gaoua's caves and to Mont Koyo at Doudou. They're a committed lot in Gaoua, so hopefully most of this will be up and running by the time you arrive.

Around Gaoua

Sunday is the day for transport into or out of Gaoua, though **Loropeni** and **Nako** are best reached on their own market days, when vehicles usually leave early in the morning and return in the evening. There's usually something to **Doropo** in Côte d'Ivoire (see p.798), especially on its market day, Thursday, where you'll probably have to change for other Ivoirian destinations. Often there's also a vehicle or two to DIÉBOUGOU, where you may have to change for Bobo and HAMALE. **X9** runs a thrice weekly service to Bobo, weekly to Ouaga, all via Diébougou. There's also a weekly flight to Bobo and Ouaga, from the airstrip 6km out of town on the Diébougou road. If all else fails, try **hitching** from the police post 2km out of town on the same road.

KAMPTI, en route between Gaoua and Loropeni, (the direct route being out of commission), isn't especially compelling, though it has its own ruins nearby. There's a mass of food stalls, about a kilometre from the *autogare*/junction, and, if you get stuck, the locals will probably put you in the *Consolatrice*, a place sometimes used for dances.

NAKO has its market always the day after Loropeni's. You may find yourself there if taking the short cut into Ghana via Lawra, for which you'll need a lift 11km to BONKERO and then a *pirogue* ride across the Black Volta. Be sure to go to immigration in Nako to get stamped out of Burkina or the Ghanaians will send you back.

Loropeni

Better known for its **market** than its **ruins**, **Loropeni** is an easy excursion from Gaoua on trading day, when transport is certain – although you can get there, and back, on other days too, if you're lucky. En route from Gaoua, look out for monkeys and gazelles, which are often seen, and for elephants, which aren't but which you wouldn't miss.

The only **rooms** in **LOROPENI** are at a very basic place opposite the *autogare*. There are no real restaurants but plenty of **food stalls** doing roast meat, rice and sauce or meat "soup" though, tea and coffee become a scarce commodity after breakfast. Most of the *cabarets* are behind the hostel and there's a bar next door. The **market**, held every five days, is a bustling throng of colour. You can buy fruit, hot food, chillis, multi-coloured ground spices and peanut paste, and watch flip-flops being made out of old tyres, and enamel bowls being re-bottomed with bits of vegetable oil tins (furnished by the people of the USA). You might meet Ghanaians selling worming tablets (armed with lurid photographic displays), or Gan women, from the west, often wearing brown string mourning bands on their heads, arms, necks and ankles. You can change, and use, **cowries** here, though the rate of one per CFA franc may have changed.

The ruins

To get to Loropeni's enigmatic **ruins**, head out of town on the BANFORA road. After about 2km you come to a small hill at the top of which is a track leading off to the right. Follow it for 200m to the ruins, a rust-coloured mystery looming out of the bush.

Though not massively impressive, these are among West Africa's very few stone remains. They rise up out of the scrub like some lost temple in a Hollywood movie. Unlike the great stone ruins of East Africa and Zimbabwe, they don't get many visitors, and since their origin and the identity of their builders are still viable mysteries, your ideas about them are as good as anyone else's. The ruins are more or less rectangular, some 50m long, by 40m wide, by (originally) 6–7m high, and noticeably lack any doors or windows. Inside, like other rectangular Lobi ruins, they're divided into two enclosures, one large and one small, connected by a door and each divided into chambers.

The **Gan country** a few kilometres north and west of Loropeni habours more archaeological oddities if you can get the transport. There are some near Yerifoula, others near Oyono and Lokosso, and some large relics at Loghi.

Diébougou

Lying outside the Lobi country proper, **DIÉBOUGOU**'s people are mostly Lobi-Gan and Dagara (Dagarti). It doesn't have a lot of interest but it's friendly, full of kids and has better transport connections than Gaoua (but note that **no banks** change money).

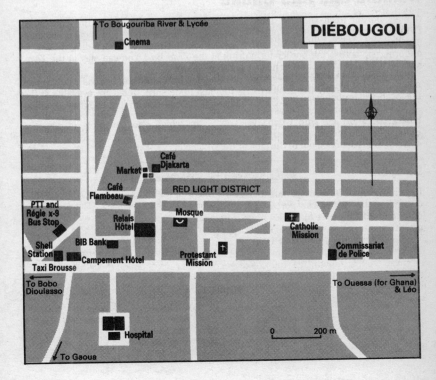

There are two **hotels**, both near the *taxi brousse* and bus stops. The *Campement Danabone* has rooms in not too bad a state, some with fans; and it's also a bar, disco and pick-up joint with generator electricity in the evenings. There's a rather mucky shower and sink for each pair of rooms. The nearby *Relais la Bougouriba* is slightly smarter with a shower in every room and fans too – if they can fix them. Rooms are cleaner and more expensive and worth it. It too has a generator, a bar and plenty of atmosphere. The *Caiman* at the east end of town is closed but may reopen. The only restaurants are at the hotels, with rice, guinea fowl, steak and the usual solid stuff. Outside there's a run of food stalls around the market and lots of *cabarets* to slake your thirst. Deserving of a mention is the *Flambeau Cafe*, a breakfast joint with real coffee, tea, omelettes and the rest. Passing an evening in Diébougou you'll likely gravitate to the hotels' **sounds** or possibly the cinema.

During the wet season there are **crocodiles** (though not, it's important to point out, sacred ones) in the swamp that forms at the eastern end of town, near the *Caiman Hotel*. They're best observed around dawn, if you can manage it, when coolness keeps them calm and visible. Older folk can be overheard complaining that they don't have swamps like they used to; needless to say, the crocodiles are diminishing in number.

Transport out of Diébougou isn't much problem; there are **X9 buses** five times a week to Bobo, four times to Gaoua, twice to Ouessa and Hamale and once to Ouagadougou. Other transport east to Hamale often comes in late at night from Bobo.

Hamale and into Ghana

A busy border town and the main crossing point into Ghana from Bob-Dioulasso, **HAMALE** rarely has much to offer – at least when beer supplies in Ghana are satisfying demand. When Ghana goes dry, periodically, Ghanaians, including police in uniform, pop across the border for a drink at the *Zodo Bar*. You can stay at the *Zodo*, but you might as well spend a cheaper night in Ghana.

Burkinabe border formalities take place at OUESSA, where you visit police and customs, and probably the gendarmerie too, just to be sure. Cedis are available at the ordinary (poor) border rate of CFA1000 to ₵800, a rate beaten just about everywhere else.

Transport on the Ghanaian side, almost all goes to LAWRA and WA, including the twice daily STC bus (see p.867).

LIMITED LOBI

The simplest Lobi greeting is *Me foaré* ("Hello") to which the normal response is *Monicho?* ("How are you?") and the reply to that *Michor* ("Fine thanks"). "Thank you" is *Ferehina foaré*.

FOOD

water	*ñyoñi*	meat	*nuni*	yam	*puri*	tomorrow	*kyo*
chicken	*yolo*	maize	*wologyo*	today	*ni*	yesterday	*gye ale*
egg yolo	*pala*	millet	*gyo/di*				

NUMBERS

1	*Biel*	5	*Yamoi*	9	*Nuor biri pero*	100	*Tama*
2	*Yenyo*	6	*Maado*	10	*Nuor*	1000	*Bulani*
3	*Yetter*	7	*Makonyo*	20	*Kpuele*		
4	*Yena*	8	*Makotter*	50	*Kpalanyo nuor*		

index

MAURITANIA

MAURITANIA

Scanning a map of West Africa, it's easy to see the vast obscurity of **Mauritania** as nothing but sand. Simple, too, to turn scraps of information on the country into preconceptions – of an austere, almost medieval nation, powered by Islam, riven by racial hatred and flayed by drought. These stark images certainly have some foundation in reality, yet Mauritania comes as a revelation to most travellers: pleasantly laid-back, spacious and physically comfortable because dry, scenically dramatic in several regions and culturally complex, with its rock paintings, thousand-year-old mosques and deep-rooted class structure.

Although the southernmost region of the country – made up of the **Chemama** flood plain along the river and the hilly savannah triangle of **Gorgol-Guidimaka** – extends south to the same latitude as Dakar, this anomalous "green" region covers less than five percent of the territory and is progressively being nibbled away by the advancing desert. Apart from the rocky uplands of the north and centre – the **Adrar**, **Tagant** and **Assaba** massifs – the rest of Mauritania, the most *Saharan* of countries, is indeed largely sand.

FACTS AND FIGURES

The **République Islamique de Mauritanie** (often shortened to R.I.M.) covers over a million square kilometres, more than four times the size of Britain and nearly as big as California and Texas combined. The **population** of about two million gives it the lowest density in the world, but the eastern third of Mauritania is designated as "zone vide" (empty quarter) and there's heavy migration to the towns, to the south, and abroad. Mauritania's **foreign debt** is currently over £1 billion (not such a huge figure when compared, for example, with the similar cost of adding a new runway to London's Gatwick airport). The **government** is presently the *Military Committee for National Salvation* (CMSN), under Colonel Ould Taya.

People

The country's name comes from its dominant ethnic group, the traditionally nomadic **Moors**, who speak the **Hassaniya** dialect of Arabic. The Moors are broadly divided into "white" **Bidan**, who claim ancestors from north of the Sahara, and "black" **Haratin**, whose physical ancestry lies in Saharan and sub-Saharan Africa and who were subjugated and "Arabised" by the Bidan. The Haratin, traditionally, were vassals to the noble classes, but some Haratin elevated themselves into an independent caste which owed no tribute. The formal abolition of slavery in 1980 decreed that all "ex-slaves" (usually called Abid) were henceforth to be known as "Haratin" – a source of offence to "real Haratin" and of confusion to outsiders.

This characterisation oversimplifies the make-up of a very diverse and multifaceted population. **Social status** in Mauritania is considerably more than a question of skin colour. The white Moor community is divided broadly into Hassanes (noble families), Zouaya (or Tolba, the pious maraboutic caste) and Zenaga vassals (herders and cultivators). Status among black Moor families tends to be determined by their length of association and degree of intermarriage with white Moors. Within Hassaniya-speaking Moorish society, intermarriage has blurred racial distinctions and skin colour is ignored in many social contexts anyway.

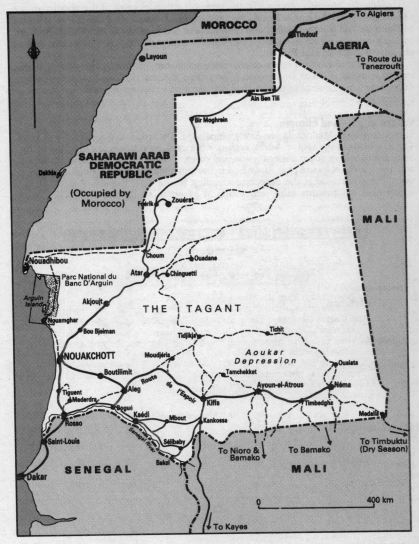

You can get a quick initial fix on the social complexities of Moorish society from the **position of women**, which is less rigidly defined than in most Arabic-speaking countries. Women may travel alone, drink tea with men, take an active part in male-dominated conversations and breast-feed their children in public; they rarely cover their faces, though always cover their hair. The Berber and African heritage is apparent in these freedoms, which indicate the relative superficiality of the country's Arabic culture. But, in matters economic and political, women's freedom to act is widely curtailed.

Outside the Moorish community, the remaining forty percent of the population are southerners – *Soudaniens* in Mauritanian phraseology – speaking **Fula** (Pulaar), **Wolof** or **Soninke** and mostly farming and herding near the Senegalese and Malian borders. In Mauritania, the Fula-speakers of the Tukulor (Toucouleur) and Fula ethnic groups are known jointly as **Hal-Pulaar**.

In addition, Mauritania has a considerable population of African **immigrant workers**, from as far afield as Guinea and Niger, many of them working in the iron-mining districts around Zouérat in the north. Their position in the country, after 1989s racial conflict, looks tenuous.

Where to go – and climate

Travel targets in Mauritania are easily pinpointed. Two roads cut across the country. The first leads to the central **Adrar region**, where a rugged landscape softened by rolling dunes shelters some ancient towns and oases – Oujeft, Chinguetti and Ouadane – and a rich archaeological past, embodied in the stone tools and rock paintings found all over. The other road is the desperate-sounding **Route de l'Espoir** (Road of Hope), which runs out towards other **old cities** in Mauritania's inventory: Tidjikja, in the

AVERAGE TEMPERATURES AND RAINFALL

NOUAKCHOTT

	Jan	Feb	Mar	Apr	May	June	July	Aug	Sept	Oct	Nov	Dec
Temperatures °C												
Min (night)	14	15	17	18	21	23	23	24	24	22	18	13
Max (day)	29	31	32	32	34	33	32	32	34	33	32	28
Rainfall mm	0	3	0	0	0	3	13	104	23	10	3	0
Days with rainfall	0	1	0	0	0	1	1	3	3	1	1	0

NOUADHIBOU

	Jan	Feb	Mar	Apr	May	June	July	Aug	Sept	Oct	Nov	Dec
Temperatures °C												
Min (night)	12	13	14	14	15	16	18	20	20	19	16	14
Max (day)	26	28	27	27	28	30	27	30	33	30	28	25
Rainfall mm	0	0	0	0	0	0	0	0	8	12	3	10

ATAR

	Jan	Feb	Mar	Apr	May	June	July	Aug	Sept	Oct	Nov	Dec
Temperatures °C												
Min (night)	12	13	17	19	22	27	25	26	26	23	17	13
Max (day)	31	33	34	39	40	42	43	42	42	38	33	29
Rainfall mm	3	0	0	0	0	3	8	30	28	3	3	0

Tagant region, and Tichit and Oualata, further east on the fringe of the country's empty quarter. Dotted with ragged, newer, settlements on its way, the Route de l'Espoir is tarred its full eleven hundred kilometres, and a good (if roundabout) route to Mali if you're driving from Senegal.

Nouakchott, the capital, is a nearly inevitable but unremarkable transit point, while **Nouadhibou**, the second largest town and much more European, is relatively cut-off and hardly more enticing. The train that links it with central Mauritania makes an unusual trip, but Nouadhibou is not much of a destination unless you're heading for Europe – ships and flights to the **Canary Islands** aren't excessively expensive from here. Nouakchott and Nouadhibou both have **beaches** that go on forever.

Wherever you go, you'll find a release from the freneticism of lands further south, and **travel conditions** generally more peaceful than elsewhere in West Africa. The worthwhile goals make it attractive, and the desert journeys are a fair substitute for crossing the Sahara. Alcohol is effectively banned, though one or two hotels serve drinks. Other travellers are fairly rare.

When to visit is conditioned more by burning temperatures than disruptive rainfall. The coast is cooled by sea breezes, but you'd probably want to avoid the interior between April and October – see the table for Atar, and remember the daytime figures are averages: the thermometer often pips 50°C in the shade. The **southwest** gets oppressive humidity and occasional cloudbursts between July and October. At this time earth roads can be cut – especially near the Senegal river – and transport off the paved highway can be very difficult. Nouadhibou and the **north** get an occasional shower during the European winter, and very occasionally a summer torrent if the clouds drift far enough north. Otherwise rain is a very scarce commodity.

Arrivals

Cut off to travellers from the north since 1975 by Morocco's greedy war over Western Sahara (see "History"), Mauritania doesn't represent an obvious overland arrival point in West Africa. Despite Morocco's virtual elimination of the Saharawi opposition to its rule, and Mauritania's withdrawal from the conflict, the alluring route south along the coast from Morocco is still not open, even though signposts in southern Morocco mark road distances to Dakar and you may well find you can get as far as Dakhla.

The route from Algeria, however, is reported to be now open. Polisario forces apparently allow vehicles through **Tindouf**, the Algerian town that is their capital in exile, and some French overland tours are taking advantage of a fast route to Dakar.

■ Flights

Apart from the obscure monthly flight on *Aeroflot* between **Bissau** and Nouadhibou, continuing to **Casablanca** and Moscow, inter-West-African flights are all via **Nouakchott**. There are direct services from **Bamako** and **Nioro** (Wed, *Air Mauritanie*), **Freetown** (Wed, *UTA*), **Ndjamena** and **Niamey** (Tues, *Air Afrique*), **Casablanca** (Mon, *Air Mauritanie*; Tues & Thurs, *Royal Air Maroc*), and **Algiers** (Wed & Sat, *Air Algerie*). Daily direct flights from Dakar are currently suspended until the conflict with Senegal is resolved – travellers from Senegal can fly from **Banjul** (The Gambia).

From **Las Palmas** in the Canary Islands, there are *Air Mauritanie/Iberia* flights on Tues, Thurs and Sat to Nouakchott (via Nouadhibou on Tues & Sat).

■ Overland

Background on entering Mauritania **from Algeria** is given in Part One, "The Algerian Sahara"; details of access from Mali and Senegal are given below. You'll find Mauritanian **border officials** generally straight dealing, occasionally pedantic but not often ostentatiously corrupt. There's a gauntlet of police and customs checks along the Rosso–Nouakchott highway but they rarely bother tourists. Across the rest of the country, *postes de contrôle* are few.

From Mali

From Mali, routes into Mauritania are only from **the south**: there are no official border crossings on the long eastern frontier. The principal crossing is Bamako–Nioro–Ayoun, with a less-used route running Bamako–Nara–Néma (or Timbedgha). Few travellers use these, and you'll find little preparedness for nationals of countries other than Mali and Mauritania. You should therefore hasten to a police *commissariat* at Néma, Timbedgha or Ayoun and make sure you get the stamp you need. The lack of banks in eastern Mauritania makes it hard to operate the closed economy, so you will have to change money unofficially one way or another (see "Money, Banks and Costs", below).

From Senegal

The main crossing point **from Senegal** is Rosso, a frontier that has seen the worst effects of the crisis in relations between the two countries. The car ferry over the Senegal River was out of action in 1990 and the border itself closed. In normal circumstances this is a swift crossing, except between noon and 3pm, when the ferry takes a lunch break – as does the "bank". (*Pirogues* continue to cross the river, though.) Other possible border crossings from Senegal are covered in that chapter. All land frontiers between the two countries are liable to sudden closure under the present uneasy climate.

Red Tape

Visas for Mauritania are required by most nationalities except West Africans, French and Italians. Getting a visa abroad, you'll probably have to provide a letter of introduction from your own embassy before one will be issued. Some Mauritanian embassies will direct you to get a visa from the "country of embarkation" (ie the one you'll be leaving immediately before entering Mauritania).

Visa prices and durations vary considerably from embassy to embassy and even from one applicant to the next, but they are generally valid from the date of issue for a limited period only. Ask the price, get a receipt, and check what you've paid against the fiscal stamps used in your passport. In several embassies, a little discussion about Mauritania's historic sites can quickly break the ice and you may find some room for manoeuvre over the price of the visa, which otherwise can easily run to CFA1000 per day of your stay.

Mauritanian **embassies** in West Africa are in Dakar (handled during the crisis by the Kuwaiti embassy), Bamako, Abidjan, Lagos and (uncertainly) Banjul. It's useful to know, however, that French embassies' **visa services** are usually authorised to cover Mauritania, wherever there's no Mauritanian embassy. In this case, the whole procedure is generally cheaper and quicker.

Visas for Onward Travel

There's **no Malian embassy** in Nouakchott. If you're heading straight for Mali but not equipped with a visa, it's probably worth trying the border anyway – which is unsophisticated, and a couple of days' drive from Bamako – and sorting things out when you get to the capital. Otherwise, you'd have to detour to Dakar first.

Money, Banks and Costs

Mauritania's currency is the Ouguiya/Uguiya Mauritanien (UM, Oug, Ug), divided into 5 khoums (which you never see). It has slipped in value against the CFA franc, on which it was based originally (1 khoum = 1 franc CFA), but has remained fairly stable at around UM120 = £1 increasing to UM140 = £1 over the last few years, with inflation low. Although the economy is closed, so that export/import of Ouguiya is prohibited, there's little or no black market. Notes come in convenient denominations of UM100, UM200 and UM1000, with coins of UM1, UM5, UM10 and UM20.

At the airports and at Rosso you'll be given a **currency declaration** form to complete. This is usually demanded on departure but rarely checked. At minor borders you may not be given one, and it's best to straighten your affairs at the first large town rather than risk a potential problem on departure. Notionally, there is a UM1000 minimum daily expenditure requirement.

Outside of Nouakchott, **banks** are few and very far between. Nouadhibou, Atar, Rosso, Bogué, Kaédi, Kiffa, Ayoun el Atrous and Néma all have banks. The biggest network, with six branches, is the *Banque Internationale pour la Mauritanie* (*BIMA*), the Mauritanian division of the West African *BIAO*. There is no *American Express* representative and **credit cards** are accepted only by a few airlines and hotels in the capital. You can't get credit card cash advances.

There are no exchange facilities on the border with Mali. Therefore, if you're coming from Nara, in Mali, for example, you give whatever CFA you want to change to an official in the *gare routière*, who gives you a ticket for the sum of Ouguiya you're due in Timbedgha or Néma – sounds dubious, but it seems to work.

■ Costs

Daily living costs are somewhat lower than in Senegal or Mali, but Mauritania is an **expensive** country to travel in, as distances are long and there are virtually no cheap hotels. If you're content to sleep on a mattress under the stars, in a tea house or, most obviously, in someone's home, you'll find costs bearable. For more on accommodation, see below.

There's no avoiding high **transport costs**, though these may fluctuate with the cycle of date harvests and pastoral migration. (Prices generally escalate if you travel *away* from the attraction.) You can quite easily spend £20 (say US$30–35) on a day's travel. As a broad guide, expect to pay around UM300 per 100km on tarred roads and up to two to three times as much on dirt roads and desert *pistes*. Prices are fixed on what could be considered "scheduled runs", and you won't be overcharged. Baggage, as usual, is another matter. And if you want to get to out-of-the-way sites and towns, transport costs can quickly become exorbitant. The cheapest option is to wait for a vehicle that's going anyway.

Maps and Information

The *IGN* 1:2,500,000 (1980) map of Mauritania is too small a scale to be useful for serious exploration, and not really much better than the Michelin 953. However, the *IGN* 1:1,000,000 topographical surveys published in the 1960s are still available from their French headquarters (107, rue de la Boétie, 75008, Paris) and might be obtained, or ordered, through one of the map suppliers listed in *Basics* on p.34.

There are no Mauritanian tourist offices, indeed no ministry that ever holds responsibility for tourism for more than a year or two. *Air Afrique* and *UTA* both publish tourist material which includes some details on Mauritania.

Health

Mauritanian officials are quite keen on health certificates and may ask you to show your yellow fever certificate at checkpoints.

The most critical feature of travel in Mauritania from a health aspect, however, is the size of the country and the **isolation** of most towns and villages. You'll often be *very* far off the beaten track, and here, more than anywhere else in West Africa, you must have **repatriation insurance** in case of accident or sudden illness. Beware, too, of dangerous vehicles being used for relatively rough desert and mountain passages: a British woman died in 1987 after the Land Rover she was in rolled over on the way to Chinguetti. In the north and east, spare parts for vehicles are very hard to obtain and the scarcity of vehicles keeps many in use long after their safe life.

Treat **water** with suspicion – reserves are usually low, and domestic animals depend on them too. It's good practice to carry a five-litre container and refill it at every opportunity.

Fresh camel or goat's **milk** (*zrig*) is often offered to guests and it's probably best to limit your consumption: although tuberculosis is a very minor risk (even in the case of fresh Zebu cow's milk), brucellosis and hepatitis A can be contracted from infected milk. Your hosts' health is probably the best criterion for deciding.

The **malaria** risk is generally slight, except along the river, where it's as high as anywhere. Roughly north of a line from Nouakchott to Tidjikja it's not reckoned to occur at all, but unless you're based in the north for a long period, there's no point in breaking your course of anti-malarial pills.

Hospitals and treatment facilities outside Nouakchott are strapped. Some of the southern towns have regional hospitals/health centres, but the north, apart from Atar and Nouadhibou, has almost no health provision.

Getting Around

Most transport in Mauritania is by Land Rover, though taxis brousse operate on the few main highways. Otherwise, air travel is a useful option. The railway system – a single iron ore line in the far north – is more of an adventure than an ordinary form of transport, but still a useful link between Nouadhibou and the rest of the country.

■ Road Transport

The main **public transport** between Rosso and Nouakchott, along the *Route de l'Espoir* to Néma, and north to Atar, is **Peugeot 504**, carrying nine passengers (six to Rosso). Be prepared for long, dust-blown journeys, frequent breakdowns, lack of water, and no toilet stops. Riding in the back of trucks, along these same routes, is slower, but hardly less comfortable, and a good deal cheaper. Fares are normally paid in advance, so if there's a breakdown you have to stick with the vehicle until it's fixed or the driver buys a place for you in another.

Between Nouakchott and Nouadhibou, trucks and Land Rovers run along the shore to Nouamghar, then turn inland to follow the railway line for the last 100km.

In the south, south of the paved *Route de l'Espoir*, a conventional *taxi brousse* network operates on most roads, most of the year. The vehicles are generally *404 bâchés*, but Peugeot 504 drivers work on some routes, especially between Rosso and Kaédi. The new tarred road from Aleg to Bogué is transforming that part of the river's flood plain.

PUBLIC TRANSPORT ROUTES
Nouakchott–Rosso: frequent, 3–5hr;
Nouakchott–Atar: up to 12 daily, 8–12hr;
Atar–Choum: 3–6 daily, 4–5hr;
Atar–Chinguetti (4WD and trucks only): 3–6 weekly, 4–7hr;
Nouakchott–Kaédi: several daily, 7–8hr;
Nouakchott–Ayoun el Atrous: 1 or more daily, 16–20hr;
Nouakchott–Nouadhibou (4WD and trucks only): 2–6 weekly, 30–50hr;

Road journeys **off the main routes** are arduous, with soft sand the recurring problem. Conditions are detailed in the main guide section. If you're driving yourself, you should treat Mauritania north of the *Route de l'Espoir* exactly as you would a trans-Saharan *piste*. In many respects, because of the scarcity of other travellers, the routes are tougher and more **dangerous**. The *piste* between the Tagant plateau and the Adrar (connecting Tidjikja with Atar), and the myriad tracks along the coast, are notorious. If you've no room to carry local people to guide you (never a problem to find), don't set off on little-trodden trails into the desert. The Mauritanians are not as used to tourists' follies as the Algerians or Nigériens are, and you may not be prevented from going – or searched for if you don't arrive.

Car hire, available only in Nouakchott, is as expensive as you'd expect. Since there's pressure to take a driver at little extra cost, it's often indistinguishable from a personalised safari arrangement. Keep your fuel tanks and spare jerry cans full. Off the main route axes, **petrol**, when available, is around UM60–70 a litre.

■ Rail and Air

Alternatives to road travel are worth using if the opportunity arises. If your point of arrival in Mauritania is Nouadhibou, the **trains** from there to Zouérat are a good way into the country, and you can hop off in Choum, a relatively short journey from the Adrar plateau and a further day's travel down to Nouakchott (details in the guide).

Air travel makes sense if time is short (the longest flight is under 2hr), but fares are around twice the price of land transport. *Air Mauritanie*'s current domestic schedule runs approximately as follows (with returns mostly same day):

Nouakchott to:
Atar, Mon, Thurs, Sun;
Tidjikja, Kiffa: Tues, Fri ;
Ayoun el Atrous: Mon;
Kaédi, Selibaby: Wed and Sun;
Nouadhibou: twice daily;
Nouadhibou to:
Zouérat: Sun, Thurs;
Atar: Sat, Mon, Thurs;
Ayoun el Atrous–Nema–Nouakchott, Mon.

Sleeping

Mauritania's hotels generally resemble Moroccan or Middle Eastern establishments and are fine if you're not short of money. Minimum price for a room is UM1000, with a general cost of upwards of UM2000. Payment is always in advance, and you leave your passport with reception. Nouakchott has half a dozen or more hotels, most other large towns just one or two, if that.

Travellers tend to rely on the **hospitality** of Mauritanians or expatriate residents. Moorish hospitality is legendary and you'll be well looked after by taxi drivers and other casual acquaintances across the country. Money will rarely be accepted as a gift, so you may want to carry cigarettes and lighters, pens and watches, tea and instant coffee.

Several Catholic **missions** have, in the past, been exceptionally helpful to travellers, and one or two are still generous, but they're all gradually pulling out of the Islamicising country. The **Peace Corps**, who run a high-profile programme in the R.I.M., may put you up. Several of their *Maisons de Passage* are open to outsiders, at slightly higher prices (still extremely cheap), on the understanding that they aren't hotels and volunteers always have preference.

Camping out, as long as you have access to water, is always a fine option. A tent is rarely necessary.

Eating

Mauritania doesn't come up with much food that's memorable, but Live Aid images of desolation have been shunted aside since the late 1980s. Saudi Arabian direct food aid has turned the Mauritanian economy inside out. Regular shipments bring white flour, UHT milk, pasteurised fruit juices, canned tomatoes and fish, and healthy supplies of rice. (Before the ethnic conflict, a profitable smuggling trade saw surpluses sold off to Senegal in an obscene "trickle-up" effect.)

The food situation is liable to change rapidly, of course, and as fewer and fewer Mauritanians contribute to the country's food supply, the underlying problems can only become graver. But for travellers with money, there's no need to worry about stocking up with food supplies for a trip to Mauritania, but within the country, you'd certainly want to take in some provisions for longer trips off the beaten track. Shops with any variety are limited to a few main towns.

Restaurants don't exist much outside Nouakchott and Nouadhibou, though there are chop-house eateries in most towns, often run by immigrants from other parts of West Africa.

Bread (French style) is usually in good supply. Main meals are invariably **rice**-based. Towns with flourishing gardens often have potatoes, carrots and onions. **Mutton, camel** meat and **chicken** are standard fare, as too is **fish**, usually dried and re-cooked. More expensive eating houses tend towards Moroccan couscous dishes and *tajine* stews. If you eat with Mauritanians, **milk** (fresh, as *zrig* – often diluted and sweetened – or curdled) often figures prominently.

As for fruit, **dates** are cheapest after the August or September harvest; Middle Eastern imports are generally better quality, and more expensive. Other fruit is limited to what comes over the border from Senegal or Mali (seasonal shipments of mangoes and more frequent truck-loads of oranges) and what's grown in the far south of Mauritania itself – the whole range of tropical fruit from bananas to papaya and sugar cane – little of which finds its way to Nouakchott or elsewhere. Vegetarian travellers in Mauritania have quite a hard time of it – quantities of **eggs** are used in homes and restaurants.

Drinking is a serious business – not alcohol, which has ceased to be sold in public places since economic agreements with Saudi Arabia were drawn up, but **tea**. Moors take their green tea often and earnestly. Even more than in Mali or Niger, a few small glasses of scalding, bitter-sweet yellow froth are part of the daily round. There's always a shortage of glasses: throw yours back to the tea-maker as soon as you've drained it. Despite the insistence of the tourist literature, it's only rarely drunk with mint. Travelling by taxi, the driver will usually foot the small tea bill for his passengers at rest-stops.

Language, PTT and Media

Mauritania's most widespread languages are Hassaniya Arabic and French. Other languages are mostly concentrated in the non-Moorish regions of the far south and include Fula or Fulfulde (see box p.576), Wolof (see box p.360) and the old Mande tongue known as Soninke or Sarakole. For more immediate communications, the main PTTs are in Nouakchott and Nouadhibou, and there's not much of a telecommunications service outside these towns – Zouérat, Atar and Kaédi are passable exceptions. Nouakchott's PTT is open every day.

Poste Restante is reliable but slow. Phoning abroad (not yet IDD) is reasonably efficient but expensive, at UM500/minute to Europe, UM800/minute to the USA) and no reverse charge calls.

■ Media

In a country which lists the *Bulletin of the Chamber of Commerce* as one of its four national periodicals, you know the press is pinned to the ground. *Chaab*, the only daily paper, is eight pages of generally dull African and World news and rambling articles about Mauritanian development. Page two carries a few useful directory services.

You'll find French newspapers and magazines around town, but only second-hand copies of

---

A MAURITANIAN GLOSSARY

Aftout Seasonal water course or flood zone

Aklé Zone of jumbled, live dunes

Barkane Very mobile, crescent-shaped dune with characteristic "crest"

Barrad Teapot

Boubou Loose cotton shirt or cloak

Chemama Flood plain of the Senegal River

Dahr/dhar Fault line (cliffs or escarpment)

Darrah Boubou

Erg Shifting ('live') sand dunes

Girba Goatskin waterbag

Guelb Isolated mountain or peak

Guetna Date harvest

Hal-Pulaar Fula-speaking, including Fula and Tukulor

Houli Man's headscarf, turban

Kas Drinking glass

Kedia Long tableland, mesa

L'msal Prayer ground

Mehlafa Women's long upper wrap/headscarf

Nsara Nazarene/Christian: white person (pl. Nsarani)

Reg Flat gravel, windblown sand plain

Rifi Hot wind from the north

Sebkha Dry, salt plain

Sirwal Loose, cotton pantaloons

Tabel Tea tray

Tishtar Dried meat, usually gazelle

Tell Hill covering the ruins of a former settlement

Zrig Sweet, diluted milk

English language ones. The *Novotel* sometimes carries them.

The state-run *ORTM* radio and TV network broadcasts radio in French and Hassaniya with some programmes in Fula, Wolof and Sarakole/ Soninke. You can catch the colour TV on one of Nouakchott's thousand-odd sets – nice for a change to see the news read by someone not wearing a shirt and tie – but elsewhere in the country you're unlikely to see TV at all.

HASSANIYA – SOME BASICS

Hassaniya, the language of the Hassanes and the sole language of the Moors, is a strongly Berberised form of Arabic. It's recently, and controversially, become the official language of the country, usurping less divisive French for many purposes.

Moorish Mauritanians have an elaborate greeting ritual which they go through with resignation or enthusiasm depending on whether they're late for work or not. Farewells, on the other hand, are brief and free of sentiment.

GREETINGS

Iyak la bas – Hope you have no bad.
La bas – I have no bad (usually followed by numerous *Iyaks*, eg *Iyak mo a vin* – Hope you have no sickness).
If you want to end the *Iyak* sequence try:
Mar Abah, they should get the picture.
Mah Salaam – Goodbye.
Sh'halak is an informal "How are you?" that doesn't lead to anything much.

Il hum did Illai – Praise be to God. Stick it on the end of sentences – something like *Insh Allah* when talking about the future. *Ilhumdidillai* rolls off the tongue. You'll hear it a lot if you listen out.
Salaam Alaikum Peace be with you.
Alaikum Salaam And also with you .
Sho'kran – Thank you (hardly used).
Please is never used.

OTHER PHRASES

Where is?	*Mynayn?*	I am English	*Ana min Ingletra*
What time is it?	*Waqt shin hoo?*	Hotel	*Vondeg*
Thats OK/enough (if someone's serving you something for example)	*Kavi*	Do you have?	*An dak?*
		Is there?	*Halig?*
		Water	*Ilma*
Before eating or starting something one says "In the name of God"	*Bismalai*	Food	*Lukil*
		White person/ tourist	*Nasrani*
		Good	*Zaiyn*
Yes	*Ahey*	Very good	*Hutt zaiyn*
No	*Abdei*	Not good	*Mal zaiyn*
No, by God!	*Walahi!* or *Man Allah!*	How much is?	*Kem?*
Come here	*Wahai*	A little less (to knock down the price)	*Ingus Shwei*
Tomorrow	*Subh*		
Yesterday	*Yemes*	A little (as in response to "Do you speak Hassaniya?")	*Shwei Shwei*
Today	*Ilyom*		
I am going to Nouakchott	*Ana nymshee shawr Nouakchott*	I am full	*Ana stuk fai*
		I am tired (male)	*Ana v'tran*
I am going to the market	*Ana nymshee shawr marsa*	I am tired (female)	*Ana v'trana*
		Take it easy	*Beshar*

If you're very pissed off with something or someone, try *Gassa Ramarak* ("May God shorten your life"); use carefully, it's used a lot with disobedient kids.
Ski (with a short "i") is an expression of satisfaction, usually followed by a hand slap.

NUMBERS

1	*Wahid*	3	*Ethnayn*	5	*Hamsa*	7	*Seb'a*	9	*Tesa'a*
2	*Athlath*	4	*Arba'a*	6	*Setta*	8	*Thimayna*	10	*Ashara*

Arts and Culture

Independent artistic expression is rather rare in Mauritania, where "culture" is expected to reflect state religion (hence the Ministry of Culture and Islamic Orientation).

Cinema has a beacon in the shape of exiled director **Med Hondo**. His 1969 film *Soleil Ô* was a bleak and somewhat plodding mix of *cinema verité* and weird set pieces dealing with African immigrants in France; more recently, with Burkinabe backing, he made the impressive historical epic *Sarraounia*, about a queen who resisted both the conialists and the Muslims.

Theatre is non-existent, as is any accessible **literature** (certainly none in English translation). There's a little more hope for **musical culture**, though at present it's not a lively scene. The Moorish griot caste – the Igaouen – traditionally played the *tidinit* (three- or four-stringed lute played by men), *ardin* (ten or fourteen stringed kora, women), *tebeul* (drum) and *zozaya* (flute). Music is traditionally dominated by female groups. At best, it combines soulful, Araby singing with complicated picking and rapid clapping that makes the Berber antecedents of flamenco music clear. A group of performers headed by **Dimi Mint Abba** and **Seidoum Ould Eide** made a first ever – and disappointingly lacklustre – tour of the UK in 1989, but you'd have to be unusually lucky to catch a show in Mauritania itself.

Wildlife and National Parks

Mauritania's **wildlife** has been depleted by hunting and the spread of the desert. Formerly, the south had a good cross-section of West African savannah animals, including elephants, giraffes, cheetahs, leopards, lions, and several species of antelope. The giraffes, cheetahs and lions have gone, but there are still a few **leopards** and there are said to be small numbers of **elephants** (small in stature too), hiding out in the hilly bush country between Kaédi and Ayoun el Atrous.

The uninhabited eastern desert is one of the last refuges of the endangered **addax antelope**, an extraordinary survivor, which, with careful husbandry could become a source of domestic protein in an otherwise empty environment. Other species include **mouflon** (wild sheep) in the Adrar, and gazelles and oryx antelope scattered through the north; the occasional family of ostriches in the southeast; and very rare **monk seals** at Nouadhibou. You'll see plenty of **camels**, but these, like all of Africa's dromedaries, are domesticated.

For naturalists, the country's biggest potential attraction is the migratory **birdlife** of the isolated sandbanks and seashore in the country's only national park – the **Parc National du Banc d'Arguin**, south of Nouadhibou. This is one of the world's great bird breeding sites, with millions of water birds nesting and raising their chicks here from April to July and October to January. The migrants include greater (and, uncommonly, lesser) **flamingos**, both grey and white **pelicans**, white-breasted **cormorants**, several species of **heron** and **egret**, European **spoonbills**, grey-headed and unusual slender-billed **gulls**, Caspian, royal and gull-billed **terns** and several species of waders. **Turnstones** come here in winter to scavenge the eggs of tropical birds. Fortunately for the birds (regrettably for birders) the national park is highly inaccessible and requires a major outlay in funds for the 4WD vehicles, boats and guides necessary to visit it. If you're really determined, contact M. Khattry Ould Seguane Dah Ould Cheikh, Ministre de la Pêche et de l'Économie Maritime, BP 137, Nouakchott (☎252 476, telex 595).

Directory

AIRPORT DEPARTURE TAX UM500.

CRAFTS AND MARKETS Mauritania is famous for stylishly refined **carpets**, woven in Nouakchott. Sadly these are impractical purchases for most travellers, as are the brass-fitted, dark stained **wooden chests** and **camel saddles**. But there's quite a desirable selection of **jewellery** in silver (cheap) and amber (not so), tobacco **pipes** and pouches, **sandals**, and printed cotton cloth (good value). In the Adrar and Tagant, children and market sellers hawk neolithic stone **arrow heads** and tools. You can turn up medieval glass **trading beads** as well, though these are becoming internationally sought after and increasingly rare. Be prepared to find bargaining hard work: jocularity doesn't always hit the right mark.

HOLIDAYS Apart from those decreed by the **Islamic lunar calendar**, which are followed everywhere, Mauritania's public holidays are: **January 1, February 26** (National Reunification day), **May 1** (Labour day), **May 25** (African Liberation day), **July 10** (Army day), **November 28** (National day) and **December 12** (anniversary of the 1984 coup). **December 25** is an office holiday, but you'll find most commercial doors open. Don't forget the week starts on Sunday, with Friday and Saturday the weekend.

NAMES You'll quickly notice almost all Moors retain traditional names. *Ould* and *Mint* mean "son of" and "daughter of" in Hassaniya: hence Mokhtar Ould Daddah, Dimi Mint Abba.

OPENING HOURS The office day is usually 7.30/8am–1.30/2pm. Banks are open for changing money Sunday to Thursday only until 12.30pm (2.30pm for other business). Shops close for a long break and open again in the late afternoon, until about 7.30pm.

PHOTOGRAPHY There is no photography permit. People tend to be suspicious of cameras and prefer not to have their pictures taken, but the reaction is not normally heavy. Be especially careful in Nouakchott, check before snapping and avoid all broad, street scenes – there's often an upset. Film in Nouakchott is expensive and unreliably stored.

POLICE AND TROUBLE Mauritania is **report-to-the-police** territory. Large towns have control posts on the entrance roads where your particulars will be recorded. Smaller places don't, and it's up to you to find the man on duty and proffer your *pièce*. If you fail to do so, you could have an uncomfortable dressing down when they apprehend you. If you're **driving**, you may have your vehicle very thoroughly searched; searches are otherwise rare. **Alcohol** is theoretically illegal, except in controlled upmarket bars and hotels. **Drugs** aren't much of an issue though some expensive grass finds its way in from Mali.

SEXUAL ATTITUDES In the Moorish community, there is more openness than you might at

first expect. Younger women are rapidly shaking off old values, if not always traditional costume. Urban men, too, are beginning to accept a realignment of sexual attitudes. Affairs and "love-marriages" are increasingly common in Nouakchott, and the bride price (paid to the woman or her family) is less often stipulated. Clitoridectomy is still practised, though more in the far south. Male travellers aren't very likely to be hustled by prostitutes.

WOMEN TRAVELLERS Women travellers can expect a combination of chivalry and pestering, though not too much of the latter. Covering your hair is an effective way of cooling ardour: Moorish women never let their scarves slip. Fatness in women is considered desirable by older men, though younger men insist it's no longer important to them. Sex is openly discussed among women: if you find yourself among French-speaking Moorish women, or (more likely) you speak a little Hassaniya yourself, the conversation can take remarkable turns. There is no organised women's movement in Mauritania, though Mrs Khadija Ahmed was appointed "Minister in Charge of Women, Handicrafts and Tourism" in 1988.

It's natural that you'll spend a fair amount of time, like everyone else in Mauritania, lying on mattresses on the ground. Useful to know, then, that lying either on your back or your stomach is considered highly suggestive: Moor women, you'll notice, invariably lie on their sides, supporting their head with a hand. There's reportedly a high incidence of arthritis of the elbow.

A Brief History of Mauritania

Contemporary Mauritania doesn't coincide with the ancient "Mauretania Tingitana", a region confined to present-day Morocco and Western Algeria, and annexed to the Roman Empire by Claudius in 42 AD. The events and processes that led to the creation of the République Islamique de Mauritanie are taken up here in the fifteenth century with the arrival of the first mercantile Europeans. For some further background on southern Mauritania and on political change in the French colonies, see the Senegal chapter. For some of the little-known early history of the region, see p.330, p.332, p.336 and p.339.

■ European Contact

Direct contact with Europeans began in 1445, when **Portuguese traders** set up a small *factoria* at the raised, southern tip of Arguin island.

At about the same time, the **Hassane Arabs** from upper Egypt were moving into the northern parts of the territory, subjugating the largely Berber-speaking population, spreading the use of the Hassaniya language, and creating the cultural complex that became **Moorish society**.

Early Portuguese efforts to conduct a trade in slaves and gold were not hugely successful. Instead, acacia tree gum (called "gum arabic" because it was originally exported to Europe by Red Sea Arabs) soon became the main item of commerce, most of it coming from the southwest region, near the mouth of the Senegal River.

When Portuguese commercial influence waned in the seventeenth century, the **gum trade** fuelled intense rivalry between French, Dutch and English trading houses. The Dutch pulled out in 1727, but Anglo-French competition (and war) continued until 1857, when the British withdrew from the region in exchange for the French ceding them Albreda island in the Gambia River. Even alone, the **French** had forcibly to impress their control over the gum trade on the Moors in order to hold a profit.

Throughout the seventeenth and eighteenth centuries, the French had also been more successful than the Portuguese in whipping up the slave trade. From their main base at **St-Louis** in Senegal, they sent foreign goods up-river, ensuring a supply of slaves from the feuding and rigidly class-stratified societies of the interior. Mauritania's involvement in this trade was heavy, and the class structure of the southern agricultural districts was set in aspic by the culling of non-Arabic-speaking peoples, who were sold by their captors in exchange for firearms, cloth and sugar.

But the slave trade didn't account for the slow **decline in trans-Saharan commerce**. This came about through the increasing imposition of Arab (later Arab-Berber) rule throughout the territory during the seventeenth century. By 1800, most of today's Mauritania was divided into competing **"Emirates"** – Trarza, Brakna, Adrar and Tagant – highly organised internally, but with little in the way of constructive foreign relations, and inimical to commercial links between their domains. The French at St-Louis were thus able to take advantage of the divisions, and actively promoted **civil war** in order to divert ordinary trade, as well as the slave victims of battle, in their direction.

French expansion up the Senegal river (the fort at Bakel in Senegal was built in 1818) and gathering French interest in Morocco and Algeria led, towards the end of the nineteenth century, to the strategic penetration of the Mauritanian interior, with "protection" and "pacification" sounded as the key-notes to local people. The **assassination of Xavier Coppolani**, a French commander and Arabist, at Tidjikja in 1905, ended a period of relatively peaceful expansion and brought down a five-year reign of terror in the territory. The Adrar was occupied in 1908, the Hodh (in the southeast) in 1911. The next year, France reached an agreement with Spain over respective spheres of influence in the western Saharan region, and in 1920 **La Mauritanie** became a colony of French West Africa. "Police actions" against nomadic guerrilla resistance continued throughout the north until 1933, when complete "pacification" was finally achieved.

■ The Path to Independence

Mauritania was used by the French as a **buffer zone** protecting their more valuable assets in Senegal and Soudan (Mali), and as a place of internal exile for political agitators from their other colonies. Since the end of commercial slavery in 1820, only gum arabic and potential mineral wealth had provided any economic justification for occupying the territory. They invested almost nothing in Mauritania's future, administering it as a part of Senegal and counting on nomadic conservatism to look after the population in traditional ways.

As late as 1946 there was still no political party in Mauritania. In that year, administrative apathy seems to have allowed **Horma Ould Babana**, a socialist, to become the first Mauritanian deputy to the National Assembly in Paris. In the view of the French administration, he was a dangerous radical whose presence on the National Assembly was intolerable.

Blatant interference in the 1951 National Assembly elections duly secured support for the pro-French nomadic chiefs from the 26 percent of the population who were registered to vote (one polling station controller declared "if a dog had come before me with a voter's card I'd have made him vote"). **Sidi el Mokhtar**, a member of the Gaullist *Rassemblement du Peuple Français*, and a puppet candidate of the white Moors, was duly appointed deputy.

In the Territorial Assembly elections of 1952, the Mauritanian representatives were still not seeking independence from France – indeed Mauritania, still party-less, had no effective branch of the *Rassemblement Démocratique Africaine* – the affiliation of French West African parties led by Houphouët-Boigny of Côte d'Ivoire which was in the forefront of nationalist demands.

Although the 1956 National Assembly elections were free of adminsitrative interference, and many French territories elected nationalist deputies, Mauritania again elected Sidi el Mokhtar, who stood with Gaullist support but then transferred his allegiance to the *Mouvement Républicaine Populaire*, a French Christian Democrat party.

In the same year, significantly, **Morocco** achieved independence. King Hassan V's ruling group was opposed, principally, by *Istiqlal*, a party of conservative expansionists who wanted to see the reconstruction of a **"greater Morocco"** that included much of Mauritania. The King outflanked *Istiqlal* by taking up the expansionist cause. The claims naturally had repercussions in Mauritania, where an extreme, Moorish, irredentist movement took shape, fighting to hive off part, if not all, of Mauritania to

Morocco which it believed was the true homeland of all Moors.

In the 1957 Territorial Assembly elections (the first with universal suffrage), the unaffiliated *Union Progressiste Mauritanienne*, Mauritania's first indigenous political party, won 33 out of 34 seats. **Mokhtar Ould Daddah**, a young, white Moor lawyer with considerable French support (he was de Gaulle's son-in-law), was elected vice-president of Mauritania's first governing council (the French governor was president). Ould Daddah, too, was territorially ambitious, calling on the people of the **Spanish Sahara** to unite with his own in a "great economic and spiritual Mauritania".

On November 28, 1958, Mauritania became an autonomous republic within the French community and the **République Islamique de Mauritanie** was proclaimed. A national election held in 1959 gave Ould Daddah the post of prime minister, after his party (the *Parti du Regroupement Mauritanien*) won every seat in the new National Assembly, and on November 28, 1960, Mauritania became an **independent nation state**, with Ould Daddah as president. Its entry into the United Nations, however, was vetoed by the Soviet Union, because Morocco (which then had a pro-Communist foreign policy) still claimed Mauritania.

■ Mokhtar Ould Daddah

With the founding of the new capital of Nouakchott, the development of the Fëdérik iron ore mines and the completion of the railway to Nouadhibou in 1963, Mauritania's economic future looked fairly bright. But at the same time Ould Daddah set about eliminating **political opponents**. In December 1961, the four main political parties became one, the *Parti du Peuple Mauritanien* (**PPM**). Within three years, the *de facto* one-party state had been enshrined in law.

In the south and among the **black, non-Arabic-speaking population**, expectations raised by independence from France gave way to resentment and indignation. In 1966, Arabic was made the compulsory teaching medium in schools. Ensuing **riots in Nouakchott** were summarily suppressed and laws swiftly enacted to ban all discussion of racial conflict. The country had come close to civil war, but Arabisation continued, with a 1968 law putting **Hassaniya** on a co-footing with French as dual official languages.

The government was intent on integrating the trade union movement into the PPM, a move which angered **teachers** and **miners** particularly and led to strikes and demonstrations in 1968, 1969 and 1971. For two months in 1971 there was a complete shut-down of iron ore production. The force of government repression, and the determination of the ruling party to silence the opposition led to the creation of clandestine political movements and a simmering groundswell of anti-government feeling. Through much of this first decade of independence, however, foreign affairs issues served to dampen the opposition.

Through the 1960s, support from the **other Arab states** for Morocco's claim over Mauritania had resulted in very few of them recognising the Islamic Republic. Ould Daddah's hope that the country would be seen as a bridge between Africa and the Arab world failed to materialise as his dependency on French military and economic support consolidated. Thus, with the Arab World largely left out of Mauritania's picture, the southerners' deepest fears had been partly abated during the first decade of independence.

But in 1969 came **Morocco's formal recognition of Mauritania**. Increasing Islamic radicali-

WESTERN SAHARA AND THE POLISARIO WAR

The colony of Spanish Sahara was acquired by Spain in a succession of Franco-Spanish conventions between 1886 and 1912. The motivation for coveting this 266,000-square-kilometre wedge of gravel plains and low hills (about the size of Britain) sprang from a desire to join in the "scramble for Africa", a sense of wounded imperialist pride at the loss of the South American colonies, and the proximity of the Spanish Canary islands.

Villa Cisneros (Dakhla) and La Guera were the only Spanish bases until 1934, when the first base was established in the interior. **Smara**, an abandoned Arab town, was reoccupied, at France's behest, to help control nomadic anti-colonial resistance still swirling around the region at the time. *Africa Occidental Española* had no apparent economic potential and **General Franco** didn't waste money on it. By 1952 there were only 216

civilian employees, 24 telephones and 366 school children in the entire territory. Until Franco's death, the *Provincia de Sahara* (as it became) with its capital El Ayoun (constructed 1940), was ruled as a military colony where, as in Spain, independent political expression was ruthlessly crushed.

In 1966, the United Nations insisted on the right to self-determination for the colony. But a survey of Spanish Sahara's **phosphate reserves** in the early 1960s had indicated vast deposits of up to ten billion tonnes, and Spain was soon digging in.

Although there had been armed resistance to Spanish occupation in the late 1950s, in the wake of Morocco's independence, **urban anti-colonial demonstrations** began only in June 1970, when troops fired on marchers in El Ayoun and hundreds more were arrested — and subsequently disappeared.

THE POLISARIO

The **Polisario Front** was born in Zouérat in Mauritania, on May 10, 1973, spurred into existence not just by Spain's continued occupation, but also by the threats posed by competing claims from Mauritania and Morocco. For two years Polisario acted as self-sufficient guerrillas, with no outside support, but then in May 1975 thousands of Polisario supporters emerged in the Sahara to meet the United Nations mission of inquiry.

Meanwhile, as the world witnessed the breakup of Portugal's African empire in 1974, Spain was planning a process of decolonisation and independence to thwart Polisario's growing influence, with blueprints for limited self-rule, a referendum, and a state-sponsored Sahrawi National Unity Party of Sahrawi moderates. But King Hassan put pressure on Spain to reconsider, came to an agreement with Mauritania over partitioning the terri-

tory, and then managed to persuade the International Court of Justice to consider some rather arcane questions of nineteenth century Saharan history. This last plea was turned down and the ICJ upheld the right to self-determination. Within three weeks, 350,000 Moroccans were marching, Korans in hand, into the Western Sahara, to claim their country's historical right to the territory. Then Franco died.

Spain agreed to **pull out** of Western Sahara, leaving the territory to Morocco, Mauritania and the Spanish-installed *Djemaa* council — a body of conservative, urban Sahrawis through whom they had ruled. Although the UN continued to uphold the resolutions on Western Sahara, a UN visit in early 1976 decided that the scale of upheaval was so great that there was no way the Sahrawis could be properly consulted. The guerrilla war now

sation, a slackening of ties with France coupled with growing Algerian support, and a clear state socialist programme seemed natural consequences. The huge MIFERMA (*Mines de Fer de Mauritanie*) iron ore complex at Fdérik/Zouérat was nationalised and the country withdrew from the CFA franc zone to bring in its own, Arab-bank-supported currency. There was wide backing for these moves in the Arabic-speaking community and, by 1975, broad government confidence. Although the **drought** of the early 1970s had left the country reeling, the worst affected were the largely Arabic-speaking nomads of the north and

centre. Now, with trade unions and students in Nouakchott appeased, the problem of the disenfranchised southerners, who had found some voice through these groups, was less urgent.

Spain's decision to withdraw its garrisons from the Western Sahara plunged Mauritania into a **war with the Polisario** (Popular Front for the Liberation of Sagia el Hamra and Rio de Oro; see box). The war, over the small and economically worthless piece of territory ceded to Mauritania by Spain, proved the downfall of Ould Daddah. Even with a massive increase in military spending, and a tenfold expansion of the army,

---

began in earnest, and more than half the population fled the country – old people, women and children to Algerian refugee camps around Tindouf,

men to join Polisario. The **Sahrawi Arab Democratic Republic** (SADR) was proclaimed – in exile in Tindouf – on February 27, 1976.

MAURITANIA AT WAR

Mauritania was never an enthusiastic ruler of the desert plain it called **Tiris el Gharbia**, nor was it prepared for a long and costly war. From the beginning Polisario concentrated on knocking Mauritania out of the picture, thus breaking the Morocco-Mauritania alliance. Mauritania's army was never sufficient to look after the new territory, let alone defend the bulk of the country from highly motivated Polisario incursions. There were repeated, humiliating losses: the iron ore railway was under constant threat; foreigners working at the mines were kidnapped; and twice, in June 1976 and July 1977, Polisario mounted daring **raids on the outskirts of Nouakchott** itself, and shelled the presidential palace.

In 1978 a desperate President Ould Daddah agreed to the stationing of 9000 **Moroccan troops** in the Saharan territory, and they were soon routinely skirmishing with Polisario in Mauritanian terrain. France too was heavily involved in defending Mauritania, President Giscard d'Estaing sending Jaguar bombers to blitz Polisario encampments and a steady stream of personnel to shore up Mauritania's flagging army. Mauritania was crippled by debt, doubt and drought, and its war was an undignified fiasco. For President Ould Daddah, the situation had become untenable, and he was relieved of his post in July 1978. The **new regime** sued for peace with Polisario the following year.

STALEMATE

The war between Morocco and Polisario has now lasted over fifteen years. Arms-dealing nations (including France, Britain and the USA) continue to supply Morocco, while maintaining token support for the UN resolutions on the Sahrawis' rights to self-determination. Despite this military support, Morocco has been incresingly stretched and, since the early 1980s, has pulled back its front line to the **northwest** area of Western Sahara (the so-called "useful triangle" containing the phosphate fields) and **Dakhla**, while building immensely long, defensive, earthworks that now enclose almost 90 percent of the territory. Polisario chips away, but a stalemate has now dragged on since 1986.

Meanwhile, the **Tindouf refugee zone** has grown into a state-in-exile, a stable and relatively prosperous republic which, though heavily dependent on international donations, has built a reputa-

tion for its agricultural efforts and welfare services.

The resumption of diplomatic relations between **Algeria and Morocco** in May 1988 didn't result in the crisis for the Polisario that might have been expected. King Hassan is no longer calling the Polisario "Algerian puppet terrorists" and there seems a real possibility of a **referendum** for the people of the territory (and the 170,000 refugees living in the four Tindouf camps), after the first **direct talks** between Sahrawis and Moroccans in January 1989. That said, Morocco has already "West Banked" the sectors of the Western Sahara it holds, pumping resources – and 100,000 **Moroccan settlers** – into the region, in order to outwit a democratic solution. Another possibility – that the plight of the Sahrawis might slip into obscurity – is also real.

popular support was so low in Mauritania that the war was clearly unwinnable.

■ The Lieutenant-Colonels

On the night of July 9, 1978, a quiet and bloodless **military coup** ousted Mokhtar Ould Daddah. The officers dissolved the PPM party and announced the formation of a *Comité Militaire de Redressement National* (CMRN) – "to save the country from ruin and dismemberment" – under the chairmanship of Chief of Staff Lt-Col **Moustapha Ould Salek**.

Ould Salek tried to bring Polisario and Morocco together for a negotiated settlement, but the terms suited neither party. When Polisario's kidnapping of a Mauritanian prefect pushed Mauritania into a **peace treaty** with Polisario in August 1979, Morocco immediately moved into the territory vacated by Mauritanian troops. Morocco and Mauritania consequently have had an uneasy relationship ever since. Meanwhile, at home, Ould Salek was confronted by outbreaks of racial conflict, student agitation, and factional strife in the *CMRN* – upgraded, desperately, in April 1979, to the Military Committee for National *Salvation* (*CMSN*). Ould Salek resigned and was replaced as president by Lt-Col **Mohammed Louly**, whose prime minister, Lt-Col **Mohamed Khouna Haidalla**, in turn staged another palace coup in January 1980, to take control of government.

Haidalla's five years as head of state saw an overall improvement of foreign relations, but a deterioration in the domestic situation. The continuing war between Polisario and Morocco repeatedly spilled onto Mauritanian soil, hindering rapprochement with Morocco and delaying Mauritania's recognition of the state of the Sahrawi Arab Democratic Republic.

Internally, Mauritania's most dramatic event – as far as the rest of the world was concerned – was the formal **abolition of slavery** in 1980. This may have been intended to forestall links between the Dakar-based black opposition and supporters of exiled white Moor groups in Paris, and also to divert attention away from the increasingly blatant racial discrimination against the *Soudanien* southerners, but the effect of the pronouncement was to focus world attention on a repressive military dictatorship. Mauritania's law did indeed guarantee freedom from chatteldom, but not freedom from hunger, dispossession or political repression.

For a short time in 1980/81, President Haidalla experimented with **political relaxation**. He formed a civilian government led by prime minister Ahmed Ould Bneijara, and drew up a draft constitution recommending a democratic multi-party system. But rumours of a **Libyan-backed plot** (part of the ripple of Libyan-inspired insecurity that passed through West Africa at that time), and then a genuine **coup attempt** by the *Parti Islamique* of former government ministers operating from Morocco, shook the democracy idea apart. Having executed the coup leaders, the CMSN appointed a new prime minister, Lt-Col **Maawiya Ould Sid'Ahmed Taya**, and re-militarised the government.

Despite this clampdown, another **military coup** was foiled in February 1982, involving Ould Salek and the just-deposed Ould Bneijara. In a surprise display of clemency, the instigators were given ten-year jail sentences.

Through the early 1980s, Mauritania's prospects failed to improve. Severe drought in 1983 brought tens of thousands of famine-struck nomads virtually to the door of the Presidential Palace in Nouakchott; opposition groups continued to fight a war of words in France, Morocco and Senegal; and Haidalla's recognition of the SADR early in 1984 brought further insecurity to the country as Morocco seemed more than ever determined to oppose any referendum in the Western Sahara – increasing the tension between Morocco and Mauritania. In August, Morocco entered a bizarre pact of union with Libya, unsettling the Mauritanians. The prime minister, **Colonel Ould Taya**, who was already concerned about government corruption and inaction, deposed President Haidalla on December 12, 1984, in yet another, gentlemanly palace coup.

■ Ould Taya: Progress and Reaction

President Ould Taya wasted no time. With World Bank and IMF support he adopted a programme of economic recovery with heavy emphasis on fishing and agriculture. Targets were set, and reached, and creditors were evidently impressed by Taya's abandonment of some of the capital-intensive industrial schemes set up by Haidalla to the detriment of basic infrastructure and rural development. Iron ore is still a major source of foreign exchange (reserves have been variously estimated at between 500 and 2000 million tonnes, which at the present rate of extraction would last up to 200 years), though variations in foreign demand make it an uncertain guarantee of prosperity. In the late 1980s **fish** came to be seen as a more flexible resource, and looks set to become established as the country's biggest earner.

If Ould Taya's government can get round the problems of wealth distribution, Mauritania may yet avoid self-destruction. On assuming power in 1984, he released all political prisoners and talked of a policy of democratisation. And at the end of 1986, democratic municipal elections had been held – the first for twenty years.

As Mauritania enters its fourth decade of independence, however, the **prospects for political stability** are looking worse than ever before. The current predicament hasn't emerged unexpectedly. Ould Taya has striven to reach a reconciliation with what, until very recently, he perceived to be his strongest opposition – the *Alliance pour une Mauritanie Démocratique* (AMD) led by ex-president Mokhtar Ould Daddah, who'd been released into exile under French pressure in 1979. Several of Ould Daddah's ministers have served under Ould Taya and an open invitation exists to the ex-president himself to return home.

The Southern Mauritanians

Unity within the Moorish community will not solve (and may well aggravate) a far more pressing and much neglected issue – the severe discrimination against the **non-Arabic-speaking southerners**. In fairness, there are several non-Moorish ministers on the ruling council, and Fula- and Wolof-speakers have been given government posts (though they are not always very effective in isolated Moorish communities in the desert) – but it is not enough.

In 1986, a tract in French entitled *Manifesto of the Oppressed Black Mauritanian: From Civil War to National Liberation Struggle; 1966–86* made the rounds among students, lecturers, journalists and staff at the National Language Institute. It was reportedly the work of Tene Youssouf Gueye, a member of the Dakar-based **African Liberation Forces of Mauritania** (FLAM). Twenty prominent southerners were arrested and jailed on charges of "undermining national unity". Widespread rioting and destruction subsequently took place in Nouakchott and Nouadhibou, and thirteen of those involved were also jailed, in March 1987. Strict **Islamic law** was introduced.

In October 1987, 51 Fula-speaking Tukulor officers were arrested on charges of insurrection. According to the Interior Minister, "this plot was more than an attempt to overthrow the government, it was a crime against the whole nation". Three officers were executed (the first death sentences imposed by Ould Taya's regime) and 41 more were given long prison terms. Bitterness among Tukulor in the army and gendarmerie later led to a **purge of Tukulor officers**, with over 500 dismissals. The executions were condemned by the Senegalese Human Rights Federation, in Senegal's pro-government daily, *Le Soleil* – a humiliating snub to the Ould Taya government.

Tension coninued through 1988. In June, two Moors and a Senegalese taxi driver were murdered in Nouakchott. Police described the stabbing of the two Moors as "ordinary assassinations", but FLAM claimed that racial grievances were the spark. They pointed out that the "sensitisation programme" being carried out by the government in the **Senegal River flood plain** region wasn't appeasing local people, who bitterly resented the influx of Moorish and Arab land-buyers and the pressures on them to make way for alien **development projects**.

Towards the end of 1988, it was reported that a number of southerners serving terms for political crimes, including the author of the Black Manifesto, had died in **Oualata prison**. The allegations were denied by the government, who sent the Mauritanian League of Human Rights to confirm their falsehood. They found several Oualata inmates were, indeed, still alive.

■ The Race Riots: What Hope?

Events finally boiled over in April 1989, triggered by an incident on the border with Senegal. **Border incidents** over farming and grazing rights are quite common, because the river's level changes all the time, and new dams downstream are creating new islands. Most disputes are between members of the same language group or even the same extended families, and without the presence of outsider armed forces, feuds might be settled by negotiation, or even fratricidally. With the intervention and protection of personally uninvolved police or soldiers, however, violent escalation and racial strife is always a possible consequence.

In this instance, trouble began with a comparatively minor incident on the disputed island of **Ndounde Khore** in the Senegal River, near

Bakel, in which Mauritanian camels were supposed to have plundered Senegalese vegetable gardens. During an argument, Mauritanian border guards were said to have opened fire on the Senegalese, killing two people. Thirteen Senegalese were then captured and taken to Selibaby where they were effectively kept hostage, which led to attacks on Mauritanian shops in Bakel.

Within days, violence had spread to Senegalese towns and dozens of Mauritanians had been stoned to death and thousands driven out as their shops and homes were ransacked. In Dakar, thousands of Mauritanians sheltered in the Grande Mosquée and in the compound of the Mauritanian embassy.There were savage **reprisals** against Senegalese and other black Africans in Mauritania. (Some reports stated the atrocities *began* in Mauritania, as news reached Nouakchott of looting in Senegal.) Groups of Haratins, and even security forces, were said to be lynching southerners. Curfews were enforced in Nouakchott and Nouadhibou but neither government took rapid action to control the violence, and both were slow to condemn killings by the other side.

A massive dual **evacuation by air** began as it emerged in early May that at least two hundred Senegalese had died in Nouakchott. The army remained on the streets of Dakar as accusations were levelled against President Ould Taya that he had virtually declared war on Senegal.

As the exodus went on, it became clear that some of those leaving Mauritania were southern Mauritanians – whom the regime now routinely refers to as "Senegalese" – and many were being forcibly expelled. The government, it seemed, was taking the opportunity to banish up to 20,000 **potential opponents**, reduce the impact of the returning Moors and to lessen the numbers of non-Moorish Mauritanians, who have claimed for several years that they are now in the majority. Conspiracy theories about white Moor supremacism have been revived: the purge of Tukulor officers in 1987 falls all too neatly into place.

The future for Mauritania looks extremely grim. The country's returning citizens can only add to problems of unemployment and swelling slums, while its long-established ties with the West African Economic Community are close to breaking point. Relations with Morocco are still strained over Western Sahara, leaving Mauritania distressingly isolated. The likely result of current racial policies will be civil war, and perhaps attempted secession of the south, along the Senegal River – the most important region for the country's unified future. This would bring Senegal into conflict with Mauritania, a prospect which – despite joint talks held in Bamako after the riots – both countries would seem prepared to face. Hope can only lie in far-reaching **government concessions** to black opposition demands and the less tangible withering away of Moorish culture's most chauvinistic aspects.

NOUAKCHOTT

Mauritania's capital, **NOUAKCHOTT,** is the biggest city in the Sahara, a modern, dusty sprawling place of half a million inhabitants – over a quarter of the country's population. Once you're settled in, it's hard to dislike; you can wander around more or less unhassled, and there's a certain ease in the wide, tree-lined streets of crushed sea-shells, with their drifts of sand. And yet there's something soulless about this commercial and self-interested city, with its brutally severe state buildings and its dearth of things to do. For most itinerants, a couple of nights are enough before moving on.

A short history
The site of the new city of Nouakchott – whose name may mean "Place of Wind" or "Place of Floating Seashells" – was nominated by Bidan elders in 1957, who chose to raise it near a French military post on the **Piste Impériale**, the old Imperial road. The buildings were constructed on fixed dunes, in an attempt to give protection from the flooding of the Aftout es-Saheli seasonal watercourse, which nearly surrounds it – the original Ksar settlement had been seriously damaged by floods in 1950. With funds limited and formal independence pressing, the city was hastily planned and constructed – medina, residential blocks, schools, ministries – for an anticipated population of 15,000. It was already 20,000 by 1969, when the first great Sahel drought tipped the country into crisis. By 1980 the immigrant influx had pushed it past 150,000, and since then it has more than tripled again.

Arrival and practicalities

Arriving by **taxi brousse** from Senegal or landing at the **airport** are probably the most usual introductions to the capital. At the *gare routière* or the airport exit, a scene of scruffy lanes, wind-blown rubbish, wasted palm trees and perfunctory shops seems to confirm worst fears. Whipped by dust storms for nine months of the year, Nouakchott seems to be drowning under a sea of sand. But Nouakchott is a sprawling city and the *gare routière* and airport are in the old part of town, the pre-capital "Ksar", 3km from the centre. This is also the slightly sleazy area where most of the garages and service stations are located (see "Directory"). There's an exchange counter at Nouakchott airport, and car hire available, but few other facilities. Ordinary **taxis** charge around UM300 to the *centreville*, possibly less if you haggle. There's no airport bus, and Nouakchott city bus services extend to about two blue *STPN* vehicles. Best is to share a taxi for UM30–100 or find a green and yellow *Transports Urbaines* minibus (UM10–20). Once in the real city centre, and assuming the dust has settled, impressions do improve. Note, however, that you'll find the city lifeless if you arrive between noon and 3pm. And during Ramadan, that's the normal condition during daylight hours.

Orientation
The **lay-out** of Nouakchott can be confusing at first, and there are no heights from which to get your bearings. **Le Ksar** is on the east side of town, from where the slums spread north along the Atar highway and east along the Route de l'Espoir. From the paved roads, there's no indication of their vast extent.

The city's main street, **Avenue Abd El Nasser**, runs east–west from just south of the Ksar, through **La Capitale** and out to the beach, 5km away. Cutting across it at right angles is **Avenue Kennedy**, which connects the affluent, ambassadorial quarter on the northern edge of La Capitale to the Medina and the extensive commercial districts of the *cinquième arrondissement* in the south (Nouakchott is divided into numbered **arrondissements** and alphabetical blocks called **îlots**).

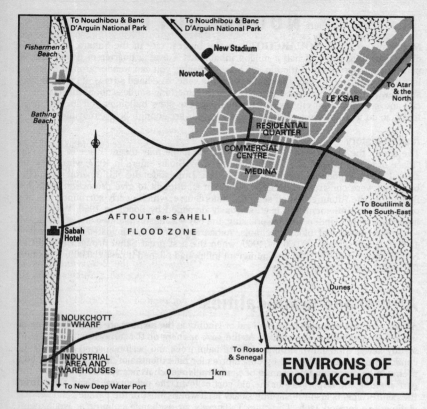

ENVIRONS OF NOUAKCHOTT

Most hotels, restaurants and shops are within a short walking distance of the Kennedy-Nasser intersection and this district is likely to be the main focus for the time you're in town.

Accommodation

The cheapest **rooms** in Nouakchott start at around UM1000, but there's a very limited choice of hotels, and places in the lower price brackets are often full. The Catholic Mission has gone, and the Peace Corps' *Maison de Passage* doesn't usually admit outsiders either. All the places listed below are in the Capitale (see map): an alternative in the **Ksar quarter** of the city is *Auberge de Ksar* (☎522 711). In the other direction, price-wise as well as geographically, the uninspiring *Sabah Hôtel* (BP 452; ☎251 552, telex 821; UM3200/3700) is the only one on the beach. **Camping** on the beach is relatively safe, but to stay more than one night would be likely to invite official attention.

Le Stade, 2km out of town, past the *Novotel*. Not really a hotel, and there's no guarantee you'll get a room, but polite persuasion and a promise to leave after one night might get you in. It's often full of new Peace Corps recruits, foreign technicians or students. Clean, airy, S/C, non-AC rooms from UM1200/1600 (negotiable).

Hôtel Adrar, travellers' focus and flophouse bordello, scruffy and unhygienic, but convenient and friendly enough. Nominally S/C rooms from UM1000, UM200 supplement for AC.

Hôtel Oasis, (BP 4; ☎252 011). Cheapest of the rest at around UM2000/2500 S/C non-AC B&B. Adequate, but nothing about it merits the price.

Park Hôtel (BP 50; ☎251 444). Nice enough place with S/C AC rooms from around UM2600/3200 B&B.

Hôtel El Amanne (BP 13; ☎252 178, telex 544). Arguably the best hotel in Nouakchott, from UM2600/3200 S/C AC B&B. Usually packed with businessmen; pretty courtyard restaurant.

Hôtel Chinguetti (BP 541; ☎251 320). Fairly smart but way overpriced at UM3000/4000 AC B&B.

Hôtel Marhaba (BP135; ☎252 094/252 124). Upmarket place, now eclipsed by the *Novotel*.

Novotel (☎253 526). Architecturally Nouakchott's best, but not the most rewarding way of spending US$100.

Food

Eating in Nouakchott is a slightly more hopeful adventure than the pursuit of a cheap room: several restaurants have been firmly established for many years, and even the odd new one opens occasionally. Cheapest deals are around the main Marché Capitale, where you can get a *plat* of rice or pasta for UM70–140: try the *Restaurant Mena*, on the first floor of the market, but avoid the dirty and unappetising *Sindibads*. All the places listed below are marked on our map.

Phenicia and **Rimal**, both popular standbys, have good menus (UM250–400) and decent service; the former is especially renowned for its mounds of couscous.

Friscos is a more pretentious new arrival, providing American food and pizzas to an air-conditioned expatriate and well-connected Mauritanian crowd (UM300–700).

Zoubeida, a Moroccan restaurant, hugely popular with less well-connected people, recommended for an evening out. The set-up here is piles of cushions and carpets, shoes off, TV in the corner, conversational opportunities – and endless food. Wonderful value.

Winding Mali Booli, near the Marché Cinquième, is clean and not overpriced, and its name infects it with a levity unusual in Mauritania.

In town and around

It's quickly apparent that Nouakchott doesn't spill over with **things to see and do**. Apart from checking out the **markets** and various **artisanal centres**, the only obvious destination is the **beach**.

There are several spots around the city where you can study tourist bric à brac and while away some hours in bargaining – such as outside the *El Amanne* and *Novotel* hotels. The main **Centre Artisanal**, however, is a walk or taxi ride out of town on the Rosso road. Though bulky items like camel saddles, silver-inlaid chests and carpets make up much of the most impressive stuff, **jewellery and silverware** is also worth close inspection – silver, at UM22/gramme, is remarkably cheap. Don't buy stone arrow heads here: they're much cheaper in the regions where they're found (see "The Adrar", below).

Set up as a womens' income development initiative, the **Centre National du Tapis**, in the Ksar quarter, produces finely woven **rugs and carpets** in subtle, deserty colours with rigorous geometrical patterns – sadly, they are out of range of most pockets. There's another women's centre in the Capitale, behind the Grand Marché, where the speciality is **embroidery**. If this appeals, try to track down the **Soninke tie-dye/batik workshops**.

NOUAKCHOTT: 'LA CAPITALE'

To New Stadium & Novotel

0   500 m

Cathédrale St. Joseph

L

M

E

F

Presidential Palace

H

K

J

G

D

RUE AHMED OULD MAMMED

AVENUE KENNEDY

RUE OULD GENERAL DE GALLE

RUE MAMADOU KONATE

RUE ABOUBAKER

RUE ALIOUNE

RUE GATAH

RUE OMAR

RUE ABOUBAKER

AVENUE DE L'INDEPENDANCE

RUE MOHAMED LEMINE SAVIO

10

Hospital

To Fishermen's Beach Sabah Hôtel and Noudhibou
AVENUE DE LA DUNE

Beach Taxis

N

Fish Market

Wrestling Arena

Mosque

Taxis

3

4

Grand Marché

2

5

R

8

9

Post Office

6

P

AVENUE ABD EL NASSER

Commissariat Central

A

RUE BAKAR AHMED

Marché Ilot 'H'

B

C

RUE HEMMOUNE OULD BOUCIF

AVENUE DE L'INDEPENDANCE

RUE MOHAMED EL HABIB

RUE MOHAMED LEMINE SAVIO

AVENUE KENNEDY

RUE AHMED OULD MAMMED

11

RUE ELY OULD MHAMO

Stadium

Vegetable Gardens

Marché Cinquième

RUE MAKAYUDDA

12

Creeping san invading the

To Centre Artisanal, Rosso & Senegal

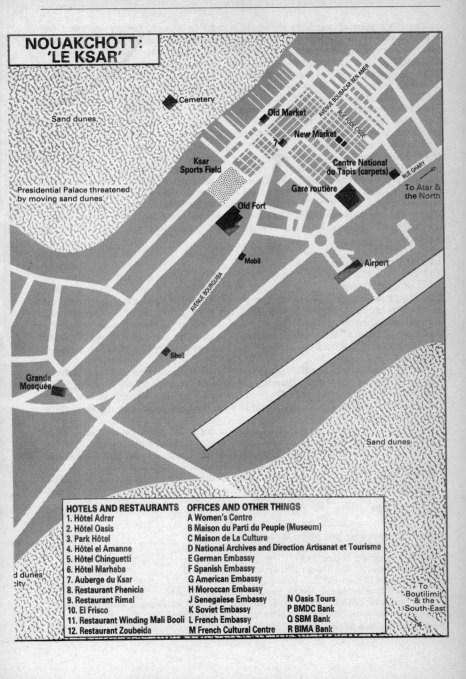

NOUAKCHOTT: 'LE KSAR'

Cemetery

Sand dunes

Old Market

New Market

AVENUE BOUBACAR BEN AMER

RUE FODE ISSE

Ksar
Sports Field

Centre National
du Tapis (carpets)

RUE GHARY

Presidential Palace threatened
by moving sand dunes

To Atar &
the North

Old Fort

Gare routière

Mobil

AVENUE BOURGUIBA

Airport

Shell

Grande
Mosquée

Sand dunes

d dunes
city

To
Boutilimit
& the
South-East

HOTELS AND RESTAURANTS	OFFICES AND OTHER THINGS	
1. Hôtel Adrar	A Women's Centre	
2. Hôtel Oasis	B Maison du Parti du Peuple (Museum)	
3. Park Hôtel	C Maison de La Culture	
4. Hôtel el Amanne	D National Archives and Direction Artisanat et Tourisme	
5. Hôtel Chinguetti	E German Embassy	
6. Hôtel Marhaba	F Spanish Embassy	
7. Auberge du Ksar	G American Embassy	
8. Restaurant Phenicia	H Moroccan Embassy	
9. Restaurant Rimal	J Senegalese Embassy	N Oasis Tours
10. El Frisco	K Soviet Embassy	P BMDC Bank
11. Restaurant Winding Mali Booli	L French Embassy	Q SBM Bank
12. Restaurant Zoubeida	M French Cultural Centre	R BIMA Bank

The city's **general markets** are worth wandering around, though you'll not find much of note in the purpose-built Grand Marché/Marché Capitale, or in the Marché Ilot H. Instead take a taxi/bus down to the **Marché Cinquième**, where you can shuffle the sandy lanes for as long as you can stand the heat. If you really dig through the reams of nylon and piles of plastic sandals you'll find a wealth of fine fabrics down here, including exceptionally fine-weave lightweight muslin in attractive prints. A clutch of medicine and *gri-gri* sellers, with their displays of monkeys' and birds' feet and lizards' and turtles' heads making for macabre browsing.

Across Kennedy from the Marché Cinquième, you'll find other **commercial districts** – a whole street devoted to dried dates for example. Ironically, they're almost as expensive here as in supermarkets at home, and the presence of imported dates from Saudi Arabia seems breathtakingly perverse, even by the standards of Mauritania's misshapen economy. If you fancy buying some dates anyway, go for the smooth, dry, pale brown quality: these should be hard but chewable, like toffee.

There's a **fish market** over to the west (the beach scene is far more interesting – see below) and, near it, the **wrestling arena**, which holds bouts on Saturday afternoons. The city **museum**, the collections of which are assembled in the gaunt Maison du Parti du Peuple, is no longer open to the public. Somewhere, too, there's reportedly a **zoo**.

La Plage

The **beach** is the main event in Nouakchott. Once you've crossed the slums and garbage dumps separating the city from the sea, there's a solid phalanx of dunes behind it, and then an impressively straight sweep of fine sand stretching north and south to the horizons. The **Plage des Pêcheurs** is fairly busy all the time, mostly with Senegalese fishermen, though the scene is no longer as animated as before the departure of most of the black immigrant communities. The boats come in around 5pm, when there are cold drink kiosks and stalls selling freshly fried fish with hot sauce.

Five hundred metres south from here the beach is nearly deserted, and perfectly clean – come either early in the morning and have it to yourself, or late afternoon when there's a scattering of other swimmers and strollers. There's no shade, and beware the strong current and occasional swarms of jellyfish. Despite these hazards, the bathing here is lovely.

Surprisingly perhaps, you can often meet young Bidan Moor couples strolling or making tea on the beach, especially at weekends (Friday and Saturday). Among Mauritania's alcohol-deprived and unemployed urban youth, it looks like the *mehlafas* and *darrahs* might be concealing a new rebellion founded on sex and drugs.

If you have to take a taxi by *déplacement* to the beach, you'll pay up to UM500. Coming back though, there's rarely any problem squeezing in a *bâché*.

Directory

Airlines The following have offices in Nouakchott:
Air Afrique (BP 51; ☎252 084/252 545); accepts *Visa* cards;
Air Algérie av Abd El Nasr (☎252 059);
Air Mauritanie av Abd El Nasr (BP 41; ☎252 212/252 472);
Iberia av Abd El Nasr (BP 727; ☎252 654);
Royal Air Maroc Immeuble SMAR, av Abd El Nasr (☎253 564);
UTA Immeuble SMAR (BP 662; ☎253 916/251 808); accepts *Visa* and *Amex* and offers under-25 discounts; Paris one-way fares otherwise from UM45,000.
American Express Not represented.

Banks The *Société Mauritanienne de Banque* (BP 614; ☎252 602), the *Union des Banques de Développement* (BP 219; ☎252 061), and the *Banque Internationale pour la Mauritanie* (BP 210; ☎252 363) seem the surest, but they can take ages. All are open Sun–Thurs 7.30am–12.30pm; out of hours, your best bet is the airport bank or the *Novotel*.

Bars The only places to get a drink are the *Hôtel Marhaba*, *Novotel*. and the *Racing Club*, an ex-pat hang-out (☎252 418).

Car hire and travel agents include:
Oasis Tours (BP 926; ☎251 717, telex 531), the most organised tour agent, will take you anywhere in the country, at a price;
Agence Nouvelle d'Auto Location has cars from around UM5000/day for use around the city, and from UM4000/day plus UM15/km for paved highways outside it. 4WD vehicles are about UM9000/day plus UM20/km, and generally come with a driver.
Ets. Memoudy (BP 1774; ☎251 788) is another firm – it may be able to beat these prices. Naturally, you should bargain your mouth off.
Hertz (BP 1163; ☎253 787, telex 506) and *Europcar* (BP 791; ☎251 136, telex 853) are also represented.

Car parts and main dealers include *Nosoco* for Land Rover (☎252 352) and *Lacombe* for Citroën and VW (☎252 194), both in the Ksar. *Peyrissac* for Peugeot and Nissan (☎252 213) is on av Abd El Nasr in the Capitale.

Cinemas The *Oasis* and the *El Mouna* show Westerns, Kung Fu and occasional French and Egyptian movies. There's a couple more screens in the Ksar – the *El Jouad* and the *Sahara*.

Embassies Consulates for **Belgium** (near the Ksar stadium), **Switzerland** (on the road to the beach, near the hospital) and **Great Britain** (across the ring road from the French embassy, ☎252 337) seem to have lapsed. Britain apparently has no representation: nearest diplomatic help is the American embassy or the British embassy in Dakar. Note that there is **no Mali embassy** in Nouakchott. The visa service at the **French embassy** handles visas for **Côte d'Ivoire, Burkina Faso, Chad, Togo** and **Centrafrique**.
  Algeria (telex 871);
  France, rue Ahmed Ould Mahmed (BP 231; ☎251 740, telex 582);
  Gabon (BP 38; ☎252 919, telex 593);
  West Germany (BP 372; ☎251 032, telex 555);
  Morocco (BP 621; ☎251 411, telex 550);
  Nigeria (BP 367; telex 869);
  Senegal, av du Général de Gaulle (BP 611; ☎252 106);
  Spain (BP 232; ☎251 028, telex 563);
  Tunisia (BP 681; ☎252 871, telex 857);
  USA (BP 222; ☎252 660, telex 558);
  USSR, rue Abdou Baker (BP 251; ☎251 973);
  Zaire (BP 487; ☎252 836, telex 812).

Emergencies Police ☎17, Hospital ☎252 135. The hospital is helpful and not too expensive.

French Cultural Centre The usual pleasant, chauvinistic retreat.

Postcards An underwhelming selection of Mauritanian views at several school supplies/bookshops and a handful of street stalls. "Ministry Buildings" and "Pelican Wounded in the Sands" are two examples worth obtaining.

Post Office The PTT on av Abd el Nasser is theoretically open daily 8am–12.30pm & 2–6.30pm. Collecting mail from *Poste Restante* depends on the availability of the bureau clerk but is otherwise efficient and costs UM24/item. There's also a public telex.

Swimming pools Only at the *Hôtel Marhaba* and the *Novotel*. The former is open only to annual subscription holders; brazen entry has the best chance of success at the latter.

Telephoning Calls abroad are most easily made at the *Novotel*.

Tourist office Make enquiries direct with the *Direction Artisanat et Tourisme* (BP 246), near the Présidence.

Visas Visa "prolongation" is possible at the *Commissariat Central*.

SOUTHERN MAURITANIA

Southern Mauritania is the most densely populated part of the country, its major settlements connected by the Brazilian-built **Route de l'Espoir**. The one thousand and ninety-nine kilometres of paved *transmauritanienne* highway have certainly opened up the isolated southeast, bringing the far-flung regional capital of **Néma** within less than three days' drive of Nouakchott. There's a grim irony to the name, though. Instead of spreading wealth to the provinces, the Road of Hope has sucked them dry, offering swift escape from the parched countryside to the even less hopeful Nouakchott shanties – where the nomads and impoverished farmers can only sit and wait.

Roughly south of the Route de l'Espoir the population is largely non-Arabic-speaking and the land is dry savannah and bush, with irrigated rice and millet lands near the river. Shabby **Rosso** is a first glimpse of Mauritania for most travellers arriving from Senegal, but **Bogué** and **Kaédi**, further up-river are more interesting towns. Along the road, **Boutilimit** is worth a stop, as are **Ayoun el Atrous**, **Timbedgha** and Néma itself. Off the road to the **north**, the Moorish citadels of **Tidjikja** and **Tichit** are spectacularly isolated and tough destinations – Tichit up to five days' travel from Nouakchott. **Oualata**, north of Néma, is also highly recommended if you've time. Making for Bamako in Mali, the *piste* to the border crossing south of Timbedgha passes near the site of **Koumbi Saleh**, plausible capital of the ancient kingdom of Ghana.

Rosso and north to Nouakchott

Arriving on the north bank of the Senegal river, there's nothing to hold you in **ROSSO**, and no accommodation. Rarely would you be stuck for transport to Nouakchott however. The *gare routière* is 500m out of town, an arrangement that seems to have been designed to allow the *calèche* drivers the opportunity of giving you a ride in their horse-drawn buggies. *Peugeots* do the run up to Nouakchott in three to four hours along a coastal highway which for most of the year runs through dry dunes and sand hills with a scattering of trees. With rain, the dunes become gentle, grass-spiked hills, dotted with goats and camels and planted with the flapping white tents of nomads – looking strangely out of place, like a Lancastrian army encamped before battle.

If you have your own 4WD, you could deviate from the highway some 20km outside Rosso to visit **MEDERDRA**, an old gum arabic centre at the heart of the defunct kingdom of Trarza, now renowned for wood and silver craftsmanship.

Boutilimit

An unengrossing two-hour drive from Nouakchott, **BOUTILIMIT** is the first major settlement along the road, a Moorish caravanserai and site of one of the earliest French military bases in the country, with a large, permanent **market**. It was the birthplace of Mokhtar Daddah, Mauritania's first president. The religious capital of the country, Boutilimit is renowned for the literary collection of its *medrassa*, and for its crafty fabrications – goat and camel hair rugs, and silverware. Nowadays the town is very much under economic thrall to Nouakchott.

To Kaédi

From the anonymous town of ALEG a brand new paved road leads 60km down to the river and the Chemama (flood plain) town of BOGUÉ. You can get across the river by *pirogue* to the Isle à Morfil in Senegal (p.407) from here, but the car ferry may no longer be operating. A rough road (often flooded in summer) continues to KAÉDI, Mauritania's third largest town, and a major market centre (a good place to buy cloth). In the late 1970s a meat-freezing plant was built here, with the intention of culling some of the over-grazing herds of the south and air-freighting the meat to Europe. But the land immediately around Kaédi is barren, and offers no grazing at all to cattle driven there, so the herders continue to drive their cattle for slaughter down to the coast. A high percentage of Kaédi's people are settled (or semi-settled) Tukulor, whose white, long-horn zebu cattle can be seen roaming everywhere in the Gorgol and Guidimaka districts, to the southeast.

The Tagant

The **Tagant** is a region of sear, stony plateaux, the remote location of some of Mauritania's oldest towns and notoriously hard of access. By 4WD it takes between a day and a half and two days to reach **Tidjikja**, geographically almost the dead centre of Mauritania. The final 200km of *piste* is very variable, and petrol supplies north of the *transmauritanienne* are unreliable, so fill your tank and jerry cans at every opportunity. Coming by **public transport**, you should fix up a vehicle for the whole journey in Nouakchott. Hop by *taxi brousse* if you like, but distances are long, junctions often deserted and scorching, and **local transport** (from Aleg or MAGTA LAHJA, for example) is very uncertain. Many local people prefer to fly to Tidjikja: planes depart every Tuesday and Friday, and cost about UM4500, twice the road fare.

Tidjikja – and Rachid

A three-hundred-year-old bastion of conservative Bidan ideology, **TIDJIKJA** was founded by Moorish exiles from the Adrar, who planted the *palmeraies* for which it's still famous. In common with several other towns in this area, the sprawling mess of Tidjikja is split by a sizeable **wadi**, which runs wet for a few days at most each year. On the southwest side of the town, where you arrive, are most of the modern administrative blocks. After something of a tourist "boom" in the 1970s (dozens every year, before the banning of alcohol), Tidjikja doesn't expect many *Nsarani* visitors any more.

The interest, though, lies up the slope on the northeast bank of the wadi, a fifteen-minute walk away, where the old city surrounds the Friday mosque, with palm groves and a jumble of houses spreading on either side. The **architecture** of the Tagant region is clear to see here, even if many of the houses appear unoccupied – and many are falling apart. Most are in fact owned by somebody. **The houses**, massively constructed out of dressed stone, cemented with clay, sometimes clad in clay, with flat roofs and palm-trunk waterspouts to drain storm water, display the ornamental *kefya* – triangular niches – that can be seen in various forms right across the Sahelian belt. Rooms are narrow, owing to the lack of long, strong beams, and focus inwards on interior courtyards.

As for **accommodation**, there are no commercial lodgings in Tidjikja, but police and drivers will help. There's a bank of sorts, a PTT, market, shops, a smart new Kuwaiti-built hospital, fuel, kids aplenty and a lake where nobody swims because they drown.

On to Rachid

The caravan route **from the Tagant to the Adrar** – a journey of 470km from Tidjikja to Atar – is still viable but best undertaken with high clearance vehicles (two in preference). Guides are essential. It's easier to go in this direction than the reverse, because you're travelling "with the sand".

RACHID you can visit more easily – it's only 35km north of Tidjikja. Four-wheel-drive vehicles can be hired in Tidjikja for UM5000 a day, and it might even be possible to hire a camel. Rachid, perched high on the west side of the wadi, is an eighteenth-century Kounta Bedouin citadel, from where piratical tradesmen would prey on the

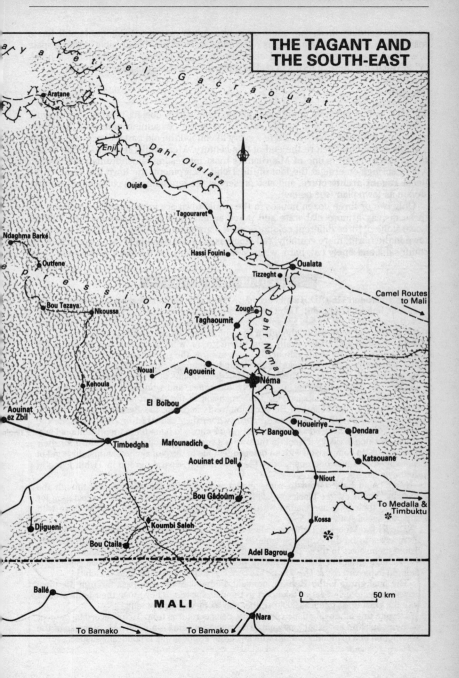

THE TAGANT AND
THE SOUTH-EAST

caravans wending their way south from the Adrar massif to Tidjikja. It still has a magnificent, dense *palmeraie* and is referred to as Tidjikja's "beauty spot". After a spate of visitors they're getting excited about tourism and talking about building a hotel. What you'll find there in terms of real facilities is uncertain. Most likely nothing.

Tichit

TICHIT, too, is radically unprepared for tourism, which doesn't prevent them having piles of gear ready to sell, just in case. Such is the consuming nature of the dunes swamping the town, however, there's every likelihood the old part will cease to exist as a viable community before the end of this century. Meanwhile, if you have the means to get there, Tichit is one of Mauritania's most interesting sites: dramatically located where springs emerge at the foot of the Tichit escarpment, the town has some of the finest **Tagant architecture**, and also preserves the remnants of a complex ethnic division in its town plan (see below).

Only two or three dozen houses in the whole town are in reasonable condition, but these display a more elaborate and purer architecture than what's seen in Tidjikja. Local stone of three different colours is used – greenish stone for the Chorfa quarter of town in the north; more crumbly, red stone used in the ruinous Masena quarter on the south side; and finely cut, hard, white stone, used only for the most prestigious build-

---

PEOPLE OF TICHIT

Founded around 1150 AD, Tichit once had a population variously estimated at between six and one hundred thousand. Tichit's people now number about 500, as more families leave each year, and more houses are smothered by the sand. But the basic ethnic divisions are still visible, and encapsulate, though in an atypical way, the complexity of Mauritania.

The biggest and economically most active group, who call themselves **Masena**, are concentrated on the south side of the town, towards the modern administrative quarter. The Masena traditionally speak Aser, a Mande language closely related to the Soninke spoken in eastern Senegal. They're probably descendants of the black peoples who lived all over the Sahara in earlier, more propitious times, and who were pushed south into oases like Tichit (and Oualata) by the expansion of the desert – and by the Berbers. Masena society has absorbed Berber immigrants and, like the Berber Tuareg, wealthy Masena families still keep slaves (*captifs*), whom they call **Abid** or **Bella**. Despite the formal freeing of the slaves in 1980, most *captifs* chose to hang on to their traditional way of life, working six days a week in the owner's gardens or household, in return for their basic needs. In comparison with an independent life in the Nouakchott slums, this kind of captivity seems less onerous. Today the Abid form a separate group in Tichit, living in their own quarter.

Many Abid have mixed to some extent with Tichit's **Haratin** Moors, though the Haratins' status as free black ex-slaves is much longer established. Their reputation for piety and their long association with the Bidan Moors continues to endow them with superior social status.

The **Bidan** Moors in Tichit are called **Chorfa** – from *Sharif*, those families who believe themselves to be direct descendants of the prophet. Arabised Berbers who had established themselves in these parts by the ninth century, the Chorfa were originally part of the **Zenaga** group of Berber-speaking peoples from whose name the word Senegal is thought to have derived. The Chorfa are concentrated on the north side of Tichit.

The final group is the **Rehian**, nomadic Bedouin Arabs who pass through the town occasionally, to sell meat or take part in the date harvest. They move their tents around with the grazing, as much as 200km either way along the escarpment.

Despite this ethno-linguistic complexity, census returns from Tichit record 99 percent of the population as "Moor", meaning Hassaniya-speaking – a reflection, perhaps, of the assumption that to identify oneself with any other ethnic group is politically suspect.

ings. The *kefya* ornamental niches are intricate, and the doors of a few of the old residences are still marvellously solid, with heavy, hob-nailed bolts and latches made of wood from Mali. Sadly the skills necessary to maintain the buildings are fading, and few people are prepared to make the investment of time and energy. The red clay that was once used to plaster interior walls is hardly ever seen today, and only the mosque is regularly repaired.

The best time to be in Tichit, if you can bear the heat, is shortly before or during the July **date harvest**. The palm groves extend south of the town, between the houses and the ancient lake bed of Aoukar. Until about 1000 BC this was a vast reed-covered lake of some 50,000 square kilometres, supporting a large population of farmers, hunters and fishers on its shores. Today, the surface near the town is encrusted with **salt** which blows into the palm groves and coats the dates, making them inedible – and so the people of Tichit spend the last two months of the ripening season painstakingly washing the crop with well-water. The consequent joy and relief of the actual harvest make Tichit one of the best places to be at that time – even if the district, though reliant on the crop, isn't famous for dates in the same way that Tidjikja is.

Travel practicalities

If you're **driving to Tichit**, you **must take a guide**: heading out of Tidjikja, the route is clear enough to the Rehian stronghold of LECKCHEB (a few windblown huts, some tents and a military post), but then the *piste* deteriorates. To the west of Tichit, the line of cliffs peters out and there's a waste of dunes in which to get stuck and lost. Eventually the track descends to the prehistoric lake floor of the **Aoukar depression**, where it winds along the base of the scarp.

Alternatives to your own 4WD vehicle are chancy. Getting a lift from Tidjikja isn't likely, except possibly after the plane from Nouakchott arrives on a Tuesday. And hiring a vehicle for this expedition is an expensive business, even in a group – allow up to UM20,000, but bargain furiously. *Air Mauritanie* has ceased operating scheduled flights to Tichit, but at the prices you're liable to pay for surface transport, it would be worth enquiring about a chartered continuation of the Tuesday Nouakchott–Tidjikja flight. Obviously, you've every chance of getting stranded in Tichit, unless you go there by 4WD vehicle. You couldn't ask for much more adventure.

Unless, that is, you're determined to go further and make a full circle by taking on the three days and 400km of *piste*-driving **from Tichit to Oualata** (see below). This represents a major desert crossing, and the police in Tichit will make sure you take a guide. The *piste* follows the old caravan route around the Tichit and Oualata escarpments, with good wells at fairly regular intervals – Toujinet, Aratâne, Oujaf, Tagourâret, Hâssi Fouîni. The *piste* is mostly sandy, occasionally ascending the scarp to a kind of "Lost World" scene on top. You're unlikely to see other vehicles along the way and there are barely any wrecks to indicate much traffic in the past.

A less daunting forty-kilometre run east of Tichit leads to the nearly deserted and sand-swamped ruins of AGRIJIT – showing what Tichit itself is doomed to become.

The Far Southeast

East of the Route de l'Espoir's high point on the Tagant plateau – the Passe de Djouk – is the scrappy administrative town of KIFFA, where you can stay at the Peace Corps *Maison de Passage*. Deviating northeastwards from here, there's 120km of *piste* to another post, TAMCHEKKET (transport most days), enticing only if archaeological dedication drives you to find the ruins of **Aoudaghost** (see overleaf), poking from the rocky ground in the **Massif du Rkiz**, some 40km further east. This is one for motorised travellers only.

AOUDAGHOST AND GHANA

Aoudaghost (modern name Tegdaoust) was formerly a great trans-Saharan trade city on the edge of what was then grassland. Its inhabitants were probably speakers of a Mande language like Soninke. From perhaps 500 BC, caravans of horses and bullocks were arriving from Marrakech and the Roman Empire's Mediterranean shores. By the third century AD, the domestication of the **camel** had improved the viability of the trans-Saharan trade and Aoudaghost flourished on the commerce through most of the first millennium AD, in later years repulsing Berber Almoravid attempts to subjugate and convert it to Islam. The rapidly expanding empire of Ghana – focused on Oualata and Koumbi Saleh – captured the town around 1050, but within a decade Ghana's Muslim western neighbour, **Tekrur**, had helped the Berber Almoravids to invade and convert Ghana. By early in the twelfth century, the Berbers were leaving again, and over the next century both Tekrur and Ghana were swallowed by the mightier empire of Mali to the east. Aoudaghost was rebuilt in the sixteenth and seventeeth centuries, and then definitively deserted. Today, it's only as interesting as the most recent excavations, and not easily visited (because so hard to find), unless a dig is in progress.

Ayoun el Atrous

Little **AYOUN EL ATROUS** is a more interesting town than most others along the road, and buildings of dressed sandstone plus a nice UM1200-a-night hotel (the *Ayoun*) make it an attractive place to stop. If the sand-sweepers on the highway have been doing their stuff, you might just do the drive from Nouakchott in one dawn-till-late day; public transport takes two days over the 800-odd kilometres. If you're into collecting old trade beads, you'll enjoy Ayoun's **market**. The first of the three principal *pistes* to Mali starts at Ayoun, a two-day trip to Bamako by *taxi brousse*.

Timbedgha and Koumbi Saleh

If you're bent on visiting the ruins of Koumbi Saleh, and can find someone who knows exactly where they are, press on to TIMBEDGHA (Timbedra) and aim for the Malian town of Nara from there.

The site is some 50km from Timbedgha, close to the main route, and there seems to be a good chance of getting there by ordinary *taxi brousse* bound for the border, as long as you're prepared to pay a little extra for the diversion.

KOUMBI SALEH, the putative capital of the Ghana empire, is the most important medieval site in West Africa, and the archaeologists have barely scratched its huge extent. The town is estimated to have had a population of about 30,000, which would have made it one of the largest cities in the world at the time. The Arab geographer Al-Bakri, writing in 1067, described a conurbation of two towns, a northern one with twelve mosques, and, 10km to the south, the royal town of **al-Ghala**, with huts arranged concentrically around a palace. Between the two, along the royal road, was a continuous "suburb" of houses. Curiously, although traces of the royal part of Koumbi Saleh have been found, the royal quarter doesn't appear to have been constructed in stone. The main part of town is more impressive, successive excavations having uncovered massive stone houses, an enormous mosque and flagstone floors covering a more ancient layer of buildings.

Néma and Oualata

The *transmauritanienne* ends with a whimper at **NÉMA**, where the architecture – stone clad with clay – intimates that of Oualata, 90km north. Vegetable gardens, like Ayoun's, prettify Néma at the end of the brief rainy season, but for some reason hospitality here tends to be perfunctory. If you have your own 4WD vehicle, a guide can be

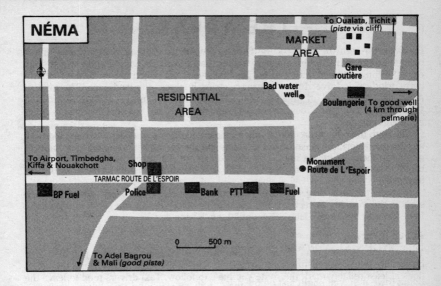

NÉMA

MARKET AREA

To Oualata, Tichit
(piste via cliff)

Gare routière

Bad water well

RESIDENTIAL AREA

Boulangerie To good well
(4 km through palmerie)

To Airport, Timbedgha, Kiffa & Nouakchott

Shop

TARMAC ROUTE DE L'ESPOIR

Monument
Route de L'Espoir

BP Fuel   Police   Bank PTT   Fuel

0   500 m

To Adel Bagrou
& Mali *(good piste)*

hired for the deep desert drive from Néma to Tidjikja (4–5 days), and right up to Chinguetti (10 days) for around UM20,000–25,000 plus UM2–3000 for his travel costs home again. A quarter of the fee is payable up front to his family.

There are fairly frequent vehicles to **OUALATA**, though not every day. Best chances are on **Sunday** (when the plane comes up from Ayoun el Atrous to Néma, and returns to Nouakchott), **Friday**, when the Nouakchott–Ayoun flight is sometimes extended to Néma, or **Wednesday**, when it usually lands at Nioro in Mali, en route to Bamako. If you're in Néma by mid-morning on one of these days, you may strike lucky with vehicles passing through to Oualata.

Oualata's superficial glamour comes from the amazingly beautiful bas-relief **ornamentation** of its house walls. The decorations, of gypsum, white and red clay, and indigo, are designed and applied by the women, and although they're all unique, personal works, they share certain motifs and a thorough-going exuberance. The old town is partly abandoned and fewer and fewer households bother with decorating outside. Inside the houses, if you get the opportunity to look, the effects created can be stunning. Oualata's **doors** are highly stylised as well – the best ones studded with copper and silver.

Oualata's past is a fairly glorious one, and its present momentum as a viable community rests on its worldwide eminence as a centre of **Islamic scholarship**, the basis of long-term rivalry with Timbuktu. There are only twenty places in its Koranic school, creating a permanent waiting list of anything up to ten years. Less illustriously, Oualata, like Tichit, is also known as a place of internal exile, where outspoken political dissidents are detained.

You don't just show up in Oualata and wander around. Much as you'll have come to expect, a **visit to the police** is important, more so here than elsewhere. The Oualatans don't take kindly to Land-Rovies using their town as a photo backdrop, but allow some time for introductions and tea-drinking, and a day or two here can be rewarding. Such formalities are necessary, in any case, if you want somewhere to stay.

THE ADRAR

Breaking through the sands of the Sahara, the **Adrar Plateau** is Mauritania's most outstanding region. Though nowhere higher than 1000m, the gaunt, multi-brown scenery is strikingly clawed into deep **gorges** and sheer, cliff-edged mesas. In the southern parts, wind-carried **live dunes** stream ceaselessly across the landscape. The town of **Atar**, plus a handful of villages, and the ancient settlements of **Chinguetti** and **Ouadane**, account for almost all the population; camels and oases of date palms determine the economy.

Although the options are fairly limited unless you devote considerable time, the wildness of the desert, the isolation of the towns and the somewhat precarious feasibility of getting to them, make it a rewarding area to explore. The ubiquity of **neolithic stone tools** – some of them remarkably small and beautiful – adds further, acquisitive interest.

If you're taking a *Peugeot* taxi to Atar from Nouakchott's *autogare*, get to the Ksar early in the morning to secure a seat, preferably before dawn; you could otherwise be forced to wait until much later, even until the following day.

The route to Atar

Though the tarmac road **from Nouakchott to Akjoujt** is badly potholed and repeatedly sand-covered (the only scenery of note is plentiful, snowy white dunes), it does at least reliably mark the route you have to follow. Taxi drivers tend to leave the road for their own, sandy deviations, or else drive with two wheels on the tarmac and two in the sand. They normally take about five hours to Akjoujt, with a tea, pee, and prayer stop at BOU RJEIMAT en route. Careful motorists might need eight hours or more to get there.

After 250km of empty desert, **AKJOUJT** is a frightful place. Constructed in 1949, this artificial town is even more desolate now that it has ceased to be a copper-mining centre, which at least gave it a veneer of prosperity during the 1970s. The "technical reasons" blustered for the failure turned out to be simply the depletion of what little ore was worth digging. Old mud-brick buildings mix with newer miners' housing in desert-utilitarian style. Around the main *place* you'll find a scattering of barely awake shops and eating houses which service a few dozen people a day. They always have fuel.

Beyond Akjoujt, which signals the end of the tamac, the **piste** varies from firm gravel and rocks to swervy sand, rapidly obliterated in the wind. If you become lost, the low relief to the north, from where the wind usually prevails, can make for more excitement than you really want as other wheel marks are quickly erased. About 130km from Akjoujt the landscape begins to fracture, and you're soon climbing gently on the redefined track, with the village of AIN AHEL ET TAYA a stony rest stop at the edge of the plateau.

If you are driving, you could check out the reasonably accessible **springs** at TERJIT, 12km from the main route, signposted about 5km before Ain Ahel Et Taya. A hot spring and several cool ones water a tight little oasis of exceptional beauty, crouching like moss between the cliffs.

Continue a tough 35km further south and you come to OUJEFT – another very lush oasis. Like many localities in the Adrar, Oujeft harbours archaeological and palaeontological relics: there's a gigantic human footprint impressed in a mudstone rock nearby (the Peace Corps volunteer should be able to tell you where it is). It's difficult, however, to get down this route without your own 4WD; occasional vehicles make the trip from Atar.

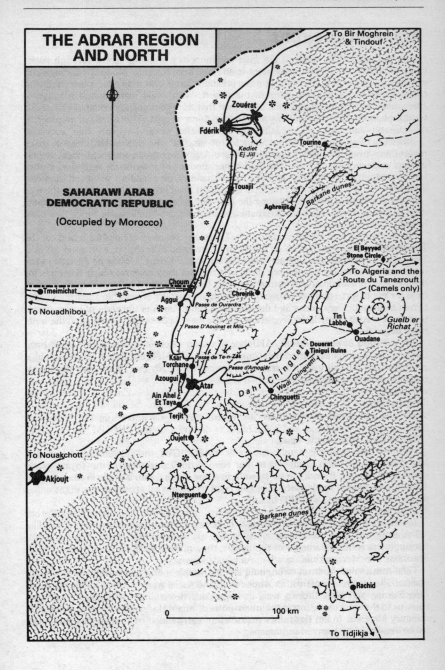

THE ADRAR REGION AND NORTH

To Bir Moghrein & Tindouf

SAHARAWI ARAB DEMOCRATIC REPUBLIC

(Occupied by Morocco)

Zouérat

Fdérik

Kediet Ej Jill

Tourine

Touajil

Aghreijit

Barkane dunes

El Beyyed Stone Circle

To Algeria and the Route du Tanezrouft (Camels only)

Choum

To Tmeimichat

To Nouadhibou

Aggui

Passe de Ourardra

Chreirik

Passe D'Aouinat et Mlis

Tin Labbe

Guelb er Richat

Ksar Torchane

Passe de Te-n-Zak

Azougui

Passe d'Amogjâr

Atar

Dahr Chinguetti

Douerat Tinigui Ruins

Ouadane

Ain Ahel Et Taya

Terjit

Wadi Chinguetti

Chinguetti

Oujeft

To Nouakchott

Akjoujt

Nterguent

Barkane dunes

0   100 km

Rachid

To Tidjikja

Atar and environs

From the edge of the plateau the road commences a winding ascent through rocky hills to **ATAR**, the largest settlement in the northern interior. Modern buildings and offices are fairly few, but this is a surprisingly large and energetic place, drawing business from the deepest parts of the desert. With lively markets and a fringe of *palmeraies* and irrigated gardens, it's a town that travellers quickly come to like, and a really pleasant base for looking around the Adrar region. There's a fair number of shops and *boutiques*, all focusing on the market area, but only one specialist leather-working shop. A whole *quartier* of smiths (the Maalemine caste) make everything from jewellery to saddle fittings. Atar's reputation for handicrafts at first seems exaggerated, but you can find a fair amount of interesting stuff if you nose around. Much of it – Moorish clothing, camel saddles, pipe holders, belts and sandals – is designed and manufactured for local use. Apart from browsing, the standard thing to do is take a walk before sunset along the dike that separates the town from the gardens and *palmeraie* and holds back the rushing waters of the Séguélil wadi, which flow once a year at most.

Arrivals into Atar are often after dark. There are two main options for a **bed** for the night. One is the newish *Hôtel de Marie*, in a converted French fort, with good AC S/C rooms at UM2500/3000. The alternative is the Peace Corps' *Maison de Passage* in the older part of town, across the big main square from the *autogare*, which has rates for non-volunteer travellers, and normally gives a happy welcome, as long as there's room. If you elect to go to the hotel, beware the common mistake of marching into the nearby French Army officers' mess and demanding a room. Such is the state of international relations in Atar, some local people assume the mess is the "white" hotel, and the hotel the "black" one.

In the **food** line, you'll find a number of cheap eateries in the older part of town where a bowl of rice and dried fish comes for around UM80, and camel steak and chips for under UM200. Try the *Moderne*. Fix your price in advance; some establishments will take advantage otherwise.

Around Atar

Ten kilometres east of Atar there are **stone circles** (volunteers at the *Maison de Passage* may have details), and 20km north of the town, on the CHOUM road, is KSAR TORCHANE, an attractive oasis.

But the best local trip is up to the ruins of **AZOUGUI**, the old Almoravid capital of the Adrar, about 15km northwest of Atar beyond the Tarazi pass, in the Tayaret wadi. During the winter, it's not too far to **walk** in a day if you fix up a guide in Atar, though unless you make a really early start you need to reckon on spending the night under the stars. Otherwise, it's a 4WD trip.

Azougui (the Azokka of medieval Arab writers) was the eleventh-century Berber base from which the Almoravid jihadists launched raids on the Ghana empire satellite of Aoudaghost, and the Ghana cities of Oualata and Koumbi Saleh. Having swept through the southern fringes of the desert, they turned north for their second great invasion, into Morocco and decadent Andalusian Iberia.

The remains of the main stronghold are still visible today, a relatively small **citadel** (about 50 metres square) within whose walls the social framework of medieval southern Europe and North Africa was, in large part, determined. A couple of hundred metres to the west of the fort is the **necropolis** of Imam Hadrami – one of the eleventh-century jihadists. Imam Hadrami's mausoleum, surrounded by tombstones, continues to be venerated by many Mauritanians.

Chinguetti, Ouadane and beyond

Chinguetti is probably the single most visited site in the country, though tourists in the broadest sense are still counted in handfuls each month. In itself, the town's mosque and jealously guarded library hardly add up to a compelling draw, yet the town does have picturesque qualities and the journey, through a landscape stripped to essentials, is emphatically worthwhile. **Ouadane**, possibly more interesting, bears comparison with Tichit in its remoteness. Neither is particularly easy to get to, and the upper *piste* to Ouadane reportedly still harbours Polisario mines.

The route from Atar

Occasional **supply trucks** do trudge through the sand and up the passes from Atar to Chinguetti, but their departures are barely advertised and by no means regular. More likely a lift will come from one of the battered **Land Rovers** that whirl around Atar. If you join a vehicle that's making the trip, the fare will be around UM1000, depending on whether you sit in the cab or bounce in the back. If you hire a vehicle to get you there and back, allow up to UM10,000, returning the next day; you're best advised to take along someone who knows the route, as several sections are hard to follow – there'll be no shortage of demand for a free lift.

There are two alternatives, with the new "road" following a less scenic but safer and more direct course. The **old route** runs first through flat, grey rock and sand, then for several kilometres past high, yellow dunes above a *palmeraie* tucked into a wadi, then between high, dry mesas and finally in a steeply twisting series of hairpins to the head of the Amogjar wadi, a gorge which gives out to a further incline and the **Amogjar Pass**. It's common practice to get out and walk the steepest ascents and descents: don't hesitate to ask the driver to stop. Among the sandstone massifs you can see gun emplacements and the remains of military posts from the Polisario war. Up at the top squats the incongruous shell of the fake "Fort Sagane", built for the movie of that name in 1985.

Rock paintings – and lizards

Up at around 800m, a couple of kilometres after the final climb, you pass a conical rock stack on the left, fifty metres or so in height. Under an overhang near the top of the stack there are some intriguing **rock paintings** (*gravures rupestres/les dessins*), not hard to find even unguided. While they're not up to Algerian or southern African standards in terms of size or confidence of execution, and give little more than hints about the people who sketched them, they're worth stopping for, and photographing. There are several red-coloured lanky figures, though it's not possible to make out the animals that some books refer to. The curious circular design on the left, with its four inner circles and radiating strokes, looks like Von Daniken spaceship material – but the Paris–Dakar rally has passed this way, so it's perhaps unwise to assume authenticity.

More figures are to be found on rocks directly by the road, on the right, about 6km further on, but these have been disfigured by Arabic graffiti. The figures are different from those on the hill: the frog-like heads (or headdresses) and massive thighs, could mean anything, though several resemble pygmies most of all. Thousands of examples of such rock art exist in the Adrar: only those near the roads have been seen, or disturbed, by outsiders.

The road now levels out and ploughs once again through soft sand. Look out for the heavily built, tortoise-headed, half-metre-long black Dhub (or Dhab) **lizards**, which scamper into their holes and crevices as you pass. Harmless vegetarians, they subsist between rainfalls by drawing on reserves of fat in their spiky, club-like tails, which they use to guard their tunnels. If you find yourself with an hour or so in the desert, they adore the colour yellow, and bananas send them . . .

Chinguetti

The route passes the turning for the upper route to Ouadane, 10km before entering the "modern quarter" of **CHINGUETTI**. On this side of the town, the main building – in fact Chinguetti's most striking – is the abandoned Foreign Legion **fortress**, used in the movie *Fort Sagane*, about the Legion's exploits in Algeria. The fort doubled as set and film crew accommodation, and the air-conditioning and other facilities they installed made it the best hotel outside Nouakchott for a while. All is now deserted, but you can still climb onto the ramparts for fine views across the town (beware some very fragile sections). Other notable buildings on this side of town are the Gendarmerie, where you should check in on arrival, a Polisario-shot-up generator house hard by (electricity may have been restored by now) and a defunct solar water pump.

The oldest parts of the town lie across the broad football-kicked and goat-trailed wadi to the south, and to the west, where you'll also find the official **accommodation**. Ask for the *Maison de Bien Être*, where you'll get a basic spot to set down for the night for about UM500. **Eating** in Chinguetti is a matter of luck in the market, and one or two perfunctory shops. There seem to be no eating houses, but you will find cold cokes at one or two *boutiques* with fridges.

Chinguetti's most venerable quarter, on the west side, dates from at least the thirteenth century. The town was established rather quickly, by exiles from the oasis of ABWEIR, just 4km down the wadi. Most of the buildings are made of stone, including the fine old **mosque**, off-limits to Nazarenes. Fortunately you can still get good views of it – complete with the five ostrich eggs atop its squat minaret and much of the interior courtyard – from surrounding dunes and piles of rubble. The "donnez-moi un cadeau" brigade are out in some force in the neighbourhood, but will show you to the *Maison de Bien Être* and the main **Koranic library**. The latter has been the object of some conservation work, and the most prized manuscripts are now contained in filing cabinets, opened only on payment of rather large sums. Families round about may have kept some of their own documentary heirlooms, and it's worth asking if you're interested. Chinguetti is the most venerated city in Mauritania, and was once rated as one of Islam's holiest cities, along with Jerusalem, Mecca and Medina.

Relics of a much more ancient history can be bought in the **market**. Extraordinarily fine **flint arrow heads** seem to be two a penny, as do the **barbs** that may have been used for fishing in a long-ago Adrar of forests and streams. They are apparently collected by children in the dunes. Weightier implements – beautifully shaped and much-worn cleavers and scrapers, for butchering meat and preparing skins – also appear occasionally. But they too are curiously small, and must have been used by small hands.

To Ouadane

The main route **to Ouadane** branches off the Atar–Chinguetti road, 12km outsaide Chinguetti, and most transport there will call at Chinguetti first. But Ouadane-bound vehicles are few, so unless you've loads of time you're best advised to get a lift that's coming back again. The southern route to Ouadane, marked on the *IGN* map of Mauritania, is a sandy, wadi-course for high-clearance 4WDs only – but recently favoured after the discovery of mines on the other. If you're driving, neither route should be undertaken without a local guide.

Ouadane

OUADANE is a town of stones camouflaged in a landscape of stones. The place is quite extraordinary, collapsing in ruins amid the jumble of rocks from which it was constructed eight hundred years ago. So complete is the chaos that, arriving in the middle of the day, with no shadows to define the buildings, you don't even notice them stacked along the steep scarp until you're almost among them. Modern Ouadane – not a lot of it – perches above, on the plateau's edge. There was a rest house some years ago, but it's fallen into disuse, and you'll probably have to rely on hospitality, or maybe camp in the *palmeraie* beneath the town.

Ouadane was founded in the twelfth century by **Berbers** of the Ida-u-el-Hadj tribe, and some of the present-day inhabitants still speak Berber rather than Hassaniya Arabic. Its huge reputation as a **caravan crossroads** and trading centre for gold, salt and dates – secure beyond the limits of the West African empires – lasted nearly four hundred years. There was even a **Portuguese trading post** here at the end of the fifteenth century, busily intercepting the trade for the main Portuguese base on the coast at Arguin island. Ouadane's fortunes waned, unevenly, as it succumbed first to the onslaught of the sixteenth-century Saadian prince, Ahmed el Mansour of Morocco, who took control of the trans-Saharan trade and diluted much of the town's influence, and then lost its remaining economic power when the Alaouites invaded, also from the north, two centuries later.

Tin Labbé

Only 7km northwest of Ouadane, on the *piste* that curls round the mountain of Guelb er Richat, lies the semi-troglodyte village of **TIN LABBÉ**, where natural rock shelters and crevices have been incorporated into the cluster of stone and mud houses. If you've made it all the way to Ouadane, it would seem a shame not to walk up the wadi to see it. Among the tumble of huge boulders down by the vegetable gardens you can find more rock paintings, and writing too, both in Arabic script and in the archaic Tifinar script of the Tuareg, a writing that traces its roots to a Libyan alphabet of the fourth century BC.

THE NORTH

For travellers flying in from Europe, **Nouadhibou** comes as an unlikely first taste of West Africa, and it's not a place on which to base any firm ideas of the region. Coming from the south, only a perverse determination to set foot in the northernmost corner of West Africa could really provide motivation for heading so far out of the way. But the immensely long iron ore trains that rumble daily between the mines at **Zouérat** and the coast do at least offer a straightforward way of getting to Mauritania's second city, which has no road connections with the rest of the country. And if you're in the Adrar region, with a few days in hand before returning to Nouakchott, you can make a satisfyingly complete circuit either by flying from Nouadhibou to Nouakchott, or by joining a truck convoy along the sandy *piste* that follows the coast.

The Ore Train

One or more trains go from ZOUÉRAT to Nouadhibou every day, the most convenient one passing through Choum, on the border of Western Sahara, at about 5.30–6pm. Two others may come through late at night, or early morning. All of them are **iron ore trains**, carrying thousands of tons of crushed rock in a chain of wagons up to three kilometres long. Their schedules and frequencies depend partly on the speed of extraction at the mines, and on unpredictable hold-ups – damaged rails, engine failure and even, in the past, attacks by Polisario guerrillas from over the border.

The Choum taxi drivers in Atar keep abreast of the news and will get you to the train on time. If you're driving yourself, there is the possibility of loading your vehicle aboard, but **at the railhead**, not at Choum. Before setting off, buy food for the journey, and take as much fresh water as you can – supplies on the train vary from limited to non-existent.

Daily taxis run **from Atar to Choum** in four or five hours, a fine trip with beautiful scenery much of the way. There's a habitual tea stop halfway, a cool and friendly place of massive rocky outcroppings where camels are watered.

Choum and onwards

CHOUM consists of a string of restaurants and crash-out houses where passengers snooze through the afternoon, waiting for the train's arrival. Leave your bags in the taxi: you'll be driven alongside the train when it arrives, to meet the passenger wagon. Only the middle of the train actually stops at Choum and it often sets off again within minutes. The fare in the passenger wagon is around UM500, with a supplement for a fold-down bunk. Riding on the ore wagons is free – and you'll discover why, as the dust works its way into your soul. If you do go for this option, take a *houli* to wrap round your head, and have something warm for later in the night, when it can get remarkably cool.

The journey generally passes without incident these days, and there are no police checks. Restful dune scenery accompanies the trip for the last hour or two of daylight. There's generally one stop at TMEIMICHATT (or *trois cents dix neuf* – kilometre post 319), to allow the empty train going the other way to pass. If you pick the right compartment you can find yourself sharing endless cups of tea and learning Fula or Hassaniya. At this point the interest outside the carriage, even on a clear moonlit night, is nil, and daylight brings no improvement, except hints of the sea as you approach the Nouadhibou peninsula. The usual journey time is around fourteen hours.

Nouadhibou and the Cap Blanc peninsula

Arriving by train, the chain of wagons finally stops at PORT MINÉRALIER, a full half-hour after passing through Nouadhibou itself. Peugeot *camionettes* clamour to take you back into town. On the way, you stop for the gendarmerie outside the dockers' lifeless dormitory town of CANSADO, and then the police at the entrance to Nouadhibou. The gendarmes can be difficult, so be prepared for a hostile reception. They're closed from noon to 3pm, but don't let them keep your passport: tell them you'll return in the afternoon.

Arriving by air, the airport (no facilities) is a twenty-minute walk, or a UM40 taxi ride, to the town centre. Leaving Nouadhibou, most days there are two *Air Mauritanie flights* to Nouakchott (UM5000). Or if you want to go north, check out *Iberia's* flights to the Canary Isles and Spain; their office is in boulevard Median (☎45 255).

The landscape roundabouts is lunar, the peninsula a finger of desert pointing into the sea. **NOUADHIBOU** (Jackals' Well) is fittingly colourless, a pale, flat, industrial city-satellite of Mauritania, where bars are permitted (or rather, alcohol is blind-eyed) and the mix on the streets is heavily European, Oriental, and Mediterranean. Nouadhibou's wealth, and purpose, come not just from shipping iron ore, but also from **fishing**, with Japanese and Korean fleets especially active. The southward sweep of the chill Canary current makes the waters here among the best fishing grounds in the world. Foreign fishing vessels are obliged to land and process a percentage of their catch in Mauritania.

The problem in Nouadhibou is **where to stay**. Unlike Nouakchott there are *no* cheap hotels. The *Sabah*, on the north side of town near the airport, is, like the same-named hotel on the beach at Nouakchott, expensive and uninspiring (BP 285; ☎2377, telex 508; UM3500/4000). The *Hôtel des Imraguens* (BP 160; ☎2180/2272) is even costlier. Failing these, you're pretty much down to hooking up with residents of the city or seeking suitable shade for your tent.

The **supermarket** opposite the police often has a wide selection of imports. Food, otherwise, is hit and miss – local fish can be frustratingly unavailable and the selection of produce in the market is meagre. But there is a fair number of cheap **restaurants** near the modern market. A place worth highlighting is *La Cabana*, run by charming Algerians down by the Port de Pêche Moderne. Prices aren't the cheapest, at UM300–600, but the food is excellent – fish, *frites*, salads and homemade ice cream. Get there from the town centre by going south under Nouadhibou's main street archway, then turning left after a couple of blocks and continuing to the wharf, where you turn left again and walk for five minutes. The proprietors can fill you in on what's happening in Nouadhibou, though it's only fair to say that the town's reputation as a slightly Bogartian port of call is exaggerated.

Beaches and other interesting things

More positively, there are wonderful **beaches** on both sides of the peninsula. **LA GOUERA** (Laguéra, La Guera), a run-down Spanish fishing town almost swamped by sand, is technically part of Western Sahara, but is now administered by Mauritania – a head-scratching arrangement that applies to the whole west side of the peninsula. Apart from a police post on the road, there's no *contrôle*. Flaking whitewash and collapsed houses are

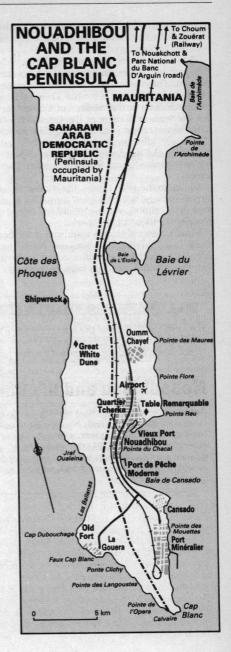

NOUADHIBOU AND THE CAP BLANC PENINSULA

↑ To Choum & Zouérat (Railway)

To Nouakchott & Parc National du Banc D'Arguin (road)

MAURITANIA

Baie de l'Archimède

SAHARAWI ARAB DEMOCRATIC REPUBLIC (Peninsula occupied by Mauritania)

Pointe de l'Archimède

Côte des Phoques

Baie de L'Étoile

Baie du Lévrier

Shipwreck

Oumm Chayef — Pointe des Maures

♦Great White Dune

Pointe Flore

Airport ✈

Quartier Tcherka

Table Remarquable

Pointe Reu

Vieux Port Nouadhibou
Pointe du Chacal

Jraf Oualeina

Port de Pêche Moderne
Baie de Cansado

Cansado

Les Ballenas

Pointe des Mouettes

Port Minéralier

Cap Dubouchage

Old Fort

La Gouera

Faux Cap Blanc

Ponte Clichy

Pointe des Langoustes

0   5 km

Pointe de l'Opera

Cap Blanc

Calvaire

the main sights, but there's good swimming here in the sheltered bay behind **Faux Cap Blanc**. With perseverance, you might even find a room in La Gouera, but there are no commercial lodgings.

Three kilometres due north is the dune-backed bay of **Las Ballenas**, which may still harbour a breeding colony of very rare Mediterranean **monk seals** (*phoques moines*). They look something like young elephant seals, and the males grow to over two-and-a-half metres in length. Their valuable oil and skin has almost certainly led to their extinction further south, but hunting them is now forbidden. You're most likely to see the seals at the bay of Las Cuevecillas (La Baie des Phoques). Northwards from here the west coast is mostly rough and rocky, with cliffs.

Thirteen kilometres from Nouadhibou, on the **east side** of the peninsula, there's delightful, sheltered swimming in the almost enclosed **Baie de l'Étoile**. There's an *Air Afrique*-operated game fishing lodge here, where you could presumably get a drink or a meal.

Closer to the town centre, the wind-sculpted *table remarquable*, just east of the main airport runway, is a geological formation worth investigation (if you can get to it). And west of the airport, you might still find traces of the **Village Canarien**, once the Canary islanders' settlement of Tcherka.

Finally, intrepid birders could call at the head office of the **Banc d'Arguin National Park** (see "Wildlife and National Parks" on p.310), located on Nouadhibou's main street. Check the possibilities out with them; but it seems even harder to get there from Nouadhibou than it is from Nouakchott.

THE IMRAGEN – LIFE IN THE DESERT WITH DOLPHINS

The Banc d'Arguin National Park contains the seven villages of the **Imragen**, an isolated group of 500 **Bedouin fishing people**. Their traditional harvest of yellow mullet is caught in November – the period when huge shoals of fish spawn amid the sea grass in the warm shallows. By a remarkable feat of human-animal cooperation, which started nobody knows when (or how), the catch is brought to shore with the assistance of dolphins. Somehow summoned by the Imragen beating the water surface, the dolphins drive the fish to the beach, where the mullet provide a feast for them and a tremendous haul for the villagers. It's an extraordinary event, a spectacular chaos of leaping fish, thrashing cetaceans and ducking fishermen. Other Imragen fishing methods are less successful: they aren't skilled boatbuilders and they only have six small vessels. Their survival on this barren shore is entirely dependent on an extractive economy, and even water has to be trucked into the villages from Nouakchott or Nouadhibou. The best windfalls are provided by ships scuppered offshore for insurance purposes. There are literally hundreds of these, providing fuel, building materials and occasionally more interesting bounty for the Imragen.

index

SENEGAL

SENEGAL

Senegal can seem more French than France. In 1658 it became the first part of West Africa to be colonised by the French, and there's an enduring relationship between the two countries: Gorée, Casamance and St-Louis are prominent names in a flourishing cultural empire whose emblems are the Paris–Dakar rally and *Gauloises* cigarettes. Partly as a result of this pervasive Europeanism, you could breeze through Senegal and hardly notice anything distinctive about it. A land of contrasts it is not, and while there's some scenic variety to be sure, at the touristic level the country is worthwhile only in parts – despite which it's the biggest holiday destination in West Africa, hauling in over two hundred thousand annually, mostly French and Germans.

But as soon as you start scraping away the French skin, a far more fascinating creature is revealed. The **Muslim marabouts** wield exceptional power in Senegal, commanding block votes at elections and even directing the course of the economy by their injunctions to followers. Although Islam in Senegal is quite different from its North African counterpart, the idea of a future Islamic state doesn't seem wholly fanciful. **Touba**, the holy city of the most powerful Muslim brotherhood, is a name you'll see everywhere.

This combination – French style and deeply felt Islam – coexists with extraordinary success, though both elements are relatively recent introductions to most of Senegal. Islam did not have a wide reach until the end of the nineteenth century, while the French, although long-established in key towns on the coast, finally subdued parts of the interior as recently as the 1920s.

Country and People

Senegal is one of the **flattest** countries in West Africa, rising to barely 500m in the Fouta Djalon foothills. Two main rivers, the Senegal and the Casamance, roughly mark the north and south limits of the country, and the southern region is sliced through by The Gambia – the result of a colonial carve-up that was seen as asinine even when it was being done in the 1890s.

The people of Senegal are dominated by the biggest language group, the **Wolof**, who figure prominently in government and business and control the Mouride brotherhood. Middle class Wolof **women,** stunningly attired in yards of shining fabric, make a sensational visual impact in Senegal's cities. A clutch of Wolof kingdoms used to cover the heart of Senegal – an area now largely under fields of all-important **groundnuts** – in a highly stratified society based on class and caste differences. But it was the **Tukulor** and closely related **Fula** – people whose kingdom was in the northeast – who were Senegal's first Muslims. The **Mandinka**, too, were widely converted to Islam before the Wolof. In the southwest, the **Serer** (Sérère) and **Jola** resisted Islam until the twentieth century – in parts still do – and maintained more egalitarian, clan-based societies than the Wolof or the Muslim peoples. Christian missions have had a limited impact.

Today, most language groups are increasingly subject to **"Wolofisation"** and a national Senegalese identity is emerging as people move to Dakar and other towns. More resilient have been the people of the south – the Jola and other scattered, largely non-Muslim, communities of Bassari, Bainuk, Konyagi and Jalonke.

Where to go

Senegal is easy to get around, more organised than several of its neighbours, and familiar with (and officially supportive of) **independent travel**. Recent events notwithstanding, it's also one of the freest countries in West Africa, which adds to the sense of ease in travel.

The south of Senegal, effectively screened from Dakar by The Gambia, provides the biggest attraction for travellers. The forests and mangrove creeks of the **Basse Casamance**, and some exceptional **beaches** along the short southern coastline, are what increasing numbers of people come for – these and the largely non-Muslim culture of the Jola. In the southeast, **Niokolo-Koba National Park** is one of the best game reserves in West Africa, and particularly worth the effort if you can go right beyond it into the remote southeast corner of the country.

The attractions further **north** are round the edges: that's to say along the coast or up the Senegal river. **Dakar** – probably unavoidable, definitely two-faced – is a place to enter with some caution. Yet for all its tough character, there are rewards in the city itself, and a number of good trips round about. **St-Louis** is another ambiguous case, charged with atmosphere or depressingly run down, as it strikes you. The up-river towns are small outposts along the Mauritanian border, and are more likely to figure as part of your travel plans – if the border with Mauritania re-opens – than as ends in themselves.

FACTS AND FIGURES

The Wolof have an apocryphal account of the derivation of the **name** *Senegal*, in which a witless explorer points across the Senegal river and asks some fishermen what it is called. "That's our boat" they reply – *li suñu gal le*. In fact the name probably derives from the **Sanhaja** Berbers who frequently raided the river region and were known by the early Portuguese explorers as *Azanaga*.

Today **La République du Sénégal** has a **population** of about seven million and an **area** of 196,000 square kilometres – roughly the size of England and Scotland combined. The country's **foreign debt** totals about £2.5 billion, colossal in this context but rather less than the projected cost of the now abandoned high speed rail link in southern England. Senegal's **political system** is a presidential democracy; it's the only practising multi-party democracy in West Africa, but the ruling moderate *parti socialiste* has never been defeated. Senegal's on-off **Senegambia confederation**, a political pact with the tiny country it surrounds, is currently off.

Climate

Senegal's **climate** is one of West Africa's better ones, with a short rainy season (*l'hivernage*) between June and September – or October in the south – and a period of dry weather between December and April. The winds turn with the seasons, blowing warm and humid from the southwest, then fiercely hot, dry and dusty from the northeast and the Sahara (the *harmattan*). Early in the dry season, in December and January, Dakar and St-Louis can be surprisingly cool, especially at night. Through the rains however, Dakar's combination of high humidity and city pollution can be pretty oppressive.

The weather needn't alter your travel plans as a rule, but you'll find some of the **National Parks** closed during the wet season, and sometimes remaining closed until tracks become passable.

You'll find a temperature and rainfall box on p.350.

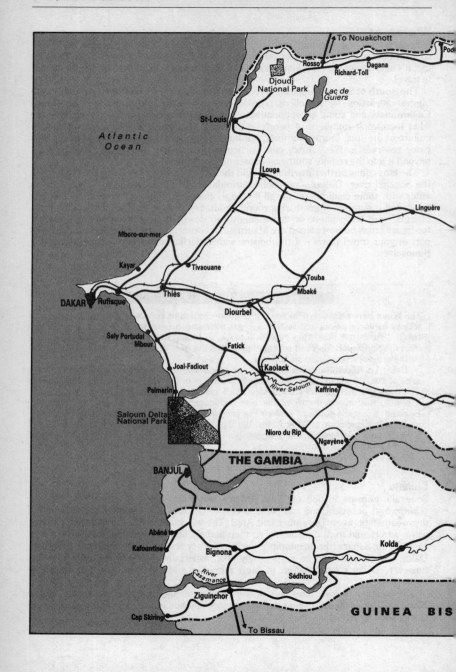

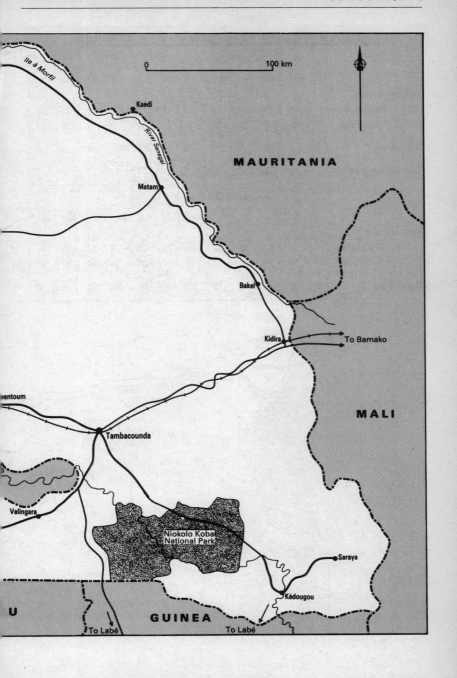

AVERAGE TEMPERATURES AND RAINFALL

DAKAR

	Jan	Feb	Mar	Apr	May	June	July	Aug	Sept	Oct	Nov	Dec
Temperatures °C												
Min (night)	18	17	18	18	20	23	24	24	24	24	23	19
Max (day)	26	27	27	27	29	31	31	31	32	32	30	27
Rainfall mm	0	0	0	0	0	18	89	254	132	38	3	8
Days with rainfall	0	0	0	0	0	2	7	13	11	3	0	1

ZIGUINCHOR

	Jan	Feb	Mar	Apr	May	June	July	Aug	Sept	Oct	Nov	Dec
Temperatures °C												
Min (night)	17	17	19	20	22	24	23	23	23	23	21	18
Max (day)	33	34	35	35	35	33	31	30	31	31	32	31
Rainfall mm	0	3	0	0	12	142	406	559	338	160	8	0

Arrivals

Dakar is a common starting and finishing post for overland travels, and in many ways the city feels like a stepping stone between Africa and the West. This section primarily gives details on getting to Senegal. For more information on getting into other countries from Senegal, refer to the "Practical Information" sections for those countries. For details of getting around Senegal, see "Getting Around" below.

■ Flights from Africa

From **North Africa** there are direct flights from Casablanca (*Royal Air Maroc, Air Afrique* and *Tunis Air*), Tunis (*Tunis Air*) and Algiers (*Air Algérie*).

There's at least one direct flight to Dakar weekly from every capital city in **West Africa**, most of the non-stop ones on *Air Afrique*. From **Banjul** in The Gambia there's a twice-daily weekday service on the *Gambia Air Shuttle*, once on Sat & Sun.

Some details about **cheap flights out of Dakar** are given in the Dakar "Directory".

■ Overland

A natural terminus on the trans-Africa and trans-Saharan routes, Dakar has for a number of years been literally the end of the road, with flying out the only onwards option. As we go to press (May 1990), Senegal is in conflict with Mauritania and not on the best of terms with The Gambia, so that some of the long-established routes that follow may prove temporarily closed or impeded.

Via the Sahara and Mauritania

Morocco would like to open the routes **across the Sahara** through Mauritania, but the route through Moroccan-held Western Sahara past **Dakhla** is closed for military and practical reasons: the Polisario are still prepared to fight and there's no *piste*. In recent years, one or two organised overland groups from France have used the **Tindouf route** (Algeria, Mauritania).

From Mali by Rail

For the present, the great majority of overland travellers arrive **from Mali**, mostly on the *Océan-Niger* **railway**. Departures from Bamako are scheduled for **8am Wed & Sat**; the Sat train is

the Senegalese one and more comfortable – you're strongly advised to avoid its Malian counterpart. Scheduled arrival time into Dakar is 1.30pm the following day, but the usual delays mean you're likely to arrive after dark. **From Dakar**, current schedules are Wed (Senegalese train) & Sat, dep. 8am, arr. 30–36hr later.

An alternative is take the train from Bamako only as far as **Tambacounda** (where it should arrive 3–4am): thereafter it's a hot, uninteresting journey and quicker by road – which also gives the option of going down to Basse Casamance or The Gambia before confronting Dakar.

Fares to Dakar range from around CFA12,000 2nd class, CFA19,000 1st class to CFA29,000 sleeper. There are small **student reductions** in 2nd class, which on the Senegalese train is not very dissimilar from 1st: it's worth paying the difference only if you want more leg-room and fewer companions. It's possible to upgrade to **sleeper class** once you're on the move, assuming there are berths available (double cabins only), but the protracted border formalities take place during the night and require your active participation outside the train, so you don't get much sleep in any case. A buffet has snacks and drinks, and the stations come alive with **street food** – bean fritters, rice and fish, meat stew sandwiches, fruit. **Water** supplies aren't good, so take plenty.

Beware that **Muslim holidays**, and particularly the *Magal* (see Islamic calendar p.53), can alter train timetables. In recent years, for example, stranded pilgrims have stoned the train in frustration as it passes through Diourbel, forcing the *Regie* to send trains through there.

From Mali by Road

Driving, in any manner of vehicle, **from Bamako to Dakar** is reckoned to be a feat of skill and endurance: the section from Bamako to Kayes is virtually impassable most of the year and the Falémé river on the Mali-Senegal border unfordable between July and February. You can put your vehicle on the train.

Coming from Mali with your own wheels, you might do better, in normal circumstances, to drive **via Mauritania** (the usual motor route to Kayes goes via Nioro anyway, close to the Mauritanian border). In this case you connect with the tarred highway running west to Nouakchott, then turn south and follow the coast to Dakar. This route, or a variation, is also quite practical if you're using public transport (see Mauritania, p.304).

If you want to avoid the highways you've several possibilities for **entering Senegal across the river**, well off any beaten track. You might try Sélibabi to Bakel or Bogué to the Ile à Morfil. But all these Mauritanian possibilities are probably out of the question while the cross-border conflict persists.

From Guinea-Bissau and Guinea

Two main routes cross the border **from Guinea-Bissau** – São Domingos to Ziguinchor and Farim to Tanaf – and both are easiest by public transport (what there is of it) rather than your own. Entering Senegal **from Guinea**, Koundara to Tambacounda is the usual crossing. A couple of spidery routes further east make the Labé to Kédougou crossing increasingly viable. Rainy season road problems are the only reason for lengthy delays; you can expect daily transport otherwise. Further details are given on p.601.

From The Gambia

After the break-up of the Senegambia confederation in 1989, the Gambia Public Transport Corporation bus service described below has been temporarily suspended. You may have to change vehicles at the border. Also note that goods bought in The Gambia may be subject to duty. Explain they're not for resale and ask them to write the details in your passport if they're concerned.

To Dakar, there are normally two *GPTC* buses each morning from the ferry dock at Barra, meeting the 8am & 10am boats from Banjul dock. Assuming no serious delays, the trip takes about six hours. *GPTC* has its own bus park in Dakar at Place Leclerc close to the Kermel Market. The border crossing at **Karang/Amandlai** tends to be mildly chaotic if you're travelling by bus.

From Banjul **to Ziguinchor** there's a variety of bush taxis from the main taxi park in Serekunda market – three hours by Peugeot 504, up to all day by *car rapide* coach. The border crossing at **Séléti** is fairly efficient and there's usually little hassle: make sure The Gambia stamps you in the right direction though – *Arrival* or *Departure*. Again, through services may not be operating if Senegal and The Gambia are unhappy with each other.

If you're really short on time for Senegal, you can fix something up on a *charter* basis with a taxi driver – prices to popular destinations are posted outside the beach hotels. **Cap Skiring**, though offered as a day-trip, is too far to be

worthwhile. For a one-day trip to Casamance, stick to the north side of the Casamance river.

Red Tape

French, Italian and West German passport holders do not need visas. Other EC passport holders too, should be exempt, but some officials may not be aware of this, and may try to insist you have a visa – in which case buy one at the airport or border. As of 1990, the embassy in London no longer stipulates tourist visas for UK passport holders.

Non-EC passport holders definitely need visas, but they're usually for multiple entry (ask) and can be issued quickly. Visa requirements are normally minimal and, in West Africa, visas can be obtained from Senegalese embassies or consulates in virtually every country.

As for **health certificates** you must have yellow fever (and you're advised to have cholera) even if you're flying in direct from Europe: there's sometimes a negotiable line between what's stipulated by the Ministry of Health and what's demanded by the official at the arrivals desk.

Duty free allowances don't include any spirits, though in practice this may be overlooked.

For visas for **onward travel**, Dakar has embassies for most West African countries. Addresses and selective visa information are given in the Dakar "Directory".

Money and costs

Senegal's currency is the CFA franc. (CFA50 always equals 1 French franc; CFA450-500 = £1.) Despite all its visitors and westernisation, changing money in Senegal can be very difficult, so be sure to have French francs on you. Senegal is also one of West Africa's more expensive countries. Hotels – even cheap ones – will easily cost you CFA10,000/ day in Dakar (£20, US$35), and not much less outside the capital. A room for under CFA5000 is rare. Travelling costs, when you've taken baggage into account, usually exceed CFA1200/100km.

The system of *campements rurals integrés* in Casamance improves the county's affordability, and a tent can be a boon. An *ISIC* card is useful for reduced entry fees and possibly discounted travel (trains and planes are worth trying).

■ Money

As in other CFA countries, carrying your money in **French franc travellers' cheques** makes most sense, but carrying some francs in cash is useful too, because although Dakar is one of the region's main financial centres, banks are scarce outside the capital and foreign currencies unfamiliar. Shop around for the best **rates** if you're changing other currencies, especially if the foreign exchange markets are volatile: the benefits on large sums can be significant.

If you're staying in Senegal some time, or basing yourself in Dakar for your travels, opening a **bank account** with one of the main banks is effective but not simple, despite the business-like climate of Dakar. It's better to have your bank open an account for you in advance – then you can take your account number to the bank in Senegal on their letter.

Apart from Dakar airport's **twenty-four hour exchange counter** (which is sometimes closed), the only other out-of-hours change facilities are the normally exploitative hotel desks. Banks tend be closed from 11.30am until 2.30 or 3pm.

Credit cards are of more use than in other countries, with *Visa* and *Amex* leading the field for tourist services, car hire, fancy restaurants and flashier shops. **Visa cash advances** can be arranged through the *SGBS*, *BICIS* and *BICICI* banks, subject to certain restrictions. *BICICI*, for example, takes an hour or two and won't handle less than CFA50,000.

Health

One of the most comfortable countries in West Africa, Senegal doesn't pose too many health problems for a first-time visit. It's mostly dry, seasonally mild (at least along the coast), and has a relatively well developed health care infrastructure.

Having said which, a recent Department of the Environment study reported 600,000 Dakarois with year-round colds and the country's highest typhoid levels – attributed to exhaust fumes, industrial air pollution and the 1200 tonnes of rubbish produced every day. **Dakar** used to be the place to convalesce from the diseases of the interior. If you're getting over something, perhaps you should find a resting-up spot away from the city.

Staying some time in the Dakar area, especially during the cool, dry season from December to March, you may prefer to forget about **malaria** prophylaxis. Local doctors often insist it's more harmful than beneficial, and many expatriate residents don't bother – certainly the mosquito problem is minimal at this time of year. Most travellers, however, will move on. As soon as you go into the back country, especially in forested or watered areas, you expose yourself to risk again, a risk that is higher if you've broken your course.

Town **water** from taps is normally fine, though the Senegalese have taken to *Evian* and their own *Celia* bottled water with enthusiasm. From shops it's not too expensive; from hotels and bars usually a rip-off. Like the other Sahel countries, seasonal drought means insufficient washing water. Away from large towns try to keep tabs on the provenance of the water used (if any) to wash your plate and glass in eating houses.

Water-borne *schistosomiasis* (**bilharzia**) poses no threat in the brackish tidal waters of the lower Casamance, Saloum and Senegal rivers. Make sure you're sufficiently down-river for it to be salty before plunging in.

Senegal has a higher than usual incidence of **diptheria**. If you're not sure whether you were immunised as a child (possibly not if you were born after 1970), check with your doctor.

In the north along the river, especially around Rosso, there have recently been outbreaks of **"arbovirus"** diseases – similar to yellow fever but with no antivirus available. Check locally. All you can do is try to avoid being bitten by insects.

The **incidence of Aids** is reckoned, currently, to be relatively low. A number of 1988 "cases" subsequently proved to be incorrect diagnoses. Even so, there's a massive anti- *Sida* campaign.

Maps and Information

The London embassy has a few, quite informative, leaflets, not all aimed at package tourists. The Paris office is of course the big one and they can supply whatever's available. Addresses include:

BRITAIN Senegalese Embassy, 11 Phillimore Gardens, London W8 7QG (☎071/937 0925);

ITALY Ufficio di Promozione Turistica del Senegal, Centro di Cooperazione Internazionale, Largo Africa, 20145 Milano (☎49 97 450);

WEST GERMANY Fremdenverkehrsamt-Senegal, Münchener Strasse 7, D-6000 Frankfurt/M (☎069/23 26 91/92);

FRANCE Office du Tourisme, 30 ave George-V, 75008 Paris (☎47 20 40 70).

In the tourist offices, and Dakar itself, it's always worth picking up a copy of the free monthly listings and ads pamphlet *Le Dakarois*. Also in Dakar you can go along to the Ministry of Tourism – in the defunct *Village des Arts* – and collect whatever they've got.

For **maps**, you're best advised to get what you can before you arrive in Dakar, because the availability and price of these is none too good in the country. The *IGN* **Senegal** map at 1:1,000,000 is very useful if you'll be spending any time in the country (though it's already out of date) and its companion 1:10,000 **Dakar** is invaluable. There are also some moderately useful **regional survey maps** that you'll only find in specialist shops.

Getting Around

Senegal offers easy travelling compared with many parts of West Africa: bush taxis will get you nearly everywhere; plane, train and even boat are all viable options, and hitching is possible in some areas. With over 4000km of tarmac, Senegal has one of West Africa's better road networks. For the rest, flat landscapes make for lots of passable, if monotonous and dusty, tracks.

■ Bush Taxis and Buses

Most **public transport** is by bush taxi (*taxi brousse*) – either a Peugeot 504, *camion bâché* (covered pick-up van) or *car rapide* (often decrepit, always slow, box-like minibuses). Prices descend in this order, but you'll travel considerably faster by 504.

There are increasing numbers of Japanese minibuses (*cars*) on the roads too, though they tend to charge higher prices for their "comfortable seats" than the improvement warrants – but at least you will get a seat of your own, which isn't the case in 504s.

Autogares, or *gares routières* are usually well organised, and waiting times on the main routes short enough. Most of the motorable roads on the *IGN* map of Senegal get at least one vehicle of some description every day.

Real **buses** are few and, apart from the Gambian buses that normally run between Dakar and Banjul (twice daily in each direction) and Dakar's excellent bus system, they are not likely to figure much in your travels.

Routes and frequencies

Dakar is unusual in having just one main *gare routière*. The *autogare* at the end of rue Malick Sy is fairly together, though not any less intimidating for that if you're not used to shouting in French at four people simultaneously while beggars pull at your clothing and the fumes from a hundred idling engines fill the air. Don't **pay** unless it's half full and others have done so. In Senegal it's usual to pay before the journey has finished, and often enough before it's even started.

What follows is a summary of transport availability out of the capital and around Senegal. The busiest road in the country is the **Dakar–Kaolack–Ziguinchor** route, part of which forms the *transgambienne* highway. For years this has been bedevilled with chronically unreliable **ferries** over the Gambia river between Farafenni and Soma, but now it seems two new large ferries have arrived from Japan and the crossing will be effected in five minutes. Droves of *taxis brousse* use this route – departure before noon, journey time seven hours plus.

The old route to **Ziguinchor via Barra and Banjul** (4 ferries daily each way; approx. 9am, 11am, 3pm & 7pm from Barra; duration 1hr) is likely to become less important. Two *GPTC* buses depart each morning from Place Leclerc in Dakar for Barra – check the night before – arriving at Barra in time for the last two ferries. If there's a delay, motor *pirogues* also make the crossing to Banjul. From Banjul to Ziguinchor see "Arrivals From The Gambia" (above).

Thiès is an important transport hub, with a constant stream of vehicles running up from Dakar (1hr) until late in the day. With a morning departure from Dakar you can also go straight through to **St-Louis** (3hr plus) and **Rosso** (5hr plus).

St-Louis is the north's transport focus. There are departures all day for **Rosso**, **Richard Toll** and **Dakar**, but destinations further up-river are served only by a few early morning departures.

Eastwards, few vehicles make a living on the **Tambacounda** road because the train takes so much of the business. But you can make it there in a day if you get down to the Dakar *autogare* at dawn. Continuing to the **Kédougou** district you'll be relying solely on Tambacounda vehicles, and they are not numerous.

The **Tambacounda–Ziguinchor** road is mostly quiet – and on this route too you'll need an early start to make miles in either direction.

Finally, **Basse Casamance** transport is detailed in that section of the guide: despite its popularity, it's a remote region, where you'll have to be prepared to walk, cycle or wait.

SAMPLE FARES

Dakar–Thiès (surfaced; 70km) CFA725 by 504, CFA585 by minibus.

Dakar–St-Louis (surfaced; 266km) CFA2400 by 504, CFA1800 minibus.

Dakar–Rosso (surfaced; 366km) CFA3400 by 504, CFA2900 minibus.

Dakar–Ziguinchor (surfaced; 440km) CFA4480 by 504, CFA3600 minibus.

Dakar–Banjul (surfaced; 300km) CFA2500 *GPTC* bus.

Mbour–Joal (surfaced; 30km) CFA375 by 504, CFA275 minibus.

Ziguinchor–Serekunda/Banjul (surfaced; 175km) CFA2000 by 504.

Ziguinchor–Elinkine (part surfaced; 70km) CFA700 *car rapide.*

Most fares are fixed, but the crews make money on **baggage**; they will ask for a supplement of up to 25 percent per pack – which you should haggle over vigorously.

■ Car Hire

A spectacularly expensive means of getting about, **car hire** in Senegal is really only worth considering for special targets which might otherwise be inaccessible (eg national parks), and even then most realistically as a group of three or four travellers. The **main agents** for *Avis* (the biggest), *Hertz* and *Europcar* (one or more in Dakar, Ziguinchor, Cap Skiring and St-Louis) provide the guarantee of a name and the chance to pay on plastic, but the **all-in cost** for a Renault 5 or something similar, assuming 1000km and including petrol, will work out around **£500 per week** and isn't negotiable. Daily rates are fractionally more than *pro rata*, a weekend slightly less. There's a ban on driving on tracks and a minimum age of 25. National driving licences held for one year are sufficient, but don't be surprised if an international drivers' licence is specifically demanded if you're stopped.

It's really worth checking out some of the **local car rental places** which are usually willing to negotiate a little, can often be persuaded to give you unlimited mileage and aren't so fussed about off-road driving. They may work out less than half the price of the big agencies. A weekend is frequently the best deal, and the most useful duration. Don't forget possible extras (*frais non-inclus*): collision damage waiver, 17 percent tax.

■ Hitching

Because of the number of private vehicles, ex-patriates and, relatively, the volume of tourist traffic too, **hitching** on some of the main routes is an option worth trying. In decreasing order of feasibility, there are reasonable chances of lifts around the **Dakar suburbs**, to destinations on the coasts **south and north of Dakar**; in **Basse Casamance**, and from **Tambacounda to Dakar** and **into Niokolo-Koba National Park**.

If you're stuck on a minor turn-off, attempting to wave down passing vehicles is at least more promising than simply waiting for the day's bush taxi service.

■ Trains

There are two main railway lines: the northern Dakar to St-Louis route and the eastern *Océan-Niger* line.

The daily Mon–Sat run **from Dakar to St-Louis** departs Dakar at 3pm, arrives St-Louis 7.40pm, and departs St-Louis 6.30am, arriving Dakar 11.10am (Sun dep. Dakar 5.30pm arr. St-Louis 10.10pm, dep. St-Louis 3pm, arr. Dakar 7.40pm). Extra trains are often laid on during holidays. The route goes via Rufisque, Thiès, Tivaouane and Louga.

Despite a recent World Bank study which found this service uneconomic, its future looks fairly secure. And certainly it's the best way of getting between the towns, with immaculate first class AC seats under CFA3000 and second class less than CFA2000. Only the fastest bush taxis (comparable prices) cover the distance more quickly.

Dakar has its own commuter service now (*les petits trains bleus*) running to and from **Rufisque** several times during morning and evening rush hours. As a result, the schedules below may have altered.

On the *Océan-Niger* line from Dakar, the Bamako service via Thiès, Diourbel and Tambacounda is covered in "Arrivals: From Mali by Rail", above. In addition, there's an **express service** (dep. Dakar 5.20am daily plus 7.25am Tues, Thurs & Sat) to Thiès (1hr 15min) Diourbel (2hr 40min) and Kaolack (4hr 10min), and a daily

slow train (dep. Dakar 6.20am) to Thiès (2hr 20min), Diourbel (5hr) and branching to Touba (6hr 30min). There are daily **connecting services from Diourbel** (dep. 9.05am) **to Kaolack** (3hr) and **Guinguinéo/Kaolack junction** (dep. 2.40pm) **to Tambacounda** (7hr).

In the reverse direction, the Dakar-bound express leaves **from Kaolack** at 5.40am via **Diourbel** and **Thiès** (plus 3.10pm Tues, Thurs & Sat) and the slow train to Dakar leaves **from Touba** at 2.10pm daily. The daily connecting services are **from Tambacounda** (dep. 5.30am) to Guinguinéo and **from Kaolack** (dep. 2pm) to Diourbel. On all of these routes, prices hold well against road travel, but don't expect the luxury standards of the St-Louis train — and be no more surprised at delays than you would on the road.

■ Internal Flights

Air Senegal operates a few flights round the country from Dakar, but it's not a frequent enough service to offer much competition to bush travel. Services include: **Ziguinchor** every morning, returning immediately, except Sun, when the return flight leaves in the evening; **Ziguinchor and Kolda** on Mon morning, and back to Dakar; **Tambacounda** and **Kédougou** on Fri, calling at **Simenti** in the Niokolo-Koba National Park on the way back to Tambacounda and Dakar; **Cap Skiring** on Wed and Sat, returning immmediately, and on Thurs, Fri, Sun, returning in the evening; **along the Senegal river** on Wed, calling at **St-Louis**, **Richard Toll**, **Podor**, **Matam** and **Bakel**, and returning the same way.

Most flights depart from Dakar between 8am and 9am. One-way fares in the single (economy) class are: Bakel CFA27,000; Cap Skiring CFA24,000; Kédougou and Simenti CFA30,000; Kolda CFA21,000; Matam CFA24,000; Podor CFA19,000; Richard Toll CFA15,000; St-Louis CFA12,000; Tambacounda CFA24,000; Ziguinchor CFA22,000.

■ Other Options

The *Casamance Express* **steamer** — which used to do a regular run between Dakar and Ziguinchor — has recently come back into operation, and should be offering at least a weekly service. Smaller and more exclusive pleasure boats ply the waters of the Saloum and Senegal deltas, and if you're interested, staying in the right hotels in those areas will give you rapid access. There's no steamer service higher up the Senegal

or the Casamance though you can usually cross by *pirogue*. If you want to travel by river there's ample opportunity to arrange it locally. The Senegal is navigable by small boats all year as far up as Bakel; the Casamance past Sedhiou.

A characteristically Senegalese form of transport is the horse- or mule-drawn two wheel buggy called a **calèche**, which you'll see all over the north and centre but not south of The Gambia (because of tsetse fly). They're often used as town taxis in smaller places, ferrying goods and people from the *autogare*. In St-Louis they've taken on a more touristy function as well.

At several locations in Basse Casamance you can hire **bicycles** — not very rideable ones, admittedly, and mostly they don't have refinements such as gears, but they make a welcome change of pace. Buying a bicycle in Senegal will cost around CFA70,000; there are much cheaper countries, but on the other hand it's the flattest country in West Africa.

Sleeping

For the most part, accommodation in Senegal is sophisticated and wide-ranging. With the exception of youth hostels, most other overnight options are available.

■ Hotels

Most large towns have several decent **hotels**. Coming overland from one of its neighbours, Senegalese establishments seem, on the whole, plush and heavily Europeanised. In the higher price brackets, if they're not actually part of a chain, they're very often French or Lebanese-owned or managed. And a surprising number of quite modest places turn out to have French hands behind the scenes.

Not surprisingly, a room in Senegal is generally expensive: CFA5000 about the bottom line for the most basic lodging and CFA10,000 a typical price for often unremarkable amenities. And there's a **tourist tax** too, currently set at CFA400 per person per night, sometimes included in the room charge, more often added to the bill afterwards.

■ **Campements Rurals Integrés**

An important and gratifying exception to the ordinary hotels is the network of **campements rurals integrés** (*CRIs*) established by the Ministry of Tourism over the last ten years to cater for lighter budgets and less mainstream requirements. Built by villagers with loans from central funds, often in a traditional architectural style, the *campements* bring tourist money into parts of the rural economy that don't usually benefit.

Run by local people, the *campements* provide about the best commercial opportunity for sampling village life. In the better ones you'll feel thoroughly integrated, and eat with your hosts; in one or two a straightforward "cheap hotel" feel begins to creep in, but the extent to which it does so is up to the visitors as much as the village owners.

Facilities at the *campements* are streamlined in the most basic fashion – European plumbing, cold running water, kerosene lighting, three-course meals, and cold drinks from a gas fridge. They provide mosquito nets and foam mattresses, but no bedding, so you need a sheet sleeping bag. At night some *campements* can be uncomfortably hot as the mud brick walls release the day's heat. For the same charge you can always camp outside. Prices are the same at all *campements* and you can pay for accommodation only, or as many meals as you want. New prices were set for 1990, and should stick for a couple of years: bed – CFA1500; breakfast – CFA700; meal CFA1400.

A number of cheaper hotels in touristic areas also style themselves *campement*, but they're normally more refined and rarely as cheap or as fun as the *CRIs*.

For more details, and where to book (many *CRIs* fill up over the Nov–Feb peak season), see the Ziguinchor "Directory".

■ **Other accommodation**

Camping out in the bush is normally okay in Senegal, where there's a fairly indulgent attitude to the eccentricities of foreigners: the French community has been doing it for years. Be sure, though, that you're out of any urban "zone of influence" where you might conceivably be putting yourself at risk of robbery. The Dakar region, and the towns in the groundnut basin – Thiès, Diourbel and Kaolack – are areas to avoid, as are the beaches. There are no formal campsites.

Staying with people frequently comes out of efforts to camp on their land – even if it's not demarcated. Rewarding areas for such contacts lie throughout southern Senegal east of Ziguinchor – a region which, except for the Niokolo-Koba park, gets very few visitors, and virtually none who stay.

Eating and Drinking

Senegal has some of West Africa's best food and you can do everything from serious dining out to street food experimentation. Drinks are equally diverse.

■ **Restaurants**

You can eat well in Senegal, though **restaurants** in the larger towns and main hotels incline towards French style, offering a *menu* (four courses or more, and usually a choice) and a *plat du jour* (main dish only). Predictably there's lots of tough steak and chips, heavy sauces, imported canned food. And if they haven't caught up with French cooking trends, their prices are up-to-date: for a *menu* expect to pay CFA3000–5000, and upward of CFA2000 for the *plat*. There are some decent French restaurants, and various other exotic species as well, but with a few exceptions they're an unmemorable lot. The better value venues are covered throughout this guide. **Interesting food** is Senegalese: you can often eat best – certainly in Dakar – by going to some of the cheapest places, where you simply order dishes from the list.

■ **Dishes**

North African influences are melded in **Senegalese cooking**, which is strong on seafood, mutton and Middle Eastern snacks. The basics, as everywhere, are starch – usually rice – and spicy sauces, though the key word is aroma rather than pungency.

If you've been travelling elsewhere you'll also notice the near absence of plantains and root crops, and palm oil is used much less than in the southern coastal countries.

The national dish is **chep-bu-jen** (spelled variously as *cep-bou-dien* and *tiéboudienne*), Wolof for rice-with-fish. This can be anything from plain rice with boiled fish and a few carrots to a glorious kind of paella with spiced rice and half a dozen vegetables. There's no recipe.

Stuffed fish (**poisson farci**), which is an ingredient of the best *chep-bu-jen*, is associated with St-Louis and sometimes denoted *à la saint-louisienne*. Done properly, the result can be delicious. The mullet (usual species) is filleted and flayed, leaving the skin whole: the flesh is then chopped finely, spiced and herbed, sewn up inside the skin and the whole package baked.

Varieties of **yassa** – a Casamançais dish – are characteristic of most menus too. Traditionally it uses **chicken**, but any animal ingredient qualifies so long as it is marinated at length in lemon juice, pepper and onions.

Riz Jollof – a mound of vegetables and meat in an oily tomato sauce on rice, named after the old Wolof kingdom – is found all over West Africa and has more or less escaped into international status.

Mafe and **Domodah** are stewy, soupy sauces based loosely around tomatoes and groundnuts. The latter, so peanutty in The Gambia, is sometimes nut-less in Senegal. Both are best with beef or fish.

Couscous (or *basi-salete*) is fairly common too, though traditionally considered a festive meal and eaten at the Muslim New Year; comprising steamed grains of millet flour with a smothering of vegetables, mutton and gravy, it's best by far when you're very hungry. **Méchoui**, a whole roast sheep, is one for *Tabaski* – the *Fête des moutons*.

Fruit tends to be expensive imports away from the main growing areas in the south: oranges from Morocco, Ivoirian pineapples and French apples. Even a papaya will be CFA400 in Dakar. Hold out for Casamance and look for unusual wild tastes (see box).

■ Breakfast and Snacks

The great French bequest, as always, is their **bread**, consumed in vast quantities and almost always delicious when fresh. *Pain beurre* and *café au lait* is the ubiquitous **breakfast** and roadside snack, often with real butter. Be warned, though, that the *Nescafé* is often unrelated to what you'll find in, say, Mali, Burkina or Niger, as it's made with an infusion like weak tea, from a shrub called **kenkeliba**. Mild and indifferently nutty on its own or mixed with sweet milk, it acquires a revolting flavour when mixed with *Nescafé*. Specify "made with water" if you want *Nescafé*.

WOLOF FOOD TERMS

The list below will help you ask for and identify food in out of the way places. For a little more Wolof, see overleaf.

bey/siket	goat	*lem*	honey	*nxar*	mutton
chep/malo	rice	*lemnad*	soft drink	*nyam dunde*	food
chwi/genar	chicken	*makande*	corn	*nyebe*	beans
darr	butter	*mar*	thirst	*sangara*	alcohol,
dom/garap	fruit	*mbam*	pork		spirits
dugup	millet	*mbum*	spinach/boiled	*sobele*	onions
gejieu	dried fish		leaves	*sohu*	sour milk
gerte	groundnuts	*mburu*	bread	*sukar*	sugar
jen	fish	*mehu*	fresh milk	*suna*	bulrush millet
jeo	water	*nak*	beef	*tomat*	tomato
jere	couscous/millet	*nene*	egg	*xif*	hunger
jernat	sorghum millet	*nex-na*	good (referring	*xorom*	salt
kani	hot pepper		to food)	*yap*	meat

There are various **wild fruits**, sold seasonally in the markets:

ditak	oval, pebble-like fruit, with thin, dry skin and aromatic, acid green flesh surrounding a fibrous seed, sometimes made into a drink: very common in Casamance	*solom*	brown, pea-sized berry, with furry (edible) skin and a black seed
		cerise	tart, green "cherry'"
		nyul	"black", a small black fruit
		dimbu	small, black, soft fruit with a vegetable taste and staining flesh red

For **snacks** in towns you'll often end up in a *shawarma* bar. *Shawarma*, like kebabs, are shreds of barbecued compressed mutton cut from a roll, wrapped in a *pita* bread or French loaf sandwich. They're normally a dependable standby at around CFA500. Middle Eastern alternatives are *merguez* (spicy sausage), *kofta* (meat balls), *fataya* (meat pies), *nems* (like a pancake roll made of vermicelli pastry) and of course **brochettes**.

In the suburbs and countryside the *dibiterie* takes over. Roadside or market stalls, *dibiteries* are really butcher's shops, where you choose your flank of flesh and have it chopped and barbecued on the spot. Flies are attracted to the best cuts, it's said, so take their choice as a recommendation. Go armed with a French stick (usually sold next door) and a couple of beers and you have a picnic.

■ Drinking

Flag is Senegal's **beer**, and not at all bad. It comes in two-thirds and third-litre bottles, and the price depends on where you buy it – any bar that sells only the small size is expensive. A quite acceptable alternative, assuming you're in need of refreshment rather than intoxication, is the far less alcoholic *Gazelle* (large size only), which tends to be one of the cheapest bottled drinks you can buy.

Wine is available in groceries in most town centres, and tends to be about twice the French price. **Palm wine** costs next to nothing but you need to be in Casamance and friendly with the owner of a tree.

Non-alcoholic alternatives to bottled sodas and mineral water are plastic bags of iced **hibiscus syrup** (*bisap*), ginger water, sherberty baobab juice or tamarind juice. If you're interested in unusual tastes, seek out *njamban* – a concoction of tamarind juice, smoked fish, salt and cayenne pepper. Something mellower is **thiacry**, a mixture of couscous, sour milk and sugar that's closer to a dessert than a drink, or **lakh** – millet, sour milk, sugar and orange water. And in many parts Sahelian **tea** – tongue-liftingly strong and sweet – is a much-loved refreshment.

Communications – Post, Phones, Language and Media

Post offices (*PTT*), normally open Mon-Fri 8–noon & 3–6pm plus Sat morning, operate with grinding, morose efficiency. Senegalese mail is expensive, and delivery from Dakar (where the central *PTT* has long hours) to Britain is slow – Banjul is much faster as it goes on the next *BA* flight.

Getting mail at **poste restante** may require infinite patience: letters commonly take two to three weeks to find their box in the Dakar *poste restante*, and are then only held for a month.

Phoning home is costly, £8 for three minutes to Britain and US$18 to the USA, with extra minutes *pro rata*. Americans, in common with several other nationalities, can make collect calls (*PCV*) – a service not available to Britain. One minute of **telex** is around CFA1500.

■ Language

Though only twenty percent of the population has any fluency in the colonial tongue, communication will rarely be a problem if you speak French to some degree, and you'll frequently be able to hold conversations. (English alone won't get you far.) If you know some **Wolof** however, you're on the way to a different level of experience. It's not an easy language, but making the effort to say even a few simple greetings will gratify people out of all proportion to your ability (see overleaf).

Though it's become Senegal's African lingua franca and continues to gain importance, Wolof is not the whole story. The important minority vernaculars include: **Fula** (*Pulaar*), spoken by the Tukulor and Fula (*Peul*); **Serer**, spoken by the partly Christianised people of the same name; **Kriyol**, a Portuguese creole spoken by up to

ELEMENTARY WOLOF

Wolof (sometimes *Ouolof* or *Volof* to the French) is understood by an estimated fifty percent of Senegalese. Perhaps two-thirds of these are ethnic Wolof, the rest are mother tongue speakers of other languages, all of which are losing ground. Wolof is growing in importance all the time and there are regular calls for it to be adopted as the official national language. Wolof is classified as a "West Atlantic" language, in the same large basket of "class languages" as Fula and Serer, quite different from the "non-class" Mande languages like Mandinka, Bambara and Dyula. The main criterion for this classification is the grammatical system of Wolof, which groups nouns into fairly arbitrary classes something like genders. There's the usual confusion over **spellings** created by British and French transcribers using their own norms, but the following selection should be as pronounceable as possible. The letter "x" denotes a throaty sound like the ch in loch, but even rougher.

GREETINGS

All purpose greeting...	*Salam malekum*	How are your family/	*Ana sa wa ker?*
...and response	*Malekum salam*	home/people? (very	
How are you? (literally:	*Nanga def? Jam*	informal)	
Do you have peace?)	*ngaam?*	Well, thank you (all	*Jam dal*
I'm just around here	*Mangi fi rek/Jamarek*	purpose)	
(Nothing but peace)		What's your name?	*Naka nga sant?*
Thank God	*al xamdulilay*	My name is Dave	
Good morning (lit. did	*Jamanga fanan?*	Warne	*Tuda Dave santa Warne*
you sleep well?)		Goodbye (I'm off)	*Mangi dem*
How are you all? (formal)	*Naka waa keur ga?*		

GENERAL PRACTICALITIES

I don't speak	*Man deguma*	Where are you	*Fanga dem nile?*	Please	*Su la nexe*
Wolof/French	*Wolof/Faranse*	going?		I don't mind/I	*Ana sema yon*
Please repeat	*Wahat ko del*	The road to ...	*Di yon wi demi ...*	don't care	
Yes	*Wow*	Right	*Chamong*	When?	*Sar?*
No	*Dedet*	Left	*Ndejor*	No problem	*Du problème*
Perhaps	*Xey na*	Far	*Sore*	(No) thank you	*Jere jef*
Where is ...?	*An na...?*	Slowly	*Ndank*	Wife	*Djabar*

PLACES

Market	*Jebe*	Room	*Neg*	Field	*Toll*
Village	*Deuke*	Bed	*Lale*	Forest/bush	*Alle*
House	*Ker*				

DAYS

Today	*Tei*	Monday	*Altine*	Thursday	*Alxemes*
Saturday	*Aser*	Tuesday	*Telata*	Friday	*Ajuma*
Sunday	*Diber*	Wednesday	*Alarba*		

BUYING

Give me/sell me...	*Mai man/jai man*	Cheap	*Yombe na*
I want.../I don't want...	*Bugema.../buguma ...*	Expensive	*Jafe*
Enough	*Doi na*	Not...	*Do...*
More, again	*Ati*	Money	*Xalis*
A little	*Sin tut*	Lower the price (a	*Wanil ko (tuti)*
Lots of	*Lol/bare*	little)	
Full	*Fes*	You're killing me!	*Hey! Yangi ma rey!*
That's all	*Mom rek*	Leave me alone, I'm	*Baye ma, dama son*
How much is that?	*Bi nyata le?*	fed up/tired	
It's too much	*Defa jafe torop.*	Gift	*Nexeul*

OTHER NEEDS

Please give me some water	*Mai man ndox su la nexe*	I've got a stomach ache	*Suma biir day metti*
I'm hungry	*Damaa xiif*	Show me the way to the post office	*Won ma post bi*
What would you like to eat?	*Loo begga lekk?*	What would you like?	*Lan nga bugg?*
I'm sleepy	*Damaa gemmeentu*	Do you have a little bit of aspirin?	*Amuloo tutti aspirin?*
I'm going to sleep (now)	*Maangi nelawi waay*	Do you smoke?	*Dinga tix?*
Where are you going?	*Foo jem?*	Do you drink palm wine?	*Dinga naan sung?*
Are you going to the market?	*Dangay dem marse?*	I don't have any money	*Awma xalis*
I feel ill	*Damaa feebar*	Someone's waiting for me	*Am naa ku may xaar*

EMERGENCIES

Thief!	*Sachu kat!*	Call the police/ a doctor quickly!	*Uho police/medecin gahu!*
S/he's ill!	*Dafa fun ope!*		

NUMBERS

1	*bena*	7	*jerom nyar*	21	*nyar fuka bena* (etc)	80	*jerom nyeta fuka*
2	*nyar*	8	*jerom nyeta*	30	*nyet fuka/fanver*		
3	*nyeta*	9	*jerom nyenent*	40	*nyenent fuka*	90	*jerom nyenent fuka*
4	*nyenent*	10	*fuka*	50	*jerom fuka*		
5	*jerom*	11	*fuka bena* (etc)	60	*jerom bena fuka*	100	*temer*
6	*jerom bena*	20	*nyar fuka/nit*	70	*jerom nyar fuka*	1000	*june*

TREES

Baobab	*Gui*	Raffia palm	*Bari*	Locust bean	*Netetu*
Silk-cotton (kapok)	*Bentenki*	Oil palm	*Tir*	Mandingo kola	*Tabu*
		Custard apple	*Jorut*		

ANIMALS

Horse	*Fas*	Monkey	*Golo*	Pelican	*Jagabar*
Camel	*Gwilem*	Elephant	*Nye*	Crocodile	*Jasik*
Goat	*Bei*	Hippopotamus	*Leber*	Chameleon	*Kakatar*
Pig	*Mbam*	Large antelope	*Koba*	Monitor lizard	*Mbeta*
Cow	*Nak*				
Bull	*Yek*	Hyena	*Buki*	Gecko	*Onka*
Lion	*Gawnde/daba*	Porcupine	*Sav*	Snake	*Jan*
Leopard	*Tenev*	Ostrich	*Baa*	Tortoise	*Mbonat*

50,000 along the coast south of Dakar; **Jola**, spoken in various dialects in the Casamance region; the **Mande** languages (Mandinka/ Malinké, Bambara and Sarakole/Soninké), spoken in scattered communities across the south and east; and the languages of the **Tenda** group – Konyagi, Bedik, Bassari. All are a major component of ethnic identity, especially in the case of Jola.

◼ Media

Language politics are reflected in Senegalese **radio** which is divided into two *chaines* – a French language station, and a vernacular station broadcasting in Wolof with extra transmissions in Fula, Serer, Mandinka, Jola and Sarakole/ Soninke. **TV**, exclusively in French, is watched mostly in Dakar.

Radio Sénégal (ORTS) on about 750mMW and *Radio Inter*, about 1350mMW, both carry Dakar information and, on Friday afternoons, news about music and shows.

The paltry Senegalese **press** seems extraordinarily undeveloped given the country's record on freedom of speech. *Le Soleil* – the "independent" paper of the *Parti Socialiste* but

SENEGALESE TERMS – A GLOSSARY

Common words and expressions, French and Wolof

Bana Bana wandering street vendor

Baye Fall zealous disciples of Mouridism, dressed in brilliantly coloured patchwork cloaks, often seen collecting money for their marabout

Borom *patron*, chief, owner

Boubou long gown worn by men and women

Ceddo traditional Wolof warrior caste

Damel pre-Islamic Wolof kings

Daxa pioneering settlements of Mourid disciples

Djigeen woman

Dibiterie roadside butcher and barbecue artist

Fatou domestic servant, commonly also means "woman" or "lady"

Filao casuarina tree; a kind of weeping fir

La Fleuve "The River" – the Senegal river

Fromager silk-cotton tree or kapok

Gewel griot; praise singer, musician storyteller

Goor man/male

Gue ford, river crossing

Hajj/El Hajj the pilgrimage to Mecca/one who has been

Herbe Qui Tu grass, cannabis

HLM "Habitations à Loyer Modérés" – council flats

Jeu de Dames draughts, checkers; a more competitive game than *wure*

Keur/kerr/ker place, home

Maquis cheap eatery

Magal annual mass pilgrimage to Touba

Marabout religious leader accredited with magical powers; they hold enormous sway

Mbalax music – modern expression of traditional roots rhythms

Mouridiya the most powerful of the Islamic orders; headquarters at Touba

Planton orderly, watchman, dogsbody

PDS *Parti Démocratique Senegalaise*, the main opposition party

PS *Parti Socialiste*, the ruling party; curious name

Radio Kankan public rumour

Sayisayi provocative dancing

Sandarma gendarme

Sopi "Change", the slogan of the main political opposition alliance

Talibe disciple of a marabout

Teranga hospitality, generosity; sums up the Wolof code of behaviour to strangers

Tijaniya numerically the largest Islamic brotherhood divided into dynasties, some of which are fundamentalist in nature

Touba not just the holy city east of Dakar; also means "happiness"

Tubab/Toubab foreigner, usually white foreigner; from the Wolof "to convert"

Wure the game of pebbles/seeds and holes

Yamba cannabis

---

effectively the voice of government – is the country's only true daily and always short on readable news, though not for lack of newsprint. The same house may still be putting out the weekly *Senegambian Sun*. Most of the dozen or more political parties publish their own sheets more or less regularly, but they tend towards the turgid.

For something oppositional, look for the *PDS'* weekly *Sopi*. If your French is up to it, *Le Politicien* is a monthly breath of fresher air – nicknamed *Le Cafard Enchaîné* after the Parisian satirical mag. For an angle on the Islamic brotherhoods pick up the Islamic weekly *Wal Fadjri* (in French).

Entertainment

Unlike a number of countries where organised entertainments can be somewhat inaccessible to outsiders, Senegal has plenty of spectator sport, as well as musical performers, theatre and cinema.

■ Sport

La lutte – wrestling – is the most popular sport country-wide, and consists of furious jostling of oiled and charm-laden poseurs trying to get each other down in the dust: fun to watch, but best at a small venue. Casamançais style is less violent than the mainstream brawls.

Football is popular too, and set to become even more so after Senegal took fourth position after Algeria, Nigeria and Cameroon in the 1990 African Cup in Algiers.

■ Culture

Theatre doesn't make much impression, though there is a small, active theatre community based around the Senegal National Theatre Comapany and the institutional *Théâtre Daniel Sorano* in Dakar. A leading figure was **Doura Mane**, who split from the National to form the *Ballets de Casamance*; they visited Britain in 1972, two years after their founder's death. Foreign cultural centres in Dakar, St-Louis and Ziguinchor may have something worth a look.

Cinema, sadly, is mostly imported mush. Senegal's own directors, notably Ousmane Sembene, Pape B. Seck, Djibril Diop Mambety and the woman *cinéaste* Safi Faye, struggle for funds despite – in Sembene's case – international critical acclaim.

Music is another story. Senegalese music is revelation after the foreign imports heard in other countries. While traditional **griots** are less and less to be seen, on a different level Senegal is in the vanguard of African music's sweep through Europe and the rest of the west – even Japan. **Youssou N'dour**, for the complex **Mbalax** style he developed with his band **Super Etoile de Dakar**, and for his singular presence in the World Music firmament, is the best-known musician, but he's just one of very many. Major stadium **gigs** are held in Dakar, Ziguinchor and elsewhere, while you can pick up on even the big names in the Dakar clubs. (More detail and background is given in *Contexts*.)

Holidays and Festivals

Apart from international Christian and Islamic holidays, during which all official and most business doors will be closed (see p.53), there are also holidays on April 4 (Nationality day), May 5 (Labour day) and June 20 (Independence day).

There's also considerable unofficial disruption to normal hours and services at the time of **Magal** – the annual pilgrimage to Touba, which falls on the 18th of Safar, 48 days after the Islamic new year – ie on approximately **Sept 6,** **1990**, **Aug 26, 1991** and **Aug 15, 1992**. Public transport all over Senegal is severely affected in the days before and after *Magal* with many drivers preferring to do pilgrim business only.

The other major event of the year is the **Paris– Dakar Rally** (Dec 26–Jan 15), an international motor industry spree that brings wild scenes of celebration to Lac Rose, and later at the finish in Dakar. In recent years the increasingly cumbersome line-up – over 500 vehicles at the start – has come via Mali, Mauritania and St-Louis for a final tear-up along the beach to Dakar. 1988 saw at least five onlookers killed and the usual spate of spectacular accidents; the organisers now face mounting opposition from the *Pa'Dak* association ("*Paris–Dakar pas d'accord*") and the future of the race is in doubt. If it's on, there'll be accommodation problems in the second half of January, especially in Dakar and St-Louis.

■ Traditional Festivals

A St-Louis and Gorée institution is the **Fanals** parade, featuring the decorated lanterns (*fanals*) that slaves used to carry in front of wealthy mixed-race women (*signares*) on their way to Christmas mass. Competition developed between *quartiers* to produce the most elaborate lamp, the rivalry becoming so intense that the parades were banned in 1953 after violence between the teams. But they were revived in St-Louis in 1970, and you can should be able to see them around Christmas. Impressive **pirogue races** also take place from time to time, notably in St-Louis.

But it's in **the south**, in Basse Casamance and in the Bassari country beyond Niokolo-Koba park, where a **seasonal cycle of festivals** and ritual events still dominates the cultural sphere, though to a diminishing extent. Whether or not they continue to be enacted in earnest, the events in the following list are all worth checking out if you're placed and timed right; most take place towards the end of the dry season.

Olugu March: jubilant entry of Bassari initiates who underwent *Nit* the previous year, signifying their reintegration as adults.

Fityay March–April: ritual appeasement of the spirit Beliba, supplicated to look after the people of Essil (the region around Enampore) through the dry months.

Nit end of April: ritual battle in the Bassari villages of Ebarak, Etiolo and Kote, with masked attackers (*lukuta*) of boys undergoing initiation.

Ufulung Dyendena May: throughout the kingdom of Essil this ritual propitiation of rain spirits takes place before and after rice planting.

Synaaka May: "circumcision" of Jola girls, during which the initiates are instructed in retreat for a week; widespread partying.

Zulane May–June: festival of the royal priest of Oussouye.

Futampaf May–June: initiation of adolescent Jola boys into adulthood; lasts two to three weeks, commencing and concluding with major celebrations.

Kunyalen May–June: three days of ritual performed to ensure Jola female fertility and the protection of new-born infants.

Ekonkon June: (Oussouye), traditional dances.

Bukut June: takes place in each Jola village roughly every twenty years.

Wrestling June–July: takes place all year, but the start of the rains is a traditional time in Essil.

Homebel October: after the rains, girls' wrestling bouts around Oussouye.

Beweng or ***Epit*** November–December: a two-day harvest festival in Base Casamance when the spirits are asked to sanction the transfer of the rice crop to the granaries. Each head of household donates a sheaf.

Ebunay every two years: a festival in the Oussouye district involving all the women of the village holding it; female (*Bugureb*) dances in the first week, followed by the enthronement of a ritual priestess.

Directory

AIRPORT DEPARTURE TAX CFA2000–5000 depending on destination.

BEGGARS In downtown Dakar and in *gare routières* and train stations all over, you'll see plenty of beggars. Without exception they're handicapped, usually with leprosy, polio or blindness. The police keep them on the move. Fifty francs makes all the difference. Giving money to *Baye Fall* begging for their marabout is altogether different.

CRAFTS AND OTHER PURCHASES Senegal doesn't stand out as a country to buy handicrafts, but you'll find a number of hole-in-the-wall **curio shops** in Dakar, where some musty old relics can be unearthed and argued over. Officially sanctioned *centres artisanals* tend to be touristic set-ups, where you can see the stuff being made (carved statues and masks, model *pirogues*, paintings on glass, sand paintings) but where you might not want to buy it. **Cloth** pagnes are generally cheaper than in The Gambia, with Dakar's suburban markets being the best places for a good deal. Jewellery, in variety and notably in silver, is usually a good buy.

DRUGS Grass (*yamba*) is cultivated mostly in the south and not used very widely away from there. Popular attitudes are ambivalent as usual, but there's strong official condemnation.

EMERGENCIES ☎17 seems to be the best bet if you require the **police** in a hurry. Always shout like hell if you need help.

OPENING HOURS Normal business hours are Mon–Fri 8am–noon & 2.30/3–6pm, Sat 8–11am/noon (except banks and most embassies). The long lunch break is popular and nothing happens then. Many establishments, including some restaurants, also close one day a week – museums usually all day Mon & Wed morning.

PHOTOGRAPHY Officially there are few problems: you can even take pictures of the presidential guards and palace, though you should ask first. But you'll certainly hurt people's feelings if you take their pictures without permission. In many areas, high prices will be demanded.

POLICE Law enforcers are of two main types – machine-gun-toting, brown-uniformed *gendarmes* – with whom you shouldn't have much to do –and blue-togged *agents de police* – who operate the occasional countryside road blocks. The **police**, though generally not into bothering tourists, will pull you in if you're not carrying any identification. You can be held for 24 hours and fined – it happens, often. If you're out at night and would rather not take your passport, keep a photocopy and another piece of ID with you. **SEXUAL ATTITUDES** are unremarkable in any sphere, and as transparent and hedonistic as in most countries. The Wolof tend to be exceptionally beautiful people, and unafraid of marrying out of their own communities, which tends to strengthen their already dominant position. **Prostitution** has a rather lower profile than, for example, in The Gambia. **Gay attitudes** seem relaxed: Avenue Georges Pompidou in Dakar is a well-known cruising strip for *gor-digen*, and Ngor beach north of Dakar is another area to know about.

STUDENT CARDS You can usually get reduced rate at the museums, sometimes on the trains and they're always useful for student air fares (worth trying).

TROUBLE Be **security**-conscious on first arriving in Dakar: although it's spelt out in detail in the Dakar section, it can't be over-stressed that this is a city where too many new arrivals are robbed – usually in a snatch and run attack. The rest of the country is as safe as anywhere.

Don't aggravate street peddlers by looking at their gear if you're really not interested, or by bargaining for fun when you've no intention of buying. In Dakar this can give rise to serious offence. *Always* ignore the guy who gets an item out of his pocket to sell you; this is a set-up for a mugging.

On a wider front, despite some political detentions, Senegal prides itself on **freedom of speech**: domestic politics aren't taboo and you can converse openly without fear of offending or unnerving anyone.

WILDLIFE Senegal isn't well-endowed with **large animals**. In Basse Casamance National Park you're not likely to see anything larger than a monkey. In the north there may still be elephants along remoter parts of the river, though you're likely to see large numbers of camels up there – there's currently a population explosion. In Niokolo-Koba National Park, on the other hand, you can see a few elephant, lion, buffalo and western giant eland, plus several troupes of chimpanzees at the northernmost point of their range, and quantities of crocs and hippos. If you're an ornithologist, the **birdlife** is more satisfying: the coast boasts some of the best spots in the world for watching palearctic migrants in the winter. (For animal names in Wolof, see p.361.)

WOMEN'S MOVEMENT Long-standing and continued French influence has been superficially helpful to women in terms of career opportunities: three out of twenty-eight members of the Council of Ministers are women. Dakar's fairly active **movement** is coordinated through the *Fédération Sénégalaise des Groupements Féminins*. The central issue of institutional female genital mutilation – still performed in some communities – is being tackled by a pan-African organisation who have their headquarters in Dakar – the *Commission Internationale pour l'abolition des mutilations sexuelles*, Villa 811, SICAP Baobabs, Dakar (bus#4 from the train station).

WORK Dakar is one place where you'll quite possibly find a job if you're prepared to settle in for a while. The most likely openings are English **teaching** (approach the British-Senegalese Institute or look on notice boards; see Dakar *Directory*) and – if you have very good French – secretarial and other office jobs, or working in glamorous shops. All are strictly unofficial – making friends with the expatriate communities will help. If you're a sailor and want to do some crewing, Dakar is port of call for trans-Atlantic yachts and other vessels. There are bars and restaurants where you'll make contact.

A Brief History of Senegal

The earliest deductable history of Senegal comes from the oral accounts of the aristocracy of the Wolof kingdom of Jolof (from about 1300) in the centre of the country. Jolof fragmented into a number of small Wolof kingdoms which, together with Casamance, had frequent contacts with Portuguese traders after 1500. In 1658, the French settled on an island at the mouth of the Senegal river, which they named St-Louis, after Louis XIV. This account picks up the story from there. For the history of Islam in Senegal, see the feature box on p372.

■ French Inroads

By 1659 the trading fort of **St-Louis** was established, buying in **slaves** and **gum arabic** – the first a product of up-river raids, the second a valuable extract from acacia trees, used in medicine and textile manufacture.

The permanent French presence at St-Louis stimulated the slave trade to a level at which it began to dominate the Senegal valley's economy, prompting a frenzy of warfare for profit in the region's indigenous states. Wolof rulers (the *damel*) and their warriors (the *ceddo*) were spurred to raid their own peasantry for slaves. In the 1670s a popular *jihad* by Muslim marabouts, rebelling against the social cannibalism of the traditionalist Wolof elite, was suppressed with the help of French soldiers and guns. Henceforth Wolof of all classes found themselves trapped between Islamic reformers and mercenary Europeans.

St-Louis in the Eighteenth Century

Through the eighteenth century St-Louis thrived and increasingly absorbed the Wolof people of Walo state, which occupied the area between Richard Toll and the coast. The Wolof had not been converted to Islam: on the contrary, the intermarriage of Wolof women and French Catholics created an exclusive miniature society, to a large extent run by the mixed race matriarchs known as *signares*.

By the time of the French Revolution, St-Louis had a population of 7000, of whom a large proportion, including the mayor, were *métis* (mixed race). In deference to French blood, but also to post-revolutionary notions of the rights of man, the people of St-Louis and Gorée were accorded most of the privileges of **French citizenship**, including, after 1848, the right to elect a deputy to the National Assembly in Paris – a right later extended to the mainland *communes* of Rufisque and Dakar.

Futa Toro and Omar Tall

In the interior, developments were underway that would shape the future of the modern state. In 1776 a league of **Tukulor marabouts** from north of the river overthrew the Fula dynasty of Denianke in **Futa Toro** on the south bank, a region the dynasty had ruled for over 250 years. They were replaced by a reforming government of Muslim clerics (known as *almamays*) who, with fundamentalist zeal, dispatched warrior-missionaries to spread Islam across the western part of the subcontinent.

The greatest of these expansionists was **Omar Tall**. On his way to Mecca in the 1820s Tall was initiated into the **Tijaniya brotherhood**, which was founded in Morocco in the late eighteenth century. He was appointed the Tijani chief khalif for the region and travelled extensively, gathering a huge following. By the early 1850s Tall had carved out a vast **empire** centred on **Ségou** in present-day Mali and stretching as far east as Timbuktu. Westwards, his ambitions to expand to the coast were soon thwarted by the French.

■ French Conquest

In the 1820s, after the abolition of slavery, Governor Baron Roger had tried unsuccessfully to develop agriculture up-river at Richard Toll with a view to French settlement. **Louis Faidherbe**, appointed governor in 1854, saw no mileage in that approach to imperialism. Instead he annexed the Wolof kingdom of **Walo**, and brutally subjugated the Mauritanians of Trarza, who had long frustrated French ambitions to control the gum trade. To pay for the military campaigns, the first harvests of **groundnuts** were being shipped to French soap and oil factories. In 1857 a deal was struck with the head man of the Lebu village of **Dakar** – which became the administrative capital of French West Africa for the next 100 years – and further settlements were established along the coast at Rufisque and elsewhere. Faidherbe founded the *Tirailleurs sénégalais* (West African Infantry), who became the firepower of France's "civilising mission" across West Africa. He also strengthened the forts along the river at **Podor**, **Matam** and **Bakel**, which repulsed Al Haj Omar Tall's repeated attacks and provided bases for the French expansion across the Sahel.

Omar Tall was killed in 1864, besieged in the Bandiagara escarpment in present day Mali, his empire still land-locked and Ségou itself lost to the French. His son **Amadu Sefu** continued his reign.

Muslim Conquest

After Omar Tall's death, **Ma Ba** – a senior disciple – carried on the work of the Tijaniya with a clutch of Soninke (Sarakole) followers. They led and sponsored *jihads* against non-Muslim Mandinka along the river Gambia (see **"The Soninke-Marabout Wars"**, p.445), and also converted most of the Wolof kings to Islam, goading them into individual armed resistance against the French. But a united front of Wolof states proved impossible to achieve. In 1867 Ma Ba died in a battle with the **Serer**-speaking state of Sine, marking a temporary halt in the advance of Islam and leaving the Serer to a different evangelical fate with the Christian missions.

As Wolof leaders were converted however, and pushed their people – or were sometimes pushed by them – into accepting Islam, so **conflict with the French** became, with increasing clarity, a conflict between Muslims and infidels. Humiliated by their 1871 defeat in the Franco-Prussian war, the French found new reserves of aggression. And despite the marabouts' powers of mobilisation, the French grip on the territory grew tighter every year through the 1880s. The Wolof armies were defeated one by one, and the old authority structures – already weakened by the imposition of Islam – were dismantled as each kingdom was annexed to France.

Wolof Collapse

By now the French were irreversibly committed to making Senegal pay for itself and to directly administering the whole of their West African territory. When **Lat Dior**, the ruler of **Kayor**, appealed to the French not to build the Dakar to St-Louis railway through his kingdom, he was ignored, and the railway was opened in 1885,

despite sabotage by Lat Dior and his *ceddo*. The same year the **Berlin congress** divided the African spoils among the European powers, splitting Senegal by the creation of The Gambia and formally ratifying France's sovereignty over her possessions. Lat Dior was killed at Dekhlé the following year, becoming one of the country's folk heroes.

Another Wolof *damel*, **Alboury of Jolof**, at first allied himself with the French at St-Louis against Amadu Sefu's empire to the east, even undertaking to facilitate the building of the ambitious, and never-completed, railway to Bakel. But, along with his distant cousin Lat Dior, Alboury had been converted to Islam in 1864, and he was secretly in contact with Amadu Sefu. He later became violently opposed to French expansion, allying his kingdom with the Ségou empire, leading fanatical attacks and trying to expand Ségou even further to the east. His own kingdom, whose capital was Yang Yang, was formally annexed by the French in 1889; Ségou fell in 1893; and Alboury died in Dosso, Niger in 1902.

■ French Administration

As everywhere in the early years of *Afrique Occidentale Française* (AOF) the French stressed their *mission civilatrice* – their peaceful aim to bring French civilisation to black Africa. Only in Senegal was this accompanied by any real manifestation of assimilationist ideals. And even here, it was only in the four *communes* that French citizenship was available. Through the rest of Senegal and AOF, most people had the status of *sujet* – subject and were at the mercy of the hated *indigénat* "native justice" code, under which they were ruled by the local *commandant* – the equivalent of a district commissioner – who could impose summary fines and imprisonment. The *indigénat* and a mass of oppressive legislation, including tax provisions, compulsory labour and restrictions on movement, were mostly operated through *chefs de canton* ("district chiefs") nominated by and answerable to the *commandant*. The chiefs were frequently corrupt and almost always regarded as collaborators. Legitimate leadership in the countryside came from the **marabouts** only (see p.372).

Blaise Diagne and the Marabouts

In marked contrast, Dakar, Gorée, Rufisque and St-Louis elected a territorial assembly – the *conseil général*, which controlled the budget for the whole of Senegal – and a deputy to the Paris National Assembly. In 1914 **Blaise Diagne**, a customs official from Gorée, became the first black deputy, a post he was to hold until his death in 1934.

The tone of Diagne's career was set early on when he offered to recruit Senegalese soldiers for the French war effort in exchange for legislation guaranteeing the political rights of the black *commune* residents – rights which the colonial administration was keen to erode. Laws were passed confirming that they were in fact full citizens of France. As far as Diagne was concerned, only further **assimilation** could better the lot of the Africans. He saw Senegal's fate as inextricably linked to France's.

Outside the *communes* the Senegalese still had hopes of redemption through their marabouts, but the warrior evangelists of the nineteenth century were gone. In their place, men like **Amadou Bamba** – founder of the Mourid brotherhood – and **Malick Sy** – leader of the biggest Wolof dynasty of the Tijaniya – bought their religious independence by co-opting their followers in the colonial process, organising recruitment drives and providing support to Senegalese politicians in the *communes*: Blaise Diagne's election owed much to support from the Mourid brotherhood, who counted on him to raise his voice on their behalf. The marabouts also encouraged the **cultivation of groundnuts** a crop that quickly exhausted the soil, was totally dependent on the rains, forced farmers to buy food they would otherwise have grown for themselves and – as groundnut prices fell while others rose – led to falling living standards. In return the marabouts were given the administration's support in their land disputes with Fula cattle herders. By the end of the 1930s a system of **reciprocal patronage** betwen marabouts and government was established, and two out of three *sujets* were growing groundnuts.

Political Developments

Diagne was succeeded as deputy by Galandou Diouf, a less enthusiastic assimilationist. His main rival was **Amadou Lamine Guèye**, Africa's first black lawyer, who came to prominence by demanding the extension of citizenhood to the *sujets*. Already elected mayor of St-Louis in 1925, he forged strong links with the French Socialist party and, in 1936, founded the Senegalese

branch of the *Section Française de l'Internationale Ouvrière* (*SFIO*), Africa's first modern political party. When the French Socialists came to power and conceded some limited rights to non-citizens – the right to form trade unions for example – he began organising among *sujets* in the back-country towns.

■ World War II

With the outbreak of **World War II**, political life virtually ceased as the citizens' rights in the *communes* were abrogated, the country was scoured for supplies and the social advances of the pre-war government were swiftly negated. The Allies blockaded Vichy-ruled Dakar as Churchill and de Gaulle's **"Operation Menace"** attempted to rally the AOF to the war. Senegal was starved of imports, causing enormous suffering in the groundnut regions. Peasants were forced to switch to subsistence crops, and for the first time were encouraged by the colonial administration to do so.

After two years of Vichy control, the colonial administration did turn to the Allies and for the rest of the war the country was an important logistical base for the Free French – though political rights were not restored until 1945. During the Allied occupation an agricultural campaign – **"Battle for Groundnuts"** – was launched, which extracted more from the country, economically, than Vichy had.

Promises and Blunders

The **Brazzaville Conference** of 1944 prepared the ground for major changes in France's relations with its colonies. A fairer deal for Africans, allowing them more administrative involvement, was the main theme, partly in recognition of the part played by them during the war, partly because France's credibility as a great and munificent nation was in question. The underlying aim was the reconstruction of postwar France and the incorporation of all its territories as integral parts of the Republic. The possibility of independence was explicitly ruled out.

Yet there was a clear call for "Equal Rights for Equal Sacrifices", a reference to the 200,000 Africans who were recruited to the war, the 100,000 who fought and the 25,000 who died.

Events in Senegal brought citizens and *sujets* closer together. At the end of 1944 at **Camp Thiaroye**, outside Dakar, demobilised West African soldiers just returned from Europe refused to be transported to Bamako without their back pay. When a general was taken hostage, French soldiers were ordered to open fire. Forty Senegalese were killed, as many more injured and a number of survivors sentenced to long jail terms.

Then in 1945 the **vote for women** was finally won in France, but in the four *communes* only white women were enfranchised, a discrimination that under Blaise Diagne's 1915 guarantee should have been impossible.

Although the woman's vote decision was shortly repealed, both these events sullied relations with France and added fuel to growing demands for radical reforms.

■ The Rise of Senghor

To speak of independence is to reason with the head on the ground and the feet in the air; it is not to reason at all. It is to advance a false problem.
L.S.Senghor, Strasbourg, 1950.

Early in 1945 a commission was set up to look into ways of organising a new Constituent Assembly for the French colonies. One of the two black Africans to sit on it was a 38-year-old Catholic Senegalese, **Leopold Sédar Senghor**, who was chosen because, despite having lived almost continuously in France since 1928, he was the first African to achieve the rank of *agrégé*, (the highest teaching qualification) and was also a war veteran and a *sujet*. Moreover, he was a Christian Serer rather than a Wolof and had close contacts with the French administration.

In October 1945 **elections** were held to two electoral colleges of the Assembly, one for citizens and one for *sujets*. **Lamine Guèye**, now mayor of Dakar and seen as the most experienced black politician in AOF, successfully rallied various political groups to form a popular front and was elected to the first electoral college. **Senghor**, fresh back from France, was easily voted to the second college – even though few Senegalese knew who he was.

Reforms and Advances

Though not without hindrance, **reforms** were rapidly pushed through: the *indigénat* was abolished, as was forced labour. Even more significant, Lamine Guèye succeeded in raising the status of all *sujets* to that of citizen.

Senghor meanwhile was emerging from Lamine Guèye's political tutelage within the SFIO, campaigning to extend the role of the peasants in the interior, for increased financial credits and improvements in health and education in the overseas territories, and supporting the 1947–48 **railway workers' strike** for non-racial pay differentials on the Dakar-Bamako line. In 1948 Senghor formed his own party, the ***Bloc democratique sénégalais***, and became leader of an association of African deputies – the *Indépendents d'Outre-Mer*.

The postwar reforms and the rise to power of the *BDS* in the early 1950s soon transformed Senegalese **politics**, even if the economy remained heavily dependent on the fickleness of the groundnut harvest. Senghor's party capitalised greatly on its leader's ex-*sujet* status and the credibility this brought him with the newly politicised peasantry. Senghor also took advantage of maraboutic favour to impress on business interests his influence over the groundnut economy. The **marabouts**, formerly an important behind-the-scenes factor, were becoming political focal points themselves. Lamine Guèye's *SFIO* meanwhile struggled for support in the urban centres beyond the four *communes* and continued to ignore the countryside, to his party's cost.

The third political grouping, a loose association of **Marxist intellectuals**, trade unionists and students, tended to see the established politicians as too closely wedded to Paris. Their calls for independence were drowned by the clamour for fairer assimilation.

The ***Loi Cadre*** ("Blueprint law") of 1956 was a step in both directions. Self-government was instituted for each of the overseas territories. But there was not to be the widely desired **federation** of territories with a capital in Dakar. And defence, higher education and currency would still be issues debated in Paris.

This was transparently an attempt to **balkanise** French Africa. It's been argued, and was at the time, that it gave more Africans the chance to participate in government than would have been the case had they been answerable to Dakar instead of their own capitals. In that sense it was a device to cloud over the real issue – independence.

The UPS and the 1958 Referendum

Senghor continued to build a power base, drawing his support from the marabouts, the business community and **Mamadou Dia**'s socialist movement. He also attempted to make an alliance with Felix Houphouet-Boigny's *Rassemblement*

Démocratique Africain in Côte d'Ivoire, arguing the need for federation. When this was blocked by Houphouet, the *BDS* moved left and changed its name to *Bloc populaire sénégalais*, taking with it the *Mouvement autonome de Casamance* – the regional independence movement for Casamance which had grown out of the final "pacification" in the region little more than a decade earlier. Mamadou Dia became prime minister in the new territorial government of 1957 after the defeat of Lamine Guèye's *SFIO*. His party subsequently merged with the *BPS* and the *Union Progressiste Sénégalaise* was born.

The *UPS* was soon split by **de Gaulle's coming to power** in 1958 and his intransigent offer of immediate independence and severance from the French Union or continued self-government within the French Union. It was a critical choice and one that Senghor was unwilling to make. Mindful of French economic clout as well his support among the marabouts and their mistrust of the party left wing, he ultimately sacrificed a section of young *UPS* radicals (who immediately formed their own party) and made sure that Senegal's vote to continue the Union was **Yes**. With this Lamine Guèye and even Mamadou Dia were in accord. But trade unionists, intellectuals and Casamance separatists were mostly alienated and disappointed at the submission to de Gaulle. Modern opposition politics have their roots in the 1958 referendum.

Independence

Senghor still favoured an independent, Dakar-led federation of states. Working with the ex-territory of Soudan (now Mali) and others, the **Mali Federation** was formed to further this end; but by the time it was constituted in April 1959, the federation's members were reduced to Mali and Senegal – an unworkable alliance given the influence of Dakar. But it was pursued nonetheless.

Lamine Gueye was now elected president of the new territorial assembly. Modibo Keita of Mali was elected president of the Federal Government and Mamadou Dia vice-president. In September, inspired by Guinea's secession, the Mali Federation lobbied France for independence. And in a *volte-face* which amazed most observers, de Gaulle conceded that total independence should not, after all, deny a country the right to remain within the French Union. On April 4, 1960 (now "National Day") the principle of indepen-

dence for the Mali Federation was declared; and on June 20 **independence** was proclaimed.

On August 20, 1960, the Mali Federation suddenly broke down over the election of a president. The Senegalese had insisted on Senghor for this role, having begun to distrust Bamako's rigorous Marxist policies. Senegal proclaimed its **independence from Mali** the same day, arresting Modibo Keita and sending him back to Bamako in a sealed train wagon. Mali refused to recognise the new **Republic of Senegal**: for three years the Dakar–Bamako railway was unused.

The Senghor Years

Senghor took the presidency of the new republic, keeping Mamadou Dia as his prime minister. Senghor's formulation of **négritude**, Senegal's nationalism, blended with his motto "Assimiler, pas être assimilés", urging Africans to assimilate European culture, not be assimilated by it. On this foundation, Senghor and the *UPS* built the ideology of **African socialism**, which amounted to a tacit defence of the status quo in its emphasis on consensus. Dia, whose own politics remained to the left of Senghor, failed to find a balance between the business community and the radical left, and succeeded only in irritating the French. In 1962, Senghor had him arrested (he was sentenced to life imprisonment after an alleged coup attempt in which the army came to Senghor's rescue), and relations with France began to prosper.

The One Party State

The rest of the decade saw the government growing increasingly right-wing. In 1963 a **revised constitution** was appproved, strengthening the role of the president and effectively forcing radical opposition underground. Cheikh Anta Diop's *Bloc des masses sénégalaises* was the most powerful group the opposition could legally muster and this was smashed by a massive and disputed *UPS* victory in the elections of that year. **Riots** in their aftermath were put down by troops, with many deaths – the first serious smear on Senegal's hitherto spotless reputation. The *BMS* was banned; the remaining opposition had by 1966 been forced into the *UPS* or harassed out of existence.

Farmers were badly hit by the abolition of French subsidies for groundnut prices in 1967, while most town dwellers were no better off than they had been before independence. In May 1968 **trade unionists** and **students protested** at the government's complacency, confronting it with the charge of neo-imperialism. Senghor confronted the protesters with the **army**. Further strikes were followed by some concessions, then the government tried to force the unions into its own muzzled national confederation of workers (the *CNTS*). Some, like the teachers, resisted.

Repeated crises slackened off at the end of the decade when Senghor revived the post of prime minister – given to Abdou Diouf in 1970 – and, after further university unrest in 1973, banned the teacher's union and jailed some of the activists. The party was renamed the *Parti socialiste*, a cosmetic alteration that convinced few.

Democratic Reforms

In 1974, a cautious new liberalism was initiated with the release of ex-PM Mamadou Dia from twelve years in detention. Soon after, Abdoulaye Wade's *Parti démocratique sénégalais* was allowed to register and by 1976 various brands of liberal and social democracy were on offer, as well as a legal Marxist-Leninist party, which attracted a small number of radicals. A flood of political handouts and news sheets hit the streets. Anta Diop and Mamadou Dia were banned from forming parties, but not excluded from discussion.

By 1978, with Senghor now in his late sixties and spending more time on poetry and the *Académie française* than running Senegal, he began to groom his vice-president, **Abdou Diouf**, for leadership. Diouf was already taking responsibility for executive decisions and his status grew as he gained support from the major aid institutions for his austerity management of the economy.

A bizarre sideshow in the late 1970s was the **militant Tijaniya dynasty** of Ahmet Khalif Niasse. Niasse went into exile in Libya allegedly intending to organise for an Islamic state in Senegal, which led to the cutting of diplomatic relations. The Libyan connection resurfaced across the border in The Gambia, where the "coup attempt" of November 1980 reportedly had the same roots. President Jawara invoked the two countries' historic relationship, and Senegalese troops were sent in.

■ Diouf in Power

Senghor, the first African president to retire voluntarily, passed the presidency to Diouf on January 1, 1981. At first it was feared that Diouf's uncharismatic style would be insufficient to carry him, but **opposition groups** were hopeful he would lift remaining restrictions on political activities and their hopes were soon fulfilled. Cheikh Anta Diop's *Rassemblement national démocratique* (*RND*) was legalised, Dia founded the *Mouvement démocratique populaire* (*MDP*), and there were several others. Wade's *PDS* relinquished its role as the focal point of opposition and actually lost a few members in a purge of pro-Libyan sympathisers.

Diouf increased his popularity by launching an **anti-corruption drive** focusing on his own cabinet and firing Senghor's "barons". And traditional supporters of the government – the moderate Muslim masses – were gratified to have a president at last who spoke Wolof as his mother tongue and peppered his speeches with Koranic references.

The July 1981 coup in **The Gambia** was the severest test of Diouf's nerve in his first year in office. President Jawara called him from London to ask Senegal to restore him to power, which the Senegalese army accomplished with considerable bloodshed. A detachment stayed in The Gambia until recently.

However, the spectre of an unfriendly and destabilising power taking control in The Gambia galvanised Diouf to do something about the dormant **Senegambia confederation**. In December 1981 an agreement was ratified and a Senegambian parliament met for its first session in 1983. The Gambia, with no army and little to offer Senegal except a headache and its river, was always likely to be the passive partner in a relationship that finally collapsed in 1989.

The Casamance question

On the other side of The Gambia, demonstrations in **Casamance** in December 1982 led to detentions without trial. The region is poorly developed and substantially non-Muslim: the charge that it's ignored because it produces less groundnuts and can't muster heavyweight marabouts is not baseless. **Elections** the following year gave an embarrassingly resounding victory to the *PS* and left the eight opposition parties which had a substantial power base in Casamance, in frag-

ISLAM IN SENEGAL

Ligey si top, yala la bok – "Work is part of religion"
Amadou Bamba, founder of Mouridism

Any insight into modern Senegal requires an understanding of the country's extraordinarily influential **Muslim brotherhoods**. You won't stay here long without noticing – in the names on the bush taxis, the signs on the village shops and the flocks of multicoloured Hare Krisna-like disciples – that something very unusual lies in the dusty heart of Senegalese society.

ORIGINS

The Muslim **brotherhoods** are in conflict with original, Arabian Islam, which says everyone has a direct relationship with God. They resulted from the religion's spread to the Berber peoples of northwest Africa, the brotherhoods flourishing in these class-based societies, where it was natural to think that certain men should be gifted with divine insight, able to perform miracles and bestow blessings.

One of the earliest dynasties of Moroccan Muslims to make permanent contact with the people south of the desert was the *Almoravid* (whence *Marabout*: holy leader/saint) who, in the twelfth century, made conversions in the kingdom of Tekrur in northeast Senegal. In the fifteenth century, the **Qadiriya** brotherhood was introduced south of the Sahara and, by the end of the eighteenth century, was firmly based near Timbuktu. Stressing **charity**, **humility** and **piety**, Qadirism

made no exclusive demands of its followers and recruited from all ethnic groups. A local Qadiri offshoot, the **Layen** brotherhood, was founded in the late nineteenth century as an exclusively Lebu-speaking order in the Cap Vert district.

Another order, the **Tijaniya**, crossed the desert early in the nineteenth century and was spread over Senegal by the proselytising warlord Omar Tall. Tijaniya laid less stress on humility than earlier orders. Indeed, its Moroccan founder Al-Tijani had claimed direct contact with the Prophet Muhammad and, as a consequence, his followers were forbidden allegiance to any other orders. The brotherhood rapidly recruited the mass of Tukulor speakers in northeast Senegal. Tukulor marabouts – notably the forefathers of the hugely influential **Sy** and **Mbacke** families – were largely responsible for the later conversion of the Wolof.

MARABOUTS AND THE FRENCH

The interplay between **the brotherhoods and the French** was complicated. Allegiances often cut through ties of birth and language, so that, typically, peasants found themselves in alliance with the marabouts against their own, traditional rulers who tended to conspire with the French. Moreover, "pacification" by the French often resulted in more fertile ground for the spread of Islam. By the early 1900s, with the conversion to Islam of even the

most resistant traditional rulers, a new establishment of **vested interests** had been founded uniting the French and the marabouts. Although the Tijaniya traditionally had a core of fundamentalist, anti-French sentiment, the order soon adjusted to the material realities of colonialism. The latest and greatest brotherhood, the **Mouridiya** – exclusively rural and Senegalese – came, in practice, to be a bastion of the status quo.

MOURIDISM

The Mouridiya was founded in 1887 by **Amadou Bamba**, nephew of the Wolof king Lat Dior, and a member of the influential Mbacke family. An offshoot of the Qadiriya brotherhood, Mouridiya initially attracted many former anti-colonial fighters inspired by its discipline and dynamism, and by the charisma of Bamba. Rumours of an armed insurrection from his court at Touba terrified the French ("We cannot tolerate a state within a state") and Bamba was twice exiled by the authorities – banishments that only increased his standing.

Mouride folk history places great emphasis on Bamba's anti-colonial credentials, but soon after his return to Senegal in 1907 (a return celebrated in the annual *Magal* pilgrimage), he was striking deals with the authorities and trusting in the slow wheels of political reform. He was also amassing a personal fortune.

One of Bamba's early disciples, **Ibra Fall**, was personally devoted to the marabout, but he was a poor Koranic student. Bamba gave him an axe and told him to work for God with that. Sheikh Ibra Fall went on to found the fanatically slavish *Baye*

Fall; these dreadlocked devotees in patchwork robes now have their own khalif but they are exempt from study and even from fasting at Ramadan.

The founding of *Baye Fall* signalled a radical shift in religious thought, making **labour** a virtue and bringing Mouridism into the very heart of contemporary life. Among Mourides (whose name means "the hopeful") there's a universal belief that hard work is the key to paradise. Bamba is credited with announcing "If you work for me I shall pray for you" and even the five daily prayers are less important than toiling in the groundnut fields. The colonial authorities and the Mouride marabouts – mostly from wealthy, landed families – soon found areas of agreement.

THE BROTHERHOODS TODAY

Many senior and middle-ranking Mouride disciples today form a **new business class**. Even French-educated businessmen would rather become disciples of respected marabouts than short-cut the system. Over a dozen Mourides are multi-billionaires in CFA francs (worth anything from £10 million to £100 million) and Lebanese entrepreneurs find that business is increasingly out of their hands.

Illegal traffic has been profitable too, not least in the Mouride capital **Touba** itself, where the absence of government agents brought **racketeering** on a grand scale. All the hardware of Western consumerism, and even alcohol and arms, was widely available until the chief khalif, under pressure from Dakar, admitted that Mouridism was in danger of losing its soul, and allowed *gendarmes* into the holy city. The black market is clandestine again, but still funnels huge quantities of money and goods between Senegal and The Gambia.

Cooperation between the government and the brotherhoods – and more pointedly between the ruling *parti socialiste* and the Mourides – has continued, seamlessly, into the independent era. Yet the relationship remains one of latent mistrust, and even if many of those involved profit through it, the potential for a reactionary and anti-secular revolt against the government has always been there, as the Mouride brotherhood is conservative, overwhelmingly Wolof-speaking and rigorously hierarchical. The former chief khalif, **Abdoul Ahad Mbacke**, presided over a firmly united brotherhood from 1968 until his death in June 1989.

Successions to the position of chief khalif are times of crisis in all the brotherhoods, since the relationship between the voters and the elected government hangs very heavily on the words of the marabouts. The new Mouride chief khalif, the senior surviving son of Amdaou Bamba, **Abdoul Khadre Mbacke**, is considered to be less interested in worldly matters and therefore less likely to throw his weight behind the government's posturing and campaigning. This is a worry for the government, which is voicing a growing concern about the rise of a more **fundamentalist** strand of Islam in Senegal.

Economically, the Mouride-groundnut connection remains solid, with the **religious elite** supported by the harvest and the boundless offerings of their followers. With marginal exceptions the brotherhoods have rooted firmly in the safest political ground. The government, while insisting that the state and political process is strictly secular, lavishes publicity and patronage on the marabouts for delivering votes. In 1968 the chief khalif instructed Mouride university students to disobey the strike call. Twenty years later, the **general election** was won overwhelmingly by Diouf after the usual maraboutic injunctions and the same can be expected in 1993.

The *Magal* pilgrimage to Touba looks set to continue as the occasion when the state president reiterates his support for the Mourides and his appreciation of the benefits they've brought Senegal. In turn the chief khalif emphasises to his two million followers the sanctity of the groundnut harvest, the importance of not rocking the boat and their duty to support stable government, implying that a vote against the *parti socialiste* would be a vote against him, and therefore against God. The Tijaniya **Gamou** gatherings in Tivaouane and Kaolack are smaller-scale versions of the *Magal*, and similar back-slapping are the orders of the day.

But there's been an interesting recent development. President Diouf's arch-enemy **Abdoulaye Wade** – who is a Mouride, whereas Diouf is a follower of Tijaniya – has indicated that Abdoul Khadre Mbacke, the somewhat austere new chief khalif, is "his" marabout. Hitherto, maraboutic allegiance seemed to be given automatically to the government, and it's long been an irony of Senegalese politics – and frustrating for the country's left wing – that Senegal, with its highly developed democratic structures, should find democracy repeatedly brushed aside by the mass of its people in exchange for the grace of God. Although a wayward chief khalif wouldn't necessarily punch a hole in the ruling party, it does suggest the possibility of a rent in the almost hermetic Mouride-*parti socialiste* relationship.

mented disarray. With the question of **autonomy** in Casamance off the government agenda, anti-government groups announced the formation of a "shadow government" and a boycott of the nine seats won by them.

Diouf's new cabinet was announced in April 1983 and the prime minister's post abolished once again. Violently suppressed demonstrations in Casamance in December 1983 left over 100 people dead and hundreds in detention. Similar incidents have continued sporadically in the Casamance ever since.

Economic woe

The **economy**, meanwhile, continued to decline. Although the state groundnut-buying monopoly, *ONCAD*, was dissolved in 1980 after years of corruption and inefficiency, low prices and disastrous harvests that year and in 1984 meant no perceptible improvement for the peasant farmers. **Fishing** was pushed into first place as a foreign exchange earner, with **tourism** second and groundnuts third. Agricultural diversification is desperately needed: as subsidies on fertiliser and seed are phased out, soil exhaustion and poor harvests are the prospect for the future.

▓ Recent Events

An event that brought Senegal unwanted international attention in recent years was the 1987 **police strike** and Diouf's immediate decision to sack the whole force. The initial cause of the strike was the jailing of seven policemen for torturing to death a robbery suspect, but the trouble was exacerbated by resentment of the much better paid and equipped gendarmerie, who took over their functions until they were reinstated.

The **1988 election** was hardly any less dramatic, an ominously quiet polling day being followed by the biggest disturbances in Dakar since the "Mamadou Dia affair" in 1963. Diouf declared a **state of emergency**; tanks and tear gas came on to the streets; a dusk to dawn curfew was in force for three weeks; and **Abdoulaye Wade,** who claimed to have been defeated by a rigged poll, was arrested. His trial and conviction on charges of incitement to subvert the state triggered further unrest, quelled by his own and Diouf's conciliatory remarks.

Diouf, however, later withdrew any inference of a pact between him and Wade and set about making **changes to the electoral system**, ostensibly to guarantee fairer elections. In practice these adjustments have delayed local elections and enraged Wade and the main opposition alliance, *Sopi* ("Change"), who accuse Diouf of perpetuating the distortion of the democratic process by vested interests and vote-buying.

In foreign affairs, the government has recently fallen out both with **Guinea-Bissau** (see p.548) over disputed offshore areas believed to contain oil reserves, and with **The Gambia**, over what Diouf saw as the failure of the country to move towards full integration with Senegal.

But the biggest news to come out of Senegal in recent years has been the **flight of the Mauritanian community** (some 300,000 strong) in the immediate aftermath of savage intercommunal strife in Senegal and Mauritania against each other's immigrant nationals. The subsequent war of words has once or twice become a war of guns across the disputed Senegal River frontier. There's more detailed coverage of the conflict in Part Six: "Mauritania", p.317.

STOP PRESS

● The independence movement in Basse Casamance seems to be gathering momentum – there have been a number of deaths in attacks on government targets and over one hundred people are in political detention. Oussouye and Bignona are considered separatist hotbeds. So far, travel and tourism are unaffected.

● The border with Mauritania shows no signs of re-opening.

DAKAR, CAP VERT AND CENTRAL SENEGAL

West Africa's westernmost point and one of its most westernised capital cities, **Dakar** wields a powerful influence. Its pull extends well beyond Senegal's borders, drawing in migrants from across the Sahel and expatriates from overseas – especially, still, France. The city swarms with newcomers caught up in the neocolonial whirlpool, and its undoubted attractions are tempered by all this hustle and by the sheer size of the place. But the physical setting is striking and the city has undeniable style, epitomising the residue of French colonialism in Africa.

Out of Dakar, **Gorée island** is a major draw, while the peninsula of **Cap Vert** offers beaches and out-of-town amusements. A more sheltered coast is **la petite côte** to the south of the city, which beyond the dubious tourist magnet of **Joal-Fadiout** merges into the creeks and islands of the **Sine-Saloum** region, adjoining the Gambian border.

Inland, the travel options from Dakar are harsher and the attractions scarcer, the focal points being the shady rail hub of **Thiès** and the much more distant Islamic hothouse of **Touba**. If you're interested in the culture of the **Islamic brotherhoods**, some suggestions are made at the end of this section, along with details on the Sine-Saloum **stone circles** complex.

Dakar

A giant of a city in African terms, with over a million inhabitants, **DAKAR** can be hard work. The shock of arriving after a long overland trip can be intense: it's incredibly dynamic, sophisticated and wretched in equal measure, and a severe test of will if your budget is tight. **French** influence is inescapable, especially in the downtown **Plateau** area, with the architecture and the whole feel of the place constantly reinforcing the impression of southern France transplanted to Africa.

And the results can be quite beautiful, without question. Between sprouting skyscrapers, the terracotta rooftops and deeply shaded, tree-lined avenues of the older quarters give Dakar an elegant maturity shared by few other African capitals. Unfortunately some of the most attractive parts of town swarm with vendors and hustlers, but you'll find there are some quieter places, easily reached when you need to escape the sometimes overbearing pressure of life in the centre. The **Isle de Gorée**, **Hann Park**, and the beaches at **Ngor** and **Yof** all provide degrees of space and seclusion. And if, rather than retreat, you'd prefer a more human participation, most of Dakar's teeming **suburbs** are a lot more open and easy-going than experiences in the city centre might lead you to imagine.

How it all began

Gorée island was first settled by European merchant adventurers in the fifteenth century, whereas the fortress-like peninsula of **Dakar** was not established until 1857 – nonetheless the oldest European city in West Africa. The name Dakar was first used in the eighteenth century and is supposed to derive from the Wolof for tamarind tree – *daxar* – or refuge – *dekraw*.

The town's development really began towards the end of the last century, with the decline of St-Louis as a port, and the opening of the Dakar to St-Louis **railway** in 1885 (the first in West Africa), which gave a boost to groundnut farmers along its route. By the turn of the century the population numbered 15,000. With considerable dredging and port construction, Dakar became a **French naval base** in the early 1900s and the **capital** of Afrique Occidentale Française in 1904. It was also a calling port on the

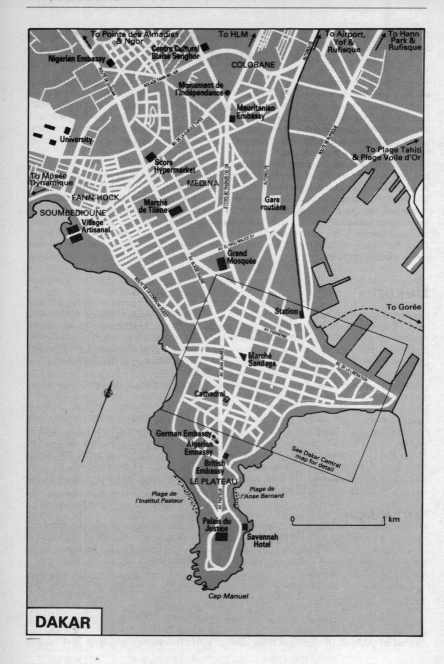

To Pointe des Almadies & Ngor
To HLM
To Airport, Yof & Rufisque
To Hann Park & Rufisque
Nigerian Embassy
Centre Cultural Blaise Senghor
COLOBANE
ROUTE DE OUAKAM
ROCADE FANN BEL AIR
Monument de l'Indépendance
Mauritanian Embassy
University
AUTOROUTE
RD DE LA GUEULE TAPÉE
ROUTE DU GÉNÉRAL DE GAULLE
ROUTE DE RUFISQUE
To Plage Tahiti & Plage Voile d'Or
Score Hypermarket
To Musée Dynamique
MEDINA
FANN-HOCK
Marché de Tilène
SOUMBEDIOUNE
Village Artisanal
Gare routière
ROUTE DE LA CORNICHE OUEST
AV EL HADJ MALICK SY
Grand Mosquée
Station
To Gorée
AV FAIDHERBE
AV BLAISE DIAGNE
Marché Sandaga
AV JEAN JAURÈS
RD DE LA LIBÉRATION
Cathedral
German Embassy
Algerian Embassy
See Dakar Central map for detail
British Embassy
LE PLATEAU
Plage de l'Anse Bernard
Plage de l'Institut Pasteur
AV PASTEUR
0   1 km
Palais du Justice
Savannah Hotel
Cap Manuel

DAKAR

routes to South America and West and South Africa runs, and throughout the hundred years of colonial occupation, Dakar's cosmopolitan reputation as the first call on "the Coast" went before it. On the opening of the Dakar–Bamako line in 1923, Dakar was easily the most important city in West Africa.

The original Lebu and Wolof inhabitants of the Plateau district were forced out to the new town of Medina in the early Thirties, when the Depression coincided with rent increases imposed to pay for improvements to their houses. Yet the white settlers who moved in were often poor – a rigorous colour bar prevailing over economic reality – and even today you'll see elderly French, some running small businesses, hanging onto very modest existences.

Orientation, arrival, transport and survival

Dakar is built on the twin-pronged **Cap Vert peninsula**. The southern spur contains the city's heart, with cliffs and coves along the ocean side and Cap Manuel, and the main port area along the sheltered eastern flank. The suburbs spread out north and west towards the **airport** and the other prong of **Pointe des Almadies**, Africa's most westerly point.

It can take a day or two to tune in to the size of Dakar, but the **city centre** is a relatively manageable two square kilometres of tightly gridded streets, with the **railway station** to the north, the **museum** to the south, **av Jean Jaurès** on the west and the **Kermel market** and **PTT** to the east. In the middle is the big, sloping centrepiece of **Place de l'Indépendance**, from where **av Georges Pompidou** runs out to cut the district into a northern, heavily commercial quarter and a southern, more affluent, more residential one – the **Plateau**. Most of the grand buildings of state and several important embassies are located south of this central district, where the street pattern breaks into graciously radiating avenues and looping clifftop corniches.

One slight and not unexpected source of confusion is the **renaming** of streets, replacing European with African heroes: we've tried to be as up-to-date as possible but occasionally the signs themselves have yet to catch up. Route de Rufisque is now officially *Boulevard de la centenaire de la commune de Dakar 1887–1987*. It's a long street, but even so.

Arriving

Arriving by air, you emerge into the milling confusion of **Yof Airport**, 12km north of the city. Track down your luggage and hang onto it: the supervision of the arrivals hall is pretty relaxed and not all the "porters" are honourable men. There's a **"24-hour bureau de change"**, that usually closes after the last flight . Until mid-evening, you've the option of *SOTRAC* **buses** #7 or #8, which take you either along the west coast of the peninsula through fairly exclusive suburbs to Place Leclerc (#7) or through the mishmash of Grand Dakar, past the University and right through the centre of the Plateau to the Palais de Justice (#8) – but you can hop off at any stop. If you get in late at night you'll have to take a taxi into Dakar (hard bargaining might get the price down to CFA3000). Spending the night at the airport isn't advisable.

Arriving by road you'll probably end up at the swarming **gare routière** at the head of the autoroute that funnels suburban traffic into the city. From here it's a two-kilometre walk to the centre: much easier to take a taxi (CFA300–500) or a bus from across the railway tracks behind the *autogare*. Arriving **from Banjul** on the *GPTC* bus, the terminus is Place du Maréchal Leclerc in the centre, below the PTT.

Trains come in at the old, Art Deco station, right by the centre and just ten minutes from the closest cheap hotels and restaurants. The train from Bamako usually gets in after dark, so make sure you're wide awake.

Transport

One of Dakar's great pluses is an excellent **bus system**. The *Société des Transports en Commun du Cap Vert* has fast, frequent and cheap buses which run from dawn till late evening. They're numbered and carry destination signs, and they charge a flat fare. You can get anywhere by bus, though during rush hours the squeeze – and the heat – are sapping. For long stays you'd do well to obtain a copy of the *SOTRAC* route map from the *SOTRAC* Direction Commerciale at Route de Front de Terre (bus #6).

Cars rapides – big orange and blue minibuses, usually sporting marabout monikers – are a poorer, and mostly private, version. Destinations are shouted by the fare collector, and although they're more erratic than the buses, you're at least guaranteed a seat.

As for **taxis**, supply seems to keep ahead of demand so that you can always argue a fare. In theory most operate meters, but whether you trust the clock or pre-bargain a fair fare is something of a gamble. Daytime journeys in the town centre should be no more than CFA300 and trips to the suburbs roughly CFA200/km; after dark (officially from midnight to 4am) the tariff doubles. Keep some change and small notes handy for when drivers don't have any.

The **railway** isn't a very functional way of getting in or out of the city, but there is a new commuter service to Rufisque, well out of town and sometimes used by travellers as a base. Called *les petits trains bleus*, the trains run about three times morning and evening in each direction, and seem to be highly successful.

Security

It's worth deciding quickly on an initial destination rather than wandering in hope. The question of **personal safety** is one you can't afford to be casual about, particularly when you first arrive. Be aware that Place de l'Indépendance and av Georges Pompidou are notorious tourist-hunting reserves, that a few gangs of organised **thieves** operate with extraordinary daring and that, burdened with luggage, you're an easy and valuable trophy. Paranoia isn't in order, but common sense dictates you keep valuables, purses and wallets completely out of sight. Don't be deflected or distracted – keep up a steady pace and get where you're going.

Once you've found a base you'll soon make up your own mind about the relative safety of Dakar. As a **general rule** however, avoid carrying anything you'd hate to lose and *never* keep purses or wallets in pockets. Carry a camera only in order to take pictures, not out of habit. During banking hours the pavements around the Place de l'Indépendance can be threatening and though it's not really necessary to wear mirror shades and a Clint Eastwood sneer, it may seem appropriate if you've just come out of a bank.

At the risk of sensationalising, the current favourite group **technique** is to stop you by offering a bangle, hold your legs together from behind and grab your shirt sleeves. By the time you've realised what's happening, they're off down the street with your wallet. If they bungle it, they may try again tomorrow – the police never seem to be in the right place at the right time.

If you lose anything of personal value (as opposed to just money or expensive items), it's worth making a visit to the market in Kolobane – the so-called *marché aux voleurs* – 500m east of the Monument de l'Indépendance, where, if you keep asking and manage to make the right connections, you may be able to buy it back.

Accommodation

Dakar has dozens of **hotels** and standards are generally high, with corresponding prices. Finding a room for less than CFA6000 is virtually impossible, and in December or January finding one at all can be difficult. For the real bargains you'll have to look well out of the city centre: middle-class suburbs like Dieupeul, Castors and Liberté can be fruitful. **Camping** isn't an option unless you're prepared to leave the greater Dakar region altogether, as there are no city campsites. The only alternative to hotels is meeting someone who's prepared to put you up, but while this can work well, the attendant risks are obviously high.

The city makes no more concessions to **apartment** hunters than any other, and a decent place is likely to go for more than the price of a modest hotel. If you are planning a long stay, you could try *Regie Immobilier Mugnièr et Compagnie*, 11 rue Muhammad V (☎21 03 74).

The following **hotel listings** give the best value rooms in each price range. The majority of cheap ones are located within a few blocks of Place de l'Indépendance.

BOTTOM BRACKET

Hôtel du Marché, 3 rue Parent (☎21 57 71). An old stand-by, recently renovated with a pleasant courtyard; S/C and non-S/C rooms. Handy for Gambia buses, PTT and Marché Kermel.

Auberge Rouge, corner of rue Jules Ferry/rue Mousse Diop ex-Blanchot (☎21 72 56). Perennially popular and usually full. Five rooms only, above the restaurant. Worth booking – BP 1033, Dakar.

Hôtel Mon Logis, corner of av Lamine Guèye/rue Galandou Diouf (☎22 03 71). Rather a dive, down an alley next to a mosque. Variable rooms, but cheap.

Hôtel du Grasland, (ex-*Coq Hardi*) corner of rue Grasland/rue Raffenel (☎22 55 22). Renovated old favourite with a new owner. Clean, quiet, well kept and low-key. No S/C rooms and no frills. Nice courtyard.

Hôtel du Prince, 49 rue Raffenel. Unmarked, bordello-ish place, but S/C and passably clean rooms for under CFA5000.

Hôtel Provençal, 17–19 rue Malenfant (☎22 10 69). The cheapest place to stay with a possible view of the Place de l'Indépendance. Rooms both S/C and non-S/C, some with AC too. Cleanish and well lit, but obviously a brothel downstairs.

AROUND CFA12,000

Hôtel St-Louis, 68 rue Felix Faure (☎22 54 23). Popular for its patio restaurant, but actually pretty basic and noisy. Prices for the ordinary rooms are virtually bottom-bracket level, but you pay dear for the dingy AC ones in the annexe across the street.

Hôtel Atlantic, 52 rue de Docteur Thèze (☎21 63 80). Very good value, as all rooms are S/C and AC. A rambling old place, clean and secure.

Hôtel Continental, 10 rue Galandou Diouf. Reasonable value, but the annexe at 57 rue Mousse Diop (once *Mon Logis*) is better; airy, light rooms with balconies.

Hôtel Central, 16 av Georges Pompidou (☎.21 72 17). Apart from its expensive address, unremarkable; but cheap AC & S/C rooms if you need comforts.

Hôtel de la Paix, 38 rue El Hadj Amadou Assane Ndoye (☎22 29 78). Modernish, clean place with a whole variety of rooms from cheap and pokey to large and half luxurious.

Hostellerie du Chevalier du Boufflers, Gorée Island (☎22 53 64). If you don't mind commuting by hourly *chaloupe* – or you just want to get out – this earns its place at the top of the price range; rooms with fan and breakfast. Often full, so call to check.

OVER CFA12,000

Hôtel Miramar, 25–27 rue Felix Faure(☎21 55 98/22 20 97). New, cool and comfortable, a three-star place and best value in town if you're going to spend over twenty pounds. Good breakfasts included.

Hôtel le Plateau, 62 rue Jules Ferry (☎22 15 26, telex 3252). A posh location but a little too expensive for what you get.

Hôtel Farid, 51 rue Vincens (☎21 67 19). Clean and fairly upmarket.

Hôtel Nina, 43 rue de Docteur Thèze (☎21 22 30). A good place with odd-shaped rooms, if rather over-priced.

Hôtel Albaraka, 32 rue El Hadj Abdoukarim Bourgi (☎22 55 32). Well over CFA10,000 here, with seasonal rates. New and fresh with huge bathrooms, TV and video. A surprisingly pleasant place with a really nice patio garden.

OVER THE TOP

Hôtel Indépendance, Place de l'Indépendance (BP 221; ☎23 10 19, telex 234). Curiously quiet, bland and absurdly overpriced at around CFA30,000, but the views are brilliant.

Hôtel Lagon II, Corniche de l'Est. Tucked below the French Embassy in a superb setting; a stylish place to dispose of large sums of money.

Teranga Hôtel, Place de l'Indépendance (BP 3380; ☎23 10 44, telex 469). *Teranga*? What *teranga*? Extortionate and obnoxious. Prices from around CFA32,000.

Novotel, bd de la Défense (BP 2073; ☎21 88 49, telex 3363). Chez-eux pour les français. A better place to dispose of an expense account than the *Sofitel Teranga*, and a shade cheaper.

The Town

Dakar is every inch a capitalist capital with **consumption** as conspicuous and contradictory as you'd expect. Lepers, polio cripples and other beggars are a common sight, and you may find the contrasts repugnant, especially along the café-lined avenue Georges Pompidou, where the police spend more time harassing the destitutes than the thieves. But unless you're going to do your necessary business as fast as possible and get out, you might as well resign yourself to participation and expenditure.

The city has some worthwhile non-consuming activities as well – notably the IFAN **museum** – and merely walking the avenues and exploring the backstreets is rewarding, especially during the comfortable winter months.

For a wonderful **bird's-eye view** of Dakar, go up to the seventeenth-floor swimming pool and roof terrace of the *Hôtel Indépendance* – just buy a coke to get access. From this height the old red-tiled quarters and the main avenues of dark green foliage stand out clearly.

The Museum and the Plateau

Dakar's cultural showpiece, the **IFAN (Institut Fondamental d'Afrique Noir) Museum** (Tues–Sun 8am–12.30pm & 2–6.30pm), does not make a great first impression: thousands of objects from all over West Africa, many of them visibly decaying, are pinned to the walls or lying in glass cases with little in the way of background information. Yet take your time, and you'll appreciate the visual simplicity of the display.

On the **ground floor** look out for the **white man mask**, obviously modelled on a moustached colonial officer with a wrinkly neck. **Circumcision instruments**, the giant **thighbone** of an unidentified but hopefully prehistoric animal, and a large assortment of **Senoufo** (Cote d'Ivoire) initiation and ancestor ethnographia compete for attention. Games of **pebbles-and-holes** (called here *Dodoi* and *Aji*), hundreds of **ancestor figures** and some fine **cattle and hippo masks** from Guinea-Bissau are also prominent. There's a fascinating account too, presented through a collection of printing blocks, of the development of a kind of African swastika, a stylised lizard or crocodile motif.

The **first floor** collections are slightly easier to distinguish, though there are **masks** everywhere. In the three central halls there are examples of **bark cloth** and the instruments used to beat it out, dyed and woven **strip cloth**, an entire case of spindles, whorls and looms, and the **costumes** of kings and lesser mortals. One especially striking outfit is the Gerze mask-wearer's costume from southeastern Guinea, which with its all-in-one gloves and feet could come from an operating theatre: notice how worn and red-mudded the feet are. The Fula (*Peul*) **circumcision costume** also stands out: it's virtually identical to the white "Phrygian caps" worn by newly circumcised boys on the streets of Dakar.

Dogon headdresses from Mali, now almost a commonplace image of West African art, are on show at the far right-hand end. Their remarkable geometric appearance, as if constructed from set squares, looks like the result of a stylistic evolution when compared with the more representational masks from Mali in the middle hall (first entry on the right as you come upstairs). The latter look much more like four-legged animals and the common "swastika" motif is clear.

Chairs and tableaux from the **Benin courts** (Nigeria) and illustrations of the arrival of the Europeans fill the central hall. Over in the big room on the right, the **sewn canoes** are interesting, while the lovely **balafons** – which you can play – make a glorious sound.

Outside, the main state buildings of the **Plateau** are obvious enough, and you can see them all – if you want to – in an hour or so, by wandering around the Parisian quarter centering on Place Tascher. On the *place* itself, across from the museum, is the **Assemblée Nationale**; along avenue Courbet stands the appalling **"Building Administratif"** a mega-block of ministries with a vulture topping; and then on the right down avenue Roume is the refreshingly high-profile **Presidential Palace**, with its be-fezzed and unfazed presidential guards.

The Central Markets

Down towards the port stands the circular **Marché Kermel** which, though designed in the style of an old southern French covered market, was actually built as the city bandstand. Later famous for **flowers** and **birds**, it's developed into a full-blown tourist market, a quarrelsome and unrelaxing place, its offerings including stacks of basketry, faddish fashions, carvings and other **souvenirs**, plus a cornucopia of expensive produce for the old-style *colons* still living in the quarter. Beware of dastardly sales psychology – don't accept "gifts" or, if you do, insist on paying. Repeated visits improve the atmosphere as the pushers get used to your face, but it takes courage to leave without buying something – if you do, you may hear *libanais* hissed after you in contempt.

You should experience less aggressive merchandising below Kermel, along the portside **boulevard de la Libération**, where an active street market has operated for some years. Don't come down here after dark though, as it's dodgy territory.

More workaday than Kermel is the **Marché Sandaga** at the end of avenue Georges Pompidou. This is Dakar's big *centreville* market, an unpretentious two-storey emporium with a tremendous variety of fruit, vegetables and dry foods, and lots of beautiful fish in the morning. You can buy just about anything here, from avocadoes to bootleg cassettes and attaché cases made out of beer cans. Hassles are fewer than at Kermel, but there's such a crush that everyone runs a gauntlet of pickpockets, and there's still a certain amount of hussle around the fringes of the building, where extra care is needed. Sandaga has been almost completely taken over by Mouride traders, about whom more can be read on p.372–373.

The **Mauritanian silversmiths'** yard has long been located at 69 avenue Blaise Diagne – 500m downhill from Sandaga. Whether anything much will be going on here is hard to say, in view of the Mauritanian exodus of 1989. Some of their jewellery was stunning, but less appealing objects were on sale too, including ivory.

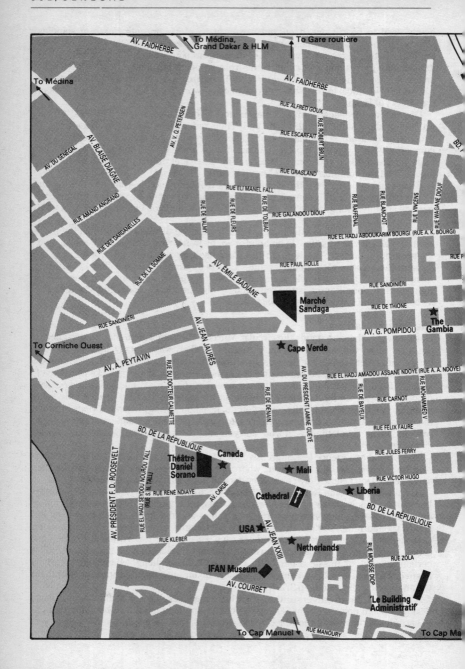

To Médina,
Grand Dakar & HLM

To Gare routière

AV. FAIDHERBE

To Médina

AV. FAIDHERBE

RUE ALFRED GOUX

RUE ESCARFAIT

RUE ROBERT BRUN

AV. DU SENEGAL

AV. BLAISE DIAGNE

AV. V. O. PETERSEN

RUE GRASLAND

RUE AMAND ANGRAND

RUE ELI MANEL FALL

RUE DE VALMY

RUE DE FLEURS

RUE DE TOLBIAC

RUE GALANDOU DIOUF

RUE RAFFENAL

RUE BLANCHOT

RUE VINCENS

RUE WAGANE DIOUF

RUE DES DARDANELLES

RUE EL HADJ ABDOUKARIM BOURGI (RUE A. K. BOURGI)

BD. I

RUE DE LA SOMME

RUE PAUL HOLLE

RUE P

AV. ÉMILE BADIANE

RUE SANDINIÉRI

Marché
Sandaga

RUE SANDINIÉRI

RUE DE THIONE

★ The
Gambia

AV. JEAN JAURÈS

★ Cape Verde

AV. G. POMPIDOU

To Corniche Ouest

AV. A. PEYTAVIN

RUE DU DOCTEUR CALMETTE

RUE DU PRÉSIDENT LAMINE GUÈYE

RUE DE DENAIN

RUE EL HADJ AMADOU ASSANE NDOYE (RUE A. A. NDOYE)

RUE DE BAYEUX

RUE MOHAMMED V

RUE CARNOT

RUE FÉLIX FAURE

BD. DE LA RÉPUBLIQUE

RUE JULES FERRY

AV. PRÉSIDENT F. D. ROOSEVELT

Théâtre
Daniel
Sorano

★ Canada

RUE EL HADJ SEYDOU NOUROU TALL
(RUE S. N. TALL)

RUE RENÉ NDIAYE

AV. CARDE

★ Mali

RUE VICTOR HUGO

★ Liberia

Cathedral †

BD. DE LA RÉPUBLIQUE

RUE KLÉBER

USA ★

AV. JEAN XXIII

★ Netherlands

RUE MOUSSE DIOP

RUE ZOLA

IFAN Museum

AV. COURBET

'Le Building
Administratif'

To Cap Manuel

RUE MANOURY

To Cap Ma

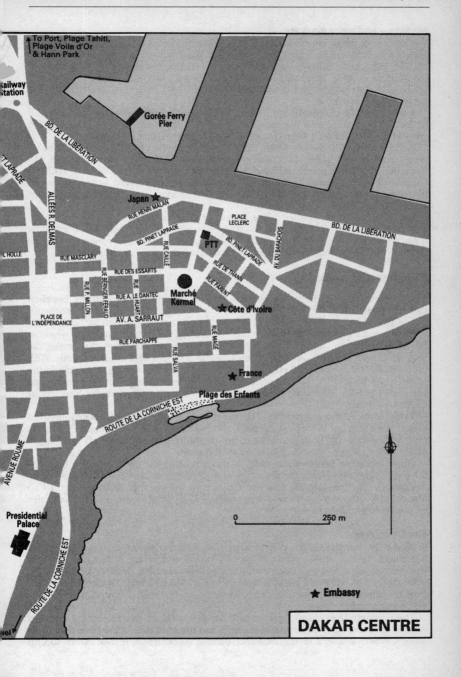

To Port, Plage Tahiti, Plage Voile d'Or & Hann Park

Railway Station

BD. DE LA LIBÉRATION

Gorée Ferry Pier

ALLÉES R. DELMAS

T LAPRADE

Japan ★

RUE HENRI MALAN

PLACE LECLERC

L'HOLLE

RUE MASCLARY

BD. PINET LAPRADE

RUE CAILLE

PTT

BD. PINET LAPRADE

AV. DU BARACHOIS

BD. DE LA LIBÉRATION

RUE DES ESSARTS

RUE DE THANN

RUE BÉRENGER FÉRAUD

RUE P. MILLON

RUE A. LE DANTEC

RUE HUART

Marché Kermel

RUE PARENT

★ Côte d'Ivoire

PLACE DE L'INDÉPENDANCE

AV. A. SARRAUT

RUE PARCHAPPE

RUE MAGE

RUE SALVA

★ France

Plage des Enfants

ROUTE DE LA CORNICHE EST

AVENUE ROUME

0   250 m

Presidential Palace

ROUTE DE LA CORNICHE EST

★ Embassy

DAKAR CENTRE

Medina – and more markets

You can't miss the **Grande Mosquée**, over to the northwest of Sandaga (bus #2 or 4). Finished in 1964 and built after the style of the Muhammad V mosque in Casablanca, it's truly impressive, with seventy-metre minaret standing out above the low rooftops of the **Medina** quarter. Non-believers are strictly barred most of the time, so your only option is to peer in through the windows. One day they'll put in the lawn that's crying out to be sown around it.

A trip to the **Marché de Tilène**, a short distance north, brings you down to earth with its football-pitch-sized food market. This is certainly the place to come for a massive array of **produce**, and it's where you can absorb ordinary Dakar life most easily.

Going a good deal further north, there's a vast array of **cloth** at the best possible prices in the market in the old African quarter of **Bène Tali** (bus #3 from Sandaga, #13 from Place de l'Indépendance), and more textiles at the less traditional **HLM V** ("Council Flats 5") market in the middle class suburbs out between Grand Dakar and the autoroute (buses #3 and 13 again). This last market has a recommended bar/ grocery just behind it – *Chez Moraira*.

Lastly, if you go out further to the suburb of **Castors**, there's perfectly humdrum general market (buses #3, #13, #18, #6) where you can wander in complete tranquility. A place to buy food, spices, traditional remedies, cheap cassettes, second-hand clothes and so on, it's somewhat cheaper than the central markets and easier bargaining.

Beaches and walks

There's plenty of opportunity for physical pursuits around Dakar, with the **beaches** naturally coming top. The best town beaches are *Tahiti* and *Voile d'Or* on the sheltered Pointe de Bel-Air, on the east side of the city; bus #6 passes the sign to *Tahiti plage*, from where it's a five-minute walk to the entrance gates. Unfortunately the whole of Bel-Air is a French military base, whose only saving grace is that they make the beaches as safe as you could wish (entry CFA200–300, less with a student card). With the *militaires* on one side and chemical and groundnut plants fuming on the other, the scene could be prettier, but the sand and sea are clean enough, and the palms and sunshades provide additional compensation. There are windsurfers for hire too, at CFA3000 per hour.

Tahiti is the nearer and smaller of the two; the adjoining **Voile d'Or** is definitely the better, stretching out to rocks at the point, and has beach cabins for around CFA10,000 (S/C with electricity). Both beaches get crowded at weekends; come early and bring a bite to eat and water – the beach bars are too expensive.

Other possible beaches are south of the port along the corniches (see below) – the pretty *plage des enfants*; the deep cove at Anse Bernard (crowded with local kids at weekends); and the *plage de l'Institut Pasteur*, on the rougher Atlantic side of Cap Manuel. All of them are to some extent unsafe, but if you obviously have no valuables on you there's nothing to worry about.

The Corniches

Walking the corniches also carries some risk, both having acquired reputations for bag snatching and various kinds of assault. Violent attacks are in fact rare, but you shouldn't go alone and under no circumstances take valuables. Both the Corniche Est, from the end of boulevard de la Libération to Cap Manuel, and the Corniche Ouest, from the Ministry of Tourism right up to Mermoz, are fine walks, mostly on the clifftop, with some stunning views.

The **Corniche Est** (4km) runs through dense vegetation, past the back gardens of various embassies and diplomatic residences and the front gate of the German ambassador's bizarre house, a kind of Sudanic-Teutonic construction. It then climbs to **Cap**

Manuel via Dakar's most picture-postcard viewpoints over the city and Gorée. You pass the self-consciously tropical *Hôtel Savanna* – a good place for a break and a drink – and from the forbidding yellow slab of the nearby **Palais du Justice** you can bus back into town. As you go, look out for the beautiful **Aristide le Dantec maternity hospital** – Sudanic architectural influences and two shades of baby pink.

The **Corniche Ouest** (8km), windswept and wave-ripped and racing with traffic and joggers, has a far less intimate feel. A lot of city tours come out here for the **Village Artisanal** on Soumbedioune bay, but it's frankly a rip-off arena, with high prices and loads of pressure. However, as long as you're not carrying anything of value it's fun to go down on the ant's-nest-busy **beach** to watch the day passing in **Lebu** style. The Lebu are fishing people, related to the Wolof, from whom they broke away at the end of the eighteenth century. Most belong to the Tijaniya brotherhood rather than the Mourides, but a few are Layen, an exclusively Lebu fraternity. Lebu villages have borne the brunt of the burgeoning greater Dakar.

The **Musée Dynamique**, on the far side of the bay, is not especially dynamic but art exhibitions are occasionally hosted there. Beyond, you come to FANN: more diplomatic and ex-pat residences with guard dogs and iron gates, and armies of dakarois youth working out on the skyline – the **University** is nearby, and physical fitness is a big thing these days. Any time you get tired of walking, bus #10 follows this whole route.

Hann Park

One part of the city that doesn't yet appear to suffer the problems of the corniches – though perhaps you should be cautious nonetheless – is **Hann Park**, eighty hectares of woodland and swamp with a **zoo** and a network of paths. It's a pleasant place for a stroll, again full of joggers and keep-fit fanatics in the hour before dark, and a good complement to the beaches at Bel-Air (same bus #6). It's quite attractive to ornithologists, too, who can find several different habitats here. The **Parc Zoologique** (Tues–Sun 10am–noon & 3–6.30pm), on the other hand, is moderately disgraceful, a small collection of listless mammals and a large one of birds – not counting the vultures littered ominously on the branches of trees outside. If you want to do it the Dakar way, you go armed with sweets and groundnuts and feed everything; but maybe it's best shunned.

Restaurants, bars and nightlife

The capital has a blaze of **restaurants** worth trying, and some that are even affordable. Don't be misled by the charmless parlours along av Georges Pompidou – you need to explore the safer side streets to find good food at sensible prices.

In addition, there are dozens of **shawarma joints** scattered across the city, and in the suburbs you'll find roadside **stalls** selling fruit, bread, roast or fried plantain, groundnuts and boiled eggs. Some stalls are more elaborate **snack bars** – one such is the *Diamelaye* near the Monument de l'Indépendance, opposite the Mauritanian embassy. The following listings mix the cheap and good with the more expensive but worth it.

Touba Restaurant, corner of rue de Denain/rue El Hadj A.A. Ndoye. A busy, clean lunchtime eatery with generous helpings of Senegalese food (fish and rice, *mafe*, couscous). Pay as you enter; CFA400–700.

Restaurant le ? ("Restaurant l'Intérogatif"). Two highly recommended venues with the same name and owner, both on rue A. A. Ndoye. Usually open. Long menus of Senegalese food, mostly around CFA600 – outstanding value.

Diarama, 56 rue Felix Faure. Cheap and popular but with unpredictable hours.

Chez Loutcha, 101 rue Mousse Diop. An exceptional Cape Verdean restaurant where you can splurge without wrecking your budget. Typically enormous meals; wonderful tuna salad and insurmountable three-course menu under CFA2000. Good for breakfast too. The room on the left is air-conditioned. Closed Sun.

Buffet de la gare, Railway station yard. Recommended for the *poisson farci* at around CFA700; otherwise an ordinary eating house, a little pricier than similar ones, but still good value for money.

Club de Presse, Place Soweto. Cheap beer in a bar frequented by Senegalese journalists. Daily dishes in the dining room, around CFA700.

La Buvette de la Chaloupe, Gorée wharf. A busy French place, bursting with tourists and ex-pats. Could be any French quay. *Plats* for CFA2000, *menus* for CFA3000.

L'Auberge Rouge, corner of rue Mousse Diop/rue Jules Ferry. Consistent Antillean specialities; on the pricey side, but usually first rate, and a nice ambience.

L'Oasis, 8 rue des Essarts. More *bonne ambiance* on the rear patio, and reasonably priced French food.

Hostellerie du Chevalier de Boufflers, Ile de Gorée (☎22 53 64). Seafood specialities in a romantically charged setting on the island's waterfront. Book a table, and take a friend and CFA10,000.

Keur Ndeye, corner of rue Sandinieri/rue de Vincens (☎21 49 73). Upmarket Senegalese with kora minstrels; meals nicely served but contents much the same as in a *gargotte*. CFA6000 for two, with wine. They also do a vegetarian option.

La Palmerie Diogonal, 20 av Georges Pompidou. Nothing to do with Senegal; delicious crêpes and wonderful ice cream. Air conditioned. Bring money.

Le Bilboquet, 29 av Roume. Air-conditioned French restaurant with impressive style and manageable prices. Drinks come with hors d'oeuvres. Large beers.

Bar Ponty, av Pompidou south side. Chips, burgers and *shawarma* from the pavement counter. Good, fresh and not too pricy.

L'Impériale (aka "Robert's Bar"), Place de l'Indépendance, corner of Allée R. Delmas. Popular refuge for toubabs escaping the *Indépendance* hustle. Expensive fresh fruit juices.

Etoile Bleu, rue de Thann. Cheap grocery and sandwiches near the PTT and Kermel market. Bargain breakfasts too.

After dark

In view of the city's impeccably cosmopolitan credentials, Dakar's **nightlife** is less exotic than one might anticipate. There is no shortage of **nightclubs**, but few of them are really appealing. If you want a fairly unpredictable night out, most in the following list of bars and clubs will do the business – but there are one or two stinkers in the middle. For money-burning venues with real action, head to one of the **big discos** or **music clubs**, few of which warm up before midnight.

Note: if you're going to check out several places and move by taxi, anticipate spending at least CFA20,000 between two, and that's without many drinks. Going in a group is cheaper and more fun. Take IDs but leave all valuables.

BARS AND CLUBS

Le Colisée, av Lamine Guèye. Lively bar, pinball and video games, swarming with *militaires*. CFA600 beer. A regular setting-off point.

Le Marseille, rue Felix Faure. Bar/disco/pick-up joint.

Saraba II, corner of rue Robert Brun/rue Escarfait A nice blues club; no cover; beers CFA700; food. Closed Sun.

Yang Yang, corner of av Jean Jaurès/av Emile Badiane. Indescribable, but loud and steamy will do. No cover. Beers CFA700, softs CFA400.

La Plantation, 42 rue Docteur Thèze. Recently refurbished and terribly pleased with itself. Good *dancing*. Expensive.

Le King's Club, 32 rue Victor Hugo. Flashy.

Le Harry's Club, bd de la République. Flashy and pricey.

Tropicana, 55 rue A. K. Bourgi. Disco. CFA1500, more at weekends.

Le St. Germain, rue Victor Hugo. Full of French prostitutes.

Chez Vous, rue Wagane Diouf. No different.

Imperator, 42 rue Wagane Diouf. Same sleaze.

Black and White, rue de Bayeux. Bar/disco. Drinks CFA 1000.

Jazz Bar Tamango, bd de l'Est, Pointe E. Could be in Paris. Clean in all senses, with occasional live jazz but otherwise discreet background piping and civilised ambience. Rarely any cover, beers not expensive.

DISCO PALACES

Ngalam, bd de l'Est, Pointe E (☎23 02 27). Covers CFA2500 Mon–Thurs, CFA3000 weekends; drinks the same price.

Le Sahel, Route de Ouakam/bd de la Guele Tapée (☎21 21 18). Taxi drivers know it as "Sam", because it's next to the *Hypersahm* supermarket. A flashy place, used for fashion shows and pop video recordings. CFA3500 cover.

LIVE MUSIC

These are the places to hit at weekends – or even around which to plan a stay in Dakar. *Relais*, *LT* and *Liberté Bar* are a short walk apart.

Kilimandjaro, Corniche Ouest, Soumbedioune (☎21 62 55). The best-looking nightclub in Dakar, with a hot sound system, chic clientele and little tack. Regular artists include Youssou Ndour and Ismael Lô. Fri disco cover of CFA2000 includes a drink; Sat & Sun entry CFA2000–2500, drinks extra (CFA100–2000). Check press.

Thiossane, rue E. H. D. Coulibaly (ex Dial Diop) (☎24 35 10). Everyone plays here, including famous names. Notice board ouside hails forthcoming events. *American Bar* features videos. On band nights (entry CFA2500, beer CFA1000), the scruffy interior contrasts with a cool, style-merchant crowd (to their delight).

Relais, Route de Ouakam, near the university. A student venue with cheap drinks (entry CFA2500, beers CFA500) and an open-air dance area. Small outside stage (check press for gigs) and good sound system encourage a lively young crowd paying more attention to moves than clothes. Not to miss if there's a band playing.

L.T. Horoscope, Route de Ouakam. A cracking place, though at first inspection not very promising. Four "venues" consist of a fast food outlet at street level, an upstairs bar-restaurant with "traditional" balafon serenades, a sleazy *American Bar* video lounge, and a tiny but red-hot night club with a formidable twelve-piece house band who play every night from midnight till 4am. An unusual, tiered stage crams them in the corner and makes room for luminaries like El Hadj Faye of Etoile de Dakar and Etoile 2000 fame, Dou Dou Sow from the Star Band de Dakar and a rising *vedette*, Alias Jalo. Drinks CFA1000. If any other plans fall through, you can always count on the *LT*.

Liberté Bar, Rte de Ouakam. Adjoining the right side of the Liberté Theatre, the regular Fri night venue for the re-formed Orchestre Baobab. Balla Sidibe, the host, mixes a mellów and friendly atmosphere to match a less pretentious crowd than most of the competition, reflected in the low prices – CFA1000 cover, beers CFA1000, softs CFA500.

Le Warref, route de Rufisque, Dagoudane-Pikine. A long taxi ride, but a cheap club at last when you get there (CFA500–1000 entrance, CFA300 beer). Live music and perspiration – try it.

Directory

Airline offices The main ones are:

Aeroflot 2 place de l'Indépendance (☎22 48 15);
Air Algérie 2 place de l'Indépendance (☎22 55 48);
Air Afrique place de l'Indépendance (☎23 10 45);
Air France 47 av Albert Sarraut (☎22 48 15);
Air Gabon 27 av Georges Pompidou (☎22 24 05);
Alitalia 3 place de l'Indépendance (☎22 21 29);
Air Sénégal 45 av Albert Sarraut (☎21 09 70);
Air Zaire 47 av Albert Sarraut (☎23 10 77);
Gambia Air Shuttle 15 rue Sandiniéri (☎21 21 12/22 54 22);
Ethiopian Airlines 16 av Roume (☎21 99 13);
Iberia 3 place de l'Indépendance (☎22 74 47/21 34 77);
Royal Air Maroc 1 place de l'Indépendance (☎22 32 67);
Sabena 2 place de l'Indépendance (☎21 49 71);
Saudia 12 av Georges Pompidou (☎22 63 00);
Swissair 3 place de l'Indépendance (☎22 48 48);
TACV (Cape Verde) 102 rue Mousse Diop (☎21 39 68/22 06 07);
Tunis Air 24 av Roume (☎21 14 35).

Others include *Ghana Airways* and *Air Mauritanie*. *Nigeria Airways* has closed its office. For **cheap flights out of Dakar**, check out *Aeroflot* if you're headed for Europe (around CFA140,000; with a few nights at their expense in Moscow; five days' wait for the visa), and *Air Afrique* for African destinations (good discounts).

American Express At *SOCOPAO Voyages*, 51 rue Albert Sarraut (☎22 22 79/22 24 16).

Banks Head offices all on Place de l'Indépendance west: **BIAO**, bad rates; **BICIS**, efficient, average rates; **Bank of Credit and Commerce International**, good rates, small and quick, open to 6.30pm; **Citibank**, good rates.

Barbers Men can get their hair cut cheaply at the outdoor barbers' stalls on av Jean Jaurès (corner of av André Peytavin), though the barbers aren't too familiar with straight hair.

Boats to Casamance operated by *SEMALINES* above the Tourist Office on Place de l'Indépendance.

Books *Librairie aux Quatre Vents*, 91 rue Mousse Diop, is probably the best bookshop in West Africa and they also sell books in English, a surprisingly rare commodity. There are several good shops in the av Georges Pompidou area.

Car Hire Main agents are:

Hertz, 64 rue Felix Faure (☎22 20 16);
Avis, 71 rue Mousse Diop (☎21 32 32);
Europcar (☎22 17 80).

Good value at:

Car Afric, rue de Bayeux. Air-conditioned Mitsubishi Lancer for CFA110,000/week (including 1000km free). You can pay twice as much elsewhere.
Dakar Auto, 7 rue Masclary (☎21 55 48), just off allées Robert Delmas; CFA30,000/weekend for a Toyota Starlet, with unlimited mileage.

Cassettes Stacks of bootlegs at stalls around Sandaga market and from street sellers in the vicinity. Beware of buying from the pavement cruisers down av Georges Pompidou. Prices should be close to CFA1000, normally less – buy for CFA500 and the quality will be dreadful. For "legitimate" recordings expect to pay up to CFA2000. For browsing and listening in a more controlled and relaxing atmosphere, head out to a suburban market such as Castors.

Cinemas The *Paris* on Place de l'Indépendance, and the *Vog* and *Plaza* on av Georges Pompidou show familiar American or European movies either *v.o.* (*version originale* with subtitles if not in French) or *v.f.* (*version française* with French sound track). Smaller and/or suburban cinemas show mostly martial arts films.

Cultural centres The **American cultural centre**, Place de l'Indépendance (☎22 01 24); air-conditioned retreat for looking at *Herald Tribune* and a selection of mags; good library;

Mon–Fri 8am–noon & 2.30–6pm. The **British-Senegalese Institute**, 18 rue de 18 Juin; caters to the small British community; library and film shows; membership fee; Mon–Fri 9am–12.30pm & 4–7pm, Sat 10am–noon. **Centre culturel Blaise Senghor**, rue 10, Place de l'O.N.U., Cerf Volante (buses #2 & #9); named after the film director and UNESCO ambassador, the centre hosts arty events and shows movies; closed in the summer vacation. **French cultural centre** rue de Bayeux/rue Carnot. **Goethe Institute** 2 av Albert Sarraut.

Curios For the real thing, visit *El Hadj Traoré*, rue Muhammad V, between rue Carnot and rue Felix Faure – a fine musty collection. There are more further north on Muhammad V, on the left before av Pompidou. Avoid flashy "galleries"– unreasonably expensive and not special.

Doctors If you need an emergency consultation try one of the following practitioners:

Dr D. Tap, 16 rue Victor Hugo (☎21 51 19/21 06 70);

Dr F. Coulibaly (Mme), 69 rue Mousse Diop (☎22 19 78);

Dr M. Kaouk, 144 rue de Bayeux (☎22 56 12);

Dr Chignara, 5 rue Parchappe (☎22 15 66);

Dr Benoît Marie Louise Correa, 25 av Georges Pompidou (☎22 00 59).

Embassies include:

Algeria, 5 rue Mermoz (BP 3233; ☎22 35 09, telex 3173);

Belgium, Corniche Est (BP 524; ☎22 47 207, telex 265);

Cameroon, 157–59 rue Joseph Gomis, (BP 4165; ☎21 33 96, telex 1429);

Canada, 45 bd de la République (BP 3373; ☎23 92 90, telex 51632);

Cape Verde, 1 rue de Denain (BP 2319; ☎21 18 73/21 29 91, telex 3128); Mon–Fri 8am–noon & 3–5pm; visas take up to 3 weeks to clear through Praia, with notification received in Dakar on a Wed or Mon (when the plane comes in), but visas can sometimes be issued in 48hr if you present your ticket); visa valid for duration of intended stay; CFA3000;

République Centrafricaine, Amitié 2 (☎22 25 71) – take bus #4;

Côte d'Ivoire, 2 av Albert Sarraut (BP 359; ☎21 01 63, telex 3170); Mon–Fri 8am–1pm & 4–6pm; allow 48hr to clear visa for up to three months stay; CFA3500 single entry, CFA5000 multiple entry;

Denmark, km2 route de Rufisque (☎21 30 43);

Egypt, 45 av de la République (BP 474; ☎21 24 75, telex 697);

Ethiopia, 24 bd Pinet-Laprade (BP379; ☎21 27 63, telex 413);

France, 1 rue El Hadj A. A. Ndoye (BP 4035; ☎21 01 81, telex 597);

Gabon, 36 rue A A Ndoye (BP 436; ☎21 15 29, telex 475);

The Gambia, 11 rue de Thiong (BP 3248; ☎21 44 76); Mon–Thurs 8am–3pm, Fri & Sat 8am–1pm; immediate processing of visas; ask for multiple entry; up to 6 months stay; CFA4000;

Guinea, km4.5 Route de Ouakam (BP 7123; ☎21 86 06, telex 3242); Mon–Fri 9am–3pm; not issuing visas at latest enquiry;

Guinea-Bissau, rue 6, Pointe E (BP 2319; ☎21 59 22, telex 243) – take bus #7/#12; Mon–Fri 8am–noon & 4–6pm (visas mornings only); 24hr to process; CFA5000 single entry (cheaper and less fuss in Banjul, or Ziguinchor);

Italy, rue El Hadj Seydou Nourou Tall (BP 348; ☎22 05 78, telex 641);

Japan, 2 rue Henri Malan (BP 3140; ☎21 01 41, telex 677);

Kuwait, 36 rue du Docteur Calmette (☎21 98 81; telex 3327); handling Mauritanian visas during the diplomatic crisis.

Liberia, 20 bd de la République (☎22 53 72);

Mali, 46 bd de la République (BP 478; ☎22 04 73, telex 429); Mon–Thurs 8am–2pm, Fri–Sat 8am–noon; 24hr for visas; one month stay, valid three months; CFA5000;

Mauritania, 37 bd Général De Gaulle (☎21 43 43); assuming normal relations are resumed with Senegal (see "Kuwait") Mon–Thurs 8.30am–12.30pm & 3.30–6.30pm, Sat morning only; introductory letter required from your own embassy for a visa; 24–48hr to process; prices vary with status and length of projected visit, and should be negotiated;

Mexico, immeuble Sorano, 45 bd de la République (BP 3830; ☎21 51 23, telex 51235);

Morocco, route de Ouakam (BP 490; ☎21 69 27, telex 21 69 27);

Netherlands, 37 rue Kléber (BP 3262; ☎22 04 83, telex 610);

Niger, km5 route de Ouakam (☎22 54 01);

Nigeria, rue 1, Pointe E (BP 3129; ☎21 69 22, telex 404); bus #7 /#12; Mon–Fri 8am–2.30pm; "issue of visas all depends on circumstances"; 3 days to process; CFA6215, but prices vary according to nationality; one month stay;

Norway, rue de Dr. Thèze (☎22 39 32);

Portugal, 5 av Carde (BP 281; ☎21 58 22, telex 61134);

Sierra Leone, consul at the *Clinique Croix Bleu*, rue 13 Castors (bus #3/#13/#8/#20); Mon–Fri 8.30am–noon; 24hr to process visas; CFA3000. Ask first at the UK embassy.

Spain, 45 bd de la République (BP 2091; ☎21 30 81, telex 415);

Sweden, av Albert Sarraut (☎22 30 74);

Switzerland, rue El Hadj Seydou Nourou Tall (BP 1772; ☎22 58 48, telex 411);

Tunisia, rue El Hadj Seydou Nourou Tall (BP 3127; ☎21 47 47, telex 561);

United Kingdom, 20 rue du Dr. Gillet (BP 6025; ☎23 73 92, telex 21690);

USA, av Jean XXIII (BP 49; ☎23 42 96, telex 517);

West Germany, 43 av Albert Sarraut (BP2100; ☎22 48 84, telex 542);

Zaire, Fann Résidence (BP 2251; ☎21 13 20, telex 254);

Zimbabwe, km6, Route de Ouakam (BP 2762; ☎23 03 25, telex 3231).

Flight information Yof International Airport, ☎22 40 60.

Language courses Private and group courses in French and Wolof at the *Alliance Franco-Senegalaise*, 2 rue Assane Ndoye (☎21 08 22).

Maps *Service Géographique National*, 14 rue Victor Hugo. Large maps of Dakar and Senegal.

Newspapers If you can't read French you'll have to make do with an occasional *Herald Tribune*, *Time* or *Newsweek* from newsstands along av G. Pompidou and the Place de l'Indépendance end of Albert Sarraut. *West Africa* magazine is usually in by Friday.

Notice boards Many supermarket exits have pinboards for buying or selling – cameras, cars, whatever. See addresses below.

Pharmacies There are lots. Each day's 24-hour one is given on the information page of *Le Soleil*.

Police Commissariat Central, rue de Docteur Thèze/rue Sandinièri (☎22 23 33).

Post/telephones Main PTT open Mon–Sat 7am–7pm. For **poste restante** you must present your passport or other ID (CFA165 per item). International **telephones** service 7.30am–10pm daily. PCV calls available to several countries, but not Britain.

Parcels can be sent from *Colis Postaux* office at Place d'Oran, at the junction of av El Hadj Malick Sy and av Blaise Diagne.

Shipping lines *Smith et Kraft* at Somicoa, 17 rue Huart (BP 55; ☎23 39 83, telex 51495, fax 214911), are port agents for *Grimaldi Lines*, which run regular passenger-carrying cargo ships to Europe. See also "Boats to Casamance" p.388.

Supermarkets *Hypersahm*, the city's biggest hypermarket (closed Mon) is out on route de Ouakam/bd de la Gueule Tapée. More convenient but pricier is *Au Ranche Filfili* on bd de la République/rue Mousse Diop.

Swimming pools Roof terrace at *Hôtel Indépendance*; fee-paying, Olympic-sized and thoroughly tropical at the *Savannah*, Cap Manuel; chic but slightly cheaper at the *Afritel*, av Faidherbe/rue Raffenel.

Tailoring For a job done well and not too expensively, try Ndiaga Ndiaye at Marché Sandaga no. A119, av Emile Badiane (☎22 97 84).

Theatre *Théâtre Daniel Sorano* is the place where things happen, often but not nightly; they sometimes have big name music shows here.

Trains Tickets from Dakar **to Bamako** go on sale at 3pm the day before departure – though first class reservations can be made from 8am two days before. Second class is always full.

Travel agents For general bookings and tours in Senegal try *SOCOPAO Voyages*, 51 rue Albert Sarraut or *Nouvelles Frontières*, at the corner of rue Sandiniéri/rue de Vincens.

Tourist office The *Délégation au Tourisme*, Place de l'Indépendance is pretty washed up. Visit the **ministry** itself in the defunct *Village des Arts* off av André Peytavin (BP 4029; ☎22 22 26): they have various leaflets.

Wrestling *La lutte* can be seen all over the city, with regular Sun evening shows at the *Stade Demba Diop* attracting the big stars (CFA2000). Wandering around Medina and Grand Dakar at weekends you can find amateur – and kids' – bouts. Around the Monument de l'Indépendance seems a popular venue.

Gorée Island

Just twenty minutes by *chaloupe* from the city lies the tiny **Ile de Gorée**, a mere 800m end to end and 300m across at its widest point. Its **slave-trading** history makes it more or less a required visit for all but the most unmovable – but it would be a compelling retreat without this historical dimension, and many people come back to it repeatedly. UNESCO has declared the island one of its World Heritage Sites.

The island bristles with old buildings. Apart from the famous **House of Slaves**, there's the excellent new **Museum of the Diaspora** in the horseshoe-shaped Fort d'Estrées, the less impressive **Maritime Museum**, the old **church** of St Charles Barromée, and, at the southern end, the **Castle** topping a warren of bunkers and underground passages from where there are colourful views over the island and across to Dakar.

Down in the town, dozens of flaking **houses** are virtually concealed from the street behind high walls and wrought iron: the president and the Aga Khan both have villas here. There's a cluster of fine and more easily viewed Gorée houses at the northern end. The sheltered harbour **beach**, backed by a row of low-key **restaurants** and bars, is a draw in itself.

History

The first Europeans on Gorée were the **Portuguese**, who first used the island as a trading base in the mid-fifteenth century. **Dutch** adventurers captured it in 1588 – naming it *Goede reede* (good roadstead) – but the Portuguese regained control, before again losing the island, this time to the **French**, in 1678. This date marked the beginning of the golden age of the **signares**. Daughters of white colonists and slave women, the *signares* of Gorée wielded extraordinary power in a largely matriarchal, slave-worked society.

Gorée was fought over between the French and the **English**, who repeatedly captured and recaptured Gorée from each other – the score for the eighteenth century being France 5, England 4. The island prospered despite the changes of ownership: by the 1850s there was a population of 6000 – ten times the present figure. The first fortifications of Dakar in 1857 signalled the start of Gorée's slow, graceful demise.

GORÉE ISLAND

Chaloupe to Dakar

Fort d'Estrées
(Museum of
the Diaspora)

Hostellerie du
Chevalier de
Boufflers

Beach

Maritime
Museum

Police
Station

Maison
des Esclaves

Place du
Gouvernement

Jardin
Publique

Eglise
St. Charles

Mosque

Le Castel

0   100 m

Around the island

For a day trip, it's best to take an early *chaloupe* to beat the crowds, and you should try to avoid weekends, especially in the high season; Mondays are quiet, but the museums are closed. Early in the morning you may be the only visitor, and the pastel colours of the old buildings and the bougainvillea draped through the narrow alleys make it particularly beautiful at this time of day.

The **House of Slaves** (10.30am–noon & 2.30–6pm; closed all Mon & Wed morning; free) is the sole survivor of a number of buildings once used to store "pieces of ebony" before they were shipped to the New World. A visit could be anticlimactic, though – especially if you've ever seen film of weeping black Americans visiting it. Unfortunately, some of the more famous of these, as well as showbiz and political figures from all over, have marked their visits with personal impressions felt-penned onto pieces of paper by the site director – whose own reflections have also been pasted up everywhere. If you can imagine the house without the festoon of posters, then its walls, dark chambers and slit windows, speak very well for themselves. This is a mournful and numbing reminder of the first major phase in the European exploitation of Africa. Scarcely believable though it seems, whites lived in some style above the warehouse, where there are well-proportioned rooms, a balcony and a reconstructed eighteenth-century Dutch kitchen.

The cleverly designed **IFAN Museum of the Diaspora** (same hours) takes you on an instructive tour through the island's complicated past. The **Marine Museum** (again, same hours) makes a more singular contribution, being in large part devoted to the life cycle of the dogfish – note the human foot in a preserved stomach. The oldest building on the island is the seventeenth-century police station, believed to be built on the site of a Portuguese church dating from 1482. But the great pleasure of Gorée is just wandering the sandy, quiet lanes and soaking the place up.

Practicalities

Chaloupes make about a dozen journeys daily from the Embarcadère de Gorée, off bd de la Libération; with very few exceptions, the return departure time from Gorée is half an hour later than departure from Dakar. The weekday departures from Dakar are as follows, with the Sunday and holiday times in brackets: (12.45am), 6.30am (7am), 7.30am (9am), 10am (10am), 11am (noon), 12.30pm (2pm), 2.30pm (4pm), 4pm (5pm), 5.30pm (Mon, Tues, Thurs & Fri during school terms only; 6.30pm), 6.30pm (7.30pm), 8pm (8.30pm), 10.30pm (10.30pm), 12.30am (Mon & Fri, and days after public holidays). Departures are prompt; return fares are CFA2000 for visitors and CFA1000 for residents – summon a French accent and slur "billet resident s'vous plaît". You'll notice that the *chaloupe* swings round a buoy just before arriving – it's avoiding the wreck of a British warship sunk during the bombardment of Vichy-held Dakar in 1943.

Commercial **accommodation** on Gorée appears limited to the often heavily booked *Hostellerie du Chevalier de Boufflers* (☎22 53 64) with double B&B around CFA10,000; it has a good seafood menu too (see "Restaurants", above). An alternative is to ask around town or at the beach cafés about the possibility of **private rooms**, which shouldn't work out more than CFA1000–2000 a day per person.

Iles des Madeleines

A trip to the uninhabited **Madeleines Islands** is popular with naturalists, and ornithologists in particular. Now a National Park, the Madeleines are the habitat of a number of interesting **plants** – including a dwarf baobab and American wild coffee – and many species of indigenous and migratory **birds**: the tropic bird (*Phaëton aethereus*), recognised by its bright red bill and immensely long pointed tail, is found only here. There's little coral in the seas around, but the clear waters harbour a rich variety of **fish**. Half an hour by motor *pirogue* from Soumbedioune Bay, this is a good outing too for anyone in need of a day of solitude.

Sarpan

The island of **Sarpan** – the only one at which a boat can anchor -is best visited between September and November, before the seas become too rough and the anchoring point in the cove inaccessible. It's necessary to obtain a park permit (CFA1,000 each) from the office on the Corniche Ouest past the Musée Dynamique. **Pirogue hire** can be sorted out on Soumbedioune beach. You should get them down to below CFA12,000 but the answer is to form a group. Occasionally the *British-Senegalese Institute* arranges a trip and it's worth contacting them first (see Dakar "Directory". Take food and drink as well as binoculars and a snorkel and mask if possible.

You'll almost certainly have the Gorée-sized island to yourselves. It slopes from 30m cliffs at its northern end to a gentler southern shore where the boats moor. Although no-one lives here, it hasn't always been completely deserted, as occasional finds of **stone tools** indicate. In more recent history however it's acquired a malevolent reputation and "L'îlot Sarpan" (named after a French soldier banished here in punishment) was soon corrupted to "L'île aux Serpents", of which it has none. The Lebu traditionally believe that a number of sea spirits live on the island: their own efforts to settle on it several centuries ago were met with strange weather and violent seismic effects and they settled instead on Gorée.

North and East of Dakar

An easy and much-vaunted trip out of town is the ride to the beaches of **Ngor** and **Yof**. From Dakar, bus #7 takes you up past the two rounded hills of **Les Mamelles** and the turn-off to **Pointe des Almadies** – Africa's Land's End – which, admittedly, isn't totally smothered by its *Club Méditerranée* holiday camp. Bus #7 then goes on to Yof, while bus #8 goes direct to Yof up the autoroute, without passing Ngor.

Public transport to **Lac Retba** and **Keur Moussa** can be unpredictable, and in truth neither need come high on your list. At the bottom of the list is **Kayar**, further up the coast – once a fishing village, it's now a tourist-trapping reserve of the most oppressive kind, where groups are brought to see the fishermen coming in. You can see the same thing, less intrusively, all along the West African coast.

Ngor

NGOR has blown away any charm it may once have had with the unbelievably hideous *Méridien Hotel* and a rash of beach clubs, restaurants and sporting facilities between here and Yof airport. The hassles for would-be relaxers are obvious and tedious. There are two options: hide in the *Méridien's* secure zone, or take a *pirogue* out to the **Ile du Ngor** (CFA300, payable on your return) – which is probably the best, if not the only, reason to come here.

The **island** is mostly divided into small plots for private beach houses, pretty enough retreats between the casuarina trees, but hardly idyllic. An old military assault course adds nothing to the cliff tops on the island's northern side. There's a couple of small beaches on the landward shore, but not much space when the tide comes in. For sustenance you have a half-reasonable restaurant/snack bar. There's no **accommodation** at all, but off-season you might get an empty bungalow for CFA3000–5000 a night.

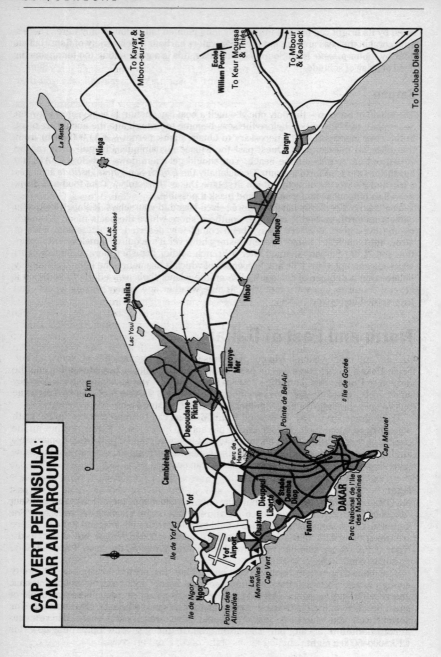

CAP VERT PENINSULA:
DAKAR AND AROUND

Yof

The village of **YOF** – a maze of houses, boats on the beach, children everywhere – has a sense of community that Ngor has lost. The beach is the start of a continuous strand that reaches to the mouth of the Senegal river. There's also a tiny island just offshore, given over mostly to goats but yours for the exploring: a *pirogue* will take you over, though at low tide you can almost wade across.

Yof is also a focus for the **Layen** brotherhood, an exclusively Lebu fraternity whose most venerated shrine is the **mausoleum** of the founder Saidi Limamou Laye and his son Mandione Laye. For members of the brotherhood, this slightly templish building is the holiest of sites, and it attracts vast crowds at the end of Ramadan; if the festoon of vultures perched on its roof doesn't put you off climbing the steps, respect should. A nearby grotto contains perfumed sands and is believed to be where Muhammad's spirit dwelt for a thousand years before being reincarnated as the sect's founder.

If you want to get *into* something – though you won't be the only *tubab* on the scene – come to Yof on a Thursday afternoon when **spirit possession dances** (*Ndeup*) are organised by traditional psychiatrists with the mentally ill – who come with their relatives from all over Senegal.

The Pink Lake

The popular Dakarois picnic spot of **Lac Retba** – also known as Lac Rose – is certainly a remarkable spectacle, but a trip out here is worthwhile as much for the opportunity to get right out of Dakar and look at the Côte Sauvage as for the lake itself. The pinkness of the soda lake is caused by the action of bacteria that excrete red iron oxide; for maximum effect, watch the lake as the sun goes down, when it turns from coral to mauve and violet. Salt is collected by women from the lake – which is almost as salty as the Dead Sea and just as hard to swim in – and packed into sacks by men at the far end. The lakeshore is a beach of bleached shells, with banana plots and casuarina trees greening up an otherwise harsh landscape. Over the soft **dunes** north of the lake is the Atlantic, rough and swirling and definitely only for strong swimmers.

Getting to the lake, about 40km from Dakar, take a #15 bus to Rufisque (see below) and then a bush taxi to NIAGA. The *campement* here – the *Ker Kanni* – has concrete thatched huts and a nice, local atmosphere (around CFA8000 S/C double B&B). It's then a twenty-minute walk to the lakeside and another, more expensive, *campement*.

Keur Moussa

The Benedictine monastery of **Keur Moussa**, up in the hills off the Thiès road 50km from Dakar, has acquired a reputation for its *messes africaines* – rather touristy affairs now, with koras, balafons and tam-tams, and plenty of stuff for sale afterwards. Sunday morning mass at 10am is the best. **Getting here** without your own car, you'll need early transport towards Thiès (hitchable) and a drop-off at the junction 5km past SEBHIKOTANE, from where it's another 5km to the monastery. Don't confuse Keur Moussa with Keur Massar, which is on the #21 bus route, much closer to Dakar. The coincidence causes lots of frustration.

South of Dakar

Once you get out of the city centre and onto the busy **coast road** heading southeast, there's still forty or more kilometres before the edges of the capital finally give way to open, baobab-dotted contryside. Road and railway go through the agglomeration of DAGOUDANE-PIKINE/GUEDIYAWE, a huge spill-over of city workers and refugees from the interior: already larger in area than the rest of greater Dakar, the sprawl is fast encroaching on the shifting dunes of the north Cap Vert coast.

RUFISQUE – the Portuguese fifteenth-century Rio Fresco – is the last Dakar suburb, and is already provincial in feel. A scruffy seafront town, it's more human in scale than anything closer to the city (you'll see *calèches* here, for example). There are also several wholesalers of **exotic birds** along the road – middle men between the poverty-stricken peasants and a market in the west which will pay the equivalent of a year's labour for a parrot.

If you're beach-hunting, there's little difficulty in travelling down this way by bush taxi, and it's one area you might **hitch** successfully. It's worth making the slight extra effort to get to **Palmarin**'s near deserted shore (see opposite) – especially if **Fadiout** leaves a sour taste in your mouth. And before reaching Mbour, check out the "Serer pyramids" in the Bandia forest.

La Petite Côte

At the small resort of BARGNY, the **Petite Côte** commences and road and railway turn inland to the junction for Thiès, Touba and St-Louis (see below). Heading south, you pass several turnings to **resort beaches**; if you've transport and a flexible budget, you may want to check some of these out – TOUBAB DIALAO and POPENGUINE (the two least developed), SOMONE, NGAPAROU and SALI-PORTUDAL, the last, especially, beautiful if a little sterile in its tourist ghetto pretensions.

Away from this coastal swing, the scrub-and-baobab **Forêt de Bandia**, to the east of the main highway (1km south of Sindia, 23km from the Thiès junction), is the site of an interesting archaeological site: the **burial mounds** of the vanished Serer village of Tay, and a **burial baobab**, where Serer griots were once entombed. The baobab still has a collection of skulls and bones at its small entrance. The site has only recently come to outside attention, but already a **replica** has been built of the burial huts which lie beneath the hardened earth mounds, and a guided tour is on offer. There are plans for developments here, including even a game park.

Though dusty, unattractive and crammed with tourists in season, **MBOUR** is the obvious base for this part of the coast. For **accommodation**, cheapest of the touristy places is *Relais 82* at the turn-off to the town centre – around CFA6000 and nothing special. The main alternative in town, a kilometre or so down the road, is the *Centre Touristique de la Petite Côte*, right on the shore next to the Préfecture, which at twice the price is unlikely to be money better spent. Take a look instead at *Le Filao* pizzeria, which has a few rooms for CFA5000 – the drawback here is that they give onto the *Jardin des Rêves*, which gets noisier as the evening progresses.

Mbour has a fair offering of bars and small **restaurants**: *Restaurant d'Islam* has been popular for some years, with meals for CFA1000. The town has a **PTT** and a *BICIS* **bank**, and there's even a bit of a **tourist office** along avenue El Hadj Malick Sy. But the town depends first on fishing, not tourism; the beach is dirty and littered with fishy remains, and the sea is uninviting anyway – usually calm and tending to weediness. The **gare routière** is in front of the tree-shaded **marketplace**.

The road continues south past NIANING and a couple of exclusive holiday villages – *Domaine de Nianing* for the French on the landward side, and *Club Aldiana* for German packagers on the sands. Substantial **birdlife** through the remains of the **Forêt de Nianing** keeps it all fairly pleasant and the shore scene, with scattered palm trees, is pretty enough.

Joal-Fadiout

Next stop is **JOAL**, the underrated town where president Senghor was born. It's another old Portuguese settlement, with a few old houses still standing, including the Senghors'. If you arrive at the end of the day, the hauling-in of the fish is as diverting as anywhere.

But apart from a visit to *Chez Senghor* and a pat delivery from the on-tap *gardien*, the big draw is a wander over to **FADIOUT**, the fishing village on the shell-bank **island** in the estuary facing Joal. By virtue of a wicked combination of attractive features – proximity to the tourist camps up the coast, houses built of crushed shells, granary huts on stilts like a field of mushrooms, and fishermen's cemetery on a neighbouring island – Fadiout is one of the most aggressive hustler haunts in Senegal. Down at the bridge to the island there's a gauntlet of obnoxious teenage "guides" to be overcome: if you spurn their *pirogues* and persist in walking over, they'll follow you waving sea and turtle shells for sale and making uninviting offers of cheap *logements*.

Fadiout is fascinating though, a **"shell midden"** entirely composed of the refuse from centuries of shellfish consumption. It takes about an hour to trail around the houses and Serer cemetery, which is about as long as you'll be able to sustain resistance to all the pestering.

If you would actually like to do a **pirogue trip**, get into top bargaining gear and make sure you know how long you're going to get. Note, too, that the grain store island, a few hundred metres to the southeast of Fadiout, is virtually empty before the harvest and not very impressive at that time.

For **food and accommodation**, look to Joal. Probably you'll want to avoid the *Hôtel le Finnio* right by the bridge: the tour groups call in here, and it shows. Leave the Catholic mission alone too, even if you're broke: they have absolutely no interest in putting you up. Instead, make for the centre of town and check out the well-signposted *Relais 114*, run by a Guinean family who insist on having nothing to do with "guides". Clean non-S/C doubles are around CFA4000 and there's a pleasant balcony with hammocks. The *Relais* makes a big thing of its lobster, but much cheaper eats are to be had in omelette and shawarma bars around town. **Beaches** in this area are all too crowded and hustly for abandonment to the sun, sea and sand. On the fishing beach near the town centre you can mingle with the masses at the end of the day and normally be ignored, but about the only place you might consider for a peaceful **swim** is the sandy, casuarina-covered bar to the south, past the school and football pitch.

The Saloum Delta

Situated between Dakar and The Gambia, the delta of Senegal's third river – the **Saloum** – tends unjustly to get bypassed. Visiting the maze of islands and creeks by *pirogue* from the landward side – the usual way – can work out expensive; the best solution is to get a vehicle down from Joal to **PALMARIN** – but be prepared to wait several hours and possibly to change vehicles at KEUR SAMBA DIA. Going back again is harder, but there's always space when a vehicle comes: as one passer-by commented, cryptically, "La voiture du sous-développement est jamais pleine". And if rains have washed the road out completely, you'll hear of it.

Palmarin has a wonderful **campement** – an outpost of Casamance's system of *campements rurals intégrés* (see p.357) – right on the beach, a short distance from the village itself. Thatched, twin-bed huts among the palms and a gas refrigerator full of cheap cold beer are all you really need. Kerosene lamps, shared washing and loos and communal dinner and breakfast are included at the current *CRI* rate of CFA3000 a day.

Around the delta

The **campement** owner is helpful with arrangements to hire a **pirogue** for the day, most easily done at **DJIFERE**, south of Palmarin – but getting here by *bâché* will involve a wait. Prices for the day need serious discussion, but you shouldn't pay more than CFA10,000 for six hours' worth of boat and crew.

DIONEWAR and NIODIOR on the **Ile de Guior** are laid-back villages, little affected by the gradual advance of tourism. Nearer the Gambian border and inside the **Parc**

National du Delta du Saloum, the **Ile aux Oiseaux** has variably interesting birdlife – time of day and time of year are both critical. Early evening tends to yield better bird-watching, and palearctic migrants swell numbers from October to March. Turtles are common; dolphins often seen too.

From Djifere it's possible to take a trading *pirogue* down to Banjul, which is the closest large town by boat – they go several times a week (daily, some claim), and cost about CFA2000. The journey – 60km along the shore – takes around six hours.

Other departure points for the delta are **FOUNDIOUGNE**, below **KAOLACK**, 33km from the main highway at **PASSI** (also accessible by road from **FATICK** and then a ferry); **NDANGANE**, reachable from Joal or from the main highway east of THIADAYE; and **TOUBACOUTA**, conveniently just 2km from the highway and 25km from the Gambian border. All three places have fairly luxurious holidaying set-ups.

Thiès and onward

The great garrison town and rail hub of colonial days, and now Senegal's second largest town, **THIÈS** is close enough to Dakar (70km) to be an easy visit, and also lies en route if you're journeying by train to other parts of the country. **Arriving** by bus or taxi you'll almost certainly be left at the *gare routière*, 3km out of town – a good reason to come by train. The railway is still the pivot of much of the town's life, whose rhythms are adjusted to the comings and goings on the track. Thiès has restaurants and a scattering of **places to stay** – let us know if any shine.

Thiès retains much of the character of a French town, with parks and wide shady avenues, solid brick and tiles, a remarkable old Sudanic-style cinema, and even the odd rampart from an earlier period of "pacification". Its history, even in recent times, has been punctuated by violent episodes, notably the 1947 strike by railway workers – "God's Bits of Wood" of Sembene Ousmane's novel.

The Tapestry Factory and the Museum

Main points of interest if you're passing through are the small **museum** and the very impressive **tapestry factory**, both reached from the centre of town by following the railway (on your right) in the St-Louis direction. At the junction by the level crossing (fortifications on your left), head off left.

The **Manufactures Senegalaises des Arts Decoratifs** (Mon–Fri 8am–12.30pm & 3–6.30pm, Sat 8am–12.30pm; entry charge), opened in 1966, focuses the output of many of Senegal's artists and has an enormous influence on younger painters. Having work painstakingly redrawn and fabricated into glowing tapestries – many for exhibition and sale abroad – is an accolade providing a rare incentive.

Since its foundation, the Thiès school has produced fewer than 400 pieces: its annual output working out at around 300 square metres, each tapestry being produced in an exclusive edition of eight. Prices are accordingly high – around CFA400,000 per square metre. The workmanship is the very finest, and there are few centres – if any – in West Africa which match Thiès for sheer impact. Common themes are village life, nature, history and myth, executed in dazzling, graphic style. Look out for the stunning *Rendezvous au Soleil* by Jacob Yacouba, a giant ten-metre version of which was purchased by Atlanta airport. Yet a lot of the designs suggest some fresh ideas are needed in the selection criteria, and as more commercially oriented foreign painters begin commissioning the Thiès workshops to weave their own work for them, there's a danger the centre will lose its creative edge.

Try to get to see all the stages of work, from drawing up the original paintings to dyeing the wool and the rapid but careful process of weaving itself. You should be allowed to take photos in the workshops, but perhaps not in the exhibition hall.

Across the way is the **Museum** (Mon–Fri 8am–noon & 3–6pm, Sat 8am–noon), housed in the fort, first built in 1871. Aside from a number of interesting photos and a good deal of commentary on Senegalese history, there's a special concentration on the role of the marabouts. Near the museum there's a small **art workshop** where a number of artists work and sell their paintings.

Inland from Thiès

Heading onwards from Thiès, there are a number of diversions if you have time to do things slowly. Moving north, you might visit **Tivaouane** if you're gripped by the fascination of the Islamic brotherhoods. Or, heading south, you could go to **Kaolack** via **Diourbel**, from where you might strike out to **Touba**, the big Mouride stornghold with the country's most impressive mosque. From Touba there's the option of following the dusty N3 highway northeast, onwards via **Linguère** to **Matam** on the Senegal river. Lastly, if you're heading through the **Sine-Saloum region**, either south on the *trans-gambienne* or east on the N1 to Tambacounda, you might take time out to look at some of the Iron Age **stone circles** .

Independent transport is the best way to visit these places, though with the possible exception of the stone circles and Touba during *Magal*, you'll normally find public means to the towns.

Tivaouane

TIVAOUANE, 5km off the main N2 to St-Louis, is the seat of the **Sy** dynasty of the **Tijaniya** brotherhood, the largest brotherhood in Senegal. The grand North African style mosque is best seen during *Gamou*, the Tijani pilgrimage, or *Maulidi*, the prophet's birthday, when thousands of believers pour into the town. Accommodation, which seems pretty minimal at the best of times, is impossible to find during these times.

Diourbel and Touba

DIOURBEL, with its huge domed mosque, is one of the principal saintly towns of the Mourides, and capital of the region of the same name, the heart of the groundnut basin.

Fifty kilometres east, following the Sine valley, lies **TOUBA**, the burial place of the founder of Mouridism, **Sheikh Amadou Bamba Mbacke** (1850–1927), and thus the high holy place of the brotherhood. The extraordinary 87-metre-high mosque – built over the family tomb in 1963 and visible from miles away – is the largest and one of the finest in West Africa, and the most important religious shrine in Senegal.

Amadou Bamba's triumphal return home in 1907, after years of detention by the French, is celebrated annually in the festival of **Magal** (see the Muslim calendar on p.53 for dates). Up to half a million pilgrims flock here from all over Senegal and The Gambia, and public transport – hard to find anywhere (in The Gambia even the state-owned *GPTC* buses are roped in) – is virtually suspended on routes to and from Touba. *Magal* is the manifestation of a religious fervour whose only equal in Africa is found in northern Nigeria.

Senegalese authority is minimal here: the **maraboutic militia** is responsible for law and order, which includes absolute bans on tobacco and alcohol anywhere in the town precincts. Searches – especially of *tubabs* – aren't uncommon, and you will be fined and your drugs confiscated if found out. Photography, too, isn't likely to please many. Despite these considerations, Touba can be an irresistible challenge. If you're going there for *Magal*, expect to spend the night awake with the crowd of *talibes* disciples: you'll almost certainly have found companions on the journey. Be warned, though, that **accommodation** isn't likely to come your way if you don't get invited.

Rooms might be available 10km away in **MBACKE**, a kind of secular counterpoint to Touba, where the maraboutic laws don't apply. And you could get stranded there for the big night anyway, as Mbacke goes into partying hyperdrive, diverting attention from the devotions at Touba and increasingly reducing *Magal* to a Christmas-style commercialism.

Coming with your own vehicle, you may end up jammed in pedestrian traffic or directed to leave your vehicle in a designated zone and walk. However you manage it, don't confuse piety with honesty. Touba has plenty of "guides" and during *Magal* a nimble army of hustlers and pickpockets filters the crowds.

To Linguère

With stamina you could continue from the Touba area to Linguère and Matam (see p.408). This route, the N2, goes right through the heart of the Fula **Réserves Sylvo-Pastorales** (wild grazing reserves), a fragmented cluster of badlands (virtually tribal reserves), glumly conceded to the pastoralists and always under threat from the expanding Mouride groundnut enterprises. With improved irrigation and increases in population, agriculture encroaches on all sides except the east, where the *Réserves de Faune du Ferlo-Nord* and *Ferlo-Sud* – areas in which no grazing is permitted – create a barrier between the cattle herds and the potentially rich Senegal river valley.

LINGUÈRE is the main town of this region, surrounded by the reserves and not a place of great interest, it would seem. But there must be somewhere to stay; let us know. If you've transport, or a dogged persistence coupled with a devotion to obscure archaeological sites, you might move down the Ferlo river course from Linguère to the ruins of the **fortress** of Alboury Ndiaye – the last independent ruler of the Wolof kingdom of Jolof (see p.306). The site is located to the north of the road before the village of YANG-YANG.

From Linguère the road to the river Senegal at Matam follows the normally dry upper course of the Ferlo, between the faunal reserves. Transport is limited and departures early.

Kaolack

A big, noisy interchange town, hub of five road routes (but not on the main railway line), **KAOLACK** is not a place where you'll particularly want to stop over. If you do, take a look at the brand new mosque, a splendid creation by all accounts, paid for partly by Saddam Hussein of Iraq. The Niasse dynasty of the Tijaniya brotherhood – based here – is bent on founding an Islamic republic, a movement which is also reportedly funded by Libya. Kaolack has a venerable and bustling market and a number of reasonable hotels.

Sine-Saloum Stone Circles

Part of the same cultural complex as the circles in The Gambia (see p.471), the **megliths** scattered across the plain between Nioro du Rip on the *transgambienne* N4 and Tambacounda are vestiges of a prehistoric society about which virtually nothing is known. Including some unimpressive circles that you'd not glance twice at, they number approximately **one thousand** in this region. Associated with them are burial sites which have yielded a number of skeletons and a certain amount of weaponry, pots and copper ornaments. Seeming to date from before the twelfth century, they bear no sign of any Islamic impact.

The most impressive site is the one known as **Djalloumbéré**, at **NGAYÈNE**, hard against the Gambian border. Over eleven hundred individual pillars here make up fifty-two stone circles – some of them the sites of mass burials. It's hardly more inaccessible than Wassu in The Gambia, but it's virtually impossible without your own transport, turning left 9km south of Nioro du Rip to Kaymor (17km) on a decent track, then continuing southeast another 15km via Tène Peul and Keur Bakari to Ngayène. From here you can head straight back to the main road at MEDINA SABAK, 28km from Nioro.

In the middle of this "circuit", 10km due south of Kaymor, is the village of PAYOMA, where stones from the local circles have been uprooted to support the buildings – including the mosque. Numerous other circles are visible at various points along these tracks.

Assuming you've got wheels or you're using a *taxi brousse*, there are more easily accessible sites along the Tambacounda highway, at **MALÈME HODAR** (right by the road) and **KEUR ALBÉ** and **SALI**, respectively 9km and 20km southwest of KONGHEUL on a minor road to The Gambia. This road crosses the border just north of Wassu (see p.471): if you're enraptured by the circles and your papers are in order, you could cross over for further observations and stay in Kuntaur or Georgetown.

THE NORTH AND EAST

Northern Senegal is the least populated part of the country, with few large towns and a landscape whose main interest derives from its harsh marginality. Northeast of Cap Vert stretches the **Sahel**, where the desert's southward advance is ever apparent. But there are two conspicuous attractions in the north: the **Senegal River**, forming the border with Mauritania and feeding a continuous flood plain up to 30km wide; and the old French port of **St-Louis**, tucked behind the bar at the mouth of the river. Two **national parks** – the Parc National des Oiseaux du Djoudj and the Parc National de la Langue de Barbarie – provide mostly ornithological inducements.

Should you be **heading north** to Mauritania and – if they're reopened – the western routes across the Sahara, St-Louis is a natural break in the journey, a few hours by *taxi brousse* from Dakar, slightly longer by train. To **follow the river**, however, you have to be a little more determined: transport withers away as you leave the main centres behind and push deep inland to **Matam** and **Bakel**. Going this way, you'll intercept the Dakar-Bamako train at **Kidira**, on the border, where there'll be a crush to find space on board. Driving in the other direction, into Senegal from Mali, the river course is a much preferable route to the coast: following the direct line of the railway there's very little to detain you.

The main **ethno-linguistic groups** of the north are Wolof, concentrated around St-Louis and along the lower reaches of the river, and **Tukulor** higher up, who speak a dialect of Fula. In the far east, around Bakel, there are **Sarakole** (Soninke/Serahuli) speakers, while communities of semi-nomadic **Fula** live in the scorched region of Futa Toro.

St-Louis and around

The oldest French settlement in West Africa and capital of Senegal and Mauritania until 1958, **ST-LOUIS** is something of a world apart. In later colonial times its *commune* status – shared with Gorée, Rufisque and Dakar – meant its inhabitants were considered citizens of France; today the town's striking eighteenth- and nineteenth-century European architecture and its white- and blue-draped Wolof and Moorish inhabitants maintain the culture clash. Like Gorée too, St-Louis is a UNESCO-protected World Heritage Site. If decay, abandonment and the ghosts of slaves and fishermen attract you, then you'll enjoy this town. Just don't expect to discover much truth behind the "Venice of Africa" handle.

Practicalities

St-Louis' wonderfully ornate **railway station** is in the mainland quarter of **Sor**, close to the end of the iron Pont de Faidherbe; the **gare routière** is right by the tracks. It's a hectic area, thronged with stalls and vendors – and of course dark by the time the train gets in. The oldest part of St-Louis is the **island** of the same name, a ten-minute walk away across the bridge (which, incidentally, spanned the Danube until 1897).

Places to Stay

St-Louis doesn't get hordes of visitors, so **accommodation** choices are fairly limited. Easily the nicest place is the locally famous *Hôtel de la Poste*, right by the river on the other side of the bridge; at around CFA12,000 for a double, it's pretty good value. If you can afford to eat there too, the food is outstanding. In the event of its being full (not unlikely), try one of the following, given in descending order of price and amenities: *Hôtel du Palais*, a big old house, tattier than the *Poste*, but the only place that accepts *Visa* cards; *Hôtel de la Résidence*, fairly new and unatmospheric, due to be refurbished into something trendier; or *Hôtel Battling Siki*, which has much the cheapest rooms (around CFA4/5000), but no AC or S/C ones – the amenable *patronne* will negotiate sleeping space on the roof if you want. The bar at the *Battling Siki* is lively – cheap *Gazelles* – and the house rules loose.

Apart from the beach – not recommended for either comfort or security – the **cheapest** place in town is the *Maison du Combattant*, a run-down tenement opposite the hospital. For CFA1000 you can get a hospital bed and possibly clean sheets, and share nightmare toilets, showers and intermittent water with fellow guests – mostly people visiting relatives in hospital, if not actually patients.

Eating

There's an excellent but expensive menu at the *Hôtel de la Poste*, but St-Louis has a surprising dearth of good cheap **places to eat**. You'll likely fall back on *O Kane* several times: they do mountainous Senegalese dishes every day for around CFA1000 and have wine at less than CFA2000 a litre. Apart from these you could also check out the *Aziz* (budget tourist class, high-season only) and *Signare* (faintly French-style *café-pâtisserie*), and probably make do at a number of omelette and **shawarma shops** – a better one is the *Arafa*, just along from the *Hôtel de la Poste*. For **street food** you'll do well only by getting off the island, either back to the mainland or out into the less refined quarters on the Langue de Barbarie peninsula.

The Town

Spending time at St-Louis, your pace will slow to the sedate local stroll. It gets furiously hot here, so don't over-plan. If you can fix a good price (CFA1000/hour), engage a **calèche** for part of your explorations – you'll find them in Sor and on the peninsula.

The Island

You can foot round the **island** *–Ndar* in Wolof – in about an hour and a half. Shuttered windows, occasional balconies and flaking yellow paint are the abiding impressions. Some of the best houses – which, as in Gorée, tend to conceal their interiors from snooping strangers – are to be found around and just north of the hotels, especially rue Blanchot and rue Pierre Loti. *Maurel et Prom* was a slave market, and the *Hôtel de la Poste* started as a gum arabic warehouse. The old houses characteristically have interior courtyards, warehouses on the ground floor (mostly now converted) and first-floor, inward-facing living quarters.

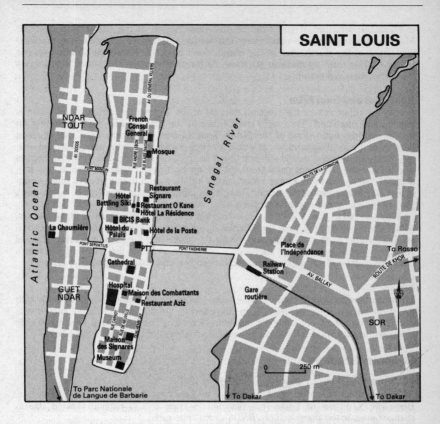

At the Place de Lille, named after St-Louis's twin city, notice the plaque commemorating the town's most celebrated citizen, Mbarick Fall, who as **Battling Siki** became the first world professional boxing champion in 1925 (his remains are shortly due to be returned from New York by the World Boxing Council). Heading south round the corner from here, beneath a wonderful old silk-cotton tree, you come to the **Place Faidherbe,** with a bust of the eponymous French governor in the middle, and government and military buildings round about.

At the southern tip of the island, the **Museum** is worth a look if you're here – and if it's open (in theory daily 8am–noon & 3–6pm). The palm trees outside have been beheaded and carved – an appropriately bizarre introduction to a collection in dire need of attention. Downstairs there are stuffed animals and fish, cases of dried insects ravaged by the living, and various Wolof, Fula and Moor ethnographic bits. Most interesting is the end room, with its documented history of St-Louis, showing how the shape of the land has changed in the last few centuries. Faded photos and forgotten fossils on dusty shelves complete a dismal ensemble (note the puzzling picture of a cow and dead calf on wooden legs). Upstairs, masks, carvings and weaponry dominate; look out for impressive statuary at "Fecundity" and a life-size Fula dwelling with a pervasive smell that suggests it's due for re-thatching.

From the museum, if you head up the eastern side of the island, you pass the **Maison des Signares**, a particularly impressive example of St-Louisienne architecture. Back at the **north end** of the island, don't miss the **Palais de Justice** on rue Brière de l'Ile, with its massive staircase. At the northern tip, the island deteriorates into dereliction and marsh.

Ndar Tout and Guet Ndar

Across the other arm of the river on the spit of the Langue de Barbarie, the scene is much more animated. Turn right over either of the bridges and you're strolling on avenue Dodds, main drag of the **Ndar Tout** quarter. This was once the Champs Elysées of the local *signares* set, at a time when there were 4000 French *colons* and military based in St-Louis, and is still just about imaginable as such. Tall, gracious houses rise behind the pavement palm trees. At the far north end, again, ruination sets in – skeletal buff and red remains of French army buildings and then a marker pillar designating the **Mauritanian frontier**. There's no official border crossing here, so don't plan on hiking up the spit to Mauritania.

Action in Ndar Tout focuses on the **market** and sandy **Place de la République**, which gives out straight onto the Atlantic down avenue Servatius, itself ankle deep in sand. From here you can walk south along the shore into the fishing quarter of **Guet Ndar** – rewarding in the late afternoon – and down as far as the Islamic fishermen's cemetery, a net and stake graveyard with the familiar and disquieting vulture retinue.

Sor

The **mainland** area of St-Louis – **Sor** – is the part of town whose population swells with every downward cycle of drought in the interior. On the whole it's an anonymous district, though there are some old buildings here, too. The **Ecole des Fils des Chefs** is housed in a distinctive Portuguese house on the way out towards Richard Toll.

St-Louis Directory

Air Afrique/UTA place Franchet-d'Espérey (☎61 13 63).

Artisanal village At the far end of the route de la Corniche in Sor.

Bank *BICIS,* on rue de France/rue Blanchot (8–11am & 2.30–4.30pm) seemed able to change money in the afternoon only. *BNDS* weren't interested.

Car hire *Hôtel la Résidence* is the *Avis* agent (☎61 12 60). The *Hôtel de la Poste* can also arrange it for the day.

Cinemas Kung Fu and Indian epics dubbed into French at the open-air *Vox* and *Rex*. A good laugh, with the bonus of armchairs (CFA250).

Food Many of the smaller shops on Ndar island have slow-moving stock. Open and check to avoid returns, or bring your own supplies.

French cultural centre All the usual stuff.

Guide book There's a semi-legible pamphlet available around town, printed by the diocese of St-Louis. If you're staying for a while it might prove more useful than frustrating.

Nightclubs *La Chaumière* in Ndar Tout, which belongs to the *Hôtel de la Poste* (free to guests), is a classy joint charging CFA1/2000 at the door, with ordinary bar prices. It gets into gear after midnight. Or simply cut across the Servatius bridge and let your ears track down the action: community events are easily located.

Pharmacies *Sayegh* and *Kandji* at rue André Lebon/rue Henri Louis Guillabert.

PTT A grand affair opposite the Faidherbe bridge. Poste restante.

Tours *Hôtel de la Poste*, as the longest established tourist venue in town, offers excursions all around St-Louis for those who are not strapped financially. They'll also take you down to the beach in the morning and pick you up at the end of the day – at a price. You may make cheaper – if also somewhat less organised – arrangements through the *Hôtel du Palais*.

Trains Mon–Sat departure from St-Louis at 6.30am, arriving Dakar 11.10am, Sunday dep 3pm, arr 7.40pm. To be sure of seats, buy tickets from the ticket office the night before, when the train arrives from Dakar.

The Langue de Barbarie and its Parc National

If you've a 4WD vehicle you can usually drive the entire length of the **Langue de Barbarie**, dodging the waves and hundreds of thousands of crabs as you go. The trip starts in Guet Ndar, passing the ruins of a psychiatric hopital (ex-leprosarium) and the remains of the **Hydrobase**, the seaplane centre used as a staging post by the early airmail service between Europe and South America. The first South Atlantic crossing took off from here in 1930; the *Hôtel de la Poste* in town is full of momentoes.

Casuarina trees were first planted here by Governor Faidherbe, when the Langue was called *La Piste des Cavaliers*. Although tree cover is extensive in places, many of the trees have since perished, and it's an often melancholy beachscape. At the tip of the spit you look across the estuary to the area protected by the National Park, and there's a good chance of seeing cormorants, pelicans and turtles down here.

The **Parc National de Langue de Barbarie** (daily 7am–6pm; CFA1000) covers twenty square kilometres of estuarine islands and waterways around the southern end of the Langue. Its main entrance is on the landward side, after the village of GANDIOL, which is accessible by occasional bush taxi from the Sor *autogare* at St-Louis. The quantity of birds depends on the time of year and on an element of luck: flamingos and pelicans are the obvious species – rarer ones require more patience. On firmer ground you can see warthogs and, in a fenced enclosure, a pair of giant tortoises and a herd of deer – gift of King Juan Carlos of Spain.

In a 4WD vehicle it's possible to **follow the beach** the entire distance from Gandiol to Dakar, a 150-kilometre drive of five hours plus, depending on tides. The Paris–Dakar rally sometimes comes down this way. If you need to get back on the main N2 highway, there are half a dozen routes leading up from the shore along the way.

Parc National des Oiseaux du Djoudj

Situated in the heart of the Walo delta of the Senegal River, and considerably bigger than the Langue de Barbarie park, the **Parc National des Oiseaux du Djoudj** (daily 7am–7pm; CFA2000 for 72-hr entry) is Senegal's ornithological showcase, rated the third most important **bird reserve** in the world. If you're at all into birds and are here during the palearctic migrants' season between November and April, you should make the effort to get in. The track into the park is signposted to the left off the Rosso/ Richard Toll road near the village of NDIOL; once in the park, however, restricting yourself to the tracks will give only half the picture. Try to get a good price for a **pirogue trip** (aim for CFA1000 each per hour) across the shallow expanses, for it's here that you'll get close enough to the wildlife to take good pictures.

The Djoudj is West Africa's best bird reserve, its estimated 100,000 **flamingos** and 10,000 **white pelicans** among the world's largest concentrations. January is probably the ideal time to visit, with the migrants in residence but the water levels already receding. Flamingos prefer the high alkalinity – and the reduced water surface tends to concentrate the birds, making them easier to spot. Crowned cranes are among the park's more ostentatious inhabitants. You should also keep a look out on the water surface for the eyes and snout of **crocodiles**, especially visible in the dry season.

For those without their own transport, **trips to the Djoudj** can be arranged with *Hôtel de la Poste* (around CFA15,000 each for the day, minimum five people; cheaper en masse), or with the owners of the *Hôtel du Palais*, who do a similar trip for around CFA10,000 per person, which includes entrance fees, a two- or three-hour *pirogue* ride and unlimited stops en route to the park. Taxis waylaid in town can also be persuaded to spend the rest of the day taking you there and back, but you'll pay at least CFA12,000, and you've little room to protest if the trip is cut short. At the park entrance, the *Air Afrique*-run *Campement du Djoudj* offers superior S/C huts for CFA14,000 per double.

Along the Senegal River

From St-Louis, **transport up-river** is easy as far as Rosso (for Mauritania) and Richard Toll. Thereafter, vehicles from St-Louis are scarcer, so chances are you'll have to hop your way along the bank from town to town. Podor has opportunities for short, unofficial trips into Mauritania; Matam and Bakel are much further up-river and perhaps only worth visiting in passing.

The Lower River

Between St-Louis and Richard Toll, the scene varies sharply with the time of year: in the dry season from November to May, you'll see the oblong, wicker huts of migrant Fula herders who've moved from the higher, drier lands of the interior. Signs of human habitation include the practice of planting old car tyres in the mud to stake a land claim – common all over West Africa.

Around the turn-off to Rosso, and all along the six-kilometre causeway road to it, you see thousands of hectares of **sugar cane**, a project intended not only to feed Senegal's considerable sugar consumption but also, eventually, to produce fuel alcohol to offset the high cost of oil imports. In the irrigation ditches, **nile monitor lizards** abound, growing enormous on a diet of insects, frogs and rodents – we saw a two-metre specimen waddling across the road.

Rosso
ROSSO is a pretty dreadful place. Its recent vitality was the result of a flourishing minor **smuggling** industry, not – as you might imagine – from relatively thriving Senegal into drought-stricken Mauritania, but the reverse, from aid-saturated Mauritania into IMF-austere Senegal. Until the border reopens, however, that industry, together with the following details, can be considered to have lapsed.

The road curls through desperate shacks past official buildings to a tongue of land from where a barge regularly crosses the brown flow to Mauritania (see p.326 for the continuation of the journey to Nouakchott). If you're **crossing the river** – and there's little point in coming up here if you're not – remind the driver to drop you at the first flag-poled white building on the left, where your passport gets stamped out of Senegal. If you're on foot you can get across the river easily enough using *pirogues* for about CFA50. Between noon and 2/3pm this is the only way to traverse – it's lunchtime for the barge crew. The border closes at 6pm.

Richard Toll
Meaning "Garden of Richard", **RICHARD TOLL** is named after the ambitious regional development planned by the French planter Richard in the 1820s. Roger's **colonial mansion**, built on an island in the River Taouey – which flows into the Senegal on the east side of town – is Richard Toll's one notable building, but utterly unspecial. It's surrounded by the remains of his ornamental park – now a dusty and overgrown jungle. There are a couple of **accommodation** options. The informally run *Gîte d'Etape*, right on the river at the west end of the town near the St-Louis *gare routière*, is pleasant enough but costs around CFA10,000 for a double (S/C & AC). The *Hôtel Keur Massada* is in the dull town centre, a kilometre or so further.

Lac de Guiers

There's a more attractive scene at the **Lac de Guiers**, some 30km southwest of Richard Toll. This is a wild area, and swarms with most of the birds present in the Djoudj, with the exception of flamingos. Warthogs are common and if you find a way to get out on the water you might even see **manatees** – strange, aquatic mammals which hold onto a precarious existence here. **People** of the area include Tukulor and Black Moor fishermen, and Fula herders at certain times of year. Protected from the Senegal river's brackish contamination by a dam in the River Taouey at Richard Toll, the lake supplies much of Dakar's drinking water, which is purified at GNIT on the western shore and piped 300km to the capital. You can't get right round the lake – it's best seen from the village of MBANE, on the eastern shore. The reedy western shore is accessible only from the St-Louis–Dakar road or a track which leads off south from the N2, 10km west of the Rosso junction.

The Middle River

After DAGANA – an old gum arabic entrepôt on the Senegal, with colonial buildings and semi-intact nineteenth-century fort – you leave traditional Wolof country. From here on most of the people you'll see are **Tukulor** and **Fula**, and the atmosphere is more laid-back – the friendliness no longer verging on aggressiveness, and commerce no longer quite such a feature.

Podor

In **PODOR**, a 24-kilometre north-bound sidetrack from the highway, the kids soon find you, but the demands for *cadeaux* have ceased and they seem genuinely pleased to have strange faces in town. Indeed the whole place is delightfully friendly, and everyone pauses to say hello. Podor is a very old town, getting its name from the gold (*or*) which used to be brought down here from up-river regions. Given character by its fort (1854) and relicky, mud-built houses, Podor is situated on the western tip of the **Ile à Morfil** (Island of Ivory), a long slug of floodlands (120km by 10km) between the main course of the river and the meandering Doué. At one time the island had a large population of **elephants**, supported by the covering of dense, silt-fed woodland. It's still a good wildlife district, with monkeys and crocodiles numerous and a proliferation of birdlife, but elephants haven't been regularly seen since the 1960s and it's doubtful if any survive.

The slightly grotty **campement**, at CFA3000 a double (meals available), is the cheapest and more or less the only place to stay in Podor. The mosquitos can be trying, so be prepared. Neither of the two missions is keen to put travellers up, but local people sometimes offer – the children will pull you home anyway. What makes Podor a

---

THE STATE OF TEKRUR

The Ile à Morfil lay at the heart of the **state of Tekrur** (whence *Tukulor*), which was at its most powerful in the eleventh century, when it became a major sub-Saharan trading partner with the Almoravid Arabs of north Africa. The Tukulor claim, as a result, that they were the first west Africans to adopt Islam, and went on to evangelise, among others, the Fula – with whom they share a common language and much else. Their own state was annexed by ancient Ghana, with its power base to the east at Koumbi Saleh, in present-day Mauritania. When the Almoravids attacked Ghana, Tekrur helped the invaders, only to fall shortly afterwards to the Mali empire.

There's a fair number of villages with Sudanic-style **mosques** scattered along the island's one main track as far as SALDE, the furthest east, where you can ferry back to the main road 90km short of Matam. If you can find transport the length of the island, it's a far preferable alternative to following the main N2, which is unremittingly dull.

nice stop-over is that you can take a *pirogue* ride across the river and visit Mauritania for a few hours – relations permitting. Until the conflict, the small checkpoint was only interested in customs duty, and would only bother you if you intended bringing back large quantities of tomato purée or other desirable goods; a visa wasn't necessary for a short visit – transport into Mauritania would, in any case, be difficult from this frontier.

The Upper River

From the up-river part of the N2 highway, there are two routes to the river crossing **into Mauritania** at Kaédi (see p.326), though both of them are liable to flooding. After Rosso, Kaédi is the best bet for a crossing into Mauritania, with regular transport on to the southeast of the country as well as up to Nouakchott.

Matam

MATAM – 10km east of the highway – marks the start of bushier, hillier terrain. The town was a Tukulor **slave trading** station, which until the late nineteenth century profited through raids conducted by the Fula. The name Matam is supposed to derive from the Tukulor word for debt settlement, referring to the demands made by Fula creditors on their slave-buying partners. A century or more ago, the town had a cosmopolitan reputation, a place where deals were struck and scores settled. It's all pretty quiet now: even the old French fort which helped "pacify" the district was swept away in a flood a few years back.

Bakel and onward

Approaching **BAKEL**, the road follows close to the river and the flood plain narrows before disappearing between steeper banks. Bakel is larger than Matam and still has its **fort**, built in 1818 on a promontory above the water. The town is the stronghold of Senegal's **Sarakole** people (or Serahuli or Soninke), who farm and fish but are principally traders. In some villages it seems most of them are away in France; "staying abroad is better than dying" is the Sarakole response to drought and hard times. Again, you could formerly cross to Mauritania here: a 50km *piste* runs to SELIBABI, the country's southernmost town and Mauritania's Soninke centre.

From Bakel, the track to the **railway line** at KIDIRA on the **Malian border** cuts sixty kilometres or so straight across country. Transport connects with the trains. By road Kidira is 105 barely passable kilometres from KAYES in **Mali**, starting with a ford across the Falémé river that is rarely negotiable between July and February. Road transport can't be relied on and most people use the train.

NIOKOLO-KOBA AND THE SOUTHEAST

Senegal's number one **National Park** and the flag-bearer for the country's conservation policies, **Niokolo-Koba** covers 8000 square kilometres of savanna, forest and swamp – a little smaller than the area of The Gambia. It's an undulating wilderness, straddling the Gambia river and two major tributaries in the gentle uplands of **Sénégal Oriental**.

The park is open only during the **December to June** dry season (exact dates fixed according to the weather), when animals gather along the water courses. The park closes for the rest of the year, as tracks are cut by rising water and large areas flooded. If you check in the right places – detailed in the text and on the map – you've a chance of seeing most of the larger species.

Aside from Niokolo-Koba, which is visited by around 5000 people a year, **southeast Senegal** is on the whole little affected by tourism. This is the area where you're most likely to find strongly traditional ways enduring, even though hunting as a livelihood took a severe blow from the park's opening, which displaced a large, scattered population of Mandinka, Bassari and Fula. Tourists' excursions to **Bassari country**, beyond the park, have been running in a small way from Tambacounda for some years, but to reap the high rewards of this part of the country, you must be prepared to hike and be self-sufficient.

Heading coastwards from the southeast, few people slow down on their way through the regions of **Haute Casamance** and **Moyenne Casamance**, and to be honest the main towns of **Velingara** and **Kolda** don't have much to offer. Although there are interesting corners to explore, access can be a problem. There are, anyway, big enticements in **Basse Casamance**, a region covered in the section after this one.

Tambacounda

Getting to Niokolo-Koba is a serious business, feasible without your own transport only if you're prepared to put in some considerable time waiting for a ride, probably at **TAMBACOUNDA**, 80km from the park entrance. Tambacounda is eastern Senegal's major transport hub, the big station on the Dakar-Bamako railway after Kayes in Mali. There's little to recommend staying here, but if you're travelling without your own car you almost inevitably will. Even if you have a vehicle, it's still a likely night and supply-stop, 460km from Dakar, 400km from Ziguinchor and 500km from Banjul.

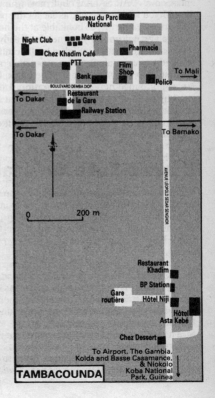

The centre of town is bunched around the station, where **trains** from Bamako are scheduled to arrive around 5am on Thursdays and Sundays, and those from Dakar around 8pm the same days. Trains are always packed, so be prepared for some difficulty getting on.

For **accommodation** you've a limited choice, all on the other side of the tracks. The unimpressive *Hôtel Niji* charges about CFA6000 for a room with fan; the very comfortable *Asta Kebé* offers the works for impressive prices (CFA15,000 and up); and at the charmingly off-the-wall *Chez Dessert* – opposite the sign to the *Asta Kebé* on the way out of town heading south – a bed or floor space courtesy of the fairly keyed-up owner costs CFA2000 a head, with breakfast for CFA500. You'll need to ask the way.

There's **cheap eats** at the *Resto de la Gare* and slightly better cooking at the new, blue *Restaurant Khadim* near the BP station – not to be confused with *Chez*

Khadim, near the market, which is your place for sandwiches. The *Asta Kebé* does a *menu* for around CFA4000 – a place to celebrate if you see any lions. No excuses needed – or sufficient – to visit the dingy **nightclub** near the market (CFA500).

Into the park from Tambacounda

Your best move for a **lift to the park** is a CFA500 investment in a day at the *Asta Kebé's* swimming pool, where there's usually a contingent of French tourists to chat up. The one-day **organised excursions** from the *Asta Kebé's* are too brief to be worthwhile. Cost is the main drawback of their other deals: a two-day safari costs CFA60,000 each for a minimum group of four, and a four-day trip, including the Bassari country south of the park, will set you back CFA120,000. Even a 4WD vehicle hired from the hotel costs around CFA60,00 a day.

As usual, you can always find a **taxi** driver who's willing to spend the day – possibly even longer – driving you round. The advantage is the price – negotiable down to realistic levels of CFA10–12,000 per day, plus expenses. But be sure the driver knows what he's about, that the vehicle is sound and has spares, and that you pay for petrol separately, otherwise your game-viewing is going to be limited indeed. Note that diesel isn't always available in the park.

Finally, one or two daily *taxis brousse* serve villages down the road to the park entrance at DAR SALAM, but moving on from there can prove virtually impossible. Should you manage to get as far as the park headquarters at Simenti you'll find bearably priced game drives bookable at the hotel.

If you've not got all your needs already, stock up on supplies in Tamba, as there's really nothing but a handful of restaurants in the park itself. There's a couple of wellstocked *épiceries* along avenue Senghor and another shop selling film on boulevard Demba Diop, near the station. The **bank**, **PTT**, **pharmacy** and a disappointing **market** are also grouped here, and the **national park office** is just a little further behind. You can buy park entry permits in advance at the same price as on the gate (CFA2000 per person per day, plus CFA10,000 per car per visit). You'll need a means of carrying **water** in the park, as you'll be spending a lot of time far from habitation – five litres each should be enough.

Niokolo-Koba National Park

Within the park, **accommodation** at the main centres of **SIMENTI** and **NIOKOLO-KOBA** is expensive, the *campements* being almost indistinguishable from hotels, with restaurants, fuel supplies and swimming pools (non-guests can pay a fee for a swim). Simenti has an excellent location above the Gambia river and a good game-viewing **hide**. BADI, not far from Simenti in the western part of the park, has a much more basic set-up.

In addition you should be able to **camp** at the guard posts at Badi, Malapa, Dienoum Diala, Bangaré, Gué de la Koulountou and, if you can get to it, Mont Assirik (see map); at dusk the rangers can't really refuse, as driving isn't allowed after dark, and if you've brought a bottle or two to share with them, so much the better. Such encounters can also yield good animal-watching opportunities – we were led to nearby waterholes on foot, an experience not normally on the tour groups' itineraries. It's not a bad idea to hire a guide at some point anyway, as they can often show you things you would never have found alone.

You'll find it a considerable help to learn some French animal names – the **Haltenorth and Diller** field guide is useful (see "Books", in *Contexts*).

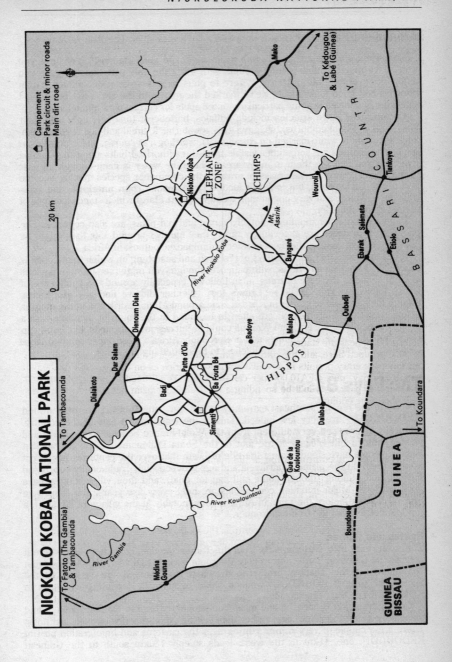

Around the Park

Niokolo-Koba's tracks are mostly well maintained, and good signposting ensures you won't have much trouble getting around; with 4WD the only part that will gave you difficulties is around Mont Assirik. **Where to go** is far less a matter of confidence than hunches and good luck. Again, we've marked the map with the areas we found most satisfying and keyed in some particularly noted spots for certain park inhabitants.

Commonest large species include buffalos, hartebeest (uniquely ugly with their long faces and hooked horns), shaggy Defassa waterbuck, timid and fast-moving bushbuck (beautifully white-marked on russet coat), warthogs, of course, and crocodiles in the rivers. **Hippos** are sometimes visible from the authorised halts along the Gambia river, but you can see them in many areas where the water is deep enough all year round. Don't ignore the less massive grazers: the commoner species quickly become part of the background, but look out for the large, maned **roan antelope**, and especially for the huge and very uncommon **western giant eland** which stands a couple of metres at the shoulder.

Baboons and other monkeys, notably vervet and red patas, are also common. The park's **chimpanzees** are exceedingly rare – they number around 150; they might be observed east of Assirik, the most northerly chimpanzee outpost in Africa.

It has to be said that the four days of research and searching on which this section is based failed to clock any **lions**; with patience, though, you might see them in pockets of deep shade at the base of trees, or in hollows, especially around the confluence of tracks known as Patte d'Oie – "Crow's foot". Neither did we find any **elephants**, though they are said to gather in a broad zone around Mont Assirik and in the months before the rains (March–May) are often to be found in the south of this area – so a drive between Bangaré ford and Worouli could be successful. **Leopards**, like lions, can range outside the park's confines and are probably Africa's most under-counted large predator; very rarely seen, they are likeliest to be spotted high in a tree.

The Pays Bassari

Visitors to the remote southeast extremity of Senegal – the **Bassari country** around **KÉDOUGOU** – are very few indeed. This is the least known part of the country, ethnically diverse and very different from the Wolof-Franco Senegal to the north and west. Living in hill villages at the foot of the Fouta Djalon mountains, the ancient Bassari people have stood against the tide of Islam that over the centuries has swept around them on the plains. Matrilineal and age-grouped, they traditionally subsist on farming and hunting (though some still pan for gold), and their villages often have good markets. Major initiation ceremonies are held every few years, and there's an **annual festival** before the rains in April or May, notably at the village of ETIOLO, a few kilometres from the Guinean frontier.

Routes into Guinea

The main route **into Guinea** parts from the Tambacounda–Ziguinchor road where it scrapes the Gambian border. From here the route is via MEDINA-GOUNAS (a devout community of the Tijaniya brotherhood, where the women are veiled) to the Senegalese post at BOUNDOU, whence 55km of normally terrible track leads to KOUNDARA on the Guinean side.

Getting transport is fairly hit and miss. You should try hard in Tambacounda to find something going the whole way, rather than setting off on a series of bush taxi hops. There are a couple of very **minor routes** near the customs and immigration post of KÉDOUGOU: one, 11km to the **west**, leads steeply 120km south to the Guinean village of Mali (see p.601); the other, 11km east of Kédougou, winds for over 200km to the major town of LABÉ, right in the heart of the Fouta Djalon (p.599). You might be lucky with transport on the first route, which is also by far the most scenic. On the second, the Gambia River crossing in Guinea is particularly uncertain. Both are supposed to have Guinean entrance formalities on the border itself.

BASSE CASAMANCE

Basse Casamance – the lower reaches of the Casamance river – is the most seductive part of Senegal. Wonderfully tropical, with dense forest, winding creeks, rice fields and quiet back roads shaded by massive silk-cottons, the district seems to have little in common with the Senegal of Islamic brotherhoods, groundnuts, cattle and dust.

For centuries the mostly **Jola**-speaking population of Basse Casamance resisted the push of Islam (most successfully on the south bank of the river), while the Portuguese maintained a typically torpid presence. The ceding of the region to the French in 1886 didn't precipitate any great social shifts. Changes are now underway, despite an isolation in which villages and language groups are cut off even from each other, but there's

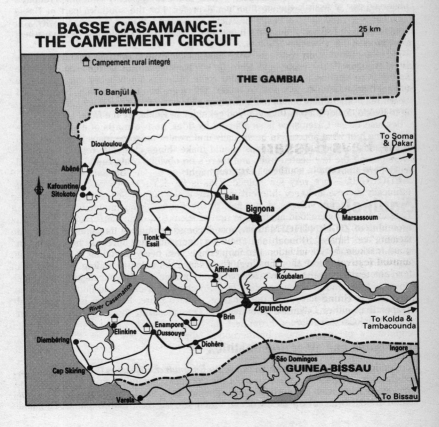

a resolve to maintain some degree of self-determination. Since independence, the **Casamance question** and the apparent threat to Wolof-speaking, French-abetted metropolitan Senegal, has been a prickly one. Casamance provides the bulk of the country's rice crop and, furthermore, without its full participation in national affairs, the issue of confederation with The Gambia – an even more troublesome thorn in Senegal's side – will never be resolved.

Staying in Basse Casamance – and getting around

While the region gets thousands of **holiday-makers** flying in direct from France for winter sun on the Cap Skiring beaches, there's more off-beat appeal in the network of **campements rurals integrés**, which offer a chink in the wall of an otherwise mono-lithic tourist industry. Ziguinchor is a natural base for visiting the *campements*, many of which are ends in themselves for their locations and architectural interest. The fact that all ten of the Casamançais *campements* charge the same low rates (bed CFA1500; breakfast CFA700; meal CFA1400) and are bookable in Ziguinchor is further recom-mendation. Rates and facilities are variable at the handful of other, similar places in the region; only the official *campements* are marked on the map below.

Unless you have your own transport, getting to the *campements* sometimes requires perserverance or more expense than you'd prefer. For the southern part of Basse Casamance a **bicycle** is a really practical option, and there's no reason why you shouldn't take it further, though it's more than 100km from Ziguinchor to the furthest *campement* in the network – Sitokoto.

There are three **main roads** to Basse Casamance: from **Banjul**; from **Dakar** on the faster *transgambienne* route; and from far-off **Tambacounda** in the east. If you're coming from Mali on the train, this third route makes a much better introduction to Senegal than an after-dark arrival in Dakar. There are two or three daily Peugeot 504 departures from Tambacounda to Ziguinchor, all leaving early; the alternative is chang-ing in **Kolda**, making a longer day. If you get stuck in Kolda, try the *Hôtel Hobbe*.

Because Basse Casamance is so affected by tides, no two **maps** of it ever look the same: much of what appears to be virtually underwater on some maps is actually firm ground most of the time. Our maps should make things clear.The region has many diversions off the few beaten trails and there's no obvious route round. Allow several weeks here if possible – it's likely to be a highlight.

Ziguinchor

Something of **ZIGUINCHOR**'s exotic appeal comes through in its name, pronounced "Sigichor" or "Sichor" by most Jola. There's a luxuriant sense of repose here, found in no other Senegalese town of its size. Surprisingly, you need reminding of the fact that Ziguinchor is on – and of – the River Casamance: its colonial trading houses don't stand out, and the river port isn't likely to figure prominently in your meanderings. It's a town of trees and avenues, roosting birds, orchestral crickets and fluttering bats at dusk, with a strong flavour of the Guineas. What's more, life here is a good deal cheaper than either Dakar or The Gambia. Less pleasant, though, is the attention lavished by local mosquitos.

Orientation and other practicalities

Coming into Ziguinchor **up the river** on the *Casamance Express* is the best approach, and the ship deposits you at the heart of the town, two minutes from the main hotels. Arriving **by road** from the north or from Tambacounda, ask to be dropped at the *Total* station in the town centre – all the action's then on your right (shops, banks, PTT and

THE JOLA

The people of Basse Casamance are predominantly **Jola** (or Diola; no relation to the Diola/Dyula of Côte d'Ivoire) – broadly divided by the river into Buluf and Fonyi on the north bank and Huluf (or Fulup) on the south. From around the sixteenth century they gradually displaced earlier Casamance inhabitants called the Banyun, who used to be great traders and still live among them. Where the Jola came from nobody seems to know, but their dialects are closely related to the Manjak spoken in Guinea-Bissau, and indeed the Jola generally claim to come from the south. They never developed a unified state, and their fragmentation has resulted in some **Jola dialects** being mutually unintelligible. In fact the idea of a Jola "tribe" is mostly a colonial one: only contact with outsiders has given the term any meaning for the people themselves. The word is supposed to derive from the Manding *jor la* – "he who avenges himself".

A distinctive style of **wet rice farming** has been practised for at least 600 years in the reclaimed land between the creeks. **Dikes** are built around new fields so that the rains will flood them and leach out the sea salt, which runs away through hollow tree trunks in the dikes while the fields lie fallow. Once the field is flooded, the drains are blocked and the rice plants brought out from the nurseries and planted, one by one, in the mud. After three or four months of weeding and dike care by the men, the women gather the **harvest** in November or December. For the first half of the year, though, there's little work in the rice fields and increasingly this is a time when young people drift away to Ziguinchor, The Gambia or Dakar. Many don't return for the next season. Later in the year, you'll see villagers walking to the fields early in the morning with the amazingly long, iron-tipped hoes called **kayendos**.

Traditionally, rice was never sold. Having huge numbers of granaries full of it, often for years, brought the kind of **prestige** every Jola man wanted. Consequently, conflicts over **land rights** have always been close to the surface and still occasionally erupt, as in 1976, when troops were sent in to crush a "rice war" that was being settled with guns and machetes in Affiniam and Diatok, across the river from Ziguinchor.

Islam has made little headway among the Jola, but an erosion of traditional values has been brought about by **groundnuts**. Introduced to the region in the early nineteenth century, the crop provided a commercial alternative to rice that could earn ready money, with relatively little labour, on land that had hitherto been unplanted bush. Now grown on raised ground all over the region, the groundnut crop has resulted in deforestation, soil degradation and reliance on imported food. "He who wears a *boubou* can't work in the rice fields" goes the Jola saying, ironically excusing the way things increasingly are in terms of Islam's stress on the individual.

JOLA WORDLIST

Jola is a diverse language, comprising a number of dialects: the following words and phrases may be helpful in Basse Casamance, but don't be surprised if not all of them provoke immediate recognition.

Safi	Bonjour, hello	*Nyukul*	Funeral
Gasumai	Yes, hello, welcome (a universal response)	*Ebuk/Sibuk*	Mosquito/s
		Ekumba	Pig
Ça gasse?	How is it? (French Jola) Ça va?	*Bunuk*	Palm wine
		Hank/fank	Interior courtyard of house
Furi	To eat (rice)		
Emano	Rice	*Gutep*	Surrounding private areas
Niankatang	Rice cooked in palm oil	*Kafat*	Private kitchen gardens
Epit	Rice harvest (the season, Nov–Jan)	*Butog*	Family (nuclear)
Bekin	Fetish	*Eyi*	King, but literally priest or religious leader

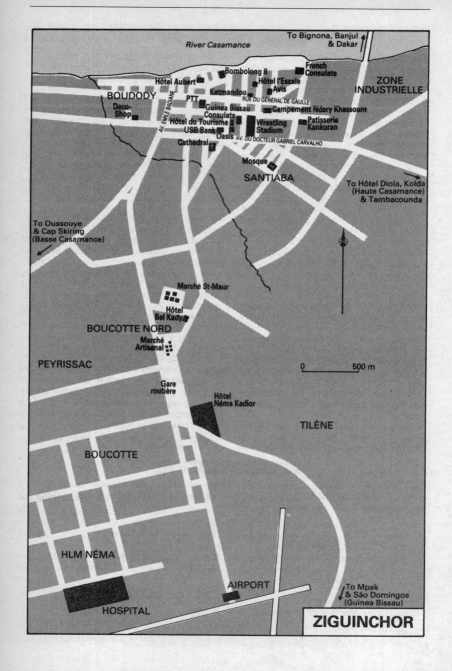

other business). The only reason for getting off at the **gare routière and the markets**, 1.5km south of the centre, is if you're looking to install yourself right away in the cheapest place you can find – or else heading for the *Nema Kadior*, which is the opposite. If you arrive **by air** you're a kilometre further south on the same road – but a taxi ride won't break the bank.

Accommodation

Best value in the **town centre** is *Hôtel du Tourisme*, basic yet slightly stylish, with a popular, though not dead cheap, restaurant – check in early (CFA5/6000 S/C, AC extra). The *Hôtel Aubert* looks like the place where the visiting parents of French *co-opérants* stay – a no-nonsense *auberge* with a nice pool and a good atmosphere, and well over CFA10,000. There's excellent food here if you're ready to splash out CFA4000 each. Priced between these two is the *Hôtel Bar l'Escale*, which seems quiet and a little run down. Still central, cheapest of the bunch is the family run *Campement Ndary Khassoum*, where rooms around a central courtyard are under CFA4000 – though again the place has an air of desertion about it.

Moving away from the river and into less salubrious quarters, the *Hôtel Bel Kady*, (☎91 12 22), ten minutes' walk from the *gare routière*, is an established stand-by, faintly bordello-ish and non S/C, but only CFA3000 a room, and less for singles; the good cheap restaurant – with a beer licence – is worth the walk out. In the same vicinity but offering different standards, the *Hôtel Nema Kadior* is really only for the rich or reckless, but its pool, landscaped gardens and mosquito-proofed AC rooms (close to CFA20,000 a double) are a tempting option. Lastly, if you have transport you might want to check out the newish *Campement Touristique ZAG*, 2km out of town on the OUSSOUYE road, where you can camp or stay cheaply in a pleasant, pastoral setting (less than CFA2000 a head, but they have "local" prices too).

Eating

Food in Ziguinchor is unremarkable – with the exceptions noted above. The *Tourisme*'s restaurant is always lively, with music many evenings. Round the corner at the *Oasis* you can eat more cheaply, at CFA1500 a *plat*. Getting more down-to-earth, the *gare routière* has the usual sprinkling of fly-blown greasy spoon huts. And for very cheap home cooking, seek out *Bamba Dinka*. You might also check out *Keur Clara*, a place that used to get lots of praise as a jazz bistro – but service here can be unbearably slow. If you're motivated by cream cakes and pastries, look into the *Patisserie Kankuran*. For fruit and veg in the town centre, there's usually a fair selection near the water, next to the *Bombolong II* nightclub.

In and around town

There's not a great deal to keep you scurrying around Ziguinchor, but just hanging out is pleasure enough. In the old quarter of the town centre, there's a string of public gardens, heavily shaded, with park benches and – sign of a non-Islamic region – rootling piglets. Large birds congregate in the trees, however, making this an unpredictable place to relax.

For guaranteed unwinding, try the *Hôtel Aubert*'s **swimming pool** and busy terrace – non-guests are allowed in for CFA1000, unless it's very busy or they don't like your appearance. Or go out to the *Nema Kadior* for a whiff of tropical package holidays, French-style; the pool here is larger than the *Aubert*'s, though the price is the same, and the attractive gardens with their labelled trees are acquiring a reputation among bird-watchers.

Both **markets** – the **artisanal** and the **St-Maur-des-Fossés** (named after the southeast Paris suburb with which Ziguinchor is twinned) – are worth visiting, and neither is much hassle. The huge municipal *St-Maur* is divided into zones of merchandise and always heaving with activity, while the *artisanal* stall holders really are working at their crafts. The office of the *campements rurals integrés* is at the latter, and you can make reservations with the helpful, overworked *chef* M. Adama Goudiaby; in the high season advance booking is recommended – contact Coordinateurs régional, Centre Artisanal, Ziguinchor (☎91 12 67/68).

If you're in shopping mood, take a look at the *Deco Shop*, in an attractive house in the old quarter of town – it sells various batiks, tablecloths and other unlikely confections.

Wrestling
There's West African **wrestling** at the *Stade* near *Hôtel du Tourisme* every Sunday (5–7pm; CFA500, CFA1000 to sit). If you've not seen it before, and won't get the chance again, give it a whirl. And take fast film. But the fun and informality of the competitions in The Gambia (see p.459) make them more enjoyable – and they're cheaper.

River Trips
Excursioning further afield, you can take a *pirogue* past the mangroves to the **Ile aux Oiseaux**, bookable at the *Uniclam* desk at the *Hôtel du Tourisme*. By recent accounts there's not at lot of birdlife to be seen, but it's doubtless a seasonal sight.

More reliable – if also more money – are the trips **across the river** to DILAPAO and up the serpentine Marigot de Bignona to AFFINIAM. Dilapao offers two-storey mud brick houses and palm wine tasting, while Affiniam's large **case à impluvium** (see "Enampore", below, for background) is one of the oldest *campements* in the *rural integré* circuit. These river trips, and others, can be fixed up in most of the hotels. There's a regular Monday, Wednesday and Friday service to Affiniam leaving at 9.30am (fare CFA250 one way) and between times you can also reach an agreement direct with the *piroguiers* on the waterfront. This is a good way of starting a tour round the north bank dry land region of **Buluf**, as an alternative to taxiing straight out of Ziguinchor.

Nightlife
After dark, Ziguinchor smoulders. *Le Bombolong II* and *Katmandou* have been *the* places to visit for a number of years, both repaying the CFA1000 entrance fee with hot music – lots of *zouk* – and as many chance enounters as you want. *Le Bombolong II* has a new interior and scores highly with the French community, as well as passing *tubabs*. *Katmandou* has a greater head of steam and a largely local crowd: the patio behind is a vital cooling-off area. At *Katmandou* expect to pay around CFA1000 for a *Flag*, CFA700 a soft; slightly more at *Le Bombolong II*.

Ziguinchor Directory

Air Senegal At the airport (☎91 10 81). There's a daily flight to Dakar (Mon–Wed 9.45am, Thurs & Sat 9.30am, Fri 10.45am, Sun 5pm), CFA22,000.

Banks The *BIAO* don't change money. *Union Senegalaise de Banques* (Mon–Fri 8.15–11am & 3.15–5pm, Fri closes 4.30pm) can be unnervingly inefficient. *SGBS* can arrange *Visa* cash advances. Go early in the day and plan to come back later.

Bicycles For **hire** from the *Avis* agency (☎91 10 38) – CFA2,000/day – and *Hôtel du Tourisme*. For **sale** at several locations for around CFA65,000.

Black Market At the *gare routière* you'll get lousy rates for your spare Gambian dalasis (75 percent of bank value), but you may be able to buy Guinea-Bissau pesos for CFA. The official rate for the peso has been improving however, so black market changing is no longer an important consideration. Check with one who knows the latest situation – some of the dealers at the *autogare* are sharks.

Car hire Not much choice. *Avis*, at CFA12,000/day plus CFA120 per km for a Renault 5, is an expensive business for fewer than four.

Cinemas Occasionally watchable movies at the *Rex*, opposite *Hôtel du Tourisme*, and the *Vox*, near the cathedral.

Doctor Dr. Maouad (☎91 13 85).

French Consulate (☎91 10 30).

Guinea-Bissau The Senegalese border post is at Mpak (18km); the Guinea-Bissau post is at São Domingos (25km). There's a *taxi brousse* most mornings from outside the *Hôtel Bel Kady;* departure times vary. Plan for an early start. Guinea-Bissau **visas** from the consulate, next to *Hôtel du Tourisme*, Mon–Fri 8/9am–noon & 2/4–6pm (☎91 10 46). Three months multiple entry delivered on the spot: one photo, CFA5,000. Due to strained relations between Senegal and Guinea-Bissau visas are sometimes unobtainable.

Police ☎17. Sûreté in Ziguinchor may refuse to extend Senegalese visas.

The Northern Region

Coming over **the border from Banjul** at SÉLÉTI used to be a simple business. For a while after the collapse of Senegambia confederation in 1989, however, there were rather heavy formalities and, more recently, there have been some sinister hold-ups in which drivers have had to pay to proceed.

If you have independent means of transport, you may like to take a look at the **waterholes** along the course of the Allahein (San Pedro) stream. They're located 500m after the frontier line itself: a large pool on the left before the bridge over the stream, a smaller one on the right just after it. At dawn and dusk you've an excellent chance of some good, natural observations of birds and monkeys here.

It's a CFA200 *taxi brousse* ride from Séléti to **DIOULOULOU**, the first large Senegalese village – assuming you're not ploughing straight through to Ziguinchor. Diouloulou, a sleepy community, is focused on its roundabout: the main N5 runs across the tidal flats of the *marigot* to Ziguinchor, and to the west lie some fine unspoilt **beaches**. Transport down the latter road is infrequent; so position yourself comfortably on the roots of the tree which serves as a taxi stand, and wait.

An aspect of the **local economy** recently made a front-page headline in *Le Soleil*. "Yamba", it read, "12 tons seized: a whole village cultivating 'the grass that kills' ". The paper reported that a gendarme had opened the door of a shed in nearby Donbondir and been promptly overcome by fumes from the sacks of cannabis stored inside. With the specialist assistance of the Gambian police, more plants were found growing in the fields nearby. The seized *yamba* burned for four hours.

The beaches

There are two main **beach destinations** west of Diouloulou – Abêné (18km) and Kafountine (24km). Neither is very easy to get to, though a *bâché* comes up from Bignona and runs down to Abêné every afternoon: other traffic comes through sporadically. The road is tarred right down to Kafountine, but for Abêné you turn off on a winding, pretty track signposted to "Kalissai". Sand makes it hard going if you're cycling, and the village of **ABÊNÉ** itself is ankle deep.

The Abêné *campement* – a kilometre or two further down a narrow, and undrivable track – makes it all worthwhile. Nestling in the dunes a short walk from the sea, it's a fine place to flop out for a day or two – a large house with a family atmosphere, good food, cold beer and a delightful beach. The campement is called *Campement Samaba* after the first *chef du village*, Samaba Diabang; *Abêné* means the "call" to form a village, in this case to gather as a defensive measure.

Up the coast, the altogether different *Hôtel Village Kalissai*, run by the *Aubert* in Ziguinchor, is beautifully sited right by the beach with a landscaped (!) mangrove creek; it's accessible from Abêné village, 2km away. Even at CFA14,000 a double, menus for CFA5000 and small Flags for CFA700, this beats much of what's on offer in the fast lane at Cap Skiring. But it's not exactly *integré*.

KAFOUNTINE is 7km south along the beach from Abêné; it's most easily walked at low tide, or you could get onto the road from Diouloulou and hitch. Bigger than Abêné, the village has a couple of shops, but is less rural in feel. Its new *campement rurale integré* is Sitokoto, 500m off to the right before you hit the beach, at present fairly basic but nicely situated on the dunes. A longer established base is the private *Campement le Filao*, in a grove of casuarinas at the end of the road, with some S/C bungalows at around CFA3000/4000, but slightly run down. Kafountine's is a working beach, planted with fuel pumps for motor *pirogues* and strewn with boats and nets.

On to Ziguinchor

By land there's no way through towards Ziguinchor from Kafountine, so you'll likely have to backtrack again to Diouloulou. An adventurous alternative would be to strike out southeast to the hamlet of HILOL, about 15km and walkable at low tide, from where you might take a *pirogue* through the maze of islands out to the main body of the Casamance or across the Diouloulou *marigot* to the Buluf district.

The continuation of the Banjul–Ziguinchor route south of Diouloulou (and points off) is usefully sprinkled with **campements** – at BAILA, TIONK ESSIL and AFINIAM in the district of Buluf, and at KOUBALAN southeast of Bignona (see below). Cycling to any of them is pretty straightforward, though if you intend turning west off the N5 highway into the Buluf district at Baila, try to ascertain the condition of the track. It's easier to get a lift into Buluf from Bignona than waiting at one of the trackheads off the main road.

From Affiniam you could get a *pirogue* over to Ziguinchor (Mon, Wed & Fri). If you've time, try to visit **NIAMONE**, either by *pirogue* from Affiniam, or by making a side trip from south of Bignona: it's one of the last Banyun–speaking villages in the region, inhabited by the people who were almost certainly the main group along the Casamance before the Jola arrived on the scene.

BIGNONA itself is a large route focus, frequently the scene of changes of vehicle, paid for by the taxi-driver you thought was taking you all the way to Ziguinchor. If you're staying the night, try *Le Palmier* (☎94 11 47). There's an impressive backdrop of tall jungly trees as you enter town over the Bignona creek from the north. The tropicality of Basse Casamance is vivid all over, with tall grasses bordering the road, monitor lizards shooting across it and the odd chameleon anxiously wobbling through the traffic.

West of Ziguinchor

Between Ziguinchor and the coast lies the boxing-glove-shaped heart of the **southern Basse Casamance**, a district of tall hardwood forest and rice fields cut by three major creeks and their fringes of mangrove flats. It's an ideal region for **cycling**, with the longest distance between significant places just 34km. You can hire bikes at **Oussouye** – the expanding village capital of the district – to get down to the underrated and little-visited **Basse Casamance National Park**, but it's probably better to hire them from Ziguinchor, having negotiated a week or ten days' worth (a week should cost under CFA12,000). Apart from having a water bottle (minimum capacity two litres) and devising a way to carry your gear (much of which you can probably leave at a hotel in Ziguinchor), there are no special practical problems in cycling around. Alternatively, you may be able to hire a mobylette.

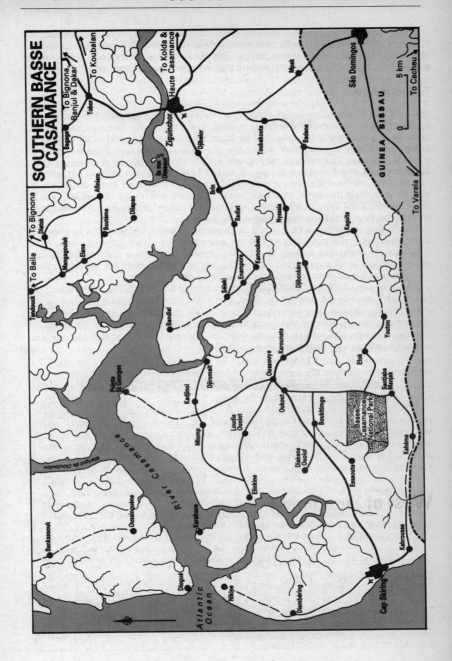

If you have no vehicle and choose to forgo the pleasures of peddling or tending a mobylette, then you should anticipate some **public transport difficulties** in reaching one or two slightly out-of-the-way places. The *campement* at **Enampore** is the most problematic, but the **Elinkine** campement may require some patience too.

To Enampore

Climbing the gentle valley out of Ziguinchor, the road passes through the remains of the **forest** that once covered the entire area. The magnificent thirty-or forty-metre trees, strung with vines, are inhabited by large numbers of birds and small animals – though you'll only see monkeys where the trees are close enough together to form arboreal highways. Examples of the region's wildlife can be observed at the signposted **farm/orchard** about 4km out of town at **DJIBELOR**, opposite a tropical agriculture research station. Near the river are several hectares of fruit trees and a collection of animals including monkeys, tortoises, monitor lizards and dwarf crocodiles. You'll likely be welcomed by Julie, a large but exceptionally tame chimpanzee, who may insist on a ride on your shoulders as she shows you round.

BRIN, 6km further, is where you'll be dropped if you're taking a taxi brousse to Enampore, and you're not likely to find any more transport. It's a four-hour walk, best done as early in the day as possible. If you're cycling you'll know the junction by the sharp left-hand bend across from a large church, and by the soda bar on the corner, where they're bound to wave you in the right direction.

It's 13km from here to **ENAMPORE**, with a left-hand fork at ESSIL after 6km. The Enampore **campement** is one of the best, a beautiful *case à impluvium* (see box) with a welcoming, familial atmosphere, excellent meals and cold drinks. The house is wonderfully constructed and a pleasure just to be in, especially during the hot hours of the day; however familiar you become with the region's *impluvium* architecture, the simplicity and calm of Enampore are memorable.

CASES À IMPLUVIUM AND FETISH SHRINES

Case à impluvium translates as "rain reservoir hut", a somewhat demeaning term that tells only half the story. The design is doughnut-shaped, with entrances into a shared, circular courtyard and internal doors into private rooms that are built as individual units. There's a stunning quality to the light reflected off the clean-swept courtyard floor to illuminate the living space. The thatched, saddleback roof circling above the living quarters is built like a funnel to allow rain to drain into a central reservoir, from where it runs outside through a drain.

In the past the *impluvium* was good insurance in times of war or drought, but since pure water wells have been dug all over, few *impluvium* houses are being built these days. Yet they make wonderful homes, and undoubtedly more Jola family heads would build new *cases à impluvium* if they could afford to – but the increasing nuclearisation of families means that few can find the necessary money or labour.

Although it's often written that the only other examples of *impluvium* architecture are found in New Guinea, similar houses were traditional in Guinea-Bissau and parts of southwest Côte d'Ivoire, and also in parts of southern Nigeria, where they were square in plan.

In the bush around, you'll also come across isolated miniature huts in the briefest of clearings. Often just a forked stick under a thatched roof, these are **fetish shrines**, the earthly visiting rooms of spirits that hold power over rain, fertility and illnesses. They are consulted less frequently than in the past, but there are still matters about which many Jola feel the traditional spirits know more than modern science or medicine. You should be careful not to disturb them or take photos.

At certain times of the year, usually in the vicinity of cattle, there's an awful lot of small **flies** around during the day; larger than the sweat flies you encounter in many places, they settle on your face and arms and are a ceaseless torment. They don't bite, but their presence can deter you from exploring the actual village, where an older, inhabited *case à impluvium* can be visited for a small payment.

If the flies are about, you could get away from the forest and head to SÉLEKI, at the end of the road; from there you can continue across the **dikes and rice fields** to ETAMA and then – if you've plenty of time – on to BANDIAL (15km there and back from Enampore). There's interesting architecture en route, and they don't get many foreign visitors out on the mud flats, so they'll be pleased to see you .

To Oussouye

From Brin, the road turns south, looping away from the river to cross the **Kamobeul Bolong** creek on a new bridge. Oussouye, the next major focus, is 34km away, across scrub, open mangrove flats and more scrub – good for birds west of the bridge, otherwise unenthralling. If you're cycling, you may be interested in three accommodation possibilities which have sprung up in recent years.

Four kilometres out of Brin, in the vicinity of DAR SALAM, the *Ranche des Routards* is signposted off to the left (with what looks like a Malian *SMERT* sign), then 2.5km down forest paths, bearing right at the forks. This orchard/*campement* project was looking promising; let us know.

The rurally integrated *Campement Diohère*, signposted 10km further on, is one of the latest in the family. Despite its unaccountable location, it has all the usual facilities; the hosts are particularly welcoming, and there are some wonderful creek excursions very nearby. If you want a cycle back to Ziguinchor, the eastward route from Diohère through farms and forest to the Ziguinchor–Guinea-Bissau road is idyllic.

Another 10km down the main road to Oussouye you come to the **Case à Impluvium chez Theodore Balousa**, signposted left a little after a sign for "Niambalang"; go 800m along the track and it's just after the well. A *case à impluvium* dating from the 1980/81 dry season, it has a well-lived-in feel and the family charge less than the going rate for bed and board. Scuttling with children and chickens, the house itself is a lot livelier than Enampore's, for example.

OUSSOUYE is the centre of these parts, sitting on the largest patch of dry land around. Once the seat of a line of Jola **priest-kings**, the town is still an important and growing place, but royalty is no longer much in evidence. Although the market is dull, there are one or two shops, and keen hagglers can make for the artisanal centre, and for some more evidence of Jola architectural innovation, take a look at the inspiring all-wood church, on the road out to Cap Skiring.

The best place to hang out in Oussouye while you wait to move on is the *Restaurant du Sud*, near the roundabout – cheap, agreeable and unpredictable. Or you could try the *Restaurant Noflaye* ("tous les délices à votre disposition"), also near the roundabout and run single handedly by its woman owner. If you're staying the night, the regal **campement**, 1km out on the forest path towards Elinkine, is the largest in the chain, a two-storey affair that boasts something of a forest view from the balconies at the back. Occasionally overrun by tour groups, it's otherwise wonderful, especially if you get an upstairs room. From the campement you can do an all-day excursion to the Basse Casamance National Park for around CFA5000 per person (minimum group of four).

Moving on from Oussouye

There are **five routes** out of Oussouye – to Ziguinchor, to Elinkine via Mlomp, direct to Elinkine, to the Basse Casamance National Park, and to Cap Skiring. Transport along all except the Ziguinchor road has its problems.

The daily car rapide from Ziguinchor **to Mlomp and Elinkine** passes through Oussouye around 4pm, but may well be full. More than likely there'll be other vehicles, but there's no guarantee. The **direct route to Elinkine** has been undriveable for several years and it doesn't look like the small bridge in the middle is going to be repaired; for cyclists and keen walkers it's an exciting and unbeaten track. The forest road to the park (the village of SANTIABA MANJAK is a handy label) varies in condition but it's never easy to find transport; if you intend continuing to **Cap Skiring**, note that at present there's no way a motor vehicle can get through. Even on the main road to Cap Skiring you can wait hours for a lift.

Should you despair of getting a lift – or simply need a change of pace – hire a bicycle from Youssouph Diallo in the market (CFA 1500/day).

Mlomp and Pointe St Georges

A wide, newly graded piste swoops in through the forest from Oussouye to **MLOMP**, a place which is preposterously overplayed. However, the pair of two-storey banco cottages with their amazing grove of silk-cotton trees are worthy of some attention – so long as you can be there when the tourist minibuses aren't. Two-storey buildings are uncommon in traditional African architecture, and it's hard to think of explanations why Mlomp should have them: nobody here can give any. They're reminiscent of Ashanti houses from Ghana and the possibility exists that the earlier Banyun traders of Casamance brought the innovation back from their travels. The *patron* will show you round one of them, and a postcard from home is much appreciated: pictures of the Empire State Building, Windsor Castle and the Arc de Triomphe adorn the walls.

Mlomp is getting a campement, on the road to Elinkine: it'll be a good place to stop over, as the interest of the village doesn't end with the two-storey houses: there are other attractive buildings around as well.

The Pointe

Mlomp is a departure point for **Pointe St Georges**, the Casamance's last elbow before it reaches the sea. You can walk or cycle the 10km from a point just east of the T-junction up from Oussouye, or there's the "main" road from KAGNOUT, 5km west of Mlomp and not on our map. Both tracks are reportedly terrible. Most of Pointe St George's visitors come by launch from Ziguinchor or Cap Skiring to stay at the *Village-Hôtel*. This commercial venture, owned in partnership with the *Hôtel du Tourisme* in Ziguinchor (and bookable there), apparently coexists harmoniously with the real village alongside. "Pool, tennis, exoticism, adventure" goes their blurb, but domesticated adventure does not come cheap – CFA20,000 per person per day.

Elinkine and Karabane

From Mlomp, a flat, straight route leads 12km to the creek-side village of **ELINKINE**, with several stands of huge silk-cottons giving way to monotonous, open country beyond the turning to Pointe St Georges. A much more interesting route is the one direct from Oussouye, a narrow track which year by year is returning to the forest. For the moment it's an enchanting and easy 14km by bike, but allow two hours.

Elinkine is more fun getting to than staying at. The village consists of very little, and the *campement* is the least *sympa* of all the *CRI*s, with very average food (served rather than shared), tatty facilities and poor security. Until their act improves, perhaps it would be better to stay at the more animated and cheaper *Le Fromager* in the village itself – the place where everyone fetches up after getting off the daily bus from Ziguinchor.

Karabane Island

The only thing worth doing in Elinkine is a trip to the history-laden island of **Karabane** in the river mouth. The most readily available transport is a CFA5000 *pirogue* trip, but there are more affordable possibilities if you can invest a day or two seeking them out. By all accounts it should be possible to get there for CFA1000 or so.

The island, or rather the headland where the settlement sits, was an early offshore trading base with the interior (like St-Louis and Gorée), and the first French toehold in the Kasa Mansa – the kingdom of the Kasa, one of the ancestral Jola peoples. Slaves, ivory, gum and hides were exported from here, paid for with cloth, alcohol and iron bars. There's a large Breton-style church, partly in ruins, dating back to the earliest days of the Holy Ghost Fathers, and a number of crumbling merchant houses. The beach is beautiful, with 10km of salty River Casamance in front and coconuts behind, but if you visit for only a few hours the whole place can feel slack with isolation and irrelevance.

Staying the night, the trip becomes more worthwhile, although neither hotel shines: one is an ugly mission money-earner (*Hôtel Karabane*), the other a very basic *campement*. But once everyone else has left and you can walk along the beach in peace, Karabane quickly becomes a place that's hard to leave.

A dubious alternative to the Elinkine approach is a day-trip from the creek behind Cap Skiring (9am–5.30pm) – around CFA7000 from *Le Paradise* or *Mussuwam* and maybe twice as much from *La Paillotte* (see p.427). Despite the price difference, you get the same fish and rice lunch and probably ride in the same pirogue. The trips normally take in the Ile des Feticheurs, an Ile aux Oiseaux or two, Elinkine and Karabane. That's a lot of messing around on the river among low mangroves, which cast little shade, so you're strongly advised not to go without suntan lotion, a hat and sunglasses – the brownest of *toubabs* lose their skin on these gentle excursions and bad burns can make travel impossible for several days.

Basse Casamance National Park

Hard up against the Guinea-Bissau border, the **Parc National de Basse Casamance** is forty square kilometres of streams, marshy savanna and partly untouched primary forest. Large mammals such as forest buffalo, leopard, hippo and bushbuck are rarely seen here, it's true; but there's wonderful **monkey-spotting** from several of the paths and lookout towers (*miradors*), there are **crocs** in the creeks, and the deep forest harbours species of **birds and insects** you're unlikely to come across anywhere else in Senegal. The best time to visit is well into the dry season, when, even in this relatively moist part of the country, waterholes dry up and sources become good spots to watch animals.

Practicalities

Getting to the park by public transport is difficult. The only possibilities lie with park staff or villagers going to Santiaba Manjak (see "Cap Skiring and Around", below). Oussouye is the place to try, the road from the coast being impassable – and of course this inaccessibility is part of its appeal. Unless you make your own way there on foot or bicycle, the only other possibility is an organised trip from the Oussouye campement (see above), but this means rushing it too much.

The park (CFA1000 per person per day) is not a place to visit in a single day: in order to get anything from it you'll need to stay for at least one dusk and dawn. The only accommodation in the park is a very pleasant *case à impluvium* campement near the entrance, with a newly renovated eating area; it's not a *campement rurale integré*, but it charges similar rates and does excellent meals. You could presumably camp here.

Animals, watchtowers and circuits

To maximise your chances of seeing animals, get out on the forest paths by about 6am. For animal-watching at the end of the day, come out at 4pm, install yourself somewhere comfortable, and wait. You can also look around at night, preferably in a vehicle or using a powerful torch. The hot, middle part of the day is quiet and often unrewarding.

The **Mirador du Buffle**, one of half-dozen observation platforms scattered through the park, is the best spot in the dry season, but only if you're early. The 2.5km of the *Circuit Houssiou*, which runs past it, meanders into tall grass and near its end reaches the *Mirador des Oiseaux*, on the main track; this circuit is only negotiable by bike (just) or on foot.

Monkeys are everywhere, especially in certain trees during their fruiting seasons – they adore the sharp *ditak* fruits. The *Circuit Djiban Epor*, which terminates in a rangers' encampment, is a good path for monkeys, having many high trees along it.

Don't be alarmed by noises in the undergrowth – they're most often caused by small duiker antelope and occasionally by bushbuck. Noisier – and heavier – movements are forest buffalo, relatively small and not dangerous; you're more likely to see their dung. Leopards are exceedingly shy and silent, and you would be fortunate indeed to see one; there are no records of any attacks. Crocodiles, particularly the dwarf (one-metre) species, are common enough if you're patient at the waterfront miradors. The *Mirador des Crocodiles* is easily reached off the main track, which terminates about 7km from the park entrance on the creek shore – with a jetty and picnic site.

Cap Skiring and Around

The immediate environs of straggling and undistinguished **CAP SKIRING** have nothing to recommend them: a minimal market, plus one or two small shops and snackeries. Of course if you're inside the *Club Méditerranée* honey pot, that isn't likely to make any difference: apart from organised excursions, the high barbed wire and soldiers guarding the *plage privé* discourage any independent roving outside the reserve.

The beaches here are pretty, the more deserted sections spectacular, and the sea warm and safe. The arrival of *Le Club* heralded the opening up of a new resort – with The Gambia and the coast of Côte d'Ivoire, one of the top three in West Africa. This is hedonistic territory and lacks much of deeper interest. Find a room, peel off your clothes and get down to the beach.

Places to Stay

Accommodation pickings aren't as slim as you might expect. In the village, *Hôtel Kassoumaye* and the *Campement Fogny* are for travellers straight off a vehicle and anxious to get settled: both are cheap and insalubrious, and the closest bits of non-*Club* beach none too great. Better options are found south of the Ziguinchor junction, so it's a good idea to get off your transport there rather than in Cap Skiring itself. At the junction is *La Paillotte* (☎93 14 14, fax 93 17 17) – big, expensive and joint-owned with the *Aubert* in Ziguinchor. If you're splashing out, this is the one to go for, with really comfortable rooms, hospitable staff and wonderful food; twin-bed bungalows go for under CFA20,000, but reckon on CFA18,000 per person HB. *Hôtel Emitai*, next one along, is pleasant but hasn't been open year-round lately; it charges around CFA15,000 per double, S/C and AC.

The bargains are bunched together a short walk south. Oldest is the *Campement Mussuwam* (☎93 14 84), a *Bel Kady* (Ziguinchor) venture that is seriously in danger of losing any bargain credibility: half board is around CFA15,000 for two (non-S/C, non-AC). Off-season prices may be lower, but with *Uniclam* and *Nouvelles Frontières* clients noisily occupying the restaurant, it looks like the Mussuwam has been "discovered".

The main bar/restaurant has a terrace overlooking quite a nice beach front and evenings come steamily to life with local people turning up to dance in an atmosphere like a youth club social. The neighbouring *Campement Paradis* (huts and a new *case à impluvium*) again deals in obligatory half board, but at around CFA4000/CFA7000 it's reasonably good value as long as they've solved their terrible security problems. The *Auberge de la Paix*, on the *Mussuwam*'s other side, is the newest of the three and a bargain-basement establishment, with facilities just about adequate. Clean, white-washed cubicles (with use of a single shower/toilet) go for CFA2500/CFA5000 HB, and the management are *sympa*. It shares the same beach as the *Paradis*, the *Mussuwam* and *La Paillotte*. As for food, a recommended break from the hotel restaurants is *La Pirogue*, a starlit walk from the *Mussuwam* and good value.

Further south, the *Houback* (☎93 14 36) is fairly new and touristy, used by *Enterprise holidays*, and around CFA14,000 per person HB.

Sea and sand

Bronzing and bathing are the main daytime occupations, though the more expensive hotels have windsurfers at around CFA3000/hour – there's almost always a good breeze. The *Mussuwam* and a few other places rent out bicycles for CFA2000 per day, better value than a car at CFA20,000 or a 4WD vehicle for CFA45,000.

By **bicycle** you can easily get up to Diembering (see below) in an hour or two along the beach at low tide when the sand is firm; the main motorable track through the bush is very sandy. Don't venture onto the *Club Med*'s stretch: it is ostensibly a public right of way but there are armed *militaires* at each end where the fence goes into the sea. Most people follow the fence down to the beach on its northern side then cycle from there, passing through the sunbed obstacle course in front of the *Hôtel Savanna* (dirty looks but no force of arms), and then climbing over a jumble of low rocks for a magnificent sweep of sand. Shortly after this point there's an interesting and apparently recent open-air mosque – or possibly a church? – built into the cliffside. And a kilometre further, you come to a derelict beach house between sea and forest. Obviously once a wonderful spot, surrounded by coconut palms, with picnic tables and showers, it's now inhabited by spiders and the floorboards are rotten.

Diembering

DIEMBERING lies deep behind the dunes, 8.5km further. The obvious retreat from Cap Skiring, this is a satisfying village, as traditional as you could expect, living from fishing and livestock and by no means entirely dependent on its three privately owned campements. The most striking thing about Diembering is the hill that rises from the centre of the village, a steep and ancient dune crowned and stabilised by a grove of venerable silk-cotton trees. It's no more than thirty metres high, but in Basse Casamance it looks like a mountain, and there's no escaping the strong and mysterious sense of place.

Between the trees is the *Campement Aten-Elou*, named after a local priestess who at one time acted virtually as village chief. The biggest and highest *campement* in Diembering, its prices are just a little higher than the *CRI*s. The rooms, in quartered, circular thatched huts with terraces, are scattered between the silk-cotton buttresses, and they lock up properly; the food is pretty good, and it's a lively and popular place, with a wonderful beach visible through the trees, a twenty-minute walk away. *Campement Albert Sambou*, down the hill beneath the trees, is smaller and cheaper (CFA3000 per person HB), but not open all year round; a prettily located *case à impluvium* with a marvellous atmosphere, family-run and nicer than the *Aten Elou*, this is definitely the place to try first. The other campement, the *Asseb*, at the entrance to Diembering if you arrive by road, is clean and new, but there's little else positive to say about it. The small, rectangular S/C rooms are hot and uninviting, with no view; you'd want to stay only if the others were full.

If you get tired of the crowds even at Diembering, you could walk or cycle – again, preferably at low tide – up to NYIKINE, a village at the very mouth of the Casamance. It's a place of coconuts and seclusion, recommended by some of the boys hanging around in Diembering, and possibly worth visiting in their company.

Inland from Cap Skiring

The 25km **from Cap Skiring to the Basse Casamance National Park** has to be done on foot or bike, because although the ferry over the inland creek may be transporting cars, the track beyond it is impassable.

South of Cap Skiring, the road turns through the village of **KABROUSSE** – a scattered community of farmers. There's one last tourist hotel here (*Hôtel Kabrousse*), and nothing in the way of *campements* until you get to the park. It was here that a major anti-colonial rebellion was instigated during World War II under the leadership of Alinsitoé, a famous Jola visionary from Kabrousse. Aged only twenty, she spearheaded a revolt provoked by the tax burden placed on the Jola peasantry by the government. After a vicious battle at Efok (see below), Alinsitoé was arrested and exiled to St-Louis, then to Timbuktu, where she died. Her name is evoked whenever the question is raised of Casamance secession from northern Senegal.

The forest path to the park

The tarmac goes into Kabrousse but fails to come out again, so make sure you pick the right path. It's rare for a motor vehicle to head out across these fields, understandably when you get to the creek, 6km on, and see the remains of the ferry. But a bicycle can make it easily. A *mobylette* is less suitable, because you may have to load it onto a *pirogue* for the creek crossing, and take it through patches of deep sand later.

On the eastern side of the creek the path continues along the Guinea-Bissau border, clear enough but frequently bicycle-width only, and sometimes degenerating into sandy oblivion, where you'll have to push. Although the total distance to the park gate is only some 22km from Kabrousse, it can feel longer. Not that it's a pain, as long as you allow a full morning or afternoon, because the entire route is blissfully uncontaminated by tourism. You pass through family hamlets where frank stares of astonishment meet you. Much of the way is heavily overgrown, with thickets of bamboo and forest filling the gaps between farm plots and compounds.

SANTIABA MANJAK is the largest village you pass through before the park gate; 2km further, a right turning leads off to the Alinsitoé battle village of EFOK (5km) and equally isolated YOUTOU (10km). Efok's main public place is supposed to have a huge war drum, confiscated during the rebellion, while at Youtou similar drums are apparently still being made.

THE GAMBIA

THE GAMBIA

The Gambia could easily be dismissed as an inconsequential little tourist trap. A tiny and frail country, eking out its existence along the banks of the Gambia River, it relies heavily on the December to April influx of British and European visitors taking a step beyond Spain and the Canaries. Out of season the **beach resort** hotels go to sleep or close down, and Gambians turn their attentions inland to the groundnut – peanut – harvest. The feeling of nothing much happening can be acute, and if you've already travelled widely in West Africa, The Gambia isn't going to knock you out.

But after a major overland trip it's a congenial enough place to rest up. Equally, it's an easy **access point** from which to embark on more extensive African wanderings, with the flight from Europe taking less than six hours. Should you want to stay put, you can spend a week or two here in **package-holiday** style for less than what you'd pay in many European resorts – and of course you can do it in mid winter. The beaches are good – though they get a lot better the further you go from the hotels – and the sea is unfailingly warm.

The Gambia's surest appeal lies in its **smallness**: with a population about the same size as Berkshire's or Delaware's, there's a rapidly acquired feeling of knowing everyone. Pomp and exclusivity are hard to maintain and you can find yourself in conversation with cabinet ministers without even realising it.

Where and when to go

While a surprising drabness characterises the capital **Banjul**, and organised excursions can be unrewarding, West Africa does reveal itself if you make an effort to leave the crowds and visit the interior. Dominated by the daily cycle of tides and the annual swing

THE GAMBIA AND SENEGAMBIA

The country is officially designated *The* Gambia, a device that has a certain cachet but only tends to emphasise the fact that the Gambia river is all there is to it. The country's population, rising steadily towards one million, lives in a strip of only 11,300 square kilometres of river bank, making The Gambia one of the smallest and most densely populated countries in Africa. Since independence in 1965, the country's leader has been Sir Dawda Jawara – head of the ruling People's Progressive Party and president of a nominally multi-party democracy. The politically expedient Senegambia Confederation, linking the country with big Senegal, came to an end in 1989 when Senegalese troops were withdrawn.

of flood and drought, the **Gambia River** has a compelling life of its own. Once you get beyond **Brikama**, the villages and the main "up-country" centres of **Georgetown**, **Bansang** and **Basse Santa Su** are little affected by the coast's tourism. Animal and **birdlife** is diverse and exotic (and ornithologists will recognise many wintering migrants); there are coconut trees, rice fields, mangrove swamps and dugout canoes in the creeks. And the country's borders need not limit your explorations: encircling **Senegal**, vast in comparison, is accessible without a visa for many nationalities.

Deciding **when to go**, if you've the choice, is basically a question of avoiding the rainy season. If you're going on a package you'll quickly see that there's nothing much on offer from **June to October**, which is when The Gambia gets up to 1300mm of rain – about fifty percent more than Britain's annual average. There's a degree of regional variation: on the coast the rains don't begin in earnest much before July, but inland they can start in May; up-river they may finish by the end of August, down at Banjul often not until October. August is usually the wettest month, making north bank roads impassable for days on end. The period from **March to May** is normally rainless, but dust and wind from across the Sahara can be a torment, and the haze can even block out the sun. The ideal period for a visit is **December or January**, when you can expect dry, hot days and mild – even cool – nights.

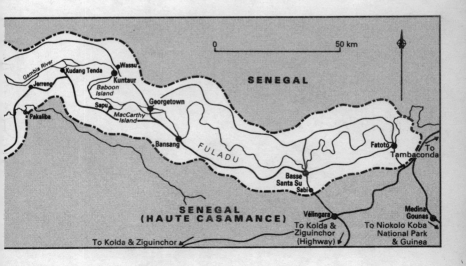

BANJUL: AVERAGE TEMPERATURE AND RAINFALL

	Jan	Feb	Mar	Apr	May	June	July	Aug	Sept	Oct	Nov	Dec
Temperatures °C												
Min	15	16	17	18	19	23	23	23	23	22	18	16
Max	31	32	34	33	32	32	30	29	31	32	32	31
Rainfall mm	3	3	0	0	10	58	282	500	310	109	18	3
Days with rainfall	0	0	0	0	1	5	16	19	19	8	1	0

Arrivals

As a first taste of West Africa, The Gambia is an easy arrival point. It's also the first choice for a fair number of expatriate workers looking for a short holiday in the region. Flights and package deals from Europe are covered in the *Basics* section at the front of the book.

■ Flights from West African Cities

The main airlines into Banjul are *Ghana Airways* and the *Gambia Air Shuttle*. *Ghana Airways* flies in four times weekly from **Accra** via **Abidjan** and **Monrovia** – plus stops in **Freetown** and **Conakry** on three of the flights. They also run Wed & Sun flights down from **Dakar**. The *Gambia Air Shuttle*, together with *Air Senegal*, fly at least daily between the two capitals. The *Gambia Air Shuttle* also operates Tues & Thurs flights from **Bissau**, a Mon flight from **Bamako** and a Fri link from **Sal** airport on the Cape Verde Islands (possibly discontinued). *Nigeria Airways* operates a weekly service from **Lagos** via Cotonou, Abidjan, Monrovia and Conakry. Lastly, *British Airways* connects Monrovia and Freetown with Banjul every Tues & Sat.

Flights **from other African capitals** to Banjul usually connect through Dakar, though the *Zambia Airlines* Lusaka–Monrovia flight (Mon & Fri) is worth remembering.

■ Overland Entry

Whichever way you travel overland, you'll arrive first in **Senegal**, with which The Gambia's relations have recently become a little strained since the demise of the confederation. Some hassle can now be expected at border posts which used to process travellers swiftly .

From **Dakar to Banjul** there are theoretically two Gambian state buses daily, and from **Ziguinchor to Serekunda** (outside Banjul) a number of Peugeot 504 bush taxis every morning. Until relations between the two countries improve, however, you're likely to have to change vehicles at the border, which isn't much of a problem.

You're unlikely to save time or money by coming direct **from Bamako** and entering The Gambia at its eastern end, but this route to Banjul is more enjoyable than the dreary highway through Senegal to Dakar. Break your journey at Tambacounda, make your way to the Gambian border crossing at Fatoto and pick up a Gambian state bus from there to Banjul (two each morning) – or bush taxi-hop your way down the river.

Red Tape and Visas

Most Commonwealth and European Community passport holders don't require a visa. French, Belgian, US and Japanese nationals are among those who do. If you're simply traversing the country, from northern to southern Senegal, visas aren't required by any nationality.

For all visitors, the important document is a **ten-year passport**, valid at least six months past your stay. For package-tour visitors from Britain, a yellow fever certificate is no longer needed. **Flying in** you'll normally be given as long as you request – up to three months if you have a return ticket. If your flight is one-way only, you might be required to show evidence of sufficient funds, though this isn't common. Immigration is somewhat different at the land borders. Regardless of nationality or wishes, most **overland** entrants are given a maximum of one week to sort themselves out and report to the Immigration Office in Banjul, where it's necessary to apply for an extension.

For **onward travel** from The Gambia, you can obtain visas in Banjul for Senegal, Guinea-Bissau and Sierra Leone. Visas for Nigeria, Mauritania and Liberia may be available too, if harder to obtain. There's no French embassy, so no francophone country visa service.

Money and Costs

Gambian currency is the *dalasi* (D), divided into 100 *bututs* (approximately D13.5=£1). Outside The Gambia dalasis aren't officially convertible, so go easy and only change what you need. The currency is weak, though it hasn't fared badly over the years.

If you're arriving in the country from Senegal, you might want to bring CFA francs to change rather than using your dollars or European currency. CFA francs are much in demand and you should end up better off. There is no currency declaration form.

There are **banks** in Banjul, Bakau, Serekunda and Basse, usually open Mon–Thurs 8am–1pm, Fri 8am–11am. The *Standard Chartered* in Banjul

will cash personal cheques on British bank accounts with a cheque guarantee card. There is normally no commission at banks. The airport *bureau de change* appears to be an exception.

The open **black market** – about as laid-back as you'll find anywhere in West Africa – normally offers a marginally better rate than the banks (for £ sterling, US dollars, CFA and French francs), and is useful anyway outside banking hours. In Banjul, check down by the Barra ferry terminal. Avoid changing money at the hotels if you can – they do a brisk rip-off trade with diabolical rates.

Credit Cards

Credit cards (notably *Amex*, but *Visa* and *Access/Mastercard* to some extent also) are handy if you're staying in one of the main beach hotels, but they're not of much use in Banjul itself, or anywhere else in the country. *Access/Mastercard* can't be used for cash advances.

■ Costs

Costs tend to be somewhat lower than northern Senegal's and overall rather higher than in the Basse Casamance region of southern Senegal. But the two countries are not really comparable: away from Banjul and the coast there simply isn't much to spend your cash on. Ordinary market produce and grocery store fare isn't going to break your budget. Beer and soft drinks get pricey up-river and away from main centres. The same broad rule applies to petrol, which varies from around D7 per litre from pumps at licensed stations to D50 per "gallon" from jerry cans up-river. If you're staying on the coast, you'll soon discover which hotels charge D12 or more for a beer and where you can find one for less than half that.

Accommodation costs are very much up to you – anything from D60 to a small fortune for a room in Banjul or the coastal resorts, depending on whether you want full tropicalised comforts or a very basic bed for the night. Up-river, D120 is probably the most you'd pay.

Information, Maps, Guides

It's worth visiting a Gambia National Tourist Office before you leave. The London office (at the High Commission) is efficient and helpful. Good, free maps of the country are available plus ideas on packages, flights and the rest.

In The Gambia itself things are a bit different: you can pick up the same maps – at a price – from the Ministry of Tourism/Tourist Office above the *Apollo Hotel* in Banjul. They should also be able to advise about car hire and river travel possibilities. For more **detailed maps**, you need to visit the Survey Department in the ominously named "Half Die" quarter of Banjul, open week-day office hours. The 1:250,000 sheet (1980) covers the country but there's also a nice 1:50,000 series (1981) based on aerial photographs that seems to show every compound. They're hard to obtain outside the country.

■ Guides

There are two **guidebooks** to The Gambia you may come across. **Michael Tomkinson**'s *The Gambia – a holiday guide* (1983, Michael Tomkinson Publishing) is not often in print and superseded now by his coffee table re-vamp *The Gambia* (1987). Both books contain nice pics and a wealth of interesting detail – if you can swallow the smartass style – but the first no longer has much practical utility. **Terry Palmer**'s *Discover The Gambia* (1988, Heritage House) has various odd gaffs, but it's better than Tomkinson as a practical guide.

As for general works on The Gambia, and fiction by Gambian writers, the in-print choice is very limited. There is a selection in "Books" in the *Contexts* section at the back of the book.

Health

Apart from a yellow fever vaccination certif-icate, which is no longer compulsory unless you're visiting Senegal, it's a good idea to have the whole range of jabs unless your stay is a simple package.

You must take **anti-malaria tablets** even if you're holidaying for a week. The disease is more resistant in areas like The Gambia, where malarial parasites have long been combatted with the drugs used by tourists. Given the greater virulence of the parasites here, the risks if you don't bother with tablets are consequently higher. That said, while Banjul and the river are mosquito-prone all year round, the hotel areas on the Atlantic coast are mostly free by the middle of the season. The insects themselves aren't often a persistent menace.

As for health care, there are two principal **hospitals** in The Gambia: the Royal Victoria in Banjul, with its crowded wards and mosquito-netted patients visible from Marina Parade, and the more reputable Bansang Hospital, 300km up-river. If you're seriously ill, contact a hotel or, up-river, the nearest dispensary or foreign aid worker. Emergency services are rudimentary.

Water in The Gambia is considered safe when it comes from taps or pumps. You shouldn't hesitate to drink tap water in your hotel: plastic bottles of Senegalese *Celia* mineral water are expensive and only worth it if you're in Africa for a short time. If you must buy it, get it in bulk from one of the supermarkets at a fraction of the hotel price.

A health concern of some importance in the Banjul area is the **sewage** system – or rather the lack of one. An EC-aided project has been digging up the capital for some time to install a plumbed-in service to households on the rates register. This means about one in five, but it's expected that many more will connect themselves unofficially, resulting in a chronic overload and the prospect of two or three times more raw sewage flowing out into the estuary than planned for. Hotels on the north-facing section of coastline will suffer most unless a solution is found.

Lastly, the **AIDS** position. By the end of 1987, twelve people were known to be suffering from – or had died from – the disease. Male and female prostitutes work in the Banjul region, though prostitution is principally a diversion of the beach hotels, some of which are fairly lax about their policy on visits by non-guests.

Getting Around

The Gambia's internal transport system is not complicated by air, sea or rail routes, and neither is the river used any longer as a significant means of transport. There are ferry services across it but none along, and what ought to be an asset is seen as a hindrance to north–south communications. Principal car ferry crossings are at Banjul–Barra and Yelitenda–Bambatenda, the trans-Gambian highway crossing between Soma and Farafenni.

Cross-river **ferries** have recently improved with the arrival of new ships, and Banjul–Barra and Yelitenda–Bambatenda are now much more reliable. The Georgetown–north bank and Basse ferries remain unpredictable, as does the one across Jowara Bolong at Kerewan on the north bank. Other ferries are for passengers only.

As to **roads**, there's one main, hard-surfaced artery from Banjul to Basse Santa Su ("Basse"), along the south bank of the river; it's in terrible condition as far as Serekunda, and not a great deal better until Soma, but fine after that. North bank roads are entirely of laterite, mud, sand or rock, apart from the short stretch from Barra into Senegal.

The country is held together by the efforts of the **GPTC** (*Gambia Public Transport Corporation*) recently much improved by a fleet of new buses. The main route, **between Serekunda bus depot and Basse**, has six services daily, at 6.45am, 7.40am (to Gambisara, 10km short of Basse), 8am (express), 8.30am, 10.20am and noon. The 2pm departure terminates in Dankunku, the 3.45pm in Soma. Departures and schedules depend somewhat on demand. The express service (D40 as compared with D30 for ordinary speed) aims to roar into Basse at 3pm. The north bank *GPTC* services (three daily in each direction) concentrate on linking the villages between Barra and Georgetown with the transport hub of **Farafenni**.

In addition, privately operated **bush taxis** known as "cars" (mostly Japanese vans, pick-ups, a few saloons and goods trucks) fill in the gaps (especially in the coastal hinterland) and feed the bus routes, and can often get you out of a corner. Around the touristy parts, ordinary **taxis** are touted by their drivers and are unlikely to overcharge if you start with some good-natured bargaining: fares to various local points are usually displayed outside the main hotels.

■ Car Hire

Car hire is very undeveloped, with the international agencies unrepresented and just a handful of local operations meeting demand – and often preferring to provide drivers. Self-drive deals are generally only available in the Banjul/ resorts area, and start from around £30 per day all-in in the low season. Some suggestions are included in the Banjul "Listings" section. Petrol at about 60p a litre makes up for relatively low prices.

■ Cycling

Fat wheel **motortrikes** are on hire from several coast hotels, as are **bicycles**. If you'd prefer to bring your own bike, The Gambia is quiet, safe and flat terrain for a first try at cycling in Africa, with ample opportunity for leisurely sidetracking to the river. In the dry season, a complete circuit of the country (inland on the south bank, back to Banjul on the north) would take a couple of weeks assuming about 75km a day. Mountain bikes would be best, but you'd get away with well set-up ordinary tourers on a short trip.

Sleeping

The vast majority of visitors have hotels pre-booked for the duration of their stays, which works out relatively cheap. The hotels guide on p.458 gives some idea of what to expect.

None of these – except those block-booked by tour operators – is closed to you if you arrive by independent means and feel the urge to splurge. But the outlay is likely to be heavy unless you visit out of season or turn up a special deal: The Gambia's tourist hotels do operate seasonal tariffs. The hotels ignored by the tour operators are of course more affordable, but the number of hotels in The Gambia is very small and away from the tourist areas there are practically none. Even including the most basic establishments and various government or development organisation **rest houses**, there's barely a handful throughout the entire up-river region.

With so few lodgings, **camping** makes a lot of sense. There are no campsites, but pitching a tent is unproblematic if you have your own transport: despite a fairly high population density, you're likely to find secluded spots off the main road where you can peg out for a night and enjoy the bush. Carrying a tent on your back there's less opportunity, as always, to find that good pitching place. You're going to have to ask to camp on people's land – which will often lead to invitations to stay with them instead.

Eating and Drinking

Restaurants are no more numerous than hotels – even the sort of chop-house establishments you may have come to expect from wider travels are largely absent – and with everything on such a tiny scale it's not altogether remarkable that no significant national cuisine has emerged.

Gambian dishes do not differ much from Senegalese, as they are all **Wolof dishes**. The tourist hotels' Gambian "standard" is *Yassa Chicken*, delicious when prepared well, but often just casseroled fowl with a searing sauce of chile and onions. *Domodah*, if you like groundnuts, is invariably good (the thicker the better), usually with chicken, sometimes beef, always rice. *Mafe* is another peanutty variation.

A serious rice dish is *Benachin*, the "Jollof Rice" of African restaurants abroad, served with beef (or sometimes fish), tomato puree and vegetables (sweet peppers, aubergine, carrots and squash) – the emphasis is on the palm oil that stains the rice red and goes down your chin.

The best feature is quantities of fresh **seafood**: shrimps, ladyfish (like sole), barracuda if you're in luck, and excellent chowders and bisques in a few places. But this is effectively to recommend a clutch of decent eating houses near Banjul and the resorts. If you leave the coast, you really have to get to Basse before restaurants appear again in just about recognisable form.

Fortunately, you'll find quite good French-style **bread** all over. **Pies** – resembling Cornish

MANDINKA FOOD AND DRINK TERMS

bread	mburo	groundnut oil	dulino	water	jio
rice	mano	palm oil	tulussy	hibiscus tea	honjo
meat	subo	onion	jabo	green tea	ataya
fish	nye	aubergine	patanse	soft drink	lemnato
millet (grain)	nyo	orange	lemuno	palm wine	tenkuolo
groundnut (peanut)	teo	water melon	sarro	alcohol	dolo
groundnut paste	deke				

pasties – seem to be a leftover British influence: found in meat and fish varieties, they are often surprisingly tasty. And **fruit** you can get just about everywhere – especially bananas and papayas at any time (though the latter aren't often sold and you'll have to ask in the country-side), and mangoes, guavas, avocados, water melons and oranges in season – the last often imported from Morocco.

■ Drinking

For **drinking**, you'll have to get used to The Gambia's **lager** – *Julbrew* – which is fairly strong but not one of West Africa's better-tasting beers, and fizzy drinks (**"softs"**) from the same enterprise. Bottled Guinness is a colonial relic, sold quite widely, but rarely cold and perhaps verging on the medicinal in the view of most Gambians. Soda water – seltzer – is usually obtainable in larger places. Plastic bottled "spring" or "mineral" water from Senegal is catching on fast, but it's a pricey way of avoiding contamination. Tap water is generally very healthy.

Try the homemade plastic-bag **juices**, or ices, which are popular because they're so cheap, and are on sale wherever people can get hold of plastic bags. Tasty but sticky sweet, they come in three main kinds – white, brown and red – made from baobab fruit, ginger and hibiscus flowers (*bisap*). Coffee for breakfast from roadside stalls isn't as common as in the French-speaking countries; green tea – known here as "Gambian tea" – is fairly widespread though, especially in Fula areas up-river.

Palm wine – which of course you'll be told is a Gambian speciality – is usually tapped from oil palms and is pretty well universal: the speciality lies in getting the tourists plastered on it during "bush and beach" excursions. As everywhere it varies considerably in taste and strength depending on when it was tapped and what it's been

stored in – and as usual, it's tolerated but not strictly legal.

Language, Communications and Media

The Gambia's main language is English, fairly widely spoken in Banjul and the resorts, but often not understood outside the metropolitan areas or up-river. Krio, still spoken by the descendants of freed slaves who moved from Freetown, is heard less and less. The African language you'll most often hear around Banjul is Wolof (see the Senegal chapter for some words and phrases), but the language with the strongest claim to be the country's traditional tongue is Mandinka, very widespread up-river, especially on the south bank.

There's a large **Fula**-speaking contingent also, particularly on the north bank. Other languages you may come across include **Jola** towards the Casamance to the south and **Serahuli/ Sarakole**, originally from far to the northeast. Around the Bakau and Fajara resort areas many young people speak some **French**, now the fastest-growing language.

Radio comes in two versions. There's *Radio Gambia*, broadcasting in English and the main national languages on 670m MW; it does news, announcements ("will all members of the national football squad please get in touch with the coach...") and endless request shows – there can be very few Gambians who haven't at one time or another said hello to everyone who knows them. The other is *Radio Syd* (329m and 900m MW; PO Box 279, ☎26490), a privately owned commercial station operating on the Serekunda highway at the end of Bund Road; started by a Swede, it specialises in good music

MINIMAL MANDINKA

The Mandinka of The Gambia is a fairly mainstream dialect of the large **Mande** language group. As usual in languages of Islamic peoples, there's a scattering of Arabic. Mandinka is not difficult to get your tongue round, though grammatically, of course, it's unfamiliar. The "kh" sound is the "ch" of loch. A characteristic of spoken Mandinka is the omitted final vowel, lending a "clipped" quality to the language.

GREETINGS AND USEFUL PHRASES

How are you? (do you have peace?)	Khaira be?	Where do you come from?	Bota min to ley?
		Sit down	Si gi
How are you all?	Al be khairato?	White person	Toubab
I'm well (I've peace)	Khaira dorong	Black person	Morfula
How is everyone in the compound?	Sumo ley?	Where are you going?	Kata min?
		I'm going to Basse	Nkata Basse
They're well	Ibi jay	Let's go	Alingta
All OK? (general, further greeting)	Kortanante?	Goodbye (sing/pl)	I si kontong/Al si kontong
All OK	Tanante	Clear off! (to cheeky children)	A cha!
How's the work? (if you're passing by)	Nimbara? (pl Alnimbara?)	I'll beat you! (beware!)	Be buteka!
The work's OK	Nimbara, nimbara		
Thank you	Abaraka	I want some bananas	Banano sanye
Is Musa at home?	Musa ley?	Five dalasis	Dalasi lulu
Yes (I'm here)	Naam	Too much!	Alcoleata!/Adajoiata!
What's your name?	Ito ndi?		
My name is Kaba	N to Kaba	Lower the price!	Atala/Njauiata

NUMBERS

1	kiling	5	lulu	9	kononto	20	moang		
2	fula	6	woro	10	tang	35	tang saba ning lulu		
3	saba	7	worowula	11	tang ning kiling	100	kemi		
4	nani	8	sei						

and mundane adverts – "Remember *Chellarams* for all your paint and household requirements . . . we are best". DJ Ebrahima at Syd is always happy to meet visitors with good sounds.

If you want to tune in to what's really going on you need the BBC on short wave. There's no TV in The Gambia, but there are televisions: *RTV Sénégal* is partly responsible for the growing francophone element in national life.

As for the print media, Gambian **newspapers** are a little hard to track down. People say the government's *Gambia News Bulletin* appears "each week". *The Nation* certainly appears fortnightly, spouting with wonderful forthrightness and at considerable length on a variety of topics. *The Torch* is another small thorn in the government's side, its editor recently escaping conviction for libel after arraigning several ministers for corruption. And there's the newish, leftish *Foroyaa*.

You're unlikely to get **foreign papers** in Banjul: the *Atlantic Hotel* might have something, or you could try the beach hotels. *Time* and *Newsweek* are obtainable if you want them, though often late. *West Africa* magazine is available the week after publication.

■ Post and Phones

Keeping in contact with home is relatively easy if you're down on the coast: up-river is altogether another matter. Aerograms are the cheapest way of writing, if the Banjul GPO has any, but ordinary post isn't expensive. **Poste restante** facilities at Banjul are not especially efficient compared to, say, Dakar. There's a small charge.

Phoning home, on West Africa's best international telecom system, is good value, especially to the UK. Dialling is direct, charged at a rate of approximately D20/minute (take a watch). You can phone internationally from the new call

GLOSSARY OF GAMBIAN TERMS

This list includes Wolof and Mandinka terms and a number of suffixes used in place names.

Alkali Village elder

Ba Big, as in Tenda-ba (big wharf)

Bantaba Mens' communal siesta platform in every village

Banto faro River flood lands

Bengdula/la Craft market/s

Car Minibus

Duma Lower

Fodi Teacher/marabout

Kafo Traditional "youth club"

Kerr/Keur Place

Koto Old

Kunda Place

Kuta New

Lumo Weekly (or regular) rural market

MOJA-G A proscribed organisation – the Movement for Justice in Africa-Gambia

Nding Small

PPP People's Progressive Party

Santa Upper

Su Home

Tenda Port, wharf

Tesito Self-reliance, a government slogan

boxes – reputedly solar powered! – dotted around the country. If you can make contact by **telex**, that works out to about D25/minute.

Entertainment

While for the majority of visitors entertainment means the hotel formula-mix of "folkloric dance troupes" and homestyle discos, it's easy enough to escape the dross and find real Gambian musical entertainment. To be fair, the hotels do sometimes host worthwhile gigs – the country's kora players (see below) have all played to tourist audiences.

The best time to be in the Banjul area for **music on stage** is the end of the month, when people can afford tickets for the bands that occasionally visit from abroad, usually Senegal. There are normally two or three gigs – the first a more expensive **"dance"** at the Banjul City Council on Independence Drive (D30 or more, starting around 11pm and going on to 3 or 4am) and the next night a more proletarian **"show"** at the big Bakau stadium (tickets from D10, hordes of people, arrive early to get a seat or you'll never see the musicians).

The Gambia's own main electric band is **Abdul Kabir**, led by Laye Ngom – brother of UK-based percussionist **Sagar Ngom** and ex-Super Diamono singer **Moussa Ngom**. Abdul Kabir play the Serekunda and Bakau clubs fairly often. As the only creative, amplified group working in the country, they're major stars on their own patch. Most Gambian groups (**Ifang Bondi** a classic example) gravitate inevitably to Dakar, if not to

Europe, as soon as they reap a measure of success. Musically, Dakar is The Gambia's real nerve centre.

The Gambia however is more distinguished for its Mandinka-speaking **kora musicians**. The most famous talents – **Dembo Konte**, **Kausu Kouyate**, **Foday Musa Suso**, **Jali Nyama Suso**, **Malamini Jobarteh** and junior **Pa Jobarteh** – are as likely to be playing in a British folk festival as in a compound in Brikama or at a wedding in Serekunda. **Wolof drummers** often perform at "private" functions too. Keep your ears open and drop in politely. If you're into the idea of participation, rather than merely being part of the audience, there's a box of details at the end of the Banjul section. And for pre-departure inspiration, there's a growing list of Gambian kora records available in Britain, including most of the artists above.

Lastly, with cinema and theatre not happening at all, spectator sports are the other principal entertainment in the country. Football is popular and even cricket gets played once in a while, but the big sport is **wrestling**, an exciting way of spending a few hours – see p.459.

Women Travellers

Sexual hassles in the resort areas are generally not a problem – certainly no more so than in neighbouring countries – though you may find the frank scrutiny unnerving. And of course sexual interest isn't exclusively one-sided – which can make life harder for women not in search of adventures.

If you find your freedom is being seriously compromised by the ubiquitous presence of **"guides"**, it's probably best in the long run to give in – to *one* of them; you may need to be ruthless in your choice and quite frank about your intentions. He'll act as your chaperone and, tipped occasionally or given the odd souvenir or present from home, may become a real friend for the duration. It's hard and not necessarily helpful to generalise, but the average age of the guides around Banjul is probably no more than 16. They are sometimes amazingly well-informed.

Up-river, foreign **women travelling alone** are a rare sight and will arouse enormous curiosity. Disappointingly, your contacts with Gambian women may not prove any more fruitful than if you were to travel in male company.

The *Women's Bureau*, located just inside the gates of State House, is the main organ of the Gambian **Women's Movement**. It's concerned primarily with establishing financial stability for women and developing non-traditional income sources, especially crafts cooperatives. Emancipation is a long way off, with polygamy still the norm and six children commonly planned (even in middle-class marriages). Clitoridectomies, performed not infrequently at the Royal Victoria Hospital, are common. **Contraception**, for those men or women who want it and make the effort, is free, but there's little in the way of campaigning for family planning.

DRESS SENSE

While topless bathing is fine on most of the beaches, appearing elsewhere less than well-covered, particularly from the waist down, is provocative. An idea of the prevailing conservative morality can be inferred from this 1985 letter from the *Women's Bureau* to the National Tourist Organisation:

Dear Sirs,
A BRIEF COUNSEL ABOUT THE APPEARANCE OF TOURISTS IN THE GAMBIA
The staff of the Women's Bureau would like to express its concern about the effects of the tourist season on citizens and residents of The Gambia. While walking through Banjul or Kombos area it is apparent that many of the tourists are unaware of the local dress standards. Scantily clad men and women walking into public places can be an embarrassment for both Gambians and expatriates living and working in The Gambia. Perhaps if the tourists were made aware of cultural and religious customs they would not mind wearing more discreet clothing away from the confines of their hotel. We would therefore urge that some information be presented to the tourists either at the hotels or at the airport, so that they could be informed in a nonoffensive way about local standards of dress. Perhaps a poster could express the message (i.e. cover up a bit when you're about in the town), and allow the tourists to make an informed choice on how to dress. It would still be their choice, of course, but once they are made aware of Gambian customs they may be less likely to walk around in outfits that elicit stares and whispers, tempt young boys to approach unaccompanied women, and contribute to the more negative impact of tourism.
Welcome to The Gambia and thank you for your kind consideration of this matter.
Yours sincerely,
The National Women's Bureau

Which really seems the height of reasonableness.

Directory

AIRPORT TAX Airport tax of £10 (but reportedly US$11 and CFA8000) payable on departure.

"ANY PEN?" In the 1960s the first Swedish tour groups brought **biros** with them to help The Gambia's education system. Children now teach toddlers the catch phrase. It does no harm to take some Bics yourself – there's no accounting for what happens to them all.

FESTIVALS AND HOLIDAYS The Gambia is predominantly Muslim and, with the exception of tourist services, everything comes to a halt on Muslim holidays. Christmas and Easter are also observed, with banks, offices and most shops closed around Banjul and the coast and a few other places. Otherwise, the principal annual days off are January 1, February 18 (Independence Day) and May 1 (Labour Day). The biggest **festival** of the year is the Christmas day **Lantern Parade** in Banjul – a competitive float festival with many similarities to the parades held in Freetown, St-Louis and Bissau.

Other times to know about include the president's annual "Meet the Farmers Tour" in Sept/Oct (all those blue pennants are PPP supporters' flags), the Dec/Jan groundnut sales that put money in farmers' pockets once a year, and the miserable April/May "hungry season" that follows.

GAY LIFE Although there's nothing in the way of a gay scene as such (and The Gambia's laws on homosexuality are the fossilised edicts inherited from the British at independence in 1965) there's a broad acceptance of gay male visitors and several very low-key haunts in the resort area. Gay women won't find the same.

OPENING HOURS Most places open at 8am and close at noon or 1pm. Shops and some offices (but not banks) reopen in the afternoon at 2pm or 3pm. Shops tend to close at 5pm. Fri and Sat are half-days. Most doors are closed Sun. If you want to get things done, start doing them by 9am: the small scale of everything in The Gambia can slow business down.

PHOTOGRAPHY You'll have very few problems. Gambians don't, in general, mind being in the viewfinder, and cameras aren't objects of suspicion in the Banjul and resort areas. The "security" angle is rarely played up by police – though, as usual, you should avoid photographing them without their permission, or snapping anything "stately". Up-country attitudes vary from clear hostility to enthusiasm. Just ask. There's no colour processing in Banjul. Film should be bought from a hotel shop, not in town.

SHOPS AND CRAFTS Banjul and the Kombo peninsula is the only area you'll find either. The "crafts" tradition isn't a spectacular one. "Ebony carvings" rarely are, and anyway, as with dry land mahogany, the trade encourages deforesta-tion. At the *bengdulalu* crafts stalls, go for cheaper softwood carvings, gaudy cloth (including batik), jewellery and leather.

TROUBLE Trouble with the police – who are unarmed and among the nicest in West Africa – is unusual, though motorised overlanders occasionally report problems over vehicle import duty, which strictly speaking you're not liable to pay. If you're going to smoke dope, be as discreet as you would anywhere – it's not "semi-legal" as some authorities have suggested. The most trouble you're likely to encounter is with "tourist guides" whom you fail to shake off and who later expect payment for the services you didn't want. Tell them you're not going to pay at the very beginning and they'll soon give up.

WILDLIFE AND NATIONAL PARKS The Gambia is wonderful for ornithologists, but a disappointment to anyone expecting big game. Despite President Jawara's much-vaunted "Banjul Declaration" in support of wildlife conservation, the faunal heritage diminishes while the human population expands. But monkeys and baboons are common enough; there are hippos up-river and small crocs in the streams; warthog are common but overhunted; hyenas, aardvarks and leopards are nocturnal, their status uncertain. Many southern Senegalese animals occasionally range towards the river.

The Abuko Nature Reserve (the country's only park) includes a small collection of imported, caged big beasts. Baboon Island National Park is a chimpanzee rehabilitation centre, not open to the public, but accessible to serious visitors.

A Brief History of The Gambia

The earliest people of the Gambia valley may have been the Jola, who traditionally keep very limited oral history. By the fifteenth century, most of the valley was under the control of small Mandinka kingdoms founded by immigrants from the Mali empire. The first European settlers of the late fifteenth and sixteenth centuries were mostly Portuguese and tended to set themselves up in partnership with headmen of the locality, marrying their daughters and trading cloth for slaves. The descendants of the mixed unions were important figures (see Part Nine "Cape Verde" for more details). From the mid-seventeenth century, English, Dutch, French and Baltic merchant adventurers shared and fought over trading rights from the restricted and neighbouring bases of Fort James Island and Albreda. The British won lasting influence after the Napoleonic wars, declaring a Protectorate along the river in the 1820s and in 1888 establishing a Crown Colony that comprised Banjul Island, the district of Kombo St. Mary and MacCarthy island (Georgetown). In the same year, the territory ceased to be governed from Freetown, Sierra Leone, and was given its own government.

■ The Gambia: Colony and Protectorate

In the second half of the nineteenth century, while the British hesitated and focused their attentions elsewhere, the French were battling their way deep into the Soudan, actively engaged in a mission to conquer (see Part Seven, "Senegal"). From 1850 to 1890 the whole of the Gambia region was in a state of social chaos as the **"Soninke-Marabout Wars"** repeatedly flared up (see box), eventually forcing the British to consolidate in the region or else lose it to France.

The Gambia's acquisition by Britain, which was formally agreed at the Paris conference of 1889, stemmed less from commercial ambitions than from **imperial strategy**. The intention was to pawn the country off in exchange for some better French territory; Gabon was one chunk favoured by the British – they'd already turned down the offer of the Ivory Coast sea forts. But the temporary expedient of holding the river became permanent when, having failed to agree on an exchange, the British succeeded merely in delimiting a narrow strip of land on each side of the Gambia, into the heart of French territory. Yet Britain wasn't really reconciled to its responsibilities along the Gambia River until after World War I – thus The Gambia's era of effective colonialism lasted little more than forty years.

The imposition of **British hegemony** wasn't impressive. Beyond the limits of the Colony, the country's headmen and chiefs, some of whom were appointed by the Crown, were allowed to rule their people little disturbed by the two "travelling commissioners" to whom they were answerable. Two or three African representatives from Bathurst (the future Banjul) were nominated to the Legislative Council after 1915, but there was no representation of the 85 percent of the population who lived in the Protectorate.

The main relationship between **the people and the government** devolved around the issue of **taxes**. Yet two-thirds of the Gambia's revenue was accounted for in the salaries of the colonial administration. The remainder was insufficient to develop the country's infrastructure, education or health systems. "Benign neglect" is about the best that can be said of the administration's performance. It started to improve only after World War II, though the government was gravely embarrassed by the financially disastrous **Yundum egg scheme,** which fowl pest made an unredeemable fiasco costing £500,000. **Groundnuts** (peanuts) have been the country's main export crop since the middle of the nineteenth century – Gambia is a classic monoculture – and until the 1970s it was also self-sufficient in food. There were minor advances in education and medical services: by 1961 for example, the country had five doctors and there were 37 up-country primary schools.

Financial pressures on the Colonial Office in the 1950s, and mounting international demands for decolonisation were as much instrumental in **the push to independence** as Gambian nationalism. Britain was perhaps even more anxious to rid itself of the financial liability as the country's own senior figures (they were barely yet leaders) were to take power. From Britain's point of view, there was no reason to delay the country's return to independence – except, perhaps, a measure of concern over the fate of such a small and unprotected nation. Colonial civil servants were in broad agreement that Gambia would be forced to merge with Senegal, but chose to defer the move.

■ The Gambia's Road to Independence

The progression to independence was not an heroic one. In a manner similar to that of many other countries in West Africa, the men who led Gambia into the neo-colonial era were not so much nationalists as pragmatic and ambitious politicians.

Although the **Bathurst Trade Union** had been founded in 1928 and struck successfully for workers' rights, the first **political party** wasn't formed until shortly before the Legislative Council

elections of 1951. Through most of the 1950s, the Gambian parties were reactive, personality-led interest groups rather than campaigning, policy-making, issue-led organisations. The Rev. John Fye founded the **Democratic Party** as a vehicle for the civic ambitions of his Bathurst coterie; I.M. Garba-Jahumpa founded the **Muslim Congress Party** in an attempt to align religious consensus behind a political movement; and Pierre S. N'Jie founded his largely Catholic **United Party**, which maintained close relations with up-country chiefs. All these early-1950s parties were Wolof- and Colony-based and highly sectional. Gambia had to wait until 1960 before a party with a genuinely grassroots programme emerged. This was the Protectorate People's Party (quickly relabelled **People's Progressive**

THE SONINKE-MARABOUT WARS

Mandinka civil war along both banks of the Gambia began in the 1850s. Local holy leaders – the **marabouts** – influenced by the great Muslim expansionist Omar Tall, called for the overthrow of the traditional Mandinka kings known as **Soninkes**, whose adherence to Islam was greatly tempered by indigenous religion and alcohol. The marabouts aimed to install a puritanical Islam and to capture local states (best described as manors) and trading networks.

Most of the "wars" consisted of battles, skirmishes and feuds between villages, which disrupted trade and agriculture year after year. Serer and Jola mercenaries were bought in on both sides to bulk out the limited armies. The main areas of unrest were: **Kombo**, south of the tiny British enclave at Bathurst, where a wild young marabout called **Fodi Kabba**, spread serious anarchy; **Baddibu** and **Niumi** on the north bank, where a renegade Soninke-turned-marabout, **Ma Ba**, caused massive destruction; and **Fuladu**, upriver on the south bank, where **Fula marabouts** from the southeast, right outside the region, swept the local Mandinka aside with great savagery.

By the mid-1870s, all of the Kombo district was under maraboutic control. Religious imperatives had been forgotten as purely political and economic considerations pitted one leader against another. Acting under financial constraints laid down in London the **British** avoided interference whenever possible, refused requests for protection from besieged Soninke leaders and only went into battle to defend the Colony or British subjects. Only when there seemed to be a risk that the fighting might jeopardise British commercial interests did the Governor try to impose a truce.

But in the **1880s**, the British were unable to avoid being drawn into the conflicts. In Baddibu the wars had now become an internal affair between competing marabouts, and they spilled over into French-occupied Senegal. The French, in hot pursuit on behalf of their Sine-Saloum chiefs (the French were much more actively involved in protection than the British) chased the marabout army back into "British" territory as far as Barra. The British were forced to arrest the marabout in question, **Said Mati**, to forestall any further French advances. Mati's removal led to a power vacuum in Baddibu, which the French began to fill with their own appointees. The British had no choice but to enter into binding protection agreements with as many Gambian chiefs as possible.

A period of relative peace broke out, but in the Kombo and Foni regions Fodi Silla and Fodi Kabba kept up **continued resistance** against the now-expanding British. With the country's borders fixed and support at last from London, the British moved against **Fodi Silla** in 1894, occupying all the towns of Kombo – Gunjur, Sukuta, Brikama – and pushing Silla into Senegal, where he was captured and exiled to St-Louis.

Fodi Kabba pursued the struggle, killing a travelling commissioner and his entourage at Sankandi on the border in 1901. The British and French moved swiftly and in concert, "pacifying" the region in imperial style and killing Fodi Kabba, a campaign which marked the end of the Soninke-Marabout Wars.

Party), led by an ex-veterinary officer from the MacCarthy Island Division, **David Jawara**. The PPP looked to the Protectorate for support, but was distinctly anti-chief. It spoke for the rural Mandinka and others in their resentment against corrupt chiefdoms and for disenfranchised and younger Wolof of the Colony.

The administration overhauled the constitution in 1951 and finally, after consultation with senior Gambian figures, produced a complicated new constitution in 1954. This gave real representation to the Protectorate peoples for the first time, but precipitated sharpened demands for greater responsibility for Gambian ministers in the government. It also put extraordinary power in the hands of the chiefs, who were, for the most part, supporters of the colonial status quo. To avoid a crisis, another constitution was formulated in 1959 which abolished the Legislative Council and provided for a parliament – the House of Representatives.

In the run-up to the **1960 elections**, the Democratic and Muslim Congress parties merged as the **Democratic Congress Alliance**, but couldn't shake off the popular impression that their nominees were all puppets of the administration. As a result the DCA took only three seats, while the United Party of P.S. N'Jie (with whom the governor had recently fallen out) and David Jawara's PPP took eight seats each. The Governor, in a move to placate the Protectorate chiefs, offered the post of Prime Minister to P.S. N'Jie, to the consternation of Jawara, who became Education Minister.

But the 1959 constitution was bound to give rise to further indecisive election results. More talks resulted in yet another constitution, providing for a 36-seat House of Representatives with 32 elected seats and just four chiefs nominated by the Chiefs' Assembly.

The balance of power now shifted against the United Party. Jawara and the Democratic Congress Alliance found room for cooperation and, in the **1962 elections** – which were to determine the political configuration for full self-government – the two parties contested seats in concert to squeeze out the United Party. The results of this electoral alliance were highly successful for the PPP, who won 17 out of the 25 Protectorate seats and one of the 7 Colony seats. The DCA, however, managed to gain only one seat in the Colony, and couldn't shift the UP from its urban power base. As a result, with the support of

the DCA's two elected members, Jawara had an absolute majority in parliament and his party has remained in control of the country ever since.

Subsequently, Jawara entered into a coalition with the experienced P.S. N'Jie to form the first fully independent government. Independence Day came on 18 February 1965, with **The Gambia**, as it was henceforth known, admitted to the Commonwealth as a constitutional monarchy with the Queen as titular Head of State.

■ Independent Gambia

In 1966 N'Jie took his United Party out of government to lead the opposition. Four years later, on April 24, **The Gambia** became a republic and prime minister Dawda Jawara (now using his Muslim name) became president. At every election, the PPP continued to win the vast majority of seats, and P.S. N'Jie to claim that each election was rigged. The PPP, however, despite its roots in the Mandinka villages, managed to establish credible support across the country.

The **first fifteen years of independence** were peaceful, and the groundnut economy fared better than expected thanks to high prices on the world markets. But by 1976 prospects for the government were less favourable. Two new opposition parties had formed: the somewhat Mandinka-chauvinist **National Convention Party**, led by dismissed vice-president Sherif Mustapha Dibba, and the more left-wing **National Liberation Party** of Pap Cheyassin Secka. And as groundnut prices fell in the late 1970s, so The Gambia experienced a string of disastrous harvests.

This economic recession, and political opposition to the government – perceived increasingly as incompetent and corrupt – partly account for the conditions that led to the formation of two new **Marxist groupings** in 1980 and an **attempted coup** in October of that year. Senegalese troops were flown in under a defence agreement and the leaders of the **Gambia Socialist Revolutionary Party** and the transnational **Movement for Justice in Africa-Gambia** (MOJA-G) were arrested and their organisations banned.

A far more **serious coup attempt** on July 30, 1981 (while Jawara was at a royal wedding in London), resulted in a force of 3000 Senegalese troops arriving with a group of SAS soldiers from Britain, to put down sporadic, bloody fighting and disorder around Banjul. The trouble lasted a week and cost up to a thousand lives. **Kukoi Samba Sanyang**, the self-styled revolutionary who led the plot – "we do not believe in elections, we wanted a radical transformation of the entire socio-economic system" – escaped to Guinea-Bissau and thence to Libya.

It's hard to find an altruistic justification for a coup in The Gambia. Though the country does not have an unblemished human rights record, it remains one of Africa's very few multi-party democracies. Opposition parties are consistently frustrated at elections but the evidence for vote-rigging is limited. The complete control of the government apparatus which the PPP enjoys, however, coupled with firm ethnic allegiance among the rural Mandinka, make alternative results unlikely.

The 1981 insurrection shook the government and immediate steps were taken to maintain Senegal's support. The subsequent **Senegambia Confederation**, ratified on December 29, 1981, assured The Gambia of Senegal's protection while ostensibly assuring Senegal of The Gambia's commitment to political union.

Treason trials in the wake of the attempted coup led to long terms of imprisonment but, with the increasingly important tourist industry to consider and international opinion reminding the country of its reputation, there were no executions.

A popular **presidential election** in 1982 gave Jawara a personal vote of 137,000 and Sherif Mustapha Dibba, who was in detention at the time, 52,000. A 1984 cabinet reshuffle brought in some popular, reformist MPs, and in the following year public opinion was heeded in the dismissal of several ministers after allegations of corruption.

With Dibba released, the National Convention Party mounted a serious challenge at the 1987 general and presidential elections. However, it was a new opposition grouping, the **Gambia People's Party**, led by the respected former vice-president **Hassan Musa Camara**, that made the most impact on the government. President Jawara's own vote was reduced from 72 percent to 59, but though his party's share of the vote was also reduced, the PPP still managed to win 31 of the 36 elected seats in the House, with the NCP holding the remaining five. Supporters of the GPP, particularly in its Fula- and Serahuli-speaking strongholds up-river, were left frustrated, as were supporters of the new social-

ist party, the **People's Democratic Organisation for Independence and Socialism**, a party with close ties to the banned MOJA-G.

Another **coup plot** – really a long-running, conspiratorial rumble – was uncovered a year after the elections, in February 1988. The conspiracy involved both Gambian leftists and Casamance separatists from Senegal. It was suggested at the trials that the Senegalese opposition leader, **Abdoulaye Wade**, had been involved in planning it, along with Kukoi Samba Sanyang, but attempts to implicate Libya directly were treated with scepticism abroad.

■ The Gambia today – and in the future

In 1985, the government embarked on an **Economic Recovery Programme** designed to encourage aid donors. The privatisation of various state enterprises, a public expenditure squeeze and cutbacks in subsidies to farmers led to increasing hardship in the countryside. At the Independence Day celebrations in Banjul in 1986, a teenager, **Baboucar Langley**, staged a solitary protest before the presidential platform declaring that "the people are dying of starvation". He was arrested and sentenced to eighteen months imprisonment.

Four years on, with the ERP still grinding through its measures, the country is faced with widespread malnutrition, insufficient schools for enrolled students and mounting evidence of high levels of corruption and mismanagement. Senior ministers, bankers, customs officials and heads of the Produce Marketing Board (GPMB) and the Utilities Corporation responsible for the intermittent electricity supply have all been investigated. President Jawara routinely "cleans out" public offices, but accountability is not enforced with tough sanctions, and a prevailing sense of stagnation and recycled rhetoric hangs over Banjul.

On the broad economic front, the recent **liberalisation of groundnut sales** removed the GPMB's monopoly and allowed farmers to sell their harvest to the highest bidding private trader. Although this may force *down* the price in remote areas, the net effect should be to keep more of the crop from being smuggled to high-paying Senegal. Tourism, too, is benefiting from the sale of the state's hotel interests and an increased profile abroad, with more than 100,000 tourists now visiting every year. In terms of prosperity, The Gambia is now moving into the middle bracket of West African countries.

But the wider future has been marred by the **breakdown of the Senegambia Confederation** (officially dissolved on September 30, 1989), as a result of Senegal's frustration at the slow pace of moves towards union. Senegal, in its latent conflict with Mauritania, withdrew the troops which provided The Gambia's security (and indeed President Jawara's personal security), saying they were needed at home.

The end of the Senegambia confederation leaves a huge question mark over The Gambia.

It's been the national controversy for the best part of a decade, supported by the mostly urban Wolof but generally mistrusted by the Mandinka, who would stand to lose their dominant position in the country. For The Gambia's opposition parties and minorities of all ethnic groupings, the prospect of a greater Senegambia was always a provocative one which left many doors open. It now looks as if those doors have been closed and The Gambia's anachronistic borders and domestic political stalemate will stay as they are.

BANJUL AND THE
KOMBO PENINSULA

Banjul and its hinterland, fronted by 50km of broad beaches, are all that most visitors to The Gambia ever see. A good number of the country's best points and virtually all the hotels are located here.

The **beaches**, naturally, are the big attraction for the tour operators, with good ones in the **Bakau** and **Fajara** resort areas and some truly spectacular strands as you head south. Inland, in **Kombo North**, **Kombo South** and **Kombo Central** districts, dozens of small, back country villages set in the random patchwork of forest, savannah and farmland, are accessible on foot, by bicycle or hired car, or by bush taxi or bus.

For **naturalists**, and especially ornithologists, the region is a rewarding one. The maze of mangrove-festooned **creeks** behind Banjul and the justly popular **Abuko Nature Reserve** have great appeal, and even walks in the bush near the hotels can yield delightful discoveries – monkeys, parrots, chameleons, tortoises.

A large and expanding proportion of the population of The Gambia lives in this district, but **Banjul** itself, sited on a low island jutting into the mouth of the **Gambia River,** is a sleepy, desultory town and increasingly a daytime city only. At dusk, truck- and bus-loads of workers pour back over the bridge to the relative metropolis of **Serekunda** and the leafier districts around **Bakau**, behind the hotels. There's not a lot to draw you to Banjul and nothing that could hold you longer than a day. Arriving **over- land** from Senegal, however, or **flying in** to start a trip through West Africa, the capital is likely to figure to some extent in your plans. Details of places to stay and eat are included below, with a few ideas on how to pass the time if you're picking up visas, waiting for mail or money, or otherwise treading water. While it may grow on you after a few days, Banjul's attractions are indeed limited, so you may prefer to mingle with the sun-worshippers out by the hotels and commute into town if necessary. Even the president does.

Banjul – the town

At no time of year is **BANJUL** a prepossessing place: chokingly dusty in the dry season, it becomes a chaos of red mud and gigantic puddles during the rains. Dilapidated architecture of corrugated iron and peeling paint, vast potholes and a reek- ing lattice of open drains – with no slopes for them to drain down – complete a very melancholy picture.

As a national capital, Banjul (or Bathurst as it was known to the colonial British) was doomed to failure by its site. It was acquired by Britain in 1816 to defend the river from slavers and to control trade with the interior, but its size was restricted to the area of land that could be kept free of flooding from the creeks and swamps behind. **Bund Road** dykes the city on its present small patch, and further expansion is impossible. Hot and confined and seething with mosquitoes, Banjul is not a town where many choose to live. The exodus after business hours is understandable, and nightlife all but nonexistent.

If you have to be here, compensations are scant. With a population of barely 60,000 and probably shrinking, Banjul is too small to offer any of the ordinary facilities and diversions of a capital – though at least whatever you need to accomplish can usually be done safely, and on foot. Walking gets you anywhere and the paranoia of some West African capitals is absent.

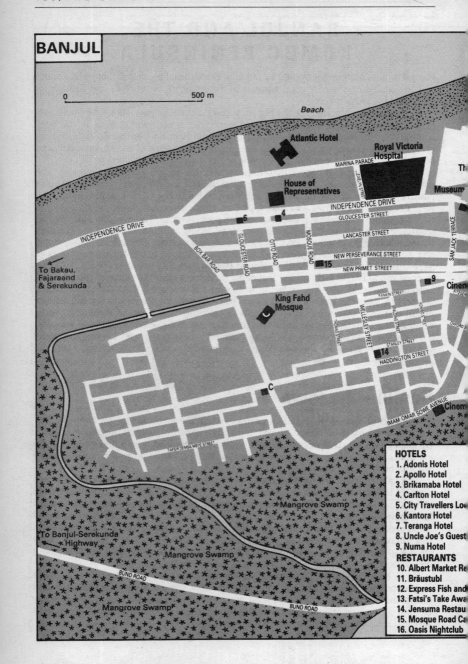

BANJUL

0   500 m

Beach

Atlantic Hotel

Royal Victoria Hospital

MARINA PARADE

BREZN STREET

House of Representatives

The

Museum

INDEPENDENCE DRIVE

INDEPENDENCE DRIVE

GLOUCESTER STREET

6

4

LANCASTER STREET

SAM JACK TERRACE

To Bakau, Fajaraand & Serekunda

BOX BAR ROAD

GLOUCESTER ROAD

OTTO ROAD

MOSQUE ROAD

NEW PERSEVERANCE STREET

15

NEW PRIMET STREET

9

Cinem

King Fahd Mosque

RANKIN STREET

DAILING STREET

DOBO STREET

WELLESLEY STREET

JONAS STREET

OXFORD S

STANLEY STREET

14

HADDINGTON STREET

C

IMAM OMAR SOWE AVENUE

Cinem

TAFSIR IRIMBA MOVE STREET

Mangrove Swamp

To Banjul-Serekunda Highway

Mangrove Swamp

BUND ROAD

Mangrove Swamp

BUND ROAD

HOTELS
1. Adonis Hotel
2. Apollo Hotel
3. Brikamaba Hotel
4. Carlton Hotel
5. City Travellers Lod
6. Kantora Hotel
7. Teranga Hotel
8. Uncle Joe's Guest
9. Numa Hotel

RESTAURANTS
10. Albert Market Re
11. Bräustubl
12. Express Fish and
13. Fatsi's Take Awa
14. Jensuma Restau
15. Mosque Road Ca
16. Oasis Nightclub

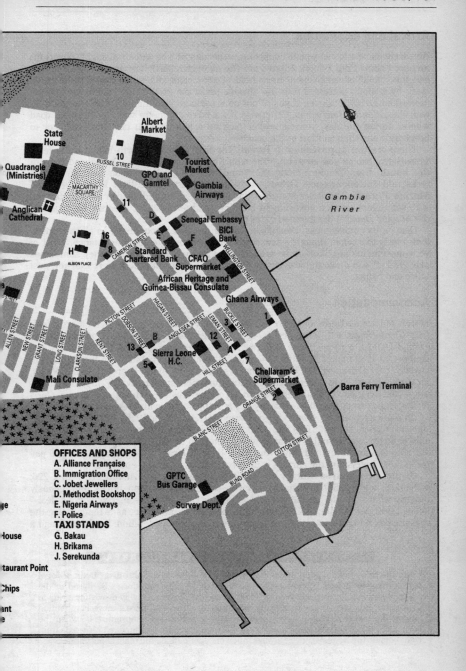

State
House

Quadrangle
(Ministries)

Albert
Market

10

RUSSEL STREET

MACARTHY
SQUARE

Anglican
Cathedral

GPO and
Gamtel

Tourist
Market

Gambia
Airways

*Gambia
River*

11

D

16

8

CAMERON STREET

ALBION PLACE

J

H

Senegal Embassy

E

F

BICI
Bank

Standard
Chartered Bank

CFAO
Supermarket

WELLINGTON STREET

African Heritage and
Guinea-Bissau Consulate

Ghana Airways

HAGAN STREET

PICTON STREET

ALLEN STREET

NEW STREET

GRANT STREET

LONG STREET

CLARKSON STREET

KENT STREET

DOBSON STREET

ANGLESEA STREET

LEMAN STREET

BUCKLE STREET

1

3

B

13

12

Sierra Leone
H.C.

5

A

HILL STREET

7

Chellaram's
Supermarket

ORANGE STREET

2

Barra Ferry Terminal

Mali Consulate

BLANC STREET

COTTON STREET

OFFICES AND SHOPS
A. Alliance Française
B. Immigration Office
C. Jobet Jewellers
D. Methodist Bookshop
E. Nigeria Airways
F. Police
TAXI STANDS
G. Bakau
H. Brikama
J. Serekunda

GPTC
Bus Garage

BUND ROAD

Survey Dept.

ge

House

taurant Point

Chips

ant
e

Arrival and orientation

Air arrivals are low-key and confusing, especially if you get in at night. **Yundum airport** (24km from Banjul, 18km from the nearest resort) has virtually no facilities, and the "bank" is rarely open. Keep hold of your bags, otherwise they'll be whisked away by zealous porters. From the airport, **taxis** are predictably expensive (pay no more than D100), but even if you're not on a package you should be able to get a lift with the *Atlantic Hotel*'s bus. Otherwise it's a three-kilometre walk to the main road where, during the day, you can either pick up a bus or bush taxi into Banjul or to Serekunda and then another to the beaches.

There are two **approaches** to Banjul. The first, from the north bank on the ferry from Barra, brings you straight to the wharf by the town centre. The second is **from the south**, from Yundum along the brand new Banjul–Serekunda highway, which forks into **Independence Drive** – considerably less grand than it sounds – and **Marina Parade**. The latter is one of Banjul's pleasanter and shadier streets, fringed with somnolent wooden government buildings and terminating, after the hospital and the *Atlantic Hotel*, at the guarded gates of **State House**.

Despite its compactness, Banjul's layout can be initially confusing as all the streets look much the same, though a few street-name plates give some assistance. Most of your movements are likely to be around **MacCarthy Square** (where they sometimes play cricket) and down the waterfront Wellington Street, with the **Albert market**, post office and banks.

Accommodation

Hotels at Banjul's **budget** end are at best mediocre and there's not much choice. *Uncle Joe's Guest House, City Travellers' Lodge, Teranga Hotel, Brikamaba Hotel* all charge around D60 for a room. *Uncle Joe's* (☎28191) is very decrepit, and the demise of the landlord in 1989 makes its future uncertain; it's only really habitable in the dry season anyway. *City Travellers'* is a brothel; the *Teranga* is just okay. There's also the *Numa*, on Rankin Street, with decent facilities – mosquito nets, fans, hot water, modern plumbing – and charges around D90/120. Best of the cheapies, though, is *Duma Guest House*, Hope Street (parallel to Stanley St.) at D100 double with breakfast.

In a pricier bracket, *Adonis* is good value (D120/145 for B&B; ☎27262), while the *Apollo* (PO Box 219l; ☎28184) and *Kantora* (☎28715) are tatty but cleanish and reasonable enough (the second is probably the quietest in town). The *Carlton* (PO Box 639; ☎27258) is uninspiring and way overpriced. Fans or air conditioning are what you pay for in these hotels, but the current is frequently off for hours on end.

Of the three **tourist hotels** in the Banjul area, only the *Atlantic* (PO Box 296; ☎28601/2, telex 2250) is actually in town, and its high-season prices outrageously outstrip what's on offer; in the low season however, it can be a remarkably good deal – about D140 per person (B&B). Although the food is mediocre, as a Banjul base the *Atlantic* has no real competition if money's not a first consideration: lovely staff, and a

---

TRANSPORT AROUND THE BANJUL AREA

From Banjul to Bakau/Serekunda/Fajara, you've got the choice of **tourist taxis** or **local transport** – ie shared jalopies or buses. A clutch of taxis can always be found at the *Atlantic Hotel*, but prices are fixed for set trips and you'll pay relatively dearly for a ride to Fajara, for example. If you're already out near the beaches, there's more competition among the taxi drivers and better opportunities to achieve a compromise between the high cost of taxis and the inconvenience of other transport. In Bakau, don't hire taxis from right outside the hotels – they're always much cheaper outside the main supermarket.

bar that's popular with Banjul's men of influence and something of a focus for anything that's happening in the country. In-house generators ensure the 24-hour rumble of air conditioning. The *Palm Grove* (PO Box 2475; ☎28631/2) is a smaller, unfussy package place with off-season rates worth checking out. *Wadner Beach Hotel* (PO Box 2377; ☎98199) has been closed rather a lot in recent years, and is now co-owned with the *Hotel Fajara*.

Eating, drinking and nightlife

The opportunities for **eating and drinking** are about as exciting as those for passing a comfortable night. If you're seriously into having a good meal out you'll quickly gravitate to *Braüstubl*, 277 Leman St (☎28371) – the only convincing **restaurant** in town. For D70 and upward, they do well-prepared but not notably Germanic dishes – excellent *domodah* (often unavailable in the cheaper places that advertise it) and fish soups. In season, the *Oasis* nightclub at the top of Clarkson Street (☎26996) usually turns out reasonably good meals at around D30 a dish – and their groundnut soup is something else. But the whole place has a slightly exploitative, hello-tourists feel, and you may not be wild about the piles of small crocodiles dormantly on display in the restaurant fountains.

Looking for **cheap eats** in Banjul is a strangely thankless task. The following shortlist covers most options:

Albert Market Restaurant Point (Mon–Sat 7.30am–7pm). *The* cheap place to eat in comfort, patronised by market people who can afford it. Remarkably together, clean and bright with the usual greasy spoon offerings (D20 for a fry-up) and at least one Gambian dish every day (D10).

Jensuma Restaurant (usually open), Stanley St. A very limited choice but clean, friendly and dead cheap if you need a rice and sauce fill-up.

Mosque Road Café, Mosque Rd. Stock up on good fish pies and meat pies for next to nothing.

Express Fish and Chips, Leman St. Long-established, with very good fish 'n' chips (D12) and a variety of other dishes.

Fatsi's Take Away, Dobson St (open after 8pm). A popular place specialising in submarine sandwiches (steak, salad and potatoes in half a French loaf for D8).

African Heritage, 16 Wellington Street (☎26906). A cool waterfront place that's the best retreat in town. There's a daily menu, reasonably priced beer and softs, and a 4–6pm "Happy Hour". Danish-run, it has a gallery and crafts shop where you can sometimes find interesting works and ethnographic bits and pieces.

Nightlife

Nightlife in Banjul itself isn't up to much, and you should be a little bit careful wandering around after dark with valuables. The *Oasis* nightclub is lively in the high season though it's hard to know whether it'll be worth the D20–30 entrance. The *Red Gate Bar* opposite is a nice place to ponder whether you'll hit the *Oasis* or not – sit outside in the lumber yard with a cool beer and the works of owner/artist Colley to admire.

At least one new club springs up each season in Banjul, but few survive and prospects aren't good. You could check if anything watchable is showing at either of the two **cinemas**, the *Eros* or the *Ritz* – they show mostly Indian movies.

Around Banjul – museum, market and walks

There's a dearth of things to do in Banjul. The **Museum** (Mon–Thurs 8am–4pm, Fri & Sat 8am–12.30pm) doesn't contain a wildly exciting display, but they haven't the funds to keep up the present collection, let alone improve it. A great deal of mouldering ethnographia – mostly the remains of private collections and not all of it Gambian – and a lot of old anthropological "type" photos are the predominant features. But there are a few rediscoveries to be made if you take time to peer into some of the dark corners. Excellent *warri* boards (see p.34), fascinating maps and documents and generally informative stuff about the wars and migrations of the Senegambia region are all worth going for. There's an impressive array of palm wine-tapping and drinking equipment, and don't leave without a look at the early Iron Age wood drill with its Black & Decker bit. The curator, Mr Sidibe, is interesting if you both have time.

African Heritage deserves a mention again here; its **gallery** houses miscellaneous *objets d'art*, carvings, paintings and more, all for sale, including some amazing old guns.

Albert Market

Market business is one of Banjul's big pluses. After the fire which gutted the old **Albert Market** in 1986, the art of bargaining has regained its spark in the resurrected marketplace (Mon–Sat). As a relatively laid-back and rather sanitised version of what you'll find everywhere in West Africa the Albert is not bad – and you won't get lost. Nearby is the highly enjoyable **tourist market**. Take a pocketful of dalasis and argue your head off. While you're busy bargaining for D2 bangles you can eye up the better merchandise and come back later if it appeals. If you're not into parting with money at all then you're likely to feel uneasy – and free gifts of the very thing you didn't want are all part of the wearing-down process. Go in a bright mood.

Walks out of town

While the beach hotels will set you off on an organised minibus "city tour" – which really seems a little pointless – there are a number of manageable and more gratifying **walks** you can do around town. A big one for bird-watchers is the morning or evening stroll along **Bund Road**, best at high tide when the birds are very prolific and the smelly mudbanks water-covered. Allow a couple of hours.

From Banjul, Bund Road joins the Serekunda road between the prison and *Radio Syd*: turn left here and there's a short walk to the *Palm Grove* and *Wadner Beach Hotel*, the latter with really cheap beer. Walking **back to town**, there are Muslim and Christian cemeteries if you're interested: the epitaphs on some of the Christian tombstones are recommended reading. The Scout HQ and – curious find – Masonic Hall are also out here on the seafront.

If you walk **along the beach** between the *Atlantic* and the markets, go in company or carry just the bare essentials – if you're going to get robbed anywhere it might be

---

GETTING OUT OF BANJUL

The provisional timetable for the **Barra ferry** is: depart Banjul 8am, 10am, 2pm and 4pm; depart Barra 9am, 11am, 3pm and 7pm (be early). In high season, there may be extra midday sailings. Passenger fares are nominal. Large *pirogues* also operate between ferries, but they've an unsafe reputation. If you miss the last ferry back from Barra to Banjul, visit the *Café Lingaire*, by the wharf, where you can get help on accommodation.

GPTC buses to Dakar normally leave from Barra terminal after the first and second ferries have arrived, but might leave close together after the first ferry if demand is heavy.

Note that recent border problems have led to the occasional suspension of services.

For journeys out **to Bakau, Serekunda, Brikama and along the Atlantic coast**, get a *GPTC* bus from the Banjul depot in the southern Half Die district. It's worth the walk to be sure of a seat – by the time it reaches the northern part of town it'll be full. Alternatively, take a minibus or Peugeot from the Serekunda or Brikama taxi stands off Albion Place. Or simply walk out to the end of Independence Drive and hitch. For bus journeys **inland along the south bank**, see "Getting Around" (p.437).

here. Which is a shame, as it's a fine walk, especially in the early evening when hundreds of boys are out doing exercises, playing football, developing their Kung Fu skills and jogging. Between the shore and Albert Market, fishing boats smother the beach: this is where to come to negotiate a private creek trip (see p.462).

Bakau, Fajara and around

The Gambia's **tourist strip** runs for 10km or so of relatively unobtrusive development along the sandy cliffs of the Atlantic coastline: barely a dozen hotels account for virtually the whole package industry. At times you wonder how so many people used to support themselves down here. Fishing and farming no longer figure a great deal, and apart from palm wine collecting, there can't have been much else before the first plane loads of tourists arrived from Sweden twenty-odd years ago.

Tourism has transformed the area utterly. It's only remarkable that Gambians who live here have retained such an equable regard for visitors who generally pay them such scant attention. As always where the poor world meets the holidaying rich, the stories of locals who made good by marrying abroad fuel hopes and dampen the inevitable resentment. More positively there's considerable enthusiasm for having a good time and it's not impossible to meet local people in the bars and discos or on the beach without the question of patronage creeping in.

The area splits into two districts. **BAKAU** is the older touristically, and retains a closer, more established feel. **FAJARA** is harder to locate – unless it's the big golf club. In any character competition Bakau would win hands down; its "old" town is a swarming village of dirt streets and noisy compounds, home to many of the hotel staff. Bakau "new" town is more villas and lawns.

Settling in: hotels in Bakau and Fajara

Arriving for a couple of weeks in the sun, few people have much idea of what to expect from their **hotels**: a rough guide to the main package venues is outlined further below. If you've entered independently from north or south Senegal you're more likely looking for reasonably **cheap places** to flop out for a few days. The area doesn't go overboard on these and, in the high season, you'll need to persevere to find a good-value room – assuming you find any space.

LOW BUDGET LODGINGS

Francisco's (PO Box 2609 Serekunda; ☎95258), corner of Fajara and Pipeline Roads (D250/300 B&B). The best and most expensive "budget" hang-out, a popular tropical garden restaurant with a clutch of pleasant rooms in a nice setting, 5min from a quiet stretch of beach. Increasingly block-booked by perceptive tour ops, so worth advance booking.

Sambou's (☎95237), Old Cape Road, Bakau (D200). Noisy and convivial drinking place with new rooms in front and old at the back (with balconies).

Friendship Hotel (☎95829), Bakau Stadium, well visible (D140/220). Like so many others in Africa, the stadium was built by the People's Republic. Functional and impersonal, this sports hostel may mellow with time, though it's too far from the beach to be really useful without transport.

Leybato Guest House, 1km down Pipeline Road on the right (D80/140). No fans but a nice, together place and about the cheapest out here.

Hotel Serekunda (PO Box 384 Serekunda; ☎92780) in the heart of Serekunda, just after the *Arts Cinema* on the right coming from Banjul (D150/200). A totally different kind of hotel offering house video in each room and every convenience apart from a peaceful night. Good for cultural immersion, hopeless for the beach.

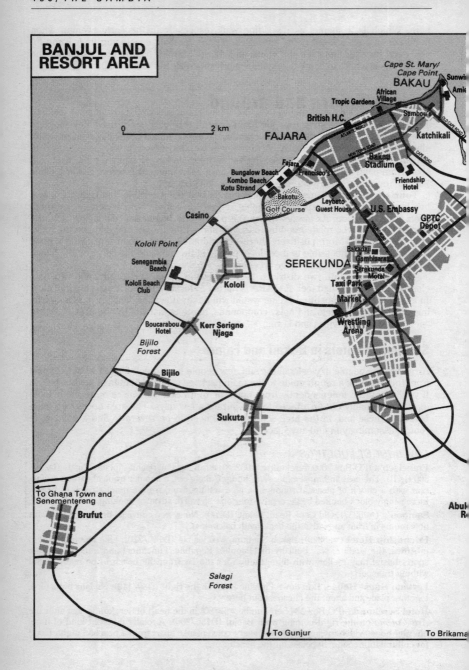

BANJUL AND RESORT AREA

0   2 km

Cape St. Mary/
Cape Point

BAKAU

Sunwi

Amie

Tropic Gardens

African Village

British H.C.

Sambou

FAJARA

Katchikali

Bakau Stadium

Fajara

Francisco's

Bungalow Beach
Kombo Beach
Kotu Strand

Bakotu Golf Course

Leybato Guest House

Friendship Hotel

Casino

U.S. Embassy

GPTC Depot

Kololi Point

Bakadaji

Gambisara

Senegambia Beach

SEREKUNDA

Serekunda Motel

Kololi Beach Club

Kololi

Taxi Park

Market

Boucarabou Hotel

Kerr Serigne Njaga

Wrestling Arena

Bijilo Forest

Bijilo

Sukuta

To Ghana Town and Senementereng

Brufut

Abuk
R

Salagi Forest

To Gunjur

To Brikama

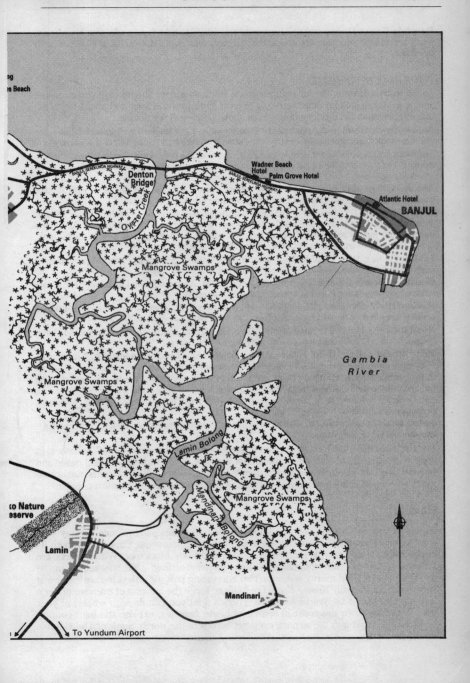

People's Guest House (☎91965) opposite the *BICI* bank in Serekunda, is a brand new, small place with nice sounds and a roof terrace, and only D150 night per person with breakfast.

TOUR BROCHURE HOTELS

As for **tourist hotels**, the following north-to-south summary should help you choose if you're perusing holiday brochures, or even if you're on the spot and about to splash out. High season B&B prices range from about D400–600 per double.

Amies Beach Hotel and Apartments. Brand new in 1989, modern with good facilities, but vile atmosphere and not on the best beach – strictly speaking at the mouth of the estuary.

Sunwing (PO Box 2638; ☎95428, telex 2220). High season only. On Cape Point, with beach-fronts at the mouth of the estuary and on the ocean side. Excellent reputation, with lots to do and well organised.

African Village (PO Box 2475; ☎95307). High season only, an old favourite with double B&B from around D350. Brilliant pool bar. Recommended.

Tropic Gardens (PO Box 2475; ☎95369). Slightly costlier sister hotel of the *African Village*, lives luxuriantly up to its name but lacks a proper beach beneath its clifftop site. Ambitious kitsch in its mediocre "marine" restaurant surrounded by aquaria and a huge turtle tank. Good atmosphere wins through but still has occasional water problems.

Fajara (PO Box 2489; ☎95351). High season only. Not a very attractive site but conveniently central between Bakau and other hotels. Many British clients.

Bungalow Beach (PO Box 2637; ☎95288, telex 2318). Apartment hotel with competitive low season long-stay rates. Popular, attractive and highly rated.

Bakotu Hotel (PO Box 2532; ☎95555). High season only. Swedish-run, informal, relaxed service, keen prices. Small place back from the coast with no beach of its own.

Kombo Beach Hotel (PO Box 694; ☎95465/8, telex 2216). One of the French *Novotel* chain. Expensive and classily impersonal with a strong French accent.

Kotu Strand Village Hotel (PO Box 957; ☎95609). Small and unpretentious. Nice atmosphere and good management with excellent low-season rates.

Senegambia Beach Hotel (PO Box 2373; ☎92717/9, telex 2269). Fairly new and gigantic but recommended. Called a "club" for its isolated location well away from the others on a good beach. High standards, excellent food, lots of action. The co-owned *Kairaba Hotel,* next door, opened in 1990.

Kololi Beach Club (☎91757). Rather anaemic new establishment of serviced beach villas – mostly sold off on timeshare.

For the **beach** itself, the strip between the *Fajara* and the *Kotu Strand* becomes, in season, the demonic heartbeat of the tourist industry. If you want any kind of peace and quiet, this patch should be avoided. A number of beach bars and restaurants mushroom every autumn with the first arrivals: *El Mondo* is cheap and seems the most popular.

Daylife

Before venturing into the **sea** you should make sure your patch is safe – every year sees several swimmers swept out. Cape St Mary (also known as Cape Point), with its cross-cutting tidal and river currents, is the notorious blackspot. **Watersports** are reasonably priced – for example, D40/hour for windsurfing – but snorkelling in the usually turbulent and murky water isn't an interesting pastime. **Bicycles** are on hire at several hotels (notably *Kombo Beach*) or you can forgo the benefits of exercise under a hot sun and hire a fat-tyre **motortrike**. There's a lot you can do with wheels of your own – trundle down the coast in search of better beaches, explore the back-country between the coast and the airport, even get across to the **north bank** of The Gambia on the first ferry.

Bakau botanical garden and the crocodile pool

Closer at hand, the small **botanical garden** in Bakau (daily, dawn to dusk) is a shady and rather beautiful hideaway just off the main road, naturally greenest and most impressive after the rains. The gardener will show you round, enthusiastically naming plants and offering scents to your nose. Note the fairy-tale teak tree and the prehistoric cycads.

The **crocodile pool** of Katchikali is just a ten minute-walk from here in the heart of Bakau, a path leading almost straight to it from the junction of Atlantic and Old Cape Roads. Ask for "crocodiles" or, more determinedly, *bambo*, the Mandinka name. There's usually a small payment to visit the poolside. And there are, in fact, some crocodiles – none too big and strangely white among the dense covering of lilies. No-one fears these crocs: you can approach quite close even when they're out of the water and they have a magical effect on the pool, ensuring pregnancy for women who wash in it. Not that there's very often much water. Every few seasons it's necessary to call a work party together to dig a little deeper, and sometimes to introduce new crocodiles.

Serekunda

As a confirmation that there's more to town life in The Gambia than the terminal dullness of Banjul, **SEREKUNDA** deserves a visit at least. This is where the energy of the country is concentrated and if you're travelling nowhere else, Serekunda gives at least a flavour of modern, urban West Africa – a choking racket of diesel engines, half collapsed wooden trolleys, bricollaged stalls selling a riot of dust-covered imports, music blaring from the hundreds of cassette players and radios. The focus of all this is the town's central lorry/taxi park and market, but you can sit under the shades of the Texaco station café and just watch the life go by; they may even have a cold drink.

Wrestling

To add purpose to your wanderings you could aim, on a Saturday or Sunday afternoon, for the **wrestling arena**, some 2km down the main road through town after the Banjul junction. People will point you to the place when you get close (wrestling: *nyororu* in Mandinka, *boreh* in Wolof) – if you can't hear the noise, that is. Entrance is cheap and the advertised time is usually 5pm, though nothing much is happening then. Drumming and whistling teams keep up steady competitive rhythms as the action builds slowly, the first few wrestlers pacing around the court flexing their muscles and psyching themselves up. The referee starts whistling the men into order and gradually the opponents pair off to start their bouts. Contestants are evenly matched, it being forbidden for small wrestlers to take on bigger men, however much the crowd roars its approval. At the Serekunda arena, teams are effectively divided along ethnic lines – Jola and Fula for example. The chunky Jola are renowned for winning most of the time, and for losing with good grace.

The **object** is to land your opponent on his back as cleanly as possible. Dust flying, bodies bound with *grigis* and slicked with sweat and charmed potions to weaken the opponent's grip, this usually takes a few seconds. But bouts can last for several minutes, as contestants bluff and threaten, facing each other with backs bent and hands trailing in the dust to make a good grip. Dozens of bouts take place during the afternoon and judges keep track of results. The winner of each bout takes a triumphal turn around the edge of the arena, accompanied by his drum team, and counting on collecting a few dalasis in appreciation as he goes. Take at least D10 in small change.

If you want to take **photos** there's no problem – it's expected – but you'll need a telephoto lens and fast film to capture the excitement as the contest develops and the sun goes down.

Eating, drinking and nightlife

In addition to the main hotels, most of which have several **bars and restaurants**, there are some independent places, whose number increases – like the prices – in season. But these are year-round standbys:

Sambou's, Bakau. Perenially popular though now taken over by Tjaereborg groups. Good food and very cheap beer (even cheaper during happy hours, 5–7pm plus Sun noon–2pm).

Bamba Dinka, Atlantic Road, Bakau. Nice place, sometimes with live music in the high season. Meals from D35, happy hour 8–10pm. Often has live music in season.

Ali Baba's, by *Tropic Gardens Hotel*, Bakau. Wonderful prawns.

Francisco's, Atlantic Road, Fajara. Consistently good, though not cheap (D150–200). Worth it for the exotic garden setting.

Gambisara, bottom of Old Pipeline Rd, Serekunda. Good and filling dishes for D40–50. Not licensed for alcohol.

Bakadaji, midway between Casino and Kololi Pt. on the coast road. Recommended, if touristy, Gambian restaurant with good value Sat and Thurs buffets for around D60.

Bamboo and **Rice Bowl**, the first signposted off Old Pipeline Road, the second off Old Cape Road, Bakau. Both Chinese and both good – at least D100 for two.

Tropic Smile, Bakau. English-run in a pleasant garden setting, and English food, unless you order Gambian in advance.

Rasta Dragon, Old Bakau. Local food at D10 a dish. Top value.

Nightlife

After-dark action is livelier in Bakau-Fajara or Serekunda than in Banjul. Recommended **hotel spots** are the *Sunwing* (in the high season), the *Kombo Beach's Bellengo Disco* (Fri & Sat nights) and especially the *Tropicana* outside the *Senegambia Hotel*, which draws big crowds of Gambians as well as tourists. It would be *the* place to go on a Saturday night, if it weren't for the *Afro Inn*. This is probably the best **local nightclub**, heaving and swaying till at least 4am, with an entrance fee of almost nothing and great sounds. Track it down during the day and you'll find it again after dark: it's signposted, left, off New Town Road, 200m from the Cape Road end.

For **drinking**, look out everywhere for cut-price drinks during **"Happy Hours"**, often twice a day. As for specific places, *Marie's*, opposite *Sambou's* in Bakau, is smaller than the latter, and with a stickier club feel. It has no draught beer – an indication of the glass-breaking clients they get – but it's an engaging little *boîte* with occasional live music. Jali Nyama Suso plays his kora here at the drop of a hat. *Revelation*, in Atlantic Road, Bakau, is tatty but friendly, with pounding reggae. Downtown Serekunda has a number of divey clubs where you may not feel so comfortable: *Eddies* is in at the moment, with hot music in the evenings, though the food is dire. Or check out the *Monte Carlo* on Mosque Road during the day and see what you think . If you want to hold your own party, there's **palm wine** for sale by the grove of tall palm trees on the landward side of Fajara golf course; take a bottle and you'll pay around D10 per litre.

Lastly, you might go a little further and check out the two **discos** in Brikama, 20km from Serekunda (see p.467). For night-time mobility you'll need **taxis**. It's often easiest to get a group together and hire one for the whole evening, specifying roughly where you want to go and how long you expect to be. Waiting time will be taken into consideration but this system usually works out cheaper than hiring a taxi for each trip.

Banjul and Area Directory

Air Freight *DHL*, Wellington St; around D300 per package plus D75 (UK), D90 (USA) per 500g. *British Airways* has a minimum charge of D500, but this allows up to 15kg. Alternatively, take your items, unwrapped, to Yundum airport well before the flight.

Airline Offices *Air Gambia*, 7/9 Cameron St (☎27824/5/6, telex 2255, fax 29354).

Gambia Airways (handling agents only, not an airline), City Terminal, PO Box 268, 68–69 Wellington St (☎27778-9, ☎28861/2) provide forms for airline student reductions, and handle bookings for *Gambia Air Shuttle*, *Air Senegal*, *British Airways* , *Sabena* and *Gam-Air*, as well as tickets for *Ghana Airways*. The *Ghana Airways* office in Wellington St (☎28245) makes reservations only.

Nigeria Airways 11–12 Buckle St (☎27438), offers 40 percent student discount.

Alliance Française at 2 Hill Street, operates as a cultural exchange and exhibition centre as well as promoting francophilia.

Art Gallery The Gambian Black Art Club is an active vehicle for the careers of a number of Gambian artists. They have an Art Centre in Serekunda, struggling towards completion.

Banks *Standard Chartered*, PO Box 259, 8 Buckle St, Banjul (Mon–Thurs 8am-13.30 Fri 8am-11am; ☎28681, telex 2210). *BICI* in Banjul has good rates (Mon–Thurs 8am-13.30, Fri 8am-11.30). *BICI* in Bakau is open late.

Batiks Take a look at the brilliant batik workshop, *Gena Bes Batiks*, in Bakau on Bakau Salong St (☎95614). See the whole process in action under the supervision of owner Queen Amie. Batiks and clothing for sale.

Bicycles Several beach hotels hire them out at around D30–40/half day, D60/day. Available to buy at one or two shops in town, but expensive at D800–1800. Mopeds, however, are around D10,000.

Birds The Gambia Ornithological Society (PO Box 757, Banjul) runs slide evenings and bird walks and excursions for members; temporary membership is available.

Books and Maps *Methodist Bookshop* Mon–Fri 8.30am–noon & 2–4.30pm, Sat 8.30am–noon. A few imported books and magazines, plus local publications by the *Book Production and Material Resources Unit*. Survey maps are available from the Survey Dept., Cotton St, Half Die, Banjul.

Car Hire The international agencies aren't properly represented and self-drive isn't common. Land Rovers with driver start at around D500/day. Call at the Tourist Office above the *Apollo Hotel* in Banjul for information on local companies, or try direct:

Crocodile Safaris, PMB 347 Serekunda (☎96068). First-class company with outstanding staff. Highly recommended, especially if there are border hassles going south to Ziguinchor.

West African Tours in Bakau (☎95258).

Gambia Tours, based at the *Senegambia* (☎95717/9), or from *Spot* in Serekunda (☎92657).

Black & White Enterprises through *Wings* or *Select* reps at the hotels (head office PO Box 201 Banjul; ☎92815).

Cassettes Best shop in Banjul is in New Primet St; in Serekunda it's *Derwali Sounds* in Mosque Rd behind the taxi garage.

Crafts and clothes First call in town is the **Tourist Market** near Albert Market or the **bengdulala** at most hotels, eg off-season at the *Atlantic* on Tuesday evening. **Jewellery** at *Jobet*, Box Bar Rd, a reputable place with nice gold. Best value, as Senegalese women know, is in **cloth and tailoring**; there's no shortage of importers and exponents – try Joseph in Picton St, opposite the No. 99 lamppost.

Doctors Royal Victoria Hospital, Banjul (☎28223/7); West Field Private Clinic, Serekunda (☎92213).

Embassies and High Commissions The main ones are:

France (Hon. Consulate), c/o *CFAO*, Wellington St, Banjul.

Great Britain, PO Box 507, 48 Atlantic Rd, Fajara (☎95133/95433, telex 2211).

Guinea-Bissau, Wellington St, by *African Heritage*, Banjul. Mon–Thurs 8am–3pm, Fri 8am–12.30pm: visas issued in 24 hours (same day on Fri) with no form and no photos needed.

Mali Honorary Consulate, corner of Lasso Wharf/Grant St, Banjul, irregular hours and seems likely to have closed down.

Mauritania 12 Clarkson St (☎27690), status uncertain.

Nigeria Garba-Jahumpa Ave, New Town Rd, Bakau (☎95803/5); visas issued with letter from your embassy only.

Senegal, 10 Cameron St, Banjul (☎27469). Mon–Thurs 8am–4pm, Fri 8–11.30am; visas take at least two working days.

Sierra Leone, 67 Hagan St, Banjul (☎28206); visas are expensive (UK nationals from D240).

USA PO Box 596, Pipeline Rd, Fajara (☎92858).

Emergencies Ambulance ☎16, Police ☎17, Fire service ☎18.

Excursions If you're lazy or timid, there's a range of half- and one-day trips you can do from any of the hotels. Prices start at around D150.

Immigration Ministry of the Interior, 71 Dobson St (☎28611).

Pharmacy Main one is the *Banjul Pharmacy* on Independence Drive (☎27470).

Photocopies *Electro Hall* Wellington St, D1.5.

Post Office Russel St (Mon–Fri 8.30am–noon & 2–4pm, Sat 8.30am–noon).

Supermarkets *CFAO*, Wellington St, Banjul & Bakau shopping centre (Mon–Thurs 9am–12.30pm & 2.30–5.30pm, Fri 9am–1pm & 3–5.30pm, Sat 9am–1.30pm). *Chellaram's* in Wellington St is similar.

Taxis Main private taxi ranks are outside the big hotels. In Banjul go to the *Atlantic Hotel*, where a fares list is displayed.

Telephone and telex *Gamtel* offices in Russel St, Banjul, and at the bottom of Pipeline Rd, Serekunda, are both open 24hr a day in principle.

Tourist Office Located in the *Apollo Hotel* building (☎28472, telex 2204).

Travel agents and tour operators These are mostly covered under Airline and Car Hire details but, again, give **Crocodile Safaris**, PMB 347 Serekunda (☎96068) a try – they're exceptional by any standards.

Trips around Banjul

In the high season **boat trips** can be arranged in just about any hotel lobby for around D150 per person, and many hotel guests end up on organised excursions with titles like "Creek Tour", "Abuko Nature Reserve", "Roots", "Bush 'n' Beach". However, it's easy enough and considerably more satisfying to take off on your own explorations in the coastal region.

Up the creeks

The usual destination for self-organised creek trips is the village of **MANDINARI**, reached up the snaking Lamin and Mandinari *bolongs*. The cheapest way of doing it is to get a group together and fix up boat hire yourself with the fishermen on the shore behind the Albert Market in Banjul. Prices depend on demand and what the boatmen reckon they could earn from a day with the nets, but don't expect much of an outing for less than D300, and maybe substantially more in the high season. While it's always useful to have a "guide" acting as intermediary, try to establish exactly what is going to be provided and make sure the crew know what they're about. Being stranded up a dead-end *bolong* at low tide, miles from anywhere, in the middle of the day – or worse, with the sun going down – may give you more of the mangrove experience than you want. Take plenty of water and food, clothes and hats to cover up with, and binoculars.

The **mangroves** are beautiful, eerie and surprisingly tall – up to 20m – and their birdlife is quite prolific if unspectacular. Fiddler **crabs** beckon maniacally on every mudbank, herding in silent, jostling droves as the boat approaches. The quicksilver, dun-coloured hopping things are **mud-skippers** – fish seemingly intent on becoming amphibious – which always seem to have gone by the time you've noticed them. Occasional, and odder, inhabitants of the mangroves are **monkeys**, bounding through the foliage, presumably taking refuge from persecutors on the farm plots inland. Hippos, incidentally, don't circulate this far downstream – though this isn't because the brine interferes with their buoyancy control (hippos live in salt water off the coast of Guinea-Bissau, see Part Nine), but because of over-hunting in the past.

Mandinari, with one or two small shops where you can get warm softs and something to eat, is a thirty-minute walk from where the boats tie up. The path goes through rice fields and seasonally lush jungle foliage, jewelled with a mass of birdlife that makes the creek look dead in comparison. From Mandinari you've the choice of going back to Banjul by road, or doing the whole journey back down the creek again.

Abuko Nature Reserve

Certainly one of The Gambia's best bits, the vaunted **ABUKO NATURE RESERVE** (daily, dawn to dusk; D10, half-price off season) is barely two square kilometres in extent, but within its carefully protected confines it preserves a patch of tropical riverine woodland that's becoming increasingly rare in West Africa. For Gambia holidaymakers it's an unmissable visit and is still very worthwhile for overlanders. Most attractively, you have to walk through it: vehicles aren't allowed in.

The **Lamin stream** and its remarkable necklace of rainforest was noticed in 1967 by Eddie Brewer, father of The Gambia's conservation movement, and was fenced the following year. The barrier is there to keep domestic animals and hunters out, rather than anything in – Abuko's 200-odd bird species and dozens of small mammals and reptiles need no encouragement to stay. Apart from pond-dredging, path-clearing and hide-building, the reserve is left more or less natural, and the strongest impression is imposed by the magnificent **forest trees** themselves, spiralling up from the webbed fingers of their buttress roots through a canopy of trailing creepers and epiphytes to create dark cathedrals of vegetation.

Organised excursions tend to destroy the sense of place. Go alone, in the early morning or late afternoon, and the forest exerts real fascination. Abuko is situated right by the main road and you can take the Brikama bus or any passing bush taxi to the reserve front gate easily enough. The office has some good booklets and leaflets about plant and wildlife, and you can leave bags safely – or even camp the night if you're dead keen to be in the woods at the crack of dawn. Take drinks and food – there's nothing much in this line at Abuko – and bring mosquito repellent, as they can be a serious menace.

The whole walk around takes a couple of hours, but it could easily turn into half a day depending on your interest in the various bird species (more often heard than seen) and your curiosity about the more bizarre life forms of the forest floor. Don't count on spending long at the "animal orphanage" at the top of the circuit, though; it's a smelly adjunct for penned lions, hyenas and apes. It's easy to work out how far you've gone: there are numbered markers on the trees at 20m intervals.

From the primate world you can expect to see **patas** and **green monkeys** and beautiful, acrobatic **western red colobus**. You'll also be delighted, or else unnerved, by the amazing numbers of **Nile monitor lizards** which dart across the path and claw their way through the undergrowth. Most are small, but they can grow as long as two metres. There's normally a number of **crocodiles** to be seen at the "bambo pool", from the "education centre" look-out. Watch for two distinct species: the larger, pale Nile crocodile and the small, dark **dwarf crocodile**, a threatened species. **Snakes** are very

---

BIRDS OF ABUKO

Well over **200 species of birds** are the chief animal delight of Abuko. This is the closest patch of tropical forest to Europe, and each winter it attracts thousands of bird-watchers as well as a host of **palearctic migrants** (willow warblers, chiff chaffs, black caps, melodious warblers) to swell the numbers of its native species. Most obvious are the water birds – a couple of photo hides overlooking the stream and pools are usually occupied by murmuring birders. Look out for **kingfishers** (blue-breasted, Senegal, malachite and pied), the "umbrella fishing" **black heron** and two great bird-watcher's sights – the **painted snipe** (the male, remarkably, incubates the eggs) and the stunning **red-bellied paradise flycatcher**, with its thirty-centimetre tail feathers. You can generally see **hammerkops** around the bambo pool at the start of the trail; in flight, their swept-back crest of feathers and pointed beaks make them look exactly like miniature pterodactyls. In the clearings, wait to see **Fanti rough-winged swallows** flitting through the light and, above the forest canopy, **hooded vultures**, **black kites**, **palm nut vultures** and swooping **bee-eaters**.

---

rarely observed, though the fact there has never been a single "incident" involving a tourist isn't likely to convince snake phobics, especially after reading the slightly gloating notes on sale at the office.

Out-of-the-way beaches

Given transport, preferably 4WD, you could get to virtually any part of **the coast** between Cape Point and the mouth of the Allahein (San Pedro) River, where anglo-Gambia finishes and franco-Senegal takes over. And equipped for a few days' self-sufficiency, it's perfectly possible to walk the entire length of the Gambian coastline – less than 50km from Fajara to Kartong. More realistically, most people will have to rely on **buses** and **lifts**, hired **motortrikes** or some vigorous leg-work on **bicycles**.

To **GUNJUR** there's a daily *GPTC* bus direct from the Bund Road station in Banjul. This goes via BRIKAMA and continues on to KARTONG – The Gambia's southernmost village, with a crocodile pool like Katchikali's at nearby FALONKO, and a fantastic beach. **Gunjur beach** is a working fish shore, a messy, active seafront where fish are more important than tourists and you'll probably be ignored. For serenity head back north on the pretty track towards Sanyang and Tujering. **Sanyang beach** is fabulous, a broad, smooth sweep of firm sand backed by coconuts. Deserted wooden stilt houses from some forgotten tourist beach camp stand among the trees. Unfortunately they're really too far gone to be a very secure place to stay, but there's nothing to stop you using them as a base or shelter – supposedly, water is available from the well of a farm plot nearby. **TUJERING**, some 4km inland, is a very pleasant old village that owes nothing of its character to tourism or colonialism: whitewashed mudstone houses, and a central crossroads with meeting place, mosque and market.

Along the forested and palm-planted stretch of track between TANJI and Ghana Town, are several species of monkeys – saving the harvest down here is a nightmare for farmers. **GHANA TOWN** is a community of Ghanaian fish driers and smokers, not an uncommon coastal phenomenon in many parts of West Africa. If you're curious you can stoop inside the long, low huts where the racks of blackening fish cure over smouldering wood. The finished product – basically kippers, often good – can be seen all over.

The holy site at **SENEMENTERENG** is a marvellously meditative spot around a craggy old baobab tree on the clifftop, the air wafting with incense. Local people come here for cures, consultations and peace; it's a good place to come at sundown, though not really improved by the carved inscription of "Scotland forever" at the base of the baobab, half obliterated now by a cankerous growth. A steep path leads to another superb beach.

Barra, Juffure, Albreda and James Island

The visit to **Juffure** used to be a necessary business, when the *Roots* industry was at its peak and thousands of black Americans made the pilgrimage to see the village they believed **Alex Haley** had been describing. So convincing was the hype that the author himself seems to have believed the same thing – pictures of Haley with an elderly Kinte descendant are part of the myth of modern Gambia, used to boost the small country's respectability on the world stage. As an excuse for a trip to the **north bank**, the visit to the supposed birthplace of Kunta Kinte is still an enjoyable day, but unless you do one of the organised *Roots* tours you'll find **transport** problematic. Cycling is a possibility, but the 70-odd kilometres there and back can be hard work, despite their flatness, and are well-nigh impossible if the earth road is wet.

Initial target is the 8am Barra **ferry**, a wonderful crossing at this time of day, with dolphins often plunging in the bow-wave and a chance to be the important first customer of the day for a marketeer going to Dakar or one of the weekly north bank *lumos*.

BARRA, old capital of the Mandinka kingdom of the same name, no longer has much of interest except for the squat hulk of **Fort Bullen**, neglected on the grassy shore. In the time of Mungo Park, the indefatigable eighteenth-century Scottish explorer, the kingdom produced "great plenty of the necessaries of life". Times change. In the village is the unspeakable *Rest House*, which unlucky travellers are forced to resort to if they miss the last ferry, at around 6.30pm.

Two *GPTC* **buses** call each day at Juffure en route to points further east and you can usually count on one or two bush taxis also. But for the most part the red ribbon of the road is empty, a swathe of well-graded laterite through quiet farm and savannah lands, with women (and men) in the fields and, before the harvest, small boys armed with bows and catapults in the monkey watchtowers.

Albreda and Juffure

You come first to **ALBREDA**, down on the shore. The settlement, also known as Albadarr, still has its old trading house with dangerously leaning walls and an immovable cannon pointing fiercely out over the river. **JUFFURE**, a short walk away from the river, isn't distinguished by any such monuments and, apart from a very basic sign, looks much like any other Mandinka village – a gathering of thatched, mud-brick cottages, *bantabas* and goat pens.

Even as an individual traveller your requirements are clear enough as far as local people are concerned: "You want to meet the Kintes and get some photos right?" Speak now if you don't. First you pay a few dalasis to the elderly headman of the village, Bakaari Taal, very decrepit now but still the guardian of the Juffure maintenance fund. Accompanied by a gang of children you proceed on a brief tour, winding up at the **Kinte**'s compound to meet whoever's in, usually the senior lady, Binta Kinte, and various sons, daughters and grandchildren. Photos are allowed, but postcards or return photographs would be as acceptable a payment as money.

It's hard to understand why this particular Juffure (a widespread place name) or these Kintes (a common Mandinka family name) should have been chosen by Haley as his roots. According to the book, the griot he met here told the same story as the one passed down through his family. But it was a simple and familiar history. And it seems Haley had already written his Africa passages when he came here, and his account of Juffure seems unrelated to the location of today's village. In the book Kunta Kinte is surprised by a slave-raiding party, yet Juffure is only a few hundred metres from the Gambia River and close by the sites of the trading stations of Albreda and Fort James, which would have been there throughout Kunte Kinte's childhood. But villages can move of course, and eight or ten generations have passed since he went out to collect firewood and never came back.

You can't be sure who is taking whom for a ride – the story has been a winner for both Haley and the Juffure griots – but it's worthwhile participating in the pretence only if you've plodded through *Roots'* 600 pages to the line "That baby was me!".

James Island

Less questionable history is out mid-river on **James Island**, but the *pirogue* ride costs at least D80 per person, and the very ruined ruins of **Fort James** are probably only for enthusiasts. Originally constructed in 1651 by agents of the Duke of Courland (now Latvia and Lithuania), Fort James rode the usual roller-coaster of occupations, routings, sackings, desertions and rebuildings. It was seized by **Britain** in 1661 when the Royal Adventurers of England Trading into Africa bundled out the Baltic occupants and set themselves up under the Royal Patent of Charles II, buying gold, ivory, peppers, hides and of course **slaves** for the American colonies – Britain's first imperial exploit in Africa. In one mercantile guise or another, the British and the **French** fought over the fort for more than a century. France held the trading "factory" of Albreda on the shore and continued slaving long after the British had opted for a new role as anti-slavers at the end of the eighteenth century. After 1779 James Island was rarely inhabited. Today the remains of the old walls and the strewn cannon are dominated by a grove of large baobabs.

UP-RIVER GAMBIA

To travel **up-country** is to travel up-river: the **Gambia River** is the national life-line and the country's very definition. With its headwaters 500km from Banjul in the Fouta Djalon highlands of Guinea, it snakes down in typically West African fashion, heading any direction but seawards most of the way.

Repeatedly doubling back on itself, the river's course is paralleled by the **Senegalese frontier**, which was drawn by compass at a cannon shot's distance from the river bank. Inland, this extraordinary artificiality is madly apparent. Senegal, never more than 10km from the road, breathes all around it, creating an increasing osmosis of francophone language, customs, food and music. At one point in the country's thin form the Dakar-Ziguinchor highway cuts clean across it – a traverse that, but for border formalities, would take only twenty minutes. A cultural equivalent of the always unbalanced and uneasy Senegambia confederation looks set to enhance Senegal's influence, whether the Gambians like it or not.

While you might expect an entirely frontier feel along the length of the country, there are plenty of short **sidetracks** off the main road, which quickly get you into traditional village life – districts of creeks and bushland where the concerns of fuel smuggling into Senegal and black market currency are still secondary.

The principal **towns** of Brikama, Soma/Mansa Konko, Bansang and Basse are all on the south bank. Georgetown is on MacCarthy Island in mid-river. The **north bank** is altogether bushier, with no hard-surface roads apart from the two that cross the country into Senegal, little transport or electricity, and only a couple of important centres at Kerewan and Farafenni. If you've time to explore, it's interesting territory, with much to be discovered and bearable walking distances. Most often visited are the strange **stone circles** at Wassu, reached easily from Georgetown and the south bank highway.

Practicalities

The pity is you can no longer do the obvious thing and go up the river **by boat**, unless you shell out for an expensive, private yacht cruise on one of the two Banjul-based charter vessels – *Spirit of Galicia* or *Spirit of Africa* – or buy into such a trip with your package. The *Lady Chilel Jawara*, last in a long line of ill-fated steamers, lies in the mud off

Banjul and there's no plan for a replacement. Come through at the right time of year and you might be lucky with a groundnut barge or even a small launch, but such vessels are few: apart from the fantastical ferries at the main **crossing points**, the Gambia is not a busy waterway.

Since the demise of the steamers, few people make the effort to go up-country. Unless you're heading anyway for Tambacounda and the Niokolo-Koba National Park in Senegal, or else down into eastern Guinea, the interior of The Gambia is a bit of a cul-de-sac. Still, it's a relatively easy and easy-going region, and if you're just starting your travels in West Africa, not a daunting introduction.

For **road travel** the main tarred route along the **south bank** is the only straightforward option. There's not much transport (notice how few dead animals are on the roads) and you'll need to rely mostly on the *GPTC* buses. If you've the money, hiring a car for a few days will get you just about anywhere, though you'll need 4WD during the wet season; otherwise, to do any sort of diversion you have to hope for an occasional bush taxi, or walk.

The Lower River

Out of the Serekunda conurbation, first town you hit is **BRIKAMA**, until a few years ago The Gambia's second largest. Excursion groups are often brought here to visit the **wood-carving centre**, to be charged up to ten times the going rate for carvings and musical instruments. (Get in touch with local people and you'll be offered uninflated prices.) Much better deals can be had in **bespoke clothes** – bring your chosen cloth from Serekunda and there are several tailors' shops that will make up almost any pattern very cheaply. *Uprising Tailorshop* and *Zion Tailoring*, both on the main road to the mosque, are recommended. But what makes Brikama really stand out – first appearances notwithstanding – is that several celebrated **kora musicians** have compounds near the secondary school, and are happy to see devotees (see the box over the page).

You might also make a special trip to Brikama for some rural **nightlife**. Unlike one or two of the earthier joints in Serekunda, there's no disquiet in Brikama, which is as safe after dark as the night sky. Hire a taxi to bring you out to the *Sifari*, a fairly informal club with a reasonably good PA, which means you can actually hear the music. Entrance is around D5, beers D6. Another Brikama club, the once laid-back *Club 1990*, has fizzled out completely and become a bordello.

There's a fifteen-kilometre track from Brikama down to the Senegalese **border** at DARSILAMI, while the new main road to Senegal branches off right at MANDINABA, a small place distinguished by a large, four-towered mosque. A couple of kilometres further, near the river at KULORO, is **Saidou Barry's Bird-Watchers' Compound**, a rural holiday village idea well worth checking out. The enterprise has British money behind it and, if successful, should be offering regular ornithological holidays from the UK (details in *Basics*. p.8).

Villages in Western Division

BULOK has a transient claim to fame: an old Fula resident – Bari Bulok – has a nation-wide reputation as an expert thief and housebreaker. A criminal phenomenon, he's repeatedly evaded all efforts by the police to catch him, always getting away as if by magic. Perhaps not a place to stay the night.

The ruins at **BEREFET**, mentioned on the Tourist Office map, are all but obscured by vegetation much of the year, and there's nothing to see of the "long-abandoned European trading post" which supposedly exists. Local people know of the site and call it "Marco", but they'll be pretty surprised if you make the six-kilometre effort down the sandy track to look for it. More ruins at **BINTANG** are equally invisible. Either place however, is a good excuse to get down to the river – or rather creeks off it. They're building a rather grand mosque at Bintang and are delighted to have visitors.

BWIAM, just off the main road amid a superb grove of silk-cotton (*bantango*) trees, has a real curiosity in the form of its *Karelo*. The word is Mandinka for cooking pot, but Bwiam's inverted **iron cauldron** resembles nothing so much as a gun turret poking out of the ground. By all accounts it is quite unmovable (Europeans of course have tried), and its origins and function are obscure. It's considered good luck to leave something on the pot and take something away. The old man we talked to was certain it had always been there, occasionally drifting round to face a new direction. The aperture on one side faces a large grove of mangoes and a glimpse of the river. Let us know if it's moved.

In the wet season or after the rains, brilliant emerald **rice fields** mark the shallow wooded valleys inland. At the end of the growing season in August and September, anti-monkey watchtowers are dotted among the rows of groundnuts and bush on the ridges between. There are other signs of a more rural way of life too. The largish concrete block and corrugated-iron roofed houses that set the scene on the coast are increasingly replaced with more attractive straw thatch and mud-brick compounds. And the tripod water pumps supplied by Saudi Arabia over German bore-holes become a familiar sight in every village.

As the road turns north over the head of **Bintang Bolong** you're passing to the west the region designated as the new **Kiang West National Park**. The 750 square kilometres between river and bolong, of which the park has a quarter share, is the wildest, least-explored region in the country. Well supplied for a few days in the bush, you could head off down the track to the left, just after the village of JATABA. There are further hamlets scattered an hour or so apart along the path that follows the low ridge through the district. In the middle, at KENEBA, the Medical Research Council has a tropical disease field station. Disappointingly, the National Park exists only on paper and, while it may harbour representatives of most of The Gambia's dwindling fauna, getting in to see them doesn't look very practical.

Tendaba Camp

One place where you might see a fair bit of wildlife – or at least have fun trying – is **Tendaba Camp**. Five or six kilometres off the main road, this is the only "tourist class" hotel up-river and it's close enough to the Kiang district for monkeys, crocodiles, hyenas and even – they insist – leopards to be around.

The Swedish owners never let their **whisky** bar drop below eighty varieties; they shoot warthog for dinner; and their idea of a "creek trip" is a dawn speedboat race through the mangroves, fortified with schnapps. If hunting, fishing and drinking appeal, you'll probably love it, though the slightly Viking atmosphere, briny outside showers and various caged animals put some people off. The setting on a bluff over the river is fine, however, and the bird-watching really something.

The mosquito-netted chalets at D100 per person and meals at D40–60 are fair value out here, and if you were to turn up with a bottle of *Hankie-Bonnister* or *Sheep Dip* you might well be given a special discount. Evenings are not formal: staff and guests crowd round the video on the patio and when there's sufficient enthusiasm, women from the village put on a dancing show or someone sets up a disco. There might be a certain tackiness to it, but with so many types of scotch, it's not a persistent worry.

Without you own wheels, there's a five-kilometre walk from the main road to Tendaba and little chance of a lift. For ornithological encouragement, a group of silk-cotton trees at KWINELLA, near the main road, is the habitual roost and nesting site of hundreds of **pelicans** – a cacophonous and extraordinary sight close up.

MUSICAL HOLIDAYS

In recent years, as **West African music** has made increasing impact abroad, enthusiasts are now travelling to hear and study the traditional **kora, guitar, drums, balafon and singing**. You can now make music the whole point of a trip by taking a kind of music workshop package holiday through the innovative German operators *Cool Running Tours* (Kiesstrasse 9, D-6000 Frankfurt 90; ☎069/70 86 75). *Cool Running Tours* have helped build the *Boucarabou Hotel and Music School* at **Kerr Serigne Njaga**, about 2km south of Kololi, 1km from the sea. Built as a compound, the hotel is simple and comfortable. It'll naturally help if you speak some German, though most of the German guests speak English. You can stay here as a straightforward guest (about D250/night per person HB) or take music tuition as well (around D150/day). Tuition is partly by Malamini Jobarteh, artistic director of the Gambian National Troupe and renowned kora player and recording artist.

You can be less organised, and more frugal, by fronting up to one of several compounds in **Brikama** and staying indefinitely on a house guest basis, paying an agreed contribution and learning as much about Mandinka music and culture as you want. **Malamini Jobarteh** has a particularly pleasant and peaceful compound in Brikama and relations are very good-humoured. You might expect to pay around D50–60/day to stay there, including shared meals. Should you want to write to forewarn them, the address is "Jobarteh Kunda", Sanchaba, Brikama Town, Western Division, The Gambia. On arrival in Brikama, follow the path along the left side of the mosque until you pass the communal tap on the right. Turn right here and the Jobarteh compound is three hundred metres on the left. Malamini's eldest son Ebrima is a musician too and a local "pop star" in Brikama: children in the district can tell you where the family lives if you ask for him by his popular name of Tata Din Din.

It's inevitable that **contacts** such as these will become somewhat debased over the years, but local enthusiasm for music and insistence that people should visit, require their inclusion. Don't bother going unless you share the enthusiasm and don't be upset if your reception is fairly nonchalant at first (though ecstatic might better describe it if you turned up with some second-hand mikes or speaker units – they are virtually unobtainable).

Toniataba and around Soma

Before the trans-Gambian highway's halfway mark at SOMA/MANSA KONKO, you pass the unremarkable village of **TONIATABA**: unremarkable that is, except for the grass-thatched and enormous **circular house** in the compound of Fatikunda ("Fati's place"). Fatikunda is the home of the Fati family, and the present family head, Alhaji Fodali Fati, is one of the district's most senior religious leaders, or **marabouts**. First constructed in the nineteenth century by Fodali's father Sheikh Othman, the house is believed to be one of the largest traditional homes in The Gambia, at around sixty metres in circumference. It's not exactly unknown, but nor are the Alhaji's family or his house a tourist attraction, and unless you speak Mandinka you'll probably feel easier with a guide to introduce you. Take your shoes off if you're invited in, and come with some gifts – postcards or other souvenirs from home are very welcome. The old man is generally delighted to get visitors. The house itself is of unusual design, its outer wall surrounding an interior house divided into separate rooms. In the middle is an inner sanctum, a private area reserved for family prayers.

A few minutes down the road and you're hit by the trashy, sprawling contrast of **SOMA**, where there's the opportunity to turn either left over the river into northern Senegal for Kaolack and Dakar or south into the Casamance district. You can also escape southwards further up-river, but this is the furthest point you can easily turn north into Senegal.

Soma is just a bustling truck stop, a charmless string of gas stations, cheap restaurants, bars and shops where you can get all sorts of Senegalese imports. Buses stop here, and bush taxis whirl up the dust, collecting passengers for the short ride down to the ferry crossing for the north bank and Farafenni. **Mansa Konko** ("King's Hill"), a couple of kilometres away, is the administrative quarter, quiet and uncommercial in exact proportion to Soma's racket. Neither centre has any special interest, but if you're driving, it's important to know that Soma is about the **last guaranteed source of fuel** – certainly of pumped petrol – up-country.

Crossing the river northwards, **FARAFENNI**'s big day is Sunday, when the weekly *lumo* is held. *Eddy's Hotel*, with S/C rooms (and AC when feasible) from around D100/150, is the best on the north bank.

The Upper River

Back on the south bank, the road's condition improves dramatically from potholed oyster-shell mix to hot black macadam as you pass through a fairly wild stretch of bush land, where you're likely to see baboons and other monkeys. If you're on the water, you can start looking out for **hippos** from this point on, where the estuarine part of the river ceases and the mangroves peter out. The no longer appropriately named Elephant Island in mid-stream appears to be their lowest grazing ground.

The village of BUIBA is the site of a long-established traditional curing centre for the mentally ill, but the first real punctuation in the new up-river scene is **PAKALIBA**, a village by the Sofanyama bolong on the district boundary between Lower River and MacCarthy Island Divisions. It's an attractive place, marked by a ridge of small rocky hills that are surprising in the undulating savannah; a sort of cultural holiday camp called **Sofanyama Kampo** is planned here. Pakaliba is the source of a fable about a crocodile hunter called Bambo Bojang, who learned to control the Sofanyama crocodiles, after being attacked by them; he's now the patron saint of the *bambo*, and his descendants live in the area. If you've time, you could track down Lalo Kebba, a famous kora player, and persuade him to sing the whole story.

Heading on through mostly flat and open grasslands, the only place you're likely to be detained is **JERRENG**, where they make an impressive – and very cheap – range of bamboo beds, chairs and other furniture.

If you're interested in learning about The Gambia's economy, you might like to side-track 3km down to **KUDANG TENDA** , on the river, where giant sheds hold hundreds of tonnes of groundnuts. When we visited, ninety percent of the mountain was weevily and abandoned, for lack of barges to get it down to the coast. Under the hot corrugated-iron roofs thousands of birds and rats fattened themselves on another wasted harvest.

There's a convenient and quite good place to stay in this area – the Gambia Agricultural Research and Diversification Rest House at **SAPU**, on the river bank some 3km down the slope from the road village of BRIKAMABA. With AC, fans, a kitchen and only eight beds, it does get booked up. Spare beds are normally available to outsiders only after 8pm, but they're unlikely to turn you away; if you manage to get in, you can look forward to some interesting development conversations.

Across the river is BARAJALI, birthplace of President Jawara, for which reason it was declared a national monument in 1985. A few kilometres downstream is the off-limits **Baboon Island National Park**, where chimpanzees have been reintroduced to the wild. If you're really intent on getting there (and by travellers' accounts it's very worthwhile), you'll need to contact Eddie Brewer in Banjul, or the Ministry of Water Resources, Fisheries, Forestry and Wildlife (5 Marina Parade, Banjul; ☎27431, telex 2204) and convince them of your impeccable motives. How you actually get there is another matter – it's only feasible if you've made contacts.

Georgetown

GEORGETOWN, though located midstream on MacCarthy Island, suffers no problem of access: one arm of the river is barely 100m wide, and is crossed by a hand-hauled ferry from the south bank. During the steamboat era, Georgetown was The Gambia's second town, a relatively thriving administrative outpost and a major up-river trading centre. The prestigious Armitage High School is still in business, but dismiss any notions of nostalgic, tropical languor conjured up by the colonial names: backwaters don't come much further back than this. On the north side there's a whole quarter of the town that's like an open museum of the old trading days, with tiled floors and ornate plaster work disintegrating behind an onslaught of tropical vegetation. The big roofless barn usually labelled a "slave house" was probably no such thing, more likely a warehouse for perishable goods. Much of Georgetown's significance was lost in the 1970s after the completion of the main south bank highway and its fate was sealed by the closure of the riverboat service. Judging by the closed shops and clubs, it's obvious that the islanders are continuing to leave. Georgetown remains the site of the country's main **prison**, a place so grim that a number of prisoners recently died of malnutrition.

It's not all bad though. Ask for *Tide's Bar* – warm company and cold beer. And if you're intent on **staying** in Georgetown, check out the *Government Rest House*, which has intermittent electricity powering its fans and AC, somebody to cook (if you provide the food) and a fine location beneath large shady trees; it costs around D50 per person, less in a group. You may be required to book your room at the divisional commissioner's office opposite – a tedious operation. But as long as the market continues to tick over, the rest house makes Georgetown a viable and quiet place to unwind. The quietness may change drastically, though, if the new Tendaba-style **safari lodge** on the river's north bank just upstream of Georgetown attracts tourists in large numbers.

Stone circles

You'll probably need to pass through Georgetown if you're interested in getting to the **Wassu stone circles**. With wheels of course, you just wait for the ferry to the north bank of the river and drive thirty minutes – in theory. In fact, the ferry is sublimely unpredictable, breaking down all the time, running out of fuel in mid-channel, snapping its rudder cable and spinning helplessly, or simply running aground. Anticipation runs high, and it seems a shame when the crossing goes smoothly. By **public transport**, from the north bank landing (Lamin Koto), there are *GPTC* buses two or three times a day, connecting Georgetown with Farafenni. For a return day trip from Georgetown to Wassu however, an early start by bush taxi is essential.

First stop is **KUNTAUR**, approached down a low earth causeway across the rice fields of a broad *banto faros* – good bird country, but a murderous road after rain. It's a busy little town, purring with mosquitoes and set low by the water's edge, with a new Italian-aid-supported health centre. From Kuntaur you cut back to the main road for Wassu – an hour or so's walk on tracks over the marsh.

In the dry season, with the bush thin, you may see the reddish pillars of **WASSU** on the north side of the road from a distance; otherwise ask for "stone circles". Wassu is The Gambia's prehistory lesson, but it's no Stonehenge, so adjust your expectations accordingly. The hardened laterite pillars, clustered in loose rings, vary from mere stumps to veritable menhirs weighing several tonnes and standing 3m high. They were apparently levered into place and then jammed upright with packed earth, hence their tendency to fall out of the circle. The burial places of senior personages, they have obscure cultural origins. Carbon dating has pinpointed some of them to 750 AD, but recent research indicates that the burials had taken place long before the circles were erected, suggesting the sites themselves were sacred. You're not likely to illuminate the mystery by asking local people – nobody seems to know anything. It's considered good form to leave rocks on top of the pillars, though again, no-one knows why.

The white huts at Wassu are a rest house. While it's not really operational, you could probably camp here and use it as a base. One hut is given over to a very half-hearted attempt at an information centre. If you're captivated by the antiquity of Wassu, you may want to go on to explore **other stone circle sites** on the north bank: there are stones on each side of the road at NIANI MARU, the largest stones (up to ten tonnes) at NJAI KUNDA, and nine circles of pillars, including a bizarre V-shaped one, at KERR BATCH. And you could pursue the quest for the stones into Senegal (see Part Seven).

A different kind of pillar sits in isolation on the river bank at **KARANTABA TENDA**. A 20m obelisk marks the site of the former village of Pisania, whence Mungo Park set out on his last adventure, in the course of which nearly everyone either died or went missing. It's really not worth the struggle to get there unless you're passing by anyway. One reason you might be is in search of the so-called Monkey Court, a natural rocky amphitheatre on the north bank, and a favourite socialising spot for baboons.

The Eastern Bends: Bansang and Basse

Before getting into the eastern tail end of The Gambia – Upper River division – you pass through **BANSANG**, where the main highway cuts within sight of the river for the first and only time between Banjul and Basse. Bansang is located on a magnificent bend, with easily scrambled hills behind the town providing excellent views. To Gambians, Bansang means the **hospital**, The Gambia's second and only one up-river (and apparently the one to choose), which admittedly does largely determine the town's character. If you're staying the night here, try the *Bunyadu Hotel* at the Basse end of town, scruffy but reasonable enough at D40. A favourite volunteers' hang-out is *Mrs Keru's Shop*, but the best nightspot is the *Konkaduma* – with cold beer and Friday and Saturday discos.

Basse

BASSE – Basse Santa Su – is The Gambia's last town, a surprisingly animated centre that gets its energy from its proximity to Senegal. Only 20km from VELINGARA across the border, its shops tend to be full and there's usually some bottled petrol available. It's a major Peace Corps and VSO posting, and a popular one, with banks, bars and hotels.

The current economic climate is apparently so auspicious that a brand new **hotel** has just been completed behind the main market. With over a dozen rooms and bar/restaurant it's an ambitious affair, but it's hard to see where all the new business will come from. It might be the classiest bordello in Basse. The *Apollo* on the main street isn't bad, with fans or AC in the rooms (D50 and D80 respectively), but like the rest of the town centre its electricity is sporadic. For administrative reasons, electricity is only guaranteed in the administrative quarter of Mansajang, a kilometre out of town near the junction for Sabi and Fatoto. Here you can get a bed at the pleasant and roomy Government Rest House (D30), where they may be surprised to see you; take food along and someone will do the cooking. The problem here is the walk back into town if you want to take refreshment at the locally famous *Uncle Peacock's Fuladu Bar* ("a bar of principle no music" he says enigmatically) and *Finch's*. In the dry season, try to be in Basse on a Thursday morning when a major **lumo** is held, mostly earthenware from the nearby villages of Alunghari and Sotuma.

After Basse, it's just dirt track to FATOTO, with its derelict trading station on the higher than usual river bank. For a big change of tempo, TAMBACOUNDA lies an hour or two to the east by bush taxi, in Senegal. Or, if you're determined – and lucky – there's the passenger **ferry** to the north bank and the return loop to Banjul by whatever transport you can find. This might take a few days.

THE CAPE VERDE ISLANDS

THE CAPE VERDE ISLANDS

From a traveller's viewpoint, and indeed a West African one, the archipelago of Cabo Verde is barely on the map. If you ever hear of the **Cape Verde Islands**, it's usually as an offshore supplement to the grim process of desertification on the African mainland, 500km away. An Atlantic world apart, the Cape Verdes fall in more neatly with the Azores, or even the Canary Islands. They consist of nine main islands in two groups, the **Barlaventos** (Windwards) and the **Sotaventos** (Leewards). Six of them – **Santiago**, **Fogo**, **Brava**, **São Nicolau**, **São Vicente** and **Santo Antão** – are volcanic and inspiringly scenic while three to the east – **Maio**, **Boa Vista** and **Sal** – are flat and sandy.

Despite their **isolation**, the islands are not difficult to get around – once you've arrived – using the good internal air service and ferries. There's usually a place to stay – a small hotel or *pensão* – and prices are reasonable. **Practical hurdles** are the **cost** of the flight and the **time** required to sort out a visa in Dakar – the usual embarkation point for the very few travellers who make the effort. But the islands are, emphatically, worth the hassle.

The Cape Verdes were uninhabited until first colonised by the **Portuguese** in 1462. The first Portuguese immigrants, who in the sixteenth century made the islands an Atlantic victualling station and entrepôt for the trade in African produce and **slaves**, were a mixed population of landless peasants, banished malefactors, adventurers and exiles. The islands were soon being cultivated by the slaves and freed slaves who rapidly made up the bulk of the population. But while the mixed race population that emerged was considered "assimilated" – accepted as Portuguese by Lisbon – the islanders suffered in various degrees from oppressive and racist policies. In Cape Verdean society there was great emphasis on skin colour, the criterion by which "real Portugueseness" was measured.

Commercial planting was mostly of cotton, woven into the *panos* prized along the Guinea coastlands. Catastrophic **droughts** brought despair and neglect however; for nearly the whole of their colonial period the islands remained a largely ignored backwater of the Portuguese empire. Over the last 150 years, tens of thousands of poor Cape Verdeans have left the islands for São Tome, Guinea-Bissau, Senegal, Europe and the USA. The **New England connection** is especially strong, with *americanos* remitting the hard currency which the island families need and flights recently started (but are currently suspended) between Boston and Sal – the island with the country's main international airport.

CAPE VERDE – CABO VERDE

The islands' **name** is derived from their geographical position off "Cap Vert"– the Dakar peninsula in Senegal. Their total **land area**, just over 4000 square kilometres, is about the same size as Kent. Less than 400,000 Cape Verdeans (under half the total) now live on the islands, with the remainder living or working abroad. Cape Verde's **government**, probably the freest in West Africa, is a popular democracy led by President Aristides Pereira. Cape Verde's **foreign debt** is a severe test of the country's strappped resources, yet at barely £100 million, a trifling figure compared with chemical giant ICI's half-year profits in 1990 which were nearly £800 million.

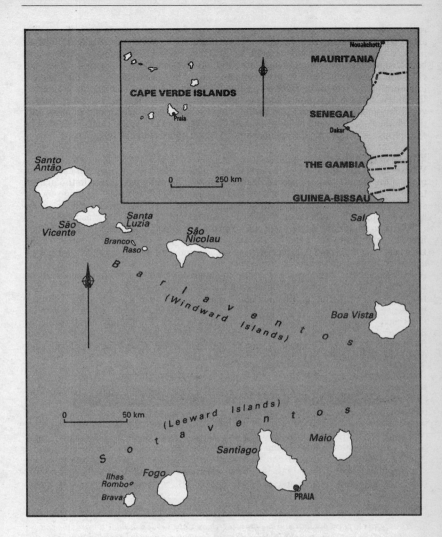

Visiting the islands

The **feel** of the Cape Verde Islands is unplaceable – not quite African, scarcely European, but Portuguese mannered and Kriolu- (an African/Portuguese creole) speaking. The islands are no tropical paradise, so banish any Caribbean associations. The most recent **drought**, which lasted from the early 1970s to 1985, brought malnutrition and hardships which only worsened the country's economic plight in the first decade of independence. But some good rainy seasons in recent years have seen the islands increasingly green – especially on their northern windward slopes. Several have interiors resembling anything but deserts, with towering, cloud-drenched peaks and ravines choked with vegetation. The **coasts** vary from white sands against metallic azure blue to full-tempered, Atlantic seas on black cliffs. Inland, the **roads** are for the most part steep, winding and cobbled, as if harking back to pre-motor days; **trees** are baobab and breadfruit, coconut and date palm; the **livestock** pigs and goats, ducks and chickens. **People** distil *grog* from sugar cane, fish for huge tuna, and strum out laments in mournful *mornas* on the right occasions. Rip-offs and hustle seem almost unknown. In the few small, tidily colonial **towns** clustered around a central square – the *praça* – you'll find restless teenagers perched on mopeds, widows in black going to mass and potted plants on the window ledges. Most Cape Verdean towns are referred to simply as *povoação* – "the town". Except on Santiago island, there could be no other.

Where to go and when

Where to go in Cape Verde is a fairly simple matter – in a few weeks you can get to most of the islands and see a good deal of each one. If you've any choice in the matter try to allow time to spend longer than you'd planned. Some islands – Santiago for its size, Santo Antão and Fogo for their stunning scenery, Boa Vista for its beaches – may hold you longer than others; but they're all small enough to be quickly graspable.

When to visit can be more specific. You'd want to avoid, if possible, a trip in the first five months of the year before the anticipated July to October summer rains. Between December and March it can be unpleasantly windy, especially in the northeast part of the archipelago, as *harmattan* winds blow across from the Sahara. From April to June, the higher reaches of the mountainous islands are often blanketed in cold fog. If the rains come, splendid thunderstorms and torrents of water across the roads are the norm, though they shouldn't hinder your travels if you're visiting during this season. But the best time is probably **October and November**, when the vegetative results of a successful rainy season are truly verdant, the islands' name suddenly no longer ironic. One exception to the rule would be a special visit to São Vicente for the annual Mindelo *Carnaval*, a riot of Rio-style street entertainment, floats and costumes which takes over the town every February.

AVERAGE TEMPERATURES AND RAINFALL												
PRAIA												
	Jan	Feb	Mar	Apr	May	June	July	Aug	Sept	Oct	Nov	Dec
Temperatures °C												
Min (night)	20	19	19	20	21	22	23	23	24	23	22	20
Max (day)	27	28	29	29	30	30	30	30	31	31	30	27
Rainfall mm	2	0	0	0	0	1	8	76	102	30	10	2

It's only fair to point out that much of the research on Cape Verde was done towards the end of one of the best rainy seasons in decades: some descriptions need to be read in that light.

Arrivals

The Cape Verde islands are remote. Apart from the monthly ferry service from Dakar, flying to the islands is the only way of reaching them – unless you have an ocean-going yacht.

■ Flights from Europe and North America

Getting to Cape Verde from Europe you've strictly limited options. Cape Verde's airline, *TACV*, fly Sundays from **Sal to Paris and Amsterdam**, then **back to Sal** overnight; cheapest Apex fares from about £800. *TAP Air Portugal* fly from **Lisbon to Sal** once a week with an extra departure in holiday periods. *TAP* connections out of London don't tie in with these flights, however, and you'd have to spend a night in Lisbon. Excursion fares ex-London start from around £700. *TACV* fly once a week from Lisbon to Sal (about £350 return for an excursion purchased in Lisbon; the same price as *TAP* ex-Lisbon). *Aeroflot* fly **Moscow to Sal** every Sunday with a midday connection out of London. Yearly returns can be found for under £400 and one-ways for a lot less. It may also be worth checking out the cost of flying **via Dakar** (monthly excursions from around £400 and yearly fares for less than £500; try *Air France* and *Sabena*) and then connecting out to the islands – see below. Lastly, out of **Boston**, USA, *TACV* formerly flew fortnightly to Sal. This service is currently suspended.

■ Flights from West Africa

The twice weekly, fifty-seater flight from **Dakar to Praia** is always full and usually overbooked. It's operated jointly by *Air Senegal* and *TACV*. *Air Senegal* flights leave Dakar at noon on Saturday, returning from Praia at 2pm; *TACV* fly on Tuesday, departing Praia at 8am and Dakar at noon. *TACV*'s flights, however, have lately been suspended and the traffic surplus taken by ferry (see below). Fares are CFA47,000 one way, CFA66,000 one month excursion. If you may be staying longer than a month then think about waiting to buy the Praia–Dakar leg in Cape Verde: it works out a little cheaper purchased in escudos. In any case, make a **booking** as soon as you can – you don't have to pay up front – and be sure to reconfirm your seat a couple of days before – or to make a strong impression in the office in Dakar. If you're not confirmed you'll have to hustle hard at the airport on the day of the flight. Note that because of an unreliable reservations system for these flights, "confirmed" seats on a ticket purchased in Europe are no guarantee. Check when you get to Dakar.

It's also possible to fly from **Bissau to Praia** on *TAGB* (Wednesday) at comparable prices; though you may find that Guinea Bissau's weak peso makes it cheaper than flying out of Senegal.

■ Ferries

The *Companhia Nacional de Navegação* runs a **monthly ferry service** between Praia and **Dakar**. Departures are normally first Saturday of the month and fares are CFA35,000 deck class, CFA41,000 cabin: tickets from 18 rue Rafenel, Dakar. There's also a service **from Las Palmas** in the Canary Islands.

There are further possibilities (though fairly remote ones) of getting a berth on board a merchant vessel out of **Lisbon**, **Las Palmas** or **Rotterdam** – at least one a month from each – to Mindelo. If you're interested try: *Joaquim Pio & Martins Lda* Rua da Vitoria 7–0, 1100 Lisbon (☎877181/2); *Yuba de D. Juan Cardenas Guerra*, Arco 16, Las Palmas, Gran Canaria (☎243704); *Viagens Cabo Verde B.V.* Rochussenstraat 395, 3023 DK Rotterdam, Netherlands (☎258054).

Red Tape

All nationalities require visas. Cape Verde's consulates are few and scattered: there's no diplomatic representation in Britain.

Addresses in Europe – **Paris**, **Rotterdam**, **The Hague**, **Bonn** and **Lisbon** – are given in *Basics*. Other consulates are in the USA, at 3415 Mass. Ave NW, **Washington** DC 20007 (☎202 965 6820) and 535 Boylston St (2nd floor), **Boston** 02116 (☎617 353 0014). In West Africa the only consulate is in **Senegal**, at 1 rue de Denain, Dakar (☎21 18 73).

Visas can take some time to come through, commonly up to three weeks in Dakar. Notification comes in the diplomatic bag from Praia with each flight so check Mondays and Wednesdays only: some gentle pressure may get you an early result. Note that buying your plane or ferry ticket beforehand and taking it with you to the embassy seems to speed up the issue of your visa.

If you intend applying in advance in Europe, write first for application forms and send your passport by registered mail. Rotterdam and Paris are both fairly efficient, but you may be asked for references. You should be given your requested duration, up to a month or so. Overstaying by a few days doesn't excite much concern – by the nature of the flights out it happens a lot.

There's a simple rule on **duty free allowances** of alcohol and tobacco; none. The principle is not rigorously adhered to however and reasonable personal quantities are probably fine. There's rarely much of a customs check anyway.

Costs and Money

Cape Verde is one of the less expensive West African countries and comes as pleasant relief if you've been in Senegal. Cape Verde's currency is the Cape Verdean escudo (CV$) which on the islands you'll normally see written thus – 500$00: five hundred escudos. Centavos account for the zeros but you're not likely to see smaller than a 50 centavo piece. The exchange rate is fairly stable, currently CV$122 = £1.

A *conto* is a thousand escudos. Escudos are not convertible outside Cape Verde but you should be able to buy some in Dakar if you want, or on the ferry. Arriving at Praia there's no bank at the airport; Sal has one. The *Banco de Cabo Verde* is the only bank and most towns – and all island capitals – have a branch. They normally take travellers' cheques in all major currencies and service is efficient. The **black market** which is said to exist isn't worth bothering yourself (or Cape Verde's balance of payments) over, in order to add ten percent to your spending power.

You won't save much by **bargaining** either; the practice is considered a little unworthy and most people prefer to stick by their starting price even if it means losing the sale. This is hard to accept at first if you've grown accustomed to a noisy exchange of mock outrage every time you buy something. But it makes life more relaxed and seems entirely appropriate in Cape Verde's almost hassle-free environment.

Credit cards don't help much on the islands. The three or four top hotels take Amex, but they're about the only establishments that will.

■ Costs

Your **outlay** will very much depend on how and how much you travel between islands. While the flight network looks inexpensive, you're going to

be spending at least £15–£20 on most hops and travel costs can quickly break out of even fairly generous budgets. Ferries are cheaper but they don't offer the same flexibility. Land travel, at least on the islands which have buses, is inexpensive; but the costs of exploring those islands which don't have buses soon mounts up. A basic room in a *pensão* will cost upwards of £5 and a straightforward three course meal from about £2, with individual dishes in fancier establishments for about the same.

In three weeks, visiting half a dozen islands and keeping flights to a minimum, staying in the cheapest *pensões* and restricting yourself to one restaurant meal a day, a rough estimate of spending would be around £500, somewhat less if you're sharing and much less if you spend any time hiking and camping. **Prices** vary considerably from island to island and of course are much lower outside the few main towns; reading through you'll get a good idea of where is most expensive. Prices tend to be lower where much food is locally produced (Santiago, Santo Antão), and higher where there are international connections or a whiff of tourism (Sal, Praia itself, São Vicente, Fogo).

Health

Arriving direct from outside Africa, you don't need any inoculations. Coming from the mainland, cholera and yellow fever certificates are routinely demanded, though you may get away without a yellow fever certificate if you're connecting straight through to São Vicente, Sal, Maio or Boa Vista.

One of the health successes of independent Cape Verde has been the virtual elimination of **malaria.** Until the nineteenth century a posting to the islands from Portugal was viewed as one step short of a death sentence. Now, all planes arriving from Africa get insect-sprayed before any passengers are allowed off and all visitors are issued with a health card asking them to report any fever they get on the islands. Only parts of Santiago are reckoned to have a malaria risk and in practice few people use anti-malaria pills. If you're on Cape Verde for a short time only, however, and planning to return to the mainland, you shouldn't break your course.

Water from the tap is almost always good but water shortages mean that you'll sometimes be drinking water that's been stored or sold, so beware. And be sparing too: the normal water rate is CV$14 per 100 litres, but big increases are common during droughts. Bottled Portuguese brands are widely available.

Health care on the islands isn't bad and while infant mortality is still high, life expectancy, at 63, is impressive. **Leprosy** is still a big problem on Fogo, but not one that will affect your own health. Surprisingly few people **smoke** – though it's a habit enjoyed in pipes by elderly ladies in rural Santiago. Litter bins and enjoinments to **social responsibility** are features of urban life and Praia is a refreshingly clean capital. If, on your travels, you had the misfortune to get hepatitis, Cape Verde would be a fine place to **convalesce**. Low humidity, sea breezes and clear skies are the norm.

There are **hospitals** in Praia and Mindelo with adequate facilities for ordinary problems. Dispensaries, cottage hospitals and pharmacies (*farmacia*) in most towns or, failing these, *postos venda medicamentos*, should fulfil basic needs.

Information and Maps

As you'll soon discover, Cape Verde has no tourist offices abroad and the few embassies have either nothing or the most limited leaflets.

As for **maps** there's a good general travel sheet of the whole archipelago – which you may come across on office walls in Cape Verde – but it's been out of print for some time and isn't generally available either in the country or abroad. A British Admiralty naval chart based on nineteenth-century soundings (available from *Stanfords* in London) shows quite a lot of topographical detail but is hopelessly out of date – despite twentieth-century updating – on roads and villages.

Single island sheets published in 1982 for a *Food Strategy* survey are still available in one or two bookshops in Praia and Mindelo – but stocks are mostly limited to the less interesting islands like Maio and Sal. If you can get hold of them, they're useful, particularly for hiking. Town plans of Praia and Mindelo are still in print, and worth obtaining.

In the absence of anything else, the Cape Verde **telephone directory** contains a wealth of surprisingly useful information that includes a map of each island.

Getting Around

The most important inter-island connections are by plane, with ferries providing a good alternative if you have more time. Except on Santiago, road transport on the islands is very limited.

■ Domestic Flights

All the inhabited islands except Brava are now linked by **internal flights** run by *Transportes Aereos de Cabo Verde*. Fares range from CV$1000–3000 – no special reductions. It's important to book in advance as flights are usually full (though sometimes cancelled) and to reconfirm your seat if it's been booked for more than 24 hours. It's often possible, even when there's no direct flight, to get where you want to on the same day with a little island hopping. Note however that international arrivals delayed into Sal airport can sometimes knock the whole domestic service out of joint, as planes are taken off minor routes to deal with inbound passengers.

■ Ferries

Two new German **ferries**, *Barlavento* and *Sotavento*, run weekly schedules through the islands on a four-weekly cycle. The home port is Mindelo on São Vicente, and the **itinerary** is either from Mindelo to São Nicolau, Sal, Praia, Fogo and back to Mindelo or in the other direction from Mindelo to Fogo, Praia, Sal, São Nicolau and Mindelo. On this latter route, the ferries also call on alternate voyages at Brava and Boa Vista.

The voyages start in Mindelo on Mondays and terminate there on a Friday or Saturday. The big question is which itinerary is operating in any given week. If you want to plan ahead before arriving in Cape Verde, the *Companhia Nacional de Navegação "Arca Verde"* (CP 41 Praia; ☎61.10.35/61.10.60/61.14.21, telex 6067 ARCAV CV) are good at providing their latest details, but even they may not know which itinerary will be in force more than a month in advance.

Inter-Island Ferry Practicalities

Deck berths – with the reclining seats and inaudible TV so familiar to Greek island hoppers – are cheap and insalubrious. Cape Verdeans are surprisingly poor sailors and the seas usually rough, occupying the crew with mops and buckets. For a small supplement, there are comfortable four-berth **cabins** with basins and secure lockers. You'll find that cabin berths are often left unsold, gving you a private cabin and, in effect, a budget cruise. With a little planning you can spend the days visiting islands and nights aboard the pitching, rolling vessel. This kind of travel doesn't give you much time ashore but its great advantage is cheapness and – assuming you can handle the seas – an unexpected degree of luxury.

A few considerations: there's **no food** for sale on board the ferries (though you can usually buy cold beers from the crew), no recommended **drinking water** (make provision) and **no showers**, so be inventive with the hand basins.

Other Principal Ferries

The *Porto Novo* runs daily (except Tuesday, but twice on Saturday) between **Mindelo** (São Vicente) and **Porto Novo** (Santo Antão) with a special itinerary out to **Tarrafal de Monte Trigo** (Santo Antão) on the third Wednesday of every month. And the *Furna* operates the rather impenetrable timetable shown in the box below between **Praia, Porto de Vale** (Fogo) and **Furna** (Brava).

FURNA TIMETABLE			
Mon	dep. Brava noon	**Thurs**	arr. Praia 6am
	arr. Fogo 1pm		dep. Praia 9.30pm
	dep. Fogo 6pm	**Fri**	arr. Brava 6am
Tue	arr. Praia 2am		dep. Brava noon
	dep. Praia 9.30pm		arr. Fogo 1pm
Wed	arr. Fogo 6am		dep. Fogo 5pm
	dep. Fogo 5pm		arr. Brava 6pm.
	arr. Brava 6pm		
	dep. Brava 8pm		

■ Buses and Taxis – and Hitching

Compared with getting between them, **getting around each island** is relatively straightforward: the longest land journey is less than 100km, on Santiago, and most trips take under an hour. On Santiago the national bus network, *Transcor*, is fairly well developed. Of the smaller islands, São Vicente and Santo Antão also have buses but services are fewer. Where *Transcor* has buses on other islands, they usually tie in with plane and boat arrivals (for example on Santo Antão) and are unpredictable at other times. Prices, except for local runs, are very low, around CV$1–2 per kilometre.

The alternative to buses are **carrinhos** (bush taxis), which operate widely wherever there's sufficient demand. It's not always easy to tell which of these are licensed and which are private (or government) vehicles, but official ones usually carry a sign in red, usually marked **aluguer** – "for hire". Prices tend to be fixed at fifty percent or more above the bus fare. **Particular** ("private") taxis or cars are expensive, but the drivers are usually willing to bargain. For inaccessible places on the smaller islands they can be a viable option.

Hitching, when there are any vehicles, is easy and drivers *simpatico* – though habitually reckless. The lack of traffic gives some drivers a vivid sense of immortality, but the combination of tortuous bends and precipices with cobbled roads is perilous. Be confident in saying "devagar" ("slow down") if you start shaking. It's normal to pay for lifts when hitching, though it won't always be expected – agree in advance.

■ Car Hire – and bringing your own vehicle

The one or two local **car hire** places in Cape Verde don't impress much, but at least they're not overpriced: the international companies haven't yet heard of the country. The only outlets are in Praia and Mindelo – unfortunately there's no motorcycle or moped hire which would be really useful here.

It's possible of course to **bring your own bike** by ferry from Dakar, a recommended option if you have one with you on the mainland. Local ferries are used to loading and unloading motorbikes, but do check that petrol is available before crossing over to the next island – some of the less populous ones have very few vehicles and unreliable fuel supplies. Lastly, Cape Verde is wonderful **cycling** territory for the fit and fanatical and, in

view of the gradients, not to mention the cobble-stone roads, obviously suited to mountain bikes. Perhaps a cycling trip more than any other visit to the islands ought to be made shortly after the rains when the countryside is in full flush.

Sleeping

Putting your head down for the night is a simple business and over most of the country Portuguese-style *pensões* (plural of *pensão* – "pension") provide clean, down-to-earth accommodation – often with a fan – for CV$500–1000.

Ask to see several rooms and perhaps suggest *Tem um quarto mais barato?* (which slips off the tongue and means "Do you have a cheaper room?"). Full-scale **hotels** – with hot water, private bath, air conditioning and restaurants – are restricted to Praia, Sal, Mindelo and São Filipe, with rooms starting from around CV$1000 and rising to CV$5000 or more.

In smaller towns you may have to ask to locate your accommodation: tourism is still of such minor importance that people tend to assume everyone knows where to stay, and elementary signs are often missing. Assumptions are also made that you'll know about the **twelve o'clock checkout rule**, sometimes applied quite ruthlessly. Hotels, especially, will try hard to make you pay an extra half or whole day if you've not vacated on time.

If you want to spend a while in one place, there should be little difficulty in arranging **private accommodation**.

Cape Verde has no youth hostels nor any campsites and, surprisingly perhaps, truly wild country suitable for **camping** – as opposed to marginal agricultural land – isn't plentiful. Still, as an eccentric foreigner you'll be happily tolerated if you camp in the neighbourhood. You're likely, anyway, to have an opportunity to ask permission when you collect water.

Eating and Drinking

It would be surprising if Cape Verde had an extensive and flourishing cuisine: with severe malnutrition and famines that killed thousands still remembered, the question of food has tended to concentrate on the number of calories – and in respect of variety most mainland countries can do a lot better than the islands. Still, the dishes on offer are a wholesome and always filling selection, probably little changed since the sixteenth century.

Apart from the big hotels in Sal, Praia and Mindelo, and a handful of restaurants where you'll get a decent variety of unremarkable international fare as well as local dishes, the choice is always strictly limited. In smaller towns the *pensões* usually serve meals somewhere in the building, but a **casa de pasto** (dining room, diner) is the standard, and often unmarked, place to eat. You eat what they have, which as often as not will be *cachupa*, the national dish (believed to derive from the same African term that resulted in catsup/ketchup).

Staples include rice, potatoes (Irish and sweet), beans, maize, squash, pork and – inevitably – tuna. Meals always start with a solid vegetable broth and finish with fruit, occasionally *pudim* (crème caramel).

■ Drinking

When it comes to drinking, Cape Verdeans usually think first of **grog** or **canna** (sugar cane distillates known collectively with other spirits as *aguardente*), which get consumed – and apparently made at home – in large quantities. A cautious approach is recommended: liquor often comes from anonymous bottles and sacking-wrapped jars and you're never quite sure what the effect will be. There are "new" (*novo*) and "old" (*velho*) varieties and diffrent degrees of smoothness. It's usually clean, but even so can be quite deadly, gasping stuff. "Punch" – a concoction of dark rum, honey and lemonade – is, like *aguardente*, often on sale over the counter in rural shops. It's not an ideal midday quencher.

Beer (*cerveja*) is still largely imported – *Heineken, Stella* or what have you – but Praia has recently acquired its first brewery and cans of *Ceris* are now out in the bars and cafés. They also make soft drinks. For juices ask for **sumo –** *de laranja, limão,* etc.

Wine has some potential on the islands as a significant industry, but the lethally dry, red product of Fogo's volcanic slopes doesn't inspire much enthusiasm just yet. Unreasonably expensive **imports** of Portugal's favourites can be found in most bars and groceries.

Coffee, when it's not instant, is usually terrible, either utterly tasteless or swimming with over-roasted grounds. Angola once supplied a lot, but, again, Fogo's own contribution isn't that great. Often it just seems to be stale or mixed with chicory.

Communications – Language, Media and CTT

The day-to-day language of Cape Verde is **Kriolu ("Creole"), quite distinct in structure and in much of its vocabulary from Portuguese (Cape Verde's official language): the two are not mutually intelligible. Kriolu contains many elements of Fula and Mandinka and a wide range of adopted vocabulary from archaic sea-faring**

PORTUGUESE AND KRIOLU FOOD TERMS

Beans	Feijões	Jam/	Marmelade	Shellfish	Mariscos
Bread	Pão	Marmalade		Soup/broth	Sopa
Bread roll	Bolho	Maize/corn	Milho	Squash	Abóbora
Butter	Manteiga	Meat	Carne	Sugar	Açúcar
Cheese	Queijo (always	Milk	Leite	Tea	Chá
	goat)	Pork	Carne de	Tuna	Atum
Coffee	Café'		Porco	Vegetables	Legumes
Eggs	Ovos	Potatoes	Batatas	Water	Agua
Fish	Peixe	Rice	Arroz	Yams	Inhames
Food	Comida	Salt	Sal		

DISHES

Cachupa	A mash of beans and maize, sometimes with bacon and sausage, eaten at breakfast.	Feijoada	Beans and salt pork
		Frango	Chicken
		Langosta	"Lobster"; strictly crayfish
Cachupinha	Similar to cachupa, with green bits	Lapas	Tiny mussels, usually in a spicy sauce
Caldeirada de Peixe	Fish stew	Licuda/linguiça	Sausage
Carne de Vaca	Beef	Linguado	Sole
Coelho	Rabbit	Polvo	Octopus
Doce	Sweet/dessert	Prato do Dia	Dish of the day
Espadarte	Swordfish	Tubarão	Shark

TERMS

Assado	Roasted	Frito	Fried
Bife	Steak or cutlet, as in Bife de Atum	Molho	Sauce
		Piri piri	Hot sauce
Cozido	Boiled	Doce	Dessert/sweet

FRUIT AND SNACKS

Banana	Banana	Melão	Melon	Croquetes	Fish cakes
Goyaba	Guava	Papaya	Pawpaw	Gelado	Ice cream
Laranja	Orange	Tâmaras	Dates	Iorgurte/Yaourt	Yoghurt
Manga	Mango	Toranja	Grapefruit	Pasteles	Pies – usually
Melancia	Watermelon	Frutapão	Breadfruit		savoury

Portuguese and other European languages including English.

If you speak **Portuguese** – and it's one of the easiest languages to pick up, particularly if you're familiar with Spanish or Italian – you'll find you can get by easily everywhere. Even in rural areas everyone speaks some: papers, signs and radio are all in Portuguese and education is largely conducted in it. Learning Kriolu is another matter: Cape Verdeans tend to slip in and out of Kriolu and Portuguese, and Kriolu takes some time to tune into.

While a little Portuguese goes a long way, if you don't have any you'll be falling back on **French** and **English**, neither of which is spoken very widely outside the main towns. In most places, though, you'll run into younger people who've learned them at school as well as returnee emigrants from Europe, Senegal or the USA who speak them fluently.

KRIOLU – A BEGINNER'S GUIDE TO NOT-PORTUGUESE

BASICS

Hello	*Bon dia*	God go with you	*Deus ta kunpaño-lo*
How are you?	*Kuma ño sta?*	Please	*pur fabor*
I'm fine	*N sta ben*	Thankyou	*brigod*
What's your name?	*Kali e bo nómi?*	Today	*oshi*
[or more formally] What is your (masc/fem) name ?	*Kal e nómi di ño/di ña?*	Tomorrow	*mañan*
		Yesterday	*ónti*
My name is Caroline	*Ña nómi é Caroline*	Before	*ántis*
Do you have/is there any...?	*Ño ten...?*	After	*dipos*
		Near	*pértu*
Goodbye	*Bon dia/te lóg*	Far	*lonzi*
See you soon/sometime	*Te lóg/te dipos di mañan*	Here	*li*
		There	*la*

TRAVELLING

I'd like some water	*N kre agu*	Is there a cheap hotel near here?	*Ten penson li pértu*
How do I get to Tarrafal?	*Kma N pode bai pa Tarrafal?*	I'd like a room for one person/two people	*N Kreba kuartu pa un psoa/dos psoa.*
Is this the bus stop for Tarrafal?	*Undi e paraza di otukaru pa Tarrafal?*	Is there a toilet/ bathroom?	*Ten kasa di bañu li?*
What time does the plane leave/arrive?	*Ki óra avion ta sai/ tchga?*	What is it?	*Kuse e es?*
Where are you (masc./ fem.) going?	*Undi ño/ña ta bai?*	I don't know	*N ka sabe*
		We don't speak Kriolu	*Nu ka ta papia kriolu*
We're going to Praia	*Nu ta bai pa Praia*	Open	*abert*
How much is it?	*Kal e presu?*	Closed	*fetchod*

NUMBERS AND DAYS

1	*un*	11	*ónzi*	21	*vinti y un*	200	*duzéntus*
2	*dos*	12	*dozi*	30	*trinta*	500	*kiñéntus*
3	*tres*	13	*trezi*	40	*korenta*	1000	*mil*
4	*kuatu*	14	*katorzi*	50	*sinkuenta*	Monday	*segunda-feira (2ªF)*
5	*sinku*	15	*kinzi*	60	*sasenta*	Tuesday	*terça-feira (3ªF)*
6	*sais*	16	*dizasais*	70	*satenta*	Wednesday	*quarta-feira (4ªF)*
7	*séti*	17	*dizaséti*	80	*oitenta*	Thursday	*quinta-feira (5ªF)*
8	*oitu*	18	*dizóitu*	90	*novénta*	Friday	*sexta-feira (6ªF)*
9	*nóvi*	19	*dizanóvi*	100	*sén*	Saturday	*sábado (S)*
10	*dés*	20	*vinti*	101	*sén-t y un*	Sunday	*domingo (D)*

■ The Media

Radio and TV are important tools in Cape Verde and while you're not likely to see much of the latter (an eclectic mix of Brazilian soap operas and right-on documentaries), *Radio Nacional de Cabo Verde* is a good station, with an insidiously catchy signature tune and an enlightened play list. The BBC is hard to get hold of in mid-Atlantic and signals wander.

The **press** consists of the solitary, twice-weekly *Voz di Povo* ("Voice of the People") which, even without alternatives, is really not bad, covering a fair selection of local and international news. In Mindelo there's also the monthly *Notícias*. And in any bookshop you can get *Africa*, the Time Magazine of the Lusophone states. Portuguese is easier to read than to speak; just as well, as foreign papers are virtually unobtainable.

■ Post and Phones

Both post and telephones in Cabo Verde are run by the **CTT**, or simply *Correio*. There's at least one CTT on each island, open Monday to Friday 8am to noon and 2.30 to 5.30pm, and sometimes Saturday and even Sunday mornings. **Post**, both outgoing and incoming, is generally efficient and honest though not especially swift. For *poste restante* have your mail marked "Lista da Correios". If you have **urgent mail** to post from one of the more isolated islands try taking it to

the local airstrip for the next flight to Sal, or even ask them at the local *TACV* office if someone could give it to the pilot: people are usually understanding.

Telephoning locally isn't likely to crop up much during your stay (though for some emergency telephone numbers see "Directory" below) as there are very few phones on the islands – two call boxes in Mindelo, three in Praia, a total of 100 telephones on Fogo and until recenty just one phone on São Nicolau. **Phoning abroad**, the IDD automatic system is supposedly largely complete by now (you dial 0 then the country code) but outside of Praia, Mindelo and Sal you're not likely to have much joy with this – which is a pity because it's cheaper. Prices to the UK and Europe (except special rate Portugal) are CV$230 per minute IDD and CV$280 per minute (minimum three minutes) by operator; to the USA CV$300 and CV$360 repectively. The international operator is on 111. You can't normally reverse charges.

Entertainment

There's little in the way of an organised leisure industry – less than a handful of cinemas in Praia and Mindelo, no theatre (though see below), and the "sport" of bull-fighting didn't travel from Portugal.

A GLOSSARY OF CAPE VERDEAN TERMS

Americano	Cape Verdean living in America
Badiu	peasant from rural Santiago descended, according to tradition, from runaway slaves
Bairro	suburb, outskirts of town
Branco	white – or wealthy – person
Camâra	town hall
Cidade	city, town
Conto	one thousand escudos
Criança	child
Crise	drought, community crisis
EMPA	*Empresa Publica do Abastecimento*, the public provisions company, like a nationalised wholesale grocers
Festa	feast, festival, party
Funco	round, stone, thatched house
Grog, Grogo, Grogue	sugar-cane firewater, *aguardente*
Igreja	church
Lenço	traditional headscarf worn differently by women of each island
Liceu	secondary school
Morabeza	kindness, gentleness, considered to be a peculiarly Cape Verdean quality
Morna	the heavy hearted music of the islands, sweet-sounding, nostalgic and very characteristic
PAICV	African Party for the Independence of Cape Verde
Pano	cloth, *pagne*
Paragem	bus stop
Pelourinho	pillory, the slave auction post
Povoação	"town", the local town
Praça	square, *place*
Praia	beach
Quinta	estate, owned by a landlord; rare today
Quintal	courtyard of a house
Ribeira	stream, river or rivercourse
Seca	drought
Vila	town

■ Music

There are a few nightclubs (*boites*) and a clutch of them are regular **live music** (*musica ao vivo*) venues. The commonest entertainments though are strictly home-spun – births, baptisms, confirmations, marriages and deaths providing occasions for gathering together. In the evenings it's quite the thing for young people to meet in the town square (*praça*) with a guitar or two. The best-known Cape Verdean forms are guitar and fiddle songs – the ***morna***, a mournful lament reminiscent of Portuguese *fado*, and the more upbeat and very danceable ***moradeira***, music with a wonderful muscular rhythm. Many songs are love songs – addressed to the islands – and powerfully sentimental. An exponent who's released a record available in Europe is **Cesaria Evora**; check out her lovely LP, *La diva aux pieds nus*, on the *Lusafrica* label. And try to hear her in Mindelo.

In the past, in smaller towns and rural areas, you might have heard soneone playing the *cimbó* or the *berimbau*, old **one-stringed instruments** of African origin producing plangent, ancient sounds – either with a bow on the *cimbó*, or plucked and resonating in a sound box, or the mouth, with a *berimbau*. Both have virtually fallen into the realm of folklore, though in parts of Santiago you might still be lucky.

■ Other Pastimes

The **game** of *orzil* or *oril* (the hole and pebble mindbender common all over Africa in different versions, see p.34) is popular everywhere, as is draughts or chequers. **Theatre** is usually community-based and party-led, normally carrying ideas to the people rather than straight entertainment .

Directory

AIRPORT TAX None.

CONTRACEPTIVES Free to Cape Verdeans, you can get condoms (*camisas de vênus*) from most pharmacies and *postos venda medicamentos*.

EMERGENCIES There are fortunately very few in Cape Verde. If you can find a phone you can call the **police** on ☎132 in Praia, Sal, S. Nicolau and Santo Antão. On Fogo they're on ☎81.11.32; Mindelo ☎31.46.31; Boa Vista ☎51.11.24. **Medical emergencies** require a hospital: in Praia, Sal and S. Nicolau ☎130; on Santo Antão

☎21.11.30; Mindelo ☎31.23.55; Fogo ☎81.11.77; Boa Vista ☎51.11.13. If you have an emergency on Maio or Brava, shout for help.

OPENING HOURS AND PUBLIC HOLIDAYS Most shops and businesses are open from about 8am to noon and again from 3 to 7 or 8pm. Lunch hours are long and lazy and *everything* closes, even – curiously and frustratingly – many bars and cafés. Cape Verde follows the main **Christian holidays** with some exotic additions (Dec 8, Immaculate Conception; Jan 1, Circumcision of Our Lord) plus Jan 20, National Heroes; Mar 8, Mothers' Day; May 1, Labour Day; June 1, Childrens' Day; July 5, Independence; and Sept 12, Nationality Day. There are also a host of other days off – any number of saints' days, annual municipal festivals in most towns and a major ***Carnaval*** every February in Mindelo, emulated in the same month by Praia.

PHOTOGRAPHY doesn't usually pose any problems. There are very few subjects which would get you in trouble and most people are uninterested where you choose to point your camera. Taking pictures of Cape Verdeans, ordinary courtesy is your only restraint: you'll rarely be asked for payment.

PLACE NAMES AND RIVALRIES On the islands, Cape Verde is called Cabo Verde – or Cáu Berde in Kriolu – the people Caboverdianos. It's not uncommon on Santiago, however, to hear people referring to *Cabo Verde* when they mean Santiago, as if it was the mainland, while referring somewhat dismissively to the other Cape Verdes as *as Ilhas* – the islands. There's a good deal of **rivalry** between the islands, with competition between the people of the Barlaventos – who see themselves as more urbane and metropolitan – and the Sotaventos where, in Santiago particularly, a larger proportion of the population are descended from slaves. There are subtle cultural variations from island to island too, with differences in the local form of Kriolu. Look out too, as you travel, for the characteristic women's headscarf style – tied differently on each island.

Many towns and villages are called Ribeira something, which just means River – understandable where fresh water is so important. Tarrafal is another common name. Every island seems to have its Tarrafal – which makes it useful to know which one's being referred to.

RELIGION Mostly Catholic, although American Protestant churches have made some headway since independence. There's probably quite a lot to be learned about the process of Islam's arrival and spread in West Africa from the fact that it's completely unknown in the Cape Verdes. It's likely that Islam hadn't made much impression in the peasant communities from which slaves were commonly taken.

TAMPONS Usually available from larger general stores, but not on the smaller islands or outside the main towns.

TROUBLE It's hard to imagine getting into any in Cape Verde. Drug use, in the close-knit island communities, carries a strong stigma and doesn't go unnoticed. While quite a few youngish men smoke home-grown weed, you could expect a barrel-load of trouble if seen by the wrong people. Nudity and topless bathing are pretty well out of the question and particularly ill-advised for unaccompanied women. Cape Verde is a tolerant country and etiquette has grown out of the combination of Latin manners and Wolof, Fula and Mandinka social convention that you'd expect. You're just as unlikely to be a victim of trouble. While theft is not unknown, the islands are one of the safest places in the world for absent-minded travellers. Even long-term expatriates agree on this, which must say something – though they tend to single out Praia as an exception.

WATERSPORTS There's some good **snorkelling** in places and exciting **diving** in a number of wreck-strewn shallows, notably off Boa Vista and Sal. Cape Verde's **windsurfing** is some of the ocean's most challenging. The big centre (though not, in fact, big at all) is Santa Maria on Sal island – details there. Addresses are also given in the Praia "Directory" on p.503.

WILDLIFE Cape Verde's native fauna is a meagre show, with no large mammals and few outstanding birds. Herpetologists are excited by *Tarentola giganta* (the giant gecko) and the Cape Verde Island skink (another relative giant) but disappointed at the total absence of snakes. Birdwatchers might want to go out of their way to spot the Razo Island lark (p.521) but it's fairly uninteresting for non-specialists. The seas are more rewarding with good chances of seeing dolphins, whales, turtles and amazing flying fish.

WOMEN TRAVELLERS AND THE WOMEN'S MOVEMENT Women travellers will find the Cape Verde islands relaxed after continental West Africa. While **sexual attitudes** do contain an element of machismo, it's normally expressed as nothing much stronger than winks, whistles, stares and strong expectations that you *will* dance. It can also come across as absurdly innocent: heavy sexual pestering is unusual. Younger women, travelling without men, may find that their "unmarried condition" gives them almost adolescent social status, which can be frustrating. But the islands are too small for problems to last long.

As for the lives of **Cape Verdean women**, little seems to have changed despite the government's on-paper commitments to reducing sex discrimination and promoting their rights and welfare. Yet there are good reasons why change is needed: the continued emigration involves mostly men, and there are now 108 women for every 100 men, leaving many rural women *de facto* household heads. The *Organização das Mulheres de Cabo Verde* (Rua Unidade Guiné-Cabo Verde, Praia, ☎61.24.55) is quite active and the main contact-making body.

A Brief History of the Cape Verde Islands

The Cape Verde Islands blew out of the Atlantic in a series of volcanic eruptions during the Miocene period some 60 million years ago – though Maio, Sal and Boa Vista may be a geological extension of the African mainland. The islands were uninhabited (so far as is known) until 1462, making the country unique in West Africa. In the gloriously clumsy eloquence of Adriano Moreira, Portugal's Overseas Minister from 1961–2, the Cape Verdes were "islands asleep since the eve of time, waiting to be able to be Portugal". After five centuries of such paternalism, the turn of recent events has been remarkably peaceful.

■ Discovery and Colonisation

Although African sailors may have visited the islands in earlier centuries, it was a Genoese navigator, **Antonio da Noli**, working for Prince Henry of Portugal, who discovered and first documented Santiago (which he called São Tiago – St James) and four other islands, some 500km off Africa's Cap Vert, in 1455. Three more in the northwest (Santo Antão, São Nicolau and São Vicente) were reached by Diogo Afonso in 1461. Santiago, by far the biggest prize, was split between the two navigators, who were granted a captaincy each: da Noli set himself up at **Ribeira Grande** in the south and Afonso made his headquarters in the northwest. Slaves were brought from the African mainland to work the parcels of land alotted the handful of immigrants and in the capital, Ribeira Grande, work began on a cathedral. The Portuguese crown viewed the new extension of empire – 2500km from Lisbon – with indifference; but the archipelago could serve as a stepping stone to exotic riches, and it would certainly do as a penal colony.

Fogo was settled in the 1480s and its western region was singled out as one of the most likely productive areas on the islands – rolling, partly wooded country, with substantial rainfall in most years. But Fogo islanders were forbidden to trade with foreign ships – a right reserved by Santiago – and the island was considered a hardship post for the Portuguese officials sent there. By the end of the sixteenth century its population had barely reached 2000 and there were appeals to Lisbon for more settlers – petitions which were met with the arrival of convicts and political undesirables (*degredados*) from Portugal and the internal banishment, from nearby Santiago, of certain offenders.

The tiny volcanic pimple of **Brava** attracted its first colonists in the early 1540s. They kept much to themselves: climatically the island was one of the easiest to survive on, yet it was very remote. It was only when large numbers of families escaped here from Fogo in 1680, after volcanic eruptions and an earthquake, that Brava became heavily populated. It has had the densest population of the islands ever since.

The big island of the far northwest, **Santo Antão**, got its first inhabitants in 1548 but its large size, with remote and rugged interior valleys and craters, and its distance from the main shipping lanes, kept it very isolated and unknown for at least 200 years. Among its settlers were Jewish families fleeing the Inquisition and subsequent European persecutions. The village of Sinagoga is a reminder.

São Nicolau offered fewer opportunities to adventurous migrants and only its northwest valleys – even these with uncertain rainfall – made colonisation viable in the middle of the sixteenth century. The town of Ribeira Brava became an important literary and ecclesiastical centre and was the seat of the Cape Verdean bishopric from the end of the eighteenth century until the beginning of the twentieth.

São Vicente, one of the driest islands, was virtually uninhabited until the start of the nineteenth century when the sheltered bay at Porto Grande (the best harbour in the islands) was chosen as the site of a British coal bunkering station for steamships on the Brazil and East Indies runs.

The "flat islands", **Boa Vista**, **Maio** and **Sal**, were also late in being fully colonised. Maio and Boa Vista had small numbers of herders and poor farmers, most of them freed or escaped slaves, and Maio eventually became the virtual private fiefdom of a freed slave family, the Evoras.

An early plan, conceived by Genoese merchant adventurers, was to create on Santiago a major **sugar** industry, following its success in Madeira. With the conquest and colonisation of tropical lands, Europe could begin to grow the crop for itself instead of relying on expensive imports. But

THE CAPE VERDEAN SLAVE TRADE

As the New World opened across the Atlantic in the sixteenth century, the **trade in slaves** gathered momentum and the islands – now important stepping stones to Brazil and the Caribbean – became an emporium for their trans-shipment and taxation.

Although they were more expensive, slaves at **Ribeira Grande** (the main entrepôt) were better value than those bought directly on the Guinea coast: they tended to be healthier, as the sick had already perished; they spoke some Portuguese and some had even been baptised (the Portuguese were keen on finding religious justifications for their slave-trading, safeguarding the captives from purgatory). And for the slave ships, buying at Ribeira Grande was a much safer option than sailing directly into the creeks of Guinea to barter for slaves.

Roughly between 1600 and 1760 (the peak years) anything from a few dozen to several thousand slaves were sold annually through Ribeira Grande, most of them exported to the Spanish West Indies and Colombia. Large numbers were shipped off in years of bad drought on Santiago, when planters would sell their **farm slaves** to traders when they couldn't afford to feed them. This was prohibited in law: the only slaves supposed to be exported from Cape Verde were those just imported from the coast under licence.

From the earliest years of the colony, Lisbon had passed a succession of **trade laws**, ruling that the resale of slaves and foreign trade partnerships were illegal. In 1497 the sale of iron to Africans was banned, and between 1512 and 1519 further crushing edicts – equally unenforceable – were issued: outlawing the much-in-demand Indian and Dutch cloth from the islands; banning the commissioning of *lançado* adventurers to trade on the mainland; and ruling that all legally contracted slave ships bound for the Americas should first detour to Lisbon because Ribeira Grande could not be trusted to extract duty honestly.

The people involved as **trading partners** in the complex mesh of buying, selling and bartering were a mix of European merchant adventurers (sometimes merely pirates) and various mixed race labourers and entrepeneurs (see below) as well as bona fide licensed contractors waving charters from Lisbon or Madrid. But the trading networks rarely operated in a free market. For most of the time, Portugal tried to ensure that as many profits and tariffs as possible accrued to the crown, even if that meant making ordinary trade illegal and relegating much business to the status of **smuggling** – from which the crown received nothing.

Successive **governors** of the islands, who generally viewed their postings with misgivings if not actual horror, succumbed to the inevitability of **corruption** (if they survived malaria and other diseases long enough to care). Some succumbed too enthusiastically for the likes of the islands' clergy, aldermen, court and treasury officials – whose own commerical interests they threatened – but most governors managed to amass reasonable wealth while leaving space for smaller operators to do business.

The banes of Lisbon – the *lançados* – eventually became totally estranged from Portugal and even at times from Santiago. Once fully acculturated in Guinea, and unable to return to Portugal (on pain of death), they had no need to worry about the rules, as the contract holders were obliged to, and could trade with the Dutch, English and French boats which sailed around the Atlantic in growing numbers. In this way they kept a good selection of merchandise for purchasing slaves and other African goods, while contract holders were obliged to buy the limited range of goods for resale and barter offered by the state supply monopoly.

LANÇADOS, TANGOMAUS, GRUMETES AND LADINOS

A number of distinctly defined groupings were involved in the slave trade:

● **Tangomaus** (dragomans); cosmopolitan Africans who traded in the Guinea interior and did much of the initial negotiating for slaves but who were familiar with Portuguese ways.

● **Lançados**, ("sent outs"); originally white or part-white Cape Verdeans who had familiarised themselves with African ways on the mainland and had settled in African communities to trade and transport goods along the coast. They eventually became indistinguishable from *tangomaus*.

● **Grumetes**; African or mixed race deckhands and carriers working for the traders.

● **Ladinos**; slaves or other Africans who could speak Portuguese or Kriolu.

the Cape Verdean climate proved unsuitably dry and, although the **rum** which normally came as a by-product of sugar production was found to be useful for **slave trading** along the Guinea coast, the sugar farms at Ribeira Grande never really took off and by the late sixteenth century were already eclipsed by the vast quantities being produced in Brazil.

Instead, the Cape Verde islands found themselves in the middle of a growing network of **trade routes** – between Europe and India, between West Africa and the Spanish American colonies and between Portugal and Brazil. They took on the function of **victualling stations** for the trading vessels, supplying fresh water, fruit, salted and dried meat, and carrying on a trade of their own in commercial goods – salt, hides, cotton *pagnes* and slaves.

■ 1640–1775: Cloth and the Crown Monopolies

With the **break-up of the union between Portugal and Spain** in 1640 business went into the doldrums for a number of years. Several governors were denounced to Lisbon after they monopolised what trade there was or even started applying the rule of law in order to confiscate and penalise foreign trading ships for their own gain. The islands were at a severe disadvantage because international demand for slaves had saturated the Guinea coastlands with **iron bars**, the principal currency, causing huge increases in the price of slaves. Portugal, which produced very little iron and forbade its export, was unable to compete.

Cotton, though, had become Cape Verde's main commercial crop, grown especially on the estates of Fogo. Slave women spun it; men wove it into strip cloth, dyed it with cultivated indigo and native *orchilla*, and sewed the strips together into *pagnes*. Some of the material found its way to Brazil but most was traded – generally for more slaves – on the Guinea coast. Throughout the sixteenth and seventeenth century and for much of the eighteenth – until slave trading began to be threatened by abolitionists – Cape Verdean cotton *panos*, in a multiplicity of inventive designs, were the prized dress material of the West African coast, traded as far east as Accra and as valuable as iron bars in many districts. The value of Cape Verde cloth became so universal in the region that it was also the usual currency of the archipelago: administrative

officials were commonly paid with it and accumulated vast hordes of the stuff, a soft currency which only had real value locally, not in Portugal.

In the **second half of the seventeenth century**, after the split with Spain, the private contracts system fell out of use. Portugal's African territory and trade routes were seriously depleted and for some years only the most recklessly optimistic merchants had been willing to purchase the expensive rights on slaving in those parts. With wily Cape Verdeans stealing the trade from under their noses and the price of slaves going up all the time it was difficult to make contracts pay.

Instead, in 1675 the first of the **Crown Monopolies** – the *Companhia de Cacheu* – was set up, reserving for itself sole rights to trade in foreign goods with the coast and outlawing (again) the trans-shipment of slaves through Santiago. Cape Verdeans were only allowed to export their own produce. Bitter feelings were aroused in Santiago. When a new company, *The Company of the Islands of Cape Verde and Guinea*, was formed, and bought a fat contract to supply 4000 slaves a year to the Spanish West Indies, the governor of the islands was placed on the company payroll. His salary was doubled and he was expressly forbidden from engaging in any commercial activities. With their governor now effectively playing for the opposition, the islanders were more disgruntled than usual. And true to form, the new company did nothing for their prosperity, stockpiling goods to inflate prices, under-supplying vital commodities and levying high freight charges for their meagre exports.

With the **War of the Spanish Succession** from 1701–13, which Portugal was pulled into against Spain and France, the company's valuable slaving contract was lost and in 1712 Ribeira Grande itself was comprehensively sacked and plundered by a French force. The **cathedral**, a century and a half in the building, had only been completed nineteen years earlier. About this time, serious attention began to be given to creating a new and better fortified capital at Praia. Ribeira Grande was in steep decline from the middle of the eighteenth century and **Praia** was eventually dedicated as the seat of island government in 1774.

The first half of the eighteenth century had witnessed a great **relaxation of trade embargoes**. But Lisbon's persistent and neurotic attempts to prevent the trans-shipment of slaves and the sale to non-Portuguese of Cape Verdean cloth (which in the economic climate amounted to much the same thing) mystified foreign traders, especially English and Americans, who broke the laws without compunction. Apart from its triumphant (but peaking) textiles industry, the archipelago was in a state of **economic ruin** and the population too poor and too isolated to worry much about Lisbon's laws even if some did carry the death penalty.

With the foundation in 1757 of the *Companhia de Grão Para e Marnahão*, which had the sole purpose of providing slave labour to the states of the new Brazilian empire, a twenty-year era of unparalleled cruelty and hardship began for the islands. The **annexation of political control** which had begun with the last company was taken to its logical conclusion, so that the Company now effectively *owned* the islands; while in Lisbon, a clique of English gentlemen maintained discreet but weighty capital interest in its enterprises.

Apart from the utter destitution which the enforced **bypassing of trade** brought to the archipelago, a severe **drought** struck from 1772 to 1775. By this point in the islands' history the population had grown too big to be able to survive such disasters on whatever came to hand – as they had during the famine of 1689 in Santiago when they ate horses and dogs. In the face of **starvation** throughout the islands, the Company was implacable – it held back food supplies, pushed up prices and milked the islanders of every last resource. In return for food, hundreds were abducted abroad and forced into slavery by English and French traders. Smuggling, of course, had never been so essential nor so profitable. The famine left an estimated 22,000 dead – out of a total population of less than 60,000.

◼ Into the Nineteenth Century: Famine and Emigration

By the time the rains returned in 1777, the Company's charter had expired and it went into merciful liquidation. At the beginning of the **nineteenth century** the Cape Verdes faced a quite different future. The harsh Company regime had battered the textile industry with enforced low prices while drought had extinguished the cotton crop as well as many of the field slaves and textile workers. The emergence of the newly independent **USA** as a major economic power

began to be more important than the distant historical links which tied the islands to Portugal. Lisbon, in any case, was too distracted by Napoleonic strife at home, and tail-and-dog upsets with Brazil about who ruled who, to be much concerned with the insignificant islands and their irrepressible flouting of trade laws. Moreover Angola and Mozambique held far more promise.

New England whalers began calling at the Cape Verdes from the end of the eighteenth century, to take on supplies and crew and to do a little trading. Goatskins were a profitable sideline back in the States and, once the practice had become established, the Americans arrived each year with holds full of merchandise. Brava, Fogo and São Vicente were the main islands of contact and from these a steady trickle of impoverished Cape Verdeans escaped to New England through the closing decades of the nineteenth century.

Slavery in the nineteenth century was contained by the British and (ironically) by the American presence. While the trade in slaves from the Guinea coast was forbidden from 1815, slaves were still sold, by weight, well into the 1840s. Only with the end of the American Civil War and with pressure from Britain (to whom Portugal owed a debt going back to the Napoleonic era) was an abolition process set up on the islands. Slaves were not formally emancipated until 1869 and then they had to work for their ex-owners as indentured labourers for a further ten years.

Drought and the Cape Verdean diaspora

A series of disastrous **famines** hit the islands during the nineteenth century. In the first of these, from 1830–33, an estimated 30,000 people died. No relief of any kind came from Lisbon, but America, on this and several other occasions, sent large consignments of relief aid, though towards the end of the century it was generally wealthy emigré Cape Verdeans who organised it.

While the dispossessed of the Sotaventos moved to Praia or tried to emigrate, the poor of the Barlaventos headed to the new "city" of **Porto Grande** (Mindelo) on São Vicente to find work at the British-run **coaling station** or in the shops, bars and bordellos.

At the peak of its importance at the end of the nineteenth century the port of Mindelo was servicing over 1300 ships every year – and tens of thousands of sailors. The latter industry had a far-reaching effect on the culture of the islands, introducing even more of a racial mixture and enriching Kriolu with words like *ariope* (hurry up), *fulope* (full up) and *troba* (trouble).

Meanwhile, Portugal's first efforts at "humanitarian relief" took place during the drought of 1863–5 (another 30,000 death toll). It seemed an ideal time to profit from the availability of labour eager for food by engaging the people in civil engineering projects. The islands' first **cobbled roads** date from this famine, when peasants were rounded up to work for starvation wages. A more sinister method of dealing with famine was **enforced migration** to the "Cacao Islands" of São Tomé and Principe. For a number of reasons, the abolition of slavery in São Tomé and Principe led to serious labour shortages. In the Cape

CAPE VERDEAN SOCIETY TO 1950: THE POTENTIAL FOR REVOLT

The **slave estates** had varied in size from small landholdings run on paternalistic lines, where landlord and slave led similar lives, to extensive plantations (especially on Santiago) where wealth differences were extreme. The traditional *morgadio* system of land tenure, in which inheritance was strictly by **primogeniture** (inheritance by the eldest son), produced a growing population of landless aristocrats and tenant farmers on marginal land. Under the system, land could not be bought or sold. The **estate slaves** were often tied closely to the landlord's family, occasionally by blood. Over the centuries, intermarriage blurred the distinction between slaves and share-cropping peasants, the only practical difference being that the share-croppers were always in debt to the landlords, a life in many ways as arduous as slavery. Freedom for slaves – an act of "charity" periodically undertaken by some landlords, or else an economic necessity when food supplies were exhausted in a famine – was no release from the cycle. If they ran into debt as share-croppers, freed slaves lived on the sufferance of the landlord.

This, together with the fact that the islands are too small to offer much refuge, meant that **slave rebellions** were rare and provoked only by the most savage treatment. Among the landed families there were real fears, principally because they themselves were divided (the morgadio system created bitter feuds) and sometimes engaged in fierce vendettas with their rivals. At one time many slaves were armed by their masters and gangs of pistol-toting slaves are known to have clashed on occasions, even in Praia. There was a certain insecurity about what might happen if the arms were turned against the elite. In the Santiago interior there was a large underclass of freed and escaped slaves, the *badius*, partly independent of the estates. And on Santiago relations were less paternalistic and the estates often owned by absentee landlords. A group of slaves did organise a stand against their particularly oppressive landlord in 1822 and there was an aborted general **slave revolt** in Santiago in 1835 (given passive encouragement by the administration's ragged armed forces). But that was about the extent of resistance, and it was largely brought about by anticipation in the run-up to the abolition of slavery.

As for **political resistance** which might eventually culminate in an independence movement, there isn't a great deal of early evidence for that either. Conditions on the estates in the **twentieth century** became worse. With the old *morgadio* system discredited and abandoned, and the landlords themselves in debt to the *National Overseas Bank*, much of the land was bought up by a new class of absentee landlords, often returned United States emigrants. Coaling labourers mounted **strikes** for increased pay at Mindelo in 1910 and again in 1911, but they were defeated.

Opportunities for **dissent** on the islands in the fascist **"New State"** of Portugal's prime minister Salazar (1932–68) were limited to the private publication and distribution, among a small intellectual circle, of poetry and subtly nationalistic Kriolu **literature**. Organised demonstrations of opposition were impossible, and even further ruled out by the chronic plight of the islands during the famine years of World War II and the labour migrations of the early Fifties. Debtor peasants were treated as criminals and could claim nothing from the state until their debts had been repaid. **Political dissidents** found themselves imprisoned in the notorious detention centre at Tarrafal, alongside victims ejected from Portugal, and interrogated by the Gestapo-modelled **PIDE** political police.

To make the possibility of grass roots resistance even less likely, Cape Verde has an **alcoholism** problem going back to the earliest years of the sugar industry. Never viable as a major export, cane was still grown in vast quantities for distilling *grog*, on land that could otherwise have provided food crops. The national addiction to *grog* was such that in the drought years of the 1960s sugar was imported to satisfy demand.

Verdes the shortages were of land. Offered apparently huge bonuses by the recruiting agencies when (and if) they returned, thousands of poverty-stricken Cape Verdeans were persuaded to "go south" over the next ninety years to a system of equatorial plantation labour that was little better than ordinary chattel slavery. Like the monopoly companies of a century before, Portugal's **cocoa industry** found drought on the Cape Verdes was easily turned to its advantage.

Right from the first use of this system, measures were taken to limit the number of Cape Verdeans emigrating to a life of relative security in the USA: a heavy departure tax was imposed, beyond the means of those who desperately needed to go, and travel permits and passports were made almost impossible to obtain. Nevertheless, the trickle of emigrants to New England became a flood between 1910 and 1930 when an estimated 34,000 people left the islands. This mass exodus was to become enormously significant after World War II when the emigrants were able to send back substantial **remittances** to the islands and after independence when the economy became largly dependent on them. The USA however began to make literacy a condition for emigration from 1913 and after 1922 the door to new immigrants was progressively closed.

Drought in the twentieth century has continued to be the single most important factor shaping the lives of Cape Verdeans. Only following the drought of 1959–61 were genuinely compassionate measures taken to alleviate the suffering and these seem likely to have been initiated mostly by international outrage at the colonial labour migration policies. Earlier, there were four big *crises*: 1902–4 (15,000 dead), 1920–22 (17,000), 1940–43 (25,000) and 1947–48 (21,000 lives lost). The drought of the Second World War was probably the worst catastrophe in Cape Verde's history. Brava and Fogo suffered appallingly when they had to cope with a surge of re-emigrants returning from the American depression, because the "rainy" years of the Thirties had lulled islanders into a false sense of security. And during the war years remittances from American relatives dried up completely. Older people of Furna and São Filipe remember walking into town and finding corpses fallen at the roadside.

When the last major wave of **emigration** took place as a result of these famines, the authorities were ruthless in their efforts to

prevent flight to the USA. As a result, sixty percent of applicants ended up in São Tomé and Angola. There was a small number, however, who emigrated to **Guinea-Bissau**, not out of destitution, but with ambitions. Since the opening of *liceus* (the colleges of São Nicolau in 1866 and São Vicente in 1917), about two-thirds of mainland Portuguese Guinea's teachers and civil servants were Cape Verdeans. It was principally from their ranks that organised **agitation and resistance** to Portuguese rule first germinated.

■ Organised Resistance and the Portuguese Revolution

In response to what they described as a "wall of silence" around the islands, a group of mostly Cape Verdean intellectuals led by **Amilcar Cabral** – and including Luiz Cabral and **Aristides Pereira** – met secretly in Bissau in 1956 to form the **PAIGC** (*Partido Africana da Independencia da Guine e Cabo Verde*). When peaceful representations to the colonial government were met with indifference and more repression (culminating in the massacre of striking dockers in Bissau – see p.543), the PAIGC began planning for a **guerrilla war on the mainland**, with the declared aim of liberating both Guinea-Bissau and Cape Verde. After four years of preparation and fairly continuous efforts to negotiate a peaceful alternative, war began in 1963. The Cape Verdes became a massive Portuguese military base, swarming with Portuguese troops drafted to the front in Guinea-Bissau – and in Angola and Mozambique, where wars of independence had also begun.

On the Cape Verdes themselves, the question of a violent uprising was purely academic. The small, barren and isolated islands are unpromising ground for guerilla warfare. Yet the island government and police force (with help from the military and the *PIDE*) were acutely sensitive to the possibility of open revolt: every subversive indication was examined and squashed, and activists sent to Tarrafal or worse places in Angola. On Santiago, a *badiu* religious cult movement, known as the **rebelados**, was labelled communist for criticising the corrupt, state-run Catholic church, advocating the hands-together system of community help (the *juntamão*) and resisting outside interference, especially the anti-malaria campaign, which tried to spray members' homes. The movement virtually deified Amilcar Cabral. Its leaders were brutally interrogated and deported to other islands. But their threat was no more politically coordinated or potentially subversive than that posed by the **Nazarene church**, whose American-led, puritan-inspired clergy were also subject to repression for their denunciations of the Salazarist church. Cultural opposition was the only kind available and cultural repression the inevitable response. **Kriolu**, unintelligible to ordinary Portuguese-speakers, was considered subversive in itself and its use banned from state property.

Thousands of **women** emigrated in the early 1970s to find work as domestics in Portugal, France and Italy. But the sex ratio on the islands remained unbalanced, with women far outnumbering men.

On the mainland, **the war** was drawn-out but successful. Only the **assassination of Amilcar Cabral** at his headquarters in Conakry on January 20, 1973 (partly inspired by jealousy of the Cape Verdean role in Guinea-Bissau's revolution) deflected it from a well-planned and predictable course. In September 1973, with most of the the territory controlled by the PAIGC, the party proclaimed *de facto* independence. Portugal withdrew from Bissau the following year after the *Armed Forces Movement's* (*MFA*) on April 25, 1974 **overthrow of the dictatorship** in Lisbon.

On the islands, the pre-coup government continued in office, even after the *MFA* had swept away the basis of their power. But the tide was coming in fast. In less than a week, the clandestine fragments of Cape Verde's own PAIGC cells had coalesced, and a **public meeting** was held in Praia on May 1. The Tarrafal detainees were released and the PAIGC took its message around the islands, agitating semi-legally for the independence that was almost at hand. The "wall of silence" had caved in. There were other parties, hatched and nurtured by the administration, which tried to promote the idea of some kind of "shared independence" between the islands and Portugal. They were maintained by small groups of wealthy activists and had supporters in Senegal, who mistrusted the aims of the PAIGC. None of them convinced many islanders.

Lisbon sent a new governor in August 1974, charged with asserting Portuguese **continuity** in Cape Verde. He was shouted out of Praia and back to Lisbon within a month. Another arrived with a heavier hand. His troops shot into a demonstration in Mindelo in September. But with Guinea-Bissau already independent, the **demonstrations** only grew larger. By October, with "continuity" sounding increasingly hollow, the Portuguese were negotiating with PAIGC leaders. In December, a meeting in Lisbon agreed on a transitional government consisting of three PAIGC members and two from the *MFA*. The Portuguese capitulated by allowing a general election the following June. With a landslide of votes, **Aristides Pereira** took office on **July 5, 1975** as president of the new republic.

■ Independence and the split with Guinea-Bissau

Cape Verde and Guinea-Bissau were united by a common colonial experience. The war which began in Bissau culminated in the **liberation** of all Portugal's colonies and the emergence of democracy in Portugal itself. Amilcar Cabral had been obsessive about the importance of **Cape Verde-Guinea unity** and Aristides Pereira continued to emphasise it. But the most significant political event in the first fifteen years of Cape Verdean independence has been the 1980 **coup** in Bissau which overthrew **President Luiz Cabral**, Amilcar's half brother, and led to the formal separation of the two countries.

After the liberation war there was a lingering unease within the PAIGC in Guinea-Bissau. Luiz Cabral, though a close friend of party leader Aristides Pereira, was not a statesman of the same rank, and he became an increasingly isolated figure, mistrustful of his own ministers and – it seemed to them – unwilling to discuss economic and social questions outside a clique in which Pereira figured too prominently. Suspicions grew that policy in Guinea-Bissau was being constructed by the two presidents in secret and that Cape Verde, which had achieved independence relatively painlessly – though at the cost of Guinean lives – was seeking to dominate the union. Furthermore, while Cape Verdeans had been instrumental in starting the independence movement, they had also formed a large proportion of the colonial civil service in Guinea-Bissau, most of whom had passively collaborated with the Portuguese. The charge of **neo-colonialism** didn't have to be made explicit.

Against Pereira's advice, Cabral modified the Guinea-Bissauan constitution to give himself more power and his nationalistic prime minister, **Nino Vieira**, less. It was Vieira who subsequently led the coup of November 14, 1980, putting himself in the Bissau presidency. Pereira, in condemning the coup, pointed out that the party constitution provided the means for dealing with factional problems. On January 20, 1981 (the eighth anniversary of the assassination of Amilcar Cabral) the Cape Verdean arm of the party renamed itself the **PAICV** and, at a summit in Maputo in 1982, a formal division of the two countries' assets ratified the split. A vague ideological union of the two countries still exists, but rapprochement has tended to come from the Cape Verdean corner.

One immediate effect of the events of 1980 was the fright it gave to **international aid donors** and partners. Since the early 1960s, support for the independence struggles against Portugal in the international community had been broad-based and confident. The high-profile style and actions of the PAIGC leadership were applauded and, after independence, both countries quickly came to rely on aid to rebuild their wrecked economies. After the 1980 coup, Pereira moved fast to allay fears about the region, successfully pursuing a diplomatic course to maintain international support not just for the islands, but for Guinea-Bissau – efforts which showed surprising good grace under the circumstances.

■ Successes and Prospects

Since 1981, with the union of the two countries a fast fading dream, Cape Verde has at least had a chance to address purely **national problems**, with remarkable honesty and success. Even the question of the very habitability of the islands has been raised, but the **economy** is now viable, a result of careful and sensitive development and a **lack of corruption** that seems remarkable in relation to other countries in the region.

The govenment has answered OAU demands that it apply the **sanctions policy on South Africa** and refuse refuelling rights to *South African Airways* with the response that it cannot afford to commit suicide by solidarity. The front line states support it in this dilemma. It has also kept open and increased the level of **aid** coming into the country and used it carefully on local projects of direct utility. Non-governmental aid is channelled through the *Institute of Solidarity*, matching foreign interests to Cape Verdean requirements. By leaving the door open for *americanos* to return, it has encourged **private investment** and maintained a high level of goodwill amongst the vast majority of the Cape Verdean

diaspora whose remittances continue to be the number one economic pillar.

Agrarian reform has been amazingly patient, seeking to alienate no-one, to adjust where necessary, to persuade and cajole landlords rather than to force change and always to avoid damaging the country's image of impeccable independence and openness in the eyes of the West. The worst effects of **drought** and flash floods have been combatted with tree-planting programmes on all the islands, and further measures like dyke building and better terracing.

Health has been a priority for the government, which reckons to spend three times as much per person as the average developing country. Mother and Child Protection and Family Planning programmes have a high profile, and they're operated by the Party at a community level, with theatre shows and public demonstrations organised to mobilise people on health issues (including breast feeding, contraception and nutrition) and encourage a preventative approach. The off-loading of unwanted First World drugs, so common in underdeveloped countries, has been avoided by setting up a national pharmaceuticals industry, which has even started exporting its products.

One hundred percent **adult literacy** as well as free and compulsory **primary education** are goals that the country has pretty well achieved – though adult literacy improves not only with the campaign, but also with the demise of illiterate senior citizens.

The **legal system** in Cape Verde is one of the most progressive in Africa. There are no political prisoners – indeed few of any kind – and no death sentence. The country has an almost spotless record on **human rights**: since independence there has been only one seriously violent incident involving the military when a soldier accompanying the Agrarian Reform Commission lost his nerve in a noisy crowd at Santo Antão and opened fire and one man was killed in the ensuing panic .

Respect abroad for the development of the Cape Verdean republic has found a new dimension with the country's recent hosting of multilateral **talks on Angola**. In future, Cape Verde's location and relative insignificance look likely to encourage this role as provider of neutral territory for delicate meetings.

Cape Verde's successes are startling on paper, but several lurking **problems** are not going to fade away. The **battle between church and** state over the issue of **abortion** on demand (eighty percent of children are brought up in mother-only families) resulted in violent demonstrations in 1987, led by church activists who felt they had not been sufficiently consulted. The Catholic journal Terra Nova has, as a result, been labelled "opposition newspaper" by the foreign press. Nor has the position of **women** in Cape Verdean society had as much attention focused on it as the (male-formulated) charter of the Organisation of Cape Verdean Women (OMCV) would suggest. Particularly since women make up over half of the population, this is an urgent issue. Some of the OMCV members took part in the anti-abortion protest. **Alcoholism,** especially in the rural areas, is a real problem – and at root a strictly male issue – triply destructive where it not only wastes productive land on sugar cane but hard earnings as well, and reduces the workforce. The government also needs to examine its

own mechanisms for **renewal**, to avoid a situation where the ex-guerrillas of the party grow old and stagnant together. Opportunities to climb the political ladder are few.

Good **rainy seasons** in the late 1980s broke a drought that had persisted on some islands virtually throughout the years of independence. If the climate continues favourably into the 1990s, the government will need all its skills to ride out the inevitable wave of **rising expectations** especially as, with the political changes sweeping through West Africa in 1990, Cape Verde too, is liberalising its political system. In August 1990, the prime minister, Pedro Pires, took over as PAICV party secretary from Aristides Pereira, in preparation for the introduction of a muti-party system. But in the slightly longer term future, the **harsh droughts** that are likely to continue to goad the islands may prove the government's best tool in maintaining resolve and unity.

THE SOTAVENTOS

Santiago, **Fogo**, **Brava** and **Maio** make up the leeward group of islands, the **Sotaventos**, with two-thirds of the population, more of the rainfall (which arrives from the south) and a good deal of the wealth.

If you're coming from Dakar, your first port of call on the islands wil be **Praia** on Santiago island, Cape Verde's capital and the nation's largest town. It's a pleasant enough place but there are no gripping reasons to spend time here: if you're stuck your time is better spent enjoying one of the easy and satisfying short **trips out of town**. The rest of Santiago offers more enticing attractions in the mountainous **central region** and the beaches in the northwest. But although it has a sizeable mountainous interior, Santiago's scenery just doesn't compare with that of São Nicolau and, especially, Santo Antão in the Barlaventos.

Fogo island is a vast and potentially active volcano, nearly 3000m high, whose last eruption was in 1951. There's a magnificent road tracking along the lava-covered eastern slopes, fine walking country in the gentler western parts, and a formidable hike into the old crater itself, now a domain of citrus orchards and farm plots.

Smallest of the inhabited islands, and the hardest to get to, is **Brava**. An airport is planned, however, and meanwhile if you're really keen there's a twice weekly boat from Praia. Cape Verdeans often rate it the most beautiful island – it's certainly the most cultivated and has a relatively benign climate – and it's long been a sanctuary for those families who could afford to flee the droughts on other islands.

Maio, one of the *ilhas rasas* or flat islands, is duller and drier. Locally famous for its cattle, which provide the country's limited milk supply, other attempts to drum up interest seem a little desperate. As one Portuguese brochure of 1970 put it: *the desolation of its landscape contrasts with the warm welcome of its people and the fine flavour of its fresh lobsters.* So there you have it.

Santiago

With half the cultivable land and half the population, **SANTIAGO** is the **agricultural backbone** of Cape Verde. And, unusually for the Cape Verdes, it takes a few hours to get from one end to the other, switchbacking through the mountains or along the jagged eastern coast. The island's main focus is the capital, **Praia**, at the southern tip. From here one main road snakes through the interior, sending secondary roads like suckers down to the coast; another forks off it to the northeast to link up the east coast fishing villages before meeting with the main route again at **Tarrafal** in the northwest – site of the best beaches. There are dozens of hamlets and villages scattered across the island, and any number of hidden coves and *ribeiras*. We've covered a few travel possibilities below, but Santiago, in common with all the islands, is little known outside the archipelago. Most of your discoveries will be very much your own.

Praia and around

The best way to arrive at **PRAIA** is by plane from Dakar. Clean air, bright sunlight and wind are constant reminders of the Atlantic: a couple of windmills rotating on the brown hills across the *ribeira*, the extraordinary tranquility of the little town on its small proud plateau, everything about Cape Verde, you can see, is going to be quite different. Cape Verdeans – and foreign residents too – tend to complain that Praia is soulless, thinks of nothing but money and has no *joie de vivre*. If you're tuned into Cape Verde's gentle sensibilities this may be relatively true. After Dakar, though, it all comes as a welcome drop in tension and the nicest possible culture shock.

The village of **Cidade Velha**, west of Praia, was the first settlement on the islands and remained the effective administrative centre until early in the eighteenth century. Praia then took over the role of capital, growing from village to town through the nineteenth century.

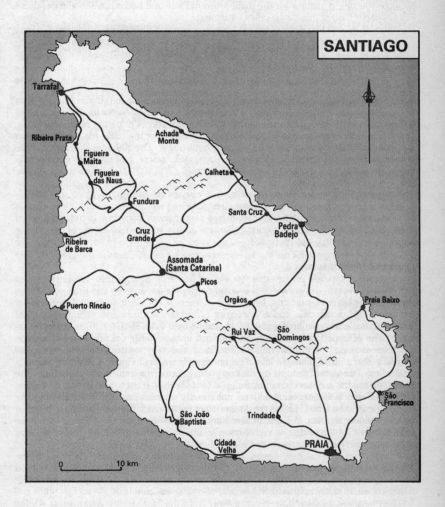

Arrival

Arrival – by sea or air – and **orientation** – on foot – couldn't be simpler. **Gago Coutinho airport** at Praia is small and, appropriately, painted green. You walk from the arrivals room to the front door and out onto the forecourt. Below is the manageable muddle of the capital, five minutes away by taxi (about CV$100). If you insist on the best **hotel** in town you'll go right the way through, which means over the rectangular block of the **Platô** (plateau) and down to the *Hotel Praia Mar* on the other side. You must be a conference delegate or about to sign a contract if you're going there. Most people head for one of the more modest *pensões*, but unless you're loaded down with luggage you might just ask for the main *praça* in Platô and hop out when you get there – it's cheaper than naming a specific destination.

Arriving by sea you dock at the pier roughly beneath the end of the airport runway. Again, it's a five-minute taxi ride to town, or a couple of kilometres on foot. The downtown part of Praia is all concentrated on the half square kilometre of the *Platô*, a neat grid of streets, simplicity to get around.

Hotels

You're best advised to track down a **room** as soon as possible and if you find one that seems okay, not to keep looking. When planes and boats come in, Praia's limited budget beds go pretty quickly. Everyone's first choice seems to be the *Hotel Felicidade*, which has street-front rooms with verandahs and others at the back, more often vacant and considerably cheaper, with or without bathrooms. The *Solmar*, although a little pricier, is clean and spacious, with a more local atmosphere, and includes good breakfasts. The *Dos Anjos* (☎61.41.78/61.42.95; around CV$1400–1600) is more expensive still, but very presentable.

For something more down-to-earth, the **cheapest rooms** in Platô are at the *Residencial Sol Atlantico*, 24 av Amilcar Cabral. Here you can get a nearly clean double for less than CV$800, though water problems plague them from time to time. If none of these has rooms, try the unexciting *Paraiso* at the top end of town, or see if the *Serjinho* in the middle has reopened.

Food and restaurants

For a capital, Praia has remarkably few **eating** houses – though this isn't unrelated to the depressed state the economy has struggled in for so long. By the time you arrive, there may be more restaurants. Best at the moment is the *Casa de Pasto Amelia*, justly popular with townspeople and a scattering of foreign workers and volunteers for its solid set meals and generous glasses of wine (open 7.30–8am, 12.30–2pm and 7.30–9pm). The *Flor de Lys* is classier, but still not unreasonably priced, with good Cape Verdean cooking – try their mussel-like *lapas* and very consumable *Molho de São Nicolau*. The *Hotel Felicidade* has a decent restaurant, and you can also get passable food at the *Panorama*, though its rooftop position is perhaps the main attraction. The *Hotel Marisol* has a deserved reputation too (order rabbit if they have it) but it's expensive (well over CV$1200 for two) and not exactly overflowing with character. In the same quarter, and also bland, is the *Restaurante Poeta* which does at least have a rather good view over the sea. You might also want to try the *Restaurante A Ponte* – Chinese of all things – by the bridge in Vila Nova, a kilometre north of the Platô. If it's closed as rumoured, there's a new one on av Cidade Lisboa.

A favourite for **breakfast** – eggs, *cachupa*, *mermelada*, papaya and the rest – is the *Restaurant Avis,* particularly on a Sunday when others tend to be closed. Another good place to start the day, *Gelados Vulcão*, has excellent homemade yoghurt, drinkable coffee for once, cakes and sandwiches, and of course ice cream.

The **cheapest places**, however, are away from the *Platô* area – *Restaurante Abolha* in Achado Santo Antonio and a good barbecue-grill, *Cantinha de São Tomé*, in Terra Branca. A basic fried fish and *cachupa* shop often appears in the evenings on av Amilcar Cabral, serving the best value food in the centre. If you really want to save money, though, use the market or one of the supermarkets and put together your own picnic.

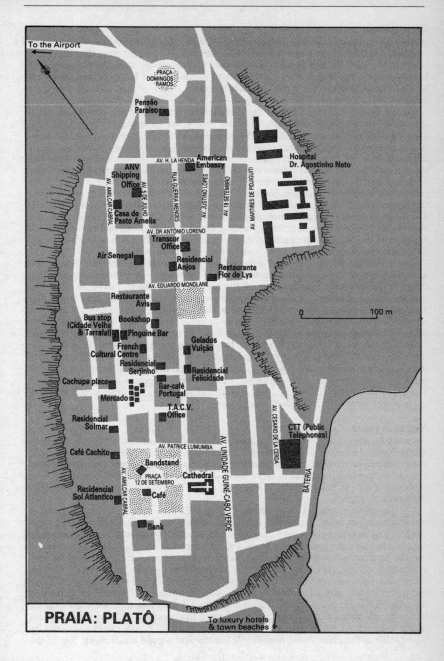

To the Airport

PRAÇA DOMINGOS RAMOS

Pensão Paraíso

AV. H. LA HENDA

American Embassy

Hospital Dr. Agostinho Neto

ANV Shipping Office

AV. 5 DE JULHO

RUA GUERRA MENDES

AV. JUSTINO LOPES

AV. 19 SETEMBRO

AV. MARTIRES DE PIDJIGUITI

AV. AMILCAR CABRAL

Casa de Pasto Amelia

AV. DR ANTÓNIO LORENO

Transcor Office

Air Senegal

Residencial Anjos

Restaurante Flor de Lys

AV. EDUARDO MONDLANE

Restaurante Ávis

Bus stop (Cidade Velha & Tarrafal)

Bookshop

Pinguine Bar

French Cultural Centre

Gelados Vulção

Residencial Serjinho

Residencial Felicidade

Cachupa place

Bar-café Portugal

Mercado

T.A.C.V. Office

AV. CESARIO DE LA CERDA

Residencial Solmar

CTT (Public Telephones)

Café Cachito

AV. PATRICE LUMUMBA

AV. UNIDADE GUINÉ-CABO VERDE

Bandstand

PRAÇA 12 DE SETEMBRO

Cathedral

BATERIA

Café

Residencial Sol Atlantico

AV. AMILCAR CABRAL

Bank

0   100 m

PRAIA: PLATÔ

To luxury hotels & town beaches

Around town . . . being here

It takes about twenty minutes to realise that Praia has almost nothing to offer in terms of sights or entertainment. Not that this is an alarming revelation – more than most this is a capital where just being here is enjoyable: the streets are friendly; the *praça* has benches and a bandstand where visting naval bands play on Sundays; and there are views from the edge of the Platô, particularly from a couple of *pensões* on the western side.

Such action as there is tends to focus around the **market** which, despite its small size (and don't forget it's the biggest in Cape Verde), brings in countrywomen from all over Santiago and, in a good year, packs surprising variety and colour; papayas, bananas, watermelons, potatoes and cassava, goat cheeses, piglets trussed in baskets, dried beans, slabs of red tuna, even potted palms. **Sugar** products are much in evidence. For the Portuguese, the islands were strategic in their efforts to dominate Atlantic trade routes in the sixteenth and seventeenth centuries: rum in particular – distilled from cane sugar – was enormously useful in the **slave trade**, commanding high prices along the Guinea coast. Cane, which grew well enough in lusher valleys on several islands, was never produced in the kind of quantities that would have led to huge commercial success. But Cape Verdeans continue to distil plenty of *grog, canna* and *aguardente* (all variants on the same theme), and to make irresistible sweets. Various kinds of sickly fudge and cup-like moulds of brown molasses crystal are always on sale.

The few large public buildings around town hold no special interest, though the Catholic **Cathedral** is quite an imposing block of a place with its potted plants and figurines. And if you're looking for seats on the plane back to Dakar, you've an excuse to visit the Prime Minister's office (do they have any unwanted seats?) – up the guarded and red-carpeted stone steps of the **Palace of the Republic**, with glimpses of an interior courtyard and gardens. Much of Praia, however, is new and drab, the scrawny suburbs crawling up boulder-strewn gulches in a barren jumble away from the plateau.

Despite the name Praia – which means **beach** – the one or two small coves near the town are none too great. The grey strip beneath where the road snakes off the end of the *Platô* is a possibility, but it tends to be used by exercising soldiers, and the pair of small crescents on either side of the *Hotel Praia Mar*'s peninsula are nothing special. You'll do much better, if you can find transport, going out to São Francisco, 13km east of Praia (see "Out of Praia", below).

Nights in Praia

Evening is when the town is at its most delightfully unhurried. Plenty of people – whole families it seems – spend an entire evening lounging in the *praça*, playing with their children or strolling past the few shops, all of which stay open. **Entertainments** need to be invented, and when you've spent one evening sipping coffee at the *12th of September Café* you'll know why Mindeloans (from São Vicente) rate their own little metropolis so highly.

For **live music** see if Os Tubarões are playing at *Di Nos*, in Achada Santo Antonio at the south end of town. The band (whose name means *The Sharks*) is one of Cape Verde's best and they play a very danceable mix of zouk and upbeat pop. *Di Nos*, partly open-air, is easily the best club in town, though there are some all-night *boites* around the Terran Branca district. If you fail in the live music hunt, excitement has to be very assiduously sought. Assuming the offering at the **cinema** leaves you in need of further stimulation then you could walk down to the *Complexe A Teia*, a surprisingly big, flash and rather snooty **nightclub** (where they refused to honour the "Free Pass" printed at the edge of the Praia town plan). Entry is around CV$400 and drinks CV$150, hardly killing by international standards, and you'll need to dress up a bit. The music at least seems to be up to Cape Verde's usually elevated standards. Another *boite* you could try is the *Pilão* at the *Hotel Praia Mar*. You'll usually find a good atmosphere, too, at the

Flor de Lys and the *Amelia* if you're simply into knocking back a few *copas*. These apart, most of the bar/cafés around town, notably a clutch down Amilcar Cabral, are basically daytime establishments only.

Praia directory

Airline offices *TACV* (☎61.32.15/61.33.89) Mon–Fri 8am–noon & 2.30–6pm, Sat 8–11.30am. *Air Sénégal* opens irregular hours (a one-person office) and is closed while the Dakar plane is in and the staff is at the airport hustling seats.

Airport There's no airport information (the *TACV* office in town knows as much as anyone) and virtually no other facilities – though a good little café does hearty Cape Verdean breakfasts upstairs. Arriving from Senegal, persuade the driver to accept some CFA francs if you're taking a taxi into town; you can't change money at the airport.

Bank One only, Mon–Fri, 8am–noon & 2.30–4pm.

Bookshop The best – nearly the only one – is the *Instituta Caboverdiano do Livro* (Mon–Fri 8.30am–noon & 3.30–6pm, Sat mornings only), which often carries whatever **maps** are available.

Buses Santiago island bus timetables are available from the *Transcor* office in Rua Guerra Mendes.

Car hire *Alucar* in Chã d'Areia, south of the *Platô*, is a bit of a joke. They offered a beat-up Lada for around CV$1400 a day.

Embassies Brazil, Cuba, China, the USSR, Portugal, France, Germany and the USA are the only countries with missions in Cape Verde. The long-established American embassy (☎61.43.63) is generally helpful to Anglophone travellers.

Ferries The *Agencia Nacional de Viagems* has all the details and even some slightly cryptic timetables.

French Cultural Centre Does the things which all *Centres Culturel Français* do. There's a library.

Illness If you need treatment the *Hospital Dr. Agostinho Neto* is adequately equipped and able to perform tests for malaria, amoebas and so on. Try to see a medically qualified person from one of the embassies first.

Post Office (CTT) Mon–Fri 8am–noon & 2.30–5.30pm.

Shipping office At the top of av 5 de Julho, *Companhia Nacional de Navegação "Arca Verde"* (CP 41 Praia; ☎61.10.35/61.10.60/61.14.21, telex 6067 ARCAV CV).

SANTIAGO BUS SERVICES

From Praia to:

Assomada 11.30am, 3.30pm, 6.15pm (90min).

Cidade Velha 6am, 12.45pm, 6.45pm (45min).

Pedra Badejo 12.15pm, 6.15pm (90min).

Praia Baixo 6am, 12.15pm, 6.15pm (75min).

São Domingos 10am, 12.30pm, 3pm, 4.30pm, 6.30pm, 8.30pm (1hr).

Tarrafal via the centre of the island 12.15pm (3hr 30min).

Tarrafal via the east coast 3pm (3hr 30min).

To Praia from:

Assomada 6am, 6.45am, 1pm (90min).

Cidade Velha 6.45am, 1.30pm, 7.30pm (45min).

Pedra Badejo 6.30am, 1.30pm (90min).

Praia Baixa 7am, 1.15pm, 7.15pm (75min).

São Domingos 6.30am, 8.15am, 10.40am, 1.15pm, 5.15pm, 7.15pm (1hr).

Tarrafal via centre 5.30am (3hr 30min).

Tarrafal via east coast 5.30am (3hr 30min).

Supermarkets The *Galerias* is the biggest shop with a fair selection, though avoid buying food that may have been on the shelf for a while. If they've now closed (as they were going to in 1990), the *Supermercado do Hotel Felicidade, Vega Minimercado* and the *Adega do Leão* are alternative standbys. Also check out the "Crioulo" market in Achado Santo Antonio.

Taxis They often don't have change, so it's worth being prepared. Prices are more or less fixed.

Telephones Mon–Fri 8am–noon & 3–5.30pm, Sat 9–11am. Cost to the UK around CV$300 per minute, no direct dialling, no collect calls.

Tourist offices and travel agents Try *Cabtur* (☎61.30.03), 4 Rua Guerra Mendes, or *Orbitur* (CP 161; ☎61.27.40), corner of av Amilcar Cabral and Rua Eduardo Mondlane. For sub-aqua, check out *Dive Cape Verde* (CP 294; ☎61.26.63, telex 4080 NOVOBEL CV).

Visas The French embassy has a visa service for a number of Francophone West African states. You may get a Guinea-Bissau visa with the help of the Cape Verdean Ministry of Foreign Affairs, Praça 10 de Maio.

INTER-ISLAND FLIGHTS FROM PRAIA

Boa Vista: 4 weekly, 45 min.

Maio: 4 weekly, 20 min.

Mosteiros (Fogo): 4–6 weekly, 30 min.

Sal: 1–6 flights a day (none Tues, Thurs).

Porto do Sol (Santo Antão): Saturday, 85 min.

São Nicolau: 4 weekly, 1hr.

São Vicente: 1–2 most days, 1hr.

Out of Praia – Southern Santiago

São Francisco beaches

Although there are a couple of half-decent beaches near the *Praia Mar Hotel*, the string of coves at **SÃO FRANCISCO** are worth the effort required to get there, to escape the odd bit of pollution and occasional hassles. There's no public transport, so head in the direction of the airport, turn left just over the bridge, walk through the *bairro* and try hitching. This is most likely to be successful on a Saturday or Sunday morning. Take food and drink; there's nothing at the beach. The track scrapes across the island's southern corner, steep and rocky, and tips you out onto a flat sandy plain by the sea. There are several **beaches** to choose from. The first is the biggest, dotted with palms and a couple of villas built further back, but the furthest to the right (south) is the best, with steps for the arthritic President to climb down for his swims. There's clean sand, good waves and 10,000km of South Atlantic to gaze across.

Cidade Velha

Heading out of town in the opposite direction brings you to the old capital – Ribeira Grande – now known simply as **CIDADE VELHA**, Old City. This is just about Cape Verde's only ancient site and in truth, while the landscape around is magnificent, the ruins aren't wildly interesting. After the dry moors on the way from Praia, you round the last bend and the village is down below. The **setting** is all, a living, moving sea, awash with foam, thundering against the black crags.

Ribeira Grande was the site of the **first Portuguese base** in Africa, founded to create a slave-trading entrepôt, selling labour to the Spanish West Indies. The most notable building today is the **Cathedral**, finished in 1693, a century and a half after the foundation of the diocese. For a few years Ribeira Grande reached a peak of prestige, until its defeat by a French force in 1712 – using the same tactics as Drake (see box) – led to a rethink by the Portuguese and the more considered development of the new capital of Praia. The cathedral at Ribeira Grande was already falling apart by 1735 and

---

RIBEIRA GRANDE – CIDADE VELHA

A relatively good anchorage – there was nothing safer in Madeira or the Azores – **Ribeira Grande** rapidly became the main mid-Atlantic victualling point for European merchant vessels in the sixteenth century. The *ribeira* almost never dried up and was dammed at its mouth to provide a permanent pool of fresh **water**. The town became a "city" in 1533 when a papal bull made it the seat of a diocese extending along half the West African coast.

In Atlantic trading circles Ribeira Grande's reputation soon spread. The English sea dog **Sir Francis Drake** caught the scent in 1585 and attacked the settlement with a force of 1000. It was not an unplanned assault – the union of Spain and Portugal meant that Cape Verde was considered enemy territory by the English – and Drake landed at Praia to sneak overland and attack Ribeira Grande from behind. The town was deserted; the inhabitants had sensibly fled inland. Drake's crew stayed a fortnight, plundering what little there was and foraying into the interior without reward. One of the force was killed and mutilated by African slaves and Drake torched Ribeira Grande in reprisal, sparing only the hospital – the *Casa Misericorde* – whose ruins are still visible to the right as you descend into the centre of the present-day village.

---

when a new bishop was appointed in 1754 he quickly left Santiago and spent the rest of his life on Santo Antão.

Nowadays Cidade Velha is badly neglected, a village of fishing people and farmers living among the ruins of sixteenth- and seventeenth-century Portugal. As the Praia town plan points out in its notes: "Birthplace of our nationality, one can find valuable patrimonial witnesses still in ruins, thus deserving restoration, good keeping and consolidation". Deserving or not, it sems that in sad reality what Drake started will be finished off within twenty years if nothing is done to prevent further collapse. Pigs and goats forage amid the fallen masonry of the cathedral and you're quite free to wander with them between the massive, roofless walls.

It's really more interesting, however, to go down to the ribeira and scramble up the other side, through cane and corn and under mango trees, to further, less explored ruins – the church of Nossa Senhora do Rosário which served as a cathedral in miniature when the diocese was first created, and the Capuchin **Monastery of São Francisco** higher up the valley. Once up there, you can admire the palm-filled valley and muse on what five centuries of Portuguese rule have brought, and taken from, the islands. When the first buildings were put up the treeless scene must have had much the barren cast of a tropical Iona: all the trees have been established since that time. Today, you're likely to come across sugar cane presses and *grog* stills as you climb through the jungly allotments – the aroma is unmissable.

Out on the southernmost cliffs, the boldest attempt at preserving the religious and military ruins in their dramatic settings has been made by a restaurateur. For better or worse, the one-time *Forte São João* is now the very picturesque *Mirimar Restaurant* with haphazard cannons on the terraces. It's empty during the week, but thronged every weekend.

Down in the town *praça* is Cidade Velha's most famous relic, the **pelourinho** or pillory, where captives were shackled on display. Today the village is mostly populated by grizzled old rustics: there are one or two general shops but no signs of anything to do with *turismo*. Though the large fleet of red fishing boats on the beach indicates more activity than you'd at first think, most of the young have moved to the mini-metropolis of Praia only twenty minutes away.

Getting back yourself can be a little problematic if you don't feel like waiting for the next bus. But you can easily fill the time drinking *grog* with the elders down in one of the village stores or, if you manage to avoid that, hiking back up the rather magnificent

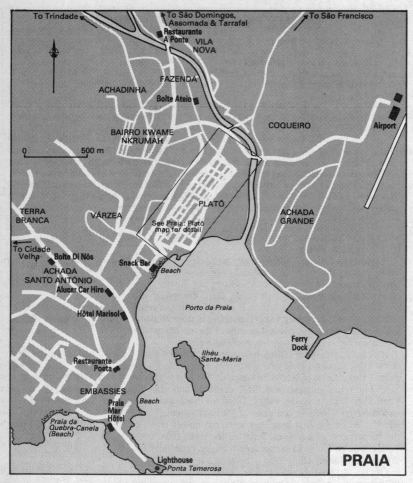

descent into town and cutting back to the left, to look over the extensive remains of the **Fortaleza Real de São Filipe** which dominates the whole of Cidade Velha from on high. Let us know if it's interesting – grogginess prevented a proper visit.

São Domingos

There's no great reason to visit **SÃO DOMINGOS**, but it's worth it for the immensely pretty **journey** – only half an hour from Praia – which takes you rapidly from the trashy outskirts of the capital into the heartland of rural Santiago. The bus plunges into deep valleys, dodging low-hanging trees. Straight-backed women grind corn with a boulder against a flat rock (a *pilão*); pigs root at the roadside; be-satchelled children walk home from school. São Domingos itself is one of the earliest settlements on the island, over 450 years old: its church has a famous boat-shaped pulpit. Drake ventured this far in

1585 and, finding the settlement abandoned like Ribeira Grande, thought better of continuing into the wild interior. There's a *pousada* here – the *Bela Vista* – which might be open for your visit. It would be a delightful place to stay, in the floor of the valley and surrounded by irrigated cultivation. Check out also the *Morenas* bar and restaurant.

The Assomada Baobab

En route to Tarrafal, if you've time and inclination, you can break your journey at ASSOMADA. The town is the second largest on the island – an interesting, lively place with a fine market and some quaint old architecture – and there should be no problem finding a place for the night here if you decide to stay. If you've only an hour or two, though, take a short walk out of town (north) and a turning right, then a steep path down into the *ribeira* to see what must be a contender for the **biggest baobab in the world**. Ask for BOA ENTRADA, the village tucked in the *ribeira*. You can't fail to see the tree standing on the slope across the valley: it's a monster.

Occasionally you'll come across postcards of this colossal baobab which make it look impossibly huge, with tiny doll-like figures at the base of a thing the size of a cathedral. It really is gargantuan. The trunk – over fifty metres round at the base – is a maze of contorted buttresses, and the massive branches are themselves the size of large trees. Towering two or three times as high as anything else, it would stand out anywhere, but in Cape Verde, land of limited leafiness, it's a fantastic sight, though frustratingly hard to get a photo that does justice to its mighty bulk. The tree has a venerable significance that surpasses mere size, and must be as old as the first generation of settlers. In 1855, according to a Rev. Thomas, chaplain to the African Squadron of the US Navy, it was "forty feet in circumference" and had been "standing where it now stands when the island was first discovered".

North and East Santiago

The main reason to go north is to visit **Tarrafal**, a beautiful fishing village that makes an ideal spot to rest up for a few days. It's right at the opposite end of Santiago from Praia, and there are two different bus routes that go there – one over the rugged spine of the island, the other along the indented east coast. The journey can make a very satisfying round trip.

The mountain route goes straight across an unexpectedly fairy-tale interior – peaks and rocky needles, soaring valleys, narrow terraces and ridges; a fine route, especially during or after the rains. There are steep climbs and some great views before ASSOMADA, then higher passes in the Malagueta range, rising to 1400m. You pass a point where you can see both coasts of the island and then, often driving through the mist of clouds at this altitude, you emerge with the broad sweep of the northwest slope in front of you, and a 10km descent on the grumbling cobbles to the sea.

Heading north by the **east coast route** you follow the same road out of Praia, then cut right at the Ribeirão Chiqueiro junction, with the village of **PRAIA BAIXA** tantalisingly visible out on the coast (three buses a day go there from Praia: it rates *Interesse Turisitico* and *Beach* symbols on the Santiago tourist map but the road is terrible, the beach uninviting and the whole area depressing). The first village you come to on the road is **PEDRO BADEJO**, with a magnificent **coconut** grove marking the entrance to the settlement and gigantic bananas on sale – if you're lucky – when the bus briefly stops. You can see *pedreiros* making cobbles here (CV$3.50), each shaded under a banana leaf on the cliff-top. It's all very floral and pleasant, with good beaches and caves, but there are no pensões. If you want to stay, make first for the *Restaurante Falucho*, order some *mariscos*, and take it from there.

CALHETA, the next stop, has a big old church on the hilltop. The dependence on rainfall in the Cape Verdes comes home to you as the road repeatedly drops to cross stoney *ribeiras* where women wash clothes in the narrow streams: when water is about, the flanks of the gulches are dense with crops – bananas, papayas, cane and cassava – and heavy rains can also bring floods that smash the cobbles in many places.

Tarrafal

TARRAFAL doesn't look much at first. You have to go right through the small town to discover the wonderful, clean white beach below its gentle cliffs. Once the site of a political prison under the Portuguese, this **beach** is now Tarrafal's main claim to fame. A restaurant sits, more or less perfectly, on a bluff above it, with palms and discreet beach houses to one side and a working fishing town atmosphere on the other. You're bound to want to stay.

Accommodation is easily fixed. Speak to the people at the restaurant and you can stay in one of the bungalows. They have big bed-living rooms with basic furniture, kitchens and bathrooms, plus electricity, water and gas – though these may well not be working. If the bungalows are full you can try the *TaTa Pensão* – to the left of the town centre, south of the market – which is perfectly OK but not half as attractive, or the row of rooms on the cliff top above the fishing beach, which some people prefer (keys for these from the *Secretaria*, the green building opposite the *mercado* on the main *praça*). Once installed it's all too easy to pass a few days – or even much longer – swimming and lounging, watching the fishing boats coming in and the children playing, drinking cold beers, and eating slabs of fresh tuna on the restaurant terrace.

The **town** has an attractive hibiscus-filled *praça* with church and marketplace (and bank, Mon–Fri 8am–noon) set traditionally around. There are one or two bars where you can drink *grog* and play *oril*. And check out the *Casa de Dona Cesário*, for discos and seafood. With the mountainous interior of the island looming behind, Tarrafal can seem incredibly isolated; yet a boy shooting down the cobbled hill on his shiny new American mountain bike is a reminder of close and important ties with the outside world. Except at weekends though, when Cape Verdean tourists and ex-patriate beach hunters zone in, it's marvellously peaceful. Walk south and you come to **further beaches** – of black sand – and more coconuts. Head north and a fine **coastal path** leads up over the cliffs above the crashing surf for as far as you like, with terrific views back. There are some tiny coves along here, with great natural swimming pools.

Fogo

First impressions of **FOGO** are of its tremendous mass – a brooding volcanic cone rising forbiddingly 2829m out of the sea. Arriving at **Mosteiros airstrip** on the dark northeast coast, the plane lands like a fly picking a spot on a black wall: the airstrip, about the size of two football pitches joined end to end, seems to occupy almost the only flattish space between the thrashing sea and sheer lava walls rising through clouds to the peak. The other airstrip, at São Filipe on the west coast (out of use for several years now), is equally precarious, perched high on the dunnish cliffs. Below it, a striking beach of baking black sand drops straight into ultramarine sea.

Although all the islands have their own distinguishing marks, it's Fogo which stands out as the great character of the Cape Verdes. It's impossible to forget you're on an active **volcano**: menacing vapours still drift from the crater. Fogo – which means "fire" – last had an eruption in 1951, when deluges of molten laval rock streamed down the steep eastern slopes. To the west, the land is gentler, the old volcanic base undisturbed by fresh explosions and cloaked, when there's been rain, by a pastoral blanket of wild flowers, low trees, farms and plantations.

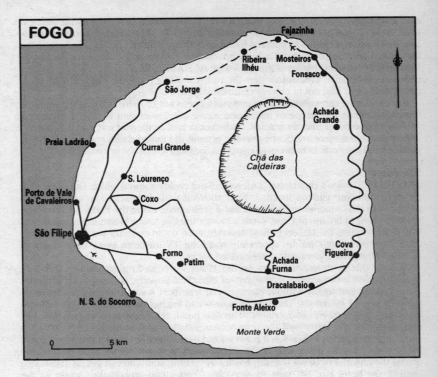

FOGO

Fajazinha

Ribeira Ilhéu · Mosteiros

Fonsaco

São Jorge

Achada Grande

Praia Ladrão

Curral Grande

Chã das Caldeiras

S. Lourenço

Porto de Vale de Cavaleiros

Coxo

São Filipe

Cova Figueira

Forno · Patim

Achada Furna

Dracalabaio

N. S. do Socorro

Fonte Aleixo

Monte Verde

0   5 km

Around the island to São Filipe

Fogo has no *Transcor* service. There used to be a bus but it was always in Praia being repaired: last time it failed to return. **Transport** therefore depends on *aluguers* and the occasional private vehicle. The south road between Mosteiros and São Filipe is the only one on which you're at all likely to get transport.

Arriving by air at **MOSTEIROS** ("Monastery") you'll normally have to walk a couple of kilometres to IGREJA ("Church") which is the nearest thing to a town centre in this part of the island. An ordinary *carrinho* ride to São Filipe shouldn't cost more than CV$600, but it's as well to know that a *particular* could cost ten times as much. If the airstrip there is open, it's probably easier to arrive and depart from São Filipe, but try to catch the spectacular eastern side of Fogo at some time if you can.

Heading **anticlockwise** out of Mosteiros, there's a breathtaking road up to the hamlet of RIBEIRA ILHEU, terrifyingly steep if you're in a vehicle. Scarcity of lifts aside, this is really worth a walk – allow a day to climb the 15km – which rewards you with stunning views, sheltered and overgrown little valleys, and a village where your arrival will cause a minor sensation. Once committed, you'll probably have to continue on foot, covering the worst portion of the round-island road, another 10km or so, as far as São Jorge, where you might (with luck) find transport on to São Filipe.

Travelling clockwise, you climb quickly from Mosteiros and skirt beneath the crater walls over a battlefield of strewn lava. The road runs high in places (looking out to sea there are clouds below the horizon and, with a fast driver, it's not a journey you'll ever forget: the cobbled highway traverses the cinder slopes in an unnerving series of undefended loops hundreds of metres above the waves. The isolated **settlements** of lava block houses have a temporary look about them – there's a menacing slag-heap darkness here. Surprisingly, it's high up on this eastern side that most of Fogo's famous (but dreadful) **coffee** is grown. And at ACHADA GRANDE there's a new experiment in cooperative **viticulture**: but the red wine they produce, although potent, is rather acidic and said not to be very commercial just yet.

Once the road curves **west** the countryside opens out to more relaxing dimensions; a mellow, rolling landscape of maize and agave takes over and there's a surprising amount of tree cover, mostly acacias. In the pockets of fertile volcanic soil that haven't been rainwashed there are beans growing around the maize stalks and squash, sweet potatoes and cucumbers between. Bananas, a Santiago speciality, are much scarcer.

São Filipe

SÃO FILIPE, Fogo's capital, has a nicely laid-out civility about it which sits oddly with its steeply sloping cliff-top location, high above the black beach. The streets link a number of small squares and gardens and a promenade along the cliffs. All São Filipe seems to lack to be one of Cape Verde's most attractive towns is sufficient population. It is deathly quiet, the streets almost deserted even on an ordinary weekday morning. After dark everyone's inside, apparently watching TV: through every open doorway there's a blue glow and a stack of silhouetted backs.

At least this is an improvement on the 1930s when an English visitor, Archibald Lyall, reported a community in the grip of diabolical poverty, isolated from Praia, let alone Lisbon, and totally without electricity or transport – small, shaggy horses were the only way to get about. The lack of **hotels** and **eating houses** that Lyall suffered hasn't altogether been put to rights. The one hotel, the *Xaguate*, is reasonably well organised, but it's pretty well the only accommodation and, at nearly CV$2000 for a single, more expensive than you'd hope for out here. They've found a good spot for it, though, over on the other side of the *ribeira* from the town centre, with good views across the channel to Brava – which blocks the setting sun. You can get an acceptable meal at the hotel too, but your money might better end up with the owner of the *Restaurant Vulção* whose wife provides enormous heaps of Cape Verdean food – heavy vegetable soups, rice, beans and squash, pork or tuna, sweet potatoes. A big cassette player gets turned on for your benefit every evening with extravagantly appropriate Cape Verdean laments to match the food and the sultry evening mood.

The atmosphere in São Filipe is always easy-going, though there are usually scuffles of excitement when a big tuna is hauled up to be portioned and sold off in the street. But **what to do** around town? Strolling through the near-deserted streets has its own quiet satisfaction: there are some fine old nineteenth-century houses and any number of small *praças* to sit in. You could also wander over to the hotel and see if there's any water in the **swimming pool** (unlikely as it's rationed).

Three or four kilometres north is PORTO DE VALE DE CAVALEIROS, where the boats come in. The walk down there is unremarkable and only the cove and mole even make the place a port. Slightly superior, for recreation, is a wander up to the airstrip a couple of kilometres south – which has been undergoing regrading for some years now – and then a bit of a scrambled **trek down the cliffs** (heading right, through a great deal of grass whose lancet seeds burrow into clothes and skin) past the ruins of a tiny church, down to a *ribeira*, where you can join a path to the beach and some fish processing works.

The **beach** itself is great if you're in the mood: a steep shelf of black sand – ferociously hot – with big waves breaking, seemingly without any fetch, directly onto it. You dive into them from the beach.

Heading back to town, take the fishermen's path and look out for the building, with arms hanging out between bars, on the cliff's very edge – São Filipe's **prison**. You'll be scolded by the guards if you engage in shouted exchanges of greetings with the prisoners across the gully. It's a mournfully picturesque spot to be jailed, gazing out across the channel to Brava and the Atlantic.

São Filipe shortlist

Aluguers From a small, mercifully shady *praça* in the centre of town.

Bank Mon–Fri 8am–noon & 2.30–4pm.

CTT Keeps similar hours.

Discoteca Open Saturday nights or on special occasions.

Electricity and water None after midnight.

Mercado Municipal A very small all-purpose market selection.

TACV the office (☎61.12.12/61.14.74) is often open during the day. Don't forget to reconfirm your flight back from Mosteiros or São Filipe – it's easy to get stranded on Fogo.

INTER-ISLAND FLIGHTS FROM MOSTEIROS

Praia: 4–6 flights weekly, 30 min.   SãoVicente: Monday, 1hr.

TACV in Mosteiros ☎61.21.21

Exploring the Volcano

If you do get left behind, accidentally or by design, the **VOLCANO** is a dominant and time-filling lure, though it's hard to **reach the crater**, and no less so for the islanders who live in it. If you ask taxi drivers about *particular* hire for the day you'll usually get quoted collossal figures – CV$6000 was one – because they genuinely don't want to do the trip: it's tremendously steep. The best plan is probably just to set off with some supplies and the time necessary to walk up if you have to. The main points of departure are ACHADA FURNA on the south side of the crater and CURRAL GRANDE on the northwest slope. You should be able to get a lift to Achada Furna – there are several *aluguers* each week from São Filipe. Once there, the crater rim is about 6km as the crow flies, but it's a 1500m climb (that's a gradient of one in four) and a good five or six hours' hike. Routes on the **north side** of the volcano are even less trafficked, if that's possible, the thirty-kilometre hike from São Filipe rolling up over some beautiful countryside to Curral Grande and the crater rim.

At the rim you may be lucky and have the whole eight-kilometre wide, 900-metre deep crater spread clearly before you, or you – and it – may be blotted out by thick cloud. Either way you'll now want to walk down **into the crater**, which is partly cultivated – the area known as CHÃ DAS CALDEIRAS. Many families in this district trace their descent from a Duc de Montrond who is said to have fled France in the nineteenth century after a duel – and thoughtfully brought vines with him. This moonscape of lava and scatterd mini craters is surmounted by the current **main cone** which rises in a cindery heap several hundred metres above the large crater floor. It's an exhausting scree-struggle to the summit, worth the effort if you have more than half a day of light left: views from the top in the right conditions can include the entire archipelago.

With lots of luck you'll have had a (rare) lift into the Chã das Caldeiras. If you're pretty fit you'll try to walk out the other side and then head off west, through the eucalyptus and conifer plantations via Curral Grande and back to São Filipe.

Lesser Sotaventos – Brava and Maio

BRAVA, the smallest inhabited island, has always been the most isolated of the Cape Verdes, properly settled only at the end of the seventeenth century after a major eruption of Fogo in 1675. Its capital, **NOVA SINTRA** – named after the royal resort of Sintra outside Lisbon – is rated one of the archipelago's loveliest towns, sedately arranged in a long-extinct crater high above the shoreline and the port of FURNA. Its stone walls overflow with lobelia and vines and clouds drift through even when the rest of the islands are parched with drought. "Mysterious" said a man on Sal, and "the most beautiful". Brava has lots of motorbikes and Cape Verde's best sunsets. Although its name means "wild", the island has long enjoyed a remarkable degree of domestication, with virtually all the land under neatly tended cultivation and the archipelago's highest population density. Bravans have a long sea-faring tradition: the American **whalers** called at this island more than any other, and the largest contingent of *americanos* comes from Brava. Sadly, much of the island's infrastructure was destroyed in 1982 by Hurricane Beryl.

Small enough to walk all over, but precipitous too, Brava is worth the **few days visit** you'll have to devote to it. This is because there's still no airstrip (1991?) and **ferry connections** are inconvenient: a boat leaves Praia Tuesday and Thursday night (Tuesday via São Filipe, Thursday direct to Brava) and Wednesday evening (direct). The channel between Fogo and Brava is notoriously rough – you may well want some seasickness pills.

Maio

MAIO was first sighted on May 1, 1460 – hence its name – but there's really nothing very spring-like about it. Early on, slaves were taken there to look after the livestock surplus of landowners on Santiago: they also produced butter. But historically, Maio was important as a **salt collecting** island. Vast quantities of evaporated sea salt – "huge heaps like drifts of snow" by Francis Drake's account – were available for the cost of the labour needed to load it on board ship. As that was often paid in old clothes or other unwanted items, the trade was a lucrative one. The English were largely in control of it and for a considerable period Maio, by Portuguese default, was in English hands.

Today, Maio is a godforsaken place, poor in agriculture, a neglected neighbour of weighty Santiago – where most of its young people soon migrate – and touristically a dead loss. It's not likely to be high on your list, but if you do take the **flight** from PRAIA (four a week: a twenty-dollar, twenty-minute hop) you're likely to be fêted as the first traveller they've seen for a while, and you'll find a place with a very distinct flavour, perhaps the least European of the Cape Verdes, with a relatively wooded, savannah-esque interior. There are no *pensões*, so you'll be looking for lodgings, or camping. To contact the *TACV* about flights back, phone Maio ☎61.33.33.

THE BARLAVENTOS

Internationally – at least in the English-speaking world – it's the **Barlaventos** that have drawn most attention to the Cape Verde islands. Among them, **São Vicente** stands out, the location of a British coal supply depot for over 100 years. Its capital, **Mindelo**, is now the **travel hub** of the Barlaventos and focus of most of what's happening, culturally, in the Cape Verdes. While the interior of the island is unbelievably waterless and barren, the town has a self-contained appeal that draws much on its evident **cosmopolitanism** and clear rivalry for civic pre-eminence with Praia.

To see Cape Verde at its most naturally glorious, hop across the channel from Mindelo for restorative **hiking** among the magnificent *ribeiras* of **Santo Antão**. The most northerly isle, Santo Antão is a splendid massif – comparable to Fogo but volcanically dormant – with an awesomely rugged interior.

São Nicolau is like a poor relation of Antão: its 400 years of human habitation seem to have been a dirge of destitution and fruitless toil and yet its town has the oldest educational and literary tradition in the country. It also offers more breathtaking scenery, as well as opportunities similar to Santo Antão's for determined walkers.

Sal, the aptly named "Salt" island, is now the site of Cape Verde's main international airport and, in an ironic neo-colonial twist, regular refuelling station for *South African Airways'* intercontinental flights. The only real reason to come here is for the **airport**, but if you happen to have time to kill there's a wonderful **beach** on the southern shore. The last of the Windward islands is **Boa Vista** – a flat island of the east. Boats call here so you may too, but once again the only possible reason to stop is for some excellent **beaches**.

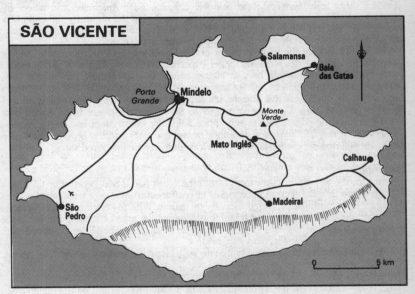

SÃO VICENTE

São Vicente – Mindelo and around

It's hard to avoid identifying **SÃO VICENTE** with its main town and indeed there's not a lot on the island that matters outside **Mindelo**. The one or two unexceptional "things to do" are best achieved by striking out from the town – there are no other significant centres of population on this hulk of moonscape.

The British had a long and influential connection with Mindelo as the operators of the **coaling station** there. From 1838 until the 1950s, Mindelo – or rather Porto Grande as the town was then called – grew from nothing to a major supply depot on the East Indies and South America runs. With the opening of the Suez canal in 1869 the shipping diminished and diesel eventually took over from coal. But by the end of World

War II, the hundred years of British presence had made some impact on the cultural life of the island. A number of English words were adopted into São Vicente Kriolu, including *blaqyefela* (blackfellow), *trôsa, ovacôte* (trousers and overcoat), *boi* (boy), *ariup* (hurry up), *djob, ovataime* (overtime) and, showing American influence, *sanababiche*.

English influence is still discernible in the architecture of some of the larger mansions. The British also introduced **cricket**, a game which no longer figures very prominently. There's still a team , however, and they still play occasionally.

Mindelo

A sense of identity has never been a problem for **MINDELO**. "Taken as a whole" thought Major A.B. Ellis of the 1st West India Regiment in 1873, "it is, perhaps, the most wretched and immoral town that I have ever seen". He stayed in the *Hotel Brasiliero* where a notice over the door proclaimed *Ici on parl Frances, Man spreucht Deutsch, Man spiks Ingleesh, Aqui se habla Español, Sabe American*, and where his room was invaded by a French farce of characters during the night. By the end of the nineteenth century, Mindelo's importance as a **coaling and victualling** station was at its peak, and less reputable ancillary industries were in top gear.

Today, while only the faintest traces of the bawdiness remain, this is the liveliest town in the Cape Verdes – and no longer especially wretched. Relatively well-provided with hotels, restaurants and bars, it buzzes contentedly after dark, its *praça* a noisy hang-out zone, its streets cheerfully animated. Mindelo is one of the few places where you can fairly often hear **live music**. It's still a small town, but it provokes good feelings in most visitors. Don't be surprised to find the atmosphere here tainted with hustle around the edges: yachts and cruise ships are intermittent and not infrequent callers (even the QE2 makes a stop once or twice a year) and the boys on the waterfront are still making escudos out of naive travellers in time-honoured ways.

Arriving

Flying in, the airstrip is 11km from town on a bleak flat at São Pedro. For CV$300 a taxi gets you to Mindelo past brave acres of **reafforestation** where windswept acacias struggle for a foothold, protected by rusty oil drums. With the *Shell* fuel-holding tanks and a strong scent of desert and trash, first appearances aren't encouraging, but these soon recede as you get into the town with its Portuguese buildings, restored pink Governor's residence and a palmy esplanade.

Arriving **by boat**, you've a twenty minute walk along the seafront to the town centre.

Hotels and places to eat

Hotels are a simple matter. The *Chave d'Ouro* (Golden Key), right on the main street, is the principal budget focus with big, airy rooms and a congenial atmosphere (CV$600/room nonS/C). Much more upmarket are the newish *Aparthotel Avenida* (CV$1500/1900) and the renovated *Hotel Porto Grande* on Praça Amilcar Cabral. Take your pick, but be warned: the front rooms at the *Porto Grande* are notoriously noisy, especially at weekends.

There are also a number of decent **restaurants** – though it's well to remember that many of them close once a week, usually on Sunday. The one in the *Chave d'Ouro* itself normally displays a suspicious emptiness, but the breakfasts there are especially nice compositions – goats' cheese, *doce* and the works. For main meals, one of the best value places is *Pica Pau* (Woodpecker): even if the bills are sometimes amazingly creative, the food is usually worth the bother. Go for seafood, not meat, or order the *Feijoada* in advance. Another recommended and even less pretentious eatery is the cheap and exellent *Bar-Restaurant 5 de Julho*. Check out also the *Café Loutcha*, 1km

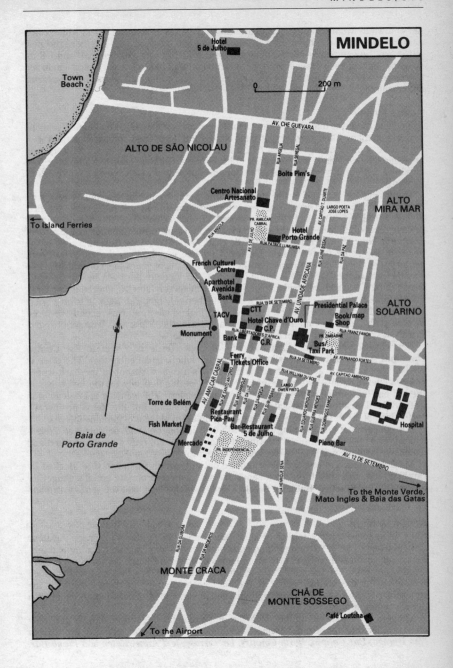

MINDELO

Town Beach

Hotel 5 de Julho

ALTO DE SÃO NICOLAU

AV. CHE GUEVARA

Boîte Pim's

To Island Ferries

Centro Nacional Artesanato

ALTO MIRA MAR

LARGO POETA JOSÉ LOPES

PR. AMILCAR CABRAL

Hotel Porto Grande

French Cultural Centre

Aparthotel Avenida

Bank

ALTO SOLARINO

RUA 19 DE SETEMBRO

CTT

TACV

Hotel Chave d'Ouro

C.P.

Monument

Presidential Palace

Book/map Shop

Bank

C.R.

PR. ZIMBABWE

Bus/ Taxi Park

RUA FRANZ FANON

AV. FERNANDO FORTES

Ferry Tickets Office

RUA 24 SETEMBRO

RUA WILLIAM DU BOIS

AV. CAPITÃO AMBROSIO

LARGO OWEN PINTO

Torre de Belém

Restaurant Pica-Pau

Fish Market

Bar-Restaurant 5 de Julho

Mercado

PR. INDEPENDENCIA

Baia de Porto Grande

Piano Bar

Hospital

AV. 12 DE SETEMBRO

To the Monte Verde, Mato Ingles & Baia das Gatas

MONTE CRACA

CHÃ DE MONTE SOSSEGO

Café Loutcha

To the Airport

0   200 m

out of town in Monte Sossego, related to the popular Cape Verdean eatery of the same name in Dakar. *O Cantinho*, also in Monte Sossego, is good too. Daytime, the best **cafés** are the competing hang-out spots *Portugal* and *Royale*, (marked CP and CR on the map), facing each other across the downtown Rua Libertadores d'Africa – unfussy, fast places where business types read *Voz di Povo*, and coffee and beers and *aguardente* are consumed.

Action by day

Mindelo is the town that Cape Verdeans resident abroad always go on about – perhaps because so many Cape Verde expatriates come from here – and compared with Praia it does have a more animated, less official feel. Helped along by the bay with its twin headlands, its esplanade and its clutter of backstreets, Mindelo feels like a holiday. The *carnaval* in February infects the town for the entire year, so it never entirely stops partying.

Exploring for yourself is the main daytime pursuit and the seafront provides an obvious anchor point. The unusual eagle-topped **monument** commemorates the first Lisbon–Rio air crossing, in 1922, by aviators Cabral and Coutinho, who spent a number of days recuperating in Mindelo after their 80mph leg from the Canaries in the airboat *Lusitania*. Nearby, the curious ornate little castle is the **Torre de Belem**, a copy of the tower of the same name outside Lisbon. That one was built in the early sixteenth century, the Cape Verdean replica in the 1920s. For many years the Torre at Mindelo was the seat of the Portuguese administator of São Vicente, but even before independence it had been abandoned and today it's a miserably smelly, shored-up and rat-infested structure which looks as if it's been deliberately ignored. Back in town a short way, the old **Governor's palace** has been well looked after and was recently restored in pale pink. Now a sometime Presidential Palace (the *Casa de Aristides*) to rival Praia's, it's clearly the object of considerable civic pride.

The closest you'll come to a museum in Cape Verde is a visit to the **Centro Nacional Artesanato** (open daily but closed for lunch, small entry fee). The place is divided into a display area and a shop, and there's also a workshop at the back where you're generally allowed to nose around: doubtless this depends on the behaviour of the last batch of cruise passengers or shore-leave sailors. The weaving is interesting to watch. The knick-knacks on sale aren't hugely appealing, but the items on display, particularly some of the pottery and tapestries, do seem old and of genuine interest.

For concerns of a consuming nature, Mindelo is about as well equipped as Praia – which means poorly – with a scattering of small **shops**, but only a poorly stocked and expensive produce market, hopeless on Saturdays and closed on Sundays.

Mindelo's **beach** is one scruffy kilometre out of town on the north side. Backed by rumbling industrial plant, the dark sands are somehow appropriate and it's altogether thoroughly unattractive. But it's a beach, it's reasonably clean, and the sea is warm and clear.

Action by night

After dark, social gravity sooner or later draws most people down to **Praça Amilcar Cabral** where a lot of excitement and somehow very Mediterranean courting and flirting go on, accompanied by enormous volumes of noise. Although Mindelo's youth are steadily deserting the town for Praia and further, it still holds a racy and sophisticated reputation for the young people of the Barlavento country hamlets. Sitting in the square is really fun: you'll quickly find yourself in some kind of conversation, tuning in to the evening grapevine.

Mindelo does have a number of *boites* and nightclubs. Though they're generally discos rather than **live music** venues, the following list is worth following up: *Galeria Nhõ Djunga, Bar Calipso, North Country, La Terrase, Je T'Aime, Katen* and *Piano Bar*.

The *Piano Bar*, down on Avenida 12 de Setembro, is recommended. Cesaria Evora sings there. And *Pims* on Rua N'Krumah is always hot and crowded. Apart from *morna*, you're most likely to come across variants of zouk, often with Senegalese influences. Unfortunately, and not surprisingly, successful singers and bands don't wait long before flying out to Lisbon where Cape Verdean audiences are larger than they would ever be in Mindelo.

Mindelo directory

Banks There are two: for changing money you want the one in the old building on Rua da Santo Antonio, south of Libertadores, open usual hours.

Boats The travel agency on the corner of Rua de Santo Antonio has tickets, timetables and a fair degree of patience.

Bookshops Try rua Franz Fanon, rua da Luz/rua N'Krumah and rua 19 de Setembro.

Car Hire You may not find *Alucar* on av 12 de Setembro. Try *Turicar* on rua do Douro, just south of the town centre. São Vicente is a good place to explore for a day by car.

CTT Mon–Fri 8am–noon & 2.30–5pm; Sat 8–11am & 3–5pm; Sun 9–11am.

Centre Culturel Français The French do work hard at their culture, even with no consulate. Worth visiting for books, mags, movies and events.

Consulates A strong team from the European Community: **Belgian**, av Marginal on the way to the port; **Danish**, Cais Acostavel near the port; **Dutch**, **Norwegian** and **Portuguese** all in rua Kwame N'Krumah; **German**, Alto Matiota past the beach; **Spanish** and **Swiss**, av 5 de Julho.

Film and photocopies *Photo Djibla*.

TACV A busy office (☎31.18.69/31.16.54/31.15.24). Availability on flights to Sal and Praia, notably those connecting with international departures, is often very bad. Plan ahead and remember to reconfirm everything.

Taxis Main ranks are in the obvious centre of town near the church (*Igreja*). Town rates are reasonable, island trips come much more expensive, but still not utterly unrealistic.

INTER-ISLAND FLIGHTS FROM MINDELO

Mosteiros (Fogo): Monday, 1hr.
Praia: 4–6 flights weekly, 1hr.
Sal: 1 flight most days, 50 min.

Porto do Sol (Santo Antão): Saturday, 25 min.
S. Nicolau: 2 a week, 30 min.

Out of town – Baia das Gatas and Monte Verde

If you don't venture **beyond the town limits** of Mindelo – wherever they are – you'll not be in a minority. The rest of the island is desperately arid, treeless for the most part and largely uninhabited – 95 percent of the 40,000 inhabitants live in the *povoação*.

For a break however, and really quite a nice **beach**, the twenty-minute drive to **Baia das Gatas** is a good trip. Transport is limited on São Vicente and you'll almost certainly have to hire a taxi unless you strike lucky, perhaps at the weekend, with a lift (walk out the length of av 12 de Setembro and wait where it bends). The cost of a taxi to Baia will depend on waiting time, as little as CV$700 for a quick dip, over CV$1000 for a prolonged lounge. It's something which is obviously cheaper and more fun if you can make a group. On Sundays, too, there's usually a bus that leaves at 9.30am and returns at 5.30pm. Baia, as it's commonly known (the reason for the *gatas* – cats – is unknown) is protected by a concrete mole and black boulders to break the thrashing surf. In the **lagoon**, the water is calm and delightfully transparent, though even with a mask there's not a lot to see. Beyond its confines the sea is more challenging and the combination of urchin covered rocks and the threat of sharks should be enough to put you off. There's a Sunday beach bar, weekend bungalows and an annual August **"Festival"** with plenty of music.

The road to Baia climbs steeply past the junction for **Monte Verde**, the dark mass commonly wreathed in clouds that rears up behind Mindelo, and the island's highest point. This too is worth an outing but it'll cost more because of the strain on the taxi: you'll need to set aside a full morning or afternoon of your time. The last section, rough in parts, gets to within a few hundred metres of the summit. It is, truly, a green mountain, covered in the once commercially important *orchil* lichen, used to produce brilliant scarlet and purple dyes. There can be stunning views down over Mindelo and Baia, but they're not to be counted on.

Further on, difficult roads lead southeast to CALHAU and due south to the island's most dramatic and isolated region, a fifteen-kilometre ridge (altitude 5–700m) paralleling the southern coast at a distance of just two or three kilometres, from which *ribeiras* plunge down to the sea.

Santo Antão

SANTO ANTÃO, the second largest of the Cape Verdes, is rugged and exciting, with the savage grandeur of a much bigger landmass and a tortoise shape cut into deep, arcing **ribeiras**. The island is also the last to suffer whenever a prolonged drought ravages the country, the northern slopes and valleys retaining a perennial verdure which is hard to believe after the desolation of Santiago and São Vicente.

But **communications** have always been difficult. The story goes that Bishop Jacinto Valente visited Santo Antão from Santiago in 1755. He crossed the island on foot and several times had to be hauled up precipices dangling from a rope. He eventually lost his nerve and had to stay put between a cliff and a chasm. The islanders went ahead, sent him back a tent and supplies, and began to construct a road for his rescue. A single **highway** now snakes up over the barren south face to edge between the peaks and abysses to the island's capital, Ribeira Grande on the north coast. Even as late as 1869, 300 years after it was first colonised, the Portuguese minister of colonies remarked that Santo Antão had "the appearance of an island that had only been discovered months ago".

Getting here today, you can **fly**, on a Saturday or Monday only, from Praia and Mindelo to the airport at Porta do Sol near Ribeira Grande. More convenient is the daily **ferry** from Mindelo to Porto Novo. The *Porto Novo* is built like a bath toy – short and proud – and, as the crossing between the islands can be surprisingly rough, you'd be wise to take seasickness tablets if you've ever suffered.

PORTO NOVO itself is an uneventful place which clearly subsists on the daily contact with Mindelo across the channel: a crowd is always down on the quay to welcome the boat. In times not so long past, it was from Santo Antão that Mindelo got almost all its drinking water – a lucrative trade that dried up with the withering of the coaling industry on São Vicente and the opening there of a desalination plant to provide fresh water.

A *Transcor* **bus** meets the ferry on its arrival and heads over the island to Ribeira Grande. Try to get a front seat on the right for the most heart-stopping views. Leaving Porto Novo (and, it appears, almost the only trees on this side of Santo Antão), the haul up the **south slope** of the island presents a pretty bleak picture to begin with: the neat and newly cobbled road snakes steeply through a lifeless mountain desert of tumbled volcanic rocks, bleached pale in the afternoon sun, the only vegetation the rows of cacti planted at the roadside. As the bus climbs, temperatures drop, views over Porto Novo become dramatic and, if it's a clear day, you can see São Vicente – a black mountain hanging, strangely, below the horizon.

But save your enthusiasm – and your film if you're snapping out of the window – for the descent down the northern side of the island. Approaching the crest, the road's contours relax as groves of coniferous trees and low herbage make an appearance. The **Casa Florestal** (Forest Station) is a sort of halfway house and, if you intend getting straight on with some serious hiking through the magnificent landscape further on, a convenient place to hop out.

Continuing by bus to the *povoação*, the landscape becomes one of competing superlatives as you sweep over the island's twisted spine and skirt the magnificent circumference of **Cova crater**. Clouds drift below the road, over the houses and sugar cane plots patched into the crater's collossal scoop. Repeatedly from this point on the bus veers over chasms of hundreds of sheer metres: immense volumes of sky and cloud open out beneath, with steep terraced slopes all around. Bishop Valente's vertigo was understandable; the scenery is awesome and even Cape Verdeans on the bus stand to gaze down – and cross themselves at the hairpins. Glimpsing the sea through the crags, it seems impossible the road can get down there in such a short distance. Indeed, even a few kilometres from the town, it tracks several hundred metres above the floor of the *ribeira*.

INTER-ISLAND FLIGHTS FROM SANTO ANTÃO (PORTO DO SOL)

Praia: Saturday, 85 min.   São Vicente, Saturday, 25 min.

TACV ☎21.18.14

Ribeira Grande town

With fortress-like cliffs and narrow streets, **RIBEIRA GRANDE** feels like a mountain town lost in a huge range, the slightly forbidding atmosphere quickly compelling and not easily forgotten. The town perches at the *ribeira*'s mouth, a cluster of close and shady houses, hemmed in by cliffs rising behind and the dark sea lashing a shingly beach. A broad *praça* fronts the Igreja de Nossa Senhora do Rosário, the formidable church intended, at one time in the eighteenth century, to be the cathedral of Cape Verde. There's a scattering of *pensões*, one or two restaurants, as well as CTT, bank and even a disco.

Finding a **place to stay** is simple, with two cheap *pensões*, the *5 de Julho* – newish and clean but rather gloomy – and the *Casa Melo*, a little cheaper at CV$700/double. Aramando Melo, the owner of the latter, will help you with your travel plans. There may also be a new, five-storey place by now. **Food-wise**, the town doesn't have a lot to offer, though the family at *Casa Melo* will come up with wholesome fare on a fresh white tablecloth if you ask. Or try the *Progreso*, which has a very solicitous owner and a nice patio dining area. Meals there are CV$300–350 with lobster at CV$500.

After dark you'll quickly track down the disco if it's still operating – and if that one isn't then another is bound to be, such is the enthusiasm of the town's teenagers. The place may well be a converted front room but the entrance fee is small, the music – mostly zouk – eminently danceable and the atmosphere ringing. A balcony gives out over the street, where on our visit a second centre of attention focused around a couple of wandering guitarists carousing under a breadfruit tree. On a moonlit night it's delightfully atmospheric and fun.

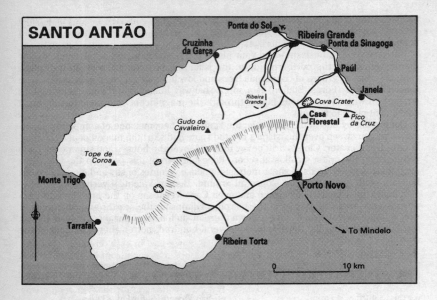

Hiking up the Ribeiras

However, the most compelling objectives are rural, not urban. Ideally, with time and energy for several days' **hiking**, you've the chance to explore all three big **ribeiras** of eastern Santo Antão – Grande, Paúl and Janela ("Big", "Swamp" and "Window").

Ribeira do Paúl is the most beautiful and densely planted of the three. Get there by finding a lift, 10km along the coast road (watch out for falling rocks). Accommodation can be fixed up through the bar/shopkeeper in Paúl, whose wife will send down very good local cooking from the kitchen higher up the *ribeira*. You can arrange a car (or if lucky a free lift) up the ribeira, but walking is wonderful. It's a riot of vegetation and, at Passagem, some 4km from Paul, there's a kind of tropical garden with a **swimming pool** and café open at weekends (CV$50).

The **hike up Ribeira Grande**, a solid morning's worth, deserves an early start and a minimum of gear – if possible simply drinking water and camera. If you're heading back to Porto Novo for the same day's ferry, then in the dry season you should take the **bus** which rattles up the *ribeira* for a few kilometres: during or after the rains, only the occasional *paragem* signs painted on the rocks indicate a bus ever comes this way, and the route has to be rebuilt every season. The owner of the *Pensão Casa Melo* is often willing to rent his car as a *taxi particular* for the day, loading your gear in the back to meet you on the road at the head of the *ribeira* and then driving you down to Porto Novo or back to Ribeira Grande town. You should expect to pay around CV$2000 for this.

If you're lucky you will see the *ribeira* cloaked in green, but unfortunately it can't be guaranteed. We hiked up the Ribeira Grande one October morning after recent heavy rains. The dirt road was slashed by a fast flowing **stream**; pools had collected big enough for children to play diving and jumping games, possible only briefly every year. Up both sides of the valley, a hothouse jungle of **cultivation** steamed in the morning sun, broken by grey stone and pastel-painted houses: on the lower slopes grew sugar cane, coconut palms, cassava and bananas, breadfruit and papaya trees, and higher up on table-sized terraces maize, beans and potatoes – sweet and Irish – were cultivated.

The route towards the trans-island road takes a left turn after a couple of flat kilometres and begins a gentle ascent. An hour from town a cobbled road drives up the valley side away from the floor and the **real climb** begins. A hamlet of cliff-clinging farm houses begins around here; there's a small shop with cold drinks and, with rain, water pipes to replenish your supply. For an hour the path creeps higher, through the same, elongated village, a riot of poinsettia and potted plants at the right time of year. People are amused to see hikers, though not completely unused to the idea – the French organisation *Le Point* ran some experimental hiking holidays a few years back, which had to cease because of the extreme drought. As the heat builds, the route becomes increasingly tough and, leaving the last houses of the village behind, finally tracks up a near vertical salient of cliff at the head of the *ribeira*. A slog, but an awe-inspiring one, follows as every twenty paces gives new and better views across the breathless vista beneath you. Houses on the lower slopes lose their dimensions as the distant contours flatten and then disappear.

Towards the top the air chills. Clouds form and drift across the canyon. There are few animals – nimble goats and the odd piglet – but no wildlife apart from small skinks flashing over the rocks and the occasional wheeling black and white eagle. Cape Verdeans, often barefoot and with heads loaded, hurry past in both directions, but one old man paused to inspect us and to offer hunks of sugar cane from his dual purpose snack and staff: a rod of the stuff, freshly cut, is probably the best sustenance to take with you.

From the impressive **summit**, where the curved horizon on the sea seems way below you, the path leads clearly on, over a rounded hillocky landscape, until it meets a dirt road leading to the tarmac in an hour or so. This hike requires the best part of a day but, if you leave by 8am and don't break too often, you can be up at the road by early afternoon.

Deserted islets: Santa Luzia, Ilhéu Branco and Ilhéu Razo

Three desert islands line up in the lee of São Vicente. The biggest, **Santa Luzia**, had a bit of a population towards the end of the eighteenth century – mostly destitute farmers from São Nicolau – but successive droughts and an impossibly harsh terrain expelled them. A more recent inhabitant was the "Governor of Santa Luzia", Francisco Antonio da Cruz, who fled there from his wife and eighteen offspring and lived as a hermit for a number of years. It's now deserted again and, unless you make special efforts by boat, out of reach. Charles Darwin called here in "The Beagle". Herpetologists know Santa Luzia as the only habitat of a large, herbivorous lizard – though it seems likely that it's extinct.

Ilhéu Branco is more of a rock, white (hence the name) from the guano deposits of generations of seabirds, and rising sheer from the sea. Its shape is supposed to resemble a ship at anchor. Ships avoid its dangerous approaches and, if you're sailing between Mindelo and São Nicolau, you're likely to get a good view of the **dolphins** which are often seen on this leg. **Flying fish** are common too – skittering things the size of a seagull which streak above the surface for several seconds at amazingly high speed.

By the time you reach **Ilhéu Razo**, you can see the jagged, cloud-protected silhouette of SÃO NICOLAU. Razo is famous – among ornithologists and conservationists – for the **Razo Island Lark**, a dun, ordinary lark that, perversely, nests only on this barren slab. The Razo lark has an extra strong beak for digging up the grubs it feeds on. It should survive until population pressure and a solution to the problem of drought bring the first human colonists to the island.

São Nicolau

Like the peaks of a submerged mountain, **SÃO NICOLAU** rises from the ocean between São Vicente and Sal. Of its **beauty** – an elegant, hatchet-shaped trio of ridges meeting in spectacular summits above the hidden capital of RIBEIRA BRAVA – there's no doubt. But the cruelly desolate slopes (this is the driest of the "agricultural" islands) testify to a history of extraordinary hardship – eternal isolation, migration and desertion.

The problem, as ever, is **water**, or chronic lack of it. In recent years efforts have been made to tap the deep underground water table – notably with the help of French *cooperants* – and a number of dams are planned, but the legacy of centuries of neglect lives on and the **drift away** from the island is continuous.

Arriving by ship at **TARRAFAL**, the island's main port, none of this meld of destitution and scenic splendour is immediately obvious. The shallow bay (giving you the chance to help the local economy by paying exorbitantly to be ferried ashore by lighter) gives on to the largest region of relatively gentle terrain on São Nicolau, from where the spectacle of the interior isn't apparent. The evident **poverty** of the village – despite the important tuna canning plant of the *Sociedade Ultramarina de Conservas* and a relative bustle about the gritty, workaday beach – isn't encouraging, but the warmth of the welcome at the *casa de pasto* and the generosity of the meals don't really signal a community under siege.

It's only when you get a lift **out of Tarrafal** to the capital that, driving through the southern countryside, you notice virtually every other house is abandoned: and between the deserted shacks lie the ruins of older dwellings, left in earlier famines. With the rains of 1987, the situation was improving; corn, planted every year, was actually growing, and water flowed from village pumps.

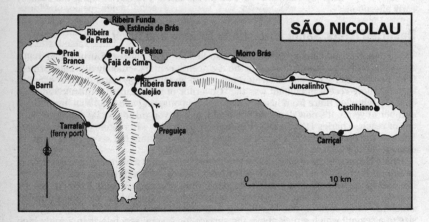

Practicalities and island sightseeing

São Nicolau is a good place to have transport of your own. If, as is likely enough, you haven't – and don't have unlimited time on the island either – you should make efforts to fix something up straightaway; the island has no bus. Certainly, if you're only here while the ferry is in port you should aim to get the first transport up to Ribeira Brava (shared *carrinhos* should charge about CV$100, chartered taxis about CV$1800) failing which a day spent waiting for the next vehicle, under the shade at the pump, is really a day wasted.

Flying in, the airstrip is just 4km from Ribeira Brava (midway between the town and the other port of PREGUIÇA), and you'll likely get a taxi into town anyway (around CV\$400). There are flights from Sal (daily except Sundays), from Praia (Wednesday, Thursday and Friday) and from Mindelo (Monday, Tuesday and Saturday).

If you get stuck at Tarrafal, you'll soon locate the good *casa de pasto* along the shore to the left of the jetty: **rooms** are also available for the asking, from Jose Gaida, and there's apparently a new *pensão* (the *Italiano*) and various tourist projects (big game fishing for example) underway.

Tarrafal's main activity is **tuna fishing** and while you'll see the great beasts hauled up on many a Cape Verdean beach, the evening business at Tarrafal seems to yield some particularly spectacular specimens, many as big as a person. People are quite happy to have you watching as the fish are wheeled into the co-op on wagons, to reappear in cans. You can also join the kids on the **swimming beach** – the hot grey sands of which are said to be good for rheumatism. A few kilometres further north, towards Barril, there are much better beaches, safe and worth snorkelling, among them the little white sand cove of Praia das Francêses.

Over the island spine

The 26km of nearly deserted cobblestone **between Tarrafal and Ribeira Brava** is another of Cape Verde's scenically outstanding routes. After a steady and satisfying pull away from the broad, southwest bay and up to around 800m, the road takes a sudden and breathtaking swing to the left and within seconds is skating above the fractured bowl of the **island's north side**. Going **by foot** from here is a good plan: there's a steep track down to the nest of the town, an hour or two's knee-wobbling on foot – negotiable also by bike they say – or, with the day before you, take the gentler descent along the main road, incised into the cliff, with the soaring needle peaks of **Monte Gordo** dominating the skyline. During the late summer months this – the *Fajãs* – can be a fabulously beautiful valley, spilling with green from the concerted efforts of farmers and hydrologists, dashed with colour from briefly flowering plants, spiked with the strange shapes of **dragon trees** – drought-resistant Nicolauan peculiarities. Behind, trailers of cloud float past the spires of Monte Gordo – higher, thinner, pointier and more Gothic than anywhere else. In front, the road winds down past the hamlets and farm plots towards a deep blue North Atlantic. Incomparable as it is, the notion of a tropical west coast of Ireland comes irresistibly forward. The walk, about 15km from the peaks down to the town via a swerving series of deep rents along the north coast, is enchanting.

Ribeira Brava

RIBEIRA BRAVA, facing out to sea on the north side, is firmly Portuguese in feel and rapidly dissolves any Hibernian associations. A delightfully pretty mesh of narrow streets and whitewash, nestled deep between towering crags, it was established in the seventeenth century, about as far inland as possible, in order to resist the attacks of pirates.

The big, sky-blue **parish church** here, the *Igreja Matriz*, was the Cape Verdean see until the twentieth century. It's supposed to hold a small museum of religious bits and pieces, among them a valuable and unusual sixteenth-century golden chalice, but it rarely seems to be open. You've a better chance at the **seminary**, a little way up the *ribeira*, which once provided a classical education for students from all over the islands. Here there's a library and reliquary attached to the chapel, and you should be able to persuade the priest to let you in. Back in town there's a fine *praça* and town hall with neatly tended gardens in front, and a memorial bust to a much loved doctor – Júlio

José Dias (1876). The site of the town hall was the birthplace in 1872 of José Lopes da Silva, a leading Cape Verdean poet. Down on the bank of the *ribeira* a shady, second *praça* hides a café and tables for serious draughts-playing and *grog* imbibing. All rather obscure attractions perhaps, but they're central to the town's appeal: Ribeira Brava, once the flourishing centre of academic and literary life in Cape Verde, quickly establishes its remote, insular identity and would be a rewarding place to while away a few days. Check out the *Bar-Restaurant Sila*, over the bridge, which has a few **rooms** for CV$600/800. Ribeira Brava also has a bank, CTT, a small *mercado* and two or three basic general stores. You may even stumble across a workshop manufacturing cups and utensils – functional and miniature – out of bamboo; a tiny part of a tiny souvenir industry. It's not enough to keep many younger people here and the flight to Mindelo, Praia and abroad is unceasing.

To get to the **rest of the island** you'll need to find someone who's driving. One of the few available Land Rovers is sometimes hired out (with owner) for around CV$4000 per day, but it's almost worth the expense for the pleasure of being able to offer lifts to dozens of otherwise stranded Nicolauans as you go.

The communities of the north west – BARRIL, PRAIA BRANCA and RIBEIRA DE PRATA – are only accessible **by track** back through Tarrafal, though you could explore the possibility of **hiking** round via the north coast fishing villages of ESTANCIA DE BRÁS and RIBEIRA FUNDA, only a few kilometres from the main road. The western road is planned to become a complete loop in the near future.

Looking east, the long axis of the island stretches 30km, narrowing at one point to less than three kilometres across. There are two principal tracks – a "ridgeway" and a north coast path – which meet high above the harbour of CARRIÇAL. You'll need to be fit and determined to hike out here – supplies are far between and very few.

INTER-ISLAND FLIGHTS FROM SÃO NICOLAU

Praia: 4–6 flights weekly, 1hr. São Vicente: 3 flights weekly, 30 min.
Sal: 5 flights weekly, 45 min.

TACV ☎31.47.24

Ilha do Sal

The Island of Salt, or just plain **SAL**, a piece of Sahara in the middle of the ocean – a real desert island and no coconuts – is the least inviting of the archipelago. Relentlessly windy and mostly flat, it's a good location for Cape Verde's main international **airport**. The majority of islanders seem to be involved with this in some way – or in the military base nearby – and the old salt-based economy looks pretty defunct. Whether you fly in from Europe or just have the good fortune to pass through during boat or plane connection, there's a high chance you'll sample Sal sooner or later. Attractions are simple to list – one beautiful white **beach**, which you're recommended to aim for without delay. There's honestly nothing else worth a pause.

Sal was one of the last islands to be colonised, early in the nineteenth century, when the Portuguese began to exploit its **salt** ponds properly and introduced purification techniques. In earlier centuries, vast heaps of salt could be loaded onto ships for the cost of the labour alone, though since it was full of donkey shit it was considered low-grade even then. Sal's salt was picked up by trawlers from England on their way to North Atlantic fishing grounds, and exported to the Newfoundland fishing towns and later to Brazil for beef preservation.

Espargos – the town

Arriving by boat you enter a drab grey bay – PALMEIRA harbour – and have to wait for a lift to **ESPARGOS**, the main urbanisation (town sounds too characterful) on the island, a couple of kilometres away. If nothing shows you might as well start walking; it's all pretty forlorn and there's unlikely to be a vehicle around anyway.

Espargos is thoroughly uninspiring – a small market, a few groceries, two or three *pensões* and a couple of bar/cafés. Sand whistles across the road, and it's hard to believe that anyone would choose to live here. If you have to stay, the *Casa Angela*'s plain and simple rooms are your best target (CV$700 non S/C) and Angela Virginia dos Santos a good-humoured hostess. There are decent evening meals for CV$400–500. The *Residencial Central* – new, rather flashy, with more rooms in construction – seems oddly inappropriate, but maybe they're expecting a tourist boom. Rooms are CV$1000–1300 S/C and you may get a good cup of coffee in the bar: the food is fairly priced. For coffee and patisseries, you could also try the *Salão Guadaloupe Café* just up from the market.

For whatever reason you're here, it's nice to get out of the town. You can do this quickly – and perhaps illicitly, so don't stop to ask anyone – by climbing to the summit of the **telecommunications hill** just five minutes' walk from the *praça*. From up there behind the dishes you have a good view of the entire, drab island; to the north a number of old volcanic hills; southwards the bleak brown wastelands fading away to the fringe of white beach at SANTA MARIA.

Send your postcards from Espargos (the CTT is an unmarked pink mansion in the middle of town; quickest mail to the outside world) and then see about transport down **to the beach**. You might catch an *aluguer* anywhere, or likely as not a free lift if you take time to walk down to the turn-off for the **airport**. This, surprisingly modern and together (in case you had any consumerist yearnings), bursts into life only when an international flight is in. Expect no fast-food joints or magazine stands. **Airline offices** – *SAA*, *Aeroflot* (☎41.11.80), *TAP* (☎41.12.55), *TAAG*, *Cubana* and *TACV* – are scattered around the tarmac.

Santa Maria – the resort

The short trip down to the south coast is a journey through a real desert, where encirclement by sea, rather than offering relief, merely seems to stress the land's dessication. **Goats**, apparently surviving off rubbish, are about the only animals you'll see: their introduction in the seventeenth and eighteenth century, before any significant human settlement, began a process of **soil destruction** which is now virtually complete. Nothing really grows, wild or cultivated. It all looks like it's just been scoured by bulldozers.

SANTA MARIA DAS DORES (St Mary of Sorrows) is practically a ghost town, though not without a desolate fascination. Ruined timber buildings in ornate style are scattered across the flats, linked by the twisted remains of a narrow gauge railway that once shifted tuna for the Portuguese and goes out to the end of the thoroughly unsafe jetty.

But the historical interest is slight. The pull is the heady shade of the *Morabeza Hotel* and the stunning flex of white sand dipping into glassy blue-green waves. The hotel is not a cheap place to stay (rooms around the CV$4000 mark) but they've a real **restaurant** with fresh salads and other surprising edibles (CV$400 and up) and there's a wide range of water sports including **windsurfing,** for which the resort is acquiring something of a reputation. Call in and you'll soon get the, unlikely, picture – *South African Airways* crews taking time out by the pool. It's a curious place to hang out for an hour or two because most of the remaining guests are made up of crews from

Cubana, Aeroflot and *Angolan Airlines* all doing the same, though it's clear that *SAA* keep to themselves. Cape Verdean reliance on South African payments would, you'd think, be a ticklish embarrassment to the socialist, popular liberation government in its relations with its Lusophone cultural and political allies in Angola and Mozambique. With the rand at the top of the the hotel reception's currency exchange list however, perhaps the pill of neo-colonial pragmatism isn't so hard to swallow. The French *Novotel*, a couple of hundred metres down the beach, seems utterly superfluous and unappealing.

Most of the crowd stay by the hotel, which is fine, giving you a perfect, private **beach** much of the time and some of the best **swimming** in the Cape Verdes. The **waves** are often considerable and the water scintillatingly clear. If you're inclined to stay over until the next day then you might find **rooms** to let in Santa Maria. A rapid survey didn't reveal any *pensões* nor any *casas de pasto* but there must be something, somewhere. There's a feeble sort of snackerette fairly near the *Hotel Morabeza* where you'll get cheapish food.

INTER-ISLAND FLIGHTS FROM SAL

Boa Vista: 4 flights weekly, 25 min.

Praia: 1–6 flights a day (none Tues, Thurs), 50 min.

São Nicolau: 4–5 flights weekly, 45 min.

São Vicente: 5 weekly, 50 min.

TACV ☎41.13.40

Another "ilha rasa" – Boa Vista

Boa Vista is said to have been productive at one time; at present it is almost a desert. Its people, of whom there are four thousand, are almost always hungry, and the lean cattle, with sad faces and tears in their eyes, walk solemnly in cudless rumination over grassless fields. In the valleys there is some vegetation. Fishing, salt-making and going to funerals are the chief amusements and employments of the people.

Life was not easy when the Rev. Charles Thomas went to **BOA VISTA** in the 1850s, but things have improved a little, at least for the cattle. With the rains of recent years, the hillocky pancake of an island is greener than in living memory. The island's struggling economy has long depended on salt and dates – there are large palm groves near the airstrip – supplemented by fishing and some livestock grazing. Boavistans seem to have made best use too of the **shipwrecks** which frequently took place in the treacherous rocky shallows on the north and northeast coasts. There are judged to be about a hundred, some quite old. The last big one was a Spanish freighter in 1968 whose cargo of car parts, garlic, rosemary and pornographic magazines was rapidly dispersed over the island. The wreck of the *Cabo de Santa Maria* is still rusting off the beach, 8km east of Sal Rei, and items from the cargo can still be found in homes around the island twenty years on. **Turtles** were grist to the Boavistan mill as well, and unfortunately still are. There are precious egg-laying sites on many beaches.

Few travellers ever make it here and, apart from a necklace of spectacular white beaches all around, there's little incentive (unless you're a **diver** and can arrange to come here with all the gear, or hire the necessary on Sal). Boa Vista is a good place to explore under your own steam however, with undemanding hills, a network of rural roads and only rudimentary public transport. *Pensões* are equally primitive, but cheap, and people graciously welcoming. The traditional *mornas* (folksongs) of the island are rated the most cheerful and upbeat in Cape Verde.

Sal Rei

SAL REI, the capital, is grubby and uninteresting, its own beach mutilated by a municipal dump. If you can find a boat, a trip out to the **Ilhéu de Sal Rei**, an islet opposite
the town, would be interesting: it holds the ruins of an old fort. Pay some attention to
the **lobsters**, which are ridiculously cheap and plentiful. To please you, people will
cook special potato dinners with expensive spuds imported from other islands, while
they make do with the local staple of lobster. So insist you want ordinary food –
"Queria comida comum".

INTER-ISLAND FLIGHTS FROM BOA VISTA

Praia: 4 times a week, 45 min.   Sal: 4 times a week, 25 min.

index

GUINEA-BISSAU

GUINEA-BISSAU

One of the smallest and least-known countries in West Africa, **Guinea-Bissau** was also the last on the mainland to regain its independence, from Portugal in 1974. It entered the world's consciousness as a highly charged symbol of colonial repression. The country's revolutionary **war of liberation** helped overthrow the dictatorship in Portugal and the revolution in Guinea-Bissau persisted after independence. Until the end of the 1970s, the country's struggle for national survival inspired progressive movements in Europe and North America, as Nicaragua did in the 1980s. Campaigns for literacy and women's freedom made progress during the war. But afterwards, political rigidity set in with economic failure, and enthusiasm for the revolution waned both in Guinea-Bissau and overseas.

Where to go

Guinea-Bissau is hemmed into a region of low-lying estuarine flats, mangrove forest, meandering rivers, jungle and grassland, with Senegal to the north and the Republic of Guinea shoving seawards from east and south. **Travelling** would be incredibly difficult were the country not so small: most journeys require at least one ferry ride, often more, and the tides determine when the ferries operate.

The **Bijagos islands** are admirably languid, dream-like destinations in their own right and worth visiting. This isn't accomplished quickly though, and you need to allow for some discomfort and inconvenience.

For the present, with the exception of one or two special, local attractions and a lovely absence of hustle, it's perhaps unfair to recommend **the mainland** very highly. The poverty and isolation seem a depressing contradiction amid – for nine months of the year – a super-abundance of greenery and evidence of unexploited agricultural potential. You'll see families eating meals that consist of nothing more than plain white rice (often imported) and parts of the country still have an atmosphere of decay and abandon. The **war's toll** surely accounts for much. Yet more subtle factors too are at work in creating the country's mood.

The Guinea-Bissauans are easily the most laid-back and effortless people to be with in West Africa. **Gentle manners** – men spend much time with their children – and a sense of personal security go with your travels everywhere. If you've been to the other ex-Portuguese colony in West Africa – Cape Verde – the cultural echoes in Guinea-Bissau are ever-present. Portugal stained its African possessions more deeply than any other colonising nation.

Lassitude aside, don't expect any longer to find Guinea-Bissau in truly dire straits. Rumours of unobtainable food supplies, and bananas being exchanged for unearthly sums, ceased to have currency in 1987. A **commercial renaissance** is underway with the large, indigenous Fula community in the vanguard. Mauritanian traders have moved in (not many returned after the 1989 Mauritania-Senegal conflict and indeed some refugee traders arrived) and Fula *commerçants* from the Republic of Guinea are mostly choosing to continue their voluntary exile, despite political improvements over the border in the Guinea Republic (see the relevant "History" sections in Part Seven "Senegal" and Part Eleven "Guinea").

Guinea-Bissau's record of change in the past few years looks impressive. The most recent development was a throng of oil industry people in Bissau City, chasing rumours of offshore discoveries. This chapter will be the fastest in the book to go out of date and you may find you rather like the place. Guinea-Bissau has the benefit of human scale, at least.

The people

The biggest of Guinea-Bissau's two dozen ethnic groups is the **Balante**, people of the southern coastal creeks and forests. Much of the area under rice cultivation has been cleared by them over the centuries. In the northwest, the smaller population of **Fulup** (part of the Jola group from southern Senegal) are also great rice farmers. **Pepel** and **Manjak** farmers from the Bissau region are heavily dependent on the city as a market, and operate a more diverse economy. In contrast, the **Bijagos**, on the islands, are mostly self-sufficient (principally on fishing and palm nut-gathering), though men increasingly find work on the mainland or abroad. The Bijagos (less than 40,000 people) have been under little pressure to change over the last 200 years. They've easily resisted Islam and Chrisitianity, and remain very attached to traditional ways. Women have relatively greater economic power than usual, as they're the owners of houses.

In the mainland interior, the biggest contingents are **Fula-** and **Mandinka**-speaking, and there's greater mixing and wider social horizons in the mostly Muslim towns and villages of the east and north. The Fula (the country's second largest language group) are, as ever, powerful players in local politics: their conservative, feudal roots can't be ignored by the government in Bissau.

A noticeable proportion of Guinea-Bissauans are mixed race **Crioulo**-speakers; mostly Cape Verdean, but also descendants of the small number of settlers and traders who came direct from Portugal. A fragmented Portuguese settler community still exists, bolstered by more recent ex-pat arrivals from Lisbon, now being encouraged by the government. But the Lebanese, so prominent in just about every other country in West Africa, seem to have passed up the country completely.

GUINEA-BISSAU – FACTS AND FIGURES

The **Republica da Guiné-Bissau** (often shortened in this chapter to "Guinea") covers 36,000 square kilometres, barely half the size of Scotland or Maine. The population is edging towards one million, but the rate of growth is slower than in most African countries. The county's **foreign debt** amounts to some £400 million, a massive figure until compared with the annual profit of electrical giant *Philips*, for example, which is rather more. The **government**, under the presidency of Commander João "Nino" Vieira, is run by the sole, ruling party, the African Party for the Independence of Guinea and Cape Verde (*PAIGC*), a name kept for ideological reasons.

Climate: when to visit

If you've any choice, the finest **time to visit** is December and January. During these months, the islands are really pleasant. The *carnaval* season in Bissau – February – is a good time to be in the capital. **Bad times**, particularly in Bissau itself which doesn't get much breeze, are the end of the rains (November), as the sun evaporates the moisture into the leaden air, and the nerve-wracking run-up to the rains in April and May when breathing seems an impossibility. All parts of the country are low-lying and humidity levels are high most of the year. In the five very wet months the air is dripping wet all the time – whether it's raining or not – like an invisible mist. See the temperature and rainfall box on p.534

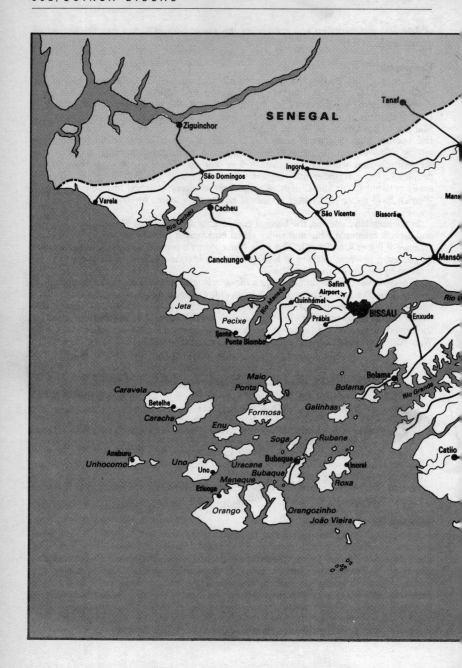

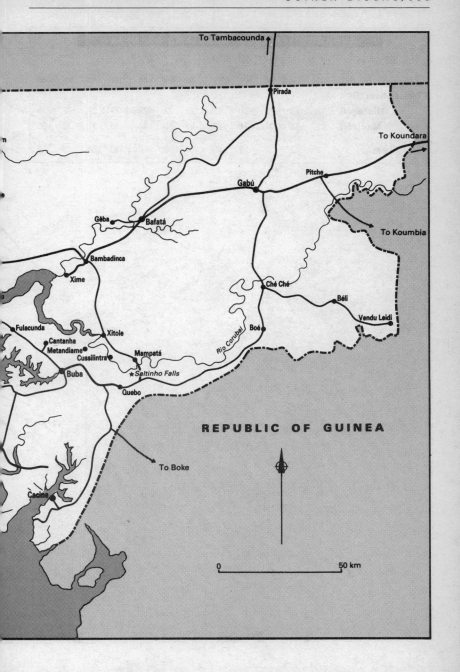

To Tambacounda

Pirada

To Koundara

Pitche

Gabú

Géba Bafatá

To Koumbia

Bambadinca

Xime

Ché Ché

Béli

Vendu Leidi

Fulacunda

Xitole

Rio Corubal

Boé

Cantanha
Metandiame
Cussilintra

Mampatá

Buba

★ Saltinho Falls

Quebo

REPUBLIC OF GUINEA

To Boke

Cacine

0   50 km

AVERAGE TEMPERATURES AND RAINFALL

BISSAU

	Jan	Feb	Mar	Apr	May	June	July	Aug	Sept	Oct	Nov	Dec
Temperatures °C												
Min (night)	18	19	20	21	22	23	23	23	23	23	22	19
Max (day)	31	33	34	34	33	31	30	29	30	31	32	30
Rainfall mm	2	2	7	15	45	200	850	900	390	180	40	5

Arrivals

It's still relatively difficult to get to Guinea-Bissau. Most people either fly in or cross the border from Senegal.

■ Flights

Flying to Bissau **from other African capitals**, your options are extremely limited. Senegal, The Gambia, Guinea and Cape Verde are the only countries with direct services: daily flights **from Dakar** (except Sun) on one of *Air Senegal*, *TAGB* (the Guinea-Bissau airline), *Africana Air* or *Gambia Air Shuttle*; **from Banjul** non-stop on Tuesday or Thursday with *Gambia Air Shuttle* or *Africana*, via Dakar on Saturday; **from Ziguinchor** on Monday or Friday with *Air Senegal*; **from Conakry** on Friday with *TAGB*; and **from Praia** on Wednesday with *TAGB*. From Morocco or Mauritania, at a pinch, there's also a monthly service on *Aeroflot* **from Casablanca** via **Nouadhibou**.

■ Overland from Senegal or The Gambia

Because of limitations on flights from Europe, many visitors fly into Dakar and either take an onward flight there, or travel **overland by public transport from Senegal**; a journey which isn't desperately difficult despite its complicated appearance on the map. The Guinea-Bissau state bus company, *Silô Diata*, should run once a week from Dakar to Bissau. Otherwise, *Peugeot 504*s go direct from Dakar to Ziguinchor, in southern Senegal. You'll have to accept an obligatory night in Ziguinchor, with an early departure for **São Domingos** the next morning and arrival at Bissau in the afternoon. Now that the **road from São Domingos via Ingoré** is paved through to Bissau, you can make this part of the journey in a couple of hours – there are only two short ferry crossings.

If you've time, the old **ferry through the creeks from São Domingos to Cacheu** is as good a way of covering kilometres as any, but only on the rare occasions when tides and ferries permit can you do this route from Ziguinchor in a single day.

From The Gambia, via Ziguinchor, you can usually make the trip to Bissau in one day, though you still need to be lucky with an afternoon vehicle going from Ziguinchor down to the border or São Domingos.

■ Overland from the Republic of Guinea

Overland **from Guinea** in your own vehicle, the fastest way between Conakry and Bissau is via Boké, Koumbia, Foula-Mori and over the border to Pitche, then via Gabú to Bissau. With a dawn start from Conakry in a tough vehicle you might just make it to the border (river crossing) in time to catch the ferry man at dusk, and so be in Bissau late at night. Normal driving time between the capitals in the dry season is not much less than 22 hours. Road conditions in western Guinea are steadily improving, but the wet season can destroy all the good work. Public transport out here is poor. The most obvious-looking route, more or less following the coast, is an arduous trek, not recommended unless you have bags of time (see Guinea "Arrivals" p.570).

■ Overland from Mali

Heading to Guinea-Bissau **from Mali**, the train as far as Tambacounda in Senegal is your best option. Tambacounda to Bissau is a perfectly feasible single day's journey by public transport, entering Guinea-Bissau at Pirada. Driving yourself, there's not much to choose, time-wise, between this route and the longer, but better surfaced one through **Guinea via Kankan and Labé**. The former route is regularly impassable in western Mali during the rains.

Red Tape

Generally easy to obtain, visas are required by nearly all nationalities apart from West Africans. Some Guinea-Bissau consulates in Europe issue visas for overland entry. At the consulates in Banjul and Ziguinchor, they're cheap and normally issued in 24 hours or less. Embassies in Dakar and Conakry are more formal. Other African embassies are in Abidjan and Algiers.

The consulate in Ziguinchor, Senegal, issues three month **multiple entry visas** on the spot. These are useful if you're in doubt about whether you'll subsequently be allowed into Guinea-Conakry for, if there's any question, Guinea-Bissau border guards won't let you leave the country without a visa allowing you to re-enter.

If you're flying into Bissau, you can also get a visa **at the airport**, though it's not recommended.

Extending your visa, once in the country, is apparently not difficult (ask at the main police station), but allowing it to expire and **overstaying** can lead to surprisingly serious problems if detected.

Visas for Onward Travel

Don't count on getting many stamps in Bissau. **Nigeria**, **Senegal**, **Mauritania** and **Guinea** are the West African states with diplomatic missions and the French Embassy can help with several others. Guinean visas are still problematic (see Part Eleven "Guinea"). Although there's a weekly flight to Praia, there's no Cape Verde Embassy.

Money, Banks and Costs

Although now part of a "free convertibility" agreement with the Portuguese escudo, the Guinea-Bissau peso (GB$) is a weak currency, almost valueless outside the country, except perhaps in Portugal. There's still a black market in foreign currency (devisas), principally CFA francs, some of which you should have when you arrive and which have recently been exchanging at CFA1:GB$9.

Although **CFA** can't be used casually (at least not openly), a number of hotels are licensed to accept — and will insist on payment in — hard currency, while setting their tariffs in pesos. Prices are often quoted in **contos**, equal to GB$1000: três contos is GB$3000. As a rough guide to **exchange rates**, the rate for the £ sterling in August 1990 was approximately GB$4000 = £1.

On entering the country you may be asked to **change some hard currency** into pesos at the official rate of exchange. At the airport, it's normally a fixed value (equivalent to about CFA20,000). At São Domingos it has lately been dropped and at many land borders it amounts more to a gift of cheap devisas to the man in charge. Only very scrupulous travellers will declare all their cash. A few thousand CFA (exchanged at an often fictitious rate actually below that of the banks) normally satisfies.

Although the peso has been massively devalued of late, losing at least two-thirds of its value in the last three years, there is still a minor **black market** offering rates for the CFA franc of about GB$10,000:CFA1000 (around 25 percent above the bank rate). The most obvious spot in

Bissau seems to be the central market itself: exchanges with stallholders are very relaxed.

Changing in **banks** will hopefully soon become the norm though it's a generally inefficient process that can take all morning. Outside of Bissau, the only recognisable banks with exchange facilities are in **Canchungo** and **Bafatá**, and on the Senegalese border at Pirada.

Credit cards are virtually useless except in Bissau — and then only for Sheraton and 24 de Setembro guests.

Costs aren't easily reckoned in advance and we give the best current estimates. Outside of Bissau, there's very little to spend your money on, so the cost of a stay in the country is generally low, and can be really minimal. Hotels are clearly the main expense, and even many of the cheaper ones now charge in CFA, and insist you pay on checking in. Prices have been comparable to Senegal's in the past, with a cheap room costing GB$30–50,000 (say CFA3–5000) and slightly better ones for maybe twice as much. Meals are usually excellent value. Transport costs, paid in pesos, are low in real terms.

Health

On purely statistical measures (numbers of cases per 100 for a range of diseases) Guinea-Bissau's relative unhealthiness is fairly low: but this probably reflects the likelihood that the worst cases die rather than go down on the record. Certainly the high humidity and bad communications mean you should take as much care as anywhere.

The only **hospitals** are in Bissau (which has 70 of the country's 130 doctors), Bafatá, Canchungo and Bolama. Out on the islands and in the south, your health problems are your own to deal with.

Bilharzia is a menace on sluggish inland waters, but the rivers are tidal far into the interior (the Gêba as far upstream as Bafatá, the Cacheu past Farim and the Corubal as far as the Saltinho Falls) and the schistosome worms can't survive in brackish water.

The World Health Organisation sponsored an anti-**Aids** song contest in Bissau in 1987 and government concern is fairly high. In September 1988, they announced 29 cases so far identified. Unofficial reports suggest the country has one of the worst Aids problems in the region and many people infected with the long incubation HIV II virus.

Maps and Information

Tourist information on Guinea-Bissau in English is almost non-existent. There are no official tourist offices, nor much of an organised government department dealing with this minor industry. Uniclam in Paris (see p.9) runs fishing, cruising and hunting holidays and may have more information available than their regular handouts.

If you want to exhaust all possibilities, write (preferably in Portuguese, or at least French) to the *Centro do Informacão e Turismo*, CP 294, Bissau, Guinea-Bissau.

The *IGN* map of the country is somewhat out of date but by far the best, if not the only one, available. You can find it abroad and occasionally in the *Casa de Cultura* in Bissau.

Getting Around

Most travel in Guinea-Bissau is ruled by the tides. On the coast there's a tidal range of over five metres, more than twice the world average. Many communities are cut off except at high tide when ferries can reach them. Departure times are therefore unpredictable, unless you've got local tide tables. Add in frequent breakdowns and the potential for delay is almost unlimited.

■ Ferries

The main ferry operator is the state line *Rodofluvial*. They supply monthly lists of dates and estimated departure times for the various routes which are, approximately:

Bissau–Enxude–Bissau: daily Mon–Fri (1 hr 15 min).
Bissau–Bolama–Bissau: out Fri/Sat, back Sun (3hr).
Bissau–Bolama–Catió–Bolama–Bissau: out Tues, back Fri (9hr).
Bissau–Bubaque–Bissau: out Sat, back Sun (4–5hr).
Bissau–Biombo–Pecixe–Biombo–Bissau: out Sat, back Sun (4–5hr).
Cacheu–São Domingos–Cacheu: daily (2–4hr).

Other destinations with at least twice monthly service include **Empada**, **Xime** and **Cacine** Additionally, the overseas national shipping line, *Guinemar* operates some domestic services parallel with *Rodofluvial*'s.

Departures can be anytime from 5am to 7pm (or the middle of the night for Pecixe), though the first daylight high tide is the usual one.

Tickets, which are quoted at two rates ("ticket office" and "on board") are usually charged at the lower rate anyway; but if you have the chance, get them in advance. Bolama is around GB$4000 one way, Bubaque GB$7500. Argue like crazy about paying for your bags: as usual, they're negotiable. Bicycles are charged at a fixed rate around two-thirds of the full fare. Note that none of these regular diesel ferries are built to transport cars.

In addition to the *Rodofluvial* ferries, there are dozens of small hand-hauled ferry bridges and *pirogue* services around the country.

■ Road Transport

The **bus** and **bush taxi** network is improving all the time, with new (and observed) road safety regulations which help to keep vehicles farily uncrowded. The state enterprise, *Silô Diata* (*Bon voyage* in Fula) is still operating, but its geriatric vehicles and under-paid staff can't provide much of a service. They run occasional (in theory daily) buses to **Bafatá**, a service to and from **Buba** connecting with the Enxude ferry, and may still operate their weekly marathon to **Dakar** (CFA12,000 at last check).

Private vehicles, known as ***kandongas***, sometimes marked **"*aluguer*"** ("for hire"), are now far more important and offer pretty good value (under GB$5000 from Cacheu to Bissau for example), but you generally have to be out and about first thing in the morning to get anywhere. Later departures can take forever to fill up.

■ Planes and other forms of transport

If *TAGB*'s international services are unreliable, its **domestic flights** are a more or less *ad hoc* operation. Towns that theoretically have an air link with Bissau include **Bubaque**, **Cacine** and **Catió**. The story recently circulating about the one airworthy DC3 was that it could only start one engine on the ground: taking off with this, the other prop would start in the wind, then it would re-land to pick up the passengers, and depart.

There are few other fruitful forms of transport. **Cycling** through Guinea-Bissau, so long as you choose your season, is an attractive option. The 500-odd kilometres of surfaced road are pleasantly quiet, flat or gently undulating, and often flanked by dense foliage and grass pouring over the road. With a week of two to spare you could explore the south and east, well off the beaten track, quite extensively. If you don't have your own bike, hiring one (or a moped) privately in Bissau isn't too difficult. You should also try to do this if you're visiting the islands as transport on them is hard to come by.

Hiring a car won't help you see the islands, but car hire possibilities do exist in Bissau city and can get you (with a driver) anywhere else in the country. Expect to pay around £30 a day, in one currency or another, plus fuel.

Hitching around might seem a hopeless task, but unless you devote your days to arranging the next bush taxi trip, you'll find you often end up walking out of the town or village and waiting for a passing vehicle. Aid worker and volunteer vehicles comprise a high proportion of traffic.

Sleeping – where to stay

Hotels in Bissau city are getting better and most can be compared with what you might find in a small town in Portugal. The family ones are known as *pensões* (singular *pensão*). Around the rest of the country, in most of the older, Portuguese-built towns – Canchungo, Bafatá, Gabú – you'll find one or two, but in more out-of-the-way places there has been no call for hotel accommodation for years, and *pensões* have barely opened their doors. During *carnaval* and possibly also during football's Amilcar Cabral Cup Final in May, you'll have trouble finding a room.

Camping is a tolerated and useful alternative: a tent is particularly helpful on the islands. But getting food and water supplies if you're in a good camping spot is always something of a problem. There are no campsites.

It's not uncommon for travellers to find **private lodging** with Guinea-Bissauans met travelling on public transport. This can be rewarding and illuminating, but most people are terribly poor and will appreciate your contributions to the evening meal.

Food and Drink

In a small country as poor and battered as this, it's no surprise to find little attention paid to gastronomy. White rice is the staple diet of nearly everyone and, for the majority, something to accompany it once or twice a week is the best they can expect.

This is unlikely to be **your diet**, at least not in Bissau city. Restaurants make the most of seafood and whatever else is available, and hotel dining rooms usually manage to produce enormous four course meals in rustic Portuguese style. Rice soup, fish, chicken, tough beef or pork and potatoes are standard fare with, invariably, a banana to finish.

If you're more used to eating **bananas** all day, then Guinea Bissau won't be a shock to your system. They, together with rather misshapen **bread rolls** or small loaves, are obtainable just about everywhere. The *Armazens de Povo* ("Peoples' Stores") set up during the war to buy crops and sell basic necessities, are no longer operating. In Bissau itself, you'll find much of what you could expect to get in Ziguinchor or Conakry, and possibly more variety than in the latter. **Small supermarkets and corner shops** are opening all the time and the markets thrive. In Canchungo, Bafatá and Gabú too, the food is in the markets. For the rest of the country, be adaptable.

THE BEER RULE

In restaurants and dining rooms, **beer** is only served with meals. If you want to drink, eat. And if you've not ordered more beer by the time you get your banana, you've missed your chance; you can only order beer with a main course.

There are few Guinea-Bissauan **specialities**. *Cachupa*, the beans, corn and pork dish characteristic of the Cape Verde Islands, is a meal for special occasions. **Monkey meat** (*carne de mono*) is common everywhere and very variable: Bissau is one of the few West African capitals where it's regularly served (though not at the *Sheraton*). Seafood is good in Bissau. *Gambas* – king prawns – are the stock in trade of the white-oriented restaurants, justifiably. **Oysters** and other shellfish are often on Bissau menus too. Don't be put off by the condition of the sea water near the capital: seafood isn't collected from nearby.

The unlabelled local **beer** – *Pampa* – is usually in good supply these days and not expensive, though none too wonderful either. They sometimes run out of bottles, in which case you may find it sold in unlabelled one-litre jam jars. Imported beer and other booze is available, in

Bissau only, at a premium. Soft drinks, all imported, are in short supply but local plastic bag juices – lime and lemon juice and wonderful **cashew juice** – can all be found for about 10p a litre. Cashews are particularly common on Bolama Island, where they make a lethal hooch – *canna* (or *kana*) *de cajeu* – from the cashew apples. The nuts themselves, as well as magnificent mangoes and a tart but not unpleasant little plum unfairly called *miseria*, help to make the end of the dry season bearable.

Communications: Post and Phones, Language and Media

Guinea-Bissau's mail, in and out, is remarkably efficient and reliable. Very little is ever lost or tampered with, and it's therefore one of the best places to post items home. But mail is expensive. Telex, telegrams and telephoning are expensive too.

For **Poste Restante**, you can have letters marked *Lista da Correios* or *Poste Restante*, CTT, Bissau. Be exceptionally pleasant to the *funcionário* in charge. Note that reverse charge calls are not possible to Europe or North America.

The main place to do all this business with confidence is the **main post office in Bissau** itself. There are functioning branches in provincial towns, but you should be prepared for expect considerable delays.

Check out the **stamps** of Guinea-Bissau while you're there. The Portuguese may have left only fifty US cents in the government coffers when they withdrew, but they bequeathed a huge stockpile of postage stamps; "Portuguese Province of Guiné", triangular and garish, denominated in *escudos*, now overprinted in *pesos*.

Collectable philately, surely. Also try to track down some of the classic armed forces **post-cards** produced after the war.

Though the telephone system is a good one and you can phone Guinea-Bissau direct from abroad, there's still no IDD dialling out of the country. Reverse charge calls are not possible.

■ Language and Media

Although the official language of Guinea Bissau is **Portuguese**, the widely used, street-friendly vernacular is **Crioulo** (or Kriolu). An old amalgam of seafarers' Portuguese with various African languages, this is very similar to Cape Verdean Kriolu, but significantly different from Portuguese. If you speak some Portuguese, Crioulo becomes only semi-intelligible. The *Casa de Cultura* bookshop in Bissau (the only one in the country) has comic books in Crioulo which will stretch your powers of interpretation to the limit. Other important languages include **Balante**, the related **Manjak** and **Pepel**, **Mandinka** and **Fula**.

Broadcasting is mainly radio, and only in Portuguese. Television broadcasting was introduced in 1989, two or three times each week, but there are very few TV sets in the country.

Looking to **the press** for news, you'll occasionally see a copy of *Nô Pintcha* (the revolutionary slogan), which is published three times a week in an edition of 10,000, only in Bissau. The other paper, *Voz da Guiné* is a new, daily title.

There are a few **foreign papers** on sale around Bissau. If you read Portuguese, popular tabloids from Lisbon are sometimes available. And if you're desperate, the *Sheraton* should have the *Herald Tribune*, *Time* and *Newsweek*.

GLOSSARY

A few terms you're likely to come across:

Assimilado in colonial times, an indigenous Guinean who, through education and connections had achieved the status of Portuguese citizen.

Armazens de Povo "peoples' stores" during the revolutionary era.

Bairro suburb, slum.

Feitoria "factory" in the historical sense of a trading post.

Kana sugar cane alcohol.

Kandonga bush taxi.

Kirintim a fence of woven brushwood (like wattle) often surrounding and identifying a bar .

Navetanes seasonal migrant workers.

PAIGC the *Partido Africano da Independência da Guiné e Cabo Verde*, the country's only political party .

Ponta small land concession or trading post in Portuguese Guinea.

Directory

AIRPORT DEPARTURE TAX CFA5000, but somewhat flexible in application.

ART AND ENTERTAINMENT Main artistic event of the year is the *carnaval* in February. Indigenous theatre and cinema are dormant. Music (see below) shows a little more promise.

BARGAINING Haggling over purchases is a brief business: few market traders will discuss for long. The last price is the last price, and quickly reached.

CRAFTS AND THINGS TO BUY A couple of spots in Bissau sell wood-carvings: the main one is rather good. Because of the lazy-sell attitude of most craft-sellers, you can choose and mull over a fair range. Animal skins – crocodile, python, even leopard and serval – are openly displayed too. The government applies no effective sanctions, though the problem is a small one at present.

DUTY FREES Strictly speaking, all alcohol brought into the country is dutiable.

HOLIDAYS New Year's Day is a big event; **January 20** Heroes' Day (assassination of Amilcar Cabral); **February** (variable dates) Bissau carnival; **February** (proposed, from 1991) annual *Lisbon–Bissau Auto Rally*; **March 8** International Women's Day; **August 3** National Day (Pidjiguiti Massacre); **September 24** Independence Day (the proclamation of the republic in the liberated zone of Boé in 1973); **November 14** Redemption Day of the Republic (1980 coup that brought the present clique to power); **Christmas Day and December 26** (a family occasion in Bissau).

Throughout the northeast, the **Islamic calendar** is observed, but a few closures and holidays aren't likely to have much noticeable effect on your travels.

MUSIC In Bissau, the band of the moment is **Super Mama Djombo**. Maio Cooperante, Manecas, Africa Libre, Dulce Mario, Justinio Delgado, Cobiana Jazz, Naka Ramiro and Jetu Katem are other names to look out for. **N'kassa Cobra** and **Kaba Mane** have both done what successful African bands tend to do and left the country for the big stages of Europe; in the case of these two, Paris. Kaba Mane sings mostly in Balante, many of his songs still firmly based in the *Koussounde* style of his roots. Kaba Mane was the first musician from Guinea-Bissau to dent the British charts, with his delightfully infec-

tious *Chefo Mae Mae* LP. His new one, *Kunga Kungake* has done even better.

OPENING HOURS Very little consistency and anyway few offices and businesses have more than one location, and that's usually in Bissau. A long lunch break is common, however, usually from 11.30 or noon to 3pm.

PETROL Outside the capital, fuel is often in short supply, or overpriced, so always plan ahead with full jerry cans if you're driving.

PHOTOGRAPHY Officialdom is very suspicious of cameras. A permit is required, in theory, but nobody can tell you where to obtain it. In Bissau, avoid the port, presidential palace and most other places with your camera. In country areas, people aren't much concerned and may even ask you to take pictures of them. Photography on the islands is relaxed. Video, and photography in general, is much easier if you're part of an aid project, or connected to one, rather than a "tourist".

PIGS Some of the scrawniest, most long-legged and hirsute hogs you'll ever see live in Guinea-Bissau: many look like dogs. It's possible the breed is a survival of the ancient pig culture of northern Africa that's mostly been obliterated by Islam. Widespread outside the Muslim regions, they perform the street-cleaning functions normally associated with goats.

SPORT African wrestling doesn't carry much kudos in Guinea-Bissau. The big sport is soccer, encouraged by the cultural ties with soccer-mad Portugal and Brazil. It's best watched at the flash new stadium outside Bissau, especially recommended if it's an African international match. There are two women's teams. Village football is often played at dusk.

TROUBLE Guinea-Bissau is one of the least uptight countries in the region, with few road-blocks, and you can easily spend several weeks here without crossing the path of a uniformed official. If you're out on the street at 8am or 6pm, however, remember that the official flag-raising and lowering, accompanied by a bugle, requires you to stand still in silence. The same rule applies when VIP convoys pass you on the road, or when a funeral procession goes by.

The laws on **drug possession** are very tough: possession of a few joints normally leads to deportation, but quite often only after a spell in jail. The maximum sentence for this offence is 25 years. Note that few nationalities have strong diplomatic representation in Bissau.

WILDLIFE Much of the indigenous wildlife was hunted out during the war years or lost its habitat to defoliants or subsequent land clearance. Still, for such a small country, the fauna can be rewarding and it's likely that thorough investigations would turn up a few species unsuspected in this part of the continent. Best areas to look are the hilly southeast, parts of the forested centre, and the outer islands. The big terrestrial animals are no longer found anywhere, but many species of monkeys and antelopes and some unusual coast dwellers – **manatees**, saltwater-dwelling **hippos** and large **sea turtles** – compensate for this. Reptile life is prolific. Guinea-Bissau has no national parks or wildlife reserves.

WOMEN TRAVELLERS AND THE WOMEN'S MOVEMENT Men and women can mix freely in Guinea-Bissau, without their association carrying implicit sexual connotations. For women travellers, this makes the country one of the most relaxed in West Africa. Guinean women fought in the war and their presence in the ranks of the revolutionary cadres made a lasting impression in the traditionally conservative and Islamic parts of the country. In these areas, the issues of female emancipation are still fairly hot ones. But the signals received by the rest of the world – that a sexual revolution was taking place in the country – have never been convincingly borne out in the communities. The movement's momentum has slowed down in the 1980s, though the structures remain. Contact the *União Democrática das Mulheres* (*UDEMU*) if you're interested (☎21 40 81/21 27 40).

The Historical Framework

Guinea-Bissau was first visited by Europeans in 1456, when Cadamosto, an Italian navigator working for the Portuguese crown, sailed as far as the Rio Mansôa and the Bijagos islands looking for the gold which figured so hugely in the trans-Saharan trade. Other sailors settled on the uninhabited Cape Verde islands over the following decades. By 1500, these communities had sprouted sub-colonies on the Guinean mainland: groups of Portuguese or mixed-race immigrants, partly absorbed into African society, trading with the interior and looking to the ocean. More about this early history of European contact is detailed in Part Nine "Cape Verde". The emphasis here is on the period of Portuguese colonialism and the brief era of independence since its demise. The story of the region's more ancient past – and of influences from within West Africa – is virtually unknown, except that it didn't result in powerful states or dynasties.

■ Crioulo Society

Through the first half of the sixteenth century, the region traded out to Europe an average of over 200,000 grammes of West African **gold** every year. But with the opening up of the "New World", from the later years of the sixteenth century onwards, much of the region which is now Guinea-Bissau, was drawn into the Atlantic **slave-trading network** which linked West Africa with Europe, the Caribbean, South and North America through the Cape Verde archipelago.

Cacheu was the headquarters: by 1600 it had as many as 1000 Crioulo (mixed-race) slave traders and employees. Portugal established a military garrison in 1616 in order to guarantee the maximum revenue to the crown, charging duty on exported slaves and sending cargoes on to the Cape Verdes where they paid further duty. Other towns were established at Farim, Ziguinchor and, later, Bissau and Bolama. But despite Portugal's efforts, the benefits of trade tended to bypass Lisbon. French and English ships could offer better trade goods and more choice. Repeated efforts by the Portuguese government to enforce **trading monopolies** in their area of influence simply pushed traders into illegal commerce. The state administrators charged with extracting taxes and levies invariably exploited their positions, so that **corruption**, **smuggling** and **state control** became inextricably tangled.

The **slaves** tended to come from the least stratified ethnic groups of farmers, fishers and hunters; Floup and Jola, Manjak and Pepel. The main **slavers** were Mandinka and, later, Fula. The Bijagos were notorious slave-hunters too, launching lethal canoe raids against the mainland. It was a circular business, however. Who was slave and who slaver depended much more on economic strength or vulnerability and on family contacts and position, than on "tribal identity". It wasn't unusual for a king or headman to sell off people under his own rule, such was the attraction of cloth and other imported goods. **Firearms** were available from the early eighteenth century to those who could afford them .

With the general **abolition of slavery** in the early nineteenth century, the slave trade from Guinea continued illicitly, given new life by the needs of Cuba's plantations. Domestic slavery (which was not abolished) was commonly used as a cover. The last big shipments, however, crossed the Atlantic in the 1840s.

Meanwhile, using labour locally, rather than selling it off unproductively, became significant with the introduction of **groundnuts**, first grown along the Gambia river at the end of the eighteenth century. Philip Beaver's attempt to start an English colony of groundnut planters on Bolama had been a disaster (see box on p.557), but local Crioulo landowners had more success. Agreements were made with Bijagos elders on Galinhas and Bolama, from where the crop was spread to the shores of the Rio Grande on the mainland. On the islands, the plantations used slaves. On the shores of the Rio Grande they called them contract labourers, with tools, transport, food, clothes and accommodation charged to the plantation workers out of their share of the crop, usually leaving nothing for wages. Portugal, however, even more than before, benefited little from the exploitation of its colonies. As much as 80 percent of the crop was sold to French trading concerns.

In 1879, Portugal's Guinean territory was separated from Cape Verde administration. The French had occupied Ziguinchor and the British claimed Bolama, so the **first capital** of "Portuguese Guinea" was established at Gêba, way up the river of the same name.

■ The Portuguese Province

The emptiness of Portugal's pride in its "colonial empire" – at least in the case of Guinea – continued through the end of the nineteenth century, and the formal carving-up of the continent. The **partition of Africa** after 1885 left Portugal with a scattering of territories, of which Guinea-Bissau was perhaps the least promising. Portuguese settlers weren't interested in going there for fear of the climate; and there appeared to be no attractive natural resources. Then, **Fula aggression** – *jihads* against non-Muslim plantation workers and raids on the foreign-run *feitoria* groundnut stations along the Rio Grande – soon led to a slump in the country's only viable export. With the region now formally annexed to Portugal, only Bolama (the capital from 1890), and the fort-towns of Bissau, Cacheu, Farim and Gêba, were in any sense under colonial rule.

Military campaigns of "pacification" took 25 years to subdue the state of general **revolt** which ensued in the 1890s. And in that time there was precious little thought in Lisbon about the administration of Guinea or the other African territories. It was somehow understood that they had always been a part of Portugal, so there was no specific colonial service, and no consideration of the purposes of colonialism, beyond furthering the greatness of Portugal and extending its benefits to those Africans who could demonstrate their "civilisation". The republican government in Portugal, wracked as it was by one military intervention after another, and by costly involvement in World War I, continued virtually to ignore Guinea.

Hut taxes were imposed and labour conscripted to help maintain the colony with as little support from Portugal as possible. Almost the entire African population was classified as *indígena* – disenfranchised, second-class noncitizens. Opportunities for education were very limited, and in practice most urbanites with prospects were Cape Verdeans, or the descendants of Cape Verdean marriages. They, together with mixed race Crioulos and a tiny proportion of **assimilado** mainlanders (less than one in 300, often Fula), formed the bulk of the civil service, as government agents and tax collectors. Cape Verdeans held many professional posts as well.

It was from this small middle class that the first calls were heard for political reform. Before World War I, a political group called the **Liga Guineense** campaigned for the interests of small traders and landowners, highlighting the abuse of powers by government agents and calling for a change in the laws favouring the big commercial enterprises. The *Liga* was outlawed in 1915 without making much impact, but it provided a background – the only indigenous political example – for the radical demands of the *PAIGC* that emerged forty years later.

The **groundnut trade** began to pick up after about 1910, though it crashed again in 1918 when a law came into force prohibiting peasant farmers from trading their crop to foreign buyers. The law was repealed, and by the 1920s, the central parts of the country, particularly around Bafatá, had become the groundnut heartland. The pressure to sell all surpluses to agents of Portugal, however, only tended to stifle production.

Despite the heavy exploitation and inequalities, there was a looseness in governing the overseas territories that failed to suppress the freedom of expression completely. The paternalistic idea of **"colonial trusteeship"** was taken seriously by some: Portuguese culture allowed a vague and distant respect for Africans stemming partly from its own infusion of African culture during the medieval Moorish occupation. But these sentiments were smothered after 1926.

Guinea under the Portuguese "New State"

The military intervention in Lisbon in 1926 was, unexpectedly different from previous ones. Instead of installing a new government and withdrawing, **General Carmona** presided over the installation of a military dictatorship which was to last until 1974, holding Portugal back and crippling her overseas territories. **António de Salazar**, a monetarist economics professor, was prime minister from 1932 until 1968. He promulgated the *Estado Novo*, or **New State**, and ran Portugal on strictly authoritarian lines. The

"Province of Guinea", along with the other parts of "Overseas Portugal" were brought to heel. The last pockets of resistance to the colonial invasion were finally "pacified" in 1936 and any chinks of progressive light from republican days were blacked out by the quasi-fascist curtain now drawn across the country.

Guinea was forced into becoming one giant groundnut and oil palm plantation with **compulsory planting and purchases**. Small traders were banned from dealing in cloth and alcohol, while Portuguese commercial agents tried vainly to interest the people in Portuguese wine and cotton clothing.

With economic repression, pass-book laws and a continuation of forced labour (reduced to only five days a year after World War II) came an unwieldy and over-staffed **bureaucracy**. All potential sources of opposition were organised into officially-sanctioned associations, from within which their members could be scrutinised by the *PIDE* – Salazar's political police force. For over four decades, there was an almost total suspension of political life.

In the 1950s, **Amilcar Cabral**, an agronomist of mixed Cape Verdean and Guinean parentage, was working in the colonial service, conducting agricultural censuses across the country. He analysed his remarkably detailed land use surveys in Marxist terms of modes of production. His conclusions convinced him that mechanisation, collectivisation, a rejection of the groundnut mono-culture and a return to mixed farming could transform Guinean society and set the country on a path to socialism. His reputation as a subversive assured, he quit the service and left the country.

■ The War of Liberation

In Bissau, the capital since 1941, a small coterie of African tradesmen and Lisbon-educated civil servants began gently agitating for independence from Portugal. On September 12, 1956 Cabral (briefly back from work in Angola) and five others met secretly and formed the *Partido Africano da Independência da Guiné e Cabo Verde* (**PAIGC**). With painstaking discretion and patience they recruited people to their ranks. Within three years they had about fifty members.

The spark for armed conflict came with a **dockworkers' strike** for a living wage in 1959. On 3 August, police confronted the strikers on the **Pidjiguiti** waterfront in Bissau (see box). When they refused to go back to work the police

"SINCE PIDJIGUITI WE NEVER LOOKED BACK"

Jose Emilio Costa now works for the Bissau Port Administration. In 1959 he took part in the Bissau dockworkers' strike that ended in a bloody massacre at the small Pidjiguiti pier. Fifty workers were killed and over a hundred wounded.

"When I started working at the docks in 1949, conditions in Guinea were difficult. Many people were without work and food was always short. Our wages were almost nothing and the work hard, but we were glad not to be starving and accepted it, more or less.

This began to change after several years. More and more Africans became aware of what colonialism was doing to our country and tried to improve the situation. At the dock we formed a club to collect money and send youngsters to study in Portugal. But the Portuguese didn't like it and one administrator, Augusto Lima, tried to stop our activities. There was also an African worker by the name of João Vaz who always spoke against what we were doing. Some people in the club weren't dockers; Rafael Barbosa, for instance, was a construction worker and Jose Francisco a sugar cane worker. They were both active in the Party and so were Caesare Fernandes, Jose de Pina and Paulo Fernandes who worked with me. But this was something very few people knew at the time.

Most of us worked for the big Casa Gouvea company [part of the giant *Companhia União Fabril*'s empire], either on the dock or on boats taking goods to and from company shops all over the country. But with our low wages, life was becoming more and more difficult. The basic wage was only ten escudos [approximately fifteen pence] a day. In 1959, after much discussion in the club and at work, we finally decided to ask for higher wages.

The manager was Antonio Carreia who had just left his post as colonial administrator to work with Gouvea. Well, he refused even to listen. Of course, this was the first time in Guinea's history that workers united to confront their boss. So, Barbosa and Augusto Laserde said that we had to go on strike and show them we were serious.

On 3 August we all gathered at Pidjiguiti, about 500 men. Nobody worked, neither on the dock nor on the boats. Carreia came down and shouted and swore, but we just looked at him without moving. At about 4.30 in the afternoon several trucks of armed police arrived. First they sealed off the gate to the street, then they ordered us back to work. When no one obeyed, they began moving slowly down the pier, now packed with striking workers.

This old captain friend of mine, Ocante Atobo, was leaning against the wall of the office shed. When the line of police reached the spot where he was, an officer suddenly raised his gun and shot

---

opened fire at point-blank range, killing fifty men and wounding more than a hundred. The massacre and subsequent police interrogations, convinced Cabral and the party leadership that peaceful attempts in the towns to bring about independence would be fruitless. Cabral, his half-brother Luiz, and Aristides Pereira went to Conakry (newly independent from France) to set up a party headquarters and training school. In Guinea-Bissau, others began organising, clandestinely, in the countryside, for **social revolution** and a **war of liberation** against the Portuguese.

Other nationalist groups were forming at the time, both inside Bissau and in Senegal. Their ideologies tended to be less well-honed than PAIGC's. They were prepared to accept a transfer of political power without a transformation in the economy, and they didn't work on behalf of the Cape Verde Islands. Nor did they approve of the Cape Verdean intellectuals who characterised PAIGC's executive. These other groups coalesced into the Front for the Liberation and Independence of Portuguese Guinea (*FLING*) based in Dakar under Leopold Senghor's sponsorship. The sum of ideological differences, at the time, between *PAIGC* and *FLING*, continues to be the fulcrum on which political life in Guinea-Bissau is balanced today.

Morocco was the first country to supply the *PAIGC* with arms. There had been scattered attacks by the Dakar-based coalition from 1961, but military action by the *PAIGC* began in earnest in January 1963. Senghor and Touré reluctantly allowed the guerrillas to launch operations from Senegal and Guinea-Conakry. In Europe, the Scandinavian countries voiced their solidarity. Internally, the most enthusiastic insurgents were the brutally exploited, rice-planting **Balante** of the southwest, around Catió. But coordination of their sabotage attacks with *PAIGC* strategy was often tenuous. At the other extreme, many **Fula** communities in the north and east – long

him point-blank in the chest. Ocante collapsed in a pool of blood. For a split second everyone froze — it was as if time stood still. Then hell broke loose. The police moved down the pier, shooting like crazy into the crowd. Men were screaming and running in all directions. I was over by my cousin Augusto Fernandes' boat, the *Alio Sulemane*. Augusto, who was standing next to me, had his chest shot wide open; it was like his whole inside was coming out. He was crying: "Oh God, João kill me, please". But it wasn't necessary; when I lifted his head from the ground he was already dead.

Now all the men were running for the end of the pier. The tide was out so all the boats and *pirogues* were resting on the beach. To hide there, however, was impossible since the police, standing high up on the dock, were shooting right into them. One officer was kneeling on the edge firing at those trying to get away in the water. All around me people were shouting "Run, run!", but I stayed beside my dead cousin. "No, if they want to kill me, let them do it right here".

I don't know how long this lasted when a *PIDE* inspector named Emmanuel Correia arived and ordered the firing to stop. The last one to die was a boatman hiding in the mud under his *pirogue*, out of sight of the police. A Portuguese merchant, however, spotted him from his apartment window and shot him in the back with his hunting rifle just after Correia had arrived. One Portuguese, Romeo Martins, always a friend of the Africans, had been trying to keep the police from shooting, but all by himself he couldn't do much.

When the massacre finally ended I saw dead and wounded men all over: on the dock, on the beach, in the boats, in the water — everywhere. Among the dead were Caesare Fernandes and Jose de Pina who had worked for the Party. Afterwards we were taken to the police for interrogation. For three straight days I had to report to the administrator, Guerra Ribeiro, who wanted to know who had organised the strike. My answer was always the same: "We all organised it; our wages were so bad we had no choice". Later, when Ribeiro had finished his enquiry, the wage went up to 14 escudos a day.

Soon after the massacre a message from Amilcar Cabral was secretly circulated among us. It said that August 3 would never be forgotten and that now we had to organise to win our independence from Portuguese colonialism. Since then we never looked back. Many other workers and I joined the Party and started the difficult work of political mobilisation here in Bissau. With experience of Pidjiguiti behind us, we knew that we had to accept the risks and sacrifices of an armed revolution to win freedom for our people."

Reprinted from Sowing the First Harvest: National Reconstruction in Guinea-Bissau (1978), LSM Press, California.

established in a feudal framework which had Islamic sanction, and positively supported by the Portuguese — resisted subversion, or tried to prevent their peasants from being politicised.

As large stretches of bush and countryside became liberated, and then the first few towns, the guerrillas of the *PAIGC* became consolidated into an effective, mobile army, clearing the way for a network of **"people's stores"**, **new schools**, **medical services** and **political institutions**. Portugal attacked their bases with weaponry purchased from **NATO**: West Germany played a key role in supporting the airforce. Napalm was used and the fighting, at times, was as intense as in Vietnam. In retaliation, the guerrilla army — the People's Revolutionary Armed Forces (*FARP*) — persuaded the Soviet Union to deliver arms on a regular basis.

While the war continued with relentless success for the liberationists, the first **internal cracks** were being felt in their upper ranks. All *PAIGC* decisions were now being taken in Conakry by the Cape Verdean leadership. Increasingly the need to coordinate a national policy came into conflict with democratic imperatives. Although Cabral enjoyed enormous support and trust, his growing stature as a world leader physically distanced him from his half million followers. In many liberated areas, there were very few democratically elected representatives between the top leadership and the people. Only at the village level were local committees elected, and then only to discuss how to implement party strategy, not to consider the strategy itself. Beyond the villages, the exigencies of war stalled and diverted elections. Party cadres with regional responsibilities were often unaccountable.

Cabral wasn't unconscious of these difficulties. In 1970, the war could have been won in a few months as heavy armaments had just been delivered from Eastern Europe. But Cabral decided to hold off the final assault on Bissau because the weapons were only usable by Soviet-trained Cape Verdeans. He thought it would only reinforce the unpopular high profile of Cape Verdean power-holders. After seven years of fighting, however, all the indications were that the mass of the people were fed up with the war and popularity would have been more likely to follow a swift end to it.

External factors intervened. In November 1970, an **invasion force of Portuguese troops** and African collaborators set off from Soga island in the Bijagos to attack Conakry, in the Republic of Guinea, with the intention of assassinating President Sekou Touré and Amilcar Cabral. They failed, and retreated in chaos (see p.583). But two years later, a more carefully planned action in Conakry, involving *PAIGC* traitors, was partially successful and led to the **assassination of Amilcar Cabral** on January 20, 1973. This was only partially successful because the party, nurtured for so long by one of Africa's most radical and humane political thinkers, did not disintegrate. Portugal's plan to install a puppet "liberation government" in Guinea-Bissau had no chance of success. Nonetheless, the damage to morale was serious and the leadership vacuum plain to see. Aristides Pereira took over as party chief and Luiz Cabral as president-in-waiting.

Major weaponry (heat-seeking SAM–7 missiles) came straight into play after Cabral's assassination. One aircraft after another was shot down. The Portuguese, in a hundred or so military camps across the country, were increasingly besieged by a confident People's Army under the general command of **João "Nino" Vieira** (later to succeed Cabral as president). In four months, through the end of the dry season of 1973, the Portuguese lost the war. With their airforce demoralised and growing evidence of discontent among their conscripted troops, rumbles of revolution began in Portugal itself.

On September 24, 1973, in the liberated village of Lugajole in the southeast, the People's National Assembly (elected the previous year in ballots held throughout the liberated zones) declared the **independence** of Guinea-Bissau. It only remained to kick out the enemy. Around the world, dozens of countries recognised the new Republic and the United Nations passed a resolution demanding Portuguese withdrawal. The **coup in Lisbon** on 25 April 1974, by army officers of the Armed Forces Movement (*MFA*), made withdrawal inevitable. Despite a summer of polit-

ical crises in Portugal, and repeated efforts by the right wing to find a way of hanging on, Portugal and the *PAIGC* signed a treaty on 10 September and the last Portuguese troops were gone within a month. **Luiz Cabral** became the new Head of State, while the party leader and senior ideologue, Aristides Pereira, became president of the new sister Republic of Cape Verde.

■ Independence: the first six years

The *PAIGC* took over a centralised and autocratic administration. Far from Amilcar Cabral's optimistic ideas of a decentralised state – of ministries scattered across a nation devoid of the usual top-heavy capital city – the party's preoccupations were almost all in **Bissau**. Realistically, with a population of 90,000 (many of whom had worked with the Portuguese to the end) the domination of Bissau city was inevitable. The urgency of the takeover, the shortage of resources (material and human) and the refugee problem in the capital, all led to government by crisis-management. The **peasants** of the liberated zones, who had supported the party and the war for so long and at such cost, were hardly consulted: nor were the **minor-ranking party cadres** who now expected to receive the fruits of independence.

> ### THE COLONIAL BEQUEST
>
> In October 1974, when real independence was achieved, Guinea-Bissau had only a handful of graduates and doctors and a population only two percent of whom, at most, were literate. The country's industrial base consisted of one brewery: there was no other manufacturing plant. There was almost no energy production. Earnings from exports barely covered a tenth of the cost of imports. And the Portuguese had left a colossal national debt.

Apart from **national reconstruction**, there was **political work** to do in Bissau. Compared with the peasants of the liberated zones, some of whom had lived under *PAIGC* government for ten years, not only were the Bissauans the least influenced by the war's ravages, they also tended to be the most cosmopolitan, the most educated and the most cynical. Now that the *PAIGC* was in control, they had to accommodate to it, but not necessarily support it down the line.

There were national **"elections"** in 1976, with voting consisting of a "for" or "against" to candidates nominated to the Regional Councils (who themselves elected the members of the National Assembly). As in 1972, there were no alternative candidates. Results showed the widest dissent in the traditionally suspicious and anti-*PAIGC* northern and eastern regions, a fifteen percent opposition in Bissau, but over ninety percent support everywhere else.

The broad approval seems surprising in light of the **difficulties** the party was having in delivering on its Independence promises to build a new society. Bissau city, for example, received over half the country's resources – justified by Cabral in terms of attracting foreign aid agencies (who poured funds into the country between 1976 and 1979) and investors. **Drought** damaged the prospects of new **agricultural projects** and efforts to become self-sufficient in food made no progress. A joint **fisheries** enterprise with Algeria was a flop. The ludicrous N'Haye **car assembly** plant was a grotesque waste of money, as was the over-massive and never finished **agricultural processing** plant at Cumeré near Bissau. Salaries in the wallowing **state sector** were eating away (in fact *exceeded*) the national budget. The **currency** was kept overvalued, and **inflation** soared while in real terms agricultural production and exports declined. In a remarkable echo of the fascist New State policy, the government tried to control the **marketing of produce**, setting **prices** at levels too low to be worth selling at and perforce encouraging a black market economy. People in the rural areas could no longer afford **basic imported goods** like soap and matches.

The persistent street rumour was that all this was the fault of the Guinea-Bissauans of Cape Verdean origin who, in many cases, had kept civil service positions since Portuguese times. Many of the "People's Stores" were run by them, too, and often corruptly. But it was their visibility, as part of the self-interested and irrepressible middle class, that made them popular scapegoats for a **failing economy**.

In November 1980, an "Extraordinary Session of the National Assembly" had discussed the unification of Guinea-Bissau and the Cape Verde Islands. Luiz Cabral, having increasingly isolated himself, refused to budge on the issue, or on the misallocation of state funds to Bissau city and prestige projects. Four days later, came the largely bloodless **coup of November 14**, which toppled his government.

■ Guinea-Bissau in the 1980s

The Commissioner for the Armed Forces, **Nino Vieira**, revoked the constitution and took control of the country. Luiz Cabral was detained on Bubaque, then allowed to fly to Cuba. Guinea-Bissau remained in the charge of the military for four years. Despite popular anti-Cape Verdean sentiment, the new "Provisional Government", formed in 1981, looked much like a rearranged version of Luiz Cabral's. Several of Cabral's Cape Verdean ministers had fled, but Vieira was adamant in his speeches that Cape Verdeans were welcome in Guinea-Bissau, and that the two countries' destinies remained linked.

One of the first announcements of the new government, was the disclosure of a series of **mass graves**, containing up to 500 bodies, in the Oio region northeast of Bissau. The story was taken up by the foreign press. Vieira's intention was to point out the summary justice meeted out by his predecessor's govenment to dissidents and those who had collaborated with the Portuguese. But counter-claims by a furious **Aristides Pereira** (the president of Cape Verde) who believed Vieira had sabotaged any chance of unification, said that Vieira had known about the murders and was even implicated. Cape Verde set up its own party, and broke relations.

As it entered its second decade of independence, prospects for Guinea-Bissau had hardly improved. And by 1982 Vieira was already repeating history, closing himself off in a tight cabal of close advisers, shuffling his cabinet according to the dictates of his personal security. **Coup attempts**, allegations of plans for coup attempts and widespread repression characterised the early 1980s. In 1984, however, there was a shift to a freer climate with new elections (of the same type as before), a rewritten constitution and a return to civilian power. But still the plots continued. Despite international appeals, (by Amnesty International and the Pope among others), **Paulo Correia** (vice-president) and five co-accused, were executed in July 1986 after a trial of over fifty people, mostly Balante, for an attempted coup the year before. Six more of the accused were said to have died in prison.

None of this, of course, helped the government to run the country effectively. Although the **IMF** and the **World Bank** had given loans, the **austerity measures** on which they were conditional were hardly followed through and, despite debt rescheduling, the country's economic plight continued to worsen. The heady years of progress in the liberated times of the 1960s seemed light years away.

In August 1986, however, the government finally agreed to the **abolition of trade laws** that had reserved all import and export licences for state monopolies. The *peso* was massively devalued, knocking the life out of the black market and encouraging potential investors. Support for Vieira's government was suddenly stronger as exports rose impressively and the domestic economy began to revive. Within a year, Guinea-Bissau was entering into long-term agreements with the IMF and World Bank to **restructure the economy**, prune the state pay-roll by a third, reduce fuel subsidies and boost agriculture, fisheries and technical training. By 1990, although the countryside still lagged behind Bissau, the fortunes of the *peso* were tied to the Portuguese *escudo* and the economic future was looking much brighter. There was even talk of revising some of the redundant revolutionary rhetoric in the constitution to take account of developments. **Cashew nuts** are now the most valuable export.

■ Guinea-Bissau today: Prospects

Guinea-Bissau's economic failure has tended to be blamed on "backward peasant cultivation" unable to integrate with the "modern economy" of Bissau city. The rural population, however, has relied, for the last half century, on its urban contacts (Bissau, Ziguinchor, Banjul and Dakar) in order to survive. And the farmers have been responsible for most of the production which supported the towns. They have been alienated by the emphasis placed by governments, both before and after independence, on **major capital projects** and **maximising export crops** through the delivery of "technical packages" to the farmers. These often unworkable **imported solutions** to the problems of underdevelopment have missed the point that "traditional" agricultural techniques work. The New State and Luis Cabral both tried to superimpose new technologies, and both failed. Vieira's regime, if it keeps the immediate needs of the rural sector in mind, if it encourages sales of surpluses inside Guinea-Bissau rather than smuggled abroad, is more likely to succeed. It's probably too late for solidarity appeals to the veterans of the liberation war. But while Guinea-Bissau remains one of the most fluid and unpredictable countries in the region, some of Amilcar Cabral's message to the people

"to live better and in peace, to see their lives go forward" may still come to be realised.

Economic update

Vieira is pushing ahead with a **"structural adjustment programme"** in order to further revitalise the economy, which is likely to lead to price increases, while pressuring the rural poor and deepening wealth differences in the fast-growing towns.

An influx of **Mauritanians**, fleshing out the burgeoning retail sector, was under way even before the recent race riots between Mauritania and Senegal. In 1989, thousands of Mauritanian refugees from the violence arrived in Bissau, apparently to an unfazed welcome by President Vieira.

The British **VSO**, a non-governmental development organisation, has started a programme in Guinea-Bissau, but it's possible that Oxfam may pull out in response to what it sees as an over-proliferation of aid agencies.

Political update: a luta continua

On the political scene, it appears that internal **opposition** has been stamped out. But intrigues continue abroad, with right- and left-wing enemies of the present government plotting from Portugal, France, Senegal and even Cape Verde. One group is called *BAFATA* (ominous in view of that town's reputation for outspoken criticism) — presumably an acronym, meaning unknown. Although there have been one or two positive steps — improvements in press freedom, permission to form professional associations — there's little sign as yet that the *PAIGC* is prepared to countenance internal opposition parties. But, in common with other African partners of the World Bank and IMF, it may soon be asked to reform its political institutions as a condition of further aid.

Meanwhile there's continuous, and apparently worsening, **friction with Senegal** over the two countries' joint border. One part of the dispute is about offshore oil-drilling rights. But lately there have been several serious incidents in which Senegalese and Guinea-Bissauan armed forces have come into conflict along the jungly border. The presence in Guinea-Bissau of **Casamance separatists**, and in Senegal of anti-Vieira opposition groups, is the main catalyst. Senegalese troops have used "hot pursuit" as an excuse to enter Guinea-Bissau and in June 1990 were evacuating several of their villages near the border.

BISSAU AND AROUND

Every year in November, after the rains, when the ground is steaming off its last sops and the sun begins to burn through, **BISSAU** is struck by a swarm of flying crickets (*grilos*). At night they zoom into lights and batter against the walls as a handful of municipal sweepers come out with hoses and brooms. In the morning they litter the pavements and float in their thousands down the gutters.

Bissau has always been one of the smallest and (away from the centre) most destitute cities in West Africa. The tarred roads, built for Portuguese colonial convenience, are padded by pedestrians, but only now being worn much by the city's fast accumulating traffic. And only since 1987, after an almost comatose decade, has the **economic life** of the capital, and hence of the small country behind it, staggered to its feet. The annual plague of *grilos* seems like a hideous goad in the right direction.

In truth, things aren't as bad for travellers as most recent write-ups – already out of date – would suggest, and they're improving all the time. The markets have produce from the countryside, imports are increasing and there's an ever-widening circle of **bars**, **restaurants** and **hotels**. While Bissau offers precious little to do, it's a safe and gentle city – almost suburban – where you can at least do it virtually hassle-free. A mild capital and not architecturally unattractive, you get a real feeling that Bissau will soon be positively appealing – if it doesn't collapse under the pressure of rural immigrants: the city's population is around 200,000 and growing rapidly. After dark, it's already a lively and pretty enjoyable place to be, though no longer especially cheap.

Bissau practicalities: arriving and staying

There's one main road into Bissau, an embarrassment of a motorway that was never needed and never completed. **Arriving** by bush taxi you'll end up at the **Bandim** transport park, in a bustling low-rent commercial quarter out near the *mercado* of the same name. If you arrive **by air**, the airport is only 11km way, but too insignificant to have much in the way of facilities. Private hire taxis meet all flights, but you can get shared transport too, or walk down to the main Safim–Bissau road and pick up a ride there: it's not far.

If you happen to arrive **by sea**, it's a question of tides. Bissau is sprawled across the right bank of the Gêba river and channels to the port are narrow. The town is directly behind the two main piers.

The **public transport** system in Bissau is fairly disorganised. There's still no bus service but there are now masses of blue and white taxis. Fares are low: expect to pay around GB$1000 a ride.

Accommodation

The **hotel** scene in Bissau is fast-changing but there's nothing really cheap and much that's often full. A standard price seems to be about CFA5000 for a cheap room. You might do well to check for private rooms with the *Ministério do Comércio e Turismo* down by the port (see *Tourist Information* in the Bissau "Directory"), but be sure to ascertain the bona fides of your landlord as there have been some recent examples of theft.

CHEAPER END

Pensão Centrale av Amilcar Cabral (☎21 32 70/71). Undoubtedly the place to make for, with solid S/C rooms for GB$60,000/100,000 FB, usually payable in CFA only. Unfortunately, rooms are always sold out to long-stayers and you'll need to win the heart of the Portuguese matron who runs it to have any chance.

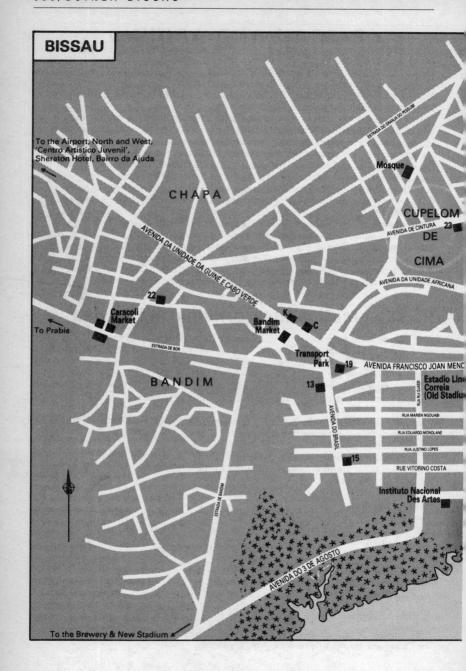

BISSAU

To the Airport, North and West,
'Centro Artistico Juvenil',
Sheraton Hotel, Bairro da Ajuda

CHAPA

Mosque

CUPELOM
DE
CIMA

AVENIDA DE CINTURA   23

AVENIDA DA UNIDADE DA GUINE E CABO VERDE

AVENIDA DA UNIDADE AFRICANA

22

Caracoli
Market

To Prabis

K

Bandim
Market   C

ESTRADA DE BOR

Transport
Park   19   AVENIDA FRANCISCO JOAN MEND

BANDIM   13   Estadio Line
Correia
(Old Stadiu

RUA MARIEN NGOUABI

RUA EDUARDO MONDLANE

RUA JUSTINO LOPES

15   RUE VITORINO COSTA

Instituto Nacional
Des Artes

ESTRADA DE BANDIM

AVENIDA DO BRASIL

RUA RUI DJASS

AVENIDA DO 3 DE AGOSTO

To the Brewery & New Stadium

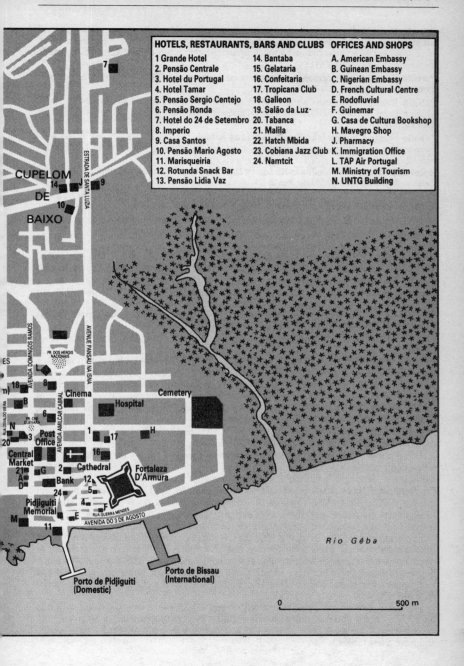

HOTELS, RESTAURANTS, BARS AND CLUBS

1 Grande Hotel
2. Pensão Centrale
3. Hotel du Portugal
4. Hotel Tamar
5. Pensão Sergio Centejo
6. Pensão Ronda
7. Hotel do 24 de Setembro
8. Imperio
9. Casa Santos
10. Pensão Mario Agosto
11. Marisqueiria
12. Rotunda Snack Bar
13. Pensão Lidia Vaz
14. Bantaba
15. Gelataria
16. Confeitaria
17. Tropicana Club
18. Galleon
19. Salão da Luz·
20. Tabanca
21. Malila
22. Hatch Mbida
23. Cobiana Jazz Club
24. Namtcit

OFFICES AND SHOPS

A. American Embassy
B. Guinean Embassy
C. Nigerian Embassy
D. French Cultural Centre
E. Rodofluvial
F. Guinemar
G. Casa de Cultura Bookshop
H. Mavegro Shop
J. Pharmacy
K. Immigration Office
L. TAP Air Portugal
M. Ministry of Tourism
N. UNTG Building

CUPELOM
DE
BAIXO

ESTRADA DE SANTA LUZIA

RUA DOMINGOS RAMOS

AVENIDE PANSAU NA ISNA

ES

PR. DOS HEROIS
NACIONAIS

Cinema

Hospital

Cemetery

AVENIDA DOMINGOS RAMOS

N

PR. CHE
GUEVARA

Post
Office

Central
Market

AVENIDA AMILCAR CABRAL

RUA OSVALDO VIEIRA

Cathedral

Bank

Fortaleza
D'Armura

Pidjiguiti
Memorial

RUA GUERRA MENDES

AVENIDA DO 3 DE AGOSTO

Rio Gêba

Porto de Pidjiguiti
(Domestic)

Porto de Bissau
(International)

0   500 m

Grande Hotel av Pansau Na Isna (☎21 34 52). A long-standing alternative to the *Centrale*, but standards of late have reportedly sagged deeper than the beds. Still clearly second best, coming across with sympathy and a touch of archaic charm too (tatty, AC, non S/C double rooms for under GB$60,000).

Pensão Tamar A considerably worse option and, at around GB$40,000–60,000 for non S/C rooms with dodgy fans, not one to target.

Pensão Ronda av Amilcar Cabral. Gloomy and run-down, this place has reportedly closed, which may be just as well. Like the *Tamar*, and similarly priced, they may insist you pay in hard currency.

Pensão Sergio Centeio (aka *Pensão Luar*) rua Antonio N'Bana 16 (☎21 29 66). A less well-known place with secure rooms around a courtyard and good prices (around GB$30,000–50,000).

Hotel du Portugal av Domingos Ramos (☎21 27 38). May be renovated, and ask about the **Pensão Proquil** (☎21 26 29) on Rua 2.

You could also try hanging out at the **Imperio** (see below) where one or two friendly, multi-lingual hustlers are usually helpful with cheap, private rooms.

LUXURY HOTELS

Leaping from the budget league there's a choice of two:

Hotel do 24 de Setembro Estrada de Santa Luzia (☎21 37 66/21 50 80). The established "top" hotel. It's way out of town and charges everything (including a glass of coke) in hard currency (from about US$40/US$55).

Sheraton Avenida 14 de Novembro CP107, 1602 Bissau CEDEX (☎21 12 24, telex 114, fax 215413). Brand new, and also out of town near the airport, the *Sheraton* is, even more than the *24 Setembro*, a place where contracts are signed between flights. Again, strictly *devisas* only, from US$105 to US$120.

Eating

Until recently getting a meal in Bissau could be a serious problem, but now it seems a new **restaurant** springs up every month. One place which has been around a long time and will hopefully stay is the *Casa Santos* – excellent for *gambas* but not so cheap. You'll need to pass by earlier in the day to book an evening meal though they can usually do an ad hoc lunch. The *Pensão Centrale* is absolutely reliable, dishing out three course meals (four if you include the banana) in a style that can't have changed much in thirty years. The beer-only-with-food rule is stringently applied and you need to be there by 8pm to be sure of getting dinner (GB$6000).

There are several lesser **permanent fixtures** all doing a variety of cobbled together snacks and drinks depending on what's available in town: the *Imperio* for watching the world go by, putting it to rights, and playing draughts; the *Marisqueira de Pidjiguiti* for the same, and occasionally good seafood dishes, run by the *Casa Santos* owners; and the big café on Praça Che Guevara. In addition the *Hotel Grande's* terrace is one of Bissau's few *rendezvous* and there's generally fresh lemon juice and sandwiches worth patronising (the *Grande's* restaurant proper is something of a joke).

Exploring **out of the centre** a little there's superb chicken and *Pampa* on draft at the *Bantaba*, not far from *Casa Santos*; tasty brochettes and brain-curling *canna de cajeu* opposite at *Pensão Maria Agosto*; monkey meat (only GB$2000) at the white house of *Pensão Lidia Vaz* near Bandim; and more good brochettes and draft *Pampa* with musical accompaniment at *Don Jose* opposite the cinema in Bairro da Ajuda on the road out of town.

There's a growing variety of sweet tooth hangouts as well: a new *Gelataria* with real Italian **ice cream** and a standby **pastries** shop – the *Confeitaria Dias & Dias* – which, even if everything does taste of coconut and margarine, really ought to serve coffee and have a few tables.

In and around Bissau

If you're in Bissau at the time of the **carnaval** – February – you'll get a lopsided view of the city's entertainment value as an endless stream of floats and elaborate *papier maché* masks is paraded through the streets. You can see the best ones (there's usually a theme, and winners) all year at the *Instituto Nacional des Artes*. Here too they've work-shops and a performance venue for occasional output by the *Ballet Nacional*. It's worth calling in if you're interested.

In town

There's very little to see in Bissau. The **museum** is homeless at present (see "Directory") though you can see the collection out on the airport road in a large school near the *Sheraton*. They've a modern collection of ethnic artefacts from around the country. The building marked as the museum on the *IGN* map of the city and country is the *UNTG* (*National Workers' Union*) building which does, at least, have some glori-ously lurid and intense paintings in the entrance hall and up the stairs.

Down by the port, you won't miss the impressive **Pidjiguiti Memorial** to the striking dockers massacred here on August 3 1959 (see p.544). And on a wall at the bottom of Avenida Pansau Na Isna you'll easily find a beautiful and unprotected tiled mural from colonial days. But this isn't compelling sight-seeing. Nor, regrettably, is the **Fortaleza d'Armura**: what ought to be an imposing monument is still a military zone and there's no way you'll get in to look around. The **mausoleum** of Amilcar Cabral is located within, but even Guineans only get to pay their respects on rare occasions – reportedly on September 24.

Beaches

If you have transport, you can explore beyond Bissau. Hiring a bicycle from a private owner is a good plan and not difficult. The nearest **sea swimming** is at PERFILIS, near PRÁBIS, where there's a bit of artificial beach – 18km from Bissau and reached by following the road past the new stadium. QUINHÁMEL (39km; follow the airport road) has a fine beach, on the creek shore, and quite possibly the best food in the country at the Portuguese-run beach restaurant, 1km down a shady track from the town. PUNTA BIOMBO (22km further), has a nice beach on the open sea but it's tiny.

GOOD TIMING

Don't bother struggling to get to the beach unless you know you'll be there at high tide. **Tide tables** are available from *Guinémar*.

Pepel people

Heading out on these short trips west of Bissau you pass through intensively farmed **Pepel** lands, the road winding characteristically, like an English country lane, in a deep trough between fenced and carefully tended raised fields. It's a curious – and likeable – landscape. The Pepel (one of the country's smaller ethnic groups, numbering about 60,000) used to take slain enemies' heads as trophies. They seem to have given that up and are more famous now as brilliant craftspeople, doing fine iron and leatherwork.

Bissau by night

After years of slumber, Bissau's **nightlife** is flexing into action again. For a popular, unpretentious and very youthful disco check out the *Tropicana* (ex-*Kora Club*) – which occasionally hosts live sounds and quite often has afternoon sessions at weekends.

Malila is a considerably flashier nightclub, with its own restaurant, but no live music. *Namtcit*, another town centre joint, has a first-floor restaurant. *Tabanca*, with resident Cape Verdean band, is a more promising venue.

You can **drink** after dark in the centre, with no danger of disturbance by sweaty bodies, at the nameless *kirintim* bar across from the *Imperio* at Praça dos Heróis Nacionais or the flamboyant *Galleon* – a Spanish-run, British "pub" set-up – which is open very late and keeps its AC high and its vibes as sophisticated as possible.

But you have to shed the relative banality of the town centre to find the worthwhile nightspots. Right on the traffic island of the Bandim transport park underneath the water tower is a tarted up *kirintim* called *Salão da Luz* which regularly hosts the N'Kassa Cobra orchestra as well as **Super Mama Djombo**, Bissau's most popular band. Heading east from here across the northern suburbs down Avenida da Unidade Africana you get into the lively district of **Cupelon de Cima** ("Upper Cupelon"). Try *Tesito* and the *Cobiana Jazz* club (residence of the band of the same name). Or walk away from town, through an increasingly dense commercial district, to *Hatch M'bida* – German-owned but the business all the same and a real *bairro* place for music and dancing.

Entry to these local clubs is normally reasonable (GB$4–5000). A taxi is worth hiring for the evening but don't leave finding one too late – and be prepared to risk some of the fare on the driver's knowledge: Bissau has plenty of action under the surface.

Bissau Directory

Airlines The following have offices in Bissau:
Aeroflot 6a rua 19 de Setembro (☎21 27 07).
Europe Aero Service (in assoociation with *TAGB*).
Gambia Air Shuttle near *Hotel Tamar*.
TAGB Transportes Aereas da Guiné-Bissau at Osvaldo Veira Airport (☎21 28 02/21 30 02)
TAP Air Portugal 14 Praça dos Hérois Nacionais (☎21 39 93, telex 242).
plus *Africana Air*, *Air Senegal* and *Cubana*.

American Express No proper agent in town. The *Sheraton* is most likely to offer help.

Bank The *Banco Nacional da Guiné-Bissau* will change your travellers' cheques and cash, after considerable delay. It's possible, according to them, to have money sent out and received in hard currency.

Bookshop The small selection of books and magazines at the *Casa de Cultura* mostly in Portuguese, includes Marx, Engels and revolutionary literature by Cabral and others; also English oddities (economics, infectious diseases) and a few cheap records – Super Mama Djombo, edited Brezhnev speeches, Chinese folk songs. The shop recently closed, future uncertain.

Car hire There's apparently a *Rentacar* on Rua 12 Setembro, but a cheaper and reasonably reliable outlet is the *Pensão Lidia Vaz* (see "Eating" above, ☎21 30 31). For private hire, a city taxi should cost around GB$50,000 per day, without petrol.

Cinema Just one main venue at the top of avenida Amilcar Cabral. One or two smaller cinemas in the suburbs.

Cloth There's been an enormous resurgence of strip-woven country cloth in the last year or two, with Pepel and Manjak the main weavers. You'll find a decent selection at Bandim market. Prices for a single *pagne* are around GB$30,000, with heavier weaves perhaps half as much again. Popular patterns include *kassav* (a check) and *volta de Bissau* (bands).

Crafts There's usually a spread of carvings and souvenirs in front of the *Grande Hotel* and there are always one or two crammed stalls in the central market, but the recommended place to browse is the *Centro Artistico Juvenil*, also known as the *Centro Padre Batista* after the Catholic priest who runs it (out of town on the avenida da Unidade de Guiné e Cabo Verde, on the right, open daily 9am–1pm & 3–7pm). This is a boys' centre producing wood carvings. Quality varies but there's some fine craftsmanship here and many pieces have real flair. Look out for telling family statuary – woman supporting kids and husband – and beautiful, cowrie-inlaid stools. Watch the carvers as long as you like: there's no pressure to buy but prices are reasonable and there's a mass of small items as well.

Cultural centres The French Cultural Centre is worth checking out if you're in town for any length of time: they often sponsor worthwhile events. The American Cultural Centre at the Embassy is less interesting. The Portuguese equivalent up in the Zona Escolar has a good library – if you speak Portuguese.

Doctors Ask your Embassy or Consulate: Cuban doctors, resident at the *Grande Hotel*, have in the past been helpful to travellers with routine stomach and malaria problems.

Duty free supermarkets For hard currency (priced in FF) these sell most of what you might be craving. Try *Mavegro* on rua Eduardo Mondlane; *Entre-loja* down on rua Guerra Mendes; *Perfila-franca* opposite the Central Market; and *Entre-franca* opposite the Ministry of Justice on a sidestreet off avenida Amilcar Cabral. There's another, behind the American Embassy, that's recommended for its cheap booze.

Embassies and consulates include:
> **Algeria** 12 rua 12 de Setembro (CP 350; ☎21 15 22).
> **Egypt** 1 rua 12 de Setembro (CP72; ☎21 36 42).
> **France** rua Eduardo Mondlane (☎21 26 33) (see "Visas" below).
> **Guinea** 9 rua 14 (CP 396; ☎21 26 81) (see "Visas" below).
> **Great Britain** Honorary Consul: Jan van Maanen, c/o *Mavegro,*, rua Eduardo Mondlane (CP 10; ☎21 15 29, telex 259).
> **Mauritania** near the *Centro Artisanal Juvenil* in Chapa.
> **Netherlands** Honorary Consul (see *Great Britain*).
> **Nigeria** avenida 14 de Novembro, off avenida da Unidade de Guiné e Cabo Verde, opposite Bandim market (☎21 27 82).
> **Portugal** 6 rua de Lisboa (☎21 30 09).
> **Senegal** near the *Presidência do Conselho de Estado* (☎21 26 36).
> **Sweden** 16 rua 13 (☎21 44 22).
> **USA** avenida Domingos Ramos (CP 297; ☎21 28 17).
> **USSR** 17 rua Rui Djassi (☎21 35 35).

Ferries and ships Details and tickets from *Rodofluvial* on avenida do 3 de Agosto. For a summary see *BASICS*. For information about **international shipping** check out *Guinémar* on rua Guerra Mendes. Bissau is a port where you might, with time and luck, find a passage: Conakry two days, Lisbon six days, Hamburg eight days.

Flight infromation From *TAGB* at the airport (☎21 30 04) or the control tower (☎21 52 72) who presumably know as much as anybody.

Immigration If you need to renew your visa, the office is opposite the Bandim market, near the Nigerian embassy.

Markets Two main venues. One is the **municipal market** in the town centre; a wide selection of stalls including fruit and vegetables, dry groceries, crafts and household goods. The other is the burgeoning area at **Bandim**, on the way out to the airport.

Museum A French Canadian team has been working on a complete catalogue of the national collections and archives. For some years, however, there's been no public exhibition. The guards in the *PAIGC* headquarters are fed up of being asked if that is the museum – a long established but groundless rumour to which they take some offence. It looks as if the museum is to be housed in the new *Compleixa 24 Setembro*.

Petrol There are two pumps on avenida Amilcar Cabral and one at Bandim transport park.

Pharmacy A reasonably stocked place on the corner of avenida Pansau Na Isna and avenida da Cintura.

Post office A safe but infuriatingly rarely opened *Lista da Correios*. Expensive mail.

Swimming pool Only at the new *Sheraton*, out of town towards the airport.

Theatre Occasional pieces are put on in the *UDIB* building – a kind of sports club next to the cinema.

Tourist information Don't run around town looking for long defunct addresses. The only official place with any information is the *Ministério do Comércio e Turismo* down by the port on avenida Domingos Ramos. Ask to see the *Secretaria de Estado do Turismo* – Secretary of State for Tourism (morning and afternoon ☎21 32 82) – who is helpful.

Visas Although a Cape Verdean ambassador is accredited to Guinea-Bissau, there's no trace of a **Cape Verde** embassy: see if the Portuguese embassy can help. Visas for **Guinea** have sometimes been issued without difficulty: the consul can be sympathetic but it may be best to avoid mention of tourism unless you're certain the rule has been relaxed (see Guinea "Red Tape"). The **French** embassy issues visas on behalf of a number of countries.

THE BIJAGOS ISLANDS

The **Bijagos archipelago** is the largest along the West African coast; at least sixteen inhabited islands in the main cluster – principal of which is **Bubaque** – plus the inshore islands of **Bolama**, **Pecixe** and **Jeta** and dozens of smaller islets.

The islands are mostly covered in dense forest, with large stands of oil palm and cashew groves, less impressive patches of cultivation and necklaces of white sand along the seashore. The islanders – predominantly Bijagos-speakers who've lived surrounded by these calm, warm waters for centuries – are remarkably autonomous: you'll see women in palm fibre skirts (*saiya*), who've never left their own island. Many of the more remote islands felt little effect from the centuries of Portuguese presence in the region (several were never, officially, "pacified" at the end of the last century when the rest of the country was being shot into line). And several still have only the most tenuous of links with the government and the outside world.

Paradise the islands are, in a way – there are even snakes in some abundance to fit – but the cost in **practical terms** is inconvenient **ferry connections** and an almost complete lack of facilities outside the two very small towns of Bubaque and Bolama. To these two islands come 99 percent of the few travellers who make it out here. Bolama, so close to the coast, is relatively straightforward to visit, though as ex-capital, the complete absence of hotels is mystifying. Bubaque has the distinction of being the country's only "tourist resort" – don't be misled by that – and it has some accommodation. You might also find a seat on the **weekly flight** there from Bissau.

Bolama

There are ferries to Bolama on the first high tide every Tuesday and Saturday, returning on Friday and Sunday. Otherwise, you can get to or from the island any weekday via ENXUDE, opposite Bissau on the mainland. From Enxude, it's a 33-kilometre bush taxi trip to São João, facing Bolama town, whence a short *pirogue* ride relays you across the channel to Bolama.

The town of **BOLAMA** is on the landward side of the island, facing the mainland barely two kilometres away. Hollow, and partly deserted, it echoes with the past grandeurs of the Portuguese empire. Solid mansions attest a century of trading in ivory and forest products and the opening up of the West African groundnut industry. Since the capital of Portuguese Guinea was transferred to Bissau in 1941, Bolama has been steadily crumbling away. The grandest buildings in town are away from the port, up the hill around the main *praça* – the old **provincial headquarters** and post office and the abandoned, Manueline-style *Hotel do Turismo*.

In more **practical terms**, today's facilities for visitors are virtually nil. There's **no hotel**, though the swimming pool, right by the harbour, does have a **restaurant** of sorts, and you can normally spend a night or two here under a *paillote* – on the understanding you buy the odd meal. Should this possibility not pan out, you may find aid workers or missionaries willing to put you up. And if you arrive on the Saturday boat, you can usually sleep on the deck (because it goes no further, returning to Bissau the next day). But you're best off with your own **tent**, preferably light and airy, and freest too, with some wheels of your own. It's really worth tracking down bicycles to hire in Bissau and bringing them with you. Exploring the island otherwise, unless on foot over an extended period, is difficult. There's no more than a handful of vehicles.

On the question of **food**, the only shops are in Bolama itself, and they don't amount to much at all. There's a limited market (in a large, walled marketplace) where a small selection of fruit and vegetables, fish, peanut butter and, usually, bread is available. Bring with you what you can from Bissau. What you don't use will find eager recipients.

Bolama's past

Curiously, the first colonial adventure attempted on Bolama was conducted by the **British** in 1792 (see box) and they tried again in 1814. But the agreements with local **Bijagos** elders on which these incursions were based were no more binding than the treaties the Bijagos had also signed with the **Portuguese**. And it was the latter – particularly the mixed race Cape Verde islanders – who survived both Bolama's fevers and the Bijagos warriors long enough to establish a real community. Throughout the nine-

---

BEAVER'S COLONY

If the **British expedition to Bolama** had resulted in a successful colony, the map of West Africa might today be radically different. **Phillip Beaver**, 26, set sail from Gravesend on April 4 1792 with 274 prospective settlers. Included among them were a ready-made Legislative Council and Governor, chosen in the Globe Tavern, London.

The first deaths occurred through smallpox before they had reached the Isle of Wight, and by the time the two ships, *Hankey* and *Calypso*, were nosing through the Bijagos islands six weeks later, half the passengers had malarial fever. Bolama, at first, seemed perfect and uninhabited, and those colonists who were well enough went ashore to chase elephants and butterflies, lie in the sun and collect oysters. Beaver was irritated at their lack of industry. They saw a Bijagos war canoe but Beaver insisted "the inhabitants were thought to be of peaceable disposition, well-inclined towards the English culture". A week later the warriors attacked, surprisingly well-armed with muskets and Solingen swords, killing and wounding a dozen people and kidnapping several women and children. The settlers' cannons had never even been unpacked.

The colony looked doomed from then on. Although the captives were released when Bolama was "bought" for £77 worth of iron bars from a pair of local headmen, over half the emigrants chose to continue to Sierra Leone in the *Calypso* in July. As the rains set in, the remaining 91 died of malaria at a remarkably even rate until by the end of the year there were only thirteen survivors. A typically laconic entry in Beavers's journal reads:

Sun 2nd Dec. Killed a bullock for the colony. Died and was buried Mr. Webster. Thermometer 92. Three men well.

Beaver and five others survived the rains of the following year and he and a companion sailed back to England in May 1794. "An ill-contrived and badly executed, though well intended expedition", he mused. The timing, arriving at the start of the rains, could not have been worse. His book was entitled "African Memoranda: Relative to an Attempt to Establish a British Settlement on the Island of Bulama on the Western Coast of Africa in the year 1792, with a Brief Notice of the Neighbouring Tribes, Soils, Productions Etc., and some Observations on the Facility of Colonising that part of Africa with a View to Cultivation; and the Introduction of Letters and Religion to its Inhabitants but more particularly as the means of gradually Abolishing Slavery". Published in 1805, and hugely readable, it's worth scanning the antiquarian bookshops for.

teenth century the British returned periodically to claim sovereignty by pulling up the Portuguese flagpoles, shouting at the settlers and shipping their domestic slaves off to liberation in the colony of Sierra Leone. But they made no serious efforts to settle permanently, or to take charge of the island, until 1860, when Bolama was annexed to Sierra Leone, hundreds of miles to the south. The Portuguese, desperate to preserve their stake in the slave trade which the British were busy trying to abolish, had formally lodged their own claim in 1830 and by the time the British annexed the island, there were 700 loyal Portuguese subjects living there. The dispute wasn't settled until 1870, when a commission headed by United States President Ulysses S. Grant found in favour of Portugal. Grant's efforts were rewarded with a statue in the town square.

Town and island

Bolama is the seat of government of Bolama Region, which includes most of the islands and a little chunk of mainland. It has its own regional president, a hospital, a nurses' school and a teacher training college. Walking around will take you all of forty minutes.

Down by the port you'll not miss the ugly **sculpture** bestowed on the island by Mussolini after an Italian seaplane crashed here in 1931 (Bolama used to be a "hydro-base" on the Rome to Rio de Janeiro seaplane route). The solid constuction of the monument means it hasn't fallen victim to the tide of nationalism which knocked Ulysses Grant off his pedestal near the bandstand in the overgrown main square. This part of town reeks of post-colonial decay, though most of the buildings, apart from the governor's residence, are still in use. The only reminder of Britain's ephemeral presence on Bolama is down to the left behind the church: the reddish two-storey ruin almost throttled by rank undergrowth is the **Casa Inglesa**, a monstrous edifice built entirely of corrugated iron. Architecturally, at any rate, the Portuguese deserved to win the island.

There's a pleasant evening stroll out of town past the secondary school and down an attractive, sandy avenue of trees, with compounds set back on both sides – surely a colonial conception, but one that's endured. Out this way too, at the start of the avenue on the left, there's a rather Gothic graveyard which is worth a look: a curious assembly of souls, including a number of middle Europeans and even one or two Britons. Rapid brown snakes shimmer out of the way as you walk.

Walks out of the town

Fork right at the end of the avenue out of the town and you soon find yourself on a delightful, narrow lane, twisting through cashew groves. There are no beaches down here, but you do pass a **cashew jam factory** which is open a few days every year – they make more deadly cashew wine than jam (out of the fruits, not the nuts) – and a cloth manufacturing plant that evidently hasn't been open from the day the looms were delivered. Passing through the hamlet of Pujangulo, the path becomes a muddy track through the mangroves at low tide, at which time it joins the main island to the Ilha das Cobras – an uninhabited islet. Exciting stuff, but watch out for snakes on the other side and don't get stranded by the tide. The walk is about 15km there and back.

There are other, shorter walks you could do in the peninsula immediately south of Bolama town. But the main interest lies **further south across the island**. Down here, unless you're prepared to set off early with food and water sufficient for a couple of days, you're really going to need transport. The dirt road cuts through pretty forest, farm and plantation lands, following the central ridge of the island (maximum elevation just 26m), never far from the sea. The people you'll meet are mostly Bijagos, though it's the women who stand out (many men are away labouring) and whose apparel is so distinctive. Although bras and cotton *pagnes* have arrived, the traditional costume of palm fibre kilt (*saya*) is still the standard wear for most women, though officially

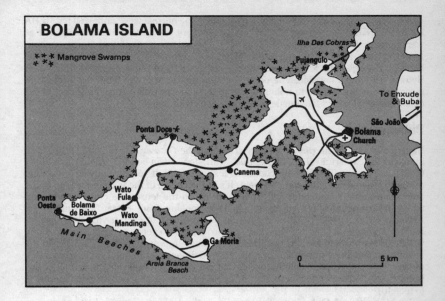

BOLAMA ISLAND

✱✱✱ Mangrove Swamps

Ilha Das Cobras

Pujangulo

To Enxude & Buba

São João

Bolama Church

Ponta Doce

Canema

Wato Fula

Ponta Oeste

Bolama de Baixo

Wato Mandinga

Main Beaches

Ga Moria

Areia Branca Beach

0   5 km

banned from the town. For the country Bijagos, tourists are a sensational novelty and you'll occasionally find children for whom such a meeting is a first.

Hamlets and clusters of compounds are, in many cases, named after ethnic groups. Some 17km from Bolama you turn left at WATO FULA and plunge into a tunnel of cashews. **Areia Branca beach** is a further 7km down here, a narrow lip of white sand dipping beneath the coconuts into a milky blue sea. It's said to be the best spot, and you're unlikely to find it anything but deserted, but there are other beaches along the southern coast. This corner of the island is very sparsely populated and you can nose around for hours completely alone. Remember, however, that coconuts are *owned*.

Bubaque

In Guinea-Bissau, tourism begins and ends in **BUBAQUE**. In colonial days the island was a Portuguese favourite, and after independence Swedish aid provided a hotel (to which excursionists from The Gambia were flown for several seasons in the late 1970s) and a tarmac road to the beach. The trips from The Gambia ceased and these days it's rare indeed to find more than a handful of guests at the *Hotel-Estância Balnear*.

The voyage

Getting there, apart from twice-weekly **flights** which often fail to materialise, involves taking the weekly *Rodofluvial* **ferry** to Bubaque on Friday or Saturday, returning Sunday (4–5 hrs), which is just enough time for a flying visit. There are also less formal possibilities: the *Vitoria*, a vessel belonging to the *Estrela do Mar* fisheries department, often makes the run for example. Prices should be the same as ordinary ferry services, but comfort (and toilet facilities) may be even more rudimentary. Take food and sufficient water for the hot and exhausting voyage.

A dirty, spume-laden sea as flat as a millpond is the normal view, until well past ILHA DAS GALINHAS (a mid-way stop where passengers are unloaded to a boat). But as you approach RUBANE, the mood improves. The intense tropicality of the green, horizontal, islands leaves a strong sense of place, reinforced as you enter the channel between Bubaque and Rubane and see the red tin roofs of Bubaque with its high pier. By now it's always low tide. The scene – children picking in the mud, the viridescent foliage of the two islands tumbling to the water, the tranquility after the racket of the diesel and what seems like bustle in Bissau – is all a bit magic.

Bubaque

Bubaque has two main **places to stay**. The first, the *Casa de Adelio* (☎82 11 26), is an immaculate, well-run shop/bar/*pensão* with four twin-bedded rooms at about GB$10,000 a room. There's the chance of a shower and, if you give advance warning, meals (the usual fish, rice and potatoes). It's in the centre of the village; walk up to the once-upon-a-time roundabout and from there it's to the left of the church and water tanks. It's sometimes full so try to phone a booking from Bissau. Staying at the *Estancia Balnear* (☎82 11 30) is a different proposition but, even paying in obligatory **hard currency** at the official rate, by no means expensive. Prices are around GB$30,000 equivalent for S/C twin B&B, with much improved meals (GB$5000) in the newly completed restaurant block on the cliff top. Rooms at the hotel suffer from a lack of fans, nets and AC, and running water and electricity are intermittent, but all of this seems likely to change for the better in the near future (probably with price increases to match).

Looking **around Bubaque** village is nice in the early morning and late afternoon. Immensely picturesque seascapes flicker through the mango boughs; oil palms in massive stands, many around the hotel, are covered in the nit-like nests of weaver birds, and resound with their chatter; butterflies and lizards dart everywhere; and the island has a reputation for mambas, though one sighting in three days doesn't seem excessive. In the village there are a couple of stalls which hardly deserve to be called a market, and one or two basic stores. You'll also find some interesting characters hanging out: a Gambian fisherman trading shark fin (to be made into shark's fin soup) to Hong Kong vessels (didn't he get lonely down here away from his people? – "Of course I do" he laughed, as if it was the funniest thing he'd heard all week); and a sober elder claiming to be the *chefe* of Bubaque who will pose reverently, having agreed a price, while you take a picture of him with his religious paraphernalia of claw-stick and basket of tricks.

The south of the island

There's a big coach at the hotel, which does a morning and evening run **to the beach** if there are enough guests. If not, there may be a rather high charge, in which case talk to any of the few drivers around the village and try to fix something up. Ideally, you'd bring a bike from Bissau or rent or borrow one on the island (GB$5–10,000 per day is the going rate).

It's certainly worth getting down to **Praia da Bruce** for at least one day, as it's practically deserted and very appealing. The 15km of heavily overgrown tarred road is dead flat; a one hour ride. There are some tall stands of wild forest still to be seen and signs, too, of old Portuguese estates and villas. The only other road users seem to be women and naked children. You can deviate from the road and call at the villages of BIJANE and BRUCE (no-one knows the derivation of that name – presumably part of the Anglo-Lusophone connection, it's also spelled Broussa).

All that's left of the hotel's **"annexe"** on the beach are rotting stools around a derelict bar, half-bald *paillotes*, bomb-struck toilet blocks and evidence of bygone picnics. But there's a beautiful pond of lilies with intriguing rustles and plenty of birdlife. The isolation down here is palpable. One or two fishermen may come by, stationing themselves in the waves with their throwing nets for hours on end, to provide a garnish for the evening rice.

The beach offers shady cashew trees and as much clean sand as you could wish for. Come here, preferably, when the tide is high. And bring drinking water, lots of it.

Other islands

Visiting the **other Guinean islands** is very much a trip into the unknown. Information is hard to obtain in Bissau: there are no regular *Rodofluvial* ferries except to PECIXE (see "Getting Around"), which does, however, have a long coastline of beaches facing the open Atlantic, usefully close to its main village, IJANTE.

Getting to other islands in the main Bijagos group, Bubaque is the best place to look for local fishing boats. RUBANE and SOGA (the latter was the island from which the 1979 Portuguese invasion of the Republic of Guinea was launched) are close by and not hard to get to, but neither offers anything beyond Bubaque's own attractions. In the dry season, Serer fishermen from south of Dakar set up temporary fishing camps on the shore.

The principal **"towns"** of the other islands are INOREI (on Ilha Roxa – also known as Ilha Canhabaque), UNO (on the island of the same name, it makes Bubaque look cosmopolitan in comparison) and BETELHE on the island of Caravela. **Inorei** has some old and attractive Bijago baked mud **architecture**. In the southeast of the island, there are natural curiosities in its population of **saltwater-dwelling hippos** that inhabit the big Meneque creek (not to be confused with the Ilha Meneque).

But it's the island of **Caravela**, facing out to sea on the archipelago's northwest periphery, that's rated outstanding and worth really persisting with to get to if you have the time. It has a string of stunning beaches on its northern, seaward coast and reportedly crystal clear water that swarms with fish. If you're in a group, the **airstrip** at Caravela suggests it might be worth enquiring of *TAGB* in Bissau how much it would cost to charter a plane: the distance from Bissau is only 80km.

After Caravela in order of wonderfulness, UNHOCOMO (a tiny three by seven kilometre islet in the far west; wild flowers, abundance of cashews, exquisite villages, main one ANABURU) and ORANGO in the south (biggest of the islands; main village ETICOGA) have had the most lavish praise from those lucky enough to visit them – usually development aid workers. Naturally we'd be pleased to hear an account of your trip, for the next edition, if you make it to any of them.

THE INTERIOR

Reserves of enthusiasm for the **Bissau hinterland** – a patchwork of low ridges, divided by the country's creeks and rivers – run pretty low once you've visited the capital and the islands. From the travel perspective, the country divides into three: a relatively busy and visited region **north and west** of Bissau towards the Senegalese border; a more inaccessible and little-known region to the **south**, fronting up against the Republic of Guinea; and the **east** of the country. The east is hardly explored by travellers either, but Guinea-Bissau's main road runs out this way, with a number of fairly important towns and villages along the line of travel.

The Northwest

The vast beach along the coast at **VARELA** is probably among the best reasons to come to Guinea-Bissau. But few people know that. The coast here is better than those across the border in the tourist ghettos of Cap Skiring, and largely empty but for local people. As a place to come for the weekend, Varela is a favourite among the country's small expatriate community; a wonderful place with gorgeous swimming, pine trees and low cliffs. There's a colonial **hotel** at Varela which, while rarely open, is always prepared to open on demand. Ask for Martinho, who's always around. Rooms are around GB$20,000 a night. There are also **houses to rent**, for a similar price, but with space for four and meals to order from the hotel. Electricity is less certain, but at busy times (Christmas and New Year for example) it's usually on.

Varela is changing. Two **new hotels** may make it easier to get to from São Domingos and may force the old establishment to close – though it's survived on little enough custom for years. A very few years could see serious competition for Cap Skiring which, if the direct jungle track across the border was opened, is only 30km away .

São Domingos and the road to Bissau

Problematically, getting to Varela means a fifty-kilometre earth road journey west of **SÃO DOMINGOS**, one of the entry points to Guinea-Bissau from Senegal. Transport down there is somewhat scarce. If you're stuck in São Domingos there's a restaurant, where they'll always rustle up a solid meal, run by one Titiche and, just opposite, a dirt cheap *pensão* (the *São Felipe*). The perennial problem at São Domingos, which is right at the head of a creek, used to be catching the **ferry to Cacheu**. This – in its many guises varying from one with room for a single car only to a small roll-on-roll-off – leaves once a day only, on the high tide, and takes a couple of hours. When it breaks down, even for thirty minutes, you're probably in for a wait until the next day. The alternative route, now much preferred since it's all been paved, goes via INGORE and a short ferry crossing at SÃO VICENTE. Buses and bush taxis run to Bissau mornings and evenings.

CACHEU, anyway, has nothing to offer. It's the site of a sixteenth-century fort, the whitewashed substance of which (only twenty metres square) is still in place, along with its guns, and more ruins to the right, down on the shore. There's no accommodation, no restaurants, and little indeed in the way of shops or food. A traditional "fair" or market is held every eight days. Stuck here the night, your only options are camping somewhere in the town or finding a friend. Notice the unusual material used on the roads in Cacheu; broken oil-palm kernel pits which are very hard-wearing, like vegetable gravel.

The next main town along the way is **CANCHUNGO**, to which several vehicles a day run from Cacheu. It looks promising from the outskirts, with a fine avenue of trees running into town, but, again, it's maddeningly listless. The central *praça* is at least moderately alive with people waiting for transport, the odd bus, a renascent market area with sellers of boiled starch and oranges, and, just off the square (really a circle) a few places where beer, meals and rooms are available. There's a regular 3pm bus from here to SAFIM, just beyond the last (short) ferry crossing of the Rio Mansôa before Bissau.

The South

The gateway to the south is **ENXUDE**, across the Rio Gêba from Bissau. A ferry links the town to the capital once a day on weekdays, and *pirogue* crossings are negotiable any time from the creek shore behind the main cemetery in Bissau. This southern region is really isolated and there's little to draw you down here unless you're determined to follow the coast as near as possible into Guinea-Conakry.

The main town of the south, **BUBA,** has almost nothing – an awful, small restaurant and possibly somewhere to stay. Nearby there are swimming beaches and waterfalls along the Rio Corubal, which separates the south from the rest of Guinea-Bissau, but even these are most easily reached from the northern part of the country via the north bank village of XITOLE. The falls are at SALTINHO, near MAMPATÁ, the only bridge over the Corubal. CUSSILINTRA, a dozen kilometres downstream and closer to Xitole, was a colonial beauty spot and is still a popular weekend excursion with good swimming nearby. Someone is evidently building a hotel and restaurant there. South of the Corubal, the villages of METANDIAME and CANTANHA, are marked on the *IGN* map as "notable sites": if you find out what's so notable about them, we'd like to know.

BOÉ, 90km east of the waterfalls along a track which skims the Guinean border, is famous as the first town to be liberated from the Portuguese by the *PAIGC*, back in 1967. It's a false reputation, though, as the first town to be liberated was in fact in Boé *district*, a place called LUGAJOLE in the deep southeast. A small plaque and hut there commemorate the occasion. Strange, hilly landscapes roundabout – the outliers of the Fouta Djalon – are a change from the maze of mangroves and mud nearer the coast.

The East: routes into Guinea and Senegal

The two main towns of the interior – BAFATÁ and GABÚ – are located along Guinea-Bissau's one, main highway. You'll find transport fairly easily along here – increasingly so – with several daily bus and *aluguer* departures between both towns and Bissau, and even reasonable hitching prospects.

It's a good and newish road most of the way, with an unremarkable scenery of tall grass and charcoal-burning villages. Before Mansôa, the road forks right for the east, and north over the Rio Mansôa for the town. **MANSÔA** has nowhere to stay, but there are a couple of restaurants: one, on the way into town, is run by a helpful Cape Verdean; the other, bang in the town centre, is a circular, thatched affair where you can drink beer, eat monkey and meet locals. The road on to FARIM (check out the *Pensão Pic-Nic*) and the Senegalese border town of TANAF, is a decent one. Farim's ferry seems to be running well these days, as much as twice an hour from 8am to 8pm.

Bafatá and around

Continuing east over the old trading river, the Rio Gêba, BAMBADINCA marks the start of the track down south to XITOLE and the riverine attractions mentioned above. The nearby port of XIME is the furthest into the interior that regular ferries run from Bissau. **BAFATÁ** comes as a surprise, its street lights offering an optimistic welcome, its brick factory apparently turning the red dust that smothers everything into the neat, tiled houses you see all round. Finding **a place for the night** is easy, and there are several **restaurants** and a flourishing market. Backtracking from here, the first capital of the Portuguese province of Guinea was **GÊBA**, 12km from the town down a side road to the north before you reach Bafatá. Now virtually a ghost town, Gêba's overgrown **ruins** are supposed to be worth a look if you're drawn to such places. Out of Bafatá, there's a well-maintained dirt **road to the Senegalese border** at PIRADA.

Gabú

From Bafatá to Gabú, unusual tall stands of bamboo flank the road. The country's eastern capital, **GABÚ** is the Fula and Muslim capital too, and perhaps the region's nicest town. It's a pleasant place to stay, an animated commercial centre prospering from its triangular trade with nearby Senegal and Guinea. There's at least one *pensão* in town (a nice place across the street from the taxi park and behind the Catholic church), as well as the flashier **tourist hotel**/hunting lodge connected to Bissau's *Hotel 24 de Setembro*.

The northern route out of Gabú to PIRADA and Senegal is another reasonable, maintained track, where you may even have luck hitching.

Into Guinea

The surfaced highway continues east to PITCHE, from where you should certainly check out the **route south into Guinea** at FOULA-MORI if you're heading for Conakry or the Fouta Djalon. On a Monday (market day in Pitche) you should find transport down this narrow track. There's a hand-hauled ferry large enough for a small truck. The route is not marked on the maps, but it's a recognised border frontier (further details in the Guinea chapter *Practical Details* under "Arrivals"). The traffic on the main road beyond Pitche is sparse and without your own wheels you may find this route, via KOUNDARA, a slower entry into the country.

GUINEA

GUINEA

S ince 1958, when it reclaimed its total independence and effectively cut itself off from France, the **Republic of Guinea** has been an isolated and secretive country. Only on the death of dictator Sekou Touré in 1984, did Guinea begin, hesitantly, to open its borders to tourists. It remains one of the least visited countries in West Africa and, despite pronouncements, it is still, periodically, very difficult to get visas.

Not just for these enigmatic reasons, Guinea holds massive appeal as a place to **travel**. It sprawls in a great arc of mountains and plains from the fuming mangrove coast to the savannah of the Niger source-lands and the montane forests on the border with Côte d'Ivoire. The great rivers of West Africa – the Gambia, the Senegal and the Niger – all rise in Guinea. And on the *Michelin* map the country has more green-bordered roads (*parcours pittoresques*) than any other – always a promising indication.

Its best-known attraction is the **Fouta Djalon** highlands, populated by settled, largely Muslim, Fula herders and farmers; a plateau region dramatically dissected into myriad hills and valleys, spouting waterfalls like a colossal rock garden. Having time to explore is the only negative consideration.

Further to the east, on **the plains** where the streams flow away from the sea, where you can already feel the cultural resonances of the Niger valley's medieval empires, scattered **historical reminders** – and towns, rather than the sparse countryside – are always the focus. To the south, another great highland region – **Guinée Forestière** – fronts up against the coastal states in a zone of wet forest and remote peoples, where liana bridges cross the rivers and pre-Islamic tradition survives. One of the biggest **weekly markets** in West Africa is held up here, at Guéckédou.

Guinea's people share a wide cultural diversity. No single language predominates and there's considerable regional variation. **Susu**, the main language of the coastal region, is currently in ascendance and the language of most of President Conté's government. Susu, as a Mande language, is related to **Kouranko** and **Malinké** (Sekou Touré's mother tongue, widely spoken in the northeast), as well as to **Kpelle** and **Loma** – minority languages of the highland forests – and to the market lingua franca known as **Dyula**.

Fula, the predominant language of the Fouta Djalon, continues to be underrepresented in national life, as it was – maliciously – under Sekou Touré. There's still deep bitterness among the Fula-speaking community who, with forty percent of the population, are the largest single ethnic group.

Overall, Guinea has extraordinary vitality and newly unleashed confidence – an energy debased only in the capital, **Conakry**, about which it's hard to be positive. The years of dictatorship were harrowing, yet they've resulted in a strong political consciousness. And outside the capital, the veneer of European culture which frequently obscures the other ex-colonies is hardly noticeable. Africa shines through very brightly.

GUINEAN FACTS AND FIGURES

The **République de Guinée** is often called Guinea-Conakry, to distinguish it from other Guineas – reflection too of the colonial preoccupation with capitals. The population at the last count (1983) was 5.4 million, with over ten percent in Conakry. The area (246,000 square kilometres) is about the same as West Germany or Great Britain. Guinea has a colossal foreign debt, estimated in excess of £1 billion, but healthy exports help. The government (since 1984) is the Military Committee for National Recovery (*CMRN*) – a military-civilian grouping. There are no legal political parties.

Climate

When you visit Guinea – and where you go – is likely to be determined in large degree by the **seasons**. Conakry, at the best of times, has an insupportable climate, with relative humidity rarely below eighty percent and July delivering the heaviest month's rainfall anywhere in West Africa, much of which, fortunately, torrents down at night.

The Fouta Djalon, on the other hand, can be truly delightful in the weeks following the rainy season – which is shorter and lighter as you head north to Labé. The southeast highlands, too, have a good spell of fine weather, though conditions vary greatly. Away from the coast, and especially in the mountains, temperatures can plummet at night: you need some warm clothes and a sleeping bag.

Off the limited runs of main, surfaced highway, most of the countryside is isolated during the rains. Many minor routes are completely impassable for days or weeks on end due to flooding. This is the Zaire of West Africa, so be prepared for plans to go awry.

The **best time to travel** is from the end of November to March. Dry season harmattan winds from the north can bring haze and dust as early as December, but poor visibility doesn't always effect regions outside the northeast.

AVERAGE TEMPERATURES AND RAINFALL

CONAKRY

	Jan	Feb	Mar	Apr	May	June	July	Aug	Sept	Oct	Nov	Dec
Temperatures °C												
Min (night)	22	23	23	23	24	23	22	22	23	23	24	23
Max (day)	31	31	32	32	32	30	28	28	29	31	31	31
Rainfall mm	3	3	10	23	158	559	1298	1054	683	371	122	10
Days with rainfall	0	0	1	2	11	22	29	27	24	19	8	1

KOUROUSSA

	Jan	Feb	Mar	Apr	May	June	July	Aug	Sept	Oct	Nov	Dec
Temperatures °C												
Min (night)	14	17	22	23	23	22	21	21	21	21	19	15
Max (day)	33	36	37	37	35	32	30	30	31	32	33	33
Rainfall mm	10	8	22	71	135	246	297	345	340	168	33	10

MAMOU

	Jan	Feb	Mar	Apr	May	June	July	Aug	Sept	Oct	Nov	Dec
Temperatures °C												
Min (night)	13	15	18	19	20	18	19	19	19	18	17	13
Max (day)	33	34	35	34	31	29	27	25	28	29	30	31
Rainfall mm	8	10	46	127	203	257	335	401	340	203	61	8

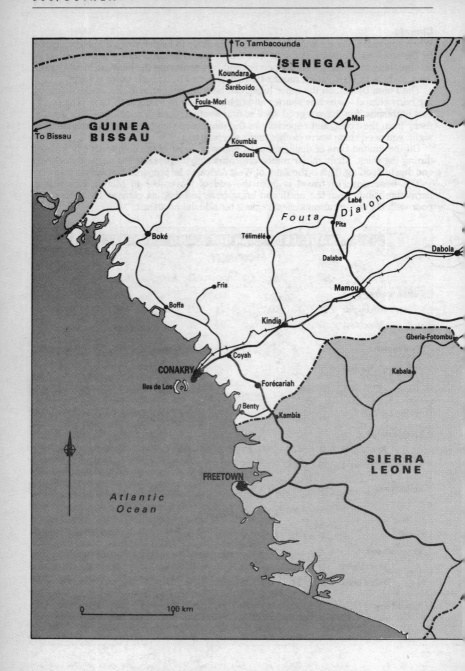

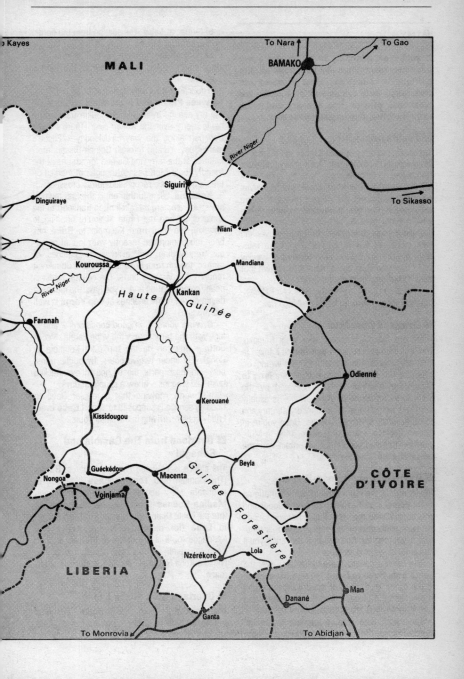

Arrivals

If you're not planning to fly in, there are overland routes into Guinea from all the surrounding countries. Most of these are endurance tests of one sort or another, but most also provide fine scenery and wild, little-travelled districts along the way.

■ Flights from Africa

There are, in theory, **direct flights** to Conakry, at least weekly, from Abidjan, Accra, Banjul, Bissau, Brazzaville, Casablanca, Dakar, Freetown, Kinshasa, Lagos, Libreville, Lomé and Monrovia. *Ghana Airways* and *Air Afrique* are responsible for most of the flights which materialize. The weekly flight from Guinea-Bissau is pretty reliable and a useful alternative to the long overland haul described below, particularly in the rainy season. *Air Guinée* usually operates a weekly flight between Hastings airfield in Freetown (not the international airport) and Conakry.

In addition, *Ghana Airways* flies Las Palmas–Conakry once a week on its West Africa run.

■ Overland from Mali

There are two main possibilities from Bamako. The first involves taking a **bush taxi** to Kankan (a long day, even assuming nothing goes wrong) or, when the River Niger is high enough, the **ferry to Siguiri or Kankan**. This – operated by the *Compagnie Malienne de Navigation* – is usually in service from August to January or February and does, at most, a weekly voyage. Once you're in Guinea the river is much narrower than in Mali, meaning that you keep in close contact with the banks. The trip is recommended.

■ Overland from Guinea-Bissau

This is one of the region's toughest international journeys and is still liable to be cut by floods and mud pools during the rains. Public transport along the way, especially in the border region, is tenuous. If you can arrange a ride in advance you'll save a lot of waiting en route.

The "direct" coastal route to Conakry, over the creeks **from Buba to Boké**, is really not a viable option except at the end of the dry season – and in any case the places along the way constitute little incentive to make the attempt.

The usual route follows the tarmac through Guinea-Bissau; thence via **Koundara** and back onto tarmac at **Labé**. The section from the border to **Saréboïdo** can be empty of traffic, but the track through the northern Fouta Djalon is rivetingly beautiful. And slow, of course. Transport is available.

You can also cross the border into Guinea **between Pitche and Foula-Mori**, connected in the dry season by a driveable 30km track and a hauled ferry over the Koliba river. There's some transport along the way on Monday – Pitche's market day. You go through Guinea-Bissau informalities at the ferry and Guinea formalities at the friendly Foula-Mori post. Although not marked on the maps, this is a recognised border crossing.

Koumbia, 80km further on, is the first town of any size; from here there's limited transport to the coast or up into the Fouta. If you're heading to Conakry, the road from Koumbia to **Boké** has been much improved recently with lots of generous regravelling and even some patches of tarmac; though from Boké to Boffa and Conakry it remains dire in many parts. The coastal forest is heady compensation and, if you have the means, a deviation out to the beaches at **Cap Verga** is well worthwhile.

Driving yourself, in good conditions – and in luck with the ferry across the wide Fatala river at Boffa – you can do the trip from Koumbia to Conakry in under twelve hours. By public transport – in these parts, mostly heavily overstacked bush taxi wagons – allow a couple of days.

It's worth knowing that a regular Gabú to Conakry service is supposed to depart **Gabú** every Friday at 8am, arriving in the small hours.

■ Overland from The Gambia and Senegal

The choice is between two main routes: **Basse** (The Gambia) and **Tambacounda** (Senegal) to Koundara (see above) by bush taxi through **Medina-Gounas** (see p.412); and **Kédougou** up into the Fouta Djalon to the village of **Mali** and on to **Labé** (for route details see p.601). The Kédougou route is the better of the two, though Kédougou itself, with its main access through the Niokolo-Koba National Park, is sometimes hard to reach.

■ Overland from Sierra Leone

The relatively busy main route connects **Freetown** with **Conakry** in a day's travel. There are one or more buses to the border every day and no shortage of *Peugeots* and other vehicles to take you on to the pretty town of **Forécariah** and Conakry. The border is normally fairly hassle-free for foreign travellers, but local people often have a hard time of it and you can expect delays on the buses.

If you've had enough travel by the time you get into Guinea, you might be intrigued to make a side trip down to **Benty** – the country's old banana port and a colonial settlement predating Conakry.

A second important route connects the high-land region in eastern Sierra Leone with **Guéckédou**, making up the fastest overland route between Freetown and Bamako (normally four days by public transport, ferries permitting). The point to make for in Sierra Leone is **Koindu** (see p.687), two days out from Freetown, from where you cross to **Nongoa** in Guinea and get transport to the tarmac at Guéckédou. Guinean visas can be obtained in Nongoa – a useful back-up but not to be relied upon. Ask the policeman at the *pirogue* wharf on the Guinean side of the river. The *pirogues* on this river border take bicy-cles and motorbikes; other vehicles have to pass through Liberia. Note that Guéckédou has no bank.

The third route from Sierra Leone to Guinea is the northern road via **Kabala** (see p.672) to **Faranah**. This is rough and steep in parts, but usually driveable: on the Guinean side it's been partly renovated. Formalities at **Gberia Fotombu** on the Sierra Leonean side are sweetly perfunc-tory and the police hospitable. There's a similar welcome at **Hérèmakono**, the first village in Guinea. You might walk this border gap – about 12km – and it's attractive, breezy country, but you'll be lucky to find transport until you hit the main road, 15km west of Faranah. Once again, note that Faranah has no bank.

■ Overland from Liberia

There's a spread of crossing points along the watershed frontier between the two countries. But with the amount of smuggling that goes on and the legacy of the two countries' historic mutual distrust, not to mention the more recent refugee problem resulting from the Liberian civil war, it's no surprise to find these borders trouble-some. Main frontiers are at **Foya–Guéckédou** (ferry), **Voinjama–Macenta**, **Ganta–Diécké**, and **Yekepa–Yalézou/Bossou** (for **Nzérékoré**).

■ Overland from Côte d'Ivoire

There are two main routes from Côte d'Ivoire. The first from **Odienné** to **Kankan** is better than it looks on most maps. The *Régroupement de Transporteurs Africain de Côte d'Ivoire* (*RTACI*) runs a weekly bus service between Bouaké and Kankan, departing Friday at 4pm, arriving Saturday night or Sunday morning (around CFA12,000).

The second important route is the lovely forest road from **Danané** to **Nzérékoré**. Sometimes you'll find taxis along here and there's always transport on a Tuesday for Nzérékoré's big weekly market. The road is normally passable throughout the year. But it can be surprisingly difficult to find transport to **Gbapleu** – where Ivoirian formalities are conducted – and from there to the Guinean frontier near **Nzo**. You might, with reason, give up a day to walk through the forest; it's magnificent.

Red Tape

Guinean visas – required by all – have for long been notoriously difficult to obtain. Occasional relaxations since 1984 have led to confusion. The situation changes constantly and you'd do well to find out as much as possible on the travellers' grape-vine before applying. When there's been a problem in recent years it's been related to directives from Conakry ordering Guinean embassies not to issue visas for the purposes of "tourism" or "visiting". The government generally takes the view that the country is "not ready for tourism". Going on business, even to conduct research, is another matter.

However, and wherever you apply, the routine at Guinean embassies in Africa is always the same. You first need a letter from a resident invit-ing you, or a **letter of accreditation** from your own embassy, who may be able to tell you the latest information. The consul will then contact Conakry for clearance. This will come back in 24 to 48 hours, or not at all. The embassies at **Bamako** and **Freetown** have lately been fairly easy. Fifteen-day single-entry visas are the norm, but you can get a month or more if you plead a little. **Bissau** and **Abidjan** seem less certain. The consulate at Banjul has closed. **Dakar** has recently been refusing non-business visas point blank. There are also embassies in **Monrovia**, **Accra** and **Lagos**.

There's no embassy in London but in Europe, the embassy in **Bonn** reportedly issues visas without demur, and not only to people with return air tickets. The embassy in **Paris** is less helpful. Enlist the services of a visa agent if you want to get your visa in advance.

■ Visas for onward travel

Apart from the embassies of the six **neighbouring countries**, Conakry has embassies of **Algeria**, **Congo**, **Gabon**, **Ghana**, **Morocco**, **Nigeria**, **Tanzania** and **Zaire**. The **French embassy** (Mon–Fri, mornings only) routinely handles visas for **Togo**, **Mauritania**, **Burkina Faso** and **Central African Republic**.

The **Sierra Leone** embassy charges FG10,000 for a visa in 24 hours, more for five-minute delivery.

If you're heading into **Liberia**, it's useful to know that for more than fifty years there has been a Liberian consulate in **Nzérékoré**.

■ Other bureaucratic business

The only **health certificate** formally required is yellow fever but it's best, as usual, to have cholera too.

If you're flying in, you may well be given a **currency declaration form**; this is unlikely at land borders. If you'll be leaving the country by air you may be required to hand the form in, in which case it must indicate bank transactions.

The **photography permit** is still required and supposedly available from the National Cinema Organisation in Conakry (see Conakry Listings). Use of the utmost discretion may be an easier course.

Other official business in Guinea has been much reduced, and most of the time you'll be left alone. However, some hotels will still try to hold your passport until you check out, even if you pay first; it's best not to allow this.

Money, Banks and Costs

Guinea uses its own *Franc Guinéan* (FG), a soft currency intended to lead the way to the country's eventual inclusion in the CFA zone. With the abolition of Sekou Touré's *syli* (elephant) currency, the Guinean franc was reintroduced at the same value as the CFA franc. It has slipped to a free market rate of FG16,000 (or more) to CFA10,000 and, if you have CFA or FF you'll commonly be able to use them for accommodation and transport. Dollars also have a little extra purchasing power on the black market. In August 1990, the official exchange rate for the US$ was approximately FG700, so for the £ sterling you could expect at least FG1200 = £1.

Other currencies are hardly known outside the **banks** – for lack of which, you may be forced to change money unofficially. The *Banque Internationale pour la Commerce et l'Industrie de la Guinée* (*BICIGUI*) is the main, and generally efficient bank (£ sterling travellers' cheques are no problem), with branches in **Conakry**, **Boké**, **Fria**, **Kankan**, **Kamsar**, **Kissidougou**, **Labé** and **Nzérékoré**. Other branches are planned, but don't count on finding banks in Kindia, Mamou, Dalaba, Faranah, Dabola, Kouroussa, Guéckédou, Macenta, Siguiri or anywhere north of Labé. If you don't have French or CFA francs you should plan ahead.

Plan ahead with your cash too, once you've got it. Guinean francs come in notes only, from filthy, damp twenty-five-franc bills to FG5000 notes which are almost unusable except in large towns. Change them down to FG1000. And convert only as much as you'll need: spare FG will be confiscated when you leave the country. With your remaining FG, you can buy CFA or other currencies in border towns – though usually at marked-up prices.

Credit cards, outside Conakry, are just so much plastic.

■ Costs

Prices compare favourably on the whole with neighbouring countries, although Conakry is considerably more expensive. Cheap hotels in most towns will be from FG3–5000 a room; rice and sauce doesn't normally cost over FG250; and you can readily get several of most kinds of fruit for FG25 or FG50. **Transport costs** are high, however, and can push up your expenditure enormously. Seat prices are fixed on the main routes but depend greatly on road conditions and vehicle – expect FG15–20/km on tarred roads in the west and anything up to FG40/km on rough roads in the east and northwest, especially those leading to the borders.

Maps and Information

There are no tourist offices, and no up-to-date official tourist information of any kind is available. As for maps, the *IGN* sheet of Guinea is definitely worth obtaining before you go, and vital if you intend doing any hiking or trail beating.

There are some colonial survey maps around (1:100,000), but you're only likely to track them down in university libraries. For long stays in Conakry, the map of the capital is also worth having, and only occasionally available at the *Novotel* in the city.

Health

Guinea provides some of West Africa's roughest travelling and it's this, rather than any intrinsic unhealthiness, which can lead to problems. Basic health care, out in the wilds, is too limited to be a safety net.

Altitude can make all the difference. Guinea is largely mountainous, and temperatures drop quickly after dark in the higher parts. Travelling by public transport, it makes good sense to keep something warm close at hand: your vehicle may roll for hours into the night with your luggage stowed inaccessibly.

Water, as usual, is a major consideration: much of what you drink, outside a few main towns, will come from wells and streams: bottled *Coyah* is rarely available outside Conakry. The huge number of rivers and streams in Guinea also means you'll likely end up wading through some of them. But try to limit this and particularly avoid slow-flowing waters and dry season pools: there's a rather high incidence of bilharzia.

Getting Around

In terms of advancing from A to B, most travellers find Guinea the toughest country in West Africa: journeys are frequently long and may follow equally long waits while seats are filled. Surfaced roads account for only 1300km or so and alternative means of transport – something of a railway line, the odd Niger steamer and a domestic air service – don't add up to much.

■ Bush taxis and trucks

Transport on Guinea's main routes is ordinarily by *Peugeot 504* with eight passengers. In the hills, they're very much faster than the clapped-out *cars* and *bâchés* with up to twenty passengers, but there are some newer **minibuses** appearing on the roads. *504*s tend to stick to surfaced and well-maintaned earth roads. Travelling along the country's less comfortable byways is down to valiant and incredibly slow open-backed **goods lorries** – *gros camions* – and, to a lesser extent, elderly jeeps and Land Rovers. More than usual, you should take some notice of the vehicles' condition and opt for the one least likely to break down or kill you. Price can be an uncanny indicator of speed and reliability.

You'll normally discuss the **price** of baggage and pay that on departure. The "head" price is payable at the end of the trip – or often just before arrival. Be certain of your fare, especially if you're setting down en route; it's very hard to argue if you've not paid.

Routes and frequencies

The busiest route is from **Conakry to Mamou** with departures until early afternoon (6hr plus). The stretch up to Kindia (3hr) is now smooth and regraded and too fast for comfort. **Mamou to Labé** (4hr) is another relatively busy road: much of the transport is local to the Fouta Djalon. From **Mamou to Faranah**, you've a fairly quiet stretch and fewer local vehicles. **Conakry to Kankan** or **Guéckédou** (14hr plus) tends to be an all-night

ROAD TRANSPORT FARES
Pamelap–Kindia (174km) FG3000 by *504*;
Conakry–Mamou (285km) FG4,000 by *504*;
Conakry–Télimélé (265km) FG3000 by *bâché*;
Pita–Labé (40km) FG700 by *504*;
Mamou–Labé (152km) FG3000 by *504*;
Faranah–Dabola (110km) FG2000 by *bâché*;
Conakry–Kankan (804km) FG15,000 by *504*;
Kankan–Malian border (217km) FG7500 by *504*;
Kankan–Kérouané (175km) FG3500 by *504*;
Kankan–Nzérékoré (383km) FG7000 by lorry;
Guéckédou–Nzérékoré (247km) FG7000 by *504*;
Nzérékoré–Côte d'Ivoire border (80km) FG3000 by *504*.

trip (and faster that way) but it's perfectly possible to make a late arrival if you start early enough. **Conakry to Nzérékoré** though (20hr or more, until the road is finished), is best contemplated with a night stop somewhere.

In the eastern and northwestern fringes of the country, most transport is long distance. You can wait days for a vehicle away from the main routes, especially during the rains.

■ Trains

The **Conakry–Kankan line** is thoroughly unpredictable. In theory only, trains run weekly, departing Conakry 8.35am Saturday, departing Kankan on Monday or Tuesday, depending on how long the up-country run takes – hopefully 24–30 hours.

Tickets for the semi-hard seats go on sale about 10am the day before departure and are always oversold. The tarif of FG9 per kilometre (Kindia 152km; Mamou 296km; Dabola 442km; Kankan 662km) makes the train, if it's operating, painfully competitive. Take as much good food as you can and plenty of water. The scenery along the way – which reputedly makes the road look dull in comparison – is fair reward.

Railway lines also go from Conakry to the Bauxite works at Fria (freight only) and from Kamsar on the northwest coast to **Boké** and **Sangaredi** (passenger service).

■ Planes

Air Guinée runs a sporadic twice-weekly service around the country. Current destinations and last known fares from Conakry: **Boké** and **Sambailo** (Koundara) FG10,000, **Labé** and **Faranah** FG13,000, **Kissidougou** FG16,000, **Kankan** and **Siguiri** FG19,000 and **Nzérékoré** FG23,000.

■ Other forms of transport

The cost of **car hire** is simply over the top. There are some outlets in Conakry, at the airport and the *Novotel* but you're unlikely to find it worthwhile except for specific targets. And there still seem to be some niggling security doubts over driving hired cars beyond the 35km city limits. Whether you like it or not, you might well find it impossible to hire a car without being obliged to hire a driver as well.

The colonial coastal cutter service that operated in thirty-six hours between Boké and Conakry is no more. But a **ferry-barge** is still running at high water times (roughly August to December) from Kankan, down a tributary of the Niger, to Siguiri and Bamako – though details vary season by season.

Guinea is wonderful territory for **hiking**, **cycling** and **motorbiking**. During the French occupation, it supported an enthusiastic fraternity of hunting and outdoor pursuit fans with an infrastructure of *campements* and guides. Today there's little back-up and you need to reckon on being self-supporting if you want to make the most of the wild country. Main requirements are a tent, water bottles, spares if you're cycling (even Africa-bought bikes are poorly serviced) and as much time as possible.

Sleeping

The recent recovery from economic coma hasn't yet precipitated a boom in hotel building, and there's very little above the basic outside Conakry. Hotels, too, are often "full" – a puzzling condition which sometimes reflects the obligation of the owner to deal with the police if foreigners are staying.

While **cheap places** (FG3–5000, more in Conakry) aren't usually up to much – electricity sporadic, water generally in buckets, though sometimes warmed for you – there is a scattering of hotels and guest houses in the east with a certain idiosyncratic appeal, all detailed under the town-by-town coverage.

In smaller towns and villages you can always ask to see the *sous-préfet* (the district officer) with a view to a night at the *Villa* – accommodation for visiting government employees. These places are often good, though they may need an airing and a broom, and you may, or may not, be asked for payment. Always leave something.

Guineans are most hospitable, aware to the point of angst of the country's shortcomings. But they may assume your needs can't be met and not think to offer an ordinary room. Once it's understood you need a roof, you'll repeatedly be offered places to stay: the only difficulty is in moving on without causing offence.

Camping, in the bush, shouldn't be a problem. Doing so near large towns is bound to cause suspicion. The law against it could be re-awakened by zealous police.

Eating and Drinking

Guinean food is based overwhelmingly on two ingredients – rice and groundnuts – but there's a terrific variety of tastes and much that's delicious. Very hot food isn't common.

International or French restaurant fare is almost restricted to Conakry, which does have a few excellent and costly joints. For the rest of the country, **street food** prevails. It's a serious business, with big pots of rice, sauces, chipped yams, potatoes and bananas hiding under an awning where you squat on a bench to eat. Choose what you want and, if you're not alone, order one at a time and share – servings are on the gigantic side.

Consistently delicious – and meatless – is *sauce de feuilles*, best made with the finely chopped young cassava leaves you see being cut in the markets. Remember, if you order *riz-sauce*, it comes with chunks of meat and gristle. Order the rice only (usually home-grown and tasty) and it will be doused with sauce anyway. *Bouillion* is usually a mutton stew made with the unappetising bits. Bananas in various shapes and sizes are very much in evidence around Kindia, while **avocados** are surprisingly popular in the southeast highlands. Taro (cocoyams), salads (a hard risk – go by first impressions), beans and other garden produce are also locally common. **Bush meat** of various kinds is mostly found in off-the-road villages: if it's monkey be certain it's deeply cooked.

Oranges are the biggest **fruit** crop. In the Fouta Djalon from November to April they're luxuriantly abundant and cheap enough to buy all day as a drink.

And as for **drinks**, Guinea's peculiarity until recently was its lack of a brewery – the only country in the region to import all its **beer**. *Skol* has just changed all that by building a new plant.

White **coffee** (*Nescafé/Café au lait*) is served as a rule with *pain beurre*, not drunk on its own. Unless *Nescafé* is specified, however, you may be served *lait concentré sucré* with weak *Lipton* poured on top – sweet tea, in other words, not coffee at all. *Café fort*, at least, is what it says.

GOOD TIMING

Beware of eating too late. The main meal of the day usually comes around 11am and by midday most street eats are finished.

Guinea's *kinkeliba* infusion is generally better tasting than Senegal's. **Sour milk**, laced with sugar and usually bulked out with starchy cassava flour, is more of a meal in itself.

Communications: PTT, Media and Language

Guinea's telecommunications network isn't promising. But Conakry's *PTT* leaves the worst impression. Forget about **poste restante** there: Kankan's is probably safer. If you must use facilities in Conakry, you're probably best off visiting the *Novotel* (phones and telex) and using your embassy or consulate for mail-holding.

Hours vary (Mon–Sat 8am–2pm in **Conakry**, 7.30am–4pm in **Kankan** and **Nzérékoré**). Other main post offices are at **Boké**, **Kindia**, **Labé** and **Faranah**. From any of these provincial capitals you can theoretically phone abroad or, when the phones are down, send a telegram.

■ The Media

Radios are prized possessions in Guinea. *Radiodiffusion-Télévision Guinéenne* broadcasts **radio** in French, English, Portuguese, Kriol, Susu, Malinké and Fula and puts out evening **TV** in French with news in six Guinean languages. Cultural programming (most shows made in Guinea) is a priority. Most of the country's TVs seem to be switched on in the capital's front yards – weather permitting – every evening. Reception isn't adequate much outside Conakry itself, however. More promising was the introduction due in 1990 of **local radio** stations in Kankan, Nzérékoré, Kindia and Labé.

The national **press** consists of *Horoya* ("Dignity") – a weekly government rag of inspired awfulness. It carries limited African news but rarely anything from outside the continent.

If you're famished for *actualités*, foreign papers and magazines are becoming more available in Conakry. In Guinea, though, more than most countries, a **short wave radio** is worth a lot.

■ Language

Although **French** is the official language, Sekou Touré virtually eliminated its teaching so that a broad generation of people speak it very badly or not at all. Since 1984 French lessons have been reintroduced into primary education.

FUNDAMENTAL FULA

Fula (technically *Fulfulde*, and sometimes called *Pulaar*) is a **class language** with 21 classes, implying the usual agreement between nouns, demonstratives, adjectives and so on. There's no tonal system. A little problematically the class agreements "mutate"; the class suffix can actually change in sound within the same class depending on the noun's root. It's all a rather complicated jump from European languages and unless you've tried learning a relatively easy class language like Swahili, probably too much trouble. There's little instructional material in English. Note that the following is based on the Fula of Fouta Djalon and the language spoken in other parts of West Africa – for example the Fouta Toro in Senegal, Massina in Mali or in Nigeria or Cameroon, can differ markedly, especially in respect of greetings.

GREETINGS

| Hello | *On jarama* | Good afternoon | *Gna léjan* |
| Good morning | *Wa léjan* | See you later | *En bimbi* |

NUMBERS

1	goo	5	joyi	9	jenayi	25	no gayi joyi
2	didi	6	jegoo	10	saapo	100	témédéré
3	tati	7	jedidi	11	sappo e goo	200	témédéré
4	nayi	8	jetati	20	no gayi		didi

USEFUL EXPRESSIONS

How much?	*Jelu?*	I don't know	*Mi anda*
It's too expensive	*No sati*	I don't understand	*Mi famali*
Where's the bank?	*Hon to bank?*	Please repeat it	*Hondu buiyu da*

SIMPLE SUSU

Susu is more straightforward in many respects, than Fula, but somewhat tonal, so that (like Chinese) the meaning of what you say depends on the tone of your voice when you say it. It bears comparison with Bambara (see p.183) and Mandinka (see p.440).

GREETINGS

Hello	*Inwali* (to one person)	Good afternoon/	*Tana mogegné*
	Wo inwali (two or more people)	evening	
Good day	*Wo mamabé*	How's the family?	*Tanamodinbayama*
Good morning	*Tana mokhi* (literally, "did noth-	See you later/good	*Won je segué*
	ing bad happen in the night?")	bye	

NUMBERS

1	keren	5	suli	9	solomanani	40	tongonani
2	firin	6	senné	10	fu	50	tongosuli
3	sakhan	7	soloferé	20	mokhein	60	tongosenné
4	nani	8	solomasakham	25	mokhein nu suli	100	kémé
				30	tongosakhan	200	kémé firin

USEFUL EXPRESSIONS

How much?	*Yéri?*	Show me the way.	*Kira ma sembé*
I'll take it (give it to me)	*A sun nyi*	I don't know.	*M'ma kolon*
It's too expensive	*Asaré khorokho*	I don't understand	*M'ma fahamukhi*
Where's the bank?	*Banque na mindé?*	Excuse me	*Diyema*
		Please repeat it	*Nakhadi*

These words and phrases are intended only as a way into further communication. Guinean women, especially, rarely speak French. For Malinké look at the Bambara language section in Part four "Mali" (p.183).

GUINEAN GLOSSARY

Alfa King (Fula).

Bowe Eroded Fouta Djalon hill (pl. Bowal).

CMRN Military Committee for National Redress.

Dougou Place (Mande languages).

FLING The anti-Touré Front for the National Liberation of Guinea.

Foté White person (corruption of "Portuguese").

Fouta Place (Fula).

Gara Indigo (and indigo cloth).

Koro Old (as in Dabolakoro – old Dabola).

Lumo Market held weekly or sometimes every four or five days.

PDG Democratic Party of Guinea, the party of the old regime.

Sofa Malinké chief (nineteenth century).

Syli Elephant (and defunct Guinean currency).

Woro Kola (Mande languages).

Public Holidays

Aside from New Year's Day, 1 May (Labour Day) and the usual shifting Islamic calendar, the principal Guinean holidays are 3 April (anniversary of the 1984 coup), 2 October (Independence Day), and 22 November ('Victory Day'; anniversary of the repulsed 1970 Portuguese invasion). Christian holidays are observed more haphazardly – in the main by large businesses and government offices.

The commemoration of other landmarks in Guinea's history depends on more ephemeral political considerations: 14 May, the anniversary of the founding of the *PDG* party, 28 September, the anniversary of the "No" vote, 9 February, National Women's Day, and 27 August, the day in 1977 when the market women revolted and forced Sekou Touré to change tack.

Regional and local **non-Islamic festivals** were attacked as sectarian and unproductive during the dictatorship and for many the generation-long repression destroyed their viability. You can still come across them if you're well-placed and timed – January to March would be a propitious season.

Arts and Entertainment

In 1969, Guinea won the *Grand Prix* at the first Pan-African Cultural Festival (FESPAC) held in Algiers. Conakry's annual *Quinzaine artistique* (Arts Fortnight) used to attract visitors from across the continent. It looks like the new regime is trying to build on the reservoir of talent with its cultural season (October to June); details at the museum in Conakry.

■ Music

Most obviously though, travelling by *Peugeot 504* across the country, you're accompanied most of the time by **music**. Driver and passengers take turns with the cassette deck and much of what you hear is Guinean – though Antillean *zouk* is increasingly popular even if only poor-quality recordings are made locally.

Guinea has nurtured some of Africa's most talented and original musicians and singers. Many are based abroad, in Côte d'Ivoire or France. There are more details and background in the "Music" piece in *Contexts*.

Mory Kante in particular has expanded into international stardom – arguably dishing his music for the sake of Europe's high street record shops – but his audience at home is still huge. Enthusiasm for some of the names that became legends in Guinea and abroad before 1984 – **Bembeya Jazz**, **Les Amazones** – is less noticeable now. Tastes in Guinea are often quite local: put on a cassette by the Fula musician **Dourah Barry** in Malinké country and you risk offending all the passengers. Music is a good way into Guinea's cultural complexities.

Live music on stage is mostly a pleasure of Conakry's clubs. Up-country, local bands play occasionally, but the big national orchestras with overseas recording contracts aren't heard much at home.

The **griots** retain a major role as entertainers in the countryside, and koras and guitars and a few beers are a common evening combination. In Guinea you can still have your praises sung for small change.

■ Other entertainments

For other cultural affairs, the best place to check what might be going on is the National Museum in Conakry which houses the "Office of National Heritage". **Theatre** is getting some encouragement with the formation of a *Théâtre National d'Enfants* and promotion of the *Théâtre National* and the *Ballet National*, but there's a lack of decent venues, even in Conakry. **Cinema** seems to be absolutely defunct, though as a creative force it never really began, and is totally disabled through lack of film stock, equipment and, perhaps, nerve. Those who wanted to create cinema – as opposed to those content with making ideologically sound documentaries – left the country long ago. Imported movies today are predictable – French, the occasional Hollywood blockbuster, and lots of cheap, cheerful violence.

In sport, wrestling is less important than in the countries further north. **Football** is hugely popular and Guinea's national team is moderately distinguished.

Directory

AIRPORT TAX FG9000.

CASSETTES Guinea's street and market vendors offer the best music deal in West Africa – about £1 each for copies.

GREETINGS Taken even more seriously in Guinea than in the rest of West Africa, traditional forms of greeting have been little diluted by European abruptness. Even in French you're expected to rattle off a few polite enquiries about family and life in general – particularly on official business. These phrases may pepper the whole conversation.

KOLA Kola nuts are a big crop in the southeast and very popular all over. Guinea is a country in which it's worth acquiring the taste. On long journeys a pocketfull of white nuts (sweeter and speedier) keeps you from nodding off and is good to share.

MUSEUMS There's a residual national structure, with museums in Conakry, Boké, and Kissidougou, and there may be others. Four new regional museums are planned.

PHOTOGRAPHY Most of the pictures you take in Guinea will be of people you know and their families, or of unpopulated landscapes when no-one is looking. Don't assume you can get out your camera as you might in neighbouring countries and with a little bluster snap away. You will cause a scene and you're quite likely to have your camera confiscated, for which a large *amend* will be payable. The *permis de photo* is hard to obtain in practice and you may as well look on it as a warning-off. In Conakry you should be very careful.

POLITICS Not completely taboo, but Guineans are often sensitive about the fact that Sekou Touré was tolerated so long; and at the same time quick to denounce neocolonialism in any form.

RELIGION As usual, the pig is a fair indication of the boundaries of **Islam**. You won't see many between the jungles of the northwest and the hilly forests in the southeast. Islam continues to consolidate and displace the indigenous religions, and its international dimension is increasingly important in shaping Guinean society. The vast majority of practising Muslims (about three-quarters of the population) are members of the Tijaniya brotherhood. Christianity is a minority religion, only significant locally around Conakry and in the southeast.

SEXUAL ATTITUDES Guinea under the old regime was moralistic and prying. Prostitution was brutally suppressed and polygamy outlawed – both in the cause of social justice. Homosexuality is presumably a crime: discretion is advised.

TOILET PAPER Very hard to obtain outside Conakry.

TROUBLE Driving in your own vehicle, you will experience repeated efforts at extortion from the police and military, ranging from mildly humorous to contemptible and hysteric. These can even affect you if you're in a taxi or other public transport, though in theory if you're all straight the driver himself is meant to soothe thirsty tempers and meet the incessant roadblock demands for a few hundred francs. The current state of affairs – especially in and around Conakry and as far up the highway as Mamou – is greatly resented, not so much because money is taken, but because the demands are deemed excessive. Most transport drivers lose a full fare on every trip.

If you genuinely break the law, you can ordinarily buy yourself out. Treat the police with caution, force out some humour, defuse them with cigarettes. Much of the pre-1984 security fabric is still, doggedly, in place and trumped-up accusations and suspicions can only be resolved in the traditional ways.

WILDLIFE Guinea has **no national parks** or game reserves. But it's one of the few West African countries which may have preserved, largely intact, a diverse indigenous fauna. It's been thirty years since any field surveys were carried out and the current position is hazy. Certainly **hunting**, rather than environmental destruction, is the main threat. Most large species – including chimpanzees, hippos, elephants, lions and buffalo – hang on, unprotected and rarely seen. Regionally, the best wildlife zones appear to be the hilly **acacia savannah in the northeast**, between the Tinkisso river and the Malian border; the undulating **bush and grassland between Mamou and Faranah** where the Fouta Djalon slopes down to Sierra Leone, and the **southeast highlands**, particularly east of the Macenta–Nzérékoré road.

WOMEN TRAVELLERS AND THE WOMEN'S MOVEMENT Women travellers have a reasonably easy time in Guinea, sheltered from some of the hassles of Mali, Senegal or Côte d'Ivoire by the lack of tourists, and frequently escorted along the way. So long as your French is just about adequate you'll find quick access to people's homes and lives wherever you go. Be prepared for – normally low-key – sexual harassment. You might prefer to describe yourself as something other than a tourist, which carries slightly pejorative connotations.

Progressive **women's organisations** in Guinea have suffered a setback though their association with Sekou Touré's deformed "socialism", the background from which they emerged. Genital mutilation is still practised in many districts. If you obtain details of contacts or addresses, we'd be interested to know.

A Brief History of Guinea

The first French expeditions into the hinterland of the Guinea coast took place from Boké, a creek-head base in contact with Europeans since the fifteenth century. Following the expansion initiated by Colonel Faidherbe across the Sahel – and to prevent the British linking The Gambia with Sierra Leone – the French commanders in "the rivers of the south" (as the Guinea region was known) forced protection treaties with dozens of small rulers through the middle of the nineteenth century. In the 1880s they came up against the first serious resistance to their invasion in the shape of the guerrilla army of the Almamy Samory Touré, a man who won headlines in the French press for two decades and became Guinea's national hero. This account follows the country's history from his defeat to the present day. Some earlier historical background can be found throughout the guide and on p.600 and p.607.

■ The French Occupation

Once Samory had been deported to Gabon in 1898, there was only relatively minor resistance to the French incursion. The **forest communities** put up a fight, and were aided by the hilly jungle in which the French couldn't use cavalry, but their political organisation was weak and the villages submitted one after another in the years leading up to the First World War.

In the early days, wild **rubber** was Guinea's main crop. By 1905 the commerce was supporting a 700-stong Lebanese community in Conakry. But the export declined after 1913 as plantation markets opened in southeast Asia.

By 1914, the French had driven a **railway** over 600km through mountain terrain to the river port of Kankan, thus linking Conakry with Bamako. This, however, was a strategic railway rather than a commercial one. Apart from limited gold and diamonds, upper Guinea didn't appear to offer much return. Better prospects lay in the forest regions to the south where **coffee** and other tropical crops were developed on French-owned plantations, and near the coast and southern foothills of the Fouta Djalon, where **bananas** – increasingly popular as an exotic fruit – flourished.

Guinea's biggest prize, though, was **bauxite** – aluminium ore – of which its vast high-grade deposits form nearly a third of the world's reserves. But the French only began to exploit them systematically in the 1950s and for most of their occupation the necessary investment wasn't attracted.

French rule in Guinea followed standard patterns except that, more so than elsewhere, the opportunities to become a privileged *evolué* were desperately few: until 1935 there was no secondary education in Guinea and, on the eve of independence, only 1.3 percent of Guinean children were receiving even primary schooling. With one singular exception, almost all the prominent Guineans before independence came from wealthy families who had sent them to the *Ecole Normale William Ponty* near Dakar.

■ The Rise of Nationalism

Ahmed Sekou Touré, a Malinké speaker from Faranah, first came to attention as a disruptive and perspicacious schoolboy in the late 1930s and then as founder of Guinea's first union – the Post and Telecommunications Workers – in 1946. In 1947 Touré and others formed the Guinean section of the *Rassemblement Démocratique Africain* (the broad alliance of French West African political groupings) and named it the *Parti Démocratique de Guinée*.

In the election for deputies to the new Constituent Assembly in 1945, the Guinean "subject" elected was **Yacine Diallo** – a Fula-speaker with the support of the Islamic old guard in the Fouta Djalon.

Guinea had made huge strides since the war with major investment in the bauxite industry at last and a rapidly urbanising workforce.

Touré meanwhile was making his name as a politician and unionist. He was a delegate to the 1947 Communist French Trade Unions (*CGT*) Congress in Dakar and, with support from the French Communist party, he backed several **strikes** in the early 1950s and produced a labour newspaper – *L'Ouvrièr*.

The most trenchant strike was the ten-week action in 1953 over the demand for a **twenty percent wage rise** to accompany a reform in the labour laws stipulating a 40-hour instead of a 48-hour week. During the strike, telegrams of instructions from Paris and Dakar to the Governor of Guinea were intercepted by radical telecommunications workers, and the strike persisted to a victory which made a lasting impression on the Guinean public and across French West Africa.

Sekou Touré's Rise to Power

By the time of the strike, Sekou Touré was the territorial assembly member for Beyla. From this platform, he and other trade unionists began a campaign to disaffiliate and Africanise the Guinean sections from the parent French unions.

Touré's career took a knock in 1954 when the Guinean **deputyship to the French assembly** came up on the death of Yacine Diallo. Convinced of his outright popularity, Touré was equally convinced that the election had been rigged when he was heavily beaten by a Fula candidate, Barry Diawadou (the Fouta Djalon was inimical territory for a Marxist Malinké). There had indeed been gross tampering by the French, and voters had even been struck off the register in areas of strong PDG support. The Minister for Overseas Territories came to Conakry to assure Guineans it wouldn't happen again. It was a debacle which many Fula had cause to regret after independence.

Instead, Touré became **mayor of Conakry** in 1955. He was just thirty-three. By 1956, with over 40,000 members in the *CGT-Guinée*, the break with the French unions was achieved and a new, African federation of labour unions created – the *Union Générale des Travailleurs d'Afrique Noire* (*UGTAN*) with Touré its first secretary general. Uniquely, in West Africa, Touré now succeeded in marrying the *PDG* party with the labour federation – an amalgam that was ratified in March 1958.

Touré's **second bid for deputy** was succesful in 1956 in an election apparently free of abuses: his vote was up 200 percent on 1954 while Diawadou's was almost identical. Sekou Touré became **vice-president** of the new Territorial Council of Government in 1957, effectively prime minister of Guinea under the low-profile Governor Jean Ramadier. Touré firmly advocated an independent West African federation of states and denounced Senghor of Senegal and Houphouët-Boigny of Côte d'Ivoire as puppets for wanting to consolidate the French connection.

One of Touré's first major acts was the **abolition of chiefs** and their replacement by party cadres. The move was particularly resented in the Fouta Djalon, where chiefdoms had some traditional legitimacy. It was accompanied by some bloody settling of scores: the groundwork for the Guinean state security network was being prepared.

With **de Gaulle's return to power** in France Sekou Touré was soon given the chance to wield full power. The new constitution of the French Fifth Republic was unacceptable to him, and the idea of a free federation of completely independent states wasn't acceptable to de Gaulle – who insisted on their giving up some of their sovereignty to the federal government.

De Gaulle's visit to Conakry to put his case was a waste of time. He would "raise no obstacles" in Guinea's path if the country chose to "secede" from the community of French states – but he would "draw conclusions". Sekou Touré replied **"We prefer poverty in freedom to riches in slavery"** and the two leaders snubbed each other at every opportunity for the rest of the visit. "Good Luck to Guinea" sneered de Gaulle on his departure.

■ Guinea under Sekou Touré

While other francophone leaders thought at first he was bluffing, Sekou Touré prepared his country to go it alone. On September 28 1958 there was a 95 percent **"No"** vote to the referendum on staying in the French community. And on October 2, **independence** was declared.

The example of Ghana under Nkrumah was an inspiration while the swift **reaction of the French** in Guinea – flight with the booty, sabotage of the infrastructure, burning of files and cancellation of all cooperation and investment – was made to seem like good riddance by the party, though the severity of the withdrawal was a vindictive blow.

The country had virtually no technical expertise and a total of six graduates. It started work from scratch, with aid from **Czechoslovakia**, the

Soviet Union and seven other Eastern-bloc countries, and solid support from the European and Third World left. Morale was high and the *PDG* organisation initially effective.

France excluded Guinea from the CFA franc zone of the newly independent francophone nations. Guinea adopted its own franc (and later the *syli*) which isolated it further from neighbouring states, and hindered what little (non-French) trade remained, but at least stemmed the drain of capital to France.

Despite Nato fears that Guinea might become a West African Cuba, United States **President Eisenhower** waited six months before even sending an ambassador to Conakry, for fear of offending de Gaulle. In 1962, a substantial American aid package was finally worked out and the Peace Corps went in. Revolution aside, **American aid and investment**, particularly in the bauxite industry, has been firm ever since.

The Teachers' Plot

The **Soviet Union** quickly fell out with Sekou Touré at the time of the Cuban missile crisis. Misjudging his prevailing ideology – which was more commitedly anti-capitalist than pro-communist – the Soviet mission was accused of "interference" when left-wing students demonstrated for a firm espousal of socialism and the dumping of Touré's "positive neutrality" (a refusal to be anyone's puppet). As a result of this **"Teachers' Plot"**, the Soviet ambassador was expelled. Diplomatic ties continued, however, and aid and expertise from the Soviet Union was never turned away – even if its usefulness was sometimes in doubt, such as in the case of the submarine base planned for the Los islands or the famous import of snow ploughs (possibly a malicious rumour as they're not much different from earth graders).

Poverty in Slavery

As the first few years of Independence unrolled, Sekou Touré, the **Pan-African** ideologue and co-author of the **OAU** charter, began to be seen in a less glamorous light as his extreme policies started to bite, and the popular enthusiasm of 1959–60 sloughed away. A planned economy without planners was taking shape (or rather not), state enterprises were extended, private business curtailed and a small but growing **middle class** was reaping illicit benefits from mismanagement and fraud.

The idea that there was a permanent, **anti-Guinea plot** obsessed the party hierarchy. The first plots had been exposed even before independence, but the climate of conspiracy thickened until virtually any action could be read as suspicious. At the height of Guinea's isolation, "citizen" and "suspect" became virtually synonymous.

For the first decade of independence, most of the "plots" originated outside the country and the party skilfully manipulated them to maintain control, timing announcements to coordinate with national events. Internal dissent was simply annihilated wherever it first breathed, usually before any chance of genuine conspiracy.

In 1969, however, the focus was shifted squarely to **internal opposition** and the Fula came under increasingly harsh attack. Touré was convinced that the densely populated Fouta Djalon was trying to secede, with the help of Senegal. Army units at Labé were purged and after the Portuguese invasion, it was the Fula who bore the brunt of his revenge.

In 1973 Sekou Touré announced the discovery of a "fifth column active in all walks of life". Again, the Fula came under concerted attack with waves of arrests, executions and disappearances. This ethnic repression culminated in 1976 with the announcement of the **"Fula Plot"** and Touré's declaration that the Fula-speaking peoples were "enemies of socialism". Diallo Telli, the first OAU secretary general, was accused of leading a CIA-backed conspiracy. He was arrested and starved to death.

If there was any real "permanent plot" during Sekou Touré's tyrannical rule — apart from mass discontent — it would appear to have been his own genocidal one against the Fula. The atrocities perpetrated fuelled the outrage of exiles: stories about human sacrifice and barbarities soon became commonplace and, true or exaggerated, eventually forced the ruling clique into a defensive posture. For the present regime of Lansana Conté, as unevenly Susu as Touré's was Malinké, the rehabilitation of Fula confidence remains a priority.

The results of the first **three year plan** weren't encouraging. Critics in the *PDG* complained the party was out of its depth in trying to control the market economy, and mistaken in extending power to the illiterate masses. Sekou Touré scolded them in a twelve-hour speech designed to weed out the party faithful from the conspirators. "Everything became rotten", he wrote later: "the elite enjoyed riding in cars and building villas".

There was a massive **market crackdown** in November 1964, with widespread harassment of traders and confiscation of assets. Limits were set on the number of traders allowed outside the state sphere and arrests, interrogations and arbitrary punishments grew in frequency. The party was moulded in Touré's image and political life stagnated. The very freedoms which lay at the heart of party policy (on paper anyway) were savagely suppressed. To many, it was clear the government was at war with the people; thousands fled the country.

In 1965 a group of opposition exiles — the *Front pour la Libération de Guinée* (*FLING*) — began to organise outside the country with tacit support from Senegal and Côte d'Ivoire and less discreet help from France. The **"traders' plot"** of 1966 — an apparent attempt to install a liberal government with capitalist leanings — resulted in the complete rupture of diplomatic relations with Paris.

But denouncing conspiracies — imagined or otherwise — couldn't improve the economy. There were chronic **shortages** and production and distribution methods failed. As American aid continued to pour in, world opinion began to see Guinea as an American stooge and — perversely — relations with the United States turned sour.

■ The Terror

Guinea now entered a dark period of isolationism and widespread **terror**. At the end of 1967 the eighth party congress had **Radicalisation of the Revolution** at the top of the agenda. To shore up its bankrupt ideology, the party formally adopted a path of "Socialism". Local revolutionary authorities (the *Pouvoirs Révolutionnaires Locals, PRLs*), were set up in every village — ostensibly to allow power to flow from the base up; in reality to extend the security blanket to every corner of the country. In the leadership, the picture suddenly became hazier, with the inauguration of a seven-member Politburo — the *Bureau Politique National* — in place of Sekou Touré alone. And as China was promulgating its bloody Cultural Revolution, Guinea — one of China's biggest African aid recipients — started its own campaign against "degenerate intellectuals".

Remarkably, in view of his political agility, the inflexible ideology which Sekou Touré carried before him wasn't abandoned for another ten years. And the elaborate and cruelly anti-human **security apparatus** that continued its triffid-like growth lost any trace of even Kafkaesque rationale. Neither was Touré totally insulated from the misery of his people. Huge sums were certainly creamed off by the Touré family's **"Faranah clan"** (see box), but ostentatious displays of wealth were avoided. The funds – and particularly hoards of **diamonds** – were siphoned abroad, while the party hierarchy lived in relatively modest style.

The **army** was kept under constant surveillance by a network of junior officers. Early in 1969 came the first big **purge** of figures close to the party leadership. Chief of Staff Kamara Diaby and the soldier-poet Fodeba Keita were the two most senior victims. Keita met his death in the prison camp he himself had built. There was an assassination attempt on Touré and more arrests in Labé the following year. As a result, the army was radically reorganised: each soldier was made a civil servant, effectively militarising a civilian regime.

THE FARANAH CLAN

Sekou Touré's quarter-century in power witnessed flagrant **favouritism** to members of his own **Malinké**-speaking ethnic group. Yet this was more a case of **nepotism** than chauvinist tribalism – indeed his wife was half Fula. The family clung jealously to their privileges. Threats from those connected to the clan by marriage were sometimes dealt with internally, but outsiders who interfered were condemned to the Boiro death camp, or simply disappeared. Sekou Touré encouraged the clan to intermarry and foresaw a long dynasty. But the paranoia that eventually touched even the president was such that the clan split into two opposing factions – the **Tourés** and the **Keitas** – each practising its own nepotism. Ismael Touré, leader of the first faction, was Sekou's half-brother and a descendant of the warlord Samory Touré (a claim also made, but vainly, by Sekou Touré himself). The Keitas were led by Mamadi Keita, the president's brother-in-law. Despite the name, the Keitas seem to have won the battle for influence with the president in his last years. The clan's reach was legendary, and supporters and beneficiaries have not all been eliminated by the new regime.

The Invasion

Although Sekou Touré had been predicting an "aggression" with more than customary conviction, the country was unprepared for the **invasion** of November 22, 1970. Four hundred troops landed from ships at night and attacked Conakry and the peninsula. This was supposed to trigger a general uprising of Guinean dissidents and the overthrow of Sekou Touré. But although three hundred defenders were killed, and a number of prisoners released by the attackers, none of the key targets (the presidential palace, radio station or airport) was taken. When the landing ships moved away 48 hours later they left behind large numbers of stranded troops who were rounded up and subjected to peoples' justice.

Reactions to the invasion proved a crucial test of party loyalty and provided the **military victory** over the forces of imperialism that Sekou Touré had always craved. It was, he wrote, "one of those sublime moments of exaltation and patriotism . . . the affirmation of collective dignity".

The **United Nations** sent a fact-finding mission. They ascertained that most of the force had been composed of Guinean exiles of *FLING* and loyalist African soldiers from Portuguese Guinea, commanded by Portuguese officers from the Caetano fascist regime, with West German logistical support. The real aim of the invasion was to destroy the base in Guinea of the *PAIGC* guerrillas fighting for independence from Portugal. It was to the lasting humiliation of the Guinea-Conakry opposition that their alliance with Caetano's fascist forces failed.

The **purge** which followed was predictably brutal. In truth, there was grass roots opposition to the Nato-backed invaders – though considerably more support for the internal rebels. Ninety-one people were sentenced to death and hundreds of others imprisoned and tortured. The hundred-stong German technical mission was expelled and dozens of Europeans spent time in jail in the aftermath.

But the popular rage whipped up by the party against imperialist aggression clouded the question of how much positive support the government still had, and obscured the **mass violations of human rights** – torture, disappearances, summary executions and detention without trial – that ravaged Guinea through the early 1970s. An *Amnesty International* report in 1978 estimated there were between 500 and 1500 political prisoners in fifteen prison camps.

In six months in 1974, however, over 250 people are believed to have been executed in Conakry's Camp Boiro alone. Tens of thousands of Guineans, particularly Fula-speakers, continued to flee the country every year.

Hanging On

As the pressures – internal and external – mounted against his regime, Sekou Touré resorted to increasingly desperate measures. **Food shortages** were worsened by the effect of the security network in hampering the normal functioning of lines of supply and communication. There was nothing to encourage farmers. Obstinately, Touré authorised the local revolutionary authorities to handle all the production and marketing of commodities. Then early in 1975 came the **banning of all private trade** and at the same time the setting up of agricultural production brigades. The borders were closed and Touré declared a **"holy war" against smugglers** who were shot if caught. In the north of the country, the **Sahel drought** added to deteriorating prospects.

Guinea struggled for two-and-a-half years, going through another purge in 1976 in response to the **"Fula Plot"** (see p.582). **Relations with France** (broken for a decade) were patched up through the new president Giscard d'Estaing, who agreed to ban Guinean dissident propaganda there. But the exodus from Guinea continued and by the end of the 1970s as many as a million Guineans were believed to be living abroad.

■ The Turnaround

The country's commercial paralysis, supervised by – and unashamedly for the benefit of – the **"economic police"** couldn't be maintained. In August 1977 **market women** in Conakry and other towns spontaneously rose up against the intolerable market situation, which made it impossible for them to afford the produce of their own harvests. It was a turning point. **Riots** flared across the country and several provincial governors were killed. Sekou Touré's resolve collapsed. He began a slow process of **economic liberalisation**. This coincided with a more pragmatic approach to government, a reduction of revolutionary rhetoric and – in response to outspoken criticism abroad – cosmetic improvements in democratic practices and human rights.

In his last few years, Touré left the running of the party and state more and more to a leading clique of ministers while devoting himself to the cultivation of an image as the grand old man of Pan-Africanism. 1982 saw the grotesque spectacle of Touré in Washington hailed by President Reagan as "a champion of human rights".

Progressive ideas were forgotten, however, as he forged close links with King Hassan of **Morocco** – whose side he took in the dispute over Western Sahara – and other bastions of the rigid right. Hassan provided money needed desperately by Touré to tide him over after the collapse of IMF negotiations in 1983, and arranged with conservative Arab states for Guinea to be the largest recipient of petro-dollar aid in sub-Saharan Africa. Touré was set to take his seat as 21st OAU chairman and had a special OAU village built (by Saudi Arabia) in Conakry, when, for administrative reasons, the summit was postponed to 1984.

In January and February of that year, groups of **soldiers** were arrested near the Senegalese border and accused of plotting against the government. At the time of **Sekou Touré's death** on March 26 1984 in a private clinic in Cleveland (whence he'd been flown in Hassan's jet), it appears that sections of the army had indeed been planning a *coup d'état*.

ACHIEVEMENTS

The litany of denunciations of Sekou Touré's regime, amongst which the 1978 Amnesty report is outstanding, has silenced most of his erstwhile supporters. In retrospect the first quarter century of independence was a tragic waste. Yet there were one or two significant **achievements** which can't be overlooked. Despite extraordinary biases in education and its own brutality, the party instilled an astute **political consciousness**: Guineans talk about "exploitation", "imperialism", "racism" and "freedom" with real feeling. There's a sense that ordinary people have political opinions about the way the country should be run. Despite that proliferation of isms, there's genuine national pride among rural people and an awareness – that can feel like touchiness – on a host of fairly abstract subjects. Sekou Touré also encouraged artistic expression in Guinea and was particularly responsible for the early creation of a proud musical tradition with the likes of the women police orchestra **Les Amazones** and the ground-breaking **Bembeya Jazz National.**

■ The New Regime

Colonels **Lansana Conté** (president) and **Diara Traoré** (prime minister) waited several days after the lavish funeral before announcing, after an almost peaceful takeover, the **dissolution of the constitution and the party**, the freeing of political prisoners, the unbanning of trade unions and the **reopening of Guinea** to private investment. Judicial reforms began and French was re-introduced as the main language of education. Most of the old party structures swiftly disintegrated. Asked why the military hadn't acted years earlier, Conté said "the spirit of the Guinean was such that he would not think. Some Guineans behaved like imbeciles. They were remote-controlled".

The *Comité Militaire de Redressement National* was given an enthusiastic welcome and ministers went on foreign tours to introduce the new Guinea and cultivate aid donors. But apart from a general liberalisation, it was hard to pinpoint the direction of the new government. Conté is a low-profile leader and his speeches have been conciliatory in tone. There was soon a split with prime minister Traoré however, and his post was abolished. Predictably, perhaps, in July 1985 Traoré and fellow Malinké officers attempted a coup against Conté.

In 1987, almost two years later, it was announced that those involved, together with a number of detainees from Sekou Touré's government, — sixty people in all — had been given **secret trials** and were to be executed. It was widely presumed, however, that most of them had died extra-judicially long before and Conté was merely setting the record straight — a presumption that hinted how close a return to state terrorism might be and, perhaps, how little Conté might be able to do to prevent it.

■ Guinea wakes up

On the economic front, Conakry was soon full of French technical advisors and business people. One of the **IMF**'s structural adjustment programmes was put in operation which, coupled with general **austerity**, state sector **job losses** and widespread civil service **corruption** and ostentation, hasn't been warmly received. Conakry boiled over in January 1988 with **street riots** over **price rises** — which, yet again, had outstripped huge wage increases designed to control the black market. The riots forced the government to back down, and commodity prices

were reduced. Foreign aid, unfortunately, has not poured into Guinea in the quantities hoped for, and there's clearly still suspicion about the country's direction.

Senegal, and especially **Côte d'Ivoire** have both been cautious in their relations with Guinea and apprehensive about its return to the French economic fold. Guinea is itching to flex its muscles. With almost limitless agricultural potential, plus its bauxite, iron and other mineral reserves, the country has the potential to become the most prosperous state in West Africa and the region's dominant francophone nation.

Political Developments

Politically, the initiative Conté lost after abolishing the post of prime minister, and the subsequent coup attempt, was recovered when he increased **civilian representation** in the government — though some of his rivals were banished from Conakry in the process. **Malinké** speakers have been particularly under-represented since the demise of the old regime and they, together with thousands of returned **Fula** exiles, are now regarded as the unofficial opposition to Conté's — predominantly **Susu** — military leadership. His close advisors, wary of giving sensitive posts to non-Susu, are alarmed at the existence of a powerful "Mandingo Union" operating out of an unspecified neighbouring country — presumably Liberia.

Ethnic **cabinet reshuffling** placated some of Conté's critics, and irked some erstwhile friends, but it's unclear whether his government will become unbalanced as a result of internal intrigues. The latest **developments** are promising however: Conté has said that it's time to draw the transitional military period to a close. A **constitutional committee**, composed of people from all walks of life, is framing a new constitution and a six-year timetable has been adopted in the run-up to free presidential elections. These are to be followed by the introduction of a two-party system, with an explicit, built-in, checks and balances function.

All this appears to signal ethnically balanced, **democratic, civilian rule** for the late 1990s. But that timescale implies a degree of patience that most people — facing growing unemployment, low salaries and inflation — may not be prepared to display. Much depends on whether Guineans can come to terms with the legacy of Sekou Touré.

CONAKRY

CONAKRY, once "the Paris of Africa" is today a city of few graces. It's certainly animated, but also morbidly dirty – with refuse, mud, dust, slicks of motor oil – and heavy with the raw noise of endless lines of jammed traffic. Vehicle carcasses rot on the verges; a scrap metal business would make a fortune. As a continuous sprawl of urbanisation claws its way off the **peninsula** and up into the hills behind the city centre, Conakry has matured into one of West Africa's least user-friendly capitals. Only Lagos could really claim to be nastier, but in Lagos at least there's a kind of manic satisfaction in the sheer, offensive, monstrosity of the place. Conakry just succeeds in driving you swiftly away, to the sweet fabled hills and grasslands of the Guinea interior.

The city is remorseless; swelteringly humid and choking with exhaust fumes. Its restaurants, cafés and other hideaways are thin on the ground and the shops you might expect in a capital city are virtually nonexistent. Conakry is expensive, soulless, unwelcoming and stressful. But, the centre at least is easily walked around with offices and businesses not far apart. The main **market** – there has to be some compensation – is bountiful and apparently growing all the time. And lastly, the **Iles de Los** are strikingly pretty and accessible.

Some History

Conakry was itself an **island** – as you can still see from the narrow causeway between the Palais du Peuple and the motorway bridge. For many years known as **Tumbo**, the island was the closest to the shore of the archipelago that provided safe haven for slavers and merchant vessels trading along the Guinea coasts.

The Portuguese, Pedro da Sintra, first set foot here around 1460 and named it Cap de Sagres, after Prince Henry the Navigator's residence in Portugal (until then the furthest point in the known world). At this time the inhabitants of Conakry were idol-worshipping (hence earning the place the name of *Idolos*, which the French turned into *Iles de Los*), skin-wearing farmers, cultivating indigenous dry-land rice and millet.

Early in the sixteenth century, the Portuguese began to anchor in the deep water on the southeast side of the island, but over succeeding centuries they and the Dutch, English and French all took turns to occupy the site and trade in slaves. By the end of the eighteenth century the Los islands were equipped as entrepôts for the transfer of slaves from the smaller coastal vessels to ocean-going merchant ships.

Yet by the time Britain, the principal contender, ceded rights over the fledgling colony to France in 1887, Tumbo island still only had four small settlements – Bulbinay and Konakiri and the non-native African toeholds of Krootown and Tumbo – with a total of maybe three hundred inhabitants. A road into the interior was started and the channel between Tumbo and the mainland was filled in. By 1904, and Britain's handing over of the Los islands, Conakry – the new capital of *Guinée française* – had its present grid pattern and a population of 10,000. The **railway** to Kankan was completed in 1914 and bananas from Kindia were the biggest export. Major developments, however, came in the brief post-war colonial period, and concentrated on improving the port for exports of newly discovered iron ore and bauxite. The last five years have seen massive **growth** and a major transformation into the consumer economy. The city – whose population numbers nearly a million – will soon cover the entire peninsula.

Orientation, arrival and practical needs

Conakry is built twenty kilometres out to sea on a **promontory**. Most of what you'll want in the way of banks, embassies, post office, hotels and restaurants is right at the end, on the two square kilometres of **city centre** where all the old parts of the town are

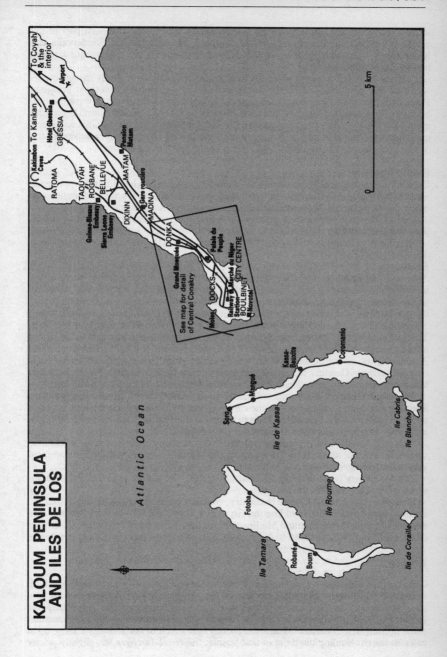

KALOUM PENINSULA AND ILES DE LOS

Atlantic Ocean

To Coyah & the interior
Airport
To Kankan
Kakimbon Caves
Hotel Gbessia
GBESSIA
Pension Niatam
RATOMA
TAOUYAH
ROGBANE
BELLEVUE
MATAM
Guinea-Bissau Embassy
Sierra Leone Embassy
DIXINN
Gare routière
MADINA
DONKA
Grand Mosquée
Palais du Peuple
See map for detail of Central Conakry
DOCKS
Marché du Niger
Railway Station
Moles
BOULBINET
CITY CENTRE
Novotel

5 km
0

Morgué
Soro
Kassa-Bauxite
Conyanaho
Ile de Kassa
Ile Cabris
Ile Blanche

Ile Tamara
Fotoba
Ile Roumé
Robané
Boum
Ile de Coraille

located. Here the grid pattern is easy once you're attuned. The northern part of the centre is business and bureaucracy; the southern part – Boulbinet, Sandervalia and Koulewondy – is mostly made up of tight-packed single-storey city compounds and still has a villagey atmosphere.

Landwards, past the huge **Palais du Peuple** and over the strategically narrow causeway onto the mainland, you hit the **autoroute** and pass under the notorious bridge at Place du 8 Novembre from which so many of Sekou Touré's condemned were publicly hanged. The **Grande Mosquée** and then, behind the Donka Hospital, Camp Boiro (the main Touré era prison camp) are over on the left. Embassies of Liberia, Ghana, Nigeria and Benin are out this way and, further on, past the up-country *gare routière*, in the Madina quarter, the embassies of Mali, Sierra Leone and Guinea-Bissau.

Public transport

Conakry has a reasonable **bus service** – basically running the length of the peninsula – but at peak hours (7–11am and 4–7pm) it can take literally hours to get from one end of the city to the other. Main terminus is the roundabout in the port area.

Taxis (allow one hour from city centre to airport) are exasperatingly hard to find off the main thoroughfares. Hustle hard. They're unmetered, charging FG100–200 for short, shared journeys in town, and FG100–200 per kilometre for a private *déplacement*.

Getting In

Arriving at Conakry **by air**, the open-plan airport is fairly organised. The introduction to Guinea is getting worse, however, with much hassle and attempts at soliciting bribes. Some airlines, *KLM* for example, normally give out currency declaration forms: if you'll be flying out it's advisable to obtain one anyway to avoid hassles on departure.

Getting into town, use the *Novotel* minibus, even if you don't plan to stay there. There are no airport buses. Alternatively, share a taxi with another arrival or go out onto the start of the *autoroute* and wave down a *taxi brousse*. If you fly in on some West African flights, or on *Sabena*'s Wednesday service from Brussels, you'll arrive early enough to leave Conakry and head up-country immediately. In that case, take a taxi towards town only as far as Madina *gare routière*, which should cost you a half fare.

Arriving at Conakry in a public vehicle **by road**, in fact, the **Madina autogare**, 6km from the city centre – is as close to the centre as you're likely to fetch up. Find a bus or taxi into town, or walk across the railway tracks to the Dixinn T-junction and try hitching a lift: a surprising number of expatriates will oblige.

However the **main up-country autogare** has recently moved to a new location, some 15km out of town. At the time of going to press, this appears to be the one most vehicles are obliged to use.

You're unlikely to be arriving **by train**. If you do, the station is in the city centre – some relief perhaps, after the journey.

However you arrive, if it's late in the day, consider pouring yourself straight into the **nearest hotel**, rather than tackling the city centre after dark. The *Pension Matam*, (see below), between the airport and Madina *gare routière* has a good reputation. The *Hôtel Gbessia* (BP 743; ☎46 11 45/46 40 40, telex 2112) next to the airport is big and expensive.

Hotels

Conakry has a dismal reputation for accommodation. Electricity and water are both unreliable and **hotels** are either overpriced and disgusting or positively in orbit and none too good. The first category contains some real stinkers. The *Hôtel Delphine* (under FG5,000/room) and the *Hôtel de l'Amitié* (same price but possibly discussable) come bottom. The *Hôtel Bar Restaurant Grillon* isn't much better and may charge up to twice as much. Hauling itself out of that league, the *Hôtel du Niger* has slightly pricier rooms, some with fan and bucket showers included. It's clean, fairly secure and in a rather good position.

Leaping into the **foreign currency only** bracket, the *Kaloum* at around US$100/ night for a double is numbingly average and undesirable – and always full of long-term renters. At the *Camayenne* (BP 1387) and *De L'Unité* (BP 683; ☎44 47 11) various repair and renovation contracts have long been in the pipeline. In the town centre, that leaves only the stylish heights of the *Novotel Grand Hôtel de l'Indépendance* (BP 287; ☎44 46 81, telex 2112) – proffer your Amex Gold Card or send home for funds.

A good solution to accommodation problems after you've spent a night of misery – or all your money – is to investigate the eastern **outskirts of the city**. *Pension Matam* (☎46 14 14, Mme. Lyde Orsolle) has been warmly recommended – out at the end of the Corniche du Sud near the Soviet Embassy. And the *Hôtel Golfe du Guinée*, a well sign-posted motel in Rogbané on the north side of the peninsula, is good value – for Conakry – with large S/C AC doubles for less than FG20,000.

The quarters of Bellevue, Rogbané and **Taouyah** may yield other good deals: this is a relatively laid-back corner of the city in which to search, and there's no shortage of small eating places, several cafés and even a half-decent *patisserie* in Taouyah.

Food

As with the hotels, strangely, so with **eating**. It's either expensive and mediocre or just poor value for money. To start with a notable exception, *Le Tinka* is quite excellent if you're feeling financially reckless. Out in the Rogbané suburb it's utterly geared to the European expat community and specialises in the kind of dishes that depend on swift air deliveries from Brussels and Paris – marinated raw beef and fish, really good cooking and bills of at least FG25,000 for two.

Assuming you're staying in town on limited means and it's not your birthday; first check out *Madame Diop's* (avenue between 8 av and 7 av at 5 bd) which has by now hopefully finished its renovations. Second, try the *Bar Restaurant Djoliba*, which is an affordable retreat with good coffee and meals from FG3–4000. And third, look into *La Palmeraie*, a Guinean businessmen's haunt with cheap coffee and inexpensive food. *La Provençale* is strictly a bar downstairs (no coffee) but they've a reasonably good first floor restaurant. The *Escale de Guinée* looks like it's been doing a quiet lunch trade on the same corner since the 1930s and, in truth, it's more worthwhile for the folks who run it than the prospect of French school dinners. But it's a good place to retreat to if you had any luck at *poste restante* down the road. Another cheapie is *La Ronda* – and, right by the station, *Le Grillon* is always worth a try. *Le Cedre* and *Le Petit Bateau* are both pricier than the aforementioned lot; the first a quite classy Lebanese (FG5000 per head or more), the second variable, but sometimes to the accompaniment of live music. A new place, in a nice setting and not overpriced, is the *Restaurant des Iles*, near the Palais des Nations.

You can, of course, eat for three figures rather than four (and if you're determined even two) out of your choice of enamel basins at any of Conakry's **markets**. After years of savage austerity (we have no potatoes, we have no rice) street food is great again. And there's a scattering of **shawarma joints** around the city – though avoid *La Touba* and instead patronise *Chez Haidar* or *Sandwiches Kiki* which are always fresh and reliable.

Spending time in Conakry

There are a dozen pleasanter West African capitals to fill the days while you wait for friends, visas, money or whatever. If you find yourself laden with spare time, you'll do best to get out of the city and explore inland. The following ideas are Conakry's best.

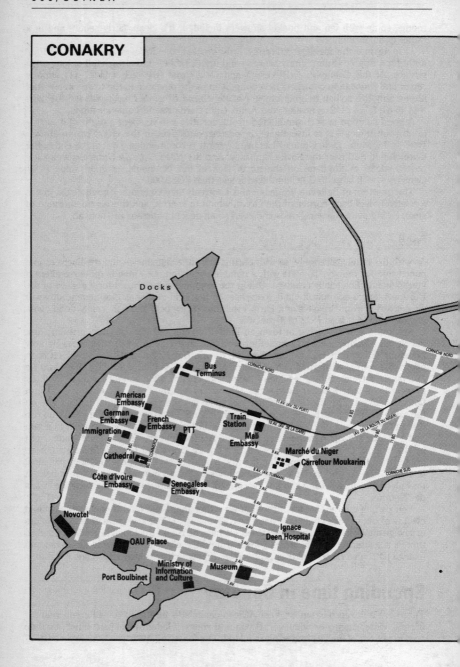

CONAKRY

Docks

Bus Terminus

American Embassy

German Embassy

French Embassy

Immigration

PTT

Train Station

Mali Embassy

Cathedral

Côte d'Ivoire Embassy

Senegalese Embassy

Marché du Niger

Carrefour Moukarim

Novotel

OAU Palace

Ignace Deen Hospital

Port Boulbinet

Ministry of Information and Culture

Museum

CORNICHE NORD

CORNICHE NORD

12 AV.

11 AV. (AV. DU PORT)

10 AV. (AV. DE LA GARE)

AV. DE LA ROUTE DU NIGER

CORNICHE SUD

9 AV. (AV. TUBMAN)

8 AV.

7 AV.

6 AV.

5 AV.

4 AV.

3 AV.

2 AV.

1 AV.

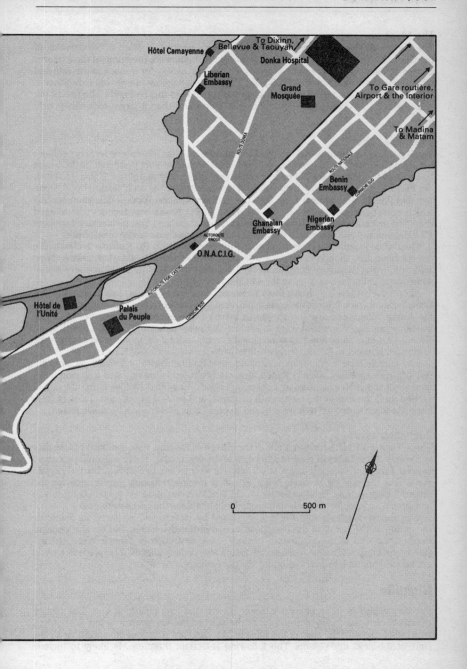

Hôtel Camayenne

To Dixinn,
Bellevue & Taouyah

Donka Hospital

Liberian
Embassy

Grand
Mosquée

To Gare routière,
Airport & the Interior

ROUTE DONKA

To Madina
& Matam

ROUTE NATIONALE

CORNICHE SUD

Benin
Embassy

AUTOROUTE
BRIDGE

Ghanaian
Embassy

Nigerian
Embassy

O.N.A.C.I.G.

AUTOROUTE FOR CAIRO

Hôtel de
l'Unité

Palais
du Peuple

CORNICHE SUD

0   500 m

The Museum

The **National Museum** – an unexceptional hour's worth – is down in Sandervalia off the Corniche Sud. The buildings, or at least part of them, were the home of the explorer Olivier de Sanderval. You might aim yourself here at midday for a snack at the café and take in whatever exhibits are on display. There was a vaguely interesting exhibition of Guinean military costume through the ages at the time of this research. The rest of the site – which has considerable potential – is little more than a large, expensive curio shop.

The Iles de Los

You'll probably want to get out to the **Los islands** quickly. There's never any problem **hiring a pirogue**, just in agreeing the price. Ask around in Port Boulbinet or the beach by the *Hôtel Indépendance* but expect some very high starting figures. If you do splash out FG15–20,000 for the day then you could really explore the archipelago, but remember that the **Ile de Tamara** is an off-limits military location (once a detention centre) which reverberates regularly to the boom of shells. Kassa was recently the alleged dumping ground for *fifteen thousand tonnes* of toxic garbage and incinerator ash from Philadelphia and Norway which the government reportedly managed to sell back.

Meanwhile – until you hear otherwise – the small, central **Ile Roume** is clearly the one to head for, though best on a weekday. Problematically, this has always been favoured by the expatriate community and is the most expensive to get to: there's even someone to collect a beach fee at the weekend.

Alternatively there's a **cheap ferry** to Kassa island every Sunday morning, returning late afternoon (pick it up at the main port). And you can get a workaday *pirogue* ride to the Kassa village of **Soro** (on the north coast) from the *Indépendance* beach. Toxic waste permitting, you might want to explore the possibilities of staying a few days on Kassa – it's 8km long and has several settlements among its monkey-packed forests. And you might get to Roume fairly cheaply from the west shore of Kassa.

The islands have a colourful, enigmatic past. Roume itself – a lavishly picturesque pair of jungle-swathed hillocks joined by a sandy-shored isthmus – was a slaving base, the site of the 1850 execution of a notorious slaver, Crawford (whose name the island carried until the end of the nineteenth century), and several of his men. Tales of their buried loot are supposed to have inspired Robert Louis Stevenson's *Treasure Island*.

Kakimbon caves

These **Grottes Préhistoriques** are in the village of Ratoma, now a suburb of Conakry at the end of the Taouyah road (north coast of the peninsula). There was until recently a **sacred forest**, a waterfall and a small **lake** as well as the two **caves**. It's not certain you'll find the site intact or to what extent it retains religious significance for the district's Baga people. Until well after World War II, it was still held in considerable awe and annual appeasement rituals to the spirit inhabitants of the caves were held.

One theory suggests that the site was used by slavers and acquired its fearsome reputation as the result of the disappearance of inquisitive locals. But several **excavations** at the end of the nineteenth century – the first such in French West Africa – yielded quantities of stone tools, arrow heads and pottery sherds. The place is easy to get to: we'd appreciate information for the next edition.

Nightlife

Conakry **nightlife** is an enjoyable scene, though an ever-changing one. The testing climate means that many clubs open at the start of the dry season before Christmas, fade out of use with the start of the rains in May, and are subsequently unusable by the start of the next dry season. The following selection, therefore, is likely to include several which have gone for good and some you may find temporarily *hors de combat*. All information for the next editon will be gratefully received and acknowledged.

TOWN CENTRE
Bembeya Club. A dive in the *Hôtel de l'Amitié*.
L'Hirondelle, opposite the Marché du Niger.
Le Petit Bateau. Exactly that, out on the Epi Nord; more of a restaurant.

PENINSULA
La Paillote Club, off route Donka, in Cameroun, just north of the autoroute bridge.
Club Jardin de Guinée, off the route nationale in Lanseboundji.
Club Le Rève, on the north side of route Donka in Dixinn-Port.
Club La Minière, 500m behind the Guinea-Bissau embassy, near the coast.
Club Hafia, almost opposite *Rogbane Cinema*.
Le Village, in Taouyah; an outdoor club, right on the corner by the main road.
Sabar Club, 1km past *Rogbane Cinema*, heading inland.

AIRPORT AREA
Zambezi, on the way in to town from the airport, just after where the *route nationale* splits from the autoroute, on the left.
Pili Pili, in *Hôtel Gbessia*.
Privilege, in the same vicinity; its ambience suggested by its name.
Le Balafon, near the airport; flashy and expensive.
Club Yehemato, well out of town, 3–4 km east of the *Cite Nord-France*.

Directory

Airline offices These are mostly clustered along the av de la République.
　Aeroflot, Air Afrique, Air Guinée (☎44 41 43, ☎44 46 07/8/9);
　Air Ivoire, at the Côte d'Ivoire embassy (address under Embassies) (☎44 50 52/3);
　Ethiopian Airlines, av de la République (☎44 25 95);
　Ghana Airways, 6 av de la République (☎44 48 13);
　KLM, Imm Banque Islamique, 6e av (☎44 44 70);
　Nigeria Airways, Imm. Somidrat, av de la Républque, (☎44 40 82/3, 44 40 92);
　Royal Air Maroc (☎44 45 59);
　Sabena, Imm. Hôtel Kaloum (☎44 34 40/44 36 10);
　UTA (☎44 36 57/8/9).
American Express No representative. The *Novotel* may help.

Banks *BICIGUI* on av de la République is the main branch for foreign exchange in Conakry. 8.30am–noon, Mon–Fri. Efficient.

British Council Out in the suburbs at Taouyah.

Car hire Outrageously expensive. One of the cheaper outlets is *Guinée Cars* (☎44 39 26/44 35 75) in av de la République. Prices per day, quoted in CFA, assuming 200km of driving and including obligatory expensive insurance start at around CFA35,000 for a runaround. You can get a week's unlimited mileage for about CFA150,000 inclusive of insurance. There's a 16 percent tax on top. The big names are at the airport and *Hôtel Indépéndance*, but they may insist on you hiring a driver for trips beyond Conakry – a leftover from the 35km restriction.

Cassettes Some of the cheapest in West Africa at two main locations in the Marché du Niger. Make up a job lot and bargain your heart out. Around FG800 each, possibly less.

Cinemas Of the ten or more in the city, the *Rogbané* in Taouyah – a fairly upmarket district – is the best, and they're beginning to show watchable films.

Curios A listless selection on the whole. Check out 4e bd between av de la République and av de la Gare, where the post office is.

DHL At over US$100 for a consignment of up to 500g you'd have to be sending home something very valuable indeed.

Embassies and consulates include:

Algeria next to Direction Garage du Gouvernement (BP 1004; ☎44 15 05);

Belgium Corniche Sud, Port de Boussoura;

Canada Corniche Sud, Coléah (BP 99; ☎46 37 37);

Congo Camayenne Corniche (BP 178; ☎46 24 51);

Côte d'Ivoire c/o 4e av and bd du Commerce (BP 362; ☎44 50 52/3);

Denmark 2e av, Hon. Consul Mr Moukarim Ossam (BP 158; ☎44 35 10/44 37 05);

Egypt Cornich Sud, Lanseboundji (BP 389; ☎46 14 25/31);

France entry on 8e av (BP 373; ☎ 44 16 55/44 17 42/44 46 52);

Gabon Dabondi, near the airport (BP 1461; ☎46 49 67);

German Federal Republic 2e bd (BP 540; ☎44 15 06/08);

Ghana Building Ex-Urbaine et la Seine, Moussoudougou (BP 372; ☎44 15 09/10);

Guinea-Bissau route de Taouyah, Bellevue (BP 298; ☎46 21 36);

Great Britain Hon. Consul Mrs Val Treitlein, near the British Council and language centre (BP 834);

Italy Pace Villa, Camayenne (BP 84; ☎46 23 32/46 13 23);

Japan Mayoré, Corniche Sud (BP 895);

Liberia Near *Hôtel Camayenne* (BP 18; ☎ 46 26 71);

Mali Corniche Sud, Madina-Port (BP 299; ☎46 14 18/20);

Morocco Corniche Nord, near the port (BP 193; ☎44 37 10);

Netherlands corner of 3e av and 4e bd;

Nigeria Corniche Sud, Coléah (BP 54; ☎46 13 43/46 14 09);

Norway opposite *KLM*, bd de la République;

Palestine av Tubman, c/o 2e bd (BP 1021; ☎44 11 32);

Senegal Madina Port (BP 842; ☎46 28 34/46 29 15);

Sierra Leone Bellevue junction (BP 625; ☎46 14 39/40/41);

Spain 2e bd, opp French Embassy;

Sweden corner of 7e av and Route du Niger;

Switzerland Rue l'Ecole de la Santé, Donka (BP 270; ☎46 26 12);

Tanzania between route de Donka and north coast, Donka (BP 189; ☎46 13 32/33);

USA 2e av (BP 603; ☎44 15 20/21/22/23/24);

USSR Matam Port (BP 329; ☎46 14 59/60);

Zaire 10e av, by the station (BP 880; ☎44 15 01/02).

Additionally among the useful addresses, **Benin** (Corniche Sud, Landseboundji) may still have an embassy but, like **Cape Verde**'s its status seems in doubt.

Photo permits These are more a theoretical than a mandatory requirement. If you're feeling frivolous enough to want to take on Guinean bureaucracy, check them out at ONACIG, by the *Sylcinéma* at Place du 8 Novembre. Otherwise, keep your lenses capped in Conakry.

Post and telephones Main PTT is open 8am–2pm Mon–Fri. Telephone section stays open on *permanence* with stamps for sale from 2–10pm.

Poste restante is neither stunningly secure nor organised.

Travel Agents The airlines act as general agents. For possible travel by ship, consult SOGUICOM (☎44 23 23, telex 22176)

THE FOUTA DJALON

Raising some spectacular cliffs just a short journey inland from Conakry and covering the greater part of the western interior, the **Fouta Djalon highlands** are Guinea's major attraction. Cut into innumerable, chocolate-bar plateaux – some denuded to *mesa*-like outcrops – the sandstone massif is the source of hundreds of **rivers**, including the Gambia and the Senegal, major tributaries of the Niger and a lattice of streams running down to the Guinea coast. After the rains, **waterfalls** spume everywhere.

Populated by now-sedentary **Fula** (Peul) herders and the remnants of the indigenous agricultural groups they invaded, the region has a fascinating ethnic history and an extraordinary variety of landscape. Lushly cultivated or **jungle**-filled **valleys** rise – sometimes with **sheer cliffs** – to scrubby high ground, bare and rocky wastelands or lightly wooded **plateaux**. Wherever the contours are gentle enough to retain the soil, swathes of **grassland** roll in the wind. It's fabulous country and needs only time, and average determination, to explore – wanderings which can be immensely satisfying.

HIKING, BIKING AND RELATED PRACTICALITIES

The Fouta Djalon is one of the best regions in West Africa for serious, stimulating **off-the-beaten-track travel**. Assuming you're armed with at least the *IGN* map of the country (the *Michelin* 953 isn't enough), there are hundreds of kilometres of, sometimes optimistically labelled, "motorable tracks" and footpaths throughout the region (see p.602 for an account of one of them). We took **mountain bikes** up here and had little trouble, on the main axes, loading them onto vehicles whenever enthusiasm waned. **Motorbikes**, with whatever reservations and hassles might accompany them – and preferably they'd need to be trail bikes – would be ideal. **Four-wheeled vehicles** (including four-wheel-*drive* vehicles) however, will run into repeated difficulties on steep and rugged terrain and you'd need the most agile and powerful machine to negotiate more than the most often-used of the minor routes. The option open to all is **footing it** and the only consideration then is whether your visa allows you the time.

You should, however, ensure minimal levels of **survivability** in the event of a breakdown or an accident. If you're on two wheels, take obsessive care: roads which seem relatively good can turn a bend and disappear without warning into a river, or lose themselves in a jumble of rocks and gullies. Have purifying tablets for water which often comes straight from the local stream; and carry some back-up **rations** for emergencies.

This is the most densely populated part of the country. The **people** of the Fouta Djalon are, in general, wonderfully kind and show a disinterested concern for the welfare of wayward *fotay* (white people). They'll nearly always get water for you when you need it. The highlands, moreover, are a major citrus-growing area and during the early dry season you'll be able to rely on oranges in their hundreds as a cheap source of fluid. Remember of course to stock up on **essentials** like toilet paper and batteries which don't grow on trees. Remember too that temperatures at night can drop below 10°C and you'll need something warm.

The approach: Coyah, Kindia and Mamou

You can get to the major Fouta Djalon centres – Dalaba, Pita and Labé – in a day's travel from Conakry on a mostly good, surfaced road. But be at Conakry's Madina taxi park early. Or check out the state of the **trains** and take *Chemin de Fer de Guinée*'s crazily precipitous route up to Mamou – you'll get the choicest scenery this way.

If you're in no hurry, start the trip with the short journey up to Coyah. Leaving Conakry, you follow the smog-laden fast lane, and the oily squalor and vitality of the city immigrants' highway-side *ateliers*, making every conceivable kind of manufacture. You pass also through a string of tedious **checkpoints**, the last of which, Kilometre 35, at the Kindia-Dubreka junction, is an outlandish scene of strutting and loafing khaki where delays, particularly heading *into* the city, are commonplace.

Coyah

COYAH (Guinea's source of bottled water) is surrounded by dense green forest and plantation, and innumerable food stalls throng its main street. The last one on the right, before the road bends left to Kindia, does a superb groundnut and cassava leaf sauce.

Out of Coyah, pale dramatic **cliffs** rise to the south from a broken plain of bush and palms. Crowned with bubbling greenery, these isolated tablelands – more or less separated from the plains by rock faces on all sides, and apparently uninhabited on top – would likely repay investigation by fairly intrepid naturalists. If you're interested and ready for a hike, stop at the village of **Tabili** and follow the left bank of the Badi upstream between the cliffs. It rises on top of the plateau.

Kindia

The road up to Kindia has recently been resurfaced – on the whole a dangerously speedy improvement. **KINDIA**, a bustling, workaday place born on the railway line in the early 1900s, has a huge market but no other obvious attractions. There are a number of decent eateries along the main road through town and a hotel or two if you're here late in the day. Roadworks and red tiles on the few remaining French mansions are the abiding impressions, together with thousands of **mango trees** (it's a wonderful place to fetch up in season, with different varieties – *chocolat*, *fini pas*, etc). The massif which rises 700m above the town to the north is **Mont Gangan**, one of the highest peaks in the southern Fouta Djalon.

Pastoria

A secondary route into the central highlands winds out of Kindia to TÉLIMÉLÉ, with onward possibilities to PITA and the far north. There's a handful of vehicles each day and the road condition is kept up fairly well. If you'd like to have a look at **PASTORIA** – the "Institut Pasteur" – which is 6km up this road, you'll probably have to *déplace* a town taxi for the trip, or take a long walk in hope. The *Institut* was founded in 1925 as a primate research centre, principally with the aim of developing various vaccines for human use. We have their consumptive **chimps** to thank for the BCG (Bacillus Calmette-Guerin) anti-tuberculosis jab. The Pasteur Institute in Paris later charged Pastoria with the collection of snake venom for anti-venene preparations and it's now heavily Soviet-funded. It's still open for visits if you call first on the director. They have a large collection of primates and snakes.

On to Mamou

After Kindia the main road drops to a broad valley, then climbs again, while the railway, creeping through the hills to the north, makes some of its most daring moves. En route you pass the **Chutes de la Santa** located in dense forest: a track turning to the right, 14km outside Kindia, leads in 7.5km to their base. Getting here without your own transport is almost certain to require a walk, but the effort is apparently more than repaid. Some sixty metres high, the falls leap from a black and yellow cliff in two streams to crash against the rockface and break into a broad fan. They're known as *Voile de la Mariée* for this "bridal veil" shape – acquired only during and shortly after the rains. Later in the dry season, as with most of the Fouta Djalon's numerous cascades, their interest diminishes with their water.

If you continue on this road, southwards, the route runs **along the foot of the southern Fouta Djalon ridges** almost the whole way to FORÉCARIAH – a beautiful and remote 120km. Any vehicles are rare.

Meanwhile, back on the main east-bound highway, the steep, hairpinning climb up to Mamou offers a sweeping panorama back over the broad tributary basins of the Kolente (or Great Scarcies) river, the border with Sierra Leone. Twenty or thirty kilometres before Mamou you'll find a couple of hamlets which have developed into sizeable "service stations" for the bush taxi traffic, providing food and prayer stalls day and night. **Madine** is the first, **Hafiya** the second and main one.

If you're in the mood for more falls – and have the means – take a side trip, 5km to the right, to the village and falls of **Konkoure**, some 25km before Mamou. There's supposed to be an old sacred wood here, containing remnant examples of trees from the ancient forest which once covered large parts of the Fouta.

Mamou

Before the building of the railway, the religious and political centre of the Fouta Djalon *almamys* (Islamic leaders) was **Timbo** – now just a village 50km northeast of **MAMOU**. Despite considerable local opposition, the French decided to bypass Timbo and set up a new railway halt and fuel depot at the hamlet of Mamou. The Fula chieftancy was transferred and, until after World War II, Mamou was the chief administrative centre for much of the highlands.

Today, piled on the hillside, the town strikes a surprisingly low-key note in its sprawl of houses and compounds. It has an agricultural college and a meat-processing industry.

If you make a late start from Conakry, Mamou is about as far as you'll get in one day. **Places to stay** are few and simple. The *Hôtel Luna* (around FG1500/2000) has spartan quarters only: if you want a half-decent wash ask the *patron* for access to his washroom, as guests' facilities are dark and fetid. The *Luna* compensates with the weekend popularity of its **terrace** among local teachers and *fonctionnaires*. Musicians and griots come here and compete against the disco on the bar radio. Pay them FG25 or 50 to sing someone's praises and you'll go down a treat. It can be quite a scene.

Onward transport from Mamou is rarely a problem. The main taxi park, surrounded incidentally by cheap little eateries, is a hive of activity from dawn to dusk.

Timbo

You'll need wheels or a little determination to reach **Timbo**, old capital of the Fula *almamys*. There should be at least one vehicle a day, probably more. Timbo apparently still has an eighteenth-century mosque – much restored – and there's a European cemetery dating back to the end of the last century when a French *résident* was installed to breath down Fula necks. You'll also come across traditional Fouta Djalon houses out here; senior figures construct fine conical beehive affairs, with solid tiers of thatching to exclude the cold.

Into the hills: Dalaba, Pita and Labe

A rough, but tarred, road winds through pretty scenery between Mamou and Dalaba. You'll notice here, if you've not done already, the many old, deformed, **telegraph poles** along the roadside. Their iron construction, with a heavy-duty confidence in their durability and permanence, and the violence with which many were later twisted out of shape in 1958 (how?), seem an eloquent summary of the French occupation.

About 15km out of Mamou the stream you cross flowing east is the Bafing, ultimate headwater of the Senegal. The road steepens after BOULIVEL (Saturday *lumo*), then drops to enter Dalaba. The town hides in a conifer-carpeted valley. Why it's called *Dalaba* – "big pond" in Malinké – is a mystery. The place, like Pita and Labé, is old.

Dalaba

DALABA gets enthusiastic praise: *the closest thing to Shangri-la in West Africa* thought a Peace Corps volunteer on furlough from the rigours of Sierra Leone. Set beautifully in the hills at 1200m, it's easy to see why the French considered the site so therapeutic – it does resemble the Maritime Alps or somewhere similar. They built a sixty-room sanatorium ("admission with medical certificate") which is no more.

The **market** has a super-abundance of produce, including, from the end of December to March, cultivated **strawberries** – a colonial bequest. It's especially worth hitting on Sunday, when it's amplified as the district *lumo*.

In **practical** terms, Dalaba breaks down easily. The market and a couple of streets around comprise the town centre, with one or two restaurant places. Try *Bar Mariam* on the street along the bottom of the market, which converts to a *dancing* on Wednesday and Saturday nights, and has cheapish eats. There's a **post office** but no bank. Away across the valley and behind the hill to the west is the administrative quarter of Etaconval – thoroughly rural and spreadeagled through the woods – and the best **place to stay**, *La Villa*. Dalaba's is one of the best *villas*, a cluster of houses on the hillside with infinite views, where you can normally sleep for FG3000. Occasionally it's full of doctors, teachers or whatever, who increasingly book it for conferences. But you can still **camp** under the pines and make use of the limited facilities and a lock-up storage room. Back towards the town centre is the *Etoile de Fouta* – restaurant and sometime *boîte* where you can usually get a *steack frites* for FG2000. But, unless they're busy, it's a mournful barn of a place (ex-French officers' club) with underwhelming appeal.

Don't fail to have a look at the odd house out among those on the hillside; a remarkable Fula chiefs' **assembly hall** – a *case de palabre* – built in the 1930s, with an inscribed floor and exceptional carving on its internal walls.

Onwards to Pita

Moving on to PITA from Dalaba by public transport can sometimes prove difficult: most vehicles are either coming full from Mamou and going on to LABÉ, or vice versa. An early start might get you a ride without having to pay the fare the whole way to Labé.

While it's not inconceivable as a **walk** – and worth it for the stunning **scenery** which at last really opens up – fifty-two kilometres is a long way for unadjusted muscles. But the first half of the route plunges down through various stages of gorgeous forest – conifer, broad leaf jungle, more open bush – and this section you might consider walking in the realistic enough hope of getting a lift further along the way. It's surely a waste to rush by jammed in a *Peugeot*.

If you have your own wheeled transport, consider a diversion down the steep grade to Tinka (right, 5km outside Dalaba). In colonial times there was an ornamental garden here – **Le Jardin de Professeur Chevallier** – but it's uncertain whether that's still there, or if the **Chutes de Ditinn**, some 30km further at the village of Ditinn, are still accessible. When there's sufficient flow, the eighty-metre falls, dropping from a perfectly vertical cliff, are very impressive.

Back on the main road, look out for the **Chutes de Piké**, hard by the road on the left just after the bridge over the same-named stream about 15km from Dalaba. These are easily accessible down a couple of short paths leading either to the pool at the top where you can stand at the precipice, or to the ledges at the bottom where you can see the ten-metre cascade: pretty, but pretty small and very unimpressive in the dry season. Still, it makes a good halt. The Fouta Djalon spurts pandemically with waterfalls, but some are more easily seen from a distance than reached. BOMBOLI's *chutes* are clearly visible about 15km before you get to Pita, several kilometres over on the right, but difficult of access.

Pita

As a place of beauty and repose, **PITA** can't equal Dalaba. But they share the same zesty atmosphere and you'll quickly grow to like it. Market day is Thursday. Pita figures in most travel plans as a place to get the necessary permission (usually free, but not always) to visit the **Kinkon Falls** – a simple matter of calling at the *commisariat* on the north side of town.

For **stays**, most people get directed to a fast-fading hotel, the *Hôtel Kinkon*, on the way out of town, just below the *commisariat*. Apparently run by a gang of young people, it's very basic but just about adequate and quite *sympa* (FG2–3000 the room). Warm water can be ordered for the self-contained washing cubicles. The adjacent black and white psychedelic nightclub is occasionally cranked into life – they have cold drinks by day.

In town there's a number of **eating** places. You might try the *Café Montréal*, or *Restaurant Djoualasso* which may still have frosty cold cans of Puerto Rican *Heineken* – puzzling. Several other places also have fridges: though you'll perhaps think them unnecessary if you're huddled round a brazier in the dark waiting for brochettes.

Another waterfall: Kinkon

The **Chutes de Kinkon** are the Fouta Djalon's best falls, a fairly easy cycle ride – but a longish walk and little chance of a lift – some 11km from Pita. A sign 2–3km along the road out to Labé sends you left (direction Touma and Télimélé, see p.602) and after a mostly downhill 7km – bearing left when in doubt – you arrive at a control post where you hand in your *laisser passer*. Here you'll be told it's 500m down to the right if you desire to inspect the dam (an unimpressive bridge across the lake; the reason for the piece of paper) and about a kilometre left for the main falls.

You can stand directly on the old **rock platform** which – before the dam was built – would have surged with water, and possibly does still during the rains. There's evidence of colonial safety measures in the broken stumps of cliff-edge railings; but nothing to stop present-day visitors plunging dramatically to their deaths – adding a risk element that makes it all fairly worthwhile. Take care: the flow is powerful. Behind, on the cliffs, is a scrappy but just-about legible list of various heads of state, with the dates of their visits. You can follow the path down below the falls to the power station on the river bank – but apart from good exercise there's absolutely no point since there's nothing to be seen.

The Northern Fouta Djalon

From Pita, the **road to Labé** loops across a mellow, pastoral landscape; an undulating grass sea, scattered with boulders and copses of oak-like *koura* trees, fringed with lines of forest along the watercourses. The district, one of the highest in the Fouta Djalon, is a watershed between the streams that flow west and the Gambia and Senegal tributaries pouring off north.

Labé

LABÉ, the historic Fula stronghold, strategically situated in the middle of this high zone, is, by contrast, a misshapen, unappealing, though evidently prosperous, town. As capital of the Fouta Djalon it's a disappointment. Sizeable – a good deal more so than Mamou, Dalaba or Pita – and ranged confusingly over a number of hills, it's a growing centre, absorbing people from the regions of Guinea and not a few from neighbouring countries. All of which delivers a rather metropolitan jolt after the surrounding horizons and makes Labé somewhat impractical as a place to stay.

Being in Labé

Arriving from Pita, you enter Labé past the sad hulk of the *Hôtel de Tourisme* – clearly a previously-grand place in vaguely Swiss-chalet style, but now somewhat decrepit and seemingly under permanent renovation. The reasonable rooms go from FG5000 and there's a bar-resto and rather commanding balcony. Taxis will deposit you at the *gare*

LOCAL HISTORY: THE RISE OF THE JIHAD STATE

The original inhabitants of the highlands were Jalonke, Baga, Nalo and **Puli** (sedentary, animist, Fula speakers). They all coexisted in relative harmony, herding on the hills and farming the valleys. The region was known then as **Jalonkadougou**, after its dominant inhabitants, and was subject to the Mali empire.

The first ripples of tension through this rural idyll were felt during the thirteenth century, when **Fula immigrants** – the superficially Muslim clans of Ba, Sow, Diallo and Bari – arrived piecemeal, in search of pasture, from Tekrur on the Senegal and Djenné on the Niger. By the fifteenth century, they were sufficiently established for one of their kings, **Koli Tengela**, to shake off Mali's rule and raid widely abroad to expand the Fula zone of influence. He later withdrew north to found the Denianke dynasty back in Tekrur.

This early Fula Muslim rule in the highlands wasn't especially zealous in its promulgation of Islam. With the demise of the Tengela dynasty, however, the increasingly fervent **Diallos** came up the Bafing and Tinkisso valleys and moved into the Labé region, spreading the faith among the Puli animists and quasi-Muslims who held local political power. Further migrations from outside the region quickened resentment of the incumbent infidel overlords. By the early eighteenth century, there was enough support for King **Karamoko Alfa Bari** to declare a jihad against the non-believers. He won a breakthrough military victory against them at Talansan in 1730.

The **Muslim Kingdom of Fouta Djalon** emerged, with Karamoko Alfa Bari as its *almamy* and its capital at **Timbo**. Karamoko's nephew, Ibrahima Sory, took power when his uncle went insane in 1767 and thereafter the **jihad state** was rapidly consolidated. The kingdom was divided into nine provinces, one of which, **Labé**, became a noted centre of learning. Labé was also a hotbed of *Alfaya* (supporters of Alfa Bari), unhappy with the rule of the nephew's line.

There were **conversions** among the animists, but many fled to less intense pastures, mostly coastwards. Those who stayed were either **"bush Fula"**, employed as herders by the Muslim aristos, or **slaves** of non-Fula origin who worked partly for their landlords and partly on their own account.

Throughout the nineteenth century, Labé drew apart from Timbo. Labé's ruler, **Alfa Yaya**, the great-grandson of Karamoko Alfa Bari, achieved his position through ruthless assassinations of his opponents. By the 1890s, with his territory extended over most of northwest Guinea, Labé constituted as powerful a state as the Timbo-based kingdom of Fouta Djalon itself. With the arrival of the French, separate treaties were entered into with both realms. Today Alfa Yaya – or Alfa Labé as he's known – is a folk hero: his **tomb** lies behind the mosque near the airstrip.

In the 1970s, the Fula population suffered heavy **repression** at the hands of Sekou Touré's terrorist dictatorship. He labelled ethnic Fula "enemies of socialism", and many thousands were killed or fled into exile.

de voitures, a few hundred metres to the right, and here you can check out some of the *Tourisme*'s competition – a couple of lodgings both called *Indépendance*. The one at the bottom of the car park is better, but often full; the other at the top very basic and even cheaper, but with comfortable kapok mattresses. There's a host of other places.

Equilibrium is probably attainable at the much superior *Hôtel Aeroport* – down at the airstrip – 2km left from the *Hôtel de Tourisme* junction. Here you can take a decent chalet room with a shower for FG4000. On the way down, you pass the National Apiculture Centre, with Fouta Djalon potted **honey** for sale.

For more substantial food, the **market** – huge, rutted and teeming – is one of Labé's strong points, though even more of a tight squeeze to walk around than usual. There's a remarkable variety of groundnut pastes on offer, and all the usual Fouta Djalon profusion of produce.

Miscellaneous *renseignements* in the centre include the only **bank** in the highlands, *BICIGUI* (open Mon–Fri 8.30am–12.30pm, 2.30–4.45pm); the **PTT**; and the *Bel Afrique* **bookshop** – owned by *Jeune Afrique* magazine, but no stronger in reading matter for that.

A good bar/café is the *Africa-Restau Restaurant Moderne* which you'll find opposite the bookshop. Lastly, look out for exquisite **gara** cloth manufactured with Czechoslovakian damask – which is tie-dyed with local indigo and beaten with clubs to a shine; it's sold, as usual, only in pairs of *pagnes*.

If, despite your other discoveries in Labé, you find yourself pining for Conakry, *Air Guinée* theoretically operates **flights** on Wednesday and Saturday – FG15,000.

Onwards from Labé

There are several **onward options** from Labé. The most obvious is to continue, off-tarmac, to the small town of MALI – at 1460m the highest Fouta settlement – and then downhill (mostly) to KÉDOUGOU in Senegal. From Mali you can also head west to KOUNDARA, though this is a diabolical road with one-in-four gradients and some dangerous hairpins and skeletal bridges. Be ready to get off the vehicle or scream for the driver to halt if it becomes too hair-raising. In Koundara, the *Hôtel Mamadou Boiron* is a good place. **Saturday night** is party night, free for residents, with great music: don't sleep, dance! The route from Labé via SÉRIBA and GAOUAL (fabulously picturesque) is the one more often used by people heading for Guinea-Bissau and Senegal's Basse Casamance. There's relatively frequent transport on this latter route and from Mali to Kédougou (at least once a day during the dries), but don't count on anything much between Mali and Koundara.

Fourteen kilometres north of Labé, the village of **TONTOUROU** formerly had, and may still have, beautiful Fula houses. It might be worth an exploratory excursion, even as a special trip out of Labé. Just a kilometre or so further, the small stream running east is the River Gambia – source nearby.

Mali

The route on to Mali switchbacks through the Fouta's loftiest parts, with a number of fair-sized villages on the way – SARÉ-KALI at 35km; the pretty hamlet of PELLAL off to the left at 65km and YAMBERING the largest, at 74km.

MALI itself (small hotel) is renowned for low temperatures – down to 3°C – and extravagant **views** at the end of the rains, particularly, however, from the summit of Mont Loura (1538m). This, the highest peak in the Fouta Djalon, is 7km north of the village. The local *curiosité*, **La Dame de Mali** – a cliff eroded into "a well-proportioned feminine profile" – is a further 7km out to the northeast, but not necessarily worth a major effort.

Going East or West

If you're heading generally **eastwards** for Mali-the-country or Côte d'Ivoire, and feeling very expeditionary, then seek out transport to TOUGUÉ and work your way off the Fouta Djalon into the Malinké savannah region and KANKAN. Generally the hills east of the main Labé–Mamou road are more sparsely populated and even tougher travelling than those to the west, though for the most part not as steep.

If you're basically **making for the coast** from Labé, a recommended alternative to the main road through Mamou and Kindia is to dive off west at Pita and steer for TÉLIMÉLÉ. For this route, however – described below – your own wheels, legs, or patience waiting for a lift are probably required.

Rough stuff: Pita to Télimélé

There must be tougher routes in the highlands, but this one (131km) fulfills every challenging requirement. For **transport** you'll really need to fish. Ask around in Labé and check with the police in Pita. Trucks may be going only as far as one of the villages en route: and they may come from the Labé or the Mamou direction. Frequency of vehicles seems to be about two or three a week in the dry season, probably none at all during the rains.

Far better to go **under your own steam**. This is an ideal route for **mountain bikes** (two days), **trail motorbikes** or high clearance **4WD vehicles** (eight hours plus) or **hiking** (four days plus). Cycling or hiking, you might try to get a lift as far as Dongol-Touma, where the thrills begin. It's worth knowing that the route in reverse is considerably less attractive, the rewards mostly westwards. East-bound you face a continuous thirty-kilometre climb.

Setting off: over the *bowe*

You can make an early start and combine the Kinkon Falls (see p.599) with this route. Access to both is from the poorly signposted turn-off 3km north of Pita. At first there's a confusion of tracks. Bear right where another sign points left to the falls; then left at a fork some way further. If in doubt, guess.

The correct **track** soon starts bucking and twisting unmistakably, with many descents to narrow streams and many wearing climbs to short level ridges. There's a fair number of Fula people about, invariably suprised to see any strangers, let alone the likes of foreign travellers. The track heads northwest, southwest, east and south before establishing a more or less westerly course on a barren hogsback of rocky land discernible on the *IGN* map. In truth, this part of the journey, across the **bowe** – the Fula name for these high, sear plateaux – isn't scenically enthralling. By December the grass torchers are out too, anticipating the *harmattan* haze which normally fogs the horizon between January and April. Come at the end of the rains in late October or November and you can at least see for miles.

The path runs over unrelenting bare rock in places, and then begins a gentle descent, with occasional wooded intervals. There's a remarkable country market (Tuesday, or possibly a non-weekly cycle) at an ill-defined spot along here where hundreds of Fula women converge to buy and sell a little, but mainly to share news. The miracle of hairstyles and print patterns is stunning and happily typical. Onwards, you reach a strung-out village focusing on the (Wednesday) *lumo* site of **DONGOL-TOUMA**, 55km from the Pita junction. Dongol-Touma, marked on the *IGN* map simply as "Touma" (and apparently marked too far west), comes at the end of the **bowe**. From here on commences a glorious **descent**.

If you see the *sous-préfet* you'll likely be able to **stay the night** in Dongol-Touma's "villa", superbly sited on a high bluff with 270 degrees of panorama. It's rarely needed for official purposes and you may receive a royal welcome and repeated donations of food and drink (something in return is appreciated the next morning).

The good part: downhill to the Kakrima river

The road snakes out of Dongol-Touma and starts a **steep descent**, with inspiring sweeps of Fouta Djalon visible through the trees now shading it. This is a breathtaking coaster, zig-zagging down a long spine and throwing up striking views of the bush country to the south, the fortress-like hills – Télimélé among them – rising in a ridge to the west, and plunging valleys right below; worth every metre of the slog from Pita. **Streams**, flecked with butterflies and overshot by parrots and hornbills, cut across the road and are quickly left behind hundreds of metres above. Giant leaves litter the ground and lianas strew overhead. Occasionally a hunter or a woodcutter emerges – always equable, if amazed, on seeing you. Monkeys, the hunters' main targets, are common. You could travel far to find a road like this.

If you're pedal cycling or motorbiking, the only effort for 26km is in keeping the brakes on. Driving a car or truck, exercise extreme caution. One section at least – a tumble of boulders and bedrock – would appear to be well-nigh impossible.

People from the immaculate mud-moulded compounds are happy, once they've got over their disbelief and exchanged greetings, to bring water from their wells or stream, and will give you handfuls of oranges and bananas as fast as sell them. Children in this isolated region may be just a little scared of white people.

At last the gradients relax and the road unwinds, through more cultivated country, towards the **Kakrima river**. The village of Dioukoum (marked on the *IGN* map) leaves no impression, but **LEMIRO** (not on the map; at a junction about 4km before the Kakrima ferry) is the second large settlement along the way. You'll find rice and the rest if you turn up early enough, or bread and sandwich-makings if not.

The Kakrima **ferry** has an engine, but it's not far across in the event of breakdown. What comes after is harder work on a bicycle, mostly flat and sandy in parts, with elephant grass jamming any view. Cars and trucks coming the other way, from the west, make it easily enough as far as Lemiro (or at least to the river), so you might pick up a lift on their return.

Sixty-one kilometres after Dongol-Touma the route hits the broad, red sweep of the maintained Kindia–Télimélé road. You'll find a lift easily enough. The final gruelling 15km to the town up the soaring flank of **Mont Louba** is noted for gut-churning accidents on the hairpins.

Télimélé

A pleasing, well-kept town, perched as if to admire its grand views, **TÉLIMÉLÉ** sees very few visitors. In the area somewhere lies **Gueme Sangan**, the ruined **fortress** of Koli Tengela, the fifteenth-century Fula warlord who laid the foundations of the kingdom of Fouta Djalon. And the whole district lifts with imposing mountain flanks and trench-like valleys. Télimélé – "the place where the *téli* grows" – is a town of orange roads, pine trees, citrus orchards and fresh air. If you're staying, there's an adequate **hotel** (FG3000) suitably elevated to give a formidable vista over the town from its terrace. It's up near the administrative quarter at the Kindia end of town. After dark its location isn't likely to be a matter for conjecture anyway, as they haul big speakers onto the terrace and obliterate the crickets with *One Night in Bangkok*. Nothing's perfect.

The road down to Kindia isn't too bad and transport plentiful, but it's worth investing a little extra for a place in a *Peugeot* rather than one of the vans. If you're up early, you can be in Conakry by the afternoon. Stay awake for the last half hour before Kindia; there are some outstanding tabular massifs, rearing like lost worlds across the valley.

THE MALINKÉ PLAINS

The great **plains** of the northeast – *Haute Guinée* – stretch, immensely vast and flat, over more than a hundred thousand square kilometres, big enough to swallow The Gambia ten times over. In this huge expanse, the few towns – Kankan the biggest, Kouroussa, Faranah, Siguiri – seem lost amid yellow grass, thorn trees and termite spires. In contrast to the Fouta Djalon and the Highlands further south, the population is sparse: most people live along the the meandering **tributaries of the Niger** which pull together in a fan in the most populous part of the region around Kankan and Kouroussa.

THE MANDE PEOPLES

The agricultural and trading **Mande**-speaking peoples are cultural heirs to the medieval empire of **Mali**, whose capital from the thirteenth to the fourteenth century was Niani, northeast of Kankan. More recently, the self-styled *almamy*, **Samory Touré**, founded and burned out two "Dyula empires" at the end of the nineteenth century and caused the French considerable grief with his determined jihad against their invasion.

The traditional Mande **names**, Touré, Traoré, Camara, Konté, Keita and Kouyateh are still the most common. Various Mande **languages** are spoken – including Bambara, Dyula and Koranko – as well as mainstream Mandinka/Malinké.

Getting around

As for **travel**, in practice, without your own means of transport you're mostly restricted to a clutch of main routes tracking through the territory. If you leave them on foot or bicycle, distances between habitation and supplies are often too long for comfort – you can go miles without seeing a soul even on the main roads. The **towns** however are mostly animated and tend to be worthwhile in themselves, while one particular journey, along the river from Kankan to Siguiri, is one of West Africa's most delightful.

Mamou to Faranah

For some distance from Mamou, the road drops, rough, through forest and hilly bush with views to pass the time. Then it flattens and the scenery breaks into pretty, but quickly monotonous, **elephant grass** and bush savannah for the rest of the journey to Faranah. The highlands are shed: the road, built after independence, arrows and loops determinedly through the flat wilderness. With time, Kouranko compounds and hamlets may gradually gather along it. **At night**, this is one of the country's most soporific journeys, with little to enliven it but the cassettes on the driver's stereo. It's worth knowing, however, that the district is one of the richest faunal areas in Guinea and your chances of seeing exciting large wild animals quite high.

Faranah

After a long, nearly uninhabited void since Mamou – of which a hot, breezy yellowness is the enduring recollection – arrival at **FARANAH** makes some impact. A parade of mighty street lights lines up to greet you on the highway into town. And the **Niger river**, which flows beneath a rattling iron bridge, looks impressive already, with 4000km of meandering still to come. The airstrip at Faranah is reportedly big enough to take international flights. The Tinkisso dam at Dabola provides electricity: a Chinese team has been improving the system to give some juice in the dry season too.

Until independence, Faranah was an unimportant village on the old road from Dabola to Kissidougou. Sekou Touré pumped money into his native village, building a large mosque, as well as the *Cité du Niger* conference centre in 1981 and a massive block of a villa for himself, now a hotel. It's a town you're bound to pass through and for practical needs by Guinean standards (apart from the lack of a bank) can't be faulted, though there's little of interest to hold you.

Faranah facts

Best **stays** are at the Touré mansion, now *Hôtel de Ville*, a repellently ostentatious four-storey pile still stuffed with hideous presidential furniture, the largest pouffe in the world and an absurd desk made of solid marble. Despite the unintentional kitsch, it's wonderfully good value (probably the best outside Conakry) and doubles as an informal Museum of President's Presents – which is what most of the trappings are. Rooms with verandah, AC, hot bath, fridge and supplies of electricity are around FG6000. Aim to secure an interesting room over the street by pointing out that they're all unoccupied – it doesn't always follow.

Should anything befall the villa (Touré's wife and son have recently been released from detention), you might need to fall back on the *Cité de Niger*, if it's standing. The rondavels sit in a great site high above the river but the whole complex is flaking away and the rooms are dismal inside (FG6000/8000, group discounts).

Back in the town centre, cheap **eateries** compete at one end of the main *gare voiture*, serving high quality street food all day, but closing at night when some vehicles come in (the boys at the café with the seats outside, round the corner, seem to maintain 24-hour service with their kettle). For more extended meals the excellent *Restaurant Gastronomique Le Regal* (around FG2000) has a full menu and a fair selection, including wine. When satisfied, spill into the nightclub across the way which has reasonably cheap beers and lots of lively clients.

Also worth noting, the **autogare** for Dabola is at the opposite end of town. Some 15km west of Faranah, a big sign on the left says *Direction Sierra Leone*, and that's the way across the border to KABALA – a road which has recently been a little improved. Finally, if you need to **phone or telegram** abroad, Faranah has an "external telecommunications centre" which makes it relatively easy.

Dabola, Kouroussa and Dinguiraye

These first two are essentially **railway towns** whose appeal lies in a certain just-past nostalgia. Dabola, in particular, was a major centre during the French occupation and carried the Conakry–Kankan road (as Faranah does today) as well as trains, until the Mamou–Faranah link was built. Kouroussa, at a rail bridge over the Niger, was also once an important centre but is now somewhat cut off. It was the birthplace of Guinea's best-known author, Camara Laye.

An earth road in fair condition cuts out of Faranah through irrigated rice fields and along the stripling Niger valley before starting a gradual ascent. There's regular transport to Dabola but considerably more difficulty going on to Kouroussa: the ferry over the Niger is often out of action and if vehicles can't get through to Kankan it's a long way back.

Dabola

DABOLA grew up after 1910 as a staging post, and it retains a slightly Wild-West feel, hemmed in by gaunt plateaux rising directly behind the town and keeping those passing through well fed and even entertained. It's not an unattractive place: in Dabolakoro ("old Dabola") neat compounds surround the small commercial centre. The less animated administrative quarter – where the ancient *Hôtel Bar Restaurant Tinkisso* still struggles along (FG1500, buckets of hot water brought to the clean S/C rooms) – is a kilometre or two in the Timbo/Mamou direction.

There are evidently two days to be in Dabola; Tuesday – market day – and Saturday, when the hotel manager's band often do a gig in town.

The **Tinkisso Falls** are well worth a short detour any time. From the hotel, a gentle six-kilometre climb on the *route de Mamou* brings you to a track (left) which drops over the railway line through a teak plantation – with drifts of huge, crunching leaves underfoot – and, forking right, to the top of the **dam** and a mass of birdlife. The **falls** themselves – which would have been impressive indeed before the dam was built – cascade over rocky shelves below. The path descends steeply to the power station and its Chinese retinue, with more views back. Continue on the same footpath downstream and you reach an immaculate Fula village and, eventually, the Dabola–Faranah road. Persistent hikers will want to do the circle – it makes a good day.

Kouroussa

KOUROUSSA is a beautiful area, although owing to a lack of transport it's somewhat hard to get to. The house of **Camara Laye**'s family, near the station, is quite well known and you'll have no difficulty tracking it down if you want to pay homage.

René Caillié, the indomitable French traveller who disguised himself and mumbled in Arabic to be the first European to return from Timbuktu, arrived in Kouroussa with a bout of malaria in June 1827:

> *We crossed the river in canoes . . . A great number of people were going across, and they were all disputing, some about the fare that was demanded, some about who should go first. They all talked at once and made a most terrible uproar.*

The ferry crossing on the Kankan road, 26km east of the town, has apparently changed little. When it breaks down in the dry season, some truckers risk fording the shallows but most *Peugeot* drivers won't.

Dinguiraye

DINGUIRAYE, isolated out in the back country towards the Malian border, was founded by Al Haj Omar Tall in 1850 and it became an important religious centre in the second half of the nineteenth century. The French post here, dating from 1896, was one of the earliest in Upper Guinea.

Omar Tall's **mosque**, an elaborate Fula-style thatched construction, was reportedly still in place a few years back. What you'll find now – and also in terms of facilities – is uncertain. The town lies on a somewhat tenuous route connecting the Fouta Djalon, SIGUIRI and Bamako – an untouched and thinly populated part of the country, renowned for its wildlife and massive granite mounds looming from the plains. You should find transport from Dabola daily.

Kissidougou

KISSIDOUGOU is composed of three distinct – but no longer easily distinguishable – villages. **Kenéma Pompo** is the oldest, a Kissi village once tucked in its sacred forest which goes back to the eighteenth century, when it was the head of a small federation of Kissi settlements. The second, **Hérèmakono** (which means roughly *Home Sweet Home*) is the administrative and commercial district built away from the forest. And the third **Dioulabou** lies on the east side, the "Dyula town" established by Samory's vanquished lieutenants in 1893. **Kissi Kaba Keita**, the ruler of the town at the time of French penetration, put up a notional resistance.

Today, this may seem just another fairly unremarkable town, but it borders the largest zone of forest in West Africa and the sense of transition is apparent in the patches of woodland. Kissidougou is also notable as the centre of Guinea's main coffee-growing area.

Practicalities and pleasures

The ensemble, flat for a change and spacious, isn't a bad place at all and it's common enough to be dumped here after one of Upper Guinea's lengthy taxi rides. **Post office** and **bank** face each other across the curve of the main street. *Le Kissi Hôtel* (let us know if you find others) is equally central, adequate and cheap enough at about FG2000/2500 for a basic non S/C room. Cold beers, steaks, omelettes, chips and the like are normally commandable.

The **market** here, in the quarter behind the central silk-cotton tree, is worth exploration. You'll find a fair selection, at fair prices, of the kind of imported stuff (Sierra Leone country cloth, Malian blankets, printed *pagnes*) that's found in greater quantities at the international markets of Guéckédou, Nzérékoré and Kankan. Goods from Mali for example, often inflated in markets there, are offered at knock-down prices.

Kissidougou is also endowed with a tiny **museum**, opposite the police and five minutes from the hotel. The two or three dozen local objects of some interest include a young elephant's and a repulsive hippo's skull – both bereft of their ivory – various bits of Kissi and Kouranko ethnographia and some domestic items currently in use. A collection of fading black and whites show scenes from *Guinée Française* at their most meaningless. The *gardien* may extract a small charge.

Strolling out on the Conakry road you'll find the largest selection of *gargottes* for street food. Worthwhile restaurants there must be also, but none that jumped out. In this quarter too (on the right) is Kissi's main cassette merchant, a lab called *Africa No. 2* (!) with a veritable recording industry going on and a wide choice of music. You can order special selections on *copie* and if prices are a little higher than usual, quality may be better too. You'll know you've missed it if you pass the **hospital** – a reassuring place to fall ill if the care lavished on the immaculate gardens extends to the patients.

Getting on

Decent surfaced roads to Faranah, Kankan and Guéckédou mean you should be able to make time on these journeys – though the latter sometimes snarls up at **Yende-Milimou** when the village beneath the giant granite mound has its Thursday *lumo*. Don't get in a vehicle going further than you want; you'll pay that fare if you do – important counsel especially if you're heading for Mamou.

Kankan

The name alone is enough to make you want to come: **KANKAN** sounds remarkably exotic and, curiously, the notion doesn't dissolve when you've been there. Of course the town is, for the most part, very ordinary. But there's a sense of place here, a depth of history that knocks spots off every other town in the country, making it by far the most alluring in Guinea.

If you're curious about the **Source of the Niger**, you can probably forget about it in Guinea. It rises at 9° 5' 0" North, 10° 47' 14" West, at an altitude of 745m. This apparently puts it 93 metres north-northeast of a frontier marker post on the border between Guinea and Sierra Leone – from where the site is probably more easily accessible. For the determined only: arrive at the village of Bambaya 30km south of the Faranah–Kissidougou road and hire guides and porters for a two-day trek. And drop us a line afterwards.

History of Kankan

The spell arises largely from the fact that Kankan is a **Malinké town**, one of the oldest and probably the biggest in the Mande region. It's really composed of a loose federation of villages which have grown into each other – a fact which goes some way to explaining its very laid-back and open atmosphere.

But it was Muslim warrior-traders, the "Soninke", speaking Sarakolé (a northern Mande tongue from the upper Senegal) who are credited with the foundation of a mini-empire centred on Kankan. They arrived at the end of the seventeenth century and set themselves up in a dozen villages along the banks of the Milo, including the embryonic – and at that time non-Muslim – Kankan. This trading empire, which was also a hub of Muslim propaganda under the rule of marabouts, was called **Baté** (Baté Nafadj 40km north of Kankan is a reminder). Kankan became its capital. By 1850 the town was walled and already sizeable: its fleets of *pirogues* were plying the Milo and Niger as far as Gao in Mali. Caravans arrived from the Sahel and the desert. From the highland forests in the south, which it largely controlled, came kola nuts, palm oil and slaves. There was another reason for Kankan's ascendance: gold. The Bure goldfields extended from north of Siguiri to far up the Milo.

Kankan's apogee didn't last long: Samory smashed the hegemony of the city in 1879 after a ten-month siege, and twelve years later the French were in occupation.

Arriving and Practicalities

The main *gare voiture* is a shady patch of dust down by the river at the edge of town: you might want to be dropped off near the **rail station** a kilometre back in town. Here you'll find the dark and unappetising hulk of the *Buffet de la Gare*. Check it out if you like, but they've a lousy reputation here (FG2000), no water and no electricity. A much better **place to stay**, and reason to be dropped off even earlier, is *Chez Madame Marie*, an excellent guest house (FG3–4000/room) about a kilometre from the station off the Kissidougou road, roughly opposite the barracks and on the right as you come in. It's not obvious but ask and you'll find it; the effort is well repaid. The Madame in question is a Vietnamese lady, related to the owners of Conakry's *La Paillote* and a Kankan institution. The place is her home and while rooms around the courtyard aren't always available at first, patience will find you somewhere. Women travellers are warmly welcomed. *Marie's* has occasional discos – join in or move out – good meals (FG1500–3000) and wine and beer in the fridge. A large new hotel is apparently being built in Kankan.

Eating in town, one of the best places is across from the PTT, but there's a host of little cafés and bars around the centre – *Café Ibis* is a pleasant and slightly bohemian venue – and also a supermarket where you can splash out on luxuries like marmalade and soft loo rolls. **Breakfast** in Kankan, as if by some magic Malian influence, is delivered with a flourish.

In passing: the **PTT** (and it has a **poste restante**) is open Mon–Sat 7.30am–4pm; the *BICIGUI* **bank** 8.30am–12.30pm, 2–4pm; and there's a branch of *SGBG* as well.

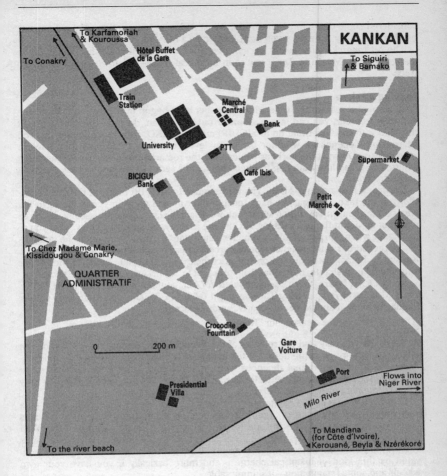

KANKAN

To Karfamoriah & Kouroussa

To Conakry

Hôtel Buffet de la Gare

To Siguiri & Bamako

Train Station

Marché Central

Bank

University

PTT

Supermarket

BICIGUI Bank

Café Ibis

Petit Marché

To Chez Madame Marie, Kissidougou & Conakry

QUARTIER ADMINISTRATIF

Crocodile Fountain

Gare Voiture

0   200 m

Port

Flows into Niger River

Presidential Villa

Milo River

To the river beach

To Mandiana (for Côte d'Ivoire), Kerouané, Beyla & Nzérékoré

Around town

Kankan has a beguiling **ambiance**. Its generous plan and long, mango-shaded avenues cast a different light: a woman on a bicyle is a rare sight in West Africa, common enough here. There's a university and lycées and lots of students, two hospitals and a considerable, scholarly, Islamic presence. The presidential palace no longer has hippos in the swimming pool, but the building itself is still there and, just across the avenue, so is the fountain where crocodiles once disported themselves.

The **markets** are really worthwhile, for the traders at least as much as for the goods on offer. The *grand marché* sells mostly clothes: both *dead mens'* and brilliantly coloured local confections that look great but would require lots of guts to wear; also myriad selections of *pagnes* and more far-flung items imported from Mali and Niger, mostly rugs and blankets; and there are a couple of stalls specialising in old bits of carving, gri-gris, amulets and mystical substances. If you're interested, by the way, in receiving some supernatural aid, then Kankan is the place to ask: **marabouts** here are considered some of the most powerful in West Africa and inscriptions and potions can be obtained easily, for a fee – you don't have to be a Muslim.

The *petit marché* sells mostly spices, vegetables and fruit. If you're in Kankan in the mango season (March to April) you're in for a real treat – the town is full of mango trees.

Leaving Kankan

At a later season, from the time when the rains have begun in earnest until about the end of November, you can take a **steamer** out of Kankan, down to the confluence of the Milo with the Niger and on to SIGUIRI and BAMAKO. How much longer this will be possible depends on whether the water levels continue to drop as they have in recent years. Down at the harbour you can see the remarkable effects of desertification where a new, and lower landing has been built and a series of steps shows the progress of the drought.

Departing Kankan by road, the **riverside route** to SIGUIRI is one of the most beautiful you can take, hugging the bank most of the way and drawing you in closer to the Niger's life than on any other section above Niamey-Gao. More prosaically, if you're planning on doing the trip to BAMAKO in one journey, be sure you know what you're paying for when you set off: many vehicles bound for "Bamako" turn out to be going as far as the border only, whence you're forced to pay for another ride to the capital. Kankan to Bamako was quoted on the price board at FG12,500. A ride to the border only should cost slightly more than half, or a seat to Siguiri just under half. Check.

For **Côte d'Ivoire** there's a scheduled *RTACI* country bus service to BOUAKÉ every Monday at 7am, arriving Tuesday night (about FG25,000). Ask at the *gare voiture* the day before – it should be in by early Sunday morning.

Siguiri

At **SIGUIRI** you may find the remains of the **French post**, established in 1888 on the hilltop over the river, at the height of the campaign against Samory Touré. At independence, parts of the original defences were still standing around the administrative district of the town. One strong factor in Siguiri's favour lies in a decent **place to stay** if you're stopping over – *Hôtel Niani*.

Niani is a village on the Sankarani river (which is the border with Mali), 80km on a very rough track southeast of Siguiri. It was here, as excavations among the baobabs have evidently proved, that **Sundiata Keita**, the legendary founding **king of the Mali Empire** (aka, most probably, Mansa Mari-Djata ca. 1205–55), installed his capital. Sites of foundries and cemeteries are dotted around the town wall alignments. If you're motivated by this kind of historical charge – and more basically if you have your own wheels and some imagination – it's unmissable.

Kankan to Nzérékoré via Kérouané

Out of Kankan, KÉROUANÉ is the limit of *Peugeot* transport southwards – fair indication of the condition of the road ahead, alongside the gaunt whaleback of the **Chaîne du Going** ridge and up into the remote and rugged region beyond BEYLA.

This is a richly historical route. On the way down to Kérouané you pass by Bissandougou, the recruiting point and eventual capital of Almamy Samory Touré's first empire. People in your vehicle will point it out to you. Whether the small cemetery with its banco wall surround is still there, is hard to tell, but the nineteenth-century fort has definitely returned to the soil.

Samory signed a treaty with the French at Bissandougou in 1887, hoping to keep them to the left bank of the Niger. But new French commanders swept the agreements aside and moved on Kankan and Bissandougou in 1890. Samory adopted scorched-earth tactics and retreated south, burning villages in his path. At Kérouané he had a fort constructed on the hilltop and from here his jihadist forces harassed the French while the holy warrior planned his next move. Samory was probably the bigges indigenous figure of nineteenth-century West Africa: other fragments of his story (which ended with capture in Côte d'Ivoire and exile to Gabon where he died in 1900) can be found on p.186 and in the *Côte d'Ivoire* section.

Kérouané

Today, the small prefecture of **KÉROUANÉ** barely hints at its place in history. The remains (and very little remains) of the **Tata de Samory** fortress are now the low hill site of the "Villa" – the administrative quarter. Archaeologically the interest is thin: a huge block of laterite bricks – part of the massive old wall of the fort which measured 170 metres across – and what looks like a gate house – a hollow hut like a honey pot near the entrance. Alongside, on the new wall, there's a faded portrait of Samory. The French **conquest cemetery** – final resting place of a number of troops of the Third Republic – is hard to find; it may have succumbed after independence.

With table-top hills rising around and the steep, bluish ridge of Going soaring to over 1\300m, it's all set in a fine **site**. Kérouané is also surprisingly lively and undoubtedly has fair appeal – though it's hard to pinpoint the attractions.

Because of the transport situation, you may well be spending a night here. **Accommodation** means basically the so-called *caravanserai* or *chambres de passage*, at one time a rather cute little *gîte* called *La Chaumière* with open-air restaurant and courtyard; now a primitive and dingy night stop. There's an outside toilet and shower (watch the world go by as you scrub off the dust) and water – which they'll warm only on request. All this for only FG500 a night and dreadful security thrown in – it can happen here.

For consuming **hunger**, there's a large market and some good rice and sauce in the street leading away from the police station. Nice *café fort* and *thé vert* can be had at a couple of licensed cafés up here on the left, with pleasant patios to loaf and meet people. From here, through the dry season, you can watch the progress of bush fires on *Mont Going* – a sombre spectacle on December and January nights as giant orange tongues leap from its flanks.

After dark, try *Djigbe's Night Club*: special dancing *soirées* on Wednesday and Saturday bring in a fair crowd, though at FG500–1000 a head it's hard to say for how much longer. And there are several video clubs.

ONWARDS TO NZÉRÉKORÉ

There's normally a truck or two out of Kérouané to NZÉRÉKORÉ early each morning – and perhaps something a great deal more comfortable if you make eager enquiries. Open back lorries, as long as they're loaded, aren't the worst travelling, but on this voyage it's important to have **warm clothes** and anticipate a very slow trip – fifteen to twenty hours – and late arrival.

THE DIAMOND ROUTE

From **Konsankoro**, there's a highly rated hundred-kilometre track over the ranges to MACENTA (see p.614) through rarely visited diamond-mining country. You could wait a long time for a ride, but there's usually a vehicle out of Kérouané on Thursday. It's reputedly a beautiful route – massive granite sugarloaf mountains and mesas pushing from the bush – which later enters the forest.

Beyla and Boola

The route south winds up over a col and into **BEYLA**, a town favoured by the French and subject of all sorts of brief colonial enthusiasms in the 1950s – "the best climate in French West Africa with 230 sunny days each year and moderate temperatures". Beyla's expatriate residents were particularly proud of their church – "adapted for the climate, it is a very good example of modern architecture with quite remarkable siting and decoration". To read colonial accounts you'd never know that Beyla was founded in the thirteenth century by Mande-speaking kola traders. If you've a tough vehicle of your own, the Beyla region is unquestionably one of Guinea's most worthwhile – with a number of tracks through the Kourando mountains, just to the northeast of the town.

Beyond Beyla the road roughens considerably: **BOOLA** lies at the foot of a bosky mountain and seems to be a regular truck stop with lots of street food. You continue, with patches of thickening forest and numerous streams, on to Nzérékoré – a couple of hours by car, four or five by goods lorry.

THE SOUTHEAST HIGHLANDS

The highland chains of the southeast, piling into the fractured border region where Guinea meets Sierra Leone, Liberia and Côte d'Ivoire, provide inducements to match the Fouta Djalon. Against their absence of towering cliffs and waterfalls, and generally lower altitudes, the highlands of **Guinée forestière** – the common name – weigh in with **ridges** still partly covered by evergreen **rainforest** and **routes** which are just as tough as the Fouta's – and remarkably muddy outside the dry seasons – and a largely non-Islamic ethnic configuration.

Climatically this is perhaps the most appealing part of the country, even if travel can be stubbornly difficult between April and November. Altitude and clouds keep it mild or warm most of the year, and while the rains are torrential, storms are accompanied by impressive electrical phenomena. There also tends to be a drier spell between the end of April and mid-June. The forest harbours significant numbers of **wild animals**, if you've the energy and resources to go looking; chimpanzees, leopards, forest elephant and buffalo, and hippos and crocs in the rivers.

The cultural background

Ethnically, this is singular territory. The region's predominant **Kissi**, **Toma** and **Guerzé** inhabitants are linguistically diverse and resolutely independent. Ancestor worship, totemism and **sacred forests** (usually a clearing *in* the forest where ritual is performed) are all important cultural elements. Islamic influences are far less pronounced than elsewhere and the stamp of colonialism was lightly impressed. Colonial subjugation – a gruelling village-by-village war of invasion – wasn't complete until 1920, having persisted bloodily since Samory's demise in 1898.

Most of the **towns** in the forest region are recent creations, dating back no further than the first French post at a suitable source of food, water and labour. Once victorious, the French maintained a thin and rather miserable presence. During the reign of Sekou Touré, many Guineans sought refuge in the relatively unpoliticised highlands, and tens of thousands more fled the country from here, especially to Côte d'Ivoire.

Guéckédou

Large but somewhat ignored, **GUÉCKÉDOU** sprawls between jungle-tufted hills. A short walk from the Liberian border and only slightly further from Sierra Leone, this proximity provides most of its livelihood and ninety percent of its character.

The vast **market** which floods the town every Wednesday is famous throughout Guinea, as the biggest in the country and one of West Africa's great commercial exchanges.

Main participants in the sales jamboree spilling along every street are Guineans, Sierra Leoneans, Liberians and Ivoirians, but you'll come across Malians, Senegalese and Gambians as well as a few Mauritanians. It's not surprising – but still a disappointment – to find though that very little of the merchandise is in any way traditional or locally made. Apart from the produce and some domestic ware, most of the rest consists of cheap imports – Philippino clothing, Taiwanese toys, Korean radios, Greek cigarettes, Japanese cloth and Chinese tools. Monrovia's free port explains a lot.

Despite the throng, hustlers and thieves seem uncommon, though ordinary **tricksters**, like the card shark with his *cherchez la dame*, clean up.

Accommodation
Clearly the best, if not the only day to visit Guéckédou is a Wednesday, but if you want to be clever go ahead of the crowds and find a room on Monday or, possibly, Tuesday morning. There's a couple of likely **lodgings**: the *Stadium Hotel*, near the bamboo-walled football ground on the road leading out to Kissidougou – FG2000 a room (all full at midday, "try again at 4pm") – and the preferable *Escale de Makona* in the same, *Sandia* quarter but more central, behind some prefectural offices, with rooms (some S/C) from FG3000 and a terrace where you can flop out with a cold beer.

Other practicalities
The town is full of **food**, but try the coffee house at the lorry park – good *cafeé au lait* and *espresso* and excellent evening meals of steak, salad and potatoes. In the same vicinity you may still find a couple of excellent, cheap **cassette** booths. Guéckédou has a **post office** but no bank: on market days you're likely to find *commerçants* willing to change money, but the nearest banks are at Nzérékoré or Kissidougou.

For a **view** of the townscape – which at times of clear visibility is quite attractive – head up to a vantage point near the hilltop mosque by crossing the Boya river on the Kissidougou road at the edge of town.

Lastly, down on the Moa (Makona) river, whose left bank forms the frontier, there are supposed to be some **beaches** – reportedly "two of the most pleasant in all of Guinea". Ascertain that the water is bilharzia-free, however, before going for a swim. If you track them down, we'd like to hear about it.

Border details
Easiest way into Sierra Leone from here is via **Nongoa**, from where *pirogues* large enough to carry motorbikes or bicycles ply the Moa river. This border closes at dusk. Cars and trucks have to go via **Foya** in Liberia, but the crossing is altogether easier from MACENTA to **Voinjama**.

Cutting through the forest: via Macenta to Nzérékoré

The route southeast from Guéckédou to Nzérékoré is an exciting one – traditionally rough and expensive at FG7000 or more for the 250km – along which for much of the way the orange ribbon of road buckles and falters and sometimes tunnels through towering green **jungle**.

Over the years parts of the road have been improved, but the latest development is a new, tarred **highway** being raised through the felled forest to link Guéckédou with

Nzérékoré in three or four hours instead of the current eight to twenty. The project – slashing through the jungle, cutting villages and, bizarrely, houses in half, bulldozing massive earthworks to canopy level – is pursued by the rains which destroy so much of the foundations each year. When it's completed the voyage through the forest will have lost most of its romance.

Up to Macenta

For the moment, it's rewarding travel, and different too. The serious forest starts with the climb from the bridge over the Makona, just beyond **Bofosso** – a large village and military post dating back to 1905. It's a steep haul up what's known, somewhat mysteriously, as the *descente des cochons*. Whether pigs, or nefarious humans are being referred to, you do indeed begin to see small hairy swine poking around at the roadside – signs of a strong non-Muslim presence.

LIANA BRIDGES AND STILT DANCERS

If you have wheels and feel like making the effort, 44km from Guéckédou a track leads left 4km to **Niagézazou**, tucked in the forest near a **liana bridge** over the Makona; and back on the main road 5km beyond the Makona iron bridge, check out the village of **Niogbozou** up a sidetrack shortly after the old mission centre of Balouma. Niogbozou, built on a rocky platform and apparently encircled with lianas, used to have a famous troupe of acrobats, dancers and stilt walkers who toured Europe several times before independence.

Passing from Kissi country into the lands of the Toma you arrive in **MACENTA**. This used to be the most important town in the highlands, chosen for its central position as a supply base for the "pacification columns" sent to the remote areas. Free Liberian troops attacked Macenta in 1906 but were fended off: it was only in 1908 that the limits of the two territories were set. The French tried to grow tea in Macenta, not very successfully. They had much more luck with **coffee**, which remains important, though much of the crop is smuggled out of the country. The biggest indigenous cash crop is **kola**.

Today, Macenta is only a moderate-sized place and quite dwarfed by Guéckédou and Nzérékoré. If you're travelling direct between those two, moreover, you'll more than likely hit Macenta at night. But by day it's a pleasing town, set amid a tumble of hills and still composed of hundreds of thatched, round house compounds. And there are fine views all around. If you find yourself **staying** in town, there's a reasonably good hotel and a number of decent eateries: if you need a coffee, or anything else, try *Dalaba Restaurant* which assures you a "rapid, honest and confidential service" (it's really quite ordinary).

Out of Macenta through the Malinké quarter, commences a wild and wonderful route to KÉROUANÉ and, ulimately, KANKAN. For several years it's been virtually impassable; which needn't necessarily stop you trying with your own vehicle, or pestering drivers at the *autogare* in Macenta for information about transport – or just setting off in comfortable shoes with three days' supplies on your back (see box, p.611).

Down to Nzérékoré

As you burrow through the jungle and over the ridges, there's a string of minor but interesting stop-offs for the self-mobile. Unfortunately, unless you pull off a ride with a very sympathetic driver you won't catch these by truck or *Peugeot*.

THE TOMA

The oldest inhabitants of the Macenta district, the **Toma**, earned respect from the French "pacification" troops for their resilience against raid upon raid on their isolated villages. Of all the highland peoples, it was the Toma who most harried the French invaders. Their last stronghold, the fortified village of Bousseedou, was attacked by two French expeditions and numerous canon before it finally succumbed in 1907.

Once battered into submission, they found favour with the French for being good scouts and solid soldiers, utterly at home in the forest. They're fairly small people and they may have distant pygmy ancestors: oral history in the forest regions recounts stories of ancient inhabitants of small stature who were decimated by the taller invaders from the north. In the case of the Toma, they lost ground to the Malinké and ulitmately mixed with Dioula Malinké to form the Toma-Manian. Today, their language – Loma – is a Mande tongue, related to Malinké.

You should look out for highly impressive **dancing** while you're in the Toma region; but you'll be lucky indeed to have the opportunity to witness one of the major life cycle celebrations. Traditionally at circumcisions, female mutilations, marriages, births and funerals, "bird men" – the *onilégagi* – danced, dressed in feathers and painted with kaolin; *lanebogué* pranced and hopped on their stilts; and *akorogi* swirled and bounded in their raffia-leaf costumes and haunted masks. Similar dances take place in Côte d'Ivoire, but generally with your attendance and money in mind.

You might stop for palm wine or food in **Sérédou** however. At 800m it straddles a col through the moist, jungly Ziama hills and most vehicles need the rest. Church bells were ringing here as we lurched out of the village: it's an old mission and quinine research station.

The stretch of road from Sérédou to Irié used to be renowned for its **butterflies**, including the giant swallowtail *Papillio antimachus*, Africa's largest butterfly, with an outrageous wingspan of up to 23cm. The males are occasionally seen around the treetops and, very rarely, sipping moisture at muddy puddles: female giant swallowtails, however, are elusive in the extreme.

Irié itself isn't much, but the side road that heads off southwest from here 100km to the border takes you to **Koyama**, the biggest **kola market** in Guinea, and the frontier town for **Zorzor** in Liberia.

Nzébéla is a traditional **music** centre, though whether you've much chance of hearing *divogi* drums and *pouvogi* trumpets couldn't be ascertained.

Immediately down the road, however, if you can just stop a while at the ferry across the Diani, there's a really enormous *pont de lianes* – a **liana bridge** – some 70m long. During the dry season, local men spend a lot of time mending this construction: when it was the only means of crossing, this was once a focal event of the year. It retains a grudging mystery: women are not allowed to witness the repairs (once even cows were banned) but the dramatic dusk-to-dawn communal effort that used to see the bridge serviceable in one night's work, (and proved the industry of the forest spirits) has been replaced with a slower and more alcoholic routine which takes some days. You'll have to make a generous contribution to the bridge fund if you want to take photos at this time.

Shortly after the village of Samoé, a path leads left to a small hamlet where a group of venerable **sacred tortoises** are kept by the community. A wide range of animals are identified with different groups of people throughout the forest region; the tortoise is a simple and popular totem. If you can't find them, maybe ask the White Fathers in Samoé.

Nzérékoré is entered down a long swoop of road, past the *First of May Forest Park* on your left.

Nzérékoré

With a very large Wednesday market and an atmosphere of thriving commerce unrivalled in Guinea, (except, competitively, on a Wednesday in Guéckédou), **NZÉRÉKORÉ** is the big town of *Guinée Forestière*.

Set amid the forest and traced through by tributary streams which feed the Mani river border with Liberia, the town's shack-lined dirt streets straggle stylelessly over hillocky ground. Yet for a back woods agglomeration, with no discernible centre, so far from anywhere (it's closer to Monrovia and even Abidjan than to Conakry) and so dependent on smuggling as a way of life, Nzérékoré is really rather an enjoyable place to be, making a good-natured exit or entrance to Guinea. Despite its size there's a more open, less cluttered feel than in Guéckédou and the scent of fresh discovery, as everywhere in the country, is here accentuated: townspeople are likely to be amazed when you show up.

SOME LOCAL HISTORY

The people of the Nzérékoré district and eastwards are **Kpelle** or **Guerzé** – related by language and some cultural elements to the Toma, and distantly to the other Mande-speaking ethnic groups. They are profoundly animist by tradition and rather resistant to Islamic influence; their mythic ancestor descended from the sky, married a local woman and settled east of Nzérékoré. Tradition relates that a man called Yegu, with a number of followers, populated the Nzérékoré district late in the nineteenth century, and these headmen were the ones in power at the time of the French arrival. It's hard to unravel the veracity of stories like these: they can easily be read as apologetics for subsequent French actions. It seems likely that the Guerzé had been around for rather longer than the French wanted to believe, and that colonial chiefs were not often pre-invasion notables.

There's no doubt about the Guerzé revolt in 1911 – abetted by free Guerzé forces from Liberia – which was put down by a Captain Hecquet. His life was abruptly ended during the campaign by a poisoned arrow.

Accommodation

So much of the impression, though, depends on where you find **lodgings**. As usual, if you discover alternatives to the following, let us know.

The outward appearance of the *Hôtel de la Forêt Sacrée* as the grandest edifice in town belies an utterly shambolic interior, squalid shared facilities and insecure rooms (FG3000). Water and electricity are in short supply throughout town, but a couple of more modest abodes on the road out to YOMOU are much better value. The first, possibly nameless, is a popular truck drivers' haunt run by a Vietnamese lady, with all the noise and distractions you'd expect. The second – *Bar Hanoi* – is further out, but the more recommended: it's clean, safe, with both well and generator, and again run by a Vietnamese, Madame Moe. Rooms (FG2500) are often full, so call in early. Arriving in the middle of the night, which, after long and unpredictable forest journeys, is sometimes unavoidable, none of these places will open for you. The **police** should help out.

Around town

Nzérékoré just has to be visited on **market day**; in which case it's a tough choice between here and Guéckédou. From the permanent market (recently renovated), stalls overflow onto the main street and the activity stretches from the hospital to the roundabout. Liberians and Ivoirians are prominent; women show off their best wraps and the atmosphere vibrates with the racket of trade – everything from multifarious qualities of palm oil and a riot of local produce to clothes (some cotton shirt bargains), Liberian

NZÉRÉKORÉ

To Gare voiture Macenta & Guéckédou

To Beyla & Kankan

To Lola & Danané (Côte d'Ivoire)

Jewellers

Hôtel du Forêt Sacrée

Medicine man

Gare gros Camions

Pharmacy

Gare voiture (Beyla, Kankan, Lola)

Gare voiture (Liberia)

Cheap Restaurants

Shoemakers

0   250 m

Boulangerie   Butchers   Bank

Tailors

Gare voiture (Yomou)

Hôtel Bar

Marché

Police Station

Cafés Silversmiths

To Liberian Consulate

Hospital

Préfecture   Obelisk

RICE FIELDS

Hôtel Bar Hanoi

To Yomou, Diéké & Ganta (Liberia)

PTT   Camp Militaire

Préfet's Residence

plastic trinkets, prints and indigo *gara* (two *lappa* for FG8000). Crafts, unless you count fabrics, are fewer, but there are good lines in leather sandals, wallets and some beautifully worked and relatively inexpensive silver. And of course you can add to your cassette collection. Traffic on Wednesday comes close to a standstill, but there's no shortage of transport afterwards.

Behind the prefect's residence, you'll find a dilapidated old *colon*'s house where a group of young men is busy on a **crafts enterprise**, weaving raffia bags and baskets and making wallets. Their goods, apparently mostly sold in Liberia and Côte d'Ivoire, require hard bargaining for a decent price. But the bags are guaranteed sturdy.

There's a fair number of **eating** houses scattered around town – several good sites are marked on the sketch map – but it's worth mentioning *Gargote Chez Mohammed Djouldé Baldé* at the Yomou *gare voiture* in the *Quartier Goniah*. When in season, the *patron* puts together wonderful avocado salads with an inimitable style of service.

Other Details

Bank *BICIGUI* open Mon–Fri 8.30am–12.30pm, 2.30–4pm, efficient service.

Herbal Remedies By no means unique to Nzérékoré, but unmissable if you've not seen them before, are the traditional pharmacists who set up on market day with a festoon of graphic boards, illustrating their range of treatments for complaints ranging from worms to impotence.

Liberian Consulate Somewhat hard to find. Mon–Thur 9am–3pm, Fri 9am–noon. Visas processed in 24 hours with two photos and FG3400 or US$10.

Music Ask about Nzérékoré's once-lauded Orchestre Nimba Jazz: they may still be around and an old compilation of theirs has just been released, available in Europe.

Post Office Mon–Sat 8am–4pm.

OUT OF GUINEA: INTO LIBERIA AND CÔTE D'IVOIRE

There are two **main routes** out of Guinea from Nzérékoré – either east via LOLA (excellent Monday market) and the foot of Mount Nimba to the **Ivoirian border** for DANANÉ and MAN, or south to DIÉCKÉ for GANTA on the **Liberian border** and tarmac to MONROVIA.

Heading for **Côte d'Ivoire**, make an early start or you'll get stuck in Lola (check out the *Rio Pongo* or one of the other clubs in town: there seems to be no hotel). Scenery along the way is unspecial until you reach NZO, from where you start to get good views of **Mont Nimba** – at 1752m Guinea's highest point. The road tunnels through impressive thickets of **giant bamboo** and tracks over precarious wooden bridges in the forest.

If you have time, or your own transport, you might be interested in visiting the village of BOSSOU, (turn right 5km east of Lola at Gogota, then continue 15km south) where **"sacred chimpanzees"** are under research by Japanese and Guinean primatologists. Ask around in Lola if you'd like to visit. You can get to YEKEPA in Liberia from here. Bossou is also the best place to start the **Mont Nimba ascent**, said to be "often difficult and sometimes perilous" (the grave of a casualty from 1951, a French geographer Jacques Richard, lies by the main road in a market village before Nzo). Perhaps the chimp researchers can advise. Stock up on rations in Nzérékoré and let us know how you get on.

As for **routes to Liberia**, (assuming peace prevails when you're in the area) apart from the Diécké routes off the Yomou road, and the Bossou track, you've a fourth option – a right turn on the reasonably fast Lola road, 6km out of Nzérékoré (signposted), which a number of taxis use to YEKEPA and SANNIQUELLIE.

---

index

SIERRA LEONE

SIERRA LEONE

For English-speaking travellers – and above all for the British – **Sierra Leone** resonates with cultural associations. Freetown, with its smoky air and net curtained windows, barrows and newspapers, Sunday church services, dirty alleys and unlit night-time streets, seems especially reminiscent of Victorian London. It strikes deep chords in some visitors. With the addition of fruit bats and mango trees, bobbing agama lizards and hot leaden air, the town seems quintessentially West African – perhaps because the Sierra Leone colony once provided a model for British schoolchildren's limited education about West Africa. It is in fact rather atypical: the only other part of West Africa that resembles Sierra Leone – and for the same reason, the freed slave heritage – is Liberia.

Any list of the country's attractions has to kick off with some of Africa's best **beaches**, couched along the mountain-flanked Freetown peninsula coast, and only matched in the region by Côte d'Ivoire. Based on their appeal, there's a small, and as yet uncertain, tourist industry, with a clutch of reasonably good international-class hotels.

But like the old British colony, the new winter invaders extend their interests little beyond the peninsula. The interior of the country, now divided into three **provinces** – what used to be the "Protectorate", as opposed to the peninsula "Colony" – is very little explored by travellers and reckoned, unfairly and dismissively, to offer nothing of interest. The attractions aren't perhaps all that thick along the way, but poor roads and accommodation are the main disincentives. **Outamba-Kilimi National Park** in the north, **Tiwai Island Nature Reserve** in the south, and some unusually high hills and mountains in the east (including the almost spectacular **Mount Bintumani**) are worthy goals. And along the remote southern coast, beyond Freetown, there are **beaches and islands** that beat even the peninsula's lotus-eating shores.

While **Freetown** and surrounding districts have up to two centuries of history behind their present, Creole appearance, this influence has hardly rubbed off on the **up-country towns** – of which the principal are **Makeni**, **Bo**, **Kenema** and **Koidu**. These have all grown from small seeds early this century. With the exception of the diamond centre, Koidu (also called Sefadu and widely known as "Kono" – the district of which it is capital), they reached some sort of zenith of development shortly after independence, since when they've increased in size, but not in stature.

SIERRA LEONE – FACTS AND FACTOIDS

Sierra Leone is a one-party republic, currently governed by the All-People's Congress (APC) under the presidency of Major General Joseph Momoh. Its **area**, about 72,000 square kilometres, is a little smaller than Scotland or Maine. The **population** is approaching five million, which gives it quite a high density. The name "Sierra Leone" (*Salon* in Krio, pronounced "Salone") has various etymologies. The idea that the Portuguese were referring to the Freetown peninsula as "Lion-like Mountain", when they called the country *Serra Leão*, seems unlikely, as nothing in the topography resembles the shape of a lion. Suggestions to do with the sound of roaring surf seem equally fanciful. The possibility that the area swarmed with lions in the fifteenth century is the most likely.

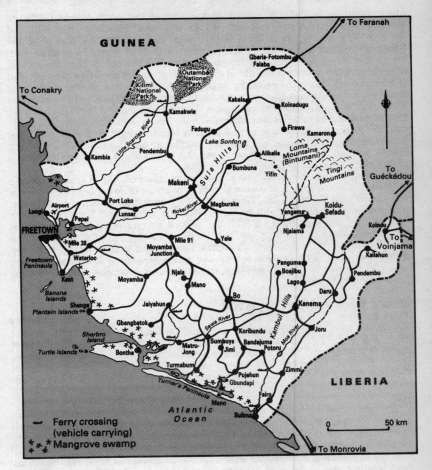

Ferry crossing (vehicle carrying)

Mangrove swamp

Country and people

Geographically, Sierra Leone is surprisingly diverse. A steep indented coast at Freetown, and shallow sand banks and mangrove swamps elsewhere, are backed by tidal creeks that penetrate far inland and make a mess of the road system in the south and west. Further up-country, the land rises through dense forest (most of it now cleared) to rolling savannah hills, rocky outcrops and mountains. The remaining patches of **rainforest**, mostly in the far southeast, beyond the Moa river, are nowadays islands in a sea of secondary growth and shifting agriculture. **Swamp rice** now covers much of the lowlands. But despite high rainfall, there are critical problems for farming, because the multitude of streams on the ridges leads to severe soil erosion.

Sierra Leone's **ethnic configuration** is unusual. In simple terms two language groups dominate: the **Temne**, who speak one of the idiosyncratic *West Atlantic* languages, are concentrated in the central north, inland from Freetown; the **Mende**, whose language is distantly related to the rest of the great *Mande* (Malinke/Mandinka) group, are strongest more to the southeast, especially around Bo and Kenema. The Mende are a many-sided group, incorporating the Komende, the Gbamende (which just means "different Mende") and the Sewa. In addition, both Temne and Mende have culturally absorbed many of the less populous groups around, often through the powerful influence of the flourishing **secret societies** (which is a bit of a misnomer). Along the coast, for example, the **Bullom** and **Sherbro**, who once spoke the same language (Bullom), now tend to speak Temne north of Freetown and Mende to the south. Smaller inland groups like the **Loko** (around Port Loko) and the **Limba**, have moved into close association with the Temne, while in the east and southeast, the **Kono** and **Kissi** have moved towards Mende culture. In the far north, the **Susu** (northwest), **Koranko** and **Yalunka** (northeast) have remained closer to their Mande (with an "a") roots. In the north and east there's also a fair scattering of Fula communities – many of them exiles from Guinea.

But what's remarkable about Sierra Leone is the influence of the Creoles – **Krios** – ex-slaves of diverse origins who were already in positions of power before the interior was carved onto Britain's plate. Numerically, they have always been a small group, confined mostly to the Freetown peninsula. With the invasion and "protection" of the interior, they lost their influence with the colonial government to British-appointed tribal chiefs, whose descendants have mostly run the country since independence. The **Krio language**, partly derived from archaic English, has made a lasting and widespread imprint on Sierra Leonean society, and is largely responsible for making Sierra Leone, to the ears of English speakers, one of the most interactive and absorbingly funny countries to travel in.

Climate: when, and when not, to visit

There are dominating climatic constraints on travel in Sierra Leone. From **May to November**, most of the country gets **heavy and prolonged monsoon rain** on most days. Only in the extreme south, around Sulima, is there a short break in the rains during July or August. While temperatures aren't extremely high, humidity usually is, above all along the coast. The lowest night-time temperature ever recorded in Freetown (19°C) is actually the *highest* record minimum temperature for any African country – indication of Freetown's altogether very uncomfortable climate much of the year.

The risk of visiting in May or November is repaid, if you're lucky, with brilliant collages of green, wonderful skyscapes and tolerable road conditions; but between these months, travel off the hard-surfaced routes varies from slow and gruelling to impossible. And the beaches never dry out sufficiently to be much fun.

In the **dry season**, a *harmattan* wind from the northeast can bring slightly cooler, dusty weather even to the coast. It's very difficult to predict clear blue skies and good visibility.

AVERAGE TEMPERATURES AND RAINFALL

FREETOWN

	Jan	Feb	Mar	Apr	May	June	July	Aug	Sept	Oct	Nov	Dec
Temperatures °C												
Min (night)	24	24	25	25	25	24	23	23	23	23	24	24
Max (day)	29	30	30	31	30	30	32	31	32	29	29	29
Rainfall mm	13	3	13	56	160	302	894	902	610	310	132	41
Days with rainfall	1	1	2	6	15	23	27	28	25	23	12	4

BO

	Jan	Feb	Mar	Apr	May	June	July	Aug	Sept	Oct	Nov	Dec
Temperatures °C												
Min (night)	20	21	21	22	22	21	21	21	21	21	21	20
Max (day)	32	34	35	34	32	31	28	28	30	31	31	31
Rainfall mm	8	16	76	130	252	368	406	536	419	325	170	38

SEFADU

	Jan	Feb	Mar	Apr	May	June	July	Aug	Sept	Oct	Nov	Dec
Temperatures °C												
Min (night)	14	17	19	20	21	20	20	20	20	20	19	17
Max (day)	32	34	35	34	33	31	29	29	31	32	31	31
Rainfall mm	10	20	96	160	228	282	269	411	401	292	145	41

Arrivals

The huge majority of visitors fly into Freetown. Land routes aren't very convenient and, for many years, Sierra Leone barely figured as an overland destination from the rest of West Africa.

■ Flights from West African cities

Nearly all flights arrive at **Lungi International airport**, across the Sierra Leone River estuary from Freetown (see the "Getting into Freetown" section). Allow plenty of time to get into the city.

The ill-fated *Sierra Leone Airlines* is currently grounded. *Air Guinée* operates a supposedly weekly service (no published schedules) from Conakry into **Hastings airfield**.

The west coast routes of *Ghana Airways* keep most of the coastal capitals connected to Freetown – four times a week from **Monrovia**, three times a week from **Abidjan**, four times a week from **Accra**, once a week from **Lomé**, twice weekly from **Cotonou** and three times a week from **Lagos**. They also operate three flights a week from **Dakar** via **Banjul** and **Conakry**. *UTA* flies in non-stop from **Nouakchott** every Wednesday. *Nigerian Airways* recently resumed weekly flights from **Lagos**. *British Airways* links **Banjul** with Freetown twice a week, and *KLM* flies **Monrovia** to Freetown every Thursday.

Other African flights

You can fly into Freetown several times a week from both **Nairobi** and **Addis Ababa** via Accra or Abidjan. Feasible conections from other east and central African cities are through Nairobi or Addis; and from North Africa through Dakar.

■ Overland from Guinea

From Guinea the principal overland route connects Conakry with Freetown, on a mostly tarred road via the new bridge over the Great Scarcies River and **Kambia**. By private vehicle, assuming no border delays, this route is about a seven- to eight-hour drive. By public transport, usually involving a change of vehicle at the Guinean side, followed by bus or *poda poda*, it's a long day's journey into night. Entering Sierra Leone at Kambia *can* be a protracted and corrupt affair; you should make every effort to anticipate your reception depending on the vigour at the time of Sierra Leone's oft-declared "state of economic emergency". Smuggling currency is

particularly to be avoided: strip-searches and friskings have recently been routine.

Less-trodden routes into Sierra Leone are more relaxed. The canoe crossing from Nongoa to **Koindu wharf** in the far east (frontier closes at 6pm) is busy but unproblematic. Note that it's not a motor vehicle route, though small motorbikes can be carried (for larger vehicles, see "From Liberia", below). The third route, from Faranah to **Falaba** in the northeast, is very little used, and there's a good chance you'll have to walk the ten no-man's-land kilometres in the middle. Most likely, you'll be given a royal welcome by the Sierra Leone Police at **Gberia-Fotombu**, from where you can arrange transport to Falaba and Kabala.

■ Overland from Liberia

From Liberia, travel into Sierra Leone is straightforward, with taxis plying **between Monrovia and Kenema** every day, and a whole string of customs and police checkpoints on both sides, payments for which are covered by your fare if travelling by *Peugeot* taxi. The border closes at 6pm. Driving yourself, be immaculately in order and never lose your cool. Bribes will be demanded. Pay up or play up.

There's a much quieter Liberia–Sierra Leone route, via the remote northern corner, **from Foya to Koindu**. It's a three- to four-day journey from Monrovia, however, and difficult in its later stages, especially in the rains. Coming **from southern Guinea in your own vehicle**, however, this is the crossing you'll have to make (unless you go north to Faranah). Cross from **Macenta** in Guinea to **Voinjama**, Liberia, from where it's a 92-kilometre drive to **Koindu** in Sierra Leone.

Red Tape

Either visas or entry permits are required by all nationalities except for *Mano River Union* nationals (Guinea and Liberia). Once upon a time, entry permits for British and most west European nationals were free on demand. No longer.

They normally cost the same as visas, except that British passport holders (in tit-for-tat response to the tightening of British immigration laws) pay more. Commonwealth citizens (including Canadians, Australians and New Zealanders) are entitled to receive visas free of charge.

Disregard references in out-of-date tourist literature to visas given on arrival at Lungi airport; there's every chance you'd be sent straight out on the first flight – or pay an unusually high sum for permission to enter.

Validity of visas and permits varies, but stays of longer than a month are rarely granted in advance, though you can extend your stay at the Immigration office in Freetown. Regardless of what your visa states, it's also common practice on overland entry to grant you just enough time to reach Freetown, where you have then to renew your permit. Avoid this hassle by pleading hard, on entering the country, for immediate permission to stay for as long as you need.

In West Africa, Sierra Leone has **embassies, high commissions, or representatives** in **Dakar** (consular representative), **Banjul, Conakry, Monrovia, Abidjan** (British Embassy), **Accra, Lagos** and **Yaoundé** (British Embassy).

Once you're in Sierra Leone, you can obtain **visas in Freetown** for all West African countries except Guinea-Bissau, Benin and Cameroon. There are no North African consulates.

TRAVELLING TO SIERRA LEONE FROM MALI AND THE DESERT

Because of the locations of Sierra Leonean consulates, if you're overlanding from the trans-Saharan routes, through Mali and eastern Guinea, you are obliged to obtain a visa in advance from a British Embassy in North Africa or from your country of origin, putting a limited time frame on your travels. Alternatively, by obtaining a Liberian visa in Nzérékoré, Guinea, and then a Sierra Leonean one in Foya, Liberia, you could go in that way. Or front up at the border and "just try", as they say: Nongoa-Koindu is your best bet.

Money and Costs

Sierra Leone's currency, devised in 1964, is called (with originality) the *leone* (Le). Like the Ghanaian *cedi*, it was introduced on par with the British pound sterling at a rate of Le2 = £1, but after 1978, the link was broken and it began sliding in value. By 1989 the rate of exchange was over Le100 = £1 and by mid–1990 around Le300 = £1. Domestic inflation (ie in Leones) was about 90 percent over 1989–90.

Despite the massive devaluation, prices are often still given, confusingly, in "pounds", worth two leones each. Notes of Le2, 5 and 10 are the commonest. Le20 notes are in short supply (hoarded, apparently). The new Le50 note (highest denomination), is likely to disappear in the same way. Le1 notes come in bundles – of 1000.

The leone has no value outside Sierra Leone, and it's illegal to import or export the currency. There has therefore been a flourishing **black market** for hard currency in recent years, with traders, and particularly Lebanese businessmen, prepared to pay up to twice the official rate for sterling, dollars or European currencies. The "state of economic emergency", first introduced in November 1987, with massive confiscations, fines and jail sentences, has more or less shut down the parallel market in foreign cash. Leone-rich businessmen are still anxious to convert their capital into hard currency, but the extra few leones per pound is hardly worth the hassle. It's important to seek out the very latest news on the situation before arrival.

On arrival at Lungi Airport and main land borders, you'll be given an **exchange contol form** "M". You're best advised to declare everything as the declaration you sign can be followed by a painstaking search. When you leave the country your balance is checked off against the banks' entries on your form. Also, on arrival at Lungi, though probably not at land borders, you're required to change US$100 into leones.

To avoid all the paranoia of dealing in illegal currency, black market money dealing in the late 1980s turned to the somewhat desperate measure of exchanging leones for **personal cheques** in foreign currency, drawn, at a later date by the dealer or a relative on the visitor's account at home. *Access, VISA* and *Amex* cards, which are not much use outside Freetown, and even then accepted only in a few establishments in the capital, could be used to the same effect. Some dealers still give a better price for cash sterling or dollars. These details may change in the near future; the economy cannot work (or continue failing to work) for much longer under such conditions.

Meanwhile, the **banks** are usually able to exchange dollars and major currencies in cash and travellers' cheques. Usually, because periodically in recent years, banks have completely run out of Sierra Leonean currency, while nervous citizens preferred to hang onto their money,

rather than trust it to them. If you're travelling up-country for a few weeks, try to take all the leones you'll need. Banks in provincial towns cannot be relied upon. The biggest networks are *Barclays* and the *Standard Chartered*.

The tourist hotels at Freetown will also exchange hard currency, though rarely for non-guests.

■ Costs

Because of the country's financial insecurity, costs in this chapter are estimated in £ sterling, **at the official rate of exchange**. With allowance for a hard currency inflation rate of five or ten percent, you should be able to ascertain approximate prices in leones, once you've arrived and discovered the rates.

Sierra Leone is not an expensive country. Even if you buy all your leones from the government, the **costs of travel** are lower than in most of the CFA zone. Away from the Freetown area, where a small number of touristy establishments charge the sort of prices that wouldn't faze you at home, there's very little that will whittle away your resources. Rest houses and provincial hotels cost from £1 for a single to maybe £10 for a double at the most. Basic chop-house meals can be had for 30–50p and more western-style food, when offered, for perhaps £1–2 a time. If you're staying in one place for a while, with accommodation taken care of, preparing your own food from the market, and living fairly frugally, you should be able to manage on £15 a week or so. **Transport**, as usual, is relatively expensive, and you pay more for travelling in some comfort at a realistic speed. Even basic transport costs may exceed £1 per 20km on the roughest roads, though the price is likely to be less than half this on busy, tarred highways.

Bargaining in Sierra Leone is important. Skill at it pays dividends. This is a country where foreigners are quite often and humorously deceived into paying unreasonable prices.

Maps and Information

Accessible information for visitors is almost nonexistent. Periodically, the Ministry of Tourism puts out a leaflet for tourists, and it's worth enquiring at embassies and high commissions if they have any. They can usually offer only a couple of hotel or tour operators' leaflets. Apart from the government tourist office in Freetown, there are no others.

Obtaining fairly up-to-date **maps** of Sierra Leone is equally difficult. *Shell Sierra Leone* recently published the first adequate tourist map of the country (1:396,000), with Freetown street plans on the reverse. It's useful for route-planning, but don't give too much credence to the crop of "Main Roads (tarred)". Read it in conjunction with the *Michelin* 953 and you won't be misled overmuch. The main problem is a lack of any relief details; even mountains are missing. And it seems to be unobtainable outside Sierra Leone: try writing to the printers *Cook, Hammond and Kell Ltd*, 35 Eveline Rd, Mitcham, Surrey, UK.

The last sheet to cover the country was published in 1976 (Sierra Leone Government, 1:500,000), an Ordnance Survey type map, at 1cm:5km, with vague roads and some odd place names. It's indispensable, however, if you're spending some time in the country. The *Tourist Map of Freetown and Peninsula* (1cm:500m) is very useful for exploring the peninsula (despite its antiquity, 1969), but hopeless for Freetown because it includes no street names. The best chance of finding these maps is from foreign map specialists, notably in Britain.

Health

Sierra Leone is distinguished by being the only country in the world where life expectancy has been on the *decrease* over the last fifteen years, due to the collapse of the once-famous health service. It used to be 44 years; it's now 42, in equal bottom place with Ethiopia and Afghanistan.

But apart from a high incidence of malaria, Sierra Leone's main **health problems** for travellers revolve around water. The lack of clean supplies is especially acute towards the end of the dry season in the north. Population densities are relatively high, and even piped water may come straight from an open tank or dam.

Freetown's water supplies are reckoned to be exceptionally healthy, as they're squeezed through porous rock before reaching the city taps. *Tutic* is the pure product, bottled, and, they say, even exported.

■ Diseases

Foreign volunteers in the lowland regions often go down with **schistosomiasis** (*bilharzia*) from contact with infected stagnant, or slow-moving water. Be careful, again, particularly in the dry season.

River blindness (onchocerciasis) is also a problem, though rarely for visitors to the country (even long-term ones). The **blackflies** which cause it fly near fast-flowing streams and waterfalls and have a painful bite, but the disease usually becomes established only after many years of infection.

Lassa fever seems to have a reservoir in Sierra Leone. Although even long-term residents are unlikely to catch it, it's a dangerous disease. The best avoidance strategy appears to be not to sleep in huts in which bush rats may have urinated in the thatch. Infection is believed to be spread by "aerosol" inhalation. A stimulating one for hypochondriacs, this.

Until 1987, Sierra Leone was denying any **AIDS** problem. But a recent random sample of 1740 people revealed 54 were carrying the HIV virus – 3.1 percent.

■ Hospitals

Medical treatment in Sierra Leone is best avoided, but in any kind of emergency, where you have a choice, the hospitals at Serabu, southwest of Bo, at Segbwema, east of Kenema and at Matru-Jong in Bonthe district have national reputations and the advantage of overseas benefactors – the places to go for appendicitis, amputations, anthrax etc.

Getting Around

First of all, two important non-services – *Sierra Leone Airlines* and *Sierra Leone Railways*. The airline is still in existence, on paper, and from time to time, a foreign carrier steps in to try operating a domestic and regional service. The last was *Aer Lingus*. The railways, however, despite the lines shown even on recent maps, ceased functioning in 1971 and are gone for ever.

■ Travelling by road

Road transport is a hectic scene. The best deals are often on the state-run blue or orange buses of the *Sierra Leone Road Transport Corporation*. The private green and yellow *City Link Express* vehicles are similar and generally reliable – if slow – once they leave, but more likely to over-fill the seats.

Schedules are hard to pin down and you should arrive early in the day to be sure of a seat, especially at the bus station in Freetown. It's not usually possible to book in advance.

Comfortable and faster **thirty-seater minibuses** come next in the order of preference, followed by **covered Toyota pick-up vans** and similar, uncomfortably converted vehicles. There's not much to choose between these two, pricewise. On certain routes only, you'll also find *Peugeot 504s*, some of which are in decent condition (on the Monrovia route for example). Seating in these, however, can be nightmarish – as many as three in the front, five in the middle and three in the back, unless you pay for some empty places.

In the far north and eastern highland districts, transport is sometimes by **goods lorries** ("Mandingo trucks") or essentially private Land Rovers. In the rains, many roads are impassable to lesser vehicles. Lastly, *poda podas* are the beat-up urban taxi-vans you'll find around Freetown, and running locally in other towns.

In Sierra Leone, you **pay** at the end of the trip, except in the big long-distance buses. Prices agreed in advance are always honoured. Bus fares on the main routes are fixed; back-country services are more negotiable. Where you can get ripped off is on the interpretation of how much baggage you're carrying. It's always extra and big items can virtually double the fare if you don't fix the price on departure. Petrol, which doubled in price overnight in 1989, is still only around £1 per gallon.

Hitching

Hitching is pretty easy in and around Freetown. There are acknowledged transport problems and private drivers are usually sympathetic. Much of the time you'll be expected to pay.

Hitching at the side of the road in the provinces, you'll find most vehicles full, but those with space will often give free lifts. It's assumed you're a volunteer worker.

■ Car Hire and Driving

Freetown's handful of **local car hire agencies** (the big internationals aren't represented) normally prefer you to take one of their drivers with you. Prices are well up, despite devaluation, and you may have to pay in hard currency.

Driving is on the right. Roads are mostly dangerous and badly signed. Be particularly careful, leaving Freetown, on the busy, narrow, winding stretch through the Occra Hills, past the Mile 38 checkpoint. Crash blackspots tend to have the final resting positions of vehicles marked on the road. And if you come across the unmistakeable chalked outline of a human being, you'll know that detectives have been at the scene of an accident . . .

■ Ferries

There are over a dozen **vehicle ferries** across rivers on the smaller roads. Most are the simple hand-hauled variety and none carries more than six tonnes. In addition, there are several diesel ferries, detailed in the guide, that ply among the creeks along the south coast. And of course the life-link Kissy–Tagrin ferry connects Freetown with the "mainland" and airport.

■ Cycling

Sierra Leone is a compact country. Although the network of less than 2000km of tarred road isn't long, it does take you to within 100km of dirt road and rough track of just about anywhere – a distance that never takes more than two days pedalling for even the most relaxed cyclist. Unvisited coastal areas and remote waterfalls and mountains become dramatically accessible.

Be aware, however, that there's little in the bike line on sale in Freetown, and parts and tools are very uncommon up-country. You're better off really with a well set-up mountain bike from home.

Sleeping

There are rather few hotels, though relative to its area, Sierra Leone isn't quite such barren territory as is sometimes suggested. Freetown has a number of cheap lodgings and several expensive places, with not much in between. Bo, Makeni, Kenema and Koidu all have one or two basic boarding houses, but nothing luxurious.

The country's economy has always been subsistence-based, and trade doesn't count to the same degree as in neighbouring countries. Without such a need for accommodation for market traders and the like, places to stay are consequently limited.

There are Peace Corps (and other) **rest houses** in a number of towns and, unless not mentioned in "The Guide", below, they normally welcome non-PCV guests, who pay slightly over the odds. Peace Corps and VSO volunteers themselves may be glad of company and put you up, but you can't just assume that you can stay.

Arriving at dusk in a strange village, it's better to ask to see the **chief** (who could be a paramount, section or village chief), and explain to him what you're doing and what are your needs. Customarily, you'll be accommodated somewhere, and your food will be cooked (see the next section). Graciousness and small return favours – kola nuts, coffee, sugar – are important.

Alternatively, if you're really out in the bush, **camping out** should be quite unproblematic. There are no campsites.

Eating and Drinking

There's an excellent range of local food in Sierra Leone. "Chop" – people's food built around rice and palm oil – is very often tasty, always fresh and filling, and only occasionally too hot to handle. Ordinary chop houses generally provide one late morning meal each day for their customers. They rarely have anything left by the afternoon.

■ Staple chop

At its simplest, chop can be just a bowl of rice with a splash of bright orange **palm oil** (impossible to keep from dribbling down your chin). But the commonest sauce – *plasas* ("palava sauce") – is made with finely shredded **leaves** of potato or cassava, gelatinous **okra** ("gumbo", "ladies' fingers"), **dried fish** and **hot pepper**, all cooked in palm oil. There are numerous variations on *plasas*; it's often served with meat, domestic or bush. Worry not about the close resemblance of *plasas* to a fresh cow pat – you soon forget.

If you're far **off the beaten track**, you won't find chop for sale, as every woman prepares her own family's. In these areas, it's quite acceptable to carry rice, palm oil, *maggi cubes* and other Sierra Leonean kitchen paraphernalia around with you and have meals cooked for you, in exchange for some of the food, or perhaps for some leones. The family meal is usually prepared late afternoon.

Stay long in Sierra Leone and you'll begin to appreciate significant differences in taste and texture between the **rice of different regions.** Upland "hill rice" is the more traditional short grain variety; the red-speckled Mende kind is the best and can be delicious. "Swamp rice" is a twentieth-century introduction that needs more work in its cultivation. But indigenous varieties always taste better than imported stuff.

Plantains are another common staple, used in place of rice.

■ Other dishes, other food

Fufu (fermented, mashed cassava stodge) and *agidi* (heavy, maizemeal stodge) are also common, though more often eaten at home than out at a chop-house. *Plasas* based on **groundnuts** is rare except in the north. You may get *egusi* sauces or soups, based on crushed squash seed.

Yebe is a good and popular breakfast dish, a kind of stew made of potato or cassava – or mangoes when in season. You buy it by the ladle in markets and truck parks between 6.30 and 8am. *Pap* , a sweet rice broth – is also nice for chilly, early starts.

KRIO FOOD AND DRINK TERMS					
agidi	corn stodge	*frut*	fruit	*omole*	hooch
airish petehteh	potato	*funde*	millet	*orinch*	orange
akara	rice and banana cake	*fresh*	new palm wine	*pamai*	red, banga nut oil
aweful	kind of fish	*gari*	cassava meal	*panapul*	pineapple
behni	sesame seed	*golik*	garlic	*pap*	porridge
bia	*Star* for example	*granat*	groundnut	*petete*	sweet potato
bif	meat, animal	*grepfrut*	grapefruit	*pia*	pear (avocado)
bush bif	game meat	*grin*	greens, used in *plasas*	*plantan*	plantain
binch	beans, peas	*jibloks/*	aubergine	*plasas*	(palava) sauce
bita	bitter leaf for sauces	*kobokobo*		*plit*	plate
		jolof	rice and *plasas* cooked together	*pongki*	pumpkin
bolgoh	bulgar wheat			*popoh*	pawpaw, papaya
biskit	biscuit	*kabej*	cabbage	*rehs*	rice
bota	butter, margarine	*kasada*	cassava	*sawa-sawa*	*plasas* made of sour leaves
		kenda	seasoning		
bonga	dried fish	*kek*	cake	*sof*	soft drink
brefos	breakfast	*kohn*	corn, maize	*sol*	salt
brefrut	breadfruit	*kondo*	basic chop	*stek*	beef
buli	jug for palm wine	*krain-krain*	slimy leaf sauce	*stu*	stew
				suga	sugar
chak	drunk	*letu*	lettuce	*sup*	soup
egusi	squash seeds used in sauces	*lif*	leaf	*tamatis*	tomato, tomato purée
		magi	maggi cube		
fis	fish	*mampama*	palm wine seasoning	*ti*	tea
fohl	chicken	*oriri*		*yabas*	onion
fud/chop/yit	food	*okroh*	okra	*yams*	yam

In the towns, **bread**, in contrast to the franco-phone pleasure of most of West Africa, tends to be white, sweetdough, and considered a luxury rather than a staple. Loaves are usually sticks, however; a popular snack is the "steak sand-wich" – slivers of kebabed meat with palm oil in bread. After dark, it can be hard to see what's cooking. Make sure your brochette sandwich really is "steak", unless you like grilled tripe.

Of the wide variety of fruit you'd expect, **oranges** are probably the cheapest; in the north, in season, you can buy five for the equivalent of five pence. Mandarins, misleadingly, are called lemons in Krio.

■ Drinks

And as for **drinking**, it all comes down to *Star* beer, usually available (brewery closures cause national consternation) and usually excellent – in fact one of West Africa's best. **Palm wine** (generally from oil palms) is very important, socially and commercially, and a pleasant way to while away an afternoon. Sierra Leonean **liquor** from Freetown distilleries, on the other hand, is a more self-destructive commodity; *Sassman* is one name to beware.

Lastly, Sierra Leone is more or less outside the green tea zone, but **coffee**, which is quite often both real and Sierra Leonean, is a pleasant surprise.

Opening Hours and Public Holidays

Offices are open Monday to Friday (rarely Saturday morning), usually 8am–noon and 2–5pm. Banks and some embassies operate a long morning with no break, closing early in the afternoon. Shops usually close by 5pm, but are open Saturday morning. Many restaurants and other establishments are closed all day Sunday.

Sierra Leone's **public holidays** follow the Christian calendar. The Islamic calendar only affects business and office opening at the end of Ramadan (see below). **April 19** Republic Day and **April 27** Independence Day are the only secular holidays.

The **Lantern Parade** takes place on **Watch Night** at the end of Ramadan, when the new moon is due to be sighted. It follows similar lines to the *fanals* of Senegal, and absorbs a complete cross section of Freetown's different language groups. Some thirty **"lantern associations"** compete to produce the best float. They set off around 3am from "Up Gun" roundabout in the East End, to walk past the Law Courts (where the floats are judged) and spill onto Lumley Beach at dawn. For the next few years, the Lantern Parade (which is in the lunar calendar) roughly coincides with the Republic Day and Independence Day holidays at the end of the dry season. See p.53 for dates.

There's also a new, annual **trade fair** (*Freefest*) in Siaka Stevens Stadium around the end of March, in which every commercially minded person in the city tries to get a stall.

Lastly, don't miss the New Year's Day "outing" in **Kabala** if you're in the country at that time.

Communications: Post, Phones and Media

The most useful thing you can do to keep in touch with events around you in Sierra Leone, is learn some Krio. Unless you're a volunteer, and have lessons, however, this isn't as easy as it might appear. Krio isn't a pidgin, so you can't guess it. You'll have to work hard too at keeping in touch with home. Sierra Leone's mail and telephone services, while showing signs of improvement, are notoriously up the creek.

■ Mail and Telecommunications

Letters posted out from the main post office in Freetown do usually arrive, but you should allow up to a month. **Aerograms**, when they have some, are the best bet, because they can't contain anything of value. Leone devaluation makes mail very cheap, and in turn almost guarantees slow delivery.

Airmail parcels are likewise cheap to send. Everything has to be checked and packed at the parcels office and, so long as it's of no value, should be safe enough. For valuable items, or anything heavy, you'd be wiser to use an air freight courier like *DHL* (see Freetown "Directory"). Posting any items abroad from the provinces isn't advisable.

Mailing things *to* Sierra Leone is even less certain. Aerograms are safest, but sealed letters and packets aren't likely to get further than Freetown. Many people working up-country use Freetown Box Numbers or Private Bags. There's a

KRIO BASICS

Krio is written phonetically. Vowels are open. Although many words look familiar, (and numbers are the same) it's a different matter to get them right in speech, and to structure your sentences correctly. Remember, too, that even with reasonable Krio, you'll still be speaking a foreign language to the nine people out of ten who are more likely to speak Mende or Temne.

Aw di bohdi?	How are you?	*A de go na Bo*	I'm going to Bo
No bad, bohdi fine	Not bad, fine	*Wan wan!/wan naya*	Let me off!/drop me here
Mohnin-o!	Good morning!		
Ivinin-o!	Good evening!	*Tap!*	Stop!
Kushe-o!	Greetings!	*A wan wata/Gi mi wata*	Can I have some water
A no sabi tok Krio	I don't speak Krio	*Ohmos foh di panapul?*	How much is the pineapple?
Usai yu kohmot?	Where are you from?		
A kohmot London	I'm from London	*Ten-ten lion*	Ten leones
Wi go si bak	Goodbye/ see you again	*(Duya) lehs mi smohl*	(Please) lower your price a little
Dehn geht hotel na dis tohn?	Is there a hotel in this town?	*Ustehm wi de go?*	When are we leaving?
A ebul slip naya?	Can I sleep here?	*Wi de go jisnoh*	Now/later/tomorrow
Dehn get chop os naya?	Is there a chop house here?	*Bai gohd in powa*	By the grace of god/ Insh'allah
Wetin na yu nem?	What's your name?	*Aw foh du?*	What can a person do? (rhetorical)
A nem Kelly	My name is Kelly		
Usai yu de go?	Where are you going?	*Nafoh bia nomoh*	Just bear it, nothing can be done

A KRIO GLOSSARY

Alagba	bigwig, personage	**"Kola"**	tip or inducement, not always of kola
Ambohg	"humbug"; bother or pester someone	**Lorry**	often a minibus or converted pick-up
APC	All-Peoples Congress, the ruling party	**Pikin**	child
Bafa	shelter made of thatch or leaves	**Porto**	European, white person
Bohboh	small boy	**Pumwe**	European (Mende)
Bruk	to wash clothes	**Salo**	Sierra Leone
Bundu	generic term for secret societies	**Titi**	small girl
Cora	Lebanese or Syrian, after the coral they used to sell	**Turntable**	roundabout, traffic circle
		Siraman	Lebanese, or other white
Gara	"indigo'", usually refers to dyed cloth	**Wetman**	"white man", can apply to anyone with a European lifestyle
Johnks	used clothes, "deadmens' clothes"		

SOME MENDE PHRASES

Mende, one of the Mande languages, is related to Susu and Mandinka. It's somewhat "tonal", so that meaning varies with the pitch of voice.

Buae! (pl)	Hello there! (response the same)	*Bi lei*	What's your name?
Wuae! (sing)		*Nya la a Kevin*	My name is Kevin
Bisye! (sing)	Thanks, greetings (said as you pass through the village)	*Pelei ji a li mi?*	Where does this road go?
Wusye! (pl)		*A li Joru*	It goes to Joru
O bi gahui?	How are you? ("Your bones?")	*Sao*	No
Kaye Ngewo ma	Response ("God can't be blamed")	*Li lele!*	Go slowly!
		Gbe jongo lo a ji	How much is this?
Ngi ya le	I am leaving	*Na bagbango, ba mayeilo?*	It's too much, can you lessen it?
Mm, ta mia, ma lo-o	Yes, OK, see you again	*Kulungoi˜*	All right

1	Yila	4	Nani	7	Wofela	10	Pu	20 Nu yila gboyongo (lit. "one
2	Fele	5	Lolu	8	Wayakpa	15	Pu mahu lolu	man finished" i.e. ten
3	Sawa	6	Woita	9	Talu			fingers and ten toes)

poste restante counter in the post office, and it's free, but again, small letters survive best.

Sierra Leone's **telephone** system is in an advanced state of disrepair (it's long been impossible, for example, to call the provinces from Freetown – or even Lumley Beach half the time) and internal phone calls are normally only possible within towns. The country is currently having its old equipment replaced by secondhand gear from Freetown's twin-town Kingston-upon-Hull, which recently upgraded its system. The deal doesn't sound that promising, but improvements are being noticed.

For **international calls**, at any rate, there's only one place to go in the country, *SLET*, the Sierra Leone External Telecommunications centre in Freetown. If you're staying in one of the big hotels, you can sometimes get them to make the connection for you – if you stay in your room half the night. The minimum charge is under £4 for three minutes, and proportionally thereafter. Reverse charge (collect) calls are possible to Britain and beyond. To make one, try calling ☎24951 (the foreign operator access code for the UK which enables you to do so). For brief messages, **telex** is more satisfactory.

AREA CODES

Some of these may not yet be installed, but Lungi, Kenema and Makeni are reportedly now obtainable by automatic trunk dialling.

Freetown ☎22	Juba ☎24
Bo ☎32	Makeni ☎52
Wellington ☎23	Lungi ☎25
Kenema ☎42	Kono ☎53

■ The Media

A proliferation of tabloid sheets, some of them just four pages long, characterises Freetown's lively **press** scene. Style varies from the establishment toadying of the *Daily Mail* to the soapbox opinions of the memorable *New Shaft*. Best of the lot at the moment are *We Yone* and *New Citizen*. Most papers appear on an occasional basis, cobbled together against extraordinary odds (late deliveries of newsprint, power cuts, censorship) and more expensive than you'd think anyone would be prepared to pay. It's all indicative of a potentially healthy industry and, while the papers seem hopeless cases individually, when bought by the handful they offer insights

and, by turns, incomprehensible and manically funny glances at Sierra Leonean life. Most are in English. A number indulge in the fictionalising of characters and events in a blatant parody of government in order to circumvent libel law. While the APC has seen fit to attack several papers, and pressurises journalists into "self-censorship", there's still hope for a freer press than in most countries.

There's little international coverage in the press (nothing, anyway, that you couldn't hear three days earlier on the BBC). For **West African news** (and probably the best hard coverage on Sierra Leone), everyone, including the government, reads *West Africa magazine*, out on sale in Freetown, and even up-country, the week after its Friday publication in the UK. British and other **foreign newspapers** are sporadically available (see Freetown "Directory").

TV and Radio, meanwhile, are going through times of severe hardship. Government broadcasting has effectively closed down. Certainly, neither service operates with anything like regularity.

Entertainment

Music in Sierra Leone is currently struggling through a recession. Cinema is, no surprise, dormant if not extinct – an unexceptional result of the economic crisis and a lack of any resources. Miserable imported movies – and of course increasingly video – are all you'll see. Film could perhaps be great in Sierra Leone, if the country's record in the field of drama is any indication.

■ Music

The best Sierra Leonean **music** is heard abroad. **S. E. (Sooliman) Rogie**, the doyen of Sierra Leonean musical entertainers, has long based himself away from Africa, first in Los Angeles and currently in London.

The Freetown recording industry died in the 1970s. While a number of dance bands do struggle on (The Surviving Survivals and various Police Bands), the only form that's really happening at the moment **inside the country** is the traditionally based **"Milo Jazz"**, a largely percussive music that requires no imported instruments or amplified sound. The leading exponent of Milo Jazz is Olofemi ("Dr Olo") Israel Cole, who has produced a number of popular cassette recordings and recently had plans to diversify with amps, guitars and keyboards. Listen out for him, and also for **Big Fayia**, an ex-military bandleader who benefits from presidential patronage.

■ Theatre

Freetown has a remarkable tradition of **popular theatre**. Some twenty theatrical groups are currently functioning, and all of them write, or translate, their own scripts.

The 1979 banning of *Poyotong Wahala*, about high level corruption, led to routine censorship of scripts. In their attempts to outwit the censors, playwrights have moved increasingly from concert party to exuberant **farce and satire**. Shows are uproarious, even rowdy. In Krio, especially, there's a strong blend of comedy and social comment in the East End "tough guys" *Rari Boys* school of theatre. Remember, however, that you just won't understand the dialogue if you don't speak any Krio. It's worth investing some time in picking some up.

The **Professionals** are currently the big rave, with sell-out audiences wherever they perform. **Tabule Theatre Group**, under director Dele Charley, is another lively downtown team. The **Shegure Players** – a Mende dance and music group – integrate Mende and Temne cultural themes in their work while the **Freetown Players** manage to slip political gestures into their songs. Watch out too for the **Ronko**, **Bai Bureh** and **Kontiki Experimental** theatre groups. Forthcoming events are usually well advertised; look out for banners, especially around Freetown's Cotton Tree.

Theatre in the provinces, is alive too, though lately it has been used less as pure entertainment than as a tool in community education, bringing together government extension workers and theatre artists.

Trouble and Police

The smuggling of what's considered the country's biggest asset – diamonds – is an ongoing problem and in mining regions, or anywhere else, you should dismiss tempting offers. Nor should you carry around undeclared foreign currency. Anything in your possession that's not on your exchange control form can land you in big trouble – a large fine and deportation. As for drugs, grass (*dhambi*, *yamba*) is widely smoked,

but not in public. Police entrapments are more likely to lead to a bribe than the pressing of charges.

■ Law enforcement officers

The **police** of the blue-uniformed SLP (Sierra Leone Police) vary from the utterly charming to the unspeakable. Between the extremes, most policemen, and women, would simply like to be paid a sufficient salary, and on time. Understand this, and you'll have little trouble at the checkpoints and roadblocks dotted round the country. Provincial police in tan uniforms are **chiefdom police** – inheritors of the much-maligned colonial "court messenger" service with civil duties, answerable to the local paramount chief. You may come across the **army** at some point, engaged in security or economic emergency duties. They're usually surprisingly nice: the army is tough to get into, and soldiers are generally respectable and educated.

■ "Tifing"

Lastly, if you're living in the country for some time, you might as well resign yourself to the problem of **"tifing"** – thieving. Everyone reckons their neck of the woods is the very worst. Unless you're prepared to live in a permanent state of paranoia, there's nothing you can do to stop small items vanishing. If you lose something precious, however, before calling in the *kopas*, make some more discreet enquiries, perhaps offer a reward and see if there's a local **"look-ground man"** (diviner) who might help. Spread the word you're going to "swear" the culprits by putting a curse on them. This only works if you have suspicions.

Women Travellers and Sexual Attitudes

Women travelling alone are often assumed to be *Piskoh* (there's a prominent Peace Corps and VSO presence) and shorts and T-shirts don't raise too many eyebrows. With exception made for Lumley Beach – where beach boys of all descriptions gather – Sierra Leone is probably one of the safest and friendliest countries for the lone female traveller.

Settle in one place to stay, or work, though, and you're bound to be persistently discomfited by inflamed egos. "When can we meet to do some loving?" is the kind of question that Sierra Leonean women have to field all the time, though the perceived cultural gap and your potential as a source of funds too, make you more vulnerable. It's possibly unfair, but broadly true, to expect more posturing in the north and less arrogant attitudes in the south.

■ Sexual attitudes

In the wider field of **sexual attitudes**, public boyfriend-girlfriend **relationships** – holding hands and walking together – are more acceptable in Sierra Leone than in most countries. Which doesn't mean husbands reserve the "right" to beat up their wives any the less. Especially in the Freetown area, "Victorian values" are still prevalent. And in the provinces, beyond the metropolising influences of the towns, female genital mutilation is widely practised within the framework of the traditional women's *Sande* society.

■ Organisations

Modern **women's organisations** are mostly Krio, and based in Freetown, which gives their concerns a slightly lopsided, Women's-Institute feel. The main umbrella organisation is the National Organisation for Women. Power for women in the provinces tends to be determined by ethnic affiliation. While there are a number of women paramount chiefs in the Mende chiefdoms, a Temne female paramount chief would be unheard of.

Directory

AIRPORT TAX US$10 payable in leones at the going rate.

CHIEFS AND MPs If you travel much in Sierra Leone you're likely to meet quite a few chiefs. These men (and women) will often be your introduction to a small town or village. Local government in the three **Provinces** (Northern, Southern and Eastern) is organised around the 146 **paramount chiefdoms**, which have local council status. These were consolidated – and invented where necessary – by the British. They're not waterproof ethnic divisions, though most have a dominant group. Beneath the paramount chiefs come section chiefs and village chiefs. Appointments are by slightly arbitrary popular vote. The **Western Area** of Freetown and the

peninsula has district councils, no chiefs. The country's 127 Members of Parliament are elected from outside the chieftaincy system.

CRAFTS Sierra Leone's best buys are **cloth** (indigo tie-dyed *gara*, rusty red and black block-printed *ronko*, soft and heavy strip-woven country cloth – single weave *barri* and double weave *kpokpoi*); **leather goods** (especially slot-together neck bags and purses); **masks** connected with the secret societies (but the made-for-tourists ones are over-priced and often crude, while the real thing is seriously expensive and requires permission to export from the museum); and *nomoli* **soapstone figurines** (with the same export caveat as masks).

PETROL Petrol and diesel are sometimes in very short supply but prices, at least official ones, are currently low at little more than £1/gallon – though it's still a desperate amount of Leones for the average Sierra Leonean.

PHOTOGRAPHY Freetown itself has a tough attitude to cameras, and on just about every street corner where you frame a scene, someone is sure to demand that you stop taking photographs – the result of acute sensitivity over the city's shabbiness. There's no permit necessary, however, and so long as you avoid getting uniforms, banks and government buildings in the viewfinder and apply due respect, you'll find that most of the country is easier than usual for photography. Often enough, people will line up enthusiastically for group portraits ("Mek yu snap wi"). Colour print film is available in Freetown, and you can get your pictures developed at reasonable prices. You need to bring slide film with you.

RELIGION Krio influence has given a broadly Christian colouration to the whole country, especially the south and west, but most deeply ingrained in and around Freetown. You'll see more mosques around the northern and eastern fringes. Indigenous religion, however, is deep-rooted and widely practised, with the powerful **secret societies** (see p.682) playing a major role in keeping it alive.

STREET ART All around Freetown and in some provincial towns too, you'll see the striking wall art of **"Amigo"** (Fode Kamura) with its repeated empathy with the lot of the people. His pictures include "Palm wine drinker: from god to man", "The beer drinker" and "Feel Free".

WILDLIFE Sierra Leone's fauna still includes **elephants** (in the Outamba-Kilimi National Park), **chimpanzees** (also in the park, but widely if thinly dispersed across the whole country) and **pygmy hippos** which are so solitary and secretive that it's hard to know what their status is.

WORKING Paid casual work isn't available. *Voluntary Service Overseas* (317 Putney Bridge Road, London SW14 2PN; ☎081/780 2266) runs a big programme in Sierra Leone for skilled volunteers, but travellers will rarely be able to involve themselves informally. A more promising avenue with less commitment would be the *Gormorgor Agricultural Development Organisation* (*GADO*), 102 Savernake Raod, London NW3, which is based out of Njala University College and takes on people from the age of 15 for farm placements in return for bed and board.

A Short History of Sierra Leone

Sierra Leone has one of the longest "modern histories" of any West African nation. The American slave trade was effectively started at the watering station by the present site of the King Jimmy market in Freetown, by Sir John Hawkins in the 1560s. Inland, at Port Loko, Afro-Portuguese *lançado* traders settled and flourished through the seventeenth century. Early British colonists gravitated to the slaving "factory" of Bunce island (downriver from Port Loko) and the coasts of Sherbro and the other islands futher south. Here, the more adventurous married into local royalty and seeded new, Creole dynasties. At the end of the eighteenth century, the first free black settlers arrived to colonise the Freetown peninsula.

■ The Province of Freedom

There were tens of thousands of **freed slaves** in Bristol, Liverpool and London in the late eighteenth century. After the outbreak of the American War of Independence in 1775, many slaves deserted to the British side from their southern plantation owners, and later made their way to London. And as early as 1772, a legal test case had ruled that, once freed, a slave could not be returned to captivity.

In 1787, the **first settlers** arrived in Sierra Leone. They were a group of 411 people, mostly "black poor" immigrants but including some sixty deported white women – "wives" for the freed slaves. Their patron, Granville Sharp, declared the mountainous shore of the peninsula "The Province of Freedom". The expedition was nearly a disaster. Sierra Leone had been chosen on the recommendation of a botanist, Henry Smeathman, who'd lived there for some years and whose private intention had been to set up plantations – using slave labour. He died before the expedition set off, but many of the putative settlers had second thoughts at the last minute and backed out. The expedition was badly managed – some

of the government funding for it was misallocated or siphoned off – and much delayed, so that the ships finally arrived just before the onset of the rains. The colonists had tents, and built makeshift huts, but within three months of living through the rainy season on the sodden hillside, a third of them were dead, of malaria or other diseases.

They bought the area of what's now Freetown from **King Tom**, a Temne headman and tributary of **King Naimbama**. But Naimbama hadn't been consulted and the area had to be bought again from him. Tom was succeeded by **King Jimmy** who resented and harassed the Bunce Island slave trading operation that was still going on. A British naval vessel, which had by coincidence arrived with new supplies for the flagging colony, torched one of Jimmy's towns – with the approval of the settlers, who had also been in dispute with him.

And there ended the "Province of Freedom". King Jimmy evicted the settlers from their homes and burnt their little colony to the ground. Those colonists that remained (it was now 1790) were absorbed into surrounding Temne villages.

■ Nova Scotians, Maroons and Temne defeat

A new consortium, the **Sierra Leone Company**, was formed to take over the assets of the defunct Province of Freedom and make a second attempt to establish a colony. Its members were **Granville Sharp** (the driving force), the liberal lord **William Wilberforce**, and a young radical, **Thomas Clarkson**.

They soon found a new group of colonists – some twelve hundred **"Nova Scotians"** – for their philanthropic experiment. These were freed slave refugees from the United States whom the British had fobbed off with a dead-end resettlement scheme in the Canadian colony. One of them went to London, where Sierra Leone was suggested to him as an alternative. The small hill farms the new settlers were allocated were not much of an improvement on Canada, but the Nova Scotians formed a viable community. They brought strong churches, and some of them became company administrators. There were further vicissitudes. French Revolutionary forces caught the ill-defended British off-guard in 1794 and ransacked Freetown. But the Nova Scotians rebuilt. The colony of Sierra Leone (as it became in 1808), owed its existence to them.

In 1795, five hundred escaped Asante slaves – the **Maroons** – who had set up an independent state in the mountains of Jamaica, were tricked into negotiations, leading to their capture and deportation, once again to Nova Scotia, and then eventually to Sierra Leone. In another historical coincidence, the Maroon settlers arrived at Freetown in 1800, just as a group of Nova Scotians, in an attempt to form their own government, were in the middle of Sierra Leone's first **rebellion**. The Maroons, and a detachment of soldiers accompanying them, came to the Governor, Thomas Ludlam's, rescue. The Nova Scotian rebels were captured; two were hanged and the rest banished. From the beginning of the nineteenth century, the settlers were given no voice in the government of Sierra Leone. Britain ruled directly.

Pushing home their new strength, the Sierra Leone Company refused to countenance claims by members of the **Temne** ethnic group that a new treaty be negotiated whenever there was a new Temne king as landlord. For the governor, the treaty of 1788 was good in perpetuity. To make the point, the British garrison built a **stone fort**, now part of State House. The Temne, led by

a new King Tom, and encouraged by a partisan Nova Scotian named Wansey, attacked it in November 1801 and were quickly repulsed. In a counteroffensive, the British ousted the Temne and their Bullom relatives from most of the peninsula and carried out savage punitive raids on many villages in King Tom's dominion. While the Temne prepared a new plan, a Susu ally of theirs arrived with his retinue to settle in Freetown. This sell-out turned the tide against the Temne. They gave up the peninsula.

■ The Crown Colony and the Recaptives

On January 1, 1808, the Sierra Leone Company, by now deeply in debt, handed over the running of the settlement to the British government and Sierra Leone became a **Crown Colony**. In the same year, Westminster passed the Abolition Act and the anti-slavery movement at last had some teeth – although the last slave ships weren't intercepted until 1864. Bunce island ceased slave-trading and the Temne country inland turned to **timber** (another non-renewable resource) to maintain its economic strength. Freetown had a naval base, charged with intercepting slave ships and **"recapturing" the slaves**. Although never precisely intended, it soon became clear that few of them could be returned to their original homes, and they were simply released at Freetown to found new villages.

Between 1808 and 1864, some 70,000 **"recaptives"** were resettled in the Sierra Leone colony. Leicester was founded by Wolof and Bambara people, Kissy by freed slaves from the "Scarcies" river and Congo Town by Congolese recaptives. In the 1820s, in war-torn Yorubaland (Nigeria), thousands of slaves of war were shipped west, in Cuban, Brazilian or American vessels, many of them to be quickly recaptured by the Freetown frigates. The "Aku", as they were called, formed the first significant **Muslim** community in the colony.

Slave-trading also continued along the southern coasts of the Sierra Leone region. Many recaptives, far from being complete strangers to the region, had roots in the territory that later became Sierra Leone the country.

After peace was achieved with the French in 1815, many of the **African soldiers** who had served in British regiments were pensioned off to the colony, where they founded villages with pugnacious names like Waterloo, Hastings and Wellington. From the interior came determined **Fula** and **Mandinka** traders who settled in Foulah Town. And much of the town's heavy labour was done by the Kru (or Kroo), who came to the coast on long residences from their homes in southeast Liberia.

In this melting pot of people, many of them traumatised by their experiences, the Church Missionary Society made headway through the early decades of the nineteenth century. Many who felt that the **Bible** had saved them from slavery were converted to Christianity. The Nova Scotians, too, were an example; African and yet European in their ways, prosperous, literate, worldly and Christian. Many recaptives adopted European names and, with intermarriage and the inevitable breakdown of many ethnic barriers, there was the gradual moulding of a new configuration – the **Creoles**, or **Krios**.

In the **interior**, the British paid kings and headmen annual stipends to try to guarantee peace between peoples whose economies had been damaged by the termination of the slave trade. Centuries of dependence upon it had left many **Temne** families, and whole districts, in disarray; while the farming peoples, like the **Limba** and the **Loko**, whom the Temne had exploited for so long, were now attacked and harassed by them. By the 1820s, the Temne had emerged as the dominant language group northeast of Freetown.

On the peninsula, recaptives began moving to Freetown from their villages. Captured cargos of **European goods** for slave-trading were auctioned off and a number of recaptive traders took advantage, selling inland, even setting themselves up in **business** in the interior, under the patronage of village headmen, who called them "white men". The timber trade declined with the introduction of iron steamships and a more easily undertaken trade in wild-collected **palm nuts**, for the burgeoning industries of Europe and the USA, spread across the country.

Further afield, the first **recaptive missionaries** began to follow the traders, not just inland from Freetown, but along the coast, and especially to Nigeria. From the 1850s onwards, the advent of steamships made Freetown the hub of the whole coast. With the return of peace in Yorubaland, large numbers of Krios returned there and went on to colonise the coast of Cameroon.

■ Expansion and Consolidation

Expansion of the Freetown colony in the 1860s took in parts of Sherbro island and the southern coast. Treaties were signed by local chiefs, forced to choose the lesser evil of British overlordship, when French traders made clear their designs on the region. Inland from the peninsula, a minor incident was used to force the "leasing" (in reality annexation) of the low-lying Koya Temne farming district around Songo – about as far inland as present-day Mile 38. Loko and Mende mercenary allies of the British helped clear the area of recalcitrant Temne.

The **end of the slave trade** in 1865 was in fact just the end of transatlantic shipments. In the interior of the country, slaves continued to be traded, for domestic work and for labour on export crops. As the pace of trade and competition increased, the British in Freetown made no effort to control slavery beyond the border of the Freetown colony, if anything recognising its usefulness and the dangers of upsetting the chiefs who profited from it.

Alongside these developments, missionaries, in particular those of the American **United Baptist Church**, aimed to create conditions in the interior that would result in the gradual dismantling of traditional ways. They spread the gospels, of course, and set a lot of store in conversions. But more significantly, they taught **new economic techniques** in their boys' schools and offered substantial credit to their graduates to set them up as traders. As more and more traders left the colony to trade outside the British customs area, so Freetown Krios, complaining of unfair competition and price wars, demanded an extension of British control to annex the whole coast. London, however, explicitly prohibited any further annexations. Indeed a parliamentary committee of 1865 had already laid out a general principal of eventual *withdrawal and self-government* for the West African colonies.

In 1882, the borders of separate **spheres of influence** with Liberia and France were settled along the coast, and Britain found itself operating a **customs area** that extended from the Great Scarcies in the north to the Mano River in the south. The purely exploitative nature of this arrangement, in which no responsibility for internal affairs was taken by the British, led to the beginning of a draining of Krio confidence in the colonial government. One incident that incensed them was the **execution of William Caulker** in

1888 for the murder of his half-brother, the disputed King of Shenge (the coast between Freetown and Sherbro). Although the king had the government's support for his succession, his enthronement had been unpopular. Krio opinion had it that such affairs could be avoided if Britain were to annex and administer the whole county, rather than simply extract duty.

The creation of the new customs area also coincided with a general recession in trade in the 1880s and repeated confrontations and battles between the trading chiefdoms along the coast and in the interior. A number of statelets, which managed to stay on the right side of the British, emerged supremely powerful in Mende country – among them **Senehun**, under Madam (Mammy) Yoko, **Panguma**, under Nyagua, **Pujehun**, run jointly by Momo Ja and Momo Kai Kai and, in the east, **Kailahun**, a new Mende-Kissi confederation under Kai Lundu.

■ Partition

With the recognition of **Freetown's importance as a coaling station** for British shipping, and a sense of urgency in Europe's attitude to Africa, a new pragmatism overcame the colonial government in the closing years of the nineteenth century. The French were chasing Samory Touré's giant *sofa* army (which was supplied with weapons from Freetown) across territory in the British zone of influence. A war between Britain and France in the region couldn't be discounted.

Hastily, the British began formulating exclusive friendship treaties with as many chiefs as would entertain them, hoping to set up a buffer zone of allies between the French and Freetown. Boundary agreements were signed with the French in 1895, a partition that forced the British to accept the **Protectorate** of Sierra Leone. The domineering governor Frederic Cardew initiated a system of **Indirect Rule** through local chiefs under European District Commissioners – a system that was later followed in northern Nigeria. All kings and queens became paramount chiefs (under Queen Victoria) and their sovereignty over their peoples strictly limited to whatever their district commissioner considered appropriate. The "treaties of friendship" they'd signed were reinterpreted as surrenders of power in the new Protectorate.

Cardew's decision to build a **railway**, based on the need to encourage trade, and the requirement that the Protectorate's administration

should not be paid for by the colony, led unavoidably to the invention of ways of paying for it. It was the first ever built and run by the British government: all previous lines had been private. Trading licences were introduced and a tax imposed of five shillings per year on every house in the Protectorate. Payments had to be forced out of people. The undisciplined **Frontier Police** force (initially mainly Krio, later largely up-country men) smashed their way across the country, effectively robbing the people to pay for the administration they had never asked for. People of the Protectorate regarded the white man's **"hut tax"** as an inversion of the proper order of things, which should have had them extracting payment from the newcomers. They assumed they were being charged rent on their houses, which had been stolen from them.

The Hut Tax War and the Mende Revolt

In the north, the Loko chief **Bai Burreh** resisted demands for the hut tax and fought a protracted **guerrilla war** against better-equipped but untrained Caribbean troops. There was support for Bai Burreh's action from the Krio, whose views about taxes concurred with his and who detested governor Cardew's arrogance.

At the beginning of the rainy season in 1898, as the collection of taxes got under way in **Mende country** and the first few lives were lost to the Frontier Police, there was a massive organised **uprising**, planned through secret society meetings. Hut tax and trading licences were the main grudges, but decades of resentment were released in unprecedented violence directed against "every man in trousers and every woman in a dress". Hundreds of administrators, traders and missionaries were hacked and bludgeoned to death. Atrocities were widespread and few escaped. The Krio traders in the Protectorate suffered most. Although there was panic in Freetown, the colony was not invaded.

Pro-British chiefs helped the government resume control in the Protectorate, although there were fierce skirmishes in several districts. Over two hundred arrests were made and 96 people were hanged. Many others, including, eventually, Bai Burreh, were deported to the Gold Coast. With a new West African regiment having replaced the West Indians, Cardew followed the crushing of the resistance with a military victory tour around the country. The Krio community was sickened. The hut tax was not repealed.

■ Krio disaffection – the Lebanese and the rise of Nationalism

The beginning of the **twentieth century** saw a new, more complex Sierra Leone. The Krios were demoralised – ignored by the government and mistrusted by the people of the Protectorate. The Protectorate people had been defeated by the government and now found themselves paying allegiance (and corruptly inflated taxes in many cases) to increasingly alienated chiefs in the pay of the British. At least the Frontier force was disbanded. Chiefdom "court messengers" were given the job of policing the Protectorate.

British policy in general moved right away from the benevolence of a century earlier. In concordance with the new authoritarian order, **racial discrimination** became policy. Blacks – whether "natives" or "creoles" – were kept in subordinate positions no matter how highly qualified. Social mixing between the races became rare and, with the discovery that mosquitoes transmitted malaria, a new whites-only suburb was created on the high ground above Freetown, Hill Station, served by its own railway. Once malaria became less of a deterrent, more and more European companies came to trade in Sierra Leone, buying out the less prosperous Krio traders and bringing venture capital with them. But it was the arrival of **Lebanese traders** in the 1890s (many, it's said, brought by unscrupulous ships' captains who told them West Africa was America) which really did for the Krio traders at the smaller end of business.

World War I and the influenza epidemic and food shortages which followed, stalled the political advances that might otherwise have taken place. Predictably, perhaps, the Lebanese (who never seemed to go short), were accused of hoarding and profiteering. Anti-Lebanese demonstrations took place and their shops were looted. Railway workers went on strike in 1919 and again in 1926, but their demands for improved pay and conditions were not met. Although an increased quota of Africans was nominated to the Sierra Leone Legislative Council, only three were elected, and then only by restricted suffrage for the literate and propertied. The voices of Africans were timid and restrained. The **abolition of slavery** as an institution came only in 1927, when the outrage from abroad became impossible to ignore. Slave-owners lost little, as most slaves preferred to stay with them as employees.

Apart from an isolated Islamic resistance movement led by a marabout, **Idara** (who was killed near Kambia in 1931, and his followers jailed), there wasn't much motion on the **political scene**. But the radical propaganda of **I. T. A. Wallace-Johnson** represented a break from conservative reformism. Organising a mass consciousness nationalist movement in the Gold Coast and Sierra Leone, he formed the West African Youth League and outspokenly denounced the government of Sir Douglas Jardine. Wallace-Johnson's use of Krio, a language more widely understood than English, was especially provocative. He was imprisoned on a charge of criminal libel, followed by years of detention though World War II, on the spurious pretext of his threat to security.

■ The Road to Independence

Only **World War II** broke the numbing spell of repression which had settled on the country since partition. By the time peace was declared in Asia and the black veterans of the Burma campaign and RAF were coming home to Sierra Leone, it was clear that profound changes could not be held off much longer.

To begin with, the colour bar was removed, opening senior civil service posts to Africans. And there was a major change in budgetary policy too, with British tax payers now funding colonial development. Independence at some point in the future was explicitly stated to be the goal. The **new constitution** of 1947 gave the Protectorate fourteen seats on the Legislative Council, and the Colony just seven, which was still a gross under-representation of Protectorate interests, despite Krio complaints that the Colony should have held a majority of seats. Wallace-Johnson bitterly opposed the new order and, making a clear distinction between Colony and Protectorate, reminded the government of the 1865 proposals to allow for self-government in the Colony, now being swept aside.

Surprised at the vehemence of the Krio attacks, the government stalled in implementing the new constitution. In the Protectorate, meanwhile, the **Sierra Leone People's Party** was being formed, the country's first. It was led by **Milton Margai**, a doctor (the first Protectorate man to receive a medical qualification) from a Bonthe business family, related to the powerful and pro-British Banta Mende chiefdom. His brother, **Albert Margai** (first lawyer) and **Siaka**

Stevens, a Vai-Limba man with a union background, were also founder members. The SLPP insisted on the introduction of the new constitution. Elections held in 1951 gave them a huge majority over the Krio-based party of the **National Council of Sierra Leone**.

The People's Party gradually took over power from colonial appointees. Margai became Chief Minister in 1954, but was in no hurry to form a government to run the country independently. "It will come" he said, "but we are not ready yet. We have not got the men to run it. We want our friends to go on helping us for some time to come".

Throughout the **1950s prosperity and confidence** grew. The diamond fields in the east were opened to private licensees and there was considerable investment in health and education, as well as general infrastructure. There were also signals of rumbling discontent at the way political reforms lagged behind growth. In 1955, price riots in Freetown and anti-chief demonstrations throughout the north drew little response from Margai, whose conservative and parochial leanings were becoming increasingly apparent.

The creation of a House of Representatives (the Sierra Leonean parliament) in 1956 replaced the Legislative Council. There was a general election, in which all tax-paying men were eligible to vote, in 1957, which returned the SLPP to power with a slightly reduced majority.

■ Independence

Albert Margai and Siaka Stevens, unhappy with Milton (Sir Milton in 1959) Margai's record, left his cabinet to form **opposition parties**. Although there was brief, ritualistic, all-party unity in the **United Front** for the **indedependence talks** held in London in 1960, there was a rapid fission of interests in the final, faster-than-expected, lead-up to independence. Stevens formed the **All-Peoples' Congress** (APC). Sir Milton Margai, now the prime minister, refused his demands for a general election before independence and went further by detaining Stevens, and several others, for over a month, throughout the transition, on the pretext that they posed a risk to the country's stability. Sierra Leone's Independence Day came on April 26, 1961. A **general election** held the following year, under universal suffrage for the first time, reaffirmed SLPP dominance, but also confirmed mass opposition support for the APC.

Dissatisfaction with the SLPP was spreading, but the death of Sir Milton Margai in 1964, and the return to the fold of his brother Albert (likewise soon Sir Albert) increased popular resentment of the government, especially in the north. The party appeared to be squandering the foreign funds that were poured into the country. It still showed scant concern to reform the corrupt and antiquated system of local government by chiefs, and too much interest in its own, Mende, power base. In **Freetown**, however, important developments were under way. Siaka Stevens was elected **mayor** from 1964–65 and he built up solid support among the disenchanted Krios, for whom independence had so far been disappointing. The general election in 1967 was a turning point. It ousted the SLPP and ushered in a period of intense instability, arguably unchanged to the present day.

■ The Coups, and Siaka Stevens

As soon as Siaka Stevens (elected leader of the victorious APC) had been sworn in as prime minister, a chauvinistic army brigadier, **David Lansana** – an eastern Mende whom Albert Margai had been grooming in a push for regional dominance – attempted a coup to retain Margai. The following day, Lansana's own officers usurped him and seized power, eventually succeeding in nominating **Andrew Juxson-Smith** to chair their army and police **National Redemption Council** (NRC).

Stevens went into exile in Guinea, with his senior supporters. At first, they had to restrain him from launching an armed invasion of Sierra Leone, with the help of Sekou Touré (Guinean president). Instead, he waited a year in exile, while the NRC's popular promises to restore the flagging economy, clean up corruption and then return the country to civilian rule came to nothing. In April 1968 a mutiny in the lower ranks, aided by junior officers, led to the arrest of the members of the NRC and the call for Stevens' return to power.

Stevens in power

Stone wey dey botam wata, no no say wen rain de cam.
A stone under the water doesn't know when it's raining.
Krio proverb

Siaka Stevens' first decade in power was characterised by a growing alienation from his political roots and the jettisoning of virtually all objectives with the exception of **"national unity"**. Publicly, he quickly ceased to be the champion of Freetown's interests. His former outward adherence to socialist principles was ploughed under by the need constantly to retrench his power base. At the same time, he was careful to shed those of his supporters who became dangerously close. He avoided clear ethnic affiliation, using his mixed background to adopt a succession of tribal identities. And all the time, he continued to accumulate a massive personal fortune.

Early after the return to civilian rule, senior ministers in Stevens' government – Mohammed Funna and Ibrahim Bash-Taqi – resigned to form the **United Democratic Party** (the UDP, banned in 1973). A **coup attempt** by the army commander, John Bangura, and two **assassination attempts** on Stevens, all led to executions and to the arrival of detachments of **Guinean troops** to protect Stevens from his own military. Repeatedly, too, **states of emergency** were imposed, which paralysed the country's fragile "democracry" and brought despair among left-leaning politicians. Sierra Leone became a republic in 1971, with *President* Stevens replacing Queen Elizabeth as head of state.

Such was the political climate by 1972 that there was no further effective opposition for nearly five years, and the House of Representatives became a discussion forum for APC members, in which the pronouncements of Pa Siaka (old man Siaka) were aired and approved. A **bomb explosion in April 1974** at the home of the finance minister gave Stevens an opportunity to smash home his dominance. Eight opponents of the regime, including the ex-APC members, Funna and Bash-Taqi, were hanged in public and their bodies desecrated.

The general election of 1977 came in the wake of student- and school pupil-led **demonstrations** across the country, amid mounting **economic disarray**. Despite vote-rigging, and violence that resulted in more than a hundred deaths, the SLPP gained fifteen seats at the expense of Siaka's supporters and, for a short period, the opposition was bolstered with new confidence. This lapsed again with Siaka's announcement that he was "obliged" to hold a referendum on the question of a **one-party state**, to save Sierra Leone from tribalist chaos. The results of this poll (officially, more that 97 percent in favour) led to the absorption of the SLPP in the ranks of the APC and the formalisation of one-party rule.

To seal his control, Siaka was lavish with his political patronage. But his appointment of the chief of the armed forces, **Major General Joseph Momoh** (from the minority northern Limba-speaking group), to the House of Representatives and the Cabinet itself as president-in-waiting – as a prelude to Stevens' retirement from politics – was a strategic bequest to the country. His two vice-presidents, Francis Minah and Sorie Koroma, were ignored.

The hosting of the 1980 **OAU conference**, which cost an estimated US$100 million, marked the end of the era of mere stagnation and rampant corruption. Food shortages, price rises and non-payment of salaries led to huge and general discontent in the towns, while in the rural areas production was depressed by, among other factors, low prices paid to producers – kept down in efforts to prevent urban protest. The black economy was tolerated, and even thrived under the bankrupt official system. A government handbook to mark the OAU conference remarked that "the nation's aims of self-sufficiency and country-wide prosperity are now on the verge of achievement". By 1985 Sierra Leone's economy was apparently on the verge of total collapse – where it was to teeter for four years.

■ Momoh in power: "The New Order"

Siaka Stevens retired in November 1985. (He died, in his mansion overlooking Freetown, on May 29, 1988, after a long and painful illness.)

The **transfer of power to Major General Momoh** was peaceful. After seventeen years of Siaka's stale and hollow rhetoric, the new man was welcomed with enthusiasm. Elections in 1986 saw many of the old guard lose their seats and some 150 new APC members installed in the House of Representatives. A number of political prisoners were released, including twelve convicted after the bomb attack of April 1974.

Momoh's **economic strategy** was to cut back on public spending, in line with IMF-imposed financial conditions. Fearful of the results of austerity measures in the already hard-pressed towns, however, he declined to follow through with a full implementation that might have satisfied the IMF. In **agriculture**, a "Green Revolution" was promulagated but, from lack of consultation with subsistence farmers, it never had much chance of success. Farmers were deserting their plots for diamond and gold prospecting in the east. And, despite an economy dominated, in human terms, by **rice** farms, self-sufficiency in rice was far from being achieved and imported sacks were hoarded to raise prices. Escalating prices resulted, early in 1987, in **student-led demonstrations and riots** and several deaths, sparked by those on government bursaries with not enough money for food. Three colleges at Bo were closed, and government-funded students were dismissed and told to re-apply. Non-academic student "activities" were banned, and remained so for three years.

The causes of growing **public disillusion** with the new government were easy to fathom. While the "New Order" tag was lauded, there was no clean sweep; a number of Stevens' old cabinet cronies were retained in senior positions. **Corruption** blazed in all corners of society, allowing the **black market** to plug the leaky system virtually unchecked. The government's economic measures bit deep, yet apparently had little effect, as Momoh still fell out with the IMF for refusing a comprehensive devaluation of the leone and insisting on retaining the petrol subsidy. Sierra Leone was working itself into a deep mire.

Political events distracted attention from the economic situation and worsened it by absorbing the government's energies. The first big crisis for Momoh's presidency came in March 1987 with the **arrest of sixty people on treason charges** and large seizures of arms. Among those arrested was first vice-president, **Francis Minah**. After a trial of inordinate length, eighteen of the alleged coup plotters were sentenced to death.

Economically, by the end of 1987, all other problems were overshadowed by the treasury's predicament in finding itself quite unable to pay the salaries of government employees, due to the hoarding of money and a consequent severe shortage of currency in the banks. Declaring a **state of economic emergency**, Momoh beefed up border controls, announced severe measures aginst diamond and foreign currency smugglers, slapped limits on the amounts of Sierra Leonean currency that could be privately held, and gave Sierra Leoneans a deadline to deposit their cash in the banks.

The emergency measures – notably efforts to get leones back in the banks – had some success. But economic performance hardly altered: indeed it continued to decline. By the end of 1988, the economy seemed to have bottomed out. It couldn't get worse. Many employees on the government payroll had not been paid for months. There was even a kind of nostalgia for the Siaka Stevens era.

■ Into the 1990s

There's a Sierra Leonean joke that when God created the world, he endowed the country with such a wealth of natural resources that the angels protested at the unfairness of his distribution. "Oh that's nothing", God replied. "Just wait and see the people I put there".

The country does have an exceptional wealth of natural resources. Diamonds and gold head the list of **valuable exports**, but iron ore, titanium (rutile), chrome, coffee and cocoa, palm oil and rice could all create the conditions for a country as prosperous as any in West Africa. President Momoh's record has been relatively good; his style – sober and perservering, even subtle – has convinced even detractors of his sincerity and desire to avoid any charges of dictatorial rule. Yet his term in office has lacked conviction. Massive corruption continues and the will to treat as criminals those who abuse their positions is lacking – not an unusual problem in West Africa. It's compounded in Sierra Leone by the skill and dedication of the **Lebanese** community who manipulate and organise the running of the economy, making use of overseas contacts and siphoning funds to the Middle East, Britain and the USA.

In May 1989, perhaps in time to prevent national breakdown, the government made the long-awaited **devaluation of the leone** to a realistic level and followed this by **removal of the petrol subsidy**. At the same time, **"ghost workers"** on government payrolls were exorcised with the help of computerisation. Average **pay rises** of seventy percent were thus awarded with an actual *cut* in costs. Tax thresholds were raised, many agricultural export taxes scrapped and the "state of economic emergency" repealed. Rewardingly, **sales of diamonds and gold** to the state monopoly have improved with the higher leone prices now being paid. Lastly, the **press**, hounded by government in 1989 for stories concerning high level corruption, has been granted a reprieve by Momoh, who genuinely appears to want a (relatively) free press after all.

Yet, as Sierra Leone turns into its fourth decade of independence, these hopeful turnarounds fade against the mounting scale of **dissatisfaction and poverty**. Government sector wages are being paid up to five months late (even those of MPs are delayed: for some time in 1989 the House was repeatedly inquorate). Then, when paid, the average wage in devalued leones is equivalent to around £10 per month: a 50kg sack of rice (the monthly requirement for a small family) is more than twice as much.

For **the future** of the country, it seems clear that the economy needs to be completely re-addressed, as if diamonds were not the export mainstay. Perhaps only massive investment in infrastructure and grass roots agricultural development can succeed in permanently improving Sierra Leone's fortunes. For without that base, precious minerals will always be subject to smuggling and drain labour from productive sectors.

Political Update: Issues and Prospects

Two issues look like exercising local journalists in the immediate future: **Israeli business interests** and the pressures being put on **Momoh's ethnic indifference** by fellow Limba-speakers.

The first story concerns the kid-glove handling of Lebanese and Israeli diamond dealers in the country. Israeli companies are accused of undermining Lebanese business, which they believe helps fund the anti-Israel war effort. Fifty-seven million leones were recently confiscated from a senior Israeli manager, so perhaps the more powerful interests have won.

The second story is more sensitive. It's widely believed that the Limba *Ekutay* society is becoming too powerful, influencing political and economic decision-making at the highest levels and incurring the wrath of Mende-speakers from the south who increasingly feel disenfranchised by the government. It's to be hoped that the president's decision in October 1989 to go ahead with the **executions** of seven of the March 1987 coup plotters – despite appeals from *Amnesty* – indicates a resolve stemming from renewed confidence in the slightly improved economic situation, rather than dictatorial determination.

Bigger than either of these issues is the question of **multi-partyism**. By mid-1990, a heated debate was going on in the country about whether Sierra Leone should follow the lead of a number of other West African nations and adopt a pluralist constitution. From his cautious pronouncements on the matter, it's clear that Momoh, while recognising the dangers it poses for ethnic harmony, isn't antagonistic to the notion of **multi-party democracy**. What's equally clear is that many high-ranking government and APC officials are furious, and determined to nip this one in the bud, raising the spectres of **anti-constitutionalism** (the present constitution allows for only one party) and **treason** at those journalists, academics and students who are prepared to speak out.

To Momoh's credit, he has unambiguously supported the right of Sierra Leoneans to hold political debates and discussions on the multi-party system. And after a three-year ban, students have once again been permitted to organise in a union.

But in May 1990, freedom of speech was blurred with **street rioting** when clashes between school students and police resulted in the deaths of at least two youths and a policeman. These disturbances, sparked off when police banned a teachers' meeting in the latest round of protests about late salaries and poor conditions, only highlight the frailty of Sierra Leone's civic order.

FREETOWN AND THE PENINSULA

FREETOWN's dilapidation is extravagant. An aged and decaying tumble of sagging streets, clapboard and cement block buildings, with a population now in excess of half a million, it fills the level areas and strains up the steep hillsides of the otherwise vegetation-flanked peninsula. Granted there are some newer, multistorey buildings, but rot and collapse are ubiquitous among the palms and mango trees, and the prevailing sense is one of teetering on the edge of chaos. Flying in fresh from Europe the impact of so much mutant tropicality run riot can damage temperate sensibilities. Simply, the place steams.

Yet, arriving from almost anywhere else in West Africa, Freetown's overall effect is enchanting, and its name appropriate. The city gurgles with twice as much atmosphere as any other West African capital. The hilly relief gives constantly changing points of view and there are photogenic street prospects in every direction.

Architecture and a real depth of **history** have much to do with it. Run-down, pastel-painted Creole houses, with rusty-red tin roofs, often propped-up on posts against steeply scaling streets, are preserved even in the city centre. The anonymous apartment blocks and broad thoroughfares of many cities are largely absent from Freetown, their place still taken by an intimate, almost nineteenth-century hubbub, instantly recognisable to anyone who's travelled in the Caribbean. After dark you catch domestic glimpses, through the burglar bars and tatty curtains, of murky interiors lit by dim light bulbs. Or by kerosene lamps. For many years, Freetown's **electricity** supply has been notoriously unruly, the short and long power cuts, and sudden runs of success, as unpredictable as downpours in the rainy season.

It would be hard to avoid a relationship with Freetown; the sheer good humour of the place compensates for high humidity and shambolic inconvenience. In practical terms, the city is easy-going, one of the least threatening to move around. There's a fair choice of places to stay and eat, and the business and embassy districts are compact and central. Sierra Leone's best **beaches** are all nearby – far enough away to ensure clean water and tranquility, but still a cheap taxi ride from the town centre and exceptionally beautiful. For many visitors they're worth a holiday in themselves. The interior of the **Freetown peninsula** is recommended too – a rugged, jungle-covered massif rising to heights of nearly 1000m. The Guma dam is a good destination, but there are also old settlements deserving a visit.

Getting into Freetown

Arriving by air and **getting into town** can be complicated, and if circumstances prove unfavourable, and you're not prepared, can turn into something of a nightmare. **Lungi International Airport** provides a variable reception, and formalities can take ages (note the advice under "Red Tape" and "Money" in the *Practical Information* section). That said, the airport business itself is gradually improving. If you need it, there's a fairly good, though by no means cheap, **hotel** nearby (see under "Accommodation" below). Curling up in a corner at the small airport until dawn isn't viable.

Hastings airfield, the old domestic airport down the peninsula half-an-hour's drive from Freetown, is now out of service except for the fickle flights on *Air Guinée*.

PRICES

As is explained in the *Practical Information* section of this chapter, all the costs in Sierra Leone have been estimated in £ sterling, **at the official rate of exchange**.

Ferries

Lungi airport is 29km north of Freetown – 12km by road, 8km by ferry, and a further 9km by road into the city centre. The optimal journey time, about ninety minutes, can easily stretch to three hours depending on the health of the ferry across the Sierra Leone River. And it's as much as a five-hour trip by road around the creeks (over 180km) if the ferry has broken down. Assuming that it hasn't, the **ferry journey** (passengers £0.10p) can be a fine scenic introduction to Freetown – there's a bar and the odd musician. The "semi-hydrofoil fast-ferry" is more often than not out of service; when available it's usually on charter (about £20).

Some if not all ferry services may by now be using the **new ferry terminal** down on the waterfront in the city centre, which takes out a great deal of the hassle of the airport journey by avoiding the need to use Kissy terminal.

Taxis and helicopters

With the exception of the *Ghana Airways* **bus** (£2), which *usually* meets each of their flights (but not any others) the main transport from the airport is **taxis**. You've a couple of options here though. One is to **charter** a taxi for the whole trip from the airport to your destination in Freetown or Lumley Beach (around £10–15 including all luggage and ferry costs). Alternatively, hop in a taxi at the airport going to the ferry dock at **Tagrin Point** (50p plus bags), then find another at **Kissy** on the Freetown side. In the daytime, this is really no problem, so long as you're not loaded with luggage. But beware the taxi drivers at the Kissy ferry terminal itself, who like to charge five or ten times the fair fare. If you're trying to save money, you may as well walk a few hundred metres up to the main road into town, where ample proletarian alternatives will be heading your way.

Lastly, you could forget all the hassle and time spent, and take the fifty-dollar option, **by helicopter** (pay in hard currency on the spot) in six minutes direct from the airport to one of the two heli-pads at Lumley Beach. The flight (sit on the left) is definitely worth considering – on its own merits as much as for ease of transport but it's more fun on departure (sit on the right), when you can look down on some of what you recognise. You are likely to be aware, by the time you take it, however, that there have been several serious helicopter accidents in recent years.

Arriving by road from up-country

There's only one **main road** into Freetown. Arriving on one of the big **bus** lines (particularly strong on the Freetown–Kenema axis), you'll come to the **central bus station**, close to the heart of the city, in the old railway station building. Most of the smaller, privately owned **minibuses and "lorries"** have drop-off/pick-up points to the east of here. The main location for those serving the north of the country (Makeni, Kono and points north) is **"Ashoebi Corner"** on Blackhall Rd at the Upgun Turntable (roundabout). You'll need to catch a taxi from here to the centre. Another transport base is the **PZ Turntable** at the eastern end of the city centre. Lastly, Conakry vehicles go from **Free St**, a couple of hundred metres uphill from here.

Orientation – and some historical background

Freetown's wonderful hills provide excellent **orientation**, but the city layout is sprawling and confusing at first, and its north-facing aspect curiously disorientating. The city begins in the east at **Wellington**, and stretches into the poor residential areas of **Kissy**, **Cline Town**, **Fourah Bay**, **Kossa Town** and **Foulah Town** (together known as **East End**) and the half square kilometre of the main **commercial and business district**, which roughly coincides with the historical centre.

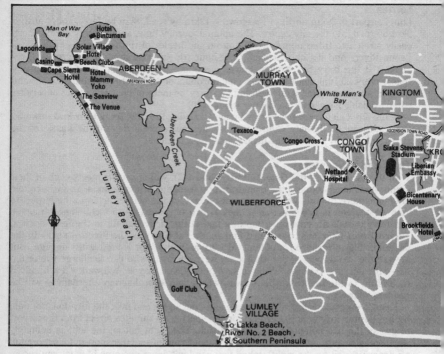

It's no longer possible to differentiate **quarters** of the city centre according to the origins of their inhabitants. But as an angle in characterising them, it's worth knowing that the oldest and most established blocks are roughly within a triangle formed by **Siaka Stevens Street** (the city's major thoroughfare), Pademaba Road and Waterloo Street, with its apex the huge and famous **Cotton Tree**. The unfortunate English immigrants of 1787 settled a few hundred metres to the north of here on the peninsula of **Kingtom**. But this triangle was home to the more successful freed slave Nova Scotians and the Maroons from Jamaica.

The **East End "towns"** were originally mostly developed by immigrants from the interior and neighbouring parts of West Africa (Temne, Mende, Limba, Kissi, Bambara, Fula, Yoruba). Some arrived in the nineteenth century looking for commercial opportunities, but many, like the Kissi and the influxes of Muslim Yoruba from Nigeria, were recaptured slaves, saved from the Atlantic crossing. The character of this side of the city thus has a less creolised flavour. Many of its founding families were traders, and a great deal of trade still goes on in the East End.

West of the centre, through a jungle of ravines, streams and sprawling shanties, stretch the more residential, less commercial areas of CONGO TOWN, MURRAY TOWN, WILBERFORCE and other nineteenth-century freed slave settlements. Down by the shore near the centre, KROO TOWN is the area which is still largely inhabited by Kru fishing people from Liberia. A new road (Motor Main/Wilkinson/Aberdeen Rd) cuts west out of the city, down the steep hillside to the sea and over a bridge to the Aberdeen Peninsula, on the far side of which lies the five-kilometre sweep of LUMLEY BEACH and the head of the road that runs south along the peninsula shore.

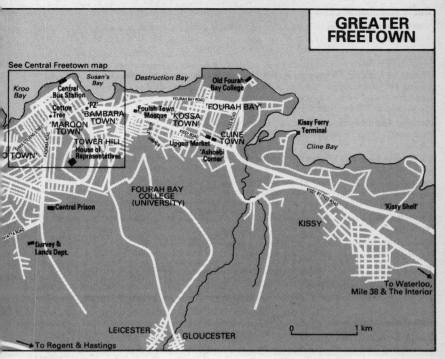

Public transport

Getting around the city, you can generally walk between most points in the centre (there's no city-centre bus service). For slightly longer trips, wave down one of the **taxis** (unmetered, yellow licence plates) going in your direction (10–15p for short hops). These run on agreed routes dropping off and picking up anywhere. If you want to hire a **private cab**, you'll pay roughly equivalent to the value of the journey to the driver, estimated on the pick-up basis (which normally adds up to around £3 for most places in Freetown, possibly more to Lumley Beach or into the hills). The main taxicab park is at the *Paramount Hotel*; most journeys have set prices. Alternatively, don't hesitate to try **hitching** a ride, especially if you're heading out to the beaches; many drivers will oblige. You can offer to pay (say twice the taxi seat fare), but you'll often get free lifts. Siaka Stevens Street at the Cotton Tree roundabout is a likely spot.

When you come **to leave the city** for up-country destinations, it's often easiest to hitch – unless you opt for the dawn scramble at the bus station. Hitching at "Ashoebi corner" is often fruitful. So too is the traffic hub of "Kissy Shell", a kilometre or so further out. In the excitement of the wait, remember to keep one eye on your bag.

Sleeping

Electricity ("light") is the limiting factor at all **hotels** and **restaurants**. Often enough, you'll have to put up with power cuts that last most of the night, ruling out electric fans and air conditioning and necessitating hot kerosene lamps. There are no campsites in Freetown (or anywhere else) and sleeping out at Lumley Beach is unsafe.

Basic Accommodation

YMCA, Fort St (PO Box 243; ☎23608). Remarkably good – elevated location with views, safe and squeaky clean and open to all (rooms non S/C, with fan £3.50/single, £5/double: with AC £6/double only). Often full; if you can book ahead, do so. Cheap beer and good dishes (£1) day and night.

Tropic of Cancer, Gloucester St. For some years the cheapest hotel in town, with a few baking hot garret rooms and one or two lower down – around £2 per person. Separate w/c and shower and uncertain security; occupied most of the time by impecunious volunteers. Good chop and cheap beer at street level.

Andy's Apartments, Rawdon St, corner of Siaka Stevens St, opposite the *Golden Bay* restaurant. Large, comfortable S/C rooms, secure and very central (around £8/double, triple).

City Hotel, Lightfoot Boston St. A nocturnal institution (immortalised, or condemned, as the cockroach-infested *Bedford* in Graham Greene's *The Heart of the Matter*), to which access, surprisingly, seems to be reserved. "Always full", it's nonetheless worth trying to get one of the extremely cheap rooms every time you're in Freetown. The often recumbent manager, and far from upright main bar and lobby, present an impression of spectacular seediness.

Homely Inn, Congo Cross. Nice-looking, new and halfway to the beach. Medium-priced and worth a check.

Dabo Hotel, Fourah Bay Rd, corner of Bombay St (☎22747). Cheap.

SK Hotel, Fourah Bay Rd near the *Dabo*. Ditto.

Leona Hotel, 1 Back St (☎23380). Reasonable S/C rooms (£8/12).

Lamar Hotel, 21 Howe St (☎24206/25903). A last resort in the cheap bracket, this is unappetising, with horrid carpets. Tolerable, but scruffy and overpriced S/C AC rooms (£10/12).

Expensive Hotels

Lungi Airport Hotel (☎23345). Self-explanatory and not exactly adventurous, but worth considering if you're flying in late (or flying out early), and a deal better than you've reason to expect – lovely garden and pool, and even a decent beach on the doorstep (around £30/45 B&B).

Paramount Hotel, Independence Ave (PO Box 574; ☎24531, telex 3257). Comfortable, establishment, city centre stand-by with large S/C, AC rooms (around £25/35 B&B with discounts for Sierra Leone residents) and big restaurant, bars and (usually) electricity. Nonetheless, it's quietly seedy.

Brookfields Hotel, Jomo Kenyatta Rd/Mereweather Rd (PO Box 1193; ☎41860/40875). The old government rest house gets much abused but is perennially popular; volunteers get special rates, the worst rooms and flat service (ordinary rates are similar to the *Paramount*'s). The pool is some compensation, as is live music every Sunday and sometimes Wednesday too.

Solar Village Hotel, Lumley Beach/Aberdeen. Self-catering establishment with reasonable rooms and good views, but no beach of its own (around £35/double). The adjoining *Old Roots New Seeds* restaurant (see "Restaurants" below) is a big bonus.

Cape Sierra Hotel (PO Box 74; ☎37266/9, telex 3367). Of the three Lumley Beach hotels, this is the one to choose. Nice S/C, AC bungalows (from around £40/55 B&B), a reasonably unpretentious atmosphere and very competent management.

Sofitel Mammy Yoko (PO Box 563; ☎37444/37459, telex 3426). The unreasonably pretentious atmosphere here is off-putting, and the prices doubly so. Small rooms (from £70/80).

Hotel Bintumani (PO Box 655; ☎37019 to 34, telex 3316). A sad case, closed for a long time recently because of a massive, outstanding electricity bill. Now reopened, and with tatty rooms, it's still a nicely positioned pile, with a really good pool.

Restaurants

The city is well endowed with **eating places**. While a number of them depend heavily on resident volunteers and aid workers, there are some good Lebanese and more authentic African chop-houses and snackeries too. Many restaurants close on Sunday. Apart from those attached to places mentioned under accommodation listings above (notably the first-class *YMCA* and the *Tropic of Cancer*), try:

Chop

Big Apple, Lamina Sankoh St. A wonderful cheap place for excellent chop, big breakfasts, bean sandwiches, whatever's going. Beer and crafts too, and a good atmosphere. Daytime only, when it's usually full of Peace Corps.

Dilly's, Garrison St. Good Sierra Leonean chop in a real sit-down restaurant. Blander international dishes too. Cold beer. Meals from £1.50.

Faiya's, near the Liberian embassy and not far from *Brookfields Hotel*. Superb. An award-winning chop house (!) with wonderful pepper chicken.

Kay's, Rawdon St. Excellent.

Subouya's, Garrison St. Really popular for its nicely positioned first-floor dining rooms. Less to rave about with the food – decent enough, but most notably, cheap.

Snacks and Fried Food

Burgerland, Siaka Stevens St. Dance floor and beer inside, sit-down and beer outside. And burgers. The street food stalls outside and round about (especially after dark) are lively competition.

International Bakery, Rawdon St. Very good croissants and *pain au chocolat* for breakfast; coffee, ice cream, fresh bread. Closes 5pm, Sat 1pm, Sun closed.

Munchies, Wilberforce St. Burgers, sandwiches, snacks and breakfasts.

Ready Foods, East St. The best take-away Lebanese sandwiches.

Rooster, Siaka Stevens St. Chicken and chips, about £2; you need to like fried chicken a lot.

Snack House, Rawdon St. Air-conditioned snack bar and beer parlour with burgers, ice-cream and smiles.

Strand Snack Bar, Waterloo St. In the heart of the night-time, downtown, street food district; good Lebanese-derived calories.

Lebanese and International

Afroditis (aka **Khadra's**), Walpole St. An American-flavour Lebanese, with fried foods, salads and sandwiches, good merguez sausages, kebeh, beer. Rather expensive. Club behind.

Alliance Française, 30 Howe St (☎23379). Unusual, outdoor venue open until dusk, with changing menu, good food (£2–5), nice juices, espresso. Live music and theatre at weekends.

Don Salvador's, Pultney St. Classy Latin eating house, with quasi-pizza, paella and shrimps. Accordingly expensive. The good-value Thursday lunch buffet is the biggest attraction.

Gem, Wilberforce St (☎23644/5). Freetown's best Lebanese, big and busy, with an extensive menu and really good coffee. From about £15 for two (on a *VISA* card if you like). Open daily, except Sunday, 8am–10.30pm.

Special Tastes

Chinese Restaurant, Wilkinson Rd. A very European Chinese, but the only one in town.

Natruj, abover the *Aeroflot* office, Wilberforce St. Great Indian food and remarkably cheap.

Old Roots New Seeds, Pademba Rd and *Solar Village*, Lumley Beach. An impeccably "ethnic" African-American roots restaurant. Excellent and original vegetarian and seafood dishes carefully prepared. *Note*: only lunches are served at the town restaurant; wonderful breakfasts and dinners are down at the beach. For main meals, allow £5–7 a head and two or three hours.

Provilac, Wilkinson Rd. The long-established African lunch buffet venue, closed evenings. Expensive, and nearly worth it.

Exploring Freetown

Wandering around Freetown is easy. You may not delay long before migrating out to the beaches, but the city's pleasant decrepitude conceals a few **sights to see**, including a **museum** and, remarkably, nearly a hundred **churches and mosques**. True, it can be murderously uncomfortable outside the cooler season (Dec to Feb). Avoid over-exertion.

An obvious place to start, and Freetown's focus, is the **Cotton Tree**, a magnificent silk-cotton older than the city itself and as tall as any of its buildings. Beneath the tree's younger branches, slaves were once sold; in 1787, in the same place, are supposed to have gathered the first colonists from England – a group of "Black Poor" immigrants and sixty white women who had been deported to Sierra Leone. The statuesque 1920s **law courts** nearby were built in the spot where the trials and adjudications of captured slave ship captains and crew took place after the British parliament had banned the slave trade in 1808.

Down **by the waterfront**, five minutes' walk away, there's a meagre clutch of **historical monuments**. At the west end of Wallace Johnson Road, the entrance to what's now the lower dispensary of Connaught hospital is formed by the **"Slave Gate"**. Slaves liberated from slave ships were detained behind it in the "King's Yards" while arrangements were made for their resettlement. It was through this gate that they walked to an unknown future in "Free Town". The sanctimonious inscription still reads:

> *Royal Hospital and Asylum for Africans*
> *Freed from Slavery by British Valour and Philanthropy*
> *A.D. 1817*

The quite inappropriately named **Portuguese Steps**, below Wallace Johnson Street near the bus station, were built the same year by Governor Charles McCarthy. They're a handsome flight to be sure, but nowadays utterly neglected and unnoticed.

The **Ruiter Stone** is an equally underwhelming monument: indeed the fact that it's buried, invisibly, "six feet below the ground just above the high water mark at King Jimmy Market" severely restricts its appeal as a tourist attraction. This 1664 **rock graffito**, scratched by bored Dutch sea captains during a lull in a military expedition against the English, was discovered in the course of drainage work in 1923. It's the oldest archaeological evidence of a European presence on the peninsula. Someone did a rubbing of the names and date;

> *M. A. Ruiter, I. C. Meppell, Vice Admiralen,*
> *Van Hollant en Westfriesland, AD 1664*

then r-buried it under the market's main drain "to protect it from the weather". A replica now takes pride of place in the museum. Possibly more interesting is another stone, yet to be uncovered, but referred to by Richard Burton in 1862, which is supposed to carry the initials of Francis Drake and Richard Hawkins.

Old Fourah Bay College

Freetown's most famous institution is **Fourah Bay College**, the oldest university in West Africa. The modern (though atrophied) university is located up at Mount Aureol, south of the city centre. But it's interesting to go and see the **original Fourah Bay building**, now a Magistrate's Court, founded in 1827 by the Church Missionary

Society, and it makes a good excuse for an exploration of one of the city's poorer, older and much-bypassed East End quarters. The old four-storey building at the end of College Road in Cline Town dates from 1845, and is made of red laterite bricks and decorated with iron fretwork. **Samuel Adjai Crowther**, the college's first student, later became the first home-grown Bishop of West Africa.

THE REVEREND KOELLE AND HIS POLYGLOTTA AFRICANA

It was at Fourah Bay College, in 1852, that a young German pastor, the **Rev. S.W. Koelle**, published an extraordinary collection of vocabularies from nearly 200 West and Central African languages, the **Polyglotta Africana**. Working with immense speed he interviewed 205 informants – most of them freed slaves – and recorded the translations of about 300 words and phrases in their natal languages. He got some curious replies: one man apparently replied "Gud-bai" when Koelle asked him to give the phrase for "I am going". But the finished book is a remarkable achievement, far in advance of anything produced until then, and still useful to linguists, and interesting to look through, today; there are copies in the University library and recent editions available abroad. Apart from giving clues about the relatedness of different West African languages, the *Polyglotta* also gives interesting cultural information. Less than a third of the informants, for example, could come up with words in their mother tongues for "butter" or "ink" and there were problems too with "book", "hell" and "soap". Missionaries must have found the blanks provocative.

Churches and Mosques

Of eighty **churches** and nearly two dozen **mosques**, the oldest place of worship is **St. George's Maroon Church**, a diminutive white chapel on the south side of Siaka Stevens Street two blocks west of the Cotton Tree. It was founded by the first freed slave settlers from Jamaica in about 1820. In construction around the same time was the colonial high temple of **St. George's Cathedral** on Lightfoot Boston Street, completed in 1828 and dedicated in 1852. Memorial plaques inside commemorate British administrators and traders who didn't survive the "White Man's Grave" to return home. The **Zion Church** on Fort Street is one to check out during a service; it's marvellously audible every Sunday morning from the *YMCA*. The Catholic community, much smaller than the reforming churches, has its relatively modest **Sacred Heart Cathedral** on Siaka Stevens Street, corner of Howe Street.

Sunday is the day when you can't fail to notice the importance of Freetown's churches, as thousands of people, and especially the Creole community, dress in their **Sunday best** – classically, men in dark suits and homburgs, women in frocks and creative hats, boys in sailor suits and girls in virginal white frills. Services are long, expressive and enthusiastic.

The oldest mosque is the **Foulah Town Mosque** on Mountain Cut, just off Kissy Road in the East End. It's surprisingly church-like in its design, possibly in deference to the concerns of colonial and Creole ruling groups in the mid-nineteenth century. There was considerable opposition to Islam from Christian freed slaves. The freed Yoruba slaves from Nigeria (known as **"Aku"** or "Oku") were predominantly Muslims. In 1832, a British lawyer, **William Henry Savage** was persuaded by his Aku servant to press for the release of a group of Aku who had been jailed for practising "Muhammedanism". In gratitude, several took the name Savage, and a mosque was built near his house, in the street now called Savage Square. Encouraged by this, other Aku built the Foulah Town mosque a kilometre further west. But opposition to Islam, and a low-key conflict between the Creoles and the Aku (who came to be considered "Muslim creoles") has kept mosques out of the commercial city centre – a quarter containing no less than sixteen churches – to this day.

Markets

Freetown's **markets** are an animated lot and you can spend many enjoyable hours just pushing though them with no definite object in mind. For specific bargaining and purchases, try the following:

King Jimmy Market Tuesday, Thursday, Saturday for fruit, vegetables and fish.

Government Wharf Market Daily, for general goods from pomade to potato peelers, including lots of "dead men's clothes".

Basket Market ("Big" Market) Daily, a covered market for quite a range of crafts, tourist bric a brac, traditional medicines and mystical materials. There are good baskets (*shuku*, *blai*), some nice musical instruments, and rather a lot of small animal skins, but you need to spend some time at the stalls to discover interesting bargains that you'd actually want to take home.

Victoria Park Tourist Market Can be fun, but keep your wits about you: a lot of people are after your custom. This is the best market in Freetown for Sierra Leonean "country cloth" and locally made-up dresses and shirts.

Kroo Town Road Fruit and vegetables.

East St/Kissy St Market A place of some commotion. good fruit and veg market, and numbers of small Lebanese trading stores of cloth and the like.

Upgun/Kennedy Street Market Also on the left, 1500 metres further east down Kissy Road, immediately before the Upgun roundabout.

Bombay Street In Kossa Town, the old Bambara quarter, not far from the shore.

Sierra Leone Museum

Mon–Fri 10am–4pm, Sat 10am–1pm, entry by donation (Curator ☎25555).

The **museum** is an institution in transition. Until 1929, a railway terminus ("Cotton Tree Station") at the foot of the "Hill railway" up to Wilberforce and Hill Station, the diminutive white building then saw service as a school, a soft drinks factory and a telephone exchange before becoming the repository of the Sierra Leonean cultural heritage in 1957.

In 1988, an extension was opened (gift of the German embassy) to mark Sierra Leone's bicentenary. Although a state of disarray tends to prevail, the collections are emphatically worth a visit: this is the country's only museum. There aren't many visitors and you're likely to get a guided tour of some kind, but much of the material is still piled in boxes and there's an endless battle with damp and termites. Donations are appreciated.

The Ruiter stone replicas are always highlighted, but the model of **Bunce island** fleshes out Sierra Leone's early slaving history more convincingly. The original 1799 Royal Charter, signed by George III, is carefully preserved. The main interest, though, lies in the **ethnographic pieces** from around the country. There's an interesting Mask Corner where some of the regalia from Sierra Leone's still lively **secret societies** is fearlessly displayed. Look out for the figure of **"Mammy Wata"**, the transmogrifying Medusa-like sea goddess (a widespread coastal icon) who can assume serpentine or human form and act for good as well as evil. Notice too, some excellent and rather rare examples of Sierra Leonean home-made **country cloth**, the unusual **instruments** of music and war and a fine old *warri* board – the pan-African game of risk and calculation played with seeds or cowries.

The statue of **Bai Bureh** is dressed in the nineteenth-century Temne guerrilla leader's own clothes and holds the cutlass with which he fought in the Hut tax war of 1898. Bai Bureh was captured and taken to the Gold Coast to die in jail. He was allowed to return in 1905 to end his years in his old kingdom. The "bullet-proof" *ronko* cloth he wore can still be bought today in Kabala, Northern Province.

Upstairs, displays of less perishable items include minerals, prehistoric stone tools and Mende *nomoli*. *Nomoli* are small, rather arcane soapstone figurines, first identified from a pair dug up on Sherbro island in the 1880s and later found in huge numbers in farmland right across the centre of the country. The Mende don't claim any connection with them, though they were traditionally revered and believed to protect the fertility of the land. Like the *pomtan* (singular *pomdo*) of the Kissi country in eastern Sierra Leone and Guinea (see p.607), they were almost certainly carved by earlier peoples as ancestor figures. The most likely artists are thought to be the **Sherbro**. Now mostly living on the island of the same name, these were displaced from the interior by the Mende around the fifteenth century. Early Portuguese sources suggest they were the best artisans in the region. Much larger figures – lifesize heads from Mende and Kono country known as *mahen yafe* ("spirit of the chief") – have also been found. Like the *nomoli* and *pomtan*, the best ones are mostly in private collections or museums abroad. Sierra Leone has a fairly flourishing tourist industry in fake *nomoli* (pay no more than £2–3), but since the export of the real thing is banned, you may have to get authorisation from the museum itself to take reproductions out of the country.

Shopping

Although it doesn't have the really big stores of a Dakar or Abidjan, Freetown has a wide variety of more modest places, and a shopping tradition that still reflects British, Indian and Mediterranean tastes. There are, however, rather frequent and unpredictable shortages. For a huge number of African stores, head out to the East End; listed below are some of the more central possibilities.

Food

Try *Goodies* in Howe Street for cheese and Lebanese fare, or *Dina's* of Wilberforce Street for Greek food, cheese, chocolates and imported fruit. *Chanrai's*, Rawdon Street, is a general delicatessen specialising in cheeses. The *China Store* in Lightfoot Boston Street sells noodles and cans. If you can't find what you want, try *Choithrams*, on the corner of Siaka Stevens Street and Krootown Road, which is a good, all-round supermarket. For fancier tastes and home-food-sickness, head out to *Atson's* on Wilkinson Road, just before "Texaco" (the Aberdeen junction), where most cravings can be remedied.

Tailors

It's possible to find skilled, cheap and astoundingly rapid workmanship all over Freetown. As ever, the ideal way of being sure that you get what you want is to take along an item of your own clothing for use as a pattern. One of the very best spots is next to *Kay's* in Rawdon Street.

Arts, crafts and junk

Check out the *National Arts Centre* on Siaka Stevens Street, opposite *Barclays Bank*. Hasan Bangura, Sierra Leone's best-known artist, sells his pen and ink and watercolour sketches of Freetown here, and this is also the base of Chernor Bah, a popular portraitist. The *King Jimmy Cultural Centre* on Lamina Sankoh Street is a good bet for little presents, postcards and cheap crafts. *Nigerian Trader*, on Gloucester Street next to the *Tropic of Cancer*, is just what it says, now one of a dimishing number. *Charlie's Curio Shop*, at the *Paramount Hotel*, isn't all curios, but not all are as expensive as you might think, either. A good place for protracted bargaining over gear from all over Africa. All the way up Howe Street, to the entrance to Victoria Park, you'll find a succession of street traders where, if you can hang on long enough, you're almost bound to get good prices. For musical instruments – *balangis*, shake-shakes and so on – try down at Lumley Beach.

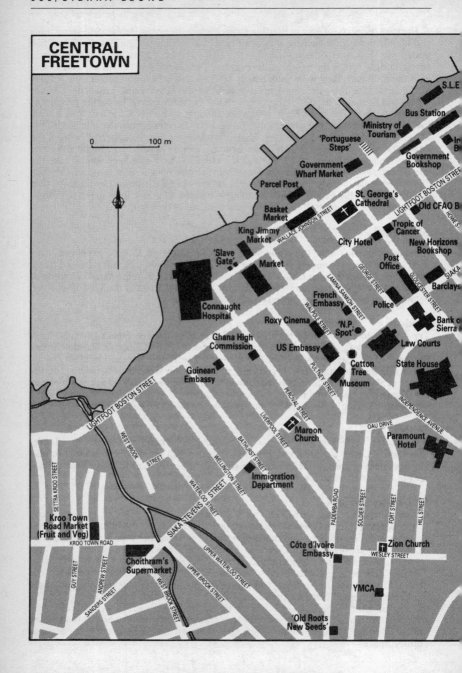

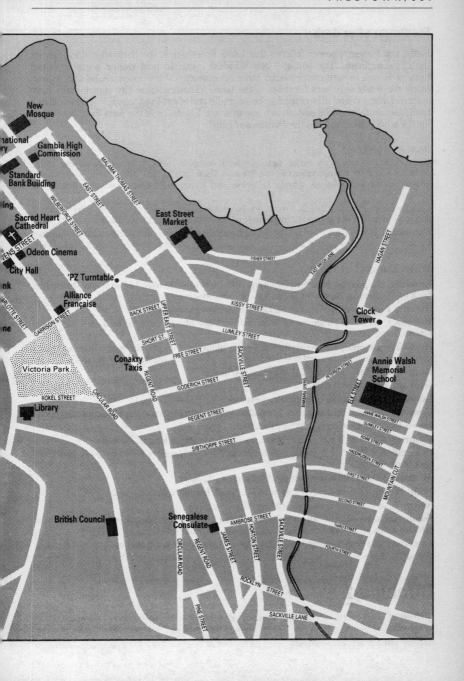

Freetown after dark

Sadly, the frequent power failures that leave Freetown in the dark after dark disrupt the city's **nightlife**. The surest – and blandest – **music and dance** scene is out at Lumley Beach, where many places have generators. Of the **town clubs** that follow, many are really only bars for most of the time. Although some city centre clubs have survived many years, others tend to be sporadic and short-lived venues. Always carry a torch (*tochlait*), or you'll end up in a storm drain. For clubs in the East End, hire a taxi for the whole evening from the *Paramount Hotel*.

BEACH NIGHTLIFE

Lagoonda The country's major entertainment complex, next to the *Cape Sierra Hotel*, includes a perfectly reasonable, air-conditioned disco palace (£3) with recent international sounds and a well-behaved, largely Lebanese and European crowd. Expensive drinks and low energy.

Casino Leone, Lumley Beach. Free entry, but not in beach wear. Lotsa slots – plus blackjack and roulette under the supervision of hopelessly untrained casino girls. Minimum bet £1.

Bintumani Hotel On a Sunday, check out Charlie Haffner and his Freetown Players as they rumble through a few festive numbers. Next time, watch their act at the *Alliance Française*!

TOWN CLUBS

Afroditis, Walpole St. Rear of restaurant club to which Michael Jacksons and Madonnas flock on Wednesday nights for the dance competitions.

Alliance Française, Wilberforce St. Live jazz and reggae at weekends.

Bennan's, corner of Pademba Rd/Bathurst St. More of a shop/bar than a club, but a cool place to hang out.

Brookfields Hotel, Jomo Kenyatta Rd. Sunday night there's a popular happy hour and polite dance; small entry charge and resident band – for a long time the Surviving Survivals.

Burgerland, Siaka Stevens St. Bop before you burger.

Cool and Cozy, Percival St.

Countdown, Sanders St (upper Siaka Stevens).

Cosmos, Kissy Rd. Famous for its "Xmastime" moonlight picnics at the Siaka Stadium pool.

Disco Isabella, Government Wharf (☎26046).

Flamingo Club, 30 Waterloo St. Finding its feet again after a long dormancy.

International Bar, Lightfoot Boston (opposite the *City Hotel*). Nice, wayward reggae bar – very pungent upstairs.

Midnight Mary Bar & Restaurant, Bathurst St.

Night Waves, Liverpool St, off Pademba Rd. Small, friendly club, tiny dance floor.

Storm, Ross Rd, Cline Town. Sometimes offers live music.

Super Kay's, Rawdon St (also a good chop-house). Every Thursday, there's the magnificent "Doctor Kitch Show", after midnight, entry about £1. Spare no efforts.

Tropicana, old Roxy Cinema building, Walpole St. A general hang-out venue as well as a bar.

Wendy's, Howe St.

Directory

Airfreight *DHL*. Delco House, Lightfoot Boston St (☎25800), offers excellent rates worldwide.

Airline offices See box overpage.

American Express Agents are *Yazbeck Tours*, 22, Siaka Stevens St (☎24423/22063).

American cultural centre At the American Embassy, library and free showings of ABC news Mon, Wed, Fri, at noon and Mon, Fri at 3pm. Air-conditioning, cold water, newspapers and magazines.

Banks include: *Barclays Bank of Sierra Leone*, 25–27 Siaka Stevens St (PO Box 12; ☎22501, telex 3220); *Bank of Credit and Commerce International*, 10 Wilberforce St (PMB 359; ☎22790, telex 3322); *Sierra Leone Commercial Bank*, 29–31 Siaka Stevens St (☎25264, telex 3275); *Standard Chartered Bank Sierra Leone Ltd*, 12 Lightfoot Boston St (PO Box 1155; ☎25021, telex 3523).

Bats In their tens of thousands, and bigger than you may be accustomed to, fruit bats hang upside-down on all the best trees by day (sleeping, or squabbling, above the city traffic) and set off in dramatic fashion every evening at sunset, for their feeding sites in the interior of the peninsula. Victoria Park has lately become vile-smelling on account of their guano.

Books European and American titles are somewhat hard to find, though occasionally you'll come across leone-bargains which have been sitting on the shelf a year or two. Try the *Diocesan Bookshop* in Lightfoot Boston St (mostly Christian), the *Government Bookstore* on Wallace Johnson and, by far your best bet, *New Horizons* on Howe St. If you're searching for something, or up at Fourah Bay College, check out the possibly surviving *College Bookshop* (☎27226), traditionally the best in the country.

British Council After a recent major refurbishment, a nice retreat from the heat. Videos, BBC broadcasts, library, events – and a very un-Sierra Leonean café called the *BBC Room*.

Bus departures If you're heading inland on one of the large buses that leave from the main bus station, make sure you're down there in the morning by 6am at the latest. Only first-comers get tickets.

Car Hire Try *Yazbeck's* or *City Travel* (addresses under "Travel Agents", below), or the *Apex Automobile Corporation*, 11 Regent Rd (PO Box 618; ☎24478/24431). *Yazbeck's* do an all-in price for a 4WD vehicle with driver of around £70/day. Or follow up car hire through J. S. Lisk (Damba Rd, north shore of Murray Town, PO Box 1314; ☎31325) who offers a Land Rover for under £60/day (and reminds you of your responsibility to provide the driver's meals). Lastly you might investigate an outfit called *Dad's Car Centre* in Lumley village, which has been recommended.

Cassettes Buy your own tapes from *New Horizons*, and have an LP recorded for less than £1. Try *Aba Tapes* in Goderich St, *Tapes International* in Regent Rd, or another, opposite *Subouya's* in Garrison St.

Cinemas The *Odeon* on Howe St, the slightly better *Roxy* on Walpole and the *Strand* on Waterloo St are the three town centre cinemas. Fuzzy videos are increasingly replacing cellu-loid. And electricity cuts are increasingly closing everything down. If there is a show, there are good opportunities to meet people on the streets outside. If you want Euro-quality cinema and ice-cold AC (take a wrap) check out the night's offering at the *Lagoonda* cinema (£1) at Lumley Beach.

Dentists Top recommendation for Dr Norman Wright, 45 Percival St. Also: Drs M. A. Rekab and R. Holst-Roness, 8 Siaka Stevens St (☎22671), or Dr George B. Morgan, 30A Wallace Johnson St (☎26536).

Doctors The embassies are helpful with suggestions, because medical facilities are gener-ally under strain. In an emergency, however, the Netland Hospital, Motor Main Road, Congo Town is certainly preferable to the Connaught Hospital. A specialist in cardiology and inter-nal medicine is Dr R. H. Eleady-Cole, 1 East St (☎24438). Dr Bernard Frazer, 11 Gloucester St (☎26788) is an excellent, and sympathetic, gynaecologist.

Flight information Talk to the airline. Be sure to reconfirm your booking in any case. Over-booking is endemic.

House of Representatives For a tour of Sierra Leone's parliament (the low, laterite stone building on Tower Hill, designed by Israeli architects in 1960) and the chance to sit in the public gallery, front up to the gate and ask for a Visitor's Pass from the Sergeant-at-Arms.

AIRLINE ADDRESSES

Aeroflot, 18 Wilberforce St (☎23328).

Air Afrique, c/o *UTA*.

Air France, c/o *UTA*.

Air Guinée, Rawdon St, by the *International Bakery*.

Air Mali, 15 Wallace Johnson St (☎24433).

British Airways, 26 Siaka Stevens St (PMB 672; ☎26559, 23050, 23534, telex 3454).

Ghana Airways, 15 Siaka Stevens St (☎24871/23428).

KLM, United States Embassy Building, Walpole St (☎24444/25254).

Nigeria Airways 11 Siaka Stevens St (☎26347/22429).

Sierra Leone Airlines, PO Box 285, 25 Pultney St.

UTA, 12 Wilberforce St (☎26075/6/7).

EMBASSIES AND CONSULATES

Austria (Hon. Consulate) King St, south of Congo Cross.

Belgium (Hon. Consulate) c/o *S.C.O.A.*, 27 Blackhall Rd, Kissy (☎50143/23941).

Côte d'Ivoire 1 Wesley St (☎23983).

Denmark (Hon. Consulate) c/o Standard Bank, Lightfoot Boston St (☎26220/25021).

Egypt *Pademba Laundry*, 37 Percival St (☎22224, telex 3300).

France 13 Lamina Sankoh St (PO Box 510; ☎22477, telex 3238) Mon–Fri 10am–noon; handles visas for Burkina Faso, Central African Republic, Mauritania and Togo. There's a flat fee for most (£6) for a validity of up to three months; thereafter more expensive. Allow 24 hours.

The Gambia 6 Wilberforce St (☎25191); visas valid for stays of up to 30 days processed in 48 hours (fee around £10).

Ghana Percival St (☎23461) Mon–Fri 8am–4pm; visas available within 24 hours, about £20.

Germany Santanno House, 10 Howe St (PO Box 728; ☎22511, telex 3248).

Great Britain Standard Bank Building, Lightfoot Boston St (☎23961–5, telex 3235) Mon–Fri 9am–1pm; mail-holding but no visa service for any other country.

Greece (Hon. Consulate) c/o *P Z*, 24 Wilberforce St (☎23087).

Guinea 4 Liverpool St (☎23080/22331) Mon–Thur 8am–3pm, Fri 8am–noon; visas tend to be issued more easily here than elsewhere. Telexes are sent to Conakry. You may have to supply a letter of introduction from your own embassy. Expect a fee of about £5, and 48 hours. If you fail, they routinely grant visas on the Guinean side

of the Koindu border, in Eastern Province.

Ireland (Hon. Consulate) 8 Rawdon St (☎22017).

Italy 32A Wilkinson Rd (PO Box 749; ☎30995, telex 3456).

Japan (Hon. Consulate), 3 Upper East St (☎26256).

Liberia 30 Brookfields Rd (PO Box 276; ☎40322, telex 3229) Mon–Fri 8am–noon, 2–4pm; you have to present cholera and yellow fever innoculation certificates. Single entry visas for stays up to two months are £5. Multiple entry visas valid one year cost £10. There's a fee for the form too (for US citizens, visas seem to be free).

Mali Old *CFAO* Building, corner of Lightfoot Boston/Howe Sts; the consul is not often in the office, but there's usually someone holding the fort who can be persuaded to issue a visa.

Netherlands (Hon. Consulate) c/o *KLM*, American Embassy Building, Walpole St (☎24444/25254).

Niger Wilkinson Rd (or c/o Côte d'Ivoire embassy).

Nigeria 21 Pultney St (☎36098, telex 3258) Tue–Fri 11am–2pm.; as a rule, you need a ticket out of Nigeria (fee around £12 for a stay up to three months).

Norway (Hon. Consulate) 1 College Rd, Cline Town (☎25124).

Senegal (Hon. Consulate) in a tailor's shop up an alley off Regent Rd.

Sweden (Hon. Consulate) Wilberforce St.

Switzerland PO Box 451, c/o *Freetown Cold Storage*, 14 Howe St.

USA Private Mail Bag, Walpole St (☎26481, telex 3509).

Immigration To extend your visa or visitor's permit, go to the Passport and Immigration Office, 2nd floor, 15 Siaka Stevens St (☎23034). It's normally necessary to register here within 48hrs of arrival. A little "kola" never hurts in this office.

Libraries The Sierra Leone Library (☎23848), corner of Rokel and Gloucester streets, near Victoria Park, is open Mon to Sat 9am–6pm. Libraries also at the British Council and the American Embassy.

Maps First try *New Horizons*, Howe St. The place to look for anything better more detailed than the *Shell* map is the Survey and Lands Department, New England, near *Brookfields Hotel* on Jomo Kenyatta Rd.

Newspapers and magazines The British Council has some of the London dailies, as does the British High Commission. To buy them, check at *New Horizons* department store, Howe St. The *Daily Mail*, 29 Rawdon St, may have some titles too. *West Africa* magazine is fairly widely available and should be sold for the price printed on the cover (unless you want to do a street boy a favour). Copies of *Time* and *Newsweek* are sometimes available too, and every now and then you may be offered an airline's copy of the *Herald Tribune*, if you want one. The main hotels don't have much, though in season the *Mammy Yoko* and *Cape Sierra* have some French news mags.

Pharmacies *City Pharmacy*, at 20 Siaka Stevens St (☎26868) and 2 Regent Rd (☎23838) is Freetown's best. Beware, everywhere, of *very* out-of-date drugs.

Photos *Rainbow Photo*, next to *British Airways* on Siaka Stevens offers good colour printing in 1 or 2 hours at not unrealistic prices. Passport photos from *Photo Centre* on Siaka Stevens St opposite the *Odeon* cinema. They also offer fast colour printing.

Police Police headquarters is in George St (☎25896).

Post office For posting **letters and cards**, the General Post Office on Siaka Stevens St is open Mon–Fri 8am–4.30pm, Sat 8am–2pm. Poste Restante is here, and free, though not renowned for its surety. Items mailed to *American Express* (see separate listing) are only held for clients. Parcels go from the separate **parcels** office on the waterfront, behind the "Basket Market". Rates are low; see "Communications: Post, Phones and Media".

Swimming pools The relatively new, public pool at the Siaka Stevens Stadium is the obvious one, though the city's water supply can't always keep it healthy. *Brookfields Hotel* may be a better bet.

Telephone, telegram and telex Sierra Leone External Telecommunications (SLET) is down on the waterfront, an affable muddle of a place with clocks for different times around the world. Truth is, although they're open 24 hours, even your presence in person doesn't guarantee a quick connection. Bring a friend, or a much-loved pastime. Mid-afternoon seems the best bet. Making a telex from upstairs is a lot swifter and comparable in cost (from around £2). You can receive telexes cheaply here too: the public telex no. is 3210 BOOTH SL.

Theatre venues The *City Hall*, which used to have one of the liveliest stages in Freetown, has been closed to theatre groups by Freetown City Council. "This is not a place of joy" decided the FCC chairman. Freetown now awaits the completion of Bicentenary House, hopefully to be converted from the old Broadcasting ministry on Brookfields Rd, for a suitably large new auditorium. The social commentary of the Tabule Theatre Group is often on stage at the *Waterfront Art Barre*, a big warehouse behind the Metropolitan Police HQ in George St. And there are performances at weekends at the *Alliance Française* restaurant. On Wednedsday nights, upstairs at the *NP Spot* (the petrol station on the corner of Lamina Sankoh/Siaka Stevens streets), you can see Krio plays and comedians. Lastly the *Lagoonda* is the unlikely, though fairly frequent setting for broadly theatrical productions – though prohibitively expensive for the smaller groups to hire.

Tourist office There isn't one, so the next best thing is to visit the Ministry of Tourism and Cultural Affairs itself, down on Government Wharf (☎25950).

Travel agents *Yazbeck Tours*, 22 Siaka Stevens St (PO Box 485; ☎24423/22063, telex 3412) are the best known, and the ones to visit first. They take most credit cards. *Yazbeck's* do a variety of half- and one-day trips around the peninsula, and a few longer ones, though all are dependent on numbers to keep prices realistic – from £10 for a few hours up to £30 for a long day. A competing spin-off of theirs, *IPC Travel*, 19 Siaka Stevens St (PO Box 1434; ☎26244, 23551, telex 348) is worth calling on too. *City Travel*, 14 Rawdon St (☎25493) is recommended, as is *Lion Travel*, 13 Howe St (☎26617), particularly for fiddly air routes round West Africa. *Kontiki Tours*, a French outfit, runs an office at the *Hotel Mammy Yoko* (PO Box 23; ☎31943, telex 3549). If you book a flight through an agent, be sure to reconfirm that reservation with the airline's own booking system.

Bunce Island

Much mentioned but less often visited – and strangely omitted or mis-sited on most maps – **BUNCE ISLAND** (pronounced Buncey) in the Sierra Leone river, is definitely worth a visit if you can find transport. *Yazbeck*'s sometimes offers day trips in the winter season, or you might be lucky on the ferry quay at Kissy, and find a motor boat willing to make the voyage. But beware the distance, over 20km, and make sure the vessel is seaworthy and the fuel, shade and water supplies sufficient. It's physically easier to get to Bunce from the village of PEPEL, on the north bank, from where it's only a couple of kilometres offshore. Pepel itself, however is more than 160km by road from Freetown.

Bunce, the country's first certified historical monument, is looked after by the Sierra Leone Monuments Commission. They kept a caretaker there for several years until his house collapsed and there was no money to rehouse him.

The flat, rocky islet is now deserted. It was first occupied early in the seventeenth century, by British traders in slaves, ivory and camwood – a local timber used to make red dye. They used the much larger Tasso Island, downstream, as an annexe, for farming. As on James Island in the Gambia river, a fort was built on Bunce – and several times rebuilt. It offered only token protection from determined sea attack. Today, the ruins are almost entirely overgrown, covered in creepers and fig trees and rather eerie to wander around.

In the 1780s, Fort Bunce was supplying an average of 3000 **slaves** a year from the interior to Danish traders alone, who sold them to the new American rice plantations of South Carolina. Some of the scattering of cannons lying about have given historians interesting insights into the complicated matrix of Afro-European relations in eighteenth- and early nineteenth-century West Africa. Most are marked GR (for George III). One, a Swedish gun dated 1780, came from a Danish slaver whose captain may have used it to complete a payment. Another, a brass one (stolen in the early 1980s), was dated *AN 2eme FN*, the second year of the French Revolutionary Calendar – 1794 – and was used in the bombardment and total destruction of Freetown and Bunce by the French in that year.

All interesting stuff, once you know it – and so much the better if only the fort and its cannons can be preserved in situ. As things stand, however, a whole team of American scientists and parks' people came over in 1989 to look into the possibilities of making the island into a "historical theme park", so it might be wise to visit soon.

The peninsula beaches

The **beaches** of the Freetown Peninsula are arguably the finest in West Africa, and certainly only those in western Côte d'Ivoire offer any competition. Lumley, the closest to Freetown, is usually the busiest, and one of the less perfect. Of Sierra Leone's five beach **hotels**, the three main ones are on or near Lumley Beach; two others nestle more engagingly on isolated strands further south.

Lumley Beach practicalities

Getting to the beach from downtown Freetown, there are buses to Aberdeen and Lumley village (note: Lumley village is *not* near the hotels) but, more reliably, you can share a taxi from the Cotton Tree to take you the 5km to "Texaco" (the garage of that name at the junction for Lumley village/Aberdeen) from where there are slightly cheaper shared vehicles to Aberdeen and the beach. But unless the heat is overpowering, it's worth walking some of the way, at least from Texaco onwards – about an hour's walk in the unlikely event of your not getting a lift.

At the first roundabout, the *Hotel Bintumani* is up on the right. Continue west and the entrance on the right leads to the triple attraction of *Alex's Beach Bar, George's Spanish Restaurant* and the *Cape Club*, three restaurant hang-outs in ascending order of sophistication. All three have fine secluded settings on Man O'War Bay. *George's* seems particularly popular with the ex-pat community if you're into all that. The small, north-facing beach is sheltered. On the left is the *Hotel Mammy Yoko* (named after the powerful nineteenth-century queen), heavily patronised by French package tourists. There's a row of chichi shops in the foyer and occasional "exhibitions" too; worth passing through at least once to see what's going on.

A second roundabout sends you, to the right, up to Cape Sierra and the hotel of the same name, to the headland **lighthouse**, and to the *Lagoonda* entertainment complex, with its bright lights glittering across Man O'War Bay after sunset. But in front of you starts the great sweep of **LUMLEY BEACH**, dotted with the odd coconut tree, but backed mostly by scrub and grass. In season, there's a cluster of **beach bars** and snack restaurants at the northern end; the oldest and the only one to stay open all year, is *The Venue*, furthest to the south, about 800m down-coast from the *Mammy Yoko*. Drinks aren't expensive, and the food, if you stick to popular lines, isn't bad. The *Seaview*, a little north, has a livelier nightlife – more Sierra Leonean, less "wetman".

The beach here is pleasant, sloping gently, with little undertow and, on occasions, half-pint waves. There are sailboards for hire (about £5/hr) and *Hobie-Cats* (mini catamarans, £10/hr) but no snorkelling worth doing. Late afternoon, the beach road from the hotels down to Lumley village makes a really nice walk, and, if you've got the equipment, an equally good run or cycle ride (it's exactly 5km to Lumley centre). A lift back again should be easy to find.

Single women – lone men too – should watch out, however, as there's a general increase in bag-snatchings and other, preferably-to-be-avoided, encounters on Lumley Beach. Bring nothing of value, and your camera only if you're going to take pictures. Ideally, go in a group. Lumley is the only beach that suffers from these problems to any degree – further south the scene gets better and better.

The southern peninsula beaches

For committed sun and sand devotees, the **southern reaches of the Peninsula** harbour some spectacular shores. If you go as far as TOMBO, there's even an occasional ferry south to SHENGE, which is an attractive alternative means of heading on down the coast.

While it's useful to have wheels of your own for getting around the peninsula, it's not absolutely necessary, so long as you don't mind hitching, or muddling along in whatever "public" transport comes your way. *Poda podas* go down this way several times a day, though not beyond York. You're more likely to score a lift at the roundabout in Lumley village, with weekenders, tourists or expatriates. On weekdays, the sand lorries that scour certain beaches for Freetown's building requirements often give lifts, but be prepared for some walking; it's a **badly (or un-) maintained road**, but pretty for most of its length. Road signs, distances and directions aren't always clear: those included below, unless indicated otherwise, are **road distances from Lumley roundabout**.

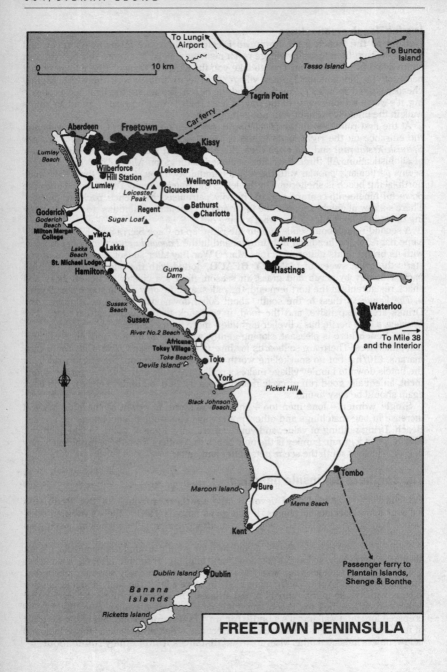

FREETOWN PENINSULA

Goderich

Out of **Lumley village**, past the quaint red-brick St Mary's Church, and Siaka Stevens' distant mansion perched high above, you cross Lumley Creek and pass the apparition of the *Let's Live Hospital*. After Juba beach, which is somewhat cluttered, **GODERICH** (3km from Lumley and 1km off the road), is the first beach, a perfectly good place to see an archetypal West-African event late every afternoon – the **return of the fishing boats** – but not one to go out of your way for if you've had the experience. Goderich village sits behind the yellow kilometre of steeply shelving sand.

Lakka

From here on, the coast road steadily deteriorates. In places the tar surface gives up completely; if you're driving, beware some dastardly potholes. A sign (4km) for the "Milton Margai Training College" indicates one access to the first really wonderful beach, **LAKKA BEACH**, which consists of a pair of long, gently shelving bays punctuated by a miniscule, rocky peninsula, two-thirds of the way down. There's little to spoil it at present. At the far north end the bay curves to face the south, beneath a riot of vegetation. Less than a kilometre south along the beach from here is the *YMCA*'s seaside branch. And beyond the rocky promontory, the second bay crescents down towards Hamilton, with a cascade of coconut jungle behind it and the select *St Michael Lodge* at its southern end.

If you don't get down to Lakka beach from "Milton Margai", continue, past the ancient colonial **Adonkia police station**, to Lakka junction (8km: if you pass the wretched-looking Lakka Isolation Hospital for TB and leprosy victims, you'll know you've gone too far). Lakka village is just down here, the beach itself ten minutes' walk away. The *YMCA* **cottages** are 2.2km (not *miles* as signed) from the junction, back *north* along a really rough dirt track behind the beach. The place appears hardly ever used, though if you talk to David and Fred at the Freetown "Y" they insist it's always necessary to book (very reasonable rates). Decent washing and toilet facilities, what looks like electricity, four-bedded rooms and a fridge in the kitchen/dining room, but no cooker (three stones available), make it a well-organised hideaway, and the resident family of caretakers seem to look after it. Regrettably the whole area surrounding is rather barren, but the beach makes a nice clean sweep right in front, and the alluring rocky cove at the northern end, with its fringe of greenery, isn't too far to stroll (less than 1km).

Back at the lower end of Lakka village, close to the rocky peninsula that divides the beach, there's a **campsite** and picnic area, though nowhere you could leave a tent untended. *St Michael Lodge* (main access road 1km past Lakka junction), is a low-key, clubby sort of place in the *Equatel* chain, right on the beach among the palms (around £50/70 HB, bookable through *Kontiki Tours*: see Freetown "Listings"). If you're splashing out, go for one of the more secluded bungalows on the beach, rather than the newer ones around the gardens.

The hamlet of HAMILTON lies on a headland, a kilometre south of the hotel. There's a small cove here, and a path to four kilometres of straight beach and rough seas, terminating in the mouth of Sussex River. There appears to be no vehicle access to this beach. Backed by scrub and mangrove, it's where the sand lorries come, and is not desperately attractive.

River No.2

The main road, meanwhile, climbs through the foothills, past the GUMA DAM turn-off/checkpoint (14km – see box) and down to SUSSEX (16km). There's another **rocky cove** at Sussex, and a pleasant beach a kilometre further at BAWBAW, but most people head on, close to the shore, to **RIVER NO.2** (19km) and the much-hyped beach of the same name. This is magnificent, Rousseau-esque country – dense, green jungle hills rising steeply behind a beach of brilliant white sand, constantly modified and redesigned by the River No.2 (Guma River) which flows behind and around it, and whose headwaters are stemmed by the Guma Dam, a few kilometres inland and 300 metres above. No.2 beach, however, while great to look at, has unstable swimming conditions, and a very steep shelf. On weekends in season, and on public holidays, it also gets busy, with "car park attendants", food stalls, even crafts, set up among the village houses behind.

GUMA DAM AND THE PENINSULA INTERIOR

Much of the interior of the Freetown peninsula is a **forest reserve**, a remarkably wild area so close to Freetown and the other nineteenth-century settlements. No road, or even established footpath, crosses the range of mountains from west to east. For some adventurous, but not too life-and-limb-risking **trail-blazing**, one or two possibilities do exist.

One potential trail, **from River No.2 beach to Hastings**, involves a climb of about 500m in just over 2km as the crow flies, and a descent of the same order to the head of a 2.5km footpath, which brings you down to the Freetown road 1.5km northwest of Hastings. You'd need a compass for this, and the 1:50,000 map of the peninsula, at least. The traverse follows stream beds on each side, through dense rainforest, to a saddle over the top. Keep to the lowest, southwest–northeast route. The starting point on the western side is a footpath that starts 400m east of the bridge over the Guma river, about 2.5km east of the turn-off for River no.2 beach.

Another possibility would be to try a hike northeast from Hamilton, up the great, tree-filled bowl of the Sussex river valley, over the **"Sugar Loaf Gap"** (600m altitude) and down to the village of Regent.

The wildest parts of the peninsula are in the **far south**, in the fragmented bulge of green-swathed mountains around **Picket Hill** (at 886m the highest point on the peninsula). But if you're thinking of hiking around in this region, beware of winding river valleys and confusing topography.

Less ambitiously, make a start in the **Guma dam** area. You need a permit to visit the site of Guma dam and reservoir, which is easily obtained from the 4th floor of the Guma Building, opposite the French Embassy in Lamina Sankoh St, Freetown (small fee). You'll have to make your own way to the dam – works vehicles go up there very infrequently. But you can get transport to the major checkpoint on the main road, from where, if you're wheel-less, you can walk easily enough up the well-maintained six-kilometre track through the jungle to the dam. Up here you're surrounded by impressive highland forest and a galaxy of bird and insect life. There's a picnic site and car park, and plenty of opportunity for local exploration, though, as yet, no trail for the obvious walk round the perimeter of the lake (8km along the water's edge, if you manage it). An advantage of making your way here on foot is the chance to return to sea level **down the course of River No.2**, a hike down a clear trail of little more than two kilometres. There's the strong possibility too (particularly at weekends in season), of finding a canoe at the creekhead below, to take you out to the coast and the beach (otherwise a 2.5-kilometre walk back along the main road). *Yazbeck's Tours* offers this as a day trip.

The **northeastern edge of the peninsula**, north of the Hill Station–Hastings road, is mostly scrubby, hilly country, and the heartland of nineteenth-century settlement – the "mountain villages". The villages along the road – REGENT, BATHURST, CHARLOTTE – and those on the way north, down to Fourah Bay College and Freetown – GLOUCESTER and LEICESTER – are agreeably pastoral and much more comfortable than the humid capital. There are *poda podas* up here from the city, and it makes a good day to walk between villages and then taxi down again. For breathtaking **views**, when the air is clear, climb **Leicester Peak** (593m), just south of Leicester. It's a steep thirty-minute hike to the top.

Toke

While at low tide you can get across the river from No. 2 beach to the much longer stretch of **TOKE BEACH**, you're then stuck until the next low, unless you walk the 3km or so to Toke village to find the track up to the main road.

A kilometre off Toke beach, **Devils Island** is reputed to be a meeting place of male *Poro* society members – which doesn't appear to dissuade tour organisers from offering the occasional boat trip there (see the box on p.682 for more details on secret societies).

Toke beach (27km) has, among a number of private chalets and villas, the last, latest, and most enticing, of the resort hotels, *Africana Tokey Village*. On a marvellous stretch of safe beach, where the forest comes right to the sands, the *Africana Toke*y is a French-run, largely French-patronised "hôtel village" of *style créole* raised bungalows, around a large, *style coloniale* villa. Half-board prices are similar to *St Michael Lodge*. It's worth remembering, if you're planning a stay here, that the drive into Freetown takes at least an hour.

York and Black Johnson

Four kilometres beyond Toke junction, you come to the pretty village of YORK (31km) at the mouth of Whale River creek. There's an **old fort** (at one time a rest house) on the other side of the village, with glorious views. York would be worth perseverance as a place to stay for a few days. From here south, all semblance of surfaced road ceases, and transport becomes very difficult.

If you're fairly self-sufficient, and don't expect to get back anywhere the same day, you could walk on to **Black Johnson beach** (36km), on Whale Bay, five hilly kilometres round the creek from York. You might also find a boat to take you the relatively short distance across the creek. Palm-fringed, remote and quite undeveloped, with clear sea, Black Johnson is an excellent area for snorkelling or diving.

Kent and the Banana Islands

At the southern extremities of the peninsula, and off the main dirt road, are **BURE** (48km) and **KENT** (52km), both of which have excitingly untouristed beaches several kilometres long. Kent's reputation for sharks in the water and cannibals inland is worth bearing in mind, though the former are the more likely contemporary worry, and even then rarely encountered. The forested MAROON ISLAND, just 300m from the shore, lies between Bure and Kent beaches. The main point of coming down to Kent, though, is to find a boat across to the **BANANA ISLANDS** 5km offshore. Prepare yourself for some vigorous bargaining. DUBLIN island and RICKETTS island are joined by a causeway and have villages of the same names at opposite ends connected by an eight-kilometre footpath. Dublin has a couple of small beaches (limpid water and some coral) on its northwest coast: Ricketts is steeper (233m high) and more densely forested. Neither has any real facilities, so take supplies and adaptability. MESMEHEUX, uninhabited, lies south west, just off Ricketts' shore.

Back on the mainland, east of Kent, on the peninsula's south-facing coastline, there's a chain of **coves and small bays**. The enterprising owner of the *Old Roots New Seeds* restaurants in Freetown, Kofi Robinson, is planning an innovative, travellers' retreat at **MAMA BEACH**. If you coincide with the ferry departure from **TOMBO** (about twice a week), you could also make your way from the peninsula to SHENGE (see p.681). The ferry calls at the spotless PLANTAIN ISLANDS.

Heading **back to Freetown or Lumley Beach** from this far south, it's quicker to make, with or without your own wheels, for WATERLOO (20km past the turn-off for Bure and Kent), where you can pick up the reasonably surfaced highway into Freetown.

THE NORTH

The **Northern Province**'s best specific attraction is **Outamba-Kilimi National Park**. Pressed around the foot of the Kuru Hills, and hard up against the Guinean border, the park is the only one in this part of West Africa, and worth the effort to visit, even without your own vehicle.

Heading northwest to Conakry, across the creek heads, the diversions are limited, though **Port Loko** is a pleasant stop, split by tumbling streams and positioned on steep slopes above Port Loko creek. It was a strategic town in the eighteenth century, when there was a significant Portuguese-speaking community. Loko slaves, from three days march to the east, were shipped from here to Bunce island. For ornitholgists with their own transport, the creeks and flats to the west offer exceptional birding.

The provincial capital of the north, **Makeni**, is animated and relatively well provided, with a famously good market, but until you head beyond Makeni for the **far north** and the town of **Kabala**, the scenic and cultural distractions aren't numerous. From Kabala, there's some exciting exploration to be done on wonderful mountainous backroads, including the trail to the top of **Mount Bintumani**. The route to Faranah in eastern Guinea, via **Falaba**, is tough on vehicles, but recommended, and is the obvious course if you're making for Mali.

Outamba-Kilimi National Park

The joint **Outamba-Kilimi National Park** was set up in 1980 after the International Union for the Conservation of Nature and Natural Resources singled the region out for urgent protection. Sensitive work with the people of the Tambakha Chiefdom (or at least with their paramount chief), led to agreements to cede land for the park and give up hunting rights. Since then, there's been steady progress, with major Peace Corps involvement and the Worldwide Fund for Nature supporting the energetic work of the people on the ground.

The park's thousand-odd square kilometres cover two great slabs of untouched, uninhabited, undulating **savannah and jungle**, in the basins of the Great and Little Scarcies rivers. Here lives a rich diversity of animal species, including most of the large West African savannah mammals (lions and giraffes excepted), and featuring a solid population of **chimpanzees** (perhaps the biggest concentration in West Africa), and twelve other primates, amomg them **red colobus, black-and-white colobus** and **sooty mangabey**. In the deepest sections of forest there are rare and scattered **bongo antelope** – magnificent, heavily built animals. And in the overgrown water margins there are **pygmy hippos**. But while you're almost bound to see the common variety, their distant pygmy relatives are secretive and rarely glimpsed. The population of **elephants** has decreased – by the worst estimates, from 500 in 1981 to less than 100 in 1990. Poachers are occasionally brought to book, only to be fined derisory sums by a legal system unconcerned with the protection of the country's natural heritage.

Happily, **birdlife**, in an ecosystem as fat and self-sustaining as this one, is prolific and rewarding. Reptiles and insects, too, are dazzlingly in evidence.

THE TAMBAKHA CHIEFDOM

The **Tambakha chiefdom** (which formerly occupied most of Outamba-Kilimi), is named after the *Tamba* – "leader" – of a successful nineteenth-century slave revolt. Slave-owning Susu were massacred by their captives, who moved to this region and set up their own, very mixed, kingdom. Susu, the slaves' customary language, was retained.

Practicalities

Few people in Sierra Leone know much about Outamba-Kilimi. Freetown tour operators have yet to run any trips and, for the moment, the place is the preserve of occasional independent visitors and volunteers on leave. **Getting there** in the dry season is a minor slog, but presents no special hassles. After the rains have set in, however, the region is more or less cut off, and access in anything except your own high-clearance 4WD vehicle (ideally with a winch) may take days. At present, **Outamba**, in the Little Scarcies basin in the east, is somewhat developed while **Kilimi**, along the Great Scarcies to the west, is quite undeveloped and more or less inaccessible.

From MAKENI, public transport takes from three to five hours to cover the 85km to **KAMAKWIE**, the closest town to the park. It's an interesting and scenic trip – though a terrible road at the best of times – passing from Loko through Temne to Limba country, with thatched roof compounds along the way and an increasingly remote feel despite the new park-direction signposts. There doesn't seem to be any commercial **accommodation** in Kamakwie – though, by the way, there is a relatively good hospital – and Peace Corps volunteers will likely put you up if you contribute.

If you've time left in the day, you could complete the last 32km to the park camp, but if you have to walk it all, it'll take a good nine hours. You should find transport most days to the park entrance at KOTO. This last stretch of the journey involves a small, unreliable, ferry across the broad, brown Little Scarcies River. Here, with exotic fan palms appearing on the scene, you're in a territory which has more in common with Guinea.

Once arrived at the main **visitors' camp** (5km from the entrance) you've got it made. Out here in the deep bush, the accommodation of four full-sized tents, tin roofed and mounted on concrete, with camp beds and bedding, lanterns and shared showers, is remarkably comfortable and excellent value (less than £2 per person per night). You'll need to bring your own **food supplies**; there's nothing available on the site, but kitchen utensils and stoves are provided. It's all kept up with great dedication.

As for **getting around Outamba**, assuming you've arrived without your own wheels, you'll have to hope for some drives with park staff: given the level of enthusiasm, this shouldn't be a wait in vain. Several trails lead through the forest and five-metre elephant grass, but accessibility – and visibility – are best after the dry season burns, which take place in January and February. Wildlife is at its most concentrated at this time, too, as the animals gather close to water sources and rivers. In the dry season, you might make a stab at climbing one of the hills dotted over the southern part of the park. **Mame peak** and **Tambara** (at 405m, the highest) rise above the south bank of the Little Scarcies.

MAMUNTA-MAYOSO NATURE RESERVE

When Outamba-Kilimi was conceived, a much smaller patch of land, in a more vulnerable locality, was also set aside for conservation purposes. However, the "reserve" on the swampy south bank of the Rokel or Seli River, 20km from Magburaka, southwest of the Makeni–Sefadu highway, was never realised and only its unsuitability for farming distinguishes it. Access is difficult, even in the dry season, though you might try getting to the village of MASAGBUL, which is approximately where the reserve begins. Latest reports suggest that attempts are being made to delimit and consolidate Mamunta-Mayoso.

Makeni

Like Sierra Leone's other provincial centres, **MAKENI** can make few credible touristic claims. It was once the terminus of the northern branch railway line, and quite a boomtown in the 1920s. Today, though still a busy **Temne** trade exchange, the momentum

has largely vanished, and you're not going to want to spend more than a night here – unless you're one of the sizeable volunteer community (many of them working in Makeni's once-vaunted education and welfare sectors) who, on the whole, rather like it. Its proximity to Freetown – under five hours on a good day – and central location are plus points to be sure.

Making do in Makeni: arrival and places to stay

Off the main highway, a spider's web of dust-clouded streets focuses noisily on what used to be a roundabout at the centre of town. The big four-minareted mosque is here, and a number of two- and three-storeyed colonial shop fronts. Most vehicles drop you at the downtown turntable, or in the lorry park itself. If you're anywhere near the point of collapse on arrival (and Makeni is *hot*), then don't carry heavy luggage far. Hire a *bohboh* with a wheelbarrow and let him take your gear to your chosen refuge.

Most travellers passing through Makeni will want to stay at the **Peace Corps rest house**, on the east side of town, which, if there's room, has a fixed rate for other volunteers and ordinary travellers. There's little space, however, and if you find it full, check out the brand new *Thinka Hotel*, on Ekes Road, or the less attractive *Gbetgbo Hotel* on Freetown Road. Both have restaurants, rooms for £3–5 and standby generators. The *Mena Hills Motel*, a couple of kilometres out of town, on the north side of the highway to Freetown, advertises rooms at £2–5 according to size and a minimum of £1 for "Short Stay". Electricity and running water aren't on offer. Still, the cleanish, bare rooms are better than nothing, in an emergency.

Making the most of Makeni: nightlife, the market and around town

Arriving in Makeni after dark, you might do just as well to settle into one of Makeni's **nightspots** and wait for events to dispose matters for you. At any of them you may run into moneyed Sierra Leoneans, Lebanese relaxers and clusters of American, British and German volunteers. Most favoured of the music bars for several years has been the *Shady Rest Bar* (a.k.a. *BP Disco*), where a healthy supply of electricity to pump the petrol also keeps the *Stars* cold and the music loud. The *Mobil Disco* is much the same (there's not much of a living to be made from selling price-controlled fuel), though currently less active. You might also call in on *Disco Kays*, behind the park. *The* place to go, however, is the *Flamingo*, which has a down-to-earth reputation and lots of energy. A popular evening hang-out for a drink is *Kargbo's Bar* on the eastern side of town near the old station. And alongside, *Usman* sets up an excellent "steak sandwich" operation every night. There are more of these up by the *Metro* **cinema** (passable movies every once in a while) and a scattering of OK chop-houses – *Sessay's* and the *Baffa* are close by.

By day, Makeni's best asset is the large and heaving **market**, from which it's practically impossible to escape without buying something. The huge attraction is the availability of reams of beautiful *gara* cloth, in a multiplicity of blue and green hues, and a huge variety of weights and finishes. With conscientious bargaining you can buy for really good prices: work at it. A pair of the standard two-yard lengths (known as a double *lapa*) normally costs around £10. Beaten damask *gara*, with a lustrous shine and heavy patterned weave, is the most expensive.

If, for whatever reason, you're spending a day or two in town, you might want to make for the higher quarters of town to the southwest, where a "Country Club" and tennis courts have been under construction (and the subject of much local rumour) for some years. From the top of **Mana Hill** there are some good, clear weather, views. This 2.5-kilometre walk from the centre of town (left after the Methodist church, then follow your nose) climbs to a couple of hundred metres above it. The hill is topped by an enormous granite boulder, also climbable: lower down, another one, weathered away underneath, threatens to topple at any moment – as it has for decades. The hill, like the other **Wusum Hill** on the north side of Makeni (climbable from the Kabala road), is the site of secret society meetings. Circles of stones testify to reserved areas. But there are also crosses among the rocks and grass. You should approach with caution to avoid causing offence, but people do regularly come for walks up here.

Heading north

Moving on to Kabala by *poda poda* there's fast tarmac stretching as far as FADUGU, and thereafter a wide graded laterite route through beautiful scenery – parts of it hilly and forested – with villages every few kilometres. Beyond Makeni, too, the architectural interest improves greatly, with small steeply conical houses of the Temne pattern, topped with an extra tuft of thatch and an entrance lobby at the front. Praying circles are all over, though sometimes, as reserved areas, they're used for drying rice or other grain.

Kabala

Ringed by a circle of hills, the highest of which leap, bold and bare, right above it to the west, **KABALA** is an attractive "highland" town with a really nice, laid-back atmosphere. The town splits roughly into two: on the way in from Makeni, the town centre is dominated by the Koranko people; across the stream on the northwest side of town, the district is more Limba. Which is only to characterise a fairly jumbled townscape – there are no real markers.

Indeed, the most noticeable Koranko element in town is probably the **ronko** cloth house, which is beyond the stream on the left. *Ronko* cloth, made by the Koranko, is deep rusty red country cloth, patterned in black block prints, sewn together from narrow strips, soft and durable and formerly vested with bullet-proof powers (a quality that's not been tested for some years). You'll always see newly dyed cloth spread out to dry (though most often it's imported cotton sheet, rather than homemade) and an assortment of garments, blankets and hats for sale. The hats are particularly nice, pillbox style, with small fringes and a tassle, and bound to become fashionable in Japan or Britain in the very near future.

Check out a couple of places if you want to **stay** in Kabala. The Peace Corps Rest House is one, and usual conditions apply for non-volunteers. The other, slightly more expensive and worth a try if the PC House is full, is the Koinadugu Integrated Agricultural Development Project (KIADP) Rest House. Kabala is small, and there's not a lot in the **restaurant** line. There's always a set of chop stalls on the north side of the market and *Anty Kay's*, behind the mosque, is good for sit-down chop, until about noon, and tea on occasions. After dark, **pleasures** are provided by *Lon's Kort* (a flashy place, for Kabala, incorporating disco, restaurant and many young blades), the *Sonfon Club*, with video shows and bar, *F.O.'s* south of the market for cold beer, and *Willy's Bar* (the *Africana*) which, as with *Kargbo's* in Makeni, is the main Peace Corps hangout. *Barclays Bank* at the turntable does foreign exchange.

The New Year's picnic

If you can manage it, be in Kabala for **New Year's Day**. It's now nationally famous for the **mass picnic** that takes place on the gaunt inselberg summit at the edge of the Wara Wara range, west of town. No-one seems to know how this started, but several hundred people – most of Kabala's youth and half Sierra Leone's volunteers – spend New Year's afternoon up there, eating, drinking and generally getting down. It's a steep climb, but not difficult or long: go in a group and take the makings of a party with you. Other than on New Year's Day, these heights are usually deserted, but always worth the hike up.

Lake Sonfon and the Bumbuna Falls

If you'd like to see **Lake Sonfon**, up in the Sula range south of Kabala, make for the small town of ALIKALIA, 64km from Kabala, approached from a turn-off on the Kabala–Makeni road, at MAKAKURA, 9km south of Kabala. You may find a guide at a closer village en route, but Alikalia, as the largest rural centre around, is a good bet. The lake (the largest in the interior) is 25km up the Pampana River valley.

Organised trips from Freetown, to the Seli river's **Bumbuna Falls**, 20km north of Bumbuna on the west side of the Sula hills, are not wildly impressive for the "falls" themselves, which really render the term "rapids" superfluous. But the area is mightily picturesque and the hills induce an extra twinge of excitement because of the presence of alluvial **gold** in them – rather a lot of it in the Tonkolili River and its tributaries south of Bumbuna, and near the village of YARE, west of Lake Sonfon. *Kontiki Tours* have their own **camp** near the Bumbuna falls, and this is currently one of the few trips to the interior being offered. The easiest approach is from Makeni and MAGBURAKA.

Onwards from Kabala: transport out and the Guinean border

For **transport out of Kabala**, vehicles for Makeni and other points south gather by the turntable near *Barclays Bank*. Vehicles for Falaba and the Guinea border road, and Koinadugu and Firawa (for Mount Bintumani) assemble, more irregularly, along the street on the northwest side of the market. You could also check by F. B. Marah's shop near the mosque. For northbound transport, generally, you need to be up and about very early. If you'd rather be out on the road, walk out at least as far as the Falaba-Koinadugu fork before waiting for a lift.

From Kabala to Falaba, the road is mostly in reasonable condition and there's transport most days. The route is pretty to begin with, with rocky massifs on the left. En route, there's an excellent chop house at the junction in SINKUNIA, 42km out of Kabala. Falaba itself shows very little signs these days of its eighteenth-century origins as a heavily fortified Yalunka (Jalonke) town, founded by non-Muslim exiles from the Guinean state of Fouta Djalon. In the 1880s the people of the town, under siege by Samory Touré's *Sofa* army, committed mass suicide by blowing themselves up with their powder store, rather than submit to the enforcement of Islam.

The best day for transport to the **Guinean border** at GBERIA-FOTOMBU (a.k.a KWENU) is Sunday, though you may get as far as LIMBAYA, 10km past Falaba, from where the road to the border climbs steeply and rockily for another 15km. Gberia-Fotombu is a largely Fula town. There's no hotel – though there are a few chop-houses – and if you arrive late in the day, you'll probably end up staying at the police station (a nice bunch).

Transport the eleven kilometres to the village of HÉRÈMAKONO (the Guinean post) is fairly rare. In the late nineteenth century, Hérèmakono was a *Sofa* base within the British "sphere of influence". The British persuaded them to leave and the French moved in, uninvited. If it looks like you'll have to walk across, it's worth knowing that a couple of vehicles a day usually run from Hérèmakono to Faranah, along a bad earth road that's being improved.

THE KORANKO

More than most of Sierra Leone's ethnic groups, the **Koranko** of the northeast have maintained a fairly distinct cultural integrity. Koranko is a Mande language, very close to the most mainstream Mande tongue, the Malinké of Guinea and Mali, and only distantly related to the more peripheral Mende of southern Sierra Leone. The Koranko are great **rice** farmers, filling the valleys with an emerald green carpet, and they grow a fair amount of **cotton**, too, for their famous *ronko* cloth.

The Koranko are also **hunters** of some repute. Traditionally, they belonged to totemic **clans**, known as "houses", called by a "surname" and each symbolised by taboo animals that were never eaten. For example, the Fona clan's totem was the royal python, the Mensereng had the monitor lizard and the lion, the Kamara's were the hippo and the chimpanzee, the Kagbo's and Sise's the crocodile and the Mara's (the most distinguished) was the leopard; not that all these animals were commonly eaten by members of other clans.

Today, an increasing contingent of the Koranko community is **Muslim**, and the old clan divisions are less significant. But the **Bundu** society initiations (*Biriye* in Koranko) are still important for young people in rural areas, with girls in seclusion for a few weeks' instruction during the rains and boys going off in the dry season. Circumcision and clitoridectomy usually take place at the same time. Another pre-Islamic activity that's pursued with enthusiasm is the making of *kamakuli* – **bamboo wine**. It's not always available, but you should try to get a taste if you're in the territory for a few days; talk to the youth of the village rather than the big men.

Mount Bintumani

Midway between Kabala and SEFADU in the east, **Mount Bintumani** in the Loma Mountains is the highest peak in Sierra Leone, and the highest mountain in West Africa, west of Mount Cameroon. The mountain is best climbed at the beginning or end of the rainy season (either in Apr–May or Oct–Nov). Dry season dust will limit visibility. Whenever you go, it can be cool at night near the summit (1945m) and you should take something warm, as well as a sleeping bag.

There are no tarred roads nearby, and **climbing Bintumani** of necessity involves some trekking from the end of the nearest motorable road. Kabala is probably the easiest base from which to go. You need transport to FIRAWA (51km), from where a five-day hike will get you to the top and back again. The small town of KOINADUGU (28km) is the most likely destination of vehicles heading this way, but your best chance of a vehicle right through to Firawa is Tuesday, when there's a major market in BUMBUKORO (misplaced on most maps) 22km along the road, from which vehicles often go on to Firawa afterwards. Of course, if you're taking a couple of weeks or more to climb Bintumani, you may want to walk the whole way from Kabala. Koinadugu's hill-top location and venerable silk-cotton trees make it a great place to stay. YIRAFILAIA BADALA (36km) is another nice village, located above a rocky bend of the Seli river. There's a sandy beach, wonderful for swimming, fishing and washing clothes. Just beware of the current if you're here at the height of the rains.

All the villages along the Bintumani trail are Koranko (for whom the mountain is **Loma Mansa** – King of the Lomas) and you'll find charming hospitality. If you want to stay in a village, ask to speak to the headman, who'll arrange overnight accommodation for you. It's important to carry some **basic provisions** – rice, palm oil, onions, salt and pepper – as supplies along the way can be short, especially in the "hungry season" before the rice harvest (August and September). Don't worry about cooking, this will be fixed for you; naturally you'll be expected to share some food. For snacks on the move (don't forget most people only cook once a day) take fruit and groundnut or benniseed cakes from Kabala. Take a supply of the freshest kola you can find, as well. This is the traditional gift in return for hospitality, though you can give leones instead. You may also want to give kola to the woman who cooks for you.

After Firawa, you'll need **a guide** to find your way down the maze of footpaths to **BANDA-KARAFAIA**, about 19km distant. This day's hike is where the trip becomes exciting and the scenery spectacular. There are usually several former students in Firawa who know some English (assuming your Koranko is limited) and are more than willing to hike up the mountain with you. There's a minimum wage, which you ought to check in Kabala before setting off, of around £1 per day, plus food. You may also want to hire a hunter (well why not?), in which case you should bring a stash of cartridges as payment. The legality of this is uncertain, however, even if the quantity of game in the hills isn't in doubt. Be aware that Mount Bintumani itself is a nature reserve.

At Banda-Karafaia, you have to sign the headman's **register** of people climbing the mountain. A cash gift is expected for this service; while there's no fixed fee, it will be made clear if it's too small. About 13km further is YALEMBE, a small village at the foot of the mountain, where you hire a guide for the final ascent.

THE SOUTH

The frustrating thing about **southern Sierra Leone**, as along much of West Africa's southwest-facing coast, is that the **coast** itself tends to be indistinct and often miles from the nearest road. The sea lies beyond vast expanses of mud, marsh and mangroves, only accessible down narrow ridges of slightly higher ground between the maze of creeks.

Sierra Leone's south coast looks in danger of separating entirely from the mainland and, indeed, **Sherbro** (with its town of **Bonthe**) and the **Turtle Islands** are already adrift in the Atlantic. Southeast of Sherbro, the surf hits a tremendous, unbroken **beach**, which stretches 110km to the little port of **Sulima** on the Liberian border. Backed by small fishing villages, this is a highly recommended week-long walk.

Inland, much of the south is sticky, palm- and bush-specked grassland, and on the whole makes for uninspiring travel. But the higher, forest areas are another matter. In the southeast, the hills come to within 50km of the sea and here, south of the provincial capital, **Bo**, there are opportunities for some of the country's most rewarding exploring. The trip to **Tiwai Island Primate Reserve**, blanketed in rainforest in a crook of the surging **Moa River**, is impressive and hugely enjoyable.

Bo

Long established as the most important town in the colonial "Protectorate" of up-country Sierra Leone, **BO** was overtaken in size some years ago by the burgeoning diamond-fed Sefadu-Koidu conurbation in the northeast. Nevertheless, and even now that the railway on which it depended for decades has gone, the town remains a relatively thriving centre. With reliable electricity, a chaotic (but not particularly interesting) market, and a number of places to stay, eat and amuse yourself, Bo holds a big, spread-out population of fifty or sixty thousand people – mostly Mende, but with a heavy Krio presence, a sizeable Lebanese community still, and the usual, noticeable, European and American volunteers and development workers.

Bo's best known institution, the **"Chief's School"** (now Bo School) north of the old railway yards, was founded in 1906, for the education of chiefs' sons from the Protectorate. It was a curious amalgam of English public school, and extended traditional instruction, intended to lend weight to the position of the chiefs, though whom the British ruled the country. The boys, divided into "houses" of Liverpool, Manchester, London and Paris, were expected to wear the customary dress of their fathers, learn improved farming and building methods, adopt "good manners" and speak "good English". The use of Krio was forbidden. Fees, of £10 a year, were extraordinarily high. The school, still a prestigious government-run establishment, now takes a wider cross-section of boarders, but the elitism and patronage remain.

Coming into Bo from Freetown, the highway is a couple of kilometres from the centre. Local Bo town taxis now operate on fixed routes. On the way in, you pass the wasteland of the old railway yards and station on the left, and skirt the town's only (indescribably ugly) landmark, the **Clock Tower**.

Bo basics

Among convenient **places to stay**, *Denby's Hotel* is cheap and dirty and, beneath it, the aptly-named *Babylon Disco* often bangs away all night. Try, by preference, the *Black and White Restaurant* in Kissi Town Road, on the north side of Bo (good if you're coming in from Makeni). The agreeable manager here is knowledgeable about the area and can help you with travel plans. Nice rooms, with AC, go for around £7–10 per night. There's a couple of other, cheaper lodgings, also along Kissi Town Rd. A fifth hotel, the *Southern Motel*, is well away from the centre on Kawusu Street on the south side of Bo.

There's a fair variety of **places to eat and drink**. The cafeteria opposite *Choithram's Supermarket* does good *plasas* – and chicken stew for well under £1. And the supermarket is a place to find food supplies you're unlikely to get elsewhere except Freetown. The *Black and White* offers reasonable western food. Out on Bo By-pass Road, check out *Mohamed Jalloh's Restaurant*, on the south side of the road. Two other eating spots, *The Villa* and *Bachelors*, have more expensive pretensions.

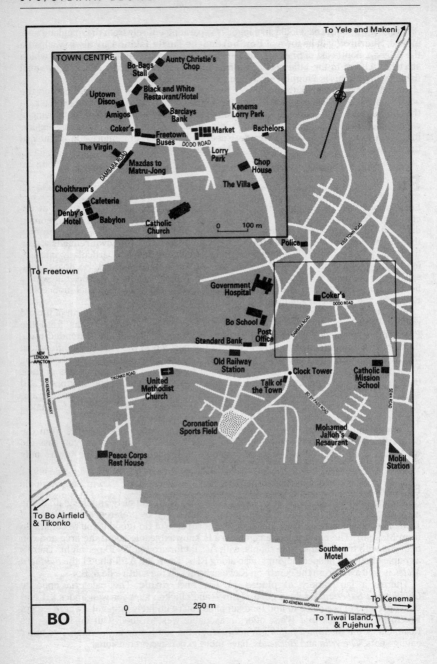

To Yele and Makeni

TOWN CENTRE

Bo-Bags
Stall

Aunty Christie's
Chop

Uptown
Disco

Black and White
Restaurant/Hotel

Amigos

Barclays
Bank

Kenema
Lorry Park

Coker's

Freetown
Buses

Market

Bachelors

DODO ROAD

The Virgin

Lorry
Park

DAMBARA ROAD

Mazdas to
Matru-Jong

Chop
House

The Villa

Choithram's

Cafeteria

Denby's
Hotel

Babylon

Catholic
Church

0   100 m

Police

To Freetown

ESS TOWN ROAD

Government
Hospital

Coker's

DODO ROAD

DAMBARA ROAD

Bo School

Post
Office

Standard Bank

NEW
LONDON
JUNCTION

Old Railway
Station

Clock Tower

Catholic
Mission
School

BO-KENEMA HIGHWAY

TIKONKO ROAD

United
Methodist
Church

Talk of
the Town

BO BY-PASS ROAD

SEWA ROAD

Coronation
Sports Field

Mohamed
Jalloh's
Resaurant

Peace Corps
Rest House

Mobil
Station

To Bo Airfield
& Tikonko

Southern
Motel

KAMUSU STREET

0   250 m

BO-KENEMA HIGHWAY

To Kenema

BO

To Tiwai Island,
& Pujehun

After dark, *Coker's* bar is the hang-out on the corner preferred by Peace Corps volunteers. Ma Coker often has nice kola nut/indigo cloth for sale. Among the Bo "nightclubs" (leaving aside the *Babylon*), you could check out *The Virgin*, *The Uptown Disco*, *Talk of the Town* and *Amigos*, all marked on our map for easy access. More vicarious pleasures can be had at any of the three cinemas. The *Rio*, near *Coker's*, has nightly features.

There's nothing of note to see in Bo, though having written off its **market**, the area is pretty wild, always crowded and sense-assaultingly smelly and noisy. You'll find limited crafts, deadmens' clothes, trinkets, *gara* and stacks of fruit and vegetables. Leather goods are available, too, if generally in short supply. Look near the *Black and White*. The slot-together, neck purses known as "Bo bags" (though in Kabala as "Kabala bags") are cheap and desirable. *Barclay's Bank* (Mon–Thur 8am–1.30pm, Fri 8am–2pm) is nearby.

Lastly, if en route for **Liberia**, you find yourself in Bo with no Liberian visa, go to the police station at the end of Dambara Rd, and ask for the immigration department.

Bo to Bonthe: Matru-Jong

Bo is a good place from which to make for BONTHE and the coast (see below). An early *Mazda* lorry leaves daily from near *Coker's* for MATRU-JONG, whence, with lots of luck and pothole avoidance (it's a dusty, gravelly road), you can pick up the morning ferry straight down the creeks to BONTHE on SHERBRO ISLAND. If you miss it, check in at the Matru-Jong paramount chief's, then go swimming in the salty creek.

Tiwai Island Nature Reserve

The **Tiwai Island Project**, run by Njala University College and the Peace Corps, has transformed a considerable island in the Moa River into a *de facto* national park. Although only covering about twelve square kilometres, the largely pristine forest-cloaked island shelters an extraordinarily rich fauna, including chimps and ten other primates, pygmy hippos, red river hogs, crocodiles and electric fish. It's fabulously sited, furthermore, and although somewhat inaccessible, the day's journey from Bo (or Kenema) is unquestionably worth making. Apart from stocking up with food, major preparations aren't involved; there are admirable facilities on the island.

Getting there

You've a couple of options for **getting to Tiwai from Bo**; first you can hang around in the main lorry park waiting for a vehicle in the PUJEHUN direction (ideally to POTORU). This may be fruitful early in the day, but if you didn't start in Bo, you might want simply to wait at the transport stop by the Pujehun junction on the Freetown highway. This is nearly 3km from the centre of Bo, down Sewa Road, so get a town taxi there. If you get a lift with a Pujehun-bound vehicle, you need to be dropped well before Pujehun itself, after 53km, at the Bandajuma construction camp, 2km south of the village of that name. From here, you'll have to hope for transport to Potoru, 25km away.

The tarmac doesn't go far south of Bo, and you're soon on a rough road. East of Bandajuma, the **forest** begins to close in; the road becomes a two-wheel track, punctuated by log bridges, and flanked by tall trees, under which cluster occasional compounds of dull rectangular mud houses. You should be able to reach Potoru by irregular *poda poda*. From here to the riverside village of KAMBAMA, where you cross to Tiwai, it's nearly 16km. You might charter a vehicle to take you, and it's rumoured there's someone with a *Honda* who offers this service quite often. If you have your own, or walk it, the route is: immediately left after the bridge on entering Potoru; just under 3km to the water tower where you turn right; then 7km to VAAMA; 3km to BAIMA; and just under 3km to Kambama, in deep forest above the river. There's a Tiwai island office here, and shelters for vehicles. Ask first to see Chief Duwai to arrange the **river crossing**. There's a shelter and safe-keeping for vehicles here.

Approaching Tiwai **from Kenema**, there's a daily truck to BAOMA-KOYA (45km). This leaves Kenema early afternoon. From Baoma-Koya (where you'll be accommodated if necessary), there's a 2km walk to MAPUMA, where you can arrange for someone to take you to the river and ferry you across. Occasionally, when the river is in full spate, during or after the rains, this can be dangerous. Once on the island, follow any east-west path to the visitor's centre on the other side of the island. The paths are laid in a grid pattern.

Tiwai Island

You glide across, typically in a canoe of the lowest and slimmest variety, to the overhanging tropical abundance on the island's bank. From the west bank, a short walk into the forest brings you to the **Visitors' Centre** – thatched communal "lounge", small library, tents under roofs with kerosene lamps, kitchen area, shower and long drop latrines. Fees are around £2–3 a night, depending on your status. If you want to be sure of accommodation, write in good time to: Tiwai Island Project Manager, Dept. of Biological Science, Njala University College, Private Mail Bag, Freetown.

Tiwai is the Africa of imagination. The air is saturated with sound – the rattle, squeak and vibrato incessance of a billion insects (listen out for the eerily ventriloqual mole cricket), the squawks and yelps of birds, monkeys, tree hyraxes, squirrels, chimpanzees and hundreds of others. The island has the world's third-highest biomass of monkeys. And it must hold some kind of record for its termites, too. In the background is the dim rush of the rapids on the Moa River, where it splits to roar around Tiwai through rocks and channels.

Guides are on hand to take you round the forest paths (in the absence of any one single path running right around the island, the chessboard of right-angles can get confusing and frustrating). Mine collected wild fruit and flowers for medicines, pointed

---

MAMMALS OF TIWAI

A complete list of the larger mammals on the island.
The leopard and giant forest hog are occasional visitors from the left bank.

Primates	**Rodents**	**Carnivores**
Demidoff's bushbaby	Beecroft's flying squirrel	African civet
Potto	Giant forest squirrel	Two-spotted palm civet
Red Colobus monkey	Red-legged sun squirrel	Genet
Olive Colobus monkey	Red side-striped squirrel	Cusimanse
Black and White Colobus monkey	Ground squirrel	Marsh mongoose
Sooty mangabey	Brush-tailed porcupine	Slender mongoose
Campbell's monkey	Giant rat	Clawless otter
Diana monkey	Cane rat ("cutting grass")	Golden cat
Spot-nosed monkey		Leopard (?)
Green monkey	**Antelopes**	
Chimpanzee	Bushbuck	**Pigs**
	Maxwell's duiker	Red river hog
	Red-flanked duiker	Giant forest hog (?)
African anteaters	Yellow-backed duiker	**Pygmy Hippopotamus**
White-bellied pangolin	Royal antelope	
Long-tailed pangolin	Water chevrotain	**Tree Hyrax**

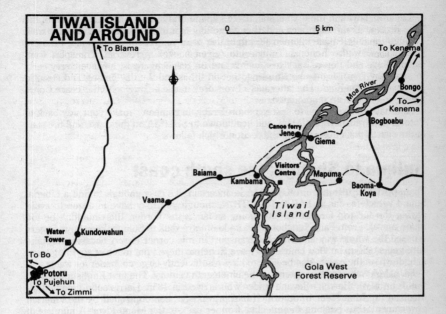

**TIWAI ISLAND
AND AROUND**

0 _____ 5 km

To Blama

To Kenema

Moa River

Bongo

To Kenema

Bogboabu

Canoe ferry
Jene

Giema

Visitors'
Centre

Baiama

Mapuma

Kambama

Baoma-
Koya

Vaama

*Tiwai
Island*

Water
Tower

Kundowahun

To Bo

Gola West
Forest Reserve

Potoru
To Pujehun
To Zimmi

out a place where a leopard had scratched for something in the ground, and tracked troupes of red colobus and spot-nosed monkeys. To be sure of seeing chimps, you'll need to devote a few days. In the dry season, they can migrate freely across the river into the Gola forest reserve to the east. Increasingly, however, they're spending time on the island as they come to appreciate the security of the local paramount chiefs' voluntary no-hunting agreement. At the local level, a lot of prestige is now attached to its succesful operation by the people on the mainland west of the reserve. People on the east side remain unconvinced.

Hog-sized **pygmy hippos** are the rarest and most secretive of riverbank denizens. Much less aquatic and sociable than their big cousins, they solitarily traipse their habitual nocturnal paths through the undergrowth, with unvarying routine. The paths – often tunnels less than a metre high – are obvious if you see one. By day, pygmy hippos lie up in thick vegetation or swamp, protecting their sensitive skin from dehydration.

From the camp, if you walk south along the path which follows the west side of the island, you come to the research camp (no public admittance), and to the right of here at the water's edge, a grove of massive bamboo stems and rocks by the water, where you can **swim** and wash clothes in the schisto-free river.

Exploring the forest after dark is highly recommended, though to do so on your own requires a little courage. The forest is a powerful presence at night and it's easy to become nervous of its immense consuming vigour. Every rotten branch creaks with termites; at every step there are things flying and jumping, and you sense the organs of detection of a million unseen creatures waving at your clumsy, illuminated figure as you stumble over the roots. It's a lot of fun if you keep cool, especially on the night of a full moon. Take a lamp with plenty of kerosene, and a torch for investigating. And mark your way as you go to avoid getting lost.

Leaving Tiwai, in the dry season, there's a land bridge to the left (east) bank of the Moa River at Tiwai's northern end, though getting to it involves a three-kilometre walk through the jungle. One kilometre north of this point you reach Giema, and from there you can follow the Kenema–Tiwai route (given above) in reverse. Transport from Baoma-Koya and Potoru back to Kenema and Bo respectively, is, however, very early to leave (by 7am). It may be simpler to get off the island the day before, and sleep in Potoru or Baoma-Koya. The latter has a two-storey house belonging to the Peace Corps where you will be accommodated.

Alternatively, with time to spare, and preferably in company, make your way back to Potoru, find transport to ZIMMI, and head down to SULIMA on the coast, and the start of the coastal walk described in the section which follows.

Sulima to Shenge: the south coast

Transport to Sulima from KENEMA is uncertain. It's easy enough to find a Liberia-bound vehicle as far as FAIRO JUNCTION, though you may have to argue to avoid paying the full trip fare (if it's only going as far as the border, this shouldn't be too much more). From Fairo Junction, it's a 24-kilometre walk to Sulima; keep your fingers crossed the whole way for a lift, but transport in this corner is *very* occasional. Make sure you stock up on food before you leave Kenema; there's not much of anything, save fish, down on the coast. Also be sure to have a sufficiently large container for water.

SULIMA was a trading station in the nineteenth century. The first Englishman here was John Myer Harris, a Jewish trader who arrived in 1855. Harris soon creamed off much of the Moa River trade, which had previously been controlled by the Liberian government, thus pushing the effective frontier back to the Mano River. A number of the old colonial buildings are still standing and fun to investigate. There's a **public rest house**, an old Siaka Stevens haunt, between the ocean and the quite amazing freshwater **lagoon**, where you can swim and wash. Apart from this rest house, there's also a private "rest house" (Pa Banya's the man) which is a lot cheaper, and comes complete with swarms of mosquitoes and incredibly uncomfortable beds. But you can base yourself at either of these two places, give someone there your food to be cooked and sleep on the beach. Sulima generally gathers an itinerant community of holidaying volunteers every Christmas. People build *baffas* (shelters) and fires on the beach.

Sulima is simply beautiful, but the surf on the open shore can be rough, and there's a rip tide. The lagoon over the sand is tranquil and clean.

Walking along the coast

If you're planning to undertake the **walk along the beach**, in order to get started you need first to ask around for a ferryman to take you across the mouth of the Moa River. The fare should be well under 50p each, but special charters are subject to rapid inflation. On the other side, the route follows the beach itself for the first 10km or so.

When you start finding boats on the beach near paths leading inland, you'll know there are villages a kilometre or two from the shore. It's actually easier to walk on the firmer (and shadier) paths that follow the coast a short distance behind the beach, though you'll be accompanied most of the time by curious children and entreated, repeatedly, to stop and accept **hospitality** in the fishing villages. A conciliatory approach to the walk works best, striking out alone along the shore in the morning, then cutting inland as the heat builds up to follow the path that links the villages, when you can slow your pace and stop to talk to people. Foreign passers-by are scarce indeed and your novelty value is immense. You can have your **food** cooked – in return for rice, *Maggi* cubes, or a few leones – then stock up on fresh **water** and return to the beach for the night – or sleep in a village.

In this way, you can follow the whole beach (110km) in a walk that takes from five days to a week without strain. This is **Turner's Peninsula**, a strip of land ceded to the British as long ago as 1825. The people are Vai, Krim and Sherbro but, increasingly, everyone speaks Mende first, Krio second and English a poor third. Houses are made from entirely natural materials – woven palmfrond walls with thatched roofs.

Instead of walking right to the end of Turner's Peninsula, you could coincide at the halfway village of MANO (one of many called that) with the **weekly launch** from GBUNDAPI (a creek head west of Pujehun) to BONTHE. It calls here at noon on Wednesday and takes seven hours to Bonthe, then returns early on Thursday afternoon, taking three hours back to Gbundapi (100km by road from Bo; first destination PUJEHUN).

If time isn't a limiting factor, you could explore the zone behind the beach and scrubby dunes. From KASI village, a fourteen-kilometre detour takes you round the landward side of **Lake Kasi** (aka Mape) to the prettily sited village of MANO BONJEMA: 4km further inland is a second lake, **Mabesi**.

Most of Turner's Peninsula is backed by low scrub, but towards the western end, coconut palms start to appear. The most attractive stretches of coast, however, are on Sherbro and the Turtle Islands. At the end of Turner's Peninsula, you should be able to find a boat for the 5km over to Bonthe from the last village, another MANO.

Sherbro Island

Though very much in ruins these days, **BONTHE**, the main town on **SHERBRO ISLAND**, is one of Sierra Leone's most appealing towns. When Frederick William Hugh Migeod (Colonial Service, retired), visited in 1924 while writing his *View of Sierra Leone*, he found "about forty Europeans there, including those on York Island, and a big gathering at tennis every evening". The atmosphere has changed somewhat in the intervening years, but Bonthe is still very pleasant. Wide sandy lanes cross the town, and many of the great old run-down buildings of the glory days are still upright. The secondary school is magnificent and the people of Bonthe charming.

There's a government **rest house** (under £1/night each). Bring your own food to be cooked and you can supplement it with fresh fish, while there's street food here too.

Bonthe is connected by daily launch to the mainland at MATRU-JONG (dep. Matru-Jong am, dep. Bonthe pm, 3hr, £1) and there are daily lorries from Bo to Matru-Jong and back. The town also has a couple of speedboats which you can reportedly charter for trips to the western end of the island, and there's an occasional (1–2 weekly) launch between Bonthe and SHENGE and TOMBO (on the Freetown peninsula), which calls at the Plantain Islands.

Except in the dry season, walking around Sherbro is pretty well impossible, as most of the island is inundated with flood water. But if your timing is right, your taste for the beach still unsatisfied, and the thought of a 55km walk to the western tip of Sherbro doesn't faze you, you'll be able to find a boat to take you over to the **Turtle Islands**. The new French beach resort, *Tisana*, on one of the islands just offshore – reportedly accessible on foot at low tide – is patronised by occasional winter season helicopter excursionists from Freetown, and may be worth gravitating towards, though an idle stay will cost a packet (bookings through *Kontiki Tours*). The Turtle Islands are idyllic and otherwise pretty well unvisited, though the entrepreneurs are hovering around. On their protected landward shores, there's wonderful swimming and goggling.

Shenge

Shenge lies between Sherbro Island and the Freetown peninsula, isolated at the end of its long feeder road from MOYAMBA JUNCTION. There's virtually no transport to Shenge. The rough road has 110 palm log bridges in its 80km stretch from Moyamba.

THE MENDE AND SECRET SOCIETIES

There is a thing passing in the sky; some thick clouds surround it; the uninitiated see nothing.
Opaque Mende proverb

The **Mende** language – the biggest language group in Sierra Leone – is supposed to have arrived from the northeast, either with people fleeing the chaotic conditions in sixteenth-century Songhai, or perhaps before the creation of the Mali empire in the thirteenth century. Ptolemy's second-century map even indicates *Purrus Campus* in about the place where the ancient Mende might have had a **"Poro Bush"** – a secret society grove. The Mende are skilled and very long-established **farmers**, trading and hunting are low priorities. Rice, sorghum and millet, root crops, oil palms and kola are the big crops. Women **fish** the streams, too, with circular nets, as much for relaxation as for the meal.

Along classic "divide and rule" principles, the British split the **Mende kingdoms** into dozens of "paramount chiefdoms", introducing a new *tribal* identity. The Mende chiefs came to see themselves as natural successors of the British, in competition – or association – with the powerful **Temne**. But the upper-class Krio families of Freetown had the same idea. The most serious of the **anti-tax revolts**, in Mende country in 1898, resulted in the deaths of hundreds of Krio traders and deepened a rift, never completely bridged, between the indigenous Protectorate peoples and the non-native Krios of the Colony. The Bo school for chiefs gave an incentive to Protectorate ambitions. Later, Mende politicians from a pro-British family of Bonthe – **Milton Margai** and his brother **Albert** – became the country's first and second prime ministers. Krio opponents attributed much of the second Margai's attachment to power to membership of the secret *Poro* society.

You can't spend more than a week in the country without hearing mysterious rumours about the **secret societies**. Among older or more traditional Mende people, enquiries get a hostile response, and the few books on the subject tend to disappear from libraries. Society graduates are sworn to secrecy and the arcane details remain hidden. But they're perhaps less sinister institutions than their reputation would suggest. It's worth knowing about them in general, because they still dominate life in Sierra Leone. Even Christians don't exclude themselves, and Islam, while opposing them, makes no purist insistence.

The general name for the societies is **Bundu**, actually a Krio word. **Poro** is the men's society (the same name is found elsewhere in West Africa, eg among the Senoufo in Côte d'Ivoire) and is by far the most powerful; the women's is called **Sande**. They're followed in almost all communities, as secret brotherhoods and sisterhoods, cutting across the family and clan divisions, maintaining stability and marking life-cycle events. *Poro* and *Sande* provide the framework for **traditional instruction** to adolescents about sex, adult behaviour and folk knowledge. Traditionally, too, the period of seclusion and endurance in the bush was when **circumcision and clitoridectomy** were performed. Boys of the same age group go through the school in the dry season, girls in the rains. Beyond the teenage rites of passage, membership of *Poro* proceeds by different stages. In addition to *Poro* and *Sande*, there's a kind of high *Poro* society called *Wunde*, and a number of other societies, some operating as professional associations of medical, psychiatric and social welfare specialists – *Humo, Toma, Njaye* – and some of entertainers and conjurers, the *Njoso*.

As an outsider, beware of "No Entry" signs in the bush, indicating a society grove, and fenced compounds outside villages. It's acceptable to witness youngsters with whitened faces, however, celebrating their new names and status.

Heavy black **Bundu masks** worn by women in the *Sande* society (and called *Sowo* by the Mende) are the most visible signs of the societies' active existence. They tell a lot about Mende ideals of feminine beauty – high-domed foreheads, elaborately-braided hair, fine-pointed features, eyes that see nothing, mouths closed. They're carved by men.

"Animal societies" – "Baboon" (chimpanzee), "Boa" (python), "Alligator" (crocodile) and "Leopard" – were always uncommon, though sensationalised. Intended to imitate attacks by wild animals, they were created in order to obtain human organs for **witchcraft**. They've tended to die out along with the animals imitated; nobody would believe a chimpanzee murder in Bo anymore.

Witchcraft is another matter.

Transfers from Moyamba Junction to **MOYAMBA** are easy enough. In Moyamba you should try to hitch a fish lorry (6–8 hr), or the odd FAO vehicle going to the big Shenge project. Genuine public transport happens about once a week. The easiest way to get to Shenge is from the Freetown side, taking the twice-weekly (though unpredictable) Tombo ferry from the village of that name, south of WATERLOO.

There's little to do at Shenge but absorb the scene and relax. The village itself is located on a hard piece of land, with low cliffs above the beaches. There's one good bar, where volunteers and locals assemble, but no official accommodation – which isn't a worry. Two small islands hard by Shenge beach – Bird Island smothered in guano, and Monkey Island with its handful of simian castaways – deserve the visit. Fishermen will give you a ride for a small fee, or you could "hijack" the FAO's demonstration outrigger canoe (more stability in rough seas). Monkey Island has a sheltered picnic cove.

EASTERN SIERRA LEONE

Diamonds and cross-border trade have made **Eastern Province** the country's most densely populated region. **Koidu/Sefadu** is now the biggest provincial town and shows an unexpected side of the country. It's a good jumping-off point for **Mount Bintumani** and, closer but rather inaccessible, the **Tingi Mountains** and the source of the Niger. **Kenema** is busy, but unexceptional, the common embarkation point for Liberia and southern Guinea. And in the salient of Sierra Leone that stretches east into hills of jungle, coffee and cocoa, with Guinea to the north and Liberia to the south, **Kailahun** and **Koindu** are the main towns, agricultural centres with good markets and very mixed populations.

Kenema and around

Basically a one-street town with a couple of extra streets, **KENEMA**'s main life stretches from the old railway station area north up Hangha Road, and out of town on the road to Tongu and Koidu. Originally a Mende settlement, Kenema grew fast on the strength of the railway and burst into development after the discovery, in 1931, of **diamonds** a few kilometres to the east, and the opening up of the Tongu diamond field to the north. Kenema's main industry, however, is logging and carpentry, with a large **Forest Industries Department** and a "Showroom" which may be open. Floods of destitute Liberian refugees, escaping from the civil war there in 1990, are likely to add new facets to the town's character.

Basic needs
If you need to get from one end of the town to the other, it's worth knowing that a blue and white *SLRTC* minibus runs from the Freetown junction up to the top of Hangha Road and back every twenty minutes or so.

Accommodation is straightforward. Unless you track down the *Pastoral Centre* out of town (for which you may need reservations; reportedly worth it, cheap and pleasant), or stay in the Peace Corps Rest House down on Blama Road, the best deal's in the shape of the *Eastern Motel* (☎042 253), which is really not a bad place (around £4/£6 non S/C, non AC). Breakfasts are good (hot fresh coffee and toast) and the kitchen does palatable food – slightly weird "salads" (baked beans, luncheon meat and sardines), burgers (between white bread) and various fried offerings. For more conventional chop, any of the places down "cheap chop" street should fill you, though as usual they're often packing up by midday: try *Hacienda Restaurant* (No.7). Also eat at *Yum-Yum's*, behind the Freetown lorry park, which does excellent salads, sandwiches and coffee.

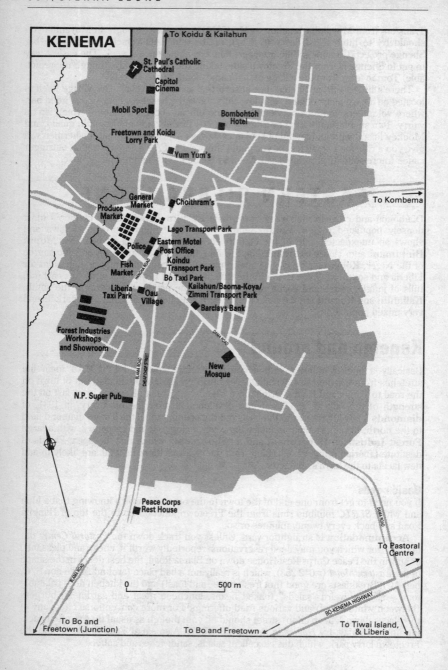

KENEMA

To Koidu & Kailahun

St. Paul's Catholic
Cathedral

Capitol
Cinema

Mobil Spot

Bombohtoh
Hotel

Freetown and Koidu
Lorry Park

Yum Yum's

General
Market

Choithram's

Produce
Market

To Kombema

Lago Transport Park

Police

Eastern Motel
Post Office

Koindu
Transport Park

Fish
Market

Bo Taxi Park

Liberia
Taxi Park

Kailahun/Baoma-Koya/
Zimmi Transport Park

Oau
Village

Barclays Bank

HANGHA ROAD

Forest Industries
Workshops
and Showroom

DAMA ROAD

New
Mosque

RIJANA ROAD

CHOITHRAM STREET

N.P. Super Pub

Peace Corps
Rest House

DAMA ROAD

To Pastoral
Centre

0   500 m

RIJANA ROAD

BO-KENEMA HIGHWAY

To Bo and
Freetown (Junction)

To Bo and Freetown

To Tiwai Island,
& Liberia

A fairly active social life seems possible in Kenema, and clearly the diamond (smuggling) industry has brought money to the town. Passing through at Christmas you might, according to the posters, have sampled

Senators Present "Bigger Boys Nite" Featuring the Crowning of Bigger Boy of the Year

or even

Senators Present "Madams' Nite" Featuring the Crowning of Madam of the Year.

Less mysterious **entertainment** is available any night at the *Mobil Spot*, Kenema's main after-dark focus, with cheap bar and a rough and noisy sound system. Avoid the disco-bordello *Bohmbohtoh Hotel* (a.k.a. *Gbongbortor*) ten minutes away on Jenneh Road unless you're feeling fierce and fickle – you'll probably be the centre of attraction. The *OAU Village* by the Monrovia lorry park on Dama Road is safe enough for a drink, even a rather good place, especially for a peaceful afternoon beer. For more serious, but no less relaxing, imbibing, stroll down to the Freetown junction where they do a nice jug of **palm wine** for £0.50p a gallon! Quaffing begins before sunset each evening.

Waanje Falls

You may be encouraged to visit the **Waanje waterfalls** outside Kenema. Unless you're up to a long walk, there's absolutely no point in making any effort to get to them without your own wheels. Once the rains have filled them out, they do become a pretty sight, but past December you'd hardly pause to look. Take the Freetown road, 5.5km from the *Eastern Motel* to BANDAMA. Turn right, up the track, crossing the railway line, past the villages of TUAHUN and KOMENDE to a bridge (4km) and the falls are audible down on your left in the valley; a series of chutes and rapids, steep rocks, boulders and vegetation. There's a clutch of nice pools where, depending on the flow, you can **bathe** (no schistosomiasis; the river tumbles out of the Kambui hills not far away).

MOVING ON FROM KENEMA

Getting out of Kenema is the usual mess. For **Bo and Freetown**, there's a Bo–Freetown lorry park/bus stop, along Hangha Road at what seems the wrong end of town (towards the *Mobil Spot*). The easiest procedure is to be down there by 5am, or around 11.30am, or hitch. You'll also find vehicles to Freetown around the used clothes market and along the parallel commercial Kingsway Street. *504*s are best for the short journey to Bo. For journeys **east or north**, check here too. "TONGU Field" – the part-way destination if you're headed for the Kono/Sefadu/Koidu conurbation or to KAILAHUN and KOINDU (with an n). As far as some way beyond LAGO, the road is surfaced; thereafter it's rough. There are usually more northbound vehicles further up Hangha Road. The **Monrovia** lorry park is distinct, anyway, at the top of Dama Road. The fare, by *Peugeot 504* (choose a good one, it's a squashed journey) is around £15.

The Kambui Hills

Scenic and festooned with tall forest, the **Kambui Hills** are worth a sidetrack if you can find a way into them. The easiest target is the forest school above BAMBAWO. From Kenema, Lago-bound vehicles can drop you at NGELEHUN on the main Kono route. Bambawo is 2km, west, up into the hills. Continue through the village a further steep and rocky 2km, past an abandoned **chrome mine** on the left (the mining camp here was used on an animal-collecting expedition by naturalist Gerald Durrell in the early 1970s) and, up at the top, seek out the head of the **forest reserve**. There are some good rest houses here, with beds and kitchen equipment (but no food). You should ideally make a booking through the Ministy of Agriculture in Freetown (☎24821), but a courteous upfront approach should secure you accommodation (under £1). There's wonderful scenery here, and an atmosphere of stillness. But, remarkably, there's also a spring-fed swimming pool. The forest school itself is only ticking over with a skeleton staff.

Not far to the north, a similar set-up at **Panguma Sawmills** now operates as an up-country tourist resort (virtually the only one), with, again, a swimming pool – though this one is more often used – and half a dozen pleasant chalets. You can take a three-day trip here from Freetown through *Yazbeck's*. But no doubt you'd be accommodated, at some expense perhaps, if you just turned up under your own steam.

Koidu/Sefadu and around

The confusion over the town's **name** is worse than a choice between two. Many locals refer to **Kono** (the district of which it's capital) when they mean the town. And the old settlement was called Sembehun, so **New Sembehun** is a fourth, pedantic, possibility.

Driving through the outskirts, scarred by alluvial **diamond diggings** and swarming with people up to their waists in water (they dig even at night, with lamps, apparently better than by day, when "the police humbug too much") you soon get the picture. Koidu is Boomtown. Over one hundred thousand people live around here. It's the one place in the country where you can make the big time without connections. Although the government has stopped granting private diamond-prospecting licenc\es, people still flock to Kono in the hope of making a fortune. After all, it only takes one lucky stone.

The results are plain to see in the **town centre** where piles of goods (children's bikes, ghetto blasters, even colour TVs) are on sale in the wide and dusty main street and posters advertise "Bionic Ninja" from the video rental shop. Arriving late at night in this distant corner of the country, the streets are excitedly illuminated, as if for a special occasion (it's easy to forget the normality of street-lighting) and villas – tightly guarded and burglar-barred – hum smugly with air conditioning.

Despite all of which, it's even harder than usual to find any decent **places to stay**. There are rooms at the nightspot near the roundabout. But they don't have overwhelming appeal at the end of a long day when you're told "they are just now all engaged . . . try to wait a small time". Instead, make your way across town to the *Masianday Hotel*; everyone knows the "Mashanday" but it's slightly hard to find, a kilometre or so from the centre. It's a big tomb of a place, but as good as you could reasonably expect: non S/C rooms (with sporadic electricity) are anything from £4–10, depending on whim. Bargain hard, and get breakfast on the verandah included.

Koidu has a major market area and, as you'll have seen, no shortage of shops. Near the centre, too, there's a large and quite organised lorry park, with *Rema's* open air "pub" to one side a popular retreat for **cold beer and snacks**.

Around Koidu

While the town's appeal is strictly as an overnighter, there are a few possible **excursions** in the area, though they are more limited attractions if you can't provide your own transport. The **waterfalls** on the upper Sewa River south of NJAIAMA-SEWAFE (*not* Njaiama) are accessible in a day if you set off early. They're an hour's hike from Njaiama-Sewafe (which is just south of the highway, 42km west of Koidu). In a similar vein, there's a fine **beach** at IKUMAH on the Bafi River, about 25km north of Koidu.

More ambitious are mountain trips, to **Bintumani and Sankanbiaiwa**. From Koidu, Bintumani is reached via YOMADU, KAIYIMA and YIFIN, the base from which to find a guide for the climb (you might also ask in KRUTO, 7km before Yifin). Practical details are much the same as those that apply if you're arriving from the north (see p.674).

Sakanbiaiwa, in the Tingi Mountains, is Sierra Leone's second highest peak (1709m) – a **botanical sanctuary** for its orchids, especially at the end of the dry season, but a much less visited area even than Bintumani. First step is transport to JEGBWEMA, 18km east of Koidu, where you turn left into the mountains. You might be lucky in the Koidu motor park, however, and get a vehicle going closer to your destination: the villages to head for are KUNDUNDU and YENGEMA (respectively, 38km and 44km from Jegbwema), along a really rough road.

The eastern corner

KAILAHUN, the district capital, is the biggest centre in the far east, but the town you're likely to be heading for in this direction is **Koindu** ("Kwindu"), where Sierra Leone meets Liberia and Guinea near the Moa River. En route, if you have the opportunity (your own transport in other words), visit the rather beautiful **Siaka Stevens Beach** at the Moa-Meli river confluence, 20km west of Kailahun.

Koindu

The best days for vehicles from Kenema to **KOINDU** are Friday and Saturday, when they load up for the **Sunday market** in Koindu. This bazaar is quite an event, rated as throughout the east – and indeed across the borders – as one of the best around. In the rains, the 180-kilometre trip can take days to complete, especially in an overloaded *Mazda* stuffed full of people and optimism. The worst stretches are beyond Pendembu. Motorbikes, Land Rovers and the three-axle trucks called "Mandingo lorries" usually make it in all weathers, eventually. But even in the dry season, it's an all-day affair.

Once in Koindu, there's a **hotel** on the Liberia road, just outside town, and no shortage of good **chop**. Try the *Ghana Restaurant*, across from the *Texaco* station, which has a helpful and knowledgeable Ghanaian owner.

Koindu was originally a **Kissi** settlement, but it's been swelling with immigrants from a wide reach for decades, and there's a notable community of Fula exiles from Guinea. The town is a sort of tradesman's entrance to Sierra Leone. Everything from rice and sugar to diamonds and human sacrifices is rumoured to pass through the town – and most of the rumours are verifiable on a Sunday. There's locally made cloth in the market (cotton is sown in with the rice and harvested afterwards), along with excellent silversmiths who specialise in filigree earrings and pendants. And you can still buy **"Kissi pennies"** here, the regional currency of pre-protectorate days, that continued to be used until World War II. Don't expect small coins, though. Kissi pennies are pieces of twisted iron rod, about 30cm long, with the ends flattened out into a T-shape. You'll need to summon all bargaining skills if you want one.

It's not surprising, given the market and the town's position, that the **currency black market** is highly developed in Koindu – as it was even seventy years ago, when Liberians came here to get British silver to pay their taxes and French Guineans would pay over the odds for silver half-crowns. These days, Koindu is in the peculiar position of being at the hub of three weak currencies. Dollars, sterling, CFA and French francs (even travellers' cheques) most impress the traders, though with the economic emergency, many, even here, have been much less keen to take the risk.

LEAVING SIERRA LEONE

Heading to Guinea, take a taxi to the Moa (Makona) River and one of the large canoes to NONGOA, where if you don't already have a **Guinean visa** you can obtain one. The immigration office closes at 6pm.

Going into Liberia, this border was closed until a few years ago to control smuggling. At the time of writing, the war in Liberia has effectively sealed it again. Under happier circumstances, lorries assemble at the *Texaco* station in Koindu for a one-day journey to VOINJAMA (first hotel) and two or three days through to MONROVIA – a considerably longer journey than the usual, checkpoint-littered day trip from KENEMA via ZIMMI. If you use this northern route, you should be able to get a **Liberian visa** at the first immigration post at FOYA.

index

LIBERIA

LIBERIA

The love of liberty brought us here
Liberian National Motto

Even early in the nineteenth century, when black settlers first arrived from America, motives less virtuous than love of liberty were also at work. Today, however, 150 years after the declaration of independence, you'll hear that people come to **Liberia** on business, to visit relatives on business, or by mistake. This is West Africa's least tourist-visited country, extraordinarily isolated behind Côte d'Ivoire, Guinea and Sierra Leone, economically under thrall to the United States and, in the social and political spheres, currently the gloomiest prospect in West Africa. If you're travelling in the region, you're unlikely to want to make a special destination of Liberia. But there are few parts of the country that aren't on one or other of the routes between Sierra Leone, Guinea and Côte d'Ivoire. And if you're coming to Liberia to work, you'll find it's far from devoid of pleasure and interest, the more so if you can get around under your own steam.

Monrovia, at any rate, hardly bears out the dismal picture. It's a functional (if not always fully functioning) capital, nefariously busy and very much the headquarters for American interests in Africa, with the sort of Kool-aid/burger culture you might anticipate. Other **coastal towns** are mostly gone-to-seed backwaters, sleepily reminiscent of their African-American roots. They perch on rocky promontories on a coast of creeks and mangroves. From the travel angle, they're mostly saved by splendid nearby beaches.

Up-country Liberia is very different. Beyond the maze of tidal creeks, the land rises onto rolling forested plateaux, split by rivers which head, surprisingly straight, to the sea. On the Guinean border in the far north, the highlands poke above 1000m and just about qualify as mountains. Nearly one fifth of the country has a dense cover of **primary forest** – the largest concentrations anywhere in West Africa – currently being lost to farmers and sawmills at the rate of five percent (450 square kilometres) each year. The **Sapo National Park,** Liberia's only one, on the Sinoe River in the remote southeast, is one of the country's major attractions for hardy travellers and determined

---

LIBERIA IN 1990 – THE INVASION AND ITS AFTERMATH

The travel research for this chapter was conducted in 1989 and writing completed on the eve of the invasion of the country by Charles Taylor's National Patriotic Front. Rather than attempt a re-write without knowledge of conditions, or leave a large blank, we have decided to leave Part Thirteen as it is. Through most of 1990, Liberia was in turmoil, tens of thousands of Liberians having fled to Côte d'Ivoire, Sierra Leone and Guinea, and all foreign residents having evacuated. The immediate future, with nothing to hold back the two groups of rebels and the dead president's remnant forces from continued civil war and tribal massacres, looks very grim. Whatever the outcome, it's certain that most of the practical details given here – especially those for Nimba county and Monrovia – will have ceased to apply by the time Liberia is able to receive visitors again. Much of Monrovia has been looted and all businesses have closed down. A special request, therefore, for feedback; please write to us. The latest details on the situation as we go to press are given in the History section on p.708.

naturalists. From January to March, canoe expeditions are organised up the Sinoe. **Towns** in the interior, apart from several along the paved highway to Ganta, are mostly very small and very undeveloped.

Liberia is divided into **counties**, like a US state, each with its "county seat". Nine small counties along the coast reflect the old centres of settler power. The four large ones in the interior – Lofa, Bong, Nimba and Grand Gedeh (pronounced Jeddah) – are the stronghold of indigenous Liberian culture.

People

Ethnically, Liberia is distinct from any other West African country. Since its foundation, the dominant ethnic group have been the **"Congos"**– descendants of freed slaves from other parts of Africa. The original settlers were American, but their numbers were increased by newly captured and released slaves taken from slave ships (many of them from the Congo region).

Of the **indigenous peoples** – often still referred to as "the tribes" (or "tribal people") – the **Kpelle** of the centre form the biggest group, some 20 percent. Like the **Mano/Dan/Gio**-speaking communities of Nimba county, the **Loma** of Lofa county and the **Vai** in the southwest, Kpelle is part of the **Mande linguistic grouping** whose languages are spoken as mother tongues by more than one in two Liberians. The purest Mande is spoken in the scattered **Mandingo** communities all over the north. Theirs is virtually the same language as the Malinké of Guinea and the Mandinka of The Gambia. They're usually responsible for bush taxi transport in Liberia and, of course, are great traders and successful business people, too.

The other big language family (35 percent) is "Kruan", of which the main language, **Kru**, is spoken all along the central coast and in fishing communities abroad as well. **Grebo**, in the far southeast, and **Bassa**, in the vicinity of Buchanan, are closely related coastal languages. **Krahn**, the language of the ruling military clique, is a Kruan language of the interior with affiliated dialects over the border in Côte d'Ivoire. **Dei** and **Belle** are minor Kruan languages of the northwest. Also in the northwest, the **Gola** and the **Kissi** speak less easily classified languages.

Fula-speakers, most of them refugees from Sekou Touré's Guinea, and **Lebanese** are almost all in business. Unlike the Lebanese in many other parts of West Africa, where they've moved into wholesale and big business, the majority of Liberia's Lebanese community continue to run general stores in small up-country towns.

Climate: when and when not to visit

Monrovia has the distinction of being not only Liberia's wettest town but also Africa's wettest capital city ,with a magnificent annual average rainfall in excess of five metres (five times as much as most of Britain). **Temperatures** are high throughout the country, most of the year round, though more extreme in the central plateau regions. But rain is the real issue.

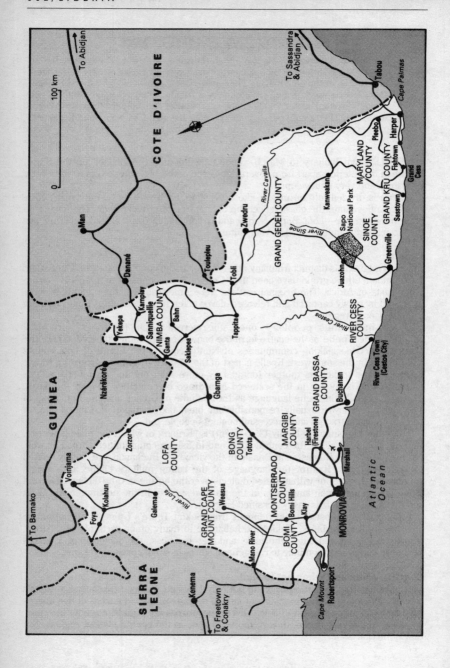

In most parts, **the rains** are heavily under way by April and there are few dry days until November. Along the coast, and inland in the south, in a year when the pattern behaves itself, you can expect some clear bright days in August (the **"middle dries"**). The middle dries become increasingly certain as you head south down the coast. Conditions in the interior are not as moist but, in the north, the middle dries don't come to the rescue. The unpredictability of the rains everywhere, together with the appalling condition of most "roads", put constraints on travel and leisure before December 1 and after April 15.

AVERAGE TEMPERATURES AND RAINFALL

MONROVIA

	Jan	Feb	Mar	Apr	May	June	July	Aug	Sept	Oct	Nov	Dec
Temperatures °C												
Min (night)	23	23	23	23	22	23	22	23	22	22	23	23
Max (day)	30	29	31	31	30	27	27	27	27	28	29	30
Rainfall mm	31	56	97	216	516	973	996	373	744	772	236	130
Days with rainfall	5	5	10	17	21	26	24	20	26	22	19	12

GANTA

	Jan	Feb	Mar	Apr	May	June	July	Aug	Sept	Oct	Nov	Dec
Rainfall mm	16	57	123	150	199	278	259	298	422	266	132	35
Days with rainfall	2	5	10	12	15	18	18	19	21	17	10	3

HARPER

	Jan	Feb	Mar	Apr	May	June	July	Aug	Sept	Oct	Nov	Dec
Rainfall mm	149	111	146	219	543	530	147	96	234	299	285	288
Days with rainfall	12	9	12	16	22	22	12	8	16	19	18	18

Arrivals

The overland routes into Liberia range from
arduous to extreme – overland access to
Liberia's neighbours being itself quite difficult. Under normal circumstances, the best
option is to fly in.

■ Flights from West African cities

In West Africa, *Ghana Airways* has the biggest
range of departures for Monrovia's **Robertsfield
International Airport**: from **Accra** via **Abidjan**
daily (and an extra non-stop Accra–Monrovia on
Wed); from **Dakar** via **Banjul**, **Conakry** and
Freetown on Wednesday and Sunday daytime;
from **Dakar** via **Freetown** on Monday; from
Dakar via **Conakry** on Friday; from **Conakry** via
Freetown on Thursday; and, with a plane change
in Accra, from **Lagos** on Saturday and
Wednesday (via **Lomé** on Wed).

Aeroflot arrives from Moscow twice a month
on Thursday via **Ouagadougou** and **Bamako**.
British Airways flies in from **Banjul** via
Freetown early Saturday morning and early
Tuesday evening.

The other airlines serving Monrovia are *Air
Afrique* (weekly non-stop flights from **Abidjan**
and **Dakar**), *Swissair* (weekly from **Accra**),
KLM (two arrivals weekly, one from **Conakry**,
one from **Freetown**) and *Nigeria Airways* (non-
stop from **Lagos** on Sun and via **Accra** on Wed).

■ Flying from the rest of Africa

Flying in from other parts of Africa, *Ethiopian
Airlines* arrives Friday from **Abidjan, Kinshasa,
Nairobi and Addis Ababa** and Mon from
Abidjan, Accra, Brazzaville and Addis.
Zambia Airways calls at Monrovia during the
night on its Monday and Friday flights **from
Lusaka** to New York.

■ Overland entry into Liberia

Road routes from any of Liberia's three neighbours are difficult. The best connections are with
Sierra Leone. From Freetown, driving yourself,
you can make it to Monrovia in the dry season in
one (long) day. If you get delayed, though, you
should put the border crossing off until the following morning; the border at Fairo junction closes at
6pm and there's nothing but a primitive hotel
there. Kenema is Sierra Leone's main transport
hub for Monrovia, with *Peugeot 504s* making the
trip daily.

Entering Liberia **from Guinea**, the fastest
land route to Monrovia is **via Nzérékoré and
Ganta** using upper Guinea's new roads. The
route is paved for all but 80km. Even from
Conakry, you may be best off coming this way if
you're trying to move fast (taking Sierra Leone
border crossings into account); it's some 1300km
compared with nearly 1000km via Freetown.

The route **from Côte d'Ivoire** is straightforward, **via Man and Kahnplay** – about 24–30hr
of travel from Abidjan. The coastal route **via
Tabou and Harper** is barely feasible unless
you've loads of time (allow at least a week from
Abidjan to Monrovia).

Red Tape

Liberia rather excels in the generation of red
tape, though many bureaucratic hassles
dissolve if you adopt the right attitude. Bring
plenty of passport photos. All nationalities,
apart from West Africans, need visas. Some
Liberian embassies are now asking for
letters confirming you aren't carrying the
HIV virus. Your embassy (or doctor) should
be able to comply.

If you're arriving with no specific address in
mind, you're strongly advised to give the **address
of a mission** in Monrovia as your destination and
base during your stay. Any of those in the
Monrovia accommodation listings should do
nicely.

Regardless of the length of stay recorded on your visa, **registration at an Immigration Office** (preferably the one in Monrovia, otherwise in a county capital) is normally required *within 48 hours*. On registering, get an extension of your stay permit *past* your anticipated visit; 60 days is standard. Supposed to be exempted from this are "tourists in possession of an entry visa and a police card who intend to stay in Liberia less than 15 days" – worth knowing if you're delayed in doing it.

Before leaving Liberia, you'll have to apply for an **exit visa**, seven days or less prior to your intended date of departure.

Photography permits are mandatory (see the "Photography" section in the Directory, below).

▓ Embassies in Liberia

As for **visas for other West African countries**, Monrovia has diplomatic or consular representatives for its neighbours plus Ghana, Nigeria, Cameroon and Mali, and the visa service of the French embassy.

Money and Costs

Financially, the country's position is parlous. Officially, the Liberian dollar (now widely known as the "Doe dollar": L$) is at par with the US dollar. The United States, however, no longer supports the currency. The largest denomination of Liberian currency is the new L$5 note, which replaces the inconvenient L$5 coin. All the coins (1¢, 5¢, 10¢, 25¢, 50¢ and L$1) are Liberian. There are no currency import/export restrictions.

US dollars ("green") are legal tender. US$10 and US$20 notes circulate freely and are now worth at least twice as much as their Liberian counterparts ("coin") – which are worthless outside the country. In addition, paying in US dollars often attracts a further large discount, so that a price of L$50 in coin might cost you US$20 in green. Prices, however, are given in L$, and you should change your US$ at the first opportunity to have coins for ordinary small puchases. Note that US$1 notes are hard to change. Travellers' cheques (in US$, preferably *American Express*) can be changed in any Lebanese shop. For most purposes, you won't need to use **banks**.

Credit cards are usable in Monrovia only, and then only in selected high-cost establishments. And remember that if you're billed in L$, you'll pay that figure in US$, plus any service charge.

Some establishments in Monrovia and all the country's main hotels insist on "tourists" **paying in US dollars** in any case. International air tickets can only be purchased in hard currency too, unless you have a resident's permit.

▓ Costs

At the black market rate of exchange (which is climbing from more than 2:1), Liberia is reasonably cheap. Even in Monrovia, on **US$20/day** for all expenses you could live reasonably well. Out in the sticks, with less to spend your money on, you're likely to find half this more than enough. Hotel rooms can be had for US$10–30 and cook shop meals for US$1 or so. Transport prices hardly push costs up: you can estimate upwards of US$1 to travel around 25 miles (40km) on dirt roads, or 30 miles (50km) on tarmac ("cold tar"). The highest fares, to the far southeast, should be under US$20 from Monrovia. Petrol ("gas") currently costs under US$2/US gallon (4 litres).

You can, and should, **bargain** for most things.

Information and Maps

Despite being an anglophone country, independent since the middle of the nineteenth century, Liberia is very little known outside its own borders. There is no tourist industry and no tourist information.

It's rumoured that the Ministry of Planning and Economic Affairs (PO Box 9016, ☎221971, telex 44374) sometimes has free literature.

There is still no reasonable **map** of the country, something Graham Greene (see "Books" in *Contexts*) might not have anticipated fifty years ago. The best widely available map is contained on the Michelin 953 sheet. A *Tourist Map of Monrovia*, published in 1980, is useful. You might still find copies in specialist suppliers abroad or possibly in Monrovia.

Health

Liberian embassies require to see your yellow fever and cholera certificates before they'll issue a visa.

Liberia doesn't have any **health problems** that you wouldn't predict from its climate and economic situation. Water-borne diseases (especially **schistosomiasis**) are a serious menace. Rabies is prevalent.

Health care facilities are almost non-existent outside Monrovia. **Phebe Hospital**, at Suakoko in Bong county, a three-hour drive from the capital, is reputable. So, too, is the German-run **Bong Mines Hospital**.

Getting Around

Travel in Liberia isn't assisted by an organised public transport system beyond the city limits of Monrovia. There are many *Toyota* **pick-ups and lorry conversions ("Mandingo money buses") operating as bush taxis. Liberia's road system is the worst in West Africa: apart from the Monrovia area, the only paved roads are to the Sierra Leone border at Mano River, to Ganta on the Guinea border, and to Robertsfield airport and Buchanan down the coast from Monrovia. Even most of the country's dirt roads are creations of the last twenty years. Many up-country towns and villages were, until the 1960s, weeks away by foot from Monrovia.**

■ Road transport

Compensating for all this, the services that are in operation, at least out of Monrovia, are fairly well run. **Tickets** are generally bought at fixed prices from ticket offices in the main transport parks, or "garages".

Much travel off the main highways is by Land Rover or motorbike, the preferred private vehicles (though amazingly, money buses do somehow get to those out-of-the-way places). If you brought a **bicycle** (by necessity a mountain bike with the widest frame/wheel clearance possible), you'd be well-equipped, even in the rains, but you wouldn't be following many others. *Bicycle Africa* (details in *Basics*) ran some tours in Liberia in 1984.

Car hire is limited to a couple of reasonably proficient Liberian operations in Monrovia. The international companies are not represented.

■ Air Travel

Missionaries and miners got around **by plane** before the roads were developed, and there are as many as 100 airfields across the country. Air travel is most important, and useful, to the south-east. Monrovia's airfield for domestic flights is Sprigg-Payne, 5km from the city centre.

Air Liberia may still fly to Cape Palmas (Harper), Sinoe (Greenville), Tchien (Zwedru), Grand Cess, Foya and Voinjama, but not to any predictable schedule. There are possibly two planes in use. Take the larger.

A better service is provided by the private charter company *Weasua Air Transport*. Prices to Sasstown/Grand Cess/Harper are around US$60–70. It's sometimes possible to get a ride with a group who have chartered a plane.

■ Other means of transport

The railway lines are strictly only for freight trains. There's hardly any more promise in the occasional **motor boats** that run along the coast, e.g. from Harbel near Monrovia to Harper.

OPTIMAL JOURNEY TIMES AND PRICE GUIDE*

MONROVIA TO:
Bomi Hills 45 miles, US$1.50 (1hr).
Robertsport 65 miles, US$2 (2–3hr).
Tallah 90 miles, US$3 (4hr).
Gbarnga 122 miles, US$4 (3hr).
Yekepa 166 miles, US$6 (7hr).
Buchanan 88 miles, US$2.50 (3hr).
Zwedru 267 miles, US$8 (10–20hr).
Sasstown 432 miles, US$17 (2–3 days).
Harper 466 miles, US$18 (2–3 days).
Zorzor 186 miles, US$6 (7hr).
Pleebo 152 miles, US$9 (12hr).
Greenville 116 miles, US$6 (10hr).

ZWEDRU TO:
Pleebo 152 miles, US$9 (12hr).
Greenville 116 miles, US$6 (10hr).

BUCHANAN TO:
River Cess 60 miles, US$2.50 (3hr).

ZORZOR TO:
Voinjama 57 miles, US$2.50 (2hr).

VOINJAMA TO:
Foya 45 miles, US$2 (3hr).

Liberians generally use miles and other US units. We've kept to kilometres in the guide.

Sleeping

There's at least one hotel of some sort in every county capital. Some are rather good, and a few face a certain amount of competition, but accommodation is generally very basic outside Monrovia. In the capital only, there's a clutch of international places. Most hotels levy a ten percent government tax. All are now obliged to charge in US$.

You may be lucky with guest houses run by development organisations like USAID and the EEC (perhaps L$10–15/night), but you shouldn't count on being able to use them. If you run into difficulties finding a place for the night, Lebanese shopkeepers can usually help with advice and directions. Because of very thick forest, **camping** is probably only feasible on the beaches (though not anywhere near Monrovia). Your reception in up-country villages will usually be hospitable.

Eating and Drinking

On a staple of upland rice (and, increasingly, swamp rice), the frog soup isn't bad, and fried bug-a-bugs (toasted termites) are okay. But in default of anything else, the national dish of Liberia is *pepper soup*, eaten all over the country.

There's terrific seasonality in food supply (worst in the rains), but generally the range and quantity is relatively high and many travellers find Liberia's food is a welcome surprise. Imports remain important, especially in Monrovia, where timid palates can stick to many familiar brands and dishes, mostly American. The same things can be bought from Lebanese stores in most towns.

■ Dishes

Various forms of **cassava stodge** are familiar basics all over. *Fufu* (fermented) is the commonest, *"G.B."* – especially popular in Nimba county – is rather coarser, and unfermented *dumboy*, popular in Vai country (and in Vai cook shops) comes somewhere between in texture. In many parts, **rice** is the preferred staple. Prepared into a *jollof*-style dish with meat, vegetables, spices, sometimes shellfish, it's *jala*; and made with chicken, it's *pela*.

Palm butter, the thick oily gravy strained from the pounded pulp of palm nuts, is one of

Liberia's more distinctive dishes, usually mixed with pepper (chili), meat, *bitter ball* (a small round aubergine) and onions – or whatever's available – and eaten as a foil with a starch base. It's especially popular in the southeast. *Tugborgee* is a fermented oil, prepared into a dish much like palm butter and commonest in Lofa county. Beans *tugborgee* is especially good.

Among the other flavours to help the starch down, ground **cassava leaves**, boiled to death with *Maggi*, palm oil, onions and meat, is widespread, and **potato greens**, not actually from Irish potatoes, likewise. **Ground pea soup** is the Liberian version of groundnut sauce/*sauce d'arachides*, based on peanut butter. **Bean gravy** is self-explanatory, and usually tasty.

All over Liberia, **cook shops** (chop houses, small restaurants) serve most of these meals.

■ Drinking

Liberia's **beer** is *Club*, in small bottles in Monrovia but the same price for large bottles up-country. There's lethal **palm wine** (usually to accompany a smoke of grass) and **"cane juice"** rum.

Communications: Language, Telecoms and the Media

Liberia's official language is English. It sounds like nothing you've ever heard before – in one traveller's opinion, "as if a punch-drunk Brando of *On the Waterfront* taught all to drop the final sounds of each word and slur the rest". You'll be understood, but you may not always understand. Liberian English is not a proper creole, however, like Krio in Sierra Leone.

While English serves you well enough in the coastal towns, people up-country are more likely to speak one of the country's twenty or so indigenous languages first, though all but the elderly speak some English. The two largest language groups speak peripheral languages of the Mande family: **Kpelle**, concentrated in Bong county and **Dan/Gio/Mano** in Nimba county. **Kru**-speakers and the linguistically-related **Bassa** in Grand Bassa county and **Grebo** in Maryland have a high profile along the coast. The **Vai**, also on the coast, have the distinction of having a script, invented in the 1820s by a Vai headman after a dream (see sample on p.720).

LIBERIAN ENGLISH: A LIMITED GLOSSARY

The trick is to recognise that correctly hearing what's said is no instant route to comprehension. Many words and phrases have different meanings from those in American or British English. You'll soon find yourself slipping into it.

Car Bus, motor bike, any kind of motor transport

Cheap-o Cheap (the -o is a characteristic suffix)

Congos Descendants of freed slaves

Dash Tip, bribe (from Portuguese, *dar-se*)

Donkahfleh Used clothes (lit. "Try it on, if you like it, buy it" – Mandingo)

Du Kor Monrovia peninsula, as referred to by inland peoples

French/French side Guinea or Côte d'Ivoire

A seh, my maa Excuse me my man

In the bush A private matter, settled privately, sometimes a chance sexual encounter

Kwi Foreign, or a foreigner/white person (e.g. Kwi food)

Merico "Americo-Liberian" or "A.L.", less common these days

Money bus Converted pick-up van or lorry with inward-facing bench seats

Of course Maybe, yes . . .

Palava Discussion, argument

Pekin Child

Reach Arrive, get to, stretch, be sufficient

Rogue Thief, to steal

Straight Straight away, immediately

Sumangama Illicit sexual behaviour

Thank you (*Thanky ya*) Congratulations! / you're welcome / I'm glad

---

■ Phones, Post and Telex

Most big towns have a **Telecommunications building** from where you can make international **phone calls**, often more easily than internal calls. The price for "station-to-station" calls is around L$15 for five minutes to Europe and L$25 to the USA. "Person-to-person" calls are a lot more. Be sure to ask for the former. Monrovia has public telephones, mainly in bars. Reverse charge (collect) calls are possible.

The **postal service** is fairly reliable from Monrovia, fairly unreliable from anywhere else. Airline offices acted unofficially as safe couriers until recently, but no longer oblige. Incoming mail is much less certain and you'd be better off having it addressed somewhere (*American Express* or your embassy) than hoping to receive it Poste Restante at one of Monrovia's two post offices.

You can send and receive **telexes** in Monrovia. The public booth numbers are 44212 and 44214.

■ Press and Radio

As for keeping in touch with events, **radio** is your best source of information. Apart from the BBC, ELBC broadcasts nineteen hours a day in Liberian English, French and sixteen indigenous languages. ELWA (dubbed "Eternal Love Winning Africa") is the short-wave station of the Sudan Interior Mission, broadcasting government-approved material only, in English and French and

forty-two African languages. **Television** is limited to a few hours a day in Monrovia only.

The press, too, currently all but silenced, shows no signs of re-establishing the reputation for outspokenness it was beginning to gain after the fall of the first republic in 1980. The government-owned *New Liberian* is what you'd expect. *The News* sticks its neck out a little, as does the best paper, the *Daily Observer*, edited by the resilient Reuters correspondent Stanton B. Peabody. *The Observer* remains permanently on probation.

West Africa magazine was banned from 1985 to 1990, but photocopies of its Liberian coverage circulated clandestinely. It seems it may now be available again.

Opening Hours and Public Holidays

Businesses and offices usually open at 8am or 8.30am and close at 4pm with a 1–2hr break. Banks are open 9am–1pm Monday to Thursday and 9am–2pm Friday. Most shops are open until 6pm and on Saturday morning. On Sunday, everything is closed by law and nothing may be bought or sold until 6pm.

Liberia has a wealth of **public holidays**, and local events augment the list (see box). Muslim holidays, however, don't figure, except at the local level.

PUBLIC HOLIDAYS

Jan 1 New Year's Day

Feb 11 Armed Forces Day

2nd Wed in March Decoration Day, when people decorate family graves

Mar 15 J.J. Roberts (First President's) Birthday

Apr 7 ◊ World Health Day

Apr 12* National Redemption Day, anniversary of the 1980 coup

2nd Fri in April Prayer and Fast Day

Easter Friday

Easter Sunday

May 5 President Doe's Birthday

May 14◊ National Unification Day

May 25◊ African Liberation Day

Jul 26 National Independence Day

Aug 24 National Flag Day

Oct 24 ◊ United Nations Day

Oct 29 ◊ National Youth Day

1st Thur in November Thanksgiving Day

Nov 29 William Tubman's Birthday

Dec 25 Christmas Day

* Don't travel on April 12. It's considered to be a sign of disrespect and the army checkpoints are out in force. Don't travel on April 13 either, as it's National Fundraising Day and they'll sting you blind.

◊ These days are working holidays: most public places and business are open. On the other holidays, all businesses are shut until sunset.

Trouble

Monrovia's crime rate is surprisingly low, and, pickpockets aside, you'll have few problems with ordinary people. Perhaps there's less laughter and more preparedness to stand ground than elsewhere.

The **police**, attired in the secondhand summer uniforms of the New York city cops, are often months late being paid and rely on extortion to get by. The reception of most white visitors by them and the various military and para-military forces is brusquely commercial. They sometimes do wind up unwary travellers to an unprecedented degree with outrageous threats and demands. If you intend to avoid repeated small payments (L$1–5), you should be prepared to adopt a very flexible attitude. You're either delayed and hassled, or you pay. Occasionally, relations can become unpleasant, but rarely is this entirely unprovoked. "Provocation" includes a lack of respect for uniforms, missing papers, flippancy. A little shrewdness can help. Humour is helpful, but only so far. African-Americans and black Europeans generally have an easier time.

Above all, there are two **places to avoid**: Camp Johnson Street in Monrovia (the road past the Executive Mansion) and Tuzon in Grand Geddeh county, President Doe's home village.

Lastly, if you're walking past a **school at around 7.45am**, listen for the whistle and stop as the flag is raised, on pain of a day in police company.

■ Women Travellers

Women experience Liberia in very divergent ways. In **Monrovia**, you're likely to be ignored, and may even find it laid-back. **Away from the capital**, women travelling alone *have* found themselves, unexpectedly, in threatening situations, detained by soldiers or police and questioned at length. Such encounters are frightening (as they are, too, for lone men), but not actually dangerous. They're most likely to occur in periods of instability and rumour, so keep in touch with events before arriving.

Entertainments

Football is big. Baseball (notwithstanding the illustration on the back of the new L$5 note) is not. There's no indigenous theatre or cinema, though in rural areas the storytelling tradition and other forms of homemade entertainment thrive. Video shows in most towns offer Kung Fu, Death and Blood.

■ Music

Liberian **popular music** is a scrappy scene at the moment. There's an eight-track studio in Monrovia and the potential for a recording industry (Kru seamen are the possible originators of highlife guitar playing) but little seems to be happening. Of the cassettes that are widely available, drossy, tinsely, Americophile soul-funksters **Dave** and **Big Steve Worjloh** seem the most popular. They compete in the bootleg stakes with slightly more African sounds – Liberian funk from **Robert Toe** and **Gedeh Rooster**, sugary reggae too from **The Vempees** and a strong commercial talent from **John Haynes** – and more interesting music from the likes of **Kplenkenten** (the best of the lot), **Nyan A Porkpan and Ben O Yini** (soukous) and **Gbesa Body**'s Kru guitar songs. By no coincidence, these last three represent a less-Americanised musical culture.

The problem with all these artists on cassette is simply dire production and a final sound that makes most West African bootleg cassettes sound clean in comparison.

Lastly, there's the relatively well-known **Miattah Fahnbulleh**, the pan-Africanist female singer with a big West African following. Her lyrics haven't always found favour at home. There's nothing available on cassette or record in Europe.

Directory

AIRPORT TAX US$20 on departure

CLOTHES Liberians are very clothes-conscious and treat dress as a mark of respect. You will cause offence all over if you dress below your perceived wealth and status. Shorts are pretty unacceptable for women except on the beach. For reasons of climate bring extra supplies of underwear if you're staying long in Liberia.

CRAFTS Liberia is not renowned. You can buy **masks** in Monrovia (best are the **Dan/Gio** ones from the northeast, the archetypal style of which is remarkably beautiful) but most are tacky exports from all over Africa. **Ganta Leprosarium** is the crafts capital – great **baskets** and **woodwork**. And you can sometimes find **"country money"** in the Kissi country in the north of Lofa county – the T-bar iron "Kissi pennies" also once used in Sierra Leone. But **tailoring** is the best deal. Two good shirt styles are "Vai" and "Paramount Chief".

DUTY Duty-free tobacco, booze, etc, are standard enough. If you're bringing in unusual or expensive items or equipment, however, you may be liable to pay duty at 75 percent. Arrange to be met, or try a diplomatic channel.

ELECTRICITY When you can find some it's a mix of American-style 110v, AC 60Hz, and European 220–240v, AC 50Hz.

HANDSHAKES Nothing to do with the Masons though it practically could be, the classic Liberian handshake ends with both parties making a deft snap of the fingers. This custom is supposed to derive from the missing fingers of freed slaves.

PHOTOGRAPHY Leave the VCR behind; ordinary cameras are hassle enough. Official attitudes to photography tend to treat it as a serious crime, especially in Monrovia. There is a photo permit, which you can obtain, in theory, from the Tourist Office there. In practice, it's best simply to avoid displaying your camera while in the capital. Upcountry, it shouldn't excite much attention and most people you meet are happy to have their pictures taken. Just ask first; it should be free.

WILDLIFE Liberia's huge tracts of primary forest remain (for the time being) one of its great natural resources, but are fast being slashed and burned for farm plots and plundered by logging. Forest **elephants**, which numbered a mere 2000 ten years ago, have been decimated. It's estimated there may be 100 remaining, probably not enough to recover as a viable population without immediate protection (little chance). The **pygmy hippo**, although rarely seen, may not be threatened. It was discovered here in 1913 and Liberia is its stronghold. Another pygmy, a **"pygmy rhino"**, was reputed to live in the mountain jungle but its existence has never been proved conclusively.

WOMEN'S MOVEMENT There's no active women's organisation in the Republic. But there is a magazine, *The Liberian Woman*, from Monitor Publications, PO Box 0136 Paynesville, Liberia (office in Gurley St, above the Liberian Technical Services next to the Commerce Ministry) that's well worth checking out.

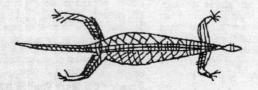

A Short History of Liberia

The very reasons that lead to Liberia being chosen for the resettlement of American freed slaves mean that its "pre-modern" history is scantily recorded and still barely known. Until the time of American colonisation, large regions were virtually stateless territory and, before the demographic shock waves set off by the collapse of the Niger River's Songhai empire in the sixteenth century, it's likely that much of what is now Liberia was dense uninhabited rainforest. True, in the northwest, where people were influenced by the urban culture of Mandingo immigrants, some fairly state-like features did emerge – and there was even a large Kpelle confederation called Kondo in the southern Lofa region north of Monrovia. But life mostly revolved around family and clan; nothing larger. Trade in the interior was largely conducted by the Mandingos. Some of the earliest *overseas contacts*, from before 1700, were between European merchant adventurers and Vai- and Kru-speaking coastal people. The Vai were a Mande-speaking group from the north; the Kru had probably migrated along the coast from the east.

■ The Colonisation

The motives that brought **freed American slaves** to the "Grain Coast" from 1822 onwards were more mixed than those that inspired the settlement of Freetown in Sierra Leone. The drive behind the repatriation of Africans was as confusedly racist as it was humanitarian, and for every Bible-inspired philanthropist there was a plantation owner with a mistrust of America's growing free black population.

The white patrons of the American Colonization Society succeeded in raising funds and in getting Congress to support their scheme. In 1822 the first emigrants were landed on a tiny island – Providence Island, now under the road bridge – at the mouth of the Mesurado River. Protracted negotiations with local Bassa and Dei headmen eventually secured the "right" (for $300 worth of trading goods) for the Americans to occupy the Du Kor peninsula on which Monrovia now stands. As in Freetown, there was a mixture of resentment of the settlers and anticipation of the material benefits they might bring.

The power of **firearms**, however, was often used to put the final seal on settlement and "protection" agreements, as the colonists continued to arrive, their numbers swelled by slaves freed from illegal slave ships in West African ports. With the approval of the white agents of the ACS, and later the first white governor of the "Commonwealth of Liberia" (Thomas Buchanan), followed by the first black governor and president (J. J. Roberts), the settlers expanded into the coastal hinterland and extended their control over communal, trust-held African land. Concepts of *ownership* of territory were, as in most of Africa,

quite alien; there was often no immediate indigenous response to what appeared from the local viewpoint to be meaningless posturing on the part of the black Americans.

Through the 1820s and 30s, Washington shirked any responsibility and refused to recognise Liberia as an American colony, despite the industry of the ACS branches in New York, Pennsylvania, Mississippi and Maryland. In 1847, when British interests in Sierra Leone directly conflicted with those of the Liberian settlers, three of the Liberian colonies issued a **"Declaration of Independence"**, drawn up on American lines and establishing Africa's first republic under the presidency of **Joseph J. Roberts**. Maryland-in-Liberia, the colony in the southeast at Cape Palmas, was annexed by the republic ten years later, but it was only in 1862 that Abraham Lincoln's government finally recognised the Liberian republic.

During its first century of existence, Liberia's main **trading partners** were not American but British, Dutch and German. The republic used British currency until 1943. The United States provided mostly symbolic support – and a stream of earnest missionaries, black and white. America made Liberia its first major loan in 1871, but high interest and embezzlement frittered it away. Serious economic development of the country was, in any case, not viable if it was to be based only on the small coastal enclaves.

■ Nineteenth-century colonial society

The **class system** of nineteenth-century Liberia bore a remarkable resemblance to that of the United States. Established **free black families** formed the social and economic elite. **Slaves emancipated** in order to go to Liberia were next in status, followed at some remove by the **"Congos"** – displaced Africans from captured slave ships who had never been to America. The Congos' position was at first marginal, but their indoctrination in American ways and the determination of the churches to keep them from returning to "barbarism" saw them rapidly assimilated in the ranks of the Americo-Liberians, a merging that was further aided by the formation of the True Whig Party in 1869. At the bottom of the social heap were the **indigenous population** – the "tribes of savages" who were the target of missionary zeal and who outnumbered the colonists by twenty to one. The "tribes", as they were called, were ruled as a protectorate, in strictly colonial fashion. Slightly adrift of this quite rigid order was a small group of **Caribbean blacks** who had emigrated from the British empire for political reasons and who were to become highly influential in government.

This social order only existed to begin with in the colonial pockets along the coast. In the interior, Americo-Liberian traders and missionaries were at the mercy of local sympathies. And until after World War I missionaries (whether white or black) were prohibited by the government from establishing churches and schools more than fifty miles into the interior, for fear of indigenous insurrection. In places there was deep hostility towards the Americo-Liberians. Right up until the 1920s parts of Kru-land openly resisted tax payments and the judicial authority of Monrovia.

But in the late nineteenth century, as the Republic of Liberia became a fact on the ground as well as on paper, the biggest threats were external. Liberia had to concede large areas of disputed territory in the 1890s and early 1900s to the French and British.

■ Forced Labour: the Firestone Republic

Where they were in complete control, the **economic practices** of the Americo-Liberians were mostly repressive. Labour was purchased from compliant chiefs; various forms of debt-slavery and "apprenticeship" served the interests of plantation owners; and in the 1920s a full-scale trade in **forced labourers**, captured at gun point, flourished with the Spanish-ruled island of Fernando Po in Central Africa. The **League of Nations** commissioned an enquiry which found evidence of high-level government complicity in the commercial activities of the Liberian armed forces.

President King and his vice-president were forced to resign and diplomatic relations with Britain and the USA were suspended for five years. During this period, international discussions over Liberia's future tended to favour the placing of the country under a League of Nations mandate (without any admission that practices as illiberal as Liberia's continued in many European-held territories). At the same time, Colonel Elwood Davis of the **Liberian army** was engaged in brutally putting down the last outbursts of anti-settler resistance from the Kru in the Grand Bassa district – a resistance emboldened by the League report.

But what had first focused world attention on Liberia was the arrival of the **_Firestone_ rubber company** in 1926. _Firestone_ was granted, on give-away terms, a concession of a million acres (4000 square kilometres) of which it still hasn't planted more than one third. _Firestone_, in boosting rubber to the country's principal commodity, turned the economy round, soaked up Monrovia's unemployed (and in the early years at least, participated in the use of forced labour) and encouraged the arrival of an array of peripheral industries. The United States, which had no small interest in the fortunes of _Firestone_, began taking a strategic commercial view of Liberia. Under the _Firestone_ loan agreement in 1927, Liberia came under American financial supervision. By the outbreak of World War II (in which Liberia was used as an allied seaplane base and communications centre), the "Firestone Republic" was clearly established. The fall of Malaya and consequent extra demand for Liberian rubber – followed, in 1943 by the adoption of the US$ currency – confirmed Africa's first neo-colonial state.

■ Tubman: 1944–71

President William V. Tubman was elected into West Africa's period of most rapid change. The nationalist demands across the borders couldn't be ignored in Liberia, and small measures of democratisation were enacted. Although paper citizenship had been granted to all Liberians in 1904, it meant little to the "tribal" majority until 1946, when they finally got the **right to vote** – or rather their chiefs did on their behalf. Even then, a property clause kept anyone who didn't own land disenfranchised.

Tubman, a lawyer by training and an astute politician, promulgated two major new policies; an **"open-door policy"** to encourage foreign investment throughout the country (foreign capital had previously been restricted to the coast in a crude economic repression of the interior); and a **"unification policy"** to improve domestic relations between the Americo-Liberians, who were beginning to see favour in African names and culture, and the peoples of the interior, who were less often labelled "the tribes". These apparently progressive moves signalled a new era in Liberia. Yet their effect was to raise expectations without delivering any substantial improvements in most peoples' lives. When foreign companies began to arrive in large numbers in the 1960s, the prizes for the elite were plain to see, but there was little to benefit the rural poor. While some advantages did come along the new roads being cut through the forests, improved communications also heralded a **land grab** that ranks with the most blatant in African history. Tens of thousands of peasant farmers were forced to sell ancestral land, or simply lost it to Americo-Liberian interests they were powerless to resist. Monrovia and other towns swelled with rural migrants forced into the coastal cash economy, while agricultural land lay fallow, or was turned over to export crops — coffee, cocoa and rubber.

Even the new political structures were very heavily biased towards the interests of the Americo-Liberians. The coastal counties, with less than half the population, had over half the seats in the upper house or Senate and no less than four-fifths of the seats in the House of Representatives. And, of course, the new migrants to the towns and coastal plantations held no land and were therefore not entitled to vote in any case. Needless to add, the opportunities to occupy senior posts for anyone not connected to a leading Americo-Liberian family were nil. Moreover, freedom of the (government-owned) press, like political freedom, was severely curtailed.

Tubman's efforts to appear reformist were further belittled by the continued deep-rooted influence of the **Masonic Order**. Almost every important and influential figure in Liberian society was a mason, and Tubman and several senior ministers took turns in office as Worshipful Grand Masters. Masonry was the medium through which flowed almost unrestricted corruption,

though Tubman was diligent in keeping his family's activities as quiet as possible.

Yet President Tubman had a large following. He was lauded among settler families and in the first two decades of his presidency there was some showing of a genuine popularity among the indigenous peoples, more so than any previous incumbent — which is perhaps not to say a great deal. While it was recognised that the lid couldn't be kept on forever (and there were a number of assassination attempts), Tubman had no popular opposition to contend with (either from within the Whig party or from outside) and there was no alternative agenda to compare with his.

But as Tubman's post-war reforms began to lose their shine, his genuine popularity became an increasingly insincere, fearful and costly **cult of adulation*** and he lost credibility. By the mid-1960s an elaborate security apparatus of "public relations officers' was informing on every disgruntled conversation; "popular" public support had to be underpinned by government inducements; and libel and slander laws were interpreted in ways which made any criticism very expensive.

Tubman died during surgery in a London hospital in 1971.

■ Tolbert: 1971–80

Tubman's successor, long-time vice-president **William Tolbert**, was a figure from a smaller mould. Tolbert, a career politician, wasn't able in the long term to camouflage his elite background. His family were enormously influential and rapacious in business, and his style was ostentatious. On first becoming president, however, he acted the part with determination, abandoning New York fashion for sober Kaunda suits and even putting on a special country accent for his up-country tours. Although he had a knack for coining platitudinous slogans ("total involvement for higher heights", "lifting the people from mats to mattresses"), he picked up Tubman's "unification policy" with more enthusiasm than the old man himself — releasing political prisoners, freeing the press and touring the country in a *VW Beetle* instead of the executive *Mercedes*.

Tolbert surprised the country. For the first few years of his rule he was frequently given the benefit of any doubts. But he had none of Tubman's charisma, counted on less support

---

*For example, workers on state payrolls found their salaries docked to pay for annual birthday presents.

within the True Whig party, and was evidently fearful throughout his life of the fate he was finally to meet, for his public appearances, once the honeymoon period was over, became few and shy. Bullet-proof limousines and a mix of paranoia and self-glorification once again became the order of the day. He spent a good deal of time, and vast sums of public money, at the presidential "city" of **Bentol**, the renamed and reconstructed Bensonville of his birth.

Liberia in the 1970s was a country open to American cultural influence, but also with its own internal momentum for social change. The customary barriers that had set the settler families against native Liberians had less and less meaning, and a new constituency of disaffected, often foreign-educated, Liberians of all backgrounds was beginning to make known its demands for root-and-branch reform and its repugnance for the status quo. Four percent of the population owned more than sixty percent of the land. **Opposition groups** began to form – the *Movement for Justice in Africa* (*MOJA*) and the *Progressive Alliance of Liberians* (*PAL*).

The Year of Ferment

By the end of the 1970s, Tolbert had lost any sense of purpose in his presidency beyond the expansion of the **Tolbert family empire**. His **chairmanship of the OAU** in 1979 climaxed with a Monrovia summit of preposterous expense. At the same time, a deepening **domestic crisis over the price of rice** caused him to vacillate dangerously between the clear need for reforms and family pressure to carry on with business as usual. In his indecision, he became increasingly alienated from even his True Whig backers and lost any vestige of support from the young dissidents and students.

Rice production, unlike that of most export crops, was not government-subsidised. The state offered no marketing help and co-operative marketing was officially discouraged for political reasons. Cash-hungry farmers were therefore forced to sell their rice harvest at a crippling discount to Lebanese wholesalers, who would later sell it back to them at the much higher government-approved price. In April 1979, at the end of the "hungry season", when the whole country was having to buy rice, Tolbert announced a hike of fifty percent in the price of a sack of rice, to encourage local planting and decrease the bill for imported rice.

He could hardly have been more provocative. The *PAL* called a **demonstration** to protest the increase and, on April 14, 2000 people led by students marched through Monrovia. The troops who'd been ordered onto the streets included many sympathisers, and they let the crowd pass peacefully. But the police lost their nerve and opened fire. In the panic, the shooting became indiscriminate and the demonstration turned into a full-scale riot which blazed through Monrovia for the whole day. Lebanese shops were particularly singled out by the crowd. President Tolbert called frantically for Guinean president Sekou Touré's help and, later in the day, MIG fighter planes from Conakry made passes over the city.

Over 100 people were killed in the **"rice riots"**, and buried en masse without ceremony. Hundreds more were arrested in the aftermath and thirty were convicted on the capital charge of treason. Press and personal freedoms that Tolbert had introduced eight years earlier were suspended, the universities were shut down, and the army increasingly found itself the tool of True Whig repression. High-profile foreign policy and Tolbert's OAU chairmanship kept international attention on Liberia, to the president's unease.

The "rice riots" marked a watershed in Liberian politics. The Old Guard was squarely on the defensive. Tolbert had become a pathetic, dithering figure. In October, *MOJA*'s leader, **Togba-Nah Tipoteh**, challenged the True Whig incumbent in the election for the Mayor of Monrovia, and would have won but for the cancellation of the poll. The *PAL* was recognised as a party and then later banned and its leaders detained. In March there was a series of arrests of army officers and ordinary soldiers. They were all released, together with other political prisoners, on the morning of April 12, 1980.

■ April 12 1980: the Coup and the PRC

A **military takeover** by the largely Americo-Liberian officers' ranks had long been thought likely. They were competent, educated men, known to be frustrated at the lack of political will on the part of the government. However, as Tolbert himself appeared to be toying with permitting an opposition, the establishment was actually more fearful of a *right-wing* putsch by hard-line reactionaries close to the president.

Instead, when **the coup** came, in the early hours of April 12, it was the army's senior enlisted soldier, 28-year-old **Master Sergeant**

Samuel Doe who with 16 others stormed into the Executive Mansion in Monrovia, slashed and shot to death President Tolbert and killed and mutilated his 26-strong executive guard. As daylight dawned and key communications centres and arsenals were captured, the entire century-old True Whig edifice collapsed across the country. Some ninety senior Tolbert officials were detained and many others were placed under house arrest or threatened.

It was not an elegant coup. By mid-morning Monrovians were dancing in the streets and rejoicing over Tolbert's body, displayed at the Kennedy Hospital. Two days later, the body, along with the remains of the murdered presidential guards, was dumped in a swampy area near the Palm Grove cemetery (the same spot where victims of the rice riots had been buried a year earlier). Across Liberia, **revenge attacks** were raging, mostly by ill-disciplined troops, on Americo-Liberian persons and property. The Masonic temple in Monrovia was ransacked. The town of Bentol was demolished. An estimated 200 people were killed.

Doe's *People's Redemption Council* (*PRC*), largely composed of Krahn-speaking soldiers, set up a military-civilian cabinet, partly of released *PAL* and *MOJA* leaders, and made the usual promises about a swift resumption of civilian rule. Meanwhile, all political activity was banned and the constitution of 1847 suspended. There was support from "revolutionary" governments abroad and silence or protests from West African neighbours and the West. But the broad popularity of the coup within Liberia wasn't in doubt. The *PRC* "tried" most of its prisoners in a hastily convened "People's Court" and, ten days after the coup, thirteen senior figures were executed.

The trials and the summary nature of **the executions on the beach** bore no significant difference from practices conducted with less fanfare under the regimes of Tubman and Tolbert. But Doe made the colossal public relations mistake of inviting the **press and foreign TV crews**. The film of the brutal shootings, dispatched with total contempt for suffering, in an atmosphere of drunkenness and confusion, has tragically become the single most indelible image of inhumanity in modern Africa.

Europe and the United States reacted to the executions with horrified hypocrisy. But after Doe's brief flirtation with the Soviet Union, the USA recognised the new regime. President

Carter's defeat by **Ronald Reagan** in October could hardly have been better timed from Doe's point of view. The United States swiftly moved to increase its aid package to Liberia tenfold, making it a larger recipient of US aid than all other African nations put together.

The end of the *PRC*'s "radical phase" (not that it had ever clearly expressed any ideology) was marked by the departure from the cabinet in July 1982 of *MOJA*'s Tipoteh and Baccus Matthews of the *PPP* (the successor to the *PAL*) and by the execution in August of five *PRC* radicals who had earned Doe's distrust, including the vice-chairman **Thomas Weh Syen**. On a positive note, a broad-based Commission worked intensively, with full public involvement, to devise a **new constitution** with the mandate of all Liberians. It was accepted by referendum in 1984.

But by mid-1983, with an unbanning of political parties to look forward to, and elections scheduled for a return to civilian rule, the *PRC* was already turning back towards the **True Whig model of government**. All the traditional **trappings of power** had long been taken on by the revolutionaries; now, **disgraced figures from the Tubman and Tolbert era** were gradually allowed back into public life. Striking workers found the *PRC* dealt with them just as Tolbert would have done, with violence and intimidation. There were **high school student riots** in Sanniquellie, Nimba county, and, in October, army commander **Thomas Quiwonkpa** (a Nimba man credited with pulling the armed forces into line since the coup) refused a downgrading and went into voluntary exile in Côte d'Ivoire, pursued by Doe's accusations that he had tried to stage a coup.

■ **The Road to "Civilian Government"**

When political rights were restored in July 1984, severe restrictions were placed on the **new parties** that emerged – including the requirement of a $150,000 deposit in order to contest the elections! The University's Dr. **Amos Sawyer** took the reins of *MOJA* in the *Liberian People's Party* (*LPP*), but it was banned. So, too, was **Baccus Matthews'** *United Peoples' Party* (successor to the *PPP* and *PAL* who had organised the 1979 rice protest). Doe's own *National Democratic Party of Liberia* was immediately registered, and three less influential opposition parties, led by a headmaster, **Gabriel Kpolleh**, and former Whig ministers with "tribal" links,

Edward Kesselly and **Jackson Doe**, were eventually registered weeks before the elections.

Attack on the University

The most restless proponents of change and reform, **the students**, had waited four years in virtual silence, patiently enduring intimidation and arrest for the least contentious remarks about the *PRC*'s rule. They justifiably felt their pressure had weakened the Tolbert regime and paved the way for the success of the 1980 coup.

The spark for the **attack on the University** was a press interview given by Amos Sawyer, Dean of Social Science, in which he criticised Doe for pre-empting the democratic process and bending his own rules. On August 22, Sawyer was arrested and the students mounted a demonstration on campus. Eye-witnesses reported a 200-strong detachment of the Executive Mansion guard stormed the University, firing into the backs of fleeing students. No official enquiry has ever been held into the attack though the government admitted 74 people had been wounded. By the number of students missing afterwards, dozens were killed. Many women were raped and horrifically tortured. The soldiers looted and destroyed some two million dollars' worth of property. The campus was subsequently sealed off for five days.

The process of return to civilian rule, from this point on, was little more than going though the motions. The credibility of the coup leaders of 1980 had been shattered. Finally, Doe's right-hand man, **Maj. Gen. Nicholas Podier**, was arrested on suspicion of treason, and then retired from the military. This left Doe the sole survivor of the original *PRC* executive.

The Elections

The run-up to the **elections of October 15 ,1985** made nonsense of the claim that they were to be "free and fair". The *NDPL* was able to pull the whole government apparatus into serving its campaign before opposition parties had even been legalised. There was widespread intimidation and coercion. The elections themselves went off peacefully, with a large turnout (though not without serious malpractice, including a bonfire of ballots outside Monrovia). But when early counting indicated a large vote for **Jackson Doe's *Action Party***, the *NDPL*-partisan "Special Elections Commission", in charge of running the election, found spurious arguments to justify ordering all ballots to be transported to Monrovia. They were counted there by an overwhelmingly biased committee of citizens, "handpicked by the Commission", consisting of Doe aids, Krahn civilians and *NDPL* supporters.

Two weeks later it was announced that Doe's party had won with a 51 percent share of the vote. The only voice that sounded a credulous note in response to this "result" was that of the U.S. Department of State. In Liberia, the victorious government banned demonstations in the aftermath "out of fear that the jubilation might get out of hand". Of course.

■ The Second Republic

The **Second Republic** got off to a bad start, with the refusal of the elected opposition to take their seats in the Legislature on the grounds that this would legitimise the fraudulent elections.

This shaky beginning was crippled by the serious **coup attempt** of November 12, 1985, led by the respected ex-*PRC* man **Thomas Quiwonkpa**. He arrived from Sierra Leone with two dozen heavily armed soldiers. The tragedy of the coup lay in the premature radio announcement that Doe had been toppled. There was mass jubilation on the streets of Monrovia. But Quiwonkpa's small force failed to strike hard enough. Doe kept control, recaptured the radio station, and set about rounding up those who had celebrated his end.

Retribution was frenzied and, for the first time, unmistakably **tribalist** in nature. Quiwonkpa himself was caught and killed, and his body taken to central Monrovia where onlookers and a TV crew witnessed hysterical soldiers tearing it apart with bayonets and consuming the flesh in a scarcely believable cannibalistic ritual. The soldiers, mostly Krahn, arbitrarily subjected non-Krahn speakers to extortion, beatings and murder. For a week, truckloads of mutilated corpses passed through Monrovia to be buried in mass graves on isolated beaches. Up-country, in Doe's Krahn homeland of **Grand Gedeh county** and in **Nimba county**, the Dan/Gio-speaking ethnic group of both Quiwonkpa and Jackson Doe was viciously harassed. A reign of terror descended, and hundreds were killed over the ensuing months. The iron-mining town of Yekepa was a particular target. Officials of the part-foreign-owned mining company that operates there refused to speak to human rights investigators about reports that company staff and vehicles were involved in summary arrests and executions.

The **United States**, Liberia's prop, refused to notice what was happening – or perhaps was too ill-informed to see – and the Liberian opposition, at home and in exile, was bitter over the administration's official bland "satisfaction" with Doe's performance and the conduct and outcome of the elections. Only Congress resolved that the current aid package should be contingent on honest elections and an improvement in human rights.

After Doe's lavish inauguration as president on January 6, 1986, there was a remarkable strengthening of nerve. The new constitution was technically now in force and the press began to speak up again. While most of the opposition seats in the Legislature were finally filled, the three opposition parties found scope for a united front in **the Grand Coalition** which served as a platform for all dissenting voices in the country. The Coalition was banned and its three leaders (Jackson Doe, Kesselly and Kpolleh) sent to the notorious **Belle Yella** prison camp in Lofa county on charges of "contempt of court" for referring to themselves as members of what was not an officially recognised body.

The seventeen experts

1987 saw Doe requesting American expertise in running his shambolic and corrupt economy. His shameless admission of failure ("I don't know who to trust any more") was, he knew, the only way to keep the funds coming in. The **17 accountancy "experts"** stayed most of 1988, acting virtually as a parallel goverment, limiting the diversion of US aid to private accounts,* overseeing tax collection and sorting out salary backlogs. But they were not empowered to veto cheques signed by Doe himself. Following a US Congressional freeze on aid, they left Monrovia before time and shaking their heads. The IMF and World Bank had by now given up on Liberia meeting its debts and pulled out.

The year was one of increasing turmoil in government, with a large turnover in senior positions and a growing lack of direction. American aid continued to decline as Liberia showed no signs of being able to service any of its debts.

---

* In 1984, Liberia accounted for one third of the $7 billion in Swiss private holdings, considerably more than the country's entire national debt of $1.36 billion at the time.

Crushing the Opposition

On the political front, a number of **opposition figures** fled to the USA where they continued their campaign to remove Doe. Liberian "justice" could claim a catalogue of abuses and deliberate misinterpretations of the law by corrupt senior judges. It was even made explicit that the new constitution was to be seen as no more than a framework on which the government might, or might not, hang its decisions.

The "Grand Coalitionists" were released from Belle Yella, but **Gabriel Kpolleh** was detained again in March 1988 and given a ten-year jail sentence on treason charges in June.

The announcement by Doe in July that an "invasion attempt" from Côte d'Ivoire, led by the exiled Nicholas Podier (one of the co-authors of the 1980 coup), had been foiled and Podier killed, was confused by another story that Podier had arrived by air at Robertsfield Airport with two black Americans. Podier's body was never displayed – an exception from usual practice.

■ Liberia into the 1990s: what next?

Liberia's ill-founded distinction as West Africa's oldest independent republic disguises the fact that, until 1980, it was simply a **colony** whose rulers had *declared* their independence. Had they been white Americans, it seems doubtful whether Washington would have permitted this (any more than Britain did Rhodesia in 1965). Liberia, ruled as a colony by a small elite caste, still retained, at the time of the coup, a property restriction on voting rights. Economic development was entirely colonial in nature. To make some sense of what has happened in the country, it's necessary to see Liberia as the **last independent nation** in West Africa, not the first. And its first ten years have been, not surprisingly, a bloody disaster.

The worst aspect of Liberia's current mess is the emergence of unregenerate **tribalism** of the kind that most of Africa has managed to dispel in exchange for something more permeable. The Liberian armed forces are overwhelmingly Krahn-speaking (a minority group from Grand Gedeh accounting for some five percent of the population). Virtually all the key military leaders are Krahn. Disproportionately, so too are the non-Americo-Liberian holders of high government office. Ordinary Krahn people of Grand Gedeh fear, with justification, the return cycle of retaliation on their ethnic community which a change of government would almost certainly bring.

Moves to fill all important posts with Krahn-speakers seem to be continuing, however. **Maj. Gen. Gray Allison**, an American-trained career soldier and Minister of National Defence until 1989, is not Krahn; he is a Grebo-speaker from Maryland county. In June of that year Allison was sacked and put under house arrest. In August he was sentenced to death for the alleged murder of a policeman whose body was found outside Allison's home.

The **United States administration** has much to answer for in the continuing support, both military and economic, which it extends to Samuel Doe. There were violent scuffles between Liberian exiles and police at a democracy rally outside the Liberian embassy in Washington to mark the tenth anniversary of the "rice riots". The rally was led by two of Liberia's most distin-guished human rights campaigners **Dr Amos Sawyer** and the economist **Mrs Ellen Johnson-Sirleaf**, a former finance minister who had been intimidated into exile in 1986.

The United States claims it does not want to jeopardise the "**special relationship**" it has with Liberia – a relationship based on outdated cold war strategy that allows the virtually free use of a giant military-commercial "**Omega**" navigation station outside Monrovia as well as the *Voice of America* transmitters broadcasting to the whole continent and the **largest American embassy** and American community in Africa. If America fails to question its backing for one of Africa's most entrenched and tribalistic military dictatorships (albeit an English-speaking one with democratic frills), then the process of real development and reform can only be delayed.

POSTSCRIPT: THE CIVIL WAR

The writing of this historical overview was completed on the eve of the **invasion of Liberia** by several hundred rebels who entered from Côte d'Ivoire on Christmas eve, 1989 and took the town of Butuo. Government troops – accompanied by US military advisors – soon lashed back in Nimba county, burning suspected rebel villages. Hundreds of **Gio and Mano civilians** were murdered by troops and thousands fled to Côte d'Ivoire and Guinea. **Mandingos and Krahns** were vicitimised by the rebels. By early January the rebels had over-run Karnplay and they were soon in control of most of Nimba county and apparently gathering strength all the time

Charles Taylor, leader of the *National Patriotic Forces of Liberia*, is a little known ex-Doe minister Charles Taylor. He's wanted by the FBI for jumping bail in Boston while waiting to be extra-dited to Monrovia to face embezzlement charges. In February he fell out with one of his senior commanders, Prince Yormie Johnson, who appears to have moved his breakaway group – the *Independent PFL* – into the northwest.

For three months, the main NPFL consolidated and continued its invasion across the country, but leaving much of Grand Gedeh county and the south-east in the control of government forces. At the end of May they took the major sea port of **Buchanan**.

In late June, as foreign governments scrambled to make evacuation plans for their nationals, the country entered a terminal phase of desperation. In **Monrovia**, Doe and several hundred of his Israeli-trained presidential guard holed themselves up in the Executive Mansion. Businesses closed, strocks of food ran down, city life came to a halt, and the people fled – many to Sierra Leone. Those who stayed, especially any who couldn't prove their unrelatedness to Gio or Mano, risked **summary execution** by troops who terrorised the city under cover of the curfew. Massacres and starvation became commonplace.

As the **community of West African states**, led by Nigeria, tried to arrange negotiations, and then a peacekeeping force, Charles Taylor's rebels moved into the eastern suburbs of Monrovia – and Prince Yormie Johnson's into the north of the city. A three-sided street battle ensued in the city centre. American **marines** were sent in by helicop-ter in August to rescue remaining American citi-zens and protect the embassy. The long awaited **West African peacekeeping force** (composed of detachments from Nigeria, Ghana, Sierra Leone, The Gambia and Guinea, finally arrived at the end of August. It proved quite incapable of separaing the rebels or imposing any ceasefire and recieved its biggest embarrassment on September 10, when Samuel Doe, who ventured out to speak to Prince Johnson and the Ecowas force, was captured by Johnson's men and killed.

In a conference in Banjul, **Dr Amos Sawyer** was handed the job of interim president. It now remains for the Ecowas force to dissolve the rebel armies – a seemingly insuperable problem in the case of Taylor.

Meanwhile, as we go to press, the long-dreaded **revenge on the Krahn** has begun.

MONROVIA

It's hard to know what to make of **MONROVIA**. A city with a population approaching half a million people, it comes across like a dull southern-states American town you'd barely leave the interstate to see. The American analogy is valid: Monrovia was named after US President James Monroe, and grew up on the hilly peninsula at the mouth of the Mesurado River as a home from home for American freed slaves. The slightly skewed emulation of southern architecture and plantation manners was inevitable.

The city spreads widely, north past the Free Port to the teeming slums of **Bushrod island** and southeast through the main suburb of **Sinkor**, the older quarter of **Congotown** ("Congo" referred to the presumed embarkation point of captured slave ships) out to the **beaches** and, eventually, the airport.

Downtown Monrovia is perhaps the least African of all West African capitals. Suburban bungalows are juxtaposed with the relics of antebellum-style grandeur and 1960s multi-storey optimism. For all of Liberia's downside, the capital at least is a pleasant city with sea views in every direction, well-supplied shops and easy to get around (by taxi), with potential, in its beaches, bars and clubs, for a good time. But it doesn't feel much like Africa.

Getting into town

Arriving by air, **Robertsfield** (or **Roberts**) **International Airport** is 60km from the city centre. There are no buses. And there's no *bureau de change*. You'll need US$ in cash to get a taxi to Monrovia. But try to fix up shared arrangements with others on the plane. Taxi hire varies from US$25 to as much as US$45 on a Sunday. Anticipate your final destination in town: if you take your taxi right through to the commercial downtown district, you've a long way to go back if you want Sinkor (where there are several cheap places to stay).

Arriving in Monrovia **by road**, you'll find yourself in one of the city's two main **transport parks**, either the one on the corner of Water and Randall Streets if you've come from Kenema, Sierra Leone, or the other at the end of Water Street by the bridge. The first of these handles all transport to the north and west of the St. Paul River, the second to everywhere else, including all destinations off the paved Ganta highway.

Getting around

There's an abundance of MTA (Monrovia Transit Authority) **buses** between 6am and 6pm, with fares of 25¢–45¢ for any distance. But the city has excellent public transport in the shape of **yellow taxis**. The average wait is about two minutes for a ride in a Japanese compact in good condition with a courteous but occasionally unintelligible driver. *Some* taxis are very bad so you can afford to be choosy. Rates on the set routes are fixed: 45¢ for up to six kilometres (from downtown, as far as 17th St in Sinkor), 70¢ up to nine kilometres. Big bags cost extra. Taxis to the airport area from the Robertsfield parking station at McDonald St/Camp Johnson Rd are around L$2 per head but a special charter to the airport is negotiable, around L$20. The fare to *Hotel Africa* is around L$2, or L$8 for the whole charter.

Accommodation

There's a fair range of places to stay but nowhere cheap that really stands out. If you're able to spend US$30 or more for a room, there are several downtown hotels that should suit. And if money's not the problem there are two major possibilities.

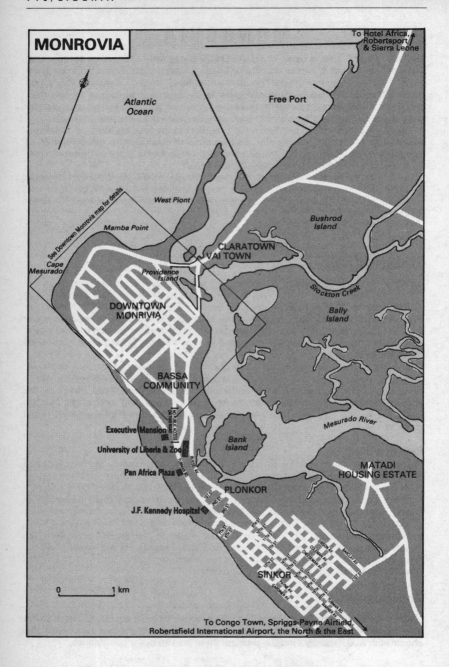

MONROVIA

Atlantic Ocean

Free Port

To Hotel Africa, Robertsport & Sierra Leone

West Piont

Mamba Point

See Downtown Monrovia map for details

CLARATOWN
VAI TOWN

Bushrod
Island

*Cape
Mesurado*

*Providence
Island*

Stockton Creek

DOWNTOWN
MONRIVIA

Bally
Island

BASSA
COMMUNITY

Mesurado River

Executive Mansion
NO PUBLIC ACCESS

University of Liberia & Zoo

Bank
Island

MATADI
HOUSING ESTATE

Pan Africa Plaza

PLONKOR

J.F. Kennedy Hospital

SINKOR

0   1 km

To Congo Town, Spriggs-Payne Airfield,
Robertsfield International Airport, the North & the East

Budget stays

YMCA, corner of Broad and McDonald Streets. Cheap and usually full.

The following are three **mission guest houses**, with cooking and laundry facilities, each located a block apart, along the seafront on Payne Avenue in Sinkor, 4km from downtown. Prices are around L$10/bed, sometimes discounted for volunteers.

Baptist Mission, 11th Street. No smoking or alcohol allowed on the premises.

United Methodist Mission Guest House, 12th St.

Lutheran Guest House, 13th St.

St. Theresa's. A convent-style place, around L$20 including meals.

Mid-range hotels

Centrally located **hotels** (most with self-contained rooms) tend to be sleazy, restless hangouts, notably the cheaper ones. Mostly from around US$25/35, they include:

Ambassador Hotel, U.N. Drive (PO Box 889; ☎223147). On the beach beneath the British Embassy.

Arizona Hotel, Gurley St.

Astoria Hotel, Carey St (PO Box 1280; ☎223667).

Carlton Hotel, Broad St (PO Box 285; ☎221245).

Christina Hotel, Sao Bosso St (PO Box 2786; ☎221158).

El Meson, 83 Carey St (PO Box 67; ☎222154).

Hotel Holiday Inn, 100 Carey St (PO Box 996; ☎222342). Not that *Holiday Inn*.

Hotel de France, 57 Sao Bosso St (PO Box 59; ☎221063). Cheapest in this range.

Julia's Hotel, 43 Gurley St (PO Box 1624; ☎224327). Run by a French woman, this is a good place for Francophone travellers and fine for English speakers, too. Good value for money.

Maxim Hotel, corner of Benson and Gurley Sts (PO Box 1152; ☎222252). One of the cheaper establishments.

Palm Hotel, Broad St (PO Box 132; ☎222964).

Paradise Hotel, Broad St, above the *Gondole Restaurant* (PO Box 318; ☎222128).

Gertylue Floral Park Motel, out of town beyond Sinkor, near the sea and close to the Catholic Hospital (PO Box 1474; ☎261342). Situated in the grounds of a commercial plant nursery, this is worth checking out for its "exotic tropical garden" and swimming pool. You could send your mum a bunch of flowers by *Interflora* at the same time.

Top addresses

Rooms at these hotels start from around US$60/80, not extortionate by international standards.

Ducor Palace, Broad St (PO Box 86; ☎224200/224301, telex 44268). Occupies the highest point on the peninsula but, prices considered, deserves a less elevated position in Monrovia's hotel listings.

Hotel Africa, OAU village, off the Bomi Hills road (PO Box 1515; ☎223992/224519, Telex 44223). If you're splurging at a hotel, this ex-OAU conference village is the one to go for, despite the 10km trip from town. Safe sea swimming, brilliant pool, Monrovia Sporting Club on site.

Eating and drinking

The city puts on a good show in this department. There are **cook shops** everywhere and **bars** in quantity. There's also a large number of mainstream American-flavour **restaurants**, many with a Lebanese or oriental edge, and various specialist eating houses, too. Many places close on Sunday.

Downtown

LIBERIAN

Doris' Cook Shop, at the Mamba Point end of Ashmun St. Famous for its baking, and palm butter every Monday.

Roseline's, 156 Carey St, between Warren and McDonald (☎222513). High-class chop at non-chop prices.

AMERICAN

Arizona Coffee Lounge, Gurley St. Reliable snacks, sandwiches and bar and good breakfasts. Air-conditioned.

Arlene's Restaurant and Bar, Warren St, opposite *Black Sugar Club*. Good, moderately priced American and Liberian food.

Diana's Restaurant, Broad St. Cheap and cheerful junk food, better burgers than most and great breakfasts.

The Rooster, Ashmun St. Inexpensive standard issue fried chicken with the tasty bonus of *Bong fries* (cassava chips).

LEBANESE

Abou-Tel-Lous/The Falafel Shop, Carey St. Cheap, Middle-Eastern sandwiches and snacks and a knock-out selection of sweets and pastries.

Beirut Restaurant, Center St, by the Immigration office (☎222891). Expensive Lebanese place but fun in a group. Open for Sunday brunch.

Gondole Restaurant, beneath the *Paradise Hotel* on Broad St (☎222128). Long and excellent value Lebanese/American menu.

INDIAN

Maharaja Restaurant, Carey St. Straight Indian and very good, but not cheap.

Parkway's, UN Drive, near Camp Johnson Rd. Indian/Liberian and not too expensive. Make up for that by playing on the slot machines.

EUROPEAN

Ambassador Hotel Restaurant, UN Drive (☎223147). Italian food – notably reputed pizzas – and not priced too high.

Casa Real, 55 Carey St (☎224641). Seafood and Portuguese menu.

El Meson, 83 Carey St (☎222154). Spanish and seafood, and usually excellent – popular expat place, expensive. Open Sunday.

Julia's, 43 Gurley St (☎224327). Nice atmosphere with French dishes (the best pepper steak in Liberia), full of ex-pats who can't afford *El Meson*, but still not cheap-o.

Salvatore's, Broad St (☎222643). Classy Italian (from around L$20).

INDULGENCE

Sweet and Sweet, Broad St. Pastries and good ice cream at a price.

Swiss Rolls, Broad St. The top place for cakes and pastries plus biscuits, chocolates and soft ice cream.

Sinkor

G.S.A. Cook Shop, Tubman Boulevard/26th St. Pleasant budget eatery with good service.

Midway Restaurant, Sinkor Shopping Center, Tubman Boulevard/13th St. Specialists in breakfasts and burgers.

The Rooster, Tubman Boulevard/10th St. Another fried fowl outlet.

La Villa, 14th St/Payne Ave (☎261235). All-Italian and not at all cheap. Homemade pasta in Monrovia còmes at a premium.

Sophie's Ice Cream Parlour, Tubman Boulevard. A good selection, and better than you've any cause to expect.

Bars and Clubs

Some of these are raunchy in the extreme, not recommended for unaccompanied women. It's rare to find live music.

Monte Carlo, Broad St/Mechelin St, by the Ministry of Finance. Booze and billiards.

Pandora's, Ashmun St/Mechelin St. Pricier and offers food, too.

The Splendid, Broad St opposite *King Burger*. Usually crowded with Monrovians; there's room to overflow in the bar behind (upstairs and straight down again).

Black Sugar, Warren St. A pick-up joint of the first order, but a popular place to dance; L$10 cover.

Lipp's, on Lynch St, offers similar distractions; cover charge.

New Innovation, again on Lynch St, is a bar with live jazz on Friday and Saturday.

Potter's Bar, behind the *China Restaurant* on Tubman Boulevard. Full of ex-pat males seeking a peaceful drink (unaccompanied Liberian women are barred – believe it!).

The Club House, Tubman Boulevard/24th St. American TV bar with snacks. Look for three palava huts and a massive satellite dish behind a bamboo fence.

Shopping

Monrovia is one of the best cities in West Africa for **cloth and clothing**, combined result of the Free Port and large numbers of self-exiled Fula tailors from Guinea. The main **garment district** is **Benson St**: the entire avenue is lined with clothing and shoe shops. For lappas, go down to the Waterside end of Mechlin St, and for lengths of **cloth cut from bolts**, to Water St at the Gurley St junction. **Saksouk** is a recommended Lebanese drapers on Water St between Gurley and Carey.

Randall St is a good, **general shopping** street, with a number of supermarkets and grocers and several gold dealers, where you might get a good deal with hard bargaining.

Around town

Monrovia's **sightseeing** interest is limited and the place is so infernally humid most of the year that traipsing about isn't high on many people's list of priorities. Providence Island, the museum and the zoo are worth targetting when you have the energy. Waterside market you'll probably find yourself in anyway, sooner or later.

Tiny **Providence Island**, in the Mesurado River on the north side of the city centre, is the site of the first settlers' landings in 1822. It's overflown by a road bridge, but the squat grey hulks of various military edifices remain at one end. Providence Island is "now a place of amusement and recreation" according to official sources – a little hard to believe when you go there.

The **National Museum** (daily, 8am–6pm), on Broad Street at Buchanan Street – housed in the mid-nineteenth-century building that was once the seat of the State Legislature – has modest collections of historical and ethnographic items, various photos and archaeological pieces, and a rather more carefully tended gift shop with arty crafts and books. Next door, on the corner of Center St, the **Providence Baptist Church**, founded in 1839, is the city's oldest. And one block north and two west, the **Executive Pavillion** on the corner of Randall and Ashmun Streets was built by the first president of the republic, J. J. Roberts.

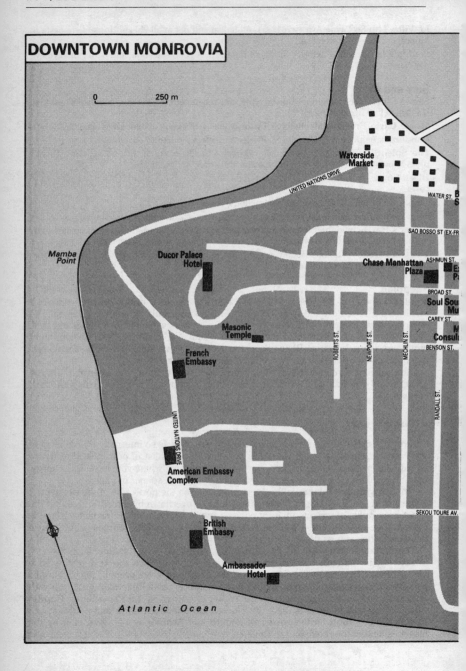

DOWNTOWN MONROVIA

0   250 m

Waterside Market

UNITED NATIONS DRIVE

WATER ST.

B S

SAO BOSSO ST (EX-FR

Mamba Point

Ducor Palace Hotel

Chase Manhattan Plaza

ASHMUN ST.

E Pa

BROAD ST.

Soul Sou Mu

CAREY ST.

Masonic Temple

Consul

BENSON ST.

French Embassy

ROBERTS ST.

NEWPORT ST.

MECHLIN ST.

RANDALL ST.

UNITED NATIONS DRIVE

American Embassy Complex

SEKOU TOURE AV.

British Embassy

Ambassador Hotel

Atlantic Ocean

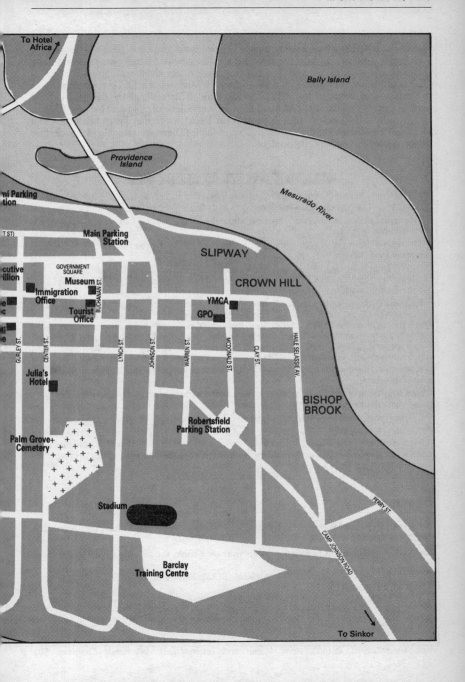

To Hotel Africa

Bally Island

Providence Island

Mesurado River

mi Parking tion

T ST)

Main Parking Station

SLIPWAY

CROWN HILL

GOVERNMENT SQUARE

cutive illion

Museum

Immigration Office

Tourist Office

BUCHANAN ST.

YMCA

GPO

GURLEY ST.

CENTER ST.

LYNCH ST.

JOHNSON ST.

WARREN ST.

McDONALD ST.

CLAY ST.

HAILE SELASSIE AV.

Julia's Hotel

BISHOP BROOK

Palm Grove Cemetery

Robertsfield Parking Station

Stadium

PERRY ST.

CAMP JOHNSON ROAD

Barclay Training Centre

To Sinkor

The **Steiner's Zoo and animal orphanage** on Airfield road has some seventy species of Liberian fauna. Pygmy hippos are the main attraction (don't be fobbed off with young common hippos: the pygmies are disagreeable, smelly animals and quite different) and other captives include leopards, golden cats, civets and chimps.

Down at **Waterside** you soon realise where all Monrovia's action is concentrated. In the market and along the top of Mechlin and Randall Streets is all the downmarket city centre commercialism (see *Listings*, below, for some details). Head off into the thick of things beyond the market and you're on **West Point**, an extraordinary bottleneck of a slum and more crowded than you'd believe possible. There are valuable pickpocketing opportunities everywhere. Be prudent.

OUT OF TOWN BEACHES

It's important to note that most of the beaches along this part of the coast are exceedingly dangerous. Tugging **rip tides** pull swimmers to their deaths with sobering frequency.

Tropicana Beach at the *Hotel Africa* has safe swimming – and safe lying about because it's not open to the public.

The rest of Monrovia's beaches string along the coastline by the road to Roberts International Airport.

ELWA Beach: a private beach operated by the Sudan Interior Mission. Weekends, missionaries only (how dull); weekdays, general public, but no alcohol permitted. A 65¢ taxi ride from town.

Kenema (Cooper's) Beach: the best one close to the city (15km) because of its shallow shelf into the ocean, with palms and junk vendors; rather busy; entrance fee. Take a 50¢ taxi ride as far as the ELWA junction, and another 50¢ ride to the beach. Kenema's advantage is the freshwater lagoon behind where you can rinse off the salt. The *Kenema Beach Restaurant* is an expensive seafood place. The *National Cultural Centre* is at **Kendeja** (a.k.a. Paynesville) nearby, though it's uncertain what you'll find there these days. The massive and mysterious **carved face** of rough-hewn stone known as *Blo Degbo* should still be sitting there.

Barnes Beach: a small beach with rougher sea and a rougher and more affordable snack bar/restaurant.

Cole's Beach: about a mile from the main road with a nice lagoon and palm groves.

Caesar's Beach: beautiful and peaceful, and worth the effort of getting to if you can, but it has a steep shelf and difficult swimming.. The *Caesar Beach Motel* is now little used and not wildly expensive. You can use the facilities there when they have any. They keep up appearances.

Directory

American Express Main agent is *Doukor Travel Agency*, Chase Manhattan Plaza, Randall St (☎221104, 224209).

Banks If you're making transactions with your own bank, the following may be the most useful:

Bank of Credit and Commerce International (*BCCI*), Randall St/Broad St (PO Box 3588; ☎224011, telex 44470).

Chase Manhattan Bank NA, PO Box 181, Randall St.

Citibank (Liberia), Ashmun St (PO Box 280; ☎224991, telex 44274).

Books *National Bookstore* at Carey/Mechlin Sts and on Broad St.

Car Hire The two main operators are: *Yes Transport Services*, 80 Camp Johnson Road (PO Box 49; ☎222970, 221403, telex 44396) and *International Automobile Company*, 301

AIRLINE OFFICES

Aeroflot, Pan-African Plaza, Tubman Bd (☎261399).

Air Afrique, 53–55 Broad St (PO Box 2077; ☎224568, 224624).

Air Liberia, PO Box 2076, Broad St (☎222144).

Ethiopian Airlines c/o *Doukor Travel*, Chase Manhattan Plaza, Randall St.

British Airways, Randall St (PO Box 1279; ☎222245, 222479).

Ghana Airways, Broad St (PO Box 788; ☎222277).

KLM Dutch Airlines, 56 Broad St (PO Box 1413; ☎222631/2).

Nigeria Airways, 75 Broad St (PO Box 1409; ☎222112/222845).

Sabena Belgian Airlines, Broad St (PO Box 2298; ☎221204).

Swissair, Broad St/Randall St (PO Box 2306; ☎2222809).

UTA, c/o *Air Afrique*.

Weasua Airlines, Spriggs-Payne Airfield.

EMBASSIES AND VISAS DETAILS

Algeria, Capitol By-pass (PO Box 2032; ☎224311, telex 44475).

Cameroon, 18th St/Payne Ave, Sinkor (PO Box 414; ☎261374, telex 44240); may need letter from your embassy for visa.

Canada, Peter Reinis (Hon. Consul), *Exchem*, Harbel, Firestone (☎721086/7).

Central African Republic, Tubman Blvd, Sinkor (PO Box 545; ☎261319).

Côte d'Ivoire, Tubman Blvd, Congotown (PO Box 126; ☎261284, telex 44273).

Denmark, Klaus Homsgaar (Hon. Consul), Denco Building (PO Box 1587; ☎225360).

Egypt (PO Box 462; ☎261953, telex 44308).

France, U.N. Drive, Mamba Point (PO Box 461; ☎221122, telex 44360); French Embassy visa service covers Mauritania, Senegal, Burkina Faso and Togo.

Germany, Tubman Blvd, Oldest Congotown (PO Box 34; ☎261516, telex 44230).

Ghana, 11th St/Gardiner Ave, Sinkor (PO Box 471; ☎261477); visas issued routinely.

Guinea, Tubman Blvd/19th St, Sinkor (PO Box 41; ☎261711, 261182); visa issue is unpredictable (see "Freetown" p.660).

Israel, Gardiner Ave/12th St, Sinkor (PO Box 257; ☎262861, telex 44415).

Italy, U.N. Drive, Mamba Point (PO Box 255; ☎224580, telex 44438).

Japan, Kapa House Building, LBDI Compound, Tubman Blvd (PO Box 253; ☎262468, telex 44209).

Mali. Visas are available from the Malian consul who runs a crafts shop on the corner of Carey/Gurley Sts.

Morocco, Tubman Blvd, Congotown (PO Box 134; ☎262767, telex 44540).

Netherlands, U.N, Drive (PO Box 284; ☎221155, 221266).

Nigeria, Tubman Blvd (PO Box 366; ☎261093, telex 44278); letter from your embassy may be required for a visa.

Poland,10th St/Gardiner Ave, Sinkor (PO Box 860; ☎261113).

Senegal (Hon. Consul). Check phone book for private address.

Sierra Leone, Tubman Blvd, Congotown, past Spriggs-Payne Airfield (PO Box 575; ☎261301, 261203). Visas are issued routinely.

Spain, Capitol Hill (PO Box 275; ☎221299, telex 44538).

Sweden, Tubman Blvd/1st St (PO Box 335; ☎261646, telex 44255).

Switzerland, Congotown (PO Box 183; ☎261065, telex 44255).

United Kingdom, U.N. Drive (PO Box 120; ☎221055, 491, telex 44287); open Mon–Fri 8.30am–12.30pm. Describes itself as a "mini mission" and no longer issues visas for other Commonwealth countries.

USA, 111 U.N. Drive, Mamba Point (PO Box 98; ☎222992–9); open Mon–Fri 7.30am–5pm.

Zaire, PO Box 1038, Spriggs-Payne Airfield (☎261326).

Memarinna Building, Sao Bosso St/Randall St (PO Box 1089; ☎222468). Self-drive rates are around L$40 per day plus 40¢ per mile. But give some thought to having a driver (extra outlay to begin with, but possibly fewer roadside negotiations).

Cinemas The *Relda* on Tubman Boulevard at 17th St is one of the city's better ones.

Dentist Dr Jupiter, 102 Broad St (☎222216).

DHL 189 Tubman Blvd (☎262676) and 14 Randall St (☎224614).

Doctors Dr. Thomas, West Side Clinic, Lynch/Broad St.

Flight information Try Robertsfield International Airport ☎721031.

Hospital If you're in need of urgent attention, the Catholic Hospital in Sinkor is excellent. JFK Hospital isn't.

Immigration Bureau of Immigration and Naturalization, Broad St (Mon–Fri 8am–4pm, Sat 8am–3pm). Remember your passport photos when you go.

Music shops Plenty in town. The best is probably *Soul Source* at Gurley and Broad.

Newspapers Nowhere in town sells foreign newspapers. You might find something at the *Hotel Africa*. *Time* and *Newsweek* are sometimes available on the street.

Pharmacies *Otter Pharmacy*, Broad/Randall Sts.

Photo processing/passport photos There's good colour print processing at three places – *Seoul Colour Lab* on Center St, and *Expo Color* and *Fast Foto* (who also repair cameras), both on Randall St. The price is high (around L$1 a print) but no complaints about the quality. Street vendors do passport photos on Randall and Broad – about L$5 for four.

Post offices There are two post offices. The main one, which deals with parcels and poste restante, is on Carey St at McDonald. The other is on Randall St at Ashmun. Hours are 8am–4pm Mon–Fri and 9am–noon on Sat.

Shipping agents If you want to try to get a berth on a ship, *Intraco*, Jamaica Rd, PO Box 1653 (☎223869, telex 44469, fax 225948) are port agents for *Grimaldi Lines*.

Swimming pools Two in downtown Monrovia are at the *Ducor Palace Hotel* and the American Embassy (the latter open daily 10am–7pm, except Tues noon–7pm). The British Embassy has a pool, too.

Telephone, telegrams and telex Telecom office off Broad St. Reverse charge ("collect") calls can be made only after 9pm, or on Sun. You can send and receive telexes from abroad on telex 44212 and 44214.

Tourist information You may find a tourist information office still on Broad St at Buchanan St. Or check out the **National Bureau of Culture and Tourism** (PO Box 3223, ☎262989) on 14th St and Cheesman Ave in Sinkor.

Travel agents If you're **flying to Europe**, Monrovia can work out one of the cheapest places from which to do it. Monrovia's agents are mostly flight agents, there not being a lot in the way of Liberian excursions to sell.

  Jet Travel, PO Box 71, 69 Broad St (☎224442) has a sound reputation.
  Also worth checking are any of the following:
  Brasilia Travel, PO Box 54, 67 Broad St (☎224998)
  Morgan Travel, PO Box 1260, 70 Ashmun St (☎222149)
  Doukor Travel, PO Box 2246, Chase Manhattan Plaza, Randall St (☎221104)
  Ophelia International Travel Services, PO Box 2126, Broad St west of Mechlin St (☎2238701).

THE COASTAL TOWNS

Apart from the settlement at Du Kor – Monrovia – the early black immigrants settled in four main clusters along the coast; north, at Lake Piso, they created Robertsport, and south of Monrovia they developed colonies at Grand Bassa (Buchanan), Greenville and Harper. These four towns remain the most attractive and atmospheric in Liberia and if you're in the country for any length of time, they're all worth making some effort to · visit. **Robertsport** isn't inaccessible and the sea and lakeside around make it close to a resort in Liberian terms. **Buchanan** is even easier to get to. **Harper** is picturesquely sited near the Côte d'Ivoire border but a long journey by road, while the logging port of **Greenville**, base for canoe trips up the Sinoe River, is very remote.

Robertsport

ROBERTSPORT is the county seat of Grand Cape Mount county and Liberia's prettiest town. At the tip of a hilly peninsula it faces the volcanic forested promontory of Cape Mount across a narrow strait at the mouth of the sizeable gulf of Lake Piso. It's a quiet, balmy place, with a beautiful beach – ideal resting-up territory in happier times.

Robertsport's **"Fanti Town"** quarter, originally populated by Fante fishermen from Ghana, has interesting architecture. You might also seek out the **Tubman Center for African Culture**, a semi-private institution that used to have a small ethnographic collection; what's become of it since 1980 is uncertain. Most travellers focus on Lake Piso's safe sheltered **swimming**, the island of **Massating** and **boating** opportunities with fishermen. Back out of town, along the road towards the Monrovia highway, **Sembuhun Beach** is secluded and idyllic, with good surf. Drivers will stop at Sembuhun, from where the beach is a 15–20 minute walk.

In practical terms, Robertsport has a couple of basic **places to stay**, but also a fairly comfortable hotel on the Atlantic side of the peninsula (the *Wakolor*). Across the lake, at **Tallah**, a small "resort" has recently been constructed. Reach there by canoe

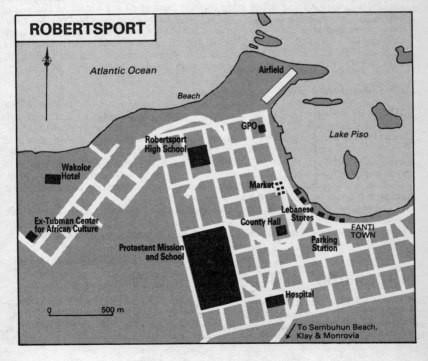

ROBERTSPORT

Atlantic Ocean

Airfield

Beach

GPO

Lake Piso

Robertsport High School

Wakolor Hotel

Market

Ex-Tubman Center for African Culture

Lebanese Stores

County Hall

FANTI TOWN

Parking Station

Protestant Mission and School

Hospital

0   500 m

To Sembuhun Beach, Klay & Monrovia

(around L$7), or come from the other direction by road, passing the Robertsport turn-off on the Monrovia highway and continuing west to a sign (left) for *Club 42*.

The Vai are a Mande-speaking group, mostly Muslim, who live along the coastal strip in western Liberia and southwest Sierra Leone. The Vai script – one of the very few indigenous scripts of sub-Saharan Africa – was invented in the early nineteenth century, by traditional accounts after a headman's dream. It was used for a number of decades but fell out of use at the beginning of this century. In World War II, Nazi intelligence officers adapted it for use as a cipher.

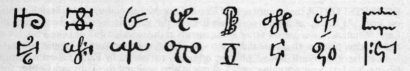

Buchanan and River Cess

Much more of an industrial centre than Robertsport, **BUCHANAN** is at the end of the iron ore railway from Yekepa and, outside of Monrovia, as bustling a town as you'll find anywhere in Liberia. It's located on the east bank of the St John River, some 5km from the open sea. Arriving from Monrovia (a straightforward 2–3 hour journey) you pass the ruins of old **Grand Bassa** on the right, then turn into the town centre to be dropped at the best organised parking station in the country. Buchanan has a **hotel** (the *Louiza*), as well as the *Lamco* mining company's **guest house** (and *Lamco* has a host of other facilities), two **restaurants** and a whole array of cook shops, three **supermarkets**, a large daily **market** which sells pretty well everything, a temperamental Telecom office, a post office open Tuesday and Friday, a cinema (the decent *Ocean Theatre*) and some good **bars**. Not far away are some of the best beaches in Liberia, notably **Silver Beach**.

River Cess (Cestos City)

Ninety kilometres east of Buchanan, on a bad dirt road, you reach **RIVER CESS TOWN**. On the west bank of the Cestos and hard by the Atlantic, it's a relaxing get-away – and may well still be, despite the civil war of 1990 – fanned by ocean breezes, with plenty of swimming places, **cold beer** (there's reliable current), a good palm wine connection and a **disco** on the beach (the *Atlantic*). Maroun, the Lebanese shopkeeper in the centre of the small town (so small there's only one cook shop), is the person to visit for practical advice. If you've loads of time, you might walk up-river from the town, 10km or so, to a district of bush trails, small villages, swimming holes and fishing streams. It's easy to find a canoe back down to the beach.

The road network of central Liberia terminates along the coast at Cess Town. There are no bridges over the Cestos River and, to reach GREENVILLE, only 80km southeast along the coast as the crow flies, you have to turn hundreds of kilometres inland via ZWEDRU.

Greenville

Remote **GREENVILLE** is a major forest industries centre, with a factory and timber mills. It's an industry that's developed from scratch over the last twenty years and there's now an exploitative momentum that seems barely in control. The fast roads round about give it all away; they're kept in fine condition by the timber extractors to provide swift exits by truck for the giant logs from the forest. If you arrive by road, you'll witness the pillaging of Sinoe county's rainforest on your way down from Zwedru – hard to believe how much of the virtually non-renewable resource is turned into ordinary plywood.

Greenville itself is doing well on the timber boom. Visit *Dennawy's* for advice on accommodation and wonderful hospitality, *Joseph & Fouad's* for biscuits and similar goodies, *Dean & Son's* for the best selection of *Kwi* foods in town and *Ramzy's* if your bike (motor or push) needs attention. There are several excellent **cook shops** – *Doris' Bakery* on the way into town on the right, *Comfort's* a little further on the right and *The Place* down on Sinoe Street. As for bars, the *Checkpoint* has its own generator, but the *Consulate* maintains a better atmosphere, if not the coldest drinks. If you're interested in local **crafts**, ask around for Morris, a would-be rasta, who's a local craftsman.

Greenville has fine **beaches** nearby, so long as you take on board the usual tide and current warnings. Scanship beach and Cove beach are both good for swimming. **Devil's Rock** beyond the port is excellent for rock exploring but not for swimming.

SAPO NATIONAL PARK

Greenville is the departure point for seasonal **river trips** by canoe up the Sinoe, one of the country's longest navigable waterways. Several trips are run each year between January and March at a cost of around US$150. Trips last three or four days and take in the **Sapo National Park**, Liberia's only effective nature reserve. The park, and the trips, are partly run by Peace Corps volunteers. You can find out more at the Peace Corps office at Tubman Boulevard/26th St in Monrovia (Mon–Thurs 8am–5.15pm, Fri 8am–4pm, ☎261112) or from the Wildlife and National Park Office, Forest Development Authority, PO Box 3010, Old Road, Sinkor, Monrovia. *Weasua Airlines* flies to Greenville for around US$60.

Harper, Maryland county and around

HARPER CITY was founded as *Maryland in Liberia* in 1834. For ten years after the declaration of the Republic, Maryland remained an independent territory. It joined Liberia in 1857 and went on to become one of the most influential parts of the country. President Tubman was a Grebo-speaker from Harper, and Maryland county benefited considerably as a result of his thirty-year stay in power.

A sense of lost grandeur still pervades the town; mould and vines smother buildings no longer kept up. The colossal Masonic temple is still in one piece and provides a good four-storey overview of the entire surrounding area. Even better views can be got from the top of the old lighthouse out on the point – wonderful sunsets.

There's a good **hotel** on the seaward side of town – the *Cape Motel and Restaurant* – with excellent food (Harper has great seafood), a collection of local animals (chimp and monkeys, turtles and peeskorps) and good rates (about L$20/night). Swimming here is safe. For a change from the hotel, walk through town to the old Kru Town quarter north of the Pléebo road and sample the **street cooking** of the Old Ma on Market Street – famous fried fish, plantain, cassava, banana and the hottest pepper in Liberia – daily, after sunset. If you intend flying to Monrovia, book as soon as possible at Cape Palmas Airfield. There are flights every day of the year.

To the north of the **port** – which was developed with Italian aid – **snorkelling** in the bay can be rewarding when the water is clear. Further north, across the channel and along the shore, there's a **shipwreck**, explorable at low tide (don't risk swimming out to it at other times).

A couple of other spots in Maryland county are worth visiting while you're here.

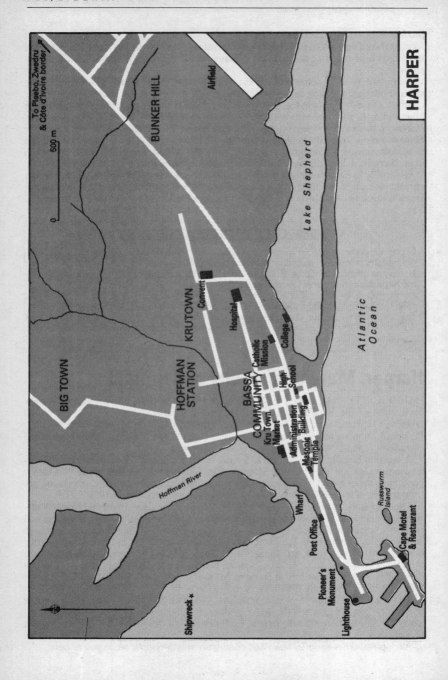

HARPER

To Pleebo, Zwedru
& Côte d'Ivoire border

500 m

0

BUNKER HILL

Airfield

BIG TOWN

KRUTOWN

HOFFMAN
STATION

Convent

Hospital

Lake Shepherd

BASSA
COMMUNITY

Catholic
Mission

College

High
School

Kru Town
Market

Administration
Building

Masonic
Temple

Atlantic
Ocean

Hoffman River

Wharf

Post Office

Russwurm
Island

Cape Motel
& Restaurant

Shipwreck

Pioneer's
Monument

Lighthouse

Around Pleebo

PLEEBO has a reputation as Maryland's "food capital", with a highly rated street meat corner. Just north of the village, to the right of the road, you might take a look at the **W.V.S. Tubman Farmhouse**, a typically Beverly Hills-style mansion of the late chief executive, vandalised and uninhabited, but still guarded by someone who'll show you round for a consideration.

A thirteen-kilometre walk or bike ride (no transport) east of Pleebo takes you through one of *Firestone's* **rubber plantations** to the **Cavalla/Cavally River,** separating Liberia from Côte d'Ivoire. There are good spots on the bank for sitting in the sun, and, in the dry season, for fishing. If you have a visa for Côte d'Ivoire, there's nothing in practice to stop you from taking one of the low-riding canoes across to "Frenchside".

The conventional **border crossing** and ferry (or dugout) over the Cavalla is 25km east of Harper (the ummarked but unmissable turn-off some 6km outside Harper). If you want to get beyond TABOU in Côte d'Ivoire, start early in the day from Harper.

Fishtown

This is the archetypal image of the West African coast – white sands shaded by drunken coconut trees. **FISHTOWN** is about 30km west of Harper; you can get a taxi there. There's a daily beach fee of 50¢ or similar payable to Fishtown's town chief as you pass through. The beach, to the west of the town, is popular with Harper's Lebanese community, though except at weekends and holidays you should have the palms and peace to yourself. Take all your needs, including water, and camp as long as your survival kit and taste for coconuts lasts. There's increasingly exciting body-surfing the further west you venture along the beach, though close to the rivermouth at the far end the waves become a little rougher than most people want.

Grand Cess and Sasstown

Lastly, if your appetite for **remote beaches** is unsatisfied, make your way from Harper, via PLEEBO and BLEBO, into Grand Kru county and to **GRAND CESS** (not related to the Cess Town further up the coast). There's a Catholic Mission here, a guest house, nice stretches of seashore, an **airfield**, and a **ferry** across the river if you want to go further to Sasstown.

SASSTOWN, about two hours' rough drive from Grand Cess, has wonderful beaches. **Kata beach** is very private and untouched and **Monkey Island** 300m offshore is a great place to spend the afternoon. Sasstown has no Lebanese shops (nor, remarkably, any beer or coke). Esther Nagbe's, on the left as you approach the main town beach, is the place to head for food and bed; she has a soft spot for travellers. If you get lost, the Catholic Mission may be able to advise.

The **journey to Monrovia** by road may take anything up to three days. But Sasstown has an airfield whence, for twice the price of all that discomfort you could, with luck, **fly** to the capital in less than an hour with *Weasua Airlines*.

THE INTERIOR

Looking inland from Monrovia, the main focus is on the fast **highway** northeast to **Gbarnga** and **Ganta**. Dirt roads branch off to the northwest corner of the country, through the hilly forests of **Lofa county** to Zorzor, Voinjama and the meeting place of Liberia, Sierra Leone and Guinea. In the central north, Ganta is the hub for the densely populated Gio-speaking region of **Nimba county**, while southeast of Ganta a road of red dust (or mud) strings through the rolling jungle-covered plateaux of **Grand Gedeh county** and down to the Atlantic at Harper and Sasstown.

Near Monrovia

If you have a couple of hours and your own wheels, or a weekend or more with public transport, the immediate **region behind Monrovia** has a few diversions that are worthwhile.

East: Firestone, chimps, Totota

The obvious place of interest near the capital is the gigantic *Firestone* rubber plantation based around **HARBEL**, beyond Robertsfield International Airport. The plantation, by various accounts the "largest" or the "third largest" in the world, is only one of several *Firestone* plantations in the country which added together amount to an area under rubber trees of some 800 square kilometres. The Harbel headquarters include an American country club and golf course.

Down the Mani River from Harbel, outside MARSHALL, there's the **Liberia Institute of Biomedical Research**, which is now conducting Aids research. There's a good beach and accommodation is offered free of charge. The **chimpanzee** reseach centre here is being closed down. Over the years attempts have been made to rehabilitate into the wild more than 100 chimps released from captivity onto six islands in the river. But, for lack of sufficient wild food, the chimps still have to be fed. On a total area of less than five hectares of what are effectively prison islands, the chimps have become violently disturbed. Food now has to be thrown onto the beaches as the chimps race to the shore screaming abuse, waving sticks and even hurling missiles. It's an extraordinary, haunting, visit.

TOTOTA, on the Ganta highway beyond the *Firestone* plantations, and the impressive escarpment of Gibi Ridge, has a major market on Wednesday and benefits from the *Top Bar and Disco* (aka *Rice and Beans Disco*), on the right, about 3km before you get to the town centre. Helpful Lebanese merchants *Haykal and Bediah* can advise on accommodation and the *Auto Parts* store in town on the right has guaranteed ice-cold soft drinks. Totota's famous **"zoo"** at **Tubman Farm**, outside the town, is rumoured to have been "restocked", its restaurant done up and its tennis courts revamped. Check it out and let us know.

West: Bomi Hills and Gola National Forest

Heading out of Monrovia in the other direction (over the Mesurado River and Bushrod Island), you arrive, after 35 miles (nearly 60km), at the **"Besao Cultural Village"** in MALEMA, a kind of living museum of Liberian ethnic architecture and lifestyles. It's just beyond KLAY on the dirt road to BOMI HILLS/TUBMANBURG.

BOMI HILLS itself is a bigger town than you'd expect, as a result of its once-important role as an iron ore centre (reserves now exhausted). If you make the effort to get up here, you'll find drum and furniture makers, weavers and wood-carvers, good bars, a cinema and even the odd disco. As usual, though, you'll need to think creatively about accommodation.

Much of the northern part of Grand Cape Mount county and the southern parts of Lofa county are nearly unexplored. The only way to get to the impressive rainforest of the **Gola National Forest**, in the far west near the Sierra Leonean border, is to head north from BOMI HILLS to LOFA BRIDGE, a journey that takes around three hours (L$6).

The Gola forest is the heart of Liberia's **diamond country**. Capital of the diamond-rush (which began in 1957 and peaked in 1973) is WEASUA, a small town in which, it's claimed, you can hear every indigenous Liberian language. It's not an easy place to reach.

Northwest Liberia: Gbarnga and Lofa

The route to the northwest is fast as far as GBARNGA. But if you have the opportunity, you may want to call at **Cuttington College** (officially now University College) in SUAKOKO, just south of Gbarnga, for the **museum** on the campus. Ask for Mr N'gele, the helpful curator. There are usually arts and crafts for sale. Cuttington is an interesting institution, long derided by Monrovians as a "country people" college, now recognised as the country's most energetic and development-orientated higher education site. If you're around long enough, you can take **Kpelle classes** here. There's also an African-American **Hebrew colony** at nearby SINYEA.

Gbarnga

GBARNGA itself is a sizeable town, the axis of Liberian road transport, with nearby rubber plantations contributing to local prosperity. Arriving in the big Monrovia Parking Station, you can walk back to the seedy *D'Afal Motel* (L$15 a room), or right through the town centre to the other side on the Ganta road for the much more salubrious *Hillcrest Hotel and Restaurant*. They only have three rooms here, priced at about L$20, L$25 and L$30, but with lovely views. The *Hillcrest* does Kwi food; you need to reserve earlier in the day. After-dark amusements include several nice **bar/clubs** – *Under the Tree, Treasure of Love, Octopus, The Court Disco* and *Ribbon's Nite* – and there are various **Kwi cook shops** (the *Charleston* is recommended) and even a reputable local radio station (KLRG) and Catholic Mission short-wave station (daily, 8–9pm). Gbarnga gets **piped water** mornings only, but luxuriates into **current** from 6.30pm to 3am every night.

There's a great trip you can do from Gbarnga to the beautiful **Kpatwe Falls**, an hour or so away. Few vehicles go out this way, so you'd have to arrange a taxi charter.

Lofa county

Lofa is Liberia's biggest county – nearly a quarter of the country's area – but has only twelve percent of the population. Most of these predominantly Mande-speaking people (Kpelle, Loma, Gbandi) live along the road which snakes its way over the ridges by the Guinean border through Lofa's main towns and villages. As you travel in Lofa, look out for the county's many **rope and liana bridges** – "monkey bridges".

Zorzor

ZORZOR, 100km from Gbarnga, didn't find a lot of favour with Graham Greene in 1935 ("the most desolate place in the Republic") but nowhere looks enticing at the very end of the dry season, and Zorzor does have one or two pluses: the **Bridal Veil Falls** on the north side of town (rainy season only); the **Thursday market**; the **leper colony** with its basket-making enterprise; and *The Explosion* **bar and disco**. Best **cook shop** in town is the *Unity*, right by the central town street triangle.

FISSEBU, just a few kilometres after Zorzor, has little to offer, though it's rumoured you can get *Rosé d'Anjou* wine at the petrol station on the Voinjama side.

Voinjama

VOINJAMA is the region's biggest town, set amid steep banks of forest and swarming with missionaries despite (or because of) serious competition from Islam. It boasts an impressive **market**. For eating, *Klubo's* **cook shop** between the Monrovia road checkpoint and the Pentecostal church, *Aunt D. cook shop* by the parking station and *Super Mandingo* cook shop in the centre are recommended, as are the *Tropical Village bar*, just before the checkpoint, and *TT's bar* in the centre between the two mosques. The best Lebanese shop for aid and advice is *Kracht*, on the left, just past the big mosque.

A LIBERIAN FOLKTALE

Liberia has a rich **oral literature**, much of it passed on these days in English. Most stories contain a moral. Many deal with animals like leopard, deer, monkey and hare, though less by fixing on real aspects of the animal's appearance or "character" than by taking as a starting point the emotional relationship of humans with the animal. Many stories were taken to America by slaves, and some subsequently returned to Liberia. Brer Rabbit's origins lie in this fusion. **Spider** is usually a crafty, avaricious person who brings trouble on others and sometimes himself. This tale, and others like it, can be interpreted to give powerful expression to social and political frustration where candid opinion is uncustomary and unwise.

SPIDER AND THE HONEY TREE

One day Spider asked a young girl from the village to help him look for food in the bush. This girl was very good in finding the sweetest foods. Spider wanted her help because he was too lazy to work hard for himself.

The girl took Spider to her secret places to find the best foods. "This plum tree," she explained, "does not have much fruit, but its plums are the sweetest ones in the bush."

Spider was just as greedy as he was lazy. As soon as the young girl showed him the plums, he rushed past her into the tree and ate all the plums. He didn't leave even one plum for the young girl.

The girl continued to show Spider her secrets of the bush. "Over there is a small patch of the very best bananas," declared the young girl. Again Spider pushed her aside and ate all of the ripe bananas. Again he left the young girl with nothing.

His belly was getting full, but Spider wanted to learn more of the secret places of the bush. Spider thought the young girl was foolish to share these places with him because he ate all the food. However, if she was willing to continue guiding him, he was willing to continue eating her food.

The young girl led Spider deeper and deeper into the bush, where people rarely went. "Over here," instructed the young girl, "is a very special tree. Deep inside a small hole is the most delicious honey you will ever find."

The young girl was not so foolish. She knew Spider loved honey and she was not surprised when he raced past her and squeezed into the hollow of the tree. He ate all of the sweet golden honey, sharing nothing with the young girl. When he had eaten his fill of the honey, he started to climb out of the tree. He couldn't get out of the hole. His stomach had grown too large.

"Help me, young girl," pleaded Spider, "for I have grown too large and cannot get out of the tree."

"You would not be so large if you had shared some of the special food with me," scolded the young girl.

"I beg you, please call for help," cried Spider.

"Help, help," whispered the young girl as softly as she could, "the foolish Spider is caught inside the honey tree. Someone come and help this greedy spider.'"

Nobody could hear the whispers. Nobody could hear Spider's cries for help from inside the tree. They were too far into the bush, where people seldom travel.

"Goodbye, Spider," called the young girl, as she left the honey tree. "I am going to get some huge cassava for my family. If you want to eat some, just follow me there."

Story narrated to **Phillip Martin**

Kolahun and Foya

KOLAHUN might be a place to stop a few days. It's really pretty hereabouts, with waterfalls, rope bridges, hills and bush-hiking opportunities and a **swimming hole** just outside town. There's a **hotel** here, two recommended bars (*Masri's* and *Kaima's*), a friendly Lebanese shop (*Fouad's*), and both a daily market and a large, separate **Monday market** (look out for country cloth). A difficult road tracks south out of Kolahun, cutting across the headwaters of the Mano River and reaching GALEMA, from where you could head for the Liberian Iron and Steel Concession (LISCO) and hike and camp, among waterfalls, in the remote **Wologesi mountains**. Peace Corps volunteers in Kolahun may be able to advise.

Last stop on the road before Sierra Leone is **FOYA**. You can tell it's a border town, and particularly on this border, by the number of Lebanese stores crowding the single main street. *Betty's* **cook shop**, opposite the Kolahun parking station, is a sure bet for good food and there are several **palm wine** vendors near the market place. Foya's **main Saturday market** is judged to be the best in the country.

Even bigger **international markets** happen in Koindu, Sierra Leone, on a Sunday and in Guéckédou, Guinea, on a Wednesday. Despite indications to the contrary on certain maps, there is a road from Foya to Guéckédou.

Nimba county

Another big county, **Nimba** has a high population density and is one of the wealthiest regions, in terms of resources. Huge reserves of **iron ore** are located here and farms are highly productive.

Centrally located and largely Dan-Gio speaking (languages of the Mande cluster again), Nimba has also been the focus both of government opposition and of heavy-handed reaction to it. Nimba people suffered severely after the 1985 coup attempt, and government mistrust of the county after a purported "invasion attempt" by an ex-vice president in 1988 was shown to be justified when Charles Taylor's invasion of 1990 developed inexorably into civil war.

Ganta

GANTA lies at the end of the paved road from Monrovia, right on the border with the southernmost tip of Guinea, only an hour's drive from the large Guinean town of NZÉRÉKORÉ. The local helpful contact is *Michael Issac's* store, in the middle of town, just past the mosque. The shop acts as a drop-off for mail.

Ganta's only **hotel** is the *Travelers' Inn*, opposite the beautiful old **Methodist church** on the north side of town. If you find it full or uninhabitable, you can also stay at the town's famous **leprosarium** where they have several inexpensive guest rooms. The Ganta leprosarium is Liberia's premier **crafts centre**, with excellent and unusual basketry and wood carvings. Prices in the gift shop are fixed, but you can haggle in the hospital lobby and around the eighty or so outpatients' houses if you prefer. There's a farm attached to the hospital. The place fairly buzzes and has a number of European and Japanese volunteers.

If you're on the prowl for **cook shops**, first check out *Aimee's*, next to the *Traveler's Inn*; it's slightly expensive but first class. *Teague's*, too, on the left on the road out to Guinea, is good and also cheap. And *Bob Dimmo's* does excellent bitter ball and palm butter. After dark, investigate the *Jupiter Club* disco, next to *Traveler's Inn*.

The day to be in Ganta is Thursday, when the **weekly ("Guinea") market** comes to town – good cheap clothing, exotic animals, snake protection and anti-poison rings from the snake man . . . There's also a good possibility of being able to cross to Guinea for a few hours, even if you don't have a visa already. And if you're down at the border early on a Wednesday morning, you might be able to spend the day at Nzérékoré's own, gigantic, weekly market.

Sanniquellie and Karnplay

SANNIQUELLIE, the next stop going north and the **capital of Nimba county**, doesn't have much to offer beyond a scattering of cook and bake shops and a few tatty reminders of its significance as the birthplace of the **Organisation of African Unity**. In 1959, the leaders of the first three independent West African nations (Liberia, Guinea and Ghana) got together here for their first summit.

Turn right at Saniquellie for **KARNPLAY** (Kahnplé, etc.) and **Côte d'Ivoire** (regular taxis, L\$3). This can be a disruptive border, so you're strongly advised to set off from Ganta early in the day. If you turn up in the cool of early morning staff are more likely to be pleasant to you, and less likely to have embarked on the long process of unwinding. If you're coming directly from further afield, spend the night in Ganta or Karnplay in order to do this. Karnplay's **hotel** is the nightclub on the other side of town on the BAHN road. **Market day** in Karnplay is Wednesday; the first big town across the border, DANANÉ, has its weekly market on Thursday.

Yekepa

Iron ore and huge foreign investments have made **YEKEPA** the largest town in Liberia after Monrovia. It's an artificial place created by the *Liberian American Swedish Minerals Company* (*LAMCO*) in a beautiful setting high in the hills. For two decades, it has been virtually a **highlands resort** for wealthy Liberians and expatriates. But a slackening of world iron ore markets in the 1980s led the USA's *Bethlehem Steel Corporation* to sell off its quarter-share in *LAMCO* to a government-owned Liberian company, and the remaining secondary partner, a Swedish mining company, is trying hard to quit also. It looks very much as though Yekepa's days as a mining town are numbered. Already the big hotel, *Mountain View Lodge*, has closed. The brightest prospect for the future is a business link between Liberia, Guinea and foreign shareholders to exploit high-grade ore on the Guinean side of the border and then export it through Liberia. So Yekepa may continue to exist. And you may still find it surprisingly comfortable and a pleasant place to stop over for a day or two.

Arriving in Yekepa by taxi from Ganta, you'll be dropped at the **Camp 4 parking station** some 7km from the town centre. Take a Yekepa taxi into town (50¢). The town is divided into areas, which without much logic are lettered A to T. It focusses on **Sandy Clark's Square**, near the river and stadium and not far from the Olympic-length swimming pool, tennis courts and church. There are Methodist and Baptist Mission **guest houses** to the north of the square and a Lutheran one between the square and the swimming pool. These are basic and very cheap. The *Traveler's Inn* in the square is a reasonable hotel with S/C rooms (about US\$20/night). The *Standard*, over in Area H on the west side of town, is pricier. **Restaurants** (Kwi and mostly expensive) include Stanley's in Area H, *Queen Burger* in the square, and *Tennis* and *Pool* restaurants where you'd expect.

If you've time in Yekepa to make contacts and arrangements, you can not only swim and play tennis but even swing **golf** clubs. Yekepa's course is supposed to be the only one in the world that straddles two countries. There's also the possibility of **horse-riding** through the meadows. And if you're feeling vigorous, the **climb up Mount Nimba** (1752m) isn't beyond most fit people's capacities, though you do need well-gripping footwear. You leave Liberia 11km due east of Yekepa, and follow the ridge, northeast, right along the Guinea-Côte d'Ivoire border for a further 10km to the summit.

If you're going **into Guinea** from Yekepa, see p.618. First base is BOSSOU, where a chimpanzee research programme is under way; first main town is LOLA, which has a big Monday market.

Southeast from Ganta: Saclepea, Bahn, Tappita

SACLEPEA (Saklepie, etc) is the first town after Ganta on the road to ZWEDRU. A **Mandingo** town, and consequently without the usual complement of Lebanese stores, Saclepea has various Mandingo shops instead, a small-small daily market and larger **Tuesday market**, foreign organisation guest houses where you can surely get a bed if they've room (the German-run Nimba County Rural Development Project charges L$15 a night, with current). For entertainment's sake, there's the *Intofawar Club*, *Chris's Bar*, *Patrick's Bar* and *Ma Vic's cold drink Spot*. And since you're here, the *Tilapia Avenue Restaurant* and *Saclepea City Tea and Bread Shop* are also recommended.

BAHN, 20km east into the diamond hills, is hardly en route to anywhere, but is nice to visit at the end of Ramadan (a Mandingo town again, Monday market) and figures as the first place on a loop from Saclepea to the Côte d'Ivoire border and back to the Zwedru road. Right on the border is BUTUO, which has a famous Friday market.

The last town before Grand Gedeh county is **TAPPITA**, where Graham Greene spent two days in the company of the notorious "Dictator of Grand Bassa", one Colonel Elwood Davis (see "History"). Tappita in the 1930s was principally a prison town. Today it has lost that dubious quality, but remains a fair-sized route junction (a rough road runs 122 miles down to Buchanan – Grand Bassa) with a **hotel** and **air strip** and a **Wednesday market**. Lebanese merchants include *Haddad's* and *Aboud's*. Tappita is also the base of Dru, an excellent wood sculptor who has exhibited in the USA and is happy to take orders if you've time in the country.

Grand Gedeh county: Zwedru and beyond

Grand Gedeh is a huge, sparsely populated territory, its people very largely Krahn (part of the Kru language family), though another Kru tongue (Grebo) is spoken in Lower Gedeh towards the coast. This part of Liberia, traditionally the major source of army recruits, received considerable attention from government funds during the Tolbert era. But, more pointedly, Grand Gedeh is the home county of the president of the Second Republic. It shows, both in the evidence of patronage, and in the heavy presence of troops. These facts needn't much affect your travels, but you'd be ill-advised to make a casual journey to the President Doe's home village of Tuzon, north of the Tappita–Zwedru road.

Upper Grand Gedeh is flattish with few horizons; lower Grand Gedeh is more hilly. **Gedeh mountain** itself rises in the **Putu Range** to the southeast of Zwedru. This region holds iron ore and was an ancient **smelting district** in past centuries. The **Grebo forest**, in Lower Gedeh, is still wild and hardly explored, with elephants in unknown, though surely diminishing, numbers. If you're zoologically inclined, you may be interested to look out for the rare **Liberian mongoose** (*Liberiictis kuhni*) which was only known from museum specimens until 1989, when the first live one (a male) was caught. Its long claws and snout are specialised for worm-digging in light soils. Conservationists are now hoping to find a female.

Zwedru and Kanweakan

Capital of Grand Gedeh, **ZWEDRU** ("headwaters of the Zwe", aka "Tchien") is also one of the most developed up-country towns, with its grid of paved streets, presidential mansions and rows of shops. Unless you make a better contact (possibly through *Brahma Fo's* store on the main street), you can **stay** at the *You and I Motel* at the entrance of town on the left. Favoured **cook shops** include the *Cool Cabin*, between the parking station and the old hospital, and *King's and Queens* on the Telecom Road. Recommended night spots: *Roots Disco*, *Travelers Disco* (both near the *Cool Cabin*), the

Checkpoint near the Telecom building, and the very good *Park* in a palm plantation near the airfield, which is definitely the best drinking hole in Zwedru – open-air dance floor and plenty of palava huts.

There's good dry season swimming in the Cavalla River, 50km from Zwedru.

Kanweakan

If you go by money bus, you need to allow up to a whole day to get from Zwedru to KANWEAKAN (Kahnwiake, etc), though with luck you could make it right through to HARPER. On the way you pass through PUTUKEN, with the largest **weekly market** (Saturday) in Lower Gedeh (mats, fish baskets, food; arrive early morning for the full array) and SABO GEEKEN (Geeken is the village, Sabo its district), where they make beautiful **country clay pots**.

KANWEAKAN, a cowboy sort of place, is the major town of lower Grand Gedeh, though it feels more like Maryland. On arrival make immediately for *Naji Azzam's* store where you'll be welcomed, advised and aided. The town market is open daily. If you've got your own wheels (and travelling round this part of Liberia is no mean feat without them), you can make a trip out of Kanweakan to JULAKEN, 45 minutes by motorbike on the Maryland road (signposted Tatoeken). This is one of the nicest roads in the entire country for a lazy bike ride – excellent rolling scenery all the way. A one-hour **hike** from Julaken brings you to the goal – a wonderful swimming hole beneath a waterfall.

CÔTE D'IVOIRE

COTE D'IVOIRE

I n many respects, **Côte d'Ivoire** seems the least African of any country in the region. **Abidjan** is a glittering capital with a highly developed service infrastructure, most of which works. Rural Ivoirians take the bus to Abidjan for jobs and dreams, though well-off Abidjanis tend to consider Paris the country's real capital and go there as often as possible.

In the reverse direction – and on the back of an economy largely dependent on **coffee and cocoa** – some twenty to forty thousand **French people** live in Abidjan, running businesses, hotels, restaurants, and even taking positions of high office in the government and civil service. Thousands of others work on French government overseas salaries across the country. There's no question of formal integration. The French expatriate presence lends Côte d'Ivoire a curious, unfinished feel, as if independence had never been returned to Ivoirians; there are far more French than there ever were in colonial days.

Surrounded by countries whose economic circumstances have ranged from hopeful to desperate, Côte d'Ivoire has stood out as a fairly shining example of the most **pragmatic capitalism** at work in independent Africa. Politically, too, it has been viewed as a close ally of the West, on the one hand willing to engage in relations with South Africa, and on the other maintaining "stability" without the kind of outright repression the word usually implies. Côte d'Ivoire has, until recently, had a generous press in Europe and America, where it has been called everything from the *African Miracle* to the *Land of Welcome*. Most of this impression hangs on a single factor – **Houphouët-Boigny**. The diminutive and soberly engaging president's word and work have determined much of the course of Côte d'Ivoire's thirty-year independent history. Ideology has been kept at bay and his avoidance of charges of tribalism has helped to keep opposition in check. Under his tutelage, Côte d'Ivoire is close to becoming an emergent industrial nation, comparable, in its atmosphere of feverish transformation, to Brazil.

The coupling of images of **skyscrapers** with shots of local **folklore** – Dan dancers or Akan kings – is part of the *National Geographic* approach to foreign relations (the magazine did a story on the country in 1982: they called it "The Ivory Coast: African Success Story" and stressed "moderate politics", "thriving capitalism" and "nonchalant grace"). H-B never passes up an opportunity to profile his country as a place where new meets old and Western economic principles get along famously with African values. It's easy to apply scorn, but glitzy development does encourage investors, and the past three decades have seen widespread prosperity and no coups or major ethnic conflicts.

IVOIRIAN STATISTICS

The **République de Côte d'Ivoire** (often shortened there to RCI) is a sizeable country of **323,000 square kilometres** – more than twice the area of England and Wales. Although long called Ivory Coast in English, the French name is now official in all languages. The **population** is estimated at over 11 million, of whom nearly a third are economic migrants from neighbouring states. Côte d'Ivoire's national debt, at over £8 billion, is the biggest in West Africa after Nigeria's (yet for some comparison, even this figure is little more than the estimated costs of building the European Channel Tunnel). The octogenarian president, **Felix Houphouët-Boigny**, has been repeatedly elected to five-year terms in office since independence. His *Parti Démocratique de la Côte d'Ivoire*, was the sole recognised political party until 1990, when nine other parties were registered.

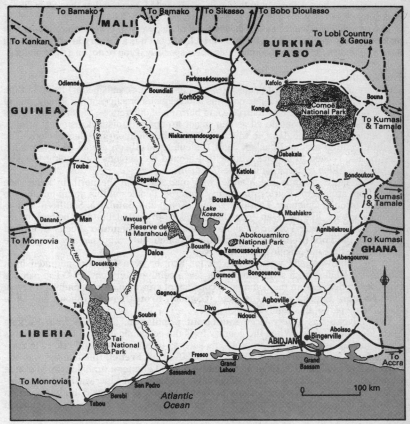

Not surprisingly, however, rapid development has exacerbated **violent tensions in the towns**, and left **granaries empty in the countryside** – failings which are perhaps felt more keenly in Côte d'Ivoire than in any other country in West Africa. The widespread prosperity doesn't have deep roots and, as successful at generating wealth as the country has been – largely on the principle that if you allow virtually unlimited foreign exploitation without closing any doors, a proportion of the cash will stay behind and multiply – some of the very worst **malnutrition** in West Africa still affects parts of northern Côte d'Ivoire, while contrasts between rich and poor in Abidjan are as stark as can be found anywhere in the world.

For these slightly voyeuristic reasons, Côte d'Ivoire is an interesting place to visit – a stage on which you can see the traditional and the modern clashing in a drama intensified by heavy capital investment and industrialisation.

Tourism is probably the most developed in West Africa. This is a country where the French come for a tropical holiday – or stay with friends and family. The government actively encourages the industry through advertising campaigns emphasing the exotic and mysterious aspects of traditional culture – images Ivoirians tend to eschew. The cultural heritage is rich and appealing, but Senoufo initiation dances or funeral ceremonies are best witnessed in the bush, as an invited guest, rather than after dinner on a hotel patio.

You're unlikely often to feel the heady thrill of discovery in Côte d'Ivoire unless you make efforts to get well off the beaten tourist trails; but it is a country in which you can have a good time, and a fairly comfortable one, especially if you're not on a tight budget.

The people

There are over sixty different peoples (*ethnies*, in French, sounds better) living in Côte d'Ivoire. Though their languages, customs and religious practices differ locally, and of course there's been wide intermarriage and blurring of differences, the diversity makes most sense if they're considered as four major groups with distinct historical origins. One of the largest is the *Akan*, to which the Asante in neighbouring Ghana belong. The **Baoulé** (centred around Bouaké), **Agni** (Indenié) and **Abron** are all Akan-speaking. They're also related to peoples who settled around the lagoons – including the **Abé** (Agboville), **Akies** (Adzopé) and **Ebrié** (Abidjan).

Another large group is the **Mande**, who migrated from the north in large-scale waves from around the fourteenth century onwards. Peoples of this group include the **Malinké** (around Odienné), **Dyula** or Dioula (Kong) and **Bambara.** Southern Mande-speaking groups like the **Dan** (near Man) and **Gouro** (Bouaflé) also belong in this ethnic configuration. **Voltaic**-speaking peoples – the **Senoufo** (focused around Korhogo), the **Lobi** (Bouna), and **Koulango** (Bondoukou) – were already living in the north by the time the Mande speakers arrived.

In the southwest and west, the **Krou** (or Kru, or even *Krumen*) migrated from Liberia and Guinea from some time in the seventeenth century onwards. The name is supposed to derive from the common occupation of crewman on sixteenth- and seventeenth-century English ships. The **Bété** (Gagnoa), **Krou** (Bereby, Tabou), and **Dida** (Lakota) are part of this family of languages.

Côte d'Ivoire has a very large **immigrant population**, especially from Burkina Faso, Mali and Guinea. When the country feels the economic pinch, these immigrants are frequently blamed for urban problems such as unemployment and crime. In addition to these African "strange workers", some 30–60,000 **French** (the number was officially reduced to 27,000 in 1986) and around 120,000 **Lebanese** (traditionally Maronite Christians but including an increasingly high proportion of Shia Muslims) are especially conspicuous minorities because of their economic clout. A very high proportion of the population lives in urban centres – Côte d'Ivoire has ten towns with a population of more than 100,000.

Roughly half the population practices traditional African **religions**, though many people – not just the other half – profess Christian or Islamic beliefs. As you'd expect, Muslims predominate in the north while smaller concentrations of various Christian sects are mainly in the south. **Harrism** – founded by William Wade Harris, a Liberian born at the turn of the century – is the oldest of these, and most developed in the Bingerville district. Other indigenous churches have also started to flourish on the preaching of a number of coastal prophets.

Where to go

Though the country is publicised as a holiday paradise, most of Côte d'Ivoire is disappointingly monotonous – a uniform plateau with few variations in altitude. The highest peak, **Mont Tonkoui**, rises to a modest 1189m in the country's most mountainous region, the far west. Waterfalls and streams in this district make for some of the country's most scenic hikes and drives.

Côte d'Ivoire's **forests,**which covered most of the southern half of the country fifty years ago, are now hugely reduced – through logging, shifting agriculture and road building which opens up remote jungle to settlement. If you're looking for adventure, the far **southwest** still contains vast districts of primary forest. Anywhere between Guiglo and San Pedro can yield barely explored valleys and ridges.

An obvious target is the **coast**, where a major system of **lagoons** is separated from the ocean by long chains of sand banks. Access is easy, either east or west of Abidjan, in a couple of hours. But swimming tends to be dangerous: when the French say *Attention la barre!* they're warning about a strong tidal race that claims many lives. For the best beaches, some with safe swimming, too, you really have to make for the **far west coast**, where West Africa's most idyllic palm-rustled strands and coves are still almost untouched. Sassandra isn't too far as a base.

Abidjan is itself part of the lagoon system. The snaking fingers of the Ebrié lagoon wind through the heart of the city, dividing a Manhattanesque urban landscape into manageable districts. If you're flying in from Europe, this first encounter with Africa is one that's only likely to shock through its superficial familiarity. Côte d'Ivoire, as show-cased by Abidjan's glass and concrete, seems the least culturally disorientating country in West Africa. And even passing through the city on long African travels can feel like a quick trip to Europe.

While still the Ivoirian metropolis, Abidjan is technically no longer the capital. That mantle has been passed to **Yamoussoukro** which, virtually overnight, changed from a colourless village to the nation's administrative centre. Home of the president, this burgeoning city with its monstrous **Catholic Basilica** lies in the heart of Côte d'Ivoire. This is the **Baoulé country**, settled in the eighteenth century by refugees from the Asante Empire. Their customs and art – in which gold plays an important symbolic role – still resemble those of their neighbours in Ghana.

The **north**, despite the heat and the endless flat grasslands, has its share of interesting sites. There's a number of moderately old Islamic centres, which relate culturally to the medieval empires of the Niger River region. Towns are fewer and further apart up here and the pace slower, while the French influence, so pervasive on the coast, is much less entrenched. This is the home of some of the country's longest-settled ethnic groups; people like the **Senoufo**, whose elaborate system of education and initiation – the *poro* – served as the social glue that held them together in the face of colonialism, and more recently has preserved their identity against the onslaught of tourism.

Also in the north is West Africa's biggest game reserve, the **Comoé National Park**, where you stand a good chance of seeing some of the Ivory Coast's remaining ivory.

Climate: when to visit

In trying to time your travels to miss the rains, efforts are complicated by the fact that Côte d'Ivoire has **two climatic zones**.

In **the south** a **long rainy season** from late April to July is followed by **short rains** in October and November, separated by a **long dry season** from December to late April, and a **short dry** in August and September. Dividing the seasons into months like this only gives an approximate idea of when to expect dry weather; "dry" seasons in the south include days of rain and dense clouds blowing in off the coast. And Sassandra, for example, which commonly has quite a dry season from July to September, received 231mm (nine inches) of rain in 24 hours one day in July 1989. Temperature-wise, the coast varies little through the year, and it doesn't cool down much at night either.

The **north** has only two seasons. Rains usually last from late May to early November. Because of the mountains, the northwest receives more rain and is generally cooler than the northeast.

The **ideal time** to visit, especially the north, is probably between February and April, late enough in the season to avoid the *Harmattan* winds that may adversely effect travel (and dust that makes photos drearily flat). Remember, too, if you're intent on visiting the **game parks**, that they close during the rains, and the dates are contingent on the weather.

AVERAGE TEMPERATURES AND RAINFALL

ABIDJAN

	Jan	Feb	Mar	Apr	May	June	July	Aug	Sept	Oct	Nov	Dec
Temperatures °C												
Min (night)	23	23	24	25	24	23	23	21	22	23	24	24
Max (day)	30	31	31	32	31	29	28	27	28	29	31	31
Rainfall mm	41	53	99	125	361	495	213	53	71	168	201	79
Days with rainfall	3	4	6	9	16	18	8	7	8	13	13	6

FERKESSÉDOUGOU

	Jan	Feb	Mar	Apr	May	June	July	Aug	Sept	Oct	Nov	Dec
Temperatures °C												
Min (night)	16	19	22	23	23	22	21	21	21	21	20	25
Max (day)	35	36	36	36	34	32	30	30	31	33	34	34

MAN

	Jan	Feb	Mar	Apr	May	June	July	Aug	Sept	Oct	Nov	Dec
Temperatures °C												
Min (night)	19	20	21	21	21	21	20	20	20	20	20	19
Max (day)	32	33	33	32	31	29	27	27	29	30	31	31

Arrivals

Abidjan, as the capital of the Côte d'Ivoire, plays a pivotal economic role in the region, and is consequently well connected to the rest of Africa. Flights in are easy, and land connections are good from Burkina, Mali and Ghana, with a main rail service from Ouagadougou. Connections with Guinea and Liberia are rougher.

■ Flights

Air Afrique and *UTA* handle most of the traffic from other West African cities. Their daily flights from Europe call (depending on the day of the week) at Dakar, Bamako, Bobo-Dioulasso, Ouagadougou, Niamey, Accra, Lomé, Freetown and Conakry. This service is complemented by national airlines. *Nigeria Airways* has a weekly flight from Lagos. *Air Guinée* has two flights a week from Conakry; *Air Mali* has two weekly flights from Bamako, one direct and the other with stops at Monrovia, Freetown and Conakry; *Ghana Airways* flies from Accra, and from Dakar with stops at Monrovia, Freetown and Banjul; and *Cameroon Airlines* has two flights a week from Douala. *Air Ivoire* itself connects Abidjan (and Bouaké) with Burkina Faso, Mali and Guinea.

From **East Africa**, *Ethiopian Airlines* operates several flights a week from Addis Ababa to Abidjan, with stops in Nairobi, Brazzaville, Kinshasa, Lagos and Accra depending on the day. *Egyptair* has a reliable Wednesday service from Cairo via Kano, Lagos and Accra.

Central Africa is primarily served by *Air Zaire* (with two flights a week from Kinshasa) and *Air Gabon* (three flights a week from Libreville via Lagos).

Abidjan is the only airport in West Africa (apart from Sal on the Cape Verde islands) that allows landing rights to the planes of *South African Airways*.

■ Overland from Burkina Faso

From **Burkina Faso**, the main road stretches from Ouagadougou all the way to Abidjan. It's in good shape really, with only one stretch – from the border to Ferkessédougou – unpaved. The border post stays open twenty-four hours a day. Back-country *pistes* through the **Lobi country** are in bad condition. Very little traffic connects the towns of **Gaoua** and **Bouna**.

■ Overland from Ghana

The principal route **from Ghana** is looking better these days. It's been paved through the border town of Elubo, meaning you no longer have to catch a ferry across the Ehi Lagoon dividing the two countries. Besides the normal formalities, there are no special difficulties at this border and the crossing is generally a quick one. If you want to slow things down, the section on Côte d'Ivoire's eastern coast explains how. The road from Kumasi is also frequently travelled and in decent condition, but for the stretch between Dormas-Ahenkro (Ghana) and Agnibilékrou (Côte d'Ivoire).

DRIVING INTO CÔTE D'IVOIRE

If you're coming in with your own vehicle, you'll most usually be given a seven-day *permis* by customs, which has to be extended in Abidjan. Don't ignore this if you're not going to Abidjan; be sure to sort the matter out before you leave the border.

■ Overland from Mali

The easiest way into the country **from Mali** is via Sikasso, crossing the border at Pogo. This gives you the possibility of joining Côte d'Ivoire's main north–south road rather quickly at Ouangolodougou.

From Bamako, heading for western Côte d'Ivoire, you can also cut down to Bougouni at which point a *piste* leads directly to Odienné although traffic along this stretch is unreliable and especially bad during the rains.

If you're coming from the region of Gao, it makes much more sense to head down to Bobo-Dioulasso from San, which then gives you the luxury of driving on paved roads all the way to the border.

■ Overland from Guinea

Travelling **from Guinea** is more problematic, owing to the bad condition of the roads.

The two most common routes are those running between Kankan and Odienné (from where regular buses head through to Bouaké) and between Nzérékoré and Man. Rains along these roads (and in particular the Sankarani ferry being out of operation on the first one) may bring traffic to a standstill.

■ Overland from Liberia

From Liberia, the road is paved between Monrovia and Ganta, leaving about 90km of tracks – well maintained and motorable year round – until you arrive at Danané. Which is fine in principle, except that it was along this road that thousands of Liberians fled the civil war in 1990. Since Liberia and Côte d'Ivoire have had edgy relations for years, this has only worsened the atmosphere at border crossings. An alternative, along the coast via Tabou and Harper, may take days if the weather is bad, but the road from Abidjan is now tarred all the way to Tabou.

Red Tape

Passport holders of European Community member states can stay up to three months in Côte d'Ivoire with a valid passport. Other nationals must obtain a visa *before* entering. You cannot get them at the border or the airport. Visas are generally easy to obtain and are issued at Ivoirian embassies, or at French consulates in those countries where Côte d'Ivoire lacks representation.

An international **vaccination card** proving you have an in-date Yellow Fever inoculation is required at the border. It will be frequently checked at police barriers when driving through the country. And make sure your arrival formalities are completed. At some borders you're expected to complete things at the first main police station. Find out. Ivoirian bureaucracy has a reputation for extra-officiousness.

All neighbouring countries – Guinea, Liberia, Mali, Burkina Faso and Ghana – are represented in Abidjan. Mali and Ghana visas are easily obtained, although the latter may take 72 hours to be issued. Embassies' addresses are listed at the end of the Abidjan section. It's worth knowing that the British Embassy handles visas for The Gambia and Sierra Leone.

Money and Costs

Ivoirian currency is the CFA franc (CFA50 always equals 1 French franc; CFA450–500=£1). The easiest place to change non-franc currencies is Abidjan, where many of the banks work in conjunction with European, particularly French, banks. *Barclays* and *Chase Manhattan* have branches here. **There are branches of the *Societé Générale de Banques en Côte d'Ivoire, Banque Internationale pour le Commerce et l'Industrie* and the *Banque Internationale de l'Afrique Occidentale* in towns across the country. Be aware, however, that they're often unwilling to change £ sterling, US$ or German marks. It's a problem that's common in Côte d'Ivoire.**

French franc travellers' cheques are the easiest and safest form of money to bring. The exception might be if you come into the country from Ghana, Guinea or Liberia and think you may have trouble changing money straight away at the border. In that case, French **notes** could come in handy and are usually accepted by taxi drivers, hotel operators and merchants in lieu of CFA. If you arrive by plane, the *bureau de change* at the airport is theoretically open round the clock.

■ Credit cards

Credit cards have made some headway. They're more use here than in any other West African country. Most big hotels now take them, as do car hire and travel agencies. In Abidjan, some of the fancier restaurants also accept them.

■ Costs

In terms of **costs**, Côte d'Ivoire is one of the most exhausting countries in West Africa, maybe even more so than Senegal. Abidjan is consistently rated one of the world's most expensive cities, and other towns, though less expensive, aren't cheap. The main problem, if you're on a budget, is the wide availability of so *much* to spend on.

Your major expense will be **accommodation**. Even if staying in the cheapest places, you should plan on averaging CFA3–5000 per day on hotels if you're on your own, slightly less if you're travelling with someone else. Decent hotels tend to be more in the CFA8–10,000 range. **Transport** is another big cost; the average trip by shared taxi costs around CFA18 per km and there's the baggage fee on top. Car hire is unbelievably expensive. **Food**, at least, is still relatively affordable; a meal in a market or motor park costs only a couple of hundred CFA. Sit-down *maquis* are slightly more expensive. Ordinary meals in mid-range hotel restaurants cost about what you'd pay for *le menu* in an average hotel in France; CFA3–5000. Indulging in a foreign restaurant in Abidjan or Yamoussoukro, however, could set you back as much as CFA20,000 per person.

Information and Maps

Despite its high profile and importance in the French-speaking world, Côte d'Ivoire is little known in Anglophone countries. If you've access to a tourist office, it's worth visiting one first. The country puts out some very attractive material, though not always giving much detail.

For tourist information contact:

In Europe: Délégation du Tourisme de Côte d'Ivoire, 24 bd Suchet 75016 Paris, (☎45 24 43 28).

In the USA: Délégation du Tourisme de Côte d'Ivoire, 117 East 55, Street, New York New York, 10022 (☎355 69 75).

As for **maps**, the best one currently available, regularly updated to take account of an active road-building programme, is the *Michelin 975 Côte d'Ivoire* which shows the country in satisfying detail at 1cm:8km and gives all *Michelin's* usual supplementary information.

Health

Health concerns aren't paramount in Côte d'Ivoire. You'll generally find adequately treated water supplies – which makes a big difference. If you're being careful, too, you can find Ivoirian bottled water everywhere, and soda water is usually stocked in shop fridges. Notwithstanding some shocking malnutrition, Côte d'Ivoire has the best record in the region in terms of percentages of people affected by various diseases.

Health care facilities, in the main towns at least, are pretty much up to international standards and, for long-term residents, there's not much that could befall you that would require evacuation abroad. The *Polyclinique Internationale Ste Anne-Marie* (☎44 51 32) in the Deux Plateaux district of Abidjan is superbly equipped.

AIDS figures released in 1989 are alarming, however; the Health Minister announced that around one prostitute in three, and one in three outpatients tested in infectious diseases wards, are HIV carriers. An AIDS prevention programme is now under way and blood screening facilities are to be introduced throughout the country by 1993.

Getting Around

Côte d'Ivoire is one of the easiest West African countries to travel around. Good internal air and road connections and the Abidjan–Niger railway give the country a fast flavour. Off the beaten track you can still get stuck, but rarely for long, even during the rains. There's no serious river transport.

■ Road transport

Côte d'Ivoire boasts eight-lane super highways – rarely seen in this part of the world. If you stuck to the motorway linking Abidjan with Yamoussoukro, or the big highway running near the coastal lagoons to Ghana, you'd have a very favourable impression of the road network. In all, however, there are barely 5000km of paved roads, and in the north and southwest dirt tracks are the rule.

Every city or town has its lorry park, or *gare routière*. Increasingly, air-conditioned coaches compete with *mille kilos* (22-seater minibuses) and *Peugeot* taxis. The big buses are usually more comfortable and cheaper, but take a long time to fill and tend to be slower than *Peugeots*.

■ By air

Air Ivoire links Abidjan to the following towns in the interior: Bondoukou, Bouaké, Bouna, Boundiali, Daloa, Gagnoa, Guiglo, Korhogo, Man, Odienné, San Pedro, Sassandra, Seguela, Tabou, Touba and Yamoussoukro. For an idea of prices, they range from CFA3000 (Daloa–Yamoussoukro to CFA21,000 (Abidjan–Odienné). Only the main routes are served daily or more. Most towns get between one and three flights a week. Note that student and youth reductions on *Air Ivoire* can reduce the cost of flying to roughly twice the road transport cost. You have to be under 32, but you need an ISIC card if you're over 26.

■ Trains

The *Régie Abidjan–Niger* (**RAN**) runs 1173km of track between Abidjan and Ouagadougou, 655km of which are in Côte d'Ivoire. With two trains a day in both directions, this is one of the most convenient ways to cross the country from north to south. The first- and second-class carriages are in good condition considering the volume of passengers they handle. Prices are competitive – even first class is cheaper than going by road. For more complete information, see *Moving On* at the end of the Abidjan section.

Hitching

There's a lot of private traffic on the roads in Côte d'Ivoire and you've every chance of success in **hitching** if you stick to the main ones. Abidjan–Man, Abidjan–Ferkessédougou and anywhere tarred along the coast shouldn't be unduly difficult. And with the high price of public transport it's a positive option if you're budgeting. You *might* also strike lucky on the approach roads to the game parks. But your timing needs to be impeccable (public holidays, weekends) to really make it worth a try.

Sleeping

Hotels are generally very good and in most sizeable towns you'll find something with air-conditioning and self-contained rooms. Unfortunately, you pay heavily for such conveniences; accommodation will be by far your highest expense unless you know people – or camp out.

In Abidjan, it's difficult to find anything appealing for under CFA5000, and prices are only slightly better in other major towns. Only in the extreme north do you start to notice lower prices, and even there prices aren't cheap compared to neighbouring countries.

Like France, Côte d'Ivoire has a **rating system** for hotels, using a star classification. Five stars, the maximum, are given to ultra-luxurious places like the *Ivoire* in Abidjan or the *Président* in Yamoussoukro – both of which have state-of-the-art gadgets in the rooms and facilities ranging from ice rinks to 18-hole golf courses. A night in one of these places starts in the neighbourhood of CFA25,000. At the other end of the scale, one-star hotels usually have S/C rooms with AC and not a lot more. They cost from around CFA6–7000 a night.

Unclassified hotels are the cheapest option. You'll find many throughout the country, their prices varying according to the region. The less respectable these are known as *chambres de passage*, and although they're often rented out by the hour and not really intended for travellers, you can stay in them, usually quite cheaply, for the night. Some take their social responsibilities quite seriously and provide clients with clean bathrooms and towels.

Staying with people is perfectly feasible. The government puts no restrictions on contacts – something of a relief if you're coming from Mali. On the other hand, nationals see a lot of travellers and tourists, most of whom appear to be in a hurry, and they tend to be regarded as part of the scenery of the modern state. You're not likely get a lot of spontaneous invitations, which isn't an indication of a lack of hospitality.

Camping out is feasible in many areas, particularly, as ever, in the more open and sparsely populated north. If you're anywhere near the big highways, or in the vicinity of one of the country's large towns, it's really better to have some security.

Food and Drink

Côte d'Ivoire has a variety of dishes more or less unique to the country. In the south, you'll find usual varieties of tubers – yams, cassava (*manioc*) – which, along with plantains, make up a large part of the diet. They are often pounded into *foutou* and eaten with a clear sauce.

Around Abidjan, cassava or manioc is commonly dried, grated and steamed. The result, called *achéké* (and also spelled *atiéké*), is often compared to couscous, although the steam makes the manioc grains stick together in a large lump. It's a heavy meal served with a soup and *poisson braisé*, for some reason, it seems to induce sleep. You can buy *achéké* ready-made in the markets – all wrapped in large leaves. Another staple is *aloko*, the local name for sliced, deep-fried plantains. In other countries this is more of a snack, but in the RCI it's the basis of a meal served with a bit of *piment* and fish.

Rice is grown in the northwest and is the main staple there, although you now find it throughout the country. In the northeast, millet and increasingly corn make up the basis of the diet. *Kedjenou* is a northern dish which has caught on throughout the country and is commonly served even in the *maquis* (small open-air restaurants) of Abidjan. It's made from chicken, steamed together with vegetables – aubergines, tomatoes and onions – and served on rice.

■ Drinking

Local **liquid refreshments** include palm wine – *banqui/bangi* – commonly found in the south. *Chapalo* (or *tchapalo*) is the millet beer favoured by northerners: Ivoirians usually drink it *pimenté*, adding hot peppers to give it an extra kick. *Mouroudji* is a non-alcoholic drink based on lemon and ginger, which is sold throughout the country, notably in town markets and motor parks. Staple internationals – *Coke* and other soft drinks and often soda water – are complemented by Ivoirian **beer**. The thought of a giant, litre bottle of ice-cold *Solibra* (*grands modèle*) has encouraged many a dusty *mille kilo s* traveller.

Foreign restaurants are commonplace in Côte d'Ivoire and, if you're homesick, this is where you'll find some of the best European eating in West Africa. In Abidjan, dining in a French restaurant costs substantially more than in Paris, but the quality compares well. Restaurants catering to the tastes of the big ex-pat community have sprouted up across the country.

Communications: PTT, media and language

Keeping in touch with home is easy, as there's a well-developed telephone system and good postal service. Mail rarely goes astray but, like the phone, you pay a lot. Poste restante tends to be held for a limited period only – better to use a private box number or the Amex representative in Abidjan.

Internal, let alone international phone calls can be fiendishly expensive (seven minutes in the afternoon from the PTT in Man to Abidjan – CFA3200). Always check the cost first. New card phones are being introduced in various towns, with cards from CFA1000–10,000. If you're travelling widely in West Africa, don't count on the Abidjan PTT as a major mail and telephone point. It's exasperating.

■ Language

The official **language** of Côte d'Ivoire (and God forbid you should call it Ivory Coast) is French. If you speak some, you'll have little trouble communicating. There are numerous national languages; the most widespread is perhaps **Dyula** (often spelled *Dioula*), a Mande language of commerce very closely related to Bambara and Malinké (in fact the three are virtually dialects, to a large extent mutually intelligible). The Akan language **Baoulé** is also widespread; Baoulé people (Houphouët-Boigny's community) account for a large chunk of the total population (fifteen percent) and are well represented in the administration. The Kru language, **Bété**, is the most widely spoken language in the southwest, while Voltaic **Senoufo** is spoken in a number of dialects across a substantial region in the north.

A SHORT GLOSSARY OF IVOIREAN TERMS

A mix of French and Ivoirian language words.

Apatam   Men's meeting shelter, palava house.

Barre   The surf barrier; on the landward side, the tidal race is often too much to swim against.

Bia   The thrones of the Akan-speaking kingdoms.

Deguerpi   Meaning "he who had to get out", it refers to people displaced by development projects, notably those forced to move when the Kossou Dam flooded the region west of Yamoussoukro.

Maquis   A French word meaning scrub or bush, and hence the French underground resistance in World War II. Formerly, local drinking places couldn't operate without authorisation so they moved to hidden courtyards, gaining the name *maquis*. Today it refers to small restaurants – now legal – that serve drinks with inexpensive Ivoirian food.

Mille kilos   22-seater, one tonne mini-buses, generally the type of vehicle to avoid at a motor park.

Papo   Palm fronds woven into roofs or fences, common along the coast.

PDCI   *Parti Démocratique de la Côte d'Ivoire* – the nation's sole political party.

Yacouba   Name commonly given to the Dan people. A misnomer, it supposedly stuck when one of the first Europeans asked what the people were called and someone responded with a sentence that started "*yacouba*", meaning "he says". Frequently the area around Man is referred to as the Yacouba country.

■ Press and airwaves

Media-wise, two major dailies, *Fraternité Matin* (commonly referred to as "Frat-Mat") and *Ivoire Soir* keep readers of French abreast of Ivoirian national and regional news, but neither has extensive international coverage. The latter has a punchier style and generally makes for lighter reading. *Frat-Mat*'s editor-in-chief is also Houphouët's Information Minister, so he's hardly famous for his searching editorials. *Ivoire Dimanche* is a weekly magazine with more in-depth articles and popular comic strips.

The RCI has one of the most together and user-friendly TV and radio services in West Africa. Colour transmissions in French on *Télévision Ivoirienne* go out eleven hours daily on two channels. *Radiodiffusion Ivoirienne* broadcasts mostly in French, plus English and several Ivoirian languages.

Holidays and Festivals

The usual Christian holidays are official, while moveable Muslim feasts affect local services only. Beyond these are New Year's Day, Labour Day (May 2), Ascension Day and Assumption Day (both variable), All Saints Day (November 1), and Independence Day (December 7).

Numerous **regional festivals** include:

January
Ancestral festival in Tiagba; Harvest festival in Dabou; Yam festival in Abengourou.

March
Carnival in Bouaké – M*ardi-gras*-like celebration.

April
Dipre Festival of the sacrifice in Gomon north of Abidjan (self-mutilation and trances); Mask festival in Behoua.

June
Lagoon festival in Yassap near Dabou.

July
Circumcision festival in Man.

August
Generation festival in Blokosso; Yam festival in Sikensi.

November
Abissa festival of the dead in Grand Bassam; Prophet Atcho Festival in Bregbo (Harrist celebration); Yam festival in Bondoukou; Mask festival in Man.

Directory

AIRPORT DEPARTURE TAX None.

FOOTBALL Soccer is the national sport, and seeing a match in the new stadium in Abidjan is recommended. Despite a relatively small number of professional players, the national squad – the **Elephants** – repeatedly shines in international competitions. The country's star player is **Youssouf Fofana** ("le petit") whose fame has spread across the continent. On a good day he can win a match almost single-handed. Unfortunately he's been whisked away; he plays left-wing for Monaco.

MUSIC Considering the fairly elaborate recording facilities and relative availablity of instruments, the Abidjan music scene is none too exciting. Live gigs are infrequent. Reggae superstar **Alpha Blondy** has lost some of his more politically aware fans abroad and opted for comfortable sell-out; crooner **Daouda** continues his gush of bilious sweet-soukous tunes; and **Ismaela Isaac et les Freres Keita** provide Blondy-esque wallpaper-music. Other names to look and listen out for include the zouky **Nyanka Bell, Adama Drame, Jane Agnimel, Beny Bezy, Fifi Dallo, Albert Doh, Maître Gazonga, Jimmy Hyacinthe, Kass Men, Ade Liz, Bailly Spinto, Thomas Tia, Woya** and **Dothy Zebro**, all of whom have released records available in Europe.

OPENING HOURS Banks open Mon–Fri 8–11.30am and 2.30–4.30pm. **Government offices** operate Mon–Fri 8am–noon and 2.30–5pm, Sat 8am–noon.

PHOTOGRAPHY No permit is required and people are generally unperturbed by picture taking. In some areas where tourism is popular, artists, dancers or local chiefs may ask for money before being photographed. Either comply or don't take the shot. Other than that, the only real restriction concerns pictures of military installations, airports, bridges and the like.

TROUBLE You're less likely than usual to get into misunderstandings in Côte d'Ivoire. The manners and customs of *les blancs* (if you're one) are quite well known and if you're young and pass for a student, there's a framework to fit you into as well. That said, police and customs officers can be surprisingly prickly and in the roadside encounters you'll have with extraordinary frequency (especially in the east towards the

Ghana border) they can be hostile and humourless — though not especially corrupt. It's as well to know that the official line on illegal drugs (in response to the threat of heroin and cocaine trans-shipments) is severe; the new *Ministry of Drug Control* isn't likely to be indulgent towards cannabis smoking.

Situations where you're clearly a victim occur most often in Abidjan, only rarely elsewhere, and some advice is given in that section. The worst pickpocketing goes on at the end of the month, when Ivoirians are carrying their salaries home. Beware, too, in this very mobile society, of being robbed as you get off a night bus half asleep.

Côte d'Ivoire – A Brief History

The early history of Côte d'Ivoire is perhaps better known than that of many other West African countries because its northern fringes were part of the vast, literate, Mande cultural domain. Several towns are estimated to have been founded as far back as the twelfth or thirteenth centuries – including Kong, Bouna and Bondoukou – though not by Mande speakers, who arrived later. By the sixteenth century, the early European presence was being felt along the coast, but trading posts were strictly temporary affairs, dependent on the supplies of ivory, hides, gold and slaves that could be extracted from the people of the interior. Early slaving "factories" – but not stone forts – were set up at São Andreas (Sassandra), Grand Lahou, Jaqueville and Assinie. During the eighteenth century, the interior was transformed with the arrival and establishment of an Akan-speaking offshoot, the Baoulé, who set up a successful planting and trading economy in the forest and savannah lands of central Côte d'Ivoire, and became the country's most important people.

■ Arrival of the French

Apart from a brief contact at Assinie around 1700, the **French** only became interested in the coast after the Napoleonic wars, when they began to buy "treaties" with local kings and chiefs along the coast. In the 1840s, they built **forts at Assinie, Bassam and Dabou**, which during the 1860s and again in 1875 were the subject of inter-governmental efforts to exchange them with Britain for the Gambia colony. But the French "resident" at Bassam, **Arthur Verdier**, had his own plans for the future of the settlements and resisted the idea, a relatively minor

obstinacy that did much to set the shape of West Africa. Verdier had already established *la Compagnie de Kong*, trading French goods far into the interior, via Bondoukou. Now, a young director of the French school at Assinie, **Marcel Treich-Laplène**, was persuaded by the governor of Senegal to make an expedition to the northeast to consolidate the districts threatened by British expansion from the Gold Coast. Treich-Laplène's, and then Louis Binger's, expeditions effectively laid claim to most of the area of today's Côte d'Ivoire. It became a colony of France in 1893, with Grand Bassam its capital.

SAMORY TOURÉ

Pressured by the French advance from the west in the 1880s, the Malinké warmongerer, jihadist and empire-builder **Almamy Samory Touré** organised a systematic scorched-earth retreat to the northern part of Côte d'Ivoire, where he set up a temporary second *Dyula Empire* stretching from Séguéla to the Upper Volta. In the process, Kong was largely destroyed (in 1897) and Bondoukou sacked. Thousands of people, especially Senoufo farmers, fled their homes, and several seasons' worth of

crops were lost. Samory was planning to hold a heavily defended mini-empire based at Katiola, against the French on one side and the British on the other. But he altered strategy on learning of the defeat by the French in a single day of the well-fortified town of Sikasso (now in Mali) and the death of his ally there, Ba Bemba. He fled west again, only to be captured at Guéoulé, near Man, on September 29, 1898. He was exiled to Gabon, where he died of pneumonia on June 21, 1900.

■ "Pacification" and anti-colonial resistance

After the **1885 Berlin conference**, France had newly aggressive competitors for African territory in Britain, Belgium and Germany. With the commencement of the Abidjan–Niger railway and the building (after Grand Bassam's yellow fever epidemic) of the new capital, **Bingerville**, the French adopted a vigorous imperialism which stressed their "mission to civilise". The exploits of Samory against the French had featured off and on in the French headlines for some years and "pacification" now became a violent series of repressions against poorly armed insurgents. Governor **Angoulvant**, whose name is still remembered in an Abidjan street name (remarkably in view of his special talents), had a reputation for using strong-arm tactics, and he made a deeper impression on the colonised Ivoirians than any other Frenchman.

There were uprisings all over the country; the Agni kingdom revolted from 1895–96, sections of the Baoulé in 1899 and the Dida and Wobe groups of Kru-speakers in 1913. But the **Abé revolt** of January 8, 1910 was one of the most violent and well organised.

The Abé, from the area around Agboville, were directly in the line of the railway. Traditionally chauvinistic, the Abé were independent to the point of hostility; but, forced to pay taxes, intimidated into labouring on the railway construction, and press-ganged from their families and villages to walk for days through the forest carrying iron rails and sleepers, they prepared secret plans for an uprising. On the chosen day, the line to the coast was destroyed in several places and every non-Abé whom the rebels encountered was killed, including a number of French settlers and engineers.

Angoulvant reacted with characteristic swift brutality, bringing in troop reinforcements and organising **manhunts** through the forest. But the Abé's guerrilla war against the railway line – and against the creeping usurpation of Abé dominance in their homeland by other groups, some of whom actively collaborated with the French – continued for several years.

■ The Côte d'Ivoire colony

Because of Angoulvant's energetic methods, the people of southern Côte d'Ivoire had to contend, in the early colonial years, with even worse treatment than was common in West Africa. Not unconnected with this was the fact that their country was also viewed as the most economically promising in French West Africa. Trade routes deep into the interior were well-established, the railway gradually drew more wealth to the coast and, most important, two crops of massive significance on the world markets – **coffee and cocoa** – flourished. Although their cultivation was at first forced on farmers, the value of coffee and cocoa wasn't lost on them and they soon began to devote most of their land to cash crops. By the 1920s, families with large holdings on good coffee or cocoa land had become an incipient middle class. Furthermore, Côte d'Ivoire was also exporting rubber, palm oil, timber and fruit crops.

Meanwhile, Bingerville had already been dismissed as a permanent economic capital and surveying and initial work at the site of Abidjan had begun in 1903, the same year the railway started its journey north. Although de facto capital and economic lynchpin since the early 1920s, Abidjan finally became capital officially in 1934.

Côte d'Ivoire was governed by decree, from Paris and Dakar. Its very attractiveness, commercially, brought hardships for those who found themselves "Ivoirians" under colonial rule. The country was almost a "type case" of French colonialism. Forced labour, "for the development of the country", was extracted through chiefs as part payment of dues and taxes. But subjects (the status of nearly all Ivoirians) were also forced to work on private plantations when it was demanded, and on these corporal punishment and privation were normal practice. Such forced labour wasn't always a local matter; with the connivance of chiefs, thousands of labourers were rounded up in the Upper Volta region and trucked south.

Chiefs were co-opted into becoming the lower ranks of the French administration, doing the dirty work of recruitment, tax collection, crop and livestock requisition (common during both wars) and enforcing compulsory cultivation. In large measure, too, the chiefs retained and increased their customary **judicial power**, now with higher authority. Where districts were quiet and taxes and harvests flowed in, the French senior administrators did little to interfere with the running, smooth or otherwise, of colonised society. The corrupting effects of the system were almost immediately apparent.

■ Nationalist stirrings

But it was injustice at a level above the grass-roots that led to the earliest clear signs of nationalist aspirations. **French plantation-owners** benefited from both a cheap labour supply and the market rate for their coffee and cocoa. **African farmers** had to rely on their own kin and community networks for labour and were obliged to accept enforced low prices for their harvests, even though the differences in quality, compared with French produce, were negligible.

Yet African unions and associations were permitted and flourished, though at this stage (the 1930s) calls for more equality and faster assimilation were heard considerably more often than demands for self-government or independence. **Felix Houphouët-Boigny**, a Baoulé doctor, trained in Dakar, became involved in the question of cocoa prices in 1932, when he first lobbied on behalf of farmers in Abengourou.

World War II delayed, as it did everywhere, much political progress, and also marked a threshold. De Gaulle's appearance on the scene, and the Brazzaville declaration of 1944 that brought an end to forced labour and accepted the need for an overhaul of administrative methods, utterly transformed the future possibilities in Côte d'Ivoire. Houphouët-Boigny had been given the job of *chef du canton* for Akoué in 1939. Now he set up, with several other wealthy farmers, the *Syndicat Agricole Africain* (African Farmers' Union), which had the support of the progressive French governor. The planters managed to persuade northern chiefs, including the Moro Naba in Upper Volta, to send labourers for their own plantations, to be paid four times the rate paid by the French planters *and* to receive a share of the crop. In the climate of conflict between settlers and *indigènes* planters, this was a serious, political step; it also put the white tribe of Côte d'Ivoire on the defensive, and pitted them against their own liberal governor, **André Latrille**.

Post-war politics

In the **1946 elections** to the French Constituent Assembly, Houphouët-Boigny was elected as peoples' deputy for Côte d'Ivoire. He won by a narrow margin: there were several other important candidates, one of whom received much support from the settlers trying to keep the African planters out of power. Houphouët's first act was to ensure that the Brazzaville recommendation on forced labour was followed through by the Constituent Assembly. The law which abolished forced labour was quickly coined the *loi Houphouët-Boigny* and the reputation of the planter from Yamoussoukro reached a new peak.

In response to clear messages of antagonism from post-war France, however, and especially the failure of the French Socialist and Christian Democrat parties to support the African cause, Houphouët, together with several other African deputies (including those from Senegal and Soudan – later Mali), formed the *Rassemblement Démocratique Africaine* (*RDA*) in October 1946 to act as an umbrella negotiating body for local political parties in French West and Equatorial Africa – in Côte d'Ivoire, for the *Parti Démocratique de la Côte d'Ivoire* (*PDCI*). The settlers in Côte d'Ivoire finally succeeded in getting rid of the pro-Houphouët Governor Latrille, whom they distrusted intensely. And, spreading the belief that the RDA was a hotbed of Soviet-backed agitators, the next colonial administration in Abidjan managed to break the ties between the Mossi chiefs in Upper Volta and Houphouët's new political power base.

Reactionary responses to political developments continued, however. During 1949 and 1950 there was a series of **"incidents"** across the country involving quarrels started by anti-RDA *provocateurs*, which provided the colonial government with pretexts to bully and arrest Houphouët's followers for having "incited" the trouble. In a large number of small disturbances there were several dozen deaths, most of them of innocent villagers killed when troops opened fire. In several cases, however, cold-blooded extra-judicial executions took place. Most of the leaders of the RDA, except Houphouët himself, were arrested and imprisoned in Grand Bassam. A year of ferment ended with the shooting by troops in Dimbokro of thirteen people on January 30, 1950 – and the decree banning all RDA activity which was issued two days later.

But the momentum for change couldn't be held back. Despite the predictable formation, under colonial auspices, of parties like the *Parti Progressiste de Côte d'Ivoire* and the *Bloc Démocratique Eburnéen*, vehemently opposed to the relatively mild and reformist goals of the PDCI-RDA, the movement made progress. Through the "dark years" of 1948–50, when over 3000 supporters were arrested, they staged **strikes and protests**, culminating in a boycott of European goods in 1950. To drive home the message of the *PDCI*'s independence to anyone who still believed its actions were being orchestrated in Moscow, Houphouët-Boigny broke off his party's tactical alliance with the French Communists which had given his critics so much political ammunition. Houphouët the Marxist had never sounded a very credible epithet.

■ Independence

The constitution of the *PDCI* declared its "struggle for the unity of the native people of Côte d'Ivoire with the French people, for political, economic and social progress following a programme of democratic claims". It didn't sound revolutionary and, when moves **towards independence**, or the possibility of it, came after the 1956 promulgation of the *Loi cadre* (blueprint law) establishing local government for each of the French colonies (but expressly heading off any calls for federalism), it was clear that Houphouët favoured retaining very close ties with France; not the kind of West or pan-African federation that Nkrumah (of newly independent Ghana), Senghor of Senegal and Sekou Touré of Guinea each envisaged in his own way.

When, in 1958, **de Gaulle** returned to power, established the "French Community", and made his famous Yes or No offer to the French colonies (self-government within the French union or complete independence outside it), there was never much doubt about which way Houphouët wanted the country to go. The idea of a French West African federation with its capital in Dakar had never appealed to the Ivoirians, whose country, already the richest in the group, stood to gain little from supporting a federal structure. On the other hand, Houphouët would certainly have countenanced a federation of states which included France on equal terms.

By 1960, with de Gaulle suddenly prepared to see independence (which really meant control over currency and defence) *within* the French union, a last-minute scramble began in some territories to try to salvage the federal ideal. Houphouët pre-empted any considerations of Côte d'Ivoire's involvement by unilaterally declaring **independence** on August 7, 1960. At the same time he formed the *Conseil de l'Entente*, consisting of Côte d'Ivoire, Niger, Burkina and Benin (and later Togo), loosely to pull together those economies which relied upon Abidjan, and further to hinder any West African federation which might seek to draw them away.

■ Independent Côte d'Ivoire: "Economic Miracle" – and crisis

The **first twenty years** bore out the hyperbole pretty well; in comparison with every other West African country, Côte d'Ivoire made staggering progress. Economic growth rates were remarkably high, though everything depended on coffee and cocoa, which together still account for over half the export earnings in most years and employ up to two-thirds of the population. There were strong developments in manufacturing, too, and the country moved into the "middle bracket" of under-developed nations.

In the late 1980s, the full-scale development of the president's showcase capital, **Yamoussoukro**, was met with muted enthusiasm at home and considerable scepticism abroad. Its positive effect in attracting new investment to the country is undoubted, but observers outside the business community have pointed to the enormous cost (some \$US200m) of constructing the mammoth basilica – and Houphouët-Boigny's scarcely credible claim to have paid for it all from private "family" wealth.

Criticism of the president or of government policies is rarely tolerated and strikes often result in the temporary banning of the union involved. But denunciation of the top-heavy role of **French expatriates** in administration and senior management is an escape valve which is generally sanctioned. Periodic reductions of their numbers, in drives for **Ivoirianisation**, are greeted with applause.

On the **political scene**, events – or the lack of them – in the 1960s and 70s seemed to bode well for the stability of the republic. Houphouët-Boigny took personal control of the country's transformation from colony to regional power, directing the French-dominated economy and avoiding confrontation with political opponents by a skilful mix of stick and carrot.

The earliest clear opposition came in the 1960s, when Kragbe Gnagbe tried to set up an alternative party with support from his Bété ethnic community around Gagnoa. This led to **mass arrests** of alleged coup plotters in 1963 – and the death in detention of one of them, **Ernest Boka**, a former head of the supreme court. The perceived threat to the government led inexorably to the bloody **Bété revolt** in 1970 in which Gnagbe was banished to his village and several hundred people died in clashes with troops.

THE COCOA CRISIS

Economically, there have been warning signals in Côte d'Ivoire for some years. By the late 1970s, cutbacks in public expenditure were becoming necessary as the country slid into serious debt, and Côte d'Ivoire's long and complacent record of success began to erode. The year of 1983, and nearly every year since, saw the country as the world's largest cocoa producer. But there's been a glut on the world market and cocoa prices (coffee too) have fallen. At first Houphouët tried to hold up the producer price paid to the farmers, and stockpile the crop in an attempt to raise world market prices. But the ploy was unsuccessful and, ultimately, Côte d'Ivoire had to agree to World Bank and IMF adjustment plans in 1988 as the country was unable to service its foreign debts. As a result, cocoa farmers are being paid in the early 1990s roughly roughly half what they received in 1989.

Any potential coup threat from the small **army** itself has been kept in check by the presence of 1000 **French troops** based at Port Bouet. Moreover the Ivoirian armed forces are generally apolitical and not ethnically unbalanced.

There's no perceivable threat, either, to Côte d'Ivoire's stability from its four neighbours and their military leaders. Relations with **Liberia** and **Ghana** have long been soured by the presence in Côte d'Ivoire of political exiles. Both countries have accused Houphouët-Boigny of allowing rebels to plan operations on his side of the border, most recently in January 1990, when President Doe of Liberia denounced him after thousands of refugees, and the leader of a Liberian coup attempt, fled to Danané. Houphouët's relations with Blaise Compraoré of **Burkina** (who is married to his niece) were put under strain by an article in *Jeune Afrique* magazine which suggested that Côte d'Ivoire had played a role in overthrowing Thomas Sankara.

■ The growth of opposition

As long ago as 1975, with the president starting his fourth unchallenged term in office and already at least seventy years old, Ivoirians were beginning to wonder when (or if) he might step down, and who might replace him. The names of several senior figures were trailed before the public. By the early 1980s, however, the post of vice-president was vacant – and abolished in 1985 – and public debate on the question of **succession** was considered almost treasonable.

In 1987, another in the growing tradition of Bété critics of the government, **Robert Gbai Tagro**, took on the establishment in his own *Parti Républicain de la Côte d'Ivoire* by apparently pitting himself as a future president against Houphouët. His party was never banned, but nor would Houphouët recognise it and, although its centre-right newsletter *La République* is still occasionally published, its first major attempt to rally support – at the proposed first congress of the party in April 1987 – was crushed and its leaders detained. Tagro, whose criticisms of the Ivoirian leadership have been polite to the point of apology, was soon released and continues to try, carefully and respectfully, to open the country to broader political debate.

A more outspoken thorn in Houphouët's side – and one the president appears wary of – is **Laurent Gbagbo** (another Bété man from Gagnoa). Long self-exiled to France and leader of the *Front Populaire Ivoirien*, he insisted he wouldn't return until a framework for multi-party democracy was established. Houphouët managed to woo him back in September 1988 and, although the president is supposed to have offered him a ministerial post to absorb his political ambitions, he turned it down and was set to pursue his academic career. Gbagbo was quickly embroiled in a new political scandal, however, as **Kobena Innocent Anaky** – a business acquaintance – was arrested and then found guilty of "financial malpractices" and given a twenty-year jail sentence. It's widely presumed, from the conduct of the case and its extraordinarily harsh outcome (for such offences normally receive somewhat different treatment), that Anaky was a likely source of funds for Gbagbo's *FPI* and that his removal from public life was more to do with the political threat he posed than with his cavalier business style.

The closest the Houphouët government may have come to falling was in the spring of 1988, when rumours surfaced of a plot within Houphouët's *PDCI* party by a clique of Dyula businessmen from Touba. With stories circulating that he was importing arms, **Lamine Fadika**, the navy minister from Touba, was dismissed. Armed forces Chief of Staff **Zeze Baròan** was given the job of ambassador to Brazil. And the Ivoirian representative in Hamburg of the government shipping organisation *SITRAM* (who was supposed to be the arms supplier) was murdered on a visit home – according to the rumours, for informing the government about the plot. Houphouët went to his funeral.

Fadika is still in circulation and the arms story seems unlikely, but it's clear at least that powerful interests that were stacking up against the president have been toppled.

■ Into the 1990s: who next?

There's no number two, three or four in Côte d'Ivoire; there's only number one . . . and that's me.
Felix Houphouët-Boigny, July 1987

From the outside, all in Côte d'Ivoire has seemed to signal dependable neo-colonialism – at least until 1990 – with enough wealth trickling down and enough progress being made to keep the pot from boiling over. In reality, the Ivoirian situation shares much in common with, for example, Kenya, though with higher regard for due process and human rights. There is no death penalty and, while political detentions are by no means uncommon, they rarely last long.

Opposition to Houphouët-Boigny's espousal of pro-Western, capitalist values – mostly from students and teachers' unions – has resulted in several of the one-on-one *dialogues* for which the old man is famous, and which temporarily serve to defuse the issues – or at least defer them – with large dollops of Houphouët charisma. To avoid anti-Houphouët resentment building up, disgraced members of his government – of whom there have been several – are sent to tread water for a spell away from the limelight before being rehabilitated elsewhere.

At the time of writing, however, the country is in the grip of **austerity measures** under an imposed "structural adjustment programme" of the kind which most of Côte d'Ivoire's neighbours have had to put up with for some years. Power worker strikes led to blackouts in February 1990. These in turn pushed **students** into marching on Abidjan city centre and finally led to the violent arrest of 150 students who had barricaded themselves in the cathedral in Abidjan. They were demanding **Houphouët's resignation**, an **end to one-party rule** and better grants and conditions on campus. **Marcel Ette** of the lecturers' union *SYNARE* (which, with the high school teachers' union *SYNESCI* has always been vocal

in support of democratic reforms) spoke out eloquently and with some courage against the "deep malaise afflicting Ivoirian society".

National turmoil

Houphouët's oft-repeated claim that "not a single drop of blood has been spilled in this country since I've been President", while not exactly true, was conclusively sunk in April 1990, when a schoolboy was shot dead as police tried to disperse a crowd of demonstrators in Adzopé, north of Abidjan. Amid rumours that Houphouët was shortly to resign, **protests** flared in a number of towns and doctors went on strike.

Under siege, the government dropped the massive **tax increases** (effectively pay cuts) due to be implemented in 1990. Although peace was restored for a few weeks, there was an unprecedented **army rebellion** in May, led by hundreds of young conscripts demanding improved conditions. They took over a radio station in Abidjan, and were soon emulated by air force personnel who staged an **occupation of Abidjan aiport**. There was a further army uprising the next day, and a state of general panic and confusion reigned in the Plateau district of Abidjan as soldiers tore through the streets in commandeered cars. Lebanese shops and businesses were attacked. While no more deaths were reported, there were dozens of other disturbances in garrison towns around the country, most of them contained by the police, who remained loyal throughout. The 1000-strong contingent of **French troops**, based at Port Bouet, was placed on alert by Paris, but not deployed.

During this period of instability, Houphouët's remaining resolve appears to have collapsed. He agreed to the **legalisation of opposition parties** and seemed to have lost the will to contest the **presidential elections** set for the end of 1990. If "Houf" – as American bankers like to call him – decides it's time to write his memoirs, then **Laurent Gbagbo**, the increasingly outspoken leader of the left-wing coalition *Front Populaire Ivoirien*, and the unionist **Marcel Ette**, are likely to be key contenders. Meanwhile, the **PDCI**, which has run the country for the last thirty years, is beginning to fragment as senior party figures – among them Houphouët's chosen successor, speaker of the National Assembly **Henri Konan Bedie**, and Defence Minister **Jean Konnan Banny** – prepare for a dogfight and a leap into the unknown of multi-party politics.

ABIDJAN

ABIDJAN has wide **avenues** with names like De Gaulle, Marseille and République; there are **pavement cafés** and **billboards** pushing *Orangina* and *L'Express* – it all seems to have more in common with Paris than with any other West African city. Downtown Abidjan looks like the work of a mad urban planner who dropped the *Little Manhattan* quarter of Paris' 15th arrondissement onto the set of the *Blue Lagoon*. Even if the coconut trees, red flamboyants and frangipanis lining the city's financial centre lend an exotic air to its supermarkets, **skyscrapers** and **traffic jams**, they barely camouflage the familiar signs of urban paranoia.

Now the second largest city in West Africa, Abidjan has grown from nothing in less than sixty years, and at an astounding pace since independence. Considering the number of **rural migrants** and **foreign workers** who've come in hope of easy money, the city has done a fair job of absorbing the influx – certainly much better than its nearest rival, Lagos. On first glance, this is a clean city, well laid-out and aesthetically appealing. For many, it's the very model of what **prosperity** can bring to Africa. But you don't have to go far outside the centre to find shocking examples of poverty and **overcrowding**. In a scenario that has played itself out repeatedly around the world, the jobless and displaced turn to illicit survival tactics. Violent crime, prostitution and drug trafficking now taint the image of the "pearl of the lagoon". Of course, you could spend a good deal of time in the city without encountering its dark side. But beneath Abidjan's glittering façade there's a whole set of problems tied to Africa's best hopes and representing its worst fears.

A brief history

The French abandoned their first capital, Grand Bassam, in 1900 because of disease. The hilly location of the new capital, Bingerville, away from the sea posed transport problems that limited its economic future. In 1934, the governor moved to a new mansion 17km to the southwest, in a spot then known as **Abidjean**.

The **European district** thus grew up on the Plateau peninsula, where administrative buildings sprang up beside trading depots, shops and villas. It was surrounded by two African suburbs – Adjamé to the north and Treichville across the lagoon to the south – although in the early days the collective population of these three districts was barely 20,000.

After 1950, however, Abidjan began to grow at a pace, and quickly took on the dimensions of a capital city. The catalyst was the **Vridi canal** which opened the Ebrié lagoon to the Atlantic and gave Abidjan the capacity to become an international **port**. Five years later, the railway line was extended from Treichville all the way to Ouagadougou, 1156km to the north. People started flocking to the town as new commercial possibilities developed. The population has jumped from 60,000 in the early 1950s to somewhere in the neighbourhood of three million today.

Though Yamoussoukro became the country's administrative capital in the mid-1980s, Abidjan remains the economic nerve centre. It's still growing at a rate of about twelve percent each year, its population more than doubling every decade.

Orientation and getting around

Abidjan's most striking physical feature is the **Ebrié Lagoon**, as one piece of tourist blurb attempts to describe: *With its capricious tentacles the lagoon spreads as it were its silvery arms into the surrounding country offering Abidjan to the gaze of the overwhelmed traveller.* They are rather murky fingers these days, dividing the city into distinct land masses. These quarters have evolved into large distinct neighbourhoods, each with its

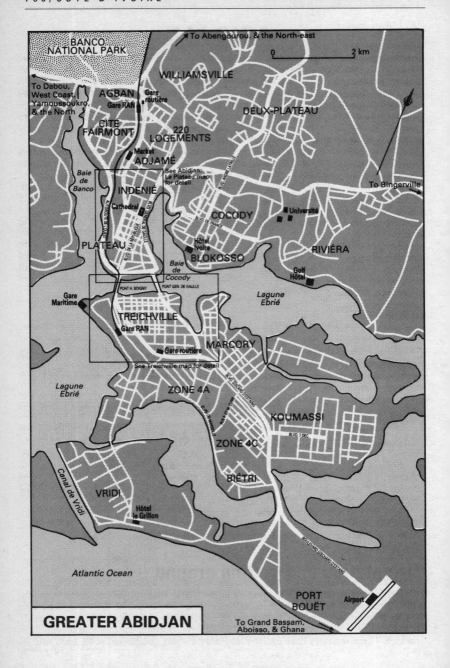

GREATER ABIDJAN

own flavour. Although there are officially ten such districts, only four are likely to figure prominently in your plans – **Le Plateau**, **Treichville**, **Adjamé** and **Cocody**.

The main **points of arrival** are the **airport**, close to the city at Port Bouet on the ocean-front, **Treichville** *gare routière* if you're coming from Ghana or the east coast, and **Adjamé** *gare routière* if you're arriving by road from anywhere else. Arriving by train, the *Gare R.A.N. Plateau* is not for passengers and the train terminates in **Treichville**.

Note that if you're arriving in the city at the end of the week with business to attend to, you might just as well shoot out again to somewhere cheaper and more relaxing like **Bingerville** (p.765), **Grand Bassam** (p.772) or **Jacqueville** (p.767) and come back bright and early on Monday morning.

Le Plateau

This futuristic financial district is the showcase of Côte d'Ivoire's economic capital. The quarter's main thoroughfare, the **Boulevard de la République**, stretches from the **Houphouët-Boigny Bridge** in the south up to the **Palais de Justice**. Along its way, the boulevard passes by the Central Post Office, the food and crafts markets, the *Hôtel de Ville* and the smart new stadium. The main **banking district** is on the Avenue Joseph Anoma, between the bd de la République and the rue Botreau Roussel. Nearby, Abidjan's most famous skyscraper, **the Pyramid** (its heavy avant-garde style has long made it controversial), commands a view of **Cocody Bay**. The city's most recent architectural curiosity, the stunning **Saint Paul's Cathedral**, lies on the northern fringe of the Plateau, off the Avenue Jean Paul II. Intimidating **administrative towers** loom up west of the church near the Boulevard Angoulvant, dwarfing the embarrassingly small **National Museum**.

Treichville

Two bridges, Houphouët-Boigny and De Gaulle, lead from the Plateau to **Treichville**. Described by those who don't live here as Abidjan's "most African" quarter, Treichville is the city centre's cheapest and poorest district. It's divided into 25 "wards", each with its own character; in Quartier Yobou Lambert, one of the poorest, you'll find an amazing mix of nationalities and ethnic groups – Ghanaian, Gambian, Sierra Leonean, Hausa, Yoruba, Wolof – and "blocks" mostly consisting of a compound with a gate onto the street. What Treichville lacks in high-cost high-rises, it makes up for in its level of activity. When the Plateau is fast asleep, this neighbourhood still moves at a frenzied clip. Treichville's grid layout, with numbered *rues* running north–south and numbered *avenues* going east–west, is dominated by the Boulevard du 6 Fevrier – a popular shopping street that leads south from Treichville's **main market**. The Avenue de la Reine Pokou, which cuts the district from west to east, is another main artery with a heavy concentration of restaurants and **nightclubs**. Abidjan's **railway station** faces the port on the Boulevard de Marseille, and off the Boulevard Giscard d'Estaing in the south-

---

A NOTE ON SECURITY

It's not a surprise to find Abidjan one of the **least secure cities** in West Africa. As usual, stories get repeated and recycled, and the true incidence of attacks on tourists has to be related to the high number of tourists and expatriates passing through. Having said which, Abidjan can be a dangerous city and violent robberies – usually at knife point – do occur, in Treichville and Adjamé, but also on the Plateau. Simply leave all your valuables behind when going out and you'll feel less threatened and be less intimidated. The notorious **blackspots** are the bridges from Treichville to the Plateau. Do not cross on foot. And one last thing – don't let anyone put you off going to Treichville market; it's brilliant.

west is one of the city's major **lorry parks** serving destinations to the east of Abidjan. Thus, your first encounter with Abidjan may very likely be via Treichville. Bordering Treichville to the east is the middle-class **Marcory** district, where you might venture in search of a moderately priced hotel.

Cocody

The Boulevard de la Corniche snakes around **Cocody Bay**, leading from the Plateau to the tropical opulence of Abidjan's foremost **residential neighbourhood**. Whatever Ivoirian reggae star Alpha Blondy may sing in his former hit song, Cocody does not rock, nor is it even vaguely rasta. The neatly landscaped streets and villas set a decidedly bourgeois tone, improved a little by the presence of the university. Cocody's major stake in tourism is the **Ivoire**, the city's biggest and most expensive hotel. A monumental architectural extravaganza when it was inaugurated in 1963, this towering high-rise is today something of a dinosaur, but it still has the best views of the Plateau's skyline; a good place for taking photos.

Adjamé

North of the Plateau, **Adjamé** is another *quartier populaire*, like Treichville but less established and urbane, swarming with recent immigrants and, because it's on the mainland in the north, expanding and evolving uncheckably. The neighbourhood **market** is one of Abidjan's biggest and is surrounded by a multitude of boutiques where you can find the widest selection of bric-à-brac imaginable. The district's **bus and lorry park** is also the busiest in the city and services the entire country, with the exception of towns along the route to Ghana.

CITY TRANSPORT

The four main districts, and the six others surrounding them, are connected by an efficient **bus service**, green and cream-coloured (just like those in Paris). The main SOTRA terminus, the *Gare du Sud*, is located on the Plateau, at the foot of the Houphouët-Boigny Bridge. Theoretically you can pick up a map of routes here, though they frequently run out. Buses cost CFA100–300 a ride and can get you virtually anywhere in the greater Abidjan area.

As an alternative, the city boasts a spiffy fleet of shiny orange **metered taxis** – one of the best in West Africa. Remarkably fast and undamaged, they can work out expensive. They operate on meters with a daytime tariff (CFA150 plus CFA100 per km) from 6am to midnight, and a higher night-time tariff *only after midnight*. Check you're paying *Tarif 1*. Fares from the airport to anywhere in Treichville or the southern half of the city shouldn't exceed CFA1200 to Plateau no more than CFA1600, to Cocody maximum CFA2100.

SOTRA also operates a **ferry service**, *bateaux bus*, to various points around the lagoon. The main *gare lagunaire* (☎32 17 37) is on the southern tip of the Plateau, near the *Gare du Sud* bus station and Houphouët-Boigny Bridge.

BUS ROUTES

A large number of bus routes run through the Plateau. The following selection is useful:

#06 Aeroport – Gare du Sud (daily from 6am–9.20pm every 10–15mins)

#86 Gare du Sud – Musée National – Adjame gare routière – Blokosso (Cocody)

#05 Gare du Sud – Treichville – Koumassi

#18 Gare du Sud – Vridi

#15 Gare du Sud – Gare Abobo

#03 Pyramide (bd Botreau Roussel) – Cité Fairmont (Banco National park entrance)

#28 Gare Sud – Hôtel du Golf

Finding a place to stay

Abidjan boasts a good choice of comfortable **accommodation** in the middle-to-upmarket price range, but budget lodgings are extremely hard to come by. As a basic rule, the closer you are to the centre, the more expensive things are – prices on the Plateau are out of sight, and accommodation here is geared mainly to business travellers and wealthy tourists.

The bottom line

You really have to scrape the bottom of the barrel to find **cheap places** in Abidjan and usually that means a *chambre de passage*. Two well-known hotels in the genre are:

Hôtel Fraternité, av 21, rue 44 (behind the *Cinéma l'Entente*). Musty rooms for CFA1500. It's not too bad for a brothel, but you have to check out every day at 6.30am and can't check back in until 8pm. In the interim, you can leave your bags at reception.

Hôtel Tourbouroux (☎32 64 48), at the corner of rue 8 and av 13.

Hôtel Plaisir is recommended for **single women**. It's on the corner of bd Giscard d'Estaing and av de Carrier (from CFA3000).

To camp, you'll probably need to go out on the Grand Bassam road. *Coppa Cabana* in Adjoufou (2–3km after you've turned left along the seafront) is reasonable. Take Bus #17.

Cheap to moderate

It's really worth looking at a number of places if you're going to be in town for a while. There's lots of choice and no guarantee of value for money. Be sure to ask first for their best room.

TREICHVILLE

L'Argiegeois, bd de Marseille. Virtually next door to the *France* (see below), this has slightly lower standards and prices but, with comfortably furnished rooms from CFA7000, it's not bad value.

Hôtel Atlanta, av 15, rue 15 (☎33 24 69). Fairly unrefined, but quite good value; from CFA5500/6500.

Hôtel California, av 23, rue 44 (05 BP6474; ☎35 55 66). It seems there's a hotel with the name in every large town and Abidjan is no exception. Not bad value – S/C rooms with AC start from CFA5000 and are decently clean.

Hôtel de France, 19 bd de Marseille (01 BP 690; ☎32 65 18), on the west side of Treichville. An older hotel, well maintained and full of charm. Single S/C rooms with AC go from CFA8500 and, given the comfort and location, that's not unreasonable.

Hôtel Mandani, av 7, rue 25. There are worse places (non S/C rooms from CFA3000–4000 for the night, depending on AC, fan included, or no fan).

Hôtel le Prince, av 20, rue 19 (☎32 71 27). Good value and not unclean. S/C AC rooms from CFA5000–7000.

Hôtel de Succès, av 14, rue 25. This place is a real old factory of a bordello – basic but OK and quite friendly. Prices from CFA2500–5500 according to height and facilities. Top-floor front rooms with AC are good value; *rez de chaussée* rooms on the wrong side are dismal, mostly used for *passages*.

Hôtel Terminus, bd Delafosse (01 BP 790; ☎32 11 98). Large rooms with fan and corner kitchen. Located across from the RAN railway station, this one's convenient if you arrive late with the train.

Treichôtel, av de la Reine Pokou (☎32 89 65). This tall hotel used to be a cheapie, but it's been re-done and now seems too much (and has more than you want – carpets, TV etc). S/C AC rooms from CFA10,000. Safe parking.

MARCORY

Konankro-I, av de la TSF (BP 4237; ☎35 61 96). Small S/C rooms with AC from CFA6000. Located in a busy part of the district, near the *Église Sainte Thérèse*.

ADJAMÉ

Relais d'Adjamé (☎37 18 56). Rooms from about CFA3500, located right next to the *gare routière*. Noisy and minimal standards of cleanliness, but one of the town's better bargains.

Hôtel La Rocade (☎37 21 51). A likeable dive near the *220 Logements* district, with rooms for CFA3000.

Hôtel du Nord (09 BP 230; ☎37 34 53). Conveniently situated in the *220 Logements* part of Adjamé, just north of the Plateau. Well-maintained AC rooms from CFA6000 – good value.

KOUMASSI

Hôtel Seleki, bd 7 Dec, Koumassi. A nice, no-nonsense hotel in a quieter part of town, not far from the airport. Clean S/C AC rooms from CFA6000/7000.

ZONE 4C

Le Stop, 38 rue Pierre et Marie Curie, Zone 4c (01 BP 1947; ☎35 71 17, telex 3341). A smartish place in an upmarket neighbourhood, again convenient for the airport. S/C, AC rooms from 10,500.

VRIDI PLAGE

Hôtel Le Grillon, Vridi Plage, near the S.I.R. refinery (01 BP 2393; ☎ 35 52 60). Clean and quiet and fairly close to the airport but a long way into town. S/C, AC rooms from CFA7500–10,000.

PLATEAU

Grand Hôtel, bd Général de Gaulle/rue Montigny (01 BP 1785; ☎32 12 00, 32 64 38, telex 3807). Near the Pont Général de Gaulle and the lagoon, looking out onto Treichville. Newer and showier hotels have forced the *Grand* to keep its prices low (from CFA11,000) in order to remain competitive – though the standards here are very high.

Hôtel Sports, av Général de Gaulle. The only hotel in the Plateau that approaches the inexpensive/moderate range, the *Sports* has S/C, AC rooms starting at CFA8500.

Expensive

There's generally a very high standard in the expense account bracket. Many travellers staying at the following may have had little choice in the matter. But if you can afford to be selective, the options are wide-ranging.

MARCORY

Hibiscus, bd du Gabon (☎35 38 78). Part of the *Ibis* chain, this is classy and relatively expensive with comfortable AC rooms from CFA16,000. Pleasant garden restaurant under *paillotes*.

COCODY

Hôtel Ivoire, bd de la Corniche (08 BP 8001; ☎44 10 45, telex 23555). Abidjan's pride and joy, this *Intercontinental* hotel is really a city within the city, with everything from a bowling alley and car hire to West Africa's only **ice rink**. Cinema, sauna, casino, nightclub, swimming pool and tennis courts add to the razzle-dazzle, but jaded business travellers find it all a bit much. Rooms start at CFA35,000. Numerous restaurants include the *Toit d'Abidjan* (☎44 10 45) on top of the tower – elegant and expensive French dining with the city's best view.

Golf-Hôtel, Riviera (08 BP18; ☎43 10 44, telex 2368). Just east of Cocody near the golf course and Lagoon. More intimate than the *Ivoire* but almost as classy, the *Golf-Hôtel* has an attractive residential setting. Well-cropped lawns sweep down to meet the clear pool. Garden *terrasse-bar*, restaurant and water skiing in the lagoon. Rooms from CFA27,000.

PLATEAU

Hilton, av Delafosse (01 BP 4081; ☎32 26 00, telex 2636). Poshest and one of the newest on the Plateau with famous service and lagoon views. Very convenient for the city centre and much more personal than you might expect. Pool, sauna and massage parlour count among the perks. Prices start around CFA33,000.

Ibis Plateau, 7 bd Roume (☎32 01 57, telex 22608). More affordable luxury and one of the better bargains among the international class options. Rooms with TV, video and phone from CFA18,000.

Novotel, av Général de Gaulle (BP 3718; ☎32 04 57, telex 3264). An imposing hotel and a great location (rooms with everything from CFA27,000). Swimming pool, of course.

Tiama, bd de la République (04 BP 643; ☎32 08 22, telex 23494). Located in the ministerial district and favoured by journalists and business people, rooms (from CFA23,000) on the upper floors look out onto the lagoon. Restaurant, *brasserie*, shops and car hire.

BIETRY

Le Wafou, Kilometre 7, bd de Marseille (☎36 84 40, telex 42199). A village built on stilts, the *Wafou* attempts to combine traditional style (mud-like walls, thatched roofing) with modern convenience (rooms with phones, TVs and minibars). A cross between Disneyland and Club Med (from CFA20,000).

VRIDI PLAGE

Palm Beach, rue de l'Ocean, Vridi (01 BP 2704; ☎35 42 16, telex 42236). A beachfront hotel with *paillotes* and S/C AC rooms. An older establishment, the place has charm and is well kept up. Saltwater pool and excellent restaurant. Rooms start at CFA15,000.

Eating

The variety of **restaurants** in Abidjan seems endless and you can find food from just about any corner of the world, so the following listings are but a small selection of good spots. The city has carved out a deserved reputation for good eating although some of the classier Asian, European and African restaurants are prohibitively expensive. To save money, you can still find good **street food** at the markets of Treichville, Adjamé, Cocody and even on the Plateau – Senegalese rice with a thick vegetable sauce is common fare. Also inexpensive are the *maquis* scattered about town. Though you'll find them in every district, they're most numerous in Treichville, notably along the Avenue de la Reine Pokou. On the plateau there's also a good clutch of street café *gargotes* across from the PTT near the Gare du Sud bus station (telephones, too). Typical dishes include stewed chicken or fish, chicken *kedjenou* or brochettes.

Inexpensive – and snacks

Abidjan's expensive reputation obscures a lot of reasonable places to fill up, where the competition helps keep prices down.

Barakiss. Cross between a pavement café and a *maquis* ,located in the park across from the *Hôtel de Ville* in Plateau. Inexpensive meals, cold drinks and an endless parade of shoe-shiners.

Chawarma Caravelle 2 A good shwarma joint, not too pricey, clean and busy – a place to stop for a drink too.

Maquis du Stade ("chez Tantie Youyou"), av du Docteur Crozet. An excellent lunchtime *maquis*, shadey and convenient, somewhat slow, but delicious on final arrival – plaintain *foutou*, rice, meat, fish, sauce and quite excellent *kedjenou* (around CFA750).

Restaurant de Bah, av de la Reine Pokou, Treichville, opposite the *Treichotel*. Cheap, clean, tasty and unpretentious.

Super Chicken, d owntown near the Pyramid and on av 20, rue 13 in Treichville. Abidjan's answer to fast food – a cross between Colonel Sanders and Ronald McDonald.

Snackorama, adjoining the bowling alley of the *Hôtel Ivoire*. Burgers, milk-shakes and sundaes served to the sounds of crashing pins. Inexpensive Americana.

Tehran Express, av Terrasson de Fougères, bd de la République. Popular and cheap meals (CFA4–800) and nice "special yoghurt".

Moderate

There's a good range of pricier restaurants where presentation and ambience count for as much as the cuisine. Prices for lunch or dinner at most of these start around CFA4000 a head.

Attoungblan, av 21, Treichville (☎35 20 41). African specialties like *foutou*, *riz sénégalais* or *couscous*. Closed Tues.

Le Calalou, av 2, rue 6, Treichville (☎22 70 99). Togolese fish and dishes from Senegal and Côte d'Ivoire. Inexpensive, but good.

Chez Mamie, SICOGI Arras building, av 21, Treichville (☎22 61 93). *Riz sénégalais* and other African specialties.

Maison des Anciens Combatants, Allée des Anc. Combatants, off rue Jesse Owens, Plateau (☎22 77 24). Relatively inexpensive and very popular four-course set lunches – healthy servings of French and African dishes and nice service and atmosphere (around CFA4000).

Café de Paris, 11 av Marchand, Plateau (☎22 83 91). French – *steak au poivre, escalope de veau à la crème* and the like.

Chez Babouya, av 7, rue 7, Treichville (☎32 39 28). Thoroughly enjoyable experience with Mauritanian specialities. Set-price dinner might be *pigeon aux dattes* or excellent couscous. Cushions on the floor and Bobouya's incomparable self are the extra attractions. Meals from CFA3500.

Expensive

At the expense account end, Abidjan tends to lay on the style somewhat thick. The best of these are excellent by any measure, but you'd be wise to garner the latest reports before risking important occasions on them.

AFRICAN

Chez Cakpo, rue du Canal Vridi (☎35 29 78). African specialities served by the waterfront. Excellent lobster and grilled prawns.

Climbié, av Chardy and Rue Lecouer, Plateau (☎32 71 63). Upmarket African restaurant.

Aboussouan, bd Giscard-d'Estaing, Treichville (☎22 37 14).

Le Marrakech, av 21, rue 13 Treichville (☎32 51 64). Moroccan *tagines, couscous pastilla* and *brochettes* – well prepared and not too pricey.

ANTILLEAN

La Créole, av Delafosse, av 7, Treichville (☎22 21 06). Original Antillean recipes including West Indian black pudding, stuffed crab and *colombo de poulet*.

Le Madiana. Restaurant of the *Hôtel California* featuring Caribbean cooking.

EUROPEAN

Le Nid de Cigognes, 20 av Noguès, Plateau (☎32 30 46). Bar/restaurant featuring *choucroute* and other Alsatian specialities.

Le Grenier, rue Crosson Duplessis, Pleateau (☎32 34 94). Refined French cuisine, like *riz de veau bordelaise* and seasoned escargot. Closed Sun.

Lagon Bleu, bd Général de Gaulle and av Chardy, in the lagoon (☎32 84 68).

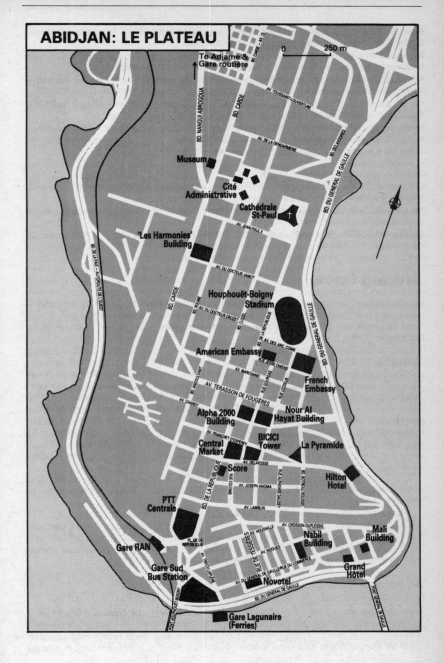

ABIDJAN: LE PLATEAU

0   250 m

To Adjamé &
Gare routière

BD. NANGUI ABROGOUA

BD. CARDE

AV. TOUSSAINT-LOUVERTURE

AV. DE LA GENDARMERIE

BD. DES AXOKOMS

BD. DU GÉNÉRAL DE GAULLE

BD. DE LA PAIX — AUTOROUTE DE L'OUEST

Museum

Cité
Administrative

Cathédrale
St-Paul

AV. JEAN-PAUL II

'Les Harmonies
Building

AV. DU DOCTEUR JAMOT

BD. CARDE

BD. ROUME

AV. DU DOCTEUR CROZET

RUE CLOZEL

Houphouët-Boigny
Stadium

RUE DE LA RÉPUBLIQUE

AV. DES ANC. COMB

American Embassy

RUE JESSE OWENS

French
Embassy

RUE LYCURGANT

AV. MARCHAND

N/E GOURGAS

R/E LECOEUR

AV. TERASSON DE FOUGÈRES

AV. CHARDY

Alpha 2000
Building

Nour Al
Hayat Building

AV. FRANCHET D'ESPEREY

BICICI
Tower

La Pyramide

Central
Market

AV. DELAFOSSE

Score

RUE BOURGOIN

AV. JOSEPH ANOMA

RUE ALPHONSE DAUDET

RUE DU COMMERCE

Hilton
Hotel

PTT
Centrale

BD. DE LA RÉPUBLIQUE

AV. LAMBLIN

AV. CROSSON DUPLESSIS

Mali
Building

Gare RAN

PL. DE LA
RÉPUBLIQUE

RUE DU GÉNÉRAL DE GAULLE

RUE DE TESSIÈRES

RUE THOMASSET

BD. ROUDAILLE

AV. NOGUES

Nabil
Building

Gare Sud
Bus Station

AV. DU GÉNÉRAL DE GAULLE RUE DU COMMERCE

Novotel

Grand
Hôtel

PONT HOUPHOUÊT-BOIGNY

BD. DU GÉNÉRAL DE GAULLE

PONT GÉNÉRAL DE GAULLE

Gare Lagunaire
(Ferries)

Tout Va Bien, Kilometre 2, bd de Marseille, Treichville (☎32 18 37). Swiss specialtiies like fondue and *gratin dauphinois* plus Italian pasta and pizza.

Brasserie Abidjanaise, bd de la République (☎32 92 35). Long rated one of the best French restaurants in town. Correspondingly high prices. The menu changes weekly.

Le Chalet Suisse, av Chardy, Plateau (☎32 54 80). Popular spot for fondue or interesting French and Swiss specialities. Less expensive than many upmarket restaurants; book a table.

Chez Valentin, av Jean Paul II, Plateau (☎32 47 16). Intimate restaurant serving French food (including pastries and ice cream) and African specialities.

Santa Maria, bd de Marseille (☎35 75 85). Very good seafood restaurant with *terasse* overlooking the lagoon. Book early to get a seat. Closed Tues.

Pizza Di Sorrento, Kilometre 6, bd de Marseille (☎35 57 75).

ASIAN

L'Oriental, bd de Marseilles (☎32 36 85). The best Lebanese cooking in town and belly dancers to go with it.

La Grande Muraille, av Terrasson de Fougères (☎32 25 06). Very good, and not outrageously priced, Chinese food.

La Baguette d'Or, bd Carde (☎22 60 70). One of the best places for Vietnamese eating, open daily 7.30–10.30pm.

Around town

On the surface, there's not a lot of **sightseeing** to do in Abidjan. You may be satisfied simply to absorb the energy of one of West Africa's busiest urban centres and, if your heart is gladdened by concrete and glass, to contemplate the merits of some of the city's more daring high-rises.

One of the first was the **Nour al Hayat** building, built in 1966 on the Avenue Chardy. A landmark of sorts, the modest tower has since been humbled by more recent skyscrapers erected nearby, like the **Alpha 2000** building, whose 21 floors filled with shopping galleries, offices and the headquarters of the *Société Ivoirienne de Banque*, made it the largest commercial centre in West Africa when it opened in 1977. Other recent additions include the **BICICI building** with its fifteen storeys of tinted glass and, of course, the **Pyramid**, on the corner of the av Franchet d'Esperey and av Botreau-Roussel. Designed by Italian architect Olivieri, the eighteen floors of this building, with the upper levels inclining trapezoidally, were shocking to many when it opened in 1973, and the highly unusual lines continue to make it one of the most talked about buildings on the Plateau and an easy landmark.

The trend towards modernism continues, notably in the form of the **Cathedral**, erected in the north of the Plateau in 1985 with the futuristic **Tours Administratives** serving as a backdrop.

Abidjan cosmopolitanism hasn't obliterated one or two other distractions. The **national museum** houses a fine collection of Ivoirian art, and the district **markets** make for interesting shopping. You could even get back to nature with a quick trip to the **Banco National Park** or the **Parc Zoologique**, both of which are located a short distance from the city centre, north of Adjamé.

The National Museum

Open daily except Monday, 9am–noon, 3–6pm, free, donations anticipated.

Set in the shadows of Abidjan's sparkling ministerial towers, the **National Museum** is a bleak colonial building which seems inexplicably paltry given the fantastic collection of Ivoirian art it contains. The present facilities have long been recognised as inadequate for the collection of several thousand pieces – many of which are kept in storage due to lack of exhibition space – and there's been talk for years of eventually moving the museum to a new site. Meanwhile, don't be put off by the bad lighting and crowded exhibits.

Many of the works in the museum are **wood carvings**, including religious statuary, Senoufo sculpted doors, and the symbolic sceptres of the Agni chiefs. An impressive collection of **masks** spreads over the walls, representing the ritualistic art of nearly every ethnic group in the country. Though fascinating as works in themselves, they're unfortunately not accompanied by explanations of their ceremonial significance.

Musical instruments from throughout the country make up a sizeable portion of the collection. You'll find sacred objects used in various ancestral cults and **pottery**, too, including vases and water containers as well as Agni figurines.

Also on display are beautiful **bronze weights** used for measuring gold and other bronze objects made by the Akan-speaking peoples (especially the Baoulé) using the *cire perdue* or lost wax method (see the box on p.775).

The markets

The **fruit and flower market** on the Boulevard de la République provides a burst of traditional colour in the heart of the Plateau high-rises. It's a good place to come not only for food shopping, but also to take a break in one of the bars or restaurants housed in the market building – a relaxing vantage point from which to watch the lively commerce. Nearby, the **Marché Artisinal** (also called *marché sénégalais*) targets tourists and is expensive. This doesn't mean you can't find well-made sculptures, bronze objects or cloth, but you'll have to brave the aggressive salesmen. Of course, if you're going to travel on, you'll get better buys on Ivoirian crafts in towns such as Man, Bouaké or Korhogo.

Much bigger is the **Treichville Market** which displays myriad goods from throughout the western continent on its two milling floors: handwoven and dyed cloth; traditional sandals and leather bags; basketwork and pottery. Locally made goods still rival electronic equipment from Japan and European imports.

Even larger, the **Adjamé Market** spreads over several blocks near the railway station. Cocody too has a good **food market** located near the intersection of the bd de France and the bd Latrille.

The Cathedral

Mass: daily 7pm, and Fri 12.15pm, Sun 8am, 9.30am, 11.15am. Buses #10 and #12 from Gare du Sud.

It's an impressive and moving church, yet never far from tasteless, too. The $15m bill is hard to forget. When the **Cathédrale Saint-Paul** was inaugurated on August 10 1985 by Pope Jean Paul II, nearly 100,000 Ivoirians turned up for the christening. At the time, it was one of the largest cathedrals in the world (though now there's also the Basilica in Yamoussoukro . . .). You really need to be standing over on the waterfront in Cocody to grasp the significance of its extraordinary design: it's a human figure, presumably representing St Paul himself, arms outstretched to the north, his robe trailing lavishly behind to accommodate 3500 seated worshippers and another 1500 standing.

You enter under the back of the robe and it would be hard not to be impressed; the ceiling cleaves away and upwards with stunning grace. If its construction endures, the Italian architect Aldo Spirito's cathedral will one day rate as classic twentieth-century church architecture. The lines pull you into the heart of the building, soaring fifty metres or more above the altar. Breathtaking **stained glass tableaux** depict Paul's conversion on the road to Damascus, black slaves in his retinue; and, on the right, the arrival of the paddle steamer "Dahomey" with its contingent of French fathers come to spread the gospels in Africa. This picture is glorious, even if it does show unrealisti-

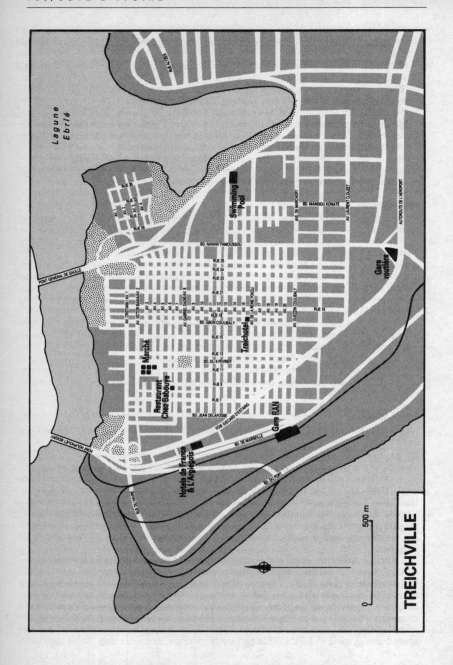

Lagune Ebrié

RUE 14 (RO)

RUE 29

RUE 27
AV. 8
RUE 13
AV. 6
AV. 4

RUE 25

PONT GENERAL DE GAULLE

BD. NANAN YAMOUSSOU

RUE 26

RUE 24

RUE 23

RUE 21

Swimming Pool

AV. DE MARCHARY

BD. MAMDOU KONATÉ

AV. LAURENT CLOUZET

AUTOROUTE DE L'AÉROPORT

Gare routière

AV. CRISTIANI (AV.) 1
AV. VICTOR BIABAANT 2
AV. 3
AV. 4
AV. 5
AV. 6
AV. 7
AV. GABRIEL DADIE AV. 8
AV. 9
AV. 10
AV. 11
AV. 12
AV. 13
AV. 14
AV. DE LA REINE POKOU
AV. 15
AV. 17
AV. 19
AV. 18
AV. 20
AV. DEZZIN COULIBALY

RUE 19

BD. GBON COULIBALY

Treichotel

RUE 15

Marché

RUE 13

BD. DU 6 FÉVRIER

RUE 11

Restaurant Chez Babouya

RUE 9

RUE 7

BD. JEAN DELAFOSSE

VOIE GISCARD D'ESTAING

Gare RAN

PONT HOUPHOUET-BOIGNY

BD. DE MARSEILLE

Hotels de France & L'Arpegois

RUE DU HAVRE

BD. DU PORT

500 m

0

TREICHVILLE

cally enthusiastic pagans rushing to the shore with welcoming smiles and baskets of fruit. Across the other side, a ship guided by Paul braves a storm, again, with Africans on board and Roman soldiers cutting loose the lifeboat. Other panels show the baptism of Jesus and sundry Afro-Biblical scenes.

Nightlife

Sightseeing done, there's a little nightlife to look forward to. Go out on the town with enough cash only, no jewellery and no watch. You can get around easily by **taxi** (you may even be lucky with an informed driver). Don't try to go clubbing on foot.

•**La Canne à Sucre**, av 7, rue 7, Treichville, not far from *Chez Babouya*. Abidjan's liveliest club; flashy, expensive (CFA5000 cover includes drink). Not up to much Mon–Wed but warms up nicely from midnight onwards, Thur–Sun, and sometimes has a real live *ochrestre*.

•**La Cabane Bambou**, av 15, rue 12, Treichville. Similar, but less conveniently located.

• If these don't excite, or you're not quite up to that kind of money, try the cluster of slightly cheaper **night haunts** on av 12, around rue 7–rue 11 (*Jannick Bar* seems to be the focus), and spilling onto bd Jean Delafosse. All are rowdy and heaving with hookers.

• Naturally enough, all the big hotels have sanitised **disco-clubs** of their own. If you're in the right frame of mind, and not skint, you could visit the *Ivoire*. Try also the *Golf-Hotel*, *Hilton* and, especially, *Le Wafou* (addresses under hotel listings above).

Directory

Airfreight *DHL* are efficient. Main office is on rue Pierre et Marie Curie, near bd Marseilles, in Zone 4C (☎35 90 39). Open Mon–Fri 8am–6.30pm, Sat 8am–noon.

Airlines See box overleaf.

Airport information ☎36 71 83.

American Express Main agents are *Socopao Voyages*, Immeuble Alpha 2000, av Chardy (01 BP 1297; ☎32 35 54/22 70 05).

Banks The Plateau is the main banking district where you'll find, all on av J Anoma:
  Banque Africaine de Développement (☎32 07 11);
  Banque Internationale de l'Afrique de l'Ouest (01 BP 1274; ☎32 07 22, telex 23641);
  Societé Général de Banques en Côte d'Ivoire (01 BP 1355; ☎32 03 33, telex 23437);
  Chase Manhattan Bank , Imm. B.A.D. av Joseph Anoma (☎33 10 41);
  Citibank, Imm. Amci, av Joseph Anoma (☎32 46 10).
  Elsewhere on the Plateau are:
  BICICI, av Franchet d'Espérey (01 BP 1298; ☎32 03 79, telex 23651);
  Barclays, Imm. Alpha 2000, bd de la République (☎32 28 04) gives some of the best rates for non-franc currencies.

Beaches Past the industrial zone in the south of the city, **Vridi Plage** is the closest beach to the city. Bus #18 runs here from the Plateau *Gare Sud*.

Books *Librairie de France*, Imm. Alpha 2000, av Chardy, is the city's biggest bookshop.

Car hire agencies
  Avis (☎32 04 57) at the *Novotel* and airport;
  Budget , rue Dr Blanchard (☎35 60 11) and airport (☎35 63 54);
  Europcar, rue Dr Colmette, agencies at *Ivoire*, *Tiama* and *Sebroko* hotels and airport;
  Hertz , bd Giscard d'Estaing (☎35 73 56) and airport (☎36 89 43).

Charter flights *Air Transivoire* (☎36 84 15, telex 22323) offers five-seater Cessnas, and up, from around CFA130,000 per hour.

Cinemas The two big ones on the Plateau are *Le Paris* with two screens in Imm. Le Paris on av Chardy (☎32 64 96) and the huge five-screen *Les Studios* on bd de la République *and* Rue Gourgas (☎32 38 97). There's usually something worth watching, though not always in *v.o.*

AIRLINE ADDRESSES

Air Afrique, 3 av Anoma, Plateau
(☎32 09 00/32 05 00).

Air Burkina Air Gabon, Imm. Nabil, av
Noguès (☎32 55 06/32 74 29).

Air Guinée, Imm. Général, bd Botreau
Roussel (☎32 66 47).

Air Ivoire, Imm. SIDAM, av Houdaille
(☎32 34 39).

Air Mali, Imm. M. du Mali, av Général de
Gaulle (☎22 62 96).

Air Zaire , Imm. BNDA, av Joseph
Anoma(☎32 54 49/33 22 31).

British Airways , Tour BICICI, rue Gourgas
(04 BP 827; ☎32 11 40, telex 23237).

Cameroon Airlines , Imm. Pyramide, av
Franchet d'Espérey (☎32 19 19).

Ethiopian Airlines, av Chardy (☎32 52 84).

Ghana Airways, Imm. Général, av Général
de Gaulle (☎32 27 83).

Iberia, av Delafosse, rue Alphonse Daudet
(☎33 19 91).

Nigeria Airways, 28/40, av Général de
Gaulle (☎22 39 36).

Sabena, Imm. Nour Al Hayat, av Chardy
(☎33 29 36).

Swissair, Imm. F. d'Espérey, av Franchet
d'Espérey (☎33 55 72, 32 51 27).

TAP Air Portugal , 25 bd Botreau Roussel,
Imm, Botreau Roussel (☎32 17 55).

UTA , Imm. BNDA, av Joseph Anoma
(☎33 22 31).

EMBASSIES

Algeria, 53 bd Clozel (01 BP 1015; ☎32 32
40, telex 23243).

Benin, rue des Jardins, Cocody (09 BP
238; ☎41 44 84, telex 23922).

Burkina Faso, 2 av Terrasson de
Fougères (01 BP 908; ☎32 13 13, telex
23453).

Cameroon, Imm. Général, bd Botreau
Roussel (01 BP 2886; ☎32 33 31).

Canada, Imm. Trade Center, av Noguès
(01 BP 4104; ☎32 20 09, telex 23593).

Central African Republic, rue des
Combattants (01 BP 3387; ☎32 36 46, telex
22102).

Denmark, Imm. Le Mans, bd Botreau
Roussel, av Noguès (01 BP 4569; ☎33 17
65, telex 23871).

France, rue Lecoeur/rue Jesse Owens,
(17 BP 175; ☎32 67 49, telex 23699). Togo,
CAR, Chad visa service.

Gabon, Imm. Les Hévéas, bd Carde (01
BP 3765; ☎33 23 12, telex 23561).

Germany , Imm. Le Mans, bd Botreau
Roussel (01 BP 1900; ☎32 47 27, telex
23642).

Ghana, Résidence de la Corniche, bd
Général de Gaul (01 BP 1871; ☎33 11 24).
Single entry visas issued overnight.

Guinea, Imm. C Duplessis, av Crosson
Duplesis (08 BP 2280; ☎32 86 00, telex
22865). Allow two days for visas.

Italy, 16 rue de la Canebière, Cocody (01
BP 1905; ☎31 11 70, telex 26123).

Liberia, Imm. La Symphonie, av Général
de Gaulle (BP 2514; ☎22 23 59, telex
23535).

Mali, Imm. Mason du Mali, rue du
Commerce (01 BP 2746; ☎32 31 47, telex
23429).

Mauritania, Rue Pierre et Marie Curie
(01 BP 2275; ☎35 20 68, telex 22371).

Netherlands, Imm. Les Harmonies, bd
Carde (☎22 77 12, telex 23694).

Niger, 23 av Angoulvant (01 BP 2743; ☎35
50 98, telex 43185).

Nigeria, 35 bd de la République (01 BP
1906; ☎22 30 82, telex 23532).

Norway, Imm. N'Zarama, bd Général de
Gaulle (01 BP 607; ☎22 25 34, telex
23355).

Senegal, Résidence Nabil, av Général de
Gaulle (08 BP 2165; ☎33 28 76, telex
23897).

Switzerland, Imm. Alpha 2000, rue
Gourgas (O1 BP 1914; ☎32 17 21, telex
23492).

United Kingdom, Imm. Les Harmonies,
av Docteur Jamot/bd Carde (01 BP 2581;
(☎22 68 50–3/32 82 09, telex 23706).
Consular dept. Mon–Fri 8am–12.30, issues
visas for The Gambia and Sierra Leone.

USA, 5 rue Jesse Owens (01 BP 1712; ☎32
09 79, telex 23660).

(original soundtrack, undubbed). Cocody's *Ivoire* (44 10 45) and Treichville's *Plaza* (☎22 20 21) are worth a try, too.

Crafts All over the place. But, ironically, the *Hôtel Ivoire* offers the best and most unusual selection at amazingly cheap prices (cheaper than the street) and you can check the stuff out without the usual hassles. There's also a charity outlet that merits some support. It's the *Fraternité des Artisans Handicapés, Vente d'Artisanat Local* on the corner of bd de la République and av Docteur Jamot – normally open Mon–Fri 9am–noon & 3–5pm, Sat 9am–noon only.

Cultural centres The *American Cultural Centrer*, with its AC reading library featuring US newspapers and magazines, is in Cocody on the bd de la Corniche. The expansive *Center Culturel Français* is on the Plateau, next to the Pyramid building. There's a strong flavour of Paris' *Beaubourg* about its high-tech interior design and sunken front courtyard. Relax amid shade and plants and simply sit. There's a library, conference centre and cinema, and the centre is a live performance venue with plenty going on.

Economists' corner For a revealing look at how Côte d'Ivoire manages its accounts, check out the *DCTGX* (*Direction Contrôle des Grands Travaux*) in the old *Hôtel de Relais* building off the Corniche in Cocody before the *Hôtel Ivoire* , where every payment from a truck repair to a bill for hotel construction is checked and multi-checked. Visits permitted.

Emergencies Police ☎170; Ambulance ☎35 36 88; Fire service ☎180.

Ferries From *Gare Lagunaire* to Abobo-Doumé (not much use unless you live over there) and Treichville, every ten minutes (don't walk across the Houphouët-Boigny bridge). The *Promenade* is more interesting. For CFA1500, you get 90min on the lagoons with a stop on l'Ile Boulay (departs Wed 3pm, Thurs 9am & 3pm, Sat, Sun and holidays 11am & 2pm). *Special trips*, including lunch go Sat, Sun and holidays 11am & 2pm (CFA8000).

Gay Abidjan Well, not really. But gay men and women could try *Chez Oscar*, a bar on the junction of rue Pierre et Marie Curie and the bd Giscard d'Estaing autoroute. *Hôtel Le Stop*, further down rue Pierre et Marie Curie on the left, is happy to welcome gay as well as straight guests. The public areas of the *Ivoire*, by virtue of its stylish pretensions, make it probably the city's biggest pick-up and cruising spot.

Hospitals and dental treatment University Hospital Cocody (*CHU Cocody*; ☎43 90 24); University Hospital Treichville (*CHU Treichville*; ☎36 91 22). Best place to be ill is the Polyclinique, av J. Blohorn (BP 1453; ☎44 51 32, telex 26195), near *Hôtel Ivoire*, which has a near legendary reputation among sick ex-pats in West Africa. Outpatients clinic ☎44 62 83/4/5.

Newspapers and magazines Several outlets for foreign journals and papers, including the large hotels. *West Africa* magazine is always available outside the *PTT*.

Post and telephones The *Poste Centrale* is above Place de la République at the southern end of the Plateau. A trip here won't likely be your most pleasant as the *fonctionaires* are generally obnoxious. The telephone cabins for local calls are often out of order (and you can't get change anywhere); the *poste restante* charges CFA300 per letter and those not collected within three weeks are either returned or destroyed.

Rail information ☎32 02 45.

Supermarkets One of the most convenient is *Score* across from the *Marché du Plateau* on bd de la République.

Swimming pools The big hotels all have pools, including the *Ivoire*, the *Hilton*, the *Novotel*, the *Palm Beach* and the *Wafou*. The *Golfs* is probably the most alluring. Most of them charge about CFA1000 for non-residents. In addition, there's a pool at the *Aquarium* on the bd Général de Gaulle (☎32 19 95) and the *Piscine municipale de Treichville*.

Tourist information Generally, you're best off getting information on excursions and places to visit at one of the travel agencies listed below. They are much better prepared to field questions and make travel arangements than either the *Office National du Tourisme*, Imm. Pyramide 7th floor (☎32 00 88) or the *Ministère du Tourisme*, located in the *Cité Administrative*, Tower E (☎29 20 00).

Travel agents include:

> *CATH Voyages* , Imm. Alpha 2000, av Chardy (01 BP 2636; ☎32 70 73, telex 23780) is big and one of the best, good for Comoé air safaris if you're splashing out;
> *SOCAPAO Voyages* , Imm. Alpha 2000, av Chardy (01 BP 1297; ☎22 83 84) are helpful;
> *Afric-Voyages*, Imm. Le Paris, av Chardy (☎33 29 51);
> *SOAEM Voyages*, rue de Senateur Lagarosse, opposite *UTA* (01 BP 1727; ☎32 75 03);
> *Covitour*, Imm. Le Paris, av Chardy (☎33 29 51) are agents for *Nouvelles Frontières;*
> SITRAM (*Société Ivoirienne de Transports Maritimes*) offers berths on freighters to Europe and other parts of West Africa.

Weather forecast Believe it! ☎36 71 71.

Outside the city

You don't need to spend much time in Abidjan to feel like getting **out of the city** – a little goes a long way. The **zoo** isn't exactly a big escape, but **Banco National Park** can be a good breather, if sometimes rather crowded. Getting further out of town, **Bingerville**, on the shore of the Ebrié lagoon, 17km east of Adjamé, does make a pleasant break. A former colonial town now settled into comfortable obscurity, it's an interesting place for a slow-paced day trip and, whether you have your own transport or not, can lead to an easy weekend round trip if you include Grand Bassam on the way back.

The Zoo

Just north of town on the Williamsville Road is Abidjan's **Parc Zoologique** (daily 8am–noon & 2.30–6.30pm; small entrance fee). Though now quite extensive, the town zoo was started many years ago by a French animal lover who raised chimpanzees in his backyard and crocodiles in his bathtub. Gradually his collection of beasts grew and was taken over by the state's National Park Service. Today you'll find hippos, crocodiles and tortoises, as well as lions, buffaloes, elephants, monkeys and various birds. This is one of Africa's better zoos and some attempt has been made to create a natural environment for the luckier animals. Others sit in bare cages.

Banco National Park

Just three kilometres from the noise and traffic of the city, the **BANCO NATIONAL PARK** comprises thirty square kilometres of dense forest which have been set aside as a natural reserve. Though it's said that a wide variety of animals still lives in the park, they stay well hidden in the woodlands and you're likely to see no more than perhaps a monkey or two skirting along the main paved road leading to the lake in the middle.

Despite the apparent absence (or invisibility) of fauna, Banco's **towering trees**, over-sized **ferns** and **hanging vines** make for a satisfying day trip – a reminder of the thick rainforests that once spread along the entire coast. The best way to visit is by car; to get there, take the road towards Dabou from Adjamé. Or you can catch a #3 bus to Cité Fairmont and walk the last few hundred metres to the entrance. Ideally, take a mountainbike. The main road criss-crosses the river as it leads to the lake in the heart of the park. From here various **foot trails** lead through the forest, passing through small villages which survive in the park interior.

Early morning at the park entrance there are unlimited opportunities for photographing one of Abidjan's classic scenes, the *fanicos*, or **Banco washer men**. The small Banco River runs by the park entrance, and along it hundreds of immigrant workers squeak out a living thrashing clothes against their rocks jammed in truck tyres in the stream. There's a lot of competition for this work.

By road

The main *gare routière* is in **Adjamé** at the junction of the roads to Dabou, Abobo and Bingerville. **Taxis** here service the entire interior of the country – Abengourou, Bouaké, Yamoussoukro, San Pedro, Korhogo – and through to Mali and Burkina Faso. **Buses** head to the same destinations. Those heading to towns along the railway lines are only slightly more expensive than the trains and much quicker.

The *gare routière* in **Treichville** handles eastbound traffic to Grand Bassam, Assinié, Aboisso and coastal towns in Ghana.

By train

The *RAN* railway company (☎32 02 45) runs two trains a day from Abidjan to Ouagadougou. They call at Dimbokro, Bouaké, Ferkessedougou, Ouangolodougou, Niangoloko, Banfora, Bobo Dioulasso and Koudougou. The *Gazelle* is usually preferred, as it leaves Treichville at 8am and arrives the next morning in Ouaga at 7.10am – slightly less than a 24-hour trip. The slower *Express* leaves at 4.45pm, arriving the following evening at 7.15pm. Prices for the *Gazelle* are Ouaga-Abidjan CFA19,800 1st class, CFA13,800 2nd class. The *Express* is some CFA4000 cheaper. First-class ticket holders can pay a supplementary CFA4500 for a couchette.

Additional *Omnibus* trains run from Abidjan to Bouaké and Dimbokro. Remember that at certain times of the year (before school starts) an International Student ID card may get you up to a 50 percent discount on second-class fares.

By plane

Air Ivoire (address in listings) connects Abidjan to major cities in the interior, including Bouaké (daily flights), San Pedro, Abengourou, Bondoukou, Yamoussoukro, Man, Touba, Odienné, Boundiali and Korhogo.

Bingerville

Set in the hills that rise between the Ebrié and Aguien lagoons, **BINGERVILLE** is today a quiet town in a rich agricultural region (bananas, pineapple, oil palms). This was an early capital of the French colony, but you'll find surprisingly few vestiges of that era. Today, the town has been utterly eclipsed by Abidjan (a mere 20-minute drive away) and, with its *lycée*, military academy, psychiatric hospital and catholic seminary, almost has the feeling of a distant suburb. It's an appealing, intriguing place, lapsed and restful.

Frequent shared **taxis** to Bingerville leave from the Adjamé motor park. To continue by transport to Grand Bassam you need a ride, 15km further, to the **Eloka ferry** where you cross the Ebrié lagoon, with another 10km to Grand Bassam on the other side.

Background and sites

Bingerville – which retains the name of Côte d'Ivoire's first colonial governor, Louis-Gustave Binger – was known as Adjamé-Santey when it was an **Ebrié settlement** in the early part of the nineteenth century. Around 1850, the villagers first came into contact with Europeans, and by the end of the century they had signed a treaty with the French which paved the way for the creation of a colonial post. The first government buildings went up in 1901, after disease drove the French out of Grand Bassam.

Bingerville thus became the colony's second political capital, but due to its hilly inland setting it never attained the economic importance of Grand Bassam. In 1931, a new wharf was built at Port Bouët and, from then on, Abidjan grew to become Côte d'Ivoire's major town. The capital was transferred in 1934.

Vestiges of the past

Reminders of the colonial period are fewer than you might expect. One of the most striking is the beautifully restored **Governor's Palace**, which now serves as an orphanage. Near the palace is the *jardin d'essaie* – a vast **botanical garden** where the French carried out agricultural experiments. Entering through a walk with giant bamboos forming a natural archway, you discover a wide variety of regional plants, trees and spices in the gardens, though the original layout today is rather overgrown and unkempt.

At the bottom of the steep grade that shelves to the lagoon (following the Eloka Road) is the small **Musée Charles-Combes**. Combes was a French merchant who founded the *Ecole d'Art Moderne Africain* in Bingerville, where he taught until his death in 1968. The giant **sculptures** he left behind consist mainly of idealised busts of Ivoirian women from various ethnic groups. They're a bit much really and, not very African, they suggest rather more about the artist than his subjects. There's no charge to visit the museum, but donations are appreciated. In the grounds, students chisel out copies of Combes' works as well as more original creations.

Places to stay, food and other practicalities

Bingerville doesn't offer much in the way of **accommodation**. The main place to stay is the *Bakona Hôtel*, a short distance from the *gare routière* as you walk towards the botanical gardens. Simply furnished rooms here start from CFA4000. The hotel also has a restaurant that serves French and African food. Some of the bars in town also rent cheap and rudimentary rooms. One such place is the *Obounon Bar*, with two dingy *chambres* at CFA2000 a night. Find it by heading down to the museum, turning left at the junction just before the housing blocks and continuing about 200m.

For **cheap eats**, women prepare *foutou*, rice and other local dishes in small restaurants grouped around the *gare routière*. You'll also find stalls for *bangi* (palm wine), tapped freshly in the district.

THE WEST COAST

The longest and most unexploited stretches of coast reach **westward from Abidjan**, and curve south to the remote Liberian border at Cape Palmas. Along the way, the string of **lagoons and sand bars**, scattered with the vestiges of old trading stations, gives out to a solid, forest-backed strand. Here, **Sassandra** is the first of the accessible

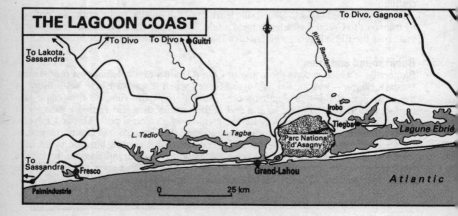

towns; **San Pedro** and **Tabou** lie beyond, alluring in their names alone, but offering some of West Africa's very best beaches if you're prepared to make the effort.

Inland, in the far west, lies the country's remotest region and one of West Africa's most secure zones of primary **tropical forest**.

West of Abidjan: the lagoon coast

West of Abidjan, the coast is shattered into a string of **lagoons and canals** for nearly 200km. If you make the right connections, you can find outboards in Treichville to take you along here, to **Jacqueville**, **Tiegba**, **Grand Lahou** and **Fresco**. There's also meant to be a regular midnight *pinasse* to Grand Lahou (arrives 9am).

Dabou, the jumping-off point if you're heading out this way by road, isn't interesting. But as you survey the bucolic passing scene of oil palm plantations and banana groves, consider the local legend of red hairy dwarves. As recently as the 1940s, there were reports of "little men with long reddish fur", rarely seen in the daytime. One sighting – of a small, hairy figure between the roots of a silk-cotton – took place in 1947 at the O.R.S.T.M science research station at Adiopodoumé, just a few kilometres from Abidjan. More reports of sightings, and stories of captures, come from further west, especially in the high forest now within Tai National Park and northwards (more later). Well it's something to ponder as you lie on the beach; more exciteable scientists like to dwell on the possibility of ape-men surviving into the modern era.

Jacqueville

Something of a resort town after the style of Grand Bassam (see p.772), **JACQUEVILLE** is located out on the ocean front sandbar which encloses the Ebrié lagoon, some 50km west of Abidjan (plus a 5-km ferry ride from the mainland). You can get here by bush taxi from Adjamé via the DABOU road, or take a ferry across the Vridi canal to the south of Abidjan and then bush taxi along the ocean shore for 45km. Either way, when you get to Jacqueville (once Grand Jack – an English slaving port), there's little sense of history in the modern town. Old buildings have been left to collapse. The *SIETHO* chain's *Hôtel M'koa* (BP 4375 Abidjan; ☎22 74 74) is nice enough and not over-priced, set on the shore of a small pretty lagoon now sealed off behind the town on the sandbar. **Toukouzou**, 44km west along the beach, is the headquarters of one of the coast's most famous *Harrist* bible prophets – Papa Novo. Ask if anything by way of celebration is going on while you're in Jacqueville; a visit is said to be quite something.

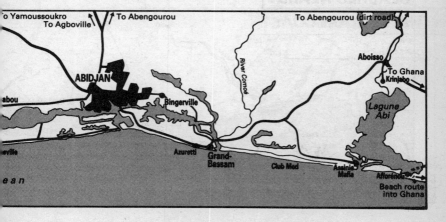

Tiegba

TIEGBA is a village on an island in the northwest corner of the Ebrié lagoon. It's a **stilt village** – or used to be, many people having moved to the mainland – which should be warning enough for anyone who has visited similar places like Fadiout in Senegal or Ganvié in Benin. You're likely to be so overcome by pestering children that any appreciation of the place is flattened in the effort to survive without losing your temper. Go in an organised group and you might as well forget the whole point of the visit. Try an individual approach and things seem a lot different. Tiegba is accessible by *mille-kilos* from DABOU (about 60km of rough track, probably impassable after rain). There are rooms on the mainland near where the *pirogues* take you over the hundred-metre channel.

Grand Lahou and Assagny National Park

Particularly confusingly, **GRAND LAHOU**'s old town is on the narrow strip of a sand bank *beyond* the main sand bar. A ferry goes from the new and developing modern town on the mainland proper. Grand Lahou is similar in every respect to Grand Bassam – both of them trading stations at the mouths of major rivers – but Grand Lahou's old sea-front buildings, in a variety of styles according to the nationality of the owners – Dutch, English, German and only later French – are almost completely abandoned.

There's a fairly expensive and long-established safari-style *campement* on the eastern tip of the old town sand bank, some kilometres from the centre. But there must be accommodation to be had in town, too, if you ask around. In season, the *campement* offers *pirogue* rides all over the place, especially to the **Parc National d'Assagny**, a few kilometres up the Bandama River. The park is renowned for buffaloes and elephants, ideally observed from tree-house viewing platforms. There's no network of tracks in the park so walking, accompanied by rangers, is allowed. Another entrance, more practical if you're not about to splash out on the excursion, is from the mainland side at IROBO, where you might get a lift with rangers *into* the park, if not around it.

Fresco

Another old trading "factory", old **FRESCO** is completely deserted, under the high **cliffs** (rich in fossils) across the lagoon from the new town. It's all pretty inaccessible without your own wheels, but you might find water transport from Grand Lahou, along the lagoons and canals, or even from Abidjan. Road transport from DIVO (130km) is

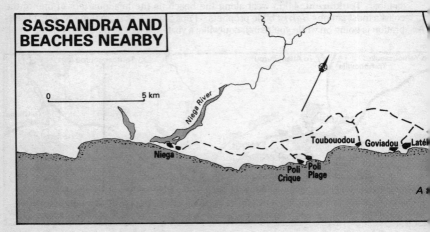

SASSANDRA AND BEACHES NEARBY

really no easier than finding a vehicle in Sassandra (100km), though the tracks through the forest on the latter route are really unpredictable – lots of fun with a trail bike.

Sassandra and around

SASSANDRA has *really* beautiful beaches nearby and they're the best reason, if not quite the only one, for coming here. Unusually, though, along the West African coast, there's also some topographical relief in the district as low cliffs extend most of the way to the Liberian border.

Getting to the town from Abidjan is no problem, but the trip, via DIVO, will take most of a day and, until the road is finished, you'll complete the 380-odd kilometres ready to drop. There are daily buses (*cars*) from Adjamé at 8am as well as 22-place *Renaults* and more expensive *504s*. There are also several **flights** a week – an option that makes some sense if time is limited and especially if you can claim a reduction as a youth (under 26) or student (under 31 plus an *ISIC* card), which reduces the fare by forty percent, making it just double the road transport cost. Expect to walk or hitch the 7km into Sassandra from the airstrip.

The town itself is built at the mouth of the Sassandra River, so what with rivermouth islands and lagoons there's lots of water about and pretty pictures in every direction. The **best beaches** are out west, the first – Batelébré I, II and III – about 2km from town, further ones – Yeseko, Grand Drewin, Lateko, Gade, Poli-plage and Niega – requiring transport and defined only by the roads and tracks that lead to them. You can make Sassandra a base and do some beach-hopping. Sleeping out is quite viable and for sustenance there are always coconuts . . .

Around town

The **Portuguese** named the site of *São Andrea* at the mouth of the same-named river and there was a permanent French settlement here after 1730. The town became really important, though, only in the years leading up to independence, when it was the main port used by Soudan Français (later Mali) and a timber port for the forests of the Ivoirian southwest.

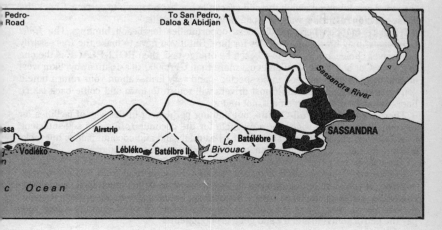

It's a small enough place to stroll happily for an hour or two, where you can't miss the tall yellow **waterfront monument** to the British victims of the *SS Oumana*, sunk by a German submarine on Christmas Day 1943; nor, after dark, the massive bordello called the *Bateau* ("because it has so many cabines"), where the Nigerian management boasts of "one hundred girls".

A visit to the hospital is recomended for the **view**, less for the *bloc opératoire*. It's located high above the river mouth. Go up the hill past the Ghanaian fish-smokers. It's worth coming up here really early in the morning to watch local Neyo (Kru-speaking) and migrant Fante fishermen pushing out to sea.

For **food**, apart from the good hotel restaurants, the market (largely run, again, by Ghanain Fante) is quite lively – you can get really cheap eats there. Also try the *Terminus Bar-Rest* for good African food ("chez Adama"). After dark, you'll find a whole row of typical Ivoirian *maquis* for *café complet*, omelettes and the rest.

Accommodation in town

The most popular and cheapest **hotel** is the *Hôtel de l'Ouest* (BP 349; ☎72 04 64), on the right before you reach the town centre coming from Abidjan or San Pedro. Rooms verging on the clean with shower and occasional water are CFA4000/double (with fan) and CFA6000 (with AC). The *patron* knows his way around town and, if you stay a while, will help you to appreciate Sassandra's attractions as much as he does. He has a citrus plantation on the other side of the Sassandra River a few kilometres upstream (with a camp where guests can stay). The *Ouest*'s menu is good value, too – at least it is if you're fond of lobster and homemade marmalade (served separately). Alternative lodgings are the *Hôtel Grau* (☎BP 168; ☎72 01 79), further down in the town direction on the left (similar prices), and the more expensive, unspecial, less popular *Hôtel Campement* on the seashore near the river's embouchure (S/C, AC rooms CFA8000/9000).

Beaches

The owner of the *Hôtel de l'Ouest* has an essentially private beach at the disposal of his guests, about forty minutes' walk from the hotel, west along the coast. Here, there's what he calls *Le Bivouac* – a Robinson Crusoe affair of basic huts and shelters where you can stay for CFA1000/night per person (you'll need to be suitably equipped). The beach is pretty and the sea safe, so it's an ideal spot. There's even a mangrove-shrouded creek behind which the odd crocodile has been known to surface. Check the latest situation regarding water supplies and staff at the site.

If you're mobile, there are limitless opportunities for beach hunting. The *Hôtel Campement* may have some vehicles for hire. But if you have to make the (necessarily expensive) choice and go out to a beach by orange taxi, then **POLI-PLAGE** is the one to go for. Out and back shouldn't cost more than CFA5000 (it's 16km away, 9km west of the airstrip), but you need to be specific – and very firm – about your return time if you've any transport to catch (most drivers will return to town and come back later). Fares are arrived at by agreement, not meter.

There's a village at **Poli-Crique**, but nothing permanent in the way of facilities for visitors, so take some water (or a machete for the coconuts). If you're self-sufficient, then Poli-Plage is heaven to camp out at – beautiful sand and coconut palms; hot rocks and a clear blue sea; tropical vegetation, dugout canoe-makers, total peace.

You can fix up a trip anywhere along the coast with the taxi drivers in Sassandra. NIEGA, some 3–4km beyond Poli, is as far as the rough road from Sassandra goes, however. If you start getting into private *déplacements* to points much further down the coast (the stunning, sheltered cove at **Monogaga**, for example, which is 65km away via the San Pedro road), you're talking about a lot of money. Instead, arrange a *daily rate*, pay the petrol yourself, and try and get a group together.

San Pedro and beyond

Until a few years ago, **SAN PEDRO** was earmarked for serious development as a timber exporting port. Thousands of immigrant farmers moved here and now crowd a vast shanty area called *Bardo* on the north side of the town. These days, San Pedro is just about ticking over, and much of the energy devoted to its expansion remains fixed on the ground among the unfinished building sites and semi-deserted timber yards. If you come in by public transport, you'll arrive at the *gare routière* in the northern Séwéké quarter, 4–5km from the town centre.

It's a pretty dull place in the centre, though it livens up considerably in the evenings. Make for the *quartier triangle* district. There's no shortage of **hotels**, but they're all rather more expensive than you're used to, even for Côte d'Ivoire. Best deal seems to be out of town to the west at the *Campement Ponty*, 7km in the direction of the lagoon; ask for the village of DIBOUÉ. They've got a really nice terrace here, a good cheapish restaurant and fine beaches nearby.

The **lagoon** was once planned to be surrounded by the future city of San Pedro – not an attractive image – but with the effective town centre some 6km away, that doesn't look likely. Plans are still alive, however, to develop "touristically" the area around Pointe Taki on the inaccessible west side of the lagoon.

There are daily **flights** between Abidjan and San Pedro. Unscheduled drop-offs in Sassandra are often possible.

Tabou, Grand Bérébi – and Tai National Park

Now joined to San Pedro – and thus to Abidjan – by tarmac, **TABOU** is reachable in a day from the capital (or there are 2 or 3 flights a week). There's a **hôtel campement** on the beach (around CFA4–5000 for plain S/C rooms) but problems with the water supply. Beaches round about are good, of course, but rough and dangerous for swimming. For that, visit **GRAND BÉRÉBI** midway between Tabou and San Pedro – a brilliant east-facing beach with an expensive, ex-patish hotel and restaurant. Getting down here the 10km from the main road shouldn't be too difficult now the highway is completed.

Into the interior – Tai National Park

There are virtually no facilities for visits to the **Parc National de Tai**. It's a conservation area, at present, rather than a wildlife park. But if you want to try and get into the forest, the most promising approach is from the west and the small town of **Tai** itself, 202 rough kilometres north of Tabou, following the Cavally River frontier with Liberia through thick forest most of the way. The road is hardly used, and if you're relying on

---

AN IVOIRIAN MYSTERY

The huge area of almost uninhabited forest south of the road from Guiglo to Toulépleu (northwest of Tai National Park) is the most frequently mentioned haunt of mysterious, half legendary, ape-men creatures inhabiting the twilight zone between animals unknown to science and mythical human ancestors. The Ngere (or Guere) people of the district used to call them *Séhité* and told how they had a system of barter with them, in which they left cultivated food and manufactured goods in the forest and received forest fruits in exchange. They claimed hardly to know who the *Séhité* were themselves. Anthropologists have suggested the stories may be part of a folkore about the pygmy people who are presumed to have lived throughout West Africa several thousand years ago. And the cultural memory may have been mixed with the existence until quite recently (possibly still) of a large, sometime bipedal primate with a superficially human appearance. This may have become extinct without ever being given a formal zoological identification.

mille kilos you'll need a lot of luck: best to plan on a week or more for the trip and expect to hop from village to village with whatever vehicles are moving. There's a track into the park (and possibly rudimentary accommodation) from PAULEOULA, a village 10km before Tai. Write and let us know how you get on. People who've been into the Tai forest rate it highly: human pressures on it are relatively light and it contains all the essentials to be West Africa's most important rainforest reserve.

THE EAST COAST

East of Abidjan, the coastal highway runs through fine coconut groves broken by the occasional fishing village. Curio and crafts stalls dot this touristy stretch of road and become particularly dense just before **Grand Bassam** – a picturesque weekend retreat popular with Abidjanis. Further east, towards the Ghanaian border, **Assinie** lies in another resort area renowned for its **beaches** and exclusive holiday clubs. **Crossing into Ghana** is a straightforward procedure if you use the straightforward route: more adventurous routards can experiment with shoreline hikes and obscure lagoons.

Grand Bassam

If you're based in Abidjan, **GRAND BASSAM** makes an excellent excuse to get out of the city – it's a good day trip. And if you're leaving Abidjan for Ghana, or you've just arrived from there, it's a gentle place to spend the night. Some travellers, too, find Abidjan's pace so frenetic that they stay in Grand Bassam, and go into the city as they need or want to.

Founded in the early nineteenth century by the Nzima people, the original village derived its name from the word *bassam*, meaning "coastal settlement". Easily the most attractive town on the Ivoirian coastline, Grand Bassam is one of the oldest settlements of the European era and the **first capital** of the colony of Côte d'Ivoire from 1893 to 1900. Yellow fever decimated the town in 1898–99; the French evacuated, almost overnight, and the capital was transferred to Bingerville, considered healthier. For three more decades, Grand Bassam survived and developed as an active commercial centre and the country's number one port. But the cutting of the Vridi canal opened Port Bouët and Abidjan in 1950, and the old centre of Grand Bassam has been in decline ever since. Many of the town's graceful administrative buildings remain, however, and the hotels and seafood restaurants bask in the derelict elegance of their surroundings.

In contrast, the mainland part of the town seems to get livelier every year.

The Route de Bassam and arrival

From Abidjan, there's a good paved road to Grand Bassam. Taxis and *mille kilos* leave frequently from the **Treichville motor park** and take little more than half an hour to arrive. Or take a #17 bus as far as it goes, then hitch the final 20km. The route also makes a great half-day **cycle ride** – with the exception of Togo, the only strip of main highway actually *on the shore* along the entire West African coast.

The *Route de Bassam*, which first skirts the airport, is a seemingly endless coconut *bidonville* jammed with **artisans' stalls**, "motels", bars and hotels (some offering "room service"). Stalls sell a wonderful variety of useful and useless craftiness, especially "home decor" in the form of toys, ships, gaudy model motorbikes, and basket-work – everything from table mats to double beds. Further on, the roadside shacks fade at the end of the misnamed *autoroute* and the coconut trees begin to rustle in earnest. Between them are the *concessions* of numerous *guérissseurs traditionnels* (heal-

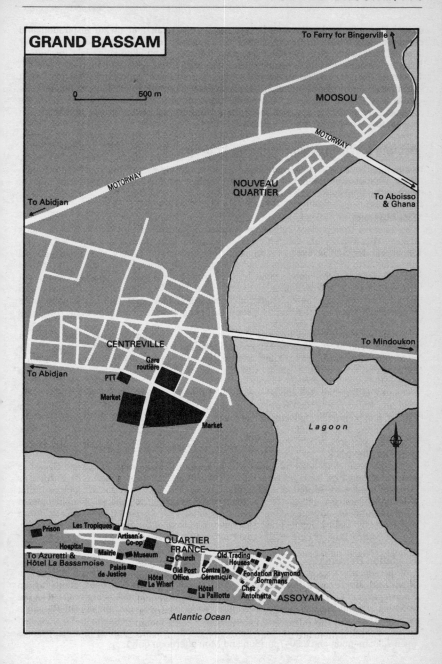

GRAND BASSAM

0   500 m

To Ferry for Bingerville

MOOSOU

MOTORWAY

MOTORWAY

To Abidjan

NOUVEAU
QUARTIER

To Aboisso
& Ghana

To Mindoukon

CENTREVILLE

Gare
routière

To Abidjan

PTT

Market

Market

Lagoon

Prison

Les Tropiques

Artisan's
Co-op

Hospital

Mairie

Museum

QUARTIER
FRANCE

Church

Old Trading
Houses

To Azuretti &
Hôtel La Bassamoise

Palais
de Justice

Old Post
Office

Centre De
Céramique

Fondation Raymond
Borremans

Hôtel
Le Wharf

Chez
Antoinette

Hôtel
La Paillotte

ASSOYAM

Atlantic Ocean

ers) offering guaranteed cures, long-distance witchcraft and divine inspiration and support: *"La Maison du Tout Puissant"* (the House of the All Mighty) seems a popular epithet. Look out, too, for the village specialising in building materials for huts – bamboo reinforcements, thatching grass, *papo* palm frond strips and the rest.

Grand Bassam you enter down a gauntlet of souvenir and craft shops (the most striking stuff on offer is imitation Ghanaian *kente* cloth). Arriving by taxi, you'll be let down at the *gare routière* in **Nouveau Bassam**, the modern district north of the lagoon. The market is down on the right. From here, follow the bridge that spans the lagoon to the **old town**, and the **France** district.

Around town: museum, ruins and co-ops

Swimming isn't really a recommended pastime on this part of the coast (people who think otherwise are swept out all the time) so the town itself is likely to occupy most of your active hours – if you have any.

The Museum

The obvious first port of call is the **museum**, housed in the restored Governor's Palace. This *Musée National du Costume* (Tues–Sun 9am–noon & 3–5.45pm, entry free, donations desired) is worth visiting not only for a good variety of Ivoirian national dress but also for some genuinely old and handmade bark and raffia cloth, for painted Senoufo *toiles* and for some serious hunters' outfits bedecked with *grigris*. Though not large it's a lively and well-presented collection. The Yacouba, Malinké, Senoufo and Baoulé costumes are mostly *pagnes* in variations of blue, grey and black, sometimes made locally from broad strips. The southeast peoples have gear made of narrow strips in a very wide variety of colours.

Around the main room housing the costumes, a corridor contains some excellent models of Ivoirian regional **architecture**, including a beautiful miniature of one of the mud and wood mosques at Kong and models of Dida houses from the area around Divo, which are almost identical to the famous *cases à impluvium* from Casamance in Senegal.

On the walls, there are some revealing old **photos** of Côte d'Ivoire in colonial times (did you know that 16,000 Ivoirians fought in World War I or that the forced labour system had men felling silk-cotton trees with axes?), including scenes of suave moustachioed young officers with their boots up, surrounded by crowds of bemused *indigènes*. There are pictures, too, of the Abidjan–Niger railway in construction; the **Abé revolt** prevented the track from reaching Bouaké until 1912.

The museum sells a useful leaflet which details the background of Grand Bassam's **old buildings**. Few have yet been taken over for renovation by Ivoirians or Europeans (though most were inhabited until the tidal wave of 1965) and it doesn't look as if that will happen soon enough to save the ones which are about to collapse. The dilapidated condition of older structures like the monumental *hôtel des postes*, the *palais de justice* and the early trading depots projects a haunting sense of the march of time, but some, like the *mairie* (and, of course, the governor's palace), have been beautifully restored.

Fondation Borremans

One person who clearly feels Grand Bassam deserves some serious re-colonisation is **Raymond Borremans**, nicknamed *"le vieux pecheur"*, who has been compiling an *Encyclopedia of Côte d'Ivoire* for decades and whose dream is now being realised as the volumes start to appear. He has set up a *Fondation Borremans* on one of Bassam's street corners in a much modified old house. It's really just a bookshop in the front part of his home, but he's quite a character if you get the chance to meet him; his place is open 7.30am–noon and 2.30–7pm (Sun and Mon afternoon only).

Other Bassam visits

Other reminders of the colonial period include the melancholic **Monument des Morts** (a weary white *France* holding her dead), the **old cemetery** (where many victims of the yellow fever epidemic were buried) and the **prison**. Following rioting on February 6, 1949, the French arbitrarily arrested leaders of the *Parti Démocratique de Côte d'Ivoire* and held them in this prison. In protest, the women of Abidjan marched here to demand the end of the incarceration and of political oppression.

Much better than you might expect is the **Coopérative des Artisans d'Art** on the lagoon side of the town (Mon–Fri 8am–5pm, Sat & Sun 8am–6pm). This huge warehouse has a vast selection of carvings, fabrics and other crafts to choose from. Prices are fixed and not outrageous. Around the hall and outside you can watch dozens of co-op members fashioning their merchandise.

Nearby, there's a **memorial pillar** to Marcel Treich-Laplène (1860–90), founder of the colony of Côte d'Ivoire and *Résident de France à Grand-Bassam 1889*. T-L was also first *explorateur* of Indenié in 1887 and of Abron and Bondoukou in 1888 – an active young fellow in his short time.

A much less worthwhile craft centre is the *Centre de Céramique* co-operative (8am–noon, 3–6pm, Sun opens 9am). They have an uninteresting selection of pots and plates. And unfortunately they've got the measure of the ceramics market with their globby little pottery fishes.

To get out of colonial (or neo-colonial) France and find Africa again, strike off east of this quarter, through the heart of the old commercial district with its rambling trading houses, and you'll enter **Assoyam**, a fairly traditional fishing quarter.

CIRE PERDUE

The *cire perdue* ("lost wax") process used in the co-operative at Grand Bassam for metal-casting is one of West Africa's oldest crafts techniques. Everything from the intricately ornate to the mundanely obscene starts as a model in wax. This is dipped repeatedly in washes of clay-water, each allowed to dry, and then finally wrapped with a thick coat of clay and fired, in which process the wax exits through a hole. Through this same hole, molten metal is poured and the clay "wrapping" is later chipped off to reveal the cast.

Accommodation

If the old town provides the backdrop for nostalgic weekend walks, **the beach** is still Bassam's main draw and most of the **hotels** face the seafront. The budget possibilities are not unlimited. Most of the places are clean and comfortable, often European-run and catering to European tastes, with obligatory HB in the high season.

A place in the **cheap range** to try first is *Chez Ton Ton Léon*, located near the bridge on the north side of the lagoon. Rooms are just four walls and a bed, but at only CFA3500 with fan, they seem cheap here. Over the bridge, on the right, check out *Les Tropiques*, where the dark, smelly, nominally S/C rooms may have improved (and would need to have done for CFA4000). *Chez Antoinette*, closer to the beach in the old commercial district, is the best choice, once you've found it. The price will depend on you and Antoinette but it's certainly the cheapest, quite possibly the nicest abode in town, though there are no fans or S/C rooms.

Of the **weekenders' hotels**, *La Paillote* (BP 196, Gd Bassam; ☎30 10 76), with very ordinary S/C, AC rooms starting at CFA9000, is one of the least expensive right by the sea. Nearby, *Le Wharf* (☎30 15 33) has chintzy double rooms for CFA10,000. Both have excellent seafood restaurants. The most luxurious lodgings are at *La Bassamoise* (☎30 10 16), a colonial-style set-up with a terrace restaurant overlooking the ocean. Spacious

S/C rooms with AC start at CFA22,000. Although they're on the sea, it's far too danger-ous for swimming – a pity. *La Paillote* has a saltwater pool in compensation. As at *La Basssamoise*, non-residents can pay for a day by the pool.

Moving on

When you're ready to leave, **public transport** is back over the bridge again. Two or three possibilities present themselves. If you're returning to Abidjan, you can make your way (9km north) to the ferry across the Ebrié lagoon for the Bingerville track (18km on the other side), and return that way, rather than using the coast highway (you should find transport every morning). Or, if you're heading for Ghana, there are taxis and other transport all the time to ABOISSO. Or if you've time and feel like doing some beach walking (or even cycling), you can cross the border through the lagoons at ASSINIE MAFIA.

But before leaving Bassam, take a look at an old Ivoirian quarter of the town – **Moosou** – once a village and further inland from the new town centre beyond the high-way bridge that crosses the lagoon. There are a few cheap places to eat here (you'll be hungry if you walk, it's 4km from the museum), a nice welcome and an elaborate, angel-topped mausoleum in the main street. If you're on foot, you don't have to walk all the way back: climb up onto the highway and wave down a vehicle.

On to Assinie

From Grand Bassam eastwards, it's all **pineapples** and **coconuts**, pockets of secon-dary forest, a few old trees still standing, plantations of wispy, temperate-looking **rubber trees**, punctilious police and rather more military gendarmes.

East of Grand Bassam, too, the coast gets more exclusive. At the town of Abrobakro, a secondary road leads down to the **Assinie canal**, which stretches along the coast to connect the Ebrié and Abi lagoons. On the other side of the canal, ASSINIE has gained fame for its **unspoiled beaches**. Many wealthy Abidjanis own private bungalows along the seafront for use as weekend getaways.

This coastal strip is also the domain of **packaged vacations** and features two **resorts** as luxurious as they're antiseptic. *Club Méditerranée* (☎Abidjan 30 07 17, telex 50101) has a "village" in a coconut grove here with 200 AC rooms and the usual combination of sports facilities and other diversions like a disco, boutiques and organised excursions. *Les Palétuviers* (BP 4375; Abidjan ☎30 08 48) is even more ambitious. This club (with a gay emphasis, though not exclusively) is a complex with 338 luxury AC rooms and facili-ties for water-skiing, riding, volleyball and most other things. Both places attempt to recreate a natural feel with thatched roofs and shady gardens, but know their clients are more interested in sun and sand than cultural contact. Open from October to April, these are mostly filled with tour groups flown in direct from Europe. Even if you wanted to, you could only stay by booking in advance via the above reservation numbers in Abidjan. A night in either will cost some CFA35,000 a head.

Into Ghana

Most travellers and nearly all vehicles go via ABOISSO (see p.803) to the **main inter-national frontier** at ELUBO. Alternatively, and quite legitimately, you can cut off south, east of Aboisso, for a 22-kilometre secondary road to FRAMBO, where you complete exit formalities and whence a ferry connects regularly with JEWI-WHARF in Ghana for about CFA600. From Jewi-Wharf, see p.849.

Alternatively again, but it seems with less legitimacy, you can take a small ferry-*pirogue* across **from Assinie-Mafia** to a sand bar which is connected by land only to Ghana (although it is part of Côte d'Ivoire). There's fairly frequent transport from Abrobakro to Assinie-Mafia, calling at Assinie-Terminal, where the *Club Med* crowd cross the lagoon to their paradise prison.

From the other side of the less exclusive lagoon crossing at Assinie-Mafia, it's about 16km to the Ivoirain post at AFFORÉNOU and 32km more to the first small town along the beach in Ghana – HALF ASSINI. Note that JEWI-WHARF in Ghana is located not, as the maps indicate, on the ocean, but on the lagoon. NEWTOWN, which looks on maps to be a Ghanaian border village at the far western end of the road, is no such thing: it's just a border control.

The slightly dodgy factor in all this is the ease with which **you can miss the Ivoirian border post** (not to mention the uncertainty of its being staffed), and thus get apprehended by Ghanaian soldiers or officials later without ever having officially exited from Côte d'Ivoire. If you show up near Jewi-Wharf or further east with no Ivoirian exit stamp, you'll be sent back on the ferry across the lagoon to the official exit point at Frambo in order to get a stamp and return again – it's no way to spend a day in West Africa.

If you decide to come along the beach: make sure you **exit properly from Côte d'Ivoire**; beware of the fact that the strip is used by smugglers; and be prepared to explain yourself once or twice. That said, it's a beautiful journey so long as there's no sea mist. A tractor and trailer runs a laborious shuttle service from the end of the sand bar (where the little ferry moors) to Newtown post, and the fantastically wrecked *Peugeots* scudding up and down the beach will give you a ride further on if you can stop one.

THE BAOULÉ COUNTRY

The **Baoulé** live in the centre of Côte d'Ivoire, where the northern savannahs meet the southern forests. Related by language and culture to the other Akan-speaking peoples of the east and Ghana, their prosperity formerly derived from trade in **gold**. Ancient mines can still be seen at **Orumbo Boka** (south of Toumodi) – the Baoulé's **sacred mountain**.

In the south of the Baoulé country, **Yamoussoukro** recently became the nation's administrative **capital**, a slice of architectural artifice that now just needs a couple of hundred thousand more inhabitants to lend it a real sense of city. Further north, the country's second largest town, **Bouaké**, is a bustling centre of trade and industry that attracts a diverse mix of people from throughout the country.

In addition to these **urban centres**, the Baoulé region also contains much unspoilt countryside. Though flat and unvaried landscapes are normally not cause for excitement, they lend themselves well to **game viewing**. The **Marahoué National Park** near the town of BOUAFLÉ could be a chance to take in wildlife ranging from elephant to antelope. But the president's new safari land, **Abokouamikro National Park**, within limo distance of Yam, is a more likely bet, if it's up and running – and if the animals (imported at huge cost from South Africa) are settled in.

Yamoussoukro

In the 1950s, few people had heard of the small village of **Ngokro** except for the 500 or so who lived there. One of those residents was Nana Yamoussou, whose son Felix became the president of Côte d'Ivoire. That fact permanently altered the hamlet's history, since Houphouët-Boigny has tirelessly used his influence to turn his birthplace into a present for his family and ancestors. In honour of his mother, he changed its name to **YAMOUSSOUKRO** and devised a plan to transform the town into a glittering metropolis. Many of the **monumental buildings** now dotting the cityscape are indeed impressive. Besides the imposing *Hôtel Président*, Yam boasts modern college **campuses**, government buildings like the *Maison du Parti*, the *Hôtel de Ville* and, completed in 1990, a colossal **basilica** – a virtual replica of Saint Peter's in Rome, only a fraction smaller than the grand original.

But in between these isolated pockets of pomp are vast stretches of nothingness – large open fields and vacant lots waiting for people to breathe some life into them. Like Abuja in Nigeria, this capital lacks a certain spark. The vast layout is confusing and impersonal and the grandiose dimensions of the futuristic buildings further diminish the human scale. The place is worth visiting as a phenomenon, but don't expect warmth or spontaneity.

Historic changes

As early as the 1960s, Houphouët-Boigny already planned to convert Yamoussoukro to the nation's capital. He moved ahead cautiously, however, slowly putting the necessary infrastructure in place so as not to incite criticism. One of the first moves was to build a system of roads capable of handling traffic for a vast metropolis. Wide **paved avenues** were traced through the emptiness of the countryside and **multi-laned highways** were laid out, linking the village to Abidjan, Bouaké and Man. By the mid-1970s, the incandescence of 10,500 streetlights flooded the quiet nights of the burgeoning town whose population had still only grown to around 30,000.

Prestige projects followed. The lavish *Hôtel Président*, a brash combination of reinforced concrete and marble, rose up in the south of town and was surrounded by what must be the continent's most-watered **golf course**. Dominating a nearby hill, the gilded *Maison du Parti* became a showy symbol representing the power and grandeur of the nation's only political party. Houphouët-Boigny then set out to create in Yamoussoukro the nation's **educational centre**. No expense was spared on the town's two outstanding *écoles superieures* – the INSET and INSTP – both blessed with beautiful **campuses** of inspired architecture and state-of-the-art facilities (permission to visit obtainable at the *Hôtel de Ville*). A Moroccan-style mosque established a sense of religious legitimacy as did the neo-classical Saint Augustine church – built in honour of one of the president's brothers. The crowning glory, however, is the granite and marble *Basilique de Notre Dame de la Paix*, planned to be the largest cathedral in the world and entirely financed out of the president's own pocket – a claim far from politic, even were it true, in a country as poor at the grass roots as this.

By 1983, Yamoussoukro had sufficient trappings to back up its international pretensions. The president's private dream became a public reality when the National Assembly voted to transfer the political capital here from Abidjan and it became Côte d'Ivoire's fourth capital.

The power and the glory

While spending on his hometown, the president didn't neglect his own fancies. The large **presidential palace** imposes itself on the city centre, but is enclosed by a high fence and off-limits to visitors – unless you happen to be one of the heads of states *le Vieux* commonly receives here. Bordering the palace are the man-made **sacred crocodile ponds** filled with snappers given as a gift by the former president of Niger. You can watch the reptiles being fed by Bozo caretakers, brought in from Mali specially for the job. Behind the palace is the president's private **plantation**, which spreads out over 2000 hectares, making it one of the largest in West Africa. Experimental methods of farming national crops like rubber, coffee, cocoa, pineapples, avocadoes and yams are carried out here.

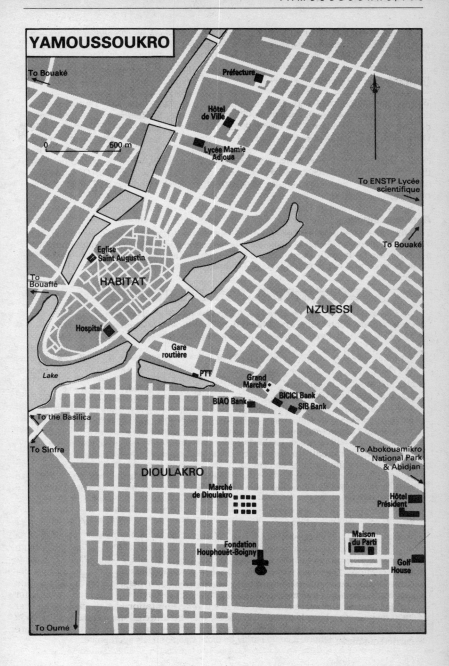

The latest enhancement to personal glory is the *Fondation Houphouët-Boigny* – a vast historical and cultural complex soon to be opened in the south of town not far from the *Maison du Parti*.

Orientation and practicalities

With a population now estimated at a more respectable 100,000, Yamoussoukro comprises four main neighbourhoods. The first of these, **la Résidence**, is the private domain of the president. The administrative centre is known as **l'Habitat**, while **Dioulakro** is a residential district located behind the mosque. The town's **main market** is held in the **N'Zuessi** neighbourhood, which is where you'll find the commercial centre. The principal trading day is Wednesday, when people come from the surrounding countryside. Major **banks** like the *BICICI* and the *BIAO* are on the main street near the market. On the same street, you'll also find the **PTT** and the *gare routière*.

Accommodation

You might expect a wider variety of **hotels** for a town of such pretensions, but Yamoussoukro doesn't boast a great choice. Some recent additions have recently sprung up, notably in the inexpensive range, but the focus seems to be on the flashy *Hôtel Président* – another reason why you probably won't feel compelled to stay long if operating on a budget.

THE BASILICA: H-B'S "DEAL WITH GOD"

When they built St. Peter's, were there no hungry people in Rome? When England after the Great Fire built itself St. Paul's, were there no poor or homeless in London?
Ivoirian craftsman, quoted in the Sunday Times, December 2, 1989

On a clear day, **the Basilica** stands out from miles away on every approach road to Yamoussoukro. It was built between September 1986 and January 1990, in conditons of immense secrecy, by a labour force of **1500 men**, working continuously in two shifts a day between 7am and 2am, and paid CFA5000 a month, greatly above average wages. It has cost an estimated **£100 million**. Among other barely comprehensible statistics, the Basilica required the equivalent of an entire year's supply of French white cement; each of its **7000 seats** has individual air-conditioning; it can hold another 12,000 people standing; and on its "piazza" and surrounding areas of Italian marble, there's space, in theory, for 300,000 more – a crowd that's unlikely ever to be tested as it surely exceeds the country's Catholic population. There are thirty-six **stained glass windows**, in 4000 shades, each 30 metres high, covering an acreage of glass greater than that at Chartres cathedral. And, although the dome is a little lower than St. Peter's in Rome – which the whole enterprise has so slavishly imitated – it is surmounted by an immense cross of gold soaring to **168 metres** above the savannah, which makes it 23 metres taller than St. Peter's.

In September 1990, **Pope John-Paul** finally consecrated the Basilica – though with evident unease, and only after receiving assurances that a new hospital would be built too. Far from being a resounding success, the Pope's visit triggered a wave of protest and has only served to increase Côte d'Ivoire's domestic political crisis and foment rumours of financial scandal. Houphouët claims the Basilica was inspired and made possible because "I did a deal with God, and you wouldn't expect me to discuss God's business in public, would you?" Unfortunately for him, growing numbers of Ivoirians do expect that, and are looking ahead to an era beyond the almost medieval trappings with which the republic's first president has dressed his office.

In 3000 years Egypt's pyramids may still be standing. Strange to think the Basilica of Yamoussoukro, already looking faded in places, may be lucky to last a tenth, even a hundredth, as long. As a symbolic target – one day – for those whose lives the town, and its founder, currently ignore, it could hardly be more vaingloriously appropriate.

INEXPENSIVE

They may be grubby and unenticing, but in a town where accommodation tends to be expensive, hole-in-the-wall hotels or **chambres de passage** could be a welcome relief if money's tight. They start around CFA4500, but you can sometimes bargain down the price, especially if staying a couple of days.

Near the *gare routière* :

Hôtel de la Paix. Affordable squalor with rooms from CFA1500.

Hôtel Akouaba (☎64 07 61), north of the motor park, is more respectable and slightly more expensive.

Hôtel Belier, over in the Dioulakro district near the mosque, is much cleaner and more comfortable though rooms are correspondingly pricier.

Hôtel Confidences, in the same neighbourhood, near the cinema, is cheaper and run-down, but not too dirty.

Le Cameo, across from the mosque, is also worth trying.

MODERATE

Relais Shell (☎64 00 24). The cheapest of the petrol station hotels surrounding the Abidjan motor park and the one with the least frills. S/C AC rooms start at CFA6500.

Mobil Oil (☎64 00 61). Very similar to the *Shell* in price and comfort. Bar and restaurant.

Hôtel AGIP (BP 9; ☎64 00 39). Considered the nicest of this bunch, the *AGIP* is also the most expensive. They have clean S/C rooms with AC (from CFA7500), a good bar and restaurant specialising in French food.

Le Paysan (☎64 00 31). An unassuming hotel near the mosque with simple S/C rooms from CFA7500. Some suites also available. Extra charge for TV.

Hôtel Résidence, Quartier Résidentiel (BP 84; ☎64 02 48). A cut above the others, the *Résidence* has spacious AC rooms with TV, plus its own bar, restaurant and nightclub. A single here costs CFA10,000.

OWN LEAGUE

Hôtel Président (BP 1024; ☎64 01 81, telex 72104). Part of the *Sofitel* chain, this is one of Côte d'Ivoire's poshest hotels – 284 rooms (including 18 suites), all with colour TV and telephone. You can get a sauna (and another one in the town if you try to go sightseeing), play squash and tennis, and cool off in one of the two pools. The 18-hole golf course adjoining the hotel is rated one of the best in West Africa. There are 3 restaurants and four bars, including one on the top floor with striking **panoramic views** of the city. All this, plus the disco, cinema and shops, just for you and the management (or so it may seem). Rooms start at CFA30,000.

Food

Like Abidjan, Yam has numerous **maquis** where you can get tasty Ivoirian food without spending a lot of money. A good one is *Les Cocotiers*, located in the *Habitat* district overlooking the lake. They serve large portions of *poisson à la braise* and other local specialities and offer a selection of European dishes. Another well-known one is the *Wayofe*, also located in *Habitat*, near the market. There are many more *maquis* in the area around the motor park.

Almost all the hotels above have their own **restaurants**. Other places to try in town include *The Yellow House* (American) and *Tout Va Bien*, an outdoor French restaurant.

Nightlife

The emphasis is on chic as you'd expect, and Yamoussoukro's nightlife is expensive. Such is the case at the *Hôtel Président's* disco – the *Kokou* – where moneyed hopefuls pay a CFA2000 cover only to find that few other people had the same idea. At weekends there's usually more of a crowd. A more popular venue, *Klimbli*, is equally flashy . Another-well known place is the *Paillote*, especially popular with expats.

ONWARDS FROM YAMMOUSSOUKRO

Frequent transport from the **gare routière** heads to Abidjan (266km), **Kossou** (43km) and **Man** (233km) – all accessible on paved roads. Taxis and *cars* also head regularly to Bouaké and Korhogo in the north.

Yamoussoukro's **airport** was designed to be large enough to receive any visiting heads of state who might need to fly in urgently by Concorde. More mundane traffic goes via *Air Ivoire* which has daily flights to Abidjan and Bouaké and four flights a week to **Korhogo** and **Odienné**.

The Marahoué National Park and Kossou Dam

Set aside in 1968 to preserve wildlife in the relatively populated area of the Baoulé country, the **MARAHOUÉ NATIONAL PARK** spreads across 1000 square kilometres. In environmental terms, that's really not much (a fraction of the size of the Comoé Park further north) and the variety of animals you can see here isn't overwhelming. Bordered by the namesake **Marahoué River**, the park does, nonetheless, still harbour various **antelope** species and different kinds of **monkeys**. The main *piste* leading off towards **Mont Saninlego** leads through a valley where you can sometimes spot **elephant** or **buffalo**. **Hippos** still live in the rivers.

The park entrance is at the village of **Goazra**, near BOUAFLÉ which is 59km west of Yam. Since the park has no accommodation, you can sleep in Bouaflé at the *Campement Hôtel*. While in town, you can also pick up an authorisation to **camp** in the park at the *Eaux et Forêts* office. Inquire, too, about the possibility of getting a guide.

The road to the park from Yam passes just south of the **Kossou Dam**, built where the White Bandama River joins the Marahoué (or Red Bandama). The hydroelectric dam created the nation's largest **lake**, which spreads, indented like an insect-eaten leaf, over 1700 shallow square kilometres, and which doubled the country's production of electricity when it opened in 1972. It also flooded numerous villages and displaced an estimated 100,000 people, most of whom were resettled in new towns. The paved road to Bouaflé passes near many of the sad concrete and aluminum *AVB* villages which were built to replace the traditional settlements of local Baoulé fisherpeople and farmers by the *AVB* – the Bandama Valley Development Authority.

Bouaké

The antithesis of Yamoussoukro, **BOUAKÉ** lacks glamour and a sense of overall planning. But it's not altogether surprising if the town seems at times chaotic. Bouaké has grown dramatically in the last fifty years, to become Côte d'Ivoire's **second largest town**. As workers and traders from throughout the country flocked to this commercial crossroads on the major north–south route, neighbourhoods grew up willy-nilly, attaching themselves loosely to the districts laid out by the colonials. The diversity and dynamism of the peoples who've come together here make Bouaké an exciting place to visit, although the town is visually unappealing and there's admittedly not much to see. The highlight of any trip here is a visit to the **market** – one of the biggest and most colourful in the country.

Some background

Sometimes called the capital of the Baoulé country (a title which more accurately belongs to **Sakasso**, 42km southeast near the lake, where the successors to Baoulé **Queen Pokou** still reside). Bouaké was already an important commercial centre at the

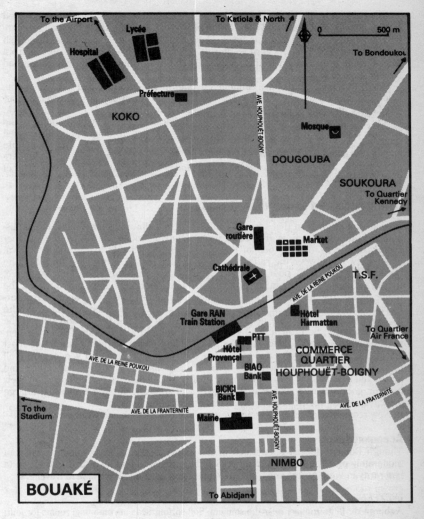

end of the nineteenth century when the French established a **military base**. It was used to launch attacks against the armies of **Almamy Samory Touré**, then sweeping into the region from the northwest. When Samory Touré finally surrendered at Gouelemou, the colonials once again sought to open up trade routes to the north. Bouaké soon regained prominence as a **centre for trade** in cloth, gold powder, indigo and tobacco.

An added boost was given to commerce when the French brought the **railway** line up from Abidjan in 1912, eventually extending it all the way to Ouagadougou. That same year, **industry** was launched in the interior when a cotton seeding plant was opened in Bouaké. In 1919, Robert Gonfreville, a French agriculturalist, opened a textile factory – the first in *Afrique Occidentale Française*.

As maritime trade dwindled during World War II, the railway line took on added importance and Bouaké found itself in the centre of a wartime trade boom. The country's food supply rolled into this town – beef cattle from the Upper Volta, dried fish from Mali, rice from the western territories, peanuts and sheep from the north – from where it was redistributed to the regions. By the end of the war, the population had swelled beyond 25,000.

Since 1945, immigrants have continued to pour into the town so that today the population has shot up to over 350,000. The continued growth of industry (brewery, cigarette factory, improved textile mills) has attracted many rural people in search of work. Part of the influx was spurred by chronic rural dislocation caused by the building of the **Kossou dam** in 1972. Though many people were resettled in villages specially created along the lake, many migrated to the towns. Today, Bouaké's wide **mix of people** includes Malinké and Sarakolé, Dyula (Dioula), Bambara, Senoufo and large numbers of Burkinabé. The original Baoulé inhabitants today only account for about a quarter of the total population.

Orientation and somewhere to stay

Bouaké is a large town that spreads confusingly in a thousand directions. The undisputed centre, however, is the **Commerce District**, today known as the *quartier Houphouët-Boigny*. This is one of the oldest neighbourhoods in the modern town, which grew up between the **railway station** and the *mairie*. It is where you'll find the **banks** (*BIAO, BICICI*), **post office** and administrative buildings. North of Commerce, the *gare routière* is located in the **Koko District**, a principally Baoulé quarter. Near the motor park is one of the town's few buildings of monumental proportions, the **Saint-Michel cathedral**, built in a heavy modern style. The expansive **grand marché** spreads over three separate neighbourhoods east of Koko – **Dougouba** (site of the *grande mosquée*), **Soukoura** (also known as the *quartier Dioula*) and **TSF** (a residential area with large villas and shaded streets). The Bouaké market is one of the most fascinating in Côte d'Ivoire and brings together over four thousand vendors from all parts of the country. In addition to the food items like fruit, vegetables, cereals and spices you'll find a variety of locally-made **crafts**. The Baoulé have a reputation for their **leather goods** (snake- and lizard-skin bags and wallets), but you'll also find a large selection of **jewellery** if you'd prefer to leave the reptiles in the bush.

New residential areas to the southwest include **Air France** and **Kennedy**.

Accommodation

Though Bouaké doesn't offer much in the luxury range, it has a good selection of moderately priced **hotels**. Overlanders will be pleased to find a **youth hostel** here (a real rarity in West Africa) and a couple of missions that sometimes take in travellers.

INEXPENSIVE

Auberge de la Jeunesse, near the stadium. Soft-sprung beds in communal rooms for four; showers and fans included in the price of CFA1000. Taxis to the centre are CFA100. Also try the **Mission Protestante** in the Commerce district near the *mairie* (town hall), and the **Mission Catholique** in the Nimbo district on the Abidjan road – both of which are said to take in travellers.

Hôtel Bakolé, Koko district (behind cathedral). Relatively cheap for the centre and not too run down. Rooms with fan cost CFA2500.

Iroco, Kamonikro district (☎63 34 95). This is a newer place, clean and well-run though far from the centre. S/C rooms with AC run CFA5000.

Aklomaibla, av de la Fraternité, near *Centre Ivoire* cinema, Air France. Plain, grotty quarters, but the price is right and the place is within walking distance of the Commerce district.

MODERATE TO EXPENSIVE

Hôtel Eléphant (☎63 25 24). Not bad value (AC rooms from CFA5600–8000) and near the market in the residential Air France district.

Phoenix, rue du Commerce, Commerce. A large place in the heart of town with basic S/C rooms for around CFA8500.

Hôtel Provençal, Commerce, behind the PTT (☎63 34 59). Fifties-style hotel run by Belgians and conveniently located. Spacious and clean rooms with AC for CFA8000–10,000. The restaurant here is very good and the outdoor *terrasse* a nice place to come for a drink.

Hôtel du Centre, Commerce (☎63 34 95). In the upper moderate level, rooms here come with AC and bath and cost from CFA8500. The hotel has its own restaurant and nightclub, plus a crafts boutique.

Hôtel de l'Aïr, route de l'Aeroport (☎63 28 15).Twenty-two comfortably furnished rooms with AC and bath. Clean and not overpriced with doubles for CFA8000. There's a good restaurant, too, but it's a taxi ride from the centre.

Hôtel Harmattan (☎63 39 95). Bouaké's stab at international accommodation, this is an unpretentious, modern hotel with nightclub, conference centre, craft shops and pool. Comfortable AC rooms with TV and phones start at CFA15,000.

Ran Hôtel, next to the railway station (☎63 20 16). Newer and a touch classier than the *Harmattan*, this has 60 rooms with all the trimmings from CFA16,000. The *Ran* also has a popular restaurant and bar and Bouaké's best pool.

MOVING ON FROM BOUAKÉ

The *gare routière* is easy to find, in the Koko district across from the market. **Coaches** and **taxis** head from here in all directions – Man, Abidjan, Korhogo, Odienné. As an alternative, you can catch the **train** which leaves twice daily for Abidjan and FERKESSÉDOUGOU (continuing to OUAGADOUGOU).

Air Ivoire operates daily **flights** to Abidjan and other urban centres. If you're in a hurry – or suddenly get sick of the whole Ivoirian scene – weekly flights also link the town, at some considerable expense, with Ouagadougou, Bamako and Conakry. For flight information, contact *Bouaké Voyages* (☎63 34 91).

If you're moving on to **Burkina Faso**, you should be able to get a visa from the consulate (☎63 31 70) in Bouaké, though they're more used to dealing with the *papiers* problems of the many Burkinabe who live in the district.

Katiola

Although small, **KATIOLA** enjoys fame throughout Côte d'Ivoire for its **pottery**. It's a puzzle why the jugs and *canaries* made here attract such wide attention when no one seems to pay much mind to those produced elsewhere in the country. Chalk it up to a strange quirk of fate, but it's one that has drawn a lucrative **tourist trade** to the town – or at any rate capitalised on the traffic passing through.

The traditional jugs the women here turn out are, in truth, rather nice. They're almost perfectly symmetrical, but shaped without a wheel. The women smooth the surfaces with their hands and use a special tool to cut out ornamental motifs. If you want to watch them work these days, you're probably going to have to pay for it. Photos are extra and the price of the real thing – mainly sold through a co-operative – is downright expensive.

In Katiola, you can stay at the *Hôtel Hambol* (☎65 47 25) – a modern place with African-style archways lining the façade. Rooms have AC and there's a good restaurant, swimming pool and nightclub. Cheaper accommodation can be found at the *Hôtel Makarwa* – a grimy but affordable place in the town centre – or the *Hôtel de l'Amitié*.

WESTERN CÔTE D'IVOIRE

The big attractions of **western Côte d'Ivoire** are high forest-strewn ridges and valleys, and the relatively intact traditional culture in the Dan (or Yacouba) speaking people. **Man** is the main town, and **Danané** – close to both Guinea and Liberia – is also important. **Touba** to the north, on the road that winds off the mountains into the drier savannah lands, was originally a Malinké town founded in the 1870s by immigrants from Timbuktu. But the country here was *Toura* (people related to the Dan) before that, and the Toura, whose reputation as sorcerers has stayed with them, today live southeast of Touba, especially around the steep village of Zala.

Although the main centres of the west are accessible enough at any time, the **rains** fall heavily in the region from March to October, and getting to some of the more out-of-the-way sites can be difficult. Lulls between showers provide fantastic conditions for photography, however; this is an area that needs clear air to be appreciated.

Daloa

The first western town you hit along the great central highway, **DALOA** is a good place to break your trip to MAN. This is a coffee-growing area – which brings the district substantial wealth – and, although it doesn't figure much on the tour itineraries, Daloa is one of the country's oldest and most important towns, solid, well-planted and industrious.

There's a variety of accommodation options, with *Les Ambassadeurs* (BP 754; ☎78 32 19) the most upmarket (from CFA9000/11000). But the best value place to stay is the impeccably clean *Roc Hôtel*. Rooms with shower start from only CFA3000, there's a nice bar-resto and the English-speaking owner is friendly. Just down the road is the *Billy Bob* disco, and there's plenty of other nightlife if you're not starting early in the morning.

Man

MAN, a large commercial centre of some 60,000 people, is a rather hideous town in beautiful surroundings. Most of its appeal derives from its spectacular geographical setting. Often called the **"town of eighteen peaks"**, it spreads over a valley with mountains rising up on all sides and from the end of its wide streets. There's an American feel here; there are towns in Colorado like Man and though the horizons inspire, the town itself is a muddled confusion of districts that leaves little impression. Still, it's a lively place with much activity focusing around the market and adjoining *gares routières*.

Practicalities: food, accommodation, moving on

Man consists of numerous districts, most of which you probably won't get the time to visit. The centre of town is occupied by the *quartier commercial*, where you'll find the large town **market** and the *gare routière*. If you're interested in buying masks from the region, there's a wide selection sold on the upper level of the market along with numerous other **crafts**. Nearby are countless shops and small businesses, and branches of the major **banks** – BICICI, BIAO, BCEAO and BNDA. Note, however, that there's sometimes a major problem changing non-franc currencies in Man. No bank would touch sterling travellers' cheques when we tried.

There's **food** everywhere in Man – lots of places near the market. *La Prudence*, on the other side of the main street towards the *PTT*, does wonderful salads if your stomach is feeling robust. It's clean and fresh and not expensive, and they also serve good chips and other meals, and cold beer.

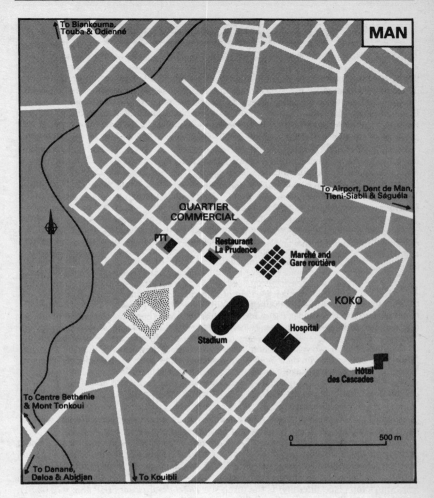

MAN

To Biankouma,
Touba & Odienné

To Airport, Dent de Man,
Tieni-Siabli & Séguéla

QUARTIER
COMMERCIAL

PTT

Restaurant
La Prudence

Marché and
Gare routière

KOKO

Stadium

Hospital

Hôtel
des Cascades

To Centre Bethanie
& Mont Tonkoui

0   500 m

To Danané,
Daloa & Abidjan

To Kouibli

Rooms

Thanks to its popularity with tourists, Man has a decent choice of **accommodation**. If
you're on a budget, you might consider the beautifully sited *Centre Bethanie*, 3km out
of town on the Mont Tonkoui road, which in the past has put up travellers in a guest
house with clean dorm rooms. They charge about CFA2000 a night. In town, one of the
cheaper options is the *Hôtel Fraternité* (☎79 06 89). You can get a room with or without
fan; nothing special but, at CFA3000, good value.

Moving slightly upmarket, the *Virginia* (☎79 06 91) is a comfortable place in a quiet
residential neighbourhood, a taxi ride out on the Daloa road (argue if you're quoted a
tourist rate for the taxi). Rooms are nicely furnished; most have AC, but some relatively
cheap ones (CFA3500) are without. Friendly management takes good care of the
guests, providing them with toilet paper, soap and towels. More central, the *Hôtel*

THE MAN DISTRICT IN HISTORY

Hidden in the forests of the western mountains, the **Dan** (also known as Yacouba), lived in almost complete isolation since the beginning of their migration from the Guinea and Liberian regions in the fourteenth century. Other peoples of Côte d'Ivoire – the Akan, Senoufo and Malinké – had little contact with them, while the Europeans, who had been along the coast since the early 1700s, only made it to Man in 1897. It was largely the military victories of **Samory Touré** that drew the French to the region; they finally tracked down the most serious threat to their colonialist ambitions in 1898, capturing him in the village of Guéoulé, northwest of Man. They built a military post at Man in 1908 and used the town for regional administration.

DAN CULTURE

So the Dan remained cut off from outside influences – African or otherwise – until relatively late. They base their traditions and religion on a single God, **Zran**. Creator of the universe, *Zran* contains elements of both good and evil. Part of traditional education involves **secret societies**. After passing a first initiation, boys and girls enter these societies where they gain more profound religious instruction and learn to assume their adult roles. Members of the *gor*, for example, are charged with administering justice. They ultimately gain the power of turning themselves into animals, notably the leopard, in order to pass unnoticed as they survey the forces of good and evil at work in the community. **Masks** are important symbols in initiations and other ceremonies. Dan masks, unlike many others, characteristically have smooth, delicate lines and gentle, even sensual, human features. They're easily recognised and well known throughout the entire country.

Dance is another important element of Dan culture, and the region is famous for it. One of the most unusual is the **stilt dance** (*Zekre Touli*). Dressed in grass skirts and covered with cowrie shells, the masked performers make beguiling, inexplicable movements on stilts up to six metres in height. Also impressive is the *Menon* or **juggling dance**. Young girls, about four years old, are specifically chosen for this dance and undergo a special two-year initiation. During this period, they live with the dance troops and have no contact with their families until puberty. They learn to do death-defying acrobatics (and that's no exaggeration) – even being tossed into the air to land on knife blades held by their adult partners. These dances are now performed in slightly sanitised form throughout the country and versions of them are frequently staged in large hotels.

Leveneur (☎79 00 39) is just a couple of minutes' walk from the market. Rooms with AC start at CFA6000. The French restaurant here is rated one of the best in town.

More upmarket, the *Beausejour "Les Masques"* (☎79 09 91) is popular despite being 3km from the centre on the Mont Tonkoui road. The *paillote*-like bungalows around the attractive courtyard have AC and TV. A night costs an average of CFA11,000, though smaller non-AC rooms cost half that. It's recommended, especially if you have a car. Man's top place (literally) is the three-star *Hôtel des Cascades* (BP 485; ☎79 02 51). Perched on a hill, it commands a brilliant view of the town and the surrounding mountains. AC rooms overlook the swimming pool, gardens and tennis courts.

GETTING OUT OF MAN

Express buses leave for **Abidjan** morning and evening (CFA4000 plus luggage) with middle of the night stops in **Yamoussoukro** to delay arrival in Abidjan until 6am. For **Odienné** on the route to **Bamako**, *TRAMOCI* offers the cheapest bus fares. *Peugeot 504s* run north to **Touba** and south to **San Pedro** (CFA5000). Heading west to **Guinea**, *504s* and *mille kilos* go to **Danané**, whence a few taxis a day drive to **Gbapleau** (no shops or facilities). Going into **Liberia** from Man and Danané – in the wake of the messy invasion of January 1990 – is probably not recommended. Try to use an alternative route. Find out about the situation on the ground in any case.

Around Man

The bold, green **mountain scenery** around Man lends itself well to day trips. For some of the longer destinations, you'll need transportation (car or taxi), but if you're feeling in shape, there are rewarding outings within hiking distance. Kids around town may approach you to offer their services as guides (some try to pass themselves off as representatives of the tourist office) and are generally quite helpful. To avoid bad feelings, come to an agreement on payment before you head off. Some of the most popular excursions are outlined below; if you want more information or are interested in organised tours contact the *Délégation Régionale du Tourisme*: BP 613, Man (☎79 09 41).

The cascade

One of the easiest trips, and one you won't regret taking, is to the **cascade**, only 5km from the centre along the road to Mont Tonkoui. There's a motorable road almost the entire distance (by car you'll have to park nearby and walk down a steep footpath to the base of the falls), but it's perfectly feasible to hike. Depending on how much mud you have to contend with, it won't take much over an hour, and the road winds its way through beautiful mountain scenery. You're likely to find yourself stopping frequently just to admire the views. The last stretch passes through a thick bamboo grove where you hear the rush of the stream in the valley below, but can't see it through the greenery. Walk towards the top of the waterfall and continue until you see a painted signboard indicating where you scale down the cliffs to the bottom of the falls. In full view for the first time, they're magnificent, with the white water crashing down a stair-like rock formation.

A nice **restaurant** has been built at the base of the falls and is run by the same owner as the popular *paillote* in town. Though slightly expensive, the food is good and the setting – outdoor decks shaded by thick trees with the *cascade* churning away behind you – is spectacular. Spanning the river near the restaurant is a **hanging bridge** – a copy of those for which the region is famous. Although real vines are woven into it, this one is supported by thick metal cables put in place by the French. From a distance it looks authentic enough for atmospheric photos, with the falls tumbling in the background.

Mont Tonkoui

Its name deriving from the Dan word *tonkpi*, meaning big mountain, **Le Mont Tonkoui** is the tallest mountain in Côte d'Ivoire. You can see it clearly from Man, its summit now marked by an unsightly **television transmitter**. A *piste* leads northwest from town (the same tracks that pass the *cascade*) and continues about 20km to the mountain. The road winding its way up to the peak adds another 12km to the total distance. The TV relay station on the summit is off-limits to unauthorised personnel, but about two-thirds of the way to the top tracks lead off to a guest house – formerly the *villa du gouverneur* – used occasionally by visiting dignitaries. From here you get a magnificent panoramic view of the mountain chains and **thick forests** of the region. On a clear day, it's said you can see 150kms, beyond the **Nimba Mountains** on the Guinean border.

La Dent de Man

Aptly named, this bald rock formation rises, incisor-like, 12km northeast of Man. The Tooth of Man is the most identifiable mountain you can see from Man and is practically a town totem. Some say it has special protective powers – a spiritual sentinel watching over the townspeople. If you're without transport, take a taxi from town to the village of **Glongouin**, at the foot of the mountain. Here you can find a kid to lead you up the *dent*, guiding you through the maze of footpaths and, hopefully, finding the easiest way up the steep parts. It's a hard climb in areas – you'll get hot – but you don't have to be in spectacular shape to make it. The view from the top is worth the effort.

Tieni-Siabli and Fakobli

TIENI-SIABLI, 14km east of Man, has become a common target for travellers, though there's nothing of essential interest. Tieni was the original settlement, built atop a cliff. Most of the inhabitants, however, live below in the uninspiring new town of Siabli. Few of the old-style huts left on the hill are still lived in. You can visit them, but must ask permission from the town chief first. The authorisation will cost you money.

Ten kilometres further down the same road, you arrive in **FAKOBLI**. It's a quiet town which lies at the foot of numerous mountains. A branch of the **Sassandra river** flows within a couple of kilometres, keeping the surrounding countryside especially green. Fakobli, however, is best known as home of the *tematé* dance, performed by young girls around harvest time.

Danané and around

If you arrive in Côte d'Ivoire from southern Guinea or Liberia, **DANANÉ** is likely to be your first Ivoirian town. It sprawls across a great valley and you can find yourself doing a lot of walking. The *gare routière* for arrivals from the west is on the west side of town. Ask the driver to drop you by the police station in the centre if possible. Here you need to get a *tampon* (stamp) from the *chef* to finish off your entry formalities. Don't go on to Man without it; you'll have to come back.

The best of the very few **places to stay** in town is the *Hôtel Tia Etienne* – well out on the east side of town – but on the Man road, and only 500m from the *gare routière est*. It's a nice enough place, with simple S/C rooms from CFA3–5000 (depending on your choice of air) and quite good meals for around CFA1500. Arriving from either of Côte d'Ivoire's western neighbours, the prospect of so much comfort (AC, wine, TV in the bar) seems positively over the top.

The liana bridges

So long as you have your own transport to get around, Danané's **liana bridges** are worth the trip: authentic old swinging constructions that span the Cavally River south of town at DRONGOUINEAU (15km), LIEUPLEU (26km) and VATOUO (30km), all off the main road to TOULÉPLEU. Like others in the region in Guinea and Liberia, considerable mystique attaches to these bridges (which also makes them paying attractions) and they're supposed to be reconstructed when necessary in a single night – something that women and outsiders are not allowed to witness. The bridges at Lieupleu and Vatouo are the easiest to visit by *504* from Danané (you'll have to walk 4–5km from the main dirt road).

THE NORTH AND EAST

Northwestern Côte d'Ivoire is sparse, mostly flat country, yellow and dusty for eight months of the year. While **Odienné** may figure only as a night stop en route to or from Mali, it offers an unusual and beautiful route into Guinea via Beyla. **Korhogo**, more central, is certainly worth a detour if you're heading up the country's main transport axis. You can jump train or bus at Ferkessédougou and spend a rewarding two or three days in the Senoufo country.

The **northeast**'s great attraction is the **Comoé National Park** – the largest in West Africa. For most travellers this is a fairly inaccessible reserve and doesn't always repay the expense and effort of getting there. But if you're travelling south from Burkina (or north from Abidjan), and you've some spare days, it's worth making a big loop through the northeast, calling in at the old Dyula capital of **Kong**, following the boundary of the park around its eastern side, and using an unusual back-country route through the Akan centres of **Bondoukou** and **Abengourou** – nice untouristy towns the pair of them. Or else you can cut across the border to Ghana at one of several frontier posts and make for Kumasi.

This is a much more interesting prospect than the monotonous highway through the centre of Côte d'Ivoire. And at the northwest corner of the park there are opportunities for worthwhile, and just about affordable, **game-viewing trips** out of Kafolo.

The far northeast is **Lobi country** and you'll see Lobi hunters, tracking through the dry bush with bows and hunting tackle. But the **Koulango**, whose language is close to Lobi, have long had a more settled farming lifestyle and are the *de facto* land holders in the region.

Eastern Côte d'Ivoire is the least tourist-frequented part of the country. The hilly central east, close to the Ghana border, is the heartland of the **Agni** and **Abron**, which, culturally and linguistically, have much in common with the Ashanti in Ghana.

Odienné

ODIENNÉ is the focus of the most scenic district in the northern grasslands. To the west, the **Dienguélé range** ripples over to the Guinean border. Another set of hills follows the road to BOUNDIALI, peaking near Tiemé with **Mont Tougoukoli** which rises to over 800m. Although it's a historic town, Odienné has few reminders of the days when it was capital of the **Kabadougou Empire**, founded by the local hero Vakaba Touré, whose modest grave can still be seen on one of the town's main streets near the post office. In the 1970s Odienné was scheduled for radical **urbanisation**, but the scheme only went far enough to give an anonymous this-could-be-almost-anywhere feeling to the agricultural town of some 30,000. Though the old quarters were knocked down, the new city never came, and the former charm of the traditional houses and shady streets has long since been forgotten.

Some background

A Muslim fief, Odienné was originally founded by the Senoufo. But as early as the sixteenth century, Mande migrations had pushed all the way to Touba, and over the next two centuries their movements slowly displaced the Senoufo. Odienné remained in Senoufo control until the mid-1700s, but eventually the native people were overwhelmed by the newcomers and made peace with the Malinké.

Soon after, the townships of **Samatiegla** and **Tiéma** became important Muslim centres along with Odienné. By the mid-nineteenth century, the town had also become a commercial stop on the **caravan routes** linking Bougouni (Mali) to Touba and Seguéla. Salt and horses from the north were traded here against gold and kola nuts from the south. And, as the town prospered, it grew to become the capital of a sizeable kingdom led by **Vakaba Touré**, who expanded his empire east to Boundiali. Vakaba's son, **Maagbé Mandou**, was later to marry one of the daughters of **Samory Touré**. Odienné thus became an important ally of Samory, whose hegemony extended over the town until it was captured by the French in 1893.

Accommodation and transport

Though there's nothing to get excited about in the way of **hotels**, Odienné does have a decent *campement* with rooms that have basic furnishings and fans. They start at CFA4000. There's an inexpensive bar/restaurant in the place as well. For something a bit more lavish, try the three-star *Hôtel Les Frontières* (BP 135; ☎80 02 03). It's arranged in attractive bungalows though the swimming pool is dry and the electricity unreliable.

If you're heading north, Odienné is a springboard **to Mali**. **Taxis** run to BOUGOUNI, though the tracks are often bad. *Pistes* are well maintained east as far as KORHOGO where the tarmac to Abidjan begins. The road to MAN is paved.

Boundiali

The short drive from Odienné to **BOUNDIALI** passes through a hilly agricultural region before entering the flat plains of the **Senoufo country**. The town name means "drum dried in the sun", and it was an old settlement founded around the twelfth century by a Senoufo ancestor, a hunter named Nambaga Ganon. Eventually, it was incorporated into Vakaba Touré's empire, and it's said that René Caillié, the first explorer to be recognised for reaching Timbuktu and returning again to recount the tale, stayed here on his way to the "mysterious city".

Now the town has an attractive **hotel** – the *Dala* (BP 90; ☎82 00 41) – run collectively by a community association. It's laid out like a small village with comfortable S/C accommodation in round thatched huts. The venture has been quite successful at attracting tourism, with the villagers organising events like dancing (troops from throughout the region come to perform) and excursions. As an experience, it is of course contrived, but the villagers at least seem sincere in their desire to demonstrate local customs.

THE PORO

Senoufo society is regulated by a process of **training** (sometimes called initiation) that may last an entire lifetime. Young men normally go through three phases of this training, known as **poro** (the same name as a similar institution found far to the west, especially in Sierra Leone), each of which lasts seven years. Girls go through an initial phase that ends when they get their first period. After their menopause, women are considered asexual and may begin the training again. If they live long enough, they become fully initiated.

Traditionally, the *poro* served as the basis of Senoufo government. Communities were led by elders who had reached the highest level of the training. These elders themselves chose the members of their ranks from the brightest and most talented initiates, thus ensuring that the governing body was composed of the most able leaders. Though effective, this system of ruling broke down somewhat when Malinké invasions sparked the need for village elders to relinquish some of their authority to a central chief – the most famous of which was **Gbon Coulibaly.**

But the initiation lived on and is today still practised throughout the Senoufo country. Yet exactly what is learned during the seven-year cycles is unknown by outsiders, since it is a highly guarded **secret** considered vital to the survival of *poro* and thus to Senoufo society. In very general terms, initiates receive religious and professional education and learn about social obligations. Part of the training takes place in the **sacred forest**. Among other things, initiates in the same seven-year cycle learn to communicate in a special language.

Various stages in the initiation are marked by festivals – a sort of graduation ceremony. One of the better known is the **dance of the leopard-men**, celebrated after a group of initiates returns from the sacred forest having learned to master religious forces. Similar celebrations may mark a birth or a death, and since the whole community participates, the whole community takes part symbolically in the important stages of an individual's life. Many of these dances are now acted out in major regional hotels (the *Mont Korhogo* or, in Boundiali, at *Le Dala*). This may be your best shot at experiencing such an event (or at least a commercially staged version thereof), but if you stay any time in the region and get to know some people, it's not unrealistically difficult to accompany them to one of the celebrations. They leave a lasting impression.

Korhogo

Côte d'Ivoire's third largest town, **KORHOGO** is capital of the Senoufo country. The original settlement was founded in the thirteenth century by a soldier named **Nengué** who had been in the service of the ruler in Kong. This is the most touristy of Côte d'Ivoire's northern towns, famous for its rough, unusual, painted *toiles*, examples of which seem to hang in every hotel and expat home in the country. Fortunately there's more to the town and its district than this pretty, but somewhat debased, art form. Senoufo culture finds its firmest expression in the district and there's every possibility, if you make some effort to meet people, of witnessing some of the frequent ceremonial events that take place (see opposite). These dances aren't easily confused with what you might be served as after-dinner entertainment in some of the hotel lounges.

Accommodation and practicalities

The cheapest relief for overlanders seeking **accommodation** is at the *Mission Catholique* which has a limited number of well-kept rooms. If they're not being used by people working with the mission, the staff doesn't object to putting you up, charging CFA1500/bed; you may be asked to share a room. Equally cheap, but a lot less wholesome, you'll find a number of *chambres de passage* in town, often unmarked. There's a couple over in the Koko district; if you ask at any of the crafts *ateliers* someone will point you in the right direction, though they'll laugh if you're loaded down with luggage. Near the large **central market**, the *Hôtel Pelerin* is not a bad buy, with S/C rooms from CFA3000.

The *Motel Agip* (☎86 01 13) is one of the better bets in the **medium price** bracket and is centrally located near the market. It's a small place, where the rooms (from CFA5500) are kept spotlessly clean. The *Agip's* French restaurant is one of the town's better eating places. Also fairly central, the *Hôtel du Nord* (☎86 08 58) is not as smart as the *Agip* though the price of a night is about the same. Another good find is the *Hôtel des Avocats* (☎86 05 69), though it's located outside town just off the Ferkessédougou road. Nicely furnished AC rooms start at CFA7000. Also some way from the centre as you go towards Mont Korhogo, the *Kafiledjo* (☎86 09 88) has pleasant AC rooms, a pool, restaurant and bar.

In the more **expensive range**, the *SIETHO* chain's *Le Mont Korhogo* (BP 263; ☎86 04 00) is the town's plushest, ideally located near the market – to which you may be dragged anyway by one of the crafts vendors (many of whom are Senegalese), who sell their wares along the street at the hotel entrance. All rooms are S/C and have air-conditioning; average price, CFA15,000. The hotel has a pool, restaurant and bar and they **hire cars**, though not cheaply.

Some miscellaneous pointers: **change money** at one of two banks – the *Société Générale* or the *Société Ivoirienne de Banques* – both located in the town centre. Due to the large number of visitors, there's also a **tourist office**, the *Délégation du Tourisme* (☎86 05 84), located near the Mairie. *Air Ivoire* is represented at the *Hôtel Kedjona*. You can fly daily to Bouaké and Abidjan and four times weekly to Odienné (the latter flight giving an eagle's-eye view of the savannah for only CFA4000).

Korhogo sites

Since Korhogo is today famous for its **crafts**, a good place to head for an introduction is the new *Centre Artisanal*. To get there, go to the roundabout of the Mairie and walk towards the **municipal pool**, from where you can already see the large conical thatching of the centre's rooftop. Inside, there's a wide selection of local artwork – weaving, carving, basketry. The quality is strictly controlled and artists receive a take of the (non-negotiable) selling price.

You can get better buys in the **Koko district**, where many craftsmen have set up workshops. Here you have to bargain the price of sculpted masks and wooden objects and must be your own judge of the workmanship; it varies from good to shoddy. This district borders the *fôret sacrée* – where *poro* initiates go through secret training. The forest is fenced off, however, and you'll not be allowed in.

Near Koko, you'll see the new **Grande Mosquée**, built in 1980 in a style similar to the mosque at Yamoussoukro. On Fridays, men turn out in large numbers for the afternoon prayer. And in the distance, the mountain looming up with its **sacrificial rocks** recalls a different religious tradition. In former days, when a chief died, his slaves were sacrificed on these rocks and he was buried on a bed of their skulls. You'll hear people insist that in remote villages the practice still continues.

If you haven't got transport, but want to visit some of the **surrounding villages** described below, it's possible to do so by arranging an excursion through the *Délégation du Tourisme*. Their office is located on the same roundabout as the Mairie and they'll organise day trips for around CFA25,000/day, transport costs and guide included.

Around Korhogo

Many of the crafts you see in town – at the *Mont Korhogo* hotel or the *centre artisinal* – are made in the surrounding villages, which could make for easy **daytrips**. Formerly, it was a lot more interesting to see the artisans at work and cheaper to buy from them directly, but in recent years so many people have followed the idea that neighbouring villages have become suspiciously touristy and prices have risen to the point where you can probably find better buys in Korhogo itself from sellers undercutting each other.

Still, one of the easiest to get to – and therefore one of the most visited – is **Waraniéné**, noted for its weavers (*tisserands*). Now, in addition to the rough hand-woven cloth, you can buy embroidered tablecloths with matching napkins – one suspects tourism has affected local production. Waraniéné lies only 6km southeast of town on the road to Sirasso, close enough to hire a taxi or even try hitching if you've no other means of transport.

Other villages lie along the southern road which leads to DIKADOUGOU. At **Tioroniaradougou**, turn left towards **Fakaha** (35km from Korhogo), where painted fabric (*toiles peintes*) is produced. These are all over Korhogo town itself and, indeed, you can see them in markets throughout West Africa. The designs represent scenes from folklore and local legends; the colours are made from mud and vegetable dyes. Originally these fabrics were made for costumes used in *poro* ceremonies and had geometric patterns. If you get the chance to go to a funeral or initiation, you'll still see dancers wearing them. Now, however, they're mostly made into wall hangings for tourists. Note that those in black and white retain their colours fairly well, but the multi-toned patterns fade almost immediately and the slightest moisture will cause the dyes to run. Because of the demand, prices are steep. Taxis head here from Korhogo's *grand marché*. The nearby town of **Napéolédougou** also produces the same fabric.

Ferkessédougou

Whatever you do **in the northeast**, you're likely to pass through **FERKESSÉ-DOUGOU**. It's an unexceptional road town, but nice enough anyway after the hours of travel that it generally takes to get there.

Ferké, as it's known, stretches a couple of dust-blown kilometres along the highway, with turnings west towards KORHOGO and east to COMOÉ PARK and KONG. It's only worth stopping the night here for the **market on Thursday**, though, if you've come up by public transport from Abidjan, Ferké is about as far as you'll get in one day.

In-town practicalities

Ferkessédougou's **Thursday market** is enjoyable but not special. All morning the 22-place lorries come in loaded with farmers with tomatoes, yams, hot peppers and whatever's in season. The whole town is caught up in the action. Stalls selling more interesting items – straw hats and other domestic crafts – spread out down the long shady avenue towards the RAN (railway) **station**.

One of the cheapest **accommodation** options is the *Hôtel Campement* right here by the teak trees near the station. It's pretty basic and gloomy – they promise a fan brought to the room and you can do better than this (CFA3000/room) in town. For the early train north, however (the ordinary *express* as opposed to the *rapide* which arrives later), it is convenient.

Best value is the decent and friendly *Hôtel Koffikro*, to the south of the *Shell* station and west of the highway. Rooms are CFA2500 (simple), CFA3000 (with fan) and CFA4000 (with shower). The AC, S/C *Hôtel Refuge*, also on the west side of town, but north of *Shell*, is slightly more expensive, but it boasts a popular bar and restaurant. *Relais de Senoufo*, directly behind the *Shell* station, which used to pack them in, is defunct. Most upmarket in Ferké is *La Réserve*, a kilometre or two south on the Bouaké road (take a taxi maybe). This is a very comfortable place with an interesting menu if you want to splurge (CFA7000/10,000 S/C AC, CFA3000 *plat*, CFA4000 menu). A shame the pool is such an unappetising lurid green.

There are several little **eateries** in Ferké. Try the *Oasis* (you'll need to ask: taxi drivers are helpful) which seems to be staffed by Ghanaians – a nice place with cold beer but somewhat limited menu (good river fish).

Ferké has *PTT* and banks. The *SIB* bank changes non-franc currencies.

TRANSPORT ONWARDS

If you're heading north and have your own wheels, it's worth mentioning here the lovely ancient little mosque at KAUARA, 15km beyond OUANGOLODOUGOU. It's just off the road to the left and deserves a look.

Ferkessédougou's *gare routière nord* is opposite the *PTT*. Prices to BOBO DIOULASSO seem high considering the distance. The train is a lot cheaper, but has its own, special disadvantages: it's often been attacked in the border region by thieves – not usually dangerous, but you might want to pay special attention to the concealment of valuables. *Gare routière est et Abidjan* is behind the market to the east of the town centre on the way out to the railway station. Here you'll find daily transport to KONG (CFA1200) and KAFOLO/BOUNA (CFA2500/4500).

Kafolo (also known as "Petit Ferké") is where you should head for *Comoé Safari Lodge*, the northwest part of the park and the Lobi country. For Kong and Kafolo only the following two vehicles per day can be relied upon: Kong, usually mid-afternoon (3hr); and Kafolo normally before 10am (3–5hr), arriving in Bouna much later (8–10hr). Lastly, note that throughout this great tranche of Côte d'Ivoire, there is no tarmac. **Roads** are not too badly potholed, but are every bit as corrugated as you'd expect.

Kong

Known and visited for its old Sudanic mosques – sloping *banco* walls on a wooden frame with characteristic protruding joists – **KONG** is worth a side trip from Ferkessédougou if you're really interested and/or have some spare time, and especially if you've not seen the much more impressive architecture in Mali. It's not easy to hit Kong en route to anywhere else. Occasional vehicles come up from some of the Djimini Senoufo villages to the south (from DABAKALA. for example), but this means a diversion in any case; and several times a week something goes from Kong to KAFOLO, up on the main Ferké-Bouna northeast axis.

Otherwise you're pretty much limited to one or two vehicles a day from Ferké, and the same back again. This isn't a bad trip (3hr, CFA1200), with a foretaste of Kong's architecture at NAFANA, 22km before it. But you'll see some of the poorest villages in Côte d'Ivoire around here and, at the end of the dry season, when the granaries like giant egg-cups are empty, you come face to face with the awful downside mundanity of the country's economic "miracle" – seriously malnourished people. With heavy dependence on hunting, and the flight to the Comoé park of much of the game, the people here are suffering partly as a result of wildlife conservation policies which have ignored their needs.

In Kong

Be prepared for **"guides"** when you get to Kong. Ask the price before submitting to their company – you won't escape freely otherwise. They're hardly needed in any case, as what there is to be seen is standing before you. The large **Friday mosque** dates from the seventeenth century (though most of it was rebuilt in 1905 after its destruction by Samory Touré) and the smaller one to the south, behind the houses on the main square, from the fourteenth century. This latter has white painted coconuts on its turrets which you'll be told are ostrich eggs from Mecca. Both are impressive enough relics in an environment largely devoid of monuments, but neither is accessible to non-Muslims and, having circumnavigated each one, you may feel ready to go back to Ferké.

The **other sites** to which guides will haul you are really hardly worth bothering about. There's the rubbish-strewn grave of a certain *Voyageur Moskowitz* who succumbed here in 1894 while on Marchand's expedition, and the *Maison du Binger*, of dubious authenticity, which stands in dilapidated ruins some way off as memorial to the French expansionist who based himself in Kong for a while in 1889.

If you end up **spending the night** here you should know that food and drink is concentrated up by the town centre, opposite the petrol pump, and what's there is about all there is (the occasional cold *Solibra* has been procured there in the past). Sleeping usually means the *campement*, which is straight down the road through town about 800m and then up on the left. There are basic S/C chalet rooms for about CFA3000.

THE KINGDOM OF KONG

The town of **Kong** was founded, probably in the twelfth or thirteenth century, by Voltaic-speaking ancestors of the Senoufo. But the town was relatively unimportant until its commercial invasion by Muslim Mande-speaking **Dyula merchants** at the end of the seventeenth century. Islamic scholarship followed in the footsteps of mercantile success, and the town became the capital of a **trading empire** that stretched south and east to the Baoulé- and Akan-speaking farmers of the hills and north to the edge of Ségou's domain near the Niger River, while the **mosques and Koranic institute** extended its reputation. But, although the Dyula exerted a powerful influence in Kong, it was another hundred years before **Sekou Ouattara**, chief of one of the most influential Dyula families, seized power in a bloody coup directed against the ruling **Falafala-Senoufo** incumbents. The new kings of Kong were constantly in dispute with the Bambara of Ségou and the peoples of the south. As a political entity, Kong ceased to have much cohesion by the early nineteenth century. But it was still a prestigious centre as late as 1897, when Samory Touré swept in – and then moved on having all but destroyed the town in his scorched-earth flight from the French.

Comoé National Park

Open December to the end of May (check in Ferké, Katiola or Bondoukou before setting off).
Entry through Kafolo, Ouango-Fitini, Gansé, Kakpin, Toupé and Bania.

The **PARC NATIONAL DE LA COMOÉ** is the largest in West Africa – 11,500 square kilometres of rolling, tsetse-ridden, savannah and bush with patches of forest in the south. As late as the 1950s colonial maps marked the region "uninhabited". While this wasn't quite true (the Lobi and Koulango hunted and planted there, and continue to do so despite the rangers), it's basically wild animal territory. And the animals know it.

The main feature of the park (which is also known as the *Réserve de Bouna*) is the broad and twisting **Comoé River**, flanked by stretches of riverine forest. Seasonal streams flow in from the north and the generous scattering of lakes and pools across the park provides further dry season animal-viewing targets. The zones to concentrate on are westwards, however; the eastern borders of the park are included more as a buffer against human encroachment than as recommended game country.

Comoé practicalities

The best trips to Comoé are done in **private cars**, with a ranger on board to navigate and scan for wildlife. There are no facilities inside the park, so you need to plan ahead to avoid re-tracing your route, or else aim to cross the park, most rewardingly north to south, or vice versa. While the east may be worth exploring at the beginning of the park season, when the animals are dispersed, if you're here after the end of January you're best advised to stay fairly close to the main river.

If you've **no wheels of your own**, Kafolo, in the north, is the place to head for. The visit is still likely to cost you dear, but there are one or two money-saving devices.

Kafolo

KAFOLO is hard by the Comoé bridge right on the park boundary. *Comoé Safari Lodge* is the only, expensive, accommodation. The place is nicely set and pretty good, if you can afford around CFA35,000/night double HB (no room-only tariff), with cool, pyramid-shaped rooms, a fine swimming pool and some imaginative cooking (homemade bread what's more). But at CFA1800 for breakfast and CFA6000 for lunch it all adds up. As an alternative (and you might try to persuade them to waive the obligatory dinners), Kafolo has a few snack and cheap chop sellers where your food may come wrapped in the chits you signed at the lodge. Beer and other drinks are a good deal cheaper, too, and, given the thrice-daily-only electricity at the lodge, hardly any less chilled. Incidentally, the building of the lodge disturbed some old middens: you can find potsherds and other scraps of domestic Lobi life all around the perimeter. Some may be quite old.

If the lodge is right out of your pocket and you succeed in finding a place to put your head in the village (talk to the staff if nothing else comes up), you'll still want a game-drive round the northwest corner. Subject to four or more takers, these run every morning (CFA10,000). What you see is very dependent on luck but on a good run you should see buffalo and elephants and possibly lions. Hippos are nearly guaranteed (and there are opportunities to get closer to them in afternoon *pirogue* rides – CFA5000). On a disappointing trip you'll get antelope (great numbers of hartebeest), warthogs and monkeys only. Persuade the driver to make a diversion to Lake **Dalandjougou** – a major dry season watering place. They do try. You'll be out from 6am until at least 11am, so take fluids and something to eat.

If you're without a car, and decide to make the Comoé trip *quand même*, you may well strike lucky with a lift with motorised visitors. They don't see many backpackers out here. There's at least a good chance of a ride out again with tourists or a tour group.

Gansé and Kakpin

The focal points of **Gansé** and nearby **Kakpin** are on the southwest perimeter of the park, and not at all easy to get to without your own vehicle. Access from the southeast is from BONDOUKOU, some 170km away, and from the southwest from BOUAKÉ (180km) or, with less *piste* , KATIOLA (160km).

The big draw in the **"Kakpin trianglé"** (150 square kilometres of bush and forest between Kakpin, Gansé and the river) is the singular presence of **lions**. There's a good network of tracks here, too. You need sharp eyes, binoculars and patience. Keep stopping to scan around (remember to look behind you) and take notice of the behaviour of prey animals like hartebeest and warthog.

Kakpin's **accommodation** is a simple *campement*, a favourite of Jaques Verrier in Bondoukou (see p.801), with S/C huts and a sometime bar-restaurant. Gansé has the *Comoé Sogetel*, an all-in lodge along the same lines as *Comoé Safari Lodge* and similarly priced, but styled, with cubist abandon, on local architecture.

The Lobi country and Bouna

Traditional **Lobi territory** begins somewhere along the road from Ferkessédougou. Until you reach Kafolo, however, you won't see any Lobi compounds, as the whole area is part of the Muslim domain of Kong.

The easiest shot of Lobi life comes with an excursion from *Comoé Safari Lodge* up the road to **Bolé** village. On Saturday there's a market here and wonderful diversity in the people (mostly women) who come to buy and sell. Among the Dyula, Koulango and Senoufo, you'll even meet a few Fula women – though perhaps not all year round.

But the highlight of the *Tour Lobi* (CFA8000) is a visit to a compound – a **soukala** – on the way to Bolé (usually one where the guide has friends or family); the chance to look around the organically sculpted, rectangular, mud-built houses around a central courtyard; and the opportunity to meet some Lobi people – including elderly ladies who dutifully arrive, lip plugs in place, to sit and be photographed. You get to poke around in private homes and climb up notched tree trunks on to the roof terraces. The whole event reeks of forced welcomes and the manipulating power of money. And the impression of smiling French tourists hurling sweets at the naked children through the windows of the minibus (an established ritual) is hard to stomach. Yet the same crowd left *bic* biros and enthusiasm in the primary school at Bolé. If you're not set up for independent travel well off the beaten track between Kafolo and BOUNA (the Lobi heartland), then the four-hour tour is probably worthwhile. Take a Polaroid camera if you can.

The **heartland of the Lobi region** in Côte d'Ivoire lies to the north of the Bouna road (the people and their style and culture are covered in more depth in Part Five, "Burkina Faso"). At the park ranger post at TEHINI, try for a vehicle on a Wednesday, or early Thursday morning up to DOROPO, whose Thursday market and location on a crossroads close to the Burkinabe border make it a major rural centre. The time to get the most out of a trip up here would be the *Djoro* – the movable initiation of boys to men which takes place every six to ten years for all the uninitiated boys who are big enough to stand the rigours (and whose parents don't want to wait another six years or more). The rites of passage are fairly secret, but there's no mystery about the celebration that concludes them, when the boys return home decked in cowrie-covered costumes.

Bouna and beyond

BOUNA, although very much a workaday Koulango town, suffers and benefits from being the country's remotest outpost. Not only chokingly dusty in the dry season but so muddy in the wet it's almost cut off, Bouna has never quite recovered from the savagery of Samory Touré's full frontal assault in 1892. Today it's a garrison town and capital of the country's biggest *département*. Bush taxis pull into the central *place* surrounded by single-storey shops and *gargotes*. There seems to be just the one **hotel**, the *Eléphant*, bang in the centre, only a few years old, clean, fresh and not unreasonable (CFA5000/7000 S/C, AC). Also on the plus side, Bouna's permanent **market** is busy and interesting and offers a lot of unusual trinketry and magical paraphernalia as well as the usual pots and pans and a rather limited selection of fruit and vegetables (seasonal commodities this far north).

If you're staying for a day, there are some particularly good examples of Lobi architecture at **POUON**, 18km northeast of Bouna. You should be able to get transport there several times a week, or charter a taxi. But you won't make it across the Koulda river (tributary of the Volta Noire) in the rainy season – and even if you do, you might not get back again.

South from Bouna, the road along the eastern boundary of the Comoé park (transport to Bondoukou every morning for around CFA3000) passes through desolate regions cleared of human inhabitants. Run-down and abandoned Lobi *soukalas* seem to indicate mass migration or expulsion from the area. This was the dry season, however: perhaps many people were away on Lobi business. Traditionally the Lobi were quite nomadic, returning to their homesteads only periodically. Between the park ranger posts at BANIA and KOUOUBA, however, the road tracks dustily through wild bush, with never a compound.

Continuing south, the desolation of the far northeast is left behind. Beyond the village of SALEYE, the land begins to rise and the road passes through fine, hilly forest and dense cultivation on the approach to Bondoukou. On the east side of the road, some 10km beyond YÉZIMALA, a group of impressive **Abron tombs**, inhabited by life-size plaster figures, signals the start of a new cultural zone. If you're coming in by public transport, Bondoukou's northside *gare routière* is just a few minutes beyond here.

Bondoukou

Set amid rising hills which hint at the forests further south, **BONDOUKOU** has a distinctive flavour, a long-established centre of Islamic studies with an old Koranic university and now some forty mosques. The town is also heavily infiltrated by Ghanaians (not altogether unexpectedly if you've just come from Ghana, but more of a surprise otherwise) who, along with the culturally related Abron community, help to knock off some of the Ivoirian brashness and also provide strong alternative religious counterpoints to the town's Islam. Despite its dust (or mud) and a real shortage of decent places to stay, it's a likeable town and worth a day or two.

Practical matters

Arrivals by transport from the north, or Ghana, are dampened by the fact that the respective *gares routières* are well out of the town centre and you have to pay again for a ride of several kilometres by orange taxi. From Abidjan and the south, however, the transport park is dead *centreville*.

Accommodation options are strictly limited. Best in purely functional terms is the *Hôtel Mont Zanzan* (BP 132; ☎92 54 14), atop the hill of the same name on the north side of town, about thirty minutes' walk from the centre. The pool is usually empty and the whole place is beginning to look shabby, but at CFA7500/room (S/C, AC) it could be worse. In town, the choice seems to rest between two basic *maisons de passage – La Bahia* (sometimes spelled *Baya*) and *Hôtel Nord Est. La Bahia* is slightly more respectable, but note that the AC rooms are scruffier than the simple ventilated ones

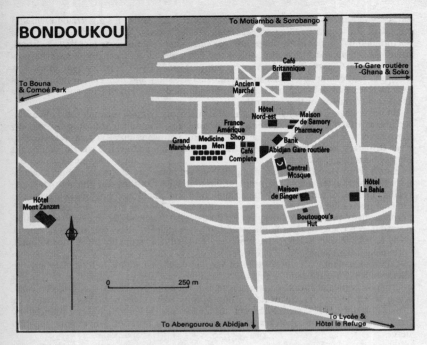

BONDOUKOU

To Motiambo & Sorobango

To Bouna & Comoé Park

Café Britannique

To Gare routière -Ghana & Soko

Ancien Marché

Hôtel Nord-est

Maison de Samory

France-Amérique Shop

Pharmacy

Grand Marché   Medicine Men

Bank

Abidjan Gare routière

Café Complete

Central Mosque

Maison de Binger

Hôtel La Bahia

Hôtel Mont Zanzan

Boutougou's Hut

0   250 m

To Abengourou & Abidjan

To Lycée & Hôtel le Refuge

(CFA2500–4000 S/C) and the place is a real thrash at weekends. As for the *Nord-Est*, it's pretty dismal but at least centrally located and cheap (CFA2500/room). Lastly, you could check out the *Complexe Hôtelier Le Refuge*, right out of town on the southern side, near the *lycée*. But it's hard to see what might draw you apart from TV and videos in the S/C AC rooms (CFA7000). The unappealing ordinary rooms go for CFA4000.

As for **eating**, Bondoukou offers plenty of street food, but nothing more sophisticated for a sit-down meal than a few *maquis* (unless you count the gloomy restaurant at the *Mont Zanzan*). Try the *Café Britannique* on the road to the Ghana *autogare*. Agriculturally this is a lively region and there's a good variety of produce; the central *place* beneath the pretty main mosque turns into a kind of street salad market every evening around sunset. For a good *café complet*, patronise the shack on the corner across from the *Shell* station. And for really cold beer visit the *France Amérique* grocery store, just along from here towards the *grand marché*.

The market

The best day to visit the **marché** is Sunday, when people come from the dozens of farming villages in the hills around to do their stuff. For the rest of the week the market, though imposing in its purpose-built two-storey hall, is like any other. Well, not like any other in *West Africa*. It's full of the most amazing selection of secondhand clothes. You might not be scouring West Africa for a pair of *Benetton* trousers, but you can find them here, hardly worn, and hardly any cheaper than brand new in London.

Nearby, there are some interesting traditional "pharmacists" (**medicine men** is probably a fair term), whose stalls overflow with a cornucopia of python skins, baby crocodile and viper heads, dried chameleons, baboons' feet (the big clawed hands), shrivelled bats, hideous hyenas' genitals, skins of countless small mammals, turtle shells, bones, tails, tufts, feathers and beaks; and then leather *grigris*, amulets, bracelets, beads, bark, fibres, stones, crystals and powders. They even have old British coins (Victorian shillings, for example) from Gold Coast days. But these traders rarely speak French, and bargaining with tourists isn't their strong point.

Bondoukou buildings and history

For a serious appreciation of Bondoukou – if you've time and preferably a good command of French – go and see M. Jacques Verrier (BP 63 Bondoukou) at the big corner pharmacy. A Frenchman with an immense and infectious enthusiasm for Africa, he's usually delighted to fill travellers in on places of local interest. If you hit it off, and preferably have your own wheels, you might arrange to do a trip with him.

Architecturally, Bondoukou's most striking attribute is the pink **ancien marché** building, in the centre of town and exotically in view all the way up the long straight approach road from Abidjan. Enquiries about it are disappointing, however. It was built in the colonial *style soudanais* by the French in 1952, and it's currently under consideration as the site of a civic museum.

The town has enough historical interest to support the endeavour. Track down the **Maison de Samory** (yet another) which was not actually one of the leader's abodes, but was inhabited by a fellow Touré. It has a massive, fortress-like appearance and a flat roof, reached up a flight of steep stairs (watch your step). Below, in the street, **metal workers** turn out bracelets and rings for local consumption – painstaking and surprisingly earnest labour.

Other surviving historical fragments are the **Maison de Binger**, a Mali-style *banco* house with characteristic saw-tooth roof edges and window slits like radioactivity symbols, where the French explorer stayed during his 1888 Indénié expedition. There's also the hut of **Goudougou** or Boutougou, a curious mud *case* in a large

BONDOKOU IN HISTORY

Whatever the real date of the first settlement here (probably in the fifteenth century), the **mosques** began to be built quite a lot later with the arrival in the seventeenth century of Mande-speaking Dyula from the north. Few of today's are older than the turn of this century and many have gone up since World War II, as the town's **old quarters**, each with its own **gate** and built entirely in the style of the Touré house, have been progressively replaced by concrete and *tôle*. (At one time, there was even a cloth-dyers quarter, with dye pits and all). The oldest surviving mosque in town is the one with a square minaret, a portion of which stands behind its modern-day descendant in a slumped lateritic pyramid, like a termite hill. This relic goes back to the eighteenth century and may be the last of the mosques of the Dyula era.

Around this time, Akan-speaking people – the **Abron** – began arriving from the east. With some administrative and military efficiency they succeeded in establishing themselves as the region's overlords. Unusually, however, many families adopted **Islam** and the language of the Koulango inhabitants. The Abron kingdom is one of the most Islamicised and deracinated of all the Akan societies.

By the end of the nineteenth century, **King Ardjoumani** of the Abron was in contact with the rulers of the British Gold Coast (flushed with their victory over the Asante – see p.850). But the French, as usual, were quicker to take the initiative, and they entered into agreement with the Abron and later annexed the kingdom for France. Meanwhile, **Samory Touré**'s gale-force transit through Bondoukou in 1895 largely wrecked the district's economic stability; thousands of families fled east and south out of his way. Bondoukou never fully recovered its pre-eminent position, and was left in the economic wilderness by its proximity to the British frontier and the new **railway**, which had reached as far as Bouaké by 1912 and which sucked trade away.

fenced compound down below the Abidjan *gare de voitures*. Goudougou, the semi-mythical founder of Bondoukou, was a Lobi or Loron-Koulango hunter. The hut, according to Bondoukou civic tradition, has been preserved to this day.

Out of town
The **tombs of Abron notables** (mentioned earlier at the end of the Bouna section) are worth a taxi ride out of town to see. But there are several worthwhile **short excursions** in the surrounding countryside.

Most famous is the village of **SOKO**, right on the Ghanaian border, 8km from Bondoukou. Soko is a monkey village, where the local vervets are especially tame and demanding and nobody harms them – much less eats them. The story goes that in 1895, with Samory's forces ransacking the district, the people of Soko turned to their fetish priest for help in escaping a massacre. He transformed them into monkeys but he himself was killed by the invaders and the monkeys were powerless to become humans again. Tradition requires that the people of Soko now treat the monkeys as their relatives. It's interesting to guess at how such a story came to be invented: the likeliest explanation is that most of the inhabitants fled the village, or were killed or sold into slavery, and the pride of survivors demanded an alternative explanation.

If you're coming to Soko you must have your passport, as you have to go through part of the border control. Take some food for the monkeys as well. The best time is early morning.

In the northeasterly direction out of Bondoukou, **MOTIAMBO** (8km on the SOROBANGO road, turn right at the "lion house") is a good village to visit for local pottery. A big funeral was going on here when we arrived, so the potters weren't potting and intrusion was not in order. But the potting technique is the great thing; work is done by hand, not on a wheel, and they *dance* around the work to fashion it. Potting is generally done on Wednesday and Thursday and firing on Friday in time for Bondoukou's Sunday market. If you go on to **SOROBANGO** (29km from Bondoukou), you'll find more potters, Koulango weavers, an old mosque and (somewhere) plates embedded in the walls – an Islamic style rarely found in this part of Africa.

Akan country: Abengourou and beyond

Travelling from Bondoukou to ABENGOUROU you should try and get a front seat. It's a brilliant, twisting forest route and you'll see more of the amazing figurative Akan tombs. There's a fine set down on the left of the road (beyond a cemetery on the right) as you leave the village of APROMPRONOU, 25km south of AGNIBILEKROU. Such precise details are worth having; if you have wheels, stop and look.

Abengourou

ABENGOUROU is solidly Akan – both culturally and linguistically. Royal capital of the **Agni** kingdom of **Indénié**, it's of the south, firmly engaged with metropolitan Côte d'Ivoire and, if you've come from sparser northern regions, offers a first taste of a big Ivoirian town.

The Agni left the Akan homeland around Kumasi in the eighteenth century and moved west to set up a new community with its capital at ZARANOU, 40km south of the present site. Abengourou seems to have been established by a part of the royal family about a hundred years ago in a zone of good hunting country they named *N'pekro* ("I don't like chatter") for its peacefulness, from which the present name was Frenchified. The current king of Indénié (the official title) is **Bonzou II**, who succeeded from his uncle, political heavyweight **Amoa Kon Dihié II**, in 1965.

Practicalities

To begin with, none of this royalty is very apparent. The town spreads widely, though its heart is compact. **Accommodation** is easy enough. The *Hôtel L'Indénié* (BP128; ☎91 31 59) has good doubles for around CFA8000 with shower, CFA9000 with bath and a CFA3000 menu (*plat* for CFA2000) – and the swimming pool is usually in order (but costs CFA1000 to use if you're not staying). Alternatively, the best value in town is the very central *Forêt* (☎51 36 16), on the main street (the *route principale d'Abidjan*), which has some rooms with balconies overlooking the action (doubles CFA3500 with fan, CFA6000 AC). There's a nightclub downstairs, a reasonable Chinese-Vietnamese restaurant and amiable staff, too. You can also go right downmarket with the *Hôtel Asi* between the market and the royal palace, which is riddled through with character and costs CFA2500 *jusqu'au matin*. Or try the *Hôtel Bezzerebla* in the Agnikro Nouveau Quartier.

Street **food** and *gargotes* are all over. Abengourou's market is great, a (never threatening) warren of tight-packed stalls and dark alleys and masses of possibilities if you're looking for crafts and locally manufactured items – from the smallest size of *daba* (digging hoe) forged virtually before your eyes to children's play-kitchen sets made of old tuna cans, and very cheap leatherwork.

Around town

The **royal palace** (built 1883, restored 1980, further restored 1988) is not far from the market and easily accessible. The house itself, a big oblong villa with wooden balconies running right round, isn't a splendid sight on its own. The large partially-covered courtyard in front, however, is the scene of serious ritual and festivity each year in December or January, when the **Yam Festival** (*la fête des ignames*) takes place and astonishing quantities of gold and finery are on display. And at any time you really can arrange **audiences with the old king**. It's preferable, if you want to do this, to have a day or two in hand to make an appointment, to dress as smartly as circumstances allow, and to take something as a gift: postcards of other royal families (English, Dutch, Danish, Spanish?) seem appropriate and welcome but a bottle of Scotch goes down well. If the king is in, the best time for an audience is usually between noon and 3pm.

Abengourou's other site of interest is the **museum/art gallery** (Mon–Sat 8am–noon and 3–6pm, Sun 8am–2pm) near the *Hôtel Indénié*. Run by a French husband and wife foundation (Charles and Marguerite Bieth), this has ambitions to be an important regional showcase, and certainly some money has been invested. But the utter banality of putting masks and statues around a room strikes forcibly. Out of context they lose most of their meaning. Many of the pieces need some woodworm treatment anyway. Most interesting of the ethnographia are the Senoufo crime detection statuettes with headdresses and swivelling arms for seeking out culprits, though it's not quite clear how they worked.

Many of the paintings derive from the art school which the foundation runs across the way. Most are uninspiring and many appear to be copies, but some of the "naïf" works are more absorbing, with interesting details.

Onwards from Abengourou

Heading to Abidjan, scheduled buses of several companies leave all day from the main bus station (4hr). Having bought your ticket, you can wait in a waiting room with a television for the next departure.

Since the road was tarmacked, the **alternative route**, via ABOISSO, is no longer much used except by local traffic. But if you make an early start from Abengourou, this dirt road, which stays on the east side of the Comoé close to the Ghanaian border, has some fine sights along its way in jungle scenery and the old Indénié capital of **ZARANOU**. If you've more time to make this trip down from Abengourou, you might think of spending a night here. There's a small museum, originally conceived as a memorial to Binger, who spent a total of three years in Zaranou.

The nice little town of Aboisso itself – site of France's earliest (*Louis quatorze;* late seventeenth century) base in the country – is also worth a stay. **KRINJABO**, 9km south of Aboisso on the Bia lagoon, is the capital of another Agni kingdom, **Sanwi**, whose king is often roped into packaged tourist-visit audiences. By all accounts he's as happy, if not more so, to meet independent travellers.

index

GHANA

GHANA

G **hana** was the first African country to retrieve its independence, in 1957. At the time it was one of the richest nations on the continent – the world's leading **cocoa** exporter and producer of a tenth of the world's **gold**. But since Kwame Nkrumah's optimistic start it has suffered a hornet's nest of setbacks. Repeated coups, food shortages and sapping corruption for years combined to make Ghana a place to be avoided.

No longer. Conditions have improved almost out of recognition since the terminal bottoming-out in 1979 and the country is firmly back on its feet and pursuing a vigorous course of IMF rehabilitation with the grudging approval of most Ghanaians – and so far with huge success as far as the international development agencies are concerned. From a traveller's point of view, this means low prices, but limited luxury.   Compared with the other Anglophone countries in West Africa, Ghana offers a **transport and accommodation** infrastructure that's second to none; a **cultural mix**, inevitably stressing the **Asante** nation's rich and vibrant lifestyle, that's every bit as rewarding as Nigeria's (without that country's immense size or intimidating reputation); and better **beaches** than The Gambia. The Ghana government has an enthusiastic commitment to tourism, with a number of regional tourist offices set up and plenty to engage visitors. Ghana also offers respite from the pervasive and sometimes touristy *Francophonie* of Mali, Togo and Côte d'Ivoire.

But visiting Ghana is by no means a compromise: this is a country with a distinctive personality and more claim to a **national character** than any other in the region. Ghana has had long contact with European cultural forms. School education has had a major impact, going back four generations now, and there's a high level of literacy and an inventiveness with language (both written on signs and in the press and spoken in repartee) that hints at a creativity as yet barely unleashed in Africa. Ghanaians are hospitable and generous to a fault and there's more warmth to be experienced in Ghana than in either of its coastal neighbours.

The country – and where to go

Ghana is compact and mostly flat. With the exception of the striking **scarp system** that curves through the country from the Gambaga escarpment in the northeast, round to the Wenchi scarp west of Lake Volta, and southeast as the Mampong scarp through the forest, there are few striking highland regions. But there are some attractive rolling green landscapes and, in the central regions, away from the **cocoa** plantations and the **goldfields**, several large districts of dense **rainforest** with giant hardwoods and palms vying for space. The biggest impact, however, is made by the enormous stretch of **Lake Volta**, an artificial lake created in the wooded savannah in 1966, which has totally

---

GHANAIAN STATISTICS

Known as the **Gold Coast** during the colonial era, **Ghana** took its present name from the former West African empire far to the northwest with which it has only legendary connection. With a **population** of around 15 million and an **area** of 240,000 square kilometres – about the same size as Britain – Ghana is one of the region's most densely populated states. The foreign debt stands at around £2 billion – for some sense of scale, that's just half Britain's annual expenditure on armaments research. Since 1981, Ghana has been led by the Provisional National Defence Council, with Flight-Lieutenant Jerry Rawlings firmly at the controls.

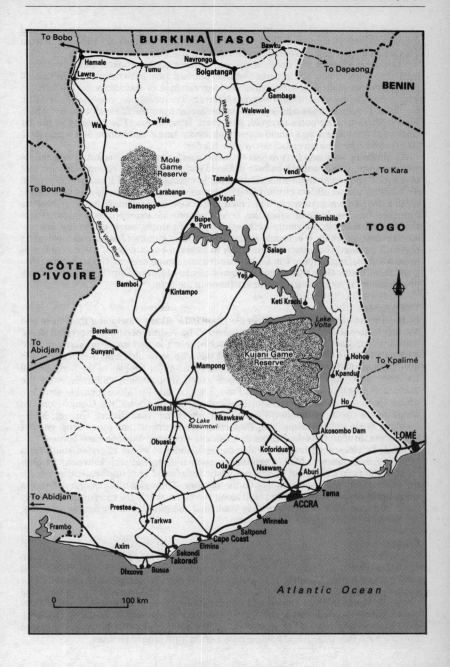

changed the anatomy of the country – not to mention the lives of the thousands of rural dwellers its waters displaced. In the east, the hills of the **Akwapim range** roll in from Togo to create a region of verdant green valleys and gentle peaks.

The **Accra district** and much of the surrounding bushy, **coastal plain** is surprisingly dry – almost desolate in parts – with an unusual local sub-climate, but the coastal road to the west runs at least within striking distance of the shore for much of its length and the beaches themselves are alluring. The coast has a special dimension, too, in its European **forts and castles**, some dating from the fifteenth century, which were built as trading posts for gold, ivory and, later, slaves. The beaches of the far southwest are backed by lowland forest and patchy jungle agriculture in a scene similar to most of the Ivoirian coastline over the border.

As to **where you go**, don't expect to spend much time in the capital **Accra**, unless you're drawn to the music clubs over the weekend and are lucky enough for your visit to coincide with some live shows. The capital is manageable, and friendly enough, but it's bustling and scruffy – a city tarnished by years of neglect that residents with means try to leave as often as possible. The **coast** to the west is exceptional, however, and the European **castles**, most of which can be visited, provide excellent focuses for beach-hopping. **Kumasi**, in the centre of the country, has a strong sense of identity, and the forest region of which it is capital is scenically and culturally Ghana's most appealing region. The **north** is quite different, both in landscape and people, but its climate is more tolerable and, if there's not a lot that demands to be seen as you pass through – apart from **Mole Game Reserve** – there's plenty of interest in the region's ethno-grapic history if you've more time or are based in the area.

The people

Of the myriad ethnic groups that people Ghana, the **Akan** – including the **Fante** and **Asante** (also spelled Ashanti) – predominate. The Asante occupy the central forest, and in pre-colonial days their empire stretched into the regions of present-day Côte d'Ivoire and Togo. The **Ga-Adangme** and **Ewe**, who probably came from Yorubaland in Nigeria, settled mainly in the east and south. The major peoples of the north are all speakers of Voltaic languages and share much in common, culturally, with the Burkinabe over the border in Burkina Faso. They include the More-speaking southern Mossi kingdoms of **Mamprusi** and **Dagomba** in the northeast, the **Gonja** (some of whom speak the Grusi tongue, Wagala, and others the Akan dialect, Guang), More-speaking **Wala** and Grusi-speaking **Dagarti** in the northwest, and other Grusi peoples – **Kassena**, **Frafra**, **Sissala**, **Builsa** and **Talensi** – near the Burkina Faso border.

Islam is widespread among the northerners, some of whom migrated south from Muslim communities in Mali. **Christianity**, of course, spread with European involvement in the Gold Coast, but non-monotheistic beliefs and ancestor veneration remain the most widely practised religions in the country. Throughout the country there's a remarkable degree of syncretism and, along the coast, you'll see extraordinarily decorated ancestor shrines, incorporating tradtional motifs as well as figures of Jesus, angels, djinns and more mundane icons.

Climate

Ghana has a lot more **climatic variation** than most of West Africa. Central and southern Ghana, south of Tamale, is unusual in having **two distinct rainy seasons**, the first lasting roughly from March to June and the second from September to October. The far southwest gets heavy rains, but Accra's tend to be light and day after day of torrential downpour is uncommon. The central rainforest regions tend to be wetter and slightly cooler (though you wouldn't know it because of the high humidity) and the north is basically hot and dry most of the year, with a climate much like that of Ouagadougou in Burkina Faso (see p.246), and a single rainy period from June to October.

AVERAGE TEMPERATURES AND RAINFALL

ACCRA

	Jan	Feb	Mar	Apr	May	June	July	Aug	Sept	Oct	Nov	Dec
Temperatures °C												
Min (night)	23	24	24	24	24	23	23	22	23	23	24	24
Max (day)	31	31	31	31	31	29	27	27	27	29	31	31
Rainfall mm	15	33	56	81	142	178	46	15	36	64	36	23
Days with rainfall	1	2	4	6	9	10	4	3	4	6	3	2

TAMALE

	Jan	Feb	Mar	Apr	May	June	July	Aug	Sept	Oct	Nov	Dec
Temperatures °C												
Min (night)	21	23	24	24	24	22	22	22	22	22	22	20
Max (day)	36	37	37	36	33	31	29	29	30	32	34	35
Rainfall mm	3	3	53	69	104	142	135	196	226	99	10	5
Days with rainfall	1	1	1	6	10	12	14	16	19	13	1	1

Arrivals

Ghana is well connected and a good starting point for longer travels. Though it can
seem more of a bureaucratic hassle than
one or two of its Francophone neighbours,
you won't be constantly asked for identity
papers. The deplorable state of roads in the
early 1980s fostered a bad image, but they
are much improved of late. Travelling on the
north-south axis, however, still takes longer
than through Togo or Côte d'Ivoire.

■ Flights from Africa

From other parts of West Africa, Accra can be
reached by direct flights from **Abidjan** (daily on
Ghana Airways, Air Afrique or *Swissair*);
Conakry (4 flights a week); **Cotonou** (3 a week);
Dakar (5 a week); **Freetown** (4 a week); **Lagos**
(daily); **Lomé** (2 a week); and **Monrovia** (daily).
Most flights are with *Ghana Airways*.

Ethiopian Airlines provides the link with **East
Africa** with direct flights from **Nairobi** (once
weekly) and **Addis Ababa** (4 flights a week).
There are no direct flights from **North Africa**.

Ghana Airways flies every Monday night from
Harare, Zimbabwe.

■ Overland from Burkina Faso

Beware that the **Ghana embassy in
Ouagadougou** can be very unwilling to issue
visas to British passport holders resident in the
UK, who, they say, should get their visas in
London. Try to plan ahead or think creatively.

Roads are now reasonably good **from
Ouagadougou into Ghana**. Coming from the
Burkina capital, you have several possibilities:
taking a **bush taxi** or **bus** to the border at Paga,
or getting transport through to Navrongo,
Bolgatanga or direct to Accra. Going by bush taxi
you'll make better time on the road but the buses
are more comfortable and generally get through
the border and various checkpoints more quickly.
If you're lucky with connections, it can sometimes
work out cheapest and fastest to change transport at the border, which is generally amicable.

You can also cross between Léo and Tumu
and at Hamale. Transport is patchy on both sides
of the border, and there's no direct through transport to speak of in either case – your prospects
are much better on market days.

The **fast route to Accra** goes via Tamale,
Kintampo and Kumasi; the other route, involving

a Lake Volta ferry or canoe crossing between
Makongo and Yeji, is not practicable for cars.

■ Overland from Togo

The road from Lomé to Accra has recently been
re-surfaced. The quickest way between the two
capitals is by **bush taxi** but you'll save some
hassle if you first get yourself to the border on
the west side of Lomé, cross on foot, to Aflao and
then continue by bush taxi or bus. The border
closes at 6pm and, depending on relations
between the two countries, can sometimes be
rather a pain. It takes about three hours to Accra.

■ Overland from Côte d'Ivoire

The coastal stretch between Abidjan and Accra is
in good condition, and Ghanaian *STC* **buses** –
not to mention fleets of **bush taxis** – connect
the two capitals in a day. Buses leave from
Abidjan's Treichville quarter, near the hospital.
There's also a fast route direct to Kumasi via
Abengourou – a journey of identical length.

Red Tape

Visas are required by all non-
Commonwealth nationals. Commonwealth
citizens need an entry permit. Ghana visas,
valid for a maximum stay of one month, are
among the most expensive in West Africa,
costing CFA10,000 in most neighbouring
countries.

Entering the country, you will be asked how
long you plan on staying and your reply is noted
in your passport. If you say a week, that's your
limit, even if you have a one-month visa. It's wise
to get the longest possible stay, since extensions
are in practice only delivered in Accra and are
sometimes difficult to obtain. You'll also be
asked at the border for a Ghanaian address so
have a hotel in mind. Additionally, you'll be given
a form at the border which you must fill out and
submit (along with two passport photos) to the
Secretariat of Internal Affairs within 48 hours
of your arrival. At the Secretariat, you'll again be
asked your address and it should be the same
one you gave on entry. It all sounds intimidating
but Ghanaian bureaucracy is rarely transacted
without good humour.

International **certificates of vaccination**
are required for yellow fever (and sometimes
cholera) and are closely checked at the borders.

Another piece of paper to worry about is the T5, or **currency declaration form**. In theory, you must declare all your currency at the border and have the form stamped every time you change money. In practice, this form is often not checked when leaving the country and customs agents may forget to give it to you when you enter. Occasionally you'll still find it in use but it's likely to be ignored much of the time.

■ Visas for onward travel

Ghana's three neighbours issue **visas in Accra** as do most West African countries. For addresses and details see the Accra "Directory".

Health

Yellow fever vaccinations are required in Ghana. Cholera epidemics occur, especially in isolated regions with limited sources of clean water; you'd be well advised to get vaccinated for the disease as a precaution. Bilharzia is another concern; stay away from stagnant ponds or slow-running streams – especially in savannah areas. Lake Volta is notorious.

In large towns, **tap water** is always drinkable. In smaller places, and villages, the well or stored rain water isn't always the purest and you may want to try some combination of boiling (not always practical), filtering or adding purifying tablets.

Main **hospitals** are in Accra and Kumasi. Smaller hospitals and clinics can be found in towns throughout the country, but for a major medical problem you may prefer a private clinic. For a reference, consult an embassy.

Ghana has a surging **AIDS** problem, as much as – though presumably no more than – any other country in the region, with hundreds of cases reported and thousands of HIV carriers.

Maps and Information

There's not really any official tourist information supplied outside the country – though Ghana clearly needs some good PR to convince sceptics of its attractions and security. You can get to know the country quite well, however, through the detailed weekly coverage of *West Africa* magazine.

Map availability is dire, and you won't find any decent, up-to-date single sheets of the whole country. In Accra, the best place to find detailed regional and **national maps** is at the *Survey Office* (Cantonments, PO Box 191, Accra ☎77.73.31) on Giffard Road near the airport – the only place in the country with a dependable supply. They sell **town maps** for a number of places outside the capital. An Accra city map is available here, or you can get it free at the *KLM* office in town on Nkrumah Ave.

The *Ghana Tourist Board* has an office **in Accra** and a number of branches in larger towns throughout the country (Kumasi, Bolgatanga, Takoradi). A new office is supposed to be opening in Tamale. The tourist offices sometimes arrange organised tours, and can give you the latest information on transport and the possibility of visiting various regional sites.

Money and Costs

Ghana's currency is the cedi (₵). Formerly, one cedi was divided into 100 pesewas, but inflation long ago rose well past the point at which pesewas had any value. Even ₵10 notes are rare and the biggest bill is ₵500, which is worth less than £1. New ₵10 and ₵ 25 coins are likely to be introduced soon.

The official **exchange rate** (currently roughly ₵600 = £1) is set every week in an auction of foreign exchange in Accra. This has resulted in an annual inflation rate running at about 25 percent, but dropping. There is no black market.

In other countries market women tie up their money in their skirts, but in Ghana they keep it in huge plastic bags. You'll find yourself walking around with huge **wads of money** that don't add up to much. But don't destroy any – a tourist was recently fined ₵200,000 and jailed for a month for lighting a cigarette with a ₵100 note.

For changing money you'll find **foreign exchange (forex) bureaux** in Accra, Kumasi and other major towns, and new ones springing up all over the country, including Aflao on the Togo border. Shop around for the best rates; they offer around 10–20 percent more than the banks, not all of which change money anyway. **Cash US dollars** are the premium medium of exchange, with sterling and all travellers' cheques worth less. You can also buy hard currency from forex bureaux.

If you're stuck for a forex bureau the most likely banks are *Ghana Commercial Bank, Barclays* and *Standard Chartered*, which have branches pretty well throughout the country. **Banking hours** are Monday to Thursday 8.30am to 2pm, Friday until 3pm.

Credit cards are accepted in major hotels in Accra and Kumasi and at some travel agencies. Outside the main cities they won't get you far.

You can have **money sent to you** easily enough at the *Bank of Ghana*, Thorpe Road, Accra (PO Box 264; ☎66.69.02), through *Ghana Commercial Bank*, 69 Cheapside, London EC2P 2BB or *Midland Bank International*, 110–14, Cannon St, London EC4N 6AA.

■ Costs

Cedi devaluations make it difficult to gauge **costs** but in real terms prices have come down recently – even in Accra – to levels that are relatively low compared with neighbouring countries, making Ghana currently one of the cheapest countries in West Africa. **Accommodation** in Accra can run as low as ₵2000 and cheaper still in the interior. Prices are government-fixed and fairly steady in real terms. Although Ghanaians find even street **food** expensive on their salaries, it will seem cheap enough to you – staples like *kenkey* and fish, for example, run ₵300 or less. The other major cost, **transport**, is also cheaper in Ghana than surrounding countries, especially if you travel by *State Transport Corporation* buses.

Getting Around

The government has recently made an effort to improve a transportation system that was sinking into a miserable state. They've re-surfaced roads, bought new trains and expanded the country's now highly efficient bus service. Buses, in fact, are the most convenient means of travelling round the country and you'll find them a real luxury after the battered bush taxis you may have grown accustomed to using elsewhere.

■ Buses

The *State Transport Corporation*'s **coach service** provides the cheapest and most hassle-free way to get around the country with a minimum of waiting at roadside checkpoints. They service all towns of any size and the buses are safe, comfortable and run on fixed schedules – a welcome relief if you've been travelling widely and become used to spending hours waiting in motor parks for vehicles to fill with passengers. It's always a good idea to book seats in advance with *STC*, especially if you're heading for popular destinations like Accra, Kumasi or Tamale. The State Transport yard in each town usually adjoins the main motor park. In some parts you'll also find *Omnibus Services Authority* (*OSA*) buses operating alongside. Remember, they're all now non-smoking.

■ Bush taxis and *tro-tros*

Minibuses (*tro-tros*) and **Peugeot 504s** ("caravans") are less comfortable than the coaches, but they leave more frequently and travel faster. They're notoriously overloaded in Ghana and, if you're out to enjoy the ride, should be used only if you're not going far or can't get on a bus. Worse than the bush taxis are the **lorries**, or mammy wagons, which you'll only want to consider as a last resort. These squeeze as many people as can possibly fit onto wooden planks in a boarded-up truck. You'll see nothing on the way and collect lots of bruises to boot.

It's useful to know that a 1990 safety ban on minibuses driving beyond a **30km radius** of their home town has resulted in greater pressure on the government bus services. If you're using bush taxis to hop from A to B, be sure you know where you'll be dropped. Upper West Region, the capital of which is Wa, has recently abandoned the ban as *STC* couldn't meet long-distance needs.

■ Trains

Trains are the cheapest way of travelling and, since the government bought new rolling stock in the 1980s, they're actually quite comfortable. As a Peace Corps volunteer summed it up, "Trains in

Ghana are great when they don't derail!" You shouldn't rule out this eventuality. The three main lines run from **Accra to Takoradi**, from **Accra to Kumasi**, and from **Kumasi to Takoradi**. Unfortunately, the Accra–Takoradi line bypasses the coast and most of the interesting stone castles. In terms of scenery, therefore, the road is better along this stretch. On the other hand, the beaten-up condition of roads through the forest between Takoradi and Kumasi makes rail the best mode of transport direct from the coast to the Asante country.

There's an average of at least one service per day on each route (often overnight), with first-class sleeper fares around ₵2000.

■ Planes

Ghana Airways connects Accra with northern points like Kumasi, Tamale and Sunyani. Schedules change frequently, but there are daily flights to Kumasi and Tamale and twice weekly to Sunyani. Students get a 25 percent discount through *SYTAG* (see Accra "Directory"). All internal flights are non-smoking.

■ Other forms of transport

You can cover a good deal of the country by boat, as a Lake Volta **ferry service** links the southern town of Akosombo with various ports in the north. En route, the ferry calls at Kpandu and Keti-Krachi. There are more departures than those listed at the Ghana Tourist Board in Accra, since besides the temperamental passenger service, cargo vessels also make the trip. For current information, check at the hotel in Akosombo. The trip takes two to three days but the scenery is not as exciting as you might expect – long stretches of dead tree trunks sticking up through flooded landscapes.

Outlets for **car hire** are still limited, though Accra has a number of possibilities, including some licensed outlets for the big international groups. Driving in a hired car, or **your own vehicle**, Ghana's roads are improving all the time (though there's a lot still to be done in the north) and **fuel** is cheap – the price recently rose to around ₵400 a gallon (5 litres) for petrol and diesel.

Lastly, Ghana is a good country for **cycling**, offering a moderate scale (two weeks or less from north to south), immense scenic variety and minimal endurance requirements – if you start in the north it's all basically downhill.

Sleeping

Although luxury accommodation is rare in Ghana (a fact that stands out if you're arriving from Côte d'Ivoire), major towns have decent hotels – run by the government or privately – which are in general comfortable if lacking in conveniences. Running water and AC can be had in most places, but may only work sporadically. Added to your bill is a ten percent state hotel tax, included in our estimates of room prices. Special mention should be made of the handful of forts along the coast which have been converted to rest houses. They offer exceptionally cheap and characterful accommodation, though they have limited space so are often full in high season. Cape Coast Museum and SYTAG in Accra – see p.839 – may help with bookings.

■ Staying with people

Travellers are still comparatively rare in the country, especially in the north. Ghanaians are generally curious to meet you, and if you're on your own, you may be surprised how many offers you get to **stay with people**. (For organised home stays, see p.8.) It can be rewarding, especially since they are generally prompted by a sincere interest and sense of hospitality. You should be extremely conscious, however, when accepting such offers, of the expense your stay imposes, and be aware that even for salaried government workers a bottle of beer may be a luxury they rarely treat themselves to. Be as generous as your host; pay at the cinema, bars or discos, and, if you go to the market together, pay for the food. Ghana's **cost of living** is incredibly high relative to local wages (in 1990, the daily minimum wage could only buy two eggs) and most people are barely scraping by, and generally doing so outside the money economy.

■ Camping

If you have your own transport, of course, you have the freedom of getting off the beaten tracks to many of the small towns and villages where accommodation doesn't even exist. **Camping** is feasible in the bush, though in practice it's most pleasant in the north, beyond the damp forest zone. In villages ask the chief if and where you can spend the night, and he'll make the arrangements.

Eating and Drinking

In southern Ghana, the most common staple by far is *kenkey* – fermented maize flour balls, steamed and wrapped in maize leaves. You'll see it in markets everywhere. The sour taste takes a while to acquire, and you don't often get much sauce to help it down – just a splash of ground tomatoes, onions and peppers and deep fried fish. But it does, eventually, taste good. In the north, *TZ* (or *tozafi*) takes over – a mush made from millet (occasionally maize) flour, and commonly eaten with palm nut or okra soup.

Plantains are used a lot in Ghanaian cooking and, together with beans, groundnuts, rice, fresh and dried fish, guinea fowl (especially in the north) and grasscutter (the large, tasty rodent hunted mainly in the south), supply the basis of one of West Africa's best national cuisines.

If you're adventurous, there are other flavours, including clay-baked **lizard** (in Dagomba country; the skin comes off with the clay) and giant forest **snails** – even rat, cat and dog.

Ghana has a lot of good **chocolate**, available everywhere and not expensive, but it's not popular with Ghanaians. The country's outstanding fruit is the **pineapple** – notably along the coast

– and this is the cheapest part of West Africa to buy them. **Coconuts**, too, are terrifically cheap and surprisingly good for you.

■ Drinking

Ghana was the first West African country to possess a brewery and it now has a wide range of beers. One of the most popular, perhaps because it's also got the highest alcohol content, is **Gulder**. Other brands include **Star** (a personal favourite and great encouragement at times during this research), **ABC**, **Club** and bottled **Guiness**. Non-alcoholic **minerals** include the usual *Coke* and *Fanta* varieties. **Refresh** comes in orange and pineapple and, with 25 percent juice, it's not bad. A more acquired taste is **Supermalt**, dark and sugary with a burnt caramel flavour. Homemade drinks include **Taka Beer** (a ginger drink) and **Ice Kenkey** – sweetened, fermented maize flour in water, a taste you may not acquire. **Pito** is the millet-based beer commonly drunk, from shared bowls, in the north. As you'd expect, it varies greatly but it's not hard to get a liking for. In the south, the favourite local brews are naturally fermented **palm wine** (known in Akan as *ntunkum* when it's fresh and low in alcohol and *nsa* when it's winey) and **akpeteshie**, a potent firewater, also called "VC10" or "Kill-me-quick".

GHANIAN FOOD TERMS AND DISHES

Abenkwan	Palm nut soup (Akan)	*Koko*	Corn or millet porridge with milk and sugar
Aduane	Food (Akan)		
Akawadu	Banana (Akan)	*Kontumbre*	Cocoyam leaves
Akokoh	Chicken (Akan)	*Kyinkyinga*	Beef with vegetable sauce (Hausa)
Amadaa	Fried, ripe plantain (Ga)		
Ampesi	Plantain and yam mash	*Kokonte*	Cassava meal (Akan)
Banku	Corndough, good with groundnut soup	*Momone*	Sun-dried fish (Akan)
		Nsuomnam	Fish (Akan)
Boflot	Doughnut (north)	*Nuhuu*	Cocoyam porridge (Akan)
Borode (kokoo)	(Ripe) plantain (Akan)	*Ode*	Yam (Akan)
Borodo	Bread (Akan)	*Omo tuo*	Mashed rice balls with soup or stew, usually served Sundays only (also written *Emo* or *Amo tuo*)
Ekwei bemi	Boiled, sweetened corn kernels		
Enam	Meat (Akan)		
Fufu	Yam mash		
Gari	Cassava flour	*Rice water*	Rice pudding, often for breakfast
Gari foto	Gari dish, mixed with palm oil and other ingredients		
		Shito	Pepper soup (Ga)
Kalawule	Spicy fried ripe plantain with stew	*Suya*	Small shish kebab
		Tatare	Ripe plantain, pounded and fried
Klaklo	Ripe plantain dough, deep-fried	*TZ (Tozafi)*	Millet mush (north)
Khosay	Bean cakes (north)	*Waachi*	Rice and red beans

Communications: Post, Phones, Language and Media

Ghana's postal services are inexpensive and relatively efficient to Europe. Letters take a week to ten days to Britain and slightly longer to North America, although to neighbouring West African countries they can take up to two months! Postal pilfering used to be a problem, but has lately been heavily censured and is now much improved.

Accra's poste restante service is free and reliable. Telephones, on the other hand, are pretty bad. No matter where you ring from your call must

MAIN TELEPHONE CODES	
Accra – no code required	Kumasi – 051
Bolgatanga – 072	Takoradi – 031
Cape Coast – 042	Tamale – 071

pass through Accra, and you can literally take days to get through. There's now a handful of new card-operated public phones, in Accra. International direct dialling was due to become operational from these by the end of 1990.

■ Languages

Ghana's official language is English and you can use it without much trouble throughout the coun-

TWI PHRASE LIST

Twi, pronounced somewhere between "Twee" and "Chooi", is the name commonly given to the language of the Asante and Fante people. It's a difficult tongue to master, with a complex tonal system – and anyway most people you meet will have some English – but a few words and phrases in Twi always go down well. Note that it's usually written with the somewhat impenetrable orthography mentioned above, but we've gone for a simple transliteration that should sound okay.

GREETINGS

Hello, you are welcome	*A kwaaba*	Good evening	*Mma adjo*
Response	*Yaa*	Response	*Ye Muu*
Good morning	*Mma ache*	Anyone home?	*Ebi wo fie?*
Good afternoon	*Mma aha*		

BASIC CONVERSATION

How are you?	*Wo o te sen?*	Thankyou	*Meda ase*
I'm fine	*Me ho ye*	Response (you're welcome)	*Mme enna ase*
Come here (children)	*Bra*	Do you speak English (lit. white language)?	*Wote Borofo anna?*
Go away (kids again)	*Koh*		
Yes	*Aan*	I don't understand	*Mnta se*
No	*Dabe*	I'm married	*Ma ware*
Please (lit. I beg you)	*Me pawocheo*	(Please) give me water	*Ma me nsuo*
What's your name?	*Ye ferew sen?*	I want/like	*Me pe*
My name is	*Ye fere me*	I am not well	*Me nti apoh*
Where do you come from?	*Wo fri he?*	I'm hungry	*E komdeme*
I come from	*Me fri*		

TRAVEL

I'm going	*Me ko*	Today	*Enne*	Yesterday	*Enrah*	Lorry	*Lore*
We're going	*Ye ko*	Tomorrow	*Echina*	Tonight	*Annajoh*	Bus stop	*Bossogyinabea*

NUMBERS

1	*Biako*	7	*Asong*	30	*Aduasa*	500	*Ahannum*
2	*Abieng*	8	*Awotwe*	40	*Aduanang*, etc	600	*Ahansia*
3	*Abiesa*	9	*Akrong*	100	*Oha*	700	*Ahansong*
4	*Anang*	10	*Du*	200	*Ahannu*	800	*Ahangwotwe*
5	*Anum*	11	*Dubiako*, etc	300	*Ahasa*	900	*Ahangkron*
6	*Asia*	20	*Aduonu*	400	*Ahannang*	1000	*Apem*

GHANAIAN TERMS – A GLOSSARY

Adinkra Cotton, funeral cloth with printed black symbols worn by Akan mourners.

Agbada Large embroidered robe, usually white, worn on special occasions.

Akan The language that includes dialects spoken by the Fante and the Asante.

Asante Standard spelling of the Kumasi-based ethnic group.

Ashanti Popular European spelling and name of the administrative region.

Burglar Means rip-off artist in general, including con-merchant.

Chop Food, or "to eat".

Colo Ingratiating, "colonial" behaviour.

Concert party Popular entertainment that started in the villages. When people couldn't afford to go to clubs, they began "concert parties" with a theatrical performance – usually humorous – and highlife music.

Dash From Portuguese for to give, it means a gift or bribe. It can also function as a verb as in "How much you dash me?"

Durbar Not the horse rally of northern Nigeria, this is the occasion that climaxes traditional festivals when chiefs receive distinguished guests.

ERP Economic Recovery Programme.

Ghana Ancient Ghana was based in what's now southeast Mauritania. It never reached the borders of modern Ghana.

Highlife "Big Band Highlife" is Ghana's best-known dance music form, but Ghanaians use the term to refer to a much broader range of music which is no more homogenous than, say, rock.

How be? Common greeting meaning "How are you?"

Kalabule Corruption and palm greasing.

Kente Multi-coloured, woven strip fabric, sometimes silk, made by the Asante.

Kotoko Porcupine, symbol of the Asante. The animal's countless sharp quills stand for boundless Asante bravery, reflected in the saying "Kill a thousand porcupines and a thousand more will come" (*Kotoko wokum apem, apem beba*).

Obroni wawu Imported second-hand clothes (lit. "A white man has died").

Oware The game of pebbles and holes (see p.34).

Paa "Very", for example "It's expensive, paa", very expensive.

PDC People's Defence Committees – regional political bodies designed by Rawlings to increase local participation and awareness.

PNDC Provisional National Defence Council – governing body founded and currently chaired by Rawlings.

Posu Ancestor shrine.

Silly Pejorative term implying an insult to one's intelligence – stronger term than in Britain.

Tro-tro Collective taxis, usually lorries, derived from the Akan for "Three pesewas, three".

Wee Marijuana.

Weeding, or Weeding-off, is the collective grave-tending ceremony that takes place some time after a funeral.

---

try, although you'll likely need a period of adjustment before completely understanding the broader **pidgin** accents. If English is not your first language, you might be misunderstood.

The two main language "families" into which Ghanaian languages fall are Kwa in the south and Voltaic to the north.

The great **Twi** group of Kwa languages and dialects includes **Akan**, spoken by the Asante and Fante, **Ewe**, the traditional language of the Accra region, spoken in the southeast (see box in Part Sixteen, "Togo" practicalities section), and **Ga**, or Ga-Adangme. Important Voltaic languages include the big **More** (or Mole) cluster – including **Dagomba** and **Mamprusi** – and various **Grusi** tongues, **Frafra** and **Nunumba** among them.

A number of Ghanaian languages have long been written with unfamiliar **orthography** and you'll see satisfyingly exotic-looking spellings used in many hand-painted signs; a curly backward "c" (pronounced "o" as in "cost"); a backward "3" (pronounced "e" as in "men"); an "n" with a tail (pronounced "ng" as in "sing"); and a Y with a looped stem (pronounced as a very soft "h").

■ Media

Ghana has an established and respected press, but for much of the independent era its freedom has been severely curtailed. However, press freedom is currently improving and there are dozens of weekly or monthly magazines and reviews, most of them light.

The main **newspapers** are the *People's Daily Graphic*, the *Ghanaian Times* and the critical Kumasi-based *Pioneer*. They stick fairly close to the government line (*Graphic* and *Times* are both government-owned), but often have interesting coverage of national and regional events. International news is barely scratched by them, but the *Graphic's* "Tit Bits" column is a bizarre collection of snippets from around the world – worth the price of the paper alone.

As for **foreign press**, there's normally a small selection of British papers available at Accra airport and the posher hotels, and *West Africa* magazine, which provides probably the best regular coverage of the country in English, is always on sale.

There's colour **TV** broadcasting and three state-owned GBC **radio** stations, plus an external service in French and English. GBC FM plays current pop and covers news and the social scene.

Entertainment

Ghana has a satisfying cultural life, with theatre, cinema and especially music all accessible. If you're in Accra in June, you'll catch notice of the annual Entertainment Critic and Reviewers Association of Ghana awards.

Theatre

Although a national theatre is being set up, and the School of Performing Arts at Legon University produces no shortage of talent and occasional staged productions in Accra, the more traditional, "Concert Party" form is the type of light social comment musical-comedy-drama you're most likely to come across. *Akpeteshie* is the drink and the party typically goes on all night. Many itinerant bands cover the village and small town circuit. You might get a taste, if you can't attend a show, by tracking down a Concert Party cassette, like the one by the stand-up comic "Waterproof" (on the local *"Q" Production* label).

Cinema

Ghanaian **cinema** has a wealth of unexplored potential (there's talent in the wings, held back by financial constraints, and more in exile, held back for different reasons), but you're still more likely to get a helping of Bond or Stallone than something from top Ghanaian director **Kwaw**

Ansah. Video shows, in any case, are fast taking over from fleapit cinemas. There's more background in the "Film" piece in *Contexts*.

Music

While Ghana is famous for **highlife**, the country has an active tradition of **rural music and dance** that continues to influence urban sounds. Look out for forthcoming shows by groups like the award-winning **Ntiri Buoho Nwonkoro** and **Upper East Buzio Group**.

Although "big band" highlife declined in 1970s with the frequency of coups, curfews and power cuts, these technical problems didn't really affect guitar highlife which can still be heard all over. Concert parties and, delightfully, **gospel highlife**, took off in the 1970s and are still thriving.

Many "name" stars migrated to Europe, but especially to Nigeria, where they've kept a highlife spark burning. Those currently based in Ghana include **Kwame Ampadu and the African Brothers**, still one of the nation's top electric guitar bands after nearly three decades, **Daniel ("Koo Nimo") Amponsah** and his "palm wine", "Afro-Spanish", accoustic **Adadam Band**, the irrepressible **Alex Konadu** – a gig of whose you might catch just about anywhere in the country – and the almost dangerously popular **C.K. Mann**, whose 1989 song "Adjoa Yankey" got banned from the airwaves by the GBC because its title, associated with a popular type of batik cloth, was taken up as a jeer by traders in other kinds of fabric to ridicule those wearing batik. Strange, but true.

Some of the other prominent names in Ghanaian music, at home and abroad, are given more space in the music feature section in *Contexts* at the back of the book.

Look out for the weekly *Hit Parade* magazine if it's still being published.

The Ghanaian Year: Holidays and Festivals

The main Christian and Muslim holidays are celebrated in Ghana, though the impact of Islam is patchy and strongest in the northwest. Shops and businesses also close down for Independence Day (March 6), Revolution Day (June 4), Republic Day (July 1), and the Anniversary of the Second Revolution (December 31).

THE GHANAIAN FESTIVAL YEAR

In addition to the official public holidays, many **regional celebrations** or festivals (*afahye* in Twi) animate the country throughout the year. Dates often vary. This **selective listing** covers most of the country but there are very many more. Note that dates are approximate in most cases and, in some, the local name of the occasion just means "festival".

FESTIVAL (DATE)	LOCALITY
JANUARY	
Kwafie (early)	Berekum
Ntoa Fokuokese (10th)	Nkoranza, west of Ejura, Ashanti Region
Kpini-Kyiu (22nd)	Wa, Upper West Region
Danso Abaim Afahye (end)	Techiman, 130km north of Kumasi
Tengbana	Tongo, Upper East Region
Jimbenti A period of purification and pacification of the gods. An all-day festival, *Jimbenti* ends at sunset when burning sticks are thrown into the eastern sky to scare away unknown demons.	Tumu (Sissala people)
Adae Kese Asante festival culminating in the purification of the ancestral stools.	Kumasi and other Asante towns
FEBRUARY	
Damba	Wa, Upper West Region
Amu Harvest festival including ritual *Asafo* dances and other cultural displays.	Vane Avatime near Ho, Volta Region
MARCH	
Kotokyikyi (first Friday)	Senya Beraku, west of Accra
Kyiu Sung (7th)	Throughout Upper West and Upper East
Golgu (around Easter)	Bolgatanga
Lalue Kpledo (10th)	Prampram, east of Accra
Ogyapa (end March, early April)	Senya Beraku
Sigi Sheep and chickens are slaughtered and *pito* offered to God through the ancestors in a thanksgiving and harvest celebration that includes drumming and dancing.	Navrongo
APRIL	
Dam and *Bugum* festivals	Tamale and around
Godigbeza Celebrations to commemorate migration from the Ewe ancestral lands at Notse (Togo) include drumming, dancing, ceremonial costumes.	Aflao
Aboakyer antelope-hunt (late April early May) More commonly known as the Deer-Hunting Festival, this famous event involves two hunting groups competing to bring back a live antelope. The first to present it to the chief and elders is proclaimed champion.	Winneba, Central Region.
MAY	
Don (14th)	Wa, Bawku and Bolgatanga
Sallah	Tamale and Tumu
Chimisi	Bawku, Upper East Region.
JUNE	
Dzimbenti or *Bugum* (11th)	Throughout Upper West and Upper East

Apiba	Senya Beraku, west of Accra
Fire festival	Tamale and Bawku
Dongu	Wa, Upper West Region

JULY

Bakatue Festival (first Friday)	Elmina, coast
Damba (last week or early August)	Dagomba people, Northern Region
Yam festival	Tamale
Edjodi	Senya Beraku west of Accra
Bugumlobre	Bongo, Upper East Region.
Jimbanti	Tumu, Upper West Region.
Dzumbanti	Wa, Upper West Region

AUGUST

Asafotufiiam (first week)	Ada, coast east of Accra
Akumasi (second week)	Senya Beraku, coast west of Accra
Damba (12th)	Tamale
Odwira Thanksgiving festival held any time between August and February.	Held througout the Asante country and by most Akan people
Bontungu Five days of drumming and dancing in which villagers clear all superfluous or undesirable objects from their homes and ask God for good health and prosperity in the coming year.	Anomabu, near Saltpond,wes of Accra
Homowo (Aug/Sept). Traditional festival of the Ga people including street processions of twins and offerings of ceremonial *kpokpoi* food to the gods.	Accra, Prampram and surrounding districts

SEPTEMBER

Yam Festival (all month)	Volta Region.
Oguaa Fetu Afahye (first Saturday) A big, dressy occasion lasting several days (see p.843).	Cape Coast
Kobina (15th)	Lawra, Upper West Region.
Black Stool Festival (25th)	Seikwa, north of Berekum
Yam Festival (last week or early October)	Effiduasi, Ashanti Region.

OCTOBER

Daa (1st–12th)	Tongo, Upper East Region.
Sebre dance (9th)	Lawra, Upper West Region.
Akonedi (9th–13th)	Larteh, 56km north of Accra
Boaram (28th)	Tongo, Upper East Region.
Yam Festival	Ejura and Effiduasi, Ashanti Region
Fijyiiyna/Monomene Bayere Afahye	Nkoranza, west of Ejura

NOVEMBER

Atweaban (second week)	Ntonso, northeast of Kumasi
Yam Festival	Ejura, northeast of Kumasi
Afahye	Agogo, 100km east of Kumasi
Yango	Bawku, Upper East Region.
Boaram	Tongo, Upper Region.
Hotbetsotso Commemoration of the Anlos' migration from a tyrannical kingdom to their homeland.	Anloga, on the Atlantic shore southwest of Keta

DECEMBER

Fao (1st)	Navrongo, Upper East Region.
Kwafie (over the New Year)	Berekum
Kpini guinea fowl festival	Dagomba and Gonja people

Directory

AIRPORT TAX US$10, in hard currency only.

CRAFTS AND OTHER PURCHASES Ghana has a wide variety of arts and crafts, still widely made for local consumption. Accra is good for imported printed cloth. The Asante region is a prolific producer and well known for it's *kente* and *adinkra* cloths. These can be bought in villages around Kumasi or at the town's cultural centre. The region is also famed for its carvings – especially of stools made in Bonwire. The north specialises more in leather goods, rough cotton weaves and basketry, all of which are found at the Bolgatanga market. Perhaps the best place for selection is in Accra where art from all over the country – and from throughout West Africa – comes together at the crafts market.

DRUGS *Wee* (**marijuana**) is technically illegal, though widely available. The main areas of production are around Ejura in the Asante region and Nsawam north of Accra. Generally looked upon more as a bad habit than a dangerous drug, consumers aren't likely to run into big trouble, though discretion is always advisable.

EDUCATION Ghana has traditionally been known for a relatively high level of education and the country has three universities – the University of Ghana, near Accra; the University of Science and Technology, Kumasi; and the University of Cape Coast. Students have been one of the more vocal groups of opponents of Rawling's policies and, as a result, universities were closed in 1983 for nearly a year. They've since re-opened, but the student population remains volatile. Primary school is compulsory, and figures from the mid–1980s reported well over two million pupils. There were about 150,000 secondary students at that time.

GOLD This is the country all right, but you'll be hard pressed to find much sign of the precious metal away from the big goldfields, around Tarkwa and Obuasi, southwest of Kumasi. Visits are not difficult to make, in practice but there's been some understandably defensive posturing from the *Lonhro*/Government-owned Ashanti Goldfields Corporation in reponse to accusations from the Anti-Slavery Society that young men are working, almost naked for security reasons, in cyanide cleaning pools.

OPENING HOURS Government offices are open Monday to Friday 8am–12.30pm and 1.30–5pm. Most businesses operate Monday to Friday 8/9am–noon and 2–5.30pm. Many shops also open on Saturday, from around 8am to 1pm. Shops are closed on public holidays, without exception – it's the law.

PHOTOGRAPHY You don't need a **permit** to take pictures in Ghana, though the usual regulations against snapping military installations and strategic points are rigorously enforced. This includes the Akosombo Dam and the nearby bridge spanning the Volta River – both of which are rather photogenic. Resist the temptation or be absolutely sure no one's watching to avoid problems. Especially sensitive is Osu Castle in Accra which is now the seat of government. Taking pictures anywhere in the vicinity could lead to the confiscation of camera and film, if not arrest.

SMOKING A major anti-smoking drive was recently started by the government, with no smoking on any Ghana Airways domestic flights, or STC buses and health warnings on all packets.

STUDENT CARDS May entitle you to discounts on *Ghana Airways* and *STC* buses if you get necessary authorisation from *SYTAG* (address in the Accra "Directory").

TROUBLE Muggings aren't a problem in Ghana, not even in Accra, though this may change if the city becomes a transit point for hard drugs, as seems to be happening. Ordinary **pickpocketing** is probably worst in Kumasi market.

Police sometimes stop travellers (and Ghanaians) and pretend to be really angry about a minor infraction (such as jaywalking, which is illegal at certain places including Kwame Nkrumah Circle in Accra). Customs and immigration officers employ similar tactics. They are almost certainly angling for dash, and you may have to pay up, but large amounts aren't necessary and politeness and smiles will help.

WILDLIFE Ghana's native fauna is not in as desperate a position as you might expect. Mole Game Reserve is a functioning and well-stocked park with the full complement of bush-savannah mammals. Newly amended conservation laws ban hunting for food or sport (except as part of a traditional festival) and even trade in game meat – edicts which may prove impossible to enforce in the present economic climate. Along the coast, the British RSPB has been effective in helping to curb the killing of **sea birds** for sport and food – especially the very rare and now protected **roseate tern**, which migrates to these shores every winter from northern Europe. Ghana **Friends of the Earth** (PO Box 3794, Accra, ☎71.26.13) is an active group, one of the few such in Africa.

WOMEN TRAVELLERS AND GHANAIAN WOMEN Most travellers experience great kindness and there are few special problems for women – indeed, many rate Ghana one of the most hassle-free countries in West Africa. However, even more than in other parts, Ghanaian men and boys are likely to respond with unrestrained lewdness to what may be seen as provoc-ative clothing or inappropriate behaviour in a woman (riding a bicycle, for example) – nothing remarkable about that.

As for women in Ghanaian society, the Akan-speaking people (but not all other groups) are mostly **matrilineal** – a system in which men inherit from their maternal uncles, rather than their fathers – but the impact on women's status is, if anything, reduced as a result and there is firm government pressure against this form of inheritance. Genital mutilation isn't practised much in Ghana. If you're interested in making contacts, write to the *Ghana Assembly of Women* (PO Box 459, Accra) or the *Federation of Ghanaian Women* (PO Box 6326, Accra).

A Brief History of Ghana

By the early nineteenth century the Gold Coast interior had developed a complicated network of northern states – Gonja, Dagomba, Mamprusi and Nanumba – and, in the south, smaller confederations (the Fante for example) and statelets (Ga, Ewe, Nzima). In the central region, the Asante confederation was rapidly mushrooming. Given time, the empire might have conquered and assimilated most of the smaller political units in the surrounding territories which were later to come under French rule. Such a scenario, however, was thwarted by the colonial experience which began in earnest in the nineteenth century. But European involvement in the region began much earlier than the dramatic British conquest of the Asante empire in 1874.

■ European arrival

Searching out new trade routes and a way to obtain the gold of the trans-Saharan caravans closer to source, the first **Portuguese** ships came to Ghana in 1471. By 1482 they had returned to build a fort at **Elmina** ("the mine"), using a mixture of persuasion and threats to gain the consent of the local ruler. The region turned out to be rich in gold, ivory, timber and skins, and other Europeans followed the Portuguese. Over the next 400 years, sea powers like the Dutch, Danes and British competed heavily for the trade. With the European colonisation of America, this expanded to include **slaves.**, in exchange for which the Europeans brought hard liquor and manufactured goods like **clothing** and **weaponry**. Guns eventually helped the **Asante** – the principal traders with the foreigners – to expand their influence over the region's interior and to apply pressure to the **Fante** middlemen through whom they'd been dealing with the British since the 1600s.

■ The British colony

By the early nineteenth century, the British had emerged as the strongest foreign power on the "Gold Coast". In 1807, they abolished the slave trade in the region and began looking for other exploitable resources. Over the next 100 years, palm oil, cocoa, rubber, gold and timber were developed as exports. These products drew the British – hitherto content to remain in their coastal forts – increasingly into the hinterland, which they had previously ignored.

The stage was set for the outright **conquest** of the interior when the Asante invaded the Fante confederation in 1806. The Fante had long resisted the attempts of their powerful northern neighbours to dominate them, thanks in large part to their role as preferential trading partners with the Europeans. Now the British rallied to the aid of their Fante "allies", even offering them protection in one of their coastal forts.

Hostilities flared and **tenuous treaties** were reached between the two Akan factions throughout the first half of the century. But, as competition increased for the control of trade, the British decided there could be only one victor. They ultimately found the excuse they needed to invade the interior when war again broke out between the Fante and Asante in the 1870s. The British marched on Kumasi and sacked the capital in 1874. Subsequent **Asante wars** followed in 1896 and 1900, when the ruling Asanthene was finally exiled (see p.850).

By that time Germany, France and Britain had already agreed on borders for the areas they would control. The British introduced elements of **indirect rule** in their new colony, even allowing the Asante confederation to be re-established under the Ashanti Confederacy Council – a government agency – in 1935. After World War I, part of German Togoland was integrated into the British colony.

The rise of Nationalism

Nationalist movements were created early in the colonial period, with one – the Aborigines' Rights Protection Society – dating as far back as 1897. Other parties sprang up during the 1920s and 1930s and, by 1946, concessions to African demands for representation had led to an African majority in Ghana's Legislative Council, although the executive branch – and effective rule – was still in the hands of the British Governor. In 1947, **J.B. Danquah** formed the United Gold Coast Convention, which favoured the principle of a gradual shift to self-government and independence. The same year, the party invited **Kwame Nkrumah** to join its ranks as party secretary in an effort to broaden a base that consisted mainly of the educated elite – civil servants, lawyers, businessmen and doctors.

In the aftermath of the 1948 **Accra riots** (see Accra history, p.827) Nkrumah lost patience with conservatives in the UGCC and split from it to form his own party, the **Convention People's Party** – campaigning slogan, *Self-government now.* He gained prominence among the masses as a result and the British detained him when he

called for a national strike in 1950. The CPP, meanwhile, won the Legislative Assembly election of 1951, and the governor, Sir Charles Arden-Clarke, prudently released Nkrumah and invited him to help form a govenment. Thus, in 1952, Nkrumah became the first African prime minister in the Commonwealth. He went on to win the elections of 1954 and 1956 – a period during which his CPP party shared power with the British. On August 3, 1956 the legislative assembly passed a unanimous motion calling · for complete independence.

■ Heady days: independence

When **independence** was ultimately returned on March 6, 1957, the future looked bright for the first African country to break colonial bonds. Ghana was then the world's leading cocoa exporter and produced a tenth of all the world's gold. Other valuable resources, of which the country had many, included bauxite, manganese, diamonds and timber. Perhaps Ghana's greatest asset was a high percentage of educated citizens who seemed well qualified to run the new nation (25 percent of the population was literate, compared, for example, to an estimated 1 percent in Portugal's colonies).

Nkrumah became a larger than life figure, respected throughout Africa and the African diaspora and highly regarded in the West. He was an eloquent advocate of **pan-Africanism** and the **non-aligned movement**. His economic principles looked sound, too, as he sought to create an industrial base that would reduce dependence on foreign powers while improving social services throughout the country (hospitals and clinics, universities and schools were part of his legacy). The port city of **Tema**, with its smelting and other industrial plants, was constructed as this time as was the ambitious **Akosombo Dam**, built to supply hydro-electric power.

And disaster...

Nkrumah's economic strategy was, however, extremely costly, and with thirty years of hindsight it seems painfully clear that his biggest mistake was to over-emphasise **prestige projects** at the expense of a solid agricultural base. Worse still, many of the projects held no prospect of any economic return: Accra's showy conference centre – designed to be the headquarters of the OAU, which based itself instead in Addis Ababa – and symbolic monuments like

Black Star Square and the vainglorious State House were the dizzy results of a belief in the invincible right of ideals. Foreign currency reserves dwindled at a frightening rate and the country instead accumulated a debt running to hundreds of millions of pounds.

As the economic situation turned suddenly bleak, political discontent rose. Despite concern for his international reputation, Nkrumah responded with increasing repression at home where his support was dwindling. Government suppression of a 1961 workers' strike had already seriously alienated Nkrumah from the working class and the educated elite had long been disillusioned with his expensive brand of scientific socialism. When the world price of cocoa plummeted in the mid–1960s, Ghana's hopes for economic self-sufficiency – and long-term stability – were dashed.

By 1964, Ghana was legally a **one-party state.** As the CPP tried measures to stamp out opposition, the government increasingly arrested those it feared under the Preventive Detention Act which allowed for "enemies" of the regime to be held for up to five years without trial. Public gatherings were strictly controlled, press censorship became commonplace and an extensive network of informants was developed by the party central committee. Such measures were effective in crushing opposition, or at least in driving it deeply underground, but Nkrumah still had to contend with the military. Suspicious of the army's loyalty, he lost his nerve and made policy decisions that were bound to antagonise officers – placing limits on recruitment and hedging military procurement procedures with elaborate safeguards. Isolating himself still further from the support of the military, he formed an independent **presidential guard**, accountable only to him.

In the light of such developments, western nations increasingly criticised **governmental corruption** and recognised a **personality cult** surrounding Nkrumah, where previously they'd seen a charismatic figure. Nkrumah was forced to abandon his non-alignment and turn to the Soviet bloc for support. By then he had totally lost the backing of the military and almost every other element of society. Only a blind sense of impunity could have allowed him to travel abroad. On February 24, 1966, while on a visit to Peking, he was overthrown in a bloodless coup by British-trained officers. He died in exile in Conakry in 1972.

■ Coups and "kleptocrats"

Following Nkrumah's flight, Lietenant-General **Joseph Ankrah** was appointed head of the National Liberation Council (NLC) that ruled until 1969. The conservative junta went on a witch-hunt, arresting left-wing ideologues, banning the CPP and harrassing its leaders. The junta's **economic direction** seemed promising to the West, however, as they privatised many state enterprises and broke off relations with the Soviet Union and its allies. But for all the promises made to better the economy, life for most people without special connections grew steadily worse.

From its inception, the NLC viewed itself as a provisional government and much of its period of rule was spent preparing for a return to civilian democracy. A bill of rights was drawn up, and safeguards implemented to ensure the independence of the judiciary – measures intended to stop the reconstitution of an autocratic one-party state. In May 1969, political parties were legalised. The **Progress Party**, headed by Kofi Busia – an Akan who represented the traditional middle-class opposition to Nkrumah's rule – was counterbalanced by the **National Alliance of Liberals** led by Komla Gbedemah, an Ewe and one-time associate of Nkrumah who had broken with the leader and gone into exile.

In September 1969, Ghanaians gave democracy another try, and elected **Dr Kofi Busia** prime minister. But the new leader struggled to wade through the economic mess. Cocoa prices dropped again in 1971, sparking a new crisis and, at the same time, mismanagement and racketeering led to shortages in food production, supplies and foreign exchange. Under mounting pressure, Busia took the necessary but politically dangerous step of **devaluing the cedi**. Massive price increases followed and the public enthusiasm that had ushered in the new regime faded almost immediately. Busia was overthrown on January 13, 1972.

General corruption

From 1972 to 1979, Ghana was led by a series of juntas with remarkably **corrupt generals** at the helm. One of the most flagrant offenders was **General I. Acheampong**, who headed the National Redemption Council (NRC) from 1972 to 1975 and then the Supreme Military Council until 1978. During his period in office, Ghanaians coined the term "kleptocracy" – rule by thieves –

as the official economy moved closer and closer to complete collapse. The **black market** thrived, meanwhile, as basic goods like bread and eggs became unattainable for the poor. Production declined even further and what few agricultural goods emerged onto the market were smuggled abroad to Togo and Côte d'Ivoire, where they fetched higher, hard currency prices. The educated elite – doctors, teachers, lawyers – led a brain drain to Nigeria and overseas where they had some chance of supporting themselves.

The basis of Acheampong's economic policy was **"self-reliance"**, symbolised through programmes such as "Operation Feed Yourself", launched in 1972. Moderate successes were achieved in the early years of the NRC, but by the mid–1970s the economic outlook was so grim that the professional middle class, and especially the Ghana Bar Association, demanded a return to party politics. Acheampong sought a compromise by proposing a **"union government"** where power would be shared between civilians, the armed forces and – radically – the police. The opposition viewed UNIGOV as a mechanism to keep the military in power and reacted cynically when Acheampong pushed his idea through on the back of a trumped-up referendum held in 1978.

As criticism grew, so did **repression**, and hundreds of opposition leaders were jailed without trial. Viewed increasingly as a tyrant, Acheampong withdrew into isolation. He was quietly deposed in a coup led by **General William Akuffo** on July 5, 1978. Akuffo established the "Supreme Military Council II" and eventually set a date for elections in June 1979, but little else changed and widespread discontent in the country now spread to the ranks of the military.

■ A New Age: Rawlings Mark I

There can be no peace where there is no justice – and there will be no justice unless everyone can be made to answer for his conduct
                                    Jerry Rawlings, 1979

On May 15, 1979, there was a bungled uprising of junior ranks in the army, led by a 32-year-old flight lieutenant of mixed Scottish–Ghanaian parentage – **Jerry Rawlings**. He was captured and imprisoned but freed by fellow soldiers and they made a second, successful, attempt to take power on **June 4, 1979**.

Rawlings made it clear that his coup would be different, that he was out to eliminate corruption and restore national pride to an economic order neglected in fifteen years of waste. The title of his governing **Armed Forces Revolutionary Council** set the tone – Rawlings envisaged a "moral revolution" based implicitly on socialist principles of an economy for need rather than profit. He took a hard line, sending high-ranking officers to the firing squad (including Acheampong and Akuffo) and approving a purge of public figures under suspicion of fraud. At the same time he pledged that the AFRC would work quickly to restore order and return the reins of power to a civilian government.

The world community noted little more than another coup d'état in Ghana, but, in a remarkable departure (no African military ruler had ever voluntarily relinquished power before, except arguably, Eyadéma in neighbouring Togo), the promise was kept. Following elections held on June 18, 1979, the newly elected president, **Dr Hilla Limann** took office in September and the soldiers returned to their barracks barely three months after leaving them.

Limann rode in on a wave of popularity at home and in the West where his conservative politics won respect. But despite his best intentions, the economy continued to slide – production dropped further, the cedi remained overvalued (fearing unpopularity, the president refused to devalue the currency and thereby cost his country a major IMF loan) and the country's infrastructure became hopelessly eroded. And despite the moral high ground captured by the Rawlings clique, and Rawlings' own shadowy behind-the-scenes presence, **corrupt practices** had been re-established by the end of 1980 in virtually every sphere of public life.

■ Rawlings' second coming

On December 31, 1981, Rawlings led a **second successful coup**, toppling the Limann government, abolishing the entire "democratic" framework, and placing the government in the hands of a **Provisional National Defence Council**. As before, he justified the action by the urgent need to halt corruption and put Ghana's wrecked and abused economy in order. This time, however, no plans were made to restore the country to civilian rule. Rather, the PNDC decided to put into practice the leftist populist principles of the original coup.

Early moves were made to democratise the decision-making process and to de-centralise political power. This was done through **People's Defence Committees** (PDCs), which replaced district councils and which were intended to increase local participation in the revolution while raising political consciousness at the grass roots level.

The political orientation of the second revolution proved too much for large sections of the army, particularly northerners, and there were several **coup attempts** in 1982 and 1983, including a nearly disastrous attempt mounted from Togo (see "Foreign Affairs", below). Meanwhile, the revolution itself provided excuse enough for a few hard-line radicals to undertake terrorist attacks under the guise of "popular justice". There were calls from several quarters for a complete overhaul (even abolition) of the judiciary and there was worse in June 1982 with the kidnap and **murder of three senior judges**. Unfortunately for Rawlings, the trial and conviction of the two murderers wasn't sufficient to clear all elements of the PNDC of any involvement and it was forced into a public position of greater moderation.

Like Thomas Sankara, who arrived on the scene in Burkina Faso two years later, Rawlings has enjoyed huge popularity among the masses fed up with government lies and excesses. But he has worked against any personality cult and even insisted that photos of him should not be displayed in homes and businesses. With his battle cry of **"accountability"**, he has proved sincere in the **war against corruption** and, although the economy continued to slide during his first years as head of state, he has since managed to produce results that indicate a **turnaround** is possible (by 1984, the economy was showing a five percent growth rate, the first upswing in ten years), and he has achieved this, moreover, in the face of such setbacks as the forced **return of a million Ghanaian economic migrants** from Nigeria in 1983.

Despite Rawlings' penchant for revolutionary rhetoric, his early friendship with the Libyan leader Colonel Gaddafi and his ties with Cuba and Eastern Europe, his pragmatic economic approach – including taking the risky political step of drastically devaluing the cedi – have earned him high marks with the IMF, which has started once again to provide sizeable loans to the country.

In the mid-1980s, administrative reorganisation took place and the PDCs were replaced by **Committees for the Defence of the Revolution** (CDRs). The move was partially designed to increase the level of popular participation in the government and, in 1986, Rawlings announced that the PNDC would seek a national mandate through district council elections. Ninety percent of the population registered to vote in 1988 when the elections were finally held, though the government disappointed expectations when it decreed that the ban on political parties would not be lifted.

Foreign affairs

Relations with **Burkina Faso** were extremely close while Sankara was alive, and at one point the countries even envisaged a common currency. Plans were also made to co-ordinate their energy, trade, transportation and education programmes which shared many similarities of emphasis.

Predictably, more conservative regimes have been less receptive to Rawling's style of government. Relations with **Britain**, **Côte d'Ivoire**, and especially with **Togo** have been, at best, cool. All three countries harbour Ghanaian exiles, some of whom maintain links with **dissident opposition** groups in Ghana. In 1983 this secret opposition came dangerously close to toppling the government as they infiltrated Accra from Togo and briefly took over the GBC broadcasting station before being apprehended by the army. More recently it was a 1986 coup attempt against Togo's President Eyadema which triggered new tension between the two counties. The rebels were said to have entered Lomé from Ghana. In recent years the border has frequently been closed. The PNDC has ample reason to worry about its security, as there have been further land- and sea-borne efforts to ovethrow it.

Rawlings is an eloquent critic of the world's **commodity markets**, pointing out, for example, that the tyranny of cocoa price-setting in determing Ghana's earning power (and thus the living standards of its people) quite over-shadows what he views as the necessary curtailments on personal freedom in a society effectively under siege.

Such denunciatory justifications have earned Rawlings' revolutionary style little respect with the **British and American governments**. In 1985, relations with the United States deteriorated when a distant relative of Rawlings was arrested in America on charges of passing classified CIA information to the PNDC. Ghana retaliated by arresting two people on spying charges. An exchange of prisoners was eventually arranged and Reagan scrapped his plan to cancel American aid to Ghana in 1986.

■ The present – and the outlook

Now more than ten years in power, Rawlings has made much of what seemed to be a hopeless situation. But he's had a difficult time straddling different elements in Ghanaian society and although most rural dwellers and many wage earners have remained loyal, he has suffered scrapes with the ambitious **middle class**, who loath his socialist rhetoric and raise the banner of human rights, and with **students and academics**, to many of whom (especially the more radical Marxists) he appears to have sold out to the IMF. Certainly, the charge that he presides over an increasingly **neo-colonial state** is one that's hard to refute. And yet he has stayed and Ghana has not stood still.

The key to success for Ghana's governments has always been attention to the **economy**. Here, Rawlings has created breathing space by entering into remorselessly pragmatic agreements with the IMF, which now views the country as a shining example of its structural adjustment policies. Ghana has recorded the highest consistent rates of economic growth in Africa since 1983. But as the economic situation has improved under the Economic Recovery Programme, so too have the expectations of Ghanaians, who are demanding better **wages** and living conditions. Though inflation has been reduced and food supplies increased, while foreign investment is being encouraged, real wages at the beginning of the 1990s were still only two-thirds of their 1970s value (the minimum legal wage in 1990 was ₡218 a day, worth less than CFA200). Perhaps the ERP's biggest obvious success has been the **defeat of the currency black market**, so that the prices of goods, at least, are no longer distorted by differential access to foreign exchange among consumers.

Ghana entered the 1990s against the background rumble of the **Quarshigah Affair** – apparently yet another attempt to murder Chairman Rawlings and overthrow the PNDC. Major Courage Quarshigah and six other middle-ranking officers were, at the time of writing, still in detention in connection with the alleged plot. One of them was found hanged in his cell, and Amnesty International has adopted the others, who have not been charged. Rawlings took direct command of the armed forces at the end of 1989 and it's to be hoped that impatience with subversion (if such the "affair" turns out to have been) doesn't lead the PNDC into murky, extra-judicial waters. If nothing else, the Quarshigah "affair" is evidence of continuing dissatisfaction with the way things are going from several quarters in the armed forces.

The **future** must depend much on Rawlings' ability to maintain the pace of economic advances. In the light of events elsewhere in the socialist world, he faces increasing demands for a pluralistic, party political system and growing frustration from the alienated middle classes both on the right and left – especially from those in exile who might contribute much to the country.

ACCRA

Flat, sprawling and aesthetically verging on disaster, the cityscape of **ACCRA** is blighted by heavy concrete stacks harking back to the early years of confident independence. An absence of more modern steel and glass – the pride of capitals like Abidjan and Lagos – indicate the two decades of economic tailspin in which Accra was caught following the heady days of hope in the 1960s. With a population of over a million, it's still one of Africa's biggest cities and hasn't been spared the urban problems of traffic, noise and overcrowding, especially now that the economy is on a steady rise. Despite some uninspiring images – and open drains and sewers that add a malodorous emphasis to the general feeling of decay – the city's **trees** makes it exceptionally green. And it has bags of energy. Rush hours are dynamic and the streets thronged with a racket of vehicles and people. Accra is making a rapid comeback, especially after dark when its club scene is one of the liveliest in West Africa.

THE HISTORY OF ACCRA

Accra's **Ga founders** arrived in the region some time before 1500, setting up their capital at Ayawaso ("Great Accra") some 15km inland, and building a "Small Accra" on the coast for trade with the **Portuguese**, who put up a fort here in the sixteenth century. Trade – of slaves, gold and palm oil for guns – increased over the next hundred years with the building of the Dutch **Fort Ussher**, Danish **Christiansborg** and the British **Fort James**.

Accra originally consisted of **seven quarters** – the Ga quarters of Asere, Abola, Gbese, Sempi and Akunmadzei; Otublohu, the Akwamu quarter; and Alata, which later became the core of the British-protected area of Jamestown. Other quarters placed themselves under Dutch protection and became Usshertown. Much later, in 1840, the chief of Abola was chosen as the military leader (*Ga Mantse*) for the whole city, and treated by the British as the Ga king. Nowadays he is considered the Ga paramount chief.

Akwamu expansion from the north led to victory over the Ga in 1660 (Chief Okai Koi, defeated by treachery, put a curse on Accra that it should remain disunited against its enemies ever after) and to the destruction of Ayawaso, now just a tiny village. But the Ga regained much of their independence in 1730, when Akwamu fell to the Akim state of Akwapim, which now took over control of the **"notes"** (documents issued by African rulers giving Europeans the right to trade) for the Accra forts. These "notes" later passed to the Asante, who gained control at the beginning of the nineteenth century, but gradually lost it in a series of wars with the British. Battle was averted in 1863 when British and Asante armies were both struck by dysentery and too ill to fight, but a decisive victory in 1874 led to the British taking over and setting up the Gold Coast Colony with its capital at Accra after 1877.

Since then the city has expanded considerably, despite serious earthquakes in 1862 and 1939. After the introduction of **cocoa**, Accra became a major export port, also shipping out gold, palm oil and rubber and, from 1933, boasting West Africa's first brewery (*Club*). The municipality, set up in 1896, was expanded east to include Christiansborg and, in 1943, to bring in the ancient, walled, farming and salt-producing village of Labadi.

In February 1948, major **anti-colonial riots** in the city centre followed British police shootings at a demonstration at the junction of Rowe, Castle and Christiansborg roads. Twenty-nine protestors died and 237 were wounded in an outburst that caused £2 million worth of damage.

Arrival and orientation

Despite the urban sprawl, downtown Accra is neatly contained by the **Ring Road**. Two main thoroughfares – Nkrumah Avenue and Kojo Thompson Road – run through the city centre from the old **Jamestown** district in the south to **Kwame Nkrumah Circle** in the north, lined by shops and the main commercial and business premises. Shady **Independence Avenue**, sprinkled with embassies and business headquarters, also leads from the south of town to **Redemption Circle** in the northeast and on out to the airport. Cutting east–west through the city centre are the main arteries of **Castle Road**, **Liberia Road** and **Kinbu Road** .

The core of Accra stretches from High Street near the waterfront to the **Makola market** – a colourful hive of activity that overflows into the surrounding streets. In between, the ample proportions of the stately colonial **Parliament** and **Supreme Court** give an idea of the importance the British placed on their Gold Coast Colony.

It's worth noting – in case you were wondering – that Accra's **port** is at the separate town of **Tema**, some 30km east of the capital.

PUBLIC TRANSPORT

The main group of **parking stations** in town is at the corner of Barnes and Kinbu Roads. These, together with other main bus, taxi and *tro-tro* parks and the destinations they serve, are marked on the schematic public transport map.

Taxis in Accra can be hired outright for the journey, in which case they're **"charter"** (¢300 in town or double at night, but confirm the price before setting off), or you can share **collective taxis**, known as **"dropping"**, for around ¢30–50. Dropping taxis roll along fixed routes, often from circle (roundabout) to circle, servicing virtually the whole city. Vans (*tro-tros*) are less expensive than saloon cars. Tourists are generally assumed to be chartering, so make it clear if you're not.

Arriving in Accra

If you're arriving by road, entering Accra can be a confusing business, with little in the way of landmarks to indicate where you are. Chaotic and dusty (or muddy) as it has been for years, the approach is usually from the north.

If you're arriving by public transport, it's more than likely you'll want to hop out before it reaches its terminus. Scanning our *Accra Public Transport* map should help, so long as you know where you're coming from.

It shouldn't escape your notice, if you're **coming in by train**, that the station puts you right in the heart of the city, a short taxi ride from just about anywhere central.

Airport arrivals

At **Kotoka International Airport** there's generally a crowd of **"official porters"** in yellow T-shirts trying to handle your luggage and earn a dash. Keep cool and nominate one, or make it clear you'll do it yourself. **Customs** tend to be slow and the currency declaration form delays procedure further. You can **change money** with the officials – legally – but their rate is even worse than that at the forex bureau in the arrivals hall, which in turn is worse than places downtown. Change only sufficient to see you to the better rates at the bureaux in town.

There's no airport bus into town and **taxi drivers** converge on you as soon as you leave the terminal building. They can be quite heavy and stories circulate about menacing demands. It's all bark: stay cool and do nothing until someone calms down. The fare should be clearly agreed before you go, and in any case be no more than ¢1200 even at night. The city centre isn't far, about 8km away.

Alternatively, you can walk out of the airport zone to the main road, and pick up a dropping taxi for around ¢50 to Kwame Nkrumah circle, close to most of the low-budget accommodation.

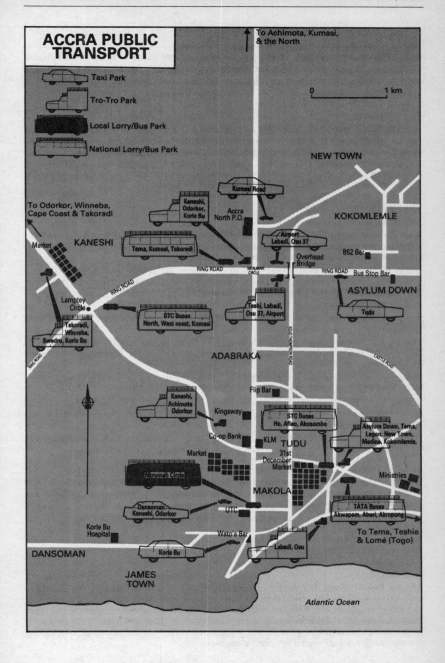

Sleeping

Beds in Accra are relatively cheap and vary from dorm space to luxury hotel rooms. Problems with power cuts and water shortages are diminishing. The prices given here are best treated as a basis for comparison; they tend to inflate with alarming speed as the cedi progressively devalues.

The bottom line

The **YMCA** and **YWCA** (both located on Castle Rd near the National Museum) still seem to take in travellers, although they're reportedly perpetually booked with student groups. If you want to economise, it's worth stopping by to check out the situation since their dormitory rooms are the cheapest in town. You might also try the **Presbyterian Guest House** on Salem Rd a couple of minutes north of Mission St. The last known cost here was under ₵1000; but church people get priority over travellers for rooms.

Cheap places

ADABRAKA

Kwame Nkrumah Memorial Hotel, Kojo Thompson Rd. Walls are thin, rooms generally filthy, but the location is great and there's even an occasional disco. What's curious is the very good food, with *Omo Tuo* on Sundays. Singles from ₵2200.

Hotel de California, intersection of Kojo Thompson and Castle roads (PO Box 7337; ☎22.61.19). Extremely popular with travellers, and the best prospect in the quarter, this place has clean, non-S/C rooms with fan (no. 3 is the best) at ₵2200/3300. Try to book ahead.

Crown Prince Hotel, across from the *California* in a colonial house. Non-S/C rooms are smaller and less comfortable than the *California*'s, but the staff are friendly. Rooms from ₵2200.

The Date, 100 metres west of Kojo Thompson Rd on the second street south of Castle Rd (PO Box 3407; ☎22.82.00). Similar to the above although standards (and prices) are lower: doubles for ₵2000.

Kyekyewere Behind Avenida Hotel. The name alone is enough to make you like this place, but the price is right, too – clean and cool doubles with fan from ₵3000.

Station View Hotel, Kinbu Rd, 25m east of Kojo Thompson Rd, opposite lorry park. Quite nice for the price and location; reasonably clean rooms with fan from ₵1500. Bar and restaurant with rice and *fufu* type dishes.

Hotel Tropicana, Tudu Rd 20m west of Kojo Thompson Rd (PO Box 1927; ☎66.62.91). Ideally located in the heart of town, S/C rooms from ₵2500/₵4500.

ASYLUM DOWN

Lemon Lodge, off Mango Tree Ave, between Burkina embassy and *Korkdam Hotel*. Good value in a quiet, leafy neighbourhood; clean rooms with fan (₵3000) or AC (₵4500) and breakfast (tea, coffee, milk, with bread and eggs) included.

Mavis Hotel, Mango Tree Ave. A bit austere (religious images in reception) but reasonably priced, with singles from ₵2300.

Newhaven Hotel, east of Overhead bridge and north of the Ring Road Central. This is good value – ₵2200/3300 for S/C rooms with fan.

Mid-range

Riviera Beach Hotel, Marine Drive, Victoriaborg (PO Box 4226; ☎66.24.00). The name suggests something more exotic than the hotel delivers. S/C, AC rooms (from ₵9000) are in fact rather run-down, but the location on the water – beautiful panoramic views of the coastline – makes up for shortcomings in service and comfort. They still vaunt their swimming pool, although it hasn't had water for years. Excellent terrace bar and restaurant overlooking the sea; worth a detour even if you don't sleep here.

Penta Hotel, Cantonments Rd near Danquah Circle (PO Box 7354; ☎22.83.06). Slightly more expensive than the Riviera, the Penta has recently been renovated and seems to have ironed out problems with AC and water supplies.

Avenida Hotel, Kojo Thompson Rd (PO Box 756; ☎22.13.21). A more upmarket hotel in the lively Adabraka neighbourhood, with spacious S/C doubles with fan from ₵5000.

Korkdam Hotel, 18 2nd Crescent, off Mango Tree Ave, Asylum Down (PO box 4605; ☎22.67.94). From ₵5000–9000 for S/C singles with hot water and fridges to executive suites with the works (phones, TV, AC).Variable standards.

St George's Hotel, Amusudai Rd, opposite Methodist School, Adabraka (☎22.46.99). In a restored colonial home, this hotel has charm plus conveniences like fridges, phones, TV and AC in posh S/C rooms from ₵10,000. Clean, comfortable and personal with a great location near the museum.

Expense account

Novotel, Barnes Rd, north of Kinbu Rd (PO Box 12720; ☎66.75.46, telex 2532). Accra's only new, really international establishment provides a free airport shuttle for guests. Amex cards accepted, and probably needed (from US$120).

Shangri-La, 1.5km from the airport (PO Box 9201; ☎77.69.93/4, telex 2561). More intimate than the *Novotel* and somewhat cheaper (though still take Amex). More local in feel but deservedly popular with ex-pats. Great pizzas at reasonable prices.

Ambassador Hotel, Independence Ave (PO Box 3044; ☎66.46.46). Recently restored colonial pile near the city centre. Now government-run, the *Ambassador* boasts a list of amenities including tennis, swimming pool, casino, restaurants and coffee shops, boutiques, secretarial services, travel agencies and car hire, some of which may well be available. From US$60, credit cards accepted.

Continental Hotel, Liberation Rd (PO Box 5252; ☎77.73.61). The second State Hotels Corp hotel, located near the airport and much the same price as the Ambassador. Showing its age although some of the rooms have been renovated. Closed for further work over 1990–91.

Marriot International Hotel, Agbawe St, Ako Adjei, in Osu (PO Box 0608; ☎77.45.42). Accra's Marriot is a small hotel and has no connection with the American chain. S/C, AC rooms with music and video.

Eating

In addition to the pricier restaurants listed below (including a shoal of Chinese ones, many of them good) cheap **street eats** are available in the motor parks, markets and in certain districts. Adabraka, for example, has many cheap eateries and, if you're staying in one of the neighbourhood's inexpensive hotels, you'll find numerous *kenkey* and fish vendors in back streets running between *The Date* and the *Hotel de California*.

Inexpensive

Variety Chop Bar, Kojo Thompson Rd, 50m north of Tudu Rd. Good Ghanaian food at reasonable rates – palm nut soup for ₵200. Recommended.

Time Square Restaurant, Mango Tree Ave, Asylum Down (south of Mavis Hotel). Bar/restaurant doing Ghanaian and European food Mon–Sat. *Omo Tuo* on Sundays.

Toledo, Cantonments Rd, about 1km from the *Penta Hotel*. Ice cream, burgers, chicken and *shawarma* at moderate prices.

Bus Stop, Ring Road Central, near the Agricultural Development Bank (☎22.30.90). Varied menu with snacks (sandwiches, kebabs), European specialities, ice cream and cheap beer.

Ghana National Museum Snack Bar (aka *Edvy Restaurant*), Barnes Rd. A fine afternoon retreat, in the cool museum gardens dotted with modern statues. Good value Chinese and Ghanaian set meals plus meat pies, sandwiches and kebabs. Top rating.

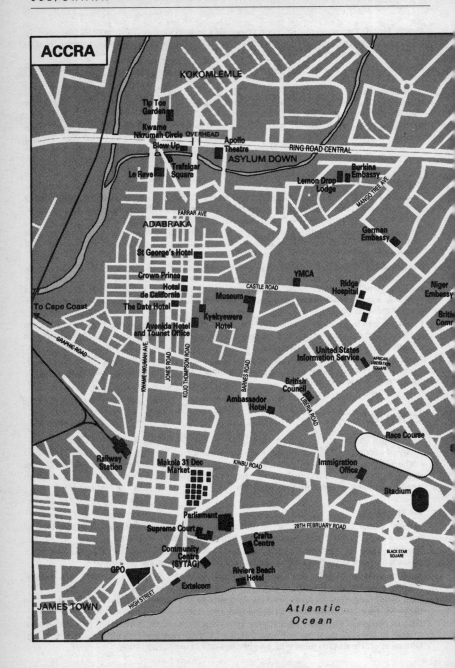

ACCRA

KOKOMLEMLE

Tip Toe
Gardens

Kwame
Nkrumah Circle   OVERHEAD

Blow Up   Apollo
                   Theatre   RING ROAD CENTRAL
Trafalgar   ASYLUM DOWN
Le Reve   Square   Burkina
                                                    Embassy
                                 Lemon Drop
                                 Lodge   MANGO TREE AVE

                  FARRAR AVE
      ADABRAKA
                                                    German
                                                    Embassy

      St George's Hotel
                                        YMCA
      Crown Prince   Ridge   Niger
      Hotel   CASTLE ROAD   Hospital   Embassy
      de California
                         Museum   Britis
To Cape Coast   The Date Hotel   Comr
                         Kyekyewere
                         Hotel
      Avenida Hotel
      and Tourist Office

         GRAPHIC ROAD   United States
                                        Information Service   AFRICAN
                                                               LIBERATION
                                                               SQUARE
                                    British
                                    Council
                         Ambassador
                         Hotel

                                                    Race Course

      Railway
      Station
            Makola 31 Dec   KINBU ROAD
            Market   Immigration
                                          Office
                                                    Stadium

                  Parliament
            Supreme Court   28TH FEBRUARY ROAD
      Community
      Centre   Crafts   BLACK STAR
      (SYTAG)   Centre   SQUARE
   GPO
JAMES TOWN   Extelcom   Riviere Beach
                                Hotel
            HIGH STREET
                                    Atlantic
                                    Ocean

To Airport & Lomé

Survey Dept.

Liberian
Embassy

WEB Dubois
Centre

A

Zoo

CANTONMENTS

French
Embassy

LIBERATION ROAD

SECOND CIRCULAR ROAD

Afrikiko

Redemption
Circle
(Sankara)

Nigerian High
Commission

Togo Embassy

Canadian High
Commission

INDEPENDENCE AVE

CANTONMENTS ROAD

ABDUL NASSER AVE

RINGWAY
ESTATES

Danquah
Circle

American
Embassy

Penta Hotel

RING ROAD EAST

Algerian Embassy

Côte d'Ivoire
Embassy

SALEM ROAD

ouse

CHRISTIANSBORG

0   500m

To Tema

LABADI ROAD

Osu Castle

More expensive

GHANAIAN

Afrikiko, Independence Ave, near 31 December Revolution Circle (towards airport). A very nice place and popular volunteers' hangout, known for cheap beer and standard African dishes. There's often a dance at weekends.

After "8", New Town Rd, Kokomlemle (☎22.50.08). Ghanaian specialities in attractive setting.

CHINESE AND INDIAN

Trafalgar Square, Nkrumah Circle. A pseudy, flashy sort of place with "cool" London pretensions, slightly pricey Ghanaian and Chinese dishes, but pots of tea to be had if you ask politely.

Pearl of the East, 15th Lane Osu, behind Penta Hotel (☎77.63.37). Perhaps the best Chinese restaurant in Accra, with authentic specialities and great vegetables (daily except Sun, noon–3pm and 7–11pm).

Hinlone, in Labone, off Ring Road East, first left and left again 500m south of the American embassy. Wonderful Chinese with very fresh selections of premium quality vegetables, meat and seafood.

Mandarin Ring Rd, west of Danquah Circle. Another highly rated Chinese restaurant, with a surprisingly varied menu (evenings until 10pm). Fridays best, with live music.

Rickshaw , at the *Ambassador Hotel*, Independence Ave (☎66.46.46). Great Chinese cooking (egg rolls, won tons, sweet and sour pork). Under separate management from the hotel (daily from noon–3pm and 7–11.30pm).

Maharaja, Cantonments Rd, below Danquah Circle. Accra's best Indian restaurant is excellent and justifiably expensive.

LEBANESE

Uncle Sam, Kojo Thompson Rd, near *Ghana Airways* (☎22.56.68). Despite the American ring to the name, this popular restaurant features Lebanese and French specialities (Mon–Fri noon–3pm and 7pm–midnight)

Tropicana, Salem Rd, Kuku Hill, Osu (☎77.66.31). Lunch and dinner service featuring Middle Eastern and European specialities.

EUROPEAN

Club 400, Cantonments, near National Film and Television Institute (☎77.58.47). Varied menu with European specialties at moderate prices (Mon–Fri for lunch and dinner; Sat dinner only; closed Sun)

Terra Nova, Nkrumah Circle (☎22.22.83). Outdoor dining under thatched cover. Conveniently located near the city's main nightclub circuit.

Los Amigos, Nkrumah Ave, opposite GNTC Technical (☎22.56.16). Spanish and European (daily noon–3pm and 7–11pm; weekends evenings only).

Time in the city

Accra doesn't especially lend itself to scenic walks and sightseeing and, by day, there's not much in the way of **things to see**. The main diversion is simply absorbing the energy of an African urban centre. Even the coast and lagoons aren't shown off to any real advantage and, from most places in town, you're barely aware that Accra lies right on the seafront. **Jamestown**, a bustling centre of small commerce at the heart of the colonial town, is an exception, though **Fort James** itself is to be avoided – it's a prison.

Osu Castle, the former Dutch Christiansborg on the cliffs, is today the seat of government, and called simply "The Castle". All surrounding streets are tightly barricaded, so you can't get anywhere near this historical curiosity.

A wander around **Independence** (or **Black Star**) **Square** is worthwhile – an Nkrumah-era monument built to herald African liberation, it looms behind the Castle in somewhat totalitarian **heroic dimensions**. The square itself is a giant parade ground, site of the Eternal Flame of African Liberation, lit by Nkrumah, and in the foreground rises the **Triumphal Arch** where national celebrations take place. Nearby are the **ministries** and **National Stadium**. A few hundred metres to the east stands the first president's proudest legacy, the monumental **State House** and adjoining **Kwame Nkrumah Conference Centre**, built in 1965 to serve as headquarters of the OAU.

A visit to the interesting National Museum is also in order, as is a quick trip to the WEB Dubois memorial centre (see below). Otherwise – markets, shopping, eating and shouting for taxis aside – save your energies for the evening, when it's cooler.

The National Museum of Ghana

Accra's **National Museum** (daily except Mon 9am–6pm; ₵300), on Barnes Road near the junction with Castle Road, houses one of West Africa's best ethnographic, historical and art collections, with exhibits from Ghana and across the continent. You could conceivably visit the entire museum in a morning or afternoon, but because of the variety and eclecticism of the exhibits, it's perhaps best to pop in several times to avoid cultural fatigue. The exhibits are well displayed, though poorly explained, and it's worth investing in the excellent **museum handbook**, with numerous black and white photos and detailed descriptions.

The museum is dedicated in large measure to **local crafts** that still thrive in Ghana, and, in addition to the numerous examples of clay water-coolers, bowls and lamps, calabash drums, iron clappers and wooden zithers, ornamental brass pots and implements, complementary exhibits show the **technology** behind cottage industry artwork. You can see how iron is forged (still common in the north), how brass weights, once used for weighing gold, are cast, and how glass beads are manufactured.

Interesting, too, are the **ceremonial objects** so common to the Akan and other peoples of the country. Gilded umbrella tops, carved royal stools, metal swords of state and intricate *kente* cloth are charged with a social and religious significance that the displays help illuminate. Artefacts from further afield in Africa (Zaire, South Africa, Angola) are interspersed among the national exhibits. Upstairs, dusty **archaeological relics** trace the country's history back to the late Stone Age.

The WEB Dubois Memorial Centre for Pan African Culture

House no. 22, 1st Circular Road, Cantonments (near airport).
The home where **WEB Dubois** – black American champion of pan-Africanism – died in 1963 has been turned into a cultural centre with a research library and gallery full of manuscripts and other Dubois memorabilia. Photographs and brief biographies of other black world leaders line the walls of his living room and study. The centre contains facilities for lectures and other educational and cultural programmes. It's not ostentatious, but a highly informative and inspiring monument to pan-Africanism and its vanguard.

What's left of the zoo

Kanda Ave, past the Ring Road; Mon–Sat 9.30am–5.30pm, Sun 9am–5.30pm
If you generally dislike **zoos**, you'll hate the one in Accra. Very little is left of it, and perhaps the best reason to visit is to scold the staff into questioning why it's so awful; that, and to pay a visit to the deeply disturbed monkeys in their solitary confinement, most of whom respond pitifully to a little stroking through the bars. Moribund reptiles and rather a lot of parrots (probably destined for the pet shops of New York and

Frankfurt) are the main inmates. Any zoo that thinks fit to prop a shelf in a monkey cage with the stuffed, decaying carcase of a very small elephant needs closing down immediately.

The crafts market

Downtown on High Street, near the *Riviera Hotel*, the **crafts market** is a huge parking-lot depot for artwork from throughout West Africa. Buying here isn't as satisfying or cheap as searching out such goods in the regions where they're manufactured, but if you've got no time or just like one-stop shopping, this is the place. You'll find everything from **Asante sandals** and **kente cloth** to **leatherwork** from the north, woven cotton fabric and glass beads, any of which can easily be bought more cheaply elsewhere. The wood crafts on the other hand – **masks, carvings** and **boxes** – and the **brasswork** are somewhat harder to find. Expect heavy pressure to buy; bargaining tends to be a battle of wits here and not a great deal of fun. If you buy anything that looks like an antique, you might take the precaution of obtaining an exemption certificate from the museum (₵50) so you won't be hassled when you take it out of the country.

Swimming

There's only one safe area for sea-swimming in Accra – "Labadi Pleasure Beach", directly below the International Trade Fair site. There are lifeguards at Labadi, occasionally called upon to rescue swimmers swept out by the strong undertow. Taxis and *tro-tros* run here from Nkrumah Circle. You can also take a dip below the *Riviera Beach Hotel*, but take nothing of value (and be seen to have nothing of value). The best **pool** is the new one at the *Shangri-La* – ₵1000.

Bars and clubs

Nightlife in Accra is an ever-changing, ever-evolving scene. More than most lively cities, Accra's clubs and dives change hands almost as often as shifts. Most get going late, if at all, during the week. Thursday, Friday, Saturday and Sunday are the days to reckon on resting up in preparation. But at weekends you can party most of the daytime, too, if you choose your venue.

Flip, Liberia Rd. Thatched rooftop bar with highish prices but views of the city to match.

Wato's, opposite the GPO in Jamestown. *Wato* stands for West African Trading Organisation (among other things). A serious watering hole with okay food to keep you going.

Blow-up, Nkrumah Circle. No longer *the* place to go, but still a place to go, early, before moving on somewhere hotter.

Star Hotel, 4th Circular Rd, Cantonments (☎77.77.28). This hotel doesn't have regular live music any more, but promoters sometimes hire it for performances (usually weekend). Check the listings in the *Daily Graphic*.

All that Jazz, off Cantonments Rd, near Danquah Circle. Not a club, but a very popular pub where you'll bump into ex-pats – if you want to. Music, but no dancing and cover only at weekends.

Le Reve, Nkrumah Ave, Nkrumah Circle (☎22.68.66). A popular European restaurant, *Le Reve* (open 8pm–3am daily) is also one of the town's hotter clubs. The action gets going after 11pm.

Piccadilly Circus, south of Nkrumah Circle. Outdoor bar with occasional live music.

Tip Toe Garden, north of Nkrumah Circle. Open-air with stage and large dance floor. Changes hands often and is just as frequently at the mercy of Accra trend-setters. Most of the time a good, well-mixed crowd of locals and foreigners enjoying plenty of live musical variety, including highlife and "copyright bands" (playing cover versions).

Apollo Theatre, Ring Road Central east of Nkrumah Circle. Similar set-up to *Tip Toe* and also open-air, so comfortable. Doesn't close till the last punters have left. A good place to meet down-to-earth local people.

African Heroes Hotel, Nima, Accra Newtown, just north of Ring Road Central. Again, similar to *Tip Toe* and the *Apollo*, but rougher; the African Brothers stronghold with some hardcore regulars and underworld vibes. "Now you're on the borderline of where angels fear to tread". Remember they warned you.

● If you're still not satisfied, ask a taxi driver to take you to one of these:

Balme Taverne – a cramped executive haunt at Kaneshie with Sunday highlife bands.

Cave du Roi – firmly-established disco palace for couples.

Crystal Palace Disco on Link Road – good dance club, with roof-top video lounge and Sunday afternoon hops from 4–11pm (free entry for "ladies").

Club Keteke – central location, dark inside, what's known as a "lights off" club, one not to be seen at, in other words, with whoever you take or meet there. Good Friday music nights.

Must – food and dance.

Next Door – on the seafront, good at weekends (especially Sunday afternoons), but dead on weekdays.

The Village – a cool place to hang out it seems, with listenable music.

Directory

Air freight *DHL* will send precious items home; Anmawuel House, 9 Sobukwe Rd (Farrar Ave), Adabraka (☎22.16.47).

Airline offices:

Aeroflot , 57 Kojo Thompson Rd (PO Box 9449; ☎22.52.89);

Air Afrique, Cocoa House, Kwame Nkrumah Ave (PO Box 539; ☎22.83.28);

Air Mali, Mona House;

Balkan Bulgarian Airlines, 37 Kwame Nkrumah Ave (☎22.20.97);

British Airways , Tudu Road (PO Box 2087; ☎66.62.22);

Egyptair John Holt Bartholomew Building, opposite UTC Dept Store (☎66.48.50);

Ethiopian Airlines , Cocoa House, Nkrumah Ave (PO Box 3600; ☎22.23.56);

Ghana Airways , Ghana House, near GPO (PO Box 1636; ☎66.48.56/7);

KLM , Republic House, Nkrumah Ave (PO Box 2223; ☎22.40.20);

Nigeria Airways, Danawi Building, Kojo Thompson Rd (PO Box 9068; ☎22.37.49/ 22.47.35);

Swissair, Nkrumah Ave (PO Box 1808; ☎66.64.88);

UTA c/o *Ghana Airways*.

American Express represented by *Scantravel*, High St (PO Box 4960, ☎66.31.34/66.42.04).

Banks Major banks are on High Street near the intersection of Bank Lane and include: *Bank of Ghana* (☎66.69.02); *Barclays Bank* (☎66.49.01); *Ghana Commercial Bank* (☎66.49.14); *Standard Chartered Bank* (☎66.66.81).

Books For secondhand books, try the southeast corner of Kinbu and Kojo Thompson roads.

British Council Independence Ave, near the *Ambassador*. Excellent library, British papers.

Car hire *Avis* through *Speedway Travel and Tours*, 5 Tackie Tawia St, Adabraka (PO Box 214; ☎22.87.99, telex 218); *Hertz* through *Allways Travel Agency* (PO Box 1638; ☎22.45.90), in *Kingsway* on Nkrumah Ave. Also try *Vanef* in Sobukwe/Farrar Ave, Adabraka. The big hotels can usually help, too.

Cinemas *Orion Cinema* Liberation Circle (☎22.22.92); *Globe* Adjaben Road; *Rex Cinema*, behind Parliament House; *The Bukom*, Continental Hotel; *Film Corporation Theatre*, off Independence Ave (near the French Embassy).

Embassies and consulates include:

Algeria, off Cantonments Road, Christiansborg (8am–2pm; PO Box 2747; ☎77.68.28);

Australia, 2 Milne Close, near airport (PO Box 2445; ☎77.79.72);

Benin , no. C175 Odoi Kwao Crescent no. 2 (8am–3pm; PO Box 7871; ☎22.57.01);

Burkina Faso, 772/3 Asylum Down, off Mango Tree Ave (7.30am–2pm; PO Box 651; ☎22.19.88, telex 2108). Visas available in 24hr, the fee is CFA6000 or $20 (no cedis) for a three-month multiple entry visa;

Canada, 46 Independence Avenue (8am–12.30pm and 1.30–4pm; PO Box 1639; ☎22.85.55, telex 2024);

Côte d'Ivoire, 9 8th Lane, Christiansborg (7.30am–2.30pm; PO Box 3445; ☎77.46.11). Visas are issued within 48hrs, although for certain nationalities (Australians, for example) they can take up to three weeks with telex exchanges to Abidjan;

Denmark (☎22.77.15);

Egypt, House F805/1, 3 Jawaharlal Nehru Ave, off Cantonments Road (9am–1pm; PO Box 2508; ☎77.67.01);

France, 12th Road, off Liberation Ave (10am–1pm except Tues 8.30am–12.30pm; PO Box 187; ☎22.85.71, telex 2101). Visa service for most unrepresented Francophone countries;

Germany, Valldemosa Lodge, 7th Ave Extension, North Ridge (7.30am–2pm; PO Box 1757; ☎22.13.11, telex 2025);

Guinea, 11 Osu Badu Street, Dzorwulu (8am–3pm; PO Box 5497; ☎77.79.21);

Italy , Jawaharlal Nehru Rd (PO Box 140; ☎77.56.21, telex 2039);

Japan, 8 Rangoon Ave, off Switchback Rd (8.30am–2.30pm; PO Box 1637; ☎77.56.15, telex 2068);

Liberia, Switchback Close, Cantonments (8.30am–noon; PO Box 895; ☎77.56.41, telex 2071);

Mali, Crescent Road, Block 1 (7.30am–2pm; PO Box 1121; ☎66.64.21, telex 2061);

Netherlands, 89 Liberation Road, Redemption Circle (8am–2pm; PO Box 3248; ☎22.16.55, telex 2128);

Niger Independence Ave (☎22.49.62);

Nigeria, Rangoon Ave (8am–3pm; PO Box 1548; ☎77.61.58, telex 2051). Visas delivered Tues only, apply am, pick up pm. No reference required;

Spain, Airport Residential Area, Lamptey Ave Extension (8am–2pm; PO Box 1218; ☎77.40.04);

Switzerland, 9 Water Rd, North Ridge (7.30am–1.30pm; PO Box 359; ☎22.81.25, telex 2197);

Togo, Togo House, near Cantonments Circle (7am–noon and 1–4pm; PO Box 4308; ☎77.79.50, telex 2166). Visas (48hr maximum duration, extendable in Lomé) require two photos and three days to issue;

United Kingdom, Abdul Nasser Ave (7.45am–3.45pm; PO Box 296; ☎22.16.65, telex 2323);

USA, Ring Road East (7.30am–12.30pm and 1.30–4.30pm; PO Box 194; ☎77.53.46).

Foreign exchange bureaux For the best rates try *BHC Bank* on the corner of Kojo Thompson and Tudu roads (open to 5pm, but takes forever). Two others by the GPO – *Kumas* and *Ladars* – are quicker.

Immigration office Registration ("within 48 hours") is done at the Secretariat for Internal Affairs (☎66.54.21) on Kinbu Road (8am–12.30pm & 1.30–5pm) in a few minutes. Two photos needed. Visa extensions can also be arranged here.

Maps The *KLM* office gives out free city maps. You can also get them at the *Survey offices* on Giffard Rd near the airport, which has national and regional road maps on sale, too

Markets Makola 31 December market is the city centre's retail pulse. These days it contains just about everything in the food and domestic line, including cheap glass beads. Huge, and a must.

Phones Main hotels are the best bet, or use the P&T External, on the seaward side of High Street or the new card-phones if they're in operation.

Photos If you want decent quality passport photos, head to a studio (there's a 24-hour one on the corner of Kojo Thompson and South Liberia Rd). Otherwise, you can get fuzzy wooden box photos done more cheaply in five minutes on Kinbu Rd, across from the lorry park.

Postcards Good selection at the museum.

Poste Restante At the GPO and open 8am–4.30pm Mon–Fri. No charge.

Shipping agents If you want to try gettig a berth on a ship, *Umarco Ghana Ltd*, PO Box 215, Harbour Area, Tema (☎0221 4031/5, telex 2037), are the Port Agents for *Grimaldi Lines*.

Student discounts Students can sometimes get discounts on *Ghana Airways* and *STC* coaches. To qualify, you must present your international student card or a letter from your university to the *SYTAG* office in the Accra Community Centre on High St. They also have student accommodation at various points throughout the country. For more information, contact: Patricia Ansah, *SYTAG*, PO Box 14337, Accra.

Supermarkets *Kingsway*, on Nkrumah Ave near *KLM*, often has wholemeal bread. *UTC* is the biggest store, with just about everything, including cheap books.

Swimming pools Canadian nationals can use the bar and pool at their High Commission. Others should head to the pool at the *Ambassador Hotel* which non-guests can use for a small fee. The swimming pool at Kaneshie sports complex is out of use.

Travel agents Check out the car hire recommendations for general agents. For cheap flights to Europe, *Aeroflot* is likely to be most promising. You might also try the *Balkan Bulgarian* agents, *Secaps Holiday Travels Ltd*, Vanderpuye-Orgle Building, 46 Sobukwe Rd (Farrar Ave), or *Egyptair* if you can put up with a long flight. *Scantravel*, High St (PO Box 4960; ☎66.31.34/66.42.04) is an efficient general travel agent and the Amex representative.

Tourist Information The Ghana Tourist Board on Kojo Thompson Rd (☎22.89.23) has been re-organising and come out with updated pamphlets on general information, hotels and restaurants. They may also be offering regional tours, as well as trips to the Mole Game Reserve.

North and east of Accra: short excursions

Getting **out of the city** for a while, especially at the hottest and most humid times of the year, from January to June, can be a relief, especially if you head north towards the hills.

Legon and Aburi

LEGON, 14km north of Accra, is the headquarters of the **University of Ghana**, described by the tourist board as "a showpiece of Japanese architecture" – judge for yourself! There's a good bookshop but, as usual, less opportunity to meet students than you might wish.

You can visit the university's botanical garden in the grounds, but there are older, more interesting and extensive gardens at **ABURI**, on Akwapim Ridge, 23km further north, with potentially magnificent views north over the forest and south to the city when the air is clear. Aburi, several hundred metres above the plain, was a colonial hill station and site of a sanatorium (now a hotel), and the gardens still bear the well-tended hallmarks of landscaped colonial taste, with hundreds of tree specimens from all over the tropical and sub-topical regions. There's a pleasant restaurant in the gardens as well as a snack bar. The **hotel** – S/C bunglows from ₵1200 or you can camp – is frequently full, so an excellent alternative is the little English-run place in Aburi village called *May & Lodge* with fine views from its S/C rooms (around ₵2000 a double).

A further 19km beyond Aburi brings you to **LARTEH** and the **Akonedi Shrine**, a centre of Ga traditional religion with an exotic assembly of priests and practitioners. The tourist office in Accra used to run trips up here so the place acquired a slightly debased atmosphere. Nowadays, though, it doesn't get a lot of tourist visitors, and you can still go yourself, armed with suitable, alcoholic offerings. By far the best time to visit is early October, when the annual **Akonedi festival** takes place.

Tro-tros from Tudu run frequently to Legon, and **buses** from Tudu bus station take about an hour to Aburi. If you're driving yourself, continue past the airport to Tetteh Quarshie Circle, then take the Akosombo road until it forks right, and you fork left and start climbing.

East of Accra: beaches

Looking **east of Accra** towards Togo, the quiet beach at **PRAMPRAM**, distinguished by the French **Fort Vernon,** is reputed to be Ghana's best. Beyond Prampram, watersports resorts of sorts at **ADA**, in the mouth of the Volta, and **KETA.**, out on its delta, are popular with Ghanaians: both provide first-class bird-watching. Some 25km to the north are the **Shai Hills**, with bizarre volcanic formations and the small **Shai hills game reserve**, which may still be offering horseriding. Any of these destinations is likely to be less patronised by travellers than the sweep of coastline to the west of Accra, which is beginning to attract attention.

THE COAST WEST OF ACCRA

The scenic coastline stretching from **Accra** to the Côte d'Ivoire border is one of the most obvious tourist targets in the whole of West Africa. The big attractions are the densest concentration of European **forts and castles** anywhere on the continent – twenty-nine of them, some over 500 years old – and innumerable, unspoiled Fante **fishing villages** tucked between links of sandy, coconut-backed beaches. It's an irresistible combination, and not one you'll be alone in discovering. Although tourism dropped off drastically in the late 1970s, it has since been revived and the trend is likely to continue. You'll have to come on a weekday or out of season to have much hope of finding your own isolated paradise. Despite which, few places are ever more than quietly humming with tourist business. This is not The Gambia.

For a little urban stimulation, **Cape Coast** – the former British Gold Coast capital – and **Takoradi** are the main coastal towns, where you'll have the best luck finding forex bureaux, long-distance transport and diversions lacking in the smaller villages.

From Accra to Cape Coast

Leaving Accra, the highway at first stays well inland, running through scrubby bush and farming country, hot and unyielding. Just 16km west of Accra is the first break, at **KOKROBITE**, a beach resort with a dance and music school (*Academy of African Music and Arts Ltd*, PO Box 2923, Accra) which doubles as a hotel and bar (look out for the "A.A.M.A.L." sign on the main road). There are free music and dance displays most afternoons between 2pm and 6pm, especially at weekends, and they offer courses in African dance and drumming. The hotel, though quite swanky in a Ghanaian way, isn't too expensive – ₵3000/5000.

The first fort along this coast is **Fort Good Hope** at **SENYA BERAKU**. To get here from Accra, take a bush taxi to Awutu junction (not Senya junction, from where you won't easily get onward transport). From here, you can get another taxi down to the village. The village is dull, but the setting is scenic, and the trip interesting mainly for the fishing activities of the Fante inhabitants (remember, the Fante don't fish on Tuesdays). You get sweeping panoramic views from the fort which hangs over the sea; staying the night costs ₵500, bucket showers included. Senya Beraku is the site of a number of **festivals** throughout the year (see p.818).

THE FORTS

Soon after the Portuguese found the maritime routes to the Gulf of Guinea in the fifteenth century, they began setting up trading posts. Rumours of the vast wealth of the region filtered back to Europe and it wasn't long before other nations established themselves on the coast, building sturdy fortresses to protect their interests in the trade of gold, ivory and, later, slaves. By the end of the eighteenth century, 37 such forts dotted the coastline. Eight of them have been completely destroyed, but after independence several of the survivors were converted to guesthouses. Many ceased taking in travellers in the early 1980s, but renovations are in motion at a number and it's possible to sleep at the rest houses (RH) in at least four of them. Along the coast from east to west, the **major forts** include:

• **Prampram** *Fort Vernon* built in 1756 by the French and taken by the British in 1806.

• **Accra** *Christianborg* built by the Danish in 1659. Earlier a Swedish, and probably also Portuguese fortress stood on the same spot. *Ussher Fort* built by the Dutch in 1642. Ten years later it was taken by the French and named "Fort Crevecoeur", then passed through the hands of the Dutch and finally the British who rebuilt it in 1868. *James Fort* mid-sixteenth-century Portuguese fort taken by the English and rebuilt in 1673.

• **Senya Beraku (RH)** *Fort Good Hope* taken by the Dutch in 1704, date of origin unknown.

• **Apam (RH)** *Fort Leydaasmheim* built in 1697 by the Dutch. Occupied by the British (who named it Fort Patience) in 1782 and retaken by the Dutch three years later. It was abandoned around 1800.

• **Anomabu** *Fort William* founded by the Dutch around 1700 and occupied by the British in 1753.

• **Mouri** *Fort Nassau* built by the Dutch in 1598. It went back and forth between the British and Dutch until it was finally abandoned in 1815.

• **Cape Coast** The original castle was founded by the Swedish then taken by the Danes and finally the English in 1662. It was renovated in the mid-nineteenth century when it lost its original design.

• **Elmina** *Saint George's Castle*, the oldest European monument in sub-Saharan Africa, built by the Portuguese in 1482 with dressed stones brought from Europe. The original castle was expanded by the Dutch in 1637. *Fort São Iago* (**RH**) is also fifteenth-century Portuguese and was taken by the Dutch in 1683.

• **Komenda** *Fort Vredenburg* built by the Dutch in 1688, taken by the British in 1782 and abandoned three years later. *Fort English* in the same town was founded by them in 1663.

• **Shama** *Fort Sebastian* founded by the Portuguese around 1560 and occupied by the Dutch in 1640.

• **Sekondi** *Fort Orange* built by the Dutch in 1640; British after 1872.

• **Dixcove (RH)** *Fort Metal Cross* occupied by the English in 1691, of unknown origin. Rebuilt in 1749.

• **Princestown** *Grossfriedrichsburg* built in 1683 by the German Brandenburgers and taken by the Dutch and later British. In ruins at independence, the fort has since been restored.

• **Axim** *Fort Saint Anthony*, the second Portuguese fort on the coast, built in the fifteenth century. Taken by the Dutch in 1642 and rebuilt on several occasions.

WINNEBA, the main town in these parts, is reached from **Swedru junction** on the main coast highway. It's famous in Ghana as the site of the *Aboakyer* or **"deer-hunting festival"** which takes place at the end of April or early May (see p.818). The town perches on raised ground between the Muni and Oyibi lagoons and offers an alternative, as yet not very well known, to Dixcove further west. Stay here, right on the beach on the other side of the town, at the *Sir Charles Tourist Centre*, from about ₵3000 a night. They do good food and there's a saltwater pool for swimmers who don't want to struggle with the dangerous sea. *SYTAG* in Accra can help lower the cost (see Student discounts in the Accra "Directory"). Out of the hotel on the right you can watch **drag fishing**, with music and singing, and fifty men hauling the net rope. In the other direction is **the town**, en route to which an amazing *posu* **shrine** is watched over by a genial priest who'll go out of his way to explain his job. Past the *posu*, at the edge of town, there are women smoking fish – then the town proper with canoes, noise and lots of bustle, especially at dusk.

Some 20km further you can also stay at **Fort Patience** in **APAM** and if you've time in the day, this is a fine alternative. At the entrance to town is another imposing *posu* which was beautifully restored in 1988. Colourful statues of Africans mounted on horseback decorate the three-storey affair which is topped by a white Jesus (for an explanation of this type of religious architecture, visit the museum in Cape Coast). **Getting there** requires taking a taxi to the Apam junction and changing. Fort Patience is beautifully sited and you can sleep at the fort for ₵250 or less, with well water for bathing and occasional electricity. Food is limited pretty much to the market, unless you can persuade someone to cook for you, but there are a couple of bars in town where you can get a drink.

The next town along, **SALTPOND**, offers precious little reason to call in (a bypass skirts the town) though it vies with Winneba for importance. If you fetch up here for the night, be sure to avoid the obnoxious *Nkrubem Motel*. Give the *Palm Beach* a try instead.

The last place of note on this stretch is the idyllic crescent of sand and coconuts at **BIRIWA,** 10km beyond the Winneba exit road. It's right beneath the main highway for a change, which makes it both accessible and a little too popular at weekends. Time was it sheltered the odd semi-resident hippy in wood shacks at the village end of the beach, but those days have passed and there's now a European-run **restaurant** on the sands and a fair-sized crowd on the beach at weekends. There are still good beach camping possibilities, though, with supplies available in the village above the rocky bluff.

Cape Coast – the town

British capital of the Gold Coast until 1876, **CAPE COAST** is a relatively large town with a solid infrastructure. The site of the nation's first university and major secondary schools, your chances of running into Ghanaian students here are good. The major attraction is, of course, the seventeenth-century **Cape Coast Castle** and museum. There are no very recreational beaches nearby. And note that through traffic doesn't go via the town, but round its north side on a **bypass**, off the frame of our map.

The castle and museum

Perched on a rocky ledge that juts out over the ocean, **Cape Coast Castle** is today a classified monument open to the public. Originally a Swedish and then a Danish fort, it was taken in 1662 by the British who made it their Gold Coast headquarters until 1876. In the nineteenth century, the building was enlarged to its present dimensions. A guided tour (₵200 plus a supplement if you want to take pictures) takes you through the maze of damp, suffocating **dungeons** where slaves were held before being shipped to Europe. The tour also includes a visit to the adjoining **museum** – naturally very small compared to the one in Accra – with scattered examples of Ghanaian pottery, carvings and other artistry mixed with historical exhibits documenting the slave trade. There's background on local indigenous religion, however, that gives a few clues about the fascinating *posu* architecture and symbolism. And don't leave without seeing the Governor's wardrobe.

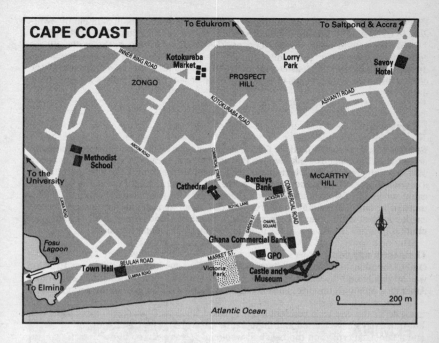

Accommodation and practicalities

Centrally located near the beachfront in the west of town, the *Savoy Hotel* in Ashanti Rd (☎042.28.66) isn't bad value at ₵2500 for clean rooms with fan. It's often full, in which case you could try *Dan's Paradise* ("*Dans Pee*", PO Box 57; ☎042.18.02), a popular disco with accommodation featuring large AC rooms with double beds from ₵3000. The other main hotel is the much dumpier *Palace*; slightly cheaper than the others with non-S/C rooms. If you're a student, *SYTAG* in Accra can, once again, help with accommodation arrangements, perhaps even in the castle. It's certainly possible to find a bed at the

---

THE OGUAA FETU HARVEST FESTIVAL

Although many harvest festivals are held in the region, one of the biggest bashes is Cape Coast's **Oguaa Fetu Afahye**, which takes place the first Saturday in September. Traditional chiefs from throughout the surrounding districts parade in sumptuous kente-cloth togas bedecked with gold crowns and medallions. The most important rulers are carried in canoe-like stretchers balanced on the heads of four manservants and shaded by huge parasols. They're accompanied by the **queen mothers**, wearing bracelets, necklaces and rings of solid gold, with more gold ornaments in their beehive coiffures. Fetish priests dance through the procession dispensing good fortune and collecting payment; palm wine flows freely. The parade lasts most of the day, terminating in **Victoria Park** for speeches by the chiefs and government representatives. Later, the streets fill up again and the party continues through the night with orchestras and dancing. This carnival atmosphere reigns for a couple of days and if you can time your trip right, it's worth making a detour. Come early and try and book a hotel in advance – most are crammed solid for the duration.

University of Ghana Cape Coast Campus **Halls of Residence**, about 3km out of town – around ₵750 a night. For night-time diversions, try the *Starlight* and *The Big Apple*.

When it's time **to move on**, the lorry park and STC yard are near the castle and can connect you with Accra, Takoradi or Kumasi. *Peugeot* pick-ups and station wagons also depart regularly for the fourteen-kilometre-trip to Elmina, the nicest stretch of the coastal highway, where it runs directly above the beach through endless swaying coco-nut trees.

Elmina

ELMINA, now a small but active fishing town, was one of the first European toe-holds on the West African coast: its name is Portuguese, and means "The Mine". The princi-pal attractions remain the **Portuguese castle and fort**, although the slow pace makes it a rewarding place to relax and absorb the rhythms of a coastal town. But it's not all calm; when the fising boats come in, Elmina can be spectacularly vibrant, and its unusual layout is arresting, counterposing the ocean against the lagoon and the two castles against each other. There are also a number of interesting *posu* shrines and, photographically, this is one of the most gratifying places along the coast.

The castle and fort

One of the oldest standing buildings in West Africa, the castle of **St George El Mina** was originally built by the Portuguese in 1482 – ten years before Columbus discovered America – although the original stockade was barely half the size of the present struc-

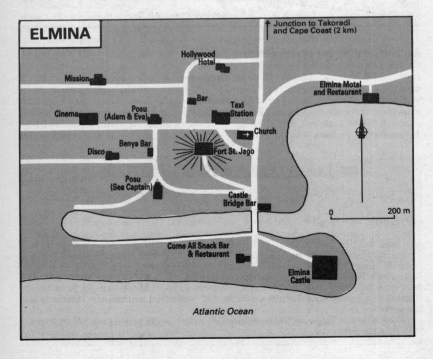

ture. It served as the **Portuguese headquarters** in West Africa for over 150 years until it was captured by soldiers of the Dutch West Indies Company in 1637. By that time, Saint George had grown roughly to its present size. In the courtyard, you'll notice a **Catholic church** built by the Portuguese. The protestant Dutch transformed this place of worship into a mess hall and **slave market** – an onerous image that poignantly drives home the barbarity of the trade. In 1872, the British bought Elmina castle, along with Holland's other possessions on the Gold Coast.

Given its age, the castle has held up well, but parts are beginning to deteriorate rapidly, notably the **Governor's kitchens** and the **officer's mess**, whose beautiful arched facade dates from the eighteenth century. Restoration work may already be under way. Extremely good tours of the castle cost ₵500, photos extra.

Across from the castle and atop a steep, partly artificial hill, is **Fort St Jago** (São Iago), also dating from the fifteenth century and built to protect Elmina. It was taken by the Dutch in 1683. Formerly a resthouse and – if only on account of its dramatic position – one of the best places to stay in Ghana, it has been under renovation for several years, but should soon be open again.

Accommodation and practicalities

The cheapest **place to stay** is likely to be Fort St Jago (due open in 1992). Alternatively, you can try the good *Hollywood Hotel*, a family-run establishment with non-S/C rooms with electricity around a lovely courtyard (from ₵2000). The more upmarket *Elmina Motel* has comfortable S/C chalets with individual terraces near the beachfront – fresh linen and comfortable beds start at ₵7500; the breakfasts in the restaurant are excellent. Beyond here again is the *Oyster Bay* , with rooms for a little less.

A first-rate cheap **place to eat** in town is the *Come All Snack Bar*, near the castle. Here you can get inexpensive omelettes, rice and chicken or fish. Behind the street-front snack bar is a sit-down restaurant, and they sell pastries and drinking water, too. The best place to park a weary body and unwind over a beer is the *Castle Bridge Bar*, built on the water by the fishing port amid all the action.

Takoradi

If you're just in from the glitter of Côte d'Ivoire and **TAKORADI** is your first Ghanaian town, take heart – it's probably the least inviting. By no stretch of the imagination is this another scenic coastal stop. Primarily an industrial centre, the ungainly sprawl has few redeeming features but, as home of the nation's second **port**, the town has a certain vitality and it's a convenient springboard for places as far afield as Abidjan, or as near as Dixcove. Takoradi is often referred to as Sekondi-Takoradi, SEKONDI being the naval base 10km to the east, with which you're unlikely to have much contact.

Orientation and practicalities

The **main market**, completely encircled by an enormous roundabout, is Takoradi's nerve centre. Liberation Road leads from Market Circle south to Sekondi Road, which continues down to **Takoradi harbour**. All the major **banks** are on Liberation Road, as are several forex bureaux and the regional **tourist office** where you can pick up a city map and information on travel in the Western Region. Minibuses ply between the market and the harbour district where the **GPO**, hospital and **railway station** are all located.

When **leaving Takoradi**, the main **motor park** is within Market Circle (transport to Cape Coast, Accra, Dixcove and Abidjan), and the **STC yard** is nearby on Axim Rd.

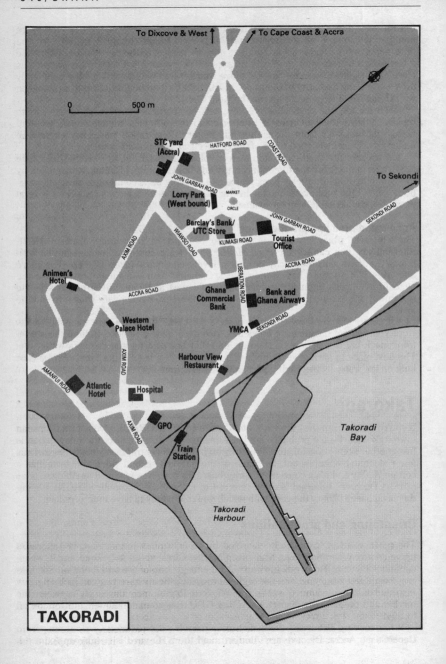

To Dixcove & West

To Cape Coast & Accra

To Sekondi

0   500 m

STC yard
(Accra)

HATFORD ROAD

COAST ROAD

JOHN GARBAH ROAD

Lorry Park
(West bound)

MARKET
CIRCLE

JOHN GARBAH ROAD

SEKONDI ROAD

Barclay's Bank/
UTC Store

WIAWSO ROAD

KUMASI ROAD

Tourist
Office

AXIM ROAD

ACCRA ROAD

Animen's
Hotel

ACCRA ROAD

Ghana
Commercial
Bank

LIBERATION ROAD

Bank and
Ghana Airways

Western
Palace Hotel

YMCA

SEKONDI ROAD

AMANFUL ROAD

AXIM ROAD

Harbour View
Restaurant

Atlantic
Hotel

Hospital

Takoradi
Bay

AXIM ROAD

GPO

Train
Station

Takoradi
Harbour

TAKORADI

The airport is further north on Axim Rd (*Ghana Airways* has an office on Liberation Ave for tickets and flight information). If you're heading **to Kumasi** you may be better off taking the **train** since the main road route to the interior makes a sweeping detour via Accra. It's apparently also possible to take a **boat** from here to Winneba.

Accommodation and food

If you have to spend the night, there are several convenient **places to stay** around the triangular town centre, all alright but none outstanding. The *Alor Hotel*, near the motor park, has exceptionally clean S/C rooms with fresh linen from ₵2200; some have AC. There's slightly cheaper accommodation at the *Zenith* on Califf Ave, with a unique circus decor that looks like something out of a Fellini film. It's plain and a bit dirty, but a room with fan is only ₵1500. Cheapest of all is the **community workers' camp** in lovely green surroundings not far from the GPO.

The more upmarket *Western Palace Hotel* off Axim Rd on Chapel Hill (☎031.24.15) has airy rooms with AC or fans from ₵3000. Pushed as the best hotel in town (at least the one always full of Aid workers and other ex-pats) is the *Atlantic* – near the main hospital and port (PO Box 273; ☎031.33.00) – with everything from **car hire sevices** to a conference centre. The AC rooms, however, are run-down, and the place is famous for shortages of electricity and water (from ₵5000). The *Ahenfie Hotel* on Axim Rd (PO Box 0608; ☎031.29.66) is less formal, but has large AC rooms, a video lounge, restaurant and disco. Takoradi's best is the smart and newish *Animen's Hotel*, off the bottom of Axim Road, where AC rooms go from at least ₵6000.

Street food abounds in the area around the *Zenith* between Califf Ave and Liberation Road if you're in need of a night-time fix of *kenkey* and fish. For more formal surroundings try the *Chez Connie* restaurant and bar, next to the *Alor*, serving moderately priced European and African food. Slightly more exciting offerings – including spring rolls – are served up at the *Harbour View Restaurant*, a nice place to sit outside where you can snack on a hill above the sea. Otherwise, prowl the hotel dining rooms, and drop us a line if you like what you find.

Dixcove and Busua – and beyond

Sheltering behind Ghana's southernmost headland, Cape Three Points, the twin villages of **DIXCOVE** and **BUSUA** have long been a favourite overlanders' hideaway. There are two principal attractions: first the cute, whitewashed hilltop **Fort Metal Cross** at Dixcove, overlooking the exceptionally animated fishing village and its deep, forest-bound, circular bay; and second the long strand of **Busua beach**, with safe swimming and a very reasonable beach bungalow set-up operating behind. Dixcove and Busua are no longer isolated retreats, though. Since the new highway was completed between Ghana and Côte d'Ivoire, it's easy to make the small diversion en route, and the area draws people from Abidjan as well as Accra.

If Busua does get a little crowded at weekends, and particularly in season from December to February, it doesn't detract much from the area's intrinsic appeal – the quintessential Ghana **beach scene**. It's hard to feel anything less than equable about a place where you can be met on arrival with the words "Hi friend, welcome to Busua, my name is Possible". More disappointing is the dying coconut forest all around, attacked by a morbid blight (see box).

Arriving from Côte d'Ivoire, AXIM is more or less en route and worth a stop – most buses call there – as too is PRINCESTOWN. Both have fine castles and magnificent views. But neither is likely to drag you away from Dixcove and Busua once you're settled in there.

Arrivals

Dixcove and Busua are about 13km from **Agona junction** on the main highway and there's little transport from east or west going down there. Change vehicles at Agona for "Discov" or "Bushwa". If you're independently mobile, there's a fork 6km down the road to the coast: left to Busua or right to Dixcove. It doesn't matter greatly which you dsecide to take, as the two are connected by a twenty-minute walk through the coastal bush.

Dixcove

Fort Metal Cross is, in principle, open as a rest house: but in practice, like most others, it has been closed more often than open over the years. Still it's been renovated since 1988 and, if you're lucky, there are four rooms at ₵250 with erratic water supplies and electricity. Its site, otherwise eminent, is regrettably marred by a monolithic block of flats of surpassing ugliness right in front of it. If you're not staying, you can look around the British fort for ₵300 or so.

If you don't find accommodation at the Fort, there's still every opportunity of staying in a private house in Dixcove. Eat at the *Ekmac* (rice and sauce, cheap and simple), a small place midway between the **motor park** and the shore on the tarred road. Dixcove is a happy and engaging fishing community with an intimate feel, strongly focused on the waterfront. If you're more intent on lying in the sun and swimming, however, you'll need to be on Busua beach.

Busua beach

Although you can get to **Busua** by taxi from Dixcove, it's just as fast to walk, via the bush-farm footpath that leads off, northeasterly, from behind the fort. Once you get up the rise, you can practically see Busua, but ask directions as you'll never find your way the first time out. There's the shallow Busua River to ford on the Busua side and you walk past the fishing beach and right though the village to reach the unmissable *Busua Pleasure Beach Hotel* (PO Box 7, Dixcove), on the sands. The spartan **chalets** go from about ₵1500–2500 a night, depending on size and facilities. Camping is allowed (₵500) but, because of thieving, not encouraged. There's no electricity or running water: you have to purify **drinking water** – which is fine by the hotel as they sell more **beer** –and there are drums of washing water on each porch. They also do lasting breakfasts and other meals to order on their terrace, or you can have them cook whatever you find for sale in the village – most famously lobsters, now getting rather pricey.

Improvements may come but the *Pleasure Beach* has been running like this for years and it's often full. The beautiful sands and equally clean, surfy sea are together a very big plus, though how much longer the nude bathing will go on is another matter. It's a place to meet travellers, swap tales, and maybe find companions.

Again, there are **rooms** available in Busua, and you can also eat very cheaply on the street. The village is a viable alternative if the hotel is full or if you're determined to avoid the inevitable overlanders' "scene" which tends to build up around the chalets.

DEAD COCONUTS AND CAMEL CORPS

If only the **coconut trees** weren't dying rapidly, Busua would be an even more enticing prospect. "Airborne bacteria" and "old age" were two theories competing for adherents in the village. Coconut trees, runs the second theory, are emotional and sympathetic souls and the sight of so many of their relatives dying fills some of them with such grief that they pine away and succumb as well. Whatever the cause – and scientists have traced a nasty blight – the trees are to be replaced with resistant varieties at some stage. Meanwhile, the remaining forest of trunks is a miserable cemetery. Many were cut down by the group from *Camel* cigarettes who stormed across the Sahara a couple of years back on a corporate image-building spree, painted the chalets in their colours and left parasols and thousands of cigarettes.

A multitude of short **walks** are possible in the area, either west to Cape Three Points, 5km beyond Dixcove, or east along Busua Beach, cutting over the headland and down to BUTRE, just a kilometre beyond the beach, which used to have a fort of its own – **Fort Batenstein** – now completely in ruins.

Further forts: west to the Ivoirian border

In 1681, Prince Friedrich Wilhelm of Brandenburg sent an expedition to the area of what is now **PRINCESTOWN** in an effort to break the seventeenth-century Portuguese, British and Dutch hold over West African trade. This led to the founding of **Fort Grossfriedrichsburg**, within whose walls the Brandenburgers soon fell victim to malaria and repeated attacks by the Dutch and British. They abandoned the citadel in 1708, turning it over to the Ahanta-Pokoso chief **Johnny Konny**, who earned the dubious title "Last Prussian Negro Prince". The Dutch stormed the fort in 1748 and renamed it Hollandia. It was finally abandoned around 1800.

Today, the fort can be visited and has spectacular views, but it doesn't serve as a guesthouse and there's nowhere obvious to stay in the village. The road down to Princestown from the highway used to be unthinkably bad and periodically impassable in the rainy season, but it has now been repaired. If it deteriorates again you may well have to walk one way or both.

Axim – and into Côte d'Ivoire

The last of the forts along the Ghana coastline is **Santa Antonia** in the small town of **AXIM**. Built by the Portuguese, probably in the fifteenth century, it was taken by the Dutch in 1642. Today it houses government offices, but if you ask in the right way you should be allowed to visit it. There's a very basic hotel on the edge of town (*San Marco*) with no running water or electricity. The staff provide lanterns and buckets.

Onward travel into Côte d'Ivoire is simple from Axim. There are daily buses through to the border at ELUBO – change at MPATABA junction if want to tackle the seashore route into Côte d'Ivoire. Details of this route in reverse are given on p.777. First (or last) money changing facilities in Ghana are at a big new branch of the *Ghana Commercial Bank* in HALF ASSINI.

KUMASI AND AROUND

The **central part of Ghana** covered in this section is one of the country's most attractive regions. The road from Accra, skirting past the northeast fringe of the old **Asante heartland**, is scenic and hilly. Around, and out of, the great hub of **Kumasi** itself, a clutch of different **routes** radiate through steep scarp and forest country. Much of this has long been under cultivation – especially **cocoa**, which brings a dark, gloomy silence to the woods – but plenty is still jungle-swathed, stacked with impressive, buttress-rooted forest giants, and scattered with misty hillside villages. These, misty grey-green in the chilly mornings, sticky and brilliantly coloured in the afternoons, are the key elements in an area to savour. Travel is easy, and the cultural heritage as rich as anywhere.

Kumasi – the town

History hangs heavy in **KUMASI**. You feel it walking through the streets where monumental **colonial buildings** – a reminder of half a century of British domination – have become worn with time and painted with water-stained layers of ochre-red dust. Foreign edifices have taken on an African look in a town that oozes with the traditions and customs of the **Asante** – one of the most powerful nations in West Africa at the end of the nineteenth century. A combination of the old order and hectic modernity makes this extremely active commercial centre one of Ghana's most satisfying cities.

THE RISE OF THE ASANTE

The Asante trace their **origins** to the northern regions of the savannah belt. Along with other Akan peoples, they came to this region around the eleventh century and settled in the area of **Lake Bosumtwi**, carving farms from the wild rainforest. These districts contained rich gold fields and trade in the metal gradually developed, at first to the north, supplying the Saharan caravans. By the fifteenth century, however, the Akan also had commercial links with the Portuguese and, by the seventeenth century, they were organised into dozens of small states, each vying for control of the mines and the slave-supplying districts in the far interior where European merchants hadn't ventured.

FOUNDING OF THE ASANTE NATION

In the 1690s, **Osei Tutu** – the first great **Asante king**, or *Asantehene* – brought together a loose confederation of states into a single nation under his rule. **Kumasi** was chosen as the site of the new capital on the advice of Osei Tutu's most trusted adviser, **Okomfo Ankoye**, an extremely powerful fetish priest. Okomfo planted the seeds of two *kum* trees in separate locations, one of which sprouted, indicating where the Asante seat was to be established; under the *kum* tree – "*kum asi*". Having received this sign, the priest evoked the **Golden Stool** from the heavens. This "throne" descended from the clouds to alight upon Osei Tutu, and thereby became the single most important symbol of national unity and the authority of the king. The Asante nation was born.

EXPANSION AND CONSOLIDATION

Osei Tutu set about expanding his empire. One of his most important early victories was against the Denkyira king, **Ntim Gyakar**, under whom the Asante had traditionally lived as vassals. They captured, tried and killed Ntim Gyakar in 1699. Other rival powers fell in their turn, each **conquered state** left intact, but owing allegiance and taxes in goods and labour to the Asante. Gradually the kingdom grew to include most of present-day Ghana and Côte d'Ivoire, with only the **Fante** states of the coast putting up realistic resistance, using European allies to their advantage.

The sheer size of the Asante kingdom spawned a royal **bureaucracy** and **judicial system**. **Administrative functions** were transferred from the hereditary nobility to a new class of appointed functionaries controlled by the king. Even **commoners** could fill lower court offices which included linguists and commissioners or governors sent to oversee vassal states. The Asantehene himself was chosen by the queen mother, who

Orientation

Even in its early days, Kumasi was an imposing capital. Today it spreads widely over the hills, and is home to close on a million people. The heart of the downtown district is marked roughly by **Kejetia Circle**, a large roundabout with a wonderfully kitsch replica of the **golden stool** rising from its centre. Nearby, the **central market** – the largest in Ghana and one of the very biggest in Africa – spills over the railway tracks to fill a hollow in the city centre. Despite the tumbledown appearance of rambling, rusty, corrugated-iron-clad stalls, it's a fantastic place to while away your time, searching out corners filled with everything from **Asante crafts** (cloth, sandals, leather goods, pottery) to spare car parts and plastic imports. A large section is devoted to fruit, vegetables and provisions.

Just west of the market, the **Adum district** is the commercial centre where you'll find **forex bureaux**, major **banks**, supermarkets and department stores, and the post office. Up the hill, northwest of Adum, **Bantama district** takes over. This is the site of the expansive **Ghana National Cultural Centre**, with museum, model Asante village, cocoa farm, palm wine "factory", crafts centre, library and performance facilities for music and dance. It's a good place to make for on arrival (₵200 by taxi from Kejetia), since it gives you an immediate fix on what Kumasi is all about, and supplies city maps.

consulted with advisors before making her decision (in the matrilineal system, successors were chosen from the king's brothers or his sisters' offspring). Though his power was nearly absolute, an unworthy Asantehene could be "destooled" – removed from the throne – by the royal family.

THE FALL, AND WAR WITH THE BRITISH

The Asante empire had reached its apogee by the year 1800 when **Osei Bonsu** ascended to the throne. The borders of the country now extended well beyond the present-day borders of Ghana, and Kumasi was a capital with a population of 700,000. In the vast market in the heart of town, trade was so healthy that the king's servants periodically sifted the sand to collect loose gold dust. Despite the prosperity, **rebellion** was fomenting among Asante refugees who took shelter in the Fante confederation of the coast. In 1806, Osei Bonsu launched a full-scale attack against the Fante and invaded their lands. The attack marked the beginning of the last phase of the great conquests.

The coastal **Fante** had traditionally traded directly with the British, and Osei Bonsu's invasion thus led to direct **conflict between the British and the Asante**. As early as 1824, on the death of Osei Bonsu, the British were anxious to squash this main obstacle to the control of Gold Coast trade. Hostilities simmered through the nineteenth century, erupting in 1824 in the **First Anglo-Asante war**. War broke out again in 1826 when the Asante were heavily defeated and Britain assumed the role of "Protector" along the coast and as far as 130km inland. A third war, in 1863, was inconclusive, though Asante history relates it as a victory, with a strong invasion force from Kumasi holding the British back for a few years. After some preparation, the British marched on Kumasi in the **Fourth Asante War** (1874), but found the palace empty since the Asantehene and his retinue had fled to the forest. The British troops took whatever treasure they could find in the palace (most of which was later auctioned in London) and then blew it up. The rest of the city was razed to the ground.

By the end of the nineteenth century, the British had annexed the Asante country as part of their Gold Coast colony. They sought to humiliate and demoralise the nation by publicly arresting the young Asantehene, **Prempeh**, and exiling him to the Seychelles. The final slap in the face came in 1900 when the new colonial governor, Sir Frederick Hodgson, demanded the Golden Stool be handed over for him to sit on. Having foreseen such a scenario, astute royal court members had made a fake golden stool and concealed the real one, which was only discovered by accident much later, in the 1920s. Nobody, not even the Asantehene, had ever sat on it. To do so would have violated national unity.

AKAN NAMES

People are named according to the day of the week in which they are born.

	GIRLS' NAMES	BOYS' NAMES
Monday	Ajoa	Kojo
Tuesday	Abena, Aba	Kwabena, Kobina
Wednesday	Akua	Kweku
Thursday	Yaa	Yao, Ekow
Friday	Efua	Kofi
Saturday	Ama	Kwame, Kwamena
Sunday	Esi	Kwasi

Accommodation

Although Kumasi lacks any really luxurious **accommodation**, inexpensive lodgings abound, getting cheaper the further you move from the centre. In vacations, the University halls of residence are often open to volunteers and travellers. **Unity Hall**, on the campus, is one such. It's pleasant there, with a pool, gardens and no lack of company. For more comfort, Kumasi has S/C, AC hotel rooms, but you won't find anything on a par with four-star international chains.

Inexpensive city centre lodgings

Hotel de Kingsway, Prempeh II Rd, Adum district (PO Box 178; ☎2441). Handily situated in the commercial centre, this is the big favourite. The restaurant, bar and occasional night-club assure a lot of activity here; rooms with fans from ₵3300.

Montana Hotel, Adum district (PO Box 1416; ☎2366). Smaller than the *Kingsway*, but same central location in easy walking distance from points of interest downtown. Non S/C rooms with fan from ₵3300.

Menka Memorial Hotel, 24 February Rd, Amakom district (PO Box 3371; ☎6432). Large hotel about 2km from centre; S/C and non S/C rooms with fan from ₵2200. Lively bar and restaurant.

Ayigya Hotel, 24 February Rd (PO Box 3515). Further out than the *Menka*, near the University junction. Clean rooms with common or private baths and fan start at ₵1650 for a single. They have a restaurant, bar and car park.

Pollux Hotel, New Tafo district opposite the motor park (PO Box 4464; ☎6355). "Decent accommodation – no problem" is their motto, backed up with small, furnished S/C rooms from ₵5000. Near the *Santos* and *Subin* nightclubs; bar and food "on request".

Cheap places in Dichemso

One of the heaviest concentrations of cheap hotels is in this district in the north of town. Collective taxis leave from the market (at Antoa Rd) and terminate in Dichemso, near the *Hotel de Plaza*.

Hotel de Plaza (PO Box 1741; ☎3716). Popular with people from other West African countries. Simple and relatively clean (the collective toilets are dubious), with rooms from ₵1650. "Our thriller disco solves your night problem of boredom", they boast. The *Phase One* across the street is under the same management.

Hotel de 77 (PO Box 3590; ☎4202). A large "storey building" opposite the *de Plaza* with similar accommodation and clientele.

Fabulous Hotel (PO Box 4556; ☎5521). A small, homely place with extremely good service. Clean rooms, some S/C, with fans from ₵1650.

Hotel de Côte d'Ivoire (PO Box 3736). Well known by Ivoirians in Kumasi, this hotel near the *Fabulous* is bigger and has non S/C rooms (some with balcony) from ₵2200.

Hotel de France (PO Box 830). The big rooms with fans aren't bad but the water supply is erratic, especially on the top floors (go down a level to shower). Guests mainly from northern Ghana. Friendly management.

Abidjan Hotel (PO Box 3053; ☎5539). A smaller place with only twelve non-S/C rooms, from ₵1650. Ivoirian clients and French spoken.

Moderate hotels

Roses Guest House, Ridge District (PO Box 4176; ☎4072). A small place with a few tidy S/C rooms from ₵5000 double. Although the accommodation is fine, *Roses* is better known as a restaurant.

Noks Hotel, Asokwa district (PO Box 8556). One of the better hotels for comfortable S/C rooms and efficient service. Some of the rooms have AC and carpets, starting from ₵5000. They have a restaurant, bar and car park.

Nurom Hotel, Suame district (PO Box 1400; ☎4000). Wins the prize for best design, from the colourful statue of the chief in front, to the Asante symbols on the modern facade. S/C rooms with fan or AC from ₵4000.

King's Hotel, Ahodwo district (PO Box 8803; ☎4490). Small garden hotel in a quiet residential neighbourhood. S/C rooms have AC and phones and there's a car park and a bar and restaurant that "welcomes you with finger-licking meals".

Closest thing to luxury

City Hotel, Harper Rd, Ridge district (PO Box 1980; ☎6210/3298). Owned by the State Hotels Corporation, this is ostensibly the best in town, although it's now showing its age badly. All the amenities are here – casino, disco, cinema, laundry – but it doesn't feel much like a luxury hotel: from ₵7500.

Catering Resthouse, Ridge district (PO Box 3179 ☎3656). The second State hotel, the *Catering Resthouse* doesn't have the *City Hotel*'s pretensions and, perhaps for that reason, is good value for money: furnished rooms, some with phone and AC, start from ₵5000 for a single. Convenient for downtown.

Restaurants and eating

Kumasi is a fine place for **street food**, which you'll find throughout town, notably in the motor parks and markets. If you stay in the Dichemso neighbourhood, numerous **chop bars** serve rice dishes, *fufu* or plaintains with sauce. Streetside coffee men whip up two-egg omelettes with Nescafé and sweet Ghana bread for around ₵400 at breakfast time. Some of the recommended **restaurants** in town are :

Family Restaurant, Prempeh II Road, Adum district (☎2441), above the *Hotel de Kingsway*. Inexpensive European and Lebanese cuisine in the middle of the commercial district (lunch noon–4pm, evenings from 7pm). Excellent.

House of Lords, Bompata district, behind Prempeh Assembly Hall. European and Oriental food served to jazz and African music. Wine available with meals (11am–11pm).

Chopsticks, Nyiaeso district, near the golf club (☎3221). Consistently one of the best restaurants in town and usually crowded, but not expensive (noon–3pm and 6.30–10pm)

Hit Parade Restaurant, Ntomin Rd, Adum district (☎6405). Formerly the venue of the *Golden Key Disco*, this now serves good, cheap Ghanaian food (11am–9pm).

Milkmaid Cafeteria, opposite the railway station in the Adum district. Inexpensive pastries with juices – or they have a bar. Also "snacks to meet your pocket" (useful if your pocket hasn't made other acquaintances).

YMCA, Adum district, out of the *Kingsway*, left, then first right, first left. No rooms, but open for lunch from noon–2.30pm

Sweet and Low Chop House, 28 February Road, near the *Menka Memorial Hotel*. Serves wonderful breakfast *chop*.

Copa Cabana, Fanti New Town District. A good place if you're fed up with *chop* houses. Chicken, rice and salad from ₵1000.

Sightseeing around town

Kumasi is one of the rare West African towns where you can go **sightseeing** in the formal sense. In addition to the **museums**, other historic points of interest, like the **palace** of the Asante king, dot the cityscape, and you could easily spend a few days just checking them out. The large **central market** alone merits a couple of trips to explore hidden corners with unusual finds.

Prempeh II Jubilee Museum and the National Cultural Centre
Open daily 9am–6pm, closed Mondays
In the grounds of the **Ghana National Cultural Centre**, this small museum of **Asante culture** holds a rich collection of artefacts housed in a reproduction of a traditional Asante regalia house, few examples of which remain since the nineteenth-century wars with the British. Such buildings served both as palaces and **shrines**; note the characteristic mural decorations on the lower walls. The designs, like those found on the **adinkra cloth** for which the region is famous, symbolise proverbs commenting on Akan moral and social values.

Among the many historical articles inside the museum is the **silver-plated stool** that the Denkyira chief Nana Ntim Gyakar was supposedly sitting on when captured in a surprise attack by the Asante in 1699. This victory marked the expansion of the Asante empire and the stool, with its intricate carving and design, became an important symbol of liberation and power. Also on display is the fake **golden stool**. The real one remains guarded in the Manhyia Palace, and is only brought out for special occasions. The replica was designed at the beginning of the century to deceive the British, who demanded that the most sacred of all Asante symbols be handed over to them.

Notice, too, a **treasure bag** on display that was presented to the Agona king by the fetish priest Okomfo Anokye. No one knows what the leather sack contains, for according to tradition to open it would bring about the downfall of the Asante nation. Other articles include examples of traditional dress, jewellery, furniture and musical instruments.

In addition to the museum, the grounds of the cultural centre contain a **crafts centre** where you can see how **kente** and **adinkra fabrics**, traditional sandals, brass weights and pottery are produced. You won't find the best buys in the country here, but there's a wide selection, and it's interesting to take a look. Don't miss the centre's small **library** with numerous works dedicated to Asante civilisation.

The Kumasi Fort and military museum
Housed in a British-built fort dating from 1820, the **military museum**'s collections have a heavy emphasis on modern **weaponry** captured by Ghanaian troops in World War II's East Africa and Asia campaigns. Far more interesting, but less extensive, are the exhibits documenting the **Anglo-Asante wars**, with period photographs and mementoes. **Fort Kumasi** itself is an intriguing structure where, as part of the guided tour, you'll be locked in a dark dungeon, to experience briefly the manner in which the British dealt with rabble-rousers. Those who went in rarely came out alive, and a few seconds is plenty to impart a sense of the terror the condemned must have felt.

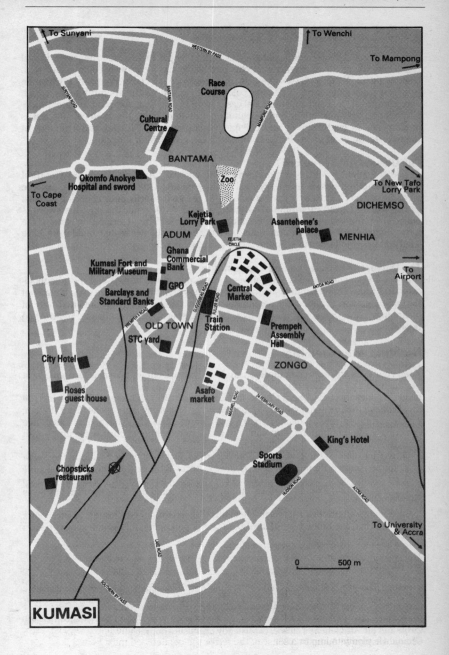

KUMASI

Manhyia: the Asantehene's Palace

Open weekdays 9am–5pm.

The traditional **Asantehene's palace** was sacked by the British, and the present royal residence, where the Asantehene and his family live, has a curiously colonial look to it. Completed in 1926, it first served as the residence of Nana Prempah I when he returned from exile. Until 1956, the palace also served as the **Asantehene's court**, where criminal, civil and constitutional cases were heard. Even today a traditional council presides over customary and constitutional matters here: the Prempeh dispenses judgements on land disputes and chieftancy matters every Monday and Thursday at the unusual hours of noon–2pm. The museum can give further details.

The Okomfo Anokye sword

Across the street from the cultural centre, the **Okomfo Anokye Teaching Hospital** contains another sacred Asante symbol in its grounds. This is the **Okomfo Anokye sword** that Osei Tutu's fetish priest planted on the spot shortly after choosing Kumasi as the Asante capital in around 1700. According to the legend, the day this sword is pulled from the ground, the Asante nation will collapse. The deteriorating state of the heavy metal blade seems an ominous portent, but locals swear that bulldozers have tried and failed to budge it – though they don't explain why.

The University of Science and Technology

When it first opened in 1952, this university was one of the largest and most sophisticated in Africa. The beautifully landscaped grounds are still impressive even if many of the buildings and facilities are beginning to show their age. A self-contained "city of technology", the university has its own hospital, sports facilities, banks, library and bookshops.

Nightlife, weekend life

Keep your eyes and ears open for **live music** in Kumasi; shows take place irregularly at the main hotels. The *City Hotel*'s *Nsadwase Disco* (☎6210), for example, has occasional bands, as does the *Old Timer's Club* at the *Kingsway* (☎2441). Other possibilites include the *Cultural Centre*'s *Anokyekrom programme* on Saturday afternoons from 1–7pm, which combines music, dance, poetry and drama. And they have occasional **live concerts** – often of highlife – on Sundays, and less recreational **choral evenings** with church choirs, especially on Wednesdays.

Otherwise, among the **clubs**, the *Star Nightclub*, just west of the Stadium, the *Subin* on Okomfo Anokye Rd in New Tafo, *Hedonist*, Accra Rd near the University and *Club 600*, on Mampong Rd near Kumasi Girl's Secondary School, are all worth following up by taxi if you're in the mood to move – though bear in mind the clubs open and close as often as Accra's.

On Sunday afternoons it's worth checking if there's a **soccer match** at the Sports Stadium. When the home team (**Kotoko**, meaning porcupine, the Asante symbol) plays it's wild: tickets go for ₵300.

Directory

Cinemas The two best cinemas in town are the *Rex Cinema*, near the Prempah Assembly Hall, and the *Odeon*, near the cultural centre. Others include the *Roxy* in Manhyia; the *Rivoli* in Bantama; the *Royal* in Asawasi; and the *Romeo* in New Tafo.

Forex bureaux There are lots around town, but the *Sweet Money Forex*, between Kejetia Circle and the Asantehene's palace, consistently offers superior rates.

Ghana Airways In Adum (☎2633).

Gold Mines The Ghana goldfields mines are at Obuasi (see below).

Kente cloth Kumasi central market is probably the best place to buy *kente* cloth and it's worth paying a child to take you to the one row of stalls where it's actually stored – they're easily missed otherwise. Prices are high and range from ₵20,000–30,000 for twelve yards (eleven metres) of single weave, or from ₵45,000–70,000 for double weave. To add a further complication, there's *kente* woven from imported rayon and real silk. It's all wonderful, though. You can sometimes buy just a small piece, or even a souvenir strip.

Supermarkets Supermarkets and department stores – *UTC, GNTC, UAC* and *Kingsway* – are concentrated in the Adum neighbourhood.

Tourist information The *Ghana Tourist Board* (☎2633, x12), adjacent to the museum in the Ghana National Cultural Centre, has complete guides to hotels, restaurants and sights in the Asante Region, plus large-scale Kumasi city maps and friendly and enthusiastic staff.

MOVING ON

Several major **lorry parks** service Kumasi if you're heading out **by bush taxi or tro-tro**. They include: *New Tafo Park*, in the north, for vehicles to Tamale, Wa, Bolgatanga, Navrongo and Yendi; *Asafo Park*, by the Asafo market, for Konongo Koforidua, Accra and Takoradi; and *Kejetia Park* for Mampong, Sunyani, Berekum and Abidjan. It's worth knowing that the direct route to Takoradi and Cape Coast is very rough and liable to be impassable in the rains.

By **rail**, there are daily sleeper trains, in theory, from Kumasi to Accra at 8.30pm, arriving early the next morning. And there are two services every other evening (at least) down through the forest to Takoradi, leaving at 6pm and 9pm – an 8–9-hour trip. The first arrives too early on the coast for convenience.

The obvious and comfortable alternative is to **fly out** of Kumasi: daily to Accra, twice a week to Tamale. Book as far ahead as possible.

Around Kumasi

Venturing into the **rainforest hills** around Kumasi, you can discover numerous villages that offer a less urbanised glimpse of Asante lifestyles. Many villages – **Bonwire** to the northwest and **Pankrona**, **Ewiha** and **Ntonso** along the road to Mampong – are known for the **traditional crafts** industries for which the entire region is famous, and best treated as day trips. **Bosumtwi**, however, has a well cared for resthouse on its pretty lake shore, and makes a good retreat. If you have your own transport, even a bicycle, **the road past Mampong** to the shore of Lake Volta – once the main route through Ghana, but now very much a back road – offers some exciting travel. An obvious, but little explored, theme around Kumasi, however, is a visit to the **goldfields**.

Obuasi gold mines

The gold mines at **OBUASI**, 70km southwest of Kumasi, are a relatively easy trip from town. You might want to seek out prior information in Kumasi (or even contact *Lonhro* in London before departure) but it seems you can also approach the offices in Obuasi and arrange a visit: Thursdays and Fridays to see the gold being smelted or Sundays and Tuesdays to go underground and witness the mining itself. Tours are enjoyably informative and conducted, at present, free of charge. Apparently at least thirty percent of the product is reckoned to disappear through one leak in the system or another, but don't expect to walk away with gold filings under your fingernails – there are metal detectors everywhere you look. Obuasi is full of English and Italian ex-pat technicians and managers who may be able to advise on accommodation if you want to stay. Otherwise, there's little in the way of hotels.

KENTE CLOTH

Kente dates from the early days of the Asante empire. The dazzling patterns are intended to enhance their owners' status as kings, queens and nobles. Court designs took on the name of the clan or individuals by which they were commissioned (a common pattern known as *mamponhema*, for example, derives its name from the Queen of Mampong). *Asasia* designates a pattern and type of cloth worn only by the Asantehene. Kente, like most African cloth, is woven in narrow strips, later sewn together. The highest quality pieces are made entirely of silk threads, which in former times were unavailable to the Asante. To satisfy the demands of royalty, the craftsmen therefore unravelled imported silk fabric and rewove the threads into kente patterns. In addition to the name denoting their owner, the most valuable cloths bore another name – *adweneasa* – a technical term indicating that the already complicated pattern contained an additional inlaid design. The word means "my skill is exhausted" – in other words the weaver has made his ultimate effort.

Bonwire

A frequent target for tourists, **BONWIRE** is a traditional Asante village and principle home of the famous **kente cloth**. Along the streets in town you can still see weavers working hand-operated looms to turn out the long strips of intricately patterned material. *Kente* is still the usual dress of Asante people on special occasions and great significance is placed on the cloth which, for this and because of its complex design, is also very expensive – especially here. Bonwire is just over 20km from Kumasi, southeast of Ntonso on the road to Effiduasi. Taxis go to the town regularly from the Kejetia motor park. The quickest route if you're getting there under your own steam is down the Accra road, then turn left near Kumasi airstrip.

Bosumtwi

Only 27km south of Kumasi, **LAKE BOTSUMTWI** fills a crater surrounded by steep green hills that rise nearly 400m above sea-level. With a diameter of 8km, this is the largest natural lake in Ghana. You can get here by taking a Benz bus or *tro-tro* from the Asafo lorry park to the town of KUNTANSI (a half-hour drive that costs almost nothing): from here you can either catch another vehicle or walk the remaining 5km to ABONO via the resthouse.

The lake itself lies in the midst of lush greenery: a superbly relaxing scene in which to unwind, simply hanging out and doing nothing as you slow down from Kumasi's pace. Traditional boats are still used to fish the lake, propelled by fishermen with calabashes cupped in their hands to serve as paddles. Formerly, the spirit of the lake forbade other forms of transport but, as one villager commented, "people used to be scared, but we don't believe in that nowadays." Clearly not, because ex-pats and rich kids from Kumasi come to water-ski and there are now motor boats buzzing over the lake.

NTONSO DYE STAMPS

Nyame biribi wo soro na ma embeka mensa: "God, there is something in the sky, let me reach it"
Gye Nyame: "We have nothing to fear but God"
Dwonnin ye asise a ode n'akorana na ennye ne mben: "The heart, not the horns, leads a ram to bully"

The **resthouse** offers fantastic views of the natural setting. To stay here, you have to book beforehand at the regional tourist office in Kumasi (next to the National Museum, ☎2633). An additional hotel is under construction in Abono – and has been since 1975.

Along the Mampong Road

Within a short distance of Kumasi, the small towns along the Mampong road have developed their own reputations for artwork and handicrafts. The first you come to is **PANKRONA** (5km from Kumasi), a village known for its **pottery**, traditionally produced by the women. All kinds of clay objects, from water jugs to characteristic Asante *fufu* bowls, are piled high in front of the homes and sold at quite reasonable prices, compared to those in town.

The next stop along the road is the town of **EHWIAA**, which specialises in **wood carvings**. Numerous shops along the main road sell tables, statues and games, but the **carved stools** you'll see craftsmen sculpting in open-air workshops along the street stand out among the wares. Throughout Ghana, such stools were not merely for decoration, but were considered prime necessities. Commonly the first gift a father would give to his child was a stool, which his soul was believed to occupy until death. To this day, stools still represent one of the most important elements of a chief's regalia and symbolise his office. When he dies, a chief's stool is smeared with ash and the yoke of an egg, and the **black stool** is preserved in a special house in memory of the late owner. *Enstoolment* and *destooling* are terms often seen in the Ghanaian press.

The stools carved in Ehwiaa today are mostly made with an eye for tourism, and you may not admire the lacquers and shoe-polish dyes that give them a tawdry finish. Nonetheless, they contain many of the intricate **traditional symbols** (the carvers can explain what they mean), and there's no cause for complaint about the quality of craftsmanship. They're expensive, a result of the time involved in making them and the high demand from tourists, among whom they're extremely popular despite their weight. Ask about the types of wood used. It's worth avoiding the more expensive hardwoods – not just for the sake of the forests, but because softer wood is lighter and cheaper.

Further down the Mampong Road, **NTONSO** is the famed home of **adinkra cloth**. Not quite as prestigious as *kente*, it's made of cotton material (often a deep red colour) covered with black patterns. These are produced with stamps carved from bits of calabash and dipped in a tree-bark dye. Craftsmen use a variety of such stamps, some with geometric patterns, others with stylised representations of plants or animals, but most with symbols reflecting an Asante saying. A cloth incorporating all such symbols in its pattern was known as the **Adinkrahene** and was reserved for the Asante king, but it wasn't uncommon for the ruler to wear a cloth marked by a single symbol that reflected a specific message he wanted to convey to the people. Today, you still see these cloths being worn toga-fashion throughout the Asante country, notably at funerals and on other important occasions.

Mampong and northeast

MAMPONG itself is surprisingly large and busy, perched on the lip of the Mampong escarpment. There's a number of places to stay. Beyond it, the road north curls down through formidable forest to the deep valley of the Afram River and then steeply, in a series of hairpins, up the other side to EJURA. The scenic beauty of this road is matched by the pleasure of being relatively off the beaten track. ATEBUBU, next, is a small, smoky town at the savannah's edge. Beyond, there's only the village of PRANG – which on this road, once tarred, now ragged asphalt and dirt – could hardly have a more appropriate name, and then YEJI, on the bleak Volta shore, where unpredictable small boats make the crossing to MAKONGO, 150km short of TAMALE (for which town, see p.863).

THE EAST: HO, AKOSOMBO AND AROUND

Eastern Ghana is home of the **Ewe**, who have traditionally been farming and fishing people. Formerly part of German Togoland, the region has periodically provided a bone of contention between the governments of Ghana and Togo and those who favour the reunification of the Ewe. The administrative capital is at **Ho**, a large town in the middle of an agricultural area rich with cocoa plantations. The Akwampim mountains add to the beauty of the fertile landscapes, but the outstanding geographical feature of these parts is artificial – the vast body of **Lake Volta**, created when the ambitious dam and hydro-electric plant was built at **Akosombo** in the mid-1960s. This region provides an interesting alternative **route to northern Ghana**, either through the remote eastern border region or straight across the great lake to Tamale Port by ferry.

Ho

Despite its prestigious designation as the Volta Region's capital, **HO** remains a quiet, rural community. Set in a green valley dominated by **Mount Adaklu**, Ho is graced with a tidy tracing of narrow **paved roads** winding through the trees, a large **hospital**, and **banks**, and even an interesting **regional museum** – some surprise in a rather remote corner like this.

The **Ewe people** are primarily involved in maize and yam farming, with cocoa plantations adding a further cash crop stimulus to the region.

Around town

The road leading from AFLAO, on the coastal border with Togo, constitutes the main street in town. It heads from the *Texaco* and *BP* filling stations in the south, past the **regional police office**, on to the **central market** and out to the main **lorry park** on the north side of town. Main **banks** are on this street but there are no forex bureaux. Changing cash or travellers' cheques is possible here but it takes ages while they phone to Accra for current rates.

Along this same road, you'll find a large roundabout near the **post office**. The road leading off west from here runs down to the **hospital**, behind which are the grounds of the **Volta Regional Museum** (daily except Mon 8am–6pm). Well presented and little frequented, the museum is worth a visit to see exhibits of ceremonial objects (Akan "spokesmen" staffs and swords), traditional **musical instruments,** and carved **stools** from various regions. **Colonial relics** complement the ethnic displays, including some dating to the district's **German Togoland period.**

Sleeping, eating and practicalities

One of the cheapest **places to stay** is the (unmarked) *Tasa Hotel*, off the main street behind the *Ghana Commercial Bank*. Accommodation is basic, but rooms are incredibly cheap. A step up is the clean and comfortable *Alinda Guest house*, near the museum, with rooms from ₵1500 and a decent bar and restaurant. Another possibility is the *Peace Palace Hotel* (☎567), set in a quiet residential area about 1km from the centre. Rooms here, some S/C with AC, start at ₵2200. It's also possible to stay at the *E.P. Church Social Centre*, a kilometre from the centre at the church headquarters, where S/C rooms are ₵1100 and dormitory space is available for next to nothing.

Street food is readily available near the main lorry park: a traditional Ewe dish is cat, often advertised rather graphically. In the same vicinity you'll find the *Cotopaxi Restaurant* (inexpensive Ghanaian fare) and the irresistible *Doris Day Restaurant* on Housing Road. In the evenings several places show videos, notably *Foxtrot Video Theatre* along the main drag.

Akosombo

Besides generating much-needed foreign exchange for Ghana, the giant **Akosombo Dam** was also responsible for **Lake Volta**, the largest artificial lake in the world. Nkrumah's pet hydro-electric project at the once insignificant village of **AKOSOMBO** provides electricity for the greater part of Ghana, with some left for export to neighbouring countries. Amid the landscape of hills and water, the general interest lies more in the **scenic beauty** – and it is beautiful – than in the traditional lifestyle of the people here, who are a broadly cosmopolitan mix of employees from all over Ghana.

PHOTOGRAPHY – A WARNING

Note that both the **Akosombo Dam** and the **Atimpoku Bridge** are considered strategic installations and it's therefore illegal to photograph them. If you're seen taking pictures, your film will be confiscated and you'll have some explaining to do. The numerous police and military personnel in the area are serious about this.

Atimpoku – arrivals and cheap lodgings

Akosombo's **lorry park** is 5km south of the town in the district of **ATIMPOKU**, a quiet locality on the main Accra road in the shadow of the large bridge spanning the **Volta River**. Taxis ply regularly from here (or walk up the road to the fire station and get a lift) to the lower part of Akosombo town proper. Most of the **cheap accommodation**, however, is here in Atimpoku. The *Delta Queen*, across the street from the motor park, has cheap and simple rooms, or the *Benkum* is another basic hotel where rooms start at around ₵1000 and you pay extra for a fan. The *Lakeside Motel* is a pleasant, slightly more upmarket place (rooms from ₵2500), just south of Atimpoku. **Street food** abounds; they do oyster kebabs and smoked shrimp to go with *abolo*, the slightly sugary, but not unpleasant, dumpling commonly eaten in the region. Across from the motor park, the *Royal Spot* chop bar serves inexpensive *fufu* and palm nut soup along with cold drinks.

Around Akosombo

Akosombo proper consists of two communities, both of which emerged in the 1960s when workers flooded here to fill demand for labour. The first perches on a hillside, whence it commands a magnificent view of **Lake Volta** and the mountains around. The

---

LAKE VOLTA FERRIES

Lake transport has been unpredictable for years. This deters many travellers, but while it's true that transport is erratic and timetables unreliable (there are generally less options than theoretically available), it's also true that the trip is highly enjoyable. If you're setting out from Akosombo, there'll always be some kind of vessel in a day or two.

The official **ferry** is the *Akosombo Queen*, which plies betwen **Akosombo** and **Kete Krachi** once a week. Departures from Akosombo have in recent years been Tuesday mornings, arrival at Kete Krachi around twelve hours later. Midweek, the vessel runs a shuttle between Kete Krachi and Kpandu. Unfortunately, it's often out of commission.

When the passenger ferry isn't running, **cargo barges** – the *Yapei Queen, Yeji Queen*, the excellent *Volta Queen*, and the even more modern *Buipe Queen* – also make the trip, but rarely run on fixed schedules. They sometimes go as far upriver as **Yapei** (Tamale Port) on the White Volta's course in the north, but this port is sometimes out of reach at the end of the dry season, in which case the port of **Buipe**, on the course of the Black Volta further to the west, is used as the northern terminus. En route there are usually stops at **Kpandu, Kete Krachi** and **Yeji**.

The voyage to the north end of the lake takes between one and two days (and nights) and you sleep on the deck. Normally, you should stock up on **food** for the trip: water and cooking facilities are provided. If the passenger ferry is running, there are meals available.

For all details, enquire at the *Lake Volta Hotel* on arrival or make advance contact with the *Volta Lake Transport Company* in the *Ghana Commercial Bank* building in Akosombo (PO Box 75, Akosombo; ☎0251.686 ext. 204).

---

spot was too scenic to resist putting in a tourist hotel, yacht club and public **swimming pool** among the luxurious ex-pat and executive **villas**. The second community, in the valley below, is a working-class neighbourhood for employees of the Volta Power Authority – no hotel, but there is a **community centre** with library, bar and the *Dam Video Theatre*. Buses run between the two districts during daylight hours.

The hotel and other practicalities

The government-run *Volta Hotel* (PO Box 25; ☎0251.753) is ideally situated on the hill with a bird's eye view of the lake and dam.Unfortunately most of it was knocked down recently in anticipation of major renovations. If it has re-opened, rooms here are likely to be expensive, from ₵6000. Even if you don't sleep here, a meal, or at least a drink in the terrace **restaurant** overlooking the lake, is a must – the views are terrific. If you want to **visit the dam** itself, for which you need authorisation, you're only likely to get a lift at weekends. Hang around at the **site office** down the road from the hotel.

NORTHERN GHANA

Coming either from the coast and Kumasi, or up the country's eastern fringe, you'll be struck by the changing landscape, as the central forests give way to arid, low-lying **grasslands**. Due to the harsher, unpredictable climate and, to this day, the effects of the slave trade (from which the inhabitants of the open plains and plateaux lacked natural protection), the region is sparsely populated, characterised by traditional **compound agriculture**. The few urban centres like **Tamale** or **Bolgatanga** seem more subdued than their counterparts to the south.

The main peoples of the north include the More-speaking **Dagomba**, with their capital at Yendi, and the **Mamprusi** people, based around Nalerigu. The **Gonja**, with their capital at Damongo, are an interesting ethnic group, formed partly of the remants of sixteenth- and seventeenth-century Mande-speaking migrant invaders from Songhai in the north, and partly of local Voltaic-speaking peoples. As a result, the Gonja, who are mostly Muslim, speak different languages according to their class – the nobles using a dialect of Akan known as Guang, and the commoners speaking Wagala. **Sudanic influences** have been important in this region, reflected in architecture, customs and dress – *boubous* for the men and long veils for women, draped over their heads. In short, the north is a completely different world and, with the exception of the popular **Mole Game Park** – easily visited and well set up for inexpensive stays – a region where you're unlikely to run into throngs of fellow travellers.

Tamale

Capital of the **Northern Region, TAMALE** is a large commercial town and junction on the main roads leading from Burkina Faso in the north, Togo in the east and Accra or Kumasi in the south. Despite its size and importance, it lacks the slightest cosmopolitan spark, and you're not going to want to spend an inordinate amount of time here. Still, as a stopover en route to other destinations you could do worse, and there are a reasonable number of hotels and diversions.

Around town

The centre of town wraps around the motor park and *STC* station, easily recognised by the towering telephone transmitter that juts up next to it and that can be seen from almost anywhere in town. The **central market** (good for locally woven cloth) and major **banks** are an easy walk away. Next to the market is a shaded **public garden** that makes a good place to read the *Daily Graphic* (usually a day or so late in these northern parts) or watch the adept draughts players who gather here daily for lightning-quick tournaments. A paved road leading out from the west of the market heads down past the *Social Security Bank* and a **small market** before arriving at a large **classified forest** – a rather unusual thing to find in the middle of an important administrative town. But the shade of the teak trees makes for an excellent place to retreat from the afternoon heat, which reaches oppressive levels on the exposed avenues downtown.

The **Ghana Tourist Board** may by now have opened their regional office in Tamale. It's something to keep a lookout for as they envisage excursions to the Mole Game Park and around the region. Ask at the *STC* yard when you arrive to see how progress is developing.

Sleeping, eating and amusing yourself

Accommodation in Tamale tends to be basic. Some places run to S/C rooms with AC, but problems with running water are perennial. If you're out for something cheap and central, you can't do better than the *Hotel Al Hassan* (PO Box 73, across from *Ghana Commercial Bank*; ☎2834). It's a vast box of a place with large, balconied rooms (from ₵1200/1600) grouped around a central courtyard. None too clean (especially in the shared showers) and rarely quiet, it's nonetheless liveable, if you can ignore the rats in the shadowy corridors after dark. Its proximity to the motor park, plus the restaurant and video theatre in the hotel, make it a bit of a caravanserai where you might run into other travellers.

Other places to stay are much further out. Topping the list is the *Catering Resthouse* (Regional Office Rd; ☎2702) in a residential area about 1km from the centre, with the

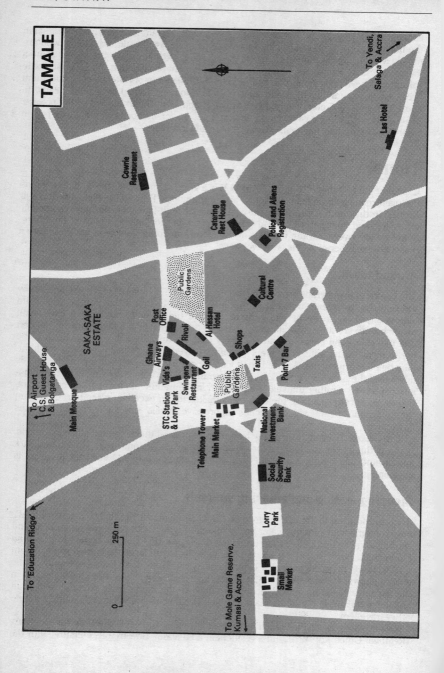

TAMALE

To Yendi,
Salaga & Accra

Las Hotel

Cowrie
Restaurant

Catering
Rest House

Police and Aliens
Registration

Public
Gardens

Cultural
Centre

Post
Office

Al Hassan
Hotel

Ghana
Airways

Rivoli

Shops

SAKA-SAKA
ESTATE

Vida's

Swingers
Restaurant

Golf

Taxis

Point 7 Bar

To Airport,
C.S. Guest House
& Bolgatanga

Main Mosque

STC Station
& Lorry Park

Telephone Tower

Main Market

Public
Gardens

National
Investment
Bank

To 'Education Ridge'

Social
Security
Bank

Lorry
Park

250 m

0

Small
Market

To Mole Game Reserve,
Kumasi & Accra

best AC rooms in town (from around ₵3000) and a very good **restaurant**. The *Christian Services Guest House* is recommended, too, and a little cheaper. The *Inter Royals Hotel* (Kalpuni Estates; ☎2247) is not so well kept, but has cheaper rooms, some with AC, plus an in-house restaurant and disco. The *Atta Essibi Hotel* (St Charles Seminary Rd; ☎2564) lies in the southern fringes. In the same class as the *Al Hassan*, it has reasonable if dingy rooms, some S/C. A cut above, and correspondingly more expensive, the *Las Hotel* (off Salaga Rd; ☎2277) has comfortable S/C rooms with fans, plus its own bar and nightclub.

There are plenty of **places to eat** apart from the hotels. All around the *Goil* station after about 6pm there's a mass of street food, especially guinea fowl. The *Cowrie Restaurant* (Kalpuni Estates) is a popular and straightforward spot for European and Ghanaian food and *Vida's* and, especially, *Swingers* both do good **chop**. But the best place at the moment is the *Picorna* which does great kebabs and has a popular **disco**.

For **passing the time**, *Point 7* (with music) and the *Continental Bar* (opposite the *Al Hassan*) are reasonable for a cold beer and you can have a pleasant afternoon on "Education Ridge" (ask for Tamasco, the Tamale Secondary School) in the *Drop In* bar, or in any of the *pito* bars around town. Check out, too, the **National Cultural Centre**, near the central market, off the Yeji Road. The building is in a horrific state of repair, but they organise sporadic performances of **regional music and dance** and, in the afternoons, you can sometimes catch a rehearsal. You can also watch some excellent football on Sunday afternoons, when major Ghanaian teams play at the main stadium on Catering Rest House (CRH) Road.

For less vicarious **sporting activity**, hire a bicycle in town (hotels seem able to help) and take it up to Education Ridge, off the northwest road out of town on our map. There's a fine ride commencing behind the Polytechnic and running for about 8km through lovely villages, coming back the same way. When you get back, check out the **swimming pool** at Kamina barracks (small entry fee), about 3km out of town on the Bolgatanga road.

As for **evening entertainment**, the *Rivoli Theatre* is a big crush, shows dated movies (Hindi, Kung-fu, Rambo), and competes with a rash of **video** theatres throughout town – look out for the street-corner blackboard announcements. The *Catering Rest House* is usually worth a visit on a Saturday night, when it quite often bursts into life.

MOVING ON

As the north's major city, Tamale is the springboard for **Burkina Faso** via BOLGATANGA on a decent paved road; for **Accra and Kumasi**, via YEJI where you cross Lake Volta; and for SAWLA in **western Ghana** via DAMONGO, which is also the point of entry to **Mole Game Park**. *STC* and *OSA* **buses** head in all these directions as do *tro-tros* and taxis. Tamale also has a **ferry** link with Akosombo and the south. The boat leaves from Tamale Port (YAPEI) to which there are buses from Tamale motor park. Full ferry details are given on p.862. In addition to all this, there are **flights** nearly every day to Accra on *Ghana Airways*, with a stop in Kumasi on Mondays.

Mole Game Reserve

Set in the savannah country of northern Ghana, the 2000-square-kilometre **MOLE GAME RESERVE** (open throughout the year, entrance ₵400) protects a wide variety of fauna – including elephants, lions, leopards, buffaloes and numerous species of antelope, monkeys and birds – in an environment little differentiated but for the Konkori escarpment, which runs northeast–southwest. Although the concentration of animals is not as high as in some other West African parks, Mole's striking advantage, if you don't have your own transport, is **ease of access**. Christmas is the best time to visit, when animals are most visible and the mosquitoes least oppressive (at other times it's vital to have repellent). From the lodgings inside the park, armed rangers run inexpensive foot safaris to track the game. A network of tracks criss-cross the park and in the dry season, you can also cover a lot in an ordinary car.

Getting to the park from Tamale couldn't be less complicated, since an **STC coach** leaves regularly from the transport yard (last known schedule was 2pm daily except sometimes Sunday, but check at the station to be sure) and takes passengers all the way into the park, dropping them off at the **motel**. If you're coming from any other direction, most obviously BOUNA in Côte d'Ivoire or WA, you can wait for this bus at DAMONGO, where it makes a stop before continuing into the reserve. Driver and bus stay the night in the reserve, and return to Tamale at 5.30 am. If you want to leave the reserve at any other time, you'll have to get to LARABANGA (an invariably hot six-kilometre-walk for which the rather beautiful old mosque only slightly compensates). From there a local lorry can get you to Damongo, whence you should pick up the Wa or Sawla bus on its way back to Tamale or, heading to Wa or northern Côte d'Ivoire, find transport westwards easily enough.

Accommodation and other park practicalities

At the park's entrance, the *Mole Motel* perches on a bit of a hill dominating an artificial water hole where animals gather to drink in the dry season. The twin bed chalets are spacious and clean with large bathrooms and screened verandahs overlooking the water hole. Electricity doesn't work (you get lanterns which help set a rustic safari tone) and the water is sporadic – don't delay your shower unless you see the swimming pool is full – but the whole place is great value (around ₵2200–3300 depending on the position of the chalet; plus a cheap bunkhouse). The motel has its own **restaurant**, but you have to order in advance for meals and there's little choice. If you're arriving by bus in the evening, eat before leaving Tamale or bring your own food: you won't get anything much until next morning's breakfast.

In addition to the motel, two **camps** may still be open (no provisions; bring your own bedding and food). **Lovi** is in the centre about 30km from the motel and **Konkori** is in the northeast, near the scarp.

Reservations can be made through the Senior Game Warden, Mole National Park, PO Box 8, Damongo, Northern Region, or through The Chief Game and Wildlife Officer, Dept of Game and Wildlife, PO Box M.239, Accra. In the dry season – especially during weekends or holidays – you should be sure to reserve in advance as the place is often booked. During the rains, this doesn't seem to be much of a problem.

Game viewing

When you check in at the motel, book a ranger to wake you in the morning for a **walking safari**. They charge around ₵300 per hour and they know where to find what's around, if anything. Your chances of seeing **elephant, antelope** and **buffalo** near the water hole are relatively good.

To have any real chance of seeing other large animals, like **lions**, you'll need a vehicle. The motel has Land Rovers for hire, and their rates aren't unreasonable, but their normal condition appears to be broken down. In the absence of other transport, you might therefore try your luck with other park visitors. You're still recommended to take a ranger to help in the quest for animals.

Note that in the wet season animals are dispersed, the grass much thicker and visible game may be virtually non-existent.

Wa

Capital of the Upper Western Region, **WA** is a predominantly Muslim town as the many **mosques** dotting the townscape attest. Although noticeably poorer than towns in the south, shortages of food and other goods no longer pose the problems they did a few years ago. The **market** near the lorry park is large and well supplied.

Wa is home of the **Wala** people who migrated from Mali. Upon arrival in Ghana, they chased the resident Lobi population to the west and converted the Dagarti inhabitants to **Islam**. The **traditional chief**, the Wa Na, still lives in a large white palace built in the Sudanese style. You can visit the palace (located behind the government transport yard), but if you do so you're expected to greet the Wa Na. Courtiers outside will arrange this; ask permission before taking photos. Apart from his ceremonial role, the Wa Na still ajudicates disputes between his subjects.

Besides local people, a number of office workers have come from outside to work in local administrative posts. Even so Wa feels remote from Accra, and even Tamale seems positively metropolitan in comparison. Life here is slow, and a short visit is enough to be convinced there's nothing happening. You might investigate the **museum**, which apparently exists behind the roundabout, near the long-defunct *Adonis Cinema*. Failing that, Wa is still a good town in which to wander without special aim.

Where to sleep and eat

The cheapest place in town is the *Sawaba Guest House* – no electricity or water, but the plain rooms with lumpy mattresses are tidy and under ₵1000 – and they can help you get on the *STC* bus out of town again. The brand new *Upland Hotel* is the nicest in town (₵6600) and has its own restaurant. The *Catering Rest House* no longer takes in travellers, but anyone can eat the traditional regional food in the dining room. Other than that, **meals** are pretty much limited to the many **chop bars** located around the market and transport park. And take a cold beer in the *Meet Me There*.

MOVING ON FROM WA

STC buses leave daily for Tamale (twice), Kumasi, Tumu, Lawra and Hamale (twice) and three times a week for Bolgatanga. **Minibuses** in Wa are known, somewhat morbidly, as "18 condemneds" following a spectacular recent accident, which hasn't stopped people from using them quite cheerily.

AROUND THE UPPER WEST REGION: A BRIEF ROUND-UP

Travelling in the region, it's useful to know the market cycles are mostly six days
North of Wa, the crossroads town of **Tumu** (market day 1) has a couple of places to stay (*Catering Rest House* and *Wobille Rest House*, both under ₵1000) and a few *chop* stalls near the bus stop: otherwise there's little here of note, apart from a profusion of silk-cotton trees. You can usually find transport across the border to the Burkina Faso town of **Léo**, but except on market days (see below) there's virtually no transport from here to Hamale. **Lawra**, between Wa and Hamale, is well known locally for its **musical instruments**, notably its *balafons*. Lastly, **Hamale** itself (market day 2), in Ghana's far northwest corner, is a regular crossing point for Burkina and has a couple of places to stay. The one near the petrol station offers occasional highlife bands. For more on the Burkinabe side, see p.296.

On the Kumasi road **south of Wa**, there are interesting mosques at **Sawla**, **Maluwe**, and especially at **Bole** and **Banda Nkwanta** (one of the oldest in the district). They all date from the sixteenth-century Gonja conquest.

Navrongo and around

Coming south from Ouagadougou on the main highway, **NAVRONGO** is the first Ghanaian town over the border. In the middle of a vast but undeveloped **agricultural region** (where crops include rice, millet and yams), it has a distinctive rural flavour. The people here are mostly **Kassena** farmers, part of the closely related Gourounsi group.

Navrongo enjoys a reputation in the north as a centre of education because of its large secondary school. It was also one of the first towns in the region to have a church built, in around 1920. This, now a **cathedral**, was done in the traditional style with *banco*, and the interior decorations reflect regional art and cultural values. Today it's one of the few "sights" in town and definitely worth a visit, Sundays especially.

Navrongo nearly received a major commercial boost when construction began on a resplendent **"cultural centre"**, complete with cinema, hotel and Olympic-size pool. That was in 1975 when Acheampong was president. Subsequent governments decided the project was not a priority for national development, and for over fifteen years the building has remained an unfinished cement carcase. Rumour has it that a scaled-down version of the centre has been approved and that work will start again. In the meantime, Navrongo remains a dusty farmers' town largely overshadowed by BOLGATANGA to the south.

Sleeping, eating and other practicalities

Navrongo still has very **limited facilities**, which make it less convenient as a stopping point than Bolgatanga, but the *Catholic Social Centre* does have good clean rooms for a remarkable ₵660. It's about 300m behind the market and any kid can show you the way.

Numerous **chop houses** and bars crowd around the market and adjoining motor park. *Pito* bars are also plentiful. Evenings you have your choice of several **video theatres** showing "action" and "brutal" films.

Moving on – and sites outside outside Navrongo

When it's time to **move on**, daily *STC* **buses** link Navrongo to Bolgatanga and Tamale, and they now service **Burkina's** capital, Ouagadougou, several times a week as well, although **taxis** are more frequent and faster. Heading west, the buses stop at TUMU, from which point you can get onward transport to Wa and Côte d'Ivoire.

Some 6km from the town itself, down a turning off the Tumu road, is the *Tono Guest House*, built on the edge of **Tono Lake**. Sometimes referred to as the "Akosombo of the Upper Region", the lake resulted from a dam designed to create a massive irrigation project for sugar production, run by *Tate & Lyle*. There's a pool, sports facilities and first class birdwatching on the dam lake nearby. The **guest house** is one of the best in the north, though there's no guarantee you'll be offered a room.

Twenty kilometres further west, beyond CHUCHILIGA, are the **Chiana-Katiu caves**, 1km out of Chiana village. They feature natural rock formations that appear, eerily, to be of human construction – though no one seems to know much about them..

Paga

PAGA, only 5km north of Navrongo on the Burkina border, has become a popular destination for its **sacred crocodile pool**. This is now something of a fleecing operation, where you'll pay more than it's worth to have your picture taken with the reptiles. As soon as you arrive someone will offer to take you to the lake (of course expecting money), but it's in fact quite easy to find on your own, a five-minute walk east of the village. When you approach the lake, a hustler brandishing **chickens** runs up to prevent you from getting too close without paying. He'll demand at least ₵1000 (for the chicken: you may be able to beat him down a little) and, money in hand, will ask for another ₵1000 for your right to take pictures.

After you've paid, the crocs are summoned by whistling and a long clicky sound – *Nnn-kii-kikikikiki*. You pose for snaps holding their tails or squatting lightly on their backs. Finally the chicken is fed to them. Expect to feel ripped off – it's not so much the amount you pay, but the way they grab it. In spite of it all, you'll be hard pressed to get an account of what, apart from their money-making abilities, makes the crocodiles sacred.

Pick-ups run regularly up to Paga from Navrongo. In Paga there's a small **catering resthouse** – the *Paga Hotel* – if you want to spend the night.

Bolgatanga and the Upper East

As capital of the Upper East region and of the Grusi-speaking **Frafra** people, **BOLGATANGA** is much larger and faster-growing than Navrongo. Growing too fast, perhaps, for it's own good – it looks a real mess. Impressions aside, if you're entering the country from Burkina it's also a better place to take care of **business**, change money or find decent accommodation. The large town **market** is a good place to hunt for local **handicrafts** – leather and hats – and there are a number of interesting sites nearby.

Around town

The main feature downtown is the **central market**, walled in around large boulder formations. Many goods are still hand-made in the market itself. **Leather items** (a local speciality), **basketwork** and clothes are all produced here and have their own sections. Beautiful examples of hand-made smocks – sewn from locally woven material and commonly worn by men throughout the region – are still sold more for local consumption than for the tourist market. Main market day is Friday.

Bolgatanga should now have a brand new **museum**, under construction at the time of this research. The building, in the administrative block behind the Catholic social centre, should be exhibiting the region's cultural, historic and ethnographic heritage. If it's open by the time you get to Bolga, let us know your impressions. In the same general area is a small town **library** where you're free to browse. In front of it, a scale-model of a **Frafra compound** – through which, Gulliver-like, you can wander – gives an insight into the way the houses of the region are divided into spaces for sleeping, cooking, animals and fetishes.

The **Ghana Tourist Board** has a regional office near the Catholic social centre. Only recently opened, they're still in a state of disarray, but are beginning to compile information about little-known regional sights. They eventually plan to organise excursions in the north and are extremely receptive to enquiries.

Accommodation, eating and other pursuits

The cheapest **accommodation** in town is at the *Catholic Social Centre*, which has clean and secure individual non-S/C rooms, plus a welcoming management. Across the street from the market is the *Central Hotel*, ideally located as the name suggests and with reasonably clean S/C rooms for ₵2200. Next to the *Central* is the ramshackle *Super Service Hotel* with basic rooms from ₵1500. They have a video theatre at night. The *Oasis Hotel*, in a quiet area a couple of hundred metres from the *STC* station on the Kumasi road, offers clean, furnished rooms (bucket showers) for ₵2200/3000. The old *Black Star Hotel* is a reasonable standby, though it has dirty water all year round: loads of good atmosphere compensates.

A pleasant **restaurant** is the *Comme Çi Comme Ça* where, if you're lucky (the name was well-chosen), you can get excellent guinea-fowl with rice and salad for around ₵1000 – a price most locals find expensive. *Top in Town* is a smaller version of *Comme Çi Comme Ça* at the edge of town on the Navrongo road, while *Sand Garden*, in similar vein but cheaper, is behind the fire station. If you want inexpensive eating, an alley of cheap **chop stands** and **pito bars** runs behind the *Black Star*, near the Catholic Social Centre. The favourite local dish is *T.Z.*, often eaten with *kino* sauce made from bitter green leaves. A more specialised Bolga taste is **hot dog**, available as very spicy kebabs from stalls at the Tamale taxi station, and only appreciated by strong constitutions.

Look into the **Bolgatanga library** if you're dead from heat. It's a cool retreat on Navrongo Road, with a decent selection of language and cultural works – not much in the way of Ghanaian fiction though. To do something more active about cooling off, go for a swim in the Canadian Aid (CIDA) compound's **pool** (small charge) opposite the Bolgatanga girl's school on Navrongo road – it's a little oasis in the searing afternoon heat.

MOVING ON

Lots of **taxis and tro-tros** leave Bolgatanga daily for Ouagadougou, Kumasi and Accra. Smaller villages in the vicinity (see below) are also served. Vehicles for Tamale leave from a separate motor park near the police station. *STC* **coaches** have regular departures for Accra, Kumasi, Sunyani, Tamale and Wa.

Around Bolgatanga and the Upper East Region

Bolgatanga has quite a hoard of **local interest** if you're here for a few days. If you don't have transport of your own, it's worth enquiring in town about **hiring a bicycle** to get you around the closer sites. The following destinations are ordered clockwise.

North of Bolgatanga

For a market with a diffference, **SAMBRUNGO**, 8km out of town on the Navrongo road, has a **night market**, on a Friday like Bolga's, offering an atmospheric – romantic even – stroll through the lanterns in the cool, evening air. Trouble is that it's not easily accessible by public transport so you may have to walk or hitch (or cycle) back to Bolga afterwards.

Heading out of town **to the northeast**, the turning to the left (which takes you to the *Sand Garden* restaurant) is the BONGO road, running out towards the Burkinabe border and to the village of the same name 15km away. Two drinking spots on the outskirts of Bolga, another *Meet Me There* and *Monkey No Fine*, are worth a pause en route. The goal at Bongo is the Bongo Hills and notably **Bongo Rock**, which, when thumped, makes an appropriately resounding boom that can be heard all over the district.

Along the Bawku road

The Bawku road **east from Bolga** takes you through the villages of NANGODI, with sacred fish and a disused gold mine, ZEBILLA, with beautifully decorated houses (try to get invited: hospitality is superb), and on to the (black) market town of **BAWKU** itself, right on the Burkinabe border and only 30km from Togo. Apart from smuggling, now on the wane, Bawku is a centre for the manufacture of *fugu* shirts, the north's characteristic costume. Look out for the **Naba's palace** and, again, geometric designs on the houses.

Around Tongo

Southeast of Bolga, the hills around the Talensi village of **TONGO** just a few kilometres from Bolgatanga are interesting – though not that easy to get to. Apart from their natural beauty, they're the site of **Tenzugu**, a famous religious shrine in a rocky cavern. The British destroyed it in 1911 and again in 1915, but couldn't prevent people from going there. Tongo is two bus rides away from Bolga – either 6km along the Bawku road to ZWERUNGU then 10km south, or 10km along the Tamale road, then 6km east – and has its market day on a Friday (again, the same as Bolgatanga). The people are very friendly here, including the chief, who can arrange for someone to guide you on the hefty hike through the hills to Tenzugu. If you're doing this, you should take some *akpeteshie* with you. Between Zwerungu and Tongo is the village of BARE, where the sacred **bat tree** makes a change from crocodile pools and holy fish ponds. The best time to visit the Tongo area would be for the **Sowing Festival** around Easter or the **Harvest Festival**, usually in September or October. Both reflect a curious blend of old and new – iron-bangled dancers shaking radios, tennis racquets and rubber dolls.

Further to the south and southeast

South of Bolga, WALEWALE is the site of a venerable mosque, the **Nakora. GAMBAGA**, 50km east of here, is famous for its scarp, stretching out towards the Togolese border and up to 300m high in places. The town is also the old **Mamprusi capital** and the site of current excavations investigating the origins of the Mamprusi kingdom (see box). The modern Mamprusi capital now stands at **NALERIGU**, 8km east of Gambaga, where you can see the palace of the Mamprusi kings as well as remains of the defensive walls built around the town when it was founded in the seventeenth century. **NAKPANDURI,** 30km further, is situated high on the scarp. The **government resthouse** here (incredibly cheap) is superbly sited, with a magnifcent view north over Burkina and some nice walks nearby through rocky outcrops.

HISTORY IN THE UPPER EAST

The Upper East Region is the traditional domain of the More-speaking peoples. Their history goes back to a thirteenth-century chief named **Gbewa** who founded a kingdom at **Pusiga**, east of Bawku on the Togolese border (where his tomb can still be seen). His sons fought over their inheritance and founded a number of mini-states in the region which grew from the fourteenth century and remained essentially intact until the nineteenth – **Mamprusi**, founded at Gambaga, **Dagomba**, and the other "Mossi" kingdoms mentioned in Part Five "Burkina Faso" (genealogy on p.258). These nations are now the names of distinct ethnic groups speaking dialects of More. Dagomba's first king, or *Ya Na*, founded a capital at **Yendi Dabari** (Dipali), north of Tamale, where ruins were unearthed in 1962. That capital was abandoned for **Yendi** (100km east of Tamale) after the sixteenth-century Gonja invasions. The Ya Na's palace is still there. At **Bagale**, in the remote country south of Gambaga, is the Dagomba Nas' mausoleum. The house built over it is the abode of the spirits of all departed Ya Nas.

TOGO

TOGO

lthough little known outside the region, **Togo** has a lot to offer in a small and accessible space. With a coastline even shorter than The Gambia's, it's only a narrow wedge of a country, but packs satisfying **scenery** – including real **highlands** and accessible **beaches** – and a vigorous **culture** differentiated into over a dozen linguistic and ethnic groups. There are decent **roads** and a surprisingly modern **service infrastructure** – startlingly conveyed if you fly into **Lomé at night** and see the glittering contrast with Ghana, the border of which demarcates the western city limit. Prices are way below those in other Francophone countries, urbanisation and accompanying neuroses have yet to make a sizeable impact and most travellers don't need a visa to enter. Togo is fast becoming one of West Africa's most popular destinations and a draw for flaked out trans-Saharans weary of dust and *piste*. You'll hear reports from returning overlanders of the country's virtues – the ocean, the proliferation of exotic fruit, the welcoming people. In the isolation of the desert, it's enough to make you want to head straight for Lomé, which is exactly what a large number of desert crossers do. True, during the Christmas and summer holidays, Lomé and the whole **coast** attract an influx of German and French vacationers, but they're easily absorbed by the population and much of the time the Togolese seem casually unaware of them.

Travel in Togo

The country's small size brings the benefits of easy **transport connections**. The main *Route National*, which shows off the country's **cultural and geographical variety**, runs north from Lomé to Dapaong, and even the most isolated villages lie within 100km of its path. Besides linking major towns, the highway also cuts through the **Kéran National Park**, where early morning travelling provides glimpses of **elephant** and **antelope**. Of course the tourist pamphlets' *All of Africa on a small scale* is a facile exaggeration, but not completely baseless since a short time in Togo can give you a substantial overview of West African scenery, wildlife and lifestyles.

Modern districts have recently sprouted in **Lomé**, but much of the capital seems like part of a provincial town where, tuned to the shuffling pace of crowded narrow streets, goats and chickens share space with the occasional *Peugeot* taxi. The **city centre**, bursting with commerce, has its own convincing momentum, yet falls restfully short of the frenzied tempo you expect from most big cities in the region. It adds up to one of West Africa's best capitals – laid-back but not chaotic, stylish but thankfully not Abidjani – and a place where you can happily adjust to West Africa or even base yourself for further travels.

TOGO VITAL STATISTICS

The **République Togolaise** is a strip of a country and one of the stranger legacies of colonial nation-carving. The name Togo means "By the water" in Ewe. At 56,000 square kilometres – hardly bigger than Switzerland – its population is estimated at under five million, with some 500,000 living in the capital, Lomé. There's a foreign debt of about £600 million, a relatively small amount even in West Africa. Government is conducted through a single party, the *Rassemblement du Peuple Togolais* (*RPT*). President Gnassingbé (formerly Etienne) Eyadéma has been in power for over twenty years.

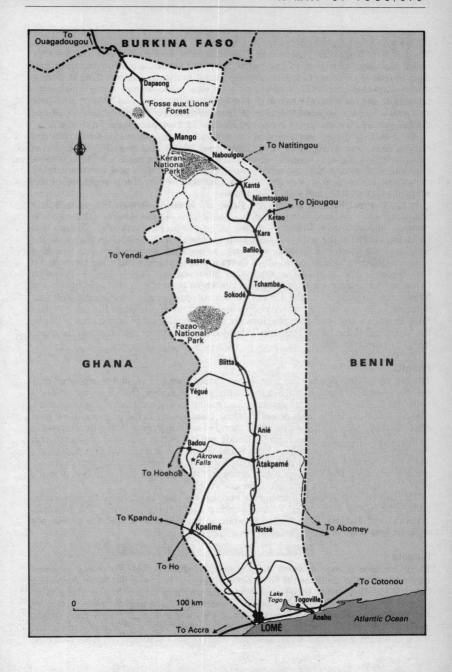

Once you leave Lomé, don't rush along the **coast**: it's worth savouring, not just for the palmy villages rustling between the lagoons and the Atlantic, but also for **Voodoo**. The towns of **Togoville**, **Aného** and **Glidji**, in their fetishes, shrines and festivals, reveal a lot about a religion no less bizarre than the **Catholicism** with which it is strikingly interwoven. Followers are usually open about *vaudau* and often willing to discuss it with interested travellers – surprisingly so in view of the secrecy under which traditional religions are often shrouded. If your African touch down was Lomé, here is one area you'll feel the unjaded strength of the continent. As a new experience, it can compensate for air-conditioned banks and Michael Jackson booming from the bars.

Northwest of Lomé stretches the mountainous and extremely fertile **plateau region**. Never exceeding 1000 metres, the peaks of this area give the impression of being somehow higher, especially when climbing the twisting roads leading to **Badou**, **Kpalimé** or **Atakpamé**. These three towns delineate the **coffee and cocoa** triangle – the richest agricultural area in the country, characterised by **thick vegetation** interspersed with fruit trees and palm plantations.

In the **Central Region**, Sokodé and Bafilo are **Muslim** strongholds, while Bassar and Kara have retained predominantly traditional religious beliefs (although the customs and religious practices in the latter two differ markedly). Mango and Dapaong, located in the semi-arid **savannah region** of the far north, already evoke the Sahel and the spectre of drought. But Kara, as home of the president, has benefited from a number of industrial and other **development projects** that have catapulted it into "second city" status. The enormous influence of "The Guide" – President Gnassingbe Eyadéma – is unmistakeable. His ample presence on photos in homes and businesses, on posters, on the TV and radio, is ubiquitous and overbearing. You may perceive Togo as a country where people are especially jumpy when the conversation turns to politics and, until recently, it rarely did, especially not in public places. But by the beginning of the 1990s, Togo was at last looking with more confidence at the possibility of a pluralistic state.

People

The big groups in Togo are the **Ewe** (often spelled Ewé or Evé, and pronounced midway between Ehveh and Eyway) in the south, and the **Kabyé** (Kabyié, Kabré, Kauré) of the north. The Ewe, who are divided into a multiplicity of local and district communities, are traditionally the most powerful ethnic constituency in the territory. They have linguistic and cultural affiliations with other Twi-speaking peoples like the Akposo in central Togo, the Asante and Fante in Ghana and the Fon in eastern Togo and Benin. The Ewe diaspora – especially in France and Ghana – is a source of firm opposition, while the Ghanaian border, which splits the Ewe into two regions, is the butt of considerable frustration. The Togolese Ewe, particularly the Mina, are the producers of much of Togo's export earnings, through coffee and cocoa.

The **Kabyé and related Tamberma** peoples are poor subsistence farmers in the north who, along with other Voltaic-speaking northerners including the Kotokoli, Tchamba and Bassari, have tended to unite to some extent behind the president's regional development plans (he himself is a Kabyé).

Climate

Togo's **climate** is another factor in its popularity with travellers. The **rainy seasons** vary from north to south, but if you have any choice, they need not be an overriding factor in deciding when to go. Lomé and the southern region has its "long rainy season" from March to June and a period of short rains some time between September and November. Sokodé and the north get a single – and less predictable – rainy season between April and September. Note, though, that there's not a lot of rain, even in the south (baobabs grow right down to within 10km of the coast) and the table for Lomé given here is an average, so that some years are very dry. Except in small villages off the paved road, notably in the Tamberma Country or the areas around Bassar and Tchamba – where steep muddy tracks can be demanding – the weather won't greatly hamper your travels.

AVERAGE TEMPERATURES AND RAINFALL
LOMÉ

	Jan	Feb	Mar	Apr	May	June	July	Aug	Sept	Oct	Nov	Dec
Temperatures °C												
Min (night)	23	24	25	24	24	23	23	22	23	23	23	23
Max (day)	31	31	32	31	31	29	27	27	28	30	31	31
Rainfall mm	15	24	52	118	145	224	71	8	35	61	28	10
Days with rainfall	1	2	4	8	9	12	5	1	5	9	2	1

Arrivals

Togo is more commonly the terminus for overland travel than a place to begin a West African trip. This was especially true when Ghana and Nigeria closed their borders a few years back, making it impossible to continue by road. That situation has now changed, and flights from Europe to Lomé – traditionally among the most expensive in West Africa – are now priced at more reasonable levels. Entering the country overland, the routes are mostly paved, and especially busy along the coast.

■ Flights from Africa

Air Afrique provides most of the flights from capital cities in **West Africa** to Lomé. They have several flights a week from **Abidjan** and **Dakar** plus at least one a week from **Bamako**, **Cotonou**, **Douala**, **Lagos** and **Ouagadougou**. Some of these same destinations are also serviced by *Air Mali*, *Air Burkina* (which also links Lomé to Bobo-Dioulasso) and *Nigeria Airways*.

Air Afrique also provides the most common link from **Central Africa**, with a couple of flights in every week from **Brazzaville** and **Libreville**. In addition, *Air Zaire* has a weekly flight from **Kinshasa**. Flights from **East Africa** on *Ethiopian Airlines* are from **Addis Ababa** and **Nairobi** via Lagos.

■ Overland from Burkina Faso

The road from Ouagadougou is sealed all the way to Lomé (with minor exceptions in Togo where stretches are undergoing repairs). Border formalities pose no special problems on either side of this well-travelled route, although the posts close at 6pm. Coming from Ouaga **by bush taxi**, you can save money by going as far as Dapaong and changing vehicles there. This alternative, however, is likely to add a lot of time to your trip (and note that "express taxis" take 22 hours to complete it with a minimum of stops). You could spend a day or longer in Dapaong waiting for a Lomé-bound taxi to fill.

■ From Ghana and Benin

The international highway that follows the coast is in good condition throughout the route from **Abidjan to Lagos**. There's a lot of traffic between both Accra and Cotonou, and catching bush taxis from Cotonou or buses from Accra is no problem.

Between Cotonou and Lomé, the Dutch airline *KLM* runs a bus each way Tues and Fri (enquire at their office; address in the Cotonou Directory, p.950).

Coming from Ghana, borders close at 6pm, but otherwise present no special difficulty. Don't take a vehicle to Lomé itself, however. Instead get transport to the Ghanaian border town of Aflao and walk into Lomé. The Hilakondji border post between Togo and Benin is open day and night.

Red Tape

Nationals of Great Britain, the USA and Canada need no visa to enter Togo and can stay up to three months. The same holds true for nationals of Belgium, Denmark, France, West Germany, Holland, Italy, Luxembourg, Norway and Sweden and ECOWAS members. All others need a visa or transit permit before entering the country. Where Togo has no diplomatic representation, you can usually get one at the French consulate.

Whether you enter by air or overland, customs and immigration officials usually give you little grief and will certainly permit the maximum stay. Sometimes you may be asked how much money you're carrying, but the amount is rarely verified. The only other piece of paper you'll need is a yellow fever certificate. The **exit visa** which gets mentioned in much literature on Togo – official and otherwise – hasn't been a requirement for a number of years.

■ Visas for onward travel

Lomé has only a limited number of **West African embassies and consulates**. You can get visas for Ghana and Nigeria, and visas for some Francophone countries, including Burkina Faso, from the French consulate – addresses are given in the Lomé directory. Benin visas are issued at the Hillakondji border.

Money and Costs

Togo's currency is the franc CFA (CFA50 equals 1 French franc; CFA450–CFA500 = £1). Coming overland, you're likely to have some CFA but, arriving by air from Europe, it's a good idea to bring some French francs in cash as they are generally acceptable for

taxis, services and hotels. The airport banks close at 6pm: arrive later than this and you'll find it difficult to change money.

Changing other major **international currencies** (traveller's cheques or cash) is no problem in Lomé, Kara or Sokodé. In smaller towns, **banks** are likely only to accept francs or dollars but not pounds sterling or deutschmarks. Banking hours are short and inconvenient: Monday to Friday 7.30–11.30am and 2.30–4pm.

■ **The Black Market**

Lomé has the biggest **currency black market** in West Africa, near the old Cotonou taxi station and Grand Marché, and all along the aptly named rue du Commerce. The quarter is notorious throughout the region and the free market operates here quite openly. You can buy **Nigerian Naira** and **Ghanaian Cedis** but also **CFA** (useful if you get caught without when the banks are closed) and other international currencies. Though you're not breaking any (Togolese) law, you should strongly bear in mind the advice given under the heading of Money and Costs in Part Eighteen "Nigeria" and Part Fifteen "Ghana".

Streetwise **money-changers** are very adept at sleight of hand tricks, so go with a friend, pay attention, and only carry the money you want to change. In general, it's advisable to avoid the sharks on the street who'll perform magic before your eyes, and deal with one of the bigger bosses at a shop front; doing the actual exchange inside the shop. Hand over nothing until you've verified your deal note by note. Much cooler exchanges are often to be had with resident expatriate money-dealers who have legal currency businesses and will give better-than-bank rates if you're buying CFA. Ask around.

■ **Costs**

The **cost of living** in Togo is substantially below that in other Francophone countries, but if you plan on living and eating à *l'européenne*, you'll pay dearly for imported goods that would be cheap at home. **Hotel rooms** in Lomé run anywhere from CFA2500 to CFA30,000 but the interior of the country is less expensive and you can find good rooms for under CFA5000 nearly everywhere. Ready-cooked **street food** is quite cheap and market produce likewise, especially in the productive southeast. **Restaurants** serving European food generally do meals from about CFA1500. Beer and soft drinks are very inexpen-

sive, although the big hotels and tourist hangouts knock the prices up as you'd expect. In a local bar, prices are the same from the north to south (CFA140 for a beer, CFA75 for soft drinks). **Petrol** costs about CFA205 per litre for super but you often find it sold more cheaply in jerry cans along the Ghanaian border – notably on the road to Kpalimé.

Health

In common with the rest of West Africa, a yellow fever vaccination certificate is compulsory; the full gamut of other shots is recommended. Malaria tablets are another must and chloroquine resistance has been reported, so extra care is needed.

Towns and large villages have either a hospital or – more likely – a **dispensary**, but these are characteristically overcrowded and lack adequate supplies. If you get seriously ill, it's best to get to your embassy (never very far in Togo) or one that speaks your language. They'll be able to refer you to a specialist or decide if you wouldn't be better off flying back home to get the help you need.

As in other countries, official reports invariably say that only a handful of **AIDS** cases have been registered in Togo and of course they're all prostitutes and foreigners – something that's very hard to believe.

Maps and Information

The best travel map of Togo is the large sheet produced by the French *IGN*, with its optimistic scattering of animal life. The *Office National Togolais du Tourisme* in Lomé also sells large national maps, but the *Michelin 953* of West Africa is more useful than they are.

The *ONATT* also have **brochures** (like *Passeport Pour Le Togo*) with pretty pictures, but only sketchy travel information.

North Americans can get **preliminary information** from the Togo Information Service, 1625 K Street N.W. Suite 102 Washington D.C. 20006. ☎(202) 659-4330. The embassy in London has very little literature to give away, but they're helpful if you visit. Europeans can also try writing to the *Office National Togolais du Tourisme*, 23 rue François 1er, 75008 Paris.

Getting Around

Getting around Togo is most easily done by road. The very limited railway network in the south dates from the era of German occupation and is universally slow and uncomfortable. There's no domestic air service.

■ Bush taxis and car hire

There are few bus services in Togo and most of the time you'll be using privately run **taxis**. Every year Japanese vans gain ground on the traditional *Peugeot 504s*: the *Nissans* and *Hiaces* are new and comfortable. Laws against overloading are enforced more often than in the past – though the number of passengers a driver will take usually depends on how many policemen he thinks he'll meet on the road, and whether the fines he pays will cancel out the extra fares.

Togo, small country that it is, has good roads on the whole and you can drive on tarmac to all the neighbouring capitals. But while Lomé and Kara have **car hire** agencies, prices are prohibitive.

■ Trains

The Germans built **railway lines** to Aného (for freighting out the coconuts), Kpalimé (for coffee and cocoa) and Blitta (for cotton) and the system, which is antiquated, and enthused over by rail buffs, only goes to these towns. If you're in no hurry the wooden carriages with shutters and colonial styling seem rather fine, and train travel is the cheapest form of transport. But the slow runs are travel for fun, not convenience. Schedules are given in appropriate sections of the guide.

Sleeping

Outside of Lomé and Kara, each equipped with showy five-star hotels, Togo has little in the way of luxury accommodation. From north to south, however, it does have an adequate number of modest hotels, either privately owned or government run. Accommodation is usually adquate and good value compared with neighbouring Francophone countries, although amenities like air-conditioning, TV and phones are exceptional.

Togo has little in the way of youth hostels or mission accommodation, though the *Affaires Sociales* government rest houses will always put you up cheaply if they've room. It's also useful to know that a large number of hotels allow **campers** to pitch on their grounds for CFA1000 or CFA2000 a night.

There are several organised **camping** sites east of Lomé and a limited number of other sites throughout the country. If you have your own transport, you can discreetly pull off the road away from the big towns and put up for the night just about anywhere, especially in the centre and north.

Staying with people is officially frowned upon unless you make a declaration at the town *préfecture*. Lomé is big enough that you can usually skip this formality with little risk of the authorities finding out, and many travellers do rent rooms or villas here from private individuals on a short-term basis – a possibility that works out much cheaper than a hotel. Best place to catch word of offers is in the bars around the Kodjiavakope neighbourhood. Outside the capital, police will soon learn your whereabouts and, if you're not staying in a bone fide hotel, may drag you into headquarters to reprimand you and make you fill out endless forms. Sheer misery.

Eating and Drinking

Togo has a reputation in West Africa for some of the best cooking in the region. Small restaurants or street stands as far as Niamey, Bamako and Abidjan are often run by Togolese women. The secret of their success lies in their sauces, which tend to be less greasy than usual and contain more vegetables. Not that you'll necessarily love Togolese food right away; some of it will seem unappealing at first (slimy gumbo – or okra – can be a real turn-off until you get used to it) and all of it's guaranteed to be heavily laced with hot peppers.

■ Staples and Dishes

Staples vary across the country: in the south, **cassava** (manioc) predominates, along with **palm oil** and **maize**. Cassava is often grated and steamed as *atieke*. In the plateau region, the diet contains more tubers – **yams**, **cocoyams** and **sweet potatoes** – boiled, grilled, steamed or fried. **Plantains** are another favourite staple, commonly pounded into **fufu** (which can also be made with cassava or yams). In the north, **shea-nut oil** is commoner than palm oil and **rice**, **millet** and **sorghum** (ground, boiled and served as a mash) are eaten more frequently than towards the coast.

Vegetables include tomatoes, gumbo, aubergines (yellowish and smaller than those of northern climates), squash and beans. These are used in **sauces** with cassava, baobab or taro leaves and mixed with fish, shellfish, meat or poultry. Common **spices** are ginger, peppers, anis, garlic, basil and mustard.

The south and plateau region have the most **fruit**, although even in the extreme north you'll find a good variety. **Pineapples**, **mangoes**, **papayas**, all the **citrus**, **avocados** and **guava** are plentiful in the markets (depending of course on the season) and downright cheap in the south.

Supplements to the basics include *agouti* (the large herbivorous rodent known in Ghana and Nigeria as "bush rat" or "grasscutter") and *koliko* (deep fried yam chips). Togo's best known dishes are *moutsella* (a spicy fish and vegetable dish), *adokouin* (shellfish with a prawn sauce known as *azidessi*), *djekoumé* (chilli chicken), and *gboma* (a spinach and seafood based dish). You're most likely to sample these at an important private gathering, or as part of the *Cuisine Togolaise* menu in one of the more expensive restaurants. But Togo has a great line in **street food** and, even in the smaller **village markets**, women sell exotic as well as fairly familiar food – rice, refried beans, macaroni – from basins, by the portion, and all served with a very hot sauce.

If such a variety of dishes isn't already enough, the large towns all have restaurants serving **European food**, but tend to be relatively expensive, especially if you want wine with your meal.

■ Drinking

Togo has its share of local drinks, similar to the other common intoxicants of West Africa. **Palm wine** is big in the south: the juice that flows from the trunks is already fermented and ready to drink, the frothier the fresher. A hard liquor can be produced by further distilling the wine. Though illegal, this highly potent "African gin", or *sodabi*, flows freely in the coastal region. Northern Togo specialises in millet beer, known locally as *choucoutou* (or *tchoucoutou*) – a taste

somwhat reminiscent of dry cider. Filtering it produces *chacbalo* (or *tchacbalo*), which is clear and slightly sweeter than *tchouc*.

Togo's modern brewery pumps out a wide selection of more familiar drinks. The **beer** here is excellent and cheap. *Bière du Benin* (referred to as "BéBé") is the standard lager. *Eku* is more potent. *Guinness* is also available, served cold. There's a wide range of soft drinks, good *Lion Killer* lemonade, soda water, tonic and the rest – even a splendidly fruity *Cocktail de Fruits* – a carbonated mixture of passion, apple, pineapple and mangoes. They all come in large and small bottles and they're all refreshingly inexpensive.

Communications

The official language of Togo is French. Communications with Europe are relatively good, at least from Lomé, and in comparison with domestic post and phones. The local media is limited, but papers and magazines are imported, and you won't feel out of touch with the news in Lomé.

■ Staying in Touch: PTT and telex

Post is fairly inexpensive – CFA200 for airmail letters to Europe (except France which is slightly cheaper) and America. Surface mail packages cost over CFA1000 per kilo and a small fortune by airmail. Lomé's *Poste Restante* is the most helpful and reliable one-man service in West Africa. **Phoning home**, reverse charge calls are only possible to France, and normal calls are pretty expensive (CFA1500 per minute to America and most of Europe, CFA800 to France) with telex even pricier. In Lomé, the telephone and telex office is located behind the central post office. There are now some phone boxes in Lomé whence you can phone abroad on IDD, assuming you've enough CFA100 pieces.

■ Language

French, the official language, is widely spoken in Togo. Due to the commerce with Ghana and Nigeria, many traders speak rudimentary **English,** especially in the area around Lomé, but it would be an exaggeration to suggest it's spoken widely spoken.

There are some fifty **African languages** and dialects, the most widely spoken among them being **Mina** (closely related to Ewe, a written

MINIMAL MINA AND ESSENTIAL EWE

Mina is spoken by about a third of the population in Togo, making it the most common language in the country. You'll run into it mostly along the coast, including in parts of Ghana and Benin. Unlike **Ewe**, to which it is closely related, Mina is not written. Both languages are tonal rather than phonetic, so that meaning varies (as in Chinese for example) with the pitch of the voice. They're therefore rather hard languages for speakers of European tongues to come to grips with, and the following words and expressions can only be a very rough guide to pronunciation.

MINA GREETINGS AND BASICS

Good day	*Sobaydo*	Have a nice day	*Nkekay anenyo*
Reply	*Dosso*	Yes	*Aaaaa*
How are you ?	*O foihn?*	No	*Ow*
Reply ("fine")	*aaaaa* (as in cat)	Come here (to a child)	*Va*
Thank you	*Akpay*	See you later	*Sodé* or *Sodaylo*
Thank you very (very) much	*Akpaykaka (kaka)*	Until we meet again	*Mia dogou/mia dogoulo*
		See you tomorrow	*Ayeee'soh*

MINA NUMBERS

1	*Dekaa*	5	*Ametón* (high tone)	8	*Ameni*
2	*Amevé*	6	*Amadé*	9	*Amesidiké*
3	*Ametòn* (low tone)	7	*Ameadrreh*	10	*Amewo*
4	*Amené*				

EWE GREETINGS AND BASICS

Good morning	*Nngdi*	I don't understand	*Nye mese egome o*
Good afternoon	*Nngdo*	Goodbye	*Hede nyuie*
Good evening	*Fie*	I'm a stranger	*Amedzro menye*
Good night	*Do agbe*	Please	*Taflatse*
Welcome	*Woe zo*	What is your name ?	*Nko wode?*
How are you?	*E foa?/ Ale nyuie?*	My name is...	*Nngkonyee nye...*
I'm fine	*Mefo/Meli nyuie*	I am leaving Ewe land	*Mele Evegbe srom*
Pleased to meet you	*Edzo dzi nam be medo go wo*		

EWE NUMBERS

1	*Deka*	7	*Aderen*	20	*Blave*
2	*Uhve*	8	*Enyee*	30	*Blatòh* (low tone)
3	*Etoh*	9	*Asiekee*	40	*Blana*
4	*Enah*	10	*Ewo*	50	*Blatóh* (high tone)
5	*Atoh*	11	*Wedekee*	60	*Bladee*, etc
6	*Adee*	12	*Weuhve*, etc	100	*Alohfa deka*

language). Mina is spoken by 30 percent of the population in the coastal region and into Ghana. Government reports list **Kabyé** (also known as Kabré or Kauré) as being the second most common language in the country. To arrive at this claim, they include a host of related **Tem** dialects in the Voltaic group, spoken in the Kara region, since **Kotokoli** – the language of Sokodé and environs; see box on p.917 – is certainly more prevalent than Kabyé. Other languages include **Bassari**, in the area around the town of Bassar, the **Tchamba** in the east, **Moba** around Dapaong and scattered communities of **Hausa, Fula and Mossi** in the extreme north.

■ The Media

Radio Togo, the national station, broadcasts news in French, Ewe, Kabyé and English (endless reports of telegrams the president received that day followed by an often interesting wrap-up of West African events). At noon endless obituaries are read while the tune of *Jesus Loves the Little Children* drones as a funeral dirge in the background. Libreville's **Africa Numero Un** and

A GLOSSARY OF TOGOLESE TERMS

Anasara In the northern parts, a white, derived from Nazarene, or Christian.

Authenticité Programme initiated by Eyadéma to instill pride in "authentic" roots, requiring French names to be exchanged for African and proficiency in Ewe, Mina or Kabyé for all school children.

Auto-suffisance alimentaire Food self-sufficiency, which, in non-drought years, Togo just about has.

Evala The annual wrestling matches in the president's hometown of Kara.

RPT *Rassemblement du Peuple Togolais* – the single party in the country.

Soukala A compound of round huts connected by a wall, found in the north.

Vaudau/Vodu Generic names for the spirit children of God – Mawu-Lisa in Ewe.

Yovo White person (Mina).

Radio France Internationale are better music stations with more comprehensive coverage of international events. National TV broadcasts about five hours every evening – news in French and local languages plus old French movies.

The single newspaper, **La Nouvelle March** ("The New Step"), in French, with Ewe and Kabyé pages, has at best sketchy international coverage, but articles on national or local events are often interesting. As part of the democratisation process, there are supposed to be a couple of new "comment" magazines of a slightly analytical or critical nature. You'll find international **English-language papers** like *The Herald Tribune*, *Time* or *Newsweek* at the airport and the big hotels. Eyadéma is proud of his claim that since his accession to power, Togo has never banned a foreign paper or journal.

Holidays

Both Muslim and Christian holidays – including Catholic festivals like Pentecost, Ascension and Assumption (the former two variable and the latter on August 15) – are celebrated in Togo, along with New Year's Day. National holidays are: January 13 (National Liberation); January 24 (anniversary of the president's plane crash at Sarakawa and the subsequent nationalisation of phosphate production); February 22 (Eyadéma's "Triumphal Return"); April 24 (Victory Day); May 1 (Labour Day): July (Evala – see below) which, with so many Kabyé employees granted leave, is increasingly a public holiday.

There are many **traditional holidays** celebrated in the different regions, many with corresponding celebrations in Ghana and Benin. Notable among them are:

July

Evala is an initiation celebration in the Kabyé country with wrestling matches (*lutte traditionnelle*). The tournaments in Kara are now televised nationally and attended by the president, a former champion. **Akpema** is the young women's initiation ceremony for in the Kabyé country.

August

Kpessosso is the Gun harvest festival celebrated in the region of Aného and marked by traditional dances (*Adjogbo* and *Gbékon*). **Kpessosso** is an element in the week-long **Yékéyéké**, or *Yakamiakin* festival (see Glidji after Lomé). **Ayize** is the bean harvest festival celebrated by the Ewe, particularly in the region of Tsévié.

September

Agbogbozan is the festival of the Ewe diaspora celebrated on the first Thursday in September and especially colourful in Notsé. In Bassar, the **Dipontre**, or yam festival, is celebrated the first week of September.

Directory

AIRPORT TAX None.

CRAFTS There are numerous points throughout the country where crafts are plentiful. The principal one in Lomé is the Passage des Arts – a small street near the market with nothing but art vendors selling sculptures, bronzes, jewellery and textiles from across West Africa. Near Kpalimé, the *Centre Artisinal de Klouto* is a noble attempt to keep regional crafts alive and traditional forms of **pottery**, **calabash decoration** and **wood carving** have here taken on a more modern and commercial flavour. Kpalimé itself is a good place to buy **kente cloth** which is woven in the town

streets. Traditional cloth is also woven in Bafilo and can be purchased directly from the *coopératives des tisserands* in the town centre. A sad, bad footnote is the firm presence of **ivory** in Lomé's craft shops and a flourishing ancillary trade in fake ivory bangles.

EDUCATION Elementary school is compulsory for children aged six to twelve, though only about seventy percent make it this far. Fewer than a quarter get through secondary school. Togo has one university, the *Université du Benin* in Lomé, which has some 5000 students.

EMERGENCIES In Lomé, the emergency number for the **police** is ☎17; for an ambulance, dial ☎21.20.42; or the hospital, ☎21.25.01.

FOOTBALL A popular sport in Togo, with particularly fierce competition between Semassi, the team from Sokodé, and Gomido from Kpalimé.

MUSIC In the world of **pop music**, Togo's sole international star is **Bella Bellow**, who was "discovered" by Cameroon's Manu Dibango and who had a successful career before her death in a car accident. Some of her cassettes can be found on the market in Lomé. More recent musicians who've made a name for themselves include **Itadi K. Bonney** and **Afia Mala**. But

probably Togo's biggest star is **Jimmy Hope**, a rock/blues musician with a huge following who often plays around Lomé.

OPENING HOURS Administrative offices and most **businesses** are open from 7.30–noon and from 2.30–4.30pm. **Banking hours** vary slightly from one institution to the next, but are roughly 7.30–11am and 2.30–4pm.

PHOTOGRAPHY No photography permit is required in Togo, though the usual restrictions apply to taking pictures of military installations and strategic points. People generally tend to be less camera-shy than in some African countries and children in particular are eager to have their pictures taken. Polaroids are popular.

WILDLIFE PARKS Of several game reserves and national parks in Togo, foremost is the **Parc Nationale de la Kéran** that straddles the northern highway. The other large park is the **Parc Nationale Fazao**, west of the highway, near Sokodé. Smaller reserves include **Abdoulaye**, to the east of the route nationale, opposite Fazao; **Togodo**, hard up against the Beninese border east of Notsé; and three areas north of Kéran – **Oti**, in a remote district along the river of the same name in the northeast, **Galangachi** just west of Sansanné-Mango, and the small **Fosse aux Lions** ("Lions' Den") just southwest of Dapaong.

WOMEN: THE FEMINIST MOVEMENT Women have considerable economic clout in Togo, particularly in the south where well-organised women merchants – known in Lomé as the *Nanas Benz* – are a political force to be reckoned with. Partly in consequence, the government recognises and sanctions the *Union Nationale des Femmes Togolaises*. Women do have access to all administrative functions and professions but the reality is that education, though compulsory for all children, is less likely to be received by girls than boys (54 percent compared to 80 percent) and there are few women with high-level government and business positions. Tradition, in rural areas especially, dictates a strict sexual division of labour.

A Short History of Togo

For centuries, Togo has been on the fringes of several empires – Mali, Asante, Benin, Mossi – but the centre of none. The country – which formed part of what was once called the slave coast – came into contact with Europeans in the fifteenth century as the Portuguese made their sweep of the African continent. Porto Seguro (Agbodrafo) and Petit Popo (Aného) evolved to become important trading posts where slaves were exchanged for European goods. By the end of the nineteenth century, trade had shifted to "legitimate" products – principally palm oil, used in soap manufacture in Europe. French and German companies competed along the coast in their dealings with the Mina people.

■ The Colonial Period

In 1884, **Gustav Nachtigal** sailed into Togo and signed a treaty with a village chief that made the country a **German protectorate**. In the following years, **Togoland** developed into the Reich's "model colony" as the Germans tried to force the country to produce economic miracles. Railways and roads were laid, and forests cleared for coffee and cocoa plantations. A direct radio link with Berlin was established and wharves were built.

The beginnings of an ill-defined educational system tried to create Christians and wage labourers out of reluctant farmers and fishermen. It took the Germans until 1902 to "pacify" the people of Togo, relying on forced labour and other repressive measures to push through their progress.

Despite the colony's economic importance, German military presence in Togoland was weak. When World War I broke out, the British and French easily overran the territory, forcing the Kaiser's soldiers to capitulate at **Kamina** on August 26, 1914. The tiny village was thus the site of the Entente Powers' very first victory. After the war, a **League of Nations mandate** placed a third of the territory under British administration and two-thirds (corresponding to the present country's borders) in the hands of the French.

The Way to Independence

Both **France and Britain** showed only half-hearted interest in their new acquisitions which technically were not colonies. The British quickly attached western Togo (today the Volta Region in Ghana) to the Gold Coast, but the French administered eastern Togo as an entity separate from its other holdings in West Africa. Thus several of Togo's peoples – the Adele, Konkomba and especially **Ewe** – suddenly found their communities divided by a border. Reunification was an early political theme, but one the European powers looked on unfavourably. A "Pan-Ewe" vision, championed by early nationalist leaders like

Sylvanus Olympio, was dealt a severe blow in 1956 when people of West Togo voted in a referendum to amalgamate with the Gold Coast, then preparing for independence.

At the same time, the French were grooming eastern Togo for independence. In 1956, Togo became an autonomous republic, with **Nicolas Grunitzky** as prime minister. Two years later, Olympio took over the role and, when Togo became fully independent on April 27, 1960, he was elected the nation's first president.

■ A Shaky Start

Olympio aspired to the ideals of early nationalists such as Nkrumah, Touré and Senghor, although he never achieved their stature. In any case, even as he ushered in a new era, the stage was set for his own demise. In a scenario all too common to the former colonies, the Germans and later French had groomed a class of coastal peoples to be civil servants and the educated elite. After independence, these peoples inherited political power and, as a consequence, economic advantages. It was a formula guaranteed to result in **ethnic tension** in countries where unity should have been of primary importance.

In the case of Togo, Olympio, an Ewe from Aného, represented the **elite minority**. He tended to put reunification with the Ewe in Ghana ahead of Togolese national unity and was openly contemptuous of the northern Togolese, whom he called *petits nordistes*. Increasing repression and disregard for the poor north didn't help to broaden his already narrow political base.

Meanwhile **Nkrumah of Ghana**, who had supported Olympio's efforts for Togo's independence, had apparently intended the territory to be integrated with Ghana and, that objective thwarted, actively harrassed Olympio's new government with border closures and trade sanctions. But the worst blow to Olympio's prestige came in 1963, when **returning Togolese**

soldiers who had fought for France in the Algerian war of independence, were refused permission by him to join Togo's national army, since in his eyes they had betrayed the African liberation movement. For the troops, in the main Kabyé men from the north, it was a humiliating snub, and seemed to be proof that Olympio was determined to exclude them from participation in the new nation.

On January 13, 1963, a group of disenfranchised soldiers, including a young Kabyé sergeant named **Etienne Eyadéma**, staged the first coup in independent Africa. They stormed the president's home and, according to the official version, shot Olympio while he was trying to escape by scrambling up the wall from his residence and into the grounds of the American embassy where he had hoped to seek refuge.

The soldiers set up a civilian government and placed Grunitsky, who had returned from exile, at its head. The new president lasted four ineffectual years and, as the country's increasing problems outstripped his competence to deal with them, he was replaced, in a bloodless coup staged by Eyadéma, in a symbolic style that became his hallmark, on January 13, 1967, four years to the day after Olympio's assassination.

■ The Eyadéma Years

After his second coup Eyadéma seized power "at the insistence of the people", suspended the constitution, dissolved political opposition and set about, much after the style of Zaire's President Mobutu, protecting his political future through the powerful mechanism of the single party he himself controls – the *Rassemblement du Peuple Togolais* or *RPT*. By 1972, he was secure enough to hold a referendum on his future as president, in which voters held up one colour card to indicate a "yes" vote and a different colour for "no" as soldiers guarded the booths. A landslide 99 percent of the population thus expressed its desire for Eyadéma to remain the national leader.

Two years later, the president profited from a bizarre series of events that seemed to give supernatural backing to the demonstration of popular support. It started in 1974 with what has gone down in Togolese political legend (actively encouraged by the president) as the "**Three Glorious Days**". On January 10, Eyadéma announced that a 51 percent share of the French-operated phosphate mines (one of the country's principal resources) would be nationalised.

Exactly two weeks later, January 24, the president's private plane crashed over **Sarakawa**, but Eyadéma walked away from the wreck virtually unmarked. An international plot was suspected, and, without any real proof, the world was led to believe this was a classic case of capitalist meddling – an assassination attempt on the man who had dared to liberate his country's economy.

After recovering, the president made a drawn out journey from Kara to Lomé, and throngs of people came to look at the man who had become a myth. On February 2, Eyadéma made his **triumphal return** to the capital and announced that the phosphate industry was henceforth one hundred percent in Togolese hands.

The incident turned into a political windfall that made Togo look like the mouse who roared. **Eyadéma's anti-imperialist record** was enshrined in myth. He began an "**authenticity**" campaign, again modelled closely on Mobutu's in Zaire, abolishing French names (and re-naming himself Gnassingbe) and introducing Kabyé and – with a little shrewdness – Ewe into the school schools as languages of instruction. Phosphate money helped build a few modern buildings in Lomé and Kara and ambitious projects like an oil refinery, steel plant and cement factory near Lomé. But rather than creating jobs, these simply lost money, forcing the country to bend to IMF pressure to denationalise as the economy slumped badly in the 1980s. The irony of Togo's position ever since Sarakawa is that it has been one of the most pragmatically **pro-Western** countries in the region.

■ International Affairs

Despite economic decline, Eyadéma has managed to keep a high diplomatic profile and created a new larger-than-life image for himself, based on his role as **West African peacemaker**. At one point he served as an intermediary between combatants in the Chadian war and helped smooth over relations between Nigeria and the Francophone countries that had backed Biafra. More recently he has provided another African platform for **Israel**, with which Togo opened diplomatic relations in 1987.

On an economic level, Eyadéma has championed ECOWAS (the West African common market, known in French-speaking countries as the CEDEAO). Along with Nigeria, Togo was a major sponsor of the organisation, established in 1975 when fifteen regional nations signed the

Treaty of Lagos. Lomé is today the headquarters of the ECOWAS Fund for Co-operation, Compensation and Development. Eyadéma has also used his influence to launch smaller groupings linking politically opposite regimes such as the *Communauté Electrique du Bénin* (Ghana, Togo, Benin) and the *Ciments de l'Afrique de l'Ouest* (Ghana, Togo, Côte d'Ivoire). But his proudest achievement was hosting the meeting that resulted in the signing of the **Lomé Convention**, giving third world nations in Africa, the Caribbean and the Pacific preferential treatment from the EC and linking the name of Lomé with co-operation in development policy.

Relations with Ghana, Burkina and Benin

Relations with **Ghana** have traditionally been rocky, partly as a result of the early pan-Ewe movement that gripped the country at the end of the colonial era and which continues in a more subtle form today. The ideological opposition of Rawlings' and Eyadéma's regimes has also led to serious tensions between the two neighbours.

Following the Ghana-**Burkina Faso** rapprochement during Thomas Sankara's period in power, Togolese relations with its northern neighbour also chilled, although they improved rapidly after Sankara's death and Compaore's assumption of power in 1987. Eyadéma was the first African head of state to recognise the new Burkinabe government, and he did so just hours after the overthrow was officially announced.

Ideology has also been a source of conflict with **Benin** – a country periodically charged by Togo with giving refuge to politically active exiles. During the 1980s, the Togo–Benin border was frequently closed.

■ At Home: Opposition and Outlook

Eyadéma, who helped to orchestrate two **coups** and has been witness to numbers of others in the three states neighbouring his own, has been careful to nip **opposition** in the bud. Although the president personally launched a recent human rights campaign and claims to have no political prisoners, Togo refused a 1986 Amnesty request to send representatives to investigate allegations of torture. Dissent does exist, and it rises to the surface in periodic **eruptions of violence** that are quickly snuffed out and hushed up.

In 1984, when the papal visit was focusing international attention on the country, a series of **bombings** rocked Lomé. But the closest thing to a successful **coup** occured in a 1986 shoot-out with armed rebels who got perilously close to the presidential residence. The coup was put down, but French paratroopers and **troops** from Zaire had to be called in to assure the revolt was hammered out. The attempted takeover was blamed on the **Mouvement Togolais pour la Démocratie** – an exiled movement led by the sons of former president Olympio. The Togolese government accused both Ghana and Burkina Faso of involvement in the attempted coup, saying that the two countries harboured and trained the captured "terrorists". Thirteen people were sentenced to death (including the son of the former president, Gilchrist Olympio, who was tried *in absentia*) and another 14 sentenced to life imprisonment. The date of the aborted uprising – September 19 – is today celebrated as a national holiday. Like most of those who have received the death sentence during Eyadéma's reign, the rebels' punishments were later mostly commuted to life imprisonment, or they were released at the president's prerogative. Such acts of magnanimity have tended further to consolidate his power base.

After more than two decades in power, Eyadéma still holds a tight reign over Togo. While fostering the **cult of personality** that has grown around the dictatorship, however, he has allowed a certain amount of democratisation within the RPT. In May 1985, the constitution was amended, allowing deputies to be elected to the National Assembly by direct universal suffrage, without being proposed by the party. In 1987, multi-candidate elections were held on a local level, the first time since Eyadéma took power. The president was himself re-elected for another seven-year term in December, 1987. As sole candidate, he received 99.5 percent of the vote. Still in his fifties, he is likely to have a continuing influence for years to come, even as French backing is increasingly tied to progress on human rights, and stirrings of inevitable change are being felt deep beneath the fault lines of Togolese society.

As the new decade opens, Eyadéma has been speechifying about the need for political maturity but seems prepared to consider the possibility of a return to a **multi-party political system**, such as existed before 1969. The unbanning of the main, French-based opposition movement, the *Mouvement Togolais pour la démocratie (MTD)*, would be a helpful start. The prospects, if this and other liberalising measures can be achieved, look promising.

LOMÉ AND THE COAST

LOMÉ is small for a capital city, but has its own convincing momentum. Though the administrative district is well planned, with majestic avenues and a flickering of flashy skyscrapers, much of the town's activity centres around the bustling **market** and surrounding **commercial district** – a pleasantly archaic area laid out by the French. These days, the narrow streets and old colonial buildings seem barely able to contain the crowds and commerce, but even in this busy section of town, the pace falls restfully short of the frenzied tempo you find in other big cities of the region and it's all remarkably tidy and clean. This mix of urban sophistication and rural informality combine to make Lomé one of West Africa's most enticing capitals – a place where you can happily adjust to the continent, or even base yourself for further travels.

East of Lomé, you'll find just fifty kilometres of coastline wedged between the Ghanaian and Benin borders. The surf is notoriously rough (even dangerous at times), yet the whole **Atlantic shorefront** is picture-postcard perfect, with its coconut groves, white sand beaches and **fishing villages** – none more than an hour's journey from the capital. On a less superficial level, the towns of **Togoville**, **Aneho** and **Glidji**, in their fetishes, shrines and festivals, reveal a lot about local voodoo customs.

These towns also served as the spearhead for the German colonial invasion which began in 1884 – the year when Gustav Nachtigal landed in Togoville and signed a treaty placing the chief under the Kaiser's "protection". Soon after, Aneho became capital of German Togoland. Today, the **coastal villages** are full of colonial vestiges. In varying states of dilapidation, they stand in sharp contrast to the predominating voodoo culture.

Lomé – the city

Although **the city** spreads in a wide radius, Lomé's population – a manageable 500,000 – is hardly enough to push it into the major metropolis category. The heart of the downtown district sweeps around the old **grand marché** which attracts traders from neighbouring Ghana, a short walk over the border and from all over West Africa, even as far afield as Zaire. In the immediate vicinity, throngs of **shoppers and street vendors** press through a maze of narrow avenues and sandy streets lined with two-storey colonial buildings – the domain of Lebanese shopkeepers and small import-export businesses. The whole area is dominated by the **beach** and pervaded by an ocean breeze ambience. Only along and beyond the Boulevard Circulaire (now called bd 13 Janvier) do you encounter the broad streets and high-rises that attest to the city's increasing **modernisation.** Industry is pleasantly out of sight, about ten kilometres from the city beyond the port.

Recent government attempts to decentralise Lomé have had only a marginal impact. Despite the congestion of the small streets around the market and the deteriorating state of some of the older buildings, merchants are loathe to leave one of the busiest commercial centres on the coast, even to set up shop in the more modern quarters of the city.

The growth of Lomé

The settlement of Lomé was originally founded by Ewe people fleeing a tyrant ruler in their homeland of Notsé in the eighteenth century. By the end of the nineteenth century, the Germans had moved the capital of their newly-declared colony from Aného to Lomé. Reminders of their rule, like the **neo-gothic cathedral** or the **old wharf** near the *grand marché*,, are still visible. Lomé remained the capital of the French protect-orate after World War I, but Togo had lost its former importance, and development was minimal compared with other colonies. Much of the infrastructure of the old part of town dates from the colonial period and has proved to be inadequate in coping with recent rapid growth.

Modernisation has continued at a slow but steady pace since independence. The first area to be affected was the administrative centre just west of the *grand marché*. Wide tree-lined avenues were traced here, and the capital's first skyscraper – the *Hôtel du 2 Février* – erected. Built in the middle of nowhere, this 37-storey marble and glass tower was part of Eyadéma's bid to have the Organisation of African Unity's headquarters transferred to Lomé. The plan failed and, despite government PR, the hotel – one of the most luxurious in Africa – is virtually empty for most of the time. Nothing daunted, a seven-metre bronze **statue of General Eyadéma** stands sentinel nearby, his arm outstretched in benediction of other expensive symbols built to promulgate his glory and Togo's entry into the twentieth century – the ultra-modern **convention hall** of the *RPT* and the gold-tinted glass **ministries**.

Recently, **development** has begun in the city's northern and eastern fringes, areas that only a few years ago were part of the bush. The Avenue Jean Paul II and the Boulevard Général Eyadéma lead to neighbourhoods that promise to be the centres of future economic activity. For the moment, however, the **Nouveau Marché**, the **Lomé 2000 conference centre** and the new taxi stations at **Agbalepedo** and **Akodessewa** still feel isolated from the city centre.

Arrival and orientation

Coming in **by taxi brousse**, you're likely to be let off at one of two *gares routières*. Vehicles **from Ghana, Benin and Nigeria** are mostly handled by the new **central station** at **Akodessewa**, about 3km east of the city centre. From here, you can take a taxi into town , most easily to the **grand marché** *autogare* right in the middle of things, from which you're within walking distance of a number of hotels if you're not piled down with luggage. **Taxis within town** cost around CFA200 per trip, or you can flag down *collectives* for about CFA50 per hop. There's **no bus system** in Lomé.

If you're arriving **from Ouagadougou and northern Togo**, most vehicles terminate at the **nouvelle station** in the Agbalepedo neighbourhood, a good 10km from the centre. The lack of activity tends to confirm first impressions as you turn off the Route d'Atakpamé and head down a series of dirt roads – you're being let off in the boondocks. To get to the centre of Lomé, hire a cab (CFA500–1000), or pile into a collective taxi. These ply from the station to the market for around CFA100.

If arriving **from Kpalimé**, you will wind up (unless your driver continues to the centre) at a small station on the route de Kpalimé in the Casablanca neighbourhood, about 5km from the central market. Again, there are collective taxis waiting to take you into town.

By train or plane

From the **railway station**, on the rue de la Gare between the market and the bd Circulaire, taxis are usually available to get you to your hotel. If not, flag one down at the roundabout in front. For rail schedules, see "Moving On" (p.903).

Lomé's **airport** is small, but one of the most modern in West Africa and one of the least traumatising places to arrive on the continent (customs and immigration are thorough, but not intimidating). It's not far from town, but the 7km to the centre is a bit much to walk. Unfortunately, there's no airport bus service, so you'll have to rely on taxis. Expect to pay around CFA1000 – after bargaining. During the daytime, you can often get collective taxis by flagging them down on the main road outside the airport.

Orientation

Getting around Lomé isn't difficult if you think of the *grand marché* as being the axis from which all the major roads shoot out like spokes. This makes things convenient if you're coming in by car, since the international roads from Ghana and Nigeria, as well as the national highways from Atakpamé and Kpalimé, all converge here, leaving you right in the centre of things. The convenience soon subsides as you try to drive around or find somewhere to park. Hotels, restaurants, banks and shops are within walking distance.

The different residential areas and commercial centres ripple out from this heart in concentric semi-circles, the first of which is hemmed in by the bd 13 Janvier (formerly named and still commonly referred to as the **Boulevard Circulaire**). West of this artery, and just after the administrative quarter as you move away from the market, the **Kodjoviakopé** neighbourhood was hardly more than a fishing village as little as fifteen years ago and still moves to a slower rhythm than the busy city centre. Many travellers attracted by the calm opt for one of the beachfront hotels here, or alternatively rent a room in a house – a choice that's becoming increasingly popular.

All the main arteries are served by CFA50-per-hop taxi-vans and cars running on set routes – for example clockwise around the bd 13 Janvier to Bé and back again, or up and down the main "spokes". But travelling far across the city like this can be an exhausting journey if you have to change vehicles more than once.

Beyond the Boulevard Circulaire

To the north, the **Amoutivé** neighbourhood – the home of the traditional chief of Lomé, a descendant of the the city's founder – is presently one of the most active quarters in town. Streets here are always packed at night and the area throbs with some of the liveliest discos in town. **Bé**, to the east, is another active neighbourhood that was formerly a village in its own right. Although it's still a stronghold of **voodooism**, the external signs of the religion are increasingly rare (even the neighbourhood **fetish market** has been moved, to Akodessewa). Flagpoles bearing a white banner in certain homes in the area indicate the presence of a fetish priest.

North of **the lagoon**, another semi-circle unfolds. Important localities such as the *CHU hospital*, the *Université du Benin* and the *Lycée* are situated beyond this natural barrier among the unpaved streets and vacant lots of the essentially residential **Tokoin** district, accessible both by the Atakpamé or Kpalimé roads.

The beaches

Although the **beach**, a stone's throw from the city centre, looks pretty enough at first glance, closer inspection soon indicates a less inviting prospect, and (unless you use private hotel zones) you're obliged to go east out of the city several kilometres before you can be fairly sure of clean sands and the opportunity to swim. Out here, too, are located Lomé's famous beach **camping sites** – see below for more details.

Accommodation in Lomé

Lomé has dozens of hotels, but most people head to the **beachfront** when seeking out places to stay. Along the *route internationale*, from the Ghana border to the eastern outskirts of town, you'll have no trouble finding a place to fit your taste and price range. In general, the **budget hotels** tend to be towards the western side of town, while the business-class establishments – including the luxury *Hôtel Sarakawa* and the *Hôtel de la Paix* – are concentrated in the east. **Camping sites** are located beyond the port, also east. If you're hoping to stay in Lomé for a while and want to take a **house**, the best plan is to present yourself at the embassies and see what they suggest. There's a sizeable expatriate community and they like their homes to be occupied when they're absent.

Camping

Outside Lomé, about 10km from the market, *Robinson Plage* (BP9149) and *Ramatou Plage* (BP 1256, ☎21.08.75) offer places to camp or *paillotes* to sleep in. Both of these places are okay, but nothing special, particularly considering they're barely out of range of the industrial zone (the air can be smelly round here). *Alice Plage*, 4km further east in the vicinity of the village of Baguida, is a good 300m from the seashore; it swarms with Germans and has become something of a roadside holiday camp. A better place can be found just 800m down the road from *Alice's*. Camping places go for CFA500-700 per person, and *paillotes* (and as many friends as you want can share) from around CFA3000–5000.

Camping out here is ideal if you've got your own vehicle, but if you're without transport, collective taxis can get you out here for around CFA100. Unfortunately, the immediate vicinities of the beach camping sites are the few parts around Lomé where you stand a substantial chance of being the victim of a **robbery**. Take precautions if you're carrying valuables and be especially careful after dark.

Cheap to moderate hotels

Hôtel Lily A stone's throw from the border and the beach, with a mostly African clientele and a sprinkling of European travellers. Spacious rooms and reasonable rates (starting from CFA4500; choice of fan or AC), but a bit far from the centre.

Pavillion Castel Towards the market, this is also on the waterfront but is a more modest affair. A nice courtyard, but minimum comfort. Non S/C rooms starting at CFA3500; fans only.

Hôtel California (directly behind the German embassy). One of the neighbourhood's only "storey buildings", the S/C rooms here are clean with AC, but the CFA7000 price seems a little steep. Pleasant, well-stocked bar and restaurant.

Paloma, rue du Grande Marché, corner of rue de la Gare. Scruffy and window-less cells for under CFA3000 per night. Bargain hard. It's very central – but, apart from the price, this is the only attraction.

Le Maxime, bd de la République, near the bd du 13 Janvier (BP 1909, ☎21.74.48). Good if you don't mind paying a bit extra for comfort (AC, S/C, terrace restaurant overlooking the sea). Rooms start at CFA7000. The shady *paillotes* and spectacular view (fishing canoes, coconut trees, sunsets) from the outdoor bar and restaurant attract mainly younger travellers, making this an excellent place to meet people and possibly work out a ride or find out about rooms to rent in the neighbourhood.

L'Abri (☎21.35.84), opposite to and comparable with *Le Maxime*, although standards are slightly lower. Same price range, but the management is sometimes willing to negotiate rates. Good seaview rooms.

Le Galion, rue Professeur Lassey, Kodjoviakopé (☎21.65.64), via rue Houndjagoh, the small street running between *Le Maxime* and *L'Abri*. Immaculate rooms in a refurbished home with landscaped courtyard cost CFA4500 with fan or CFA6500 AC. Stylish design and attentive staff make this excellent value.

Hôtel de la Plage (☎21.32.64). Right on the beach and only a short walk from the market, this hotel has long been *the* haunt of budget travellers. The brightly painted white exterior belies rather squalid rooms inside, but for the prices (starting at CFA2500 with fan) and the location, you can't complain. One of the best addresses for meeting fellow travellers.

Hôtel Ahodikpe Eboma, 45 bd 13 Janvier (BP 7025, ☎21.47.80). S/C rooms with AC starting at CFA5000. Big plus of this place is its location right next to the very likeable *Bar 50/50*.

Foyer des Marins, near the port, 5km east of the town centre (BP 1499, ☎21.41.26). Pool, excellent outdoor restaurant, bar and snack bar (CFA6500 and up for AC, S/C). A popular place with travellers.

Expensive hotels

Secourina Hôtel, 63 route d'Aného (with annex 100 metres down the street). Brand new, with rooms starting at CFA9000. For hotels in the price range, it's good value; clean S/C rooms, AC, hot water, phones etc. Creature comforts without chain-hotel sterility.

Hôtel du Golfe, rue de Commerce (BP 36, ☎21.51.41). An older but well-kept establishment. Extremely central, with high standards of service. Rooms with AC and phones from around CFA12,000.

Miramar, 3km east of the city, on the seafront (BP502, ☎21.61.41/2). Run-down and a bit of a mess, considering the CFA11,000 starting price.

Hôtel Le Bénin (BP128, ☎21.24.85, telex 5264), on the seafront, corner of av du Générale de Gaulle. Good pool, atmosphere and location, with competitive prices (from CFA14,000).

Hôtel de la Paix Frantel, 3km east of the city centre, set back from the sea (BP 3452 ☎21.52.97, telex 5252). The most pleasant of the top addresses, with its own beachfront.

Hôtel Sarakawa PLM, 3km east of downtown (BP 2232, ☎21.65.90, Fax 21.71.80) with huge pool, TV and phones in every room. Irreproachable (if perfectly predictable) international hotel with bills starting at around CFA 27,000/30,000 per night.

Hôtel 2 Février Sofitel, place de l'Indépendence (BP131, ☎21.00.03, telex 5348). Not the one you'd be likely to choose, and not the most expensive, but a mad folly with nearly 400 rooms and a handful of guests knocking around inside like seeds in a calabash. Impeccable views are the most it has in its favour.

Around Lomé: markets, fetishes, museum and other sites

There's not really a lot in Lomé to go out of your way to see, but there's plenty to take in as you wander through town. At some stage in your stay, try and take in the **Hôtel du 2 Fevrier**, built to commemorate the president's "Triumphal Return" after his plane crashed near Sarakawa (see "History"). On clear days, you get a splendid panoramic view of Lomé, Ghana and the coastline from the top-floor restaurant and bar. Even a small drink will set you way back, but it's not bad for a splurge.

But the focal point of the city, the **Grand Marché**, occupies a full city block near the ocean and may occupy a lot of your time. There are numerous other market districts specialising in everything from bicycle parts to fetish paraphernalia. Apart from these broadly commercial attractions, however, only the modest **museum** seeks to showcase Togolese culture.

The Grand Marché

Commerce spills over into all the surrounding streets from Lomé's **Grand Marché** as merchants (mostly women between the ages of three and 103) zig-zag through the crowd to hawk everything from rat poison to greetings cards. It's not an attractive building but it's about the only place you need to go for provisions, presents, in fact purchases of any kind – real one-stop shopping. The **ground floor** is filled with food – fruit and vegetables, meat, poultry, fish, and staples like yams, rice, cassava and pasta, spices, peanut butter and canned food, not to mention shopping baskets. Sellers have a flare for display and fruit and vegetables are invariably arranged in eye-catching pyramids of colour. Quality is generally very good, though if you're cooking it's best to buy meat first thing in the morning, for obvious reasons.

Up on the **first floor**, the celebrated, and extravagantly proportioned, **"Nana Benz"** (which, roughly translated, means "Mercedes Mamas", a reference to the cars they often drive) lounge around fanning themselves in the decadent style befitting their reputation as some of the richest and most adept business people in the country. They monopolise the sale of **cloth** and journey as far as Europe and Saudi Arabia to assure a stock that attracts buyers from the whole region. **"Made in Holland" Dutch wax**

prints are the most expensive and prestigious items in their selection, but you'll also find **English and African prints**, hand-woven **Kente cloth** from Ghana, **Ewe strip cloth**, naturally dyed **indigo wraps** from Guinea and Mali and rough **cotton weaves** from the Sahelian region. Generally you'll have to buy in relatively large quantities here (material is sold by *la piece*; *une piece* means six *pagnes*; and a pagne is roughly an armspread – or about 1.8m, the length of a wrap). The smallest length you can hope to buy in the market is a *demi-piece* or three pagnes' worth, which should cost little over CFA4000. For single cloths, try the rue du Commerce (see below). Prices are marked and, although you may be able to get the vendor to come down slightly, bargaining never gets you very far here.

The **second floor** at the top is a hodge-podge emporium of goods – everything from bicycle tyres to wigs, envelopes and Chinese enamel basins to plastic dolls (white as well as black). Mountains of cosmetics – lotions, shampoos, make-up – swamp an entire section. This is also where you can buy the cheapest cigarettes in town, by the carton.

The Bé and Amoutivé markets

The **Bé market**, on the rue Pa de Souza, lost much of its charm when walls went up around it in the early 1980s and the adjoining **fetish market** was moved to Akodessewa (see below). Now Bé is mainly a neighbourhood market with food items and a scattering of pottery, calabashes (rapidly losing ground to "Made in Nigeria" plastic ware) and other household items. The **Amoutivé market**, on the rue Mama Ndanida is similar.

The Nouveau Marché

Only opened in 1988, the **Nouveau Marché** (off the av Jean Paul II in the *Lomé 2000* quarter), has had trouble getting off the ground. The architecture is modern and attractive, but the place is terribly far from anything (collective taxis leave from the av Mama Ndanida near the Grand Marché). Traders, especially the headstrong Nana Benz, would rather stay in town, where the nearby international *gare routière* and numerous shops and businesses guarantee a constant flow of customers and suppliers. In a showdown with government authorities and city planners, many market people have simply refused to move to the new site. In the near future, though, it's bound to gain importance and by the time of publication, the *grand marché* may already have seen much of its business migrate north.

Handicraft markets

Crafts from all over West Africa filter into Lomé and there are several locations in town to look for them. The main selling venue is the **Passage des Arts** in the shadow of the old cathedral. You'll find a large selection of carvings, batiks, sculpture and other handicrafts here, although the majority come from Nigeria, Cameroon, Ghana and even Kenya; there's little in the way of typically Togolese art. Beware of "antiques": they almost never are. Prices are steep and the pressure to buy can be unpleasant, but the urgency of the vendors gradually gives way to something more bearable if you hang on for a few minutes, especially if you make a purchase, even of something small.

Opposite the cathedral on the rue du Commerce, the handmade **sandals** sold on the streetside are comfortable and sturdy, qualities that have made them popular throughout West Africa. The kind with the cushioned soles and toe loop go for about CFA1400 and worth every franc. On the same street, you'll also find cloth, and you can buy just short lengths of one or two *pagnes* here.

On the rue de la Gare, next to *Bopato*, you'll find the biggest selection of batiks and some vaguely African-looking tie-dyed dresses and shirts mixed together with carvings and other bric à brac.

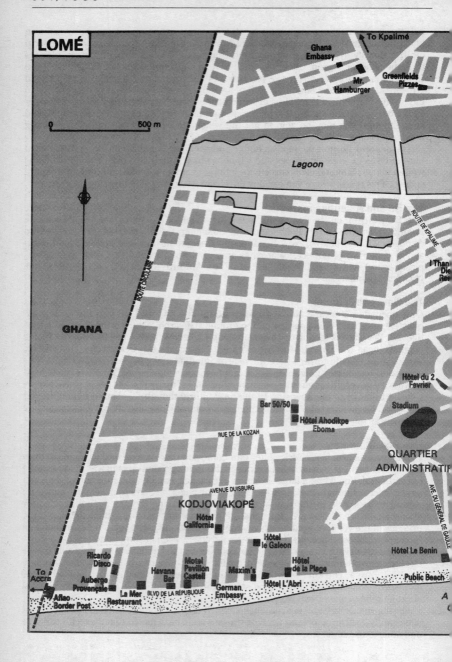

LOMÉ

To Kpalimé

Ghana
Embassy

Mr.
Hamburger

Greenfields
Pizzas

0   500 m

Lagoon

ROUTE DE KPALIME

GHANA

ROUTE CIRCULAIRE

I Than
Die
Res

Hôtel du 2
Février

Stadium

Bar 50/50

Hôtel Ahodikpe
Eboma

RUE DE LA KOZAH

QUARTIER
ADMINISTRATIF

AVENUE DUISBURG

KODJOVIAKOPÉ

AVE. DU GÉNÉRAL DE GAULLE

Hôtel
California

Hôtel
le Galeon

Hôtel Le Benin

Ricardo
Disco

Motel
Pavillon
Casteli

Maxim's

Hôtel
de la Plage

Public Beach

To
Accra

Havana
Bar

Auberge
Provençale

La Mer
Restaurant

BLVD DE LA RÉPUBLIQUE

German
Embassy

Hôtel L'Abri

Afleo
Border Post

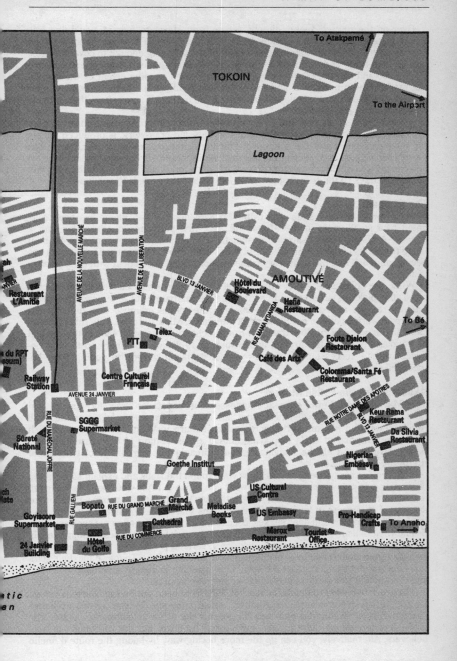

Over on the route d'Aného, directly across from *Marox* restaurant, you'll find brilliantly patterned **blankets** – mainly from Mali and Niger. These are handmade and expensive, but patient bargaining gets results. Something big enough to cover a double bed or look huge and striking on a wall should ultimately cost somewhere between CFA15,000 and CFA20,000, though price is determined to some extent by the state of the market, the time of year and the number of profligate punters in town. Another regular treasure trove of blankets is laid out on the pavement across from the *Goyiscore* supermarket on rue Gallieni.

Just down the street from *Marox*, the **tourist information office** has a showroom for regional crafts. This art, including batiks, carvings and brasswork, is produced mainly for aesthetic appeal and the traditional function of the masks and other objects has pretty much ceded to the desire to please souvenir-hunters. Prices are marked here, so you can get a rough idea how much things are going for. A similar **pro-handicap crafts centre** operates on the corner of the bd 13 Janvier and the av de la République.

The museum

The **National History Museum** (Mon–Fri 8am–noon & 3–5.30pm) has been relegated to a small room in the *Maison du RPT* (the party headquarters) for over a decade. A display inside shows a design for a grandiose cultural centre to be built along the banks of the lagoon. The display has been there so long it seems the plan has been abandoned and the temporary museum looks more permanent with each passing year.

While the collections are clearly displayed and the show-cases well lit and uncluttered, the pickings are decidedly slim. **Musical instruments** and religious objects (statues, masks and ceremonial dress) give the merest glimpse into the material cultures of various ethnic groups such as the Kabyé, Mina and Ewe. One room is dedicated to the **colonial period**, tracing it from Nachtigal's landing in 1884 to the division of Togoland between the French and British in 1914 and ploddingly on to independence, with a succession of pictures of moustachioed governors puffing their bemedalled chests.

Akodessewa: the Fetish Market

The **Marché des Féticheurs** at Akodessewa is a popular draw for visitors and Loméans alike, despite its distance, some 8km from the city centre. Adjoining the small Akodessewa food market in the northeastern suburb is West Africa's largest fetish market – a myriad of stalls displaying animal skulls, rotting bird carcases, statues, bells, powders and all the imaginable and unimaginable ingredients of **traditional medicine and religion**.

Children are always pestering to show you around the stalls and explain some of the charms or **gris-gris** – as usual, explain what you'll give (CFA50–100) before setting off, and make the most of what they know. Mostly they'll try to interest you in a talisman for safe travel or success in love – inexpensive items that it's disarmingly easy to take an interest in. Scorpions and dead snakes, used to make potions for ailments such as arthritis and rheumatism, have a more ghoulish and less user-friendly appeal. Though fetishers won't hesitate to make a quick sell, it's a serious profession, still handed down jealously from generation to generation. The reputation of the Togolese for their spiritual gifts is widespread. A little time spent here listening to tales of supernatural healing and therapy will sow seeds of doubt in the most rational mind.

There are two ways to get to the market. First is to head out on the Nouvelle rue de Bé or the rue Notre Dame des Apôtres, which converge by the old **Fôret Sacré** (Sacred Forest, on the left) and pass the former site of the fetish market at **Bé**. The forest is a remarkable little jungle, surrounded by town, but out of bounds to non-believers. Alternatively, you can go the more boring way, by taking the route d'Aneho

---

Alphonse and Felix were brothers who lived in Lomé, both Catholics. When we met, Alphonse was taking driving lessons to become a taxi driver while Felix had just passed the rigorous baccalauréat exam and planned to continue studying in Europe. Neither had travelled outside Africa but they were aware of, and involved in, many Western social and cultural themes – fashion, music, movies, politics. We seemed to have much in common.

We went to their mother's home village in the hills near Badou to visit relatives. On arrival they underwent a subtle transformation. People greeted them on the street as Koffi and Kwami and and they swopped T-shirts and jeans for loose tops and printed pantalons.

One morning Felix described how he had seen the light of a "vampire" coming towards the house in the night. Vampires are ordinary villagers who transform themselves into monstrous creatures at night, stalk their victims and eat their souls. You can recognise them by the bright light that shines from their anuses, but if they see you first, they hide in the bushes and cover their light. We had been asleep in one of the small rooms built around an open courtyard in the house of Alphonse's uncle when Felix suddenly jumped out of bed. He had seen such a light in the courtyard and a beam had penetrated the room through a crack in the shutters. For a moment, we had been in real danger. He started rummaging through his suitcase. He slipped a ring on and put some powder on the doorstep. The protective ring came from his uncle, while the powder, acquired at great expense from a fetisher in Benin, guaranteed that vampires could not enter. He considered it a good investment.

Both brothers were certain that vampires exist and Alphonse was absolutely convinced his father – who had died almost exactly a year before – had been killed by one. Even the problems of the village – a drop in the standard of living caused by the fall in cocoa prices – could be attributed to their nefarious work. These were realities as much a routine part of their lives as other occurrences that took place while they were living in Lomé. They hadn't divided the world into Western and African ideas or city ways and country ways. The two simply co-existed for them without contradiction. They didn't even give it much thought.

---

along the coast, past the *Hôtel Sarakawa*. At the rond point du port, 6km from central Lomé, turn left and follow the paved road for a kilometre and a half. If you're getting to Akodessewa by private taxi, expect to pay over the odds for the distance.

En route, you'll pass Loméans heading to the market on bicycles – or in air-conditioned Mercs. The powers of the *féticheurs* are sought after by all classes. In Togo, the overwhelming majority still practises traditional ("animist") religions and even the Christian and Muslim minorities commonly incorporate traditional practices into their beliefs. But the reputation of Akodessewa also attracts people from all over West Africa, and from as far away as Gabon and Zaire.

Eating and drinking

Cheap eats are found mainly around the different markets in town. At the *grand marché*, women serve delicious salads from stands directly opposite the taxi park. They'll throw anything that strikes your fancy onto the bed of lettuce – tomatoes, macaroni, avocadoes, even grilled chicken or Guinea fowl – and top it off with a tangy vinegar sauce. It's an excellent meal, so long as your system is acclimatised to somewhat insanitary conditions. Behind these stalls women sell *fufu*, or *akoume* (fermented white corn mash) with different sauces and meat (beef, goat, chicken). But this is daytime eating only. Similar food can be found in the *Amoutivé* and *Bé* markets.

For cheap eating **after dark**, try in front of the popular *50-50 bar* on the bd Circulaire next to *Hôtel Ahodikpe-Eboma*. At breakfast time, keep your eye out for *les* *caféman*. Scattered about town, they serve cheap omelettes with Nescafé and bread. There's a noted purveyor round the corner from the *50-50 bar*.

Lomé's workaday bars aren't expensive but there's one in particular – the *Jungle Bar* by the *Goyi Score* supemarket – where the draught *B de B* is not only exceptionally inexpensive, but it's served in an atmosphere of advanced mayhem. If you're looking to off-load some funds on the other hand, and more conservatively, Lomé can easily oblige: the selection of more expensive restaurants given below could be greatly extended.

Low-cost eateries

Increasingly, street stands are being augmented by **small restaurants** with rudimentary furnishings and predictable menus (rice with sauce, spaghetti, salads) which are good value if not very imaginative.

L'Amitié, 17 rue du Grand Marché, near the market, is the most popular eatery in the genre (not to be confused with the other *Amitié* by the bd 13 Janvier – see below).

Paplov, next door, attracts the same overland crowd (mostly French and German with the occasional passing Peace Corps volunteer), but it's wise to check the bill here carefully.

Restaurant Senegalais, rue du Commerce, is less of a thoroughfare and serves reasonable meals on a pleasantly shaded street terrace.

Bopato (across from the *BIAO* bank on the rue de la Gare) serves sandwiches and snacks in the outdoor café – and invariably miscount the change. The tourist custom assures a steady flow of hawkers who try to pass off plastic as real ivory (remind them it would all be confiscated on your return). Tedious, but still a good place to meet people and one of Lomé's main rendezvous.

Fouta Djalon, 238 bd 13 Janvier, east, is a good-value Guinean restaurant where you can eat for CFA300–1000.

Restaurant de la Paix, north of bd 13 Janvier, northeast, near the *Hôtel du Boulevard*, is likewise excellent value – *steack-frites*, omelettes, couscous, *lait caillé*.

Restaurant Hafia, north of bd 13 Janvier, completes this trio of bargain Guineans.

L'Amitié, north of bd 13 Janvier. Another restaurant by this name, it's a pleasant place to sit, with a bar, simple, inexpensive food and no pretentions. Local musicians often drop by.

I Thank Jehovah – Dieu Merci, bd 13 Janvier, near the Kpalimé road, has a huge range of interesting bean dishes, yam stew, things fried and boiled – a diversity of tastes and incredibly inexpensive. You pay by the portion, average CFA50–150. It's not slick, but for real food, well cooked, it's one of West Africa's best eating houses. Take your food across the road if you like, to the *Oncle Ben Bar*, where in the evening you can drink.

Moderate restaurants

Santa Fe Bar and Restaurant, 217 bd 13 Janvier (☎21.75.88), has developed into a major meeting place for ex-pats and travellers and stays open really late. Excellent brochettes and French fare like steak *à la crème*, plus soups, salads and fast food. Meals run CFA1500; drinks are slightly dearer than in local bars.

4ème Zone, bd du 13 Janvier, east of the Santa Fe, offers something a little different (and quality is somewhat inconsistent), serving Vietnamese dishes – shrimp with soya sauce, pork with bamboo shoots – for around CFA2000, or African specialities, including *fufu*, *gboma*, and *atieke* , from CFA 500.

Mr Hamburger, on the Route de Kpalimé, is an American hamburger restaurant doing the real thing for about CFA1000, with old *Newsweeks* to read and set the tone.

Rabile, near the Santa Fé also serves sandwiches and grilled meat, but its location on one of the busiest intersections in town makes for a loud and exhausting lunch.

Café des Arts, 229 bd du 13 Janvier, is a popular evening rendezvous; unusual milkshakes and *pression* beer.

Marox restaurant, near the market, always pulls in a crowd, mainly ex-pat and showy Togolese. It's run by Germans and does a big trade in sausages and meat dishes with fries and salads from around CFA 1500. In front, some of the best fresh produce in town fills a couple of small stands, although prices are high and geared mainly to the same *Marox* set.

Lakshmi, 64, route d'Aného. A new restaurant doing everything – European and African specialties plus Indian food, sandwiches and a *plat du jour*.

Relais de la Poste, av de la Libération, does good French food at not unreasonable prices. Only fifty metres from the post office, it's also a good place for breakfast while you read your mail.

Expensive restaurants

AFRICAN

It can be a pleasure to pay a little more to eat African food in restaurants rather than squatting on the street or at a makeshift table. Two very good ones are:

Keur Rama, 290 bd du 13 Janvier (☎21.54.62). Delicious fricassé of bush rat ("grasscutter" or *agouti*) and a long *carte* of other African specialities. Highly recommended and shouldn't cost more than CFA6000 a head.

Pili Pili Bar, route de l'Ocam. This has local food like yams and *akoume* served with sauces, including crab and shellfish with spinach. Popular with volunteer workers in Lomé; expect to pay around CFA4000 per person.

CHINESE/VIETNAMESE

Golden Crown, bd du Mono (around corner of bd 13 Janvier, route d'Aného). A first-class restaurant with wonderful dishes and not over-priced from CFA4000 a head.

ITALIAN

Au Petit Cabanon, av Duisburg in the Kodjoviakopé neighbourhood. Good pizza and lasagne in the open air for around CFA2500.

Greenfields, rue de Cebevito Tokoin-Hôpital, just east of the Route de Kpalimé, serves similar stuff (notably good pizza) in a pleasant garden.

Da Silvia, 298 bd 13 Janvier, is much more formal and expensive .

FRENCH

Apart from the restaurants in the big hotels (all of which serve refined French cuisine at elevated prices) other French restaurants in town include:

L'Auberge Provençale, bd de la République, at the border(☎21.16.82). A flashy place to spend a lot of money, preferably someone else's. Wonderful bouillabaisse and other seafood, plus couscous and paella (specialities need advance ordering).

La Vague, bd de la République, just behind the *Hôtel de la Plage*. Franco-Lebanese, and over-priced for such ordinary food.

La Mer, further towards Ghana on the beach road, serves good fresh fish dishes. Accommodating owner and prices not over-inflated; expect to pay around CFA3500.

Nightlife

Lomé still offers plenty of places to have fun at night without spending a fortune. **Cinemas** range from dingy fleapits with Bruce Lee dubbed into French over a crackling sound system to air-conditioned venues showing the latest French and American films. **Discos** run the gamut, from popular spots where you pay no entrance and drinks are hardly more expensive than in daytime bars to high-class joints with complicated light shows and DJs hyping up the crowd. There's a number of cheap places towards the Ghana border in Kodjoviakopé. For a good bar to kick the evening off, or soak it all up if you don't get it together to go anywhere, the *Fifty/fifty* (*50-50*: see map) is perenially popular and doesn't draw an especially touristy crowd.

Clubs and Discos

Café des Arts, 229 bd du 13 Janvier. More of a bar and rendezvous than a club, but another popular departure point for the evening. They have occasional live music here.

Ricardo's Disco has long packed in a young crowd of Loméans and Ghanaians attracted by cheap beer and blasting pop (Madonna, Michael Jackson, Lionel Richie) mixed with African/ Antillean hits (Kassav, Bébé Black, Jimmy Hyacinthe). Unfortunately, its proximity to the Ghanaian border only two blocks away means frequent police controls and closing as early as 11pm weekdays and 1am Fri and Sat nights.

African Queen, route d'Atakpamé, in Tokoin, is similar, but more perennially popular since it always stays open late.

La Camionette, route de Kpalimé, in the Casablanca neighbourhood, is another good outdoor disco with similar music and small cover charge. Slightly older clientele.

Maquina Loca, 8 av de Calais (☎21.75.55), is currently the most popular Western-style disco. Full sound and light show plus a heavy emphasis on European and American disco-pop. CFA2000 entrance and a similar price for drinks.

Oro Night Club, in the Bé neighbourhood at 85 rue de la Paix, 300 metres from bd 13 Janvier, is another favourite in this style.

L'Abreuvoir (☎21.64.88) and **Domino**, both in rue de la Gare, are popular nightspots, but again, drinks are not cheap.

Fever, 6 rue du Commerce (☎21.50.77).

Tabou bd 13 Janvier, corner of route de Kpalimé (☎21.02.85).

Blue Night, Route de Kpalimé, just north of the Lagoon (CFA2000 entrance).

Live music venues

A number of places have recently started staging **live music**. Among them are:

Chez Alice, Alice plage camping at Baguida, Wed and Sat nights.

Café Atlantique, near the *Sarakawa*, Fri.

Santa Fe, 217 bd 13 Janvier (☎21.75.88)

Hôtel Ifé, near the CHU Hospital in Tokoin.

Lomé Directory

Airlines include:
Aeroflot, 7 av 24 Janvier, (☎21.04.80);
Air Afrique, 12 rue du Commerce (☎21.20.42/44);
KLM, Immeuble TABA, 1 rue du Commerce (☎21.63.30/31);
UTA, 20 rue du Commerce (☎21.69.10) offers a number of special fares in West Africa and to Europe;
Ghana Airways, 16 rue du Commerce (☎21.56.91/ 21.72.91);
Lufthansa, Agents, 9 route d'Aného (☎21.31.51);
Swissair, 9 route d'Aného (☎21.31.57);
Nigeria Airways, Imm, Vendome, rue du Maréchal Foch, by the Passage des Arts (☎58.26.32/54);
Sabena, Immeuble TABA, 1 rue du Commerce (☎21.73.33/21.75.55).

American Express The representative is upstairs in the STMP building, 2 rue du Commerce, (☎21.26.11).

Artists There are many commercial artists in Lomé doing paintings which all look much the same – *pirogues*, huts, dancers, palm trees etc – but a few go way beyond this to produce work of genuinely independent expression. Check for exhibitions at the French Cultural Centre and *Gattobar*, both on av 24 Janvier in the centre of town.

Banks include:

> *BIAO* , on the corner of the rue du Commerce and rue de la Gare, Mon–Fri 7.30–11.30am, 2.30–4pm (☎21.32.86);
> *UTB* 20, rue du Grand Marché, Mon–Fri 7.45–11.30am, 2.45–5pm;
> *BTCI*, bd du 13 Janvier near av de la Libération, Mon–Fri 7.30–11.30am, 12.30–4pm (☎21.46.41, Fax 21.32.65).

Beaches In town you're limited to stretches of shore in front of *Hôtel de la Paix* and the old *Hôtel du Benin*, the latter more popular, especially at weekends, but they're dirty, not very safe and the sea has a fearfully strong undertow. Out of town past the port, *Robinson Plage* draws a large weekend crowd. The sand bar makes for safe swimming and the shipwreck adds a certain something.

Books and magazines Foreign newspapers (though no British ones) are sold at the airport. You'll sometimes find *Time*, *Newsweek* and even *West Africa* hawked around town. *Maladise* (see map) has a good selection of books and foreign newspapers – from *Jeune Afrique* to the *Herald Tribune* and *Der Spiegel*. *Librairie Bon Pasteur*, corner of rue du Commerce and av de la Libération, has a wide selection of French papers and mags plus fiction and non-fiction in French. For second-hand books in English, try the ambulant pedlars along the rue du Commerce.

Car hire A number of outlets, including:
Africom, 37 bd 13 Janvier (☎21.13.24);
> *Avis*, 252 bd 13 Janvier (☎21.10.33);
> *Budget Rent-a-Car*, Kodjoviakopé (☎21.09.31);
> *Hertz*, rue du Commerce, (☎21.50.52), branches in *Hôtel 2 Février* and *Hôtel Sarakawa;*
> *Loc-Auto*, bd 13 Janvier (☎21.42.50).

Clinics and Hospitals The *Centre Hospitalier Universitaire* (CHU) in the north of town in Tokoin is the main hospital. There's a good Chinese-run clinic, the **Bon Secours**, across from the American Embassy on Rue du Maréchal Foch and there are many othe private clinics (see "Pharmacies", below, or the free publication, *Scoop*, which lists them).

Embassies include:
> **Belgium**, 165 rue Pelletier Caventou (BP 7643; ☎21.03.23, telex 5363);
> **Denmark**, Honorary Consulate (BP 2708; ☎21.34.45);
> **Egypt**, route d'Aného, (☎21.24.43);
> **France**, 51 rue du Colonel de Roux, (☎21.25.71, telex 5202), issues visas for Burkina Faso, Côte d'Ivoire, Mauritania and Senegal;
> **Gabon**, Tokoin Super-Taco (BP 9118; ☎21.47.76, telex 5307);
> **Germany FR**, Marina, route d'Aflao (☎21.23.38, telex 5204);
> **Ghana**, 8 rue Paulin-Eklou, Tokoin Ouest (BP 92; ☎21.31.94);
> **Italy**, Honorary Consulate (BP 2105; ☎21.08.61);
> **Netherlands**, Honorary Consulate (BP347; ☎21.63.31);
> **Nigeria**, 311 bd 13 Janvier (BP 1189; ☎21.39.25/21.34.55);
> **Norway**, Honorary Consulate (BP 34; ☎21.07.13);
> **Sierra Leone**, Honorary Consulate, private address, check phone book;
> **Sweden**, Honorary Consulate (BP 34; ☎21.07.13);
> **Switzerland**, Honorary Consulate (BP 495; ☎21.02.11);
> **United Kingdom**, Honorary Consulate, c/o *Agence Maritime Atlantic du Togo SARL*, 1 rue l'Hôtel Miramar, Ablogame 2 (BP 60958; ☎21.40.82);
> **USA**, corner of rue Pelletier Caventou and rue Vauban (BP 852; ☎21.29.91);
> **Tunisia**, rue de Mélinas (BP 2983; ☎21.26.37, telex 5356);
> **Zaire**, 325 bd 13 Janvier (BP 102; ☎21.51.55) .

Immigration The Sûreté National on the rue du Maréchal Joffre (near *SGGG*) handles requests for residency permits and visa extensions.

Libraries and Cultural Centres The *American Cultural Centre* at the corner of rue Caventou and rue Vauban (across the street, north of the embassy) has a free library with

American magazines and papers (Mon–Fri 9am–12.30pm and 3–6pm, Sat 9am–noon), ABC TV news and free movies every Fri afternoon at 3pm and 6pm respectively. The *Centre Culturel Francais* on rue 24 Janvier also has a library with the best of the French press, but in theory you have to be a member to use it. There are movies on Tue and Thur in the open-air theatre. The German equivalent, the *Goethe Institut* (see map), is also worth visiting for shows and events.

Mechanics Professional and reliable service at *Turbo Garage* (☎21.16.28), rue Rhodes, Kodjoviakopé, near *Ricardo's*. Ask for Frank Johnson.

Notice boards and messages All the supermarkets have free notice boards – worth scanning for buying and selling, lifts, accommodation, employment and forthcoming events. Another source of information is the little pamphlet – *Scope*, not to be confused with the free *Scoop* – put out weekly by *Maladise* bookshop.

Pharmacies Open Mon–Fri 8.30–noon, 3–6.30pm, Sat 8am–noon. The *Nouvelle Marché* newspaper has a list of pharmacies open out of hours. *Togopharma*, towards the ocean from the Sûrete Nationale (☎21.32.47), *Pharmacie Akofa*, av Mama N'Danida, (☎21.00.97), *Pharmacie du Benin*, av de la Libération near the post office (☎21.29.64), *Pharmacie Populaire*, 27 rue du Commerce (☎21.47.65), *Pharmacie du Grand Marché* , 39 rue du Grand Marché (☎21.26.36). The *Pharmacie pour Tous,* Route de Kpalimé, also has a clinic (X-rays and much other medical attention).

Phone Telephone and telex service behind the central post office. Direct dialling to Europe and America costs around CFA 1500/minute and connections are generally very good. International reverse charge (PCV) calls to France only, which is much cheaper anyway. Calls can also be made from major hotels (more costly), from the *Foyer des Marins* and now from an increasing number of phone boxes.

Photocopies Several points around town. One of the cheapest is next door to *Bopato* on rue de la Gare.

Photo developing and film Best-equipped place is *Colorama*, bd du 13 Janvier, next to the Santa Fé restaurant. *Magic Photo*, rue du Commerce, offers more expensive one-hour development and on-the-spot passport photos. There's a new photo booth on the rue du Commerce, next to the *Librairie Evangelique*.

Post office Main post office is on Av de la Liberation, near the bd du 13 Janvier. Mon–Fri 8am–noon, 2.30–5.30pm, Sat 7.30am–12.30pm. *Poste restante* is famously helpful and reliable. There's a small fee per item.

Shoes If you're a size 11 or bigger, you're in luck. The used shoe market, a couple of blocks west of the American Embassy, offers a huge variety of huge footwear – thankfully not all with platform soles.

Supermarkets

Goyi Score, rue Maréchal Gallieni, near the Grand Marché, has a good dairy department, wines, cheeses, just like in France, but twice the price.

SGGG (pronounced "S-trois-jay", the *Societé Générale du Golfe du Guinée*)has several stores at the corner of rue Gallieni and rue de la Gare selling everything from plumbing fixtures to children's clothes. Supermarket similar to *Goyi Score*.

Marox, on the Route d'Aného, next to the restaurant. More expensive and not as well stocked, but the best place for meat, sausages and deli fare.

Swimming pools The nicest and most expensive are at the *Hôtels 2 Fevrier* and *Sarakawa* (CFA1200 for non-guests). The *Hôtel de la Paix* and *Foyer des Marins* also have pools, the latter being the cheapest in town.

Taxis Stations for *collective taxis* are scattered at various points around the vicinity of the Grand Marché. In the absence of a bus system, these can get you nearly anywhere in town. Stations for Kodjiavekope, Tokoin, Casablanca and Agbalepedo are west of the market; Amoutivé and Lomé 2000 are to the north on av Mama N'Danida. Bé and Ablogamé are to the east.

Telex Public office round behind the post office, open daily 7am–6pm. The public telex number in Lomé is 5200 PUBLIC.

Travel agents and tour operators include *Togo Palm Tours*, *Hôtel Sarakawa* (☎21.57.84); *Gazelle Tours*, 13 rue de la Gare, (☎21.17.69); *Togo Tourisme*, 9 rue du Commerce (☎21.09.32. telex 5050), who are also agents for *Nouvelles Frontières; Togo Voyages*, 13 rue du Grand Marché (☎21.12.77); and *Afrique Excursions*, 1 rue Gallieni, (☎21.02.68). This last agent can often offer cheap air fares as can *Cagesco*, 142 bd 13 du 13 Janvier (BP12416; ☎21.56.36), who are agents for *Nord-Suda Benin* which operates cheap flights to France out of Cotonou. Tours are also arranged by The High Commission of Tourism on the Route d'Aného (☎21.43.13).

MOVING ON

The two main *gares routières* are the **nouvel autogare at Akodessewa** and the **auto-gare in Agbalepedo** district on the north side of town. The former handles transport on the coastal routes, including direct taxis to Accra, Cotonou and Lagos. Agbalepedo handles northbound traffic to Sokodé, Dapaong and Ouagadougou. For Kpalimé and towns along the Kpalimé road, there's a separate station in the Casablanca neighbourhood, about 5km from the centre on the route de Kpalimé.

The **train** schedules out of Lomé for the three main destinations are:

BLITTA	**KPALIMÉ**
5.45 am daily (6hr) via **Atakpamé** (3hr 30min).	6.30am daily (4–5hr). 2.45pm daily (4hr).
7.20am Mon, Wed and Fri (11hr).	
8.00am Wed and Fri (express).	**ANÉHO**
1.20pm Sat.	Daily at 7am, 11.45am, 4.10pm (1hr).

Around Lomé

The short drive from Lomé to the Benin border passes along the coastal highway, with alternating views of the **lagoon** and **the Atlantic**. The villages along this stretch are peopled by Mina and Gun (or Guin), who migrated from Ghana at the beginning of the nineteenth century. Today, people along the coast make their living principally from fishing, coconut planting and small-scale cultivation. Main towns like **Togoville** and **Aného** are interesting combinations of colonial relics and fetish symbolism and move to a slower rhythm than the capital.

The **coast road** itself is mostly uninteresting, but parallel to it is the **old road**, now reverting through cracked and broken asphalt to sand and bush, but picturesque and ideal if you're riding a moped or motorcycle or, at a pinch, a bike.

Togoville and Lake Togo

Perched atop a hill on the north shore of the lagoonal Lake Togo, **Togoville** is most easily reached by *pirogue* from behind the main coast road. First step is a taxi, 30km to **AGBODRAFO**. This latter village was formerly known by its Portuguese name, Porto Seguro, and was the site of a small coastal fort similar to those in Ghana. Today it's ruled by one **Fio Adjete Sedo Assiakoley IV** who keeps the royal sceptres, thrones and weapons that have symbolised his family's authority in the region for 150 years.

Pirogues ply regularly between Agbodrafo and Togoville, leaving from a lagoon landing about 100 metres from the highway; any kid can point you there. You can hire a *pirogue* by paying the round-trip fare (at a price you negotiate) and arranging to be picked up in Togoville at a specified hour or, alternatively, simply wait for the boat to fill up with market women and pay the normal collective fare, an option that involves a

---

EWE NAMES

As in the Asante country in Ghana, Ewe people usually take at least one name after the day of the week on which they were born.

	GIRLS' NAMES	BOYS' NAMES
Monday	Adzo	Kodjo
Tuesday	Abla	Komla
Wednesday	Aku	Kokou
Thursday	Ayawa	Yao
Friday	Afi	Koffi
Saturday	Ami	Komi
Sunday	Kosiwa or Essi	Kossi

lot of hanging around on both shores. From the waterfront the silhouette of the cathedral in Togoville stands out on the hill across the lake.

On your right, windsurfers, boaters, and swimmers disport themselves in the schisto-free waters in front of *L'Hôtel Le Lac*. There's no **hotel** in Togoville itself and the *Hôtel Le Lac* (BP 201) is quite a fancy place with high prices (from CFA10,000) but a pleasant pool and, of course, the watersports facilities. Don't confuse it with the nearby *Auberge du Lac*, which offers simple rooms geared to more **modest budgets**, with good food and an excellent setting on the lake.

Checking in with the chief

Once you dock in **TOGOVILLE**, your itinerary is pretty much determined by boys waiting at the shorefront to be hired as semi-obligatory guides. You might as well go with the flow. They're nice enough and very adept at showing strangers the more interesting local curiosities. The first order of business, and one you can't refuse, is to **visit the chief** and advise him of your arrival. The chief will greet you personally if he's in and show you his memorabilia, including photographs of his ancestors and copies of the famous document signed with the Germans. With great pomp you'll be asked to sign the **"Golden Book"** and a small gift is expected at this point.

The present ruler is a direct descendant of **Mlapa**, the village king who signed the treaty that made the Germans protectors of the region (at which time the town was known simply as Togo, meaning "beside the water"). The contract signed with this tiny village was the basis on which the colonial government incorporated all of present day Togo and much of Ghana. A trip here serves to illustrate just how deceitful and far-fetched those early "treaties" were.

Fetish shrines and other sites

Formalities completed, you can wander at your leisure. The children take you first to the **Catholic Cathedral**, built in the early part of the century by the Germans. Notice the interior murals of African martyrs being burned at the stake, and a shrine to the Virgin who was seen walking on the lake in the early 1980s. This miracle reportedly inspired the Pope's 1986 visit to Togoville.

Despite the work of the Catholic church, Togoville remains essentially animist. Walking through the narrow back streets, you'll be shown several fetishes, hopefully including two **fertility shrines** – one of a formidably endowed man and the other of a well-rounded woman with spikes protruding from her body. Photographs are permitted provided you leave a small offering. Beyond the small market, on the north side of town, a modern statue marks the centenary of the **Germano-Togolese** treaty, celebrated in 1984.

Aného

Of all Togo's towns, the colonial presence is most strongly and most eerily felt in **ANÉHO**. The Portuguese were the first to come to the spot – a pleasing natural setting with sea and lagoon vistas – which soon developed as a major slave market. Current African family names like de Souza and the light skin of the people are surprising reminders of this "Brazilian" period, further reflected in the history and culture of Ouidah (see Part Seventeen, "Benin").

Many buildings, too, bear witness to the days when "Anecho" was the capital of Kaiser Wilhelm's prize African possesion – among them, the **Peter and Paul Church** (1898), close to being washed by the ocean, the thick-walled **préfecture** near the bridge, the intereresting **German cemetery**, and the finely restored **Protestant church** (1895) on the route de Lomé. Other buildings are reminders of the French presence, including a number of grandiose villas used by colonial administrators when Aného was capital of the protectorate.

Aného has been in a slow decline for decades. Walking the streets, there's a feeling that residents are too entrapped in their daily routines of farming, fishing and trade to have any illusions of grandeur – or much opportunity to bring the old town to life. It's a small community, completely overshadowed by Lomé and with no hope of reviving its former commercial importance. All of which is a source of frustration for the young, most of whom migrate to the capital to seek their fortunes. But they leave Aného a satisfyingly moody place for travellers. The main **market** day is Thursday – and there's a small fetish selection: monkey heads, dead and alive crabs, various skulls . . .

In contrast to the crumbling reminders of European occupation, Aného's **voodoo culture** thrives. Fetish priests are highly respected members of the community and are often more trusted than doctors practising Western medicine. Sacrifices are offered to shrines guarding many of the homes, and regular festivals are dedicated to the cult.

Practicalities and accommodation

It isn't hard to find your way around Aného since the town virtually stretches along the **route de Lomé/Cotonou.** The **market, railway station**, post office, bank, prefecture and most shops are along this street between the Protestant church and the bridge. A more residential neighbourhood, and the area where you'll find all the major **hotels and restaurants**, lies across the bridge.

The first **hotel** you come to as you cross the bridge towards Cotonou is the *Oasis* (BP 171; ☎31.01.29), with the best views of the sea and lagoon in town. Even if you don't stay, have a drink at the thatched terrace restaurant and watch the fishermen cast their nets into the shallow lagoon waters. S/C rooms start at CFA4000, most with AC. The slightly cheaper and much more soulful *As de Pique*, on a small side street off the route de Cotonou in Adidjo quarter, was sadly closed at the last check – as, too, with less regret, was the *Hôtel Atlantique,* on the route de Cotonou.This leaves the more upmarket *Hôtel Royal Holiday* (☎31.00.27), which is still reasonable, with rooms from CFA4500 and up, depending on optional AC.

Eating and entertainment

The **market** is the place for cheap eating; otherwise try one of the hotels listed above. For drinking, check out *La Paillotte* on the route de Lomé, which has an ordinary bar, but good music and ambience. The *Jardin Mama N'Danida*, in front of the Protestant church, serves cold drinks and food during the day in a shady, relaxing garden. Popular discos include *Le Maquis*, 500m from the Atlantic hotel (CFA200 entrance and drinks slightly pricier than usual), and the *Riveros* in the *Royal Holiday* (no cover charge, but small drinks cost CFA300).

Glidji

On the surface, **GLIDJI**, 4km northeast of Aného, looks just like any other Mina village. You'll notice the same *banco* huts with thatched roofs and the same narrow sandy streets found all along the coast. Yet the town is symbolically important since the present chief is a direct descendant of **Foli-Bebe** – the first ruler of the region and the man responsible for the political organisation of the Gun and Mina into independent chiefdoms after these peoples migrated from the Accra area in the early seventeenth century. Before starting off through town, you should pay a **visit to the chief**. To do so, you have to fill out a request at the royal secretariat. If the chief is around, and not otherwise occupied, he will receive you.

Glidji is also important from a religious perspective, since all the major sanctuaries to the principal **voodoo deities** are found in this town. You won't have trouble finding a boy to take you around to visit the different **fetish shrines** and voodoo **meeting places**. Ask to see the **temple of Egou**, the deity who is traditional protector of the Mina people.

THE PLATEAU REGION

Some of the country's most beautiful and fertile **rural back country** is located in the **plateau region** in the southwest quadrant of the country along the Ghanaian border – Togo's most agriculturally significant district. With its mountain vistas, thick vine-strewn forests and streams leaping in cascades from ragged clifftops, this corresponds to a stereotyped image of the jungle – especially if you've been brought up on Tarzan-type images. The wild country is as much a part of the region's scenery as the lush plantations of coffee, cocoa and fruit crops that make it so important economically.

Just a few hours from Lomé, the whole area is wonderfully accessible too, ethnically diverse and full of opportunities for hiking and discovery. The **coffee and cocoa** triangle, hemmed in by the towns of **Kpalimé**, **Badou** and **Atakpamé**, is home to several ethnic groups who came here from Ghana and the coast. Kpalimé and surrounding villages retain essentially Ewe populations but Badou and Atakpamé are regional melting pots of agricultural peoples.

Kpalimé

Capital of the *pays cacao* – the **cocoa country** – and of the entire fruit-growing region, **KPALIMÉ's** inordinately busy market is your first hint of its importance. Early on in their brief rule, the Germans recognised the agricultural potential of this mild and attractive zone. Once the plantations were established, they wasted no time in driving a **railway** through the forested hills to the town, and since that time Kpalimé has never been long out of the news in Togo. It was a stronghold of Olympio support in the early days after independence and even now is considered to be a hotbed of, at the very least, independent thinking.

Arrival and practicalities

Arriving by taxi, the *autogare* is near the market, off the road leading to Klouto. The **railway station** (this is the end of the branch line form Lomé) is right on the market square, on a hilltop in the town centre. Standing here, mountains rise in all directions around you. To the east, a television tower rockets up from a distant peak to interrupt the harmony of the setting but helps you spot Togo's highest summit – Mount Agou (1000m). Closer to hand, most immediate needs can be met in the area around the market. **Banks** (UTB and BTCI: Mon–Fri 7.30–11.30am, 2.30–4pm), **shops** (including an *SGGG* supermarket), cheap **restaurants** and a **hotel** line the streets that box in the market area. The **post office** is on the north side, towards the Catholic church.

Accommodation

The cheapest and one of the most hospitable places to stay is the *Hôtel Solo*, five minutes' walk (signposted) from the market towards Mount Agou. You sleep here in modest rooms with thatched roofing and few creature comforts beyond fans and electricity. The owner's home adjoins the hotel and, when you're ready to eat, he brings in food prepared by the family. Kids pass by regularly and will show you around town if you want (M. Solo will tell you how much to pay for a guided tour before you set off) and one or two speak English. Rooms start at CFA1500. In the north of town, *Domino* has rooms for CFA2500 with fan or CFA5000 with AC. It's also a popular bar–restaurant and close by the taxi park. The *Mini-Brasserie*, centrally located on the market square next to the railway station, has clean and comfortable S/C, AC rooms (starting at CFA4000) and an excellent, but moderately expensive French restaurant. Lastly, the *Grand Hôtel du 30 Aout* (BP 85; ☎21.95.97), at the entrance to town as you arrive from Lomé, is a government-run **luxury hotel**, with comfortable rooms, restaurant and a crafts centre. On the downside, it's over-priced and far from the centre.

You could also stay in the *campement* at the pretty nearby town of KLOUTO (see the following account), but, despite the beautiful scenery, you're likely to feel stranded there if you don't have your own car. Rates are around CFA1500 to camp or CFA4500 for a room.

Sites and sights

There's enough to see and do around Kpalimé to keep you happily busy for a couple of days and longer if you're into **trekking** – the nearby mountains are open territory. But the town is small and, should you be rushed for time, you can still get a good feel of the place in a day.

The start of any visit should of course be the **market**. For produce, this is one of the best in the region. **Citrus fruit** abounds and you'll find beautiful oranges, grapefruit and mandarins – green-skinned, juicy and sweet. Avocados as big as boats sell for next to nothing and likewise bananas, pineapples and lesser-known fruits are all available in abundance. Tubers – yams, coco yams and cassava – also thrive up here and are sold quite cheaply at the market, though there's less temptation for the average traveller with no kitchen. Inside the market building, you'll find more food, plus woven **kente cloth** and other fabric on the top floor. Kpalimé is known for its weavers and the quality of the material is very good – it's said President Eyadéma's official ceremonial wrap was made here. A giant **statue** of the President, just south of the market, throws a long shadow over the town. It's there to commemorate the founding of the nation's single party, the RPT, which the president announced in a speech made here on August 30, 1971.

Down the rue du Général Eyadéma near the stadium, **weavers** work foot-operated looms at the roadside. They'll be happy to chat if you want to stop, never breaking the rhythm of their movements in the course of conversation. It's not hard to appreciate the time involved in making cloth and why it's so expensive. You can order directly from the weavers, but you have to be prepared to wait several days (or even weeks) for the bespoke products of their skill.

The **Centre Artisanal de Kpalimé** (Mon–Fri 7am–noon & 2.30–5.30pm; Sat 8.30am–noon & 3–5pm; Sun 8.30am–1pm), on the route de Klouto, a couple of kilometres from the town centre, offers more immediate fulfilment. This crafts centre is a whole complex, run by the state to encourage the arts. Much of the work consists of modern interpretations of conventional forms – calabashes carved into delicate lamp-shades, pottery ashtrays or decorative statues and batiks (the origins of the latter are completely un-African) depicting ceremonial masks or village scenes. The wood carvings, such as the chairs and tables sculpted out of single tree trunks, represent a more traditional – though less portable – type of expression. Brilliant, but impossible to take with you if you've come with anything smaller than a truck. Weavers make kente cloth as well, but prices are higher here than at the market.

Lastly, on the northeast side of town, the towering steeple of the **Eglise Catholique** dominates the skyline. Built by the Germans in 1913, this makes every effort to appear to be a *kirche* from somewhere in the Bavarian countryside. And, while incongruous, the building imposes a beauty and calm of its own, and it's worth strolling up to have a closer look.

MOVING ON

From the **motor park** in Kpalimé, **taxis** run to the **Ghana border**, **Lomé** (1hr 15 mins) and **Atakpamé** – the latter a pretty route skirting the Danyi plateau. Although **Badou** looks quite close on the map, the "direct" route from Kpalimé peters out in a remote corner of Ghana, and you'll have to go via Atakpamé, where you change vehicles. For Lomé, **trains** leave at 6.10am daily, and at 12.45pm on Tue, Thur, and Sat and 1.20pm on Sun, Mon, Wed, and Fri; journey time 4hr 30 mins; fare CFA600. Should you be heading to, or just arrived from Ghana, **money-changers** openly convert CFA to cedis and vice-versa – but try to get an idea of the street rate in advance. And bear in mind the money details given in Part Fifteen, "Ghana", on p.811.

Around Kpalimé

Some 9km from Kpalimé, **KLOUTO** (also spelled Kloto) is a mountain retreat and site of an old **German hospital** built before World War I. The road up here from Kpalimé is nothing short of spectacular. Carved out by the Germans, it snakes up steep slopes through cocoa plantations and burrows through the dense **Missahohe Forest** where tree branches form a complete tunnel over the road in certain areas.

Collective taxis run pretty regularly from the Kpalimé station, but your best chances are on market days. They drop you off at customs (the Ghana border is just over the other side of the hill) where, after showing your passport to the officials (don't leave it behind in Kpalimé), you'll have to walk the rest of the way up the hill to the **Klouto campement**. Kids are always eager to show you the way, but if none are around follow the road that continues up the hill to the left from customs. To the right, you'll see the entrance to the **Chateau Viale** – a stone fortress of medieval aspect built during World War II by a French lawyer, Francois-Raymond Viale. It became state property in 1971 and is now used by the president, so you can forget about visiting it. Photography is forbidden for security reasons.

Once you've arrived at the campsite, you'll notice, amid the rolling hills and woodlands, the old **colonial buildings** now used for accommodation, plus a large *paillote* where you can order food and drinks. This is above all a "back-to-nature" retreat. Beyond the *campement*, a path bordered by huge mango trees leads out to **Mont Klouto** (741m). In theory, before you set off, there's a CFA500 fee to pay to the *gardiens* who keep the paths clear. From the mountain, you can see across into Ghana and may even be able to make out the shining, artificial expanse of the dammed **Lake Volta** 35km away to the west. Numerous rural villages are hidden in the forest around the *campement*, and the kids will be happy to take you around to see any of them or other curiosities in the area, including streams, waterfalls (nothing spectacular) or Prosper the butterfly collector, who's become something of a local celebrity. Of course, you're expected to dash them something but, for finding your way around the wilds, there's really no better way.

On market days, it's also possible to catch taxis to villages on **Mont Agou** and to hike around its 1000-metre peaks. For more information, ask at the *Hôtel Solo* in Kpalimé. You'll have to plan on setting off at dawn and returning early, or risk missing the last taxi back to Kpalimé. If you have a car, a good road leads all the way to Mont Agou's 986m summit.

From Kpalimé to Atakpamé: the Danyi plateau

The road **from Kpalimé to Atakpamé** runs along the base of the sheer cliffs of the **Danyi plateau**. About 10km out of Kpalimé, you can see the **Kpimé falls** from the roadside, a couple of kilometres up on the left (the driver or other passengers will likely point them out if you're in a taxi). These tumble a hundred metres off the cliffside, though in the dry season they are little more than a trickle. The results of the hydroelectric dam built in the late 1970s haven't done much for the site's aesthetic appeal.

Mostly, though, it's a picturesque drive, passing through numerous **Akposso** villages where you could easily stop and have a look around if you have your own transport. At **DZOGBÉGAN** (turn off the road at ADETA 30km from Kpalimé) no one will even be surprised to see you since there's a **Benedictine monastery** here that has become something of a local attraction. Their chapel, built entirely of local materials – teak, iroko, mahogany, bamboo – is unusual, but the real interest is more gastronomic. The monks run an orchard and produce jams from the exotic fruit as well as yogurt and other comestibles not so often found in these regions. As an added attraction, the area has Togo's freshest climate.

Atakpamé

Situated in the mountains, **ATAKPAMÉ** has historically been a place of refuge. The **Ewé** were the first to arrive, from Notsé, in the seventeenth century. They were followed by the **Ana** – a people related to the Yoruba who came from the east in the nineteenth century – and then by the Akposso who came down from the surrounding mountains in the early part of this century to farm the **fertile plains**. Today, Atakpamé's central location on the main roads to Lomé, Badou and Kpalimé and the measure of **industry** in the area – a nearby **textile works**, a **sugar refinery** 20km to the north in Anié and the new **hydro-electric power station** – have all helped it maintain its status as a regional hub and, incidentally, an ethnic melting pot.

Around town: practicalities

The most scenic approach to Atakpamé is **from Kpalimé** via HIHÉATRO, just a couple of kilometres west of the town. After this village, the road winds its way up one last steep hill and turns a bend to lead you right to the middle of Atakpamé's market place before you were really aware the town was anywhere nearby. If it happens to be Friday – **market day** – the commotion is sensational.

Although it's at the edge of town, the market is still substantial enough to be considered the town "centre". Arriving from Badou or Kpalimé, you're likely to be let off here, in which case you could hire a town taxi or walk to the east side of town to find lodgings. But if you're coming from Sokodé or Lomé, the **main autogare**, where you'll be dropped, is quite a distance from here, by the *route national*. Because it's hilly all around, the lie of the land is confusing, and it's tricky deciding which direction to set off for the market. The local neighbourhoods – scattered haphazardly in the bumpy valleys or on the rocky hillsides – have grown up wherever people found it possible to build. If you're planning on staying the night, however, most of the **hotels** are just around the *autogare* and you'd be well advised to drop off your bags in one of them before going into the town.

The route de Lomé is the major thoroughfare in town, although it doesn't really pass through the centre. The taxi station, main hotels and **post office** are along this street, with **banks** (*BIAO* and *BTCI*: Mon–Fri 7.30–11.30am & 2.30–4pm) and **shopping** around the market on the other side.

To get back to the main *gare routière*, head left down the road at the other side of the market, where you see the Mobil filling station and the **SGGG supermarket**, towards the Eglise Evangelique, whose modern bell tower can be seen for some distance. Take another left after the *Solidarité Bar*, go past the railway station, and you're back on the route de Lomé. If you walk this loop, you'll have seen pretty well the whole of Atakpamé town centre.

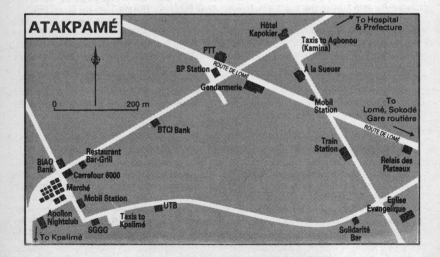

Accommodation

Of **places to stay**, the cheap *chambres de passage* at the *Le Retour* bar, located very near the taxi station off the route de Lomé, offer the minimum of comfort and lots of late-night noise, but it's not fair to complain when it costs under CFA2000. The *Relais des Plateaux* (☎40.00.31) has long been a travellers' favourite. Rooms available with or without AC and S/C; cleanliness has traditionally been adequate. Prices should start around CFA 3000. Moving towards the centre, the *Hôtel Kopokier* is just off the route de Lomé on the hospital road. More luxurious than the former, the S/C, AC rooms here start at CFA 4500. The most expensive address in town, the government-operated *Hôtel Roc* (BP 266; ☎40.02.37/90.00.01), located behind the taxi station on a hill overlooking the entire town, has S/C, AC rooms from around CFA7000/9000.

Food and nightlife

A la Sueur – "By the sweat (of my brow)" – is a terrible name for a watering hole, but this place, right on the route de Lomé near the post office, is good, clean fun. *Brasserie du Bénin* drinks are sold at normal prices and outside on the street women do food – cheap rice and spaghetti dishes, avocado, tomato and egg salads, kebabs and bread – which you can take into the bar. At weekends, the tables are removed to make room for dancing. The *Solidarité* near the Eglise Evangelique also does African food at reasonable prices, is popular with local volunteers and, again, rates at least one star for evening drinking and music. For ice cream and yogurt, visit *Fan Milk*, just down the street. Opposite the market, a large sign indicates another eatery, simply called *Restaurant, Bar, Grill* – French meals of the *steack frites* variety and good barbecued meat and kebabs on an attractive first-floor thatched terrace, from around CFA2000.

Apart from Sweat and Solidarity, Atakpamé has little excitement **after dark**, but there are several other bars and *dancings* if you're in the mood. One of the most popular clubs is *Carrefour 6000*, directly across from the market, with a young crowd and usually only full at weekends (when they charge a nominal entrance). Behind the market, *Apollon* (open nightly but again liveliest at weekends) has a huge outdoor dance floor with *paillotes* and a good atmosphere.

Kamina

You'll probably hear a lot about **KAMINA** – a major German military post in the colonial era, complete with airstrip. Today there are some old buildings dating from the end of the nineteenth cenury to remind you of the German occupation, but they're now used to house a boys' reform school. (The idea of such a school is quite revolutionary in this part of the world, and you might find it more interesting to visit than the town's historical remnants, which are hardly spectacular.)

Assuming you don't have access to a vehicle, the only way to get to Kamina is by collective taxi to AGBONOU on the *route national* from the small motor park in Atakpamé, just across the street from *A la Sueur* bar. From Agbonou you can hire a local taxi to take you along the 4km or so of dirt *piste* to Kamina.

Along the route, you'll notice the chief military officer's headquarters. Now in a ruinous state, it's still called the "first house" by locals, since it was the first cement building to go up in the area. Across the street is the grave of a German soldier dating from 1914. In Kamina itself, there are two buildings formerly used as barracks and now as school offices. Other than some cement pylons that once hooked up to a giant wireless transmitter linking Togo direct with Berlin, this is all that's left of the German presence. Most of the pylons have been reclaimed by the bush, but take a closer look at the only one visible near the school and you'll see a hole chiselled into its base. Local folk history relates how the French put dynamite inside when they captured the colony and tried to blow the thing up. When the dust settled, the pylon was still standing.

Badou and around

BADOU is the smallest, most isolated and most distinctly rural of the three towns of the coffee and cocoa triangle. Most of its people are cash crop farmers and, despite the small size of the average farm, cocoa and coffee have brought a measure of prosperity to the people of the region. In neighbouring Akrowa they've even managed to pay for all their streets to be paved. But there have been setbacks in recent years with the falling price of cocoa on the world market. Recent gluts of both crops have wreaked economic havoc in the quiet forest districts around Badou, and many young people are pinning their hopes on salaried jobs in the towns.

Practicalities: around town and lodgings

You'll get your **bearings** pretty quickly, since Badou has only one hotel, one bank and one restaurant, all located near the market. Taxis let you off at the town entrance at the junction of the Atakpamé and Tomegbé roads. To get to the **market**, head down the road that leads to Ghana, across a small bridge and past the *Toyota Bar*. Further along this same thoroughfare, you'll come to another fork marked by the *Carrefour 2000 bar/ dancing* – Badou's liveliest place at night – which offers *chambres de passage* for CFA 2000 a night, the best bargain in town. Turning left at this junction, you pass the post office on the way to Badou's fanciest accommodation – the government-run *Hôtel Abuta* (☎16), fully air-conditioned with single rooms from CFA5000 – or you can stay for CFA1000 per person if you camp in the hotel grounds – and an over-priced European-style restaurant. The **UTB bank** is right next door, but there's no guarantee they'll change your money – best to take care of that in Atakpamé. Badou's **pharmacy** is just behind the hotel.

Young boys like to earn a few *sous* showing visitors round their town and its surrounds; although Badou itself doesn't merit this treatment, you might want someone to take you to nearby hamlets. They'll sometimes even offer lodgings *en famille*, a cheaper and more enjoyable option than staying in a *chambre de passage*.

Around Badou

One of the main **attractions around Badou**, and one well worth taking the time to discover, is the **Akrowa Falls**, 11km away. Getting there, you first need a taxi along the Tomegbé road to the village of AKROWA. At its entrance, you'll see a hand-painted sign advertising the Falls and a bar-restaurant. This is the official starting point for the Falls hike up the mountain, but the taxi whizzes by to drop you off in the centre. You're supposed to ask permission to climb the hill from Akrowa's chief, and are required to pay for the privilege.

And this is where it may pay to bring a **guide from Badou**, since he can probably get you around these formalities by simply sneaking you up the paths that lead off from behind the church. There are about as many paths up the hill as there are people who hike them and they all criss-cross over streams and fallen foliage. The **climb** to the falls is strenuous, but you don't have to be especially fit – just determined. In any case, it's hard to resist dawdling through the cool, dark underbrush of the forest. After forty minutes or so of hiking through the dense vegetation, you arrive at the Falls – a drop of over thirty metres from the granite cliff. You can swim in the pool at the base of the Falls and it's said the waters are therapeutic. If you've come with someone from the area, ask him to tell you about **Mammy Wada** – the spirit that guards the water – or about the numerous other supernatural forces in the forest. Only a couple of generations ago this whole area was off limits to lay people.

SOKODÉ AND THE CENTRAL REGION

In the semi-daze of a long and comfortless taxi ride, you could miss the many signs indicating the shifts in peoples and lifestyles as you move from the balmy south of Togo to the central and northern regions. Gradually, however, you take in the change from the traditional square buildings of the south to the round, thatch-roofed **banco huts** of the interior. Around these are fixed silos of baked earth, used to store millet and corn. North of the coffee and cocoa zone, **subsistence farming** is the major economic activity of the people, and, along the roadside, the earth is pushed up into small mounds planted with yams, groundnuts and cassava. Traditional **African religions** retain a tight hold on the inhabitants of **Bassar** and **Tchamba**, two major towns in the region. The place of the church in southern Togo, however, is increasingly taken by **Islam** as you head north. And by the time you reach **Sokodé**, a long day's travel from Lomé, the whole environment – natural, cultural, social – has changed.

The predominant ethnic group of the central region are the **Kotokoli**, a people who migrated south from Mali in the late eighteenth or early nineteenth century. They brought **Islam** with them and Sokodé is now the most devoutly Muslim town in the country. Numerous **mosques**, in faded pastel colours and crowned with the star and crescent moon, attest to their faith. So, too, does **dress-style**, especially the flowing *boubous* and skull-caps commonly worn by men. Women don't wear veils, but they do drape a long, transparent scarf over their heads, wrapping it around their necks and letting it fall over their backs to flap on the ground when they walk. In accordance with the strict code of manners, people bow to one another in greeting and children even go down on their knees when greeting parents or elders.

Sokodé

In terms of numbers, **SOKODÉ** is easily Togo's second largest town, with around 50,000 inhabitants. But development has been slow in coming. There are only three paved roads in town, including the Lomé–Dapaong *route national* and the road to Bassar, both of which run through the centre. Sokodé's position at the focus of the routes assures it a certain vitality despite obvious lack of government interest in stimulating the local economy. A good number of homes in the heart of town are still made of banco and thatch and most of the people are involved in trade and subsistence routines.

Around town

Although the town is quite large, it has a definite centre of gravity around the market place. Despite official efforts to move the bustle out of town, coming in by taxi you are still let off in the *autogare* just behind the market. Drivers have been reluctant to move to the **new taxi station**, on the route de Lomé near the customs post, but the crowded market *autogare* is obviously too small to handle the traffic and the town planners may get their way in the end.

The international highway that runs through Sokodé – known as either the route de Lomé or the route de Kara depending on whether you're heading south or north – could be considered the main street. Numerous bars and restaurants jostle for custom along this two-kilometre thoroughfare through town. In the middle of it all is the large, two-storey **market building**. On the same roundabout, an independence statue at its centre and the *SGGG* supermarket to one side, is the filling station where every taxi passing through stops to refuel. Passengers with five minutes to spare mill around the market buying presents and provisions, and there's an incessant barking from hawkers desperate to sell their gear before the driver pays the petrol station *pompiste*, yells his passengers back into the sweat-box again and hits the road once more.

One block south of the turmoil, the route de Lomé intersects with the route de Bassar – Sokodé's other main street. The brand new *UTB* bank and the **PTT** (with *poste restante* that works, incidentally, if you really reckon you'll be staying here) face each other at this junction. Turning to the right, the paved road leads to the Tchaoundja neighbourhood and passes by the police station, the hospital, the *Affaires Sociales*, and the modern-looking *BTD* bank (sorry, no change). Turning left, the dirt road leads down to the town's main **mosques**, the **cinema** and the **stadium**. If you happen to be in town during a soccer match, be sure to get a ticket: **Semassi**, the home team, is one of the nation's best and, even if football isn't up your alley, the intense crowd reaction would give anyone a buzz. Near the stadium is the site of Sokodé's new **Grande Mosquée**. The Saudis have apparently promised to send funds for the building's completion, but have run low either on money or motivation, as work has barely advanced for years. The old Grande Mosquée, located a couple of streets southwest of the post office, is beautiful for its simplicity. It's completely devoid of ornamentation – you could walk right by and not even see it – but the humble architecture has a tolerant and undogmatic appeal.

Back at the independence roundabout the dirt road next to the mosque heads down to the **Zongo neighbourhood**. This is the site of the **Petit Marché**, which is more traditional in flavour than the market in town. Everything from charcoal to yams to used shoes and clothing is sold under thatched stalls winding their way through the narrow streets of the quarter. Across the street from the small market, *X Brothers Photos* is a good address should you need passport pictures or a quick bit of development done.

Somewhere to stay

Down by the stadium, the *Hôtel Alhamdou* has about the cheapest rooms in town – non S/C and nothing fancier than fans, but clean, friendly and only CFA2000. If it seems far from the centre when you take a taxi there from the station, it's an easy walk once you get your bearings. Up on the route de Bassar, *Les Affaires Sociales* has rooms for only CFA1000 or so, but civil servants get first priority here. Across from the old taxi station on the route de Bassar, the *Hôtel Tchaoudjo* is also cheap and couldn't be more central, but it can feel seedy. In the same quarter and price range is the *Hôtel Konidji*.

On the route de Lomé, *Le Relais* is a cut above all these, but it's not wildly expensive (rooms start at CFA3500) and it has a well-run restaurant and popular local bar on a shady terrace, plus a boutique full of ethnic knick-knacks. The *Campement*, off the

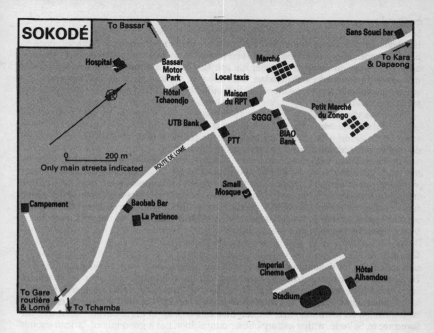

SOKODÉ

To Bassar

Hospital

Bassar Motor Park

Sans Souci bar

To Kara & Dapaong

Marché

Local taxis

Hôtel Tchaondjo

Maison du RPT

UTB Bank

SGGG

Petit Marché du Zongo

PTT

BIAO Bank

0   200 m
Only main streets indicated

ROUTE DE LOMÉ

Campement

Baobab Bar

La Patience

Small Mosque

Imperial Cinema

Hôtel Alhamdou

Stadium

To Gare routière & Lomé

To Tchamba

route de Lomé near the *prefet's* residence, is an old colonial building set on a wooded hill overlooking the town. The place hasn't been kept up (rooms start at CFA2500; or camp on the grounds) but it has a pleasant bar and restaurant. At the expensive end of the scale, the *Hôtel Central* (BP37; ☎50.01.03/23) is anything but central. Although fully self-contained and air-conditioned, it tries to catch business – like a number of other state-run hotels – by being at the entrance to town as you come in from Lomé. It's popular with ex-pats, but *La Bonne Auberge* (on the Kara road) and *Les Trois Fontaines* also cater for foreign tastes and are both cheaper.

Eating, drinking and nightlife

Budget travellers naturally head for the market. Local specialities include *watche* (rice and beans boiled together with onions and hot peppers), *kadadia* (mash made from finely ground cassava mixed with millet or corn) and *wagassi* (locally made cheese either served plain or deep-fried). Lamb kebabs are sold in the evening around the market. For snacking, be sure to try *kosse* (bean batter deep-fried in peanut oil) or *koliko* (yam chips), both local favourites.

Besides the hotel restaurants, a good place for casual sit-down meals is *La Patience*, located off the route de Lomé behind the *Baobab bar* where they do Europeanised dishes and salads for CFA1000 and up; try the grilled guinea fowl – tough but tasty. Similar food – served outside under the mango trees – is also on at *Mama J'ai Faim* near the intersection of the Lomé and Tchamba roads. *Sans Souci* is a popular bar up on the route de Kara and they also serve some of the best kebabs in town. In the evenings, *Les Affaires Sociales* runs an outside bar in a courtyard giving onto the route de Bassar. If you want to soak up the beer, there's a regular cluster of women on the street, serving salads and rice dishes to the boozers.

Festivals

Sokodé is well known for its **festivals**, most of which revolve around Muslim religious holidays. During these occasions, the town breaks from its normal lethargic pace to become surprisingly animated – and even prospects of another bleak year for the economy don't seem to dampen the people's spirits. One of the most important festivals is that marking the **end of Ramadan**. The day this month-long religious fast ends, the entire male population of the city – decked out in embroidered *boubous* – gathers at the stadium for a collective prayer. Afterwards, the day dissolves into feasting and dancing.

The **Fête du Tabaski** – celebrating Abraham's sacrificing the lamb in place of his son – takes place two months later. Several days prior to this festival, the streets in town begin filling with sheep and goats, which on the day of *Tabaski* are slaughtered en masse, roasted and shared out among the community.

The **Knife Festival**, or *Adossa*, mixes Muslim elements with a custom that certainly pre-dates the introduction of Islam into Kotokoli society and has many parallels in other West African societies. On this occasion – marking Muhammad's birthday about three months after *Tabaski* – the men drink a potion specially prepared by a marabout which renders their skin impenetrable. In public dances, they then proceed to cut one another with knives. It's even said that babies who have been administered the potion are rolled over broken bottles with no harm coming to them.

Clubs

Cheaper clubs for dancing usually attract a young teenage crowd. Popular ones include *La Gaîté* in the Kpandidjio neighbourhood (off the route de Lomé near *La Patience*); open weekends, nominal entrance. Near the the *Alhamdou Hôtel, la Cachette* has a large dance floor open at weekends and private bamboo booths discreetly closed off with curtains for *les amoureux*. A different class of joint is the *Zinaria* – currently the fave rave in Sokodé, with a sweaty indoor dance floor and a good mix of African sounds and Euro-pop. There's a small entrance fee here and slightly elevated drinks prices. *Le Relais* also has a popular weekend disco and occasionally even features live music – not an event which would be likely to escape your notice if your visit to Sokodé coincided.

There's one **cinema** in town – *L'Impériale* – down by the stadium. The fleas outnumber the customers but neither seem to be bothered by the crackling sound system and dated flicks. Lastly, the *Permanence du RPT* recently started showing nightly films and is a good deal more popular at the moment than *L'Impériale*, although the quality is about the same. Billboards outside the post office announce the day's feature at both venues.

MOVING ON

Taxis de brousse head in **all directions from Sokodé** and leave from the main *gare routière* (either still behind the market or moved to a new location on the route de Lomé). The exceptions are taxis heading to **Bassar**, which have their own *autogare* on the route de Bassar near the *Hôtel Tchadjou*. **Roads** are paved south to Lomé and north to Bassar and Dapaong (with a small *piste* deviation around Pya). If you're making the long haul north, there are no direct taxis to **Ouagadougou**. Direct vehicles come up from Lomé and are already full. Get as far as Dapaong and change – or preferably stop over.

North and west out of Sokodé

The mountainous scenery and good roads around Sokodé provide opportunities for some easy excursions. Big spenders can take in the **Fazao National Park** on an organised tour, but even if you don't have a lot of money, with a little luck and a helpful

A LITTLE KOTOKOLI			
Welcome, bonne arrivée	*Nodé*	Yes	*Mmm*
		No	*Ay*
Bonjour (5–8am)	*Nyavinakozo* (pl. *Mivinekozo*)	How are you/Ça va? (" in health?")	*Alafyaweh?*
Bonjour (8am–4pm)	*Nawsé* (pl. *Minawose*)	Fine/Ça va ("fit")	*Mumumum*
Bonsoir (4–7pm)	*Neda nana* (pl. *Minadananga*)	Fine / Ça marche ("the work")	*Kokani*
		How much?	*Ngyinidé?*
Good night (may God wake you well)	*Esofesi*	Money	*Lidé*
		Five	*Byé*
See you tomorrow/ later	*Blabtcheri* or *blabtesi*	Ten	*Byefu*
		Twenty-five	*Tchente*
Thankyou (for a gift), (for help or work completed)	*Eesobodi* *Natimaré*	One hundred	*Alfa*
		Two hundred	*Alfa nolé*
		One Thousand	*Milé*

taxi driver you'll see the wildlife anyway. The hilly and forested **road to Bassar** passes right along the game park boundary, offering glimpses of shy **monkeys** scampering as soon as they hear the car coming, and, on rare occasions, some of Togo's few hundred remaining **elephants**.

The road to **Bafilo** runs through equally striking scenery including the famous **Faille d'Aledjo** – a relatively dramatic chasm blown out of the cliff through which the highway passes. Pictures of it help keep the Togolese postcard industry alive. Skull and crossbones warning signs line the twisting and looping road as it works its way over the mountains: if you're driving, the wrecked vehicles strewn in the valleys below are evidence they should be taken seriously. If you're a bush taxi passenger, ask the driver to *allez doucement!*

Bafilo

Surrounded by mountains, **BAFILO** is the Kotokoli's second largest town and another Muslim fief – you'll see the large white **mosque** some distance before arrival. Bigger than any of the mosques in Sokodé, this place of worship was built by the funds of a single **alhadji** (one who's been to Mecca), a wealthy merchant and native son. Bafilo is a small town, easily visited in a day and famous for its hand-weaving industry.

Looking around town

The route de Kara is the only paved road and village life centres around the taxi station and adjoining market place. The main dirt road leads from the station down to the mosque. About halfway between these landmarks, a small road (nearly a path) leads down to the **weavers' yards**. You can spot them easily enough by the looms they operate in the middle of the street, and by the skeins of yarn stretched out along the roadside. If you don't see these tell-tale signs, ask someone to take you *chez les tisserands*. The quality of their work has brought them wide distinction throughout the country, and prices, depending on your bargaining skills, are as low here as you'll find anywhere. They sell either strips of woven cloth, complete *pagnes* or ready-made clothes direct from their shops near the looms.

The **Bafilo Falls** are the other major attraction around the town. Located about 4km from the centre, you can get to them easily enough by continuing down the main road past the mosque. After about a kilometre, turn right through the fields of corn, groundnuts and beans and head for the mountains. You'll see villagers out tending the fields at most times of year and you can ask them to point you to *la cascade*. Small kids may even offer to accompany you, in which case a modest dash at the end (value dependent on how old they are) will bring smiles and peals of laughter – they're not too mercenary here, yet. A concrete staircase leads to the top of the falls where a small dam assures a **swimming hole** filled with fresh spring water. It's a great escape and perfect for a break in the middle of your travels. If you wanted to stay longer, there are two other waterfalls located a bit further from town to which the kids, or the hotel, can give directions.

Where to stay

The choice is simple since there's only one hotel, the *Maza Esso* ("I thank God"). Bang on the route de Kara, this extremely clean and well-managed establishment looks expensive, but the prices are wonderful, considering the quality, with rooms starting at CFA 2500 (fans and even AC available in higher-priced rooms). The restaurant does ordinary European food but good, reasonably priced breakfasts with coffee, toast and the works.

Bassar

Culturally, the **Bassari** (no relations of the people of southeast Senegal) are worlds apart from the Kotokoli – and linguistically they belong to another cluster of Voltaic languages, **Gurma**, while the Kotokoli speak **Tem**. Traditional African religious beliefs reign supreme, and the people are known for their many and varied festivals and powerful fetishes. Traditionally the Bassari were the iron smelters for the region – indication enough, if you've travelled at all widely, of their special status – and traces of their smelting furnaces can still be seen in some of the villages neighbouring **BASSAR**.

The Bassari **fire dance** is still celebrated in Bassar and the surrounding villages. Staged versions are sometimes organised by the hotel in town, but only spirits can determine the dates for the real thing by speaking through a member of the community, who enters the arena in trance.

Bassar – the town

The paved road coming in from Sokodé runs right up to the town **market place** – where it suddenly stops. A dirt road runs in a ring round the market and functions as the high street. To the right where the tarmac ends is the **école centrale** and, just after, the *BP* station with, hard behind it, the **autogare** and PTT nearby. Continuing, you pass *Shell*, the *SGGG* and the *Cascade* bar, before coming to a huge carbuncled **baobab**, revered by the Bassari, and thus tolerated in the middle of the street. Beyond it there's not a lot – unless you count a couple of small bars – until you get back to the paved road, having by now completed the circle. Note there's no bank in town.

Accommodation, food, hopefully a cold beer or two

There's a **campement** off the paved road in the Kebedipou neighbourhood (near the *préfecture*)with basic rooms from little over CFA1000, some of them S/C and *ventilé*. The friendly staff here have all sorts of ideas for things to see in the area. The *Hôtel de Bassar* on the other hand is part of the state-run network, relatively expensive (CFA6000/CFA8000, menu from CFA2000) and somewhat dull, but nicely sited on the hilltop overlooking the town.

For cheap **eating**, the market provides the best sources of tasty calories. And for unwinding after dark, two **bars** not far from here – *Le Palmier* and *Le Bassanto* – usually run spirited discos at a small charge. They face each other, a hundred metres down the dirt road that runs out, left, from the market as you enter from the Sokodé direction.

KARA AND THE NORTH

Relatively harsh geography and climate make the north **Togo's poorest region** and probably one where you're not likely to spend much time. Much of the area is open savannah where the ochre grass of the dry season paints a disquietingly **arid** picture, portending Sahelian hardships. During the rains, however, green shoots quickly and briefly cover the hilly countryside, lending a startlingly lush appearance to the region.

The region contains Togo's highest densities of **wild animals**, concentrated in the **Kéran National Park**. Further north, the classified forest of **Fosse aux Lions** (Lion's Den) no longer harbours any big felines, but with its natural lake serving as a water hole, this is the easiest place in the country to spot **elephants**. The people, mainly small farmers of the Voltaic language group, including Tamberma, Lamba, More and Kabyé, grow staple crops of millet and, in isolated areas, rice. Cotton – an important cash crop – is grown around **Dapaong**. But the only town of any size north of Sokodé is **Kara**, which is gradually becoming the nation's administrative capital. The **Kabyé country** spreads over a rocky, mountainous area where the people acquired a reputation as renowned agriculturalists despite the hostile setting. This is the homeland of President Eyadéma – who, not unexpectedly, has made great efforts to develop his district and to transform its humble city, **Kara**, into the capital of the north. Other towns – **Sansanné-Mango** and **Niamtougou** – are extended villages with markets of local importance.

Despite a feeling of stagnation hanging heavy like a heat wave, the north offers a number of interesting sites. The **Tamberma Country**, in the valleys around **Kanté**, is famous for its remarkable architecture, each home being built like a small fortress. Until very recently, this region remained quite isolated, and to this day certain Tamberma communities have little contact with the outside world. As a result, the traditional **folk-lore**, **festivals** and **customs** of the Tamberma people have changed little over time.

Kara

KARA doesn't impress as a major metropolis and, taking the town in for the first time, you start to realise why the hype about "Togo's second city" is so necessary. Even if the town retains a provincial, not to say rustic, flavour, it has come a long way in under two decades, since when it was still a rural village called Lama-Kara. Prime political considerations have favoured Kara's development and in the space of a few years it has become the nation's second most important centre for administration and manufacturing industries. Today, incontestably the main town of the north, its infrastructure and continued growth promise to help it maintain that position for a long time to come. Some of the institutions here are worthy of a city of international pretensions, including the four-star *Hôtel Kara*, the imposing Banque Centrale, the sophisticated radio broadcasting station and especially the grandiose Maison du RPT – the party headquarters. The town also boasts more paved roads than anywhere outside Lomé and flashy illuminated road signs just like those in Paris. But the biggest boost has come from new regional industries (*Brasserie du Bénin* brewery, textile mill and sheanut oil refinery) which have been the driving force behind the expansion. Not that Kara's future is entirely rosy – the textile mill was standing idle in mid-1990, having been sold by the government at the knock-down price of US$10 million to a Hong Kong businessman.

Around town

Kara is a town with a lot going on, a lively market and pleasant setting. The centre is marked by the **Marché Moderne** and the adjoining *gare routière* for town vehicles – the main *autogare* has moved to the east of town at the intersection of the main Lomé-

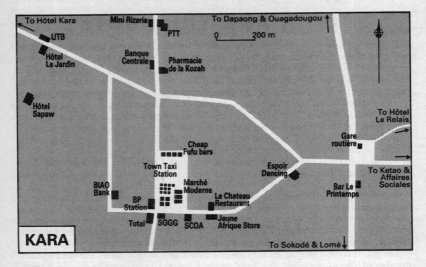

Dapaong highway and the Kétao road. It's a chaotic place with constant flow of passengers and traders swarming about frenetically, despite the heat. To escape this, most of your needs can be met in the immediate vicinity – banks, PTT, shops, bars and restaurants.

At the western end of town, a road heads from the market to the *Hôtel Kara* through a residential area. The small corrugated iron-roofed homes here stand in strange contrast to the luxury hotel with its rough stone and beam facade vaguely reminiscent of a hunting lodge. The hotel (BP 5; ☎60.60.20/21/22, telex 7204) is as expensive as it looks (from CFA18,000), but there's faultless service and all the extras you'd expect – and its **swimming pool** (open to all: CFA1000) is an obvious place to beat the heat. Near the *Kara*, you'll find the posh **UTB bank**, a convenient place to change money. The other major bank in town is the *BIAO*, one block west of the market. At weekends you can change money at the *Hotel Kara's* reception desk, though they don't offer the best rates.

Budget accommodation

Budget travellers should take advantage of the *Affaires Sociales* on the route de Kétao. Dorm rooms here are cheap at CFA1200 per bed with clean showers and baths down the hall, or there are also private rooms, some AC. Their restaurant serves inexpensive European dishes and good continental breakfasts. In a quiet part of town in the same general area (inconveniently far from the centre, off the Kétao Road to the north), *Le Relais* is a new and exceptionally clean hotel built around a pleasant courtyard with *paillotes* and exotic plants. It's not bad value with non-S/C rooms from CFA3000, or (CFA6500 with AC) and the restaurant features a long menu of European and African meals (CFA3000–4000). You can also **rent bicycles** here – a nice way to explore the town and some of the surrounding Kabyé country – and the manager is full of ideas for local trips.

Across on the other side of town, off the road to the *Hôtel Kara*, the *Sapaw* is the other budget lodging. The popular neighbourhood bar and restaurant lend a family-like atmosphere here and the rooms are good value at CFA2000–5000. Across from the UTB bank nearby, the *Hôtel le Jardin* is in similar style and receives similar custom to the *Relais*, though standards are slightly lower and prices higher.

Eating

Despite Kara's rapid modernisation the town still has many **traditional elements** like the old street-side restaurants: you'll find the majority of these chop houses around the taxi station and market. At the northern end of the station, stalls have been set aside as *fufu bars* and this is where you'll get the best calorie-to-money ratio in town. Nearby, women also sell tastier things – rice, beans, macaroni, etc – and you can go for your *choucoutou* fix round the corner.

Besides the hotel restaurants, there's a couple of other places worth mentioning. One of the most popular is the *Mini Rizerie*, located across the street from the post office. Rare treats like pizzas, hamburgers, salads and sandwiches make it popular with foreign volunteers. Expect to pay between CFA500 and CFA2000. Next to the market, *Le Chateau* is a brand new restaurant – at once casual and indubitably classy and clearly trying to up the tone in town. The terrace dining, overlooking one of the liveliest streets, has well-prepared European dishes from CFA2500 up.

MOVING ON

The taxi station near the market is the largest in the north and you can get transportation to any point between Lomé and Dapaong. If you're heading to **Bassar**, there are direct taxis that go via a good *piste*, saving you the trouble of changing taxis in Sokodé.

The northern extremities

The route north from Kara leads through the Kabyé country, dotted with characteristic *soukala* – round banco houses covered with conical thatched roofs, commonly called *tatas* by outsiders. The picturesque road, with its striking **mountain vistas**, continues as far as Kanté, the departure point for travel in the **Tamberma country**. After Kanté, it passes through the heart of the **Kéran National Park** and the village of **Nouboulou** wherein are located the reserve's lodgings. Finally the road stops off at Dapaong, the last major town before Burkina Faso.

There's currently a deviation in the road that takes you around **Pya** – the president's birthplace just north of Kara. From the *piste* you've been relegated to, you can see an odd building on a distant hilltop, with monumental dimensions that might lead you to mistake it for a modern cathedral. That's the general's humble abode and the reason why you're making a detour.

Kanté and the Tamberma Country

KANTÉ (also spelled Kandé) would surely have faded into obscurity had it not been on the nation's main *route national*. There's not much of anything in this tiny **Lamba** town where even the surrounding countryside is hardly conducive to farming anything more than the bare staples of millet and yams. There's a small **taxi park** in the middle of town, with vehicles mostly to Kara, and one or two women selling food in the vicinity. On the north side there's also a modest *campement* (rooms from CFA2000) and a decent restaurant.

Kante would be easily overlooked if it weren't the starting point for excursions into the **Tamberma country**. The region was settled by the Tamberma in the seventeeth century as they sought refuge from the King of Abomey on the coast, who raided far and wide in his quest for slaves to trade with the Portuguese. This explains the amazing fortress-like construction of Tamberma houses and the deep-rooted suspicion of outsiders.

Because these people have lived so long in isolation, their customs have remained largely unadulterated by outside influences. For that reason, if you get the chance to visit one of the villages, it can be a fascinating experience. On the other hand, this region is no longer a well-kept secret and the Tamberma country has long figured on the route of tour buses driving up from the luxury banalities of Lomé. This in turn has whetted people's appetite for tourist money and reduced their fear of foreigners. You may be invited into a Tamberma home only to find, as soon as you enter, the women ripping off their tops, sticking bones through their lips, lighting up pipes and grinding millet. Meanwhile the men are rounding up bows and arrows, clay pipes, carvings and anything else that looks like something a tourist might buy. It's all about as spontaneous as a circus perfomance, and probably not as traditional, but you can take pictures, of course, as long as you pay.

These reservations apart, however, the **homes** are indeed remarkable, self-sufficient communities, both aesthetic and functional, built some distance from each other with millet fields planted around each one. Their large central entrances were originally designed to store animals in case of attack, while grain was stockpiled in the towers and everything necessary for preparing and cooking food kept inside the house. The roof doubled as a look-out post, with rooms for sleeping built into those towers not being used as silos. With **fetishes** dotted around the house and built into the walls, the Tamberma, in short, had everything necessary in their homes to allow them to withstand long seiges. While the threat that led to the creation of such fortresses no longer exists, their architectural style has nonetheless remained unchanged.

Getting into Tamberma country

Unfortunately, if you're without your own car, **getting to the Tamberma country** can be mightily difficult, unless you **walk**. Since the first village is some 25km from Kanté that idea may not appeal – and remember this is raw bush and hotels and even *buvettes* are unheard of. The alternative is to hire a taxi in Kanté, but drivers will charge as much as they can get away with and are unlikely to take you at all for much under CFA15,000-20,000. One possibility is to hang around Kanté in the hopes of striking up a friendship with someone who'll invite you to a village – an idea that may seem implausible, but which is perfectly feasible. You'll probably end up walking anyhow, but at least you have a local companion and you'll know there's a place to sleep and eat when you arrive.

If you do have a vehicle of your own, the *piste* from Kanté leads all the way to **Natitingou** in Benin – although at times it's hard to tell if you're still on the road or in the middle of a millet field, and the one possibility may not exclude the other. If you see people walking along the road, don't hesitate to stop and give them a lift. It could lead to that first contact you've been waiting for. Kids flagging down cars along the roadside are invariably looking for tourists and, if you stop, they'll show you inside their homes and expect you to pay. It's a cringing notion, perhaps, but it's the easiest way to see inside a home and, as long as vast sums aren't laid out, doesn't do the Tamberma economy any harm.

GETTING OUT OF KANTÉ

From Kanté, there is no taxi station for **Sansanné-Mango** (also called Mango, or Nzara, and nothing to recommend it), **Dapaong** or other towns in the far north. To get there, you have to wait on the roadside by the customs post (where all traffic is obliged to stop) near the *campement*. The customs agents will find you a place in a vehicle if you ask. Usually, it's best to go in the early morning when there are more cars and when you're most likely to spot animals in the game park. If you're heading south, catch a taxi to Kara at the *place* in the centre of town, and change there.

The Kéran National Park

Anybody who takes the highway between Kanté and Mango "visits" the **PARC NATIONAL DE LA KÉRAN** as the road passes through the reserve, and there's a speed limit of 45kph. You will be clocked in and out and speeding drivers are subject to heavy fines – a serious business. In the early morning you've a good chance of seeing **baboons** or **antelopes** along the road. If you're lucky enough to see **elephants**, it's likely to be after you've already left the park on the road to Dapaong, especially in the small reserve known as the **Fosse aux Lions** – though there are few enough of those – just south of Dapaong.

Inside the park, there's a **game lodge** just outside the village of **NABOULGOU** on the highway, so a practicable stay if you're using public transport. Built in the style of a Kabyé village, this *Motel de Naboulgou* has ten AC bungalows, a dining hall and a bar. Twin rooms are CFA9000 (CFA7000 without shower) and you can hire extra mattresses for CFA1000 or camp in the grounds for the same price. Meals aren't over-priced and, compared with most game park *campements* in West Africa, this adds up to rather good value. But while the park's birdlife is prolific, considering the limited number and variety of animals you're likely to see (various antelope species, warthogs, buffaloes, monkeys and possibly elephants), Kéran is far from being the most exciting park in West Africa. Chances of seeing game increase dramatically in the dry season and the hotel shuts down in September and October. Land Rovers with drivers are available through the *chef forestière.*, though this, of course, is costly – a trip through the park around CFA16,000, sharing with others if you like. Private cars aren't allowed on the park trails.

If you're **arriving by public transport**, ask your driver to let you down at the *douane*, just outside Naboulgou. It's about a 1.5km walk down a *piste* to the hotel. The *chef forestière* has his office in a group of buildings about 200m from the customs post, so if you're thinking about renting a Land Rover, ask before heading to the hotel or you face that kilometre and a half back again to make arrangements.

Dapaong

Togo's last town in the north, **DAPAONG** (also spelled Dapaongo and Dapango) is home to a mixture of peoples of whom the **Gourma**, immigrants from the Burkina region, are the most numerous. This is a **farming district** with cotton and rice important crops. **Cattle ranching** is also prevalent, owing to the presence of a sizeable Fula (*Peulh*) population, who came down from the Mossi Country in Burkina in the mid-nineteenth century. Dapaong is a very pleasant town, a route focus and reasonable enough stop-over.

Around town

The *autogare* is at the entrance to Dapaong, some 2km south of the centre. Normally, if you come in by taxi, you should be let off in town, but if you do get dropped at the station either walk north along the paved road (it leads directly into town) or hire a town taxi to the centre. *Taxis brousse* coming into town usually stop where the road forks around the *douane*, with the *Hôtel de Ville* and hospital off to the west. From here it's an easy walk to any of the hotels, most of which are within a 500m radius.

The **market** (main market days Wed & Sat) is just east of the *douane*, down the dirt road opposite the *Hôtel de Ville* and past the popular *Relais des Savannes* bar. Besides the usual bric à brac, you'll find handmade farm tools, pottery and cheap woven gear like the broad-rimmed hats that are so common in the region. And there's no shortage of millet beer bars where you can whet your whistle if the shopping gets too heavy. Around the market square are several small *boutiques* and the inevitable *SGGG* supermarket. And on the hill behind the market, the *UTB bank* is the only place in town where you can change money.

Bed and board

For such a small town, Dapaong has very decent **lodgings**. One of the cheapest places, and certainly the most central, is the *Cercle de l'Amitié*, directly on the market square. They have rooms for all price ranges including dorm beds (CFA2000), private S/C rooms with AC (CFA5000) and an attractive restaurant with French cuisine. Just a short way behind the hospital (signs indicate the way from the *douane*), the *Hôtel le Ronier* offers rooms from CFA3000. *Le Campement* – a rather mundane name for one of the more pleasant hotels in Togo – is a colonial-style building on the hill overlooking Dapaong. Clean rooms with fan or AC are between CFA4000 and CFA6000. The courtyard bar and restaurant, shaded by thatched arcades, serves excellent French food and beer on tap but the swimming pool lacks a vital ingredient – water. Between the *campement* and the taxi station on the Mango road, the *Hôtel Lafia* has rooms at CFA3000, or CFA6000 with AC. It's clean and friendly, but a bit far from the centre.

There is plenty of the usual **street food** around the market, including coffee and omelettes in the morning, but an unusually **good place to eat** is *Le Flamboyante*, directly behind the *douane*. They claim to have everything from guinea fowl with peanut sauce to pizza, hamburgers, and sausages and chips – and it's remarkably inexpensive. Unfortunately they're often out of what you really fancied, but just like in America you can always fall back on a good tossed salad. Their terrace bar is a big Dapaong meeting point.

GETTING OUT OF DAPAONG

Heading south, you can get **taxis** to Kara, Sokodé and Lomé from the main *gare* on the Mango Road. If you want to get off before Kara (for example in Mango, the park hotel at Naboulgou, or at Niamtougou or Kanté), you still have to pay the full fare to Kara. Many people up from Lomé heading for **Ouagadougou** change taxis in Dapaong because it's cheaper than going direct. In fact, you can save about 30 percent on your fare by changing vehicles here. But if you're expecting to jump out of one taxi and into another you've another think coming. You'll almost certainly wait several hours for a Ouaga-bound vehicle at the *autogare*, if not a day or two, which tends to cancel out any saving. There are periods when traffic is particularly slow at this depot, so even if you're planning to stay in town before moving on to Burkina Faso, check the transport forecast from time to time and be set to go if something looks ready.

---

index

BENIN

BENIN

Benin is the Gulf of Guinea's least-known nation, the result of seventeen reclusive years of struggle through one of West Africa's least successful revolutions. The political climate inched westwards throughout the 1980s, but since 1990 this momentum has rapidly increased. The revolutionary rhetoric has been thrown out and Benin is in the vanguard of states adjusting to new orders, in most cases partly imposed by France. There is every indication that, by the middle of the 1990s, Benin will have adopted a multi-party democracy and, for better or worse, a liberal economic system.

Benin's years of seclusion have left it an intriguing place to travel, considerably more open than you might suspect, its people mostly warm and mild in their dealings with outsiders but quick to strike up conversations on real issues – especially now that freedom of expression is generally acceptable. But several outstanding factors distinguish the country. First, a number of sophisticated indigenous states developed here, the largest and most urbane of which was the Fon kingdom of **Dan-Homey**, whose capital, in the heartlands of the southern savannah, was **Abomey**. It was this well-organised and prosperous kingdom that was heavily responsible for one African corner of the triangular slave trade that flourished in the hinterland of what the Europeans called the "Slave Coast" from the sixteenth to the nineteenth century. The trade wasn't finally ended until 1885, when the last Portuguese slave cargo steamed out of Ouidah. But by then, a considerable amount of imported wealth had been amassed in the country. Secondly, it was in colonial Dahomey that French Catholic **mission schools** were most influential in the old empire of Afrique Occidentale Française. Thousands of highly qualified students graduated from its secondary schools, giving the country a dynamic intellectual reputation that has coloured its personality deeply.

BENIN BASICS

Known as **Dahomey** during the colonial period (after the old empire), the **République du Bénin** adopted the name of the ancient West African kingdom located in present-day southern Nigeria, after the 1972 coup led by notherner Mathieu Kérékou, the nation's most durable president, who was intent on imposing some unity, or at least some stability, on a deeply divided and unsettled country. The **population** is under five million, a good tenth of whom live in Cotonou, the largest city and the *de facto* capital. The official capital remains Porto Novo, a much smaller coastal town that served as the colonial administrative centre. Until March 1990, government was conducted through the single party – the *Parti de la Révolution Populaire du Bénin* – overseen by the president. But with the first steps towards multi-party democracy, the People's Republic has become a simple Republic, the dictatorship has collapsed and the country is in a state of flux.

The country – and travel

Benin is mostly thinly wooded savannah, part of the **open country** that comes more or less to the coast between the rain forests of Nigeria and Ghana and which accounts somewhat for the different shifts of history that have taken place here – easier travel and trade, more successful armies and faster conquests.

A flat sandy plain runs the whole length of the **coast**, broken up by a string of picturesque **lakes and lagoons**. The coast offers little enticement in the sea (rough and terrifyingly dangerous) but the **old towns** – including **Porto Novo**, Benin's crumbling

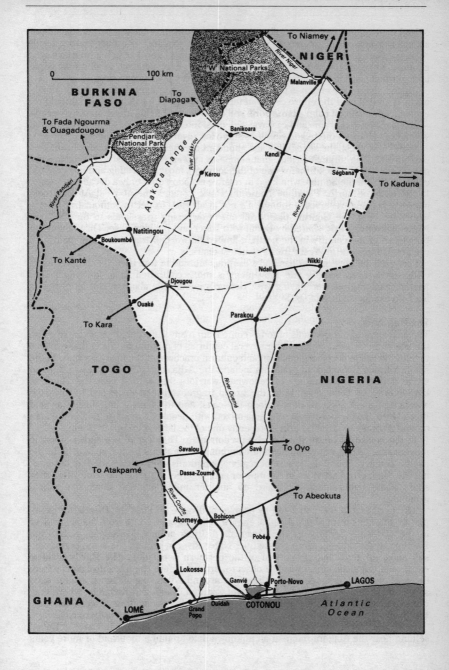

official capital, and the old Brazilian quarters of **Ouidah** – have a certain flaked-out appeal and are full of interest if you have time to explore. The over-exploited stilt village of **Ganvié** is the coastal site of which you're most likely to catch a (tourist's eye) glimpse, while dismal and austere **Cotonou**, which, unfortunately, is all most people take in when passing through the country, leaves a very poor impression.

Inland, the improvement is palpable and rapid, as a gentle **plateau** slopes gradually north to spread over the entire centre of the country in a rich patchwork of agriculture. Coffee, cotton and oil palm **plantations** collide with small fields of **subsistence crops** – maize, millet, rice, yams and cassava. The most interesting town is **Abomey** – capital of the Dan–Homey empire and site of its surviving royal palaces and museum.

In the northwest, the sheer cliffs and abundant greenery of the **Atakora mountains** rear up in a long, dramatic ridge that stands in impressive contrast to the plains and provides a striking backdrop for one of the country's most interesting and inaccessible cultures, that of the Somba, who lived in relative isolation until only a decade or so ago. In the extreme north, **Pendjari National Park** is rated one of West Africa's most interesting faunal reserves – though it's not at all easy to get to without transport – while east of it, the Gourma plains roll out in sweeping grasslands to the **"W" du Niger National Park**, shared by Benin with Niger and Burkina Faso. Throughout the broad part of the country in the north, a limited network of tracks and one main road can get you to some of West Africa's remotest districts.

For years the government has had a cautious attitude to **tourism.** It has never especially encouraged visitors and movement is more controlled than you might like. Neither camping out nor staying with Béninois is officially allowed. But all of this is likely to change soon, and fast.

The Béninois

The ancestors of the Béninois of today come from many different areas and arrived on the site of the present country after several centuries of migrations, a fact that explains the differences in social organisation and cultural practices of the many peoples. In the south, various Ewe-speaking peoples include the **Adja**, one of the earliest groups to arrive, formerly a community of renowned warriors that settled near the Togolese border town of Tado. Over time, the group fragmented and dispersed to form the **Xwala** and the **Xuéda** (Ouidah) along the coast and the **Gun** a little inland around Porto Novo. To the northwest, the Adja mixed with peoples already settled in the area around Abomey to form the **Fon** – presently one of the largest groups in Benin.

In the centre and east, the **Yoruba** predominate. They came in a series of vague movements, setting out on family and community migrations from Oyo and Ife in the twelfth century. Founding important regional kingdoms, they often ended up dominating the commercial activities of the interior and, together with the Fon with whom they share some cultural affinity, make up another influential and distinctive ethnic grouping.

The northeast is also populated by peoples of diverse origins. The **Dendi**, for example, are migrants from Mali's Songhai empire, who migrated south from the Niger river in the sixteenth century to the savannah districts around Malanville, Kandi and Djougou. **Fula** cattle herders crossed the Niger River at around the same period and still make up a sizeable proportion of the northern population. The **Bariba**, whose ethnic and linguistic affiliations are obscure, arrived before the fifteenth century from the northwest Nigeria region. Settling first around Nikki, population pressure soon spread their communities to the districts of Parakou, Kandi and Kouande, where they came to dominate predecessors like the **Bussa**, speakers of another obscure language (probably a relic Mande tongue), who had also migrated west from northern Nigeria.

In the northwest, the **Betammaribe** were one of the first peoples to arrive in Benin, settling near the Atakora range at an unknown date around a thousand or more years ago. Living in relative isolation, these people, commonly known as the **Somba**, resisted changes inflicted by the spread of Islam and the French invasion. Until quite recently, they lived in the seclusion of their fortified *tatas* and farmed their lands, wearing no more than the traditional *cache sexe* of their ancestors. Although their subsistence way of life had been ignored for centuries, in the 1970s they were exposed to the raw glare of the French press – delighted to have located a rare example of "real Africa". Stung by the sensational reports of naked tribesmen, the government ran a campaign to force the Somba to wear clothes. As a result of this humiliation and other insensitivities, the Somba remain a very private, reserved people, and outside of the main towns, such as Natitingou – where traditional ways are fast breaking down – it's difficult, and perhaps from no one's point of view very desirable, to penetrate their tight-knit communities.

Most Béninois adhere to traditional African **religious beliefs**. Along the coast, **voodooism** is common, particularly among the Ewe-speakers In many ways, their practices are similar to those of the Yoruba and Fon, each of which believe in a single supreme God who created the universe (*Orisa* in Yoruba or *Mawu-Lisa* in Fon) On earth, lesser divinities are charged with power over thunder (*Xebioso* or *Cango*), iron and war (*Ogun* or *Gu*), land and disease (*Sakpata* or *Cankpana*), and so on. Their help can be solicited through the work of priests.

Islam was brought from the north by Arab, Hausa and Songhai-Dendi traders. It extended as far south as Djougou, and even into the Yoruba country. Perhaps as much as fifteen percent of the population are Muslim. **Christianity** came with the Europeans and spread principally along the coast and the central plateau.

Climate

Given the generally bad condition of roads in Benin, the weather can have a very adverse effect on travel and it's best to avoid the rainy seasons, which, in the southwest can be prolonged and oppressive. In the **south**, there are two **rainy seasons** (a long one from April to July and a short one from October to November) and two **dry seasons** (a short one from August to September and a long one from December to March). Temperatures fluctuate little throughout the year.

In **the north**, the year divides simply into the rainy season, which lasts from late May to October, and the dry season, which lasts from November to early May. Temperatures vary more dramatically than in the south. When the *harmattan* wind blows in December, nights can be quite cool. The rainy season is sometimes extended in the Atakora region and in Natitingou, for example, it continues virtually uninterrupted from April to November.

AVERAGE TEMPERATURES AND RAINFALL											
COTONOU											
	Jan	Feb	Mar	Apr	May	June	July	Aug	Sept	Oct	Nov	Dec
Temperatures °C												
Min (night)	23	25	26	26	24	23	23	23	23	24	24	24
Max (day)	27	28	28	28	27	26	26	25	26	27	28	27
Rainfall mm	33	33	117	125	254	366	89	38	66	135	58	13
Days with rainfall	2	2	5	7	11	13	7	3	6	9	6	1

Arrivals

Despite being so centrally placed in the region, Benin is not a country to which many travellers make initial flights into West Africa. Cotonou airport is the most poorly served on the coast. Entering overland is straightforward enough from Togo or Niger, but the routes down from Burkina Faso are little used, and the way in from Nigeria can be a hectic hassle.

■ Flights From Africa

Most **direct flights** from neighbouring countries in **West Africa** are handled by *Air Afrique* which flies to Cotonou from Abidjan, Accra, Bamako (via Abidjan), Dakar, Douala, Lagos, Lomé, Niamey and Ouagadougou. Complementing the regional service, ***Nigeria Airways*** also flies from Abidjan, Banjul, Conakry, Dakar and Lagos. Another airline to note is ***Ghana Airways*** which flies from Accra, Freetown and Monrovia (via Accra), and Lagos.

From **East Africa**, possibilities are pretty much limited to *Ethiopian Airlines* flights to Lagos (three times weekly) or Accra (weekly) continuing to Cotonou with *Ghana Airways* or *Nigeria Airways*. **Central Africa** is serviced by *Air Afrique* flights out of Brazzaville and Libreville.

■ Overland from Nigeria

By far the most common point of entry is via the **Badagri** coastal road from Lagos. The Nigerian border post is much less harrowing when leaving Nigeria than when entering, but there are always crowds and it may take you a while to get through the formalities. Your bags will be given a perfunctory search, but it's not likely your currency declaration form will even be checked. Customs and immigration at **Kraké** on the Benin side present no special problems.

■ Overland from Niger

From Niamey, the road is sealed all the way to the border post at **Gaya**. Here a bridge spans the Niger River and leads to the Benin customs at **Malanville** (open daily 7am–7.30pm). There's nothing especially difficult about the formalities here, but often you have to prove you have sufficient money to support yourself by showing travellers cheques, cash or other funds. As at other border posts, you must state where you plan on staying. Give the name of any hotel, whether you intend to stay there or not. They have a list you can choose from.

From Malanville, the main road is good as far Parakou; from here to Bohicon it's been scheduled to be paved for years. If it has not been sealed before publication, this section is in awful shape with bone-rattling washboards and deep pits over a 250-kilometre stretch.

■ Overland from Burkina Faso

Most people coming from Burkina take the sealed road through Togo and branch over to Benin either at Kara or Lomé, as described below. Some vehicles do, however, leave with irregular frequency from Fada Ngourma to Natitingou. You may have to transfer at Pama.

■ Overland from Togo

Taxis whiz regularly along the **coastal highway from Lomé to Cotonou**. Although there's no Béninois embassy in Togo, **visas** are issued on the spot at the border post of Hila Kondji – providing you come with two passport photos and CFA2000. Though customs operate here around the clock, the visa section only works during business hours (Mon–Fri 8am–12.30pm & 3–6.30pm, Sat 8am–12.30pm). Note that this is the only border post where you can expect to enter Benin without acquiring a visa beforehand.

From the north of Togo, a good gravel road (possibly paved by the time you read this) leads from Kara to the border post at Kétao. Customs and immigration agents here are generally quite good-humoured and the *piste* leading on to Djougou in Benin is well-maintained if a bit slippery when wet. Alternatively, if you have your own vehicle you could take a very minor and neglected *piste* that branches off the main road at Kanté and heads **through the Tamberma country**. Little traffic uses this route and you're not likely to be aware that you've crossed the border until you arrive at the main road to Natitingou. When you arrive at this latter town, go to the police and customs to get your passport stamped.

Red Tape

French, Germans, Danes, Swedes and Italians don't need visas to enter Benin. Most other nationalities, apart from Ecowas member states, do. Israeli passport holders are prohibited entry.

In most cases, visas are only issued for a 48-hour period. This is not a major problem if you arrive in the south, since extensions of up to a month are easily obtained at the immigration office in Cotonou: you'll need two passport photos and CFA7000. If you arrive by road from the north, however, you'll have to rush your trip to get to the coast within two days – an obvious headache if you'd planned on taking in sights along the way.

Within the country, the **police** makes their presence felt: **spot checks** are frequent along the roadside, and even covering a distance as short as Cotonou to Bohicon, you're likely to be asked to show your passport three times or more. However, the police aren't particularly intimidating: they tend to be friendly through the formalities, providing that you approach them in the right way. Arriving in most large towns – for example Parakou, Djougou and Kandi – you are expected to stop at the police station and get your passport stamped. If you fail to do so, you could have troubles further on down the road and might be sent back.

■ Visas for Onward Travel

Cotonou is a good place to pick up a visa if you're going to **Nigeria**. You can generally get your stamp within 24 hours and without hassle, though usually for only a brief initial stay. The **Ghana** embassy issues visas within 48 hours, but, headed that way, there is really no reason not to wait until you arrive in Lomé. Ghanaian and Nigerian visas cost around CFA10,000.

Money and Costs

Benin uses the CFA franc (CFA50 = 1 French Franc; CFA450–CFA500 = £1) and is relatively expensive to travel through. Accommodation tends to be pricier than in neighbouring countries and you have to stay in hotels (see "Sleeping" overleaf). The price of petrol is slightly cheaper than in neighbouring countries (except Nigeria): public transport by bush taxi works out around CFA15 per kilometre.

Changing money in Benin, especially anything but French Francs, can be problematic outside of Cotonou. Two banks – the *Banque Béninoise de Développement* (the *BBD*) and the *Banque Commerciale du Bénin* (the *BCB*) – have branches in the larger towns of Parakou,

Natitingou, Abomey and Kandi. Their opening hours are usually 8am–12.30pm and 3.30–7pm.

Health

Yellow fever is currently the only vaccination required for travel to Benin, though doctors may also recommend cholera and typhoid inoculations. Malaria is widespread and, like neighbouring Togo, this is an area where the parasites are tough, and are apparently building up resistance to commonly-used drugs like chloroquine and nivaquine. Some doctors are starting to advise patients to take drugs like Fansidar or Mefloquine.

You should avoid swimming in fresh water streams and lakes in Benin, and don't walk barefoot in the grass surrounding them. They are almost invariably infested by schistosomiasis parasites which transmit **bilharzia**. Outside Cotonou, some sort of **water purification** is recommended.

Hospital facilities throughout the country are meagre, with drugs and equipment in short supply. In Cotonou, the most obvious place to head for medical problems is the *Centre Naional Hospitalier et Universitaire* in the Patte d'Oie district (☎30.01.55). The privately-run *polyclinic* (☎30.14.31), in the Cocotiers district, however, has a better reputation.

Maps and Information

The best map of Benin is the *IGN* national road map (1cm to 6km) which includes detailed *pistes* and topographical material, and is especially useful in the confusing lagoon areas along the coast. If you're not planning on staying long or travelling much off the beaten track, however, the *Michelin* map of West Africa (#953) is adequate.

There aren't any overseas tourist offices, but the embassy in Paris and the London honorary consulate do have limited supplies of leaflets and brochures. In Benin, offices of the tourist agency *ONATHO* – notably the one in Cotonou – have sketchy pamphlets about travel, but not much **information** you can sink your teeth into. Any *librairie* in the country has a hundred-page reader called *Le Bénin* which gives a good overview of the nation, intended for school children, with colour photographs and chapters on administration, industry, peoples, rural activities and a variety of other official subjects.

Getting Around

Benin's system of transport is about the worst in the region. Roads are much less reliable than in Togo, and certainly far worse than those in Nigeria – which are superb in comparison. Trains provide some alternative in the south, though the network dates from the colonial period, and it feels like it. The domestic air service is very limited.

■ Road transport

The Béninois have remained faithful to the *Peugeot* – a make still prefered to the new, lightweight Japanese models among **bush taxi** drivers. *504 famillliales* – nine-seater estate cars – are the common mode of transport for most people. Police checks are numerous along the roads and you have to show your *pieces* often, so have your passport handy when travelling.

The government also runs a regular **bus service** to all major towns between Malanville and Cotonou. The system is by no means as well developed as that in Ghana, and the buses are mostly old and battered. Still, seats are cheaper than bush taxis and run on regular schedules. They usually leave from the same *gare routière* as the *taxis brousse*. Ask in advance for times and arrive early, as they tend to fill quickly.

Routes

The main **national highway** runs for 742km from Malanville to Cotonou. It's paved between Malanville and Parakou and between Cotonou and Dassa. The miserable *escalier*-infested gap between Parakou and Dassa has been scheduled for repair for years and work has started several times, only to be stopped for lack of funds. Hopefully the latest effort, begun in 1988, will soon be complete, thereby greatly facilitating international travel between Cotonou and Niamey.

Other main **north–south** routes include a paved road stretching 80km from Grand Popo to Abomey via Lokossa (interrupted by stretches of well maintained *piste* and a few *escaliers*) and a 110-km paved road linking Porto Novo to Kétou in

the east. From Dassa, a 454-km road runs up the west of Benin to Porgo on the Burkina Faso border, paved to Savalou. After this town, the tracks aren't in good shape, and there's very little traffic along this stretch. By taxi, you may have to settle for rides to Bassila, Djougou and Natitingou before continuing on to Burkina. This road too, it's claimed, will soon be paved all the way to Fada Ngourmam in Burkina.

On the **east–west** axis, there's not much to be thankful for outside the very good international highway running the whole way beteen Abidjan and Lagos which, in Benin, stretches for 177km between **Hilakondji and Klake**. A secondary road, all *piste* except for a small section between Azove and Bohicon, links **Aplahoue** on the Togolese border with **Kétou** near Nigeria. Further north, the best cross-Benin route is a well-maintained laterite track running between **Parakou and Djougou**. Many Togo-bound vehicles pass along this stretch and transport is no problem.

■ Trains

The national **railway** company, *l'Organisation Commune Bénin-Niger des Chemins de fer et Transports*, operates three railway lines in Benin. Built between 1900–39, the ageing network consists of three tracks.

Firstly, the **northern line**, which covers 438km from Cotonou to Parakou, via Bohicon, Dassa and Savè. The trip to Parakou takes over ten hours; it's possible to reserve a *couchette* on a night train. Despite the time involved, many Béninois prefer riding by rail over this stretch since the road between Dassa and Parakou has long been a nightmare. Plans have been kicking about for years to extend this line to Niamey, via Malanville and Dosso: don't, however, expect anything to materialise in the immediate future. Secondly, the **eastern line** runs for 107km, from Cotonou to Pobè, passing through Porto Novo. Lastly, the **western line** links Cotonou with Ouidah and continues a total of 60km to Sègbohoué.

■ Planes

Interior **air transport** is handled by the domestic airline, the *Société des Transports Aériens du Bénin*. They have regular flights from Cotonou to Parakou, Kandi and Natitingou but they don't fly abroad and are not listed in the ABC world timetables.

Sleeping

A good network of hotels hasn't yet been developed in Benin. Cotonou has its *Sheraton* **and a scattering of lesser luxury, and Natitingou – the president's birthplace – has found itself with a three-star wonder in the French** *PLM* **chain. Such international-class establishments, however, are the exception rather than the rule.**

More typical (and realistic) accommodation is at the basic end of the market: sparsely furnished rooms, usually with electricity (and sometimes a fan), but not necessarily with private toilets or even running water. Despite which, **accommodation** is relatively expensive in Benin and you can't expect to pay much less than CFA4000 for even a modest single room – on top of which there's a two percent government **tax.**

Staying with people is strictly forbidden. Police rigorously enforce this law, and in most towns of any size, you have to check in with them and declare your address. Though people are hospitable and may invite you around for meals, because of the strict law, they aren't likely to invite you to spend the night. What the French call *camping sauvage* (pitching your tent in an unofficial site along the roadside or beach, for example) is also illegal. It seems most probable that both these laws will be rescinded in the near future as the structures of the repressive pseudo-socialist regime start to be dismantled.

Eating and Drinking

Food in Benin largely resembles that of neighbouring Togo and for background and details on local staples and popular dishes, refer to the food section in the previous chapter. Cotonou has a variety of European restaurants, even if the city doesn't have any gastronomic reputation in West Africa. In the provinces, such restaurants are rare indeed and are replaced mainly by small *buvettes* **specialising in rice,** *pâte* **(the generic term for pounded starch),** *moyo* **(like semolina) or macaroni served with sauce.**

One of Benin's leading industries is the *Société Nationale des Boissons* which produces the national beer, *La Béninoise*, and a variety of carbonated soft drinks. These are the cheapest drinks sold throughout the country, though both beer and fizzy pop imported from Togo are widely

available and generally better tasting. Along the coast, **palm wine** is plentiful, as is the lethal African firewater known as *sodabi*. In the north, beer made from millet, known as *chapalo* or *tchacpalo*, is more common.

Communications: PTT, Media and Language

The scope for communication isn't promising. Cotonou is the place to go for phones and mail. There's little on the airwaves and just one daily paper (but more promised). Of the host of local languages none stands out as being widely useful across the country.

■ Staying in Touch

If you're just passing through, Cotonou is the only reliable place to receive **mail**. The post office is fairly efficient and the *poste restante* service good. International **phone calls** can be made either from the PTT in Cotonou, or from the *Sheraton Hotel*, although the latter is twice as expensive and you've no way of knowing if the operator isn't adding an unofficial commission.

■ The Media

There's only one daily **newspaper**, the government organ *Ehuzu*, and even that's not as visible as the press in other countries, with a circulation of just 10,000 copies. The daily *L'Aube Nouvelle* ("New Dawn") seems to have faded away, but *La Gazette Du Golfe* and *Tam Tam Express* are just two of twenty new privavely-funded journals. The state-run *Office de Radiodiffusion et de Télévision du Bénin* has **radio** broadcasts in French, English and 18 national languages.

■ Languages

Benin's official language is **French**. The fifty or so Béninois ethnic communities speak about as many different national languages or distinct dialects. Some languages have become regional *lingua franca*: in the south, **Adja** and **Fon** are widely spoken (both are closely related to Ewe and Mina under the "Ewe group" umbrella and limited word and phrase lists are boxed in Part Sixteen "Togo") and are probably the most useful languages to have a few phrases in. In the centre and east, **Yoruba** takes over (see box in Part Eighteen "Nigeria"). **Bariba**, a Voltaic tongue, is the common language of Parakou and the north-

BÉNINOIS GLOSSARY

Amazon From Greek words meaning "without a breast", and referring to a race of Scythian female warriors who supposedly carried out mastectomies to facilitate use of their longbows, *Amazon* was the name given to female Fon soldiers by visiting Europeans. Portuguese explorers thought they saw the same kind of people on the banks of South America's biggest river.

Camarade Common Béninois term of address in keeping with socialist philosophy. *Bonjour camarade* is more likely than the *bonjour chef* of other countries.

Féticheur Traditional religious leader.

ONATHO *Office National du Tourisme et de l'Hôtelerie*, the national tourist board.

PRPB *Parti de la Révolution Populaire du Bénin*– the single party in Benin.

RPB *République Populaire du Bénin*.

Tata Fortress–like houses built by the Somba in the region of Natitingou.

Vaudou/Vodu "Divinity" in Fon. Voodoo, the religion of the coast. spread from these parts to Haiti with the exile of slaves.

east, while the old Songhaic language, **Dendi**, is spoken in the extreme north near the banks of the Niger. **Hausa** and **Fula** are also widely used in the north. Because of the proximity and influence of Nigeria and the importance of commerce, some Beninois speak a kind of mercantile **English**, though it's not likely to get you very far.

Directory

AIRPORT TAX CFA2500.

BUSINESS HOURS Most business are open 8am–12.30pm & 3.30–7pm. Government offices are open Mon–Fri 8am–12.30pm & 3–6.30pm.

HOLIDAYS Christian holidays and New Years' day are public holidays. Muslim celebrations are less formally observed, though everything shuts down in the north for them. Ramadan, however, isn't conspicuously disruptive. In addition there are secular holidays on **May 1** (Labour Day), **August 1** (Independence Day), **October 26** (Armed Forces' Day), **November 30** (Benin Day) and **December 31** (Harvest Day).

MUSEUMS Benin has several museums which have recently benefited from foreign-funded refurbishments. By far the best is housed in the former Dan-Homey palace in **Abomey**, which has undergone massive renovations with the help of UNICEF funds. **Porto Novo** also has two museums, one in the former residence of King Toffa. The museum in **Ouidah** is dedicated primarily to the Voodoo religion.

MUSIC There's little thriving musical culture in Benin though every indication that with economic liberalisation, a less insecure government and relaxations on censorship, there'll be more musi-

cal instruments, better facilities and greater freedom of expression in the future (see the "Music" section in *Contexts*).

PETROL Notoriously cheap petol (under CFA100 per litre), smuggled from Nigeria, is available by the bottle at the roadside all over, or was until very recently. The official price is CFA175/litre.

PHOTOGRAPHY In theory, you need no permit to take pictures in Benin but photographing people can be a very sensitive issue, especially in Somba country. People in touristed areas like Ganvié and Ouidah are more likely to demand money, and snapping away without permission can lead to problems. Don't take pictures in towns unless it is manifestly obvious that your subject is "touristic" – rarely so – as the security forces are notoriously, and to some extent justifiably, paranoid about espionage and conspiracies.

WILDLIFE Although densely farmed and populated in the south, Benin's northern regions spread into a broad zone of thinly populated savannah and uplands – one of West Africa's best game-viewing areas. There are significant concentrations of wildlife, especially in the Pendjari and "W" du Niger national parks, including some hundreds of elephants.

WOMENS' ISSUES The position of women in Benin has been little improved by the revolutionary 1970s and 80s. Despite the existence of the *Organisation des femmes révolutionnaires du Bénin*, Béninoise women have even less involvement in politics and decision-making than elsewhere.

Women travellers report Béninois men generally pleasantly reserved and low-key and there's relatively little sexual harassment.

A Short History of Benin

The earliest history of the territory that is now Benin is obscure. The far north was under thrall to the Niger river's Songhai empire by the end of the fifteenth century (see p235). Meanwhile, in the south, having built the fort at El Mina in Ghana, in 1482, the Portuguese continued along the coast and began trading with local rulers from the 1520s. Porto Novo and Ouidah developed through the sixteenth and seventeenth centuries into important commercial centres where slaves were traded for European cloth and guns. The British, Dutch and French, seeking labour for their American colonies, soon joined the Portuguese in the traffic, establishing their own coastal forts and commercial depots in the seventeenth century. By the 1690s, some 20,000 slaves were being shipped annually out of Ouidah and lesser ports.

■ The Slave Coast

By as early as the beginning of the seventeenth century, the **Dan-Homey Kingdom** (though itself a vassal of the great Yoruba Oyo empire to the east) dominated the political arena in the region. One of Dan-Homey's rulers, **Agadja** (in power from 1708–1740), subjugated the districts south of his capital Abomey, and finally took Ouidah itself. With access to the coast, his empire was now poised to control international trade – primarily in slaves. But he had exceeded the terms of his license with Oyo and a protracted conflict ensued which resulted in Oyo's definitive conquest of Dan-Homey. There followed a period of desperate slave-hunting as the Dan-Homey king **Tegbesu** tried to rebuild his country's war-shattered economy (more background on p.957).

After the French Revolution, however, a wave of **anti-slavery sentiment** began to sweep Europe. In France, the *Decret du 16 pluviôise an II* (February 4, 1794) abolished the trade, though it was later reinstated by Napoleon. In 1802, Denmark became the first European nation to abolish the slave trade permanently. Britain followed in 1807 and from 1819–1867, British ships patrolled the coast, arresting slave ships and resettling the captives in Freetown, Sierra Leone. France outlawed the trade in 1818.

These moves coincided with a severe shortage of slaves in the region, in large part because of excessive human sacrifices in Abomey. A Brazilian mulatto, **Francisco Felix de Souza**, whose career had been helped by **Prince Ghezo** of Dan-Homey, entered into a blood pact with the young man and supplied the guns for Ghezo to overthrow the incumbent of the stool (throne) in Abomey in return for which he was granted a monopoly over the slave trade (and became the "Viceroy of Ouidah", see "Books" in *Contexts*).

But already by the 1830s, the nature of most commerce in the region had fundamentally changed and **palm oil** became the primary export. The French soon gained the upper hand in the regional oil trade when representatives from Marseille soap-making companies arrived in Ouidah in 1843 and travelled to Abomey where they signed a contract with the Dan-Homey king, the same **Ghezo**, granting them trading rights at Ouidah. In 1861, Lagos became a British colony. **King Toffa** of Porto Novo had claims on the town of Badagary which the British now controlled. Worried that their influence would spread westward, Toffa called on the French for support and in 1863, Porto Novo became a **French protectorate**. In 1868, the new **King Glele** of Abomey ceded rights to Cotonou to the French who had by now established themselves as the most prominent European power along Benin's coast.

■ French Conquest

But the good relations between France and the Dan-Homey kingdom soured by the end of the century. In December 1889, a new sovereign, **Behanzin**, was enstooled. He adopted a more combative attitude to the French who were beginning to look less like trading partners and more like a force of occupation. He refused to recognise French rights over Cotonou and was angered that the foreigners had allied themselves with one of his bitterest enemies, King Toffa of Porto Novo. After funeral ceremonies for his father Glele, Behanzin ordered an **attack on Cotonou**. On March 4, 1890, some five to six thousand Dan-Homey warriors marched on the city and withdrew only after inflicting numerous casualties. A month later, the army surrounded Porto Novo and clashed with the French at Atchoukpa on the northern outskirts of the city.

Other skirmishes followed and in April, 1892, Behanzin sent the following message to French authorities:

I warn you that if one of our villages is touched by the fire of your cannons, I will march directly to crush Porto Novo and all the villages belonging to Porto Novo. I would like to know how many independent French villages have been overtaken by me, King of Dan-Homey. I request you to keep calm and do your business in Porto Novo. That way, we can remain in peace as it was before. But if you want war, I am ready. I will not finish it. It will last a hundred years and will kill 20,000 of my men.

The threat was taken seriously by the French who knew that Behanzin possessed more than 5000 modern firearms and was still being supplied by the Germans and the British. The government in Paris sent a distinguished commander to handle the situation, **Colonel Dodds**, a mulatto from Saint Louis in Senegal.

In August 1892, Dodds began his northern march to conquer Abomey. Accompanied by Senegalese and Hausa infantry, the French went to the Ouemé River and followed its course. Although the army was sporadically engaged by Dan-Homey troops, including divisions of Amazons — skilled female warriors specially trained to use the new Martini-Henry rifles — it was the Dan-Homey who received the heaviest casualties in the clashes. By November 1892, when the French arrived at Cana — the village where Dan-Homey kings were traditionally buried — Behanzin's army had lost 4000 dead and twice as many wounded.

The king prepared himself for a **last stand**. He recruited every warrior capable of carrying a gun and the massed ranks of his Amazons — even those specialised in hunting. And he got the nation's slaves to join the battle, promising them freedom in return. But the effort was in vain; the army was defeated and Behanzin was forced to retreat with meagre reserves. On November 16, 1892, Dodds marched on Abomey to find the city already in flames, torched by the retreating army. It took another two years for the French to track down and capture Behanzin (betrayed by the newly French-enstooled Fon king) and he was transported to exile in Martinique.

The Colonial Era

Their main rival in the region at last conquered, the French went on to subdue the north of the country, which they now called **Dahomey**. Colonial frontiers were drawn up in agreement with Britain to the east and Germany (which held Togo) to the west. In 1901, the present borders were fixed and, in 1904, Dahomey became part of AOF (French West Africa).

French policy in Dahomey was partly shaped by the influence of Catholic missions which sent large numbers of envoys into the territory in the 1920s and 1930s. Catholic seeds had been sown from a very early period, with the arrival in the eighteenth century of influential **Brazilian** families and Christian **freed slaves**. Moreover, the climate, open country and dominant voodoo religion of the south were not strongly antithetical to missionary activity. The result was that early in the colonial period, Dahomey aquired a reputation for mission-educated academics and administrators. By the 1950s, many middle-ranking posts in the French colonial service — right across West and Central Africa — were occupied by Dahomeyans, most of whom were Fon or Yoruba from the relatively prosperous south.

With few mineral resources — no gold or other precious metals — Dahomey's economy depended very heavily on its **oil palm plantations**. In addition, there were close commercial relations with Nigeria, both legal trade and illicit smuggling.

■ Independence

No single, national leader rose to pre-eminence during the fifteen-year post-war period on the road to independence. Instead, an ethnic and regional competition developed in which three prominent figures jockeyed for political prominence. They were: **Hubert Maga** representing the north, **Migan Apithy** of the southeast, and **Justin Ahomadegbe** from the southwest. On the eve of independence, the three managed to form a coalition, the *Parti Progressiste Dahoméen*, but unity was superficial. Each commanded the loyalties of about one third of the country's population and distrusted the others. After some seventy years of French rule, the **Republic of Dahomey** became independent on August 1, 1960.

In December, 1960, **elections** were held in which Maga's *Parti Dahoméen de l'Unité* won. The northerner became the nation's first president. But an uneasy dissatisfaction prevailed in the south where supporters of Apithy and Ahomadegbe suspected the new leader was trying to consolidate his position and eliminate his two most formidable rivals. By 1963, unrest had led to **political riots** as students and workers took to the streets of Cotonou. Truckloads of angry northerners descended on the town to confront the protestors.

■ Years of Instability

The situation had got out of hand and it was clear that serious violence would ensue if Maga stayed in power. At the same time, it also seemed possible that the north would try to secede if either of Maga's rivals took over the presidency.

The impasse was resolved in October 1963 when Maga was deposed in a **military coup** led by **Colonel Christophe Soglo**. The takeover was not a sudden or unexpected event, however. For two days prior to the coup, Soglo met with Maga and Apithy (who was vice-president) and members of the trade unions and the army. His ascent to power seemed the only way to maintain order. Soglo never mobilised the army and no shots were ever fired. After taking over the leadership, he immediately set about restoring civilian rule. A new constitution was adopted and, in January 1964 transparently undemocratic **"elections"** took place.

During the period of military rule, **Apithy and Ahomadegbe** had formed a coalition party which received 99.8 percent of the vote. Maga had meanwhile been jailed on charges of conspiracy to assassinate the two southern leaders. Apithy thus became the new president and Ahomadegbe took on the job of prime minister. Under a false guise of unity, the two men worked against one another, each trying to consolidate his own position within the party. The **exclusion of the north** from the political process led to more riots and bloodshed in Parakou and there were more political detentions for conspiracy to overthrow the government. But what brought the two southern leaders to loggerheads was a law concerning the appointment of members to the Supreme Court – Maga happened to be on trial at the time – which placed the judiciary in conflict with the government. Ahomadegbe, with the party behind him, demanded President Apithy's resignation. The president refused. Chaos within the party was coupled with widespread public discontent from outside its ranks, which reached fever pitch with the announcement of a 25 percent salary cut for civil servants to try to reduce the country's bugeoning deficit. In its distress, the government was virtually unable to act and normal adminstration began to break down. The military again intervened, and Colonel Soglo forced both Apithy and Ahomadegbe to step down.

A provisional government, headed by **Tahirou Congacou**, who was president of the National Assembly, released Maga from prison and set about writing a new constitution with the joint consultation of all three leaders. Elections were to be held in January 1966, but campaigning never began as, still posturing for position, Maga and Apithy allied themselves against Ahomadegbe in a move which triggered trade union protest. On December 22, 1965, Soglo intervened for a third time, and on this occasion assumed power as the head of a **military regime**. Maga, Apithy and Ahomadegbe exiled themselves in Paris.

Soglo remained head of state for two years, but his term soon met with criticism. He was accused of mishandling Dahomey's affairs and of presiding over a military structure that was rife with **corruption**. In 1967, workers went on strike to protest against intolerable economic conditions. The subsequent and predictable ban on union activity led to yet another, equally predictable **coup**, led by **Major Maurice Kouandété**, and supported by junior officers including one **Captain Mathieu Kérékou**.

■ Continuing Coups

After protracted disputes and negotiations, the army chief of staff **Alphonse Alley** took over as head of state, with **Major Maurice Kouandété** his prime minister. The military government had a strong, northern cast. Kouandété drew up another constitution and scheduled new elections for May 1968. Many politicians were banned from participating, however, including the elder statesmen, Maga, Apithy and Ahomadegbe. The trio, reunited in their exclusion, called for a boycott, and on the day of the elections, only 26 percent of the eligible voters turned out. An unknown doctor, **Basil Akjou Moumuni**, won the presidency, but the elections were immediately annulled, and the military instead conferred the presidency on a low-profile former Foreign Minister, **Emil Derlin Zinsou**.

In December 1969, sixteen months into his term, Zinsou was himself overthrown by the same man who had put him in power, **Kouandété**. The newest coup was spurred by divisions within the military and seemed to have more to do with corruption and personality differences than with ethnic tensions. Though there was no special crisis to justify the military takeover, it was the first time force was used. Zinsou's car was sprayed with bullets in downtown Cotonou, but the president escaped with his life.

Fellow officers prevented Kouandété taking power himself. Instead, a **Military Directorate** was established with Lieutenant-Colonel **Paul Emile de Souza** in charge. Once more, elections were set and this time the three old-guard politicians were allowed to participate. Maga was set to win in his loyal Atakora region, but not to receive a majority over Apithy and Ahomadegbe combined. De Souza cancelled the Atakora poll. Declaring that the north would secede if the Military Directorate refused to accept his presidency, Maga pushed the country to the brink of civil war. Apithy upped the stakes by stating his region would attach itself to Nigeria if Maga was instated. In a last-ditch compromise to save Dahomey from self-destruction, a **Presidential Council** was formed in which the three men would rotate power every two years. Maga was the first to serve as president, replaced in 1972 by Ahomadegbe.

The system seemed to be working when, in 1972, internal rivalries within the army triggered two mutinies at the Ouidah military camp. Though they were put down, more than twenty high-ranking officers, were arrested, and six of them, including Kouandété, sentenced to death. That move prompted one last coup, led by a man who, like Kouandété, was a northerner from Natitingou – **Major Mathieu Kérékou**.

■ Stability at last – and a step to the Left

At the time of Kérékou's takeover on **October 26, 1972**, Dahomey had suffered nine changes of government in twelve years. Adminstration had grown used to the notion of government by crisis control and the nation had struggled with no clear lead and almost continual uncertainty.

Although remarkable **stability** marked the next and most recent phase in the country's history, it seemed at first that the pattern of biennial coups might continue. In **1973**, the national radio, "The Voice of the Revolution" reported that top-ranking military officers had been arrested for trying to overthrow the government. Later that year, some 180 student organisations were banned following demonstrations and strikes.

1975 was another bleak year for the government. Finance Minister Janvier Assogba was arrested after it was disclosed he had documents allegedly linking the president and other important government members in a financial scandal. In March, former president Zinsou was sentenced to death in absentia (he had been living in Paris where he headed the outlawed *Parti Democratic Dahoméen*) for allegedly planning to assassinate Kérékou. And in May, Captain Aikpe, the Minister of the Interior, was shot to death by a Kérékou bodyguard when the president allegedly caught him *in flagrante delicto* with Mme. Kérékou.

In **1977** there was another dramatic **coup attempt** when a group of **mercenaries** landed at Cotonou airport and, after trying to shell the presidential mansion, were forced to retreat (events on which some of Frederick Forsyth's thriller *The Dogs of War* are said to have been based). Most of the mercenaries, led by the notorious thug Bob Denard, were French and, afterwards, already dismal Franco-Béninois relations sank to a new low. Morocco, Gabon and the *Mouvement de la Rénovation du Dahomey* – an exiled political party based in Brussels – were all implicated. A personal experience of the events is described by Bruce Chatwin, in typically laconic fashion, in "A Coup" (*Granta 10: Travel Writing*, Penguin, 1984).

Kérékou's revolution

Kérékou has weathered all the storms. Two years after his coup, the new leader announced that Dahomey would engage in a **popular revolution**, embarking on a socialist path based on Marxism-Leninism. The country established relations with the People's Republic of China, Libya and North Korea and received the blessing of Sekou Touré of Guinea. Benin also moved closer to the Soviet Union and its tributary states

Also in 1975, Kérékou changed the country's name from Dahomey to the **République Populaire du Benin** and launched the single political party, the *Parti de la Révolution Populaire du Benin* (PRPB). The new course instigated significant changes. Schools were nationalised, the legal system was reorganised and committees were established round the country to stimulate participation in local government. In 1977, a *Loi Fondamentale* established new political structures including the *Assemblée Nationale Révolutionnaire*. In 1979, the assembly's 336 members were selected by the party and approved by 97 percent of the voters. Later in the year, the party selected Kérékou as the sole presidential candidate and the assembly unanimously elected him in February 1980.

The 1980s

It would be hard to assert that Kérékou was ever a committed Marxist. Certainly it was a late conversion which only became clear after he took power and which was only defined in 1974. While the **centralised economy** has hardly produced miracles for the nation, the revolutionary stance has probably been a major contributing factor in maintaining stability since the 1970s. In the first place, it has significantly reduced the regional disputes that continuously brought down early governments, by shifting political argument from ethnic loyalties to issues of social and economic ideology. It has also helped to appease Benin's radical intelligentsia. For a long time, Benin's dissatisfied intellectual elite (the French called the country the "West African Latin Quarter") were unable to find work in the stagnant economy. Their calls for radical reforms in the early days of independence were popular with unions and student groups and helped to topple more than one president.

But while rhetorically supporting the revolution, Kérékou began gradually to embark on a path of **liberalisation**. By 1982 the government was busy selling off or reforming its unproductive and corrupt state-run companies and *sociétés*. Under IMF and World Bank pressure, Cotonou also began retraining officials and adopting measures to encourage private investment. In 1985, the government asked the IMF for assistance – a policy, it said, designed to "exploit the positive factors of capitalism".

The former leaders, Maga, Apithy and Ahomadegbe had been relesed in 1981 and many other political prisoners were pardoned (though those implicated in the bitterly resented "mercenaries invasion" of 1977 remained behind bars). The country also began fostering **relations with the west.** The relationship with France improved after the Socialists came to power in 1981, especially following President Mitterrand's official visit to Benin in 1983. Three years later, Kérékou made a series of trips to West European nations urgently seeking more aid and better debt terms. He has also moved closer to conservative African nations, repairing old rifts with Togo, Côte d'Ivoire, Cameroon and Gabon.

Most of the policy reforms of the early 1980s were prompted by the deteriorating state of the economy and a scramble to find new sources of foreign aid. **Oil**, discovered off the coast, began to be exploited in 1982. It provided some relief to the government as the country was able to produce sufficient for its own consumption and to export small quantities. Bright prospects, however, turned gloomy as the world price of oil dropped and ambitious plans for increased exploration and drilling were scrapped. With few other viable resources, the economy still relies heavily on the agricultural sector – cotton and, especially still, palm oil. A measure of the government's desperation was the risky agreement it entered into in 1988 to import highly dangerous **toxic waste** (some of it possibly radioactive) for dumping in a two-square-kilometre landfill site near the railway line not far from Abomey. The Nigerian government, which had a problem with a private commercial agreement along the same lines in Nigerian territory, was outraged at the danger to the region and the Béninois had to to renege.

Economic woes had already forced the government to devise extreme austerity measures, announcing in 1985 that it would no longer guarantee **jobs to graduates**. That decision sparked bloody rioting and widespread arrests. Kérékou quickly removed the Minister of Education, who was a Fon, thereby isolating himself from that ethnic community. When the border with Nigeria closed that year and relations with Benin's powerful neighbour deteriorated, resentment also grew among the Yoruba-speaking communities in the southeast, diminishing still further Kérékou's political stock in the eyes of southern Béninois. His resignation from the army seems to have impressed no one.

In 1987, student riots again broke out in protest at non-payment of government allowances. Further unrest, in January 1989 – when the government diverted public funds to pay the military in the wake of two coup attempts by disillusioned left-wing army officers – led to spontaneous oubursts of **violent anti-government protest** in Cotonou, where public buildings were vandalised and shops looted.

■ Prospects for Democracy

Lénin n'aura plus de chance au Bénin
Slogan of revolting students in Cotonou, December 1989

The revolutionary slogans and Marxist vocabulary that lined government buildings and punctuated political speeches until very recently are fast disappearing. Although the Béninois may go on calling each other "camarade" and getting their news from the government daily *Ehuzu*, the climate by the **eve of the 1990s** had changed remarkably.

There were **demonstrations** in **December 1989**, unprecedented since Kérékou's coup of 1972, with public demands for his resignation, for the adoption of a multi-party system and for a complete purging of entrenched, corrupt economic practices. Students and civil servants hadn't received allowances or pay for four months, absenteeism had reached epidemic proportions and the country was in a state of muddle, discontent and stagnation not witnessed since the 1960s. Because of the **fear of coups**, most of the armed forces were no longer armed, and for several days in mid-December anti-riot police stood by in Porto Novo and Cotonou as tens of thousands of protesters roared for Kérékou's downfall. In the middle of all this, Kérékou decided to go on a walkabout in the poor quarters of Cotonou. He got a mixed response, state radio reporting his progress at one stage as taking place "amid ovations and stone-throwing".

The events were inevitably compared to the similar scenes being played out in **Eastern Europe**, and certainly the Béninois were encouraged by the limited news from there that filtered through. But it had been abundantly clear for many years that Benin's wasteful command economy was not working and that the human resources at the country's disposal – some of the best-trained **administrators, teachers and intellectuals** in West Africa – were being squandered by a top-heavy and grossly inefficient bureaucracy.

After the events of December 1989 – which coincided with an agreement by the IMF and World Bank to bale out Kérékou one more time, and pay some of the salary backlog – the Marxist-Leninist ideology was dropped: this was a condition of French economic support. By March 1990, a **multipartite national conference** had been held to establish a framwork for the country's future – and to decide what role Kérékou might play. Fifty-two different political groups were represented, but the newly legalised **Communist Party of Dahomey**, whose leader, **Pascal Fatondji**, has been put forward by some radicals as a new president, chose to boycott the first relatively democratic forum in the country's history. Presidential elections were scheduled for January 1991 and Amnesty International commended Benin for releasing all its political prisoners.

The immediate result of the conference was a totally new cabinet, headed by a new prime minister, **Nicéphore Soglo** and a major reduction of presidential powers for Kérékou, whose presidency for the remainder of 1990 was, however, accepted.

There is a giddy sense of renaissance in Benin. With the referendum of August 1990 overwhelmingly supporting the conference's draft multi-party constitution, the way forward seems opitimistically set for a country which has had a particularly rough time over the last thirty years. There is, too, an international factor at work. Benin is now seen as the **barometer of West African democratisation** and its success or failure in the early 1990s is likely to be interpreted as an omen to the rest of the region.

COTONOU AND THE COAST

COTONOU is one of West Africa's least enticing cities. Though the population is under half a million, it spreads over a considerable reach of monotonously flat, lagunal landscape, clogged with residential, commercial and administrative *quartiers* that run chaotically into each another. Laid out in a grid, the cratered, grubby tedium of the streets is accentuated at rush hour, when a seemingly endless tide of rattling *mobylettes* kicks up clouds of dust and exhaust fumes. You might expect the **waterfront** to add a picturesque backdrop to this bleak environment, but the harbour view is unfortunately blocked by the **modern port** – located right in the heart of town and redolent of export produce that's waited too long in the sun. To cap it all, with not a hill or geographical landmark in the whole of Cotonou, it's difficult to get your bearings on first arriving in the smoggy clamour. Which is a pity, as your most probable desire will be to find a way out.

But the city is something of an African melting pot, with a still intact intellectual reputation. And its immediate saving grace is its fantastic **markets**. For want of other things to do by day, you could spend a good deal of your time in town shopping and browsing. Cotonou **nights**, admittedly, are thoroughly enjoyable by any standards, buzzing with people out to enjoy the cool air, and vendors crowding through the streets. There's a clutch of surprisingly good **nightclubs** where you can hear music till late.

Three of the country's biggest, if not best, attractions are each less than an hour out of the city. **Ouidah**, of Bruce Chatwin's *Viceroy* fame, can strike a slightly hollow note in its "fetish tourism", and the stilt village of **Ganvié** is a thorough rip-off – though none the less striking for that – but the official capital of Benin, **Porto Novo**, has a proud gravity that no amount of superficialising could rub out. It's well worth spending a day or two here, in the nicest town on the Dahomean coast.

If you're heading to Lomé, however, or coming in from the west, aim to stop a night at the virtually derelict old trading town of **Grand Popo**. There are magnificently picturesque lagoons and coconut groves and a renovated, and, by all accounts, very pleasant hotel-restaurant that's not expensive to stay at.

Cotonou

Though it's a large city, you'll spend most of your time in Cotonou's **centre**, hemmed in by three main paved roads – Boulevard Saint Michel in the north, Avenue Sekou Touré in the east and Avenue Clozel in the south. The **port** forms a natural barrier that marks the centre's fourth boundary. Many of the hotels and restaurants listed below are within the confines of these streets, as are the major **businesses**, the **post office** and the **banks**.

To the east, Boulevard Saint Michel stretches to the **lagoon** that cuts Cotonou in two, and to the **Nouveau Pont** that crosses over to the **Akpakpa district**. At the foot of the bridge extends the vast **Marché de Dan Tokpa**, one of the largest markets along the West African coast. Avenue Clozel, in its turn, crosses the river via the **Ancien Pont** and continues east to join the Porto Novo road.

West of the centre, Boulevard de la Marina follows the coast to the classier **Cocotiers district**. Along the way, it passes near the French and American embassies and the imposing Presidential Palace, or **Présidence**, a modern pile encircled by a seriously large fence with television cameras peering from every corner. Continuing along Boulevard de la Marina, you eventually arrive at the uninspiring, but completely luxurious, **Benin Sheraton** and the **airport** in the **Cadjehoun district**, 5km from downtown.

On the north side of town, Avenue de la République leads east from the Nouveau Pont up to the **Place de l'Etoile Rouge** – a monumental square (complete with torch-bearing cast-iron statue rising up from the giant red star at its centre) commemmorating the country's now lapsed revolution. For more, grandiose, sino-socialist architecture, continue from Etoile Rouge by the westbound road that joins the main highway to Ouidah and Lomé. At the city exit, the **Terrain Omnisports** dominates a vast expanse of the **Kouhounou district**. It's another Chinese-built "Friendship Stadium" – the **Stade de l'Amitié** – with a not typically Béninois **pagoda** at the entrance.

Arrival and getting around

The **airport** is 5km from the centre and you need to take a taxi to get into town. Though the fare is officially fixed at around CFA1000, few drivers are keen to take you for this amount: try and get an idea of the going rate, and bargain strenuously.

Coming in by **bush taxi**, you're most likely to be let off in the town centre, within walking distance of many of the hotels listed below. Arriving from Lomé or Lagos, for example, you end up at the **Jonquet autogare** right in the heart of the downtown district (coming from Lomé, if you intend staying at the *Hôtel Babo*, get dropped off there before Jonquet). Other towns in Benin have their own *autogares* in Cotonou (see "Moving On" below), most conveniently on or near one of the three main streets marking the centre – bd Saint Michel, av Sekou Touré or av Clozel. If you happen to arrive from the north by train, the **railway station** is also centrally located, near the port.

Within town, **taxis** are shared and cost CFA100–200 for most destinations; there are no buses. If you're in doubt about the fare, a list of tariffs is almost always handpainted on the dashboard.

Accommodation

From dirt cheap *chambres de passage* to luxury money temples, Cotonou has accommodation for everyone. **Campers** weren't catered for until recently, but there are now several sites to the west of the city on the Lomé road – *Camping Cocotomey* at 5km and *Ma Campagne* at 12km. Pitching your tent in an isolated spot along the beach, on the other hand, is not only illegal but also unsafe. If you're squeamish and not penniless, avoid the low-budget places where the level of hygiene is about as low as the prices: there's a number of very decent mid-range lodgings which aren't excessively priced.

Cheap

Le Muguet Hard to say why this was so called (it means lily of the valley – or thrush, and not the singing variety). A stinking dark hovel but cheap and central. Rooms go for under CFA3000.

Restaurant Guinéen Opposite the *Muguet*, has similar rooms above the eatery.

Jonquet autogare union building (the Lomé/Lagos motor park). Reasonably clean, ventilated rooms with shower sometimes available from CFA3000.

Hôtel Babo, rue Agbeto Amadore (☎31.46.07). In shades of pastel green and cream, this is visible from bd Saint Michel (easy to spot as it's the tallest building around), and represents a better bargain than the preceeding lot. Grotty, but tolerable upper rooms (on the 4th and 5th floors) and well located. Rooms with shower and balcony start at about CFA3200 for a single, and run up to CFA5000 for four beds.

Moderate

Hôtel Atlantique, near the railway station. Extremely clean with landscaped garden in front and American-style bar as you enter. A couple of small rooms are as cheap as CFA4000, although most are more spacious and cost CFA7000–8000. Recommended.

Hôtel de l'Union, bd Saint Michel (☎31.27.66). Spacious rooms with fan or AC from under CFA6000 for a single. Good location across from the *Hall des Arts* and reductions if you stay several days.

Hôtel le Concorde, av Sekou Touré near *Vog* cinema (☎31.33.13). Different categories of rooms, all AC, of which the non-S/C ones are cheapest at CFA7000 for a single.

Hôtel Pacifique, av Clozel (☎33.17.60). Good value, though outside the town centre: cross the *Ancien Pont* towards Porto Novo and it's not far from the bridge. Cheaper non-S/C rooms start at CFA4000 (fan extra); they're spacious and some look out towards the lagoon.

Upmarket

Hôtel de la Plage (☎31.25.60). Near the town centre and the fishing port, this colonial-style place has a good share of old-world charm still holding together, plus a pool and private beach all nicely furnished with coconut palms. All rooms have AC and start at around CFA11,000.

Hôtel du Port (☎31.44.43). Not in the most attractive part of town, but the AC rooms and bungalows are spacious and well kept. Rooms around the courtyard come with balconies overlooking the pool and, surprisingly, there's a garden restaurant.

Hôtel du Golfe, av Clozel, Akpakpa district (BP 37; ☎33.09.55). Clean and roomy quarters with AC, from around CFA10,000. The hotel is near some of the town's better beaches though far from the centre. Restaurant, disco and – more novel – a gym.

La Croix du Sud, facing the beach on the landward side of the bd de la Marina (BP 280; ☎30.09.54). Creeping towards luxury class, but more informal than the expense-account guzzlers below, this has rooms divided between a main block and a complex of bungalows clustered round a big pool, and all the trappings – *boite*, bars and cinema. From about CFA14,000 – not bad value if you've got the cash.

Immoderate

Hotel Sheraton, bd de la Marina (BP1901; ☎30.01.00/30.12.56, Fax 30.11.55), 4km from the centre, near the airport. The best of the international lot, the *Sheraton* has 200 luxury rooms and bungalows (some with hazy ocean outlooks), all fitted out with colour TV, video and phone. The hotel is right on the beach with a popular poolside bar and a flourish of restaurants, including one with first-class breakfast buffets. There's also a disco, sauna, crafts shop, travel agency and bank. The idea is to save guests the hassle of even going into the city, which most – here strictly on business – seem to appreciate. Rooms start around CFA34,000 B&B.

Hôtel PLM Alédjo, on the other side of town, 4km from the centre (BP 2292; ☎33.05.61, telex 5180). A dull modern hotel in a twenty-hectare tropical park, the *Alédjo* finally found a place in history as the venue of the March 1990 democracy conference. There's a pool and the hotel is right next to a protected ocean bay with windsurfing and horse riding. Rooms from CFA22,000.

Eating

Cotonou doesn't have much of a high culinary reputation as far as European and Asian cuisine goes. Local food, on the other hand, is quite good and the Béninois have a flare for tasty sauces made with plenty of vegetables and seafood or meat. There's also a busy clutch of Senegalese restaurants around the Jonquet *autorgare*. For **street food**, try around the markets and motor parks. In the centre, especially the area around the rue des Cheminots, you'll also find the ubiquitous West African *caféman*, serving up fried omelettes and instant coffee on streetside tables.

Cheap

Restaurant Guinéen, opposite Lomé/Lagos motor park. Not the most exciting meals in town, but cheap dishes like rice and peanut sauce for CFA300 will fill you up.

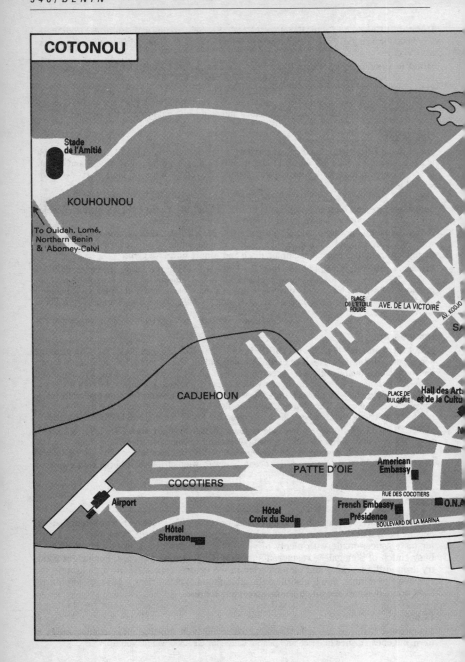

COTONOU

Stade
de l'Amitié

KOUHOUNOU

To Ouidah, Lomé,
Northern Benin
& Abomey-Calvi

PLACE
DE L'ETOILE
ROUGE

AVE. DE LA VICTOIRE

AV. KODJO

SA

CADJEHOUN

PLACE DE
BULGARIE

Hall des Art
et de la Cultu

N

American
Embassy

PATTE D'OIE

COCOTIERS

RUE DES COCOTIERS

Airport

O.N.A

French Embassy

Hôtel
Croix du Sud

Présidence

BOULEVARD DE LA MARINA

Hôtel
Sheraton

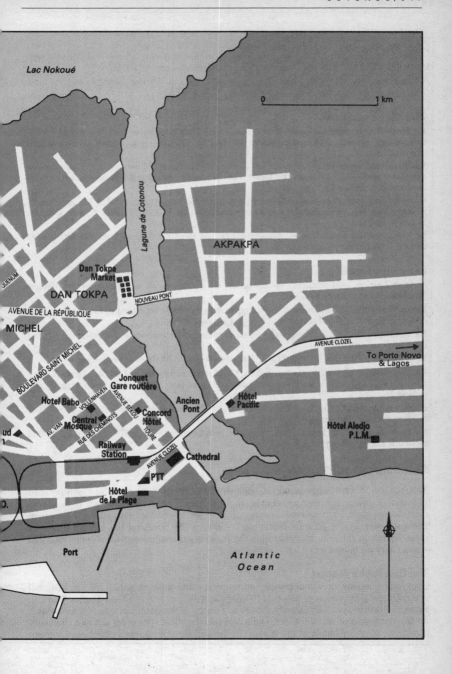

Restaurant Sénégalais, near the *Guinéen*. Rice and fish or *steack frites* from around CFA500.

Gargoterie, bd Saint Michel at the corner of av Sekou Touré. Cheap and friendly with specialities like yam *pâte* with sauce of meat, veg or fish for around CFA200.

Chez Fatou, just off the av Sekou Touré, opposite the *Cinéma Vog*. Senegalo-Ivoirian food. Rice or *moyo* with mutton, CFA500; *moyo* with chicken, CFA800.

Mid-range eateries

La Gerbe d'Or, near the post office on av Clozel. Best pastries in town since way back – rum babas, eclaires and custard slices for around CFA200. Also serves croissants and sandwiches.

La Caravelle, intersection of av Clozel and av Sekou Touré. More pastries, slightly more expensive and not so fresh as the *Gerbe d'Or*. A popular ex-pat rendezvous, however, with food and beer on the upstairs terrace.

Cotton Club, just off bd Saint Michel, between the *Hall des Arts* and the St Michel church. Chicken and rice, steak and chips or tongue and chips for CFA1500. Omelette with salad for around CFA600.

Le Village, off av Sekou Touré, opposite *Air Gabon*. Béninois food such as *pâte* with a wide variety of sauces for around CFA1000.

Expensive meals

African Queen, av Clozet. Pricey restaurant for African meals and eastern curry dishes. Weekend set menu for CFA5000.

Edelweiss (☎31.31.38). Unusual combination of specialities where sauerkraut mixes with African fish dishes. Good service and pleasant atmosphere.

La Verdure (☎31.21.32). Moderately-priced French cuisine and seafood specialities. Behind the *CFAO* supermarket.

Le Calao, av Sekou Touré (☎31.24.26). Intimate French and Lebanese restaurant.

La Fourchette, a block west of av Sekou Touré, six blocks south of bd St. Michel. Classy French cooking which is well-prepared but expensive. One of the city's best for real *haute cuisine*.

Hibiscus. Another well-known French restaurant with good beef and fish dishes. A bit out of the centre in the Akpakpa-Dodome district.

La Pagoda, av Sekou Touré. Showy Chinese restaurant with attractively served food amid authentic decor, but expect a big bill.

Cotonou: spending time in the city

Without too much exaggeration, the only really exciting thing to do in Cotonou is to get out of town. By way of **sights**, there's a **cathedral** built in an Italian neo-renaissance style, but making a special effort to see it – or for that matter, the **central mosque** over by the Jonquet motor park – seems like scraping the bottom of a very small barrel. In the end, it's really only the **markets** that will leave a lasting impression – and Cotonou boasts some very good ones.

The Dan Topka Market

Everyday, a steady stream of people can be seen skirting down Boulevard Saint Michel and over the Nouveau Pont towards the Akpakpa district and the **Dan Topka Market**. From the bridge, you can already sense the energy of the commerce as you look down on the confusion of taxis, traders, stalls and merchandise spreading out in a thousand directions near the banks of the lagoon. In the middle of it all stands the heavy cement shoe-box structure of the **market building**, inside which are the cloth boutiques and stands of merchants. But business goes on for hundreds of metres around this site and is undeterred by the gaping puddles, slippery mud and moist piles of rotting debris that recent rains have left in their wake.

The ground level of the market building is the food hall, devoted to everything from locally grown tubers and grain to boxes of canned *Milo* and *Nescafé*. Other floors have their own ranges of goods. One large section is filled with Nigerian-made cosmetics – skin lotion, shampoos, hair softeners and soaps. *Savon de Marseille* and assorted soap powders crush against Chinese enamel bowls and Nigerian plastics. **Cloth** is an especially important item. Colourful Parakou prints are quite reasonable, though less prestigious than the expensive Dutch wax designs. **Clothes** and **shoes** – flip-flops, plastic sandals, *Bata*-style loafers and imitation Italian dress shoes – also have their own specialist domains and dealers.

San Michel market

The **Marché San Michel**, between the church and Dan Tokpa, is a small, pleasant area, on the edge of which you'll find people selling books – in English as well as French.

The crafts market

Down by the *ancien pont*, the **marché des arts** provides the best location in town to shop for Béninois handicrafts. The market amounts to a series of stalls spread out near the lagoon, where you'll find familiar specimens of traditional national art – for example, the colourful **patchwork cloths** that originate from Abomey and that once were used as the banners of that city's kings. Stitched into their designs are symbolic birds, fish, lions and other emblems designating former rulers. Wooden carvings and **masks** from the various regions are also common, as are **bronze castings**, including the inevitable imitations of the famous Benin busts from the southern Nigerian kingdom of the same name. The **rue du Commerce** nearby is lined with Lebanese- and Indian-run shops.

Nightlife

For a cheap night on the town, **rue des Cheminots** is a lively introduction. In addition to the many restaurants and boutiques that stay open late, a couple of good clubs have made this one of Cotonou's best after-dark centres.

Lido, rue des Cheminots, is top of the list – an old establishment still going strong. Despite the relatively high price of drinks (CFA1000–1500), it attracts a younger crowd looking for music and romantic encounters.

Playboy Club, nearby, is slightly sleazier, and aptly enough named, as the main occupation of male clients is leering at the women as they wind their bodies around a *Makossa* rhythm. It tends to lead to *kolé-seré* (a "stick-together" dance similar to the *Lambada*), and singles rarely leave alone. Outside this area, other places to look out for in town include:

Number One, bottom of av Sekou Touré, is resolutely upmarket with the proper combination of bright lights and dark corners. The CFA2500 cover charge guarantees a well-off clientele, but it's an appealing and lively place nonetheless, especially at weekends.

Mermoz Bar is a lower-key night spot diagonally opposite the *Hôtel Babo* on rue Agbeto Amadore.

Le Memphis, out of the centre in the Cadjehoun district. Lively bar and disco after 10pm.

Hall des Arts, bd Saint Michel. Not a club, but more of a cultural centre where you can catch evening performances of music and theatre (or even magic). Admission is usually around CFA500–1000.

Cotonou Directory

Airline Offices

Aeroflot, Cocotiers, G-24 (BP 032014; ☎30.15.74); flights to Moscow and on to European capitals, twice a month, approximately CFA140,000;

Air Afrique, av Clozel, (☎31.21.07);

Cameroon Airlines,119, bd Sekou Touré, (31.52.17);

Ghana Airways, behind *CFAO* (ex Monoprix) (☎31.42.83);

KLM agent is *SNCI Tours*, place de Bulgarie (☎30.06.02, 31.27.02). KLM operates a bus to and from Lomé, Togo, every Mon & Fri;

Nigeria Airways, av du Gouveneur Ballot (BP221);

Sabena, place des Martyrs (BP 2622; ☎30.03.55);

TAB (Transports Aériens du Bénin), Place des Martyrs (BP 824; ☎30.07.97). Internal flights to Parakou, Natitingou, Djougou and Savè;

UTA, av Clozel (BP 905; ☎31.45.13).

Banks Not a wide choice. In the centre, the best bank for changing money is the *BCB*, opposite the *Air Afrique* building (BP85; ☎31.33.87). Also try the *BBD* on the rue des Cheminots (BP300). Apart from that, the only reliable place to change money is at the bank in the *Sheraton Hotel*.

Beaches Most of those around the city are filthy and, in any case, dangerously prone to the Golfe de Benin undertow. The best strands are in front of the hotels, notably the *Sheraton* and *Croix du Sud*, which are cleaner than those of the *Hotel du Port*. Near the *Aledjo*, the protected cove known as *La Crique* is popular among ex-pats and townspeople since swimming is relatively safe. Don't take valuables on to any beach – *La Crique*, especially, is notorious for rip-offs.

Car hire The major companies – *Hertz* (☎30.19.15), *Avis* (☎31.51.38) and *Europcar* – have branches at the airport. *Hertz* is also represented at 157 av Sekou Touré (BP 8128; ☎30.19.15, telex 5178) and at the *Sheraton*. Smaller firms often work out substantially cheaper, though their cars and conditions may not be as dependable. These include *ONATHO* (☎31.26.87), *Locar Benin* (BP 544; ☎31.38.37), *Sonatrac* (BP 870; ☎31.23.57), and *Locauto* (BP117; ☎31.34.42).

Cinemas The *Cinéma Vog* downtown on av Sekou Touré is good for dated adventure movies and Kung-fu action. Similar stuff is shown over at *Le Bénin* on bd Saint Michel. For more recent films in an AC cinema, head to the *Hôtel Croix du Sud*.

Embassies and consulates:

Algeria (BP 1809; telex 5030);

Egypt (BP 1215; telex 5274);

France, Route de l'Aviation, Cocotiers district (BP 966; ☎31.22.24, telex 5209), issues visas for Togo, Burkina Faso and a number of other Francophone countries;

Germany, 7 Route Inter-Etats (BP 504; ☎31.29.67, telex 5224);

Ghana (BP 488; ☎30.07.46);

Niger (BP 352,; ☎31.40.30, telex 5271);

Nigeria, Lot 21, Patte d'Oie district (telex 5247);

United Kingdom Honorary Consul, M. Inchelin, *Sobepat* (BP 147; ☎ 31.33.42). A consular officer from the British High Commission in Lagos is also available every alternate Monday from 10am–2pm at the Sheraton;

USA, rue Caporal Anani (BP 2021; ☎30.06.50);

Zaire (BP 130; ☎30.19.83).

Hospitals The privately-run *Polyclinic* (☎30.14.31), in Cocotiers, has the best reputation, though the most obvious place to head for with medical problems is the *Centre Naional Hospitalier et Universitaire* in the Patte d'Oie district (☎30.01.55).

Passport photos and film developing Passport photos for your visa extension or onward visas done quickly at: *Photo Minute*, on av Clozel near the GPO, *Lab E Hazaimé* opposite, *SAPEC*, bd Saint Michel opposite the church, and *Zoom Service*, av Sekou Touré near *Cinéma Vog*. The price is around CFA1000 depending on speed (five minutes to two days). Across the street from *Zoom Service* is a place that does one-hour film developing.

Post and phones The main PTT is off av Clozel, near the port. The *poste restante* service seems reliable here. International calls can be made most easily from the **Hotel** *Sheraton*.

Supermarkets In the centre, try *CFAO*, near the intersection of av Clozel and Sekou Touré (opposite the *Number One* club), or *SOMICO*.

Swimming pools The cheapest and most central pool is at the *Hotel du Port*, which non-guests can use for CFA500. Though much nicer, the *Sheraton's* pool costs a stiff CFA2000. The *Aledjo* has a smaller but equally expensive pool.

Tourist information At av des Cocotiers, near the *Hôtel du Port* (BP 89; ☎31.26.87). The *Office National du tourisme et de l'Hôtellerie* (*ONATHO*) occasionally has the *IGN* Benin map available. Otherwise, they won't be able to do much for you unless you're looking to rent a car or join an organised excursion to places like Ganvié or the Pendjari National Park.

Travel agents Smaller car hire companies include travel agents. The most useful address in Cotonou is *Nord-Sud Bénin*, quartier Zongo, near the *Cinéma Le Bénin* (BP252; ☎31.54.57, fax 31.57.55), open Mon–Fri, 8am–12.30pm, 3–6.30pm and Sat 8am–noon. Flights to Paris once a week, usually Sun morning, via Ouagadougou; fare approx CFA125,000.

MOVING ON FROM COTONOU

Long-distance Taxis
Travelling **along the coast**, the main international station is the Jonquet *gare routière:* located near the central mosque, vehicles depart regularly to both **Lomé and Lagos**. The commonest vehicles are *Peugeot 504* saloon and estate cars, which fill quickly before taking off. For **Porto Novo**, head to the *autogare* near the old bridge (across from the cathedral) from where cars and minibuses head out to the nominal capital. Towns in the north – including **Abomey** and **Parakou** – are serviced from a separate station located between av Sekou Touré and the lagoon (near the *Vog* cinema). Note also that the Dutch airline, *KLM*, operates a **bus to and from Lomé** every Mon & Fri.

By Rail
Heading north **by train**, the station is downtown, near av Clozel. One train leaves daily in each direction – the northbound departure for Parakou calls at Bohicon, a short distance from Abomey. Trains also go to Porto Novo and to Sebohoué (60km northwest of Cotonou) via Ouidah. Check at the station for schedules and prices.

By Air
Flights into the interior are all handled by the domestic airline, *Transports Aériens du Bénin*. There are regular flights from Cotonou to Parakou, Kandi and Natitingou.

Ganvié

GANVIÉ, said to be Africa's largest **lake village**, is an extraordinary sight. The entire town spreads across the shallow, grey-green waters on the northwest side of **Lac Nokoué**, opposite Cotonou, with wood and thatch houses built on tall stilts rising above the rippling surface and "grooved", as the tourist leaflet puts it, "not by gondolas like in Venice but by graceful *pirogues* or heavy boats loaded to the boards". Ganvié is only accessible by boat, and the water is crowded all around this part of the lake with bumping log jams of vessels – even the market is held on the water, with women selling wares from their canoes. Not altogether surprisingly, the stilt village has become stilted – overrun with tourists whose presence has encouraged a commercial free-for-all in the little town, destroying the initial impressions of a tranquil aquatic idyll. This seems to be the way with stilt or maritime villages throughout West Africa – Fadiout in Senegal and Tiegba in Côte d'Ivoire have responded to outsiders' interest in precisely the same way. If you have a low tolerance for this sort of thing, best avoid Ganvié altogether.

Some background

As the **slave trade** expanded after the Portuguese arrival in the sixteenth century, armies of the Dan-Homey king swept the surrounding countryside, rounding up people to trade with the Europeans for exotic goods such as cloth, gin and guns. Insecurity led to the widespread migration of weaker communities, and it was in this manner that the ancestors of the **Tofinu people**, who now inhabit Ganvié, came to settle in the area around Lake Nokoué. The earliest may have arrived in the sixteenth century, although at the end of the seventeenth century, an exodus of peoples from Tado near the Togolese border is known to have settled at the site of the present village, where they found sufficient space for grazing and farming. More importantly, the people were safe from invasion since, for religious reasons, the Dan-Homey were forbidden to extend their attacks over water. The name Ganvié probably derives from the Tofinu words *gan*, meaning "we are saved", and *vié* or "community".

Today the town is home to some 15,000 people who make their living primarily from **fishing**. In the shallow lake waters, they plant branches that form a network of underwater fences known as *akadja*. Trapped inside, the fish can either be caught and eaten or sold, or kept for breeding.

Getting there: how to dispose of time and money

The departure point for Ganvié is ABOMEY-CALAVI, 18km north of Cotonou. **Taxis** leave from the Akpakpa market station, but the tourist demand is such that drivers may insist you take a whole vehicle for CFA7000 or more; **collective taxis** make the trip for around CFA500 per person. Once you've arrived in Abomey-Calavi, motorised boats operated by *ONATHO* (some are also privately run) will take you on a two-hour tour of Ganvié – at a price of CFA5000 or so. Some of the villagers also run *pirogue* trips, through their own watery backyards, allowing people to take photos of kids standing on porches yelling "Cadeau!" A bit depressing really – you need to adopt a robust sociological approach to find it an enlivening experience. If, instead of stopping at Abomey-Calvi, you continue 5km up the northern highway to AKASSATO, you can approach Ganvié from behind and at much less cost. *Pirogues* punt you south 4km or so through the creeks and marshes to the edge of the lake and the stilt village.

Sleeping and eating

Tourist facilities have been set up in **ABOMEY-CALAVI**, including decent lodgings at the *Ganvié Bungalow Hotel* (☎36.00.39). It's a small place with comfortable AC rooms from around CFA8000. As an unusual, cheaper alternative, villagers often put up people in their homes and seem to get away with it. Ask around at the dock; someone will make contact. A lakeshore restaurant near the hotel, *La Pirogue* (☎36.00.40), offers an over-priced Béninois and international menu. The *menu-fixe* costs around CFA4000 and there's a couple of bars and a crafts shop nearby.

Ouidah

Hauntingly quiet after centuries of dynamic history, **OUIDAH**, on a back road off the main highway to Togo, works a wonderful spell, exactly as you'd expect. This is, after all, a **voodoo** stronghold and its eerie influence penetrates as deeply as the salt air blowing off the ocean. Clearly, the cult has survived, its power outliving that of the **Portuguese fort**, now a museum, and the streets of French **colonial architecture** – all cracked facades and sagging wooden porches and shutters – now dwelt in by poor families. The **python temple** adds a kitsch touch, but the use of snakes is part of authentic fetish practice – never mind the fact that they get rather more of a workout than they did in the days before tourism. There are plenty of other altars and temples scattered about the town, keeping the faith alive without the touristic overtones.

Some history

Back in the days when the shore of the *Golfe de Bénin* was known as the **Slave Coast**, some of the largest trading posts and slave markets were sited here. Grand Popo, Porto Novo and Ouidah were synonymous with the trade and thus have infamous origins. Ouidah was captured by the "Amazon" warriors of **King Agadja** of Abomey in the early eighteenth century and, in the following years, the town grew into one of the foremost trading posts between Europe and the Dan-Homey empire. The **Portuguese**, who arrived at the spot, then known as Ajuda ("Help"), in 1580, waited over a century to build the fort of **São João Batista**. Part of their story is told in Bruce Chatwin's *The Viceroy of Ouidah* (see "Books" in *Contexts*) and another version in Herzog's quirky film *Cobra Verde*. Nearby, the **Danes**, **English** and **French** also built forts as they tried to gain their share of the growing trade with Africa. The Danish and English bastions today house businesses, while the *Place du Fort Français* now features a small outdoor theatre. Ouidah remained an important coastal city while under French dominion, but in the early twentieth century the colonials built a new and larger port at Cotonou. From then on, the old town went into a slow decline.

The museum, python temple and other sights

The **Ouidah Museum of History** (daily 9am–noon & 4–6pm; enquiries ☎34.10.21) is housed in the Portuguese fort of **Sao João Batista**, built in 1721. Remarkably enough, a Portuguese flag waved symbolically over the building right up to Dahomey's independence in 1960, although the rest of the town was in French hands. The present museum traces the history of European exploration and exploitation of the Slave Coast region, and follows the dispersal of its people to the Caribbean and Brazil. The documentation includes displays of enlarged maps juxtaposed with period photographs and engravings. Many of the exhibits concentrate on the spread of the **Voodoo religion** to Haiti, Cuba and Brazil, with examples of religious fetishes and pictures of rituals.

Across from the large **cathedral** – itself a formidable monument dating from the beginning of the century – the **python temple** guards the secrets of Ouidah's snake cult. For visitors there's no mystery, however. The key to the secret of the fetish serpents of Ouidah lies in the strength of your donation to open the temple doors. It costs about CFA500–1000 for a python pose – wrap-around snakes believed to give vitality and protection over your person. But on days when the reptiles are, understandably, tired, your payment may get you no more than a peek into the room where they're kept. Ever been had?

Accommodation

The sole **hotel** in town, on the main highway to Lomé, is the *Gbena* – state-run, clean and comfortable. At around CFA10,000, however, the rooms are expensive and, by way of an alternative, some of the town's numerous bars rent out much cheaper (and accordingly more basic) rooms.

Porto Novo

Capital of Benin, but only in name, **PORTO NOVO** has two attributes Cotonou lacks – a geographical setting of some presence and a place in **history**. Sprawling over the hills surrounding a sizeable lagoon, the town was formerly the centre of a large kingdom of the Gun people, and the palace of the rulers has been restored. More recently it served as capital of the French colony of Dahomey – the **colonial buildings** are reminders of this period – and the town was, and remains, the centre of the country's intellectual life and something of a barometer of political opinion in Benin.

Around town

Porto Novo consists of four main parts. The **old town** in the centre is characterised by tortuous dirt roads and banco-built houses. It runs into the **commercial centre** with the *grand marché* and surrounding businesses that stretch down to the lagoon on the southern flanks of the town. In the east, the **administrative district** is the location of the former **Governor's Palace** as well as a couple of ministries and office buildings while, scattered around the margins, the zone of new **residential quarters** is inhabited by those who've moved to the city in recent years.

Despite a population of around 150,000, Porto Novo seems much smaller. Perhaps this is because of its coherent layout, but the narrow streets and absence of modern structures also add to the provincial, passed by, feeling: most of the architecture in town harks back to the colonial and pre-colonial periods. To get around, people simply flag down passing *mobylettes*, which, in the absence of cabs, are the taxis of Porto Novo. If the driver's heading in your direction, you can hop on the back – it's one of the many perils of being a moped owner in Porto Novo – for which you'll be charged about CFA100.

Accommodation, eating and practicalities

Although this is the capital, for **banking** and just about every other business, you'll find Porto Novo limited indeed. Everything happens in Cotonou, and Porto Novo doesn't even benefit greatly from Lagos traffic and trade, as it's off the main coastal highway. Even accommodation is pretty limited. The cheapest place is the *Hôtel La Détente*, near the bridge leading into town, and it's not very central – basic, but not unbearable, with fans to help keep the mosquitoes at bay. A cut above the *Détente* is the *Beaurivage* (☎21.30.38) – comfortable S/C rooms, some with AC – in a nice location overlooking the lagoon. The hotel also has a good bar and disco. Porto Novo's best lodgings are at the *Hôtel Dona* (☎21.30.52), a modern place on rue Cachi, near the water tower, with well-furnished S/C, AC rooms from CFA8000.

A recommended restaurant for moderately-priced **eating** is *La Royale* (open 7am–midnight daily) in the Agbokomey district near the *Palais Royale*. This *boulangerie/patisserie* recently added a snack bar and grill where you can get good sandwiches, pastries and ice cream – all reasonably priced – and there's a daily menu for more substantial meals as well.

Museums and sights

Porto Novo's superb **ethnological museum** (see map, open daily 9am–12.30pm and 3–6pm) recently received a welcome facelift from French funds. While quite small, it contains a wealth of well presented artefacts – material culture from all Benin's peoples, but concentrating on the southeastern Fon and Yoruba communities – each item accompanied by explanations and insights. The visit kicks off at the entrance with a pair of beautifully **carved doors** from the palace of the King of Kétou, 100km north of Porto Novo. The rooms inside are each organised around cultural themes – one dedicated to **masks** and other carvings of religious significance, including fetishes used in the voodoo cult, another devoted to **local arms**, with examples of old rifles and poisoned spears, another containing a large collection of Dahomeyan **musical instruments**. A large section of the museum is dedicated to **regional history** and the treaties signed by local rulers that led to Porto Novo's transformation into a major slave trading centre.

East of the market, the **Honme Palace** (or Palais du Roi Toffa) has also been recently restored and can be visited. It's an impressive maze of baked mud and thatch divided into the private residences of **King Toffa** and his entourage and public assembly halls. For the moment, this *Palais Royale* is rather empty except for a few rare mementos of the local kings, but plans are underway to turn it into a fully-fledged museum of local history and art. Recently, too, the Porto Novo *Palais de Culture* was substantially refurbished after a public collection raised CFA20 million on the occasion of the visit by a Council of Europe cultural delegation. It might now be looking rather good.

The market
The **market** is held every four days in Porto Novo, in keeping with the traditional calendar. It's a colourful affair that spreads over a large central square, with stalls selling agricultural goods from the surrounding countryside and fish from the nearby lagoon. Dominating the scene, the curious Brazilian-style building painted in muted pastel colours was built in the nineteenth century as a church, but is today the central mosque.

A side trip to Adjarra
Another important market – also held every fourth day – takes place in ADJARRA, 8km to the east. This small village has a reputation for its **drum-makers** and produces over fifty different types of *tam-tams* varying in construction, material (wood or clay) and

colour. Their quality attracts many buyers from Nigeria. Alongside fruit and vegetables, the market also sells a selection of useful fetishes, medicinal herbs and *gris-
gris*, as well as locally made pottery and hand-woven cloth.

CENTRAL BENIN

Benin's interior is a relatively homogeneous series of **plains** dominated by low, sloping
hills. This was the site of early kingdoms, most notably that of the **Fon** founded at
Abomey. The **Yoruba** also established a number of chiefdoms in the area, while
further north, the **Bariba** carved out a small territory – the **Borgou country** – in the
region of **Parakou**. These are still the main peoples of central Benin, an area of intensive agricultural production and small industries.

Driving north **from Cotonou to Abomey**, the road swings west, then northeast,
then at Sèhouè back northwest again. For the next twenty-odd-kilometres the road
passes through the **Lama depression**, a low-lying swampy region of clay soils,
patches of rain forest and a designated forest reserve, the **Forêt de Ko** or **Lama**. If
you have your own wheels and the will to explore, then turn off left at the **maison
forestière**, 18km from Sèhouè and make for **Koto**, 5km south into the forest.

Abomey

Capital of one of the great West African kingdoms in pre-colonial times, **ABOMEY**
boasts a fascinating history and counts as one of Benin's greatest attractions.
Commercially the town is overshadowed by BOHICON, of which Abomey is essentially the ancient precursor, and which has benefited from its position on the rail line
and main north–south highway (the French deliberately laid the railway to the east of
Abomey to reduce the commercial power of the Abomey royal dynasties). Despite
Bohicon's immense market, however, the town is another chaotic sprawl with little that
could tempt you to stay for a prolonged period. Most people skip it altogether and head
straight out to Abomey, 9km from the highway, which is more manageable and, with
the **Dan-Homey palace and museum**, infinitely more interesting.

The royal palace and museum

In the three hundred years of the Dan-Homey empire, the kings built a magnificent
palace in the centre of Abomey. In fact, it was a vast complex of many palaces, since
the sovereign never occupied the residence of his predecessor, but built a new one next
to the old. By the time the French attacked the city in 1892, there was thus a honey-
comb of twelve **adjoining palaces**, ten of which were soon destroyed by the invading
army. Today, only two – those belonging to Guezo and his successor Glegle – remain
intact, but even these have suffered badly from the effects, ultimately no less brutal, of
the climate. They're being restored with the help of funds from UNESCO. Work carried
out so far shows up magnificently the pomp and grandeur of the royal court – and
there's no doubt that this will be a spectacular site when restoration is completed.
There are even plans to rebuild the ten ruined palaces – eventually – though this would
seem to be a lifetime's work.

In the meantime, you can visit the first two renovations, though it's disappointing to
find rusty corrugated iron, rather than old-style thatch, used to cover the **animist
temples** (where the kings communicated with their ancestors), the **throne room** and
other ceremonial buildings. It's all impressive nonetheless, with the massive walls of
the complex clad in brilliantly coloured symbolic bas relief designs, and as you take the

THE DAN-HOMEY KINGDOM

From as early as the sixteenth century, much of the present Béninois territory was coalescing into small, socially stratified **states** – a string of them along the coast (including Grand Popo and Ouidah) and a cluster of less clearly defined smaller states inland. A more powerful (though still very small) city-state had developed around the town of **Allada**, just 40km from the coast, which was renowned for its slave-trading. At the end of the sixteenth century, three princes were in dispute over the rule of this little empire. The first, **Meidji**, eventually wrested power from his father. Of his two brothers, **Zozerigbe** headed south to Porto Novo where he founded the Hogbonou kingdom; **Do Aklin** went north where he founded the kingdom at **Abomey** in the early seventeenth century.

In 1654, one of the descendants of Do Aklin, **Ouegbaja**, killed the sovereign of Abomey, a king named **Dan**. Ouegbaja then built his palace over the body of the deceased monarch and his kingdom came to be known as Dan-Homey, meaning "from the belly of Dan". In the succession of kings, one of the greatest was **Agadja** who ruled from 1707–1732. He conquered the surrounding mini-states of Allada, Savi and Ouidah and, in expanding his empire to the coast, earned the title *Dé Houito*, or "man of the sea". Having gained a gateway to the Atlantic, the empire embarked on a period of direct trade with Europe, a trade dependent above all on slaves. Meanwhile, however, the powerful Yoruba state of **Oyo**, (to the east, in present-day Nigeria) was increasingly bent on retaining as much as possible of the trade for its own benefit, and through the middle of the eighteenth century, repeatedly intimidated and attacked Dan-Homey, which, after 1748 was formally a vassal state of Oyo.

The Dan-Homey state became a dictatorship under the reign of **Ghezo**, who overthrew the previous king in 1818 and ruled bloodily for forty years. He ceded his monopoly rights in the slave trade to his right-hand man in Ouidah – the Brazilian **Francisco Felix de Souza** – and increasingly preyed on his own subject peoples. His autonomy was only limited by the duty he owed to Oyo. He reorganised the army into a powerful unit comprising 10,000 soldiers and 6000 female "Amazon" warriors, who were better armed than their male counterparts. Trained to use rifles as well as bows, they were reputed to cut off one of their breasts if it impaired their ability to shoot – an apocryphal story that probably sprung from the reactions of European visitors to the sight of well-drilled women soldiers.

The Dan-Homey kings amassed a stockpile of weapons through trade with the Europeans. By the end of the nineteenth century, the royal arsenal was full of modern weaponry and the stage was set for an intense conflict as the French started out in conquest of the interior. Hostilities were high and fighting had already broken out between the French and the Fon when **King Behanzin** led an attack against the forces of **Colonel Dodds** as they advanced on Abomey. Behanzin lost the battle, and the capital of the Dan-Homey kingdom fell to the French on November 17, 1892. Abomey was already in flames as the colonial army marched into the city.

guided tour, the history of this powerful, energetic, brutal society comes alive. All the stools of the kings are guarded in the throne room with their individual banners – including that of Guezo, built on top of four human skulls, a symbol of his conquests and domination over weaker peoples. The banners, which are known as the **royal tapestries**, are themselves remarkable and commonly seen in "best of Benin" type photos – vivid patchworks sewn with symbols and emblems relating the qualities of the various kings.

Part of the collection of the **museum** – housed in one of the palaces – is devoted to the **treasures of the kings**, including gifts they were offered by European royalty and merchants. Mixed in with examples of silver jewellery are wood and iron sculptures, though some of the pieces on exhibit are copies, the original works of art stored in French museums since colonial times.

Attached to the palace, the **centre artisanal** is an effort to keep alive the craftsmanship that was the pride of the Abomey kings. The artisans were formerly constrained to produce their works for the royal court only. They still churn out crafts that were popular with the kings – brightly decorated tapestries, bronze statues made from the *cire perdue* method, jewellery – although the quality required by tourists is rather less than that demanded by the royalty. You can get some good buys here since you're not dealing with middlemen and prices are wide open to discussion.

Staying in Abomey

Most of Abomey's **accommodation** is out of town, the exception being the *Hôtel La Lutta* (BP 2009; ☎50.01.41). From the centre, follow the signs to this pleasant African-style abode with plain but decent twin rooms for CFA3000 with fan and shower. The management here is very friendly and will give a reduction for stays of more than three days.

Many other hotels are grouped about 2km from the centre, near the *préfecture*. Cheapest among them is the *Foyer du Militant*, where pretty miserable S/C rooms cost CFA3000 (no fan). In a similar price range, is *Chez Monique*, an exotic restaurant with pet monkeys in the yard. It's about 500m past the *préfecture* – continue straight ahead where the tarmac turns left. *Monique* has cleaner S/C rooms with fan and a good restaurant. The town's nicest lodgings are also in this area – the state-run *Motel d'Abomey* (☎50.00.68). Spacious S/C rooms with AC start at a not unreasonable CFA6000 for a single.

Another quarter for inexpensive accommodation is the Goho district, also about 2km from the centre. *L'Auberge du Roi* is a friendly and busy bar with music and cheap beer and good chicken and salad or omelette-type things for a few hundred CFA. They also have basic rooms with shower and fan for about CFA2500. In the same neighbourhood, the *Auberge de la Simplicité* is an unambiguous pick-up joint, again featuring cheap beer and music, and especially frenetic on Friday and Saturday nights when they open at 11pm and shake until dawn. Here, very basic bed chambers with showers run to CFA2000 or so, but it's very noisy.

North from Abomey: Dassa and rough routes in the west

The most straightforward way north is by paved road to Dassa and then the rough and ready "paved" **trans-Benin highway** to Parakou. Alternatively you could fork left at Dassa to follow the western *piste* leading directly to DJOUGOU (see p.961). **DASSA**, a village tucked in a landscape of heavy boulder formations and thick greenery, has nothing of essential interest, with the possible exception of the *grotte de Notre Dame de l'Arigbo* – a cave which has become the site of a pilgrimage for local Christians. It's perhaps not a place to stop over, as the only hotel in town charges CFA5000 for a room without a fan.

The western route beyond SAVALOU is little travelled, and involves longer waits for transport. It's difficult going, too, especially the washboard-infested stretch up to **BASSILA** – the first town along the way where you'll find **accommodation** and, perhaps more importantly, a *buvette* with the possiblity of cold drinks. There's a small *chambre de passage* next to the petrol station, run by a very friendly family.

The west is an agricultural region hemmed in by the forests of the Monts Kouffé and Agoua, and was the location of an early **Yoruba** kingdom, conquered in the eighteenth century by the **Maxi** (related to the Fon). These are still the main peoples of the area although numerous smaller groups result in a variety of regional building styles and customs. Despite the relative difficulties in getting about along this stretch it can be rewarding to travel off the beaten track, and you're likely to find contacts with people warm and immediate.

Parakou

Formerly a station on the caravan routes, Parakou, with a population of about 70,000, is today the largest northern town. Its importance still derives from its position on the major roads and on the **railway** which terminates its snail-like trail here. Recent investment in local industry – a brewery, and sheanut oil mill – have brought about rapid growth in the last couple of decades and Parakou is now the undisputed commercial centre of the interior. It's a town of little enduring interest, but abuzz with the activity of hundreds of small businesses, bars and by-passing traders.

Accommodation, eating and practicalities

Parakou has nothing in the way of fancy **accommodation**, but there's plenty of small comfortable hotels and one or two cheaper alternatives. You can actually sleep at the *gare routière*, where the rooms for rent are cleaner than you might expect, and cost under CFA1000 a night. A recommended hotel is *Les Canaris* (☎61.22.94), which has different categories of rooms ranging from non-S/C low-comfort quarters to fully furnished AC rooms with private bath. They start from CFA3000 and are grouped around two shady courtyards with a mascot monkey chained to a tree in front. If you persist, you may be able to sleep outside on the terrace for around CFA1000, though the management is not at all keen on this. Another cheap place is the *Hôtel du Bon Gout*, which shows its "good taste" through comfortable non-S/C rooms with fans starting from CFA3000. The owners are pleasant and run a good **restaurant**.

Moving upmarket, one of the town's classier places is the *Hôtel Routière* (☎61.21.27), with AC rooms from CFA7000, the price of which allows you use of the **swimming pool** and – if you're quite mad – the tennis courts.

THE NORTHERN UPLANDS AND PARKS

Parakou is the last big town on the main road. Beyond it, in the **northeast**, the only main centres of activity are **Kandi** and **Malanville**, small towns bolstered by agriculture and trade. The **northwest**, though harder to travel through, is a region of striking natural beauty dominated by the country's only serious highlands, the **Atakora Range**, and populated by a relatively ancient people, the **Somba**. Two towns of size, **Natitingou** and **Djougou**, are the bases for discovering this outback region. Lastly, northern Benin has some of West Africa's best faunal areas in the **Pendjari National Park** and, in the extreme north, the **"W" du Niger National Park**, which spreads across the frontiers of Niger and Burkina Faso. Access to Pendjari is relatively straightforward and there are several places to stay, but the Benin sector of the "W" park is extremely inaccessible (most promisingly out of Kandi) and probably has abundant wildlife as a result.

The Niger Basin: Kandi and Malanville

The northeast is characterised by relatively unvaried, north-facing, woodland savannah scenery, broken by a series of small rivers (the Mekrou, Alibori and Sota) that descend gradually to join the Niger. It's the least densely populated region of the country, the principal peoples being the **Bariba**, the **Dendi** and the **Fula**. Despite the important highway running through the region linking Cotonou with Niamey, the Niger Basin remains economically undeveloped. Cotton is a big cash crop, but industrialisation hasn't penetrated much beyond a cottonseed plant in Kandi and a rice-shelling factory in Malanville.

Kandi

Like Parakou, **KANDI** was formerly a stopping point on the caravan routes and grew to become a sizeable chiefdom – a vassal state of Bariba rulers in Nikki to the south-east. A small town, it relies heavily on farming, a livelihood with which young people are becoming increasingly disenchanted. They've been leaving in numbers that are unsettling to the local economy and heading east to Nigeria, linked to Kandi by a well-traveled *piste* that heads through Segbana. You may question the attractions of a place from which even the townspeople are engaged in a mass exodus and, it's true, apart from the **sacred house** of the fetisher where you can pick up protective *gris gris* (on the main road near the Catholic church), there's not a lot of note. Still, it's a convenient highway stopover and, with its dusty mango-shaded streets, not entirely charmless.

Practicalities and accommodation

If you're spending the night in Kandi, you have to check in with the **police** and get your passport stamped. Their office is just across the main paved road from the **grand marché** and the formality should only take a few minutes. As district headquarters, the town has such embellishments as a post office, *AGP* supermarket and *BCB* bank. **Accommodation** is limited to the *campement*, about a kilometre from the centre on the Malanville road. Rooms are inexpensive by Benin standards, starting at CFA2000 for a single, and come with bucket showers only if you ask ahead – a pail of warm water left by your door morning and night. Cheap *buvettes* for **drinking and eating** are scattered around the market place.

Malanville

Tucked in the northeast corner near the Nigerian and Nigérien borders, **MALANVILLE** is a trading town par excellence where you can run into people from all over West Africa. The **market** is Benin's largest after Cotonou and large-scale regional rice-planting attracts wage-hungry labourers from as far afield as Mali. The presence of many foreigners, mixed with the Fula and Songhai-speaking Dendi locals who form the base of the town's inhabitants, makes for an upbeat atmosphere that's worth checking out, although the lack of good accommodation and notable sites means you're not likely to want to make an extended stay.

Formalities – and finding a room

Border formalities usually present no problem here. If you're **entering the country at Malanville**, you have to state your destination and intended address. The immigration officers have a list of all hotels in the country – pick any one, there's no obligation. If you only managed to get a 48-hour visa before entering the country, you'll have to head quickly to Cotonou, the only place where you can get it extended. In theory, if you don't take care of this within the two days, you can face a fine of CFA25,000, but illness or another plausible excuse should get you off if you're a day or two late.

The only **accommodation** in Malanville is the *camepement* located near the police and customs post at the town entrance. It's pretty rudimentary, but not too expensive. Numerous **street food** stands line the paved road near the *autogare*, churning out cheap meals for travellers. You'll also find a host of *buvettes* with cold drinks.

When **moving on**, remember that in addition to the many taxis waiting in the central *gare routière*, cheaper state-run **buses** also head south to Kandi and Parakou, but usually quite early in the morning.

"W" du Niger National Park

The **PARC NATIONAL DU "W" DU NIGER** (open early December to late May) spreads over 10,000 square kilometres of wild bush in Niger, Burkina Faso and Benin – an area, virtually without human habitation, almost as big as Devon and Cornwall combined. Though nearly half the park is in Benin, the easiest viewing trails, and all the park lodgings and *campements*, are in Niger and Burkina (see p.152 and p.273).

Most of the big plains game is here, however, if you can find a way in. Although the **buffalo** herds are apparently thinning out and the buffalo is now a comparatively rare animal, **elephants** can still be spotted in the Béninois sector – notably in the Mékrou valley – while in the Mékrou's waters, unmistakeable herds of snorting **hippos** are fairly plentiful. All the cats are found in the "W" as well – **serval, caracal, leopard, cheetah** and **lion** – but you can visit repeatedly and never see a single individual. Most commonly encountered are a good number of **antelope** species – bushbuck (*guibs harnachés* in French), the cobs or waterbucks (*cob de buffon, cob defassa*), reedbuck (*redunca*) and the red-fronted gazelle (very similar to an East African "Thommie") – and, of course, **warthogs** and **baboons**. Aardvaarks (*oryctéropes* in French) are around, too, but their strictly nocturnal habits ensure they're rarely spotted.

Getting there

You more or less need your own 4WD vehicle to visit this park, at least on the Benin side. Even with one, there are very few motorable *pistes* until you cross the borders. The most common way to get to the park is up from Kandi to BANIKOARA, a small town where you'll find the last **accommodation** (a small *campement*) before entering the reserve. From here, it's a short drive to KÉRÉMOU – one of the main gateways to the park in Benin. The area that's most often visited is the 400-square-kilometre triangle formed by the Kérémou–Diapaga road, the Mékrou river (which it crosses) and the Benin-Burkina Faso border. There's a *piste* along the left bank of the Mékrou that leads up to the **Koudou Falls**. A plan is apparently under consideration to build a bridge across the Mékrou at this point and to develop tracks that would follow the Benin side of the river all the way to Pekinga near the confluence with the Niger. In the meantime, you have to cross over to Burkina Faso near the falls to keep on motorable tracks.

The Somba Country

The **northwest** is home to some of the oldest **civilisations** to migrate to Benin – a number of which groups lived for long periods with virtually no interaction. The best known are the **Somba** (more accurately the Otammari, or Betammaribe), famous for the fortress-like houses known as *Tatas-Somba* that they built to protect themselves from the slave raids of Dan-Homey warriors. They still live in largely isolated villages scattered along the base of the **Atakora Mountains**, though the young people are increasingly inclined to migrate to urban centres such as NATITINGOU – the Atakora provincial capital. Further south, Somba give way to the Yowa, part of the same cluster of related Voltaic-speaking peoples, and the Songhai-speaking Dendi who live in the region of DJOUGOU, a large commercial town on the main road to Togo.

Djougou

With a population of some 30,000, Djougou is a large town and surprisingly busy considering it's only accessible by *piste*. But the town's importance as a major regional market has been assured by its position on the main roads linking Natitingou to Savalou and Parakou to the Togolese border and through to Kara.

Accommodation, eating and moving on

Accommodation is pretty much limited to the *Motel du Djougou*, where rooms cost CFA4000 or so. Before checking in, however, you should stop at the **police**, fill out a form and get your passport stamped. Apart from the motel restaurant, the **market** is the obvious place for **eating** – and besides the numerous vendors selling local staples, there's a number of small restaurants and bars surrounding the market square.

Djougou's large *gare routière* adjoins the market and you shouldn't have any problem finding transport to Natitingou and Parakou. Many vehicles also head to Kara via the border post at Kétao in Togo.

Natitingou

Hometown of the president, **NATITINGOU** hasn't received the degree of patronage extended to Yamoussoukro in Côte d'Ivoire or Kara in Togo, but even if Kérékou hasn't attempted to turn his birthplace into the national capital, he hasn't forgotten it either. Though it's only a small centre, Natitingou has received the beginnings of an industrial base with the implementation of a *SONAFEL* juice factory and rice- and peanut-husking factories. You're more likely to notice other manifestations of the president's munificence in the town's modern bank, cinema and beautiful luxury hotel. But despite the perks, the real draw of the town lies in the countryside that surrounds it – a magnificent region of hills dotted with the *Tata-Somba* homes that have become as famous as anything in Benin.

Accommodation, eating and nightlife

The cheapest **accommodation** in town is at the guesthouse-*campement* on the main paved road on the southeast side of town (in the Djougou direction). They have basic, non-S/C rooms with twin beds (you may wind up with a room mate) for CFA2500. Slightly upscale, the comfortable *Hôtel Nantho* – on the main road half-way between the police and the PTT – charges from CFA5000 for S/C rooms with fans, grouped in a courtyard around a central lobby and restaurant. Natitingou also boasts a classy hotel in the French *PLM* chain – the *Tata Somba* (☎21.65.90) – with AC rooms from CFA13,000, doubles CFA18,000.

In the quest for meals, in addition to the hotel **restaurants** and the market, the *City Coffee*, on the main road down by the guesthouse, is good for omelettes and fry-ups. It's also a place to meet young people from the region and possibly work out an arrangement to visit some of the Somba countryside.

Natitingou has a good **cinema** at the south end of the main street. You'll also find a couple of **discos** in town including one built into a "Somba-style" house at the *Tata Somba* hotel. Another popular place for dancing (less expensive and more convincingly authentic) is the open-air *Le Village*, located in the centre of town.

The surrounding countryside

Rather than forming large communities, the Somba built their homes about 500m from one another – the distance a man could throw a spear, you'll be told, which is pretty amazing considering the current javelin world record is less than 100m. Whatever the brawn of their throwing arms (it seems more likely that 500m is the maximum dangerous range of an eighteenth-century musket), this defensive safeguard was adopted during slave-raiding days and the custom has carried over. Houses are still built like fortresses with round turrets for grain storage and internal animal pens. During slave raids, families could hole up in these houses for days on end until the marauding Dan-Homey armies went off in search of easier prey (see the "Tamberma Country" section in Part Sixteen "Togo").

The *Tatas-Somba* still dot the countryside around the Atakora region and it's worth a trip through these parts to take in the unusual architecture, though contact with the people – who tend to shy away from all foreigners, even fellow Béninois – is limited at best. Coming in by bush taxi from Djougou, you'll see some of the architecture from the roadside, notably along the stretch between **Perma** and Natitingou. One of the highest concentrations of *Tatas-Somba* is found further west, however, along the road from Natitingou to the border town of BOUKOUMBÉ. If you have your own vehicle, you could cross the border to Togo near Boukoumbé and drive to KANTÉ (Togo) via a tiny *piste* that leads through the region of the **Tamberma**, a people closely related to the Somba. Though difficult, it's one of the most beautiful drives in this part of West Africa.

Pendjari National Park

The **PARC NATIONAL DE LA PENDJARI**, spreading over 2750 square kilometres of woody savannah north of the Atakora range, is one of the best in West Africa for game-viewing. **Lions** still stalk these parts and your chances of seeing some are relatively good. Other large game you've a chance of spotting include **elephants** (notably in the south of the park) and **buffalo** which roam in large herds. **Hippos** and **crocodiles** (*caïmans* in colloquial French) are widespread in the river, while the same species of **antelope** found in the "W" park, plus **warthogs** and **monkeys**, are pretty sure bets, though as usual, all animals are most easily and abundantly seen at the end of the dry season, when dry conditions constrain their movements by the proximity of water. If planning a trip here, remember that the park is only open from mid-December to the end of May. Permits to visit may be obtained from the *postes forestiers* in Porga, Batia, Kandi and Natitingou,x but for complete information, contact the *ONATHO* tourist office in Cotonou.

Getting there

From Natitingou, the usual overland route goes north through TANGUIETA, a village at the edge of the reserve. There's a small *campement* here (though it's recently been closed) and two waterfalls in the area, both on the road to Batia – the *cascade de Tanguieta* near the village of Nanebou, and the larger *cascade de Tanougou* .

At Tanguieta, the road divides. Most people continue northwest to the border town of PORGO, one of the main entry points into the park. You can theoretically rent Land Rovers here though you may have to book before coming (check with the tourist office in Cotonou or the *poste forestier* in Natitingou), but it's definitely possible to stay at the **campement** – rooms, dormitory space and a bar–restaurant. If you've made it this far without your own transport, you might hope to tag along with tourists heading into the park at Porgo, though it seems your chances would be just as good if you hitched from Natitingou. Stop by the hotel *Tata Somba* to see if anyone is heading to the reserve. Alternatively, aim northeast from Tanguieta to BATIA, where there's also a park entrance, though significantly, no accommodation.

Inside the park, **accommodation** can be found at the *Hôtel de la Pendjari*, located near the river and the Burkina Faso border. They have AC bungalows and twin rooms plus a restaurant, bar and, miraculously, a swimming pool. **Camping**, under the supervision of rangers, is permitted at the **Mare Yangouali** and the **pont d'Arli**, where you can cross the Pendjari River into Burkina Faso and the Pendjari's extension there – **Arli National Park** (a little more detail in Part Five, "Burkina Faso").

index

NIGERIA

NIGERIA

"Listen to Nigerian leaders and you will frequently hear the phrase *this great country of ours*. Nigeria is *not* a great country. It is one of the most disorderly nations in the world. It is one of the most corrupt, insensitive, inefficient places under the sun.... It is dirty, callous, noisy, ostentatious, dishonest and vulgar. In short it is among the most unpleasant places on earth."

Chinua Achebe

W
hy build your hopes up? Nigeria is a country many people feel needs no introduction: corruption, military dictatorships and urban violence seem to be its very definition. And if Chinua Achebe – one of the country's most humane and respected writer-philosphers – can describe Nigeria thus, then seeking to defend it may look perverse.

But in truth, Nigeria's notoriety is unduly influenced by its *de facto* capital, **Lagos** – a city of incalculable population and urban distress. If you can handle the Lagos tempo its one big compensation is fine musical opportunities – no other city in West Africa is as blessed with night energy. If not, then leave the city – for **Oyo, Oshogbo, Ife, Benin**, or even giant **Ibadan** – and Lagos soon seems an anomaly. These hinterland towns, where growth has been less dizzying and local traditions not yet bulldozed into oblivion, still show you hints of the greatness of the old Yoruba and Benin kingdoms in their palaces and museums, festivals and sacred sites.

To the **east** – beyond the natural and cultural dividing line of the **Niger River** – the forests and plantations of the **Igbo Country** stretch out behind the vast fan of the **river delta.** This region has made a remarkable recovery since the civil war of the late 1960s, caused by its attempted secession, and its creek and waterfront towns – **Onitsha, Warri, Port Harcourt, Calabar** – have gained a new prosperity with their oil reserves. They're mostly busy, self-interested cities and faintly anonymous until you root around a little, but the engaging old trading base of Calabar is immediately attractive and probably the country's most easy-going city. There's a conservation focus, too, in this corner of the country, since the rediscovery in 1987 of **gorillas**, long thought to have been extinct, now protected in the wilds of the **Oban Rainforest National Park.**

Central Nigeria is a region of lower population, higher ground and some inspiring scenery, dotted with outcrops and massive stone inselbergs. It is very much the best part of the country to travel around and its main city, **Jos**, is an established old hill station with a rare line in museums. Nigeria's three other **wildlife reserves – Borgu** in the northwest, the new **Sabon Birnin Gwari** and the long-established **Yankari** with its remarkable natural swimming pool are all located in this central region. And the **eastern highlands** against the Cameroon border, are some of the most beautiful and unexplored mountains in Africa, abutting Cameroon's much better known Rhumsiki region.

The north of the coutry is **Hausa-Fulani** territory, predominantly Islamic, like the neighbouring regions of the French-speaking Sahel. There's a more comfortable climate at these latitudes and the cities are manageable, but it's the region's history – embodied in the **walled Old Towns** of Zaria, Katsina and the big metropolis of Kano – that gives northern Nigeria a special slant. While they can't compare for flavour and historical atmosphere with the old cities of North Africa or the Middle East, these emirates do have their special character. In the afternoon crush of the **Kurmi market** in Kano, or wandering through Zaria's striking **architecture**, or witnessing any of the amazing Sallah **durbar** festivals at the end of Ramadan, a much bigger and more rewarding view of Nigeria begins to emerge than the one most visitors bring with them.

Nigeria: the country

Nigerians outnumber the combined populations of all other West African nations. Among its neighbours, the country has an almost mythic status: a "giant" land where the roads are paved and petrol is as cheap as water; where there are four international airports and construction plants for cars, eight TV stations, dozens of kinds of beer and huge hoardings to advertise them; where homes are filled with consumer goods, and the shops and markets with even more; and all lit with electricty that's on more often than not. Illegal immigrants from Ghana, Togo, Niger and Benin see Nigeria as a land of infinite promise – and even when disabused of the myths, they tend to stay on.

Europeans and other foreigners from outside Africa are more of a curiosity. Large parts of the country, especially in the centre and east, are too remote to have had any experience of expatriate workers, while travellers are a distinct rarity. In general, you'll be treated with courtesy and – leaving aside Lagos, some of the other big cities and the legendarily dangerous expressways – you should enjoy the experience.

NIGERIAN FACTS AND FIGURES

The **Federal Republic of Nigeria** is the most populated country in Africa, with an estimated 110–140m nationals (there has been no census since 1963); its land area of 924,000 square kilometres is nearly four times as big as Britain.

The country consists of twenty-one states, each with a governor and legislature. **Lagos**, the largest city (at least 8m inhabitants) is the country's economic and cultural hub; administration, however, is slowly being transferred to the federal capital territory of **Abuja**, in the centre, which became the country's nominal capital in 1976. Principal **exports** are oil, cocoa, palm products, rubber, timber and tin – and money (the foreign debt is in the order of £20 billion, in a major league compared with the relatively small sums owed by most African nations).

Nigeria is currently governed by the **Armed Forces Ruling Council**, headed by **Major General Ibrahim Babangida**. Elections are planned for 1992, when the country is scheduled to return to civilian rule.

The people

Geographically, Nigeria has been profoundly shaped by its two great rivers – the **Niger** and the **Benue** – which flow together in a Y-shape at Lokoja. This isn't the centre of the country, but socio-politically it exactly corresponds to the meeting place of the three great cultural spheres which dominate Nigerian life – the southwest (**Yorubaland**), southeast (**Igboland**) and north (**Hausaland**).

The **ethnic differentiaion** of these regions is a convenient way of coming to grips with exceptionally complex cultural and linguistic groupings, but it does the country's "minorities" – several of which number in the millions and could be in the majority anywhere else in West Africa – a profound injustice. Nigeria in fact has no fewer than 250 peoples, speaking nearly as many languages in perhaps a total of 400 dialects, making it one of the world's most linguistically complex regions.

The **Nupe** are a major group in the central part of the **southwest** and are culturally somewhat assimilated to the Yoruba. Other non-Yoruba speakers include **Edo**, **Urhobo**, **Itsekeri** and **Ijaw**.

In the **Southeast**, the Igbo have cultural affiliations with the **Tiv** and **Jukun**. They are almost matched in numbers by people who speak **Ibibio**, **Efik**, **Ekoi** and **Kalabari** – among dozens of other languages.

In the **north.**, the great Hausa-Fulani configuration, has tended to obscure groups such as the **Gwari**, as well as the **Bauchi area** languages. In the northeast the picture is very fragmented and who speaks what and who claims common ancestry with whom

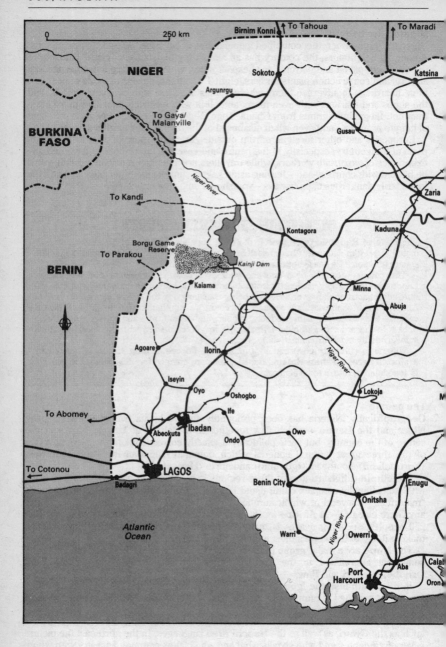

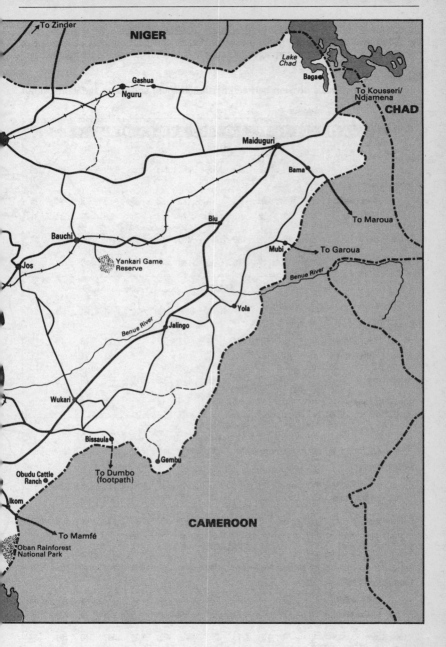

are questions still largely unanswered in many mountain districts where languages of the **Adamawa** and **Chadic groups** are spoken. In the far northeast people speak mainly **Kanuri** – a Saharan language that is the legacy of an independent imperial past.

Climate

There's a clear climatic division between north and south and many variations within the two major zones.

AVERAGE TEMPERATURES AND RAINFALL

LAGOS

	Jan	Feb	Mar	Apr	May	June	July	Aug	Sept	Oct	Nov	Dec
Temperatures °C												
Min (night)	23	25	26	25	24	23	23	23	23	23	24	24
Max (day)	31	32	32	32	32	29	28	28	28	29	31	31
Rainfall mm	28	46	102	150	269	460	279	64	140	206	60	25
Days with rainfall	2	3	7	10	16	20	16	10	14	16	7	2

KANO

	Jan	Feb	Mar	Apr	May	June	July	Aug	Sept	Oct	Nov	Dec
Temperatures °C												
Min (night)	13	15	19	24	24	23	22	21	21	19	16	13
Max (day)	30	33	37	38	37	34	31	29	31	34	33	31
Rainfall mm	0	0	3	10	69	117	206	310	142	13	0	0
Days with rainfall	0	0	0	1	8	8	14	19	12	1	0	0

JOS

	Jan	Feb	Mar	Apr	May	June	July	Aug	Sept	Oct	Nov	Dec
Temperatures °C												
Min (night)	11	12	15	17	17	16	16	16	16	16	13	11
Max (day)	31	33	34	34	33	30	28	28	29	31	31	31
Rainfall mm	3	3	27	85	205	226	330	292	213	41	2	3

CALABAR

	Jan	Feb	Mar	Apr	May	June	July	Aug	Sept	Oct	Nov	Dec
Temperatures °C												
Min (night)	23	23	23	23	23	22	22	22	22	22	23	23
Max (day)	30	32	32	31	30	30	28	28	29	29	30	30
Rainfall mm	43	76	153	213	312	406	450	405	427	310	191	43

Rains in **the north** fall during a single season, roughly between May and September. Usually this amounts to no more than 500mm (20 inches), most of it falling in the months of July and August. Typically the hottest months are March and April, when the *Harmattan* winds have blown their course and the rains not yet begun; at this time, temperatures often rise above 45°C.

In the **southwest**, the long rains bucket down from March to July with the wettest months usually May and June. There's a short lull, usually sometime in August (the "little dry") then more heavy rain from September to October. Yearly rainfall averages around 1800mm (72 inches). In the **southeast**, however, the total amount can exceed 4000mm (160 inches – about five times London's annual average) and there is a continuous and somewhat depressing rainy season from April to October, with rarely much of a drying off in the middle. Temperatures tend to be lower in the south despite the region's proximity to the equator, but the humidity can be really oppressive. The best time to be in Lagos is December and January; on the Plateau, November to February; in Kano, November and December; and in Calabar, December.

CURRENCY

The Nigerian Naira (₦) is steadily decreasing in value. We have therefore given prices in £ sterling rather than ₦.

Arrivals

While Nigeria's big urban centres hardly provide an easy introduction to the continent, the flights from London to Kano can be convenient for starting your travels in West Africa (see p.1061). Note also *Egyptair's* regular flights from Cairo and *Sudan Airways'* from Khartoum. If you're flying into Lagos, it helps to be met on arrival.

Overland routes into Nigeria are good if you're coming across the Sahara via Tamanrasset and Agadez. There are also fast connections along the coast from Togo and Benin to the west, but somewhat poorer road links with Cameroon.

■ Flights from West Africa

Within **West Africa**, you can fly to Lagos from every mainland capital except Niamey, Nouakchott, Bamako and Bissau. *Nigeria Airways* usually handles a good share of the traffic (it occasionally suspends routes), followed by *Air Afrique*.

The most frequent flights originate in **Abidjan**, **Accra** and **Douala**, with daily connections to Lagos. Other capitals have at least one, and in many cases several, flights a week, though Ouagadougou's weeky *Air Afrique* flight takes rather a roundabout route via Abidjan.

■ Other African air links

From **Central Africa** there are several flights each week to Lagos from **Kinshasha**, **Libreville** and **Brazzaville** and a weekly flight on *Iberia* to and from **Malabo**, Equatorial Guinea. *Nigeria Airways* runs two or three flights a week linking **Libreville**, **Douala**, **Calabar** and **Port Harcourt**.

From **East Africa**, *Cameroon Airlines* and *Ethiopian Airlines* each fly from **Nairobi** twice weekly via Douala and Addis Ababa respectively.

The only direct flight from **southern Africa** is *Balkan Bulgarian's* weekly haul from **Harare**.

■ Overland from Cameroon – and Chad

The main route frontier crossing from Cameroon is **Mamfé to Ikom**, over the Cross River bridge. Customs and immigration for Cameroon are in Ekok, on the east bank of the Cross (open daily 8am–7pm), whence you walk over the bridge to Mfum, the Nigerian post.

From here, catch another taxi to **Ikom** and onwards to **Calabar** or **Enugu**. The heaviest traffic is at dusk and dawn, when it can take hours to get through (many drivers stay overnight in Ekok), but because of the geography on the Cameroonian side it's almost impossible to time your arrival during the day.

There's a less used but viable and more direct route from Mamfé to Calabar, turning off south (left) from the "main" Ikom road at **Eyumajok**, after 48km. Note, however, that the Mamfe–Ikom road is frequently impassable on the Cameroonian side during the rainy season. For further details see the box on p.1117.

Further north, out of the Bamenda Highlands, you can cross on foot from **Dumbo to Bissaula** (see p.1050 and p.1132), and there are minor crossings all the way along the mountainous border, but few see much traffic.

The rough route from **Garoua–Yola** is a little busier, as is the route from **Mora to Banki**, a village half in Cameroon and half in Nigeria. Customs and immigration here are generally low-key, but the small post is hardly equipped to cope with the flow of people from Central Africa and waits are sometimes long. On the Nigerian side, officials seem lonely in this remote outpost and eager to chat in English. If you slip them CFA500 that you just happen to have left over, they'll be especially helpful. Taxis are generally no problem from here to Maiduguri.

Finally, there's the northernmost crossing from **Kousseri to Fatokol** (Cameroon formalities) and **Gamboru** (Nigerian post). This is your likely way into Nigeria coming from Ndjamena in Chad. If you're transiting Cameroon like this, the Cameroon customs will issue you with a free one-day transit visa at the immigration post in Kousseri. Further details on p.1059.

■ Overland from Niger

Coming **from the Sahara**, two main routes will get you to **Kano**. The first is from **Maradi**, and the second from **Zinder**. The latter route is preferable since Zinder is a beautiful Hausa town with outstanding architecture and a giant market. This route is also quicker now that a surfaced road goes direct from **Agadez** to Zinder. Coming from Maradi, however, would allow you to take in the old emirate of **Katsina**. You can also cross from **Birni Nkonni to Sokoto**. All three routes are practicable by bush taxi.

■ From Ghana, Togo and Benin

The **coastal route** from **Accra** and **Lomé** to **Lagos** is normally a six- to eight-hour drive in a private vehicle. It follows a well-surfaced road and takes in picturesque coastal scenery (palms, creeks and beaches). It would be a quick trip by public transport too, if it didn't entail three customs/immigration posts with endless loading and unloading of vehicles.

You can get taxis direct to Lagos from **Accra**, **Lomé** or **Cotonou**. They're relatively cheap these days, but you can cut further on costs by taking the taxi to the **Kraké** frontier post and finding another vehicle on from there.

If you're intent on **avoiding Lagos** altogether, get yourself to **Porto Novo** in Benin, from where you can enter Nigeria at the Idi-Iroko fontier post, continuing from here on the A5-1 to meet the main A5 Lagos–Abeokuta road 10km north of Ikeja.

Red Tape

Visas are requried by all except Ecowas nationals and Nigeria is not used to the idea of foreigners visiting the country for tourism. Some land borders – notoriously Mfum-Ikom in the southeast – can be heavy.

At all posts, you may well be asked to pay customs duty. And if your passport or any other details indicate you have ever been in South Africa, you are most unlikely to be granted a visa.

■ Nigerian Visas

In general visas are most easily obtained **in West Africa**, where they are relatively cheap. In **Yaoundé**, and **Accra** for example, visas are delivered the same day and cost under CFA1000.

Elsewhere, Nigeria has embassies or high commisions in virtually all major capitals. **Visas issued in Europe** cost around £30; you are likely to be asked to show travellers' cheques – not cash or photocopies – equivalent to some £40 for *each day* you intend to stay – along with an onward air ticket, or a description of the land route you intend to take, with any visas required already in your passport.

Note that **British passport holders** are at a disadvantage since the imposition of tough regulations on Nigerians visiting Britain. UK nationals are now subject to bureaucratic

obstruction at certain embassies and high commissions.

■ Vehicle Documents

The AA maintain that it's impossible to get information about Nigeria and that because of this they will not issue a **Carnet de Douane** covering it. Drivers are, however, sometimes asked for a carnet when leaving the country. If you have one, be wary of giving it up, as the authorities are not very particular about documents and may not return their copy of the document to your national motorists' association as required, thereby holding up the release of your funds from bond.

As for **insurance documents**, you may find, as have many travellers, that the *Campbell Irvine* certificate, which specifically excludes third-party risks in Nigeria, is acceptable to the police, even though it doesn't cover you. However, as ten days' worth of local Nigerian insurance costs only a few pounds at the frontier, it seems foolhardy not to buy it.

■ Other Red Tape

Entering Nigeria, **jewellery, artworks or expensive crafts** bought on your travels should be entered on the Exchange Control Form. As it's illegal to export antique works of art, there's full scope for anything that looks old to be confiscated when you come to leave. Anything you buy in Nigeria that looks like art or an antique is best sent home through an air or sea freight agency. Nigerians are anxious to keep hold of the few antiques left after 200 years of looting.

You may be told it's forbidden to take **photographs** in Nigeria without a permit (on the other hand you won't have much luck obtaining a permit as no such thing exists). You can expect to be quizzed by the police on your departure, although they may accept your word that you haven't taken any. If you stay long enough, you might have some photos printed to show how innocuous your subject matter is. But remove film from your camera, and repack it, as a precaution, before the border. If you fly out, there's no problem.

Leaving Nigeria, you'll be required to show your **currency declaration form** (the blue *Nigeria Exchange Control Form TE*), and may be asked to count out money and bank or forex bureau receipts for what you've exchanged. Export/import of Naira is limited to ₦52 – any more may be confiscated.

■ Visas for Onward Travel

While it is possible to get visas for neighbouring countries – Benin, Niger and Cameroon – in Lagos, it's useful to know that **Cameroon visas** can also be got at the consulate in **Calabar**, and generally with less hassle than in Lagos, where a letter of reference from your embassy is required.

You can get **Niger visas** at the consulate in **Kano**. Most **other West African countries** have representatives in Lagos. Cape Verde and Guinea Bissau do not; for these, a visit to the **Portuguese Embassy**, one of the few in West Africa, might be worthwhile. For addresses, see Lagos "Directory".

Money and Costs

Nigeria's currency is the **Naira (N)**, divided into 100 kobo. There are coins of 5 and 10 kobo, and notes of 50 kobo, and 1, 5, 10 and 20 Naira. The 50k and N1 notes are being replaced by coins and a new N50 note is due soon. The naira's value has been steadily declining since 1986 when it was heavily devalued, and Nigeria ceased to be expensive (in hard currency tems) overnight. Since 1986, you've been required to change the equivalent of N100 at the border, a figure that's likely to increase. Current official exchange rate is approximately **N15 = £1**.

■ Exchange

When entering the country, you have to declare all your funds on the **Exchange control form**. In practice, these forms may not be looked at when you leave, especially at land borders. Still, be sure to ask for a form even if nobody offers you one – at Gamboru, for example, they have been known to write them out by hand.

Changing money can take ages but is rarely a problem in Lagos. In other towns, banks generally demand the Exchange control form and can also be fussy about traveller's cheques, sometimes asking to see bank receipts from the place of issue. US$ and £ sterling are easiest to change. FF and CFA francs are acceptable in the cities, but smaller branch banks often won't take them.

As regards **banks**, you'll generally have best luck changing francs at the *International Bank of West Africa (IBWA)*. The other main banks – *First Bank* and *Union Bank* – have branches in large towns throughout the country. Recently, a number of privately operated forex bureaux – similar to those in Ghana – have opened.

■ The Black Market

Much of the steam was taken out of the **black market** after the devaluations. You can still change hard currencies on the streets of Lagos and other cities close to the borders, but it hardly seems worth the risk and hassle. Currency smuggling and illicit dealing is treated as a serious offence.

Remarkably few people in Nigeria smoke, so it's one of the few countries in Africa where *Marlboro* is not hard currency.

■ Costs

Although the Naira has been fairly stable over the last couple of years, anything may happen over the next two and, accordingly, we have generally avoided listing prices in the guide.

You should find costs quite cheap – even quite decent hotels can be found for under £10 a night and travel over long distances is a real bargain. But beware that recent government measures, notably lifting the subsidy on petrol, have started an upward spiral of prices.

Health

Vaccination certificates for yellow fever are mandatory and occasionally required for cholera; malaria, however, is the prime concern.

Water is good and drinkable from the taps in most towns across the country; in isolated rural areas, it requires filtering or purification tablets. In the dry season, rural areas are often short of water and poeple have to make great efforts to keep supplied, so if you're travelling in the sticks in March or April don't be surprised if there's a certain reluctance to fill your water bottles, at least for free.

Hospitals are reasonably well equipped in comparison to neighbouring countries. In Lagos, the **Akimbola Awoliyi Memorial hospital** is one of the better places to go for treatment (see Lagos "Directory"). Also recommended is the **Sacred Heart Hospital** in Abeokuta, 100km north of Lagos. In a case of a serious illness, contact your embassy.

Information, Maps, Guides

Tourist offices and local branches of the Ministry of Information can be found throughout the country – and are listed in the guide. There are no overseas tourist offices but embassies and high commissions abroad (see p.18–22) often have pamphlets on land, people and economy.

As for **maps**, the *Michelin #953* is largely accurate and constantly improving. This apart, there is little worth acquiring, though in Nigeria you'll find several larger scale national **road maps** – published by *Spectrum*, *Peugeot* and the *Nigeria Mapping Company* all at 1cm:15km. *Macmillan Nigeria* has recently come out with a new map (also 1:1.5m), but it's disappointingly featureless and quite at odds with the *Michelin* map. The same applies to the *Bartholomew* map (1:1.5m), though it does at least have a little topographical detail.

In the north, **city maps** of **Kano** and **Jos** are available at their respective tourist offices. And for a bigger map of **Abuja** than ours, try the bookstores of the city's major hotels.

■ Lagos Guides and Streetfinders

For a **long stay in Lagos**, get hold of a copy of the annual *Guide to Lagos* by Philippe Dupriez and Jacques Soulillou (in French and English, published by the French Cultural Centre in Lagos). This has complete, map-keyed listings of hotels, nightclubs and travel details, plus considerable cultural information and masses of listings. The guide's "streetfinder" is better than adequate, but for greater legibiity and real detail, get the *Winnay Lagos Street Atlas* (Macmillan, 1985), an admirable full colour A–Z.

A more general **resident's guide** is *Survive Lagos* by Elizabeth Cox and Erica Anderssen (Spectrum 1984), a lot blander than its title suggests and very out of date, but useful nonetheless and with some countrywide coverage.

Getting Around

Nigeria has some 115,000km of roads, about half of them paved. Road transport is easily the fastest in West Africa – often dangerously so. Trains, very slow in comparison, connect the northern and southern extremities of the country. River travel on the Niger and Benue unfortunately isn't developed commercially. Domestic air services are fairly good and reasonably priced at current exchange rates (£30 for the longest flight).

■ Bush Taxis and buses

Bush taxis are quick and – worries about driving notwithstanding – comfortable. Overcrowding is the exception rather than the rule, with a choice usually between a *Peugeot 504* estate or saloon. The seating arrangement is normally one passenger in front, and three in the back, with two more at the far back in an estate. There's rarely a long wait in the motor parks of major cities.

Buses ("luxury buses" as the companies like to call them) also link major cities and usually run to fixed schedules.

■ Hitching

Hitching in Nigeria isn't especially difficult but you need to be confident of your abilities to tell a bad driver from a fast driver, and to act decisively on your conclusion – much better to be stranded on the highway than spread over it. Truck drivers are your best bet, and they'll often want payment, which is fair enough.

It's helpful to know where vehicles are going. The following two letter state codes are the vehicle **registration prefixes**:

AK Akwa Ibom (capital Uyo, near Calabar)
AN Anambra (capital Enugu)
BA Bauchi (capital Bauchi)
BD Bendel (capital Benin City)
BN Benue (capital Makurdi)
BO Borno (capital Maiduguri)
CR Cross River (capital Calabar)
FC Abuja Federal Capital Territory
GG Gongola (capital Yola)
IM Imo (capital Owerri)
KD Kaduna (capital Kaduna)
KN Kano (capital Kano)
KT Katsina (capital Katsina)
KW Kwara (capital Ilorin)
LA Lagos (capital Lagos)
NG Niger (capital Minna)
OD Ondo (capital Akure)
OG Ogun (capital Abeokuta)
OY Oyo (capital Ibadan)
PL Plateau (capital Jos)
RV Rivers (capital Port Harcourt)
SO Sokoto (capital Sokoto)

ON THE ROAD

DRIVING IN NIGERIA

Nigerian petrol is about the cheapest in the world, still only 60k a litre (or about £0.20pence/gallon!). Rates are cheaper still for commercial vehicles, which have separate petrol stations –though these are technically out of bounds for foreigners.

Nigerian **oil** is of high quality and multigrade petrol and diesel engine oils are readily available and cheap. Gearbox fluid (*Hypoy*) and automatic or power steering transmission fluids are harder to come by, though, and even in large towns you might need to spend several hours cruising round petrol stations to find what you need. In extremis, most motor parts shops sell oils loose by the litre.

If you're on a long overland trip, it's worth **stocking up** with two or more complete fluid changes. You won't be taxed at the border and it'll be four times as expensive in the surrounding franc zone countries (and possibly unavailable for days or weeks in the Sahel and Sahara). Beware of taking large quantities of petrol into Cameroon: there's a major trade in smuggled Nigerian petrol, which is sold, often watered down, by the roadside.

Nigerian **motor parts** are good quality and available for a wide range of Japanese, French, British and German cars. Prices are about the same as in Britain but it's well worth knowing the list price of any parts you might need, as the first price may be twice what the item is worth in large towns accustomed to travellers. Small town parts traders will bargain, but usually start off with a sensible price. Many spare parts travel back and forth across the Sahara for years before they're fitted, passing from traveller to trader to traveller again. Original manufacturers' parts, as everywhere, carry a premium.

The main **sale and exchange of parts** (outside Lagos) is in Kano, in the streets around Ogbomosho ave in the Sabon Gari district. As soon as you pull up you'll be offered whatever you want by a young man who doesn't own a shop but operates on commission. It's generally quicker to go directly to a dealer in your make and check his stock personally.

ROADS AND ROUTES

Nigerian **main roads** are superb, and very well signposted. If you're in a hurry in the dry season, it's probably safe to rely on the roadsigns warning you of collapsed sections with a skull and crossbones followed at 100m intervals by 60, 50, 40 and 30 *"Slow Down"* signs. In the wet season, however, a recently collapsed road may not yet have been signposted. Take care.

Along all main roads there are regular roadside **marker stones** marked with the first three letters of the name of the next and previous major towns, and the distance in kilometres.

CAR HIRE

The cost of **car hire** has gone down in recent years, but it's still quite pricey as a **driver** often comes with the vehicle. Many Lagos outlets insist on this – and it's preferable if you're new to the city; elsewhere you may be able to drive yourself. The distinction between chauffeur-driven car hire and taxi hire is blurred; be clear that you will pay for fuel.

■ Trains

Trains, although the cheapest form of transport, are painfully slow – a drawback that's especially frustrating in a country where everything else goes so fast. They're not really recommended, except perhaps along the stretch from **Jos to Kafanchan** (at which point you can continue all the way down to **Port Harcourt**, or cut over to **Kaduna**), where the escarpment scenery makes the snail's pace almost pleasant.

Two main lines run through the country. The first goes from **Lagos to Kano**, calling at Abeokuta, Ibadan, Oshogbo, Ilorin, Minna, Kaduna and Zaria, with a branch line connecting **Zaria** and **Gusua**. The other goes from **Port Harcourt to Maiduguri,** calling at Enugu, Makurdi, Lafia, Kafanchan, Jos and Bauchi. The two lines are connected by a strip of track running from Kafanchan to Kaduna. Thus to go right through from **Lagos to Maiduguri**, you'd have to change at Kaduna, a trip of over 48 hours.

■ Planes

Nigeria Airways links Lagos, Abuja, Benin City, Calabar, Enugu, Jos, Kaduna, Kano, Maiduguri, Makurdi, Port Harcourt, Sokoto and Yola. Tickets are cheap and on some routes there are several flights a day to and from Lagos. Reservations normally aren't taken so get to the airport early even though your plane is likely to leave late.

Although *Nigeria Airways* theoretically has a monopoly, a couple of private companies, **Okada Air** and **Kabo Airlines** (☎934 404), operate from Terminal 2, Domestic Airport, Ikeja. And the new **Express Airways Nigeria**, who are now listed in the ABC world timetable, fly a couple of routes out of Kaduna (Kaduna–Minna–Lagos and Kaduna–Enugu–Port Harcourt) that complement, rather than compete with, *Nigeria Airways*.

■ River Transport

River transport is mainly bulk goods traffic rather than passengers. But boats do operate along some 6500km of waterways in Nigeria: a network fifty percent comprised by the **Niger** and **Benue** rivers. During the rainy season, boats go up the Benue all the way to Garoua in Cameroon.

Since the completion of the **Kainji Dam and Resevoir**, the Niger is apparently navigable above it to Niamey, though below it, only as far upstream as Jebba. Whether you can get transport along these stretches is uncertain. Contact the *Central Water Transportation Division Company* in **Onitsha**, the main river port.

Boats also operate along the **creeks and lagoons** of coastal towns. See details in the Lagos, Port Harcourt and Calabar sections.

■ Cycling

The perspective you get on the country from a **bicycle** saddle is unlike any other. Everyone you meet will think you're mad but the rewards of cycling in Nigeria are as big as the country itself and the supposed dangers fade to a manageable scale among all the pleasures – of magnificent landscapes, bush camping, village markets, small town evenings, off-road explorations.

For safety, you should keep off the main highways as much as possible, but you'll never be ignored, so the fear of being hit is diminished. Be sure to have a mirror nonetheless, and be careful when camping off the road (see below).

Sleeping

In the 1970s and 80s, international hotels started springing up everywhere from Lagos to Maiduguri, Calabar to Sokoto. Although multinational chains are represented, some of the newer hotels, notably in the *Arewa*

chain, are Nigerian owned and operated, cheap by standards of neighbouring countries and very comfortable. Two important, general points to note: all hotels levy a fifteen percent tax and they are wont to charge severe penalties to guests who leave the taps turned on during a cut-off – and subsequently flood the room.

Upmarket hotels have AC, hot water, phones, TV, fridges, minibars, the lot. Some also have tennis courts and pools. Water and electricity go out often and unpredictably, but most bigger places have generators to cope. At present, the price of such establishments is much cheaper than in neighbouring countries, with double rooms from about £25.

Rooms in privately operated **budget hotels** (£2–20) may range from a bed with four walls to gadget-filled abodes cluttered with TV, rattling AC units and leaking fridges. Prices vary according to the perks, which are becoming more and more common. In towns of any size, rooms without electricity and facilities are becoming rare. The term **"single"**, incidentally, refers to the number of beds in the room. The price you pay is for the room, and you'll often find the single bed is over six foot wide.

If you have a vehicle it's always a good idea to go for a **hotel with a compound**, where the gates are locked and usually guarded through the night. There's no extra charge.

■ Missions

In addition to the small hotels, the Evangelical Church of West Africa (**ECWA**) runs a series of **mission guesthouses** throughout the country, often in association with the Sudan Inland Mission (**SIM**). They're very cheap – and VSOs and other volunteers get a further discount. Rooms are generally tidy and spartan but in the better guesthouses – as in Jos, for example – come quite well equipped.

■ Camping

If you do have your own transport, **camping** can be a good option – but the further off the beaten track the better. You should be very wary of camping within 30km of the urban centres and it's wise to stay right away from the more congested parts of the south. Don't camp anywhere near busy roads with a car or other large vehicle, as the attention you'll attract spreads rapidly and isn't always welcome.

Eating and Drinking

European, Lebanese and Asian restaurants are found in pretty much any large town, and most hotels also have their own restaurants for either Nigerian or European meals (often with two menus). Beware that Nigerian food in the south is usually eaten firey hot with a devotion to chilli that makes a vindaloo seem mild by comparison. Many hotels also serve English breakfasts of eggs, toast, marmalade, tea and juice – a pleasant change from the *baguette* and coffee round of the francophone countries.

Assuming you're eating in **local restaurants and chop houses** – *buka* in Yoruba – there's a wide range of foods and dishes you'll come across (see box). In addition, chicken and chips, and omelette and chips are universally available (in cheaper places the price of an omelette includes bread and "Lipton's").

Vegetarians have a moderately difficult time in restaurants, as many apparently vegetarian items on menus should be understood as "plus a bit of meat" – usually goat. But salad vegetables are often crisp and fresh, and delicious once you overcome any worries about them having been washed in unsterilised water. Good transport helps to provide fresh fruit and veg even to dry regions and parts of the country where they would otherwise be out of season.

Travelling cheaply – cycle camping, for example – it's easy enough to **live on the basics**.

NIGERIAN NOSH

THE BASICS

Eba	Moist ball of steamy **gari** (cassava flour), overwhelmingly the favourite national dish, bland on its own and extremely heavy but always eaten with a hot sauce.	*Pounded yam*	Boiled yam that's been pounded to a wonderful, glazey, aerated blob – which can be delicious when you're really hungry. Commonly eaten in the south, often with a palm oil or groundnut-based soup.
Amala	Yams ground before boiling – the finished product has a brown colour of little initial appeal.	*Fufu*	Fermented pounded cassava.

THE TASTY PART

Soup	Any stew, often thick, often hot.	*Igbin,*	Large forest snails; they taste rubbery and are usually eaten with an extremely hot sauce.
Dodo	Fried plantains.		
Begiri	Yoruba bean soup.		
Bitter leaf	Not far from spinach.	*Eja gbigbe*	Yoruba smoked fish on a stick .
Egusi	Oily soup based on pounded melon seeds, usually containing stock fish or meat and green leaves (bitter leaf or pumpkin leaf).	*Akara*	Beans (cow peas or *Ogbono*), "draw soup"; Igbo soup which "draws" (ie it's mucilaginous or viscous) , made from ground Ogbono seeds.
Moin–moin	A delicious steamed bean cake snack with a slightly gelatinous texture, found mainly in the south.	*Stock fish*	Air dried fish, usually cod (from Norway) soaked and cooked.
		Jollof Rice	Rice cooked with palm oil, served with vegetables and meat.
Suya	Grilled kebabs of beef, mutton or occasionally camel, sold everywhere but especially in the north. In the Yoruba and Ibo countries you'll find a variation on these kebabs made from black-eye peas, or fried bean fritter.	*Okro*	Gumbo, okra, ladies' fingers.
		Cowleg . . .	Well, that's what shin of beef is.
		Bushmeat	Any kind of game meat, including antelope but the most valued is grass-cutter (or cutting-grass), the giant herbivorous rodent also known as cane rat and, euphemistically in French, as *agouti* (an unrelated animal).

Bread and *Blue Band*, hard-boiled eggs, portions of deep-fried fish (with or without scalding chilli sauce), bananas and salted roast peanuts make for a reasonably balanced diet that's obtainable in the remotest parts of the country. While supplies of milk are less reliable than in neighbouring countries, you can find milk powder all over (pushed by the drug companies for baby feed) which mixes well with chocolate powder (also widely available). The worst aspect of the diet is the bread – sweet, brick-shaped, often coloured yellow or pink and plastic bagged.

■ Drinking

Nigerians are great **beer** drinkers. Every state has its own breweries and their advertisment hoardings are one of the countries' most pervasive symbols. A widely available brand is *Star* – light lager relatively low in alcohol. Other of thirty-odd brands include *Gold*, *Rock*, *Gulder* and *Double Crown*. Beware cheaper brands, which tend to provoke treacherous hangovers and, so many people maintain, diarrhoea. And be cautious with Nigerian *Guinness* – which is an impressive eight percent alcohol by volume.

Palm wine, tapped from oil palms, is drunk in the south and pasteurised bottled versions have appeared recently, although their taste is a far cry from the frothy sweetness of the bush brews. Distilled, the wine becomes potent *ogogoro*, also common but usually more discreetly sold.

Coke, *Sprite*, *Fanta* and *Doctor Pepper* figure prominently in a long list of minerals manufactured in Nigeria. You can find them cold from fridges all over the country.

Languages, Post, Phones, and Media

Nigeria's official language is English and in the larger cities – especially those with universities – it's spoken widely and with accents you'll adapt to easily. Pidgin English, however, which is spoken as a lingua franca everywhere, especially in the smaller towns and rural areas, will initially throw you. Keep trying, though; ask people to repeat phrases, and before long most people find their own speech punctuated with pidgin expressions.

The three most widely spoken ethnic languages are **Hausa** (see box p.134), **Yoruba**

and **Igbo** (see boxes overleaf). Next to these, there are some 400 separate dialects representing twelve language families. The linguistic situation in central and southeast Nigeria is one of the most complicated in the world and on the islands of the Delta region there are villages a few kilometres apart with mutually incomprehensible mother tongues.

Keeping in touch

Mail is unpredictable and letters to and from Europe can take anything from a couple of days to a fortnight or more. The *poste restante* in Lagos, however, despite its disorganised state – all letters are thrown in a pile and tied together with string – works relatively well. Kano and Kaduna also seem reasonable places to receive mail. **To send mail out**, many people still use courier firms or friends flying abroad.

Telephones are run by NITEL. **Phoning abroad**, you can dial directly from Lagos and a couple of other cities; the best lines are from Kaduna. Connections are usually good, but you may be cut in the middle of a conversation for no apparent reason. To make a reverse-charge (collect) call abroad, dial the foreign operator, access code ☎191.

■ The Media

Nigeria is a country where it's fun to read the **newspapers**. They're outspoken and informative and there are lots of them. Coming from Cameroon, Benin or Togo, the press seems remarkably free and the frankness of the editorials and bite of political cartoons is refreshing. Of course there are limits to how far criticism can go (as Dele Giwa, the murdered editor of

YORUBA

Yoruba is a difficult, tonal language, a cluster of close dialects in the Kwa grouping. Because meaning is so dependent on tone, messages can be easily understood with little vocalisation. Talking drums were (and still are) literally able to transmit messages. And you don't have to listen to much of Sunny Ade's music to realise how easily this is accomplished. The "diacritics" in the following words and phrases are not accents but indicate the tone of the sound – either rising (´), or falling (`). E is pronounced "Eh" or "Ey" and O is pronouced "Or" or "Oh". E is the plural or formal prefix.

GREETINGS

Good morning	*E káàárò*	Greeting someone just arriv-ing or returning	*E káàbò*
Response	*E káàárò*		
Good afternoon	*E káàsán*	Greeting someone who is working	*E kúushé*
Response	*E káàsán*		
Good evening	*E káalé*	Response (lit. thank-you)	*Adúpé*
Response	*E káalé*	How are you?, how's life?	*Shé alááffà ni*
On entering a house	*E kúulé*	Response (lit. thank-you)	*Adúpé*
Response	*E káàbò*	Goodbye	*Ó dàbò*

PERFUNCTORY CONVERSATION

I want	*Mo féé*	Money	*Owo*
I don't want	*Mi ò féé*	Please, reduce the price	*E dín owó lori e*
Which one	*È wo?*	Give me	*E fún mi*
This is the one	*Eléyìí*	All right, okay	*Ó dáa*
Take (it)	*E gbà*	Please	*E jòó*
Water	*Omi*	Don't be annoyed	*E má bínú*
Meat	*Eran*	What's your name?	*Kini oruko ré?*
Palm wine	*Emmu*	My name is Dayo	*Dayo ni oruko mi*
Thank you (on receiving it)	*E sheé*	Greetings/commiserations	*Pèlé*
How much is (it)?	*Èló ní?*	I don't understand Yoruba	*Mi ò gbo Yoruba*
It's X naira	*Naira X ni*	No, (not) at all	*Rárá*
To pay	*Sanwó*	My friend	*Òré mi*

NUMBERS

1	ookan	9	mesan	17	metadinlogun	30	ogbon
2	méjì	10	mewa	18	mejidinlogun	40	ogoji
3	méta	11	mokanla	19	mokondinlogun	50	adota
4	merin	12	mejila	20	ogun	60	ogota
5	marun	13	metala	21	mokan le logun	70	aadorin
6	mefa	14	merinla	22	meji le logun	80	ogorin
7	meje	15	mèedogun	25	mèd ogbon	90	adorun
8	mejo	16	meridlogun	26	meridin logbon	100	ogorun

Newswatch found out too late), but there is a real range of styles and opinions.

Most of **Nigeria's papers** are privately owned ventures (though *Daily Times Publications* is a government-owned company).

Some fifteen percent of the population reads the news regularly and the major dailies have circulations ranging from 150,000–400,000. New titles appear on the stands all the time, but of the 100 or more tabloids printed throughout the country, six national dailies dominate – *The Guardian, Daily Times, The Punch, New Nigerian, Vanguard* and *National Concorde.* The *Guardian* and *Concorde* provide the most complete economic and political analysis (the *Daily Times* has far and away the biggest circulation) but none of the papers is particularly strong on international news. There are some big circulation Sundays, too – with the *Sunday Times* weighing in with a readership of 500,000 – and some twenty weekly news magazines are also published, including *Newswatch*.

IGBO

Igbo is also a tone language and part of the great Kwa grouping – but it is not intelligible to Yoruba speakers.Again, be prepared to squeeze your mouth a little to get an intelligible vowel sound.

GREETINGS

Hi/How are you?	*Kèdú/Kèdú ka í mère ?*	Welcome (to one who	*Nnòo*
How are the children?	*Kèdú maka umú-àka?*	has arrived)	
I'm fine	*Ó dì nma*	Keep up the good	*Jisie ike*
Good morning?	*Ututu òma?*	work/well done	
Good night	*Ka chíí fò*	Thank you	*Daalu/Imèela*
		Good bye	*Ka e mesia*

BASIC CHAT

Please	*Bikó*	How much?/how much	*Olé?/ Egó olé?*
Sorry (commiserations)	*Ndó*	money?	
What's your name?	*Kèdú àha gí?*	Give	*Nyé*
My name is	*Áhà m bu Theodora*	Give me	*Nyé m*
Where are you from?	*E bèè ka ísì?*	Come	*Byá*
I'm from Scotland	*E sim Scotland*	Go	*Jé*
Where are you going?	*E bèè ka í na-ijè?*	Come in	*Bhàta*
I'm going to Enugu	*Á na m èje Enugu*	Good	*Ézí*
I want	*Á chorò m*	This soup's tasty	*Ófé tòrò èto*
I want to go to the market	*Á chorò m ije ahia*	It's good	*Ó dè úmá*
I want to buy	*Á chorò m ego*	Meat	*Áné*
This one	*Nke á*	Pepper	*Ose*
How much is this?	*Nka á bù olé?*	Water	*Mmírí*

NUMBERS

1	*ótu*	9	*itenanì*	17	*irí na asáà*	50	*irí ìsé*
2	*abúo*	10	*irí*	18	*irí na asáto*	60	*irí ìsí*
3	*àtó*	11	*irí na ótu*	19	*irí na itenanì*	70	*irí asáà*
4	*ànó*	12	*irí na abúo*	20	*irí abúo*	80	*irí asáto*
5	*ìsé*	13	*irí na àtó*	21	*irí abúo na ótu*	90	*irí itenanì*
6	*ìsí*	14	*irí na ànó*	22	*irí abúo na abúo*	100	*nari*
7	*asáà*	15	*irí na ìsé*	30	*irí àtó*	1000	*puku*
8	*asáto*	16	*irí na ìsí*	40	*irí ànó*		

Political affiliations are shifting as the elections approach. The *Guardian*, which used to be noted for its objective independence, is now a platform for its publisher who has politcal aspirations. *Concorde* is owned by Muslim Yoruba millionaire M. K. O. Abiola and kowtows to his line on everything. The *Tribune* is Awolowo's (see p.988) paper. The *Vanguard*, at least, is still a small and committed outfit, with some excellent columnists.

Television

The government runs a tight monopoly on **television** through **NTA** – the Nigerian Television Authority. In addition, eight state-run TV stations broadcast regional programmes, interspersed with the national programmes (news, serials, talk shows) and foreign productions. Programmes are in English and national languages (Igbo, Yoruba, Hausa).

Radio

Radio is organised much like television with the **FRCN** – Federal Radio Corporation of Nigeria – being the national body that corresponds to *NTA*. Individual stations for the different states also broadcast their own medium-wave programmes. The *FRCN* puts out three short-wave programmes in English and national languages nationwide.

You can also receive *Voice of Nigeria* transmissions – in English, French, German, Spanish, Hausa, Arabic and Swahili – abroad.

NIGERIAN TERMS – A GLOSSARY

Abule Hamlet or small village (Yoruba).

AFRC Armed Forces Ruling Council.

Agbada Yoruba cloak for men.

Alhaji One who has been to Mecca.

Amingo White person (from Portuguese), used in Cross River State.

Ariya Enjoyment, having a good time.

Babanriga Long Hausa tunic.

Batoure White person (Hausa).

Buba Yoruba shirt.

Buka Chop house (Yoruba).

Chiroma Traditional title of the far northeast.

Dash Bribe or payment for service rendered or simply a gift (verb and noun).

Durbar Staged horse gallops in which senior men pay homage to an emir in the Muslim regions.

FCT Federal Capital Territory (Abuja).

FESTAC Festival of Arts and Culture hosted in Lagos in 1977 at incredible cost. Legacies from this event include the National Theatre and the housing project of Festac Town.

Galadima Traditional title of the far northeast.

Go-slow Traffic jam.

GRA Government reserved area, civil servants housing district.

IBB President Ibrahim Badamosi Babangida.

Ileto Village (Yoruba).

Ilu Alade Big town (Yoruba).

Ilu Oloja Small market town (Yoruba).

Kabu kabu Unlicensed taxis.

Lappa Casual loin cloth (men and women).

Mai Traditional Kanuri ruler.

Master Polite and respectful address, a little perturbing to liberal ears, especially when combined with the common phrase "I beg".

Moto Any car – a term you'll hear a lot if travelling by bush taxi.

NEPA Nigerian Electric Power Authority – also translated *Never Electric Power Always*.

Oba Traditional Yoruba king. The Nigerian government has allowed traditional rulers to keep their titles and in some cases has even supported regional monarchies. Although the *obas* have less *de jure* power than they once did, they still enjoy considerable prestige and often mediate in local disputes. In some cases, they've taken on official government functions to complement traditional roles.

Off To turn/switch something off.

On To turn/switch something on.

Onyeocha White person (Igbo).

Oyinbo White person (Yoruba).

Sabi To know (Pidgin, from Portuguese).

Sabon Gwari Foreigners' town (Hausa).

SAP Economic Structural Adjustment Programme

Shehu Chief, big man (Hausa).

Sisa "Sixpence" in Hausa, ie 5 kobo.

Sokoto Yoruba trousers.

Sule "Shilling" in Hausa, ie 10 kobo.

Touts Hyperactive youths who take it upon themselves to escort you through customs, health, immigration and currency declaration at airports or land borders, or onto vehicles in the motor parks. Much as they can be a pain, they're usually very hard to shake off. Use them, since, if you let them hang on, they'll demand payment anyway.

WAI The Buhari government's much ridiculed War Against Indiscipline campaign, now defunct.

Yellow Fever popular name for traffic control cops in Lagos, after the colour of their uniforms.

The Nigerian Year: Holidays and Festivals

Nigeria's official public holidays include Christian and Muslim celebrations plus New Year's day, May Day and Independence Day (October 1). Muslim holidays marking the end of Ramadan (*Sallah*), Abraham's sacrificing of the sheep (*tabaski*) and Muhammad's birthday are based on the lunar calendar (see p.53 for dates). In the north, these often climax with specatular "durbar" cavalry displays. A number of non-Islamic festivals are also celebrated in the different regions throughout the year. In the south, the most famous of these is the terrifyingly exciting *Egungun*.

MAIN TRADITIONAL FESTIVALS

Pategi Regatta A regatta held every other year in February–March at Pategi, 100km downstream from Jebba, the big crossing point on the Niger, 70km from Ilorin. This is one of the country's best known events, and includes horse racing, swimming, dancing and music.

Fishing festival February. Argungu, near Sokoto (see p.1071).

Egungun Usually April. A whole host of Yoruba ancestor festivals. The one at Ibadan draws huge crowds – also the town of Okene, on the A2 between Benin City and Lokoja. Masquerades and sporting events accompanied by exhilarating dancing and drumming.

Ofala December. Festival in Onitsha and other towns along the Niger to honor the traditional ruler who appears before his people.

Ogun Between June and August. Yoruba festival in honour of the god of iron with singing, dancing and drumming. Held in numerous towns of the region.

Oshun August/September. Festival in honour of the river godess and guardian spirit of the people of Oshogbo. Another well-known celebration, but much of the week-long event is considered too sacred to be shared with visitors.

Igue December. Procession of the Oba of Benin. The ensuing celebration lasts several days and includes traditional dancing and a lot of drinking and eating.

Sekiapu. October. Masquerades, regattas and a great deal of merriment in Rivers and Cross River States.

Trouble

Nigeria's dreadful reputation for trouble is fifty percent unfair and unfounded. But security is not something to take lightly in Lagos and other large cities. Lagos gangs are active and well organised. Even more disturbing is the huge number of handguns and other weapons in private possession and the widely presumed implication of some police in criminal activities. While outlaws may "control" entire neighbourhoods of the mainland, however, you're most unlikely ever to see one, or anyone out of uniform carrying a gun. Leave valuables behind when you go out and you'll be fine.

If you spend much time in ex-pat circles in **Lagos**, you'll hear an awful lot of recycled gossip about the **security problems**. There seems little point in exaggerating the issue. Despite mandatory death sentences for armed robbery, burglaries are common and night watchmen do get killed. But visitors, even long-term ones, are rarely at risk. Be alert, not paranoid.

You're unlikely to get into real trouble yourself in Nigeria unless you cross someone with serious influence. There are a lot of **drugs** floating around Lagos, however and if you become involved you could easily find yourself in deep water. **Marijuana** is cultivated in the south and commonly smoked. It became popular in the army during the civil war but its use is officially considered a serious offence. The Indian Hemp Decree of 1966 provides for ten-year jail sentences for smokers and the death sentence for cultivation or import. Lorry drivers have long used amphetamines (made in France, smuggled through Benin) but Lagos' pivotal position in the worldwide transportation of **hard drugs** (see p.57) is bringing heroin onto the domestic market and also cocaine. Cocaine, popular with the Shagari era elite, is now sold on street corners across Lagos. Stay very clear.

FOR DRIVERS: TROUBLE ON THE ROAD

If you have **your own vehicle**, be careful where you leave it. Overlanders coming down from the Sahara encounter no special problems in northern Nigeria but in the south some take a lesson from residents who carve their licence numbers on all windows and use crook locks. Never park in an unguarded area and leave nothing of value in your car at any time.

There are virtually no **roadblocks** in central Nigeria, but they appear with increasing frequency towards the borders (seven, for example in the last 21km before Ikom). Most have oil drums staggered across the road, or two nail-studded planks, and they're illuminated by torches at night. Very occasionally a roadblock will consist of just a piece of string. Although often privately on the make, the officials are there to maintain law and order and, sometimes only a few hundred yards apart, may be staffed 24 hours a day by police, army, customs, the Agriculture Ministry or detectives, each with their own particular interest in your documents, movements and motivations. Any of them may wave you through, but it's always advisable to slow down to be sure. When stopped, remain inside until told what to do, as half the officials will want you to stay put, the other half will want the passengers to assemble outside, and it's impossible to predict which.

The Nigerian **police and civil service** has its quota of thugs and morons but the jobs themselves are respected occupations, and many officers, even in the lower ranks, are educated and well read. You'll meet senior officers who've been to university in Britain or the USA. Often posted far from home, they may welcome a chat about books or politics. They may also be waiting for a lift and the minor inconvenience of an extra passenger is far outweighed by the ease with which one passes through subsequent roadblocks.

Nigerians' **sense of humour** varies greatly. Generally, officials in the north are restrained and courteous while in the south it seems to be a great joke for a soldier to storm up to a foreigner shouting about illegal parking, the wrong colour of number plate or some other misdemeanour. When you've been adequately embarrassed or terrified, there's a hearty thump on the back, and an invitation to share the joke and offer an opinion on Manchester United's chances next Saturday (try to be polite!). It's worth pointing out that the police – and others in uniform – keep abreast of the news and know full well that expatriates and other foreigners break the law and indulge in criminal activities from time to time. Rumours circulate fast among the police. Your behaviour may be impeccable, but they don't know that. In a country as big and hard to control as this, it's important you find every last ounce of tolerance.

Lastly, it's not unknown for enterprising traders, or even highway **bandits**, to pose as a roadblock by setting up their wares on a couple of oil drums. Sometimes it's hard to tell. Nigerian detectives are always in plain clothes but they invariably show their ID as soon as you pull up. Bandits really do exist. Their ingenious exploits are faithfully reported in all the tabloid newspapers.

There's a happy and ironic footnote to all this: the number of roadblocks in towns and on the roads has been officially reduced since mid-1990, and armed robbery and road accidents have dropped significantly – surely some connection.

Entertainment: Culture and Sports

Nigeria has a thriving and complex cultural scene. Music, of course, is a massive industry. Theatre is lively and inventive and now getting TV cross-fertilisation. Cinema is somewhat under a cloud of financial incapacity (see *Contexts*). Nigerian literature is of world importance – there's a clutch of great writers, including Nobel prize winner Wole Soyinka (who spends much time in the USA) and the renowned and more accessible author and opinion-moulder Chinua Achebe (who's often in Britain) as well as a new generation of writers – the most well known in Britain being Ben Okri, Adewale Maja-Pearce – who choose to live permanently abroad (see "Books" in *Contexts*). In sports, football and athletics are the big crowd-pullers.

■ Music

Lagos feels the heartbeat of Nigerian music and you can hear all the styles here and stand a good chance of seeing international stars – **Fela Kuti**, son **Femi Kuti**, **King Sunny Ade**, **Victor Uwaifor**, **Sonny Okosuns**, **Victor Olaiya** – at any of three dozen or so clubs and hotel dance floors. In other cities around the country you may be lucky, but more likely in the south – Ibadan, Benin, Enugu, Port Harcourt or Calabar. For further background and insights, see the "Music" section in *Contexts*.

■ Theatre

Nigeria has a 400-year old theatrical tradition with the **Yoruba language** its outstanding vehicle. The **Alarinjo Theatre** was the court entertainment of sixteenth century Oyo. Once allowed by the rulers to become a popular form, it spread and travelled from city to city among the old kingdoms. By the nineteenth century it was a major cultural influence but it waned with the penetration of Christianity, only to resurge again in the 1940s, when players performed biblical scenes before church congregations.

Duro Lapido, **Kola Ogunmola** and **Hubert Ogunde** were the most famous names in the travelling theatre genre. They took plays from town to town, giving voice to the changing social and cultural scene in southern Nigeria, right through the pre-independence era and successive federal governments since. You may be lucky and catch one of the noisy, half-improvised productions. But these days many groups are more involved with making their own **films** (see *Contexts*), which are popular well beyond southeast Nigeria.

As for **English language drama** groups, they're mostly attached to the universities, don't attract any state or federal support and inevitably don't have a mass audience. **Wole Soyinka**, **John Pepper Clark**, **Femi Osofisan**, **Ola Rotimi** and **Bode Osanyin** are some of Nigeria's best-known playwrights. In Lagos, check how the **Pec Repertory Group** is faring. They're the first full-time professional rep group, established by John Pepper Clark (see Lagos "Directory" p.1013).

■ Football

With 100,000 licensed players, Nigeria's footballing skills are highly respected in Africa, though setbacks spoiled the chances of the national side – **Super Eagles** – in the 1990 African Nations Cup and in the World Cup, from both of which they were knocked out of the qualifying rounds by Cameroon. Current star players are defenders **Stephen Keshi** and **Sunday Eboigbe** (aka Andrew Uwe). Sixteen Nigerian players appear in Belgian first and second division teams and, without them, the national side is always at a disadvantage.

Successful regional teams include **Shooting Stars** of Ibadan and **Enugu Rangers**. Matches are well attended and crowds often enormous.

Women In Nigeria

Most foreign women working in Nigeria don't feel comfortable travelling alone in the Islamic-dominated north (pay special attention here to covering arms and legs) but the southern half of the country doesn't pose any gender-related problems for most women: flirtatious sexual harassment may occur in clubs and at parties, but not on the street.

In a country where the change from traditional to urban-industrial values is taking place remarkably quickly, women have achieved larger real gains here than elsewhere in West Africa. But while they occupy positions in business, government and increasingly in the universities, there's still a lot or ground to cover. Two groups – the *National Committee for Women and Development* formed in the early 1980s, and the *National Council of Women Societies* twenty years older – aim to fight for more equitable integration in all spheres. A radical alternative to *NCWS*, **Women in Nigeria** (*WIN*), was founded in 1985 in the male bastion of Zaria. It now has groups nationwide. Counterposing *WIN* is the *Federation of Muslim Women* (*FOMWAN*), a northern fundamentalist grouping. And lastly there's *Nigerwives*, for foreign wives of Nigerian men. The national group of *Nigerwives* meets the last Saturday of every month at 3pm at St. Saviour's church on Tafawa Balewa Square in Lagos. Their contact address is PO Box 54664, Falomo, Lagos. More about being a woman in Nigeria (married or not) can be found in Jane Bryce's piece on the joys and fears of **expatriate life** on p.994.

Directory

AIRPORT DEPARTURE TAX ₦50.

BUYING THINGS Nigerian manufactured goods of interest to the traveller – car parts, hand tools, etc – are widely available, and are of a quality to be exported to the surrounding Franc zone countries. On the provisions front, the country's large city markets and chains of supermarkets have most things you'll ever need.

CRAFTS Nigeria has a fantastic wealth of things worth aquiring – both utilitarian and aesthetic and sometimes both. Jewellery (including the cylinidrical multicoloured glass beads that are now getting expensive, leatherware, carved calabashes, bronze figures (lost wax method), handwoven cloth and woodcarvings are the most obvious. You're likely to be offered ivory from time to time and various other animal products – lizard, snake and crocodile skin bags and belts – but you'd encounter difficulties trying to bring most of them back home. Rightly so. Possibly the best value and lasting interest is to be had from **musical instruments**, which you'll find if you look beyond the souvenir stands at the big hotels. Talking drums, the expressive *iyaalu* tension drum, which so unerringly imitates the Yoruba voice, are particularly worth looking out for. A number of other Nigerian instruments are covered in the "Music" section in *Contexts*.

EMERGENCIES If you run into trouble, the police emercency number is ☎199. But help doesn't always come in a hurry.

MUSEUMS Nigeria has more museums than anywhere in West Africa. The main ones are in **Lagos**, **Kano**, **Ife**, **Jos** and **Calabar**, but just about every town of any size has a museum of some sort. They tend to focus either on history, art or customs., though there's also an **oil museum** in Oloibiri (50km from Port Harcourt) and a **mining museum** in Jos.

OPENING HOURS Banks open Mon 8am–3pm and Tues–Fri 8am–1.30pm. Shops usually open Mon–Sat 8am–5pm.

PHOTOGRAPHY Although *no permit is required*, photography is something police and security agents are extremely touchy about. You're best off not taking pictures on Lagos Island where there are many government buildings (if one of them unwittingly works its way into your picture, it's a good way to get your film and possibly camera confiscated) and only discreetly in other neighbourhoods of Lagos. Photographing people in traditional costume, at country markets and the like, is likely to incur wrath among interfering types who may report you. Unfortunately, police are usually convinced your sole intention in taking such pictures is to assault the national image.

UNIVERSITIES Nigeria has far more universities – 26 in all, one or more in each state – than all the other countries in West Africa put together. They include the **University of Lagos** (Unilag) and the **University of Ibadan**, the nation's first, founded in 1946. Nsukka, Ife, Zaria and Benin are other large campuses. There's still quite a community of ex-pat visiting scholars and teachers.

WILDLIFE AND NATIONAL PARKS There's still a fair bit of wildlife to be seen in Nigeria, though little in the big game league. Monkeys and gazelle are the animals you'll most likely see from the road. If you make the effort to go to **Yankari** or **Borgu Reserves** or the newly created **Sabon Gwari Reserve**, all in the north, you can see elephants, hippos and larger antelopes, and there's the remote possiblitiy of glimpsing lions or other big cats. More exciting, in a way, is the recent discovery of **gorillas** in the thick forests of the southeast, and the decision to create the **Oban Rainforest National Park** in Cross River State, an initiative that ties in with the development of the Korup National Park over the border in Cameroon. The Nigerian Conservation Foundation is making valiant efforts to rouse Nigerians from a complacent attitude to the wildlife heritage.

Nigeria's History

Nigerian history is the most complex and also one of the most ancient in West Africa. The earliest indications of the use of iron in the region come from the Nok Culture (after the Jos plateau village where much of the evidence was found) and date back to 300BC. For reasons unknown, this civilisation faded, and the next discoveries date from over a millennium later. The development, by the ninth century, of mineral wealth in the Yoruba and Igbo regions of the south, led to long-lasting and sophisticated political structures. In the north, kingdoms arose at much the same time – first the Bornu Empire in the ninth century, then, not long afterwards, the Hausa City States – and they became powerful stations on the trans-Saharan caravan routes, and supplying many of the exotic requirements of medieval Europe.

The slave trade and, much later, colonial invasion, wreaked havoc on these indigenous states, as well as on the weaker, stateless communities living among them.

Since the end of the nineteenth century, the colnial protectorates and then the federation of modern Nigerian states, have been the setting for a huge tapestry of events and characters woven into a familiar screen of poverty, booming population and almost continual crisis. Unlike most smaller West African nations, a substantial and expanding literarture exists on the history, sociology and political science of Nigeria (see "Books" in *Contexts*). The following summary is only the simplest historical framework.

■ The Arrival of Europeans

The **Portuguese** were the first Europeans to reach the Benin Gulf, in 1472, and within a short time they had made contact with the kingdom of **Benin**. Trade soon began, initially centred on pepper, ivory and other exotic goods. It was not until the second half of the seventeenth century, when the Americas had been widely colonised and plantations needed increasing supplies of labour, that the focus shifted to slaves.

The early Europeans had few permanent forts or settlements, basing themselves instead on offshore "hulks" near the ports. These, by the 1660s, were highly developed, sparking off an explosion of competitive slave-trading at ports like **Lagos**, **Warri**, **Calabar** and **Bonny**. Much of the dynamic for the trade, which was exploited by local chiefs, came from the insecurity of a West African arms race for the latest European muskets and canon. In exchange for weaponry, the French and British, who had supplanted the Portuguese and Brazilians by the eighteenth century, were scarcely interested in buying anything except slaves.

The Colonial Grab

At the beginning of the nineteenth century, things appeared to change, as the newly republican **French** sent warships to the southeast Nigerian coast to break up the slave trade. To French cries of *Liberté, Egalité, Fraternité*, the British added their own hollow *Christianity, Commerce and Civilisation*. In fact, slaves no longer made economic sense; instead, in the wake of the European industrial revolution, **markets** were needed for manufactured goods and there was a massive demand for supplies of raw materials – cotton, sugar and the rest.

In 1851, the British shelled Lagos, ostensibly to quicken the demise of the slave trade, in practice to impose a puppet regime and improve the newly important oil palm trade. The slave trade went underground, and slavers hid out in the lagoons around Lagos from where they would sneak out their cargo to Brazil, which was still an importer. Meanwhile the British seized Lagos Island in 1861 – which then became Lagos colony, the first particle of Nigeria.

After the European Powers' **Berlin Conference** of 1885, the London-based **Royal Niger Company** was granted exclusive trading rights in the basin of the Niger River. With the Germans expanding to the east, and the French to the north and west, the British government took over the RNC in 1899 and began pushing it in all directions.

By 1900 they'd succeeded in drawing borders around a vast region of diverse peoples, who found themselves under the ultimate authority of northern and southern protectorates. In 1914 a federation was formed – in preference to a united colony – and named **Nigeria**, a term coined by the wife of Lord Lugard, the British colonial commander in the region.

Indirect Rule

From the beginning, Nigeria was an ill-matched association and it was clear that conflict would arise between the conservative, largely Muslim and feudal **north**, and the more outward-looking **south** – with its Christian missions and, in the southeast, lack of rigid social hierarchies. At the very least, problems would be caused by the new territory's southward-looking orientation, away from the old Saharan routes and towards the ports and European trade.

The British, however, pressed ahead with their system of "**indirect rule**", which in the **north**, worked easily enough to the benefit of both the Hausa-Fulani emirs (who carried on much as before) and the British administration. Lord Lugard simply took over the role of regional over-lord from the Sultan of Sokoto, whose functions were perforce purely religious and ceremonial.

But indirect rule was a disaster in the **southeast**, where decisions and judicial processes were traditionally applied by consent among groups of senior men. In **Igboland**, the "Warrant Chiefs" commissioned by the British had no mandate for their authority, and on the contrary were usually independent minded status-seekers who had acquired a mission education.

In **Yorubaland**, another variation was imposed. The British held Yoruba traditional rulers, with British "advisors", accountable for their decisions. But the British had failed to understand the fabric of Yoruba politics and perceived in their centralised **government of obas** and the traditional ceremonial-executive titles of the **Alafin of Oyo** and the **Oni of Ife**, simple dictatorships somewhat akin to the emirates of the north. Disregarding the fact that the Yoruba offices were posts given to selected senior men by others of high rank, Lugard tried to control the selection of pliant chiefs by men who, again, had no mandate to enforce his requirements. And he actively connived to empower Yoruba elements who posed least threat to white prestige, to turn the clock back so far as possible to his own, avowedly racist vision of an Africa untainted by progress.

While British rule led to internal schisms in Yorubaland, the region benefited from the fastest imput of technology and **modern infrastructure**. There was electricity in Lagos by 1898, bridges between the islands and a rail link with Ibadan by 1900. All of which was to prove another source of division for north and south to deal with after independence.

■ The Road to Independence

Nigerians became involved in the political process relatively early, by the standards of other African colonies. In 1923, the first Africans, led by **Herbert Macaulay**, a Yoruba whose father had returned from slave captivity in Sierra Leone, were elected to a legislative advisory council in Lagos. But local parties really only developed after the experience of World War II, when Nigerians returned from fighting for European ideals like "self–determination" and "liberty".

In 1944, the **National Council for Nigeria and the Cameroons** was formed by Herbert Macaulay and **Dr Nnamdi Azikiwe**, an Igbo. Four years later, **Chief Obafemi Awolowo**, a Yoruba, founded a second party, the **Action Group**. By the end of the decade, the northerners also had their own party, the **Northern People's Congress**, with **Tafawa Balewa** at its head.

Predictably, these three parties came to represent the **regional interests** – the NPC for the north, the NCNC for the east, and the AG for the west. As they jockeyed for position to rule an independent nation, the parties agreed on nothing, delaying the process of reform in the process. In a dispute over the date for self-rule, suspicious northerners walked out of the colonial assembly in 1953, and bloody **riots in Kano** followed. Members from each region felt sure the other two were conspiring to dominate, and there was talk of dividing the country into several smaller political units in an effort to relieve the tension. The British argued such a measure would only stall independence further, an argument in which they were supported by the northern region, which had to have a friendly route to the sea.

Finally, in 1957, it was decided the nation would be formed of the three rival regions. **Tafawa Balewa** became the head of the new central government and Nigeria had its independence returned to it on October 1, 1960.

■ Independence: the early years

The early 1960s were characterised by an **uneasy coalition** between the **north** and the **southeast** against the powerful **southwest** region dominated by the Yoruba. The latter thus saw its worst fears realised and its leaders panicked when a bogus census in 1963 suggested the north had four million more inhabitants than the rest of the nation combined. The threat of Muslim domination in the political arena now seemed very real.

The southeast eventually slipped out of the coalition and Chief Awolowo raised angry cries against government tinkering with the country's structure. He was tried for treason and jailed. **Early chaos** seemed to be gaining momentum and in January 1966 the army toppled the government – killing Tafawa Balewa in the process – and set about trying to restore order.

Military Rule

The new **military government** was headed by **Gen. J. Aguiyi-Ironsi**, an Igbo. Northerners rioted in reaction to his radical early reforms that abolished the federation and imposed a unitary government dominated by Igbos. Fighting broke out within the army and, after only six months, Ironsi was killed in another **coup**, this time led by northern officers. As many as 7000 Igbos living in the north were massacred in the aftermath and up to half a million fled to the east.

But the military's new leader was different from his predecessors. **Yakubu Gowon** was a Christian northerner, a young and charismatic figure, who restored the tripartite federation and released Awolowo and other Action Group leaders of the west. But the southeast region, led by the military governor, **Lt-Col. C. Odumegwu-Ojukwu**, who rejected Gowon's leadership, pushed instead for a loose confederation.

In September 1966, elements of the Northern army began the systematic **killing of Igbos** who had remained in the north. Official reports placed the deaths at 5000, though Igbos claimed that as many as 30,000 were massacred. The pogrom was a decisive blow to the shaky federation. High ranking Igbo civil servants began returning from Lagos to the regional capital at Enugu and pressuring Ojukwu to secede.

National politics in the early part of 1967 were completely dominated by the **question of the future of the Federal Republic**. The Ghanaian government attempted to mediate between the sides and, in January 1967, leaders of the federal government met with Ojukwu in Aburi. The meetings produced no acceptable compromise; nor did subsequent government moves to appease the east with conciliatory measures and guarantees.

At the last minute, Gowon announced the **division of the federation** into twelve separate states in an attempt to undermine the overweening north and disarm his critics from the ethnic minorities, especially in the southeast, who had long sought greater autonomy. It was too late.

Fearing the Igbo constituency would be pushed permanently into the margins of national politics, Ojukwu unilaterally withdrew the Eastern Region from the federation and declared the independent **Republic of Biafra** on May 30, 1967.

The Biafran War

In July 1967, Biafran troops marched into the Western Region in an attempt to surround Lagos. Federal troops responded by blockading eastern ports and by attacking Biafra from the north and west. Despite a lack of manpower and resources, Biafra scored a number of military successes in the early days of the war, but by the end of 1967, the conflict had degenerated into a brutal **war of attrition**. Fighting was vicious and confused. Most of the major towns changed hands several times. Federal forces captured a number of coastal towns, reducing Biafra to an enclave in the Igbo heartland. Federal military atrocities, of which many were reported, further convinced the Igbos that they were engaged in an all-out war for survival.

Biafra gained considerable sympathy in the international press: for the first time, public opinion in the rich world was mobilised against third world poverty. Yet few countries gave official recognition to Biafra, and French military and technical aid seemed suspiciously self-interested. The war dragged on for three years, claiming the lives of at 100,000 soldiers, but many more Igbo civilians, of whom between half a million and two million are estimated to have perished as a result of the government's policy of **blockade and starvation**. Supported by British aid and Soviet arms, the Federal government finally captured the last rebel-held town of Owerri and quelled the rebellion in December 1969. Much of the southeast was ravaged.

▪ Reconstruction

The gaping wounds of the war healed with remarkable apparent speed. Gowon, who was still in power after four years, was careful not to humiliate the defeated and bereaved easterners or exclude them from the new federation. In fact, he offered an **amnesty** to all who had fought on the Biafran side, and vowed to rebuild the east while furthering the economic development of the entire country.

Reconstruction didn't take place overnight, but it is remarkable today how little evidence of the war remains, even in cities that were virtually destroyed. The number of roads, bridges and industries now largely exceeds pre-war levels.

Gowon was aided in the early days of reconciliation by **oil revenues** that flooded into the coffers in the early 1970s as Nigeria became one of the world's ten largest producers. But as blatant corruption became a national issue, and Gowon began dragging his feet on promises of a return to civilian rule and devoting most of his energies to international image-building, he was ousted, after nine years in power, in a bloodless coup led by **General Murtala Muhammed** in July 1975.

Murtala Muhammed

Of all Nigeria's leaders, Murtala Muhammed has been without doubt the most popular. Even today, his name is referred to with a reverence not normally reserved for politicians. Another northerner with considerable charisma, he structured all his policies around the return of power to an elected leadership and devoted himself to wiping out corruption.

Shortly after coming to power, Muhammed instigated **"Operation Deadwoods"** – a policy of forced dismissal or retirement of public officials on a whole range of charges from corruption to "infirmity". In all, more than 10,000 civil servants – police officials, senior diplomats, university professors, even military officers – were relieved of their posts. Swift action was taken against embezzlement of public funds. Assets were confiscated. Appointees were sacked for reasons as simple as a conflict of interests. It was a breath of fresh air in a stagnating and counterproductive bureaucracy and brought the government huge popularity.

By the end of 1975, Muhammed had concluded the purge and announced a four-year countdown to return the country to civilian rule. He had come to be regarded as a politician who made promises and kept them, and drew attention to the future and away from the divisive tragedy of the past. Nigerians felt they were leaders in a liberalising movement that would sweep the continent and break the cycle of totalitarianism in Africa.

It's difficult to know if posterity would have been so kind to Muhammed had he lived to see his programmes carried out. After only six months of reshaping the country he was assassinated in a hail of bullets, by disgruntled members of the military, while his car was in a Lagos traffic jam.

■ The Second Republic

The counter-coup was effective only in eliminating Muhammed, for the plotters were rounded up and with the help of Major General Ibrahim Babangida, power was smoothly transferred to Muhammed's chief of staff, **Olusegun Obasanjo**, a Christian Yoruba.

Obasanjo pledged to adhere to Muhammed's schedule for the return to civilian government and continued reshaping the civil service. A new constitution, based on that of the USA, was drawn up, and political parties were unbanned in September 1978.

Five **political parties** were finally approved, but four were headed by familiar old names, had vague right of centre programmes and seemed to indicate the persistence of regional divisions. Both **Awolowo** and **Azikwe** (now in their seventies) headed parties largely representing the west and the east, or at least their personal power-bases in those regions – the *Unity Party of Nigeria* and the *Greater National People's Party* respectively. The *GNPP* was a breakaway group from the *National People's Party*, led by a northern businessman, **Alhaji Waziri Ibrahim**. The *National Party of Nigeria*, based on Kaduna and led by **Alhaji Shehu Shagari**, claimed to cut across regional loyalties but was essentially the old *NPC* northern party, controlled as ever by the Fulani oligarchy. Shagari, himself a Fulani from a leading northern family, had been a member of the first civilian government and had served under Gowon's military regime. Lastly, in opposition to the NPN, another northern party had also been formed – the the *People's Redemption Party*. Led by **Alhaji Aminu Kano**, it had radical socialist leanings and was explicitly committed to the cause of inter-ethnic cooperation.

In the complicated elections that spread over six weeks in 1979, all the parties achieved some representation, but **Shagari** won the all-important **presidential election**. He rode out his first term in Nigeria's new "Second Republic" on a wave of genuine popularity and public relief that the long period of military rule was over. But the new president didn't survive long untarnished. **Crackdowns on the press** – which had begun reporting government corruption, and even daring to point fingers at Shagari and his Kaduna clique – clearly signalled his insecurity, and he faced serious challenges from other northern parties and eastern allies in his unstable coalition.

The **economy**, too, was slipping badly. The oil boom had peaked in 1980. In December of that year serious **riots** broke out in Kano, prompted by the popular "jihadist" teachings and calls for social justice of Mai Tatsine. As foreign currency reserves dwindled and the external debt skyrocketed, the standard of living for most Nigerians rapidly declined, while government officials, cabinet ministers and the president himself, made fortunes, indulging in what came to be known as "squandermania". Further, serious **riots in Maiduguri** in October 1982 were dismissed by Shagari as "religious agitation", and in February 1983, some two million immigrant workers –from Ghana, Cameroon, Chad and Niger – were expelled as economic scapegoats.

Despite these various obstacles, Shagari managed to get elected to a second term in October 1983, a sounder win, in fact, than his first, though achieved with less than sound methods.

■ Another coup: a new military regime

The inevitable happened barely three months after the 1983 elections, when another northerner – **Major General Mohammed Buhari** – staged a bloodless takeover of power and suspended the 1979 constitution. Explaining his actions, the new leader announced shortly after the takeover: "The economic mess, the corruption and unacceptable level of unemployment could not be excused on the grounds that Nigeria was a practising democracy."

Buhari announced the "voluntary retirement" of high ranking military officers and the inspector general of the police, all of whom were implicated in financial mismanagement and corrupt practices on a gigantic scale. Prominent members of Shagari's party were arrested, as was the president. Through such moves, Buhari sought to associate his regime with the purist popularity of Muhammed. Important elder statesmen from the martyred president's administration were brought into the new government, including former head of state Obasanjo.

The attack on graft – the **"War Against Indiscipline"** – even crossed international borders. One of the most wanted offenders was the former transport minister **Alhaji Umaru Dikko**, who was living in luxurious exile in London, from where he openly criticised the new government. In one of the more bizarre instances of abuse of diplomatic privilege, Dikko was kidnapped, drugged and bundled into a crate, ready to be shipped off as diplomatic baggage from Gatwick airport. The plot was only aborted when British customs officials queried the contents of the crate. Buhari's government quickly denied any responsibility, although the Nigerian High Commission was strongly implicated in the abduction. Diplomatic relations between the UK and Nigeria nearly broke over the incident and subsequent British immigration policy has tended to keep relations cool.

Buhari, however, seemed serious in his efforts to wipe out corruption, and as a result was initially quite popular with people fed up with government abuse. But it soon became apparent that members of Shagari's Kaduna clique were not prominent among those convicted on corruption charges. In addition to the accusation of partialitiy, it was not long before Buhari himself was gaining a reputation as an unbending **autocrat**. As those accused of corruption were given sentences of as much as 72 years, Buhari arrested many of his regime's critics and suppressed the Nigerian media in ways Shagari had not dared. On the discovery of an alleged coup plot in 1984, he swiftly executed a group of some forty soldiers. And two government decrees, reflecting the new hard line, proved extremely unpopular with the masses. The first, known as Decree 2, allowed for detention without trial of citizens regarded as a threat to the state. Decree 4 imposed press controls by insisting journalists verify the "truth" of their reporting.

Even more unpopular were **austerity measures** adopted by Buhari in 1984 as he sought to remedy the country's growing economic problems. Strong opposition to his rule grew as resulting price increases and shortages of consumer goods jolted the nation – especially its poorer citizens. Buhari tried to deflect criticism, as Shagari had done, by blaming the country's economic woes on foreign workers robbing Nigerians of jobs. **Mass expulsions of immigrants** were instigated and, in May 1985, up to a million foreigners – again many of them Ghanaian – were shipped out in chaotic conditions. Relations soured with Nigeria's neighbours which, facing economic crises of their own, suddenly found a flood of displaced and unemployed refugees on their doorsteps.

None of Buhari's drastic measures worked, partly because there was virtually no popular support for the man behind them and principally because the Naira was overvalued and worthless. With the economy hardly performing any better after his two years at the top, and a foreign debt of some £12 billion pulling the country down, a new coup was orchestrated, in August 1985, by close associates of Buhari in the Supreme Military Council, led by army chief of staff **Major General Ibrahim Babangida**.

■ The "Period of Transition": Ibrahim Babangida

Within a short time of taking office, **Babangida** and his new Armed Forces Ruling Council had released many of the political prisoners from Nigerian jails and a new sense of freedom began to be felt. Not without misgivings, though, for in December 1986, ten officers from Benue State, who, Babangida alleged, had been conspiring to overthrow him, were executed. This was a new departure in Nigeria. It had always been understood that conspiracies, or bloodless coup attempts, were not punishable by death. Babangida had established that he could not be overthrown in the normal way, since failure meant execution.

Babangida began, however, once again preparing the country for national elections, with the declared intention of handing over power to the civilians on October 1, 1990. Such political moves have gone down well at home, though his economic policies have been tough and unyielding. Shortly after taking power, he declared an **economic state of emergency** and assumed almost total control over the economy. In late 1985, he broke off loan negotiations with the IMF that had been in the process for three years under the Shagari and Buhari regimes – a move that met with popular nationalistic support. But enthusiasm waned when the president imposed austerity measures of his own. He went on to devalue the Naira some fourfold, in the hope of attracting investors, and began privatising unprofitable public enterprises and lifting government subsidies, notably of petrol.

Periodic **demonstrations and strikes** have resulted from the measures and, although conflict tends to be sparked by economic causes, **ethnic and religious tensions** are still an issue to contend with. In 1986, Babangida announced that Nigeria had joined the Organisation of the Islamic Conference. Despite stressing this had been done for cultural and religious reasons – and not political ones – non-Muslim southerners were outraged and voiced the fear that the government and its northern powerbase was trying to impose Islamic rule on the whole country. There were **campus protests** and a number of deaths in northern universities in 1986 and, in 1987, **religious riots** broke out between Muslims and Christians in Kaduna State, leading to the deaths of dozens of people, the arrest of over a thousand and the banning of religious organisations at schools and universities. Adding to economic frustrations, in 1986, Babangida had announced that the return to civilian government would now not take place until 1992.

May 1989 saw some of independent Nigeria's worst **civil disturbances** as, for nearly a week, Lagos boiled with street rioting, looting and running battles between students, unemployed youths and police and army squads. At least fifty people were killed.

Babangida, however, remains firmly in power. He has said he will step down voluntarily by 1992 and not contest the elections on his own account. In some quarters he is trusted in this – though he has also acquired the nickname Maradona for his unfailing political instincts and dexterity – and for his luck.

Meanwhile, Babangida has been as much an autocrat as any of his predecessors. He was unable to satisfy public opinion on the issue of the murder of **Dele Giwa**, the editor and publisher of the outspoken *Newswatch* magazine who was killed in 1986 by a letter bomb which purportedly came from the president's office. He also wasted no time in smashing the **Nigerian Labour Congress**, foisting his own leadership on it and reducing it to a condition of paralysis. Further, he has attacked the Academic Staff University Unions and encouraged an odious student network to report on the doings of politically active teaching staff. There have been no serious investigations into the hundreds of deaths that have taken place under police and army fire in demonstrations. And in a disconcerting development that seems to indicate a total lack of will, a statement in March 1990 by Lagos State governor Colonel Raji Rasaki explicitly encouraged **lynch mob justice** where thieves were caught red-handed. It was condemned by the Nigerian Civil Liberties Organisation but met with profound silence from more powerful quarters.

■ Into the 1990s: third time lucky?

Babangida came to power on a human rights ticket but it soon became apparent that he could be as repressive as his predecessor Buhari, if more subtle. He lifted a six-year ban on civilian politics in May 1989 but the people he appointed to draft the new constitution were mostly related to discredited former politicians. After a deluge of applications to **register political parties**, of which two were to be chosen, Nigerians were dismayed by Babangida's announcement that none of the new groupings showed any genuine departure from those of the Shagari era.

He decreed that, instead, there would be **two parties** in Nigeria and he would set them up – one "a little to the left" (the Social Democratic Party) and one "a little to the right" (the National Republican Convention), or, as Nigerian commentators like to point out, a "Yes" party and a "Yes Sir" party. Babangida tightened the screws still further in January 1990, sacking a number of senior Christian officers – some of whom, including his popular defence minister Lieutenant General Domkat Bali, had helped him topple Buhari in 1985 – and replacing them with officers of his own Islamic faith, while retaining the defence ministry portfolio for himself.

The bad blood thus made has pushed his credit to the very limit and now risks nullifying Nigeria's status as a constitutional non-religious state. There's a widely held belief that Babangida the power-broker is preparing the ground for his own political role after the handover of power in 1992, and doing so in collusion with the very forces overthrown by Buhari in 1983.

The first response came on April 22, 1990, when a group of junior, Christian officers **attempted a coup** by trying to seize Dodan barracks in Lagos. Their coup message rambled disparagingly about the administration and then stated "This is not just any coup but a well-conceived revolution by middle-belt and southern parts of the country" and that five northern states were "excised" from the federation.

The coup attempt, mercifully, was a failure, though in the ensuing fiasco, hundreds of people were killed in street fighting between army, rebels, and opportunist rioters, and at least forty people suspected of being involved in the attempt were executed some weeks later. Had the coup been successful it would have led to civil war that would almost certainly have torn the country apart – irreparably.

Babangida the pragmatist has achieved something of a reputation as an anti-ideologue. Athough his stubborn determination to continue with the SAP **austerity programme** is unpopular, people seem grudgingly to accept that a future elected government must have strong economic foundations to have any chance at all. Many are uncertain they're not being fooled yet again. For the moment, political commentators in Nigeria are focusing on the form a Nigerian civilian democracy might take after the much anticipated elections. The **two party system** is supposed to realign political debate on ideological issues rather than ethnic loyalties. But this is a gamble, even if it had the necessary support of good will, for ideological differences need not preclude ethnic or religious ones – and there's little doubt about which way the country will divide up under the proposed two party structure. There's already enomous scepticism about the chances for Nigeria's survival as a federal two-party democracy with a population of perhaps 150 million people.

Expatriate Nigeria: A Living Guide

Nigeria has by far the largest English-speaking expatriate community in West Africa but, before arrival, many are apprehensive about the prospect of living and working there. This specially commissoned piece sheds a positive light on the experience. Jane Bryce first went to Nigeria on a Commonwealth Scholarship to do research on African women writers. She stayed for five years, mostly around Lagos, and married a Nigerian. They now live in London.

Middle-class Nigerians tend to regard London as an extension of Lagos. Though the days are gone when every bride routinely shopped for her wedding dress on Oxford Street and a trip to London was the reward for favours rendered, the connections are still strong. Thousands of Nigerians went there to train and take degrees in the 1960s and their offspring born in the UK now have British passports. So people still move freely between Nigeria and London, spending a year or two working in Britain – in the civil service, on the buses, serving burgers, driving mini-cabs, working in petrol stations, schools and offices – before going home to get serious about life.

So on one level, Nigeria isn't strange at all. Whichever part of the world you come from you'll meet Nigerians who've lived there. There are Nigerian communities in Australia, Saudi Arabia, the United States, Canada.

"The best strategy is to get in on the act and ham it up"

As a foreigner, black or white, visiting Nigeria or taking up a contract there, you're automatically part of the elite, part of an estimated two percent of the population who are western educated, literate, professional people – which means in most communities you all know each other. Almost anything can be achieved by personal contact. In the cities, you live in one of the exclusive residential areas, where water runs and electricity is supplied, at least on a part-time basis. You have a driver to steer you through the hectic traffic, and take the strain of longer journeys. And with foreign exchange,

you're rich. The equivalent of £1 in Naira buys you a decent meal at an upmarket Nigerian restaurant. But you pay the price in other ways.

One of these – the one I found most difficult to come to terms with – is that you can never be invisible. This is obviously so if you're white, but if you're black, you'll meet it to some extent too. The universal cry of *oyinbo* follows you everywhere in the southwest, like *batoure* in the north and *onyeocha* in the east. You can never be anonymous, never blend into the background. There were times when I felt dehumanised by my skin colour, robbed of my identity, with a host of stereotypes foisted onto me. As a woman, one of these was "sexually available". As a foreigner another was "rich beyond our wildest dreams". As a freelance journalist and researcher with a small scholarship living hand to mouth, I found it very galling. But finding yourself at the centre of an impromptu drama, with a chorus of children or market women improvising around you, can also be very funny. The best strategy is always to get in on the act and ham it up a bit. The worst thing is to get defensive or irritable, which, of course, I often did too.

"Any Sunday you can see red-faced oyinbos being ferried to beaches as exclusively white as any in South Africa"

Theatre is an intrinsic part of Nigerian culture. People are self-confident and expressive. Foreigners nearly always feel underdressed at functions, where women glitter in gold jewellery and flaunt the latest lace fabric or designer dress.

Traditional dress lends itself to ceremony and display. A man wearing a voluminous Yoruba agbada, worn over matching tunic and trousers will perpetually be throwing the folds back over his shoulders with an air of "look at me". If you can join in by learning to wear traditional dress yourself, you'll be surprised at the effect it has on people. Despite the pleasure and pride people take in their own culture, they're surprised and flattered when a foreigner shows the same interest. When I wore the Yoruba woman's buba and wrapper, strangers would come up and tell me how fine I looked.

All too many expatriates seem content to live self-contained lives in a little world of ex-pat parties and activities isolated from the wider community. People who do this merely reinforce their own prejudices about Nigerians and Nigerians' prejudices about them. Any Sunday in Lagos you can see boatloads of red-faced *oyinbos* being ferried to Tarkwa Bay, where they frequent beaches which are as exclusively white as any in South Africa. Living in Ikoyi or Apapa in comfortable bungalows in big gardens surrounded by walls and guarded by a Hausa gateman, it takes an effort to drag oneself out of the hectic whirl of barbecues, squash, tennis, sailing, bridge and dinner parties. But it's worth it.

Nigerian culture – both traditional and contemporary – is rich, varied and accessible. Because the elite is so small, personal introduction can open almost any door. Never have I met the generosity with time and information that I encountered in Nigeria, both as a researcher and a journalist. I was literally adopted by one newspaper and given carte blanche to contribute to the arts and features pages. Later on, another paper gave me a column to write twice a week, with the only brief to "write about anything you want". This could never happen to a Nigerian making the reverse transition. I was able to interview artists, writers, dramatists, professors, actors, designers, sports-people, doctors and bankers with much greater ease than would be the case with such people else-where. You don't have to be a journalist to get the benefit of this kind of treatment. One ex-pat man I knew who worked for a multinational, proudly displayed the cap and stick of a Rivers State chief in his Lagos drawing room – the emblems of his own chieftaincy.

"Dancing to old highlife under a starlit sky has to be among life's best experiences."

But you shouldn't overestimate the extent to which a foreigner can enter and be part of the society. Unless you live in Nigeria long-term and speak a Nigerian language, or marry a Nigerian and acquire status as a member of the family, you'll ultimately remain an outsider. People are valued for where they come from and whom they're associated with, as much as for their individual merits. This breeds a kind of tribal herding instinct and partly accounts for why expats stick together to the extent they do.

While the Nigerian elite in Lagos, Kano or Enugu spend their weekends on an interminable social round of naming ceremonies, weddings, funerals, thanksgivings and birthday parties, what will you be doing? The answer is to join in. Whether you like the fact or not, it's considered some sort of a status symbol among a lot of Nigerians to have whites at your party. Accept the invitations. Dress up, go prepared for lots of sitting about with nothing much happening, and enjoy the social spectacle. This is an essential facet of life in Nigeria – the celebration of life itself. It can pall, as such parties tend to follow a formula of tarpaulin, plastic chairs, warm Fanta, jollof rice and speeches from the high table – or at the casual end, frilly dresses, disco music and heavy competition for the best catch – but occasionally it can be magical. Dancing to old highlife under a starlit sky with a crowd of people whose only thought is enjoyment is among life's best experiences.

If you don't participate, you'll never understand what drives Nigerian society. In the intricate social network, the observation of convention and the physical presence of people at each other's celebrations, lies the secret of Nigerian culture. A major source of that living history is festivals, which may be on a grand scale in the cities, attracting thousands of visitors, or small and local.

In the oldest part of the Lagos, Isale Eko, the home of the original Lagosians, there's a yearly masquerade festival celebrating the spirit of the city and the origins of its people. Called "Eyo", it's an occasion of eye-opening contrasts between ancient and modern.

I once unknowingly took a bus on Eyo day into the very part of the city where it was being celebrated. As it drew up at the stop, a band of stick-wielding figures emerged from a side-street, curiously inhuman in appearance, almost sinister. They wore wide-brimmed hats with white, shroud-like veils. Since no part of an Eyo masquerade is supposed to be seen, they had covered their hands with socks, giving them a strange, fingerless look. As they surrounded the bus, chanting and shaking their sticks, the other passengers hurriedly took off their shoes and stepped onto the street barefoot. No-one objected, or regarded it as an inconvenience. Through that simple gesture of respect for tradition, they became, not observers, but participants in the ritual.

"Like most ordinary Nigerians, police and soldiers are underpaid and hungry"

Nigeria has a reputation for being dangerous, and this is a real cause of anxiety for many visitors. It's true that living in Nigeria seems an unhealthy enterprise at times, but the dangers and violence now prevalent arise from the socially destructive effects of Structural Adjustment, from which ex-pats are largely insulated. The austerity measures demanded by the IMF are a well-known cause of distress and Nigeria is dangerous for its citizens because it's poor, because the leadership is undisciplined and unprincipled, and because the vast majority of the population live on the margins of survival, while a few ostentatiously enjoy their wealth. Such conditions breed crime, and there's been a marked increase in the incidence of armed robbery since 1985.

It's not all at the level of the famous Anini, whose name became a national password for trickery in the months he managed to make fools of the police as they tried to catch him a few years ago. On a recent occasion, a driver wound down his window in the Lagos traffic and held a ₦10 note out to a newspaper vendor. A passerby coolly lifted the note from his fingers and strolled away with the words "I no get money for chop and you wan buy newspaper".

The shock of this has to be seen in the context of a society where the sanctions on stealing are swift and drastic. If the cry of *ole* goes up, the thief knows he'd better run for his life, or he'll have a tyre doused in paraffin over his head and someone will strike a match. This, in turn, has to be seen in the light of a largely corrupt and incompetent police force, slow to show up at the scene and as likely to make trouble for the innocent as the guilty. Drivers have learnt not to carry accident victims to hospital. Too many have found themselves accused of being responsible for the death of a person they meant to help, and have had to buy their way out.

Like most ordinary Nigerians, police and soldiers are underpaid and hungry. The question "Wetin you get for me?" is a routine one at police and army checkpoints, and no wonder. It means, "I know you want to get where you're going, so I'll delay you till you get fed up and give me something". Money, you'll find, can get you out of most situations. Whether you want to collude in the system is up to you. But never show anger or impatience. Stay calm, crack a joke, offer a couple of cigarettes. Don't pull rank or threaten. It's a certain formula for escalating the tension and causing you real difficulty.

Apart from armed robbery and official intimidation, the biggest danger comes from the state of the roads and the vehicles that use them. Empty coffers mean minimal road maintenance, road surfaces pot-holed or simply disintegrating, no traffic lights and floods in the rainy season. A shortage of foreign exchange for imports means a scarcity of spare parts which anyway are very expensive, which in turn means a majority of cars with bald tyres, faulty headlights, water for brake fluid and so on.

These factors are a lethal combination – not helped by the conviction on the part of most drivers that it's essential to drive as though they've overdosed on kola nuts. The best advice is to hire a reputable car and driver from one of the international hotels, and insist that the driver keep his speed down to 80mph on the expressway and doesn't overtake on blind corners. Or drive yourself. Try to avoid travelling in the Peugeot estates which ply between towns. They're known as flying coffins and, they've become progressively more unsafe.

"Society itself is catching up with fiction"

If you're travelling north–south or vice versa, I'd recommend the train, which is slow but safe. Travel first class and you'll have a private compartment with a door you can lock and sheets you can hire for a good night's sleep. It's a wonderful opportunity just to sit and stare out of the window and gives you a striking impression of the sheer size and diversity of the country. The landscape shifts from coast to rainforest to savannah, and the tantalising glimpses of a world never seen from the road – backyards, marketplaces, vast stretches of farmland dotted with lonely peasant cultivators, and the distinctive enclosed circular villages of the north with their mud houses and thatched roofs and traditional granaries. The stations are an experience in themselves, as a multitude of hawkers all try at once to sell you oranges, eggs, cigarettes, soft drinks, bean fritters, fried fish, bread, garden eggs, groundnuts, chewing gum and bananas.

The famous novelist, Chinua Achebe, said on the publication of his most recent novel *Anthills of the Savannah* "Soon we won't be able to write novels because anything you can concoct has already been surpassed yesterday. Our society itself is catching up with fiction." This encapsulates a truth about Nigeria which lies at the heart of its fascination: the only thing you can be sure of is that you don't know what's going to happen next. In place of a working infrastructure and reliable public services, it offers unpredictability and confusion.

The pressure to survive in the face of extreme insecurity has made Nigerians phenomenally resourceful. No-one is content to be pigeon-holed. Businessmen write plays, teachers trade, lawyers are dress designers, executives import toilet paper and toothbrushes, doctors run shops or playschools. There isn't much leisure as we understand it: life is too hard and too fast for spare time. Drama, music, fashion, food and seduction are part and parcel of life itself.

The pages of the newspapers are an unending serialisation of the bizarre and unexpected. A publisher is killed by a letter bomb said to come from the president's office. A betrayed wife goes to the workplace of her husband's lover and tips a pot of soup over her desk. Ludicrously wealthy men donate fabulous sums of money to schemes of self-glorification. A popular musician whose songs annoy the government is put in prison for almost a year. A small boy walks to Lagos from the east to ask the Minister of Education to pay his school fees. The president declares a public holiday because the national football team is playing. Politicians make announcements which read with all the veracity of fairy tales.

Nigeria is a country of poverty, danger, theatre, ritual, creativity and humour. If you can relate to any of these elements – and if you can put your own relatively privileged life in perspective and sometimes find it funny too – you'll find you can cope.

LAGOS

If you're reading nervously, you wouldn't be the first traveller to approach **Lagos** with a sinking feeling of despair and trepidation, convinced you're going to hate the place – should you live through it. Lagos has grown too big too fast. Long ago, the city over-flowed from the **islands** at its heart, and the urban sprawl on the mainland has mush-roomed alarmingly. Its eight million inhabitants, whose number may double in the next decade, are living under siege. Of the infrastructure – housing, roads, public transport, water, electricity and sewerage – only the new expressways show any sign of keeping up (cars, as everywhere, getting priority). Pollution, squalid overcrowding, violent crime and a twenty-four hour din are the inevitable results of the shortfall. And there's a feeling that never leaves you, of traumatised lives, surviving by guile and instinct on a razor's edge – a feeling somewhat reminiscent of the street scenes in the film *Blade Runner*. There's a lot here to keep you on your toes.

But you just may be surprised. It's the **international airport** – the whole, dreadful business of arrival or connecting planes there – that's to blame for much of the terrible first impression. And having approached the city with a caution verging on paranoia, you may find rather less chaos – and more to excite. For Africa's foremost metropolis is, at the very least, a city of intense, voluble personality and breathtaking dynamism. Ships from around the globe berth at its **ports** of Apapa and Tin Can Island, and the **skyscrapers** that spike from Lagos Island house a swarm of international firms.

A more immediate sign of "success" is the commuter traffic packing the **flyovers**, regularly grinding to a halt in rush hour "go-slow" traffic jams, to be exploited by thou-sands of irrepressible **street vendors** trying to sell anything from imported apples to bathroom scales. And beyond the non-stop, unrestrained commercialism on the streets, universities, museums, galleries and the national theatre all attest to a thriving **intellectual and cultural life**.

SOME HISTORY

About all that can be deduced about the swampy mangrove zone around Lagos before the Portuguese arrived is that it was inhabited by small Ga fishing communities. Rainforest and marshes probably prevented large scale settlement. **Sequestra** and other **Portuguese mariners** first arrived at the islands around Lagos in 1472 and named the place *Lago de Curamo*, but it wasn't until much later that the area became an important port of trade.

In the sixteenth century, **Yoruba settlers** came to Iddo and later moved onto Lagos Island – which they named Eko – and beyond. The settlement was eventually incorpo-rated into the **Benin Kingdom** which at the time extended all the way to the Cotonou district. In the early eighteenth century, the ruling Oba granted a trade monopoly to the Portuguese whose main export was, of course, **slaves**. In the early nineteenth century, the French and British governments began sending warships to break up the slave trade. Lagos was used as a hideout by profiteers who made advantage of the many creeks and rivers to hide their human cargo. In 1851, the **British** shelled Lagos and eventually forced the Oba to abandon the slave trade. Soon after, they captured the islands and formed Lagos colony.

Early this century, Lagos grew into an important commercial centre thanks to the port and the **railway line**, begun in 1896 and opened through to Kano in 1912. It became the capital of the southern Nigerian protectorate and later of the entire Federation when north and south were merged. After independence, Lagos maintained its role as capital until 1976 when Abuja assumed the title. The city is still the country's undisputed commercial, industrial, cultural and diplomatic centre, capital in all but name.

While it would definitely be misleading to downplay its problems, Lagos is no more of a hell hole than any other gigantic, seething, impoverished city with a military administration and an intolerable climate. Travel with as much confidence as you can muster and you may well have a good time . . . and debunking some myths and surviving the experience unscathed, as nearly everyone does, carry their own satisfaction.

Arriving and practicalities

Lagos spreads over some 200 square kilometres and comprises myriad **neighbourhoods**. But the heart of the city, where you're likely to spend most time, is tucked onto **Lagos and Ikoyi Islands** – now merged – and **Victoria Island**, to the south.

By whatever means you come to Lagos, however, the **mainland** is your point of entry. Although there are bland neighbourhoods here (like the administrative district of Ikeja), most are populated by the city's working class and poor – and they can feel distinctly heavy. In reality, while this is where many Lagos horror stories are located, that's mostly because richer people don't live there. As a temporary visitor you're no more likely to run into serious, violent trouble on the mainland than anywhere else in Lagos (perhaps, in truth, less). Still, if you can arrange to be **met from the airport**, do so – any of the travel agents detailed on p.1015 offer this service.

THE TAXI DRIVERS ACTUALLY SCREAM

"Well, it's true one must fight to pay a normal taxi fare. For women, including Nigerian women, it's harder. The taxi drivers actually scream at you if you try to pay the regular price. But the regular price is the regular price and you can pay it after a fight (verbal) and all is well. This didn't bother me, but then I spent fourteen years living in New York City. By comparison Lagos is a gentle place."

Arriving by air

Arriving by plane at **Murtala Muhammed Airport** could be the most harrowing experience you'll have in Lagos – indeed it's probably the most unpleasant way to spend an hour or two anywhere in West Africa. Customs agents are routinely aggressive and unsubtle ("What are you going to dash me?") and the whole entrance process – verification of visa and health certificate, issue of currency declaration form, luggage search, body search and so on *ad nauseum* – is enough to put you off the city forever.

Unfortunately, unless there's just been one of the state government's irregular clampdowns on people hanging arond the airport area, things don't get any better when you step outside to find an **airport taxi** (only limited numbers of taxis are licensed to trade at the airport, and there are no buses out here). The way the drivers fight for your business, you'd think your mere presence had triggered a war, but the battle really begins when you start talking prices. You might as well concede from the outset that you'll probably pay much more than the going price (there are set rates usually posted in the airport and in the taxis themselves, currently the Naira equivalent of around £6). If it's after dark, your main concern, rather than worrying about saving a little money on the fare, should be to get out of the airport and into a hotel. There, the worst is over. If you're lucky enough to be flying in during daylight hours, you could, alternatively, walk down the airport road about 2km and pick up a shared taxi or a bus – but most people don't.

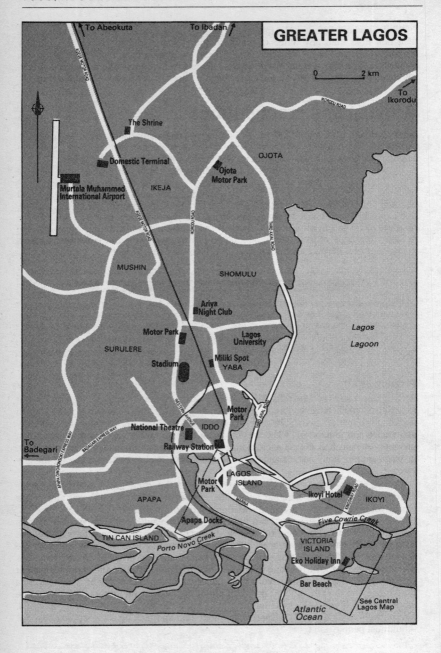

GREATER LAGOS

To Abeokuta
To Ibadan

0   2 km

To Ikorodu

The Shrine

Domestic Terminal

Murtala Muhammed
International Airport

IKEJA

OJOTA

Ojota
Motor Park

MUSHIN

SHOMULU

Ariya
Night Club

Motor Park

Lagos
University

Lagos
Lagoon

SURULERE

Stadium

Miliki Spot
YABA

Motor
Park

National Theatre   IDDO

Railway Station

To
Badegari

LAGOS
ISLAND

Motor
Park

APAPA

Ikoyi Hotel

IKOYI

Five Cowrie Creek

Apapa Docks

TIN CAN ISLAND

Porto Novo Creek

VICTORIA
ISLAND

Eko Holiday Inn

Bar Beach

Atlantic
Ocean

See Central
Lagos Map

GETTING AROUND

Transport is a nightmare. Getting around Lagos, unless you have unlimited time or patience (or your own car and driver as many expatriates do) it is basically down to **taxis**. Fares are inexpensive, and you'd need to be down on your luck (or just curious) to use the complex array of buses and minibuses. The plan in the 1980s for a **metro system** that was to have come to Lagos' rescue, has been shelved. For the northern suburbs, trains are an option, but hardly very practicial – and there are limited boat services, too.

Taxis

Lagos taxis are usually yellow *Peugeot 504s* with black stripes. The drivers like to "pick" people as they go, effectively running a share-taxi service, often on the route of their choice, and ignoring the regular fares (a table of which they're obliged to display) and the protests of passengers. You hail them by yelling out your destination.

Use some discretion over where you say you're going (be prepared to get out and walk a hundred metres) as it can affect the fare, which you should discuss and agree on first. Stand in the door till you're sure the driver knows the price is agreed. Try also to have the notes ready (if possible wave them in the driver's face) to emphasise the fare you're prepared to pay. Change is a rare thing in any case. The kinds of fares you'll end up paying vary from around Naira equivaents of 20–30p for district-to-district hops and £1–2 for lengthy cross-city jobs. If you want to **charter**, rather than wait for a share, shout "Drop!" and it'll be understood, but you'll pay much more – £1 for short hops, £2–3 for cross-city journeys. The official "standard" fare for a drop at the end of 1990 was still ₦25, but they'll tell you much more.

Minibuses and buses

Lagos public transport makes you nostalgic for Dakar or Abidjan, or even Douala. The system is fraught, exhausting and unpredictable. There's a struggling fleet of red and white, Lagos State Transport Corporation midi- and minibuses and *Mercedes* buses (*oluwale*). But they're far outnumbered on the mainland by motley swarms of privately owned midi- and minibuses – either VW or Japanese kombis, or local *Merc* or *Bedford* conversions known as *molue* (large, with aisles) or *danfo* (small, seat only). Privately owned vehicles in this league aren't officially allowed off the mainland.

Maximum fares (private or LSTC) are low, 50kobo or ₦1 for long hauls, but the discomfort and hair-pulling frustration and slowness of them can undermine the resolve of even the staunchest city survivor.

Commuter trains

Commuter trains seem quite a good idea once you've ridden a few *molue*. The Nigerian Railways Corporation runs 13 pairs of diesel hauled **trains** on weekdays only, between the railway terminal in **Iddo**(by Lagos Island) and **Ifo**, 48km out of the city on the **Abeokuta/ Iseyin** road. En route, they pass through **Oshodi** and **Ikeja** (by the airport) and **Agege**, on the northern edge of the city. Fares are low and they even do monthly season tickets.

Ferries and boats

There's a lot more **ferrying about** that could be done with all that water and creek front-age. At present, the main water route consists of an hourly ferry service in a big, hundred-seater vessel, from midway along **Marina** across Lagos Harbour to Apapa and "Mile Two", on a canal west of the Apapa-Orowonsoki Expressway, about 1km south of the Badagari Expressway.

You can also get ferries from **Victoria Island to Tarkwa**. *Tarzan Boats* across from the Italian embassy, run to Tarkwa Bay and other local beaches.

Most boat trips **out to the beaches** (the best ones all to the west) tend to be a private affair. Lagos is a place where it very much pays to have, or make friends, quickly. A lot of boats take off every weekend from the Motor Boat Club at the west end of Awolowo Rd on Five Cowrie Creek.

Arriving by long-distance taxis

By **long-distance taxi**, you'll arrive at one of several points on the mainland – Mile Two, Yaba, Ojota or Iddo. From these places, battered yellow private buses or state-run red and white buses (see "Getting Around") will drop you at Lagos Island whence you can hire a cheap taxi to a hotel. Unless you're really strapped for cash, it's really worth the extra money to hire a taxi.

Arriving by rail

If you happen to come in **by train** you'll arrive at Iddo, a small island near the north tip of Lagos Island. This is a tough area but more peaceful zones are close at hand and the recommended plan of action is to hire a taxi directly to your destination.

Arriving by ship

These days it's unusual to arrive by ship. But a number of cargo lines do still offer berths. If you're interested in leaving this way, follow up the address in the Lagos "Directory" on p.1015 (see under "Getting out of Lagos"). Ships berth at Apapa, opposite Lagos Island.

Orientation

From a traveller's point of view, Lagos consists of four main areas: the Mainland, Lagos Island, Ikoyi and Victoria Island. If your stay is going to be any longer than a day or two, it's worth getting hold of the excellent *Winnay Lagos Street Atlas*, published by Macmillan, either before you arrive, or as soon as possible in Lagos.

THE TROUBLE WITH LAGOS

While the risks of **muggings and pickpocketing** in Lagos are naturally high, most people get through their stays safely. Perhaps more than any other city in the world, Lagos induces an immediate response. The fact that so many visitors fear and detest it has more to do with its formidable expanse and chronic, threatening mess than with personal experience of real danger – as you'll soon find out if you listen hard, for example, to expatriate residents, for whom it's home to one of the largest communities in West Africa. And at the risk of sounding mysterious, reactions to Lagos depend a lot on the way you feel and act – see the section on "Trouble – Getting in and out" on p.56–58.

The mainland

A vast reach of working-class districts, industrial zones and shanty towns heaves over the mainland for miles.

At it's northwest edge is the **international airport**, while rising above it all near the creeks to the south, the **National Theatre** vaunts its modernistic architecture in an area that reeks of destitution. Built for the 1977 FESTAC cultural festival it's a classic example of the kind of high-prestige, low-reward development that faces increasing criticism in Africa. Whatever your personal feelings, since the complex exists, you may as well take advantage of the facilities which include the **National Gallery of Modern Art**, the **Centre for Black and African Arts and Civilization** (see "Museums") and the **National Gallery of Crafts and Design**.

Nigeria's **National Stadium** is located on Western Avenue in the nearby **Surulere** neighbourhood. Surulere is a vibrant quarter and contains some of Lagos' most popular nightspots, but watch yourself at night.

Lagos Island

Lagos Island is the commercial centre and site of the towers that provide the city's striking skyline. Many of these highrises – including most of the bank headquarters and **Nitel House**, Africa's tallest skyscraper – are on the south side of the island behind **Marina Street**, which used to run along the waterfront. Today, Marina is several hundred metres back from the water, shadowed by the zooming split-level expressway of **Apongbon Street**. But it retains some buildings of note, including the former **State House** – residence of the British governors – the infamous headquarters of **NEPA** (electricity corporation) headquarters, with the bronze statue of Shango the thunder god before it, Lagos' **main post office** and the eighteenth-century **Anglican church**.

Broad Street, which runs parallel to Marina, is another well-known thoroughfare with more banks and markets and some fairly upmarket shops. It runs into **Tinubu Square**, a landscaped roundabout, with a perpetually defunct fountain, in one of the busiest parts of town. Nearby, the **markets** of **Jankara, Isale Eko, Ebute Ero** and **Balogun** all run into one another, filling the western part of the island with frenetic small-scale commerce. The **Brazilian quarter**, founded by former slaves brought back from Brazil, is concentrated in the area around Campos Square and Campbell Street, while the **Oba's palace** lies on the northern tip of the island on Upper King Street.

The eastern end of Marina is dominated by the great scar of **Tafawa Balewa Square**, with its monumental equine statues rearing up at the entrance in memory of the old racetrack that used to be here. Now, the north side of Tafawa Balewa is where almost all the major airlines and travel agencies have their offices. The south is shops and cheap restaurants. Just up the road is the **Onikan National Museum**.

Ikoyi

The swamps formerly dividing **Ikoyi** from Lagos Island have been filled in, and today the two sections of town are separated only by a tangle of motorway flyovers. But Ikoyi still retains its individual flavour. Its main artery, **Awolowo Road**, links Lagos Island with Victoria Island via the **Falomo Bridge**. Awolowo is all chic **boutiques** – many operating out of converted private homes – high-priced **restaurants**, a sprinkling of embassies and the **Polo Club**, a reminder of the days when Ikoyi was the poshest colonial neighbourhood. The **Falomo Shopping centre** crowns Awolowo Road at the junction to Kingsway Road near the bridge.

The centre of Ikoyi, dominated by the **administrative district**, includes the **Federal Secretariat**, where most of the ministries are housed, and the present State House. Further west, **Obalende** is a vibrant working-class neighbourhood with a large market, numerous chop bars (good places for authentic pepper soup or suya) and watering holes where locals come to drink and dance. As Dodon Barracks and the Presidential Lodge border this neighbourhood, it is well policed and one of the safest low-income areas in town. However, it's still a good idea to go accompanied at night.

Victoria Island (V.I.)

The principal new residential area of Lagos, **Victoria Island**'s bleak and shadeless sandy wastes are now divided into thousands of expensive plots, many of them taken up by foreign **embassies**. **Bar Beach**, the city's closest strand, runs along the island's southern flank and, nearby, the **Eko Holiday Inn** – the newest (late 1970s) and nicest big hotel in Lagos – rises up behind the oceanfront.

To the west of the island, on Ahmadou Bello way, the **Federal Palace** has taken a dive in recent years though it used to be the city's premier hotel. The lagoon-side bar still affords a **panoramic view** of the Lagos Island skyline (good place for photos) and ships docking at the ports of Apapa and Tin Can Island.

Near the **Independence Bridge** to Lagos Island, **Eleke Crescent** has the highest concentration of diplomatic missions – including those of Britain and the USA – of any street in town. On the northeast corner of the island, **"1004"**, a vast housing project with a thousand and four apartments, is Lagos' first tasted of massive-scale urban housing, a maze of buildings and parking lots.

Accommodation

There's no shortage of **hotels** in Lagos, and most of them are on the mainland. While it may be more convenient to be on the islands, there's a persistent notion that the mainland is a more dangerous area. There's complete disunity of opinion on this among expatriates and frequent visitors. But it's worth knowing that those who actually enjoy aspects of Lagos life aren't intimidated by the mainland – most of the music clubs are there for example. Moreover the islands do have the lion's share of what's worth robbing. We've listed four mainland hotels and would welcome further recommendations for the next edition.

Even **upmarket hotels** are at present reasonably priced in Lagos, and downright cheap if you've come west from Cameroon. If you've been waiting to relax your fiscal controls, this is a good place to splurge and budget travellers won't be disappointed either as **cheap hotels and hostels** are also available. The following places are reliable, safe and central; they are listed (by area) in roughly ascending order of price.

Ikoyi

YMCA, 77 Awolowo Rd (☎680 516). The cheapest accommodation in town (though for men only: the YWCA is on Lagos Island – see below) and conveniently equidistant from Lagos and Victoria islands. Rather scruffy non S/C 4–bed dorms with fan. Nigerians and refugees from throughout Africa board here, however, and can be a big help showing you around the city if you strike up a friendship. Often full; book ahead. Under £2.

Beneshade Restaurant and Guest-house, 15 Sumbo Jibowu St. Directly behind the YMCA, this is a small hotel in a house conversion in a good, safe area. There's a garden bar and African restaurant; rooms (some S/C) are clean and moderately priced.

Ikoyi Hotel, Kingsway Rd (PO Box 895; ☎603 202, telex 22632). Once a colonial institution and top-notch hotel, but it's taken a slide – tatty carpets and furniture and usually out-of-action pool pump so you have to swim elsewhere (Ikoyi club for example). At low exchange rates though, it's still reasonably good value and the other amenities are all there.

Lagos Island

YWCA, George V Street, corner of Moloney St. Clean, cheap dorm rooms for women only. But apart from the gender specificity, the only advantage of this Y is its proximity to the National Museum. The locks on the lockers don't lock and loud bells ring at 6am to turf you out for the day. Under £2.

Hotel Wayfarer, 52 Campbell St (☎630 113), by Lagos Island Maternity Hospital. Moderate and in the town centre, with simple but adequate and safe S/C, AC rooms. One of the cheapest places for couples, with a small restaurant. Nice management. Book ahead. Under £5.

Ishaga Inn, off Balogun St, at the western end of the island. Another reasonably priced hotel. Clean and in a colourful area hemmed in by a cloth market. Note, however, that this end of Lagos Island is not the safest after dark.

Bristol Hotel, 8 Martin St (PO Box 1088; ☎661 201/207/242, telex 21144). Like the *Ikoyi* and *Federal Palace*, a lapsed old standby and well-known pre-independence middle-class African joint. You could do a lot worse in Lagos, though it's moderately expensive and (along with its immediate, claustrophobic surrounds) is now almost synonymous with money changers, prostitutes and drug dealers. Never a dull moment, but in truth not dangerous.

The Regent, 23 Abibu Oki Street (☎662 527). A similar, but danker, hotel near the *Bristol*.

Victoria Island

B-Jays Guesthouse, 12 B Adeola Hopewell St (☎612 391). A small, moderately priced hotel with AC, S/C rooms. Clean, friendly service and a safe residential neighbourhood.

Federal Palace Hotel, Ahmadou Bello Rd (PO Box 1000; ☎610.031, telex 21432). *The* hotel in Lagos until the late 1970s, the *Federal Palace* still harks back to the first flush of independence. But faulty plumbing makes bucket showers obligatory in older rooms and while the new wing is better, there's no water in the pool, the furniture is falling apart (etc.). It's scheduled for renovation, but meanwhile take a couple of beers and you can almost imagine what it used to be like – and then it's okay. The bar built over the lagoon is accessible from the new building, from where spectacular views can be had of ships nosing out into harbour. Poolside dancing to live music (pop-schlock) on weekends is tacky but again okay if you're in the right mood – and company. Moderate to expensive.

Eko Meridien Hotel, Kuramo Waters (Private Bag 12724; ☎615 000/695, telex 22650, fax 615 205). The sparkling white tower – rising a short distance from the open Atlantic – is the best and most expensive hotel in downtown Lagos (from £60) and definitely the place to book if you're travelling on someone else's account. Complete comfort in all departments, including a crystal-clear pool.

Mainland

Ritalori, Animashawun St, off Eric Moore Rd, Surulere. A highly recommended Nigerian hotel in a lively area with a pool and friendly management. Not too expensive.

Kolex, off Fola Agoro St, Shomulu. Small, quiet, comfortable and modern. Disco and a useful shop. Transport available. Around £7–£16.

Airport Hotel, Obafemi Awolowo Rd (☎901 001/5, 901 040). Large, plush pile gone to seed but not at all bad and not expensive or anonymous compared with the competition by which it's recently been overtaken.

Sheraton, 30 Airport Rd, Ikeja (PMB 21189; ☎900 930, telex 27202/3). Lagos' newest and smartest hotel, American-run and right by the airport, caters for business people whose contacts come to them, with everything on hand and no need even to go into the city. From around £70 per night.

Around the City

The effort of getting **around the city** is the only thing that really detracts from its worthwhile sites. It can literally take hours to accomplish journeys that, in retropsect could probably have been walked more quickly. Don't be afraid of venturing out on foot duing the day. So long as you have nothing of value on you, you've nothing to fear – apart from the drivers.

Museums

Lagos is almost alone among West Africa cities in having more than a single **museum**. The **National Museum** is highly recommended and, if you've time or opportunity, make an effort to visit the **National Theatre** and see what's on view at its cultural centre and galleries; the local press will have details.

The National Museum

Nigeria's foremost museum (see map for location; open daily, 9am–6pm), is a required visit, especially worthwhile if the travelling exhibition, "Treasures of Ancient Nigeria", happens to be home for a rest from world touring.

The **"Treasures"** traces 2500 years of Nigerian art from the earliest terracotta figures from **Nok** on the plateau, through extraordinarily intricate and sophisticated

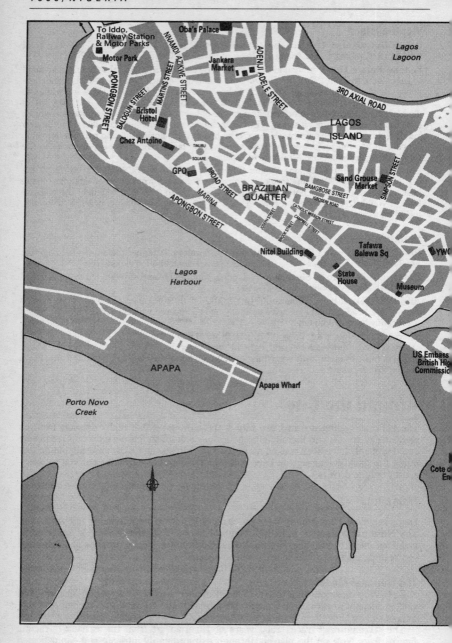

To Iddo,
Railway Station
& Motor Parks
Motor Park
Oba's Palace
Jankara
Market
*Lagos
Lagoon*
NNAMDI AZIKIWE STREET
MARTINS STREET
ADENIJI ADELE STREET
3RD AXIAL ROAD
APONGBON STREET
BALOGUN STREET
Bristol
Hotel
LAGOS
ISLAND
Chez Antoine
TINUBU
SQUARE
GPO
BROAD STREET
MARINA
APONGBON STREET
BRAZILIAN
QUARTER
BAMGBOSE STREET
Sand Grouse
Market
SIMPSON STREET
IGBOSERE ROAD
CATHOLIC MISSION STREET
JOSEPH STREET
BROCK STREET
CAMPBELL STREET
Nitel Building
Tafawa
Balewa Sq
YWC
State
House
Museum
*Lagos
Harbour*
APAPA
Apapa Wharf
US Embass
British Hig
Commissio
*Porto Novo
Creek*
Cote d
En

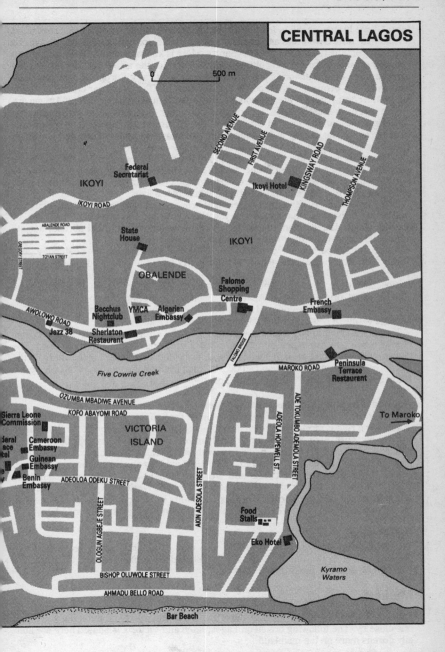

CENTRAL LAGOS

0   500 m

IKOYI

Federal
Secretariat

Ikoyi Hotel

SECOND AVENUE

FIRST AVENUE

KINGSWAY ROAD

THOMPSON AVENUE

IKOYI ROAD

ABALENDE ROAD

OKOKR STREET

TOYAN STREET

State
House

IKOYI

OBALENDE

Falomo
Shopping
Centre

French
Embassy

AWOLOWO ROAD

Becchus
Nightclub

YMCA

Algerian
Embassy

Jazz 38

Sherlaton
Restaurant

FALOMO BRIDGE

MAROKO ROAD

Peninsula
Terrace
Restaurant

Five Cowrie Creek

OZUMBA MBADIWE AVENUE

KOFO ABAYOMI ROAD

Sierra Leone
Commission

VICTORIA
ISLAND

To Maroko

ederal
ace
tel

Cameroon
Embassy

Guinean
Embassy

Benin
Embassy

ADEOLOA ODEKU STREET

ADE TOKUMBO ADEMOLA STREET

ADEOLA HOPEWELL ST.

AKIN ADESOLA STREET

OLOGUN AGBEJE STREET

Food
Stalls

Eko Hotel

BISHOP OLUWOLE STREET

Kyramo
Waters

AHMADU BELLO ROAD

Bar Beach

Igbo-Ukwe bronze castings from southeast Nigeria to the almost Hellenic realism of the later **Ife and Owo** brass and terracotta busts – which provide a glimpse into Yoruba court life from the twelfth to fifteenth century. More is known about the **Benin** kingdom than any of Nigeria's other old cultures, because besides the art works, there is also the corroboration of oral histories and written accounts by early European explorers. The famous **Benin bronzes** were made exclusively for the Oba by master craftsmen working for the court. These represent some of the greatest masterpieces of West African art.

The **permanent exhibits** are divided into four galleries. The **Ethnographic Gallery** is designed to give an overview of the cultural materials of Nigeria's diverse ethnic groups. The display of **Masquerades**, common to a range of peoples, shows off one of the oldest forms of cultural and artistic expression. In Nigeria, masquerades not only served to provide a link with the realm of the dead but were important in instigating other art forms like music, dance and drama. Other exhibits range from decorated **pottery and calabashes** from the different regions to **shrines** and household gods reflecting the importance of the supernatural in people's lives.

The **Benin Gallery** contains a selection of bronzes and ivory carvings, including the well-known waist mask that appears on the Naira note and was symbol of the *FESTAC* festival. Unfortunately, many masterpieces of Benin art are still held abroad, despite numerous requests for their return from the Nigerian government.

An additional permanent exhibition – **"Nigerian governments: Yesterday and Today"** – traces the political history of the country from the slave trade to the present. The post-independence section acts as a visual *aide-mémoire* in figuring out the rather complicated train of events since the days when Abubakar Tafawa Balewa became Nigeria's first prime minister. Amid the displays recounting the coups and governments that followed, President Murtala Muhammed's bullet-holed car pays menacing homage to one of Nigeria's most popular assassinated leaders.

If you're looking to buy crafts, check out the **crafts shop** in the museum for an idea of how much you can expect to pay for artwork in Lagos – prices here are fixed. The chances are you won't actually find a cheaper price outside the big hotels where all the gear is often laid out. Lastly, you can take a break from all the culture in the very good **Museum Kitchen** (see "Cheap Eating", p.1010).

National Theatre Exhibitions and Spaces

The National Theatre is more a cultural complex than simply a theatrical venue, which is actually a role it rarely has the chance to play. The main ancillary site is the **Centre for Black and African Arts and Civilization** (Mon–Sat 7.30am–3.30pm) which contains archives, a library and a museum with periodically changing exhibits, all dedicated to black culture. The original *FESTAC 1977* exhibits should still be on show.

The **National Gallery of Crafts and Design** (Mon–Fri 10am–5pm, Sat 10am–4pm; ☎830 200) displays traditional Nigerian handicrafts. The **National Gallery of Modern Art** at Entrance B of the Theatre complex (Tues–Fri 10am–3pm, Sat & Sun noon–4pm, closed public holidays) is an exhibition space for the work of young Nigerian talents.

Didi Museum

The **Didi Museum** on Victoria Island is a new exhibiution space featuring fresh Nigerian talent in the fine arts. Local press should have more details, or ask at the National Museum or the National Theatre.

Markets

Lagos lacks nothing in the **market** department and wherever you fetch up, you'll find one close by. The following are all on Lagos, Ikoyi and Victoria Islands. There are literally dozens more on the mainland.

Jankara market on Lagos Island. The prime site and one of the cheapest places for new **clothes** or second-hand garments, general **hardware, traditional musical instruments, cassettes, jewellery** and **trading beads, magical materials** (jujus, skins, powders), and, if you look hard, examples of **adire** – local tie-dyed indigo cloth.

Isale Eko market, further west between Adeniji Adele Rd and Ebute Ero St. Specialises in food, crocks and baskets. You can also find some ready-made clothes here. In the same area, near the old Carter bridge, is an **"Ogogoro market"** with scorching local spirit for sale.

Balogun market, centred on the street of the same name. The best place for **cloth**. In the rambling maze of alleys you'll find mostly imported material, including damasks, plus a wide range of African prints. A little to the east, around Nnamdi Azikwe St, you can find batiks and ready-made clothes, plus records and cassettes.

Sand Grouse, between Lewis St and Simpson St on the eastern end of the island. The best bet for **food** – fresh fish, shrimps and huge snails, as well as more conventional provisions.

Obalende, in Ikoyi. Again, mostly food, usually with a good selection of fruit and veg.

Bar Beach market, towards the end of Ahmadu Bello Rd on Victoria Island. Another food market. In view of all the money and expatriates on the island, it's no surprise to find some arts and crafts here, too – including basketry, batiks and even Tuareg leather chests.

Parks and architecture

Lagos Island is the oldest part of the city. Between the highrises and the market shacks and the exhaust emissions and the rains, a few old buildings from more peaceful times have survived. As too, have one or two slightly secluded, city centre retreats.

Tafawa and Ikoyi Parks
Tafawa Balewa Square is a big grassy dusty patch, but hardly a park. Go to **Ikoyi** if you're looking for some space within walking distance. Many of the residential avenues are shady and attractive. **Ikoyi park,** partially wooded behind the bay at the northeast end of the island, east of Kingsway Rd, goes right down to the shore and provides a passable few acres for bird-watching.

Brazilian architecture
As for Lagos' famous old **Brazilian-style architecture,** very little survives – and that which does is falling apart and jealously guarded against photographers. The Oba's palace, in particular, is completely unimpressive.

Still, if you're keen on a hunt, the following, all on Lagos island, may still be worthwhile: **Chief's House,** Ado St; **Ebun House,** 85 Odunfa St (300m east of Tinubu Sq), a great pile of a place dating from 1914; **Brazilian House,** 29 Kakawa St, off Marina; **Da Silva House,** Odufege St; and the comely **Shitta Mosque** on Martins St, with its Brazilian tilework.

Beaches

Bar Beach, on Victoria island, was always unattractive and shadeless, but the closest spot to swim in the sea – and also a meeting place for Christian sects. Now they, and you, will have to find somewhere else, as the beach was swept away on an exceptional spring tide in August 1990. Barring a sudden change in wind and wave patterns it probably won't be seen again. The 300,000 inhabitants of Maroko slum lost their homes in the flood – or more precisely they were bulldozed away after the event when the state government couldn't deal with the crisis.

Badagary, to the west of Lagos, is a good area to head for beaches, but somewhat far. **Lekki Beach,** 10km east of town off the Lagos Expressway past the vast dumpscape of Maroko, is lined with coconut palms that improve the mood considerably.

Take a taxi to Gbara village and walk 2km down the sand road leading from the Expressway to the beach, or arrange to be dropped directly at the beach; settle the cab price beforehand. You can hire horses quite cheaply here and food and drink are on sale.

Eating, drinking and nightlife

Lagos is heavily geared to slavish spending: flashy restaurants, bars, clubs and discos abound – as do more tacky establishments. With the Naira cheap, it's a city where you can have a good time on a low budget. So pick and choose. And if you're thinking you might go out on the town later, assume you will; and accordingly leave all but the necessary minimum of possessions in your hotel.

Restaurants

By day, numerous **snack bars** line the southern edge of Tafawa Balewa Square on Lagos Island. All serve similar fare of meat pies, sausage rolls or pizza – nothing fancy, but quick and inexpensive. Over on Marina St, the supermarkets all have cafeterias for reasonable lunches. Most of Lagos' **pricier restaurants** are on Lagos Island and Ikoyi and even the expensive places aren't unreasonable at current exchange rates. A number are quite formal, however, and you'd do well to book.

Cheap to moderate

LAGOS ISLAND

L&S Superstore. One of the best supermarket restaurants, serving inexpensive snacks and salads, overlooking the harbour.

Mr Biggs, in the former Kingsway building on Marina St. This restaurant looks like a *MacDonald's*, (and is recommended for nostalgic Americans) but the meat pies are better value than the shriveled Big Mac effigies. You'll find another branch on Tinubu St behind the post office.

Musuem Kitchen, National Museum grounds. Extensive selection of reasonably priced standbys – *eba, moin-moin, fufu, dodo, egusi, ogbono* – plus a daily regional speciality dish. Highly recommended.

IKOYI

There's a favourite small **restaurant** near the YMCA (left down Raymond Njoku Rd when coming from the Y, then 300m) marked only by two *7 Up* signs at the entrance. They do plain Nigerian food – *eba*, rice and beans, *dodo* and *amala* with cold beer and minerals. The best cheap eats in the neighbourhood.

Josephine's restaurant, Keffi St near the junction with Awolowo Rd (also near the YMCA), serves reasonable meals of the rice and fish type.

On the west side of Ikoyi, the **Obalende** area is full of **cheap restaurants and outdoor stands** where you can buy fish, *suya* (kebabs), rice and so on. Don't miss the pepper soup, a speciality of this quarter.

VICTORIA ISLAND

Cheap street food is available from a small side street directly opposite the *Eko Meridien*. Boiled yams, beans and rice, fufu with meat or fried fish. Eat here and then have a drink in the *Eko* for rapid culture contrast.

Expensive

LAGOS ISLAND

The Phoenecia, 35 Martin St, near the Bristol Hotel (☎663 156). A popular evening retreat with European food and a cover charge, African house bands and late night service.

Chez Antoine, 61 Broad St (☎664 881). More casual restaurant with French and Lebanese cuisine and sandwiches at lunchtime. Cool and relaxing after the heat and bustle of the street.

Tam Tam, 16 Market St (☎660 273) and **Tabriz**, behind the Bristol at 90 Breadfruit St (☎662 328). Two other downtown restaurants with Franco-Lebanese menus.

Cathay 88 Broad St (☎664 926). Quite good Chinese food, in a dodgy-looking building. Open daily.

Quo Vadis, Western House (17th floor), 8 Broad St (☎635 132). This restaurant has excellent seafood and Lebanese dishes and a view of the harbour. Men need to put on a tie. Closed Sundays.

Club Bagatelle, 208 Broad St, (☎662 410). Old established eating house with a Middle East flavoured international menu. Fourth-floor harbour view with bar and dancing; again, ties required for men.

IKOYI

Deja Vu, Falomo shopping centre. A reasonable if rather short menu – European food and burgers – but great cocktails and beer on tap.

The Sherlaton 108 Awolowo Rd (☎681 914). One of Lagos' best Indian restaurants and not over-priced or ostentatious.

Bacchus, 57 Awolowo Rd (☎681 653). A popular European restaurant with music and dancing. Dress up and be ready to pay a cover.

VICTORIA ISLAND

Imperial, in the *Federal Palace Hotel* (☎614 225). The city's top-notch Chinese, with higher standards than its host establishment.

Peninsula, Plot 8, Ozumba Rd, on the lagoon facing the 1004 flats (☎616 911). Terrace restaurant right on the water, serving good Chinese meals in a really nice ambience – for Lagos. Even if you're not hungry, you can come for a drink and the view.

MAINLAND

Art's Palace 280 Murtala Muhammed Way, Yaba (☎860 827). Art's own Brazilian family house. European and African dishes with jazz and highlife accompaniment and art exhibitions.

Club Panache *Mainland Hotel*, 2 Murtala Muhammed Way (☎ 800 300). Good Chinese food in an extravagantly decorated seting, with music and dancing. Closed Sunday.

Nightlife

Lagos is famous as a **music** centre, and the styles that have originated and evolved here – **Highlife, Juju, Fuji** and **Afrobeat** – are as legendary and international as any in Africa. Lagosians are proud of this and prefer listening to their own music than to the anodyne trans-Atlantic pop that's current over so much of West Africa. The daily *Evening News* normally has details of what's on across a span of forty or fifty venues, where you can dance till dawn and often see live performances. The following clubs (mostly selected for their live show pedigrees) are all, with the notable exception of **Jazz 38**, on the mainland. Don't be intimidated. Get a taxi and get on down.

IKOYI

Jazz 38 38, Awolowo Rd, Ikoyi (☎684 984). Owned by Fela Kuti's niece, Frances, and her husband, Tunde Kuboye, this open-air place is also known as the *Dental Club* (after the surgery next door). Afrobeat devotees crowd in on Fri, Sat and Sun, when the Kuboyes' "Extended Family Jazz Band" is often accompanied by Fela. He usually plays his sax for an hour or more, and doesn't hog the limelight. But he's also been known to come on chomping a cigar-sized joint, snarl at the crowd, sing for ten minutes and then leave again – irresistible stuff.

SURULERE

Stadium Hotel, 27 Iyun Rd, just west of the National Stadium (☎833 593). Home of highlife supremo Victor Olaiya and boasting a fantastic floorshow with dancers and contortionists. Friday nights feature **Sir Shina Peters and group**, the latest item on the Lagos scene, hotter than Alligator pepper. (You can of course stay at the Stadium afterwards, but bring your own sheets, at least).

APAPA

Bank Hotel, 20 Achakpo St, off Kirikiri Rd, Apapa-Ajengunle district. This is something of a focus for eastern Nigerian musicians like Nico Mbarga, Sonny Okosuns. Well worth checking out.

Faslax Nightclub, opposite NNPC, Apapa. Orlando Owoh, grand-daddy of highlife plays here every Thursday.

YABA

Ariya Night Club, 12, Ikorodu Rd, at Jibowu St, Yaba. Belongs to juju maestro King Sunny Ade, who plays here on Wednesdays or Saturdays, when he's not touring. Closed for renovations. as at the end of 1990.

Art's Palace, 280 Murtala Muhammed Way, corner of Petgrave St (☎860 827). Home of the Nigerian Jazz Club, highlife, everything.

Kariba Tavern, 2 Igbobi College Rd, a few minutes walk northwest from *Ariya* (☎821 898). Good jazz music and environment.

Fantasy Night Club, 17A Commercial Ave (☎862 082). Restaurant and nightclub with live bands on Thursdays.

Gab Willy Hotel, Fawehinmi St, Onike district. Local resident bands play juju and highlife – used to be "Late" Ade Ade and His Federal Orchestra and Chief S.O. Atolagbe.

Lay Torino, 24 Abeokuta St, Ebute Metta. Live fuji music.

Miliki Spot, 23–25 Olonade St (☎860 205). Live music from Chief Ebenezer Obey. Closed for renovations as at the end of 1990.

SHOMULU

Ikosi Hotel, 18B Ubani St, Bariga district. Disco with fuji, juju and apala.

Banana Club, 48 Salami Bolaji St, just west of Ikorodu Rd, Musin, 2.5km north of the *Ariya*. Fuji bands.

Samav Hotel, 4 Igbehinadun St, Mushin-Pedro district. Live fuji and juju bands nightly till midnight and weekends to dawn.

Standard Hotel, 13 Ogooluwa St. Fuji from Mon–Thurs, and juju at weekends. A long established Yoruba music spot.

IKEJA

The Shrine, Pepple St (no ☎) This is it. Fela Kuti's club, not far from the *Sheraton*, near the airport. It's one to rest up in preparation for. Get there no earlier than 11pm and be prepared for Fela to come on sometime after 2am and play till 4am or later.

Lagos Directory

Air Freight *DHL* at 1 Sumbo Jibowu St, Ikoyi (☎681 106).

Banks all open Mon–Thurs 8am–3pm, Fri 8am–1pm, including: *National Bank of Nigeria*, 82–86 Broad St, (☎661 561); *First Bank of Nigeria*, 37 Marina St; *International Bank for West Africa* (IBWA), 94 Broad St (☎662 301); *Societe Generale Bank of Nigeria*, 126 Broad St (☎660 315); *Union Bank*, 40 Marina St (☎661 810); *United Bank of Africa*, 97 Broad St.

Bookshops Lagos has the best English-language bookshops in West Africa. Besides the hotels (good selections in the *Eko Meridien* and the *Federal Palace*), try *Best Seller* in the Falamo Shopping Centre or the bookshops on Broad St, including *S.S. Bookshop* at the intersection with Odunlami St. Check out also *New World Bookshop* on Tafawa Balewa Sq.

Car hire There are many agencies in Lagos but they nearly all insist on renting a driver with the vehicle. The major ones – *Hertz, Europcar, Budget* – have branches at Murtala Muhammed Airport. In town ask at large hotels. The main offices are *Avis* 225 Apapa Rd, Iganmu (PMB 1155; ☎846 336, telex 21324); *Europcar* (PO Box 6569; ☎662 572); *Hertz* agents are *Mandilas* 96–102 Broad St, Lagos Island (PMB 35,; ☎663 514, telex 21383).

Clubs The Ikoyi Club, near the Ikoyi Hotel, isn't terrifically expensive for a short membership, though you have to be introduced by a member. Playing squash in Lagos feels like you've had six games before you've started.

Dentists Dr E. Solarin, Flat 2, Block D, Eko Court, Kofo Aboyomi, V.I. (☎610 917).

Doctors Dr Williams, 13 Airport Rd, Ikeja (☎933 482); Dr M. and Dr D. Semaan, St Francis Clinic, Keffi St, Ikoyi (☎684 125).

Hospitals Akimbola Awoliyi Memorial Hospital, 183 Bamgbose St, Lagos Island (☎631 520, ☎930 916) is one of the best, with a 24-hr casualty service. Near the airport there's Maryland Clinic, Abida Close, Maryland Estate, Ikeja (☎962 348).

Libraries and cultural centres
   National Library, 4 Wesley St (☎656 590), open Mon–Fri 7.30am–3.30pm, is a reference library with books and periodicals.
   British Council, 54 Okunola Martins Close, Ikoyi (☎680 008).

AIRLINES

Aeroflot, 36 Tafawa Balewa Sq (☎637 223); 8am–4pm.

Air Afrique, 18 Tafawa Balewa Sq (☎634 775); 8.30am–4pm.

Air Mali, Tafawa Balewa Sq (☎635 136); 8.30am–4pm.

Alitalia, 2 Martins St (☎662 468); 8am–5pm.

Balkan Bulgarian Airlnes, 39–41 Martins St (☎661 974/102).

British Airways, Unity House, 37 Marina St (☎662 669); Mon–Fri 8am–5pm, Sat 9am–noon; and Commerce House, 1 Idowu Taylor St, V.I. (☎613 004); 8.30am–5pm.

Cameroon Airlines, 11a Tafawa Balewa Sq (☎630 909); 8.30am–4.30pm.

Egyptair, 39–41 Martins St (☎661 974).

Ethiopian Airlines, 20 Tafawa Balewa Sq (☎637 655, 632 690).

Express Airways Nigeria, 84 Awolowo Rd, Ikoyi (☎686 048).

Ghana Airways, 17 Martins St (☎661 808); 8am–4.30pm.

Iberia, 17 Tafawa Balewa Sq (☎636 950); 8am–5pm.

KLM, Mandilas House, 96 Broad St, (☎661 452); and NUJ Building, Adeyemo Slakija St, V.I. (☎619 406).

Lufthansa, 150 Broad St (☎664 430).

Nigeria Airlines, Tafawa Balewa Sq (☎631 003).

Sabena, 23–25 Martins St (☎664 133); 8am–5pm.

Swiss Air, Hamburg House, 31–33 Martins St (☎662 299).

UTA 1 Davies St (☎664 909).

EMBASSIES AND CONSULATES

Algeria, 26 Maitama Sule St, Ikoyi (PO Box 7288; ☎683155, telex 21676); 9am–2pm.

Australia, plot PC43, off Idowu Taylor St, V.I. (PO Box 2427; ☎618 875, telex 21219).

Belgium, 1A Bank Rd, Ikoyi (PO Box 149; ☎603 230, telex 21118); 8.30am–13.30pm.

Benin, 4 Abudu Smith St, V.I. (PO Box 5705; ☎614 411, telex 21583); 8am–3pm.

Burkina Faso, 15 Norman Williams St, Ikoyi (☎681 001).

Cameroon, 5 Femi Pierce St, V.I. (PMB 2476; ☎614 386, telex 21343); 8am–2.30pm.

Canada, 4 Idowu Taylor St, V.I. (PO Box 54506; ☎612 382,, telex 21275); 7.30am–3pm.

Central African Republic, Plot 137 Ajao Estate, New Airport, Oshodi (☎682 820); 8am–noon.

Chad, 2 Goriola St, V.I. (PMB 70662; ☎613 116, telex 21414); 8am–2pm.

Côte d'Ivoire, 3 Abudu Smith St, V.I. (PO Box 7780; ☎610 963, telex 21120).

Denmark 4 Eleke Crescent, V.I. (PO Box 2390; ☎610 841, telex 21349); 8am–2pm.

Egypt, 81 Awolowo Rd, Ikoyi (PO Box 538; ☎681 867); 8am–2.30pm.

Equatorial Guinea, 7 Bank Rd, Ikoyi (PO box 4162; ☎683 717); 8am–2pm.

Ethiopia, Ahmadu Bello Rd, V.I. (PMB 2488; ☎613 198).

Finland, 13 Eleke Crescent, V.I. (PO Box 4433; ☎610 916, telex 21796); 7.30am–2pm.

France, 1 Queens Drive, Ikoyi (PO Box 567; ☎603 300, telex 21338); 9am–2.30pm.

Gabon, 8 Norman Williams St, Ikoyi (PO Box 5989; ☎684 673, telex 21736); 8.30am–2.30pm.

The Gambia, 162 Awolowo Rd, Ikoyi (PO Box 8037; ☎682 192).

Germany FR, 15 Eleke Crescent, V.I. (PO Box 728; ☎611 011, telex 21229); 8am–2pm.

Ghana, 21 King George V Rd (PO Box 889; ☎630 015); 8am–2.30pm.

Guinea, 8 Abudu Smith St (PO Box 2826; ☎612 206); 8am–2pm.

Ireland, 31 Kofo Abayomi Rd (PO Box 2421; ☎615 224, telex 21478); 8am–1pm.

Italy, 12 Eleke Crescent, V.I. (PO Box 2161; ☎614 066, telex 21202); 8am–2pm.

Japan, 24 Apese St, V.I. (PMB 2111; ☎614 929, telex 21364); 8am–3pm.

Kenya, 53 Queen's Drive Ikoyi (PO Box 6464; ☎682 768, telex 21124).

Liberia, 3 Idejo St, off Adeola Odeku St, V.I. (PO Box 70841; ☎618 899, telex 23361).

Mauritania, 1a Karimu Giwa Close, Ikoyi (☎684 439); 9am–1pm.

Morocco, 27 Karimu Katun St, V.I. (☎611 682, telex 21835).

Netherlands 24 Ozumba Mbadiwe Av, V.I. (PO Box 2426; ☎613 510, telex 21327); 8am–2.30pm.

Niger, 15 Adeola Odeku St, V.I. (PMB 2736; ☎612 300, telex 21434); 8am–noon.

Norway, 3 Anifowoshe St, V.I. (PMB 2431; ☎618 467, telex 21429); 8am–2pm.

Portugal, Olukunle Bakare Close, V.I. (☎619 037, telex 22424).

Senegal, 14 Kofo Abayomi Rd, V.I. (PMB 2197; ☎614 226, telex 21398); 8am–3pm.

Sierra Leone, 31 Alhaji Waziri Ibrahim St, V.I. (PO Box 2821; ☎614 666, telex 21495); 8am–3pm.

Spain, 21c Kofo Abayomi Rd, V.I. (PO Box 2738; ☎615 215, telex 22656); 9am–2pm;

Sweden, 26 Moloney St (PO Box 1097; ☎630 688, telex 21318); 7.30am–2.30pm.

Switzerland, 7 Anifowoshe St, V.I. (PO Box 536; ☎613 918, telex 21597); 7.30am–noon & 12.45–3.45pm;

Tanzania, 45 Ademola St, Ikoyi (PO Box 6417; ☎682 757).

Togo, Plot 976, Oju Olobun Close, V.I. (PO Box 1435; ☎617 449, telex 21506); 8am–3.30pm.

United Kingdom, 11 Eleke Crescent, V.I. (PMB 12136; ☎619 531); 8am–3pm, consular section at Chellarams Building, 54 Marina (☎667 061, 666 413, Fax 666 909); 8am–3pm.

USA, 2 Eleke Crescent, V.I. (☎610 097).

Zaire, 23a Kofo Abayomi Rd, V.I. (PO Box 1216; ☎656 289, telex 21365).

Zambia, 11 Keffi St, Ikoyi (PMB 6119; ☎680 991).

Zimbabwe, 6 Kasumu Ekemode St, V.I. (PO Box 50247; ☎619 328, telex 22650).

United States Information Service, 1 Kings College Rd (☎635 665).

Goethe Institut, (☎610 717) and *Centre Culturel Français*, (☎615 592) both at plot PC14, off Idowu Taylor Rd, V.I.

Newspapers International press and news mags (*Economist, Time, Newsweek, Herald Tribune*) are available at the airport and hotels and *West Africa* magazine all over.

Photocopies Numerous places throughout town, all quite cheap. Try the southern side of Tafawa Balewa Square.

Post and telephones The main GPO (Mon–Fri 8am–noon, 2–4pm, Sat 8am–noon) is on Marina St; branches in **Ikoyi** (Awolowo Rd) and **Victoria Island** (Adeola Odeku St) are closed Saturdays. Phone calls can be made around the clock from the NITEL Building on Marina St or from 7am–8pm at Falomo Shopping Centre.

Swimming pools The big hotels have pools, but those at the *Ikoyi* and *Federal Palace* (in theory open for a fee to non-guests) usually don't have water. The *Eko Holiday Inn* has the cleanest water, but it's reserved for residents only. There's also a public pool across from the museum which has relatively grimy water.

Travel agents and tour operators Many agencies are grouped around the racecourse. Other important firms include:

Bitts Travel and Tours E7 Falomo Shopping Centre (☎684 550). Organise excursions for groups to various tourist destinations.

Tours and Trade International Limited 4 Adeyemo Alakija Street, PMB 70047, Victoria Island (☎618 665). Trips to the game parks, Obudu Cattle Ranch and other sites.

Transcap Travel CFAO Building, 1 Olap Davies St (PO Box 2326; ☎660 321, 665 063). Agents for *Thomas Cook*.

GETTING OUT OF LAGOS

Bush taxis

The main motor park for the **southwest** – Ibadan, Oshogbo, Ilorin, Ilesha and other towns in Yorubaland – is the **Ojota station** on Ikorodu Road, near the junction with the airport road in the Ojota district (take a taxi). For the **north** – including Kaduna and Jos as well as Zaria, Sokoto and Kano – the park is in the **Iddo** district on Murtala Muhammed Way near the railway station. Taxis heading for the **east** – Onitsha, Benin City, Port Harcourt and Calabar – depart from Oju Elegba junction in Surulere district. Taxis for destinations **outside Nigeria** – including Lomé, Porto Novo and Cotonou – leave from the end of Eko Bridge at the tip of Lagos Island.

Trains

The **railway station** is on Murtala Muhammed Way, near the Carter Bridge in Iddo. There are daily departures for **Kano**, arriving up to 40 hours later, and four trains a week for **Jos**. To go by train to **Maiduguri**, take the Jos train and change at **Kafanchan**. This is a 48-hour trip – two nights on board. There are three classes: it's best to avoid third class, especially when covering long distances. For information, try enquiries at the Nigerian Railway Corporation head office in Ebute Metta (☎802 000/4).

Domestic flights

Nigeria Airways, go from the domestic terminal, off to the east of Murtala Muhammed Airport. There are, in theory, flights **every day** to: **Abuja** (2), **Calabar, Enugu** (2), **Jos** (2), **Kaduna** (2 on Mon, Wed, Thur), **Kano** (2 daily, 3 on Tues, Thur), **Maiduguri** (2 on Tues, Thur, Sat), **Port Harcourt** (2 daily, 3 on Sat) and flights to **Benin City, Sokoto** and **Makurdi** on Mon, Wed, Fri and Sun. *Express Airways Nigeria* runs a more limited service, flying daily out of Lagos for **Kaduna via Minna**.

Ships

Panalpina, 4 Creek Rd, Apapa (☎803 440/4, telex 21346), are port agents for the Italian *Grimaldi Lines*, which runs some quite smart vessels on regular voyages to Europe.

YORUBALAND

There's a common assumption, certainly in the expatriate community, that if you visit anywhere in Nigeria you go to the north – and that anywhere south of Jos is barely worth a pause. Don't believe it: the towns and rural parts of **Yorubaland** have an exceptional wealth of cultural interest and natural beauty, and once you move out of Lagos, you leave behind most of the heavy baggage of Nigerian travel. Other cities certainly have their share of blight and bluster, but none really compares.

The **Yoruba** people created one of the most powerful empires on the West African coast of pre-colonial times – and the area is still charged with reminders. Most of the larger towns, for example, still have ruling **Obas**, or kings, who wield a good deal of political clout despite limitations imposed on them by the the modern Nigerian system of a federal government. The Obas continue, too, to live in **royal palaces**, many of which – including that in **Oyo**, former capital of the Yoruba empire of the same name – can be visited.

Much of what is now known about the area's more distant past is the result of excavations carried out in **Ife**. The brass and terracotta statues found here gained international attention and suggest a sophisticated civilisation dating back to at least the ninth century. According to Yoruba custom, however, Ife is even older – the first place in the world to be created. It has naturally enjoyed a position as the holiest place in the Yoruba realm, a sort of Mecca of Yoruba religion. Here and throughout the region, the living wood of the **old religion** still breathes beneath a thin veneer of Islamic or occasionally Christian belief. You'll see shrines and temples in almost all the towns, and at **Oshogbo** a whole **Sacred Forest** has been set aside as a reserve for worshippers, or **"fetishers"**; the shrines here are vast and amazing and the worshippers only too eager to show visitors around – definitely a Nigerian highlight.

Ibadan

Nigeria's second largest city, **IBADAN** (pronounced as in "pardon") is the modern capital of Oyo State – a vast metropolis that sprawls so far you think it's never going to stop. Its cityscape comprises few Lagos-style highrises but instead a plethora of corrugated iron-roofed two-storey houses, spreading like an urban fungus over the low hills. People here assert Ibadan has the biggest population of any city in Africa – twenty million people, some say; the real figure is probably around five million, but, in the absence of a census for two decades, who knows.

Somehow the crowds, congestion and noise are especially oppressive, and as the city lacks a real centre, a shambolic, unfocused tumult is about the only lasting impression. However, coming from Lagos, this is likely to be your first stop in Yorubaland and, with its numerous hotels, banks and other facilities, it is a convenient base for visiting other sites in the region.

Some history

Originally founded by Yoruba renegades, at the end of the eighteenth century, Ibadan occupies a strategic position between the forest and the plains – its name derives from *Eba Odan*, meaning "field between the woods and the savannah". The settlement began to grow after 1829, when it became an important Yoruba military headquarters and a refuge for people dispossessed in Fulani raids on northern Oyo. By the time the British forced it into a treaty of protection in 1893, it was already extraordinarily large for its time, with an estimated population of 120,000.

In colonial times, Ibadan went on to become an important trading centre, which it remains. And it is also a major educational centre. The **University of Ibadan**, founded in 1948, was the first in the country and is still considered one of West Africa's best. The **University College Hospital** and the world-renowned **International Institute of Tropical Agriculture** (5km north of the University) add to Ibadan's academic prestige.

Orientation – and around the town

Given the city's unwieldy dimensions, it's hard to pinpoint Ibadan's heart (note the very small scale of our map, more than 15km from the north, by the university, to the south by the line of the old city wall). By default, however, you'd have to say it beats around the **Dugbe Market** – one of Nigeria's largest. Characteristic of the city as a whole, the streets running through this area seem to wind at will, so your chances of getting lost are high. Should that happen, look for the the strange **Bower Memorial Tower** on **Mokola Hill** to the east, a good viewpoint to climb and a reference point for orientation anywhere in the city.

The tower of **Cocoa House**, south of the market, is another guide for the disoriented. One of the few skyscrapers in town, and nearly lost in 1985 when it was severely damaged by fire, Cocoa House is evidence of the regional importance of a vital export crop and marks Ibadan's commercial centre. You'll find **banks** in the area (*IBWA*, *First Bank*, *Nigeria Central Bank*; all Mon–Thur 8am–3pm, Fri 8am–1pm), and, for more predictable shopping than at the market, *Leventis* and *UTC* **supermarkets** nearby. A couple of hundred metres to the west of this area on Abeokuta Rd is the already old-looking **New GPO** (Mon–Fri 8am–noon & 2–4pm). The **railway station** is directly across the street.

On the north side of town on Oyo Rd, the campus of the **University of Ibadan** is a microcosm of student life and activities. You can meet and mix with people here at the **cafeteria, coffee shop** or **swimming pool** (the refectories are open to all, the pool is ostensibly students only, but you should be able to talk your way in). The university **bookshop** (Mon–Fri 8am–4pm, Sat 8am–noon) is larger and better than any you'll find in Lagos. The **Institute of African Studies** building also houses a small **museum** (Mon–Fri 10am–3.30pm) with bronze statues and carvings. Finally, the university has a **zoo** (daily 7am–7pm), where you can see various antelopes, gorillas, crocodiles and a pretty good selection of other animals.

The **International Institute of Tropical Agriculture** (IITA) is 5km beyond the University campus on the Oyo road. With rich foreign sponsors and an international

---

IBADAN AREA MARKETS

Most of Ibadan's **markets** work on a four-day cycle, which is fine as long as you know where you are in it: check local papers such as the weekly *Irohin Yoruba* for details.

Most of these markets are identified on our map.

Dugbe, daily, near the railway station. A massive general market.

Mokola, daily, 3km north of Cocoa House. Food, pots and baskets.

Oje, sixteen days, near Mapo Hall, east of Bere Rd. A big cloth market (they sell the *Aso-oke* strip cloth made in Iseyin), trade beads, coral.

Bode, eight days, near Molete bridge. Beads.

Sako, daily, near the Friday mosque. The big food and domestic market, sells good pounders (if you're looking for a good pounder).

University. Daily souvenir market.

Ojoo, eight days, 2km north of University, west of the Oyo road.

Onidundu, eight days, 14km north of IITA, west of the Oyo road. Spices, herbs, mats and baskets.

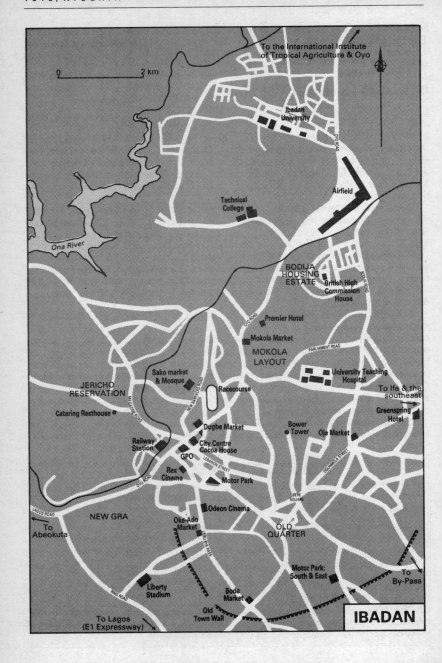

To the International Institute
of Tropical Agriculture & Oyo

Ibadan
University

Airfield

Technical
College

Ona River

BODIJA
HOUSING
ESTATE

British High
Commission
House

Premier Hotel

Mokola Market

MOKOLA
LAYOUT

PARLIAMENT ROAD

Sako market
& Mosque

JERICHO
RESERVATION

Racecourse

University Teaching
Hospital

To Ife & the
southeast

Catering Resthouse

Greenspring
Hotel

Dugbe Market

Bower
Tower

Oje Market

Railway
Station

City Centre
Cocoa House

GPO

LEBANON STREET

Rex
Cinema

Motor Park

BERE
SQUARE

Odeon Cinema

NEW GRA

Oke-Ado
Market

OLD
QUARTER

To
Abeokuta

LAGOS ROAD

OYO ROAD

Motor Park:
South & East

To
By-Pass

Liberty
Stadium

RING ROAD

Bode
Market

Old
Town Wall

To Lagos
(E1 Expressway)

IBADAN

team of staff, this is like a slice of California and a welcome respite from the hurly burly of Ibadan. You obviously have to know someone to get in, but it's surprising how easily such contacts are made. There's a crystal clear pool, ice cream, hot dogs and guest chalets if you have an introduction. If you're going to be passing through, or staying in Ibadan, you might write to the IITA (PMB 5320, Ibadan) requesting their introductory information about Ibadan, provided for newly arrived staff.

Accommodation

One good thing that can be said for Ibadan is its selection of **hotels**, ranging from cheap hostels to AC palaces with pools. The recommendations below are in ascending order of price.

CUSO guesthouse, 836 Adelabu Rd, Iyaganku GRA (PMB 5297; ☎315 484). The Canadian volunteers organisation guesthouse is open to all. Recently renovated, it's clean and cheap, but a little hard to find. From Abeokuta Rd, take Ring Rd towards the *Challenge* bookshop. Turn left on Olaniyan Fagbemi Rd and continue past Ring Rd Restaurant. The *CUSO* office is off this latter road to the right, and the guesthouse to the left.

Pastoral Institute Hostel (commonly referred to as "P.I."). Way across town, near the university, on Bodija Rd . The non-S/C rooms are immaculately clean with fans and mosquito nets. Breakfast is included; other meals can be had in the cafeteria.

British High Commission (BHC) Rest House, Bodija. An air-conditioned breather out of Lagos for the staff, but others may use it subject to availability. Bookable at the High Commission in Lagos. Inexpensive.

Alma Guest House, 19 Oyo–Ibadan Ave, Bodija, near the customs post. Small, quiet and clean, with a bar and restaurant. Cheap to moderate.

Green Spring Hotel, Old Ife Rd (☎713 796). An older, hotel with AC, S/C bungalow-style rooms and a pool. Good bar and restaurant for evening distractions. Moderately priced.

Influential Hotel, (☎414 894), towards the centre of town on Mokola Hill. Another moderately priced hotel in a very handy location.

Catering Guest House, behind the railway station in the Jericho Reservation. Pleasant colonial-style building in a quiet neighbourhood, with reasonably priced AC, S/C rooms and a Nigerian-European restaurant.

University of Ibadan Conference Centre, right by the Staff Club, (see below). Adequate accommodation.

Lafia Hotel (PO Box 5353; ☎416 750, telex 31175). Boasts features like colour TV and, more desirably, a swimming pool, but at a price and some distance from the city centre in Apata Ganga.

Premier Hotel, Mokola (PO Box 1206; ☎623 409/400 340, telex 31174). The most expensive-looking place in town. Actually very reasonable, and rather good. You can relax in relative style here with all the amenities, including a pool. There's also a Chinese restaurant – one of the few such in town.

Food

Apart from the hotel restaurants, there is nothing out of the ordinary. For really cheap, quick calories, **chop bars** – serving *eba*, *amala* and pounded yam with the usual *egusi* and other soups and stews – line Magazine St near the junction with Abeokuta Rd close by the railway station. And up on Mokola Hill, there are *bukas* doing *begiri* (traditional bean soup) and *amala*.

If you're at the university, use the **student cafeteria** – bland but cheap food, and a good place to meet students. There's also the **Staff Club** here, the meeting place for people who work on campus, with a pool and restaurant.

Near the CUSO hostel, there's the *Ring Road* and the *Joyce-B* restaurants for unfancy Nigerian and European fare. And in the **Dugbe market quarter**, there are plenty of **Lebanese** restaurants, offering similar dishes at similar prices. *The Cabin*, on Lebanon street, stands out, in an air-conditioned steakhouse sort of way.

MOVING ON: SOME TRANSPORT DETAILS

● **Long-distance taxis** Vehicles heading to Oyo and on further north leave from the **Sango taxi station** southeast of the GPO (get a taxi there). The **Gate taxi station** is the departure point for Ife and the southeast, located down in the southeast of town.

● **Trains** leave for Lagos via Abeokuta and Jos via Oshogbo. Check schedules at the station.

● **Flights** *Nigeria Airways* has offices at Lister House, Southwest Ring Road, Agbowo Shopping Complex, Jaja Rd, University of Ibadan (☎462 550) but no schduled flights out of Ibadan – the closest large airport is Lagos. *British Airways* is at the C. Zard Building, 6 Lagos By-Pass (☎413 967), *UTA* has an agency at 7 Lebanon St (☎410 280) and *KLM*'s representative is *Airlink Travel Agency*, Jubilee House, Ring Rd (☎315 098).

Oyo

OYO is a relatively small town by Nigerian standards, with only a quarter of a million inhabitants, and its characteristic rust-stained roofscape looks like an Ibadan that never quite took off.

While by no means desolate, the town is hard to imagine as once having been the capital of the namesake Yoruba-speaking empire that stretched as far as present-day Togo (including in its hegemony such vassal states as Dan-Homey). In fact, the site of the old city was to the north, not here. At its apogee in around 1700, Oyo was probably the most powerful state in West Africa.

OYO HISTORY

Oyo was founded in the northern Yoruba savannah, some time between the eleventh and thirteenth centuries by **Oranmiyan**, the youngest of the Ife princes (sons of Oduduwa). It was strategically located in a part of the savannah relatively free from tse-tse flies – and so could use **horses** for transport and war.

From its old capital in **Oyo-Ile**, Oyo began to expand southwards in the sixteenth century, using its highly efficient horsemen to extend its power to the coast. Until the end of the eighteenth century, it had not been directly concerned with the slave trade on a large scale, most of its wealth coming from the control of the trade routes between the coast and the north. By the late eighteenth century, however, the courts of **Lisbon and Oyo** were increasingly involved as partners in the slave trade. The name "Yoruba" is a corruption of "Yooba", meaning "the dialect of the Oyo people." The fact that missionaries applied the term to all the peoples of the region attests to the city's once far-reaching power. Decline set in when internal revolt from vassal states (see p.957) and war with the Mulim jihadists from the north, spelt the end of the empire in the nineteenth century.

The present town of Oyo was founded in the 1820s, when the old capital Oyo-Ile, fell to the Muslim raiders. The *alafin* attempted to re-establish the grandeur of the old capital at **Ago**, a market town south of Oyo-Ile, which he named Oyo. The only remaining evidence of its grand past is a sign welcoming visitors to "The City of Warriors". Today, Oyo is more noted for leatherwork, calabash-carving, weaving and a famous night market.

Orientation – and sights

Everything in Oyo centres around **Abiodun Atiba Hall** (also called Town Hall), perched high on a hill top. If you're walking from one of the hotels, you can see this monumental ochrous building from a kilometre away. When you arrive at the Hall, you will see the **market** spreading out before you on Palace Road. Besides the usual provisions and various household goods, you can find wonderful **leatherwork** and intricately **carved calabashes** – a local speciality, carved at the market in small ateliers. Another speciality are **"talking drums"** – *dundun* – and these too are made and sold in market workshops.

Oyo's main point of interest is the **Alafin's Palace**, situated near the market on Palace Road. Townspeople will tell you that the present ruler is still head of all the Oba of Yorubaland, although the Oni of Ife is also considered to hold the title. In fact a raging dispute – going back to colonial times when the practice of rotating the Chair of the Council of Obas was upset – has occupied attention for years and the two leaders are effectively at daggers drawn. The Oni of Ife, however, is more a spiritual leader, the descendant of Oduduwa, and thus not open to challenge by earthly office-holders.

Whatever the respective virtues, the Alafin of Oyo is one of the nation's most influential traditional rulers. His residence is a curious compound with numerous low buildings roofed in the ubiquitous rusty corrugated iron. Some of the buildings are decorated with traditional symbols and statues and carvings line the grounds. You'll have to get a guide at the gate before visiting the grounds, and put all thoughts of seeing inside the palace out of your head. You won't. Money is never discussed, but at the end of the tour you're expected to dash something.

Accommodation, meals, things to attend to

The two **hotels** of note are both located at the entrance to town as you arrive from Ibadan, and are both moderately priced. The *Labamba* is the main one and most expensive but the *International Hotel* is good too. The *Merry Time*, with clean S/C rooms and optional AC, is across from the *Agip* petrol station on the Ibadan road – a bit cheaper and very convenient if you arrive by taxi, as you'll probably be dropped here. It has a great bar with huge armchairs and a lively atmosphere after dark; you can order meals or snack on *moin-moin* – delicious bean cakes. For other cheap **eating**, you'll find plenty of chop bars in the market place, and you can wash down meals with frothy palm wine. Don't leave town without sampling **gbegiri** (bean soup) and **wara** (curd cheese). You can buy cheese in Akesan market.

The **Post Office** is directly opposite the market. There are also branches of *First* and *National* **banks** on Atiba St where, in theory, it's possible to change money. You may encounter problems, though, especially if you have traveller's cheques in anything other than sterling or dollars. You'll really be better off changing your money in Ibadan.

Ife

According to Yoruba legend, **IFE** (also known as **ILE IFE**) was the first Yoruba city, and indeed, the first city in creation. Custom says it was at this spot that **Olorun** – Supreme God – threw an iron chain from the heavens into the waters below. He then instructed his son **Oduduwa** to climb down the chain. Oduduwa carried with him a calabash full of sand, a chicken and a palmnut. He dumped the sand on the water and let the chicken loose. The bird began scratching in the sand, causing dry earth to appear, and meanwhile the palmnut produced a tree. The sixteen fronds of the palm tree represented the sixteen crowned rulers of Yorubaland.

More prosaic **excavations** indicate that Ife was probably founded in the ninth century. They also reveal a lot about the lifestyle of the royal court and many of the brass and terracotta sculptures from the digs are today on display in the **Ife museum.** Although Ife was already in political and economic decline by the early 1500s, the town remained a spiritual focus and is still an important symbol of Yoruba nationhood. In addition, it has had a post-independence renaissance as a modern cultural centre with Nigeria's most extensive **university campus**. The thousands of students add more than a spark of energy to what might otherwise be a rather sleepy town.

The sights

Unlike other Yoruba towns, you won't be able to visit the grounds of the **Oba's Palace** in Ife, so you'll have to console yourself by walking around the high walled, front court-yard – statues and important looking people milling about, even penetrating the royal sanctuary, but nothing very special to see.

Museums

Next door, however, and not to be missed, is the **Ife Museum** (daily 7am–7pm; free entry). As much as a millennium ago, the Oni of Ife wielded great political and spiritual powers. He commanded a whole army of servants, including indentured artists who made brass castings for him and his retinue – staffs, chest ornaments, and miniature pieces in abstract designs or animal shapes. The most precious treasures are the magnificent **brass and bronze heads** of the Oni and other senior royal figures, made by the lost wax method. The king's sculptors worked pure copper and copper alloys of various composition – either with more tin (bronze) or more zinc (brass) – in a realistic mode of expression that is relatively uncommon in African art. They were clearly tech-nical virtuosos of enormous skill, producing heads of rare grace, scored with the fine lines of scarification indicating royal rank. But there is an imperious, remote, vanity about these heads, and the sense of duty – and proscribed creativity – in the artist's craft, is self-evident; a strong sense of order, verging on an obsession with formal ways of doing things, comes though. The museum also contains cast metal and terracotta works dating from the tenth to the thirteenth centuries.

There's also a small **Pottery Museum** in town, over on More Street – two floors of dusty pottery works including musical jars (like skinless drums), coolers and cooking jugs. Entrance is free, but you can make a contribution at the end. In an unmarked garden in the middle of town, the **Oranmiyan Staff** – a carved and decorated stone monolith about five metres high – symbolises the sword of the first Alafin of Oyo.

The University

Obafemi Awolowo University was established by the government of Western Region (the post-independence division that was later sub-divided into Oyo, Ogun, Ondo, Bendel and Lagos States) and renamed after the first premier of the region when he died in 1988 – a nametag that didn't meet with unanimous approval. The 1960s architec-ture looks very dated now, but the scope of the grounds and facilities is impressive indi-cation of the stress laid on higher education by the governments of the early independent era.

The university also has its own **Museum of Natural History** (Mon–Fri, 8am–6pm, Sat & Sun 11am–6pm) and a rather unspectacular **Zoo** (daily 10am–5.30pm). To get there, you need to take a taxi or bus from town to the **campus gate**, which is really only half way to the university and then catch another bus or flag down students driv-ing into college. The **student union** and other buildings are a long way from the entrance, in the middle of the third largest campus in the world.

YORUBA RELIGIOUS CULTS

Aje The malevolent and destructive aspects of womanhood.

Efe Male masks.

Egungun Masks to honour family ancestors, worn during the annual festival of the secret, male society of the same name. Some Egungun are put on just for entertainment, to mock police, prostitutes, avaricious traders, people with deformities or anyone who unsettles the community. Many come from Abeokuta, reflecting that town's links with Sierra Leone.

Ekiti Masks of the eastern (Ekiti) Yoruba kingdoms. Best known is the Ekiti *Epa* mask, a wooden helmet surmounted by a carved figure.

Eshu Messenger of the gods – the *orisha* – and the divine trickster responsible for everything that goes wrong in the world. Every market place has a shrine to him, often a simple pillar of sun-baked mud, over which the priests pour daily libations to preserve harmony in the market and in the community. His devotees keep wooden scupltures in their houses.

Gelede The Gelede society is found only in some of the western Yoruba kingdoms. Its job is to appease female witches by entertaining them.

Ifa The oracle consulted by those afflicted by disease or madness, or by anyone with a problem to solve. A series of sacred texts – poetic sayings – are interpreted by the *babalawo* or "father of secrets" using the Ifa board and cowries, seeds or stones thrown in a pattern. Powerful and respected.

Ijebu masks The Ijebu kingdoms of southern Yoruba have imported some of the delta region societies, like Ekine, from the Ijo. Their masks tend toward the formalistic cubism of Ijo sculpture, quite distinct from the naturalistic lines of northern Yoruba sculpture.

Shango God of thunder and lightning, identified with one of the very earliest Kings of Oyo.

Osanyin God of medicine, responsible for the magical therapeutic action of leaves, herbs and other ingredients. There's a fundamental relationship between Osanyin and all other cults since devotees use appropriate medicines in order to enter into a close relationship with their chosen *orisha* during their initiation and subsequent life in the cult.

Ibeji Twins. If twins die, an image is carved of the dead child.

Obatala (or Orishanla) Responsible for the creation of each individual human form, to which Olurun, the Supreme God, gives life and destiny. Obatala's devotees wear white beads and on ceremonial occasions dress in white cloth.

Ogboni The Ogboni society, to which all chiefs, priests and senior men belong, is the cult of the earth. It also has a judicial role, being responsible for all cases of human bloodshed – which are an offence against the earth – and a political one, in providing a forum for discussion free of outside interference. Meetings take place in a cult house, where the society rites and discussions are kept secret from non-members.

Ogun God of iron, whose devotees include all those who use iron or steel to make a living or who drive on roads or fly planes.

Orisha Oko God of the farm.

Oshun Goddess of the river which flows through Oshogbo, the patron deity of the town and bringer of fertility to women.

Accommodation and practicalities

There's a string of **hotels on the Ibadan road**. The nicest, the *Diganga*, is out by the university. Videos in the S/C, AC rooms make this an expensive place, but it's not excessive and the bar–restaurant fills with students in the evening (though *Folabot*, next door, serves cheaper African meals if the hotel restaurant is out of your price range). During the day you won't have trouble finding buses going to the town centre, but at night, when you'll have to rely on rare taxis, it can be a problem.

The cheaper and older *Motel Royal*, compensates for being slightly run-down by having a swimming pool and tennis courts. Another Ibadan road hang-out, the *Transmotel*, is a standard government-issue resthouse with moderately expensive AC, S/C chalets. It's also possible to sleep at the *University Conference Centre*. The accommodations are good and you have access to staff facilities – pool, tennis courts – but the place is pricey and far from the campus centre (there's a short cut through the gardens at the back that makes it a lot closer – if you can find it).

Of the **hotels in the town centre**, the *Mayfair*, at the junction of the Ondo and Ibadan roads, is the budget option, with very average standards but a good location – walking distance from Ife centre. Out on the Ondo road, the *Hotel Olympique* is similar to the *Mayfair*, but a little smarter.

Food

As for **eating**, there's a couple of good restaurants in Ife, notably the *Samtad* on the Ondo junction. The garden restaurant and bar features Nigerian and continental food in a relaxed atmosphere – a good place for a few beers, if you're not eating. Over on the Ondo road, the *Beacon Disco and Restaurant* does inexpensive Nigerian food – including great fish pepper soup – and has been known to get lively at night. The owner, Mr Sutton, is full of ideas of things to see in the area.

For **cheaper eating**, try the *Modern Food Centre* at 14 Aderemi Rd (behind *Prof. Ojulari's Pool Agency*) for *eba* and pounded yam with soup, or the host of cheap eateries on or around the campus. Apart from the a whole areas of *bukas* doing hot food all day, *Forks and Fingers* in the student union offers a pretty good and inexpensive greasy spoon selection, and you can get chicken and chips in Oduduwa Hall or eat in the more expensive staff club restaurant. *Banwill* is a "Chinese" restaurant with a decent reputation on the Ibadan road..

Oshogbo

Despite a population close on half a million and an important modern sheetmetal plant, **OSHOGBO** (or Osogbo) seems somehow smaller and more traditional than either Ife or Oyo. **Traditional religion** is perhaps no more prevalent here than in other Yoruba towns, but it's more superficially obvious, at least. Ironically, the renaissance of the religion and art of the town, was in part due to an influx of European artists and philosophers who moved here in the 1950s, the most notable of whom was **Suzanne Wenger**, an Austrian painter and sculpter.

The Sacred Forest

Suzanne Wenger was interested in the beliefs and language of the Yoruba as inspiration for her painting, but she soon became a follower of **Obatala** – the Yoruba God of Creation – and, as local women came to appreciate her charismatic "artistic power", became a priestess of the religion in the 1960s. She has been a prime mover in restoring Oshogbo's **Sacred Forest**, which is devoted to the female water deity **Oshun**. With the help of Nigerian artists, she set about rebuilding the broken-down shrines, places of worship and sculptures using modern cement on wood and steel frames and a style that combined traditional elements with her own inspiration. The results are spectacular, mysterious and unique.

The **forest** is on the outskirts of town. It's not far to walk – about 2km from the centre – but you're better off taking a taxi there the first time. From the roadside, you can make out various shrines and an elaborate fence confining the retreat, before arriving at the gate. Here you'll find followers waiting by the road. To visit, you have to be accompanied by one of these disciples, and it's just as well, as none of the site would make much sense otherwise.

The first place you'll be shown is the **Oshun Temple** – the main place of worship and said to be the first building of the old town (Oshogbo used to be on this site until Oshun said she couldn't live with people any more and sent them off to found the new town). If you go into the temple, you'll see shrines dripping with palm oil and will be asked to make a **sacrifice**. Make sure you've plenty of small change, and don't pull out wads of bills; your guide will say something like, "Make a small contribution, you know, like ₦50," when you know a couple of Naira would do the trick. The money is supposedly used by **priestesses** to buy things for a sacrifice in your name. If you don't use discretion from the outset, though, you'll find yourself paying an arm and a leg for kola nuts which you'll have to "sacrifice" every time you blink. The offering taken, prayers will be made by the priestesses and your fortune told. You may be asked to kneel in front of the shrines and pray yourself – quite what you do at this point is up to you, though a rendering of the Lord's prayer or any humble invocation would be quite adequate.

Afterwards, you will be taken down to the **river** – the sacred domain of Oshun, the water goddess. Having had the surrounding shrines explained, you may be handed a calabash full of murky river water. It makes a big impression if you drink it and you probably won't die if you do, but you know best how your body is likely to react. Do what you have to. You're unlikely to cause offence.

Walking through the forest, you'll be shown shrines depicting a myriad of deities, all of whom are represented by statues at the **site of the market** of the old town. The god of creation, **Obatala**, is portrayed riding on an elephant. He is the moulder of human beings, but when his penchant for palm wine leads him to drink too much, he's apt to create deformed people. **Oshun** is the goddess who showed all the other deities the way down to earth when they were sent to pull the world together. Other representations at the old marketplace include **Ogun**, master of iron, **Shango**, who controls thunder and lightning (he's been coopted by *NEPA*, the electricity board), **Iyamapo**, goddess of women's crafts, including weaving and dyeing, and **Nanabuku**, who controls the wind.

Other temples in the forest include **Ontoto's Building**. Ontoto is the son of Obatala and this building is a place for prayer. Designed by Wenger, the architecture forces you into the world of the fantastic – one of the rooms is in the shape of an ear so that those who pray will have their prayers heard. The **Ontoto Conference Hall** – a meeting hall for initiates – has an entrance way consisting of a gigantic statue of Obatala on his elephant.

Around town

In Oshogbo town itself, try and visit the **Oba's Palace**, on the junction of Catholic Mission St and Okeoshun St. Besides the old and new palace buildings, the grounds contain a temple to Oshun with traditional wall paintings and sculpted wooden pillars. Aged priestesses guard the inside of the temple and will say prayers for you in exchange for an offering. To see the Oba in person, you must write in advance – Oba's Palace (Alafin), Oshogobo.

Directly across from the palace is one of the most interesting buildings in town – the meeting place for elders and **"King Makers"** – decorated with carved wooden totems and abstract paintings at the front and with a tree growing out of the back. And flamboyant Brazilian houses with wild ornamentation and bright colours line the whole length of Catholic Mission St.

The **King's Market** spreads out opposite the palace. Besides the wide selection of fruit and vegetables, which grow easily in this fertile part of the country, you'll notice a lot of juju, sacred pots and other ritual articles. **Suzanne Wenger's house**, is over on Ibokun St and it's worth having a look at from the outside for the imaginative architecture and ornamentation replete with traditional imagery and symbolism. If the priestess is in, you may be able to meet her. She has a shop with artefacts for sale inside the house.

THE OSHOGBO SCHOOL

Oshogbo is the site of a famous **artists' workshop**, set up as an offshoot of Ibadan's Mbari Club in the 1960s, by writer Ulli Beier (previously married to Suzanne Wenger) and artist Georgina Beier. They ran it for three years, attracting a collection of locals and performers involved in the Duro Ladipo Travelling Theatre. Nigerian artists such as Twins Seven Seven, Muraina Oyelami, Jimoh Buraimoh, Rufus Ogundele, Adebisi Fabunmi and others learnt from Georgina Beier the new techinques to which they'd previously had no access. Some of these names are now world famous and rich and influential at home.

Each of the studios can be visited and you can meet the artist and buy his work (they're almost all men), as well as batiks, which are a speciality of Oshogbo. **Twins Seven Seven** is a particularly entertaining, maverick character, who has determinedly made his art the most commercially successful (if you and he are talking money, talk hard!). **Jimoh Buraimoh** works with beaded collage, beads being traditionally a part of royal insignia on the Yoruba beaded crown. Jimoh's murals adorn public buildings all over Lagos and, in 1990 he exhibited at the Africa Centre in London.

A new cooperative gallery/workshop recently opened with a permanent collection of the Oshogbo School's works. It's on Station Rd; you can't miss the green and white sign.

Lastly, Nike Davies (a former wife of Twins77), has set up the new **Nike Centre** for young artists on Iwo Rd (take a taxi from the Oke Fia garage and if the driver doesn't know it ask for the Dada estate and look out for the signpost). It's booming with creativity, and heavily into batik, painting, carving and even quilt making.

Staying in Oshogbo

There are many places to stay in town. Best is Jimoh Buraimoh's *Heritage Hotel*, with a bar, restaurant and art gallery. It's signposted, on a small road off the Ibadan–Ife road, on the outskirts of town. On Ede Road, the refurbished government guesthouse,*Trans Motel*, has a nice colonial air to its architecture and is airy and secluded. Two slightly more expensive places are the modern *Moeje Hotel* and the *Hotel Terminus*, both with S/C rooms with AC. Oshogbo's best hotel is the *Osun Presidential Hotel*, at the north end of town, with comfortable AC rooms, plus a nightclub, cinema and **car hire** facilities.

After dark, the *Laro Disco* and *Rasco Cinema*, both together on Oke Fia Rd, give you something to do if want to do that kind of thing – dance to Yoruba music and watch Hindi, Karate and Yoruba movies.

MOVING ON FROM OSHOGBO

The main **motor park** is outside town on the Ilesha road.

Other towns in Yorubaland

Although Ibadan, Oyo, Ife and Oshogbo are the main points of interest in Yorubaland, you may pass through one or other of the towns below. If you feel more should be said about any of them, please let us know!

Abeokuta

ABEOKUTA, north of Lagos, on the old road to Ibadan, is Wole Soyinke's "Ake". The captial of Ogun State, it was founded in the early 1800s as a site for freed Yoruba slaves, some of whom were being liberated by the British Royal Navy, and some of whom had made their own way back to their homeland from Freetown and elsewhere. It's an attractive town, with a spectacular, and easily climbable, outcrop of gigantic granite boulders overlooking it.

The town's top hotel is the mid-range *Ogun State Hotel*, Kobape Rd (PO Box 30; ☎200 130/231 574, telex 24670), but the *Alefin Guest House* in Oke Ilewo district, or the *Frontline* in Onikolobo are a good deal cheaper.

Iseyin – and towards Benin

North of Abeokuta, there's 60km of unfinished pavement and then red washboard leads to the small town of **ISEYIN** – famous locally for its wonderful **night market** and cashew trees. It's also one of the main centres for **Aso-oke** strip cloth – most of its weaves come from here.

Between Iseyin and the border of Benin, there's a wealth of beautiful countryside dotted with old Yoruba **hill forts** – if you've got your own transport visit **Ado-Awaiye**, 26km south of Iseyin and Saki(Shaki), and **Ogboro**, respectively 87km and 105km to the north of Iseyin, both off the Agoare-Kaiama road that leads north through the Oyo and Kwara back-country to **Borgu Game Reserve** (see p.1043). Returning east to the main A1 highway north, much of the road from Iseyin to Oyo is rough until you cross the bridge over the Ogun river.

Ogbomosho

OGBOMOSHO, mid-way between Oyo and Ilorin, is a large industrial centre and one of the biggest towns in the region. It's ferociously busy, horrible in every way, massively congested and in a state of permanent commercial mayhem along its manic main road, bottlenecked with traffic, fumes and dust. But if you can bear to stop, it has a large market with a reputation for Yoruba cloth.

If you decide or need to **sleep here**, try either the *Catering Resthouse*, the *California Hotel* or *Hotel Terminus* (☎710 032) at the Igbo Market.

Ilorin

ILORIN, capital of Kwara State, lies at the edge of the Yoruba cultural domain, its strong Muslim flavour the result of **Usman dan Fodio**'s nineteenth-century jihad. Again, it's basically a workaday trade and market centre – and not too enticing for passing punters. The colossal, white and blue **Mosque** with its four spiring minarets and the Emir's palace, lighten the dust and noise somewhat. The **Sallah festival** is celebrated with a vigour that's unusual for a southern town – it's a good place to be, in fact, for any Muslim festival.

Among the **hotels**, the *White House* on Lagos Rd is pleasant and reasonably priced. Others include the *Fisayo* and *Niger*, both on Niger Rd, and the *Unity* on Murtala Muhammed Way. The *Kwara*, at 9 Ahmadou Bello Avenue, is the best place in town, though unfortunately that's not to say very much . . .

THE SOUTHEAST

East of Ife (see p.1021), the usual route through the rainforest is via **Ondo** and **Ore**, at which point you hit the expressway. At Ondo it's also possible to branch towards **Akure** and **Owo**, a final Yoruba town with its own Oba's palace and museum. Midway between Ondo and Akure, on the old road, is **Idanre**, a town surrounded, extraordinarily in these sticky lowlands, by stern granite massifs with steep cliffs. Old Idanre, up on top, is a sacred sight of some significance and, more immediately, a good base for some wonderful walks and scrambles, though you would need to give up a day or two to do it justice. There are rooms at the *Idanre Tourist Centre* in "Hilltop".

Once you cross over into **Bendel State,** it's a short distance to **Benin**, once a formidable kingdom though already in decline by the time the British arrived. Faced with the modern town of the same name, you may be hard pressed to conjure up images of the former empire, but there are vestiges of the past, including ruins of the **great wall** that formerly surrounded the city and more formal reminders in the numerous bronze and ivory **sculptures** housed in the city's renowned museum.

Further east, you arrive in what's often called the **Igbo Country** (see box), although numerous other peoples also live in the region. The **Niger River** – major geographical feature of these parts – passes through **Onitsha**, an industrial port city heavily damaged during the **Biafran conflict**. Although it has now regained a dominant commercial position in the area, you won't find much of interest any more and even the market – home and source of Nigeria's "market literature" and the hometown of Cyprian Ekwensi – has lost its verve (practical details on Onitsha and **Owerri**, to the south, are covered briefly after Benin City, p.1032). To the northeast, **Enugu** survived the civil war largely unscathed. As capital of the fledgling republic of Biafra, however, strategically placed on the railway line, it was continually under threat and more or less turned into a ghost town. It has since bounced back and is now a vital economic centre and home to many international firms.

THE IGBO

Igbo speakers have played an important role in the uncertain history of Nigeria. Unlike the Yoruba of the southwest, or the city-state political systems of the centre and north, the people of the southeast forest country have traditionally maintained much more clan-based socities with fewer social hierarchies. Largely spurning slavery in their own culture, these comunities fell easy prey to it when it was imposed from outside from the sixteenth to the nineteenth centuries. Later, having few cumbersome political structures to set up barriers, they quickly adapted to the new ideas of colonial society – its stress on personal achievement, on virtue earned through work and self-advancement, on business acumen and the creation of wealth. By the time World War II was over, the Igbo were clearly dominating the roles allowed to native Nigerians by the colonial government. Their success was partly responsible for the bloody trauma of **Biafra** – the still-born Igbo republic declared in 1967 – which resulted in civil war and a federal blockade which brought widespread starvation. And their continued dynamism is still the source of frustration among other groups in Nigeria – in particular the Muslims of the north, Hausa and especially Fulani. It has tended to earn southeast Nigerians a reputation as survivors. After all, they have the oil. And, having relatively poor representation in the Federal Republic's formal political structures (and those representatives often corrupt and rarely called to account), has meant an acknowledged deficit of infrastructure and social services in the southeastern states. The image of the Igbo in Nigeria is a cruelly contradictory one which has parallels with many commercially successful peoples around the world.

As it approaches the coast, the Niger River fans out into the endless meandering channels of the **Delta region.** The major town in the area, **Port Harcourt** is another modern town that's grown quickly since independence. You'll understand why when you see **oil flares** belching black smoke and flames on the seaward horizon: this is the heart of Nigeria's oil country. But it's also a good place for exploring **creek villages** and towns like nearby **Bonny Island** off the coast. **Calabar**, relaxing and scenic, spreads over a high hill overlooking the Cross River in the very far southeast. This town, once a big slave port now turned to palm oil, is one of Nigeria's most enjoyable.

Benin City

Long before Europeans arrived on the West African coast, **BENIN**, now the capital of Bendel State, was capital of a powerful empire with a **divine king.** A direct descendant of this line, the **Oba**, still rules over his kingdom, even in the restrictive context of federal government. Today the city is as business-like as any in Nigeria – feverish, dirty, noisy and crowded – it has a wretched climate, no coast, and little in the way of open spaces to escape to; yet its remarkable history, traced in the **Benin National Museum**, have made the town into something of a cultural centre. If you're here anyway, you might as well make the most of it.

Finding your way around: palace and museum

Although Benin is a big city with some 300,000 inhabitants, it's well laid out and not especially difficult to get to grips with. Everything centres around **King's Square** (popularly known as Circle Rd), a roundabout at the heart of town. As the name, if not the square's various bronze statues, would suggest, this is where you'll find the **Oba's Palace**. You may have to ask someone to point it out among the various buildings along the square, because the bland exterior doesn't shout to be noticed. You can visit the palace – the dun facade of which masks a rather grand interior – but you have to write for an appointment first (addressing yourself most respectfully to *The Secretary to Oba, Oba's Palace, Benin City, Bendel State, Nigeria*). The Oba himself never makes public appearances except for festivals or important court or civil state occasions. Since you have to state the date you want to visit and provide a return address, this seems like a real hitch if you're only passing through. Try writing on arrival in Nigeria, give your return address as a hotel in Benin and privately hope the Oba can be flexible on the date.

The **Benin National Museum** (daily 9am–6pm; free) in the middle of Circle Rd – when the traffic's heavy, it's a life-risking manoeuvre getting to it – contains many sacred royal treasures and some of the legendary artworks of the former empire. Most of the kingdom's treasures were stolen and taken abroad following the British invasion of 1897, so that today Benin can claim only the world's third largest collection of Benin art – after London and Berlin. It's an impressive collection nonetheless and very well displayed: there are examples of the **bronze plaques** that lined the palace interior together with masks, ivory works and a series of heads representing the three distinct periods of an art form that spanned five centuries.

Also on Circle Rd is the **Oba's Market**, once one of the largest and most animated in the region. It burned down in 1983, but reconstruction should now be complete. The major **banks** are also on this roundabout.

Akpakpava St, which runs out of Circle Rd, is the location of a number of hotels and the **post office.** The best place for buying **crafts**, naturally including replica bronze busts, is on Igun St. If you're interested in seeing vestiges of the **old city wall**, ruined morsels of it can still be seen on Sakoba Rd on the outskirts of town.

When you go into it you enter a great broad street, which ... seems to be seven or eight times broader than the Warmoes street in Amsterdam ... and thought to be four miles long ... The houses in this town stand in good order, one close and evenly spaced with its neighbour ... They have square rooms, sheltered by a roof that is open in the middle, where the rain, wind and light come in ... The king's court is very great ... built around many square shaped yards ... I went into the court far enough to pass through four great yards ... and yet wherever I looked I could still see gate after gate which opened into other yards.

From O. Dapper, *Description of Africa*, recorded in 1602, published in Amsterdam 1668

Benin is west of the Igbo country, and mainly peopled by the **Edo** or **Bini** (hence "Benin") who according to their own oral history migrated from the east – perhaps, some would still dare say, Egypt, a fairly common origin myth, until recently presumed Biblical, that may turn out to have a deeper and more ancient grain of truth as more is learnt about the black roots of pharaonic civilisation. Whatever the case, the Edo settlement in West Africa was founded by **Ere**, a man credited with being the inventor of order and instigator of traditions.

Sometime around 1300, the chiefs impeached their king and for some years were governed by a democratically elected ruler. But this system also failed and the chiefs threw up their hands and appealed to Ife to send over a capable monarch. The Yoruba prince **Oranmiyan** arrived and married a local woman. Their son **Eweka** became the first Oba and the royal palace was built during his reign.

From Oranmiyan's time onward, **bronze** achieved status as an important symbol. The very notion of kingship seemed to reside in this alloy of local tin and copper imported at great expense. When an Oba died, it was customary to send his head to Ife to have a portrait cast, but in the mid-fourteenth century, a metalsmith from Ife moved to Benin. From then on, the Edo became bronze-workers themselves. This artform, however, was reserved strictly for the court. A smith foolish enough to waste his talent on anyone other than the Oba was quickly executed.

The kingdom enjoyed its **golden era** between the fifteenth and seventeenth century. One of the greatest rulers was **Oba Ewuare** who ascended to the throne around 1440. He expanded the empire through conquests and his exploits brought new wealth – slaves, ivory, livestock – rolling into the city. Ewuare also greatly enlarged the capital, adding wide avenues and nine new gates each manned by a tax collector. When the **Portuguese** first arrived here, as early as 1485, they encountered a vast capital – the heart of a capable kingdom.

Other Europeans – English, Dutch, Florentines – quickly followed the Portuguese to the Bight of Benin. Their requirements were slaves, ivory, pepper, leather and handmade cloth. The Oba, **Ozula the Conqueror**, had plenty to offer from a string of fruitful conquests but, after only a few seasons of trade, he refused to sell slaves after 1516. He willingly exchanged his stocks of pepper and ivory, however, for metals, silk and velvet cloth, mirrors and European horses – most of which quickly succumbed to sleeping sick-

Benin practical business: hotels

Benin has a number of conveniently located hotels near Circle Rd. The **inexpensive** *Central Hotel*, 76 Akpakpava St (☎200 780), is a little run-down, but perfectly acceptable with AC, S/C rooms. Further away from Circle Rd on Akpakpava St, the *Hotel Jenik* is similar and in the same price range but shabbier. The *7 Sisters*, 112 Akpakpava St, is cheaper still, but now sleazy with it ("you mean you want to rent a room for the whole night?"). They don't have running water, but will fetch you all the buckets you require.

ness. Ambassadors were exchanged with several European nations in the sixteenth century and the Oba's court acquired a Portuguese cultural veneer.

The Oba became interested in **guns**, but the Pope had forbidden traders to sell weapons to heathens. Oba Ozula sent a son to Portugal to be converted and promised to build churches in his kingdom. He never built any, but he got the guns. The Vatican looked the other way. Trade flourished. Copper and copper alloys became plentiful and the Oba could afford to commission unlimited metal plaques to line his palace walls. Heady from the booming business, the trade partners even fought side by side, as when Portuguese mercenaries aided the Edo in their war against the neighbouring kingdom of Idah to the northeast, at the end of the sixteenth century. The Portuguese did very well out of the trade, even though they only succeeded in overturning the sanction against slave-trading out of Benin's dominions in the eighteenth century – even then, the Obas placed strict limits on the numbers sold.

By the late nineteenth century, the **British** Empire had become the Benin kingdom's principal partner and London was increasingly determined to develop new commodity sources and expand her markets for manufactured goods. The Oba's council increasingly perceived the calculating Europeans as a threat, while the Oba himself tried hard to find ways of negotiating a peaceful takeover that would allow him maximum power. His council sabotaged his plans and, while civil war was averted, they still attacked and slaughtered a British negotiating team. Benin retreated behind the massive city walls to concentrate on metaphysical ways of dealing with the impending disaster of invasion.

Creating an image of savagery was in Britain's interest, since public opinion at home would accept relatively painless war and invasion as long as it was linked to a "civilising mission". In any case, when the British Army launched a retaliatory "punitive expedition" to crush and seize Benin in 1897, they apparently found the Oba had made one last desperate effort to save the city in the only way he knew, and had ordered human sacrifices on a massive scale. They reported corpses lying everywhere and the pervasive stench of death in the town. The king himself had escaped, but was captured in the forest and sent into exile. His palace was pillaged. The great art treasures were sent to England – where they remain to this day, many in the Museum of Mankind in London. Others were sold to private collections.

The stories of sacrifice undoubtedly had some basis in fact – the Oba's efforts to appease the spirits and ward off the encroaching white men were by no means extraordinary – but there was certainly sensationalist reporting too. Writing in the *Evening News* forty years after the event, Major James F. Ellison referred to a "14 hours running fight with the fleeing enemy" all around the city walls. Inside,

> *Benin ran with blood. Human sacrifices were everywhere. Some of the human beings who were in chains were still alive, speedily to be liberated. Around a huge tree in the centre of the city were erected poles on which were cross-pieces. On these were bodies, remains of those who had been sacrificed. In the Valley of the Skulls were hundreds of human heads and bones.*

After the campaign, the British press referred to Benin as the City of Blood and Crucifixions. Whatever the magnitude of the barbarities carried out on the kingdom's own slaves and convicts, however, there can't be much doubt about where the responsibilty for the greatest bloodshed lay.

The nearby *Jajat* is similar. Lastly, another cheapie, but a decent one, is the *Victory Hotel* at 2 Victory Rd off Lagos Rd, with AC, S/C rooms, friendly staff, even a car park.

Also on Lagos Rd in the Uselli neighbourhood is the more **medium range** *Etin Osa Motel*. Near the coach station in Iyaro district, the *Goodwill Hotel*, Urubi St offers clean, moderately priced S/C rooms with fan or AC and even a video option.

Benin's **expensive** hotel is the *Motel Benin Plaza*, 1 Reservation Rd, (☎201 430) in a quiet neighbourhood. The *Benin Plaza*'s chalets are grouped around a swimming pool, and there's a pleasant bar and a restaurant serving Nigerian or European dishes.

Eating in Benin

Almost all the hotels listed have their own restaurants, but they're rarely very exciting and never offer the best value. Not that Benin's other eating places are up to much really, but if you want to venture out on the town, try the following low budget possibilties. One of the best markets for street food is **New Benin Market**. You can get some of the town's best fruit here during the day and cheap finger food (*suya*, grilled chicken) at night when this turns into a very active area and many shops and bars stay open late. A smaller market in similar vein near Circle Rd is the *Agbadan Market*, on Akpakpava St just next to the *Central Hotel*. The *Asumufoashi Restaurant*, opposite, does inexpensive Nigerian dishes – *amala*, *eba*, *dodo*, rice. The *T.J. Hamburger Restaurant*, on Circle Rd near the museum, might satisfy a craving for American flavours – they also do Nigerian dishes, including snails, though not snail burgers yet. Over on Sapele Rd, you can get decent, moderately priced Chinese food at the *Right Time* .

After all this, if you're lucky of an evening, you may catch the famous highlifer, Victor Uwaifo, at the *Paradise Nite-Club* (ask a taxi driver).

MOVING ON FROM BENIN

Vehicles to **Onitsha** and the east leave from Auchi Rd at the station near Ramat Park on Ikpoba Hill. **To Lagos** and the west, the station is on New Lagos Rd, before the University as you head out of town. **Coaches** – cheaper and slower than taxis – leave from a row of service stations on Urobi St in the Iyaro neighbourhood. Departure times and destinations need careful advance checking.

If you're **driving**, the main A232 goes east to Onitsha, from where you branch either to Enugu by the new expressway link, or south on the A6 to Owerri and Port Harcourt. You'll hear dire warnings about this route, as it holds something of a record for accidents in Nigeria: and that says a lot. If you're going directly to Port Harcourt, you might want to consider the A2 rainforest route via Sapele and Warri. Look for palm wine sellers along the roadway, but don't even inhale near the stuff if you're behind the wheel.

There are **flights** from Benin on *Nigeria Airways* (7 Forestry Rd, ☎241 766, 241 841) on Mon, Wed, Fri and Sun **to Makurdi** and, on the same days, **to Lagos**. The **travel agency** at 63 Akenzua St (☎222 806, 244 724) handles Lagos bookings on *BA*, *KLM* and others.

Travelling through the South: Onitsha and Owerri

ONITSHA, about halfway between Benin City and Enugu was almost completely destroyed during the Biafran conflict, and the town has since been rebuilt. Famous as the location of the earliest indigenously published literature in Nigeria (novels and tracts from 1949, under the label "Onitsha Market Literature"), it's still a highly energetic place, though there's no compelling reason to stay here except for a night stop. In that case, the very cheap and dingy *AP2 Hotel* near the renowned town market is in the bottom bracket. More recommended places include the *Traveller's Palace Hotel* (☎211 013), very near the taxi park, or Onitsha's best place in the middle price range, the *Nkisi Palace*, Old Nkisi Rd, GRA (☎211 711–9). The *Bolingo Hotel*, Zik Ave (☎210 877) is more upmarket, and has a pool.

The **Igbo-Ukwu** site, one of the earliest bronze age sites – ninth-century – is near Onitsha. Enormous bowls have been discovered here, only 1–2mm thick, indicating a *tour de force* of lost wax casting at a time when other civilisations were still hammering their wares into shape. Evidence of old copper mines has now been found in the region.

Owerri

About 100km south of Onitsha, **OWERRI**, the capital of **Imo State** is famous for its oil fields and its pottery – but it's a quiet town for its size. Places to stay include the *Executive* (☎230 100) and the smaller *Ivory Hotel* (☎230 902), northeast of town on the Okigwe Road. The flashiest place in town is the *Imo Concorde* (☎231 111) with restaurant, nightclub, pool and tennis courts.

Enugu

In sharp contrast to Benin, **ENUGU**, capital of Anambra State and the effective capital of Igboland, is a town without a long history. It was founded in 1909 when **coal deposits** were discovered in the area, some time later a considerable amount of iron ore was also located, and when the railway came through in 1916, the town's economic future was sealed. It became capital of the Eastern region in the 1930s (which marks the arrival of the large government buildings) and later was the headquarters of **Biafra**. Although the town was all but deserted during the civil war, it has since rediscovered its old vitality. Industry has taken off and there's even a *Mercedes* assembly plant which must be some crude indication of local prosperity.

There's a decent selection of hotels in Enugu, and although there's no gripping reason to go out of your way for it, should you be heading north (to Jos, for example), this town makes a good stopping-off place. Enugu displays a certain colonial charm and the odd, shady open space, and it's certainly better than the congestion and commercial frenzy of Onitsha. But with mines, railway tracks, smoky factories and a population pushing past half a million, it's hardly a garden city and you'll need to work hard to really like it.

Finding your way

You can take care of most of your business in the area around Okpara St, along which *First Bank*, *Union Bank* and *IBWA* are good for changing money. The **post office** is just off this road – on Post Office Avenue – and Enugu's vast **administrative district** straggles off behind it. Another main strip is Ogui Rd, where the railway station is located. At number 9, you'll find offices for the **National Museum**. Oddly enough, there's no museum as yet, but plans are in hand to build one in the future. You might stop by and check on progress. A number of **parks** dot Enugu, including the Murtala Muhammad Park across from the bustling new market. Jacaranda and other flowering trees make it a pleasant place to relax in the afternoon heat. At the eastern end of town, the **zoo** also has nice gardens, but the animals (those few of them that remain) look neither particularly happy nor healthy.

Accommodation and food

The *Hotel de Placia*, 25 Edinburgh St (☎331 565), is a very well kept older hotel in the older part of town – Ogui district. You have your choice of rooms with S/C, AC and optional TV, with prices ranging from low to moderate. They have a good restaurant and bar. Another inexpensive place, the *Dayspring*, 178 Ogui Rd (☎257 591), isn't quite up to the standards of the *Placia*, but it's conveniently located on one of the town's main roads. Even more central, the *Hotel Metropole*, 13 Ogui Rd, near the railway station, falls into a more upmarket bracket, with flamboyant decor and a lively **nightclub**. The *Modotel*, 2 Club Rd, off Garden St near the post office (☎338 870), is a sparkling, expensive, international class set-up with a surprisingly pleasant restaurant and bar. Behind the administrative quarter, the *Pan Afric* (☎335 248) has quite elegant gardens and reasonably priced rooms.

A good place for cheap eating is the *MOWLT canteen* across from the New Market. They serve pounded yams, *eba*, rice and beans along with beer and minerals, and it's always full and noisy. In the administrative area, you might try the *Cool Spot Canteen* for cold beer and snacks. Or, next to the *Hotel Metropole* on Ogui St, there's a *Danny Boy Fast Food* with meat pies, "mega burgers" and samosas. It's not the freshest food, but quite okay. *Chicken Danny's* is just next door.

ENUGU: SOME AIR TRAVEL DETAILS

There are twice daily **flights** (once on Sun) on *Nigeria Airways* to **Lagos**, and flights to **Kaduna** and **Port Harcourt** on Mon, Wed and Fri with *Express Airways*.

British Airways, 5 O'Connor St, Asata (☎334 806).

KLM, Chuben Travel Agency, 35a Ogui Rd (☎339 586).

Nigeria Airways, 23 Okapara Ave (☎252 881).

UTA, 11 Ogui Rd (☎257 785).

Port Harcourt

Capital of Rivers State, **PORT HARCOURT** ("Po-ta-ko" in pidgin) tries to promote its image as the "**Garden City**." Given its location in the rainforest, it might be remarkable if it *wasn't* green. Port Harcourt first came to prominence early in its history during World War I as a result of military operations mounted from here against German Kamerun. But the fortunes of the modern city are thanks primarily to the **oil wells** that have sprouted throughout the region since 1956 when commercial quantities were discovered in **Oloibiri**. The first shipload of Nigerian crude was exported from Port Harcourt in 1958 and the country was launched on a new economic course that promised rapid industrial development and prosperity in the new era of independence. As a side benefit, Port Harcourt has acquired a strikingly **modern aspect**, with wide avenues, flyovers and highrise blocks easily outshooting the last of the giant forest trees left standing in the city limits. Yet the **"Old Township "** (founded in 1913) has survived the rapid growth and if you were to limit your time to this district, you could come away believing that Port Harcourt is still a small town with a good deal of charm.

For a traveller using public transport, the main problem in the city is its **size**. You're likely to be dropped at Diobu Mile 3 motor park, which is a good 5km from the most appealing parts of town. And if you have to get around a lot, then taxi fares from one end of the city to the other are high.

Around town: orientation, sights and practicalities

Port Harcourt is divided by the **flyover** – a freeway overpass that's something of a monument and symbol of the town's modernity – into two distinct zones, the new town to the north and the old town to the south.

The **Aba Expressway** runs clean through the new part of town, from the air force base down to the flyover. Expressway is no exaggeration since cars seem to be out to break speed records as they scream down the motorway; the pedestrian overpasses that get across it intact are few and far between. Banks line the expressway as do various governmental buildings including the Rivers State **Ministry of Tourism** (35–37 Aba Expressway; ☎334 901) – their offices are chaotic, but the staff are friendly and helpful within the limits of available information, and they've been putting together a River State travel guide which may exist by now. For more information , including how

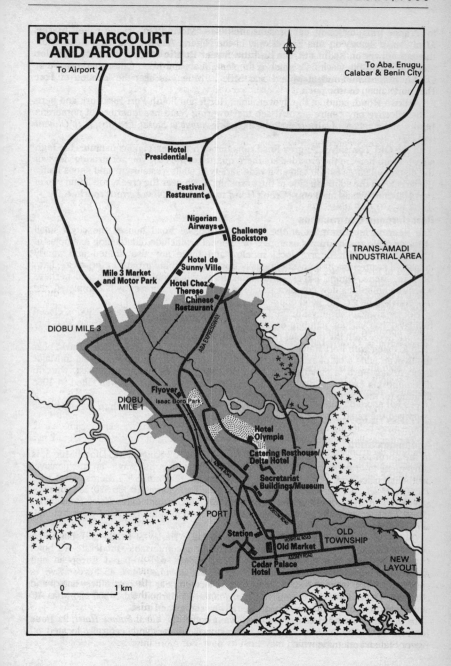

PORT HARCOURT
AND AROUND

To Airport

To Aba, Enugu,
Calabar & Benin City

Hotel
Presidential

Festival
Restaurant

Nigerian
Airways

Challenge
Bookstore

TRANS-AMADI
INDUSTRIAL AREA

Hotel de
Sunny Ville

Mile 3 Market
and Motor Park

Hotel Chez
Therese
Chinese
Restaurant

DIOBU MILE 3

ABA EXPRESSWAY

Flyover

DIOBU
MILE 1

Isaac Boro Park

Hotel
Olympia

Catering Resthouse/
Delta Hotel

ABA ROAD

Secretariat
Buildings/Museum

PORT

Station

Old Market

OLD
TOWNSHIP

HOSPITAL ROAD

NEW
LAYOUT

Cedar Palace
Hotel

0   1 km

to arrange trips to Bonny and Brass islands (see "Moving On", facing page), try the *Ideal Travel Agency* on Aba Expressway in the Nigeria Airways Building. Nearby, off the expressway on Kaduna St, the **Kaduna Street Public Market** is a good place for food, including the fresh fish which is so plentiful around here. Other markets are in **Diobu neighbourhood** at Mile 1 and Mile 3. Mile 3 is also the location of Port Harcourt's main **motor park**.

Azikwe Road, south of the flyover, links North and South Port Harcourt, and here – the effective city centre – you'll see the towering State headquarters of numerous **banks** and a galaxy of **supermarkets**, including *Supabod Stores, Leventis, G.B. Olivant* and *UTC*.

In the **Old Township**, Aggrey Road runs through the heart and constitutes the high street. From here, in the crowded southern quarter of the city, you get striking views of the distant oil flares as you take in a wide variety of stalls, restaurants and shops lining the street. On the southern side of the township, down near the creek, you'll find two of Port Harcourt's main markets – **Creek Road market** and **New Layout market**.

Port Harcourt's attractions

The **Secretariat Complex** at the bottom of Azikwe Road houses the city's small **ethnographic museum**. Its examples of regional art include outstanding examples of the colourful, often bizarre local **masks**, and there are also limited and poorly displayed scatterings of domestic utensils from major ethnic groups in the area – Ijaw, Ikwerre, Etche, Ogoni, Ekpeye and Ogba. Its worth a look even now, and perhaps when the ambitious new complex proposed for the Aba Expressway is completed, the museum will be a really good one.

Not far away, on Bonny Rd, the **Cultural Centre** (Mon–Sat 7.30am–3.30pm, closed holidays) has various exhibits on handicrafts and canoe building. You can also buy artwork here. Both the **port** and **railway station** are nearby.

In keeping with Port Harcourt's image as a garden city, the **Isaac Boro Park**, near the flyover, adds a bit of extra green to the city centre. The park is dedicated to Major Isaac Adaka Boro, a champion of the **minority peoples** of the southeast, who, in defending his cause against Governor Ojukwu's Igbo domination, was killed in 1968 fighting for the Federal forces during the civil war.

Finally, in the north of town the **zoo park** contributes a wild touch to the otherwise relentless **Trans-Amadi Industrial Area.**

Accommodation

In the north part of town, *The Mary Dok Guest House*, 27 Sangana St, Diobu Mile 3, is convenient to crawl into from the motor park just across the way – an inexpensive, brothelish place with bucket showers, and clean AC (but non-S/C) rooms, some with TV. The *Hotel Chez Therese* at 3, Udom St, off Aba Expressway (☎330 820) is spotless – a proper and moderately priced place with S/C, AC rooms. The *Hotel Presidential* (PMB 5141; ☎300 260), on Aba Expressway, is the city's international class hideout, with pool, tennis, casino even.

On the south side of the flyover, *Delta Hotels Ltd*, 1 Harley St (☎225 052), has taken over the catering resthouse and has turned it into a comfortable, moderate AC hotel (twin rooms very good value). The restaurant does well-prepared European and African dishes, and good breakfasts. Nearby, the *Olympia Hotel*, 45 Forces Ave, is smart, but much less expensive, conveniently located near the post office, banks and museum. The moderately expensive *Cedar Palace*, 11 Harbour Rd (☎300 180), has AC and TV in the rooms and is very near the railway station and port.

In the Old Township near the large Civic Centre, the *Civic Palace Hotel*, 31 Potts Johnson St (☎335 086), is a beautifully restored old building, centrally located off Aggrey Rd and not overpriced.

Restaurants

For inexpensive eating in the Old Township, try the *Black and White* restaurant at 54 Aggrey Rd, a trendy place that serves fry-ups – chicken, sausages, chips, hot dogs, fried rice. It's friendly, and the food's pretty good value and well prepared. It's also a good place to come for a drink. The *Beverly Café* at the bottom of Aba Expressway near the roundabout, is another casual place with good meat pies, sausage rolls, burgers and other fast food. More expensive eating places include a couple of Chinese restaurants – the *Golden Phoenix* and the *Chinese* at 27 and 97 Aba Expressway. Up near the *Presidential*, the *Festival Restaurant* serves European and African specialties.

Nights

As you would expect in a town the size of Port Harcourt, there are numerous night-clubs that cater, Thursday to Sunday, to all (male) tastes. The best – the only – way to find out which is currently most fancied and most likely to have a group playing, is to ask around. The *Manatee* on Kaduna St, off Aba Expressway, is a favourite old standby. In this same, new part of town, the *Presidential* and the nearby *Aquarius*, 205 Aba Expressway, have their own flashy mirror-and-lights discos.

In the old part of Port Harcourt, have a look at the *Orupolo Night Club* at 31 Harold Wilson Drive, or the *Tropicana* in the Cedar Palace.

Of the numerous **cinemas** around town, the one in the *Hotel Presidential* is best.

MOVING ON FROM PORT HARCOURT

● The **Mile 3 motor park** has vehicles to everywhere – Port Harcourt is literally at the end of the road, or at least the Old Township is – and transport isn't hard to find, though a driver without suicidal inclinations may be (if you're Enugu-bound, don't forget the 270km of motorway when selecting your vehicle).

● As for **trains**, there's supposed to be a weekly service to Maiduguri (change at Kafanchan for Kano and Lagos) but, as ever, you'll have to ask at the station. Don't plan on boarding further up the line at sub-stations in north Port Harcourt either. Get a seat at the terminus in the Old Township.

● You can travel by irregular motorboat to **Bonny and Brass islands** (three and six hours respectively) or by much slower goods boats, from the **local wharf** next to the larger harbour in town. Bonny and Brass were the first fifteenth-century Portuguese toe-holds in Nigeria, and later missionary gateways (St Stephens on Bonny is one of the oldest Anglican churches in the country), but are now devoted to the oil industry. There are still some wonderfully ornate Victorian tombstones and monuments and some great old houses. Local chiefs tend to wear Edwardian shirts with tucked fronts and top hats. There are no hotels.

● **Flights** on *Nigeria Airways* to **Lagos** (two to four times daily) continue to **London** on Wed. They fly direct to **Libreville** on Wed too, en route from Lagos. Finally, flights to **Enugu and Kaduna** are on Mon, Wed and Fri with *Express Airways*. Helicopter flights to Bonny and Brass for oil industry personnel: check at the tourist office for how to hitch a ride.

Airlines (and agents) addresses:

British Airways, Rivers State Tourist & Hotels Corp Building, Aba Expressway (☎331 986).

KLM, Leventis Stores Building, Liberation Drive (☎331 055).

Nigeria Airways, 6 Bank Rd (☎229 931).

Sabena, Mr. Nwosu, 14 Udom St (☎333 505).

UTA, 13 Azikwe Rd (☎333 534).

Calabar and Cross River State

It's not just its position high on the hills overlooking the Cross River that makes **CALABAR** such a pleasant town to visit. There's a general ambience created by its compact size and the outgoing nature of the Efik and Ibibio people. The port area sums up the elegantly run-down, colonial feel of the place. Apart from Lagos, Calabar is the only large Nigerian city actually on the coast and the tension that crackles in so many other large towns is absent, as if whisked away on the ocean breeze. Calabar also has the best **culinary reputation** in the country, with lots of good, and varied, traditional cooking.

If you've any choice about when you visit, October is **masquerade month** in Calabar, the time when cultural values and traditional beliefs are most in evidence. The masquerades – **Sekiapu** – include not only continous **drumming and dancing**, sculpted **masks** and elaborate and dazzling **costume personalities**, but regattas of huge, fabulously decked, competitive society **canoes**.

Outside Calabar, a large proportion of Cross River State, of which it's the capital, is still covered in dense **rainforest**. The new **Oban reserve** on the Cameroon border, and **Obudu cattle ranch** in the northeast of the state, are worthy travel targets.

CALABAR'S HISTORICAL BACKGROUND

The **Efik** and **Efut** people – predominantly fishers and subsistence farmers – were the first to settle in the Calabar area. Later migration brought the **Qua** (or Ekoi) who came from the northern woodlands and were principally hunters and farmers. The Portuguese arrived in the closing years of the fifteenth century and the economic orientation of the local people slowly shifted to **trading**. By the seventeenth century, the Efik were in control of the lucrative export of **slaves**. Efik settlements on the estuary of the Calabar river developed into trading **city-states** that dealt with the Portuguese, Dutch, French, German and English. Rich and powerful, the rulers took European names to emphasise their importance – the Dukes, the Jameses, the Henshaws – and welcomed **missionaries** despite their opposition to the slave trade. Calabar thus became a centre of education and religion, and local rulers gained further advantages with the European trading partners, since the Efik forbade missionaries to come into contact with ethnic groups in the hinterland. With their understanding of the ways of the west, the Efik made the transition as smoothly as anyone could have expected when trade shifted from slaves to **palm oil** and later when Nigeria became a colony and the Efik were ruled "indirectly", through their chiefs. At the end of the nineteenth century, Calabar became the capital of Southern Nigeria and during the **Biafran war**, the town was recaptured from the secessionists and served as an important federal forces naval base.

Staying in Calabar: arrival, transport, bed and board

Calabar is a great place to **rest up** for a day or two – a fine introduction to the nicer facets of Nigerian life and, if you're heading east, a good place to prepare yourself for upbeat Cameroon and the rigours of Central Africa.

It's an easy town to get around. **Taxis**, even cheaper **buses** and **motorcycles** together provide nearly 24-hour mobility. There's a bus park right by Watt market in the centre of town where you're likely first to land up. The buses run on set routes but will usually stop if you wave them down. The "cyclists" charge the same as a shared taxi for a single drop, though it may be double this for long transits across town. But they drive like maniacs and often try to cheat you blind, so use them with caution and fix a firm fare in advance. Like taxi fares, prices double after dark, though you may be able to negotiate two up on the bike for a discount on the single drop price.

Accommodation

There's a host of pleasant, small, **family-run hotels**, many of which have air conditioning and TV at completely affordable prices.

Hotel de Achiv, 3 Clifford Lane (the small unpaved street that runs alongside the *Iteecee (ITC) Supermarket*), off Calabar Rd. Near the market in the centre of town, the *Achiv* is one of the town's cheaper establishments. The S/C, double rooms with fans much better than singles and only slightly more expensive. It's not exactly of good repute, but the people are very nice and they have a bar/TV room with snacks – try the snail kebabs, a local delicacy.

Centralway Hotel, 27 Bedwell St, near the *Achiv*. Larger and slightly more expensive with AC, S/C rooms.

Redemption Hotel, 18 Mary Slessor St, off Bedwell St. In the same area, moderately priced, clean and with attentive staff. They've an excellent restaurant doing inexpensive African dishes. Breakfasts here are especially good – tea, eggs, fruit salad.

Ayimo Hotel. Away from the centre, an older place which has worn well – the double rooms are quite reasonable for two, but slightly pricey if you're on your own. The Cameroon consulate is nearby, at 21 Marian Rd.

Paladium, 106 Marian Rd. Still further out of the centre, this has been around for twenty years or more and is showing its age, but still reasonably priced and welcoming.

Nsibuk Sea Side Hotel, 45 Edem St (☎228 443), right on the waterfront down by the port. Keeps up a modern-looking front, and despite the faded interior is still comfortable and the S/C, AC rooms relatively inexpensive. The top floor bar is enclosed by huge bay windows for a beautiful view of the river and town.

Rolsol Guest House, 91 Palm St. Good value doubles with fan.

The Metropolitan, Calabar Rd (PO Box 1071; ☎220 911/ 222 257). Calabar's international class place, with all the usual amenities, and a swimming pool.

The **CUSO hostel** on King St is now reserved for Canadian and British volunteers only.

Food and drink

Calabar soup with periwinkles is famous in Nigeria. Nigerians say that if a Calabar woman cooks for you, you'll never leave the town. But as usual, if you're willing to prepare it, the cheapest place to get **food** is at the market. *Watt Market* in the centre has a wide range of foodstuffs, including fresh fruits and vegetables and the usual tins of sardines or corned beef. You'll also find numerous chop bars in town. Near the Centralway, one of the best is the *Eno Abasi Eating and Drinking House*, serving inexpensive African meals (*gari*, rice and beans, *dodo*) and always packed. Another place to try in town is *Mr Magic* on Marian Rd. The Lebanese restaurant next to *La Luna* club (see under "Nightlife") also serves excellent meals although it's slightly expensive. If, in walking through the streets, you pass houses with cages full of mangy looking dogs in front, don't think the mutts are there to mount guard. These places are dog meat restaurants – a local delicacy. Not everyone can redefine those ideas of man's best friend and try some, but it's not bad.

You could spend your days in Calabar just wandering from **bar to bar**. There are many good ones and you shouldn't hesitate to try them. For their inimitable ambience, the *Monkey Bar* on M.C.C. Rd and *The Champion* on New Airport Rd near Calabar Polytechnic are both recommended. Many of the bars also serve today's (or yesterday's) palm wine. It's good and even cheaper than beer.

Nightlife

A number of zesty **clubs** enliven Calabar nights and, since this is one of the southern Nigerian cities where you can feel relatively safe after dark, it's fun to wander around checking them out. *Paradise City*, 87 Akekong Drive, off Marian Rd (☎221 234), is one of the flashiest and most popular at the moment. It has live music (reggae or high-life) on Fridays and Saturdays and charges a modest entrance fee. *La Luna*, Fosbery Rd, also has regular live music at weekends and is slightly cheaper than *Paradise. City*. If you want something reassuringly mainstream and unsurprising, the *Metropolitan* has an ordinary disco that always packs them in. For something at the other end of the scale, the small *Jazz Club* on Target Rd has a very nice music selection.

Calabar has two downtown **cinemas** – the *National* on Target Rd, opposite the motor park, and the *Patsol*, 22 Bedwell St. The *Patsol* is the better of the two, as it's nigh impossible to make out the soundtrack at the National – not that it matters a great deal as most of the movies are Hindi dramas or Kung-fu. For the chance of something better, try the Calabar University Campus

Looking around Calabar

The centre of town is marked by **Watts Market**. Calabar Road runs through the middle of this market dividing foodstuffs on one side from cloth and household goods on the other. Also on Calabar Rd, between the market roundabout and the international class *Metropolitan Hotel*, you'll find the **post office** and major **banks**.

There's still a good deal of **colonial architecture** in the older parts of town, especially around the districts of Henshaw town, Dukes town and down by the port. The **port area** has one of the highest concentrations of old colonial buildings, many of them still inhabited despite their dilapidated condition. The **old courthouse** is a good example of period design.

The Museum

On the hill overlooking the port, **Calabar Museum** (daily 9am–6pm, ☎223 476) is housed in the **Old Government House**, the former residence of the colonial governor. The building, which was actually built in Glasgow and shipped over in pieces, has been beautifully restored.

The museum concentrates on the **history** of old Calabar, rather than on ethnography or art, and the collections are well thought-out, and clearly documented and displayed. In fact, there's almost too much to contemplate here in one visit, with a mass of details on trading, missionary activities and colonial administration. It's a remarkable collection spanning pre-colonial days and continuing through the slave and palm oil eras, British invasion and later anti-colonial resistance to end with the path to independence. The museum also contains a **craft village** and shop and there's a good outdoor bar with wonderful views over the town. The small **bookshop** has interesting material on the history and culture of the region.

Creek Town

From the port, you can catch a "fly boat" (motor boat) to nearby **Creek Town** (also spelt Greek Town – even residents seem to have lost track of the correct name) a 45-minute ride down the Cross River, with dense mangrove greenery reminiscent of scenes from *African Queen*. On arrival, there's nothing much to visit as such, but you can wander around and absorb the intimate creekside village atmosphere. Some of the houses still have small "factories", where they produce **palm oil** using antiquated nineteenth century mills from Britain. If you express interest, people are surprised but happy to show you their production methods. The town has a small **market** and numerous **palm wine bars** – look for the tell-tale phallic gourds that serve as cups, hung in front of the bars – where you'll find the beverage much fresher, and therefore much less alcoholic and more quaffable, than in Calabar town itself. It's often served with grilled **monkey meat** – not a bad accompaniment if you can maintain the frame of mind the wine will ultimately induce anyway.

Cross River State

The natural vegetation of **Cross River State** is almost entirely **rainforest**, though large reaches have been cleared for oil palm plantations since the turn of the century.

Oban Rainforest

One of the most exciting wildlife and conservation projects in Africa is currently under development along the A4-2 Calabar to Ekang road, northeast of Calabar. This is the **Oban Rainforest National Park**, an amazingly rich biosphere sponsored by the Worldwide Fund for Nature. On paper, there's a Cross River National Park, but the Oban division (Oban village is about 60km along the road) is the current focus of world attention for its recently discovered **gorilla** denizens. It was thought the gorilla had disppeared from most of West Africa in the last century, and from Nigeria and western Cameroon several decades ago, but the WWF has located at least four separate gorilla populations, and it's thought they may number several hundred individuals in the park. The Oban reserve, which is about the size of Cambridgeshire, abuts the Korup National Park in Cameroon and shares similar flora and fauna (including the gorillas). At present, there's little in the way of facilities for visitors. If you don't have any luck with information in Oban village, continue along the road towards Ekang and try to make your way to Mkpot, 15km west. Better still, write in advance to WWF (Panda House, Weyside Park, Godalming GU7 1XR, UK) and see if you can be put in touch with field workers.

Obudu Cattle Ranch

The other relatively well-known attraction in Cross River is **Obudu Cattle Ranch** in the north of the state. This is a kind of hill resort cum cattle station in the beautiful folds of the grassy Sonkwala range, over 1500m above sea level, spread across the north-facing slopes of Oshie Ridge. In the 1960s and 1970s Obudu Ranch was a fashionable place to stay, popular with oil industry ex-pats escaping from the maddening climate of the delta oil fields, as it offered a virtually European climate and exotic fresh garden produce like strawberries and cauliflowers. The *Ranch* (PO Box 40; Obudu, Cross River State) may have gone downhill a little, but it still offers chalet accommodation, with **walking** opportunities all round – and possibly still riding (it's outside the tse-tse fly zone). A path leads from the hotel about 6km to a striking waterfall.

Also in the area is a natural spring – "the grotto". Getting up here is difficult without your own transport and the maps are inconsistent. Make for OGOJA, whence it's over 100km via the village of OBUDU, now all on a new tarmac road. It gets busy during holidays and advance bookings are always advisable – most Nigerian travel agents can help. You're not likely to be turned away, however, if you make it here under your own steam and want to camp. Remember the altitude: it does get cool here at night, so bring something warm.

Ikom

The border town of **IKOM** by no means counts as a Cross River attraction but it's tolerable enough. If you need to **stay** there are two decent hotels – the *Lisbon*, at 70 Calabar Road, and the *Unima* – both of which have compounds for safe parking. The *Lisbon* is clean enough but rather tatty with less than perfect mosquito netting. Ikom has banks (though you'll not be able to buy Central African CFA, even if newly arrived travellers can exchange them for Naira) plus a number of shops, and the usual services, but there's little nightlife aside from the quiet bars. If you arrive early enough in Ikom, it's preferable to move straight on to the border – there are regular taxis the 26km to Mfum.

CROSS RIVER TRAVEL DETAILS

Out of Calabar

● Most vehicles go from the **Watt Market Motor Park** – regular transport to **Port Harcourt, Ekang** (for Oban Rainforest Reserve and Cameroon) and **Ikom** (for Cameroon and northern Cross River State). Go to the other Nigerian extreme from Calabar to **Jos** – *Crosslines* runs a daily bus service that takes all day, plus some.

● **Flights** out of Calabar (on *Nigeria Airways*) include daily flights to Lagos and weekly flights to Douala, Cameroon and Libreville, Gabon, both originating in Lagos. With the current exchange rate, the Calabar–Douala flight is less than £30.

● **Airline agents and adresses:** *British Airways*, 164 Ndidem Usang Iso Rd (☎224 466); *KLM*, Tripton Travel Agency, 1 White House St (☎224 488); *Nigeria Airways*, 45 Bedwell St (☎222 504).

Into Cameroon

● **Cameroon Consulate**, 21 Marian Rd – any taxi driver or *cyclist* can take you there. Even if your application was refused at the Lagos embassy, your chances of getting a visa here are good. Bring two passport photos, and you can normally get it the same day.

● The **most direct frontier** from Calabar is Ekang–Otu, at the end of the Oban Rainforest road. Cross River State's **main crossing point**, however, is Mfum–Ekok. Taxis stop a few hundred metres from the customs and immigration posts. Here, "guides" will try to show you the way, which isn't really necesary. Allow a few hours for customs and immigration at **Mfum** (open 8am–7pm). In the past officials here have been oppressive in the extreme – confiscating used film for example – and it may require full reserves of humour on your part to rescue the situation. "Yes sir" is important, and you'd better mean it. Once you've filled your Nigerian exit forms and been questioned, searches are usually fairly limited. You can soon be on your way across the bridge into Cameroon (see p.1087).

● Ekok, the first centre in Cameroon, is a lively place to stay the night, with bright lights(mainly kerosene), loud music, hotels, burgers and a Wild West feel. Note that once you get here, however, there's no bank for changing money into Central African CFA. French francs would be best. Naira are acceptable currency for the short journey to Mamfe, but the price will be a lot more than you're officially allowed to export from Nigeria. The first large town of Mamfe has banks – see p.1117.

● Alternatively, various **boats to Cameroon** leave from **Oron** in Akwa-Ibom State, 25km southwest of Calabar across the mouth of the Cross River – boats there are fairly frequent from Calabar, a ninety-minute voyage – for a 150-kilometre sea voyage around the creeks and mangroves to **Limbé**. If you intend going this way, try to have your passport stamped for an exit from Nigeria, either in Calabar or Oron. And don't use the overloaded cargo vessels that are obviously smuggling goods. These boats from Oron to Cameroon are commonly taken by local people, but you may be dropped on the coast almost anywhere and then run the risk of missing official entry procedures to Cameroon. Pay more for a passenger boat with a turn of speed otherwise the voyage will take days. And make sure your passport is stamped as soon as possible after arrival. Note: going through the creeks does seem to be a good way of getting to the **Korup National Park** from Calabar, presumably by boat up the Akpa Yafe river that forms the border, from the creekside village of **Ikang**, 25km southeast of Calabar by taxi.

CENTRAL NIGERIA

The huge area that is **"Central Nigeria"** is an artificial division, and really consists of the middle margins of the country's more natural divisions into southwest, southeast and north. However, the centre has quite a concentration of interest. If the new federal capital of **Abuja** has nothing to offer but projections for the future, the same cannot be said of one of the country's most favoured towns, **Jos**, on its fine, high plateau of almost Mediterranean climate. **Bauchi** is less attractive, though pleasantly spacious, while **Yankari Game Reserve**, not far away, is the country's best organised park and its amazing **Wikki Warm Springs** a pristine attraction in their own right. On the way north, you might consider striking out to the **Borgu Game Reserve** – something that's a lot easier to do with your own vehicle.

Kainji Dam and Borgu Game Reserve

Scenically, climatically and culturally, this area feels more like a part of northern Nigeria, but it's remote and far to the west, and most commonly and easily approached from the south.

Ilorin to the Kainji Dam and New Bussa

North of Ilorin (see previous section) you leave Yorubaland and enter a drier and less mono-ethnic environment, populated by a mix of Nupe, Bussa, Bargu, Kamberi, Fulani and Hausa communities. After some 70km you reach **JEBBA** (off the road to the right) and cross the Niger on a fine, low bridge. At **MOKWA**, 38km further, the road to the Kainji Dam, New Bussa and Borgu Game Reserve sweeps off to the northwest. There are few towns up here amid the wild bush and dry patchy farmlands. **ZUGURMA** (24km from Mokwa), however, is a pretty halt, with a fine, jungly stream running past (nice wild camping) and, beyond, you're sure to see some wildlife – monkeys at least, if you've not spotted them before in Nigeria.

Kainji dam is impressive, though you probably won't be allowed to go onto it (the road runs past, below it). It was just north of here, at Old Bussa (which has now been submerged by the artificial Kainji Lake) that the Scottish explorer Mungo Park was killed in 1805 by people on the bank – who apparently thought he was a party of raiding Fulani jihadists.

The local town, **NEW BUSSA** is a dull, scruffy town, as you'd expect of a settlement created to house displaced persons whose homes and land lie under water. There's little of interest save the *Kainji Tourist Motel* – a modestly superior, fairly expensive establishment a little way out of town, with old-fashioned but comfortable S/C chalet rooms and a safari atmosphere – not to mention a wonderful swimming pool (bookable through *Tourist Resources*, PO Box 3336; 3 Hussey St, Yaba, Lagos). It accommodates frazzled ex-pats up from Lagos for the weekend and is the only base for the Borgu Game Reserve (headquarters at WAWA) whose boundary is 20km west of here. A lot cheaper beds can be had at the *Student Hostel* in town.

Borgu Game Reserve

BORGU doesn't get a lot of visitors, and it's doubtful if it has a lot of wildlife – in fact it looks certain that much has been poached out. However it's uninhabited by humans, and its 4000-odd square kilometres do contain plentiful numbers of various **antelope** species and there are several families of **hippos** in the pools of the somewhat seasonal Oli River which flows through the reserve.

The roads through Borgu tend to be well maintained, though that won't help much if you don't have a vehicle of your own. Still, if you pressed on up here using available transport, that won't deter you, and vehicles can be hired – as can rangers, compulsory companions to your game drive; they are to be found up at the guard post in Wawa, where you also pay your entrance fee.

Abuja

ABUJA has a beautiful setting, with a backdrop of stunning stone inselbergs and a good deal of greenery. But that's about it. There are landscaped boulevards with wonderful views across the savannah, an empty ring road called Ring Road 1, which skims miles from the centre in a great lemon-shaped thirty-kilometre loop, a scattering of snappy adminstrative and commercial buildings, spaces for city parks – and lots more spaces to be filled by new businesses – and a few uneasy international hotels writing off empty rooms against a less and less promising future. The new **federal capital**

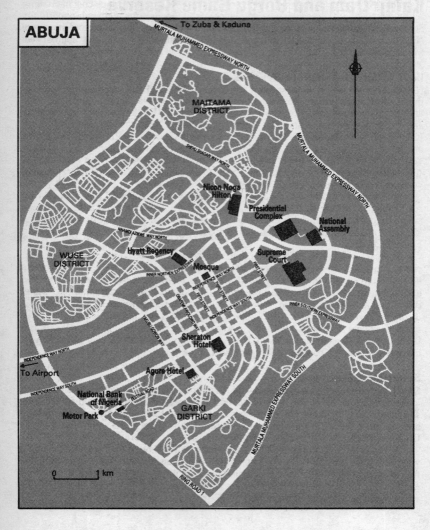

is Nigeria's only well-planned modern city and one day may develop into something exciting. Meanwhile, it's just a great, soulless blueprint on the plains.

The new capital

The federal government's decision to create a new capital dates from 1976 when the experience of the civil war made it clear that Lagos, with a seventy-five percent Yoruba population, was not conducive to relieving ethnic tensions. Besides, Lagos had already outgrown its capacities. Work on the new capital began in 1981 and, almost overnight, the peaceful setting of this hitherto sparsely populated corner of the Niger State was transformed into Africa's biggest ever construction site. The enormous cost of creating a city from scratch, especially one with such ambitious designs and such opportunity for misappropriation, led to serious economic difficulties for the civilian presidency of Shehu Shagari and after the 1983 coup, which deposed him, the project came to an abrupt standstill. Although the capital has now officially been moved, Abuja remains unfinished and, in these austere times, progress continues at a snail's pace.

As a result, Abuja is not very appealing. You can walk for blocks in areas of town without passing a single building – nothing but vacant plots and stilled construction sites. Many of the proud boulevards lead nowhere and flyovers fail to fly right over. Indeed half the time, it's hard to believe anyone could still lay their hands on any plans. Ambitious building projects remain at the foundation stage and although the city is designed with a population of three million in mind, there are as yet precious few signs of an influx. At times there's an uncanny feeling everyone must be away.

A more basic personality disorder results from the lack of an indigenous population or culture. Don't expect to meet an "Abuja local." People living and working here come from all parts of the country and no one considers Abuja home. Except perhaps the **Gwari**, the original "sparse population". Partly village based and partly nomadic, they were unceremoniously evicted from their ancestral lands in the cause of federal glory, in a casting aside that points up both the ruthlessness of the power elite and the disregard of the urban middle classes for other Nigerians living according to customs eroded elsewhere by westernisation. It's sad – and ironic in view of the unifying purpose of the Abuja plan in the first place. Today, the Gwari have nearly disappeared as a distinct ethnic and linguistic (Kwa-speaking) community.

Around town – and accommodation

If you have a passion for visiting the bars of **international hotels**, you'll love Abuja. Otherwise, you'll have to be especially interested in urban planning or the sociology of development to find any reason to want to stay. In the continued absence of the projected **National Museum**, or any other worthy distraction, many travellers resign themselves to one of the air-conditioned cocktail lounges in the **Nicon-Noga Hilton** (PMB 200, PO Box 81; ☎523 1811, Fax 523 1839). With 817 rooms and a huge conference centre, this is said to be the largest hotel in Africa. They feature a happy hour from 6–7pm – a good pretext for people watching.

For similar diversions you could try the nearby *Hyatt Regency* or, assuming it's opened, the *Sheraton* (there are indications it may be a while yet). The only other thing you might want to go out of your way to see is the **Central Mosque**, with its large golden dome and fairy tale minarets.

Cheap **lodging** doesn't yet exist in Abuja, though the most promising reaches of town are down in the south in Garki district. About the best you can do is the *Sunny Guest Inn* (PO Box 199; ☎523 1881), across from the motor park, or the *Baguda Suite Hotel*, Festival Rd (PMB 326; ☎523 1563), also near the motor park, in what looks like a rundown tenement in the Garki district – you could easily walk by without noticing it. Despite the AC, TV and fridges, both of these are modest places, but a night at either costs more than in the *Federal Palace* in Lagos. At an intermediate stage, you might also try the *Agura Hotel* in Festival Rd (☎523 1753), which has all the perks of the big hotels – pool, tennis, shops, nightclub – but is a notch cheaper and several degrees less pretentious.

MOVING ON FROM ABUJA

The main **motor park** is on Festival Rd near the junction with Ring Road 1. Considering this is the federal capital, traffic is limited. Cars and buses leave pretty regularly for **Kaduna**, but departures are rare for other destinations, even Lagos. There is a regular service to **Suleija**, one of the original settlements now swamped by the FCT, which has a much more active motor park. It's often a good plan to go out there if you have trouble getting long-distance transport from Abuja.

If you're in a hurry, there are twice daily **flights** on *Nigeria Airways* to Lagos (1hr), the second of which goes via Jos (30 min). There may be an office in Abuja but it doesn't advertise itself. Ask at a hotel front desk.

Bida

If you're coming up to Abuja from the west by road, from Ibadan/Ilorin, you'll pass through the old Nupe capital of **BIDA**. Nupe was an early kingdom, contemporaneous with the Hausa emirates, that lasted from around 1400 through its submission to Fulani rule after the nineteenth century jihads. The Nupe people (who speak a Kwa language related to Yoruba) are still renowned crafts experts and Bida has something of a reputation as a place to buy locally made cloth, metal jewellery, and cylindrical coloured glass "trading beads" whose style is supposed to have originally derived from the markets of medieval Venice.

Jos

Set 1200m above sea level, **JOS** enjoys a mild climate that has long attracted Europeans weary of the coastal humidity and northern heat and dust. Purposefully laid-out in a beautiful, rocky landscape, the hill resort grew up around **tin mines** exploited by the British at the turn of the century – and still partly managed by expatriates. Jos' history, though, can be traced back much further to the **Nok Culture** (named after the Jos plateau village of the same name) which spread throughout central Nigeria 2500 years ago. Terracotta artefacts left behind by this civilisation were discovered quite accidentally in the mines and are today housed in the **Jos Museum**.

This is only one of many sites in a town that seems to have been intentionally designed for visitors. Another diversion is the **Zoo**, which contains perhaps the best collection of animals in the country. Another original idea was to create the **Museum of Traditional Nigerian Architecture**, where lifesize replica buildings from Zaria, Kano, Katsina and other cities have been completely reconstructed. Here you can visit the gems of traditional architecture which, all too typically, have largely fallen into disrepair or disappeared altogether in their native cities.

Orientation and basics

The **Main Market** is an unmistakable landmark, covering a large area in the middle of town. Built after the the old market burned down in 1975, it's a massive modern structure with a wild, colourful design – and it's well-stocked to boot.

From the market, **Ahmadu Bello Road**, one of the town's main thoroughfares, runs down towards the **Post Office**. Along it, you'll find a number of **supermarkets** –

notably *Chellarams* – and several **banks**, although the major ones are behind the post office around Bank Rd. Near the post office, **Beach Road** ("The Beach") runs parallel to the railway tracks, across from the main goods yard. Vendors line this street selling a variety of **local crafts**, with a heavy emphasis on leather and basketwork. A pedestrian bridge leads over the tracks to **Murtala Muhammad Way**, another major thoroughfare, which runs from the **railway station** back down to the main market.

Around Town: the Museums and Zoo

From the post office, follow the road leading uphill past Bank Rd and Noad Ave. When you reach this second street, the road winds back down to a vast recreational area where the various museums and the zoo are located.

Jos National Museum

The first building you come to is **Jos National Museum** (daily 9am–6pm; free), created in 1952 to house the **Nok terracotta figures** first found in the tin mines near Nok in the 1920s. These pieces are complemented by exhibits showing aspects of the art and culture – masks, weaving, medicine, ceremonies – of central Nigerian peoples. The collections are extremely well presented and the brief explanations are helpful. At the end of the museum (notice, as you're leaving, the massive gate from the ancient wall around Bauchi), an extensive **pottery collection** is displayed in a cool courtyard with fountains, ponds and trees. Part of the exhibition is contained in a reproduction Hausa home, and more in a Nupe hut. **Crafts** are sold in a small shop across from the museum and leatherwork, pottery and weaving is carried out in nearby workshops.

The Zoo and Light Railway

The **Zoo** (daily 7.30am–6pm) adjoins the National Museum, spread over a large park with trees and streams. There's an impressive collection of animals here – antelopes, monkeys, crocodiles and birds – caged in environments designed to resemble their natural habitats. (Note, though, that the "Rock" lion is not so-called because he lives in precipitous areas, but because he was donated by *Rock Beer*.) Even if you're not normally an afficionado, this is a relaxing place to while away an afternoon.

Near the zoo, several old locomotives and carriages from the **Bauchi Light Railway** (which closed in 1957), serve as a home for a collection of recent paintings and drawings by Nigerian artists. There's nothing special about the works and they really only serve as a pretext to climb over the **antiquated steam engines** and wander through the compartments of trains dating from the early part of the century.

Also nearby, the **Tin Mining Museum** (daily 7.30am–6pm) is dedicated to the history and technology of mining in the area. It was closed for renovations at the last check but should by now have reopened. If you're minded to find out more about how the metal is extracted – it's a wet and messy, open-cast business requiring considerable land rehabilitation – try contacting the *Nigerian Tin Mining Company Ltd* (PMB 2036, Jos; ☎80632) for a **guided tour**. People here are generally quite amenable.

Traditional Architecture

Probably the most unusual museum, and one well worth spending some time to discover, is the **Museum of Traditional Nigerian Architecture** (MOTNA), which covers a vast area behind the zoo. Full scale reproductions of the country's most impressive monuments have been built on the site. You get a better idea of the magnitude of the **Kano Wall** here than you do in its city of origin, especially if you climb the narrow staircase leading to the top. The **Zaria Friday Mosque** with its impressive vaulting is a revelation of the highly sophisticated technical skills of the Hausa. There are also smaller copies of the **Katsina Palace** and the **Ilorin mosque**. In addition to

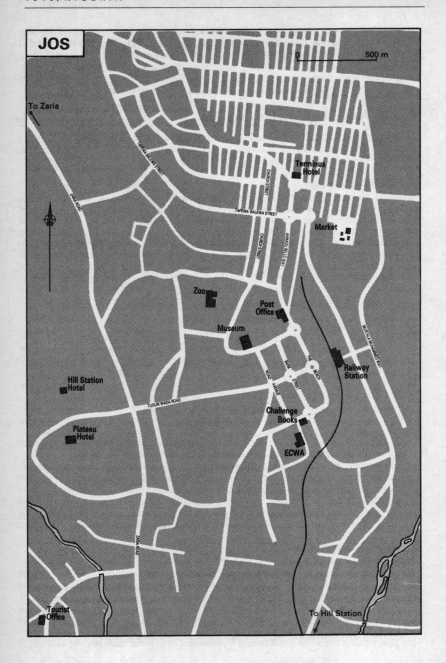

these masterpieces, humbler examples of traditional housing styles are slated to be built on the grounds to create "a miniature architectural map of Nigeria." A few compounds are in place, but nothing much else for the moment.

Sleeping and eating

Accommodation is pretty easy to find in Jos, with a range of choice at all budget levels. There is a treat on the meal front, too, at the *Bight of Benin* (see below). And Jos' own *Rock* beer, a German-award-winning brew is highly recommended.

Hotels

SIM/ECWA Guest Inn, off Kano Rd – behind *Challenge Books* (a short distance from the museum). Clean and safe, this is the cheapest place in town and often used by travellers (volunteers get a reduced rate); rooms at various prices, some S/C with hot water. The restaurant serves solid helpings of solid meals like Irish stew and two veg.

Colin and TEKAN guesthouses. Two missionary-orientated places off Bank St; they will usually put you up if they have room.

Terminus Hotel, Ahmadu Bello Rd. An attractive, timeworn colonial building overlooking the main market. Though it can feel somewhat sleazy, the rooms are clean and comfortable – and it's a real bargain for the price (low) and central position.

The Universal, 11 Pankshin Rd. Great value – and has hot baths!

Moonshine Hotel, Atili St (☎55645). Similar to the Universal and equally good value rooms – plus a decent restaurant. A bit far, however, from the centre.

Tati Hotel, Zaria Rd (☎52554). This is in a pricier league, with extras like phones and a popular weekend nightclub. The comforts come with friendly service.

Plateau Rock, Tudun Wada Rd (☎55740); **Jos Hotel**, Zaria Rd (☎55381). The two state-run hotels, both well maintained if a little overpriced for the standards.

Hill Station Hotel, Tudun Wada Rd (PO Box 72; ☎52808 or 55399, telex 81130). The big hotel in town, with a pool (small fee for non-residents), shops and the works. It's an attractive building overlooking the hills, a refreshing place to come for a cold drink even if you don't envisage staying the night. And it's something of a focus for the remains of Jos' ex-pat community – call in and you'll get a feel for the town's curious, slightly lapsed colonial mentality.

STAYING ON THE PLATEAU

If you want to get into the **Jos Plateau** countryside, take a taxi or minibus out to Bukuru from the end of Tafawa Balewa St, near the market. Get out somewhere en route and **camp** or stay in the very nice *Yelwa Club* in Bukuru, which has a pool and is surprisingly cheap.

For **camping**, the VOM area to the southwest of Jos is pretty, with plenty of good grassy spots amid boulders and groves of gum trees. **Vom** itself has a mission and veterinary labs servicing its dairy – fresh Friesian milk at next to nothing a litre and wonderful cheese.

Restaurants

If you're visiting the museum and zoo, the *Bight of Benin* restaurant is an excellent place to eat, housed in an exact replica of a Benin noble's house and serving different specialties from throughout the country at reasonable prices. The interior is beautiful (traditional red paint is made by mixing fine Benin sand with ground snail shells; the overhead beam is Iroko wood) and provides a cool place to take a break.

Among the better known restaurants in the town centre, the *Cedar Tree* on Bukuru Road, serves excellent, expensive Lebanese food, the *Sharazad*, also on Bukuru Rd, is another popular place and, for a Chinese meal, check out the *Palace Restaurant* in the *Hill Station Hotel*.

MOVING ON: SOME JOS TRANSPORT DETAILS

Buses to **Calabar** are operated daily by a *Crosslines* bus service at 7am. Office and embarkation point is by the Bauchi road taxi park. Bus services to **points northeast** are run by *Yankari Express*, next to *Crosslines*, who cover several routes including Bauchi/Maiduguri.

The **railway** (Jos is on a branch line) is not a predictable means of transport. Check in the station what's supposed to be departing for Maiduguri or Kafanchan (where you would change for Kaduna/Kano, Lagos, or Port Harcourt).

There are twice daily **flights to Lagos** on *Nigeria Airways*, but none to Kano. **Airlines offices in Jos:**

British Airways, 41 Murtala Muhammed Way (☎53547);
KLM, Plateau Hotel (☎52185);
Nigeria Airways, 6 Bank St (☎52298/9).

Off the Plateau: routes into Cameroon

Heading south from Jos the topography is complicated and travel delightful. Forests of gum trees spread around **PANYAM** and from here on the road (surfaced, whatever the maps may say) drops in a breathtaking escarpment through coniferous woods and Mediterranean landscapes to **SHENDAM** and **YELWA**. It's fine cycling country – if you happen to have a bike. Otherwise, apart from one or two exhausting through bus services to, for example, Port Harcourt, road transport becomes chancy as you get into this eastern part of Central Nigeria.

One of the major peoples of the plateau is the Tiv, highly regarded for their brilliant **puppet theatre** tradition. See it if you can by asking in the museum in Lagos or at the theatre arts department in any university city.

Wukari to Cameroon – the Dumbo Trek

If you're travelling south on this road into Gongola State, you're in a position to make an unusual **entry into the North West Province of Cameroon**.

From the bustling market town of **WUKARI** (try the *Catering Rest House*, or *Ishaku* or *Taraba* hotels), head for **TAKUM**, where the highlands ahead begin to make their presence felt. Takum is at the southern end of the paved road and beyond it, looping into the green hills, with bananas and fleshy jungle plants increasingly conspicuous, there is just a earth track, mostly in reasonable condition, passing over innumerable frog-filled streams up to the village of **BISSAULA** (also spelled Bissuala). You'll get transport as far as here, though don't miss any vehicles that are going, as they're not numerous.

The Michelin map used to mark as a "recognised track" the route that snakes from Bissaula to **DUMBO** on the Bamenda Higlands Ring Road: a bit of an optimistic gesture, as it consists only of the roughest footpath, the first few kilometres of which scale a steep, rocky, root-entangled, forest smothered escarpment, inaccessible to any vehicle. If you are into a **trek**, though, it's a winner: a moderately tough two-day hike (about 60km) that takes in towering trees, squealing parrots, leaping monkeys, thatched hut hamlets in smokey forest clearings, rope bridges and lines of porters (mostly portering on their own accounts, beer, cigarettes and cloth). When you reach the top, it seems half of southern Nigeria is spread out below.

You shouldn't set off trekking on your own – orientation here is impossible! – but for about CFA10–15,000 you can hire a porter to walk up to Dumbo with your luggage (the Nigerian immigration post will stamp you out and write "Footing" in your passport). Be aware that the Cameroonian post at Dumbo isn't frequently blessed with tourists and may try hard to extract presents from you. And if you take photos on the trek, try to be discreet – it's a slightly sensitive border area – and remove film before you get to Dumbo.

The A3 to Cameroon: Makurdi

The more direct route south from the Jos Plateau follows the A3 into southern Cameroon, a regular driving route bringing you to Mamfé and the highway for Douala.

MAKURDI lies half way down the route, on the south bank of the Benue River on the fringes of Igboland. It's a fair sized town with several small and medium **hotels**. Although there may not be much to choose between them, the *Dolphin* – part of a complex of cinemas, restaurants and lodgings in Secretariat Road to the north of town – is clean, welcoming and inexpensive. If you need a **travel agent** in Makurdi, *Chuben*, 35A Bank Rd (☎32060) is reliable.

Bauchi and Yankari Park

Northeast from Jos, the road drops down from the plateau in a spectacular curving hill, turns east and then runs across featureless plains to **BAUCHI**, capital of the state of the same name. Bauchi is a large impersonal place with wide avenues and ranks of office buildings, though it has a more exotic air – a little wild west if Fulani herders are pushing through the area – if approached from the north down the A3 Kano/Maiduguri route, which lines up a grand assembly of inselbergs known as the Belo Hills, shortly before you reach town.

After the Fulani jihad, in the 1840s, an Emirate was established at Bauchi. But despite the **Emir's palace**, the **old mosque** and the large **Mausoleum** of Tafawa Balewa, Nigeria's first prime minister, the town has little of enduring interest. It is, however, the nearest big centre to **Yankari Game Reserve** and if you don't have transport you'll very likely have to spend a night here before getting to the reserve.

Bauchi accommodation and practicalities

For **inexpensive lodging**, try the *Derkerker Lodge* on Murtala Muhammed Road. The *Karama Hotel*, across from the **Gombe motor park**, also has reasonably priced accommodation and is conveniently located if you're planning to catch an early taxi to the park. The expensive hotels in town are the *Awalah* (☎42344) which has a swimming pool, tennis and AC rooms with colour TV and the *Zaranda* (☎42155), featuring similar luxuries. The *Zaranda* is also where you book for *Yankari Lodge*.

For **flights** on *Nigeria Airways*, the closest airport is **Jos** – enquiries and bookings, hopefully, at 40 Kobi St, Bauchi (☎42800).

Yankari Game Reserve

YANKARI GAME RESERVE was the first animal park in Nigeria and it remains the most popular. It covers over 2200 square kilometres of protected area, but despite the best efforts, poaching is still widespread and for seeing game, the park is not exceptional even by West African standards. You'll likely see herds of **gazelle and antelope,** and **elephants** with a little luck, but **lions,** which still hunt in the park, are getting increasingly shy and elusive. Other animals include, warthogs, hippos, waterbuck, buffalos, several species of duiker, hartebeest, various monkeys and crocodiles.

In addition to the animals, **Wikki Warm Springs** provides reason of its own to come to the park. If you have problems organising game-viewing trips at the lodge, you probably wouldn't be unhappy spending your time in its crystal-clear waters.

Getting there

There is no longer any regular transport for the 105km from Bauchi to **Yankari**. If you're without a car you can take a **collective taxi** from the Gombe station on the east side of Bauchi. These vehicles go to neighbouring villages and will let you off right in front of the park gate en route. Having got this far, you're still 40km from the camp and you will then have to hitch the rest of the way with incoming visitors (if you inform the guards at the gate you're looking for a ride into the park, they're usually pretty good about asking the cars on their way in). Note that in the middle of the week and on certain off weekends, the park may be devoid of visitors, in which case you could be really stuck. For that reason, avoid setting off from Bauchi in the late afternoon, hoping to make it all the way to the campsite. Another way of getting to the campsite is to **charter a taxi** in Bauchi and arrange a price with the driver. This will be mighty expensive.

If you happen to be **cycling**, the path from Bauchi to Wikki is a fine and exciting day's ride in the park, with no access problems, and no serious worries about animals.

The way it works: Yankari practicalities

If you're planning on visiting the park during weekends or any major holiday, it's a good idea to make advance **reservations**. You can do so by contacting the Yankari Game Reserve and Tourism Company Ltd direct (PO Box 12, Bauchi; ☎42174 or 43675), by enquiring at the *Zaranda Hotel* in Bauchi, or by fixing things up several days before hand with a local travel agency.

Yankari has recently been taken over by a private company but, although prices have gone up substantially, it's still relatively inexpensive. There's a small entrance fee at the gate, then, arriving at the camp, a choice of accommodation ranging from a **campsite** (with toilets and showers) to **luxury rooms** in the lodge. Besides the campsite (you can **hire tents** here – though double check on that before striking out), the cheapest place to sleep is in a **double chalet**, which costs about twice the price of a moderate hotel in Bauchi though water and electricity go out even more frequently, and routinely at a set time late each evening.

For food, the **restaurant** near the lodge serves European meals at reasonable prices – and it could be a lot worse considering there's no alternative. If you really want to save money, bring provisions from Bauchi and do your own cooking. A pleasant **outdoor bar** overlooks the savanna and the lodge has a small **natural history museum**, full of local tales, open free of charge.

Game-viewing

Game-runs are organised at the lodge. If you don't have your own car, you can go on one of the camp vehicles for a fee, provided they get enough people together to form a worthwhile group. If you have your own vehicle, you must take one of the rangers – which isn't a bad idea, anyway, as they're most likely to know where to see animals and can direct you to other sites like the **Marshall Caves**, believed to have once been inhabited, or to the **Borkono Falls.**

Wikki Warm Springs

Below the restaurant, a steep path leads down to **Wikki Warm Springs.** It's hard to imagine any site in West Africa more completely satisfying from a hedonistic point of view. Twelve million litres a day of perfectly clear, utterly clean water at a steady ideal temperature of 31°C comes bubbling up from a dark hole at the bottom of a deep pool, at the base of a steep, sheltering cliff. Nothing, save perhaps the persistent hassles of monkeys and baboons, detracts from the site's beauty. From its source, the water flows out for a hundred metres or more past steep banks of overhanging foliage, over a bed of glistening sand. It's almost too pretty, especially at night when it's lit by floodlamps – like an elaborate bit of New Age interior design.

The access side of the steam is concreted over, which keeps it clean, and there are parts shallow enough for toddlers to enjoy, and deeper areas for bigger swimmers. Downstream, camp staff wash clothes and bathe. Access is free if you're staying at the camp but there's a charge if you're just here for the day – as, at weekends, rather a lot of people are. If you take food or valuables down there, watch out for those monkeys.

THE NORTH

Formerly a conglomeration of disunited and often warring emirates, the **Hausa country** spreads over the arid **savannah** of the northern plateaux and comprises the largest geographical entity in Nigeria. In this vast region, Hausa makes sense as a linguistic grouping rather than an ethnic one, since there are many different northern peoples. The religious and in many respects political head of all the Hausa city states is in fact a Fulani – the **Sultan of Sokoto** – and has been for nearly 180 years. Thanks to the common faith of **Islam** and the *lingua franca* of Hausa, however, a bond has been created among northerners that puts them politically at an advantage over the south.

The area near **Lake Chad** in the northeast of the country is peopled by the **Kanuri**, who, around the ninth century, migrated from the northern, desert regions of Kanem to form the new empire of Bornu which grew rich on the **trans-Saharan trade**. In the context of the current Federal Republic, this kingdom translates roughly into the **Borno State** with its capital in **Maiduguri**, the only major town in the rather depressed northeast. Further west, the **Hausa city states** (the *Hausa Bokwai*: Gobir, Katsina, Kano, Zaria, Daura, Rano and Biram), developed into powerful emirates from around the eleventh century and had partially converted to Islam by 1400. Old walled cities from this era still exist in **Katsina**, **Zaria** and **Kano**: Kano has today developed into a major **urban centre**, with international airport and diverse industries.

HAUSA ORAL HISTORY: THE ORIGIN OF THE SEVEN STATES

The Hausa have a rich oral literature outside the overweening influence of more recent Islamic tales. In folk history, the origin of their states is traced to **Bayajida**, son of the king of Baghdad, who fled his homeland afer a bitter dispute with his father. After years of wandering he arrived in Bornu and was recognised as a natural leader by the *Mai* or king, who married one of his daughters to the boy. Bayajida fell out with his father-in-law too, and fled again, with his pregnant wife, to a place called Garun Gabas. He left his Bornu wife here, where she gave birth to a son, **Biram**, who later established the first of the *Hausa Bokwai*, named after him, in the area to the east of Kano. Meanwhile Bayajida had taken off again for the west and, in the middle of one night, fetched up at Daura, a place east of Katsina that was ruled at the time by a dynasty of queens. He stopped an old woman, Ayana, to ask for water and was told it was the wrong day of the week: the snake who owned the well only allowed people to draw water on a Friday. Nobody had been able to kill the snake. Bayajida, of course, went straight to the well, woke up the snake and chopped its head off. Then he drank his fill, pocketed the head and moved on. The next day was Friday and the queen wanted to know who had killed the snake. Ayana told her about the stranger and the queen sent messengers to catch up with the restless Bayajida, who agreed to return – and then asked her to marry him as a reward. They had a son, **Dawo**. Following the death of Bayajida, Dawo's own six sons went on to found the remaining towns of the Hausa Bokwai – Daura, Katsina, Kano, Rano, Gobir and Zaria.

Development has come more slowly to the conservative Islamic stronghold of **Sokoto**, the spiritual capital of the north, while **Kaduna** is a much more anonymous, modern town neatly laid out by the British colonials as an uncontroversial adminstrative capital of the somewhat disunited north.

If you're driving north towards Kaduna on the A1 and A125, you go through the town of SABON BIRNIN GWARI. There's a new **Wildlife Reserve** here with the not unconnected *Birnin Gwari Hotel* just outside. If you're interested, the Forestry Division in Kaduna (PMB 2181 Kaduna) may be able to supply further details of the reserve, or you could simply turn up and ask to have a look around – it's only been open a year or two and certainly until very recently was allowing people access on foot. It looks set to rival Yankari in terms of accessibility and visible game and has a mass of birdlife.

Kaduna

With no palace (the town was formerly a fief of the Zaria Emirate), no city wall and no ancient mosque, **KADUNA** is essentially a **modern town** of broad avenues, with its own oil refinery, a good smattering of other industries and a bustling business environment. It's not the kind of place you'd want to spend weeks or even days discovering (indeed there's not much to find), but hitting upon this kind of cosmopolitan atmosphere, second only to Kano in the north, is not completely disagreeable either, especially after crossing the desert.

Coming up from southern Nigeria, Kaduna is usually looked on as the first town of the north. This is a slightly misleading assumption since it doesn't have much in common with the other towns in this section. It's a place, however, that on any major travels through Nigeria, you're unlikely to avoid.

Note that the area shown on our map is commonly referred to as "Kaduna North"

A short history

Originally conceived as the capital of the Northern Region, and perhaps the entire federation, Kaduna represents one of the best examples of a town created to be the seat of government. The original **northern capital** was at Zungeru, on the Kaduna river 150km southwest of Kaduna, but when **Sir Frederick Lugard** became governor of the amalgamated colonial federation in 1912, he shifted the site to the small town of Kaduna which had the advantage of being near a good water supply and on the line of the newly constructed railway. Within easy striking range of all the former emirates, the spot was also strategically important. The West African Frontier Force moved here from Zaria in 1912, and in 1917 the civil administration was transferred from Zungeru.

Kaduna lost its role as capital of northern Nigeria when the states were created in 1967, but it has continued to thrive as a centre for the army (in 1965, 28 percent of the city's area was taken up by the armed forces) and industry. Near Nigeria's main cotton growing region, Kaduna contains several textile mills, a vast oil refinery, the *Peugeot* assembly plant, a brewery and an ordnance factory.

Around town

Kaduna's spacious and purposeful layout reflects it's former function as seat of government. **Administrative buildings** line Independence Way, one of the principal tree-lined avenues, including, at the northern end, the monumental **Lugard Hall** with its impressive dome – now government offices – the GRA for senior officers, various administrative buildings and the junior staff quarters. The golf course and racecourse are nearby.

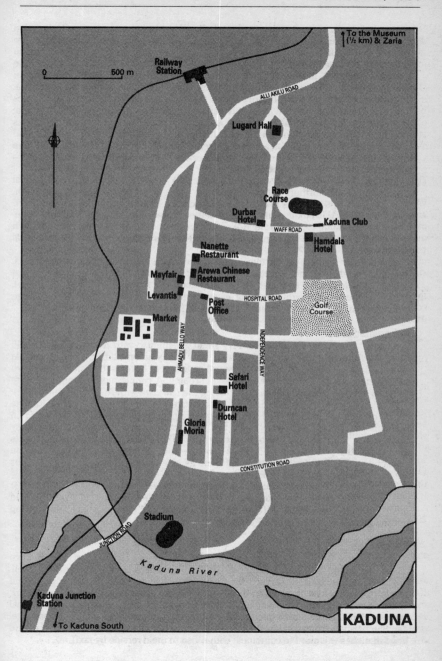

To the Museum
(½ km) & Zaria

Railway
Station

0   500 m

ALLI AKILU ROAD

Lugard Hall

Race
Course

Durbar
Hotel   Kaduna Club

WAFF ROAD

Nanette   Hamdala
Restaurant   Hotel

Mayfair   Arewa Chinese
           Restaurant

Levantis   HOSPITAL ROAD   Golf
           Post   Course
Market   Office

AHMADU BELLO WAY

INDEPENDENCE WAY

Safari
Hotel

Durncan
Hotel

Gloria
Moria

CONSTITUTION ROAD

Stadium

JUNCTION ROAD

Kaduna   River

Kaduna Junction
Station

To Kaduna South

KADUNA

The main **commercial axis**, Ahmadu Bello Way, runs in a north–south direction parallel to Independence Way. Main offices and businesses are along this street as are most of the **banks**, restaurants and hotels. In the extreme north of town, Ahmadu Bello Way becomes Alli Akilu Road. Past the State House on this thoroughfare, the **Kaduna National Museum** (daily 9am–6pm; free) houses a small collection of masks, musical instruments, leather and brass work and miscellaneous ethnographia. Its **Gallery of Nigerian Prehistory** traces the country's past back to neolithic times (the New Stone Age ended in parts of Nigeria, as in diverse other parts of West Africa, only over the last two thousand years), and examples of Nok terracotta and bronzes from Ife and Benin also figure in the exhibition. It doesn't take very long to look round the museum, but the exhibits are well presented and documented. Behind, a **Hausa village** has been recreated, and **traditional crafts** – weaving, forging, leatherwork – are carried out in the different buildings.

Kaduna's large **market** is also off Ahmadu Bello Way, in the centre of the commercial area. As in many northern cities, it's a good place to get leather goods and cloth, although most of the area is dedicated to plastic ware, clothes and other more modern goods. There's a good food section in back of the market with a range of fruits and vegetables. Further south, Ahmadu Bello Way changes names to become Junction Rd, then crosses over the bridge spanning the **Kaduna River** to Kaduna South – the industrial side of town.

If you fancy getting out of town a little, the **riverside** is a recommended area, though somewhat difficult to get to. Get a town taxi and ask for Malali village – or just "village" and get out near Malali "GTC" on Rabeh Rd. A walk parallel to the school, then over the hill through a housing estate, brings you down to the river. You can watch fishermen and lounge around on the rocks in relative peace and quiet.

Accommodation

For budget travellers, *ECWA* has a very small guesthouse with **dorm rooms** on Alli Akilu Rd. Although reserved for their staff, they'll let you have a bed if one's available (ask at *Challenge Books*). About the cheapest near-decent **hotel** is the *Safari*, downtown on Argungu St (☎211 838), which offers AC rooms. A couple more cheap places are dotted around on nearby Katsina St, including the *Durncan* with AC rooms and TV.

Hotels in the **moderate range** are concentrated in the southern part of Kaduna North, down more towards the Kaduna river. One popular place is the *Gloria Moria* on Junction Rd (☎214 501) with clean S/C, AC rooms and restaurant. On nearby Constitution Rd, the *Fina White House* (☎216 418/211 852) has two establishments near each other, with quite well set-up rooms – and TV and fridge to boot. Also on Constitution Rd, the *Kimbo Hotel* is not quite as nice as the others, but its AC rooms are decent enough and quite a bit cheaper.

There are two **upmarket hotels** in town, the *Hamdala* (PO Box 311; ☎201 440/3) and the more expensive and newer *Durbar*, near the junction of Waff Rd and Independence Way (PMB 2218; ☎211 001/8, telex 71134). Both have **swimming pools** (open to non-guests for a fee) and garden bars.

Restaurants

If you're a *suya* fan, there's a big spot for them outside the *Dubar Hotel*. For sit-down meals, the *Nanet Restaurant*, 6 Ahmadu Bello Way, offers mostly African food "well-prepared and attractively served" they say. They rise to their publicity, with solid meals, not overpriced or overspiced, served in a large, fresh dining area. The *Mayfair*, further down Ahmadu Bello Way on the other side of the road, is slightly more formal and expensive, but recommended for a hot breakfast of omelettes, chips and sausage. *Les Boro*, Rabeh Rd extension, Malali village, serves moderately priced Nigerian and English dishes (it's good to combine it with a visit to the riverside by taxi).

For more **expensive eating**, you could try the Chinese restaurant in the *Hamdala Hotel*. However, the *Arewa China Restaurant* on Ahmadu Bello Rd is generally considered to have the best oriental food in Kaduna and they do a splendid buffet on Saturdays. *La Cabana*, Junction Rd opposite the railway station, serves Lebanese and French food and is popular with ex-pats. This place also runs a good **disco** at nights and can be quite a laugh. Lastly, if you have transport, try the *Jakaranda Farm and Pottery* on Mile 20 on the Katchia road (southeast of the town, beyond the Kaduna refinery) – a surprisingly beautiful garden restaurant with crocodile pool, landscaped water garden and fruit orchards. They manage to create excellent African and European food out here, and serve all sorts of exotic cocktails. And they operate a **pottery**, as will hardly escape your notice.

Kaduna Directory

Airlines and agents include:
British Airways, Development House, 18 Ahmadu Bello Way (☎212 815, 217 315);
Express Airways Nigeria; ask locally for current address;
KLM, Philips House, 4 Alli Akilu Road (☎212 419, 217 228);
Nigeria Airways, 26 Ahmadu Bello Way (☎210 174, 210 298);
Sabena, Development House, 18 Ahmadu Bello Way (☎210 034).

Banks The banking district is around the intersection of Ahmadu Bello Way and Hospital Rd. You'll find main branches here and should have no trouble changing major international currencies (though preferably dollars or pounds) either in cash or travellers' cheques.

British Council Hospital Rd near Ahmadu Bello Rd. In theory you have to be a member to use the library, but if you explain you're passing through and want to catch up on the western press, you're likely be allowed in. They also show films and run occasional exhibitions.

Consulates
British Deputy High Commission, 2/4 Lamido Road (PMB2096; ☎201 380/2);
German Consulate, 22 Ahmadu Bello Rd (☎223 696);
American Consulate, 2 Moska Rd (☎213 074).

Phoning home Kaduna is the best place in Nigeria to get a reasonable telephone line.

Post office The GPO is on Hospital Rd in the heart of the banking district. Poste Restante is reasonably reliable.

Supermarkets There's a large *Chellarams* and a *Leventis* on Ahmadu Bello Rd near the intersection with Hospital Rd

Tourist information The *Tourist Information Centre* is on Wurno Rd, near the KSBC Radio station, at the northern end of town, off Alli Akilu Rd.

MOVING ON FROM KADUNA

● The town's main **motor park** is adjacent to the market, but note that Kaduna is bypassed by the main highway (A1, A125) between Lagos and the north. The fastest route to Jos is north out of Kaduna and via the A11 and A236.

● The **railway station** is just over the bridge. Kaduna grew up with the railway and is Nigeria's major railway town, with services, in theory, to Maiduguri, Kano, Port Harcourt and Lagos.

● According to the (not altogether reliable) schedules there are at least **daily flights to Lagos** from Kaduna on *Nigeria Airways* with two flights on Mon & Sat and three flights on Tues, Thur and Fri. Depending on demand, there are two flights a week to **Yola**. In addition, *Express Airways* operates a daily flight to **Lagos**, via **Minna**, and two flights each on Mon, Wed & Fri to **Kano** (the only flights there from Kaduna). Also currently Mon, Wed & Fri they operate a single flight to **Port Harcourt** via **Enugu**.

Zaria

One of the *Hausa Bokwai* or seven legitimate Hausa states, the old town of **ZARIA** has withstood the tests of time rather better than most of the other emirates. The **ancient wall** has largely crumbled away, but some of the old gates have been restored and are most impressive. The **Emir's palace**, with its elaborately decorated facade, is a beautiful example of traditional architecture. Nearby, the **Friday Mosque** was formerly one of the most magnificent in the entire region. It's now enclosed by a plain-looking modern structure, but the inside vaulting remains intact. Almost all the homes in the old town are built in the traditional style and many display the detailed exterior decoration for which the town is famous.

Zaria is also famous for **religious factionalism** and for the **radical student life** of Ahmadu Bello University. Over the years it has been the scene of several violent clashes with the security forces.

Orientation and staying in town

After the British arrived, a **new town** was built up some three kilometres north of the walled city, across the **Kubani River**, and this is the quarter, known as **Sabon Gari**, where you'll arrive if you're coming from Sokoto or Kano. In the centre the **railway station** and the main **motor park** stand next to each other on Main St. This is also the part of town where, early this century, Yoruba and Igbo traders settled near the tracks. The new town's **main market** is in this neighbourhood, with **banks** and major businesses nearby around Crescent Rd and Park Rd. Hospital Rd leads south across the bridge to the **Tudan Wada** neighbourhood where most of the infrastructure is located – the hospital, schools and teacher training colleges.

Lodging and eating in Zaria

In the moderate price range, the *Kuta Hotel* (☎33268) is well located off Hospital Rd, between Zaria old town and Sabon Gari. A **hotel** of character with a restaurant (but no alcohol) it has AC non-S/C rooms with balconies giving onto an inner courtyard. The *Beauty Guest Inn*, on Sokoto Rd, also has clean, moderately priced AC rooms but to its disadvantage it's a bit far from the town centre. Even further out on the Sokoto road, the *Zaria Hotel* (☎32820/9) has clean AC rooms, restaurant and bar in a quiet (dead) neighbourhood. The nicest hotel in the centre is the *Kongo Conference Hotel* on Old Jos Rd (PO Box 1068; ☎32872) which aims for complete comfort with its pool, tennis courts, restaurants and bar. It's one of the few places in town to get a cold beer at any time of year, even during Ramadan.

One of the best **restaurants** in town, and inexpensive, is the *Shagarikun* on Kongo Rd. Formerly in a banco house, the restaurant is now in a modern "storey building", but they've thoughtfully kept a section where visitors can eat on the floor. Just a couple of doors down from the *Shagarikun*, the *Zami* is a tiny and very cheap eatery with African dishes. They keep anthologies of African literature on the tables to feed your mind while you stuff your face.

Around the old town

The main centres of activity in the **old town** are the **Emir's palace** (*Gidan Sarki*) and the **market**, which, as in the other northern cities, are set well apart from one another. The houses and stores of traders and the craftsmen's ateliers (including leatherworkers, tailors and **dye pits**) are scattered around the market. You can still visit many of these workshops today.

The palace is south of the market and is surrounded by a high walled enclosure. The main entrance, the **Kofar Fada**, faces a large square where ceremonies, including the annual **durbar** cavalry charges are held. The **Friday Mosque**, disappointingly hidden behind a modern facade, dominates one side of the square. According to the story, the architect who designed it was put to death so he would never create a more beautiful building elsewhere – which surely indicates how far from traditional, retributive religion the rumour-mongers of Zaria have strayed. The architecture is outstanding, and an exact replica of the mosque exists in Jos, where, ironically, you get a better idea of what the building looks like. In the vicinity in Zaria are the offices of court counsellors and the homes of leading citizens.

Zaria town tours

There is also a **tourist information office** on the square and if you want to visit the old town it's a good idea to take advantage of its services. To visit the palace on your own you have to make a request at the secretary's office next door, and if you're not a Muslim this will almost certainly be refused. Other places around the market you could ostensibly visit, but you're not likely to find much of interest if you don't know where to look and you're almost bound to feel something of an intruder as you wander around the streets of the old town. The tourist office, however, can set you up with a guide to show you around the different sites – **dye pits**, **tanning workshops**, **weavers**, **mosque**, **palace** and **main city gates** (including the Kofar Doka and Kofar Kuyumbana). You pay something for the tour and, if you don't have a car, they'll ask you to hire a taxi for a couple of hours (not as expensive as you might imagine), but it's worth it: unless you know someone from town who can show you around there's not really much alternative. How rewarding it turns out is very much up to you: at the most superficial level it should at least allow you to take photos without harassment.

Kano

The largest city in the north, and effectively Nigeria's second city (despite being smaller than Ibadan), the ancient Hausa metropolis of **KANO** is a strange mixture of modern and traditional, with the former gaining ground and invading the latter every year. The **international airport** assures daily flights to Lagos and several direct flights each week to Europe and the Middle East, while growing **industrialisation** in the region continues to draw people from the countryside to a city over a thousand years old that strews apparently unchecked over the dusty savannah and is now home to more than two million inhabitants. Kano is committed to growth and to the future, but there's a distinct feeling that much more could be done to preserve the ties with its great past, especially to look after the **old city wall** that resisted British colonial invaders with greater success than it has the elements in recent years. Although a few of the great **gates** that once protected the emirate still stand, much of the wall has now become huge lumps of rain-smoothed mud, and people still dig away at it to make bricks for new homes. The **Gidan Makama Museum**, however, is a beautiful effort to protect Kano's heritage, housing historical exhibits of Kano and environs in a former Emir's palace, completely restored to show off the intricacy and technical excellence of the ancient architecture: the present **Emir's palace** and the **central mosque** are nearby. Other reminders of the past include the **old market** and the **dye pits** where, beside a busy multi-laned avenue, cloth is still soaked in indigo in the gloriously messy way it's been done for centuries.

Note that the Old Town of Kano is a very **traditional Musim centre** and women should be careful to dress appropriately – no exposed skin or jeans.

Downtown and around – modern Kano

The intersection of Murtala Muhammed Road and Lagos/Airport Road is the centre of modern Kano, the heart, at any rate, of its main commercial district. Many **banks** – *IBWA*, *First*, *Union* and *Bank of the North* (Mon–Fri 8am–2pm, Sat 8am–noon) – are located just south of this junction around the intersection of Lagos and Bank roads. Continuing south on Lagos Rd brings you to Post Office Rd and the **GPO** (8am–5pm). Local and **international calls** can be made further down Lagos Rd, near where it runs

---

KANO'S HISTORY

Kano's history (its courtly history at any rate) has been preserved in the *Kano Chronicles*, which give the most detailed account of any Sudanic nation with the exception of Songhai. A compilation of brief histories of the region, the Chronicles originated in the mid-seventh century, shortly after the introduction of Arabic. The first settlement of Kano was founded on **Dala Hill**, where archaeologists have uncovered furnaces and slag heaps indicating ironworking on the spot from as early as the sixth century; this settlement was later conquered by the descendants of **Bagauda** – one of the six sons of **Dawo** whose offspring founded the *Hausa Bokwai* – the seven legitimate Hausa states.

Kano was fortified at the beginning of the twelfth century during the reign of **Gijimasu**. Later, under **Yaji** (1349–85), it developed a powerful army that used new technology – quilted armour, iron helmets and chainmail – to overthrow its adversaries. The city become independent of its neighbours and gained control of the trans-Saharan trade in gold and salt. It thus acquired wealth and power to rival Timbuktu and Gao. Additions to the walled city were made in the fifteenth century under **Muhammed Rumfa**, who had converted to Islam and who transformed Kano from a local miltary chiefdom to an Islamic sultanate with close links across the Sahara and to Arabia.

Contact with Europe came in the mid-sixteenth century. **Portuguese** attempts to establish a trading centre were thwarted, but settlers from Ragusa (now Dubrovnik in Yugoslavia) maintained a presence in Kano throughout the 1560s and 1570s, under the protection of the North African-based Turkish Ottoman sultan.

Over the next two centuries, Kano warred continuously with the neighbouring states of Borno and Katsina. At the same time, European maritime powers on the coast slowly undermined the trans-Saharan routes that were the basis of Kano's power and autonomy. Although the textile and leather **industries** kept the economy going (the indigo-dyed cloth and soft red leather, known as "Moroccan", were exported as far afield as Europe), the state's political structure was fragile. When the Fulani, led by Usman Dan Fodio, waged their religious war, or **jihad**, Kano was unable to resist: the city fell in 1807. A new era of hostilities followed, and it was during this period that **European explorers** reached Kano – Clapperton in 1824, Barth in 1853 and Monteil in 1891. By the end of the nineteenth century, British **imperial designs** posed a direct threat to the emirate. Kano refortified its walls and prepared to resist, but in 1903 the city fell to British troops.

Kano effectively became a laboratory for testing the theories of colonial rule. The British appointed a compliant Emir in order to try out a system of **indirect rule** – successful in colonial terms, but a disastrous precursor to independence. The railway was opened in 1911 and the airport in 1937 and Kano's future as the dominant city of northern Nigeria, and the biggest in the Sahel, was sealed. After World War II, Kano became the centre of a renewed Islamic nationalism in Nigeria, intent on resisting the power of the southern regions of the country as much as, if not more than the British who were clearly intent on pulling out. The rift with southern Nigeria, especially with the Igbo community in the southeast, continued after independence, through the Biafran war and into recent years. As recently as 1980, a mad Kano prophet, Maitatsine, whipped up a frenzy among landless and unemployed peasants against Nigerian armed forces in the city, in an uprising that left dozens of casualties.

into Ibrahim Taiwa Rd. The **railway station** is also very nearby on Fagge Rd. Up on Club Rd, the **Central Hotel** makes a good place to stop for a cold drink: even if you don't stay here, you can pay to use the **pool**, though the water is often murky. The **Kano Club**, just up the street, used to sell weekly memberships quite cheaply which allowed use of their pool and other facilities, but on last checking the pool was dry and the ex-pat community not exactly falling over backwards to use the place. Across from the *Central*, vendors sell various **crafts**, mainly for the hotel guests. The quality is not at all bad, and while prices start high, patient bargaining can reduce them to realistic levels.

North of Murtala Muhammed Rd, the **Sabon Gari** ("New Town") neighbourhood is home to mainly Igbo and Yoruba workers and has a distinct southern Nigerian flavour. with flocks of **cheap hotels** and energetic bars – something of a relief after the more austere "dry" areas of the old city and particularly animated after dark. The recently rebuilt **Sabon Gari Market** always draws a lot of colour and crowds. Get your food and other odds and ends here, but for traditional crafts head to the old town.

Slightly out of town on the Zaria road, the **Audo Bako Zoo** has an exotic collection of animals, including a kangaroo – nothing to go out of your way for but a good excuse for a late afternoon stroll if you've nothing else to do. There's also a beer garden.

The old town

Most of Kano's special appeal lies beyond the modern commercial centre in the **old town**, down Kofar Mata Road from the modern centre. Disappointingly the fortified **town wall** has all but disappeared, but some of the original **city gates** (*Kofar*), have been restored and are worth a look. The ones in best shape are all on City Road in the south of town – Kofar Na Isa (Jesus' Gate), Kofar Dan Agundi and Kofar Sabwar. Just outside these gates you'll see the **groundnut pyramids**, the harvest of the Kano countryside.

As you walk round the old town, be on the lookout for examples of **traditional Hausa exterior decorations**. Particularly beautiful is the "masque" style of house facade (see picture on p.986), but if you have the chance to travel widely, you'll notice how much dirtier the Kano houses are than similar buildings in, say, Zinder in Niger, where the destructive combination of rain, exhaust fumes and industrial pollution is that much less. There's a fine "masque" house just past the dye pits on the left as you head into the old town.

FLYING IN FROM EUROPE

Kano is quite a good **place to start West African travels** – reasonably lively but not so intolerably frenetic and intimidating as to put you right off – and well placed for Niger and Mali or for Cameroon. If your journey is specifically to visit **friends or relatives in Nigeria**, or you want to visit Nigeria anyway, Kano is really a far better city to fly into than Lagos, and even if your eventual destination in Nigeria is far from here, you can at least arrive in Kano without feeling thoroughly daunted by the prospect of having nobody to meet you at the airport. **Aminu Kano International Airport** is only 8km from the central Sabon Gari quarter of the city, an inexpensive taxi ride.

● Serving **airlines** are currently:
British Airways from London (Wed & Sun, arriving early evening);
KLM from London and Amsterdam (Mon & Fri, early evening arrival);
Nigeria Airways from London (Mon, Wed & Sun, overnight, arrival at dawn);
Egyptair from London via Cairo (Tues & Sat, overnight in Cairo, arrive next afternoon).

● For **departures**, see "Moving on from Kano" on p.1067.

To Katsina & Zinder (Niger)

Kofar
Mazugai

Dela Hill

OLD CITY

Orion
Cinema

Kofar
Wambai

KOFAR WAMBAI ROAD

Cloth
Market

Kurmi
Market

Kofar Mata
Dye Pits

KOFAR MATA ROAD

Central
Mosque

Emir's
Palace

Kof
Nassarav

Gidan Makama
Museum

Kofar
Sabwar

Kofar
Na Isa

Kofar
Dan Agundi

KANO

Dye pits

Inside the modern Kofar Mata gate into the old town (small hillocks indicate where the wall used to be), you'll see the **dye pits** on the right. They soak cloth here in natural indigo as they have for hundreds of years, using great basins of indigo buried in the hard ground: Kano fabrics once clothed most of the people in the Sahara region and were highly valued. You can buy material or ready-made clothes here, or even have some of your own clothes dyed. But beware: if you take a picture, you'll be asked for a dash (the demanding upturned palms are plain to see on most snaps of the dye pits).

The Central Mosque and Emir's Palace

Continuing down Kofar Mata Rd, the **Central Mosque** is large and stately, but not the most noteworthy building architecturally. It has, however, been of enormous importance as a focus for the Islamic nationalism that has so bedevilled successive federal governments. With proper authorisation you can climb one of its two minarets for fine views over the city (enquire at the secretary's office at the entrance to the Emir's palace). Behind the mosque, the **Emir's Palace** spreads out over a huge acreage, and approaching from this direction its traditional architecture blends easily with the buildings of the old town albeit on a rather larger and more stately scale. The front is far more modern and obviously palatial. Unfortunately, whichever way you approach, you can't visit it.

Kurmi market and Dala Hill

North of the Emir's palace, **Kurmi (City) market** forms an impossibly tight maze of alleys and stalls. They're pressed together to exclude the heat, but there are so many people milling about, it gets claustrophobic and sweaty anyhow. The market swarms with petty hustlers and **"guides"**. If you can bear to come to terms with just one boy, accept you'll have to pay him something and be prepared for a little transparent salesmanship at certain stalls of his acquaintance, you may find the visit a lot more enjoyable. Once you've got to know each other, a guide can be instructive and helpful and his presence saves you from the others – the one thing that mars a visit to Kurmi is forever trying to shake off would-be assistants.

The busiest and best time to visit is any afternoon except Friday. The market retains a strong **traditional flavour**, although certain sellers with an eye on tourist bucks turn out shoddy and not very traditional junk. As always, you have to try and confront the chimera of "authenticity", but it's not yet too common a dilemma, and **leather**, **cloth**, **brass**, **silverwork** and **beads** are still good value.

Dala Hill, site of the original settlement in Kano, rises up to the north of the Kurmi market, pretty well in the centre of the old town. You can walk up there – it involves finding your way through narrow alleys and backstreets – and can usually find a kid to take you for a dash, but remember to fix the price first.

The museum

Across the square in front of the palace, the grandiose building is the **Gidan Makama Museum** (daily 10am–4pm; free). Formerly a palace itself, the building is as interesting for admirers of **architecture** as the exhibits inside. Fittingly, the displays in the first room explain the technological and decorative aspects of traditional Hausa building styles. Rooms two to six trace the **history of Kano** and the other Hausa states through drawings, photographs, documents and reconstructions spanning a thousand years – a dense and informative chronology, though not for the faint-hearted. The coming of Islam to Kano and the Muslim tenets are laid out in the seventh room. Finally, rooms eight and nine are dedicated to a less demanding selection of **traditional arts** – music, weaving, brasswork etc. Set aside a couple of hours to visit, as it's well worth the time – you may want to come back.

Staying in Kano: accommodation

Kano has a wide range of places to stay, ranging from camping grounds (in the middle of town!) or dorm rooms to international class hotels. Whatever your taste or means, you can get what you're looking for here. A number of reasonably inexpensive **small hotels** ("Moderate") are concentrated in the Sabon Gari district.

Inexpensive

Kano Tourist Transit Camp, Club Rd between the *Central Hotel* and the Kano Club. Camping places, dormitory space and private rooms, bucket showers and fans, all at reasonable rates. It's safe, friendly and central. There's a **tourist information office** here (it's a key trans-African travellers' haunt) that can organise excursions around the city or to nearby sites.

SIM/ECWA Guest House, Tafawa Balewa Rd between Mission Rd and Zaria Ave. Very clean rooms and friendly staff, but its "budget" prices are almost up to the small hotel range. Family atmosphere, but you have to be on your best behaviour.

Baptist Guest House and Restaurant, France Rd. Offers twin rooms (if you're alone, you may end up with a roommate) with fan and fridge. Very simple, but clean and about the cheapest you'll find in Kano.

Moderate

TYC Hotel, 44 France Rd (☎627 491). At the junction of France Rd and Ibo Rd, with a range of options from single rooms (moderately priced) to more elaborate suites with colour TV and fridge. They run a good restaurant serving full Nigerian meals – or just pepper soup or sandwiches – and they've a "roof garden" that's unbearably hot during the day, but a nice place for drinks while looking out on the lights of Sabon Gari at night.

Rolling Hotels 82 Church Rd (☎620 097). Slightly cheaper, but also has clean S/C rooms with AC and its own restaurant.

Universal Hotel, 86 Church Rd (the street is actually now called Awolowo Rd although the old appellation seems to have stuck). Once popular with travellers, but now a brothel. If you're feeling hardy, it's probably worth checking to see if it's reverted to more licit business.

Mikela De Hotel 29–31 Church Rd (☎627 009). Excellent value lodgings with reasonably priced rooms that include AC, TV and even a fridge. They also have a pleasant bar and restaurant. The annex across the street has simpler, cheaper accommodation.

Challenge Guest Inn 87 Yoruba Rd, and **Duniya** 12 Fesling Rd, are two other inexpensive places in the district.

Upmarket hotels

Kandara Palace Hotel Unity Rd, near the old town (☎623 073). Nice place with clean enough AC rooms, very kind and friendly service and moderate rates.

Central Club Rd (☎625 141). The main international class hotel, looks like it could use a new coat of paint (among other things), but has a pool (small fee for non-residents use), tennis courts and, above all, an air-conditioned bar – popular ex-pat rendezvous.

Daula (☎625 311). The other expensive hotel in town, newer than the Central with its own swimming pool.

Places to eat

Cheap

Galaxy Restaurant, 139 Murtala Muhammed, not far from the Tourist Camp. Ask others before eating here – there have been some upset tummies. They used to have good omelettes and chips for breakfast, and dishes like rice with chicken or beef stew later in the day. It's in an old cottage with outdoor terrace for drinking at night.

Choice Restaurant & Takeaway, 40a Niger St, by the International Clinic. Excellent simple meals – plantains, omelette and meat, for example – for a few Naira.

A cheap outdoor restaurant hides in the Mallam Kata Square off Yolawa Rd – good helpings of rice with sauce and cold minerals served in the shade of the garden.

Hotel restaurants are generally reliable too: *The Tourist Camp* and *TYC* are both reasonable, and the *Akija Hotel*, Murtala Muhammad Rd, serves moderately priced Nigerian food.

Not cheap

Big hotels – the *Central* and the *Daula* – have expensive restaurants serving not always very wonderful European food.

Fellowship Hotel, Niger St. European food.

Brick Castle Restaurant, 20 Ahmadu Bello Way. Lebanese and European food and a nightclub adjoining.

Lebanese Patisserie, Ahmadu Bello Rd opposite *Chellarams*.

Lebanon Street is full of patisseries and Lebanese restaurants – real cakes, real ice cream.

Magwan Water Restaurant, Audo Bako Way.

Chinese

Peking Chinese Restaurant, 14 Ahmadu Bello Way.

The Pink Peacock, Dantata Rd.

Great Wall, Bompai Rd.

China Restaurant in the *Central Hotel*.

In Kano after dark

The place to be is **Sabon Gari**, the old city being pretty quiet in the evenings. Cinemas and bars are the main diversions, though there's the odd **disco** too – *Lilywhite*, next to the *Galaxy* on Murtala Muhammed at the bottom of Club Rd, is a positively outrageous example, named ironically. The bars of the *Central* and *Dubar* hotels are usually quite animated too, but as you'd expected there are frequent and fickle shifts of favour among customers between them. Calmer evenings can be spent drinking on the *Rooftop Bar*, opposite Sabon Gari market. For something still more comatose, explore the possibilities of Kano Club.

Kano Directory

Airlines
  British Airways, Hafsatu House, 7 Bompai Rd (☎626 040, 624 834/5);
  EgyptAir 16c Murtalla Muhammed Rd (☎624 027);
  Express Airways Nigeria; ask locally for current address;
  KLM, 17 Airport Rd (☎600 240);
  Nigeria Airways, 3 Bank Rd (☎623 891, 623 041);
  Sabena, Central Hotel, Bompai Rd (☎621 364)
  UTA, Murtala Muhammed Rd near the Kano Club (☎627 721).

British Council Between Kofar Nassarawa Gate and the Museum, a good place to catch up on the news – they even take *The Face*.

Cinemas Lots of places throughout the city, including the *Plaza Cinema* on Kofar Mata Rd, the *Orion* on Kofar Wambai Rd, the *Eldorado* on Lagos Rd near Mission Rd and the *Rex* and *Sheila* along Murtala Muhammed Rd.

Changing money You can queue for literally hours at the banks. If you're slightly impatient, take a taxi to the airport where there are several bureaux de change, a bank in the car park and hardly ever any queues. The best place though is the *Criss Cross Bureau* on City Rd, effectively offering official black market rates, *and* your yellow form stamped.

Consulates
British Liaison Officer 64 Murtala Muhammed Rd, weekday mornings;
Niger Consulate Alu Avenue, near the racecourse;
There are no consulates for Cameroon or Chad.

Dentists Dr J.P. Rossek, Kowa specialist clinic, Club Rd (Mon–Fri 8.30am–noon, Sat 9am–12.30pm); Ahmadiya Clinic, Club Rd (Mon–Fri 8.30am–12.30pm, Sat 8am–1pm).

Doctors Dr K. Khouri, Club Rd (Mon–Fri 8.30am–12.30pm & 3–6pm, Sat 8.30am–12.30pm); Bompai Rd clinic (Mon–Sat 8am–8pm ; 24-hr emergency cover).

Poste Restante Free, reliable and relatively swift because of international air services.

Telephones Office for international calls is down Lagos Rd, beyond the post office, near the corner of Ibrahim Taiwa Rd. A good line is hard to get.

Tourist information You can get maps and a "Kano State Hotel Guide" at the *Ministry of Home Affairs and Information*, New Secretariat, Zaria Rd, or at the *Tourist Information Centre* in the Airport. The *Tourist Transit Camp* on Club Rd has free city maps and organises tours of Kano and the district at reasonable rates. You can also sometimes buy maps at the bookstore of the *Central Hotel*.

MOVING ON FROM KANO

● Long-distance taxis and minibuses to **Jos and Lagos** leave from the **Zaria road motor park** (a minibus hop from Sabon Gari). Buses and minibuses towards the **Niger border**, and to Niger itself, go from the **Kofar Ruwa motor park**, north of the old city off the Katsina road. Vehicles heading, broadly, east – to northern parts of **Cameroon** and to **Maiduguri** and the Chad border – leave from **Murtala Muhammed Rd** near the Sabon Gari market.

● There should be **trains** to Lagos, Jos and Port Harcourt. Check at the station, as there have been many cancellations and suspended services of late.

● *Nigeria Airways* has **flights** to **Maiduguri** (Tues, Thur, Sat), **Sokoto** (Mon, Wed, Fri, Sun), **Port Harcourt** (late Wed night) and **Lagos** (2–4 flights daily). *Express Airways* flies to **Kaduna** six times a week (twice each on Mon, Wed & Fri), the morning flights connecting with their flights to **Enugu** and **Port Harcourt**.

INTERNATIONAL DIRECT FLIGHTS

British Airways to **London** (Tues & Sat nights, arrives early morning);
KLM to **Amsterdam and London** (Mon & Fri nights, arrives early morning);
Nigeria Airways (flights originate in Lagos) to **London** (Mon, Tues & Thur, arrives evening); to **Rome** (Wed, arrives evening);
Egyptair to London via Cairo (Mon & Thur, overnight in Cairo, arrives next afternoon).

Katsina

Tucked in the extreme north, **KATSINA** flounders in the dry Sahelian badlands. Recent efforts to pump some life into the region, notably through the installation, in 1982, of a steel plant, have so far brought few noticeable signs of development beyond a few strands of paved road. Vestiges of the once powerful **Katsina emirate** – one of the oldest of the seven Hausa states – have hardly fared better. One or two of the original city gates still stand in varying states of ruin, but the fortifications that once surrounded the town have been all but flattened. Reminders of the past remain in the **Emir's palace** and the **Gobarau Tower** that once served as a sentry post. You can visit these, but the real pleasure of Katsina perhaps lies more in simply wandering the dusty streets, absorbing the atmosphere of a Hausa city that has changed little in recent years.

Around town

"Downtown" Katsina spreads along Kano Rd between the **Kofar Daura**, a recent stone gate built to replace an older *banco* one, and the **Central Mosque** with its onion-domes. Along this road, you'll find the major **banks**, the post office and the big trading stores. The main **motor park** is also down this stretch. Just beyond the mosque, Kano Rd veers to the left and continues to the **Emir's Palace**. The entrance way to this building looks more recent than you might expect and sports a bizarre clocktower in apparent imitation of a mittel-European castle. Inside, the large compound is a hodge-podge of old *banco* and new cement buildings that pile into each other unharmoni-ously. If you want to visit the palace, you must make advance arrangements at the **Ministry of Information** building on Kano Rd.

Following the paved road to the west, the **Central Market** is a short way from the palace. You'll find a few fruits and vegetables here (mangoes in season, oranges, toma-toes, onions and okra), decorated calabashes and pottery with a bronzey glaze, cereals (corn and different kinds of millet) and livestock including goats, donkeys and the occasional camel. Notice the open-air "butcher's shop" and Fulani women selling milk from calabashes.

To the north of the market, you can make out the **Gobarau Tower**. To reach this minaret – built in the seventeenth century as a lookout post – follow the unmarked street called Gobarau road on the eastern edge of the market. The tower later served as the muezzin's platform in pre-loudspeaker days. A guide will take you to the top and explain the history for a small dash. From the minaret, Hospital Rd leads past a walled graveyard, with unmarked graves pushing up the red earth, to the **Kofar Uku**. This gate "of the three doors" was formerly attached to **Katsina Teacher College**, the first institute of higher learning in town. It was built, say the residents, in the seventeenth century and is now falling into ruins. Other gates of note include the **Kofar Guga** and, at the end of Nagogo St, the **Kofar Durbi**, where you can still see part of the old wall.

Practical details

Most of the **hotels** are on Kano Rd outside the Kofar Daura. The *Siamond Hotel* and the *Abuja Hotel* are both typical Nigerian establishments, comfortable and reasonably priced. Right near the Kofar Kaura, the brand new and slightly more expensive *Maikudi*, 3 Kano Rd (☎065 690), is very clean with pleasant staff and has a good AC **restaurant** serving Nigerian and European food. In the same general area, you'll also notice signs for the *New City Hotel* and the *Liberty Hotel*. These two aren't for lodging as much as dancing, drinking and other forms of recreation.

Sokoto

Until the beginning of the nineteenth century, **SOKOTO** was a small town of small import, surrounded by the Hausa city states. It only gained its present status as **relig-ious capital** of the north after Usman dan Fodio's Islamic jihad led to the creation of the **Sokoto Khalifate** in 1807. The present Emir is to this day leader of all other Hausa emirates and effective spiritual leader of Nigeria. Modernisation came slowly to this region as development goals conflicted with the Khalif's own ideas about what "civilisa-tion" should entail. Thus, at the wish of the Khalif, the railway line that pushed north-wards as far as Kaura Namoda in the 1920s was never extended to Sokoto. The town's isolation from corrupting outside influences was thus preserved.

SOME SOKOTO HISTORY

The **Fulani** of Sokoto are thought to have migrated from Mali in the thirteenth century and to have settled in **Gobir**, then a powerful ancient kingdom. Known as *Fulanin Gida* (town Fulani as opposed to pastoral nomads), they were mainly traders and highly regarded Muslims. The most learned were welcomed into the Hausa Emirs' courts as advisors, where some succumbed to lives of indolence; others kept on the move and preferred a more ascetic lifestyle, teaching and speaking on behalf of the poor. **Usman dan Fodio**, from Gobir, was of the latter mould, preaching energetically against the corrupt influence of high office and the lax ways of the traditional non-Muslim (or quasi-Muslim) Hausa Emirs. There was much support for his stand, which called for the retrenchment of the widely ignored or circumvented *sharia* legal code. And naturally there was also plenty of resentment of his politicking piety on the part of traditionalists with a lot of stock in the status quo. By 1804, the tension had led to the birth of a radical reform movement and to civil war in Gobir, where the traditionalist Emir first used arms against the reformers. Dan Fodio was a reluctant warrior and, while he agreed to be appointed Amir al-Muminin ("Commander of the Faithful"), the military leadership of the **holy war**, or jihad, was handled by his brother Abdullah and son Muhammadu Bello.

Weakened from centuries of warring, the Hausa emirates fell quickly and, over the space of four years, with growing popular support, dan Fodio became the uncontested ruler of the entire north. Although often characterised as a war of pious Muslim Fulani against corrupt Hausa, the reality was considerably more complicated and very much determined by people's economic position – the jihad promised a more equitable distribution of wealth and the reduction of taxes and levies. In 1809, dan Fodio's son, **Bello**, who later became the second Sultan, established Sokoto as the *Sarkin Musulmi*, the spiritual and political capital of the empire. By the time of Bello's death in 1835, Sokoto was effectively the capital of Islam for the whole of West Africa.

The **social consequences** of the jihad were many. Dan Fodio had created, for the first time in the region, a single state with a central government controlling the entire north (with the exception of Bornu) and extending deep into present-day Cameroon and south into the Yoruba country which up to then had resisted Islam. As a result, trade was facilitated throughout the region and the Arabic language and writing spread with the teachings of the Koran. When the **British** conquered Sokoto in 1903, they took advantage of the highly stratified and unified government system to implement their policy of indirect rule.

Around town: echoes of the past – and the market

Despite Sokoto's rich history and its position as spiritual capital of the north, this is no sightseeing Mecca. The city's *raison d'être* is of course the **Sultan's Palace** and the nearby *Masallachin Shehu*, or **Shehu's Mosque** (on Sultan Bello Rd). These buildings, with their Sudanic aura, are pleasant enough to look at, but you cannot go in. About halfway between the palace and the mosque is the *Hubbare*, the former home of Shehu Usman dan Fodio (located off Sultan Bello Rd, it's a bit tricky to find; if you're near the mosque, ask any kid and he'll take you there). Inside the house is the **Shehu's Tomb**, where dan Fodio is buried with his companions. Take off your shoes before entering and be as respectful as possible. People from throughout the region still make pilgrimages to this spot to pay homage. Not far from the palace as you head down Sultan Abubakar Rd), the **Sokoto Museum** is housed in a small building opposite the Federal Prisons, but doesn't have a great deal to offer. The few exhibits are poorly maintained and you're not likely to find much of interest – unless you count some bashed up musical instruments, Arabic scripts and letters from members of the ruling family. A much larger and more comprehensive **History Bureau and Museum Complex** has been under construction for some time on By-Pass Rd next to the **Sokoto University Teaching Hospital**; this should be open by now.

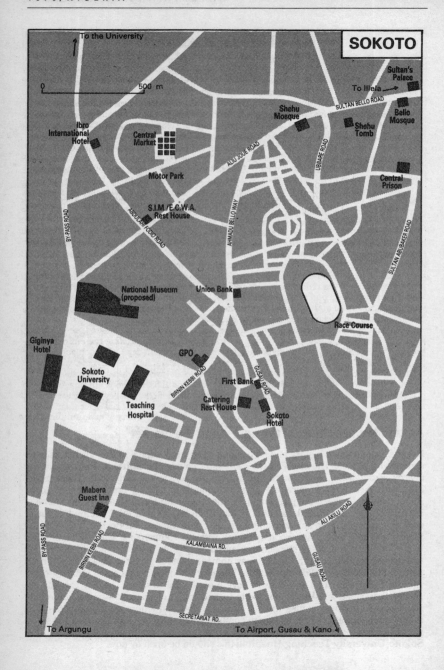

SOKOTO

To the University

0   500 m

Sultan's Palace

To Illela →

Ibro International Hotel

Central Market

Shehu Mosque

SULTAN BELLO ROAD

Bello Mosque

Shehu Tomb

Central Prison

Motor Park

S.I.M./E.C.W.A. Rest House

ALU JOUE ROAD

UBARE ROAD

AHMADU BELLO WAY

ABDULLAH FODIO ROAD

BY-PASS ROAD

National Museum (proposed)

Union Bank

Race Course

SULTAN ABUBAKER ROAD

Giginya Hotel

GPO

First Bank

Sokoto University

BIRNIN KEBBI ROAD

GUSAU ROAD

Catering Rest House

Sokoto Hotel

Teaching Hospital

Mabera Guest Inn

BY-PASS ROAD

BIRNIN KEBBI ROAD

KALAMBAINA RD.

ALI AKILU ROAD

GUSAU ROAD

SECRETARIAT RD.

To Argungu

To Airport, Gusau & Kano →

You won't, or shouldn't, be disappointed by Sokoto's **Central Market**, adjacent to the **central motor park**. It's one of the biggest and best stocked in the entire Sahel Region – an amazingly well-planned, clean, modern site with a startling abundance of flowers and trees planted throughout. And for what seems like such an isolated city there's a remarkable variety of stuff here – if you're lucky, you could find a **produce** selection ranging from pineapples, coconuts and mangoes to millet, sorghum, a mass of vegetables and all the usual proliferation of spices and condiments. There's a large **cloth emporium** with busy tailors who sew to order on the spot. And when you're tired of drifting around, a pleasant and inexpensive **outdoor restaurant** has been set up round the large, green-and-white tower that dominates the whole area.

Accommodation, food and other necessities

Sokoto doesn't have an overwhelming selection of **hotels**, especially in the lower price range. The *SIM/ECWA Rest House*, conveniently close to the motor park and market, will normally let you stay quite cheaply; otherwise one of the cheapest places in town is the *Sokoto Catering Rest House* (☎232 505) on Gusau Rd behind the more expensive *Shukura* (see below). They have rooms at various prices depending on whether you want them S/C and with or without AC. The place is run-down, but liveable. Slightly more expensive (but still not bad value) is the *Mabera Guest Inn*, Mabera Layout(☎233 205), which is cleaner and in a more lively part of town.

Moving into a pricier range, the *Ibro International Hotel*, Abdullahi Fodio Rd (☎232 510), is in an excellent location next to the central market and motor park. You may not need all the luxuries of AC, TV and hot water, but with the current exchange rate it's really not over the top compared to what you'll pay in Niger if you're going that way. There's a good restaurant in the hotel as well, and a small **supermarket** across the street. In a similar price range, and with a good restaurant and bar, AC rooms and swimming pool, the *Sokoto Hotel*, Gusau Rd (PO Box 1193; ☎232 412), is an ageing modern pile but has a travel bureau. Just down the road, the *Shukura Hotel* (☎232 126) is still the town's best (though the four star *Giganya Hotel* being constructed on By-Pass Rd will usurp it if it's ever completed). New and very efficient with comfortable AC rooms, the *Shukura*'s prices are competive with the *Sokoto* and the AC video bar (!) and restaurant are popular.

Sokoto's main commercial district runs along Gusau Rd, where you'll find the major **banks** and hotels. The **GPO** is on Birnin Kebbi Rd, not far away.

MOVING ON FROM SOKOTO

The main **motor park** in the north of the city handles regular transport for **Kano** and **Illela** (the border town facing Birni Nkonni in Niger). Vehicles to **Argungu** (and on to the Nigeria/Niger/Benin border at Gaya/Malanville) are less frequent, as too are vehicles heading south down the A1 to **Yelwa and Kontagora**.

If you want to make a quick getaway, *Nigeria Airways*, Gusau Rd (☎232 252) flies Mon, Wed, Fri and Sun to **Kano and Lagos** – always very heavily booked. For more long-distance travel arrangements, the *Sokoto Hotel* has an accredited travel agency that can make airline bookings

---

A side trip to Argungu

Ninety-nine kilometres southwest of Sokoto by good paved roads, **ARGUNGU** makes for an interesting excursion. Well known for its annual fishing festival in February – a photo library shot of which has been reproduced on countless occasions – the town also has the excellent **Kanta museum** with historical relics and traditional artefacts, and an impressive **Emir's Palace**. You can sleep here at the *Government Catering Resthouse* and there's a new hotel either in place or on its way – the *Grand Fishing Hotel*.

Some history

Argungu has an illustrious place in the annals of West African history. The **Kingdom of Kebbi**, which had formerly been an outlying province of the **Songhai empire**, was founded near here in the early sixteenth century by **Muhammadu Kanta**, a general in the army of the Songhai emperor Askia Muhammed (see p.235). When the Songhai invaded the Hausa states between 1512 and 1517, Kanta revolted against his overlords, and established himself as an independent ruler of the area between the Niger and Sokoto rivers. The capital of his kingdom was Argungu.

Later, Argungu was one of the pockets of traditionalist resistance to the Fulani jihad led by Usman dan Fodio, and was never successfully conquered by Sokoto. An apocryphal account even derives the town's name from the Fulani moan *Ar sunyi gungu* ("Oh dear, they've regrouped"), since their invasions were repeatedly repulsed. The Kebbi kingdom fell to the British at the beginning of the century and became part of the Northern Nigeria protectorate.

The fishing festival

In late January or February (sometimes even as late as March), the **fishing festival** takes place in a stretch of the **Sokoto River** known as *Matan Fada*, where it braids into a multitude of channels. Here, thousands of huge *giwan ruwa* fish (some weighing as much as 100kg) are penned in a confined, shallow lake. On the chosen day, the signal is given and hundreds of fishermen plunge into the waters watched by thousands of onlookers. Using only hand-held "butterfly" or clap nets called *homa*, and hollowed calabashes with an opening at the top, they thrash around among their prey. Fishing is banned for the rest of the year in this part of the river and rituals are performed to try to ensure the biggest possible catches. The fish hunt, however, is only the climax of a festival that spreads over three days and includes a long list of other sporting activities and competitions (boxing, archery, camel and donkey races), punctuated with endless speeches by commissioners of Sokoto State government, local leaders and sponsors. If you want to see the festival, it's imperative to make room reservations in advance through the Ministry of Information, Secretariat Rd, Sokoto, since rooms at the available accommodation in Argungu get solidly booked.

Maiduguri

The north's closest major town to the Cameroon border, **MAIDUGURI** is the first (or last) stop in Nigeria for many overlanders. The town is incredibly flat and hot, and has that quiet, nothing-happening feeling characteristic of so many places in the arid Sahel regions. If it wasn't for the **neem trees** lining the neatly laid-out avenues and providing a bit of respite from the merciless sun, you might find it unbearable. But as capital of the **Borno State**, it has a good infrastructure and makes a reasonable resting point for further travels in the arid north. The **people of Borno** are largely **Kanuri**, and women, especially, are elegant dressers and hairstylists and often wear nose rings. If you spend a night here – or more – you may also come to appreciate a second level of life in Maiduguri, as experienced by the many students from all over Nigeria, who live on the Maiduguri univeristy campus and probably feel almost as much strangers in this northwest outpost as you do.

SOME HISTORY

The rise of the **Kanem-Bornu empire** was a consequence of the spreading Sahara and the subsequent migration of nomadic peoples who concentrated in the **Lake Chad** basin, in districts that had been covered in lake water in earlier times. Conflicts flared between the newcomers and established communities. The **Kanuri** (a people of distinctively Saharan origins, with a language quite unrelated to Hausa, whose distant ancestors are presumed to have farmed and hunted in the era of Saharan fertility) eventually gained the upper hand in the struggles, out of which arose the **Sefawa dynasty** which ruled over **Kanem** – the concretion of mini-states to the northeast of Lake Chad – from about 850AD.

Oral historical records claim the founder of the dynasty was **Sayf Dhi Yazam**, and say he was of Arabic origin. It is possible, and more likely, that the first dynastic family had Berber connections rather than Arab. Whatever the truth, the authority of the *Mai* (as the kings of the dynasty were known – they converted to Islam in the eleventh century) gradually spread over nomadic peoples, and the *Mai* came to be accepted as a divine ruler. In Mecca, a special guesthouse was built for Kanem pilgrims and in Spain, the court of El Mansur (1190–1214) in Seville, had renowned Kanem poets.

A new series of conflicts arose in the thirteenth century that incited **Mai Umar bin Idris** to emigrate west to Bornu. The new empire – now effectively Bornu, rather than Kanem – remained unstable until the end of the fifteenth century when **Mai Ali Gaji** came to power, put an end to dynastic squabbles and established a new capital at Gazargamo, the first permanent residence in more than a century.

A new golden era was thus launched that reached its peak under the best known of the Bornu rulers – **Idris Aloma** – who ruled until 1603. He was a zealous Muslim reformer under whose reign Islam became the basis of Bornu ideology and who also achieved military advances by importing Turkish mercenaries and military advisors to instruct his troops in the use of muskets. Although the empire was among the most severely affected by the decline in trans-Saharan trade, Bornu was the only northern power to repulse dan Fodio's invasion. The Fulani did manage to attack the capital city and sent the king into retreat, but a Bornu *malam* (teacher) named Al-Kanemi organised a counter-offensive that successfully drove out the enemy. As a result, Al-Kanemi became the Bornu ruler and his sons started a new dynasty, drawing to a close the dynasty of the Sefawa, which, with its origins in the ninth century and a final date of 1846, may have been the world's most enduring line of royal rulers.

Maiduguri gained its importance as a regional capital only after 1907 when the British reinstated the Shehu in the new town where they had established a military base. It wasn't until after independence, however, that the town was linked to Kaduna by rail and thus gained a slight advantage for its beef, leather and peanut exports.

Around town

Thanks to its fairly modern origins, Maiduguri is a well-planned city and easy to get around. Its characteristic landmarks are the **roundabouts** which have come almost to designate neighbourhoods and are thus convenient markers for orientation. The major ones include **"West End"**, with three large cast iron fish in the middle, **"Banks"**, a large spikey phallic symbol, **"Welcome"**, a green and white concrete statue, **"Post Office"** near the GPO, **"NEPA"** near the market, **"Customs"** near the museum, and **"Eagle"**, with a large eagle statue in the south of town (just off our map). The easiest way to get around town is by collective taxi to one of these roundabouts, walking from there to your destination. For example, when going to the market, hail a cab going to the NEPA roundabout and walk up Amadu Bella Way from there.

Maiduguri doesn't have much in the way of sights, and any exploring, at almost any time of year, should be done in the early hours before the town gets intolerably hot. An obvious place to start is at the **Shehu's Palace**. A colonial-style building with clock

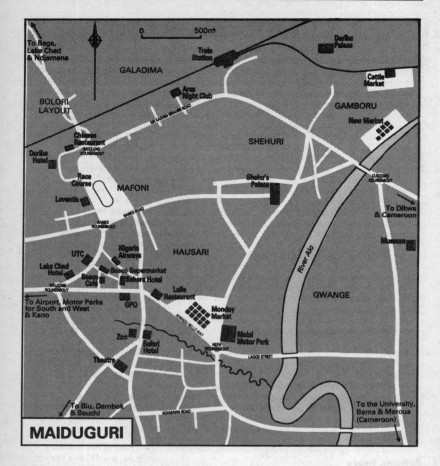

MAIDUGURI

tower, the palace has no organised tours, but if you tell the guards in front that you're interested in visiting they usually try to arrange it. Inside, the emphasis is more on modern administration than Bornu history: after taking off your shoes, a guide trails you from one scorching patio to the next, making a point of showing you every room with a typewriter or leatherette armchairs.

Much better for a historical overview is the small **museum**, near the customs warehouse on Bama Rd, which provides a useful introduction to the customs of different peoples living in Bornu State. Artefacts – pottery, jewellery, mats, utensils – are well displayed with accompanying texts. In the courtyard there's an interesting reproduction of a "Arab" tent with characteristic furnishings.

Maiduguri's colourful **Monday Market** now takes place in a covered cement building in the commercial centre of town. The New Market sprouted a few years back in the Gamboru district near Customs roundabout. Apart from all the usual gear, it's well known locally for its attractive handwoven **mats** made of Lake Chad reeds.

The **Zoo**, located across from the *Safari Hotel* at the end of Shehu Lamisu Way (Mon–Fri 9am–noon & 3–6pm, Sat & Sun 9am–6pm), is actually not bad, whatever your feelings about zoos. Many of the animals are captives without cages, and are kept in place by large ditches surrounding reproductions of their habitats. From a distance, it looks like they are running loose. Shaded in a forest of neem trees, the zoo and park are excellent places for a picnic, and the whole town seems to turn out here on Sundays.

When the afternoon sun begins to drum down, head to one of the town's two **swimming pools**. The best is at the *Deribe Hotel*, which has crystal clear water, but unfortunately serves no beer. The more central *Lake Chad Hotel* has murkier water and more people, but there is a poolside bar.

Bed, board and living it up

Maiduguri has all kinds of **accommodation** ranging from cheap bordellos to hotels with international standards. Among the nicest of the latter is the *Deribe Hotel*, Kashim Ibrahim Rd (☎232 445), with pleasant AC rooms and the town's best pool. It's kept in better condition than its nearest competitor, the *Lake Chad*, Kashim Ibrahim Rd (☎232 746), which is looking slightly worn despite extras like the pool, tennis courts and TVs. The old *Catering Rest House* has been converted into the new *Borno State Tourist Centre*, Talba Rd, down to Eagle roundabout and turn right (beneath the Maiduguri label on our map) with bar, restaurant and accommodation in chalets.

For **moderate lodging** try the *Merry Joe Guest Inn*, Bolori Layout (☎232 872), which has rooms with or without AC that start at less than half the price of the upmarket places. It's clean and pleasant and there's a good bar and inexpensive restaurant. Similar hotels in the Bolori Layout include the *Safecon Hotel* behind the *Merry Joe* and the *Aceta International Hotel* (☎232 871). Along Kashim Ibrahim Rd in the Galadima area, the *Horizontal Hotel* is slightly more expensive, but more central. The *D'Accord Hotel* (☎232 535) has also been recommended although it's a bit far from the centre, near the airport.

For really **cheap accommodation**, there's a "hotel colony" off Kashim Ibrahim Rd near the railway tracks. A lively neighbourhood known for discos and cheap restaurants in addition to the hotels, the whole quarter is seething with ill repute. If you really want to save money you'll find the *Traveller's Hotel*, the *Peace and Charity*, the *Benue Annex Hotel*, the *Rockefeller Plaza*, and the *End Well Hotel*, all squalid, within about a four-block radius of each other.

Eating

There are a couple of inexpensive restaurants on Bama Road, east of the museum. The first you come to is the *De Bee Restaurant*, which is pleasantly AC and serves very good European and Nigerian dishes. Also nearby, the *Li Sandra* is popular with students as it has AC and serves cold beer (alcohol isn't allowed on campus) and reasonably priced food. Close to the Monday market on Ahmadu Bello Way, the clean and friendly *Lalle Restaurant* also specialises in inexpensive Nigerian food. The nearby *Nefertiti 2000* has

---

KANURI PHRASES

It's nice to be able to say a few things in Kanuri, though this list won't get you very far.

Good day	*Ndawatu*	Come in	*Are*
I'm fine	*Kalewa sule*	Sit down	*Namne*
Hello	*Wooshe* (pronounce carefully: *Wus!* is an expression of disgust in Hausa)	I have it	*Fi*
		I don't have it	*Ma fi*

inexpensive dishes like rice and chicken or beef and boiled yams. The *Bosco Café* is another popular place for inexpensive Nigerian chop. For **Chinese** food, *Chopsticks* has a cheap takeaway service.

Nightlife

Because of the strong Muslim influence, nights in Maiduguri tend to be tranquil. But the presence of the university, which has a large proportion of students from the less Islamic regions of the south, means there are a lot of young people out to drink and have a good time, and a few decent clubs to dance away the nights. One of the most popular is the *Chez Coan Nightclub* behind the Federal Lowcost Housing Estate in Galadima. It's young and lively and also features a half decent restaurant. *Ares Club*, off Sir Kashim Ibrahim Rd, is another rowdy spot that's currently in. In addition to these clubs, the *Alliance Française*, behind *Leventis* and the *Deribe*, has a regular *disco-soirée* with a good mix of music, that attracts ex-pats and some of the Unversity crowd.

MOVING ON: NIGERIA

Several **motor parks** are spread throughout Maiduguri. **To Kano**, Dambon and Biu, the station is just outside the town gates along airport road. **To Baga**, Geidam and Gashua, the park is just up from the West End, past the railway tracks. **To Bama**, the station is after the customs roundabout on Ring Road.

Trains There's supposed to be a weekly departure for Kafanchan junction, where you change for Lagos.

Flights Daily early morning flights to **Lagos** on *Nigeria Airways* with additional afternoon departures on Tues, Thur and Sat via **Kano**. *Nigeria Airways* is at 19 Hospital Rd (☎232 743).

MOVING ON: CAMEROON AND CHAD

For the short crossing of Cameroon to **Ndjamena**, Chad, the **Gamboru motor park** is in the district of Maiduguri, on the northeast side of town. You won't need a Cameroon visa if you're simply passing through this narrow neck of the country en route to Chad. Four- and six-seater taxis shuttle to the village of Gamboru (Nigerian exit formalities). From **Fotokol** on the Cameroonian side (where you'll have to seek out the *douaniers* and gendarmes 1km away, but they're pleasant enough) you take a much more expensive ride to **Kousseri**, 100km away. For Kousseri and onward details into **Chad**, see p.1058.

Around Maiduguri and into Gongola State

Although Maiduguri feels like the end of the road – and certainly most Nigerians consider the town is already at the back of beyond – it is still 100km further to the borders of Niger, Chad or Cameroon. If you're driving in far northwestern Nigeria, it's as well to know that it's an area of some political sensitivity where you should notify the authorities of your movements before setting off from each town or village.

To Lake Chad

Getting to **Lake Chad** is somewhat difficult, and police are suspicious of people who want to go to the region whether they've come by their own means or with public transport. They've apparently been known to confiscate ID cards and to generally harass travellers. An additional problem is the total retreat of the lake itself from Nigerian territory over the last few years. The place to go if you want to check out the situation is **BAGA**. Taxis head here from Maiduguri. When you get into town, check in with the police, who won't take long anyhow to discover your arrival. There's a customs and immigration post at Baga and, if the water is high, foot travellers may be able to get a boat across into Chad: the village of Baga Sola is 76km away to the northwest, about three days by pole and paddle or a full day by outboard. If not, there's accommodation at the *Baga State Hotel*. If the lake has dried up, the small village of **DORO**, 2km away, may be more interesting.

South of Maiduguri

The great wedge of **Gongola State** spreads from the Sahel near Maiduguri south along the mountainous Cameroon borderlands to the fringes of the Cross River rainforest. It's a huge and very little travelled region, even in comparison with just about every other state in the federal republic, and if you can devote the necessary time offers some of Nigeria's best rewards in terms of landscapes and traditional rural communities.

BAMA, on the main road from Maiduguri to Cameroon (still in Borno state), is a Kanuri town with a large market – Saturday the big day. There's a good *Guest House* on the southern side of town, which features occasional gatherings with dancing and *brukutu*, locally made Guinea-corn beer.

Thirty-two kilometres south of Bama, **GWOZA** lies on the western flank of the **Mandara Mountains**, hardly visited in comparison to the rather touristy villages a short distance away in Cameroon. Market day in Gwoza is Sunday, and there's a trade fair in March with demonstrations of local crafts like calabash-carving and mat-weaving. From Gwoza you can hike east through the mountains (a four-hour trek) to another village, **NGOSHE**, where there's a government resthouse, numerous chop houses and a small market. The mountain footpath is the quickest way between the two towns, but very hard to find, especially coming from Gwoza to Ngoshe. It's less difficult in the other direction and many people use it on market day. In either case, ask people to point it out to you. If you have time, this trip makes for a rewarding excursion. The scenery is perhaps less impressive than on the Cameroon side, but the contact with the mountain people is much less contrived. There is regular transport to both Gwoza and Ngoshe from Bama.

Gongolan wanderings

South of Gwoza you enter Gongola State and the scenery starts to become spectacularly spiky and volcanic. There are terrific hikes up into the **Mandara mountains** east of the Madagli–Mubi road. One route starts off from CHAMBULA, about 12km southwest of Madagli, and goes some 10km southeast (and up) to MILDO JUNCTION. Some 5km further up a near invisible path you reach a school (keep asking, preferably in Hausa – unless you've got any Adamawa dialects) from where you can expect or hope to be taken around the district. Bring food and flexibility. The place where a few travellers before you have been is SUKUR, the seat of a once powerful mountain kingdom. There's a remarkable stone causeway – product of ancient civil engineering – from the school up to this village. You'll meet people wearing a lot of red make-up, calabashes as hats and little else except on market days. You can walk right along the Cameroon/Nigeria border, though the track doesn't appear to be marked on any map.

Further south, KAMALE is a village with an amazing **volcanic plug** nearby – accessible from MICHIKA, 20km south of Chambula. This whole area has everything in common with its Cameroonian counterpart and mountain people don't generally draw much of a boundary line (see p.1077).

The Gongola State capital is **YOLA**, an unexceptional, flat, spacious town near the banks of the Benue. It's fairly accommodating, but its cheaper hotels tend to be a little more expensive than usual. Best value are the *Ise Hotel* (☎24810), the *Palace* (☎25204) or the *Bridge Hotel* – in that order. If you need to travel fast, there are daily flights out of Yola on *Nigeria Airways* to Lagos and Maiduguri and Thursday and Sunday flights to Kaduna and on to Lagos. Their office (☎24713) is on Main St, **JIMETA**, the new suburb on the riverbank 7km from the city centre. If, by chance, you find yourself in NUMAN, 60km west of YOLA and an older town somewhat left behind by the state capital's surging modernism, don't stay there. Both hotels are dreadful.

If you're travelling on the A345 **Yola–Numan–Bauchi road** be sure to do so by day, and if you're going by public transport, get a window seat on the left. Numan to Gombe is a superb stretch of scenery and, if you've got your own transport, there are some fantastic **hikes and climbs** in the Mouri mountains. **Tangale Hill** near KALTUNGO, is another steep and stunning volcanic plug and a brisk three-hour climb, but you'll need permission from the Emir of the little town and help from local men in guiding you up.

Further dramatic **highland regions** fill the southern part of Gongola State – the **Alantika range** southeast of Yola, the **Shebshi mountains** (with 2042m Vogel Peak) to the southwest, and the green, cloud-drenched **Mambila range** around GEMBU in the very far southeast of the state (two hikes/4WD routes lead up into Cameroon from here, but ascertain driving viability locally). Also in the south is BISSAULA and the start of the Dumbo trek up to the Bamenda Highlands Ring Road in Cameroon (see p.1050).

index

CAMEROON

CAMEROON

The **landscapes of Cameroon** are exceptional. The country stretches from the fringes of the Sahara in the north to the borders of Congo and Gabon in the south and takes in every African variation, from equatorial rainforest (some of the continent's most unexploited tracts) to moist, tree-scattered savannah; from dry grassy plains to bucking volcanic ranges flecked with crater lakes; from gaunt rocky massifs to the swampy basin of Lake Chad; and, just for good measure, the highest mountain on this side of the continent – the 4095 metres of Mount Cameroon – rising direct from the ocean shore to an impressive cloud-wreathed summit. Beyond the scenic and alfresco incentives, the country has some entrancing beaches and several large parks, rewarding quantities of wildlife, including species found nowhere else in West Africa. At the simple level of tourism, it's hard to oversell Cameroon – it's simply the most dramatic country in West Africa.

But there's another side to Cameroon in its hugely stimulating cultural environment. Only to highlight the most striking ethnic distinctions: the Muslim sultanates of the north are reminiscent of northern Nigeria and also have strong Arab connections, but exist alongside the avowedly non-Muslim people of the mountainous Rhumsiki district; in the forests of the far south, the so-called "Pygmies" – the original inhabitants – still live a hunting and gathering life largely untroubled by the concerns of the modern nation state; and in the mountains and pasturelands of the country's western "bulge", a remarkable complex of kingdoms has developed, speaking dozens of Bantoid languages. This is the only country in West Africa with a large Bantu-speaking population, which culturally gives the south much in common with the central African region.

Cameroon has a colonial past of German, French and British occupation. With the current division between Francophone and Anglophone in every aspect of national life, it all means that a sense of national identity is profoundly lacking – and impressions of contrast and fragmentation are never far away. Coupled with its natural diversity, it's a country that, for once, can claim to embody elements of the entire continent.

CAMEROON – FACTS AND FIGURES

The **Republic of Cameroon** (or *République du Cameroun* to Francophones) covers 475,000 square kilometres, an area twice the size of Britain, with a population estimated at eleven million. The name derives from *camarões*, the Portuguese for prawns, which the first European visitors found in large quantities in the Wouri river. The common reference to **"Cameroons"** is a legacy of the colonial division into two Cameroons – French and British – a dual heritage preserved in the official bilingualism, (easily dominated by French). The country has been ruled since 1982 by **Paul Biya** who heads the sole political party, the Cameroon People's Democratic Movement (CPDM/MDPC).

Cameroon is divided into ten administrative **Provinces** with Governors appointed by the president. They are much referred to and you may find their names confusing at first, in that for example the South West is further north than the Centre; the logic is that the South West and North West provinces are the southern and northern regions of the West, not of the whole country. The provinces are:

Centre/Centre (capital: Yaoundé)
South/Sud (Ebolowa)
East/Est (Bertoua)
Littoral/Littoral (Douala)
South West/Sud Ouest (Buéa)

West/Ouest (Bafoussam)
North West/Nord Ouest (Bamenda)
Adamawa/Adamaoua (Ngaoundéré)
North/Nord (Garoua)
Extreme North/Extrême Nord (Maroua)

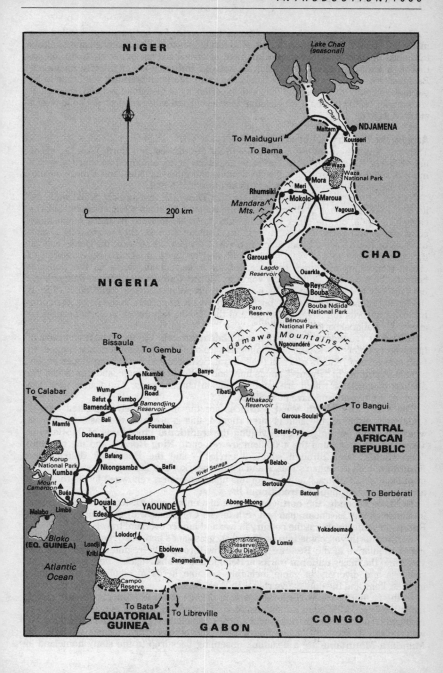

The increasing importance of tourism as a source of foreign exchange has led to a marked improvement in official attitudes to foreign visitors. The searches and controls that once dogged visitors from the moment of arrival are no longer anything like so thorough and aggressive. That said, the **tourist industry** is commitedly upmarket. Backpackers who sleep in class D hotels and cram into bush taxis are still prone to be put down as *pauvres blancs,* and may well experience the disdain of local law officers. If you wander off the beaten tracks leading to selected and sanctioned sites, you may well attract suspicion.

Around the country: where to go

The main **English-speaking regions** are in the South West and North West provinces near Nigeria. Broadly, the **Francophone areas** are better equipped for tourists, with a more developed infrastructure of roads, hotels and other facilities, and a more cosmopolitan feel. **Anglophone** regions tend to be more traditional.

Neither of the two main cities, **Douala** and **Yaoundé**, is especially worthwhile for its own sake. Douala, a seething, sweltering metropolis, makes few converts, but the capital Yaoundé, on the other hand, is more bearable to work in and a much more comfortable and relaxed place to rest up. Outside Douala, the nearby black sand beaches of **Limbé** are a good, quick getaway. Between the strands, the dense vegetation pushes right to the water's edge, although it has increasingly been cleared to create plantations of coffee, bananas, rubber trees and oil palms, in the rich soil beneath the mountain. Still actively volcanic, **Mount Cameroon** offers a challenging – but perfectly possible – ascent. Its last, minor, eruption occurred, fortuitously, during the filming of the Tarzan movie *Greystoke*. Around the mountain, to the north, the country drops towards the Nigerian border and the **Korup rainforest**, soon to become an accessible national park.

Inland to Yaoundé and beyond, a vast **plateau** stretches to the east. Huge tracts of hardwood rainforest – sapele and mahogany, iroko, obiche – has been little logged (in both senses) and renders much of the Central, Southern and Eastern provinces impenetrable. A number of **"Pygmy"** bands hunt and gather in the jungle, and this is also the domain of **gorillas**, which are quite prolific in certain areas. The Campo and Dja reserves are remote and have no facilities.

The **West and North West** provinces are the most densely populated area of Cameroon. Although the land is often rugged, this is probably the easiest region in which to strike out on your own, visiting the **traditional chiefdoms** of the Bamoun Tikar and others around the 400-kilometre red earth **Ring Road** – and the beautiful **"Grassfields"** area through which it circles – and the **Bamiléké district** and **Foumban**, with its Sultan's Palace and a crafts market that attracts buyers and sellers from throughout Africa. The whole of this upland region is renowned for its **thatched architecture** and animated **traditional life**.

North of Yaoundé, the northern sectors of Central and Eastern provinces are an immense, empty savannah, patched with forest. Combined with the gaunt **Adamawa Range** they effectively cut the country in two and hinder overland travel.

Further north you come into pre-Sahelian grasslands and dusty bush country. The upper tributaries of the **Bénoué** (Benue) flow through the region and this is where you'll find the major **national parks** of Bénoué and Bouba Ndjida. There's a wonderful richness and diversity of game including sizeable herds of elephants and buffalo, giraffes, lions and the only native rhinos in West Africa.

In the far north, **Waza National Park** in the flat plains is Cameroon's outstanding faunal reserve, with good conditions of visibility at the end of the dry season, for elephants, lions, giraffe, ostriches and a host of antelope species clustering around the waterholes. To the west, a few hours away, the otherworldly volcanic plugs of the **Mandara Mountains** are a beautiful, unsettling backdrop to the stony homeland of the "mountain people". The northernmost tip of the country, leading up to what's left of **Lake Chad**, is usually dry, but floods under the waters of the **Logone** and **Chari** rivers during the brief, annual rains.

Cameroon's people

The oldest group of people to have lived in Cameroon are the **"Pygmies"** of the south and southeast forests. Although forced onto the defensive by the expansion of the Bantu (many have settled in small villages, notably in the area around Kribi), most of these people have opted for the traditional independence of the impenetrable rainforest where they live by the hunt.

Although over the best part of two thousand years, there had been a gradual southeasterly spread of **Bantu-speaking** populations through the Cameroon region into central Africa, Bantu-speaking communities migrated in strength from the Adamawa range and settled along the coast from about the fifteenth century. The first to migrate were the **Bassa** and **Bakoko**, followed by the **Douala**. In the nineteenth century, pushed in a chain reaction by migrations engendered after the Fula Sokoto invasions in Nigeria, the **Fang**, **Ewondo** and **Eton** came from the plateaux in the east to settle in the central southern region around Yaoundé.

In the west of the country, waves of northern immigration between the sixteenth and nineteenth centuries saw the installation of **"Semi-Bantu"** peoples. The first to arrive were the **Tikar** who probably came from the area near Ngaoundéré and who today live in semi-autonomous chiefdoms throughout the Grassfields. In the eighteenth century a splinter group broke away from the Tikar country to form the powerful **Bamoun** empire a little to the east. The **Bamiléké** – a fusion of peoples from the north, east and southwest whose arrival spread over three centuries – settled in the plateau region south of the Noun River. Now the country's largest single ethnic group, the Bamiléké are also numerous in Douala where they have come to control a good deal of the national economy.

The predominant group in the north is the **Fula** (Foulbé or Peul) who settled in *lamidats* or principalities around the early nineteenth century, bringing Islam with them. But the mountains of the far northwest are inhabited by staunchly non-Muslim groups known collectively as *Kirdi* – which just means "infidels". Pushed to these desolate extremities by the Muslim invasions of Dan Fodio, they comprise numerous Adamawa and Chadic-speaking peoples: the **Podoko**, **Fali**, **Kapsiki**, **Mafa** and **Bata**. Principally farmers, they grow millet in terraced gardens on the rocky slopes of the mountains.

The northern plains near Lake Chad are peopled by the **Choa**, semi-nomadic peoples of Arab origin, who share these open spaces with the **Kotoko** – descendants of the ancient Sao culture – who live from fishing and growing a few cereals. Near the Logone River live the **Toupouri**, **Massa** and **Mousgoum**, people of pre-Islamic belief who are increasingly becoming Islamised.

Climate

The region around Mount Cameroon and the western mountains has the dubious privilege of one of the highest levels of rainfall in the world: Debuncha is the second wettest place on earth, after Cherrapungi in India. The general pattern here and in the south can be divided into three approximate seasons: a period of relatively light but persistent rains from March to June; the long rainy period from July to October; and the **dry season from November to February**. Travel can involve great waits during the rains, especially when involving those towns accessible only by track, such as Mamfé. Roads around the Grassfields are often unmotorable during the rains when even four-wheel-drive vehicles can have problems. The grasslands further north choke towards the end of the dry season with fine red laterite dust, blown up by the northerly *harmattan*. Plants and crops turn rusty red, while cameras – and lungs – seize up.

Northern Cameroon, north of the **Adamawa Plateau** has a different weather pattern, characterised by a long rainy season from May to October. Although travel in the north doesn't present any special problem during this period, note that the national parks do close, roughly between May and December. Overall, the ideal time to visit the country, taking into account different regional patterns, is December and January.

AVERAGE TEMPERATURES AND RAINFALL

YAOUNDÉ

	Jan	Feb	Mar	Apr	May	June	July	Aug	Sept	Oct	Nov	Dec
Temperatures °C												
Min (night)	19	19	19	19	19	19	19	18	19	18	19	19
Max (day)	29	29	29	29	28	27	27	27	27	27	28	28
Rainfall mm	23	66	147	170	196	152	74	79	213	295	117	23
Days with rainfall	3	5	13	15	18	17	11	10	20	24	14	4

DOUALA

	Jan	Feb	Mar	Apr	May	June	July	Aug	Sept	Oct	Nov	Dec
Temperatures °C												
Min (night)	23	23	23	23	23	22	22	22	22	22	23	23
Max (day)	30	30	30	30	30	28	27	27	27	27	29	29
Rainfall mm	46	94	203	231	300	539	742	693	531	429	155	64
Days with rainfall	4	6	12	12	16	19	24	24	21	20	10	6

KOUSSERI

	Jan	Feb	Mar	Apr	May	June	July	Aug	Sept	Oct	Nov	Dec
Temperatures °C												
Min (night)	14	16	21	23	25	24	22	22	22	21	17	14
Max (day)	34	37	40	42	40	38	33	31	33	36	36	33
Rainfall mm	0	0	0	3	31	66	170	320	119	36	0	0
Days with rainfall	0	0	0	1	6	10	15	22	13	4	0	0

Arrivals

Getting to Cameroon is facilitated by the fact that *Cameroon Airlines* is one of Africa's best. Flying in, however, suffers the disadvantage of arrival in the uncomfortable and rather heavy city of Douala. Arriving overland from the east, Cameroon feels like the threshold of a new region, which it is, as you leave the confines of the central African rainforest and enter West Africa.

◼ Flying from Africa

Cameroon's one **international airport** is not in the capital, Yaoundé, but in the rival (and larger) city of Douala. *Cameroon Airlines* has a good international network, connecting Douala with most major African cities. Capitals in **West Africa** from which it flies include: **Abidjan** (daily flights, shared between *Cameroon Airlines* and *Air Afrique*); **Cotonou** (twice weekly); **Ouagadougou** (weekly via Abidjan); and **Lagos**. They also operate regular flights from **Malabo**, Equatorial Guinea.

Nigeria Airways flies several times a week from **Lagos**, including one flight via Calabar and two via Port Harcourt.

Air Afrique flies from **Cotonou** (twice weekly); **Dakar** (twice weekly); **Lagos** (twice weekly); and **Lomé** (several flights a week).

Close political and economic ties ensure that Cameroon has good air links with its neighbours in **Central Africa**. Between *Air Afrique* and *Cameroon Airlines*, direct flights originate in **Brazzaville** (several a week) and **Kinshasa** (twice weekly); and from **Libreville** on *Air Gabon*.

From **East and Central Africa** *Cameroon Airlines* flies twice a week from **Nairobi** (heavily booked), once via **Kigali** and **Kinshasa** and once via **Bujumbura** and Kinshasa. There's also a weekly direct flight on *Ethiopian Airlines* from, **Nairobi**, originating in **Addis Ababa**. *Ethiopian Airlines* also services **Southern Africa** with a weekly flight from **Harare** (overnight in Addis).

The long-scheduled upgrading of the airport at Yaoundé to receive international flights showed little sign of completion at the time of going to press.

◼ Overland from Nigeria

The two main overland routes from Nigeria lead to **Mamfé** in the west of Cameroon and to **Molo** in the north. Coming in via the north is much more direct if you're arriving from the Sahara, but if you don't already have a Cameroon visa you may be forced to head south (see "Red Tape").

The **southern route** is straightforward and involves getting a bush taxi from **Calabar to Ikom**. From here small taxis leave regularly to the busy border, where after completing Nigerian customs formalities, you walk over the bridge spanning the Cross River and up the hill to Cameroon customs at **Ekok**. The tarmac ends abruptly at the border, and the taxis from **Ekok to Mamfé** rattle along bumpy tracks through a beautiful but tortuous mountain region. There are a couple of variations on this route, one via the Oban Rainforest National Park and one using boats through the creeks (see p.1042).

The main **northern route** leads from **Maiduguri to Bama** over a good flat paved road, where taxi drivers love to get up a bit of speed. Forty kilometres separate Bama from the border post at Banki. From here you can get taxis across the unpaved plains (look out for antelope) to **Moro** and on to Maroua or up to Waza National Park.

◼ Overland from Central African Republic

A reasonable, graded road leads to **Bouar** in the west of CAR and a more deteriorated route on to the border post at **Beloko**, 10km short of Cameroon. After the Cameroonian border town of **Garoua Boulai**, the road deteriorates further to become a difficult, bone-shaking track, travelling the 500-kilometre length of which, via **Bertoua** to Yaoundé, will wipe you out for 24 hours on arrival. To minimise the *piste*, head north to **Meidougou** to join the paved N6 road to **Ngaoundal**, from where you can take the **railway** southwest to **Yaoundé** or north to **Ngaoundéré**.

◼ Overland from Equatorial Guinea and Gabon

The main road from **Bata** in **Equatorial Guinea** heads far inland to **Ebebiyin**, at the point where Gabon, Cameroon and Equatorial Guinea all meet. From here, you travel via **Ambam** to **Ebolowa**, where there's the choice of heading either direct to Yaoundé or taking the roundabout but more scenic coastal route via **Kribi**.

You'll use this same arrival point (Ambam) if you come up from **Gabon**, reached from **Libreville** by heading to **Oyem**, where you can pick up transport to Ambam.

■ Overland from Chad

There is now a bridge between **Ndjamena** – the capital of Chad – and **Kousseri** in Cameroon, open from 6am to 5.30pm. Visas for Cameroon are issued on arrival here. Details of this border are given on p.1158.

Red Tape

All passport holders (other than Germans and certain African nationals) need visas to enter Cameroon. In the past these have only been given with reluctance at Cameroon embassies abroad apart from in your country of residence.

In West Africa, **Calabar** and **Lagos** are the only places west of Cameroon – apart from **Dakar**, **Monrovia** and **Abidjan** – which have embassies or consulates. You should try in **Algiers**, but there are no embassies or consulates in the Sahel states. The embassy in Algiers (see p.83) has recently been refusing visa issue to transient travellers, and insisting *categorically* that visas can be issued on the Nigerian border at reorganised posts at Fotokol and Banki (near Maiduguri) and Belel/Demsa (near Yola).

Broadly, **visas** are expensive, valid for three months, and must be activated within one month of issue. They're generally issued for an initial stay of twenty days. The main requirements are either a return air ticket, or proof of your intended onward route – including any other relevant visas. Stays are hard to extend (virtually impossible in Yaoundé so don't fetch up there on day 19), and impossible to prolong beyond the validity of your visa.

If you are travelling from Cenrtal or East Africa, there are Cameroonian **embassies** in **Central African Republic**, **Equatorial Guinea** (Malabo), **Congo** (Brazzaville, ☎83.34.04), **Zaire** (1175 av Tombalbaye, Kinshasa; ☎22505) and **Ethiopia** (Bole Rd, Addis Ababa). There's no representation in **Chad**, but you can normally get a visa at the Ndjamena–Kousseri border post.

For more red tape, see the "Roadblocks" box overleaf, and "Photography" on p.1095.

■ At the border

When you arrive in Cameroon – especially if you come in overland – immigration officers may well want to check that you have what they consider to be **sufficient funds** to stay in the country. If your visa is in order, you shouldn't have difficulties getting in. The rule about departure being by the same mode of transport as arrival has apparently been rescinded.

Health certificates are frequently checked on the road, and must be presented at the border. Yellow fever is always obligatory, and cholera when there are epidemics. It's a good idea to have this latter vaccination just in case.

Money and Costs

Although Cameroon uses the CFA franc (CFA50 always equals 1 French franc; CFA450–CFA500 = £1), it is part of the Central African economic zone. West African CFA are exactly equivalent in value, but the bills for the two regions are different and people on the streets will refuse West African notes. The two currencies are easily exchanged in banks.

The best way to carry your money is in French franc **travellers' cheques**. There tends to be a flat fee for changing money (CFA1130 in the case of the *Standard Chartered* bank), rather than a percentage, so it may make sense to change all your money at once. One or two banks (or possibly certain branches of them) seem to levy no fee – try BIAO and BICIC first. Pounds and dollars are easily converted in Yaoundé, Douala and one or two other big towns, but in smaller places, you are likely to encounter great difficulties changing them and may not be able to make a transaction at all.

Outside the two major cities, banks frequently run out of money, especially around payday (at the end of the month).

There is no limit on importation of cash in any currency. There's a CFA20,000 **export limit** unless you're going to a franc zone country, in which case there's no limit. Any CFA you have left over when leaving Cameroon can, in theory be exchanged at the fixed rate – if you can find a bank with French francs.

■ Costs

Cameroon is one of the three or four most expensive countries in the region. Living cheaply, you can probably expect to average CFA3000–4000 daily for **accommodation**. Douala is by far the country's most expensive city for lodging and even budget accommodation here is no bargain.

Fortunately, there are numerous missions throughout the country that take in travellers, expecially in the Anglophone North West and South West provinces. The country's **luxury hotels** charge over CFA20,000 per night.

Travel is more expensive in Cameroon than in its neighbours to the west. Travel costs average over CFA12 per kilometre – often more in the north or along unpaved *pistes*.

Health

Cameroon poses no exceptional health problems. Malaria prophylaxis is essential throughout the country and there are multi-drug resistant strains. It's generally okay to drink the tap water in major towns. If you have doubts, you can find bottled water everywhere except in small villages, but it becomes increasingly expensive the further north you go.

Cameroon, like most countries in West Africa, has a serious **schistosomiasis** (bilharzia) problem though it's usually safe enough to use free-flowing stream water in the highlands, especially after recent rain. There's a major regional initiative based in Cameroon and assisted by USAID which may help to eradicate the disease from large areas of the country in the near future.

Accurate statistics on **AIDS** are unobtainable, but it would be foolish not to take the same precautions you would anywhere.

■ Health Care

Medicines, well within their sell-by date, are available over the counter in most pharmacies. Dental care in Douala and Yaoundé is excellent; a filling costs about CFA10,000. Hospital care is also very good in the capital, although the poly-clinics in the rest of the country are generally poorly stocked with medicines and equipment, and often very dirty. You're expected to supply your own food in hospital. If you're travelling alone, the British Embassy may be able to help.

Information and Maps

Abroad, tourist pamphlets and information are best obtained at the *Cameroon Airlines* offices listed in the box below. The embassies too, may have some information, though probably the same stuff (see p.18–22).

■ Maps

It's well worth getting hold of some maps before leaving. Much the best is the recently produced *Macmillan* road map of Cameroon (with road surfaces indicated), which has excellent city maps for Douala and Yaoundé (indicating hotels and sites of interest) on the flip side. In Cameroon, the *Institut Géographique National* also sells detailed national and city maps, though they date to the late 1970s. In Yaoundé they are on the Avenue Monseigneur Vogt (☎22.34.65); in Douala *IGN* maps are sold at 36 rue Joffre in the Akwa neighbourhood (☎42.02.75). The *Shell* map, drawn up in the early eighties and available from *Shell* garages for CFA2000–3000, is helpful for showing the infrequent petrol stations. The *Michelin* #953 has tended to be a little enthusiastic in its portrayal of surfaced roads that aren't finished. What's more annoying, though not remediable, is the fact that you need the #955 as well if you want coverage of the southernmost hundred kilometres of the country.

CAMEROON AIRLINES OFFICES IN EUROPE

UK 44 Conduit St, London W1 (☎071 734 7676).

France 12 bd des Capucines, Paris 75009 (☎47.42.78.17); and 55 place de la République, Lyons (☎78.92.87.89).

Germany Langer Kornweg 19, 6092 Kelsterbach Main, Frankfurt (☎61 07 60 37).

Italy via Bissolati, Rome (☎474.51.33).

Switzerland 12 quai Gi Gruisan, Geneva (☎20.28.44).

Getting Around

The main choice for travelling around Cameroon is between road and rail. The roads can be okay, though the good-quality paved sections are often separated by endless kilometres of rough dirt track, while the trains only cover certain very limited routes – barely venturing for example into the north or the west. *Cameroon Airlines* covers a good deal of the country, though at a price.

If you prefer to have your arrangements made for you, *Socatour*, the national travel agency, arrange tours throughout the country. However, their primary aim is to process (mainly French) tourists at enormous cost to a small number of destinations. They may well decline altogether to organise a complicated itinerary, and independent travellers have tended not to find them much use.

■ By Road

Although 35,000km of roads criss-cross Cameroon, only about 3000km are paved. Even those are often in decay, with sections washed out by floods or pitted with potholes. Less-used dirt roads in particular can also be blocked for several days by overturned vehicles.

That said, the roads around and between **Douala** and **Yaoundé** are always reliable, as are those from Douala to **Bamenda** or **Foumban** via Bafang and Bafoussam (though not via **Mamfé**, which some maps show as the main road).

Western Cameroon has a reasonable network (the Bamenda highlands Ring Road is being surfaced) and the north is well served by the highway which runs between **Ngaoundéré** and **Maltam,** past the four national parks in the north.

The entire **centre** of the country, however, lacks a good system, the **Adamawa Plateau** providing a formidable obstacle. Between **Yaoundé** and **Ngaoundéré**, where the dirt roads are quite appalling, you'd be wiser taking the train – in fact you can even take a car on the train, for about 45,000CFA for two people. In the east of the country, the overabundant forest is another barrier to overland travel, and there are no good paved roads.

The far **south** – pretty well everywhere south of Yaoundé apart from the 170km to Sangmélima – is held together by dirt roads and tracks through the forest.

A couple of **dangers** peculiar to road travel in Cameroon: firstly the law that forbids motorists involved in an accident to move their cars until the police have inspected the site – meaning that all traffic may be held up for a couple of hours (quite apart from the implicit danger of hanging around if you are the party at fault); and secondly the behaviour of Cameroonian hitchhikers, who often attempt to stop cars by standing in the middle of the road with both arms outstretched. Stopping is an implicit offer of a lift, so they tend to stand just round a blind corner where cars will be forced to screech to a halt to avoid killing them.

Taxis

In the absence of a national transport system, most Cameroonians rely on *taxis de brousse*. Within cities, taxis cost CFA200 for any distance – one of the few real bargains in Cameroon. Taxi drivers generally don't attempt to overcharge – it's hard to imagine why not.

ROADBLOCKS

The one hazard even the most careful driver can't avoid in Cameroon is **police roadblocks**. These are usually on the outskirts of towns, often outside a bar or café. They're not easy to spot, as they may consist of no more than a policeman fast asleep in camouflage fatigues, and a piece of string lying on the road.

Cameroonian police are less troublesome to foreigners than they were a few years ago, but can still be drunk, abusive, surly, and alarmingly casual about pointing submachine guns at your stomach.

The best precaution you can take is always to travel with a full clutch of documents, whatever current regulations may say – better to show an International Medical Certificate ("carte jaune") than to insist that you aren't required to carry it.

As a foreigner, you're permitted to move about with a certified photocopy of your passport, which avoids the fear of having it confiscated at a police check. Take the original and copies of the first five pages (as well as your visa) to any main police station, where it will be stamped and signed for CFA500.

Car Hire

Car hire rates border on the outrageous. This is especially true of the main operators – **Hertz** and **Avis** – which at least back up their high prices with reliable cars and services. You will find car hire agencies only in the larger towns (Douala, Yaoundé, Garoua, Maroua, Ngaoundéré, and Kousseri); their addresses are in the "Directory"sections of the guide. Hire charges are higher in the north, and you'll be charged extra for any *piste* driving as opposed to street driving. If you hire on a daily basis, expect to pay upwards of CFA9000/day for a European or Japanese compact, with taxes, insurance, the kilometre charge and, of course, petrol on top.

■ By Rail

The **Régifercam** operates nearly 1200km of track, along two main routes. First is the **western line** from **Douala to Nkongsamba** (172km, up to eight hours travelling time), which branches to **Kumba** at **Mbanga**.

The substantially longer *Transcamerounais* line links the country's two major cities with Ngaoundéré in the north. *Transcam I* covers the 308-kilometre stretch from **Douala to Yaoundé** for about CFA2500 return. Given that this train takes over seven hours (and up to twice as long if the train derails, as is pretty common) it's more convenient to go via road, especially now that the paved highway has been completed. *Transcam II* forges on over 620km from **Yaoundé to Ngaoundéré**. This is actually a fairly quick trip – roughly twelve hours assuming there are no delays. Certainly you couldn't expect to get through the country any more quickly by road. There are reductions with **student cards**.

Carriages are relatively comfortable, with couchettes (linen, blankets and pillows provided) available on the Transcam routes if you book the morning of the day you're leaving. Second-class carriages have seats only and are often crowded. Food is available from vendors in the stations, but you ought to take your own water for the trip.

Like the airline, the railway authorities are extremely sensitive about foreigners taking **photographs**, and it would be wise to pack your camera deep inside your bag during the journey.

■ By Air

Cameroon Airlines operates a reasonably efficient domestic service connecting **Douala** and **Yaoundé** with each other and **Bafoussam**, **Bamenda**, **Batouri**, **Bertoua**, **Garoua**, **Koutaba**, **Maroua**, and **Ngaoundéré**. Flights are not all that cheap – Yaoundé to Garoua costs over CFA30,000 one way – but they do obviously save a lot of time. Note that on the routes to Maroua, Garoua and Ngaoundéré, they offer **30 percent reduced price** on 3–7 day excursions and group return fares (at least 4 people, max. 30 days); and **40 percent reduction** for students (ISIC card or letter) and weekend excursions (available to all, out Fri or Sat, back Sun or Mon). Thus you could do a weekend excursion from Yaoundé to Garoua for CFA37,000 or a one-way student fare to Maroua for around CFA24,000.

Five or six daily flights connect Yaoundé and Douala. Most other links have services varying from three times a week to daily. Note that flights are often overbooked; arrive early and hope for the best.

Sleeping

Hotels in Cameroon are officially classified from A to D. The luxury ones – those with AC rooms containing bath and shower and extras like swimming pool, tennis courts et al, fall into the A category. After that, it's hard to discern how hotels are classified, especially since in the cheaper *auberges*, some rooms may have AC or fans, while others little more than four walls and a barely sleepable bed.

Ratings take into account only the facilities and not considerations like cleanliness and service, which you may find more important than finding a toilet that doesn't flush in your grimy private "vaysay". In the west and south, the most expensive regions, you can expect to pay anything from CFA4000–24,000 a night (for class D to A).

■ Other Accommodation

If you have your own transport, **camping** away from the major urban centres is a fine alternative to hotel living. The game parks and natural reserves are restricted, but that only excludes a small chunk of the north. Elsewhere, there are tens of thousands of square kilometres of wild country.

The **missions** scattered throughout Cameroon will often put up travellers, but they don't have to – and don't always want to. In Douala and Yaoundé, the religious institutions are a real godsend if you're on a budget. In the face of ever-increasing demand, however, many missions are starting to turn away all who are not on church business.

There's a large European presence in Cameroon, so you won't be thought special or exotic. Travellers are treated with nonchalance and you're unlikely to receive many offers to **stay with people**, even if you're on your own. You may find exceptions in the north, where the rocketing price of accommodation in out-of-the-way villages such as Mokolo has given enterprising young people the idea of "inviting" travellers to spend the night in their homes. If you stay a couple of days, they can earn a month's income, even for a contribution that is negligible compared to what you'd pay in a hotel. You might find this blend of commerce and camaraderie a little difficult to handle, but it's a solution that benefits both parties. Be clear about prices before agreeing to any such arrangements.

Eating and Drinking

Cameroon has a rich and varied cuisine, with a heavy emphasis in the south on cassava, yams and plantains and in the north on maize, wheat, millet and groundnuts. Fruit and vegetables are probably the best in the whole of West Africa and the variations in climate and altitude mean you can get nearly everything all year round – except the luscious and varied types of mangoes, in which Cameroon excels and which are at their best from February to May.

In common with much of Francophone West Africa, however, French cuisine dominates in the big hotels and expensive restaurants – though all the glitter is no guarantee of special food. When you're paying CFA10,000–20,000 (the price per head in many Douala and Yaoundé restaurants), you don't expect tough meat and soggy vegetables.

Beware that in Douala and especially Yaoundé it can be very difficult to **eat cheaply** in the city centre. Even restaurants serving what seems like typical Cameroonian dishes, may be charging the earth for *Plats Typiques*. Still, though you're unlikely to find such specialised regional treats as fried termites, grasshoppers, dog, snake or cat in Yaoundé, you can taste a wide variety of national dishes without leaving the capital.

In "bush bars" and country town cafés, an item such as "omelette" (about CFA400–600) is

likely to include toast or bread, a cup of tea or soft drink, chilled water, and perhaps chips or peas.

All over, especially in the north, you'll find the tasty little snack kebabs known as **soya**, exactly like the *suya* of Nigeria. With French bread they make a good meal.

■ Dishes

Cameroonian cooking varies radically by region. In the equatorial south, plantains and tubers such as yams and manioc (cassava) dominate the diet. These can be boiled, pounded or even grilled, but invariably turn out bland – a characteristic which may put you off at first, but that complements the fiercely peppered sauces quite nicely. **Atchu** is the Grassfields version, made from small, quite tastey, cocyams. **Bobolo**, a heavy, nearly translucent cassava preparation, comes in a miniature *baguette* shape, while **miondo** is fermented cassava served wrapped up in banana leaves. The most widely eaten southern dish is **ndolé**, made from a boiled bitter leaf pounded into a paste. Seasoned with hot oil and spices, it's eaten with fish or meat. The similar **kwem** is made from pounded cassava leaves and usually eaten with a red, palm oil sauce. Such meals are served throughout the south in small restaurants known as *chantiers* (worksites), run by *veuves joyeuses* (merry widows) or *tantes* (aunties). **Millet**, most commonly ground and made into a stodge, and **rice**, are the staples of the north.

■ Buying your own food

If you plan to buy food to cook for yourself, expect to pay the same for vegetables as in Europe. A wide range is available in the markets, and basic vegetables like potatoes, cereals, onions, yams are roughly the same price throughout the country. Fruit and vegetables for export such as pineapples and mangoes vary enormously by growing area and season. At harvest time in a growing area you can buy a sack of ten pineapples for CFA1000; you often see the roof rack of a *taxi de brousse* with half a dozen sacks on top, perhaps to be sold in a mango-growing district down the road.

Good bread and *patisseries* are available throughout the country at fixed prices – CFA90 for a *baguette*, CFA70 for *pain batard*.

One final bargain, wherever you might be in Cameroon, is superb local **chocolate**, at CFA175 for a big bar.

Drinking

The *Brasseries du Cameroon* represents (for better or worse) one of the country's most important industries, so drink up. Although relatively expensive, **"La 33"** is real prestige beer, often associated with French-style affluence. Other brands include *Guinness*, *Gold Harp* and *Special*. If you're not into alcohol, the brewery also manufactures minerals (*sucreries*) in sickly-sweet orange, yellow, brown and colourless. If it's hot (and they're cold), you may even enjoy these syrupy carbonates. Mineral water can be had in the big hotels, and at Douala and Yaoundé supermarkets.

Palm wine (*mimbo*) is available throughout the south and west, where the best quality is said to come from raffias. After distillation, it becomes **arki**, or "African gin". Other indigenous drinks include millet beer and corn beer (*kwatcha*).

Communications – PTT, Language and Media

In this area, again, Cameroon is a real mixture, with sophisticated telecom systems in the metropolitan areas and virtually no communications in parts of the far south and remote centre. Linguistically it's very diverse – easily the most complex and interesting country in Africa. In the field of the media, there's much less to be proud of, through no fault of the journalists.

Staying in touch

Post offices keep the same hours as other bureaux, Mon–Fri 8am–noon and 2.30–5.30pm,

and Sat 8am–1pm. Letters to Europe take a week to fourteen days. The **poste restante** service seems to operate well enough in Yaoundé and Douala.

Douala and Yaoundé have a sophisticated modern **telephone** system which is generally reliable between the two cities and with IDD to Europe. First-try connections are common. Phoning up-country is considerably less reliable, and for booking a hotel, telex is preferred (which also provides useful physical evidence for disputes over double-booking). You can telex from hotels and travel agents, at variable costs.

Language

Uniquely in Africa, Cameroon has **two official languages**, French and English, and a difficult but worthy policy of bilingualism in the civil service and education. In practice, French has always had the upper hand. The majority of the country is Francophone, and only 22 percent (corresponding to the populations of North West and South West provinces) is Anglophone. This of course does not mean that most people speak one or the other language, although you might get that impression in the big towns. In North West and South West provinces, people in major towns usually speak **Pidgin English**, which doesn't come easily to an outsider – though you'll recognise a few words.

Of the four generally accepted groups of **African languages** (Afro-Asiatic, Nilo-Saharan, Niger-Congo, and Khoisan – divisions that contain languages as diverse as those found within the Indo-European group) all but Khoisan-related tongues are spoken in Cameroon. In all, some 160 different dialects are spoken, repre-

A CAMEROONIAN GLOSSARY

Auberge Cheap hotel or maison de passage.

Ba- Means "people of" in the Bantu and Semi-Bantu languages, widely extended (by European geographers) to indicate their towns and vilages. Place names are a good deal easier to remember if this prefix is mentally dropped.

Boukarou In hotel jargon, bungalow-like huts with thatched roofs.

Chantier Literally a construction site. In Yaoundé's popular jargon "street food stands".

Fon In western Cameroon, a chief or king.

Kirdi Collective name for the mountain people of the Mandara range. It means pagan, since most of these people are non-Muslim and non-Christian.

Lamidat Equivalent to a sultanate in the north. The sultan is the *Lamido*.

Mayo In the north, a river or dried river bed.

Ramassage "Collection" or "pick up". You take a taxi *en ramassage*, meaning you share it (and the fare) rather than hire it individually.

Saré Sudanic-style huts common in the north.

Sauvetteurs Wandering vendors, hawkers.

Stationnement Motor park.

senting seventeen different language families. In the face of such diversity, some languages have become *lingua francas*. In the south, **Douala** and **Bassa** are often used as vehicular languages, while in the north **Pulaar** (the Fula tongue) has taken on that role.

■ Media

The press looks quite limited in Cameroon, especially if you've just come from print-mad Nigeria. The *Cameroon Tribune*, a daily published in French and English editions, represents the laconic, voice of the government – with so few lines to read between it's hard keeping informed. The weekly *Canard Libéré* represents the closest thing to a satirical paper you'll find. *Radio Cameroon*, broadcast from Yaoundé in French, English and main Cameroonian languages, repeats, between programmes of African music, everything you could have read in the paper.

Arts and Entertainment

Cameroon has produced a number of highly regarded dramatists, film-makers and novelists, of whom the best known are cinéaste Jean Pierre Dikongue-Pipa and writers Mongo Beti and Ferdinand Oyono (see *Contexts*). But it's the country's musicians who have most successfully put Cameroon on the map for a world audience.

By repute and commitment, **Francis Bebey** – multi-talented artist in the broadest sense – is Cameroon's honorary cultural ambassador to the world. But more familiar in the record shops is the tireless Makossa star **Manu Dibango**. Makossa – derived from *kosa*, to strip off – is Cameroon's biggest dance music, a sexy fast-paced rhythm, now increasingly underscored by thunderous bass and, with the influence of Paris, only a squeeze away from Zouk. **Sam Fan Thomas** and **Moni Bile** are the two other best-known exponents out of hundreds (more coverage in *Contexts*).

But the biggest thing to have happened on the Cameroonian music scene of late is **Les Têtes Brulées**, whose wild cross-cultural appearance (day-glo "tribal paint", shaved and sculpted hair and the clumpiest trainers they could find) and an album of the same name, has stirred up a whirlwind of excitement abroad and confusion and controversy at home. Their music is based on a hyperactive version of the mad, nervy (but nonetheless traditional) **bikoutsi** rhythms of their Beti

background in Southern Province, an ethnic affiliation shared with President Paul Biya. If Yaoundé has a new wave scene, the *Têtes* are it. Look out for them, they just might be playing at home.

Directory

AIRPORT TAX CFA450.

ARTS AND CRAFTS It's illegal to take antiques and certain works of art out of the country without special government authorisation. That still leaves a wide variety of arts and crafts to choose from. The most famous region for art is the Bamoun-Bamiléké district, known for its intricately carved statues, masks and *bas reliefs*. The long tobacco pipes used by the Tikar and other peoples of the region have become popular tourist items and are widely available. The north is more renowned for leather and jewellery, fashioned primarily by the Fulani. Samples from all the regions can be found at the *marché artisinale* in Yaoundé.

Many antiques are smuggled down the Gamana and Donga rivers from Nigeria, which has strict views about the export of its heritage, and harsh penalties for smugglers. If you are continuing north from Cameroon, don't buy anything that looks old; it will almost certainly be confiscated by Nigerian customs officers, who are no more likely than you to be able to tell the difference between a copy and an original.

There's not likely to be a problem exporting artworks through Douala airport, as the rules on export are loosely observed. Doubtless many treasures slip through amongst the replicas. If you want to check, call the Ministry of Economic Planning Cultural Affairs Division in Douala on ☎22.51.89.

CRIME Douala is especially dangerous after dark and stabbings are common, with money the main motive. But rape is almost unheard of – which is not to say that it doesn't happen. Cameroonian justice is rough. The death penalty exists even for minor thefts, though few get as far as the courts. They may be dealt with by a roughing-up behind the police station or, if the cry of "Voleur" is heard, by a beating from an angry crowd.

EDUCATION Somewhat surprisingly for a country as well off as Cameroon, the country has only one university to date. Founded in 1961, the **University of Yaoundé** now has an enrolment of 15,000 students. The University has specialist facutlies at Douala, Dschang, Buéa and Ngaoundéré. Students from South West and North West Provinces commonly head to Nigeria to pursue higher education.

FOOTBALL After the **Indomitable Lions'** mighty result in the 1990 World Cup (they reached the quarter-finals against odds of 100:1), there's not much more to be said. Cameroon certainly has some of Africa's, and the world's, finest players, though regrettably for home games, many have given their careers to European clubs. Always a wildly popular sport in Cameroon, the status of soccer is now close to religious. Go to a match. The big teams are **Canon** and **Tonnerre** of Yaoundé and **Union**, **FC Rail** and **Dynamo** of Douala.

HOLIDAYS AND FESTIVALS Shops and administrative services all shut down for the major **Muslim and Christian holidays**. The most important of the **official holidays**, the *Fête Nationale*, takes place every May 20. On this day, parades and speeches commemorate the 1972 approval of the referendum for a united Cameroon. Other holidays include **Labour Day** (May 1) and **Youth Day** (February 11).

OPENING HOURS Most businesses, banks and offices are open Mon–Fri 7.30–11am and 2–5pm, with Sat a half-day.

PHOTOGRAPHY Although you're now theoretically allowed to take pictures openly, photography is hedged about with restrictions. These go beyond the usual military and "national security" taboos to include anywhere the president is likely to stay when travelling, parades and festivals and anything "likely to cause a decline in morality and damage the country's reputation". The interpretation of this law is left to the person who decides to take you to task for breaking it. Taking pictures in Yaoundé and Douala, all over the forest zone and in Muslim areas in general, is likely to lead to trouble unless you're very discreet or very charming.

But there's more: Cameroon used to issue **photography permits** (see Yaoundé "Directory", p.1141). These appear to have lapsed, but you may not convince a provincial busybody who may want to see an *authorisation d'exemption* – your permit exempting you from having a permit. Anything covered in signatures and stamps is a good item to have, but there's a final twist. Authorisations from provincial capitals will only carry weight in that province.

The use of **movie or video cameras** may still attract a licence fee of CFA30,000.

POSTCARDS Look out for the the hanpainted and screenprinted cards by local artists, available in bookshops and at the *Seamen's Mission* in Douala.

RELIGION Officially, Catholics, Protestants and Muslims all number about a million, but this estimate sounds too fortuitous to be true. Given that the country's population is now about eleven million, it seems clear at least that an overwhelming majority still practices traditional African religions.

WILDLIFE Cameroon is blessed with a wonderful natural heritage, as Gerald Durrell discovered in the 1950s. Fortunately, it seems the government is fairly committed to saving some of it – even at the expense of lucrative logging contracts and difficult decisions over local development. There are enough national parks to validate the country's safari claims and the latest initiative, in league with the powerful Worldwide Fund for Nature, is the Korup National Park in a remote corner of rainforest in the southwest on the Nigerian border. Details are given on p.1116 but, as yet, it's still hard to visit as a non-specialist traveller or tourist. In Cameroon's other parks, however, you can do the closest to an East African safari available on this side of the continent. Cameroon is the only country in West Africa that has rhinos. These, along with most other African big game, including one of Africa's largest elephant counts, can be seen in several localities. Sensitive souls beware, however, that Cameroon actively encourages paid-up hunting, as part of its conservation strategy.

WOMEN TRAVELLERS AND CAMEROONIAN WOMEN Any foreign woman considering marriage to a Cameroonian man should be aware of the law that requires a husband's written permission for his wife to leave the country. The law applies equally to foreign nationals, and even to those with work visas. It's not strictly enforced for holders of tourist visas leaving through Douala, but an unaccompanied wife can't guarantee being able to exit the country without her husband at her side. Worth knowing.

There's not been a great deal of progress for women in Cameroon, though there is a Ministry – of Social Affairs and Women – which you might write to (c/o PTT Centrale, Yaoundé, or telephone ☎22.41.48) if you're keen to make contact with groups in the country.

A Concise History of Cameroon

In the southern half of the Cameroon region, the first Bantoid-speaking peoples had moved in by 200–100BC from the Nigerian plateau, displacing the original inhabitants (the people of small stature known as "Pygmies") and pushing them deep into the forests. But the earliest clearly defined presence in Cameroon is that of the materially advanced *Sao* culture, which developed around Lake Chad, and left archaeological evidence of works in bronze and terra-cotta – human and animal figures – coins, dishes, jewellery and funeral jars. From the eighth century the Sao evidently began mixing with peoples pushed southward by the powerful empire then forming in Kanem (the Kotoko who live along the banks of Lake Chad and the Logone river are thought to be their descendants). Today, Cameroon is a complicated mixture of peoples, none of which is really predominant. As an archetypal example of an artificial state its present configuration derives in large part from the imposed colonial history of the last hundred years, a legacy from which it is still struggling to break free.

■ The Arrival of the Portuguese

In 1472, the Portuguese navigator **Fernando Po** led an expedition around the Bay of Biafra and was the first European to penetrate the estuary of the **Wouri River**, which he called *Rio dos Camarões* ("Prawn River"). From this time on, the coastal region gained unprecedented influence, taking over from such northern powers as the **Bornu Empire** (which extended down to the Benoué in the sixteenth century). The centre of trade shifted to the regions around Douala, Limbé and Bonaberi where local chiefs signed consecutive trade agreements with the Portuguese, Dutch, English, French and Germans. These chiefs rounded up slaves and ivory which they traded against cloth, metal and other European products.

Although commerce flourished over the ensuing four centuries, the Europeans didn't settle on the Cameroonian coast until the nineteenth century, when British missionaries began to protest against the **slave trade**. Britain was pushed to the forefront of the anti-slavery crusade. In 1845, an English pastor, **Alfred Saker**, founded the first European settlement in Cameroon at Douala. Although he set up churches and schools Saker was hardly a liberator. He recognised early on the strategic importance of **Douala** and **Victoria** and pushed for them to become Crown colonies.

With the arrival of British, German and French **commercial houses**, trade shifted to "legitimate" exports of palm oil, ivory and gold. But the **Douala chiefs** became increasingly worried they would lose their role as middlemen between interior peoples and the Europeans and sought British guarantees that would have led to a protectorate. Queen Victoria hesitated. By the time she finally sent an envoy to make an arrangement, the Germans had beat her to it. On July 12 1884, **Gustave Nachtigal** signed a treaty with the Douala chiefs **Bell**, **Deido** and **Akwa**, who willingly ceded their sovereignty to Kaiser Wilhem in exchange for trade advantages.

■ The German, French and British Occupations

In 1885, Baron von Soden became the first governor of *Kamerun*, and spent the next ten years trying to quell **rebellions** in the interior. He was replaced by **von Puttkamer** who relied on forced labour and brutality to carve out the colony's first **railway line** in 1907. But the promising economic results of the German activities, which included building some roads, hospitals and schools, came to an abrupt halt with the outbreak of **World War I**. In 1916, after a long, arduous and bloody campaign, the Allies wrested control of the territory from Germany and, in 1922, it was officially placed under French and British mandates – with only about one fifth of the area ceded to Britain.

The **British Cameroons** were joined to Nigeria in an administrative union, but lay outside the framework of development plans for Nigeria, and received only minimal funding. Ironically, much of the growth in the region after World War I was spurred by the **Germans** who returned as private citizens to develop the plantations around the Victoria plains. (When, in the 1930s, many of them rallied to the call of Nazism, they were expelled and their private development efforts consolidated into the *Cameroon Development Corporation*, today the country's second biggest employer.) The **French** were more active in developing the infrastructure. Cultivation of the main export commodities of cocoa, palm oil and timber increased dramatically. French plans, however, relied heavily on exacting taxes and forced labour (in lieu of tax), to extend the road network, enlarge Douala's port and build up the vast plantations. Arising from such methods, well-founded grievances grew up over French rule.

■ The Beginnings of Nationalism

After World War II, the United Nations renewed the French and British mandates. The **British sector** continued – essentially – to be ruled from Nigeria. On the eve of independence, two camps emerged; the first pushing to become a state within the Nigerian federation, and the second calling for reunification with "the other" Cameroon.

In the **French territory** the call for reunification was also voiced. Political parties began to form, including the **Union des Populations Camerounaises** (UPC) and the less radical **Bloc Democratique Camerounais** of northerner **Ahmadou Ahidjo**.

The UPC was the first party to call both for unification of the two separate Cameroons and for **independence from France**. Prevented by force of oppostion from attaining these demands legally, it organised a **revolt** in the larger towns of the French colonies in 1955. The uprising was put down, but at the cost of hundreds of lives and huge economic waste and destruction. The UPC, using increasingly extreme and violent liberation tactics, was banned in 1956 by the French government, but its influence barely diminished, especially in the **Bamiléké country** and **Sanaga region** where rebellion continued to foment and was brutally suppressed.

The UPC's actions acted as a catalyst to Cameroonian nationalism and focused the attention of more conservative parties on developing specific policy. Its influence was felt by leaders such as Ahidjo, who was still working within the political mechanism put in place by the French. In 1958 he founded a new party, **l'Union Camerounaise** and became the Prime Minister of the *Assemblée Legislative du Cameroun*. His platform called for reunification, total independence and national reconciliation.

■ Independence

Ahidjo met his first aim when he proclaimed **independence** on January 1, 1960. The next year, his goal of reunification was also partly satisfied. Following a United Nations plebiscite,

the northern half of the former British territory voted to join Nigeria, while the southern British Cameroons voted to join the francophone territory. But national reconciliation proved more difficult as the UPC problem dragged on and it took a further twelve years before Ahidjo (with continued French assistance) prevailed over the rebels when their last members were executed. In remarkably astute political manoeuvring, he then neutralised much of the internal opposition by integrating it into his government and the enlarged party, **l'Union Nationale Camerounaise**.

As the political wrinkles were being ironed out (symbolised through the adoption of a new constitution, the dissolution of the federal system and the formation of the **United Republic of Cameroon** in 1972) progress was also being made on the economic front. Like Houphouët-Boigny in Côte d'Ivoire, Ahidjo focused first on developing agriculture and then moved on to basic industry. Thanks in part to the discovery of oil, the country's GNP nearly doubled in the first twenty years of independence. By the end of the 1970s, Cameroon was thus shaping up as one of the rare stable countries in the region. If reports of **political prisoners** and repression trickled out of the country, and **Anglophone students** (to single out just one obvious group) were supremely dissatisfied with the way Cameroon was going, the west turned a blind eye on the autocratic excesses of a reliable friend.

■ A Change of Regime

Yet, as the years dragged on, it looked as though Ahidjo was settling into a pattern all too familiar in post-independence Africa – that of the powerful political leader who refuses to relinquish power or look to the future. He had been president for 22 years when he rather unexpectedly stepped down in 1982, citing ill-health as his reason. Just as Senghor had done in Senegal, he passed the sceptre to a young prime minister of his own grooming, from a different background – the 49-year-old bilingual southerner, **Paul Biya**. Recognised for his honesty and competency, Biya had barely been in office a year when his reputation, and that of Cameroon, took a beating in the international press.

Trouble started in 1983 when Biya fired the prime minister and several members of his cabinet, on the grounds that he had uncovered a **treasonous plot**. Ahidjo resigned as UNC party boss and, from his residence on the French Riviera, he openly criticised his heir, claiming that Biya was turning Cameroon into a police state, and asserting that he had been tricked into relinquishing power by faked health reports (it seems the former president was resentful that Biya would not allow him to transfer his vast fortune out of Cameroon, and was sensitive to Muslim worries that the balance of power had shifted to southern Christians). The showdown had begun, but Biya seemed to have all the cards. Ahidjo was sentenced to death in absentia.

Although Biya then pardoned his predecessor, things went from bad to worse in 1984, when units of the presidential guard formed by Ahidjo (and still loyal to the ex-president) revolted in Yaoundé. They were only put down by the army after three days of **fighting in the streets** of the capital and an unknown death toll that has been estimated at as many as 1000. Ahidjo denied any involvement, but Biya cracked down on dissidents and dozens of guard members were secretly tried and executed. Since then, calm has returned and Biya has consolidated his position, but the incident showed the world that, even in Cameroon, stability is fragile.

■ Consolidation of Power

For months after the coup, Biya rarely left the presidential palace. Indeed, many observers expected a further attempt to overthrow him, and it was widely believed an irreparable rift between the north and the rest of the country had been opened. But after a series of purges within the government, military and public sector, the president seemed to gain confidence.

As the nation prepared for the five-year congress of the UNC, in 1985, expectations ran high that Biya would announce sweeping reforms, including the revival of a multiparty system. Such hopes were disappointed when the president directed that no legal opposition to the ruling party would be allowed. Furthermore, he announced he was changing the UNC's name to the *Rassemblement Démocratique du Peuple Camerounais* (RDPC), apparently a move to distance the political body from its association with Ahidjo. At the same time, he moved towards a **cautious democratisation** within the party, and in 1986, elections were held for members of RPDC bodies from the village level up to the *départements* (which saw the emergence of a lot of new blood).

On an **international level**, relations improved with the west, and in 1985 Biya made a much-publicised official visit to France. This was viewed as a conciliatory move, as the two countries had been on bad terms due to the widely-believed French complicity in the attempted coup of 1984. Shortly afterwards, Biya travelled to Britain, and in 1986, to West Germany, the Vatican City and Canada. Also in 1986, Cameroon became the fourth African nation, after Zaire, Liberia and Côte d'Ivoire, to restore diplomatic relations with Israel, partly in response to the wishes of the American government, with whom he was seeking closer ties after the cooling of relations with France.

These events, however, were largely overshadowed by the worst **natural disaster** in the nation's history. In late 1986, an eruption of underwater volcanic gases escaped at Lake Nyos, a crater lake in the grassfields of North West Province. A cloud of deadly chemicals leaked into the atmosphere, suffocating at least 2000 people almost instantly and killing thousands of head of livestock. It caused great insecurity among local people who depend heavily on the crater lakes for fish and drinking water. Even some of the Anglophone intelligentsia persisted in the belief that a crude American or Israeli experiment in chemical warfare had been carried out at the lake site. Rumour aside, Lake Nyos served to bring Cameroon under the international spotlight once again.

At the end of 1986, Biya once again reshuffled the government and replaced key senior officials. Increasingly confident, he announced that **elections**, scheduled for early 1989, would be brought forward to April 24, 1988. The RDPC approved 324 candidates for 180 seats, and after the voting, the National Assembly had been filled with technocratic members of the new "young guard". Biya, the sole presidential candidate, was "elected" to a new term by 98.75 percent of the votes, a bit of a dip since his 99.98-percent win in 1984.

■ The 1990s

At the end of the 1980s, Biya's position appeared secure. Some dissent still remained from Army officers loyal to Ahidjo, and in 1989 there were rumours of minor insurrections and firefights in the districts bordering Nigeria. However, Biya's great strength – apart from skill at political manoeuvre – lies in the relative stability of the economy. Cameroon has moved to the middle-bracket status of underdeveloped nations, its gross national product per person much above West Africa's average. When coffee and cocoa prices dropped in the early 1980s, Cameroon was able to fall back on its rapidly growing oil exports, which actually pushed foreign trade into a surplus. Only now that the oil is running out is the need to attract foreign investment – and tourists – inducing Biya to curry favours abroad and to relax the previous somewhat xenophobic atmosphere at home. And even now, Biya may be in luck, as there were fresh oil discoveries in Littoral Province in 1990.

Pro-democracy - anti people?

Politically, Cameroon's prognosis is less healthy. In July 1990, Biya's address to the conference of his party, now renamed the **Cameroon People's Democratic Movement** (CPDM) indicated a willingness to go down the road to a multiparty system. "One can imagine things will go quite fast in the coming months", he said. But, apart from **Amnesty International**'s much publicised concern on political detentions and mistreatment, and steady pressure from Paris on reforms, explicitly tied to **debt relief**, this announcement of measures to liberalise politics looks like a response from the government to unexpected events, rather than a planned programme of political reform.

Two events in particular have detonated the political bedrock in the country as it enters its fouth decade of independence. The first was the arrest and trial of the respected former president of the Cameroonian Bar Association **Maître Yondo Black**. Black, from Douala, was arrested with a number of others early in 1990 and sentenced, by a specially convened military court, to three years in prison on charges of showing contempt for the president and planning, with others, ways and means of introducing a multiparty political system. There was an immediate and vocal response from the **Cameroonian legal community** and 200 lawyers went on strike to demand Black's release. He was finally freed in August – significantly, after Cameroon's surprise success in the **World Cup** had once again renewed the government's confidence, but also focused world attention on the country.

The other event that pushed Biya into talking about democracy was catalysed by the Black affair. The newly formed, but unlicenced **Social Democratic Front** – the vanguard of the pro-

democracy movement – proceded, despite a government ban, with its inaugural rally in Bamenda on May 26, 1990. In the run-up, **troops** were massed in the town. The organisers managed to get over 30,000 people onto the streets. After a peaceful demonstration, attempts to disperse the crowd met with stone-throwing and, in the ensuing rout, troops shot into fleeing marchers, killing six people and injuring dozens more. On the same day in Yaoundé, the university campus was the scene of brutal attacks on students supporting the rally.

In the Bamenda area, **harassment** of potential opposition figures continues. Fons have been provocatively stopped and searched at random in a fashion calculated to cause the maximum offence to traditional office-holders.

The suppression has been partly effective. Leaders of the SDF, not all of whom are from the Anglophone region, have claimed the Anglophone districts are being treated like a colony by the Francophone and that "the opposition has been silenced".

It's clear that support for the government in the North West and South West provinces has bottomed out. The Bamiléké of Western Province – powerful in Cameroon commerce – have also lost enthusiasm since the shooting dead of a senior lawyer **Pierre Bouobda** at a Bafoussam roadblock on the day of Black's conviction. The ill will from the west added to continued resentment from the north about the treatment of Ahidjo and his barons, amounts to a heavy show

In the aftermath of the Bamenda killings, the government and ruling CPDM are looking increasingly divided. There have been a number of key replacements and resignations and clear messages of **protest** as senior figures have sought to distance themselves from the clampdown. There seems to be solid support for the government in the senior ranks of the army, however; some southern commanders have profited considerably from the high profile of southerners in government.

Cameroon's **economic prospects** are good. Oil, coffee and near self-sufficency in food are a healthy combination. Private investment was on the rise until recently too. But it may require a monumental change of pace at the top – and a lot more than words – to convince a dissatisfied and impatient people that respect for human rights and a real measure of democratisation are at the top of the government's agenda.

DOUALA AND
SOUTH WEST PROVINCE

As **economic capital** of Cameroon, **DOUALA** is a vast and energetic city. The driving force behind its growth has been the **port**, which handles 95 percent of the nation's maritime traffic and has stimulated regional development in **industry** and trade. But despite Douala's activity and relative prosperity, the cityscape is a relentless urban jungle distinguished neither by traditional flavour nor modern flashiness. Urban planners have concentrated their efforts on Yaoundé in the interior, with the result that Douala suffers from overpopulation and a worn-down and inadequate infrastructure. It's all a bit depressing – and aesthetically disastrous.

Fortunately, a variety of natural highlights are within easy reach of the metropolis. On a clear day in Douala, you can just about make out **Mount Cameroon** – West Africa's highest peak. The colonial town of **Buéa** is only 70km away, 1000m up the slopes of the mountain, and makes a good base for climbing expeditions. Continuing north, **Kumba** – a vibrant commercial town located near **Lake Barombi** – a beautiful crater lake – makes a good stopover on the way to Nigeria. Here is where you head out from to visit **Korup National Park**. But for simple rest and recuperation, you can't beat the **black sand beaches** of **Limbé**, a small town with a distinctly British flavour tucked against wooded mountains on the ocean.

Douala

Despite its status as the nation's largest city and economic capital, **DOUALA** is hardly dazzling. The architecture is unspectacular (few modern buildings and barely a highrise to rival Yaoundé), and the streets in the major commercial and administrative quarters lack character. With certain exceptions, notably the lively market area around the **Lagos neighbourhood,** it would be unlikely to fill you with a wild desire to explore, nor tempt you to stay long enough to figure out its complex patchwork of peoples – even if it were not also a somewhat unsafe place. The population has skyrocketed in recent years and may now have passed the million mark, an influx which, in conjunction with a scarcity of jobs, has brought about acute social malaise. Crime is rampant and certain areas of the city – those around the port, for example – are just plain dangerous.

Some history
Like so many settlements on the West African coast, the Douala area was once home to small fishing communities, who first came into contact with Europe when the **Portuguese** made contact at the end of the fifteenth century. Although trade between local rulers and seafarers continued for many centuries – especially in slaves – Europeans didn't settle on the shores of the Wouri (or Cameroons) River until the nineteenth century. The first were **English missionaries** led by **Alfred Saker** who, in 1845 founded a small community at the site where the *Eglise du Centainaire* stands today. By that time, the **Douala** (who probably arrived in the estuary at the beginning of the seventeenth century) were established into two groups united around the **Bell** and **Akwa** families.

German trading companies followed in the footsteps of the missionaries and quickly persuaded Bismarck to protect their interests in the region. The German chancellor thus sent **Gustav Nachtigal** to claim the lands in the name of the Kaiser. In July 1884, Nachtigal signed treaties with the chiefs Bell, Akwa and Deido, who ceded all administrative and legal rights. With the flick of a pen, British designs in the region were wiped out and the Douala chiefs had ceded legal rights to the territory (at least they had by German law). In 1885, a German governor was appointed and **Kamerunstadt** became the capital. The name stuck until 1907 when it was changed to Douala.

After World War I, Douala became part of the French protectorate. Although it was no longer capital of the territory, the French began large-scale urban construction, and enlargement of the port. Industry followed and Douala forged ahead to become the economic engine of the whole country.

Arrivals and transport

The **airport** at Douala remains the only arrival point for **international** flights to Cameroon, until such time as the one under construction at Yaoundé is finally operational. Douala's *nouvel aéroport* handles a large quantity of air traffiic, but it's already showing signs of age after only ten years, and can seem surprisingly small-time. From the airport, you can get a **taxi** to the town centre for around CFA2000. But it's no problem to catch a **bus**, by turning left out of the airport and walking down to the "SOTUC Terminus". From here, the #11 (costing under CFA100) takes you straight to the middle of the Lagos Market – a sure way to get radical culture shock if you're arriving direct from Europe.

If you happen to arrive **by train** from Yaoundé, the new station is just off Boulevard de la République in the northeast part of the city centre (and just off our map, roughly under the "Douala" label). The old Gare de Douala Port has been closed for serveral years. The **New Bell Railway Station** has been in use while the city's modern *gare ferroviaire* has been under constrution.

Coming into Douala **by bush taxi**, the main **gares routières** are in the Yabassi and Deido neighbourhoods (the latter just off our map to the north), from either of which it's best to take a cab to the centre. Long-distance drivers sometimes continue all the way into the centre, letting off passengers along the way. If this happens, ask to be dropped at the Akwa post office, which is central and within walking distance of hostels and moderate hotels.

Getting around Douala

The quickest way to get around town is **by taxi share** – around CFA200 for any distance within cities (even to Douala airport).

Douala also has a very good **bus system**, at a flat fare (still under CFA100) and covering virtually the whole town, including the airport, on eleven routes. Run by *SOTUC*, (the *Société des Transports Urbains du Cameroun*) the buses aren't as convenient as taxis – and the crowds can be murder if you've got lots of luggage – but they provide a reliable means of getting around town.

Some bookshops sell the Douala street map for CFA2500, but many streets are unnamed both on the map and on the ground. Locals and taxi drivers give directions by landmarks – hotels, nightclubs, water towers – rather than by street names. You might be better off spending the money on ten taxi trips.

Accommodation

Cheap accommodation doesn't really exist in Douala – even the missions charge premium rent on rooms. There are a few good hotels in the moderate category, but the city seems to belong to the international hotels.

The bottom line: missions

Eglise Evangelique, also known as the *Temple du Centenaire*. Near the port, this church has a guesthouse (*centre d'accueil*) with very clean rooms from CFA2500. It's probably the

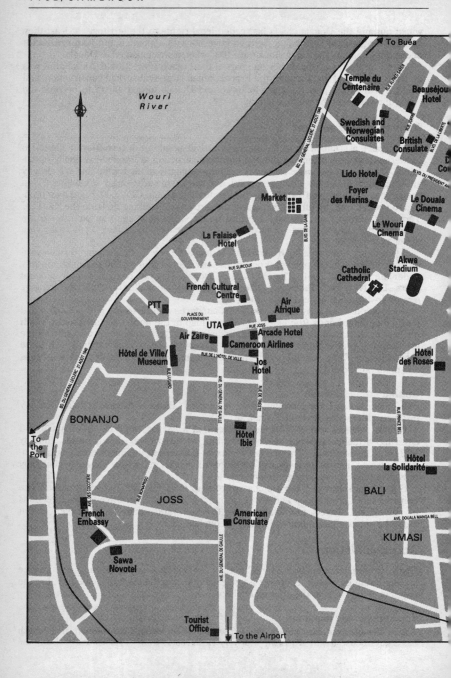

To Buéa

Wouri
River

Temple du
Centenaire

Beauséjou
Hotel

Swedish and
Norwegian
Consulates

British
Consulate

Lido Hotel

Foyer
des Marins

Le Douala
Cinema

Market

Le Wouri
Cinema

La Falaise
Hotel

RUE SURCOUF

Akwa
Stadium

French Cultural
Centre

Catholic
Cathedral

PTT

PLACE DU
GOUVERNEMENT

Air
Afrique

UTA

RUE JOSS

Air Zaire

Arcade Hotel

Cameroon Airlines

Hôtel de Ville/
Museum

RUE DE L'HOTEL DE VILLE

Jos
Hotel

Hôtel
des Roses

BONANJO

To
the
Port

Hôtel
Ibis

Hôtel
la Solidarité

BALI

JOSS

French
Embassy

American
Consulate

KUMASI

AVE. DOUALA MANGA BELL

Sawa
Novotel

Tourist
Office

To the Airport

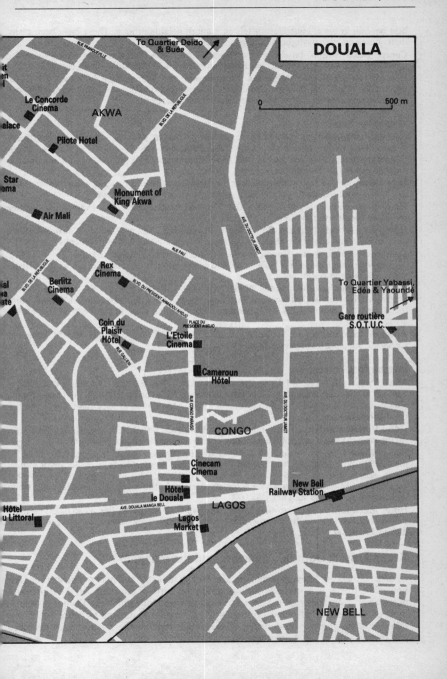

DOUALA

best bargain in town, but unfortunately in a tough neighbourhood. There have been many thefts here and even daylight muggings.

Centre Baba Simon, bd de la Liberté across from the Cathedral. Dormitory space for CFA4000 a night (try to bargain) hardly seems worth it for such rudimentary conditions.

Procure Générale des Missions Catholiques, rue Franqueville in Akwa (BP 5280; ☎42.27.97, telex 5728). Very comfortable (AC in rooms, swimming pool) and reasonable, but missionaries get first priority. The place is often full as a result.

Moderate hotels

Foyer des Marins, rue Galliéni (BP 1594; ☎42.27.94) off bd de la Liberté near the *Wouri* cinema. One of the best bargains in town although really reserved for seamen. From CFA8000 per night for S/C rooms with AC. Swimming pool on premises and many ex-pats, perhaps due to the draught beer.

Lido Hôtel, rue Joffre (☎42.04.45), near the *Foyer des Marins*. In a quiet area, this hotel has S/C rooms with AC starting at CFA8500, plus its own bar and restaurant.

Hôtel Kontchupe, rue Alfred Saker (BP 558; ☎42.68.52), near Eglise Evangelique. Rather run-down considering the CFA7500 starting price of rooms, but it's central.

Hôtel du Littoral, 38 av Douala Manga Bell, Bali (BP 1389; ☎42.24.84). Not the classiest place in town, but one of the cheapest with rooms from CFA6000. Near the Lagos market.

Cameroun-Hôtel, 3 rue Congo Parriso, Carrefour des Flèches (BP 5412; ☎42.17.67). African-style hotel in a lively quarter near the mosque and market. Rooms with AC from CFA7500. Bar and restaurant.

Hôtel de Douala, bd Ahmadou Ahidjo prolongé (BP 780; ☎42.54.78), across from the market on the Huatole intersection. Very near the bus stop, so convenient for arrivals from the airport. AC rooms (CFA7000), bar and restaurant and right in the heart of the market area.

Hôtel de la Maturité, bd de l'Unité (BP 2207; ☎42.71.46). A large hotel with AC rooms at CFA8000, but not a lot of personality.

International class

Akwa Palace, 52 bd de la Liberté (BP 4007; ☎42.26.01, telex 5322). The oldest of the international hotels, still boasting an older wing in all its colonial pomp. Pleasant pool and gardens plus restaurant and bar. If CFA15,000 for a room is too much, at least have a drink in the popular *café terrasse*.

Hôtel Parfait Garden, bd de la Liberté near Akwa Palace (BP 5350; ☎42.63.57, telex 5716). All the services of a 3-star hotel but lacking charm. Rooms begin at CFA15,000.

Sawa Novotel, av de Verdun, off av de Gaulle in Bonanjo (BP 2345; ☎42.08.66, 42.14.70, telex 5532). With four stars, the *Novotel* offers complete comfort and extras like video, tennis, sauna, and poolside barbecue. Coffee shop and restaurant with European food, plus banks, car rental and boutiques – a whole complex. A stand in the foyer sells artefacts and some good jewellery. Rooms start at CFA23,000.

Hôtel Méridien, av des Cocotiers (BP 3232; ☎42.46.29, 42.90.44, Fax 42.35.07). The most expensive hotel in town. It has everything: real class and really expensive, with rooms starting at CFA28,000.

Around town: Douala's quarters and the museum

Douala sprawls out in every direction. Much of its industry and many of its workers are housed on the far side of the Wouri bridge (to the north of our map), on the right bank of the river. Nonetheless, the various distinct quarters into which the town is divided – most of them named after local ruling families – aren't too difficult to figure out. If you take the town *quartier* by *quartier*, orientation is much easier, and Douala becomes less overwhelming and more interesting.

Akwa: the modern centre

As the main commercial area, the **Akwa neighbourhood** is more or less the centre of the modern city. Its lifeline is the boulevard de la Liberté, with the **Cathédrale Catholique** something of a landmark at its southern end. Built in the 1930s, this is one of the few attractive edifices in town, even if its neo-romanesque style is a bit incongruous in this sweltering climate.

Just opposite the church, the **Stand Municipal Artisanal** is a market for a wide range of **crafts**. Foumban (see p.1125) has a reputation for being the best place in Cameroon to buy authentic artefacts (and high quality reproductions), but this rates a good second. They sell good quality jewellery as well as both real and fake antiques – and regrettably local ivory carvings too. The masks, both new and old (and it's pretty hard to tell which is which) are imported from all over West Africa, and are the same as those on sale in London or Paris at ten to twenty times the price. There's more about buying and exporting crafts in the *Practical Information* section (p.1094), and in the account of Foumban.

Continuing north, you pass the Akwa post office and the *Wouri* cinema before arriving at the wide tree-lined boulevard du Président Ahmadou Ahidjo. Here, numerous department stores, supermarkets, boutiques and outdoor cafés provide an upmarket commercial backdrop for the vendors selling clothes, shoes and accessories on the streetside.

Turning towards the river on boulevard Ahidjo (away from the shops) takes you past the **Eglise Evangelique** (or *Temple du Centenaire*, built to commemorate the 100th anniversary of Alfred Saker's arrival) and down the hill to the **port**. The surrounding area is run-down and has a dangerous reputation, so it might be worth skipping this detour and instead continuing north on boulevard de la Liberté to the **Akwa Palace**. This old colonial hotel (now with a modern extension) was for long Cameroon's ultimate in luxury accommodation and still retains a certain charm. The outdoor café in front is a popular meeting place for ex-pats. Beyond the hotel, businesses become more sparse on boulevard de la Liberté as it leads on to the **Wouri Bridge** and over to the industrial **Bonabéri** neighbourhood.

Bonanjo and the administrative district

Heading the other way from the Cathedral, the boulevard de la Liberté curves to the west and becomes rue Joss – a street that leads downhill to **place du Gouvernement**. This is the heart of the administrative quarter and the **Bonanjo** district. The **Poste Centrale**, with a large monument commemorating the World War II exploits of General Leclerc, dominates the square. On one corner, you'll see the pagoda-shaped colonial house which was once the **palace** of Prince Rudolf Manga Bell. The grandson of a Douala signatory of the German treaty, the prince was later killed by them for treason. East of the square, the main branches of all the major **banks** congregate around avenue du Général de Gaulle.

The Museum

Mon–Fri 8am–noon & 2.30–5.15pm, Sat 8am–1pm; free.

The rather forlorn **Musée de Douala** is housed in the **Hôtel de Ville**, off rue Lugard behind place du Gouvernement. It's not marked anywhere, so don't worry about just walking into the City Hall and heading upstairs to find the museum on the first floor.

It consists of a dusty collection of national art, poorly presented, inadequately explained, and looking as if no one has paid it any attention in years. But if you're going to be travelling around the country, the museum gives a generous overview of regional art, and has one or two rare pieces. Visits start in a sort of entrance hall, framed by posts from the famous **Bandjoun chiefdom**. Here the whole **history** of the nation, from the **paleolithic** (old stone) age via the **slave trade** to the **colonial era**, is represented by a somewhat haphazard assortment of articles. This room also contains a couple of **Bamoun statues**, some of clay and one beautiful bronze cast, to draw your attention from the clutter.

The other four rooms of the museum are much more coherent. The **Salle du Sud** represents art from the forests of southern Cameroon. Wooden objects dominate, such as **Fang statues** and colourful sculpted Douala decorations for the bows of *pirogues*. A Basso cloak made of hammered tree bark is especially striking and there are also various musical instruments and games. The **Salle du Nord** is military, with an emphasis on Fula arms, such as a suit of mail and helmet together with spears, saddles and harnesses. In the **Salle Bamoun**, dedicated to the Bamoun culture, is a series of coloured drawings evoking the Cameroon region's history, up to the reign of the great innovator and statesman Sultan Njoya (see "Foumban", p.1123). Njoya created the alphabet used in the writings alongside. Numerous sculptures adorn the room, including a magnificent **bas relief** depicting the sultan returning from war. Lastly, the **Salle Bamiléké** contains a collection of thrones, and statues representing of the chief and his servants. Notice the sculpted wooden posts – a traditional part of Bamiléké architecture used to decorate the house of a chief.

Lagos and Kassalafam

From Bonanjo, avenue Douala Manga Bell leads east through the **Bali quarter** to the district known as **Lagos**. This area is the site of the **Marché Central** – the biggest market in the country. You reach it at the level of the **mosque** in front of which assorted barks, seeds and powders – the essential ingredients of the **African pharmacopoeia** – are on sale. Nearby on rue Congo, the **Marché Congo** specialises in African and imported fabrics. Across the railway tracks from place de l'Indépendance, the **Lagos market** unfolds, stretching up boulevard des Nations Unies where it merges with the **Marché de Kassalafam**. These are two of the liveliest neighbourhoods in town, well worth visiting even if you don't want to buy anything.

Eating and Drinking

Although you should find something suitable in the following lists, eating in Doula is shockingly expensive. Be warned, however, that, even if you decide you can afford them, some restaurants close in July and August when the rain comes bucketing down and people stay in.

If you're basically living from the markets and the odd *chantier* bite, Douala's restaurants can seem inhuman. It also flaunts a number of Paris-style pavement cafés, however, where shoppers retire for a break and business people do their deals. You can relax in their air-conditioned comfort for as long as you like for the price of a coffee (which is about CFA800). *Akwa Palace*, *le Delice* and *Gourmandaise* take turns at being the in place of the moment. If you're feeling flush or homesick, splash out CFA1500 on one of their superb pastries.

Cheaper restaurants: up to CFA5000

La Sanaga, next to the *Douala* cinema on rue Gallieni. Copious meals – spaghetti, rice and beans, *steack frites* or chops for CFA500–1500. Try *un peu de tout*. One of the best bargains in town.

Bar Express, next to the *Wouri* cinema on bd de la Liberté. A cross between an American coffee shop and a French café. Burgers, pitta sandwiches and salads for around CFA800–1500. Not a place to go if you're starving, but decent snacks.

Pizzeria, av de Gaulle, identified by the illuminated Fiat 500 on the roof. Authentic Italian pizzas for CFA2000 (plate-sized) to CFA5000 (tray-sized model).

Le Touristic, corner of bd de la République and bd de la Réunification (☎42.40.88), way out from the centre. Outdoor restaurant serving Cameroon specialties like grilled fish or chicken. Very reasonable by Douala standards, with meals running about CFA5000.

The Marina, down a dirt track off the airport road, on a jetty in the not-too-clean Wouri river (take a taxi, and ask the driver to come back later). A limited menu, specialising in prawn or meat brochettes, but to a consistent standard, and with probably the cleanest toilets in Douala. Relaxed, friendly atmosphere improved further by the cool evening breeze. More than adequate starters for CFA2000, main courses CFA5000; drinks cheaper than in town.

Expensive

Le Phaco, near the *Sonel* building at Koumassi on Le Circuit. Every bit as vibrant and rumbustious as the warthog it's named after – and much friendlier. The boisterous owner, always makes sure there's something going on. The food is basic; tasty fish and chicken cooked on charcoal or any way you ask for it, served on wooden tables in the open air. Superb chocolate mousse. You can spend CFA10,000 and come out stuffed, or CFA5000 and restrict yourself to chicken and chips (and plantain, of course).

L'Auberge, bd de la Liberté (☎42.36.23). A reputation built on excellent French and European cuisine, but with meals running at CFA20,000, this "quaint" restaurant isn't for everybody.

Il Canasta, off av de Gaulle. Good Italian food for about CFA25,000 for two, with wine.

Le Coq Noir, not far from the *Akwa Palace*. White-uniformed waiters serve upmarket African food on linen tablecloths to wealthy Cameroonians and visiting French dignitaries and nightclub stars. The ambience is Parisian gentility, the live music totally African. Food is Cameroonian (crocodile and snake are best ordered in advance). CFA15–20,000 a head.

Feu de Bois, deep in Akwa (☎42.37.78). African decor, with woodcarvings on the wall. Good solid African food and lots of it, but few concessions to European tastes. CFA10–15,000.

Lotus, rue Kitchener. More or less Vietnamese, as far as ingredients will allow; excellent food, but the portions are not overgenerous. Allow CFA15,000 per person if you don't want to go home hungry.

Le Marieke, rue Tokota, off rue Bonapriso. A friendly family-run place offering good hearty North French cuisine at CFA10,000 each.

La Porte Jaune, corner of rue Franqueville and av King Akwa (☎42.98.54). Original African cooking with dishes as provocative as crocodile, boa and porcupine. Wild and well served; expect to pay around CFA12,000 per person.

La Tête de l'Art, near the British Consulate in rue Pau. Lives up to its name with elegant decor and regular exhibitions of paintings. Excellent French cuisine, good wines, friendly service. CFA15,000 a head.

Douala after dark: nightclubs

Douala's **clubs** open, close down and change hands even more frequently than restaurants and the information below will inevitably date quickly. However, as the clubs tend to be in the same area, it's easy to cruise around by taxi until you find a goood one. The driver will be able to locate the club of your (or his) choice even if it's in an apparently derelict warehouse. All the clubs open around 11pm or midnight, with the exception of *Café des Sports*, which sometimes opens at 10pm. They close when they get quiet, sometime between 3am and 5am.

Entry prices vary enormously for foreigners and locals, men and women, but once in, you rarely come under pressure to spend. Drinks cost CFA3000–5000, regardless of alcohol content, but you can nurse one for as long as you wish, or buy a bottle of whisky for about CFA12,000 to be kept for you behind the bar.

For women, alone or in groups, nightclubs are almost completely hassle free and safe. The worst that can happen is a man asking you to pretend to be his wife for the evening (or sometimes the whole night).

Safari, rue de la Motte Piquet (☎42.61.99), off rue Surcouf. Fairly up-to-date pop chart and African music. Generally quiet on weekdays. There's seating around a minuscule dance floor, barely larger than the enormous video screen and a mostly white crowd – and often very young, particularly during school vacations. Soft drinks are cheaper than shots here, so if you're staying it's a good place to buy a whole bottle of spirits.

Café des Sports (☎42.09.52, also called *Le Kontchoupé*), near the British Consulate. Chart and African music, and a tiny dance floor. As the *Café* opens around 10pm, it is used mainly by those warming up for a long night. The one place where foreign women might feel threatened by the local bar girls.

Top Ten. Up-to-date music, largely African, with a relatively large dance floor for serious movers. Spacious seating areas, and a good mix of customers.

Le "78". Douala's newest nightclub, run by ex-pats, and with a large ex-pat clientele. Modern imported light and sound systems, and mainly up-to-date Western music.

St Hilaire, rue Alfred Saker. Fairly small bar, with dancing to (not particularly up-to-date) chart music. This is something of a pick-up joint (with a gay reputation, too), and has very dark seating areas. Usually the most crowded nightspot, the last to open and the last to close.

Le Night Spot (☎42.23.03). Western and African music, small dance floor, limited seating.

Lastly, various **cabaret bars** offer live music, occasional acts, cocktails at CFA3000–5000 and a relaxed atmosphere.

Magnetic Terrace is open all day, with music 10pm–1am and a mostly Cameroonian clientele.

Café Equateur, frequented mainly by ex-pats and a well-heeled Cameroonian set, is open from 11pm until the early hours.

Pacific Pallisades is also open from 11pm.

Douala Directory

Airfreight Precious and express items can be sent and received through *DHL*, Soms Building, rue Drouot (☎42.98.82).

Banks Major branches in the Bonanjo neighbourhood: *Banque Internationale pour l'Afrique Occidentale*, av Charles de Gaulle, (☎42.80.11); *Banque des Etats de l'Afrique Centrale*, av de Gaulle (☎42.84.55); *Banque Internationale pour le Commerce et l'Industrie*, rue Kitchener (☎42.84.31); *Société Camerounaise de Banque*, rue Joss (☎42.98.60).

The best place for **changing money** is *Standard Chartered* in bd de la Liberté. Althought *BICIC* charges no commission, the *SC* has few or no queues, and always seems to have money, changed for a flat fee of CFA1130.

Car rental The major firms are at the airport and in the larger hotels: *Hertz, Sawa Novotel* (BP 2345; ☎42.99.18, telex 5532); *Avis, Hôtel Meridien* (BP3232; ☎42.61.36, Fax 42.35.07); *Locauto, Akwa Palace* (☎42.26.01); *Europcar*, bd de la Liberté across from *Akwa Palace* (☎42.18.79).

Chemists The *Pharmacie du Centre* , 38 bd de la Liberté (☎42.14.30) is well stocked and central.

Cinemas The two big AC cinemas are *Le Concorde* on rue Lapeyrère and *Le Wouri* on bd de la Liberté (☎42.19.47). Smaller movie houses showing old re-runs include *Le Douala* on rue Gallieni, *The Rex* on bd Ahidjo and *Le Toula* on rue Kitchener.

Hardware Campers, bikers, and motorists will appreciate Douala's wide selection of hardware shops. If you spend more than a couple of thousand CFA on these kind of supplies you should be able to negotiate a ten- or fifteen-percent cash discount, but even then goods aren't cheap, around twice the London price.

Libraries *Centre Culturel Français*, rue Ivy (☎42.69.96); *Centre Culturel Africain* in the college Liberman, rue des Écoles (☎42.28.90). They also have African language courses. *USIS* has closed its library in Douala.

Post office The *Poste Centrale* is near the banks in the Bonanjo neighbourhood, on the place du Gouvernement (☎42.40.25). Branches include: *Poste d'Akwa*, bd de la Liberté (☎42.25.30);

AIRLINE ADDRESSES

Most of the airlines are in the Bonanjo neighbourhood or in Akwa along bd de la Liberté.

Air Afrique, bd de la Liberté (☎42.42.22).

Aeroflot, 83 bd de la Liberté (☎42.79.91).

Alitalia, pl du Gouvernement (☎42.36.08).

British Airways, Standard Chartered building, 61 bd de la Liberté (☎42.01.47, 42.38.73).

Cameroon Airlines, 3 av de Gaulle (☎42.32.22).

Ethiopian Airlines, bd de la Liberté (☎42.47.04, 42.47.86)

Iberia, (☎42.14.50).

Lufthansa, bd de la République (☎42.57.76).

Nigeria Airways, 17 bd de la Liberté (☎42.62.34).

Sabena, 60 av de Gaulle (☎42.05.15).

Swissair, 33 bd de la Liberté (☎42.29.29).

UTA 1 place du Gouvernement (☎42.80.20).

CONSULATES

These countries maintain consular offices in Douala, with main embassies in Yaoundé:

Belgium, 13 av de la Marine, (BP 263; ☎42.47.50).

Equatorial Guinea, bd de la République (BP 5544; ☎42.26.11).

Denmark, (BP 215; ☎42.64.64).

France, rue des Cocotiers (BP 869; ☎42.62.50); francophone country visa service.

Italy, rue de l'Hôtel de Ville (☎42.36.01).

Nigeria, (BP 1553, ☎42.71.44).

Norway and Sweden (BP 320; ☎42. 02. 88).

Spain, (BP1102; ☎42. 23. 95).

United Kingdom, rue Pau (BP 1016; ☎42.21.77, 42.81.45).

USA, 21 av de Gaulle (☎42.34.34).

Poste de New Bell, av Douala Manga Bell (☎42.13.30); *Poste de Deido*, rue Dibombé (☎42.17.70).

Shipping agents *SOCOPAO*, 30 quai de Dion Bouton (☎42.64.54, telex 5319) are agents for *Grimaldi Lines*, which operates regular cargo services, with comfortable cabins, to Europe.

Stolen documents The one-legged beggar who sits outside *Monoprix* is said to be able to discover the whereabouts of any stolen passport. For a small consideration.

Supermarkets *Monoprix* and *Aux Bonnes Courses* stock French delicacies flown in regularly from Paris – lobsters, caviar, champagne, patisseries, and fresh exotic vegetables all available at something less than twice the Champs Elysées price. The *Mysan Market* supermarket has American goodies. If you're travelling north across the Sahara, and expecting to use whisky and Marlboro as hard currency, stock up at *Monoprix*. You won't find them as cheap again – if you find them at all – before Marseille.

Swimming pools Non-guests can use the pools at the *Akwa Palace* and the *Novotel* for a fee. They're both expensive, but nice and worth it when the humidity gets too much.

Tourist information The *Service Provincial du Tourisme* (☎42.14.22) is located on av de Gaulle beyond the tennis club. They have **city maps** of Douala and Yaoundé for CFA2000 and the usual pamphlets for travel in the different regions.

Travel agencies *Emil Travel* in bd de la Liberté (BP 5393; ☎42.55.59) has a reputation for reliable bookings, with telex connections throughout the country.

Others **in Akwa** include: *Jully Voyages* (BP1868, ☎42.32.09); *Camvoyages*, corner of bd de la Liberté and rue des Écoles (☎42.31.88); *Mory and Co Voyages*, rue Joffre (BP 572; ☎42.61.66, 42.04.66).

There is a further selection of travel agencies **in Bonanjo**: *Transcap Voyages*, rue de Trieste (☎42.92.91); *SATA Voyages*, rue Lugard (☎42.68.77); *SOAEM*, av de Gaulle (☎42.02.88); *Delmas Voyages*, rue Kitchener (☎42.11.84); *West African Alternatives*, *Meridien Hotel* (BP 3232; ☎ 42.46.29, Fax 42.35.07).

ONWARDS FROM DOUALA

● If you're continuing **by bush taxi**, the main motor park is the **Yabassi gare routière** at the junction of av Japoma and rue Nassif (bus #2). This *autogare* handles traffic for the west (Bafang, Bafoussam and Bamenda) and Yaoundé, Edéa and Kribi. The smaller **Deido gare routière** is near Wouri bridge (bus #6) with vehicles for Limbé and Buéa.

● Moving on **by train** on the *Transcam 1* line, the new station is in the northeast part of the city centre, off the bd de la République. Until it's finished, New Bell Station is standing in. The gare de Douala Port is closed to passengers. Enquiries to **Régiefercam**, BP 304, Douala (☎42.91.20). You can buy tickets to Yaoundé, and possibly still to Nkongsamba and Kumba.

Intercity:	**Omnibus service, all stations:**
Dep. Douala 6.15am, arr. Yaoundé 9.40am.	Dep. Douala 8.25am, arr. Yaoundé 5.50pm.
Dep. Douala 6.45pm, arr. Yaoundé 10.10pm.	
	Douala–Edéa "shuttle" service (*Navette*):
Express-Autorail, stopping service:	Dep. Douala 3.30pm, arr. Edéa 6.10pm.
Dep. Douala 1pm, arr. Yaoundé 4.55pm.	

● **By air**, *Cameroon Airlines*, 3 av de Gaulle (☎42.32.22) has flights to:

Bafoussam and Bamenda: Tues, Fri, Sun.	**Garoua:** daily.
	Ngaoundéré: daily except Sun.
Batouri and Bertoua: Mon, Thur and Fri.	**Maroua:** daily except Thur.
	Koutaba: every Sun.

● **By sea**, if you're heading back to Europe, see under *Shipping Agents* in "Directory".

Limbé

LIMBÉ, still labelled with its pre-1983 name of "Victoria" on certain maps, is everything Douala isn't – small, scenic and reposeful – with the mass of Mount Cameroon looming to the north. Limbé is the nearest settlement to Douala on the open ocean, and owes its popularity primarily to the surrounding beaches along the shore of **Ambas Bay**. There's a holiday feel to it, with historical touches added in its well-preserved German and British **colonial buildings**, the distinctive Creole elements of its **Caribbean past** and its shady **botanical gardens**. Yet despite the influx of holidaying ex-pats and weekenders, Limbé is not the expensive and overdone resort town you might expect. There's enough economic stimulus in the old **port** and the market, plus the nearby oil refinery and various agricultural projects, for the town not to rely wholly on its tourist industry, and it has retained an authentic provincial feel.

Incidentally, the Limbé area is host to a specially virulent and untreatable form of malaria. Avoid being bitten.

Accommodation

Most hotels are oriented to the affluent from Douala who flock to Limbé at weekends. But given the standards of accommodation, prices are not outrageous and even seem reasonable if you've just come from Douala. There's budget accommodation to be had alongside the pricier places.

Hôtel Atlantic Beach (BP 63; ☎33.32.32, telex 5845) is in a converted military hospital once used by the Kaiser's imperial army. Restored almost to the point of luxury, thishas AC rooms at around CFA17,000 and a sea-view restaurant in which the highlight is a CFA7000 lunch buffet, with masses of fresh and beautifully presented Cameroonian and French food. The pool is filled from the sea, and collects a fair amount of effluent from the oil wells up the coast, while the tennis courts look as though the last players used hand grenades.

Park Hotel Miramar, about 2km from the centre, is co-managed with the *Atlantic* and much cheaper. However, from its hilltop position it offers beautiful views of Ambas Bay and its islands, and also has a pool, and a good disco.

Bay Hotel, near the main roundabout in town, is also in a restored colonial building commanding spectacular views of the bay. The fully AC rooms start at CFA7000.

Victoria Guest House (BP 358; ☎33.24.46), next door to the *Bay*, offers rooms with or without AC, some S/C, starting at CFA5000.

Mansion Hotel, up on Church St, is one of the cheapest in town. Rooms with fan start at CFA2500. They're clean but rudimentary (and often rented by the hour).

Eating

Away from the more expensive European food in the hotel restaurants, there are a few good cheap places in town. Church Street has many "off licence" bars and inexpensive restaurants, among which the *Guinness Club* is a popular outdoor bar with some of the best *soya* in town – try them grilled with a coating of ground peanuts. Another casual place on Church Street is the *Café Cameroon* by the *Agip* filling station. They serve excellent avocado salads as well as more filling dishes like rice and beans, and omelettes, coffee and fresh bread make it a good breakfast stop, too. Turning left at the *Agip* station and heading down the paved road towards the ocean, you'll come to the

THE CURIOUS HISTORY OF VICTORIA

Limbé was originally created by the **London Baptist Missionary Society**, after they were chased from Fernando Po by the Spanish in the mid-1850s. The missionaries turned to **Alfred Saker** – a former navy engineer converted to missionary work – and asked him to get them a foothold on the mainland. Saker bought the lands around the **Ambas Bay** from the Isubu king, **William of Bimbia** and, in 1858 founded Victoria.

The first inhabitants of the town were mostly **freed slaves** from Jamaica, Ghana and Liberia, and converted Bakweri and Bimbia (indigenous peoples related to the Douala). From 1859, these townspeople were governed by their own tribunal, headed first by a Jamaican and then by a Sierra Leonean recaptive and Victoria was effectively an African Christian colony. At first, the town centred around the church, the school (established in 1860), and the missionary residences. But by the 1870s, English and German **commercial enterprises** – *John Holt*, the *Ambas Bay Trading Co.* and the *Woermann Co.* – had established their own set-ups alongside the church. Contrary to Saker's wishes, the site was neither turned into a British naval base, nor declared a colony of the British crown. It was left to the Baptists to administer.

British holdings in Cameroon were ceded to the Germans on May 7, 1875. Victoria however posed a special problem, as it belonged technically to the missionaries and not the crown. The problem was solved in 1887 when Presbyterian missionaries from Basle purchased the land, and incorporated it into the Kaiser's colony. The town then became an important urban centre surrounded by the industrial plantations of the **West Afrikanische Pflanzung Victoria**. By the beginning of the twentieth century, the Victoria–Buéa–Douala triangle had become the political and economic nerve centre of German *Kamerun* , and Victoria grew to become the colony's second port, exporting vast quantities of cocoa and other agricultural products. Although the Victoria territory became part of the British protectorate in 1915, German companies swiftly regained economic control of the region by buying back their old concessions.

But with the outbreak of World War II, the Germans once again saw their lands confiscated. In 1947, the British founded the **Cameroon Development Corporation**, and the vast regional plantations – dense stands of cocoa, bananas, oil palms and rubber trees still to be seen as you drive through – spurred Victoria into a new period of expansion. After independence, the CDC was partly taken over by the government, but the British government retains a commercial stake in it. It remains the region's biggest employer.

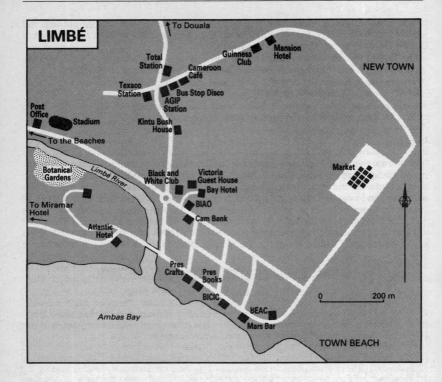

LIMBÉ

Kintu Bush House after about a hundred metres. Put together with rough planks, this has a treehouse feeling enhanced by airy windows and views over the town. You can eat cheap meals here, or simply enjoy a cool drink.

The ocean takes regular bites out of the shoreline at Limbé, nowhere more so than in the corner of the esplanade where the *Mars Bar* perches precariously at the edge of the road. For as long as the building stands they aim to continue serving snacks, meals and drinks in comfortable armchairs (chicken and chips CFA2000).

Around town

The beachfront is the obvious place to start a visit, with a main thoroughfare running along the shoreline from the **Town Beach**, and the nearby **fish market**, over to the *Atlantic*. In between are many of the town's major **banks**, and the *Prescraft* centre where you can buy regional **artwork**. Looking out over Ambas Bay from either the Town Beach or the *Hôtel Atlantic Beach*, you can see a group of small islands, the biggest of which is **Bota**. Now uninhabited, it's possible to get across to it if you can strike a deal with one of the fishermen at the port. West of the *Atlantic Beach*, an old paved road winds between the sea and rocky hills up to the *Miramar*. It's a pleasant walk along the coast, and even if you don't stay here, it makes a nice excursion with a cold drink at the bar overlooking the bay a satisfying payoff.

North of the *Atlantic Hotel*, the westbound road shooting out from the main rounda-bout leads to the **post office**, oddly remote from the centre. Across the street, the

Botanical Gardens were originally laid out by the Germans for agricultural experimentation. Now this is a big pleasure park with hundreds of varieties of trees and the **Limbé River** flowing through the middle. It makes a relaxing spot to spend an afternoon. The **main market** is in the east of town.

Along beach road

Although **Town Beach** is a convenient place to frolic in the water and catch some sun, its proximity to the port means it gets pretty dirty; and in any case it feels a little odd to disport yourself under the gaze of the fishermen. But west of Limbé, a whole string of beaches awaits. Like the one in town, they all have fine **black sand** (actually, a deep bitter-chocolate colour) – result of the ocean's grinding of ancient **lava flows** from Mount Cameroon. The combination of lush tropical vegetation with sea and mountains produces a paradisiacal landscape, often enriched with the brooding purple and yellow of an impending storm or the green and gold of a recent downpour. Furthermore, the waters around here are calm – unlike most places along the West African coast – and perfect for swimming. The beach scenes of the film *Chocolat* were shot here.

You can get **transport to the beaches** from in front of the stadium, near the post office. There's a small motor park and you can either hire a cab (roughly CFA1000) to your destination, or take a collective taxi (CFA200) with people heading to neighbouring villages along the coast. To get to the most popular beach, ask to be dropped at **Mile 6**, where a signboard points through 500m of palm groves to the sea. Mile 6 is a public beach with a guardian, so you have to pay a small entry charge to use it. The nearby oil refinery spoils the view a bit, but it's still not a bad place.

If you'd rather be watching fishing boats, you might head two miles further on to **Batoké**, a fishing village with a stunning (free) beach surrounded by mountains that drip with vegetation. If you have your own car, the paved road continues all the way to **Ideano** and passes by numerous other unspoiled beaches.

Buéa and Mount Cameroon

Once briefly the capital of *Kamerun*, BUÉA is located on the slopes of **Mount Cameroon** some 70km from Douala. Perched on the slopes more than 1000m above the ocean, the town breathes in a relatively cool climate – something the Germans were always keen to seek out during their colonial days. Like Limbé, it's a popular retreat for sagging city folk from Douala looking for calm and natural beauty.

BACKGROUND TO BUÉA

In 1895, with the arrival of colonial governor **Jesco von Puttkamer**, the Germans began establishing military outposts in their new protectorate. Buéa was one such spot, and was made capital in place of Douala from 1901 until 1909. It still has many reminders of its **colonial past**, including administrative buildings, an old school, numerous villas built on piles and a magnificent **palace** built as von Puttkamer's residence. Today this German *schloss* is used by the president – you could be arrested for taking pictures.

During British rule, Buéa was under the authority of the Lieutenant Governor of the Southern Provinces of Nigeria. On the eve of independence, the town had dwindled to 3000 inhabitants and was primarily a colonial resort. But Buéa once again found its prestige as an administrative centre when it became capital of the English-speaking West Camerooon, in the post-independence federation. Over the next ten years, it received substantial public investment in the form of government buildings and the population grew rapidly. Since then, Buéa has been demoted to capital of South West Province only, and expansion has once more given way to calm stagnation.

Accommodation

The cheapest place to stay in town is the *Hotel Mermoz*. It's looking a little shabby these days and is used a lot for carousing, but costs only CFA5000 for a S/C room. Surprisingly, the *Parliamentarian Flats* (☎32.26.46), up the hill and looking right out on the slopes of the mountain, is an only slightly more expensive address than the *Mermoz* – despite being a lot cleaner and more comfortable. The flats have a pleasant restaurant that also looks out on the mountain.

At the **top of the line** is the more atmospheric three-star *Mountain Hotel* (BP 71; ☎32.22.51) with pool, tennis court and an excellent garden restaurant. Rooms are around CFA12,000/4,000.

Climbing Mount Cameroon

Thousands of visitors over the years have used Buéa as the starting point for their ascent of the dormant volcano **Mount Cameroon**. Despite being over 4000m high, it's not an exceedingly difficult climb, and although oxygen gets noticeably thin above 3000m you don't have to be super fit to make it to the top. You do need to know, however, that it's forbidden to climb Mount Cameroon in the rainy season, so you have to plan to go during the "dry" season, roughly from November to April. If you get the chance contact the Buéa Mountain Club on ☎32.22.68.

Not surprisingly, a whole little industry has developed around the climb. Officially, you must now arrange your hike at the **tourist office** in Buéa (PO Box 92; ☎32.32.34). For CFA7000 per day, they will provide you with a guide and porter (though you have to bring your own food). It's hard to get going without a guide in any case, since the start of the trail is somewhat obscure. It takes a good ten hours or more to reach the volcanic crater, and the same to get back down, so you should allow at least two full days.

The ascent starts at **Prison Farm** (also know as Upper Farm) a couple of kilometres up the moutain behind Buéa. Along the ascent, which is mostly marked by white blazes, there are three **chalets** for sleeping: the first at an elevation of 1830m (9km from town and the only one with beds); the second at 2780m; and the third at 3950m. Fako peak itself is 4095m.

As for **equipment**, you should certainly wear hiking shoes for the steep and usually muddy paths. The sub-zero temperatures and strong winds in store on the summit mean you'll want warm waterproof clothes and something dry to change into, and don't go without a good sleeping bag. You'll also need cooking gear, food and water.

For some sense of scale, Mount Cameroon is about four times as high as Mount Snowdon and only 1000m lower than Mount Kenya. Like Kenya, despite its equatorial latitude, Mount Cameroon's highest slopes get freezing rain and occasional snow.

THE MOUNT CAMEROON RACE

Since its inception in 1973, the annual Guinness Mount Cameroon Race has achieved a reputation as one of the toughest athletic events in the world. It's held in February, with a field of about 350 runners (selected from 100 entries) slogging 27km over tortuous terrain from the jungly lower slopes up to the chilly summit. If it rains, the course becomes a slippery quagmire. Although Cameroonians dominate the competition – and the £2,000 first prize represents a small fortune here – they have been joined by an international array of athletes including Europeans and representatives of most African countries. An Englishman, Mike Short was the winner in 1989. Fifty thousand spectators watch the proceedings, with the men's winner usually completing the event in around three hours fifty minutes and the women's winner in about five hours fifty.

Kumba

The first of the major towns of western Cameroon that you come to heading north from Buéa or Douala is **KUMBA**, an agricultural and commercial centre. Although the town itself is large and uninspiring, with a population approaching 60,000, it's at least in the middle of a beautiful region. **Lake Barombi** is a picturesque crater lake just 5km out of town – a shortish walk and you're in another world.

Around town

If you find yourself terribly disorientated upon arrival in Kumba, don't worry. Low-lying houses (built of wooden planks, they look like something out of a Western movie) spread in all directions and the town has no real centre; or rather it has too many. But there's a very big **market** here, and if, like most travellers, you're only passing through, that's where you should direct your attention. With the main **motor park** next door, the market is in a modern covered building and specialises in goods imported from Nigeria (there's a large Igbo immigrant community in Kumba). East of the market, you'll find the **post office** and **banks**.

The main **administrative quarter** is located a good 4km from the market. And another centre has grown up around the **train station**.

Accommodation

As you'd expect in a busy market centre such as this, there's a host of reasonably cheap hotels. The *Hôtel Authentique* recently reopened and has clean S/C rooms and friendly staff. Hot water is the other selling point, and rooms start at CFA5000. The nearby *Star Hotel* is also nice, although its well-kept S/C rooms, with fans, are a little pricy at CFA6000. There's a couple of decent hotels behind the market – the *Western Inn* on Kramer St which has very clean S/C rooms with fans from about CFA6000 and, close by, the *Queens Inn* on Endeley St with ventilated non-S/C rooms starting at CFA3500, which isn't bad value. Over by the post office, the *Lido Hotel* is another cheap place, although its non-S/C rooms, at CFA3000, are on the squalid side. The place has a disco with occasional live music.

Lake Barombi Mbo

Lake Barombi is only an hour's walk from the main part of town, and quite close to the administrative quarter, but there are no signs marking the way and the paths that lead there are rather obscure. The best way to proceed is simply to take a taxi from town to the *gendarmerie nationale*. From here, follow the dirt road leading past the

---

THE ECOLOGY OF BAROMBI MBO

The Barombi people of the lake shores are completely dependent on the lake and seem to have lived in a harmonious symbiosis with it for hundreds of years. The fish they catch are an obscure series of small cichlid species (mouth breeding fish) called *pundu, kululu, dikume* and *pingu* – and a single type of catfish. All of them live only here, some at depths scientists haven't been able to account for in terms of normal fishy physiology. Traditional hand-woven gill-nets and basket traps select only larger fish, ensuring their continued survival. Traditionally, the Barombi took further care, by actively appeasing the lake at their Ndengo cult grove. More and more young people, though, are installing themselves down in Kumba or futher afield and leaving the old ways behind. Kumba itself is now drawing not just people but the lake's very water, piped to the town system

colonial-looking government buildings for about a kilometre. At this point, a small and inconspicuous footpath leads off to the left. If you have doubts, ask anyone for directions. Once on the path, you continue up and over the slippery hills for about another kilometre before arriving at the lake.

The dense forest of the area crowds right down the inside of the crater to the lakeshore, providing an unbelievable green backdrop. The lake – 2.5km across and 110m deep – is crystal clear and perfect for swimming. You'll see a couple of fishing boats when you arrive, and if their owners are around, they'll paddle you around the lake, or take you across it to the small village of Barombi on the other side. The price of the trip is negotiable.

North towards Nigeria

The main overland route from Cameroon to Nigeria passes through the somewhat isolated enclave of **Mamfé**, in the middle of a dense forest about 65km short of the border. Only Nigeria-bound travellers are at all likely to visit Mamfé. If you drive up from Douala, much the quickest way is via Nkongsamba and Dschang.

The direct road, via Kumba, is one of the most undriveable in Cameroon, frequently impassable even to four-wheel drive vehicles in the wet season. This road has been the focus of a surfacing project for a number of years but it may still not be finished. Meanwhile, if you can cope with its difficulties, it's quite a trip. The road passes through dense rainforest, and occasionally yields spectacular views as it detours around a mountainside. This region has its own unique flora and fauna, and the Cameroonians are making the district between the road and the Nigerian border into a national park, with British and European assistance.

Korup National Park

The **KORUP NATIONAL PARK**, which adjoins Nigeria's **Oban Rainforest National Park** (see p.1041) harbours one of the richest remaining equatorial ecosystems in Africa. The whole Korup project covers an area ten times the size of greater London, stretching across most of the area west of the Kumba–Mamfé road – but the core protected area, where no logging or agriculture is permitted, is just 1250 square kilometres. It contains one quarter of all the primate species known in Africa, including gorillas, 250 species of birds and 400 different kinds of tree. In the wild rivers flowing through the park – the **Cross**, the **Ndian** and the **Munaya** – many varieties of fish previously unknown to zoologists have recently been discovered. And new finds in natural pharmacological products are being made all the time. The governing principle of the Korup project is an innovation, but obvious enough: it is that the people of the area should be involved in all the decisions relating to its management, and that their own needs – hunting and gathering, farming and trading – should be respected as an integral part of the forest system.

Despite the wealth of wildlife, Korup only achieved the status of a national park in 1986 and, until more funds are provided, has yet to be fully developed. In the absence of decent roads through the densely foliaged landscapes, access is extremely difficult. If you're interested in visiting, the *World Wide Fund for Nature* is currently working with the Cameroonian government to turn the park into an educational and recreational area for Cameroonians and foreigners alike. For information on how to visit, contact Frances Sullivan, WFN, Weyside Park, Godalming, Surrey GU7 1XR (☎0483/426 444). If you happen to be already in Cameroon, make for the main village of MUNDEMBA – you'll soon make contacts and figure things out, though there are hardly any facilities and this isn't a national park in the routine safari sense.

Mamfé

MAMFÉ is basically a stopover point for travellers or traders, many of whom use the town as a base to unload goods they have smuggled from Nigeria on small boats brought clandestinely down the **Cross River**. The constant comings and goings add energy to the otherwise sleepy town, but makes it rather anonymous as well. This could be almost anywhere in West Africa.

Today the administrative headquarters of the Manyu district of South West Province, Mamfé (the name is a corruption of Mansfield, the settlement's first German district officer), was later part of the British Cameroons and subject to the policy of **"indirect rule"** expressed through the creation of Native Authorities. When it was administered as part of Nigeria, it was an important town. In 1959, the town hosted the **Mamfé Conference** which tried unsuccessfully to establish voting rules for the upcoming UN plebiscite. In 1961 its inhabitants voted for unification with the Cameroon Republic, since when its status has fallen.

Considering its remoteness, the town has a reasonable infrastructure – district buildings, hospital, petrol station, missions. If you've just arrived from Nigeria, you may be relieved to discover there are two **banks** here – *BICIC* and the *Bank of Cameroon* and, if you've made it this far without CFA, you can get them here. You'd do best to change travellers' cheques in French francs (or West African CFA), as the banks don't usually have current rates for dollars or pounds.

Accommodation and food

Accommodation seems pretty expensive in Mamfé, especially once you see what you actually get for your money. And fresh in from Nigeria, Cameroonian prices come as a shock. The *African City Hotel*, right near the motor park, but unmarked except for a sign reading "hotel" is one of the town's cheaper places, with clean, basic rooms (non-S/C) for CFA4000. At night, there are numerous small shacks nearby for cheap eating. The *Great Aim Hotel* is also near the motor park, with a good bar and restaurant and non-S/C ventilated rooms from CFA3000. Near the Catholic church, the much nicer *Little Paradise* has S/C rooms with fan (CFA6000). The *Inland Hotel* (☎34.11.28) is top of the line in Mamfé. Away from the centre on the route to Bamenda, it's a well-appointed colonial pile, and the pleasant garden – where you can eat or have a drink and pass the time of day with the hotel's chimpanzee – looks onto forested hills and valleys.

TO THE BORDER

Two or three hours west of Mamfé is the border town of **EKOK**. The gates on the Nigerian side close at 7pm so you have to clear Cameroon customs with ten minutes to spare unless you're willing to sleep in the muddy lorry park in no-man's-land. Otherwise, stay in Ekok – a brash, noisy place, with an authentic frontier-town feel. There are several hotels almost always full of overnighters waiting for the border. Rock music blares from every stall, kerosene lamps dazzle, and street sharks besiege you with all kinds of nefarious suggestions. Many Cameroonians visiting Nigeria come here by taxi, and the drivers hang around until 7pm or 8pm hoping for a fare back to Mamfé (costing about CFA2000).

THE BAMENDA HIGHLANDS

As you head inland, the topography of Cameroon's mountainous west is overwhelming. Landscapes range from the **volcanic hills** of the **Grassfields** to sheer cliffs with **waterfalls** and **crater lakes** hidden behind dense vegetation. This area is additionally interesting from a cultural point of view, with many of its old chiefdoms still surviving into an era when increasing agricultural prosperity has brought one of the fastest rates of development in the country. The area divides up fairly clearly into the **Bamiléké country** in the south and the **Bamoun country** in the north. There's a wealth of sights and towns in the Bamenda Highlands; it's an exhilarating area you could spend weeks, or months, exploring.

The main town in Bamiléké country – and the capital of West Province – is the rapidly growing centre of **Bafoussam**. Formerly its wealth was based on coffee production, but in recent years, industrialisation has come fast and it's not a very soulful place. Situated on a junction of good paved roads, though, it's a convenient springboard for visiting other, more characterful regional towns. **Bandjoun**, for example, retains the traditional flavour of its old chiefdom, and boasts the best preserved **palace** in the region. While **Dschang**, situated in the mountains at an elevation of 1400m, has a mild, almost European climate that's led to something of a tourist boom, focused on its luxury hotel and the cultivation of a Club-Med ambience.

In the neighbouring Bamoun country, to the north, the cultural and historical highpoint is **Foumban**, a town with a remarkable turn-of-the-century palace, notable museums and a thriving crafts industry. For all its rich past, however, Foumban takes an economic backseat to **Bamenda**, capital of North West Province. From here, you can travel around the **Ring Road** which dips and bends through the mountainous **Grassfields**, passing through a number of **Tikar chiefdoms** and Fula settlements.

Bafoussam

The **administrative capital** of the Western Province, with a population that has mushroomed in the last two decades to approach the 150,000 mark, **BAFOUSSAM** is a noisy and unwieldy centre of commercial hyperactivity. It owes its prosperity largely to **Arabica coffee**, which flourishes in the surrounding hills. **Industry**, spurred on by earnings from the coffee crop, has also made deep inroads in recent years. The *Union des Coopératives du Café de l'Ouest* set up a coffee processing plant in the 1970s and since then, a *Brasseries du Cameroun* brewery, a cigarette factory and a printing press have all gone into operation. It marks the edge of the francophone zone (the Gallic influence is fairly unmistakable if you've just arrived from "Anglo" Bamenda). Despite its traditional **chefferie**, the numerous **crafts workshops** and an ever-so-tiny **museum**, Bafoussam lacks basic appeal. Its basic homogeneity – the Bamiléké may move and trade all over the country but they never sell their land so newcomers rarely integrate – means that it doesn't have the vital mix of culture and language so common in Cameroon's livelier towns.

Staying in town

Bafoussam also lacks, surprisingly, the wide range of accommodation you might expect from a town of its size, but there are a number of **moderate hotels**, and one "luxury hotel".

Foyer Culturel Evangelique always used to put up travellers for a pittance, and claims still to do so. On the last check, however, no one could find the caretaker with the only set of keys, and the place was dirty and run-down.

Hôtel Fédéral, near the market on route de Foumban (☎44.13.74). Cleanish, non-S/C rooms start at CFA4000-odd; they've a good restaurant (meals at CFA2000) and a video bar.

Hôtel de la Mifi (☎44.11.81). Another moderate place, in the Tamdja neighbourhood across from the gendarmerie and very near the post office. Rooms start at CFA5000, and the bar and nightclub attract a younger crowd, often including overlanders.

Hôtel Continental, on route de l'Hôpital (BP 136; ☎44.11.81, 44.14.58). More expensive, but newer and more comfortable than the *Mifi*, with a good restaurant and bar.

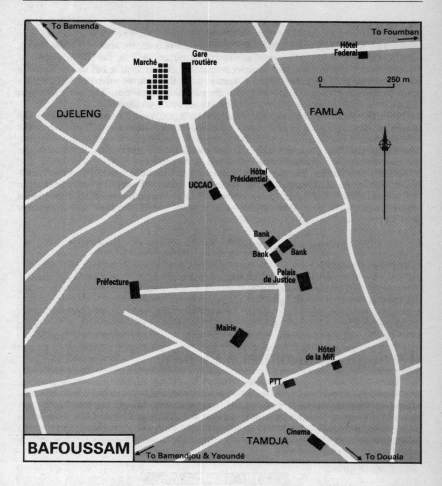

Hôtel Le Président (BP 78; ☎44.11.36). The biggest hotel in town, with AC rooms (from around CFA11,000), and a nightclub. It's not new, though, and can't really be considered luxurious anymore.

Résidence Sare Hôtel (☎44.25.99). Recently built and well-maintained chalets around a bar and restaurant complex. Hot showers and working AC in every chalet (from CFA18,000).

Restaurants

A number of **cheap eating** places line the route de Foumban near the *Hôtel Fédéral*. Try the *Relais Africain* or the *Intercontinental* for healthy portions of rice, beans and veg for not a lot. There are similar places on the streets surrounding the market. *La Tour* is a popular restaurant directly opposite the market where you can get *steack frites* type meals for around CFA2000.

Around town

Bafoussam's dual functions, administrative and commercial, are reflected in its layout. The broad avenues of the **administrative quarter**, where the **Résidence du Gouverneur**, **Préfecture**, and **Mairie** are neatly gathered on a hill in the **Tamdja neighbourhood**. The **post office** is nearby, as is the **tourist office** (☎44.11.89; it's next to the *gendarmerie nationale*) with its adjoining **museum**. The old **chiefdom** headquarters or *chefferie* is to the southeast, off the route de Douala.

From the roundabout where the Mairie stands, av Wanko heads downhill to the north, passing the *Palais de Justice* and most of the town's **banks** (you'll find the major ones including *BIAO*, *BICIC*, and *SCB* either on or around this street) as it leads to the **market**. Occupying its own small hill, the **market** (held every four days) is in the middle of the older **commercial neighbourhoods** known as Djeleng and Famla. The main **gare routière** is right alongside, ensuring a maximum amount of noise and activity. A wide range of **crafts** can be bought in the market, although it's better to head to the street in front of *Hôtel Le Président* (parallel to av Wanko). Here you'll find numerous workshops where artists carve decorative wood panels, furniture and sculptures, and it's possible to bargain directly with them.

ONWARDS FROM BAFOUSSAM

The **gare routière** is right next to the market and has bush taxis to most destinations. An exception is **Foumban**, for which taxis leave from in front of the *Shell* station down the street (it's very near the *Hôtel Fédéral*). Taxis to **Bamenda** leave from the route de Bamenda near the Catholic Cathedral.
By plane, there are flights for Douala via Yaoundé every Tues, Fri and Sun afternoon. For schedules and prices, check with *Cameroon Airlines* in town (☎44.15.03).

Through the Bamiléké Country

Starting at Bafoussam, the **Bamiléké country** is roughly a triangle, circumscribed by the road that passes through Bandjoun, Bangangté, Bafang, Dschang and Mbouda. These towns are all accessible by taxi and have **accommodation**. The area has numerous **chiefdoms** and natural sites including **crater lakes** and **waterfalls**. Tourism is quite developed – it's an important supplementary money earner in the district – which unfortunately means things are generally expensive; three-star hotels are not uncommon even in the smaller towns.

THE BAMILÉKÉ

Most populous of the Cameroon Highlanders (also called semi-Bantu, a collective term for the Bamiléké, Tikar, Bamoum and many others – peoples often associated with one another because of their similar histories and cultures) the **Bamiléké** migrated from the north in a series of migrations and settled in the plateau areas southeast of the Bamboutos Mountains probably around the early seventeenth century. The prefix Ba is a characteristic Bantu word, simply meaning "people of". They organised themselves into a multitude of chiefdoms with populations ranging upwards from fifty to 30,000. Social organisation revolved, of course, around the **chieftancy**. The chief is the titular owner of all land, dispenser of justice, and religious leader. Under these rulers comes a quite rigidly stratified hierarchy of notables, freemen and (in the past) slaves. These groups were further organised into age-grade associations and **secret societies**, most of which still operate within the limitations imposed by the Cameroonian state. Admission of fraternities is controlled by the local chiefs who are themselves heads of the societies.

Bandjoun

Twenty kilometres south of Bafoussam, **BANDJOUN** is the largest and best preserved of the Bamiléké chiefdoms. If you arrive by taxi, walk to the **chief's compound**, situated on the route de Bangangté 3km from the Hôtel de Bandjoun and the *gare routière*.

Bandjoun is the ideal place to admire traditional Bamiléké architecture at its best (see box below). Traditionally, the chief's compound was the largest in town, incorporating several huts encircled by a bamboo fence. Inside were rooms and granaries for the chief and each of his wives, who could be quite numerous. Larger public buildings used for assemblies, judicial gatherings and dispute settlements or meetings of secret societies also figured in the compound. Commonly, a large square preceded the entranceway to the "palace" and served as a market (market day in the Bamiléké country traditionally falls every eight days).

The Bandjoun chieftancy follows this basic pattern more faithfully than others in the region, where cement and corrugated metal sheeting are replacing traditional building materials. Even here, the chief lives in a **modern palace**, but the overall effect of the compound is an impressively large and harmonious ensemble of bamboo and thatch. You have to pay an entrance fee to visit the grounds, and there's a further charge if you have a camera. Included in the price of admission is a visit to the **"treasury"** where you can see the chief's collection of carved thrones, arms, pipes and other memorabilia.

The *Hôtel de Bandjoun* is near the motor park. New and very comfortable, it's also quite expensive (from around CFA10,000). If money's tight, you'll be better off staying in Bafoussam.

BAMILÉKÉ ARCHITECTURE

Characteristic Bamiléké houses consist of a square room topped with a conical roof covered with a thick layer of thatch. Although the principle seems simple enough, an elaborate framework is necessary to make the conical roof sit on square walls. These walls are built of palm fronds or bamboo filled in with mud. A circular platform is then made and set on top of the walls. Finally, a pyramid-shaped frame is constructed on top of the platform and the thatch added. The exteriors of the buildings are often decorated with bamboo and intricately carved wooden boards. There are some wonderful old photos and details in *African Traditionl Architecture*, by Susan Denyer (Heinemann 1978).

From Bangangté to Bafang

There's a direct paved road all the way from Bafoussam to **BAFANG**, but the *piste* that heads south from Bandjou to **BANGANGTÉ**, while making for a much more circuitous route to Bafang, is worth experiencing in its own right. The most spectacular stretch comes after Bangangté, as it passes over the **Bana Col**, a depression in the mountains that offers panoramic views of the Bamiléké country.

Bangangté itself is a fairly large town, with its share of administrative buildings and a wide divided avenue that leads from the préfecture down to the recent *Maison du Parti*. But there is also a **chiefdom** here that has recently been renovated. In the chief's compound, modern buildings have been replaced with traditional Bamiléké structures, and the complex promises eventually to rival that of Bandjoun. You can stay in Bangangté at the moderately expensive, partially AC, *Auberge de Ndé*. Next to the hotel there's a small **crafts centre** and the town also has a **post office** and **banks**.

The *piste* leading from Bangangté to Bafang is motorable for normal cars (taxis also ply regularly between the two towns) and passes by another traditional chiefdom, the **chefferie de Bana**, located off the main road.

Bafang

A line of small businesses at a major intersection on the Foumban–Douala road marks the centre of **Bafang**. This could be a convenient stopping point, although there's no exceptional reason to spend a long time here and **accommodation** is mostly expensive. Especially steep is the three-star *Hôtel la Falaise* (BP 143; ☎48.63.11) across from the *Palais de Justice*. It's fully AC, has a bar, restaurant and nightclub, and charges CFA15,000 for a room. The *Grand Hôtel le Paradis* (☎48.63.62) has fourteen non-AC rooms and despite being cheaper than *La Falaise*, is still overpriced. The *Auberge du Haut-Nkam* has more **moderately priced** rooms, some of which are S/C, plus a nightclub.

Around Bafang

The scenery around Bafang is striking, with numerous **waterfalls**. One of these, the **chute de la Mouenkeu**, is only a kilometre outside the town (on the Nkongsamba road). A sign points to the falls, which you can see by walking a short way into the woods.

More spectacular (and more famous) are the **Chutes d'Ekom**, 30km farther down the Nkongsamba road. The falls are not marked from the road; assuming you have your own car, you turn off the main road, heading southeast, at the sign indicating the **chefferie de Bayong**. From here, it's about 10km to the falls, though you have to walk the last bit. If you're unsure about the directions, you can ask at the village of **Ekom Nkam**; they'll know what you're looking for even before you tell them. In a beautiful forest setting, the **Nkam River** plunges dramatically 80m from the clifftop to the valley below.

From Bafang to Dschang

The paved road continues directly south from Bafang to DOUALA, though if you're travelling by taxi you may have to go to NKONGSAMBA and change vehicles there. If heading north, the quickest way to Bafoussam is via the paved road, but you can also go by way of Bangangté as just described.

Alternatively, you can go via the small town of **DSCHANG** by taking the route des Mbo which winds its way through the coffee and cocoa **plantations**. Dschang is above all a colonial town founded by the Germans in 1903. In the 1940s, Europeans forced by the war to stay in Africa all year round built an *ersatz* **vacation colony** in this region, attracted as ever by its cool climate. The resulting complex, the *Centre Climatique* (BP 40; ☎45.10.58, telex 7016), still attracts numerous tourists with its pool, tennis, volleyball and riding stables. The centre's hotel is the nicest in the region and consists of luxury bungalows in a landscaped garden, with rooms from CFA13,000/16,000. Even the smaller hotels are expensive. One of the "cheaper" ones is *Le Constellation* (BP22; 45.10.61) which sometimes has special rates on rooms in the back courtyard. Other small hotels include the *Menoua Palace* and the *Auberge de la Menoua*.

Around Dschang

Unless you too have been drawn here by the cool climate and hotels, Dschang doesn't have much to offer apart from its colourful **market**, one of the biggest in the area. But the surrounding countryside is well worth exploring if you have a car. From the place de l'Indépendance the route to **Fongo-Tongo** leads through a series of hills and valleys, passing by two waterfalls. The first, the **Cascade de Lingam**, is signposted, ten kilometres from Dschang. The more impressive **Chute de la Mamy Wata** is roughly 10km past Fongo-Tongo and is reached by a small side road that ends at the top of the falls.

Foumban

Capital of the Bamoun people and seat of their **sultan**, the town of **FOUMBAN** is charged with history and culture. You're reminded of it at every turn as you pass monuments like the outstanding **Royal Palace**, built at the beginning of the century, the **Musée des Arts et des Traditions Bamoun** or the *ateliers* of the talented **craftsmen** who churn out works in bronze, ebony and a host of other materials. These elements, have given Foumban a touristy feel uncommon in the west. You get endless offers from children who want to be your guide, shouting claims to be "sons of the sultan"; with such a prolific ruler, there may be an element of truth to many of them. There's definitely an unusual pressure to spend money at every turn – "come in to my shop, just for the pleasure of your eyes". Such an atmosphere, however, shouldn't deter you from visiting Foumban. Delving into its history and culture is a rewarding step towards an understanding of the whole region.

SOME FOUMBAN HISTORY

The Bamoun Empire dates from the eighteenth century and was founded by **Nshare Yen**, the first of seventeen kings in the present dynasty. Son of a Tikar chief, Nshare led a faction of rebels away from the main territory and settled in the eastern country known as Pa-Mbam. Here he consolidated his power and proclaimed himself king, establishing **Mfom-Ben** (whence Foumban) as his capital. The subsequent history has been carefully recorded, and, today, the accomplishments of all Nshare's successors are known in detail.

One of the most remarkable was **Mbuémbué**, a giant of a leader (he is said to have been 2.6m tall) whose first words were, "I will make the borders of the kingdom with blood and black iron; borders made with words are inevitably erased". Speaking at a normal level, his voice carried 2km, but when he shouted, he could be heard for a radius of 15km. Not surprisingly, people listened. He fortified his capital (ruins of the old walls can be seen today), withstood Fulbe (Fula) invasions and pushed back his Tikar and Bamiléké rivals, thus expanding the empire.

Of all the kings, however, the greatest was **Ibrahim Njoya** (sixteenth in the dynasty, reigning from 1895–1924) under whose rule Bamoun culture had a golden age. A remarkable figure, he masterminded numerous inventions, not the least of which was the **Bamoun alphabet** (one of only two in the whole West African region: the other was the Vai script, p.720). Shumom, the language of the Bamoun, consists largely of monosyllabic roots, so Njoya's 348 original signs were easily converted, in 1909, into a syllabary and later refined into a true alphabet.

Once the alphabet was created, Njoya founded schools throughout the kingdom to teach the new writing. He also tried, less successfully, to design a printing press, and set about recording Bamoun tradition. It is thanks to his *History and Customs of the Bamouns* that so much is known about the empire (or, to be exact, about his account of it, as related through oral tradition). Njoya also drew up a map of his kingdom, invented an electric mill and designed the outstanding **royal palace**.

Having converted to Islam he proclaimed himself Sultan of Bamoun, but with the arrival of Christian missionaries, he attempted to create a **new religion** that fused Muslim, Christian and traditional beliefs. The secular state (first colonial, later independent) tended to restrain this development, but Bamoun **court music and theatre** still reflect it and Islam, especially, is a strong influence on Bamoun sculpture. Njoya was deposed by the French in 1924, and eventually exiled to Yaoundé where he died in 1933, his pro-German views still mistrusted by the French. The present sultan is Seidou Njimoluh Njoya.

Accommodation and food

Due to the heavy tourist presence, hotels tend to be slightly expensive in Foumban – though things could be a lot worse, especially by Cameroonian standards. The *Beauregard Hotel* (☎48.21.82) is in a fantastic location on the main commercial street, near the palace, the museums and the market. They have different categories of rooms, most S/C and some with AC that are priced accordingly. They may not tell you straight away about the cheaper rooms so be sure to ask. The hotel has its own bar and restaurant. Rooms come a bit cheaper (under CFA4000) at the *Prunier Rouge* (☎48.23.52), which is located in the west near the préfecture, still within walking distance of the centre. It's an older place with considerable charm (the namesake plum tree grows through the roof of the restaurant) and friendly management, and you get picturesque views of the town from the upstairs rooms.

For **food**, apart from the hotel restaurants, you might try the *Snack Touristique*, a popular bar with terrace restaurant on the main street next to the *Beauregard*.

The sites

While the administrative quarter – with the town hall, post office, hospital and préfecture – is grouped in the west of town, the sites more likely to draw your attention are all in the centre, within walking distance of the **royal palace**. Built in 1917 by King Njoya, the old palace (the present sultan lives in a new one) is a notable architectural achievement, unique in Africa. The townspeople may tell you the king conceived his design in a dream, but he must have done some studying to enable him to combine assorted elements of German Baroque with such pure Romanesque forms. He was greatly influenced by a visit to Buéa, where he saw the German castle.

The Palace and Sultan's Museum

You approach the palace by means of a vast **courtyard** lined with *rônier* palms, tempering its blue tones with long shadows. Constructed entirely of locally made bricks, the mass is supported by strong pillars, the walls are carried by arcades and the structure embellished with balconies worked with intricately carved wood. As you enter the building, you can't help but be impressed by the grandeur of the entrance hall, the armoury and the reception hall with its ceiling supported by four majestic columns.

Tickets are on sale in the reception hall (CFA500) to visit the **Sultan's Museum**, upstairs on the first floor. A private collection of memorabilia from the long line of kings, this gives an interesting, very personal, overview of Bamoun history. Among the eclectic assortment of objects there are thrones decorated with beadwork, masks, shields and weapons made from hides and woven raffia palms, and a large collection of **sculptures**. One room contains the personal possessions of Mbuémbué – his pipe, shields, and dagger, and a calabash decorated with the jawbones of his enemies. Writings by Njoya are also on display – including the famous *History and Customs of the Bamouns* in the *Shumom* script he invented, still taught today.

The Museum of Art and Tradition

Tues–Thurs 8am–noon & 2.30–5.30pm, Sat & Sun 8am–noon & 3–6pm, closed Mon & Fri.

It's a short walk from the palace to the five small rooms of the **Musée des Arts et des Traditions Bamoun**. You enter through two ornate carved doors, and begin your visit in the **Salle Mosé Yeyap** (Mosé Yeyap was a patron of the arts at the time of Sultan Njoya, and this museum started off as his private collection). Along the walls, a series of intricately carved wooden plaques portray important events in Bamoun history. Beside these are jugs for heating palm wine, **clay masks**, and samples of natural-dyed cloth. Notice the collection of clay and bronze pipes (some up to 2m long) used by dignitaries in traditional ceremonies, as well as the **engraved gongs** which the sultan would present to military heroes. The **Salle du Guerrier** contains military relics recalling the many clashes between the Bamoun and their Bamiléké, Tikar and Fula neighbours. You'll see spears, engraved *coupe-coupes*, protective charms and a calabash decorated with a skull and jawbones that was used in victory celebrations. In the **Salle du Notable**, a carved bed and table, weapons for fighting and hunting, and riding gear evoke the lifestyle of the Bamoun elite. The **Salle du Danseur** is dedicated to music and dance, with costumes and unusual instruments including a xylophone with carved snake heads. The Sultan's **court orchestra** still play these instruments to accompany elaborate set theatrical pieces, and have toured abroad (including Britain in 1989). The final room, the **Salle de la Cuisine Bamoun**, contains cooking utensils – pottery, baskets for smoking meat, mortars – used by Bamoun women.

The attendants at both museum and palace are welcoming and helpful, not importunate but always ready to answer any questions; and happily you're positively encouraged to take photographs.

The Village des Artisans

Don't listen to the small boys in Foumban's main square, who insist that the handful of little artisan shops clustered round the palace entrance constitute the town's main craft market. In fact the real **Village des Artisans**, a major distribution centre for crafts and antiques from all over Cameroon and neighbouring countries, is about 2km away. Go east for five hundred metres down the Bafoussam road, and turn left at the roughly scrawled signpost. At the bottom of a hill the road forks to the right. Each of the twenty or thirty houses lining the short road up to the village square is a workshop, where you can watch craftsmen from all over the country casting and beating metals, and carving kola wood, mahogany and, at the time of this reseach, ivory.

The biggest range of artefacts is in Ndam Ismaila's *Galerie Prince*, at the top of the hill on the left as the street widens. Don't bother with the "Exhibition Centre" in the square, which asks CFA200 to look at items you can see for free down the road.

Some of the finished artefacts are bright and new-looking, some tarnished to suit European tastes for elusive "authenticity", but there's little attempt to fool you that you are buying a valuable antique when you can see identical items being manufactured alongside. Nevertheless, some shops do also sell genuine antiques, mainly smuggled from Nigeria, and you need some expertise or wit to tell the difference.

HINTS ON BUYING

The diversity of buyers who come to the Village des Artisans is such that the sellers have little idea of what prices they can get away with. An item which might sell for CFA1000 to a dealer from Douala could equally be bought for a hundred times that by an American tourist. The mainly Muslim dealers will be happy to discuss prices for an hour or three, usually in French, which is the only European tongue spoken by most artisans. The exchange of courtesies is an integral part of the process; offer a coke or a cigarette to help the process. Anything you can to do to give the impression that you're not just an ignorant foreign sucker is worth trying; local knowledge, or signs of a long-term stay such as local car number-plates, will be noted and respected. What you're hoping to achieve is to pay the *prix de brousse* – the bush, or local, price. While it's a mistake to imagine you're doing the local economy a favour by paying more than the lowest price acceptable – it's a free market and local inflation can be very damaging – still, the bottom line on buying, has to be that if you like something, and can afford it, buy it for its intrinsic beauty and the hours of skilled craftmanship it represents; not because you hope to flog it at home for ten times the price.

ONWARDS FROM FOUMBAN

From the main **motor park** next to the market, vehicles head to Kumbo, Nkongsamba, Bafoussam and Bamenda. Although the route looks direct enough **to Ngaoundéré** and the north, there's no direct transport and you will have to count on two or three days of travel to get there from Foumban. To do so, first take a taxi to **Banyo**. If you miss the afternoon's taxi from here to **Tibati** you will have to spend the night (Banyo has a couple of CFA3000 hotels near the market). From Tibati, get another taxi to **Ngaoundal** (paved road at last), and from Ngaoundal, trains run to **Ngaoundéré** twice daily.

Bamenda and around

BAMENDA, capital of North West Province, is really two towns – one administrative and the other commercial – separated by a steep scarp. The **government buildings** perch high on the clifftop in a neighbourhood known as **Upper Station** (or Supply Station). With its sweeping views and cooler air, this used to be a spot favoured by the Germans and British, and even today it remains a high-class **residential area**, the stomping ground of ex-pats, civil servants and the local business elite. Arriving from the cities of the south in this part of town, as you do, Bamenda seems to be nodding off, almost suburban. From Upper Station, a tortuous road – carved out by the Germans at the beginning of the century – snakes its reluctant way to the hot valley, 300m below and the main motor parks.

Downtown Bamenda is a vast conglomeration of small businesses and working neighbourhoods and it's here that most of the town's life happens. A mid-morning stroll down Commercial Avenue, with its dual carriageway of ateliers and ghetto blasters, is as fit an introduction to the real heart of town as any. Two things stand out, apart from the glorious pines-and-bananas scenery; an excellent **handicrafts** reputation and some wild **nightclubs**.

Around town

Commercial Avenue, the main street downtown, is a good place to get your bearings. The **tourist office**, at the extreme north of this thoroughfare, may be able to provide you with a town map and some ideas for local excursions. They organise some regional tours themselves. All the major **banks** – *BIAO, BICIC, SGBC* – line this road and will change travellers' cheques or cash without demur. Moving to the southern end of the street, the **Main Market** is one of the biggest in the west and offers cheap deals on goods smuggled in from Nigeria – nice for you, tough on Nigeria. Local crafts are also sold here, but before you get into bargaining mode you may want to check out the **Prescraft centre** next door(Mon–Fri 8am–noon, 2.30–5pm, Sat 8am–1pm). There, you'll find a good selection of fixed price bronzes, carvings and basketwork. Another crafts centre is located in the eastern end of town, along the road that climbs to Upper Station and the popular *Skyline* **terrace restaurant**. It's worth going to Upper Station just for the views – early in the day the valley can be smothered in mist, the conifers poking though like a northern winter scene. But while you're up here, ask around for the **Atanga Museum**.

Accommodation, food and fun

Bamenda offers every imaginable description of lodging, from mission dorms and cheery brothels to luxury hotels, so it's a good base for trips out to nearby districts. Whatever your budget, you'll find suitable sleeping quarters.

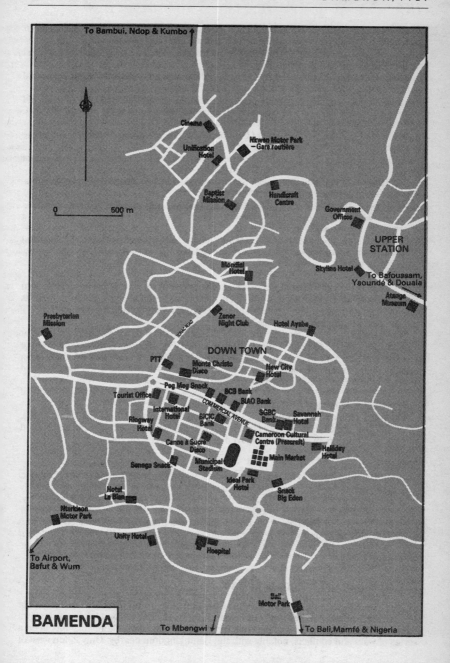

To Bambui, Ndop & Kumbo ↑

0   500 m

Cinema

Unification Hotel

Nkwen Motor Park – Gare routière

Baptist Mission

Handicraft Centre

Government Offices

UPPER STATION

Mondial Hotel

Skyline Hotel

To Bafoussam, Yaoundé & Douala

Atange Museum

Presbyterian Mission

Zenor Night Club

Hotel Ayaba

DOWN TOWN

PTT

Monte Christo Disco

New City Hotel

Peg Meg Snack

Tourist Office

BCB Bank

BIAO Bank

International Hotel

COMMERCIAL AVENUE

SGBC Bank

Savannah Hotel

Ringway Hotel

BICIC Bank

Cameroon Cultural Centre (Prescraft)

Canne a Sucre Disco

Holiday Hotel

Senega Snack

Main Market

Municipal Stadium

Ideal Park Hotel

Snack Big Eden

Hotel La Bien

Ntarkison Motor Park

Unity Hotel

To Airport, Bafut & Wum

Hospital

Bali Motor Park

BAMENDA

To Mbengwi ↓

To Bali, Mamfé & Nigeria ↓

Presbyterian Mission, in the north of town, has dorm rooms with beds (and clean sheets) for around CFA2000. It's well kept and friendly, but a bit far from the centre.

Baptist Mission, more central, at the foot of the road leading down from Upper Station, has similar, slightly pricier accommodation.

International Hotel, Commercial Ave, very near the tourist office, is both extremely central and reasonable, with rooms starting around CFA6000.

Ringway Hotel, four streets south of Commercial Ave (BP 126; ☎36.12.98), is an old standby, perhaps a bit expensive considering its age and wear – but no less friendly for that, with a good restaurant.

Halliday Hotel, at the southern end of Commercial Ave, is in the same price bracket as the *International*, though standards are slightly inferior.

New City Hotel, also near Commercial Avenue (about 100m east of the stadium), is one of the cheapest in the centre – a choice of rooms, some S/C.

Ayaba Hotel (BP 315; ☎36.13.21, telex 5387) is central, modern and comfortable, presumably the one you'd choose on an expense acccount.

Skyline Hotel (BP 11; ☎36.12.89), Upper Station. The tremendous cliff-edge perch overlooking downtown Bamenda, makes it the favourite luxury hotel. Rooms start at 15,000; there's a swimming pool and a really good restaurant.

A mixed bag of others includes, from north to south, the **Unification Hotel**, the **Mondial** (☎36.18.32), the **Ideal Park** (☎36.11.66), **Hôtel Le Bien** (BP 69; ☎36.12.06), and the **Unity**.

Eating

Street eating is good in Bamenda. Besides the **finger food** like *soya* and grilled corn cobs available all around town, more solid meals can be had at any of the numerous **roadside restaurants**. The heaviest concentration is along Sonac Rd between the PTT and the *Zenor* nightclub.

Several slightly more formal sitdown restaurants offer more westernised fare at **reasonable** rates. Among the most popular is the *Peg Meg*, on Commercial Avenue across from *Cambank*. They do salads, fish, steak and chips (around CFA1500) in an upstairs dining room overlooking the busiest street in town. For the best chicken, head to the *Ringway Hotel*'s small restaurant. The *Snack Concorde* near the *Roxy Cinema* is a good place for salads and the like, while *Senega Snack*, five blocks south of Commercial Avenue, features very good fish dishes.

The **high class restaurants** are in the big hotels. For good food and atmosphere, you can't beat the *Skyline* in Upper Station, a taxi ride from downtown. European food and the best burgers in town, best enjoyed in the garden restaurant.

Nightlife

Clubs in Bamenda tend to be expensive and they're all noisy, but they're very popular. The *Zenor Nightclub* on Sonac Rd, for example, is an underground affair, deafeningly loud and over-priced, but it still packs them in and you can't fault it for low energy. Near the municipal stadium, *Canne à Sucre* is another popular place, with a much older clientèle. The *Ayaba Hotel* also has a nightclub where the point is to be seen spending money lavishly on young women (or have money spent on yourself). The *International Hotel* and the *Ideal Park Hotel* attract a younger crowd for a less expensive, less pretentious night out.

A side trip to the Kingdom of Bali

Of the region's main chiefdoms – **Bafut, Bali and Nso** – only **BALI** is not accessible by the Ring Road. A **Chamba settlement**, (the Chamba are part of the Adamawa linguistic grouping) it was founded relatively late, around 1830. Its history has been a series of wars and conflicts, notably with the Bafut kingdom nearby. Only 20km west of

Bamenda by taxi, Bali makes for a satisfying excursion, offering the opportunity to visit not only the **Fon's palace**, but also the town's **crafts centre**. A good many of the artefacts sold in Bamenda (notably those at *Prescraft*) are made in Bali; the difference is that here you get to see the artists at work. Prices may be no less.

Lake Awing

Another possible excursion from Bamenda is to **Lake Awing**, a crater lake very similar to Lake Nyos (the lake which erupted with devastating effect in 1986 – see p.1098). Just before (north of) SANTA on the N6 Douala/Yaoundé road, a signpost to the west points to a forestry reserve open to the public. Bamenda ex-pats come here to swim, and Cameroonians to fish, although many prefer to steer clear of it altogether. In the evening you can see will-o'-the-wisps rising from the water – miniature eruptions of methane, or possibley the still unidentified gas of Lake Nyos. By day the lake is often mirror smooth, and shows a perfect reflection of the surrounding woods. Climb for about an hour up the adjoining peak and you can take in a view of the Bamenda plateau, and of other crater lakes in various stages of geological formation.

ONWARDS FROM BAMENDA

Three **motor parks** service Bamenda. The biggest is *Nkwen Park* where you get vehicles to Yaoundé, Bafoussam and Douala. In the northwest of town, *Ntarikon Park* is the place to get transport to Mankon, Bafut and Wum and where to start if you're continuing around the **Ring Road**. Finally, *Bali Park* has vehicles for Bali, Batibo and Mamfé, en route to Nigeria.

The small **airport** at Bali connects Bamenda to **Yaoundé** and on to **Douala** on Tues, Fri and Sun afternoons. One-ways to either are around CFA14,500. For more information, contact *Cameroon Airlines*, FONADER Building, Sonac Rd, Bamenda (☎36.11.62, telex 5052).

The Ring Road

The **RING ROAD** circles around 360km of difficult red earth road – in the rainy season a vicious streak of orange mud and rocks inadvisable in anything but four-wheel-drive vehicles and tough-going even then – through some of the finest scenery in Africa. Despite the demanding road conditions (and the road is currently being surfaced; a job which may take several more years), this is a highly recommended route, bucking and swerving through the verdant pasturelands of the **Grassfields**. Not that these are rolling savannahs – for the most part the Grassfields are just that – hilly meadows of rank herbage between stands of hardwood forest and patches of shifting agriculture. Natural sites in the region include the thundering **Menchum Falls**, a number of volcanoes such as **Mount Oku** (3008m) and nearly forty clear **crater lakes**, many of them sacred, and at least one of them (Nyos) off-limits and dangerous. Terraced farmlands defy the steep slopes; the mountain soils, ploughed along the contours, sustain crops like cocoyams, maize and plantains. Cash crops such as coffee grow at higher altitudes. **Fula herders** roam the pastures to graze their cattle.

The best way to tour the Ring Road is by car – a possibility that allows you the freedom to stop between the route's main centres; **Bamenda**, **Wum**, **Nkambé** and **Kumbo**. These last three are all accessible by bush taxi from Bamenda and in Wum and Kumbo you can be sure of accommodation. But many of the most interesting sites outlined below are off the main road and you'll have to forego them if travelling by what little public transport creeps around the ring. Using bush taxis also means it's very difficult to camp as you travel; camping in the countryside – when you can find a flat space – is one of the Ring Road's greatest pleasures. Should you choose to **cycle** some of the way round, beware that any rain will stop your machine dead in its tracks, horribly clogged with mud. In dry conditions, though, this is outstanding mountain-bike territory. However you go, try to have a larger scale **map** than the Michelin; there's a certain frustration in trying to follow a twisting, village-spotted route at 40km to 1cm. It's also a good idea to bring some Dutch *Key Schnapps* or even just a stash of *Becks Beers*, available in Bamenda, to present to the kings, or fons, if you visit any of the palaces in the various chiefdoms.

Bafut

The first stop along the Ring Road, heading in a clockwise direction from Bamenda, is the chiefdom of **BAFUT**, which acquired a little international fame in the 1950s and 1960s as the site of two animal-collecting trips by naturalist, Gerald Durrell. His account of the first, *The Bafut Beagles* (a reference to the team of hunters he assembled) makes amusing reading, though Bafut today feels a far cry from those slightly mythologised days of Assistant District Commissioners and pink gins.

Bafut is a **Tikar community** – people who migrated to Bafut from the northern regions of Lake Chad. It's the most powerful of the traditional kingdoms in the Grassfields, divided into 26 **wards** along a ten-kilometre stretch of the Ring Road that trails along a ridge above the Menchum valley (more than one map puts the road on the west side of the valley, instead of the east side as is the case). The current fon – **Abumbi II** – is a Paramount fon, titular overlord of a large number of lesser fons in the region. Still in his early thirties, Abumbi was chosen from his father's 100-odd offspring to ascend to the throne when the aged fon died in 1971. Although he was educated in Yaoundé, he was allowed to succeed his father – in theory on pain of death if he broke local tradition. In **religion**, although the Tikar have long been dominated by intrusive Fula Muslims, and thus heavily Islamised themselves, they've also (perhaps not coincidentally) been the subjects of intense Presbyterian missionary work, so you'll meet a fair few intense Christians too.

Taxis from Bamenda cost CFA400 for the sixteen-kilometre trip. There's no accommodation, but you could go for the day and return to Bamenda.

Exploring Bafut

Unless you do get transport here, the centre of Bafut can seem elusive. It's at the southern end of the "town" that Bafut spreads into something more than roadside compounds. The main attraction is the **Fon's palace**, a large complex laid out in a quiet pattern of dark interiors and bright courtyards. The fon himself lives in a large villa overlooking the grounds. The most sacred building in the complex is the **Achum,** the previous fon's palace, with its striking, pyramidal thatched roof. Dedicated to the ancestors, only the fon and other notables are allowed to enter this shrine. A visit to the royal compound and grounds costs CFA1000.

Bafut also boasts the liveliest **market** in the Grassfields and people come from all over the region for its selection of fruits, vegetables, spices, meat and animals. Hard by the market lives a local celebrity, Peter Fu, the **snake charmer**. A magician of sorts, Peter has no fear of serpents, holding cobras and green mambas in his bare hands and keeping a wide variety in cages in his home. He's been bitten so many times (scars cover his arms and legs) that he claims he's now immune to the strongest venom. He is highly respected in the community for his power over the reptiles, and you're in for a memorable experience if you get to meet him.

More dependable, however, is the yearly **grass-gathering ceremony**, still performed much as it was in the 1950s when described by Durrell. The entire community goes into the grasslands at the end of the dry season, to collect bundles for rethatching the Achum and other important buildings. They troop before the fon with their offerings. It's a confirmation of community spirit and always ends with tremendous eating and drinking. Huge quantities of palm wine – *mimbo* – are consumed.

Wum and around

The next significant town along the Ring Road is **Wum**. Travelling onwards from Bafut, the vegetation grows increasingly dense as the road follows the course of the **Menchum**. About 20km before Wum, the **Menchum Falls** plunge spectacularly down a rocky cliffside, but they're set slightly off the road (on the west side) and you could easily pass right by without noticing them. If you have your own car, start looking out about 30km north of Bafut and listen for the thundering sound of falling water. At the exact spot, you'll probably see tyre marks where cars have pulled off the road. There are mercifully no "tourist facilities" of any kind here, nor anything to stop you boulder hopping across the river in the dry season – except common sense; a French woman was swept over the edge in 1990 doing just this.

When you get to **WUM**, the staff at the **tourist office** have little information (in fact they barely seem to know the area), but they're eager to help and should develop more expertise as people call. **Hotels** in town, in roughly ascending order of price, include the tumultuous *Happy Day Lodge* near *Ambassador Books*, the *Lake Nyos City Hotel*; and the new, well-maintained, *Gay Lodge* at the entrance to town. Rooms range from CFA3000–5000. These hotels have no **restaurants**, but you can usually arrange to have food prepared for you. Don't leave Wum without eating at the *Peace, Unity and Hygienic* restarant. If it's gone, the *New Deal* near *Ambassador Books* is a popular "off-licence" where you can also buy food.

Three kilometres from the town centre, **Lake Wum** is a beautiful crater lake nestled in the hills, which are patchily cultivated from the peaks right down to the water's edge. Fula herders graze their cattle in the open fields and bring them down to the lake to drink. The banks are a bit muddy but you can swim here; the cool, green waters are immensely deep. Just outside Wum on the road to We, you can catch a glimpse of **Lake Nyos** by climbing a high hill to the east.

Wum to Nkambé: the highlights

Northeast of Wum, the Ring Road branches at **WE** (last chance until Nkambé of pumped water, market produce and chop-house food). If you head to the right (south), you get back to Bamenda via the "small ring road" and the town of FUNDONG. The left branch continues on to the wildest stretch of the road which switchbacks up from We into a broad valley.

Up here, the population drops right away, and, if you're travelling under your own steam, you can go for kilometres without seeing a soul. The landscapes are astonishingly beautiful, though at their pristine best when the **rains** have started in April. At this time, when the region is so inaccessible, there are vistas of startling colour, complexity and dimension in every direction; before an afternoon cloudburst, great swathes of reflected, glistening light bounce off the scenery in a gigantic celestial performance; the land stirs from heavy torpor to meet the deluge and clouds become magnificent, solid creations of sculpted mist like slow-moving, shadowy meteorites blowing through the sky.

You won't notice many villages along this part, but will understand fully why the area has acquired the name Grassfields. Frequent burning on the slopes favours the growth of grass over shrubs and bushes. It makes for excellent grazing and you're likely to see more Fula and their cattle along this stretch.

A baleful interlude: Lake Nyos

The dead village of **NYOS** is on the Ring Road about 20km from We (not, as marked on some maps, south of the road). The notorious **Lake Nyos** itself is a couple of kilo-metres south. Nyos is a deep, crater lake, now in a Restricted Zone, understandably out of bounds since the gas eruption on August 21, 1986 which killed up to 3000 people enveloped in a cloud of suffocating gas – probably carbon dioxide – that poured off its surface downhill to the west, and was blown north to Su-bum. The cause of the disaster is still unknown. There were no indications of a volcanic eruption and some scientists have postulated a weird reaction between warm and cold waters in the lake depths. But some victims appeared to have suffered chemical burns – and volcanic sulphur seems the most likely cause. Whatever the geo-chemical explanation, the people of the area suffered their worst disaster in passed-down history. The crater lakes are supposed to be the homes of the spirits of the fons.

SU-BUM (Soumbon) – a scattering of houses and smoke-stained compounds looped along the valley about 20km from We – is now the only settlement of any size in the area. It too suffered a number of casualties from the gas disaster. More happily it boasts quite spectacular avocadoes.

The north of the Ring Road

Some 60km from We, you enter the **Kimbi River Game Reserve**, which straddles the road, marked by a large signboard. The most abundant animals here are said to be **waterbuck and buffalo**, though one night camped in the reserve revealed only a lone and disoriented kob antelope crossing the road. The few **leopards** that still roam the wilds here are now exceptionally rare, and you've no chance of spotting one. There's a **rest house** of doubtful standard in the reserve (CFA1000), but you have to have your own 4WD transport to head out in search of the fauna. Ask at the tourist office in Wum.

Seventy-four kilometres from We at **MSENJE**, (small, pleasant market and village square, seemingly no rooms), a branch road heads north to DUMBO (17km) and the start of an exceptional trekking route – strictly foot traffic only – into Nigeria, covered on p.1050. Customs and immigration are in Dumbo, and may need gentle handling.

Nkambé to Kumbo

NKAMBÉ itself is a large town by Grassfield standards, with petrol stations and numerous eating and drinking houses. Beyond, the route continues south and south-east at an altitude of between 1500 and 2000m and soon becomes more densely popu-lated again. Among the settlements through which it passes is the chiefdom of **MBOT**, which has its own fon and palace. **NDU**, a couple of kilometres further, is the site of Cameroon's largest tea plantation, an enterprise begun by the British in the 1950s. A rough road leads east from here to SABONGARI, whence some sort of track allegedly connects with GEMBU in Nigeria. Don't count on it being motorable or negotiable by any kind of vehicle.

Kumbo and the Nso

KUMBO stands on a plateau 2000m above sea level. One of the biggest towns in the Grassfields, it has no shortage of accommodation, banks and other attributes, including two of the best hospitals in the region. But it's also the seat of another powerful **chief-dom** – as important as those of Bali and Bafut. Kumbo is in the heart of the Nso-speaking (the language is "Lamnso") region of Bui and the fon here lives in a **palace** with both old and new sections (the latter with a decidedly Muslim flavour, witness his recent conversion to Islam). Though predominantly now a Catholic commu-nity, the Nso are traditionalists. Don't offer traditional office-holders your hand when greeting, nor drink in their presence, nor pass the traditional policeman (the *Ngwerong*) on his left. The Nso were defeated by the Germans in 1906, and their fon executed in Bamenda – bitter history with which they have never been completely reconciled

There's a large **market** in Kumbo, and, every eight days, an animal market. *Guinness* has recently started sponsoring an annual **horse race**. Fula from throughout North West Province assemble here for the event, which usually takes place in November – the Nso Cultural Week. If you can plan it right, it's exhilarating to watch their daredevil bareback ride through the streets. On a slightly more off-beat note, but just as interesting, there's a cave about a half-kilometre east of Kumbo which is the resting place of a number of old skulls from long-ago traditional feuds. Find someone to take you.

As for **accommodation**, the bottom line is the *Baptist Mission Catering Rest House*, which puts up travellers for a small fee. Inexpensive hotels include the *Travellers Lodge* near the cathedral, and the *Merryland Hotel*. The *Bonni Hotel* and the *Tourist Home Hotel* (☎48.12.02) are just a little more expensive.

A side trip to Oku

From Kumbo, you can deviate off the Ring Road to visit **OKU**, a traditional village high on the mountain of the same name. There is a motorable road to the village, but it's a difficult climb to Mount Oku's summit, where you'll find pasturelands and a spectacular crater lake about 3000m up. For the sake of protocol, you should ask the fon's permission before setting out to **Lake Oku** (which in any case is not accessible by car, and is most easily found with the help of a guide). To do so, go to the **fon's palace** at the far end of town, with its myriad of huts, many decorated with carved posts representing symbolic leopards, chameleons and soldiers. Here you will be given permission to see the lake and someone may well be assigned to lead you there. Lake Oku is sacred and tradition forbids fishing and swimming, though exceptions are sometimes made for foreigners. There's a very uninviting "tourist chalet" up here, though no good reason to stay in it. Below, the lake is a deep green pool, perhaps 2km wide and several long, encircled by splendid, dark rainforest. The area has a diverse avifauna and in the **Kilum Mountain Forest Project** you may see the very local and unmistakeably red-headed **Bannerman's Touraco** and the rare **Banded Wattle-Eye**.

Kumbo to Bamenda

The stretch from Kumbo to Bamenda is the most populated district along the Ring Road. South to **JAKIRI** it affords panoramic views of the **Ndop Plains** that stretch out to the east, forming a bed for the vast waters of the dam lake, **Lake Bamendjing**. You'll notice many **crafts** being sold along the roadside around here, including baskets sold by an old blind man, Waïnama. Other stands sell carved calabashes and root figures. There's a small *Auberge* in Jakiri if you want to spend the night: a spectacular range of hills rears up near the town. This was the headquarters of British troops from 1958–61 when South Cameroons was on the verge of independence.

From here, you can branch off on a direct road, 75km southeast to FOUMBAN (see p.1123) although it's usually quicker to reach this town by returning to Bamenda and going via tarmac and BAFOUSSAM on the N6. The main Ring Road continues on through **Ndop** and **Bambui** whence it's a twelve-kilometre hop back to Bamenda.

YAOUNDÉ AND THE SOUTH

As the capital of Cameroon, **Yaoundé** (the name is a corruption of *Ewondo*, the local language) has been consciously developed as a showcase, but remains essentially a shanty town interspersed with prestige buildings, not all of them finished. Still, all the recent building does give the place a modern air; the feel of the place is a lot more tolerable than fetid Douala; you'll find most of the facilities you need; and mercifully the population remains comparatively low.

Only a few hours away to the southwest (on a good day), spectacular **beaches** dot the Atlantic coastline between the fishing village of **Londji** and **Campo**, on the border of Equatorial Guinea. In between, the nation's second port, **Kribi**, has become something of a holiday centre where the well-to-do from the capital head for the weekend.

Thick rainforest covers the southern interior and there are few decent roads, making travel difficult. Even with determination and time, you could only begin to explore the incredible forests, by heading out from towns like **Ebolowa** or **Mbalmayo** as bases.

Yaoundé

Comparisons between the rival cities of **YAOUNDÉ** and Douala are inevitable; most visitors prefer Yaoundé. It lies amid magnificent natural surroundings, heavy with green vegetation, and with a range of peaks, including **Mont Fébé**, as a backdrop. At an altitude of some 700m, it also enjoys a cooler climate. The city's man-made attributes add to the overall visual effect. New buildings, especially in the administrative quarter, give at least a superficial feeling of upward momentum lacking in Douala. Yaoundé thus feels the part of a **capital city**, but what it's gained in credibility, it has perhaps lost in colour and spontaneity; somehow it all seems a bit stiff. Since 1989, too, there have been chronic **water problems**, with supplies on a rota basis around the city districts five days in every week. The situation seems to be getting worse.

> ### YAOUNDÉ HISTORY
>
> The site was originally founded by the **Ewondo**, whose history has them crossing the **Sanaga River** on the back of a giant snake before settling on the hilltops of the site of present-day Yaoundé. When the **Germans** criss-crossed the country at the end of the nineteenth century, setting up military posts to affirm their influence in the new protectorate, they established a small presence here. The first commercial enterprises followed in 1907. After World War I, the French chose the budding settlement as capital of what was now their territory; the British had claims to the former capital, Buéa, so Yaoundé became the administrative centre more or less by default. It has continued in that role ever since (except for a brief period during World War II), although its population and industry remain far behind Douala's.

Arrival and Getting Around

The most likely place to arrive by **road** in Yaoundé is the *SOTUC* **bus station** and main *autogare*, on Boulevard de l'OCAM about 100m south of the city's main square, place Ahmadou Ahidjo. This throws you right into the heart of things, and is the central focus of an excellent local bus system; every bit as good as the one in Douala, it can get you all about town, except the furthest points, like Mont Fébé, for very little money. Buses run from 6am to 9pm. Only if you come in from West or North West Province – Bafoussam, Foumban and Bamenda – may you find yourself dropped off further out; these vehicles tend to stop at the **Messa bus station** near the Messa market.

Arriving by rail, the **railway station**, just off place Elig-Essono, is about a kilometre north of place Ahidjo. Ideally, you should have a clear idea of where you want to stay; several of the cheaper accommodation options are located north of the station, away from the centre.

The **airport** (no international flights at present) is roughly 3km south of place Ahidjo down Boulevard de l'OCAM.

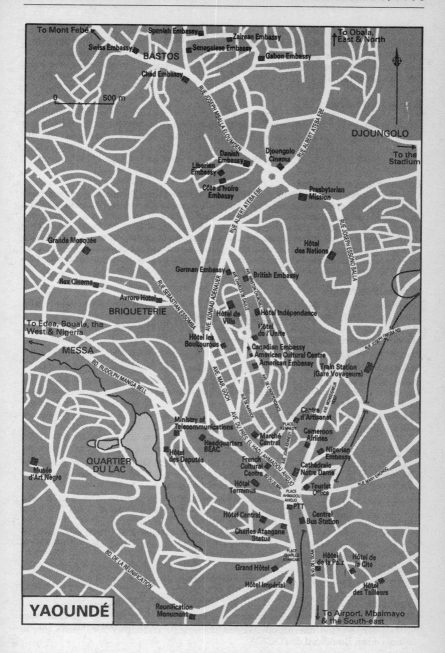

YAOUNDÉ

Unless you have transport or a healthy budget, you'll probably find yourself dependent on the buses for the time you're in Yaoundé. With its undulating hills spreading
over an area of some eight kilometres by five, it's not an easy town to get around on
foot. Sinuous roads convulse up, over and all around; straight streets and square junctions are exceptional.

Accommodation

While Yaoundé has the **luxury hotels** you'd expect in a capital city, it's also got a
reasonable network of moderate accommodation. Small hotels here are about half the
price of those in Douala. If you're on a budget, but can't get a bed in the excellent
mission, you still have a pretty good selection of inexpensive lodgings to fall back on.

Bottom bracket lodgings

The cheapest place to stay is the **Presbyterian Mission** in the Djoungolo neighbourhood
(take bus #4 to the terminus at rue Albert Ateba Ebe roundabout, and walk 200m uphill to the
east). They have a colonial-style guesthouse with individual or shared rooms. Missionaries
get first crack and so the place is often full. Rooms (starting at CFA2500) are clean and the
staff friendly. If you're utterly broke, it's also worth trying the **Centre Jean XXIII**, Mission
Mvolye (*La Source*), a Catholic mission on the south side of the city (follow the road past the
Hôtel Impérial then climb to the right) where you may still be able to sleep in the dorm of the
old *SEPAC* building for CFA500 or something – shower and toilets nearby.

Inexpensive hotels

Hôtel des Nations, directly behind the Presbyterian Mission, off rue Joseph Essono Balla.
Offers rudimentary but well-kept rooms starting at CFA4000.

Hôtel Idéal, rue Albert Ateba Ebe roundabout (☎22.03.04). The *Idéal* has a large selection
of rooms. It is clean and friendly, and, conveniently, both #2 and #4 bus lines stop in front.

Aurore, rue Sebastian Essomba (BP 152; ☎23.08.06), is another relatively cheap place.

● A number of slightly pricier places are in the south of town near the *SOTUC* bus station.

Hôtel de la Paix, off bd de l'OCAM (BP 106; ☎23.32.73) lacks basic comfort and won't win
any hygiene awards, but it's in a good location near place Ahidjo, and with rooms at
CFA4000, it's very affordable.

Casino, off bd de l'OCAM (BP 246; ☎22.22.03).

Hôtel Tailleur, place Nkondongo (BP 576; ☎22.41.00).

Moderate

Hôtel de l'Unité, place de l'Indépendance (BP 1034; ☎23.18.26). Ideally located near the
Hôtel de Ville for exploring the commercial district on foot. Rooms with fans cost about
CFA8000. It has a good, rather expensive garden restaurant.

Hôtel Impérial, av Charles Atangana (BP 977; ☎22.35.66). A charming older hotel, popular
among overlanders, especially Germans. Nostalgic rooms with AC start at CFA12,000. It has
a good restaurant and bar on the outdoor terrace.

Hôtel Le Progrès, rue Nana Tchakounté near the Messa market (BP 1005; ☎22.49.06), far
from the centre in the lively Messa neighbourhood. It has a good reputation with comfortable AC rooms (starting at CFA12,000) and friendly service.

Grand Hôtel, bd de la Réunification (☎23.04.77). Another hotel dating from the colonial era,
the *Grand* was recently restored. S/C rooms with fans or AC start at CFA14,000.

Expensive

Hôtel des Députés in the administrative quarter near the lake (BP 24; ☎22.49.65, telex
8341). A bland modern hotel with AC rooms (around CFA20,000); bar and restaurant too.

Hôtel Les Boukarous, rue Narvick (BP 1295; ☎22.47.48). A nice garden hotel in the quiet Lake Quarter, the *Boukarous* has AC rooms for around CFA17,000. Pleasant outdoor restaurant.

Indépendance Hôtel, av Winston Churchill (BP 474; ☎23.32.65). Very good hotel in a central location with forty AC rooms. The bar and restaurant get lots of praise.

Sofitel Mont Fébé (BP 711; ☎23.01.07, 23.40.02, telex 8263). This is the city's most expensive five-star place (CFA28,000 and upwards). It has a swimming pool, 18-hole golf course, shopping boutiques, banks and car rental service. At 6km from the centre, it's a bit far, but offers peace and prime views of the capital and surrounding hills.

Eating

The surest way of guaranteeing yourself **cheap eating** is to buy food supplies from the well-stocked **marché central**, or other neighbourhood markets such as that in the Messa quarter. For inexpensive snacking, the commercial area is full of *soya* sellers. Vendors also tempt you with cool pineapple slices stored on ice packs. Should you be staying at the Presbyterian Mission, there are numerous **small eateries** on rue Onembele Nkou and rue Joseph Essono Balla. They serve good breakfasts of omelettes and *Nescafé* in the morning, and filling rice and bean dishes in the afternoon and evening.

French-style cafés

For relatively inexpensive eating in town, a meal in one of the popular pavement cafés near avenue Kennedy might suggest itself. One of the best known (and they're all well known) is *L'Ane Rouge* on place Kennedy. They serve home-style French dishes such as *côtes de porc, haricots* or *steak frites* for around CFA2000. Have a beer on the perennially popular outdoor terrace and watch the people mill through the busy *quartier*. Next to the *Ane Rouge*, a small bar, *La Gargotte*, sells beers for about half the price of its neighbour. You can get cheap brochettes here as well. On rue Marie Goker, *The Pussy Cat* serves bistro-style food for around CFA3000–5000. While often crowded due to its central location, the food isn't exceptional and the service not up to *Ane Rouge* standards.

Slightly upmarket, *Le Cintra*, av Kennedy (☎22.33.88) is another *café terrasse* with French cuisine and rather elevated prices. *La Saladière* (☎22.15.15), just down the street, is from the same mould.

European food: expensive

Le Dauphin, route de l'Aviation (☎23.12.54). Well known and liked for excellent French food – but at a fiendish price (up to CFA20,000 a head).

La Trappola, near the Swiss Embassy on route du Mont Fébé (☎23.06.85). Very good Italian food at around CFA15,000.

Le Mont Fébé, at the *Sofitel* (☎22.43.24). One of the best restaurants in town for French cooking and one of the most expensive. There is a cheaper coffee shop in the hotel and a poolside buffet.

Oriental food: moderate to pricey

Grand Muraille de Chine, next to the German Embassy on av Charles de Gaulle. Chinese vegetables, egg rolls etc, for as little as CFA1500 and up. A good place for lunch.

Aux Baguettes d'Or (☎22.39.29). Good Chinese food at moderate prices.

Chez Wou, route du Mont Fébé near the Swiss Embassy. This Chinese restaurant features authentic decor and terrace eating. A good place for a special dinner, but expensive.

Nightlife

Yaoundé has none of Douala's **after dark** energy. There are a few places attached to the hotels but these, apart from a few bars, and small places in Briquetterie and Messa are about all the city can offer. Some taxi drivers (you'll need taxis to get you about at night) may have better pickings to suggest. Let us know.

Le Balafon, *Sofitel Mont Fébé*'s disco, pretty well exclusively white. CFA5000 cover.

Super Paquita, Mvog-Ada *quartier*, east of place Ahmadou Ahidjo. Supposed to be highly animated.

Katio Reputedly good, but expensive.

Le Pacha, basement of Imm. Hajal Massad, av Foch. Disco palace.

Black and White, rue Gocker, near place Kennedy. Similar.

La Saladiere, av Kennedy (☎22.15.15). Occasional live music.

Exploring Yaoundé

There are not all that many specific targets to aim for in your explorations of Yaoundé, beyond the usual pleasures of pavement cafés and the main market – though it's well worth checking out the **artwork** on sale at the *Centre d'Artisanat*.

In the midst of all the recent building, there's been talk of creating a national museum worthy of a great capital, but the project has yet to get off the ground and you'll have to be content with two, small private collections – the jumble of clobber in the **Musée d'Art Negre** and the immaculately presented **Musée d'Art Camerounais**.

The commercial centre

Despite its difficulties for pedestrians, Yaoundé does have a walkable centre, its heart at **place Ahmadou Ahidjo**. The most startling of the many buildings grouped around this square is the very 1950s **cathedral**, with a sloping roof that goes on forever. Across the square from the church is the **main post office**. Several government buildings also surround the square, including the **Commisariat Général du Tourisme** – Yaoundé's main source of tourist information .

The city's main arteries shoot out from place Ahidjo. To the east, avenue Monsigneur Vogt runs uphill past many of the city's major **banks**. Avenue du Président El Hadj Ahidjo leads north of place Ahidjo up to the colourful **marché central**, while avenue Kennedy, off avenue Ahidjo, is one of Yaoundé's classier streets. With its **sidewalk cafés** and upmarket shops, it flaunts a distinctly French flavour. This street ends in place Kennedy where you'll find the town's biggest crafts depot – the **Centre d'Artisanat**. Avenue de l'Indépendance leads from place Kennedy and passes the **Canadian Embassy** and **American Cultural Centre** before ending at place de l'Indépendance, dominated by the futuristic **Hôtel de Ville**.

The Lake Quarter and Melen

Most of the administrative buildings in town congregate to the east of place Ahidjo, between boulevard du 20 Mai and the **town lake**. Known as the *Quartier du Lac*, this tranquil neighbourhood with imposing avenues has long been a construction site for experiments in **modern architecture**. Buildings such as the **Ministère des Postes et Télécommunications** or the imaginative headquarters of the **Banque des Etats de l'Afrique Centrale** have gone a long way towards changing Yaoundé's look and self-image in recent years. On boulevard de la Réunification, which marks the southern fringe of this *quartier*, the **Monument de la Réunification** rises up in a helter-skelter spiral as it commemorates the coming together of Cameroon's French and English-speaking components.

In the middle of this neighbourhood, the lake itself hardly provides the serene natural backdrop you might imagine. It's more like a stagnant pond – and a perfect mosquito breeding ground. The **Club Nautique et Piscine** is now defunct, the grimy swimming pool drained.

Le Musée d'Art Negre

Daily 8am–noon & 2–6pm; free entrance, but you can slip the caretaker some money.

Although this museum is relatively close to the centre, in the *Quartier du Lac*, it's still difficult to find. Get there by taking bus #4 to place Melen and walking down rue de Melen. After about 100m, follow a sign reading *Centre Aumonerie Catholique Universitaire* down a small path to the right leading to the museum. The works here come from the private collection of the Jesuit founder and are arranged haphazardly. Arty, African odds and ends include masks from Zaire, a Benin bronze, Bamoun pipes – and a crown from Thailand thrown in for good measure – but there's nothing to link them together. The museum is dark and dusty and not really worth making a big effort to see, although it does contain an interesting **library of African history** with archives of transcribed oral histories and some period photographs.

Mass at Ndjong-Melen

This is a famous tourist outing, but not done for tourists. Every Sunday from 9.30am to noon the congregation in the **Catholic church** in the quarter of Ndjong Melen, just west of the *Musée d'Art Negre*, works itself into a state of high excitement during the Ewondo language service – wonderful music and dancing and high-energy drumming and everyone in their most colourful outfits.

The northern suburbs

Yaoundé's poor and working-class districts are usually tucked away in the valleys, hidden from sight by the hill tops. Such neighbourhoods include the **Briqueterie**, with the town's **Grande Mosquée**, and **Messa**, which has one of the liveliest markets outside the centre. In the extreme north of town, the **Bastos** neighbourhood is the most exclusive residential area. Site of the nation's first factory (making the *Bastos* cigarettes which gave the quarter its name), this area is now better known for its many **embassies** and the modern – and top-heavy – **presidential palace**. You pass through here on your way to the country's largest hotel, the **Sofitel Mont Fébé**, and to the **Musée d'Art**.

Le Musée d'Art Camerounais

Thurs, Sat & Sun, 3–6pm; free entrance, but you are encouraged to leave a donation.

Situated in a **Benedictine monastery** on Mont Fébé (above the *Sofitel*), this museum is way out of the centre and accessible by taxi (the alternative is to take bus #5 to the end of the line and hike up the mountain). A narrow flight of steps takes you up to the museum from the main road (and continues to the *Novotel*). Ring the bell when you arrive at the monastery; a monk will lead you to the exhibit.

Like a monument to minimalism, the museum's interior is completely stark, with clean whitewashed walls and appropriate lighting to force your attention on the displays. Although the collection is small, it contains many masterpieces, notably from the western provinces. First of all is a display of pipes (in ivory, wood and terracotta) including some amazing **Bamoun bronze pipes**. Another room features **masks**, mainly from the Grassfields, and a fantastic wooden **bas relief** depicting a market scene. Notice too a carved wooden bed for a king, and intricate wooden panels showing scenes from the hunt. A third room contains **Tikar bronzes** and includes pipes, bells used to call the ancestors, and a king's throne. The remarkable **maternity statue** is a gentle tribute to motherhood.

Yaoundé Directory

Airfreight *DHL* (☎23.13.58).

Airlines The international companies have their offices in Douala. In Yaoundé, *Cameroon Airlines* is on av Monseigneur Vogt, behind the cathedral (☎23.40.01, 22.39.74).

Banks The main banks are near place Ahmadou Ahidjo. Those on av Ahidjo include: *BIAO* (BP182; ☎23.41.35), recommended for having money sent to; *BICIC* (BP 5; ☎23.41.30). Many others are on av Monseigneur Vogt: *SGBC* (BP 244; ☎23.41.25); *SCB* (BP 145; ☎23.41.20).

Bookshops *Librairie Hermes Memento* (☎22.12.39), *Librairie Moderne Hachette*, av Kennedy(☎23.16.88).

Car hire As reliable as it is expensive, *Hertz* has its office in the *Mont Fébé Novotel* (☎23.40.02). Other agencies include: *Jully Auto*, av Ahidjo (BP 6064; ☎22.39.47, telex 8331); *Neuilly Auto*, av de l'Indépendance (BP 375; ☎22.15.35); *P.Z. Motors Europcar*, at the airport (☎22.33.44) and on av Ahidjo (BP 198; ☎22.11.47).

Cinemas The nicest cinemas, with the most up-to-date films, are *Le Capital*, on av Ahidjo (☎22.49.77), and *L'Abbia* on rue Nachtigal (☎22.31.66). Other neighbourhood cinemas include: *Le Djoungolo*, rue Albert Ateba Ebe; *Le Fébé*, in the Messa quarter on rue Sultan Njoya; *La Mefou*, place Awae, off bd de l'OCAM; *Les Portiques*, av John Kennedy; *Le Rex*, in the Briqueterie quarter on rue de la Briqueterie.

Cultural centres:
  British Council office and library, av Kennedy.
  United States Information Service, av Nachtigal (☎23.16.33).

EMBASSIES AND CONSULATES

Algeria Bastos Quarter (BP 1619; ☎23.06.65, telex 8517).

Belgium Bastos Quarter, Mban Building (BP 816; ☎22.27.88, telex 8314).

Canada Imm. Stamatiades, av de l'Indépendance (BP 572; ☎23.02.03, telex 8209).

Central African Republic (BP396; 22.51.55).

Chad rue Joseph Mballa Eloumden, Bastos Quarter (BP 506; ☎22.06.24, telex 8352).

Congo (BP 1422; ☎23.24.58, , telex 8379).

Côte d'Ivoire Imm. Ndende, Bastos Quarter (BP 203; ☎22.09.69, telex 8388).

Equatorial Guinea (BP 277; ☎22.41.49).

France, av de Gaulle (BP 1631; ☎22.02.33, telex 8233).

Gabon Bastos Quarter off bd de l'URSS (BP 4130; ☎22.29.66, telex 8265).

Germany av de Gaulle, near the Hôtel de Ville (BP 1160; ☎23.05.66, telex 8412).

Israel (BP 5934; ☎22.16.44, telex 8632).

Italy Bastos Quarter (BP 827; ☎22.33.76, telex 8305).

Morocco (BP 1629;☎22.50.92, telex 8347).

Netherlands (BP 310; ☎22.05.44, telex 8237).

Nigeria off av Monseigneur Vogt (BP 448; ☎22.34.55, telex 8267); follow small side road at *Cameroon Airlines* junction to the east; the Embassy is 100m on.

Senegal Bastos Quarter (BP 176; ☎22.03.08, telex 8303).

Spain Bastos Quarter (BP 877; ☎22.41.89, telex 8287).

Sweden bd Edjoa Mbede (BP 830; ☎23.38.54).

Switzerland route du Mont Fébé (BP1169; ☎23.28.96, telex 8316).

Tunisia rue de Rotary (BP 6074; ☎22.33.68, telex 8370).

United Kingdom av Winston Churchill (BP 547; ☎22.07.96, telex 8200); Mon, Wed, Fri 8.30am–noon, 2.30–4.30pm, Tues & Fri 8.30am–noon; issues transit visas for Ghana and tourist visas for The Gambia, Sierra Leone, Kenya, Zambia, Malawi, Uganda, Zimbabwe and Botswana at a flat fee of CFA16,500 each.

USA rue de Nachtigal (BP 817; ☎23.40.14, telex 8223).

Zaire Bastos Quarter (BP 632; ☎22.51.03, telex 8317).

Centre Culturel Français, av de Gaulle, (☎23.40.13).
Goethe Institut, av Kennedy (☎23.38.74).
Chinese Cultural Centre, near the embassy off route de Ngousso.

Doctors Polyclinic André-Fouda (☎22.24.64) route de Ngousso, east of the railway tracks.

Emergencies Police ☎17, Fire ☎18.

Maps The *Institut Géographique National*, on av Monseigneur Vogt (☎22.34.65) has city and national maps. For less detailed versions, try the tourist office.

Newsline English news of the day ☎22.90.00, French ☎22.80.00.

Pharmacies Among the best stocked and most central is the *Pharmacie Française* (☎22.14.76) on the corner of avs Kennedy and Ahidjo.

Post offices The main post office (Mon–Fri 8am–noon & 2.30–5.30pm) is on place Ahidjo. The poste restante service costs CFA200, but they don't hold letters very long.

Photography permits No longer needed, in theory, but if you want to check for yourself, visit the Ministry of Information and Culture (BP 1588; ☎22.31.85, telex 8215), bureau 206, on the 2nd floor.

Supermarkets *Prisunic*, av de l'Indépendance (near USA cultural centre) is one of the cheapest.

Telephones CFA1500 per minute to the UK, CFA2000 to USA and Australasia.

Tourist information. *Secretariat d'Etat du Tourisme*, place Ahidjo (☎22.44.11).

Travel agencies:
Antoniades Travel Agency(ATA), place Kennedy (BP 419 ☎23.14.88).
Camvoyages, av de l'Indépendance (BP 606; ☎23.22.12).
Cameroun Publi-Expansion (CPE) Imm. Les Galeries (BP 1399; ☎23.39.21).
Intervoyages, place Hôtel de Ville (BP 127; ☎22.03.61).
Transcap Voyages (BP 153; ☎23.12.96).

ONWARDS FROM YAOUNDÉ

● Most **buses** and **taxis** leave from the **bus station** on boulevard de l'OCAM. For the western towns of Bafoussam, Foumban, Bamenda and so on, head to **Messa bus station** near Messa market.

● **Trains** leave daily **to Ngaoundéré** via **Belabo** and **Ngaoundal** (for road routes to Centrafrique) from the railway station by place Elig-Essono (enquiries ☎23.40.03), and there's a night train with couchettes. You can also get trains **to Douala**, although for this stretch, the speed of the excellent paved road makes the train journey a bit pointless unless you're an enthusiast.

TRANSCAM I	TRANSCAM II
"Intercity" service:	"Express Autorail" (stopping) service:
Dep. Yaoundé 6.50am, arr. Douala 10.20am.	Dep. Yaoundé 7.10am, arr. Ngaoundéré 6pm.
Dep. Yaoundé 7.20pm, arr. Douala10.50pm.	"Trains couchettes" service:
"Express Autorail" (stopping) service:	Dep. Yaoundé 6.40pm, arr. Ngaoundéré 6am.
Dep. Yaoundé 12.45pm, arr. Douala 4.50pm.	"Omnibus" all stations service:
"Omnibus" all stations service:	Dep. Yaoundé 8.25pm, arr. Belabo 12.30pm.
Dep. Yaoundé 7.45 am, arr. Douala 4.05pm.	

● If you want to travel **by air**, check with *Cameroon Airlines* for up-to-date schedules and prices. There are 1–3 flights daily to Douala; flights to Bafoussam and Bamenda on Tues, Fri and Sun; to Bertoua and Batouri on Mon, Thur and Fri; to Ngaoundéré daily except Sun; to Garoua daily; and to Maroua daily except Thur.

Southwest: Kribi and the Province du Sud

As an escape from the swelter of Douala or the rigours of overlanding, Kribi and the white sand beaches of the "south coast" are hard to beat. At present, too, access is still enough of an effort to deter the less determinedly hedonistic beach seekers.

The quickest route from Yaoundé to **Kribi** is via **EDÉA**. This attractive and well provisioned town, has always made a good living from the passing Douala–Yaoundé–Kribi trade at the lowest bridge over the broad **Sanaga River**, but especially since the completion of the N3 highway brought a mass of new traffic. It's also responsible for much of the country's electric power generation. If you're staying over, the *Foyer* and *Auberge* are reasonable, *Hôtel La Sanaga* (BP 54; ☎46.43.11) better and more pricey.

Alternatively, it's possible to make your way to Kribi through the forests of Le Province du Sud, along tracks which, in the dry season at any rate, are passable by normal cars. There are two main routes from the capital; in either case the first stage is to **Ebolowa**, then either via **Lolodorf** or **Akom II**. Travel can be painfully slow along these stretches, but the roads take in lush scenery punctuated with the occasional waterfall, and skirt a number of **"Pygmy" villages**. Note, however, that the finest beaches in the Kribi area are to the north of the town, on the Edéa road.

Kribi is Cameroon's second-largest port, but has long remained in relative isolation. Since 1987 the Germans have been building a new paved road to connect this potential commercial centre and resort to Edéa and Cameroon's two main cities. When it's finally completed – and be wary of maps that already show it – the road is intended to give a much needed economic boost to the region – though at the expense of opening the tourism floodgates.

Yaoundé to Ebolowa

Heading towards Ebolowa, the N2 highway brings you in 50km to MBALMAYO, a prosperous logging town with accommodation, banks and post office. You can actually get as far as Mbalmayo by train, but the road is so good (and so frequently served by **taxis**) that there's little point.

From Mbalmayo, the paved road continues southward to **SANGMÉLIMA**, another large town in the forest region, centre of the president's Beti ethnic group (his home town is Mvomeka, 50km northeast). There's modest accommodation here at the *Auberge Jeanine* and the *Hôtel Astoria*. The **Gabonese border** at NSAK is 150km away to the south. Eastward, you could strike out at the rarely visited rainforest zone of the **Réserve du Dja**.

To get to the coast, however, take instead the good-quality track that leads via NGOULEMAKONG to **EBOLOWA**. This lively provincial capital amid the forest is an important cocoa marketing centre. There are several small **hotels** (you're not likely to get much further in a day, even with you own wheels), the nicest being *Hôtel La Jungle* (☎28.35.73) where doubles go for around CFA6000. Le Ranch is another reasonable abode (BP 670; ☎28.35.31). More rudimentary places include *Hôtel Splendid*, *L'Ane Rouge* and *La Cabane Bambou*; most have restaurants and *bar/dancings* that make for rather wild nights in the jungle. Ebolowa also has a **bank** (*BIAO*), **post office** and hospital.

Around Ebolowa

The environs of Ebolowa harbour a number of interesting natural curiosities, though to see them you really have to have your own transport. One of the best known is the **Trou des Fantomes** (Phantoms' Cave), reached by taking the Sangmélima route out of town and following it 20km to the village of **NKOÉTYÉ**. Ask there for directions to the yawning chasm, where a chained monster is reputed to live. And drop us a line about the outcome if you survive.

Given time for an even longer excursion, you could conceivably get as far as the **Menvé Elé Falls**, over 150km away towards the Campo Game Reserve. This trip leads into the heart of the Cameroonian wilds, far from the world of hotels, restaurants and even petrol stations (except in MÉYO, and even there the pumps are sometimes dry). You therefore need to be equipped with survival provisions, and take all the petrol you'll need for the 300-odd-kilometre roundtrip. Although the falls are marked on the maps near NYABESSAN, the most difficult part of the trip is yet to come. At Nyabessan, you have to ask the chief's permission to visit the area, and he'll make sure you get a guide (at this point you'll have to settle on a price, and it won't be a trifling sum). You then hike with your guide through 7km of forest (and cross two rivers by *pirogue*) to the village of EBIANEMEYONG. Here you again need the chief's permission (and dash some more money) to continue. There are 4km more of forest to bash your way through before you reach the **Ntem River**, once more crossed by *pirogue*. From here, follow the river up to a series of seven cascades, the highest crashing down from a height of fifty metres. It's all the getting there that makes the falls – modestly impressive – really worthwhile.

Via Lolodorf to Kribi

From Ebolowa, it's another 73km by decent *piste* to **LOLODORF** (its name about the only such reminder of the German presence – Lolo's village – as most towns were renamed by the French), where you may be able to fill up with petrol, but won't find any accommodation. Only 110km separate Lolodorf from Kribi, but the tracks that wind through the hilly tropical forest make for a long trip. As a payoff, however, this route does pass by numerous "Pygmy" villages where, unlike in the extreme east of the country, the people have adopted a sedentary lifestyle. The worst stretch of road comes in the first 34km to the village of BIDJOKA, from where you can walk to the **Bidjoka Falls**. Ten kilometres further on is the larger village of BIPINDI whence it's another 66km to Kribi.

The town's name is said to come from the word *kiridi*, which roughly translated means "short men". It's a reminder that you're in "Pygmy" country – these were the original inhabitants of the district. Now, however, Bantu-speakers like the **Batanga** and **Bakoko** predominate, and you might not see a single convincing "Pygmy". The "Pygmies", of course, don't call themselves by that term and every community is part of a small cluster of bands, traditionally nomadic, but increasingly sedentary these days, and more and more dependent on the larger economy of Cameroon, beyond the forest. The main groups of the western part of equatorial Africa are the Binga, Beku, Baka, Jelli, Koa, Kola, Kouya, Rimba and Yaga. All Africa's people of small stature have completely lost their original languages and now speak the local language of the dominant people – in this area Bassa.

Kribi

As a backdrop to the daily activity of commerce, fishing and foresting, colonial reminders abound in **KRIBI**, creating a quiet nostalgic feeling. The hometown of the Bassa, Kribi was a noted hotbed of UPC radicalism in the 1950s. The **port** at the centre of town was built by the Germans and is today too shallow for larger vessels to enter the harbour: from the nearby hillside, crowned with its colonial **cathedral**, you can see ships anchored a few kilometres offshore as their cargo is transferred by lighter. The former **German administrative buildings** lining the beachfront in the northwest of town now house government offices such as the préfecture and the **tourist office**.

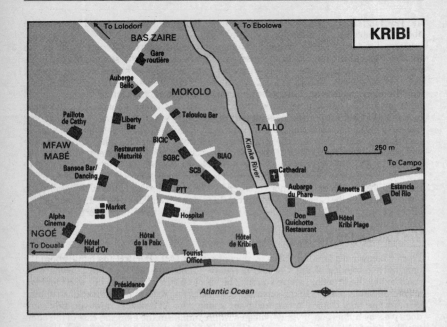

Accommodation

Because of the relatively heavy tourist influx, **accommodation** tends to be expensive in Kribi, though there are still a few relatively cheap places to stay. About the best you can do money-wise is the *Hôtel de la Paix* in town near the post office junction. Their simple rooms, some with fans, run from CFA4000–5000. The nearby *Auberge Annette I* (BP 53; 46.10.57) also has inexpensive lodgings. If they're full, as thy might well be at weekends, you might want to enquire about the *Auberge Bello*, two blocks from the *gare routière* in the New Bell neighbourhood, or the nearby *Paillote de Cathy* in Afan Mabé quarter.

Most of the other hotels are at the southern end of town, past the bridge. Down by the port, the *Auberge du Phare* (☎46.11.06) is a reasonable place, clean and well-managed, with rooms for around CFA6000 and a restaurant. The *Hôtel Kribi Plage* (☎46.11.23) is small with ventilated rooms, conveniently located near the beach – expect to pay around CFA9000 for a double. Slightly more casual, the *Annette II* (BP 53; ☎46.10.57) also enjoys an ideal beachfront location that justifies relatively high prices considering it's only an *auberge*.

A brief rundown of Kribi's more expensive options:

Hôtel de Kribi (BP 118; ☎46.12.76). In the centre of town, this stylish colonial hotel was recently revamped. It's bound to be very expensive, and it used to be essential to book in advance for weekends – and probably still is.

Hôtel Centre d'Acceuil (BP 142; ☎46.16.35). A brand new hotel on the route de la Lobé, the *Centre d'Accueil* has attractive ocean-front rooms with unnecessary AC from CFA13,000. There's a fine bar-restaurant looking out on the water.

Estancia del Rio (BP 353; 46.16.22). Outside of Kribi, on the route de Campo, this luxury hotel on the beach is something like a honeymooners' paradise – complete comfort and correspondingly high prices.

Along the coast

The beaches along this southern stretch of the coast, north and south of Kribi, are, with their wild vegetation, white sand and calm waters, among the most beautiful anywhere in Africa. They stretch over 100km, from the small village at Londji to the town of Campo on the border of Equatorial Guinea. Beach bums will be in their element, though the paradise is far from being a well-kept secret.

Londji and the beaches to the north

North of Kribi, the Edéa road hugs the coastline as it skirts some of the most picturesque strands. It passes the village of MPALLA and, after 15km, Cocotier Plage (a beautiful beach where there are rudimentary bungalows for rent) before arriving at LONDJI. Some 25km from Kribi, this small fishing town spreads round a large bay with calm, warm water, white sands and coconut trees. Two rustic hotels without water or electricity offer perfect repose (you won't miss modern conveniences in the beautiful natural setting) and you can fill up in town on fish, *brochettes d'escargot* and rice. A couple of local bars sell beer, minerals and freshly tapped palm wine.

After midnight, fishermen set out in wooden canoes across the bay, stirring up luminous phosphoresence in the water as they paddle towards the deeper ocean. You may be able to persuade one to take you along, though it's not always an eventful experience. On arrival *au large* – out at sea – they cast their nets, which are hundreds of metres long, and simply wait until dawn (in daylight, fish can see the nets and avoid getting caught). When they arrive at shore in the morning, buyers from surrounding villages are already waiting at the beach to see the night's catch.

Staying in Londji is as relaxing as the fishing technique, but despite its position on the main *piste* it does feel isolated and if you're lookin for bars with *dancings*, restaurants and the like, this is not the place. Although Kribi isn't far, taxis there are rare and if you want to go for a day, you'll spend most of the time waiting for transport – with the distinct possibility of being stuck for the night in Kribi if you don't head back early enough in the afternoon.

The southern beaches to Campo

Another *piste* follows the coastline southwards from Kribi to the Guinean border, passing still more beaches, all exotically named – Marseilles, Océan Amérique, Azure. Seven kilometres from town, just before GRAND BATANGA, a small signpost points down to the Chutes de la Lobé where the river of the same name comes thrashing over a rocky descent as it plunges directly into the ocean. The force of these rapids stirs up an unappealing brownish foam in the bay, but the surrounding beaches are clean and have excellent swimming. A small and rather pricey restaurant at the foot of the falls serves grilled fish specialities under a pleasant *paillote*. You could walk down here from Kribi, but would probably want a lift back again.

You certainly need transport to continue to the fishing village of EBOUNDJA, 20km south of Kribi, where the local chief authorises camping on the beach, and will arrange meals, fishing boat excursions and more complicated trips up the Lobé to visit "Pygmy" villagers. Some 25km further south, a rocky land formation, the Rocher du Loup – photo unfailingly included in the tourism literature – rises dramatically, but not very wolf-like, from out of the water. Beyond here, you're getting into very remote reaches: the road passes yet another fishing village, EBODJE, before petering out at the two-bit border town of CAMPO. You can expect customs and immigration checks in the vicinity. The big Réserve du Campo, 3000 square kilometres of gazetted but apparently unmanaged rainforest, doesn't currently aim to attract visitors. Still, there's a network of tracks into the forest east of Campo, and, in your own vehicle, you could venture forth. The town beach stretches south out to the **Ntem River**, on the other side of which lies Equatorial Guinea. There's no cross-border route here – passage by boat for local pedestrian travellers only.

Bertoua and the Province de l'Est

Three hundred kilometres of *piste* separate Yaoundé from **Bertoua**, the capital of Eastern Province and one of the few towns of any size in the region. The tracks are relatively good and pass through **Nanga-Eboko** (accommodation at the *Etoile d'Or de Nanga*). Situated on the border of the savannah and the forest, Bertoua has grown rapidly in recent years, thanks to improved transport. The airport was opened in 1976 and provides regular flights to Yaoundé. Also, Bertoua is only 80km from BELABO on the Transcam railway; buses link the two towns. Trains depart Belabo daily at 5.15am for Ngaoundéré and 6am for Yaoundé.

With a population upwards of 20,000, **BERTOUA** has a solid industrial base, and its new three-star hotel – the *Mansa Novotel* (BP 285; ☎24.13.33) – seems to be a symbol of recent economic expansion. Despite the **banks** (*BIAO, BICIC*), cinemas and bars, however, it's an uninspiring place to visit. Besides the expensive *Novotel*, the town has a number of moderate hotels including *Hôtel de l'Est* (☎24.11.28), *Hôtel BP* (☎24.10.03), and the smaller *Hôtel Goldman*. If you're in a hurry to get out of Bertoua, *Cameroon Airlines* (☎24.12.78) flies Monday, Thursday and Friday to Yaoundé and Douala (CFA16,000 to Yaoundé).

Moving on from Bertoua to the **Central African Republic**, the main road shudders northeast to **GAROUA-BOULAI**, a long journey through a great swathe of jungle and grassland to a busy crossing point and marketplace on the savannah fringes of northern Cameroon. Lots of Fula herders pass through here. The American mission may allow you to camp in their grounds.

NORTHERN CAMEROON

Northern Cameroon is remarkably detached from the rest of the country by a vast, almost trackless region in the centre. This huge expanse of rolling savannah and forests – as big as Scotland – is thinly populated and crossed by just three *pistes*, and the railway.On its northern edge, the **Adamawa Mountains** cut across the centre of Cameroon, and as you cross this barrier, it's striking how effectively it divides the country into two distinct parts. It's a tough journey by road from Yaoundé or Bamenda to the first town of northern Cameroon, Ngaoundéré. It's a good reason to use the train. Beyond, a flat plateau stretches over much of the north, where light forests and grasslands replace the south's thick vegetation, indicating that the climate is harsher and nature less generous. But there's more variety to the scenery than you might detect from the mostly flat sealed highway, running from **Ngaoundéré** all the way to **Kousseri**, which makes this one of the easiest regions to travel through.

No less than four **game parks** are situated in the north, ranging from the hilly **Bouba Ndjida** reserve, where there's still some chance of spotting the (increasingly rare) **black rhinoceros**, to the popular **Waza National Park**, where the flat savannahs are ideal for seeing herds of giraffe and elephant, as well as lions and numerous other species. In the extreme northwest, the volcanic **Mandara Mountains** have been scoured by thousands of years of *harmattan* winds and the people of the region squeeze their livelihood out of the dry rocky slopes. Although this region has been "discovered" by travel operators, if you're determined enough you can work your way off the more beaten tracks and away from such overrun sites as **Rhumsiki** to villages which may not be any more authentic but are at least less tainted by package tourism.

The mountain people of the northwest have retained traditional **religious beliefs**, but the rest of the region bears the stamp of **Islam**, brought by Fula migrants who established principalities called **lamidats** in the eighteenth century. The **Muslim influence** is especially noticeable in towns such as **Garoua** and **Maroua**, which seem unusually large and dynamic in a region where you might expect climate and geography to reduce energy to a minimum.

Ngaoundéré

Coming from the south, **NGAOUNDÉRÉ**, with its mango-shaded streets and the mild climate resulting from its 1400-metre elevation, proves a satisfying introduction to the north. Though rapidly growing, the **old Fula settlement** is well contained in the neighbourhood around the **Lamido's palace**, where the architecture of the houses and mosques and the dress of the people bear witness to a Sudanic tradition that is very much alive.

NGAOUNDÉRÉ HISTORY

The first people to settle around Ngaoundéré were the **Mboum**, whose claims to the area were lost to the **Fula** after a military siege in the early 1830s. By 1835, **Ardo Ndjobdji** had established the Muslim **Lamidat** and the Mboum became Fula vassals. A large town of some 10,000 at the end of the last century, the city was surrounded by a protective wall in 1865; its influence extended over a vast territory to the south and east. Even during the colonial period, the traditional town changed little, and it wasn't until the **Trans-Cameroonian Railroad** was extended here in 1974 that a real boom occurred. In the early 1970s, the population paused briefly at around 20,000, but by 1983 it had rocketed to nearly 60,000 and may be close to 100,000 people by now. New *quartiers* have grown up all around the old centre – adding a sense of vitality to the traditional core. Improved transportation also facilitated regional economic activity that today includes an industrial slaughterhouse (livestock is a regional mainstay), a tannery, and intensive wheat production led by the *Sodeblé* company.

Bed and board

The Catholic Mission no longer puts up travellers, but the nearby *College Catholique Mazenod* apparently provides low-cost dorm space. Other than that, one of the cheapest places to stay is the *Auberge Le Château de Adamaoua* where no-frills non-S/C rooms without fans start at CFA4000. You can eat at their restaurant for CFA500–1500. Near the Presbyterian church (in the **Joli-Soir** neighbourhood), the *Auberge de la Colombe* has reasonably priced rooms with showers. Slightly upmarket, and more central, the *Hôtel le Relais* (BP 47; ☎25.11.38) behind the *Cinéma Le Nord* has non-AC rooms starting at CFA8000 for a double. One place formerly popular with travellers, the *Hôtel des Deux Plateaux*, has closed.

The *Hôtel du Rail* (BP 319), near the railway station has clean and very comfortable S/C rooms, costing slightly more than at *Le Relais*. But the most expensive place in town is the three-star *Hôtel Transcam* (BP 179; ☎25.10.41), a showy place next to the railway station where rooms are CFA14,000: excellent service, tennis courts, a bar, restaurant and nightclub.

Eating

You'll find numerous cheap eating places around the gare routière. For something a little fancier, try *La Girafe* (on av Ahidjo near the Catholic mission) which is popular among ex-pats and volunteers for the attractive shaded *terrasse*, and good food at fair prices. At lunchtime they produce grilled fish, pork chops, kebabs or lamb with *frites*, fried plantain or rice for around CFA1500. Evening meals cost a touch more. Also try *Le Snack*, a fast-food place in the station and a popular rendezvous for the youth of Ngaoundéré.

Things to see

The **old town** centres around the **Lamido's Palace**, which is a **saré** – the Hausa word for this style of housing, made of *banco* huts and with vast straw rooftops that swoop down nearly to the ground. A large wall surrounding the compound keeps the maze of courtyards, private dwellings and public rooms out of view from the street. For an **inside visit**, ask at the Lamido's *secretariat* at the palace entrance, or go to the **tourist office** on av Ahidjo. They'll phone and make a booking for you.

For pageantry, time your visit for the weekend, in time for the **Friday prayer.** Dignitaries in brightly coloured *boubous* – magnificent accents of orange and red against the ochre tints of the townscape – come to pay their respects to the Lamido who leads a procession to the mosque. Similar displays take place on Saturday and Sunday.

Ngaoundéré's **marché central** is just down the main avenue from the palace, and is surrounded by an arcaded wall. The **gare routière** adjoins the market. The main avenue from the market leads to the commercial centre with its **banks**, post office and boutiques.

Listings

Banks *BIAO* and *BICIC* (the only one that will change travellers' cheques) are on the main avenue between the Lamido's palace and the tourist office.

Car and moped hire If you want to hire a car, to visit the game reserves for example, it's very expensive. The going rate is around CFA13,000 per day, which doesn't include the kilometre charge, normally CFA50–100 per km; and of course there's petrol on top of that. Prices for more than a day are more negotiable. Try the *Garage Adamaoua* (☎25.13.15) or the *Socaret Garage* (☎25.11.26). **Mopeds** come much cheaper, from numerous points around town – opposite the *Hôtel le Relais*, for example.

Cinemas The *Cinéma Adamaoua* (☎25.13.04) and the *Cinéma du Nord* (☎25.10.04) are in the centre of town.

Hospital If you need medical help, head first to the Norwegian Mission's hospital (☎25.11.95).

Tourist information The small tourist office on av Ahidjo has enthusiastic staff with good regional travel tips. They can also recommend places to eat and sleep in town and aren't snooty about directing you to the cheaper *auberges* if you emphasise you're on a budget.

Around Ngaoundéré

Should you have your own transport – or make yourself mobile by **hiring a moped** – you're well positioned to take some easy side trips in the environs of Ngaoundéré. The nearest site of scenic interest is **Lac Tison**, just 10km from town. Take the MEIGANGA road south and, after 6km a signpost points east to the crater lake, 3km further on. It's a pleasant ride along a *piste* bordered by awkward boulder formations, and the lake is deep in the woods, but forget swimming, as bilharzia is a real risk. Back on the Meiganga road, the **Chute de la Vina** is a well-known, if rather unspectacular waterfall, just past the village of **Wakwa.**

Further afield, you could conceivably go as far as the **Chutes de Tello** by moped, although to attempt the fifty-odd kilometres of track might be pushing your luck. To get there, follow the MBALANG road out of Ngaoundéré 22km to the village of **Mbalang Djalingo.** (A side trip from here could be the 2km to **Lac Mbalang,** a crater lake around a wooded island.) The road branches after the village, and it's the right fork you need to take, towards **Tourningal.** After a further 28km, turn off the main tracks and follow a small side *piste* 2.5km to the Tello Falls.

ONWARDS FROM NGAOUNDÉRÉ

● Heading south, the best bet is the **train.** The modern **Gare de Chemin de Fer** (enquiries ☎25.13.77) is a kilometre from the centre. Trains leave daily **to Yaoundé** and thrice-weekly night trains offer the luxury of a couchette. It's also possible to load a car on the train, should you want to avoid the long trek around the Adamawa range.

● The **gare routière** is next to the central market. Vehicles can take you from here to **Tibati,** on the long and rugged road to Foumban; to **Tchollíré,** between the Benoué and Bouba-Ndjida parks; to **Meiganga** on the main overland routes to Yaoundé and Central Africa; and of course up the road 300km to **Garoua.**

● If you want to get south fast, *Cameroon Airlines* (☎25.12.95) have daily **flights** (except Tues) to Yaoundé and Douala, Tues and Thur flights to Garoua, and Mon, Tues, Fri and Sat through to Maroua. You can confirm these by calling the airport (☎25.12.84).

Rey Bouba

One of the most influential and traditional of the Fula *lamidats*, **REY BOUBA** makes a worthwhile excursion, albeit a time-consuming one if you lack your own transport. To get here from Ngaoundéré, take a bush taxi to TCHOLLÍRÉ, along a road which gives you a welcome opportunity to see a bit of the Bénoué game park. At Tchollíré – where if necessary you can spend the night in a rudimentary **guesthouse**, the *Campement de Djiré* – find a vehicle going on the 35km to Rey Bouba. Your best chance is on Friday – market day.

Rey Bouba was founded by **Bouba Njida** in 1804. For thirty years, this religious zealot led a regional *jihad* to subdue the animist peoples of the region. While extending his authority over a vast territory, he also freed the area from domination by the powerful **Yola Emirate** (whose capital was in what is now Nigeria). By the time of Bouba Njida's death in 1864, he had created the most powerful and prestigious *lamidat* in northern Cameroon, a position Rey Bouba upholds today.

Built on the banks of the **Mayo Rey**, and only a few kilometres from the shores of the large Lagdo Reservoir, the village is a conglomeration of ochreous *saré* with straw roofs grouped around the **Lamido's Palace**. You won't be allowed into this fortified compound, where the spiritual leader of the region lives with his concubine, counsellors and servants, without the approval of the Lamido himself, and, even if he consents, you may have to wait several days before the reception. Subjects are not allowed to look at the face of the "prince", who wears a veil in public. At night, you can sleep on a mat on the floor of a traditional resthouse reserved for travellers. If you do stay, you wash in the river and eat food served in a calabash. It's all quite rootsy though also fairly exploitative.

THE NATIONAL PARKS OF THE NORTH

Northern Cameroon has some of the best **game viewing** in West Africa, with the **Waza National Park** (see p.1155) heading the list of attractions. Unfortunately, you can't get around them if you don't have transport, so assuming you're not taking an air tour out of Douala or Yaoundé, you're left with the painfully expensive option of **renting a car** in one of the main towns (Ngaoundéré, Garoua or Maroua), or the painfully slow and uncertain option of hitching a lift in with mobile tourists. To stay at any of the *campements*, you should reserve in advance, maybe even a couple of weeks or months during weekends or holidays when the places fill up. Contact the *Provincial Tourism Service*, BP 50, Garoua (☎27.10.20). Note that the entrance fees below are good for the whole season, so if you leave the parks and re-enter later, a new pass is not necessary each time. Note that Cameroonian conservation policy makes special provision for big game hunting, with macabre head prices on every species, from CFA100,000 for an elephant, down to CFA3000 for a monkey. Hunting blocks are well-defined and the paths of camera- and gun-users don't cross.

Faro Reserve

Comprising over 3000 square kilometres, **Faro** is the largest parcel of land under goverment protection in the north. Though slated to become a proper national park, this rugged, mountain-dotted slab of bush is currently nigh impossible to visit as it has virtually no usable tracks. The only facilities are the rudimentary quarters at the *Campement Hippopotames* on the Faro river outside the reserve near the village of Voko. It's a pity, because the wildlife in Faro is reputed to be prolific and if you could look round, you would supposedly see much large game that's hard to see elsewhere. In the absence of any infrastructure, tourists or a proper ranger service, however, and in its location hard up against a remote sector of the Nigerian frontier, it's no suprise to hear how much poaching goes on.

Bénoué National Park

Open all year round, entrance fee CFA2500; guide obligatory.

Coming north from Ngaoundéré, you can enter the **BÉNOUÉ PARK** either at **Mayo Alim** or **Banda**. From both of these towns, tracks lead through the park to the *Campement du Buffle Noir* (BP 49, Ngaoundéré). Situated on the banks of the Bénoué River, this camp has S/C rooms grouped in *boukarous* that are simple and comfortable. **Buffalo** and **eland** predominate in the park, where you may well also see **waterbucks**, **reedbucks**, **hartebeeste** and other species of antelope. **Elephants** and **lions** are neither as prolific nor as easily spotted here as at Waza but **hippos** and **crocodiles** are common in the river. **Hunting** is popular in the park, especially from the *Campement du Grand Capitaine*, the Bénoué's second resthouse which lies on the main road leading from Guidjiba to Tchollíré.

Bouba Ndjida National Park

Dec–May; entrance fee CFA2500; guide obligatory.

The main access to the **BOUBA NDJIDA PARK** is via **Tchollíré**. Cameroon's largest reserve, the Bouba Ndjida was created in 1968 to protect the increasingly rare herds of **rhinoceros** and **Derby eland** which still inhabit the area. A salt lick was created to attract the rhino, and there's a good chance of seeing them, along with **elephant** and **buffalo**. You may also spot **lion**, which are quite plentiful and even approach the resthouse. The rugged landscape with rivers and relatively thick vegetation makes this one of the country's most beautiful parks, but the vast space (2200 square kilometres and 450km of track) and thick bush means that the animals are more dispersed and not as visible as in Waza, for example. The *Bouba Ndjida camp* is 40km inside the camp and faces the Mayo Lidi river.

Garoua

Capital of Northern Province, **GAROUA** has grown rapidly since independence. Surprisingly, for a town situated so far into the interior, it has the country's third largest port, on the banks of the **Bénoué (Benue) River**. This has helped smooth the way for local **industrialisation** – not that the fact that the town was former president Ahidjo's birthplace was any hindrance: he has always been ready to invest in it. As the principal administrative and economic focus of the north, Garoua's more traditional aspects have been eclipsed to a large extent by its heterogenous blend of northern Cameroonians, Nigerians and Chadians. Traditional *saré* buildings – quite common up to the 1960s – have ceded to cement homes with tin roofs; the centre of town is dotted with modern blocks. Growth of course has meant increased facilities – with convenient banks, hotels and tourist information – but you're unlikely to miss its swarming crowds and oppressive heat when you leave.

THE FULA CONNECTION

Fali and Bata people were the first to settle along the banks of the Bénoué, in the eighteenth century. They were followed by **Kilba Fula** – herders who came in the early nineteenth century. After Dan Fodio's *jihad* (see p.1069) the Fula built a fortification (*ribadou*) around the town they called Ribadou-Garoua, to stave off Fali invasions. Other Muslims – Hausa, Bornu and Choa Arabs – arrived in the second half of the nineteenth century, lending an early urbanism to the settlement. The present **Lamidat** dates from 1839.

The **Germans** subjected Garoua in 1901 and set up a small port (British steamers from the *Niger Company* had been trading in ivory, salt and cloth since 1890). Enlarged in 1930, the port served as a vital link between Cameroon, Chad, and Nigeria, even though the port has only ever been able to function during the rainy season, from mid-July to mid-October. Garoua became an important international focus and has always had a large expatriate community. After independence, the roads were improved, and investments increased in the various industries relying on cotton, the regional cash crop. Factories producing thread, cloth and cotton seed oil were in time joined by a brewery and soapworks. The hydroelectric plant at **Lagdo** has a capacity larger than those of the south but the much vaunted **airport** – supposed to have been an international one – has lost that potential to the one being built up at Yaoundé. With a population of over 100,000, Garoua is easily the north's most dynamic town.

Staying in Garoua

Two **inexpensive** *auberges* face the taxi park; very convenient if you arrive after dark. The first is the *Salam* (☎27.22.16), with a dingy exterior that belies the clean rooms in the courtyard, grouped in whitewashed bungalows. Rooms start at CFA3000, and the outdoor showers are perfect for the hot climate. A couple of doors down, *The Auberge Chic* offers rooms with AC or fans for upwards of CFA4000 – nothing fancy, but it's clean. In the **middle price range**, the *Relais Saint Hubert* (BP 41; ☎27.13.21) is a popular standby. Well located near the commercial centre, it has S/C *boukarous* (many with AC) from around CFA9000. The restaurant (reckon on CFA4000) and bar are decent value. The most **expensive** hotel in town, *Novotel La Bénoué* (BP 291; ☎27.12.04, telex 7625) offers three-star comfort plus a **pool**, tennis courts and – for the mostly French guests – *pétanque*. In a well-shaded area away from the main commercial centre, it also features a restaurant with really good French food (though over CFA5000) and a nightclub. Rooms are upwards of CFA17,000.

Eating

Cheap restaurants grouped around the taxi park include, *L'Etoile*, *La Camerounaise* and *Le Bénoué*. All similar, they serve rice, plantain, yams or macaroni with beef sauce for CFA500–1000. Across from the **Marché Central** (near the *Shell* station) two more eating places – *Super Restaurant* and *Restaurant Moderne* – serve the same sort of hunger-stoppers, along with freshly blended fruit juices (pineapple, banana, lemon, orange). For something a little upmarket, *Le Berry* (across from the *Ribadou* cinema) serves excellent French food, but a full meal costs upwards of CFA8000.

Around town

There's nothing around town worth visiting, apart from the huge **central market**, best at weekends. Next to it are the **botanical gardens and zoo**, but they tend to be rather shrivelled and the animals haven't fared much better. The lonely giraffe is so bored he'll do anything to try to rub his snout on you, while a nearby buffalo appears terminally tired as he seeks the shade of a eucalyptus. On the other side of the market, the commercial centre spreads out with its **banks** (*BIAO, BCD, BICIC, SGBC* all within 100m of the **post office**), and administrative buildings such as the *Service Provincial du Tourisme* (☎27.10.20) and the **city hall**, with the obligatory fountain in front.

ONWARDS FROM GAROUA

Car hire *Hertz* is represented at the Novotel (☎27.12.04). Also try *Esgreg Voyages* (BP 210; ☎27.11.20); *Sorileges Voyages* (BP 133); *Renault Cameroon* (☎27.11.34); or *Jean Despotakis*, av du Port, (☎27.12.11).

Flight information Daily flights to Yaoundé and Douala, and, in theory, regular flights to Ngaoudéré and Maroua. Precise information and reservations available by calling *Cameroon Airlines* (☎27.10.55) or **the airport** (☎27.14.81/3).

Gare routière Transport out of Garoua is straightforward. The main **gare routière** is near the *marché central*, and has regular vehicles **to Maroua** and the north or **to Ngaoundéré** and south. There are also less frequent *taxis brousse* to Gaschiga (customs and immigration) and Demsa for Yola in Nigeria. It's a bad road.

Tourist information Contact the *Service Provincial du Tourism* Garoua (BP 50; ☎27.10.20) This is the place to book **lodgings in the game parks**.

Maroua

One of Cameroon's few pre-colonial cities, **MAROUA** already had a population of some 25,000 when French administrators took their first census in 1916 and 100,000 people lived in a twenty-kilometre radius of the town. Today it remains the largest northern city, and has retained a much more traditional flavour than its main rival Garoua. The old neighbourhoods of Maroua spread out on both banks of the **Mayo Kalliao**, run through with streets shaded by sweet-smelling *neem* trees.

Practical matters: lodgings and food

The cheapest place to stay in town (and for that matter, one of the cheapest in the whole country) is the *Baptist Mission*, near the market on the same street as the *SGBC* bank, where a night costs under CFA1000. There's no electricity or water in the dark and poorly maintained rooms of the courtyard, but you will be given a lantern and bucket for washing. You may prefer to put your mattress outside, as the rooms are as comfortable as ovens at night – you can practically hear the heat escaping from the

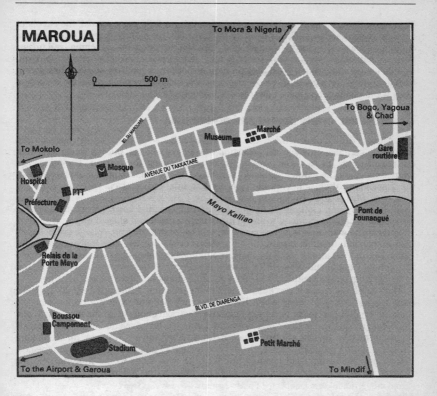

walls. Alternatively, several **inexpensive** *relais* can be found on the south side of the river near the stadium – but they're a bit of a trek from the gare routière. These include the *Auberge Maidjiguilao Domayo*, which has simple rooms with showers and a helpful staff, and the *Campement Bossou*, where the *boukarous* have fans and cold showers. It's clean and not too expensive. Moving up to the **moderate** range, *Le Relais de la Porte Mayo* (BP 112; ☎29.11.98) offers comfortable AC *boukarous* in a garden near the river. The hotel is a popular *rendezvous* for expatriates and volunteers.

Topping the list of **expensive hotels**, the *Mizao Novotel* (BP 205; ☎29.13.00, telex 7639) makes up for in comfort what it singularly lacks in character. Rooms start at around CFA17,000 and the hotel has its own tennis courts, video club and **swimming pool** (open to non-guests for CFA800). The restaurant serves mostly French cuisine (CFA5000);and there's the usual Novotel *boîte de nuit*. *Motel Le Saré* (BP 11; ☎29.12.45) is just as commodious, but far more likeable, in a large shaded garden with its own pool and crafts centre. The spacious rooms here are close to CFA20,000 for a twin.

Eating

A large number of cheap restaurants cluster near the *centre artisanal*. Directly opposite, *Chez Hanza* serves up rice, yams and macaroni with sauce, omelettes or *steak frites* for CFA500–1500. The nearby *Restaurant des Sportifs* is similar, as is the *Restaurant de la Jeunesse* on the road leading from the market to the bridge. On the other side of the river, *Chez Justine* is a cheap eatery across from the stadium and within walking distance of the surrounding *auberges*. For something a little more formal, the excellent outdoor restaurant of *Le Relais de la Porte Mayo* fills up nightly with an ex-pat crowd chatting noisily in French, English and German to the clink of china and glass. Vendors sidle between the tables selling local leatherwork and other crafts – but you wouldn't expect to strike a good bargain here, especially when they see you forking out CFA4000–7000 for a meal. *Le Saré* also has a very good restaurant in their garden. They serve continental food – upwards of CFA8000 a head.

The museum, crafts centre and other sites

The **Musée du Diamaré** (Mon–Sat 8am–noon & 2.30–5.30pm; free entrance but tip the guide) contains only a small collection of regional objects, but it's worth checking out nonetheless. It's in a rosy Sudanic-style building near the market. They don't get many visitors, so the *gardien* is usually very eager to provide thoughtful explanations of the assortment of objects from the **Sao civilisation**, and artefacts collected from the Toupouri, Massa and Mousgoum peoples. The **Fula** are represented by carved calabash, jewellery and clothing, including a beautifully crafted *boubou* worn by a *lamido* for special occasions. Notice the shield made from a dried and shaped elephant ear.

The **centre artisanal** is in a separate wing of the same building. A large crafts supermarket with innumerable stands, the emphasis is on the locally made **leather goods** for which Maroua is famous (sandals, bags, round floor cushions) but you find goods from throughout Central and West Africa as well. Jewellery and handwoven cloth can be good value here but bargain astutely and take your time choosing; there's a vast selection.

Maroua's large **market** spreads out next to the museum. Although it's held daily, the main market day is Monday when **Kirdi** ("pagan") peoples from the region come to trade. Everything, from car parts and Japanese electrical goods to locally made cloth and traditional medicines, is sold here. From the market, a broad avenue leads east, several hundred metres, to the **Founangué Bridge**. Alternatively, avenue du Takkatare stretches southwest nearly 2km to the very colonial **PTT** and **Préfecture**. From the post office roundabout, the road heading uphill to the west leads to the **hospital** and the *Novotel*, while the bridge spanning the Kalliao crosses to the *Relais de la Porte Mayo*.

Maroua shortlist

Banks *BIAO, BICIC, SCB* and *SGBC* are in the immediate vicinity of the market. Changing money is no problem.

Car hire Contact *Norcamtour* (☎29.10.48). That's also the number for **tourist information**, as they organise excursions to the Mandara Mountains and **Waza National Park**.

Flight information In theory there are flights to **Yaoundé** and **Douala** daily, to **Garoua**, daily except Thurs and Sat, and to **Ngaoundéré** on Thurs and Sun. For latest information, contact *Cameroon Airlines* (☎29.10.50) or call the **airport** (☎29.10.21).

Mokolo, Mora and the Mandara Mountains

Beautiful and haunting, the denuded volcanic plugs of the **Mandara Mountains** rise up to the west of Maroua like stony brown fingers. They form the backdrop to some of the country's most fascinating, desolate scenery, and are home to communities who have come to be known as the "mountain people" – staunch non-Muslims who were pushed to the extremities of the inhabitable areas during the Muslim wars of the nineteenth century. Today the region highlights Cameroon's most striking contrasts in the cultural clash of Kirdi, Fula and Choa Arabs from the far north. In its ethno-linguistic complexity, highland site and stone buildings – as well as the rise of organised adventure tourism – the Mokolo district bears superficial similarities to the Dogon country in Mali.

WAZA NATIONAL PARK

Nov 15–June 15; CFA 2500 entrance fee payable at the gate; guide obligatory.

With a minimum of vegetation, **WAZA** spreads over 1700 square (and flat) kilometres, and is probably the single best site for viewing game in the whole of West Africa. The main park entrance, just outside the small town of Waza, is marked by two Mousgoum huts. Pay your fee here, before heading to the nearby *Campement de Waza* (BP 361, Maroua), or reserve through any *Novotel*). It's an excellent camp set on a hill with comfortable AC *boukarous* equipped with running water and electricity. As you'd expect, **accommodation** is not cheap; rooms are around CFA16,000. But you can camp near the park entrance and there are informal options in Waza village itself.

Guides are obligatory (an added expense), but are useful anyhow for locating the maximum amount of wildlife. Among the park's star attractions, **giraffes** are quite plentiful here, and congregate near the gate. There's a substantial **elephant** population, too, which you should have no problem seeing with a decent guide. Your chances of finding **lions** are also pretty good. **Ostriches** tend to be shy but herds of **buffalo** and **antelope** fill the scene often enough. Since Waza is the most popular of the game parks, it's also the one you have the best chance hitching into.

There is **no bank** in Mokolo nor in any of these villages and towns; change money in Maroua. Smuggled **petrol** is usually sold cheaply along the roadside, but it's safest to try and get up-to-date information from travellers before setting off with an empty tank.

Mokolo and around

The main point of entry to the region, **MOKOLO**, is the capital of the **Mafa** people (also called Matakam by the Fula) – one of the most populous groups in the mountains. Mokolo, however, is a quiet town (perhaps "village" is more accurate) with round houses of stone with thatched roofs, a market, motor park and not much else. You can sleep at the *Campement du Flamboyant* (BP 22 Mokolo; ☎29.51.16) which has AC *boukarous* and, since the recent rise in tourism, very inflated prices. There's a good restaurant and bar here, but with the price of rooms starting near CFA10,000, it seems very expensive. Unfortunately, the *Catholic Mission* on the hill behind the motor park no longer puts up travellers, but there's a bar on the main paved road that does (on the opposite side of town from the *Flamboyant*). Even the rudimentary rooms in this place start at CFA5000. As a cheaper solution, some people in town will put up travellers for a negotiated fee; if you want to find them, call at *Rex Photo* on the main road. It's run by a Nigerian who loves to talk English, and some of his younger employees have in the past been able to make arrangements for accommodation. The **centre artisanal** in the village of **DJINGLIYA**, 15km from Mokolo, also puts up travellers for a small fee.

Mokolo's small **museum** occupies a square off the motor park, but it keeps odd hours. Besides visiting the exhibition of **local crafts**, ask the guardian about the possibility of getting a guide to take you through the region. The idea may not have instant appeal, but the level of tourism in the mountains to the west is such that you can't really avoid this sooner or later, and it might just as well be initiated by you. At the major attractions such as **Rhumsiki** you'll wind up with a guide whether you like it or not, and villages off the beaten track are unfindable (even if you do manage, you'll need someone to interpret and make arrangements for sleeping and eating). Be clear about the itinerary and price (probably not less than CFA4000/day) before setting off. A walking trip through the area could last anything from a day to a week or more. And check out the alternative possibility of **renting a moped** around the market. On the highest paths, you can cross undetected and unmolested into Nigerian territory (see p.1077) but you should be wary of going on into Nigeria without making a formal exit from Cameroon.

Rhumsiki

A brief visit to **RHUMSIKI** (Roumsiki), 50km from Mokolo, is these days very much a standard item on Cameroon's increasingly web-like tourist circuits. This, despite the fact that it's a small and fairly ordinary village in itself. The appeal of the visit is largely to get a taste of the "real" Cameroon, and the built-in flaw is that the more people come, the more distorted and unreal life in the village becomes. However, there's one over-whelming reason why it is genuinely worth making the trip. Wherever you look, the scenery is breathtaking. Rhumsiki lies deep in the mountains, surrounded by magnificent time-worn peaks, the highest of which is much-photographed **Kapsiki**. Houses built of local stone in the traditional style blend in with the gothic backdrop, changing shades of ochre and orange to umber and russet as the sun moves over the horizon.

You have no option arriving at Rhumsiki other than to allow the little kids who greet you to act as your guides (unless you brought a paid companion with you from Mokolo. They follow their own rigid programme in showing you what they imagine every tourist wants to see. There's no point resisting their help and trying to explore the village on your own; you'll just be made to feel like an unwelcome voyeur. So let the boys show you the **féticheur** who tells your future by watching the way a river crab moves pieces of wood; the **weavers** who make cloth by hand; the **potters** and the **blacksmiths**. They explain how the huts are made and tell you about local customs and history. In the evening, they even accompany you to a nearby peak to get a better view of the sunset. Your every question, in fact, is answered before you ask it. It's all quite interesting on a superficial level, but it's about as personal as watching a television documentary. The bottom line is definitely money, and you'll just have to accept that.

You can sleep in the village (its inhabitants are called **Margui** or often **Kapsikis**, "those who have grown tall") at the new *Campement de Rhumsiki* (BP 27, Mokolo) – a tastefully rustic cluster of *boukarous* with beautiful mountain views, every bit as expensive as you might imagine (from CFA12,000). Alternatively you can arrange to sleep in people's homes; ask the little kids, but do so before the last taxi heads back to Mokolo. Once they know you can't escape, prices rise.

From Mokolo to Mora

On market days (Wednesday for Mokolo and Sunday for Mora) you can get a bush taxi to **MORA** via **Koza** – a picturesque track road that cuts through the heart of the **Mafa Country**. Even on these days, you will have to leave Mora very early in the afternoon to get back to Mokolo with the last taxi. Other days, you'll probably have to go by the less scenic route that passes through Maroua.

Mora – the market and practicalities

Capital of the **Wandala** (also called *Mandara*) – a people who accepted Islam in the late seventeenth century after their contact with the Bornu Empire – Mora is especially known for a **market** which attracts a wide range of peoples from throughout the region. Muslim Fula, Wandala and Choa women sell their goods alongside the traditionalist mountain people – **Podoko**, **Guizica** and **Mofou** – who retain their own firm views on suitable dress and headgear. It's a colourful mixture of cultures and produce from goat's milk to mangoes and millet. Donkeys and goats are sold in the **animal market**. You'll find also jewellery and carved calabashes. Directly across from the market, you can get cold drinks and a bite to eat at the *Bana Bar*.

Accommodation in town is limited and rather over-priced. The *Campement du Wandala* charges CFA8000 for its AC rooms arranged in bungalows. In theory rooms have running water, though it seldom is. Behind the *Total* station at the entrance to Mora (route de Maroua), the *Auberge Sanga Le Podoko* is slightly cheaper.

An excursion to Oudjilla

Mora is the departure point for the eleven-kilometre trip to the village of **OUDJILLA** in the mountains, a spot which, like Rhumsiki, has become a magnet for tourism. You can barely set foot in Mora without a posse of gushing teenagers racing up to you on motor bikes and asking, "Mistah, tu vas où, a Oudjilla?".

Oudjilla is an authentic **Podoko village**, though once again your experience there may seem a bit contrived. You're led on arrival to the *saré* of the chief, who lives in a walled compound with over fifty wives and countless children. For an incredible price, you get to visit the chief's compound and see the hut that serves for public deliberations; another where the chief's father is buried and where jugs of millet beer are stored; and the sacrificial pen where the chosen **cow** awaits slaughter during the harvest festival. You're taken into the hut of one of the wives to see the **kitchen** and the utensils used for pounding millet, storing water and so on. At the end, you are "invited" to take pictures of the chief and some of his wives with **shaved heads** and bare chests. For just a little more money, the wives might even do a harvest dance. It makes for the kind of photographs that put postcards to shame, but at the same time is liable to leave you feeling rather empty. To get beyond the performance, however, would take more time and dedication than most people have. But there's nothing to stop you putting your feelings back in balance by exploring some of the other roads in this region; or by trying, "Non, merci, Oudjilla ne m'intéresse pas, mais pourrais-tu me diriger à . . .?" (then picking a small name from the map).

Kousserri and north

At the confluence of the **Logone** and **Chari** rivers, **KOUSSERI** lies directly opposite the war-scarred capital of Chad – NDJAMENA. The new bridge and *pirogues* that link them are the main *raison d'être* for a town that otherwise would be right off the beaten track.

Principal sites in town include the **port** and **market** where, not surprisingly, fish is the mainstay (market day is Thursday). There are two **hotels**, but nowhere cheap now that the mission is turning people away. *Le Relais du Logone* (☎29.41.57) has rooms (some with AC) from around CFA8000 a double. The *Moderne* (☎29.40.91) charges about the same or a touch less, but they can be persuaded to give verandah space if you plead a good case. Neither of the two **banks** – *BICIC* and *SCB* – can be relied on to change money, not even French francs, in a hurry. A good road now links Kousseri to the south via Maroua. Boats still provide an important link with **Ndjamena** but the new bridge downstream from the centre of Kousseri is an easier crossing.

Heading north via Kalamaloué Park

Accommodation facilities don't exist **north of Kousseri**. In the towns that lie between Kousseri and **Lake Chad**, you're therefore at the mercy of the local authorities (police or sultans) – even when arriving in the bigger places such as MAKARI or GOULFEY. They're not always hospitable and some overlanders have been turned back. If possible, check the latest information with other travellers in Kouserri. If you find out more details, we'd be interested in hearing.

The smallest and most recently created of Cameroon's northern reserves, the **Parc National de Kalamaloué** is something of a budget park. Some 100km north of Waza, it stretches along the road from Kousseri to MALTAM. There's a rudimentary *campement* that costs only a fraction of the one at Waza and although the animals aren't as abundant, you still see herds of **elephant**. You can take guided **walking tours** to see **crocodiles** and **hippos** in the Chari River that borders the park and separates it from the outskirts of Ndjamena on the opposite bank.

HEADING INTO NIGER, NIGERIA OR CHAD

● If you're continuing into **Nigeria**, Fotokol is your last destination in Cameroon: Gamboru, over the border in Nigeria, is 140km short of Maiduguri (see p.1072–1076).

● If you happen to be travelling **direct from Ndjamena to Maiduguri** in Nigeria, you shouldn't need a visa to transit across the 100km or so of Cameroonian territory from Kousseri to Fotokol.

● Making for **Niger** *circumventing* Nigeria, you've a number of options for where to cross the border into Chad for the short detour around the lake to Nguigmi (see p.169), but if you're in Kousseri, you should cross here to Ndjamena, rather than risk going further north and finding yourself in a difficult position with nobody authorised to process your entry. If you're driving and intending heading the same way, Ndjamena is your most northerly reliable crossing point in any case.

● From Kousseri, **entry into Chad** – directly into its captial, Ndjamena – across the new bridge, can be a protracted affair and a potentially expensive arrival unless you're prepared to be patient and understanding. Once over the bridge (and it closes at 5.30pm), you have to visit three *contrôle* huts, in any order. In Ndjamena, you have to recollect your passport the next day from the Gendarmerie Central, then take it across the road to Immigration. Be prepared to give them your exact address – room no. and BP no. Accommodation is terrifyingly expensive in Ndjamena. Expect to pay at least CFA12,000 at the *Metropole*. The *Hirondelle* is a little cheaper. You may still be able to camp at the faded *Hôtel Tchadienne* , but it's not very secure.

index

PART TWENTY

THE
CONTEXTS

MUSIC IN WEST AFRICA: AN INTRODUCTION TO THE FEAST

There's nowhere in the world that can match the rhythm, melody and musical colour of West Africa. You can hardly fail to come back with at least one tune in your head, and probably a handful of tapes in your luggage.

The question is: where to start? You'll usually hear the cassette stalls when you arrive in any town, and if you want to meet local musicians you'll often find artists glad to play if you can pay something. Your interest may surprise people – so let them know!

Notices about dances and concerts are often posted up but they're most likely to take place around the end of the month – when people have some money in their pockets – and at public holidays, especially Christmas and Muslim feasts.

This introduction to West African music jumps off with a section devoted to Manding music, which has had a major influence in the region. It's followed by pieces on Mali and the other countries in the order they appear in the book, with the exceptions of Cape Verde and Guinea-Bissau (see p.487 and p.540) and Niger (a short piece appears on p.1171). Additionally there are boxes on the music of the Hausa, Tuareg and Fula.

The division of each country section into "folk" and "modern" categories is somewhat arbitrary – and much of what you might hear played by local musicians is likely to fall somewhere in between – but it serves as a useful cut-off point. "Folk", embedded in traditional society, whose artists don't as a rule have record deals or tour Europe, includes much that's disappearing; "modern" includes the whole gamut of recording artists, most with devoted local followings. But it also includes a number of styles and performers tearing away from their roots in the attempt to present music that stands alone.

MANDING MUSIC

"Manding" music is about sweet melodies and hypnotic rhythms. You'll find this broad genre from The Gambia to Mali and down through Guinea – an area roughly corresponding to the spread of the Mande languages. The music of the Mande-speaking peoples (the Malinké, Mandinka, and a number of others; see p.69) is largely untouched by western influences and has a swing to which you can either dance or daydream.

Manding musicians are easy enough to track down. Only certain families – notably Konté/h, Kouyaté/h and Diabaté/Jobarteh (note the French/English variations) carry the title of *jali* or hereditary musician, often called a *griot* in French. Traditionally, most instruments are restricted to them. They've been around since the thirteenth-century origins of the Mali empire under **Sundiata Keita**.

A jali's **reputation** is built upon humility and correct behaviour as well as his knowledge of history and family genealogies. Originally, the job was to do with the preservation of oral history. Mostly, this meant singing the praises of the noble and wealthy (no occasion – a wedding or child-naming ceremony for example – would be complete without a jali), but now they're just as likely to have business or civil service patrons. Jali, moreover, are personalities who have the ears of the people and any corrupt politician or civil servant has to reckon with them.

Jali call on a great **repertoire of songs**. If you have the chance to hear a number of artists, however, you'll start to recognise lyrical variations on common melodic themes. Songs like *Sundiata*, *Kaira*, *Duga* and *Tutu Jara* are heard time and time again. A jali's skill lies in the improvised flourishes and ornamentation – the *birimintingo* – that he brings to the recurrent theme or core melody, called the *kumbengo*.

In Mande-speaking society **men** always play the instruments. **Women artists** are considered the better singers and often receive extraordinary gifts – planes and houses aren't unknown – especially in Mali. Even at "ordinary" live shows, women commonly receive gold. Moved by a particular song, people in the audience just shed their jewellery there and then.

Traditional Manding music is a lasting influence on the modern music of Mali and Guinea. **Mory Kanté**, **Salif Keita** and **Kasse Mady** all derive artistic sustenance from it, and popular bands like **Bembeya Jazz** and **Les Amazones** reinterpret Manding songs.

MANDING INSTRUMENTS

Kora 21-stringed harp-lute made with a large decorated half-gourd covered with a skin. The strings – which used to be twisted leather, but tend now to be various gauges of fishing line – are attached with leather thongs to a rosewood pole put through the gourd. The top of the body has a large sound hole that doubles as a collection point for money from the audience.

Balo Rosewood xylophone with between 17 and 20 keys, known to have been around since the fourteenth century.

Kontingo Small, oval lute with five strings.

Bolom (or *bolombato*) Lute with 3 or 4 strings and an arched neck that used to be played for warriors going into battle. It's now an instrument played by men who are not jali.

THE MANDING JALI

There are hundreds of wonderful jali in the region, though **Dembo Konte and Kausu Kouyateh**, are, after numerous visits, probably the best known in Britain. Dembo is the son of the late great **Alhaji Bai Konte**, one of The Gambia's most revered jali, several of whose albums are available – the best on *Rounder*.

● **Sidiki Diabaté**, from Mali, toured with his ensemble in 1987, when they recorded a beautiful LP, *Ba Togoma*, which features the talents of **Kandia Kouyaté**, **Djeli Mady Sissokho**, **Mariama Kouyaté** and Sidiki's son, **Toumani** – who has also made a name for himself as a soloist, with an album of solo *kora*, *Kaira*.

● **Sékou Batourou Kouyaté**, probably the most famous of all Malian *kora* players, has released two albums; *Mamaya*, on *Disques Kouma* and *Keme Bourama*, which is only available in Mali.

● **Jali Musa Jawara** made one of the all-time classic African albums with *Fote Mogoban*, on *Oval*.

● **Ousmane Sacko** and his wife, **Yiakare Diabate**, are from the family which has the title of Chief Jali of Kayes, in western Mali. They have a superb double album recorded in France and issued on the *Ocora* label, which contains many classics including the autobiographical *Ousmane Sacko dans Ousmane Sacko*.

● **Tata Bambo Kouyaté**, is one of Mali's leading female vocalists. She claims that everything she has – and she has a lot – came to her because of her voice. She's one of the new breed of jali who travel between patrons with a portable P.A. system. Her album of traditional music, *Jatioui*, released by *Globestyle* in 1989, is more traditional (and accessible) than her more electric album in French.

● Other great female singers worth looking out for include **Kandia Kouyaté** and **Djena Doumbia**, especially Djena Doumbia's version of *Maniaba*.

MALI

Mali's music is steeped in tradition. Even in the modern popular music there's very little influence from cultures outside Mali. The musics of the Mande-speaking Bambara and Malinké, Fula, Songhai and Dogon have all helped to give today's Malian music its flavour and colour.

After **independence**, there was a renaissance of popular music in Mali. The bands, who had for many years been playing latin styles, became aware that people wanted to hear music from their own cultures. The government supported this search for roots and a number of groups received state sponsorship. Orchestras were at last able to afford modern instruments. *Janfa*, a popular song of the time, recorded by the **Orchestre National Formation "A"**, made a plea to people not to betray their traditions.

One of the most famous venues in Mali is the *Buffet Hôtel de la Gare* in Bamako, a venue which emerged from the hotel's quest for financial salvation. The director of Mali's state railway in the sixties, **Djibril Diallo**, was crazy about music and decided to create a station orchestra. The *Buffet Hôtel* soon became the hottest spot in Bamako and the **Rail Band**, as they became known, rapidly acquired legendary status, mixing Islamic vocal styles over traditional Manding rhythms played with electric instruments.

Over the years the Rail Band – still going today – has provided a launch pad for many talented musicians, including **Salif Keita** and **Mory Kanté**. There are two highly recommended Rail Band albums in the **Mali stars** series.

● **Salif Keita** has become huge in Europe – his album, *Soro*, is reported to have sold over 100,000 copies in Europe alone. An albino, he started out singing in bars for loose change, evidently to the disgrace of his family. In 1970 he joined the Rail Band, which gave him an opportunity to modernise traditional songs. After being ousted from the *Buffet Hôtel* by the then *balafon* (xylophone) player Mory Kanté, Salif joined the **Ambassadeurs** – who had immediate success with hits like *Primpin* – and recorded three albums for *Safari Ambience*. In 1978 he moved to Abidjan and, with **Kanté Manfila**, formed **Ambassadeurs International**, who recorded the wonderful song *Mandjou*. Then he left for Paris, international stardom and outer space with the high-tech *Soro* and *Ko-Yan* albums.

● **Kasse Mady Diabaté**, one of the leading vocalists of modern Manding music, made his name playing with **National Badema** for twelve years. There's a great album from this period – part of the *Mali stars* series released by *Syllart*. Kasse Mady's latest album, *Fode* has seen a move into the big sound of Paris production but the next promises a return to more traditional Malinké roots. Keyla, where Kasse Mady Diabaté was born, is a Malinké village in the west of Mali, almost entirely inhabited by jali of the **Diabaté** family. If you go there you won't want for good musicians.

● **Zani Diabaté and the Super Jatta band** are currently hot property in Mali. Although from a famous jali family, Zani draws inspiration for his rhythms from the songs of **Bambara hunters** and **Bozo fishermen** and laces it with Peul and Manding melodies and an almost psychedelic guitar style which brings to mind Jimi Hendrix. Although the group have been around since 1969 there's only one album available in Europe, released in 1985 on the French *Milady* label and three years later by *Mango*. Listen to the wonderful *Fadinga Kouma* which introduces the *balo* to electric instruments. You may find other albums in Senegal or Mali. The **Black Album** – much less refined than the European LP – is worth hearing.

● **Super Biton** have been around since the early Sixties under the leadership of trumpeter **Amadou Ba**. They've made two records – *Balandzan* on the *Tangent* label, and *Super Biton de Ségou*, part of the *Mali stars* series.

● **Sory Bamba** is a singer who has taken Dogon musical folklore and adapted it using modern instrumental arrangements. There are two albums on *Sonafric* (the most recent is *Yayoroba*) and one on *Safari Ambience*.

● **Ali Farka Touré** is an oddity, as he'd be the first to admit. Not from one of the traditional families of hereditary musicians, he started playing purely for his own pleasure and doing so in a style which – although he had never heard the blues until he was already firmly established – resonates with American blues affinities. He caused a sensation when he came to Europe a few years back. There are six records on *Disques Esperance* (for which he has never been paid) and a couple of very good ones on *World Circuit*. His vow is to give up music when he is fifty, so catch him while you can. One of a kind and never to be repeated.

BURKINA FASO

Very little Burkinabe music reaches the ears of other West Africans, let alone Europeans. Yet the country has a rich musical heritage and an annual percussion festival in Bobo-Dioulasso.

FOLK MUSIC GROUPS
A few **traditional groups** have made tours of Europe. Dance is an important part of their acts so they tend to get booked at outdoor festivals.

● One such group is the **Coulibaly Twins** whose ethnic background is **Bobo Bwa** – Voltaic-speaking people from around Burkina's second largest (and nicest) town, Bobo-Dioulasso. They play together as a duo or as part of the renowned dance and music group the **Kouledafourour Band**.

● The other famous group is drum and dance troupe **Farafina**. They were formed in 1978 by **Mahama Konaté** (also from Bobo) who is rated one of the best balafon players in West Africa. Apart from the balafon they also use the *jembe, tama* (the Wolof hourglass drum), *bara* (calabash drums) and flutes.

● The only other major artist is **Hamidou Ouédraogo**, a Peul singer and accordionist, and master of the *Gumbe* dance. He has released two solo albums on *Sonafric*.

BURKINABE INSTRUMENTS

Goni Like a miniature *kora*.
Dudumba A large metal drum beaten with a stick.
Jembe A conga-like drum.
Suku A one-string fiddle.

MAURITANIA

Until the ethnic conflict of 1989, it was easier to hear Mauritanian music in Senegal than in its homeland. This situation has now changed but it's still true that very little Mauritanian music is heard outside the region.

MAURITANIAN FOLK MUSIC

The professional musical caste in Mauritania are called *igaouen* or *iggiw*. In the past they depended, like the jali, on the patronage of big men and nobles. The more flexible modern *igaouen* repertoire includes complex songs of Middle-Eastern character and others simple enough to be taken up in chorus by the audience. The music is based on a sophisticated modal system – sometimes referred to as the "black and white ways" – derived from Arab musical theory.

There are a few **albums** of traditional music available: two of *Ocora's* feature the black and white ways on the double album **Hodh Oriental**, and a variety of sounds on **Musique Maure**. Three *Safari Ambience* albums featuring **Saidou Ba** – a musician who plays the *hadou* or African guitar in a bluesy style – are harder to find.

You may also see a group of performers led by **Dimi Mint Abba** and **Seidoum Ould Eide**, who made their first tour of the UK in 1989.

MAURITANIAN INSTRUMENTS

Tidinit Lute with two long strings on which the melody is played, and two short ones which give a fixed drone-like rhythm; played by men.
Ardin Ten- to fourteen-stringed women's harp.
Tbol Large kettledrum.
Daghumma Less common, a slender, hollowed-out gourd with a necklace, which acts as a rattle.

MODERN MUSIC FROM MAURITANIA

● There's very little **modern music** coming out of Mauritania, but one singer – **Tara** – is worth listening out for. Her eerie vocal style is given a funky backing on a record available in Paris – but so far not in Britain.

SENEGAL AND THE GAMBIA

Senegal and The Gambia share a common musical heritage and are heavily influenced by the traditions of the Mande heartland to the east. You're most likely to hear Wolof, Fula, Tukulor (Toucouleur) and Serer music north of the Gambia river, and Mandinka, Jola and Balanta music in The Gambia itself and the Casamance region of southern Senegal.

WOLOF AND TUKULOR INSTRUMENTS

The most widespread instruments are plucked **lutes**, known generically in Wolof as **khalem** or *xalam*.
Molo The most common variety, a single-string lute with a half-gourd, skin-covered soundbox.
Diassare Five-stringed, roughly boat-shaped lute with a carved wooden soundbox.
Bappe and **ndere**, often played as a pair, are similar to the *diassare*.
Riti Single-stringed Wolof lute played with a bow.
Gnagnour, The Tukulor *riti*.
Paly-yela, Sets of gourds of different shapes and sizes, bumped on the ground to produce different notes and tones to accompany Tukulor women's songs.
Tama Small, hourglass-shaped talking drum, which produces an amazing series of tones.
Sabar Large, free-standing cylindrical drums.

FOLK MUSIC OF SENEGAMBIA

In the south, listen out for the huge double xylophone or *balo* of the **Balanta**, played by two people facing each other. If you hear them, you may have difficulty seeing them, because they're invariably surrounded by a jostle of whooping and clapping women.

The best known **drums** are the **Wolof** *tama* and *sabar* (both used to great effect by Youssou Ndour and his band). Drums of all shapes and sizes are in great abundance in the Senegambia region and are the only instruments that can played by absolutely anyone.

Wrestling matches are fine opportunities to hear a bit of first-class drumming – in snatches. The wrestlers bring their own drummers to support them and the drum teams jog and pace around the arena, competing with each other with cacophonous dedication.

MODERN SENEGAMBIAN MUSIC

Modern music in the region is essentially Senegalese, largely because of the country's cultural dominance over the tiny Gambia and the inevitable magnetism for musicians of Dakar's big audiences and big money.

● The scene has been dominated for some years by the soaring voice of **Youssou Ndour and the Super Etoile de Dakar**. Although Youssou's popularity in Africa has waned slightly since his music became more Westernised, his series of fourteen early cassettes (distributed by *Saprom*) are nearly all classics. Volumes 1 to 12 cover his best music. As a starting point try volume 12, **Jamm – La Paix**, which includes the wonderful *Sabar*, a song dedicated to the drum and its rhythm. Youssou plays *mbalax*, a style rooted in the Wolof tradition, featuring frenetic rhythms with bursts of *tama* (battered by **Assane Thiam**) and complex time signatures.

● **Baaba Maal** is the new rising star of Senegalese music. He sings in the Tukulor language (a dialect of Fula) and has at least eight cassettes available; electric ones with **Dande Lenol** (which means "The Voice of the Race") and **Wandama**, and acoustic tapes with guitarist **Mansour Seck**. The only records in the UK are **Dande Lenol** so far available in the UK are the over-produced **Wango** and **Taara**. If you can find **Souka Nayo**, it's far better.

● **Orchestre Baobab** were formed in 1971 by saxophonist **Issi Cissokho** and vocalist **Laye**

M'Boup. They were one of the first groups to use Wolof and Mandinka songs as the basis for electric music. *World Circuit* have released the legendary 1982 sessions, but if you find any other old Baobab tapes, buy them; you won't be disappointed. One you should find easily enough is **Diarra Bousso** released by **Studio 2000**. **Thione Seck**, the one time singer with Baobab has been building a reputation in Europe for his rousing, hysterically up-tempo *mbalax*.

● **Super Diamono de Dakar** call their style **Afro-feeling music**. Quite different from *mbalax*, Super Diamono go for a much harder sound with heavy bass and powerful kit drums. Try to hear an early album, **Ndaxona**, which features the wailing vocals of **Omar Pene**. Their most recent is **Borom Daarou** released in Africa by *Studio 2000*.

● **Ismael Lô** was a member of Super Diamono during their early days in the late 1970s. He has released four albums so far, the latest of which – **Diawar** – was produced in Paris and goes for a predictably hi-tech sound.

● **Pascal Diatta and Sone Mane** are from the Balanta country in the Casamance region. Pascal plays guitar and his rhythms and melodies are based around patterns used on the *Balanta balo*. An album is available in the UK on *Rogue* records.

GUINEA

Guinea is the home of some of Africa's most exciting musicians and singers. Although many are now based abroad, especially in Cote d'Ivoire and France, there's still a lot of good music to be heard.

GUINEAN FOLK MUSIC

Traditional music in Guinea can be roughly divided into four geo-cultural areas.

In the lowland coastal forest of the west the musics of the Mande-speaking **Susu** and **Jalonke** are related to the **Manding** tradition.

The Fouta Djalon highlands of the centre and north are mainly inhabited by the **Fula** (see box on p.1168). In the northern Fouta, near the frontier with Senegal the **Konyagi** people play a variety of wind instruments. Long flutes are made out of bamboo cane and they also play short flutes, usually in pairs, and a stick-zither, similar to a mouth bow.

The eastern savannah, towards the Niger river, is mainly occupied by the **Malinké**, whose cultural domain spreads into eastern Mali. But the Guinean Malinké use a number of instruments not usually associated with Manding tradition (though possibly more traditional, as this is the area where the Mali empire first emerged) including **slit-drums** (usually a hollowed log with a single longitudinal gash) – and **ground bows** (in which a hollow in the earth acts as the soundbox), now only used as child's toy.

In the southeast highland forest region the **Kissi**, **Toma**, **Guerze** and **Kono** use single and double-headed drums, slit-drums and xylophone-drums. Xylophone-drums are made either from hollowed logs or from bamboo stems, slit to prduce vibrating "keys" of different lengths.

MODERN GUINEAN MUSIC

With independence in 1958 and Sékou Touré's **Authenticité** campaign, modern musical styles developed, using electric instruments but based on traditional music. Local radio was directed to play authentic Guinean music, and the government sponsored national festivals which became a focus for the new Guinean sound. Lots of new bands appeared including **Bembeya Jazz**, **Les Balladins** and **Les Amazones**. *Syliphone* have recently been re-issuing albums by the **regional bands** of the late 1970s and early 1980s. Three well worth listening to are the **Tropical Djoli Band**, **Orchestre Nimba Jazz** and, especially, **Tele-Jazz de Télimélé**.

● **Bembeya Jazz**, the Guinean vanguard, were formed in 1961 by singer **Aboubacar Demba Camera**. They mixed Malinké praise songs with Congolese musical threads and Islamic traditions with Cuban rumba. The death in 1973 of Aboubacar Camera robbed Africa of one of its greatest singers. The band is now led by lead guitarist, "Diamond Fingers" **Sekou Diabate**. They've recorded a stack of albums for *Syliphone*; perhaps kick off with *Mémoire de Aboubacar Camera*.

● **Les Amazones**, also formed in 1961, featured between fifteen and twenty female musicians – all of them suposedly members of the Guinean police force. There's an album available on *Syliphone*, **Au Coeur de Paris**. **Sona Diabate**, guitarist, singer and *balafon* player with Les Amazones, and **Mmah Sylla**,

vocalist, have both released solo albums on the same label. And the best tracks of these have been compiled by *Triple Earth Records* to make one stunner of a record, **Sahel**.

● **Mory Kanté** started playing music at the age of seven, later joining the Rail Band in Bamako before embarking on a stupendously successful solo career playing what he describes as **kora funk** on the albums *À Paris* and *Akwaba Beach*. He even broke into the singles charts all over Europe with his ebullient version of *YekeYeke*; different interpretations of which feature on both *À Paris* and *Akwaba Beach*. Loathed by purists, his music has a global village feel that makes him a star of the world stage. He still plays the occasional solo *kora* piece as part of his stage show and he played kora on **Kanté Manfila's *Tradition***.

Although relatively small, Sierra Leone has a rich variety of music and its influence, through the spread of people and ideas from Freetown over the last 200 years, has been large. Elements of early highlife can be traced back to the prewar Krio dance halls. Inland, a much less cosmopolitan scene still prevails, and it's here that Sierra Leone's older music can sometimes be heard. Folk music is closely connected with dance, storytelling and drama. Praise songs are also widespread and one unusual characteristic is that male soloists tend to sing in a high register while women sing in low voices.

SIERRA LEONEAN FOLK MUSIC

To list the enormous number of Sierra Leonean **instruments** would take pages. **Thumb pianos** are common in the north, among the Temne, Limba and Loko. **Xylophones and**

SIERRA LEONEAN INSTRUMENTS

Kondi Small thumb piano with about ten keys.

Kongoma Larger thumb piano, with only five or six keys, which picks out the bass rhythms.

Balangi Xylophone, similar to the Mandinka *balo*.

Kondingi Small three-stringed lute,

Kondene Harp-lute, used in Yalunka hunting songs.

lutes are used in the north by the Susu, Mandingo, Yalunka, Temne and Koranko. A good selection of traditional music is available on the *Ocora* label.

MODERN MUSIC OF SIERRA LEONE

In popular music the two main styles, which developed during the Fifties, were acoustic guitar *palm-wine music* (music for drinking with) and *maringa* a peculiarly Krio style. The maringa singer **Ebenezer Calender** was one of the most popular; he played guitar and trumpet and wrote all his own songs. A wonderful selection of music has been garnered on *Sierra Leone: West African gramophone records recorded at Freetown in the 1950's and early 60's*, with extensive notes by Wolfgang Bender, on the *Gema* label.

While the Freetown recording industry died in the Seventies, a number of **dance bands** struggle on in concert parties and at public holidays and the odd hotel residence. Local percussive sounds are still popular (see p.634) but today the best music is heard abroad.

● **S. E. Rogie**, the doyen of Sierra Leonean musical entertainers, has recently had sell-out gigs in Britain, confirming the enduring appeal of his palm-wine style. Picking up the trail led by the effortless style of two great guitarists, **Ekundaio** and **Joboynor**, he had hits in the 1960s all along the West African coast with *Koneh Pehlawo*, *My Lovely Elizabeth* and the gently raunchy *Go Easy With Me*. His albums are available in the UK on *Cooking Vinyl*, *Special Delivery* and *Workers Playtime*.

● **Abdul Tee-Jay's Rokoto**, based in London, is the other big name currently making music outside the country, with a high-energy live show and great debut album on *Rogue Records*, *Kanka Kuru*, meaning "God save us from parasites". They sing in all Sierra Leone's major languages.

LIBERIA

Liberian music can be put into three rough and ready groups: music of the indigenous people, music from the freed slave tradition of repatriated Africans, and modern, more de-cultured, popular music. The "Congos" – people with connections with the freed slave heritage, sing a lot of religious music, which bears close comparison with American gospel.

LIBERIAN FOLK MUSIC

Most indigenous Liberian peoples incorporate "music" within a broader term that describes an event involving music, dancing and celebration. The **Kpelle** call this the *pelee*, and its songs the *wule*. In traditional **Kpelle** and **Gio** culture, a wide variety of flutes, xylophones and drums are used. The coastal **Kru** people also play the guitar and may have been partly responsible for the creation of highlife guitar playing.

MODERN LIBERIAN MUSIC

Liberian **popular music** was in a parlous state of disarray even before the **war**. For some idea of what you might find, see p.699.

CÔTE D'IVOIRE

Côte d'Ivoire, with Abidjan's high-quality studios, has long been a musical centre for the Francophone states, but has very few stars of its own. The country's own musicians reflect this mixed salad of musical influences and it's hard to come up with any that aren't making very derivative music. Even the top artists are aiming for a market in the Francophone world – even in France itself – which is not really their own. But Ivoirians have no lack of traditions to call upon. In the north the Senoufo and Lobi people are famous for their xylophone music; while in the centre and east, the Akan peoples – Baoulé, Abron, Agni, and Atié – together with the Bété of the southwest, have produced most of Cote d'Ivoire's popular musicians and all have strong, if under-recognised folk-music heritages.

MODERN IVOIRIAN MUSIC

In the 1940s there were **Akan street groups** who played a traditional dance called *Akpombo*. Gradually they started introducing guitars and accordions to their line-up. After independence it was these street groups that became the first popular dance bands. In the 1960s these bands would play cover versions of European and American hits over traditional rhythms like the Bété *gbegbe*. The best known groups of the day were **Agnebi Jazz, Souers Comoé, Anoma Barou Felix** and, much later, **Ernesto Djedje**, who updated the Bété dance, the *ziglibithy*.

● **Sery Simplice** is one the chief modernisers of *gbegbe* music and has made about a dozen records. Try to hear his second and third albums *Gbolou* and *Atrikakou*, on which he tells people to stop playing funk and reggae and listen to the sound of their own culture.

● **Alpha Blondy** has become one of West Africa's most successful musical exports – whatever Simplice might call it – with his form of reggae. His top-selling album *Apartheid is Nazism* is probably his best to date – a mostly on-target album from a sometimes very off-beam artist.

● **Nyanka Bell** is a singer who has turned to the French West Indies for her inspiration. After a period churning out ballads to disco funk backing, she has now started to include more and more zouk-flavoured songs in her repertoire.

● **Daouda**, singer and composer, mixes Zairian *soukous* with Cameroonian *makossa* and local rhythms. He's recorded a string of albums in London and Paris including, on *Sterns*, **Le Sentimental** – slick, mushy music from a superstar crooner. The track *La Femme de Mon Patron* (a massive hit all over West Africa, later covered in English) is its one redeeming feature.

FULA MUSIC

The **Fula** are commonly called **Fulani** in Nigeria where they form a very large and powerful community. This name has tended to be used as the standard form in English. The same people, however, are **Fullah** in Sierra Leone, **Peul** or **Peulh** in Senegal and Mali and **Pulaar** in Mauritania. Nomadic Fula groups in Niger include the **Bororo** and the **Wodaabe**, while in Senegal, the **Tukulor** are a Fula-speaking ethnic group who have been Muslims for nearly a thousand years.

With their wide geographical distribution and considerable cultural diversity (most fundamentally between the traditional cattle herders – the Fula stereotype – and the urban communities) it's hard to generalise about **Fula music**. There are, however, two distinct genres. The first is pure Fula music, composed and played by them or their recognised professional musicians; the second consists of the hymns and songs which, though mostly still in the Fula language, have been passed down and evolved from the Islamic tradition.

TRADITIONS AND INSTRUMENTS

There are three **classes of professional musician** in Fulani society. The **wammbaabe** and the **maabube** were, and in some cases still are, court musicians, singing the praises of chiefs and wealthy patrons and telling tales of their ancestors and epic stories of the Fula past. The **awlube** are less closely associated with the court and more often found praising and entertaining the people in general, using a wider frame of reference and using a wider range of **instruments**. The instrument used most by the *wammbaabe* and *maabube* is the **hoddu**, a three-stringed lute. The *wammbaabe* also play the **nyaanyooru**, a one-stringed fiddle. The **awlube** play everything, but their main instruments are drums.

In some areas – for example The Gambia, where Fula live in proximity to Mandinka – you also find a three- or four-stringed lute, the **bolon**, very similar to the Mandinka *bolombato*. At the other end of West Africa, in Cameroon, the instruments used in court music are similar to those used by the **Hausa** court musicians of Nigeria.

Professional troupes – and the Fula are famous for their bands of entertainers, which play in all communities – nearly always use a **percussion** instrument or two. The most common is the *horde*, a half-gourd vessel with a rattling metal plate attached inside. The player holds the open end towards his chest and beats the outside with his hands or uses rings on his fingers. The *horde* player is usually the acrobat of the troupe.

Another percussive instrument is the **lala**, a pair of L-shaped stick-rattles. Each one has three or four calabash discs which move up and down on the stick.

Lastly, the **instruments of the pastoral Fula** – flutes of wood, bamboo or corn stalks, two-stringed lutes, single-stringed fiddles and jew's harps – are mainly played for their own enjoyment. They have a range of songs for pleasure, similar to that of many other African peoples – work songs, lullabies, love songs and herders' songs (often in praise of cattle, sung at them as they graze).

Of modern Fula music, try to hear the stunning voice of **Sali Sidibe** from Mali and **Dourah Barry** from Guinea. Sali Sidibe uses traditional instruments like the *nyaanyooru* and *bolon*, which create a hypnotic bass beat, together with what sounds like a Casio keyboard complete with drum machine. Her super tape is available in Europe from *Syllart*.

Ghana's "town music" is well known abroad but the country has a strong and living tradition of rural music still commonly performed, which continues to influence urban sounds.

GHANAIAN FOLK MUSIC

The main types of music you can hear are **court music** played for chiefs, **ceremonial music** and **work songs** – and, of course, music for its own sake. It's probably clearest to explain traditions region by region.

Northeastern Ghana is home to a cluster of Voltaic-speaking peoples – best known of which are the **Dagomba**, **Mamprusi** and **Frafra**. In this area you find mostly fiddles, lutes and wonderful hourglass talking-drum ensembles. It's customary for musicians to perform frequently for the local chief – in the Dagomba country each Monday and Friday. In towns like **Tamale** and **Yendi** you might find something going on, because professional musicians, although attached to chiefs, regularly perform for the general public. Dagomba drummers are always a great spectacle, their flowing tunics fanning out as, palms flying, they dance the *takai*.

In the northwest, the main instrument of the **Lobi**, **Wala**, **Dagarti** and **Sissala** is the xylophone – either played alone or with a small group of drums and percussion instruments. Finger bells and ankle bells are often worn by the dancers.

The **Ewe** are the main people of eastern Ghana. Their music is closer to the traditions of

Togo and Benin than to that of other Ghanaian peoples and with their enthusiasm for music associations and dance clubs they've developed many different kinds of recreational music.

In the southern part of central Ghana the **Akan** peoples, notably the **Asante** and **Fante**, have an elaborate court music using large drum ensembles and groups of horns. Another great spectacle is huge log xylophones played in *asonko*, a form of recreational music.

PALM-WINE MUSIC OF GHANA

Palm-wine is the popular music of the Asante. Primarily solo guitar music, it originated in the palm-wine bars – usually under a big tree. A musician would turn up with his guitar and play for as long as people wanted to buy him drinks. This is very much good-time music and such palm-wineists tend to be comedians as well as parodists of the local scene. If you buy him a drink you may well find your name included in the current song.

Palm-wine guitar music is slowly dying out partly because musicians are being enticed into the guitar bands and concert party groups, and partly due to the lack of instruments in Ghana. In any town someone will be able to point you in the direction of a palm-wine player but you may have to find an instrument for him to play on.

GHANAIAN HIGHLIFE

Highlife originated in Ghana and Sierra Leone and has proved to be one of the most popular, enduring (and broad) African styles. Originally a fusion of traditional percussion and melodies, with European influences like brass bands, sea shanties and hymns, it started in the early 1920s with the growth of major ports along the West African coast. The term itself is no more than a reference to the kind of European-derived evening of dressing up and dancing (the "highlife") to which new immigrants to the towns of West Africa between the wars were quite unaccustomed – but which they soon made their own.

The first 78rpm records were released in the 1930s and highlife's international reputation started to grow. There are about a dozen **different styles of highlife** but the two main ones are played by the *guitar bands* and the *concert party* groups. The guitar bands are the real dance bands, while the concert party is a mixture of storytelling, comedy, music and dance. There's a wonderful highlife variation in

---

NORTHEAST

Gonge One-stringed fiddle.
Kologo Two-stringed lute.
Donno Talking drums, in an ensemble.

EWE

Sogo and **Kidi** Drums.
Atsimewu Master drum.
Axatse Rattles.
Gankogui Double bells.

ASANTE

Atumpane Sets of twin drums.
Ntahera Ensemble of ivory horns.

"Gospel Highlife" – do everything possible to hear something by the **Genesis Gospel Singers**.

● **E. T. Mensah** was the unchallenged "king of highlife". Mensah had a musical childhood and developed his skills on the guitar, organ, sax and trumpet. During World War II he came into contact with British and American styles like **calypso**, **swing** and **cha-cha**, and in 1948 he formed the **Tempos Band**, then the only professional dance band in Ghana. After a string of hits, including *Donkey Calypso, School Girl* and *All for You*, the group went international with frequent tours of West Africa – a golden age of highlife. Soon there were hundreds of bands imitating their style and, in the 1950s and 1960s, a host of exciting groups including **The Uhurus**, **Broadway** and the **Black Beats**. Mensah's popularity declined during the 1970s, but he made a comeback towards the end of the decade, with an album, *The King of Highlife Music* recorded on the *Afrodisia* label. In 1986, he released *All For You*, a compilation of classics and a good introduction to his unique style.

● **African Brothers International Band**, formed in 1963 by **Nana Kwame Ampadu**, are still one of the country's most innovative and enduring guitar groups. They had their earliest and one of their best-loved hits in 1967 with *Ebi Tie Ye* – a plea for democracy in the dark days following the fall of Nkrumah – and had released over 100 discs before 1970 and the release of their first LP, *Ena Eye A Mane Me*. Since then they've released over twenty albums and countless singles. Always a group to mix street wisdom with thinly veiled political comment, they never let this interfere with good music, and are forever trying something new. During the 1970s they experimented with a variety of styles including reggae, rumba and what they called *Afro-hili*, a James Brown-inspired beat which was a challenge to **Fela Kuti's** *Afrobeat*. In recent years they have returned to a more refined highlife with strong rhythms and sparkling guitars.

● **Daniel Amponsah**, aka **Koo Nimo**, is a guitarist who has done as much as anyone to enrich and preserve Ghana's traditional guitar music. Now in his late fifties, he still performs regularly at concerts and festivals with his all-acoustic **Adadam band** and commands huge respect among Ghanaians at home and abroad.

There are two albums available in Ghana: a good place to start is *Odonson Nkoaa* on the *Phillips* label.

● **A. B. Crentsil's Sweet Talks** were one of Ghana's most successful highlife bands in the 1970s. Originally based at Tema's *Talk of the Town* club, the group gained national popularity after a string of hit albums, the first of which was *Adam and Eve*. In 1978 they went to the USA and recorded their classic *Hollywood Highlife Party*. Soon after the group split, Crentsil formed the new **Ahenfo Band**. International acclaim came with the group's first British release, *Tantie Alaba*, in 1984.

● **Asabia**, one-time singer with the **Sweet Talks**, went to Côte d'Ivoire to record her first solo LP, *Wamaya* (available on the American *Makossa* Label) – one of the most popular ever to come out of Ghana.

● **Pat Thomas** is one of the nation's premier highlife vocalists. He sang with many of Ghana's great dance bands in the 1970s before going solo in the 1980s. He subsequently gained international recognition with the release of several albums, including the 1986 *Highlife Greats*.

● **Osibisa** were formed in London by three Ghanaians, **Teddy Osei**, **Mac Tontoh** and **Sol Amarfino**. Their Afro-rock singles climbed the British charts in the 1970s with three of them, *Dance the Body Music, Sunshine Day* and *Coffee Song*, rising to the top ten. Perhaps they were five years too early, but by the time Sunny Ade was making headlines with undiluted *juju*, they had melted away.

● **Highlife International** are another London-based band that enjoyed British success. They have released two albums on *Stern's*; *Travel and See* (1983) and *Na Wa For You* (1985).

● **Kantata**, a Berlin-based combo led by Ghanaian guitarist **George Darko**, have released a number of successful albums of dance floor music including *It's High Time*. The single *Slim Lady* was a huge success in Ghana.

● **Alex Konadu** is today the uncrowned king of guitar band highlife. He plays music firmly rooted in Ghanaian traditions and has enjoyed massive sales all over West Africa. It's claimed he has played in every town and village in Ghana. He has released about a dozen albums including the 1989 release on *World Circuit* – *One Man Thousand – Live in London*.

TOGO

Traditional music tends to split into two: Kabyé in the north and Ewe/Mina in the south (see Ghana).

TOGOLESE FOLK MUSIC

The **Kabyé** have a rich musical culture. Some of the most interesting instruments are only used for special celebration like the **picancala**, a xylophone-like instrument made of stones and rocks — a "lithophone" — and the unusual **water flutes**. There's music played on horns, flutes and whistles and even a trumpet — the **xokudu** — made from the fruit of the baobab tree.

Ocora has an album of Kabiyé music. There's a less recherché selection on *Togo: Music from West Africa* on *Rounder Records*, which has a good mixture of traditional and modern styles and features some nice acoustic guitar songs from **Ali Bawa**.

MODERN MUSIC OF TOGO

Modern music in Togo has not thrown up any great stars and most of the few singers seem content to imitate external styles. Togo's urban music has been greatly influenced by Congolese styles during the 1960s and 1970s and reggae, soul, highlife and Latin music have all dominated the local scene at some time or other.

Bella Bellow was the leading singer in the late 1960s. She toured Europe and America and made an album, with the help of **Manu Dibango**, *Album Souvenir* which is on *Safari Ambience*. **Afia Mala** recorded an album in 1984 called *Lonlon Viye*. A couple of other local stars are included in the Togo "Directory" on p.884.

BENIN

Benin has a variety of cultures and a diverse musical tradition, with the Hausa, Kabyé and Bariba in the north, and the Yoruba, Gun and Fon people in the south. The music of the Fon played a crucial ceremonial role in the court at Abomey, capital of the country's major pre-colonial state Dan-Homey. The Gun people use a wide variety of instruments including a huge double log xylophone, percussion pots and raft zithers.

MODERN MUSIC FROM BENIN

Modern music of Benin mixes indigenous rhythms and melodies with Congolese styles. During the 1970s Benin's popular music scene was severely impeded by government curfews, but orchestras carried on somehow, the most successful being **Orchestre Poly-Rythmo, Disc Afrique** and **Les Astronauts**. Poly-Rythmo, led by horn player **Ignace de Souza**, have one record released on the French *Tangent* label entitled *Zero + Zero*.

● The only **musical export** from Benin in recent years has been **Wally Badarou**, whose album *Echoes* was released by *Island* in 1986, but on the whole the 1980s have failed to produce any noticeable artists or groups. If the processes described on p.942 bear fruit, the 1990s may bring a new wave.

NIGER

Not much is heard in Europe about music from Niger. A few records of traditional music are available, but none of its modern music travels far. They do however have a "Top of the Pops"-type television programme where the miming seems to be as bad as everywhere else in the world.

FOLK MUSIC OF NIGER

Niger's major ethnic groups are the **Tuareg** (see box overleaf), **Bororo**, **Songhai** and **Hausa**. The Bororo are nomads closely related to the Fula. They have no musical instruments and all their songs are for voices only.

There's a good instrumental ensemble in **Niamey**, which features musicians from all the major ethnic groups, and a national dance troupe called **Karaka**.

Two recordings of traditional music are available on *Ocora*: one, *Nomades du Niger*, is of Tuareg and Bororo music; the other, *La Musique des Griots*, features sounds of the Songhai, Hausa and Tuareg.

MODERN NIGÉRIEN MUSIC

Popular artists you may well hear include Hausa singers **Mahaman Garba** and **Yan Ouwa** — both use mostly percussive backing — and the African reggae of **Amadou Hamza**. Best of Niamey's bunch is female singer, **Madelle Iddari**.

TUAREG MUSIC

Although Tuareg men and women both make music, they have separate forms and styles. Women's songs include *tinde nomnas* (praise songs), *tinde nguma* (songs of exorcism) and *ezele* (dance songs). The *tinde*, used to accompany women's songs, is a drum made from a goat skin stretched over a mortar.

Other instruments used by women include the *assakhalebo* water drum, made from a half-gourd floating upside down in a bowl of water, and the *tabl* – a kettle drum (traditionally a battle drum) with a broad camel-skin top.

The men's songs – *Tichiwe* – are, in striking contrast to the women's, essentially lyrical. They sing about the beauty of the women they love or celebrate some happy event. The songs are performed by soloists – whose virtuosity lies, as ever in improvisation – either with or without an accompaniment. This is usually provided by a single-stringed fiddle, the *inzad*, which consists of a half-gourd, goatskin-covered resonator and a horsehair string stretched over a bridge in the form a small wooden cross.

The Tuareg also use an end-blown **flute**, called the *sarewa*, constructed from a sorghum stem in which four holes are made, with leather thongs tied round its body for ornamentation and protection.

HAUSA MUSIC

The **Hausa**, whose communities are concentrated in the cities of Niger and northern Nigeria, have spread right across West and Central Africa, setting up shops in the smallest towns, content to live among strangers. They have long been famous for their art and music which has flourished since the sixteenth century and the fall of the Songhai empire, with whose music Hausa has many parallels.

Hausa music splits into **rural music** and **urban music** of the court and state. State ceremonial state music – *rokon fada* – still plays a great part (though not a very musical one) in Hausa traditions, while court praise singers still play for the amusement of emirs and sultans, usually in private. The emirates of **Katsina** and **Kano** together with the sultanate of **Sokoto**, and to a lesser extent **Zaria** and **Bauchi**, are the major creative centres.

THE MUSICIANS

The instruments of **ceremonial music** are largely seen as prestige symbols of authority, and ceremonial musicians tend to be chosen for their family connections rather than any musical ability. They don't present the most dulcet of tones. **Court musicians**, on the other hand, are always chosen for their musical skills. Exclusively dependent on a single wealthy patron, it's hardly surprising that the most talented players are rarely seen in public.

The greatest praise singer was **Narambad**, who lived and worked in Sokoto: he died in 1960 and it's doubtful if you can still get his recordings.

THE INSTRUMENTS

The most impressive of the state **instruments** is the elongated state trumpet called *kakakai*, which was originally used by the Songhai cavalry and was taken by the rising Hausa states as a symbol of military power. Kakakai are usually accompanied by *tambura*, large state drums. Lesser instruments include the *farai*, a small double-reed woodwind instrument, the *kafo*, an animal horn, and the *ganga*, a small snare drum. Ceremonial music can always be heard at the *sara*, the weekly statement of authority which takes place outside the emir's palace on a Thursday evening.

The principal instruments accompanying praise songs are percussive – small kettledrums, *banga* and *tabshi*, and talking drums, *jauje* and *kotso*.

RURAL HAUSA MUSIC

Traditional **rural music** appears to be dying out in favour of modern popular music which still draws inspiration from the traditional roots. The last expressions of rural music are to be found in traditional dances like the *asauwara*, for young girls, and the *bori*, the dance of the spirit possession cult, which dates back to a time before Islam became the accepted religion and continues to thrive parallel with the teachings of the Koran. Zaria is its main stronghold.

MODERN HAUSA MUSIC

Popular music thrives in town and countryside and although very little seems to be of interest outside Hausaland, musicians can still make a good living satisfying local needs and, as ever, expressing, and sometimes moulding, public opinion.

The leading Hausa singer, **Muhamman Shata**, is always accompanied by a troupe of virtuoso drummers who play *kalangu*, small talking drums. There's a fair number of other worthy artists such as **Dan Maraya**, leading exponent on the *kontigi* one-stringed lute, **Ibrahim Na Habu**, who popularised a type of small fiddle called the *kukkuma*, and **Audo Yaron Goge** who plays (not surprisingly) the *goge* or fiddle.

There are two excellent records available on *Barenreiter Musicaphon*.

NIGERIA

As far as the music industry is concerned, Nigeria is the centre of African Music. The industry is well developed here, with numerous recording studios and pressing plants and, in spite of recession and poverty, a huge home market. Of more intrinsic interest, Nigeria also has a big enough population to sustain artists who sing in regional languages and experiment with indigenous styles. Drawing from traditional sources and outside influences, three main types of modern music have developed – *juju*, highlife and *fuji*. Both *juju* and *fuji* are almost entirely sung in local languages, principally Yoruba.

IGBO MUSIC

The Igbo people of the southeast have always been receptive to cultural change. This ease is reflected in their music and in the incredible variety of instruments played in Igboland. No local occasion would be complete without musicians and you should find them at any event associated with the *obi* (chief). The other major occasions would be seasonal festivals, wrestling matches, a visit by a high-ranking official or the funeral of a prominent citizen.

In more traditional communities, royal music is played every day, when the *ufie* slit drum is used to wake the chief and to tell him when meals are ready. A group, known as *egwu ota*, which consists of slit-drums, drums and bells, performs when the *obi* is leaving the palace and again when he returns.

One of the most pleasing Igbo instruments is the *obo*, a thirteen-stringed raft zither, which can heard at many a nostalgic palm-wine drinking session.

YORUBA MUSIC

Yoruba instrumental traditions are mostly based on drumming. The most popular form of traditional music today is *dundun*, played on hourglass tension drums of the same name. The usual *dundun* ensemble consists of tension drums of various sizes together with a small kettledrums called *gudugudu*. The leading drum of the group is the *iyaalu* ("mother of the drums"), which talks by imitating the tone patterns of Yoruba speech. It's used to play out praise poetry, proverbs and other oral texts. Another important part of Yoruba musical life is

music theatre, which mixes traditional music with storytelling or live drama.

JUJU

The origins of *juju* music are not very clear but, it's said to have emerged as a Lagosian variation of palm-wine music. The word *juju* is thought to be a corruption of the **Yoruba** word *jo jo*, meaning "dance" – or may just be a dismissive epithet coined by colonial officers. The first records of this dreamy style started coming out in the early 1930s but it really took off just after World War II with the introduction of amplified sound. The major stars of the pre-war period were **Irewolede Denge** ("grandfather of *juju*") and **Tunde King**; and after the war, **Ayinde Bakara** and the **Jolly Orchestra**.

The **1960s** saw the emergence of a great number of new *juju* singers and bands. Three came to dominate the scene; **I.K. Dairo, Ebenezer Obey** and, in the later 1960s, **Sunny Ade**. During and after the Nigerian Civil War (1967-70) *juju* thrived at home as highlife artists from the eastern region either went to Biafra or fled abroad, and highlife as a whole lost its popularity.

In the 1980s, as *juju* fractured into several strands, Yoruba pop music – **Yo-pop** – crashed onto the scene, in the person of **Segun Adewale**. All speed, thunder and lightning, Yo-pop has found a huge young audience, especially in Lagos. The latest star in this evolution is **Sir Shina Peters**.

● **I. K. Dairo** had been playing in bands for a good part of his life when he formed the **Morning Star Orchestra** in 1957. By 1961, he set up the popular **Blue Spots** and rose to become the best-known *juju* player in Nigeria. He has released albums over his thirty years in music, mostly on *West Africa Polydor*. A taster of his early music can be heard on *Juju Music of I.K. Dairo* released by *Decca West Africa*. Although Dairo was overshadowed on the international scene with the rise of Obey and Ade in the 1970s, he continued to make a solid contribution with hit albums like *Kekere*. The 1980s have also seen a string of successes including *Iyo Mi Iyo* and *Easy Motion* and he still performs in Lagos, notably at the *Ariya* club.

● **Ebenezer Obey** formed his first group, **The International Brothers**, in 1964. Since then the man-mountain has released over fifty LPs.

Early records include *In London, Board Members* and *Aiye Wa A Toro*. The success of his blend of talking drums, percussion and guitar had already caught on by the time he renamed his group **The InterReformers** in 1970. *Murtala Muhammed* and *Immortal Songs for Travellers* were among albums he was turning our at a staggering rate in the late 1970s, with guaranteed advance sales of over 100,000 records. In 1980 he went international with *Current Affairs* followed by *Je Ka Jo* on *Virgin* and *Solution* on *Sterns*.

● **King Sunny Ade** started his musical career playing with highlife bands in Lagos before making the transition to *juju*. He went solo in 1966 when he formed **The Green Spots**, and struck gold with *Challenge Cup* the following year. He changed the name of the group to **African Beats** in 1974 and released hit albums including *The Late General Murtala Muhammed*, *Sound Vibration* and *The Royal Sound*. By the end of the decade, Ade was one of the most popular musicians in the country. In the 1980s he broke into the intenational scene with tours of Europe, Japan and the USA, and signed to *Island* records, with whom he released three albums, easily the finest of which is *Juju Music*. This album included many of his best songs including *365 is My Number*, a great version of which takes up a whole side on the 1978 release *Private Line*. In 1984 he formed a new band, **Golden Mercury**.

APALA AND FUJI

Though never knowing the international success that both *juju* and highlife enjoyed, *fuji* has still been extremely popular in Nigeria since the 1970s. It has its roots in the Yoruba styles of *apala* and *sakara*, themselves products of Muslim influence on older musical forms in northern Yorubaland. Some of *fuji*'s leading exponents include:

● **Haruna Ishola**. One of Nigeria's greatest *apala* performers, Ishola's music helped pave the way for *fuji*. Before he died in 1983, he had produced some 25 LPs and opened his own recording studio. It's still relatively easy to find many of his later records like *Apala Songs* or *Haruna Ishola and his Apala group*.

● **Sikiru Ayinde**, better known as **Barrister** by his fans, is the leading Yorubal *fuji* singer. He started singing *were*, Muslim music performed at Ramadan celebrations, at the age

of ten. After a brief army career, he turned back to music and, in the early 1970s, formed the **Supreme Fuji Commander**, a 25-piece outfit. They soon became one of Nigeria's top bands, firing off a battery of hit records, including *Iwa*, *Igo Olomo*, *Fuji Vibration* and *Elo Sona*.

● **Ayinla Kollinton** is ranked second in the *fuji* popularity stakes behind Barrister. He's very much the source of social commentary in the Yoruba Muslim music scene. His lyrics can be razor sharp – though he rarely puts himself on the front line with Fela Kuti. He released over a dozen albums in the 1980s, including *Motun De Pelu Ara* and *Knock-out Special*.

NIGERIAN HIGHLIFE

Highlife came to Nigeria from Ghana in the 1950s, but it was quickly moulded by indigenous styles and influences from Cameroon and the Congo so that it came to have a flavour that was unmistakeably Nigerian. Western instruments – brass sections, electric keyboards and guitars – and polish were added to homegrown rhythms and, by the 1960s, highlife was in the forefront of popular urban music. It lost its universal appeal during the civil war, when it retained mass popularity only in Igboland, and quite quickly lost ground to juju among the Yoruba.

● **Bobby Benson**: One of the pioneers of Nigerian highlife, Benson switched to this style after hearing Ghana's E. T. Mensah. In the 1950s, he created **Bobby Benson and his Combo** whose early hits went a long way to popularise the style at home.

● **Rex Lawson**: Lawson began playing trumpet in bands at the age of twelve, and when highlife took off in the 1950s, he worked with many of the greats. In the 1960s, his 11-piece group, **Mayor's Dance band** produced successive hits including *Jolly Papa* and *Gowon Special*. Lawson died suddenly in 1976, at the height of his career. Many of the classics can be heard on his *Greatest Hits* album on *Polydor Nigeria* – though you'll be hard-pressed to find it.

AFRO-BEAT

Afro-beat was almost solely the creation of one extraordinary musician, **Fela Anikulapo-Kuti**. The style has its own distinctive beats and rhythms which provide a flexible vehicle for

Fela's political lyrics and call-and-response vocal style. He chose to sing in the lingua franca of pidgin English to avoid limiting his audience, and it's worked. His eruptive performances and defiant lifestyle have found him huge following and brought him into constant conflict with the Nigerian authorities. Since the release of his first album, **Why Black Men Dey Suffer**, in 1971, he has released a steady stream of hits including **Black President**, **Perambulator**, **Coffin for Head of State** and **Expensive Shit**.

Fela has always had a precarious relationship with the police. During his periods in jail, his bands, first **Africa 70** and then **Egypt 80**, have carried on, led by his son Femi and others. **Femi Kuti** has now launched a career of his own, to escape from the shadow of Fela. There is a fascinating biography available in Europe, *This Bitch of a Life* by Carlos Moore (Alison & Busby).

CAMEROON

In Cameroon there are hundreds of ethnic groups, many of them with a distinctive musical culture and dances. More than two hundred different dances are still performed on a whole range of occasions and the majority are accompanied by instrumental ensembles.

FOLK MUSIC

In the south the **Bakweri**, **Bamiléké**, **Bamoun** and **Beti** have mostly xylophone or drum ensembles and their masked dance dramas are well worth seeing. The Sultan of Bamoun's Musical Theatre (see p.1125) is a remarkable institution. Also in the south live the **Bulu**, **Fang**, **Eton** and **Mvele**, who play a wide diversity of musical instruments including the *ngkul*, a slit-drum formerly used to send messages but now only to accompany the *ozila* or initiation dance; the *mendzan*, a small xylophone; and the *mvet*, a long stick zither (*mvet* refers not only to the instrument but also the pantomime and dances associated with it).

Northern Cameroon is mainly occupied by Fula and Hausa people (see boxes).

● The career of **Francis Bebey** won't fit into any category. Multi-talented, Bebey is a writer and storyteller, film-maker and musician. As a guitarist and composer, he sings in English, French and Douala, experimenting with styles ranging from classical guitar and traditional rhythms to *makossa* and plain pop. He has released some twenty albums since 1969 and you never know what you'll find on any of them. He's also the author of a seminal book, *African Music; A People's Art* (see box on p.1178).

MAKOSSA

Makossa, the popular music of Cameroon, was created in the 1950s but has its roots in the 1930s. Mission schools created their own bands to usher the pupils into assembly, using xylophones and percussion instruments. These bands performed at dances outside school hours, playing a mixture of western and local styles. Guitars were introduced before the war and guitarists would perform accompanied by a bottle player. There were three main dance styles at the time: *asiko* – percussion and xylophone music; *ambasse bey* – a guitar based dance with much faster rhythms; and the fledgling *makossa*, a popular folk dance.

● *Makossa* gained international appeal with the coming of **Manu Dibango**. A sax-player, composer, singer, pianist and arranger, Dibango's inspirations are diverse. He has lived and recorded in Brussels, Paris, Zaire, the United States, Jamaica and Côte d'Ivoire. He started a whole wave of urban popular music with the release of his album **Soul Makossa** in 1973. This record paved the way for a new generation of artists who now rely on a combination of traditional inspiration and high-tech recording facilities to produce the highly exportable dance music that has turned Douala into one of the dynamos of African music. Now in the superstar class – nearly thirty years after his first single – Manu Dibango is one of the few African artists guaranteed to draw a full house anywhere in the world.

● **André Marike Tala** is a singer/songwriter discovered by Manu Dibango. Blind since the age of thirteen, this didn't stop him going to France where he recorded several singles that became hits in Cameroon – **Potaksima** and **Sikata**. Mixing traditional and modern styles, he is also recognised for the creation of the *tchamassi* rhythm. His albums include **Black Woman**, **Mother Africa** and **Je Vais A Yaoundé**.

● **Sam Fan Thomas** recorded with Tala for over eight years before going solo in 1976. He recorded several albums with minor hits, but had to wait until 1984 and the release of *Makassi* to achieve a wider reputation. The album's single *African Typic Collection* instantly ignited his reputation when it became an international dance hit.

● Thomas and **Moni Bile** have ignited in the 1980s to become the hottest *makossa* singers in Cameroon. Using the best session men, Bile is known for his sophistication and driving dance melodies. His albums include *Chagrin d'Amour* and *African Melody*.

● **Anne-Marie Nzie**, "La voix d'or du Cameroun", started singing at the age of eight and was a national star by the 1950s. Though no longer a chart-topper, she remains one of the most respected and popular female singers in the country. 1984 saw the release of her latest album, *Liberté*.

● **Bébé Manga**, another great female singer, started her career with the group **Douala** as a nightclub artist before going to Paris in the early 1980s to record her first album *Amie*. Although this excellent LP contained solid

makossa and Congalese rhythms, it was the accessible title track that became an international hit.

● **Toto Guillame** was Cameroon's most sought after session guitarist in the1970s. He made a splash with his band **The Black Styles** and progressively earned himself a reputation as a *makossa* wizard. He has backed just about everybody on some of the country's hottest albums and is now one the main engineers of the explosive affair between Antillean *zouk* and African music. His own hit releases include *Toguy*, *Makossa Digital* and *Elimbi Na Ngoma*.

● **Lapiro de Mbanga** has not been around long but how can any singer go wrong when cutting an album with Jean-Claude Naimro (of Kassav), Jimmy Cliff and Toto Guillame? *No Make Erreur* was a fitting title for the 1986 chart-topper that catapulted him into the limelight. But he can also stand alone and is comfortable with a range of styles from *makossa* to Zairian *soukous*.

RECOMMENDED DISCOGRAPHY

Jali Musa Jawara, *Fote Mogoban* (*Oval* OVLP511), **Guinea**. Gently produced kora, guitar, balo and beautiful backing voices with a version of *Yeke Yeke* very different from Mory Kanté's. A must in any collection.

Kanté Manfila, *Tradition* (*Tangent* 470171, and subsequently remixed by **Sterns**), **Guinea**. Former Ambassadeur with his second solo album. An all-acoustic line-up similar to Jali Musa Jawara's. The earlier French mix is slightly more atmospheric.

Télé-Jazz de Télimélé, *La Fête au Foutah* (*Syliphone* SLP 70), **Guinea**. Vintage Guinean sounds of the early 1980s. Guitar, bass and drums augmented with brass and balafon. *Dyarama* based on a Manding tune, is a classic.

Tropical Djoli Band de Faranah, *Style Savane* (*Syliphone* SLP 70), **Guinea**. Another of the series of regional bands, not as immedi-

ate as Télé-Jazz but worth hearing for the wild polyrhythms and brass.

Bembeya Jazz National, *Mémoire de Aboubacar Camara* (*Syliphone* SLP 65), **Guinea**. Vintage 1973, still available and rightly so. Garage production which only enhances the weaving guitar and soulful vocals. Contains two wonderful songs, *Alla Lake* and *Ballake*, both based on Manding songs and bursting with emotion.

l'Ensemble Instrumental, *Medaille d'Or au Festival Culturel Panafricain d'Alger* (*Musicaphon* BM 30 L 2504), **Mali**. Traditional ensemble of 29 singers and musicians playing some of the most popular Malinké songs. Lively and invigorating.

Cordes Anciennes (*Musicaphon* BM 30 L 2505), **Mali**. Featuring two of Mali's finest kora players, Sidiki Diabaté and Sékou Batourou Kouyaté playing a selection of the most popular Manding songs.

Sidiki Diabaté and Ensemble, *Ba Togoma* (*NSA/Rouge* FMS 001), **Mali**. Sidiki and Toumani Diabaté with some of Mali's most famous singers, Kandia and Mariama Kouyaté plus Djeli Mady Sissoko. Well produced.

Rail Band (with Salif Keita and Mory Kanté) (*Mélodie* 38750-2), **Mali**. Recorded in the 1970s, this still sounds very good, with two different versions of *Sunjatta*/*Sundiata* that last over forty minutes plus two other classics. If you understand the words it's even more interesting because Keita and Kanté claim descent from the two opposing leaders in the legendary battle surrounding Emperor Sundiata Keita in the early thirteenth century.

Orchestre National "A" de la République du Mali (*Musicaphon* BM 30 L 2605), **Mali**. Features guitarist **Kélétigui Diabaté**, who now plays *balo* with Salif Keita. They were the state orchestra for a number of years, listen to *janfa* and *duga* and you'll find out why.

Sabougnouna (7488; try *Sterns*), **Mali**. A compilation tape of electric and acoustic tracks that includes some of Mali's finest singers including Ami Koita, Tata Bambo Kouyaté, Kandia Kouyaté and Djelimady Sissoko. Djelimady's Sory Kandia is the pick of the crop.

Sali Sidibe (*Syllart* SYL 8362), **Mali**. Yet to be released in the UK but available in Africa and France. Hypnotic *balafon* and funky *bolom*, meandering fiddles and soaring vocals, all sizzling over an echo machine.

Dembo Konte, Kausu Kouyateh and the Jali Roll Orchestra, *Jali Roll* (*Rogue* FMSD 5020), **The Gambia, Senegal and UK**. Dembo and Kausu have two all-acoustic albums available but on this one they're augmented by the rhythm section from 3 Mustapha 3, a mysterious brass player and a well-known button accordionist. A strange mixture but it works irresistibly.

Baaba Maal and Mansour Seck, *Djam Leelii* (*Rogue* FMSD 5014), **Senegal**. An impeccable, near-acoustic set from the gifted singer Baaba and blind guitarist Mansour. Recorded in 1985 but only recently released in Europe, this is a wonderful, spacious sound with occasional *balafon*, electric guitar and percussion.

Youssou Ndour et Super Etoile de Daker, *Volumes 1–12*, **Senegal**. Forget *The Lion* and other European-produced albums, these are the ones to go for. Soulful brass, funk guitar, attacking *tama* and *sabar* and Youssou's unique voice. Buy all twelve if you can.

Pascal Diatta and Sone Mané, *Simnade* (Rogue FMSL 2017), **Senegal**. A simple, beautiful album of voice and Balanta guitar music.

Une Journée chez les Bassaris (*Playasound* PS 33519), **Senegal**. An unusual album of traditional Bassari music from southeast Senegal. A strange, nice touch is that every track is linked by a natural sound of some sort.

Kabe Mane, *Chefo Mae Mae* (ESP 7519) **Guinea-Bissau**. Great zouk-flavoured dance music. Paris production, with thrusting brass over delectable guitars.

The Music of the Senoufo (*Barenreiter Musicaphon* BM 30 L 2308), **Côte d'Ivoire**. A good selection of short pieces (perhaps too short) with a variety of folk instruments. The xylophone orchestras and the ensemble of one stringed harps are two of the best.

Sierra Leone: Musiques Traditionelles (*Ocora* 558549), **Sierra Leone**. A wide variety of styles and instruments with two great examples of Fula music, *Praise Song for Independence* and a Fula flute solo. Also features Mandingo, Limba, Mende and Koranko music .

Sierra Leone Music (*Gema records*), **Sierra Leone**. Outstanding selection of 1950s and 1960s Salonean styles. Ebenezer Calender and other Krio musicians on side one; a diverse range of up-country talents on side two. Worth buying just for Calender's *Double Decker Buses*.

Abdul Tee-Jay's Rokoto, *Kanka Kuru* (*Rogue* FMSL 2018), **Sierra Leone**. A great debut album from the finest British-based African band. Abdul's sweet guitar style over pulsating rhythms and a liberal helping of horns all help to make tracks like *Salima Yako* shine brilliantly.

Musiques du Pays Lobi (*Ocora* OCR 51), **Burkina Faso**. Side one is mostly xylophone music with sweet melodies; side two more varied, with some Gan music for mouth bow and some nice Dagarti xylophone tracks.

Musiques Bisa (*Ocora* OCR 58) **Burkina Faso**. Thumb pianos, fiddles, lutes, flutes and a wide range of percussion gear blended together under unique quavering vocals. Very interesting.

E. T. Mensah, *All For You* (*Retroafic* 1) **Ghana**. All the classics from the 1950s are here, including the wacky *Inflation Calypso*,

Sunday Mirror and the title track. Never mind the crackles, everyone likes it.

Fela Anikulapo-Kuti and Africa 70, *Perambulator*, **Nigeria.** One of Fela's most accessible albums. The title track has lovely guitars weaving around crazed organ playing.

King Sunny Ade, *Private Line* (Sunny Alade) **Nigeria.** A version of *365 is my Number* appeared on the *Juju Music* album but the track here is longer, sharper and looser. If the Velvet Underground had been African they might have sounded like this.

Musique Kabiyé (*Ocora* OCR 76), **Togo.** Traditional music from the north. Features the curious *picancala* "rock xylophone" together with women grinding millet, a rain dance and a musical bow. What more could you ask?

Musiques du Cameroun (*Ocora* OCR 25), **Cameroon.** Music of the Bakweri, Bamiléké, Bamoun and Beti. Side one opens with a stunning piece of Beti music for five xylophones of different sizes and closes with a beautiful Bamoun piece for *mvet*. Side two features mainly drum tracks.

MUSIC BOOKS

Frances Bebey *African Music: A People's Art* (Lawrence Hill, 1975). First published in French in 1969, this is an excellent and well-illustrated ethnomusicological survey, concentrating on Francophone Africa.

Ronnie Graham *Stern's Guide to Contemporary African Music* (Pluto Press, 1989). An invaluable, country-by-country survey of styles, artists and releases. Very strong on Ghana and Nigeria. New edition on the way.

Chris May and Chris Stapleton *African All Stars: the Pop Music of a Continent* (Paladin, 1989). An indispensable, and highly readable, account of the development of African music's many and diverse strands.

John Collins *Musicmakers of West Africa* (Three Continents Press, 1985). A collection of articles and interviews, mostly on highlife and its offspring, by a committed veteran of the Ghana music scene.

Jenny Cathcart, *Hey You!* (Fine Line Books, 1989). A detailed biography of Youssou Ndour, with translations of many of his lyrics.

John Miller Chernoff, *African Rhythm and African Sensibility* (University of Chicago Press, 1980). A travelogue and easy-to-read analysis of Ghanaian drumming, music's spiritual meaning and the place of Art in African society. Beautifully written.

Samuel Charters, *The Roots of the Blues* (Quartet 1982). A bit of a classic, Charter's serendipitous journey (The Gambia, Senegal, Mali) aimed to find the Blues' roots in West Africa. While he failed, his other discoveries make great reading. Two illustrative LPs were released with the book.

CINEMA

West African cinema provides a stimulating way into the complexities of the region's culture and concerns. This short introduction maps out its brief history and highlights some of the better known films and film-makers.

THE BEGINNINGS

In 1963 a short film by the acclaimed novelist **Ousmane Sembène** – *Borom Sarret* – managed to get onto the screens of Africa and Europe. Well received by the critics, this work laid the foundations for what, by the end of the 1960s, had become a great cinematic movement south of the Sahara. In 1968, Sembène released *Mandabi* (*Le Mandat*), the first movie by a Black African to reach a large audience; critics also hailed the film, which won the Silver Lion at the 1969 Venice Film Festival.

The success of *Le Mandat* inspired a whole generation of West African film-makers, and the 1970s turned out to be the region's most prolific decade. Early directors, many of them trained in the Soviet Union, were aware of their power to reach the masses and of Lenin's assertion that "the most imortant of all the arts is cinema". From the beginning they perceived their craft as a functional art form, which could break down stereotypes by giving a realistic portrayal of Africa from an African perspective, and could take an active part in national development by adapting film to the needs and aspirations of their newly independent countries.

Though early West African films were the products of many different cultures and looked at the continent in various historical, political and social stages, they were remarkably similar in their **themes**. Most commonly, they dealt with the conflict that arose from traditional values and those that had been imported from the west. Typically, the opposition between the old and the new is expressed by the opposition between **the city and the country** – the implication being that the process of rural migration has contributed to a loss of cultural identity. Among numerous examples of films of this type are *Kwami* by Quenum Do-Kokou from Togo (1974), *Sous le signe de Vaudou* by Pascal Abikanlou from Benin (1973), and *Le Bracelet du Bronze* by Tidiane Aw from Senegal (1974). Other topics include the **alienation** faced by African emigrants abroad, the **exploitation** of the masses by a corrupt and unscrupulous elite, the weight of **social traditions**, and the **injustices** of colonial or neo-colonial systems.

African film-makers also struggled with the limitations imposed by a film language that has evolved in the west. Thematic inspiration that derived from **African tales and legends** necessitated a new style capable of breaking down a story, of using digression to accept the irrational within the logical structure of a tale. There has thus been a tendency to move away from the slow-paced linear narrative of early films in order to forge an authentic African aesthetic, based on the conventions of oral literature.

As the cinematic movement progressed, **Upper Volta** (now Burkina Faso) emerged as the "capital" of African cinema. In 1969, Ouagadougou hosted the first *Festival Panafricain du Cinema* (FESPACO), a forum for African film-makers held every other February. Winners of the "Yenenga" – the African oscar – have increasingly achieved international plaudits, and though participation in the main event is limited to Africans, an increasing number of entries from the diaspora – the United States, Latin America and the Caribbean – have gained recognition through presentation in a special category. Burkina Faso has produced its own notable directors too: **Gaston Kaboré**, whose *Wend Kuni* (*Le Don de Dieu*) won the Grand Prize at the 1985 FESPACO; **Samon Emmanuel**, who won acclaim for his 1985 film *Dessé Bagato*; and **Idrissa Ouédraogo**, whose *Yaaba* earned a prize at the 1989 Cannes festival.

PRESENT SETBACKS

Throughout West Africa, the remarkable creativity that characterised the 1970s, began a **decline** by the end of the decade that continued into the 1980s. A major reason for the stagnation can be found in the system of film production and distribution. With few exceptions, films are made with state subsidies, which limits creative possibilities in countries where the treasury doesn't give high priority to cinema. Most people in business consider film a risky investment – although movie-going is popular in towns, the gate receipts are small, and imported **videos** are increasingly driving cinemas out of business. Adding to the frustration, most countries lack film industries of a technical level that would permit post-production control (laboratories, synchro, editing). Most post-production work for African-produced films is still carried out in Europe.

Distribution has proved a further stumbling block. Although nationalised in most West African countries, distribution companies still depend on larger European and American firms which control the African screens. Sadly, they exhibit minimal enthusiasm for national products, and films made in Africa have little or no chance of being shown in their countries of origin. Today, in fact, it is easier to see African films in Paris, London, Rome and New York than in Abidjan, Conakry, Lagos or Lomé.

Despite these obstacles, independent film continues to progress, and the early pioneers are being followed by a hopeful new generation.

OUSMANE SEMBÈNE

Senegal's **Ousmane Sembène**, a marxist whose films are explicitly political, remains the "papa" of West African cinema. Since his debut in 1963, he has made over a dozen films, of which several are considered classics. Besides *Borom Sarret* ("Cart-driver", 1963) and *Mandabi* ("The Money Order", 1968), his most famous works are *Xala* (1974) – a satire (that gets darker and darker) about a corrupt Dakar bureaucrat who loses touch with the people and thereby becomes impotent – and the less accessible, *Ceddo*, which deals with the three-way conflict in the the nineteenth century between the jihadists, the traditionalists and the French. More recently, he has made *Camp Thiaroye* (1986), the story of a massacre, by French troops, of African soldiers who had mutinied on their return from fighting for France during World War II.

SOULEYMANE CISSÉ

Another giant is **Souleymane Cissé** from Mali, who, like Sembène, was trained at the famous Moscow film school. Since the early 1970s, he has been as prolific as Sembène and has made a good number of films which have gone on to commercial and critical successes in Africa and Europe. Unlike Sembène, however, his craft always leads his message, not the other way round.

In addition to well-known early works like *Cinqs jours d'une vie* (1972) and *Baara* ("The Porter",1977), he has made perhaps the two best films to come from the continent: *Finyé* (*Le Vent*, "The Wind", 1983) , a film about the overweening pressures of seniority on youth, and **Yeelen** (*La Lumière*, "Brightness" 1986). The latter film, the story of a conflict between father and son, each trying to preserve "knowledge" in pre-colonial Africa, went on to win the *Grand Prix du Jury* at the 1987 Cannes Film Festival. With its deft visual impact and atemporality – and a deliberate ambiguity about the level of reality at which the images operate – the metaphysical world of the old West Africa comes alive and is as real as any drought or slave trade. For this lyricism – which made the film an arthouse hit in the West – Cissé is inevitably running into criticism from those who would prefer a more realist cinema that talked more of exploitation, colonialism and repression.

GHANA

The wave of productivity that swept the Francophone countries generally bypassed the English-speaking states, only two of which – **Ghana and Nigeria** – have gone beyond government-sponsored documentaries to create an independent cinema. In Ghana, independent film-makers like **King Ampaw** and **Kwaw Ansah** began producing features that combined comedy and melodrama.

Ghana is rated the best equipped of the West African states and the government branches of the film industry have left their mark on some of the country's top film-makers. The documentary style of the state-run Ghana Film Industry Corporation, for example, has influenced the style of such well-known directors as **Sam Aryete** (*No Tears for Ananse*, 1968), **King Ampaw** (*They Call It Love*, 1972; *Kukurantumi*, 1983 and *Juju* 1986), **Kwate Nee Owo** (*You Hide Me*, 1971; *Struggle for Zimbabwe*, 1974; and *Angela Davis*, 1976), and **Kwaw Ansah** (*Love Brewed in the African Pot*, 1982). But unlike other African countries, Ghana's film industry does not rely wholly on state funding and some of the best-known filmmakers finance their projects through local and international backing. Kwaw Ansah, for example, produced his latest film, *Heritage Africa* — which won the grand prize at the 1989 FESPACO — with the backing of the Ghana Commercial Bank, the National Investment Bank and other financial institutions.

The films of these more independent directors have produced a good box-office return both in and outside Ghana. ***Love Brewed in the African Pot***, for example, conveys its narrative through musical performances, wedding ceremonies and sports events — all popular with African audiences — and drew record attendances not only in Ghana, but also in Sierra Leone, Liberia, Kenya and, naturally, Nigeria.

NIGERIA

Francis Oladele was one of the producers of Nigeria's first film, *Kongi's Harvest*, based on the play by Wole Soyinka. He also co-produced *Bullfrog in the Sun*, adapted from Chinua Achebe's novels *Things Fall Apart* and *No Longer at Ease*. Because of the sensitive political subject matter, this latter film was never properly distributed in Nigeria.

Another director, **Eddie Ugbomah** also draws his inspiration from current political events but turns them into Hollywood-style popular movies. In *The Rise and Fall of Dr Oyenusi* (1977), he considers the true story of a Lagos gangster who was arrested and publicly executed in the early 1970s. *The Mask* (1979) follows the adventures of a Nigerian secret agent sent to Britain to take back a Benin mask stolen by the British and housed in a London museum. *The Death of a Black President* (1983) treated the events that led to the traumatising assassination of the much-loved General Murtala Muhammed.

Other Nigerian directors include the late **Hubert Ogunde** whose films, such as *Aiye*

(with Ola Balogun) and its sequel *Jaiyesinmi*, often deal with witchcraft or with the significance of tradition. Ogunde set up a "film village" at Ijebu Ososa near Lagos, to encourage Nigerian film-makers. And in the field of comedy, **Moses Olaiya** — better known as Baba-Sala — is a new arrival from the world of Nigerian TV, now making a name for himself in cinema with films like *Orun Mooru* ("It's not Easy") and *Mosebolatan* ("I thought my wealth was finished").

The most prolific film-maker in West Africa is Nigeria's **Ola Balogun**, who has released a steady stream of documentaries and feature films since the early 1970s. His 1975 production of *Amadi* was the first film in the Igbo language, while the 1976 *Ajani Ogun* was the first in Yoruba.

Yoruba cinema emerged in the early 1970s out of the Yoruba theatre tradition (see p.985). Its success was partly due to the huge home market — over twenty million Yoruba-speaking Nigerians in the southwest of the country — rather than to the broader appeal which English or French language films must draw on. Films in mother tongue languages are still a novelty in Africa. In 1978, Balogun's film, *Black Goddess*, dealt with the African-Brazilians who returned to Nigeria after being freed from slavery. But some of Balogun's biggest hits in Nigeria draw their inspiration directly from Yoruba popular theatre. In 1976, *Ajani Ogun* starred one of the country's top theatre performers, **Ade Folayan**, in a story about a young man who runs up against a conniving rich buffoon as he struggles to keep both his fiancée and his inheritance. The popularity of *Ajani Ogun* led to *Ija Ominira* (1977), a popular tale of a tyrannical king in which Ade Folayan again starred. Outside Africa, films such as *Cry Freedom* (1981) and *Money Power* (1982) have secured Balogun's international reputation.

NIGER

Nigérien cinema has been dominated by three film-makers. **Oumarou Ganda** began his career as an actor in Jean Rouch's *Moi, un Noir*, after he was discovered by the noted French *cinéaste* on the docks in Abidjan. After appearing in other Rouch films, notably *La pyramide humaine*, he went on to become a film-maker in his own right and one of the great cultural archivists of African cinema, with works such as the autobiographical *Cabascabo*, *Wazzou polygame* (1971), *Saitane* (1973) – which looks critically at the authority of the Muslim marabouts – and *L'Exilé*. In 1981, he died unexpectedly at the age of 46, while filming his last work, *Gani Kouré, le vainqueur de Gourma*. Reflecting a distribution problem faced by most contemporary African film-makers, you're more likely to see his works abroad or possibly at Niamey's Franco-Nigérien Cultural Centre than in any ordinary Nigérien movie theatre.

Rouch also inspired another relatively well-known film-maker, **Moustapha Alassane**. After studying at the *Institut Nigérien de Recherche en Sciences Humaines*, Alassane made a number of shorts, including *Aouré* (1962), and *La Bague du Roi Koda* (1963). His most famous feature film is *Femme, Villa, Voiture, Argent* (1972) a popular comedy dealing with the issue of cultural identity.

The third director to gain international acclaim is **Djingary Maïga**, producer of *l'Etoile Noire*, in which he also starred. Like many early African film-makers, Djingary's movies deal with the clash between western values and traditional wisdom.

CAMEROON

Jean-Paul Ngassa was one of the pioneers of Cameroonian cinema with his production of *Aventures en France* in 1962, followed by *La Grand Case Bamilékeé* in 1965. After *Une Nation est Née*, in 1970, Cameroonian production went into a lull until **Daniel Kamwa** brought a new spark with his 1972 prize-winning short *Boubou Cravatte*. The 1977 production of *Pousse Pousse* – a comical look at the conflict between traditional customs and modern urban lifestyles as expressed through the dowry – established him as a producer with wide public appeal, even if the movie got a mediocre reception in Europe. *Pousse Pousse* was seen by some 700,000 movie-goers, making it one of the most popular African films of the period. The success was followed by *Notre Fille* in 1980.

During the same period **Jean Pierre Dikongue-Pipa** began making waves. *Muno Moto*, made in 1975, won encouraging reviews in France although it was hardly as popular at home as *Pousse Pousse*. Pipa's other productions include *Prix de la Liberté* (1978), *Badiaga* (1983), and *Music Music* (1983).

Although Kamwa and Dikongue-Pipa are still the best known Cameroonian producer/ directors, a new generation seems to be emerging. After studying at the *Ecole supérieure d'etudes cinématographiques* in Paris, **Louis Balthazar Amadangoleda** made his first full-length film, *Les trois petits cireurs*, in 1985. Based on the novel of the same name by Francis Bebey, it looks at delinquency and its consequences.

A former professor of literature, **Arthur Si Bita** turned to film in 1978 and made a couple of shorts, including *No Time to Say Goodbye* shot in Ouagadougou. His first feature-length film, *Les Cooperants* traces the adventures of six youths from the city who decide to return to the village.

With his first feature-length film, *L'Appat du gain* (1982), **Jules Takam** breaks away from common themes of dowry, marriage and traditional custom and offers instead a fast-paced political intrigue based in Paris.

Jean-Claude Tchuilen came out with a promising first feature film in 1984 – *Suicides* – a well-paced psycho-drama set in Paris. It was banned for being inflammatory when first released in Cameroon and commercially never bounced back after the ban was lifted.

Lastly, **Jean-Marie Teno** is considered one of the brightest prospects of the new generation. Though he has yet to make a full-length feature, his short films, including *Schubbah* (1984), *Hommage* (1985) and *La caresse et la gifle* (1987) have been highly acclaimed.

VIDEO CENTRE

If you want to obtain videotapes of African movies, the **African Video Centre**, 7 Balls Pond Rd, Dalston, London N1 4AX (☎071 923 4224) can oblige. They're particularly hot on Yoruba releases and music videos.

BOOKS

While there's a substantial volume of reading material on West Africa, its subject matter and authorship is very unevenly distributed. By far the largest body of literature in English comes from Nigeria, with its hundreds of novelists and academics. By contrast, many of the francophone nations have scant coverage other than in French. For pre-departure reading, probably the best foretaste is provided by West African fiction – much of which is available in paperback in Heinemann's *African Writers Series* or Longman's *African Classics*.

The following recommendations are divided first by subject matter across the region, and then country-by-country in the order in which they appear in the book. French works have been included only when there is little alternative in English.

SERIES PUBLICATIONS

Aujourd'hui, (Editions Jeunes Afrique). The *Aujourd'hui* series – *Togo Aujourd'hui*, etc – is available in English translation for Algeria, Niger, Mali, Senegal, Guinea-Bissau, Côte d'Ivoire, Togo and Cameroon. They're tourist-office oriented but good for an initial browse. Check publication dates, as the books are updated sporadically.

Jeune Afrique and **Hachette** both do one or two country guides of a more practical nature, in French only, to most of the francophone countries. *Jeune Afrique* also publishes an excellent and affordable series of thematic **atlases** on the francophone countries.

African Historical Dictionaries, (Scarecrow Press, Metuchen, New Jersey). If you're seriously looking to find out about a country, the Scarecrow series is what you need. They have titles on virtually every African country, covering names, places and events in detail.

Heinemann African Writers Series AWS books are the vanguard of African publishing in Britain and add regularly to their list – now some 300 titles, though kept erratically in print. Catalogue from Heinemann, Halley Court, Jordan Hill, Oxford, OX2 8EJ (☎0865 311 366).

Longman also publishes a good, though much shorter, series of *African Classics*. Catalogue from Longman UK, Fourth Ave, Harlow, Essex, CM19, 5AA (☎0729 29655).

TRAVEL AND GENERAL ACCOUNTS

Mary Kingsley, *Travels in West Africa* (1897; reprinted Virago, 1982). The title is misleading these days, as Kingsley's dauntless travels in search of fetishes and fish took her – with a quick hike up Mount Cameroon – principally to the region of Gabon. But a terrific book: funny, intelligent and a worthy classic.

Mungo Park, *Travels into the Interior of Africa* (1799; reprinted Eland Books, 1983). Absorbing and short-winded account of the then youthful Scottish traveller's two journeys – in 1795–1797 and 1805 – along the Niger.

Elspeth Huxley, *Four Guineas* (1954, o/p). This account of Huxley's trip through the four anglophone colonies on the eve of independence is full of credible conversations – and the occasional lapse into racist angst.

Geoffrey Gorer, *Africa Dances* (1935; Penguin, 1986). Enduring account of a journey from Dakar to Dahomey and back with Feral Benga, an African dancer from Paris.

Patrick Marnham, *Dispatches from Africa* (Penguin, 1980). Although now a decade old, this journalism remains devastatingly sharp – especially on the aid industry. Notable essays on Senegal, Mali and The Gambia.

David Lamb, *The Africans* (1984; Mandarin, 1989). There's really no choice between Marnham and Lamb, *LA Times* hack, for a contemporary view of the continent. *The Africans* has been almost a best-seller, but Lamb's fly-in, fly-out technique is a statistical rant couched in cold war rhetoric – and, even when ostensibly uncovering a pearl of wisdom, he can be rebarbatively offensive.

Michael Asher, *Impossible Journey: Two Against the Sahara* (Viking Penguin, 1987). Adventurous Mauritanian and Nigérien foretastes in this account of a first-ever west to east Saharan crossing. Asher, an ex-SAS man, travelled with his wife, plus camels, from Chinguetti to the Nile. **Geoffrey Moorhouse**'s *Fearful Void* (Penguin, 1974) details his own, unsuccessful, earlier attempt.

Geoff Howard, *Wheelbarrow across the Sahara* (Alan Sutton, 1990). Somewhat bizarre account of a 2000-mile hike with a specially adapted wheelbarrow . . .

HISTORY

Most histories cover the whole continent, and, inevitably, jump from place to place: Davidson, Buah and Ajayi are the most easy-to-follow, and well complemented by various historical and cultural atlases.

THE AFRICAN CONTINENT

Basil Davidson, *Africa in Modern History* (Penguin, 1978). Lucidly argued and readable summary of Africa's dominant nineteenth- and twentieth-century events.

A. E. Ahigbo, R. J. Gavin, R. Palmer, E. A. Ayandele and J. D. Omer-Cooper, *The Making of Modern Africa, Vol 1 C19th, Vol 2 C20th* (Longman, 1986). A more detailed, illustrated guide, putting West Africa in the continental context up until the first big changes after independence.

Christopher Hibbert, *Africa Explored: Europeans in the Dark Continent, 1769–1889* (Penguin, 1984). Entertaining read, devoted in large part to the "discovery" of West Africa.

Cheik Anta Diop, *Pre-Colonial Black Africa* (Lawrence Hill, 1987). A quest, in part, for the lost roots of European culture in Africa.

WEST AFRICA

Basil Davidson, F K Buah and J F A Ajayi, *A History of West Africa 1000–1800* (Longman, 1965). Clear, wide-ranging and readable.

J. B. Webster et al, *West Africa Since 1800: The Revolutionary Years* (Longman, 1980). An excellent follow-up companion to the above.

A. G. Hopkins, *An Economic History of West Africa* (Longman, 1973). Well-written grounding offering an invaluable economic perspective.

Patrick Manning, *Francophone sub-Saharan Africa 1880–1985* (Cambridge University Press, 1988). A rare book on the subject in English.

ATLASES

Colin McEvedy, *Penguin Atlas of African History* (Penguin, 1980). Useful for placing West Africa, and the whole continent, in context, and for getting to grips with some of the names and themes. Fifty nine maps of Africa with facing text.

Jocelyn Murray, ed, *Cultural Atlas of Africa* (Phaidon, 1981). An attractive, highly polished book, if also an inevitably over-simplified view of the continent.

Brian Catchpole and L. A. Akinjogbin, *A History of West Africa in Maps and Diagrams* (Collins Educational, 1984). A remarkable encapsulation of the region's history from ancient times to the 1980s. Its only flaw is an utterly inadequate index.

LAND, PEOPLE AND SOCIETY

R. J. Harrison Church, *West Africa* (Longman, 1979). The standard geography reference – traditional in approach but much updated from its 1957 original edition, excellent and unexpectedly absorbing.

Donal Cruise O'Brien, *Contemporary West African States* (Cambridge University Press, 1989). Recent survey of Burkina Faso, Cameroon, Chad, Côte d'Ivoire, Ghana, Liberia, Nigeria and Senegal.

John S. Mbiti, *African Religions and Philosophies* (2nd edition, Heinemann, 1989). A good compendium.

Adewale Maja-Pearce, *The Press in West Africa* (in *Index on Censorship* Vol 19, No. 6, 1990). Probing report into the health of the anglophone press in West Africa.

Pierre Alexandre, *Languages and language in Africa* (Heinemann, 1972). Surprisingly entertaining tour of the arcane world of African linguistics, led by a magnificently enthusiastic French professor.

Claudia Zaslavsky, *Africa Counts: Number and Pattern in African Culture* (Lawrence Hill, 1979). A unique, extraordinary book, with a chapter on "Warri" games (see p.34).

Colin Turnbull, *The Forest People* (1961; Grafton, 1979). An account of the Ituri forest

Bambuti ("Pygmies") in Zaire; the best writing in English on the oldest African people. Essential, delightful reading for forest stays in Cameroon.

Keletigui Mariko, *Les Touaregs Ouelleminden* (Karthala, 1984). French survey of the Tuareg nomads who live in Algeria, Niger and Mali.

ARTS

Most works dealing with the arts cover the whole continent. For books on West African music, see the box on p.1178.

Susan Denyer, *African Traditional Architecture* (Heinemann, 1982). Rewarding study, featuring hundreds of photos (most of them old) and a wealth of detailed line drawings.

Werner Gillon, *A Short History of African Art* (Penguin, 1984). A substantial study despite the name, though inevitably still very selective.

Frank Willett, *African Art* (Thames and Hudson, 1988). A cheaper, more accessible and better illustrated volume.

Jan Vansina, *Art History in Africa* (Longman, 1984). Readable theorising by an interesting French anthropologist.

Michael Huet, *The Dance, Art and Ritual of Africa* (Random House, 1978). Remarkable photos of ceremonies and costume, captured with an exceptional clarity and power.

Geoffrey Williams, *African Designs From Traditional Sources* (Dover, 1971). A designer's and enthusiast's sourcebook, from the copyright-free publishers (several of the illustrations have been used in this *Rough Guide*).

Roy Braverman, *Islam and Tribal Art* (Cambridge University Press 1974). A useful if somewhat specialist paperback text.

COUNTRY BY COUNTRY

ALGERIA

For general reading, it's hard to find much in English that's accessible. If you can read French, however, check out some of the country's fine novelists – most of whom are published in Paris.

Caren Caraway, *African Designs of the Congo, Nigeria, The Cameroons and the Guinea Coast* (Stemmer, 1986). Black and white designs from masks, fetishes and textiles.

Margaret Courtney-Clarke, *African Canvas* (Rizzoli, 1990). Sumptuous colour photos bring out vivid details of exterior and interior house painting by women in a number of countries.

Esi Sagay, *African Hairstyles* (Heinemann, 1988). What they're called, and how to do them; a wonderful little book.

FOOD

G. B. Masefield, M. Wallis, B. E. Nicholson and S. G. Harrison, *The Oxford Book of Food Plants* (Oxford University Press, 1976). A good, traditional guide, covering most of the fruit and veg that will come your way.

Frances Bissel and Christine Hanscomb *Sainsbury's Book of Food* (Websters, 1989). This also has photos of the majority of the exotic foodstuffs you're likely to come across, together with pertinent facts and opinions.

Daniel K. Abbiw, *Useful Plants of Ghana* (ITP 1990). Unusual reference guide to plants, organised by use – as food, fuel, medicine. Highly recommended for impoverished volunteers.

NATURAL HISTORY

The following field guides are invaluable.

W. Serle and G. Morel, *A Field Guide to the Birds of West Africa* (Collins, 1977).

T. Haltenorth and H. Diller, *A Field Guide to the Mammals of Africa* (Collins, 1980).

John G. Williams, *A Field Guide to the Butter-flies of Africa* (Collins, 1969).

Frantz Fanon, *Studies in a Dying Colonialism* (1959; reprinted with a new introduction by A. M. Babu, Earthscan Press, 1989). A classic of liberation literature and incisive reading on the Algerian revolution as a focus for north–south relations.

Nina de Voogd, *The Passionate Nomad: the Diary of Isabelle Eberhardt* (trans. Virago/Beacon Travelers, 1987). One of the nineteenth century's most exceptional adventurers – a brief life, ecstatic and self-destructive. Dressed as a man Eberhardt mixed freely with Algerians, even gaining admission to one of the fiercely protected Muslim Brotherhoods. An excellent, small selection of her writings, translated by Paul Bowles, is published as *The Oblivion Seekers* (City Lights, 1972).

Touatti Fettouma, *Desperate Springs: Lives of Algerian Women* (The Women's Press, 1987). Follows the life of one girl growing up in a traditional Berber family.

Bound and Gagged by the Family Code in Miranda Davies, ed, *Third World − Second Sex* (Zed Books, 1987). An interview with an Algerian feminist, Marie-Aimée Hélie-Lucas, that details the restrictions imposed on women by an increasingly fundamentalist culture.

NIGER

Published material in English on Niger is really limited: if you want more than the handful of volumes devoted to the country, you'll need to read French.

Finn Fuglestad, *A History of Niger 1850–1960* (Cambridge University Press, 1983). Somewhat inaccessible but there's no English alternative.

Politique Africaine: Le Niger (Karthala, 1990). Survey of Nigérien politics, aid and economics − and the Sahara.

Carol Beckwith and Mario Van Offelen, *Nomads of Niger* (Collins, 1984). Superbly illustrated essay on the Wodaabe Bororo.

Paul Stoller and Cheryl Olkes *In Sorcery's Shadow: a Memoir of Apprenticeship among the Songhay* (University of Chicago Press, 1987); *Fusion of the Worlds: An Ethnography of Possession among the Songhay of Niger* (University of Chicago Press, 1987). Stoller is a kind of Nigérien answer to Carlos Castaneda. All interesting stuff.

Boubou Hama was one of Niger's most prolific writers, publishing numerous historical works on the empires of Gao, Gobir and Songhai. A former president of the *Assemblé Nationale*, he also wrote works on politics, philosophy and folklore.

FICTION

French readers might like to dip into:

Ibrahim Issa, *Grandes Eaux Noires*. The first Nigérien novel to be published (before independence), this manages to describe humorously the travails of second century BC Mediterranean explorers south of the Sahara. A later book, *Facéties*, is a collection of poems, including long paeans to African heroes from Samory Touré to Steve Biko.

More recent writers include:

Idé Oumarou, *Gros Plan*. This won the *grand prix de l'Afrique Noire* award in 1978.

Halilou Sabbo Mahamadou, *Abokki ou l'Appel de la Côte*, *Les Caprices du Destin*.

Amadou Ousmane, *Quinze ans, ça suffit*. Certain aspects of contemporary Nigérien society illumintated. Kicks off with the food aid-hoarding scandal (see p.138).

MALI

There's very little accessible writing in English from, or about, Mali.

Stephen Pern and Bryan Alexander, *Masked Dancers of West Africa: The Dogon* (Time-Life Books, 1982). Fine photography and good text. Highly recommended pre-visit (or even carry-around) reading.

Richard Trench, *Forbidden Sands* (John Murray, 1978). Stodgy travelogue, but an unusual route: Tindouf–Taoudenni–Timbuktu.

William Seabrook, *The White Monk of Timbuctoo* (Harrap, 1934). It's worth checking libraries and second-hand bookshops for this biography of Père Yakouba, a white priest who married a Timbuktu woman and changed his vocation.

Ibn Battuta, *Travels in Asia and Africa* (Routledge, 1983). Selections from the writings of the great fourteenth-century wanderer, including his travels along the Niger.

Brian Gardner, *The Quest for Timbuktoo* (Cassell & Co, 1968). An easily digested, though old-fashioned and not altogether reliable, collection of explorers' biographies; can often be found in second-hand bookshops.

Pascal James Imperato, *Mali* (Dartmouth, 1989). The author of the *Historical Dictionary of Mali* (Scarecrow) here devotes himself even more extensively to history, society, economy and politics.

FICTION

You'll be lucky to find much of the following in English translation but Malian literature in French repays the effort.

Yambo Ouologuem is Mali's only writer to have achieved international recognition. In *Bound to Violence* (trans. Ralph Manheim, Heinemann, 1971), his treatment of brutality and deceit in an invented African empire, Nakem, insists that West African society rests on foundations as bloody and self-destructive as any other and screams for a new, re-humanising look at the liberal romantic version of black history – a position that upset the earnest negritude movement. Most of Ouologuem's works excite controversy – he specialises in unabashed plagiarism, pornography (*Les Mille et une Bibles du Sexe*, 1969) and cudgel-like satire – but he can also be very funny (see the poem on p.230). He's been out of circulation for a number of years.

Fily-Dabo Sissoko was one of Mali's earliest contributors to written literature. *Crayons et Portraits* (Mulhouse, 1953) recounts his idyllic childhood in rural Soudan; *La Savane Rouge* (Presses Universelles, 1962) offers further reminiscences; *Sagesse Noire* (Editions de la Tour du Guet, 1955) is a collection of over 500 African proverbs and axioms.

Amadou Hampate Ba, *Fortunes of Wangrin* (New Horn, 1987). An administrative interpreter tells of the colonial period from 1900 to 1945, and his successfully collusion with it. Hampate Ba, born in Bandiagara, is a Fula academic and transcriber of oral literature. His *Kaïdara*, an esoteric Fula cosmological epic poem, has also been translated into English (Three Continents Press, 1988).

Seydou Badian, *Le Sang des Masques* (Laffont, 1976). Nightmarish vision of the city, in this follow up to Badian's earlier novel *Sous l'Orage* (Paris, Presence Africaine, 1963) in which the young generation – formed by Western education – criticise traditional practices of religion and authority.

Moussa Konaté, *Le Prix de l'Ame* (Présence Africaine, 1981). Also set in the here and now – in the modern city.

Mandé-Alpha Diarra, *Sahel! Sanglante Sécheresse* (Présence Africaine, 1981). The story of a doomed village schoolboy through the drought in a kind of documentary fiction.

Mamadou Kouyaté, *Sundiata: an Epic of Old Mali*, transcribed into French and annotated by **D. T. Niane** (translated into English by G. D. Pickett, Longman, 1988). Slim and fascinating transcription of a griot's history of Mali.

BURKINA FASO

There is next to nothing published in English on Burkina – and nothing very digestible in French either . . .

Joan Baxter and Keith Somerville, *Benin, Congo and Burkina Faso* (Pinter Publishers, 1989). Part of the excellent Marxist regime series; includes fifty pages on Burkina.

Pierre Englebert, *La Révolution Burkinabé* (L'Harmattan, 1986). Thorough look at the country's recent history by a political scientist.

Thomas Sankara Speaks (Pathfinder Press, 1988). Collection of the revolutionary's speeches – worth dipping into to see where the revolution was supposed to be going.

Politique Africaine Retour au Burkina (Karthala, 1989). Survey of changes since the death of Sankara.

Ben O. Nnaji, *Blaise Compaoré: The Architect of the Burkina Faso Revolution* (Spectrum, 1989). Unashamedly propagandist offering, with some general information on the country.

MAURITANIA

Literature in English on Mauritania is minimal.

Peter Hudson, *Travels in Mauritania* (Virgin, 1990). Recent tale of a two-month trek.

Catherine Belvaude, *La Mauritanie* (Karthala, 1989). Describes peoples, the state, religion, economy, fishing, arts, and society. The French reader's essential starting point.

Odette du Puigaudeau, *Barefoot in Mauritania* (Routledge, 1937). The author and his female companion took camels across "the land of death" – an entertaining ramble through a Mauritania that hardly knew it existed. A biography of Odette du Puigadeau, who lives in Morocco, is being written.

Tony Hodges, *The Western Saharans* (Minority Rights Group report No. 40, 1984). Trenchant background on the situation in Western Sahara.

SENEGAL

There are several books by Senegalese writers in the Heinemann and Longman series. Other, mostly academic English-language works, are only likely to be available in libraries. In French, there's a

very wide range of literature – by both French and Senegalese – and a steady output of glossy tomes to whet travelling appetites.

Sheldon Gellar, *Senegal – An African Nation Between Islam and the West* (Gower, 1982). A condensed and very readable survey.

Lucy C. Behrman, *Muslim Brotherhoods and Politics in Senegal* (Harvard, 1970). Fascinating, though dated study with interesting statistical information about the marabouts at the turn of the century.

Michael Crowder, *Senegal: A Study of French Assimilation Policy* (Oxford University Press, 1962). Concise, fairly unacademic look at how the French colonised African minds.

Donal B. Cruise O'Brien, *Saints and Politicians: Essays in the Organization of a Senegalese Peasant Society* (Cambridge University Press, 1975); *The Murides of Senegal: The Political and Economic Organization of an Islamic Brotherhood* (Oxford University Press, 1971). This last work is the definitive text in English on the Mouride brotherhood.

Rita Cruise O'Brien, *White Society in Black Africa: the French of Senegal* (Northwestern University Press, 1972); *The Political Economy of Underdevelopment: Dependence in Senegal* (Sage, 1979).

Maureen Mackintosh, *Gender, Class and Rural Transition* (Zed Books, 1989). An alternative view of the effects of development, agribusiness and the food crisis.

Janet G. Vailant, *Black, French and African* (Harvard University Press, 1990). The latest biography of Léopold Senghor.

Christian Saglio, *Sénégal* (Petite Planète, Editions Seuil, 1980). The best available introduction to the country, if you read French, full of incisive commentary. Saglio was instrumental in setting up the *campement intégré* network.

FICTION

Mariama Bâ, *So Long a Letter* (Heinemann, 1981; Virago, 1988). Dedicated to "all women and to men of good will", this is the story of a woman's life shattered by her husband's sudden, second marriage to a younger woman. Bâ's second book, *The Scarlet Song* (Longman, 1986) – published posthumously, eloquently

traces the relationship between a French woman and a poor, Senegalese man.

Nafissatou Diallo, *A Dakar Childhood* (Longman, 1982). Short and sweet; a middle-class girl growing up in the postwar years. Illuminating on family life.

Birago Diop, *Tales of Amadou Koumba* (Longman, 1966). A collection of short stories based on the tales of a griot, and rooted in Wolof tradition.

Aminata Sow Fall, *The Beggars' Strike, or the Dregs of Society* (Longman, 1981). The mental health of the Dakar elite when their consciences can no longer be salved . . .

Cheikh Hamidou Kane, *Ambiguous Adventure* (Heinemann, 1963). The autobiographical tale of a man torn between Tukulor, Islam and the West. Recommended.

Ousmane Sembene, *God's Bits of Wood* (1960), *Xala* (1973), *The Last of the Empire* (1981), and others; all published by Heinemann. A committed, political and very immediate writer (and film-maker, see "Cinema" p.1180) who can also be very funny, as in *Xala*, the satirical tale of a wealthy Dakarois' loss of virility. The best of these, by far, is *God's Bits of Wood*, the story of the rail strike of 1947.

Leopold Sédhar Senghor, *Nocturnes* and *Prose and Poetry* (Heinemann, 1969). Collection of poems and writings by the country's ex-president, and member of the Académie Française.

THE GAMBIA

For general works on The Gambia, and fiction by Gambian writers, the in-print choice is limited, if not quite zero.

J. M. Gray, *History of The Gambia* (Frank Cass, 1966, o/p). This aquarium-style account (peering in from the outside) is heavy going and finishes before World War II.

Berkeley Rice, *Enter Gambia: the Birth of an Improbable Nation* (Houghton, Mifflin Co, 1967, o/p). A more digestible work, but marred by an unpleasantly derisory tone.

Patience Sonko-Godwin, *Ethnic Groups of the Senegambia* (1985, Book Production; also, Material Resource Unit, Banjul). A brief and graspable social history of the region.

Alex Haley, *Roots!* (1976; Arrow, 1990). Good honest "faction", and a reasonably entertaining

American saga to read on the beach, though only the first few dozen pages are set in Kunta Kinte's semi-mythical Gambian homeland.

Mark Hudson, *Our Grandmothers' Drums* (Minerva, 1989). Rich, absorbing story of Hudson's stay in the village of Dulaba (Keneba) in the proposed Kiang National Park area.

FICTION

William Conton is a writer from the colonial era, heavily influenced by his Sierra Leonean upbringing. *The African* (Heinemann, 1960) is a classic rags-to-premiership story.

Ebou Dibba, *Chaff in the Wind* (Macmillan, 1986). Highly accomplished author, now living in Britain, decribes lives and loves in the 1930s. *Fafa* (Macmillan, 1989) tells of goings-on at a remote trading post on the Gambia River.

Lenrie Peters, *Selected Poetry* (Heinemann, 1981). *The Second Round* (Heinemann, 1966) is a readable, if slightly downbeat, story.

CAPE VERDE

Cape Verde is one of the least documented countries in the world. Sources of information in English are few, and most are technical, research-based studies that you'll find only in university libraries.

Basil Davidson, *The Fortunate Isles – a Study in African Transformation* (Hutchinson, 1989). The most recent book on Cape Verde by one of its most ardent supporters, this is a positive and not unduly critical survey, mixing impression with historical accounts to the present.

Colm Foy, *Cape Verde: Politics, Economics and Society* (Pinter Publishers, 1988). The first and only contemporay survey of Cape Verde, readable, bang up-to-date and very comprehensive on politics and economics, sparser on society.

Anne Hammick and Nicholas Heath, *Atlantic Islands* (RCC Pilotage Foundation, Imray, Laurie, Norie and Wilson, 1989). A comprehensive sailors' pilot, with a healthy chunk on the Cape Verdes and plenty of navigational charts and photos.

Archibald Lyall, *Black and White Make Brown: An Account of a Journey to the Cape Verde Islands and Portuguese Guinea* (Heinemann, 1938). Very hard to obtain – but well worth trying.

Deidre Meintel, *Race, Culture and Portuguese Colonialism in Cabo Verde* (Maxwell School of Citizenship and Public Affairs, Syracuse University, New York; 1984). An expanded PhD thesis, this fascinating study of race and self-image gets right inside the psychological effects of Portuguese colonialism.

Antonio Carreira, *The People of the Cape Verde Islands* (Hurst, 1982). An indigestible analysis of a very important subject – the forced labour policy of the Portuguese in Cape Verde.

A. B. Ellis, *West African Islands* (1885). Adventures from Madeira to Ascension with a couple of lively chapters on "St. Vincent" and "San Antonio". Entertaining stuff.

GUINEA-BISSAU

Again, works in English are extremely sparse – and there's no Guinea-Bissauan literature in translation.

Rosemary E. Galli and Jocelyn Jones, *Guinea-Bissau: Politics, Economics and Society* (Pinter Publishers, 1987). A well-researched, rather gloomy survey, which finds parallels between the independent governments and the fascist New State regime in their alienation of the rural people. The best general text but already out of date (written in 1986).

Basil Davidson, *No Fist is Big Enough to Hide the Sky: The Liberation of Guiné and Cape Verde* (Zed Books, 1981). Enthusiastic, quirky account of the war and its aftermath. Davidson's close and sympathetic involvement with the liberation fighters, particularly Amilcar Cabral himself, gives a rosy picture, tarnished by subsequent events.

Stepanie Urdang, *Fighting Two Colonialisms: Women in Guinea-Bissau* (Monthly Review Press, 47 Red Lion Street, London WC1R 4PF; 1979). Journalistic essays on escorted travels through the liberated zones and after the war. Detailed and interesting but with much wishful thinking.

Ole Gjorstad and Chantal Sarrazin, *Sowing the First Harvest: National Reconstruction in Guinea-Bissau* (LSM Press, PO Box 2077, Oakland, CA 94604, USA; 1978). Dated and somewhat rhetorical; but sounded good at the time. See extract on p.544.

Carlos Lopes, *Guinea Bissau: From Liberation Struggle to Independent Statehood* (Zed Books, 1987) A recent survey that brings the story up to the end of the period of stagnation

Amilcar Cabral, *Unity and Struggle* (Heinemann, 1980). The man himself speaks well. And such was Cabral's immense popularity, there seems little doubt his assassination marked a point of turning back for the country, and for West Africa.

Joch McCulloch, *In the Twilight of Revolution: the Political Theory of Amilcar Cabral* (Routledge & Kegan Paul, 1983). Provides some analysis.

Walter Rodney, *A History of the Upper Guinea Coast 1545–1800* (Oxford University Press, 1970). An Afro-centric history covering the region from the Casamance to Sierra Leone, dealing in depth with the area the Portuguese moved into and providing a mass of fascinating material on its social complexity.

GUINEA

There's again little published in English, though libraries may reveal some of the following.

Ladipo Adamolekun, *Sékou Touré's Guinea: an Experiment in Nation Building* (Methuen, 1976). One of the less credulous studies, but too old to be very useful as a retrospective.

Anonymous, *Sékou Touré* (Panaf Great Lives Series, 1978). Read now, a naïve tribute to an obsessive despot, yet interesting for putting the rúler's case better than he himself did. Clearly and readably delivered.

Politique Africaine, *Guinée: L'après-Sékou Touré* (Karthala, 1989). A useful collection of articles (in French) looking at political and economic change since the death of Sékou Touré in 1984.

FICTION

Camara Laye, *The African Child* (1954; Fontana, 1989). One of the best known books by an African writer, these sweet-scented memoirs of a privileged rural childhood are a homage to the author's parents. Other translations of works by Laye include *The Radiance of the King* (1954, 1956), *A Dream of Africa* (1966, 1968) and *The Guardian of the Word* (1978).

Alioum Fantouré, *Tropical Circle* (1972; Longman, 1981). A "novel" about Guinea between the end of World War II and the reign of terror. The build-up to independence is a muddle but the second half is illuminating, despite a dire, anglicised translation.

SIERRA LEONE

Sierra Leone has never had as much literary or scholarly attention as its anglophone neighbours, Ghana or Nigeria, though there are works to be found if you're prepared to scour libraries.

BACKGROUND AND TRAVELOGUES

Graham Greene, *The Heart of the Matter* (1948; Penguin). Set in Freetown during World War II, Greene's novel uses Freetown as a seedy web in which his protagonists struggle. No great insights on Sierra Leone, but it touches illuminatingly on the racism and repression then present in the colony. Enduring, and still worth reading as wry introduction or in-situ mental scenery. *Journey without Maps* (1936; Penguin) includes several dozen atmospheric pages narrating Greene's progress towards the Liberian border in 1935.

Christophe and Emmanuel Valentin, *Sierra Leone* (Editions Xavier Richer, 1 quai aux Fleux, 75004 Paris; 1986). *The* coffee table book of Sierra Leone. Nice pictures, mostly of Freetown and the peninsula (some interesting older B&Ws, too) but the feeble French/English text is at tour brochure level.

F. W. H. Migeod, *View of Sierra Leone* (1926, o/p). Fascinating and readably scatty account of a six-month trek through the country, with interesting appendices on secret societies and Mende songs.

HISTORY AND SOCIETY

Joe A. D. Alie, *A New History of Sierra Leone* (Macmillan, 1990). A recent, accessible and copiously illustrated general history from early times to the present. Explores social and economic as well as political developments.

Christopher Fyfe, *A Short History of Sierra Leone* (Longman, 1979). Secondary school text for West Africa, useful as an introduction, good on the nineteenth century but hazy post-independence, and deliberately written down to pupils.

Adelaide M. Cromwell, *An African Victorian Feminist – the Life and Times of Adelaide Smith Casely Hayford 1868–1960* (Frank Cass, 1986). A remarkable, epoch-bridging biography on a figure from the Krio elite (see p.1192).

John W. Nursley, *Moving with the Face of the Devil* (University of Illinois Press, 1987). A sociology of Freetown's contemporary masquerade societies – brilliant photos complement.

Sylvia Ardyn Boone, *Radiance from the Waters: Ideals of Feminine Beauty in Mende Art* (Yale, 1986). Circumspect account of the Mende women's Sande society by an art historian who promised not to reveal all.

Olayinka Koso-Thomas, *The Circumcision of Women – a Strategy for Eradication* (Zed Books, 1987). Just what the Sande matriarchs would prefer to avoid seeing discussed in public. Focusing on Sierra Leone, and in the Sande context, this includes detailed survey results.

E. Frances White, *Sierra Leone's Settler Women Traders* (University of Michigan Press, 1987). A study of the central economic role of Freetown's "Big Market" women in the nineteenth century.

FICTION

Robert Wellesley Cole, *Kossoh Town Boy* (Cambridge University Press, 1960, o/p). Classic novel of a childhood in pre-World-War-I and early 1920s Freetown.

Syl Cheney-Coker, *The Last Harmattan of Alusine Dunbar* (Heinemann, 1990). American-educated professor's first novel – a black comedy of life in a neo-colonial state. Honesty versus Ali Baba and his forty thieves.

R. Sarif Easmon, *The Feud* (Longman Drumbeat Series, 1981). A dozen short stories.

Yulisa Amadu Maddy, *No Past, No Present, No Future* (Heinemann, 1973). Three Sierra Leonean boys in Europe make up for, and make the most of, their different backgrounds. Maddy's *Obasai and Other Plays* (Heinemann, 1971) is worth looking out for too.

People's Educational Association, *Fishing in Rivers of Sierra Leone* (PEA, 1987: Private Mail Bag 705, 50 Siaka Stevens St, Freetown). A work of the German-funded organisation, this is a major collection of oral literature – stories and songs – from 13 Sierra Leonean language groups with hundreds of colour and B&W photos of the performers in action. Highly recommended.

LIBERIA

Liberia does have a modest literature, but much of it is American socio-political and development analysis – and hardly screaming out to be read.

Graham Greene, *Journey without Maps* (1936; Penguin). Acid account of the author's walk in 1936 from Foya to Buchanan, via Ganta. He was accompanied by a cousin (hardly mentioned) and a line of porters.

Barbara Greene, *Too Late to Turn Back* (Penguin, 1990). Revenge of the above-mentioned cousin. "It sounded fun", she writes (but evidently it wasn't).

Alice Walker, *The Color Purple* (The Women's Press, 1983). Part of the story offers an oblique glance at the conditions that led to the creation of America's Liberian colony.

John Gay, *Red Dust on Green Leaves: a Kpelle Twin's Childhood* (Thompson CN, Interculture Associates, 1973). Recommended background.

Liberia: a Promise Betrayed (1986, Lawyers Committee for Human Rights, New York). Gives another background, deeply disturbing, on the nature of the Liberian state under Doe, setting the present crisis in its bloody context.

J. G. Liebenow, *Liberia: The Quest for Democracy* (Indiana University Press, 1987). A detailed, if rather dry political history.

COTE D'IVOIRE

Books in English on – or deriving from – Côte d'Ivoire are few, though the French publishers *Karthala* (22–24 Bd Arago, 75013 Paris) publish a number of titles.

Marcel Amdonji, *Félix Houophouët-Boigny: L'envers d'un légende* (Karthala, 1985). A hard look at the man.

Abdou Touré, *Les petits métiers d'Abidjan: L'imagination au secours de la "conjoncture"* (Karthala, 1985). A series of lucid interviews giving a remarkable inside view of survival strategies on the city's streets.

Laurent Gbagbo, *Histoire d'un Retour* (L'Harmattan, 1989). Critique of the government of Houophouët-Boigny, putting the case for an alternative future politics.

V. S. Naipaul, *Finding the Centre: Two Narratives* (Alfred A. Knopf, 1984). Includes a long, characteristically interesting and perceptive essay – *The Crocodiles of Yamoussoukro*.

FICTION

Bernard Dadié, *Climbié* (1956; Heinemann, 1971). A sedately elegant portrayal of growing up in colonial Côte d'Ivoire and Senegal, shot through with occasional flashes of bitterness against the colonisers. Dadié, who was for many years the Minister of Cultural Affairs, has also edited *The Black Cloth* (1968; University of Massachusetts Press, 1987), a collection of tales from the oral tradition.

Ahmadou Kourouma, *The Suns of Independence* (Heinemann, 1981). A very African novel, full of imagery and suspended reality.

Jean-Marie Adiaffi, *The Identity Card* (Zimbabwe Publishing House, PO Box 350, Harare; 1984). Less compelling; a pursuit for identity in colonial Côte d'Ivoire.

GHANA

Ghana has an established literary tradition with a number of widely available works.

HISTORY AND SOCIETY

F. K. Buah, *History of Ghana* (Macmillan, 1980). A basic text, with a fair amount of illustration.

Donald I. Ray, *Ghana: Politics, Economics and Society* (Marxist Regimes Series, Pinter, 1986). A useful overview, but not one of this series' better volumes, partly because it doesn't take account of the significance of one man – Jerry Rawlings – in Ghana's "revolution", nor of the fact that he has no time for Marxists.

Emmanuel Hansen and Kwame A. Ninsin eds., *The State, Development and Politics in Ghana* (Codesria, 1989). An essential recent collection of essays on labour, women, the IMF, foreign policy, land, food, export agriculture and health care.

Eboe Hutchful, *IMF and Ghana* (Zed Books, 1987). Collection of original IMF documents . . . displaying the Fund with its pants down.

Jeff Crisp, *Story of an African Working Class: Ghanaian Miners' Struggle* (Zed Books, 1984). Epic struggle retold.

FICTION

Joseph Casely-Hayford, *Ethiopia Unbound* (1911, o/p). Generally considered the first West African novel, *Ethiopia Unbound* treats a theme that later became familiar in African literature: the student who goes to study in London, and returns home to find he's a stranger. Early suggestions of what later became "negritude".

Ama Ata Aidoo, *The Dilemma of a Ghost and Anowa* (Longman, 1965). Aidoo, one of Africa's relatively few female writers, deals in *Dilemma* with the unusual theme of a black American girl married into a Ghanaian family and in *Anowa* with a Ghanaian legend about a girl who refuses her parents' chosen suitors. *No Sweetness Here* (Longman, 1970) is a collection of short stories, most of which handle the theme of conflict between traditional and urban life in Ghana. *Our Sister Killjoy* (Longman, 1977), Aidoo's first novel, explores, in an experimental fashion, the thoughts and experience of a Ghanaian girl on a voyage of self-discovery in Germany.

Ayi Kwei Armah, *The Beautiful Ones Are Not Yet Born* (Heinemann, 1968). An insightful story of politics, greed and corruption in newly independent Africa, seen through the life of a railway clerk; Armah beautifully captures the sense of frustration and crisis that befell Ghana after the fall of Nkrumah. Armah's second novel, *Fragments* (Heinemann, 1970), is the story of a young African who comes home to Ghana after five years in the USA. *The Healers* (Heinemann, 1978), a compulsive historical novel set in the Asante empire at the time of its demise, retains an optimistic vision.

Amu Djoleto, *Hurricane of Dust* (Longman, 1987). A vital, rap-paced tale, set in a post-coup Accra.

Maya Angelou, *All God's Children Need Travelling Shoes* (Virago, 1986). The story of black activist Angelou's emigration to newly independent Ghana and her growing sense of disillusion, picked out in dialogue.

TOGO

Comi M. Toulabor, *Le Togo sous Eyadema* (Karthala, 1986). A solid discussion of recent politics – and about the only one to appear.

George Packer, *The Village of Waiting* (Sceptre, 1990). An informative book, recounting the experiences of a Peace Corps volunteer in the Corp's favourite West Africa country.

Tete Michel Kpomassie, *An African in Greenland* (Washington Square Press, 1989). The narrative of a Togolese explorer on a whimsical journey among the Innuit. Never quite transcends the basic oddity of its theme, and begs a few questions along the way, but entertaining nonetheless.

FICTION

David Ananou, *Le Fils du Fétiche* (Nouvelle Editions Latine, 1955). Intended to combat the racism of its time by a portrayal of a typical Togolese family, the effort is confounded by Ananou's rejection of traditional beliefs for the "lofty" tenets of Christianity.

Yves-Emmanuel Dogbé, *La Victime* (Paris, Editions Akpagnon, 1979). A treatment of the inter-racial theme in West Africa. White girl's parents come to recognise the error of their prejudice, but too late.

BENIN

Bruce Chatwin, *The Viceroy of Ouidah* (Picador, 1980). Without a doubt the first book to read on Benin – gripping, in Chatwin's inimitable style, from the prologue on.

Patrick Manning, *Slavery, Colonialism and Economic Growth in Dahomey 1640–1960* (Cambridge University Press, 1982). Heavy scholarship, but well done.

Dov Ronen, *Dahomey: Between Tradition and Modernity* (Cornell University Press, 1975). Unfortunately, the publication date means the Kérékou era is largely left out.

Robert Cornevin, *La République Populaire du Bénin* (Editions G-P Maisonneuve et Larose, 1984). A complete, if dryly chronological, history, with a French nationalist slant.

FICTION

Maximilien Quenum, *Légendes Africaines* (1946). One of the earliest African writers inspired by the early doctrine of "negritude". The legends include an account of the founding of the Dan-Homey empire along with that of kingdoms in Côte d'Ivoire and the Soudan (Mali).

Paul Hazoumé *Doguicimi* (Larose, 1938). The essence of the Dan-Homey kingdom is again

captured in this carefully documented work of realist-romantic fiction, unfortunately not yet translated from French.

Olympe Bhêly-Quénum, *Snares Without End* (trans. Dorothy S. Blair, Longman 1981, from *Un Piège sans Fin*, 1978). The only Béninois writer available in translation.

NIGERIA

There's a vast body of books on and from Nigeria in print – and more being published all the time . . .

COUNTRY AND STATE

Peter Holmes, *Nigeria: Giant of Africa* (Oregon Press, 1985). Coffee-table format with nearly 200 photos. Detailed and interesting notes; nothing else on Nigeria of this type compares.

Nigeria, the Land, its Art and its People (Studio Vista, 1977). A brief, good-value anthology of prose, with photographs.

Adewale Maja-Pearce, *In My Father's Country* (Heinemann, 1987). A curiously flat and brief travelogue. Maja-Pearce (back in Nigeria for the first time in a long while) seems afraid of commitment, travelling to Maiduguri "only to be able to say I'd been there".

William D. Graf, *Nigerian State: Political Economy, State, Class and Political System in the Post-Colonial Era* (J. Currey, 1988). An overview analysing political, social and economic shifts over the last 25 years.

T. Falola, *Rise and Fall of Nigeria's Second Republic 1979–1983* (Zed Books, 1985). Scrutiny of the exceptionally corrupt Shagari regime.

Chinua Achebe, *The Trouble with Nigeria* (Heinemann, 1983). A brief and immensely useful insight into the complexity of Nigerian society and politics.

ART AND PEOPLE

J. S. Boston, *Ikenga* (Ethnographica Press, 1977). Explores the symbolism of carvings amongst varied peoples of Nigeria.

Bryna Freyer, *Royal Benin Art* (Smithsonian Institute, 1987). Illustrated and informative catalogue from a major exhibition of the art of the Benin Empire.

G. I. Jones, *Ibo Art* (Shire, 1989). Well-illustrated survey of arts and their role in Ibo (Igbo) society.

Henry J. Drewal and John Pemberton III, *Yoruba: Nine Centuries of African Art and Thought* (Abrams, 1989). Sumptuous and terribly expensive – a majestic, detailed photo and essay documentary on various Yoruba states and their individual artistic traditions.

T. J. H. Chappel, *Decorated Gourds in North Eastern Nigeria* (Ethnographica Press, 1977). A substantial survey of their use, decoration and symbolism.

Barry Hallen and J. O. Sodipo, *Knowledge, Belief and Witchcraft* (Ethnographica Press, 1977). A survey of Yoruba philosophical ideas.

Berkare Gbadamosi and Ulli Beier, *Not Even God Is Ripe Enough* (Heinemann, 1968). Full of amusing stories.

LANGUAGE

Teach Yourself Yoruba, **E C Rowlands**, and **Teach Yourself Hausa**, **Charles H Kraft and H. M. Kirk-Greene** (Teach Yourself Books, 1989). Serious application required.

FICTION

Nigeria's post-colonial literature has been the continent's most prolific and most outspoken, its writers enjoying a greater liberty than most of their African counterparts. One of the greatest impetuses to national writing was Onitsha Market Literature, which emerged between 1947 and 1966. At the time, Onitsha was one of Nigeria's most important commercial centres, with a long history of mission education and cosmopolitan influence. Dozens of spare-time writers – teachers, office clerks and journalists – turned out some 200 books that were printed in the market itself. Today, by far the most influential Nigerian writers are Chinua Achebe and the Nobel prize-winning novelist and playwright Wole Soyinka.

Olaudah Equiano, *The Life of Olaudah Equiano* (1789; Longman, 1988). Classic autobiography and one of the earliest West African books. Equiano was born in Igboland in 1745 and captured by slavers at the age of ten. Highly recommended reading.

Amos Tutuola, *Palm Wine Drinkard* (Faber, 1952). This, the first West African novel, is heavily under the spell of Yoruba oral tradition as it recounts a journey into the "Dead Towns" of the supernatural. It was followed by *My Life in the Bush of Ghosts* (Faber, 1954).

Chinua Achebe, *Things Fall Apart* (1958), *No Longer at Ease* (1960), *The Arrow of God* (1964), *A Man of the People* (1966), *Anthills of the Savannah* (1987); all published by Heinemann. One of Africa's best known novelists, Achebe gained international fame with his classic first novel *Things Fall Apart*, which deals with the encounter, at the turn of the century, between missionaries, colonial officers and an Igbo village. Okwonkwo, a self-made man, rises to respected seniority, then falls, inexorably and tragically. It's a brilliant, moving book – universal in what it says on pride, and on fathers and sons. With it, the three following novels form part of a loose quartet: in *No Longer at Ease*, Okwonkwo's grandson, Obi, is a corrupt Lagos civil servant, trapped in his head between home and ambition; in *Arrow of God*, set in the 1920s, there's direct confrontation between an Igbo priest and a colonial officer; and in *A Man of the People*, Achebe adopts a more satirical approach, setting up an idealist against a rogue and showing how close their paths run. Achebe's characters bend and sweat with life and develop unexpected traits just as you thought you had the measure of them. His last novel, a humanist fable, *Anthills of the Savannah*, was shortlisted for the Booker Prize.

Wole Soyinka. When Soyinka won the Nobel Prize for Literature in 1986, he not only gained international recognition for himself (becoming the first African to be so honoured), but for the writers of his continent. Known primarily as a playwright, his early works include *The Lion and the Jewel* (1963), *A Dance of the Forests* (1963) – an exercise in demythologising Africa's historic idyll – and *Kongi's Harvest* (1967). Both Oxford University Press and Methuen publish editions of his plays. He later published poetry, sketching beautiful images in *Idanre, and Other Poems* (Methuen, 1967). He has also delivered substantially as a novelist with *The Interpreters* (Heinemann, 1965) – in which a group of young intellectuals living in Lagos attempts to "interpret" its role in traditional and modern Nigeria – and the luminous, dream-like *Ake* (Arrow, 1982) – an autobiographical account of his childhood in Abeokuta. *Isara: A Voyage around Essay* (Methuen, 1990) is his latest book – a biographical account of Nigeria in the times of his father, the memorable schoolmaster "Essay" from *Ake*. As a writer of equal prominence to Achebe, Soyinka's work is denser and less easy-going.

Simi Bedford, *Yoruba Girl Dancing* (Heinemann, 1990). A British Nigerian's depiction of early life in Nigeria, adjustment to the UK, and the getting of wisdom.

T. M. Aluko, *One Man, One Wife* (Heinemann, 1967). Entertaining tale of a Yoruba village's disillusionment with the missionary's God and its return to traditional worship. *One Man, One Matchet* (Heinemann, 1965) is written in a similarly crafted and satirical style as it portrays conflict in a Western cocoa community. *Chief the Honourable Minister* (Heinemann, 1970) is the less amusing story of a schoolmaster appointed minister in a corrupt government.

Tafawa Balewa, *Shaihu Umar* (Longman, 1968; translated from the Hausa). Portrayal of a Hausa family at the turn of the century by Nigeria's first Prime Minister.

Flora Nwapa, *Efuru* (Heinemann, 1966). The first novel by a woman published in Africa. As in the later *Idu* (Heinemann, 1969), Nwapa looks at women's roles – not always in a traditional way – in a society precariously balanced between the traditional and the new.

Buchi Emecheta, *Slave Girl* (Fontana, 1979), *Second Class Citizen* (Fontana, 1977), *In The Ditch* (Fontana, 1988), *Head Above Water* (Fontana, 1986), *Joys Of Motherhood* (Heinemann, 1979), *Double Yoke* (Fontana, 1984), *Bride Price* (Fontana, 1978) and *Rape Of Shavi* (Fontana, 1989). Emecheta writes, with a humour that refuses to be submerged, about the struggle to be a Nigerian woman and an independent person – in Nigeria and the UK.

Zainab Alkali, *A Virtuous Woman, The Stillborn* (Longman, 1984). Another writer focusing on women, Alkali is unusual in being from the conservative north of the country. "I see myself as a typical Nigerian woman who wants to get married, raise a family and live according to the expected norms of the society. . . . A woman can never be anything else but a woman".

John Pepper Clark, *A Reed in the Tide* (Longman, 1965), *Casualties* (Longman, 1970), a lament written during the civil war, and *A Decade of Tongues* (1981) are poetry collections with which Clark first gained recognition. He is now better known as a playwright – for *Ozidi*, a play based on an Ijaw saga, *State of the Nation*, a piece of social criticism written in 1985, and *America, Their America*, a biting

indictment of values in the United States where he studied in the early 1960s – Clark is established in Lagos with the influential Pec Repertory company.

Cyprian Ekwensi, *Jagua Nana* (Heinemann, 1961). Superbly captures the life and rhythm of 1950s Lagos using a style resembling that of the traditional storyteller. *Burning Grass* (Heinemann, 1962) is set in the north among Fula herders (an unusual departure for Ekwensi). Now one of Nigeria's most popular novelists, Ekwensi started his writing career at Onitsha market. *Lokotown and other stories* (Heinemann, 1966) is a collection of short tales, again set in the city, while *Survive the Peace* (Heinemann 1976) is his most recent, most political novel, set in the aftermath of the defeat of Biafra, a secession he had supported.

Vincent Chukwuemeka Ike, *Toads for Supper* (Fontana, 1966), *The Naked Gods* (Fontana, 1970), *Chicken Chasers* (Fontana 1980) and *Sunset at Dawn* (Fontana, 1976). A series of entertaining, critical novels by a brilliant comic writer.

Eddie Iroh, *Forty Eight Guns for the General* (Heinemann, 1976), *Toads of War* (Heinemann, 1979) and *The Sirens in the Night* (Heinemann, 1982). Three thrillers that rode in on the wave of writing following the Biafran War.

Adewale Maja Pearce, Loyalties (Longman, 1987). Evocative short stories and vignettes of a society on the brink of chaos by a writer based in Britain.

Festus Ijayi, *Violence* (Longman, 1979), *Heroes* (Longman, 1986). A committedly political writer, Ijayi was detained in 1988 for protesting the govenment's human rights abuses. *Violence* is a howl of anguish at the inhumanity of urban survival in Africa. *Heroes* is set in the dark backyard of Nigeria's soul, the civil war.

Ben Okri, *Flowers and Shadows* (Longman, 1980). Okri's excellent first novel was published when he was only twenty. The short story collections, *Incidents at the Shrine* (Fontana, 1986) and *Stars of the New Curfew* (Penguin, 1988) propelled Nigerian literature into a new wide audience with their angry, hallucinatory short stories. Okri, like Ijayi, one of Nigeria's "new realists" (based in Britain), provides razor-sharp dialogue and settings, fine evocations of character (male and female) and an angular wit.

CAMEROON

A fair number of books dealing with Cameroon have been published, and the country has the literary advantage of a dual linguistic heritage which has inspired a relatively rich literature, though predominantly in French.

GENERAL/TRAVELOGUES

Gerald Durrell, *The Oveloaded Ark* (Faber, 1953), *The Bafut Beagles*, (Penguin, 1954), *A Zoo in my Luggage* (Penguin, 1960). Durrell's animal-collecting exploits in the British Cameroons — first freelance, and then for his Jersey Conservation Trust zoo — are delightfully recounted and still funny, with exceptions made for an unexceptionally colonial attitude to quaint native behaviour. But it's hard indeed to recognise the present town of Mamfé — even less Bafut — in his misty pictures.

Nigel Barley, *Innocent Anthropologist: Notes from a Mud Hut* (Penguin, 1986), *A Plague of Caterpillars* (Penguin, 1986). The books that did for anthropology what Durrell did for animal collecting — and infuriated anthropologists.

Dervla Murphy, *In Cameroon with Egbert* (Arrow, 1990). Murphy is not at her best in this unenthralling and unperceptive travelogue.

HISTORY/POLITICS/ART

Mark DeLancey, *The Cameroons* (Dartmouth, 1989). Up-to-date survey of history, economics and politics.

T. E. Mbuagbaw, R. Brain, R. Palmer, *A History of Cameroon* (Longman, 1987). Useful school text.

Joseph Sheppherd, *Leaf of Honey* (Bahai, 1988). An American anthropologist's study of the Ntuumu people of Cameroon, laced with their proverbs and their views about life.

Albert Mukong, *Prisoner without a Crime* (Nubia, 1989). The darker side of political life under Biya, this tells the story of six years of imprisonment with graphic details of arbitrary justice, brutality and torture. Leave at home.

Philippe Gaillard, *Le Cameroun* (L'Harmattan 1989, two volumes). General political and economic survey in French from colonial times to the present

Tamara Northern, *Art Of Cameroon* (Smithsonian Institute, 1984). Large-format colour illustrated survey of regions and their art.

FICTION IN ENGLISH

Ferdinand Oyono, *Houseboy* (trans. from *Une Vie de Boy*, Heinemann, 1956). Oyono was one of the first satirical writers of the anti-colonial period to break from an autobiographical form in this scathing satire about colonialism. *The Old Man and the Medal* (trans. from *Le Vieux Negre et la Médaille*, Heinemann, 1967) is less caustic, but equally effective, both in its criticism of colonial insensitivity, and of blind adherence to tradition. Oyono is now Minister of Housing and Town Planning.

Guillaume Oyônô-Mbia, *Three Suitors, One Husband* and *Until Further Notice* (Methuen, 1968). Comic masterpieces, written in English. His later play in French, *Notre Fille ne se mariera pas*, like *Three Suitors*, deals with the familiar theme of the dowry in a changing African society. It was made into the 1980 film *Notre Fille* by Daniel Kamwa (see p.1182).

Mongo Beti, *The Poor Christ of Bomba* (trans. Heinemann, 1971). One of the senior figures of African literature — living in exile since 1959 — Beti's novels combine political satire with more basic human conflict. *Poor Christ*, the most cynical of his novels, deals with the perverse efforts of a French priest to convert the whole village, with disastrously ironic consequences. Later works, *Mission to Kala* (trans. from *Mission terminée*, Heinemann, 1957) and *King Lazurus* (trans. from *Le Roi Miraculé*, Heinemann,1960) established his mastery of social satire. After independence, Beti embarked on a long period of silence until the publication of his critique of the Ahidjo regime — *Main basse sur le Cameroon* (F. Maspero, 1972), which he followed with *Remember Ruben* and *Perpetua and the Habit of Unhappiness* (trans. John Reed and Clive Wake, Heinemann, 1974).

Francis Bebey, *Agatha Moudio's Son* (trans. from *Le fils d'Agatha Moudio*, Heinemann, 1971). Better known as a musician (see p.1177), this was Bebey's first novel, a tragi-comic study of human relations in a traditional village society.

Ndeley Mokoso, *Man Pass Man!* (Longman, 1987). A string of darkly funny short stories. The subject of the title tale — maraboutic meddling on the football pitch — couldn't possibly account for Cameroon's success in the 1990 World Cup. Could it?

FICTION IN FRENCH

René Philombe, *Lettres de ma Cambuse* (Editions CLE, 1964). Life in the urban slums described – even on the basis of personal experience – with humour. Subsequent work includes an inspired collection of short stories *Histoires queue de chat: quelques scènes de la vie camerounaise* (Editions CLE, 1971).

Benjamin Matip, *Afrique nous t'ignorons* (1954). Matip contemplates the past from a young African's perspective – separated from tradition by Western education and World War II. The novel also hits at the exploitation of Cameroonian planters: it contributed to an outpouring of anti-colonial literature in the 1950s. Matip's *A la Belle Etoile: Contes et nouvelles d'Afrique* (Presence Africaine, 1962) is a classic collection of folk stories.

Léon-Marie Ayissi, *Contes et Berceuses Béti* (1966). A satisfying collection of Beti folktales.

Jacques Mariel Nzouankeu, *Le Souffle des Ancêtres* (Edit CLE, 1965). Tales that illustrate the conflict between humans and the metaphysical forces that dominate their destinies.

BOOKSHOPS AND LIBRARIES

Useful **bookshops** and **libraries** for obtaining African (and out of print) books are detailed on p.34. Any UK resident can make use of the **Inter-Library Loans** system to obtain even the most obscure titles – given time.

For **books in French**, *La Page* French bookshop (7 Harrington Rd, London SW7; ☎071/589 5991) may be able to help. The best African bookshop in Europe, however, is *L'Harmattan* in Paris (16 rue des Ecoles, 5e).

TRAVELLER'S FRENCH

Apart from some specialised vocabulary, there's little that non-fluent speakers will find characteristic about West African French beyond the accent. It's generally a lot easier to understand than French as spoken in France, because it's more vigorously pronounced. And the French colonists encouraged the use of French far more than the British, so that, assuming you have at least some French, there are fewer language problems in the *pays francophones*.

As with English spoken as a second language, you'll hear in West African French the rhythmic and tonal colouring of the speaker's mother tongue.

WEST AFRICAN FRENCH: A TRAVELLER'S GLOSSARY

This is a mix of pertinent words and expressions together with some French and West African street slang and a few historical terms that have found their way into West African French.

amende	fine, penalty
atelier	workshop, studio
bâché	pick-up van, (lit. "tarpaulined")
balise	beacon or cairn, usually in the desert
banco	mud and straw mixture for building
barrage	road block, barrier
barraquer	to stop, rest awhile, camp
berline	saloon car
bic	disposable pen
biche	doe, gazelle, pet
bidonville	slum, shanty town
bonne arrivée	favoured greeting in francophone Africa
bord	fortress (Arabic)
bordelle	prostitute, pick-up
borne	kilometre marker, "kilometre"
bouffer	to eat
break	estate car, station wagon
bricolage	the art of preserving equipment or making something out of nothing
brousse	countryside, the bush
buvette	outside bar, refreshments stall
cadeauter	to give a present; children may tell you, "il faut me cadeauter"
caféman	coffee, bread and omelette man
campement	budget motel or country guest house

canari	clay pot for storing cool water
carte d'identité	identity card
carte routière	road map
case	hut, small house
chef	boss, chief
chômer	to be unemployed.
cinq cent quatre	Peugeot 504
climatisée	air conditioned (room)
colon	a colonial
commander	ask someone to do something
contrôle	checkpoint
coupe-coupe	machete
dancing	dance floor, disco
depuis	a long time
devises	money or (hard) currency
dépannage	breakdown service
discuter	to discuss, negotiate
doux	good (even a hot pepper soup, far from mild, can be doux)
eau potable	drinking water
en panne	out of order, broken down
escalier	washboard road surface
escroc	swindler, con-man
exigé	required, demanded
faisable	feasible, do-able
féticheur	religious man with a knowledge of the ways of the spirits
fiche	form, document to fill in
flic	cop, policeman
fréquenter	to go to school

BASIC FRENCH WORDS AND PHRASES

today	*aujourd'hui*	this one	*ceci*
yesterday	*hier*	that one	*celà*
tomorrow	*demain*	open	*ouvert*
in the morning	*le matin*	closed	*fermé*
in the afternoon	*l'après-midi*	big	*grand*
in the evening	*le soir*	small	*petit*
now	*maintenant*	more	*plus*
later	*plus tard*	less	*moins*
at one o'clock	*à une heure*	a little	*un peu*
at three o'clock	*à trois heures*	a lot	*beaucoup*
at ten-thirty	*à dix heures et demie*	cheap	*bon marché*
at midday	*à midi*	expensive	*cher*
man	*un homme*	good	*bon*
woman	*une femme*	bad	*mauvais*
here	*ici*	hot	*chaud*
there	*là*	cold	*froid*

fric	cash, dosh	*palu/paludisme*	malaria
frequenter	to go to school	*patron*	boss, chief, mister
fromager	silk-cotton (kapok) tree	*phacochère*	warthog
garé	parked, not in use	*pièces*	identity papers
gare routière	motor transport station	*pirogue*	dugout canoe
gare ferroviaire	railway station	*piste*	track, trail
gargote	cheap restaurant or chop-house	*préfet/sous-préfet*	administrative prefect/assistant prefect (equivalent of District Commissioner and assistant)
gaté	spoiled, broken, needing repair		
gênant	bothersome, a hassle		
gîte (d'étape)	boarding house, inn (staging post)	*quatre-quatre*	four-wheel drive
		récolte	harvest
goudron	tar, tarmac	*régler*	to sort out, settle up, pay up
gri-gri	charm, amulet, juju	*renseignements*	information, details
griot	traditional musician, storyteller, court minstrel	*route bitumée*	surfaced road
		sapeur	one who is well dressed-up, usually for discos and hanging out; from Sape, the fictitious Société des ambianceurs et persons élégants
hivernage	rainy season		
HLM	"low rent housing" (council flats)		
insh'allah	if God wills it (hopefully)		
intéressant	good, enjoyable; eg a film or the food you're eating.		
		sofa	Nineteenth-century Muslim cavalry
lampe tempête	hurricane lamp, kerosene lamp		
livres sterling	pounds sterling	*source (d'eau)*	spring, water source
machin	thingimajig, whatsitsname	*sous*	money
mairie	town hall, city hall	*sucrerie*	mineral or soft drink
maison de passage	boarding house used as a brothel	*sympa/sympathique*	nice, friendly
marigot ←	creek	*tampon*	rubber stamp
marque	make or brand (eg vehicle or spare part)	*tata*	fortress (Mande)
		tôle ondulée	corrugated iron, washboard road
mec	guy, fellow	*tourner*	to go out, go dancing, hang out
moustiquaire	mosquito net/mosquito screen	*triptyque*	triptych; a document in three folds
occasion	a seat or place in a bush taxi		
ornières	wheel ruts	*trop*	more often means "very" than "too much"
paillote	straw hut, sunshade, thatched awning		
		truc	thing, whatsit
palétuviers	mangroves	*ventilée*	"ventilated" – a room with a fan

TALKING TO PEOPLE

Excuse me	*Pardon*	please	*s'il vous plaît*
Do you speak English ?	*Vous parlez anglais ?*	thank you	*merci*
How do you say it in French ?	*Comment ça se dit en Français ?*	hello	*bonjour*
		goodbye	*au revoir*
What's your name ?	*Comment vous appelez-vous ?*	good morning/ afternoon	*bonjour*
My name is . . .	*Je m'appelle . . .*	good evening	*bonsoir*
I'm English/	*Je suis anglais[e]/*	good night	*bonne nuit*
Irish/Scottish	*irlandais[e]/écossais[e]/*	How are you ?	*Comment allez-vous ?/ Ça va ?*
Welsh/American/	*gallois[e]/américain[e]/*		
Australian/	*australien[ne]/*	Fine, thanks	*Très bien, merci*
Canadian/	*canadien[ne]/*	I don't know	*Je ne sais pas*
a New Zealander	*néo-zélandais[e]*	Let's go	*Allons-y*
yes	*oui*	See you tomorrow	*à demain*
no	*non*	See you soon	*à bientôt*
I understand	*Je comprends*	Sorry	*Pardon, Madame/ je m'excuse*
I don't understand	*Je ne comprends pas*		
Can you speak slower ?	*s'il vous plaît, parlez moins vite*	Leave me alone (aggressive)	*Fichez-moi la paix!*
OK/agreed	*d'accord*	Please help me	*Aidez-moi, s'il vous plaît*

FINDING THE WAY

bus	*autobus, bus, car*	I want to get off at . . .	*Je voudrais descendre à . . .*
car	*voiture*		
train/taxi/ferry	*train/taxi/ferry*	the road to . . .	*la route pour . . .*
boat	*bâteau*	near	*près/pas loin*
plane	*avion*	far	*loin*
What time does it leave ?	*Il part à quelle heure ?*	left	*à gauche*
		right	*à droite*
What time does it arrive ?	*Il arrive à quelle heure ?*	straight on	*tout droit*
		on the other side of	*l'autre côté de*
a ticket to . . .	*un billet pour . . .*	on the corner of	*à l'angle de*
ticket office	*vente de billets*	next to	*à côté de*
how many kilometres ?	*combien de kilomètres ?*	behind	*derrière*
		in front of	*devant*
how many hours ?	*combien d'heures ?*	before	*avant*
on foot	*à pied*	after	*après*
Where are you going ?	*Vous allez où ?*	under	*sous*
		to cross	*traverser*
I'm going to . . .	*Je vais à . . .*	bridge	*pont*

OTHER NEEDS

doctor	*médecin*	chemist	*pharmacie*
I don't feel well	*Je ne me sens pas bien*	bakery	*boulangerie*
medicines	*médicaments*	food shop	*alimentation*
prescription	*ordonnance*	supermarket	*supermarché*
I feel sick	*Je suis malade*	to eat	*manger*
headache	*J'ai mal à la tête*	to drink	*boire*
stomach ache	*mal à l'estomac*	bank	*banque*
period	*règles*	money	*argent*
pain	*douleur*	with	*avec*
it hurts	*ça fait mal*	without	*sans*

QUESTIONS AND REQUESTS

The simplest way of asking a question is to start with *s'il vous plaît* (please), then name the thing you want in an interrogative tone of voice. For example:

Where is there a bakery ?	*S'il vous plaît, la boulangerie ?*
Which way is it to Bobo ?	*S'il vous plaît, la route pour Bobo ?*

Similarly with requests:

We'd like a room for two	*S'il vous plaît, une chambre pour deux*
Can I have a kilo of oranges	*S'il vous plaît, un kilo d'oranges*

Question words

Where ?	*où ?*	When ?	*quand ?*
How ?	*comment ?*	Why ?	*pourquoi ?*
How many/how much ?	*combien ?*	At what time ?	*à quelle heure ?*
		What is/which is ?	*quel est ?*

ACCOMMODATION

a room for one/two people	*une chambre pour une/deux personnes*	second floor	*deuxième étage*
a double bed	*un lit double*	with a view	*avec vue*
a room with a shower	*une chambre avec douche*	key	*clef*
		to iron	*repasser*
Can I see it ?	*Je peux la voir ?*	do laundry	*faire la lessive*
a room on the courtyard	*une chambre sur la cour*	sheets	*draps*
		quiet	*calme*
a room over the street	*une chambre sur la rue*	noisy	*bruyant*
		hot water	*eau chaude*
first floor	*premier étage*	cold water	*eau froide*
		breakfast	*le petit déjeuner*

DAYS AND DATES

January	*janvier*	November	*novembre*	August 1	*le premier août*
February	*février*	December	*décembre*	March 2	*le deux mars*
March	*mars*			July 14	*le quatorze juillet*
April	*avril*	Sunday	*dimanche*	November 23	*le vingt-trois novembre*
May	*mai*	Monday	*lundi*		
June	*juin*	Tuesday	*mardi*		
July	*juillet*	Wednesday	*mercredi*	1991	*dix-neuf-cent-quatre-vingt-onze*
August	*août*	Thursday	*jeudi*		
September	*septembre*	Friday	*vendredi*	1992	*dix-neuf-cent-quatre-vingt-douze*
October	*octobre*	Saturday	*samedi*		

NUMBERS

1	*un*	11	*onze*	21	*vingt-et-un*	95	*quatre-vingt-quinze*
2	*deux*	12	*douze*	22	*vingt-deux*	100	*cent*
3	*trois*	13	*treize*	30	*trente*	101	*cent-et-un*
4	*quatre*	14	*quatorze*	40	*quarante*	200	*deux cents*
5	*cinq*	15	*quinze*	50	*cinquante*	300	*trois cents*
6	*six*	16	*seize*	60	*soixante*	500	*cinq cents*
7	*sept*	17	*dix-sept*	70	*soixante-dix*	1000	*mille*
8	*huit*	18	*dix-huit*	75	*soixante-quinze*	2000	*deux milles*
9	*neuf*	19	*dix-neuf*	80	*quatre-vingts*	5000	*cinq milles*
10	*dix*	20	*vingt*	90	*quatre-vingt-dix*	1,000,000	*un million*

A CHRONOLOGICAL INDEX

This chronology aims to provide a sense of a timescale and a basis for comparing historical events and developments in West Africa until the partition of the region by the colonial powers at the end of the nineteenth century.

Entries below preceded by a bullet (•) refer either to events and processes of imprecise date or to those completed by the end of the century in question. Italic numbers are page references for further information. The "Western Region" comprises the coastal states from Guinea-Bissau to Ghana and including Burkina Faso; the "Sahara and Sahel Region" comprises Algeria, Niger, Mali, Mauritania, Senegal and The Gambia; and the "Eastern Region" is Togo, Benin, Nigeria and Cameroon.

Date	Western Region	Sahara and Sahel Region	Eastern Region
6000BC		**6000–500 BC** Hunting, Herding and Chariot eras *111* **1000 BC** Desiccation of Lake Aoukar *331* **500 BC** Saharan Camel era *111* **500 BC** Start of Aoudaghost's trans-Saharan trade *332* **300BC** Sanga people in Dogon region *224* **300BC** Founding of Djenné-Djeno *217* **C6th** Arrival of Kawkaw fishermen at site of Gao *234* **C7th** Ancestors of Songhai arrive from the S. *176* **C7th** Foundation of Songhai *234* **750** Founding of Ghana *332* **750** Wassu stone circles **800** Founding of Djenné *214* **C10th** Assodé, Tuareg capital *161*	**300BC** Earliest evidence of Nok civilisation *987, 1046* **100BC** Early Bantu-speakers migrate from Nigeria; display "Pygmy" people *1096* **C6th** Evidence of iron-working on site of Kano city *1060* **C7th** Earliest date in Kano Chronicles *1060* **C8th** Sao civilisation; advanced material culture *1096* **850** Sefawa dynasty at Kanem 1073 **C9th** Founding of Ife *987, 1022* **C9th** Igbo-Ukwu archaeological site *1032*
1000AD	• Arrival of Akan people around Lake Bosumtwi *850*	**1009** Songhai King Za Kossoi converts to Islam *234* **1014** Founding of Ghardaïa by Mozabites *96* **1050** Capture of Aoudaghost by Ghana *332* **1067** Description of Koumbi Saleh, capital of Ghana *332* • Sine-Saloum stone circles *400* • Berber base of Azougui used to raid Aoudaghost *332* • State of Tekrur, N.E. part of Senegal *407* • Tuareg in control of Timbuktu *218* • Start of occupation of Dogon region by Tellem *224*	• Founding of Hausa emirates *1053*

Date	Western Region	Sahara and Sahel Region	Eastern Region
1100	**1130** Arrival of Kurumba/Fulse in N. Burkina region *275* • Founding of Kong by Senoufo *796*	**1150** Founding of Tichit by Mande speakers *330* • Islamisation of Tekrur *372* • Islamisation of Ghana *332* • Annexation of Tekrur and Ghana by Mali *332* • Founding of Ouadane by Berbers *339*	**1190–1214** El Mansur of Seville (Spain) boasts of Kanem poets in his court *1073* • Founding by Yoruba people of Oyo *1020* • Earliest Walls of Kano *1060*
1200	**1205–55** Sundiata Keita lived at Niani *610* • Gbewa, traditional father of the Mossi peoples *257* • Founding of Korhogo by Senoufo *793* • Founding of Odienné by Senoufo people *791* • Fula Muslims arrive in Fouta Djalon *600* • Founding of Beyla by Mande-speaking Dyula kola traders • Founding of Mali empire, first capital Niani, near Kankan *604* • Rise of Mossi peoples *871*	• Founding of Chinguetti *338* • King of Djenné adopts Islam *214* • Sundiata Keita King of Mali *200*	• Migration of Kanuri from N.E. of Lake Chad to Bornu *1073* • Migration to Sokoto area of "Town Fulani" people from Mali, to establish trade *1069*
1300	**1330** Sacking of Timbuktu by forefathers of the Mossi of Yatenga *275* • Nomoli stone figurines, originating with the forest-dwelling ancestors of the Kissi *607* • Dan people arrive in Man district *788* • Emergence of Mamprusi, Dagomba and other Mossi states *871*	**1300** Founding of Wolof Kingdom of Jolof *366* **1325** Djenné becomes part of Mali empire *214* **1325** Annexation of Gao by Mali empire *234* **1327** Djingereber mosque in Timbuktu *221* **1330** Start of control of Timbuktu by Mali *218* • Founding of Agadez *154* • Banyun and Jola people living in Casamance *415*	**1350–1700** Golden age of Benin bronze workers **1360** Start of Kano's era as a military power to rival Gao and Timbuktu *1060* • Founding of Benin City *1030* • Start of settlement of Calabar by Efik and Efut people *1038* • Establishment of Bornu empire *1073*
1400 (cont)	**1450** Beginning of Mossi power in the region *275* **1456** First Portuguese visit to Bissau area *541* **1460** Arrival of Portuguese *586* **1470** Founding of Kingdom of Zandoma *277* **1482–1756** Coastal forts of European powers *841* **1482** Fort St George El Mina *844* • Fouta Djalon Fula leader Koli Tengela declares independence from Mali *600*	**1400** Sidi Yahya mosque in Timbuktu *221* **1445** Portuguese at Arguin Island *312* **1449** Agadez becomes Tuareg capital *154* **1460** Portuguese at Gorée *391* **1468** Occupation of Timbuktu by Songhai *235* **1470** Bandiagara escarpment invaded by Songhai *225* **1473** Djenné occupied by Songhai empire *214* **late C15th** Resumption of Tuareg rule in Timbuktu *218*	**1472** Lagos visited by Portuguese *998* **1472** Arrival of Portuguese at the mouth of the Wouri river *1100* **1485** Arrival of Portuguese at Benin City *1030*

Date	Western Region	Sahara and Sahel Region	Eastern Region
1400 (cont)	• Sherbro people displaced onto islands by Mende migrants from the N. *655* • Founding of Bondoukou *801* • Founding of Bobo-Dioulasso *285* • Start of Akan links with the Portuguese *850*	**late C15th** Portuguese trading post in Ouadane *339* **late C15th** Arrival of Portuguese settlers on Gambia river *444* • First Hausa language *135* • First Emperor of Songhai *235* • Dogon people arrive on Bandiagara escarpment *224* • Qadiriya Islamic brotherhood spreads from Timbuktu *372* • Gambia valley occupied by Mandinka kingdoms *444*	• N. parts of "Benin" region under Songhai hegemony *937* • Portuguese coastal toe-holds of Bonny and Brass islands *1037* • Portuguese arrival in Calabar district *1038* • Partial conversion of Hausa emirates to Islam *1053*
1500	**1500** Founding of Accra *827* **1500** Portuguese settlers in Bissau area *541* **1500** Founding of Kingdom of Ouagadougou *258* **1500** Founding of Po *283* **1540** Founding of Kingdom of Yatenga **1560** Start of American slave trade *637* **1591** Start of colonisation of forest by refugees from the collapse of the Songhai empire *701* • Kpelle confederation of Kondo, Liberia *701* • Emergence of Gonja state *863*	**1500–91** Agadez: northernmost Songhai vassal *154* **1500–1827** Algeria controlled by Ottoman empire *90* **1591** Timbuktu, Gao-Songhai invaded by Morocco *218, 235* **1591** First use of firearms S. of Sahara *218, 235* **1591** Start of "Arma" rule of Djenné, Timbuktu *214, 218* • Capture of Ouadane by Moroccan Prince Ahmed el Mansour *339*	**early C16th** Founding of Kingdom of Kebbi *1072* **1512–17** Songhai invasion of Hausa states *1072* **1516** Minimising of Benin slave sales to foreign traders *1030* **1517** Revolt of Songhai ruler of Kebbi: establishment of kingdom of Argungu *1072* **1550** Portuguese trading base at Kano pre-empted *1060* **1560** Dalmatians in Kano *1060* **1580** Start of Portuguese/ Brazilian contact with Aného, Ouidah *905, 937, 953* • Introduction to Bornu of Turkish mercenaries and Islamic ideology *1073* • Decline of Ife *1022* • Expansion S. to Lagos of Oyo Yoruba *998, 1020* • Maximum S. extent of Bornu empire to Benue river *1096* • Lagos incorporated into Benin Empire *998*
1600	**1600** Dyula displacement of Odienné Senoufo begins *791* **early C17th** Founding of Kankan by Sarakolé speakers *608* **early C17th** Start of Bunce Island trading base *662* **late C17th** Invasion of Kong by Mande-speaking Dyula *796* • Gourounsi people established in present homeland *281* • Portuguese trading settlements: Sierra Leone area *637* • Arrival in Bondoukou of Mande-speaking Dyula *801* • Contact between Europeans and Vai and Kru *701* • Gonja mosques *867*	**1651** Fort James, James Island, Gambia river *466* **1659** Founding of St. Louis (*366*), start of *Age of the Signares* on Gorée and St. Louis *391, 401* **1680** Founding of Tidjikja by Arabic speakers *327* • Foundation of Bamako *191* • Foundation of Ségou *204* • Foundation of Dyula kingdom of Kénédougou *207* • Bozo people in Mopti district *209*	**early C17th** Founding of Dan-Homey kingdom *937, 957* **early C17th** Arrival of Bamiléké in present homeland *1120* **1654** Rise of Dan-Homey *957* **1668** Dutch description of impressive Benin City *1030* **late C17th** Settlement of Atakpamé by Ewe *909* **late C17th** Start of Efik-Portuguese slave trade *1030* • Kano engages in wars with Bornu and Katsina *1060* • Settlement of Tamberma country by refugees from Dan-Homey slave-hunting *921*

Date	Western Region	Sahara and Sahel Region	Eastern Region
1700	**1700** "Asante confederation" of King Osei Tutu, at Kumasi *850* **early C18th** Yako raiders threaten Ouagadougou *259* **1730** Alfa Bari's jihad in Fouta Djalon *600* **1730** French at Sassandra *769* **1754** Acquisition of firearms by Mossi of Yatenga *277* **1754** Start of Naba Kango's rule of terror in Yatenga *277* **1757** Ouahigouya founded *277* **1787** Start of settlement of freed slaves at Freetown *637, 652* **1792** British colony on Bolama island *557* **1795** "Maroons" deported from Jamaica to Freetown *638* • Founding of Falaba by refugees from Fouta Djalon *673* • Kong powerful *796* • Founding of Zaranou by Agni people from Kumasi *802* • Arrival in Bondoukou of Akan-speaking Abron from E. *801*	**1712** Firearms acquired by Ségou King Biton Coulibaly *204* **early C18th** Invasion of Bandiagara escarpment by Ségou kingdom *225* **1750** Start of Dutch, English, French and Baltic trade disputes *444* **1776** Jihad sweeping through Tekrur *366* **1795** Mungo Park's departure from Pisania on his first expedition *472* • Zinder, capital of Damagaram *166*	**1707–32** Reign of Agadja in Dan-Homey, expansion of the empire *957* **early C18th** War between Dan-Homey and Oyo *957* **1740** Start of Dan-Homey's demise *937* **1748** Dan-Homey henceforth a vassal state of Oyo *957* **late C18th** Founding of Ibadan *1016* **late C18th** Courts of Lisbon and Oyo in slave-trading partnership **late C18th** Resumption of slave exports from Benin City *1030* **late C18th** Holy war-mongering of Usman Dan Fodio *1069* **late C18th** Arrival in Sokodé of Kotokoli from the N.W. *913* • Founding of Lomé by Ewe refugees from Notsé tyranny *888* • Founding of Bamoun *1123* • Settlement of non-Muslim Fali and Bata people along the Benue river *1151*
1800 (cont)	**early C19th** Founding of Grand Bassam by Nzima people *771* **early C19th** Asante control of Accra *827* **1800** Peak of Asante power *850* **1808** Sierra Leone becomes a British crown colony *639* **1815** Emergence of Krio *638* **1822** Start of colonisation of Liberia by freed slaves *701* **1824** 1st Anglo-Asante war *850* **1825–34** Yatenga wars of succession *277* **1826** 2nd Anglo-Asante war *850* **1827** Caillié in Kouroussa *606* **1830–1900** Samory Touré, Malinké warlord *579, 604, 608, 610, 611* **1847** Independence of Liberia from United States *702* **1850** Founding of Djinguiraye by El Hadj Omar Tall *606* **1850** Ebrié people at Bingerville meet Europeans *765* **1853** Heinrich Barth in Dori *274* **1855** Founding of Jewish-Vai trading base at Sulima *680* **1863** 3rd Anglo-Asante war *850*	**early C19th** Mopti, an outpost of Amadou Lobbo's jihad state of Masina *209* **1810** Djenné controlled by Amdou Lobbo *214* **1820** The Gambia valley under British control *444* **1824** Start of European explorers "rush" for Timbuktu *219* **1825** El Hadj Omar Tall appointed Tijani chief khalif *366, 372* **1827** French take power in Algeria *90* **1827–47** Algerian anti-colonial resistance of Abd-el-Kader *90* **1830** Bandiagara escarpment invaded by Amadou Lobbo of Masina *225* **1850** Explorer Heinrich Barth in Zinder and Agadez *137, 155* **1850s** Start of the Soninke–Marabout wars *372, 445* **1852–1890** Tukulor expansion *186* **1857** Founding of Dakar, end of *Signares*' culture *375*	**early C19th** Founding of Abeokuta *1027* **early C19th** European anti-slavery laws *937* **1804** Civil war in Gobir *1069* **1804** Founding of sultanate of Rey Bouba *1149* **1805** Mungo Park killed at Bussa on Niger river *1043* **1807** Kano falls to Usman Dan Fodio's jihad *1060* **1807** Argungu resists Usman Dan Fodio's jihad *1072* **1807** Bornu repulses Usman Dan Fodio jihad *1073* **1809** Sokoto established as capital of Islamic empire *1069* **1818** Start of King Ghezo's tyranny in Dan-Homey *957* **1820** Founding of new Oyo *1020* **1824** Clapperton in Kano *1060* **1829** Ibadan a Yoruba military HQ and refugee camp *998* **1830s** Start of "Amazon" army regiments in Dan-Homey *957* **1835** Death of Sultan Bello of Sokoto *1069* **1835** Ngaoundéré subjected by Fula jihadists *1147*

Date	Western Region	Sahara and Sahel Region	Eastern Region
1800 (cont)	**1865** End of Atlantic slave trade *638* **1870** Anglo-American rights dispute on Bolama *558* **1874** 4th Anglo-Asante war *850* **1879** Kankan conquered by Samory Touré *608* **1880** Founding of Abengourou by Agni from Zaranou *802* **1880s–93** Odienné controlled by Samory Touré *791* **1880s** Falaba under siege by Samory Touré: mass suicide of inhabitants *673* **1892–97** Attacks on Bouna, Bondoukou, Kong by Samory Touré *799, 801, 802, 796* **1890s** Liberian territory conceded to France, UK *702* **1890s** Start of French rule in Burkina region *253* **1898** Anti-colonial resistance in Sierra Leone *640* **late C19th** Djerma raids on Gourounsi *281* • Demise of independent Mossi states/kingdoms *871* **1900** Samory Touré captured *788* **1900** Asante empire annexed to British Empire *850* **1933** W. Africa's first brewery *827*	**1857** British cede Mauritania region for Albreda Is, Gambia river *312* **1860** Bandiagara escarpment invaded by El Hadj Omar *225* **1862** Start of Djenné's occupation by El Hadj Omar's Tukulor army *214* **1864** Islam starts to spread widely in N. Senegal *367* **1864** Start of serious French penetration of N. Senegal *367* **1870** Sikasso becomes Kénédougou's capital *207* **1880s** Mopti: Tukulor warlord El Hadj Omar's military HQ *209* **1887** Founding of Mouridiya brotherhood by Amadou Bamba *372* **1889** Fall of Yang-Yang, Wolof's last independent state *401* • Anti-Muslim resistance of the Maouri-Hausa people in Niger *163*	**1839** Fortification of Garoua *1151* **1845** First European settlement at Douala *1100* **1851** British shell Lagos *998* **1853** Explorer Barth visits Kano *1060* **1858** Founding of Victoria as freed slave colony *1111* **1861** Lagos a British colony *998* **1884** Purchase of Togo treaty by Germany *885* **1884** Purchase of Cameroon treaties by Germany *1100* **1884–1911** German occupation of Togoland *885, 911* **1884–1916** German occupation of Kamerun *1100* **1891** Explorer Monteil visits Kano *1060* **1892** Fall of Dan-Homey to the French *957* **1895** Start of Ibrahim Njoya's reign of Foumban *1123* **1897** British Punitive Expedition to Benin City *1030* **1903** Kano falls to British troops *1060*

INDEX

This index includes italicised references to topics covered in *Basics* and *Contexts* and all the place names mentioned in each country index. For more details of various topics, historical events, the names of ethnic groups and languages, etc, refer to individual country indexes.

KEY:
(A) Algeria
(B) Benin
(BF) Burkina Faso
(C) Cameroon
(Cd'I) Côte d'Ivoire
(CV) Cape Verde Islands
(Gam) The Gambia
(Gh) Ghana
(GB) Guinea-Bissau
(Gui) Guinea
(L) Liberia
(M) Mali
(Mau) Mauritania
(Ni) Niger
(N) Nigeria
(S) Senegal
(SL) Sierra Leone
(T) Togo

NEW WORLDS OF FINE WRITING

The African Writers Series